THE SPORTS ILLUSTRATED

1994 SPORTS ALMANAC

By the Editors of Sports Illustrated

LITTLE, BROWN AND COMPANY

Boston   New York   Toronto   London

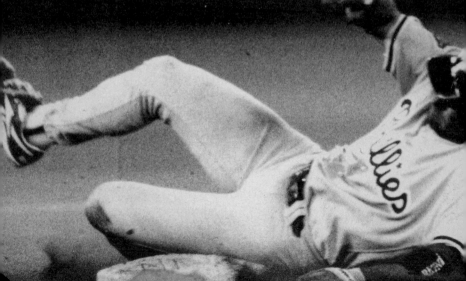

Sports Illustrated

1994
SPORTS
ALMANAC

CONTENTS

Expanded Contents

Expanded Contents *(Cont.)*

Expanded Contents *(Cont.)*

Expanded Contents (Cont.)

SOURCES

In compiling the *Sports Illustrated 1994 Sports Almanac*, the editors would like to thank Natasha Simon and Linda Wachtel of the Sports Illustrated library for their invaluable assistance. They would also like to extend their gratitude to the media relations offices of the following organizations for their help in providing information and materials relating to their sports: Major League Baseball; the Canadian Football League; the National Football League; the National Collegiate Athletic Association; the National Basketball Association; the National Hockey League; the Association of Tennis Professionals; the World Tennis Association; the U.S. Tennis Association; the U.S. Golf Association; the Ladies Professional Golf Association; the Professional Golfers Association; Thoroughbred Racing Communications, Inc.; the U.S. Trotting Association; the Breeders' Cup; Churchill Downs; the New York Racing Association Inc.; the Maryland Jockey Club; Championship Auto Racing Teams; the National Hot Rod Association; the International Motor Sports Association; the National Association for Stock Car Auto Racing; the Professional Bowlers Association; the Ladies Professional Bowlers Tour; the American Professional Soccer League; the National Professional Soccer League; the *Fédération Internationale De Football Association*; the U.S. Soccer Federation; the U.S. Olympic Committee; USA Track & Field; U.S. Swimming; U.S. Diving; U.S. Skiing; U.S. Skating; the U.S. Chess Federation; U.S. Curling; the Iditarod Trail Committee; the International Game Fish Association; the U.S. Gymnastics Federation; the Lacrosse Foundation; the American Power Boat Association; the Professional Rodeo Cowboys Association; U.S. Rowing; the American Softball Association; the Triathlon Federation USA; the National Archery Association; USA Wrestling; the U.S. Squash Racquets Association; the U.S. Polo Association; and the U.S. Volleyball Association.

The following sources were consulted in gathering information:

Baseball   *The Baseball Encyclopedia*, Macmillan Publishing Co., 1990; *Total Baseball*, Warner Books, 1991; *Baseballistics*, St. Martin's Press, 1990; *The Book of Baseball Records*, Seymour Siwoff, publisher, 1991; *The Complete Baseball Record Book*, The Sporting News Publishing Co., 1992; *The Sporting News Baseball Guide*, The Sporting News Publishing Co., 1993; *The Sporting News Baseball Register*, The Sporting News Publishing Co., 1993; *National League Green Book—1992*, The Sporting News Publishing Co., 1991; *The 1992 American League Red Book*, The Sporting News Publishing Co., 1991; *The Scouting Report: 1993*, Stats, Inc., Harper Perennial, 1993.

Pro Football   *The Official 1991 National Football League Record & Fact Book*, The National Football League, 1991; *The Official National Football League Encyclopedia*, New American Library, 1990; *The Sporting News Football Guide*, The Sporting News Publishing Co., 1992; *The Sporting News Football Register*, The Sporting News Publishing Co., 1992; *The 1992 National Football League Record & Fact Book*, Workman Publishing, 1992; *The Football Encyclopedia*, David Neft and Richard Cohen, St. Martin's Press, 1991.

College Football   *1991 NCAA Football*, The National Collegiate Athletic Association, 1990.

Pro Basketball   *The Official NBA Basketball Encyclopedia*, Villard Books, 1989; *The Sporting News Official 1992–93 NBA Guide*, The Sporting News Publishing Co., 1992.

College Basketball   *1993 NCAA Basketball*, The National Collegiate Athletic Association, 1992.

Hockey   *The National Hockey League Official Guide & Record Book 1991–92*, The National Hockey League, 1991; *The Sporting News Complete Hockey Book,* The Sporting News Publishing Co., 1992; *The Complete Encyclopedia of Hockey,* Visible Ink Press, 1993.

Tennis   *1993 Official USTA Tennis Yearbook*, H. O. Zimman, Inc., 1993; *IBM/ATP Tour 1993 Player Guide*, Association of Tennis Professionals, 1993; *WTA Official 1993 Media Guide*, Women's Tennis Association, 1993.

Golf   *PGA Tour Book 1993*, PGA Tour Creative Services, 1993; *LPGA 1993 Player Guide*, LPGA Communications Department, 1993; *Senior PGA Tour Book 1993*, PGA Tour Creative Services, 1993; *USGA Yearbook 1993*, U.S. Golf Association, 1993.

Boxing   *The Ring 1986–87 Record Book and Boxing Encyclopedia*, The Ring Publishing Corp., 1987. (To subscribe to *The Ring* magazine, write to P.O. Box 768, Rockville Centre, New York 11571-9905; or call (516) 678-7464); *Computer Boxing Update*, Ralph Citro, Inc., 1992.

Horse Racing   *The American Racing Manual 1992*, Daily Racing Form, Inc., 1992; *1992 Directory and Record Book*, The Thoroughbred Racing Association, 1992; *The Trotting and Pacing Guide, 1992*, United States Trotting Association, 1992; *Breeders' Cup 1992 Statistics*, Breeders' Cup Limited, 1992; *NYRA Media Guide 1992*, The New York Racing Association, 1992; *The 118th Kentucky Derby Media Guide, 1992*, Churchill Downs Public Relations Dept., 1992; *The 118th Preakness Press Guide, 1992*, Maryland Jockey Club, 1992; *Harness Racing News,* Harness Racing Communications.

Motor Sports   *The Official NASCAR Yearbook and Press Guide 1993*, UMI Publications, Inc., 1993; *1993 Indianapolis 500 Media Fact Book*, Indy 500 Publications, 1993; *IMSA 1993 Yearbook*, International Motor Sports Association, 1993; *1993 Winston Drag Racing Series Media Guide*, Sports Marketing Enterprises, 1993.

Bowling   *1993 Professional Bowlers Association Press, Radio and Television Guide*, Professional Bowlers Association, Inc., 1993; *The Ladies Pro Bowlers Tour 1992 Souvenir Tour Guide*, Ladies Pro Bowlers Tour, 1993.

Soccer   *Major Soccer League Official Guide 1991–92*, Major Soccer League, Inc., 1991; *Rothmans Football Yearbook 1993–94*, Headline Book Publishing, 1993; *American Professional Soccer League 1992 Media Guide*, APSL Media Relations Department, 1992; The *European Football Yearbook*, Facer Publications Limited, 1988; *Soccer America,* Burling Communications.

NCAA Sports   *1992–93 National Collegiate Championships*, The National Collegiate Athletic Association, 1992; *1992-93 National Directory of College Athletics,* Collegiate Directories Inc., 1992.

Olympics   *The Complete Book of the Olympics*, Little, Brown and Co., 1991.

Track and Field   *American Athletics Annual 1992*, The Athletics Congress/USA, 1992.

Swimming   *6th World Swimming Championships Media Guide*, The World Swimming Championships Organizing Committee, 1991.

Skiing   *U.S. Ski Team 1992 Media Guide / USSA Directory*, U.S. Ski Association, 1991; *Ski Racing Annual Competition Guide 1991–92*, Ski Racing International, 1991; *Ski Magazine's Encyclopedia of Skiing*, Harper & Row, 1974; *Caffä Lavazza Ski World Cup Press Kit*, Biorama, 1991.

Scorecard

OCTOBER 18, 1993 · $2.95 (CAN. $3.95)

Sports Illustrated

JORDAN 23

Why?

A summary of late Fall 1993 events

AUTO RACING

Dale Earnhardt all but clinched his sixth NASCAR points title on Oct. 31., when a sway bar broke on Rusty Wallace's Pontiac, knocking him from seventh place—right on Earnhardt's tail—all the way back to 19th at the finish of the Slick 50 500, in Phoenix. Earnhardt finished fourth, behind winner Mark Martin.

That made for a rather anti-climactic end to what was becoming a thrilling duel between the two drivers. The previous week Wallace had won the Delco 500 in Rockingham, N.C., to pull within 72 points of Earnhardt. The win was Wallace's ninth of the season and fourth in six races, but since Earnhardt finished second he did not lose much of his overall lead. "Doggone it, everytime I look around, Earnhardt's on my bumper," said Wallace after his Delco win. No longer. With Earnhardt carrying a 126-point lead into the final on Nov. 14 at the Atlanta Motor Speedway, he needed only to finish in the first 34 in what is expected to be a 42-car field.

Also on Oct. 31, at the NHRA finals at the Pomona (Calif.) Raceway, Rance McDaniel earned the first Top Fuel victory of his career, clocking 4.875 seconds at 295.37 MPH to beat Jimmy Nix (4.969). In the Pro Stock category Warren Johnson beat his son, Kurt, in a battle of Oldsmobile Cutlasses. The elder Johnson had a run of 7.113 seconds at 194.67 mph to top Kurt's run of 7.154 seconds at 193.29 mph. Jim Epler won the Funny Car competition when his final-round opponent, Al Hoffman, got his car jammed in forward during his pre-race burnout and was unable to get back to the starting line for staging.

BASEBALL

Mike Piazza, the Los Angeles Dodgers' catcher, was unanimously voted the National League Rookie of the Year on Oct. 27. The 13th Dodger to win the award, Piazza is only the sixth unanimous choice in the 47 years the award has been given, but he certainly earned the distinction, hitting .318 with 35 homers and 118 RBIs. Those numbers were unprecedented. Piazza's 35 homers were the most ever hit by a rookie catcher, and no previous winner had ever driven in more than 100 runs.

Tim Salmon, who was named American League Rookie of the Year on Oct. 28, was almost as impressive. Like Piazza, the California Angel outfielder won a "rookie triple crown," hitting .283 with 31 homers and 95 RBIs. He too was a unanimous choice.

Piazza was a unanimous Rookie of the Year selection in the NL.

V.J. LOVERO

PRO BASKETBALL

The rumor flew around Comiskey Park on Oct. 5. even as Michael Jordan was preparing to toss out the first ball of the American League playoff series: Jordan was retiring. He made it official the next morning. "I just feel that I don't have anything else to prove," said Jordan, who leaves the game with the highest scoring average (32.3 points per game) in NBA history, plus seven straight scoring titles, three straight playoff MVP awards and three straight team titles.

But the long term impact of Jordan's retirement remains to be seen. Along with Magic Johnson and Larry Bird, he had done an extraordinary job of lifting the fortunes of both the NBA and of its players. That much was clear from the enormous contracts many NBA players signed in the fall. Charlotte Hornet forward Larry Johnson got $84 million for 12 years. That makes some sense: Johnson, after all, is a player of proven value, the 1991 NBA Rookie of the Year.

But even rookies were commanding figures that looked like the GNPs of small countries: Anfernee Hardaway of the Orlando Magic was given $65.3 million for 13 years; Jamal Mashburn of the Dallas Mavericks, $32 million for seven; Chris Webber of Golden State Warriors, $74.4 million over 15 years; and Shawn Bradley of the Philadelphia 76ers (who hasn't even played college ball for the past two seasons) $44.2 million over eight.

With numbers like that flying around, it's no wonder that Derrick Coleman, a true franchise player for the New Jersey Nets who will become a free agent at the end of this year, turned his nose up at the paltry sum the Nets were offering him. "We're just so far apart," said Coleman's agent, Harold MacDonald of his negotiations with the Nets. "They issued an offer that we knew would not be acceptable." The figure? Sixty-nine million dollars for eight years.

BOXING

WBO heavyweight champion Tommy Morrison, who had impressed everyone in beating George Foreman on June 7, got a rude surprise on Oct. 29, when he was knocked down three times in the first round of his title fight with Michael Bentt, in Tulsa. When referee Danny Campbell stopped the fight after just 93 seconds, Bentt, a 28-year-old from Queens, New York, fighting only his 12th pro bout, had taken Morrison's title and improved his record to 11–1, with six

Bradley (with Sixers assistant Jeff Ruland) now has a contract as lofty as his 7'6" frame.

knockouts. The defeat was a costly one for Morrison, who had already signed to fight WBC champ Lennox Lewis in March for a guaranteed $7.25 million—if he did not lose before then.

The following night, in Phoenix, Oscar de la Hoya, the lone U.S. gold medalist at the 1992 Olympics, came back from a quick knockdown to stop Narciso Valenzuela of Mexico at 2:25 of the first round. That improved de la Hoya's record to 11–0 with 10 knockouts. On the same card, Michael Carbajal successfully defended his IBF and WBC world titles, stopping Domingo Sosa of the Dominican Republic in the fifth round.

The first sanctioned bout between two women took place on Oct. 30, in Lynnwood, Wash. Dallas Malloy, a 16-year-old high school dropout, beat Heather Poyner, a 21-year-old former high school cheerleader, in three, two-minute rounds.

JOHN BIEVER

Ward scampered for this two-yard TD in Florida State's 28–10 win over Miami in September.

COLLEGE FOOTBALL

On Nov. 1, two-thirds of the way through the college football season, the Florida State Seminoles were looking a lot like one of college football's alltime great teams. Led by quarterback Charlie Ward, their Heisman Trophy candidate and point guard on their basketball team, the Seminoles were 8–0 and beating opponents by an average of 39 points. Through eight games Florida State's defense had given up just 38 points. The Seminoles' biggest win came against their cross-state rivals, the Miami Hurricanes, whom they beat 28–10.

By Halloween, there were still five other teams that were both unbeaten and untied. Among them were such perennial powers as Nebraska at 8–0 and Notre Dame, which seemed to gather inspiration from the controversy surrounding the publication of *Under the Tarnished Dome: How Notre Dame Betrayed Its Ideals for Football Glory*. Written by Doug Looney and Don Yeager, the book suggested that under coach Lou Holtz the Notre Dame program may be no worse, but is certainly no better than any other big time college football program. Circling the wagons, the Fighting Irish won their first nine

games and were looking ahead to a Nov. 13 showdown with top-ranked Florida State.

There were also some surprises. Auburn, under rookie coach Terry Bowden, was 8–0. West Virginia (7–0) climbed as high as number 2 in *The New York Times* computer poll. Wisconsin beat Michigan 13–10 to improve its record to 7–1.

But the biggest surprise was Ohio State. The Buckeyes had not finished a season in the top 20 since 1986. Indeed, in four years under coach John Cooper, their record against ranked opponents was a dismal 3-13-2, and Cooper was having to re-think his strategy. "We've begun to realize that if we're going to compete with the big boys, we're going to have to recruit speed," said Cooper. He did. Paced all season by speedy stars like tailback Butler By'not'e, wide receiver Jeff Galloway and outside linebacker Craig Powell, the Buckeyes beat Penn State 24–6 on Oct. 30 to run their record to 8–0. Said Raymont Harris, who rushed for 151 yards and one touchdown against the Nitanny Lions, "I can smell a very faint smell of roses."

Ward was looking like a lock for the Heisman. He bruised his ribs in Florida State's 54–0 trouncing of Wake Forest on Oct. 30, but the injury was not expected to halt the tremendous season he was having.

Not only was Ward routinely posting awesome numbers for an undefeated team—168 of 241 passes for 2,011 yards and 16 touchdowns with just one interception—but many of his rivals had lost some of their early lustre, victims not so much of their own disappointing play but of playing for teams which under-achieved. Most notable of these was the star of last year's Rose Bowl, Michigan running back Tyrone Wheatley. Wheatley had carried 152 times for 835 yards, an average of 5.5 per carry, but at 4–4 the Wolverines had fallen right out of the polls. Two-time Heisman finalist Marshall Faulk was averaging 118.3 yards per game and had 16 scored TDs, but the Aztecs were just 6–3 and no one was paying all that much attention to Faulk.

PRO FOOTBALL

Several important NFL milestones were reached on Oct. 31:

• Green Bay defensive end Reggie White passed Lawrence Taylor as the alltime sacks leader, getting two in the Packers 17–3 defeat of the Bears to run his total to 130½.

• Kansas City quarterback Joe Montana completed the 3,000th pass of his career, a milestone reached by only Fran Tarkenton, Dan Fouts and Dan Marino, in the Chiefs' 30–10 loss to the Miami Dolphins.

• And in the same game Miami coach Don Shula tied George Halas as the winningest coach in NFL history. Shula's overall record in his 31 seasons with the Baltimore Colts and the Miami Dolphins is 324–152–6, a winning percentage of .678.

Shula's milestone win came without the services of quarterback Dan Marino, whose string of 145 straight starts at quarterback ended on Oct. 10, when he severed his Achilles tendon in a bizarre non-contact injury. Marino's was just one of a disturbing number of serious injuries that marked the early season, including a broken leg left suffered by Philadelphia quarterback Randall Cunningham in the Eagles' 35–30 win over the Jets on Oct. 3.

But a troubling number of the more serious injuries came not from vicious hits but from contact with the Astroturf, which was beginning to seem almost as dangerous. Wendell Davis of the Chicago Bears and Mike Sherrard of the New York Giants are both out for the season following weird non-contact injuries. Indianapolis Colt linebacker Steve Emtman, the top pick in the 1992 NFL draft, tore tendons and ligaments in his right knee so violently that he may not be ready for *next* season.

Shula's Dolphins had the best record in the NFL at 6–1. But there were some surprises. The Seattle Seahawks had already doubled their 1992 wins, going 4–4 under rookie quarterback Rick Mirer. The Giants, under Dan Reeves, were 5–2. And the Cleveland Browns, despite some confusion at quarterback, were looking like a formidable team, especially Eric Metcalf. On Oct. 24 Metcalf tied an NFL record by running back two kicks for touchdowns against the Pittsburgh Steelers. He returned the first a team-record 91 yards, the second 75 yards to give the Browns a 28–23 win and a record of 5–2.

A month before burying the Steelers, Metcalf scored the game-winner against the Raiders.

RICHARD MACKSON

Still, things hadn't changed all that much. The best team in the NFL remained the Dallas Cowboys. Sure, they had two losses midway through the season, but both came before the re-signing of running back Emmitt Smith, who sat out the first two games in a contract dispute with Cowboy owner Jerry Jones. They came to terms on Sept. 16, and with Smith back in the lineup, the Cowboys once again looked a lot like Super Bowl contenders. They beat the Philadelphia Eagles 23–10 on Oct. 31 as Smith romped for 237 yards, a franchise record and the sixth most yards ever gained in a single NFL game.

And football fans in Charlotte, North Carolina, celebrated wildly on Oct. 26 when the NFL owners awarded the next NFL franchise to their city. The Carolina Panthers will join the league in 1995, playing their first season in Clemson, S.C.

while the city of Charlotte builds a new 72,000-seat $160 million stadium. The owners delayed awarding the second new franchise until Nov. 30.

GOLF

The Ryder Cup has become one of the most exciting events in all of golf, and this year's battle between the top U.S. and European pros more than lived up to expectations. Galleries at the Belfry in Sutton Coldfield, England, were treated to some exhilirating golf. Nick Faldo got a hole-in-one in Sunday's match play. Faldo and Paul Azinger traded birdie for birdie in Friday's four-ball match, with Faldo making seven and Azinger six. After Joakim Haeggman of Sweden hit a half wedge four feet from the cup, his partner, Jose Maria Olazabal, asked him to mark the ball, then proceeded to hit the pin with his own wedge shot.

Midway through Sunday's 12 singles matches, the Europeans held a 12½ to 10½ point lead. The Cup would turn on the match between Constantino Rocca, a roly-poly, 36-year-old former plastics worker from Italy, and Davis Love III. "The tension," Rocca said later. "Very big." It sure looked that way. Rocca matched Love's two pars with a pair of bogeys, and the U.S. had a clutch 15–13 win.

Elsewhere in England, in the final of the World Match Play championship, which concluded Oct. 24 at the Wentworth Club in Virginia Water, Corey Pavin beat defending champion Nick Faldo of England, one up. The victory was particularly satisfying for Pavin, who had led this summer's British Open by a stroke after 54 holes only to get trampled by Greg Norman in the final round and finish fourth. Pavin is also the first American to win the World Match Play since Bill Rogers did in 1979.

The PGA tour concluded on Oct. 31, with the TOUR Championship, at the Olympic Club in San Francisco. The event

STEPHEN MUNDAY/ALLSPORT

Love's six-foot putt on the 18th clinched the win for him and the Ryder Cup for the U.S.

Potvin has been a central figure in the quick start for the Maple Leafs in '93.

provided yet another stage for poor Greg Norman to collapse on. The failures of this enormously talented player are becoming painful to watch.

Leading Jim Gallagher by two strokes with seven holes to play, Norman consistently found ways to sabotage his chances. He bogeyed both 12 and 13. He hit his approach shot into a bunker on 16 and had to settle for yet another bogey. On the 347-yard 18th, needing a birdie to beat Gallagher, Norman hit an eight iron into the rough behind the green and got down in three. Bogey. Norman called the round "a pathetic mental performance," and it was hard to disagree with him.

"It was his tournament to win," said Gallagher, who shot a 277 to win the $540,000 first prize. "I'd run out of holes. It turned out I was lucky."

ICE HOCKEY

The Toronto Maple Leafs were the big story in the first month of the NHL's 77th season. The Leafs won their first 10 games to set a record for consecutive wins at the start of a season. The previous best of eight straight had been set in 1974 by the Buffalo Sabres.

Among the stars for Toronto were center Doug Gilmour and veteran scorer Dave Andreychuk, who was obtained when Grant

Fuhr was traded to Buffalo. But brightest of all was 22-year-old goaltender Felix Potvin. Toronto's front office had taken a chance last year in trading away Fuhr, their veteran goalie and a perennial All Star. They were banking on Potvin and he has not let them down. In last season's playoffs Potvin had a superb 2.84 goals-against average and has played this year with the same stinginess. Through 11 games his goals against average was 2.20 and in win Number 10, a 4–2 defeat of the Chicago Blackhawks on Oct 29, Potvin stopped 46 shots.

The Leafs' streak came to an end on Oct. 30, when the Stanley Cup champion Montreal Canadiens beat them 5–2 on the strength of Vincent Damphousse's hat trick. The Canadiens got some practice in ending streaks earlier in the season, when they snapped the New Jersey Devils' season-opening win streak at seven.

The two new NHL franchises began play. Through Oct. 31, the Mighty Ducks of Anaheim were barely keeping their heads above water at 2-7-2, while the Florida Panthers were a respectable 4-5-3.

The league's two biggest stars had different debuts. Wayne Gretzky signed the richest contract in NHL history, a three-year deal worth $25.5 million. And if anyone doubted whether the 32-year-old Gretzky was worth it, he gave convincing proof by leading the league in points through Nov. 1, with 29 points. With eight goals in the Kings'

Next year will be the last in Navratilova's glorious career.

first 13 games, Gretzky seemed to stand a good chance of reaching Gordie Howe's alltime NHL record of 801 goals this season.

The league's other top star was not so lucky. Mario Lemieux had back surgery in late July and had to sit out the Penguins' first 10 games. He returned on Oct. 28, with two assists in a 7–3 loss to Quebec. But playing aggravated Lemieux's back again, and he missed Pittsburgh's next game.

MARATHON

On Oct. 31, in San Sebastián, Spain, Wang Junxia of China led three of her countrywomen across the finish line first in the World Marathon Cup. Wang's time was 2:28:16, making her an easy winner over Zhang Linli, who ran 2:29:42.

"We all feel tired," Wang said, alluding to her astonishing runs at the World Championships in mid-August and then at China's National Games three weeks later. "We just ran it as our coach planned, not very fast in the beginning and keeping pace with the other runners."

Richard Nerurkar of England won the men's race in 2:10:03.

TENNIS

Martina Navratilova announced on Sept. 29 that next year will be her last on the circuit. The 37-year-old Navratilova said simply that it was "time to move on": "I shouldn't say I'm looking forward to leading a normal life, because I don't know what normal is. This had been normal for me." But extraordinary by any one else's standards. Navratilova is the alltime women's leader in both career earnings, with $19,065,633, and in tournament wins, with 165, including 18 Grand Slam singles titles.

In a ruling that some people found irresponsible and others found downright bizarre, Judge Elke Bosse of the Hamburg District Court gave Günter Parche, the man who stabbed Monica Seles in the back during a match in April, a suspended two-year sentence on Oct. 13. That meant, incredibly, that Parche walked out of the courtroom a free man.

In explaining her decision, Bosse said that she believed Parche's contention that he meant only to disable Seles for a brief period of time, not kill her. She also said she took into account his apparent remorse and testimony from a psychiatrist that Parche had a highly abnormal personality. Said Navratilova, who happened to be in Germany when the decision was announced, "You guys need some serious help with the laws here in Germany."

TRIATHLON

Mark Allen won his record fifth straight Ironman Triathlon in Kailua-Kona, Hawaii, on Oct. 31, finishing the 2.4-mile swim, 112-mile bike and 26.2-mile run in a record eight hours, seven minutes and 46 seconds. He caught eventual runner-up Pauli Kiuru of Finland 16 miles into the run. Paula Newby-Fraser won her sixth women's race (8:58:23).

The Year in Sport

Super Showdown: Buffalo and Dallas

Emmitt Smith Leads the Cowboys To Pasadena

JOHN W. McDONOUGH

THE NCAAs What A Week!

Jason Kidd And Cal Dethrone Duke

JOHN BIEVER

BIONIC BO JACKSON'S BIG BLAST
BERNHARD LANGER: MEISTER AT THE MASTERS

Miracle On Ice

Mario Lemieux fights back from cancer and powers Pittsburgh to a record winning streak.

DAVID E. KLUTHO

EMMITT'S BACK AND SO ARE THE COWBOYS

Smokin'

The red-hot bat of Ron Gant ignites the Braves

CHUCK SOLOMON

9

A Losing Season

Despite some stirring performances, 1993 was above all a year of deaths and departures | **by RON FIMRITE**

WHERE IS GABRIEL HEATTER now that we need him? Heatter, mature readers will recall, habitually began his nightly radio newscasts of long ago with the cheerful announcement, "Ah, yes, there's good news tonight." He insisted on this sunny opener even in the bleak days immediately following Pearl Harbor, when just about the only good news was that Adm. Yamamoto's battleships had not anchored in San Francisco Bay, although that prospect seemed imminent. Heatter, alas, is no longer among us, but the sporting world of 1993 could surely have used someone of his unquenchable optimism in a year when good news was a rare and precious commodity.

There was, sadly, no shortage of bad news, and the National Basketball Association had more than its share of it. During the playoffs in June, Drazen Petrovic, star guard of the New Jersey Nets, was killed in an auto accident in Germany. Later that month the parents and sister of Miami Heat guard Brian Shaw were killed in another car

crash. In July popular Boston Celtic guard Reggie Lewis, who had collapsed during the season and whose condition thereafter was the subject of medical controversy, died of heart complications. And on Aug. 3, the body of Michael Jordan's father, James, was discovered in a South Carolina creek; he was the victim of a murder apparently committed by two mindless teenage thugs. On Oct. 6, Jordan, 30, announced his retirement from the NBA, thus depriving the Chicago Bulls of a chance for a fourth straight championship and basketball fans worldwide of the game's stellar attraction.

Within a single year the NBA had lost Magic Johnson, Larry Bird and Jordan, the equivalent, say, of baseball losing, all at once, Babe Ruth, Henry Aaron and Willie Mays. Johnson is HIV-positive and the aging Bird was injured, but Jordan was at the very peak of his abundant powers, so his departure came as a much greater jolt to fan sensibilities. Not that he didn't have good reason to pack it in. He scarcely had time to recover from the shock of his father's death. He was irritated by persistent references in the press to his gambling. He had, he said,

Jordan announced his retirement on Oct. 6, leaving Shaquille O'Neal as Air apparent.

no more worlds to conquer in his sport. And he just wanted a little peace and quiet for a change. Who can blame him? Still, the loss was a big one for all of sport.

It was, in fact, a year of terrible loss. In February, tennis's best ambassador, Arthur Ashe, succumbed finally to his long struggle with AIDS, his death bringing on a mourning worldwide that transcended sports. In baseball's spring training, Cleveland Indian pitchers Tim Crews and Steve Olin were killed in a Florida boating accident that left a third Indian pitcher, Bob Ojeda, with severe injuries to body and psyche. Two of auto racing's most successful and popular drivers, Alan Kulwicki and Davey Allison, were killed, not on road or track, but in separate aircraft accidents: Kulwicki on April 1 in a private plane crash and Allison on July 13 when a helicopter he was piloting went out of control just before landing.

Horse racing's Triple Crown was marred by two fatal spills. In the Preakness, won by gelding Prairie Bayou, another horse, Union City, broke down and had to be destroyed. And then, in the Belmont Stakes, Prairie Bayou himself took a bad step on the backstretch and fractured a foreleg so severely that he, too, had to be put down. The two fatalities precipitated renewed demands for greater control over the pain medications administered to horses. Julie Krone, who became the first woman jockey to win a Triple Crown race — the Belmont, aboard Colonial Affair— had precious little time to enjoy her historic triumph, injuring a leg so badly in a fall on the last day of the Saratoga racing season that a surgeon likened her injuries to those suffered by a plane crash victim.

And to complete this litany of woe, there was the stabbing of tennis queen Monica Seles by a crazed German fan during an April tournament in Hamburg, Germany. Seles survived the stab in the back, but her

assailant, an unemployed lathe operator named Günter Parche, accomplished his avowed purpose, which was to return Steffi Graf to the No. 1 ranking in women's tennis. Seles was unable to compete for the remainder of the year, and Graf, who was horrified by the attack, swept nearly every tournament in sight, albeit not without some humility and embarrassment. After winning the U.S. Open, Graf pointedly made reference to the absence of her chief rival. In a final irony Parche was freed of felony charges by a German court that ruled he was not in control of his faculties at the time of the attack.

So now, as Heatter would say, on with the good news. The baseball season was eventful and ultimately thrilling. There were milestones aplenty. Dave Winfield joined the exclusive 3,000-hit club. George Brett stole his 200th base, joining Mays and Aaron as the only major league players to have had more than 3,000 hits, 300 homers and 200 stolen bases. Brett announced his retirement the last week of the season, join-

ing Nolan Ryan among 1993's distinguished retirees. Carlton Fisk might also be included in the august number, although he didn't quit voluntarily, the White Sox having released him after he set the record for most games caught at 2,226.

Lee Smith, who started the year with the Cardinals and finished it with the Yankees, set a new career record for saves with his 401st. No-hitters were thrown by Chris Bosio of the Mariners, Darryl Kile of the Astros and Jim Abbott of the Yankees. Abbott rates special mention because he was born without a right hand and therefore becomes the only one-handed no-hit pitcher. Met pitcher Anthony Young set a record, too, but it's not one he's likely to relate to his grandchildren, since, during the season, he lost his 27th consecutive game.

The Cardinal's Mark Whiten didn't actually set any records, but he tied a bunch when, on Sept. 7, he had the most productive day of any batter in history, hitting four homers and driving in 12 runs in the second

Prairie Bayou (5) broke down badly in the Belmont.

game of a doubleheader in Cincinnati. The four homers in one game tied him with 11 other hitters—among them Mays and Lou Gehrig—but none of those sluggers drove in as many as a dozen runs, a feat accomplished only once before, in 1924, by another Cardinal, Sunny Jim Bottomley. And by driving in yet another run in the first game that day, Whiten also tied the record of 13 RBIs in a doubleheader; set in 1972 by the Padres' Nate Colbert. "You can't even do what he did in batting practice," said Whiten's understandably amazed teammate Todd Zeile. Whiten, by the way, was hitting a mere .248 before his big game.

The two league batting champions also emerged from relative obscurity. Andres Galarraga of the expansion Colorado Rockies was a .267 career hitter before 1993, and though he had consecutive .300 seasons in 1987 and '88, he hadn't hit higher than .257 since. But in '93, though plagued by injuries, he hit a rousing .370 to become the first expansion team player ever to win a batting title. The Rockies, meanwhile, set a major league attendance record of 4,483,350, averaging an astonishing 55,350 per game at Denver's Mile High Stadium. In the American League, Toronto's John Olerud had been discussed mainly in terms of that elusive quality: potential. He had always had a sweet swing, and in '92 he had hit a commendable .284, but his career average for four seasons, three full, was a mere .269. In 1993 he batted .363, his 200

Abbott celebrated one of three no hitters pitched in the major leagues this season.

hits including 54 doubles, the most in either league in 16 years.

Sparked by Olerud and by his new teammate Paul Molitor, who finished second in the batting race, the Blue Jays handily won the AL East and then terminated the White Sox in the playoffs. But the best race was in the National League West, where the Braves and the Giants were tied at 103 wins apiece going into the last game of the season. The Giants, losers of 90 games in '92 and apparently headed for Florida before a group of local investors saved them for San Francisco, had led by as many as 10 games in late July. But an eight-game losing streak in September handed the lead over to the red-hot Braves. The Giants recovered, however, winning 14 of 16 to catch the Braves in the last week of the season. But on that fateful last day, the Braves beat the Rockies 5–3, and the Giants got clobbered by arch foe Los Angeles 12–1. One hundred and three wins were not enough. Neither, as it developed, were 104, because the Braves

were upset by the roughhouse Phillies in the playoffs.

The World Series, played under the dome in Toronto and in the rain in Philadelphia, was mostly a slugfest, highlighted by a preposterous 15–14 Toronto win in Game 4, the highest-scoring game in Series history. The Jays won it all, 8–6, in Game 6 on Joe Carter's climactic three-run homer in the ninth, only the second time a Series had ended with a home run. Bill Mazeroski did it the first time, beating the Yankees in 1960, the year Gabriel Heatter retired from network broadcasting.

The National Football League crowned the Dallas Cowboys, formerly "America's Team," champions in January after they demolished the Buffalo Bills 52–17 in Super Bowl XXVII at the Pasadena Rose Bowl. It was the third straight Super Bowl loss for coach Marv Levy and his increasingly frustrated team and the first NFL title for coach Jimmy Johnson, who as recently as 1989 had endured a 1–15 season.

The NFL also took some positive steps toward joining the 21st century, reducing the college draft to eight rounds and granting players the privilege of free agency after five years of service. The new free agency boosted the average player's salary to $643,000, three times what it had been only six years earlier. The owners, however, hope to stave off bankruptcy with the new salary caps, which are projected to average $31 million to $35 million per team.

Rule changes in 1993 gave passers greater freedom in grounding the ball or throwing it away when threatened, but quarterback-bashing continued unabated, the most celebrated victim being Dan Marino, who never before suffered a debilitating injury in his 11-year career. Actually, Marino tore his Achilles tendon without being sacked, but the Oct. 10 injury ended his season. A bad back ended Eric Dickerson's 11-season career, the last few years of which have been characterized by trade demands,

complaints about coaching and all-around grousing. Dickerson retired as the league's second leading career rusher.

By trouncing Miami 34–13 in the Sugar Bowl, Alabama became the reigning college champion, but Florida State and Notre Dame emerged as potential successors in '93. A national title would be the first for Florida State's Bobby Bowden in 27 years of coaching.

Despite the Sugar Bowl defeat, Miami's Gino Torretta won the Heisman Trophy, and though pretty much snubbed in the draft, moved on to the NFL. The early 1993 Heisman favorite, Marshall Faulk of San Diego State, suffered a couple of sub-100-

A bad back forced Dickerson (29) to retire after 11 seasons and 13,259 yards.

yard games in the early season and quickly dropped out of the race, despite a midseason surge against lesser opponents than the likes of Cal and UCLA.

Michael Jordan may be gone, at least for now, and Charles Barkley may be threatening to leave after the '93–94 season, but the NBA still has wunderkind Shaquille O'Neal, who not only made the All-Star Game as a rookie, but also threatens to steal some of Jordan's commercial air time, so adept is he before a camera. And for comebacks it would be hard to beat Chris Webber's. Webber was the Michigan star who called that illegal timeout in the closing seconds of the NCAA championship game at the Louisiana

Superdome in April, thereby drawing the technical foul which clinched North Carolina's 77–71 win. "I cost us the game," a disconsolate Webber admitted afterward. His grief was assuaged some six months later when he signed a record $74.4 million, 15-year contract with the Golden State Warriors. Talk about good news.

The women's NCAA basketball championship was won by Texas Tech, which defeated Ohio State 84–82 in the title game behind forward Sheryl Swoopes's 47 points. Sheryl Swoopes, I submit to you, is every bit as congenial a name for a basketball player, male or female, as Gabriel Heatter is for a newscaster. And her 47 points set a scoring

JIM GUND

Swoopes (center) got a record 47 points and a hug from her Texas Tech teammates.

record for an NCAA championship game, men's or women's, topping Bill Walton's 44 for UCLA against Memphis State in 1973.

The National Hockey League got off to a somewhat fresher start under new commissioner Gary Bettman, a former aide to NBA commissioner David Stern. Bettman vowed to eliminate senseless brawling as an NHL attraction, and he realigned the conferences, ditching such quaint division names as Norris and Smythe for regional designations. New teams were also added in Miami (the Florida Panthers) and in Anaheim, Calif. The Anaheim franchise is owned by the Disney Corporation, plays within sight of Disneyland itself and is called the Mighty Ducks for the simple reason, says Disney chairman Michael Eisner, that "we made a movie about a hockey team called the Mighty Ducks. It did $50 million at the box office." Reason enough.

And 1993 showed that athletic versatility is not limited to the Bo Jacksons and Deion Sanderses of this planet. How about Walter Ray Williams Jr., the big money winner on the professional bowling circuit who is also a five-time national champion at horseshoes? Williams was on his way to setting a tour record for wins on the bowling circuit when he interrupted his schedule to compete in the World Horseshoe Tournament in Spearfish, N. Dak. He finished 12th. Must've gotten those grips mixed up. The question is: can this guy play the outfield?

Boxing had a dull year in comparison with bowling and horseshoes. The sport's showcase fight between Pernell (Sweet Pea) Whitaker and Julio César Chávez for both Whitaker's WBC title and the right to be called the best fighter pound-for-pound ended in a highly debatable draw. Whitaker, who abandoned his usual clowning for this fight, appeared to be the clearcut winner, but two of the three judges scored it a draw, and though the third judge had it for Whitaker, the official verdict came down as a "majority draw." Whitaker kept his title, and Chávez, as consolation, remained undefeated, although 87-0-1 doesn't exactly have the panache of 88–zip.

The two principal heavyweight champions did little to advance their stagnant reputations. Riddick Bowe hardly worked up a decent sweat disposing of tubby Michael Dokes in one round and 36-year-old journeyman Jesse Ferguson in two. Lennox Lewis, meanwhile, appeared awkward and amateurish in whipping tired veterans Tony Tucker and Frank Bruno. Tommy Morrison, the WBC champ, may finally have terminated the decades–long career of George Foreman by winning a 12-round decision from the old-timer.

At the World Track and Field Championships in August in Stuttgart, Germany, some gratifying performances were turned in by a quartet of 1992 Olympic Games flops. Sergei Bubka, the Ukrainian pole vaulter who failed to clear the qualifying height in Barcelona, won his fourth world title to become the only athlete with a perfect record in these meets. Dan O'Brien, who failed to make the U.S. Olympic team when he no–heighted in the pole vault at the decathlon trials, successfully defended his world title by scoring 8,817 points. Michael Johnson, who, afflicted with food poisoning, didn't reach the Olympic finals in the 200 meters, won the 400 in 43.74 at the Worlds and then ran the fastest 400 in history— 42.97— in anchoring the U.S. 4X400 relay team to a world record 2:54.29. And Noureddine Morceli, a seventh place finisher in Barcelona, won the world 1,500 in 3:34.24 and then, on Sept. 5 in Rieti, Italy, broke Steve Cram's record for the mile by nearly two seconds with a clocking of 3:44.39.

But the most astonishing times of all were recorded in China where 20-year-old Wang Junxia ran a reported 29:31.78 10,000 meters, which beat the world record for women at this distance by nearly 42 seconds. And then she and countrywoman Qu Yunxia broke the women's 1,500 record. Both women were trained, Chinese officials claimed, on a diet of turtles, worms and caterpillar fungi. Skeptics suspect something more chemically stimulating. Further suspicion may have been aroused when seven Chinese women swimmers broke one minute in the 100-meter butterfly, a time previously achieved by only 19 swimmers. The Chinese women athletes seem to be supplanting the former East Germans as supercharged international champions.

Nobody suspects golfers of ingesting anything more complicated than gin and vermouth, but scores in 1993 dipped to new lows. Greg Norman, returning to championship

Things were just ducky when the NHL opened its latest franchise in Anaheim.

ROBERT BECK

form after a seven–year drought, won the British Open at Royal St. George's with a record 13-under-par 267, finishing with a final round of 64. The British Open scores were so low that Ernie Els of South Africa became the first player in the history of the tournament to shoot four rounds in the 60's and lose. Three players—Nick Faldo, Payne Stewart and Vijay Singh— shot rounds of 63 in major championships during the year; only 12 had ever done it before. The Masters was won by Bernhard Langer, shooting 11 under; the U.S. Open by Lee Janzen at eight under. "Pars aren't good enough anymore in major championship golf," lamented Jack Nicklaus, who won his second Senior Open. Maybe so.

In tennis 22-year-old Pete Sampras won Wimbledon and the U.S. Open, unseating Jim Courier as the No. 1–ranked player. But he couldn't shake his image, perpetuated by the British press, of being as dull as warm beer. Nobody ever accused Andre

Lalas (22) scored the second goal in the U.S.'s shocking 2–0 defeat of England.

Agassi of being boring—tasteless, maybe, but never boring—and when he showed up at Wimbledon with Barbra Streisand in tow, his rakehell reputation soared once more. Sampras, Courier and Agassi all refused to play in the Davis Cup, prompting team captain Tom Gorman to resign in justifiable disgust.

The U.S. soccer team needs all the help it can get, but it did bring off an international shocker on June 9 when it defeated England 2–0 in a U.S. Cup match at Foxboro (Mass.) Stadium. The upset inspired one British newspaper to headline its game story as THE END OF THE WORLD. As in World Cup. The U.S. Cup series drew crowds averaging 47,793. "No one should say Americans don't like soccer," a grateful Guido Tognoni of the game's international ruling body declared. He'll know more about that in '94 when the World Cup starts here in June.

So you see, dear Gabriel, there's good news after all. If not tonight, surely tomorrow.

The Year in Sport Calendar

compiled by John Bolster

Baseball

Oct 27, 1992—Don Baylor is named the first manager of the expansion Colorado Rockies.

Oct 30—The Cincinnati Reds name ex-Red Tony Perez as their new manager.

Nov 3—Los Angeles Dodger first baseman Eric Karros, who hit .257 with 20 homers and 88 RBIs, is named National League Rookie of the Year.

Nov 9—Lou Piniella is named manager of the Seattle Mariners.

Nov 10—National League club owners reject the San Francisco Giants' proposed move to Tampa Bay by a vote of 9–4, one short of the 10 votes required for approval.

Nov 10—Oakland Athletic reliever Dennis Eckersley, who saved 51 games, is awarded the American League Cy Young Award.

Nov 11—Greg Maddux of the Chicago Cubs, who went 20–11 with a 2.18 earned run average for a team that lost more games than it won, is named the winner of the National League Cy Young Award.

Nov 12—Arbitrator George Nicolau overturns the lifetime ban imposed by Commissioner Faye Vincent on Yankee pitcher Steve Howe for his repeated drug use.

Nov 18—Barry Bonds wins his second National League MVP award in three years. Bonds, who hit .311 with 34 home runs and 103 RBIs, wins easily over the man who edged him out for the award in '91, Terry Pendleton of the Braves.

Dec 4—The New York Yankees acquire 25-year-old lefty Jim Abbott from the California Angels in exchange for three minor league prospects.

Dec 4—Kirby Puckett signs a five-year contract with the Minnesota Twins worth $30 million, turning down bids from other clubs that would have earned him at least $5 million more.

Dec 7—Joe Carter signs a three-year, $19.5 million contract with the Toronto Blue Jays.

Dec 8—National League MVP Barry Bonds closes a six-year deal worth $43.75 million with the San Francisco Giants. Averaging $7,291,667 a year, the contract makes Bonds the richest player in baseball. David Cone signs a three-year contract with the Kansas City Royals for $18 million, making him the game's highest paid pitcher.

Dec 9—Greg Maddux signs a $28 million, five-year deal with the Atlanta Braves, spurning the New York Yankees, who had offered him $37 million for six years.

Feb 11, 1993—Nolan Ryan announces that he will retire at the end of the 1993 season, his 27th in the game.

Mar 1—George Steinbrenner officially returns to baseball after a 30-month suspension.

Mar 22—Cleveland Indian pitchers Steve Olin and Tim Crews are killed and Bob Ojeda is severely injured when their aluminum fishing boat hits a dock jutting out onto Little Lake Nellie, about 25 miles west of Orlando.

Mar 24—The Chicago White Sox exercise the option on Bo Jackson's contract for $910,000, plus a possible $1.05 million in incentives.

Mar 31—A House judiciary committee begins hearings on legislation to revoke baseball's antitrust exemption. Bud Selig, chairman of major league baseball's executive committee, is grilled on subjects such as Faye Vincent's forced resignation and the decision to keep the Giants in San Francisco.

Apr 5—Opening Day! In debuts by expansion teams, the Florida Marlins win their first game, 6–3 over the Los Angeles Dodgers, at sold-out Joe Robbie Stadium. The Colorado Rockies are shut out 3–0 by Dwight Gooden and the Mets at Shea

RONALD C. MODRA

Bonds' contract made him baseball's richest.

BRUCE KLUCKHOHN

Winfield is the 19th player to get 3,000 hits.

Stadium. Bret Barberie had the first hit for the Marlins, Andres Galarraga the first for the Rockies.

Apr 8—Carlos Baerga of the Cleveland Indians become the first man to hit home runs from opposite sides of the plate in a single inning. Batting right-handed, he hits the first off the Yankees' Steve Howe; batting lefty, he hits the second off Steve Farr.

Apr 9—In his first at bat in 18 months, Bo Jackson hits a pinch hit home run off Yankee Neal Heaton. Still, Chicago loses to New York 11–6.

Apr 9—The Colorado Rockies set a major league record by drawing 80,220 fans to their home opener. They pull 65,268 on Saturday and 66,987 Sunday to set an attendance record for a three-game series, with 212,475.

Apr 15—Andre Dawson hits his 400th homer, off the Indians' Jose Mesa.

Apr 15—Sparky Anderson gets his 2,000th win as a manager, as the Detroit Tigers beat the Oakland A's 3–2.

Apr 22—Chris Bosio of the Seattle Mariners pitches the first no-hitter of the season, shutting down the Red Sox 7–0.

May 19—The New York Mets, off to a 13–25 start, fire manager Jeff Torborg and replace him with Dallas Green.

May 24—The Cincinnati Reds, 20–24, fire rookie manager Tony Perez and name Davey Johnson as their new skipper.

May 27—Dale Murphy announces his

retirement. Murphy, who hit 398 homers and won two MVP awards in his 16 seasons, was batting just .143.

June 2—A ban on the use of all tobacco products is announced for the minor leagues.

June 9—The disintegrating San Diego Padres dismiss Joe McIlvaine, their general manager.

June 17—Baseball's owners vote 26–2 in favor of doubling the number of teams that make the playoffs. The first round will be a best-of-five series.

June 22—White Sox catcher Carlton Fisk catches his 2,226th game, passing Bob Boone in major league games caught.

June 22—New York Mets' general manager Al Harazin resigns.

June 23—John Olerud's consecutive game hitting streak comes to an end at 26 when he goes 0–4 against the New York Yankees.

June 23—Jay Buhner becomes the first player in the 17-year history of the Seattle Mariners to hit for the cycle, going 4 for 7 in an 8–7 win over Oakland.

June 24—The financially strapped San Diego Padres trade National League batting champion Gary Sheffield to the Florida Marlins for three pitchers.

June 27—Hapless pitcher Anthony Young of the New York Mets loses his major league record 24th straight decision, 5–3 to the St. Louis Cardinals.

June 28—Carlton Fisk is released by the Chicago White Sox.

July 2—The Philadelphia Phillies and the San Diego Padres play, on and off, for 12 hours. They start the first game of a scheduled doubleheader at 4:35 P.M. It ends, with Philadelphia losing 5–2, at 1:03 A.M. They start Game 2 at 1:28. It goes 10 innings and ends at 4:40 A.M. with the Phillies winning 6–5.

July 13—At Baltimore's Camden Yards the American League All-Stars defeat the National League All-Stars 9–3. Jack McDowell of the White Sox gets the win, and Minnesota's Kirby Puckett is named the MVP.

July 24—New York Met outfielder Vince Coleman throws a firecracker from a car as he leaves Dodger Stadium. It injures 2½-year-old Amanda Santos, whose parents file a suit against Coleman.

July 28—Anthony Young finally wins when the Mets score with two out in the bottom of the ninth to give him a 5–4 win over the Florida Marlins. Young's streak of losing decisions had reached 27 before the win.

July 28—Seattle slugger Ken Griffey Jr. homers off Minnesota's Willie Banks, making this the major league record-tying eighth straight game in which Griffey has hit a home run. Dale Long of

Pittsburgh achieved the feat in 1956 and Don Mattingly of the Yankees did it in 1987.

Aug 1—Reggie Jackson has the spolight to himself as he is inducted into the Hall of Fame.

Aug 2—The Baltimore Orioles are purchased at auction for $173 million by a group of investors headed by Baltimore attorney Peter Angelos.

Aug 3—Vince Coleman is charged with a felony for throwing an explosive device and takes a leave of absence from the Mets.

Aug 4—U.S. District Court judge John Padova rules that baseball's seven-decade antitrust exemption applies only to player contracts. Padova rules that the buying and selling of franchises was not covered by the 1922 Supreme Court decision.

Aug 16—Cleveland Indian pitcher Bob Ojeda gets a standing ovation as he starts a game for the first time since getting severely injured in the boating accident that took the lives of his teammates Steve Olin and Tim Crews. After giving up two first inning homers, Ojeda settles down and pitches four scoreless innings, but loses 4–1.

Aug 22—Jack McDowell of the Chicago White Sox becomes baseball's first 20-game winner when he beats the Minnesota Twins.

Aug 26—Fred Wilpon, the CEO of the New York Mets, announces that the club has put outfielder Vince Coleman on administrative leave and promises that he will never again play for the club.

Aug 31—The New York Yankees acquire alltime saves leader Lee Smith from St. Louis.

Brett retired after 20 thrilling seasons.

JOHN BIEVER

Sep 1—The charging Atlanta Braves whip the Chicago Cubs 8–2 to pull within four games of the San Francisco Giants. It is the Braves 16th win in their last 19 games.

Sep 4—Jim Abbott of the New York Yankees no-hits the Cleveland Indians. It is the first no-hitter by a Yankee pitcher in 10 years.

Sep 7—St. Louis Cardinal Mark Whiten ties three major league records in the Cards' doubleheader with Cincinnati. He gets four homers and 12 RBIs in the nightcap and 13 RBIs in the doubleheader.

Sep 8—Darryl Kile of the Houston Astros beats the New York Mets 7–1 with a no-hitter.

Sep 11—The red-hot Atlanta Braves beat the San Diego Padres 13–1 to move into sole possession of first place in the National League West.

Sep 15—The Pittsburgh Pirates, who have won a record nine Eastern Division titles, agree to move to the Central Division in 1994 in order to create a deep-South rivalry between the Atlanta Braves and the Florida Marlins in baseball's new alignment.

Sep 16—Minnesota Twin Dave Winfield, 41, becomes the 19th player in major league history to get 3,000 hits. Winfield's historic hit comes off the Oakland Athletics' Dennis Eckersley in the ninth inning.

Sep 17—The Philadelphia Phillies, who as late as August 20 were leading the National League East by nine games and the Montreal Expos by 14½, travel to Montreal to play the red-hot Expos, whom they lead by just five games. The Phillies win one of three and see their lead shrink to just four games.

Sep 19—Tom Glavine of the Atlanta Braves gets his 20th win of the season, beating the New York Mets 11–2. The win also makes Glavine the first National League pitcher to have three straight 20-win seasons since Ferguson Jenkins had five in a row between 1967 and '72.

Sep 22—In Seattle Texas Ranger pitcher Nolan Ryan faces just three Mariner batters before hurting his right elbow and leaving the last major league game of his great career. The Ryan legacy includes 324 wins, 5,714 strikeouts and seven no-hitters. The last two are major league records.

Sep 22—The Colorado Rockies play their final home game, defeating the Cincinnati Reds 12–7. The attendance of 70,069 at Mile High Stadium brings the Rockies' home attendance in their inaugural season to a major league record 4,483,350. Previously only the Toronto Blue Jays had topped the 4 million mark.

Sep 25—George Brett, 40, announces his retirement after 20 major league seasons, all of them with the Kansas City Royals.

Sep 27—Bo Jackson hits a three-run homer to power the Chicago White Sox to a 4–2 win over the

DAVID LIAM KYLE

Molitor was named Series MVP for hitting .500.

Seattle Mariners and to clinch the American League West.

Sep 27—The Toronto Blue Jays beat the Milwaukee Brewers 2–0 to win the American League East for the third straight year.

Sep 28—The Philadelphia Phillies beat the Pittsburgh Pirates 10–7 to clinch the National League East. The big blow for the Phillies is Mariano Duncan's grand slam home run in the seventh inning.

Sep 29—Gary Sheffield signs a four-year, $22.5 million contract with the Florida Marlins.

Sep 30—The Philadelphia Phillies' record of 174 straight games without getting shut out ends when the Pittsburgh Pirates beat the Phillies 5–0 in Pittsburgh.

Oct 2—Andres Galarraga of the Colorado Rockies goes to the plate four times, giving him the 502 at bats needed to qualify for the National League batting title. Galarraga wins it with an average of .370. John Olerud wins the American League crown, with an average of .363. Second and third are his teammates Paul Molitor (.332) and Roberto Alomar (.326). It is the first time this century a league's top three hitters are teammates.

Oct 3—The Atlanta Braves clinch the NL West on the final day of the season, defeating the Colorado Rockies 5–3 and then waiting for the Los Angeles Dodgers to finish off the San Francisco Giants, 12–1, in L.A.

Oct 3— A sellout crowd of 72,390 gathers to watch the last game to be played in Cleveland

Stadium. The Indians lose to the Chicago White Sox 4–0. The only consolation for the Tribe is that over the weekend they set an attendance record for a three game series, with 216,904.

Oct 5—The American League playoffs begin in Chicago, with the Toronto Blue Jays beating the White Sox 7–3.

Oct 6—The National League playoffs begin in Philadelphia, with the Phillies topping the Atlanta Braves 4–3 in 10 innings.

Oct 12—The Toronto Blue Jays beat the Chicago White Sox 6–3 to win the American League pennant, four games to two. The Blue Jays had a 3–2 lead going into the top of the ninth, when Devon White homered and Paul Molitor hit a two-run triple. Dave Stewart is named the series' MVP.

Oct 13—The Phillies beat the Braves 6–3 to win the National League pennant four games to two, ending Atlanta's bid to become the first NL team to win three straight pennants since the Cardinals of 1942–44. Curt Schilling, who did not win a game but allowed just three earned runs in 16 innings, while striking out 19, is named series MVP.

Oct 16— The 90th World Series opens in Toronto's SkyDome with the Blue Jays beating the Phillies 8–5. Juan Guzman is the opening pitcher for Toronto, Curt Schilling the opener for Philadelphia.

Oct 20— In the longest nine-inning game in postseason baseball history (4:14), Toronto beats Philadelphia 15–14. Among the records set in this weird game are those for total runs scored in a game, at bats (85) and total bases by both teams (65, 20 of them on seven doubles). Tony Castillo was the winning pitcher, Mitch Williams the loser.

Oct 21—In dramatic contrast to the previous game, Philadelphia's Curt Schilling shuts out Toronto 2–0, and the Series heads back to Toronto with the Blue Jays leading three games to two.

Oct 23—With one out in the bottom of the ninth and Toronto trailing Philadelphia 6–5, Toronto right fielder Joe Carter hits a three-run homer off Phillie reliever Mitch Williams to give the Blue Jays their second straight World Series title. Paul Molitor, who hit .500 with two homers, 8 RBIs and a slugging percentage of 1.000, is named Series MVP.

Oct 25—Gene Lamont, who managed the Chicago White Sox to a 94–68 record this season, is named Manager of the Year in the American League. The following day San Francisco Giant manager Dusty Baker is named National League Manager of the Year. Baker took the Giants from 72–90 last year to 103–59 this year.

Oct 26— The Chicago White Sox sign slugging first baseman Frank Thomas to a four-year contract worth $42 million.

Nov 13, 1992—Riddick Bowe beats Evander Holyfield at the Thomas and Mack Center in Las Vegas to become boxing's undisputed heavyweight champion. The win improved the new champion's career record to 32–0, with 27 knockouts, while the loss was Holyfield's first in 29 bouts.

Nov 23—In his pro debut Oscar de la Hoya, the only U.S. boxer to win a gold medal at the 1992 Olympics, pounds Lamar Williams into submission. The knockout comes at 1:42 of the first round of their lightweight fight at the Great Western Forum.

Feb 6, 1993—Riddick Bowe makes his first title defense, knocking out flabby Michael Dokes in the first round of their fight in New York City.

Feb 20—WBC super lightweight champion Julio César Chávez knocks down Greg Haugen twice before their fight is stopped in the fifth round, in Mexico City. On the same card Terry Norris, the WBC super welterweight champion, stopped Maurice Blocker in the second round.

March 6—Pernell Whitaker takes Buddy McGirt's WBC welterweight title in a unanimous decision.

March 13—Michael Carbajal KOs Humberto Gonzalez at the end of seven to add Gonzalez's WBC light flyweight crown to the IBF one he already owns.

March 21—Russian lightweight Sergei Artemiev is hospitalized with a blood clot on the surface of his brain after losing to Carl Griffith in Atlantic City.

May 8—Lennox Lewis successfully defends his WBC heavyweight crown with a unanimous 12-round decision over Tony Tucker, in Las Vegas. On the same card Gerald McClellan wins the WBC middleweight title with a fifth round TKO of Julian Jackson, and Julio César Chávez keeps his WBC super lightweight crown with a sixth-round TKO of Terrence Alli.

May 22— Riddick Bowe retains his heavyweight title by destroying hapless 36-year-old Jesse Ferguson in 3:17.

June 7—Twenty-four-year-old Tommy Morrison scores a unanimous 12-round win over George Foreman, who is 20 years his senior.

June 21—Terry Norris gets decked in the second round of his fight with Troy Waters but proceeds to pummel Waters, forcing the Australian's corner to throw in the towel after the third round.

June 27—Evander Holyfield fights for the first time since losing his heavyweight title to Riddick Bowe the previous November. He outscores Alex Stewart over 12 boring rounds.

June 29— Heavyweight contender Ray Mercer pleads not guilty in New York City to charges that he tried to persuade Jesse Ferguson to take a dive for $100,000 during their fight in February.

RICHARD MACKSON

Neither Whitaker (left) nor Chávez lost. Or won.

July 17—Michael Carbajal KOs Kwang-Sun Kim at 2:23 of the seventh round of their fight in Las Vegas to retain both his IBF and WBC world light flyweight crowns.

Aug 6—Mike Tyson's request for a new rape trial is turned down by an Indiana appeals court by a 2–1 vote.

Sept 10—In the Alamodome in San Antonio, Pernell Whitaker and Julio Cesar Chavez fight to a rare majority draw, a result that virtually everyone but Chavez's camp finds highly unsatisfactory. Two judges—Mickey Vann of England and Franz Marti of Switzerland—score the fight 115–115, while the third, Jack Woodruff of Dallas, scores it 115–113 Whitaker.

Sept 22—The Indiana Supreme Court denies Mike Tyson's request for a review of an appeal court's refusal to grant him a new trial.

Oct 2—Lennox Lewis successfully defends his WBC heavyweight title against Frank Bruno, knocking out his fellow Briton in the seventh round.

Oct 16—Tracy Harris Patterson, son of ex-heavyweight champion Floyd Patterson, retains his WBC super bantamweight title with a seventh-round TKO of Daniel Zaragoza of Mexico, in Poughkeepsie, N.Y. The win improves Patterson's career record to 48-2-1, with 35 knockouts.

Nov 27, 1992—Indiana beats Seton Hall 78–74 to win the Preseason NIT. Calbert Cheaney scores 36 points for the Hoosiers and is named the tournament MVP.

Dec 5—In a rematch of last season's championship finalists, the Duke Blue Devils beat Michigan 79–68.

Dec 7—Mike Krzyzewski gets his 300th win at Duke in his 410th game, as the Blue Devils crush Northeastern 103–72.

Feb 14, 1993—Louisville stops UNLV's homecourt winning streak at 59, beating the Runnin' Rebels 90–86. The streak had been the nation's longest.

Feb 23—Ohio State upsets top-ranked Indiana 81–77 in overtime.

Feb 25—Vermont breaks the NCAA Division I women's record for consecutive regular season wins when it gets its 50th straight win, beating Northeastern 50–40.

Feb 28—Lamar sinks 23 three-point shots, an NCAA record, in a 113–76 win over Louisiana Tech.

Mar 6—Georgia upsets the top-ranked Lady Vols of Tennessee, 73–72, in the SEC women's tournament.

Mar 6—Seton Hall beats St. John's 92–73 to finish first in the Big East. Terry Dehere leads the Pirates with 36 points, pushing his Big East career total to 1320 and breaking Chris Mullin's Big East career scoring record.

Mar 8—The Viriginia women's team beats Maryland 106–103 in triple OT to win the ACC title. Vanderbilt, now ranked number one, defeats Georgia 78–64 to win the SEC.

Mar 14—Georgia Tech surprises number one ranked North Carolina 77–75 to win the ACC.

Mar 18—Santa Clara, a 20-point underdog, pulls off one of the biggest upsets in NCAA tournament history, beating Arizona 64–61. It marks the second straight year that the Wildcats have been ousted from the tournament in the first round.

Mar 27—Kansas beats top-seeded Indiana 83–77 to win the Midwest Regional and advance to the Final Four. Also advancing is Kentucky, which wins the Southeast Regional by beating Florida State 106–81.

Mar 28—North Carolina wins the East Regional by beating Cincinnati 75–68 in OT. Also advancing to the Final Four is Michigan, which beats Temple 77–72 to win the West Regional.

Mar 31—Minnesota beats Georgetown 62–61 to win the 56th National Invitational Tournament.

JOHN W. McDONOUGH

Webber (4) starred early, but called a costly timeout.

Apr 2—Shawn Bradley, the 7' 6'' BYU center who has spent the past two years on a Mormon mission to Sydney, Australia, announces that he will enter this year's NBA draft.

Apr 3—In NCAA semifinal games at the Superdome in New Orleans, Michigan beats Kentucky 81–78 and North Carolina tops Kansas 78–68.

Apr 3—Sheryl Swoopes scores 47 points—a championship game record—to lead Texas Tech to an 84–82 win over Ohio State in the NCAA women's final.

Apr 4—North Carolina beats Michigan 77–71 to win the NCAA tournament. Sophomore Donald Williams leads the Tar Heels, scoring 25 points, including five three-pointers. But the game's great drama comes with 11 seconds left when, with Michigan trailing by two points, Chris Webber calls a timeout the Wolverines don't have. Michigan is assessed a technical foul.

College Basketball (Cont.)

Apr 14—The NCAA votes to reduce the shot clock from 45 to 35 seconds and to stop the game clock after a basket in the last minute.

Apr 28—Jim Valvano, who led North Carolina State to the NCAA title in 1983 and more recently has worked as a TV analyst, dies of bone cancer at 47.

May 5—Michigan forward Chris Webber announces that he will enter the NBA draft.

June 8—The University of Kentucky extends Rick Pitino's contract through the 1999—2000 season.

June 30—Chris Webber is the first player chosen in the NBA draft, by the Orlando Magic who immediately trade him to Golden State for Anfernee Hardaway and first round draft picks in 1996, 1998, and 2000. Shawn Bradley is taken second, by Philadelphia, and Hardaway third, by Golden State.

Sept 4—Southern Cal names Cheryl Miller, who led the school to national titles in 1983 and '84, as its new women's basketball coach.

College Football

Nov 5, 1992—The University of Washington suspends Husky quarterback Billy Joe Hobert for the upcoming game against Arizona after learning that Hobert received $50,000 in loans from a friend's father-in-law the previous spring.

Nov 7—After losing its quarterback two days before, Washington loses its unbeaten status, its No. 1 rating and, as becomes clear later, its shot at a national championship, in a 16–3 defeat to Arizona at Tucson. Arizona has knocked off Stanford and Washington and come within a point of Miami. Stanford prevents Southern California from moving into a tie with Washington for first in the PAC-10 with a 23–9 home victory.

Nov 7—Ninth ranked Boston College brings its 7-0-1 record to Notre Dame for its first test of the season on the national stage and suffers its third worst defeat in school history, 54–7.

Nov 10—Quarterback Billy Joe Hobert is declared ineligible to play intercollegiate athletics by the University of Washington after athletic director Barbara Hedges says an investigation determined that the $50,000 in no-interest loans he received from the father-in-law of a friend were improper. The school is later absolved of responsibility in the matter.

Nov 14—San Diego State's Marshall Faulk runs for 300 yards and four touchdowns, breaking out of a four game slump as his team defeats Hawaii 52–28 to delay the 24th-ranked Rainbows' clinching of the Western Athletic Conference title.

Nov 14—The Crimson Tide of Alabama rolls to its 20th consecutive victory with a 30–21 defeat of Mississippi State and clinches a spot in the inaugural Southeastern Conference championship game.

Nov 21—Columbia University wins its second in a row, 34–28, over Brown, for its first two-game winning streak since 1978.

Nov 23—Ron Dickerson becomes the only current African-American head football coach in

Division I-A when Temple University signs him to a five-year contract. The former defensive coordinator at Clemson, Dickerson has his work cut out for him as the Owls have had eight losing seasons in the last 10, including a 1–10 mark this year.

Nov 25—On the eve of his team's annual "bragging rights" showdown with Alabama, Auburn coach Pat Dye resigns, citing poor health and a pending NCAA investigation into his program. Dye's tenure at Auburn included four Southeastern Conference titles but ended with nine charges of rules violations by the NCAA. The next day the Tigers are shut out by Alabama for the first time since 1975, gaining only 20 yards rushing in a 17–0 defeat.

Nov 28—The Miami Hurricanes conclude their second consecutive undefeated regular season and their fourth in the last seven years with a 63–17 rout of San Diego State.

Dec 5—On the strength of Antonio Langham's 26-yard interception return for a touchdown with 3:25 remaining, Alabama wins the Southeastern Conference championship game 28–21 over Florida, to post a 12–0 regular season record and set up a showdown with 11–0, No.1-ranked Miami in the Sugar Bowl.

Dec 10—Alabama coach Gene Stallings, who played for Bear Bryant at Texas A&M and was on his staff at Alabama, wins the Bear Bryant award as the college football coach of the year.

Dec 11—Johnny Majors returns to the head coaching post at Pittsburgh, where he guided teams to three bowl appearances and one national championship from 1973–1976. In November, he learned he'd be ousted after the season from the head coaching position he'd held for 16 years at his alma mater, Tennessee, where he had gone 63-23-5 since 1985.

Dec 12—Miami quarterback Gino Torretta wins the 58th Heisman Trophy as the nation's top college football player. Sophomore running back Marshall Faulk of San Diego State finishes

DAMIAN STROHMEYER

Ward (17) was a shifty opponent in two sports.

second and Georgia junior Garrison Hearst, also a running back, is third.

Dec 12—Jacksonville (AL) State takes the NCAA Division II title with a 17–13 victory over Pittsburg State. Wisconsin-LaCrosse wins the Amos Alonzo Stagg Bowl for the Division III Championship with a 16–12 win over Washington & Jefferson.

Dec 14—Earle Bruce, dismissed Nov. 23 as coach at Colorado State, reaches a contract settlement with the school that will pay him an estimated $110,000 in salary and benefits. The university detailed charges against Bruce of mental and physical abuse of players and NCAA violations after the community rallied around him.

Dec 19—Playing at their home stadium in Huntington, WV, Marshall University overcomes an impressive rally by Youngstown State to win the Division I-AA national championship game by a 31–28 score. Youngstown State comes back from a 28–0 deficit to tie the game late in the fourth quarter, but Marshall wins it on Willy Merrick's 22-yard field goal with 10 seconds left.

Jan 1, 1993—Stanford secures its first 10-victory season in 52 years, beating Penn State 24–3 in the Blockbuster Bowl. In the Cotton Bowl, Notre Dame crushes unbeaten Texas A&M, 28–3, spoiling the Aggies national championship hopes.

Michigan avenges last season's Rose Bowl defeat with a 38–31 win over Washington, and Florida State wins 27–14 over Nebraska in the Orange Bowl. Syracuse takes an exciting 26–22 win from Colorado in the Fiesta Bowl.

Jan 1—Alabama stuns Miami with 14 third quarter points in the Sugar Bowl on the way to a lopsided 34–13 victory, ending the Hurricanes' 29-game winning streak and completing a perfect 13–0–0 season to capture its first national title since 1979.

Apr 3—University of Houston coach John Jenkins resigns amid allegations that there had been violations of NCAA rules, among them rules that limit practice time and others concerning payments to recruits.

May 25—KRIV-TV in Houston reports that two more Texas A & M players—linebacker Jesse Cox and wide receiver Brian Mitchell—will be suspended for taking money for work not performed on summer jobs. That brings to seven the total of A & M players suspended.

May 25—Saying he feels foolish and embarrassed, Stanford coach Bill Walsh apolgizes to the University of Washington for telling a group of Stanford alumni that Washington runs an outlaw football program that does not care for players' academic development.

June 29—Citing health problems, Dick Sheridan, 51, resigns as coach at North Carolina

State, where he had a seven year record of 52-29-3. Sheridan is replaced by Wolfpack quarterback coach Mike O'Cain.

Aug 10—Rutgers quarterback Bryan Fortay files a suit in federal court in Newark, N.J., seeking $10 million from the University of Miami for hurting his chances of a pro career by not keeping a promise to make him a starter.

Aug 18—Auburn University suffers the stiffest penalties imposed on a major football program in years. Among other penalties, Auburn is barred from postseason play for two years and from appearing on television for one. The NCAA's Committee on Infractions found Auburn guilty of six "major" violations, many of them based on a recording made by former Auburn player Eric Ramsey.

Aug 22—Don James, the University of Washington's head football coach for 18 years, angrily quits after the Husky program is found guilty of 15 rules violations and hit with harsh sanctions, including a two-year ban on post season competition. Under James, whose overall record at Washington was 153-57-2, the Huskies won the last three Pac 10 titles. James is replaced by defensive coordinator Jim Lambright.

Aug 28—In the Kickoff Classic at Giants Stadium, top-ranked Florida State shuts out Kansas 42-0.

Aug 28—Former sports agent Lloyd Bloom, whose 1989 conviction for racketeering was eventually reversed, is found murdered in Malibu, Calif. No weapon is found, and there appears to be no forced entry.

Aug 29—In John Robinson's deja vu debut as USC coach, the Trojans fall to North Carolina 31-9 in the Disneyland Pigskin Classic in Anaheim, Calif.

Sep tk—*Under the Tarnished Dome: How Notre Dame Betrayed Its Ideals for Football Glory*, a book about the Fighting Irish football program by Don Yaeger and *Sports Illustrated's* Doug Looney is published. Among the book's allegations are that since 1985, when Lou Holtz became head football coach, there had been widespread

steroid use and callous treatment of players. Notre Dame stands firmly behind Holtz.

Sep 4—San Diego State's Marshall Faulk, the 1992 Heisman Trophy runnerup, opens his season with 170 yards rushing and three TDs in the Aztecs' 34-17 defeat of Cal State-Northridge. One of Faulk's chief rivals for the 1993 Heisman, Florida State quarterback Charlie Ward, passes for 272 yards and two TDs in the Seminoles' 42-7 win over Duke.

Sep 11—Notre Dame upsets Michigan 27-23 in Ann Arbor. Irish quarterback Kevin McDougal leads the way, passing for 208 yards and rushing for another 56. Top-ranked Florida State slams Clemson 57-0.

Sep 25—All around the country, there are brawls in college football. Twelve players are ejected from the Miami-Colorado game, four from both the Maryland-Virginia Tech and Duke-Virginia games, two from the Tennessee-LSU game, and one from the UNC-N.C. State game. In that game two assistant coaches—Ted Cain of N.C. State and Donnie Thompson of North Carolina—are also suspended.

Oct 7—Nebraska beats Oklahoma State 27-13 in Stillwater, Okla., to give Cornhusker coach Tom Osborne his 200th career victory. Among active Division I coaches, only Joe Paterno and Bobby Bowden have more wins than Osborne, whose overall record is now 200-46-3.

Oct 9—Florida State beats Miami 28-10, in Tallahassee. Seminole quarterback Charlie Ward, who by now is the easy leader in the Heisman race, completes 21 of 31 passes for 256 yards and a TD.

Oct 16—Undefeated Auburn shocks Florida 38-35 on Scott Etheridge's 41-yard field goal with 1:21 left to play. That gives Terry Bowden, Bobby's son, a 7-0 start as Auburn's head coach. In other Southeastern Conference action, Alabama and Tennessee play to a 17-17 tie in Tuscaloosa. Elsewhere, Florida State rolls over No. 14 Virginia 40-14.

Golf

Dec 13, 1992—Ray Floyd shoots a final-round 65 to win the Senior Tour Championship by five strokes. Floyd's score of 197 is 19 strokes under par, equalling the Senior Tour record.

Jan 31, 1993—Arnold Palmer sinks a 22-foot birdie putt to win the Senior Skins Game. Palmer claims $190,000 of the $450,000 purse to beat Lee Trevino, Jack Nicklaus and Ray Floyd.

Feb 14—Tom Kite wins the Bob Hope Chrysler Classic, finishing the five rounds in 325, an astonishing PGA-record 35 strokes under par.

Mar 28—Helen Alfredsson of Sweden becomes the first foreign woman since 1988 to win a major when she takes the Nabisco Dinah Shore by two strokes.

JOHN IACONO

Nicklaus won the U.S. Senior Open by a stroke.

Mar 28—Nick Price wins the Tour Players Championship by five strokes over Bernhard Langer.

Apr 11—Bernhard Langer wins his second Masters, shooting an 11-under-par 277 to finish four shots ahead of runner-up Chip Beck.

June 13—Patty Sheehan comes from behind in the final round to win her third LPGA Championship, at Bethesda Country Club, in Bethesda, MD. Sheehan shoots a nine-under-par 275 to finish one stroke ahead of Lauri Merten.

June 20—Lee Janzen outduels Payne Stewart down the stretch to win the 93rd U.S. Open, at Baltusrol Country Club, in Springfield, NJ. In winning his first major Janzen ties two venerable Open records: Jack Nicklaus's low total of 272 and Lee Trevino's four straight rounds in the 60's.

July 12—Jack Nicklaus, 53, wins the U.S. Senior Open by one stroke over Tom Weiskopf. Nicklaus's total of 278 is six under par.

July 18—Greg Norman shoots a final round 64 to win the British Open at Royal St. George's, in Sandwich, England. Norman, whose only other major title was the 1986 British Open, shoots a British Open-record 267 to beat runner-up Nick Faldo by two strokes.

July 25—Lauri Merten wins the U.S. Women's Open with a final-round 68 at Crooked Stick Golf Club, in Carmel, IN. Merten's 280 is eight under par and holds up as several players crumble in the final round.

July 31—Tiger Woods, 17, beats Ryan Armour in 19 holes to win his third consecutive U.S. Junior Amateur title. To do so, Woods survives a dormie situation with two holes left, birdying twice, before claiming the title when his 16-year-old opponent three-putts the 19th hole.

Aug 14—Jill McGill beats Sarah Ingram 1 up to win the U.S. Women's Amateur at San Diego Country Club in Chula Vista, CA.

Aug 15—Paul Azinger wins the 75th PGA championship—his first major—when Greg Norman three putts from 20 feet on the second hole of their playoff. To reach the playoff, Azinger and Norman both shot 12-under-par 272 to beat Nick Faldo by a stroke.

Aug 29—Fulton Allem shoots an amazing 62— eight strokes under par—for the final round to win the NEC World Series of Golf at the Firestone Country Club in Akron, OH.

Aug 29—Brandie Burton, all of 21 years old, beats Betsy King on the first playoff hole to win the du Maurier Classic at the London Hunt and Country Club in London, Ontario. Both players finish regulation at 277, 11 under par.

Aug 29—John Harris defeats Danny Ellis 5 & 3 to win the U.S. Amateur title, at Champions Golf Club, in Houston, TX.

Sept 26—The United States keeps the Ryder Cup, coming from behind in the singles matches to beat Europe 15 to 13 at the Belfry in Sutton Coldfield, England. The Cup is clinched when Ryder Cup rookie Costantino Rocca, a 36-year-old Italian who was still making boxes in a plastics factory at the age of 25, finishes bogey-bogey to lose to Davis Love III.

Hockey

Oct 5, 1992—Mario Lemieux celebrates his 27th birthday by announcing that he has signed a seven-year contract with the Pittsburgh Penguins.

Reportedly worth $42 million, it makes Lemieux the highest paid player in hockey history.

Nov 21—Toronto center Doug Gilmour breaks

Tomas Sandstrom's arm with a two-handed slash. Gilmour is suspended for eight days by NHL president Gil Stein and ordered to forfeit eight days' worth of his salary, or $29,000. But because suspensions for first-time offenders apply only to non-game days, Gilmour misses no games.

Dec 10—The NHL Board of Governors awards conditional expansion franchises to south Florida and Orange County, CA. Blockbuster video magnate H. Wayne Huizenga puts up $50 million to own the Florida Panthers, while Walt Disney Co. spends the same for the as-yet unnamed southern California franchise. On March 1 the Disney team becomes the Mighty Ducks of Anaheim.

Jan 5, 1993—Mario Lemieux plays what turns out to be his last game for eight weeks, as he is first bothered by a sore back and then diagnosed with Hodgkin's disease, a form of cancer.

Feb 1—Gary Bettman, the NBA's former senior vice president and general counsel, takes over as the NHL's first commissioner.

Feb 2—The Toronto Maple Leafs trade goaltender Grant Fuhr and two future draft picks to the Buffalo Sabres for left wing Dave Andreychuk, goalie Daren Puppa and the Sabres' first pick in the 1993 draft.

Feb 6—The Wales Conference beats the Campbell 16–6 in the NHL All-Star Game.

Feb 14—The San Jose Sharks edge the Winnipeg Jets 3–2 to avoid becoming the first team in NHL history to lose 18 straight games. As it is, San Jose's streak of 17 losses equals the league record set by the Washington Capitals in 1974–75.

Mar 2—Mario Lemieux completes his final radiation treatment in the morning in Pittsburgh, then flies to Philadelphia, where that night he scores one goal and assists on another in a 5–4 Penguin loss to the Flyers.

Mar 3—ABC announces that it will carry five Sunday NHL divisional games. They will be the first NHL games (other than the All-Star Game) on network television since 1980.

Mar 5—Pittsburgh goon Ulf Samuelsson hammers injured Mark Messier into the boards with his stick in the second period of the Penguins' 3–1 loss to the Rangers. Messier, who has his sore ribs wrapped in a flak jacket, retaliates, and both players are ejected.

Mar 6—Brett Hull signs a new contract with the St. Louis Blues. He gets $19 million for four years, plus an option fifth year, making him the second highest paid player in the NHL, behind Mario Lemieux.

Mar 10—Norman Green, owner of the Minnesota North Stars, announces that he will move his team to Dallas, starting with the 1993–94 season. The franchise will be known as the Dallas Stars.

Mar 17—The New York Rangers trade center

DAVID E. KLUTHO

The astonishing Lemieux won the scoring title.

Doug Weight to the Edmonton Oilers for defenseman Esa Tikkanen just hours before the two teams play each other in Madison Square Garden.

Mar 23—Teemu Selanne has two goals and an assist in the Winnipeg Jets' 5–4 loss to the Toronto Maple Leafs. Those three points give the Finnish rookie 111 for the season, breaking the rookie record set by Peter Stastny in the 1980–81 season.

Mar 30—The Ottawa Senators tied an 18-year-old NHL record when they lose their 37th straight road game, 6–4 to the Pittsburgh Penguins. The old record was set by the Washington Capitals in their expansion season, 1974–75.

Apr 9—The Pittsburgh Penguins beat the New York Rangers 10–4 for their 16th straight win, a league record. The Penguins run the streak to 17 the next night, when they beat the Rangers again, 4–2.

Apr 12—The New York Rangers, who had the best regular season record in the NHL the previous season, lose to Philadelphia 1–0 and lose their chance of going to the 1993 playoffs.

Apr 13—The Minnesota North Stars play their final game at the Met Center, losing to the Chicago Blackhawks 3–2.

Apr 22—The Pittsburgh Penguins win their 14th straight playoff game, an NHL playoff record, beating the New Jersey Devils 4–3. Three nights later the Devils stop the Penguins' streak, beating them 4–1.

Apr 28—Dale Hunter of the Washington Capitals nails Pierre Turgeon, the New York Islanders' leading scorer, separating his shoulder. Hunter is suspended for 21 games by new NHL commissioner Gary Bettman and loses $150,000 in salary.

May 14—The Los Angeles Kings beat the Vancouver Canucks 5–3 to reach the Campbell Conference finals for the first time.

June 1—Herb Brooks resigns as head coach of the New Jersey Devils, saying only that he wants to explore other opportunites. In Brooks's only season at the helm, the Devils won a franchise record 40 games.

June 1—The Stanley Cup final begins, as the Los Angeles Kings beat the Montreal Canadiens 4–1 in Montreal.

June 1—The Montreal Canadiens beat the Los Angeles Kings 4–1. It is their fourth straight win over the Kings and gives them their 24th Stanley Cup title. Patrick Roy, who made 19 saves in the final game, is awarded the Conn Smythe Trophy as the most valuable player in the playoffs. The postgame celebration turns into a riot, with 168 people injured, 115 arrested and damage done worth an estimated $10 million.

June 15—The Detroit Red Wings name former Penguin coach Scotty Bowman as their new head coach.

June 16—Kevin Constantine is named head coach of the San Jose Sharks. At 34 he is the youngest coach in the NHL.

Roy (center) was named MVP of the Stanley Cup.

June 22—Eddie Johnston is named head coach of the Pittsburgh Penguins.

June 26—Alexandre Daigle, a French Canadien center, is the top player chosen in the NHL draft. He is taken by the Ottawa Senators and given $12.5 million for five years.

June 28—The New Jersey Devils hire Hall of Famer Jacques Lemaire as their new coach.

June 30—Ron Wilson, who has been a Vancouver Canuck assistant coach for the past three seasons, is named the inaugural coach of the Mighty Ducks of Anaheim.

Aug 17—Arnold Burns and L. Yves Fortier, independent counsel appointed by rookie NHL commissioner Gary Bettman, announce that they have found that former NHL president Gil Stein "improperly manipulated the process" in gaining election to the Hall of Fame. Stein announces that he has already decided to withdraw his nomination.

Aug 19—Bruce Firestone, former chairman of the Ottawa Senators, dismisses as "hogwash" allegations that the franchise deliberately lost its final game last season in order to secure the first pick in the NHL draft.

Sept 20—Former league presdient Gil Stein, who has been the center of controversy for the circumstances of his election to the Hall of Fame, announces that he will be resigning his post as special advisor to the commissioner.

Sept 21—Wayne Gretzky, 32, agrees to a three-year, $25.5 million contract with the L.A. Kings that makes him the NHL's highest paid player.

DAVID E. KLUTHO

Horse Racing

Feb 1, 1993—Jockey Kent Desormeaux, 22, wins his third Eclipse Award. Other Eclipse winners are trainer Ron McAnally, breeder William S. Farish III, and A.P. Indy, the 3-year-old colt who later in the week is named 1992 Horse of the Year.

March 6—Sir Beaufort, with Pat Day up, wins the Santa Anita Handicap, beating Star Recruit by a nose.

Apr 3—The Grand National in Aintree, England is declared void after a horribly botched start results in eight horses completing the 4½ mile course, nine others waiting at the start and the rest of the 40 horse field wandering aimlessly around the course. Wagers totalling $115 million must be returned.

March 20—Bull inthe Heather, a 29-to-1 long shot, wins the Florida Derby by two lengths over undefeated favorite Storm Tower.

Apr 11—Prairie Bayou wins the Blue Grass Stakes, beating previously undefeated Dixieland Heat.

May 1—Sea Hero, with Jerry Bailey up, wins the 119th running of the Kentucky Derby by 2½ lengths over the favorite, Prairie Bayou. Sea Hero goes off at 13-to-1. It is Bailey's first triumph in the Run for the Roses, as it is for both 85-year-old owner Paul Mellon and 71-year-old trainer Mack Miller.

May 15—Prairie Bayou, with Mike Smith in the saddle, wins the Preakness Stakes in 1:56⅜, the race's slowest winning time in 25 years. Cherokee Run finishes second by half a length. Union City breaks down on the backstretch and has to be destroyed.

June 2—Commander In Chief wins the English Derby in Epsom by 3½ lengths before a crowd of 250,000.

June 5—Julie Krone becomes the first female jockey to ride a winner in a Triple Crown race, when she guides Colonial Affair to a 2½ length victory in the 125th Belmont Stakes. But tragedy overshadows Krone's achievement as Preakness winner Praire Bayou missteps, breaks several bones in his left leg and has to be destroyed.

July 10—American Winner wins the Yonkers (N.Y.) Trot by 10½ lengths over Armbro Lexicon.

Mellon (left) won the first Derby of his career.

The 3-year-old colt clocks 1:56⅜, a world record for a half-mile track.

Aug 17—Strike Cambest, a 5-year-old pacer, breaks the world mile record by finishing a time trial at the Springfield (IL) Fairgrounds in 1:46¼.

Aug 21—Sea Hero wins the $1 million Travers Stakes, beating runnerup Kissin Kris by two lengths.

Aug 29—Laffit Pincay Jr. gets his 8,000th win aboard El Toreo in the seventh race at Del Mar. Pincay is already the leading career money winner, with $17 million in purses.

Aug 30—Julie Krone takes a bad spill in the third race at Saratoga, breaking her right ankle, cutting her left elbow severely and suffering a bruised heart. After operating on Krone two days later, Dr. Frank Ariosta says she will most likely not ride again for at least six months.

Sept 6—Treacherously's bid for a quarter horse triple crown ends when he finishes third in the All American Futurity at Ruidoso Downs in New Mexico.

Sept 23—Life Sign ends Riyadh's bid to complete the triple crown of pacing, by winning the third leg, the Little Brown Jug, by half a length.

Motor Sports

Nov 15, 1992—Richard Petty drives in the last race of his 35-year career, the Hooters 500. A fiery crash ends his chances of going out a winner.

Nov 25—Bobby Rahal is named 1992 Driver of the Year, beating out NASCAR drivers Davey

Allison and Alan Kulwicki.

Jan 31, 1993—Toyota gets its first win at the 24 Hours of Daytona, averaging 103.503 miles per hour for 698 laps and 2,484.88 miles.

Feb 14—Dale Jarrett uses an inside move on the last lap to pass Dale Earnhardt and win the

GEORGE TIEDEMANN

Mansell made his rookie season on the CART circuit a winner.

Daytona 500. Jarrett's car is owned by Washington Redskin coach Joe Gibbs.

Feb 28—Rusty Wallace dominates the Goodwrench 500 NASCAR race at Rockingham, N.C. Wallace took the lead in his Pontiac on the 275th lap.

Mar 7—Davey Allison wins the Pontiac Excitement 400, averaging a record 107.709 miles per hour in his Texaco/Havoline Ford.

Mar 14—In the opening race of the Formula One season, Alain Prost wins in Johannesburg, South Africa while Michael Andretti's Grand Prix debut ends when he stalls shortly after the start. Prost averages 115.825 miles per hour and finishes the 190.6-mile race in one hour, 38 minutes, 45.082 seconds.

Mar 21—Briton Nigel Mansell wins his first IndyCar race, the FAI Australian Grand Prix. Driving a Lola-Ford, Mansell wins the 65 lap, 181.675-mile race in one hour, 52 minutes, 2.886 seconds at a record average speed of 97.284 miles per hour.

Apr 1—Alan Kulwicki is killed in a private plane crash near Bristol, Tenn.

Apr 11—For the second race in a row, Michael Andretti crashes on the first lap. This time it's the European Grand Prix in Donington, England, which is won by Ayrton Senna.

Apr 25—Rusty Wallace wins his third straight NASCAR race, the Hanes 500 at Martinsville (Va.) Speedway.

May 23—Tim Hensley and Michael Hussey become the first U.S. team in 14 years to win the Camel Trophy for four-wheel drive vehicles, in Borneo.

May 24—Ayrton Senna wins the Monaco Grand Prix for the sixth time, one more than the late Graham Hill did.

May 30—Emerson Fittipaldi wins the Indianapolis 500, the second Indy title of his career.

June 7—Chip Hanauer, driving *Miss Budweiser*, wins a record ninth APBA Gold Cup Unlimited Hydroplane title, on the Detroit River.

June 13—Alain Prost retakes the lead in the Formula One world championship by driving his Williams-Renault to victory in the Canadian Grand Prix, in Montreal.

June 27—Juan Manuel Fangio II, driving a Toyota, wins the Camel Continental X at Watkins Glen, New York, for his six straight IMSA triumph.

July 11—Alain Prost wins the 50th Formula One race of his career, taking the British Grand Prix in Silverstone, England.

July 13—Davey Allison dies the day after the helicopter he is piloting crashes while attempting to land in a parking lot at Talledega Superspeedway in Alabama.

July 25—Dale Earnhardt wins the crash-filled Diehard 500 at Talladega Superspeedway, edging Ernie Irvan by six inches. Stanley Smith is in very critical condition after a seven-car crash that sends Jimmy Horton's Chevrolet up and over the wall and 50 feet down the embankment on the other side.

Aug 1—Nigel Mansell wins the second 500 mile race of his IndyCar career, the Marlboro 500 at Michigan International Speedway. With the win, Mansell regains the IndyCar-PPG Cup points lead from Emerson Fittipaldi, who finished 13th.

Aug 8—Nigel Mansell celebrates his 40th birthday by winning the New England 200 at Loudon, N.H.

Aug 15—Damon Hill, son of the late Graham Hill, becomes the first second generation winner of a Formula One race when he drives his Williams-Renault to victory in the Hungarian Grand Prix in Budapest.

Sept 5—Mark Martin wins his fourth consecutive NASCAR race, the Southern 500, at Darlington International Raceway.

Sept 19—Nigel Mansell clinches the PPG Cup title with a runaway win in the Bosch Spark Plug Grand Prix, in Nazareth, Pa. The 40-year-old Englishman becomes the first rookie in the rookie in the series' 82-year history to win the points championship.

Sept 19—Shelly Anderson becomes the fourth woman in NHRA history to win a national event in the pro category, when she claims the Top Fuel title at the Keystone Nationals in Mohnton, Pa.

Sept 26—Just two days after announcing that this season will be his last, Alain Prost clinches his fourth Formula One title by finishing second in the Portuguese Grand Prix to Michael Schumacher of Germany.

Olympics

March 16, 1993—Atlanta mayor Maynard Jackson announces the signing of an agreement to build a $209 million stadium for the 1996 Olympic Games.

May 11—The USOC announces an expansion of its Operation Gold program. Under the expanded plan athletes who win an Olympic gold medal will earn $15,000, while athletes who win a gold medal in a major championship in a non-Olympic year will get $5,000.

May 12—Needing to raise $1,200 in order to make ends meet, U.S. Olympic kayaker Eric Jackson dons his Olympic uniform, drags his kayak to a busy Washington , D.C. intersection and asks passersby for money.

June 14—The decision-making counsel of the International Skating Union grants reinstatement to all figure skaters who'd sought it for the 1994 Winter Olympics. The ruling makes those skaters eligible to qualify for their country's Olympic team.

June 21—U.S. senator Bill Bradley, who won a gold medal playing basketball for the U.S. in the 1964 Olympics, writes a letter to IOC president Juan Antonio Samaranch urging him to reject Beijing's bid for the 2,000 Olympics.

July 7—The U.S. State Department refuses to grant entry visas to the Libyan delegation hoping to compete in the World University Games in Buffalo.

July 26—By a vote of 287–99, the U.S. House of Representatives passes a resolution opposing Beijing's bid for the 2,000 Olympics.

July 27—NBC pays $456 million for the television rights to the 1996 Olympics.

Sept 23—Sydney, Australia, is awarded the 2000 Summer Olympics, tallying the required 45 votes on the fourth ballot. Beijing, the candidacy of which had caused controversy for months, finishes second with 43 votes after leading Sydney on each of the first three ballots.

Pro Basketball

Nov 2, 1992—Magic Johnson retires for a second time just four days before he is scheduled to resume his NBA career. His decision is apparently the result of increasingly vocal concern by other NBA players about their chances of contracting the disease from him.

Nov 12—Alonzo Mourning ends his holdout and signs a six-year deal with the Charlotte Hornets worth $26 million.

Nov 20—The Detroit Pistons suspend forward Dennis Rodman without pay for an indefinite period for his failure to rejoin the team after he getting medical clearance to play.

Dec 8—Dominique Wilkins of the Atlanta Hawks sinks 23 free throws without a miss, an NBA record, in Atlanta's 123–114 defeat of Chicago.

Jan 25, 1993—Salt Lake City police confirm that they are investigating allegations of possible sexual misconduct by members of the Portland Trail Blazers. The incident involved three "underaged females" who attended a party at the downtown Marriott Hotel.

Feb 21—The West wins the NBA All-Star game 135–132 in Salt Lake City, as Utah Jazz teammates Karl Malone and John Stockton share MVP honors.

Feb 22—The Seattle SuperSonics trade center Benoit Benjamin and the rights to unsigned first-round draft pick Doug Christie to the Los Angeles Lakers for veteran forward Sam Perkins.

Feb 23—Officials of Japan's women's pro league announce a ban on foreign players, putting more than 30 U.S. players out of a job.

Mar 1—New Jersey Net Kenny Anderson is placed on the injured list after he breaks a bone in his left hand following a flagrant foul by the Knicks' John Starks. The Nets initially think they've lost their point guard for two weeks, but in the end he's gone for the season.

Mar 4—The Dallas Mavericks, 4–50 this season, make two big moves. They hire Quinn Buckner as their new coach and finally sign their top draft pick, Jim Jackson.

Mar 7—The Philadelphia 76ers fire coach Doug Moe, who had coached the team to a 19–37 record this season. Moe is replaced by one of his assistants, Fred Carter.

May 1—The Phoenix Suns and New York Knicks have a bench-clearing brawl in the Suns' 121–92 rout of the Knicks. Twenty-one players are fined a total of $160,500, the second largest amount ever imposed. Knick Greg Anthony is fined the most ($20,500) and is suspended for five days. Anthony's teammate Doc Rivers is suspended for two games, as is Kevin Johnson of Phoenix.

Apr 2—Cleveland guard Mark Price hits seven straight free throws against Charlotte to tie Calvin Murphy's NBA record of 78 consecutive free throws made, then misses the shot that would have broken the record.

Apr 8—Miami guard Brian Shaw makes 10 three pointers, an NBA single-game record, in the Heat's 117–92 defeat of Milwaukee.

Apr 25—Minnesota's Micheal Williams is 10 of 10 from the line to run his streak of successful free throws to 84, six more than Calvin Murphy's NBA

record. Since this is the Timberwolves' final game of the season, Williams will have to wait until next season to add to it.

Apr 29—Boston forward Reggie Lewis collapses during the Celtics' opening playoff game, against the Charlotte Hornets. Tests reveal cardiac abnormalities and it is decided that Lewis will not play the rest of the season.

May 2—The surprising Los Angeles Lakers take their second straight playoff game from the Phoenix Suns, 86–81.

May 6—Orlando center Shaquille O'Neal is named NBA Rookie of the Year, receiving 96 of 98 first place votes.

May 9—The Phoenix Suns make history by becoming the first team to lose two playoff games at home and then come back to win three straight. They do it the hard way, trailing the pesky Lakers by four points with a minute to play before pulling out the game 112–104 in OT.

May 10—Julius Erving leads this year's class of inductees to the Basketball Hall of Fame in Springfield, Mass. Also going in are Bill Walton, Walt Bellamy, Dan Issel, Dick McGuire, Calvin Murphy, Ann Meyers and Ulyana Semenova.

May 10—Reggie Lewis is cleared to resume his NBA career by doctors who conclude that the neural condition he suffers from—in which the nerves become confused trying to signal the heart to speed up or slow down—can be treated by medication.

May 17—New York Knick coach Pat Riley edges Houston's Rudy Tomjanovich 32–31 in voting for NBA coach of the year. It is the closest vote in the award's 31-year history.

May 20—Peripatetic coach Larry Brown resigns as coach of the Los Angeles Clippers with two years remaining on his contract.

May 23—For the second straight year the Orlando Magic win the top pick in the NBA lottery.

May 25—Phoenix forward Charles Barkley is named the NBA's most valuable player, receiving 59 of 98 first places votes. Hakeem Olajuwon of

MANNY MILLAN

O'Neal (right) made a colossal impact on the NBA as a rookie.

Houston finishes second, Michael Jordan third.

May 24—Michael Jordan, his father and some friends travel by limousine from New York City to Atlantic City. They depart the casinos, depending on whom you believe, either late on the night of the 24th or early the morning of the 25th. In any case, the Knicks beat the Bulls convincingly in the first two games of their series, and Jordan, infuriated by questions about the trip, clams up.

June 1—Phoenix guard Dan Majerle hits eight three pointers—several from two or three steps behind the line—to lead the Suns to a 120–114 win over Seattle in the fifth game of the Western Conference finals.

June 3—Richard Esquinas, a San Diego businessman, claims that Michael Jordan lost $1.252 million over 10 days golfing with Esquinas in 1991. Jordan admits knowing Esquinas but denies the amounts.

June 4—The Chicago Bulls beat the New York Knicks 96–88 to win the Eastern Conference finals four games to two.

June 5—The Phoenix Suns finally dispose of the surprising Seattle SuperSonics 123–110 in the seventh game of the Western Conference finals.

June 7—Larry Brown is named coach of the Indiana Pacers, the fifth NBA team he has coached.

June 7—New Jersey Net guard Drazen Petrovic, 28, is killed in a car accident outside Munich, Germany, where he has been playing for Croatia in the qualifying tournament for the European basketball championship.

June 13—The Phoenix Suns, in one of the longest games in NBA finals history, beat the Chicago Bulls 129–121 in triple overtime. Dan Majerle hits six three pointers for Phoenix to tie an NBA finals single game record. The Suns now trail the Bulls by two games to one.

June 16—Michael Jordan scores 55 points in leading the Bulls to a 111–105 win and a three games to one lead over Phoenix.

June 20—The Chicago Bulls beat the Phoenix Suns 99–98 to win their third straight NBA title, a feat that had not been accomplished since the Boston Celtics won eight championships in a row

from 1959 to 1966. For a record third straight time, Michael Jordan is named MVP, rising above a maelstrom of controversy to average an NBA-record 41 points over the six games.

June 30—At the NBA draft the Orlando Magic use the top pick to take Chris Webber, then trade him almost immediately to Golden State for Anfernee Hardaway and three future first round picks. Philadelphia, picking second, chooses Shawn Bradley.

July 19—Toni Kukoc, the 6' 11" Croatian who can play both inside and out, signs a multiyear contract with the Chicago Bulls for an undisclosed amount.

July 27—Boston Celtic captain Reggie Lewis dies after collapsing while shooting baskets at Brandeis University. Lewis was 27.

Aug 12—James Jordan, Michael Jordan's father, is reported missing when his car is found stripped about 10 miles outside Fayetteville, N.C. The following day a body that had been discovered on August 3rd is identified as James Jordan's.

Aug 15—Funeral services are held for James Jordan. Police arrest two 18-year-olds, Larry Martin Demery and Daniel Andre Green, and charge them with first degree murder.

Sept 21—Turner Broadcasting announces a new $352 million, four-year deal with the NBA.

Sept 30—The NBA's expansion committee votes to place the league's 28th franchise in Toronto. The franchise, which will be the first based outside the U.S., is headed by Toronto businessman John Bitove.

Oct 5—Michael Jordan throws out the first ball in the American League Championship Series between Chicago and Toronto amid rumors that he will announce his retirement the next day. He makes it official the next morning.

Oct 5—Larry Johnson signs a 12-year contract with the Charlotte Hornets guaranteeing him $84 million. Two days later rookie Anfernee Hardaway signs a 13-year deal with the Golden State Warriors worth $68 million.

Pro Football

Nov 1, 1992—The Pittsburgh Steelers improve to 6–2 and complete a regular-season sweep over the Houston Oilers as Al Del Greco's 39-yard field goal attempt with six seconds remaining misses wide left and the Steelers cling to a 21–20 lead. The 1–6 Phoenix Cardinals upset the San Francisco 49ers 24–14 in Sun Devil Stadium, the site of their 23-point comeback win over the 49ers

in 1988. The San Diego Chargers win their fourth straight, 26–0 over the Colts, after dropping four to start the year.

Nov 8—All-Pro N.Y. Giants linebacker Lawrence Taylor ruptures his Achilles' tendon during a 27–7 home victory over Green Bay and declares that his career is over. By Monday, however, Taylor moderates this statement, saying he hasn't decided whether or not to retire.

Nov 15—Hit after a five-yard scramble that sets up a game-winning score, Houston quarterback Warren Moon breaks his left arm and is lost to his team for five games. It is the third consecutive week that Moon is injured and replaced by backup Cody Carlson.

Nov 15—Steve Young throws an eight-yard touchdown pass to tight end Brent Jones with 46 seconds remaining to lift the 49ers to a 21–20 victory against the New Orleans Saints and a sweep of the season series against the Saints.

Nov 16—Buffalo recovers from a 14–3 deficit to defeat Miami 26–20 at Joe Robbie Stadium and even the season series between the AFC East rivals. The win gives them the division lead by one game over the Dolphins.

Nov 23—The injury-plagued defending champion Washington Redskins drop to 6–5 with a 20–3 defeat at New Orleans. It is their third loss in the past four games and the fifth consecutive week in which they've failed to score an offensive touchdown in the first half.

Nov 27—Citing the advice of "a million doctors" in the wake of, by his count, the ninth concussion of his career, suffered on Nov. 8 against Denver, N.Y. Jets wide receiver Al Toon announces his retirement after eight seasons in the league.

Nov 29—New York Jets defensive lineman Dennis Byrd fractures his fifth vertebra in a full-speed collision with teammate Scott Mersereau. The injury leaves him partially paralyzed. Already this season almost 500 NFL players have been hurt seriously enough to miss at least one game.

Nov 29—Led by quarterback and game-MVP Doug Flutie's 480 passing yards, the Calgary Stampeders win the Canadian Football League's Grey Cup, 24–10, over the Winnepeg Blue Bombers, in the Toronto SkyDome.

Nov 29—Pittsburgh's Barry Foster breaks Franco Harris's club records for yards rushing and yards from scrimmage in a season when he rushes for 102 yards in the Steelers 21–9 victory against Cincinnati. It is his ninth 100-yard game of the year, two more than the previous franchise record, also set by Harris.

Dec 6—San Francisco wide receiver Jerry Rice sets a career mark for touchdown receptions, besting Steve Largent with his 101st scoring catch—a 12-yarder from Steve Young in the fourth quarter of a 27–3 drowning of the Miami Dolphins.

Dec 6—Dedicating the game to defensive lineman Dennis Byrd who suffered a broken neck in the previous week's game, the New York Jets defeat the heavily-favored Buffalo Bills, 24–17 in Buffalo.

JOHN BIEVER

Smith won his second straight rushing crown.

The victory stops the Jets 10-game losing streak against the Bills dating to 1987.

Dec 20—With a 36–14 triumph over the Raiders in Los Angeles, the San Diego Chargers (10–5) become the first team in league history to make the playoffs after starting 0–4.

Dec 27—The Buffalo Bills lose quarterback Jim Kelly, the AFC East title and critical home-field advantage through the playoffs in their last regular-season game, a 27–3 loss to Houston in the Astrodome.

Dec 27—Emmitt Smith gains 131 yards in the Dallas Cowboys' 27–14 win against Chicago to become the ninth player to win consecutive NFL rushing titles, besting Pittsburgh's Barry Foster by 23 yards. His 1,713 yards break Tony Dorsett's club record of 1,646, set in 1981. The Cowboys' 13 wins are a franchise regular season record. By contrast, the Bears' 5–11 record makes this their worst full season since 1973. The game is the last for two great Bears: veteran linebacker Mike Singletary, who retired after playing 12 years for Chicago, and Mike Ditka, who will be relieved of his duties nine days later after 11 stormy seasons as the Chicago coach.

Dec 27—Sterling Sharpe makes six catches to bring his season total to an NFL-record 108, two more than the previous record set by Art Monk. Unfortunately for the Green Bay faithful, the Packers lose the game, 27–7 to the Minnesota Vikings, and are eliminated from playoff contention.

Dec 28—After leading Denver to three Super Bowl appearances in 12 years, Broncos coach Dan Reeves is dismissed. Wade Phillips is hired on Jan. 25 to fill the vacancy. Reeves is tabbed Jan. 26 by the N.Y. Giants to succeed Ray Handley, who is let go on Dec. 30.

Jan 3, 1993—In the greatest comeback in NFL history, the Buffalo Bills recover from a seemingly insurmountable 35–3 third quarter deficit to snatch a dramatic 41–38 overtime victory from the Houston Oilers in the AFC wild-card playoff game.

Jan 5—Chicago favorite Mike Ditka is dismissed as head coach by the Bears after a 5–11 season. Dallas Cowboy defensive coordinator Dave Wannstedt becomes his successor on Jan. 19.

Jan 10—In divisional playoffs, the 49ers beat the Redskins 20–13, and the Bills down Pittsburgh 24–3.

Jan 11—Miami shuts out San Diego 31–0, and Dallas blitzes Philadelphia 34–10 to complete the final four.

Jan 17—The Buffalo Bills defeat the Miami Dolphins 29–10 in Joe Robbie Stadium to win their third straight AFC championship, and the Dallas Cowboys surprise the San Francisco 49ers at Candlestick Park by a 30–20 score to reach the Super Bowl just three years after going a woeful 1–15.

Jan 31—The Dallas Cowboys hand the Buffalo Bills a record-setting third straight Super Bowl loss with a 52–17 shellacking in Super Bowl XXVII in Pasadena, Calif. Cowboy quarterback Troy Aikman throws for 273 yards and four TDs and is named the game's MVP.

Feb 25—In an NFL strategy to offset the vagaries created by free agency, ten teams designate their "franchise players." Among the players designated are 49er quarterback Steve Young, San Diego defensive end Leslie O'Neal and Redskin linebacker Wilbur Marshall.

Mar 5—The New York Giants sign quarterback Phil Simms, 37, to a two-year contract worth $5,050,000.

Mar 5—Citing health and personal reasons, Joe Gibbs retires after 12 seasons as coach of the Washington Redskins. Redskin defensive coordinator Richie Petitbon replaces him.

Mar 8—John Elway signs a four-year-contract worth $20 million with the Denver Broncos, making him the NFL's highest paid player. But free agency is clearly enriching the players in the trenches too. The Minnesota Vikings sign offensive lineman Brian Habib to a three-year deal worth $4.2 million, the most ever paid to an offensive lineman.

Mar 10—U.S. District Judge David Doty rejects an appeal by Washington Redskin linebacker Wilbur Marshall to drop the "franchise player" category from the NFL's new free agency system.

Mar 17—Boomer Esiason becomes a New York Jet when Cincinnati trades him away for two draft picks, a No. 3 and a conditional No. 2.

Mar 22—The NFL formally awards Super Bowl XXX, to be played Jan. 28, 1996, to Phoenix.

Mar 23—At league meetings in Palm Desert, Calif., NFL owners do the following: decide to add two teams; vote to allow teams to carry 53 players, with 45 of them eligible to play each week; cut the interval between plays from 45 to 40 seconds; and reject a proposal to move the kickoff from the 35-yard line to the 30-yard line to encourage more runbacks.

Mar 28—Salary offers to offensive lineman continue to escalate, as Indianapolis signs former Minnesota center Kirk Lowdermilk to a three-year deal worth $6 million, and the following day sign Buffalo tackle Will Wolford to a three-year deal worth $7.65 million.

Mar 31—The Cleveland Browns sign free agent quarterback Vinny Testaverde.

Apr 6—Reggie White, the former Philadelphia Eagle All-Pro defensive end, signs a four-year, $17 million contract with the Green Bay Packers.

Apr 12—Lawrence Taylor ends his brief retirement, signing a two-year, $5.05 million contract with the New York Giants.

Apr 20—The San Francisco 49ers trade quarterback Joe Montana, safety David Whitemore and a 1994 third round draft pick to the Kansas City Chiefs for a first round pick in the NFL draft.

May 6—The NFL and its players' union agree to a seven-year contract, six years after the last one expires.

May 24—NFL owners extend commissioner Paul Tagliabue's contract through May 31, 2000.

May 25—The NFL sets $140 million as the price for an expansion franchise.

June 9—Marcus Allen signs a three-year contract with the Kansas City Chiefs worth a reported $4.5 million.

July 6—The New England Patriots sign Drew Bledsoe, the No. 1 pick in the NFL draft, to a contract worth nearly $15 million over six years.

July 14—San Francisco 49er quarterback Steve Young signs the richest contract in the NFL, a five-year deal worth $26.75 million.

July 21—Thurman Thomas signs a four-year contract with the Buffalo Bills worth $13.5 million, making him the highest paid running back in the league.

Pro Football *(Cont.)*

July 26—The Canadian Football League announces that it will field an expansion franchise in Las Vegas for the 1994 season.

Aug 30—Raghib Ismail, the receiver/returner who played the last two years with the Toronto Argonauts of the CFL, signs a two-year, $3 million contract with the Los Angeles Raiders.

Sep 12—Dan Marino throws for 286 yards in the Miami Dolphins' 24–14 home loss to the New York, making him the fourth NFL quarterback to top 40,000 yards, with 40,024. Morten Andersen of the New Orleans Saints sets an NFL record by kicking his 25th straight field goal, a 27-yarder in the first quarter of a 34–31 defeat of the Atlanta Falcons.

Sep 16—Emmitt Smith signs a four-year, $13.6 million deal with the Cowboys and thus replaces Thurman Thomas as the NFL's highest paid running back.

Sep 19—San Diego Charger kicker John Carney is successful on all six of his field goal attempts—as he was the previous week—to

break Morten Andersen's NFL record for consecutive field goal conversions. Carney's six give him 29.

Oct 3—The Philadelphia Eagles lose quarterback Randall Cunningham to a broken left fibula in the Eagles' 35–30 win over the New York Jets.

Oct 10—The Miami Dolphins lose quarterback Dan Marino when he tears his right Achilles tendon in Miami's 24–14 win at Cleveland. The injury ends Marino's streak of 145 straight starts.

Oct 17—The New Orleans Saints are the last team this season to fall from the ranks of the undefeated, losing to the Steelers 37–14.

Oct 22—The NFL owners award an expansion franchise to Charlotte, North Carolina. The team, which will begin play in 1995, will be known as the Carolina Panthers. The Panthers will play home games in Clemson, S.C., for one season.

Tennis

Nov 22, 1992—Monica Seles beats Martina Navratilova 7–5, 6–3, 6–1 to win the Virginia Slims Championships.

Nov 22—Boris Becker beats Jim Courier 6–4, 6–3, 7–5 to win the ATP Tour World Championship.

Dec 6—Jim Courier beats Jakob Hlasek of Switzerland 6–3, 3–6, 6–3, 6–4 to clinch the Davis

Graf won three majors, including the U.S. Open.

Cup for the United States. The team score is 3–1.

Dec 15—*Sports Illustrated* names Arthur Ashe its Sportsman of the Year for 1992.

Jan 1, 1993—At the start of the year Jim Courier and Monica Seles are the number-one ranked men's and women's players in the world.

Jan 30—Monica Seles defeats Steffi Graf 4–6,

6–3, 6–2 to win the Australian Open for the third straight year.

Jan 31—Jim Courier successfully defends his men's title at the Australian Open by beating Stefan Edberg 6–2, 6–1, 2–6, 7–5.

Feb 6—Arthur Ashe dies of AIDS-related pneumonia, at 49.

Feb 21—Martina Navratilova beats Monica Seles 6–3, 4–6, 7–6 (7–3) at the Paris Open to become—at 36 years, three months and 29 days—the oldest person to beat a number-one ranked player.

Feb 24—Kraft General Foods, one of the major sponsors of women's pro tennis, announces that it will discontinue its support after the 1994 season. On Sept. 16 it is announced that Kraft will relinquish its sponsorship even earlier, at the end of the 1993 season.

Feb 24—Tracy Austin upsets second-seeded Katerina Maleeva 6–2, 2–6, 6–3 in the second round of the Matrix Essentials Evert Cup. It is the first time since 1983 that Austin has beaten a top player.

Mar 28—The United States suffers the ignominy of becoming the first Davis Cup defender to lose in the first round, when Australia beats the U.S. 4–1.

April 30—Monica Seles is stabbed in the back by an unemployed German lathe worker named Günter Parche during a change over in her match with Magdalena Maleeva at the Citizen Cup tournament in Hamburg, Germany. Parche's nine-inch serrated boning knife barely misses Seles's spinal cord, but does tear muscle, doing what turns out to be more damage than originally thought. Seles spends two nights in Hamburg's Eppendorf Hospital before returning to the United States. She spends most of the year in seclusion and Parche achieves his sick aim: Graf replaces her atop the rankings.

June 1—Jim Pierce, father of number-12 seed Mary Pierce, is removed from the stands at the French Open and his credentials are confiscated.

June 5—Steffi Graf, who has replaced Monica Seles as the top-ranked woman player by beating Anke Huber in the semis, defeats Mary Joe Fernandez 4–6, 6–2, 6–4 to win the French Open.

June 6—In a huge upset, Sergi Bruguera of Spain, the number 10 seed, beats two-time defending champion Jim Courier 6–4, 2–6, 6–2, 3–6, 6–3 to win the French Open.

June 17—Citing its "dishonorable or unprofessional conduct" rule, the Women's Tennis Council votes unanimously to bar Jim Pierce, the father of ranked pro Mary Pierce, from the remaining tournaments on the 1993 Kraft Tour.

July 3—Steffi Graf retains her Wimbledon singles title, beating Jana Novotna 7–6 (8–6), 1–6, 6–4.

July 4—Pete Sampras defeats Jim Courier 7–6 (7–3), 7–6 (8–6), 3–6, 6–3 to win his first Wimbledon title.

July 25—Spain wins the Federation Cup, defeating Australia 3–0 in the final, in Frankfurt, Germany.

Sept 11—Steffi Graf beats Helena Sukova 6–3, 6–3 to win the U.S. Open.

Sept 12—Pete Sampras defeats Frenchman Cedric Pioline 6–4, 6–4, 6–3 to win the U.S. Open. In doing so, Sampras regains the No. 1 ranking he'd lost to Jim Courier in August.

Sept 29—Martina Navratilova, 36, announces that the 1994 season will be her last.

Oct 4—John McEnroe withdraws as a candidate to replace Tom Gorman as captain of the U.S. Davis Cup team, citing "personal considerations."

Oct 12—Tom Gullikson is named the U.S. Davis Cup captain for 1994.

Other Sports

Nov 28, 1992—Just five days after winning the NCAA cross country title, Indiana University senior Bob Kennedy wins the U.S. cross country title, coming from behind to nip Todd Williams at the finish. Kennedy is the first person to win both the collegiate and open national titles since Al Lawrence did it in 1960. Lynn Jennings wins her seventh straight U.S. title, her eighth overall.

Nov 29—Julie Parisien of the U.S. wins the slalom at the opening race of the World Cup season, in Park City, Utah.

Dec 3—Judge Joseph Kinneary of the U.S. District Court in Columbus, Ohio, awards Butch Reynolds $27.3 million in his suit against the IAAF, $6.8 million of it in lost earnings and the remainder

in punitive damages for the body's "malice" in its handling of Reynolds's drug suspension.

Dec 6—The University of Virginia Cavaliers beat the University of San Diego Toreros 2–0 to win their second straight NCAA men's soccer title. Though Nate Friends and Erik Imler score the two Cavalier goals, their teammate Claudio Reyna is named offensive MVP.

Dec 13—Benson Masya of Kenya wins the Honolulu Marathon in 2:14:19, while 40-year-old Carla Beurskens of the Netherlands takes the women's race in 2:32:13.

Dec 13—Rai scores twice to lead Sao Paulo to a 2–1 win over FC Barcelona in the Toyota Cup final, matching the top European club against the top South American club.

Jan 24, 1993—The U.S. Figure Skating Championships come to a close in Phoenix. Scott Davis is the men's champion, Nancy Kerrigan the ladies'.

Jan 24—Addis Abebe wins $500,000 for breaking the world 10K road record at the Bob Hasan 10K in Jakarta, Indonesia. Abebe, a 22-year-old Ethiopian, clocked 27:40, one second under Arturo Barrios's seven-year-old world best.

Feb 1—Marco Van Basten of the Netherlands and AC Milan is named FIFA World Player of the Year for 1992.

Feb 10—At the World Alpine Championships in Morioka-Shizukuishi, Japan, where the weather conditions are atrocious, Kjetil-Andre Aamodt of Norway picks up his second gold medal, this one for the Giant Slalom.

Feb 11—AJ Kitt of the U.S. wins the bronze medal in the downhill at the World Alpine Championships.

Feb 14—Hungarian chess prodigy Judit Polgar beats former world champion Boris Spassky when they agree to a draw in their ninth game.

Feb 14—Falko Zandstra of the Netherlands wins the world speedskating title, beating Ohann Olav Koss in front of his home crowd in Hamar, Norway.

Feb 15—Demer Holleran wins her fifth national title at the U.S. National Hardball Squash Rackets Championship in Philadelphia. Hector Barragan wins his fourth men's title.

Feb 21—Sergei Bubka pole vaults a world record 20' 2" in his hometown of Donetsk, the Ukraine. It is the 34th world record of Bubka's career.

Feb 26—Forty-year-old Eamonn Coghlan of Ireland runs the mile in 4:01.39 at the U.S. Indoor Championships in Madison Square Garden to break his own world master's (40+) record.

Feb 27—Ron Palombi Jr. bowls a 237 to beat Eugene McCune and win the PBA National Championship.

Mar 5—Canadian sprinter Ben Johnson is suspended from track and field for life after testing positive for testosterone at an indoor meet in Montreal.

Mar 6—Walter Ray Williams Jr. defeats Ron Williams 214–193 at the PBA Flagship City Open. It is the first bowling tournament Williams has won in the U.S. in six years.

Mar 7—Joseildo Rocha of Brazil wins the Los

SIMON BRUTY/ALLSPORT

Parisien won the opening slalom of the World Cup season.

Angeles Marathon in 2:14:29. The women's race is won by Lubov Klochko of the Ukraine, in 2:39:49.

Mar 8—Speedskater Bonnie Blair, who won gold medals in the 500- and 1,000-meter events at the 1992 Winter Olympics in Albertville, France, is given the Sullivan Award as America's top amateur athlete of 1992.

Mar 10—Canada's Isabelle Brasseur and Lloyd Eisler end nine years of Russian domination when they win the pairs title at the World Figure Skating Championships in Prague.

Mar 11—Kurt Browning of Canada wins the men's title at the World Figure Skating Championships.

Mar 12—Gail Devers of the U.S. beats world record holder Irina Privalova of Russia in the 60-meter dash at the World Indoor Track and Field Championships, in Toronto. Her time of 6.95 seconds is an American record.

Mar 13—Fifteen-year-old Oksana Baiul of the Ukraine wins the ladies' title at the World Figure Skating Championships. The top American, Nancy Kerrigan, finishes fifth.

Mar 13—The Arkansas Razorback men's track and field team wins its 10th straight NCAA indoor championship, an NCAA Division I record for consecutive national titles. LSU takes the women's crown.

Mar 14—Butch Reynolds wins the 400 meters in 45.26 at the World Indoor Track and Field Championships, in Toronto, and also anchors the U.S.'s victorious 4 x 400 team. Dan O'Brien sets a world record in the heptathlon, with 6,476 points.

Mar 14—Dan Jansen of the U.S. clinches the 500-meter World Cup speed-skating title in Heerenveen, the Netherlands. Qiaobo Ye of China takes the women's 500-meter title, edging Bonnie Blair of the U.S.

Mar 14—The U.S. men's soccer team loses to Japan 3–1 in the Kirin Cup, extending to seven the U.S.'s winless streak.

Mar 17—Jeff King of Denali, Alaska, sets a record in winning the Iditarod Trail Sled Dog Race, his time of 10 days, 15 hours and 38 minutes easily beating the mark set last year by Martin Buser. Runnerup DeeDee Jonrowe and third place finisher Rick Mackey also beat Buser's record.

Mar 20—The University of Iowa Hawkeyes win their third straight—and 14th overall—NCAA wrestling title. Iowa's 123.75 points tops Penn State (87.50). Hawkeye Terry Steiner is named the tournament's outstanding wrestler, beating Troy Sunderland 8–7 in the 150-pound class.

Mar 20—Stanford successfully defends its NCAA Division I women's swimming and diving championship, topping runner-up Florida 649.5 to 421. The Division III title goes to Kenyon for the 14th straight time.

Mar 21—Parma scores a shocking 1–0 win over AC Milan in Rome, ending the longest undefeated streak in Italian soccer league history at 58 games.

Mar 27—Stanford repeats as the NCAA Division I men's swimming and diving champion.

Mar 28—Anita Wachter of Austria wins the overall World Cup women's skiing title, at Are, Sweden.

Mar 28—William Sigei of Kenya wins the world cross country title, covering the 7.3-mile course in Amorbieta, Spain, in 32:51. Four of his Kenyan teammates follow him over the line, giving the Kenyan men the team victory with just 25 points, leaving runnerup Ethiopia far behind, with 82. It is the Kenyan men's eighth straight win. Albertina Dias of Portugal wins the women's race by nine seconds over Catherina McKiernan of Ireland. U.S. champ Lynn Jennings finishes third.

Apr 3—The Black Bears of the University of Maine score three third-period goals to beat defending champion Lake Superior State 5–4 in the NCAA men's ice hockey championship. Assists on two of those goals came from Maine freshman Paul Kariya who the day before had been given the Hobey Baker Award as college hockey's top player.

Apr 3—Janet Evans wins her third event, the 1500-meter freestyle, at the U.S. Indoor Swimming Championships, in Nashville. The win gives the 21-year-old Evans her 33rd national title, placing her third on the alltime list behind Tracy Caulkins

and Johnny Weismuller. The meet's high point scorer is Jenny Thompson with 77 points.

Apr 6—Swimmer Matt Biondi, who won eight gold medals in his Olympic career, retires.

Apr 9—The U.S. men's soccer team ends its winless streak at 10 games, beating Saudi Arabia 2–0 on second-half goals by Joe-Max Moore and Janusz Michallik.

Apr 10—Del Ballard Jr. wins the BPAA U.S. Open, rolling a 237 in the final to top Walter Ray Williams Jr.'s 193.

Apr 10—The Buffalo Bandits beat the Philadelphia Wings 13–12 for the Major Indoor Lacrosse League title.

Apr 12—Jeff Rouse sets a world record in the short-course 100-meter backstroke, clocking 51.43 at the Optrex World Challenge in Sheffield.

Apr 16—Shannon Miller wins the all-around title at the world gymnastics championships, in Birmingham, England.

Apr 18—Katrin Dorre of Germany pulls off a small upset in the London Marathon, her winning time of 2:27:09 beating pre-race favorites Lisa Ondieki (2:27:27) and Liz McColgan (2:29:37). Eamonn Martin wins the men's race in 2:10:50.

Apr 19—Unknown Kenyan Cosmas N'Deti comes from way back to win the 97th Boston Marathon in 2:09:33. Olga Markova repeats as women's champion, winning easily in 2:25:27.

Apr 20—*Commodore Explorer*, an 85-foot French catamaran skippered by Bruno Peyron, sets a world record for sailing around the world,

Speedskater Blair won the 1992 Sullivan Award.

MANNY MILLAN

finishing the global circuit in 79 days, 6 hours, and 16 minutes to win the Trophee Jules Verne.

Apr 21— Carrie Zarse wins her first national diving title, edging Mary Ellen Clark in the women's one-meter springboard at the U.S. diving championships in Austin, Texas. Clark comes back to successfully defend her platform title. Russ Bertram takes the men's platform title.

Apr 24—George Branham III becomes the first black bowler to win a PBA triple crown event, when he beats Parker Bohn III 227–214 to win the Tournament of Champions.

Apr 28—Seventeen members of the Zambian national soccer team die when their team plane crashes into the Atlantic Ocean off the coast of Gabon. All 30 people on board die in the crash.

Apr 28—England and the Netherlands play to a 1–1 draw in a World Cup qualifying match in London. Elsewhere, Ireland ties European champion Denmark 1–1 in Dublin, Portugal whips Scotland 5–0 and Russia beats Hungary 3–0.

May 1—Bruce Baumgartner wins his 11th consecutive national title, beating Joel Greenlee 6–0 in the 286-pound division at the U.S. National Wrestling Championships, in Las Vegas.

May 5—The Canisius softball team beats Niagara 11–1 for its 34th consecutive win, an NCAA Division I record. Central (Iowa) wins boths ends of a doubleheader with Wartburg (Iowa) to set a Division III record for consecutive wins, with 28.

May 6—Simona Koch wins the one-meter springboard title at the Alamo International diving meet in Fort Lauderdale.

May 9—Mexico becomes the first country to play into the 1994 World Cup soccer field by beating Canada 2–1 in Toronto.

May 9—Lan Wei of China scores the only perfect "10" of the Alamo International diving championships on her way to winning the three-meter springboard title.

May 15—Sheffield Wednesday midfielder John Harkes becomes the first American to play in an FA Cup final, setting up David Hirst's tying goal in Wednesday's 1–1 draw with Arsenal.

May 16—Raul Alcala of Mexico wins the Tour DuPont in dramatic fashion, winning the final stage—a 36.5-mile time trial—to beat Lance Armstrong of the U.S. in the overall standings by 2:26.

May 16—Virginia wins the NCAA women's lacrosse title, beating Princeton 8–6 in overtime.

May 16—Texas upsets Stanford 5–2 to win the NCAA women's tennis title.

May 20—Lisa Raymond of the University of Florida beats North Carolina's Cinda Gurney 6–3, 6–1 to win her second straight NCAA women's tennis title.

May 23—Greece earns its first World Cup soccer berth, tying Russia 1–1 in Moscow.

May 26—The U.S. men's soccer team plays to a scoreless draw with Peru, in Mission Viejo, Calif.

May 31—Syracuse wins its fourth NCAA men's lacrosse title in six years, edging North Carolina 13–12 on Matt Riter's goal with eight seconds left to play. Syracuse goaltender Chris Surran is named the tournament MVP for making 20 saves in the title game and 15 in the Orangemen's 15–9 defeat of defending champion Princeton in the semifinal game.

May 31—Arizona capitalizes on an error by UCLA shortstop Kristy Howard to score the game's only run and win the College Softball World Series. Despite losing the championship game, UCLA's ace pitcher Lisa Fernandez finishes her career with a record of 93–7.

June 3—Arkansas junior Erick Walder jumps a world-leading 28' to win the long jump at the men's NCAA track and field championships in New Orleans. Walder and his Razorback teammates amass 69 points to top runners-up LSU and Ohio State, who tied with 45. Indiana State's Holli Hyche won both sprints, while the LSU women more than doubled the score of runner-up Wisconsin, 93 points to 44.

June 6—Lance Armstrong completes a sweep of the Thrift Drug Triple Crown by winning the CoreStates USPRO Cycling Championship. For his triple crown win Armstrong collects a cool $1 million.

June 9—The U.S. men's soccer team shocks England 2–0 in the U.S. Cup, in Foxboro, Mass. Thomas Dooley scores the first goal on a header in the 42nd minute and Alexi Lalas adds the second in the 71st. U.S. goaltender Tony Meola makes 15 saves and is named the game's MVP.

June 12—Louisiana State University beats Wichita State 8–0 to win the College World Series. LSU's freshman pitcher Brett Laxton strikes out a championship game-record 16 and does not allow a single batter to reach third base. Laxton's teammate, second baseman Todd Walker, is named the tournament's outstanding player, hitting .350 with three homers and 12 RBI.

June 12—At the 12th National Collegiate Rowing Championships at Bantam, Ohio, Brown's unbeaten men's crew wins the varsity eight championship by a length over Penn.

June 12—Marion Jones, a senior at Thousand Oaks (Calif.) High School, sets three meet records at the Golden West Invitational track and field meet. Jones win the 100 (11.31), the 200 (23.01) and the long jump (20' 9"). The following weekend she wins the same three events at the California state high school meet.

BRUCE ZAKE

Branham rolled a 227 to win the Firestone.

June 13—Miguel Indurain of Spain wins his second consecutive Tour de Italy, beating Piotre Urgumov of Latvia by 58 seconds overall.

June 13—The U.S. men's soccer team loses 4–3 to Germany in the U.S. Cup, in Chicago.

June 17—Andre Cason, who had to be carried off the track with a torn calf muscle at last year's Olympic trials, wins the 100 meters in a windy 9.85 at the U.S. Outdoor Track and Field Championships in Eugene, Oregon. Also qualifying for the World Championships in the 100 are Dennis Mitchell and Carl Lewis. Dan O'Brien fights through a groin problem to win the decathlon with 8,331 points.

June 19—David Chapman, 17, becomes the youngest man ever to win the pro singles title at the U.S. Handball National Championships, in Baltimore.

June 20—President Clinton names Florence Griffith Joyner and Tom McMillen to replace Arnold Schwarzenegger as head of the President's Council on Physical Fitness and Sports.

June 20—Michael Johnson wins a sizzling 400-meter showdown at the U.S. Track and Field Championships. Johnson's winning time of 43.74 is the fastest ever run on U.S. soil and beats world record holder Butch Reynolds (44.12) and Olympic champion Quincy Watts (44.24). Also, Annette Peters completes a triumphant 1,500/3,000 double.

July 10—Yobes Ondieki of Kenya becomes the first person to break 27 minutes for the 10,000, clocking 26:58.38 at the Bislett Games in Oslo.

July 14—Cuba beats the U.S. 7–2 in baseball at the World University Games, in Buffalo, New York.

July 15—Dennis Conner skippers the *Winston* to a win in the inaugural Gold Cup Transatlantic Sailing Race, reaching Southampton, England 12 days, eight hours and 14 minutes after leaving New York City.

July 25—Miguel Indurain rides into Paris in total command of the Tour de France. Only the fourth rider to win three straight Tours, the 29-year-old Spaniard finishes in 95 hours, 57 minutes, and nine seconds.

July 25—Mexico's men's soccer team beats the U.S. 4–0 in the final of the Gold Cup, in Mexico City.

July 27—Javier Sotomayor of Cuba breaks his own world high jump record by half an inch, clearing 8′ ½″ at a meet in Salamanca, Spain.

July 28—Eric Namesnik sets an American record in the 400-meter individual medley, touching in 4:14.50 at the U.S. Swimming Long Course Championships in Austin, Texas.

Aug 3—Karoly Guttler of Hungary sets the only world swimming record of 1993, clocking 1:00.95 in the qualifying round of the 100-meter breaststroke at the European Championships, in Sheffield, England. He wins the final in 1:01.04.

Aug 4—UCLA, faced with a projected budget deficit of $9 million over the next seven years, announces it will cut its men's swimming and men's and women's gymnastics programs.

Aug 8—Franziska van Almsick of Germany wins a record-tying sixth gold medal at the European Swimming Championships, touching in 25.53 in the 50-meter free.

Aug 8—In the final of the CONCACAF tournament, the U.S. women's soccer team beats Canada 1–0 on Joy Fawcett's unassisted goal. The U.S. women finish the tournament 3–0.

Aug 14—On the opening day of the World Track and Field Championships, Mark Plaatjes, a former South African who, after years of seeking it, finally obtained U.S. citizenship on July 24, wins the world marathon title, in Stuttgart, Germany. Plaatjes, whose time was 2:13:57, is the first American man to win a championship marathon since Frank Shorter did so at the 1972 Olympics.

Aug 15—Betsy Dougherty scores twice in 38 seconds to lead the United States to a 4–1 victory over England in the World Cup women's lacrosse championship.

Aug 15—Thirty-three-year-old Linford Christie of England wins the world 100-meter title in Stuttgart, Germany, clocking 9.87 to beat U.S. champ

Andre Cason (9.92), Dennis Mitchell (9.99) and Carl Lewis (10.02).

Aug 15—Jenny Thompson of the U.S. wins three gold medals to bring her total to six at the Pan Pacific Swimming Championships, in Kobe, Japan.

Aug 16—Gail Devers wins the women's 100 at the World Track and Field Championships, edging Merlene Ottey of Jamaica. Both runners are timed in 10.82.

Aug 19—Sally Gunnell of Great Britain breaks the world record in the 400 hurdles, running 52.74 to edge Sandra Farmer-Patrick of the U.S., whose 52.79 also broke the old record. Sergei Bubka wins the pole vault, clearing 19' 8¼" to become the only person to get a gold medal at all four world outdoor championships. And Merlene Ottey of Jamaica, whose collection of Olympic and world championship medals includes eight bronzes and two silvers, finally earns a gold, holding off Gwen Torrence in 21.98 in the 200 meters.

Aug 20—At the World Track and Field Championships, Colin Jackson of Wales sets a world record in the 110-meter hurdles, his time of 12.91 snipping .01 from Roger Kingdom's four-year-old record. Dan O'Brien fights off several challengers before successfully defending his world decathlon title, with 8,817 points. And Carl Lewis avoids a medal shut-out by finishing third in the 200, behind Frankie Fredericks of Namibia and John Regis of Great Britain.

Aug 22—The U.S. 4 x 400-meter relay team of Andrew Valmon, Quincy Watts, Butch Reynolds and Michael Johnson smashes the world record with a time of 2:54.29. Johnson's anchor leg is the fastest ever, a 42.97.

Aug 26—John Roethlisberger of the University of Minnesota wins the all-around title at the national gymnastics championships, in Salt Lake City. Roethlisberger also wins the still rings.

Aug 27—Shannon Miller wins the all-around title at the U.S. Gymnastics Championships, in Salt Lake City. She also wins the uneven bars and the floor exercise.

Aug 27—A U.S. District Court in Alexandria, Virginia, awards Butch Reynolds $691,667—the amount the Mobil Corporation owes the International Amateur Athletic Federation for the period May 21 to August 27—as the first installment of the $27.3 million the IAAF owes Reynolds.

Aug 27—Long Beach (Calif.) beats Panama 3–2 to win the Little League World Series. Long Beach, powered most of the tournament by slugging shortstop/pitcher Sean Burroughs, wins when pinch hitter Jeremy Lewis, batting .167 for the week, hits a bases-loaded , two-out line drive to

the wall in the bottom of the sixth. Long Beach is the first U.S. team to win the title two straight years.

Aug 28—The U.S., which has finished second or third every year since 1979, wins the Freestyle Wrestling World Championship, in Toronto. Led by gold medalists Bruce Baumgartner in the 286-pound class, plus twins Terry and Tom Brands in the 125.5 and 136.5 pound classes, respectively, the U.S. accumulated 75 points to easily beat Russia (53) and Turkey (51).

Aug 29—Lance Armstrong wins the pro road race at the World Cycling Championships in Hamar, Norway. The 21-year-old from Plano, Texas, beats Tour de France winner Miguel Indurain by 19 seconds. Rebecca Twigg wins the 3,000-meter pursuit.

Aug 29—Jan Zelezny of the Czech Republic breaks his own world record in the javelin throw with a toss of 313' 10", in Sheffield, England.

Sept 5—Noureddine Morceli of Algeria smashes the world mile record in Rieti, Italy. Morceli's time of 3:44.39 lowers Steve Cram's eight-year-old mark of 3:46.32 by 1.93 seconds, the largest margin the mile record has been broken by since 1966, when Jim Ryun broke it by 2.3 seconds.

Sept 8—At China's National Games in Beijing, Wang Junxia starts the greatest binge of track and field record-setting ever by hacking almost 42 seconds off Ingrid Kristiansen's seven-year-old world record for the 10,000. Junxia's time is 29:31.78. Over the next five days Junxia breaks the existing world record for the 1500—she runs 3:51.92 but finishes second to countrywoman Qu Yunxia's 3:50.46—and the 3,000 *twice*, clocking 8:12.19 in the heats and 8:06.11 in the finals.

Sept 9—Diego Maradona signs with Newell's Old Boys of Argentina's First Division.

Sept 16—The Cherry Creek (Colo.) High School boys' tennis team beats Denver's Mullen High School 7–0 for its 248th consecutive dual-match win since 1971. That's the nation's longest.

Oct 2—Taifour Diane scores the game-winning goal in OT to help the Colorado Foxes beat the Los Angeles Salsa 3–1 for their second straight American Professional Soccer League title.

Oct 13—The Netherlands scores two second half goals to beat England 2–0 and all but eliminate the Brits from the 1994 World Cup. In World Cup action elsewhere, Italy beats Scotland 3–1; Israel shocks France 3–2; Spain beats Ireland 3–1; Portugal edges Switzerland 1–0; and Norway beats Poland 3–0.

Oct 13—The U.S. men's soccer team ties Mexico 1–1 on Cobi Jones's goal in the 83rd minute.

Baseball

THE WORLD SERIES

Sports Illustrated

NOVEMBER 1, 199

O Happy Jays!

Toronto
Hero
Joe Carter

JOHN IACONO

Jays Again

The Toronto Blue Jays became the first team in 15 years to repeat as World Series champions | by **TIM KURKJIAN**

THE 1993 BASEBALL SEASON, A historic one filled with drama, indelible marks left by star players and high-octane offense, ended as it should have: with a cleanup hitter blasting a home run in the ninth inning against a top pitcher, turning defeat into victory and leaving us all to shake our heads at baseball's greatness.

Blue Jay rightfielder Joe Carter made Game 6 one for the ages and the World Series one that will never be forgotten, by hitting a three-run home run in the bottom of the ninth off the Phillies' Mitch Williams for a remarkable 8–6 win. Carter's bolt gave Toronto its second consecutive world championship, making it the first team to accomplish that feat since the 1977–78 Yankees. "It was a storybook ending," said Carter, who romped around the bases as 52,195 at the SkyDome, and the entire nation of Canada, celebrated with thunderous applause. "It couldn't have had a better script."

No World Series had ever before ended with a team that had been trailing at the time, winning with a home run. But this was no ordinary World Series. It was loaded with records, 13 in all, and not all of them for sterling play. In the middle of most everything significant that occurred in the Series was the Blue Jays' Paul Molitor, 37, who

won his first championship in his 16th major league season. Molitor was named the Series MVP, hitting .500, slugging 1.000 and driving in eight runs. As he raced around the field hugging teammates after Game 6, he was crying. Who could blame him?

At the parade the following day, which drew an estimated 300,000 fans to downtown Toronto, Blue Jay manager Cito Gaston choked back tears as he spoke at the podium. It wasn't an easy season for the Blue Jays, who lost eight key players from their 1992 championship team, struggled with their pitching and had to fight off the Orioles, the Yankees and the Tigers most of the season. But this team was able to turn on the switch and play well whenever it had to. Gaston, the first manager since Cincinnati's Sparky Anderson to win back-to-back World Series, said, "This team had more heart than any team I've been with in my life."

Yet their heart was no bigger than that of the Phillies, that lovable mob that became the third team in this century to go from last place to first place in one year. In the end, however, they ran into a team that was more talented and had just as much character. "It's over. Toronto's the better ball team," said Phillie centerfielder Lenny Dykstra, who had a brilliant Series, hitting .348 with four home runs. "That's it. Uncle."

That wasn't clear, however, until the

There was no place like home after Carter's dramatic blast won the Series for Toronto.

ninth inning of Game 6. The Phillies entered the inning with a 6–5 lead, forged by a five-run seventh inning that included a three-run homer by Dykstra off Blue Jay starter Dave Stewart. Williams started the ninth, his first appearance since losing Game 4, an incredible 15–14 defeat that turned the Series and made Williams the subject of death threats. Williams started by walking Rickey Henderson on four pitches. After Devon White had flied out, Molitor singled Henderson to second. Both scored when Carter drilled a 2–2 fastball over the leftfield fence. "I blew two World Series games," Williams said. "I have no excuses. Ain't nobody in the world feels worse than I do. I feel terrible for my teammates, who battled so hard. Don't pity me. I won't commit suicide. I just didn't get it done."

The Phillies' pitching staff didn't get it done against Toronto's relentless offense.

Philadelphia pitchers posted a 7.57 ERA, and gave up eight or more runs in each of the four losses. The Blue Jays won the Series opener 8–5 at SkyDome by shelling Phillies starter Curt Schilling for eight hits and seven runs in 6⅓ innings. The Phillies bounced back in Game 2, winning 6–4 on the strength of a five-run third off Stewart. The big blow was a three-run homer by Jim Eisenreich. Terry Mulholland got the win, Williams a nervous save.

The Series shifted to Philadelphia for Game 3, which meant no designated hitter for the Blue Jays. John Olerud, the AL batting champion, was benched against lefthander Danny Jackson so Molitor, a righthanded hitter, could play first base. It was only the third time in Series history that a batting champ was benched for a Series game. It didn't matter. Molitor hit a two-run triple in the first inning and a home run in the third, sending Toronto to a 10–3 win behind Pat Hentgen.

That was nothing, however, compared to

RICHARD MACKSON

Dude was rude to postseason pitchers, hitting six homers and driving in 10 runs.

Game 4, which will go down in history as the most memorable, most bewildering, most incredible game in World Series history. The Blue Jays won 15–14 with six runs in the eighth inning to take a 3–1 Series lead. It was the highest-scoring game (by seven runs) in World Series history. It was also the longest nine-inning game (four hours and 14 minutes) in postseason play. It marked the first time in Series play that the losing team scored more than nine runs. It was more runs than were scored by *both* teams in 16 different Series. It marked the third time in Series history that a team came back to win from a five-run deficit. The Jays trailed by five runs twice, including a 14–9 deficit with none on and one out in the eighth.

"I've never seen anything like it ... ever," said Phillie catcher Darren Daulton.

No one ever had. There was the hilarious attempted slide by Blue Jay pitcher Todd Stottlemyre in the second inning, a flop that almost knocked him out and bloodied his chin. That was almost as comical as Stottlemyre walking four batters in the first inning, helping to turn a 3–0 lead into a 4–3 deficit. There was the malfunctioning of the phone in the Toronto bullpen, leading to total confusion, including bringing in the wrong

reliever, Mark Eichhorn, instead of Tony Castillo, who hadn't even been warming up. And in the seventh there was the amazing decision by Gaston to let Castillo hit even though the Jays were down 13–9 and the bench and bullpen had plenty of bodies. "They gave up when they left that pitcher in," said Dykstra. "But we couldn't put them away."

Leading 14–9 behind two homers and four RBIs by Dykstra and five RBIs by Milt Thompson, the Phillie bullpen fell apart. Larry Andersen started the inning, got one out, then gave up a single to Carter, a walk and a double to Molitor. In came Williams. Tony Fernandez singled to make it 14–11. After pinch hitter Ed Sprague struck out, Henderson lined a two-run single to center, and White followed with a two-run triple to right center for a 15–14 lead. Toronto reliever Duane Ward retired the final four hitters to end it.

Such a loss would devastate most teams. Not the Phillies. Schilling threw a masterful five-hit shutout in Game 5, sending the Series back to Toronto. It marked only the second time that the Blue Jays were shut out this year, the first time a righthander had done it since Aug. 23, 1992.

The Phillies' drubbing of the Braves was one of the biggest upsets in NLCS history. Atlanta, the two-time defending league champions, entered the series with 104 wins, three Cy Young candidates and three 100-RBI men. But the underrated starting pitching of the Phillies stifled the Braves in four of the six games.

In the opener in Philadelphia, Schilling, who won the series MVP without winning a game, pitched eight overpowering innings but saw his 3–2 lead slip away in the ninth on a leadoff walk by closer Mitch Williams, a throwing error by Kim Batiste (a defensive replacement) and a ground out. Batiste atoned in the 10th with the game-winning hit for a 4–3 win.

The Braves rocked Phillie starter Tommy Greene in Game 2, rolling to a 14–3 victory behind four homers. When the series shifted to Atlanta for Game 3, Mulholland was cruising with a 2–0 lead, but the Braves scored five runs in the sixth and four in the seventh to win 9–4. A third straight Brave pennant seemed certain.

Then the series turned weird. In Game 4, the Phillies left 15 men on base, struck out 15 times (tying an NLCS record), went 1 for 12 with runners in scoring position and didn't score an earned run. But they still won 2–1, thanks to Jackson's gritty 7⅔ innings and a miraculous save by Williams.

Game 5 was the pivotal game. Schilling took a 3–0 lead into the ninth but was removed after a walk to Jeff Blauser and another error by Batiste. In came Williams. Fred McGriff's single, a sacrifice fly and singles by Terry Pendleton and Francisco Cabrera (the Game 7 hero of the 1992 NLCS) tied the score and put the winning run on third with one out. But Williams struck out Mark Lemke and got Bill Pecota to fly out. In the 10th inning Dykstra homered off Mark Wohlers for a 4–3 win.

"Dude is the greatest," said Phillie reliever Andersen of Dykstra. "I don't like the word *destiny*, but we were destined to get here. I know what this team has in common with destiny—Dude and destiny start with the letter D."

Guzman won two games, struck out nine and had an ERA of 2.08 in the ALCS.

Darren Daulton is DD. In Game 6 in Philadelphia, Daulton's double off Greg Maddux in the third gave Philadelphia a 2–0 lead that it never lost. A two-run homer by Dave Hollins in the fifth and a two-run triple by Mickey Morandini in the sixth finished Maddux, who had not allowed six runs in a game in his previous 94 starts. Meanwhile, Greene threw seven strong innings, and David West and Williams finished up a 6–3 victory that sent the Phillies to the World Series for the third time since 1950.

There was no sense of destiny—just good pitching and timely hitting—for the Blue Jays in whipping the White Sox, four games to two, in the ALCS. Toronto won all three games at Chicago's Comiskey Park, winning the first two of the series, then, after losing two of three at SkyDome, winning Game 6 on the road to wrap it up. The ALCS MVP was Toronto pitcher Dave Stewart, now 8–0 in LCS play. Stewart won Games 2 and 6, outdueling Alex Fernandez. The LVP— least valuable player—of the series was White Sox ace Jack McDowell, who was 0–2 with a 10.00 ERA in two starts.

McDowell, the probable AL Cy Young award winner this year, was hammered for 13 hits—the most ever allowed in an LCS— in a 7–3 loss in the opener. Blue Jay DH Molitor, the oldest player to lead the major leagues in hits (211) in a full season, had four more, including a two-run homer that wrecked McDowell. It was a bad night all

BILL SMITH

CHUCK SOLOMON

Thomas led the White Sox into the ALCS, batting .317 with 41 homers and 128 RBIs.

over Chicago: Word leaked out that Michael Jordan was retiring.

Chicago's defense had a bad series. In Game 2 second baseman Joey Cora and first baseman Dan Pasqua (playing because Frank Thomas was limited to DH duties the first two games because of a sore right shoulder) made critical mistakes, handing Stewart a 3–1 victory. Down 2–0 the White Sox began to unravel. Bo Jackson, who didn't play in the first two games, said the team "was playing a man short." (Which prompted Chicago shortstop Ozzie Guillen to ask, "Who's the one, Babe Ruth?") DH George Bell, who batted .217 in the regular season, also hadn't played in the first two games. He said he had no respect for manager Gene Lamont, adding that "48 percent" of the team felt that way.

Whatever, the White Sox, left for dead as they left for SkyDome, won Games 3 and 4 to even the series. Wilson Alvarez, Chicago's best pitcher down the stretch, stopped Toronto's turbocharged lineup in Game 3,

winning 6–1. In Game 4 White Sox center-fielder Lance Johnson, who in the regular season had the most at bats of any player who didn't hit a homer, homered to key a 7–4 win. With McDowell going in Game 5, things were looking up for Chicago.

But McDowell was awful again, this time lasting 2⅓ innings and leaving the Sox a 3–0 deficit. Juan Guzman beat him again, allowing one run in seven innings. The series moved back to Comiskey, but the Chicago defense was again atrocious. Cora's relay throw on what should have been a routine double play in the third short-hopped to Thomas, who couldn't dig it out, allowing the go-ahead run to score. Toronto took that 3–2 lead into the ninth when Devon White (.444 in the series) homered off Scott Radinsky and Molitor (.391) added a two-run triple for a 6–2 lead.

That won a trip to the Series for Toronto. "They were just better than we were," said Lamont. "We still had a great season."

It was a great regular season throughout baseball. It was a season for milestones. Minnesota's Dave Winfield, who played against the now 62-years-old Willie Mays, became the 19th player in history to collect 3,000 hits. Carlton Fisk set the record for most games caught in a career (2,226) but was released a week later by the White Sox. St. Louis's Lee Smith became the alltime save leader but was traded Aug. 31 to the Yankees. The Mets' Anthony Young lost his first 13 decisions, giving him 27 straight, a major league record.

It was a monster year for offense—some claim the ball was juiced, others blamed expansion—but most agreed that there are some great hitters, and even more really bad pitchers, playing today. Five players hit 40 homers, led by Texas's Juan Gonzalez (46), and 22 players hit at least 30 homers. Gonzalez was one of 25 players to drive in 100 runs, led by Cleveland's Albert Belle with 129. On Sept. 7, Cardinal outfielder Mark Whitten became the 12th player to hit four home runs in one game and the second player to drive in 12 runs in a game. Seattle's Ken Griffey Jr. tied a major league record by hitting a home run in eight straight games. Colorado's Andres Galarraga (.370) and Olerud (.363) took their leagues' batting titles. The Blue Jays became the first team in this century to have the top three hitters in a league batting race (Molitor finished second at .332, Robbie Alomar was third at .326).

There was some good pitching. Five pitchers won 20 games, topped by the White Sox's Jack McDowell's 22. The Cubs' Randy Myers's 53 saves set an NL record. Seattle's Randy Johnson became the first lefthander since Steve Carlton in 1972 to strike out 300, fanning 308, including 14 or more in a game five times. Seattle's Chris Bosio, the Yankees' Jim Abbott and Houston's Darryl Kile tossed no-hitters.

The final season for Nolan Ryan, the no-hit king and alltime strikeout leader, ended Sept. 22 when a tendon snapped in his right elbow, a sad finish to one of the longest, most remarkable careers in baseball history. Ryan and Fisk weren't the only future Hall of Famers to say goodbye. Kansas City's George Brett retired after 20 seasons, leaving with 3,154 hits, three batting titles and thousands of sprints to first base on routine ground outs.

It was a fabulous first season for Dodger rookie Mike Piazza, who became the fifth catcher ever to hit .300 (.318) with 30 homers (35) and 100 RBIs (112) in a season. Angel outfielder Tim Salmon became the first AL player since Reggie Jackson in 1968 to win the "rookie triple crown," hitting .283 with 31 homers and 95 RBIs.

It was a season of unpredictability. Especially surprising was the way bad teams suddenly got good and good teams suddenly got bad. Before this season only five teams had ever gone from 90 wins one year to 90 losses the next: This season three teams turned that trick—the A's, the Brewers and the Twins—and the Reds almost did, losing 89. Oakland became the second team ever to go from first place one year to sole possession of last the next season. The Mets, contenders in spring training, rekindled memories of the '62 expansion Mets by, among countless indignities, losing 103 games and going 65 days without two wins in a row.

Then there were the Phillies. Since winning the NL pennant in 1983, Philadelphia had been 98 games under .500, and had been the only NL team not to finish .500 in any season since 1985. But the '93 Phillies came flying out, winning 44 of their first 61 games to lead by 11½ games on June 14. Theirs was the zaniest clubhouse in sports, housing a long-haired, unshaven group of renegades, rejects and recalcitrants. "You can't get on this club without a letter from a psychiatrist," said Schilling.

The Cardinals and the Expos challenged the Phillies in August and September. But the Phillies, despite being reminded daily about the colossal collapse of the '64 Phillies, persevered and survived.

It wasn't nearly as easy for the Blue Jays. They lost eight players from their 1992 world championship team, opening the season with question marks at several positions. They trudged through the first four months, bludgeoning opponents, but never establishing their pitching. After being swept at home by Oakland Sept. 11–13, the Jays were tied for first place with the Yan-

JOHN BIEVER

The burly, bearded Kruk was a model Phillie, batting .316 in the regular season.

good reason most experts picked the Giants to finish fourth or fifth. But the signing of free-agent outfielder Barry Bonds in December, coupled with the team's improved pitching, led by 20-game winners Bill Swift and John Burkett, made San Francisco a new team. The Giants shocked the world by opening a 10-game lead on the supposedly unbeatable Braves on July 22. Bonds was playing at a level not seen since Mays in his prime, while Atlanta was having major offensive woes.

The Braves began their turnaround by taking advantage of the season-long fire sale run by the cash-strapped San Diego Padres, trading them three minor leaguers for power-hitting first baseman Fred McGriff, who played his first game as a Brave on July 20. On that night the luxury boxes at Atlanta–Fulton County Stadium caught fire, and so did the Braves. McGriff hit a three-run homer to help wipe out a 5–0 deficit against the Cardinals. Led by McGriff the Braves went 54–19 after the All-Star break—the third best second half in major league history.

By Sept. 17, Atlanta had beaten the Giants five times in six meetings down the stretch to help open a four-game lead, virtually assuring San Francisco of becoming the fourth team in this century not to win a division or league that it had led by 10 or more games during that season. But the courageous Giants battled back to tie the division entering the final three games of the season. The Braves were at home against the Rockies. The Giants were in Los Angeles to play a four-game series against the hated Dodgers. Atlanta swept its three-game series. Bonds hit two three-run homers and drove in seven runs on Oct. 1 in one of the greatest big-game performances of all time, sparking an 8–7 win. But on the final day of the season the Dodgers smashed the Giants 12–1, relegating them to second place despite their gaudy total of 103 wins. With expanded playoffs in place for 1994, the Giants will be remembered as the last great team not to reach the playoffs.

kees and only two games ahead of the Orioles. But Toronto won 16 of its next 18 to win by seven games.

The White Sox stumbled through the first two months but never dropped below first place after June 20. On Aug. 13 the Royals had pulled within 2½ games and were ahead 4–2 entering the eighth inning with their ace reliever, Jeff Montgomery, on the mound. Chicago scored three runs, the last two on a mammoth homer by Frank Thomas, to win 5–4. "It doesn't get any bigger than that," said Gene Lamont. That home run started the White Sox on a 16–6 run that all but sealed the division.

The NL West race wasn't sealed until the final day—the first time in major league history that two teams with as many as 103 wins apiece had gone to the last day tied for first. For the Giants this was an astonishing turnaround. In 1992 the team lost 90 games, finished 26 games out of first place and got 27 homers from their outfielders. With

FOR THE RECORD·1993

Final Standings

National League

EASTERN DIVISION

Team	Won	Lost	Pct	GB	Home	Away
Philadelphia	97	65	.599	—	52-29	45-36
Montreal	94	68	.580	3	55-26	39-42
St. Louis	87	75	.537	10	49-32	38-43
Chicago	84	78	.519	13	43-38	41-40
Pittsburgh	75	87	.463	22	40-41	35-46
Florida	64	98	.395	33	35-46	29-52
New York	59	103	.364	38	28-53	31-50

WESTERN DIVISION

Team	Won	Lost	Pct	GB	Home	Away
Atlanta	104	58	.642	—	51-30	53-28
San Francisco	103	59	.636	1	50-31	53-28
Houston	85	77	.525	19	44-37	41-40
Los Angeles	81	81	.500	23	41-40	40-41
Cincinnati	73	89	.451	31	41-40	32-49
Colorado	67	95	.414	37	39-42	28-53
San Diego	61	101	.377	43	34-47	27-54

American League

EASTERN DIVISION

Team	Won	Lost	Pct	GB	Home	Away
Toronto	95	67	.585	—	48-33	47-34
New York	88	74	.543	7	50-31	38-43
Baltimore	85	77	.525	10	48-33	37-44
Detroit	85	77	.525	10	44-37	41-40
Boston	80	82	.494	15	43-38	37-44
Cleveland	76	86	.469	19	46-35	30-51
Milwaukee	69	93	.426	26	38-43	31-50

WESTERN DIVISION

Team	Won	Lost	Pct	GB	Home	Away
Chicago	94	68	.580	—	45-36	49-32
Texas	86	76	.531	8	50-31	36-45
Kansas City	84	78	.519	10	43-38	41-40
Seattle	82	80	.506	12	46-35	36-45
California	71	91	.438	23	44-37	27-54
Minnesota	71	91	.438	23	36-45	35-46
Oakland	68	94	.420	26	38-43	30-51

1993 Playoffs

National League Championship Series

Oct 6 ....Atlanta 3 at Philadelphia 4 (10 innnings)
Oct 7 ....Atlanta 14 at Philadelphia 3
Oct 9 ....Philadelphia 4 at Atlanta 9
Oct 10 ....Philadelphia 2 at Atlanta 1

Oct 11 ....Philadelphia 4 at Atlanta 3
Oct 13 ....Atlanta 3 at Philadelphia 6

(Philadelphia wins series 4-2)

GAME 1

Atlanta	0	0	1	1	0	0	0	0	1	0	—3
Phila	1	0	0	1	0	1	0	0	0	1	—4

WP—Williams; **LP**—McMichael; **BS**—Williams.
E— Philadelphia: Batiste (1); **LOB**— Atlanta 11, Philadelphia 8. **2B**— Atlanta: Nixon (1), Olson (1), Avery (1); Philadelphia: Dykstra (1), Kruk (1), Hollins (1), Chamberlain (2); **HR**— Philadelphia: Incaviglia (1). **S**—Atlanta: Belliard (1); **SF**—Atlanta: Justice **GIDP**—Philadelphia: Hollins; **A**—62,012.
Recap: After striking out the side in the first, Curt Schilling held the Braves in check for eight innings, scattering seven hits. The Phillies' Kim Batiste made up for a ninth inning, lead-blowing error by doubling home John Kruk with the game winner.

GAME 2

Atlanta	2	0	6	0	1	0	0	4	1	—14
Philadelphia	0	0	2	0	0	0	0	0	1	—3

WP—Maddux; **LP**—Greene. **E**—Philadelphia: Morandini (1). Stocker (1); **LOB**—Atlanta 6, Philadelphia 8. **2B**—Atlanta: Nixon (2), Gant (2). **HR**—Atlanta: Blauser (1)..McGriff (1), Pendleton (1), Berryhill (1); Philadelphia: Dykstra (1), Hollins (1), **SB**—Philadelphia: Morandini (1). **CS**—Atlanta: Nixon (1); **A**—62,436.
Recap: Atlanta shooed Tommy Greene (10–0 in 16 consecutive starts at Vet Stadium) with a six run third that featured Damon Berryhill's three-run shot to right.

GAME 3

Philadelphia	0	0	0	1	0	1	0	1	1	—4
Atlanta	0	0	0	0	0	5	4	0	x	—9

WP—Glavine; **LP**—Mulholland.
E—Philadelphia: Duncan (1). **LOB**—Philadelphia 7, Atlanta, 7. **2B**—Philadelphia: Chamberlain (3), Stocker (1), Eisenreich (1); Atlanta: Blauser (1), McGriff (1) Justice (1), Lemke (1);. **3B**—Philadelphia: Duncan (2), Kruk (1); **HR**—Philadelphia: Kruk (1), . **SB**— Philadelphia: Hollins (1); **CS**— Atlanta: Nixon (2); **A**—52,032.
Recap: Atlanta's five-run fifth broke open a tight game and chased Philadelphia starter Terry Mulholland.

GAME 4

Philadelphia	0	0	0	2	0	0	0	0	0	—2
Atlanta	0	1	0	0	0	0	0	0	0	—1

WP—Jackson; **LP**—Smoltz; **S**—Williams.
E—Philadelphia: Williams (1); Atlanta: Lemke (1). **LOB**—Philadelphia 15, Atlanta 11. **2B**—Philadelphia: Thompson (1); Atlanta: McGriff (2), Pendleton (1), Lemke (2); **CS**—Atlanta: Gant (1), **S**—Atlanta: Nixon (2); **SF**—Philadelphia: Stocker. **GIDP**—Atlanta: Gant. **A**—52,032.
Recap: Danny Jackson shut down the Atlanta offense, allowing just one run over 7⅔ innings, then provided some offense of his own, driving in what proved to be the decisive run in the fourth inning.

National League Championship Series *(Cont.)*

GAME 5

Philadelphia	1	0	0	1	0	0	0	1	1—4
Atlanta	0	0	0	0	0	0	0	3	0—3

WP—Williams; **LP**—Wohlers; **S**—Andersen; **BS**—Williams. **E**—Philadelphia: Batiste (2); Atlanta: Gant (1) **LOB**—Philadelphia 5, Atlanta 6. **2B**—Philadelphia: Kruk (2); **HR**—Philadelphia: Dykstra (2), Daulton (1); **S**—Philadelphia: Schilling. **SF**—Philadelphia: Chamberlain, Atlanta: Justice. **A**—52,032.

Recap: Curt Schilling tossed eight scoreless, 4-hit innings at Atlanta, only to watch his three-run lead disappear as a Kim Batise error and ineffective pitching by Mitch Williams allowed the Braves tie the game in the ninth. Fortunately for the Phillie faithful, Lenny Dykstra drove a ball deep into the centerfield seats in the tenth for the game-wining margin.

GAME 6

Atlanta	0	0	0	0	1	0	2	0	0—3
Philadelphia	0	0	2	0	2	2	0	0	x—6

WP—Greene; **LP**—Maddux; **S**—Williams. **E**—Atlanta: Justice (1), Lemke (2), Maddux (1); Philadelphia: Thompson (1). **LOB**—Atlanta 6, Philadelphia 9. **2B**—Philadelphia: Daulton (1). **3B**—Philadelphia: Morandini (1). **HR**—Atlanta: Blauser (2); Philadelphia: Hollins (2); **S**—Atlanta: Maddux (2).; Philadelphia: Greene (2). **GIDP**—Atlanta: Berryhill. **A**—62,502.

Recap: Darren Daulton hit a two-run double that was fair by inches in the third, Dave Hollins homered in the fifth and, an inning later, Mickey Morandini tripled in two more.Tommy Greene atoned for his Game 2 showing with seven strong innings, and Wild Thing Williams closed with uncharacteristic ease.

American League Championship Series

Oct 5 ....Toronto 7 at Chicago 3	Oct 9 ....Chicago 7 at Toronto 4
Oct 6 ....Toronto 3 at Chicago 1	Oct 10 ....Chicago 3 at Toronto 5
Oct 8 ....Chicago 6 at Toronto 1	Oct 12 ....Toronto 6 at Chicago 3

(Toronto wins series 4-2)

GAME 1

Toronto	0	0	0	3	0	2	0	0	0—7
Chicago	0	0	0	3	0	0	0	0	0—3

WP—Guzman; **LP**—McDowell. **E**—Toronto: Olerud (1); Chicago: Cora (1). **LOB**—Toronto 12, Chicago 13. **2B**—Toronto: Olerud (1); Chicago: Burks (1). **3B** — Toronto: Sprague **HR**—Toronto: Molitor (1). **SB**—Chicago: Raines (1), Guillen (1) **CS**—Chicago: Raines (1) **A**—46,246.

Recap: Paul Molitor went 4-for-5 with three RBI, John Olerud added three hits and three RBI and Toronto starter Juan Guzman overcame his own control problems to post the win for the Blue Jays.

GAME 2

Toronto	1	0	0	2	0	0	0	0	0—3
Chicago	1	0	0	0	0	0	0	0	0—1

WP—Stewart; **LP**—Fernandez; **Save**—D. Ward **E**—Chicago: Cora (2), Pasqua (1) **LOB**—Toronto 6, Chicago 10. **2B**—Toronto: Molitor (1); Chicago: Johnson (1). **GIDP**—Toronto: Alomar, Sprague; Chicago: Johnson. **A**—46,101.

Recap: Toronto's Dave Stewart, Mr. October of the mound, recovered from first inning wildness and cruised through the sixth, fanning five. His Chicago counterpart, Alex Fernandez, pitched well for eight, but two unearned runs made the difference.

GAME 3

Chicago	0	0	5	0	1	0	0	0	0—6
Toronto	0	0	1	0	0	0	0	0	0—1

WP—Alvarez; **LP**—Hentgen **E**—Toronto: Henderson (1). **LOB**—Chicago 10, Toronto 5. **2B**—Chicago: Raines (2); Toronto: Henderson (1). **SB**—Chicago Johnson (1), Toronto Henderson (1); .**CS**—Chicago: Burks (1), Toronto: White (1). **S**—Chicago: Cora. **SF**—Chicago: Ventura. **GIDP**—Toronto:Sprague, Fernandez. **A**—51,783.

Recap: Coming to the White Sox' rescue was Wilson Alvarez, who pitched a complete game, allowing just one hit and two baserunners in the last five innings.

GAME 4

Chicago	0	2	0	0	0	3	1	0	1	—7
Toronto	0	0	3	0	0	1	0	0	0	—4

WP—Belcher; **LP**—Stottlemyre; **S**—Hernandez. **LOB**—Chicago 7, Toronto 11. **2B**—Toronto: Alomar. **3B**—Toronto: White (1); Chicago: Johnson (1). **HR**—Chicago: Thomas (1), Johnson (1). **GIDP**—Chicago: Burks, **A**—51,889.

Recap: Chicago's Lance Johnson homered and drove in four runs and five different pitchers contained the Blue Jays after their three-run outburst against Chicago starter Jason Bere in the third inning.

GAME 5

Chicago	0	0	0	0	1	0	0	0	2—3
Toronto	1	1	1	1	0	0	1	0	x—5

WP—Guzman; **LP**—McDowell. **E**—Chicago: McDowell (1),. **LOB**—Toronto 12, Chicago 3. **2B**—Toronto: Henderson (2), White (1), Molitor (2); **HR**—Chicago: Ventura (1),.Burks (1);**SB**—Toronto: Henderson (2), Alomar (3) Borders (1); **CS**—Toronto: Henderson (1); **GIDP**—Toronto: Olerud, Chicago: Guillen; **A**—51,375.

Recap: Using his tricky changeup and wicked slider, Juan Guzman kept Chicago guessing, while the Sox' Jack McDowell flopped again, allowing Toronto to win their first game at home.

GAME 6

Toronto	0	2	0	1	0	0	0	0	3—6
Chicago	0	0	2	0	0	0	0	0	1—3

WP—Stewart; **LP**—Fernandez; **S**—D. Ward. **E**—Chicago: Cora (3), Ventura (1), Radinsky (1). **LOB**—Toronto 10, Chicago 7. **2B**—Toronto: Borders (1); Chicago: Guillen (1). **3B**—Toronto: Molitor (1) **HR**—Toronto: White (1), Chicago: Newson (1). **SB**—Toronto: Alomar (4),. **A**—45,527.

Recap: A two-run triple from Molitor, a solo HR from White and another strong performance from Dave Stewart produced Toronto's second straight AL crown.

Composite Box Scores

National League Championship Series

ATLANTA

BATTING	AB	R	H	HR	RBI	Avg
Bream	1	1	1	0	0	1.000
Cabrera	3	0	2	0	1	.667
Avery	4	1	2	0	0	.500
McGriff	23	6	10	1	4	.435
Nixon	23	3	8	0	4	.348
Pendleton	26	4	9	1	5	.346
Olson	3	0	1	0	0	.333
Pecota	3	1	1	0	0	.333
Blauser	25	5	7	2	4	.280
Maddux	4	1	1	0	0	.250
Berryhill	19	2	4	1	3	.211
Lemke	24	2	5	0	4	.208
Gant	27	4	5	0	3	.185
Justice	21	2	3	0	4	.143
5 others	8	1	0	0	0	.000
Totals	215	33	59	5	32	.274

PITCHING	G	IP	H	BB	SO	ERA
Smoltz	1	6⅓	8	5	10	0.00
Stanton	1	1	1	1	0	0.00
Mercker	5	5	3	2	4	1.80
Glavine	1	7	6	0	5	2.57
Avery	2	13	9	6	10	2.77
Wohlers	4	5⅓	2	3	10	3.38
Maddux	2	12⅔	11	7	11	4.97
McMichael	4	4	7	2	1	6.75
Totals	6	55	59	22	54	4.75

PHILADELPHIA

BATTING	AB	R	H	HR	RBI	Avg
Batiste	1	0	1	0	1	1.000
Chamberlain	11	1	4	0	1	.364
Dykstra	25	5	7	2	2	.280
Duncan	15	3	4	0	0	.267
Daulton	19	2	5	1	3	.263
Jackson	4	0	1	0	1	.250
Kruk	24	4	6	1	5	.250
Morandini	16	1	4	0	2	.250
Thompson	13	2	3	0	0	.231
Hollins	20	2	4	2	4	.200
Stocker	22	0	4	0	1	.182
Incaviglia	12	2	2	1	1	.167
Eisenreich	15	0	2	0	1	.133
6 others	10	1	0	0	0	.000
Totals	207	23	47	7	22	.227

PITCHING	G	IP	H	BB	SO	ERA
Mason	2	3	1	0	2	0.00
Jackson	1	7⅔	9	2	6	1.17
Schilling	2	16	11	5	19	1.69
Williams	4	5⅓	6	2	5	1.69
Rivera	1	2	1	1	2	4.50
Thigpen	2	1⅔	1	1	3	5.40
Mulholland	1	5	9	1	2	7.20
Greene	2	9⅓	12	7	7	9.64
West	3	2⅔	5	2	1	13.50
Andersen	3	2⅓	4	1	3	15.43
Totals	6	55	59	22	54	4.75

Overreaction Alert

Once an anti-owners guy, always an anti-owners guy—that's one way to make sense of the silly attack that U.S. Representative Jim Bunning (R., Ky.) leveled at baseball last week. Acting commissioner Bud Selig had offered each of the 535 members of Congress a chance to buy—that's right, *buy*—two tickets to the July 13 All-Star Game, in Baltimore, and Bunning, a conservative who's ordinarily pro-business, accused the owners of trying to bribe—that's right, *bribe*—the pols not to scrap the game's antitrust exemption.

The charge, which Bunning made in a letter to his Capitol Hill colleagues headed BRIBE ALERT, indicates that he still distrusts the owners, just as he did while winning 224 games as a big league pitcher from 1955 to '71. Bunning was a players' union firebrand who was instrumental in setting up the players' pension fund and hiring Marvin Miller as president of the increasingly militant union. But the suggestion that baseball can curry favor with members of Congress by offering to sell them tickets—Selig called the offer a "courtesy"—is laughable in light of the large sums of money that political action committees lavish on the legislators in hopes of influencing policy. Indeed, Bunning himself received $439,491 in PAC contributions in 1992, which ranks him among the top 10% of House members.

THEY SAID IT

Joe Torre, St. Louis manager: "When we lose, I can't sleep. When we win, I can't sleep. But when you win, you wake up feeling better."

American League Championship Series

TORONTO

BATTING	AB	R	H	HR	RBI	Avg
White	27	3	12	1	2	.444
Molitor	23	7	9	1	5	.391
Olerud	23	5	8	0	3	.348
T. Fernandez	22	1	7	0	1	.318
Alomar	24	3	7	0	4	.292
Sprague	21	0	6	0	4	.286
Carter	27	2	7	0	2	.259
Borders	24	1	6	0	3	.250
Henderson	25	4	3	0	0	.120
Totals	216	26	65	2	24	.301

PITCHING	G	IP	H	BB	SO	ERA
Cox	2	5	3	2	5	0.00
Castillo	2	2	0	1	1	0.00
Eichorn	1	2	1	1	1	0.00
Stewart	2	13⅓	8	8	8	2.03
Guzman	2	13	8	9	9	2.08
Leiter	2	2⅔	4	2	2	3.38
Timlin	1	2⅓	3	0	2	3.86
Ward	4	4⅔	4	3	8	5.79
Stottlemyre	1	6	6	4	4	7.50
Hentgen	1	3	9	2	3	18.00
Totals	6	54	46	32	43	3.67

CHICAGO

BATTING	AB	R	H	HR	RBI	Avg
Grebeck	1	0	1	0	0	1.000
Raines	27	5	12	0	1	.444
Thomas	17	2	6	1	3	.353
LaValliere	3	0	1	0	0	.333
Burks	23	4	7	1	3	.304
Guillen	22	4	6	0	2	.273
Johnson	23	2	5	1	6	.217
Ventura	20	2	4	1	5	.200
Newson	5	1	1	1	1	.200
Cora	22	1	3	0	1	.136
Karkovice	15	0	0	0	0	.000
Jackson	10	1	0	0	0	.000
Pasqua	6	1	0	0	0	.000
Totals	194	23	46	5	22	.237

PITCHING	G	IP	H	BB	SO	ERA
Hernandez	4	4	4	0	1	0.00
McCaskill	3	3⅔	3	1	3	0.00
Alvarez	1	9	7	2	6	1.00
A. Fernandez	2	15	15	6	10	1.80
DeLeon	2	4⅔	7	1	6	1.93
Belcher	1	3⅔	3	3	1	2.45
Radinsky	4	1⅔	3	1	1	10.80
McDowell	2	9	18	5	5	10.00
Bere	1	2⅓	5	2	3	11.57
Totals	6	53	65	21	36	3.57

World Series

Oct 16 ....Philadelphia 5 vs. Toronto 8
Oct 17 ....Philadelphia 6 vs. Toronto 4
Oct 19 ....Toronto 10 vs. Philadelphia 3
Oct 20 ....Toronto 15 vs. Philadelphia 14
Oct. 21 ....Toronto 0 vs. Philadelphia 2
Oct. 23 ....Philadelphia 6 vs. Toronto 8
(Toronto wins series 4-2.)

GAME 1 (AT TORONTO)

Philadelphia	2	0	1	0	1	0	0	0	1—5
Toronto	0	2	1	0	1	1	3	0	x—8

WP—Leiter **LP**—Schilling; **S**—D. Ward. **E**—Philadelphia: Thompson (1); Toronto: Alomar (1), Carter (1), Sprague (1). **LOB**—Philadelphia 11, Toronto 4. **2B**—Toronto: White (1), ALomar (1) **3B**—Philadelphia: Duncan (1) **HR**—Toronto: White (1), Olerud (1), Sprague (1) **SB**—Philadelphia: Dykstra (1), Duncan (1); Toronto: Alomar (1). **CS**—Toronto: Fernandez (1) **GIDP**—Philadelphia: Thompson, Toronto: White.
Recap: The offense to come in this series was foreshadowed in Game 1 as the two teams battered each other's starters early. John Olerud wristed a home run in the sixth, giving the Jays a 5–4 lead, to which they added three in the seventh. Al Leiter and Duane Ward silenced the Phillie bats in closing.
T—3:27. **A**—52,011.

GAME 2 (AT TORONTO)

Philadelphia	0	0	5	0	0	0	0	1	0—6
Toronto	0	0	0	2	0	1	0	1	0—4

WP—Mulholland; **LP**—Stewart; **Save**—Williams. **LOB**—Philadelphia 9, Toronto 5. **2B**—Toronto: White (2). Molitor (1), Fernandez (1). **HR**—Philadelphia: Dykstra (1),. Eisenreich (1) , Toronto: Carter (1) **SB**—Toronto: Molitor (1), Alomar (2), **CS**—Philadelphia: Stocker (1), Toronto: Henderson (1), Alomar (1)
Recap: In the third inning with two men on base, Jim

Eisenreich hit an 0–2 pitch over the fence in right-center to power Philadelphia to an early 5–0 lead. Toronto chipped away until Mitch Williams allowed two baserunners in the eighth, then caught Roberto Alomar in a foolish attempt to steal third. Williams earned the save by inducing a game-ending double-play grounder from Pat Borders.
T—3:35. **A**—52,062.

GAME 3 (AT PHILADELPHIA)

Toronto	3	0	1	0	0	1	3	0	2—10
Philadelphia	0	0	0	0	1	1	0	1—3

WP—Hentgen **LP**—Jackson.
E—Toronto: Carter (2). **LOB**—Toronto 7, Philadelphia 9. **2B**—Toronto: Henderson (1); Philadelphia: Kruk (1). **3B**—Toronto: White (1), Molitor (1), Alomar (1) **HR**—Toronto: Molitor (1), Philadelphia: Thompson (1). **SB**—Toronto: Alomar (3); **SF**—Toronto: Sprague, Fernandez, Carter; **GIDP**—Philadelphia: Hollins, Chamberlain.
Recap: Using a total of 13 hits from six different batters, Toronto pounded the Phillies in rainy, chilly Veterans Stadium to take a 2–1 series lead. Roberto Alomar, making up for his baserunning gaffe in Game 2, went 4-for-5 with 2 RBI.
T—3:16 (plus 1:12 rain delay in first.)
A—62,689.

GAME 4 (AT PHILADELPHIA)

Toronto	3	0	4	0	0	2	0	6	0—15
Philadelphia	4	2	0	1	5	1	1	0	0—14

WP—Castillo; **LP**—Williams; **Save**—D. Ward.
LOB—Toronto 10, Philadelphia 8. **2B**—Toronto: Henderson (2), White (3), Carter (1), A. Leiter (1); Philadelphia: Dykstra (1), Hollins (1), Thompson (1). **3B**— Toronto: White (2); Philadelphia: Thompson (1) **HR**—Philadelphia: Dykstra 2 (3), Daulton (1) **SB**—Toronto: Henderson (1), White (1); Philadelphia: Dykstra (2), Duncan (2).
Recap: The highest scoring game in the 532-game history of the World Series, this four-hour, 14 minute, rain-sprinkled slugfest set or tied 13 Series records. Pitchers appeared to be throwing batting practice, surrendering 31 hits, including seven doubles. Trailing 14–9 in the eighth, the Blue Jays scored half-a-dozen runs off relievers Larry Andersen and Mitch Williams to take the outrageous affair.
T—4:14. **A**—62,731.

GAME 5 (AT PHILADELPHIA)

Toronto	0	0	0	0	0	0	0	0	0—0
Philadelphia	1	1	0	0	0	0	0	0	0—2

WP—Schilling; **LP**—Guzman. **E**—Toronto: Borders (1); Philadelphia: Duncan (1). **LOB**—Toronto 6, Philadelphia 8. **2B**—Philadelphia: Daulton (1), Stocker (1); Toronto: Borders (2). **SB**—Philadelphia: Dykstra (3). **CS**—Toronto: Alomar (2). **GIDP**—Toronto: Alomar, Guzman; Philadelphia: Duncan.
Recap: Night to the previous day's game, this game saw the ever-reliable Phillie pitcher Curt Schilling put out the Toronto offensive fire with a complete game, a

five-hit shutout, staving off elimination for Philadelphia.
T—2:53. **A**—62,706.

GAME 6 (AT TORONTO)

Philadelphia	0	0	0	1	0	0	5	0	0—6
Toronto	3	0	0	1	1	0	0	0	3—8

WP—D. Ward; **LP**—Williams; **Blown Save**—Philadelphia: Willams, 2; Toronto: Cox,1. **E**—Toronto: Alomar (2), Sprague (2). **LOB**—Philadelphia 9, Toronto 7. **2B**—Philadelphia: Daulton (2); Toronto: Olerud (1), Alomar (2). **3B**—Toronto: Molitor (2). **HR**—Toronto: Molitor (2), Carter (2). Philadelphia: Dykstra (4). **SB**—Philadelphia: Dykstra (4), Duncan (3). **SF**—Philadelphia: Incaviglia; Toronto: Sprague, Carter.
Recap: With one out in the bottom of the ninth and the Phillies leading 6–5, Joe Carter faced Mitch Williams with Paul Molitor on first and Rickey Henderson on second, 2–2 the count. He hit a low, inside fastball over the fence in left and, with fireworks detonating in the dome, made an ecstatic, leaping tour around the bases to deliver the Jays their second straight world title. It was only the second time in the 89-year history of the Fall Classic that a series had been ended by a home run.
T—3:27. **A**—52,195.

World Series Composite Box Score

TORONTO

BATTING	AB	R	H	HR	RBI	Avg
Leiter	1	0	1	0	0	1.00
Molitor	24	10	12	2	8	.500
Butler	2	1	1	0	0	.500
Alomar	25	5	12	0	6	.480
Fernandez	21	2	7	0	9	.333
Borders	23	2	7	0	1	.304
White	24	6	7	1	7	.292
Carter	25	6	7	2	8	.280
Olerud	17	5	4	1	2	.235
Henderson	22	6	5	0	2	.227
Sprague	15	0	1	0	2	.867
4 others	7	0	0	0	0	.000
Totals	206	45	64	6	45	.311

PITCHING	G	IP	H	BB	SO	ERA
Timlin	2	2⅓	2	0	4	0.00
Eichhorn	1	⅓	1	1	0	0.00
Hentgen	1	6	5	3	6	1.50
Ward	4	4⅔	3	0	7	1.93
Guzman	2	12	10	8	12	3.75
Stewart	2	12	10	8	8	6.75
Leiter	3	7	12	2	5	7.71
Castillo	2	3⅓	6	3	1	8.10
Cox	3	3⅓	6	5	6	8.10
Stottlemyre	1	2	3	4	1	27.00
Totals	6	53	58	34	50	5.77

PHILADELPHIA

BATTING	AB	R	H	HR	RBI	Avg
Greene	1	1	1	0	0	1.000
Schilling	2	0	1	0	0	.500
Dykstra	23	9	8	4	8	.348
Kruk	23	4	8	0	4	.348
Duncan	29	5	10	0	2	.345
Thompson	16	3	5	1	6	.313
Hollins	23	5	6	0	2	.261
Eisenreich	26	3	6	1	7	.231
Daulton	23	4	5	1	4	.217
Stocker	19	1	4	0	1	.211
Jordan	10	0	2	0	0	.200
Morandini	5	1	1	0	0	.200
Incaviglia	8	0	1	0	1	.125
3 others	4	0	0	0	0	.000
Totals	212	36	58	7	35	.274

PITCHING	G	IP	H	BB	SO	ERA
Thigpen	2	2⅔	1	1	0	0.00
Mason	4	7⅓	4	1	7	1.17
Schilling	2	15⅓	13	5	9	3.52
Mulholland	2	10⅔	14	3	5	6.75
Jackson	1	5	6	1	1	7.20
Andersen	4	3⅔	5	3	3	12.27
Williams	3	2⅔	5	4	1	20.25
Greene	1	2⅓	7	4	1	27.00
Rivera	1	1⅓	4	2	3	27.00
West	3	1	5	1	0	27.00
Totals	6	52⅓	64	25	30	7.57

National League Batting

BATTING AVERAGE

Galarraga, Col	.370
Gwynn, SD	.358
Jefferies, StL	.342
Bonds, SF	.336
Grace, Chi	.325
Bagwell, Hou	.320
Piazza, LA	.318
Kruk, Phil	.316
Merced, Pitt	.313
Thompson, SF	.312

HITS

Dykstra, Phil	194
Grace, Chi	193
Grissom, Mon	188
Bell, Pit	187
Jefferies, StL	186
Blauser, Atl	182
Bonds, SF	181
Butler, LA	181

TRIPLES

Finley, Hou	13
Butler, LA	10
Bell, Pit	9
Morandini, Phil	9
Coleman, N.Y.	8
Martin, Pit	8

ON-BASE PERCENTAGE

Bonds, SF	.458
Kruk, Phil	.430
Dykstra, Phil	.420
Merced, Pitt	.414
Jefferies, StL	.408

HOME RUNS

Bonds, SF	46
Justice, Atl	40
Williams, SF	38
McGriff, Atl	37
Gant, Atl	36
Piazza, LA	35
Bonilla, NY	34
Plantier, SD	34

RUNS SCORED

Dykstra, Phil	143
Bonds, SF	129
Gant, Atl	113
McGriff, Atl	111
Blauser, Atl	110
Williams, SF	105
Grissom, Mon	104
Hollins, Phil	104

TOTAL BASES

Bonds, SF	365
Williams, SF	325
Gant, Atl	309
Dykstra, Phil	307
Piazza, LA	307

STOLEN BASES

Carr, Fla	58
Grissom, Mon	53
Nixon, Atl	47
Jefferies, Stl	46
Lewis, SF	46

RUNS BATTED IN

Bonds, SF	123
Justice, Atl	120
Gant, Atl	117
Piazza, LA	112
Williams, SF	110
Daulton, Phil	105
Zeile, StL	103
McGriff, Atl	101
Murray, NY	100
Plantier, Phil	100

DOUBLES

Hayes, Col	45
Dykstra, Phil	44
Bichette, Col	43
Biggio, Hou	41
Gwynn, SD	41
Gilkey, StL	40
Grace, Chi	39
Bonds, SF	38

SLUGGING PERCENTAGE

Bonds, Pit	.677
Galarraga, Col	.602
Williams, SF	.561
Piazza, LA	.561
McGriff, Atl	.549

BASES ON BALLS

Dykstra, Phil	129
Bonds, SF	126
Daulton, Phil	117
Kruk, Phil	111
Butler, LA	86
Blauser, Atl	85

National League Pitching

EARNED RUN AVERAGE

Maddux, Atl	2.36
Rijo, Cin	2.48
Portugal, Hou	2.77
Swift, SF	2.82
Avery, Atl	2.94
Harnisch, Hou	2.98
Candiotti, LA	3.12

SAVES

Myers, Chi	53
Beck, SF	48
Harvey, Fla	45
L. Smith, StL	43
Wetteland, Mon	43
Mitch Williams, Phil	43

WINS

Glavine, Atl	22
Burkett, SF	22
Swift, SF	21
Maddux, Atl	20
Portugal, Hou	18
Avery, Atl	18

GAMES PITCHED

Jackson, SF	81
Beck, SF	76
West, Phil	76
McMichael, Atl	74
Murphy, StL	73
Myers, Chi	73

STRIKEOUTS

Rijo, Cin	227
Smoltz, Atl	208
Maddux, Atl	197
Schilling, Phil	186
Harnisch, Hou	185
Benes, SD	179
Greene, Phil	167

INNINGS PITCHED

Maddux, Atl	267
Rijo, Cin	257⅓
Smoltz, Atl	243⅔
Glavine, Atl	239⅓
Drabek, Hou	237⅔
Schilling, Phil	235⅓

COMPLETE GAMES

Maddux, Atl	8
Drabek, Hou	7
Gooden, NY	7
Greene, Phil	7
Mulholland, Phil	7
Schilling, Phil	7

SHUTOUTS

Harnisch, Hou	4
R. Martinez, LA	3

American League Batting

BATTING AVERAGE

Olerud, Tor	.363
Molitor, Tor	.332
Alomar, Tor	.326
Lofton, Cle	.325
Baerga, Cle	.321
Thomas, Chi	.317
Greenwell, Bos	.315
Phillips, Det	.313
O'Neil, NY	.311
Johnson, Chi	.311

HOME RUNS

Gonzalez, Tex	46
Griffey, Sea	45
Thomas, Chi	41
Belle, Cle	38
Palmeiro, Tex	37
Carter, Tor	33
Palmer, Tex	33
Tettleton, Det	32
Salmon, Cal	31
Tartabull, NY	31

RUNS BATTED IN

Belle, Cle	129
Thomas, Chi	128
Carter, Tor	121
Gonzalez, Tex	118
Fielder, Det	117
Baerga, Clev	114
Davis, Cal	112
Molitor, Tor	111
Tettleton, Det	110
Griffey, Sea	109

HITS

Molitor, Tor	211
Baerga, Cle	200
Olerud, Tor	200
Alomar, Tor	192
Lofton, Cle	185
Puckett, Min	184
Fryman, Det	182
Griffey, Sea	180

RUNS SCORED

Palmeiro, Tex	124
Molitor, Tor	121
Lofton, Cle	116
White, Tor	116
Henderson, Tor	114
Griffey, Sea	113
Phillips, Det	113

DOUBLES

Olerud, Tor	54
White, Tor	42
Palmeiro, Tex	40
Valentin, Bos	40
Puckett, Min	39
Greenwell, Bos	38
Griffey, Sea	38

TRIPLES

Johnson, Chi	14
Cora, Chi	13
Hulse, Tex	10
Fernandez, Tor	9
McRae, KC	9

TOTAL BASES

Griffey, Sea	359
Gonzalez, Tex	339
Thomas, Chi	333
Palmeiro, Tex	331
Olerud, Tor	330

SLUGGING PERCENTAGE

Gonzalez, Tex	.632
Griffey, Sea	.617
Thomas, Chi	.607
Olerud, Tor	.599
Hoiles, Balt	.585

ON-BASE PERCENTAGE

Olerud, Tor	.473
Phillips, Det	.443
Henderson, Tor	.432
Thomas, Chi	.426
Hoiles, Balt	.416

STOLEN BASES

Lofton, Cle	70
Alomar, Tor	55
Polonia, Cal	55
Henderson, Tor	53
Curtis, Cal	48
Johnson, Chi	35

BASES ON BALLS

Phillips, Det	132
Henderson, Tor	120
Olerud, Tor	114
Thomas, Chi	112
Tettleton, Det	109
Ventura, Chi	105

American League Pitching

EARNED RUN AVERAGE

Appier, KC	2.56
Alvarez, Chi	2.95
Key, NY	3.00
Fernandez, Chi	3.13
Viola, Bos	3.14
Finley, Cal	3.15
Langston, Cal	3.20

WINS

McDowell, Chi	22
Johnson, Sea	19
Hentgen, Tor	19
Key, NY	18
Appier, KC	18
Fernandez, Chi	18

STRIKEOUTS

Johnson, Sea	308
Langston, Cal	196
Guzman, Tor	194
Cone, KC	191
Finley, Cal	187
Appier, KC	186
Eldred, MII	180

SAVES

Montgomery, KC	45
D. Ward, Tex	45
Henke, Tex	40
Hernandez, Chi	38
Eckersley, Oak	36

GAMES PITCHED

Harris, Bos	80
Radinsky, Chi	73
Fossas, Bos	71
Nelson, Sea	71
D. Ward, Tor	71
Frohwirth, Balt	70

INNINGS PITCHED

Eldred, Mil	258
McDowell, Chi	256⅔
Langston, Cal	256⅓
Johnson, Sea	255⅓
Cone, KC	254
Finley, Cal	251⅓

COMPLETE GAMES

Finley, Cal	13
Brown, Tex	12
Johnson, Sea	10
McDowell, Chi	10
Eldred, Mil	8

SHUTOUTS

McDowell, Chi	4
Brown, Tex	3
Johnson, Sea	3
Moore, Det	3
Doherty, Det	2
Finley, Cal	2
Key, NY	2

1993 Team Statistics

National League

TEAM BATTING	BA	AB	R	H	TB	2B	3B	HR	RBI	SB	BB	SO
San Francisco	.276	5557	808	1534	2373	269	33	168	759	120	516	930
Philadelphia	.274	5685	877	1555	2422	297	51	156	811	91	665	1049
Colorado	.273	5517	758	1507	2329	278	59	142	704	146	388	944
St. Louis	.272	5551	758	1508	2192	262	34	118	724	153	588	882
Chicago	.270	5627	738	1521	2327	259	32	161	706	100	446	923
Pittsburgh	.267	5549	707	1482	2179	267	50	110	664	92	536	972
Houston	.267	5464	716	1459	2235	288	37	138	656	103	497	911
Cincinnati	.264	5517	722	1457	2185	261	28	137	669	142	485	1025
Atlanta	.262	5515	767	1444	2248	239	29	169	712	125	560	946
Los Angeles	.261	5588	675	1458	2138	234	28	130	639	126	492	937
Montreal	.257	5493	732	1410	2118	270	36	122	682	228	542	860
San Diego	.252	5503	679	1386	2140	239	28	153	633	92	443	1046
New York	.248	5448	672	1350	2126	228	37	158	632	79	448	879
Florida	.248	5475	581	1356	1897	197	31	94	542	117	498	1054

TEAM PITCHING	ERA	W	L	Sho	CG	SV	Inn	H	R	ER	BB	SO
Atlanta	3.14	104	58	16	18	46	1455.0	1297	559	507	480	1036
Houston	3.49	85	77	14	18	42	1441⅓	1363	630	559	476	1056
Los Angeles	3.50	81	81	9	17	36	1472⅔	1406	662	573	567	1043
Montreal	3.55	94	68	7	8	61	1456⅔	1369	682	574	521	934
San Francisco	3.61	103	59	9	4	50	1456⅔	1385	636	585	442	982
Philadelphia	3.95	97	65	11	24	46	1472⅔	1419	740	647	573	1117
New York	4.05	59	103	8	16	22	1438	1483	744	647	434	867
St. Louis	4.09	87	75	7	5	54	1453	1553	744	660	383	775
Florida	4.13	64	98	5	4	48	1440⅓	1437	724	661	598	945
Chicago	4.18	84	78	5	8	56	1449⅔	1514	739	673	470	905
San Diego	4.23	61	101	6	8	32	1437⅔	1470	772	675	558	957
Cincinnati	4.51	73	89	8	11	37	1434	1510	785	718	508	996
Pittsburgh	4.77	75	87	5	12	34	1445⅔	1557	806	766	485	832
Colorado	5.41	67	95	0	9	35	1431⅓	1664	967	860	609	913

American League

TEAM BATTING	BA	AB	R	H	TB	2B	3B	HR	RBI	SB	BB	SO
New York	.279	5615	821	1568	2444	294	24	178	793	39	629	910
Toronto	.279	5579	847	1556	2434	317	42	159	796	170	588	861
Cleveland	.275	5619	790	1547	2296	264	31	141	747	159	488	843
Detroit	.275	5620	899	1546	2438	282	38	178	853	104	765	1122
Texas	.267	5510	835	1472	2377	284	39	181	780	113	483	984
Baltimore	.267	5508	786	1470	2276	287	24	157	744	73	655	930
Chicago	.265	5483	776	1454	2256	228	44	162	731	106	604	834
Minnesota	.264	5601	693	1480	2185	261	27	121	642	83	493	850
Boston	.264	5496	686	1451	2170	319	29	114	644	73	508	871
Kansas City	.263	5522	675	1455	2194	294	35	125	641	100	428	936
Seattle	.260	5495	734	1429	2232	272	24	161	681	91	624	901
California	.260	5364	684	1399	2048	259	24	114	644	169	564	930
Milwaukee	.258	5525	733	1426	2091	240	25	125	688	138	555	932
Oakland	.254	5543	715	1408	2184	260	21	158	679	131	622	1048

TEAM PITCHING	ERA	W	L	Sho	CG	SV	Inn	H	R	ER	BB	SO
Chicago	3.70	94	68	11	16	48	1454	1398	664	598	566	974
Boston	3.77	80	82	11	9	44	1452⅓	1379	698	609	552	997
Kansas City	4.04	84	78	6	16	48	1445⅓	1379	694	649	571	985
Seattle	4.20	82	80	10	22	41	1453⅔	1421	731	678	605	1083
Toronto	4.21	85	67	11	11	50	1441⅔	1441	742	674	620	1023
Texas	4.28	86	76	6	20	45	1438⅓	1476	751	684	562	957
Baltimore	4,31	85	77	10	21	42	1442⅔	1427	745	691	579	900
California	4.34	71	91	6	26	41	1430⅓	1457	770	690	550	843
New York	4.35	88	74	13	11	38	1438⅓	1511	761	695	552	899
Milwaukee	4.45	69	93	6	26	29	1447	1547	792	716	522	810
Cleveland	4.58	76	86	8	7	45	1445⅔	1591	813	735	591	888
Detroit	4.65	85	77	7	11	36	1436⅔	1547	837	742	542	828
Minnesota	4.71	71	91	3	5	44	1444⅓	1591	830	756	514	901
Oakland	4.90	68	94	2	8	42	1452⅓	1551	846	791	680	864

National League Team-by-Team Statistical Leaders

Atlanta Braves

BATTING	BA	G	AB	R	H	TB	2B	3B	HR	RBI	SB	BB	SO
Pecota, Bill	.323	72	62	17	20	24	2	1	0	5	1	1	5
Blauser, Jeff	.305	161	597	110	182	260	29	2	15	73	16	85	109
McGriff, Fred	.291	151	557	111	162	306	29	2	37	101	5	76	106
Sanders, Deion	.276	95	272	42	75	123	18	6	6	28	19	16	42
Gant, Ron	.274	157	606	113	166	309	27	4	36	117	26	67	117
Pendleton, Terry	.272	161	633	81	172	258	33	1	17	84	5	36	97
Justice, David	.270	157	585	90	158	301	15	4	40	120	3	78	90
Nixon, Otis	.269	134	461	77	124	145	12	3	1	24	47	61	63
Bream, Sid	.260	117	277	33	72	115	14	1	9	35	4	31	43
Lemke, Mark	.252	151	493	52	124	168	19	2	7	49	1	65	50
Berryhill, Damon	.245	115	335	24	82	128	18	2	8	43	0	21	64
Cabrera, Francisco	.241	70	83	8	20	35	3	0	4	11	0	8	21
Beillard, Rafael	.228	91	79	6	18	23	5	0	0	6	0	4	13
Olson, Greg	.225	83	262	23	59	81	10	0	4	24	1	29	27

PITCHING	ERA	W	L	G	GS	CG	SV	INN	H	R	ER	BB	SO
Bedrosian, Steve	1.63	5	2	49	0	0	0	49⅔	34	11	9	14	33
McMichael, Greg	2.06	2	3	74	0	0	19	91⅔	68	22	21	29	89
Howell, Jay	2.31	3	3	54	0	0	0	58⅓	48	16	15	16	37
Maddux, Greg	2.36	20	10	36	36	8	0	267	228	85	70	52	197
Mercker, Kent	2.86	3	1	43	6	0	0	66	52	24	21	36	59
Avery, Steve	2.94	18	6	35	35	3	0	223⅓	216	81	73	43	125
Glavine, Tom	3.20	22	6	36	36	4	0	239⅓	236	91	85	90	120
Smoltz, John	3.62	15	11	35	35	3	0	243⅔	208	104	98	100	208
Smith, Pete	4.37	4	8	20	14	0	0	90⅔	92	45	44	36	53
Wohlers, Mark	4.50	6	2	46	0	0	0	48	37	25	24	22	45
Stanton, Mike	4.67	4	6	63	0	0	27	52	51	35	27	29	43
Freeman, Marvin	6.08	2	0	21	0	0	0	23⅔	24	16	16	10	25
Borbon, Pedro	21.60	0	0	3	0	0	0	1⅔	3	4	4	3	2

Chicago Cubs

BATTING	BA	G	AB	R	H	TB	2B	3B	HR	RBI	SB	BB	SO
Hill, Glenallen	.345	31	87	14	30	67	7	0	10	22	1	6	21
Grace, Mark	.325	155	594	86	193	282	39	4	14	98	8	71	32
Sandberg, Ryne	.309	117	456	67	141	188	20	0	9	45	9	37	62
Wilkins, Rick	.303	136	446	78	135	250	23	1	30	73	2	50	99
Smith, Dwight	.300	111	310	51	93	153	17	5	11	35	8	25	51
May, Derrick	.295	128	465	62	137	196	25	2	10	77	10	31	41
Vizcaino, Jose	.287	151	551	74	158	197	19	4	4	54	12	46	71
Sanchez, Rey	.282	105	344	35	97	112	11	2	0	28	1	15	22
Rhodes, Karl	.278	20	54	12	15	28	2	1	3	7	2	11	9
Buechele, Steve	.272	133	460	53	125	201	27	2	15	65	1	48	87
Sosa, Sammy	.261	159	598	92	156	290	25	5	33	93	36	38	135
Wilson, Willie	.258	105	221	29	57	77	11	3	1	11	7	11	40
Jennings, Doug	.250	42	52	8	13	24	3	1	2	8	0	3	10
Lake, Steve	.225	44	120	11	27	48	6	0	5	13	0	4	19
Yelding, Eric	.204	69	108	14	22	32	5	1	1	10	3	11	22
Roberson, Kevin	.189	62	180	23	34	67	4	1	9	27	0	12	48
Maldonado, Candy	.186	70	140	8	26	40	5	0	3	15	0	13	40
Shields, Tommy	.176	20	34	4	6	7	1	0	0	1	0	2	10

PITCHING	ERA	W	L	G	GS	CG	SV	INN	H	R	ER	BB	SO
Bautista, Jose	2.82	10	3	58	7	1	2	111⅔	105	38	35	27	63
Myers, Randy	3.11	2	4	73	0	0	53	75⅓	65	26	26	26	86
Boskie, Shawn	3.43	5	3	39	2	0	0	65⅔	63	30	25	21	39
Assenmacher, Paul	3.49	2	1	46	0	0	0	38⅔	44	15	15	13	34
Hibbard, Greg	3.96	15	11	31	31	1	0	191	209	96	84	47	82
Morgan, Mike	4.03	10	15	32	32	1	0	207¾	206	100	93	74	111
Bullinger, Jim	4.32	1	0	15	0	0	1	16⅔	18	9	8	9	10
Guzman, Jose	4.34	12	10	30	30	2	0	191	188	98	92	74	163
Scanlan, Bob	4.54	4	5	70	0	0	0	75⅓	79	41	38	28	44
Plesac, Dan	4.74	2	1	57	0	0	0	62⅔	74	37	33	21	47
Castillo, Frank	4.84	5	8	29	25	2	0	141⅓	162	83	76	39	84
Harkey, Mike	5.26	10	10	28	28	1	0	157⅓	187	100	92	43	67

Cincinnati Reds

BATTING	BA	G	AB	R	H	TB	2B	3B	HR	RBI	SB	BB	SO
Mitchell, Kevin	.341	93	323	56	110	194	21	3	19	64	1	25	48
Kelly, Roberto	.319	78	320	44	102	152	17	3	9	35	21	17	43
Morris, Hal	.317	101	379	48	120	159	18	0	7	49	2	34	51
Larkin, Barry	.315	100	384	57	121	171	20	3	8	51	14	51	33
Howard, Thomas	.277	38	141	22	39	65	8	3	4	13	5	12	21
Sanders, Reggie	.274	138	496	90	136	220	16	4	20	83	27	51	118
Milligan, Randy	.274	83	234	30	64	95	11	1	6	29	0	46	49
Brumfield, Jacob	.268	103	272	40	73	114	17	3	6	23	20	21	47
Sabo, Chris	.259	148	552	86	143	243	33	2	21	82	6	43	105
Branson, Jeff	.241	125	381	40	92	118	15	1	3	22	4	19	73
Roberts, Bip	.240	83	292	46	70	86	13	0	1	18	26	38	46
Oliver, Joe	.239	139	482	40	115	185	28	0	14	75	0	27	91
Varsho, Gary	.232	77	95	8	22	34	6	0	2	11	1	9	19
Samuel, Juan	.230	103	261	31	60	90	10	4	4	26	9	23	53
Costo, Tim	.224	31	98	13	22	36	5	0	3	12	0	4	17

PITCHING	ERA	W	L	G	GS	CG	SV	INN	H	R	ER	BB	SO
Rijo, Jose	2.48	14	9	36	36	2	0	257⅓	218	76	71	62	227
Spradlin, Jerry	3.49	2	1	37	0	0	2	49	44	20	19	9	24
Ruffin, Johnny	3.58	12	8	31	30	5	0	213⅔	210	72	64	41	138
Reardon, Jeff	4.09	4	6	58	0	0	8	61⅔	66	34	28	10	35
Service, Scott	4.30	2	2	29	0	0	2	46	44	24	22	16	43
Belcher, Tim	4.47	9	6	22	22	4	0	137	134	72	68	47	101
Luebbers, Larry	4.54	2	5	14	14	0	0	77⅓	74	49	39	38	38
Browning, Tom	4.74	7	7	21	20	0	0	114	159	61	60	20	53
Cadaret, Greg	4.96	2	1	34	0	0	1	32⅔	40	19	18	23	23
Pugh, Tim	5.26	10	15	31	27	3	0	164⅓	200	102	96	59	94
Ayala, Bobby	5.60	7	10	43	9	0	3	98	106	72	61	45	65
Smiley, John	5.62	3	9	18	18	2	0	105⅔	117	69	66	31	60
Roper, John	5.63	2	5	16	15	0	0	80	92	51	50	36	54

Colorado Rockies

BATTING	BA	G	AB	R	H	TB	2B	3B	HR	RBI	SB	BB	SO
Galarraga, Andres	.370	120	470	71	174	283	35	4	22	98	2	24	73
Bichette, Dante	.310	141	538	93	167	283	43	5	21	89	14	28	99
Hayes, Charlie	.305	157	573	89	175	299	45	2	25	98	11	43	82
Girardi, Joe	.290	86	310	35	90	123	14	5	3	31	6	24	41
Clark, Jerald	.282	140	478	65	135	212	26	6	13	67	9	20	60
Sheaffer, Danny	.278	82	216	26	60	83	9	1	4	32	2	8	15
Jones, Chris	.273	86	209	29	57	94	11	4	6	31	9	10	48
Young, Eric	.269	144	490	82	132	173	16	8	3	42	42	63	41
Boston, Daryl	.261	124	291	46	76	135	15	1	14	40	1	26	57
Cole, Alex	.256	126	348	50	89	106	9	4	0	24	30	43	58
Castilla, Vinny	.255	105	337	36	86	136	9	7	9	30	2	13	45
Mejia, Roberto	.231	65	229	31	53	92	14	5	5	20	4	13	63

PITCHING	ERA	W	L	G	GS	CG	SV	INN	H	R	ER	BB	SO
Ruffin, Bruce	3.87	6	5	59	12	0	2	139⅔	145	71	60	69	126
Reynoso, Armando	4.00	12	11	30	30	4	0	189	206	101	84	63	117
Holmes, Darren	4.05	3	3	62	0	0	25	66⅔	56	31	30	20	60
Reed, Steve	4.48	9	5	64	0	0	3	84⅓	80	47	42	30	51
Harris, Greg	4.59	11	17	35	35	4	0	225⅓	239	127	115	69	123
Blair, Willie	4.75	6	10	46	18	1	-	146	184	90	77	42	84
Wayne, Gary	5.05	5	3	65	0	0	1	62⅓	68	40	35	26	49
Bottenfield, Kent	5.07	5	10	37	25	1	0	159⅔	179	102	90	71	63
Nied, David	5.17	5	9	16	16	1	0	87	99	53	50	42	46
Sanford, Mo	5.30	1	2	11	6	0	0	35⅔	37	25	21	27	36
Leskanic, Curt	5.37	1	5	18	8	0	0	57	59	40	34	27	20
Parrett, Jeff	5.38	3	3	40	6	0	1	73⅓	78	47	44	45	66
Painter, Lance	6.00	2	2	10	6	1	0	39	52	26	26	9	16
Fredrickson, Scott	6.21	0	1	25	0	0	0	29	33	25	20	17	20
Moore, Marcus	6.84	3	1	27	0	0	0	26⅓	30	25	20	20	13
Grant, Mark	7.46	0	0	20	0	0	1	25⅓	34	24	21	11	14
Smith, Bryn	8.49	2	4	11	5	0	0	29⅔	47	29	28	11	9

National League Team-by-Team Statistical Leaders *(Cont.)*

Florida Marlins

BATTING	BA	G	AB	R	H	TB	2B	3B	HR	RBI	SB	BB	SO
Cotto, Henry	.296	54	135	15	40	56	7	0	3	14	11	3	18
Sheffield, Gary	.294	140	494	67	145	235	20	5	20	73	17	47	64
Conine, Jeff	.292	162	595	75	174	240	24	3	12	79	2	52	135
Magadan, Dave	.286	66	227	22	65	89	12	0	4	29	0	44	30
Barberie, Bret	.277	99	375	45	104	139	16	2	5	33	2	33	58
Arias, Alex	.269	96	249	27	67	80	5	1	2	20	1	27	18
Carr, Chuck	.267	142	551	75	147	182	19	2	4	41	58	48	74
Weiss, Walt	.266	158	500	50	133	154	14	2	1	39	7	79	73
Destrade, Orestes	.255	153	569	61	145	231	20	3	20	87	0	58	130
Renteria, Ruch	.255	103	263	27	67	89	9	2	2	30	0	21	31
Carrillo, Matias	.255	24	5	4	14	20	6	0	0	3	0	1	7
Felix, Junior	.238	57	214	25	51	85	11	1	7	22	2	10	50
Santiago, Benito	.230	139	469	49	108	178	19	6	13	50	10	37	88
Natal, Bob	.214	41	117	3	25	34	4	1	1	6	1	6	22
Whitmore, Darrell	.204	76	250	24	51	75	8	2	4	19	4	10	72
Briley, Greg	.194	120	170	17	33	48	6	0	3	12	6	12	42

PITCHING	ERA	W	L	G	GS	CG	SV	INN	H	R	ER	BB	SO
Harvey, Bryan	1.70	1	5	59	0	0	45	69	45	14	13	13	73
Carpenter, Cris	2.89	0	1	29	0	0	0	37⅓	29	15	12	13	26
Turner, Matt	2.91	4	5	55	0	0	0	68	55	23	22	26	59
Lewis, Richie	3.26	6	3	57	0	0	0	77⅓	68	37	28	43	65
Aquino, Luis	3.42	6	8	38	13	0	0	110⅔	115	43	42	40	67
Rodriguez, Rich	3.79	2	4	70	0	0	3	76	73	38	32	33	43
Rapp, Pat	4.02	4	6	16	16	1	0	94	101	49	42	39	57
Hough, Charlie	4.27	9	16	34	34	0	0	204⅓	202	109	97	71	126
Bowen, Ryan	4.42	8	12	27	27	2	0	156⅔	156	83	77	87	98
Armstrong, Jack	4.49	9	17	36	33	0	0	196⅓	210	105	98	78	118
Hammond, Chris	4.66	11	12	32	32	1	0	191	207	106	99	66	108
Klink, Joe	5.02	0	2	59	0	0	0	37⅔	37	22	21	24	22
Weathers, Dave	5.12	2	3	14	6	0	0	45⅔	57	26	26	13	34

Houston Astros

BATTING	BA	G	AB	R	H	TB	2B	3B	HR	RBI	SB	BB	SO
Bagwell, Jeff	.320	142	535	76	171	276	37	4	20	88	13	62	73
Gonzalez, Luis	.300	154	540	82	162	247	34	3	15	72	20	47	83
Biggio, Craig	287	155	610	98	175	289	41	5	21	64	15	77	93
Bass, Kevin	284	111	229	31	65	92	18	0	3	37	7	26	31
Cedeno, Andujar	.283	149	505	69	143	208	24	4	11	56	9	48	97
Finley, Steve	.266	142	545	69	145	210	15	13	8	44	19	28	65
Caminiti, Ken	.262	143	543	75	142	212	31	0	13	75	8	49	88
Donnels, Chris	.257	88	179	18	46	70	14	2	2	24	2	19	33
James, Chris	256	65	129	19	33	63	10	1	6	19	2	15	34
Taubensee, Eddie	250	94	288	26	72	112	11	1	9	42	1	21	44
Anthony, Eric	.249	145	486	70	121	193	19	4	15	66	3	49	88
Uribe, Jose	245	45	53	4	13	14	1	0	0	3	1	8	5
Servais, Scott	244	85	258	24	63	107	11	0	11	32	0	22	45
Candaele, Casey	.240	75	121	18	29	40	8	0	1	7	2	10	14

PITCHING	ERA	W	L	G	GS	CG	SV	INN	H	R	ER	BB	SO
Reynolds,Shane	0.82	0	0	5	1	0	0	11	11	4	1	6	10
Hernandex, Xavier	2.61	4	5	72	0	0	9	96⅔	75	37	28	28	101
Portugual, Mark	2.77	33	33	1	0	1	0	208	194	75	64	77	131
Harnisch, Pete	2.98	16	9	33	33	5	0	217⅔	171	84	72	79	185
Edens, Tom	3.12	1	1	38	0	0	0	49	47	17	17	19	21
Jones, Todd	3.13	1	2	27	0	0	2	37⅓	28	14	13	15	25
Osuna, Al	3.20	1	1	44	0	0	2	25⅓	17	10	9	13	21
Kile, Darryl	3.51	15	8	32	26	4	0	171⅔	152	73	67	69	141
Drabek, Doug	3.79	9	18	34	34	7	0	237⅔	242	108	100	60	157
Swindell, Greg	4.16	12	13	31	30	1	0	190⅓	215	98	88	40	124
Jones, Doug	4.54	4	10	71	0	0	26	85⅓	102	46	43	21	66
Williams, Brian	4.83	4	4	42	5	0	3	82	76	48	44	38	56
Juden, Jeff	5.40	0	1	2	0	0	0	5	4	3	3	4	7
Agosto, Juan	6.00	0	0	6	0	0	0	6	8	4	4	0	3
Bell, Eric	6.14	0	1	10	0	0	0	7⅓	10	5	5	2	2

National League Team-by-Team Statistical Leaders *(Cont.)*

Los Angeles Dodgers

BATTING	BA	G	AB	R	H	TB	2B	3B	HR	RBI	SB	BB	SO
Hansen, Dave	.362	84	105	13	38	53	3	0	4	30	0	21	13
Piazza, Mike	.318	149	547	81	174	307	24	2	35	112	3	46	86
Butler, Brett	2.98	156	607	80	181	225	21	10	1	42	39	86	69
Goodwin, Tom	.294	30	17	6	5	6	1	0	0	1	1	1	4
Mondesi, Raul	291	42	86	13	25	42	3	1	4	10	4	4	16
Reed, Jody	.276	132	445	48	123	154	21	2	2	31	1	38	40
Offerman, Jeff	.269	158	590	77	159	195	21	6	1	62	30	71	75
Snyder, Cory	.266	143	516	61	137	205	33	1	11	56	4	47	147
Sharperson, Mike	.256	73	90	13	23	33	4	0	2	10	2	5	17
Hernandez, Carlos	253	50	99	6	25	36	5	0	2	7	0	2	11
Karros, Eric	.247	158	619	74	153	253	27	2	23	80	0	34	82
Webster, Mitch	244	88	172	26	42	58	6	2	2	14	4	11	24
Harris, Lenny	.238	107	160	20	38	52	6	1	2	11	3	15	15
Davis, Eric	.234	108	376	57	88	147	17	0	14	53	33	41	88
Wallach, Tim	.222	133	477	42	106	163	19	1	12	62	0	32	70
Rodriguez, Henry	222	76	176	20	39	73	10	0	8	23	1	11	39
Strawberry, Darryl	.140	32	100	12	14	31	2	0	5	12	1	16	19

PITCHING	ERA	W	L	G	GS	CG	SV	INN	H	R	ER	BB	SO
Gross, Kip	0.60	0	0	10	0	0	0	15	13	1	1	4	12
McDowell, Roger	2.25	5	3	54	0	0	2	68	76	32	17	30	27
Gott, Jim	2.32	4	8	62	0	0	25	77⅔	71	23	20	17	67
Martinez, Pedro	2.61	10	5	65	2	0	2	107	76	34	31	57	119
Candiotti, Tom	3.12	8	10	33	32	2	0	213⅔	192	86	74	71	155
Martinez, Ramon	3.44	10	12	32	32	4	0	211⅔	202	88	81	104	127
Astacio, Pedro	3.57	14	9	31	31	3	0	186⅓	165	80	74	68	122
Hershiser, Orel	3.59	12	14	33	33	5	0	215⅔	201	106	86	72	141
Trlicek, Rick	4.08	1	2	41	0	0	1	64	59	32	29	21	41
Gross, Kevin	4.14	13	13	33	32	3	0	202⅓	224	110	93	74	150
Wilson, Steve	4.56	1	0	25	0	0	1	25⅔	30	13	13	14	23
Daal, Omar	5.09	2	3	47	0	0	0	35⅓	36	20	20	21	19
Worrell, Todd	6.05	1	1	35	0	0	5	38⅔	46	28	26	11	31

Montreal Expos

BATTING	BA	G	AB	R	H	TB	2B	3B	HR	RBI	SB	BB	SO
Grisson, Marquis	.298	157	630	104	188	276	27	2	19	95	53	52	76
DeShields, Delino	295	123	481	75	142	179	17	7	2	29	43	72	64
Lansing, Mike	287	141	491	64	141	181	29	1	3	45	23	46	56
Alou, Moises	286	136	482	70	138	233	29	6	18	85	17	38	53
Frazier, Lou	286	112	189	27	54	66	7	1	1	16	17	16	24
Walker, Larry	.265	138	490	85	130	230	24	5	22	86	29	80	76
Berry, Sean	.261	122	299	50	78	139	15	2	14	49	12	41	70
White, Rondell	.260	23	73	9	19	30	3	1	2	15	1	7	16
Fletcher, Scott	.255	133	396	33	101	150	20	1	9	60	0	34	40
Colbrunn, Greg	.255	70	153	15	39	60	9	0	4	23	4	6	33
Ready, Randy	254	40	134	22	34	47	8	1	1	10	2	23	8
Cordero, Wilfredo	248	138	475	56	118	184	32	2	10	58	12	34	60
Vander Wal, John	.233	106	215	34	50	80	7	4	5	30	6	27	30
Spehr, Tim	.230	53	87	14	20	32	6	0	2	10	2	6	20
Bolick, Frank	.211	95	213	25	45	70	13	0	4	24	1	23	37
Marrero, Oreste	.210	32	81	10	17	27	5	1	1	4	1	14	16
Laker, Tim	.298	43	86	3	17	21	2	1	0	7	2	2	16

PITCHING	ERA	W	L	G	GS	CG	SV	INN	H	R	ER	BB	SO
Wetteland, John	1.37	9	3	70	0	0	43	85⅓	58	17	13	28	113
Fassero, Jeff	2.29	12	5	56	15	1	1	149⅔	119	50	38	54	140
Rueter, Kirk	2.73	8	0	14	14	1	0	85⅔	85	33	26	18	31
Rojas, Mel	2.95	5	8	66	0	0	10	88⅓	80	39	29	30	48
Scott, Tim	3.01	7	2	56	0	0	1	71⅓	81	28	24	34	65
Hill, Ken	3.23	9	7	28	28	2	0	183⅔	163	84	66	74	90
Martinez, Dennis	3.85	15	9	35	34	2	1	224⅔	211	110	96	64	138
Heredia, Gil	3.92	4	2	20	9	1	2	57⅓	66	28	25	14	40
Nabholz, Chris	4.09	9	8	26	21	1	0	116⅔	100	57	53	63	74
Shaw, Jeff	4.14	2	7	55	8	0	0	95⅔	91	47	44	32	50
Barnes, Brian	4.41	2	6	52	8	0	3	100	105	53	49	48	60
Henry, Butch	6.12	3	9	30	16	1	0	103	135	76	70	28	47

National League Team-by-Team Statistical Leaders *(Cont.)*

New York Mets

BATTING	BA	G	AB	R	H	TB	2B	3B	HR	RBI	SB	BB	SO
Murray, Eddie	.285	154	610	77	174	285	28	1	27	100	2	40	61
Orsulak, Joe	.284	134	409	59	116	163	15	4	8	35	5	28	25
Coleman, Vince	.279	92	373	64	104	140	14	8	2	25	38	21	58
Gallagher, Dave	.274	99	201	34	55	89	12	2	6	28	1	20	18
Kent, Jeff	.270	140	496	65	134	221	24	0	21	80	4	30	88
Bonilla, Bobby	.265	139	502	81	133	262	21	3	34	87	3	72	96
Landrum, Ced	.263	22	19	2	5	6	1	0	0	1	0	0	5
McKnight, Jeff	.256	105	164	19	42	53	3	1	2	13	0	13	31
O'Brien, Charlie	.255	67	188	15	48	71	11	0	4	23	1	14	14
Thompson, Ryan	.250	80	288	34	72	128	19	2	11	26	2	19	81
Bogar, Timothy	.244	78	205	19	50	72	13	0	3	25	0	14	29
Burnitz, Jeromy	.243	86	263	49	64	125	10	6	13	38	3	38	66
Johnson, Howard	.238	72	235	32	56	89	8	2	7	26	6	43	43
Hundley, Todd	.228	130	417	40	95	149	17	2	11	53	1	23	62
Fernandez, Tony	.225	48	173	20	39	51	5	2	1	14	6	25	19
Walker, Chico	.225	15	213	18	48	72	7	1	5	19	7	14	29
Saunders, Doug	.209	28	67	8	14	16	2	0	0	0	0	3	4
Jackson, Darrin	.195	31	87	4	17	21	1	0	1	7	0	2	22
Housie, Wayne	.188	18	16	2	3	4	1	0	0	1	0	1	1
Baez, Kevin	.183	52	126	10	23	32	9	0	0	7	0	13	17

PITCHING	ERA	W	L	G	GS	CG	SV	INN	H	R	ER	BB	SO
Fernandez, Sid	2.93	5	6	18	18	1	0	119⅔	82	42	39	36	81
Saberhagen, Bret	3.29	7	7	19	19	4	0	139⅓	131	55	51	17	93
Gooden, Dwight	3.45	12	15	29	29	7	0	208⅔	188	89	80	61	149
Maddux, Mike	3.60	3	8	58	0	0	5	75	67	34	30	27	57
Jones, Bobby	3.65	2	4	9	9	0	0	61⅔	61	35	25	22	35
Young, Anthony	3.77	1	16	39	10	1	3	100⅓	103	62	42	42	62
Hillman, Eric	3.97	2	9	27	22	3	0	145	173	83	64	24	60
Innis, Jeff	4.11	2	3	67	0	0	3	76⅔	81	39	35	38	36
Draper, Mike	4.25	1	1	29	1	0	0	42⅓	53	22	20	14	16
Tanana, Frank	4.48	7	15	29	29	0	0	183	198	100	91	48	104
Telgheder, David	4.76	6	2	24	7	0	0	75⅔	82	40	40	21	35
Franco, John	5.20	4	3	35	0	0	10	36⅓	46	24	21	19	29
Schourek, Pete	5.96	5	12	41	18	0	0	128⅓	168	90	85	45	72

Philadelphia Phillies

BATTING	BA	G	AB	R	H	TB	2B	3B	HR	RBI	SB	BB	SO
Stocker, Kevin	.324	70	259	46	84	108	12	3	2	31	4	30	43
Eisenreich, Jim	.318	153	362	51	115	161	17	4	7	54	5	26	36
Kruk, John	.316	150	535	100	169	254	33	5	14	85	6	111	87
Dykstra, Lenny	.305	161	637	143	194	307	44	6	19	66	37	129	64
Jordan, Ricky	.289	90	159	21	46	67	4	1	5	18	0	8	32
Pratt, Todd	.287	33	87	8	25	46	6	0	5	13	0	5	19
Duncan, Mariano	.282	124	496	68	140	207	26	4	11	73	6	12	88
Batiste, Ken	.282	79	156	14	44	68	7	1	5	29	0	3	29
Chamberlain, Wes	.282	96	284	34	80	140	20	2	12	45	2	17	51
Incaviglia, Pete	.274	116	368	60	101	195	16	3	24	89	1	21	82
Hollins, Dave	.273	143	543	104	148	240	30	4	18	93	2	85	109
Thompson, Milt	.262	129	340	42	89	119	14	2	4	44	9	40	57
Daulton, Darren	.257	147	510	90	131	246	35	4	24	105	5	117	111
Morandini, Mickey	.247	120	425	57	105	151	19	9	3	33	13	34	73

PITCHING	ERA	W	L	G	GS	CG	SV	INN	H	R	ER	BB	SO
Andersen, Larry	2.92	3	2	64	0	0	0	61⅔	54	22	20	21	67
West, David	2.92	6	4	76	0	0	3	86⅓	60	37	28	51	87
Mulholland, Terry	3.25	12	9	29	28	7	0	191	177	80	69	40	116
DeLeon, Jose	3.26	3	0	24	3	0	0	47	39	25	17	27	34
Williams, Mitch	3.34	3	7	65	0	0	43	62	56	30	23	44	60
Greene, Tommy	3.42	16	4	31	30	7	0	200	175	84	76	62	167
Jackson, Danny	3.77	12	11	32	32	2	0	210⅓	214	105	88	80	120
Schilling, Curt	4.02	16	7	34	34	7	0	235⅔	54	114	105	57	186
Mason, Roger	4.06	5	12	68	0	0	0	99⅔	90	48	45	34	71
Rivera, Ben	5.02	13	9	30	28	1	0	163	175	99	91	85	123
Williams, Mike	5.29	1	3	17	4	0	0	51	50	32	30	22	33
Thigpen, Bobby	6.05	3	1	17	0	0	0	19⅔	23	13	13	9	10

Pittsburgh Pirates

BATTING	BA	G	AB	R	H	TB	2B	3B	HR	RBI	SB	BB	SO
Merced, Orlando	.313	137	447	68	140	198	26	4	8	70	3	77	64
Bell, Jay	.310	154	604	102	187	264	32	9	9	51	16	77	122
Van Slyke, Andy	.310	83	323	42	100	145	13	4	8	50	11	24	40
Slaught, Don	300	116	377	34	113	166	19	2	10	55	2	29	56
King, Jeff	295	158	611	82	180	248	35	3	9	98	8	59	54
Smith, Lonnie	.286	94	199	35	57	88	5	4	6	24	9	43	42
Tomberlin, Andy	286	27	42	4	12	17	0	1	1	5	0	2	14
Martin, Al	281	143	480	85	135	231	26	8	18	64	16	42	122
Clark, Dave	271	110	277	43	75	123	11	2	11	46	1	38	58
Garcia, Carlos	269	141	546	77	147	218	25	5	12	47	18	31	67
Foley, Tom	.253	86	194	18	49	71	11	1	3	22	0	11	26
Young, Kevin	.236	141	449	38	106	154	24	3	6	47	2	36	82
McClendon, Lloyd	.221	88	181	21	40	59	11	1	2	19	0	23	17
Prince, Tom	.196	66	179	14	35	55	14	0	2	24	1	13	38

PITCHING	ERA	W	L	G	GS	CG	SV	INN	H	R	ER	BB	SO
Dewey, Mark	2.36	1	2	21	0	0	7	26⅔	14	8	7	10	14
Johnston, Joel	3.38	2	4	33	0	0	2	53⅓	38	20	20	19	31
Belinda, Stan	3.61	3	1	40	0	0	19	42⅓	35	18	17	11	30
Toliver, Freddie	3.74	1	0	12	0	0	0	21⅔	20	10	9	8	14
Cooke, Steve	3.89	10	10	32	32	3	0	210⅔	207	101	91	59	132
Hope, John	4.03	0	2	7	7	0	0	38	47	19	17	8	8
Minor, Blas	4.10	8	6	65	0	0	2	94⅓	94	43	43	26	84
Wagner, Paul	4.27	8	8	44	17	1	2	141⅓	143	72	67	42	114
Smith, Zane	4.55	3	7	14	14	1	0	83	97	43	42	22	32
Tomlin, Randy	4.85	4	8	18	18	1	0	98⅓	109	57	53	15	44
Ballard, Jeff	4.86	4	1	25	5	0	0	53⅔	70	31	29	15	16
Otto, Dave	5.03	3	4	28	8	0	0	68	85	40	38	28	30
Neagle, Danny	5.31	3	5	50	7	0	1	81⅓	82	49	48	37	73
Wakefield, Tim	5.61	6	11	24	20	3	0	128⅓	145	83	80	75	59
Walk, Bob	5.68	13	14	32	32	3	0	187	214	121	118	70	80
Petkovsek, Mark	6.96	3	0	26	0	0	0	32⅓	43	25	25	9	14

St. Louis Cardinals

BATTING	BA	G	AB	R	H	TB	2B	3B	HR	RBI	SB	BB	SO
Jefferies, Gregg	.342	142	544	89	186	264	24	3	16	83	46	62	32
Perry, Gerald	.337	96	98	21	33	50	5	0	4	16	1	18	23
Jordan, Brian	.309	67	223	33	69	121	10	6	10	44	6	12	35
Gilkey, Bernard	.305	137	557	99	170	268	40	5	16	70	15	56	66
Smith, Ozzie	.288	141	545	75	157	194	22	6	1	53	21	43	18
Brewer, Rod	.286	110	147	15	42	56	8	0	2	20	1	17	26
Alicea, Luis	.279	115	362	50	101	135	19	3	3	46	11	47	54
Zeile, Todd	.277	157	571	82	158	247	36	1	17	103	5	70	76
Pappas, Erik	.276	82	228	25	63	78	12	0	1	28	1	35	35
Zeile, Todd	.257	126	439	51	113	160	18	4	7	48	7	68	70
Pagnozzi, Tom	.258	92	330	31	85	123	15	1	7	41	1	18	30
Pena, Geronimo	.256	74	254	34	65	103	19	2	5	30	13	25	71
Whiten, Mark	.253	152	562	81	142	238	13	4	25	99	15	58	110
Lankford, Ray	238	127	407	64	97	141	17	3	7	45	14	81	111

PITCHING	ERA	W	L	G	GS	CG	SV	INN	H	R	ER	BB	SO
Perez, Mike	2.48	7	2	65	0	0	7	72⅔	65	24	20	20	58
Guetterman, Lee	2.93	3	3	40	0	0	1	46	41	18	15	16	19
Lancaster, Les	2.93	4	1	50	0	0	0	61⅓	56	24	20	21	36
Osborne, Donovan	3.76	10	7	26	26	1	0	155⅔	153	73	65	47	83
Arocha, Rene	3.78	11	8	32	29	1	0	188	197	89	79	31	96
Tewksbury, Bob	3.83	17	10	32	32	2	0	213⅔	258	99	91	20	97
Olivares, Omar	4.17	5	3	58	9	0	1	118⅓	134	60	55	54	63
Cormier, Rheal	4.33	7	6	38	21	1	0	145⅓	163	80	70	27	75
Smith, Lee	4.50	2	4	55	0	0	43	50	49	25	25	9	49
Watson, Allen	4.60	6	7	16	15	0	0	86	90	53	44	28	49
Urbani, Tom	4.65	1	3	18	9	0	0	62	73	44	32	26	33
Murphy, Rob	4.87	5	7	73	0	0	1	64⅔	73	37	35	20	41
Magrane, Joe	4.97	8	10	22	20	0	0	226	127	68	64	37	38

National League Team-by-Team Statistical Leaders *(Cont.)*

San Diego Padres

BATTING	BA	G	AB	R	H	TB	2B	3B	HR	RBI	SB	BB	SO
Gwynn, Tony	.358	122	489	70	175	243	41	3	7	59	14	36	19
Clark, Jerald	.313	102	240	33	75	119	17	0	9	33	2	8	31
Gardner, Jeff	.262	140	404	53	106	144	21	7	1	24	2	45	69
Bell, Derek	.262	150	542	73	142	226	19	1	21	72	26	23	122
Bean, Billy	.260	88	177	19	46	70	9	0	5	32	2	6	29
Gutierrez, Ricky	.251	133	438	76	110	145	10	5	5	26	4	50	97
Teufel, Tim	.250	96	200	26	50	86	11	2	7	31	2	27	39
Cianfrocco, Archi	.243	96	296	30	72	123	11	2	12	48	2	17	69
Plantier, Phil	.240	138	462	67	111	235	20	1	34	100	4	61	124
Shipley, Craig	.235	105	230	25	54	75	9	0	4	22	12	10	31
Higgins, Kevin	.221	71	181	17	40	46	4	1	0	13	0	16	17
Stillwell, Kurt	.215	57	121	9	26	33	4	0	1	11	4	11	22
Geren, Bob	.214	58	145	8	31	46	6	0	3	6	0	13	28

PITCHING	ERA	W	L	G	GS	CG	SV	INN	H	R	ER	BB	SO
Martinez, Pedro	2.43	3	1	32	0	0	0	37	23	11	10	13	32
Harris, Gene	3.03	6	6	59	0	0	23	59⅓	57	27	20	37	39
Benes, Andy	3.78	15	15	34	34	4	0	230⅔	200	111	97	86	179
Whitehurst, Wally	3.83	4	7	21	19	0	0	105⅔	109	47	45	30	57
Hoffman, Trevor	3.90	4	6	67	0	0	5	90	80	43	39	39	79
Mauser, Tim	4.00	0	1	36	0	0	0	54	51	28	24	24	46
Sanders, Scott	4.13	3	3	9	9	0	0	52⅓	54	32	24	23	37
Davis, Mark	4.26	1	5	60	0	0	4	69⅔	79	37	33	44	70
Seminara, Frank	4.47	3	3	18	7	0	0	46⅓	53	30	23	21	22
Brocail, Doug	4.56	4	13	24	24	0	0	128⅓	143	75	65	42	70
Worrell, Tim	4.92	2	7	21	16	0	0	100⅔	104	63	55	43	52
Eiland, Dave	5.21	0	3	10	9	0	0	48⅓	58	33	28	17	14
Taylor, Kerry	6.45	0	5	36	7	0	0	68⅓	72	53	49	49	45
Ashby, Andy	6.80	3	10	32	21	0	1	123	168	100	93	56	77

San Francisco Giants

BATTING	BA	G	AB	R	H	TB	2B	3B	HR	RBI	SB	BB	SO
Bonds, Barry	.336	159	539	129	181	365	38	4	46	123	29	126	79
Carreon, Mark	.327	78	150	22	49	81	9	1	7	33	1	13	16
Thompson, Robby	.312	128	494	85	154	245	30	2	19	65	10	45	97
McGee, Willie	.301	130	475	53	143	185	28	1	4	46	10	38	67
Williams, Matt	.294	145	579	105	170	325	33	4	38	110	1	27	80
Benzinger, Todd	.288	86	177	25	51	80	7	2	6	26	0	13	35
Clark, Will	.283	132	491	82	139	212	27	2	14	73	2	63	68
Clayton, Royce	.282	153	549	54	155	204	21	5	6	70	11	39	91
Manwaring, Kirt	.275	130	432	48	119	151	15	1	5	49	1	41	76
Reed, Jeff	.261	66	119	10	31	52	3	0	6	12	0	16	22
Lewis, Darren	.253	136	522	84	132	169	17	7	2	48	46	30	40
Scarsone, Steve	.252	44	103	16	26	41	9	0	2	15	0	4	32
Martinez, Dave	.241	91	241	28	58	87	12	1	5	27	6	27	39
Benjamin, Mike	.199	63	146	22	29	48	7	0	4	16	0	9	23
Colbert, Craig	.162	23	37	2	6	11	2	0	1	5	0	3	13

PITCHING	ERA	W	L	G	GS	CG	SV	INN	H	R	ER	BB	SO
Beck, Rod	2.16	3	1	76	0	0	48	79⅓	57	20	19	13	86
Rogers, Kevin	2.68	2	2	64	0	0	0	80⅔	71	28	24	28	62
Swift, Bill	2.82	21	8	34	34	1	0	232⅔	195	82	73	55	157
Jackson, Mike	3.03	6	6	81	0	0	1	77⅓	58	28	26	24	70
Sanderson, Scott	3.51	4	2	11	8	0	0	48⅔	48	20	19	7	36
Black, Buddy	3.56	8	2	16	16	0	0	93⅔	89	44	37	33	45
Wilson, Trevor	3.60	7	5	22	18	1	0	110	110	45	44	40	57
Burkett, John	3.65	22	7	34	34	2	0	231⅔	224	100	94	40	145
Minutelli, Gino	3.77	0	1	9	0	0	0	14⅓	7	9	6	15	10
Torres, Salomon	4.03	3	5	8	8	0	0	44⅔	37	21	20	27	23
Deshaies, Jim	4.24	2	2	5	4	0	0	17	24	9	8	6	5
Burba, Dave	4.25	10	3	54	5	0	0	95⅓	7	49	45	36	88
Hickerson, Bryan	4.26	7	5	47	15	0	0	120⅓	137	58	57	39	69
Brantley, Jeff	4.28	5	6	53	12	0	0	113⅔	112	60	54	46	76
Brummett, Greg	4.70	2	3	8	8	0	0	46	53	25	24	13	20
Righetti, Dave	5.70	1	1	51	0	0	1	47⅓	58	31	30	17	31

American League Team-by-Team Statistical Leaders

Baltimore Orioles

BATTING	BA	G	AB	R	H	TB	2B	3B	HR	RBI	SB	BB	SO
Baines, Harold	.313	118	416	64	130	212	22	0	20	78	0	57	52
Hoiles, Chris	.310	126	419	80	130	245	28	0	29	82	1	69	94
Hammonds,.Jeffery	.305	33	105	10	32	49	8	0	3	19	4	2	16
Pagliarulo, Mike	.303	116	370	55	112	172	25	4	9	44	6	26	49
Hulett, Tim	.300	85	260	40	78	99	15	0	2	23	1	23	56
Voigt, Jack	296	64	152	32	45	76	11	1	6	23	1	25	33
Segui, David	.273	146	450	54	123	180	27	0	10	60	2	58	53
Obando, Sherman	.272	31	92	8	25	36	2	0	3	15	0	4	26
Anderson, Brady	.263	142	560	87	147	238	36	8	13	66	24	82	99
Ripken, Cal, Jr.	.257	162	641	87	165	269	26	3	24	90	1	65	58
Reynolds, Harold	.252	145	485	64	122	162	20	4	4	47	12	66	47
Devereaux, Mike	.250	131	527	72	132	211	31	3	14	75	3	43	99
Buford, Damon	.228	53	79	18	18	29	5	0	2	9	2	9	19

PITCHING	ERA	W	L	G	GS	CG	SV	INN	H	R	ER	BB	SO
Olson, Greg	1.60	0	2	50	0	0	29	45	37	9	8	18	44
Poole, Jim	2.15	2	1	55	0	0	2	50⅓	30	18	12	21	29
Mills, Alan	3.23	5	4	45	0	0	4	100⅓	80	39	36	51	68
McDonald, Ben	3.39	13	14	34	34	7	0	220⅓	185	92	83	86	171
Moyer, Jamie	3.43	12	9	25	25	3	0	152	154	63	58	38	90
Frohwirth, Todd	3.83	6	7	70	0	0	3	96⅓	91	47	41	44	50
Oquist, Mike	3.86	0	0	5	0	0	0	11⅔	12	5	5	4	8
Mussina, Mike	4.46	14	6	25	25	3	0	167⅔	163	84	83	44	117
O'Donoghue, John	4.58	0	1	11	1	0	0	19⅔	22	12	10	10	16
Williamson, Mark	4.91	7	5	48	1	0	0	88	106	54	48	25	45
Valenzuela, Fernando	4.94	8	10	32	31	5	0	178⅔	179	104	98	79	78
Sutcliffe, Rick	5.75	10	10	29	28	3	0	166	212	112	106	74	80
McGehee, Kevin	5.94	0	0	5	0	0	0	16⅔	18	11	11	7	7

Boston Red Sox

BATTING	BA	G	AB	R	H	TB	2B	3B	HR	RBI	SB	BB	SO
Naehring, Tim	331	39	127	14	42	55	10	0	1	17	1	10	26
Greenwell, Mike	315	146	540	77	170	259	38	6	13	72	5	54	46
McNeely, Jeff	297	21	37	10	11	14	1	1	0	1	6	7	9
Vaughn, Mo	297	152	539	86	160	283	34	1	29	101	4	79	130
Hatcher, Billy	.287	136	508	71	146	203	24	3	9	57	14	28	46
Fletcher, Scott	.285	121	508	71	146	203	24	3	9	57	16	37	35
Cooper, Scott	.279	156	526	67	147	209	29	3	9	63	5	58	81
Valentin, John	.278	144	468	50	130	209	40	3	11	66	3	49	77
Dawson, Andre	.273	121	461	44	126	196	29	1	13	67	2	17	49
Quintana, Carlos	.244	101	303	31	74	82	5	0	1	19	1	31	52
Zupcic, Bob	.241	141	286	40	69	103	24	2	2	26	5	27	54
Melvin, Bob	.241	77	176	13	39	55	7	0	3	23	0	7	44
Deer, Rob	.210	128	466	6	98	180	17	1	21	55	5	58	169
Rivera, Luis	.208	62	130	13	27	40	8	1	1	7	1	11	36
Riles, Ernest	.189	94	143	15	27	50	8	0	5	20	1	20	40
Pena, Tony	.181	126	304	20	55	78	11	0	4	19	1	25	46

PITCHING	ERA	W	L	G	GS	CG	SV	INN	H	R	ER	BB	SO
Dopson, Pat	4.97	7	11	34	28	1	0	155⅔	170	93	86	59	89
Russell, Jeff	2.70	1	4	51	0	0	33	46⅔	39	16	14	14	45
Sele, Aaron	2.74	7	2	18	18	0	0	111⅔	100	42	34	48	93
Viola, Frank	3.14	11	8	29	29	2	0	183⅔	180	76	64	72	91
Darwin, Danny	3.26	15	11	34	34	2	0	229⅓	196	93	83	49	130
Clemens, Roger	4.46	11	14	29	29	2	0	191⅔	175	99	95	67	160
Bankhead, Scott	3.50	2	1	40	0	0	0	64⅓	59	28	25	29	47
Minchey, Nate	3.55	1	2	5	5	1	0	33	35	16	13	8	18
Ryan, Ken	3.60	7	2	47	0	0	1	50	43	23	20	29	49
Harris, Greg	3.77	6	7	80	0	0	8	112⅓	95	55	47	60	103
Quantril, Paul	3.91	6	12	49	14	1	1	138	151	73	60	44	66

American League Team-by-Team Statistical Leaders *(Cont.)*

California Angels

BATTING	BA	G	AB	R	H	TB	2B	3B	HR	RBI	SB	BB	SO
Easley, Damion	.313	73	230	33	72	95	13	2	2	22	6	28	35
Javier, Stan	.291	92	237	33	69	96	10	4	3	28	12	27	33
Curtis, Chad	.285	52	583	94	166	215	25	3	6	59	48	70	89
Salmon, Tim	283	142	515	93	146	276	35	1	31	95	5	82	135
Turner, Chris	.280	25	75	9	21	29	5	0	1	13	1	9	16
Gruber, Kelly	.277	18	65	10	18	30	3	0	3	9	0	2	11
Polonia, Luis	.271	152	576	75	156	188	17	6	1	32	55	48	53
Correia, Rod	.266	64	128	12	34	39	5	0	0	9	2	6	20
Myers, Greg	.255	108	290	27	74	105	10	0	7	40	3	17	47
Gonzles, Rene	.251	118	335	34	84	107	17	0	2	31	5	49	45
Lovullo, Torey	.251	116	367	42	92	130	20	0	6	30	7	36	49
Perez, Eduardo	.250	52	180	16	45	67	6	2	4	305	5	9	39
Davis, Chili	.243	153	573	74	139	252	32	0	27	112	4	71	135
Snow, J.T.	.241	129	419	60	101	171	18	2	16	57	3	55	88
Di Sarcina, Gary	.238	126	416	44	99	130	20	1	3	45	5	15	38
Tingley, Ron	.200	58	90	7	18	25	7	0	0	12	1	9	22

PITCHING	ERA	W	L	G	GS	CG	SV	INN	H	R	ER	BB	SO
Butcher, Michael	2.86	1	0	23	0	0	8	28⅓	21	12	9	15	24
Grahe, Joe	2.86	4	1	45	0	0	11	56⅔	54	22	18	25	31
Frey, Steve	2.98	2	3	55	0	0	3	48⅓	41	20	16	26	22
Finley, Chuck	3.15	16	14	35	35	13	0	251⅓	243	108	88	82	187
Langston, Mark	3.20	16	11	35	35	7	0	256⅓	220	100	91	85	196
Leftwich, Phil	3.79	4	6	12	12	1	0	80⅔	81	35	34	27	31
Magrane, Joe	3.94	3	2	8	8	0	0	48	48	27	21	21	24
Lewis, Scott	4.22	1	2	15	4	0	0	32	37	16	15	12	10
Sanderson, Scott	4.46	7	11	21	21	4	0	135⅓	153	77	67	27	66
Patterson, Ken	4.58	1	1	46	0	0	1	59	54	30	30	35	36
Hathaway, Hilly	5.02	4	3	11	11	0	0	57⅓	71	35	32	26	11
Valera, Julio	6.62	3	6	19	5	0	4	53	77	44	39	15	28
Springer, Russ	7.20	1	6	14	9	1	0	60	73	48	48	32	31
Farrell, John	7.35	3	12	21	17	0	0	90⅔	110	74	74	44	45
Linton, Doug	7.36	2	1	23	1	0	0	36⅔	46	30	30	23	23

Chicago White Sox

BATTING	BA	G	AB	R	H	TB	2B	3B	HR	RBI	SB	BB	SO
Thomas, Frank	.317	153	549	106	174	333	36	0	41	128	4	112	54
Johnson, Lance	.311	147	540	75	168	214	18	14	0	47	35	36	33
Raines, Tim	.306	115	415	75	127	199	16	4	16	54	21	64	35
Guillen, Ozzie	280	134	457	44	128	171	23	4	4	50	5	10	41
Burks, Ellis	.275	146	499	75	137	220	24	4	17	74	6	60	97
Cora, Joey	.268	153	579	95	155	202	15	13	2	51	20	67	63
Ventura, Robin	.262	157	554	85	145	240	27	1	22	94	1	105	82
LaValliere, Mike	.258	37	97	6	25	27	2	0	0	8	0	4	14
Sax, Steve	.235	57	119	20	28	36	5	0	1	8	7	8	6
Jackson, Bo	.232	85	284	32	66	123	9	0	16	45	0	23	106
Karkovice, Ron	.228	128	403	60	92	171	17	1	20	54	2	29	126
Grebeck, Craig	.226	72	190	25	43	51	5	0	1	12	1	26	26
Bell, George	.217	102	410	36	89	149	17	2	13	64	1	13	49
Calderon, Ivan	.209	82	239	26	50	67	10	2	1	22	4	21	33
Pasqua, Dan	.205	78	176	22	36	63	10	1	5	20	2	26	51

PITCHING	ERA	W	L	G	GS	CG	SV	INN	H	R	ER	BB	SO
Hernandez, Roberto	2.29	3	4	70	0	0	38	78⅔	66	21	20	20	71
Leach, Terry	2.81	0	0	14	0	0	1	16	15	5	5	2	3
Alvarez, Wilson	2.95	15	8	31	31	1	0	207⅔	168	78	68	122	155
Fernandez, Alex	3.13	18	9	34	34	3	0	247⅓	221	95	86	67	169
Pall, Donn	3.22	2	3	39	0	0	1	58⅔	62	25	21	11	29
McDowell, Jack	3.37	22	10	34	34	10	0	256⅔	261	104	96	69	158
Bere, Jason	3.47	12	5	24	24	1	0	142⅔	109	60	55	91	129
Schwarz, Jeff	3.71	2	2	41	0	0	0	51	35	21	21	38	41
Radinsky, Scott	4.28	8	2	73	0	0	4	54⅔	61	33	26	19	44
Belcher, Tim	4.40	3	5	12	11	1	0	71⅔	64	36	35	27	34
McCaskill, Kirk	5.23	4	8	30	14	0	2	113⅔	144	71	66	36	65
Thigpen, Bobby	5.71	0	0	25	0	0	1	34⅔	51	25	22	12	19

Cleveland Indians

BATTING	BA	G	AB	R	H	TB	2B	3B	HR	RBI	SB	BB	SO
Lofton, Kenny	.325	148	569	116	185	232	28	8	1	42	70	81	83
Baerga, Carlos	.321	154	624	105	200	303	28	6	21	114	15	34	68
Treadway, Jeff	.303	97	221	25	67	89	14	1	2	27	1	14	21
Belle, Albert	.290	159	594	93	172	328	36	3	38	129	23	76	96
Espinosa, Alvaro	.278	129	263	34	73	100	15	0	4	27	2	8	36
Alomar, Sandy, Jr.	.270	64	215	24	58	85	7	1	6	32	3	11	28
Kirby, Wayne	.269	131	458	71	123	170	19	5	6	60	17	37	58
Thome, Jim	.266	47	154	28	41	73	11	0	7	22	2	29	36
Fermin, Felix	.263	140	480	48	126	152	16	2	2	45	4	24	14
Sorrento, Paul	.257	148	463	75	119	201	26	1	18	65	3	58	121
Jefferson, Reggie	.249	113	366	35	91	136	11	2	10	34	1	28	78
Maldonado, Candy	.247	28	81	11	20	37	2	0	5	20	0	11	18
Martinez, Carlos	.244	80	262	26	64	89	10	0	5	31	1	20	29
Howard, Thomas	.236	74	178	26	42	58	7	0	3	23	5	12	42
Hill, Glenallen	.224	66	174	19	39	65	7	2	5	25	7	11	50
Ortiz, Junior	.221	95	249	19	55	68	13	0	0	20	1	11	26

PITCHING	ERA	W	L	G	GS	CG	SV	INN	H	R	ER	BB	SO
Lilliquist, Derek	2.25	4	4	56	2	0	10	64	64	20	16	19	40
DiPoto, Jerry	2.40	4	4	46	0	0	11	56⅓	57	21	15	30	41
Plunk, Eric	2.79	4	5	70	0	0	15	71	61	29	22	30	77
Hernandez, Jeremy	3.14	6	5	49	0	0	8	77⅓	75	33	27	27	44
Wertz, William	3.62	2	3	34	0	0	0	59⅔	54	28	24	32	53
Kramer, Tom	4.02	7	3	39	16	1	0	121	126	60	54	59	71
Clark, Dave	4.28	7	5	26	15	1	0	109⅓	119	55	52	25	57
Slocumb, Heathcliff	4.28	3	1	20	0	0	0	27⅓	28	14	13	16	18
Ojeda, Bob	4.40	2	1	9	7	0	0	43	48	22	21	21	27
Young, Cliff	4.62	3	3	21	7	0	1	60⅓	74	35	31	18	31
Mesa, Jose	4.92	10	12	34	33	3	0	208⅔	232	122	114	62	118
Young, Matt	5.21	1	6	22	8	0	0	74⅓	75	45	43	57	65
Cook, Dennis	5.67	5	5	25	6	0	0	54	62	36	34	16	34

Detroit Tigers

BATTING	BA	G	AB	R	H	TB	2B	3B	HR	RBI	SB	BB	SO
Trammell, Alan	.329	112	401	72	132	199	25	3	12	60	12	38	38
Phillips, Tony	.313	151	566	113	177	225	27	0	7	57	16	132	102
Fryman, Travis	.300	151	607	98	182	295	37	5	22	97	9	77	128
Livingstone, Scott	.293	98	304	39	89	109	10	2	2	39	1	19	32
Whitaker, Lou	.290	119	383	72	111	172	32	1	9	67	3	78	46
Kreuter, Chad	.286	119	374	59	107	181	23	3	15	51	2	49	92
Barnes, Skeeter	.281	84	160	24	45	61	8	1	2	27	5	11	19
Fielder, Cecil	.267	154	573	80	153	266	23	0	30	117	0	90	125
Gladden, Dan	.267	91	356	52	95	154	16	2	13	56	8	21	50
Gibson, Kirk	.261	116	403	62	105	174	18	5	13	62	15	44	87
Davis, Eric	.253	23	75	14	19	40	1	1	6	15	2	9	17
Gomez, Leo	.250	46	128	11	32	41	7	1	0	11	2	9	17
Tettleton, Mickey	.245	152	522	79	128	257	25	4	32	110	3	109	139
Cuyler, Milt	.213	82	249	46	53	78	11	7	0	19	13	19	53
Thurman, Gary	.213	75	89	22	19	25	2	2	0	13	7	11	30

PITCHING	ERA	W	L	G	GS	CG	SV	INN	H	R	ER	BB	SO
Henneman, Mike	2.64	5	3	63	0	0	24	71⅔	69	28	21	32	58
Krueger, Bill	3.40	6	4	32	7	0	0	82	90	43	31	30	60
Boever, Joe	3.61	6	3	61	0	0	3	102½	101	50	41	44	63
Wells, David	4.19	11	9	32	20	0	0	187	183	93	87	42	139
Doherty, John	4.44	14	11	32	31	3	0	184⅔	205	104	91	48	63
Bolton, Tom	4.47	6	6	43	8	0	0	102½	113	57	51	45	66
Leiter, Mark	4.73	6	6	27	13	1	0	106⅔	111	61	56	44	70
Knudsen, Kurt	4.78	3	2	30	0	0	2	37⅔	41	22	20	16	29
Davis, Storm	5.05	2	8	43	8	0	4	98	93	57	55	48	73
Moore, Mike	5.22	13	9	36	36	4	0	213⅔	227	135	124	89	89
MacDonald, Bob	5.35	3	3	68	0	0	3	65⅔	67	42	39	33	39
Gullickson, Bill	5.37	13	9	28	28	2	0	159¼	186	106	95	44	70
Bergman, Sean	5.67	1	4	9	6	1	0	39⅔	47	29	25	23	19
Groom, Buddy	6.14	0	2	19	3	0	0	36⅔	48	25	25	13	15

Kansas City Royals

BATTING	BA	G	AB	R	H	TB	2B	3B	HR	RBI	SB	BB	SO
Gwynn, Chris	.300	103	287	36	86	111	14	4	1	25	0	24	34
Joyner, Wally	.292	141	497	83	145	232	36	3	15	65	5	66	67
Brooks, Hubie	.286	75	168	14	48	63	12	0	1	24	0	11	27
McRae, Brian	.282	153	627	78	177	259	28	9	12	69	23	37	105
Gagne, Greg	.280	159	540	66	151	219	32	3	10	57	10	33	93
Macfarlane, Mike	.273	117	388	55	106	193	27	0	20	67	2	40	83
Brett, George	.266	145	560	69	149	243	31	3	19	75	7	39	67
Wilson, Willie	.265	21	49	6	13	17	1	0	1	3	1	7	6
Pulliam, Harvey	.258	27	62	7	16	24	5	0	1	6	0	2	14
Mayne, Brent	.254	71	205	22	52	69	9	1	2	22	3	18	31
Jose, Felix	.253	149	499	64	126	174	24	3	6	43	31	36	95
Lind, Jose	.248	136	431	33	107	124	13	2	0	37	3	13	36
McReynolds, Kevin	.245	110	351	44	86	149	22	4	11	42	2	37	56
Gaetti, Gary	.245	102	331	40	81	145	20	1	14	50	1	21	87
Hamelin, Bob	.224	16	49	2	11	20	3	0	2	5	0	6	15
Rossy, Rico	.221	46	86	10	19	29	4	0	2	12	0	16	82
Hiatt, Phil	.218	81	238	30	52	87	12	1	7	36	6	16	82
Miller, Keith	.167	37	108	9	18	21	3	0	0	3	3	8	19

PITCHING	ERA	W	L	G	GS	CG	SV	INN	H	R	ER	BB	SO
Montgomery, Jeff	2.27	7	5	69	0	0	45	87⅓	65	22	22	23	66
Appier, Kevin	2.56	18	8	34	34	5	0	238⅔	183	74	68	81	186
Cadaret, Greg	2.93	1	1	13	0	0	0	15⅓	14	5	5	7	2
Cone, David	3.33	11	14	34	34	6	0	254	205	102	94	114	191
Brewer, Billy	3.46	2	2	46	0	0	0	39	31	16	15	20	28
Gordon, Tom	3.58	12	6	48	14	2	1	155⅔	125	65	62	77	143
Pihcardo, Hipolito	4.04	7	8	30	25	2	0	165	183	85	74	53	70
Magnante, Mike	4.08	1	2	7	6	0	0	35½	37	16	16	11	16
Habyan, John	4.15	2	1	48	0	0	1	56½	59	27	26	20	39
Belinda, Stan	4.28	1	1	23	0	0	0	27½	30	13	13	6	25
Gubicza, Mark	4.66	5	8	49	6	0	2	104⅓	128	61	54	43	80
Haney, Chris	6.02	9	9	23	23	1	0	124	141	87	83	53	65
Gardner, Mark	6.19	4	6	17	16	0	0	91⅔	92	65	63	36	54

Milwaukee Brewers

BATTING	BA	G	AB	R	H	TB	2B	3B	HR	RBI	SB	BB	SO
Hamilton, Darryl	.310	135	520	74	161	211	21	1	9	48	21	45	62
Surhoff, B.J.	.274	148	552	66	151	216	38	3	7	79	12	36	47
Thon, Dickie	.269	85	245	23	66	81	10	1	1	33	6	22	39
Seitzer, Kevin	.269	120	417	45	112	165	16	2	11	57	7	44	48
Vaughn, Greg	.267	154	569	97	152	274	28	2	30	97	10	89	118
Jaha, John	.264	153	515	78	136	214	21	0	19	70	13	51	109
Yount, Robin	.258	127	454	62	117	172	25	3	8	51	9	44	93
Nilsson, Dave	.257	100	296	35	76	111	10	2	7	40	3	37	36
Reimer, Kevin	.249	125	437	53	109	172	22	1	13	60	5	30	72
Listach, Pat	.244	98	356	50	87	113	15	1	3	30	18	37	70
Spiers, Bill	.238	113	340	43	81	103	8	4	2	36	9	29	51
Bell, Juan	.234	91	286	42	67	92	6	2	5	29	6	36	64
Brunansky, Tom	.183	80	224	20	41	72	7	3	6	29	3	25	59

PITCHING	ERA	W	L	G	GS	CG	SV	INN	H	R	ER	BB	SO
Lloyd, Graeme	2.83	3	4	55	0	0	0	63⅔	64	24	20	13	31
Orosco, Jesse	3.18	3	5	57	0	0	8	56⅔	47	25	20	17	67
Miranda, Angel	3.30	4	5	22	17	2	0	120	100	53	44	52	88
Fetters, Mike	3.34	3	3	45	0	0	0	59⅓	59	29	22	22	23
Ignasiak, Mike	3.65	1	1	27	0	0	0	37	32	17	15	21	28
Austin, James	3.82	1	2	31	0	0	0	33	28	15	14	13	15
Eldred, Cal	4.01	16	16	36	36	8	0	258	232	120	115	91	180
Wegman, Bill	4.48	4	14	20	18	5	0	120⅓	135	70	60	34	50
Novoa, Rafael	4.50	0	3	15	7	2	0	56	58	32	28	22	17
Maldonado, Carlos	4.58	2	2	29	0	0	0	37⅓	40	20	19	17	18
Bones, Ricky	4.86	11	11	32	31	3	0	203⅔	222	122	110	63	63
Navarro, Jaimie	5.33	11	12	35	34	5	0	214⅓	254	135	127	73	114
Henry, Doug	5.56	4	4	54	0	0	17	55	67	37	343	25	38
Boddicker, Mike	5.67	3	5	10	10	1	0	54	77	35	34	15	24

Minnesota Twins

BATTING	BA	G	AB	R	H	TB	2B	3B	HR	RBI	SB	BB	SO
Hale, Chip	.333	69	186	25	62	79	6	1	3	27	2	18	17
Harper, Brian	.304	147	530	52	161	225	26	1	12	73	1	29	29
Puckett, Kirby	.296	156	662	89	184	295	39	3	22	89	8	47	93
Knoblauch, Chuck	.277	153	602	82	167	208	27	4	2	41	29	65	44
Mack, Shane	.276	128	503	66	139	207	30	4	10	61	15	41	76
Winfield, Dave	.271	143	547	72	148	242	27	2	21	76	2	45	106
Larkin, Gene	.264	56	144	17	38	50	7	1	1	19	0	21	16
Reboulet, Jeff	.258	109	240	33	62	73	8	0	1	15	5	35	37
Meares, Pat	.251	111	346	33	87	107	14	3	0	33	4	7	52
Hrbek, Kent	.242	123	392	60	95	183	11	1	25	83	4	71	57
Munoz, Pedro	.233	104	326	34	76	128	11	1	13	38	1	25	97
Jorgensen, Terry	.224	59	152	15	34	44	7	0	1	12	1	10	21
McCarty, Dave	.214	98	350	36	75	100	15	2	2	21	2	19	80
Webster, Lenny	.198	49	106	14	21	26	2	0	1	8	1	11	8
Bush, Randy	.156	35	45	1	7	9	2	0	0	3	0	7	13

PITCHING	ERA	W	L	G	GS	CG	SV	INN	H	R	ER	BB	SO
Casian, Larry	3.02	5	3	54	0	0	1	56⅔	59	23	19	14	31
Willis, Carl	3.10	3	0	53	0	0	5	58	56	23	20	17	44
Aguilera, Rick	3.11	4	3	65	0	0	34	72⅓	60	25	25	14	59
Hartley, Mike	4.00	1	2	53	0	0	1	81	86	38	36	36	57
Banks, Willie	4.04	11	12	31	30	0	0	171⅓	186	91	77	78	138
Deshaies, Jim	4.41	11	13	27	27	1	0	167⅓	159	85	82	51	80
Tapani, Kevin	4.43	12	15	36	35	3	0	225⅔	243	123	111	57	150
Trombley, Mike	4.88	6	6	44	10	0	2	114⅓	131	72	62	41	85
Erickson, Scott	5.19	8	19	34	34	1	0	218⅔	266	138	126	71	116
Brummett, Greg	5.74	2	1	5	5	0	0	26⅔	29	17	17	15	10
Guardado, Eddie	6.18	3	8	19	16	0	0	94⅔	123	68	65	36	46
Tsamis, George	6.19	1	2	41	0	0	0	68⅓	86	51	47	27	30
Mahomes, Pat	7.71	1	5	12	5	0	0	37⅓	47	34	32	16	23
Merriman, Brett	9.67	1	1	19	0	0	0	27	36	29	29	23	14

New York Yankees

BATTING	BA	G	AB	R	H	TB	2B	3B	HR	RBI	SB	BB	SO
James, Dion	.332	115	343	62	114	160	21	2	7	36	0	31	31
O'Neil, Paul	.311	141	498	71	155	251	34	1	20	75	2	44	69
Leyritz, Jim	.309	95	259	43	80	136	14	0	14	53	0	37	59
Stanley, Mike	.305	130	423	70	129	226	17	1	26	84	1	57	85
Boggs, Wade	.302	143	560	83	169	203	26	1	2	59	0	74	49
Velarde, Randy	.301	85	226	28	68	106	13	2	7	24	2	18	39
Mattingly, Don	.291	134	530	78	154	236	27	2	17	86	0	61	42
Gallego, Mike	.283	119	403	63	114	166	20	1	10	54	3	50	65
Kelly, Pat	.273	127	406	49	111	158	24	1	7	51	14	24	68
Williams, Bernie	.268	139	567	67	152	227	31	4	12	68	9	53	106
Tartabull, Danny	.250	138	513	87	128	258	33	2	31	102	0	92	156
Nokes, Matt	.249	76	217	25	54	92	8	0	10	35	0	16	31
Owen, Spike	.234	103	334	41	78	104	16	2	2	20	3	29	30
Maas, Kevin	.205	59	151	20	31	62	4	0	9	25	1	24	32
Meulens, Hensley	.170	30	53	8	9	18	1	1	2	5	0	8	19
Williams, Gerald	.149	42	67	11	10	18	2	3	0	6	2	1	14

PITCHING	ERA	W	L	G	GS	CG	SV	INN	H	R	ER	BB	SO
Key, Jimmy	3.00	18	6	34	34	4	0	236⅔	219	84	79	43	173
Gibson, Paul	3.06	2	0	20	0	0	0	35⅓	31	15	12	9	25
Kamieniecki, Scott	4.08	10	7	30	20	2	1	154⅓	163	73	70	59	72
Farr, Steve	4.21	2	2	49	0	0	25	47	44	22	22	28	39
Abbott, Jim	4.37	11	14	32	32	4	0	214	221	115	104	73	95
Jean, Domingo	4.46	1	1	10	6	0	0	40⅓	37	20	20	19	20
Wickman, Bob	4.63	14	4	41	19	1	4	140	156	82	72	69	70
Hitchcock, Sterling	4.65	1	2	6	6	0	0	31	32	18	16	14	26
Monteleone, Rich	4.94	7	4	42	0	0	0	85⅔	85	52	47	35	50
Howe, Steve	4.97	3	5	51	0	0	4	50⅔	58	31	28	10	19
Perez, Melido	5.19	6	14	25	25	0	0	163	173	103	94	64	148
Witt, Mike	5.27	3	2	9	9	0	0	41	39	26	24	22	30
Munoz, Bobby	5.32	3	3	38	0	0	0	45⅔	48	27	27	26	33

American League Team-by-Team Statistical Leaders *(Cont.)*

Oakland A's

BATTING	BA	G	AB	R	H	TB	2B	3B	HR	RBI	SB	BB	SO
McGwire, Mark	.333	27	84	16	28	61	6	0	9	24	0	21	19
Neel, Troy	.290	123	427	59	124	202	21	0	19	63	3	49	101
Gates, Brent	.290	139	535	64	155	209	29	2	7	69	7	56	75
Steinbach, Terry	285	104	389	47	111	162	19	1	10	43	3	25	65
Aldrete, Mike	.267	95	255	40	68	113	13	1	10	33	1	34	45
Hemond, Scott	.256	91	215	31	55	89	16	0	6	26	14	32	55
Browne, Jerry	.250	76	260	27	65	84	13	0	2	19	4	22	17
Bordick, Mike	.249	159	546	60	136	170	21	2	3	48	10	60	58
Sierra, Rueben	.233	158	630	77	147	246	23	5	22	101	25	52	97
Henderson, Dave	.220	107	382	37	84	163	19	0	20	53	0	32	113
Paquette, Craig	.219	105	393	35	86	150	20	4	12	46	4	14	108
Blankenship, Lance	.190	94	252	43	48	64	8	1	2	23	13	67	64

PITCHING	ERA	W	L	G	GS	CG	SV	INN	H	R	ER	BB	SO
Smithberg, Roger	2.75	1	2	13	0	0	3	19⅔	13	7	6	7	4
Honeycutt, Rick	2.81	1	4	52	0	0	1	41⅔	30	18	13	20	21
Nunez, Edwin	3.81	3	6	56	0	0	1	75⅔	89	36	32	29	58
Jimenez, Miguel	4.00	1	0	5	4	0	0	27	27	12	12	16	13
Karsay, Steve	4.04	8	8	0	0	49	49	23	22	16	22	16	33
Eckersley, Dennis	4.16	2	4	64	0	0	36	67	67	32	31	13	80
Witt, Mike	4.21	14	13	35	33	5	0	220	226	112	103	91	131
Gossage, Goose	4.53	4	5	39	0	0	1	47⅔	49	24	24	26	40
Van Poppel, Todd	5.04	6	6	16	16	0	0	84	76	50	47	62	47
Darling, Ron	5.16	5	9	31	29	3	0	178	198	107	102	72	95
Welch, Bob	5.29	9	11	30	28	0	0	166⅔	208	102	98	56	63
Horsman, Vince	5.40	2	0	40	0	0	0	25	25	15	15	15	17
Mohler, Mike	5.60	1	6	42	9	0	0	64⅓	57	45	40	44	42
Downs, Kelly	5.64	5	10	42	12	0	0	119⅔	135	80	75	60	66
Hillegas, Shawn	6.97	3	6	18	11	0	0	60⅔	78	48	47	33	29
Campbell, Kevin	7.31	0	0	11	0	0	0	16	20	13	13	11	9
Briscoe, John	8.03	1	0	17	0	0	0	24⅔	26	25	22	26	24

Seattle Mariners

BATTING	BA	G	AB	R	H	TB	2B	3B	HR	RBI	SB	BB	SO
Griffey, Ken, Jr	.309	156	582	113	180	359	38	3	45	109	17	96	91
Litton, Greg	.299	72	174	25	52	78	17	0	3	25	0	18	30
Amaral, Rich	.290	110	373	53	108	137	24	1	1	44	19	33	54
Blowers, Mike	.280	127	379	55	106	180	23	3	15	57	1	44	98
Buhner, Jay	.272	158	563	91	153	268	28	3	27	98	2	100	144
Martinez, Tino	.265	109	408	48	108	186	25	1	17	60	0	60	45
Magadan, Dave	.259	71	228	27	59	73	11	0	1	21	2	36	33
Valle, Dave	.258	135	423	48	109	167	19	0	13	63	1	48	56
O'Brien, Pete	.257	72	210	30	54	82	7	0	7	27	0	26	21
Haselman, Bill	.255	58	137	21	35	58	8	0	5	16	2	12	19
Vizquel, Omar	.255	158	560	68	143	167	14	2	2	31	12	50	71
Boone, Bret	.251	76	271	31	68	120	12	2	12	38	2	17	52
Martinez, Edgar	.237	42	135	20	32	51	7	0	4	13	0	28	19
Sasser, Mackey	.218	83	188	18	41	58	10	2	1	21	1	15	30
Felder, Mike	.211	109	342	31	72	92	7	5	1	20	15	22	34
Cotto, Henry	190	54	105	10	20	27	1	0	2	7	5	2	22

PITCHING	ERA	W	L	G	GS	CG	SV	INN	H	R	ER	BB	SO
Charlton, Norm	2.34	1	3	34	0	0	18	34⅔	22	12	9	17	48
Johnson, Randy	3.24	19	8	35	34	10	1	255⅓	185	97	92	99	308
Bosio, Chris	3.45	9	9	29	24	3	1	164⅓	138	75	63	59	119
Hanson, Erik	3.47	11	12	31	30	7	0	215	215	91	83	60	163
Holman, Brian	3.72	1	3	19	0	0	3	36⅓	27	17	15	16	17
Powell, Dennis	4.15	0	0	33	2	0	0	47⅔	42	22	22	24	32
Nelson, Jeff	4.35	5	3	71	0	0	1	60	57	30	29	34	61
Fleming, Dave	4.36	12	5	26	26	1	0	167⅓	189	84	81	67	75
DeLucia, Rich	4.64	3	6	30	1	0	0	42⅔	46	24	22	23	48
Leary, Tim	5.05	11	9	33	27	0	0	169⅓	202	104	95	58	68
Power, Ted	5.36	2	4	45	0	0	13	45⅓	57	28	27	17	27
Cummings, John	6.02	0	6	10	8	1	0	46⅓	59	34	31	16	19
Henry, Dwayne	6.67	2	1	31	1	0	2	54	56	40	40	35	35

Texas Rangers

BATTING	BA	G	AB	R	H	TB	2B	3B	HR	RBI	SB	BB	SO
Gonzalez, Juan	.310	140	536	105	166	339	33	1	46	118	4	37	99
Palmeiro, Rafael	.295	160	597	124	176	331	40	2	37	105	22	73	85
Hulse, David	.290	114	407	71	118	150	9	10	1	29	29	26	57
Franco, Julio	.289	144	532	85	154	233	31	3	14	84	9	62	95
Redus, Gary	.288	77	222	28	64	102	12	4	6	31	4	23	35
Diaz, Mario	.273	71	205	24	56	74	10	1	2	24	1	8	13
Rodriguez, Ivan	.273	137	473	56	129	195	28	4	10	66	8	29	70
Peltier, Dan	.269	65	160	23	43	55	7	1	1	17	0	20	27
Strange, Doug	.256	145	484	58	124	174	29	0	7	60	6	43	69
Canseco, Jose	.255	60	231	30	59	105	14	1	10	46	6	16	62
Davis, Butch	.245	62	159	24	39	66	10	4	3	20	3	5	28
Palmer, Dean	.245	148	519	88	127	261	31	2	33	96	11	53	154
Petralli, Geno	.241	59	133	16	32	40	5	0	1	13	2	22	17
Lee, Manuel	.220	73	205	31	45	53	3	1	1	12	2	22	39
Dascenzo, Doug	.199	76	146	20	29	42	5	1	2	10	2	8	22
Harris, Donald	.197	40	76	10	15	20	2	0	1	8	0	5	18
Ripken, Billy	.189	50	132	12	25	29	4	0	0	11	0	11	19

PITCHING	ERA	W	L	G	GS	CG	SV	INN	H	R	ER	BB	SO
Henke, Tom	2.91	5	5	66	0	0	40	74⅓	55	25	24	27	79
Nelson, Gene	3.12	0	5	52	0	0	5	60⅔	60	28	21	24	35
Pavlik, Roger	3.41	12	6	26	26	2	0	166⅓	151	67	63	80	131
Brown, Kevin	3.59	15	12	34	34	12	0	233	228	105	93	74	142
Rogers, Kenny	4.10	16	10	35	33	5	0	208⅓	210	108	95	71	140
Whiteside, Matt	4.32	2	1	60	0	0	1	73	78	37	35	23	29
Leibrandt, Charlie	4.55	9	10	26	26	1	0	150⅓	169	84	76	45	89
Burns, Todd	4.57	0	4	25	5	0	0	65	63	36	33	32	35
Bohanon, Brian	4.76	4	4	36	8	0	0	92⅔	107	54	49	46	45
Patterson, Bob	4.78	2	4	52	0	0	1	52⅔	59	28	28	11	46
Ryan, Nolan	4.88	5	5	13	13	0	0	66⅓	54	47	36	40	46
Schooler, Mike	5.55	3	0	17	0	0	0	24⅓	30	17	15	10	16
Lefferts, Craig	6.05	3	9	52	8	0	0	83⅓	102	57	56	28	58

Toronto Blue Jays

BATTING	BA	G	AB	R	H	TB	2B	3B	HR	RBI	SB	BB	SO
Olerud, John	.363	158	551	109	200	350	54	2	24	107	0	114	65
Molitor, Paul	.332	160	636	121	211	324	37	5	22	111	22	77	71
Alomar, Roberto	.326	153	589	109	192	290	35	6	17	93	55	80	67
Fernandez, Tony	.306	94	353	45	108	156	18	9	4	50	15	31	26
Henderson, Rickey	.289	134	481	114	139	228	22	2	21	59	53	120	65
White, Devon	.273	146	598	116	163	262	42	6	15	52	34	57	127
Sprague, Ed	.260	150	546	50	142	211	31	1	12	73	1	32	85
Borders, Pat	.254	138	488	38	124	181	30	0	9	55	2	20	66
Carter, Joe	.254	155	603	92	153	295	33	5	33	121	8	47	113
Coles, Darnell	.253	64	194	26	49	72	9	1	4	26	1	16	29
Jackson, Darrin	.216	46	176	15	38	61	8	0	5	19	0	8	53
Griffin, Alfredo	.211	46	95	15	20	23	3	0	0	3	0	3	13
Ward, Turner	.192	72	167	20	32	52	4	2	4	28	3	23	26

PITCHING	ERA	W	L	G	GS	CG	SV	INN	H	R	ER	BB	SO
Ward, Duane	2.13	2	3	71	0	0	45	71⅔	49	17	17	25	97
Eichhorn, Mark	2.72	3	1	54	0	0	0	72⅔	76	26	22	22	47
Cox, Danny	3.12	7	6	44	0	0	2	83⅔	73	31	29	29	84
Castillo, Tony	3.38	3	2	51	0	0	0	50⅔	44	19	19	22	28
Hentgen, Pat	3.87	19	9	34	32	3	0	216⅓	215	103	93	74	122
Guzman, Juan	3.99	14	3	33	33	2	0	221	211	107	98	110	194
Flener, Huck	4.05	0	0	6	0	0	0	6⅔	7	3	3	4	2
Leiter, Al	4.11	9	6	34	12	1	2	105	93	52	48	56	66
Williams, Woody	4.38	3	1	30	0	0	0	37	40	18	18	22	24
Stewart, Dave	4.44	12	8	26	26	0	0	162	146	86	80	72	96
Timlin, Mike	4.69	4	2	54	0	0	1	55⅔	63	32	29	27	49
Stottlemyre, Todd	4.84	11	12	30	28	1	0	176⅔	204	107	95	69	98
Morris, Jack	6.19	7	12	27	27	4	0	152⅔	189	116	105	65	103

The World Series

Results

Year	Result
1903	Boston (A) 5, Pittsburgh (N) 3
1904	No series
1905	New York (N) 4, Philadelphia (A) 1
1906	Chicago (A) 4, Chicago (N) 2
1907	Chicago (N) 4, Detroit (A) 0; 1 tie
1908	Chicago (N) 4, Detroit (A) 1
1909	Pittsburgh (N) 4, Detroit (A) 3
1910	Philadelphia (A) 4, Chicago (N) 1
1911	Philadelphia (A) 4, New York (N) 2
1912	Boston (A) 4, New York (N) 3; 1 tie
1913	Philadelphia (A) 4, New York (N) 1
1914	Boston (N) 4, Philadelphia (A) 0
1915	Boston (A) 4, Philadelphia (N) 1
1916	Boston (A) 4, Brooklyn (N) 1
1917	Chicago (A) 4, New York (N) 2
1918	Boston (A) 4, Chicago (N) 2
1919	Cincinnati (N) 5, Chicago (A) 3
1920	Cleveland (A) 5, Brooklyn (N) 2
1921	New York (N) 5, New York (A) 3
1922	New York (N) 4, New York (A) 0; 1 tie
1923	New York (A) 4, New York (N) 2
1924	Washington (A) 4, New York (N) 3
1925	Pittsburgh (N) 4, Washington (A) 3
1926	St Louis (N) 4, New York (A) 3
1927	New York (A) 4, Pittsburgh (N) 0
1928	New York (A) 4, St Louis (N) 0
1929	Philadelphia (A) 4, Chicago (N) 1
1930	Philadelphia (A) 4, St Louis (N) 2
1931	St Louis (N) 4, Philadelphia (A) 3
1932	New York (A) 4, Chicago (N) 0
1933	New York (N) 4, Washington (A) 1
1934	St Louis (N) 4, Detroit (A) 3
1935	Detroit (A) 4, Chicago (N) 2
1936	New York (A) 4, New York (N) 2
1937	New York (A) 4, New York (N) 1
1938	New York (A) 4, Chicago (N) 0
1939	New York (A) 4, Cincinnati (N) 0
1940	Cincinnati (N) 4, Detroit (A) 3
1941	New York (A) 4, Brooklyn (N) 1
1942	St Louis (N) 4, New York (A) 1
1943	New York (A) 4, St Louis (N) 1
1944	St Louis (N) 4, St Louis (A) 2
1945	Detroit (A) 4, Chicago (N) 3
1946	St Louis (N) 4, Boston (A) 3
1947	New York (A) 4, Brooklyn (N) 3
1948	Cleveland (A) 4, Boston (N) 2
1949	New York (A) 4, Brooklyn (N) 1
1950	New York (A) 4, Philadelphia (N) 0
1951	New York (A) 4, New York (N) 2
1952	New York (A) 4, Brooklyn (N) 3
1953	New York (A) 4, Brooklyn (N) 2
1954	New York (N) 4, Cleveland (A) 0
1955	Brooklyn (N) 4, New York (A) 3
1956	New York (A) 4, Brooklyn (N) 3
1957	Milwaukee (N) 4, New York (A) 3
1958	New York (A) 4, Milwaukee (N) 3
1959	Los Angeles (N) 4, Chicago (A) 2
1960	Pittsburgh (N) 4, New York (A) 3
1961	New York (A) 4, Cincinnati (N) 1
1962	New York (A) 4, San Francisco (N) 3
1963	Los Angeles (N) 4, New York (A) 0
1964	St Louis (N) 4, New York (A) 3
1965	Los Angeles (N) 4, Minnesota (A) 3
1966	Baltimore (A) 4, Los Angeles (N) 0
1967	St Louis (N) 4, Boston (A) 3
1968	Detroit (A) 4, St Louis (N) 3
1969	New York (N) 4, Baltimore (A) 1
1970	Baltimore (A) 4, Cincinnati (N) 1
1971	Pittsburgh (N) 4, Baltimore (A) 3
1972	Oakland (A) 4, Cincinnati (N) 3
1973	Oakland (A) 4, New York (N) 3
1974	Oakland (A) 4, Los Angeles (N) 1
1975	Cincinnati (N) 4, Boston (A) 3
1976	Cincinnati (N) 4, New York (A) 0
1977	New York (A) 4, Los Angeles (N) 2
1978	New York (A) 4, Los Angeles (N) 2
1979	Pittsburgh (N) 4, Baltimore (A) 3
1980	Philadelphia (N) 4, Kansas City (A) 2
1981	Los Angeles (N) 4, New York (A) 2
1982	St Louis (N) 4, Milwaukee (A) 3
1983	Baltimore (A) 4, Philadelphia (N) 1
1984	Detroit (A) 4, San Diego (N) 1
1985	Kansas City (A) 4, St Louis (N) 3
1986	New York (N) 4, Boston (A) 3
1987	Minnesota (A) 4, St Louis (N) 3
1988	Los Angeles (N) 4, Oakland (A) 1
1989	Oakland (A) 4, San Francisco (N) 0
1990	Cincinnati (N) 4, Oakland (A) 0
1991	Minnesota (A) 4, Atlanta (N) 3
1992	Toronto (A) 4, Atlanta (N) 2
1993	Toronto (A) 4, Philadelphia (N) 2

Brewmeister

Ken Killebrew, son of Hall of Fame slugger Harmon Killebrew, remembers slugging down his father's homemade root beer as a boy in Oregon. "He made it using dry ice and root extracts all mixed up in a big bowl in the kitchen," says Ken. "I'll never forget how good it tasted." Recently Ken suggested that his pop recreate his pop for the public. The result is Killebrew, an all-natural root beer produced by the Cold Spring Brewing Co. of Cold Spring, Minn. Says Ken of the new brew, which is made from Harmon's "secret recipe": "It's as close as you can get to what my father used to make."

Most Valuable Players

1955	Johnny Podres, Bklyn
1956	Don Larsen, NY (A)
1957	Lew Burdette, Mil
1958	Bob Turley, NY (A)
1959	Larry Sherry, LA
1960	Bobby Richardson, NY (A)
1961	Whitey Ford, NY (A)
1962	Ralph Terry, NY (A)
1963	Sandy Koufax, LA
1964	Bob Gibson, StL
1965	Sandy Koufax, LA
1966	Frank Robinson, Balt
1967	Bob Gibson, StL
1968	Mickey Lolich, Det
1969	Donn Clendenon, NY (N)
1970	Brooks Robinson, Balt
1971	Roberto Clemente, Pitt
1972	Gene Tenace, Oak
1973	Reggie Jackson, Oak
1974	Rollie Fingers, Oak
1975	Pete Rose, Cin

1976	Johnny Bench, Cin
1977	Reggie Jackson, NY (A)
1978	Bucky Dent, NY (A)
1979	Willie Stargell, Pitt
1980	Mike Schmidt, Phil
1981	Ron Cey, LA
	Pedro Guerrero, LA
	Steve Yeager, LA
1982	Darrell Porter, StL
1983	Rick Dempsey, Balt
1984	Alan Trammell, Det
1985	Bret Saberhagen, KC
1986	Ray Knight, NY (N)
1987	Frank Viola, Minn
1988	Orel Hershiser, LA
1989	Dave Stewart, Oak
1990	Jose Rijo, Cin
1991	Jack Morris, Minn
1992	Pat Borders, Tor
1993	Paul Molitor, Tor

Career Batting Leaders (Minimum 50 at bats)

GAMES

Yogi Berra	75
Mickey Mantle	65
Elston Howard	54
Hank Bauer	53
Gil McDougald	53
Phil Rizzuto	52
Joe DiMaggio	51
Frankie Frisch	50
Pee Wee Reese	44
Roger Maris	41
Babe Ruth	41

AT BATS

Yogi Berra	259
Mickey Mantle	230
Joe DiMaggio	199
Frankie Frisch	197
Gil McDougald	190
Hank Bauer	188
Phil Rizzuto	183
Elston Howard	171
Pee Wee Reese	169
Roger Maris	152

HITS

Yogi Berra	71
Mickey Mantle	59
Frankie Frisch	58
Joe DiMaggio	54
Pee Wee Reese	46
Hank Bauer	46
Phil Rizzuto	45
Gil McDougald	45
Lou Gehrig	43
Eddie Collins	42
Babe Ruth	42
Elston Howard	42

BATTING AVERAGE

Pepper Martin	418
Paul Molitor	418
Lou Brock	391
Thurman Munson	373
George Brett	373
Hank Aaron	364
Frank Baker	363
Roberto Clemente	362
Lou Gehrig	361
Reggie Jackson	357

HOME RUNS

Mickey Mantle	18
Babe Ruth	15
Yogi Berra	12
Duke Snider	11
Reggie Jackson	10
Lou Gehrig	10
Frank Robinson	8
Bill Skowron	8
Joe DiMaggio	8
Goose Goslin	7
Hank Bauer	7
Gil McDougald	7

RUNS BATTED IN

Mickey Mantle	40
Yogi Berra	39
Lou Gehrig	35
Babe Ruth	33
Joe DiMaggio	30
Bill Skowron	29
Duke Snider	26
Reggie Jackson	24
Bill Dickey	24
Hank Bauer	24
Gil McDougald	24

RUNS

Mickey Mantle	42
Yogi Berra	41
Babe Ruth	37
Lou Gehrig	30
Joe DiMaggio	27
Roger Maris	26
Elston Howard	25
Gil McDougald	23
Jackie Robinson	22
Gene Woodling	21
Reggie Jackson	21
Duke Snider	21
Phil Rizzuto	21
Hank Bauer	21

STOLEN BASES

Lou Brock	14
Eddie Collins	14
Frank Chance	10
Davey Lopes	10
Phil Rizzuto	10
Honus Wagner	9
Frankie Frisch	9
Johnny Evers	8
Pepper Martin	7
Joe Morgan	7
Rickey Henderson	7

TOTAL BASES

Mickey Mantle	123
Yogi Berra	117
Babe Ruth	96
Lou Gehrig	87
Joe DiMaggio	84
Duke Snider	79
Hank Bauer	75
Reggie Jackson	74
Frankie Frisch	74
Gil McDougald	72

Career Batting Leaders (Cont.)

SLUGGING AVERAGE

Reggie Jackson	755
Paul Molitor	636
Babe Ruth	744
Lou Gehrig	731
Al Simmons	658
Lou Brock	655
Pepper Martin	636
Hank Greenberg	624
Charlie Keller	611
Jimmie Foxx	609
Dave Henderson	606

STRIKEOUTS

Mickey Mantle	54
Elston Howard	37
Duke Snider	33
Babe Ruth	30
Gil McDougald	29
Bill Skowron	26
Hank Bauer	25
Reggie Jackson	24
Bob Meusel	24
Frank Robinson	23
George Kelly	23
Tony Kubek	23
Joe DiMaggio	23

Career Pitching Leaders (Minimum 25 innings pitched)

GAMES

Whitey Ford	22
Rollie Fingers	16
Allie Reynolds	15
Bob Turley	15
Clay Carroll	14
Clem Labine	13
Waite Hoyt	12
Catfish Hunter	12
Art Nehf	12
Paul Derringer	11
Carl Erskine	11
Rube Marquard	11
Christy Mathewson	11
Vic Raschi	11

INNINGS PITCHED

Whitey Ford	146
Christy Mathewson	101⅔
Red Ruffing	85⅔
Chief Bender	85
Waite Hoyt	83⅔
Bob Gibson	81
Art Nehf	79
Allie Reynolds	77
Jim Palmer	65
Catfish Hunter	63

WINS

Whitey Ford	10
Bob Gibson	7
Red Ruffing	7
Allie Reynolds	7
Lefty Gomez	6
Chief Bender	6
Waite Hoyt	6
Jack Coombs	5
Three Finger Brown	5
Herb Pennock	5
Christy Mathewson	5
Vic Raschi	5
Catfish Hunter	5

LOSSES

Whitey Ford	8
Eddie Plank	5
Schoolboy Rowe	5
Joe Bush	5
Rube Marquard	5
Christy Mathewson	5

SAVES

Rollie Fingers	6
Allie Reynolds	4
Johnny Murphy	4
Roy Face	3
Herb Pennock	3
Kent Tekulve	3
Firpo Marberry	3
Will McEnaney	3
Todd Worrell	3
Tug McGraw	3

EARNED RUN AVERAGE

Jack Billingham	36
Harry Brecheen	83
Babe Ruth	87
Sherry Smith	89
Sandy Koufax	95
Hippo Vaughn	1.00
Monte Pearson	1.01
Christy Mathewson	1.15
Babe Adams	1.29
Eddie Plank	1.32

SHUTOUTS

Christy Mathewson	4
Three Finger Brown	3
Whitey Ford	3
Bill Hallahan	2
Lew Burdette	2
Bill Dinneen	2
Sandy Koufax	2
Allie Reynolds	2
Art Nehf	2
Bob Gibson	2

COMPLETE GAMES

Christy Mathewson	10
Chief Bender	9
Bob Gibson	8
Red Ruffing	7
Whitey Ford	7
George Mullin	6
Eddie Plank	6
Art Nehf	6
Waite Hoyt	6

STRIKEOUTS

Whitey Ford	94
Bob Gibson	92
Allie Reynolds	62
Sandy Koufax	61
Red Ruffing	61
Chief Bender	59
George Earnshaw	56
Waite Hoyt	49
Christy Mathewson	48
Bob Turley	46

BASES ON BALLS

Whitey Ford	34
Allie Reynolds	32
Art Nehf	32
Jim Palmer	31
Bob Turley	29
Paul Derringer	27
Red Ruffing	27
Don Gullett	26
Burleigh Grimes	26
Vic Raschi	25

National League

1969	New York (E) 3, Atlanta (W) 0
1970	Cincinnati (W) 3, Pittsburgh (E) 0
1971	Pittsburgh (E) 3, San Francisco (W) 1
1972	Cincinnati (W) 3, Pittsburgh (E) 2
1973	New York (E) 3, Cincinnati (W) 2
1974	Los Angeles (W) 3, Pittsburgh (E) 1
1975	Cincinnati (W) 3, Pittsburgh (E) 0
1976	Cincinnati (W) 3, Philadelphia (E) 0
1977	Los Angeles (W) 3, Philadelphia (E) 1
1978	Los Angeles (W) 3, Philadelphia (E) 1
1979	Pittsburgh (E) 3, Cincinnati (W) 0
1980	Philadelphia (E) 3, Houston (W) 2
1981	Los Angeles (W) 3, Montreal (E) 2
1982	St Louis (E) 3, Atlanta (W) 0
1983	Philadelphia (E) 3, Los Angeles (W) 1
1984	San Diego (W) 3, Chicago (E) 2
1985	St Louis (E) 4, Los Angeles (W) 2
1986	New York (E) 4, Houston (W) 2
1987	St Louis (E) 4, San Francisco (W) 3
1988	Los Angeles (W) 4, New York (E) 3
1989	San Francisco (W) 4, Chicago (E) 1
1990	Cincinnati (W) 4, Pittsburgh (E) 2
1991	Atlanta (W) 4, Pittsburgh (E) 3
1992	Atlanta (W) 4, Pitsburgh (E) 3
1993	Philadelphia (E) 4, Atlanta (W) 2

American League

1969	Baltimore (E) 3, Minnesota (W) 0
1970	Baltimore (E) 3, Minnesota (W) 0
1971	Baltimore (E) 3, Oakland (W) 0
1972	Oakland (W) 3, Detroit (E) 2
1973	Oakland (W) 3, Baltimore (E) 2
1974	Oakland (W) 3, Baltimore (E) 1
1975	Boston (E) 3, Oakland (W) 0
1976	New York (E) 3, Kansas City (W) 2
1977	New York (E) 3, Kansas City (W) 2
1978	New York (E) 3, Kansas City (W) 1
1979	Baltimore (E) 3, California (W) 1
1980	Kansas City (W) 3, New York (E) 0
1981	New York (E) 3, Oakland (W) 0
1982	Milwaukee (E) 3, California (W) 2
1983	Baltimore (E) 3, Chicago (W) 1
1984	Detroit (E) 3, Kansas City (W) 0
1985	Kansas City (W) 4, Toronto (E) 3
1986	Boston (E) 4, California (W) 3
1987	Minnesota (W) 4, Detroit (E) 1
1988	Oakland (W) 4, Boston (E) 0
1989	Oakland (W) 4, Toronto (E) 1
1990	Oakland (W) 4, Boston (E) 0
1991	Minnesota (W) 4, Toronto (E) 1
1992	Toronto (E) 4, Oakland (W) 2
1993	Toronto (E) 4, Chicago (W) 2

NLCS Most Valuable Player

1977	Dusty Baker, LA	
1978	Steve Garvey, LA	
1979	Willie Stargell, Pitt	
1980	Manny Trillo, Phil	
1981	Burt Hooton, LA	
1982	Darrell Porter, StL	
1983	Gary Matthews, Phil	
1984	Steve Garvey, SD	
1985	Ozzie Smith, StL	
1986	Mike Scott, Hou	
1987	Jeffrey Leonard, SF	
1988	Orel Hershiser, LA	
1989	Will Clark, SF	
1990	Randy Myers, Cin
	Ron Dibble, Cin
1991	Steve Avery, Atl
1992	John Smoltz, Atl
1993	Curt Schilling, Phil

ALCS Most Valuable Player

1980	Frank White, KC
1981	Graig Nettles, NY
1982	Fred Lynn, Calif
1983	Mike Boddicker, Balt
1984	Kirk Gibson, Det
1985	George Brett, KC
1986	Marty Barrett, Bos
1987	Gary Gaetti, Minn
1988	Dennis Eckersley, Oak
1989	Rickey Henderson, Oak
1990	Dave Stewart, Oak
1991	Kirby Puckett, Minn
1992	Roberto Alomar, Tor
1993	Dave Stewart, Tor

The All Star Game

Results

Date	Winner	Score	Site
7-6-33	American	4-2	Comiskey Park, Chi
7-10-34	American	9-7	Polo Grounds, NY
7-8-35	American	4-1	Municipal Stadium, Clev
7-7-36	National	4-3	Braves Field, Bos
7-7-37	American	8-3	Griffith Stadium, Wash
7-6-38	National	4-1	Crosley Field, Cin
7-11-39	American	3-1	Yankee Stadium, NY
7-10-40	National	4-0	Sportsman's Park, StL
7-8-41	American	7-5	Briggs Stadium, Det
7-6-42	American	3-1	Polo Grounds, NY
7-13-43	American	5-3	Shibe Park, Phil
7-11-44	National	7-1	Forbes Field, Pitt
1945	No game due to wartime travel restrictions		
7-9-46	American	12-0	Fenway Park, Bos
7-8-47	American	2-1	Wrigley Field, Chi
7-13-48	American	5-2	Sportsman's Park, StL
7-12-49	American	11-7	Ebbets Field, Bklyn

Results (Cont.)

Date	Winner	Score	Site
7-11-50	National	4-3	Comiskey Park, Chi
7-10-51	National	8-3	Briggs Stadium, Det
7-8-52	National	3-2	Shibe Park, Phil
7-14-53	National	5-1	Crosley Field, Cin
7-13-54	American	11-9	Municipal Stadium, Clev
7-12-55	National	6-5	County Stadium, Mil
7-10-56	National	7-3	Griffith Stadium, Wash
7-9-57	American	6-5	Busch Stadium, StL
7-8-58	American	4-3	Memorial Stadium, Balt
7-7-59	National	5-4	Forbes Field, Pitt
8-3-59	American	5-3	Memorial Coliseum, LA
7-11-60	National	5-3	Municipal Stadium, KC
7-13-60	National	6-0	Yankee Stadium, NY
7-11-61	National	5-4	Candlestick Park, SF
7-31-61*	Tie*	1-1	Fenway Park, Bos
7-10-62	National	3-1	D.C. Stadium, Wash
7-30-62	American	9-4	Wrigley Field, Chi
7-9-63	National	5-3	Municipal Stadium, Clev
7-7-64	National	7-4	Shea Stadium, NY
7-13-65	National	6-5	Metropolitan Stadium, Minn
7-12-66	National	2-1	Busch Stadium, StL
7-11-67	National	2-1	Anaheim Stadium, Anaheim
7-9-68	National	1-0	Astrodome, Hou
7-23-69	National	9-3	R.F.K. Memorial Stadium, Wash
7-14-70	National	5-4	Riverfront Stadium, Cin
7-13-71	American	6-4	Tiger Stadium, Det
7-25-72	National	4-3	Atlanta Stadium, Atl
7-24-73	National	7-1	Royals Stadium, KC
7-23-74	National	7-2	Three Rivers Stadium, Pitt
7-15-75	National	6-3	County Stadium, Mil
7-13-76	National	7-1	Veterans Stadium, Phil
7-19-77	National	7-5	Yankee Stadium, NY
7-11-78	National	7-3	Jack Murphy Stadium, SD
7-17-79	National	7-6	Kingdome, Sea
7-8-80	National	4-2	Dodger Stadium, LA
8-9-81	National	5-4	Municipal Stadium, Clev
7-13-82	National	4-1	Olympic Stadium, Mon
7-6-83	American	13-3	Comiskey Park, Chi
7-10-84	National	3-1	Candlestick Park, SF
7-16-85	National	6-1	Metrodome, Minn
7-15-86	American	3-2	Astrodome, Hou
7-14-87	National	2-0	Oakland Coliseum, Oak
7-12-88	American	2-1	Riverfront Stadium, Cin
7-11-89	American	5-3	Anaheim Stadium, Anaheim
7-10-90	American	2-0	Wrigley Field, Chi
7-9-91	American	4-2	SkyDome, Toronto
7-14-92	American	13-6	Jack Murphy Stadium
7-13-93	American	9-3	Camden Yards, Balt

*Game called because of rain after 9 innings.

Most Valuable Players

1962	Maury Wills, LA	NL
	Leon Wagner, LA	AL
1963	Willie Mays, SF	NL
1964	Johnny Callison, Phil	NL
1965	Juan Marichal, SF	NL
1966	Brooks Robinson, Balt	AL
1967	Tony Perez, Cin	NL
1968	Willie Mays, SF	NL
1969	Willie McCovey, SF	NL
1970	Carl Yastrzemski, Bos	AL
1971	Frank Robinson, Balt	AL
1972	Joe Morgan, Cin	NL
1973	Bobby Bonds, SF	NL
1974	Steve Garvey, LA	NL

1975	Bill Madlock, Chi	NL
	Jon Matlack, NY	NL
1976	George Foster, Cin	NL
1977	Don Sutton, LA	NL
1978	Steve Garvey, LA	NL
1979	Dave Parker, Pitt	NL
1980	Ken Griffey, Cin	NL
1981	Gary Carter, Mont	NL
1982	Dave Concepcion, Cin	NL
1983	Fred Lynn, Calif	AL
1984	Gary Carter, Mont	NL
1985	LaMarr Hoyt, SD	NL
1986	Roger Clemens, Bos	AL
1987	Tim Raines, Mont	NL

Most Valuable Players *(Cont.)*

1988 ....Terry Steinbach, Oak AL	1991 ....Cal Ripken Jr, Balt AL
1989 ....Bo Jackson, KC AL	1992 ....Ken Griffey Jr AL
1990 ....Julio Franco, Tex AL	1993 ....Kirby Puckett, Minn AL

The Regular Season

Most Valuable Players

NATIONAL LEAGUE

Year	Name and Team	Position	Noteworthy
1911	Wildfire Schulte, Chi	Outfield	21 HR†, 121 RBI†, .300
1912	*Larry Doyle, NY	Second base	10 HR, 90 RBI, .330
1913	Jake Daubert, Bklyn	First base	52 RBI, .350†
1914	*Johnny Evers, Bos	Second base	F.A. .976†, .279
1915-23	No selection		
1924	Dazzy Vance, Bklyn	Pitcher	28†-6, 2.16 ERA†, 262 K†
1925	Rogers Hornsby, StL	Second base, Manager	39 HR†, 143 RBI†, .403†
1926	*Bob O'Farrell, StL	Catcher	7 HR, 68 RBI, .293
1927	*Paul Waner, Pitt	Outfield	237 hits†, 131 RBI†, .380†
1928	*Jim Bottomley, StL	First base	31 HR†, 136 RBI†, .325
1929	*Rogers Hornsby, Chi	Second base	39 HR, 149 RBI, 156 runs†, .380
1930	No selection		
1931	*Frankie Frisch, StL	Second base	4 HR, 82 RBI, 28 SB†, .311
1932	Chuck Klein, Phil	Outfield	38 HR†, 137 RBI, 226 hits†, .348
1933	*Carl Hubbell, NY	Pitcher	23†-12, 1.66 ERA†, 10 SO†
1934	*Dizzy Dean, StL	Pitcher	30†-7, 2.66 ERA, 195 K†
1935	*Gabby Hartnett, Chi	Catcher	13 HR, 91 RBI, .344
1936	*Carl Hubbell, NY	Pitcher	26†-6, 2.31 ERA†
1937	Joe Medwick, StL	Outfield	31 HR‡, 154 RBI‡, 111 runs†, .374†
1938	Ernie Lombardi, Cin	Catcher	19 HR, 95 RBI, .342†
1939	*Bucky Walters, Cin	Pitcher	27†-11, 2.29 ERA†, 137 K‡
1940	*Frank McCormick, Cin	First base	19 HR, 127 RBI, 191 hits†, .309
1941	*Dolph Camilli, Bklyn	First base	34 HR†, 120 RBI†, .285
1942	*Mort Cooper, StL	Pitcher	22†-7, 1.78 ERA†, 10 SO†
1943	*Stan Musial, StL	Outfield	13 HR, 81 RBI, 220 hits†, .357†
1944	*Marty Marion, StL	Shortstop	F.A. .972†, 63 RBI
1945	*Phil Cavarretta, Chi	First base	6 HR, 97 RBI, .355†
1946	*Stan Musial, StL	First base, Outfield	103 RBI, 124 runs†, 228 hits†, .365†
1947	Bob Elliott, Bos	Third base	22 HR, 113 RBI, .317
1948	Stan Musial, StL	Outfield	39 HR, 131 RBI†, .376†
1949	*Jackie Robinson, Bklyn	Second base	16 HR, 124 RBI, 37 SB†, .342†
1950	*Jim Konstanty, Phil	Pitcher	16-7, 22 saves†, 2.66 ERA
1951	Roy Campanella, Bklyn	Catcher	33 HR, 108 RBI, .325
1952	Hank Sauer, Chi	Outfield	37 HR‡, 121 RBI†, .270
1953	*Roy Campanella, Bklyn	Catcher	41 HR, 142 RBI†, .312
1954	*Willie Mays, NY	Outfield	41 HR, 110 RBI, 13 3B†, .345†
1955	*Roy Campanella, Bklyn	Catcher	32 HR, 107 RBI, .318
1956	*Don Newcombe, Bklyn	Pitcher	27†-7, 3.06 ERA
1957	*Hank Aaron, Mil	Outfield	44 HR†, 132 RBI†, .322
1958	Ernie Banks, Chi	Shortstop	47 HR†, 129 RBI†, .313
1959	Ernie Banks, Chi	Shortstop	45 HR, 143 RBI†, .304
1960	*Dick Groat, Pitt	Shortstop	2 HR, 50 RBI, .325†
1961	*Frank Robinson, Cin	Outfield	37 HR, 124 RBI, .323
1962	Maury Wills, LA	Shortstop	104 SB†, 208 hits, .299, GG
1963	*Sandy Koufax, LA	Pitcher	25‡-5, 1.88 ERA†, 306 K†
1964	*Ken Boyer, StL	Third Base	24 HR, 119 RBI†, .295
1965	Willie Mays, SF	Outfield	52 HR†, 112 RBI, .317, GG
1966	Roberto Clemente, Pitt	Outfield	29 HR, 119 RBI, 202 hits, .317, GG
1967	*Orlando Cepeda, StL	First base	25 HR, 111 RBI†, .325
1968	*Bob Gibson, StL	Pitcher	22-9, 1.12 ERA†, 268 K†, 13 SO†, GG
1969	Willie McCovey, SF	First base	45 HR†, 126 RBI†, .320
1970	*Johnny Bench, Cin	Catcher	45 HR†, 148 RBI†, .293, GG
1971	Joe Torre, StL	Third base	24 HR, 137 RBI†, .363†
1972	*Johnny Bench, Cin	Catcher	40 HR†, 125 RBI†, .270, GG

Most Valuable Players (Cont.)

NATIONAL LEAGUE (Cont.)

Year	Name and Team	Position	Noteworthy
1973	*Pete Rose, Cin	Outfield	5 HR, 64 RBI, .338†, 230 hits†
1974	*Steve Garvey, LA	First base	21 HR, 111 RBI, 200 hits, .312, GG
1975	*Joe Morgan, Cin	Second base	17 HR, 94 RBI, 67 SB, .327, GG
1976	*Joe Morgan, Cin	Second base	27 HR, 111 RBI, 60 SB, .320, GG
1977	George Foster, Cin	Outfield	52 HR†, 149 RBI†, .320
1978	Dave Parker, Pitt	Outfield	30 HR, 117 RBI, .334†, GG
1979	Keith Hernandez, StL	First base	11 HR, 105 RBI, 210 hits, .344†, GG
	*Willie Stargell, Pitt	First base	32 HR, 82 RBI, .281
1980	*Mike Schmidt, Phil	Third base	48 HR†, 121 RBI†, .286, GG
1981	Mike Schmidt, Phil	Third base	31 HR†, 91 RBI†, 78 runs†, .316, GG
1982	*Dale Murphy, Atl	Outfield	36 HR, 109 RBI‡, .281, GG
1983	Dale Murphy, Atl	Outfield	36 HR, 121 RBI†, .302, GG
1984	*Ryne Sandberg, Chi	Second base	19 HR, 84 RBI, 114 runs†, .314, GG
1985	*Willie McGee, StL	Outfield	10 HR, 82 RBI, 18 3B†, .353†, GG
1986	Mike Schmidt, Phil	Third base	37 HR†, 119 RBI†, .290, GG
1987	Andre Dawson, Chi	Outfield	49 HR†, 137 RBI†, .287, GG
1988	*Kirk Gibson, LA	Outfield	25 HR, 76 RBI, 106 runs, .290
1989	*Kevin Mitchell, SF	Outfield	47 HR†, 125 RBI†, .291
1990	*Barry Bonds, Pitt	Outfield	33 HR, 114 RBI, .301
1991	*Terry Pendleton, Atl	Third base	23 HR, 86 RBI, .319†
1992	Barry Bonds, SF	Outfield	34 HR, 103 RBI, .311

AMERICAN LEAGUE

Year	Name and Team	Position	Noteworthy
1911	Ty Cobb, Det	Outfield	8 HR, 144 RBI†, 24 3B†, .420†
1912	*Tris Speaker, Bos	Outfield	10 HR‡, 98 RBI, 53 2B†, .383
1913	Walter Johnson, Wash	Pitcher	36†-7, 1.09 ERA†, 11 SO†, 243 K†
1914	*Eddie Collins, Phil	Second base	2 HR, 85 RBI, 122 runs†, .344
1915-21	No selection		
1922	George Sisler, StL	First base	8 HR, 105 RBI, 246 hits†, .420†
1923	*Babe Ruth, NY	Outfield	41 HR†, 131 RBI†, .393
1924	*Walter Johnson, Wash	Pitcher	23†-7, 2.72 ERA†, 158 K†
1925	*Roger Peckinpaugh, Wash	Shortstop	4 HR, 64 RBI, .294
1926	George Burns, Clev	First base	114 RBI, 216 hits‡, 64 2B†, .358
1927	*Lou Gehrig, NY	First base	47 HR, 175 RBI†, 52 2B†, .373
1928	Mickey Cochrane, Phil	Catcher	10 HR, 57 RBI, .293
1929	No selection		
1930	No selection		
1931	*Lefty Grove, Phil	Pitcher	31†-4, 2.06 ERA†, 175 K†
1932	Jimmie Foxx, Phil	First base	58 HR†, 169 RBI†, 151 runs†, .364
1933	Jimmie Foxx, Phil	First base	48 HR†, 163 RBI†, .356†
1934	*Mickey Cochrane, Det	Catcher	2 HR, 76 RBI, .320
1935	*Hank Greenberg, Det	First base	36 HR‡, 170 RBI†, 203 hits, .328
1936	*Lou Gehrig, NY	First base	49 HR†, 152 RBI, 167 runs†, .354
1937	Charlie Gehringer, Det	Second base	14 HR, 96 RBI, 133 runs, .371†
1938	Jimmie Foxx, Bos	First base	50 HR†, 175 RBI†, .349†
1939	*Joe DiMaggio, NY	Outfield	30 HR, 126 RBI, .381†
1940	*Hank Greenberg, Det	Outfield	41 HR†, 150 RBI†, 50 2B†, .340
1941	*Joe DiMaggio, NY	Outfield	30 HR, 125 RBI†, .357
1942	*Joe Gordon, NY	Second base	18 HR, 103 RBI, .322
1943	*Spud Chandler, NY	Pitcher	20†-4, 1.64 ERA†, 5 SO‡
1944	Hal Newhouser, Det	Pitcher	29†-9, 2.22 ERA†, 187 K†
1945	*Hal Newhouser, Det	Pitcher	25†-9, 1.81 ERA†, 8 SO†, 212 K†
1946	*Ted Williams, Bos	Outfield	38 HR, 123 RBI, 142 runs†, .342
1947	*Joe DiMaggio, NY	Outfield	20 HR, 97 RBI, .315
1948	*Lou Boudreau, Clev	Shortstop	18 HR, 106 RBI, .355
1949	Ted Williams, Bos	Outfield	43 HR†, 159 RBI‡, 150 runs†, .343
1950	*Phil Rizzuto, NY	Shortstop	125 runs, 200 hits, .324
1951	*Yogi Berra, NY	Catcher	27 HR, 88 RBI, .294
1952	Bobby Shantz, Phil	Pitcher	24†-7, 2.48 ERA
1953	Al Rosen, Clev	Third base	43 HR†, 145 RBI†, 115 runs†, .336
1954	Yogi Berra, NY	Catcher	22 HR, 125 RBI, .307
1955	*Yogi Berra, NY	Catcher	27 HR, 108 RBI, .272

Most Valuable Players (Cont.)

AMERICAN LEAGUE (Cont.)

Year	Name and Team	Position	Noteworthy
1956	*Mickey Mantle, NY	Outfield	52 HR†, 130 RBI†, 132 runs†, .353†
1957	*Mickey Mantle, NY	Outfield	34 HR, 94 RBI, 121 runs†, .365
1958	Jackie Jensen, Bos	Outfield	35 HR, 122 RBI†, .286
1959	*Nellie Fox, Chi	Second base	2 HR, 70 RBI, .306, GG
1960	*Roger Maris, NY	Outfield	39 HR, 112 RBI†, .283, GG
1961	*Roger Maris, NY	Outfield	61 HR†, 142 RBI†, .269
1962	*Mickey Mantle, NY	Outfield	30 HR, 89 RBI, .321, GG
1963	*Elston Howard, NY	Catcher	28 HR, 85 RBI, .287, GG
1964	*Brooks Robinson, Balt	Third base	28 HR, 118 RBI†, .317, GG
1965	*Zoilo Versalles, Minn	Shortstop	126 runs†, 45 2B‡, 12 3B‡, GG
1966	*Frank Robinson, Balt	Outfield	49 HR†, 122 RBI†, 122 runs†, .316†
1967	*Carl Yastrzemski, Bos	Outfield	44 HR†, 121 RBI†, 112 runs†, .326†, GG
1968	*Denny McLain, Det	Pitcher	31†-6, 1.96 ERA, 280 K
1969	*Harmon Killebrew, Minn	Third base, First base	49 HR†, 140 RBI†, .276
1970	*Boog Powell, Balt	First base	35 HR, 114 RBI, .297
1971	*Vida Blue, Oak	Pitcher	24-8, 1.82 ERA†, 8 SO†, 301 K
1972	Dick Allen, Chi	First base	37 HR†, 113 RBI†, .308
1973	*Reggie Jackson, Oak	Outfield	32 HR†, 117 RBI†, 99 runs†, .293
1974	Jeff Burroughs, Tex	Outfield	25 HR, 118 RBI†, .301
1975	*Fred Lynn, Bos	Outfield	21 HR, 105 RBI, 103 runs†, .331, GG
1976	*Thurman Munson, NY	Catcher	17 HR, 105 RBI, .302
1977	Rod Carew, Minn	First base	100 RBI, 128 runs†, 239 hits†, .388†
1978	Jim Rice, Bos	Outfield, designated hitter	46 HR†, 139 RBI†, 213 hits†, .315
1979	*Don Baylor, Calif	Outfield, designated hitter	36 HR, 139 RBI†, 120 runs†, .296
1980	*George Brett, KC	Third base	24 HR, 118 RBI, .390†
1981	*Rollie Fingers, Mil	Pitcher	6-3, 28 saves†, 1.04 ERA
1982	*Robin Yount, Mil	Shortstop	29 HR, 114 RBI, 210 hits†, .331, GG
1983	*Cal Ripken, Balt	Shortstop	27 HR, 102 RBI, 121 runs†, 211 hits†, .318
1984	*Willie Hernandez, Det	Pitcher	9-3, 32 saves, 1.92 ERA
1985	Don Mattingly, NY	First base	35 HR, 145 RBI†, 48 2B†, .324, GG
1986	*Roger Clemens, Bos	Pitcher	24†-4, 2.48 ERA†, 238 K
1987	George Bell, Tor	Outfield	47 HR, 134 RBI†, .308
1988	*Jose Canseco, Oak	Outfield	42 HR†, 124 RBI†, 40 SB, .307
1989	Robin Yount, Mil	Outfield	21 HR, 103 RBI, 101 runs, .318
1990	*Rickey Henderson, Oak	Outfield	28 HR, 119 runs†, 65 SB†, .325
1991	Cal Ripken, Jr, Balt	Shortstop	34 HR, 114 RBI, .323
1992	Dennis Eckersley, Oak	Pitcher	7-1, 1.91 ERA, 51 saves

*Played for pennant or, after 1968, division winner.

†Led league.

‡Tied for league lead.

Notes: 2B=doubles; 3B=triples; F.A.=fielding average; GG=won Gold Glove, award begun in 1957; K=strikeouts; SO=shutouts; SB=stolen bases.

Rookies of the Year

NATIONAL LEAGUE		AMERICAN LEAGUE	
1947*	Jackie Robinson, Bklyn (1B)	1949	Roy Sievers, StL (OF)
1948*	Alvin Dark, Bos (SS)	1950	Walt Dropo, Bos (1B)
1949	Don Newcombe, Bklyn (P)	1951	Gil McDougald, NY (3B)
1950	Sam Jethroe, Bos (OF)	1952	Harry Byrd, Phil (P)
1951	Willie Mays, NY (OF)	1953	Harvey Kuenn, Det (SS)
1952	Joe Black, Bklyn (P)	1954	Bob Grim, NY (P)
1953	Junior Gilliam, Bklyn (2B)	1955	Herb Score, Clev (P)
1954	Wally Moon, StL (OF)	1956	Luis Aparicio, Chi (SS)
1955	Bill Virdon, StL (OF)	1957	Tony Kubek, NY (OF, SS)
1956	Frank Robinson, Cin (OF)	1958	Albie Pearson, Wash (OF)
1957	Jack Sanford, Phil (P)	1959	Bob Allison, Wash (OF)
1958	Orlando Cepeda, SF (1B)	1960	Ron Hansen, Balt (SS)
1959	Willie McCovey, SF (1B)	1961	Don Schwall, Bos (P)
1960	Frank Howard, LA (OF)	1962	Tom Tresh, NY (SS)

Rookies of the Year (Cont.)

NATIONAL LEAGUE (Cont.)

1961	Billy Williams, Chi (OF)
1962	Ken Hubbs, Chi (2B)
1963	Pete Rose, Cin (2B)
1964	Dick Allen, Phil (3B)
1965	Jim Lefebvre, LA (2B)
1966	Tommy Helms, Cin (2B)
1967	Tom Seaver, NY (P)
1968	Johnny Bench, Cin (C)
1969	Ted Sizemore, LA (2B)
1970	Carl Morton, Mont (P)
1971	Earl Williams, Atl (C)
1972	Jon Matlack, NY (P)
1973	Gary Matthews, SF (OF)
1974	Bake McBride, StL (OF)
1975	John Montefusco, SF (P)
1976	Pat Zachry, Cin (P)
	Butch Metzger, SD (P)
1977	Andre Dawson, Mont (OF)
1978	Bob Horner, Atl (3B)
1979	Rick Sutcliffe, LA (P)
1980	Steve Howe, LA (P)
1981	Fernando Valenzuela, LA (P)
1982	Steve Sax, LA (2B)
1983	Darryl Strawberry, NY (OF)
1984	Dwight Gooden, NY (P)
1985	Vince Coleman, StL (OF)
1986	Todd Worrell, StL (P)
1987	Benito Santiago, SD (C)
1988	Chris Sabo, Cin (3B)
1989	Jerome Walton, Chi (OF)
1990	Dave Justice, Atl (OF)
1991	Jeff Bagwell, Hou (3B)
1992	Eric Karros, LA (1B)

AMERICAN LEAGUE (Cont.)

1963	Gary Peters, Chi (P)
1964	Tony Oliva, Minn (OF)
1965	Curt Blefary, Balt (OF)
1966	Tommie Agee, Chi (OF)
1967	Rod Carew, Minn (2B)
1968	Stan Bahnsen, NY (P)
1969	Lou Piniella, KC (OF)
1970	Thurman Munson, NY (C)
1971	Chris Chambliss, Clev (1B)
1972	Carlton Fisk, Bos (C)
1973	Al Bumbry, Balt (OF)
1974	Mike Hargrove, Tex (1B)
1975	Fred Lynn, Bos (OF)
1976	Mark Fidrych, Det (P)
1977	Eddie Murray, Balt (DH)
1978	Lou Whitaker, Det (2B)
1979	Alfredo Griffin, Tor (SS)
	John Castino, Minn (3B)
1980	Joe Charboneau, Clev (OF)
1981	Dave Righetti, NY (P)
1982	Cal Ripken, Balt (SS)
1983	Ron Kittle, Chi (OF)
1984	Alvin Davis, Sea (1B)
1985	Ozzie Guillen, Chi (SS)
1986	Jose Canseco, Oak (OF)
1987	Mark McGwire, Oak (1B)
1988	Walt Weiss, Oak (SS)
1989	Gregg Olson, Balt (P)
1990	Sandy Alomar Jr, Clev (C)
1991	Chuck Knoblauch, Minn (2B)
1992	Pat Listach, Mil (SS)

*Just one selection for both leagues.

Cy Young Award

Year		W-L	Sv	ERA	Year		W-L	Sv	ERA
1956	*Don Newcombe, Bklyn (NL)	27-7	0	3.06	1962	Don Drysdale, LA (NL)	25-9	1	2.83
1957	Warren Spahn, Mil (NL)	21-11	3	2.69	1963	*Sandy Koufax, LA (NL)	25-5	0	1.88
1958	Bob Turley, NY (AL)	21-7	0	2.97	1964	Dean Chance, LA (AL)	20-9	4	1.65
1959	Early Wynn, Chi (AL)	22-10	0	3.17	1965	Sandy Koufax, LA (NL)	26-8	2	2.04
1960	Vernon Law, Pitt (NL)	20-9	0	3.08	1966	Sandy Koufax, LA (NL)	27-9	0	1.73
1961	Whitey Ford, NY (AL)	25-4	0	3.21					

NATIONAL LEAGUE

Year		W-L	Sv	ERA
1967	Mike McCormick, SF	22-10	0	2.85
1968	*Bob Gibson, StL	22-9	0	1.12
1969	Tom Seaver, NY	25-7	0	2.21
1970	Bob Gibson, StL	23-7	0	3.12
1971	Ferguson Jenkins, Chi	24-13	0	2.77
1972	Steve Carlton, Phil	27-10	0	1.97
1973	Tom Seaver, NY	19-10	0	2.08
1974	Mike Marshall, LA	15-12	21	2.42
1975	Tom Seaver, NY	22-9	0	2.38
1976	Randy Jones, SD	22-14	0	2.74
1977	Steve Carlton, Phil	23-10	0	2.64
1978	Gaylord Perry, SD	21-6	0	2.72
1979	Bruce Sutter, Chi	6-6	37	2.23
1980	Steve Carlton, Phil	24-9	0	2.34
1981	F. Valenzuela, LA	13-7	0	2.48
1982	Steve Carlton, Phil	23-11	0	3.10
1983	John Denny, Phil	19-6	0	2.37
1984	†Rick Sutcliffe, Chi	16-1	0	2.69

AMERICAN LEAGUE

Year		W-L	Sv	ERA
1967	Jim Lonborg, Bos	22-9	0	3.16
1968	*Denny McLain, Det	31-6	0	1.96
1969	Denny McLain, Det	24-9	0	2.80
	Mike Cuellar, Balt	23-11	0	2.38
1970	Jim Perry, Minn	24-12	0	3.03
1971	*Vida Blue, Oak	24-8	0	1.82
1972	Gaylord Perry, Clev	24-16	1	1.92
1973	Jim Palmer, Balt	22-9	1	2.40
1974	Catfish Hunter, Oak	25-12	0	2.49
1975	Jim Palmer, Balt	23-11	1	2.09
1976	Jim Palmer, Balt	22-13	0	2.51
1977	Sparky Lyle, NY	13-5	26	2.17
1978	Ron Guidry, NY	25-3	0	1.74
1979	Mike Flanagan, Balt	23-9	0	3.08
1980	Steve Stone, Balt	25-7	0	3.23
1981	*Rollie Fingers, Mil	6-3	28	1.04
1982	Pete Vuckovich, Mi	18-6	0	3.34
1983	LaMarr Hoyt, Chi	24-10	0	3.66

Cy Young Award *(Cont.)*

NATIONAL LEAGUE

Year		W-L	Sv	ERA
1985	Dwight Gooden, NY	24-4	0	1.53
1986	Mike Scott, Hou	18-10	0	2.22
1987	Steve Bedrosian, Phil	5-3	40	2.83
1988	Orel Hershiser, LA	23-8	1	2.26
1989	Mark Davis, SD	4-3	44	1.85
1990	Doug Drabek, Pitt	22-6	0	2.76
1991	Tom Glavine, Atl	20-11	0	2.55
1992	Greg Maddux, Chi	20-11	0	2.18

AMERICAN LEAGUE

Year		W-L	Sv	ERA
1984	*Willie Hernandez, Det	9-3	32	1.92
1985	Bret Saberhagen, KC	20-6	0	2.87
1986	*Roger Clemens, Bos	24-4	0	2.48
1987	Roger Clemens, Bos	20-9	0	2.97
1988	Frank Viola, Minn	24-7	0	2.64
1989	Bret Saberhagen, KC	23-6	0	2.16
1990	Bob Welch, Oak	27-6	0	2.95
1991	Roger Clemens	18-10	0	2.62
1992	*Dennis Eckersley	7-1	51	1.91

*Pitchers who won the MVP and Cy Young awards in the same season.

†NL games only. Sutcliffe pitched 15 games with Cleveland before being traded to the Cubs.

Career Individual Batting

GAMES

Pete Rose	3562
Carl Yastrzemski	3308
Hank Aaron	3298
Ty Cobb	3034
Stan Musial	3026
Willie Mays	2992
Rusty Staub	2951
Brooks Robinson	2896
Robin Yount	2856
Dave Winfield	2850
Al Kaline	2834
Eddie Collins	2826
Reggie Jackson	2820
Frank Robinson	2808
Tris Speaker	2789
Honus Wagner	2789
Tony Perez	2777
Mel Ott	2734
George Brett	2707
Graig Nettles	2700

HOME RUNS

Hank Aaron	755
Babe Ruth	714
Willie Mays	660
Frank Robinson	586
Harmon Killebrew	573
Reggie Jackson	563
Mike Schmidt	548
Mickey Mantle	536
Jimmie Foxx	534
Ted Williams	521
Willie McCovey	521
Eddie Mathews	512
Ernie Banks	512
Mel Ott	511
Lou Gehrig	493
Willie Stargell	475
Stan Musial	475
Dave Winfield	453
Carl Yastrzemski	452
Dave Kingman	442

BATTING AVERAGE

Ty Cobb	367
Rogers Hornsby	358
Joe Jackson	356
Ed Delahanty	346
Ted Williams	344
Tris Speaker	344
Billy Hamilton	344
Willie Keeler	343
Dan Brouthers	342
Babe Ruth	342
Harry Heilmann	342
Pete Browning	341
Bill Terry	341
George Sisler	340
Lou Gehrig	340
Jesse Burkett	339
Nap Lajoie	338
Riggs Stephenson	336
Wade Boggs	335
Al Simmons	334

AT BATS

Pete Rose	14053
Hank Aaron	12364
Carl Yastrzemski	11988
Ty Cobb	11429
Robin Yount	11008
Stan Musial	10972
Willie Mays	10881
Brooks Robinson	10654
Dave Winfield	10594
Honus Wagner	10441
George Brett	10349
Lou Brock	10332
Luis Aparicio	10230
Tris Speaker	10208
Al Kaline	10116
Rabbit Maranville	10078
Frank Robinson	10006
Eddie Collins	9949
Reggie Jackson	9864
Tony Perez	9778

HITS

Pete Rose	4256
Ty Cobb	4191
Hank Aaron	3771
Stan Musial	3630
Tris Speaker	3515
Carl Yastrzemski	3419
Honus Wagner	3418
Eddie Collins	3311
Willie Mays	3283
Nap Lajoie	3244
George Brett	3154
Paul Waner	3152
Robin Yount	3142
Rod Carew	3053
Lou Brock	3023
Dave Winfield	3014
Al Kaline	3007
Roberto Clemente	3000
Cap Anson	3000
Sam Rice	2987

RUNS

Ty Cobb	2245
Babe Ruth	2174
Hank Aaron	2174
Pete Rose	2165
Willie Mays	2062
Stan Musial	1949
Lou Gehrig	1888
Tris Speaker	1881
Mel Ott	1859
Frank Robinson	1829
Eddie Collins	1818
Carl Yastrzemski	1816
Ted Williams	1798
Charlie Gehringer	1774
Jimmie Foxx	1751
Honus Wagner	1735
Willie Keeler	1727
Cap Anson	1719
Jesse Burkett	1718
Billy Hamilton	1692

Career Individual Batting (Cont.)

DOUBLES

Tris Speaker	792
Pete Rose	746
Stan Musial	725
Ty Cobb	724
George Brett	665
Nap Lajoie	658
Carl Yastrzemski	646
Honus Wagner	643
Hank Aaron	624
Paul Waner	603
Robin Yount	583
Charlie Gehringer	574
Harry Heilmann	542
Rogers Hornsby	541
Joe Medwick	540
Al Simmons	539
Lou Gehrig	535
Al Oliver	529
Cap Anson	528
Frank Robinson	528

TRIPLES

Sam Crawford	312
Ty Cobb	297
Honus Wagner	252
Jake Beckley	243
Roger Connor	233
Tris Speaker	223
Fred Clarke	220
Dan Brouthers	205
Joe Kelley	194
Paul Waner	190
Bid McPhee	188
Eddie Collins	187
Sam Rice	184
Ed Delahanty	183
Jesse Burkett	183
Edd Roush	182
Ed Konetchy	181
Buck Ewing	178
Rabbit Maranville	177
Stan Musial	177
Harry Stovey	177

BASES ON BALLS

Babe Ruth	2056
Ted Williams	2019
Joe Morgan	1865
Carl Yastrzemski	1845
Mickey Mantle	1734
Mel Ott	1708
Eddie Yost	1614
Darrell Evans	1605
Stan Musial	1599
Pete Rose	1566
Harmon Killebrew	1559
Lou Gehrig	1508
Mike Schmidt	1507
Eddie Collins	1503
Willie Mays	1463
Jimmie Foxx	1452
Eddie Mathews	1444
Frank Robinson	1420
Rickey Henderson	1406
Hank Aaron	1402

RUNS BATTED IN

Hank Aaron	2297
Babe Ruth	2211
Lou Gehrig	1990
Ty Cobb	1961
Stan Musial	1951
Jimmie Foxx	1921
Willie Mays	1903
Mel Ott	1861
Carl Yastrzemski	1844
Ted Williams	1839
Al Simmons	1827
Frank Robinson	1812
Dave Winfield	1786
Honus Wagner	1732
Cap Anson	1715
Reggie Jackson	1702
Eddie Murray	1662
Tony Perez	1652
Ernie Banks	1636

SLUGGING AVERAGE

Babe Ruth	690
Ted Williams	634
Lou Gehrig	632
Jimmie Foxx	609
Hank Greenberg	605
Joe DiMaggio	579
Rogers Hornsby	577
Johnny Mize	562
Stan Musial	559
Willie Mays	557
Mickey Mantle	557
Hank Aaron	555
Ralph Kiner	548
Hack Wilson	545
Chuck Klein	543
Duke Snider	540
Frank Robinson	537
Al Simmons	535
Dick Allen	534
Earl Averill	533
Mel Ott	533

STOLEN BASES

Rickey Henderson	1095
Lou Brock	938
Billy Hamilton	915
Ty Cobb	892
Eddie Collins	743
Arlie Latham	739
Max Carey	738
Tim Raines	730
Honus Wagner	703
Joe Morgan	689
Willie Wilson	660
Tom Brown	657
Bert Campaneris	649
George Davis	616
Vince Coleman	648
Dummy Hoy	594
Maury Wills	586
Davey Lopes	557
Cesar Cedeno	550

PINCH HITS

Manny Mota	150
Smoky Burgess	145
Greg Gross	143
Jose Morales	123
Jerry Lynch	116
Red Lucas	114
Steve Braun	113
Terry Crowley	108
Gates Brown	107
Denny Walling	107
Mike Lum	103
Rusty Staub	100
Vic Davalillo	95
Larry Biittner	95
Jerry Hairston	94
Jim Dwyer	94
Dave Philley	93
Joel Youngblood	93
Jay Johnstone	92

TOTAL BASES

Hank Aaron	6856
Stan Musial	6134
Willie Mays	6066
Ty Cobb	5863
Babe Ruth	5793
Pete Rose	5752
Carl Yastrzemski	5539
Frank Robinson	5373
Tris Speaker	5104
Dave Winfield	5063
Lou Gehrig	5059
Mel Ott	5041
George Brett	5044
Jimmie Foxx	4956
Ted Williams	4884
Honus Wagner	4868
Al Kaline	4852
Reggie Jackson	4834
Robin Yount	4730
Rogers Hornsby	4712

STRIKEOUTS

Reggie Jackson	2597
Willie Stargell	1936
Mike Schmidt	1883
Tony Perez	1867
Dave Kingman	1816
Bobby Bonds	1757
Dale Murphy	1748
Lou Brock	1730
Mickey Mantle	1710
Harmon Killebrew	1699
Dwight Evans	1697
Dave Winfield	1609
Lee May	1570
Dick Allen	1556
Willie McCovey	1550
Frank Robinson	1532
Willie Mays	1526
Rick Monday	1513
Greg Luzinski	1495

Career Individual Pitching

GAMES

Hoyt Wilhelm......................1070
Kent Tekulve.......................1050
Lindy McDaniel....................987
Goose Gossage.....................966
Rollie Fingers.......................944
Gene Garber.........................931
Cy Young.............................906
Sparky Lyle..........................899
Jim Kaat..............................898
Don McMahon.......................874
Jeff Reardon........................869
Phil Niekro...........................864
Lee Smith............................850
Roy Face.............................848
Charlie Hough.......................837
Tug McGraw.........................824
Nolan Ryan..........................807
Dennis Eckersley...................804
Walter Johnson.....................801
Gaylord Perry.......................777

LOSSES

Cy Young.............................315
Pud Galvin...........................308
Nolan Ryan..........................292
Walter Johnson.....................279
Phil Niekro...........................274
Gaylord Perry.......................265
Jack Powell..........................256
Don Sutton..........................256
Eppa Rixey...........................251
Bert Blyleven........................250
Robin Roberts.......................245
Warren Spahn.......................245
Early Wynn...........................244
Steve Carlton.......................244
Jim Kaat..............................237
Gus Weyhing........................235
Frank Tanana........................234
Tommy John.........................231
Ted Lyons............................230
Bob Friend...........................230

EARNED RUN AVERAGE

Ed Walsh.............................1.82
Addie Joss...........................1.88
Three Finger Brown................2.06
Monte Ward..........................2.10
Christy Mathewson.................2.13
Rube Waddell........................2.16
Walter Johnson.....................2.17
Orval Overall........................2.24
Tommy Bond.........................2.25
Will White............................2.28
Ed Reulbach.........................2.28
Jim Scott.............................2.32
Eddie Plank..........................2.34
Larry Corcoran......................2.36
Eddie Cicotte........................2.37
George McQuillan...................2.38
Ed Killian.............................2.38
Doc White............................2.38
Nap Rucker...........................2.42
Jeff Tesreau.........................2.43

INNINGS PITCHED

Cy Young.............................7356
Pud Galvin...........................5941
Walter Johnson.....................5923
Phil Niekro...........................5403
Nolan Ryan..........................5386
Gaylord Perry.......................5351
Don Sutton..........................5280
Warren Spahn.......................5244
Steve Carlton.......................5217
Grover Alexander...................5189
Kid Nichols..........................5084
Tim Keefe............................5061
Bert Blyleven........................4969
Mickey Welch........................4802
Tom Seaver..........................4783
Christy Mathewson.................4782
Tommy John.........................4708
Robin Roberts.......................4689
Early Wynn...........................4564
Tony Mullane........................4540

WINNING PERCENTAGE

Bob Caruthers.......................692
Dave Foutz...........................690
Whitey Ford..........................690
Lefty Grove..........................680
Vic Raschi............................667
Christy Mathewson.................665
Larry Corcoran......................663
Sam Leever..........................658
Sal Maglie...........................657
Dwight Gooden......................655
Roger Clemens......................655
Sandy Koufax........................655
Johnny Allen.........................654
Ron Guidry...........................651
Lefty Gomez.........................649
Three Finger Brown................649
John Clarkson.......................648
Dizzy Dean...........................644
Grover Alexander...................642
Deacon Phillippe....................639

SHUTOUTS

Walter Johnson.....................110
Grover Alexander....................90
Christy Mathewson..................80
Cy Young..............................76
Eddie Plank...........................69
Warren Spahn........................63
Nolan Ryan...........................61
Tom Seaver..........................61
Bert Blyleven.........................60
Don Sutton...........................58
Ed Walsh.............................57
Three Finger Brown.................57
Pud Galvin............................57
Bob Gibson...........................56
Steve Carlton........................55
Jim Palmer............................53
Gaylord Perry.........................53
Juan Marichal........................52
Rube Waddell........................50
Vic Willis..............................50

WINS

Cy Young.............................511
Walter Johnson.....................416
Christy Mathewson.................373
Grover Alexander...................373
Warren Spahn.......................363
Kid Nichols..........................361
Pud Galvin...........................361
Tim Keefe............................342
Steve Carlton.......................329
Eddie Plank..........................327
John Clarkson.......................326
Don Sutton..........................324
Nolan Ryan..........................324
Phil Niekro...........................318
Gaylord Perry.......................314
Old Hoss Radbourn.................311
Tom Seaver..........................311
Mickey Welch........................308
Lefty Grove..........................300
Early Wynn...........................300

SAVES

Lee Smith............................401
Jeff Reardon........................365
Rollie Fingers.......................341
Goose Gossage.....................309
Bruce Sutter........................300
Dennis Eckersley...................275
Tom Henke...........................260
Dave Righetti........................252
Dan Quisenberry....................244
Sparky Lyle..........................238
John Franco..........................236
Hoyt Wilhelm........................227
Gene Garber.........................218
Dave Smith..........................216
Bobby Thigpen......................201
Roy Face.............................193
Doug Jones...........................190
Mike Marshall........................188
Kent Tekulve.........................184
Steve Bedrosian.....................184
Randy Myers.........................184

COMPLETE GAMES

Cy Young.............................750
Pud Galvin...........................639
Tim Keefe............................557
Kid Nichols..........................532
Walter Johnson.....................531
Mickey Welch........................525
Old Hoss Radbourn.................489
John Clarkson.......................485
Tony Mullane........................469
Jim McCormick......................466
Gus Weyhing........................448
Grover Alexander...................438
Christy Mathewson.................435
Jack Powell..........................422
Eddie Plank..........................412
Will White............................394
Amos Rusie..........................392
Vic Willis..............................388
Warren Spahn........................382
Jim Whitney..........................377

Career Individual Pitching *(Cont.)*

STRIKEOUTS		BASES ON BALLS	
Nolan Ryan	5714	Nolan Ryan	2795
Steve Carlton	4136	Steve Carlton	1833
Bert Blyleven	3701	Phil Niekro	1809
Tom Seaver	3640	Early Wynn	1775
Don Sutton	3574	Bob Feller	1764
Gaylord Perry	3534	Bobo Newsom	1732
Walter Johnson	3508	Amos Rusie	1704
Phil Niekro	3342	Charlie Hough	1613
Ferguson Jenkins	3192	Gus Weyhing	1566
Bob Gibson	3117	Red Ruffing	1541
Jim Bunning	2855	Bump Hadley	1442
Mickey Lolich	2832	Warren Spahn	1434
Cy Young	2796	Earl Whitehill	1431
Frank Tanana	2761	Tony Mullane	1409
Warren Spahn	2583	Sad Sam Jones	1396
Bob Feller	2581	Tom Seaver	1390
Jerry Koosman	2556	Gaylord Perry	1379
Tim Keefe	2527	Mike Torrez	1371
Christy Mathewson	2502	Walter Johnson	1355
Don Drysdale	2486	Don Sutton	1343

Individual Batting (Single Season)

HITS

George Sisler, 1920	257
Bill Terry, 1930	254
Lefty O'Doul, 1929	254
Al Simmons, 1925	253
Rogers Hornsby, 1922	250
Chuck Klein, 1930	250
Ty Cobb, 1911	248
George Sisler, 1922	246
Willie Keeler, 1897	243
Babe Herman, 1930	241
Heinie Manush, 1928	241

BATTING AVERAGE

Hugh Duffy, 1894	438
Tip O'Neill, 1887	435
Willie Keeler, 1897	432
Ross Barnes, 1876	429
Rogers Hornsby, 1924	424
Jesse Burkett, 1895	423
Nap Lajoie, 1901	422
George Sisler, 1922	420
Ty Cobb, 1911	420
Tuck Turner, 1894	416

DOUBLES

Earl Webb, 1931	67
George Burns, 1926	64
Joe Medwick, 1936	64
Hank Greenberg, 1934	63
Paul Waner, 1932	62
Charlie Gehringer, 1936	60
Tris Speaker, 1923	59
Chuck Klein, 1930	59
Billy Herman, 1936	57
Billy Herman, 1935	57

TOTAL BASES

Babe Ruth, 1921	457
Rogers Hornsby, 1922	450
Lou Gehrig, 1927	447
Chuck Klein, 1930	445
Jimmie Foxx, 1932	438
Stan Musial, 1948	429
Hack Wilson, 1930	423
Chuck Klein, 1932	420
Lou Gehrig, 1930	419
Joe DiMaggio, 1937	418

TRIPLES

Owen Wilson, 1912	36
Heinie Reitz, 1894	31
Dave Orr, 1886	31
Perry Werden, 1893	29
Harry Davis, 1897	28
Sam Thompson, 1894	27
George Davis, 1893	27
Jimmy Williams, 1899	27
George Treadway, 1894	26
Long John Reilly, 1890	26
Joe Jackson, 1912	26
Sam Crawford, 1914	26
Kiki Cuyler, 1925	26

HOME RUNS

Roger Maris, 1961	61
Babe Ruth, 1927	60
Babe Ruth, 1921	59
Hank Greenberg, 1938	58
Jimmie Foxx, 1932	58
Hack Wilson, 1930	56
Babe Ruth, 1920	54
Mickey Mantle, 1961	54
Babe Ruth, 1928	54
Ralph Kiner, 1949	54

RUNS BATTED IN

Hack Wilson, 1930	190
Lou Gehrig, 1931	184
Hank Greenberg, 1937	183
Jimmie Foxx, 1938	175
Lou Gehrig, 1927	175
Lou Gehrig, 1930	174
Babe Ruth, 1921	171
Hank Greenberg, 1935	170
Chuck Klein, 1930	170
Jimmie Foxx, 1932	169

STRIKEOUTS

Bobby Bonds, 1970	189
Bobby Bonds, 1969	187
Rob Deer, 1987	186
Pete Incaviglia, 1986	185
Cecil Fielder, 1990	182
Mike Schmidt, 1975	180
Rob Deer, 1986	179
Jose Canseco, 1986	175
Dave Nicholson, 1963	175
Gorman Thomas, 1979	175
Rob Deer, 1991	175

RUNS

Billy Hamilton, 1894	196
Babe Ruth, 1921	177
Tom Brown, 1891	177
Joe Kelley, 1894	167
Tip O'Neill, 1887	167
Lou Gehrig, 1936	167
Billy Hamilton, 1895	166
Willie Keeler, 1894	165
Babe Ruth, 1928	163
Lou Gehrig, 1931	163
Arlie Latham, 1887	163

Individual Batting (Single Season) (Cont)

STOLEN BASES

Rickey Henderson, 1982	130
Lou Brock, 1974	118
Vince Coleman, 1985	110
Vince Coleman, 1987	109
Rickey Henderson, 1983	108
Vince Coleman, 1986	107
Maury Wills, 1962	104
Rickey Henderson, 1980	100
Ron LeFlore, 1980	97
Ty Cobb, 1915	96
Omar Moreno, 1980	96

BASES ON BALLS

Babe Ruth, 1923	170
Ted Williams, 1947	162
Ted Williams, 1949	162
Ted Williams, 1946	156
Eddie Yost, 1956	151
Eddie Joost, 1949	149
Babe Ruth, 1920	148
Jimmy Wynn, 1969	148
Eddie Stanky, 1945	148
Jimmy Sheckard, 1911	147

SLUGGING AVERAGE

Babe Ruth, 1920	847
Babe Ruth, 1921	846
Babe Ruth, 1927	772
Lou Gehrig, 1927	765
Babe Ruth, 1923	764
Rogers Hornsby, 1925	756
Jimmie Foxx, 1932	749
Babe Ruth, 1924	739
Babe Ruth, 1926	737
Ted Williams, 1941	735

Individual Pitching (Single Season)

GAMES

Mike Marshall, 1974	106
Kent Tekulve, 1979	94
Mike Marshall, 1973	92
Kent Tekulve, 1978	91
Wayne Granger, 1969	90
Mike Marshall, 1979	90
Kent Tekulve, 1987	90
Mark Eichhorn, 1987	89
Wilbur Wood, 1968	88
Rob Murphy, 1987	87

WINS

Jack Chesbro, 1904	41
Ed Walsh, 1908	40
Christy Mathewson, 1908	37
Walter Johnson, 1913	36
Jouett Meekin, 1894	36
Amos Rusie, 1894	36
Joe McGinnity, 1904	35
Cy Young, 1895	35
Smoky Joe Wood, 1912	34
Frank Killen, 1893	34

SAVES

Bobby Thigpen, 1990	57
Randy Myers, 1993	53
Dennis Eckersley, 1992	51
Dennis Eckersley, 1990	48
Rod Beck, 1993	48
Lee Smith, 1991	47
Bryan Harvey, 1991	46
Dave Righetti, 1986	46
Bruce Sutter, 1984	45
Dan Quisenberry, 1983	45
Dennis Eckersley, 1988	45
Jeff Montgomery, 1993	45
Bryan Harvey, 1993	45
Duane Ward, 1993	45

GAMES STARTED

Amos Rusie, 1893	52
Jack Chesbro, 1904	51
Frank Killen, 1896	50
Amos Rusie, 1894	50
Pink Hawley, 1895	50
Ted Breitenstein, 1894	50
Ted Breitenstein, 1895	50
Ed Walsh, 1908	49
Wilbur Wood, 1972	49
Joe McGinnity, 1903	48
Jouett Meekin, 1894	48
Frank Killen, 1893	48
Wilbur Wood, 1973	48

LOSSES

Red Donahue, 1897	33
Jim Hughey, 1899	30
Ted Breitenstein, 1895	30
Vic Willis, 1905	29
Bill Hart, 1896	29
Jack Taylor, 1898	29
Still Bill Hill, 1896	29
Duke Esper, 1893	28
Paul Derringer, 1933	27
Bill Hart, 1897	27
George Bell, 1910	27
Willie Sudhoff, 1898	27
Dummy Taylor, 1901	27
Pink Hawley, 1894	27

EARNED RUN AVERAGE

Dutch Leonard, 1914	1.01
Three Finger Brown, 1906	1.04
Walter Johnson, 1913	1.09
Bob Gibson, 1968	1.12
Christy Mathewson, 1909	1.14
Jack Pfiester, 1907	1.15
Addie Joss, 1908	1.16
Carl Lundgren, 1907	1.17
Grover Alexander, 1915	1.22
Cy Young, 1908	1.26

INNINGS PITCHED

Amos Rusie, 1893	482
Ed Walsh, 1908	464
Jack Chesbro, 1904	455
Ted Breitenstein, 1894	447
Pink Hawley, 1895	444
Amos Rusie, 1894	444
Joe McGinnity, 1903	434
Frank Killen, 1896	432
Ted Breitenstein, 1895	430
Kid Nichols, 1893	425

WINNING PERCENTAGE

Roy Face, 1959	947
Johnny Allen, 1937	938
Ron Guidry, 1978	893
Freddie Fitzsimmons, 1940	889
Lefty Grove, 1931	886
Bob Stanley, 1978	882
Preacher Roe, 1951	880
Tom Seaver, 1981	875
Smoky Joe Wood, 1912	872
David Cone, 1988	870

SHUTOUTS

Grover Alexander, 1916	16
Bob Gibson, 1968	13
Jack Coombs, 1910	13
Grover Alexander, 1915	12
Christy Mathewson, 1908	12
Dean Chance, 1964	11
Walter Johnson, 1913	11
Sandy Koufax, 1963	11
Ed Walsh, 1908	11

Thriller with Bonilla

After novelist Scott Turow threw out the first ball before a New York Met–Chicago Cub game at Wrigley Field in June, Met rightfielder Bobby Bonilla approached Turow on the field and asked him to wait a minute. Bonilla went into the dugout and returned with a copy of Turow's latest page-turner, *Pleading Guilty*. Bonilla asked Turow to autograph the book, which, as it happened, Bonilla had purchased that morning. "Tell me I won't be able to put it down, just like your other two," Bonilla said.

Turow hit a home run with his book—it shot up the bestseller list immediately after its release. After getting the author's autograph, Bonilla swatted a homer too, a two-run blast that helped power the Mets to an 11–3 win over the Cubs.

Individual Pitching (Single Season) (Cont)

COMPLETE GAMES

Amos Rusie, 1893.................50
Jack Chesbro, 1904 48
Ted Breitenstein, 1894..........46
Ted Breitenstein, 1895..........46
Vic Willis, 1902.....................45
Amos Rusie, 1894.................45
Kid Nichols, 1893.................44
Cy Young, 1894....................44
Joe McGinnity, 1903.............44
Pink Hawley, 1895................44
Frank Killen, 1896.................44

STRIKEOUTS

Nolan Ryan, 1973 383
Sandy Koufax, 1965 382
Nolan Ryan, 1974 367
Rube Waddell, 1904............349
Bob Feller, 1946 348
Nolan Ryan, 1977 341
Nolan Ryan, 1972 329
Nolan Ryan, 1976 327
Sam McDowell, 1965...........325
Sandy Koufax, 1966 317

BASES ON BALLS

Amos Rusie, 1893................218
Cy Seymour, 1898 213
Bob Feller, 1938 208
Nolan Ryan, 1977 204
Nolan Ryan, 1974 202
Amos Rusie, 1894................200
Bob Feller, 1941 194
Bobo Newsom, 1938...........192
Ted Breitenstein, 1894.........191
Tony Mullane, 1893 189

Manager of the Year

NATIONAL LEAGUE

1983	Tommy Lasorda, LA
1984	Jim Frey, Chi
1985	Whitey Herzog, StL
1986	Hal Lanier, Hou
1987	Buck Rodgers, Mont
1988	Tommy Lasorda, LA
1989	Don Zimmer, Chi
1990	Jim Leyland, Pitt
1991	Bobby Cox, Atl
1992	Jim Leyland, Pitt
1993	Dusty Baker, SF

AMERICAN LEAGUE

1983	Tony La Russa, Chi
1984	Sparky Anderson, Det
1985	Bobby Cox, Tor
1986	John McNamara, Bos
1987	Sparky Anderson, Det
1988	Tony La Russa, Oak
1989	Frank Robinson, Balt
1990	Jeff Torborg, Chi
1991	Tom Kelly, Minn
1992	Tony La Russa, Oak
1993	Gene Lamont, Chi

Individual Batting (Single Game)

MOST RUNS

6 ......Mel Ott, NY (N),   Aug 4, 1934, 2nd game
                                     Apr 30, 1944, 1st game
      Johnny Pesky, Bos (A) May 8, 1946
      Frank Torre, Mil (N)   Sept 2, 1957, 2nd game
      Spike Owen, Bos (A) Aug 21, 1986

MOST HITS

7 ......Rennie Stennett, Pitt   Sept 16, 1975

MOST HOME RUNS

4 ......Lou Gehrig, NY (A)   June 3, 1932
      Gil Hodges, Bklyn   Aug 31, 1950
      Joe Adcock, Mil (N) July 31, 1954
      Rocky Colavito, Cle June 10, 1959
      Willie Mays, SF   April 30, 1961

MOST HOME RUNS (Cont.)

4 ......Bob Horner, Atl   July 6, 1986
      Mark Whiten, StL   Sep 7, 1993

MOST GRAND SLAMS

2 ......Tony Lazzeri, NY (A) May 24, 1936
      Jim Tabor, Bos (A)   July 4, 1939
      Rudy York, Bos (A)   July 27, 1946
      Jim Gentile, Balt   May 9, 1961
      Tony Cloninger, Atl July 3, 1966
      Jim Northrup, Det   June 24, 1968
      Frank Robinson, Balt June 26, 1970

MOST RBI

12 .....Jim Bottomley, StL   Sep 16, 1924
      Mark Whiten, StL   Sep 7, 1993

Individual Batting (Single Inning)

MOST RUNS

3 ......Sammy White, Bos (A) June 18, 1953,
                                7th inning

MOST HITS

3 ......Gene Stephens, Bos (A) June 18, 1953,
                                 7th inning

MOST RBI

6 ......Fred Merkle, NY (N)   May 13, 1911 (RBIs not
                                officially adopted until
                                1920)
      Bob Johnson, Phil (A) Aug 29, 1937

MOST RBI (CONT.)

6 ......Tom McBride, Bos (A) Aug 4, 1945
      Joe Astroth, Phil (A)   Sept 23, 1950
      Gil McDougald, NY (A) May 3, 1951
      Sam Mele, Chi (A)   June 10, 1952
      Jim Lemon, Wash   Sept 5, 1959
      Jim Ray Hart, SF   July 8, 1970
      Andre Dawson, Mont Sept 24, 1985
      Dale Murphy, Atl   July 27, 1989
      Carlos Quintana, Bos (A) July 30, 1991

Individual Pitching (Single Game)

MOST INNINGS PITCHED

26 .....Leon Cadore, Bklyn   May 1, 1920, tie 1-1
Joe Oeschger, Bos (N) May 1, 1920, tie 1-1

MOST RUNS ALLOWED

24 .....Al Travers, Det   May 18, 1912 (only
major league game)

MOST HITS ALLOWED

26 .....Harley Parker, Cin   June 21, 1901
Hod Lisenbee, Phil (A) Sept 11, 1936
Al Travers, Det   May 18, 1912 (only
major league game)

MOST STRIKEOUTS

20 .....Roger Clemens, Bos (A)   April 29, 1986

MOST WALKS ALLOWED

16 .....Bruno Haas, Phil (A)   June 2, 1915

MOST WILD PITCHES

6 .......J.R. Richard, Hou   April 10, 1979
Phil Niekro, Atl   Aug 14. 1979
Bill Gullickson, Mont   April 10, 1982

Individual Pitching (Single Inning)

MOST RUNS ALLOWED

13 .....Lefty O'Doul, Bos (A)   July 7, 1923

MOST WALKS ALLOWED

8 ....Dolly Gray, Wash   Aug 28, 1909

MOST WILD PITCHES

4 ....Walter Johnson, Wash Sept. 21, 1914
Phil Niekro, Atl   Aug 14, 1979

Miscellaneous

LONGEST GAME, BY INNINGS

26 .....Brooklyn 1, Boston 1   May 1, 1920

LONGEST GAME, BY TIME

4:18 ..LA 8, SF 7   Oct 2, 1962

Note: All records after 1900. All single game hitting records for nine-inning game.

Baseball Hall of Fame

Players

	Position	Career Dates	Year Selected		Position	Career Dates	Year Selected
Hank Aaron	OF	1954-76	1982	Fred Clarke	OF	1894-1915	1945
Grover Alexander	P	1911-30	1938	John Clarkson	P	1882-94	1963
Cap Anson	1B	1876-97	1939	Roberto Clemente	OF	1955-72	1973
Luis Aparicio	SS	1956-73	1984	Ty Cobb	OF	1905-28	1936
Luke Appling	SS	1930-50	1964	Mickey Cochrane	C	1925-37	1947
Earl Averill	OF	1929-41	1975	Eddie Collins	2B	1906-30	1939
Frank Baker	3B	1908-22	1955	Jimmy Collins	3B	1895-1908	1945
Dave Bancroft	SS	1915-30	1971	Earle Combs	OF	1924-35	1970
Ernie Banks	SS-1B	1953-71	1977	Roger Connor	1B	1880-97	1976
Jake Beckley	1B	1888-1907	1971	Stan Coveleski	P	1912-28	1969
Cool Papa Bell*	OF		1974	Sam Crawford	OF	1899-1917	1957
Johnny Bench	C	1967-83	1989	Joe Cronin	SS	1926-45	1956
Chief Bender	P	1903-25	1953	Candy Cummings	P	1872-77	1939
Yogi Berra	C	1946-65	1972	Kiki Cuyler	OF	1921-38	1968
Jim Bottomley	1B	1922-37	1974	Ray Dandridge*	3B		1987
Lou Boudreau	SS	1938-52	1970	Dizzy Dean	P	1930-47	1953
Roger Bresnahan	C	1897-1915	1945	Ed Delahanty	OF	1888-1903	1945
Lou Brock	OF	1961-79	1985	Bill Dickey	C	1928-46	1954
Dan Brouthers	1B	1879-1904	1945	Martin Dihigo*	P-OF		1977
Three Finger Brown	P	1903-16	1949	Joe DiMaggio	OF	1936-51	1955
Jesse Burkett	OF	1890-1905	1946	Bobby Doerr	2B	1937-51	1986
Roy Campanella	C	1948-57	1969	Don Drysdale	P	1956-69	1984
Rod Carew	1B-2B	1967-85	1991	Hugh Duffy	OF	1888-1906	1945
Max Carey	OF	1910-29	1961	Johnny Evers	2B	1902-29	1939
Frank Chance	1B	1898-1914	1946	Buck Ewing	C	1880-97	1946
Oscar Charleston*	OF		1976	Red Faber	P	1914-33	1964
Jack Chesbro	P	1899-1909	1946	Bob Feller	P	1936-56	1962

Note: Career dates indicate first and last appearances in the majors.
*Elected on the basis of his career in the Negro leagues.

Players (Cont.)

Player	Position	Career Dates	Year Selected
Rick Ferrell	C	1929-47	1984
Rollie Fingers	P	1968-85	1992
Elmer Flick	OF	1898-1910	1963
Whitey Ford	P	1950-67	1974
Jimmie Foxx	1B	1925-45	1951
Frankie Frisch	2B	1919-37	1947
Pud Galvin	P	1879-92	1965
Lou Gehrig	1B	1923-39	1939
Charlie Gehringer	2B	1924-42	1949
Bob Gibson	P	1959-75	1981
Josh Gibson*	C		1972
Lefty Gomez	P	1930-43	1972
Goose Goslin	OF	1921-38	1968
Hank Greenberg	1B	1930-47	1956
Burleigh Grimes	P	1916-34	1964
Lefty Grove	P	1925-41	1947
Chick Hafey	OF	1924-37	1971
Jesse Haines	P	1918-37	1970
Billy Hamilton	OF	1888-1901	1961
Gabby Hartnett	C	1922-41	1955
Harry Heilmann	OF	1914-32	1952
Billy Herman	2B	1931-47	1975
Harry Hooper	OF	1909-25	1971
Rogers Hornsby	2B	1915-37	1942
Waite Hoyt	P	1918-38	1969
Carl Hubbell	P	1928-43	1947
Catfish Hunter	P	1965-79	1987
Monte Irvin*	OF	1949-56	1973
Reggie Jackson	OF	1967-87	1993
Travis Jackson	SS	1922-36	1982
Ferguson Jenkins	P	1965-83	1991
Hugh Jennings	SS	1891-1918	1945
Judy Johnson*	3B		1975
Walter Johnson	P	1907-27	1936
Addie Joss	P	1902-10	1978
Al Kaline	OF	1953-74	1980
Tim Keefe	P	1880-93	1964
Willie Keeler	OF	1892-1910	1939
George Kell	3B	1943-57	1983
Joe Kelley	OF	1891-1908	1971
George Kelly	1B	1915-32	1973
King Kelly	C	1878-93	1945
Harmon Killebrew	1B-3B	1954-75	1984
Ralph Kiner	OF	1946-55	1975
Chuck Klein	OF	1928-44	1980
Sandy Koufax	P	1955-66	1972
Nap Lajoie	2B	1896-1916	1937
Tony Lazzeri	2B	1926-39	1991
Bob Lemon	P	1941-58	1976
Buck Leonard*	1B		1977
Fred Lindstrom	3B	1924-36	1976
Pop Lloyd*	SS-1B		1977
Ernie Lombardi	C	1931-47	1986
Ted Lyons	P	1923-46	1955
Mickey Mantle	OF	1951-68	1974
Heinie Manush	OF	1923-39	1964
Rabbit Maranville	SS-2B	1912-35	1954
Juan Marichal	P	1960-75	1983
Rube Marquard	P	1908-25	1971
Eddie Mathews	3B	1952-68	1978
Christy Mathewson	P	1900-16	1936
Willie Mays	OF	1951-73	1979
Tommy McCarthy	OF	1884-96	1946
Willie McCovey	1B	1959-80	1986
Joe McGinnity	P	1899-1908	1946
Joe Medwick	OF	1932-48	1968
Johnny Mize	1B	1936-53	1981
Joe Morgan	2B	1963-84	1990
Stan Musial	OF-1B	1941-63	1969
Hal Newhouser	P	1939-55	1992
Kid Nichols	P	1890-1906	1949
Jim O'Rourke	OF	1876-1904	1945
Mel Ott	OF	1926-47	1951
Satchel Paige*	P	1948-65	1971
Jim Palmer	P	1965-84	1990
Herb Pennock	P	1912-34	1948
Gaylord Perry	P	1962-83	1991
Eddie Plank	P	1901-17	1946
Hoss Radbourn	P	1880-91	1939
Pee Wee Reese	SS	1940-58	1984
Sam Rice	OF	1915-35	1963
Eppa Rixey	P	1912-33	1963
Robin Roberts	P	1948-66	1976
Brooks Robinson	3B	1955-77	1983
Frank Robinson	OF	1956-76	1982
Jackie Robinson	2B	1947-56	1962
Edd Roush	OF	1913-31	1962
Red Ruffing	P	1924-47	1967
Amos Rusie	P	1889-1901	1977
Babe Ruth	OF	1914-35	1936
Ray Schalk	C	1912-29	1955
Red Schoendienst	2B	1945-63	1989
Tom Seaver	P	1967-86	1992
Joe Sewell	SS	1920-33	1977
Al Simmons	OF	1924-44	1953
George Sisler	1B	1915-30	1939
Enos Slaughter	OF	1938-59	1985
Duke Snider	OF	1947-64	1980
Warren Spahn	P	1942-65	1973
Al Spalding	P	1871-78	1939
Tris Speaker	OF	1907-28	1937
Willie Stargell	OF-1B	1962-82	1988
Bill Terry	1B	1923-36	1954
Sam Thompson	OF	1885-1906	1974
Joe Tinker	SS	1902-16	1946
Pie Traynor	3B	1920-37	1948
Dazzy Vance	P	1915-35	1955
Arky Vaughan	SS	1932-48	1985
Rube Waddell	P	1897-1910	1946
Honus Wagner	SS	1897-1917	1936
Bobby Wallace	SS	1894-1918	1953
Ed Walsh	P	1904-17	1946
Lloyd Waner	OF	1927-45	1967
Paul Waner	OF	1926-45	1952
Monte Ward	2B-P	1878-94	1964
Mickey Welch	P	1880-92	1973
Zach Wheat	OF	1909-27	1959
Hoyt Wilhelm	P	1952-72	1985
Billy Williams	OF	1959-76	1987
Ted Williams	OF	1939-60	1966
Hack Wilson	OF	1923-34	1979
Early Wynn	P	1939-63	1972
Carl Yastrzemski	OF	1961-83	1989
Cy Young	P	1890-1911	1937
Ross Youngs	OF	1917-26	1972

Umpires

	Year Selected
Al Barlick	1989
Jocko Conlan	1974
Tom Connolly	1953
Billy Evans	1973
Cal Hubbard	1976
Bill Klem	1953
Bill McGowan	1992

Managers

	Years Managed	Year Selected
Walt Alston	1954-76	1983
Clark Griffith	1901-20	1946
Bucky Harris	1924-56	1975
Miller Huggins	1913-29	1964
Al Lopez	1951-69	1977
Connie Mack	1894-1950	1937
Joe McCarthy	1926-50	1957
John McGraw	1899-1932	1937
Bill McKechnie	1915-46	1962
Wilbert Robinson	1902-31	1945
Casey Stengel	1934-65	1966

Meritorious Service

	Year Selected
Ed Barrow (manager-executive)	1953
Morgan Bulkeley (executive)	1937
Alexander Cartwright (executive)	1938
Henry Chadwick (writer-executive)	1938
Happy Chandler (commissioner)	1982
Charles Comiskey (manager-executive)	1939
Rube Foster (player-manager-executive)	1981
Ford Frick (commissioner-executive)	1970
Warren Giles (executive)	1979
Will Harridge (executive)	1972
Ban Johnson (executive)	1937
Kenesaw M. Landis (commissioner)	1944
Larry MacPhail (executive)	1978
Branch Rickey (manager-executive)	1967
Al Spalding (player-executive)	1939
Bill Veeck (owner)	1991
George Weiss (executive)	1971
George Wright (player-manager)	1937
Harry Wright (player-manager-executive)	1953
Tom Yawkey (executive)	1980

THEY SAID IT

John Kruk, the Philadelphia Phillies' doughy first baseman, reacting to a prediction by St. Louis Cardinal outfielder Ray Lankford that the Cards would win the National League East because they're in better shape than the Phils: "He probably looked at our media guide and saw a picture of me."

Notable Achievements

No-Hit Games, 9 Innings or More

NATIONAL LEAGUE

Date		Pitcher and Game
1876	July 15	George Bradley, StL vs Hart 2-0
1880	June 12	John Richmond, Wor vs Clev 1-0 (perfect game)
	June 17	Monte Ward, Prov vs Buff 5-0 (perfect game)
	Aug 19	Larry Corcoran, Chi vs Bos 6-0
	Aug 20	Pud Galvin, Buff at Wor 1-0
1882	Sep 20	Larry Corcoran, Chi vs Wor 5-0
	Sep 22	Tim Lovett, Bklyn vs NY 4-0
1883	July 25	Hoss Radbourn, Prov at Clev 8-0
	Sep 13	Hugh Daily, Clev at Phil 1-0
1884	June 27	Larry Corcoran, Chi vs Prov 6-0
	Aug 4	Pud Galvin, Buff at Det 18-0
1885	July 27	John Clarkson, Chi at Prov 4-0
	Aug 29	Charles Ferguson, Phil vs Prov 1-0
1891	July 31	Amos Rusie, NY vs Bklyn 6-0
	June 22	Tom Lovett, Bklyn vs NY 4-0
1892	Aug 6	Jack Stivetts, Bos vs Bklyn 11-0
	Aug 22	Alex Sanders, Lou vs Balt 6-2
	Oct 15	Bumpus Jones, Cin vs Pitt 7-1 (first major league game)
1893	Aug 16	Bill Hawke, Balt vs Wash 5-0

Date		Pitcher and Game
1897	Sep 18	Cy Young, Clev vs Cin 6-0
1898	Apr 22	Ted Breitenstein, Cin vs Pitt 11-0
	Apr 22	Jim Hughes, Balt vs Bos 8-0
	July 8	Frank Donahue, Phil vs Bos 5-0
	Aug 21	Walter Thornton, Chi vs Bklyn 2-0
1899	May 25	Deacon Phillippe, Lou vs NY 7-0
	Aug 7	Vic Willis, Bos vs Wash 7-1
1900	July 12	Noodles Hahn, Cin vs Phil 4-0
1901	July 15	Christy Mathewson, NY at StL 5-0
1903	Sep 18	Chick Fraser, Phil at Chi 10-0
1904	June 11	Bob Wicker, Chi at NY 1-0 (hit in 10th; won in 12th)
1905	June 13	Christy Mathewson, NY at Chi 1-0
1906	May 1	John Lush, Phil at Bklyn 6-0
	July 20	Mal Eason, Bklyn at StL 2-0
	Aug 1	Harry McIntire, Bklyn vs Pitt 0-1 (hit in 11th; lost in 13th)
1907	May 8	Frank Pfeffer, Bos vs Cin 6-0
	Sep 20	Nick Maddox, Pitt vs Bklyn 2-1
1908	July 4	George Wiltse, NY vs Phil 1-0 (10 innings)
	Sep 5	Nap Rucker, Bklyn vs Bos 6-0

No-Hit Games, 9 Innings or More *(Cont.)*

NATIONAL LEAGUE *(CONT.)*

Date	Pitcher and Game	Date	Pitcher and Game
1909......Apr 15	Leon Ames, NY vs Bklyn 0-3 (hit in 10th; lost in 13th)	1965......Aug 19	Jim Maloney, Cin at Chi 1-0 (10 innings)
1912......Sep 6	Jeff Tesreau, NY at Phil 3-0	Sep 9	Sandy Koufax, LA vs Chi 1-0 (perfect game)
1914......Sep 9	George Davis, Bos vs Phil 7-0	1967......June 18	Don Wilson, Hou vs Atl 2-0
1915......Apr 15	Rube Marquard, NY vs Bklyn 2-0	1968......July 29	George Culver, Cin at Phil 6-1
Aug 31	Jimmy Lavender, Chi at NY 2-0	Sep 17	Gaylord Perry, SF vs StL 1-0
1916......June 16	Tom Hughes, Bos vs Pitt 2-0	Sep 18	Ray Washburn, StL at SF 2-0
1917......May 2	Jim Vaughn, Chi vs Cin 0-1 (hit in 10th; lost in 10th)	1969......Apr 17	Bill Stoneman, Mont at Phil 7-0
May 2	Fred Toney, Cin at Chi 1-0 (10 innings)	Apr 30	Jim Maloney, Cin vs Hou 10-0
1919......May 11	Hod Eller, Cin vs StL 6-0	May 1	Don Wilson, Hou at Cin 4-0
1922......May 7	Jesse Barnes, NY vs Phil 6-0	Aug 19	Ken Holtzman, Chi vs Atl 3-0
1924......July 17	Jesse Haines, StL vs Bos 5-0	Sep 20	Bob Moose, Pitt at NY 4-0
1925......Sep 13	Dazzy Vance, Bklyn vs Phil 10-1	1970......June 12	Dock Ellis, Pitt at SD 2-0
1929......May 8	Carl Hubbell, NY vs Pitt 11-0	July 20	Bill Singer, LA vs Phil 5-0
1934......Sep 21	Paul Dean, StL vs Bklyn 3-0	1971......June 3	Ken Holtzman, Chi at Cin 1-0
1938......June 11	Johnny Vander Meer, Cin vs Bos 3-0	June 23	Rick Wise, Phil at Cin 4-0
June 15	Johnny Vander Meer, Cin at Bklyn 6-0	Aug 14	Bob Gibson, StL at Pitt 11-0
1940......Apr 30	Tex Carleton, Bklyn at Cin, 3-0	1972......Apr 16	Burt Hooton, Chi vs Phil 4-0
1941......Aug 30	Lon Warneke, StL at Cin 2-0	Sep 2	Milt Pappas, Chi vs SD 8-0
1944......Apr 27	Jim Tobin, Bos vs Bklyn 2-0	Oct 2	Bill Stoneman, Mont vs NY 7-0
May 15	Clyde Shoun, Cin vs Bos 1-0	1973......Aug 5	Phil Niekro, Atl vs SD 9-0
1946......Apr 23	Ed Head, Bklyn vs Bos 5-0	1975......Aug 24	Ed Halicki, SF vs NY 6-0
1947......June 18	Ewell Blackwell, Cin vs Bos 6-0	1976......July 9	Larry Dierker, Hou vs Mont 6-0
1948......Sep 9	Rex Barney, Bklyn at NY 2-0	Aug 9	John Candelaria, Pitt vs LA 2-0
1950......Aug 11	Vern Bickford, Bos vs Bklyn 7-0	Sep 29	John Montefusco, SF at Atl 9-0
1951......May 6	Cliff Chambers, Pitt at Bos 3-0	1978......Apr 16	Bob Forsch, StL vs Phil 5-0
1952......June 19	Carl Erskine, Bklyn vs Chi 5-0	June 16	Tom Seaver, Cin vs StL 4-0
1954......June 12	Jim Wilson, Mil vs Phil 2-0	1979......Apr 7	Ken Forsch, Hou vs Atl 6-0
1955......May 12	Sam Jones, Chi vs Pitt 4-0	1980......June 27	Jerry Reuss, LA at SF 8-0
1956......May 12	Carl Erskine, Bklyn vs NY 3-0	1981......May 10	Charlie Lea, Mont vs SF 4-0
Sep 25	Sal Maglie, Bklyn vs Phil 5-0	Sep 26	Nolan Ryan, Hou vs LA 5-0
1959......May 26	Harvey Haddix, Pitt at Mil 0-1 (hit in 13th; lost in 13th)	1983......Sep 26	Bob Forsch, StL vs Mont 3-0
1960......May 15	Don Cardwell, Chi vs StL 4-0	1986......Sep 25	Mike Scott, Hou vs SF 2-0
Aug 18	Lew Burdette, Mil vs Phil 1-0	1988......Sep 16	Tom Browning, Cin vs LA 1-0 (perfect game)
Sep 16	Warren Spahn, Mil vs Phil 4-0	1990 ......June 29	Fernando Valenzuela, LA vs StL 6-0
1961......Apr 28	Warren Spahn, Mil vs SF 1-0	1990......Aug 15	Terry Mulholland, Phil vs SF 6-0
1962......June 30	Sandy Koufax, LA vs NY 5-0	1991......May 23	Tommy Greene, Phil at Mont 2-0
1963......May 11	Sandy Koufax, LA vs SF 8-0	July 26	Mark Gardner, Mont at LA 0-1 (hit in 10th, lost in 10th)
May 17	Don Nottebart, Hou vs Phil 4-1	July 28	Dennis Martinez, Mont at LA 2-0 (perfect game)
June 15	Juan Marichal, SF vs Hou 1-0	Sept 11	Kent Mercker (6), Mark Wohlers (2), and Alejandro Pena (1), Atl at SD 1-0
1964......Apr 23	Ken Johnson, Hou vs Cin 0-1	1992 Aug 17	Kevin Gross, LA vs SF 2-0
June 4	Sandy Koufax, LA at Phil 3-0	1993 Sept 8	Darryl Kile, Hou vs NY 7-1
June 21	Jim Bunning, Phil at NY 6-0 (perfect game)		
1965......June 14	Jim Maloney, Cin vs NY 0-1 (hit in 11th; lost in 11th)		

Note: Includes the games struck from the record book on September 4, 1991, when baseball's committee on statistical accuracy voted to define no-hitters as games of 9 innings or more that end with a team getting no hits.

Out of Date

The San Diego Padres' media guide is a collector's item. The cover bears photos of Gary Sheffield, who was traded to the Florida Marlins in June, and Fred McGriff, who was unloaded to the Atlanta Braves in July as part of a relentless Padre fire sale. Ironically, for years the Padres were careful not to picture players on the guide's cover, lest those players be traded during the season, but the club's p.r. department figured that Sheffield and McGriff, the '92 National League batting champion and home run leader, respectively, were safe.

No-Hit Games, 9 Innings or More *(Cont.)*

AMERICAN LEAGUE

Date	Pitcher and Game	Date	Pitcher and Game
1901......May 9	Earl Moore, Clev vs Chi 2-4 (hit in 10th; lost in 10th)	1966......Oct 8	Don Larsen, NY (A) vs Bklyn (N) 2-0 (World Series)
1902......Sep 20	Jimmy Callahan, Chi vs Det 3-0	1957......Aug 20	Bob Keegan, Chi vs Wash 6-0
1904......May 5	Cy Young, Bos vs Phil 3-0 (perfect game)	1958......July 20	Jim Bunning, Det at Bos 3-0
		Sep 20	Hoyt Wilhelm, Balt vs NY 1-0
Aug 17	Jesse Tannehill, Bos at Chi 6-0	1962......May 5	Bo Belinsky, LA vs Balt 2-0
1905......July 22	Weldon Henley, Phil at StL 6-0	June 26	Earl Wilson, Bos vs LA 2-0
Sep 6	Frank Smith, Chi at Det 15-0	Aug 1	Bill Monbouquette, Bos at Chi 1-0
Sep 27	Bill Dinneen, Bos vs Chi 2-0	Aug 26	Jack Kralick, Minn vs KC 1-0
1908......June 30	Cy Young, Bos at NY 8-0	1965......Sep 16	Dave Morehead, Bos vs Clev 2-0
Sep 18	Bob Rhoades, Clev vs Bos 2-1	1966......June 10	Sonny Siebert, Clev vs Wash 2-0
Sep 20	Frank Smith, Chi vs Phil 1-0	1967......Apr 30	Steve Barber (8¾) and Stu Miller (⅓), Balt vs Det 1-2
Oct 2	Addie Joss, Clev vs Chi 1-0 (perfect game)		
1910......Apr 20	Addie Joss, Clev at Chi 1-0	Aug 25	Dean Chance, Minn at Clev 2-1
May 12	Chief Bender, Phil vs Clev 4-0	Sep 10	Joel Horlen, Chi vs Det 6-0
Aug 30	Tom Hughes, NY vs Clev 0-5 (hit in 10th; lost in 11th)	1968......Apr 27	Tom Phoebus, Balt vs Bos 6-0
		May 8	Catfish Hunter, Oak vs Minn 4-0 (perfect game)
1911......July 29	Joe Wood, Bos vs StL 5-0	1969......Aug 13	Jim Palmer, Balt vs Oak 8-0
Aug 27	Ed Walsh, Chi vs Bos 5-0	1970......July 3	Clyde Wright, Calif vs Oak 4-0
1912......July 4	George Mullin, Det vs StL 7-0	Sep 21	Vida Blue, Oak vs Minn 6-0
Aug 30	Earl Hamilton, StL at Det 5-1	1973......Apr 27	Steve Busby, KC at Det 3-0
1914......May 14	Jim Scott, Chi at Wash 0-1 (hit in 10th; lost in 10th)	May 15	Nolan Ryan, Calif at KC 3-0
		July 15	Nolan Ryan, Calif at Det 6-0
May 31	Joe Benz, Chi vs Clev 6-1	July 30	Jim Bibby, Tex at Oak 6-0
1916......June 21	George Foster, Bos vs NY 2-0	1974......June 19	Steve Busby, KC at Mil 2-0
Aug 26	Joe Bush, Phil vs Clev 5-0	July 19	Dick Bosman, Clev vs Oak 4-0
Aug 30	Dutch Leonard, Bos vs StL 4-0	Sep 28	Nolan Ryan, Calif vs Minn 4-0
1917......Apr 14	Ed Cicotte, Chi at StL 11-0	1975......June 1	Nolan Ryan, Calif vs Balt 1-0
Apr 24	George Mogridge, NY at Bos 2-1	Sep 28	Vida Blue (5), Glenn Abbott and Paul Lindblad (1), Rollie Fingers (2), Oak vs Calif 5-0
May 5	Ernie Koob, StL vs Chi 1-0		
May 6	Bob Groom, StL vs Chi 3-0		
June 23	Ernie Shore, Bos vs Wash 4-0 (perfect game)	1976......July 28	John Odom (5) and Francisco Barrios (4), Chi at Oak 2-1
1918......June 3	Dutch Leonard, Bos at Det 5-0	1977......May 14	Jim Colborn, KC vs Tex 6-0
1919......Sep 10	Ray Caldwell, Clev at NY 3-0	May 30	Dennis Eckersley, Clev vs Calif 1-0
1920......July 1	Walter Johnson, Wash at Bos 1-0	Sep 22	Bert Blyleven, Tex at Calif 6-0
1922......Apr 30	Charlie Robertson, Chi at Det 2-0 (perfect game)	1981......May 15	Len Barker, Clev vs Tor 3-0 (perfect game)
1923......Sep 4	Sam Jones, NY at Phil 2-0	1983......July 4	Dave Righetti, NY vs Bos 4-0
Sep 7	Howard Ehmke, Bos at Phil 4-0	Sep 29	Mike Warren, Oak vs Chi 3-0
1926......Aug 21	Ted Lyons, Chi at Bos 6-0	1984......Apr 7	Jack Morris, Det at Chi 4-0
1931......Apr 29	Wes Ferrell, Clev vs StL 9-0	Sep 30	Mike Witt, Calif at Tex 1-0 (perfect game)
Aug 8	Bob Burke, Wash vs Bos 5-0		
1934......Sep 18	Bobo Newsom, StL vs Bos 1-2 (hit in 10th; lost in 10th)	1986......Sep 19	Joe Cowley, Chi at Calif 7-1
		1987......Apr 15	Juan Nieves, Mil at Balt 7-0
1935......Aug 31	Vern Kennedy, Chi vs Clev 5-0	1990......Apr 11	Mark Langston (7), Mike Witt (2), Calif vs Sea 1-0
1937......June 1	Bill Dietrich, Chi vs StL 8-0		
1938......Aug 27	Monte Pearson, NY vs Clev 13-0	June 2	Randy Johnson, Sea vs Det 2-0
1940......Apr 16	Bob Feller, Clev at Chi 1-0 (opening day)	June 11	Nolan Ryan, Tex at Oak 5-0
		June 29	Dave Stewart, Oak at Tor 5-0
1945......Sep 9	Dick Fowler, Phil vs StL 1-0	1990......July 1	Andy Hawkins, NY at Chi 0-4 (pitched 8 innings of 9-inning game)
1946......Apr 30	Bob Feller, Clev at NY 1-0		
1947......July 10	Don Black, Clev vs Phil 3-0	Sep 2	Dave Stieb, Tor at Clev 3-0
Sep 3	Bill McCahan, Phil vs Wash 3-0	1991......May 1	Nolan Ryan, Tex vs Tor 3-0
1948......June 30	Bob Lemon, Clev at Det 2-0	July 13	Bob Milacki (6), Mike Flanagan (1), Mark Williamson (1), and Gregg Olson (1), Balt at Oak 2-0
1951......July 1	Bob Feller, Clev vs Det 2-1		
July 12	Allie Reynolds, NY at Clev 1-0		
Sep 28	Allie Reynolds, NY vs Bos 8-0	Aug 11	Wilson Alvarez, Chi at Balt 7-0
1952......May 15	Virgil Trucks, Det vs Wash 1-0	Aug 26	Bret Saberhagen, KC vs Chi 7-0
Aug 25	Virgil Trucks, Det at NY 1-0	1993......Apr 22	Chris Bosio, Sea vs Bos 7-0
1953......May 6	Bobo Holloman, StL vs Phil 6-0 (first major league start)	Sept 4	Jim Abbott, NY vs Clev 4-0
1956......July 14	Mel Parnell, Bos vs Chi 4-0		

Longest Hitting Streaks

NATIONAL LEAGUE

Player and Team	Year	G
Willie Keeler, Balt	1897	44
Pete Rose, Cin	1978	44
Bill Dahlen, Chi	1894	42
Tommy Holmes, Bos	1945	37
Billy Hamilton, Phil	1894	36
Fred Clarke, Lou	1895	35
Benito Santiago, SD	1987	34
George Davis, NY	1893	33
Rogers Hornsby, StL	1922	32
Ed Delahanty, Phil	1899	31
Willie Davis, LA	1969	31
Rico Carty, Atl	1970	31

AMERICAN LEAGUE

Player and Team	Year	G
Joe DiMaggio, NY	1941	56
George Sisler, StL	1922	41
Ty Cobb, Det	1911	40
Paul Molitor, Mil	1987	39
Ty Cobb, Det	1917	35
Ty Cobb, Det	1912	34
George Sisler, StL	1925	34
John Stone, Det	1930	34
George McQuinn, StL	1938	34
Dom DiMaggio, Bos	1949	34
Hal Chase, NY	1907	33
Heinie Manush, Wash	1933	33
Nap Lajoie, Cle	1906	31
Sam Rice, Wash	1924	31
Ken Landreaux, Minn	1980	31

Triple Crown Hitters

NATIONAL LEAGUE

Player and Team	Year	HR	RBI	BA
Paul Hines, Prov	1878	4	50	.358
Hugh Duffy, Bos	1894	18	145	.438
Heinie Zimmerman,* Chi	1912	14	103	.372
Rogers Hornsby, StL	1922	42	152	.401
	1925	39	143	.403
Chuck Klein, Phil	1933	28	120	.368
Joe Medwick, StL	1937	31	154	.374

*Zimmerman ranked first in RBIs as calculated by Ernie Lanigan, but only third as calculated by Information Concepts Inc.

AMERICAN LEAGUE

Player and Team	Year	HR	RBI	BA
Nap Lajoie, Phil	1901	14	125	.422
Ty Cobb, Det	1909	9	115	.377
Jimmie Foxx, Phil	1933	48	163	.356
Lou Gehrig, NY	1934	49	165	.363
Ted Williams, Bos	1942	36	137	.356
	1947	32	114	.343
Mickey Mantle, NY	1956	52	130	.353
Frank Robinson, Balt	1966	49	122	.316
Carl Yastrzemski, Bos	1967	44	121	.326

Triple Crown Pitchers

NATIONAL LEAGUE

Player and Team	Year	W	L	SO	ERA
Tommy Bond, Bos	1877	40	17	170	2.11
Hoss Radbourn, Prov	1884	60	12	441	1.38
Tim Keefe, NY	1888	35	12	333	1.74
John Clarkson, Bos	1889	49	19	284	2.73
Amos Rusie, NY	1894	36	13	195	2.78
Christy Mathewson, NY	1905	31	8	206	1.27
	1908	37	11	259	1.43
Grover Alexander, Phil	1915	31	10	241	1.22
	1916	33	12	167	1.55
	1917	30	13	201	1.86
Hippo Vaughn, Chi	1918	22	10	148	1.74
Grover Alexander, Chi	1920	27	14	173	1.91
Dazzy Vance, Bklyn	1924	28	6	262	2.16
Bucky Walters, Cin	1939	27	11	137	2.29
Sandy Koufax, LA	1963	25	5	306	1.88
	1965	26	8	382	2.04
	1966	27	9	317	1.73
Steve Carlton, Phil	1972	27	10	310	1.97
Dwight Gooden, NY	1985	24	4	268	1.53

AMERICAN LEAGUE

Player and Team	Year	W	L	SO	ERA
Cy Young, Bos	1901	33	10	158	1.62
Rube Waddell, Phil	1905	26	11	287	1.48
Walter Johnson, Wash	1913	36	7	303	1.09
	1918	23	13	162	1.27
	1924	23	7	158	2.72
Lefty Grove, Phil	1930	28	5	209	2.54
	1931	31	4	175	2.06
Lefty Gomez, NY	1934	26	5	158	2.33
	1937	21	11	194	2.33
Hal Newhouser, Det	1945	25	9	212	1.81

Consecutive Games Played, 500 or More Games

Lou Gehrig	2130	Frank McCormick	652
Cal Ripken Jr.	1897*	Sandy Alomar Sr	648
Everett Scott	1307	Eddie Brown	618
Steve Garvey	1207	Roy McMillan	585
Billy Williams	1117	George Pinckney	577
Joe Sewell	1103	Steve Brodie	574
Stan Musial	895	Aaron Ward	565
Eddie Yost	829	Candy LaChance	540
Gus Suhr	822	Buck Freeman	535
Nellie Fox	798	Fred Luderus	533
Pete Rose	745	Clyde Milan	511
Dale Murphy	740	Charlie Gehringer	511
Richie Ashburn	730	Vada Pinson	508
Ernie Banks	717	Tony Cuccinello	504
Earl Averill	673	Charlie Gehringer	504
Pete Rose	678	Omar Moreno	503

*Streak in progress at the end of the 1993 season.

Unassisted Triple Plays

Player and Team	Date	Pos	Opp	Opp Batter
Neal Ball, Clev	7-19-09	SS	Bos	Amby McConnell
Bill Wambsganss, Clev	10-10-20	2B	Bklyn	Clarence Mitchell
George Burns, Bos	9-14-23	1B	Clev	Frank Brower
Ernie Padgett, Bos	10-6-23	SS	Phil	Walter Holke
Glenn Wright, Pitt	5-7-25	SS	StL	Jim Bottomley
Jimmy Cooney, Chi	5-30-27	SS	Pitt	Paul Waner
Johnny Neun, Det	5-31-27	1B	Clev	Homer Summa
Ron Hansen, Wash	7-30-68	SS	Clev	Joe Azcue
Mickey Morandini	9-20-92	2B	Pitt	Jeff King

National League

Pennant Winners

Year	Team	Manager	W	L	Pct	GA
1900	Brooklyn	Ned Hanlon	82	54	.603	4½
1901	Pittsburgh	Fred Clarke	90	49	.647	7½
1902	Pittsburgh	Fred Clarke	103	36	.741	27½
1903	Pittsburgh	Fred Clarke	91	49	.650	6½
1904	New York	John McGraw	106	47	.693	13
1905	New York	John McGraw	105	48	.686	9
1906	Chicago	Frank Chance	116	36	.763	20
1907	Chicago	Frank Chance	107	45	.704	17
1908	Chicago	Frank Chance	99	55	.643	1
1909	Pittsburgh	Fred Clarke	110	42	.724	6½
1910	Chicago	Frank Chance	104	50	.675	13
1911	New York	John McGraw	99	54	.647	7½
1912	New York	John McGraw	103	48	.682	10
1913	New York	John McGraw	101	51	.664	12½
1914	Boston	George Stallings	94	59	.614	10½
1915	Philadelphia	Pat Moran	90	62	.592	7
1916	Brooklyn	Wilbert Robinson	94	60	.610	2½
1917	New York	John McGraw	98	56	.636	10
1918	Chicago	Fred Mitchell	84	45	.651	10½
1919	Cincinnati	Pat Moran	96	44	.686	9
1920	Brooklyn	Wilbert Robinson	93	61	.604	7
1921	New York	John McGraw	94	59	.614	4
1922	New York	John McGraw	93	61	.604	7
1923	New York	John McGraw	95	58	.621	4½
1924	New York	John McGraw	93	60	.608	1½

Pennant Winners *(Cont.)*

Year	Team	Manager	W	L	Pct	GA
1925	Pittsburgh	Bill McKechnie	95	58	.621	8½
1926	St Louis	Rogers Hornsby	89	65	.578	2
1927	Pittsburgh	Donie Bush	94	60	.610	1½
1928	St Louis	Bill McKechnie	95	59	.617	2
1929	Chicago	Joe McCarthy	98	54	.645	10½
1930	St Louis	Gabby Street	92	62	.597	2
1931	St Louis	Gabby Street	101	53	.656	13
1932	Chicago	Charlie Grimm	90	64	.584	4
1933	New York	Bill Terry	91	61	.599	5
1934	St Louis	Frankie Frisch	95	58	.621	2
1935	Chicago	Charlie Grimm	100	54	.649	4
1936	New York	Bill Terry	92	62	.597	5
1937	New York	Bill Terry	95	57	.625	3
1938	Chicago	Gabby Hartnett	89	63	.586	2
1939	Cincinnati	Bill McKechnie	97	57	.630	4½
1940	Cincinnati	Bill McKechnie	100	53	.654	12
1941	Brooklyn	Leo Durocher	100	54	.649	2½
1942	St Louis	Billy Southworth	106	48	.688	2
1943	St Louis	Billy Southworth	105	49	.682	18
1944	St Louis	Billy Southworth	105	49	.682	14½
1945	Chicago	Charlie Grimm	98	56	.636	3
1946	St Louis*	Eddie Dyer	98	58	.628	2
1947	Brooklyn	Burt Shotton	94	60	.610	5
1948	Boston	Billy Southworth	91	62	.595	6½
1949	Brooklyn	Burt Shotton	97	57	.630	1
1950	Philadelphia	Eddie Sawyer	91	63	.591	2
1951	New York†	Leo Durocher	98	59	.624	1
1952	Brooklyn	Chuck Dressen	96	57	.627	4½
1953	Brooklyn	Chuck Dressen	105	49	.682	13
1954	New York	Leo Durocher	97	57	.630	5
1955	Brooklyn	Walt Alston	98	55	.641	13½
1956	Brooklyn	Walt Alston	93	61	.604	1
1957	Milwaukee	Fred Haney	95	59	.617	8
1958	Milwaukee	Fred Haney	92	62	.597	8
1959	Los Angeles‡	Walt Alston	88	68	.564	2
1960	Pittsburgh	Danny Murtaugh	95	59	.617	7
1961	Cincinnati	Fred Hutchinson	93	61	.604	4
1962	San Francisco#	Al Dark	103	62	.624	1
1963	Los Angeles	Walt Alston	99	63	.611	6
1964	St Louis	Johnny Keane	93	69	.574	1
1965	Los Angeles	Walt Alston	97	65	.599	2
1966	Los Angeles	Walt Alston	95	67	.586	1½
1967	St Louis	Red Schoendienst	101	60	.627	10½
1968	St Louis	Red Schoendienst	97	65	.599	9
1969	New York (E)††	Gil Hodges	100	62	.617	8
1970	Cincinnati (W)††	Sparky Anderson	102	60	.630	14½
1971	Pittsburgh (E)††	Danny Murtaugh	97	65	.599	7
1972	Cincinnati (W)††	Sparky Anderson	95	59	.617	10½
1973	New York (E)††	Yogi Berra	82	79	.509	1½
1974	Los Angeles (W)††	Walt Alston	102	60	.630	4
1975	Cincinnati (W)††	Sparky Anderson	108	54	.667	20
1976	Cincinnati (W)††	Sparky Anderson	102	60	.630	10
1977	Los Angeles (W)††	Tommy Lasorda	98	64	.605	10
1978	Los Angeles (W)††	Tommy Lasorda	95	67	.586	2½
1979	Pittsburgh (E)††	Chuck Tanner	98	64	.605	2
1980	Philadelphia (E)††	Dallas Green	91	71	.562	1
1981	Los Angeles (W)††	Tommy Lasorda	63	47	.573	**
1982	St Louis (E)††	Whitey Herzog	92	70	.568	3
1983	Philadelphia (E)††	Pat Corrales, Paul Owens	90	72	.556	6
1984	San Diego (W)††	Dick Williams	92	70	.568	12

*Defeated Brooklyn, two games to none, in playoff for pennant. †Defeated Brooklyn, two games to one, in playoff for pennant. ‡Defeated Milwaukee, two games to none, in playoff for pennant. #Defeated Los Angeles, two games to one, in playoff for pennant. ††Won Championship Series **First half 36-21; second half 27-26.

Pennant Winners *(Cont.)*

Year	Team	Manager	W	L	Pct	GA
1985	St Louis (E)††	Whitey Herzog	101	61	.623	3
1986	New York (E)††	Dave Johnson	108	54	.667	21½
1987	St Louis (E)††	Whitey Herzog	95	67	.586	3
1988	Los Angeles (W)††	Tommy Lasorda	94	67	.584	7
1989	San Francisco (W)††	Roger Craig	92	70	.568	3
1990	Cincinnati (W)††	Lou Piniella	91	71	.562	5
1991	Atlanta (W)††	Bobby Cox	94	68	.580	1
1992	Atlanta††	Bobby Cox	98	64	.605	8
1993	Philadelphia††	Jim Fregosi	97	65	.599	3

††Won Championship Series

Leading Batsmen

Year	Player and Team	BA	Year	Player and Team	BA
1900	Honus Wagner, Pitt	.381	1930	Bill Terry, NY	.401
1901	Jesse Burkett, StL	.382	1931	Chick Hafey, StL	.349
1902	Ginger Beaumont, Pitt	.357	1932	Lefty O'Doul, Bklyn	.368
1903	Honus Wagner, Pitt	.355	1933	Chuck Klein, Phil	.368
1904	Honus Wagner, Pitt	.349	1934	Paul Waner, Pitt	.362
1905	Cy Seymour, Cin	.377	1935	Arky Vaughan, Pitt	.385
1906	Honus Wagner, Pitt	.339	1936	Paul Waner, Pitt	.373
1907	Honus Wagner, Pitt	.350	1937	Joe Medwick, StL	.374
1908	Honus Wagner, Pitt	.354	1938	Ernie Lombardi, Cin	.342
1909	Honus Wagner, Pitt	.339	1939	Johnny Mize, StL	.349
1910	Sherry Magee, Phil	.331	1940	Debs Garms, Pitt	.355
1911	Honus Wagner, Pitt	.334	1941	Pete Reiser, Bklyn	.343
1912	Heinie Zimmerman, Chi	.372	1942	Ernie Lombardi, Bos	.330
1913	Jake Daubert, Bklyn	.350	1943	Stan Musial, StL	.357
1914	Jake Daubert, Bklyn	.329	1944	Dixie Walker, Bklyn	.357
1915	Larry Doyle, NY	.320	1945	Phil Cavarretta, Chi	.355
1916	Hal Chase, Cin	.339	1946	Stan Musial, StL	.365
1917	Edd Roush, Cin	.341	1947	Harry Walker, StL-Phil	.363
1918	Zach Wheat, Bklyn	.335	1948	Stan Musial, StL	.376
1919	Edd Roush, Cin	.321	1949	Jackie Robinson, Bklyn	.342
1920	Rogers Hornsby, StL	.370	1950	Stan Musial, StL	.346
1921	Rogers Hornsby, StL	.397	1951	Stan Musial, StL	.355
1922	Rogers Hornsby, StL	.401	1952	Stan Musial, StL	.336
1923	Rogers Hornsby, StL	.384	1953	Carl Furillo, Bklyn	.344
1924	Rogers Hornsby, StL	.424	1954	Willie Mays, NY	.345
1925	Rogers Hornsby, StL	.403	1955	Richie Ashburn, Phil	.338
1926	Bubbles Hargrave, Cin	.353	1956	Hank Aaron, Mil	.328
1927	Paul Waner, Pitt	.380	1957	Stan Musial, StL	.351
1928	Rogers Hornsby, Bos	.387	1958	Richie Ashburn, Phil	.350
1929	Lefty O'Doul, Phil	.398	1959	Hank Aaron, Mil	.355

THEY SAID IT

Jeff Reboulet, Minnesota Twin third baseman, when asked, after hitting his first homer of the season, if he had pointed to the leftfield bleachers before he connected: "No, I pointed to the dugout—where I usually go after I bat."

Leading Batsmen

Year	Player and Team	BA	Year	Player and Team	BA
1960	Dick Groat, Pitt	.325	1977	Dave Parker, Pitt	.338
1961	Roberto Clemente, Pitt	.351	1978	Dave Parker, Pitt	.334
1962	Tommy Davis, LA	.346	1979	Keith Hernandez, StL	.344
1963	Tommy Davis, LA	.326	1980	Bill Buckner, Chi	.324
1964	Roberto Clemente, Pitt	.339	1981	Bill Madlock, Pitt	.341
1965	Roberto Clemente, Pitt	.329	1982	Al Oliver, Mont	.331
1966	Matty Alou, Pitt	.342	1983	Bill Madlock, Pitt	.323
1967	Roberto Clemente, Pitt	.357	1984	Tony Gwynn, SD	.351
1968	Pete Rose, Cin	.335	1985	Willie McGee, StL	.353
1969	Pete Rose, Cin	.348	1986	Tim Raines, Mont	.334
1970	Rico Carty, Atl	.366	1987	Tony Gwynn, SD	.370
1971	Joe Torre, StL	.363	1988	Tony Gwynn, SD	.313
1972	Billy Williams, Chi	.333	1989	Tony Gwynn, SD	.336
1973	Pete Rose, Cin	.338	1990	Willie McGee, StL	.335
1974	Ralph Garr, Atl	.353	1991	Terry Pendleton, Atl	.319
1975	Bill Madlock, Chi	.354	1992	Gary Sheffield	.330
1976	Bill Madlock, Chi	.339	1993	Andres Galarraga, Col	.370

Leaders in Runs Scored

Year	Player and Team	Runs	Year	Player and Team	Runs
1900	Roy Thomas, Phil	131	1937	Joe Medwick, StL	111
1901	Jesse Burkett, StL	139	1938	Mel Ott, NY	116
1902	Honus Wagner, Pitt	105	1939	Billy Werber, Cin	115
1903	Ginger Beaumont, Pitt	137	1940	Arky Vaughan, Pitt	113
1904	George Browne, NY	99	1941	Pete Reiser, Bklyn	117
1905	Mike Donlin, NY	124	1942	Mel Ott, NY	118
1906	Honus Wagner, Pitt	103	1943	Arky Vaughan, Bklyn	112
	Frank Chance, Chi	103	1944	Bill Nicholson, Chi	116
1907	Spike Shannon, NY	104	1945	Eddie Stanky, Bklyn	128
1908	Fred Tenney, NY	101	1946	Stan Musial, StL	124
1909	Tommy Leach, Pitt	126	1947	Johnny Mize, NY	137
1910	Sherry Magee, Phil	110	1948	Stan Musial, StL	135
1911	Jimmy Sheckard, Chi	121	1949	Pee Wee Reese, Bklyn	132
1912	Bob Bescher, Cin	120	1950	Earl Torgeson, Bos	120
1913	Tommy Leach, Chi	99	1951	Stan Musial, StL	124
	Max Carey, Pitt	99		Ralph Kiner, Pitt	124
1914	George Burns, NY	100	1952	Stan Musial, StL	105
1915	Gavvy Cravath, Phil	89		Solly Hemus, StL	105
1916	George Burns, NY	105	1953	Duke Snider, Bklyn	132
1917	George Burns, NY	103	1954	Stan Musial, StL	120
1918	Heinie Groh, Cin	88		Duke Snider, Bklyn	120
1919	George Burns, NY	86	1955	Duke Snider, Bklyn	126
1920	George Burns, NY	115	1956	Frank Robinson, Cin	122
1921	Rogers Hornsby, StL	131	1957	Hank Aaron, Mil	118
1922	Rogers Hornsby, StL	141	1958	Willie Mays, SF	121
1923	Ross Youngs, NY	121	1959	Vada Pinson, Cin	131
1924	Frankie Frisch, NY	121	1960	Bill Bruton, Mil	112
	Rogers Hornsby, StL	121	1961	Willie Mays, SF	129
1925	Kiki Cuyler, Pitt	144	1962	Frank Robinson, Cin	134
1926	Kiki Cuyler, Pitt	113	1963	Hank Aaron, Mil	121
1927	Lloyd Waner, Pitt	133	1964	Dick Allen, Phil	125
	Rogers Hornsby, NY	133	1965	Tommy Harper, Cin	126
1928	Paul Waner, Pitt	142	1966	Felipe Alou, Atl	122
1929	Rogers Hornsby, Chi	156	1967	Hank Aaron, Atl	113
1930	Chuck Klein, Phil	158		Lou Brock, StL	113
1931	Bill Terry, NY	121	1968	Glenn Beckert, Chi	98
	Chuck Klein, Phil	121	1969	Bobby Bonds, SF	120
1932	Chuck Klein, Phil	152		Pete Rose, Cin	120
1933	Pepper Martin, StL	122	1970	Billy Williams, Chi	137
1934	Paul Waner, Pitt	122	1971	Lou Brock, StL	126
1935	Augie Galan, Chi	133	1972	Joe Morgan, Cin	122
1936	Arky Vaughan, Pitt	122	1973	Bobby Bonds, SF	131

Leader in Runs Scored (Cont.)

Year	Player and Team	Runs	Year	Player and Team	Runs
1974	Pete Rose, Cin	110	1986	Von Hayes, Phil	107
1975	Pete Rose, Cin	112		Tony Gwynn, SD	107
1976	Pete Rose, Cin	130	1987	Tim Raines, Mont	123
1977	George Foster, Cin	124	1988	Brett Butler, SF	109
1978	Ivan DeJesus, Chi	104	1989	Howard Johnson, NY	104
1979	Keith Hernandez, StL	116		Will Clark, SF	104
1980	Keith Hernandez, StL	111		Ryne Sandberg, Chi	104
1981	Mike Schmidt, Phil	78	1990	Ryne Sandberg, Chi	116
1982	Lonnie Smith, StL	120	1991	Brett Butler, LA	112
1983	Tim Raines, Mont	133	1992	Barry Bonds, Pitt	109
1984	Ryne Sandberg, Chi	114	1993	Lenny Dykstra, Phil	143
1985	Dale Murphy, Atl	118			

Leaders in Hits

Year	Player and Team	Hits	Year	Player and Team	Hits
1900	Willie Keeler, Bklyn	208	1945	Tommy Holmes, Bos	224
1901	Jesse Burkett, StL	228	1946	Stan Musial, StL	228
1902	Ginger Beaumont, Pitt	194	1947	Tommy Holmes, Bos	191
1903	Ginger Beaumont, Pitt	209	1948	Stan Musial, StL	230
1904	Ginger Beaumont, Pitt	185	1949	Stan Musial, StL	207
1905	Cy Seymour, Cin	219	1950	Duke Snider, Bklyn	199
1906	Harry Steinfeldt, Chi	176	1951	Richie Ashburn, Phil	221
1907	Ginger Beaumont, Bos	187	1952	Stan Musial, StL	194
1908	Honus Wagner, Pitt	201	1953	Richie Ashburn, Phil	205
1909	Larry Doyle, NY	172	1954	Don Mueller, NY	212
1910	Honus Wagner, Pitt	178	1955	Ted Kluszewski, Cin	192
	Bobby Byrne, Pitt	178	1956	Hank Aaron, Mil	200
1911	Doc Miller, Bos	192	1957	Red Schoendienst, NY-Mil	200
1912	Heinie Zimmerman, Chi	207	1958	Richie Ashburn, Phil	215
1913	Gavvy Cravath, Phil	179	1959	Hank Aaron, Mil	223
1914	Sherry Magee, Phil	171	1960	Willie Mays, SF	190
1915	Larry Doyle, NY	189	1961	Vada Pinson, Cin	208
1916	Hal Chase, Cin	184	1962	Tommy Davis, LA	230
1917	Heinie Groh, Cin	182	1963	Vada Pinson, Cin	204
1918	Charlie Hollocher, Chi	161	1964	Roberto Clemente, Pitt	211
1919	Ivy Olson, Bklyn	164		Curt Flood, StL	211
1920	Rogers Hornsby, StL	218	1965	Pete Rose, Cin	209
1921	Rogers Hornsby, StL	235	1966	Felipe Alou, Atl	218
1922	Rogers Hornsby, StL	250	1967	Roberto Clemente, Pitt	209
1923	Frankie Frisch, NY	223	1968	Felipe Alou, Atl	210
1924	Rogers Hornsby, StL	227		Pete Rose, Cin	210
1925	Jim Bottomley, StL	227	1969	Matty Alou, Pitt	231
1926	Eddie Brown, Bos	201	1970	Pete Rose, Cin	205
1927	Paul Waner, Pitt	237		Billy Williams, Chi	205
1928	Freddy Lindstrom, NY	231	1971	Joe Torre, StL	230
1929	Lefty O'Doul, Phil	254	1972	Pete Rose, Cin	198
1930	Bill Terry, NY	254	1973	Pete Rose, Cin	230
1931	Lloyd Waner, Pitt	214	1974	Ralph Garr, Atl	214
1932	Chuck Klein, Phil	226	1975	Dave Cash, Phil	213
1933	Chuck Klein, Phil	223	1976	Pete Rose, Cin	215
1934	Paul Waner, Pitt	217	1977	Dave Parker, Pitt	215
1935	Billy Herman, Chi	227	1978	Steve Garvey, LA	202
1936	Joe Medwick, StL	223	1979	Garry Templeton, StL	211
1937	Joe Medwick, StL	237	1980	Steve Garvey, LA	200
1938	Frank McCormick, Cin	209	1981	Pete Rose, Phil	140
1939	Frank McCormick, Cin	209	1982	Al Oliver, Mont	204
1940	Stan Hack, Chi	191	1983	Jose Cruz, Hou	189
	Frank McCormick, Cin	191		Andre Dawson, Mont	189
1941	Stan Hack, Chi	186	1984	Tony Gwynn, SD	213
1942	Enos Slaughter, StL	188	1985	Willie McGee, StL	216
1943	Stan Musial, StL	220	1986	Tony Gwynn, SD	211
1944	Stan Musial, StL	197			
	Phil Cavarretta, Chi	197			

Leaders in Hits (Cont.)

Year	Player and Team	Hits	Year	Player and Team	Hits
1987	Tony Gwynn, SD	218	1991	Terry Pendleton, Atl	187
1988	Andres Galarraga, Mont	184	1992	Terry Pendleton, Atl	199
1989	Tony Gwynn, SD	203		Andy Van Slyke, Pitt	199
1990	Brett Butler, SF	192	1993	Lenny Dykstra, Phil	194
	Lenny Dykstra, Phil	192			

Home Run Leaders

Year	Player and Team	HR	Year	Player and Team	HR
1900	Herman Long, Bos	12	1946	Ralph Kiner, Pitt	23
1901	Sam Crawford, Cin	16	1947	Ralph Kiner, Pitt	51
1902	Tommy Leach, Pitt	6		Johnny Mize, NY	51
1903	Jimmy Sheckard, Bklyn	9	1948	Ralph Kiner, Pitt	40
1904	Harry Lumley, Bklyn	9		Johnny Mize, NY	40
1905	Fred Odwell, Cin	9	1949	Ralph Kiner, Pitt	54
1906	Tim Jordan, Bklyn	12	1950	Ralph Kiner, Pitt	47
1907	Dave Brain, Bos	10	1951	Ralph Kiner, Pitt	42
1908	Tim Jordan, Bklyn	12	1952	Ralph Kiner, Pitt	37
1909	Red Murray, NY	7		Hank Sauer, Chi	37
1910	Fred Beck, Bos	10	1953	Eddie Mathews, Mil	47
	Wildfire Schulte, Chi	10	1954	Ted Kluszewski, Cin	49
1911	Wildfire Schulte, Chi	21	1955	Willie Mays, NY	51
1912	Heinie Zimmerman, Chi	14	1956	Duke Snider, Bklyn	43
1913	Gavvy Cravath, Phil	19	1957	Hank Aaron, Mil	44
1914	Gavvy Cravath, Phil	19	1958	Ernie Banks, Chi	47
1915	Gavvy Cravath, Phil	24	1959	Eddie Mathews, Mil	46
1916	Dave Robertson, NY	12	1960	Ernie Banks, Chi	41
	Cy Williams, Chi	12	1961	Orlando Cepeda, SF	46
1917	Dave Robertson, NY	12	1962	Willie Mays, SF	49
	Gavvy Cravath, Phil	12	1963	Hank Aaron, Mil	44
1918	Gavvy Cravath, Phil	8		Willie McCovey, SF	44
1919	Gavvy Cravath, Phil	12	1964	Willie Mays, SF	47
1920	Cy Williams, Phil	15	1965	Willie Mays, SF	52
1921	George Kelly, NY	23	1966	Hank Aaron, Atl	44
1922	Rogers Hornsby, StL	42	1967	Hank Aaron, Atl	39
1923	Cy Williams, Phil	41	1968	Willie McCovey, SF	36
1924	Jack Fournier, Bklyn	27	1969	Willie McCovey, SF	45
1925	Rogers Hornsby, StL	39	1970	Johnny Bench, Cin	45
1926	Hack Wilson, Chi	21	1971	Willie Stargell, Pitt	48
1927	Hack Wilson, Chi	30	1972	Johnny Bench, Cin	40
	Cy Williams, Phil	30	1973	Willie Stargell, Pitt	44
1928	Hack Wilson, Chi	31	1974	Mike Schmidt, Phil	36
	Jim Bottomley, StL	31	1975	Mike Schmidt, Phil	38
1929	Chuck Klein, Phil	43	1976	Mike Schmidt, Phil	38
1930	Hack Wilson, Chi	56	1977	George Foster, Cin	52
1931	Chuck Klein, Phil	31	1978	George Foster, Cin	40
1932	Chuck Klein, Phil	38	1979	Dave Kingman, Chi	48
	Mel Ott, NY	38	1980	Mike Schmidt, Phil	48
1933	Chuck Klein, Phil	28	1981	Mike Schmidt, Phil	31
1934	Ripper Collins, StL	35	1982	Dave Kingman, NY	37
	Mel Ott, NY	35	1983	Mike Schmidt, Phil	40
1935	Wally Berger, Bos	34	1984	Dale Murphy, Atl	36
1936	Mel Ott, NY	33		Mike Schmidt, Phil	36
1937	Mel Ott, NY	31	1985	Dale Murphy, Atl	37
	Joe Medwick, StL	31	1986	Mike Schmidt, Phil	37
1938	Mel Ott, NY	36	1987	Andre Dawson, Chi	49
1939	Johnny Mize, StL	28	1988	Darryl Strawberry, NY	39
1940	Johnny Mize, StL	43	1989	Kevin Mitchell, SF	47
1941	Dolph Camilli, Bklyn	34	1990	Ryne Sandberg, Chi	40
1942	Mel Ott, NY	30	1991	Howard Johnson, NY	38
1943	Bill Nicholson, Chi	29	1992	Fred McGriff, SD	35
1944	Bill Nicholson, Chi	33	1993	Barry Bonds, SF	46
1945	Tommy Holmes, Bos	28			

Runs Batted In Leaders

Year	Player and Team	RBI	Year	Player and Team	RBI
1900	Elmer Flick, Phil	110	1947	Johnny Mize, NY	138
1901	Honus Wagner, Pitt	126	1948	Stan Musial, StL	131
1902	Honus Wagner, Pitt	91	1949	Ralph Kiner, Pitt	127
1903	Sam Mertes, NY	104	1950	Del Ennis, Phil	126
1904	Bill Dahlen, NY	80	1951	Monte Irvin, NY	121
1905	Cy Seymour, Cin	121	1952	Hank Sauer, Chi	121
1906	Jim Nealon, Pitt	83	1953	Roy Campanella, Bklyn	142
	Harry Steinfeldt, Chi	83	1954	Ted Kluszewski, Cin	141
1907	Sherry Magee, Phil	85	1955	Duke Snider, Bklyn	136
1908	Honus Wagner, Pitt	109	1956	Stan Musial, StL	109
1909	Honus Wagner, Pitt	100	1957	Hank Aaron, Mil	132
1910	Sherry Magee, Phil	123	1958	Ernie Banks, Chi	129
1911	Wildfire Schulte, Chi	121	1959	Ernie Banks, Chi	143
1912	Heinie Zimmerman, Chi	103	1960	Hank Aaron, Mil	126
1913	Gavvy Cravath, Phil	128	1961	Orlando Cepeda, SF	142
1914	Sherry Magee, Phil	103	1962	Tommy Davis, LA	153
1915	Gavvy Cravath, Phil	115	1963	Hank Aaron, Mil	130
1916	Heinie Zimmerman, Chi-NY	83	1964	Ken Boyer, StL	119
1917	Heinie Zimmerman, NY	102	1965	Deron Johnson, Cin	130
1918	Sherry Magee, Phil	76	1966	Hank Aaron, Atl	127
1919	Hi Myers, Bklyn	73	1967	Orlando Cepeda, StL	111
1920	George Kelly, NY	94	1968	Willie McCovey, SF	105
	Rogers Hornsby, StL	94	1969	Willie McCovey, SF	126
1921	Rogers Hornsby, StL	126	1970	Johnny Bench, Cin	148
1922	Rogers Hornsby, StL	152	1971	Joe Torre, StL	137
1923	Irish Meusel, NY	125	1972	Johnny Bench, Cin	125
1924	George Kelly, NY	136	1973	Willie Stargell, Pitt	119
1925	Rogers Hornsby, StL	143	1974	Johnny Bench, Cin	129
1926	Jim Bottomley, StL	120	1975	Greg Luzinski, Phil	120
1927	Paul Waner, Pitt	131	1976	George Foster, Cin	121
1928	Jim Bottomley, StL	136	1977	George Foster, Cin	149
1929	Hack Wilson, Chi	159	1978	George Foster, Cin	120
1930	Hack Wilson, Chi	190	1979	Dave Winfield, SD	118
1931	Chuck Klein, Phil	121	1980	Mike Schmidt, Phil	121
1932	Don Hurst, Phil	143	1981	Mike Schmidt, Phil	91
1933	Chuck Klein, Phil	120	1982	Dale Murphy, Atl	109
1934	Mel Ott, NY	135		Al Oliver, Mont	109
1935	Wally Berger, Bos	130	1983	Dale Murphy, Atl	121
1936	Joe Medwick, StL	138	1984	Gary Carter, Mont	106
1937	Joe Medwick, StL	154		Mike Schmidt, Phil	106
1938	Joe Medwick, StL	122	1985	Dave Parker, Cin	125
1939	Frank McCormick, Cin	128	1986	Mike Schmidt, Phil	119
1940	Johnny Mize, StL	137	1987	Andre Dawson, Chi	137
1941	Dolph Camilli, Bklyn	120	1988	Will Clark, SF	109
1942	Johnny Mize, NY	110	1989	Kevin Mitchell, SF	125
1943	Bill Nicholson, Chi	128	1990	Matt Williams, SF	122
1944	Bill Nicholson, Chi	122	1991	Howard Johnson, NY	117
1945	Dixie Walker, Bklyn	124	1992	Darren Daulton, Phi	109
1946	Enos Slaughter, StL	130	1993	Barry Bonds, SF	123

Classic Analysis

San Francisco Giant pitcher John Burkett was left dazed after his appearance for the National League in the All-Star Game, in which he was charged with the loss after American League batters racked him for four hits and three runs in two thirds of an inning. "That's a tough lineup," Burkett said. "It's like you were facing All-Stars out there."

Leading Base Stealers

Year	Player and Team	SB	Year	Player and Team	SB
1900	George Van Haltren, NY	45	1953	Bill Bruton, Mil	26
	Patsy Donovan, StL	45	1954	Bill Bruton, Mil	34
1901	Honus Wagner, Pitt	48	1955	Bill Bruton, Mil	35
1902	Honus Wagner, Pitt	43	1956	Willie Mays, NY	40
1903	Jimmy Sheckard, Bklyn	67	1957	Willie Mays, NY	38
	Frank Chance, Chi	67	1958	Willie Mays, SF	31
1904	Honus Wagner, Pitt	53	1959	Willie Mays, SF	27
1905	Billy Maloney, Chi	59	1960	Maury Wills, LA	50
	Art Devlin, NY	59	1961	Maury Wills, LA	35
1906	Frank Chance, Chi	57	1962	Maury Wills, LA	104
1907	Honus Wagner, Pitt	61	1963	Maury Wills, LA	40
1908	Honus Wagner, Pitt	53	1964	Maury Wills, LA	53
1909	Bob Bescher, Cin	54	1965	Maury Wills, LA	94
1910	Bob Bescher, Cin	70	1966	Lou Brock, StL	74
1911	Bob Bescher, Cin	80	1967	Lou Brock, StL	52
1912	Bob Bescher, Cin	67	1968	Lou Brock, StL	62
1913	Max Carey, Pitt	61	1969	Lou Brock, StL	53
1914	George Burns, NY	62	1970	Bobby Tolan, Cin	57
1915	Max Carey, Pitt	36	1971	Lou Brock, StL	64
1916	Max Carey, Pitt	63	1972	Lou Brock, StL	63
1917	Max Carey, Pitt	46	1973	Lou Brock, StL	70
1918	Max Carey, Pitt	58	1974	Lou Brock, StL	118
1919	George Burns, NY	40	1975	Davey Lopes, LA	77
1920	Max Carey, Pitt	52	1976	Davey Lopes, LA	63
1921	Frankie Frisch, NY	49	1977	Frank Taveras, Pitt	70
1922	Max Carey, Pitt	51	1978	Omar Moreno, Pitt	71
1923	Max Carey, Pitt	51	1979	Omar Moreno, Pitt	77
1924	Max Carey, Pitt	49	1980	Ron LeFlore, Mont	97
1925	Max Carey, Pitt	46	1981	Tim Raines, Mont	71
1926	Kiki Cuyler, Pitt	35	1982	Tim Raines, Mont	78
1927	Frankie Frisch, StL	48	1983	Tim Raines, Mont	90
1928	Kiki Cuyler, Chi	37	1984	Tim Raines, Mont	75
1929	Kiki Cuyler, Chi	43	1985	Vince Coleman, StL	110
1930	Kiki Cuyler, Chi	37	1986	Vince Coleman, StL	107
1931	Frankie Frisch, StL	28	1987	Vince Coleman, StL	109
1932	Chuck Klein, Phil	20	1988	Vince Coleman, StL	81
1933	Pepper Martin, StL	26	1989	Vince Coleman, StL	65
1934	Pepper Martin, StL	23	1990	Vince Coleman, StL	77
1935	Augie Galan, Chi	22	1991	Marquis Grissom, Mont	76
1936	Pepper Martin, StL	23	1992	Marquis Grissom, Mont	78
1937	Augie Galan, Chi	23	1993	Chuck Carr, Flor	58
1938	Stan Hack, Chi	16			
1939	Stan Hack, Chi	17			
	Lee Handley, Pitt	17			
1940	Lonny Frey, Cin	22			
1941	Danny Murtaugh, Phil	18			
1942	Pete Reiser, Bklyn	20			
1943	Arky Vaughan, Bklyn	20			
1944	Johnny Barrett, Pitt	28			
1945	Red Schoendienst, StL	26			
1946	Pete Reiser, Bklyn	34			
1947	Jackie Robinson, Bklyn	29			
1948	Richie Ashburn, Phil	32			
1949	Jackie Robinson, Bklyn	37			
1950	Sam Jethroe, Bos	35			
1951	Sam Jethroe, Bos	35			
1952	Pee Wee Reese, Bklyn	30			

THEY SAID IT

Tom Kelly, Minnesota Twin manager, explaining why he made pitcher Pat Mahomes walk off the field with him after pulling him during a 17–1 loss to the Detroit Tigers: "Then we would have to take only half the boos each."

Leading Pitchers—Winning Percentage

Year	Pitcher and Team	W	L	Pct	Year	Pitcher and Team	W	L	Pct
1900	Jesse Tannehill, Pitt	20	6	.769	1948	Harry Brecheen, StL	20	7	.741
1901	Jack Chesbro, Pitt	21	10	.677	1949	Preacher Roe, Bklyn	15	6	.714
1902	Jack Chesbro, Pitt	28	6	.824	1950	Sal Maglie, NY	18	4	.818
1903	Sam Leever, Pitt	25	7	.781	1951	Preacher Roe, Bklyn	22	3	.880
1904	Joe McGinnity, NY	35	8	.814	1952	Hoyt Wilhelm, NY	15	3	.833
1905	Sam Leever, Pitt	20	5	.800	1953	Carl Erskine, Bklyn	20	6	.769
1906	Ed Reulbach, Chi	19	4	.826	1954	Johnny Antonelli, NY	21	7	.750
1907	Ed Reulbach, Chi	17	4	.810	1955	Don Newcombe, Bklyn	20	5	.800
1908	Ed Reulbach, Chi	24	7	.774	1956	Don Newcombe, Bklyn	27	7	.794
1909	Christy Mathewson, NY	25	6	.806	1957	Bob Buhl, Mil	18	7	.720
	Howie Camnitz, Pitt	25	6	.806	1958	Warren Spahn, Mil	22	11	.667
1910	King Cole, Chi	20	4	.833		Lew Burdette, Mil	20	10	.667
1911	Rube Marquard, NY	24	7	.774	1959	Roy Face, Pitt	18	1	.947
1912	Claude Hendrix, Pitt	24	9	.727	1960	Ernie Broglio, StL	21	9	.700
1913	Bert Humphries, Chi	16	4	.800	1961	Johnny Podres, LA	18	5	.783
1914	Bill James, Bos	26	7	.788	1962	Bob Purkey, Cin	23	5	.821
1915	Grover Alexander, Phil	31	10	.756	1963	Ron Perranoski, LA	16	3	.842
1916	Tom Hughes, Bos	16	3	.842	1964	Sandy Koufax, LA	19	5	.792
1917	Ferdie Schupp, NY	21	7	.750	1965	Sandy Koufax, LA	26	8	.765
1918	Claude Hendrix, Chi	19	7	.731	1966	Juan Marichal, SF	25	6	.806
1919	Dutch Ruether, Cin	19	6	.760	1967	Dick Hughes, StL	16	6	.727
1920	Burleigh Grimes, Bklyn	23	11	.676	1968	Steve Blass, Pitt	18	6	.750
1921	Bill Doak, StL	15	6	.714	1969	Tom Seaver, NY	25	7	.781
1922	Pete Donohue, Cin	18	9	.667	1970	Bob Gibson, StL	23	7	.767
1923	Dolf Luque, Cin	27	8	.771	1971	Don Gullett, Cin	16	6	.727
1924	Emil Yde, Pitt	16	3	.842	1972	Gary Nolan, Cin	15	5	.750
1925	Bill Sherdel, StL	15	6	.714	1973	Tommy John, LA	16	7	.696
1926	Ray Kremer, Pitt	20	6	.769	1974	Andy Messersmith, LA	20	6	.769
1927	Larry Benton, Bos-NY	17	7	.708	1975	Don Gullett, Cin	15	4	.789
1928	Larry Benton, NY	25	9	.735	1976	Steve Carlton, Phil	20	7	.741
1929	Charlie Root, Chi	19	6	.760	1977	John Candelaria, Pitt	20	5	.800
1930	Freddie Fitzsimmons, NY	19	7	.731	1978	Gaylord Perry, SD	21	6	.778
1931	Paul Derringer, StL	18	8	.692	1979	Tom Seaver, Cin	16	6	.727
1932	Lon Warneke, Chi	22	6	.786	1980	Jim Bibby, Pitt	19	6	.760
1933	Ben Cantwell, Bos	20	10	.667	1981*	Tom Seaver, Cin	14	2	.875
1934	Dizzy Dean, StL	30	7	.811	1982	Phil Niekro, Atl	17	4	.810
1935	Bill Lee, Chi	20	6	.769	1983	John Denny, Phil	19	6	.760
1936	Carl Hubbell, NY	26	6	.813	1984	Rick Sutcliffe, Chi	16	1	.941
1937	Carl Hubbell, NY	22	8	.733	1985	Orel Hershiser, LA	19	3	.864
1938	Bill Lee, Chi	22	9	.710	1986	Bob Ojeda, NY	18	5	.783
1939	Paul Derringer, Cin	25	7	.781	1987	Dwight Gooden, NY	15	7	.682
1940	Freddie Fitzsimmons, Bkln	16	2	.889	1988	David Cone, NY	20	3	.870
1941	Elmer Riddle, Cin	19	4	.826	1989	Mike Bielecki, Chi	18	7	.720
1942	Larry French, Bklyn	15	4	.789	1990	Doug Drabeck, Pitt	22	6	.786
1943	Mort Cooper, StL	21	8	.724	1991	John Smiley, Pitt	20	8	.714
1944	Ted Wilks, StL	17	4	.810		Jose Rijo, Cin	15	6	.714
1945	Harry Brecheen, StL	15	4	.789	1992	Bob Tewksbury, StL	16	5	.762
1946	Murray Dickson, StL	15	6	.714	1993	Tom Glavine, Atl	22	6	.786
1947	Larry Jansen, NY	21	5	.808					

*1981 percentages based on 10 or more victories.

Note: Based on 15 or more victories.

Teddy Tunnel

In a break from tradition Massachusetts governor William F. Weld announced in October that Boston's new harbor tunnel, currently under construction, would not be named after a local politico but after Red Sox legend Ted Wiliams. In a ceremony attended by the Kid himself, Weld dedicated Ted Williams Tunnel to "the greatest hitter who ever played the game of baseball."

"Gee, I thought I was kind of a hated man here," said Williams, in a reference to past battles with the Beantown press. "This thrills me more than I can say."

Lieut. Governor Paul Cellucci's suggestion: "In the event there is a lane shift in the ... tunnel—particulary when traffic has to shift from left to right—I propose we call it the Boudreau Shift."

Leading Pitchers—Earned-Run Average

Year	Player and Team	ERA	Year	Player and Team	ERA
1900	Rube Waddell, Pitt	2.37	1948	Harry Brecheen, StL	2.24
1901	Jesse Tannehill, Pitt	2.18	1949	Dave Koslo, NY	2.50
1902	Jack Taylor, Chi	1.33	1950	Jim Hearn, StL-NY	2.49
1903	Sam Leever, Pitt	2.06	1951	Chet Nichols, Bos	2.88
1904	Joe McGinnity, NY	1.61	1952	Hoyt Wilhelm, NY	2.43
1905	Christy Mathewson, NY	1.27	1953	Warren Spahn, Mil	2.10
1906	Three Finger Brown, Chi	1.04	1954	Johnny Antonelli, NY	2.29
1907	Jack Pfiester, Chi	1.15	1955	Bob Friend, Pitt	2.84
1908	Christy Mathewson, NY	1.43	1956	Lew Burdette, Mil	2.71
1909	Christy Mathewson, NY	1.14	1957	Johnny Podres, Bklyn	2.66
1910	George McQuillan, Phil	1.60	1958	Stu Miller, SF	2.47
1911	Christy Mathewson, NY	1.99	1959	Sam Jones, SF	2.82
1912	Jeff Tesreau, NY	1.96	1960	Mike McCormick, SF	2.70
1913	Christy Mathewson, NY	2.06	1961	Warren Spahn, Mil	3.01
1914	Bill Doak, StL	1.72	1962	Sandy Koufax, LA	2.54
1915	Grover Alexander, Phil	1.22	1963	Sandy Koufax, LA	1.88
1916	Grover Alexander, Phil	1.55	1964	Sandy Koufax, LA	1.74
1917	Grover Alexander, Phil	1.83	1965	Sandy Koufax, LA	2.04
1918	Hippo Vaughn, Chi	1.74	1966	Sandy Koufax, LA	1.73
1919	Grover Alexander, Chi	1.72	1967	Phil Niekro, Atl	1.87
1920	Grover Alexander, Chi	1.91	1968	Bob Gibson, StL	1.12
1921	Bill Doak, StL	2.58	1969	Juan Marichal, SF	2.10
1922	Rosy Ryan, NY	3.00	1970	Tom Seaver, NY	2.81
1923	Dolf Luque, Cin	1.93	1971	Tom Seaver, NY	1.76
1924	Dazzy Vance, Bklyn	2.16	1972	Steve Carlton, Phil	1.98
1925	Dolf Luque, Cin	2.63	1973	Tom Seaver, NY	2.08
1926	Ray Kremer, Pitt	2.61	1974	Buzz Capra, Atl	2.28
1927	Ray Kremer, Pitt	2.47	1975	Randy Jones, SD	2.24
1928	Dazzy Vance, Bklyn	2.09	1976	John Denny, StL	2.52
1929	Bill Walker, NY	3.08	1977	John Candelaria, Pitt	2.34
1930	Dazzy Vance, Bklyn	2.61	1978	Craig Swan, NY	2.43
1931	Bill Walker, NY	2.26	1979	J.R. Richard, Hou	2.71
1932	Lon Warneke, Chi	2.37	1980	Don Sutton, LA	2.21
1933	Carl Hubbell, NY	1.66	1981	Nolan Ryan, Hou	1.69
1934	Carl Hubbell, NY	2.30	1982	Steve Rogers, Mont	2.40
1935	Cy Blanton, Pitt	2.59	1983	Atlee Hammaker, SF	2.25
1936	Carl Hubbell, NY	2.31	1984	Alejandro Pena, LA	2.48
1937	Jim Turner, Bos	2.38	1985	Dwight Gooden, NY	1.53
1938	Bill Lee, Chi	2.66	1986	Mike Scott, Hou	2.22
1939	Bucky Walters, Cin	2.29	1987	Nolan Ryan, Hou	2.76
1940	Bucky Walters, Cin	2.48	1988	Joe Magrane, StL	2.18
1941	Elmer Riddle, Cin	2.24	1989	Scott Garrelts, SF	2.28
1942	Mort Cooper, StL	1.77	1990	Danny Darwin, Hou	2.21
1943	Howie Pollet, StL	1.75	1991	Dennis Martinez, Mont	2.39
1944	Ed Heusser, Cin	2.38	1992	Bill Swift, SF	2.08
1945	Hank Borowy, Chi	2.14	1993	Greg Maddux, Atl	2.36
1946	Howie Pollet, StL	2.10			
1947	Warren Spahn, Bos	2.33			

Note: Based on 10 complete games through 1950, then 154 innings until National League expanded in 1962, when it became 162 innings. In strike-shortened 1981, one inning per game required.

Leading Pitchers—Strikeouts

Year	Player and Team	SO	Year	Player and Team	SO
1900	Rube Waddell, Pitt	133	1911	Rube Marquard, NY	237
1901	Noodles Hahn, Cin	233	1912	Grover Alexander, Phil	195
1902	Vic Willis, Bos	226	1913	Tom Seaton, Phil	168
1903	Christy Mathewson, NY	267	1914	Grover Alexander, Phil	214
1904	Christy Mathewson, NY	212	1915	Grover Alexander, Phil	241
1905	Christy Mathewson, NY	206	1916	Grover Alexander, Phil	167
1906	Fred Beebe, Chi-StL	171	1917	Grover Alexander, Phil	200
1907	Christy Mathewson, NY	178	1918	Hippo Vaughn, Chi	148
1908	Christy Mathewson, NY	259	1919	Hippo Vaughn, Chi	141
1909	Orval Overall, Chi	205	1920	Grover Alexander, Chi	173
1910	Christy Mathewson, NY	190	1921	Burleigh Grimes, Bklyn	136

Leading Pitchers—Strikeouts *(Cont.)*

Year	Player and Team	SO	Year	Player and Team	SO
1922	Dazzy Vance, Bklyn	134	1957	Jack Sanford, Phil	188
1923	Dazzy Vance, Bklyn	197	1958	Sam Jones, StL	225
1924	Dazzy Vance, Bklyn	262	1959	Don Drysdale, LA	242
1925	Dazzy Vance, Bklyn	221	1960	Don Drysdale, LA	246
1926	Dazzy Vance, Bklyn	140	1961	Sandy Koufax, LA	269
1927	Dazzy Vance, Bklyn	184	1962	Don Drysdale, LA	232
1928	Dazzy Vance, Bklyn	200	1963	Sandy Koufax, LA	306
1929	Pat Malone, Chi	166	1964	Bob Veale, Pitt	250
1930	Bill Hallahan, StL	177	1965	Sandy Koufax, LA	382
1931	Bill Hallahan, StL	159	1966	Sandy Koufax, LA	317
1932	Dizzy Dean, StL	191	1967	Jim Bunning, Phil	253
1933	Dizzy Dean, StL	199	1968	Bob Gibson, StL	268
1934	Dizzy Dean, StL	195	1969	Ferguson Jenkins, Chi	273
1935	Dizzy Dean, StL	182	1970	Tom Seaver, NY	283
1936	Van Lingle Mungo, Bklyn	238	1971	Tom Seaver, NY	289
1937	Carl Hubbell, NY	159	1972	Steve Carlton, Phil	310
1938	Clay Bryant, Chi	135	1973	Tom Seaver, NY	251
1939	Claude Passeau, Phil-Chi	137	1974	Steve Carlton, Phil	240
	Bucky Walters, Cin	137	1975	Tom Seaver, NY	243
1940	Kirby Higbe, Phil	137	1976	Tom Seaver, NY	235
1941	Johnny Vander Meer, Cin	202	1977	Phil Niekro, Atl	262
1942	Johnny Vander Meer, Cin	186	1978	J.R. Richard, Hou	303
1943	Johnny Vander Meer, Cin	174	1979	J.R. Richard, Hou	313
1944	Bill Voiselle, NY	161	1980	Steve Carlton, Phil	286
1945	Preacher Roe, Pitt	148	1981	Fernando Valenzuela, LA	180
1946	Johnny Schmitz, Chi	135	1982	Steve Carlton, Phil	286
1947	Ewell Blackwell, Cin	193	1983	Steve Carlton, Phil	275
1948	Harry Brecheen, StL	149	1984	Dwight Gooden, NY	276
1949	Warren Spahn, Bos	151	1985	Dwight Gooden, NY	268
1950	Warren Spahn, Bos	191	1986	Mike Scott, Hou	306
1951	Warren Spahn, Bos	164	1987	Nolan Ryan, Hou	270
	Don Newcombe, Bklyn	164	1988	Nolan Ryan, Hou	228
1952	Warren Spahn, Bos	183	1989	Jose DeLeon, StL	201
1953	Robin Roberts, Phil	198	1990	David Cone, NY	233
1954	Robin Roberts, Phil	185	1991	David Cone, NY	241
1955	Sam Jones, Chi	198	1992	John Smoltz, Atl	215
1956	Sam Jones, Chi	176	1993	Jose Rijo, Cin	227

Leading Pitchers—Saves

Year	Player and Team	SV	Year	Player and Team	SV
1947	Hugh Casey, Bklyn	18	1970	Wayne Granger, Cin	35
1948	Harry Gumpert, Cin	17	1971	Dave Giusti, pitt	30
1949	Ted Wilks, StL	9	1972	Clay Carroll, Cin	37
1950	Jim Konstanty, Phil	22	1973	Mike Marshall, Mont	13
1951	Ted Wilks, StL, Pitt	13	1974	Mike Marshall, LA	21
1952	Al Brazle, StL	16	1975	Al Hrabosky, StL	22
1953	Al Brazle, StL	18		Rawly Eastwick, Cin	22
1954	Jim Hughes, Bklyn	24	1976	Rawly Eastwick, Cin	26
1955	Jack Meyer, Phil	16	1977	Rollie Fingers, SD	35
1956	Clem Labine, Bklyn	19	1978	Rollie Fingers, SD	37
1957	Clem Labine, Bklyn	17	1979	Bruce Sutter, Chi	37
1958	Roy Face, Pitt	20	1980	Bruce Sutter, Chi	28
1959	Lindy McDaniel, StL	15	1981	Bruce Sutter, StL	25
	Don McMahon, Mil	15	1982	Bruce Sutter, StL	36
1960	Lindy McDaniel, StL	26	1983	Lee Smith, Chi	29
1961	Stu Miller, SF	17	1984	Bruce Sutter, StL	45
	Roy Face, Pitt	17	1985	Jeff Reardon, Mont	41
1962	Roy Face, Pitt	28	1986	Todd Worrell, StL	36
1963	Lindy McDaniel, Chi	22	1987	Steve Bedrosian, Phil	40
1964	Hal Woodeshick, Hou	23	1988	John Franco, Cin	39
1965	Ted Abernathy, Chi	31	1989	Mark Davis, SD	44
1966	Phil Regan, LA	21	1990	John Franco, NY	33
1967	Ted Abernathy, Cin	28	1991	Lee Smith, StL	47
1968	Phil Regan, Chi, LA	25	1992	Lee Smith, StL	42
1969	Fred Gladding, Hou	29	1993	Randy Myers, Chi	53

American League

Pennant Winners

Year	Team	Manager	W	L	Pct	GA
1901	Chicago	Clark Griffith	83	53	.610	4
1902	Philadelphia	Connie Mack	83	53	.610	5
1903	Boston	Jimmy Collins	91	47	.659	14½
1904	Boston	Jimmy Collins	95	59	.617	1½
1905	Philadelphia	Connie Mack	92	56	.622	2
1906	Chicago	Fielder Jones	93	58	.616	3
1907	Detroit	Hughie Jennings	92	58	.613	1½
1908	Detroit	Hughie Jennings	90	63	.588	½
1909	Detroit	Hughie Jennings	98	54	.645	3½
1910	Philadelphia	Connie Mack	102	48	.680	14½
1911	Philadelphia	Connie Mack	101	50	.669	13½
1912	Boston	Jake Stahl	105	47	.691	14
1913	Philadelphia	Connie Mack	96	57	.627	6½
1914	Philadelphia	Connie Mack	99	53	.651	8½
1915	Boston	Bill Carrigan	101	50	.669	2½
1916	Boston	Bill Carrigan	91	63	.591	2
1917	Chicago	Pants Rowland	100	54	.649	9
1918	Boston	Ed Barrow	75	51	.595	2½
1919	Chicago	Kid Gleason	88	52	.629	3½
1920	Cleveland	Tris Speaker	98	56	.636	2
1921	New York	Miller Huggins	98	55	.641	4½
1922	New York	Miller Huggins	94	60	.610	1
1923	New York	Miller Huggins	98	54	.645	16
1924	Washington	Bucky Harris	92	62	.597	2
1925	Washington	Bucky Harris	96	55	.636	8½
1926	New York	Miller Huggins	91	63	.591	3
1927	New York	Miller Huggins	110	44	.714	19
1928	New York	Miller Huggins	101	53	.656	2½
1929	Philadelphia	Connie Mack	104	46	.693	18
1930	Philadelphia	Connie Mack	102	52	.662	8
1931	Philadelphia	Connie Mack	107	45	.704	13½
1932	New York	Joe McCarthy	107	47	.695	13
1933	Washington	Joe Cronin	99	53	.651	7
1934	Detroit	Mickey Cochrane	101	53	.656	7
1935	Detroit	Mickey Cochrane	93	58	.616	3
1936	New York	Joe McCarthy	102	51	.667	19½
1937	New York	Joe McCarthy	102	52	.662	13
1938	New York	Joe McCarthy	99	53	.651	9½
1939	New York	Joe McCarthy	106	45	.702	17
1940	Detroit	Del Baker	90	64	.584	1
1941	New York	Joe McCarthy	101	53	.656	17
1942	New York	Joe McCarthy	103	51	.669	9
1943	New York	Joe McCarthy	98	56	.636	13½
1944	St Louis	Luke Sewell	89	65	.578	1
1945	Detroit	Steve O'Neill	88	65	.575	1½
1946	Boston	Joe Cronin	104	50	.675	12
1947	New York	Bucky Harris	97	57	.630	12
1948	Cleveland†	Lou Boudreau	97	58	.626	1
1949	New York	Casey Stengel	97	57	.630	1
1950	New York	Casey Stengel	98	56	.636	3
1951	New York	Casey Stengel	98	56	.636	5
1952	New York	Casey Stengel	95	59	.617	2
1953	New York	Casey Stengel	99	52	.656	8½
1954	Cleveland	Al Lopez	111	43	.721	8
1955	New York	Casey Stengel	96	58	.623	3
1956	New York	Casey Stengel	97	57	.630	9
1957	New York	Casey Stengel	98	56	.636	8
1958	New York	Casey Stengel	92	62	.597	10
1959	Chicago	Al Lopez	94	60	.610	5
1960	New York	Casey Stengel	97	57	.630	8
1961	New York	Ralph Houk	109	53	.673	8
1962	New York	Ralph Houk	96	66	.593	5
1963	New York	Ralph Houk	104	57	.646	10½
1964	New York	Yogi Berra	99	63	.611	1

Pennant Winners (Cont.)

Year	Team	Manager	W	L	Pct	GA
1965	Minnesota	Sam Mele	102	60	.630	7
1966	Baltimore	Hank Bauer	97	63	.606	9
1967	Boston	Dick Williams	92	70	.568	1
1968	Detroit	Mayo Smith	103	59	.636	12
1969	Baltimore (E)‡	Earl Weaver	109	53	.673	19
1970	Baltimore (E)‡	Earl Weaver	108	54	.667	15
1971	Baltimore (E)‡	Earl Weaver	101	57	.639	12
1972	Oakland (W)‡	Dick Williams	93	62	.600	5½
1973	Oakland (W)‡	Dick Williams	94	68	.580	6
1974	Oakland (W)‡	Al Dark	90	72	.556	5
1975	Boston (E)‡	Darrell Johnson	95	65	.594	4½
1976	New York (E)‡	Billy Martin	97	62	.610	10½
1977	New York (E)‡	Billy Martin	100	62	.617	2½
1978	New York (E)†‡	Billy Martin, Bob Lemon	100	63	.613	1
1979	Baltimore (E)‡	Earl Weaver	102	57	.642	8
1980	Kansas City (W)‡	Jim Frey	97	65	.599	14
1981	New York (E)‡	Gene Michael, Bob Lemon	59	48	.551	#
1982	Milwaukee (E)‡	Buck Rodgers, Harvey Kuenn	95	67	.586	1
1983	Baltimore (E)‡	Joe Altobelli	98	64	.605	6
1984	Detroit (E)‡	Sparky Anderson	104	58	.642	15
1985	Kansas City (W)‡	Dick Howser	91	71	.562	1
1986	Boston (E)‡	John McNamara	95	66	.590	5½
1987	Minnesota (W)‡	Tom Kelly	85	77	.525	2
1988	Oakland (W)‡	Tony La Russa	104	58	.642	13
1989	Oakland (W)‡	Tony La Russa	99	63	.611	7
1990	Oakland (W)‡	Tony La Russa	103	59	.636	9
1991	Minnesota (W)‡	Tom Kelly	95	67	.586	8
1992	Toronto‡	Cito Gaston	96	66	.593	4
1993	Toronto‡	Cito Gaston	95	67	.586	7

*Games ahead of second-place club.

†Defeated Boston in one-game playoff.

‡Won championship series.

#First half 34-22; second 25-26.

Leading Batsmen

Year	Player and Team	BA	Year	Player and Team	BA
1901	Nap Lajoie, Phil	.422	1923	Harry Heilmann, Det	.403
1902	Ed Delahanty, Wash	.376	1924	Babe Ruth, NY	.378
1903	Nap Lajoie, Clev	.355	1925	Harry Heilmann, Det	.393
1904	Nap Lajoie, Clev	.381	1926	Heinie Manush, Det	.378
1905	Elmer Flick, Clev	.306	1927	Harry Heilmann, Det	.398
1906	George Stone, StL	.358	1928	Goose Goslin, Wash	.379
1907	Ty Cobb, Det	.350	1929	Lew Fonseca, Clev	.369
1908	Ty Cobb, Det	.324	1930	Al Simmons, Phil	.381
1909	Ty Cobb, Det	.377	1931	Al Simmons, Phil	.390
1910	Nap Lajoie, Clev*	.383	1932	Dale Alexander, Det-Bos	.367
1911	Ty Cobb, Det	.420	1933	Jimmie Foxx, Phil	.356
1912	Ty Cobb, Det	.410	1934	Lou Gehrig, NY	.363
1913	Ty Cobb, Det	.390	1935	Buddy Myer, Wash	.349
1914	Ty Cobb, Det	.368	1936	Luke Appling, Chi	.388
1915	Ty Cobb, Det	.369	1937	Charlie Gehringer, Det	.371
1916	Tris Speaker, Clev	.386	1938	Jimmie Foxx, Bos	.349
1917	Ty Cobb, Det	.383	1939	Joe DiMaggio, NY	.381
1918	Ty Cobb, Det	.382	1940	Joe DiMaggio, NY	.352
1919	Ty Cobb, Det	.384	1941	Ted Williams, Bos	.406
1920	George Sisler, StL	.407	1942	Ted Williams, Bos	.356
1921	Harry Heilmann, Det	.394	1943	Luke Appling, Chi	.328
1922	George Sisler, StL	.420	1944	Lou Boudreau, Clev	.327

Leading Batsmen (Cont.)

Year	Player and Team	BA	Year	Player and Team	BA
1945	Snuffy Stirnweiss, NY	.309	1970	Alex Johnson, Calif	.329
1946	Mickey Vernon, Wash	.353	1971	Tony Oliva, Minn	.337
1947	Ted Williams, Bos	.343	1972	Rod Carew, Minn	.318
1948	Ted Williams, Bos	.369	1973	Rod Carew, Minn	.350
1949	George Kell, Det	.343	1974	Rod Carew, Minn	.364
1950	Billy Goodman, Bos	.354	1975	Rod Carew, Minn	.359
1951	Ferris Fain, Phil	.344	1976	George Brett, KC	.333
1952	Ferris Fain, Phil	.327	1977	Rod Carew, Minn	.388
1953	Mickey Vernon, Wash	.337	1978	Rod Carew, Minn	.333
1954	Bobby Avila, Clev	.341	1979	Fred Lynn, Bos	.333
1955	Al Kaline, Det	.340	1980	George Brett, KC	.390
1956	Mickey Mantle, NY	.353	1981	Carney Lansford, Bos	.336
1957	Ted Williams, Bos	.388	1982	Willie Wilson, KC	.332
1958	Ted Williams, Bos	.328	1983	Wade Boggs, Bos	.361
1959	Harvey Kuenn, Det	.353	1984	Don Mattingly, NY	.343
1960	Pete Runnels, Bos	.320	1985	Wade Boggs, Bos	.368
1961	Norm Cash, Det	.361	1986	Wade Boggs, Bos	.357
1962	Pete Runnels, Bos	.326	1987	Wade Boggs, Bos	.363
1963	Carl Yastrzemski, Bos	.321	1988	Wade Boggs, Bos	.366
1964	Tony Oliva, Minn	.323	1989	Kirby Puckett, Minn	.339
1965	Tony Oliva, Minn	.321	1990	George Brett, KC	.329
1966	Frank Robinson, Balt	.316	1991	Julio Franco, Tex	.341
1967	Carl Yastrzemski, Bos	.326	1992	Edgar Martinez, Sea	.343
1968	Carl Yastrzemski, Bos	.301	1993	John Olerud, Tor	.363
1969	Rod Carew, Minn	.332			

*League president Ban Johnson declared Ty Cobb batting champion with a .385 average, beating Lajoie's .384. However, subsequent research has led to the revision of Lajoie's average to .383 and Cobb's to .382.

Leaders in Runs Scored

Year	Player and Team	Runs	Year	Player and Team	Runs
1901	Nap Lajoie, Phil	145	1935	Lou Gehrig, NY	125
1902	Dave Fultz, Phil	110	1936	Lou Gehrig, NY	167
1903	Patsy Dougherty, Bos	108	1937	Joe DiMaggio, NY	151
1904	Patsy Dougherty, Bos-NY	113	1938	Hank Greenberg, Det	144
1905	Harry Davis, Phil	92	1939	Red Rolfe, NY	139
1906	Elmer Flick, Clev	98	1940	Ted Williams, Bos	134
1907	Sam Crawford, Det	102	1941	Ted Williams, Bos	135
1908	Matty McIntyre, Det	105	1942	Ted Williams, Bos	141
1909	Ty Cobb, Det	116	1943	George Case, Wash	102
1910	Ty Cobb, Det	106	1944	Snuffy Stirnweiss, NY	125
1911	Ty Cobb, Det	147	1945	Snuffy Stirnweiss, NY	107
1912	Eddie Collins, Phil	137	1946	Ted Williams, Bos	142
1913	Eddie Collins, Phil	125	1947	Ted Williams, Bos	125
1914	Eddie Collins, Phil	122	1948	Tommy Henrich, NY	138
1915	Ty Cobb, Det	144	1949	Ted Williams, Bos	150
1916	Ty Cobb, Det	113	1950	Dom DiMaggio, Bos	131
1917	Donie Bush, Det	112	1951	Dom DiMaggio, Bos	113
1918	Ray Chapman, Clev	84	1952	Larry Doby, Clev	104
1919	Babe Ruth, Bos	103	1953	Al Rosen, Clev	115
1920	Babe Ruth, NY	158	1954	Mickey Mantle, NY	129
1921	Babe Ruth, NY	177	1955	Al Smith, Clev	123
1922	George Sisler, StL	134	1956	Mickey Mantle, NY	132
1923	Babe Ruth, NY	151	1957	Mickey Mantle, NY	121
1924	Babe Ruth, NY	143	1958	Mickey Mantle, NY	127
1925	Johnny Mostil, Chi	135	1959	Eddie Yost, Det	115
1926	Babe Ruth, NY	139	1960	Mickey Mantle, NY	119
1927	Babe Ruth, NY	158	1961	Mickey Mantle, NY	132
1928	Babe Ruth, NY	163		Roger Maris, NY	132
1929	Charlie Gehringer, Det	131	1962	Albie Pearson, LA	115
1930	Al Simmons, Phil	152	1963	Bob Allison, Minn	99
1931	Lou Gehrig, NY	163	1964	Tony Oliva, Minn	109
1932	Jimmie Foxx, Phil	151	1965	Zoilo Versalles, Minn	126
1933	Lou Gehrig, NY	138	1966	Frank Robinson, Balt	122
1934	Charlie Gehringer, Det	134	1967	Carl Yastrzemski, Bos	112

Leaders in Runs Scored *(Cont.)*

Year	Player and Team	Runs	Year	Player and Team	Runs
1968	Dick McAuliffe, Det	95	1982	Paul Molitor, Mil	136
1969	Reggie Jackson, Oak	123	1983	Cal Ripken, Balt	121
1970	Carl Yastrzemski, Bos	125	1984	Dwight Evans, Bos	121
1971	Don Buford, Balt	99	1985	Rickey Henderson, NY	146
1972	Bobby Murcer, NY	102	1986	Rickey Henderson, NY	130
1973	Reggie Jackson, Oak	99	1987	Paul Molitor, Mil	114
1974	Carl Yastrzemski, Bos	93	1988	Wade Boggs, Bos	128
1975	Fred Lynn, Bos	103	1989	Rickey Henderson, NY-Oak	113
1976	Roy White, NY	104		Wade Boggs, Bos	113
1977	Rod Carew, Minn	128	1990	Rickey Henderson, Oak	119
1978	Ron LeFlore, Det	126	1991	Paul Molitor, Mil	133
1979	Don Baylor, Calif	120	1992	Tony Phillips, Det	114
1980	Willie Wilson, KC	133	1993	Rafael Palmeiro, Tex	124
1981	Rickey Henderson, Oak	89			

Leaders in Hits

Year	Player and Team	Hits	Year	Player and Team	Hits
1901	Nap Lajoie, Phil	229	1941	Cecil Travis, Wash	218
1902	Piano Legs Hickman, Bos-Clev	194	1942	Johnny Pesky, Bos	205
1903	Patsy Dougherty, Bos	195	1943	Dick Wakefield, Det	200
1904	Nap Lajoie, Clev	211	1944	Snuffy Stirnweiss, NY	205
1905	George Stone, StL	187	1945	Snuffy Stirnweiss, NY	195
1906	Nap Lajoie, Clev	214	1946	Johnny Pesky, Bos	208
1907	Ty Cobb, Det	212	1947	Johnny Pesky, Bos	207
1908	Ty Cobb, Det	188	1948	Bob Dillinger, StL	207
1909	Ty Cobb, Det	216	1949	Dale Mitchell, Clev	203
1910	Nap Lajoie, Clev	227	1950	George Kell, Det	218
1911	Ty Cobb, Det	248	1951	George Kell, Det	191
1912	Ty Cobb, Det	227	1952	Nellie Fox, Chi	192
1913	Joe Jackson, Clev	197	1953	Harvey Kuenn, Det	209
1914	Tris Speaker, Bos	193	1954	Nellie Fox, Chi	201
1915	Ty Cobb, Det	208		Harvey Kuenn, Det	201
1916	Tris Speaker, Clev	211	1955	Al Kaline, Det	200
1917	Ty Cobb, Det	225	1956	Harvey Kuenn, Det	196
1918	George Burns, Phil	178	1957	Nellie Fox, Chi	196
1919	Ty Cobb, Det	191	1958	Nellie Fox, Chi	187
	Bobby Veach, Det	191	1959	Harvey Kuenn, Det	198
1920	George Sisler, StL	257	1960	Minnie Minoso, Chi	184
1921	Harry Heilmann, Det	237	1961	Norm Cash, Det	193
1922	George Sisler, StL	246	1962	Bobby Richardson, NY	209
1923	Charlie Jamieson, Clev	222	1963	Carl Yastrzemski, Bos	183
1924	Sam Rice, Wash	216	1964	Tony Oliva, Minn	217
1925	Al Simmons, Phil	253	1965	Tony Oliva, Minn	185
1926	George Burns, Clev	216	1966	Tony Oliva, Minn	191
	Sam Rice, Wash	216	1967	Carl Yastrzemski, Bos	189
1927	Earle Combs, NY	231	1968	Bert Campaneris, Oak	177
1928	Heinie Manush, StL	241	1969	Tony Oliva, Minn	197
1929	Dale Alexander, Det	215	1970	Tony Oliva, Minn	204
	Charlie Gehringer, Det	215	1971	Cesar Tovar, Minn	204
1930	Johnny Hodapp, Clev	225	1972	Joe Rudi, Oak	181
1931	Lou Gehrig, NY	211	1973	Rod Carew, Minn	203
1932	Al Simmons, Phil	216	1974	Rod Carew, Minn	218
1933	Heinie Manush, Wash	221	1975	George Brett, KC	195
1934	Charlie Gehringer, Det	214	1976	George Brett, KC	215
1935	Joe Vosmik, Clev	216	1977	Rod Carew, Minn	239
1936	Earl Averill, Clev	232	1978	Jim Rice, Bos	213
1937	Beau Bell, StL	218	1979	George Brett, KC	212
1938	Joe Vosmik, Bos	201	1980	Willie Wilson, KC	230
1939	Red Rolfe, NY	213	1981	Rickey Henderson, Oak	135
1940	Rip Radcliff, StL	200	1982	Robin Yount, Mil	210
	Barney McCosky, Det	200	1983	Cal Ripken, Balt	211
	Doc Cramer, Bos	200	1984	Don Mattingly, NY	207

Leaders in Hits *(Cont.)*

Year	Player and Team	Hits	Year	Player and Team	Hits
1985	Wade Boggs, Bos	240	1989	Kirby Puckett, Minn	215
1986	Don Mattingly, NY	238	1990	Rafael Palmeiro, Tex	191
1987	Kirby Puckett, Minn	207	1991	Paul Molitor, Mil	216
	Kevin Seitzer, KC	207	1992	Kirby Puckett, Minn	210
1988	Kirby Puckett, Minn	234	1993	Paul Molitor, Tor	211

Home Run Leaders

Year	Player and Team	HR	Year	Player and Team	HR
1901	Nap Lajoie, Phil	13	1950	Al Rosen, Clev	37
1902	Socks Seybold, Phil	16	1951	Gus Zernial, Chi-Phil	33
1903	Buck Freeman, Bos	13	1952	Larry Doby, Clev	32
1904	Harry Davis, Phil	10	1953	Al Rosen, Clev	43
1905	Harry Davis, Phil	8	1954	Larry Doby, Clev	32
1906	Harry Davis, Phil	12	1955	Mickey Mantle, NY	37
1907	Harry Davis, Phil	8	1956	Mickey Mantle, NY	52
1908	Sam Crawford, Det	7	1957	Roy Sievers, Wash	42
1909	Ty Cobb, Det	9	1958	Mickey Mantle, NY	42
1910	Jake Stahl, Bos	10	1959	Rocky Colavito, Clev	42
1911	Frank Baker, Phil	9		Harmon Killebrew, Wash	42
1912	Frank Baker, Phil	10	1960	Mickey Mantle, NY	40
	Tris Speaker, Bos	10	1961	Roger Maris, NY	61
1913	Frank Baker, Phil	13	1962	Harmon Killebrew, Minn	48
1914	Frank Baker, Phil	9	1963	Harmon Killebrew, Minn	45
1915	Braggo Roth, Chi-Clev	7	1964	Harmon Killebrew, Minn	49
1916	Wally Pipp, NY	12	1965	Tony Conigliaro, Bos	32
1917	Wally Pipp, NY	9	1966	Frank Robinson, Balt	49
1918	Babe Ruth, Bos	11	1967	Harmon Killebrew, Minn	44
	Tilly Walker, Phil	11		Carl Yastrzemski, Bos	44
1919	Babe Ruth, Bos	29	1968	Frank Howard, Wash	44
1920	Babe Ruth, NY	54	1969	Harmon Killebrew, Minn	49
1921	Babe Ruth, NY	59	1970	Frank Howard, Wash	44
1922	Ken Williams, StL	39	1971	Bill Melton, Chi	33
1923	Babe Ruth, NY	41	1972	Dick Allen, Chi	37
1924	Babe Ruth, NY	46	1973	Reggie Jackson, Oak	32
1925	Bob Meusel, NY	33	1974	Dick Allen, Chi	32
1926	Babe Ruth, NY	47	1975	Reggie Jackson, Oak	36
1927	Babe Ruth, NY	60		George Scott, Mil	36
1928	Babe Ruth, NY	54	1976	Graig Nettles, NY	32
1929	Babe Ruth, NY	46	1977	Jim Rice, Bos	39
1930	Babe Ruth, NY	49	1978	Jim Rice, Bos	46
1931	Babe Ruth, NY	46	1979	Gorman Thomas, Mil	45
	Lou Gehrig, NY	46	1980	Reggie Jackson, NY	41
1932	Jimmie Foxx, Phil	58		Ben Oglivie, Mil	41
1933	Jimmie Foxx, Phil	48	1981	Tony Armas, Oak	22
1934	Lou Gehrig, NY	49	1981	Dwight Evans, Bos	22
1935	Jimmie Foxx, Phil	36		Bobby Grich, Calif	22
	Hank Greenberg, Det	36		Eddie Murray, Balt	22
1936	Lou Gehrig, NY	49	1982	Reggie Jackson, Calif	39
1937	Joe DiMaggio, NY	46		Gorman Thomas, Mil	39
1938	Hank Greenberg, Det	58	1983	Jim Rice, Bos	39
1939	Jimmie Foxx, Bos	35	1984	Tony Armas, Bos	43
1940	Hank Greenberg, Det	41	1985	Darrell Evans, Det	40
1941	Ted Williams, Bos	37	1986	Jesse Barfield, Tor	40
1942	Ted Williams, Bos	36	1987	Mark McGwire, Oak	49
1943	Rudy York, Det	34	1988	Jose Canseco, Oak	42
1944	Nick Etten, NY	22	1989	Fred McGriff, Tor	36
1945	Vern Stephens, StL	24	1990	Cecil Fielder, Det	51
1946	Hank Greenberg, Det	44	1991	Jose Canseco, Oak	44
1947	Ted Williams, Bos	32		Cecil Fielder, Det	44
1948	Joe DiMaggio, NY	39	1992	Juan Gonzalez, Tex	43
1949	Ted Williams, Bos	43	1993	Juan Gonzalez, Tex	46

Runs Batted In Leaders

Year	Player and Team	RBI	Year	Player and Team	RBI
1907	Ty Cobb, Det	116	1951	Gus Zernial, Chi-Phil	129
1908	Ty Cobb, Det	108	1952	Al Rosen, Clev	105
1909	Ty Cobb, Det	107	1953	Al Rosen, Clev	145
1910	Sam Crawford, Det	120	1954	Larry Doby, Clev	126
1911	Ty Cobb, Det	144	1955	Ray Boone, Det	116
1912	Frank Baker, Phil	133		Jackie Jensen, Bos	116
1913	Frank Baker, Phil	126	1956	Mickey Mantle, NY	130
1914	Sam Crawford, Det	104	1957	Roy Sievers, Wash	114
1915	Sam Crawford, Det	112	1958	Jackie Jensen, Bos	122
	Bobby Veach, Det	112	1959	Jackie Jensen, Bos	112
1916	Del Pratt, StL	103	1960	Roger Maris, NY	112
1917	Bobby Veach, Det	103	1961	Roger Maris, NY	142
1918	Bobby Veach, Det	78	1962	Harmon Killebrew, Minn	126
1919	Babe Ruth, Bos	114	1963	Dick Stuart, Bos	118
1920	Babe Ruth, NY	137	1964	Brooks Robinson, Balt	118
1921	Babe Ruth, NY	171	1965	Rocky Colavito, Clev	108
1922	Ken Williams, StL	155	1966	Frank Robinson, Balt	122
1923	Babe Ruth, NY	131	1967	Carl Yastrzemski, Bos	121
1924	Goose Goslin, Wash	129	1968	Ken Harrelson, Bos	109
1925	Bob Meusel, NY	138	1969	Harmon Killebrew, Minn	140
1926	Babe Ruth, NY	145	1970	Frank Howard, Wash	126
1927	Lou Gehrig, NY	175	1971	Harmon Killebrew, Minn	119
1928	Babe Ruth, NY	142	1972	Dick Allen, Chi	113
	Lou Gehrig, NY	142	1973	Reggie Jackson, Oak	117
1929	Al Simmons, Phil	157	1974	Jeff Burroughs, Tex	118
1930	Lou Gehrig, NY	174	1975	George Scott, Mil	109
1931	Lou Gehrig, NY	184	1976	Lee May, Balt	109
1932	Jimmie Foxx, Phil	169	1977	Larry Hisle, Minn	119
1933	Jimmie Foxx, Phil	163	1978	Jim Rice, Bos	139
1934	Lou Gehrig, NY	165	1979	Don Baylor, Calif	139
1935	Hank Greenberg, Det	170	1980	Cecil Cooper, Mil	122
1936	Hal Trosky, Clev	162	1981	Eddie Murray, Balt	78
1937	Hank Greenberg, Det	183	1982	Hal McRae, KC	133
1938	Jimmie Foxx, Bos	175	1983	Cecil Cooper, Mil	126
1939	Ted Williams, Bos	145		Jim Rice, Bos	126
1940	Hank Greenberg, Det	150	1984	Tony Armas, Bos	123
1941	Joe DiMaggio, NY	125	1985	Don Mattingly, NY	145
1942	Ted Williams, Bos	137	1986	Joe Carter, Clev	121
1943	Rudy York, Det	118	1987	George Bell, Tor	134
1944	Vern Stephens, StL	109	1988	Jose Canseco, Oak	124
1945	Nick Etten, NY	111	1989	Ruben Sierra, Tex	119
1946	Hank Greenberg, Det	127	1990	Cecil Fielder, Det	132
1947	Ted Williams, Bos	114	1991	Cecil Fielder, Det	133
1948	Joe DiMaggio, NY	155	1992	Cecil Fielder, Det	124
1949	Ted Williams, Bos	159	1993	Albert Belle, Cle	129
	Vern Stephens, Bos	159			
1950	Walt Dropo, Bos	144			
	Vern Stephens, Bos	144			

Note: Runs Batted In not compiled before 1907; officially adopted in 1920.

Leading Base Stealers

Year	Player and Team	SB	Year	Player and Team	SB
1901	Frank Isbell, Chi	48	1911	Ty Cobb, Det	83
1902	Topsy Hartsel, Phil	54	1912	Clyde Milan, Wash	88
1903	Harry Bay, Clev	46	1913	Clyde Milan, Wash	75
1904	Elmer Flick, Clev	42	1914	Fritz Maisel, NY	74
	Harry Bay, Clev	42	1915	Ty Cobb, Det	96
1905	Danny Hoffman, Phil	46	1916	Ty Cobb, Det	68
1906	Elmer Flick, Clev	39	1917	Ty Cobb, Det	55
	John Anderson, Wash	39	1918	George Sisler, StL	45
1907	Ty Cobb, Det	49	1919	Eddie Collins, Chi	33
1908	Patsy Dougherty, Chi	47	1920	Sam Rice, Wash	63
1909	Ty Cobb, Det	76	1921	George Sisler, StL	35
1910	Eddie Collins, Phil	81	1922	George Sisler, StL	51

Leading Base Stealers *(Cont.)*

Year	Player and Team	SB	Year	Player and Team	SB
1923	Eddie Collins, Chi	49	1958	Luis Aparicio, Chi	29
1924	Eddie Collins, Chi	42	1959	Luis Aparicio, Chi	56
1925	John Mostil, Chi	43	1960	Luis Aparicio, Chi	51
1926	John Mostil, Chi	35	1961	Luis Aparicio, Chi	53
1927	George Sisler, StL	27	1962	Luis Aparicio, Chi	31
1928	Buddy Myer, Bos	30	1963	Luis Aparicio, Balt	40
1929	Charlie Gehringer, Det	27	1964	Luis Aparicio, Balt	57
1930	Marty McManus, Det	23	1965	Bert Campaneris, KC	51
1931	Ben Chapman, NY	61	1966	Bert Campaneris, KC	52
1932	Ben Chapman, NY	38	1967	Bert Campaneris, KC	55
1933	Ben Chapman, NY	27	1968	Bert Campaneris, Oak	62
1934	Bill Werber, Bos	40	1969	Tommy Harper, Sea	73
1935	Bill Werber, Bos	29	1970	Bert Campaneris, Oak	42
1936	Lyn Lary, StL	37	1971	Amos Otis, KC	52
1937	Bill Werber, Phil	35	1972	Bert Campaneris, Oak	52
	Ben Chapman, Wash-Bos	35	1973	Tommy Harper, Bos	54
1938	Frank Crosetti, NY	27	1974	Bill North, Oak	54
1939	George Case, Wash	51	1975	Mickey Rivers, Calif	70
1940	George Case, Wash	35	1976	Bill North, Oak	75
1941	George Case, Wash	33	1977	Freddie Patek, KC	53
1942	George Case, Wash	44	1978	Ron LeFlore, Det	68
1943	George Case, Wash	61	1979	Willie Wilson, KC	83
1944	Snuffy Stirnweiss, NY	55	1980	Rickey Henderson, Oak	100
1945	Snuffy Stirnweiss, NY	33	1981	Rickey Henderson, Oak	56
1946	George Case, Clev	28	1982	Rickey Henderson, Oak	130
1947	Bob Dillinger, StL	34	1983	Rickey Henderson, Oak	108
1948	Bob Dillinger, StL	28	1984	Rickey Henderson, Oak	66
1949	Bob Dillinger, StL	20	1985	Rickey Henderson, NY	80
1950	Dom DiMaggio, Bos	15	1986	Rickey Henderson, NY	87
1951	Minnie Minoso, Clev-Chi	31	1987	Harold Reynolds, Sea	60
1952	Minnie Minoso, Chi	22	1988	Rickey Henderson, NY	93
1953	Minnie Minoso, Chi	25	1989	Rickey Henderson, NY-Oak	77
1954	Jackie Jensen, Bos	22	1990	Rickey Henderson, Oak	65
1955	Jim Rivera, Chi	25	1991	Rickey Henderson, Oak	58
1956	Luis Aparicio, Chi	21	1992	Kenny Lofton, Cle	66
1957	Luis Aparicio, Chi	28	1993	Kenny Lofton, Cle	70

Leading Pitchers—Winning Percentage

Year	Pitcher and Team	W	L	Pct	Year	Pitcher and Team	W	L	Pct
1901	Clark Griffith, Chi	24	7	.774	1924	Walter Johnson, Wash	23	7	.767
1902	Bill Bernhard, Phil-Clev	18	5	.783	1925	Stan Coveleski, Wash	20	5	.800
1903	Earl Moore, Clev	22	7	.759	1926	George Uhle, Clev	27	11	.711
1904	Jack Chesbro, NY	41	12	.774	1927	Waite Hoyt, NY	22	7	.759
1905	Jess Tannehill, Bos	22	9	.710	1928	General Crowder, StL	21	5	.808
1906	Eddie Plank, Phil	19	6	.760	1929	Lefty Grove, Phil	20	6	.769
1907	Wild Bill Donovan, Det	25	4	.862	1930	Lefty Grove, Phil	28	5	.848
1908	Ed Walsh, Chi	40	15	.727	1931	Lefty Grove, Phil	31	4	.886
1909	George Mullin, Det	29	8	.784	1932	Johnny Allen, NY	17	4	.810
1910	Chief Bender, Phil	23	5	.821	1933	Lefty Grove, Phil	24	8	.750
1911	Chief Bender, Phil	17	5	.773	1934	Lefty Gomez, NY	26	5	.839
1912	Smoky Joe Wood, Bos	34	5	.872	1935	Eldon Auker, Det	18	7	.720
1913	Walter Johnson, Wash	36	7	.837	1936	Monte Pearson, NY	19	7	.731
1914	Chief Bender, Phil	17	3	.850	1937	Johnny Allen, Clev	15	1	.938
1915	Smoky Joe Wood, Bos	15	5	.750	1938	Red Ruffing, NY	21	7	.750
1916	Eddie Cicotte, Chi	15	7	.682	1939	Lefty Grove, Bos	15	4	.789
1917	Reb Russell, Chi	15	5	.750	1940	Schoolboy Rowe, Det	16	3	.842
1918	Sad Sam Jones, Bos	16	5	.762	1941	Lefty Gomez, NY	15	5	.750
1919	Eddie Cicotte, Chi	29	7	.806	1942	Ernie Bonham, NY	21	5	.808
1920	Jim Bagby, Clev	31	12	.721	1943	Spud Chandler, NY	20	4	.833
1921	Carl Mays, NY	27	9	.750	1944	Tex Hughson, Bos	18	5	.783
1922	Joe Bush, NY	26	7	.788	1945	Hal Newhouser, Det	25	9	.735
1923	Herb Pennock, NY	19	6	.760	1946	Boo Ferriss, Bos	25	6	.806

Leading Pitchers—Winning Percentage (Cont.)

Year	Pitcher and Team	W	L	Pct	Year	Pitcher and Team	W	L	Pct
1947	Allie Reynolds, NY	19	8	.704	1971	Dave McNally, Balt	21	5	.808
1948	Jack Kramer, Bos	18	5	.783	1972	Catfish Hunter, Oak	21	7	.750
1949	Ellis Kinder, Bos	23	6	.793	1973	Catfish Hunter, Oak	21	5	.808
1950	Vic Raschi, NY	21	8	.724	1974	Mike Cuellar, Balt	22	10	.688
1951	Bob Feller, Clev	22	8	.733	1975	Mike Torrez, Balt	20	9	.690
1952	Bobby Shantz, Phil	24	7	.774	1976	Bill Campbell, Minn	17	5	.773
1953	Ed Lopat, NY	16	4	.800	1977	Paul Splittorff, KC	16	6	.727
1954	Sandy Consuegra, Chi	16	3	.842	1978	Ron Guidry, NY	25	3	.893
1955	Tommy Byrne, NY	16	5	.762	1979	Mike Caldwell, Mil	16	6	.727
1956	Whitey Ford, NY	19	6	.760	1980	Steve Stone, Balt	25	7	.781
1957	Dick Donovan, Chi	16	6	.727	1981*	Pete Vuckovich, Mil	14	4	.778
	Tom Sturdivant, NY	16	6	.727	1982	Pete Vuckovich, Mil	18	6	.750
1958	Bob Turley, NY	21	7	.750		Jim Palmer, Balt	15	5	.750
1959	Bob Shaw, Chi	18	6	.750	1983	Richard Dotson, Chi	22	7	.759
1960	Jim Perry, Clev	18	10	.643	1984	Doyle Alexander, Tor	17	6	.739
1961	Whitey Ford, NY	25	4	.862	1985	Ron Guidry, NY	22	6	.786
1962	Ray Herbert, Chi	20	9	.690	1986	Roger Clemens, Bos	24	4	.857
1963	Whitey Ford, NY	24	7	.774	1987	Roger Clemens, Bos	20	9	.690
1964	Wally Bunker, Balt	19	5	.792	1988	Frank Viola, Minn	24	7	.774
1965	Mudcat Grant, Minn	21	7	.750	1989	Bret Saberhagen, KC	23	6	.793
1966	Sonny Siebert, Clev	16	8	.667	1990	Bob Welch, Oak	27	6	.818
1967	Joel Horlen, Chi	19	7	.731	1991	Scott Erickson, Minn	20	8	.714
1968	Denny McLain, Det	31	6	.838	1992	Mike Mussina, Balt	18	5	.783
1969	Jim Palmer, Balt	16	4	.800	1993	Jimmy Key, NY	18	6	.750
1970	Mike Cuellar, Balt	24	8	.750					

Note: Based on 15 or more victories.

*1981 percentages based on 10 or more victories.

Leading Pitchers—Earned-Run Average

Year	Player and Team	ERA	Year	Player and Team	ERA
1913	Walter Johnson, Wash	1.14	1947	Spud Chandler, NY	2.46
1914	Dutch Leonard, Bos	1.01	1948	Gene Bearden, Clev	2.43
1915	Smoky Joe Wood, Bos	1.49	1949	Mel Parnell, Bos	2.78
1916	Babe Ruth, Bos	1.75	1950	Early Wynn, Clev	3.20
1917	Eddie Cicotte, Chi	1.53	1951	Saul Rogovin, Det-Chi	2.78
1918	Walter Johnson, Wash	1.27	1952	Allie Reynolds, NY	2.07
1919	Walter Johnson, Wash	1.49	1953	Ed Lopat, NY	2.43
1920	Bob Shawkey, NY	2.46	1954	Mike Garcia, Clev	2.64
1921	Red Faber, Chi	2.47	1955	Billy Pierce, Chi	1.97
1922	Red Faber, Chi	2.80	1956	Whitey Ford, NY	2.47
1923	Stan Coveleski, Clev	2.76	1957	Bobby Shantz, NY	2.45
1924	Walter Johnson, Wash	2.72	1958	Whitey Ford, NY	2.01
1925	Stan Coveleski, Wash	2.84	1959	Hoyt Wilhelm, Balt	2.19
1926	Lefty Grove, Phil	2.51	1960	Frank Baumann, Chi	2.68
1927	Wilcy Moore,* NY	2.28	1961	Dick Donovan, Wash	2.40
1928	Garland Braxton, Wash	2.52	1962	Hank Aguirre, Det	2.21
1929	Lefty Grove, Phil	2.81	1963	Gary Peters, Chi	2.33
1930	Lefty Grove, Phil	2.54	1964	Dean Chance, LA	1.65
1931	Lefty Grove, Phil	2.06	1965	Sam McDowell, Clev	2.18
1932	Lefty Grove, Phil	2.84	1966	Gary Peters, Chi	1.98
1933	Monte Pearson, Clev	2.33	1967	Joe Horlen, Chi	2.06
1934	Lefty Gomez, NY	2.33	1968	Luis Tiant, Clev	1.60
1935	Lefty Grove, Bos	2.70	1969	Dick Bosman, Wash	2.19
1936	Lefty Grove, Bos	2.81	1970	Diego Segui, Oak	2.56
1937	Lefty Gomez, NY	2.33	1971	Vida Blue, Oak	1.82
1938	Lefty Grove, Bos	3.07	1972	Luis Tiant, Bos	1.91
1939	Lefty Grove, Bos	2.54	1973	Jim Palmer, Balt	2.40
1940	Bob Feller, †Clev	2.62	1974	Catfish Hunter, Oak	2.49
1941	Thornton Lee, Chi	2.37	1975	Jim Palmer, Balt	2.09
1942	Ted Lyons, Chi	2.10	1976	Mark Fidrych, Det	2.34
1943	Spud Chandler, NY	1.64	1977	Frank Tanana, Calif	2.54
1944	Dizzy Trout, Det	2.12	1978	Ron Guidry, NY	1.74
1945	Hal Newhouser, Det	1.81	1979	Ron Guidry, NY	2.78
1946	Hal Newhouser, Det	1.94	1980	Rudy May, NY	2.47

Leading Pitchers—Earned-Run Average (Cont.)

Year	Player and Team	ERA	Year	Player and Team	ERA
1981	Steve McCatty, Oak	2.32	1988	Allan Anderson, Minn	2.45
1982	Rick Sutcliffe, Clev	2.96	1989	Bret Saberhagen, KC	2.16
1983	Rick Honeycutt, Tex	2.42	1990	Roger Clemens, Bos	1.93
1984	Mike Boddicker, Balt	2.79	1991	Roger Clemens, Bos	2.62
1985	Dave Stieb, Tor	2.48	1992	Roger Clemens, Bos	2.41
1986	Roger Clemens, Bos	2.48	1993	Kevin Appier, KC	2.56
1987	Jimmy Key, Tor	2.76			

Note: Based on 10 complete games through 1950, then, 154 innings until the American League expanded in 1961, when it became 162 innings. In strike-shortened 1981, one inning per game required. Earned runs not tabulated in American League prior to 1913.

*Wilcy Moore pitched only six complete games—he started 12—in 1927, but was recognized as leader because of 213 innings pitched.

†Ernie Bonham, New York, had 1.91 ERA and 10 complete games in 1940, but appeared in only 12 games and 99 innings, and Bob Feller was recognized as leader.

Leading Pitchers—Strikeouts

Year	Player and Team	SO	Year	Player and Team	SO
1901	Cy Young, Bos	159	1947	Bob Feller, Clev	196
1902	Rube Waddell, Phil	210	1948	Bob Feller, Clev	164
1903	Rube Waddell, Phil	301	1949	Virgil Trucks, Det	153
1904	Rube Waddell, Phil	349	1950	Bob Lemon, Clev	170
1905	Rube Waddell, Phil	286	1951	Vic Raschi, NY	164
1906	Rube Waddell, Phil	203	1952	Allie Reynolds, NY	160
1907	Rube Waddell, Phil	226	1953	Billy Pierce, Chi	186
1908	Ed Walsh, Chi	269	1954	Bob Turley, Balt	185
1909	Frank Smith, Chi	177	1955	Herb Score, Clev	245
1910	Walter Johnson, Wash	313	1956	Herb Score, Clev	263
1911	Ed Walsh, Chi	255	1957	Early Wynn, Clev	184
1912	Walter Johnson, Wash	303	1958	Early Wynn, Chi	179
1913	Walter Johnson, Wash	243	1959	Jim Bunning, Det	201
1914	Walter Johnson, Wash	225	1960	Jim Bunning, Det	201
1915	Walter Johnson, Wash	203	1961	Camilo Pascual, Minn	221
1916	Walter Johnson, Wash	228	1962	Camilo Pascual, Minn	206
1917	Walter Johnson, Wash	188	1963	Camilo Pascual, Minn	202
1918	Walter Johnson, Wash	162	1964	Al Downing, NY	217
1919	Walter Johnson, Wash	147	1965	Sam McDowell, Clev	325
1920	Stan Coveleski, Clev	133	1966	Sam McDowell, Clev	225
1921	Walter Johnson, Wash	143	1967	Jim Lonborg, Bos	246
1922	Urban Shocker, StL	149	1968	Sam McDowell, Clev	283
1923	Walter Johnson, Wash	130	1969	Sam McDowell, Clev	279
1924	Walter Johnson, Wash	158	1970	Sam McDowell, Clev	304
1925	Lefty Grove, Phil	116	1971	Mickey Lolich, Det	308
1926	Lefty Grove, Phil	194	1972	Nolan Ryan, Calif	329
1927	Lefty Grove, Phil	174	1973	Nolan Ryan, Calif	383
1928	Lefty Grove, Phil	183	1974	Nolan Ryan, Calif	367
1929	Lefty Grove, Phil	170	1975	Frank Tanana, Calif	269
1930	Lefty Grove, Phil	209	1976	Nolan Ryan, Calif	327
1931	Lefty Grove, Phil	175	1977	Nolan Ryan, Calif	341
1932	Red Ruffing, NY	190	1978	Nolan Ryan, Calif	260
1933	Lefty Gomez, NY	163	1979	Nolan Ryan, Calif	223
1934	Lefty Gomez, NY	158	1980	Len Barker, Clev	187
1935	Tommy Bridges, Det	163	1981	Len Barker, Clev	127
1936	Tommy Bridges, Det	175	1982	Floyd Bannister, Sea	209
1937	Lefty Gomez, NY	194	1983	Jack Morris, Det	232
1938	Bob Feller, Clev	240	1984	Mark Langston, Sea	204
1939	Bob Feller, Clev	246	1985	Bert Blyleven, Clev-Minn	206
1940	Bob Feller, Clev	261	1986	Mark Langston, Sea	245
1941	Bob Feller, Clev	260	1987	Mark Langston, Sea	262
1942	Bobo Newsom, Wash	113	1988	Roger Clemens, Bos	291
	Tex Hughson, Bos	113	1989	Nolan Ryan, Tex	301
1943	Allie Reynolds, Clev	151	1990	Nolan Ryan, Tex	232
1944	Hal Newhouser, Det	187	1991	Roger Clemens, Bos	241
1945	Hal Newhouser, Det	212	1992	Randy Johnson, Sea	241
1946	Bob Feller, Clev	348	1993	Randy Johnson, Sea	308

American League (Cont.)

Leading Pitchers—Saves

Year	Player and Team	SV	Year	Player and Team	SV
1947	Joe Page, NY	17	1971	Ken Sanders, Mil	31
1948	Russ Christopher, Cle	17	1972	Sparky Lyle, NY	35
1949	Joe Page, NY	29	1973	John Hiller, Det	38
1950	Mickey Harris, Wash	15	1974	Terry Forster, Chi	24
1951	Ellis Kinder, Bos	14	1975	Goose Gossage, Chi	26
1952	Harry Dorish, Chi	11	1976	Sparky Lyle, NY	23
1953	Ellis Kinder, Bos	27	1977	Bill Campbell, Bos	31
1954	Johnny Sain, NY	22	1978	Goose Gossage, NY	27
1955	Ray Narleski, Cle	19	1979	Mike Marshall, Min	32
1956	George Zuverink, Bal	16	1980	Dan Quisenberry, KC	33
1957	Bob Grim, NY	19	1981	Goose Gossage, NY	33
1958	Ryne Duren, NY	20	1982	Rollie Fingers, Mil	28
1959	Turk Lown, Chi	15	1983	Dan Quisenberry, KC	35
1960	Mike Fornieles, Bos	14	1984	Dan Quisenberry, KC	45
	Johnny Klippstein, Cle	14	1985	Dan Quisenberry, KC	37
1961	Luis Arroyo, NY	29	1986	Dave Righetti, NY	46
1962	Dick Radatz, Bos	24	1987	Tom Henke, Tor	34
1963	Stu Miller, Bal	27	1988	Dennis Eckersley, Oak	45
1964	Dick Radatz, Bos	29	1989	Jeff Russell, Tex	38
1965	Ron Kline, Wash	29	1990	Bobby Thigpen, Chi	57
1966	Jack Aker, KC	32	1991	Bryan Harvey, Cal	46
1967	Minnie Rojas, Cal	27	1992	Dennis Eckersley, Oak	51
1968	Al Worthington, Min	18	1993	Jeff Montgomery, KC	45
1969	Ron Perranoski, Min	31		Duane Ward, Tor	45
1970	Ron Perranoski, Min	34			

The Commissioners of Baseball

Kenesaw Mountain Landis ....Elected November 12, 1920. Served until his death on November 25, 1944.
Happy Chandler ....Elected April 24, 1945. Served until July 15, 1951.
Ford Frick ....Elected September 20, 1951. Served until November 16, 1965.
William Eckert ....Elected November 17, 1965. Served until December 20, 1968.
Bowie Kuhn ....Elected February 8, 1969. Served until September 30, 1984.
Peter Ueberroth ....Elected March 3, 1984. Took office October 1, 1984. Served through March 31, 1989.
A. Bartlett Giamatti ....Elected September 8, 1988. Took office April 1, 1989. Served until his death on September 1, 1989.
Francis Vincent Jr....................Appointed Acting Commissioner September 2, 1989. Elected Commissioner September 13, 1989.
Allan H. (Bud) Selig ....Elected chairman of the executive council and given the powers of interim commissioner on September 9, 1992.

THEY SAID IT

Tim McCarver, CBS baseball announcer sweltering in Philadelphia's 102° heat, recalling a bracing moment in the 1992 National League playoffs: "Where's Deion when you need him?"

Pro Football

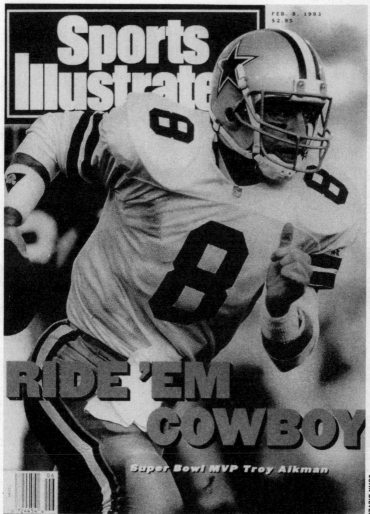

FEB. 8, 1993
$2.95

Sports Illustrated

RIDE 'EM COWBOY

Super Bowl MVP Troy Aikman

JOHN BIEVER

The Year of the Cowboy

After a four-year ascent, the rebuilt Cowboys are on top of the NFL and looking to stay awhile | **by PETER KING**

FROM THE START, JIMMY JOHNSON knew he would win. He knew after the Cowboys' 1–15 season in 1989. "We're going to build it the right way here, and we'll win. I'm sure of it," he said after that season. He knew after the Cowboys' 7–9 season in 1990, after which he said, "We're going to be good. Big-time good. There's no doubt about it." He knew after the Cowboys' 11–5 playoff season of 1991—everyone could feel it happening—and of course he knew on that beautiful Sunday evening in Pasadena in early 1993, when the rest of the world found out why Johnson never truly despaired in some of those dark early days he and Jerry Jones spent building the Dallas Cowboys back to prominence.

They were damned good.

Football is football, Johnson knew. Whether it be building college football's dominant team at the University of Miami or pro football's best with the Cowboys, he differed with many prominent football minds who thought great teams had to be huge and bulky and imposing. Johnson thought the best football on any level was played by fast and quick and intimidating men. Speedy guys. Tough guys. Brawling guys. They might give up 20 pounds to their adversaries, but they would fight like pit bulls to win. And they just loved football, the kind they played in the 1992 postseason, the kind that culminated in a 52–17 Super Bowl XXVII rout of Buffalo. It was the toughest of the three straight Super Bowl losses for erudite Buffalo coach Marv Levy and his Bills, and that's because the Cowboys were the toughest of the three Super Bowl teams that had pounded them.

Yes, Johnson, with Jones's money, built a team of speed and quickness and relentlessness with a franchise quarterback in Troy Aikman and a franchise runner in Emmitt Smith and a franchise pass rusher in Charles Haley leading the way. If pure power football—Giant football, Redskin football—was going to beat Johnson, fine. He had given it his best shot, doing it his way. But power football couldn't beat the Cowboys. Nor could anyone's finesse football. And it might not for a long time.

"We have players," Johnson said, emphasizing *players* in his Texas twang. "You know, while Marv Levy is over there reading about Truman, [defensive tackle] Jimmie Jones is on his bed, belly-laughing at Fred and Barney on the Flintstones."

Dallas did not corner the market on players in 1992, although the Cowboys did have rushing titlist Smith (1,713 yards) and a quarterback, Aikman, who emerged from a superb postseason (eight touchdowns, no interceptions, a 126.4 rating) as one of the game's very best. The 1992 season certainly will go down as the year of the Cowboy, but this wasn't a one-story season.

You want stories? Pick one. Green Bay, for instance. New coach Mike Holmgren turned a bunch of guys with 3–13 talent into 9–7, on-the-playoff-brink overachievers. The best new aerial combination in the game helped, with 23-year-old quarterback Brett Favre throwing darts to wideout Sterling Sharpe, who set an alltime NFL record with 108 catches. The Vikings won the NFC Central with another rookie coach,

The Cowboy win was sweet vindication for Dallas architects Johnson (left) and Jones.

AL TIELEMANS

Dennis Green, who somehow juggled the worst quarterback situation in the conference and piloted the team to an 11–5 finish. The 49ers (14–2) and Saints (12–4) were again the class of the West. Again the Saints found a way to lose the big ones—jittery quarterback Bobby Hebert, fired after the season, over and over again disappointed the football-starved Louisianans—and fellow disappointment Philadelphia

got blown out of the playoffs by the upstart Cowboys in the East.

In the AFC the stunning story happened in Pittsburgh, where rookie coach Bill Cowher energized the dormant Steeler fans. You kept waiting for the Steelers to fall to earth, but they never did until January, winning homefield advantage through the playoffs and losing to the Bills at Three Rivers Stadium. The Chargers started 0–4

A Fresh Start?

Chuck Schmidt looked flustered. Here was Schmidt, the CEO of the Detroit Lions, at the 1993 National Football League owners' meetings in California, dying to make anyone with a bit more bulk than the hotel janitor the highest-paid offensive lineman in NFL history. And no one, apparently, wanted his money in the new era of NFL free-agency. "We've got to get some linemen," he said, sounding determined to make up for the loss of two starting guards—Mike Utley, paralyzed in 1991, and Eric Andolsek, run over by a truck in 1992. But beefy Houston tackle Don Maggs signed with Denver before Schmidt could get his paws on him. Guard Houston Hoover of Atlanta defected to Cleveland, jilting the Lions too. The big hurt came when Miami guard Harry Galbreath picked Green Bay over Detroit, even though the Lions offered more money.

Join the frenzy, Chuck. In the first year

of unencumbered free-agency in the 74-year history of the league, offensive linemen became the glamour players. Just glance at the chart below to see what happened to the list of the ten highest-paid linemen before and after the advent of free-agency on March 1, 1993.

Interesting dynamic at work here. Not only did Lachey move from 1 to 8 in the salary standings in six weeks, but the Lions, in their desperation, had to vastly overpay for three marginal NFL linemen—Fralic, Richards, and former Kansac City guard David Lutz, who signed for $1.2 million a year for two years. "I'm afraid," said Jets general manager Dick Steinberg, "that we might be getting into an era where we're paying incredible money for .220-hitting shortstops and 4–10 pitchers."

So why did the Lions, and so many others, go out and pay filet-mignon prices for Salisbury-steak players? "There's more of a value on offensive linemen than any of us in the league ever thought there was," said Denver director of football

BEFORE FREE AGENCY		
	Player, Club	Avg. Salary
1.	Jim Lachey, Wash.	$1.35m
2.	Bob Whitfield, Atl.	$1.25m
3.	Jay Hilgenberg, Cle.	$1.051m
4.	Mike Munchak, Hou.	$1.05m
5.	Jackie Slater, Rams	$1.05m
6.	Tony Mandarich, GB	$1.03m
7.	Mike Kenn, Atl.	$1.025m
8.	Ray Roberts, Sea	$1.006m
9.	Bruce Matthews, Hou.	$1.00m
10.	Leon Searcy, Pitt.	$1.00m

AFTER ONE FREE-AGENCY SEASON		
	Player, Club	Avg. Salary
1.	Will Wolford, Ind.	$2.55m
2.	Kirk Lowdermilk, Ind.	$2.00m
3.	Bill Fralic, Det.	$1.80m
4.	Harry Swayne, SD	$1.80m
5.	Dave Richards, Det.	$1.70m
6.	Harry Galbreath, GB	$1.52m
7.	Brian Habib, Den.	$1.40m
8.	Gerald Perry, Raiders	$1.35m
	Jim Lachey, Wash.	$1.35m
10.	Houston Hoover, Cle.	$1.25m
	Bob Whitfield, Atl.	$1.25m

but won 11 of their last 12; 11–5 San Diego lost on a flooded Miami field in a second-round playoff game but made believers of the up-for-grabs AFC West. And the Bills. The poor, pathetic Bills. They struggled into the playoffs, losing in the regular season to Indianapolis and the Jets, then falling behind 35–3 in the playoffs to Houston. They won in overtime, 41–38, in the greatest football comeback ever. "I can feel it," defensive end Bruce Smith said. "This is our year."

Unfortunately for the Bills, though, the Cowboys could feel it too, and the result was a joke of a Super Bowl. "The ultimate embarrassment," linebacker Darryl Talley said before slinking off into the off-season. The Dallas defense just outquicked and outfoxed anything Buffalo's offense tried. It didn't hurt that Aikman played the

operations Bob Ferguson. "We're seeing how important it is to build a solid core of big, strong, smart and tenacious guys to set the tone for your offense."

The Broncos seemed to be the clever ones in the talent chase for linemen. "We had a plan," said Ferguson, "to overpay, get the guys we wanted, and get out of the market." Whew. Overpay? Admittedly? That's right, and it was a wise move. The Broncos judged Maggs the top tackle and Habib the top guard of the unrestricted free-agent class, and so Ferguson went to coach Wade Phillips and owner Pat Bowlen to see if he could go all-out to sign them. Phillips said he trusted Ferguson, and Bowlen handed him the checkbook.

Neither Maggs, a plodder Houston wasn't too sorry to lose, nor Habib, a first-year starter for the Vikings in 1992, had ever been a Pro Bowler. But Denver didn't have much of a choice. The Broncos' line allowed 52 sacks in 1992—only four teams gave up more—and everyone knows they're going nowhere unless John Elway has time to make things happen. After his visit to Denver, Maggs planned to make several trips to visit other prospective new teams. So what did Ferguson do? Offer Maggs, and then Habib, more money than they dreamed they'd be making, and not let them get out of town without agreeing to a contract. That done, the pressure now lands squarely on the front-office of the Broncos

for the players to perform like the million-dollar ballplayers they have become. "This is definitely not a system for the timid," Ferguson said.

"Now comes the hard part," said Kirk Lowdermilk, the new center of the Colts. He's never made the Pro Bowl, but he's making twice as much as the previously highest-paid center of all-time, Bruce Matthews of Houston. "Now it's time to justify the money and expectations."

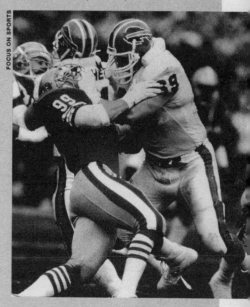

Former Bill Will Wolford will have to justify his status as the NFL's highest paid lineman.

After flirting with free agency, Smith (108 yards in the Super Bowl) stayed in Dallas.

greatest game of his life—22 of 30, 273 yards, 73% completion rate, four touchdowns, no interceptions. After a player plays a game like that, and indeed after a player plays a postseason like Aikman's, what doubt can there be that he is one of the premier players in the game?

In the rush to crown Dallas the team of the '90s, America's sporting press forgot something, though. It's a new game. No longer can general manager George Young build an offensive line for a decade with the Giants, like he tried to do in the mid-'80s. No longer can the Redskins keep a Monk–Sanders–Clark triumvirate intact to catch passes for eight or 10 years. "We're building more for the short term than we ever have before," says Jets GM Dick Steinberg, "because we don't know what tomorrow will bring." With the advent of true free agency a month after Dallas put on its crown, we can't assume that the Troy Aikman–Emmitt Smith–Michael Irvin–Erik

Williams–Charles Haley–Russell Maryland nucleus (and friends) will stay intact the way it would have in past eras.

Every great football team will have to deal with this now. As free agency showed, teams aren't building for the next six to eight years with a solid core of players. They're building for two to four years, signing aging veterans who can contribute a couple of quality seasons. And here's the critical factor: Beginning in 1994, each team will almost certainly be limited to a uniform salary cap on the amount they can spend on players, probably about $31 million. So the free-spending clubs like San Francisco and Washington will have to be relative tightwads now.

As you might expect, the Cowboys aren't daunted by the new freedom and salary restrictions. When there were rumors that Smith, the NFL's leading rusher in 1992, would be signed by another team for about $4 million a year, Johnson was asked if the Cowboys, who retained the right to match any offer to Smith, would match any contract that came down the pike. "If teams are trying to put our feet to the fire and force us to screw up our structure, they can forget it," Johnson said. "If anybody offers Emmitt that kind of money, they'd better be prepared to eat it."

"We'll figure out how to deal with free agency, like we've figured a way to deal with everything else that comes up," owner Jones said.

If they do, they'll be the team of the '90s. But who will be their competition for that title if they don't? In order, here's who will challenge Dallas as the team of the decade:

1. The 49ers. They were coming off an NFL-best 14–2 regular season in 1992, but a couple of signs early in 1993 showed they would have trouble with the looming salary cap. San Francisco, still with 1992 NFL MVP quarterback Steve Young left to sign, already lost two salary fights with great defensive players before the off-season was very old. The 49ers will have problems paying all their great players and having enough money left to pay the average guys you need to win titles. Raiders owner Al Davis said that he was stunned the 49ers allowed free-agent defensive tackle Pierce Holt—San Francisco's best defensive player— to jump to Atlanta for a guaranteed $2.5 million a year. The 49ers gambled that they could lure Reggie White for a nonguaranteed, more expensive deal and lost. This is still a great team, but a great team won't stay great for long without a continuing infusion of great players.

2. The Redskins. They were only 9–7 in 1992 to begin with, with a quarterback (Mark Rypien) who looked awful, a receiving corps (Monk–Sanders–Clark) getting old and a backfield need-

ing new talent. And then Joe Gibbs retired abruptly in March, Clark flew off to Phoenix as a free agent and the Redskins failed to land White because their offer was $3 million less than Green Bay. Now they face the same problems most teams face. Their quarterback is fallible. They have two segments of their team—receivers, offensive line—getting quite threadbare. And they can't spend Jack Kent Cooke's money like they once did to reel in a Jason Buck here, a Jumpy Geathers there. This isn't exactly a fortress that Richie Petitbon is inheriting entering the mid-'90s.

3. The Packers. Shocked to see them up this high? Don't be. Money was the primary reason that prime free-agent White chose the Packers after his March 1993

Young was the league's top-rated passer and MVP in 1993.

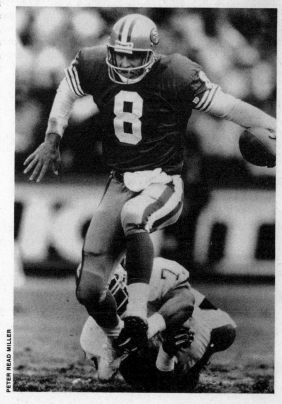

quest for a new team, but he saw things happening here. "I love the quarterback," White said in the middle of his free-agency fling. "I think he's the best young quarterback playing today." Favre came to Green Bay for a first-round pick from Atlanta before the 1992 draft, and all he did in '92 was nearly lead the Pack to the playoffs by being the sixth-rated NFL quarterback. That's better than Dan Marino, Jim Kelly or John Elway. He has Sharpe, a 28-year-

According to White, his new teammate is "the best young quarterback playing today."

JOHN BIEVER

old speedster in his prime, as his main target. The Packers beefed up their offensive line with the signing of guard Harry Galbreath and their backfield by acquiring running back John Stephens from New England. And they have the best one-two architectural punch in the NFL: G.M. Ron Wolf, who has a blank checkbook and lots of football savvy, and Holmgren, whom players respect and play hard for.

4. The Bills. Kelly's mortal. The defense will dissolve slowly through free agency, as we saw with Shane Conlan's defection to the Rams and Bruce Smith's possible defection in 1994. And the players are getting unhappy. Wouldn't you, after getting slapped in the face three straight Januaries? One more thing: G.M. Bill Polian, fired by owner Ralph Wilson, and assistant G.M. Bob Ferguson, who left for Denver, will be big losses.

5. Everybody else. The Eagles are dismantling and readying a Dallas-like run of draft choices to try to get them back on top. It's impossible to declare them serious contenders until we see who they pick in the next two drafts. The Dolphins are too myopic and not tough enough defensively; unfortunately, Dan Marino can't rush the passer. The Giants? Nah. Any team claiming to be serious about White and then contacting his agents 11 days into the free-agency period is serious all right—seriously fragmented at the top. Houston, even with Buddy Ryan, doesn't have the character. The Chargers? Now there's a bright young team. But can Stan Humphries be a prime-time quarterback, and can the defense suddenly stop aging?

One April day in 1993, almost three months after the Super Bowl, Johnson sat back in his office and mused about the near future. "No player will be more important than the team," Johnson vowed. "Free agency is going to test us on that. But I've got faith that we're going to win again, and win big."

Champions talk that way. Expect Johnson to keep talking just like that through the decade.

FOR THE RECORD · 1992 - 1993

1992 NFL Final Standings

American Football Conference

EASTERN DIVISION

	W	L	T	Pct	Pts	OP
Miami	11	5	0	.688	340	281
†Buffalo	11	5	0	.688	381	283
Indianapolis	9	7	0	.563	216	302
NY Jets	4	12	0	.250	220	315
New England	2	14	0	.125	205	363

CENTRAL DIVISION

	W	L	T	Pct	Pts	OP
Pittsburgh	11	5	0	.688	299	225
†Houston	10	6	0	.625	352	258
Cleveland	7	9	0	.438	272	275
Cincinnati	5	11	0	.313	274	364

WESTERN DIVISION

	W	L	T	Pct	Pts	OP
San Diego	11	5	0	.688	335	241
†Kansas City	10	6	0	.625	348	282
Denver	8	8	0	.500	262	329
LA Raiders	7	9	0	.438	249	281
Seattle	2	14	0	.125	140	312

† Wild Card team.

National Football Conference

EASTERN DIVISION

	W	L	T	Pct	Pts	OP
Dallas	13	3	0	.813	409	243
†Philadelphia	11	5	0	.688	354	245
†Washington	9	7	0	.563	300	255
NY Giants	6	10	0	.375	306	367
Phoenix	4	12	0	.250	243	332

CENTRAL DIVISION

	W	L	T	Pct	Pts	OP
Minnesota	11	5	0	.688	374	249
Green Bay	9	7	0	.563	276	296
Tampa Bay	5	11	0	.313	267	365
Chicago	5	11	0	.313	295	361
Detroit	5	11	0	.313	273	332

WESTERN DIVISION

	W	L	T	Pct	Pts	OP
San Francisco	14	2	0	.875	431	236
†New Orleans	12	4	0	.750	330	202
Atlanta	6	10	0	.375	327	414
LA Rams	6	10	0	.375	313	383

1993 NFL Playoffs

AFC FIRST ROUND	AFC DIVISIONAL PLAYOFF	AFC CHAMPIONSHIP	NFC CHAMPIONSHIP	NFC DIVISIONAL PLAYOFF	NFC FIRST ROUND

SUPER BOWL XXVII — January 26, 1993

Houston 38 / Buffalo 41
Buffalo 24
Buffalo 29
Pittsburgh 3

Kansas City 0 / San Diego 17
San Diego 0
Miami 10
Miami 31

DALLAS 52 / Buffalo 17

Washington 13
San Francisco 20
San Francisco 20
Philadelphia 10
Dallas 30
Dallas 34

Washington 24 / Minnesota 7
Philadelphia 36 / New Orleans 20

AFC Wild Card Games

```
Houston..................7  21   7   3   0—38
Buffalo...................3   0  28   7   3—41
```

FIRST QUARTER

Houston: Jeffires 3 pass from Moon (Del Greco kick), 9:09. Drive: 80 yards, 14 plays.
Buffalo: FG Christie 36, 13:36. Drive: 38 yards, 10 plays.

SECOND QUARTER

Houston: Slaughter 7 pass from Moon (Del Greco kick), 6:01. Drive: 80 yards, 12 plays.
Houston: Duncan 26 pass from Moon (Del Greco kick), 10:51. Drive: 67 yards, 5 plays.
Houston: Jeffires 27 pass from Moon (Del Greco kick), 14:46. Drive: 67 yards, 8 plays.

THIRD QUARTER

Houston: McDowell 58 interception return (Del Greco kick), 1:41.
Buffalo: Davis 1 run (Christie kick), 6:08. Drive: 50 yards, 10 plays.
Buffalo: Beebe 38 pass from Reich (Christie kick), 7:04. Drive: 52 yards, 4 plays.
Buffalo: Reed 26 pass from Reich (Christie kick), 10:39. Drive: 59 yards, 4 plays.
Buffalo: Reed 18 pass from Reich (Christie kick), 13:00. Drive: 23 yards, 4 plays.

FOURTH QUARTER

Buffalo: Reed 17 pass from Reich (Christie kick), 11:52. Drive: 74 yards, 7 plays.
Houston: FG Del Greco 26, 14:48. Drive: 63 yards, 12 plays.

OVERTIME

Buffalo: FG Christie 32, 3:06.

A: 75,141; T: 3:25.

```
Kansas City..............0   0   0   0— 0
San Diego................0   0  10   7—17
```

THIRD QUARTER

San Diego: Butts 54 run (Carney kick), 9:07. Drive: 74 yards, 4 plays.
San Diego: FG Carney 34, 11:27. Drive: 9 yards, 4 plays.

FOURTH QUARTER

San Diego: Hendrickson 5 run (Carney kick), 10:03. Drive: 90 yards, 10 plays.

A: 58,278; T: 3:05.

NFC Wild Card Games

```
Washington.............3  14   7   0—24
Minnesota .............7   0   0   0 —7
```

FIRST QUARTER

Minnesota: Allen 1 run (Reveiz kick), 4:55. Drive: 79 yards, 9 plays.
Washington: FG Lohmiller 44, 14:07. Drive: 6 yards, 4 plays.

SECOND QUARTER

Washington: Byner 3 run (Lohmiller kick), 5:37. Drive: 33 yards, 6 plays.
Mitchell 8 run (Lohmiller kick), 13:04. Drive: 86 yards, 10 plays.

THIRD QUARTER

Washington: Clark 24 pass from Rypien (Lohmiller kick), 14:43. Drive: 71 yards, 10 plays.

A: 57,353; T: 2:47.

```
Philadelphia............7   0   3  26—36
New Orleans .........7  10   3   0—20
```

FIRST QUARTER

New Orleans: Hayward 1 run (Andersen kick), 5:40. Drive: 73 yards, 8 plays.
Philadelphia: Barnett 57 pass from Cunningham (Ruzek kick), 11:38. Drive: 80 yards, 4 plays.

SECOND QUARTER

New Orleans: FG Andersen 35, 6:42. Drive: 71 yards, 13 plays.
New Orleans: Early 7 pass from Hebert (Andersen kick), 10:46. Drive: 53 yards, 4 plays.

THIRD QUARTER

New Orleans: FG Andersen 42, 8:32. Drive: 44 yards, 5 plays.
Philadelphia: FG Ruzek 40, 13:59. Drive: 39 yards, 9 plays.

FOURTH QUARTER

Philadelphia: Barnett 35 pass from Cunningham (Ruzek kick), 4:23. Drive: 64 yards, 9 plays.
Philadelphia: Sherman 6 run (Ruzek kick), 8:12. Drive: 26 yards, 5 plays.
Philadelphia: Safety, White tackled Hebert in end zone, 9:24.
Philadelphia: FG Ruzek 39, 12:24. Drive: 40 yards, 11 plays.
Philadelphia: Allen 18 interception return (Ruzek kick), 12:43.

A: 68,893; T: 3:02.

THEY SAID IT

Bill Belichick, Cleveland Brown coach, before a game with the San Diego Chargers: "I don't think there's anybody in this organization not focused on the 49ers.... I mean Chargers."

AFC Divisional Games

Buffalo..................0	7	7	10—24
Pittsburgh.............3	0	0	0— 3

FIRST QUARTER

Pittsburgh: FG Anderson 38, 7:46. Drive: 33 yards, 9 plays.

SECOND QUARTER

Buffalo: Frerotte 1 pass from Reich (Christie kick), 13:04. Drive: 59 yards, 9 plays.

THIRD QUARTER

Buffalo: Lofton 17 pass from Reich (Christie kick), 11:00. Drive: 80 yards, 13 plays.

FOURTH QUARTER

Buffalo: FG Christie 43, 4:47. Drive: 44 yards, 10 plays.
Buffalo: Gardner 1 run (Christie kick), 13:04. Drive: 86 yards, 8 plays.

A: 64,991; T: 2:58.

San Diego...............0	0	0	0— 0
Miami 0	21	0	10—31

SECOND QUARTER

Miami: Paige 1 pass from Marino (Stoyanovich kick), 8:30. Drive: 48 yards, 9 plays.
Miami: K. Jackson 9 pass from Marino, (Stoyanovich kick), 13:14. Drive: 37 yards, 2 plays.
Miami: K. Jackson 30 pass from Marino (Stoyanovich kick), 14:33. Drive: 42 yards, 4 plays.

FOURTH QUARTER

Miami: FG Stoyanovich 22, :57. Drive: 60 yards, 12 plays.
Miami: Craver 25 run (Stoyanovich kick), 6:41. Drive: 53 yards, 6 plays.

A: 71,224; T: 3:00.

NFC Divisional Games

Washington............3	0	3	7—13
San Francisco........7	10	0	3—20

FIRST QUARTER

San Francisco: Taylor 5 pass from Young (Cofer kick), 3:12. Drive: 83 yards, 6 plays.
Washington: FG Lohmiller 19, 10:34. Drive: 61 yards, 10 plays.

SECOND QUARTER

San Francisco: FG Cofer 23, 2:52. Drive: 76 yards, 13 plays.
San Francisco: Jones pass 16 from Young (Cofer kick), 14:36. Drive: 35 yards, 5 plays.

THIRD QUARTER

Washington: FG Lohmiller 32, 12:37. Drive: 71 yards, 14 plays.

FOURTH QUARTER

Washington: Rypien 1 run (Lohmiller kick), :24. Drive: 15 yards, 3 plays.
San Francisco: FG Cofer 33, 12:38. Drive: 59 yards, 14 plays.

A: 64,991; T: 2:58.

Philadelphia............3	0	0	7—10
Dallas......................7	10	10	7—34

FIRST QUARTER

Philadelphia: FG Ruzek 32, 7:15. Drive: 56 yards, 12 plays.
Dallas: Tennell 1 pass from Aikman (Elliott kick), 13:02. Drive: 46 yards, 10 plays.

SECOND QUARTER

Dallas: Novacek 6 pass from Aikman (Elliott kick), 14:13. Drive: 67 yards, 5 plays.
Dallas: FG Elliott 20, 15:00. Drive: 27 yards, 6 plays.

THIRD QUARTER

Dallas: E. Smith 23 run (Elliott kick), 3:44. Drive: 70 yards, 6 plays.
Dallas: FG Elliott 43, 11:43. Drive: 26 yards, 7 plays.

FOURTH QUARTER

Dallas: Gainer 1 run (Elliott kick), 11:41. Drive: 80 yards, 13 plays.
Philadelphia: C. Williams 18 pass from Cunningham (Ruzek kick), 14:10. Drive: 70 yards, 8 plays.

A: 63,721; T: 2:52.

AFC Championship

Buffalo	3	10	10	6—29
Miami	3	0	0	7—10

FIRST QUARTER

Buffalo: FG Christie 21, 9:17. Drive: 43 yards, 6 plays.
Miami: FG Stoyanovich 51, 13:03. Drive: 39 yards, 7 plays.

SECOND QUARTER

Buffalo: Thomas 17 pass from Kelly (Christie kick), :40. Drive: 64 yards, 7 plays.
Buffalo: FG Christie 33, 2:59. Drive: 2 yards, 4 plays.

THIRD QUARTER

Buffalo: Davis 2 run (Christie kick), 1:58. Drive: 24 yards, 5 plays.
Buffalo: FG Christie 21, 11:33. Drive: 67 yards, 15 plays.

FOURTH QUARTER

Buffalo: FG Christie 31, :04. Drive: 39 yards, 5 plays.
Miami: Duper 15 pass from Marino, (Stoyanovich kick), 7:28. Drive: 62 yards, 7 plays.
Buffalo: FG Christie 38, 12:23. Drive: 23 yards, 7 plays.

A: 72,703; T: 2:57.

NFC Championship

Dallas	3	7	7	13—30
San Francisco	7	3	3	7—20

FIRST QUARTER

Dallas: FG Elliott 20, 8:20. Drive: 20 yards, 5 plays.
San Francisco: Young 1 run (Cofer kick), 11:11. Drive: 48 yards, 8 plays.

SECOND QUARTER

Dallas: E. Smith 5 run (Elliott kick), 9:55. Drive: 39 yards, 7 plays.
San Francisco: FG Cofer 28, 13:41. Drive: 65 yards, 10 plays.

THIRD QUARTER

Dallas: Johnston 4 run (Elliott kick), 4:15. Drive: 78 yards, 8 plays.
San Francisco: FG Cofer 42, 8:35. Drive: 66 yards, 7 plays.

FOURTH QUARTER

Dallas: E. Smith 16 pass from Aikman (Elliott kick), 2:35. Drive: 79 yards, 4 plays.
San Francisco: Rice 5 pass from Young (Cofer kick), 10:38. Drive: 93 yards, 9 plays.
Dallas: K. Martin 6 pass from Aikman (kick failed), 11:17. Drive: 79 yards, 4 plays.

A: 64,920; T: 2:56.

Super Bowl Box Score

Buffalo	7	3	7	0—17
Dallas	14	14	3	21—52

FIRST QUARTER

Buffalo: Thomas 2 run (Christie kick), 5:00. Drive: 16 yards, 4 plays. Key plays: Tasker block of Saxon's punt from Cowboys' 16 rolls out of bounds for no gain; Tolbert's sack of Kelly on 3rd and 3 nullified by defensive holding call, giving Bills first down at Cowboys' 5. Buffalo 7, Dallas 0.
Dallas: Novacek 23 pass from Aikman (Elliott kick), 13:24. Drive: 47 yards, 6 plays. Key plays: Washington interception of Kelly's pass and 13 return to Bills' 47; Aikman 20 pass to Irvin. Dallas 7, Buffalo 7.
Dallas: J. Jones 2 fumble return (Elliott kick), 13:39. Key play: Haley 8-yard sack of Kelly forces fumble recovered by J. Jones. Dallas 14, Buffalo 7.

SECOND QUARTER

Buffalo: FG Christie 21, 11:36. Drive: 82 yards, 12 plays. Key plays: Reich, on first play after replacing injured Kelly, 7 pass to Metzelaars on 3rd and 3; Reich 38 pass to Reed. Dallas 14, Buffalo 10.
Dallas: Irvin 19 pass from Aikman (Elliott kick), 13:08. Drive: 72 yards, 5 plays. Key plays: Aikman 9 pass to Novacek; E. Smith 38 run. Dallas 21, Buffalo 10.
Dallas: Irvin 18 pass from Aikman (Elliott kick), 13:24. Drive: 18 yards, 1 play. Key play: Thomas fumble on screen pass forced by Lett and recovered by J. Jones at Bills' 18. Dallas 28, Buffalo 10.

THIRD QUARTER

Dallas: FG Elliott 20, 6:39. Drive: 77 yards, 12 plays. Key plays: E. Smith 11 run; Irvin 25 and 12 passes from Aikman. Dallas 31, Buffalo 10.
Buffalo: Beebe 40 pass from Reich (Christie kick), 15:00. Drive: 61 yards, 5 plays Key plays: K. Davis 12 run; Reed 13 pass from Reich. Dallas 31, Buffalo 17.

FOURTH QUARTER

Dallas: Harper 45 pass from Aikman (Elliott kick), 4:56. Drive: 56 yards, 2 plays. Key play: E. Smith 11 run. Dallas 38, Buffalo 17.
Dallas: E. Smith 10 run (Elliott kick), 8:12. Drive: 8 yards, 3 plays. Key play: Everett 22 interception return to Bills' 8. Dallas 45, Buffalo 17.
Dallas: Norton 9 fumble return (Elliott kick), 7:29. Dallas 52, Buffalo 17.

A: 98,374; T: 3:23.

Super Bowl Box Score (Cont.)

Team Statistics

	Buffalo	Dallas
FIRST DOWNS	22	20
Rushing	7	9
Passing	11	11
Penalty	4	0
THIRD DOWN EFF	5–11	5–11
FOURTH DOWN EFF	0–2	0–1
TOTAL NET YARDS	362	408
Total plays	71	60
Avg gain	5.1	6.8
NET YARDS RUSHING	108	137
Rushes	29	29
Avg per rush	3.7	4.7
NET YARDS PASSING	254	271
Completed-Att.	22–38	22–30
Yards per pass	6.0	8.7
Sacked-yards lost	0–0	5–46
Had intercepted	4	0
PUNTS-Avg.	3–45.3	4–32.8
TOTAL RETURN YARDS	90	149
Punt returns	1–0	3–35
Kickoff returns	4–90	4–79
Interceptions	0–0	4–35
PENALTIES-Yds	4–30	8–53
FUMBLES-Lost	8–5	4–2
TIME OF POSSESSION	28:48	31:12

Passing

BUFFALO

	Comp	Att	Yds	Int	TD
Kelly	4	7	82	2	0
Reich	18	31	194	2	1

DALLAS

	Comp	Att	Yds	Int	TD
Aikman	22	30	273	0	4
Beuerlein	0	0	0	0	0

Rushing

BUFFALO

	No.	Yds	Lg	TD
K. Davis	15	86	14	0
Thomas	11	19	9	1
Gardner	1	3	3	0
Reich	2	0	0	0

DALLAS

	No.	Yds	Lg	TD
E. Smith	22	108	38	1
Aikman	3	28	19	0
Gainer	2	1	1	0
Johnston	1	0	0	0
Beuerlein	1	0	0	0

Receiving

BUFFALO

	No.	Yds	Lg	TD
Reed	8	152	40	0
Thomas	4	10	7	0
K. Davis	3	16	13	0
Beebe	2	50	40	1
Tasker	2	30	16	0
Metzelaars	2	12	7	0
McKeller	1	6	6	0

DALLAS

	No.	Yds	Lg	TD
Novacek	7	72	23	1
Irvin	6	114	25	2
E. Smith	6	27	18	0
Johnston	2	15	8	0
Harper	1	45	45	1

Defense

BUFFALO

	Tck	Ast	Int	Sack
Bennett	8	1	0	1
Talley	6	0	0	0
Patton	6	0	0	0
B. Smith	5	0	0	0
Odomes	4	0	0	0
Conlon	3	5	0	0
Jones	3	2	0	0
Williams	3	2	0	0
Derby	3	0	0	0
Wright	3	0	0	0
Pike	3	0	0	0
Kelso	2	2	0	0
Hanson	2	1	0	0
Hale	2	0	0	0
Maddox	1	0	0	0
K. Davis	1	0	0	0
Beebe	1	0	0	0
Metzelaars	1	0	0	0
Tasker	0	1	0	0
Goganious	0	1	0	0
Awalt	0	0	0	0
Hicks	0	0	0	0

DALLAS

	Tck	Ast	Int	Sack
Norton	8	1	0	0
Haley	5	0	0	1
Washington	4	2	1	0
Edwards	4	2	0	0
Maryland	4	2	0	0
Woodson	4	0	0	0
Lett	3	0	0	1
Everett	3	0	2	1
Holmes	3	0	0	0
Casillas	2	3	0	0
Jeffcoat	2	0	0	1
Brown	2	0	1	0
J. Williams	1	0	0	0
Jones	1	0	0	0
Thomas	1	0	0	0
Ritcher	1	0	0	0
Lofton	1	0	0	0

OFFENSE

Sterling Sharpe, Green Bay	Wide Receiver
Jerry Rice, San Francisco	Wide Receiver
Jay Novacek, Dallas	Tight End
Harris Barton, San Francisco	Tackle
Richmond Webb, Miami	Tackle
Randall McDaniel, Minnesota	Guard
Steve Wisniewski, LA Raiders	Guard
Bruce Matthews, Houston	Center
Steve Young, San Francisco	Quarterback
Emmitt Smith, Dallas	Running Back
Barry Foster, Pittsburgh	Running Back

DEFENSE

Clyde Simmons, Philadelphia	Defensive End
Chris Doleman, Minnesota	Defensive End
Cortez Kennedy, Seattle	Defensive Tackle
Ray Childress, Houston	Nose Tackle
Pat Swilling, New Orleans	Outside Linebacker
Wilbur Marshall, Washington	Outside Linebacker
Junior Seau, San Diego	Inside Linebacker
Al Smith, Houston	Inside Linebacker
Rod Woodson, Pittsburgh	Cornerback
Audray McMillian, Minnesota	Cornerback
Steve Atwater, Denver	Safety
Henry Jones, Buffalo	Safety

SPECIALISTS

Pete Stoyanovich, Miami	Kicker
Rich Camarillo, Phoenix	Punter
Deion Sanders, Atlanta	Kick Returner

1992 AFC Team-by-Team Results

BUFFALO BILLS (11-5)

40	LA RAMS	7
34	at San Francisco	31
38	INDIANAPOLIS	0
41	at New England	7
10	MIAMI	37
3	at LA Raiders	20
	OPEN DATE	
24	at NY Jets	20
16	NEW ENGLAND	7
28	PITTSBURGH	20
26	at Miami	20
41	ATLANTA	14
13	at Indianapolis (OT)	16
17	NY JETS	24
27	DENVER	17
20	at New Orleans	16
3	at Houston	27
381		283

CINCINNATI BENGALS (5-11)

21	at Seattle	3
24	LA RAIDERS (OT)	21
23	at Green Bay	24
7	MINNESOTA	42
	OPEN DATE	
24	HOUSTON	38
0	at Pittsburgh	20
10	at Houston	26
30	CLEVELAND	10
31	at Chicago (OT)	28
14	at NY Jets	17
13	DETROIT	19
9	PITTSBURGH	21
21	at Cleveland	37
10	at San Diego	27
20	NEW ENGLAND	10
17	INDIANAPOLIS	21
274		364

CLEVELAND BROWNS (7-9)

3	at Indianapolis	14
23	MIAMI	27
28	at LA Raiders	16??
0	DENVER	12
	OPEN DATE	
17	PITTSBURGH	9
17	GREEN BAY	6
19	at New England	17
10	at Cincinnati	30
24	at Houston	14
13	SAN DIEGO	14
13	at Minnesota	17
27	CHICAGO	14
31	CINCINNATI	21
14	at Detroit	24
14	HOUSTON	17
13	at Pittsburgh	23
272		275

DENVER BRONCOS (8-8)

17	LA RAIDERS	13
21	SAN DIEGO	13
0	at Philadelphia	30
12	at Cleveland	0
20	KANSAS CITY	19
3	at Washington	34
27	HOUSTON	21
21	at San Diego	24
	OPEN DATE	
27	NY JETS	16
27	NY GIANTS	13
0	at LA Raiders	24
13	at Seattle (OT)	16
27	DALLAS	31
17	at Buffalo	27
10	SEATTLE	6
20	at Kansas City	42
262		329

HOUSTON OILERS (10-6)

24	PITTSBURGH	29
20	at Indianapolis	10
23	KANSAS CITY (OT)	20
27	SAN DIEGO	0
	OPEN DATE	
38	at Cincinnati	24
21	at Denver	27
26	CINCINNATI	10
20	at Pittsburgh	21
14	CLEVELAND	24
17	at Minnesota	13
16	at Miami	19
24	at Detroit	21
24	CHICAGO	7
14	GREEN BAY	16
17	at Cleveland	14
27	BUFFALO	3
352		258

INDIANAPOLIS COLTS (9-7)

14	CLEVELAND	3
10	HOUSTON	20
0	at Buffalo	38
	OPEN DATE	
24	at Tampa Bay	14
6	NY JETS (OT)	3
14	SAN DIEGO	34
31	at Miami	20
0	at San Diego	26
0	MIAMI	28
34	NEW ENGLAND (OT)	37
14	at Pittsburgh	30
16	BUFFALO (OT)	13
6	at New England	0
10	at NY Jets	6
16	PHOENIX	13
21	at Cincinnati	17
216		302

KANSAS CITY CHIEFS (10-6)

24	at San Diego	10
26	SEATTLE	7
20	at Houston (OT)	23
27	LA RAIDERS	7
19	at Denver	20
24	PHILADELPHIA	17
10	at Dallas	17
3	PITTSBURGH	27
	OPEN DATE	
16	SAN DIEGO	14
35	WASHINGTON	16
24	at Seattle	14
23	at NY Jets	7
7	at LA Raiders	28
27	NEW ENGLAND	20
21	at NY Giants	35
42	DENVER	20
348		282

LOS ANGELES RAIDERS (7-9)

13	at Denver	17
21	at Cincinnati (OT)	24
16	CLEVELAND	28
7	at Kansas City	27
13	NY GIANTS	10
20	BUFFALO	3
19	at Seattle	0
13	DALLAS	28
	OPEN DATE	
10	at Philadelphia	31
20	SEATTLE	3
24	DENVER	0
3	at San Diego	27
28	KANSAS CITY	7
7	at Miami	20
14	SAN DIEGO	36
21	at Washington	20
249		281

MIAMI DOLPHINS (11-5)

	OPEN DATE	
27	at Cleveland	23
26	LA RAMS	10
19	at Seattle	17
37	at Buffalo	10
21	ATLANTA	17
38	NEW ENGLAND	17
20	INDIANAPOLIS	31
14	at NY Jets	26
28	at Indianapolis	0
20	BUFFALO	26
19	HOUSTON	16
13	at New Orleans	24
3	at San Francisco	27
20	LA RAIDERS	7
19	NY JETS	17
16	at New England (OT)	13
340		281

NEW ENGLAND PATRIOTS (2-14)

	OPEN DATE	
0	at LA Rams	14
6	SEATTLE	10
7	BUFFALO	41
21	at NY Jets	30
12	SAN FRANCISCO	24
17	at Miami	38
17	CLEVELAND	19
7	at Buffalo	16
14	NEW ORLEANS	31
37	at Indianapolis (OT)	34
24	NY JETS	3
0	at Atlanta	34
0	INDIANAPOLIS	6
20	at Kansas City	27
10	at Cincinnati	20
13	MIAMI (OT)	16
205		363

NEW YORK JETS (4-12)

17	at Atlanta	20
10	at Pittsburgh	27
14	SAN FRANCISCO	31
10	at LA Rams	18
30	NEW ENGLAND	21
3	at Indianapolis (OT)	6
	OPEN DATE	
20	BUFFALO	24
26	MIAMI	14
16	at Denver	27
17	CINCINNATI	14
3	at New England	24
7	KANSAS CITY	23
24	at Buffalo	17
6	INDIANAPOLIS	10
17	at Miami	19
0	NEW ORLEANS	20
220		315

PITTSBURGH STEELERS (11-5)

29	at Houston	24
27	NY JETS	10
23	at San Diego	6
3	at Green Bay	17
	OPEN DATE	
9	at Cleveland	17
20	CINCINNATI	0
27	at Kansas City	3
21	HOUSTON	20
20	at Buffalo	28
17	DETROIT	14
30	INDIANAPOLIS	14
21	at Cincinnati	9
20	SEATTLE	14
6	at Chicago	30
3	MINNESOTA	6
23	CLEVELAND	13
299		225

SAN DIEGO CHARGERS (11-5)

10	KANSAS CITY	24
13	at Denver	21
6	PITTSBURGH	23
0	at Houston	27
17	SEATTLE	6
	OPEN DATE	
34	at Indianapolis	14
24	DENVER	21
26	Indianapolis	0
14	at Kansas City	16
14	at Cleveland	13
29	TAMPA BAY	14
27	LA RAIDERS	3
27	at Phoenix	21
27	CINCINNATI	10
36	at LA Raiders	14
31	at Seattle	14
335		**241**

SEATTLE SEAHAWKS (2-14)

3	CINCINNATI	21
7	at Kansas City	26
10	at New England	6
17	MIAMI	19
6	at San Diego	17
0	at Dallas	27
0	LA RAIDERS	19
10	at NY Giants	23
	OPEN DATE	
3	WASHINGTON	16
3	at LA Raiders	20
14	KANSAS CITY	24
16	DENVER (OT)	13
14	at Pittsburgh	20
17	PHILADELPHIA (OT)	20
6	at Denver	10
14	SAN DIEGO	31
140		**312**

ATLANTA FALCONS (6-10)

20	NY JETS	17
17	at Washington	24
7	NEW ORLEANS	10
31	at Chicago	41
24	GREEN BAY	10
17	at Miami	21
17	at San Francisco	56
	OPEN DATE	
30	LA RAMS	28
3	SAN FRANCISCO	41
20	PHOENIX	17
14	at Buffalo	41
34	NEW ENGLAND	0
14	at New Orleans	22
35	at Tampa Bay	7
17	DALLAS	41
27	at LA Rams	38
327		**414**

CHICAGO BEARS (5-11)

27	DETROIT	24
6	at New Orleans	28
14	NY GIANTS	27
41	ATLANTA	31
20	at Minnesota	21
	OPEN DATE	
31	TAMPA BAY	14
30	at Green Bay	10
10	MINNESOTA	38
28	CINCINNATI (OT)	31
17	at Tampa Bay	20
3	GREEN BAY	17
14	at Cleveland	27
7	at Houston	24
30	PITTSBURGH	6
3	at Detroit	16
14	at Dallas	27
295		**361**

DALLAS COWBOYS (13-3)

23	WASHINGTON	10
34	at NY Giants	28
31	PHOENIX	20
	OPEN DATE	
7	at Philadelphia	31
27	SEATTLE	0
17	KANSAS CITY	10
28	at LA Raiders	13
20	PHILADELPHIA	10
37	at Detroit	3
23	LA RAMS	27
16	at Phoenix	10
30	NY GIANTS	3
31	at Denver	27
17	at Washington	20
41	at Atlanta	17
27	CHICAGO	14
409		**243**

DETROIT LIONS (5-11)

24	at Chicago	27
31	MINNESOTA	17
10	at Washington	13
23	TAMPA BAY	27
7	NEW ORLEANS	13
	OPEN DATE	
14	at Minnesota	31
38	at Tampa Bay	7
13	GREEN BAY	27
3	DALLAS	37
14	at Pittsburgh	17
19	at Cincinnati	13
21	HOUSTON	24
10	at Green Bay*	38
24	CLEVELAND	14
16	CHICAGO	3
6	at San Francisco	24
273		**332**

GREEN BAY PACKERS (9-7)

20	MINNESOTA (OT)	23
3	at Tampa Bay	31
24	CINCINNATI	23
17	PITTSBURGH	3
10	at Atlanta	24
	OPEN DATE	
6	at Cleveland	17
10	CHICAGO	30
27	at Detroit	13
7	at NY Giants	27
27	PHILADELPHIA*	24
17	at Chicago	3
19	TAMPA BAY*	14
38	DETROIT*	10
16	at Houston	14
28	LA RAMS	13
7	at Minnesota	27
276		**296**

LOS ANGELES RAMS (6-10)

7	at Buffalo	40
14	NEW ENGLAND	0
10	at Miami	26
18	NY JETS	10
24	at San Francisco	27
10	at New Orleans	13
38	NY GIANTS	17
	OPEN DATE	
28	at Atlanta	30
14	PHOENIX	20
27	at Dallas	23
10	SAN FRANCISCO	27
17	MINNESOTA	31
31	at Tampa Bay	27
14	NEW ORLEANS	37
13	at Green Bay	28
38	ATLANTA	27
313		**383**

MINNESOTA VIKINGS (11-5)

23	at Green Bay (OT)	20
17	at Detroit	31
26	TAMPA BAY	20
42	at Cincinnati	7
21	CHICAGO	20
	OPEN DATE	
31	DETROIT	14
13	WASHINGTON	15
38	at Chicago	10
35	at Tampa Bay	7
13	HOUSTON	17
17	CLEVELAND	13
31	at LA Rams	17
17	at Philadelphia	28
17	SAN FRANCISCO	20
6	at Pittsburgh	3
27	GREEN BAY	7
374		**249**

NEW ORLEANS SAINTS (12-4)

13	at Philadelphia	15
28	CHICAGO	6
10	at Atlanta	7
10	SAN FRANCISCO	16
13	at Detroit	7
13	LA RAMS	10
30	at Phoenix	21
	OPEN DATE	
23	TAMPA BAY	21
31	at New England	14
20	at San Francisco	21
20	WASHINGTON	3
24	MIAMI	13
22	ATLANTA	14
37	at LA Rams	14
16	BUFFALO	20
20	at NY Jets	0
330		**202**

NEW YORK GIANTS (6-10)

14	SAN FRANCISCO	31
28	DALLAS	34
27	at Chicago	14
	OPEN DATE	
10	at LA Raiders	13
31	PHOENIX	21
17	at LA Rams	38
23	SEATTLE	10
24	at Washington	7
27	GREEN BAY	7
13	at Denver	27
34	PHILADELPHIA	47
3	at Dallas	30
10	WASHINGTON	28
0	at Phoenix	19
35	KANSAS CITY	21
10	at Philadelphia	20
306		**367**

PHILADELPHIA EAGLES (11-5)

15	NEW ORLEANS	13
31	at Phoenix	14
30	DENVER	0
	OPEN DATE	
31	DALLAS	7
17	at Kansas City	24
12	at Washington	16
7	PHOENIX	3
10	at Dallas	20
31	LA RAIDERS	10
24	at Green Bay	27
47	at NY Giants	34
14	at San Francisco	20
28	MINNESOTA	17
20	at Seattle (OT)	17
17	WASHINGTON	13
20	NY GIANTS	10
354		**245**

PHOENIX CARDINALS (4-12)

7	at Tampa Bay	23
14	PHILADELPHIA	31
20	at Dallas	31
	OPEN DATE	
27	WASHINGTON	24
21	at NY Giants	31
21	NEW ORLEANS	30
3	at Philadelphia	7
24	SAN FRANCISCO	14
20	at LA Rams	14
17	at Atlanta	20
10	DALLAS	16
3	at Washington	31
21	SAN DIEGO	27
19	NY GIANTS	0
13	at Indianapolis	16
3	TAMPA BAY	7
243		**332**

SAN FRANCISCO 49ERS (14-2)

31	at NY Giants	14
31	BUFFALO	34
31	at NY Jets	14
16	at New Orleans	10
27	LA RAMS	24
24	at New England	12
56	ATLANTA	17
	OPEN DATE	
14	at Phoenix	24
41	at Atlanta	3
21	NEW ORLEANS	20
27	at LA Rams	10
20	PHILADELPHIA	14
27	MIAMI	3
20	at Minnesota	17
21	TAMPA BAY	14
24	DETROIT	6
431		**236**

TAMPA BAY BUCCANEERS (5-11)

23	PHOENIX	7
31	GREEN BAY	3
20	at Minnesota	26
27	at Detroit	23
14	INDIANAPOLIS	24
	OPEN DATE	
14	at Chicago	31
7	DETROIT	38
21	at New Orleans	23
7	MINNESOTA	35
20	CHICAGO	17
14	at San Diego	29
14	vs Green Bay	19
27	LA RAMS	31
7	ATLANTA	35
14	at San Francisco	21
7	at Phoenix	3
267		**365**

WASHINGTON REDSKINS (9-7)

10	at Dallas	23
24	ATLANTA	17
13	DETROIT	10
	OPEN DATE	
24	at Phoenix	27
34	DENVER	3
16	PHILADELPHIA	12
15	at Minnesota	13
7	NY GIANTS	24
16	at Seattle	3
16	at Kansas City	35
3	at New Orleans	20
41	PHOENIX	3
28	at NY Giants	10
20	DALLAS	17
13	at Philadelphia	17
20	LA RAIDERS	20
300		**255**

American Football Conference
Scoring

TOUCHDOWNS	TD	Rush	Rec	Ret	Pts	KICKING	PAT	FG	Lg	Pts
Thomas. Buff	12	9	3	0	72	Stoyanovich, Mia	34/36	30/37	53	124
Foster, Pitt	11	11	0	0	66	Christie, Buff	43/44	24/30	54	115
Givins, Hou	10	0	10	0	60	Anderson, Pitt	29/31	28/36	49	113
Culver, Ind	9	7	2	0	54	Carney, SD	35/35	26/32	50	113
Jeffires, Hou	9	0	9	0	54	Lowery, KC	39/39	22/24	52	105
Fenner, Cin	8	7	1	0	48	Del Greco, Hou	41/41	21/27	54	104
Jackson, Den	8	0	8	0	48	Stover, Cle	29/30	21/29	51	92
Miller, SD	8	0	7	1	48	Breech, Cin	31/31	19/27	48	88
White, Hou	8	7	1	0	48	Treadwell, Den	28/28	20/24	46	88
Brown, Rai	7	0	7	0	42	Jaeger, Rai	28/28	15/26	54	73

Passing

	Att	Comp	Pct Comp	Yds	Avg Gain	TD	Pct TD	Int	Pct Int	Lg	Rating Pts
Moon, Hou	346	224	64.7	2521	7.29	18	5.2	12	3.5	72	89.3
Marino, Mia	554	330	59.6	4116	7.43	24	4.3	16	2.9	t62	85.1
O'Donnell, Pitt	313	185	59.1	2283	7.29	13	4.2	9	2.9	51	83.6
Kelly, Buff	462	269	58.2	3457	7.48	23	5.0	19	4.1	t65	81.2
Carlson, Hou	227	149	65.6	1710	7.53	9	4.0	11	4.8	65	81.2
Krieg, KC	413	230	55.7	3115	7.54	15	3.6	12	2.9	t77	79.9
Humphries, SD	454	263	57.9	3356	7.39	16	3.5	18	4.0	t67	76.4
Elway, Den	316	174	55.1	2242	7.09	10	3.2	17	5.4	t80	65.7
Schroeder, Rai	253	123	48.6	1476	5.83	11	4.3	11	4.3	53	63.3
George, Ind	306	167	54.6	1963	6.42	7	2.3	15	4.9	t57	61.5

Pass Receiving

RECEPTIONS	No.	Yds	Avg	Lg	TD	YARDS	Yds	No.	Avg	Lg	TD
Jeffires, Hou	90	913	10.1	47	9	Miller, SD	1060	72	14.7	t67	7
Duncan, Hou	82	954	11.6	72	1	Duncan, Hou	954	82	11.6	72	1
Harmon, SD	79	914	11.6	55	1	Harmon, SD	914	79	11.6	55	1
Williams, Sea	74	556	7.5	27	2	Jeffires, Hou	913	90	10.1	47	9
Miller, SD	72	1060	14.7	t67	7	Reed, Buff	913	65	14.0	51	3
Givins, Hou	67	787	11.7	41	10	Langhorne, Ind	811	65	12.5	34	1
Reed, Buff	65	913	14.0	51	3	Hester, Ind	792	52	15.2	81	1
Langhorne,.Ind	65	811	12.5	34	1	Fryar, NE	791	55	14.4	t54	4
Thomas, Buff	58	626	10.8	43	3	Givins, Hou	787	67	11.7	41	10
Burkett, NYJ	57	724	11.2	t37	1	Lofton, Buff	786	51	15.4	50	6

Rushing

	Att	Yds	Avg	Lg	TD
Foster, Pitt	390	1690	4.3	69	11
Thomas, Buff	312	1487	4.8	44	9
White, Hou	265	1226	4.6	44	7
Green, Cin	265	1170	4.4	53	2
Warren, Sea	223	1017	4.6	52	3
Higgs, Mia	256	915	3.6	23	7
Butts, SD	218	809	3.7	22	4
Dickerson, Rai	187	729	3.9	t40	2
Baxter, NYJ	152	698	4.6	30	6
Green, Den	161	648	4.0	t67	2

Total Yards from Scrimmage

	Total	Rush	Rec
Thomas, Buff	2113	1487	626
Foster, Pitt	2034	1690	344
White, Hou	1867	1226	641
Green, Cin	1384	1170	214
Warren, Sea	1151	1017	134
Harmon, SD	1149	235	914
Johnson, Ind	1109	592	517
Miller, SD	1059	-1	1060
Higgs, Mia	1057	915	142
Humphrey, Mia	978	471	507

Interceptions

	No.	Yds	Lg	TD
Jones, Buff	8	263	t82	2
Robinson, Sea	7	126	49	0
Carter, KC	7	65	t36	1
Kelso, Buff	7	21	13	0
Carrington, SD	6	152	69	1
Brim, NYJ	6	139	t77	1
Perry, Pitt	6	69	34	0
Washington, NYJ	6	59	t23	1
Prior, Ind	6	44	19	0
Gray, Hou	6	24	22	0

Sacks

O'Neal, SD	17.0
Fletcher, Den	16.0
N. Smith, KC	14.5
Thomas, KC	14.5
Cox, Mia	14.0
Kennedy, Sea	14.0
B. Smith, Buff	14.0
Childress, Hou	13.0
A. Smith, Rai	13.0

American Football Conference (Cont.)

Punting

	No.	Yds	Avg	Net Avg	TB	In 20	Lg	Blk	Ret	Ret Yds
Montgomery, Hou	53	2487	46.9	37.3	9	14	66	2	31	255
Stark, Ind	83	3716	44.8	39.3	7	22	64	0	45	313
Tuten, Sea	108	4760	44.1	38.7	8	29	65	0	56	416
Barker, KC	75	3245	43.3	35.3	13	16	65	1	35	300
Royals, Pitt	73	3119	42.7	35.6	9	22	58	1	39	308

Punt Returns

	No.	Yds	Avg	Lg	TD
Woodson, Pitt	32	364	11.4	t80	1
Verdin, Ind	24	268	11.2	t84	2
Marshall, Den	33	349	10.6	47	0
Carter, KC	38	398	10.5	t86	2
Brown, Rai	37	383	10.4	40	0

Kickoff Returns

	No.	Yds	Avg	Lg	TD
Vaughn, NE	20	564	28.2	t100	1
Baldwin, Cle	30	675	22.5	47	0
Montgomery, Den	21	466	22.2	64	0
Verdin, Ind	39	815	20.9	42	0
Ball, Cin	20	411	20.6	48	1

National Football Conference

Scoring

TOUCHDOWNS	TD	Rush	Rec	Ret	Pts
E. Smith, Dall	19	18	1	0	114
Allen, Minn	15	13	2	0	90
Hampton, NYG	14	14	0	0	84
Sharpe, GB	13	0	13	0	78
Anderson, Chi	11	5	6	0	66
Rice, SF	11	1	10	0	66
Rison, Atl	11	0	11	0	66
Watters, SF	11	9	2	0	66
Gary, Rams	10	7	3	0	60
Haynes, Atl	10	0	10	0	60
Sanders, Det	10	9	1	0	60

KICKING	PAT	FG	Lg	Pts
Andersen, NO	33/34	29/34	52	120
Lohmiller, Wash	30/30	30/40	53	120
Elliott, Dall	47/48	24/35	53	119
Cofer, SF	53/54	18/27	46	107
Reveiz, Minn	45/45	19/25	52	102
Jacke, GB	30/30	22/29	53	96
Hanson, Det	30/30	22/29	52	93
Johnson, Atl	39/39	18/22	54	93
Butler, Chi	34/34	19/26	50	91
Ruzek, Phi	40/44	16/25	50	88
Zendejas, Rams	38/38	15/20	49	83

Passing

	Att	Comp	Pct Comp	Yds	Avg Gain	TD	Pct TD	Int	Pct Int	Lg	Rating Pts
Young, SF	402	268	66.7	3465	8.62	25	6.2	7	1.7	t80	107.0
Miller, Atl	253	152	60.1	1739	6.87	15	5.9	6	2.4	t89	90.7
Aikman, Dall	473	302	63.8	3445	7.28	23	4.9	14	3.0	t87	89.5
Cunningham, Phi	384	233	60.7	2775	7.23	19	4.9	11	2.9	t75	87.3
Favre, GB	471	302	64.1	3227	6.85	18	3.8	13	2.8	t76	85.3
Hebert, NO	422	249	59.0	3287	7.79	19	4.5	16	3.8	t72	82.9
Everett, Rams	475	281	59.2	3323	7.00	22	4.6	18	3.8	t67	80.2
Chandler, Pho	413	245	59.3	2832	6.86	15	3.6	15	3.6	t72	77.1
Harbaugh, Chi	358	202	56.4	2486	6.94	13	3.6	12	3.4	t83	76.2
Testaverde, TB	358	206	57.5	2554	7.13	14	3.9	16	4.5	t81	74.2

Pass Receiving

RECEPTIONS	No.	Yds	Avg	Lg	TD
Sharpe, GB	108	1461	13.5	t76	13
Rison, Atl	93	1121	12.1	t71	11
Rice, SF	84	1201	14.3	t80	10
Irvin, Dall	78	1396	17.9	t87	7
Pritchard, Atl	77	827	10.7	t38	5
Perriman, Det	69	810	11.7	t40	4
E. Martin, NO	68	1041	15.3	t52	5
Novacek, Dall	68	630	9.3	34	6
Barnett, Phil	67	1083	16.2	t71	6
Clark, Wash	64	912	14.3	47	5

YARDS	Yds	No.	Avg	Lg	TD
Sharpe, GB	1461	108	13.5	t76	13
Irvin, Dall	1396	78	17.9	t87	7
Rice, SF	1201	84	14.3	t80	10
Rison, Atl	1121	93	12.1	t71	11
Barnett, Phil	1083	67	16.2	t71	6
E. Martin, NO	1041	68	15.3	t52	5
Moore, Det	966	51	18.9	t77	4
Clark, Wash	912	64	14.3	47	5
R. Hill, Pho	861	58	14.8	49	3
Pritchard, Atl	827	77	10.7	t38	5

National Football Conference (Cont.)

Rushing

	Att	Yds	Avg	Lg	TD
E. Smith, Dall	373	1713	4.6	t68	18
B. Sanders, Det	312	1352	4.3	t55	9
Allen, Minn	266	1201	4.5	51	13
Cobb, TB	310	1171	3.8	25	9
Hampton, NYG	257	1141	4.4	t63	14
Gary, LA Rams	279	1125	4.0	63	7
Walker, Phil	267	1070	4.0	38	8
Watters, SF	206	1013	4.9	43	9
Byner, Wash	262	998	3.8	23	6
Johnson, Phoe	178	734	4.1	t42	6

Total Yards from Scrimmage

	Total	Rush	Rec
E. Smith, Dall	2048	1713	335
Allen, Minn	1679	1201	478
Sanders, Det	1577	1352	225
Sharpe, GB	1469	8	1461
Gary, LA Rams	1418	1125	293
Watters, SF	1418	1013	405
Irvin, Dall	1387	-9	1396
Hampton, NYG	1356	1141	215
Walker, Phil	1348	1070	278
Byner, Wash	1336	998	338

Interceptions

	No.	Yds	Lg	TD
McMillian, Minn	8	157	t51	2
Woolford, Chi	7	67	32	0
Edwards, Wash	6	157	t53	1
Cook, NO	6	90	t48	1

Note: Four players tied with five.

Sacks

Simmons, Phil	19.0
Harris, SF	17.0
Martin, NO	15.5
Doleman, Minn	14.5
White, Phil	14.0
Bennett, GB	13.5
Jackson, NO	13.5
Randle, Minn	11.5

Punting

	No.	Yds	Avg	Net Avg	TB	In 20	Lg	Blk	Ret	Ret Yds
Newsome, Minn	72	3243	45.0	35.7	15	19	84	1	34	339
Barnhardt, NO	67	2947	44.0	37.7	10	19	62	0	31	218
Arnold, Det	65	2846	43.8	34.7	10	12	71	1	30	356
Landeta, NY Giants	53	2317	43.7	31.5	9	13	71	2	30	406
Saxon, Dall	61	2620	43.0	33.5	9	19	58	0	34	397

Punt Returns

	No.	Yds	Avg	Lg	TD
Bailey, Pho	20	263	13.2	65	0
Martin, Dall	42	532	12.7	t79	2
Sikahema, Phil	40	503	12.6	t87	1
Parker, Minn	33	336	10.2	42	0
Buckley, GB	21	211	10.0	t58	1

Kickoff Returns

	No.	Yds	Avg	Lg	TD
Sanders, Atl	40	1067	26.7	t99	2
Bailey, Pho	28	690	24.6	63	0
Gray, Det	42	1006	24.0	t89	1
Meggett, NYG	20	455	22.8	t92	1
Lewis, Chi	23	511	22.2	t97	1

Anthonia Who?

Do the 49ers have a bottomless pool of talent? Sure seems that way. Lose Joe Montana, plug in Steve Young. Lose John Taylor, plug in Mike Sherrard. Lose Ricky Watters, plug in Anthonia Wayne Lee. That's Amp Lee, for short. In fact, it's the league's shortest name.

But Lee was long on ability in a 20–17 win at Minnesota in December, rushing 23 times for 134 yards and scoring twice. The 49ers drafted Watters and Lee in the second round of the 1991 and '92 drafts, respectively, in the hope that one of them would develop into a long-term replacement for departed multipurpose back Roger Craig. Both might fit the bill.

Watters looked like a franchise back for the first three months of the season, but then he suffered a deep shoulder bruise against the Eagles on Nov. 29. In stepped Lee. "Several times this year I completely forgot to pick up my paycheck because I didn't feel I had done anything," says Lee. "It was like Wednesday or Thursday before I went to get it." Players are paid after games on Sunday, and after the Minmnesota game Lee picked up his check on time. No back in the league had a better day than he did.

AFC Total Offense

	Total Yds	Yds Rush	Yds Pass	Time of Poss	Avg Pts/Game
Buffalo	5893	2436	3457	28:10	23.8
Houston	5655	1626	4029	31:09	22
Miami	5500	1525	3975	30:30	21.3
San Diego	5221	1875	3346	32:02	20.9
Pittsburgh	4906	2156	2750	32:05	18.7
Cleveland	4492	1607	2885	30:13	17
NY Jets	4431	1752	2679	30:24	13.8
Denver	4430	1500	2930	28:14	16.4
LA Raiders	4384	1794	2590	29:06	15.6
Indianapolis	4368	1102	3266	28:17	13.5
Kansas City	4324	1532	2792	29:37	21.8
Cincinnati	3919	1976	1943	27:06	17.1
New England	3584	1550	2034	28:28	12.8
Seattle	3374	1596	1778	29:01	8.8

AFC Total Defense

	Opp Total Yds	Opp Yds Rush	Opp Yds Pass	Avg PA/Game
Houston	4211	1634	2577	16.1
San Diego	4227	1395	2832	15.1
Kansas City	4324	1787	2537	17.6
LA Raiders	4516	1683	2833	17.6
Miami	4583	1600	2983	17.6
Seattle	4583	1922	2661	19.5
Buffalo	4604	1395	3209	17.7
Pittsburgh	4658	1841	2817	14.1
Cleveland	4757	1605	3152	17.2
NY Jets	4880	1919	2961	19.7
New England	5048	1951	3097	22.7
Indianapolis	5074	2174	2900	18.9
Denver	5083	1963	3120	20.6
Cincinnati	5333	2007	3326	22.8

NFC Total Offense

	Total Yds	Yds Rush	Yds Pass	Time of Poss	Avg Pts/Game
San Francisco	6195	2315	3880	32:19	26.9
Dallas	5606	2121	3485	33:57	25.6
Philadelphia	4980	2388	2592	31:47	22.1
Chicago	4941	1871	3070	29:15	18.4
Atlanta	4905	1270	3635	28:36	20.4
Minnesota	4899	2030	2869	29:18	23.4
Washington	4890	1727	3163	31:04	18.8
LA Rams	4877	1659	3218	28:31	19.6
New Orleans	4806	1628	3178	31:10	20.6
Green Bay	4786	1556	3230	32:30	17.3
Tampa Bay	4771	1706	3065	29:15	16.7
Phoenix	4577	1491	3086	31:02	15.2
Detroit	4440	1644	2796	27:36	17.1
NY Giants	4412	2077	2335	29:22	19.1

NFC Total Defense

	Opp Total Yds	Opp Yds Rush	Opp Yds Pass	Avg PA/Game
Dallas	3933	1244	2689	15.2
New Orleans	4075	1605	2470	12.6
Philadelphia	4402	1481	2921	15.3
Washington	4438	1696	2742	15.9
Minnesota	4515	1733	2782	15.6
San Francisco	4787	1418	3369	14.8
Chicago	4952	1948	3004	22.6
NY Giants	5043	2012	3031	22.9
Detroit	5058	1841	3217	20.8
Green Bay	5098	1821	3277	18.5
Phoenix	5126	1635	3491	20.8
Tampa Bay	5185	1675	3510	22.8
LA Rams	5524	2231	3293	23.9
Atlanta	5549	2294	3255	25.9

Takeaways/Giveaways

AFC

	Takeaways Int	Fum	Total	Giveaways Int	Fum	Total	Net Diff
Kansas City	24	15	39	12	9	21	18
Pittsburgh	22	21	43	14	18	32	11
Cincinnati	16	17	33	17	10	27	6
Cleveland	13	20	33	16	12	28	5
San Diego	25	11	36	21	12	33	3
NY Jets	21	18	39	24	15	39	0
Miami	18	14	32	17	17	34	-2
Indianapolis	20	15	35	26	11	37	-2
Buffalo	23	12	35	21	17	38	-3
Houston	20	11	31	23	12	35	-4
Seattle	20	12	32	23	18	41	-9
Denver	15	16	31	29	15	44	-13
New England	14	15	29	19	26	45	-16
LA Raiders	12	7	19	23	15	38	-19

NFC

	Takeaways Int	Fum	Total	Giveaways Int	Fum	Total	Net Diff
Minnesota	28	14	42	15	17	32	10
Washington	23	11	34	17	7	24	10
New Orleans	18	20	38	16	13	29	9
Philadelphia	24	13	37	13	15	28	9
San Francisco	17	12	29	9	13	22	7
Dallas	17	14	31	15	9	24	7
Tampa Bay	20	13	33	20	9	29	4
NY Giants	14	12	26	10	13	23	3
Green Bay	15	19	34	15	21	36	-2
LA Rams	18	15	33	20	17	37	-4
Detroit	21	11	32	21	15	36	-4
Chicago	14	16	30	24	10	34	-4
Atlanta	11	12	23	15	14	29	-6
Phoenix	16	12	28	24	18	42	-14

THEY SAID IT

Bruce Coslet, New York Jet coach, on the NFL's new free agency system: "It's like recruiting for college, only the money's on the table instead of under it."

Conference Rankings

American Football Conference

	Offense			Defense		
	Total	Rush	Pass	Total	Rush	Pass
Buffalo	1	1	3	7	1T	13
Cincinnati	12	3	13	14	13	14
Cleveland	6	8	7	9	4	12
Denver	8	13	6	13	12	11
Houston	2	7	1	1	5	2
Indianapolis	10	14	5	12	14	7
Kansas City	11	11	8	3	7	1
LA Raiders	9	5	11	4	6	6
Miami	3	12	2	5T	3	9
New England	13	10	12	11	11	10
NY Jets	7	6	10	10	9	8
Pittsburgh	5	2	9	8	8	4
San Diego	4	4	4	2	1T	5
Seattle	14	9	14	5T	10	3

National Football Conference

	Offense			Defense		
	Total	Rush	Pass	Total	Rush	Pass
Atlanta	5	14	2	14	14	9
Chicago	4	6	9	7	11	6
Dallas	2	3	3	1	1	2
Detroit	13	10	12	9	10	8
Green Bay	10	12	4	10	9	10
LA Rams	8	9	5	13	13	11
Minnesota	6	5	11	5	8	4
New Orleans	9	11	6	2	4	1
NY Giants	14	4	14	8	12	7
Philadelphia	3	1	13	3	3	5
Phoenix	12	13	8	11	5	13
San Francisco	1	2	1	6	2	12
Tampa Bay	11	8	10	12	6	14
Washington	7	7	7	4	7	3

1992 AFC Team-by-Team Statistical Leaders

Buffalo Bills

SCORING	TD Rush	Rec	Ret	PAT	FG	S	Pts
Christie	0	0	0	43/44	24/30	0	115
Thomas	9	3	0	0/0	0/0	0	72
K. Davis	6	0	0	0/0	0/0	0	36
Lofton	0	6	0	0/0	0/0	0	36
Metzelaars	0	6	0	0/0	0/0	0	36

RUSHING	No.	Yds	Avg	Lg	TD
Thomas	312	1487	4.8	44	9
K. Davis	139	613	4.4	t64	6
Gardner	40	166	4.2	19	2
Reed	8	65	8.1	24	0
Kelly	31	53	1.7	10	1

PASSING	Att	Comp	Pct Comp	Yds	Avg Gain	TD	Int	Rating Pts
Kelly	462	269	58.2	3457	7.48	23	19	81.2
Reich	47	24	51.1	221	4.70	0	2	46.5

RECEIVING	No.	Yds	Avg	Lg	TD
Reed	65	913	14.0	51	3
Thomas	58	626	10.8	43	3
Lofton	51	786	15.4	50	6
Beebe	33	554	16.8	t65	2
Metzelaars	30	298	9.9	t53	6

INTERCEPTIONS: Jones, 8

PUNTING	No.	Yds	Avg	Net Avg	In TB	20	Lg	Blk
Mohr	60	2531	42.2	36.8	7	13	61	0

SACKS: Smith, 14.0

Cincinnati Bengals

SCORING	TD Rush	Rec	Ret	PAT	FG	S	Pts
Breech	0	0	0	31/31	19/27	0	88
Fenner	7	1	0	0/0	0/0	0	48
Ball	2	2	0	0/0	0/0	0	24
Query	0	3	0	0/0	0/0	0	18
McGee	0	3	0	0/0	0/0	0	18

RUSHING	No.	Yds	Avg	Lg	TD
Green	265	1170	4.4	53	2
Fenner	112	500	4.5	t35	7
Hollas	20	109	5.5	24	0
Esiason	21	66	3.1	15	0
Ball	16	55	3.4	17	2

PASSING	Att	Comp	Pct Comp	Yds	Avg Gain	TD	Int	Rating Pts
Esiason	278	144	51.8	1407	5.06	11	15	57.0
Klingler	98	47	48.0	530	5.41	3	2	66.3
Hollas	58	35	60.3	335	5.78	2	0	87.9

RECEIVING	No.	Yds	Avg	Lg	TD
Green	41	214	5.2	19	0
McGee	35	408	11.7	36	3
Pickens	26	326	12.5	38	1
Holman	26	266	10.2	t26	2
Rembert	19	219	11.5	27	0

INTERCEPTIONS: D. Williams, 4

PUNTING	No.	Yds	Avg	Net Avg	In TB	20	Lg	Blk
Johnson	76	3196	42.1	35.9	9	15	64	0

SACKS: A. Williams, 10.0

End Zone

For years Ron Dixon has fired a cannon on the sideline whenever the San Diego Chargers have scored a touchdown, field goal or safety in a home game. That was a busy job in the Dan Fouts era; Dixon fired the cannon 16 times at one game. But, after the Chargers went 0–3 to start the 1992 season, the club told Dixon he could fire when the team was introduced before the game. Even so, he shot the thing only six times in the Chargers' first two home games last year—two introductions, three field goals and one touchdown. "I am the Maytag repairman," he says.

Cleveland Browns

SCORING

SCORING	Rush	TD Rec	Ret	PAT	FG	S	Pts
Stover	0	0	0	29/30	21/29	0	92
Metcalf	1	5	1	0/0	0/0	0	42
M. Jackson	0	7	0	0/0	0/0	0	42
Mack	6	0	0	0/0	0/0	0	36

RUSHING

RUSHING	No.	Yds	Avg	Lg	TD
Mack	169	543	3.2	37	6
Vardell	99	369	3.7	35	0
Metcalf	73	301	4.1	31	1
Hoard	54	236	4.4	37	0
Tomczak	24	39	1.6	16	0
Baldwin	10	31	3.1	11	0

PASSING

PASSING	Att	Comp	Pct Comp	Yds	Avg Gain	TD	Int	Rating Pts
Tomczak	211	120	56.9	1693	8.02	7	7	80.1
Kosar	155	103	66.5	1160	7.48	8	7	87.0

RECEIVING

RECEIVING	No.	Yds	Avg	Lg	TD
M. Jackson	47	755	16.1	t69	7
Metcalf	47	614	13.1	t69	5
Hoard	26	310	11.9	t46	1
Tillman	25	498	19.9	52	0
Bavaro	25	315	12.6	39	2

INTERCEPTIONS: Newsome and Walls, 3

PUNTING	No.	Yds	Avg	Net Avg	In TB	20	Lg	Blk
Hansen	74	3083	41.7	36.1	7	28	73	1

SACKS: Burnett and Matthews, 9

Houston Oilers

SCORING

SCORING	Rush	TD Rec	Ret	PAT	FG	S	Pts
Del Greco	0	0	0	41/41	21/27	0	104
Givins	0	10	0	0/0	0/0	0	60
Jeffires	0	9	0	0/0	0/0	0	54
White	7	1	0	0/0	0/0	0	48
Slaughter	0	4	0	0/0	0/0	0	24

RUSHING

RUSHING	No.	Yds	Avg	Lg	TD
White	265	1226	4.6	44	7
Moon	27	147	5.4	23	1
G. Brown	19	87	4.6	26	1
Carlson	27	77	2.9	13	1

PASSING

PASSING	Att	Comp	Pct Comp	Yds	Avg Gain	TD	Int	Rating Pts
Moon	346	224	64.7	2521	7.29	18	12	89.3
Carlson	227	149	65.6	1710	7.53	9	11	81.2

RECEIVING

RECEIVING	No.	Yds	Avg	Lg	TD
Jeffires	90	913	10.1	47	9
Duncan	82	954	11.6	72	1
Givins	67	787	11.7	41	10
White	57	641	11.2	t69	1
Slaughter	39	486	12.5	t36	4

INTERCEPTIONS: Gray, 6

PUNTING	No.	Yds	Avg	Net Avg	In TB	20	Lg	Blk
Gr. Montgomery	53	2487	46.9	37.3	9	14	66	2

SACKS: Childress, 13.0

Denver Broncos

SCORING

SCORING	Rush	TD Rec	Ret	PAT	FG	S	Pts
Treadwell	0	0	0	28/28	20/24	0	88
Jackson	0	8	0	0/0	0/0	0	48
Lewis	4	0	0	0/0	0/0	0	24
Rivers	3	1	0	0/0	0/0	0	24

Four tied with 12.

RUSHING

RUSHING	No.	Yds	Avg	Lg	TD
Green	161	648	4.0	t67	2
Rivers	74	282	3.8	48	3
Lewis	73	268	3.7	22	4
Elway	34	94	2.8	9	2
S. Smith	23	94	4.1	15	0

PASSING

PASSING	Att	Comp	Pct Comp	Yds	Avg Gain	TD	Int	Rating Pts
Elway	316	174	55.1	2242	7.09	10	17	65.7
Maddox	121	66	54.5	757	6.26	5	9	56.4
Moore	34	17	50.0	232	6.82	0	3	35.4

RECEIVING

RECEIVING	No.	Yds	Avg	Lg	TD
Sharpe	53	640	12.1	56	2
Jackson	48	745	15.5	t51	8
Rivers	45	449	10.0	37	1
Marshall	26	493	19.0	t80	1
V. Johnson	24	294	12.3	40	2

INTERCEPTIONS: D. Smith and Henderson, 4

PUNTING	No.	Yds	Avg	Net Avg	In TB	20	Lg	Blk
Horan	37	1681	45.4	40.2	1	7	62	1
Parker	12	491	40.9	31.9	1	1	61	0

SACKS: Fletcher, 16.0

Indianapolis Colts

SCORING

SCORING	Rush	TD Rec	Ret	PAT	FG	S	Pts
Biasucci	0	0	0	24/24	16/29	0	72
Culver	7	2	0	0/0	0/0	0	54
Cash	0	3	0	0/0	0/0	0	18
Johnson	0	3	0	0/0	0/0	0	18
Verdin	0	0	2	0/0	0/0	0	12

Seven tied with 6.

RUSHING

RUSHING	No.	Yds	Avg	Lg	TD
Johnson	178	592	3.3	19	0
Culver	121	321	2.7	t36	7
Clark	40	134	3.4	13	0
George	14	26	1.9	13	1

PASSING

PASSING	Att	Comp	Pct Comp	Yds	Avg Gain	TD	Int	Rating Pts
George	306	167	54.6	1963	6.42	7	15	61.5
Trudeau	181	105	58.0	1271	7.02	4	8	68.6
Tupa	33	17	51.5	156	4.73	1	2	49.6
Herrmann	24	15	62.5	177	7.38	1	1	81.4

RECEIVING

RECEIVING	No.	Yds	Avg	Lg	TD
Langhorne	65	811	12.5	34	1
Hester	52	792	15.2	81	1
Johnson	49	517	10.6	t57	3
Brooks	44	468	10.6	26	1
Cash	43	521	12.1	41	3

INTERCEPTIONS: Prior, 6

PUNTING	No.	Yds	Avg	Net Avg	In TB	20	Lg	Blk
Stark	83	3716	44.8	39.3	7	22	64	0

SACKS: Banks, 9.0

Kansas City Chiefs

SCORING

	TD						
SCORING	Rush	Rec	Ret	PAT	FG	S	Pts
Lowery	0	0	0	39/39	22/24	0	105
Okoye	6	0	0	0/0	0/0	0	36
Barnett	0	4	0	0/0	0/0	0	24
Word	4	0	0	0/0	0/0	0	24

Four tied with 18.

RUSHING

RUSHING	No.	Yds	Avg	Lg	TD
Word	163	607	3.7	t44	4
Okoye	144	448	3.1	22	6
Williams	78	262	3.4	11	1
McNair	21	124	5.9	30	1
Krieg	37	74	2.0	17	2

PASSING

PASSING	Att	Comp	Pct Comp	Yds	Avg Gain	TD	Int	Rating Pts
Krieg	413	230	55.7	3115	7.54	15	12	79.9

RECEIVING

RECEIVING	No.	Yds	Avg	Lg	TD
McNair	44	380	8.6	36	1
Birden	42	644	15.3	t72	3
Davis	36	756	21.0	t74	3
Barnett	24	442	18.4	t77	4
F. Jones	18	265	14.7	56	0

INTERCEPTIONS: Carter, 7

PUNTING

PUNTING	No.	Yds	Avg	Net Avg	TB	In 20	Lg	Blk
Barker	75	3245	43.3	35.3	13	16	65	1
Lowery	4	141	35.3	32.8	0	0	39	0
Sullivan	6	247	41.2	38.2	0	2	59	0

SACKS: N. Smith, 14.5

Los Angeles Raiders

SCORING

	TD						
SCORING	Rush	Rec	Ret	PAT	FG	S	Pts
Jaeger	0	0	0	28/28	15/26	0	73
Brown	0	7	0	0/0	0/0	0	42
Gault	0	4	0	0/0	0/0	0	24
Dickerson	2	1	0	0/0	0/0	0	18
Allen	2	1	0	0/0	0/0	0	18
N. Bell	3	0	0	0/0	0/0	0	18

RUSHING

RUSHING	No.	Yds	Avg	Lg	TD
Dickerson	187	729	3.9	t40	2
N. Bell	81	366	4.5	21	3
Allen	67	301	4.5	21	2
Schroeder	28	160	5.7	19	0
S. Smith	44	129	2.9	15	0

PASSING

PASSING	Att	Comp	Pct Comp	Yds	Avg Gain	TD	Int	Rating Pts
Schroeder	253	123	48.6	1476	5.83	11	11	63.3
Marinovich	165	123	49.1	1102	6.68	5	9	58.2
Evans	53	29	54.7	372	7.02	4	3	78.5

RECEIVING

RECEIVING	No.	Yds	Avg	Lg	TD
Brown	49	693	14.1	t68	7
Horton	33	409	12.4	30	2
Allen	28	277	9.9	40	1
S. Smith	28	217	7.8	19	1
Gault	27	508	18.8	53	4

INTERCEPTIONS: McDaniel, 4

PUNTING

PUNTING	No.	Yds	Avg	Net Avg	TB	In 20	Lg	Blk
Gossett	77	3255	42.3	36.5	3	17	56	0

SACKS: A. Smith, 13.0

Miami Dolphins

SCORING

	TD						
SCORING	Rush	Rec	Ret	PAT	FG	S	Pts
Stoyanovich	0	0	0	34/36	30/37	0	124
Duper	0	7	0	0/0	0/0	0	42
Higgs	7	0	0	0/0	0/0	0	42
K. Jackson	0	5	0	0/0	0/0	0	30

RUSHING

RUSHING	No.	Yds	Avg	Lg	TD
Higgs	256	915	3.6	23	7
Humphrey	102	471	4.6	21	1
Marino	20	66	3.3	12	0
Parmalee	6	38	6.3	20	0
Paige	7	11	1.6	6	1

PASSING

PASSING	Att	Comp	Pct Comp	Yds	Avg Gain	TD	Int	Rating Pts
Marino	554	330	59.6	4116	7.43	24	16	85.1
Mitchell	8	2	25.0	32	4.00	0	1	42.7
Martin	1	0	0	0	0.0	0	0	39.6

RECEIVING

RECEIVING	No.	Yds	Avg	Lg	TD
Humphrey	54	507	9.4	26	1
K. Jackson	48	594	12.4	42	5
Paige	48	399	8.3	30	1
Duper	44	762	17.3	t62	7
Clayton	43	619	14.4	t44	3
Martin	33	319	16.8	t55	2

INTERCEPTIONS: Oliver, 5

PUNTING

PUNTING	No.	Yds	Avg	Net Avg	TB	In 20	Lg	Blk
Roby	35	1443	41.2	34.3	3	11	60	0
Stoyanovich	2	90	45.0	45.0	0	0	48	0

SACKS: Cox, 14.0

New England Patriots

SCORING

	TD						
SCORING	Rush	Rec	Ret	PAT	FG	S	Pts
Baumann	0	0	0	22/24	11/17	0	55
Fryar	0	4	0	0/0	0/0	0	24
Coates	3	0	0	0/0	0/0	0	18

Six tied with 12.

RUSHING

RUSHING	No.	Yds	Avg	Lg	TD
Vaughn	113	451	4.0	36	1
Russell	123	390	3.2	23	2
Stephens	75	277	3.7	19	2
Lockwood	35	162	4.6	23	0
Millen	17	108	6.4	26	0

PASSING

PASSING	Att	Comp	Pct Comp	Yds	Avg Gain	TD	Int	Rating Pts
Millen	203	124	61.1	1203	5.93	8	10	70.3
Zolak	100	52	52.0	561	5.61	2	4	58.8
Hodson	91	50	54.9	496	5.45	2	2	68.8
Carlson	49	18	36.7	232	4.73	1	3	33.7

RECEIVING

RECEIVING	No.	Yds	Avg	Lg	TD
Fryar	55	791	14.4	t54	4
Cook	52	413	7.9	27	2
McMurtry	35	424	12.1	t65	1
Timpson	26	315	12.1	25	1
Stephens	21	161	7.7	32	0

INTERCEPTIONS: Hurst and Henderson, 3

PUNTING

PUNTING	No.	Yds	Avg	Net Avg	TB	In 20	Lg	Blk
McCarthy	103	4212	40.9	35.4	4	18	61	0

SACKS: Tippett, 7

New York Jets

SCORING

SCORING	Rush	Rec	Ret	PAT	FG	S	Pts
			TD				
Blanchard	0	0	0	17/17	16/22	0	65
Baxter	6	0	0	0/0	0/0	0	36
Moore	0	4	0	0/0	0/0	0	24
Mathis	1	3	0	0/0	0/0	0	24
Staurovsky	0	0	0	6/6	3/8	0	15

RUSHING

RUSHING	No.	Yds	Avg	Lg	TD
Baxter	152	698	4.6	30	6
Thomas	97	440	4.5	19	0
Chaffey	27	186	6.9	32	1
McNeil	43	170	4.0	18	0
Hector	24	67	2.8	14	0

PASSING

PASSING	Att	Comp	Pct Comp	Yds	Avg Gain	TD	Int	Rating Pts
Nagle	387	192	49.6	2280	5.89	7	17	55.7
O'Brien	98	55	56.1	642	6.55	5	6	67.6
Blake	9	4	44.4	40	4.44	0	1	18.1

RECEIVING

RECEIVING	No.	Yds	Avg	Lg	TD
Burkett	57	724	12.7	t37	1
Moore	50	726	14.5	t48	4
Toon	31	311	10.0	32	2
Mathis	22	316	14.4	t55	3
Boyer	19	149	7.8	23	0

INTERCEPTIONS: Brim and Washington, 6

PUNTING	No.	Yds	Avg	Net Avg	TB	In 20	Lg	Blk
Aguiar	73	2993	41.0	37.6	3	22	65	0

SACKS: Washington, 8.5

Pittsburgh Steelers

SCORING

SCORING	Rush	Rec	Ret	PAT	FG	S	Pts
			TD				
Anderson	0	0	0	29/31	28/36	0	113
Foster	11	0	0	0/0	0/0	0	66
Cooper	0	3	0	0/0	0/0	0	18
Mills	0	3	0	0/0	0/0	0	18
Stone	0	3	0	0/0	0/0	0	18

RUSHING

RUSHING	No.	Yds	Avg	Lg	TD
Foster	390	1690	4.3	69	11
Thompson	35	157	4.5	25	1
Hoge	41	150	3.7	15	0
Stone	12	118	9.8	30	0
Mills	1	20	20.0	20	0

PASSING

PASSING	Att	Comp	Pct Comp	Yds	Avg Gain	TD	Int	Rating Pts
O'Donnell	313	185	59.1	2283	7.29	13	9	83.6
Brister	116	63	54.3	719	6.20	2	5	61.0
Foster	1	0	0.0	0	0	0	0	39.6
Royals	1	1	100.0	44	44.0	0	0	118.8

RECEIVING

RECEIVING	No.	Yds	Avg	Lg	TD
Graham	49	711	14.5	51	1
Foster	36	344	9.6	42	0
Stone	34	501	14.7	49	3
Mills	30	383	12.8	22	3

INTERCEPTIONS: Perry, 6

PUNTING	No.	Yds	Avg	Net Avg	TB	In 20	Lg	Blk
Royals	73	3119	42.7	35.6	9	22	58	1

SACKS: Lloyd, 6.5

San Diego Chargers

SCORING

SCORING	Rush	Rec	Ret	PAT	FG	S	Pts
			TD				
Carney	0	0	0	35/35	26/32	0	113
Miller	0	7	1	0/0	0/0	0	48
Lewis	0	4	0	0/0	0/0	0	24
Humphries	4	0	0	0/0	0/0	0	24
Bernstine	4	0	0	0/0	0/0	0	24
Harmon	3	1	0	0/0	0/0	0	24
Butts	4	0	0	0/0	0/0	0	24

RUSHING

RUSHING	No.	Yds	Avg	Lg	TD
Butts	218	809	3.7	22	4
Bernstine	106	499	4.7	t25	4
Bieniemy	74	264	3.6	21	3
Harmon	55	235	4.3	33	3
Humphries	28	79	2.8	25	4

PASSING

PASSING	Att	Comp	Pct Comp	Yds	Avg Gain	TD	Int	Rating Pts
Humphries	454	263	57.9	3356	7.39	16	18	76.4
Gagliano	42	19	45.2	258	6.14	0	3	35.6

RECEIVING

RECEIVING	No.	Yds	Avg	Lg	TD
Harmon	79	914	11.6	55	1
A. Miller	72	1060	14.7	t67	7
Lewis	34	580	17.1	62	4
Walker	34	393	11.6	59	2
Jefferson	29	377	13.0	51	2

INTERCEPTIONS: Carrington, 6

PUNTING	No.	Yds	Avg	Net Avg	TB	In 20	Lg	Blk
Kidd	68	2899	42.6	36.4	9	22	65	0

SACKS: O'Neal, 17

Seattle Seahawks

SCORING

SCORING	Rush	Rec	Ret	PAT	FG	S	Pts
			TD				
Kasay	0	0	0	14/14	14/22	0	56
Williams	1	2	0	0/0	0/0	0	18
Kane	0	3	0	0/0	0/0	0	18
Warren	3	0	0	0/0	0/0	0	18

RUSHING

RUSHING	No.	Yds	Avg	Lg	TD
Warren	223	1017	4.6	52	3
Williams	114	339	3.0	14	1
Gelbaugh	16	79	4.9	22	0
Mayes	28	74	2.6	14	0

PASSING

PASSING	Att	Comp	Pct Comp	Yds	Avg Gain	TD	Int	Rating Pts
Gelbaugh	255	121	47.5	1307	5.13	6	11	52.9
Stouffer	190	92	48.4	900	4.74	3	9	47.7
McGwire	30	17	56.7	116	3.87	0	3	25.8
Tuten	1	0	0.0	0	0.0	0	0	39.6

RECEIVING

RECEIVING	No.	Yds	Avg	Lg	TD
Williams	74	556	7.5	27	2
Kane	27	369	13.7	31	3
J. Jones	21	190	9.0	30	0
L. Clark	20	290	14.5	33	1

INTERCEPTIONS: Robinson, 7

PUNTING	No.	Yds	Avg	Net Avg	TB	In 20	Lg	Blk
Tuten	108	4760	44.1	38.7	8	29	65	0

SACKS: Kennedy, 14.0

Atlanta Falcons

SCORING	Rush	Rec	Ret	PAT	FG	S	Pts
N. Johnson	0	0	0	39/39	18/22	0	93
Rison	0	11	0	0/0	0/0	0	66
Haynes	0	10	0	0/0	0/0	0	60
Pritchard	0	5	0	0/0	0/0	0	30

Two tied with 18.

RUSHING	No.	Yds	Avg	Lg	TD
Broussard	84	363	4.3	27	1
T. Smith	87	329	3.8	32	2
K. Jones	79	278	3.5	26	0
Miller	23	89	3.9	16	0
Pegram	21	89	4.2	15	0

PASSING	Att	Comp	Pct Comp	Yds	Avg Gain	TD	Int	Rating Pts
Miller	253	152	60.1	1739	6.87	15	6	90.7
Wilson	163	111	68.1	1368	8.39	13	4	110.2
Tolliver	131	73	55.7	787	6.01	5	5	70.4

RECEIVING	No.	Yds	Avg	Lg	TD
Rison	93	1121	12.1	t71	11
Pritchard	77	827	10.7	t38	5
Hill	60	623	10.4	43	3
Haynes	48	808	16.8	t89	10
T. Jones	14	138	9.9	24	1

INTERCEPTIONS: Sanders 3

PUNTING	No.	Yds	Avg	Net Avg	TB	In 20	Lg	Blk
Fulhage	68	2818	41.4	33.0	3	11	56	1
Johnson	1	37	37	37.0	0	1	37	0

SACKS: Conner, 7.0

Dallas Cowboys

SCORING	Rush	Rec	Ret	PAT	FG	S	Pts
Elliott	0	0	0	47/48	24/35	0	119
E. Smith	18	1	0	0/0	0/0	0	114
Irvin	0	7	0	0/0	0/0	0	42
Novacek	0	6	0	0/0	0/0	0	36
Martin	0	3	2	0/0	0/0	0	30

RUSHING	No.	Yds	Avg	Lg	TD
E. Smith	373	1713	4.6	t68	18
Richards	49	176	3.6	15	1
Aikman	37	105	2.8	19	1
Johnston	17	61	3.6	14	0
Agee	16	54	3.4	10	0

PASSING	Att	Comp	Pct Comp	Yds	Avg Gain	TD	Int	Rating Pts
Aikman	473	302	63.8	3445	7.28	23	14	89.5
Beuerlein	18	12	66.7	152	8.44	0	1	69.7

RECEIVING	No.	Yds	Avg	Lg	TD
Irvin	78	1396	17.9	t87	7
Novacek	68	630	9.3	34	6
E. Smith	59	335	5.7	t26	1
Harper	35	562	16.1	52	4

INTERCEPTIONS: Washington and Gant, 3

PUNTING	No.	Yds	Avg	Net Avg	TB	In 20	Lg	Blk
Saxon	61	2620	43.0	33.5	9	19	58	0

SACKS: Jeffcoat, 10.5

Chicago Bears

SCORING	Rush	Rec	Ret	PAT	FG	S	Pts
Butler	0	0	0	34/34	19/26	0	91
Anderson	5	6	0	0/0	0/0	0	66
Muster	3	2	0	0/0	0/0	0	30
Lewis	4	0	1	0/0	0/0	0	30
Waddle	0	4	0	0/0	0/0	0	24

Three tied with 12.

RUSHING	No.	Yds	Avg	Lg	TD
Anderson	156	582	3.7	t49	5
Muster	98	414	4.2	35	3
Lewis	90	382	4.2	33	4
Harbaugh	47	272	5.8	17	1
Green	23	107	4.7	18	2

PASSING	Att	Comp	Pct Comp	Yds	Avg Gain	TD	Int	Rating Pts
Harbaugh	358	202	56.4	2486	6.94	13	12	76.2
Willis	92	54	58.7	716	7.78	4	8	61.7
Furrer	25	9	36.0	89	3.56	0	3	7.3

RECEIVING	No.	Yds	Avg	Lg	TD
Davis	54	734	13.6	40	2
Waddle	46	674	14.7	t68	4
Anderson	42	399	9.5	t30	6
Muster	34	389	11.4	t44	2
Jennings	23	264	11.5	23	1

INTERCEPTIONS: Woolford, 7

PUNTING	No.	Yds	Avg	Net Avg	TB	In 20	Lg	Blk
Gardocki	79	3393	42.9	36.2	9	19	61	0

SACKS: McMichael, 10.5

Detroit Lions

SCORING	Rush	Rec	Ret	PAT	FG	S	Pts
Hanson	0	0	0	30/30	21/26	0	93
B. Sanders	9	1	0	0/0	0/0	0	60
Green	0	5	0	0/0	0/0	0	30
Perriman	0	4	0	0/0	0/0	0	24
Moore	0	4	0	0/0	0/0	0	24

RUSHING	No.	Yds	Avg	Lg	TD
B. Sanders	312	1352	4.3	t55	9
Ware	20	124	6.2	32	0
Peete	21	83	4.0	12	0
Stradford	12	41	3.4	11	0

PASSING	Att	Comp	Pct Comp	Yds	Avg Gain	TD	Int	Rating Pts
Peete	213	123	57.7	1702	7.99	9	9	80.0
Kramer	106	58	54.7	771	7.27	4	8	59.1
Ware	86	50	58.1	677	7.87	3	4	75.6

RECEIVING	No.	Yds	Avg	Lg	TD
Perriman	69	810	11.7	t40	4
Moore	51	966	18.9	t77	4
Green	33	586	17.8	t73	5
B. Sanders	29	225	7.8	48	1
Farr	15	115	7.7	14	0

INTERCEPTIONS: Crockett, White, Scott, Jenkins, 6

PUNTING	No.	Yds	Avg	Net Avg	TB	In 20	Lg	Blk
Arnold	65	2846	43.8	34.7	10	12	71	1

SACKS: Scroggins, 7.5

Green Bay Packers

SCORING	Rush	Rec	Ret	PAT	FG	S	Pts
Jacke	0	0	0	30/30	22/29	0	96
Sharpe	0	13	0	0/0	0/0	0	78
Sydney	2	1	0	0/0	0/0	0	18
Thompson	2	1	0	0/0	0/0	0	18
Three tied with 12.							

RUSHING	No.	Yds	Avg	Lg	TD
Workman	159	631	4.0	44	2
Thompson	76	255	3.4	33	2
Bennett	61	214	3.5	18	0
Favre	47	198	4.2	19	1
Sydney	51	163	3.2	19	2

PASSING	Att	Comp	Pct Comp	Yds	Avg Gain	TD	Int	Rating Pts
Favre	471	302	64.1	3227	6.85	18	13	85.3
Majkowski	55	38	69.1	271	4.93	2	2	77.2

RECEIVING	No.	Yds	Avg	Lg	TD
Sharpe	108	1461	13.5	t76	13
Harris	55	595	10.8	40	2
Sydney	49	384	7.8	20	1
Workman	47	290	6.2	21	0

INTERCEPTIONS: Cecil, 4

PUNTING	No.	Yds	Avg	Net Avg	TB	In 20	Lg	Blk
McJulien	36	1386	38.5	30.2	4	8	67	2
Wagner	30	1222	40.7	35.0	5	10	52	0

SACKS: Bennett, 13.5

Los Angeles Rams

SCORING	Rush	Rec	Ret	PAT	FG	S	Pts
Zendejas	0	0	0	38/38	15/20	0	83
Gary	7	3	0	0/0	0/0	0	60
Anderson	0	7	0	0/0	0/0	0	42
Lang	5	1	0	0/0	0/0	0	36
Three tied with 18.							

RUSHING	No.	Yds	Avg	Lg	TD
Gary	279	1125	4.0	53	7
Lang	33	203	6.2	71	5
Everett	32	133	4.2	22	0
Delpino	32	115	3.6	31	0

PASSING	Att	Comp	Pct Comp	Yds	Avg Gain	TD	Int	Rating Pts
Everett	475	281	59.2	3323	7.00	22	18	80.2
Pagel	20	8	40.0	99	4.95	1	2	33.1

RECEIVING	No.	Yds	Avg	Lg	TD
Gary	52	293	5.6	22	3
Ellard	47	727	15.5	t33	3
Anderson	38	17.3	17.3	51	7
Price	34	324	9.5	25	2
Chadwick	29	362	12.5	t27	3

INTERCEPTIONS: Henley and Newman, 3

PUNTING	No.	Yds	Avg	Net Avg	TB	In 20	Lg	Blk
Bracken	76	3122	41.1	33.2	4	20	59	0

SACKS: Greene, 10.0

Minnesota Vikings

SCORING	Rush	Rec	Ret	PAT	FG	S	Pts
Reveiz	0	0	0	45/45	19/25	0	102
Allen	13	2	0	0/0	0/0	0	90
C. Carter	0	6	0	0/0	0/0	0	36
Craig	4	0	0	0/0	0/0	0	24
Jones	0	4	0	0/0	0/0	0	24

RUSHING	No.	Yds	Avg	Lg	TD
Allen	266	1201	4.5	51	13
Craig	105	416	4.0	21	4
Gannon	45	187	4.2	14	0
Henderson	44	150	3.4	12	1

PASSING	Att	Comp	Pct Comp	Yds	Avg Gain	TD	Int	Rating Pts
Gannon	279	159	57.0	1905	6.83	12	13	72.9
Salisbury	175	97	55.4	1203	6.87	5	2	81.7

RECEIVING	No.	Yds	Avg	Lg	TD
C. Carter	53	681	12.8	44	6
Allen	49	478	9.8	t36	2
A. Carter	41	580	14.1	54	2
Jordan	28	394	14.1	t60	2
Jones	22	308	14.0	t43	4

INTERCEPTIONS: McMillian, 8

PUNTING	No.	Yds	Avg	Net Avg	TB	In 20	Lg	Blk
Newsome	72	3243	45.0	35.7	15	19	84	1

SACKS: Doleman, 14.5

New Orleans Saints

SCORING	Rush	Rec	Ret	PAT	FG	S	Pts
Andersen	0	0	0	33/34	29/34	0	120
Hilliard	3	4	0	0/0	0/0	0	42
E. Martin	0	5	0	0/0	0/0	0	30
Early	0	5	0	0/0	0/0	0	30
Three tied with 18.							

RUSHING	No.	Yds	Avg	Lg	TD
Dunbar	154	565	3.7	25	3
Hilliard	115	445	3.9	22	3
Heyward	104	416	4.0	23	3
McAfee	39	114	2.9	19	1
Hebert	32	95	3.0	18	0

PASSING	Att	Comp	Pct Comp	Yds	Avg Gain	TD	Int	Rating Pts
Hebert	422	249	59.0	3287	7.79	19	16	82.9
M. Buck	4	2	50.0	10	2.50	0	0	56.3

RECEIVING	No.	Yds	Avg	Lg	TD
E. Martin	68	1041	15.3	t52	5
Hilliard	48	465	9.7	41	4
Early	30	566	18.9	t59	5
Small	23	278	12.1	33	3
Heyward	19	159	8.4	21	0

INTERCEPTIONS: Cook, 6

PUNTING	No.	Yds	Avg	Net Avg	TB	In 20	Lg	Blk
Barnhardt	67	2947	44.0	37.7	10	19	62	0

SACKS: Martin, 15.5

New York Giants

SCORING	TD Rush	Rec	Ret	PAT	FG	S	Pts
Hampton	14	0	0	0/0	0/0	0	84
Bahr	0	0	0	29/29	16/21	0	77
Willis	0	0	0	27/27	10/16	0	57
McCaffrey	0	5	0	0/0	0/0	0	30
Bunch	3	1	0	0/0	0/0	0	24

RUSHING	No.	Yds	Avg	Lg	TD
Hampton	257	1141	4.4	t63	14
Bunch	104	501	4.8	37	3
Hostetler	34	172	5.1	27	3
Meggett	32	167	5.2	30	0

PASSING	Att	Comp	Pct Comp	Yds	Av Gain	TD	Int	Rating Pts
Hostetler	192	103	53.6	1225	6.38	8	3	80.8
Simms	137	83	60.6	912	6.66	5	3	83.3
Graham	97	42	43.3	470	4.85	1	4	44.6
Brown	7	4	57.1	21	3.00	0	0	62.2

RECEIVING	No.	Yds	Avg	Lg	TD
McCaffrey	49	610	12.4	44	5
Meggett	38	229	6.0	24	2
Hampton	28	215	7.7	31	0
Ingram	27	408	15.1	34	1
Cross	27	357	13.2	29	2

INTERCEPTIONS: Jackson, 4

PUNTING	No.	Yds	Avg	Net Avg	TB	In 20	Lg	Blk
Landeta	53	2317	43.7	31.5	9	13	71	2
Prokop	32	1184	37.0	28.9	0	2	56	0
Rodriguez	46	1907	37.0	34.5	4	9	55	1

SACKS: Taylor, 5.0

Philadelphia Eagles

SCORING	TD Rush	Rec	Ret	PAT	FG	S	Pts
Ruzek	0	0	0	40/44	16/25	0	88
Walker	8	2	0	0/0	0/0	0	60
Barnett	0	6	0	0/0	0/0	0	36
Sherman	5	1	0	0/0	0/0	0	36
Cunningham	5	0	0	0/0	0/0	0	30

RUSHING	No.	Yds	Avg	Lg	TD
Walker	267	1070	4.0	38	8
Sherman	112	583	5.2	34	5
Cunningham	87	549	6.3	30	5
Byars	41	176	4.3	23	1

PASSING	Att	Comp	Pct Comp	Yds	Avg Gain	TD	Int	Rating Pts
Cunningham	384	233	60.7	2775	7.23	19	11	87.3
McMahon	43	22	51.2	279	6.49	1	2	60.1

RECEIVING	No.	Yds	Avg	Lg	TD
Barnett	67	1083	16.2	t71	6
Byars	56	502	9.0	46	2
Williams	42	598	14.2	t49	7
Walker	38	278	7.3	41	2

INTERCEPTIONS: Allen, Joyner and Evans, 4

PUNTING	No.	Yds	Avg	Net Avg	TB	In 20	Lg	Blk
Feagles	82	3459	42.2	36.9	7	26	68	0

SACKS: Simmons, 19.0

Phoenix Cardinals

SCORING	TD Rush	Rec	Ret	PAT	FG	S	Pts
G. Davis	0	0	0	28/28	13/26	0	67
Johnson	6	0	0	0/0	0/0	0	36
E. Jones	0	4	0	0/0	0/0	0	24
Three tied with 18.							

RUSHING	No.	Yds	Avg	Lg	TD
Johnson	178	734	4.1	t42	6
Bailey	52	233	4.5	15	1
Brown	68	194	2.9	13	2
Chandler	36	149	4.1	18	1
Centers	37	139	3.8	28	0

PASSING	Att	Comp	Pct Comp	Yds	Avg Gain	TD	Int	Rating Pts
Chandler	413	245	59.3	2832	6.86	15	15	77.1
Rosenbach	92	49	53.3	483	5.25	0	6	41.2
Sacca	11	4	36.4	29	2.64	0	2	5.3

RECEIVING	No.	Yds	Avg	Lg	TD
Proehl	60	744	12.4	t63	3
R. Hill	58	861	14.8	49	3
Centers	50	417	8.3	26	2
E. Jones	38	559	14.7	t72	4
Bailey	33	331	10.0	34	1

INTERCEPTIONS: Massey, 5

PUNTING	No.	Yds	Avg	Net Avg	TB	In 20	Lg	Blk
Camarillo	54	2317	42.9	39.6	2	23	73	0
Davis	4	167	41.8	36.8	1	0	52	0

SACKS: Harvey and M. Jones, 9.0

San Francisco 49ers

SCORING	TD Rush	Rec	Ret	PAT	FG	S	Pts
Cofer	0	0	0	53/54	18/27	0	107
Rice	1	10	0	0/0	0/0	0	66
Watters	9	2	0	0/0	0/0	0	66
Rathman	5	4	0	0/0	0/0	0	54
Three tied with 24.							

RUSHING	No.	Yds	Avg	Lg	TD
Watters	206	1013	4.9	43	9
Young	76	537	7.1	t39	4
Lee	91	362	4.0	43	2
Rathman	57	194	3.4	17	5

PASSING	Att	Comp	Pct Comp	Yds	Avg Gain	TD	Int	Rating Pts
Young	402	268	66.7	3465	8.62	25	7	107.0
Bono	56	36	64.3	463	8.27	2	2	87.1
Montana	21	15	71.4	126	6.00	2	0	118.4

RECEIVING	No.	Yds	Avg	Lg	TD
Rice	84	1201	14.3	t80	10
Jones	45	628	14.0	43	4
Rathman	44	343	7.8	t27	4
Watters	43	405	9.4	35	2
Sherrard	38	607	16.0	56	0

INTERCEPTIONS: Griffin, 5

PUNTING	No.	Yds	Avg	Net Avg	TB	In 20	Lg	Blk
Prokop	40	1541	38.5	34.6	1	8	58	0

SACKS: Roberts and Haley, 7.0

Tampa Bay Buccaneers

SCORING

	Rush	TD Rec	Ret	PAT	FG	S	Pts
Cobb	9	0	0	0/0	0/0	0	54
Stryzinski	0	0	0	13/13	5/9	0	42
Carrier	0	4	0	0/0	0/0	0	24
Hall	0	4	0	0/0	0/0	0	24

RUSHING

	No.	Yds	Avg	Lg	TD
Cobb	310	1171	3.8	25	9
Testaverde	36	197	5.5	18	2
Anderson	55	194	3.5	18	1
McDowell	14	81	5.8	23	0

PASSING

	Att	Comp	Pct Comp	Yds	Avg Gain	TD	Int	Rating Pts
Testaverde	358	206	57.5	2554	7.13	14	16	74.2
DeBerg	125	76	60.8	710	5.68	3	4	71.1
Erickson	26	15	57.7	121	4.65	0	0	69.6

RECEIVING

	No.	Yds	Avg	Lg	TD
Dawsey	60	776	12.9	41	1
Carrier	56	692	12.4	40	4
Ro. Hall	39	351	9.0	32	4
Anderson	34	284	8.4	34	0
McDowell	27	258	9.6	t51	2

INTERCEPTIONS: Carter, Fullington and Mack, 3

PUNTING

	No.	Yds	Avg	Net Avg	TB	In 20	Lg	Blk
Stryzinski	74	3015	40.7	36.2	11	15	57	0

SACKS: Dotson, 10.0

Washington Redskins

SCORING

	Rush	TD Rec	Ret	PAT	FG	S	Pts
Lohmiller	0	0	0	30/30	30/40	0	120
Byner	6	1	0	0/0	0/0	0	42
Clark	0	5	0	0/0	0/0	0	30
Three tied with 18.							

RUSHING

	No.	Yds	Avg	Lg	TD
Byner	262	998	3.8	23	6
Ervins	151	495	3.3	25	2
Mitchell	6	70	11.7	33	0
Rypien	36	50	1.4	11	2

PASSING

	Att	Comp	Pct Comp	Yds	Avg Gain	TD	Int	Rating Pts
Rypien	479	269	56.2	3282	6.85	13	17	71.7
Byner	3	1	33.3	41	13.67	1	0	121.5
Conklin	2	2	100.00	16	8.00	1	0	139.6

RECEIVING

	No.	Yds	Avg	Lg	TD
Clark	64	912	14.3	47	5
Clark	70	1340	19.1	t82	10
Sanders	51	707	13.9	t62	3
Monk	46	644	14.0	t49	3
Byner	39	338	8.7	29	1

INTERCEPTIONS: Edwards, 6

PUNTING

	No.	Yds	Avg	Net Avg	TB	In 20	Lg	Blk
Goodburn	64	2555	39.9	32.7	5	17	66	1

SACKS: Johnson and Marshall, 6.0

Question of Substance

The indictments in January 1993 of New York Giant guard Eric Moore and Tampa Bay Buccaneer defensive end Mark Duckens on federal charges that they possessed and intended to distribute anabolic steroids and human growth hormone (HGH) focus new attention on the use of these bodybuilding substances in the NFL. Moore and Duckens pleaded not guilty, but Drug Enforcement Administration officials in Atlanta, where the indictments were handed down, said that large quantities of steroids and HGH were seized from the pair and that arrests of other NFL players were possible.

The NFL tried to characterize the indictments as an aberration, claiming that it has administered 18,000 tests for steroids over the last three years, with no more than five positives. But HGH can't be detected through testing, and players can beat steroid tests with masking agents or by getting off the drugs in time. Also, there is reason to question

the league's testing procedures. "I had one player call me who was frantic," says Tony Fitton, a convicted steroid trafficker who now advises athletes on steroid alternatives. "He had a test that week, and he had used Winstrol V [an anabolic steroid]. He turned out negative. It makes you wonder about the validity of the testing."

The difficulty of combating the use of performance-enhancing drugs in sports was underscored by an estimate by Prince Alexandre de Merode, president of the International Olympic Committee's medical commission, that while only five of the 10,274 athletes at the Barcelona Olympics tested positive, 10% of the participants in the Games use steroids or other performance-enhancing substances. De Merode's 10% figure—and even that may be low—would mean that the IOC is catching barely one of every 200 drug users. There's no reason to think the NFL is doing much better.

1993 NFL Draft

First four rounds of the 58th annual NFL Draft held April 25-26 in New York City.

First Round

Team	Selection	Position
1. New England	Drew Bledsoe, Washington St	QB
2. Seattle	Rick Mirer, Notre Dame	QB
3. Phoenix*	Garrison Hearst, Georgia	RB
4. NY Jets†	Marvin Jones, Miami	LB
5. Cincinnati	John Copeland, Alabama	DT
6. Tampa Bay	Eric Curry, Alabama	DE
7. Chicago	Curtis Conway, Southern Cal	WR
8. New Orleans#	Willie Roaf, Louisiana Tech	OT
9. Atlanta	Lincoln Kennedy, Washington	OT
10. LA Rams	Jerome Bettis, Notre Dame	RB
11. Denver‡	Dan Williams, Toledo	DE
12. LA Raiders	Patrick Bates, Texas A & M	DB
13. Houston**	Brad Hopkins, Illinois	OG
14. Cleveland††	Steve Everitt, Michigan	C
15. Green Bay	Wayne Simmons, Clemson	LB
16. Indianpolis	Sean Dawkins, California	WR
17. Washington	Tom Carter, Notre Dame	DB
18. Phoenix##	Ernest Dye, South Carolina	OT
19. Philadelphia‡‡	Lester Holmes, Jackson State	OT
20. New Orleans***	Irv Smith, Notre Dame	TE
21. Minnesota	Robert Smith, Ohio State	RB
22. San Diego	Darrien Gordon, Stanford	DB
23. Pittsburgh	Deon Figures, Colorado	DB
24. Philadelphia	Leonard Renfroe, Colorado	DE
25. Miami	O.J. McDuffie, Penn State	WR
26. San Francisco†††	Dana Stubblefield, Kansas	DE
27. San Francisco	Todd Kelly, Tennessee	DE
28. Buffalo	Thomas Smith, North Carolina	DB
29. Green Bay###	George Teague, Alabama	DB

Second Round

Team	Selection	Position
30. Seattle	Carlton Gray, UCLA	DB
31. New England	Chris Slade, Virginia	DE
32. Phoenix	Ben Coleman, Wake Forest	T
33. Detroit*	Ryan McNeil, Miami	DB
34. Tampa Bay	Demetrius DuBose, Notre Dame	LB
35. Chicago	Carl Simpson, Florida State	DT
36. NY Jets†	Coleman Rudolph, Georgia Tech	DE
37. Cincinnati	Tony McGee, Michigan	TE
38. Atlanta	Roger Harper, Ohio State	DB
39. LA Rams	Troy Drayton, Penn State	TE
40. NY Giants	Michael Strahan, Texas Southern	DE
41. San Diego#	Natrone Means, North Carolina	RB
42. Cleveland	Dan Footman, Florida State	DE
43. Denver	Glyn Milburn, Stanford	RB
44. Pittsburgh‡	Chad Brown, Colorado	LB
45. Washington	Reggie Brooks, Notre Dame	RB
46. Dallas**	Kevin Williams, Miami	WR
47. Houston††	Micheal Barrow, Miami	LB
48. San Francisco##	Adrian Hardy, NW Louisiana	DB
49. Indianapolis‡‡	Roosevelt Potts, NE Louisiana	RB
50. Philadelphia	Victor Bailey, Missouri	WR
51. New England***	Todd Rucci, Penn State	T
52. Minnesota	Qadry Ismail, Syracuse	WR
53. New Orleans	Reggie Freeman, Florida State	LB
54. Dallas†††	Darrin Smith, Miami	LB
55. Buffalo	John Parella, Nebraska	DT
56. LA Raiders###	Passed	
56. New England	Vincent Brisby, NE Louisiana	WR

*From NY Jets †From Phoenix #From Detroit ‡From Cleveland **From Philadelphia. ††From Denver ##From Kansas City through San Francisco. ‡‡From Houston. ***From Phoenix through San Francisco †††From New Orleans ###From Dallas.

*From NY Jets †From Detroit #From LA Raiders through San Francisco ‡From Indianapolis **From Green Bay ††Kansas City exercised in supplemental draft ##From San Diego ‡‡From Pittsburgh ***From Miami †††From San Francisco through Green Bay ###From Dallas through San Francisco.

Final Standings

EUROPEAN DIVISION

	W	L	T	Pct	Pts/ Tm	Pts/ Opp
Barcelona	5	5	0	.500	104	161
Frankfurt	3	7	0	.300	150	257
London	2	7	1	.250	178	203

NORTH AMERICAN/EAST DIVISION

	W	L	T	Pct	Pts/ Tm	Pts/ Opp
Orlando	8	2	0	.800	247	127
NY/NJ	6	4	0	.600	284	188
Montreal	2	8	0	.200	175	274
Ohio	1	9	0	.100	132	230

NORTH AMERICAN/WEST DIVISION

	W	L	T	Pct	Pts/ Tm	Pts/ Opp
Sacramento	8	2	0	.800	250	152
Birmingham	7	2	1	.750	192	165
San Antonio	7	3	0	.700	195	150

Playoff Results

SEMIFINALS

Orlando 45, Birmingham 7
Sacramento 17, Barcelona 15

1992 World Bowl

June 6, 1992 at Olympic Stadium, Montreal

Sacramento	0	6	0	15—	21
Orlando	7	10	0	0 —	17

FIRST QUARTER

Orlando: Ford 10 pass from Mitchell (Bennett kick), 11:27

SECOND QUARTER

Sacramento: FG Blanchard 32, 5:16
Orlando: Davis 8 pass from Mitchell (Bennett kick), 8:12
Orlando: FG Bennett 20, 14:06
Sacramento: FG Blanchard 24, 14:59

FOURTH QUARTER

Sacramento: Green 12 pass from Archer (Stock pass from Archer), 3:33
Sacramento: Brown 2 pass from Archer (Blanchard kick), 9:16

A: 43,789.

WLAF Individual Leaders

PASSING

	Att	Comp	Pct Comp	Yds	Avg Gain	TD	Pct TD	Int	Pct Int	Lg	Rating Pts
Archer, Sacramento	317	194	61.2	2964	9.35	23	7.3	7	2.2	t80	107.0
Slack, NY/NJ	215	140	65.1	1898	8.83	12	5.6	7	3.3	68	98.2
Proctor, Montreal	193	113	58.5	1478	7.66	8	4.1	5	2.6	61	85.8
Perez, Frankfurt	147	86	58.5	985	6.70	6	4.1	5	3.4	46	78.2
Johnson, San Antonio	257	144	56.0	1760	6.85	8	3.1	6	2.3	63	78.0

RECEIVING

RECEPTIONS	No.	Yds	Avg	Lg	TD	YARDS	Yds	No.	Avg	Lg	TD
W. Wilson, Ohio	65	776	11.9	52	2	Brown, Sacramento	1011	48	21.1	t80	12
Bouyer, Birmingham	57	706	12.4	50	0	Ford, London	833	45	18.5	55	6
Johnson, Orlando	56	687	12.3	41	5	W. Wilson, Ohio	776	65	11.9	52	2
Garrett, London	55	509	9.3	35	1	Bouyer, Birmingham	706	57	12.4	50	0
T. Woods, Barcelona	51	546	10.7	t86	1	Johnson, Orlando	687	56	12.3	41	5

RUSHING

	Att	Yds	Avg	Lg	TD
Brown, San Antonio	166	767	4.6	54	7
Rasul, Ohio	136	572	4.2	36	4
Clack, Orlando	117	517	4.4	23	6
Pringle, Sacramento	152	507	3.3	22	6
J. Alexander, London	125	501	4.0	20	1

Other Statistical Leaders

Points (TDs)	Brown, Sacramento	72
Points (Kicking)	Doyle, Birmingham	64
Yards from Scrimmage	Brown, Sacramento	1011
Interceptions	Jones, Barcelona	9
Sacks	Lockett, London	14.0
Punting Avg.	Sullivan, San Antonio	41.6
Punt Return Avg.	D. Smith, NY/NJ	12.5
Kickoff Return Avg.	Burbage, NY/NJ	26.9

1992 Canadian Football League

EASTERN DIVISION

	W	L	T	Pts	Pct	PF	PA
Winnipeg	11	7	0	22	.611	507	499
Hamilton	11	7	0	22	.611	536	514
Ottawa	9	9	0	18	.500	484	439
Toronto	6	12	0	12	.333	469	523

WESTERN DIVISION

	W	L	T	Pts	Pct	PF	PA
Calgary	13	5	0	26	.722	507	430
Edmonton	10	8	0	20	.556	552	515
Saskatchewan	9	9	0	18	.500	505	545
B.C.	3	15	0	6	.167	472	667

Regular Season Statistical Leaders

Points (TDs)	Volpe, British Columbia	90
	Sandusky, Edmonton	90
Points (Kicking)	McLoughlin, Calgary	208
Yards (Rushing)	Richardson, Winnipeg	1153
Yards (Passing)	Austin, Saskatchewan	6225
Yards (Receiving)	Pitts, Calgary	1591
Receptions	Pitts, Calgary	103

1992 Playoff Results

DIVISION SEMIFINALS

Eastern: HAMILTON 29, Ottawa 28
Western: EDMONTON 22, Saskatchewan 20

FINALS

Eastern: WINNIPEG 59, Hamilton 11
Western: CALGARY 23, Edmonton 22

1992 Grey Cup Championship

Nov. 24, 1992, at Winnipeg

Calgary Stampeders	11	6	0	7—24
Winnipeg Blue Bombers	0	0	0	10—10

A: 45,863

Thanks, Al

At last March's NFL's annual meeting in Palm Desert, Calif., somebody asked L.A. Raider owner Al Davis about the remarkable resurgence of the Dallas Cowboys. Davis, who fancies himself the fount of football wisdom, correctly noted that soon after the Cowboys were sold in 1989, the team's new owner asked him for advice. "Call [Dallas owner] Jerry Jones and ask him who he copied and who he visited," Davis implored. We did just that, and Jones said, "I'm sending Al a Super Bowl ring—not for his advice but for the trades he gave us."

As Davis may be somewhat less eager to acknowledge, the Cowboys have picked his pocket as well as his brain. Trades with L.A. have given Jones's team its starting fullback Daryl Johnston (acquired in 1989, through a five-draft-pick swap with the Raiders); starting guard John Gesek (in 1990 for a '91 seventh-round choice); and backup quarterback Steve Beuerlein (in '91 for the '92 fourth-round pick).

THEY SAID IT

Jay Leno, talk-show host, after the Houston Oilers squandered a 35–3 lead to lose to the Buffalo Bills in the NFL playoffs: "No other team in history has blown a lead that large—except for the Republicans, of course."

The Super Bowl

Results

	Date	Winner (Share)	Loser (Share)	Score	Site (Attendance)
I	1-15-67	Green Bay ($15,000)	Kansas City ($7,500)	35-10	Los Angeles (61,946)
II	1-14-68	Green Bay ($15,000)	Oakland ($7,500)	33-14	Miami (75,546)
III	1-12-69	NY Jets ($15,000)	Baltimore ($7,500)	16-7	Miami (75,389)
IV	1-11-70	Kansas City ($15,000)	Minnesota ($7,500)	23-7	New Orleans (80,562)
V	1-17-71	Baltimore ($15,000)	Dallas ($7,500)	16-13	Miami (79,204)
VI	1-16-72	Dallas ($15,000)	Miami ($7,500)	24-3	New Orleans (81,023)
VII	1-14-73	Miami ($15,000)	Washington ($7,500)	14-7	Los Angeles (90,182)
VIII	1-13-74	Miami ($15,000)	Minnesota ($7,500)	24-7	Houston (71,882)
IX	1-12-75	Pittsburgh ($15,000)	Minnesota ($7,500)	16-6	New Orleans (80,997)
X	1-18-76	Pittsburgh ($15,000)	Dallas ($7,500)	21-17	Miami (80,187)
XI	1-9-77	Oakland ($15,000)	Minnesota ($7,500)	32-14	Pasadena (103,438)
XII	1-15-78	Dallas ($18,000)	Denver ($9,000)	27-10	New Orleans (75,583)
XIII	1-21-79	Pittsburgh ($18,000)	Dallas ($9,000)	35-31	Miami (79,484)
XIV	1-20-80	Pittsburgh ($18,000)	Los Angeles ($9,000)	31-19	Pasadena (103,985)
XV	1-25-81	Oakland ($18,000)	Philadelphia ($9,000)	27-10	New Orleans (76,135)
XVI	1-24-82	San Francisco ($18,000)	Cincinnati ($9,000)	26-21	Pontiac (81,270)
XVII	1-30-83	Washington ($36,000)	Miami ($18,000)	27-17	Pasadena (103,667)
XVIII	1-22-84	LA Raiders ($36,000)	Washington ($18,000)	38-9	Tampa (72,920)
XIX	1-20-85	San Francisco ($36,000)	Miami ($18,000)	38-16	Stanford (84,059)
XX	1-26-86	Chicago ($36,000)	New England ($18,000)	46-10	New Orleans (73,818)
XXI	1-25-87	NY Giants ($36,000)	Denver ($18,000)	39-20	Pasadena (101,063)
XXII	1-31-88	Washington ($36,000)	Denver ($18,000)	42-10	San Diego (73,302)
XXIII	1-22-89	San Francisco ($36,000)	Cincinnati ($18,000)	20-16	Miami (75,129)
XXIV	1-28-90	San Francisco ($36,000)	Denver ($18,000)	55-10	New Orleans (72,919)
XXV	1-27-91	NY Giants ($36,000)	Buffalo ($18,000)	20-19	Tampa (73,813)
XXVI	1-26-92	Washington ($36,000)	Buffalo ($18,000)	37-24	Minneapolis (63,130)
XXVII	1-31-93	Dallas ($36,000)	Buffalo ($18,000)	52-17	Pasadena (98,374)

Most Valuable Players

		Position
I	Bart Starr, GB	QB
II	Bart Starr, GB	QB
III	Joe Namath, NY Jets	QB
IV	Len Dawson, KC	QB
V	Chuck Howley, Dall	LB
VI	Roger Staubach, Dall	QB
VII	Jake Scott, Mia	S
VIII	Larry Csonka, Mia	RB
IX	Franco Harris, Pitt	RB
X	Lynn Swann, Pitt	WR
XI	Fred Biletnikoff, Oak	WR
XII	Randy White, Dall	DT
	Harvey Martin, Dall	DE
XIII	Terry Bradshaw, Pitt	QB
XIV	Terry Bradshaw, Pitt	QB
XV	Jim Plunkett, Oak	QB
XVI	Joe Montana, SF	QB
XVII	John Riggins, Wash	RB
XVIII	Marcus Allen, LA Raiders	RB
XIX	Joe Montana, SF	QB
XX	Richard Dent, Chi	DE
XXI	Phil Simms, NY Giants	QB
XXII	Doug Williams, Wash	QB
XXIII	Jerry Rice, SF	WR
XXIV	Joe Montana, SF	QB
XXV	Ottis Anderson, NY Giants	RB
XXVI	Mark Rypien, Washington	QB
XXVII	Troy Aikman, Dallas	QB

Composite Standings

	W	L	Pct	Pts	Opp Pts
Pittsburgh Steelers	4	0	1.000	103	73
San Francisco 49ers	4	0	1.000	139	63
Green Bay Packers	2	0	1.000	68	24
NY Giants	2	0	1.000	59	39
Chicago Bears	1	0	1.000	46	10
NY Jets	1	0	1.000	16	7
Oakland/LA Raiders	3	1	.750	111	66
Washington Redskins	3	2	.600	122	103
Baltimore Colts	1	1	.500	23	29
Dallas Cowboys	3	3	.500	164	102
Kansas City Chiefs	1	1	.500	33	42
Miami Dolphins	2	3	.400	74	103
LA Rams	0	1	.000	19	31
New England Patriots	0	1	.000	10	46
Philadelphia Eagles	0	1	.000	10	27
Cincinnati Bengals	0	2	.000	37	46
Buffalo Bills	0	3	.000	60	109
Denver Broncos	0	4	.000	50	163
Minnesota Vikings	0	4	.000	34	95

THEY SAID IT

*Troy Aikman, Dallas Cowboy quarterback, on his reaction to being named one of **People**'s 50 Most Beautiful People: "I thought, Well, they don't know that many people."*

Career Leaders
Passing

	GP	Att	Comp	Pct Comp	Yds	Avg Gain	TD	Pct TD	Int	Pct Int	Lg	Rating Pts
Joe Montana, SF 4	4	122	83	68.0	1142	9.36	11	9.0	0	0.0	44	127.8
Jim Plunkett, Raiders......2	2	46	29	63.0	433	9.41	4	8.7	0	0.0	t80	122.8
Terry Bradshaw, Pitt......4	4	84	49	58.3	932	11.10	9	10.7	4	4.8	t75	112.8
Bart Starr, GB... 2	2	47	29	61.7	452	9.62	3	6.4	1	2.1	t62	106.0
Roger Staubach, Dall 4	4	98	61	62.2	734	7.49	8	8.2	4	4.1	t45	95.4
Len Dawson, KC 2	2	44	28	63.6	353	8.02	2	4.5	2	4.5	t46	84.8
Bob Griese, Mia 3	3	41	26	63.4	295	7.20	1	2.4	2	4.9	t28	72.7
Dan Marino, Mia 1	1	50	29	58.0	318	6.36	1	2.0	2	4.0	30	66.9
Joe Theismann, Wash 2	2	58	31	53.4	386	6.66	2	3.4	4	6.9	60	57.1
Jim Kelly, Buff 3	3	95	50	52.6	569	5.99	2	2.1	6	6.3	61	51.6
John Elway, Den............3	3	101	46	45.5	669	6.62	2	1.9	6	5.9	t56	49.5

Note: Minimum 40 attempts.

Rushing

	GP	Yds	Att	Avg	Lg	TD
Franco Harris, Pitt..............4	4	354	101	3.5	25	4
Larry Csonka, Mia 3	3	297	57	5.2	9	2
John Riggins, Wash 2	2	230	64	3.6	43	2
Timmy Smith, Wash............1	1	204	22	9.3	58	2
Roger Craig, SF................3	3	198	52	3.8	18	2
Marcus Allen, LA Raiders...1	1	191	20	9.6	t74	2
Thurman Thomas, Buff 3	3	167	36	4.6	31	3
Tony Dorsett, Dall 2	2	162	31	5.2	29	1
Mark van Eeghen, Oak.......2	2	148	36	4.1	11	0
Rocky Bleier, Pitt 4	4	144	44	3.3	18	0

Receiving

	GP	No.	Yds	Avg	Lg	TD
Andre Reed, Buff 3	3	21	248	11.8	40	0
Roger Craig, SF 3	3	20	212	10.6	40	2
Jerry Rice, SF............................2	2	18	363	20.2	44	4
Lynn Swann, Pitt........................4	4	16	364	22.8	t64	3
Chuck Foreman, Minn 3	3	15	139	9.3	26	0
Cliff Branch, Raiders 3	3	14	181	12.9	50	3
Preston Pearson, Balt-Pitt-Dall ..5	5	12	105	8.8	14	0
John Stallworth, Pitt 4	4	11	268	24.4	t75	3
Dan Ross, Cin 1	1	11	104	9.5	16	2
Gary Clark, Wash 2	2	10	169	16.9	34	2

Single-Game Leaders

Scoring

	Pts
Roger Craig: XIX, San Francisco vs Miami (1 R, 2 P)	18
Jerry Rice: XXIV, San Francisco vs Denver (3 P)	18
Don Chandler: II, Green Bay vs Oakland (3 PAT, 4 FG)	15

Rushing Yards

	Yds
Timmy Smith: XXII, Washington vs Denver	204
Marcus Allen: XVIII, LA Raiders vs Washington	191
John Riggins: XVII, Washington vs Miami	166
Franco Harris: IX, Pittsburgh vs Minnesota	158
Larry Csonka: VIII, Miami vs Minnesota	145
Clarence Davis: XI, Oakland vs Minnesota	137
Thurman Thomas: XXV, Buffalo vs NY Giants	135
Matt Snell: III, NY Jets vs Baltimore	121

Receptions

	No.
Dan Ross: XVI, Cincinnati vs San Francisco	11
Jerry Rice: XXIII, San Francisco vs Cincinnati	11
Tony Nathan: XIX, Miami vs San Francisco	10
Ricky Sanders: XXII, Washington vs Denver	9
George Sauer: III, NY Jets vs Baltimore	8
Roger Craig: XXIII, San Francisco vs Cincinnati	8
Andre Reed: XXV, Buffalo vs NY Giants	8
Andre Reed: XXVII, Buffalo vs Dallas	8

Touchdown Passes

	No.
Joe Montana: XXIV, San Francisco vs Denver	5
Terry Bradshaw: XIII, Pittsburgh vs Dallas	4
Doug Williams: XXII, Washington vs Denver	4
Troy Aikman: XXVII, Dallas vs Buffalo	4
Roger Staubach: XIII, Dallas vs Pittsburgh	3
Jim Plunkett: XV, Oakland vs Philadelphia	3
Joe Montana: XIX, San Francisco vs Miami	3
Phil Simms: XXI, NY Giants vs Denver	3

Receiving Yards

	Yds
Jerry Rice: XXIII, San Francisco vs Cincinnati	215
Ricky Sanders: XXII, Washington vs Denver	193
Lynn Swann: X, Pittsburgh vs Dallas	161
Andre Reed: XXVII, Buffalo vs Dallas	152
Jerry Rice: XXIV, San Francisco vs Denver	148
Max McGee: I, Green Bay vs Kansas City	138
George Sauer: III, NY Jets vs Baltimore	133

Passing Yards

	Yds
Joe Montana: XXIII, San Francisco vs Cincinnati	357
Doug Williams: XXII, Washington vs Denver	340
Joe Montana: XIX, San Francisco vs Miami	331
Terry Bradshaw: XIII, Pittsburgh vs Dallas	318
Dan Marino: XIX, Miami vs San Francisco	318
Terry Bradshaw: XIV, Pittsburgh vs LA Rams	309
John Elway: XXI, Denver vs NY Giants	304
Ken Anderson: XVI, Cincinnati vs San Francisco	300

1933
NFL championship Chicago Bears 23, NY Giants 21

1934
NFL championship NY Giants 30, Chicago Bears 13

1935
NFL championship Detroit 26, NY Giants 7

1936
NFL championship Green Bay 21, Boston 6

1937
NFL championship Washington 28,
                  Chicago Bears 21

1938
NFL championship NY Giants 23, Green Bay 17

1939
NFL championship Green Bay 27, NY Giants 0

1940
NFL championship Chicago Bears 73, Washington 0

1941
W. div playoff   Chicago Bears 33, Green Bay 14
NFL championship Chicago Bears 37, NY Giants 9

1942
NFL championship Washington 14, Chicago Bears 6

1943
E. div playoff   Washington 28, NY Giants 0
NFL championship Chicago Bears 41,
                  Washington 21

1944
NFL championship Green Bay 14, NY Giants 7

1945
NFL championship Cleveland 15, Washington 14

1946
NFL championship Chicago Bears 24, NY Giants 14

1947
E. div playoff   Philadelphia 21, Pittsburgh 0
NFL championship Chicago Cardinals 28,
                  Philadelphia 21

1948
NFL championship Philadelphia 7,
                  Chicago Cardinals 0

1949
NFL championship Philadelphia 14, Los Angeles 0

1950
Am. Conf. playoff Cleveland 8, NY Giants 3
Nat. Conf. playoff Los Angeles 24,
                    Chicago Bears 14
NFL championship Cleveland 30, Los Angeles 28

1951
NFL championship Los Angeles 24, Cleveland 17

1952
Nat. Conf. playoff Detroit 31, Los Angeles 21
NFL championship Detroit 17, Cleveland 7

1953
NFL championship Detroit 17, Cleveland 16

1954
NFL championship Cleveland 56, Detroit 10

1955
NFL championship Cleveland 38, Los Angeles 14

1956
NFL championship NY Giants 47, Chicago Bears 7

1957
W. Conf playoff   Detroit 31, San Francisco 27
NFL championship Detroit 59, Cleveland 14

1958
E. Conf playoff   NY Giants 10, Cleveland 0
NFL championship Baltimore 23, NY Giants 17

1959
NFL championship Baltimore 31, NY Giants 16

1960
NFL championship Philadelphia 17, Green Bay 13
AFL championship Houston 24, LA Chargers 16

1961
NFL championship Green Bay 37, NY Giants 0
AFL championship Houston 10, San Diego 3

1962
NFL championship Green Bay 16, NY Giants 7
AFL championship Dallas Texans 20, Houston 17

1963
NFL championship Chicago 14, NY Giants 10
AFL E. div playoff Boston 26, Buffalo 8
AFL championship San Diego 51, Boston 10

1964
NFL championship Cleveland 27, Baltimore 0
AFL championship Buffalo 20, San Diego 7

1965
NFL W. Conf   Green Bay 13, Baltimore 10
playoff
NFL championship Green Bay 23, Cleveland 12
AFL championship Buffalo 23, San Diego 0

1966
NFL championship Green Bay 34, Dallas 27
AFL championship Kansas City 31, Buffalo 7

1967
NFL E. Conf   Dallas 52, Cleveland 14
championship
NFL W. Conf   Green Bay 28, Los Angeles 7
championship
NFL championship Green Bay 21, Dallas 17
AFL championship Oakland 40, Houston 7

1968

NFL E. Conf championship	Cleveland 31, Dallas 20
NFL W. Conf championship	Baltimore 24, Minnesota 14
NFL championship	Baltimore 34, Cleveland 0
AFL W. div playoff	Oakland 41, Kansas City 6
AFL championship	NY Jets 27, Oakland 23

1969

NFL E. Conf championship	Cleveland 38, Dallas 14
NFL W. Conf championship	Minnesota 23, Los Angeles 20
NFL championship	Minnesota 27, Cleveland 7
AFL div playoffs	Kansas City 13, NY Jets 6
	Oakland 56, Houston 7
AFL championship	Kansas City 17, Oakland 7

1970

AFC div playoffs	Baltimore 17, Cincinnati 0
	Oakland 21, Miami 14
AFC championship	Baltimore 27, Oakland 17
NFC div playoffs	Dallas 5, Detroit 0
	San Francisco 17, Minnesota 14
NFC championship	Dallas 17, San Francisco 10

1971

AFC div playoffs	Miami 27, Kansas City 24
	Baltimore 20, Cleveland 3
AFC championship	Miami 21, Baltimore 0
NFC div playoffs	Dallas 20, Minnesota 12
	San Francisco 24, Washington 20
NFC championship	Dallas 14, San Francisco 3

1972

AFC div playoffs	Pittsburgh 13, Oakland 7
	Miami 20, Cleveland 14
AFC championship	Miami 21, Pittsburgh 17
NFC div playoffs	Dallas 30, San Francisco 28
	Washington 16, Green Bay 3
NFC championship	Washington 26, Dallas 3

1973

AFC div playoffs	Oakland 33, Pittsburgh 14
	Miami 34, Cincinnati 16
AFC championship	Miami 27, Oakland 10
NFC div playoffs	Minnesota 27, Washington 20
	Dallas 27, Los Angeles 16
NFC championship	Minnesota 27, Dallas 10

1974

AFC div playoffs	Oakland 28, Miami 26
	Pittsburgh 32, Buffalo 14
AFC championship	Pittsburgh 24, Oakland 13
NFC div playoffs	Minnesota 30, St Louis 14
	Los Angeles 19, Washington 10
NFC championship	Minnesota 14, Los Angeles 10

1975

AFC div playoffs	Pittsburgh 28, Baltimore 10
	Oakland 31, Cincinnati 28
AFC championship	Pittsburgh 16, Oakland 10
NFC div playoffs	Los Angeles 35, St Louis 23
	Dallas 17, Minnesota 14
NFC championship	Dallas 37, Los Angeles 7

1976

AFC div playoffs	Oakland 24, New England 21
	Pittsburgh 40, Baltimore 14
AFC championship	Oakland 24, Pittsburgh 7
NFC div playoffs	Minnesota 35, Washington 20
	Los Angeles 14, Dallas 12
NFC championship	Minnesota 24, Los Angeles 13

1977

AFC div playoffs	Denver 34, Pittsburgh 21
	Oakland 37, Baltimore 31
AFC championship	Denver 20, Oakland 17
NFC div playoffs	Dallas 37, Chicago 7
	Minnesota 14, Los Angeles 7
NFC championship	Dallas 23, Minnesota 6

1978

AFC 1st-rd. playoff	Houston 17, Miami 9
AFC div playoffs	Houston 31, New England 14
	Pittsburgh 33, Denver 10
AFC championship	Pittsburgh 34, Houston 5
NFC 1st-rd. playoff	Atlanta 14, Philadelphia 13
NFC div playoffs	Dallas 27, Atlanta 20
	Los Angeles 34, Minnesota 10
NFC championship	Dallas 28, Los Angeles 0

1979

AFC 1st-rd. playoff	Houston 13, Denver 7
AFC div playoffs	Houston 17, San Diego 14
	Pittsburgh 34, Miami 14
AFC championship	Pittsburgh 27, Houston 13
NFC 1st-rd. playoff	Philadelphia 27, Chicago 17
NFC div playoffs	Tampa Bay 24, Philadelphia 17
	Los Angeles 21, Dallas 19
NFC championship	Los Angeles 9, Tampa Bay 0

1980

AFC 1st-rd. playoff	Oakland 27, Houston 7
AFC div playoffs	San Diego 20, Buffalo 14
	Oakland 14, Cleveland 12
AFC championship	Oakland 34, San Diego 27
NFC 1st-rd. playoff	Dallas 34, Los Angeles 13
NFC div playoffs	Philadelphia 31, Minnesota 16
	Dallas 30, Atlanta 27
NFC championship	Philadelphia 20, Dallas 7

1981

AFC 1st-rd. playoff	Buffalo 31, NY Jets 27
AFC div playoffs	San Diego 41, Miami 38
	Cincinnati 28, Buffalo 21
AFC championship	Cincinnati 27, San Diego 7
NFC 1st-rd. playoff	NY Giants 27, Philadelphia 21
NFC div playoffs	Dallas 38, Tampa Bay 0
	San Francisco 38, NY Giants 24
NFC championship	San Francisco 28, Dallas 27

1982

AFC 1st-rd. playoffs	Miami 28, New England 13
	LA Raiders 27, Cleveland 10
	NY Jets 44, Cincinnati 17
	San Diego 31, Pittsburgh 28
AFC 2nd-rd. playoffs	NY Jets 17, LA Raiders 14
	Miami 34, San Diego 13
AFC championship	Miami 14, NY Jets 0
NFC 1st-rd. playoffs	Washington 31, Detroit 7
	Green Bay 41, St Louis 16
	Minnesota 30, Atlanta 24
	Dallas 30, Tampa Bay 17
NFC 2nd-rd. playoffs	Washington 21, Minnesota 7
	Dallas 37, Green Bay 26
NFC championship	Washington 31, Dallas 17

1983

AFC 1st-rd. playoff	Seattle 31, Denver 7
AFC div playoffs	Seattle 27, Miami 20
	LA Raiders 38, Pittsburgh 10
AFC championship	LA Raiders 30, Seattle 14
NFC 1st-rd. playoff	LA Rams 24, Dallas 17
NFC div playoffs	San Francisco 24, Detroit 23
	Washington 51, LA Rams 7
NFC championship	Washington 24, San Francisco 21

1984

AFC 1st-rd. playoff	Seattle 13, LA Raiders 7
AFC div playoffs	Miami 31, Seattle 10
	Pittsburgh 24, Denver 17
AFC championship	Miami 45, Pittsburgh 28
NFC 1st-rd. playoff	NY Giants 16, LA Rams 13
NFC div playoffs	San Francisco 21, NY Giants 10
	Chicago 23, Washington 19
NFC championship	San Francisco 23, Chicago 0

1985

AFC 1st-rd. playoff	New England 26, NY Jets 14
AFC div playoffs	Miami 24, Cleveland 21
	New England 27, LA Raiders 20
AFC championship	New England 31, Miami 14
NFC 1st-rd. playoff	NY Giants 17, San Francisco 3
NFC div playoffs	LA Rams 20, Dallas 0
	Chicago 21, NY Giants 0
NFC championship	Chicago 24, LA Rams 0

1986

AFC 1st-rd. playoff	NY Jets 35, Kansas City 15
AFC div playoffs	Cleveland 23, NY Jets 20
	Denver 22, New England 17
AFC championship	Denver 23, Cleveland 20
NFC 1st-rd. playoff	Washington 19, LA Rams 7
NFC div playoffs	Washington 27, Chicago 13
	NY Giants 49, San Francisco 3
NFC championship	NY Giants 17, Washington 0

1987

AFC div playoffs	Cleveland 38, Indianapolis 21
	Denver 34, Houston 10
AFC championship	Denver 38, Cleveland 33
NFC 1st-rd. playoff	Minnesota 44, New Orleans 10
NFC div playoffs	Minnesota 36, San Francisco 24
	Washington 21, Chicago 17
NFC championship	Washington 17, Minnesota 10

1988

AFC 1st-rd. playoff	Houston 24, Cleveland 23
AFC div playoffs	Cincinnati 21, Seattle 13
	Buffalo 17, Houston 10
AFC championship	Cincinnati 21, Buffalo 10
NFC 1st-rd. playoff	Minnesota 28, LA Rams 17
NFC div playoffs	Chicago 20, Philadelphia 12
	San Francisco 34, Minnesota 9
NFC championship	San Francisco 28, Chicago 3

1989

AFC 1st-rd. playoff	Pittsburgh 26, Houston 23
AFC div playoffs	Cleveland 34, Buffalo 30
	Denver 24, Pittsburgh 23
AFC championship	Denver 37, Cleveland 21
NFC 1st-rd. playoff	LA Rams 21, Philadelphia 7
NFC div playoffs	LA Rams 19, NY Giants 13
	San Francisco 41, Minnesota 13
NFC championship	San Francisco 30, LA Rams 3

1990

AFC 1st-rd. playoffs	Miami 17, Kansas City 16
	Cincinnati 41, Houston 14
AFC div playoffs	Buffalo 44, Miami 34
	LA Raiders 20, Cincinnati 10
AFC championship	Buffalo 51, LA Raiders 3
NFC 1st-rd. playoffs	Chicago 16, New Orleans 6
	Washington 20, Philadelphia 6
NFC div playoffs	NY Giants 31, Chicago 3
	San Francisco 28, Washington 10
NFC championship	NY Giants 15, San Francisco 13

1991

AFC 1st-rd. playoffs	Houston 17, NY Jets 10
	Kansas City 10, LA Raiders 6
AFC div playoffs	Denver 26, Houston 24
	Buffalo 37, Kansas City 14
AFC championship	Buffalo 10, Denver 7
NFC 1st-rd. playoffs	Atlanta 27, New Orleans 20
	Dallas 17, Chicago 13
NFC div playoffs	Washington 24, Atlanta 7
	Detroit 38, Dallas 6
NFC championship	Washington 41, Detroit 10

1992

AFC 1st-rd playoffs	San Diego 17, Kansas City 0
	Buffalo 41, Houston 38 (OT)
AFC div playoffs	Buffalo 24, Pittsburgh 3
	Miami 31, San Diego 0
AFC championship	Buffalo 29, Miami 10
NFC 1st -rd playoffs	Washington 24, Minnesota 7
	Philadelphia 36, New Orleans 20
NFC div playoffs	San Francisco 20, Washington 13
	Dallas 34, Philadelphia 10
NFC championship	Dallas 30, San Francisco 20

All-Time NFL Individual Statistical Leaders

Career Leaders

Scoring

	Yrs	TD	FG	PAT	Pts
George Blanda	26	9	335	943	2002
Jan Stenerud	19	0	373	580	1699
Pat Leahy	18	0	304	558	1470
Jim Turner	16	1	304	521	1439
Mark Moseley	16	0	300	482	1382
Jim Bakken	17	0	282	534	1380
Nick Lowery	14	0	306	449	1367
Fred Cox	15	0	282	519	1365
Lou Groza	17	1	234	641	1349
Jim Breech	14	0	243	517	1246
Chris Bahr	14	0	241	490	1213
Matt Bahr	14	0	237	431	1142
Gino Cappelletti	11	42	176	350	1130
Gary Anderson	11	0	258	356	1130
Ray Wersching	15	0	222	456	1122
Eddie Murray	12	0	244	381	1113
Don Cockroft	13	0	216	432	1080
Garo Yepremian	14	0	210	444	1074
Morten Andersen	11	0	246	347	1085
Bruce Gossett	11	0	219	374	1031

Cappelletti's total includes four two-point conversions.

Rushing

	Yrs	Att	Yds	Avg	Lg	TD
Walter Payton	13	3,838	16,726	4.4	76	110
Eric Dickerson	10	2,970	13,168	4.4	85	90
Tony Dorsett	12	2,936	12,739	4.3	99	77
Jim Brown	9	2,359	12,312	5.2	80	106
Franco Harris	13	2,949	12,120	4.1	75	91
John Riggins	14	2,916	11,352	3.9	66	104
O. J. Simpson	11	2,404	11,236	4.7	94	61
Ottis Anderson	14	2,562	10,273	4.0	76	81
Earl Campbell	8	2,187	9,407	4.3	81	74
Jim Taylor	10	1,941	8,597	4.4	84	83
Marcus Allen	11	2,090	8,545	4.1	61	79
Joe Perry	14	1,737	8,378	4.8	78	53
Gerald Riggs	10	1,989	8,188	4.2	58	69
Larry Csonka	11	1,891	8,081	4.3	54	64
Freeman McNeil	12	1,798	8,074	4.5	69	38
Roger Craig	10	1,953	8,070	4.1	71	55
James Brooks	12	1,685	7,962	4.7	65	49
Mike Pruitt	11	1,844	7,378	4.0	77	51
Leroy Kelly	10	1,727	7,274	4.2	70	74
George Rogers	7	1,692	7,176	4.2	79	54

Touchdowns

	Yrs	Rush	Pass Rec	Ret	Total TD
Jim Brown	9	106	20	0	126
Walter Payton	13	110	15	0	125
John Riggins	14	104	12	0	116
Lenny Moore	12	63	48	2	113
Jerry Rice	8	5	103	0	108
Don Hutson	11	3	99	3	105
Steve Largent	14	1	100	0	101
Franco Harris	13	91	9	0	100
Marcus Allen	10	79	18	1	98
Eric Dickerson	10	90	6	0	96

	Yrs	Rush	Pass Rec	Ret	Total TD
Jim Taylor	10	83	10	0	93
Tony Dorsett	12	77	13	1	91
Bobby Mitchell	11	18	65	8	91
Leroy Kelly	10	74	13	3	90
Charley Taylor	13	11	79	0	90
Don Maynard	15	0	88	0	88
Lance Alworth	11	2	85	0	87
Paul Warfield	13	1	85	0	86
Ottis Anderson	13	81	5	0	86
Tommy McDonald	12	0	84	1	85

Longest Plays

RUSHING

	Opponent	Year	Yds
Tony Dorsett, Dall	Minn	1983	99
Andy Uram, GB	Chi Cards	1939	97
Bob Gage, Pitt	Chi	1949	97
Jim Spitival, Balt	GB	1950	96
Bob Hoernschemeyer, Det	NY Yanks	1950	96

PASSING

	Opponent	Year	Yds
Frank Filchock to Andy Farkas, Washington	Pitt	1939	99
George Izo to Bobby Mitchell, Washington	Cle	1963	99
Karl Sweetan to Pat Studstill, Detroit	Balt	1966	99
Sonny Jurgensen to Gerry Allen, Washington	Chi	1968	99
Jim Plunkett to Cliff Branch, LA Raiders	Wash	1983	99
Ron Jaworski to Mike Quick, Philadelphia	Atl	1985	99

FIELD GOALS

	Opponent	Year	Yds
Tom Dempsey, NO	Det	1970	63
Steve Cox, Cle	Cin	1984	60
Morten Andersen, NO	Chi	1991	60

PUNTS

	Opponent	Year	Yds
Steve O'Neal, NY Jets	Den	1969	98
Joe Lintzenich, Chi	NY Giants	1931	94
Shawn McCarthy, NE	Buff	1991	93
Randall Cunningham, Phi	NY Giants	1989	91

THEY SAID IT

Lawrence Taylor, 33-year-old New York Giant linebacker, on aging: "When you get old, everything is hurting. When I get up in the morning, it sounds like I'm making popcorn."

Career Leaders (Cont.)

Combined Yards Gained

	Yrs	Total	Rush	Rec	Int Ret	Punt Ret	Kickoff Ret	Fum Ret
Walter Payton	13	21,803	16,726	4,538	0	0	539	0
Tony Dorsett	12	16,326	12,739	3,554	0	0	0	33
Jim Brown	9	15,459	12,312	2,499	0	0	648	0
Eric Dickerson	10	15,262	13,168	2,079	0	0	0	15
James Brooks	12	14,644	7,962	3,621	0	565	2,762	0
Franco Harris	13	14,622	12,120	2,287	0	0	233	-18
O.J. Simpson	11	14,368	11,236	2,142	0	0	990	0
James Lofton	15	14,094	246	13,821	0	0	0	27
Bobby Mitchell	11	14,078	2,735	7,954	0	699	2,690	0
John Riggins	14	13,435	11,352	2,090	0	0	0	-7
Steve Largent	14	13,396	83	13,089	0	68	156	0
Ottis Anderson	14	13,364	10,273	3,062	0	0	0	29
Greg Pruitt	12	13,262	5,672	3,069	0	2,007	2,514	0
Ollie Matson	14	12,884	5,173	3,285	51	595	3,746	34
Roger Craig	10	12,812	8,070	4,742	0	0	0	0
Marcus Allen	11	12,803	8,545	4,258	0	0	0	0
Tim Brown	10	12,684	3,862	3,399	0	639	4,781	3
Lenny Moore	12	12,451	5,174	6,039	0	56	1,180	2
Don Maynard	15	12,379	70	11,834	0	132	343	0
Charlie Joiner	18	12,367	22	12,146	0	0	194	5

Passing

	Yrs	Att	Comp	Pct Comp	Yds	Avg Gain	TD	Pct TD	Int	Pct Int	Rating Pts
Joe Montana	13	4,600	2,929	63.7	35,124	7.64	244	5.3	123	2.7	93.5
Steve Young	8	1,506	908	60.3	11,877	7.89	76	5.0	42	2.8	90.4
Dan Marino	10	5,284	3,128	59.2	39,502	7.48	290	5.5	165	3.1	87.8
Jim Kelly	7	3,024	1,824	60.3	23,031	7.62	161	5.3	108	3.6	86.9
Mark Rypien	5	1,888	1,078	57.1	14,414	7.63	97	5.1	65	3.4	84.3
Roger Staubach	11	2,958	1,685	57.0	22,700	7.67	153	5.2	109	3.7	83.4
Neil Lomax	8	3,153	1,817	57.6	22,771	7.22	136	4.3	90	2.9	82.7
Sonny Jurgensen	18	4,262	2,433	57.1	32,224	7.56	255	6.0	189	4.4	82.6
Len Dawson	19	3,741	2,136	57.1	28,711	7.67	239	6.4	183	4.9	82.6
Dave Krieg	13	3,989	2,326	58.3	29,247	7.33	210	5.3	160	4.0	82.1
Ken Anderson	16	4,475	2,654	59.3	32,838	7.34	197	4.4	160	3.6	81.9
Boomer Esiason	9	3,378	1,897	56.2	25,671	7.60	174	5.2	129	3.8	81.8
Bernie Kosar	8	3,012	1,174	58.9	21,097	7.00	111	3.7	78	2.6	81.8
Danny White	13	2,950	1,761	59.7	21,959	7.44	155	5.3	132	4.5	81.7
Ken O'Brien	9	3,465	2,039	58.8	24,386	7.04	124	3.6	95	2.7	81.0
Warren Moon	9	4,026	2,329	57.8	30,200	7.50	175	4.3	145	3.6	81.0
Bart Starr	16	3,149	1,808	57.4	24,718	7.85	152	4.8	138	4.4	80.5
Fran Tarkenton	18	6,467	3,686	57.0	47,003	7.27	342	5.3	266	4.1	80.4
Dan Fouts	15	5,604	3,297	58.8	43,040	7.68	254	4.5	242	4.3	80.2
Randall Cunningham	8	2,641	1,464	55.4	18,193	6.89	126	4.8	82	3.1	79.9

1,500 or more attempts. The passing ratings are based on performance standards established for completion percentage, interception percentage, touchdown percentage, and average gain. Passers are allocated points according to how their marks compare with those standards.

Receiving

	Yrs	No.	Yds	Avg	Lg	TD		Yrs	No.	Yds	Avg	Lg	TD
Art Monk	13	847	11,628	13.7	79	63	Harold Carmichael	14	590	8,985	15.2	85	79
Steve Largent	14	819	13,089	16.0	74	100	Fred Biletnikoff	14	589	8,974	15.2	82	76
Charlie Joiner	18	750	12,146	16.2	87	65	Harold Jackson	16	579	10,372	17.9	79	76
James Lofton	15	750	13,821	18.4	80	75	Lionel Taylor	10	567	7,195	12.7	80	45
Ozzie Newsome	13	662	7,980	12.1	74	47	Wes Chandler	11	559	8,966	16.0	85	56
Charley Taylor	13	649	9,110	14.0	88	79	Stanley Morgan	14	557	10,716	19.2	76	72
Don Maynard	15	633	11,834	18.7	87	88	Roy Green	14	559	8,965	16.0	83	66
Raymond Berry	13	631	9,275	14.7	70	68	Mark Clayton	10	550	8,643	15.7	78	81
Jerry Rice	8	610	10,273	16.8	96	103	Roger Craig	10	547	4,742	8.7	73	16
Drew Hill	13	600	9,447	15.7	81	60	J.T. Smith	13	544	6,974	12.8	77	35

Career Leaders *(Cont.)*

Interceptions

	Yrs	No.	Yds	Avg	Lg	TD
Paul Krause	16	81	1185	14.6	81	3
Emlen Tunnell	14	79	1282	16.2	55	4
Dick (Night Train) Lane	14	68	1207	17.8	80	5
Ken Riley	15	65	596	9.2	66	5
Dick LeBeau	13	62	762	12.3	70	3
Dave Brown	16	62	698	11.3	90	5

Punt Returns

	Yrs	No.	Yds	Avg	Lg	TD
George McAfee	8	112	1431	12.8	74	2
Jack Christiansen	8	85	1084	12.8	89	8
Claude Gibson	5	110	1381	12.6	85	3
Bill Dudley	9	124	1515	12.2	96	3
Rick Upchurch	9	248	3008	12.1	92	8

Punting

	Yrs	No.	Yds	Avg	Lg	Blk
Sammy Baugh	16	338	15,245	45.1	85	9
Tommy Davis	11	511	22,833	44.7	82	2
Yale Lary	11	503	22,279	44.3	74	4
Rohn Stark	11	829	36,465	44.0	72	6
Horace Gillom	7	385	16,872	43.8	80	5

Kickoff Returns

	Yrs	No.	Yds	Avg	Lg	TD
Gale Sayers	7	91	2781	30.6	103	6
Lynn Chandnois	7	92	2720	29.6	93	3
Abe Woodson	9	193	5538	28.7	105	5
Claude (Buddy) Young	6	90	2514	27.9	104	2
Travis Williams	5	102	2801	27.5	105	6

Single-Season Leaders
Scoring

POINTS

	Year	TD	PAT	FG	Pts
Paul Hornung, GB	1960	15	41	15	176
Mark Moseley, Wash	1983	0	62	33	161
Gino Cappelletti, Bos	1964	7	38	25	155
Chip Lohmiller, Wash	1991	0	56	31	149
Gino Cappelletti, Bos	1961	8	48	17	147
Paul Hornung, GB	1961	10	41	15	146
Jim Turner, NY Jets	1968	0	43	34	145
John Riggins, Wash	1983	24	0	0	144
Kevin Butler, Chi	1985	0	51	31	144
Tony Franklin, NE	1986	0	44	32	140

Note: Cappelletti's 1964 total includes a two-point conversion.

TOUCHDOWNS

	Year	Rush	Rec	Ret	Total
John Riggins, Wash	1983	24	0	0	24
O. J. Simpson, Buff	1975	16	7	0	23
Jerry Rice, SF	1987	1	22	0	23
Gale Sayers, Chi	1965	14	6	2	22

FIELD GOALS

	Year	Att	No.
Ali Haji-Sheikh, NY Giants	1983	42	35
Jim Turner, NY Jets	1968	46	34
Chester Marcol, GB	1972	48	33
Mark Moseley, Wash	1983	47	33

Rushing

YARDS GAINED

	Year	Att	Yds	Avg
Eric Dickerson, LA Rams	1984	379	2105	5.6
O. J. Simpson, Buff	1973	332	2003	6.0
Earl Campbell, Hou	1980	373	1934	5.2
Jim Brown, Clev	1963	291	1883	6.4
Walter Payton, Chi	1977	339	1852	5.5
Eric Dickerson, LA Rams	1986	404	1821	4.5
O. J. Simpson, Buff	1975	329	1817	5.5
Eric Dickerson, LA Rams	1983	390	1808	4.6
Marcus Allen, LA Raiders	1985	390	1759	4.6
Gerald Riggs, Atl	1985	397	1719	4.3
Emmitt Smith, Dall	1992	373	1713	4.6

AVERAGE GAIN

	Year	Avg
Beattie Feathers, Chi	1934	9.94
Randall Cunningham, Phil	1990	7.98
Steve Young, SF	1992	7.10
Bobby Douglass, Chi	1972	6.87
Dan Towler, LA Rams	1951	6.78

TOUCHDOWNS

	Year	No.
John Riggins, Wash	1983	24
Joe Morris, NY Giants	1985	21
Jim Taylor, GB	1962	19
Earl Campbell, Hou	1979	19
Chuck Muncie, SD	1981	19
Emmitt Smith, Dall	1992	18

An American in Paris

American football has grown sufficiently popular in France that amateur leagues have begun springing up like chanterelle mushrooms. Marine lieutenant colonel Bob Parnell, who is serving a tour of duty at the U.S. embassy in Paris, coaches in a league in which all the players, except two expatriate Americans per team, are French.

At first Parnell was surprised by the slow pace of the games. There would be a burst of activity, then nothing would happen for a very long time. Just like an NFL game, in other words. Things speeded up considerably, however, when the league passed a rule against smoking in the huddle.

Single-Season Leaders *(Cont.)*
Passing

YARDS GAINED

	Year	Att	Comp	Pct	Yds
Dan Marino, Mia	1984	564	362	64.2	5084
Dan Fouts, SD	1981	609	360	59.1	4802
Dan Marino, Mia	1986	623	378	60.7	4746
Dan Fouts, SD	1980	589	348	59.1	4715
Warren Moon, Hou	1991	655	404	61.7	4690
Warren Moon, Hou	1990	584	362	62.0	4689
Neil Lomax, StL	1984	560	345	61.6	4614
Lynn Dickey, GB	1983	484	289	59.7	4458
Dan Marino, Mia	1988	606	354	58.4	4434
Bill Kenney, KC	1983	603	346	57.4	4348
Don Majkowski, GB	1989	599	353	58.9	4318
Jim Everett, LA Rams	1989	518	304	58.7	4310

PASS RATING

	Year	Rat.
Joe Montana, SF	1989	112.4
Milt Plum, Clev	1960	110.4
Sammy Baugh, Wash	1945	109.9
Dan Marino, Mia	1984	108.9
Steve Young, SF	1992	107.0

TOUCHDOWNS

	Year	No.
Dan Marino, Mia	1984	48
Dan Marino, Mia	1986	44
George Blanda, Hou	1961	36
Y. A. Tittle, NY Giants	1963	36

Receiving

RECEPTIONS

	Year	No.	Yds
Sterling Sharpe, G.B.	1992	108	1461
Art Monk, Wash	1984	106	1372
Charley Hennigan, Hou	1964	101	1546
Lionel Taylor, Den	1961	100	1176
Jerry Rice, SF	1990	100	1502
Haywood Jeffires, Hou	1991	100	1181
Todd Christensen, LA Raiders	1986	95	1153
Johnny Morris, Chi	1964	93	1200
Al Toon, NY Jets	1988	93	1067
Michael Irvin, Dall	1991	93	1523
Andre Rison, Atl	1992	93	1121
Lionel Taylor, Den	1960	92	1235
Todd Christensen, LA Raiders	1983	92	1247
Roger Craig, SF	1985	92	1016

YARDS GAINED

	Year	Yds
Charley Hennigan, Hou	1961	1746
Lance Alworth, SD	1965	1602
Jerry Rice, SF	1986	1570
Roy Green, StL	1984	1555

TOUCHDOWNS

	Year	No.
Jerry Rice, SF	1987	22
Mark Clayton, Mia	1984	18
Don Hutson, GB	1942	17
Elroy (Crazylegs) Hirsch, LA Rams	1951	17
Bill Groman, Hou	1961	17
Jerry Rice, SF	1989	17

All-Purpose Yards

	Year	Run	Rec	Ret	Total
Lionel James, SD	1985	516	1027	992	2535
Terry Metcalf, StL	1975	816	378	1268	2462
Mack Herron, NE	1974	824	474	1146	2444
Gale Sayers, Chi	1966	1231	447	762	2440
Timmy Brown, Phil	1963	841	487	1100	2428
Tim Brown, LA Raiders	1988	50	725	1542	2317
Marcus Allen, LA Raiders	1985	1759	555	-6	2308
Timmy Brown, Phil	1962	545	849	912	2306
Gale Sayers, Chi	1965	867	507	898	2272
Eric Dickerson, LA Rams	1984	2105	139	15	2259
O. J. Simpson, Buff	1975	1817	426	0	2243

Punting

	Year	No.	Yds	Avg
Sammy Baugh, Wash	1940	35	1799	51.4
Yale Lary, Det	1963	35	1713	48.9
Sammy Baugh, Wash	1941	30	1462	48.7
Yale Lary, Det	1961	52	2516	48.4
Sammy Baugh, Wash	1942	37	1783	48.2

Sacks

	Year	No.
Mark Gastineau, NY Jets	1984	22
Reggie White, Phil	1987	21
Chris Doleman, Minn	1989	21
Lawrence Taylor, NY Giants	1986	20.5

Interceptions

	Year	No.
Dick (Night Train) Lane, LA Rams	1952	14
Dan Sandifer, Wash	1948	13
Spec Sanders, NY Yanks	1950	13
Lester Hayes, Oak	1980	13

Kickoff Returns

	Year	Avg
Travis Williams, GB	1967	41.1
Gale Sayers, Chi	1967	37.7
Ollie Matson, Chi Cardinals	1958	35.5
Jim Duncan, Balt	1970	35.4
Lynn Chandnois, Pitt	1952	35.2

Punt Returns

	Year	Avg
Herb Rich, Balt	1950	23.0
Jack Christiansen, Det	1952	21.5
Dick Christy, NY Titans	1961	21.3
Bob Hayes, Dall	1968	20.8

Single-Game Leaders
Scoring

POINTS

	Date	Pts
Ernie Nevers, Cards vs Bears	11-28-29	40
Dub Jones, Clev vs Chi Bears	11-25-51	36
Gale Sayers, Chi Bears vs SF	12-12-65	36
Paul Hornung, GB vs Balt	10-8-61	33

On Thanksgiving Day, 1929, Nevers scored all the Cardinals' points on six rushing TDs and four PATs. The Cards defeated Red Grange and the Bears, 40-6. Jones and Sayers each rushed for four touchdowns and scored two more on returns in their teams' victories. Hornung scored four touchdowns and kicked 6 PATs and a field goal in a 45-7 win over the Colts.

FIELD GOALS

	Date	No.
Jim Bakken, StL vs Pitt	9-24-67	7
Rich Karlis, Minn vs LA Rams	11-5-89	7

Eight players tied with 6 FGs each.

Bakken was 7 for 9, Karlis 7 for 7.

TOUCHDOWNS

	Date	No.
Ernie Nevers, Cards vs Bears	11-28-29	6
Dub Jones, Clev vs Chi Bears	11-25-51	6
Gale Sayers, Chi vs SF	12-12-65	6
Bob Shaw, Chi Cards vs Balt	10-2-50	5
Jim Brown, Clev vs Balt	11-1-59	5
Abner Haynes, Dall Texans vs Oak	11-26-61	5
Billy Cannon, Hous vs NY Titans	12-10-61	5
Cookie Gilchrist, Buff vs NY Jets	12-8-63	5
Paul Hornung, GB vs Balt	12-12-65	5
Kellen Winslow, SD vs Oak	11-22-81	5
Jerry Rice, SF vs Atl	10-14-90	5

Rushing

YARDS GAINED

	Date	Yds
Walter Payton, Chi vs Minn	11-20-77	275
O. J. Simpson, Buff vs Det	11-25-76	273
O. J. Simpson, Buff vs NE	9-16-73	250
Willie Ellison, LA Rams vs NO	12-5-71	247
Cookie Gilchrist, Buff vs NY Jets	12-8-63	243

CARRIES

	Date	No.
Jamie Morris, Wash vs Cin	12-17-88	45
Butch Woolfolk, NY Giants vs Phil	11-20-83	43
James Wilder, TB vs GB	9-30-84	43
James Wilder, TB vs Pitt	10-30-83	42
Franco Harris, Pitt vs Cin	10-17-76	41
Gerald Riggs, Atl vs LA Rams	11-17-85	41

TOUCHDOWNS

	Date	No.
Ernie Nevers, Cards vs Bears	11-28-29	6
Jim Brown, Clev vs Balt	11-1-59	5
Cookie Gilchrist, Buff vs NY Jets	12-8-63	5

Passing

YARDS GAINED

	Date	Yds
Norm Van Brocklin, LA vs NY Yanks	9-28-51	554
Warren Moon, Hou vs KC	12-16-90	527
Dan Marino, Mia vs NY Jets	10-23-88	521
Phil Simms, NY Giants vs Cin	10-13-85	513
Vince Ferragamo, LA Rams vs Chi	12-26-82	509
Y. A. Tittle, NY Giants vs Wash	10-28-62	505

COMPLETIONS

	Date	No.
Richard Todd, NY Jets vs SF	9-21-80	42
Warren Moon, Hou vs Dall	11-10-91	41
Ken Anderson, Cin vs SD	12-20-82	40
Phil Simms, NY Giants vs Cin	10-13-85	40
Dan Marino, Mia vs Buff	11-16-86	39
Tommy Kramer, Minn vs Clev	12-14-80	38
Tommy Kramer, Minn vs DB	11-29-81	38
Joe Ferguson, Buff vs Mia	10-9-83	38

TOUCHDOWNS

	Date	No.
Sid Luckman, Chi Bears vs NY Giants	11-14-43	7
Adrian Burk, Phil vs Wash	10-17-54	7
George Blanda, Hou vs NY Titans	11-19-61	7
Y. A. Tittle, NY Giants vs Wash	10-28-62	7
Joe Kapp, Minn vs Balt	9-28-69	7

THEY SAID IT

Linebacker Mike Singletary, on the demise of the Bear defense: "Instead of having a bunch of guys flying to the ball, I go into the huddle and say, 'C'mon! Let's go!' Then I look into their eyes, and I can see it. They're just not with me."

Single-Game Leaders *(Cont.)*
Receiving

YARDS GAINED

	Date	Yds
Flipper Anderson, LA Rams vs NO	11-26-89	336
Stephone Paige, KC vs SD	12-22-85	309
Jim Benton, Clev vs Det	11-22-45	303
Cloyce Box, Det vs Balt	12-3-50	302
John Taylor, SF vs LA Rams	12-11-89	286

RECEPTIONS

	Date	No.
Tom Fears, LA Rams vs GB	12-3-50	18
Clark Gaines, NY Jets vs SF	9-21-80	17
Sonny Randle, StL vs NY Giants	11-4-62	16
Rickey Young, Minn vs NE	12-16-79	15
William Andrews, Atl vs Pitt	11-15-81	15

TOUCHDOWNS

	Date	No.
Bob Shaw, Chi Cards vs Balt	10-2-50	5
Kellen Winslow, SD vs Oak	11-22-81	5
Jerry Rice, SF vs Atl	10-14-90	5

All-Purpose Yards

	Date	Yds
Billy Cannon, Hou vs NY Titans	12-10-61	373
Lionel James, SD vs LA Raiders	11-10-85	345
Timmy Brown, Phil vs StL	12-16-62	341
Gale Sayers, Chi vs Minn	12-18-66	339
Gale Sayers, Chi vs SF	12-12-65	336

Annual NFL Individual Statistical Leaders

Rushing

Year	Player, Team	Att.	Yards	Avg.	TD
1932	Cliff Battles, Bos	148	576	3.9	3
1933	Jim Musick, Bos	173	809	4.7	5
1934	Beattie Feathers, Chicago Bears	101	1004	9.9	8
1935	Doug Russell, Chicago Cards	140	499	3.6	0
1936	Alphonse Leemans, NY	206	830	4.0	2
1937	Cliff Battles, Wash	216	874	4.0	5
1938	Byron White, Pitt	152	567	3.7	4
1939	Bill Osmanski, Chi	121	699	5.8	7
1940	Byron White, Det	146	514	3.5	5
1941	Clarence Manders, Bklyn	111	486	4.4	5
1942	Bill Dudley, Pitt	162	696	4.3	5
1943	Bill Paschal, NY	147	572	3.9	10
1944	Bill Paschal, NY	196	737	3.8	9
1945	Steve Van Buren, Phil	143	832	5.8	15
1946	Bill Dudley, Pitt	146	604	4.1	3
1947	Steve Van Buren, Phil	217	1008	4.6	13
1948	Steve Van Buren, Phil	201	945	4.7	10
1949	Steve Van Buren, Phil	263	1146	4.4	11
1950	Marion Motley, Clev	140	810	5.8	3
1951	Eddie Price, NY	271	971	3.6	7
1952	Dan Towler, LA	156	894	5.7	10
1953	Joe Perry, SF	192	1018	5.3	10
1954	Joe Perry, SF	173	1049	6.1	8
1955	Alan Ameche, Balt	213	961	4.5	9
1956	Rick Casares, Chicago Bears	234	1126	4.8	12
1957	Jim Brown, Clev	202	942	4.7	9
1958	Jim Brown, Clev	257	1527	5.9	17
1959	Jim Brown, Clev	290	1329	4.6	14
1960	Jim Brown, Clev, NFL	215	1257	5.8	9
	Abner Haynes, Dall Texans, AFL	156	875	5.6	9
1961	Jim Brown, Clev, NFL	305	1408	4.6	8
	Billy Cannon, Hou, AFL	200	948	4.7	6
1962	Jim Taylor, GB, NFL	272	1474	5.4	19
	Cookie Gilchrist, Buff, AFL	214	1096	5.1	13
1963	Jim Brown, Clev, NFL	291	1863	6.4	12
	Clem Daniels, Oak, AFL	215	1099	5.1	3
1964	Jim Brown, Clev, NFL	280	1446	5.2	7
	Cookie Gilchrist, Buff, AFL	230	981	4.3	6
1965	Jim Brown, Clev, NFL	289	1544	5.3	17
	Paul Lowe, SD, AFL	222	1121	5.0	7
1966	Jim Nance, Bos, AFL	299	1458	4.9	11
	Gale Sayers, Chi, NFL	229	1231	5.4	8
1967	Jim Nance, Bos, AFL	269	1216	4.5	7
	Leroy Kelly, Clev, NFL	235	1205	5.1	11
1968	Leroy Kelly, Clev, NFL	248	1239	5.0	16
	Paul Robinson, Cinn, AFL	238	1023	4.3	8
1969	Gale Sayers, Chi, NFL	236	1032	4.4	8
	Dickie Post, SD, AFL	182	873	4.8	6
1970	Larry Brown, Wash, NFC	237	1125	4.7	5
	Floyd Little, Den, AFC	209	901	4.3	3
1971	Floyd Little, Den, AFC	284	1133	4.0	6
	John Brockington, GB, NFC	216	1105	5.1	4
1972	O.J. Simpson, Buff, AFC	292	1251	4.3	6
	Larry Brown, Wash, NFC	285	1216	4.3	8
1973	O.J. Simpson, Buff, AFC	332	2003	6.0	12
	John Brockington, GB, NFC	265	1144	4.3	3

Rushing (Cont.)

Year	Player, Team	Att.	Yards	Avg.	TD
1974	Otis Armstrong, Den, AFC	263	1407	5.3	9
	Lawrence McCutcheon, LA Rams, NFC	236	1109	4.7	3
1975	O.J. Simpson, Buff, AFC	329	1817	5.5	16
	Jim Otis, StL, NFC	269	1076	4.0	5
1976	O.J. Simpson, Buff, AFC	290	1503	5.2	8
	Walter Payton, Chi, NFC	311	1390	4.5	13
1977	Walter Payton, Chi, NFC	339	1852	5.5	14
	Mark van Eeghen, Oak, AFC	324	1273	3.9	7
1978	Earl Campbell, Hou, AFC	302	1450	4.8	13
	Walter Payton, Chi, NFC	333	1395	4.2	11
1979	Earl Campbell, Hou, AFC	368	1697	4.6	19
	Walter Payton, Chi, NFC	369	1610	4.4	14
1980	Earl Campbell, Hou, AFC	373	1934	5.2	13
	Walter Payton, Chi, NFC	317	1460	4.6	6
1981	George Rogers, NO, NFC	378	1674	4.4	13
	Earl Campbell, Hou, AFC	361	1376	3.8	10
1982	Freeman McNeil, NY Jets, AFC	151	786	5.2	6
	Tony Dorsett, Dall, NFC	177	745	4.2	5
1983	Eric Dickerson, LA Rams, NFC	390	1808	4.6	18
	Curt Warner, Sea, AFC	335	1449	4.3	13
1984	Eric Dickerson, LA Rams, NFC	379	2105	5.6	14
	Earnest Jackson, SD, AFC	296	1179	4.0	8
1985	Marcus Allen, LA Raiders, AFC	380	1759	4.6	11
	Gerald Riggs, Atl, NFC	397	1719	4.3	10
1986	Eric Dickerson, LA Rams, NFC	404	1821	4.5	11
	Curt Warner, Sea, AFC	319	1481	4.6	13
1987	Charles White, LA Rams, NFC	324	1374	4.2	11
	Eric Dickerson, Ind, AFC	223	1011	4.5	5
1988	Eric Dickerson, Ind, AFC	388	1659	4.3	14
	Herschel Walker, Dall, NFC	361	1514	4.2	5
1989	Christian Okoye, KC, AFC	370	1480	4.0	12
	Barry Sanders, Det, NFC	280	1470	5.3	14
1990	Barry Sanders, Det, NFC	255	1304	5.1	13
	Thurman Thomas, Buff, AFC	271	1297	4.8	11
1991	Emmitt Smith, Dall, NFC	365	1563	4.3	12
	Thurman Thomas, Buff, AFC	288	1407	4.9	7
1992	Emmitt Smith, Dall, NFC	373	1713	4.6	18
	Barry Foster, Pitt, AFC	390	1690	4.3	11

Passing

Year	Player, Team	Att.	Comp	Yards	TD	Int
1932	Arnie Herber, GB	101	37	639	9	9
1933	Harry Newman, NY	136	53	973	11	17
1934	Arnie Herber, GB	115	42	799	8	12
1935	Ed Danowski, NY	113	57	794	10	9
1936	Arnie Herber, GB	173	77	1239	11	13
1937	Sammy Baugh, Wash	171	81	1127	8	14
1938	Ed Danowski, NY	129	70	848	7	8
1939	Parker Hall, Clev	208	106	1227	9	13
1940	Sammy Baugh, Wash	177	111	1367	12	10
1941	Cecil Isbell, GB	206	117	1479	15	11
1942	Cecil Isbell, GB	268	146	2021	24	14
1943	Sammy Baugh, Wash	239	133	1754	23	19
1944	Frank Filchock, Wash	147	84	1139	13	9
1945	Sammy Baugh, Wash	182	128	1669	11	4
	Sid Luckman, Chi	217	117	1725	14	10
1946	Bob Waterfield, LA	251	127	1747	18	17
1947	Sammy Baugh, Wash	354	210	2938	25	15
1948	Tommy Thompson, Phi	246	141	1965	25	11
1949	Sammy Baugh, Wash	255	145	1903	18	14
1950	Norm Van Brocklin, LA	233	127	2061	18	14
1951	Bob Waterfield, LA	176	88	1566	13	10
1952	Norm Van Brocklin, LA	205	113	1736	14	17
1953	Otto Graham, Clev	258	167	2722	11	9
1954	Norm Van Brocklin, LA	260	139	2637	13	21
1955	Otto Graham, Clev	185	98	1721	15	8
1956	Ed Brown, Chi	168	96	1667	11	12
1957	Tommy O'Connell, Clev	110	63	1229	9	8
1958	Eddie LeBaron, Wash	145	79	1365	11	10
1959	Charlie Conerly, NY	194	113	1706	14	4
1960	Milt Plum, Clev, NFL	250	151	2297	21	5
	Jack Kemp, LA, AFL	406	211	3018	20	25
1961	George Blanda, Hou, AFL	362	187	3330	36	22
	Milt Plum, Clev, NFL	302	177	2416	18	10
1962	Len Dawson, Dall, AFL	310	189	2759	29	17
	Bart Starr, GB, NFL	285	178	2438	12	9
1963	Y.A. Tittle, NY, NFL	367	221	3145	36	14
	Tobin Rote, SD, AFL	286	170	2510	20	17
1964	Len Dawson, KC, AFL	354	199	2879	30	18
	Bart Starr, GB, NFL	272	163	2144	15	4
1965	Rudy Bukich, Chi, NFL	312	176	2641	20	9
	John Hadl, SD, AFL	348	174	2798	20	21
1966	Bart Starr, GB, NFL	251	156	2257	14	3
	Len Dawson, KC, AFL	284	159	2527	26	10
1967	Sonny Jurgensen, Wash, NFL	508	288	3747	31	16
	Daryle Lamonica, Oakland, AFL	425	220	3228	30	20
1968	Len Dawson, KC, AFL	224	131	2109	17	9
	Earl Morrall, Balt, NFL	317	182	2909	26	17
1969	Sonny Jurgensen, Wash, NFL	442	274	3102	22	15
	Greg Cook, Cin, AFL	197	106	1854	15	11
1970	John Brodie, SF, NFC	378	223	2941	24	10
	Daryle Lamonica, Oak, AFC	356	179	2516	22	15
1971	Roger Staubach, Dall, NFC	211	126	1882	15	4
	Bob Griese, Mia, AFC	263	145	2089	19	9

Passing *(Cont.)*

Year	Player, Team	Att.	Comp	Yards	TD	Int
1972	Norm Snead, NY, NFC	325	196	2307	17	12
	Earl Morrall, Mia, AFC	150	83	1360	11	7
1973	Roger Staubach, Dall, NFC	286	179	2428	23	15
	Ken Stabler, Oak, AFC	260	163	1997	14	10
1974	Ken Anderson, Cin, AFC	328	213	2667	18	10
	Sonny Jurgensen, Wash, NFC	167	107	1185	11	5
1975	Ken Anderson, Cin, AFC	377	228	3169	21	11
	Fran Tarkenton, Minn, NFC	425	273	2994	25	13
1976	Ken Stabler, Oak, AFC	291	194	2737	27	17
	James Harris, LA, NFC	158	91	1460	8	6
1977	Bob Griese, Mia, AFC	307	180	2252	22	13
	Roger Staubach, Dall, NFC	361	210	2620	18	9
1978	Roger Staubach, Dall, NFC	413	231	3190	25	16
	Terry Bradshaw, Pitt, AFC	368	207	2915	28	20
1979	Roger Staubach, Dall, NFC	461	267	3586	27	11
	Dan Fouts, SD, AFC	530	332	4082	24	24
1980	Brian Sipe, Clev, AFC	554	337	4132	30	14
	Ron Jaworski, Phi, NFC	451	257	3529	27	12
1981	Ken Anderson, Cin, AFC	479	300	3754	29	10
	Joe Montana, SF, NFC	488	311	3565	19	12
1982	Ken Anderson, Cin, AFC	309	218	2495	12	9
	Joe Theismann, Wash, NFC	252	161	2033	13	9
1983	Steve Bartkowski, Atl, NFC	432	274	3167	22	5
	Dan Marino, Mia, AFC	296	173	2210	20	6
1984	Dan Marino, Mia, AFC	564	362	5084	48	17
	Joe Montana, SF, NFC	432	279	3630	28	10
1985	Ken O'Brien, NY, AFC	488	297	3888	25	8
	Joe Montana, SF, NFC	494	303	3653	27	13
1986	Tommy Kramer, Minn, NFC	372	208	3000	24	10
	Dan Marino, Mia, AFC	623	378	4746	44	23
1987	Joe Montana, SF, NFC	398	266	3054	31	13
	Bernie Kosar, Clev, AFC	389	241	3033	22	9
1988	Boomer Esiason, Cin, AFC	388	223	3572	28	14
	Wade Wilson, Minn, NFC	332	204	2746	15	9
1989	Joe Montana, SF, NFC	386	271	3521	26	8
	Boomer Esiason, Cin, AFC	455	258	3525	28	11
1990	Jim Kelly, Buffalo, AFC	346	219	2829	24	9
	Phil Simms, NY, NFC	311	184	2284	15	4
1991	Steve Young, SF, NFC	279	180	2517	17	8
	Jim Kelly, Buff, AFC	474	304	3844	33	17
1992	Steve Young, SF, NFC	402	268	3465	25	7
	Warren Moon, Hou, AFC	346	224	2521	18	12

Pass Receiving

Year	Player, Team	No.	Yds	Avg	TD
1932	Ray Flaherty, NY	21	350	16.7	3
1933	John Kelly, Brooklyn	22	246	11.2	3
1934	Joe Carter, Phil	16	238	14.9	4
	Morris Badgro, NY	16	206	12.9	1
1935	Tod Goodwin, NY	26	432	16.6	4
1936	Don Hutson, GB	34	536	15.8	8
1937	Don Hutson, GB	41	552	13.5	7
1938	Gaynell Tinsley, Chi Cards	41	516	12.6	1
1939	Don Hutson, GB	34	846	24.9	6
1940	Don Looney, Phil	58	707	12.2	4
1941	Don Hutson, GB	58	738	12.7	10
1942	Don Hutson, GB	74	1211	16.4	17
1943	Don Hutson, GB	47	776	16.5	11
1944	Don Hutson, GB	58	866	14.9	9
1945	Don Hutson, GB	47	834	17.7	9
1946	Jim Benton, LA	63	981	15.6	6
1947	Jim Keane, Chi	64	910	14.2	10
1948	Tom Fears, LA	51	698	13.7	4
1949	Tom Fears, LA	77	1013	13.2	9
1950	Tom Fears, LA	84	1116	13.3	7
1951	Elroy Hirsch, LA	66	1495	22.7	17
1952	Mac Speedie, Clev	62	911	14.7	5
1953	Pete Pihos, Phil	63	1049	16.7	10
1954	Pete Pihos, Phil	60	872	14.5	10
	Billy Wilson, SF	60	830	13.8	5
1955	Pete Pihos, Phil	62	864	13.9	7
1956	Billy Wilson, SF	60	889	14.8	5
1957	Billy Wilson, SF	52	757	14.6	6
1958	Raymond Berry, Balt	56	794	14.2	9
	Pete Retzlaff, Phil	56	766	13.7	2
1959	Raymond Berry, Balt	66	959	14.5	14
1960	Lionel Taylor, Den, AFL	92	1235	13.4	12
	Raymond Berry, Baltimore, NFL	74	1298	17.5	10
1961	Lionel Taylor, Den, AFL	100	1176	11.8	4
	Jim Phillips, LA, NFL	78	1092	14.0	5
1962	Lionel Taylor, Den, AFL	77	908	11.8	4
	Bobby Mitchell, Wash, NFL	72	1384	19.2	11
1963	Lionel Taylor, Den, AFL	78	1101	14.1	10
	Bobby Joe Conrad, St. Louis, NFL	73	967	13.2	10
1964	Charley Hennigan, Houston, AFL	101	1546	15.3	8
	Johnny Morris, Chi, NFL	93	1200	12.9	10
1965	Lionel Taylor, Den, AFL	85	1131	13.3	6
	Dave Parks, SF, NFL	80	1344	16.8	12
1966	Lance Alworth, SD, AFL	73	1383	18.9	13
	Charley Taylor, Wash, NFL	72	1119	15.5	12
1967	George Sauer, NY, AFL	75	1189	15.9	6
	Charley Taylor, Wash, NFL	70	990	14.1	9
1968	Clifton McNeil, SF, NFL	71	994	14.0	7
	Lance Alworth, SD, AFL	68	1312	19.3	10

Pass Receiving (Cont.)

Year	Player, Team	No.	Yds	Avg	TD
1969	Dan Abramowicz, NO, NFL	73	1015	13.9	7
	Lance Alworth, SD, AFL	64	1003	15.7	4
1970	Dick Gordon, Chi, NFC	71	1026	14.5	13
	Marlin Briscoe, Buff, AFC	57	1036	18.2	8
1971	Fred Biletnikoff, Oak, AFC	61	929	15.2	9
	Bob Tucker, NY, NFC	59	791	13.4	4
1972	Harold Jackson, Phi, NFC	62	1048	16.9	4
	Fred Biletnikoff, Oak, AFC	58	802	13.8	7
1973	Harold Carmichael, Phi, NFC	67	1116	16.7	9
	Fred Willis, Hou, AFC	57	371	6.5	1
1974	Lydell Mitchell, Balt, AFC	72	544	7.6	2
	Charles Young, Phi, NFC	63	696	11.0	3
1975	Chuck Foreman, Minn, NFC	73	691	9.5	9
	Reggie Rucker, Clev, AFC	60	770	12.8	3
	Lydell Mitchell, Balt, AFC	60	544	9.1	4
1976	MacArthur Lane, KC	66	686	10.4	1
	Drew Pearson, Dall, NFC	58	806	13.9	6
1977	Lydell Mitchell, Balt, AFC	71	620	8.7	4
	Ahmad Rashad, Minn, NFC	51	681	13.4	2
1978	Rickey Young, Minn, NFC	88	704	8.0	5
	Steve Largent, Sea, AFC	71	1168	16.5	8
1979	Joe Washington, Balt, AFC	82	750	9.1	3
	Ahmad Rashad, Minn, NFC	80	1156	14.5	9
1980	Kellen Winslow, SD, AFC	89	1290	14.5	9
	Earl Cooper, SF, NFC	83	567	6.8	4
1981	Kellen Winslow, SD, AFC	88	1075	12.2	10
	Dwight Clark, SF, NFC	85	1105	13.0	4
1982	Dwight Clark, SF, NFC	60	913	15.2	5
	Kellen Winslow, SD, AFC	54	721	13.4	6
1983	Todd Christensen, Los Angeles, AFC	92	1247	13.6	12
	Roy Green, StL, NFC	78	1227	15.7	14
	Charlie Brown, Wash, NFC	78	1225	15.7	8
	Earnest Gray, NY, NFC	78	1139	14.6	5
1984	Art Monk, Wash, NFC	106	1372	12.9	7
	Ozzie Newsome, Clev, AFC	89	1001	11.2	5
1985	Roger Craig, SF, NFC	92	1016	11.0	6
	Lionel James, SD, AFC	86	1027	11.9	6
1986	Todd Christensen, Los Angeles, AFC	95	1153	12.1	8
	Jerry Rice, SF, NFC	86	1570	18.3	15
1987	J.T. Smith, StL, NFC	91	1117	12.3	8
	Al Toon, NY, AFC	68	976	14.4	5
1988	Al Toon, NY, AFC	93	1067	11.5	5
	Henry Ellard, LA Rams, NFC	86	1414	16.4	10
1989	Sterling Sharpe, GB, NFC	90	1423	15.8	12
	Andre Reed, Buff, AFC	88	1312	14.9	9
1990	Jerry Rice, SF, NFC	100	1502	15.0	13
	Haywood Jeffires, Houston, AFC	74	1048	14.2	8
	Drew Hill, Hou, AFC	74	1019	13.8	5
1991	Haywood Jeffires, Hou, AFC	100	1181	11.8	7
	Michael Irvin, Dall, NFC	93	1523	16.4	8
1992	Sterling Sharpe, GB	108	1461	13.5	13
	Haywood Jeffires, Hou	90	913	10.1	9

Scoring

Year	Player, Team	TD	FG	PAT	TP
1932	Earl Clark, Portsmouth	6	3	10	55
1933	Ken Strong, NY	6	5	13	64
	Glenn Presnell, Ports	6	6	10	64
1934	Jack Manders, Chi	3	10	31	79
1935	Earl Clark, Det	6	1	16	55
1936	Earl Clark, Det	7	4	19	73
1937	Jack Manders, Chi	5	18	15	69
1938	Clarke Hinkle, GB	7	3	7	58
1939	Andy Farkas, Wash	11	0	2	68
1940	Don Hutson, GB	7	0	15	57
1941	Don Hutson, GB	12	1	20	95
1942	Don Hutson, GB	17	1	33	138
1943	Don Hutson, GB	12	3	36	117
1944	Don Hutson, GB	9	0	31	85
1945	Steve Van Buren, Phil	18	0	2	110
1946	Ted Fritsch, GB	10	9	13	100
1947	Pat Harder, Chicago Cards	7	7	39	102
1948	Pat Harder, Chicago Cards	6	7	53	110
1949	Pat Harder, Chicago Cards	8	3	45	102
	Gene Roberts, NY	17	0	0	102
1950	Doak Walker, Det	11	8	38	128
1951	Elroy Hirsch, LA	17	0	0	102
1952	Gordy Soltau, SF	7	6	34	94
1953	Gordy Soltau, SF	6	10	48	114
1954	Bobby Walston, Phil	11	4	36	114
1955	Doak Walker, Det	7	9	27	96
1956	Bobby Layne, Det	5	12	33	99
1957	Sam Baker, Wash	1	14	29	77
	Lou Groza, Clev	0	15	32	77
1958	Jim Brown, Clev	18	0	0	108
1959	Paul Hornung, GB	7	7	31	94
1960	Paul Hornung, GB, NFL	15	15	41	176
	Gene Mingo, Den, AFL	6	18	33	123
1961	Gino Cappelletti, Bos, AFL	8	17	48	147
	Paul Hornung, GB, NFL	10	15	41	146
1962	Gene Mingo, Den, AFL	4	27	32	137
	Jim Taylor, GB, NFL	19	0	0	114
1963	Gino Cappelletti, Bos, AFL	2	22	35	113
	Don Chandler, NY, NFL	0	18	52	106
1964	Gino Cappelletti, Bos, AFL	7	25	36	155
	Lenny Moore, Balt, NFL	20	0	0	120
1965	Gale Sayers, Chi, NFL	22	0	0	132
	Gino Cappelletti, Bos, AFL	9	17	27	132
1966	Gino Cappelletti, Bos, AFL	6	16	35	119
	Bruce Gossett, LA, NFL	0	28	29	113
1967	Jim Bakken, StL, NFL	0	27	36	117
	George Blanda, Oak, AFL	0	20	56	116
1968	Jim Turner, NY, AFL	0	34	43	145
	Leroy Kelly, Clev, NFL	20	0	0	120
1969	Jim Turner, NY, AFL	0	32	33	129
	Fred Cox, Minn, NFL	0	26	43	121
1970	Fred Cox, Minn, NFC	0	30	35	125
	Jan Stenerud, KC, AFC	0	30	26	116

Scoring *(Cont.)*

Year	Player, Team	TD	FG	PAT	TP
1971	Garo Yepremian, Mia, AFC	0	28	33	117
	Curt Knight, Wash, NFC	0	29	27	114
1972	Chester Marcol, GB, NFC	0	33	29	128
	Bobby Howfield, NY AFC	0	27	40	121
1973	David Ray, LA, NFC	0	30	40	130
	Roy Gerela, Pitt, AFC	0	29	36	123
1974	Chester Marcol, GB, NFC	0	25	19	94
	Roy Gerela, Pitt, AFC	0	20	33	93
1975	O.J. Simpson, Buff, AFC	23	0	0	138
	Chuck Foreman, Minn, NFC	22	0	0	132
1976	Toni Linhart, Balt, AFC	0	20	49	109
	Mark Moseley, Wash, NFC	0	22	31	97
1977	Errol Mann, Oak, AFC	0	20	39	99
	Walter Payton, Chi, NFC	16	0	0	96
1978	Frank Corral, LA, NFC	0	29	31	118
	Pat Leahy, NY, AFC	0	22	41	107
1979	John Smith, NE, AFC	0	23	46	115
	Mark Moseley, Wash, NFC	0	25	39	114
1980	John Smith, NE, AFC	0	26	51	129
	Ed Murray, Det, NFC	0	27	35	116
1981	Ed Murray, Det, NFC	0	25	46	121
1981	Rafael Septien, Dall, NFC	0	27	40	121
	Jim Breech, Cin, AFC	0	22	49	115
	Nick Lowery, KC, AFC	0	26	37	115

Year	Player, Team	TD	FG	PAT	TP
1982	Marcus Allen, LA, AFC	14	0	0	84
	Wendell Tyler, LA, NFC	13	0	0	78
1983	Mark Moseley, Wash, NFC	0	33	62	161
	Gary Anderson, Pitt, AFC	0	27	38	119
1984	Ray Wersching, SF, NFC	0	25	56	131
	Gary Anderson, Pitt, AFC	0	24	45	117
1985	Kevin Butler, Chi, NFC	0	31	51	144
	Gary Anderson, Pitt, AFC	0	33	40	139
1986	Tony Franklin, NE, AFC	0	32	44	140
	Kevin Butler, Chi, NFC	0	28	36	120
1987	Jerry Rice, SF, NFC	23	0	0	138
	Jim Breech, Cin, AFC	0	24	25	97
1988	Scott Norwood, Buff, AFC	0	32	33	129
	Mike Cofer, SF, NFC	0	27	40	121
1989	Mike Cofer, SF, NFC	0	29	49	136
	David Treadwell, Den, AFC	0	27	39	120
1990	Nick Lowery, KC, AFC	0	34	37	139
	Chip Lohmiller, Wash, NFC	0	30	41	131
1991	Chip Lohmiller, Wash, NFC	0	31	56	149
	Pete Stoyanovich, Mia, AFC	0	31	28	121
1992	Pete Stoyanovich, Mia, AFC	0	30	34	124
	Morten Anderson, NO, NFC	0	29	33	120
	Chip Lohmiller, Wash, NFC	0	30	30	120

Pro Bowl All-Time Results

Date	Result
1-15-39	NY Giants 13, Pro All-Stars 10
1-14-40	Green Bay 16, NFL All-Stars 7
12-29-40	Chi Bears 28, NFL All-Stars 14
1-4-42	Chi Bears 35, NFL All-Stars 24
12-27-42	NFL All-Stars 17, Washington 14
1-14-51	American Conf 28, National Conf 27
1-12-52	National Conf 30, American Conf 13
1-10-53	National Conf 27, American Conf 7
1-17-54	East 20, West 9
1-16-55	West 26, East 19
1-15-56	East 31, West 30
1-13-57	West 19, East 10
1-12-58	West 26, East 7
1-11-59	East 28, West 21
1-17-60	West 38, East 21
1-15-61	West 35, East 31
1-7-62	AFL West 47, East 27
1-14-62	NFL West 31, East 30
1-13-63	AFL West 21, East 14
1-13-63	NFL East 30, West 20
1-12-64	NFL West 31, East 17
1-19-64	AFL West 27, East 24
1-10-65	NFL West 34, East 14
1-16-65	AFL West 38, East 14
1-15-66	AFL All-Stars 30, Buffalo 19
1-15-66	NFL East 36, West 7
1-21-67	AFL East 30, West 23
1-22-67	NFL East 20, West 10
1-21-68	AFL East 25, West 24

Date	Result
1-21-68	NFL West 38, East 20
1-19-69	AFL West 38, East 25
1-19-69	NFL West 10, East 7
1-17-70	AFL West 26, East 3
1-18-70	NFL West 16, East 13
1-24-71	NFC 27, AFC 6
1-23-72	AFC 26, NFC 13
1-21-73	AFC 33, NFC 28
1-20-74	AFC 15, NFC 13
1-20-75	NFC 17, AFC 10
1-26-76	NFC 23, AFC 20
1-17-77	AFC 24, NFC 14
1-23-78	NFC 14, AFC 13
1-29-79	NFC 13, AFC 7
1-27-80	NFC 37, AFC 27
2-1-81	NFC 21, AFC 7
1-31-82	AFC 16, NFC 13
2-6-83	NFC 20, AFC 19
1-29-84	NFC 45, AFC 3
1-27-85	AFC 22, NFC 14
2-2-86	NFC 28, AFC 24
2-1-87	AFC 10, NFC 6
2-7-88	AFC 15, NFC 6
1-29-89	NFC 34, AFC 3
2-4-90	NFC 27, AFC 21
2-3-91	AFC 23, NFC 21
2-2-92	NFC 21, AFC 15
2-7-93	AFC 23, NFC 20

Chicago All-Star Game Results

Date	Result (Attendance)
8-31-34	Chi Bears 0, All-Stars 0 (79,432)
8-29-35	Chi Bears 5, All-Stars 0 (77,450)
9-3-36	All-Stars 7, Detroit 7 (76,000)
9-1-37	All-Stars 6, Green Bay 0 (84,560)
8-31-38	All-Stars 28, Washington 16 (74,250)
8-30-39	NY Giants 9, All-Stars 0 (81,456)
8-29-40	Green Bay 45, All-Stars 28 (84,567)
8-28-41	Chi Bears 37, All-Stars 13 (98,203)
8-28-42	Chi Bears 21, All-Stars 0 (101,100)
8-25-43	All-Stars 27, Washington 7 (48,471)
8-30-44	Chi Bears 24, All-Stars 21 (48,769)
8-30-45	Green Bay 19, All-Stars 7 (92,753)
8-23-46	All-Stars 16, Los Angeles 0 (97,380)
8-22-47	All-Stars 16, Chi Bears 0 (105,840)
8-20-48	Chi Cardinals 28, All-Stars 0 (101,220)
8-12-49	Philadelphia 38, All-Stars 0 (93,780)
8-11-50	All-Stars 17, Philadelphia 7 (88,885)
8-17-51	Cleveland 33, All-Stars 0 (92,180)
8-15-52	Los Angeles 10, All-Stars 7 (88,316)
8-14-53	Detroit 24, All-Stars 10 (93,818)
8-13-54	Detroit 31, All-Stars 6 (93,470)
8-12-55	All-Stars 30, Cleveland 27 (75,000)

Date	Result (Attendance)
8-10-56	Cleveland 26, All-Stars 0 (75,000)
8-9-57	NY Giants 22, All-Stars 12 (75,000)
8-15-58	All-Stars 35, Detroit 19 (70,000)
8-14-59	Baltimore 29, All-Stars 0 (70,000)
8-12-60	Baltimore 32, All-Stars 7 (70,000)
8-4-61	Philadelphia 28, All-Stars 14 (66,000)
8-3-62	Green Bay 42, All-Stars 20 (65,000)
8-2-63	All-Stars 20, Green Bay 17 (65,000)
8-7-64	Chicago 28, All-Stars 17 (65,000)
8-6-65	Cleveland 24, All-Stars 16 (68.000)
8-5-66	Green Bay 38, All-Stars 0 (72,000)
8-4-67	Green Bay 27, All-Stars 0 (70,934)
8-2-68	Green Bay 34, All-Stars 17 (69,917)
8-1-69	NY Jets 26, All-Stars 24 (74,208)
7-31-70	Kansas City 24, All-Stars 3 (69,940)
7-30-71	Baltimore 24, All-Stars 17 (52,289)
7-28-72	Dallas 20, All-Stars 7 (54,162)
7-27-73	Miami 14, All-Stars 3 (54,103)
1974	No game
8-1-75	Pittsburgh 21, All-Stars 14 (54,103)
7-23-76	Pittsburgh 24, All-Stars 0 (52,895)

All-Time Winningest NFL Coaches

Most Career Wins

Coach	Yrs	Teams	Regular Season				Career			
			W	L	T	Pct	W	L	T	Pct
George Halas	40	Bears	319	148	31	.672	325	151	31	.672
Don Shula	30	Colts, Dolphins	300	136	6	.685	318	151	6	.676
Tom Landry	29	Cowboys	250	162	6	.605	270	178	6	.601
Curly Lambeau	33	Packers, Cardinals, Redskins	226	132	22	.623	229	134	22	.623
Chuck Noll	23	Steelers	193	148	1	.566	209	156	1	.572
Chuck Knox	22	Rams, Bills, Seahawks	177	124	1	.588	184	135	1	.577
Paul Brown	21	Browns, Bengals	166	100	6	.621	170	108	6	.609
Bud Grant	18	Vikings	158	96	5	.620	168	108	5	.607
Steve Owen	23	Giants	151	100	17	.595	153	108	17	.582
Joe Gibbs	12	Redskins	124	60	0	.674	140	65	0	.683
Hank Stram	17	Chiefs, Saints	131	97	10	.571	136	100	10	.573
Weeb Ewbank	20	Colts, Jets	130	129	7	.502	134	130	7	.507
Sid Gillman	18	Rams, Chargers, Oilers	122	99	7	.550	123	104	7	.541
George Allen	12	Rams, Redskins	116	47	5	.705	118	54	5	.681
Dan Reeves	14	Broncos	110	73	1	.601	117	79	1	.596
Don Coryell	14	Cardinals, Chargers	111	83	1	.572	114	89	1	.561
John Madden	10	Raiders	103	32	7	.750	112	39	7	.731
Mike Ditka	11	Bears	106	62	0	.631	112	68	0	.622
Buddy Parker	15	Cardinals, Lions, Steelers	104	75	9	.577	107	76	9	.581
Marv Levy	12	Chiefs, Bills	98	77	0	.560	106	82	0	.564

Top Winning Percentages

	W	L	T	Pct		W	L	T	Pct
Vince Lombardi	105	35	6	.740	George Halas	325	151	31	.672
John Madden	112	39	7	.731	Curly Lambeau	229	134	22	.623
Joe Gibbs	140	65	0	.683	Mike Ditka	112	68	0	.622
George Allen	118	54	5	.681	Bill Walsh	102	63	1	.617
Don Shula	318	151	6	.676	Paul Brown	170	108	6	.609

Year	Team	Selection	Position
1936	Philadelphia	Jay Berwanger, Chicago	HB
1937	Philadelphia	Sam Francis, Nebraska	FB
1938	Cleveland	Corbett Davis, Indiana	FB
1939	Chicago Cardinals	Ki Aldrich, Texas Christian	C
1940	Chicago Cardinals	George Cafego, Tennessee	HB
1941	Chicago Bears	Tom Harmon, Michigan	HB
1942	Pittsburgh	Bill Dudley, Virginia	HB
1943	Detroit	Frank Sinkwich, Georgia	HB
1944	Boston	Angelo Bertelli, Notre Dame	QB
1945	Chicago Cardinals	Charley Trippi, Georgia	HB
1946	Boston	Frank Dancewicz, Notre Dame	QB
1947	Chicago Bears	Bob Fenimore, Oklahoma A&M	HB
1948	Washington	Harry Gilmer, Alabama	QB
1949	Philadelphia	Chuck Bednarik, Pennsylvania	C
1950	Detroit	Leon Hart, Notre Dame	E
1951	New York Giants	Kyle Rote, Southern Methodist	HB
1952	Los Angeles	Bill Wade, Vanderbilt	QB
1953	San Francisco	Harry Babcock, Georgia	E
1954	Cleveland	Bobby Garrett, Stanford	QB
1955	Baltimore	George Shaw, Oregon	QB
1956	Pittsburgh	Gary Glick, Colorado A&M	DB
1957	Green Bay	Paul Hornung, Notre Dame	HB
1958	Chicago Cardinals	King Hill, Rice	QB
1959	Green Bay	Randy Duncan, Iowa	QB
1960	Los Angeles	Billy Cannon, Louisiana State	RB
1961	Minnesota	Tommy Mason, Tulane	RB
	Buffalo (AFL)	Ken Rice, Auburn	G
1968	Minnesota	Ron Yary, Southern California	T
1969	Buffalo (AFL)	O. J. Simpson, Southern California	RB
1970	Pittsburgh	Terry Bradshaw, Louisiana Tech	QB
1971	New England	Jim Plunkett, Stanford	QB
1972	Buffalo	Walt Patulski, Notre Dame	DE
1973	Houston	John Matuszak, Tampa	DE
1974	Dallas	Ed Jones, Tennessee State	DE
1975	Atlanta	Steve Bartkowski, California	QB
1976	Tampa Bay	Lee Roy Selmon, Oklahoma	DE
1977	Tampa Bay	Ricky Bell, Southern California	RB
1978	Houston	Earl Campbell, Texas	RB
1979	Buffalo	Tom Cousineau, Ohio State	LB
1980	Detroit	Billy Sims, Oklahoma	RB
1981	New Orleans	George Rogers, South Carolina	RB
1982	New England	Kenneth Sims, Texas	DT
1983	Baltimore	John Elway, Stanford	QB
1984	New England	Irving Fryar, Nebraska	WR
1985	Buffalo	Bruce Smith, Virginia Tech	DE
1986	Tampa Bay	Bo Jackson, Auburn	RB
1987	Tampa Bay	Vinny Testaverde, Miami	QB
1988	Atlanta	Aundray Bruce, Auburn	LB
1989	Dallas	Troy Aikman, UCLA	QB
1990	Indianapolis	Jeff George, Illinois	QB
1991	Dallas	Russell Maryland, Miami	DT
1992	Indianapolis	Steve Emtman, Washington	DT
1993	New England	Drew Bledsoe, Washington St	QB

From 1947 through 1958, the first selection in the draft was a bonus pick, awarded to the winner of a random draw. That club, in turn, forfeited its last-round draft choice. The winner of the bonus choice was eliminated from future draws. The system was abolished after 1958, by which time all clubs had received a bonus choice.

Boom-erang

Next fall the NFL will reveal which two cities will receive expansion franchises beginning with the 1995 season. For now, fans in the five contending cities can ponder this list of likely names registered by the NFL with the U.S. Patent and Trademark Office:

Baltimore: Bombers or Cobras.
Charlotte: Panthers.
Jacksonville: Jaguars or Sharks.
Memphis: Bombers, Hound Dogs or Showboats.
St. Louis: Archers, Rivermen, Scouts, Stallions or Stokers.

One observation: In light of the terrorist attack on New York's World Trade Center, one hopes that should Baltimore and/or Memphis join the league, they'll jettison the Bombers.

Members of the Pro Football Hall of Fame

Herb Adderley
Lance Alworth
Doug Atkins
Morris "Red" Badgro
Lem Barney
Cliff Battles
Sammy Baugh
Chuck Bednarik
Bert Bell
Bobby Bell
Raymond Berry
Charles W. Bidwill, Sr.
Fred Biletnikoff
George Blanda
Mel Blount
Terry Bradshaw
Jim Brown
Paul Brown
Roosevelt Brown
Willie Brown
Buck Buchanan
Dick Butkus
Earl Campbell
Tony Canadeo
Joe Carr
Guy Chamberlin
Jack Christiansen
Earl "Dutch" Clark
George Connor
Jimmy Conzelman
Larry Csonka
Al Davis
Willie Davis
Len Dawson
Mike Ditka
Art Donovan
John "Paddy" Driscoll
Bill Dudley
Glen "Turk" Edwards
Weeb Ewbank
Tom Fears
Ray Flaherty
Len Ford
Dan Fortmann
Dan Fouts
Frank Gatski
Bill George
Frank Gifford
Sid Gillman
Otto Graham
Harold "Red" Grange
Joe Greene
Forrest Gregg
Bob Griese
Lou Groza
Joe Guyon
George Halas

Jack Ham
John Hannah
Franco Harris
Ed Healey
Mel Hein
Ted Hendricks
Wilbur "Pete" Henry
Arnie Herber
Bill Hewitt
Clarke Hinkle
Elroy "Crazylegs" Hirsch
Paul Hornung
Ken Houston
Cal Hubbard
Sam Huff
Lamar Hunt
Don Hutson
John Henry Johnson
David "Deacon" Jones
Stan Jones
Sonny Jurgensen
Walt Kiesling
Frank "Bruiser" Kinard
Earl "Curly" Lambeau
Jack Lambert
Tom Landry
Dick "Night Train" Lane
Jim Langer
Willie Lanier
Yale Lary
Dante Lavelli
Bobby Layne
Alphonse "Tuffy" Leemans
Bob Lilly
Larry Little
Vince Lombardi
Sid Luckman
Roy "Link" Lyman
John Mackey
Tim Mara
Gino Marchetti
George Preston Marshall
Ollie Matson
Don Maynard
George McAfee
Mike McCormack
Hugh McElhenny
Johnny "Blood" McNally
Mike Michalske
Wayne Millner
Bobby Mitchell
Ron Mix
Lenny Moore
Marion Motley
George Musso
Bronko Nagurski
Joe Namath

Earle "Greasy" Neale
Ernie Nevers
Ray Nitschke
Chuck Noll
Leo Nomellini
Merlin Olsen
Jim Otto
Steve Owen
Alan Page
Clarence "Ace" Parker
Jim Parker
Walter Payton
Joe Perry
Pete Pihos
Hugh "Shorty" Ray
Dan Reeves
John Riggins
Jim Ringo
Andy Robustelli
Art Rooney
Pete Rozelle
Bob St. Clair
Gale Sayers
Joe Schmidt
Tex Schramm
Art Shell
O. J. Simpson
Bart Starr
Roger Staubach
Ernie Stautner
Jan Stenerud
Ken Strong
Joe Stydahar
Fran Tarkenton
Charley Taylor
Jim Taylor
Jim Thorpe
Y. A. Tittle
George Trafton
Charley Trippi
Emlen Tunnell
Clyde "Bulldog" Turner
Johnny Unitas
Gene Upshaw
Norm Van Brocklin
Steve Van Buren
Doak Walker
Bill Walsh
Paul Warfield
Bob Waterfield
Arnie Weinmeister
Bill Willis
Larry Wilson
Alex Wojciechowicz
Willie Wood

Champions of Other Leagues

Canadian Football League Grey Cup

Year	Results	Site	Attendance
1909	U of Toronto 26, Parkdale 6	Toronto	3,807
1910	U of Toronto 16, Hamilton Tigers 7	Hamilton	12,000
1911	U of Toronto 14, Toronto 7	Toronto	13,687
1912	Hamilton Alerts 11, Toronto 4	Hamilton	5,337
1913	Hamilton Tigers 44, Parkdale 2	Hamilton	2,100
1914	Toronto 14, U of Toronto 2	Toronto	10,500
1915	Hamilton Tigers 13, Toronto RAA 7	Toronto	2,808
1916-19	No game		
1920	U of Toronto 16, Toronto 3	Toronto	10,088
1921	Toronto 23, Edmonton 0	Toronto	9,558
1922	Queen's U 13, Edmonton 1	Kingston	4,700
1923	Queen's U 54, Regina 0	Toronto	8,629
1924	Queen's U 11, Balmy Beach 3	Toronto	5,978
1925	Ottawa Senators 24, Winnipeg 1	Ottawa	6,900
1926	Ottawa Senators 10, Toronto U 7	Toronto	8,276
1927	Balmy Beach 9, Hamilton Tigers 6	Toronto	13,676
1928	Hamilton Tigers 30, Regina 0	Hamilton	4,767
1929	Hamilton Tigers 14, Regina 3	Hamilton	1,906
1930	Balmy Beach 11, Regina 6	Toronto	3,914
1931	Montreal AAA 22, Regina 0	Montreal	5,112
1932	Hamilton Tigers 25, Regina 6	Hamilton	4,806
1933	Toronto 4, Sarnia 3	Sarnia	2,751
1934	Sarnia 20, Regina 12	Toronto	8,900
1935	Winnipeg 18, Hamilton Tigers 12	Hamilton	6,405
1936	Sarnia 26, Ottawa RR 20	Toronto	5,883
1937	Toronto 4, Winnipeg 3	Toronto	11,522
1938	Toronto 30, Winnipeg 7	Toronto	18,778
1939	Winnipeg 8, Ottawa 7	Ottawa	11,738
1940	Ottawa 12, Balmy Beach 5	Ottawa	1,700
1940	Ottawa 8, Balmy Beach 2	Toronto	4,998
1941	Winnipeg 18, Ottawa 16	Toronto	19,065
1942	Toronto RCAF 8, Winnipeg RCAF 5	Toronto	12,455
1943	Hamilton F Wild 23, Winnipeg RCAF 14	Toronto	16,423
1944	Montreal St H-D Navy 7, Hamilton F Wild 6	Hamilton	3,871
1945	Toronto 35, Winnipeg 0	Toronto	18,660
1946	Toronto 28, Winnipeg 6	Toronto	18,960
1947	Toronto 10, Winnipeg 9	Toronto	18,885
1948	Calgary 12, Ottawa 7	Toronto	20,013
1949	Montreal Als 28, Calgary 15	Toronto	20,087
1950	Toronto 13, Winnipeg 0	Toronto	27,101
1951	Ottawa 21, Saskatchewan 14	Toronto	27,341
1952	Toronto 21, Edmonton 11	Toronto	27,391
1953	Hamilton Ticats 12, Winnipeg 6	Toronto	27,313
1954	Edmonton 26, Montreal 25	Toronto	27,321
1955	Edmonton 34, Montreal 19	Vancouver	39,417
1956	Edmonton 50, Montreal 27	Toronto	27,425
1957	Hamilton 32, Winnipeg 7	Toronto	27,051
1958	Winnipeg 35, Hamilton 28	Vancouver	36,567
1959	Winnipeg 21, Hamilton 7	Toronto	33,133
1960	Ottawa 16, Edmonton 6	Vancouver	38,102
1961	Winnipeg 21, Hamilton 14	Toronto	32,651
1962	Winnipeg 28, Hamilton 27	Toronto	32,655
1963	Hamilton 21, British Columbia 10	Vancouver	36,545
1964	British Columbia 34, Hamilton 24	Toronto	32,655
1965	Hamilton 22, Winnipeg 16	Toronto	32,655
1966	Saskatchewan 29, Ottawa 14	Vancouver	36,553
1967	Hamilton 24, Saskatchewan 1	Ottawa	31,358
1968	Ottawa 24, Calgary 21	Toronto	32,655
1969	Ottawa 29, Saskatchewan 11	Montreal	33,172
1970	Montreal 23, Calgary 10	Toronto	32,669
1971	Calgary 14, Toronto 11	Vancouver	34,484
1972	Hamilton 13, Saskatchewan 10	Hamilton	33,993
1973	Ottawa 22, Edmonton 18	Toronto	36,653
1974	Montreal 20, Edmonton 7	Vancouver	34,450
1975	Edmonton 9, Montreal 8	Calgary	32,454

Canadian Football League Grey Cup *(Cont.)*

Year	Results	Site	Attendance
1976	Ottawa 23, Saskatchewan 20	Toronto	53,467
1977	Montreal 41, Edmonton 6	Montreal	68,318
1978	Edmonton 20, Montreal 13	Toronto	54,695
1979	Edmonton 17, Montreal 9	Montreal	65,113
1980	Edmonton 48, Hamilton 10	Toronto	54,661
1981	Edmonton 26, Ottawa 23	Montreal	52,478
1982	Edmonton 32, Toronto 16	Toronto	54,741
1983	Toronto 18, British Columbia 17	Vancouver	59,345
1984	Winnipeg 47, Hamilton 17	Edmonton	60,081
1985	British Columbia 37, Hamilton 24	Montreal	56,723
1986	Hamilton 39, Edmonton 15	Vancouver	59,621
1987	Edmonton 38, Toronto 36	Vancouver	59,478
1988	Winnipeg 22, British Columbia 21	Ottawa	50,604
1989	Saskatchewan 43, Hamilton 40	Toronto	54,088
1990	Winnipeg 50, Edmonton 11	Vancouver	46,968
1991	Toronto 36, Calgary 21	Winnipeg	51,985
1992	Calgary 24, Winnipeg 10	Toronto	45,863

In 1909, Earl Grey, the Governor-General of Canada, donated a trophy for the Rugby Football Championship of Canada. The trophy, whic h subsequently became known as the Grey Cup, was originally open only to teams registered with the Canada Rugby Union. Since 1954, i t has been awarded to the winner of the Canadian Football League's championship game.

AMERICAN FOOTBALL LEAGUE I

Year	Champion	Record
1926	Philadelphia Quakers	7-2

AMERICAN FOOTBALL LEAGUE II

Year	Champion	Record
1936	Boston Shamrocks	8-3
1937	LA Bulldogs	8-0

AMERICAN FOOTBALL LEAGUE III

Year	Champion	Record
1940	Columbus Bullies	8-1-1
1941	Columbus Bullies	5-1-2

ALL-AMERICAN FOOTBALL CONFERENCE

Year	Championship Game
1946	Cleveland 14, NY Yankees 9
1947	Cleveland 14, NY Yankees 3
1948	Cleveland 49, Buffalo 7
1949	Cleveland 21, San Francisco 7

WORLD FOOTBALL LEAGUE

Year	World Bowl Championship
1974	Birmingham 22, Florida 21
1975	Disbanded midseason

UNITED STATES FOOTBALL LEAGUE

Year	Championship Game
1983	Michigan 24, Philadelphia 22, at Denver
1984	Philadelphia 23, Arizona 3, at Tampa
1985	Baltimore 28, Oakland 24, at East Rutherford

To Market We Go

Reduced to its essentials, the NFL labor settlement announced last January gives the players increased free agency in exchange for a salary cap for the owners. To be sure, the cap won't kick in until next year at the earliest, and free agency will be available only to veterans—at the outset those with five years' service, later those with four—and, for the most part, only during late winter and spring. In addition, each team can deny free agency to one so-called franchise player it designates and can asset the right of first refusal for two players in 1993 and one in '94. Also, the four conference finalists from last season can't sign any free agents in 1993 until they lose one or more of their own players to free agency.

Even with these restrictions, the seven-year deal is a triumph for the players. The agreement will result in higher player salaries, and its complexities will test the mettle of front offices, which will have to beef up their scouting of other teams; one team that's particularly deficient in this area is the Cincinnati Bengals.

Teams will also have to make hard decisions about their own personnel. Who, if anybody, should be designated a franchise player? Should they try to sign one player or another to a long-term contract? Who should be their right-of-first-refusal guys?

This much is clear: The NFL can now pursue plans, shelved because of the labor rancor that has dogged the league, to expand to two new cities, probably by the 1995 season. The most immediate beneficiaries, though, were a handful of players—most notably Pro Bowl defensive end Reggie White, who left Philadelphia for Green Bay—who had an antitrust suit pending against the NFL and were able to sell themselves to the highest bidder. On Feb. 1, 298 players became free agents too. One of them, Steeler linebacker Hardy Nickersen, exulted after the labor truce: "I couldn't ask for anything more basic than my basic freedom. In baseball, basketball and society in general, you can at some point of your life shop yourself around. Now I have that right, too."

College Football

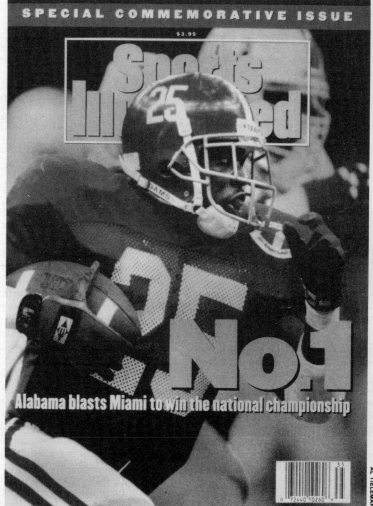

SPECIAL COMMEMORATIVE ISSUE

$3.95

Sports Illustrated

25

No. 1

Alabama blasts Miami to win the national championship

AL TIELEMANS

0 72440 10260 35

The Tide Rolled In

Alabama defeated Miami to become the national champion in a season of surprises in college football | by AUSTIN MURPHY

WIRE TO WIRE, IT WAS A season of surprises. Ask Jack Crowe, the former Arkansas coach who got the ax after a single game, a humiliating 10–3 loss to The Citadel. Ask former Washington quarterback Billy Joe Hobert, who discovered that yes, there *was* a problem with accepting no-interest, five-figure loans from a pal's relatives. Ask Lamar Thomas, the talented, loquacious Miami wide receiver who on New Year's night in the Louisiana Superdome thought he was home free.

Thomas became a symbol of his team's stunning downfall. After hauling in a pass from Gino Torretta in the Sugar Bowl, the lanky wideout had clear sailing to the end zone until—what's this?—he was run down and stripped of the ball by Alabama cornerback George Teague. Teague's larceny was college football's play of the season. It broke Miami's spirit and provided the Crimson Tide with an instant slogan for its 34–13 win over the defending national champion Hurricanes: We'll take that!

It took the Crimson Tide an even 100 years to win this, its 12th national football championship. Miami had won four from 1983 through '91 alone. The Hurricanes had also been stunned by Penn State in the '87 Fiesta Bowl with a title on the line. Thus did Alabama serve the ever braggadocious Hurricanes with their second cosmic comeuppance in six years.

Getting the nation's top two teams into a title game was an upset in itself. Before the newfangled, untested Bowl Coalition—designed to produce a No. 1 versus No. 2 matchup—could work, traditionally backstabbing bowl representatives would be forced to cooperate for the common good. Remarkably, they did ... for the most part.

While the bowl system, which had been threatened with extinction by a playoff system, was strengthened, several head coaches lost influence. Joining Crowe in the

JOE RIMKUS JR./MIAMI HERALD

When Teague stripped Thomas of the ball and a sure six points, he broke Miami's spirit.

unemployment line was 16-year Tennessee coach Johnny Majors, a former All-America halfback at Tennessee. Majors was dumped despite an 8–3 regular-season record in a rebuilding year in which he had missed the first three games while recuperating from heart surgery. Critics heaped scorn on Volunteer athletic director Doug Dickey, for such a heartless move and on Majors' replacement, assistant head coach Phil Fulmer, whom they accused—but never proved guilty—of unseemly maneuvering for the job. After Southern Cal's stunning 24–7 loss to Fresno State in the Freedom Bowl (USC's seniors had been so insulted by the prospect of having to play the lowly Bulldogs that they had to be talked out of boycotting the bowl), Trojan coach Larry Smith was sacrificed to quell alumni outrage.

Coaches were getting heat from both sides: their bosses and their underlings. Players in at least four programs fomented rebellions. After losing their first three games the Tigers of Memphis State boycotted practice one day, demanding the firing of authoritarian head coach Chuck Stobart. Stobart stayed. The Tigers won four straight. After an 0–5 start, South Carolina players called for the firing of head coach Sparky Woods. But Woods' job was saved by an earringed, longhaired true freshman quarterback named Steve Taneyhill, who guaranteed reporters that the Gamecocks would not lose another game. He was wrong—they went 5–1 the rest of the way, falling to Florida 14–9. Taneyhill has since promised that his team will go 11–0 in '93.

The off-season event with potentially the most resounding impact occurred in early February, with the stroke of an 18-year-old's pen. Scott Bentley signed a letter of intent to attend Florida State. The Seminoles finally had themselves a kicker.

Many college football followers felt that the Seminoles concluded the 1992 season playing the best football in the country. But for the second year running, Florida State had dropped a game to Miami by missing a makable last-second field goal. Which is why Florida State fans were so cheered by the news that Bentley, the top schoolboy kicker in the country, from Aurora, Colo., had snubbed Notre Dame and signed with the Seminoles. Bentley booted seven field goals of at least 50 yards in high school; 34

Dan Mowrey's Miami miss: a disaster Seminole fans hope Bentley will render obsolete.

of his kickoffs sailed through the uprights. His task will be made even easier next season by a rule change moving the hashmarks 20 yards closer to the middle of the field.

Perhaps, this Oct. 6 in Tallahassee, if the Seminoles find themselves within field goal range in a close game, Bentley will help Florida State do what it has not been able to do since 1989—beat Miami—and give Bobby Bowden the only significant achievement that has eluded him in 27 years of college coaching, a national title.

The anemia of Miami's offense in the Sugar Bowl had been prefigured by its performance over a three-game stretch earlier in the season. Against Arizona, the Hurricanes were held to two rushing yards, but eked out an 8–7 victory, thanks to a last-second Wildcat field goal attempt that missed by two feet. After squeaking past Florida State the next week, the Hurricanes flew north, to State College, Pa., where for the third straight Saturday they owed victory to an ornery defense and the vagaries of the human instep. Penn State kicker Craig Fayak had his first field goal attempt

blocked, and pulled his second, a 20-yard chip shot, wide left. Miami won 17–14.

In that three-game gantlet Torretta completed 57 of 125 passes, and the Hurricane offense scored just four touchdowns. Miami coach Dennis Erickson said he "could care less." Since the beginning of the previous season, Erickson pointed out, "Gino is 17–0." And for the second straight season the Hurricanes looked to be the best team in the country.

Only Washington could dispute that. The Huskies, with whom Miami had shared the '91 national championship, were also undefeated. It had been apparent from the beginning of the season, however, that this was an inferior edition—particularly on defense. For their '91 success Washington owed a large debt to Steve Emtman, the junior defensive tackle who left college after the season and was the first pick in that spring's NFL draft.

But it was another large debt that began the unraveling of the '92 Huskies. Two days before Washington's Nov. 7 game at Arizona, part-time starting quarterback Hobert was suspended from the team for having accepted three loans, totaling $50,000, from the father-in-law of a friend. Hobert blew the dough on guns, good times and a new Camaro, which he equipped with a $4,000 sound system. Borrowing the money "wasn't the smartest thing I've ever done, because I ended up blowing it," said Hobert. It also got him thrown off the team. Hobert's folly was thrown into even sharper relief when it was learned that his benefactor was ... a rocket scientist.

With Hobert *finito* as a Husky, part-time starter Mark Brunell had the starting job all to himself against Arizona. A swarming Wildcat defense anchored by nosetackle Rob Waldrop forced four Washington turnovers, limited the Huskies to a field goal and spoiled their hopes of repeating as national champions in a 16–3 upset. Embattled and distracted by the Hobert scandal—in addition to several other embarassments to the program—the Huskies would go on to drop two more games.

PETER READ MILLER

Hobert learned a hard lesson: Don't take no-interest loans from the family of a friend.

During 'Bama's game against Louisiana State, news of Washington's loss reached the Alabama players. The Tide poured it on, taming the Tigers 31–11, improving their record to 8–0 and leapfrogging from No. 6 in the AP poll to No. 2. By Thanksgiving two obstacles stood between the Tide and a No. 1 versus No. 2 Sugar Bowl showdown with Miami. The first was its annual Turkey Day jihad against Auburn. The Tigers gained added incentive when, on the eve of the game, 12-year head coach Pat Dye resigned, citing poor health and a pending NCAA investigation. Inspired, Auburn held Alabama to a scoreless tie at halftime. But on the first series of the second half, 'Bama cornerback Antonio Langham went 61 yards with an interception for the winning touchdown.

Langham reprised his heroics nine days later. His fourth-quarter interception return

against Florida won for Alabama the inaugural Southeastern Conference Championship Game and thus a Sugar Bowl berth. Having expanded to 12 members in 1990, the SEC split into eastern and western divisions and scheduled, beginning with the '92 season, a title game between the division champs. It was a great deal for the SEC, which reaped $6 million selling the TV rights to the game. Not all the players and coaches could muster as much enthusiasm. "We've won 11 games," said 'Bama coach Gene Stallings before beating Florida, "and we still haven't won anything."

The Hurricanes were coming off a thrashing of San Diego State, a game which had been hyped as the Heisman Bowl—featuring leading Heisman candidates Torretta (25–1 as a starter; over 7,000 career passing yards) and sophomore tailback Marshall Faulk (15 touchdowns, nation-leading 163 rushing yards per game). The game, alas, came to be known as Dud Bowl I as the Aztecs lost 63–17, with Torretta throwing for 310 yards. Faulk, nursing a sprained right knee, did not play, virtually handing the 58th Heisman to Torretta, who won it

Faulk had another fine season but finished behind Torretta in the Heisman balloting.

with 1,400 points to Faulk's 1,080. Finishing third, with 982 points, was Georgia tailback Garrison Hearst, who finished the season with an average of 6.8 yards per carry.

To the delight of the engineers of the Bowl Coalition, a No. 1 versus No. 2 matchup fell neatly into place. Once Miami and Alabama were locked into the Sugar Bowl, however, the spirit of cooperation among the fraternity of tasteless-blazer-clad Bowl reps began to fray. As Southwestern Conference champs, the 12–0, fourth-ranked Aggies of Texas A&M received an automatic invitation to the Cotton Bowl. As a member of the coalition, the raison d'être of which was to ensure better bowl matchups than in past seasons, the Cotton Bowl was obligated to invite the best team available: Florida State. After the Miami loss, the Seminoles had switched to a no-back, shotgun attack that better enabled quarterback Charlie Ward—starting point guard on the Seminole hoops team—to exploit his multiple talents. The

Seminoles started to flat out annihilate defenses.

But Cotton Bowl chairman Jim (Hoss) Brock could not resist the better television ratings his bowl would reap with an invitation to No. 5 Notre Dame. The ensuing howls of outrage from the Aggies, who saw their slim national championship hopes evanesce, gave way to whimpers of embarrassment when, a week before the game, A&M head coach R.C. Slocum was forced to suspend four players, including starting tailback Greg Hill, pending an investigation into irregularities with their school-arranged summer jobs. All the A&M national title talk rang hollow after Notre Dame's resounding 28–3 victory.

The SWC sent a meager two teams to bowl games, one less than the Big Eight and the Big Ten, which critics referred to as "Michigan and the Nine Dwarves." Among the best-represented conferences in the postseason was, surprisingly, the WAC. Five Western Athletic Conference teams went bowling. (The Pac-10 and the SEC sent six teams apiece to bowls.) The Wolverines, who won the Big Ten despite three ties, salvaged a modicum of respect for their once mighty conference by beating Washington in the Rose Bowl 38–31. Elsewhere the Big Ten took gas as usual, with Illinois losing to Hawaii in the Holiday Bowl; Ohio State lost the Citrus to Georgia 21–14, then lost junior running back Robert Smith, who announced that he would make himself available in the NFL draft. This news would not have been extraordinary—in all, 46 underclassmen made themselves eligible— had Smith not *sat out* his sophomore season after accusing coaches of encouraging him to skip classes to attend practice. Now Smith, who was taken in the first round by the Minnesota Vikings, had decided that school could wait, after all.

And in what was billed as the "Battle of the Geniuses," Joe Paterno's Nittany Lions, who commence playing a Big Ten football schedule in '93, were humbled by Bill Walsh–led Stanford, 24–3 in the Blockbuster Bowl. All-everything wideout O.J. McDuffie

was shut down by the Cardinal's cornerback Darrien Gordon, who said after the game that as McDuffie's frustration mounted, the receiver took to shouting at Gordon, "Hey man, I'm an All-American!" It was Penn State's fourth defeat in their last seven bowl appearances: The Nittany Lions should feel right at home in the Big Ten.

The Sugar Bowl would be Torretta's best chance to vindicate his Heisman electors and make believers of the large body of players, coaches and members of the media who felt that the fifth-year senior was not even the best player on his own team. The supreme overconfidence with which the Hurricanes came into the game was personified by Thomas, the mouthy receiver, who questioned the manliness of Alabama's defensive backs, who had played lots of

Reggie Brooks rambled for 115 yards in Notre Dame's 28–3 thumping of the Aggies.

DAMIAN STROHMEYER

PETER READ MILLER

Bowl. He threw three interceptions, each of which led to an Alabama touchdown. "In the second quarter he looked over at me and froze for a second," recalled Tide defensive end John Copeland. "I saw fear."

Pick No. 3 was a 31-yard interception return for a touchdown by Teague that made the score 27–6. The play was a highlight film effort, to be sure, but bloodless and uninspired next to the heroics Teague was about to perform. With less than 10 minutes left in the third quarter, Thomas, who had already lost one fumble, gathered in a pass from Torretta at the Miami 36-yard line and had clear sailing to the goal line. Teague overtook him at the Alabama 15. Not content to make the tackle, he reached over Thomas's right shoulder and stole the ball, effecting a remarkable, full-gallop fumble recovery. "Probably the worst moment I've ever had playing football," said Thomas.

Thus did Teague break the Hurricanes' spirit, just as Alabama broke the back of the nascent Hurricane dynasty. As far as cultivating a dynasty of its own, Alabama has an uphill fight. Just after 'Bama's triumph, new Auburn coach Terry Bowden announced his intention of sweet-talking the state's best recruits while the Crimson Tide celebrated. Sure enough, come signing day, two of the nation's top prospects, jumbo offensive tackle Willie Anderson of Whistler and tight end Jesse McCovery from St. Elmo, signed with Auburn.

But the best recruiting was done not by Terry Bowden, but by his old man, down in Tallahassee. A consensus of experts agreed that Bowden had reeled in the best class in the nation, including five of the top 10 players in talent-rich Florida. And one from Aurora, Colo. Beware Florida State in '93. The Seminoles finally have a kicker.

zone defense that season. "Real men play man," said Thomas. Not that he questioned the widsom of staying in safe zones against Miami's receivers, whom Thomas had dubbed the Ruthless Posse and whom he had anointed "probably the best receiving corps ever assembled."

The best receiving corps ever assembled got itself taken apart in the Superdome. When Miami had the ball the Crimson Tide put five, six, sometimes even seven defensive backs on the field. Occasionally the Tide brought all 11 men up to the line of scrimmage—a naked challenge to the Ruthless Posse: beat us deep if you can. "Sometimes we'd play man, sometimes we'd show man and drop into zone," said cornerback Tommy Johnson. "Torretta didn't know *what* was going on."

Torretta had gone 26–1 as a starter by deciphering coverages and keeping his cool. Both talents deserted him in the Sugar

Final Polls

Associated Press

		Record	Pts	Head Coach	SI Preseason Top 20
1	Alabama (62)	13-0-0	1550	Gene Stallings	7
2	Florida State	11-1-0	1470	Bobby Bowden	4
3	Miami	11-1-0	1410	Dennis Erickson	1
4	Notre Dame	10-1-1	1375	Lou Holtz	6
5	Michigan	9-0-3	1266	Gary Moeller	8
6	Syracuse	10-2-0	1209	Paul Pasqualoni	11
7	Texas A&M	12-1-0	1167	R.C. Slocum	14
8	Georgia	10-2-0	1159	Ray Goff	10
9	Stanford	10-3-0	1058	Bill Walsh	
10	Florida	9-4-0	931	Steve Spurrier	3
11	Washington	9-3-0	892	Don James	5
12	Tennessee	9-3-0	819	Johnny Majors	
13	Colorado	9-2-1	818	Bill McCartney	12
14	Nebraska	9-3-0	771	Tom Osborne	17
15	Washington State	9-3-0	618	Mike Price	
16	Mississippi	9-3-0	580	Billy Brewer	
17	North Carolina State	9-3-1	582	Dick Sheridan	
18	Ohio State	8-3-1	493	John Cooper	13
19	North Carolina	9-3-0	491	Mack Brown	
20	Hawaii	11-2-0	354	Bob Wagner	
21	Boston College	8-3-1	314	Tom Coughlin	
22	Kansas	8-4-0	183	Glenn Mason	
23	Mississippi State	7-5-0	167	Jackie Sherrill	18
24	Fresno State	9-4-0	124	Jim Sweeney	
25	Wake Forest	8-4-0	107	Bill Dooley	

Note: As voted by panel of 60 sportswriters and broadcasters following bowl games (1st-place votes in parentheses).

USA Today/CNN

		Pts	Prev Rank			Pts	Prev Rank
1	Alabama	1500	2	14	Nebraska	749	10
2	Florida State	1422	4	15	North Carolina State	572	12
3	Miami	1356	1	16	Mississippi	538	19
4	Notre Dame	1327	5	17	Washington State	495	18
5	Michigan	1231	7	18	North Carolina	450	20
6	Texas A&M	1149	3	19	Ohio State	426	14
7	Syracuse	1135	9	20	Hawaii	424	24
8	Georgia	1134	8	21	Boston College	303	16
9	Stanford	982	13	22	Fresno State	243	—
10	Washington	846	11	23	Kansas	201	—
11	Florida	845	15	24	Penn State	138	21
12	Tennessee	818	17	25	Wake Forest	128	—
13	Colorado	806	6				

Note: As voted by panel of 60 Division I-A head coaches; 25 points for 1st, 24 for 2nd, etc. (1st-place votes in parentheses).

Bowls and Playoffs

NCAA Division I-A Bowl Results

Date	Bowl	Result	Payout/Team ($)	Attendance
12-18-92	Las Vegas	Bowling Green 35, Nevada 34	150,000	15,476
12-25-92	Aloha	Kansas 23, Brigham Young 20	750,000	42,933
12-29-92	Copper	Washington State 31, Utah 28	650,000	40,876
12-29-92	Freedom	Fresno State 24, Southern California 7	650,000	50,745
12-30-92	Holiday	Hawaii 27, Illinois 17	1.5 million	44,457
12-31-92	Independence	Wake Forest 39, Oregon 35	650,000	31,337
12-31-92	Hancock	Baylor 20, Arizona 15	1.1 million	41,622

NCAA Division I-A Bowl Results

Date	Bowl	Result	Payout/Team ($)	Attendance
12-31-92	Gator	Florida 27, N Carolina St 10	1.6 million	71,233
12-31-92	Liberty	Mississippi 13, Air Force 0	900,000	32,107
1-1-93	Hall of Fame	Tennessee 38, Boston College 23	1 million	52,056
1-1-93	Citrus	Georgia 21, Ohio St 14	2 million	65,861
1-1-93	Cotton	Notre Dame 28, Texas A&M 3	3 million	71,615
1-1-92	Blockbuster	Stanford 24, Penn St 3	1.525 million	45,554
1-1-93	Fiesta	Syracuse 26, Colorado 22	3 million	70,224
1-1-93	Rose	Michigan 38, Washington 31	6.5 million	94,236
1-1-93	Orange	Florida St 27, Nebraska 14	4.2 million	57,324
1-1-93	Sugar	Alabama 38, Miami 13	3.8 million	76,789
1-2-93	Peach	N Carolina 21, Mississippi St 17	1 million	69,125

NCAA Division I-AA Championship Boxscore

Youngstown St	0	0	14	14—28
Marshall	0	14	14	3—31

SECOND QUARTER

MU: Mark Bartrum 6 pass from Michael Payton (Willy Merrick kick), 4:27.
MU: Orlando Hatchett 5 run (Merrick kick), 11:30.

THIRD QUARTER

MU: Glenn Pedro 1 run (Merrick kick), 4:47.
MU: Hatchett 22 pass from Payton (Merrick kick), 9:14.
YSU: Herb Williams 30 pass from Nick Cothran (Jeff Wilkins kick), 11:19.
YSU: Tamron Smith 4 run (Wilkins kick), 14:44.

FOURTH QUARTER

YSU: Smith 1 run (Wilkins kick), 2:56.
YSU: Smith 10 run (Wilkins kick), 12:32.
MU: FG Merrick 22 FG, 14:50.

	YSU	MU
First downs	17	26
Rushing yardage	166	185
Passing yardage	256	270
Return yardage	35	70
Passes (comp-att-int)	25-40-1	18-31-2
Punts (no.-avg)	6-41.6	5-39.8
Fumbles (no.-lost)	0-0	1-1
Penalties (no.-yards)	3-20	7-40

Small College Championship Summaries

NCAA DIVISION II

First round: Ferris St 19, Edinboro 15; New Haven 38, West Chester 26; Jacksonville St 41, Savannah St 16; North Alabama 33, Hampton 21; Texas A&I 22, Western St 13; Portland St 42, UC Davis 28; Pittsburg St 26, North Dakota 21; North Dakota St 42, Northeast Missouri St 7.
Quarterfinals: New Haven 35, Ferris St 13; Jacksonville St 14, North Alabama 12; Portland St 35, Texas A&I 30; Pittsburg St 38, North Dakota St 37 (OT).
Semifinals: Jacksonville St 46, New Haven 35; Pittsburg St 41, Portland St 38.
Championship: 12-12-92 Florence, AL

Pittsburg St	6	7	0	0—13
Jacksonville St	0	10	7	0—17

NCAA DIVISION III

First round: Mount Union 27, Dayton 10; Illinois Wesleyan 21, Aurora 12; Central Iowa 20, Carleton 8; Wisconsin-La Crosse 47, Redlands 26; Emory & Henry 17, Thomas More 0; Washington & Jefferson 33, Lycoming 0; Rowan 41, Worcester Tech 14; Buffalo St 28, Ithaca 26.
Quarterfinals: Mount Union 49, Illinois Wesleyan 27; Wisconsin-La Crosse 34, Central Iowa 9; Washington & Jefferson 51, Emory & Henry 15; Rowan 28, Buffalo St 19.
Semifinals: Wisconsin-La Crosse 29, Mount Union 24; Washington & Jefferson 18, Rowan 13.
Championship: 12-12-92 Bradenton, FL

Wisconsin-La Crosse	0	14	2	0—16
Washington & Jeff	0	0	12	0—12

NAIA DIVISION I PLAYOFFS

First Round: Central St (OH) 34, Harding (AR) 0; Central Arkansas 14, Southwestern Oklahoma 2; Gardner-Webb (NC) 28, Concord (WV) 21; Shepherd (WV) 6, Carson-Newman (TN) 3.
Semifinals: Central St (OH) 30, Central Arkansas 23; Gardner-Webb (NC) 22, Shepherd (WV) 7.
Championship: 12-12-92 Boiling Springs, NC

Central St (OH)	6	0	0	13—19
Gardner-Webb (NC)	2	14	0	0—16

NAIA DIVISION II PLAYOFFS

First round: Baker (KS) 21, Northwestern (IA) 20; Benedictine (KS) 17, Hastings (NE) 15; Findlay (OH) 32, Georgetown (KY) 14; Hardin-Simmons (TX) 42, Howard Payne (TX) 28; Linfield (OR) 26, Western Washington 0; Minot St (ND) 31, Dakota Wesleyan (SD) 21; Pacific Lutheran (WA) 37, Montan Tech 0; Westminster (PA) 28, Friends (KS) 0.
Quarterfinals: Benedictine (KS) 21, Baker (KS) 14; Findlay (OH) 13, Westminster (PA) 7; Linfield (OR) 44, Pacific Lutheran (WA) 30; Minot St (ND) 21, Hardin-Simmons (TX) 14.
Semifinals: Findlay (OH) 27, Benedictine (KS) 24; Linfield (OR) 47, Minot St (ND) 12.
Championship: 12-19-92 Portland, OR

Findlay (OH)	0	14	12	0—26
Linfield (OR)	7	0	0	6—13

Awards

Heisman Memorial Trophy

Player/School	Class	Pos	1st	2nd	3rd	Total
Gino Torretta, Miami	Sr	QB	310	179	112	1,400
Marshall Faulk, San Diego St.	So	RB	164	207	174	1,080
Garrison Hearst, Georgia	Jr	RB	140	196	170	982
Marvin Jones, Florida St.	Jr	LB	81	51	47	392
Reggie Brooks, Notre Dame	Sr	RB	42	53	62	294
Charlie Ward, Florida St.	Jr	QB	18	18	36	126
Micheal Barrow, Miami	Sr	LB	10	10	14	64
Drew Bledsoe, Washington St.	Jr	QB	6	8	14	48
Glyn Milburn, Stanford	Sr	RB/KR	5	11	10	47
Eric Curry, Alabama	Sr	DE	3	13	12	47

Note: Former Heisman winners and the media vote, with ballots allowing for 3 names (3 points for 1st, 2 for 2nd, 1 for 3rd).

Offensive Players of the Year

Maxwell Award (Player).............................Gino Torretta, Miami, QB
Walter Camp Player of the Year (Back) .....Gino Torretta, Miami, QB
Davey O'Brien Award (QB) ....Gino Torretta, Miami, QB
Doak Walker Award (RB) ....Garrison Hearst, Georgia, RB

Other Awards

Vince Lombardi/Rotary Award (Lineman) ..Marvin Jones, Florida St., LB
Outland Trophy (Interior lineman) ....Will Shields, Nebraska, OG
Butkus Award (Linebacker).......................Marvin Jones, Florida St, LB
Jim Thorpe Award (Defensive back)..........Deon Figures, Colorado, CB
Sporting News Player of the Year ....Marvin Jones, Miami, LB
Walter Payton Award (Div I-AA Player) ......Michael Payton, Marshall, QB

Coaches' Awards

Harlon Hill Trophy (Div II Player) ....Ronald Moore, Pittsburg St, RB
Walter Camp Award ....Gene Stallings, Alabama
Eddie Robinson Award (Div I-AA)..............Charlie Taaffe, Citadel
Bobby Dodd Award ....Eddie Robinson, Grambling
Bear Bryant Award ....Gene Stallings, Alabama

AFCA COACHES OF THE YEAR

DIvision I-A..Gene Stallings, Alabama
Division I-AA..Charlie Taaffe, Citadel
Division II and NAIA Division I....................Bill Burgess, Jacksonville St
Division III and NAIA Division II..................John Luckhardt, Washington & Jefferson

Football Writers Association of America All-America Team

OFFENSE

Sean Dawkins, California, Jr ....Wide receiver
Ryan Yarborough, Wyoming, Jr ....Wide receiver
Chris Gedney, Syracuse, Sr...............Tight end
Lincoln Kennedy, Washington, Sr.......OL
Will Shields, Nebraska, Sr..................OL
Everett Lindsay, Mississippi, Sr ....OL
Willie Roaf, Louisiana Tech, Sr...........OL
Gino Torretta, Miami, Sr ....Quarterback
Marshall Faulk, San Diego St, Soph....Running back
Garrison Hearst, Georgia, Jr..............Running back
Joe Allison, Memphis St, Jr ....PK
Curtis Conway, Southern Cal, Jr ....Kick returner

DEFENSE

Chris Hutchinson, Michigan, Sr...........DL
Rob Waldrop, Arizona, Jr ....DL
John Copeland, Alabama, Sr ....DL
Chris Slade, Virginia, Sr ....DL
Marvin Jones, Florida St, Jr.................Linebacker
Micheal Barrow, Miami, Sr ....Linebacker
Marcus Buckley, Texas A & M, Sr.......Linebacker
Carlton McDonald, Air Force, Sr ....Defensive back
Patrick Bates, Texas A & M, Jr............Defensive back
Deon Figures. Colorado, Sr.................Defensive back
Lance Gunn, Texas, Sr........................Defensive back
Josh Miller, Arizona, Sr.......................Punter

Division I-A

ATLANTIC COAST CONFERENCE

	Conference			Full Season			
	W	L	T	W	L	T	Pct
Florida St	8	0	0	10	1	0	.909
N Carolina St	6	2	0	9	2	1	.792
N Carolina	5	3	0	8	3	0	.727
Virginia	4	4	0	7	4	0	.636
Wake Forest	4	4	0	7	4	0	.636
Georgia Tech	4	4	0	5	6	0	.454
Clemson	3	5	0	5	6	0	.454
Maryland	2	6	0	3	8	0	.273
Duke	0	8	0	2	9	0	.182

BIG EAST CONFERENCE

	Conference			Full Season			
	W	L	T	W	L	T	Pct
Miami	4	0	0	11	0	0	1.000
Syracuse	6	1	0	9	2	0	.818
Rutgers	4	2	0	7	4	0	.636
Boston College	2	1	1	8	2	1	.773
W Virginia	2	3	1	5	4	2	.545
Pittsburgh	1	3	0	3	9	0	.250
Virginia Tech	1	4	0	2	8	0	.227
Temple	0	6	0	1	10	0	.091

Note: As it was in 1991, the Big East champion is determined by the CNN/USA Today coaches' poll. Miami was ranked the highest and thereby recognized as conference champion. Beginning in 1993, the Big East will have a full round-robin schedule to determine its champion.

BIG EIGHT CONFERENCE

	Conference			Full Season			
	W	L	T	W	L	T	Pct
Nebraska	6	1	0	9	2	0	.818
Colorado	5	1	1	9	1	1	.864
Kansas	4	3	0	7	4	0	.636
Oklahoma	3	2	2	5	4	2	.545
Oklahoma St	2	4	1	4	6	1	.409
Kansas St	2	5	0	5	6	0	.455
Iowa St	2	5	0	4	7	0	.364
Missouri	2	5	0	3	8	0	.273

BIG TEN CONFERENCE

	Conference			Full Season			
	W	L	T	W	L	T	Pct
Michigan	6	0	2	8	0	3	.864
Ohio St	5	2	1	8	2	1	.773
Michigan St	5	3	0	5	6	0	.455
Illinois	4	3	1	6	4	1	.591
Iowa	4	4	0	5	7	0	.417
Indiana	3	5	0	5	6	0	.455
Wisconsin	3	5	0	5	6	0	.455
Purdue	3	5	0	4	7	0	.364
Northwestern	3	5	0	3	8	0	.273
Minnesota	2	6	0	2	9	0	.182

BIG WEST CONFERENCE

	Conference			Full Season			
	W	L	T	W	L	T	Pct
Nevada	5	1	0	7	4	0	.636
San Jose St	4	2	0	7	4	0	.636
Utah St	4	2	0	5	6	0	.455
New Mexico St	3	3	0	6	5	0	.545
NV-Las Vegas	3	3	0	6	5	0	.545
Pacific	2	4	0	3	8	0	.273
Cal St-Fullerton	0	6	0	2	9	0	.182

Division I-A (Cont.)

MID-AMERICAN CONFERENCE

	Conference			Full Season			
	W	L	T	W	L	T	Pct
Bowling Green	8	0	0	9	2	0	.818
Western Michigan	6	3	0	7	3	1	.682
Toledo	5	3	0	8	3	0	.727
Akron	5	3	0	7	3	1	.682
Miami (Ohio)	5	3	0	6	4	1	.591
Ball St	5	4	0	5	6	0	.455
Central Michigan	4	5	0	5	6	0	.455
Kent State	2	7	0	2	9	0	.182
Eastern Michigan	1	7	0	1	10	0	.091
Ohio	1	7	0	1	10	0	.091

PACIFIC-10 CONFERENCE

	Conference			Full Season			
	W	L	T	W	L	T	Pct
Washington	6	2	0	9	2	0	.818
Stanford	6	2	0	9	3	0	.750
Washington St	5	3	0	8	3	0	.727
Southern Cal	5	3	0	6	4	1	.591
Arizona	4	3	1	6	4	1	.591
Oregon	4	4	0	6	5	0	.545
Arizona St	4	4	0	6	5	0	.545
UCLA	3	5	0	6	5	0	.545
California	2	6	0	4	7	0	.364
Oregon St	0	7	1	1	9	1	.136

SOUTHEASTERN CONFERENCE

	Conference			Full Season			
East	W	L	T	W	L	T	Pct
Florida*	6	2	0	8	4	0	.667
Georgia	6	2	0	9	2	0	.818
Tennessee	5	3	0	8	3	0	.727
South Carolina	3	5	0	5	6	0	.455
Vanderbilt	2	6	0	4	7	0	.364
Kentucky	2	6	0	4	7	0	.364
West							
Alabama*	8	0	0	12	0	0	1.000
Mississippi	5	3	0	8	3	0	.727
Mississippi St	4	4	0	7	4	0	.636
Arkansas	3	4	1	3	7	1	.318
Auburn	2	5	1	5	5	1	.500
Louisiana St	1	7	0	2	9	0	.182

*Overall record includes first SEC Championship Game in which Alabama defeated Florida, 28-21, on Dec 5.

SOUTHWEST ATHLETIC CONFERENCE

	Conference			Full Season			
	W	L	T	W	L	T	Pct
Texas A&M	7	0	0	12	0	0	1.000
Baylor	4	3	0	6	5	0	.545
Rice	4	3	0	6	5	0	.545
Texas	4	3	0	6	5	0	.545
Texas Tech	4	3	0	5	6	0	.455
Southern Meth	2	5	0	5	6	0	.455
Houston	2	5	0	4	7	0	.364
Texas Christian	1	6	0	2	8	1	.227

Division I-A *(Cont.)*

WESTERN ATHLETIC CONFERENCE

	Conference			Full Season			
	W	L	T	W	L	T	Pct
Hawaii	6	2	0	10	2	0	.833
Brigham Young	6	2	0	8	4	0	.667
Fresno St	6	2	0	8	4	0	.667
San Diego St	5	3	0	5	5	1	.500
Air Force	4	4	0	7	4	0	.636
Utah	4	4	0	6	5	0	.545
Wyoming	3	5	0	5	7	0	.417
Colorado St	3	5	0	5	7	0	.417
New Mexico	2	6	0	3	8	0	.273
UTEP	1	7	0	1	10	0	.091

INDEPENDENTS

	Full Season			
	W	L	T	Pct
Notre Dame	9	1	1	.864
Penn St	7	4	0	.636
Southern Miss	7	4	0	.636
Memphis St	6	5	0	.545
Army	5	6	0	.455
E Carolina	5	6	0	.455
Louisiana Tech	5	6	0	.455
Louisville	5	6	0	.455
Northern Illinois	5	6	0	.455
Tulsa	4	7	0	.364
Cincinnati	3	8	0	.273
Arkansas St	2	9	0	.182
Southwestern Louisiana	2	9	0	.182
Tulane	2	9	0	.182
Navy	1	10	0	.091

Division I-AA

BIG SKY CONFERENCE

	Conference			Full Season			
	W	L	T	W	L	T	Pct
Idaho	6	1	0	9	2	0	.818
Eastern Washington	6	1	0	7	3	0	.700
Weber St	4	3	0	6	5	0	.545
Montana	4	3	0	6	5	0	.545
Boise St	3	4	0	5	6	0	.455
Northern Arizona	2	5	0	4	7	0	.364
Montana St	2	5	0	4	7	0	.364
Idaho St	1	6	0	3	8	0	.273

GATEWAY COLLEGIATE ATHLETIC CONFERENCE

	Conference			Full Season			
	W	L	T	W	L	T	Pct
Northern Iowa	5	1	0	10	1	0	.909
Western Illinois	4	2	0	7	4	0	.636
SW Missouri St	4	2	0	6	5	0	.545
Illinois St	2	4	0	5	6	0	.455
Eastern Illinois	2	4	0	5	6	0	.455
Southern Illinois	2	4	0	4	7	0	.364
Indiana St	2	4	0	4	7	0	.364

Division I-AA (Cont.)

IVY GROUP

	Conference			Full Season			
	W	L	T	W	L	T	Pct
Dartmouth	6	1	0	8	2	0	.800
Princeton	6	1	0	8	2	0	.800
Pennsylvania	5	2	0	7	3	0	.700
Cornell	4	3	0	7	3	0	.700
Harvard	3	4	0	3	7	0	.300
Yale	2	5	0	4	6	0	.400
Columbia	2	5	0	3	7	0	.300
Brown	0	7	0	0	10	0	.000

MID-EASTERN ATHLETIC CONFERENCE

	Conference			Full Season			
	W	L	T	W	L	T	Pct
N Carolina A&T	5	1	0	9	2	0	.818
Florida A&M	4	2	0	7	4	0	.636
S Carolina St	4	2	0	7	4	0	.636
Howard	3	3	0	7	4	0	.636
Delaware St	3	3	0	6	5	0	.545
Bethune-Cookman	2	4	0	3	7	0	.300
Morgan St	0	6	0	2	8	0	.200

OHIO VALLEY CONFERENCE

	Conference			Full Season			
	W	L	T	W	L	T	Pct
Middle Tennessee St	8	0	0	9	2	0	.818
Eastern Kentucky	7	1	0	9	2	0	.818
Tennessee Tech	6	2	0	7	4	0	.636
Tennessee St	5	3	0	5	6	0	.455
Morehead St	3	5	0	3	8	0	.273
Austin Peay	2	6	0	3	8	0	.273
Tenn-Martin	2	6	0	3	8	0	.273
Southeast Mo St	2	6	0	2	9	0	.182
Murray St	1	7	0	2	9	0	.182

PATRIOT LEAGUE

	Conference			Full Season			
	W	L	T	W	L	T	Pct
Lafayette	5	0	0	8	3	0	.727
Holy Cross	4	1	0	6	5	0	.545
Colgate	2	3	0	4	7	0	.364
Lehigh	2	3	0	3	8	0	.273
Bucknell	1	4	0	4	7	0	.364
Fordham	1	4	0	1	9	0	.100

SOUTHERN CONFERENCE

	Conference			Full Season			
	W	L	T	W	L	T	Pct
Citadel	6	1	0	10	1	0	.909
Marshall	5	2	0	8	3	0	.727
Appalachian St	5	2	0	7	4	0	.636
Western Carolina	5	2	0	7	4	0	.636
Furman	4	3	0	6	5	0	.545
E Tennessee St	2	5	0	5	6	0	.455
Virginia Military	1	6	0	3	8	0	.273
TN-Chattanooga	0	7	0	2	9	0	.182
Georgia Southern*	-	-	-	7	4	0	.636

,*Georgia Southern did not compete for title in 1992.

Division I-AA (Cont.)

SOUTHLAND CONFERENCE

	Conference			Full Season			
	W	L	T	W	L	T	Pct
NE Louisiana	7	0	0	9	2	0	.818
McNeese St	6	1	0	8	3	0	.727
Sam Houston St	3	2	2	6	3	2	.636
Northwestern (La)	4	3	0	7	4	0	.636
N Texas	3	4	0	4	7	0	.364
SW Texas St	2	4	1	5	5	1	.500
SF Austin St	1	6	0	3	8	0	.273
Nicholls St	0	6	1	1	9	1	.136

SOUTHWESTERN ATHLETIC CONFERENCE

	Conference			Full Season			
	W	L	T	W	L	T	Pct
Alcorn St	7	0	0	7	3	0	.700
Grambling	6	1	0	9	2	0	.818
Jackson St	4	3	0	7	4	0	.636
Alabama St	3	4	0	5	6	0	.455
Southern-B.R.	3	4	0	5	6	0	.455
Texas Southern	3	4	0	5	6	0	.455
Mississippi Valley	2	5	0	4	5	0	.444
Prairie View A&M	0	7	0	0	11	0	.000

YANKEE CONFERENCE

	Conference			Full Season			
	W	L	T	W	L	T	Pct
Delaware	7	1	0	9	2	0	.818
Villanova	6	2	0	9	2	0	.818
Massachusetts	5	3	0	7	3	0	.700
Richmond	5	3	0	7	4	0	.636
Maine	4	4	0	6	5	0	.545
Connecticut	4	4	0	5	6	0	.455
New Hampshire	3	5	0	5	5	1	.500
Boston U	2	6	0	3	8	0	.273
Rhode Island	0	8	0	1	10	0	.091

INDEPENDENTS

	Full Season			
	W	L	T	Pct
Samford	9	2	0	.818
William & Mary	9	2	0	.818
Youngstown St	8	2	1	.773
Liberty	7	4	0	.636
Central Florida	6	4	0	.600
Towson St	5	5	0	.500
Northeastern	5	5	1	.500
Western Kentucky	4	6	0	.400
James Madison	4	7	0	.364

THEY SAID IT

Jim Muldoon, Pac-10 p.r. man, denigrating the record of conference champion Washington's Rose Bowl opponent, Michigan: "Eight-oh-three isn't a record. It's an area code."

Division I-A

SCORING

	Class	GP	TD	XP	FG	Pts	Pts/Game
Garrison Hearst, Georgia	Jr	11	21	0	0	126	11.45
Richie Anderson, Penn St	Sr	11	19	2	0	116	10.55
Marshall Faulk, San Diego St	So	10	15	2	0	92	9.20
Joe Allison, Memphis St	Jr	11	0	32	23	101	9.18
Greg Hill, Texas A&M	So	12	17	0	0	102	8.50
Tyrone Wheatley, Michigan	So	10	14	0	0	84	8.40
Trevor Cobb, Rice	Sr	11	15	2	0	92	8.36
Calvin Jones, Nebraska	So	11	15	0	0	90	8.18
Craig Thomas, Michigan St	Jr	11	15	0	0	90	8.18
Rusty Hanna, Toledo	Sr	11	0	26	21	89	8.09
Nelson Welch, Clemson	So	11	0	23	22	89	8.09

FIELD GOALS

	Class	GP	FGA	FG	Pct	FG/Game
Joe Allison, Memphis St	Jr	11	25	23	92.0	2.09
Scott Ethridge, Auburn	So	11	28	22	78.6	2.00
Nelson Welch, Clemson	So	11	28	22	78.6	2.00
Rick Thompson, Wisconsin	Sr	11	32	22	68.8	2.00
Rusty Hanna, Toledo	Sr	11	29	21	72.4	1.91
Tommy Thompson, Oregon	Jr	11	31	20	64.5	1.82
Eric Lange, Tulsa	Sr	11	23	19	82.6	1.73
Scott Sisson, Georgia Tech	Sr	11	24	19	79.2	1.73
Sean Jones, Utah St	Sr	11	24	18	75.0	1.64
Daron Alcorn, Akron	Sr	11	26	18	69.2	1.64

TOTAL OFFENSE

			Rushing		Passing		Total Offense			
	Class	GP	Car	Net	Att	Yds	Yds	Yds/Play	TDR*	Yds/Game
Jimmy Klingler, Houston	So	11	40	-50	504	3818	3768	6.93	32	342.55
John Kaleo, Maryland	Sr	11	106	80	482	3392	3472	5.90	22	315.64
Ryan Hancock, BYU	So	9	33	-49	288	2635	2586	8.06	17	287.33
Charlie Ward, Florida St	Jr	11	100	504	365	2647	3151	6.78	28	286.45
Gino Torretta, Miami (FL)	Sr	11	34	-24	402	3060	3036	6.96	19	276.00
Shane Matthews, Florida	Sr	12	73	-29	463	3205	3176	5.93	25	264.67
Frank Dolce, Utah	Sr	9	60	5	322	2369	2374	6.21	22	263.78
Alex Van Pelt, Pittsburgh	Sr	12	27	0	407	3163	3163	7.29	20	263.58
Drew Bledsoe, Washington St	Jr	11	78	-53	386	2770	2717	5.86	22	247.00
Trent Dilfer, Fresno St	So	12	73	82	331	2828	2910	7.20	22	242.50

*Touchdowns responsible for.

RUSHING

	Class	GP	Car	Yds	Avg	TD	Yds/Game
Marshall Faulk, San Diego St	So	10	265	1630	6.2	15	163.00
Garrison Hearst, Georgia	Jr	11	228	1547	6.8	19	140.64
Ryan Benjamin, Pacific	Sr	11	231	1441	6.2	13	131.00
Chuckie Dukes, Boston College	Sr	11	238	1387	5.8	10	126.09
Trevor Cobb, Rice	Sr	11	279	1386	5.0	11	126.00
Travis Sims, Hawaii	Sr	12	220	1498	6.8	9	124.83
Reggie Brooks, Notre Dame	Sr	11	167	1343	8.0	13	122.09
LeShon Johnson, N Illinois	Jr	11	265	1338	5.0	6	121.64
Byron Morris, Texas Tech	So	11	242	1279	5.3	10	116.27
Deland McCullough, Miami (Ohio)	Fr	9	227	1026	4.5	6	114.00

Whole Lot of W's

At the start of the 1992 season there were two Division III football teams with 500 or more wins—Wittenberg and Widener. Now there are three more. Washington and Jefferson is one of them, having joined the elite by beating Widener. Williams is another, thanks to a win over Wesleyan. The third is Franklin and Marshall, which doesn't belong in this item except that its milestone W occured at home on Williamson Field against Western Maryland.

Division I-A (Cont.)

PASSING EFFICIENCY

	Class	GP	Att	Comp	Pct Comp	Yds	Yds/Att	TD	Int	Rating Pts
Elvis Grbac, Michigan	Sr	9	169	112	66.27	1465	8.67	15	12	154.2
Marvin Graves, Syracuse	Jr	11	242	146	60.33	2296	9.49	14	12	149.2
Ryan Hancock, Brigham Young	So	9	288	165	57.29	2635	9.15	17	13	144.6
Bert Emmanuel, Rice	Jr	11	179	94	52.51	1558	8.70	11	6	139.2
Kordell Stewart, Colorado	So	9	252	151	59.92	2109	8.37	12	9	138.8
Eric Zeier, Georgia	So	11	258	151	58.53	2248	8.71	12	12	137.8
Jimmy Klingler, Houston	So	11	504	303	60.12	3818	7.58	32	18	137.6
Bobby Goodman, Virginia	Sr	11	232	130	56.03	1707	7.36	21	12	137.4
Joe Youngblood, Cent Michigan	Jr	11	278	161	57.91	2209	7.95	18	13	136.7
Trent Dilfer, Fresno St	So	12	331	174	52.57	2828	8.54	20	14	135.8

Note: Minimum 15 attempts per game.

RECEPTIONS PER GAME

	Class	GP	No.	Yds	TD	R/Game
Sherman Smith, Houston	Jr	11	103	923	6	9.36
Bryan Reeves, Nevada	Jr	11	81	1114	10	7.36
Aaron Turner, Pacific	Sr	11	79	1171	11	7.18
Ryan Yarborough, Wyoming	Jr	12	86	1351	12	7.17
Lloyd Hill, Texas Tech	Jr	11	76	1261	12	6.91
Michael Westbrook, Colorado	So	11	76	1060	8	6.91

RECEIVING YARDS PER GAME

	Class	GP	No.	Yds	TD	Yds/Game
Lloyd Hill, Texas Tech	Jr	11	76	1261	12	114.64
Marcus Badgett, Maryland	Sr	11	75	1240	9	112.73
Ryan Yarborough, Wyoming	Jr	12	86	1351	12	112.58
Victor Bailey, Missouri	Sr	11	75	1210	6	110.00
Aaron Turner, Pacific	Sr	11	79	1171	11	106.45

ALL-PURPOSE RUNNERS

	Class	GP	Rush	Rec	PR	KOR	Yds*	Yds/Game
Ryan Benjamin, Pacific	Sr	11	1441	434	96	626	2597	236.09
Glyn Milburn, Stanford	Jr	12	851	405	573	292	2121	176.75
Marshall Faulk, San Diego St	So	10	1630	128	0	0	1758	175.80
Garrison Hearst, Georgia	Jr	11	1547	324	0	39	1910	173.64
Henry Bailey, Nevada-Las Vegas	So	11	15	832	219	817	1883	171.18

*Includes interceptions return yards

INTERCEPTIONS

	Class	GP	No.	Yds	TD	Int/Game
Carlton McDonald, Air Force	Sr	11	8	109	1	.73
C.J. Masters, Kansas St	Sr	11	7	152	2	.64
Greg Evans, Texas Christian	Jr	11	7	121	0	.64
T. Drakeford, Virginia Tech	Jr	11	7	121	1	.64
Joe Bair, Bowling Green	Jr	11	7	51	0	.64
Chris Owens, Akron	Sr	11	7	49	0	.64
Corey Sawyer, Florida St	So	11	7	0	0	.64

PUNTING

	Class	No.	Avg
Ed Bunn, UTEP	Sr	41	47.68
Mitch Berger, Colorado	Jr	53	47.04
Brian Parvin, Nevada-Las Vegas	Sr	57	46.26
Sean Snyder, Kansas St	Sr	80	44.65
Jeff Buffaloe, Memphs St	Sr	52	44.56

Note: Minimum of 3.6 per game.

PUNT RETURNS

	Class	No.	Yds	TD	Avg
Lee Gissender, Northwestern	Jr	15	327	1	21.80
James McMillion, Iowa St	Jr	23	435	3	18.91
Glyn Milburn, Stanford	Sr	31	573	3	18.48
Jamie Mouton, Houston	Sr	18	278	1	15.44
Corey Sawyer, Florida St	So	33	488	1	14.79

Note: Minimum 1.2 per game.

Division I-A (Cont.)

KICKOFF RETURNS

	Class	No.	Yds	TD	Avg
Fred Montgomery, New Mexico St	Sr	14	457	0	32.64
Leroy Gallman, Duke	Sr	14	433	0	30.93
Lew Lawhorn, Temple	So	20	600	2	30.00
Chris Singleton, Nevada	Jr	17	497	0	29.24
Brad Breedlove, Duke	Sr	15	438	0	29.20

Note: Minimum of 1.2 per game.

Division I-A Single-Game Highs

RUSHING AND PASSING

Rushing and passing plays: 77—Jeff Handy, Missouri, Oct 17 (vs Oklahoma St).

Rushing and passing yards: 612—Jimmy Klingler, Houston, Nov 28 (vs Rice).

Rushing plays: 44—Kevin Galbreath, Arizona St, Oct 24 (vs UCLA).

Net rushing yards: 300—Marshall Faulk, San Diego St, Nov 14 (vs Hawaii).

Passes attempted: 75—Chris Vargas, Nevada, Sep 19 (vs McNeese St).

Passes completed: 46—Jimmy Klingler, Houston, Nov 28 (vs Rice).

Passing yards: 613—Jimmy Klingler, Houston, Nov 28 (vs Rice).

RECEIVING AND RETURNS

Passes caught: 16—Bryan Reeves, Nevada, Oct 3 (vs Cal St Fullerton).

Receiving yards: 274—Darnay Scott, San Diego St, Oct 17 (vs UTEP).

Punt return yards: 164—Deon Figures, Colorado, Oct 24 (vs Kansas St).

Kickoff return yards: 231—Leroy Gallman, Duke, Nov 14 (vs North Carolina St).

Division I-AA

SCORING

	Class	GP	TD	XP	FG	Pts	Pts/Game
Sherriden May, Idaho	So	11	25	0	0	150	13.64
Keith Elias, Princeton	Jr	10	18	2	0	110	11.00
Toby Davis, Illinois St	Sr	11	20	0	0	120	10.91
Markus Thomas, Eastern Kentucky	Sr	11	18	0	0	108	9.82
Harry Brown, Alcorn St	Jr	9	14	0	0	84	9.33
Kenny Sims, James Madison	Sr	9	14	0	0	84	9.33

FIELD GOALS

	Class	GP	FGA	FG	Pct	FG/Game
Mike Dodd, Boise St	Sr	11	31	22	.710	2.00
Scott Obermeier, Northern Iowa	Fr	11	19	17	.895	1.55
Terry Belden, Northern Arizona	Jr	11	24	15	.625	1.36
Dennis Durkin, Dartmouth	Sr	10	13	13	1.000	1.30
Mike Cochrane, Cornell	Sr	10	22	13	.591	1.30

Division I-AA (Cont.)

TOTAL OFFENSE

			Rushing				Passing		Total Offense			
	Class	GP	Car	Gain	Loss	Net	Att	Yds	Yds	Yds/Play	TDR*	Yds/Game
Steve McNair, Alcorn St	So	10	92	633	117	516	427	3541	4057	7.82	39	405.70
Doug Nussmeier, Idaho	Jr	11	97	620	211	409	333	3028	3437	7.99	28	312.45
Jay Fiedler, Dartmouth	Jr	10	80	326	140	186	273	2748	2934	8.31	31	293.40
S. Semptimphelter, Lehigh	Jr	11	107	272	288	-16	405	3190	3174	6.20	20	288.55
Jamie Martin, Weber St	Sr	11	86	200	278	-78	463	3207	3129	5.70	22	284.45

*Touchdowns responsible for.

RUSHING

	Class	GP	Car	Yds	Avg	TD	Yds/Game
Keith Elias, Princeton	Jr	10	245	1575	6.4	18	157.50
Toby Davis, Illinois State	Sr	11	341	1561	4.6	20	141.91
Carl Tremble, Furman	Sr	11	228	1555	6.8	13	141.36
Kelvin Anderson, Southeast Missouri	So	10	205	1371	6.7	13	137.10
Erik Marsh, Lafayette	So	10	284	1365	4.8	10	136.50

PASSING EFFICIENCY

	Class	GP	Att	Comp	Pct Comp	Yds	Yds/Att	TD	Int	Rating Pts
Jay Fiedler, Dartmouth	Jr	10	273	175	64.10	2748	10.07	25	13	169.4
Lonnie Galloway, W Carolina	Jr	11	211	128	60.66	2181	10.34	20	12	167.4
Wendal Lowrey, NE Louisiana	Sr	11	227	147	64.76	2190	9.65	16	9	161.1
Donny Simmons, W Illinois	Sr	11	281	182	64.77	2496	8.88	25	11	160.9
Michael Payton, Marshall	Sr	11	313	200	63.90	2788	8.91	26	11	159.1

Note: Minimum 15 attempts per game.

RECEPTIONS PER GAME

	Class	GP	No.	Yds	TD	R/Game
Glenn Krupa, Southeast Missouri	Sr	11	77	773	4	7.00
Mike Wilson, Boise St	Jr	11	76	913	2	6.91
Darren Rizzi, Rhode Island	Sr	11	74	1102	6	6.73
Yo Murphy, Idaho	Sr	11	68	1156	9	6.18
Troy Brown, Marshall	Sr	11	67	1109	11	6.09

RECEIVING YARDS PER GAME

	Class	GP	No.	Yds	TD	Yds/Game
Jason Cristino, Lehigh	Sr	11	65	1282	9	116.55
Yo Murphy, Idaho	Sr	11	68	1156	9	105.09
Vincent Brisby, NE Louisiana	Sr	10	56	1050	9	105.00
Rod Boothes, Richmond	Jr	11	47	1115	10	101.36
Troy Brown, Marshall	Sr	11	67	1109	11	100.82

ALL-PURPOSE RUNNERS

	Class	GP	Rush	Rec	PR	KOR	Yds*	Yds/Game
David Wright, Indiana State	Fr	11	1313	108	0	593	2014	183.09
Kelvin Anderson, SE Missouri	So	10	1371	171	0	253	1795	179.50
Troy Brown, Marshall	Sr	11	152	1109	101	482	1844	167.64
Keith Elias, Princeton	Jr	10	1575	98	0	0	1673	167.30
Patrick Robinson, Tennessee St	Sr	10	0	803	150	665	1618	161.80

*Includes interceptions return yards

INTERCEPTIONS

	Class	GP	No.	Yds	TD	Int/Game
Dave Roberts, Youngstown St	Sr	11	9	39	0	.82
Mark Chapman, Connecticut	Sr	11	8	67	0	.73
Don Caparotti, Massachusetts	Sr	10	7	15	0	.70
Torrence Forney, Citadel	Sr	11	7	71	1	.64
Bob Jordan, New Hampshire	Jr	11	7	35	0	.64

Division I-AA *(Cont.)*

PUNTING

	Class	No.	Avg
Harold Alexander, Appalachian St.....Sr		55	44.45
Terry Belden, Northern Arizona.........Jr		59	44.31
Rob Sims, Pennsylvania....................Sr		67	43.43
Colin Godfrey, Tennessee St ....Sr		54	42.20
Tim Mosley, Northern Iowa...............Jr		50	42.04
Leo Araguz, Stephen F. Austin ....Sr		54	42.04

Note: Minimum 3.6 per game.

Division II

SCORING

	Class	GP	TD	XP	FG	Pts	Pts/Game
David McCartney, Chadron St..........Jr		10	25	4	0	154	15.4
Ronald Moore, Pittsburg St...............Sr		11	27	4	0	166	15.1
Roger Graham, New Haven..............So		10	22	0	0	132	13.2
Chad Guthrie, NE Missouri St...........Sr		11	22	2	0	134	12.2
Larry Jackson, Edinboro..................So		10	19	0	0	114	11.4
Greg Marshall, Colorado Mines........Sr		10	18	6	0	114	11.4
A.J. Livingston, New Haven ....Jr		10	19	0	0	114	11.4

FIELD GOALS

	Class	GP	FGA	FG	Pct	FG/Game
Mike Estrella, St Mary's (Calif)..........Jr		9	27	15	55.6	1.67
Billy Watkins, E Texas St ....Jr		11	26	15	57.7	1.36
Roy Miller, Fort Hays St ....Sr		11	21	15	71.4	1.36
Ed Detwiler, East Stroudsburg ....Sr		10	25	13	52.0	1.30
Jason Monday, Lenoir-Rhyne ....Sr		10	15	13	86.7	1.30

TOTAL OFFENSE

	Class	GP	Yds	Yds/Game
John Charles, Portland St................Sr		8	2708	338.5
Thad Trujillo, Fort Lewis ....So		10	3047	304.7
John Craven, Gardner-Webb...........So		11	3216	292.4
Vernon Buck, Wingate.....................So		10	2838	283.8
Dave McDonald, West Chester........So		10	2771	277.1
Steve Smith, Western St ....Sr		10	2771	277.1

RUSHING

	Class	GP	Car	Yds	TD	Yds/Game
Roger Graham, New Haven ....So		10	200	1717	22	171.7
Ronald Moore, Pittsburg St....................Sr		11	239	1864	26	169.5
Karl Evans, Missouri Southern St...........Sr		10	327	1586	14	158.6
Thelbert Withers, N. Mexico Highlands..Jr		11	240	1621	15	147.4
Scott Schulte, Hillsdale..........................Jr		11	271	1582	16	143.8

PASSING EFFICIENCY

	Class	GP	Att	Comp	Yds	Pct Comp	TD	Int	Rating Pts
Steve Smith, Western St............................Sr		10	271	180	2719	66.4	30	5	183.5
John Charles, Portland St ....Sr		8	263	179	2770	68.0	24	7	181.3
Ken Suhl, New Haven ....Sr		10	239	148	2336	61.9	26	5	175.7
Kurt Coduti, Michigan Tech ....Sr		9	155	92	.1518	59.3	15	3	169.7
Rovell McMillien, Winston-Salem ....Jr		11	165	83	1532	50.3	14	5	150.2

RECEPTIONS PER GAME

	Class	GP	No.	Yds	TD	C/Game
Randy Bartosh, Southwest Baptist ....Sr		8	65	860	2	8.1
Rodney Robinson, Gardner-Webb ....Sr		11	89	1496	16	8.1
Troy Walker, California State Chico........Jr		10	79	874	5	7.9
Matt Carman, Livingston........................Jr		9	66	759	3	7.3
Damon Thomas, Wayne St (Neb)...........Jr		10	71	821	3	7.1
Calvin Walker, Valdosta St.....................Jr		10	71	867	8	7.1

Division II (Cont.)

RECEIVING YARDS PER GAME

	Class	GP	No.	Yds	TD	Yds/Game
Rodney Robinson, Gardner-Webb	Sr	11	89	1496	16	136.0
Johnny Cox, Fort Lewis	Jr	10	65	1331	12	133.1
Charles Guy, Sonoma St	Sr	10	64	1260	12	126.0
Randy Bartosh, Southwest Baptist	Sr	8	65	860	2	107.5
Steve Weaver, West Chester	Sr	10	53	1037	11	103.7

INTERCEPTIONS

	Class	GP	No.	Yds	Int/Game
Pat Williams, East Texas St	Jr	11	13	145	1.2
Joseph Best, Fort Valley St	Jr	11	12	129	1.1
Tom McKenney, W Liberty St	So	10	10	59	1.0
Jason Johnson, Shepherd	So	10	9	66	.9

Seven tied with .8 int/game

PUNTING

	Class	No.	Avg
Jimmy Morris, Angelo St	So	45	44.5
Eric Fadness, Fort Lewis	Sr	43	43.9
Chris Carter, Henderson St	Jr	57	43.6
Alex Campbell, Morris Brown	Fr	54	42.6
Jon Waugh, Sonoma St	Jr	46	42.5

Note: Minimum 3.6 per game.

Division III

SCORING

	Class	GP	TD	XP	FG	Pts	Pts/Game
Chris Babirad, Wash. & Jeff.	Sr	9	24	0	0	144	16.0
Trent Nauholz, Simpson	Jr	8	21	2	0	128	16.0
Greg Novarro, Bentley	Sr	10	25	0	0	150	15.0
Carey Bender, Coe	Jr	9	21	4	0	130	14.4
Stanley Drayton, Allegheny	Sr	9	20	0	0	120	13.3

FIELD GOALS

	Class	GP	FGA	FG	Pct	FG/Game
Todd Holthaus, Rose-Hulman	Jr	10	19	13	68.4	1.30
T.J. Robles, Catholic	So	10	26	12	46.2	1.20
Scott Rubinetti, Montclair St	Fr	9	14	10	71.4	1.11
Tim Dreslinski, Mount Union	So	10	17	11	64.7	1.10
Garret Skipper, Redlands	So	9	14	9	64.3	1.00
Joop De Groot, Blackburn	Sr	9	12	9	75.0	1.00
Chris DiMaggio, Alfred	Sr	10	15	10	66.7	1.00

TOTAL OFFENSE

	Class	GP	Yds	Yds/Game
Jordan Poznick, Principia	Jr	8	2747	343.4
Steve Austin, Mass-Boston	Sr	9	3003	333.7
Scott Isphording, Hanover	Jr	10	3150	315.0
Chip Chevalier, Swarthmore	Sr	9	2564	284.9
Leroy Williams, Upsala	So	10	2822	282.2

RUSHING

	Class	GP	Car	Yds	TD	Yds/Game
Kirk Matthieu, Maine Maritime	Jr	9	327	1733	16	192.6
Chris Babirad, Wash. & Jeff.	Sr	9	243	1589	22	176.6
Wes Stearns, Merchant Marine	Sr	9	247	1477	12	164.1
Trent Nauholz, Simpson	Jr	8	254	1302	21	162.8
Rob Johnson, W Maryland	Jr	10	330	1560	18	156.0

PASSING EFFICIENCY

	Class	GP	Att	Comp	Yds	Pct Comp	TD	Int	Rating Pts
Steve Keller, Dayton	Sr	10	153	99	1350	64.7	17	5	168.9
Jim Ballard, Mount Union	Jr	10	292	186	2656	63.7	29	8	167.4
Tom Miles, Grove City	Jr	9	192	113	1767	58.8	15	9	152.5
Jason Gonnion, Wisconsin-La Crosse	Jr	9	219	127	1904	57.9	17	5	152.0
John Koz, Baldwin-Wallace	Jr	10	293	182	2382	62.1	22	6	151.1

Note: Minimum 15 attempts per game

Division III (Cont.)

RECEPTIONS PER GAME

	Class	GP	No.	Yds	TD	C/Game
Matt Newton, Principia	Jr	8	98	1487	14	12.3
Sean Monroe, Mass-Boston	Sr	9	95	1693	17	10.6
Matt Hess, Ripon	Jr	9	71	1208	16	7.9
Brian Vendergrift, Rhodes	Jr	10	78	881	4	7.8
Rod Tranum, MIT	Sr	8	61	745	5	7.6

RECEIVING YARDS PER GAME

	Class	GP	No.	Yds	TD	Yds/Game
Sean Monroe, Mass-Boston	Sr	9	95	1693	17	188.1
Matt Newton, Principia	Jr	8	98	1487	14	185.9
Matt Hess, Ripon	Jr	9	71	1208	16	134.2
Eric Green, Illinois Benedictine	Sr	10	74	1189	12	118.9
Josh Drake, Swarthmore	Jr	9	67	1042	9	115.8

INTERCEPTIONS

	Class	GP	No.	Yds	Int/Game
Chris Butts, Worcester St	Jr	9	12	109	1.3
Randy Simpson, Wis-Stev Pt	So	8	8	127	1.0
Andrew Ostrand, Carroll (Wis)	Sr	9	9	91	1.0
Curtis Turner, Hamp-Sydney	So	10	9	109	.9
Brent Sands, Cornell College	Sr	10	9	163	.9
Greg Thoma, St John's (Minn)	Jr	10	9	149	.9

PUNTING

	Class	No.	Avg
Robert Ray, San Diego	So	44	42.3
Joel Blackerby, Ferrum	Sr	45	41.0
Bob Ehret, Washington & Lee	Sr	54	40.7
Andy Mahle, Otterbein	So	59	40.1
Ryan Haley, John Carroll	Jr	51	40.1

Note: Minimum 3.6 per game

1992 NCAA Division I-A Team Leaders

Offense

SCORING

	GP	Pts	Avg
Fresno St	12	486	40.5
Nebraska	11	427	38.8
Florida St	11	419	38.1
Notre Dame	11	409	37.2
Michigan	11	393	35.7
Penn State	11	388	35.3
Houston	11	378	34.4
Hawaii	12	394	32.8
Miami (Fla)	11	356	32.4
Georgia	11	352	32.0

RUSHING

	GP	Car	Yds	Avg	TD	Yds/Game
Nebraska	11	618	3610	5.8	40	328.2
Hawaii	12	630	3519	5.6	32	293.3
Notre Dame	11	555	3090	5.6	34	280.9
Army	11	667	2934	4.4	23	266.7
Michigan	11	531	2909	5.5	28	264.5
Clemson	11	580	2828	4.9	21	257.1
Air Force	11	610	2665	4.4	26	242.3
Baylor	11	570	2641	4.6	24	240.1
Colorado State	12	571	2881	5.0	25	240.1
Virginia	11	513	2589	5.0	19	235.4

TOTAL OFFENSE

	GP	Plays	Yds	Avg	TD*	Yds/Game
Houston	11	842	5714	6.8	48	519.45
Fresno St	12	881	5791	6.6	61	482.58
Notre Dame	11	808	5174	6.4	52	470.36
Maryland	11	945	5131	5.4	37	466.45
Michigan	11	806	5120	6.4	51	465.45
Florida State	11	851	5080	6.0	49	461.82
Brigham Young	12	879	5517	6.3	44	459.75
Pittsburgh	12	919	5429	5.9	35	452.42
Georgia	11	732	4954	6.8	41	450.36
Boston College	11	817	4822	5.9	41	438.36

*Defensive and special teams TDs not included.

PASSING

	P	Att	Comp	Yds	Pct Comp	Yds/Att	TD	Int	Yds/Game
Houston	11	619	368	4478	59.5	7.2	36	24	407.1
Maryland	11	514	304	3628	59.1	7.1	18	23	329.8
Miami (Fla)	11	457	259	3476	56.7	7.6	23	7	316.0
Nevada	11	497	268	3328	53.9	6.7	23	27	302.5
Brigham Young	12	405	222	3575	54.8	8.8	27	19	297.9
Colorado	11	398	232	3271	58.3	8.2	22	20	297.4
Missouri	11	442	258	3223	58.4	7.3	13	12	293.0
Pittsburgh	12	455	266	3483	58.5	7.7	23	20	290.3
Florida	12	503	290	3440	57.7	6.8	25	18	286.7
East Carolina	11	497	272	3085	54.7	6.2	27	27	280.5

Single-Game Highs

Points scored: 70—Florida St, Nov 14 (vs Tulane).
Net rushing yards: 490—Nebraska, Sep 12 (vs Middle Tenn St).
Passing yards: 654—Houston, Nov 28 (vs Rice).
Total yards: 787—Nebraska, Sep 7 (vs Utah St).
Fewest total yards allowed: 13—Arizona St, Sep 19 (vs Louisville).
Passes attempted: 77—East Carolina, Sep 5 (vs Syracuse).
Passes completed: 49—Houston, Nov 28 (vs Rice).

Defense

SCORING

	GP	Pts	Avg
Arizona	11	98	8.9
Alabama	12	109	9.1
Miami (Fla)	11	127	11.5
Ohio State	11	137	12.5
Michigan	11	140	12.7
Georgia	11	141	12.8
Washington	11	148	13.5
Toledo	11	153	13.9
Texas A&M	12	168	14.0
Louisiana Tech	11	167	15.2

TOTAL DEFENSE

	GP	Plays	Yds	Avg	Yds/Game
Alabama	12	725	2330	3.2	194.2
Arizona	11	747	2783	3.7	253.0
Memphis State	11	766	2788	3.6	253.5
Louisiana Tech	11	698	2822	4.0	256.5
Auburn	11	699	2837	4.1	257.9
Mississippi	11	775	2909	3.8	264.5
Arizona State	11	734	2957	4.0	268.8
Miami (Fla)	11	764	2979	3.9	270.8
Colorado	11	731	3058	4.2	278.0
Stanford	12	821	3369	4.1	280.8

RUSHING

	GP	Car	Yds	Avg	TD	Yds/Game
Alabama	12	395	660	1.7	5	55.0
Arizona	11	384	716	1.9	4	65.1
Mississippi	11	413	895	2.2	10	81.4
Michigan	11	369	985	2.7	6	89.5
Syracuse	11	339	1007	3.0	10	91.5
Florida State	11	400	1103	2.8	3	100.3
Memphis State	11	447	1107	2.5	9	100.6
Miami (Fla)	11	406	1118	2.8	4	101.6
Notre Dame	11	399	1222	3.1	9	111.1
Toledo	11	466	1248	2.7	8	113.5

TURNOVER MARGIN

		Turnovers Gained			Turnovers Lost			Margin/
	GP	Fum	Int	Total	Fum	Int	Total	Game
Nebraska	11	14	16	30	5	7	12	1.64
Akron	11	10	24	34	7	11	18	1.45
Miami (Fla)	11	11	18	29	6	7	13	1.45
Alabama	12	15	22	37	10	10	20	1.42
Tennessee	11	14	11	25	7	4	11	1.27
S Mississippi	11	11	19	30	6	10	16	1.27
Rice	11	12	18	30	8	8	16	1.27
Wake Forest	11	15	13	28	7	9	16	1.09
Stanford	12	16	18	34	12	9	21	1.08
Arizona	11	10	16	26	8	7	15	1.00

PASSING EFFICIENCY

	GP	Att	Comp	Yds	Pct Comp	Yds/Att	TD	Pct TD	Int	Pct Int	Rating Pts
Western Michigan	11	283	121	1522	42.76	5.38	5	1.77	15	5.30	83.16
Alabama	12	330	164	1670	49.70	5.06	6	1.82	22	6.67	84.87
Colorado	11	257	105	1461	40.86	5.68	8	3.11	18	7.00	84.87
Stanford	12	354	161	1869	45.48	5.28	10	2.82	18	5.08	88.98
Miami (Fla)	11	358	173	1861	48.32	5.20	10	2.79	16	5.93	91.15
Auburn	11	270	117	1565	43.33	5.80	10	3.70	17	4.70	92.39
Mississippi	11	362	169	2014	46.69	5.56	10	2.76	19	6.40	93.14
Southern Mississippi	11	297	143	1692	48.15	5.70	9	3.03	13	4.00	93.21
Toledo	11	325	148	1880	45.54	5.78	7	2.15	12	3.97	93.24
Georgia	11	302	151	1699	50.00	5.63	5	1.66	13	4.08	94.77

FOR THE RECORD·Year to Year

National Champions

Year	Champion	Record	Bowl Game	Head Coach
1883	Yale	8-0-0	No bowl	Ray Tompkins (Captain)
1884	Yale	9-0-0	No bowl	Eugene L. Richards (Captain)
1885	Princeton	9-0-0	No bowl	Charles DeCamp (Captain)
1886	Yale	9-0-1	No bowl	Robert N. Corwin (Captain)
1887	Yale	9-0-0	No bowl	Harry W. Beecher (Captain)
1888	Yale	13-0-0	No bowl	Walter Camp
1889	Princeton	10-0-0	No bowl	Edgar Poe (Captain)
1890	Harvard	11-0-0	No bowl	George A. Stewart
				George C. Adams
1891	Yale	13-0-0	No bowl	Walter Camp
1892	Yale	13-0-0	No bowl	Walter Camp
1893	Princeton	11-0-0	No bowl	Tom Trenchard (Captain)
1894	Yale	16-0-0	No bowl	William C. Rhodes
1895	Pennsylvania	14-0-0	No bowl	George Woodruff
1896	Princeton	10-0-1	No bowl	Garrett Cochran
1897	Pennsylvania	15-0-0	No bowl	George Woodruff
1898	Harvard	11-0-0	No bowl	W. Cameron Forbes
1899	Harvard	10-0-1	No bowl	Benjamin H. Dibblee
1900	Yale	12-0-0	No bowl	Malcolm McBride
1901	Michigan	11-0-0	Won Rose	Fielding Yost
1902	Michigan	11-0-0	No bowl	Fielding Yost
1903	Princeton	11-0-0	No bowl	Art Hillebrand
1904	Pennsylvania	12-0-0	No bowl	Carl Williams
1905	Chicago	11-0-0	No bowl	Amos Alonzo Stagg
1906	Princeton	9-0-1	No bowl	Bill Roper
1907	Yale	9-0-1	No bowl	Bill Knox
1908	Pennsylvania	11-0-1	No bowl	Sol Metzger
1909	Yale	10-0-0	No bowl	Howard Jones
1910	Harvard	8-0-1	No bowl	Percy Houghton
1911	Princeton	8-0-2	No bowl	Bill Roper
1912	Harvard	9-0-0	No bowl	Percy Houghton
1913	Harvard	9-0-0	No bowl	Percy Houghton
1914	Army	9-0-0	No bowl	Charley Daly
1915	Cornell	9-0-0	No bowl	Al Sharpe
1916	Pittsburgh	8-0-0	No bowl	Pop Warner
1917	Georgia Tech	9-0-0	No bowl	John Heisman
1918	Pittsburgh	4-1-0	No bowl	Pop Warner
1919	Harvard	9-0-1	Won Rose	Bob Fisher
1920	California	9-0-0	Won Rose	Andy Smith
1921	Cornell	8-0-0	No bowl	Gil Dobie
1922	Cornell	8-0-0	No bowl	Gil Dobie
1923	Illinois	8-0-0	No bowl	Bob Zuppke
1924	Notre Dame	10-0-0	Won Rose	Knute Rockne
1925	Alabama (H)	10-0-0	Won Rose	Wallace Wade
	Dartmouth (D)	8-0-0	No bowl	Jesse Hawley
1926	Alabama (H)	9-0-1	Tied Rose	Wallace Wade
	Stanford (D)(H)	10-0-1	Tied Rose	Pop Warner
1927	Illinois	7-0-1	No bowl	Bob Zuppke
1928	Georgia Tech (H)	10-0-0	Won Rose	Bill Alexander
	Southern Cal (D)	9-0-1	No bowl	Howard Jones
1929	Notre Dame	9-0-0	No bowl	Knute Rockne
1930	Notre Dame	10-0-0	No bowl	Knute Rockne
1931	Southern Cal	10-1-0	Won Rose	Howard Jones
1932	Southern Cal (H)	10-0-0	Won Rose	Howard Jones
	Michigan (D)	8-0-0	No bowl	Harry Kipke
1933	Michigan	7-0-1	No bowl	Harry Kipke
1934	Minnesota	8-0-0	No bowl	Bernie Bierman
1935	Minnesota (H)	8-0-0	No bowl	Bernie Bierman
	Southern Meth (D)	12-1-0	Lost Rose	Matty Bell
1936	Minnesota	7-1-0	No bowl	Bernie Bierman
1937	Pittsburgh	9-0-1	No bowl	Jock Sutherland
1938	Texas Christian (AP)	11-0-0	Won Sugar	Dutch Meyer
	Notre Dame (D)	8-1-0	No bowl	Elmer Layden

Year	Champion	Record	Bowl Game	Head Coach
1939	Southern Cal (D)	8-0-2	Won Rose	Howard Jones
	Texas A&M (AP)	11-0-0	Won Sugar	Homer Norton
1940	Minnesota	8-0-0	No bowl	Bernie Bierman
1941	Minnesota	8-0-0	No bowl	Bernie Bierman
1942	Ohio St	9-1-0	No bowl	Paul Brown
1943	Notre Dame	9-1-0	No bowl	Frank Leahy
1944	Army	9-0-0	No bowl	Red Blaik
1945	Army	9-0-0	No bowl	Red Blaik
1946	Notre Dame	8-0-1	No bowl	Frank Leahy
1947	Notre Dame	9-0-0	No bowl	Frank Leahy
	Michigan*	10-0-0	Won Rose	Fritz Crisler
1948	Michigan	9-0-0	No bowl	Bennie Oosterbaan
1949	Notre Dame	10-0-0	No bowl	Frank Leahy
1950	Oklahoma	10-1-0	Lost Sugar	Bud Wilkinson
1951	Tennessee	10-1-0	Lost Sugar	Bob Neyland
1952	Michigan St	9-0-0	No bowl	Biggie Munn
1953	Maryland	10-1-0	Lost Orange	Jim Tatum
1954	Ohio St	10-0-0	Won Rose	Woody Hayes
	UCLA (UP)	9-0-0	No bowl	Red Sanders
1955	Oklahoma	11-0-0	Won Orange	Bud Wilkinson
1956	Oklahoma	10-0-0	No bowl	Bud Wilkinson
1957	Auburn	10-0-0	No bowl	Shug Jordan
	Ohio St (UP)	9-1-0	Won Rose	Woody Hayes
1958	Louisiana St	11-0-0	Won Sugar	Paul Dietzel
1959	Syracuse	11-0-0	Won Cotton	Ben Schwartzwalder
1960	Minnesota	8-2-0	Lost Rose	Murray Warmath
1961	Alabama	11-0-0	Won Sugar	Bear Bryant
1962	Southern Cal	11-0-0	Won Rose	John McKay
1963	Texas	11-0-0	Won Cotton	Darrell Royal
1964	Alabama	10-1-0	Lost Orange	Bear Bryant
1965	Alabama	9-1-1	Won Orange	Bear Bryant
	Michigan St (UPI)	10-1-0	Lost Rose	Duffy Daugherty
1966	Notre Dame	9-0-1	No bowl	Ara Parseghian
1967	Southern Cal	10-1-0	Won Rose	John McKay
1968	Ohio St	10-0-0	Won Rose	Woody Hayes
1969	Texas	11-0-0	Won Cotton	Darrell Royal
1970	Nebraska	11-0-1	Won Orange	Bob Devaney
	Texas (UPI)	10-1-0	Lost Cotton	Darrell Royal
1971	Nebraska	13-0-0	Won Orange	Bob Devaney
1972	Southern Cal	12-0-0	Won Rose	John McKay
1973	Notre Dame	11-0-0	Won Sugar	Ara Parseghian
	Alabama (UPI)	11-1-0	Lost Sugar	Bear Bryant
1974	Oklahoma	11-0-0	No bowl	Barry Switzer
	Southern Cal (UPI)	10-1-1	Won Rose	John McKay
1975	Oklahoma	11-1-0	Won Orange	Barry Switzer
1976	Pittsburgh	12-0-0	Won Sugar	Johnny Majors
1977	Notre Dame	11-1-0	Won Cotton	Dan Devine
1978	Alabama	11-1-0	Won Sugar	Bear Bryant
	Southern Cal (UPI)	12-1-0	Won Rose	John Robinson
1979	Alabama	12-0-0	Won Sugar	Bear Bryant
1980	Georgia	12-0-0	Won Sugar	Vince Dooley
1981	Clemson	12-0-0	Won Orange	Danny Ford
1982	Penn St	11-1-0	Won Sugar	Joe Paterno
1983	Miami (FL)	11-1-0	Won Orange	Howard Schnellenberger
1984	Brigham Young	13-0-0	Won Holiday	LaVell Edwards
1985	Oklahoma	11-1-0	Won Orange	Barry Switzer
1986	Penn St	12-0-0	Won Fiesta	Joe Paterno
1987	Miami (FL)	12-0-0	Won Orange	Jimmy Johnson
1988	Notre Dame	12-0-0	Won Fiesta	Lou Holtz
1989	Miami (FL)	11-1-0	Won Sugar	Dennis Erickson
1990	Colorado	11-1-1	Won Orange	Bill McCartney
	Georgia Tech (UPI)	11-0-1	Won Citrus	Bobby Ross
1991	Miami (FL)	12-0-0	Won Orange	Dennis Erickson
	Washington (CNN)	12-0-0	Won Rose	Don James
1992	Alabama	13-0-0	Won Sugar	Gene Stallings

*The AP, which had voted Notre Dame No. 1, took a second vote, giving the national title to Michigan after its 49-0 win over Southern Cal in the Rose Bowl.

Note: Selectors: Helms Athletic Foundation (H) 1883-1935, The Dickinson System (D) 1924-40, The Associated Press (AP) 1936-90, United Press International (UPI) 1958-90, and USA Today/CNN(CNN) 1991.

Results of Major Bowl Games

Rose Bowl

1-1-2	Michigan 49, Stanford 0
1-1-16	Washington St 14, Brown 0
1-1-17	Oregon 14, Pennsylvania 0
1-1-18	Mare Island 19, Camp Lewis 7
1-1-19	Great Lakes 17, Mare Island 0
1-1-20	Harvard 7, Oregon 6
1-1-21	California 28, Ohio St 0
1-2-22	Washington & Jefferson 0, California 0
1-1-23	Southern Cal 14, Penn St 3
1-1-24	Navy 14, Washington 14
1-1-25	Notre Dame 27, Stanford 10
1-1-26	Alabama 20, Washington 19
1-1-27	Alabama 7, Stanford 7
1-2-28	Stanford 7, Pittsburgh 6
1-1-29	Georgia Tech 8, California 7
1-1-30	Southern Cal 47, Pittsburgh 14
1-1-31	Alabama 24, Washington St 0
1-1-32	Southern Cal 21, Tulane 12
1-2-33	Southern Cal 35, Pittsburgh 0
1-1-34	Columbia 7, Stanford 0
1-1-35	Alabama 29, Stanford 13
1-1-36	Stanford 7, Southern Meth 0
1-1-37	Pittsburgh 21, Washington 0
1-1-38	California 13, Alabama 0
1-2-39	Southern Cal 7, Duke 3
1-1-40	Southern Cal 14, Tennessee 0
1-1-41	Stanford 21, Nebraska 13
1-1-42	Oregon St 20, Duke 16
1-1-43	Georgia 9, UCLA 0
1-1-44	Southern Cal 29, Washington 0
1-1-45	Southern Cal 25, Tennessee 0
1-1-46	Alabama 34, Southern Cal 14
1-1-47	Illinois 45, UCLA 14
1-1-48	Michigan 49, Southern Cal 0
1-1-49	Northwestern 20, California 14
1-2-50	Ohio St 17, California 14
1-1-51	Michigan 14, California 6
1-1-52	Illinois 40, Stanford 7
1-1-53	Southern Cal 7, Wisconsin 0
1-1-54	Michigan St 28, UCLA 20
1-1-55	Ohio St 20, Southern Cal 7
1-2-56	Michigan St 17, UCLA 14
1-1-57	Iowa 35, Oregon St 19
1-1-58	Ohio St 10, Oregon 7
1-1-59	Iowa 38, California 12
1-1-60	Washington 44, Wisconsin 8
1-2-61	Washington 17, Minnesota 7
1-1-62	Minnesota 21, UCLA 3
1-1-63	Southern Cal 42, Wisconsin 37
1-1-64	Illinois 17, Washington 7
1-1-65	Michigan 34, Oregon St 7
1-1-66	UCLA 14, Michigan St 12
1-2-67	Purdue 14, Southern Cal 13
1-1-68	Southern Cal 14, Indiana 3
1-1-69	Ohio St 27, Southern Cal 16
1-1-70	Southern Cal 10, Michigan 3
1-1-71	Stanford 27, Ohio St 17
1-1-72	Stanford 13, Michigan 12
1-1-73	Southern Cal 42, Ohio St 17
1-1-74	Ohio St 42, Southern Cal 21
1-1-75	Southern Cal 18, Ohio St 17
1-1-76	UCLA 23, Ohio St 10
1-1-77	Southern Cal 14, Michigan 6
1-2-78	Washington 27, Michigan 20
1-1-79	Southern Cal 17, Michigan 10
1-1-80	Southern Cal 17, Ohio St 16
1-1-81	Michigan 23, Washington 6
1-1-82	Washington 28, Iowa 0
1-1-83	UCLA 24, Michigan 14
1-2-84	UCLA 45, Illinois 9
1-1-85	Southern Cal 20, Ohio St 17
1-1-86	UCLA 45, Iowa 28
1-1-87	Arizona St 22, Michigan 15
1-1-88	Michigan St 20, Southern Cal 17
1-2-89	Michigan 22, Southern Cal 14
1-1-90	Southern Cal 17, Michigan 10
1-1-91	Washington 46, Iowa 34
1-1-92	Washington 34, Michigan 14
1-1-93	Michigan 38, Washington 31

City: Pasadena.

Stadium: Rose Bowl.

Capacity: 104,091.

Automatic Berths: Pacific-10 champ vs Big 10 champ (since 1947).

Playing Sites: Tournament Park (1902, 1916-22), Rose Bowl (1923-41, since 1943), Duke Stadium, Durham, NC (1942).

Orange Bowl

1-1-35	Bucknell 26, Miami (FL) 0
1-1-36	Catholic 20, Mississippi 19
1-1-37	Duquesne 13, Mississippi St 12
1-1-38	Auburn 6, Michigan St 0
1-2-39	Tennessee 17, Oklahoma 0
1-1-40	Georgia Tech 21, Missouri 7
1-1-41	Mississippi St 14, Georgetown 7
1-1-42	Georgia 40, Texas Christian 26
1-1-43	Alabama 37, Boston College 21
1-1-44	Louisiana St 19, Texas A&M 14
1-1-45	Tulsa 26, Georgia Tech 12
1-1-46	Miami (FL) 13, Holy Cross 6
1-1-47	Rice 8, Tennessee 0
1-1-48	Georgia Tech 20, Kansas 14
1-1-49	Texas 41, Georgia 28
1-2-50	Santa Clara 21, Kentucky 13
1-1-51	Clemson 15, Miami (FL) 14
1-1-52	Georgia Tech 17, Baylor 14
1-1-53	Alabama 61, Syracuse 6
1-1-54	Oklahoma 7, Maryland 0
1-1-55	Duke 34, Nebraska 7
1-2-56	Oklahoma 20, Maryland 6
1-1-57	Colorado 27, Clemson 21
1-1-58	Oklahoma 48, Duke 21
1-1-59	Oklahoma 21, Syracuse 6
1-1-60	Georgia 14, Missouri 0
1-2-61	Missouri 21, Navy 14
1-1-62	Louisiana St 25, Colorado 7
1-1-63	Alabama 17, Oklahoma 0
1-1-64	Nebraska 13, Auburn 7
1-1-65	Texas 21, Alabama 17
1-1-66	Alabama 39, Nebraska 28
1-2-67	Florida 27, Georgia Tech 12
1-1-68	Oklahoma 26, Tennessee 24
1-1-69	Penn St 15, Kansas 14
1-1-70	Penn St 10, Missouri 3
1-1-71	Nebraska 17, Louisiana St 12
1-1-72	Nebraska 38, Alabama 6
1-1-73	Nebraska 40, Notre Dame 6
1-1-74	Penn St 16, Louisiana St 9
1-1-75	Notre Dame 13, Alabama 11
1-1-76	Oklahoma 14, Michigan 6
1-1-77	Ohio St 27, Colorado 10
1-2-78	Arkansas 31, Oklahoma 6

Orange Bowl *(Cont.)*

1-1-79 ....Oklahoma 31, Nebraska 24
1-1-80 ....Oklahoma 24, Florida St 7
1-1-81 ....Oklahoma 18, Florida St 17
1-1-82 ....Clemson 22, Nebraska 15
1-1-83 ....Nebraska 21, Louisiana St 20
1-2-84 ....Miami (FL) 31, Nebraska 30
1-1-85 ....Washington 28, Oklahoma 17
1-1-86 ....Oklahoma 25, Penn St 10
1-1-87 ....Oklahoma 42, Arkansas 8
1-2-89 ....Miami (FL) 23, Nebraska 3
1-1-90 ....Notre Dame 21, Colorado 6
1-1-91 ....Colorado 10, Notre Dame 9
1-1-92 ....Miami 22, Nebraska 0
1-1-93 ....Florida State 27, Nebraska 14

City: Miami.
Stadium: Orange Bowl.
Capacity: 75,500.
Automatic Berths: Big 8 champ (1954-64, since 1976).

Sugar Bowl

1-1-35 ....Tulane 20, Temple 14
1-1-36 ....Texas Christian 3, Louisiana St 2
1-1-37 ....Santa Clara 21, Louisiana St 14
1-1-38 ....Santa Clara 6, Louisiana St 0
1-2-39 ....Texas Christian 15, Carnegie Tech 7
1-1-40 ....Texas A&M 14, Tulane 13
1-1-41 ....Boston Col 19, Tennessee 13
1-1-42 ....Fordham 2, Missouri 0
1-1-43 ....Tennessee 14, Tulsa 7
1-1-44 ....Georgia Tech 20, Tulsa 18
1-1-45 ....Duke 29, Alabama 26
1-1-46 ....Oklahoma St 33, St Mary's (CA) 13
1-1-47 ....Georgia 20, N Carolina 10
1-1-48 ....Texas 27, Alabama 7
1-1-49 ....Oklahoma 14, N Carolina 6
1-2-50 ....Oklahoma 35, Louisiana St 0
1-1-51 ....Kentucky 13, Oklahoma 7
1-1-52 ....Maryland 28, Tennessee 13
1-1-53 ....Georgia Tech 24, Mississippi 7
1-1-54 ....Georgia Tech 42, W Virginia 19
1-1-55 ....Navy 21, Mississippi 0
1-2-56 ....Georgia Tech 7, Pittsburgh 0
1-1-57 ....Baylor 13, Tennessee 7
1-1-58 ....Mississippi 39, Texas 7
1-1-59 ....Louisiana St 7, Clemson 0
1-1-60 ....Mississippi 21, Louisiana St 0
1-2-61 ....Mississippi 14, Rice 6
1-1-62 ....Alabama 10, Arkansas 3
1-1-63 ....Mississippi 17, Arkansas 13
1-1-64 ....Alabama 12, Mississippi 7
1-1-65 ....Louisiana St 13, Syracuse 10
1-1-66 ....Missouri 20, Florida 18
1-2-67 ....Alabama 34, Nebraska 7
1-1-68 ....Louisiana St 20, Wyoming 13
1-1-69 ....Arkansas 16, Georgia 2
1-1-70 ....Mississippi 27, Arkansas 22
1-1-71 ....Tennessee 34, Air Force 13
1-1-72 ....Oklahoma 40, Auburn 22
12-31-72 ....Oklahoma 14, Penn St 0
12-31-73 ....Notre Dame 24, Alabama 23
12-31-74 ....Nebraska 13, Florida 10
12-31-75 ....Alabama 13, Penn St 6
1-1-77 ....Pittsburgh 27, Georgia 3
1-2-78 ....Alabama 35, Ohio St 6

Sugar Bowl *(Cont.)*

1-1-79 ....Alabama 14, Penn St 7
1-1-80 ....Alabama 24, Arkansas 9
1-1-81 ....Georgia 17, Notre Dame 10
1-1-82 ....Pittsburgh 24, Georgia 20
1-1-83 ....Penn St 27, Georgia 23
1-2-84 ....Auburn 9, Michigan 7
1-1-85 ....Nebraska 28, Louisiana St 10
1-1-86 ....Tennessee 35, Miami (FL) 7
1-1-87 ....Nebraska 30, Louisiana St 15
1-1-88 ....Syracuse 16, Aurburn 16
1-2-89 ....Florida St 13, Auburn 7
1-1-90 ....Miami (FL) 33, Alabama 25
1-1-91 ....Tennessee 23, Virginia 22
1-1-92 ....Notre Dame 39, Florida 28
1-1-93 ....Alabama 34, Miami 13

City: New Orleans.
Stadium: Louisiana Superdome.
Capacity: 69,548.
Automatic Berths: Southeastern champ (since 1977).
Playing Sites: Tulane Stadium (1935-74), Superdome (since 1974).

Cotton Bowl

1-1-37 ....Texas Christian 16, Marquette 6
1-1-38 ....Rice 28, Colorado 14
1-2-39 ....St. Mary's (CA) 20, Texas Tech 13
1-1-40 ....Clemson 6, Boston Col 3
1-1-41 ....Texas A&M 13, Fordham 12
1-1-42 ....Alabama 29, Texas A&M 21
1-1-43 ....Texas 14, Georgia Tech 7
1-1-44 ....Texas 7, Randolph Field 7
1-1-45 ....Oklahoma 34, Texas Christian 0
1-1-46 ....Texas 40, Missouri 27
1-1-47 ....Arkansas 0, Louisiana St 0
1-1-48 ....Southern Meth 13, Penn St 13
1-1-49 ....Southern Meth 21, Oregon 13
1-2-50 ....Rice 27, N Carolina 13
1-1-51 ....Tennessee 20, Texas 14
1-1-52 ....Kentucky 20, Texas Christian 7
1-1-53 ....Texas 16, Tennessee 0
1-1-54 ....Rice 28, Alabama 6
1-1-55 ....Georgia Tech 14, Arkansas 6
1-2-56 ....Mississippi 14, Texas Christian 13
1-1-57 ....Texas Christian 28, Syracuse 27
1-1-58 ....Navy 20, Rice 7
1-1-59 ....Texas Christian 0, Air Force 0
1-1-60 ....Syracuse 23, Texas 14
1-2-61 ....Duke 7, Arkansas 6
1-1-62 ....Texas 12, Mississippi 7
1-1-63 ....Louisiana St 13, Texas 0
1-1-64 ....Texas 28, Navy 6
1-1-65 ....Arkansas 10, Nebraska 7
1-1-66 ....Louisiana St 14, Arkansas 7
12-31-66 ....Georgia 24, Southern Meth 9
1-1-68 ....Texas A&M 20, Alabama 16
1-1-69 ....Texas 36, Tennessee 13
1-1-70 ....Texas 21, Notre Dame 17
1-1-71 ....Notre Dame 24, Texas 11
1-1-72 ....Penn St 30, Texas 6
1-1-73 ....Texas 17, Alabama 13
1-1-74 ....Nebraska 19, Texas 3
1-1-75 ....Penn St 41, Baylor 20
1-1-76 ....Arkansas 31, Georgia 10
1-1-77 ....Houston 30, Maryland 21
1-2-78 ....Notre Dame 38, Texas 10

Cotton Bowl *(Cont.)*

1-1-79	Notre Dame 35, Houston 34
1-1-80	Houston 17, Nebraska 14
1-1-81	Alabama 30, Baylor 2
1-1-82	Texas 14, Alabama 12
1-1-83	Southern Meth 7, Pittsburgh 3
1-2-84	Georgia 10, Texas 9
1-1-85	Boston Col 45, Houston 28
1-1-86	Texas A&M 36, Auburn 16
1-1-87	Ohio St 28, Texas A&M 12
1-1-88	Texas A&M 35, Notre Dame 10
1-2-89	UCLA 17, Arkansas 3
1-1-90	Tennessee 31, Arkansas 27
1-1-91	Miami (FL) 46, Texas 3
1-1-92	Florida St 10, Texas A&M 2
1-1-93	Notre Dame 28, Texas A&M 3

City: Dallas.

Stadium: Cotton Bowl.

Capacity: 72,032.

Automatic Berths: Southwest champ (since 1942).

Playing Sites: Fair Park Stadium (1937), Cotton Bowl (since 1938).

John Hancock Bowl

1-1-36	Hardin-Simmons 14, New Mexico St 14
1-1-37	Hardin-Simmons 34, UTEP 6
1-1-38	W Virginia 7, Texas Tech 6
1-2-39	Utah 26, New Mexico 0
1-1-40	Catholic 0, Arizona St 0
1-1-41	Case Reserve 26, Arizona St 13
1-1-42	Tulsa 6, Texas Tech 0
1-1-43	2nd Air Force 13, Hardin-Simmons 7
1-1-44	Southwestern (TX) 7, New Mexico 0
1-1-45	Southwestern (TX) 35, New Mexico 0
1-1-46	New Mexico 34, Denver 24
1-1-47	Cincinnati 18, Virginia Tech 6
1-1-48	Miami (OH) 13, Texas Tech 12
1-1-49	W Virginia 21, UTEP 12
1-2-50	UTEP 33, Georgetown 20
1-1-51	West Texas St 14, Cincinnati 13
1-1-52	Texas Tech 25, Pacific 14
1-1-53	Pacific 26, Southern Miss 7
1-1-54	UTEP 37, Southern Miss 14
1-1-55	UTEP 47, Florida St 20
1-2-56	Wyoming 21, Texas Tech 14
1-1-57	George Washington 13, UTEP 0
1-1-58	Louisville 34, Drake 20
12-31-58	Wyoming 14, Hardin-Simmons 6
12-31-59	New Mexico St 28, N Texas 8
12-31-60	New Mexico St 20, Utah St 13
12-30-61	Villanova 17, Wichita St 9
12-31-62	W Texas St 15, Ohio 14
12-31-63	Oregon 21, Southern Meth 14
12-26-64	Georgia 7, Texas Tech 0
12-31-65	UTEP 13, Texas Christian 12
12-24-66	Wyoming 28, Florida St 20
12-30-67	UTEP 14, Mississippi 7
12-28-68	Auburn 34, Arizona 10
12-20-69	Nebraska 45, Georgia 6
12-19-70	Georgia Tech 17, Texas Tech 9
12-18-71	Louisiana St 33, Iowa St 15
12-30-72	N Carolina 32, Texas Tech 28
12-29-73	Missouri 34, Auburn 17
12-28-74	Mississippi St 26, N Carolina 24
12-26-75	Pittsburgh 33, Kansas 19
1-2-77	Texas A&M 37, Florida 14

John Hancock Bowl *(Cont.)*

12-31-77	Stanford 24, Louisiana St 14
12-23-78	Texas 42, Maryland 0
12-22-79	Washington 14, Texas 7
12-27-80	Nebraska 31, Mississippi St 17
12-26-81	Oklahoma 40, Houston 14
12-25-82	N Carolina 26, Texas 10
12-24-83	Alabama 28, Southern Meth 7
12-22-84	Maryland 28, Tennessee 27
12-28-85	Georgia 13, Arizona 13
12-25-86	Alabama 28, Washington 6
12-25-87	Oklahoma St 35, W Virginia 33
12-24-88	Alabama 29, Army 28
12-30-89	Pittsburgh 31, Texas A&M 28
12-31-90	Michigan St 17, Southern Cal 16
12-31-91	UCLA 6, Illinois 3
12-31-92	Baylor 20, Arizona 15

City: El Paso.

Stadium: Sun Bowl.

Capacity: 52,000.

Automatic Berths: None.

Name Changes: Sun Bowl (1936-86), John Hancock Sun Bowl (1987-88), John Hancock Bowl (since 1989).

Playing Sites: Kidd Field (1936-62), Sun Bowl (since 1963).

Gator Bowl

1-1-46	Wake Forest 26, S Carolina 14
1-1-47	Oklahoma 34, N Carolina St 13
1-1-48	Maryland 20, Georgia 20
1-1-49	Clemson 24, Missouri 23
1-2-50	Maryland 20, Missouri 7
1-1-51	Wyoming 20, Washington & Lee 7
1-1-52	Miami (FL) 14, Clemson 0
1-1-53	Florida 14, Tulsa 13
1-1-54	Texas Tech 35, Auburn 13
12-31-54	Auburn 33, Baylor 13
12-31-55	Vanderbilt 25, Auburn 13
12-29-56	Georgia Tech 21, Pittsburgh 14
12-28-57	Tennessee 3, Texas A&M 0
12-27-58	Mississippi 7, Florida 3
1-2-60	Arkansas 14, Georgia Tech 7
12-31-60	Florida 13, Baylor 12
12-30-61	Penn St 30, Georgia Tech 15
12-29-62	Florida 17, Penn St 7
12-28-63	N Carolina 35, Air Force 0
1-2-65	Florida St 36, Oklahoma 19
12-31-65	Georgia Tech 31, Texas Tech 21
12-31-66	Tennessee 18, Syracuse 12
12-30-67	Penn St 17, Florida St 17
12-28-68	Missouri 35, Alabama 10
12-27-69	Florida 14, Tennessee 13
1-2-71	Auburn 35, Mississippi 28
12-31-71	Georgia 7, N Carolina 3
12-30-72	Auburn 24, Colorado 3
12-29-73	Texas Tech 28, Tennessee 19
12-30-74	Auburn 27, Texas 3
12-29-75	Maryland 13, Florida 0
12-27-76	Notre Dame 20, Penn St 9
12-30-77	Pittsburgh 34, Clemson 3
12-29-78	Clemson 17, Ohio St 15
12-28-79	N Carolina 17, Michigan 15
12-29-80	Pittsburgh 37, S Carolina 9
12-28-81	N Carolina 31, Arkansas 27
12-30-82	Florida St 31, W Virginia 12
12-30-83	Florida 14, Iowa 6
12-28-84	Oklahoma St 21, S Carolina 14
12-30-85	Florida St 34, Oklahoma St 23

Gator Bowl *(Cont.)*

12-27-86.........Clemson 27, Stanford 21
12-31-87.........Louisiana St 30, S Carolina 13
1-1-89.........Georgia 34, Michigan St 27
12-30-89.........Clemson 27, W Virginia 7
1-1-91.........Michigan 35, Mississippi 3
12-29-91.........Oklahoma 48, Virginia 14
12-31-92.........Florida 27, NC State 10

City: Jacksonville, FL.

Stadium: Gator Bowl.

Capacity: 82,000. Automatic Berths: None.

Florida Citrus Bowl

1-1-47.............Catawba 31, Maryville (TN) 6
1-1-48.............Catawba 7, Marshall 0
1-1-49.............Murray St 21, Sul Ross St 21
1-2-50.............St Vincent 7, Emory & Henry 6
1-1-51.............Morris Harvey 35, Emory & Henry 14
1-1-52.............Stetson 35, Arkansas St 20
1-1-53.............E Texas St 33, Tennessee Tech 0
1-1-54.............E Texas St 7, Arkansas St 7
1-1-55.............NE-Omaha 7, Eastern Kentucky 6
1-2-56.............Juniata 6, Missouri Valley 6
1-1-57.............W Texas St 20, Southern Miss 13
1-1-58.............E Texas St 10, Southern Miss 9
12-27-58.........E Texas St 26, Missouri Valley 7
1-1-60.............Middle Tennessee St 21, Presbyterian 12
12-30-60.........Citadel 27, Tennessee Tech 0
12-29-61.........Lamar 21, Middle Tennessee St 14
12-22-62.........Houston 49, Miami (OH) 21
12-28-63.........Western Kentucky 27, Coast Guard 0
12-12-64.........E Carolina 14, Massachusetts 13
12-11-65.........E Carolina 31, Maine 0
12-10-66.........Morgan St 14, West Chester 6
12-16-67.........TN-Martin 25, West Chester 8
12-27-68.........Richmond 49, Ohio 42
12-26-69.........Toledo 56, Davidson 33
12-28-70.........Toledo 40, William & Mary 12
12-28-71.........Toledo 28, Richmond 3
12-29-72.........Tampa 21, Kent St 18
12-22-73.........Miami (OH) 16, Florida 7
12-21-74.........Miami (OH) 21, Georgia 10
12-20-75.........Miami (OH) 20, S Carolina 7
12-18-76.........Oklahoma St 49, Brigham Young 21
12-23-77.........Florida St 40, Texas Tech 17
12-23-78.........N Carolina St 30, Pittsburgh 17
12-22-79.........Louisiana St 34, Wake Forest 10
12-20-80.........Florida 35, Maryland 20
12-19-81.........Missouri 19, Southern Miss 17
12-18-82.........Auburn 33, Boston Col 26
12-17-83.........Tennessee 30, Maryland 23
12-22-84.........Georgia 17, Florida St 17

Florida Citrus Bowl *(Cont.)*

12-28-85.........Ohio St 10, Brigham Young 7
1-1-87.............Auburn 16, Southern Cal 7
1-1-88.............Clemson 35, Penn St 10
1-2-89.............Clemson 13, Oklahoma 6
1-1-90.............Illinois 31, Virginia 21
1-1-91.............Georgia Tech 45, Nebraska 21
1-1-92.............California 37, Clemson 13
1-1-93.............Georgia 21, Ohio State 14

City: Orlando, FL.

Stadium: Florida Citrus Bowl-Orlando.

Capacity: 52,300. Automatic Berths: None.

Name Change: Tangerine Bowl (1947-82), Florida Citrus Bowl (since 1983).

Playing Sites: Tangerine Bowl (1947-72, 1974-82); Florida Field, Gainesville (1973); Orlando Stadium (1983-85); Florida Citrus Bowl- Orlando (since 1986). Tangerine Bowl, Orlando Stadium and Florida Citrus Bowl-Orlando are identical site.

Liberty Bowl

12-19-59.........Penn St 7, Alabama 0
12-17-60.........Penn St 41, Oregon 12
12-16-61.........Syracuse 15, Miami (FL) 14
12-15-62.........Oregon St 6, Villanova 0
12-21-63.........Mississippi St 16, N Carolina St
12-19-64.........Utah 32, W Virginia 6
12-18-65.........Mississippi 13, Auburn 7
12-10-66.........Miami (FL) 14, Virginia Tech 7
12-16-67.........N Carolina St 14, Georgia 7
12-14-68.........Mississippi 34, Virginia Tech 17
12-13-69.........Colorado 47, Alabama 33
12-12-70.........Tulane 17, Colorado 3
12-20-71.........Tennessee 14, Arkansas 13
12-18-72.........Georgia Tech 31, Iowa St 30
12-17-73.........N Carolina St 31, Kansas 18
12-16-74.........Tennessee 7, Maryland 3
12-22-75.........Southern Cal 20, Texas A&M 0
12-20-76.........Alabama 36, UCLA 6
12-19-77.........Nebraska 21, N Carolina 17
12-23-78.........Missouri 20, Louisiana St 15
12-22-79.........Penn St 9, Tulane 6
12-27-80.........Purdue 28, Missouri 25
12-30-81.........Ohio St 31, Navy 28
12-29-82.........Alabama 21, Illinois 15
12-29-83.........Notre Dame 19, Boston Col 18
12-27-84.........Auburn 21, Arkansas 15
12-27-85.........Baylor 21, Louisiana St 7
12-29-86.........Tennessee 21, Minnesota 14
12-29-87.........Georgia 20, Arkansas 17
12-28-88.........Indiana 34, S Carolina 10
12-28-89.........Mississippi 42, Air Force 29
12-27-90.........Air Force 23, Ohio St 11
12-29-91.........Air Force 38, Mississippi St 15
12-31-92.........Mississippi 13, Air Force 0

City: Memphis.

Stadium: Liberty Bowl Memorial Stadium.

Capacity: 63,000.

Automatic Berths: Since 1989, winner of Commander-in-Chief's Trophy (Air Force, Army, Navy).

Playing Sites: Philadelphia (Municipal Stadium, 1959-63), Atlantic City (Convention Center, 1964), Memphis (since 1965).

THEY SAID IT

John Routh, Miami mascot, after a stray bullet grazed his head during a Bourbon Street stroll the day before the Sugar Bowl: "It's going to take a heck of a lot more than a bullet in the head to keep me out of this game."

Peach Bowl

12-30-68.........Louisiana St 31, Florida St 27
12-30-69.........W Virginia 14, S Carolina 3
12-30-70.........Arizona St 48, N Carolina 26
12-30-71.........Mississippi 41, Georgia Tech 18
12-29-72.........N Carolina St 49, W Virginia 13
12-28-73.........Georgia 17, Maryland 16
12-28-74.........Vanderbilt 6, Texas Tech 6
12-31-75.........W Virginia 13, N Carolina St 10
12-31-76.........Kentucky 21, N Carolina 0
12-31-77.........N Carolina St 24, Iowa St 14
12-25-78.........Purdue 41, Georgia Tech 21
12-31-79.........Baylor 24, Clemson 18
1-2-81.............Miami (FL) 20, Virginia Tech 10
12-31-81.........W Virginia 26, Florida 6
12-31-82.........Iowa 28, Tennessee 22
12-30-83.........Florida St 28, N Carolina 3
12-31-84.........Virginia 27, Purdue 24
12-31-85.........Army 31, Illinois 29
12-31-86.........Virginia Tech 25, N Carolina St 24
1-2-88.............Tennessee 27, Indiana 22
12-31-88.........N Carolina St 28, Iowa 23
12-30-89.........Syracuse 19, Georgia 18
12-29-90.........Auburn 27, Indiana 23
1-1-92.............E Carolina 37, N Carolina St 34
1-2-93.............North Carolina 21, Miss. St 17

City: Atlanta.
Stadium: Atlanta Fulton County Stadium.
Capacity: 59,800.
Automatic Berths: None.
Playing Sites: Grant Field (1968-70), Atlanta Stadium (since 1971).

Fiesta Bowl

12-27-71.........Arizona St 45, Florida St 38
12-23-72.........Arizona St 49, Missouri 35
12-21-73.........Arizona St 28, Pittsburgh 7
12-28-74.........Oklahoma St 16, Brigham Young 6
12-26-75.........Arizona St 17, Nebraska 14
12-25-76.........Oklahoma 41, Wyoming 7
12-25-77.........Penn St 42, Arizona St 30
12-25-78.........Arkansas 10, UCLA 10
12-25-79.........Pittsburgh 16, Arizona 10
12-26-80.........Penn St 31, Ohio St 19
1-1-82.............Penn St 26, Southern Cal 10
1-1-83.............Arizona St 32, Oklahoma 21
1-2-84.............Ohio St 28, Pittsburgh 23
1-1-85.............UCLA 39, Miami (FL) 37
1-1-86.............Michigan 27, Nebraska 23
1-2-87.............Penn St 14, Miami (FL) 10
1-1-88.............Florida St 31, Nebraska 28
1-2-89.............Notre Dame 34, W Virginia 21
1-1-90.............Florida St 41, Nebraska 17
1-1-91.............Louisville 34, Alabama 7
1-1-92.............Penn St 42, Tennessee 17
1-1-93.............Syracuse 26, Colorado 22

City: Tempe, AZ.
Stadium: Sun Devil Stadium.
Capacity: 74,000.
Automatic Berths: None.

Independence Bowl

12-13-76.........McNeese St 20, Tulsa 16
12-17-77.........Louisiana Tech 24, Louisville 14

Independence Bowl *(Cont.)*

12-16-78.........E Carolina 35, Louisiana Tech 13
12-15-79.........Syracuse 31, McNeese St 7
12-13-80.........Southern Miss 16, McNeese St 14
12-12-81.........Texas A&M 33, Oklahoma St 16
12-11-82.........Wisconsin 14, Kansas St 3
12-10-83.........Air Force 9, Mississippi 3
12-15-84.........Air Force 23, Virginia Tech 7
12-21-85.........Minnesota 20, Clemson 13
12-20-86.........Mississippi 20, Texas Tech 17
12-19-87.........Washington 24, Tulane 12
12-23-88.........Southern Miss 38, UTEP 18
12-16-89.........Oregon 27, Tulsa 24
12-15-90.........Louisiana Tech 34, Maryland 34
12-29-91.........Georgia 24, Arkansas 15
12-31-92.........Wake Forest 39, Oregon 35

City: Shreveport, LA.
Stadium: Independence Stadium.
Capacity: 50,560.
Automatic Berths: None.

All-American Bowl (Discontinued)

12-22-77.........Maryland 17, Minnesota 7
12-20-78.........Texas A&M 28, Iowa St 12
12-29-79.........Missouri 24, S Carolina 14
12-27-80.........Arkansas 34, Tulane 15
12-31-81.........Mississippi St 10, Kansas 0
12-31-82.........Air Force 36, Vanderbilt 28
12-22-83.........W Virginia 20, Kentucky 16
12-29-84.........Kentucky 20, Wisconsin 19
12-31-85.........Georgia Tech 17, Michigan St 14
12-31-86.........Florida St 27, Indiana 13
12-22-87.........Virginia 22, Brigham Young 16
12-29-88.........Florida 14, Illinois 10
12-28-89.........Texas Tech 49, Duke 21
12-28-90.........N Carolina St 31, Southern Mississippi 27

City: Birmingham, AL.
Stadium: Legion Field.
Capacity: 75,808.
Automatic Berths: None.
Name Change: Hall of Fame Classic (1977-84), All-American Bowl (1985–90).

Holiday Bowl

12-22-78.........Navy 23, Brigham Young 16
12-21-79.........Indiana 38, Brigham Young 37
12-19-80.........Brigham Young 46, Southern Meth 45
12-18-81.........Brigham Young 38, Washington St 36
12-17-82.........Ohio St 47, Brigham Young 17
12-23-83.........Brigham Young 21, Missouri 17
12-21-84.........Brigham Young 24, Michigan 17
12-22-85.........Arkansas 18, Arizona St 17
12-30-86.........Iowa 39, San Diego St 38
12-30-87.........Iowa 20, Wyoming 19
12-30-88.........Oklahoma St 62, Wyoming 14
12-29-89.........Penn St 50, Brigham Young 39
12-29-90.........Texas A&M 65, Brigham Young 14
12-30-91.........Iowa 13, Brigham Young 13
12-30-92.........Hawaii 27, Illinois 17

City: San Diego.
Stadium: Jack Murphy Stadium.
Capacity: 60,750.
Automatic Berths: Western Athletic champ (except 1985).

Las Vegas Bowl

12-19-81.........Toledo 27, San Jose St 25
12-18-82.........Fresno St 29, Bowling Green 28
12-17-83.........Northern Illinois 20, Cal St-Fullerton 13
12-15-84.........NV-Las Vegas 30, Toledo 13*
12-14-85.........Fresno St 51, Bowling Green 7
12-13-86.........San Jose St 37, Miami (OH) 7
12-12-87.........Eastern Michigan 30, San Jose St 27
12-10-88.........Fresno St 35, Western Michigan 30
12-9-89............Fresno St 27, Ball St 6
12-8-90............San Jose St 48, Central Michigan 24
12-14-91.........Bowling Green 28, Fresno St 21
12-18-92.........Bowling Green 35, Nevada 34
* Toledo won later by forfeit.
City: Fresno, CA.
Stadium: Bulldog Stadium.
Capacity: 30,000.
Automatic Berths: Mid-American and Big West champs.
Name change: California Bowl (1981-91)

Aloha Bowl

12-25-82.........Washington 21, Maryland 20
12-26-83.........Penn St 13, Washington 10
12-29-84.........Southern Meth 27, Notre Dame 20
12-28-85.........Alabama 24, Southern Cal 3
12-27-86.........Arizona 30, N Carolina 21
12-25-87.........UCLA 20, Florida 16
12-25-88.........Washington St 24, Houston 22
12-25-89.........Michigan St 33, Hawaii 13
12-25-90.........Syracuse 28, Arizona 0
12-25-91.........Georgia Tech 18, Stanford 17
12-25-92.........Kansas 23, BYU 20
City: Honolulu.
Stadium: Aloha Stadium.
Capacity: 50,000.
Automatic Berths: None.

Freedom Bowl

12-16-84.........Iowa 55, Texas 17
12-30-85.........Washington 20, Colorado 17
12-30-86.........UCLA 31, Brigham Young 10
12-30-87.........Arizona St 33, Air Force 28
12-29-88.........Brigham Young 20, Colorado 17
12-30-89.........Washington 34, Florida 7
12-29-90.........Colorado St 32, Oregon 31
12-30-91.........Tulsa 28, San Diego St 17
12-29-92.........Fresno St 24, Southern Cal 7
City: Anaheim.
Stadium: Anaheim Stadium.
Capacity: 70,500.
Automatic Berths: None.

Hall of Fame Bowl

12-23-86.........Boston Col 27, Georgia 24
1-2-88..............Michigan 28, Alabama 24
1-2-89..............Syracuse 23, Louisiana St 10
1-1-90..............Auburn 31, Ohio St 14
1-1-91..............Clemson 30, Illinois 0
1-1-92..............Syracuse 24, Ohio St 17
1-1-93..............Tennessee 38, Boston College 23
City: Tampa.
Stadium: Tampa Stadium.
Capacity: 74,315.
Automatic Berths: None.

Copper Bowl

12-31-89.........Arizona 17, N Carolina St 10
12-31-90.........California 17, Wyoming 15
12-31-91.........Indiana 24, Baylor 0
12-29-92.........Washington St 31, Utah 28
City: Tucson.
Stadium: Arizona Stadium.
Capacity: 57,000.
Automatic Berths: None.

Blockbuster Bowl

12-28-90.........Florida St 24, Penn St 17
12-28-91.........Alabama 30, Colorado 25
1-1-93..............Stanford 24, Penn St 3
City: Miami.
Stadium: Joe Robbie.
Capacity: 75,000.
Automatic Berths: None.

Bluebonnet Bowl (Discontinued)

12-19-59.........Clemson 23, Texas Christian 7
12-17-60.........Texas 3, Alabama 3
12-16-61.........Kansas 33, Rice 7
12-22-62.........Missouri 14, Georgia Tech 10
12-21-63.........Baylor 14, LSU 7
12-19-64.........Tulsa 14, Mississippi 7
12-18-65.........Tennessee 27, Tulsa 6
12-17-66.........Texas 19, Mississippi 0
12-23-67.........Colorado 31, Miami (FL) 21
12-31-68.........Southern Meth 28, Oklahoma 27
12-31-69.........Houston 36, Auburn 7
12-31-70.........Alabama 24, Oklahoma 24
12-31-71.........Colorado 29, Houston 17
12-30-72.........Tennessee 24, LSU 17
12-29-73.........Houston 47, Tulane 7
12-23-74.........N Carolina St 31, Houston 31
12-27-75.........Texas 38, Colorado 21
12-31-76.........Nebraska 27, Texas Tech 24
12-31-77.........Southern Cal 47, Texas A&M 28
12-31-78.........Stanford 25, Georgia 22
12-31-79.........Purdue 27, Tennessee 22
12-31-80.........N Carolina 16, Texas 7
12-31-81.........Michigan 33, UCLA 14
12-31-82.........Arkansas 28, Florida 24
12-31-83.........Oklahoma St 24, Baylor 14
12-31-84.........W Virginia 31, Texas Christian 14
12-31-85.........Air Force 24, Texas 16
12-31-86.........Baylor 21, Colorado 9
12-31-87.........Texas 32, Pittsburgh 27
City: Houston.
Name change: Astro-Bluebonnet Bowl (1968-76).
Playing sites: Rice Stadium (1959-67, 1985-86),
Astrodome (1968-84, 1987).

NCAA Divisional Championships

Division I-AA

Year	Winner	Runner-Up	Score
1978	Florida A&M	Massachusetts	35-28
1979	Eastern Kentucky	Lehigh	30-7
1980	Boise St	Eastern Kentucky	3l-29
1981	Idaho St	Eastern Kentucky	34-23
1982	Eastern Kentucky	Delaware	17-14
1983	Southern Illinois	Western Carolina	43-7
1984	Montana St	Louisiana Tech	19-6
1985	Georgia Southern	Furman	44-42
1986	Georgia Southern	Arkansas St	48-21
1987	NE Louisiana	Marshall	43-42
1988	Furman	Georgia Southern	17-12
1989	Georgia Southern	SF Austin St	37-34
1990	Georgia Southern	NV-Reno	36-13
1991	Youngstown St	Marshall	25-17
1992	Marshall	Youngstown St	31-28

Division II

Year	Winner	Runner-Up	Score
1973	Louisiana Tech	Western Kentucky	34-0
1974	Central Michigan	Delaware	54-14
1975	Northern Michigan	Western Kentucky	16-14
1976	Montana St	Akron	24-13
1977	Lehigh	Jacksonville St	33-0
1978	Eastern Illinois	Delaware	10-9
1979	Delaware	Youngstown St	38-21
1980	Cal Poly SLO	Eastern Illinois	21-13
1981	SW Texas St	N Dakota St	42-13
1982	SW Texas St	UC-Davis	34-9
1983	N Dakota St	Central St (OH)	41-21
1984	Troy St	N Dakota St	18-17
1985	N Dakota St	N Alabama	35-7
1986	N Dakota St	S Dakota	27-7
1987	Troy St	Portland St	31-17
1988	N Dakota St	Portland St	35-21
1989	Mississippi Col	Jacksonville St	3-0
1990	N Dakota St	Indiana (PA)	51-11
1991	Pittsburg St	Jacksonville St	23-6
1992	Jacksonville St	Pittsburg St	17-13

Division III

Year	Winner	Runner-Up	Score
1973	Wittenberg	Juniata	41-0
1974	Central (IA)	Ithaca	10-8
1975	Wittenberg	Ithaca	28-0
1976	St John's (MN)	Towson St	31-28
1977	Widener	Wabash	39-36
1978	Baldwin-Wallace	Wittenberg	24-10
1979	Ithaca	Wittenberg	14-10
1980	Dayton	Ithaca	63-0
1981	Widener	Dayton	17-10
1982	W Georgia	Augustana (IL)	14-0
1983	Augustana (IL)	Union (NY)	21-17
1984	Augustana (IL)	Central (IA)	21-12
1985	Augustana (IL)	Ithaca	20-7
1986	Augustana (IL)	Salisbury St	31-3
1987	Wagner	Dayton	19-3
1988	Ithaca	Central (IA)	39-24
1989	Dayton	Union (NY)	17-7
1990	Allegheny	Lycoming	21-14 (OT)
1991	Ithaca	Dayton	34-20
1992	Wisconsin-LaCrosse	Washington and Jefferson	16-12

NAIA Divisional Championships

Division I

Year	Winner	Runner-Up	Score
1956	St Joseph's (IN) Montana State		0-0
1957	Kansas St-Pittsburg	Hillsdale (MI)	27-26
1958	Northeastern Oklahoma	Northern Arizona	19-13
1959	Texas A&I	Lenoir-Rhyne (NC)	20-7
1960	Lenoir-Rhyne	Humboldt St (CA)	15-14
1961	Kansas St-Pittsburg	Linfield (OR)	12-7
1962	Central St (OK)	Lenoir-Rhyne (NC)	28-13
1963	St John's (MN)	Prairie View (TX)	33-27
1964	Concordia-Moorhead Sam Houston		7-7
1965	St John's (MN)	Linfield (OR)	33-0
1966	Waynesburg (PA)	WI-Whitewater	42-21
1967	Fairmont St (WV)	Eastern Washington	28-21
1968	Troy St (MI)	Texas A&I	43-35
1969	Texas A&I	Concordia-Moorhead	32-7
1970	Texas A&I	Wofford (SC)	48-7
1971	Livingston (AL)	Arkansas Tech	14-12
1972	E Texas St	Carson-Newman	21-18
1973	Abilene Christian	Elon (NC)	42-14
1974	Texas A&I	Henderson St (AR)	34-23
1975	Texas A&I	Salem (WV)	37-0
1976	Texas A&I	Central Arkansas	26-0
1977	Abilene Christian	Southwestern Oklahoma	24-7
1978	Angelo St	Elon (NC)	34-14
1979	Texas A&I	Central St (OK)	20-14
1980	Elon (NC)	Northeastern Oklahoma	17-10
1981	Elon (NC)	Pittsburg St	3-0
1982	Central St (OK)	Mesa (CO)	14-11
1983	Carson-Newman (TN)	Mesa (CO)	36-28
1984	Carson-Newman (TN) Central Arkansas		19-19
1985	Central Arkansas Hillsdale (MI)		10-10
1986	Carson-Newman (TN)	Cameron (OK)	17-0
1987	Cameron (OK)	Carson-Newman (TN)	30-2
1988	Carson-Newman (TN)	Adams St (CO)	56-21
1989	Carson-Newman (TN)	Emporia St (KS)	34-20
1990	Central St (OH)	Mesa St (CO)	38-16
1991	Central Arkansas	Central St (OH)	19-16
1992	Central St (OH)	Gardner-Webb (NC)	19-16

Division II

Year	Winner	Runner-Up	Score
1970	Westminster (PA)	Anderson (IN)	21-16
1971	California Lutheran	Westminster (PA)	30-14
1972	Missouri Southern	Northwestern (IA)	21-14
1973	Northwestern (IA)	Glenville St (WV)	10-3
1974	Texas Lutheran	Missouri Valley	42-0
1975	Texas Lutheran	California Lutheran	34-8
1976	Westminster (PA)	Redlands (CA)	20-13
1977	Westminster (PA)	California Lutheran	17-9
1978	Concordia-Moorhead	Findlay (OH)	7-0
1979	Findlay (OH)	Northwestern (IA)	51-6
1980	Pacific Lutheran	Wilmington	38-10
1981	Austin Col Concordia-Moorhead		24-24
1982	Linfield (OR)	William Jewell (MO)	33-15
1983	Northwestern (IA)	Pacific Lutheran	25-21
1984	Linfield (OR)	Northwestern (IA)	33-22
1985	WI-La Crosse	Pacific Lutheran	24-7
1986	Linfield (OR)	Baker (KS)	17-0
1987	Pacific Lutheran	WI-Stevens Point*	16-16
1988	Westminster (PA)	WI-La Crosse	21-14
1989	Westminster (PA)	WI-La Crosse	51-30
1990	Peru St (NEB)	Westminster (PA)	17-7
1991	Georgetown (KY)	Pacific Lutheran	28-20
1992	Findlay (OH)	Linfield (OR)	26-13

*Forfeited 1987 season due to use of an ineligible player.

Awards

Heisman Memorial Trophy

Awarded to the best college player by the Downtown Athletic Club of New York City. The trophy is named after John W. Heisman, who coached Georgia Tech to the national championship in 1917 and later served as DAC athletic director.

Year	Winner, College, Position / Winner's Season Statistics	Runner-up, College
1935	**Jay Berwanger, Chicago, HB** / Rush: 119 Yds: 577 TD: 6	Monk Meyer, Army
1936	**Larry Kelley, Yale, E** / Rec: 17 Yds: 372 TD: 6	Sam Francis, Nebraska
1937	**Clint Frank, Yale, HB** / Rush: 157 Yds: 667 TD: 11	Byron White, Colorado
1938	**†Davey O'Brien, Texas Christian, QB** / Att/Comp: 194/110 Yds: 1733 TD: 19	Marshall Goldberg, Pittsburgh
1939	**Nile Kinnick, Iowa, HB** / Rush: 106 Yds: 374 TD: 5	Tom Harmon, Michigan
1940	**Tom Harmon, Michigan, HB** / Rush: 191 Yds: 852 TD: 16	John Kimbrough, Texas A&M
1941	**†Bruce Smith, Minnesota, HB** / Rush: 98 Yds: 480 TD: 6	Angelo Bertelli, Notre Dame
1942	**Frank Sinkwich, Georgia, HB** / Att/Comp: 166/84 Yds: 1392 TD: 10	Paul Governali, Columbia
1943	**Angelo Bertelli, Notre Dame, QB** / Att/Comp: 36/25 Yds: 511 TD: 10	Bob Odell, Pennsylvania
1944	**Les Horvath, Ohio State, QB** / Rush: 163 Yds: 924 TD: 12	Glenn Davis, Army
1945	***†Doc Blanchard, Army, FB** / Rush: 101 Yds: 718 TD: 13	Glenn Davis, Army
1946	**Glenn Davis, Army, HB** / Rush: 123 Yds: 712 TD: 7	Charley Trippi, Georgia
1947	**†John Lujack, Notre Dame, QB** / Att/Comp: 109/61 Yds: 777 TD: 9	Bob Chappius, Michigan
1948	***Doak Walker, Southern Methodist, HB** / Rush: 108 Yds: 532 TD: 8	Charlie Justice, N Carolina
1949	**†Leon Hart, Notre Dame, E** / Rec: 19 Yds: 257 TD: 5	Charlie Justice, N Carolina
1950	***Vic Janowicz, Ohio St, HB** / Att/Comp: 77/32 Yds: 561 TD: 12	Hank Lauricella, Tennessee
1951	**Dick Kazmaier, Princeton, HB** / Rush: 149 Yds: 861 TD: 9	Hank Lauricella, Tennessee
1952	**Billy Vessels, Oklahoma, HB** / Rush: 167 Yds: 1072 TD: 17	Jack Scarbath, Maryland
1953	**John Lattner, Notre Dame, HB** / Rush: 134 Yds: 651 TD: 6	Paul Geil, Minnesota
1954	**Alan Ameche, Wisconsin, FB** / Rush: 146 Yds: 641 TD: 9	Kurt Burris, Oklahoma
1955	**Howard Cassady, Ohio St, HB** / Rush: 161 Yds: 958 TD: 15	Jim Swink, Texas Christian
1956	**Paul Hornung, Notre Dame, QB** / Att/Comp: 111/59 Yds: 917 TD: 3	Johnny Majors, Tennessee
1957	**John David Crow, Texas A&M, HB** / Rush: 129 Yds: 562 TD: 10	Alex Karras, Iowa
1958	**Pete Dawkins, Army, HB** / Rush: 78 Yds: 428 TD: 6	Randy Duncan, Iowa
1959	**Billy Cannon, Louisiana St, HB** / Rush: 139 Yds: 598 TD: 6	Rich Lucas, Penn St
1960	**Joe Bellino, Navy, HB** / Rush: 168 Yds: 834 TD: 18	Tom Brown, Minnesota
1961	**Ernie Davis, Syracuse, HB** / Rush: 150 Yds: 823 TD: 15	Bob Ferguson, Ohio St
1962	**Terry Baker, Oregon St, QB** / Att/Comp: 203/112 Yds: 1738 TD: 15	Jerry Stovall, Louisiana St
1963	***Roger Staubach, Navy, QB** / Att/Comp: 161/107 Yds: 1474 TD: 7	Billy Lothridge, Georgia Tech
1964	**John Huarte, Notre Dame, QB** / Att/Comp: 205/114 Yds: 2062 TD: 16	Jerry Rhome, Tulsa

Heisman Memorial Trophy (Cont.)

Year	Winner, College, Position Winner's Season Statistics	Runner-up, College
1965	**Mike Garrett, Southern Cal, HB** Rush: 267 Yds: 1440 TD: 16	Howard Twilley, Tulsa
1966	**Steve Spurrier, Florida, QB** Att/Comp: 291/179 Yds: 2012 TD: 16	Bob Griese, Purdue
1967	**Gary Beban, UCLA, QB** Att/Comp: 156/87 Yds: 1359 TD: 8	O.J. Simpson, Southern Cal
1968	**O.J. Simpson, Southern Cal, HB** Rush: 383 Yds: 1880 TD: 23	Leroy Keyes, Purdue
1969	**Steve Owens, Oklahoma, FB** Rush: 358 Yds: 1523 TD: 23	Mike Phipps, Purdue
1970	**Jim Plunkett, Stanford, QB** Att/Comp: 358/191 Yds: 2715 TD: 18	Joe Theismann, Notre Dame
1971	**Pat Sullivan, Auburn, QB** Att/Comp: 281/162 Yds: 2012 TD: 20	Ed Marinaro, Cornell
1972	**Johnny Rodgers, Nebraska, FL** Rec: 55 Yds: 942 TD: 17	Greg Pruitt, Oklahoma
1973	**John Cappelletti, Penn St, HB** Rush: 286 Yds: 1522 TD: 17	John Hicks, Ohio St
1974	***Archie Griffin, Ohio St, HB** Rush: 256 Yds: 1695 TD: 12	Anthony Davis, Southern Cal
1975	**Archie Griffin, Ohio St, HB** Rush: 262 Yds: 1450 TD: 4	Chuck Muncie, California
1976	**†Tony Dorsett, Pittsburgh, HB** Rush: 370 Yds: 2150 TD: 23	Ricky Bell, Southern Cal
1977	**Earl Campbell, Texas, FB** Rush: 267 Yds: 1744 TD: 19	Terry Miller, Oklahoma St
1978	***Billy Sims, Oklahoma, HB** Rush: 231 Yds: 1762 TD: 20	Chuck Fusina, Penn St
1979	**Charles White, Southern Cal, HB** Rush: 332 Yds: 1803 TD: 19	Billy Sims, Oklahoma
1980	**George Rogers, S Carolina, HB** Rush: 324 Yds: 1894 TD: 14	Hugh Green, Pittsburgh
1981	**Marcus Allen, Southern Cal, HB** Rush: 433 Yds: 2427 TD: 23	Herschel Walker, Georgia
1982	***Herschel Walker, Georgia, HB** Rush: 335 Yds: 1752 TD: 17	John Elway, Stanford
1983	**Mike Rozier, Nebraska, HB** Rush: 275 Yds: 2148 TD: 29	Steve Young, Brigham Young
1984	**Doug Flutie, Boston College, QB** Att/Comp: 396/233 Yds: 3454 TD: 27	Keith Byars, Ohio St
1985	**Bo Jackson, Auburn, HB** Rush: 278 Yds: 1786 TD: 17	Chuck Long, Iowa
1986	**Vinny Testaverde, Miami, QB** Att/Comp: 276/175 Yds: 2557 TD: 26	Paul Palmer, Temple
1987	**Tim Brown, Notre Dame, WR** Rec: 39 Yds: 846 TD: 7	Don McPherson, Syracuse
1988	***Barry Sanders, Oklahoma St, RB** Rush: 344 Yds: 2628 TD: 39	Rodney Peete, Southern Cal
1989	***Andre Ware, Houston, QB** Att/Comp: 578/365 Yds: 4699 TD: 46	Anthony Thompson, Indiana
1990	***Ty Detmer, Brigham Young, QB** Att/Comp: 562/361 Yds: 5188 TD: 41	Raghib Ismail, Notre Dame
1991	***Desmond Howard, Michigan, WR** Rec: 61 Yds: 950 TD: 23	Casey Weldon, Florida St
1992	**Gino Torretta, Miami, QB** Att/Comp: 402/228 Yds: 3060 TD: 19	Marshall Faulk, San Diego St

*Juniors (all others seniors). †Winners who played for national championship teams the same year.

Note: Former Heisman winners and national media cast votes, with ballots allowing for three names (3 points for first, 2 for second and 1 for third).

Jim Thorpe Award

Given to the best defensive back of the year, the award is presented by the Jim Thorpe Athletic Club of Oklahoma City.

Year	Player, College	Year	Player, College
1986	Thomas Everett, Baylor	1989	Mark Carrier, Southern Cal
1987	Bennie Blades, Miami (FL)	1990	Darryl Lewis, Arizona
	Rickey Dixon, Oklahoma	1991	Terrell Buckley, Florida St
1988	Deion Sanders, Florida St	1992	Deon Figures, Colorado

Outland Trophy

Given to the outstanding interior lineman, selected by the Football Writers Association of America.

Year	Player, College, Position	Year	Player, College, Position
1946	George Connor, Notre Dame, T	1969	Mike Reid, Penn St, DT
1947	Joe Steffy, Army, G	1970	Jim Stillwagon, Ohio St, MG
1948	Bill Fischer, Notre Dame, G	1971	Larry Jacobson, Nebraska, DT
1949	Ed Bagdon, Michigan St, G	1972	Rich Glover, Nebraska, MG
1950	Bob Gain, Kentucky, T	1973	John Hicks, Ohio St, OT
1951	Jim Weatherall, Oklahoma, T	1974	Randy White, Maryland, DE
1952	Dick Modzelewski, Maryland, T	1975	Lee Roy Selmon, Oklahoma, DT
1953	J. D. Roberts, Oklahoma, G	1976	*Ross Browner, Notre Dame, DE
1954	Bill Brooks, Arkansas, G	1977	Brad Shearer, Texas, DT
1955	Calvin Jones, Iowa, G	1978	Greg Roberts, Oklahoma, G
1956	Jim Parker, Ohio St, G	1979	Jim Ritcher, N Carolina St, C
1957	Alex Karras, Iowa, T	1980	Mark May, Pittsburgh, OT
1958	Zeke Smith, Auburn, G	1981	*Dave Rimington, Nebraska, C
1959	Mike McGee, Duke, T	1982	Dave Rimington, Nebraska, C
1960	Tom Brown, Minnesota, G	1983	Dean Steinkuhler, Nebraska, G
1961	Merlin Olsen, Utah St, T	1984	Bruce Smith, Virginia Tech, DT
1962	Bobby Bell, Minnesota, T	1985	Mike Ruth, Boston Col, NG
1963	Scott Appleton, Texas, T	1986	Jason Buck, Brigham Young, DT
1964	Steve DeLong, Tennessee, T	1987	Chad Hennings, Air Force, DT
1965	Tommy Nobis, Texas, G	1988	Tracy Rocker, Auburn, DT
1966	Loyd Phillips, Arkansas, T	1989	Mohammed Elewonibi, Brigham Young, G
1967	Ron Yary, Southern Cal, T	1990	Russell Maryland, Miami (FL), DT
1968	Bill Stanfill, Georgia, T	1991	*Steve Emtman, Washington, DT
1968	Bill Stanfill, Georgia, T	1992	Will Shields, Nebraska, G

*Juniors (all others seniors).

Vince Lombardi/Rotary Award

Given to the outstanding college lineman of the year, the award is sponsored by the Rotary Club of Houston.

Year	Player, College, Position	Year	Player, College, Position
1970	Jim Stillwagon, Ohio St, MG	1982	Dave Rimington, Nebraska, C
1971	Walt Patulski, Notre Dame, DE	1983	Dean Steinkuhler, Nebraska, G
1972	Rich Glover, Nebraska, MG	1984	Tony Degrate, Texas, DT
1973	John Hicks, Ohio St, OT	1985	Tony Casillas, Oklahoma, NG
1974	Randy White, Maryland, DT	1986	Cornelius Bennett, Alabama, LB
1975	Lee Roy Selmon, Oklahoma, DT	1987	Chris Spielman, Ohio St, LB
1976	Wilson Whitley, Houston, DT	1988	Tracy Rocker, Auburn, DT
1977	Ross Browner, Notre Dame, DE	1989	Percy Snow, Michigan St, LB
1978	Bruce Clark, Penn St, DT	1990	Chris Zorich, Notre Dame, NG
1979	Brad Budde, Southern Cal, G	1991	Steve Emtman, Washington, DT
1980	Hugh Green, Pittsburgh, DE	1992	Marvin Jones, Florida St, LB
1981	Kenneth Sims, Texas, DT		

Butkus Award

Given to the top collegiate linebacker, the award was established by the Downtown Athletic Club of Orlando and named for college hall of famer Dick Butkus of Illinois.

Year	Player, College	Year	Player, College
1985	Brian Bosworth, Oklahoma	1989	Percy Snow, Michigan St
1986	Brian Bosworth, Oklahoma	1990	Alfred Williams, Colorado
1987	Paul McGowan, Florida St	1991	Erick Anderson, Michigan
1988	Derrick Thomas, Alabama	1992	Marvin Jones, Florida St

Davey O'Brien National Quarterback Award

Given to the No. 1 quarterback in the nation by the Davey O'Brien Educational and Charitable Trust of Fort Worth. Named for Texas Christian hall of fame quarterback Davey O'Brien (1936-38).

Year	Player, College	Year	Player, College
1981	Jim McMahon, Brigham Young	1987	Don McPherson, Syracuse
1982	Todd Blackledge, Penn St	1988	Troy Aikman, UCLA
1983	Steve Young, Brigham Young	1989	Andre Ware, Houston
1984	Doug Flutie, Boston Col	1990	Ty Detmer, Brigham Young
1985	Chuck Long, Iowa	1991	Ty Detmer, Brigham Young
1986	Vinny Testaverde, Miami (FL)	1992	Gino Torretta, Miami

Note: Originally known as the Davey O'Brien Memorial Trophy, honoring the outstanding football player in the Southwest as follows: 1977—Earl Campbell, Texas, RB; 1978—Billy Sims, Oklahoma, RB; 1979—Mike Singletary, Baylor, LB; 1980—Mike Singletary, Baylor, LB.

Maxwell Award

Given to the nation's outstanding college football player by the Maxwell Football Club of Philadelphia.

Year	Player, College, Position	Year	Player, College, Position
1937	Clint Frank, Yale, HB	1965	Tommy Nobis, Texas, LB
1938	Davey O'Brien, Texas Christian, QB	1966	Jim Lynch, Notre Dame, LB
1939	Nile Kinnick, Iowa, HB	1967	Gary Beban, UCLA, QB
1940	Tom Harmon, Michigan, HB	1968	O. J. Simpson, Southern Cal, RB
1941	Bill Dudley, Virginia, HB	1969	Mike Reid, Penn St, DT
1942	Paul Governali, Columbia, QB	1970	Jim Plunkett, Stanford, QB
1943	Bob Odell, Pennsylvania, HB	1971	Ed Marinaro, Cornell, RB
1944	Glenn Davis, Army, HB	1972	Brad Van Pelt, Michigan St, DB
1945	Doc Blanchard, Army, FB	1973	John Cappelletti, Penn St, RB
1946	Charley Trippi, Georgia, HB	1974	Steve Joachim, Temple, QB
1947	Doak Walker, Southern Meth, HB	1975	Archie Griffin, Ohio St, RB
1948	Chuck Bednarik, Pennsylvania, C	1976	Tony Dorsett, Pittsburgh, RB
1949	Leon Hart, Notre Dame, E	1977	Ross Browner, Notre Dame, DE
1950	Reds Bagnell, Pennsylvania, HB	1978	Chuck Fusina, Penn St, QB
1951	Dick Kazmaier, Princeton, HB	1979	Charles White, Southern Cal, RB
1952	John Lattner, Notre Dame, HB	1980	Hugh Green, Pittsburgh, DE
1953	John Lattner, Notre Dame, HB	1981	Marcus Allen, Southern Cal, RB
1954	Ron Beagle, Navy, E	1982	Herschel Walker, Georgia, RB
1955	Howard Cassady, Ohio St, HB	1983	Mike Rozier, Nebraska, RB
1956	Tommy McDonald, Oklahoma, HB	1984	Doug Flutie, Boston Col, QB
1957	Bob Reifsnyder, Navy, T	1985	Chuck Long, Iowa, QB
1958	Pete Dawkins, Army, HB	1986	Vinny Testaverde, Miami (FL), QB
1959	Rich Lucas, Penn St, QB	1987	Don McPherson, Syracuse, QB
1960	Joe Bellino, Navy, HB	1988	Barry Sanders, Oklahoma St, RB
1961	Bob Ferguson, Ohio St, FB	1989	Anthony Thompson, Indiana, RB
1962	Terry Baker, Oregon St, QB	1990	Ty Detmer, Brigham Young, QB
1963	Roger Staubach, Navy, QB	1991	Desmond Howard, Michigan, WR
1964	Glenn Ressler, Penn St, C	1992	Gino Torretta, Miami (FL), QB

Walter Payton Player of the Year Award

Given to the top Division I-AA football player, the award is sponsored by Sports Network and voted on by Division I-AA sports information directors.

Year	Player, College, Position
1987	Kenny Gamble, Colgate, RB
1988	Dave Meggett, Towson St, RB
1989	John Friesz, Idaho, QB
1990	Walter Dean, Grambling, RB
1991	Jamie Martin, Weber St, QB
1992	Michael Payton, Marshall, QB

The Harlon Hill Trophy

Given to the outstanding NCAA Division II college football player, the award is sponsored by the National Harlon Hill Awards Committee, Florence, AL.

Year	Player, College, Position
1986	Jeff Bentrim, N Dakota St, QB
1987	Johnny Bailey, Texas A&I, RB
1988	Johnny Bailey, Texas A&I, RB
1989	Johnny Bailey, Texas A&I, RB
1990	Chris Simdorn, N Dakota St, QB
1991	Ronnie West, Pittsburg St, WR
1992	Ronald Moore, Pittsburg St, RB

Career

SCORING

Most Points Scored: 423 — Roman Anderson, Houston, 1988-91

Most Points Scored per Game: 11.9 — Bob Gaiters, New Mexico St, 1959-60

Most Touchdowns Scored: 65 — Anthony Thompson, Indiana, 1986-89

Most Touchdowns Scored per Game: 1.93 — Ed Marinaro, Cornell, 1969-71

Most Touchdowns Scored, Rushing: 64 — Anthony Thompson, Indiana, 1986-89

Most Touchdowns Scored, Passing: 121 — Ty Detmer, Brigham Young, 1988-91

Most Touchdowns Scored, Receiving: 43 — Aaron Turner, Pacific, 1989-92

Most Touchdowns Scored, Interception Returns: 5 — Ken Thomas, San Jose St, 1979-82; Jackie Walker, Tennessee, 1969-71

Most Touchdowns Scored, Punt Returns: 7 — Johnny Rodgers, Nebraska, 1970-72; Jack Mitchell, Oklahoma, 1946-48

Most Touchdowns Scored, Kickoff Returns: 6 — Anthony Davis, Southern Cal, 1972-74

TOTAL OFFENSE

Most Plays: 1722 — Todd Santos, San Diego St, 1984-87

Most Plays per Game: 48.5 — Doug Gaynor, Long Beach St, 1984-85

Most Yards Gained: 14,665 — Ty Detmer, Brigham Young, 1988-91 (15,031 passing, -366 rushing)

Most Yards Gained per Game: 318.8 — Ty Detmer, Brigham Young, 1988-91

Most 300+ Yard Games: 18 — Steve Young, Brigham Young, 1981-83

RUSHING

Most Rushes: 1215 — Steve Bartalo, Colorado St, 1983-86 (4813 yds)

Most Rushes per Game: 34.0 — Ed Marinaro, Cornell, 1969-71

Most Yards Gained: 6082 — Tony Dorsett, Pittsburgh, 1973-76

Most Yards Gained per Game: 174.6 — Ed Marinaro, Cornell, 1969-71

Most 100+ Yard Games: 33 — Tony Dorsett, Pittsburgh, 1973-76; Archie Griffin, Ohio St, 1972-75

Most 200+ Yard Games: 11 — Marcus Allen, Southern Cal, 1978-81

SPECIAL TEAMS

Highest Punt Return Average: 23.6 — Jack Mitchell, Oklahoma, 1946-48

Highest Kickoff Return Average: 36.2 — Forrest Hall, San Francisco, 1946-47

Highest Average Yards per Punt: 45.6 — Reggie Roby, Iowa, 1979-82

PASSING

Highest Passing Efficiency Rating: 162.7 — Ty Detmer, Brigham Young, 1988-91 (1530 attempts, 958 completions, 65 interceptions, 15,031 yards, 121 TD passes)

Most Passes Attempted: 1,530 — Ty Detmer, Brigham Young, 1988-91

Most Passes Attempted per Game: 39.6 — Mike Perez, San Jose St, 1986-87

Most Passes Completed: 958 — Ty Detmer, Brigham Young, 1988-91

Most Passes Completed per Game: 25.9 — Doug Gaynor, Long Beach St, 1984-85

Highest Completion Percentage: 65.2 — Steve Young, Brigham Young, 1981-83

Most Yards Gained: 15,031 — Ty Detmer, Brigham Young, 1988-91

Most Yards Gained per Game: 326.7 — Ty Detmer, Brigham Young, 1988-91

RECEIVING

Most Passes Caught: 266 — Aaron Turner, Pacific, 1989-92

Most Passes Caught per Game: 10.5 — Emmanuel Hazard, Houston, 1989-90

Most Yards Gained: 4345 — Aaron Turner, Pacific, 1989-92

Most Yards Gained per Game: 128.6 — Howard Twilley, Tulsa, 1963-65

Highest Average Gain per Reception: 25.7 — Wesley Walker, California, 1973-75

ALL-PURPOSE RUNNING

Most Plays: 1347 — Steve Bartalo, Colorado St, 1983-86 (1215 rushes, 132 receptions)

Most Yards Gained: 7172 — Napoleon McCallum, Navy, 1981-85 (4179 rushing, 796 receiving, 858 punt returns, 1339 kickoff returns)

Most Yards Gained per Game: 237.8 — Ryan Benjamin, Pacific, 1990-92

Highest Average Gain per Play: 17.4 — Anthony Carter, Michigan, 1979-82.

INTERCEPTIONS

Most Passes Intercepted: 29 — Al Brosky, Illinois, 1950-52

Most Passes Intercepted per Game: 1.07 — Al Brosky, Illinois, 1950-52

Most Yards on Interception Returns: 470 — John Provost, Holy Cross, 1972-74

Highest Average Gain per Interception: 26.5 — Tom Pridemore, W Virginia, 1975-77

Single Season

SCORING

Most Points Scored: 234 — Barry Sanders, Oklahoma St, 1988
Most Points Scored per Game: 21.27 — Barry Sanders, Oklahoma St, 1988
Most Touchdowns Scored: 39 — Barry Sanders, Oklahoma St, 1988
Most Touchdowns Scored, Rushing: 37 — Barry Sanders, Oklahoma St, 1988
Most Touchdowns Scored, Passing: 54 — David Klingler, Houston, 1990
Most Touchdowns Scored, Receiving: 22 — Emmanuel Hazard, Houston, 1989
Most Touchdowns Scored, Interception Returns: 3 — by many players
Most Touchdowns Scored, Punt Returns: 4 — James Henry, Southern Miss, 1987; Golden Richards, Brigham Young, 1971; Cliff Branch, Colorado 1971
Most Touchdowns Scored, Kickoff Returns: 3 — Terance Mathis, New Mexico, 1989; Willie Gault, Tennessee, 1980; Anthony Davis, Southern Cal, 1974; Stan Brown, Purdue, 1970; Forrest Hall, San Francisco, 1946

TOTAL OFFENSE

Most Plays: 704 — David Klingler, Houston, 1990
Most Yards Gained: 5221 — David Klingler, Houston, 1990
Most Yards Gained per Game: 474.6 — David Klingler, Houston, 1990
Most 300+ Yard Games: 11 — Jim McMahon, Brigham Young, 1980

RUSHING

Most Rushes: 403 — Marcus Allen, Southern Cal, 1981
Most Rushes per Game: 39.6 — Ed Marinaro, Cornell, 1971
Most Yards Gained: 2628 — Barry Sanders, Oklahoma St, 1988
Most Yards Gained per Game: 238.9 — Barry Sanders, Oklahoma St, 1988
Most 100+ Yard Games: 11 — By nine players, most recently Barry Sanders, Oklahoma St, 1988

THEY SAID IT

Drew Bledsoe, former Washington State quarterback, after the New England Patriots made him the top choice in the NFL draft, recalling that he once thought the No. 1 pick was someone special: "But now that it's me, it loses some of its mystique."

PASSING

Highest Passing Efficiency Rating: 176.9 — Jim McMahon, Brigham Young, 1980 (445 attempts, 284 completions, 18 interceptions, 4571 yards, 47 TD passes)
Most Passes Attempted: 643 — David Klingler, Houston, 1990
Most Passes Attempted per Game: 58.4 — David Klingler, Houston, 1990
Most Passes Completed: 374 — David Klingler, Houston, 1990
Most Passes Completed per Game: 34.0 — David Klingler, Houston, 1990
Highest Completion Percentage: 71.3 — Steve Young, Brigham Young, 1983
Most Yards Gained: 5188 — Ty Detmer, Brigham Young, 1990
Most Yards Gained per Game: 471.6 — Ty Detmer, Brigham Young, 1990

RECEIVING

Most Passes Caught: 142 — Emmanuel Hazard, Houston, 1989
Most Passes Caught per Game: 13.4 — Howard Twilley, Tulsa, 1965
Most Yards Gained: 1779 — Howard Twilley, Tulsa, 1965
Most Yards Gained per Game: 177.9 — Howard Twilley, Tulsa, 1965
Highest Average Gain per Reception: 27.9 — Elmo Wright, Houston, 1968

ALL-PURPOSE RUNNING

Most Plays: 432 — Marcus Allen, Southern Cal, 1981
Most Yards Gained: 3250 — Barry Sanders, Oklahoma St, 1988
Most Yards Gained per Game: 295.5 — Barry Sanders, Oklahoma St, 1988
Highest Average Gain per Play: 18.6 — Craig Thompson, Eastern Michigan, 1992

INTERCEPTIONS

Most Passes Intercepted: 14 — Al Worley, Washington, 1968
Most Yards on Interception Returns: 302 — Charles Phillips, Southern Cal, 1974
Highest Average Gain per Interception: 50.6 — Norm Thompson, Utah, 1969

SPECIAL TEAMS

Highest Punt Return Average: 25.9 — Bill Blackstock, Tennessee, 1951
Highest Kickoff Return Average: 38.2 — Forrest Hall, San Francisco, 1946
Highest Average Yards per Punt: 49.8 — Reggie Roby, Iowa, 1981

Division I-A Individual Records (Cont.)

Single Game

SCORING

Most Points Scored: 48 — Howard Griffith, Illinois, 1990 (vs Southern Illinois)
Most Field Goals: 7 — Dale Klein, Nebraska, 1985 (vs Missouri); Mike Prindle, Western Michigan, 1984 (vs Marshall)
Most Extra Points (Kick): 13 — Terry Leiweke, Houston, 1968 (vs Tulsa)
Most Extra Points (2-Pts): 6 — Jim Pilot, New Mexico St, 1961 (vs Hardin-Simmons)

TOTAL OFFENSE

Most Yards Gained: 732 — David Klingler, Houston, 1990 (vs Arizona St)

RUSHING

Most Yards Gained: 396 — Tony Sands, Kansas, 1991 (vs Missouri)
Most Touchdowns Rushed: 8 — Howard Griffith, Illinois, 1990 (vs Southern Illinois)

PASSING

Most Passes Completed: 48 — David Klingler, Houston, 1990 (vs Southern Methodist)
Most Yards Gained: 716 — David Klingler, Houston, 1990 (vs Arizona St)
Most Touchdowns Passed: 11 — David Klingler, Houston, 1990 [vs Eastern Washington (I-AA)]

RECEIVING

Most Passes Caught: 22 — Jay Miller, Brigham Young, 1973 (vs New Mexico)
Most Yards Gained: 349 — Chuck Hughes, UTEP, 1965 (vs N Texas St)
Most Touchdown Catches: 6 — Tim Delaney, San Diego St, 1969 (vs New Mexico St)

NCAA Division I-AA Individual Records

Career

SCORING

Most Points Scored: 385 — Marty Zendejas, NV-Reno, 1984-87
Most Touchdowns Scored: 60 — Charvez Foger, NV-Reno, 1985-88
Most Touchdowns Scored, Rushing: 55 — Kenny Gamble, Colgate, 1984-87
Most Touchdowns Scored, Passing: 139 — Willie Totten, Mississippi Valley, 1982-85
Most Touchdowns Scored, Receiving: 50 — Jerry Rice, Mississippi Valley, 1981-84

PASSING

Highest Passing Efficiency Rating: 148.9 — Jay Johnson, Northern Iowa, 1989-92
Most Passes Attempted: 1,606 — Neil Lomax, Portland St, 1977-80
Most Passes Completed: 938 — Neil Lomax, Portland St, 1977-80
Most Passes Completed per Game: 23.8 — Stan Greene, Boston U, 1989-90
Highest Completion Percentage: 66.9 — Jason Garrett, Princeton, 1987-88

Most Yards Gained: 13,220 — Neil Lomax, Portland St, 1977-80
Most Yards Gained per Game: 317.8 — Willie Totten, Mississippi Valley, 1982-85

RUSHING

Most Rushes: 963 — Kenny Gamble, Colgate, 1984-87
Most Rushes per Game: 23.7 — Paul Lewis, Boston U, 1981-84
Most Yards Gained: 5,333 — Frank Hawkins, NV-Reno, 1977-80
Most Yards Gained per Game: 133.0 — Mike Clark, Akron, 1984-86

RECEIVING

Most Passes Caught: 301 — Jerry Rice, Mississippi Valley, 1981-84
Most Yards Gained: 4,693 — Jerry Rice, Mississippi Valley, 1981-84
Most Yards Gained per Game: 114.5 — Jerry Rice, Mississippi Valley, 1981-84
Highest Average Gain per Reception: 24.3 — John Taylor, Delaware St, 1982-85

Single Season

SCORING

Most Points Scored: 170 — Geoff Mitchell, Weber St, 1991
Most Touchdowns Scored: 28 — Geoff Mitchell, Weber St, 1991
Most Touchdowns Scored, Rushing: 24 — Geoff Mitchell, Weber St, 1991
Most Touchdowns Scored, Passing: 56 — Willie Totten, Mississippi Valley, 1984
Most Touchdowns Scored, Receiving: 27 — Jerry Rice, Mississippi Valley, 1984

PASSING

Highest Passing Efficiency Rating: 181.3 — Michael Payton, Marshall, 1991
Most Passes Attempted: 518 — Willie Totten, Mississippi Valley, 1984
Most Passes Completed: 324 — Willie Totten, Mississippi Valley, 1984
Most Passes Completed per Game: 32.4 — Willie Totten, Mississippi Valley, 1984
Highest Completion Percentage: 68.2 — Jason Garrett, Princeton, 1988
Most Yards Gained: 4,557 — Willie Totten, Mississippi Valley, 1984
Most Yards Gained per Game: 455.7 — Willie Totten, Mississippi Valley, 1984

Single Season *(Cont.)*

RUSHING

Most Rushes: 351 — James Black, Akron, 1983
Most Rushes per Game: 34.0 — James Black, Akron, 1983
Most Yards Gained: 1,883 — Rich Erenberg, Colgate, 1983
Most Yards Gained per Game: 172.2 — Gene Lake, Deleware St, 1984

RECEIVING

Most Passes Caught: 115 — Brian Forster, Rhode Island, 1985
Most Yards Gained: 1,682 — Jerry Rice, Mississippi Valley, 1984
Most Yards Gained per Game: 168.2 — Jerry Rice, Mississippi Valley, 1984
Highest Average Gain per Reception: 37.0 — Kenny Shedd, Northern Iowa, 1992

Single Game

SCORING

Most Points Scored: 36 — By five players. Most recently Erwin Matthews, Richmond, 1987 (vs Massachusetts)
Most Field Goals: 8 — Goran Lingmerth, Northern Arizona, 1986 (vs Idaho)

PASSING

Most Passes Completed: 47 — Jamie Martin, Weber St, 1991 (vs Idaho St)
Most Yards Gained: 624 — Jamie Martin, Weber St, 1991 (vs Idaho St)
Most Touchdowns Passed: 9 — Willie Totten, Mississippi Valley, 1984 (vs Kentucky St)

RUSHING

Most Yards Gained: 345 — Russell Davis, Idaho, 1981 (vs Portland St)
Most Touchdowns Rushed: 6 — Gene Lake, Delaware St, 1984 (vs. Howard); Gill Fenerty, Holy Cross, 1983 (vs Columbia); Henry Odom, S Carolina St, 1980 (vs Morgan St)

RECEIVING

Most Passes Caught: 24 — Jerry Rice, Mississippi Valley 1983 (vs Southern-Baton Rouge)
Most Yards Gained: 370— Michael Lerch, Princeton, 1991 (vs Brown)
Most Touchdown Catches: 5 — Rennie Benn, Lehigh, 1985 [vs Indiana (PA)]; Jerry Rice, Mississippi Valley, 1984 (vs Prairie View and vs Kentucky St)

NCAA Division II Individual Records

Career

SCORING

Most Points Scored: 464 — Walter Payton, Jackson St, 1971-74
Most Touchdowns Scored: 72 — Shawn Graves, Wofford, 1989-92
Most Touchdowns Scored, Rushing: 66 — Johnny Bailey, Texas A&I, 1986-89
Most Touchdowns Scored, Passing: 93 — Doug Williams, Grambling, 1974-77
Most Touchdowns Scored, Receiving: 49 — Bruce Cerone, Yankton/Emporia St, 1966-69

PASSING

Highest Passing Efficiency Rating: 164.4 — Tony Aliucci, Indiana (PA)
Most Passes Attempted: 1,442 — Earl Harvey, N Carolina Central, 1985-88
Most Passes Completed: 690 — Earl Harvey, N Carolina Central, 1985-88
Most Passes Completed per Game: 25.0 — Tim Von Dulm, Portland St, 1969-70
Highest Completion Percentage: 69.6 — Chris Peterson, UC-Davis, 1985-86
Most Yards Gained: 10,621 — Earl Harvey, N Carolina Central, 1985-88
Most Yards Gained per Game: 320.1 — Tom Ehrhardt, Rhode Island, 1984-85

RUSHING

Most Rushes: 1,072 — Bernie Peeters, Luther, 1968-71
Most Rushes per Game: 29.8 — Bernie Peeters, Luther, 1968-71
Most Yards Gained: 6,320 — Johnny Bailey, Texas A&I, 1986-89
Most Yards Gained per Game: 162.1 — Johnny Bailey, Texas A&I, 1986-89

RECEIVING

Most Passes Caught: 253 — Chris Myers, Kenyon, 1967-70
Most Yards Gained: 4,354 — Bruce Cerone, Yankton/Emporia St, 1966-69
Most Yards Gained per Game: 137.3 — Ed Bell, Idaho St, 1968-69
Highest Average Gain per Reception: 21.8 — Willie Richardson, Jackson St, 1959-62

Single Season

SCORING

Most Points Scored: 178 — Terry Metcalf, Long Beach St, 1971
Most Touchdowns Scored: 29 — Terry Metcalf, Long Beach St, 1971
Most Touchdowns Scored, Rushing: 28 — Terry Metcalf, Long Beach St, 1971
Most Touchdowns Scored, Passing: 45 — Bob Toledo, San Francisco St, 1967
Most Touchdowns Scored, Receiving: 20 — Ed Bell, Idaho St, 1969

PASSING

Highest Passing Efficiency Rating: 210.1 — Boyd Crawford, College of Idaho, 1953
Most Passes Attempted: 515 — Todd Mayfield, W Texas St, 1986
Most Passes Completed: 317 — Todd Mayfield, W Texas St, 1986
Most Passes Completed per Game: 28.8 — Todd Mayfield, W Texas St, 1986
Highest Completion Percentage: 70.1 — Chris Peterson, UC-Davis, 1986
Most Yards Gained: 3,741 — Chris Hegg, NE Missouri St, 1985
Most Yards Gained per Game: 351.3 — Bob Toledo, San Francisco St, 1967

RUSHING

Most Rushes: 350 — Leon Burns, Long Beach St, 1969
Most Rushes per Game: 38.6 — Mark Perkins, Hobart, 1968
Most Yards Gained: 2,011 — Johnny Bailey, Texas A&I, 1986
Most Yards Gained per Game: 182.8 — Johnny Bailey, Texas A&I, 1986

RECEIVING

Most Passes Caught: 106 — Barry Wagner, Alabama A&M, 1989
Most Yards Gained: 1,812 — Barry Wagner, Alabama A&M, 1989
Most Yards Gained per Game: 164.7 — Barry Wagner, Alabama A&M, 1989
Highest Average Gain per Reception: 28.7 — Kevin Collins, Santa Clara, 1983

Single Game

SCORING

Most Points Scored: 48 — Paul Zaeske, N Park, 1968 (vs N Central); Junior Wolf, Panhandle St, 1958 [vs St Mary (KS)]
Most Field Goals: 6 — Steve Huff, Central Missouri St, 1985 (vs SE Missouri St)

PASSING

Most Passes Completed: 44 — Tom Bonds, Cal Lutheran, 1986 [vs St Mary's (CA)]
Most Yards Gained: 592 — John Charles, Portland State, 1991 (vs Cal-Poly San Luis Obispo)
Most Touchdowns Passed: 10 — Bruce Swanson, N Park, 1968 (vs N Central)

RUSHING

Most Yards Gained: 382 — Kelly Ellis, Northern Iowa, 1979 (vs Western Illinois)
Most Touchdowns Rushed: 8 — Junior Wolf, Panhandle St, 1958 [vs St Mary (KS)]

RECEIVING

Most Passes Caught: 23 — Barry Wagner, Alabama A&M, 1989 (vs Clark Atlanta)
Most Yards Gained: 370 — Barry Wagner, Alabama A&M, 1989 (vs Clark Atlanta)
Most Touchdown Catches: 8 — Paul Zaeske, N Park, 1968 (vs N Central)

Division III Individual Records

Career

SCORING

Most Points Scored: 474 — Joe Dudek, Plymouth St, 1982-85
Most Touchdowns Scored: 79 — Joe Dudek, Plymouth St, 1982-85
Most Touchdowns Scored, Rushing: 76 — Joe Dudek, Plymouth St, 1982-85
Most Touchdowns Scored, Passing: 110 — Kirk Baumgartner, WI-Stevens Point, 1986-89
Most Touchdowns Scored, Receiving: 55 — Chris Bisaillon, Illinois Wesleyan, 1989-92

RUSHING

Most Rushes: 1,112 — Mike Birosak, Dickinson, 1986-89
Most Rushes per Game: 32.7 — Chris Sizemore, Bridgewater (VA), 1972-74
Most Yards Gained: 5,570 — Joe Dudek, Plymouth St, 1982-85
Most Yards Gained per Game: 151.8 — Terry Underwood, Wagner, 1985-88

Career (Cont.)

PASSING

Highest Passing Efficiency Rating: 153.3 — Joe Blake, Simpson, 1987-90
Most Passes Attempted: 1,696 — Kirk Baumgartner, WI-Stevens Point, 1986-89
Most Passes Completed: 883 — Kirk Baumgartner, WI-Stevens Point, 1986-89
Most Passes Completed per Game: 24.9 — Keith Bishop, Illinois Wesleyan, 1981; Wheaton (IL), 1983-85
Highest Completion Percentage: 62.2 — Brian Moore, Baldwin-Wallace, 1981-84
Most Yards Gained: 13,028 — Kirk Baumgartner, WI-Stevens Point, 1986-89
Most Yards Gained per Game: 317.8 — Kirk Baumgartner, WI-Stevens Point, 1986-89

RECEIVING

Most Passes Caught: 258 — Bill Stromberg, Johns Hopkins, 1978-81
Most Yards Gained: 3,846 — Dale Amos, Franklin & Marshall, 1986-89
Most Yards Gained per Game: 110.1 — Tim McNamara, Trinity (CT), 1981-84
Highest Average Gain per Reception: 20.0 — Marty Redlawsk, Concordia (IL), 1984-87

Single Season

SCORING

Most Points Scored: 168 — Stanley Drayton, Allegheny, 1991
Most Points Scored per Game: 16.8 — Stanley Drayton, Allegheny, 1991
Most Touchdowns Scored: 28 — Stanley Drayton, Allegheny, 1991
Most Touchdowns Scored, Rushing: 26 — Ricky Gales, Simpson, 1989
Most Touchdowns Scored, Passing: 39 — Kirk Baumgartner, WI-Stevens Point, 1989
Most Touchdowns Scored, Receiving: 20 — John Aromando, Trenton St, 1983

RUSHING

Most Rushes: 380 — Mike Birosak, Dickinson, 1989
Most Rushes per Game: 38.0 — Mike Birosak, Dickinson, 1989
Most Yards Gained: 2,035 — Ricky Gales, Simpson, 1989
Most Yards Gained per Game: 203.5 — Ricky Gales, Simpson, 1989

PASSING

Highest Passing Efficiency Rating: 203.3 — Joe Blake, Simpson, 1989
Most Passes Attempted: 527 — Kirk Baumgartner, WI-Stevens Point, 1988
Most Passes Completed: 276 — Kirk Baumgartner, WI-Stevens Point, 1988
Most Passes Completed per Game: 29.1 — Keith Bishop, Illinois Wesleyan, 1985
Highest Completion Percentage: 64.0 — Willie Reyna, La Verne, 1992
Most Yards Gained: 3,828 — Kirk Baumgartner, WI-Stevens Point, 1988
Most Yards Gained per Game: 369.2 — Kirk Baumgartner, WI-Stevens Point, 1989

RECEIVING

Most Passes Caught: 106 — Theo Blanco, WI-Stevens Point, 1987
Most Yards Gained: 1,693 — Sean Munroe, Mass-Boston, 1992
Most Yards Gained per Game: 188.1 — Sean Munroe, Mass-Boston 1992
Highest Average Gain per Reception: 26-9 — Marty Redlawsk, Concordia (IL), 1985

Single Game

SCORING

Most Field Goals: 6 — Jim Hever, Rhodes, 1984 (vs Millsaps)

PASSING

Most Passes Completed: 50 — Tim Lynch, Hofstra, 1991 (vs Fordham)
Most Yards Gained: 585 — Tim Lynch, Hofstra, 1991 (vs Fordham)
Most Touchdowns Passed: 8 — Kirk Baumgartner, WI-Stevens Point, 1989 (vs WI-Superior); Steve Austin, Mass-Boston, 1992 (vs Framingham St)

RUSHING

Most Yards Gained: 382 — Pete Baranek, Carthage, 1985 (vs N Central)
Most Touchdowns Rushed: 6 — Rob Sinclair, Simpson, 1990 (vs Upper Iowa); Eric Leiser, Eureka, 1991, (vs Concordia)

RECEIVING

Most Passes Caught: 23 — Sean Munroe, Mass-Boston, 1992 (vs Mass-Maritime)
Most Yards Gained: 332 — Sean Munroe, Mass-Boston, 1992 (vs Mass-Maritime)
Most Touchdown Catches: 5 — By 10 players. Most Recent: Sean Munroe, Mass-Boston, 1992 (vs Mass-Maritime)

Division I-A All-Time Individual Leaders

Career

Scoring

POINTS (KICKERS)

	Years	Pts
Roman Anderson, Houston	1988-91	423
Carlos Huerta, Miami (FL)	1988-91	397
Jason Elam, Hawaii	1988-92	395
Derek Schmidt, Florida St	1984-87	393
Luis Zendejas, Arizona St	1981-84	368
Jeff Jaeger, Washington	1983-86	358
John Lee, UCLA	1982-85	353
Max Zendejas, Arizona	1982-85	353

POINTS (NON-KICKERS)

	Years	Pts
Anthony Thompson, Indiana	1986-89	394
Tony Dorsett, Pittsburgh	1973-76	356
Glenn Davis, Army	1943-46	354
Art Luppino, Arizona	1953-56	337
Steve Owens, Oklahoma	1967-69	336

POINTS PER GAME (NON-KICKERS)

	Years	Pts/Game
Bob Gaiters, New Mexico St	1959-60	11.9
Ed Marinaro, Cornell	1969-71	11.8
Bill Burnett, Arkansas	1968-70	11.3
Steve Owens, Oklahoma	1967-69	11.2
Eddie Talboom, Wyoming	1948-50	10.8

Total Offense

YARDS GAINED

	Years	Yds
Ty Detmer, Brigham Young	1988-91	14,665
Doug Flutie, Boston Col	1981-84	11,317
Alex Van Pelt, Pittsburgh	1989-92	10,814
Todd Santos, San Diego St	1984-87	10,513
Kevin Sweeney, Fresno St	1982-86	10,252

YARDS PER GAME

	Years	Yds/Game
Ty Detmer, Brigham Young	1988-91	318.8
Mike Perez, San Jose St	1986-87	309.1
Doug Gaynor, Long Beach St	1984-85	305.0
Tony Eason, Illinois	1981-82	299.5
Steve Young, Brigham Young	1981-83	284.4
Doug Flutie, Boston Col	1981-84	269.5

Rushing

YARDS GAINED

	Years	Yds
Tony Dorsett, Pittsburgh	1973-76	6082
Charles White, Southern Cal	1976-79	5598
Herschel Walker, Georgia	1980-82	5259
Archie Griffin, Ohio St	1972-75	5177
Anthony Thompson, Indiana	1986-89	4965

YARDS PER GAME

	Years	Yds/Game
Ed Marinaro, Cornell	1969-71	174.6
O. J. Simpson, Southern Cal	1967-68	164.4
Herschel Walker, Georgia	1980-82	159.4
Tony Dorsett, Pittsburgh	1973-76	141.4
Mike Rozier, Nebraska	1981-83	136.6

TOUCHDOWNS RUSHING

	Years	TD
Anthony Thompson, Indiana	1986-89	64
Steve Owens, Oklahoma	1967-69	56
Tony Dorsett, Pittsburgh	1973-76	55
Ed Marinaro, Cornell	1969-71	50
Mike Rozier, Nebraska	1981-83	49

Passing

PASSING EFFICIENCY

	Years	Rating
Ty Detmer, Brigham Young	1988-91	162.7
Jim McMahon, Brigham Young	1977-78, 80-81	156.9
Steve Young, Brigham Young	1982, 84-86	149.8
Robbie Bosco, Brigham Young	1981-83	149.4
Chuck Long, Iowa	1981-85	148.9

Note: Minimum 500 completions.

YARDS GAINED

	Years	Yds
Ty Detmer, Brigham Young	1988-91	15,031
Todd Santos, San Diego St	1984-87	11,425
Alex Van Pelt, Pittsburgh	1989-92	10,913
Kevin Sweeney, Fresno St	1982-86	10,623
Doug Flutie, Boston Col	1981-84	10,579
Brian McClure, Bowling Green	1982-85	10,280

Note: Minimum 500 completions.

COMPLETIONS

	Years	Comp
Ty Detmer, Brigham Young	1988-91	958
Todd Santos, San Diego St	1984-87	910
Brian McClure, Bowling Green	1982-85	900
Eric Wilhelm, Oregon St	1989-92	870
Alex Van Pelt, Pittsburgh	1989-92	845

Note: Minimum 500 completions.

TOUCHDOWNS PASSING

	Years	TD
Ty Detmer, Brigham Young	1988-91	121
David Klingler, Houston	1988-91	92
Troy Kopp, Pacific	1989-92	87
Jim McMahon, Brigham Young	1977-78, 80-81	84
Joe Adams, Tennessee St	1977-80	81

Receiving

CATCHES

	Years	No.
Aaron Turner, Pacific	1989-92	266
Terance Mathis, New Mexico	1985-87, 89	263
Mark Templeton, Long Beach St	1983-86	262
Howard Twilley, Tulsa	1963-65	261
David Williams, Illinois	1983-85	245

CATCHES PER GAME

	Years	No./Game
Emmanuel Hazard, Houston	1989-90	10.5
Howard Twilley, Tulsa	1963-65	10.0
Jason Phillips, Houston	1987-88	9.4
Neal Sweeney, Tulsa	1965-66	7.4
David Williams, Illinois	1983-85	7.4

YARDS GAINED

	Years	Yds
Aaron Turner, Pacific	1989-92	4345
Terance Mathis, New Mexico	1985-87,89	4254
Marc Zeno, Tulane	1984-87	3725
Ron Sellers, Florida St	1966-68	3598
Elmo Wright, Houston	1968-70	3347

TOUCHDOWN CATCHES

	Years	TD
Aaron Turner, Pacific	1989-92	43
Clarkston Hines, Duke	1986-89	38
Terance Mathis, New Mexico	1985-87,89	36
Elmo Wright, Houston	1968-70	34
Howard Twilley, Tulsa	1963-65	32

Career (Cont.)

All-Purpose Running

YARDS GAINED

	Years	Yds
Napoleon McCallum, Navy	1981-85	7172
Darrin Nelson, Stanford	1977-78,80-81	6885
Terance Mathis, New Mexico	1985-87,89	6691
Tony Dorsett, Pittsburgh	1973-76	6615
Paul Palmer, Temple	1983-86	6609

YARDS PER GAME

	Years	Yds/Game
Ryan Benjamin, Pacific,	1990-92	237.8
Sheldon Canley, San Jose St	1988-90	205.8
Howard Stevens, Louisville	1971-72	193.7
O. J. Simpson, Southern Cal	1967-68	192.9
Ed Marinaro, Cornell	1969-71	183.0

Safety Patrol

All of Charleston, S.C., is hailing the heroism of Daniel Johnson, a strong safety on The Citadel football team, who in one 48-hour span in February:
• saved the life of a Citadel teammate whose throat was slashed with a broken bottle when two strangers attacked them in the street. The friend's carotid artery was cut, and as the attackers fled, Johnson stuck his fingers into the wound to stanch the bleeding;
• ran down a purse snatcher, turned the suspect over to the police and comforted the victim. Johnson even gave fair warning to the hapless thief, calling out during the chase, "I'm all-conference in track. I'm going to catch you."

Interceptions

PLAYER/SCHOOL	Years	Int
Al Brosky, Illinois	1950-52	29
John Provost, Holy Cross	1972-74	27
Martin Bayless, Bowling Green	1980-83	27
Tom Curtis, Michigan	1967-69	25
Tony Thurman, Boston Col.	1981-84	25
Tracy Saul, Texas Tech	1989-92	25

Punting Average

PLAYER/SCHOOL	Years	Avg
Reggie Roby, Iowa	1979-82	45.6
Greg Montgomery, Michigan St	1985-87	45.4
Tom Tupa, Ohio St	1984-87	45.2
Barry Helton, Colorado	1984-87	44.9
Ray Guy, Southern Miss.	1970-72	44.7

Note: At least 150 punts kicked.

Punt Return Average

PLAYER/SCHOOL	Years	Avg
Jack Mitchell, Oklahoma	1946-48	23.6
Gene Gibson, Cincinnati	1949-50	20.5
Eddie Macon, Pacific	1949-51	18.9
Jackie Robinson, UCLA	1939-40	18.8
Mike Fuller, Auburn	1972-74	17.7
Bobby Dillon, Texas	1949-51	17.7

Note: At least 1.2 punt returns per game.

Kickoff Return Average

PLAYER/SCHOOL	Years	Avg
Forrest Hall, San Francisco	1946-47	36.2
Anthony Davis, Southern Cal	1972-74	35.1
Overton Curtis, Utah St	1957-58	31.0
Fred Montgomery, New Mexico St	1991-92	30.5
Altie Taylor, Utah St	1966-68	29.3
Stan Brown, Purdue	1968-70	28.8

Note: At least 1.2 kickoff returns per game.

Single Season

Scoring

POINTS

	Year	Pts
Barry Sanders, Oklahoma St	1988	234
Mike Rozier, Nebraska	1983	174
Lydell Mitchell, Penn St	1971	174
Art Luppino, Arizona	1954	166
Bobby Reynolds, Nebraska	1950	157

FIELD GOALS

	Year	FG
John Lee, UCLA	1984	29
Paul Woodside, W Virginia	1982	28
Luis Zendejas, Arizona St	1983	28
Fuad Reveiz, Tennessee	1982	27

Note: Three tied with 25 each.

All-Purpose Running

YARDS GAINED

	Year	Yds
Barry Sanders, Oklahoma St	1988	3250
Ryan Benjamin, Pacific	1991	2995
Mike Pringle, Fullerton St	1989	2690
Paul Palmer, Temple	1986	2633
Ryan Benjamin, Pacific	1992	2597
Marcus Allen, Southern Cal	1981	2559

YARDS PER GAME

	Years	Yds/Game
Barry Sanders, Oklahoma St	1988	295.5
Ryan Benjamin, Pacific	1991	249.6
Byron (Whizzer) White, Colorado	1937	246.3
Mike Pringle, Fullerton St	1989	244.6
Paul Palmer, Temple	1986	239.4
Ryan Benjamin, Pacific	1992	236.1

Total Offense

YARDS GAINED

	Year	Yds
David Klingler, Houston	1990	5221
Ty Detmer, Brigham Young	1990	5022
Andre Ware, Houston	1989	4661
Jim McMahon, Brigham Young	1980	4627
Ty Detmer, Brigham Young	1989	4433

YARDS PER GAME

	Year	Yds/Game
David Klingler, Houston	1990	474.6
Andre Ware, Houston	1989	423.7
Ty Detmer, Brigham Young	1990	418.5
Steve Young, Brigham Young	1983	395.1
Scott Mitchell, Utah	1988	390.8

Rushing

YARDS GAINED

	Year	Yds
Barry Sanders, Oklahoma St	1988	2628
Marcus Allen, Southern Cal	1981	2342
Mike Rozier, Nebraska	1983	2148
Tony Dorsett, Pittsburgh	1976	1948
Lorenzo White, Michigan St	1985	1908

YARDS PER GAME

	Year	Yds/Game
Barry Sanders, Oklahoma St	1988	238.9
Marcus Allen, Southern Cal	1981	212.9
Ed Marinaro, Cornell	1971	209.0
Charles White, Southern Cal	1979	180.3
Mike Rozier, Nebraska	1983	179.0

TOUCHDOWNS RUSHING

	Year	TD
Barry Sanders, Oklahoma St	1988	37
Mike Rozier, Nebraska	1983	29
Ed Marinaro, Cornell	1971	24
Anthony Thompson, Indiana	1988	24
Anthony Thompson, Indiana	1989	24

Receiving

CATCHES

	Year	GP	No.
Emmanuel Hazard, Houston	1989	11	142
Howard Twilley, Tulsa	1965	10	134
Jason Phillips, Houston	1988	11	108
Fred Gilbert, Houston	1991	11	106
Sherman Smith, Houston	1992	11	103

CATCHES PER GAME

	Year	No.	No./Game
Howard Twilley, Tulsa	1965	134	13.4
Emmanuel Hazard, Houston	1989	142	12.9
Jason Phillips, Houston	1988	108	9.8
Fred Gilbert, Houston	1991	106	9.6
Jerry Hendren, Idaho	1969	95	9.5
Howard Twilley, Tulsa	1964	95	9.5

Passing

PASSING EFFICIENCY

	Year	Rating
Jim McMahon, Brigham Young	1980	176.9
Ty Detmer, Brigham Young	1989	175.6
Jerry Rhome, Tulsa	1964	172.6
Steve Young, Brigham Young	1983	168.5
Vinny Testaverde, Miami (FL)	1986	165.8
Brian Dowling, Yale	1968	165.8

YARDS GAINED

	Year	Yds
Ty Detmer, Brigham Young	1990	5188
David Klingler, Houston	1990	5140
Andre Ware, Houston	1989	4699
Jim McMahon, Brigham Young	1980	4571
Ty Detmer, Brigham Young	1989	4560

COMPLETIONS

	Year	Att	Comp
David Klingler, Houston	1990	643	374
Andre Ware, Houston	1989	578	365
Ty Detmer, Brigham Young	1990	562	361
Robbie Bosco, Brigham Young	1985	511	338
Scott Mitchell, Utah	1988	533	323

Note: Minimum 15 attempts per game.

TOUCHDOWNS PASSING

	Year	TD
David Klingler, Houston	1990	54
Jim McMahon, Brigham Young	1980	47
Andre Ware, Houston	1989	46
Ty Detmer, Brigham Young	1990	41
Dennis Shaw, San Diego St	1969	39

YARDS GAINED

	Year	Yds
Howard Twilley, Tulsa	1965	1779
Emmanuel Hazard, Houston	1989	1689
Chuck Hughes, UTEP*	1965	1519
Henry Ellard, Fresno St	1982	1510

*UTEP was Texas Western in 1965.

TOUCHDOWN CATCHES

	Year	TD
Emmanuel Hazard, Houston	1989	22
Desmond Howard, Michigan	1991	19
Tom Reynolds, San Diego St	1969	18
Dennis Smith, Utah	1989	18
Aaron Turner, Pacific	1991	18

Single Game

Scoring

POINTS

	Opponent	Year	Pts
Howard Griffith, Illinois	Southern Illinois	1990	48
Jim Brown, Syracuse	Colgate	1956	43
Showboat Boykin, Mississippi	Mississippi St	1951	42
Fred Wendt, UTEP*	New Mexico St	1948	42
Marshall Faulk, San Diego St.	Pacific	1991	42
Dick Bass, Pacific	San Diego St	1958	38

*UTEP was Texas Mines in 1948.

FIELD GOALS

	Opponent	Year	FG
Dale Klein, Nebraska	Missouri	1985	7
Mike Prindle, Western Michigan	Marshall	1984	7

Note: Klein's distances were 32-22-43-44-29-43-43. Prindle's distances were 32-44-42-23-48-41-27.

Single Game (Cont.)

Total Offense

YARDS GAINED	Opponent	Year	Yds
David Klingler, Houston ...Arizona St		1990	732
Matt Vogler,			
Texas Christian ....Houston		1990	696
David Klingler, Houston ...Texas Christian		1990	625
Scott Mitchell, Utah..........Air Force		1988	625
Jimmy Klingler, Houston ..Rice		1992	612

Passing

YARDS GAINED	Opponent	Year	Yds
David Klingler, Houston ...Arizona St		1990	716
Matt Vogler,			
Texas Christian ....Houston		1990	690
Scott Mitchell, Utah..........Air Force		1988	631
Jeremy Leach,			
New Mexico ....Utah		1989	622
Dave Wilson, Illinois ....Ohio St		1980	621

COMPLETIONS	Opponent	Year	Comp
David Klingler, Houston ....Southern		1990	48
	Methodist		
Jimmy Klingler, Houston ....Rice		1992	46
Sandy Schwab,			
Northwestern............................Michigan		1982	45
Chuck Hartlieb, Iowa ....Indiana		1988	44
Jim McMahon,	Colorado		
Brigham Young ....St		1981	44

TOUCHDOWNS PASSING	Opponent	Year	TD
David Klingler, Houston...........E. Wash		1990	11

Note: Klingler's TD passes were 5-48-29-7-3-7-40-10-7-8-51.

Rushing

YARDS GAINED	Opponent	Year	Yds
Tony Sands, Kansas.........Missouri		1991	396
Marshall Faulk,			
San Diego St.....................Pacific		1991	386
Anthony Thompson,			
Indiana..............................Wisconsin		1989	377
Rueben Mayes,			
Washington St ....Oregon		1984	357
Mike Pringle,			
California St-Fullerton ....New Mexico St		1989	357

TOUCHDOWNS RUSHING	Opponent	Year	TD
Howard Griffith, Illinois .....Southern Illinois		1990	8

Note: Griffith's TD runs were 5-51-7-41-5-18-5-3.

Receiving

CATCHES	Opponent	Year	No.
Jay Miller, Brigham Young ..New Mexico		1973	22
Rick Eber, Tulsa..................Idaho St		1967	20
Howard Twilley, Tulsa ....Colorado St		1965	19
Ron Fair, Arizona St ....Washington St		1989	19
Emmanuel Hazard,			
Houston..............................Texas Christian		1989	19
Emmanuel Hazard,			
Houston..............................Texas		1989	19

YARDS GAINED	Opponent	Year	Yds
Chuck Hughes, UTEP* ....N Texas St		1965	349
Rick Eber, Tulsa ....Idaho St		1967	322
Harry Wood, Tulsa...................Idaho St		1967	318
Jeff Evans, New Mexico St......Southern		1978	316
	Illinois		
Tom Reynolds, San Diego St ..Utah St		1971	290

*UTEP was Texas Western in 1965.

TOUCHDOWN CATCHES	Opponent	Year	TD
Tim Delaney, San Diego St ...New Mexico St		1969	6

Note: Delaney's TD catches were 2-22-34-31-30-9.

Longest Plays (since 1941)

RUSHING	Opponent	Year	Yds
Gale Sayers, Kansas ....Nebraska		1963	99
Max Anderson, Arizona St......Wyoming		1967	99
Ralph Thompson,			
W Texas St.............................Wichita St		1970	99
Kelsey Finch, Tennessee ....Florida		1977	99

PASSING	Opponent	Year	Yds
Fred Owens to Jack Ford,			
Portland ....St Mary's (CA)		1947	99
Bo Burris to Warren			
McVea, Houston ....Washington St		1966	99
Colin Clapton to Eddie			
Jenkins, Holy Cross ....Boston U		1970	99
Terry Peel to Robert Ford,			
Houston ....Syracuse		1970	99
Terry Peel to Robert Ford,			
Houston ....San Diego St		1972	99
Cris Collinsworth to Derrick			
Gaffney, Florida ....Rice		1977	99
Scott Ankrom to James			
Maness, Texas Christian .....Rice		1984	99

FIELD GOALS	Opponent	Year	Yds
Steve Little, Arkansas ....Texas		1977	67
Russell Erxleben, Texas ....Rice		1977	67
Joe Williams, Wichita St.....Southern Illinois		1978	67
Tony Franklin, Texas A&M.Baylor		1976	65
Russell Erxleben, Texas ....Oklahoma		1977	64
Tony Franklin, Texas A&M.Baylor		1976	64

PUNTS	Opponent	Year	Yds
Pat Brady, Nevada* ....Loyola (CA)		1950	99
George O'Brien, Wisconsin....Iowa		1952	96

*Note: Nevada was Nevada-Reno in 1950.

DIVISION I-A WINNINGEST TEAMS

All-Time Winning Percentage

	Yrs	W	L	T	Pct	GP	Bowl Record
Notre Dame	104	712	210	41	.761	963	12-6-0
Michigan	113	731	238	36	.743	1006	11-13-0
Alabama	97	682	236	43	.734	959	25-17-3
Oklahoma	98	650	237	52	.719	939	19-10-1
Texas	100	682	268	31	.711	981	16-16-2
Southern Cal	100	622	249	52	.702	923	22-13-0
Ohio St	103	649	264	52	.699	965	11-14-0
Penn St	106	664	289	41	.689	994	17-10-2
Nebraska	103	662	285	40	.687	991	14-17-0
Tennessee	96	627	274	52	.684	953	18-15-0
Central Michigan	92	475	249	36	.649	760	3-1-0
Washington	103	555	306	49	.637	910	12-8-1
Miami (OH)	104	542	301	42	.636	885	5-2-0
Army	103	581	323	50	.635	954	2-1-0
Georgia	99	584	327	53	.633	964	15-13-3
Louisiana St	99	568	319	46	.633	933	11-16-1
Florida St	46	304	175	16	.632	494	13-7-2
Arizona St	80	436	252	24	.629	712	9-5-1
Auburn	100	547	335	46	.614	928	12-9-2
Michigan St	96	515	322	43	.610	880	5-5-0
Minnesota	109	551	352	43	.605	946	2-3-0
Arkansas	99	545	356	39	.601	940	9-15-3
UCLA	74	429	276	37	.603	742	10-7-1
Pittsburgh	103	563	375	42	.596	980	8-10-0

Note: Includes bowl games.

All-Time Victories

Michigan	731	Georgia	584	Auburn	547
Notre Dame	712	Army	581	Arkansas	545
Texas	682	Syracuse	576	W Virginia	546
Alabama	682	Louisiana St	568	Miami (OH)	542
Penn State	664	Pittsburgh	563	N Carolina St	540
Nebraska	662	Washington	555	Texas A&M	538
Oklahoma	650	Minnesota	551	Rutgers	526
Ohio St	649	Colorado	549	California	520
Tennessee	627	Georgia Tech	549	Clemson	517
Southern Cal	622	Navy	543	Michigan St	515

NUMBER ONE VS NUMBER TWO

The number 1 and number 2 teams, according to the Associated Press Poll, have met 27 times, including 9 bowl games, since the poll's inception in 1936. The number 1 teams have a 16-9-2 record in these matchups. Notre Dame (3-3-2) has played in 8 of the games.

Date	Results	Stadium
10-9-43	No. 1 Notre Dame 35, No. 2 Michigan 12	Michigan (Ann Arbor)
11-20-43	No. 1 Notre Dame 14, No. 2 Iowa Pre-Flight 13	Notre Dame (South Bend)
12-2-44	No. 1 Army 23, No. 2 Navy 7	Municipal (Baltimore)
11-10-45	No. 1 Army 48, No. 2 Notre Dame 0	Yankee (New York)
12-1-45	No. 1 Army 32, No. 2 Navy 13	Municipal (Philadelphia)
11-9-46	No. 1 Army 0, No. 2 Notre Dame 0	Yankee (New York)
1-1-63	No. 1 Southern Cal 42, No. 2 Wisconsin 37 (Rose Bowl)	Rose Bowl (Pasadena)
10-12-63	No. 2 Texas 28, No. 1 Oklahoma 7	Cotton Bowl (Dallas)
1-1-64	No. 1 Texas 28, No. 2 Navy 6 (Cotton Bowl)	Cotton Bowl (Dallas)
11-19-66	No. 1 Notre Dame 10, No. 2 Michigan St 10	Spartan (East Lansing)
9-28-68	No. 1 Purdue 37, No. 2 Notre Dame 22	Notre Dame (South Bend)
1-1-69	No. 1 Ohio St 27, No. 2 Southern Cal 16 (Rose Bowl)	Rose Bowl (Pasadena)
12-6-69	No. 1 Texas 15, No. 2 Arkansas 14	Razorback (Fayetteville)
11-25-71	No. 1 Nebraska 35, No. 2 Oklahoma 31	Owen Field (Norman)
1-1-72	No. 1 Nebraska 38, No. 2 Alabama 6 (Orange Bowl)	Orange Bowl (Miami)

NUMBER ONE VS NUMBER TWO *(Cont.)*

Date	Results	Stadium
1-1-79	No. 2 Alabama 14, No. 1 Penn St 7 (Sugar Bowl)	Sugar Bowl (New Orleans)
9-26-81	No. 1 Southern Cal 28, No. 2 Oklahoma 24	Coliseum (Los Angeles)
1-1-83	No. 2 Penn St 27, No. 1 Georgia 23 (Sugar Bowl)	Sugar Bowl (New Orleans)
10-19-85	No. 1 Iowa 12, No. 2 Michigan 10	Kinnick (Iowa City)
9-27-86	No. 2 Miami (FL) 28, No. 1 Oklahoma 16	Orange Bowl (Miami)
1-2-87	No. 2 Penn St 14, No. 1 Miami (FL) 10 (Fiesta Bowl)	Fiesta Bowl (Tempe)
11-21-87	No. 2 Oklahoma 17, No. 1 Nebraska 7	Memorial (Lincoln)
1-1-88	No. 2 Miami (FL) 20, No. 1 Oklahoma 14 (Orange Bowl)	Orange Bowl (Miami)
11-26-88	No. 1 Notre Dame 27, No. 2 Southern Cal 10	Coliseum (Los Angeles)
9-16-89	No. 1 Notre Dame 24, No. 2 Michigan 19	Michigan (Ann Arbor)
11-16-91	No. 2 Miami 17, No. 1 Florida St 16	Campbell (Tallahassee)
1-1-93	No. 2 Alabama 34, No. 1 Miami 13	Superdome (New Orleans)

Longest Winning Streaks

Wins	Team	Yrs	Ended by	Score
47	Oklahoma	1953-57	Notre Dame	7-0
39	Washington	1908-14	Oregon St	0-0
37	Yale	1890-93	Princeton	6-0
37	Yale	1887-89	Princeton	10-0
35	Toledo	1969-71	Tampa	21-0
34	Pennsylvania	1894-96	Lafayette	6-4
31	Oklahoma	1948-50	Kentucky	13-7
31	Pittsburgh	1914-18	Cleveland Naval Reserve	10-9
31	Pennsylvania	1896-98	Harvard	10-0
30	Texas	1968-70	Notre Dame	24-11
29	Michigan	1901-03	Minnesota	6-6
29	Miami (FL)	1990-92	Alabama	34-13
28	Alabama	1978-80	Mississippi St	6-3
28	Oklahoma	1973-75	Kansas	23-3
28	Michigan St	1950-53	Purdue	6-0

Longest Unbeaten Streaks

No.	W	T	Team	Yrs	Ended by	Score
63	59	4	Washington	1907-17	California	27-0
56	55	1	Michigan	1901-05	Chicago	2-0
50	46	4	California	1920-25	Olympic Club	15-0
48	47	1	Oklahoma	1953-57	Notre Dame	7-0
48	47	1	Yale	1885-89	Princeton	10-0
47	42	5	Yale	1879-85	Princeton	6-5
44	42	2	Yale	1894-96	Princeton	24-6
42	39	3	Yale	1904-08	Harvard	4-0
39	37	2	Notre Dame	1946-50	Purdue	28-14
37	36	1	Oklahoma	1972-75	Kansas	23-3
35	34	1	Minnesota	1903-05	Wisconsin	16-12
34	33	1	Nebraska	1912-16	Kansas	7-3
34	32	2	Princeton	1884-87	Harvard	12-0
34	29	5	Princeton	1877-82	Harvard	1-0
33	30	3	Tennessee	1926-30	Alabama	18-6
33	31	2	Georgia Tech	1914-18	Pittsburgh	32-0
33	30	3	Harvard	1911-15	Cornell	10-0
32	31	1	Nebraska	1969-71	UCLA	20-17
32	30	2	Army	1944-47	Columbia	21-20
32	31	1	Harvard	1898-1900	Yale	28-0
31	30	1	Penn St	1967-70	Colorado	41-13
31	30	1	San Diego St	1967-70	Long Beach St	27-11
31	29	2	Georgia Tech	1950-53	Notre Dame	27-14
30	25	5	Penn St	1919-22	Navy	14-0
30	28	2	Pennsylvania	1903-06	Swarthmore	4-0
28	26	2	Southern Cal	1978-80	Washington	20-10
28	26	2	Army	1947-50	Navy	14-2
28	24	4	Minnesota	1933-36	Northwestern	6-0
28	26	2	Tennessee	1930-33	Duke	10-2
27	26	1	Southern Cal	1931-33	Stanford	13-7
27	24	3	Notre Dame	1910-14	Yale	28-0

Note: Includes bowl games.

Longest Losing Streaks

L		Seasons	Ended Against	Score
44	Columbia	1983-88	Princeton	16-14
34	Northwestern	1979-82	Northern Illinois	31-6
28	Virginia	1958-61	William & Mary	21-6
28	Kansas St	1945-48	Arkansas St	37-6
27	Eastern Michigan	1980-82	Kent St	9-7

Longest Series

GP	Opponents (Series Leader Listed First)	Record	First Game	GP	Opponents (Series Leader Listed First)	Record	First Game
102	Minnesota-Wisconsin	55-39-8	1890	95	Stanford-California	47-37-11	1892
101	Missouri-Kansas	48-44-9	1891	93	Navy-Army	44-42-7	1890
99	Nebraska-Kansas	75-21-3	1892	91	Auburn-Georgia Tech	47-39-4	1892
99	Texas Christian-Baylor	46-46-7	1899	92	Penn St-Pittsburgh	47-41-4	1893
99	Texas-Texas A&M	64-30-5	1894	90	Louisiana St-Tulane*	61-22-7	1893
97	N Carolina-Virginia	54-39-4	1892	90	Clemson-S Carolina	53-33-4	1896
97	Miami (OH)-Cincinnati	53-38-6	1888	90	Kansas-Kansas St	61-24-5	1902
96	Auburn-Georgia	45-44-7	1892	90	Oklahoma-Kansas	60-24-6	1903
96	Oregon-Oregon St	47-39-10	1894	90	Utah-Utah St	59-27-4	1892
95	Purdue-Indiana	58-31-6	1891				

*Disputed series record. Tulane claims 23-59-7 record.

ALL-TIME WINNINGEST DIVISION I-A COACHES

By Percentage

Coach (Alma mater)	Colleges Coached	Yrs	W	L	T	Pct
Knute Rockne (Notre Dame '14)†	Notre Dame 1918-30	13	105	12	5	.881
Frank W. Leahy (Notre Dame '31)†	Boston Col 1939-40; Notre Dame 1941-43, 1946-53	13	107	13	9	.864
George W. Woodruff (Yale '89)†	Pennsylvania 1892-01; Illinois 1903; Carlisle 1905	12	142	25	2	.846
Barry Switzer (Arkansas '60)	Oklahoma 1973-88	16	157	29	4	.837
Percy D. Haughton (Harvard '99)†	Cornell 1899-1900; Harvard 1908-16; Columbia 1923-24	13	96	17	6	.832
Bob Neyland (Army '16)†	Tennessee 1926-34, 1936-40, 1946-52	21	173	31	12	.829
Fielding "Hurry Up" Yost (Lafayette '97)†	Ohio Wesleyan 1897; Nebraska 1898; Kansas 1899; Stanford 1900; Michigan 1901-23, 1925-26	29	196	36	12	.828
Bud Wilkinson (Minnesota '37)†	Oklahoma 1947-63	17	145	29	4	.826
Jock Sutherland (Pittsburgh '18)†	Lafayette 1919-23; Pittsburgh 1924-38	20	144	28	14	.812
Bob Devaney (Alma, MI '39)†	Wyoming 1957-61; Nebraska 1962-72	16	136	30	7	.806
Tom Osborne (Hastings '59)*	Nebraska 1973-present	20	195	46	3	.805
Frank W. Thomas (Notre Dame '23)†	Chattanooga 1925-28; Alabama 1931-42, 1944-46	19	141	33	9	.795
Henry L. Williams (Yale '91)†	Army 1891; Minnesota 1900-21	23	141	34	12	.786
Joe Paterno (Brown '50)*	Penn St 1966-present	27	247	67	3	.784
Gil Dobie (Minnesota '02)†	N Dakota St 1906-07; Washington 1908-16; Navy 1917-19; Cornell 1920-35; Boston Col 1936-38	33	180	45	15	.781
Paul W. "Bear" Bryant (Alabama '36)†	Maryland 1945; Kentucky 1946-53; Texas A&M 1954-57; Alabama 1958-82	38	323	85	17	.780

*Active coach. †Hall of Fame member.
Note: Minimum 10 years as head coach at Division I institutions; record at 4-year colleges only; bowl games included; ties computed as half won, half lost.

Top Winners by Victories

	Yrs	W	L	T	Pct		Yrs	W	L	T	Pct
Paul "Bear" Bryant	38	323	85	17	.780	Warren Woodson	31	203	95	14	.673
Amos Alonzo Stagg	57	314	199	35	.605	Vince Dooley	25	201	77	10	.715
Glenn "Pop" Warner	44	313	106	32	.729	Eddie Anderson	39	201	128	15	.606
Joe Paterno	27	247	67	3	.784	Dana Bible	33	198	72	23	.715
Woody Hayes	33	238	72	10	.759	Dan McGugin	30	197	55	19	.762
Bo Schembechler	27	234	65	8	.775	Fielding Yost	29	196	36	12	.828
Bobby Bowden	27	227	77	3	.744	Howard Jones	29	194	64	21	.733
Jess Neely	40	207	176	19	.539	John Vaught	25	190	61	12	.745

Most Bowl Victories

	W	L	T		W	L	T
Paul "Bear" Bryant	15	12	2	Darrell Royal	8	7	1
*Joe Paterno	14	8	1	*Tom Osborne	8	12	0
*Bobby Bowden	12	3	1	Vince Dooley	8	10	2
John Vaught	10	8	0	*Terry Donahue	8	2	1
*Don James	10	5	0	Bob Devaney	7	3	0
*Johnny Majors	9	7	0	Dan Devine	7	3	0
Bobby Dodd	9	4	0	*Lou Holtz	9	6	2
Barry Switzer	8	5	0	Charlie McClendon	7	6	0

*Active coach.

WINNINGEST ACTIVE COACHES
By Percentage

Coach	College Years	W	L	T	Pct*	Bowls		
						W	L	T
John Robinson, Southern Cal	7	67	14	2	.819	4	1	0
Tom Osborne, Nebraska	20	195	46	3	.805	8	12	0
Joe Paterno, Penn St	26	247	67	3	.784	14	8	1
Danny Ford, Arkansas	12	96	29	4	.760	6	2	0
Bobby Bowden, Florida St	27	227	77	3	.744	12	3	1
LaVell Edwards, Brigham Young	21	191	67	3	.738	5	11	1
Dennis Erickson, Miami (FL)	11	94	35	1	.727	4	1	0
Dick Sheridan, North Carolina State	15	121	52	5	.694	5	7	0
Steve Spurrier, Florida	6	48	21	1	.693	1	2	0
Don James, Washington	22	176	78	3	.691	10	5	0

*Ties computed as half win, half loss. Bowl games included.
Note: Minimum 5 years as Division I-A head coach; record at 4-year colleges only.

Relatively Speaking

Every football season, colleges send us hundreds of slick publicity packets touting players. This year, however, two homemade packets caught our eye. One was from the mother of Penn's aptly named running back, Sundiata Rush. The other was from an aunt of Louisiana Tech offensive lineman Willy Roaf. Could this be a trend? We'll see next season.

In the meantime: "Sundi's strength is his perseverence," writes his mom, Brenda Brooks. "He is a good motivator, has good work habits, a clean character and is well liked by his teammates."

The Roaf recommendation, as penned by his aunt Mary Layton, leans heavily on his career in Pee-Wee football and on the fact that he was a choirboy at Grace Episcopal Church in Pine Bluff, Arkansas. "Willy is a big good-natured guy with the proverbial heart of gold who has never met a person he didn't like." Roaf, who is indeed big— 6' 5" and 295 pounds—will likely be a first-round pick in next year's NFL draft. When he was 13, he served as a page in the Arkansas legislature and met one person he particularly liked, the state's kid governor, another comer, named Bill Clinton.

By Victories

Coach	Won	Coach	Won
Joe Paterno, Penn St	247	Don James, Washington	176
Bobby Bowden, Florida St	227	Grant Teaff, Baylor	170
Hayden Fry, Iowa	194	Bill Dooley, Wake Forest	161
Tom Osborne, Nebraska	195	Earle Bruce, Colorado St	154
LaVell Edwards, Brigham Young	191	Pat Dye, Auburn	153
Lou Holtz, Notre Dame	182	Jim Wacker, Minnesota	146
Jim Sweeney, Fresno St	178	Bill Mallory, Indiana	147
Johnny Majors, Tennessee	176		

WINNINGEST ACTIVE DIVISION I-AA COACHES
By Percentage

Coach, College	Yrs	W	L	T	Pct*
Roy Kidd, Eastern Kentucky	29	239	84	8	.734
Eddie Robinson, Grambling	50	381	136	15	.730
Tubby Raymond, Delaware	27	223	88	2	.716
Jimmy Satterfield, Furman	7	61	24	2	.713
Houston Markham, Alabama St	6	44	19	3	.674
Andy Talley, Villanova	13	84	42	2	.675
Bill Davis, Tennessee St	14	100	51	1	.662
Bill Hayes, N Carolina A&T	17	123	63	2	.660
William Collick, Delaware St	8	56	29	0	.659
James Donnelly, Middle Tennessee St	16	119	64	1	.649

*Ties computed as half win, half loss. Playoff games included.
Note: Minimum 5 years as a Division I-A and/or Division I-AA head coach; record at 4-year colleges only.

By Victories

	Won		Won
Eddie Robinson, Grambling	381	Bill Bowes, New Hampshire	136
Roy Kidd, Eastern Kentucky	239	Willie Jeffries, S Carolina St	124
Tubby Raymond, Delaware	223	Bill Hayes, N Carolina A&T	123
Carmen Cozza, Yale	166	Don Read, Montana	120
Marino Casem, Southern-B.R.	159	James Donnelly, Middle Tennessee St	119
Ron Randleman, Sam Houston St	151	Joe Restic, Harvard	114

WINNINGEST ACTIVE DIVISION II COACHES
By Percentage

Coach, College	Yrs	W	L	T	Pct*
Rocky Hager, N Dakota St	6	59	12	1	.826
Ken Sparks, Carson-Newman	13	119	37	1	.761
Danny Hale, Bloomsburg	5	40	13	0	.755
Bob Cortese, Fort Hays St	13	106	34	3	.752
Bill Burgess, Jacksonville St	8	69	22	4	.747
Dick Lowry, Hillsdale	19	145	59	2	.709
Mark Whipple, New Haven	5	37	16	0	.698
Gene Carpenter, Millersville	24	159	69	5	.693
Tom Hollman, Edinboro	9	61	27	3	.687
Joe Taylor, Hampton	10	70	31	4	.686

*Ties computed as half win, half loss. Playoff games included.

Note: Minimum 5 years as a college head coach; record at 4-year colleges only.

By Victories

	Won		Won
Jim Malosky, MN-Duluth	223	Dick Lowry, Hillsdale	145
Fred Martinelli, Ashland	208	Douglas Porter, Fort Valley St	135
Gene Carpenter, Millersville	159	Bud Elliott, NW Missouri St	134
Ron Harms, Texas A&I	156	Claire Boroff, Kearney St	129
Ross Fortier, Moorhead St	152	Ken Sparks, Carson-Newman	119

NCAA Coaches' Records (Cont.)

WINNINGEST ACTIVE DIVISION III COACHES
By Percentage

Coach, College	Yrs	W	L	T	Pct*
Bob Reade, Augustana (IL).................................14		131	19	1	.871
Dick Farley, Williams......................................6		38	8	2	.813
Larry Kehres, Mount Union...............................7		60	13	3	.809
Ron Schipper, Central (IA)..............................32		252	61	3	.802
Lou Desloges, Plymouth St..............................7		55	14	3	.785
John Luckhardt, Washington & Jefferson............11		86	24	2	.777
Jack Siedlecki, Amherst.................................5		36	10	1	.777
Bob Packard, Baldwin-Wallace..........................12		93	27	2	.770
Roger Harring, WI-La Crosse.............................24		199	59	7	.764
Bill Manlove, Delaware Valley............................24		185	60	1	.754

*Ties computed as half win, half loss. Playoff games included.

Note: Minimum 5 years as a college head coach; record at 4-year colleges only.

By Victories (Minimum of 100)

John Gagliardi, St John's (MN)............................294		Jim Christopherson, Concordia-Moorhead...........169
Ron Schipper, Central (IA)......................................252		Frank Girardi, Lycoming...150
Jim Butterfield, Ithaca...200		Don Miller, Trinity (Conn).....................................140
Roger Harring, WI-LaCrosse.................................199		Joe McDaniel, Centre...138
Bill Manlove, Delaware Valley 185		Ray Smith, Hope 138

NAIA Coaches' Records

WINNINGEST ACTIVE NAIA COACHES
By Percentage

Coach, College	Yrs	W	L	T	Pct*
Charlie Richard, Baker (KS).........................12		107	22	1	.827
Ted Kessinger, Bethany................................17		138	31	1	.815
†Billy Joe, Central St (OH)...........................19		161	51	3	.759
Frosty Westering, Pacific Lutheran..............26		213	71	5	.746
Hank Biesiot, Dickinson St (ND)..................17		103	37	1	.734
Larry Korver, Northwestern (IA)....................26		197	70	6	.733
Max Bowman, Greenville (IL)........................6		36	13	1	.730
Jim Svoboda, Nebraska Wesleyan 6		44	17	0	.721
Dick Strahm, Findlay (OH)...........................18		127	50	3	.714
†Jim Malosky, Minnesota-Duluth.................35		216	113	10	.667

*Ties computed as half win, half loss. Playoff games included.

†Denotes Division I coach.

Note: Minimum five years as a collegiate head coach and includes record against four-year institutions only.

Victories

†Jim Malosky, MN-Duluth 216		Ted Kessinger, Bethany (KS)................................138
Frosty Westering, Pacific Lutheran (WA) 213		Dick Strahm, Findlay (OH) 127
Larry Korver, Northwestern (IA) 197		Rollie Greeno, Jamestown (ND).............................125
†Billy Joe, Central St (OH).....................................161		Bob Petrino, Carroll (MT).......................................124
Buddy Benson, Ouachita Baptist (AR)...................152		Bill Ramseyer, Clinch Valley (VA)...........................119

†Denotes Division I coach.

Pro Basketball

Thrilling Three-peat

A season of hearty hellos and fond farewells ended with the Bulls winning their third straight | by JACK McCALLUM

WHILE MICHAEL, MAGIC, Charles and Co. were alternately charming and terrorizing the world in Barcelona at the 1992 Summer Olympics, a small group of general managers and coaches were back in America gnawing on their collective fingernails. And with good reason. For months after the triumphant Dream Team returned with the gold medal, the physical and mental strain of competing almost nonstop for a calendar year had taken its toll on several of the players and therefore on their respective teams.

In New York, Patrick Ewing got off to a slow start because of a recurring ankle injury, and it was almost two months before he returned to form. In Utah, Karl Malone admitted that he and fellow Olympian John Stockton were mentally fatigued; though they played reasonably well throughout the regular season, they were unable to lift the Jazz to the status of legitimate contender. In Portland, Clyde Drexler never did recover from a season's worth of knee problems that might

not have recurred if he had rested in the summer. And in Chicago, team chemistry was disrupted when the special practice privileges extended to Olympians Michael Jordan and Scottie Pippen by coach Phil Jackson angered stalwart forward Horace Grant.

Two other Dream Teamers never made it to the starting gate, either, though their summer activities probably had nothing to do with it. Ten days after the final Olympic game, the Celtics' Larry Bird announced his retirement because of recurring back problems. Bird had limped through most of his Olympic minutes, though he showed enough flash to please the fans from time to time. And just a few days days before opening night, Dream Team captain Magic Johnson also retired, citing the distractions of trying to compete as an HIV-positive athlete. One of his Dream Teammates, Malone, had criticized Magic for trying to return, but Johnson said that had nothing to do with his decision. He said he had seen an expression of fear or at least hesitation on the faces of some opponents, and he couldn't compete under those circumstances.

Barkley found his place in the sun, leading Phoenix to its first NBA Finals since 1976.

The loss of Bird and Johnson, a one-two marketing/publicity punch the league had been enjoying since 1979, was a hard shot to the NBA's body, no doubt about that. But it was by no means a knockout punch. There were many reasons for that, but two of the biggest—and baldest—were Charles Barkley in Phoenix and Shaquille O'Neal in Orlando.

Unlike many of his Olympic teammates, Barkley came back from Barcelona excited and energized, plunging as he was into a bright new world in Phoenix. Jump on my back, he told his Sun teammates, and we'll have some fun. And so they did. The volatile Barkley and the laid-back first-year coach Paul Westphal were a perfect blend of leadership. The Suns were not strong defensively, and they lacked size underneath, but they promised a return to the Laker teams of the early '80s, offensive-oriented attackers that outran and outshot the opposition.

"You'll have to outscore us to beat us," said Barkley, "and you're welcome to try."

Super rookie O'Neal demolished backboards and defenses with equal ease.

Meanwhile, in another hot climate, O'Neal was threatening to become another Magic Kingdom all by himself. The Orlando rookie attracted enormous publicity (to match his enormous seven-year, $40 million contract), yet, incredibly, he came out to be better than advertised, becoming the first rookie to earn player of the week honors in the first week of the season. By the third week of the season, 20-point-15-rebound stat lines had become so routine for O'Neal that many observers were downright surprised when he didn't dominate Ewing, a tenacious and talented seven-year veteran, in their first meeting at Madison Square Garden, on Nov. 21. Actually, they just about neutralized each other, although the Knicks won the game 92–77.

In fact, rookies in general were a hot topic throughout the season. Tom Gugliotta drew comparisons to Bird for his inside-outside abilities in Washington. To the vast relief of the Minnesota Timberwolves, Christian Laettner proved not to be the second coming of fellow Dukie Danny Ferry but, rather, a tough, combative power forward who lived up to his status as the third pick overall. And two of the more interesting yearlings were in Phoenix, the very lean Richard Dumas and the very portly Oliver Miller. Miller spent time in a Phoenix hospital to lose weight, while Dumas spent time in mid-air, where he displayed some of the best finishing moves west of Jordan and Pippen.

Ultimately, though, no rookie, not even O'Neal, had the impact on his team that Alonzo Mourning had on the Hornets. Mourning displayed a ferocious competitiveness that drove Charlotte and provided a perfect complement to that mature second-year warrior, power forward Larry Johnson. The Hornets not only won 13 more games than they had in 1991–92 (44 as compared to 31), but, as the Knicks found out in the playoffs, they didn't wilt late in the season like young teams usually do.

The pathetic Dallas Mavericks couldn't sign their rookie, fourth pick Jimmy Jackson, which was a major reason they stumbled and bumbled their way toward the history books. They needed double figures in victories to avoid the NBA's alltime worst record of 9–73 and finally did it late in the season. They finished with 11 wins. Jackson signed his contract on March 4, which was a little like Jascha Heifetz showing up for just the final movement of the symphony.

And it wasn't just the rookie players who grabbed headlines. In San Antonio, rookie NBA coach Jerry Tarkanian lived under the microscope for 20 games before he was fired and replaced by rookie NBA coach John Lucas, an ex-player and recovering substance abuser. The Spurs responded to the change immediately, winning 14 of Lucas's first 16 games and making owner Red McCombs look like a genius.

All the talk about rookies obscured somewhat the sterling comeback play of one veteran, the Hawks' Dominique Wilkins. The 33-year-old Wilkins had missed 40 games the year before with a potentially career-ending achilles tendon injury and then, on

Dec. 15, he broke his right ring finger. But in the 71 games he did play, 'Nique was unique, averaging 29.9 points (second in the league to Jordan) and demonstrating in the process that old slam-dunk champions don't necessarily lose their springs.

And old championship coaches don't necessarily lose their touch, as Pat Riley and Phil Jackson demonstrated in New York and Chicago, respectively. Riley took a lot of heat—some of it from Jackson—for the Knicks' tough and aggressive roadhouse style. But he brought discipline and order (most of the time anyway) and won an Eastern Conference–best 60 games with a team that sometimes couldn't make a perimeter jumper to save its life. For his efforts the master of mousse was voted Coach of the Year.

Jackson, meanwhile, steered what some

Wilkins returned from a career-threatening injury to average nearly 30 points a game.

CARL SKALAK

Olajuwon led the surging Rockets with his sensational play in the pivot.

and Cleveland in four straight to reach the conference final. So devastating was the Bulls' sweep over the Cavs that Cleveland coach Lenny Wilkens resigned. In the NBA's incestuous manner, Wilkens ended up in Atlanta (where Bob Weiss was fired) and former Atlanta coach Mike Fratello (for the last three years a network commentator) ended up in Cleveland.

In the Western Conference, meanwhile, the Suns didn't exactly have a picnic. But Barkley could be spotted laying out the fried chicken and potato salad from time to time. Competitors fell away like drops of dew from a flower. The Trail Blazers suffered not only from too little Drexler (he played only 49 games) but also from too much fallout over a January incident involving four players (veteran Jerome Kersey and rookies Reggie Smith, Dave Johnson and Tracy Murray) and three underage girls during a road trip to Salt Lake City. Each of the players was fined by the club, and Johnson and Murray were also suspended for three games.

The coulda-been-a-contender Golden State Warriors were devastated by injuries to Chris Mullin, Tim Hardaway, Billy Owens and Sarunas Marciulionis, their four best players. Nay, their *only* four players. Collectively that quartet missed an incredible 149 games.

The Spurs certainly turned heads with Lucas's unusual methods, such as occasionally standing apart during timeouts and letting the team members talk things over. However, what they could have been saying to each other was: "Let's face it, guys. Besides David Robinson and Sean Elliott, we just ain't good enough to go all the way."

The Houston Rockets were a pleasant surprise, winning 55 games behind Hakeem Olajuwon, the game's best pivotman (last season anyway), rookie find Robert Horry at small forward, and the blue-collar touch of Rudy Tomjanovich, who lost Coach of the Year honors to Riley by just one vote. But they showed their backcourt deficiencies in

believed was a sinking Chicago ship through treacherous waters. Why treacherous? Well, there was the pressure of trying to become the first team in 27 years to three-peat. There was the fatigue of Jordan and Pippen, the injuries to John Paxson and Bill Cartwright and the continued (albeit restrained) dissatisfaction of Grant. Yet Jackson's Bulls finished the regular season with a 57–25 record, third best behind the Suns and the Knicks.

By the end of the season New York and Chicago were clearly the class of the East, though the Knicks had a tough first-round series with Indiana and an even tougher five-game set with the Hornets. The Bulls, however, bullied Atlanta in three straight

the playoffs and were ousted in the second round by the Seattle SuperSonics.

Ah, the Sonics. General manager Bob Whitsitt made the trade of the year on Feb. 22, when he landed versatile frontcourtman Sam Perkins from the Lakers while unloading two problems, overweight center Benoit Benjamin and unsigned rookie Doug Christie. The acquisition of Perkins augmented an already deep and talented roster and turned the Sonics from a question mark into instant contender. But.... There was always a "but" surrounding the Sonics. Even as most teams were seeking solidity before the playoffs, Seattle coach George Karl was still tinkering with his starting lineup, at times benching perhaps his two best players, Shawn Kemp and Derrick McKey, because he was upset with their inconsistent play.

Still, the Sonics grew strong in the postseason, turning back the Jazz in the first round and the Rockets in the second. To no one's surprise, their opponent in the conference final was the Suns. But what no one expected was the difficult path that Phoenix took to reach the NBA's Final Four.

It was as if all the Suns' weaknesses were just waiting to turn on them in the postseason. The Lakers, whose 39–43 record made them the weakest team to make the playoffs, extended Phoenix to five games in the first round, primarily because they dominated the Suns under the boards and showed more composure in clutch situations. And the Spurs took them to six games in the second round, largely because Phoenix could not come up with key defensive stops when they needed them. But, still, the Suns survived, and that only added to their living-on-the-edge allure.

The Suns played the same way in the conference final against the Sonics. They were sensational; they were horrible. The performance of Barkley, who was named MVP over Olajuwon and Jordan in one of the best races in history, was an accurate barometer. He scored 13 points, for example, in a 118–102 Game 6 loss, yet came back to score 44 in the 123–110 Game 7 vic-

tory that sent Phoenix into its first NBA Final since 1975–76.

Over in the East, meanwhile, the conference final was much more predictable, which is not to say uninteresting. The Knicks won the first two games at Madison Square Garden, largely because they kept Jordan in check. Even in Chicago in Game 3, Jordan made only three of 18 shots from the floor, although the Bulls coasted to a 103–83 victory to cut the Knicks lead to two games to one.

But then Jordan came alive. He scored 54 points in Game 4, and the Bulls needed every one of them in a 105–95 victory. And in Games 5 and 6, he and Pippen proved to be the best one-two punch in the game, controlling the Knicks' backcourt and making big shot after big shot. Jordan had maintained a protracted silence from Game 3 on because he was upset with press reports of a side trip he took to an Atlantic City casino between Games 1 and 2. As usual, though, his play

Vlade Divac and the surprising Lakers slowed the Suns' steady progress toward the Finals.

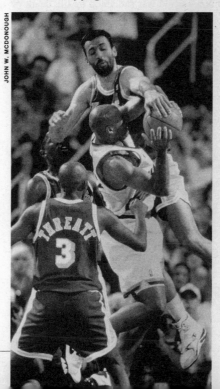

JOHN W. McDONOUGH

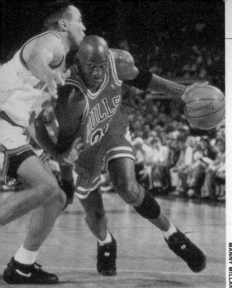

MANNY MILLAN

Jordan drove Chicago past the Knicks and their gritty guard John Starks.

same total as Jordan—it wasn't enough as the poised and mature Bulls triumphed 111–108, thus becoming the first team in NBA history to win Games 1 and 2 on the road. The Suns, it seemed, had clearly set.

Curiously, Phoenix was much more relaxed in Chicago. Perhaps the Suns just needed to get out of the heat. They engaged the Bulls in a fascinating Game 3 thriller during which they grew more confident as the game wore on. And it did nothing if not wear on, the Suns finally pulling out a 129–121 victory in triple overtime.

Jordan, by now back in a talkative mode, took control in Game 4, pouring in 55 points as the Bulls drew to within one win of a three-peat, with a 111–105 win. But, again, the Suns were the more relaxed team in Game 5, when they scored a decisive 108–98 victory to send the series back to Phoenix.

By this point the Bulls looked suspiciously like the Bulls of the late '80s—lots of Jordan and little of everyone else. That fact was borne out when Jordan was the only Bull to score through the first 11 minutes and 56.1 seconds of the final period. But with Chicago trailing 98–96, somebody else stepped up, and it happened to be Jordan's favorite point guard in all the world, Paxson. On an in-bounds play that went from Jordan to Pippen to Grant and out to Paxson behind the three-point line, Jordan's designated jump-shooter let fly with a trey that settled into the basket a split-second before the final buzzer. That gave the Bulls a 99–98 win and established them as only the third team in NBA history (after the Minneapolis Lakers of 1952 through '54 and the Boston Celtics of 1959 through '66) to win three straight titles.

Moreover, it established Jordan, who won his third straight Finals MVP award, as unquestionably the best player of his generation and probably of alltime. On July 19, the Bulls signed Croatian star Toni Kukoc, giving them, on paper at least, even more balance and depth for 1993–94.

Anyone for a four-play?

spoke volumes. The Bulls' margin of victory in the decisive Game 6 in Chicago was a comfortable 96–88, marking them as a clear, if not prohibitive favorite, even though the Suns would have the home court advantage.

Two days before the Finals began, the NBA world was saddened by the death of Net guard Drazen Petrovic in a car accident in Germany. Petrovic had come into his own as a player during the 1992–93 season and was in many ways the standard-bearer for foreign athletes who were trying to find a niche in the NBA. At the time of his death Petrovic's future with the Nets was cloudy because he was dissatisfied with their contract offer and was exploring opportunities in Europe. But two things are certain: he would have been playing somewhere in '92–93, and he would have been playing hard. That's the only way he knew how.

The championship round had many subthemes. Chicago's cool versus Phoenix's heat. The Bulls' defense versus the Suns' offense. Chicago's experience versus the Suns' new-kid-on-the-block cockiness. And, most of all, Michael versus Charles.

The first two games in Phoenix were no contest, however. Barkley came out tentative and visibly nervous in Game 1 as the Bulls won 100–92. And even when Charles responded with 42 points in Game 2—the

FOR THE RECORD·1991-1992

NBA Final Standings

Eastern Conference

ATLANTIC DIVISION					CENTRAL DIVISION				
Team	W	L	Pct	GB	Team	W	L	Pct	GB
New York	60	22	.732	—	Chicago	57	25	.695	—
Boston	48	34	.585	12	Cleveland	54	28	.659	3
New Jersey	43	39	.524	17	Charlotte	44	38	.537	13
Orlando	41	41	.500	19	Atlanta	43	39	.524	14
Miami	36	46	.439	24	Indiana	41	41	.500	16
Philadelphia	26	56	.317	34	Detroit	40	42	.488	17
Washington	22	60	.268	38	Milwaukee	28	54	.341	29

Western Conference

MIDWEST DIVISION					PACIFIC DIVISION				
Team	W	L	Pct	GB	Team	W	L	Pct	GB
Houston	55	27	.671	—	Phoenix	62	20	.756	—
San Antonio	49	33	.598	6	Seattle	55	27	.671	7
Utah	47	35	.573	8	Portland	51	31	.622	11
Denver	36	46	.439	19	LA Clippers	41	41	.500	21
Minnesota	19	63	.232	36	LA Lakers	39	43	.476	23
Dallas	11	71	.134	44	Golden State	34	48	.415	28
					Sacramento	25	57	.305	37

1992 NBA Playoffs

Eastern Conference First Round

Apr 30	Indiana	104	at New York	107
May 2	Indiana	91	at New York	101
May 4	New York	93	at Indiana	116
May 6	New York	109	at Indiana	100*

New York won series 3-1.

Apr 29	Charlotte	101	at Boston	112
May 1	Charlotte	99	at Boston	98†
May 3	Boston	89	at Charlotte	119
May 5	Boston	103	at Charlotte	104

Charlotte won series 3-1.

Apr 30	Atlanta	90	at Chicago	114
May 2	Atlanta	102	at Chicago	117
May 4	Chicago	98	at Atlanta	88

Chicago won series 3-0.

Apr 29	New Jersey	98	at Cleveland	114
May 1	New Jersey	101	at Cleveland	99
May 5	Cleveland	93	at New Jersey	84
May 7	Cleveland	79	at New Jersey	96
May 9	New Jersey	89	at Cleveland	99

Cleveland won series 3-2.

Western Conference First Round

Apr 30	LA Lakers	107	at Phoenix	103
May 2	LA Lakers	86	at Phoenix	81
May 4	Phoenix	107	at LA Lakers	102
May 6	Phoenix	101	at LA Lakers	86
May 9	LA Lakers	104	at Phoenix	112

Phoenix won series 3-2.

Apr 29	San Antonio	87	at Portland	86
May 1	San Antonio	96	at Portland	105
May 5	Portland	101	at San Antonio	107
May 7	Portland	97	at San Antonio	100*

San Antonio won series 3-1.

Apr 30	Utah	85	at Seattle	99
May 2	Utah	89	at Seattle	85
May 4	Seattle	80	at Utah	90
May 6	Seattle	93	at Utah	80
May 8	Utah	100	at Seattle	92

Seattle won series 3-2.

Apr 29	LA Clippers	94	at Houston	117
May 1	LA Clippers	95	at Houston	83
May 3	Houston	111	at LA Clippers	99
May 5	Houston	90	at LA Clippers	93
May 8	LA Clippers	80	at Houston	84

Houston won series 3-2.

Eastern Conference Semifinals

May 9	Charlotte	95	at New York	111
May 12	Charlotte	101	at New York	105*
May 14	New York	106	at Charlotte	110†
May 16	New York	94	at Charlotte	92
May 18	Charlotte	101	at New York	105

New York won series 4-1.

May 11	Cleveland	84	at Chicago	91
May 13	Cleveland	85	at Chicago	104
May 15	Chicago	96	at Cleveland	90
May 17	Chicago	103	at Cleveland	101

Chicago won series 4-0.

Western Conference Semifinals

May 11	San Antonio	89	at Phoenix	98
May 13	San Antonio	103	at Phoenix	109
May 15	Phoenix	96	at San Antonio	111
May 16	Phoenix	103	at San Antonio	117
May 18	San Antonio	97	at Phoenix	109
May 20	Phoenix	102	at San Antonio	100

Phoenix won series 4-2.

May 10	Houston	90	at Seattle	99
May 12	Houston	100	at Seattle	111
May 15	Seattle	79	at Houston	97
May 16	Seattle	92	at Houston	103
May 18	Houston	95	at Seattle	120
May 20	Seattle	90	at Houston	103
May 22	Houston	100	at Seattle	103*

Seattle won series 4-3.

Eastern Conference Finals

May 23	Chicago	90	at New York	98
May 25	Chicago	91	at New York	96
May 29	New York	83	at Chicago	103
May 31	New York	95	at Chicago	105
June 2	Chicago	97	at New York	94
June 4	New York	88	at Chicago	96

Chicago won series 4-2.

*Overtime game.. †Double overtime game.

Western Conference Finals

May 24	Seattle	91	at Phoenix	105
May 26	Seattle	103	at Phoenix	99
May 28	Phoenix	104	at Seattle	97
May 30	Phoenix	101	at Seattle	120
June 1	Seattle	114	at Phoenix	120
June 3	Phoenix	102	at Seattle	118
June 5	Seattle	110	at Phoenix	123

Phoenix won series 4-3.

Finals

June 9	Chicago	100	at Phoenix	92
June 11	Chicago	111	at Phoenix	108
June 13	Phoenix	129	at Chicago	121††
June 16	Phoenix	105	at Chicago	111
June 18	Phoenix	108	at Chicago	98
June 20	Chicago	99	at Phoenix	98

Chicago won series 4-2.

††Triple overtime.

NBA Finals Composite Box Score

CHICAGO BULLS

Player	GP	Field Goals		3-Pt FG		Free Throws		Rebounds		A	Stl	TO	BS	Avg	Hi
		FGM	Pct	FGM	FGA	FTM	Pct	Off	Total						
Jordan	6	101	50.8	10	25	34	69.4	15	51	38	10	16	4	41.0	55
Pippen	6	54	43.9	0	6	19	54.3	16	55	46	12	26	6	21.2	27
Armstrong	6	32	50.8	10	19	7	100.0	2	11	30	5	5	1	13.5	21
Grant	6	28	52.8	0	0	11	57.9	25	62	14	9	5	9	11.2	24
Paxson	6	13	61.9	9	14	0	—	4	9	5	3	1	1	5.8	12
Williams	6	13	40.6	0	0	2	28.5	12	38	10	3	8	9	4.7	9
Cartwright	6	12	40.0	0	0	2	50.0	7	19	10	3	2	1	4.3	9
Tucker	6	7	70.0	3	5	0	—	1	2	4	1	3	0	2.8	9
King	6	3	27.3	0	0	7	87.5	3	8	3	2	3	1	2.2	6
Perdue	1	0	.000	0	0	0	—	1	3	0	0	0	0	0.0	0
Walker	3	0	—	0	0	0	.000	0	0	1	0	1	0	0.0	0
McCray	1	0	—	0	0	0	—	0	1	0	0	1	0	0.0	0
Total	**6**	**263**	**48.3**	**32**	**69**	**82**	**63.1**	**86**	**259**	**161**	**48**	**77**	**32**	**106.7**	**121**

PHOENIX SUNS

Player	GP	Field Goals		3-Pt FG		Free Throws		Rebounds		A	Stl	TO	BS	Avg	Hi
		FGM	Pct	FGM	FGA	FTM	Pct	Off	Total						
Barkley	6	60	47.6	2	8	42	75.0	22	78	33	7	10	3	27.3	42
K. Johnson	6	40	42.1	0	2	23	92.0	2	18	39	8	26	2	17.2	25
Majerle	6	35	44.3	17	39	16	80.0	12	49	22	8	7	13	17.2	28
Dumas	6	44	57.1	0	0	9	77.8	15	26	6	8	6	6	15.8	25
Ainge	6	19	47.5	8	12	7	77.8	7	18	15	2	7	0	8.8	20
Chambers	6	14	35.9	0	0	12	80.0	5	18	3	1	9	3	6.7	12
West	6	13	61.9	0	0	8	53.3	12	26	4	0	5	7	5.7	11
Miller	6	12	44.4	0	1	6	75.0	10	25	8	4	7	12	5.0	8
F. Johnson	6	7	41.2	0	0	4	1.000	1	2	5	3	2	0	3.0	8
Mustaf	2	0	—	0	0	0	—	0	0	0	0	0	0	0.0	0
Total	**6**	**244**	**46.8**	**27**	**62**	**125**	**77.6**	**86**	**260**	**135**	**41**	**81**	**46**	**106.7**	**129**

NBA Finals Box Scores

Game 1

CHICAGO 100

CHICAGO	Min	FG M-A	FT M-A	Reb O-T	A	PF	S	TO	TP
Grant	44	5-9	1-1	1-7	5	2	0	1	11
Pippen	39	12-20	3-9	2-9	5	3	2	3	27
Cartwright	25	4-5	1-2	1-3	3	3	2	1	9
Armstrong	38	5-9	3-3	1-3	5	3	1	0	16
Jordan	43	14-28	3-4	2-7	5	2	5	2	31
S Williams	23	2-5	0-0	2-10	2	2	0	3	4
Paxson	16	1-3	0-0	1-1	3	2	0	0	2
Tucker	9	0-1	0-0	0-0	0	0	0	0	0
King	3	0-1	0-0	0-1	0	0	2	0	0
Totals	240	43-81	11-19	10-41	28	17	10	12	100

Percentages: FG—.531, FT—.579. 3-pt goals: 3-8, .375 (Armstrong 3-4, Jordan 0-1, Paxson 0-1, Pippen 0-2). Team rebounds: 10. Blocked shots: 8 (S. Williams 3, Grant 2, Jordan 1, Cartwright 1, Paxson 1).

PHOENIX 92

PHOENIX	Min	FG M-A	FT M-A	Reb O-T	A	PF	S	TO	TP
Barkley	46	9-25	2-3	3-11	5	4	1	2	21
Dumas	42	10-20	0-0	8-12	4	4	2	1	20
West	14	3-3	0-1	1-2	0	2	0	1	6
K Johnson	36	4-13	3-3	0-2	2	0	1	5	11
Majerle	43	6-11	3-3	3-8	2	2	1	3	16
Miller	27	2-5	2-4	1-5	3	4	1	0	6
Chambers	3	0-2	0-0	0-0	0	0	0	1	0
Ainge	20	2-4	0-1	0-1	1	3	0	0	4
F Johnson	9	4-7	0-0	1-1	1	0	0	0	8
Totals	240	40-90	10-15	17-42	18	19	6	13	92

Percentages: FG—.444, FT—.667. 3-pt goals: 2-7, .286 (Barkley 1-1, Majerle 1-4, K Johnson 0-1, Ainge 0-1). Team rebounds: 8. Blocked shots: 10 (Majerle 4, Dumas 3, Miller 3). A: 19,023. Officials: Hugh Evans, Jess Kersey, Hue Hollins.

Shaquille Bends Steel

The 7' 1", 300-pound Shaquille O'Neal put an emphatic exclamation point on his rookie season with a ferocious dunk during a late-season game at New Jersey. The slam sheared the backboard's brace supports, sending the hoop and the 24-second clock down on O'Neal and delaying the game for 46 minutes, until the backboard assembly could be replaced. Shaq now has broken three rims, shattered two backboards, and torn down two standards in two seasons at LSU and one in the NBA. No faking *that* funk.

Game 2

CHICAGO 111

CHICAGO	Min	FG M-A	FT M-A	Reb O-T	A	PF	S	TO	TP
Grant	36	10-13	4-5	5-8	2	3	2	1	24
Pippen	42	5-12	5-7	4-12	12	4	2	7	15
Cartwright	13	1-3	0-0	1-2	0	0	0	0	2
Armstrong	42	4-9	0-0	0-4	4	4	1	1	8
Jordan	40	18-36	4-5	5-12	9	2	2	5	42
Williams	36	4-7	1-4	0-1	2	4	1	2	9
King	13	1-4	4-4	1-2	0	2	1	0	6
Tucker	6	0-2	0-0	1-1	2	1	1	0	0
Paxson	12	2-3	0-0	0-1	0	1	0	0	5
Totals	240	45-89	18-25	17-43	31	21	10	16	111

Percentages: FG—.506, FT—720. 3-pt goals: 3-7, .429 (Armstrong 0-2,. Jordan 2-2, Tucker 0-2, Paxson 1-1) Team rebounds: 11. Blocked shots: 7 (Williams 3, Grant 2, Pippen 2).

PHOENIX 108

PHOENIX	Min	FG M-A	FT M-A	Reb O-T	A	PF	S	TO	TP
Barkley	46	16-26	10-12	6-13	4	3	1	2	42
Dumas	17	4-8	0-0	0-0	0	1	1	0	8
West	8	0-0	0-0	0-2	1	2	0	1	0
K Johnson	32	2-8	0-0	0-0	6	6	3	4	4
Majerle	43	4-14	2-2	1-9	4	1	2	2	13
Miller	25	4-6	0-0	2-6	2	2	2	2	8
Ainge	29	8-14	1-1	3-3	4	1	0	2	20
Chambers	26	4-9	1-3	2-7	3	4	0	3	9
F. Johnson	14	1-3	2-2	0-0	4	3	0	1	5
Totals	240	43-88	16-20	14-40	28	23	9	17	108

Percentages: FG—.489, FT—.800. 3-pt goals: 6-13, .462 (Barkley 0-1, Majerle 3-8, Ainge 3-4). Team rebounds: 6. Blocked shots: 12 (Majerle 5, Miller 3, Chambers 2, Barkley 1, West 1). A: 19,023. Officials: Jake O'Donnell, Joe Crawford, Jack Madden.

Game 3 (Triple OT)

PHOENIX 129

PHOENIX	Min	FG M-A	FT M-A	Reb O-T	A	PF	S	TO	TP
Dumas	24	7-16	3-4	3-5	1	3	3	1	17
Barkley	53	9-20	5-9	2-19	4	5	1	2	24
West	36	4-7	3-6	3-5	1	3	0	2	11
K Johnson	62	11-24	3-4	0-7	9	5	2	7	25
Majerle	59	10-17	2-2	3-7	4	0	2	0	28
Miller	11	1-1	0-0	1-2	1	4	0	3	2
Ainge	40	2-5	4-4	1-5	5	4	0	1	10
Chambers	27	5-9	2-2	2-2	0	2	1	3	12
F Johnson	2	0-0	0-0	0-0	0	0	0	0	0
Mustaf	1	0-0	0-0	0-0	0	0	0	0	0
Totals	315	49-99	22-31	15-52	25	26	9	19	129

Percentages: FG—.495., FT—.710. 3-pt goals: 9-13, .692 (Majerle 6-8, Ainge 2-3, Barkley 1-1, K Johnson 0-1). Team rebounds: 17. Blocked shots: 8 (West 2, Miller 2, Dumas, Barkley, K Johnson, Chambers).

CHICAGO 121

CHICAGO	Min	FG M-A	FT M-A	Reb O-T	A	PF	S	TO	TP
Pippen	56	12-35	2-2	5-10	9	9	1	4	26
Grant	45	6-11	1-1	8-17	1	6	2	2	13
Cartwright	20	4-12	0-0	3-3	2	2	1	0	8
Armstrong	58	10-17	0-0	0-0	7	4	0	1	21
Jordan	57	19-43	3-6	3-9	6	5	2	3	44
S Williams	46	2-8	0-0	6-14	4	3	2	2	4
King	12	0-2	0-0	2-5	2	0	0	2	0
Paxson	5	1-1	0-0	0-0	3	0	0	0	2
Tucker	14	1-1	0-0	0-1	1	3	0	1	3
Walker	2	0-0	0-0	0-0	0	0	0	0	0
Totals	315	55-130	6-9	27-59	32	29	8	16	121

Percentages: FG—.423, FT—.667. 3-pt goals: 5-13, .385 (Jordan 3-9, Tucker 1-1, Armstrong 1-3). Team rebounds: 9. Blocked shots: 6 (Pippen 3, Jordan 1 Williams 1, King 1).
A: 12,888. Officials: Mike Mathis, Ed T Rush, Bill Oakes.

Game 4

PHOENIX 105

PHOENIX	Min	FG M-A	FT M-A	Reb O-T	A	PF	S	TO	TP
Dumas	25	8-11	1-1	1-1	0	3	1	2	17
Barkley	46	10-19	12-15	3-12	10	1	3	1	32
West	19	3-5	2-2	1-4	0	6	0	1	8
K Johnson	43	7-16	5-6	0-3	4	3	0	3	19
Majerle	46	5-9	1-3	2-5	3	1	0	0	14
Miller	14	1-3	0-0	0-2	1	5	1	1	2
Chambers	23	1-9	5-6	0-4	0	4	0	1	7
Ainge	21	1-5	0-0	1-3	2	3	0	1	2
F Johnson	3	2-2	0-0	0-0	0	2	1	0	4
Totals	240	38-79	26-33	8-34	20	28	6	10	105

Percentages: FG—.481, FT—.788. 3-pt goals: 3-8, .375 (Majerle 3-5, Miller 0-1, Barkley 0-2). Team rebounds: 11. Blocked shots: 3 (Barkley, West, Majerle).

CHICAGO 111

CHICAGO	Min	FG M-A	FT M-A	Reb O-T	A	PF	S	TO	TP
Pippen	44	7-14	0-2	0-6	10	1	6	1	14
Grant	37	7-11	3-6	8-16	2	5	3	0	17
Cartwright	30	1-4	1-2	2-5	2	4	0	0	3
Armstrong	35	4-10	2-2	0-2	6	2	3	1	11
Jordan	46	21-37	13-18	1-8	4	3	0	1	55
McCray	4	0-0	0-0	0-1	0	0	0	1	0
Tucker	1	0-0	0-0	0-0	0	0	0	0	0
Paxson	18	2-5	0-0	1-3	1	2	0	1	6
King	9	1-1	1-2	0-0	0	3	1	0	3
S Williams	14	1-1	0-1	0-1	1	6	0	0	2
Walker	2	0-0	0-1	0-0	1	0	0	0	0
Totals	240	44-83	20-33	12-42	26	26	8	10	111

Percentages: FG—.530, FT—.606. 3-pt goals: 3-9, .333 (Paxon 2-4, Armstrong 1-2, Jordan 0-1, Pipppen 0-2). Team rebounds: 11. Blocked shots: 1 (S Williams). A: 12,888. Officials: D Garretson, Joe Crawford, Dick Bavetta.

Game 5

PHOENIX 108

PHOENIX	Min	FG M-A	FT M-A	Reb O-T	A	PF	S	TO	TP
Dumas	30	12-14	1-2	2-5	0	2	1	2	25
Barkley	42	9-18	6-7	1-6	6	2	0	1	24
West	33	2-4	1-2	4-9	1	3	0	0	5
K Johnson	41	10-20	5-5	0-1	8	2	1	4	25
Majerle	44	3-11	3-4	1-12	7	1	2	1	11
F Johnson	10	0-2	2-2	0-1	0	1	2	0	2
Miller	16	3-8	2-2	4-8	1	4	0	1	8
Ainge	22	3-6	1-2	2-3	1	1	0	1	8
Chambers	1	0-0	0-0	0-0	0	0	0	1	0
Mustaf	1	0-0	0-0	0-0	0	0	0	0	0
Totals	240	42-83	21-26	14-45	24	16	6	11	108

Percentages: FG—.506, FT—.808. 3-pt goals: 3-10, .300 (Majerle 2-6, Ainge 1-1, Barkley 0-3). Team rebounds: 6. Blocked shots: 4 (Dumas, West, Majerle, Miller,).

CHICAGO 98

CHICAGO	Min	FG M-A	FT M-A	Reb O-T	A	PF	S	TO	TP
Pippen	42	8-20	6-8	1-6	5	5	2	3	22
Grant	38	0-4	1-4	1-7	1	3	1	1	1
Cartwright	14	1-3	0-0	0-2	2	1	0	1	2
Armstrong	37	3-8	0-0	1-2	4	3	0	1	7
Jordan	44	16-29	7-10	1-7	7	5	0	2	41
Williams	18	2-4	0-0	2-5	1	1	0	1	4
Paxson	23	4-5	0-0	1-3	0	1	3	0	12
King	10	1-2	2-2	0-0	0	1	0	0	4
Perdue	9	0-2	0-0	1-3	0	2	0	0	0
Tucker	4	2-2	0-0	0-0	0	0	0	0	5
Walker	1	0-0	0-0	0-0	0	0	0	0	0
Totals	240	37-79	16-24	8-35	20	22	6	9	98

Percentages: FG—.468, FT—.667. 3-pt goals: 8-18, .444 (Paxson 4-5, Jordan 2-7, Tucker 1-1, Armstrong 1-3, Pippen 0-2). Team rebounds: 10. Blocked shots: 4 (Jordan 2, Pippen, Williams).
A: 18,676. Officials: J O'Donnell, J Kersey, Joe Crawford

Game 6

CHICAGO 99

CHICAGO	Min	FG M-A	FT M-A	Reb O-T	A	PF	S	TO	TP
Grant	33	0-5	1-2	2-7	3	5	1	0	1
Pippen	43	10-22	3-7	4-12	5	3	4	3	23
Cartwright	26	1-3	0-0	0-4	1	5	0	0	2
Armstrong	41	6-10	2-2	0-0	7	3	0	1	18
Jordan	44	13-26	4-6	3-8	7	3	1	3	33
Paxson	22	3-4	0-0	1-1	1	1	0	0	8
Williams	22	2-7	1-3	2-7	1	3	0	0	5
Tucker	7	4-4	0-0	0-0	1	1	0	0	9
King	2	0-1	0-0	0-0	1	0	1	0	0
Totals	240	39-82	11-20	13-39	24	26	6	8	99

Percentages: FG—.476, FT—.550. 3-pt goals: 10-14, .714 (Armstrong 4-5, Jordan 3-5, , Paxson 2-3, Tucker 1-1). Team rebounds: 9. Blocked shots: 2 (Grant 2).

PHOENIX 98

PHOENIX	Min	FG M-A	FT M-A	Reb O-T	A	PF	S	TO	TP
Barkley	44	7-18	7-10	7-17	4	5	1	2	21
Dumas	22	3-8	2-2	1-3	1	2	0	0	8
West	20	1-2	2-4	3-4	1	5	0	0	4
K Johnson	46	6-14	7-7	2-5	10	3	1	3	19
Majerle	46	7-17	5-6	2-8	2	3	1	1	21
Miller	14	1-4	2-2	2-2	0	1	0	0	4
Ainge	30	3-6	1-1	0-3	2	0	2	2	9
Chambers	12	4-10	4-4	1-5	0	2	0	0	12
F Johnson	6	0-3	0-0	0-0	0	0	0	1	0
Totals	240	32-82	30-36	18-47	20	21	5	9	98

Percentages: FG—.390, FT—.833. 3-pt goals: 4-11, .364 (Ainge 2-3, Majerle 2-8). Team rebounds: 13. Blocked shots: 9 (Miller 3, West 2, Majerle 2, Dumas 1, K Johnson 1)
A: 19,023. Officials: D Garretson, Mike Mathis, Ed T Rush.

NBA Awards

All-NBA Teams

FIRST TEAM	SECOND TEAM	THIRD TEAM
G Michael Jordan, Chicago	John Stockton, Utah	Drazen Petrovic, New Jersey
G Mark Price, Cleveland	Joe Dumars, Detroit	Tim Hardaway, Golden State
C Hakeem Olajuwon, Houston	Patrick Ewing, New York	David Robinson, San Antonio
F Karl Malone, Utah	Dominique Wilkins, Atlanta	Scottie Pippen, Chicago
F Charles Barkley, Phoenix	Larry Johnson, Charlotte	Derrick Coleman, New Jersey

Master Lock NBA All-Defensive Teams

FIRST TEAM	SECOND TEAM
G Michael Jordan, Chicago	Dan Majerle, Phoenix
G Joe Dumars, Detroit	John Starks, New York
C Hakeem Olajuwon, Houston	David Robinson, San Antonio
F Dennis Rodman, Detroit	Larry Nance, Cleveland
F Scottie Pippen, Chicago	Horace Grant, Chicago

All-Rookie Teams
(Chosen Without Regard to Position)

FIRST TEAM	SECOND TEAM
Shaquille O'Neal, Orlando	Walt Williams, Sacramento
Alonzo Mourning, Charlotte	Robert Horry, Houston
Christian Laettner, Minnesota	Latrell Sprewell, Golden State
LaPhonso Ellis, Denver	Clarence Weatherspoon, Philadelphia
Tom Gugliotta, Washington	Richard Dumas, Phoenix

NBA Individual Leaders

Scoring

	GP	Pts	Avg
Michael Jordan, Chi	78	2541	32.6
Dominique Wilkins, Atl	71	2121	29.9
Karl Malone, Utah	82	2217	27.0
Hakeem Olajuwon, Hou	82	2140	26.1
Charles Barkley, Phoe	76	1944	25.6
Patrick Ewing, NY	81	1959	24.2
Joe Dumars, Det	77	1809	23.5
Shaquille O'Neal, Orl	81	1893	23.4
David Robinson, SA	82	1916	23.4
Danny Manning, LA Clippers	79	1800	22.8

Rebounds

	GP	Reb	Avg
Dennis Rodman, Det	62	1132	18.3
Shaquille O'Neal, Orl	81	1122	13.9
Dikembe Mutombo, Den	82	1070	13.0
Hakeem Olajuwon, Hou	82	1068	13.0
Kevin Willis, Atl	80	1028	12.9
Charles Barkley, Phoe	76	928	12.2
Patrick Ewing, NY	81	980	12.1
Rony Seikaly, Mia	72	846	11.8
David Robinson, SA	82	956	11.7
DColeman, NJ	76	852	11.2
K Malone Utah	82	919	11.2

Assists

	GP	Assists	Avg
John Stockton, Utah	82	987	12.0
Tim Hardaway, GS	66	699	10.6
Scott Skiles, Orl	78	735	9.4
Mark Jackson, LA Clippers	82	724	8.8
Tyrone Bogues, Charlotte	81	711	8.8
Michael Williams, Minn	76	661	8.7
Isiah Thomas, Det	79	671	8.5
Mookie Blaylock, Atl	80	671	8.4
Kenny Anderson, NJ	55	449	8.2
Mark Price, Clev	75	602	8.0

Field-Goal Percentage

	FGA	FGM	Pct
Cedric Ceballos, Phoe	662	381	57.6
Brad Daugherty, Clev	911	520	57.1
Dale Davis, Ind	534	304	56.8
Shaquille O'Neal	1304	733	56.2
Otis Thorpe, Hou	690	385	55.8
Karl Malone, Utah	1443	797	55.2
Larry Nance, Clev	971	533	54.9
Frank Brickowski, Mil	836	456	54.5
Larry Stewart, Wash	564	306	54.3
Antoine Carr, SA	705	379	53.8

Free-Throw Percentage

	FTA	FTM	Pct
Mark Price, Clev	305	289	94.8
Chris Jackson, Den	232	217	93.5
Eddie Johnson, Sea	257	234	91.1
Michael Williams, Minn	462	419	90.7
Scott Skiles, Orl	324	289	89.2
Ricky Pierce, Sea	352	313	88.9
Reggie Miller, Ind	485	427	88.0
Kenny Smith, Hou	222	195	87.8
Drazen Petrovic, NJ	362	315	87.0
Reggie Lewis, Bos	376	326	86.7

Three-Point Field-Goal Percentage

	FGA	FGM	Pct
BJ Armstrong	139	63	45.3
Chris Mullin, GS	133	60	45.1
Drazen Petrovic, NJ	167	75	44.9
Kenny Smith, Hou	219	96	43.8
Jim Les, Sac	154	66	42.9
Mark Price, Clev	293	122	41.6
Terry Porter, Por	345	143	41.5
Dennis Scott, Orl	268	108	40.3
Danny Ainge, Phoe	372	150	40.3
Steve Smith, Mia	132	53	40.2

Steals

	GP	Steals	Avg
Michael Jordan, Chi	78	221	2.83
Mookie Blaylock, Atl	80	203	2.54
John Stockton, Utah	82	199	2.43
Nate McMillan, Sea	73	173	2.37
Alvin Robertson, Det	69	155	2.25
Ron Harper, LA Clippers	80	177	2.21
Eric Murdock, Mil	79	174	2.20
Michael Williams, Minn	76	165	2.17
Gary Payton, Sea	82	177	2.16
Scottie Pippen, Chi	81	173	2.14

Blocked Shots

	GP	BS	Avg
Hakeem Olajuwon, Hou	82	342	4.17
Shaquille O'Neal, Orl	81	286	3.53
Dikembe Mutombo, Den	82	287	3.50
Alonzo Mourning, Char	78	271	3.47
David Robinson, SA	82	264	3.22
Larry Nance, Clev	77	198	2.57
Pervis Ellison, Wash	49	108	2.20
Manute Bol, Phila	58	119	2.05
Patrick Ewing, NY	81	161	1.99
Cliff Robinson, Por	82	163	1.99

NBA Team Statistics

Offense

Team	Field Goals FGM	Pct	3-Pt Field Goals 3FGM	Pct	Free Throws FTM	Pct	Rebounds Off	Total	A	Stl	Scoring Avg
Phoenix	3494	49.3	398	36.3	1912	75.3	1141	3651	2087	752	113.4
Charlotte	3512	48.7	175	32.6	1831	77.1	1095	3603	2161	639	110.1
Golden State	3474	48.2	298	35.0	1768	71.7	1219	3603	2010	693	109.9
Portland	3361	45.8	275	32.6	1901	74.5	1226	3733	1989	770	108.5
Seattle	3473	48.8	218	35.7	1720	75.1	1222	3476	1906	944	108.3
Sacramento	3360	46.3	262	33.2	1865	76.2	1137	3418	2075	768	107.9
Indiana	3371	48.0	257	32.6	1837	76.6	1220	3675	2144	615	107.8
Cleveland	3425	49.7	283	38.1	1699	80.2	929	3425	2349	615	107.7
Atlanta	3392	46.6	382	35.5	1648	74.2	1290	3634	2084	806	107.5
LA Clippers	3544	48.4	133	27.1	1562	71.8	1183	3543	2242	847	107.1
Utah	3336	48.9	130	31.4	1907	76.5	1031	3504	2177	746	106.2
San Antonio	3311	49.0	236	34.1	1794	76.5	919	3461	2012	588	105.5
Orlando	3257	48.6	317	35.7	1821	73.0	1040	3606	1982	542	105.5
Denver	3352	46.0	138	30.4	1784	75.6	1266	3830	1735	651	105.2
Chicago	3475	48.2	244	36.5	1431	73.3	1290	3573	2133	783	105.2
Philadelphia	3225	45.6	330	35.1	1776	78.6	1031	3462	2038	672	104.3
LA Lakers	3309	47.3	187	29.9	1741	75.6	1103	3391	2013	782	104.2
Houston	3280	48.6	387	36.1	1584	75.8	985	3517	2115	682	104.0
Boston	3453	48.7	110	28.7	1486	77.7	1076	3512	1999	647	103.7
Miami	3127	45.6	333	35.4	1908	77.1	1134	3518	1688	609	103.6
New Jersey	3272	46.2	155	31.8	1732	76.7	1291	3797	1872	693	102.8
Milwaukee	3268	47.2	312	33.3	1544	74.2	1050	3163	2084	863	102.3
Washington	3302	46.7	174	30.1	1875	74.8	1031	3348	2110	673	101.9
New York	3209	46.5	193	32.0	1717	74.1	1150	3810	2125	680	101.6
Detroit	3267	45.3	292	32.2	1426	72.9	1293	3608	1941	580	100.6
Dallas	3164	43.5	283	33.8	1530	70.5	1234	3499	1683	649	99.3
Minnesota	3043	46.6	166	29.2	1794	79.8	940	3144	2001	649	98.1

Defense (Opponent's Statistics)

Team	Field Goals FGM	Pct	3-Pt Field Goals 3FGM	Pct	Free Throws FTM	Pct	Rebounds Off	Total	Stl	Scoring Avg	Diff
New York	2822	42.6	230	30.6	1949	75.5	1031	3356	657	95.4	+6.2
Chicago	3133	47.4	247	36.1	1584	77.9	1039	3304	595	98.9	+6.3
Houston	3255	45.7	242	33.2	1432	76.3	1167	3462	717	99.8	+4.2
Cleveland	3370	46.6	229	32.8	1334	76.6	1115	3494	610	101.3	+6.4
Seattle	3143	46.9	272	33.7	1746	75.9	1075	3298	655	101.3	+7.0
New Jersey	3231	46.5	201	32.5	1665	74.1	1102	3447	780	101.6	+1.2
Detroit	3321	48.1	261	33.9	1463	73.6	1099	3541	623	102.0	-1.4
Boston	3232	46.3	216	33.2	1749	77.1	1094	3472	637	102.8	+0.9
San Antonio	3290	45.8	270	36.1	1583	77.2	1082	3470	655	102.8	+2.7
Utah	3258	46.7	272	32.5	1743	74.4	1120	3434	648	104.0	+2.2
Orlando	3307	45.6	248	32.9	1692	72.9	1166	3437	715	104.2	+1.3
Miami	3232	47.6	265	33.9	1860	77.0	1032	3456	656	104.7	-1.1
Portland	3337	46.8	277	34.2	1692	76.0	1022	3549	649	105.4	+3.1
LA Lakers	3438	48.3	245	33.7	1529	74.6	1158	3569	686	105.5	-1.3
Minnesota	3323	48.8	208	36.0	1930	75.8	1122	3453	734	105.9	-7.8
Indiana	3262	46.9	216	30.6	1957	74.3	1189	3534	693	106.1	+1.7
Milwaukee	3303	48.3	269	34.4	1823	74.8	1269	3667	773	106.1	-3.8
Phoenix	3500	47.9	250	33.3	1502	72.3	1118	3434	708	106.7	+6.7
LA Clippers	3311	47.0	275	34.6	1857	76.3	1179	3616	785	106.8	+0.4
Denver	3324	46.1	222	34.3	1899	75.5	1159	3664	750	106.9	-1.7
Atlanta	3509	49.6	281	33.7	1586	75.8	1080	3493	735	108.4	-0.9
Washington	3557	49.3	239	33.6	1577	74.9	1135	3890	718	108.9	-7.0
Philadelphia	3666	48.6	280	35.8	1417	75.5	1258	3892	781	110.1	-5.8
Charlotte	3634	47.2	234	31.1	1548	74.4	1350	3753	599	110.4	-0.3
Golden State	3471	48.2	272	34.3	1881	75.5	1174	3519	824	110.9	-1.0
Sacramento	3420	48.7	213	31.3	2054	75.8	1138	3700	767	111.1	-3.2
Dallas	3401	50.1	234	35.8	2351	76.6	1063	3803	802	114.5	-15.2

NBA Team-by-Team Statistical Leaders

Atlanta Hawks

Player	GP	Min	Field Goals		3-Pt FG		Free Throws		Rebounds		A	Stl	TO	BS	Avg
			FGM	Pct	FGA	FGM	FTM	Pct	Off	Total					
Wilkins	71	2,647	741	46.8	316	120	519	82.8	187	482	227	70	184	27	29.9
Willis	80	2,878	616	50.6	29	7	196	65.3	335	1,028	165	68	213	41	17.9
Augmon	73	2,112	397	50.1	4	0	227	73.9	141	287	170	91	157	18	14.0
Blaylock	80	2,820	414	42.9	315	118	123	72.8	89	280	671	203	187	23	13.4
Ferrell	82	1,736	327	47.0	36	9	176	77.9	97	191	132	59	103	17	10.2
Graham	80	1,508	256	45.7	141	42	96	73.3	61	190	164	86	120	6	8.1
Mays	49	787	129	41.7	84	29	54	65.9	20	53	72	21	51	3	7.0
Keefe	82	1,549	188	50.0	1	0	166	70.0	171	432	80	57	100	16	6.6
Henson	53	719	71	39.0	80	37	34	85.0	12	55	155	30	52	1	4.0
Koncak	78	1,975	124	46.4	8	3	24	48.0	100	427	140	75	52	100	3.5
Rasmussen	22	283	30	37.5	6	2	9	69.2	20	55	5	5	12	10	3.2
Foster	43	298	55	45.8	4	0	15	71.4	32	83	21	3	25	14	2.9
Breuer	12	107	15	48.4	0	0	2	40.0	10	28	6	2	5	3	2.7
Sanders	9	120	10	40.0	0	0	4	50.0	12	29	6	8	11	1	2.7
Hawks	**82**	**19,830**	**3,392**	**46.6**	**1076**	**382**	**1,648**	**74.2**	**1,290**	**3,634**	**2,084**	**806**	**1,339**	**279**	**107.5**
Opponents	**82**	**19,830**	**3,509**	**49.6**	**833**	**281**	**1,586**	**75.8**	**1,080**	**3,493**	**2,189**	**735**	**1,363**	**363**	**108.4**

Boston Celtics

Player	GP	Min	Field Goals		3-Pt FG		Free Throws		Rebounds		A	Stl	TO	BS	Avg
			FGM	Pct	FGA	FGM	FTM	Pct	Off	Total					
Lewis	80	3,144	663	47.0	60	14	326	86.7	88	347	298	118	133	77	20.8
McDaniel	82	2,215	457	49.5	22	6	191	79.3	168	489	163	72	171	51	13.5
Gamble	82	2,541	459	50.7	139	52	123	82.6	46	246	226	86	81	37	13.3
Parish	79	2,146	416	53.5	0	0	162	68.9	246	740	61	57	120	107	12.6
Brown	80	2,254	328	46.8	82	26	192	79.3	45	246	461	138	136	32	10.9
McHale	71	1,656	298	45.9	18	2	164	84.1	95	358	73	16	92	59	10.7
Douglas	79	1,932	264	49.8	29	6	84	56.0	65	162	508	49	161	10	7.8
Abdelnaby	75	1,311	245	51.8	1	0	88	75.9	126	337	27	25	97	26	7.7
Fox	71	1,082	184	48.4	23	4	81	80.2	55	159	113	61	77	21	6.4
Battle	3	29	6	46.2	1	0	2	100.0	7	11	2	1	2	0	4.7
Pinckney	7	151	10	41.7	0	0	12	92.3	14	43	1	4	8	7	4.6
Webb	9	51	13	52.0	1	0	13	61.9	5	10	2	1	5	2	4.3
Kleine	78	1,129	108	40.4	6	0	41	70.7	113	346	39	17	37	17	3.3
Kofoed	7	41	3	23.1	1	0	11	78.6	0	1	10	2	3	1	2.4
Bagley	10	97	9	36.0	1	0	5	83.3	1	7	20	2	17	0	2.3
Williams	27	179	17	47.2	0	0	2	28.6	17	55	5	5	8	17	1.3
Celtics	**82**	**19,780**	**3,453**	**48.7**	**383**	**110**	**1,486**	**77.7**	**1,076**	**3,512**	**1,999**	**647**	**1,148**	**458**	**103.7**
Opponents	**82**	**19,780**	**3,232**	**46.3**	**650**	**216**	**1,749**	**77.1**	**1,094**	**3,472**	**1,971**	**637**	**1,181**	**386**	**102.8**

Charlotte Hornets

Player	GP	Min	Field Goals		3-Pt FG		Free Throws		Rebounds		A	Stl	TO	BS	Avg
			FGM	Pct	FGA	FGM	FTM	Pct	Off	Total					
Gill	79	2,906	666	46.7	25	6	284	74.5	165	402	329	154	180	46	20.5
Johnson	82	3,323	728	52.6	71	18	336	76.7	281	864	353	53	227	27	22.1
Mourning	78	2,644	572	51.1	3	0	495	78.1	263	801	76	27	236	271	21.0
Gill	69	2,430	463	44.9	62	17	224	77.2	120	340	268	98	174	36	16.9
Curry	80	2,094	498	45.2	237	95	136	86.6	51	286	180	87	129	23	15.3
Newman	64	1,471	279	52.2	45	12	194	80.8	72	143	117	45	90	19	11.9
Bogues	81	1,833	331	45.3	26	6	140	83.3	51	298	711	161	154	5	10.0
Gattison	75	1,475	203	52.9	3	0	102	60.4	108	353	68	48	64	55	6.8
Wingate	72	1,471	180	53.6	6	1	79	73.8	49	174	183	66	89	9	6.1
Bennett	75	857	110	42.3	80	26	30	73.2	12	63	136	30	50	0	3.7
Gminski	34	251	42	50.6	0	0	9	90.0	34	85	7	1	11	9	2.7
Green	39	329	34	38.2	2	0	25	80.6	32	118	24	6	20	5	2.4
Lynch	40	324	30	50.8	1	0	26	68.4	12	35	25	11	24	6	2.2
Hornets	**82**	**19,755**	**3,512**	**48.7**	**537**	**175**	**1,831**	**77.1**	**1,095**	**3,603**	**2,161**	**639**	**1,325**	**473**	**110.1**
Opponents	**82**	**19,755**	**3,634**	**47.2**	**753**	**234**	**1,548**	**74.4**	**1,350**	**3,753**	**2,277**	**599**	**1,245**	**438**	**110.4**

Chicago Bulls

Player	GP	Min	Field Goals		3-Pt FG		Free Throws		Rebounds		A	Stl	TO	BS	Avg
			FGM	Pct	FGA	FGM	FTM	Pct	Off	Total					
Jordan	78	3,067	992	49.5	230	81	476	83.7	135	522	428	221	207	61	32.6
Pippen	81	3,123	628	47.3	93	22	232	66.3	203	621	507	173	246	73	18.6
Grant	77	2,745	421	50.8	5	1	174	61.9	341	729	201	189	110	96	13.2
Armstrong	82	2,492	408	49.9	139	63	130	86.1	27	149	330	66	83	6	12.3
Williams	71	1,369	166	46.6	7	0	90	71.4	168	451	68	55	73	66	5.9
Cartwright	63	1,253	141	41.1	0	0	72	73.5	83	233	83	20	62	10	5.6
King	76	1,059	160	47.1	6	2	86	70.5	105	207	71	26	70	20	5.4
Tucker	69	909	143	48.5	131	52	18	81.8	16	71	82	24	18	6	5.2
Perdue	72	998	137	55.7	1	0	67	60.4	103	287	74	22	74	47	4.7
Paxson	59	1,030	105	45.1	41	19	17	85.0	9	48	136	38	31	2	4.2
McCray	64	1,019	92	45.1	5	2	36	69.2	53	158	81	12	53	15	3.5
Blanton	2	13	3	42.9	0	0	0	—	2	3	1	2	1	0	3.0
C. Williams	35	242	31	36.5	3	1	18	81.8	19	31	23	4	11	2	2.3
Walker	37	511	34	35.4	1	0	12	46.2	22	58	53	33	25	2	2.2
Nealy	41	308	26	37.7	27	8	9	75.0	12	64	15	12	7	2	1.7
English	6	31	3	30.0	3	0	0	00.0	2	6	1	3	4	2	1.0
Bulls	**82**	**19,830**	**3,475**	**48.2**	**669**	**244**	**1,431**	**73.3**	**1,290**	**3,573**	**2,133**	**783**	**1,103**	**410**	**105.2**
Opponents	**82**	**19,830**	**3,139**	**47.4**	**685**	**247**	**1,584**	**77.9**	**1,039**	**3,304**	**1,918**	**595**	**1,372**	**357**	**98.9**

Cleveland Cavaliers

Player	GP	Min	Field Goals		3-Pt FG		Free Throws		Rebounds		A	Stl	TO	BS	Avg
			FGM	Pct	FGA	FGM	FTM	Pct	Off	Total					
Daugherty	71	2,691	520	57.1	2	1	391	79.5	164	726	312	53	150	56	20.2
Price	75	2,380	477	48.4	293	122	289	94.8	37	201	602	89	196	11	18.2
Nance	77	2,753	533	54.9	4	0	202	81.8	184	668	223	54	107	198	16.5
Ehlo	82	2,559	385	49.0	244	93	86	71.7	113	403	254	104	124	22	11.6
Wilkins	80	2,079	361	45.3	58	16	152	84.0	74	214	183	78	94	18	11.1
Williams	67	2,055	263	47.0	0	0	212	71.6	127	415	152	48	116	105	11.0
Brandon	82	1,622	297	47.6	42	13	118	82.5	37	179	302	79	107	27	8.8
Sanders	53	1,189	197	49.7	4	1	59	75.6	52	170	75	39	57	30	8.6
Ferry	76	1,461	220	47.9	82	34	99	87.6	81	279	137	29	83	49	7.5
Battle	41	497	83	41.5	6	1	56	77.8	4	29	54	9	22	5	5.4
Phills	31	139	38	46.3	5	2	15	60.0	6	17	10	10	18	2	3.0
Lane	21	149	27	50.0	0	0	5	25.0	24	53	17	12	7	3	2.8
Guidinger	32	215	19	34.5	0	0	13	52.0	26	64	17	9	10	10	1.6
Cavaliers	**82**	**19,830**	**3,425**	**49.7**	**742**	**283**	**1,699**	**80.2**	**929**	**3,425**	**2,349**	**615**	**1,120**	**536**	**107.7**
Opponents	**82**	**19,830**	**3,370**	**46.6**	**695**	**229**	**1,334**	**76.6**	**1,115**	**3,494**	**2,109**	**610**	**1,203**	**385**	**101.3**

Dallas Mavericks

Player	GP	Min	Field Goals		3-Pt FG		Free Throws		Rebounds		A	Stl	TO	BS	Avg
			FGM	Pct	FGA	FGM	FTM	Pct	Off	Total					
Harper	62	2,108	393	44.2	257	101	239	75.6	42	123	334	80	136	16	18.2
Jackson	28	938	184	39.5	73	21	68	73.9	42	122	131	40	115	11	16.3
Rooks	72	2,087	368	49.3	2	0	234	60.2	196	536	95	38	160	81	13.5
Davis	75	2,462	393	45.5	8	2	167	59.4	259	701	68	36	160	28	12.7
Smith	61	1,524	289	43.4	4	0	56	75.7	96	328	104	48	115	52	10.4
White	64	1,433	235	43.5	42	10	138	75.0	154	370	49	63	108	45	9.7
Legler	33	635	105	43.6	65	22	57	80.3	25	59	46	24	28	6	8.8
Iuzzolino	70	1,769	221	46.2	144	54	114	76.5	31	140	328	49	129	6	8.7
Bond	74	1,578	227	40.2	42	7	129	77.2	52	196	122	75	112	18	8.0
Moore	39	510	103	41.4	67	23	53	86.9	23	52	47	21	32	4	7.2
White	65	1,021	145	38.0	27	4	124	76.5	96	236	31	31	68	22	6.4
Cambridge	53	885	151	48.4	4	0	68	68.7	88	167	58	24	63	6	7.0
Howard	68	1,295	183	44.2	7	1	72	76.6	66	212	67	55	68	34	6.5
Strothers	9	138	20	32.8	13	2	8	80.0	8	14	13	8	15	0	5.6
Hodge	79	1,267	161	40.3	0	0	71	68.3	93	294	75	33	90	37	5.0
Wiley	58	995	96	37.8	154	54	17	65.4	29	91	181	65	80	3	4.5
Palmer	20	124	27	47.4	0	0	6	66.7	12	44	5	1	10	5	3.0
Curcic	20	166	16	39.0	0	0	26	72.2	17	49	12	7	8	2	2.9
Bardo	23	175	19	30.6	6	1	12	70.6	10	37	29	8	17	3	2.2
Mavericks	**82**	**19,730**	**3,164**	**43.5**	**837**	**283**	**1,530**	**70.5**	**1,234**	**3,499**	**1,683**	**649**	**1,459**	**355**	**99.3**
Opponents	**82**	**19,730**	**3,401**	**50.1**	**653**	**234**	**2,351**	**76.6**	**1,063**	**3,803**	**2,047**	**802**	**1,273**	**520**	**114.5**

Denver Nuggets

Player	GP	Min	Field Goals		3-Pt FG		Free Throws		Rebounds		A	Stl	TO	BS	Avg
			FGM	Pct	FGA	FGM	FTM	Pct	Off	Total					
Jackson	81	2,710	633	45.0	197	70	217	93.5	51	225	344	84	187	8	19.2
Williams	79	2,722	535	45.8	122	33	238	80.4	132	428	295	126	194	76	17.0
Ellis	82	2,749	483	50.4	13	2	237	74.8	274	744	151	72	153	111	14.7
Mutombo	82	3,029	398	51.0	0	0	335	68.1	344	1,070	147	43	216	287	13.8
Pack	77	1,579	285	47.0	8	1	239	76.8	52	160	335	81	185	10	10.5
Stith	39	865	124	44.6	4	0	99	83.2	39	124	49	24	44	5	8.9
Liberty	78	1,585	252	45.0	59	22	102	65.4	131	335	105	64	79	21	8.1
Macon	48	1,141	158	41.5	6	0	42	70.0	33	103	126	69	72	3	7.5
Lichti	48	752	124	44.9	6	2	81	79.4	35	102	52	28	49	11	6.9
Plummer	60	737	106	46.5	3	0	69	72.6	53	173	40	14	78	11	4.7
Hammonds	54	713	105	47.5	1	0	38	61.3	38	127	24	18	34	12	4.6
Brooks	55	571	93	39.9	26	6	35	87.5	22	81	34	10	39	2	4.1
Hastings	76	670	57	50.9	8	2	40	72.7	44	137	34	12	29	8	2.1
Werdann	28	149	18	30.5	1	0	17	54.8	23	52	7	6	12	4	1.9
Nuggets	**82**	**19,830**	**3,352**	**46.0**	**454**	**138**	**1,784**	**75.6**	**1,266**	**3,830**	**1,735**	**651**	**1,413**	**565**	**105.2**
Opponents	**82**	**19,830**	**3,324**	**46.1**	**647**	**222**	**1,899**	**75.4**	**1,159**	**3,664**	**1,890**	**750**	**1,340**	**503**	**106.9**

Detroit Pistons

Player	GP	Min	Field Goals		3-Pt FG		Free Throws		Rebounds		A	Stl	TO	BS	Avg
			FGM	Pct	FGA	FGM	FTM	Pct	Off	Total					
Dumars	77	3,094	677	46.6	299	112	343	86.4	63	148	308	78	138	7	23.5
I Thomas	79	2,922	526	41.8	198	61	278	73.7	71	232	671	123	284	18	17.6
Mills	81	2,183	494	46.1	36	10	201	79.1	176	472	111	44	142	50	14.8
Aguirre	51	1,056	187	44.3	83	30	99	76.7	43	152	105	16	68	7	9.9
Robertson	69	2,006	247	45.8	122	40	84	65.6	107	269	263	155	133	18	9.0
Laimbeer	79	1,933	292	50.9	27	10	93	89.4	110	419	127	46	59	40	8.7
Rodman	62	2,410	183	42.7	73	15	87	53.4	367	1,132	102	48	103	45	7.5
Polynice	67	1,299	210	49.0	1	0	66	46.5	181	418	29	31	54	21	7.3
Glass	60	848	142	41.9	33	7	25	64.1	61	142	77	33	35	18	5.3
Newbern	33	311	42	37.2	8	1	34	56.7	19	37	57	23	32	1	3.6
Young	65	836	69	41.3	68	22	28	87.5	13	47	119	31	30	5	2.9
Randall	37	248	40	50.0	8	1	16	61.5	27	55	11	4	17	2	2.6
Morris	25	102	26	45.6	0	0	3	75.0	6	12	4	3	8	1	2.2
Ruland	11	55	5	45.5	0	0	2	50.0	9	18	2	2	6	0	1.1
Pistons	**82**	**19,780**	**3,267**	**45.3**	**908**	**292**	**1,426**	**72.9**	**1,293**	**3,608**	**1,941**	**580**	**1,152**	**249**	**100.6**
Opponents	**82**	**19,780**	**3,321**	**48.1**	**769**	**261**	**1,463**	**73.6**	**1,099**	**3,541**	**2,048**	**623**	**1,219**	**363**	**102.0**

Golden State Warriors

Player	GP	Min	Field Goals		3-Pt FG		Free Throws		Rebounds		A	Stl	TO	BS	Avg
			FGM	Pct	FGA	FGM	FTM	Pct	Off	Total					
Mullin	46	1,902	474	51.0	133	60	183	81.0	42	232	166	68	139	41	25.9
Hardaway	66	2,609	522	44.7	309	102	273	74.4	60	263	699	116	220	12	21.5
Marciulionis	30	836	178	54.3	15	3	162	76.1	40	97	105	51	76	2	17.4
Owens	37	1,201	247	50.1	11	1	117	63.9	108	264	144	35	106	28	16.5
Sprewell	77	2,741	449	46.4	198	73	211	74.6	79	271	295	126	203	52	15.4
Alexander	72	1,753	344	51.6	22	10	111	68.5	132	420	93	34	120	53	11.2
Spencer	20	422	73	44.8	2	0	41	75.9	38	81	24	17	26	7	9.4
Gatling	70	1,248	249	53.9	6	0	150	72.5	129	320	40	44	102	53	9.3
Grayer	48	1,025	165	46.7	14	2	91	66.9	71	157	70	31	54	8	8.8
Hill	74	2,070	251	50.8	4	0	138	62.4	255	754	68	41	92	40	8.6
Jennings	8	136	25	59.5	9	5	14	77.8	2	11	23	4	7	0	8.6
Higgins	29	591	96	44.7	37	13	35	74.5	23	68	66	13	64	5	8.3
Buechler	70	1,287	176	43.7	59	20	65	74.7	81	195	94	47	55	19	6.2
Houston	79	1,274	145	44.6	7	2	129	66.5	119	315	59	44	87	43	5.3
Pressey	18	268	29	43.9	4	0	21	77.8	8	31	30	11	23	5	4.4
Durham	5	78	6	24.0	0	0	9	75.0	5	14	4	1	7	1	4.2
Courtney	12	104	13	40.6	0	0	7	77.8	4	19	3	5	6	5	2.8
Lister	20	174	19	45.2	0	0	7	53.8	15	44	5	0	18	9	2.3
Stevens	2	6	1	50.0	0	0	0	—	2	2	0	0	0	0	1.0
Warriors	**82**	**19,905**	**3,474**	**48.2**	**852**	**298**	**1,768**	**71.7**	**1,219**	**3,603**	**2,010**	**693**	**1,451**	**383**	**109.9**
Opponents	**82**	**19,905**	**3,471**	**48.2**	**794**	**272**	**1,881**	**75.5**	**1,174**	**3,519**	**2,098**	**824**	**1,350**	**457**	**110.9**

Houston Rockets

Player	GP	Min	Field Goals FGM	Pct	3-Pt FG FGA	FGM	Free Throws FTM	Pct	Rebounds Off	Total	A	Stl	TO	BS	Avg
Olajuwon	82	3,242	848	52.9	8	0	444	77.9	283	1068	291	150	262	342	26.1
Maxwell	71	2,251	349	40.7	361	120	164	71.9	29	221	297	86	140	8	13.8
Smith	82	2,422	387	52.0	219	96	195	87.8	28	160	446	80	163	7	13.0
Thorpe	72	2,357	385	55.8	2	0	153	59.8	219	589	181	43	151	19	12.8
Horry	79	2,330	323	47.4	47	12	143	71.5	113	392	191	80	156	83	10.1
Herrera	81	1,800	240	54.1	2	0	125	71.0	148	454	61	47	92	35	7.5
Bullard	79	1,356	213	43.1	243	91	58	78.4	66	222	110	30	57	11	7.3
Floyd	52	867	124	40.7	56	16	81	79.4	14	86	132	32	68	6	6.6
Brooks	82	1,516	183	47.5	99	41	112	83.0	22	99	243	79	72	3	6.3
Garland	66	1,004	152	44.3	13	6	81	91.0	32	108	138	39	67	4	5.9
Winchester	39	340	61	43.9	19	4	17	77.3	17	49	13	10	15	10	3.7
Teagle	2	25	2	28.6	0	0	1	50.0	0	3	2	0	1	0	2.5
Rollins	42	247	11	26.8	2	0	9	75.0	12	60	10	6	9	15	0.7
Rockets	**82**	**19,780**	**3,280**	**48.6**	**1073**	**387**	**1,584**	**75.8**	**985**	**3,517**	**2,115**	**682**	**1,295**	**543**	**104.0**
Opponents	**82**	**19,780**	**3,255**	**45.7**	**730**	**242**	**1,432**	**76.3**	**1,167**	**3,462**	**1,965**	**717**	**1,228**	**327**	**99.8**

Indiana Pacers

Player	GP	Min	Field Goals FGM	Pct	3-Pt FG FGA	FGM	Free Throws FTM	Pct	Rebounds Off	Total	A	Stl	TO	BS	Avg
Miller	82	2,954	571	47.9	419	167	427	88.0	67	258	252	120	145	26	21.2
Schrempf	82	3,098	517	47.6	52	8	525	80.4	210	780	493	79	243	27	19.1
Smits	81	2,072	494	48.6	0	0	167	73.2	126	432	121	27	147	75	14.3
Richardson	74	2,396	337	47.9	29	3	92	74.2	63	267	573	94	167	12	10.4
Fleming	75	1,503	280	50.5	36	7	143	72.6	63	169	224	63	121	9	9.5
Davis	82	2,264	304	56.8	0	0	119	52.9	291	723	69	63	79	148	8.9
McCloud	78	1,500	216	41.1	181	58	75	73.5	60	205	192	53	107	11	7.2
Mitchell	81	1,402	215	44.5	23	4	150	81.1	93	248	76	23	51	10	7.2
Williams	57	844	150	53.2	3	0	48	70.6	102	228	38	21	28	45	6.1
Sealy	58	672	136	42.6	31	7	51	68.9	60	112	47	36	58	7	5.7
Green	13	81	28	50.9	10	3	3	75.0	4	9	7	2	9	1	4.8
Thompson	63	730	104	48.8	1	0	29	74.4	55	178	34	29	47	24	3.8
Dreiling	43	239	19	32.8	4	0	8	53.3	26	66	8	5	9	8	1.1
Pacers	**82**	**19,755**	**3,371**	**48.0**	**789**	**257**	**1,837**	**76.6**	**1,220**	**3,675**	**2,144**	**615**	**1,256**	**403**	**107.8**
Opponents	**82**	**19,755**	**3,262**	**46.9**	**706**	**216**	**1,957**	**74.3**	**1,189**	**3,534**	**1,987**	**693**	**1,178**	**387**	**106.1**

Los Angeles Clippers

Player	GP	Min	Field Goals FGM	Pct	3-Pt FG FGA	FGM	Free Throws FTM	Pct	Rebounds Off	Total	A	Stl	TO	BS	Avg
Manning	79	2,761	702	50.9	30	8	388	80.2	198	520	207	108	230	101	22.8
Harper	80	2,970	542	45.1	186	52	307	76.9	117	425	360	177	222	73	18.0
Norman	76	2,477	498	51.1	38	10	131	59.5	209	571	165	59	125	58	15.0
M.Jackson	82	3,117	459	48.6	82	22	241	80.3	129	388	724	136	220	12	14.4
Roberts	77	1,816	375	52.7	0	0	120	48.8	181	478	59	34	121	141	11.3
Vaught	79	1,653	313	50.8	4	1	116	74.8	164	492	54	55	83	39	9.4
Williams	74	1,638	205	43.0	53	12	70	54.3	88	316	142	83	79	23	6.6
Grant	74	1,624	210	44.1	42	11	55	74.3	27	139	353	106	129	9	6.6
Vandeweghe	41	494	92	45.3	37	12	58	87.9	12	48	25	13	20	7	6.2
J.Jackson	34	350	53	41.4	5	2	23	85.2	19	39	35	19	17	5	3.9
Conner	31	422	28	45.2	0	0	18	94.7	16	49	65	34	21	4	2.4
Spencer	44	280	44	53.7	0	0	16	50.0	17	62	8	8	26	18	2.4
Woods	41	174	23	34.8	14	3	19	73.1	6	14	40	14	16	1	1.7
Washington	4	28	0	0.00	0	0	—	—	0	2	5	1	2	0	0.0
Clippers	**82**	**19,805**	**3,544**	**48.4**	**491**	**133**	**1,562**	**71.8**	**1,183**	**3,543**	**2,242**	**847**	**1,266**	**451**	**107.1**
Opponents	**82**	**19,805**	**3,311**	**47.0**	**790**	**275**	**1,857**	**76.3**	**1,179**	**3,616**	**1,970**	**785**	**1,334**	**453**	**106.8**

Los Angeles Lakers

Player	GP	Min	Field Goals		3-Pt FG		Free Throws		Rebounds		A	Stl	TO	BS	Avg
			FGM	Pct	FGA	FGM	FTM	Pct	Off	Total					
Threatt	82	2,893	522	50.8	53	14	177	82.3	47	273	564	142	173	11	15.1
Worthy	82	2,359	510	44.7	111	30	171	81.0	73	247	278	92	137	27	14.9
Scott	58	1,677	296	44.9	135	44	156	84.8	27	134	157	55	70	13	13.7
Green	82	2,819	379	53.7	16	46	277	73.9	287	711	116	88	116	39	12.8
Divac	82	2,525	397	48.5	75	21	235	68.9	220	729	232	128	214	140	12.8
Peeler	77	1,656	297	46.8	118	46	162	78.6	64	179	166	60	123	14	10.4
Campbell	79	1,551	238	45.8	3	0	130	63.7	127	332	48	59	69	100	7.7
Edwards	52	617	122	45.2	0	0	84	71.2	30	100	41	10	51	7	6.3
Christie	23	332	45	42.5	12	2	50	75.8	24	51	53	22	50	5	6.2
Smith	55	752	133	48.4	11	2	62	75.6	46	87	63	50	40	7	6.0
Benjamin	59	754	133	49.1	0	0	69	66.3	51	209	22	31	78	48	5.7
Cooper	65	645	62	39.2	30	7	25	71.4	13	50	150	18	69	2	2.4
Blackwell	27	109	14	33.3	3	0	6	75.0	10	23	7	4	5	2	1.3
Lakers	82	19,830	3,309	47.3	626	187	1,741	75.6	1,103	3,391	2,013	782	1,266	431	104.2
Opponents	82	19,830	3,438	48.3	726	245	1,529	74.6	1,158	3,569	2,130	686	1,334	384	105.5

Miami Heat

Player	GP	Min	Field Goals		3-Pt FG		Free Throws		Rebounds		A	Stl	TO	BS	Avg
			FGM	Pct	FGA	FGM	FTM	Pct	Off	Total					
Rice	82	3,082	582	44.0	386	148	242	82.0	92	424	180	92	157	25	19.0
Seikaly	72	2,456	4TK	48.0	8	1	397	73.5	259	846	100	38	203	83	17.1
Smith	48	1,610	279	45.1	132	53	155	78.7	56	197	267	50	129	16	16.0
Long	76	2,728	397	46.9	26	6	261	76.5	197	568	182	104	133	31	14.0
Edwards	40	1,134	216	46.8	17	5	119	84.4	48	121	120	68	75	12	13.9
Coles	81	2,232	318	46.4	137	42	177	80.5	58	166	373	80	108	11	10.6
Miner	73	1,383	292	47.5	9	3	153	76.2	74	147	73	34	92	8	10.3
Salley	51	1,422	154	50.2	0	0	115	79.9	113	313	83	32	101	70	8.3
Burton	26	451	54	38.3	15	5	91	71.7	22	70	16	13	50	16	7.8
Shaw	68	1,603	197	39.3	130	43	61	78.2	70	257	235	48	96	19	7.3
Geiger	48	554	76	52.4	4	0	62	67.4	46	120	14	15	36	18	4.5
Kessler	40	415	57	46.7	11	5	36	76.6	25	91	14	4	21	12	3.9
Askins	69	935	88	41.3	65	22	29	72.5	74	198	31	31	37	29	3.3
Heat	82	20,005	3,127	45.6	940	333	1,908	77.1	1,134	3,518	1,088	609	1,287	350	103.6
Opponents	82	20,005	3,232	47.6	781	265	1,860	77.0	1,032	3,546	1,965	656	1,304	426	104.7

Milwaukee Bucks

Player	GP	Min	Field Goals		3-Pt FG		Free Throws		Rebounds		A	Stl	TO	BS	Avg
			FGM	Pct	FGA	FGM	FTM	Pct	Off	Total					
Brickowski	66	2,075	456	54.5	26	8	195	72.8	120	405	196	80	202	44	16.9
Edwards	82	2,729	554	51.2	106	37	237	79.0	123	382	214	129	175	45	16.9
Murdock	79	2,437	438	46.8	119	31	231	78.0	95	284	603	174	207	7	14.4
Day	71	1,931	358	43.2	184	54	213	71.7	144	291	117	75	118	48	13.8
Wooldridge	58	1,555	289	48.2	9	0	120	67.8	87	185	115	27	79	27	12.0
Avent	82	2,285	347	43.3	2	0	112	65.1	180	512	91	57	140	73	9.8
Lohaus	80	1,766	283	46.1	230	85	73	72.3	59	276	127	47	93	74	9.1
Roberts	79	1,488	226	52.8	29	12	135	79.9	91	237	118	57	67	27	7.6
Strong	23	339	42	45.7	8	4	68	80.0	40	115	14	11	13	1	6.8
Mayberry	82	1,503	171	45.6	110	43	39	57.4	26	118	273	59	85	7	5.2
Schayes	70	1,124	105	39.9	3	0	112	81.8	72	249	78	36	65	36	4.6
Malone	11	104	13	31.0	0	0	24	77.4	22	46	7	1	10	8	4.5
Barry	47	552	76	36.9	63	21	33	67.3	10	43	68	35	42	3	4.4
Pullard	8	37	8	44.4	0	0	1	33.3	2	8	2	2	5	2	2.1
O'Sullivan	6	17	3	60.0	0	0	3	75.0	2	6	1	1	0	0	1.5
Bucks	82	19,730	3,268	47.2	938	312	1,544	74.2	1,050	3,163	2,084	863	1,363	393	102.3
Opponents	82	19,730	3,303	48.3	783	269	1,623	74.8	1,269	3,667	2,087	773	1,476	456	106.1

Minnesota Timberwolves

Player	GP	Min	FGM	Pct	FGA	FGM	FTM	Pct	Off	Total	A	Stl	TO	BS	Avg
West	80	3,104	646	51.7	23	2	249	84.1	89	247	235	85	165	21	19.3
Laettner	81	2,823	503	47.4	40	4	462	83.5	171	708	223	105	275	83	18.2
Person	78	2,985	541	43.3	332	118	109	64.9	98	433	343	67	219	30	16.8
Williams	76	2,661	353	44.6	107	26	419	90.7	84	273	661	165	227	23	15.1
Bailey	70	1,276	203	45.5	0	0	119	83.8	53	215	61	20	60	47	7.5
McCann	79	1,536	200	48.8	2	0	95	62.5	92	282	68	51	79	58	6.3
Longley	55	1,045	133	45.5	0	0	53	71.6	71	240	51	47	88	77	5.8
Maxey	43	520	93	55.0	1	0	45	64.3	66	164	12	11	38	18	5.4
Smith	80	1,266	125	43.3	14	2	95	79.2	32	96	196	48	68	16	4.3
Spencer	71	1,296	105	46.5	0	0	83	65.4	134	324	17	23	70	66	4.1
Vetra	13	89	19	47.5	3	3	4	66.7	4	8	6	2	2	0	3.5
Blanks	61	642	65	43.3	43	11	20	62.5	18	68	72	16	31	5	2.6
Sellers	54	533	49	37.7	0	1	37	94.9	27	83	46	6	27	11	2.5
Timberwolves	**82**	**19,858**	**3,043**	**46.6**	**569**	**166**	**1,794**	**79.8**	**940**	**3,144**	**2,001**	**649**	**1,422**	**455**	**98.1**
Opponents	**82**	**19,858**	**3,323**	**48.8**	**578**	**208**	**1,830**	**75.8**	**1,122**	**3,453**	**2,144**	**734**	**1,231**	**494**	**105.9**

New Jersey Nets

Player	GP	Min	FGM	Pct	FGA	FGM	FTM	Pct	Off	Total	A	Stl	TO	BS	Avg
Petrovic	70	2,660	587	51.8	167	75	315	87.0	42	190	247	94	204	13	22.3
Coleman	76	2,759	564	46.0	99	23	421	80.8	247	852	276	92	243	126	20.7
Anderson	55	2,010	370	43.5	25	7	180	77.6	51	226	449	96	153	11	16.9
Morris	77	2,302	436	48.1	76	17	197	79.4	227	454	106	144	119	52	14.1
Bowie	79	2,092	287	45.0	6	2	141	77.9	158	556	127	32	120	128	9.1
Robinson	80	1,585	270	42.3	56	20	112	57.4	49	159	323	96	140	12	8.4
King	32	430	91	51.4	7	2	39	68.4	35	76	18	11	21	3	7.0
Addison	68	1,164	182	44.3	34	7	57	81.4	45	132	53	23	64	11	6.3
Brown	77	1,186	160	48.3	5	0	71	72.4	88	232	51	20	56	24	5.1
Williams	12	139	21	45.7	0	0	7	38.9	22	41	0	4	8	4	4.1
Mahorn	74	1,077	101	47.2	3	1	88	80.0	93	279	33	19	58	31	3.9
Cheeks	35	510	51	54.8	2	0	24	88.9	5	42	107	33	33	2	3.6
Dudley	71	1,398	94	35.3	0	0	57	51.8	215	513	16	17	54	103	3.5
George	48	380	51	37.8	5	0	20	83.3	9	27	59	10	31	3	2.5
Schintzius	5	35	2	28.6	0	0	3	100.0	2	8	2	2	0	2	1.4
Nets	**82**	**19,780**	**3,272**	**46.2**	**488**	**155**	**1,732**	**76.7**	**1,291**	**3,797**	**1,872**	**693**	**1,355**	**526**	**102.8**
Opponents	**82**	**19,780**	**3,231**	**46.5**	**618**	**201**	**1,665**	**74.1**	**1,102**	**3,447**	**1,786**	**780**	**1,304**	**416**	**101.6**

New York Knickerbockers

Player	GP	Min	FGM	Pct	FGA	FGM	FTM	Pct	Off	Total	A	Stl	TO	BS	Avg
Ewing	81	3,003	779	50.3	7	1	400	71.9	191	980	151	74	265	161	24.2
Starks	80	2,477	513	42.8	336	108	263	79.5	54	204	404	91	173	12	17.5
Smith	81	2,172	358	46.9	2	0	287	78.2	170	432	142	48	155	96	12.4
Mason	81	2,482	316	50.2	0	0	199	68.2	231	640	170	43	137	19	10.3
Blackman	60	1,434	239	44.3	73	31	71	78.9	23	102	157	22	65	10	9.7
Rivers	77	1,886	216	43.7	123	39	133	82.1	26	192	405	123	114	9	7.8
Campbell	58	1,062	194	49.0	5	2	59	67.8	59	155	62	34	51	5	7.7
Oakley	82	2,230	219	50.8	1	0	127	72.2	288	708	126	85	124	15	6.9
Anthony	70	1,699	174	41.5	30	4	107	67.3	42	170	398	113	104	12	6.6
Davis	50	815	110	43.8	19	6	43	79.6	13	56	83	22	45	4	5.4
Kimble	9	55	14	42.4	8	2	3	37.5	3	11	5	1	6	0	3.7
Williams	55	571	72	41.1	0	0	14	66.7	44	146	19	21	22	28	2.9
Anderson	16	44	5	27.8	0	0	11	84.6	6	3	3	3	5	1	1.3
Knicks	**82**	**19,930**	**3,209**	**46.5**	**604**	**193**	**1,717**	**74.1**	**1,150**	**3,810**	**2,125**	**680**	**1,296**	**372**	**101.6**
Opponents	**82**	**19,930**	**2,822**	**42.6**	**753**	**230**	**1,949**	**75.5**	**1,031**	**3,356**	**1,658**	**657**	**1,360**	**384**	**95.4**

Orlando Magic

Player	GP	Min	Field Goals		3-Pt FG		Free Throws		Rebounds		A	Stl	TO	BS	Avg
			FGM	Pct	FGA	FGM	FTM	Pct	Off	Total					
O'Neal	81	3,071	733	56.2	2	0	427	59.2	342	1,122	152	60	307	286	23.4
Anderson	79	2,920	594	44.9	249	88	298	74.1	122	477	265	128	164	56	19.9
Scott	54	1,759	329	43.1	268	108	92	78.6	38	186	136	57	104	18	15.9
Skiles	78	3,086	416	46.7	235	80	289	89.2	52	290	730	86	267	2	15.4
Royal	77	1,636	194	49.6	3	0	318	81.5	116	295	80	36	113	25	9.2
Tolbert	72	1,838	226	49.8	28	9	122	72.6	133	412	91	33	124	21	8.1
Bowie	77	1,761	268	47.1	48	15	67	79.8	36	194	175	54	84	14	8.0
Turner	75	1,479	231	52.9	17	10	56	80.0	74	252	107	19	66	9	7.0
Catledge	21	262	36	49.3	0	0	27	79.4	18	46	5	4	25	1	4.7
Williams	21	240	40	51.3	0	1	16	80.0	24	56	5	14	25	1	4.6
Green	52	626	87	43.9	10	1	60	62.5	11	34	116	23	42	4	4.5
Kerr	52	481	53	43.4	26	6	22	91.7	5	45	70	10	27	1	2.6
Wright	4	10	4	80.0	0	0	0	0.00	1	2	0	0	0	0	2.0
Kite	64	640	38	45.2	1	0	13	54.2	66	193	10	13	35	12	1.4
Magic	82	19,880	3,257	48.6	889	317	1,821	73.0	1,040	3,606	1,982	542	1,429	457	105.5
Opponents	82	19,880	3,307	45.6	754	248	1,692	72.9	1,166	3,437	2,091	715	1,119	401	104.2

Philadelphia 76ers

Player	GP	Min	Field Goals		3-Pt FG		Free Throws		Rebounds		A	Stl	TO	BS	Avg
			FGM	Pct	FGA	FGM	FTM	Pct	Off	Total					
Hawkins	81	2,977	551	47.0	307	122	419	86.0	91	346	317	137	180	30	20.3
Hornacek	79	2,860	582	47.0	249	97	250	86.5	84	342	548	131	222	21	19.1
Weatherspoon	82	2,654	494	46.9	4	1	291	71.3	179	589	147	85	176	67	15.6
Gilliam	80	1,742	359	46.4	1	0	274	84.3	136	472	116	37	157	54	12.4
Jordan	4	106	18	43.9	0	0	8	47.1	5	19	3	3	12	5	11.0
Perry	81	2,104	287	46.8	49	10	147	71.1	154	409	126	40	123	91	9.0
Dawkins	74	1,598	258	43.7	84	26	113	79.6	33	136	339	80	121	4	8.9
Anderson	69	1,263	225	41.4	120	39	72	80.9	62	184	93	31	63	5	8.1
Payne	13	154	38	42.2	18	4	4	100.0	4	24	18	5	7	2	6.5
Wilkins	26	192	55	56.7	2	0	48	61.5	14	40	2	7	17	1	6.1
Lang	73	1,861	149	42.5	5	1	87	76.3	136	436	79	46	89	141	5.3
Shackelford	48	568	80	48.8	2	0	31	63.3	65	205	26	13	36	25	4.0
Oliver	34	279	33	33.0	4	0	15	68.2	10	30	20	10	24	2	2.4
Grant	72	996	77	35.0	68	20	20	64.5	24	67	206	43	54	1	2.7
Bol	58	855	52	40.9	32	10	12	63.2	44	193	18	14	50	119	2.2
76ers	82	19,930	3,225	45.6	941	330	1,776	78.6	1,031	3,462	2,038	672	1,362	566	104.3
Opponents	82	19,930	3,666	48.6	792	280	1,417	75.5	1,258	3,892	2,406	781	1,290	431	110.1

Phoenix Suns

Player	GP	Min	Field Goals		3-Pt FG		Free Throws		Rebounds		A	Stl	TO	BS	Avg
			FGM	Pct	FGA	FGM	FTM	Pct	Off	Total					
Barkley	76	2,859	716	52.0	220	67	445	76.5	237	928	385	119	233	74	25.6
Majerle	82	3,199	509	46.4	438	167	203	77.8	120	383	311	138	133	33	16.9
K.Johnson	49	1,643	282	49.9	8	1	226	81.9	30	104	384	85	151	20	16.1
Dumas	48	1,320	302	52.4	3	1	152	70.7	100	223	60	85	92	39	15.8
Ceballos	74	1,607	381	57.6	2	0	187	72.5	172	408	77	54	106	28	12.8
Chambers	73	1,723	320	44.7	28	11	241	83.7	96	345	101	43	92	23	12.2
Ainge	80	2,163	337	46.2	372	150	123	84.8	49	214	260	69	113	8	11.8
Knight	52	888	124	39.1	7	0	67	77.9	28	64	145	23	73	4	6.1
Miller	56	1,069	121	47.5	3	0	71	71.0	70	275	118	38	108	100	5.6
West	82	1,558	175	61.4	0	0	86	51.8	153	458	29	16	93	103	4.6
Mustaf	32	336	57	43.8	1	0	33	62.3	29	83	10	14	22	11	4.6
F.Johnson	77	1,122	136	43.6	12	1	59	77.6	41	113	186	60	80	7	4.3
Stivrins	19	76	19	48.7	2	0	3	75.0	7	19	3	2	7	2	2.2
Kempton	30	167	19	39.6	0	0	18	58.1	12	39	19	4	16	4	1.9
Suns	82	19,730	3,494	49.3	1095	398	1,912	75.3	1,141	3,651	2,087	752	1,359	455	113.4
Opponents	82	19,730	3,500	47.9	750	250	1,502	72.3	1,118	3,434	2,107	708	1,328	512	106.7

Portland Trail Blazers

Player	GP	Min	FGM	Pct	FGA	FGM	FTM	Pct	Off	Total	A	Stl	TO	BS	Avg
			Field Goals		3-Pt FG		Free Throws		Rebounds						
Drexler	49	1,671	350	42.9	113	31	245	83.9	126	309	278	95	115	37	19.9
Robinson	82	2,575	632	47.3	77	19	287	69.0	165	542	182	98	173	163	19.1
Porter	81	2,883	503	45.4	345	143	327	84.3	58	316	419	101	199	10	18.2
Strickland	78	2,474	396	48.5	30	4	273	71.7	120	337	559	131	199	24	13.7
Kersey	65	1,719	281	43.8	8	8	116	63.4	126	406	121	80	84	41	10.6
Duckworth	74	1,762	301	43.8	2	0	127	73.0	118	387	70	45	87	39	9.9
Elie	82	1,757	240	45.8	129	45	183	85.5	59	216	177	74	89	20	8.6
Williams	82	2,498	270	51.1	1	0	138	64.5	232	690	75	81	101	61	8.3
Bryant	80	1,396	186	50.3	1	0	104	70.3	132	324	41	37	65	23	6.0
Murray	48	495	108	41.5	70	21	35	87.5	40	83	11	8	31	5	5.7
Johnson	42	356	57	38.3	14	3	40	67.8	18	48	13	8	28	1	3.7
Wolf	23	165	20	45.5	1	0	13	81.3	14	48	5	7	7	1	2.3
Rudd	15	95	7	19.4	11	1	11	78.6	4	9	17	1	11	0	1.7
Smith	23	68	10	37.0	1	0	3	21.4	15	21	1	4	4	1	1.0
Trail Blazers	82	19,905	3,361	45.8	843	275	1,901	74.5	1,226	3,733	1,989	770	1,215	425	108.5
Opponents	82	19,905	3,337	46.8	811	277	1,692	76.0	1,022	3,549	2,059	649	1,404	452	105.4

Sacramento Kings

Player	GP	Min	FGM	Pct	FGA	FGM	FTM	Pct	Off	Total	A	Stl	TO	BS	Avg
			Field Goals		3-Pt FG		Free Throws		Rebounds						
Richmond	45	1,728	371	47.4	130	48	197	84.5	18	154	221	53	130	9	21.9
Simmons	69	2,502	468	44.4	11	1	298	81.9	156	495	312	95	196	38	17.9
Williams	59	1,673	358	43.5	191	61	224	74.2	115	265	178	66	179	29	17.0
Tisdale	76	2,283	544	50.9	2	0	175	75.8	127	500	108	52	117	47	16.6
Webb	69	2,335	342	43.3	135	37	279	85.1	44	193	481	104	194	6	14.5
Bonner	70	1,764	229	46.1	7	0	143	59.3	188	455	96	86	105	17	8.6
Higgins	69	1,425	199	41.2	133	43	130	86.1	66	193	119	51	63	29	8.3
Causwell	55	1,211	175	54.5	1	0	103	62.4	112	303	35	32	58	87	8.2
Brown	75	1,726	225	46.3	6	2	115	73.2	75	212	196	108	120	34	7.6
Chilcutt	59	834	165	48.5	0	0	32	69.6	80	194	64	22	54	21	6.1
Conlon	46	467	81	47.4	4	0	57	70.4	48	123	37	13	28	5	4.8
Les	73	881	110	42.5	154	66	42	84.0	20	89	169	40	48	7	4.5
Rambis	72	822	67	51.9	2	0	43	66.2	77	227	53	43	42	18	2.5
Kimbrough	3	15	2	33.3	2	1	0	—	0	0	1	1	0	0	1.7
Kings	82	19,780	3,360	46.3	788	262	1,865	76.2	1,137	3,418	2,076	768	1,364	348	107.9
Opponents	82	19,780	3,337	48.7	680	213	2,054	75.8	1,138	3,700	2,073	767	1,466	551	111.1

San Antonio Spurs

Player	GP	Min	FGM	Pct	FGA	FGM	FTM	Pct	Off	Total	A	Stl	TO	BS	Avg
			Field Goals		3-Pt FG		Free Throws		Rebounds						
Robinson	82	3,211	676	50.1	17	3	561	73.2	229	956	301	127	241	264	23.4
Elliott	70	2,604	451	49.1	104	37	268	79.5	85	322	265	68	152	28	17.2
Ellis	82	2,731	545	49.9	297	119	157	79.7	81	312	107	78	111	18	16.7
Carr	71	1,947	379	53.8	5	0	174	77.7	107	388	97	35	96	87	13.1
Reid	82	1,887	283	47.6	5	0	214	76.4	120	456	80	47	125	31	9.4
Daniels	77	1,573	285	44.3	177	59	72	72.7	86	216	148	38	102	30	9.1
Johnson	75	2,030	256	50.2	8	0	144	79.1	20	146	561	85	145	16	8.7
Del Negro	73	1,526	218	50.7	24	6	101	86.3	19	163	291	44	92	1	7.4
Anderson	38	560	80	43.0	8	1	22	78.6	7	57	79	14	44	6	4.8
Mack	40	267	47	39.8	22	3	45	77.6	18	48	15	14	22	5	3.6
Cummings	8	76	11	37.9	0	0	5	50.0	6	19	4	1	2	1	3.4
Wood	64	598	52	44.4	21	5	46	83.6	38	97	34	13	29	12	2.4
Othick	4	39	3	60.0	4	2	0	00.0	1	2	7	1	4	0	2.0
Bedford	16	66	9	33.3	1	1	6	55.0	1	10	0	0	1	1	1.6
Smith	66	833	38	43.7	0	0	9	40.9	103	268	28	23	39	16	1.3
Spurs	82	19,855	3,311	49.0	692	236	1,794	76.5	919	3,461	2,012	588	1,227	516	105.5
Opponents	82	19,855	3,290	45.8	747	270	1,583	77.2	1,082	3,470	1,905	655	1,131	373	102.8

Seattle Supersonics

Player	GP	Min	FGM	Pct	FGA	FGM	FTM	Pct	Off	Total	A	Stl	TO	BS	Avg
Pierce	77	2,218	524	48.9	113	42	313	88.9	58	192	220	100	160	7	18.2
Kemp	78	2,582	515	49.2	4	0	358	71.2	287	833	155	119	217	146	17.8
Johnson	82	1,869	463	46.7	56	17	234	91.1	124	272	135	36	134	4	14.4
Payton	82	2,548	476	49.4	34	7	151	77.0	95	281	399	177	148	21	13.5
McKey	77	2,439	387	49.6	112	40	220	74.1	121	327	197	105	152	58	13.4
Perkins	79	2,351	381	47.7	71	24	250	82.0	163	524	156	60	108	82	13.1
Barros	69	1,243	214	45.1	169	64	49	83.1	18	107	151	63	58	3	7.8
McMillan	73	1,977	213	46.4	65	25	95	70.9	84	306	384	173	139	33	7.5
Cage	82	2,156	219	52.6	1	0	61	46.9	268	659	69	76	59	46	6.1
Askew	73	1,129	152	49.2	6	2	105	70.5	62	161	122	40	69	19	5.6
Paddio	41	307	71	44.7	8	2	14	66.7	17	50	33	14	16	6	3.9
Scheffler	29	166	25	52.1	0	0	16	66.7	15	36	5	6	5	1	2.3
King	3	12	2	40.0	0	0	2	100.0	1	5	1	0	3	0	2.0
Supersonics	82	19,780	3,311	48.8	610	218	1,720	75.1	1,222	3,476	1,906	944	1,267	409	108.3
Opponents	82	19,780	3,290	46.9	808	272	1,748	75.9	1,075	3,298	1,835	655	1,516	406	101.3

Utah Jazz

Player	GP	Min	FGM	Pct	FGA	FGM	FTM	Pct	Off	Total	A	Stl	TO	BS	Avg
K Malone	82	3,099	797	55.2	20	4	619	74.0	227	919	308	124	240	85	27.0
J Malone	79	2,558	595	49.4	9	3	236	85.2	31	173	128	42	125	4	18.1
Stockton	82	2,863	437	48.6	187	72	293	79.8	64	237	987	199	266	21	15.1
Corbin	82	2,555	385	50.3	5	0	180	82.6	194	519	173	108	108	32	11.6
Humphries	78	2,034	287	43.6	75	15	101	77.7	40	143	317	101	132	11	8.8
Benoit	82	1,712	258	43.6	98	34	114	75.0	116	392	43	45	90	43	8.1
Krystkowiak	71	1,362	198	46.6	1	0	117	79.6	74	279	68	42	62	13	7.2
James	10	88	21	41.2	13	3	22	84.6	7	11	1	3	7	0	6.7
Brown	82	1,551	176	43.0	1	0	113	68.9	147	391	64	32	95	23	5.7
Donaldson	6	94	8	57.1	0	0	5	55.6	6	29	1	1	4	7	3.5
Austin	46	306	50	44.6	1	0	29	65.9	38	79	6	8	23	14	2.8
Eaton	64	1,104	71	54.6	0	0	35	70.0	73	264	17	18	43	79	2.6
Crotty	40	243	37	51.4	14	2	26	68.4	4	17	55	11	30	0	2.6
Howard	49	260	35	37.6	0	0	34	64.2	26	60	10	15	23	12	2.1
Jazz	82	19,755	3,336	48.9	414	130	1,907	76.5	1,031	3,504	2,177	746	1,270	344	106.2
Opponents	82	19,755	3,258	46.7	836	272	1,743	74.4	1,120	3,434	1,928	648	1,291	468	104.0

Washington Bullets

Player	GP	Min	FGM	Pct	FGA	FGM	FTM	Pct	Off	Total	A	Stl	TO	BS	Avg
Grant	72	2,667	560	48.7	10	1	218	72.7	133	412	205	72	90	44	18.6
Ellison	49	1,701	341	52.1	4	0	170	70.2	138	433	117	45	110	108	17.4
Adams	70	2,499	365	43.9	212	68	237	85.6	52	240	526	100	175	4	14.8
Gugliotta	81	2,795	484	42.6	135	38	181	64.4	219	781	306	134	230	35	14.7
Chapman	60	1,300	287	47.7	116	43	132	81.0	19	88	116	38	79	10	12.5
Stewart	81	1,823	306	54.3	2	0	184	72.7	154	383	146	47	153	29	9.8
Smith	69	1,546	261	45.8	23	8	109	85.8	26	106	186	58	103	9	9.3
Overton	45	990	152	47.1	13	3	59	72.8	25	106	157	31	72	6	8.1
Burtt	4	35	10	38.5	3	1	8	80.0	2	3	6	2	4	0	7.3
MacLean	62	674	157	43.5	6	3	90	81.1	33	122	39	11	42	4	6.6
Johnson	73	1,287	193	47.9	3	0	92	73.0	78	195	89	36	70	18	6.5
Irvin	4	45	9	50.0	1	1	3	50.0	2	4	2	1	4	0	5.5
Corchiani	10	105	14	58.3	3	0	16	76.2	1	7	16	6	8	0	4.4
Price	68	859	100	35.8	48	8	54	79.4	28	103	154	56	85	3	3.9
Robinson	4	33	6	37.5	1	0	3	60.0	1	3	3	1	1	1	3.8
Acres	18	269	26	53.1	2	1	11	68.8	26	67	5	3	13	6	3.6
Ogg	6	29	5	38.5	0	0	3	75.0	3	10	4	1	3	2	2.2
Jones	67	1,206	33	52.4	1	0	22	57.9	87	277	42	38	38	77	1.3
Bullets	82	19,805	3,302	46.7	578	146	1,875	74.8	1,031	3,348	2,110	673	1,323	359	101.9
Opponents	82	19,805	3,557	49.3	712	239	1,577	74.9	1,135	3,890	2,062	718	1,279	425	108.9

1993 NBA Draft

First Round

1. Chris Webber, Orlando (to Golden State)
2. Shawn Bradley, Philadelphia
3. Anfernee Hardaway, GS (to Orlando)
4. Jamal Mashburn, Dallas
5. Isaiah (JR) Rider, Minnesota
6. Calbert Cheaney, Washington
7. Bobby Hurley, Sacramento
8. Vin Baker, Milwaukee
9. Rodney Rogers, Denver
10. Lindsey Hunter, Detroit
11. Allan Houston, Detroit
12. George Lynch, LA Lakers
13. Terry Dehere, LA Clippers
14. Scott Haskin, Indiana
15. Douglas Edwards, Atlanta
16. Rex Walters, New Jersey
17. Greg Graham, Charlotte
18. Luther Wright, Utah
19. Acie Earl, Boston
20. Scott Burrell, Charlotte
21. James Robinson, Portland
22. Chris Mills, Cleveland
23. Ervin Johnson, Seattle
24. Sam Cassell, Houston
25. Corie Blount, Chicago
26. Geert Hammink, Orlando
27. Malcolm Mackey, Phoenix

Second Round

28. Lucious Harris, Dallas
29. Sherron Mills, Minnesota
30. Gheorghe Muresan, Washington
31. Evers Burns, Sacramento
32. Alphonso Ford, Philadelphia
33. Eric Riley, Dallas (to Houston)
34. Darnell Mee, Golden State (to Denver)
35. Ed Stokes, Miami
36. John Best, New Jersey
37. Nick Van Exel, LA Lakers
38. Conrad McRae, Washington
39. Thomas Hill, Indiana
40. Richard Manning, Atlanta
41. Anthony Reid, Chicago
42. Adonis Jordan, Seattle
43. Josh Grant, Denver (to Golden State)
44. Alex Holcombe, Sacramento
45. Bryon Russell, Utah
46. Richard Petruska, Houston
47. Chris Whitney, San Antonio
48. Kevin Thompson, Portland
49. Mark Buford, Phoenix
50. Marcelo Nicola, Houston
51. Spencer Dunkley, Indiana
52. Mike Peplowski, Sacramento
53. Leonard White, LA Clippers
54. Bryan Wilson, Phoenix

THEY SAID IT

Don Nelson, Golden State Warrior general manager, on 7'6" Shawn Bradley, formerly of BYU and the No. 2 pick in the NBA draft : "When he sits down, his ears pop."

Five Mascot-eers

The hairy gorilla that rapells from the rafters of America West Arena and entertains the crowd with trampoline-powered dunks is former Arizona State gymnast Bob Woolf. For the past five years, Woolf has monkeyed around in his guise as the Phoenix Suns' mascot, and four of his old ASU teammates have followed him into the profession. His ex-roomate, Mike Zerrillo, is the Charlotte Hornets' Hugo, Paul Linne cheers for pay in Indiana, and Jerry Burrell and John Sweeney cavort for Houston and Seattle, respectively.

FOR THE RECORD·Year by Year

NBA Champions

Season	Winner	Series	Loser	Winning Coach
1946-47	Philadelphia	4-1	Chicago	Eddie Gottlieb
1947-48	Baltimore	4-2	Philadelphia	Buddy Jeannette
1948-49	Minneapolis	4-2	Washington	John Kundla
1949-50	Minneapolis	4-2	Syracuse	John Kundla
1950-51	Rochester	4-3	New York	Les Harrison
1951-52	Minneapolis	4-3	New York	John Kundla
1952-53	Minneapolis	4-1	New York	John Kundla
1953-54	Minneapolis	4-3	Syracuse	John Kundla
1954-55	Syracuse	4-3	Ft Wayne	Al Cervi
1955-56	Philadelphia	4-1	Ft Wayne	George Senesky
1956-57	Boston	4-3	St Louis	Red Auerbach
1957-58	St Louis	4-2	Boston	Alex Hannum
1958-59	Boston	4-0	Minneapolis	Red Auerbach
1959-60	Boston	4-3	St Louis	Red Auerbach
1960-61	Boston	4-1	St Louis	Red Auerbach
1961-62	Boston	4-3	LA Lakers	Red Auerbach
1962-63	Boston	4-2	LA Lakers	Red Auerbach
1963-64	Boston	4-1	San Francisco	Red Auerbach
1964-65	Boston	4-1	LA Lakers	Red Auerbach
1965-66	Boston	4-3	LA Lakers	Red Auerbach
1966-67	Philadelphia	4-2	San Francisco	Alex Hannum
1967-68	Boston	4-2	LA Lakers	Bill Russell
1968-69	Boston	4-3	LA Lakers	Bill Russell
1969-70	New York	4-3	LA Lakers	Red Holzman
1970-71	Milwaukee	4-0	Baltimore	Larry Costello
1971-72	LA Lakers	4-1	New York	Bill Sharman
1972-73	New York	4-1	LA Lakers	Red Holzman
1973-74	Boston	4-3	Milwaukee	Tommy Heinsohn
1974-75	Golden State	4-0	Washington	Al Attles
1975-76	Boston	4-2	Phoenix	Tommy Heinsohn
1976-77	Portland	4-2	Philadelphia	Jack Ramsay
1977-78	Washington	4-3	Seattle	Dick Motta
1978-79	Seattle	4-1	Washington	Lenny Wilkens
1979-80	LA Lakers	4-2	Philadelphia	Paul Westhead
1980-81	Boston	4-2	Houston	Bill Fitch
1981-82	LA Lakers	4-2	Philadelphia	Pat Riley
1982-83	Philadelphia	4-0	LA Lakers	Billy Cunningham
1983-84	Boston	4-3	LA Lakers	K.C. Jones
1984-85	LA Lakers	4-2	Boston	Pat Riley
1985-86	Boston	4-2	Houston	K.C. Jones
1986-87	LA Lakers	4-2	Boston	Pat Riley
1987-88	LA Lakers	4-3	Detroit	Pat Riley
1988-89	Detroit	4-0	LA Lakers	Chuck Daly
1989-90	Detroit	4-1	Portland	Chuck Daly
1990-91	Chicago	4-1	LA Lakers	Phil Jackson
1991-92	Chicago	4-2	Portland	Phil Jackson
1992-93	Chicago	4-2	Phoenix	Phil Jackson

NBA Finals Most Valuable Player

1969	Jerry West, LA	1982	Magic Johnson, LA
1970	Willis Reed, NY	1983	Moses Malone, Phil
1971	Kareem Abdul-Jabbar, Mil	1984	Larry Bird, Bos
1972	Wilt Chamberlain, LA	1985	Kareem Abdul-Jabbar, LA Lakers
1973	Willis Reed, NY	1986	Larry Bird, Bos
1974	John Havlicek, Bos	1987	Magic Johnson, LA Lakers
1975	Rick Barry, GS	1988	James Worthy, LA Lakers
1976	JoJo White, Bos	1989	Joe Dumars, Det
1977	Bill Walton, Port	1990	Isiah Thomas, Det
1978	Wes Unseld, Wash	1991	Michael Jordan, Chi
1979	Dennis Johnson, Sea	1992	Michael Jordan, Chi
1980	Magic Johnson, LA	1993	Michael Jordan, Chi
1981	Cedric Maxwell, Bos		

NBA Most Valuable Player: Maurice Podoloff Trophy

Season	Player, Team	GP	Field Goals		3-Pt FG		Free Throws		Rebounds		A	Stl	BS	Avg
			FGM	Pct	FGM	Pct	FTM	Pct	Off	Total				
1955-56	Bob Pettit, StL	72	646	42.9	–	–	557	73.6	–	1,164	189	–	–	25.7
1956-57	Bob Cousy, Bos	64	478	37.8	–	–	363	82.1	–	309	478	–	–	20.6
1957-58	Bill Russell, Bos	69	456	44.2	–	–	230	51.9	–	1,564	202	–	–	16.6
1958-59	Bob Pettit, StL	72	719	43.8	–	–	667	75.9	–	1,182	221	–	–	29.2
1959-60	Wilt Chamberlain, Phil	72	1,065	46.1	–	–	577	58.2	–	1,941	168	–	–	37.6
1960-61	Bill Russell, Bos	78	532	42.6	–	–	258	55.0	–	1,868	264	–	–	16.9
1961-62	Bill Russell, Bos	76	575	45.7	–	–	286	59.5	–	1,891	341	–	–	18.9
1962-63	Bill Russell, Bos	78	511	43.2	–	–	287	55.5	–	1,843	348	–	–	16.8
1963-64	Oscar Robertson, Cin	79	840	48.3	–	–	800	85.3	–	783	868	–	–	31.4
1964-65	Bill Russell, Bos	78	429	43.8	–	–	244	57.3	–	1,878	410	–	–	14.1
1965-66	Wilt Chamberlain, Phil	79	1,074	54.0	–	–	501	51.3	–	1,943	414	–	–	33.5
1966-67	Wilt Chamberlain, Phil	81	785	68.3	–	–	386	44.1	–	1,957	630	–	–	24.1
1967-68	Wilt Chamberlain, Phil	82	819	59.5	–	–	354	38.0	–	1,952	702	–	–	24.3
1968-69	Wes Unseld, Balt	82	427	47.6	–	–	277	60.5	–	1,491	213	–	–	13.8
1969-70	Willis Reed, NY	81	702	50.7	–	–	351	75.6	–	1,126	161	–	–	21.7
1970-71	Kareem Abdul-Jabbar, Mil	82	1,063	57.7	–	–	470	69.0	–	1,311	272	–	–	31.7
1971-72	Kareem Abdul-Jabbar, Mil	81	1,159	57.4	–	–	504	68.9	–	1,346	370	–	–	34.8
1972-73	Dave Cowens, Bos	82	740	45.2	–	–	204	77.9	–	1,329	333	–	–	20.5
1973-74	Kareem Abdul-Jabbar, Mil	81	948	53.9	–	–	295	70.2	287	1,178	386	112	283	27.0
1974-75	Bob McAdoo, Buff	82	1,095	51.2	–	–	641	80.5	307	1,155	179	92	174	34.5
1975-76	Kareem Abdul-Jabbar, LA	82	914	52.9	–	–	447	70.3	272	1,383	413	119	338	27.7
1976-77	Kareem Abdul-Jabbar, LA	82	888	57.9	–	–	376	70.1	266	1,090	319	101	261	26.2
1977-78	Bill Walton, Port	58	460	52.2	–	–	177	72.0	118	766	291	60	146	18.9
1978-79	Moses Malone, Hou	82	716	54.0	–	–	599	73.9	587	1,444	147	79	119	24.8
1979-80	Kareem Abdul-Jabbar, LA	82	835	60.4	0	00.0	364	76.5	190	886	371	81	280	24.8
1980-81	Julius Erving, Phil	82	794	52.1	4	22.2	422	78.7	244	657	364	173	147	24.6
1981-82	Moses Malone, Hou	81	945	51.9	0	00.0	630	76.2	558	1,188	142	76	125	31.1
1982-83	Moses Malone, Phil	78	654	50.1	0	00.0	600	76.1	445	1,194	101	89	157	24.5
1983-84	Larry Bird, Bos	79	758	49.2	18	24.7	374	88.8	181	796	520	144	69	24.2
1984-85	Larry Bird, Bos	80	918	52.2	56	42.7	403	88.2	164	842	531	129	98	28.7
1985-86	Larry Bird, Bos	82	796	49.6	82	42.3	441	89.6	190	805	557	166	51	25.8
1986-87	Magic Johnson, LA Lakers	80	683	52.2	8	20.5	535	84.8	122	504	977	138	36	23.9
1987-88	Michael Jordan, Chi	82	1,069	53.5	7	13.2	723	84.1	139	449	485	259	131	35.0
1988-89	Magic Johnson, LA Lakers	77	579	50.9	59	31.4	513	91.1	111	607	988	138	22	22.5
1989-90	Magic Johnson, LA Lakers	79	546	48.0	106	38.4	567	89.0	128	522	907	132	34	22.3
1990-91	Michael Jordan, Chi	82	990	53.9	29	31.2	571	85.1	118	492	453	223	83	31.5
1991-92	Michael Jordan, Chi	80	943	51.9	27	27.0	491	83.2	91	511	489	182	75	30.1
1992-93	Charles Barkley, Phoe	76	716	52.0	67	30.5	445	76.5	237	928	385	119	74	25.6

Coach of the Year: Arnold "Red" Auerbach Trophy

1962-63	Harry Gallatin, StL	1977-78	Hubie Brown, Atl
1963-64	Alex Hannum, SF	1978-79	Cotton Fitzsimmons, KC
1964-65	Red Auerbach, Bos	1979-80	Bill Fitch, Bos
1965-66	Dolph Schayes, Phil	1980-81	Jack McKinney, Ind
1966-67	Johnny Kerr, Chi	1981-82	Gene Shue, Wash
1967-68	Richie Guerin, StL	1982-83	Don Nelson, Mil
1968-69	Gene Shue, Balt	1983-84	Frank Layden, Utah
1969-70	Red Holzman, NY	1984-85	Don Nelson, Mil
1970-71	Dick Motta, Chi	1985-86	Mike Fratello, Atl
1971-72	Bill Sharman, LA	1986-87	Mike Schuler, Port
1972-73	Tom Heinsohn, Bos	1987-88	Doug Moe, Den
1973-74	Ray Scott, Det	1988-89	Cotton Fitzsimmons, Phoe
1974-75	Phil Johnson, KC-Oma	1989-90	Pat Riley, LA Lakers
1975-76	Bill Fitch, Clev	1990-91	Don Chaney, Hou
1976-77	Tom Nissalke, Hou	1991-92	Don Nelson, GS
		1992-93	Pat Riley, NY

Note: Award named after Auerbach in 1986.

NBA Rookie of the Year: Eddie Gottlieb Trophy

1952-53	Don Meineke, FW
1953-54	Ray Felix, Balt
1954-55	Bob Pettit, Mil
1955-56	Maurice Stokes, Roch
1956-57	Tom Heinsohn, Bos
1957-58	Woody Sauldsberry, Phil
1958-59	Elgin Baylor, Minn
1959-60	Wilt Chamberlain, Phil
1960-61	Oscar Robertson, Cin
1961-62	Walt Bellamy, Chi
1962-63	Terry Dischinger, Chi
1963-64	Jerry Lucas, Cin
1964-65	Willis Reed, NY
1965-66	Rick Barry, SF
1966-67	Dave Bing, Det
1967-68	Earl Monroe, Balt
1968-69	Wes Unseld, Balt
1969-70	Kareem Abdul-Jabbar, Mil
1970-71	Dave Cowens, Bos
	Geoff Petrie, Port
1971-72	Sidney Wicks, Port
1972-73	Bob McAdoo, Buff
1973-74	Ernie DiGregorio, Buff
1974-75	Keith Wilkes, GS
1975-76	Alvan Adams, Phoe
1976-77	Adrian Dantley, Buff
1977-78	Walter Davis, Phoe
1978-79	Phil Ford, KC
1979-80	Larry Bird, Bos
1980-81	Darrell Griffith, Utah
1981-82	Buck Williams, NJ
1982-83	Terry Cummings, SD
1983-84	Ralph Sampson, Hou
1984-85	Michael Jordan, Chi
1985-86	Patrick Ewing, NY
1986-87	Chuck Person, Ind
1987-88	Mark Jackson, NY
1988-89	Mitch Richmond, GS
1989-90	David Robinson, SA
1990-91	Derrick Coleman, NJ

NBA Defensive Player of the Year

1991-92	Larry Johnson, Char
1992-93	Shaquille O'Neal, Orl
1982-83	Sidney Moncrief, Mil
1983-84	Sidney Moncrief, Mil
1984-85	Mark Eaton, Utah
1985-86	Alvin Robertson, SA
1986-87	Michael Cooper, LA Lakers
1987-88	Michael Jordan, Chi
1988-89	Mark Eaton, Utah
1989-90	Dennis Rodman, Det
1990-91	Dennis Rodman, Det
1991-92	David Robinson, SA
1992-93	Hakeem Olajuwon, Hou

NBA Sixth Man Award

1982-83	Bobby Jones, Phil
1983-84	Kevin McHale, Bos
1984-85	Kevin McHale, Bos
1985-86	Bill Walton, Bos
1986-87	Ricky Pierce, Mil
1987-88	Roy Tarpley, Dall
1988-89	Eddie Johnson, Phoe
1989-90	Ricky Pierce, Mil
1990-91	Detlef Schrempf, Ind
1991-92	Detlef Schrempf, Ind
1992-93	Cliff Robinson, Port

NBA Most Improved Player

1985-86	Alvin Robertson, SA
1986-87	Dale Ellis, Sea
1987-88	Kevin Duckworth, Port
1988-89	Kevin Johnson, Phoe
1989-90	Rony Seikaly, Mia
1990-91	Scott Skiles, Orl
1991-92	Pervis Ellison, Wash
1992-93	Chris Jackson, Den

J. Walter Kennedy Citizenship Award

1974-75	Wes Unseld, Wash
1975-76	Slick Watts, Sea

Kennedy Citizenship Award (Cont.)

1976-77	Dave Bing, Wash
1977-78	Bob Lanier, Det
1978-79	Calvin Murphy, Hou
1979-80	Austin Carr, Clev
1980-81	Mike Glenn, NY
1981-82	Kent Benson, Det
1982-83	Julius Erving, Phil
1983-84	Frank Layden, Utah
1984-85	Dan Issel, Den
1985-86	Michael Cooper, LA Lakers
	Rory Sparrow, NY
1986-87	Isiah Thomas, Det
1987-88	Alex English, Den
1988-89	Thurl Bailey, Utah
1989-90	Glenn Rivers, Atl
1990-91	Kevin Johnson, Phoe
1991-92	Magic Johnson, LA Lakers
1992-93	Terry Porter, Port

NBA Executive of the Year

1972-73	Joe Axelson, KC-Oma
1973-74	Eddie Donovan, Buff
1974-75	Dick Vertlieb, GS
1975-76	Jerry Colangelo, Phoe
1976-77	Ray Patterson, Hou
1977-78	Angelo Drossos, SA
1978-79	Bob Ferry, Wash
1979-80	Red Auerbach, Bos
1980-81	Jerry Colangelo, Phoe
1981-82	Bob Ferry, Wash
1982-83	Zollie Volchok, Sea
1983-84	Frank Layden, Utah
1984-85	Vince Boryla, Den
1985-86	Stan Kasten, Atl
1986-87	Stan Kasten, Atl
1987-88	Jerry Krause, Chi
1988-89	Jerry Colangelo, Phoe
1989-90	Bob Bass, SA
1990-91	Bucky Buckwalter, Port
1991-92	Wayne Embry, Cle
1992-93	Jerry Colangelo, Phoe

Selected by *The Sporting News*.

NBA All-Time Individual Leaders

Scoring

MOST POINTS, LIFETIME

Kareem Abdul-Jabbar	38,387
Wilt Chamberlain	31,419
Elvin Hayes	27,313
Moses Malone	27,066
Oscar Robertson	26,710
John Havlicek	26,395
Alex English	25,613
Jerry West	25,192
Adrian Dantley	23,177
Elgin Baylor	23,149

MOST POINTS, SEASON

Wilt Chamberlain, Phil	4,029	1961-62
Wilt Chamberlain, SF	3,586	1962-63
Michael Jordan, Chi	3,041	1986-87
Wilt Chamberlain, Phil	3,033	1960-61
Wilt Chamberlain, SF	2,948	1963-64
Michael Jordan, Chi	2,868	1986-87
Bob McAdoo, Buff	2,831	1974-75
Rick Barry, SF	2,775	1966-67
Michael Jordan, Chi	2,753	1989-90
Elgin Baylor, LA	2,719	1962-63

HIGHEST SCORING AVERAGE, CAREER

Michael Jordan	32.3	667 games
Wilt Chamberlain	30.1	1,045 games
Elgin Baylor	27.4	846 games
Jerry West	27.0	932 games
Dominique Wilkins	26.5	833 games
Bob Pettit	26.4	792 games
George Gervin	26.2	791 games
Karl Malone	26.1	652 games
Oscar Robertson	25.7	1,040 games
Kareem Abdul-Jabbar	24.6	1,560 games

HIGHEST SCORING AVERAGE, SEASON
(Minimum of 70 games)

Wilt Chamberlain, Phil	50.4	1961-62
Wilt Chamberlain, SF	44.8	1962-63
Wilt Chamberlain, Phil	38.4	1960-61
Wilt Chamberlain, Phil	37.6	1959-60
Michael Jordan, Chi	37.1	1986-87
Wilt Chamberlain, SF	36.9	1963-64
Rick Barry, SF	35.6	1966-67
Michael Jordan, Chi	35.0	1987-88
Elgin Baylor, LA	34.8	1960-61

MOST POINTS, GAME

	Player, Team	Opp	Date
100	Wilt Chamberlain, Phi	NY	3/2/62
78	Wilt Chamberlain, Phi	LA	12/8/61
73	Wilt Chamberlain, Phi	Chi	1/13/62
73	Wilt Chamberlain, SF	NY	11/16/62
73	David Thompson, Den	Det	4/9/78
72	Wilt Chamberlain, SF	LA	11/3/62
71	Elgin Baylor, LA	NY	11/15/60
70	Wilt Chamberlain, SF	Syr	3/10/63
69	Michael Jordan, Chi	Cle	3/28/90
68	Wilt Chamberlain, Phi	Chi	12/16/67

THEY SAID IT

Scott Skiles, Orlando Magic guard, dismissing the fans' booing of him: "Basketball is like church. Many attend but few understand."

Field Goal Percentage

Highest Field Goal Percentage, Career: .599—Artis Gilmore
Highest Field Goal Percentage, Season: .727—Wilt Chamberlain, LA Lakers, 1972-73 (426/586)

Free Throw Percentage

HIGHEST FREE THROW PERCENTAGE, CAREER

Mark Price	908
Rick Barry	900
Calvin Murphy	892
Larry Bird	886
Bill Sharman	883

HIGHEST FREE THROW PERCENTAGE, SEASON

Calvin Murphy, Hou	958	1980-81
Mark Price, Clev	948	1992-93
Mark Price, Clev	947	1991-92
Rick Barry, Hou	9467	1978-79
Ernie DiGregorio, Buff	945	1976-77

Three-Point Field Goal Percentage*

Most Three-Point Field Goals, Career: Dale Ellis—882
Highest Three-Point Field Goal Percentage, Career: Steve Kerr—.475
Most Three-Point Field Goals, Season: Vernon Maxwell, Hou—172 1990-91
Highest Three-Point Field Goal Percentage, Season: Jon Sundvold, Mia—.522 1988-89
Most Three-Point Field Goals, Game: 10—Brian Shaw, Miami vs Milwaukee, 4/8/93;

*First Year of Shot: 1979-80

Steals

Most Steals, Career: 2,277—Maurice Cheeks
Most Steals, Season: 301—Alvin Robertson, San Antonio, 1985-86
Most Steals, Game: 11—Larry Kenon, San Antonio vs Kansas City, 12/26/76

Rebounds

MOST REBOUNDS, CAREER

Wilt Chamberlain	23,924
Bill Russell	21,620
Kareem Abdul-Jabbar	17,440
Elvin Hayes	16,279
Moses Malone	15,940
Nate Thurmond	14,464
Walt Bellamy	14,241
Wes Unseld	13,769
Robert Parish	13,431
Jerry Lucas	12,942

MOST REBOUNDS, SEASON

Wilt Chamberlain, Phil	2,149	1960-61
Wilt Chamberlain, Phil	2,052	1961-62
Wilt Chamberlain, Phil	1,957	1966-67
Wilt Chamberlain, Phil	1,952	1967-68
Wilt Chamberlain, SF	1,946	1962-63
Wilt Chamberlain, Phil	1,943	1965-66
Wilt Chamberlain, Phil	1,941	1959-60
Bill Russell, Bos	1,930	1963-64
Bill Russell, Bos	1,878	1964-65
Bill Russell, Bos	1,868	1960-61

MOST REBOUNDS, GAME

	Player, Team	Opp	Date
55	Wilt Chamberlain, Phi	Bos	11/24/60
51	Bill Russell, Bos	Syr	2/5/60
49	Bill Russell, Bos	Phi	11/16/57
49	Bill Russell, Bos	Det	3/11/65
45	Wilt Chamberlain, Phil	Syr	2/6/60
45	Wilt Chamberlain, Phil	LA	1/21/61

Assists

MOST ASSISTS, CAREER

Magic Johnson	9,921
Oscar Robertson	9,887
Isiah Thomas	8,662
John Stockton	8,352
Maurice Cheeks	7,392

MOST ASSISTS, SEASON

John Stockton, Utah	1,164	1990-91
John Stockton, Utah	1,134	1989-90
John Stockton, Utah	1,128	1987-88
Isiah Thomas, Det	1,123	1984-85
John Stockton, Utah	1,126	1991-92

MOST ASSISTS, GAME: 30—Scott Skiles, Orlando vs Denver, 12/30/90

Blocked Shots

MOST BLOCKED SHOTS, CAREER

Kareem Abdul-Jabbar	3,189
Mark Eaton	3,064
Wayne "Tree" Rollins	2,456

MOST BLOCKED SHOTS, SEASON

Mark Eaton, Utah	456	1984-85
Manute Bol, Wash	397	1985-86
Elmore Smith, LA	393	1973-74

MOST BLOCKED SHOTS, GAME: 17—Elmore Smith, LA Lakers vs Portland, 10/28/73

NBA Season Leaders

Scoring

1946-47	Joe Fulks, Phil	1389	1970-71	Kareem Abdul-Jabbar, Mil	31.7
1947-48	Max Zaslofsky, Chi	1007	1971-72	Kareem Abdul-Jabber, Mil	34.8
1948-49	George Mikan, Minn	1698	1972-73	Nate Archibald, KC-Oma	34.0
1949-50	George Mikan, Minn	1865	1973-74	Bob McAdoo, Buff	30.6
1950-51	George Mikan, Minn	1932	1974-75	Bob McAdoo, Buff	34.5
1951-52	Paul Arizin, Phil	1674	1975-76	Bob McAdoo, Buff	31.1
1952-53	Neil Johnston, Phil	1564	1976-77	Pete Maravich, NO	31.1
1953-54	Neil Johnston, Phil	1759	1977-78	George Gervin, SA	27.2
1954-55	Neil Johnston, Phil	1631	1978-79	George Gervin, SA	29.6
1955-56	Bob Pettit, StL	1849	1979-80	George Gervin, SA	33.1
1956-57	Paul Arizin, Phil	1817	1980-81	Adrian Dantley, Utah	30.7
1957-58	George Yardley, Det	2001	1981-82	George Gervin, SA	32.3
1958-59	Bob Pettit, StL	2105	1982-83	Alex English, Den	28.4
1959-60	Wilt Chamberlain, Phil	2707	1983-84	Adrian Dantley, Utah	30.6
1960-61	Wilt Chamberlain, Phil	3033	1984-85	Bernard King, NY	32.9
1961-62	Wilt Chamberlain, Phil	4029	1985-86	Dominique Wilkins, Atl	30.3
1962-63	Wilt Chamberlain, SF	3586	1986-87	Michael Jordan, Chi	37.1
1963-64	Wilt Chamberlain, SF	2948	1987-88	Michael Jordan, Chi	35.0
1964-65	Wilt Chamberlain, SF-Phil	2534	1988-89	Michael Jordan, Chi	32.5
1965-66	Wilt Chamberlain, Phil	2649	1989-90	Michael Jordan, Chi	33.6
1966-67	Rick Barry, SF	2775	1990-91	Michael Jordan, Chi	31.5
1967-68	Dave Bing, Det	2142	1991-92	Michael Jordan, Chi	30.1
1968-69	Elvin Hayes, SD	2327	1992-93	Michael Jordan, Chi	32.6
1969-70	Jerry West, LA	*31.2			

*Based on per game average since 1969-70.

Rebounding

1950-51	Dolph Schayes, Syr	1080	1972-73	Wilt Chamberlain, LA	18.6
1951-52	Larry Foust, FW	880	1973-74	Elvin Hayes, Capital	18.1
	Mel Hutchins, Mil	880	1974-75	Wes Unseld, Wash	14.8
1952-53	George Mikan, Minn	1007	1975-76	Kareem Abdul-Jabbar, LA	16.9
1953-54	Harry Gallatin, NY	1098	1976-77	Bill Walton, Port	14.4
1954-55	Neil Johnston, Phil	1085	1977-78	Len Robinson, NO	15.7
1955-56	Bob Pettit, StL	1164	1978-79	Moses Malone, Hou	17.6
1956-57	Maurice Stokes, Roch	1256	1979-80	Swen Nater, SD	15.0
1957-58	Bill Russell, Bos	1564	1980-81	Moses Malone, Hou	14.8
1958-59	Bill Russell, Bos	1612	1981-82	Moses Malone, Hou	14.7
1959-60	Wilt Chamberlain, Phil	1941	1982-83	Moses Malone, Phil	15.3
1960-61	Wilt Chamberlain, Phil	2149	1983-84	Moses Malone, Phil	13.4
1961-62	Wilt Chamberlain, Phil	2052	1984-85	Moses Malone, Phil	13.1
1962-63	Wilt Chamberlain, SF	1946	1985-86	Bill Laimbeer, Det	13.1
1963-64	Bill Russell, Bos	1930	1986-87	Charles Barkley, Phil	14.6
1964-65	Bill Russell, Bos	1878	1987-88	Michael Cage, LA Clippers	13.03
1965-66	Wilt Chamberlain, Phil	1943	1988-89	Hakeem Olajuwon, Hou	13.5
1966-67	Wilt Chamberlain, Phil	1957	1989-90	Hakeem Olajuwon, Hou	14.0
1967-68	Wilt Chamberlain, Phil	1952	1990-91	David Robinson, SA	13.0
1968-69	Wilt Chamberlain, LA	1712	1991-92	Dennis Rodman, Detroit	18.7
1969-70	Elvin Hayes, SD	*16.9	1992-93	Dennis Rodman, Detroit	18.3
1970-71	Wilt Chamberlain, LA	18.2			
1971-72	Wilt Chamberlain, LA	19.2			

*Based on per game average since 1969-70.

Assists

1946-47	Ernie Calverly, Prov	202	1970-71	Norm Van Lier, Cin	10.1
1947-48	Howie Dallmar, Phil	120	1971-72	Jerry West, LA	9.7
1948-49	Bob Davies, Roch	321	1972-73	Nate Archibald, KC-Oma	11.4
1949-50	Dick McGuire, NY	386	1973-74	Ernie DiGregorio, Buff	8.2
1950-51	Andy Phillip, Phil	414	1974-75	Kevin Porter, Wash	8.0
1951-52	Andy Phillip, Phil	539	1975-76	Don Watts, Sea	8.1
1952-53	Bob Cousy, Bos	547	1976-77	Don Buse, Ind	8.5
1953-54	Bob Cousy, Bos	578	1977-78	Kevin Porter, NJ-Det	10.2
1954-55	Bob Cousy, Bos	557	1978-79	Kevin Porter, Det	13.4
1955-56	Bob Cousy, Bos	642	1979-80	Micheal Richardson, NY	10.1
1956-57	Bob Cousy, Bos	478	1980-81	Kevin Porter, Wash	9.1
1957-58	Bob Cousy, Bos	463	1981-82	Johnny Moore, SA	9.6
1958-59	Bob Cousy, Bos	557	1982-83	Magic Johnson, LA	10.5
1959-60	Bob Cousy, Bos	715	1983-84	Magic Johnson, LA	13.1
1960-61	Oscar Robertson, Cin	690	1984-85	Isiah Thomas, Det	13.9
1961-62	Oscar Robertson, Cin	899	1985-86	Magic Johnson, LA Lakers	12.6
1962-63	Guy Rodgers, SF	825	1986-87	Magic Johnson, LA Lakers	12.2
1963-64	Oscar Robertson, Cin	868	1987-88	John Stockton, Utah	13.8
1964-65	Oscar Robertson, Cin	861	1988-89	John Stockton, Utah	13.6
1965-66	Oscar Robertson, Cin	847	1989-90	John Stockton, Utah	14.5
1966-67	Guy Rodgers, Chi	908	1990-91	John Stockton, Utah	14.2
1967-68	Wilt Chamberlain, Phil	702	1991-92	John Stockton, Utah	13.7
1968-69	Oscar Robertson, Cin	772	1992-93	John Stockton, Utah	12.0
1969-70	Len Wilkens, Sea	*9.1			

*Based on per game average since 1969-70.

Field Goal Percentage

1946-47	Bob Feerick, Wash	40.1	1960-61	Wilt Chamberlain, Phil	50.9
1947-48	Bob Feerick, Wash	34.0	1961-62	Walt Bellamy, Chi	51.9
1948-49	Arnie Risen, Roch	42.3	1962-63	Wilt Chamberlain, SF	52.8
1949-50	Alex Groza, Ind	47.8	1963-64	Jerry Lucas, Cin	52.7
1950-51	Alex Groza, Ind	47.0	1964-65	Wilt Chamberlain, SF-Phil	51.0
1951-52	Paul Arizin, Phil	44.8	1965-66	Wilt Chamberlain, Phil	54.0
1952-53	Neil Johnston, Phil	45.2	1966-67	Wilt Chamberlain, Phil	68.3
1953-54	Ed Macauley, Bos	48.6	1967-68	Wilt Chamberlain, Phil	59.5
1954-55	Larry Foust, FW	48.7	1968-69	Wilt Chamberlain, LA	58.3
1955-56	Neil Johnston, Phil	45.7	1969-70	Johnny Green, Cin	55.9
1956-57	Neil Johnston, Phil	44.7	1970-71	Johnny Green, Cin	58.7
1957-58	Jack Twyman, Cin	45.2	1971-72	Wilt Chamberlain, LA	64.9
1958-59	Ken Sears, NY	49.0	1972-73	Wilt Chamberlain, LA	72.7
1959-60	Ken Sears, NY	47.7	1973-74	Bob McAdoo, Buff	54.7

Field Goal Percentage *(Cont.)*

1974-75	Don Nelson, Bos	53.9	
1975-76	Wes Unseld, Wash	56.1	
1976-77	Kareem Abdul-Jabbar, LA	57.9	
1977-78	Bobby Jones, Den	57.8	
1978-79	Cedric Maxwell, Bos	58.4	
1979-80	Cedric Maxwell, Bos	60.9	
1980-81	Artis Gilmore, Chi	67.0	
1981-82	Artis Gilmore, Chi	65.2	
1982-83	Artis Gilmore, SA	62.6	
1983-84	Artis Gilmore, SA	63.1	
1984-85	James Donaldson, LA Clippers	63.7
1985-86	Steve Johnson, SA	63.2
1986-87	Kevin McHale, Bos	60.4
1987-88	Kevin McHale, Bos	60.4
1988-89	Dennis Rodman, Det	59.5
1989-90	Mark West, Phoe	62.5
1990-91	Buck Williams, Port	60.2
1991-92	Buck Williams, Port	60.4
1992-93	Cedric Ceballos, Phoe	57.6

Free Throw Percentage

1946-47	Fred Scolari, Wash	81.1
1947-48	Bob Feerick, Wash	78.8
1948-49	Bob Feerick, Wash	85.9
1949-50	Max Zaslofsky, Chi	84.3
1950-51	Joe Fulks, Phil	85.5
1951-52	Bob Wanzer, Roch	90.4
1952-53	Bill Sharman, Bos	85.0
1953-54	Bill Sharman, Bos	84.4
1954-55	Bill Sharman, Bos	89.7
1955-56	Bill Sharman, Bos	86.7
1956-57	Bill Sharman, Bos	90.5
1957-58	Dolph Schayes, Syr	90.4
1958-59	Bill Sharman, Bos	93.2
1959-60	Dolph Schayes, Syr	89.2
1960-61	Bill Sharman, Bos	92.1
1961-62	Dolph Schayes, Syr	89.6
1962-63	Larry Costello, Syr	88.1
1963-64	Oscar Robertson, Cin	85.3
1964-65	Larry Costello, Phil	87.7
1965-66	Larry Siegfried, Bos	88.1
1966-67	Adrian Smith, Cin	90.3
1967-68	Oscar Robertson, Cin	87.3
1968-69	Larry Siegfried, Bos	86.4
1969-70	Flynn Robinson, Mil	89.8
1970-71	Chet Walker, Chi	85.9
1971-72	Jack Marin, Balt	89.4
1972-73	Rick Barry, GS	90.2
1973-74	Ernie DiGregorio, Buff	90.2
1974-75	Rick Barry, GS	90.4
1975-76	Rick Barry, GS	92.3
1976-77	Ernie DiGregorio, Buff	94.5
1977-78	Rick Barry, GS	92.4
1978-79	Rick Barry, Hou	94.7
1979-80	Rick Barry, Hou	93.5
1980-81	Calvin Murphy, Hou	95.8
1981-82	Kyle Macy, Phoe	89.9
1982-83	Calvin Murphy, Hou	92.0
1983-84	Larry Bird, Bos	88.8
1984-85	Kyle Macy, Phoe	90.7
1985-86	Larry Bird, Bos	89.6
1986-87	Larry Bird, Bos	91.0
1987-88	Jack Sikma, Mil	92.2
1988-89	Magic Johnson, LA Lakers	91.1
1989-90	Larry Bird, Bos	93.0
1990-91	Reggie Miller, Ind	91.8
1991-92	Mark Price, Clev	94.7
1992-93	Mark Price, Clev	94.8

Three-Point Field Goal Percentage

1979-80	Fred Brown, Sea	44.3
1980-81	Brian Taylor, SD	38.3
1981-82	Campy Russell, NY	43.9
1982-83	Mike Dunleavy, SA	34.5
1983-84	Darrell Griffith, Utah	36.1
1984-85	Byron Scott, LA Lakers	43.3
1985-86	Craig Hodges, Mil	45.1
1986-87	Kiki Vandeweghe, Port	48.1
1987-88	Craig Hodges, Mil-Phoe	49.1
1988-89	Jon Sundvold, Mia	52.2
1989-90	Steve Kerr, Clev	50.7
1990-91	Jim Les, Sac	46.1
1991-92	Dana Barros, Sea	44.6
1992-93	B.J. Armstrong, Chi	45.3

Steals

1973-74	Larry Steele, Port	2.68
1974-75	Rick Barry, GS	2.85
1975-76	Don Watts, Sea	3.18
1976-77	Don Buse, Ind	3.47
1977-78	Ron Lee, Phoe	2.74
1978-79	M. L. Carr, Det	2.46
1979-80	Micheal Richardson, NY	3.23
1980-81	Magic Johnson, LA	3.43
1981-82	Magic Johnson, LA	2.67
1982-83	Micheal Richardson, GS-NJ	2.84
1983-84	Rickey Green, Utah	2.65
1984-85	Micheal Richardson, NJ	2.96
1985-86	Alvin Robertson, SA	3.67
1986-87	Alvin Robertson, SA	3.21
1987-88	Michael Jordan, Chi	3.16
1988-89	John Stockton, Utah	3.21
1989-90	Micheal Jordan, Chi	2.77
1990-91	Alvin Robertson, Mil	3.04
1991-92	John Stockton, Utah	2.98
1992-93	Michael Jordan, Chi	2.83

NBA Season Leaders *(Cont.)*

Blocked Shots

1973-74	Elmore Smith, LA	4.85	1983-84	Mark Eaton, Utah	4.28
1974-75	Kareem Abdul-Jabbar, Mil	3.26	1984-85	Mark Eaton, Utah	5.56
1975-76	Kareem Abdul-Jabbar, LA	4.12	1985-86	Manute Bol, Wash	4.96
1976-77	Bill Walton, Port	3.25	1986-87	Mark Eaton, Utah	4.06
1977-78	George Johnson, NJ	3.38	1987-88	Mark Eaton, Utah	3.71
1978-79	Kareem Abdul-Jabbar, LA	3.95	1988-89	Manute Bol, GS	4.31
1979-80	Kareem Abdul-Jabbar, LA	3.41	1989-90	Hakeem Olajuwon, Hou	4.59
1980-81	George Johnson, SA	3.39	1990-91	Hakeem Olajuwon, Hou	3.95
1981-82	George Johnson, SA	3.12	1991-92	David Robinson, SA	4.49
1982-83	Wayne Rollins, Atl	4.29	1992-93	Hakeem Olajuwon, Hou	4.17

NBA All-Star Game Results

Year	Result	Site	Winning Coach	Most Valuable Player
1951	East 111, West 94	Boston	Joe Lapchick	Ed Macauley, Bos
1952	East 108, West 91	Boston	Al Cervi	Paul Arizin, Phil
1953	West 79, East 75	Ft Wayne	John Kundla	George Mikan, Minn
1954	East 98, West 93 (OT)	New York	Joe Lapchick	Bob Cousy, Bos
1955	East 100, West 91	New York	Al Cervi	Bill Sharman, Bos
1956	West 108, East 94	Rochester	Charley Eckman	Bob Pettit, StL
1957	East 109, West 97	Boston	Red Auerbach	Bob Cousy, Bos
1958	East 130, West 118	St Louis	Red Auerbach	Bob Pettit, StL
1959	West 124, East 108	Detroit	Ed Macauley	Bob Pettit, StL
				Elgin Baylor, Minn
1960	East 125, West 115	Philadelphia	Red Auerbach	Wilt Chamberlain, Phil
1961	West 153, East 131	Syracuse	Paul Seymour	Oscar Robertson, Cin
1962	West 150, East 130	St Louis	Fred Schaus	Bob Pettit, StL
1963	East 115, West 108	Los Angeles	Red Auerbach	Bill Russell, Bos
1964	East 111, West 107	Boston	Red Auerbach	Oscar Robertson, Cin
1965	East 124, West 123	St Louis	Red Auerbach	Jerry Lucas, Cin
1966	East 137, West 94	Cincinnati	Red Auerbach	Adrian Smith, Cin
1967	West 135, East 120	San Francisco	Fred Schaus	Rick Barry, SF
1968	East 144, West 124	New York	Alex Hannum	Hal Greer, Phil
1969	East 123, West 112	Baltimore	Gene Shue	Oscar Robertson, Cin
1970	East 142, West 135	Philadelphia	Red Holzman	Willis Reed, NY
1971	West 108, East 107	San Diego	Larry Costello	Lenny Wilkens, Sea
1972	West 112, East 110	Los Angeles	Bill Sharman	Jerry West, LA
1973	East 104, West 84	Chicago	Tom Heinsohn	Dave Cowens, Bos
1974	West 134, East 123	Seattle	Larry Costello	Bob Lanier, Det
1975	East 108, West 102	Phoenix	K. C. Jones	Walt Frazier, NY
1976	East 123, West 109	Philadelphia	Tom Heinsohn	Dave Bing, Wash
1977	West 125, East 124	Milwaukee	Larry Brown	Julius Erving, Phil
1978	East 133, West 125	Atlanta	Billy Cunningham	Randy Smith, Buff
1979	West 134, East 129	Detroit	Lenny Wilkens	David Thompson, Den
1980	East 144, West 135 (OT)	Washington	Billy Cunningham	George Gervin, SA
1981	East 123, West 120	Cleveland	Billy Cunningham	Nate Archibald, Bos
1982	East 120, West 118	New Jersey	Bill Fitch	Larry Bird, Bos
1983	East 132, West 123	Los Angeles	Billy Cunningham	Julius Erving, Phil
1984	East 154, West 145 (OT)	Denver	K. C. Jones	Isiah Thomas, Det
1985	West 140, East 129	Indiana	Pat Riley	Ralph Sampson, Hou
1986	East 139, West 132	Dallas	K. C. Jones	Isiah Thomas, Det
1987	West 154, East 149 (OT)	Seattle	Pat Riley	Tom Chambers, Sea
1988	East 138, West 133	Chicago	Mike Fratello	Michael Jordan, Chi
1989	West 143, East 134	Houston	Pat Riley	Karl Malone, Utah
1990	East 130, West 113	Miami	Chuck Daly	Magic Johnson, LA Lakers
1991	East 116, West 114	Charlotte	Chris Ford	Charles Barkley, Phil
1992	West 153, East 113	Orlando	Don Nelson	Magic Johnson, LA Lakers
1993	West 135, East 132	Salt Lake City	Paul Westphal	K Malone, J Stockton, Ut

Members of the Basketball Hall of Fame

Contributors

Senda Abbott (1984)
Forest C. "Phog" Allen (1959)
Clair F. Bee (1967)
Walter A. Brown (1965)
John W. Bunn (1964)
Bob Douglas (1971)
Al Duer (1981)
Clifford Fagan (1983)
Harry A. Fisher (1973)
Larry Fleisher (1991)
Edward Gottlieb (1971)
Luther H. Gulick (1959)
Lester Harrison (1979)
Ferenc Hepp (1980)
Edward J. Hickox (1959)

Paul D. "Tony" Hinkle (1965)
Ned Irish (1964)
R. William Jones (1964)
J. Walter Kennedy (1980)
Emil S. Liston (1974)
John B. McLendon (1978)
Bill Mokray (1965)
Ralph Morgan (1959)
Frank Morgenweck (1962)
James Naismith (1959)
Peter F. Newell (1978)
John J. O'Brien (1961)
Larry O'Brien (1991)
Harold G. Olsen (1959)
Maurice Podoloff (1973)

H.V. Porter (1960)
William A. Reid (1963)
Elmer Ripley (1972)
Lynn W. St. John (1962)
Abe Saperstein (1970)
Arthur A. Schabinger (1961)
Amos Alonzo Stagg (1959)
Boris Stankovic (1991)
Edward Steitz (1983)
Chuck Taylor (1968)
Oswald Tower (1959)
Arthur L. Trester (1961)
Clifford Wells (1971)
Lou Wilke (1982)

Players

Nate "Tiny" Archibald (1991)
Paul J. Arizin (1977)
Thomas B. Barlow (1980)
Rick Barry (1986)
Elgin Baylor (1976)
John Beckman (1972)
Walt Bellamy (1993)
Sergei Belov (1992)
Dave Bing (1989)
Bennie Borgmann (1961)
Bill Bradley (1982)
Joseph Brennan (1974)
Al Cervi (1984)
Wilt Chamberlain (1978)
Charles "Tarzan" Cooper (1976)
Bob Cousy (1970)
Dave Cowens (1991)
Billy Cunningham (1985)
Bob Davies (1969)
Forrest S. DeBernardi (1961)
Dave DeBusschere (1982)
H. G. "Dutch" Dehnert (1968)
Paul Endacott (1971)
Julius Erving (1993)
Harold "Bud" Foster (1964)
Walter "Clyde" Frazier (1986)
Max "Marty" Friedman (1971)
Joe Fulks (1977)
Lauren "Laddie" Gale (1976)
Harry "the Horse" Gallatin (1991)
William Gates (1988)
Tom Gola (1975)

Hal Greer (1981)
Robert "Ace" Gruenig (1963)
Clifford O. Hagan (1977)
Victor Hanson (1960)
John Havlicek (1983)
Connie Hawkins (1992)
Elvin Hayes (1989)
Tom Heinsohn (1985)
Nat Holman (1964)
Robert J. Houbregs (1986)
Chuck Hyatt (1959)
Dan Issel (1993)
William C. Johnson (1976)
D. Neil Johnston (1989)
K. C. Jones (1988)
Sam Jones (1983)
Edward "Moose" Krause (1975)
Bob Kurland (1961)
Joe Lapchick (1966)
Clyde Lovellette (1987)
Jerry Lucas (1979)
Angelo "Hank" Luisetti (1959)
C. Edward Macauley (1960)
Peter P. Maravich (1986)
Slater Martin (1981)
Branch McCracken (1960)
Jack McCracken (1962)
Bobby McDermott (1987)
Dick McGuire (1993)
Ann Meyers (1993)
George L. Mikan (1959)
Earl Monroe (1989)

Calvin Murphy (1993)
Charles "Stretch" Murphy (1960)
H. O. "Pat" Page (1962)
Bob Pettit (1970)
Andy Phillip (1961)
Jim Pollard (1977)
Frank Ramsey (1981)
Willis Reed (1981)
Oscar Robertson (1979)
John S. Roosma (1961)
Bill Russell (1974)
John "Honey" Russell (1964)
Adolph Schayes (1972)
Ernest J. Schmidt (1973)
John J. Schommer (1959)
Barney Sedran (1962)
Uljana Semjonova (1993)
Bill Sharman (1975)
Christian Steinmetz (1961)
Lusia Harris Stewart (1992)
John A. "Cat" Thompson (1962)
Nate Thurmond (1984)
Jack Twyman (1982)
Wes Unseld (1987)
Robert "Fuzzy" Vandivier (1974)
Edward A. Wachter (1961)
Bill Walton (1993)
Robert F. Wanzer (1986)
Jerry West (1979)
Nera White (1992)
Lenny Wilkens (1988)
John R. Wooden (1960)

Coaches

Harold Anderson (1984)
Red Auerbach (1968)
Sam Barry (1978)
Ernest A. Blood (1960)
Howard G. Cann (1967)
H. Clifford Carlson (1959)
Lou Carnesecca (1992)
Ben Carnevale (1969)
Everett Case (1981)
Everett S. Dean (1966)
Edgar A. Diddle (1971)
Bruce Drake (1972)
Clarence Gaines (1981)

Jack Gardner (1983)
Amory T. "Slats" Gill (1967)
Marv Harshman (1984)
Edgar S. Hickey (1978)
Howard A. Hobson (1965)
Red Holzman (1985)
Hank Iba (1968)
Alvin F. "Doggie" Julian (1967)
Frank W. Keaney (1960)
George E. Keogan (1961)
Bob Knight (1991)
Ward L. Lambert (1960)
Harry Litwack (1975)

Kenneth D. Loeffler (1964)
A. C. "Dutch" Lonborg (1972)
Arad A. McCutchan (1980)
Al McGuire (1992)
Frank McGuire (1976)
Walter E. Meanwell (1959)
Raymond J. Meyer (1978)
Ralph Miller (1987)
Jack Ramsay (1992)
Adolph F. Rupp (1968)
Leonard D. Sachs (1961)
Everett F. Shelton (1979)
Dean Smith (1982)

Note: Year of election in parentheses.

Coaches (Cont.)

Fred R. Taylor (1985)
Bertha Teague (1984)

Margaret Wade (1984)
Stanley H. Watts (1985)

John R. Wooden (1972)

Referees

James E. Enright (1978)
George T. Hepbron (1960)
George Hoyt (1961)
Matthew P. Kennedy (1959)
Lloyd Leith (1982)
Zigmund J. Mihalik (1985)
John P. Nucatola (1977)
Ernest C. Quigley (1961)
J. Dallas Shirley (1979)
David Tobey (1961)
David H. Walsh (1961)

Teams

Buffalo Germans (1961)
First Team (1959)
Original Celtics (1959)
Renaissance (1963)

Note: Year of election in parentheses.

ABA Champions

Year	Champion	Series	Loser	Winning Coach
1968	Pittsburgh Pipers	4-2	New Orleans Bucs	Vince Cazetta
1969	Oakland Oaks	4-1	Indiana Pacers	Alex Hannum
1970	Indiana Pacers	4-2	Los Angeles Stars	Bob Leonard
1971	Utah Stars	4-3	Kentucky Colonels	Bill Sharman
1972	Indiana Pacers	4-2	New York Nets	Bob Leonard
1973	Indiana Pacers	4-3	Kentucky Colonels	Bob Leonard
1974	New York Nets	4-1	Utah Stars	Kevin Loughery
1975	Kentucky Colonels	4-1	Indiana Pacers	Hubie Brown
1976	New York Nets	4-2	Denver Nuggets	Kevin Loughery

ABA Postseason Awards

Most Valuable Player

1967-68	Connie Hawkins, Pitt
1968-69	Mel Daniels, Ind
1969-70	Spencer Haywood, Den
1970-71	Mel Daniels, Ind
1971-72	Artis Gilmore, Ken
1972-73	Billy Cunningham, Car
1973-74	Julius Erving, NY
1974-75	Julius Erving, NY
	George McGinnis, Ind
1975-76	Julius Erving, NY

Coach of the Year

1968-69	Alex Hannum, Oak
1969-70	Bill Sharman, LA
	Joe Belmont, Den
1970-71	Al Bianchi, Vir
1971-72	Tom Nissalke, Dall
1972-73	Larry Brown, Car
1973-74	Babe McCarthy, Ken
	Joe Mullaney, Utah
1974-75	Larry Brown, Den
1975-76	Larry Brown, Den

Rookie of the Year

1967-68	Mel Daniels, Minn
1968-69	Warren Armstrong, Oak
1969-70	Spencer Haywood, Den
1970-71	Charlie Scott
	Dan Issel, Ken
1971-72	Artis Gilmore, Ken
1972-73	Brian Taylor, NY
1973-74	Swen Nater, SA
1974-75	Marvin Barnes, SL
1975-76	David Thompson, Den
1967-68	Vince Cazetta, Pitt

THEY SAID IT

Charles Barkley, Phoenix Sun star, confiding that he mostly hangs out with people he grew up with: "I have very few friends I have met since I became Charles Barkley."

ABA Season Leaders

Scoring

		GP	Pts	Avg
1968	Connie Hawkins, Pitt	70	1875	26.8
1969	Rick Barry, Oak	35	1190	34.0
1970	Spencer Haywood, Den	84	2519	30.0
1971	Dan Issel, Ken	83	2480	29.4
1972	Charlie Scott, Vir	73	2524	34.6
1973	Julius Erving, Vir	71	2268	31.9
1974	Julius Erving, NY	84	2299	27.4
1975	George McGinnis, Ind	79	2353	29.8
1976	Julius Erving, NY	84	2462	29.3

Rebounds

1967-68	Mel Daniels, Minn	15.6
1968-69	Mel Daniels, Ind	16.5
1969-70	Spencer Haywood, Den	19.5
1970-71	Mel Daniels, Ind	18.0
1971-72	Artis Gilmore, Ken	17.8
1972-73	Artis Gilmore, Ken	17.5
1973-74	Artis Gilmore, Ken	18.3
1974-75	Swen Nater, SA	16.4
1975-76	Artis Gilmore, Ken	15.5

Assists

1967-68	Larry Brown, NO	6.5
1968-69	Larry Brown, Oak	7.1
1969-70	Larry Brown, Wash	7.1
1970-71	Bill Melchionni, NY	8.3
1971-72	Bill Melchionni, NY	8.4
1972-73	Bill Melchionni, NY	7.5
1973-74	Al Smith, Den	8.2

Steals

1974-75	Mack Calvin, Den	7.7
1975-76	Don Buse, Ind	8.2
1973-74	Ted McClain, Car	2.98
1974-75	Brian Taylor, NY	2.80

Blocked Shots

1975-76	Don Buse, Ind	4.12
1973-74	Caldwell Jones, SD	4.00
1974-75	Caldwell Jones, SD	3.24
1975-76	Billy Paultz, SA	3.05

Three-Peat Pat

During the 1988-89 season, when his Los Angeles Lakers were seeking a third straight NBA title, Pat Riley had the foresight to trademark the term Three-Peat. The Lakers didn't succeed, but Riley now figures to profit handsomely from the Bulls' successful *threpetition* since entrepeneurs who want to make Three-Peat T-shirts, hats or other merchandise will have to pay royalties to Riley. Otherwise Riley could sic the law, or maybe even John Starks, on them. Some estimates placed his potential earnings at $300,000.

THEY SAID IT

Chris Webber, former Michigan star, and the No. 1 pick in this year's NBA Draft, on the meaning of that honor: "Each year, only one guy is taken No. 1."

College Basketball

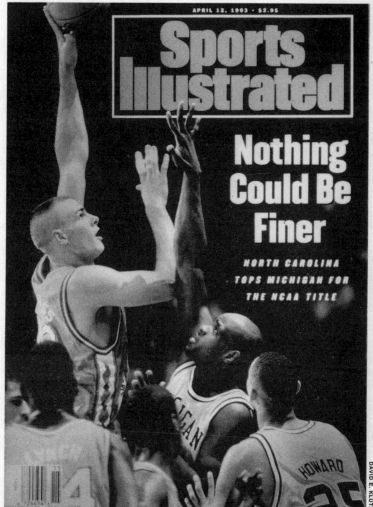

APRIL 12, 1993 · $2.95

Sports Illustrated

Nothing Could Be Finer

NORTH CAROLINA TOPS MICHIGAN FOR THE NCAA TITLE

HOWARD
25

DAVID E. KLUTHO

Grace Under Pressure

A costly gaffe, a flawless title run and an untimely death capped a bittersweet college season | by PHIL TAYLOR

WHO OF US HAS NOT PLAYED out the scenario in our minds at one time or another? The clock is running down, and we score the winning basket as time expires or hit the home run in the bottom of the ninth that wins the World Series. But buried deep in the back of our minds is the darker side of those backyard fantasies, our fear that in a clutch situation, with everything riding on us, we will fail, make the fatal error. Choke.

Michigan's Chris Webber lived that nightmare when he called the now infamous timeout in the closing seconds of North Carolina's 77–71 victory over the Wolverines in the NCAA championship game at the Louisiana Superdome in April. Michigan had no timeouts left, which meant Webber's gaffe resulted in a technical foul against the Wolverines, costing them their last chance for victory and guaranteeing the Tar Heels the national title.

Surely nothing can diminish the accomplishments of the Tar Heels, who may have turned in the most consistent overall performance in the nation from the start of the season until that night in April. But for most of us, the images that will linger far longer than that of victorious coach Dean Smith of North Carolina cutting down the net with golden scissors are those of Webber, Michigan's supremely confident—some would say arrogant—star, first with a look of panic on his face as he called the timeout with Tar Heels pressuring him on defense, and then, later, with his head bowed in defeat and embarrassment.

Maybe fans can relate better to failure than to success, because Webber's gaffe endeared him to most of the public far more than the Wolverines' 31–5 record or their two consecutive trips to the championship game. "I cost us the game," he said afterward, and there were those who agreed with him, all too happy to cruelly remind him of his mistake. He was also the

Webber's evident disappointment may be the most memorable Final Four image.

butt of more than a few jokes. Talk-show host David Letterman's list of the top 10 things overheard at the summit between President Clinton and Boris Yeltsin of Russia included this as No. 6: "What, you mean we have no more timeouts?" One fan yelled "Timeouts, timeouts for sale," as Webber walked down Bourbon Street hours after the game. But far more people applauded him for the grace with which he handled the situation. When Webber attended an awards banquet in Los Angeles a few days after the title game, his introduction was met with a standing ovation.

A month later Webber decided to forgo his final two years of eligibility and enter the NBA draft. His departure meant that the much-heralded Fab Five, as he and fellow sophomores Jalen Rose, Juwan Howard, Jimmy King and Ray Jackson were known, would never win a national championship together. The North Carolina team that denied them in New Orleans was in many ways the antithesis of Michigan. While the Wolverines were emotional and demonstrative, the Tar Heels were stoic and businesslike. Where Michigan relied to a large degree on its athleticism and ability to improvise, North Carolina stuck resolutely to coach Smith's system, which values consistency and team play over spectacular individualism.

"People say that North Carolina's system

stifles players," said Tar Heel forward Brian Reese. "But how can you argue with an approach that has been so successful and sent so many players to the NBA? Coach Smith's way of doing things didn't seem to keep [former Tar Heels] Michael Jordan, James Worthy, Sam Perkins, Kenny Smith or lots of other guys from being successful in the pros. The truth is that every player should get a chance to play under this system. It would make them better players, and it just might get them a championship."

But the Tar Heel way couldn't keep some players from grabbing the spotlight on occasion. Forward George Lynch was North Carolina's rock, its steadiest player and the leader who kept his teammates focused and prepared. Center Eric Montross provided a huge inside presence on offense and defense that most opponents couldn't handle. Point guard Derrick Phelps gamely ran the offense in a season full of injuries. And in the championship game quiet sophomore guard Donald Williams stepped forward and played the game of his life.

"He's only quiet and unassuming until he gets ready for that jumper," Reese said. "Then he turns deadly."

Williams left a trail of victims in the tournament, capping his play with a pair of 25-point games in the Final Four against

A Fine Line

There is a fine line between tough, demanding coaching and verbal or emotional abuse. When a coach screams at his team in the locker room during halftime, will his players go out for the second half feeling fired up or beaten down? There is no disputing that coaches can sometimes go too far in their zeal, but college basketball's greatest debate in the 1992–93 season was: How far is too far?

At least three coaches were judged to have crossed that invisible line during the season. Lou Campanelli of California, Kohn Smith of Utah State and Tom Miller of Army all were fired for being verbally abusive to their players. Each of the firings brought criticism from some members of the coaching community, but it was California's removal of Campanelli on Feb. 8 that brought the loudest complaints. Cal athletic director Bob Bockrath said one postgame incident, in which he accidentally overheard some of Campanelli's heated remarks to the players after a loss to Arizona, contributed greatly to his decision to give Campanelli his walking papers.

There were other incidents, as well—

Campanelli overturned several box lunches during a fit of anger after one loss and abruptly left his team at the arena without talking to the media after another—but Campanelli said he never had any indication from the Cal administration that there was the slightest dissatisfaction with his tactics. "I have done nothing wrong," he said.

"The troubling thing about it is that Campanelli was fired without being told there was a problem and being given the chance to correct it," said Duke coach Mike Krzyzewski. "He wasn't given the due process anyone in any job has the right to expect."

The Cal players, including Jason Kidd, the Golden Bears' spectacular freshman guard, didn't pretend they were sorry to see the coaching change. Some of them had even met with Bockrath before the firing to voice their displeasure with Campanelli. Todd Bozeman, Cal's 29-year-old assistant coach, took over on an interim basis, a move that so pleased the players that Cal, a disappointing 10–7 when Campanelli left, won nine of its last 10 regular-season games to earn the NCAA tournament bid that had seemed such a long shot only a few weeks earlier.

Kansas and Michigan to win the MVP award. He drilled five of seven three-pointers in both games, not to mention four crucial free throws down the stretch in the victory over Michigan. The Wolverines didn't seem terribly impressed—"It's not like he's the greatest player we ever played against," sniffed Michigan forward Ray Jackson—but that didn't matter to Williams. "It's going to take a while for this to sink in," he said. "Winning a championship is something I've always dreamed of, but getting the MVP award with it was beyond my wildest dreams."

North Carolina's victory kept the championship trophy in the state for the fourth consecutive year, following Duke's back-to-back championships. The Blue Devils struggled—at least, for a program with standards as high as theirs, it was a struggle—finishing third in the Atlantic Coast Conference and ultimately losing to upstart California (see sidebar) in the second round of the NCAA tournament. Duke coach Mike Krzyzewski gave an emotional sendoff to departing seniors Bobby Hurley and Thomas Hill in the postgame press conference, his voice trembling and tears in his eyes. Coach K received at least some consolation a few weeks later, when he signed a 15-year, $6.6 million endorsement contract with the Nike athletic footwear company.

The Bears were even more impressive once they reached the tournament, knocking off LSU 66–64 on Kidd's last-second shot, then ending Duke's quest for a third straight national championship with an 82–77 second-round win. They finally fell in the third round to Kansas, which was bound for the Final Four, but by that time Bozeman, who less than five years earlier had been making deliveries for Federal Express, had been made the permanent head coach.

That didn't keep some of his colleagues, still upset over the handling of the Campanelli situation, from being cool to him. LSU coach Dale Brown didn't shake Bozeman's hand as the two left the court after Cal's first-round victory, but did so later, out of TV camera range. Bozeman also had to deal with rumors, which he and the Cal administration denied, that he had played a part in orchestrating Campanelli's dismissal.

But in the end neither Bozeman's unlikely rise nor Cal's season-ending flourish changed anyone's mind on whether the Campanelli firing was justified. That debate will continue as long as there are coaches and administrators, as long as there is that fine line between motivation and abuse. Maybe the most constructive consequence of it all is that everyone was reminded that the line, however blurred it may sometimes become, still exists.

Campanelli's firing was popular with the players but set off a storm of controversy.

Mashburn was one of several talented players to head for the NBA.

Mashburn led the Wildcats to the Final Four, where they lost to Michigan in the semifinals. Mashburn fouled out late in the game, sealing the Wildcats' fate. Until that game the Wildcats had steamrollered through the tournament, beating their four opponents by an impressive average of 30.8 points. Among their victims was Wake Forest, but Rogers and the Demon Deacons had better moments during the season, including a win at Duke's Cameron Indoor Stadium in which Rogers so impressed Krzyzewski that he called Rogers's performance the best he had seen by an opponent on the Blue Devils' home court.

The season was marked by a great deal of movement at the top. Six different teams—Duke, North Carolina, Michigan, Indiana, Kentucky and Kansas—were No. 1 at some point in the season, but as usual some of the lesser-known teams stole the spotlight in the NCAA tournament. Little-known Western Kentucky reached the Sweet 16, upsetting second-seeded Seton Hall 72–68 along the way, with a major contribution from 5' 8" point guard Mark Bell, from a family of 18 children. Then there was Southern, with eccentric coach Ben Jobe, a onetime croquet coach in Sierra Leone who freely admitted that his mind sometimes wandered during games. Jobe and his 13th-seeded Tigers concentrated long enough to shock fourth-seeded Georgia Tech in the first round of the West Regional.

But the biggest surprise of the tournament came in Salt Lake City where 15th-

Duke's Hurley was among the many players who had an exceptional year in what turned out to be their final college season. Senior forward Calbert Cheaney of Indiana became the leading scorer in the Hoosiers' storied history and won most of the Player of the Year awards, including *Sports Illustrated's*. Indiana won the Big Ten title, beating Michigan twice by one point, but unfortunately for the Hoosiers, sophomore forward Alan Henderson suffered a knee injury late in the season that severely limited his effectiveness in the NCAA tournament, and Indiana fell to Kansas in the Midwest Regional final.

Forwards Jamal Mashburn of Kentucky and Rodney Rogers of Wake Forest, both juniors, decided after brilliant seasons that they were ready for the NBA draft.

seeded Santa Clara stunned Arizona, a No. 2 seed. The Broncos had struggled through a mediocre regular season in which they finished 18–11, and only qualified for the NCAA tournament because they managed to get hot during the Big West Conference tournament, beating heavily favored Pepperdine in the championship game to earn the automatic bid. But that upset was small potatoes compared to the win over Arizona. Only once before had a 15th-seeded team survived the first round of the tournament, and the loss added to the list of postseason indignities suffered by Arizona, the Pacific-10 Conference champions. The Wildcats had lost to 14th-seeded East Tennessee State the year before, so their loss to Santa Clara seemed to cement their reputation as a team that cruises through the regular season but crumbles in the postseason.

Even with all the upsets, fine performances and memorable mistakes of the men's tournament, perhaps the best individual effort in the postseason came during the women's NCAA tournament, where women's Player of the Year Sheryl Swoopes of Texas Tech scored 47 points in the Lady Raiders 84–82 victory over Ohio State for the national championship. Swoopes's performance can't come as much of a surprise, since she was the nation's second-leading scorer during the regular season, with an average of 28.1 points, and she scored 53 against Texas in the Southwest Conference tournament.

"You don't appreciate Sheryl Swoopes until you have to stop her," said Ohio State coach Nancy Darsch after the Buckeyes had failed to stop her. "We tried trapping in a two-three zone,

Swoopes proved unstoppable in the title game against Ohio State.

which we've never done before for an individual. We even called it '22' since that's her number. But she answered everything we tried."

Swoopes, a six-foot forward, broke the record for most points scored in an NCAA tournament championship game, women's or men's, which had been held by Bill Walton of UCLA, who had 44 against Memphis State in 1973. It was a fitting end to a remarkable career that began when she left Texas, with whom she had originally signed, after three days because she was homesick for her native Brownfield, Texas, 32 miles from Texas Tech's Lubbock campus. She went on to become such a local hero that a

JIM GUND

RONALD C. MODRA

girls' team for eight and nine-year-olds in nearby Shallowater called itself the Swoopesters.

The women's game continued to move closer to the popularity of the men's in '92–93. There was no better evidence of that than the regular-season clash between No. 1 Vanderbilt and No. 2 Tennessee in January. That game was the first in women's basketball history to be sold out more than a few days in advance. Celebrities from All-Pro defensive tackle Reggie White, a Tennessee alumnus, to Vice-President Al Gore, a Vanderbilt alum, weighed in with predictions. More than 1,000 people were turned away from Vanderbilt's Memorial Gym, including university chancellor Joe B. Wyatt.

"There are two aspects of this whole thing," said Vanderbilt coach Jim Foster. "There is the basketball game and the event." The glorious result for the women's game was that the game and the event were worthy of each other, even if the partisan Vanderbilt crowd went home disappointed at the tense 73–68 Tennessee victory. Still, as 6'10" Vanderbilt center Heidi Gillingham said before the game, "It's almost more important to play well than to win. With so many fans, many of whom are testing out women's basketball to see if they like it, we need to show them the high level at which women can play. We need to convince them they should come back." Anyone who saw Vanderbilt and Tennessee was surely convinced.

Both the men's and women's seasons were marked by an undercurrent of sadness in '92–93. Iowa was touched by tragedy twice during the season, first when William Stringer, the husband of women's coach Vivian Stringer and an exercise physiologist with the school's athletic department, died of a heart attack on Thanksgiving Day, and then on Jan. 19, when Chris Street, a 6'8" junior forward on the men's team, was killed in an auto accident.

Throughout the season, TV analyst and former North Carolina State coach Jim Valvano's battle against cancer touched everyone in college basketball and beyond. Valvano summoned the strength to work several games early in the season, but he grew progressively weaker and died on April 28 at the age of 47. He was unable to attend the Final Four, but he was never far from anyone's thoughts in New Orleans. North Carolina's Williams, the Most Outstanding Player of the Final Four, dedicated his performance to Valvano, who tried to recruit him for North Carolina State. "I don't know how anyone could fail to be inspired by the courage and the good humor with which Jimmy has handled his disease," said Krzyzewski.

Chris Webber lost a championship game. Jim Valvano lost a far greater battle. Between them they provided the overriding lesson of the 1992–93 season: how to handle whatever fate brings with grace, dignity and good humor.

NCAA Championship Game Box Score

Michigan 71

MICHIGAN	Min	FG M-A	FT M-A	Reb O-T	A	PF	TP
Webber	33	11-18	1-2	5-11	1	2	23
Jackson	20	2-3	2-2	0-1	1	5	6
Howard	34	3-8	1-1	4-7	3	3	7
Rose	40	5-12	0-0	0-1	4	3	12
King	34	6-13	2-2	1-6	4	2	15
Riley	14	1-3	0-0	2-3	1	1	2
Pelinka	17	2-4	0-0	1-2	1	1	6
Talley	4	0-0	0-0	0-0	1	1	0
Totals	200	30-62	6-7	13-31	17	18	71

Percentages: FG——.484, FT——.857. 3-pt goals: 5-15, .333 (Pelinka 2-3, Rose, 2-6, King 1-5, Webber 0-1). Team rebounds: 2. Blocked shots: 4 (Webber 3, Riley). Turnovers: 14 (Rose 6, Jackson 2, Howard 2, Webber, King, Riley, Talley). Steals: 4 (Webber, Jackson, King, Riley).

North Carolina 77

N CAROLINA	Min	FG M-A	FT M-A	Reb O-T	A	PF	TP
Reese	27	2-7	4-4	4-5	3	1	8
Lynch	28	6-12	0-0	1-10	1	3	12
Montross	31	5-11	6-9	2-5	0	2	16
Phelps	36	4-6	1-2	1-3	6	0	9
Williams	31	8-12	4-4	0-1	1	1	25
Sullivan	14	1-2	1-2	0-1	1	2	3
Salvadori	18	0-0	2-2	2-4	1	1	2
Rodl	11	1-4	0-0	0-0	0	0	2
Calabria	1	0-0	0-0	0-0	0	0	0
Wenstrom	2	0-1	0-0	0-0	0	0	0
Cherry	1	0-0	0-0	0-0	0	0	0
Totals	200	27-55	18-23	10-29	13	10	77

Percentages: FG——.491, FT——.783. 3-pt goals: 5-11, .455 (Williams 5-7, Reese 0-1, Phelps 0-1, Rodl 0-2). Team rebounds: 0. Blocked shots: 4 (Lynch 2, Montross, Salvadori). Turnovers: 10 (Phelps 5, Reese 2, Lynch, Williams, Rodl). Steals: 7 (Phelps 3, Rodl 2, Lynch, Williams).
Halftime: N Carolina 42, Michigan 36. A: 64,151.
Officials: Hightower, Harrington, Stupin.

Final AP Top 25

Poll taken before NCAA Tournament. Records entering post-season.

1. Indiana	28-3	14. Massachusetts	23-6
2. Kentucky	26-3	15. Louisville	20-8
3. Michigan	26-4	16. Wake Forest	19-8
4. North Carolina	28-4	17. New Orleans	26-3
5. Arizona	24-3	18. Georgia Tech	19-10
6. Seton Hall	27-6	19. Utah	23-6
7. Cincinnati	24-4	20. W Kentucky	24-5
8. Vanderbilt	26-5	21. New Mexico	24-6
9. Kansas	25-6	22. Purdue	18-9
10. Duke	23-7	23. Oklahoma St	19-8
11. Florida St	22-9	24. New Mexico St	25-7
12. Arkansas	20-8	25. Nevada-Las Vegas	21-7
13. Iowa	22-8		

National Invitation Tournament Scores

First round: AL-Birmingham 58; Alabama 56; Boston College 87, Niagara 83; Clemson 84, Auburn 72; Georgetown 78, Arizona St 68; Jackson St 90, Connecticut 88 OT; Miami (OH) 56, Ohio St 53; Minnesota 74, Florida 66; Oklahoma 88, Michigan St 86; Old Dominion 74, Virginia Commonwealth 68; Pepperdine 53, UC-Santa Barbara 50; Providence 73, James Madison 61; Rice 77, Wisconsin 73; Southern Cal 90, Nevada-Las Vegas 74; SW M issouri St 56, St Joseph's 34; UTEP 67, Houston 61; W Virginia 95, Georgia 84.
Second round: AL-Birmingham 65; Clemson 64; Boston College 101, Rice 68; Georgetown 71, UTEP 44; Miami (OH) 60, Old Dominion 58; Minnesota 86, Oklahoma 72; Providence 68, W Virginia 67; Southern Cal 71, Pepperdine 59; SW Missouri St 70, Jackson St 52.
Third round: AL-Birmingham 61, SW Missouri St 52; Georgetown 66, Miami (OH) 53; Minnesota 76, Southern Cal 58; Providence 75, Boston College 58.
Semifinals: Georgetown 45, AL-Birmingham 41; Minnesota 76, Providence 70.
Championship: Minnesota 62, Georgetown 61.
Consolation game: AL-Birmingham 55, Providence 52.

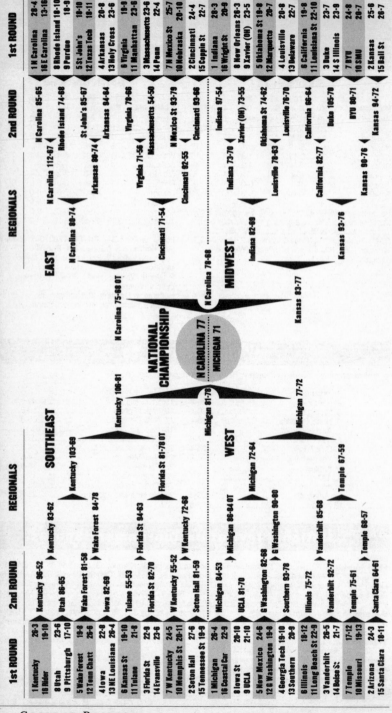

1993 NCAA Basketball Men's Division I Tournament

Assoc. of Mid-Continent

	Conference			All Games		
	W	L	Pct	W	L	Pct
Cleveland St*	15	1	.938	22	6	.786
Wright St†	10	6	.625	20	10	.667
Northern Illinois	10	6	.625	15	12	.556
IL-Chicago	9	7	.563	17	15	.531
WI-Green Bay	9	7	.563	13	14	.481
Valparaiso	7	9	.438	12	16	.429
Eastern Illinois	7	9	.438	10	17	.370
Western Illinois	4	12	.250	7	20	.259
Youngstown St	1	15	.063	3	23	.115

Atlantic Coast

	Conference			All Games		
	W	L	Pct	W	L	Pct
N Carolina*	14	2	.875	34	4	.895
Florida St	12	4	.750	25	10	.714
Duke	10	6	.625	24	8	.750
Wake Forest	10	6	.625	21	9	.700
Virginia	9	7	.563	21	10	.677
Georgia Tech†	8	8	.500	19	11	.633
Clemson	5	11	.313	17	13	.567
Maryland	2	14	.125	12	16	.429
North Carolina St	2	14	.125	8	19	.296

Atlantic 10

	Conference			All Games		
	W	L	Pct	W	L	Pct
Massachusetts*†	11	3	.786	24	7	.774
George Washington	8	6	.571	21	9	.700
Rhode Island	8	6	.571	19	11	.633
St Joseph's (PA)	8	6	.571	18	11	.621
Temple	8	6	.571	20	13	.606
West Virginia	7	7	.500	17	12	.586
Rutgers	6	8	.429	13	15	.464
St Bonaventure	0	14	.000	10	17	.370

Big East

	Conference			All Games		
	W	L	Pct	W	L	Pct
Seton Hall*†	14	4	.778	28	7	.800
St. John's (NY)	12	6	.667	19	11	.633
Syracuse	10	8	.556	20	9	.690
Pittsburgh	9	9	.500	17	11	.607
Providence	9	9	.500	20	13	.606
Boston College	9	9	.500	18	13	.581
Connecticut	9	9	.500	15	13	.536
Georgetown	8	10	.444	20	13	.606
Miami (FL)	7	11	.389	10	17	.370
Villanova	3	15	.167	8	19	.296

Big Eight

	Conference			All Games		
	W	L	Pct	W	L	Pct
Kansas*	11	3	.786	29	7	.806
Oklahoma St	8	6	.571	20	9	.690
Iowa St	8	6	.571	20	11	.645
Nebraska	8	6	.571	20	11	.645
Kansas St	7	7	.500	19	11	.633
Oklahoma	7	7	.500	20	12	.625
Missouri†	5	9	.357	19	14	.576
Colorado	2	12	.143	10	17	.370

Big Sky

	Conference			All Games		
	W	L	Pct	W	L	Pct
Idaho*	11	3	.786	24	8	.750
Boise St†	10	4	.714	21	8	.724
Weber St	10	4	.714	20	8	.714
Montana	8	6	.571	17	11	.607
Idaho St	5	9	.357	10	18	.357
Montana St	5	9	.357	9	18	.357
Northern Arizona	4	10	.286	10	16	.385
Eastern Washington	3	11	.214	6	20	.231

Big South

	Conference			All Games		
	W	L	Pct	W	L	Pct
Towson St*	14	2	.875	18	9	.667
Coastal Carolina†	12	4	.750	22	10	.688
Campbell	10	6	.625	12	15	.444
Liberty	9	7	.563	16	14	.533
Radford	8	8	.500	15	16	.484
MD-Balt. County	7	9	.438	12	16	.429
Winthrop	5	11	.313	14	16	.467
Charleston So	5	11	.313	9	18	.333
NC-Asheville	2	14	.125	4	23	.148

Big Ten

	Conference			All Games		
	W	L	Pct	W	L	Pct
Indiana*	17	1	.944	31	4	.886
Michigan	15	3	.833	31	5	.861
Iowa	11	7	.611	23	9	.719
Illinois	11	7	.611	19	13	.594
Minnesota	9	9	.500	22	10	.688
Purdue	9	9	.500	18	10	.643
Ohio St	8	10	.444	15	13	.536
Michigan St	7	11	.389	15	13	.536
Wisconsin	7	11	.389	14	14	.500
Northwestern	3	15	.167	8	19	.296
Penn St	2	16	.111	7	20	.259

Big West

	Conference			All Games		
	W	L	Pct	W	L	Pct
New Mexico St*	15	3	.833	26	8	.765
Nevada-Las Vegas	13	5	.722	21	8	.724
Pacific	12	6	.667	16	11	.593
Long Beach St†	11	7	.611	22	10	.688
UC Santa Barbara	10	8	.556	18	11	.621
Cal St Fullerton	10	8	.556	15	12	.556
Utah St	7	11	.389	10	17	.370
Nevada	4	14	.222	9	17	.346
San Jose St	4	14	.222	7	19	.269
UC Irvine	4	14	.222	6	21	.222

*Conf. champ; †Conf. tourney winner.

THEY SAID IT

Mike Krzyzewski, Duke basketball coach, after his team slipped to No. 7 in the AP Poll: "The only Pole I pay attention to is my mother."

Colonial Athletic Association

	Conference			All Games		
	W	L	Pct	W	L	Pct
Old Dominion	11	3	.786	21	8	.724
James Madison	11	3	.786	21	9	.700
Richmond	10	4	.714	15	12	.556
NC-Wilmington	6	8	.429	17	11	.607
William & Mary	6	8	.429	14	13	.519
American	6	8	.429	11	17	.393
East Carolina†	4	10	.286	13	17	.433
George Mason	2	12	.143	7	21	.250

Great Midwest

	Conference			All Games		
	W	L	Pct	W	L	Pct
Cincinnati*†	8	2	.800	27	5	.844
Memphis St	7	3	.700	20	12	.625
Marquette	6	4	.600	20	8	.714
AL-Birmingham	5	5	.500	21	14	.600
DePaul	3	7	.300	16	15	.516
St Louis	1	9	.100	12	17	.414

Ivy Group

	Conference			All Games		
	W	L	Pct	W	L	Pct
Penn	14	0	1.000	22	5	.815
Cornell	10	4	.714	16	10	.615
Columbia	9	5	.643	16	10	.615
Princeton	7	7	.500	15	11	.577
Yale	6	8	.429	10	16	.385
Dartmouth	5	9	.357	11	15	.423
Harvard	3	11	.214	6	20	.231
Brown	2	12	.143	7	19	.269

Metro

	Conference			All Games		
	W	L	Pct	W	L	Pct
Louisville*†	11	1	.917	22	9	.710
Tulane	9	3	.750	22	9	.710
VCU	7	5	.583	20	10	.667
NC-Charlotte	6	6	.500	15	13	.536
Southern Miss	6	6	.500	10	17	.370
South Florida	2	10	.167	8	19	.296
Virginia Tech	1	11	.083	10	18	.357

Metro Atlantic

	Conference			All Games		
	W	L	Pct	W	L	Pct
Manhattan*†	12	2	.857	23	7	.767
Niagara	11	3	.786	23	7	.767
Iona	9	5	.643	16	11	.593
Siena	8	6	.571	16	13	.552
Fairfield	7	7	.500	14	13	.519
Canisius	5	9	.357	10	18	.357
St Peter's	3	11	.214	9	18	.333
Loyola (MD)	1	13	.071	2	25	.074

Mid-American

	Conference			All Games		
	W	L	Pct	W	L	Pct
Ball St†	14	4	.778	26	8	.765
Miami (OH)	14	4	.778	22	9	.710
Western Michigan	12	6	.667	17	12	.586
Ohio U	11	7	.611	14	13	.519
Toledo	9	9	.500	12	16	.429
Eastern Michigan	8	10	.444	13	17	.433
Bowling Green	8	10	.444	11	16	.407
Kent St	7	11	.389	10	17	.370
Central Michigan	4	14	.222	8	18	.308
Akron	3	15	.167	8	18	.308

Mid-Eastern Athletic

	Conference			All Games		
	W	L	Pct	W	L	Pct
Coppin St*†	16	0	1.000	22	8	.733
S. Carolina St	9	7	.563	16	13	.552
N Carolina A&T	9	7	.563	14	13	.519
Morgan St	9	7	.563	9	17	.346
Florida A&M	8	8	.500	10	18	.357
MD-Eastern Shore	7	9	.438	12	15	.444
Delaware St	6	10	.375	13	16	.448
Howard	6	10	.375	10	18	.357
Bethune-Cookman	2	14	.125	3	24	.111

Midwestern Collegiate

	Conference			All Games		
	W	L	Pct	W	L	Pct
Xavier (OH)	12	2	.857	24	6	.800
Evansville†	12	2	.857	23	7	.767
La Salle	9	5	.643	14	13	.519
Detroit Mercy	7	7	.500	15	12	.556
Duquesne	5	9	.357	13	15	.464
Butler	5	9	.357	11	17	.393
Loyola (IL)	3	11	.214	7	20	.259
Dayton	3	11	.214	4	26	.133

*Conf. champ; †Conf. tourney winner.

THEY SAID IT

Rick Majerus, University of Utah basketball coach, on the major election issue of 1992: "They talk about the economy this year. Hey, my hairline is in recession, my waistline is in inflation. All together, I'm in a depression."

Missouri Valley

	Conference			All Games		
	W	L	Pct	W	L	Pct
Illinois St*	13	5	.722	19	10	.655
Southern Illinois†	12	6	.667	23	10	.697
SW Missouri St	11	7	.611	20	11	.645
Tulsa	10	8	.556	15	14	.517
Drake	9	9	.500	14	14	.500
Northern Iowa	8	10	.444	12	15	.444
Bradley	7	11	.389	11	16	.407
Indiana St	7	11	.389	11	17	.393
Wichita St	7	11	.389	10	17	.370
Creighton	6	12	.333	8	18	.308

North Atlantic

	Conference			All Games		
	W	L	Pct	W	L	Pct
Drexel†	12	2	.857	22	7	.759
Northeastern	12	2	.857	20	8	.714
Delaware	10	4	.714	22	8	.733
Hartford	7	7	.500	14	14	.500
Maine	4	10	.286	10	17	.370
Vermont	4	10	.286	10	17	.370
New Hampshire	4	10	.286	6	21	.222
Boston U	3	11	.214	6	21	.222

Northeast

	Conference			All Games		
	W	L	Pct	W	L	Pct
Rider*†	14	4	.778	19	11	.633
Wagner	12	6	.667	18	12	.600
Marist	10	8	.556	14	16	.467
Mt St Mary's (MD)	10	8	.556	13	15	.464
FDU-Teaneck	8	10	.444	11	17	.393
St Francis (NY)	8	10	.444	9	18	.333
LIU-Brooklyn	7	11	.389	11	17	.393
Monmouth (NJ)	7	11	.389	11	17	.393
Robert Morris	7	11	.389	9	18	.333
St Francis (PA)	7	11	.389	9	18	.333

Ohio Valley

	Conference			All Games		
	W	L	Pct	W	L	Pct
Tennessee St*†	13	3	.813	19	10	.655
Murray St	11	5	.688	18	12	.600
Eastern Kentucky	11	5	.688	15	12	.556
SE Missouri St	9	7	.563	16	11	.593
Tennessee Tech	9	7	.563	15	13	.536
Morehead St	6	10	.375	6	21	.222
Middle Tenn St	5	11	.313	10	16	.385
Tenn-Martin	4	12	.250	7	19	.269
Austin Peay	4	12	.250	7	20	.259

Pacific-10

	Conference			All Games		
	W	L	Pct	W	L	Pct
Arizona*	17	1	.944	24	4	.857
California	12	6	.667	21	9	.700
UCLA	11	7	.611	22	11	.667
Arizona St	11	7	.611	18	10	.643
Southern Cal	9	9	.500	18	12	.600
Washington St	9	9	.500	15	12	.556
Oregon St	9	9	.500	13	14	.481
Washington	7	11	.389	13	14	.481
Oregon	3	15	.167	10	20	.333
Stanford	2	16	.111	7	23	.233

Patriot

	Conference			All Games		
	W	L	Pct	W	L	Pct
Bucknell*	13	1	.929	23	6	.793
Holy Cross†	12	2	.857	23	7	.767
Colgate	9	5	.643	18	10	.643
Fordham	9	5	.643	15	16	.484
Navy	5	9	.357	8	19	.296
Lafayette	4	10	.286	7	20	.259
Army	2	12	.143	4	22	.154
Lehigh	2	12	.143	4	23	.148

Southeastern

EAST

	Conference			All Games		
	W	L	Pct	W	L	Pct
Vanderbilt*	14	2	.875	28	6	.824
Kentucky†	13	3	.813	30	4	.882
Florida	9	7	.563	16	12	.571
Georgia	8	8	.500	15	14	.517
S Carolina	5	11	.313	9	18	.333
Tennessee	4	12	.250	13	17	.433

WEST

	Conference			All Games		
	W	L	Pct	W	L	Pct
Arkansas	10	6	.625	22	9	.710
LSU	9	7	.763	22	11	.667
Auburn	8	8	.500	15	12	.556
Alabama	7	9	.438	16	13	.552
Mississippi St	5	11	.313	13	16	.448
Mississippi	4	12	.250	10	18	.357
TN-Chattanooga*†	16	2	.889	26	7	.788

Southern

	Conference			All Games		
	W	L	Pct	W	L	Pct
Georgia Southern	12	6	.667	19	9	.679
E Tennessee St	12	6	.667	19	10	.655
Marshall	11	7	.611	16	11	.593
Davidson	10	8	.556	14	14	.500
Appalachian St	8	10	.444	13	15	.464
Furman	8	10	.444	11	17	.393
The Citadel	8	10	.444	10	17	.370
VMI	3	15	.167	5	22	.185
Western Carolina	2	16	.111	6	21	.222

*Conf. champ; †Conf. tourney winner.

Southland

	Conference			All Games		
	W	L	Pct	W	L	Pct
NE Louisiana*†	17	1	.944	26	5	.839
Nicholls St	11	7	.611	14	12	.538
TX-Arlington	10	8	.556	16	12	.571
TX-San Antonio	10	8	.556	15	14	.517
SW Texas St	9	9	.500	14	13	.519
McNeese St	9	9	.500	12	16	.429
Stephen F. Austin	8	10	.444	12	14	.462
NW Louisiana St	7	11	.389	13	13	.500
N Texas St	5	13	.278	5	21	.192
Sam Houston St	4	14	.222	6	19	.240

Southwest

	Conference			All Games		
	W	L	Pct	W	L	Pct
SMU*	12	2	.857	20	8	.714
Rice	11	3	.786	18	10	.643
Houston	9	5	.643	21	9	.700
Baylor	7	7	.500	16	11	.593
Texas Tech†	6	8	.429	18	12	.600
Texas A&M	5	9	.357	10	17	.370
Texas	4	10	.286	11	17	.393
Texas Christian	2	12	.143	6	22	.214

Southwestern Athletic

	Conference			All Games		
	W	L	Pct	W	L	Pct
Jackson St*	13	1	.929	25	9	.735
Southern-BR†	9	5	.643	21	10	.677
Alabama St	9	5	.643	14	13	.519
Texas Southern	8	6	.571	12	15	.444
Mississippi Valley	7	7	.500	13	15	.464
Grambling St	5	9	.357	13	14	.481
Alcorn St	5	9	.357	7	20	.259
Prairie View	0	14	.000	1	26	.037

Sun Belt

	Conference			All Games		
	W	L	Pct	W	L	Pct
New Orleans*	18	0	1.000	26	4	.867
W Kentucky†	14	4	.778	26	6	.813
Arkansas St	11	7	.611	16	12	.571
SW Louisiana	11	7	.611	17	13	.567
AR-Little Rock	10	8	.556	15	12	.556
Lamar	9	9	.500	15	12	.556
S Alabama	9	9	.500	15	13	.536
Louisiana Tech	3	15	.167	7	21	.250
Jacksonville	3	15	.167	5	22	.185
TX-Pan American	2	16	.111	2	20	.091

Trans-America

	Conference			All Games		
	W	L	Pct	W	L	Pct
Florida Int'l*	9	3	.750	20	10	.667
Samford	7	5	.583	17	10	.630
Mercer	7	5	.583	13	14	.481
Stetson	6	6	.500	13	14	.481
Georgia St	5	7	.417	13	14	.481
SE Louisiana	4	8	.333	12	15	.444
Centenary	4	8	.333	9	18	.333

West Coast

	Conference			All Games		
	W	L	Pct	W	L	Pct
Pepperdine*	11	3	.786	23	8	.742
Gonzaga	10	4	.714	19	9	.679
Santa Clara†	9	5	.643	19	12	.613
San Francisco	8	6	.571	19	12	.613
San Diego	7	7	.500	13	14	.481
St Mary's	6	8	.429	11	16	.407
Portland	3	11	.214	9	18	.333
Loyola (CA)	2	12	.143	7	20	.259

Western Athletic

	Conference			All Games		
	W	L	Pct	W	L	Pct
Utah	15	3	.833	24	7	.774
BYU	15	3	.833	25	9	.735
New Mexico†	13	5	.722	24	7	.774
UTEP	10	8	.556	21	13	.618
Colorado St	9	9	.500	17	12	.586
Fresno St	8	10	.444	13	15	.464
Wyoming	7	11	.389	13	15	.464
Hawaii	7	11	.389	12	16	.429
Air Force	3	15	.167	9	19	.321
San Diego St	3	15	.167	8	21	.276

Independents

	W	L	Pct
WI-Milwaukee	23	4	.852
College of Charleston	19	8	.704
MO-Kansas City	15	12	.556
Southern Utah St	14	13	.519
NE Illinois	11	16	.407
Cal St-Northridge	10	17	.370
Central Florida	10	17	.370
NC-Greensboro	10	17	.370
Hofstra	9	18	.333
Notre Dame	9	18	.333
Central Connecticut	8	19	.296
Buffalo	5	22	.185
Chicago St	4	23	.148
Cal St-Sacramento	3	24	.111

*Conf. champ; †Conf. tourney winner.

Scoring

	Class	GP	Field Goals			3-Pt FG		Free Throws					
			FGA	FG	Pct	FGA	FG	FTA	FT	Pct	Reb	Pts	Avg
Greg Guy,TX-Pan American	Jr	19	459	189	41.2	184	67	127	111	87.4	88	556	29.3
J.R. Rider, Nevada-Las Vegas	Sr	28	548	282	51.5	137	55	236	195	82.6	250	814	29.1
John Best, Tennessee Tech	Sr	28	535	296	55.3	18	4	771	203	26.3	235	799	28.5
Vin Baker, Hartford	Sr	28	639	305	47.7	119	32	240	150	62.5	300	792	28.3
Lindsey Hunter, Jackson St	Sr	34	777	320	41.2	328	112	201	155	77.1	115	907	26.7
Alphonzo Ford, Miss Val	Sr	28	578	252	43.6	216	76	187	148	79.1	147	728	26.0
Bill Edwards, Wright St	Sr	30	556	288	51.8	114	43	176	138	78.4	289	757	25.2
Billy Ross, Appalachian St	Sr	28	536	232	43.3	230	93	170	126	74.1	162	683	24.4
Glenn Robinson, Purdue	So	28	519	246	47.4	80	32	205	152	74.1	258	676	24.1
Kenneth Sykes, Grambling	So	27	482	242	50.2	86	37	165	123	74.5	136	644	23.9
Tony Dumas, MO-Kansas City	Jr	27	487	238	48.9	127	45	170	122	71.8	148	643	23.8
Eddie Benton, Vermont	Fr	26	425	176	41.4	196	82	221	185	83.7	79	619	23.8
Tony Dunkin, Coastal Caro	Sr	32	506	263	52.0	136	64	216	169	78.2	203	759	23.7
Damian Johnson, Central Conn St	Sr	26	497	236	47.5	5	0	185	133	71.9	101	605	23.3
Stan Rose, Weber St	Sr	28	390	240	61.5	0	0	275	170	61.8	232	650	23.2
Jesse Ratliff, North Texas	Jr	26	493	207	42.0	178	60	171	127	74.3	269	601	23.1
Lucious Harris, Long Beach St	Sr	32	478	251	52.5	177	73	212	164	77.4	169	739	23.1
Darnell Sneed, Charleston So	Sr	28	494	218	44.1	85	25	186	161	86.6	177	622	23.0
Devin Boyd, Towson St	Sr	27	441	177	40.1	171	54	272	214	78.7	105	622	23.0
Anfernee Hardaway, Memphis St	Jr	32	522	249	47.7	220	73	206	158	76.7	273	729	22.8
Brian Gilgeous, American	Sr	28	419	205	48.9	111	49	211	177	83.9	201	636	22.7
Demetrius Dudley, Hofstra	Sr	26	417	184	44.1	171	81	178	141	79.2	137	590	22.7
Kareem Townes, La Salle	So	27	550	203	36.9	301	97	149	104	69.8	95	607	22.5
Calbert Cheaney, Indiana	Sr	35	552	303	54.9	110	47	166	132	79.5	223	785	22.4
Tyrone Phillips, Marshall	Sr	26	419	228	54.4	4	0	180	125	69.4	153	581	22.3
Orlando Lightfoot, Idaho	Jr	32	582	288	49.5	114	37	143	102	71.3	276	715	22.3
Devon Lake, Southeast Mo St	Sr	27	429	194	46.2	126	45	205	162	79.0	99	603	22.3
Allan Houston, Tennessee	Sr	27	454	211	46.5	198	82	188	165	87.8	145	669	22.3
Buck Jenkins, Columbia	Sr	26	433	188	43.4	146	56	193	146	75.6	84	578	22.2
Darrick Suber, Rider	Sr	30	520	246	47.3	161	63	157	110	70.1	120	665	22.2

REBOUNDS

	Class	GP	Reb	Avg
Warren Kidd, Middle Tenn. St	Sr	26	386	14.8
Jervaughn Scales, Southern-BR	Jr	31	393	12.7
Reggie Jackson, Nicholls St.	So	26	325	12.5
Spencer Dunkley, Delaware	Sr	30	367	12.2
Dan Callahan, Northeastern	Jr	28	340	12.1
Ervin Johnson, New Orleans	Sr	29	346	11.9
Carlos Rogers, Tennessee St	Jr	29	339	11.7
Malik Rose, Drexel	Fr	29	330	11.4
Michael Smith, Providence	Jr	33	375	11.4
Darren Brown, Colgate	Sr	28	317	11.3

ASSISTS

	Class	GP	A	Avg
Sam Crawford, New Mexico St.	Sr	34	310	9.1
Dedan Thomas, Nevada-Las Vegas	Jr	29	248	8.6
Mark Woods, Wright St	Sr	30	253	8.4
Bobby Hurley, Duke	Sr	32	262	8.2
Chuck Evans, Mississippi St.	Sr	29	235	8.1
Jason Kidd, California	Fr	29	222	7.7
Tony Miller, Marquette	So	28	213	7.6
Nelson Haggerty, Baylor	So	26	189	7.3
Atiim Browne, Lamar	Jr	27	195	7.2

Five tied with 7.1 assists per game

3-POINT FIELD GOALS MADE PER GAME

	Class	GP	FG	Avg
Bernard Haslett, Southern Miss	Jr	26	109	4.2
Stevin Smith, Arizona St	Jr	27	113	4.2
Mark Alberts, Akron	Sr	26	107	4.1
Keith Veney, Lamar	Fr	27	106	3.9
Doug Day, Radford	Sr	31	116	3.7
Ronnie Schmitz, MO-Kansas City	Sr	27	98	3.6
Kareem Townes, La Salle	So	27	97	3.6
Greg Guy, TX-Pan American	Jr	19	67	3.5
Matt Maloney, Pennsylvania	Jr	27	91	3.4

Four tied with 3.3 per game

3-POINT FIELD GOAL PERCENTAGES

	Class	GP	FGA	FG	Pct
Jeff Anderson, Kent	Jr	26	82	44	53.7
Roosevelt Moore, Sam Houston	Jr	25	137	73	53.3
Dwayne Morton, Louisville	Jr	31	96	51	53.1
Travis Ford, Kentucky	Jr	34	191	101	52.9
Pat Graham, Indiana	Jr	35	111	57	51.4
Bill McCaffrey, Vanderbilt	Jr	34	162	83	51.2
Brad Divine, Eastern Ky	Fr	27	85	43	50.6
Sean Wightman, Western Mich.	Sr	29	129	63	48.8
Chris Mills, Arizona	Sr	28	116	56	48.3
Sam Brown, Toledo	Jr	28	141	68	48.2

Note: Minimum 1.5 made per game.

STEALS

	Class	GP	S	Avg
Jason Kidd, California	Fr	29	110	3.8
Jay Goodman, Utah State	Sr	27	102	3.8
Mark Woods, Wright State	Sr	30	109	3.6
Mike Bright, Bucknell	Sr	29	94	3.2
Darnell Mee, Western Kentucky	Sr	32	100	3.1
Jeff Myers, St Francis (NY)	Fr	26	81	3.1
Marcus Woods, Charleston	So	27	84	3.1
Dana Johnson, Canisius	Jr	26	79	3.0
Russell Peyton, Bucknell	Sr	29	88	3.0
Terry Evans, Oklahoma	Sr	32	97	3.0

BLOCKED SHOTS

	Class	GP	BS	Avg
Theo Ratliff, Wyoming	Jr	28	124	4.4
Sharone Wright, Clemson	So	30	124	4.1
Bo Outlaw, Houston	Sr	30	114	3.8
Carlos Rogers, Tennessee St	Jr	29	93	3.2
Theron Wilson, Eastern Michigan	So	30	96	3.2
Spencer Dunkley, Delaware	Sr	30	96	3.2
Rodney Dobard, Florida St	Sr	35	111	3.2
Constantin Popa, Miami (FL)	So	27	85	3.1
Harry Hart, Iona	Sr	26	80	3.1
Shelby Thurman, Western Illinois	Jr	27	83	3.1

FIELD GOAL PERCENTAGES

	Class	GP	FGA	FG	Pct
Bo Outlaw, Houston	Sr	30	298	196	65.8
Brian Grant, Xavier (OH)	Jr	30	341	223	65.4
Harry Hart, Iona	Sr	26	231	151	65.4
Cherokee Parks, Duke	So	32	247	161	65.2
Gary Trent, Ohio	Fr	27	298	194	65.1
Mike Nahar, Wright St	Jr	30	296	190	64.2
Mike Peplowski, Michigan St	Sr	28	252	161	63.9
Jimmy Lunsford, Alabama St	Fr	22	223	142	63.7
Warren Kidd, Middle Tenn St	Sr	26	265	167	63.0
Eddie Gay, Winthrop	Sr	30	309	194	62.8

Note: Minimum 5 made per game.

FREE-THROW PERCENTAGES

	Class	GP	FTA	FT	Pct
Josh Grant, Utah	Sr	31	113	104	92.0
Roger Breslin, Holy Cross	Sr	30	111	100	90.1
Jeremy Lake, Montana	So	28	79	71	89.9
Casey Schmidt, Valparaiso	Jr	27	78	70	89.7
Scott Hartzell, NC-Greensboro	Fr	27	81	72	88.9
Greg Holman, Kent St	Sr	27	78	69	88.5
Travis Ford, Kentucky	Jr	34	118	104	88.1
Pat Baldwin, Northwestern	Jr	25	75	66	88.0
Don Burgess, Radford	Jr	31	124	109	87.9
Allan Houston, Tennessee	Sr	30	188	165	87.8

Note: Minimum 2.5 made per game.

Single-Game Highs

POINTS

49	Alphonso Ford, Mississippi Val, Jan 23 (vs Alabama St)
49	Alphonso Ford, Mississippi Val, Feb 8 (vs Southern-BR)
48	Lindsey Hunter, Jackson St, Dec 27 (vs Kansas)
47	Will Flemons, Texas Tech, Feb 15 (vs Oral Roberts)
46	Reggie Kemp, Youngstown St, Feb 6 (vs Wright St)
46	Devin Boyd, Towson St, Feb 27 (vs MD-Balt County)
45	Bill Edwards, Wright St, Dec 8 (vs Morehead)

REBOUNDS

27	Ervin Johnson, New Orleans, Feb 18 (vs Lamar)
26	Malik Rose, Drexel, Jan 29 (vs Vermont)
25	Malik Rose, Drexel, Feb 11 (vs Vermont)
25	Spencer Dunkley, Delaware, Jan 6 (vs MD-Baltimore County)
24	Todd Cauthorn, William & Mary, Dec 5 (vs Citadel)
24	Ervin Johnson, New Orleans, Jan 2 (vs Jacksonville)
24	Yinka Dare, Geo Washington, Feb 6 (vs St Bonaventure)
23	Malik Rose, Drexel, Dec 12 (vs St Francis (PA))
23	James White, Morgan St, Jan 23 (vs Bethune-Cookman)
23	Ervin Johnson, New Orleans, Feb 11 (vs TX-Pan American)

six tied with 22

ASSISTS

20	Dana Harris, MD Balt County, Dec 12 (vs St Mary's)
20	Sam Crawford, New Mexico St, Dec 21 (vs Sam Houston St)
19	Nelson Haggerty, Baylor, Feb 27 (vs Oral Roberts)
18	BJ Tyler, Texas, Dec 1 (vs Oral Roberts)
17	Gary Robb, Tenn-Chatt, Dec 29 (vs Southern-BR)
17	Bryan Parker, Pepperdine, Jan 9 (vs Oral Roberts)
17	Sam Crawford, New Mexico St, Jan 14 (vs San Jose St)
17	Gerald Lewis, Southern Methodist, Mar 6 (vs Texas)

10 tied with 16

3-POINT FIELD GOALS

11 ....Doug Day, Radford, Dec 9 (vs Morgan St)
11 ....Lindsey Hunter, Jackson St, Dec 27 (vs Kansas)
11 ....Keith Veney, Lamar, Feb 3 (vs Prairie View)
11 ....Keith Veney, Lamar, Feb 11 (vs AR-Little Rock)

STEALS

12 ....Terry Evans, Oklahoma, Jan 27 (vs Florida A&M))
11 ....Ron Arnold, St Francis (NY), Feb 4 (vs Mt St Mary's, MD)
10 ....Michael Finley, Wisconsin, Feb 13 (vs Purdue)

10 tied with nine

BLOCKED SHOTS

13 ....Jim McIlvaine, Marquette, Dec 9 (vs Northeastern)
12 ....Ervin Johnson, New Orleans, Dec 29 (vs Texas A&M)
10 ....Sharone Wright, Clemson, Dec 12 (vs NC-Greensboro)
10 ....Sharone Wright, Clemson, Jan 27 (vs Maryland)
10 ....Bo Outlaw, Houston, Feb 17 (vs Texas A&M)
10 ....Theo Ratliff, Wyoming, Feb 25 (vs San Diego St)

Five tied with nine

NCAA Men's Division I Team Leaders

SCORING OFFENSE

	GP	W	L	Pts	Avg		GP	W	L	Pts	Avg
Southern-BR	31	21	10	3011	97.1	Lamar	27	15	12	2384	88.3
Northwestern (LA)	26	13	13	2357	90.7	Alabama St	27	14	13	2378	88.1
Nevada-Las Vegas	29	21	8	2592	89.4	Kentucky	34	30	4	2975	87.5
Wright St	30	20	10	2674	89.1	Northeast La	31	26	5	2702	87.2
Oklahoma	32	20	12	2850	89.1	Tennessee Tech	28	15	13	2440	87.1

SCORING DEFENSE

	GP	W	L	Pts	Avg		GP	W	L	Pts	Avg
Princeton	26	15	11	1421	54.7	Charleston	27	19	8	1631	60.4
Yale	26	10	16	1444	55.5	Marquette	28	20	8	1692	60.4
Miami (OH)	31	22	9	1775	57.3	New Orleans	30	26	4	1835	61.2
Cincinnati	32	27	5	1871	58.5	Bradley	27	11	16	1656	61.3
Southwest Mo St	31	20	11	1813	58.5	Montana	28	17	11	1723	61.5

SCORING MARGIN

	Off	Def	Mar		Off	Def	Mar
N Carolina	86.1	68.3	17.8	Kansas	84.4	69.7	14.6
Kentucky	87.5	69.8	17.7	W Kentucky	85.1	71.7	13.4
Cincinnati	74.5	58.5	16.0	Marquette	73.8	60.4	13.4
Duke	86.4	71.2	15.2	Tenn-Chatt	85.5	72.3	13.2
Indiana	86.5	71.6	14.9	Vanderbilt	83.0	69.9	13.1

FIELD GOAL PERCENTAGE

	FGA	FG	Pct		FGA	FG	Pct
Indiana	2062	1076	52.2	Oklahoma St	1571	807	51.4
Northeast La	1946	1015	52.2	Duke	1950	989	50.7
James Madison	1634	848	51.9	Michigan St	1591	806	50.7
Wright St	1912	987	51.6	N Carolina	2407	1219	50.6
Kansas	2154	1109	51.5	Gonzaga	1435	724	50.5

FIELD GOAL PERCENTAGE DEFENSE

	FGA	FG	Pct		FGA	FG	Pct
Marquette	1613	634	39.3	Michigan St	1748	705	40.3
George Washington	1794	708	39.5	Montana	1472	595	40.4
Arizona	1776	710	40.0	Missouri	1877	759	40.4
Utah	1831	737	40.3	Seton Hall	2107	853	40.5
New Orleans	1689	680	40.3	Virginia	1947	789	40.5
				Wyoming	1794	727	40.5

FREE-THROW PERCENTAGE

	FTA	FT	Pct		FTA	FT	Pct
Utah	602	476	79.1	Iowa St	613	465	75.9
Charleston So	526	408	77.6	Seton Hall	905	683	75.5
Valparaiso	532	412	77.4	TX-Pan American	377	284	75.3
Indiana St	580	445	76.7	Creighton	543	409	75.3
Brigham Young	909	697	76.7	Cornell	553	416	75.2

3-POINT FIELD GOALS MADE PER GAME

	GP	FG	Avg		GP	FG	Avg
Lamar	27	271	10.0	Southern-BR	31	258	8.3
Kentucky	34	340	10.0	Vermont	27	222	8.2
Arizona St	28	263	9.4	Tennessee Tech	28	226	8.1
NC-Asheville	27	235	8.7	Dayton	30	240	8.0
Southern Cal	30	259	8.6	Nevada-Las Vegas	29	232	8.0
Campbell	27	228	8.4	Baylor	27	215	8.0

3-POINT FIELD GOAL PERCENTAGE

	GP	FGA	FG	Pct		GP	FGA	FG	Pct
Valparaiso	28	500	214	42.8	Louisville	31	452	188	41.6
Princeton	26	479	204	42.6	Vanderbilt	34	636	262	41.2
Indiana	35	464	197	42.5	Old Dominion	29	447	184	41.2
Kent St	27	384	162	42.2	WI-Green Bay	27	367	151	41.1
Miami (OH)	31	522	218	41.8	Utah	31	461	189	41.0

Note: Minimum 3.0 made per game.

NCAA Women's Championship Game Box Score

Texas Tech 84

TEXAS TECH	Min	FG M-A	FT M-A	Reb O-T	A	PF	TP
Kirkland	40	5-10	1-5	0-3	5	2	14
Swoopes	40	16-24	11-11	1-5	3	4	47
Clinger	19	3-5	1-1	1-5	0	5	7
N. Johnson	35	2-7	4-4	0-0	2	1	8
Scott	37	2-3	0-0	1-3	3	3	4
Atkins	21	1-3	2-2	1-6	0	2	4
Farris	8	0-1	0-0	0-0	2	0	0
Totals	200	29-53	19-23	4-22	13	19	84

Percentages: FG—.547, FT—.826. 3-pt goals: 7-17, .412 (Swoopes 4-6, Kirkland 3-6, Scott 0-1, N. Johnson 0-4). Team rebounds: 2. Blocked shots: 2 (Swoopes, Clinger). Turnovers: 13 (N. Johnson 5, Kirkland 3, Swoopes 2, Scott, Farris, team). Steals: 9 (Kirkland 3, Scott 3, Swoopes 2, N. Johnson).

Ohio State 82

OHIO STATE	Min	FG M-A	FT M-A	Reb O-T	A	PF	TP
Smith	40	11-20	5-7	5-11	4	3	28
Keyton	36	6-12	7-7	3-8	1	4	19
Howard	16	0-0	2-2	1-1	2	1	2
Burcy	31	3-15	3-4	0-5	5	4	12
Roberts	33	5-11	1-1	2-3	2	4	13
Negri	23	2-2	1-1	3-5	0	3	5
Ingwersen	4	0-0	0-0	0-0	0	0	0
A. Johnson	3	0-0	0-0	0-0	0	0	0
Sebastian	4	0-1	0-0	0-0	1	2	0
Bond	10	1-3	0-0	1-2	2	4	3
Totals	200	28-64	19-22	15-35	17	25	82

Percentages: FG—.438, FT—.864. 3-pt goals: 7-22, .318 (Burcy 3-11, Roberts 2-5 Smith 1-2, Keyton 0-2). Team rebounds: 6. Blocked shots: 0. Turnovers: 18 (Burcy 4, Negri 4, Roberts 3, Keyton 2, Howard 2, Smith, A. Johnson, team). Steals: 7 (Roberts 3, Bond 2, Smith, Burcy). Halftime: Texas Tech 40, Ohio State 31. A: 16,141 Officials: Bell, Kantner.

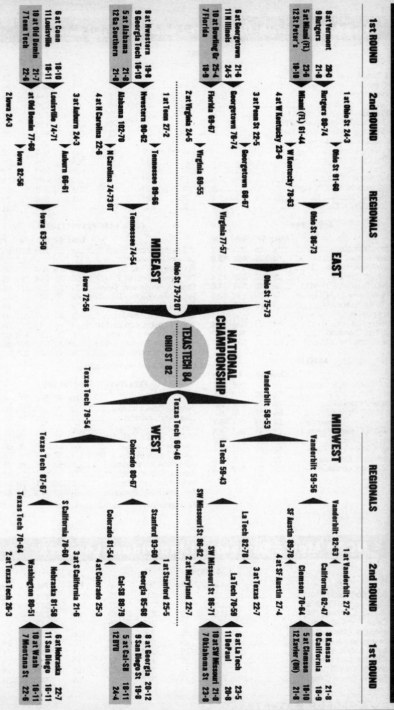

1st ROUND	2nd ROUND	REGIONALS			REGIONALS	2nd ROUND	1st ROUND

EAST

8 at Vermont 20-6 / 9 Rutgers 21-8 → Rutgers 80-74 → Ohio St 91-60
1 at Ohio St 24-3 → Ohio St 24-3

5 at Miami (FL) 23-6 / 12 St Peter's 16-10 → Miami (FL) 61-44 → W Kentucky 78-63
4 at W Kentucky 23-6 → Ohio St 86-73

6 at Georgetown 21-6 / 11 N Illinois 24-5 → Georgetown 76-74 → Georgetown 68-67
3 at Penn St 22-5

7 Florida 18-9 / 10 at Bowling Gr 25-4 → Florida 69-67 → Virginia 77-57
2 at Virginia 24-5 → Virginia 69-55 → Ohio St 75-73

MIDEAST

8 at N'western 19-8 / 9 Georgia Tech 16-10 → N'western 90-62 → Tennessee 89-66
1 at Tenn 27-2 → Tennessee 74-54

5 at Alabama 21-9 / 12 Ga Southern 21-9 → Alabama 102-70 → N Carolina 74-73 OT
4 at N Carolina 22-6 → Iowa 72-56

6 at Conn 16-10 / 11 Louisville 18-11 → Louisville 74-71 → Auburn 66-61
3 at Auburn 24-3 → Iowa 63-50

10 at Old Domin 21-7 / 7 Tenn Tech 22-6 → at Old Domin 77-60 → Iowa 82-56
2 Iowa 24-3 → Ohio St 73-72 OT

NATIONAL CHAMPIONSHIP

TEXAS TECH 84
OHIO ST 82

MIDWEST

1 at Vanderbilt 27-2 → Vanderbilt 82-63
8 Kansas 21-8 / 9 California 18-9 → California 62-47

4 at SF Austin 27-4 → Clemson 70-64 → Vanderbilt 59-56
5 at Clemson 16-10 / 12 Xavier (OH) 21-8 → Clemson 70-64

3 at Texas 22-7 → La Tech 82-78
6 at La Tech 23-5 / 11 DePaul 20-8 → La Tech 70-59 → La Tech 59-43

2 at Maryland 22-7 → SW Missouri St 86-71
10 at SW Missouri 21-8 / 7 Oklahoma 23-8 → SW Missouri St 86-82 → SF Austin 89-78

Vanderbilt 58-53

WEST

1 at Stanford 25-5 → Stanford 93-60
8 at Georgia 20-12 / 9 San Diego St 19-8 → Georgia 85-68

4 at Colorado 25-3 → Cal-SB 88-79 → Colorado 81-54
5 at Cal-SB 18-11 / 12 BYU 24-4 → Cal-SB 88-79 → Colorado 80-67

3 at S California 21-6 → S California 78-60
6 at Nebraska 22-7 / 11 San Diego 16-11 → Nebraska 81-58 → Texas Tech 87-67

2 at Texas Tech 26-3 → Texas Tech 70-64 → Texas Tech 79-54
10 at Wash 16-1 / 7 Montana St 22-6 → Washington 80-51

Texas Tech 60-46

NCAA Women's Division I Individual Leaders

SCORING

	Class	GP	TFG	3FG	FT	Pts	Avg
Andrea Congreaves, Mercer	Sr	26	302	51	150	805	31.0
Sheryl Swoopes, Texas Tech	Sr	34	356	32	211	955	28.1
Sarah Behn, Boston Col	Sr	27	227	27	203	684	25.3
Sonja Tate, Arkansas St	Sr	33	282	95	161	820	24.8
Albena Branzova, Florida Int'l	So	31	308	23	109	748	24.1
Teresa Jackson, Nevada-Las Vegas	Sr	31	278	6	156	718	23.2
Roschelle Vaughn, Tennessee Tech	Sr	29	272	1	118	663	22.9
Carol Ann Shudlick, Minnesota	Jr	26	253	0	81	587	22.6
Travesa Gant, Lamar	Jr	26	239	11	93	582	22.4
Samantha David, Niagara	Sr	27	240	0	104	584	21.6
Angie Crosby, Appalachian St	Jr	27	221	0	138	580	21.5
Natalie Williams, UCLA	Jr	23	201	0	86	488	21.2
Angela Gilbert, Illinois-Chicago	Sr	28	231	0	128	590	21.1
Latoja Harris, Toledo	Jr	28	221	0	148	590	21.1
Tonya Sampson, N Carolina	Jr	30	217	60	137	631	21.0

REBOUNDS

	Class	GP	Reb	Avg
Ann Barry, Nevada	Sr	25	355	14.2
Lauretta Freeman, Auburn	Sr	29	401	13.8
Natalie Williams, UCLA	Jr	23	310	13.5
Travesa Gant, Lamar	Jr	26	348	13.4
DeShawne Blocker, E Tenn St	So	25	326	13.0
Cammie Williams, LIU-Brooklyn	Sr	26	334	12.8
Christy Greis, Evansville	Sr	28	359	12.8
Deneka Knowles, Southeastern La	Fr	26	332	12.8
Erin Butcher, Davidson	Fr	20	246	12.3
Natasha Rezek, Pennsylvania	So	25	293	11.7

ASSISTS

	Class	GP	A	Avg
Gaynor O'Donnnell, E Carolina	Sr	28	300	10.7
Tine Freil, Pacific (CA)	Sr	26	272	10.5
Ira Fuquay, Alcorn St	So	24	223	9.3
Andrea Nagy, Florida Int'l	So	31	270	8.7
Nancy Kennelly, Northwestern	Sr	29	252	8.7
Cori Close, UC Santa Barbara	Sr	31	257	8.3
Lori Pasceri, Canisius	So	26	214	8.2
Michelle Bouldin, Duquesne	So	27	201	7.4
Niesa Johnson, Alabama	So	31	226	7.3
Ramona Jones, Lamar	Sr	26	189	7.3

FIELD GOAL PERCENTAGE

	Class	GP	FGA	FG	Pct
Lidiya Varbanova, Boise St	Jr	27	294	200	68.0
Deneka Knowles, Southeastern La	Fr	26	204	133	65.2
DeShawne Blocker, E Tenn St	So	25	294	191	65.0
Cinietra Henderson, Texas	Sr	30	325	211	64.9
Roschelle Vaughn, Tenn Tech	Sr	29	421	272	64.6
Crystal Steward, Northeast La	Jr	28	266	171	64.3
Latoja Harris, Toledo	Jr	28	347	221	63.7
Angie Crosby, Appalachian St	Jr	27	347	221	63.7
Keisha Johnson, Tulane	Jr	27	280	178	63.6
Talita Scott, Bowling Green	Jr	30	311	197	63.3
Jessie Hicks, Maryland	Sr	30	324	205	63.3

Note: Minimum 5 made per game.

FREE-THROW PERCENTAGE

	Class	GP	FTA	FT	Pct
Jennifer Cole, La Salle	Sr	27	165	150	90.9
Lisa Furlin, Indiana	Fr	27	83	75	90.4
Jen Nelson, Niagara	So	27	90	81	90.0
Shelley Sheetz, Colorado	So	31	139	123	88.5
Jennifer Clary, Idaho	So	27	86	76	88.4
Sheryl Swoopes, Texas Tech	Sr	34	243	211	86.8
Julie Powell, Vanderbilt	Jr	32	98	85	86.7
Tammie Crown, Radford	Jr	28	140	121	86.4
Helen Holloway, Penn St	Jr	28	81	70	86.4
Erin Kenneally, Syracuse	Sr	27	121	104	86.0

Note: Minimum 2.5 made per game.

NCAA Men's Division II Individual Leaders

SCORING

	Class	GP	TFG	3FG	FT	Pts	Avg
Darrin Robinson, Sacred Heart	Sr	26	313	75	130	831	32.0
Alex Wright, Central Oklahoma	Sr	28	293	97	165	848	30.3
Ray Gutierrez, California (PA)	Sr	29	235	142	165	777	26.8
David Eaker, Fort Valley St	Jr	27	257	23	176	713	26.4
Kwame Morton, Clarion	Jr	26	220	107	108	655	25.2
Terrance Jordan, Livingstone	Sr	24	214	0	166	594	24.8
Ed Wheeler, Angelo St	Jr	26	263	1	111	638	24.5
Jason Williams, New Haven	Sr	27	237	66	115	655	24.3
Terry McCord, Troy St	Sr	32	274	71	156	775	24.2
Chad Briscoe, Grand Canyon	Sr	31	278	96	95	747	24.1

REBOUNDS

	Class	GP	Reb	Avg
James Hector, American Int'l	Jr	28	389	13.9
Wayne Robertson, New Hampshire Col	Jr	33	442	13.4
Marcus Allen, Paine	Jr	26	334	12.8
Cedric Roach, LeMoyne-Owen	Jr	28	340	12.1
Fred Tyler,Central Oklahoma	Sr	29	337	11.6
Andy Uphoff, Emporia St	Sr	27	302	11.2
Ed Malloy, Philadelphia Textile	Sr	32	351	11.0
David Allen, Wayne St (NB)	Sr	26	283	10.9
Eric White, East Stroudsberg	Jr	23	250	10.9
Lorenzo Poole, Albany St (GA)	Jr	19	205	10.8

ASSISTS

	Class	GP	A	Avg
Demetri Beekman, Assumption	Sr	28	389	13.9
Hal Chambers, Columbus	Jr	24	227	9.5
David Daniels, Colorado Christian	Sr	29	264	9.1
Darnell White, California (PA)	Jr	29	249	8.6
Greg Fox, Edinboro	Sr	27	222	8.2
Chris Franklin, Lock Haven	So	26	205	7.9
Aaron Johnson, LIU-CW Post	Jr	26	205	7.9
Lamont Jones, Bridgeport	So	29	222	7.7
Warren Burgess, St Anselm	Jr	31	234	7.5
Mike Buscetto, Quinnipiac	Sr	28	211	7.5

FIELD GOAL PERCENTAGE

	Class	GP	FGA	FG	Pct
Chad Scott, California (PA)	So	28	245	173	70.6
Charles McLemore, Chaminade	Jr	28	214	148	69.2
Marcel Boggs, Francis Marion	Sr	28	278	186	66.9
James Morris, Central Oklahoma	Jr	27	269	176	65.4
Chris Jones, South Dakota	Jr	30	259	169	65.3
Wayne Robertson, New Hampshire Col	Jr	33	411	268	65.2
Antwan Stallworth, SIU-Edwardsville	Sr	25	322	209	64.9
Roheen Oats, Cal St Bakersfield	Jr	33	308	199	64.6
Sarran Marshall, Morehouse	So	25	222	142	64.0
Tyrone Davis, Cal St Bakersfield	Jr	33	288	183	63.5

Note: Minimum 5 made per game.

FREE-THROW PERCENTAGE

	Class	GP	FTA	FT	Pct
Jason Williams, New Haven	Sr	27	125	115	92.0
Chad Briscoe, Grand Canyon	Sr	31	106	95	89.6
Guy Miller, Mesa St	Sr	29	129	115	89.1
Joey Haythorn, S Colorado	Jr	28	86	76	88.4
John Brenegan, S Dakota	Sr	30	103	90	87.4
Ray Gutierrez, California (PA)	Sr	29	189	165	87.3
Kenny Warren, Cal St Bakersf	Jr	33	110	96	87.3
Kenneth Brookins, LeMoyne O	Jr	26	86	75	87.2
Scott Guldseth, N Dakota	Sr	31	176	153	86.9
Adam Cheek, Edinboro	Sr	29	111	96	86.5

Note: Minimum 2.5 made per game.

NCAA Women's Division II Individual Leaders

SCORING

	Class	GP	TFG	3FG	FT	Pts	Avg
Yolanda Griffith, Florida Atlantic	Jr	22	262	0	97	621	28.2
Paulette King Florida Tech	Sr	30	310	0	193	813	27.1
Carolyn Brown, St Augustine's	Sr	24	240	90	74	644	26.8
Julie Heldt, Northern Michigan	Sr	28	263	0	189	715	25.5
Kathy Comeaux, Henderson St	So	24	242	0	106	590	24.6
Veronica Freeman, Paine	Jr	27	251	0	134	636	23.6
Carmelia Bloodsaw, Alabama A&M	Jr	26	207	72	118	604	23.2
Lorain Truesdale, Lander	Sr	26	227	34	108	596	22.9
Kristy O'Hara, Shippensburg	Sr	26	221	35	118	595	22.9
Rachel Rosario, UC-Riverside	Sr	28	250	0	134	634	22.6

REBOUNDS

	Class	GP	Reb	Avg
Vanessa White, Tuskegee	So	25	433	17.3
Tracy Linton, Jacksonville St	Sr	29	480	16.6
Rachel Rosario, UC-Riverside	Sr	28	456	16.3
Yolanda Griffith, Florida Atlantic	Jr	22	360	16.0
Lorain Truesdale, Lander	Sr	26	404	15.5
Holly Roberts, Metropolitan St	Sr	27	349	12.9
Rebecca Hanson, Pace	Jr	30	380	12.7
Erica Taylor, Virginia St	So	26	327	12.6
Lorraine Morrissey, Dowling	So	22	269	12.2
Carrolyn Burke, Queens (NY)	Fr	25	296	11.8

ASSISTS

	Class	GP	A	Avg
Selina Bynum, Albany St (GA)	Sr	26	280	10.8
Lisa Rice, Norfolk St	So	31	305	9.8
Lori Richelderfer, California (PA)	Jr	26	239	9.2
Nikki Leibold, Northern Michigan	Sr	28	243	8.7
Tara Reardon, Queens (NY)	Sr	20	169	8.4
Beth Browning, Tampa	Sr	25	202	8.1
Paula Light, Millersville	Sr	25	201	8.0
Jody Hill, Pace	Jr	31	236	7.6
Roseann Rutledge, Saginaw Valley	Sr	29	214	7.4
Amy McMullen, Seattle Pacific	Sr	26	184	7.1

NCAA Women's Division II Individual Leaders (Cont.)

FIELD GOAL PERCENTAGE

	Class	GP	FGA	FG	Pct
Missy Taylor, Oakland City	Fr	29	385	267	69.4
Julie Eymann, Regis (CO)	Sr	27	273	186	68.1
Cynthia Bridges, Fort Valley St	So	30	226	151	66.8
Corinne Vanderwal, California (PA)	Sr	26	293	191	65.2
LaTanya Patty, Delta St	Sr	33	375	240	64.0
Kathy Comeaux, Henderson St	So	24	381	242	63.5
Yolanda Griffith, Fla Atlantic	Jr	22	415	262	63.1
Jeanette Polk, Augusta	Jr	28	453	285	62.9
Tia Glass, St Joseph's (IN)	Sr	27	365	227	62.2
Stephanie Anderson, Northern Colorado	Sr	27	243	150	61.7

Note: Minimum 5 made per game.

FREE-THROW PERCENTAGE

	Class	GP	FTA	FT	Pct
Renae Aschoff, Portland St	Sr	29	85	75	88.2
Julie Filpus, Wayne St (MI)	Jr	26	82	71	86.6
Joyce Dimond, Philadelphia Textile	Sr	25	111	96	86.5
Dawn Murphy, Hillsdale	Jr	26	135	116	85.9
Darlene Hildebrand, Philadelphia Textile	So	29	127	109	85.8
Paulette King, Florida Tech	Sr	30	226	193	85.4
Jamie Long Northwest Mo St	Sr	27	120	102	85.0
Sara Belanger, Minn-Duluth	Fr	30	98	83	84.7
Julie Krauth, Augustana (SD)	Sr	29	88	74	84.1
Keisha Bostic, Albany St (GA)	So	27	81	68	84.0

Note: Minimum 2.5 made per game.

NCAA Men's Division III Individual Leaders

SCORING

	Class	GP	TFG	3FG	FT	Pts	Avg
Dave Shaw, Drew	Sr	23	210	74	169	663	28.8
Dameon Ross, Salisbury St	Jr	26	268	84	112	732	28.2
Alberto Montanez, Rochester Inst	Sr	28	275	57	137	744	26.6
Larry Norman, Clark (MA)	Sr	24	222	10	172	626	26.1
Vaughn Troyer, Eastern Mennon	Sr	25	229	36	157	651	26.0
Mike Crnkovich, Wabash	Sr	26	272	4	111	659	25.3
Moses Jean-Pierre, Plymouth	Jr	25	190	65	169	614	24.6
Scott Fitch, Geneseo St	Jr	27	208	87	160	663	24.6
Kirk Anderson, Augustana	Sr	30	237	123	137	734	24.5
Al Pettway, Worcester St	Jr	27	239	71	93	642	23.8

REBOUNDS

	Class	GP	Reb	Avg
Steve Lemmer, Hamilton	Sr	27	404	15.0
Rolando Welch, Western Md	Jr	24	320	13.3
Jim Hoopes, Albright	Jr	22	278	12.6
Matt Cusano, Scranton	Sr	29	362	12.5
William Berry, Carthage	Sr	24	299	12.5
Jose Rodriguez, Hunter	Sr	29	357	12.3
Andrew South, New Jersey Tech	So	26	319	12.3
Shannon Cloyd, Millikin	So	25	301	12.0
Mahlon Williams, Wheaton (MA)	So	20	236	11.8
James Boykins, Chris. Newport	Sr	28	327	11.7

ASSISTS

	Class	GP	A	Avg
David Genovese, Mt St Vincent	So	27	237	8.8
Jeff Molisani, Rochester Inst	Sr	28	237	8.5
Lance Andrews, New Jersey Tech	Sr	26	217	8.3
Greg Martin, Westminster (MO)	Sr	26	211	8.1
Steve Artis, Chris Newport	Sr	28	220	7.9
Jimmy Resvanis, Baruch	Jr	24	186	7.8
Jason Franklin, Westfield St	Sr	27	203	7.5
Tres Wolf, Susquehanna	Jr	25	179	7.2
Paul Ferrell, Guilford	Jr	24	170	7.1
Steve Fleming, Hiram	Jr	25	177	7.1

FIELD GOAL PERCENTAGE

	Class	GP	FGA	FG	Pct
Jim Leibel, St Thomas (MN)	Jr	28	202	141	69.8
Gary Francisco, Utica	Sr	23	166	115	69.3
Mike Burden, Rowan	Jr	31	268	182	67.9
Marcellus Smith, Marymount (VA)	Jr	23	219	145	66.2
David Otte, Simpson	So	25	212	139	65.6
Greg Kemp, Auroroa	Jr	25	264	173	65.5
Brian Davis, Oglethorpe	Jr	24	249	163	65.5
Brett Grebing, Redlands	Sr	24	200	130	65.0
Josh Hammermesh, Amherst	Jr	23	293	189	64.5
Dan Rush, Bridgewater (VA)	So	24	249	160	64.3
James Boykin, Chris Newport	Sr	28	330	212	64.2

Note: Minimum 5 made per game.

FREE-THROW PERCENTAGE

	Class	GP	FTA	FT	Pct
Jim Durrell, Colby-Sawyer	Jr	25	72	67	93.1
Bobby Bonjean, Illinois Col	Jr	21	74	67	90.5
Pat Murphy, WI-Platteville	Sr	28	149	134	89.9
Steve Fleming, Hiram	Jr	25	146	130	89.0
Chad Onofrio, Tufts	Fr	25	89	79	88.8
Luke Busby, Johns Hopkins	Jr	26	96	85	88.5
Dennis Ruedinger, WI-Oshkosh	Fr	25	96	85	88.5
Noah Clark, Williams	So	27	77	68	88.3
Joe Levesque, MIT	So	24	85	75	88.2
Ray Cullinan, Postsdam St	Fr	23	101	89	88.1

Note: Minimum 2.5 made per game.

NCAA Women's Division III Individual Leaders

SCORING

	Class	GP	TFG	3FG	FT	Pts	Avg
Sladja Kovijanic, Middlebury	Sr	21	235	80	98	648	30.9
Annette Hoffman, Juniata	Sr	22	197	21	228	643	29.2
Tricia Rasmussen, St Mary's (MN)	Sr	24	270	2	103	645	26.9
Laurie Trow, St Thomas (MN)	Sr	26	271	0	137	679	26.1
Tricia Kosenina, Thiel	Sr	24	214	42	152	622	25.9
Renie Amoss, Goucher	Sr	25	244	39	85	612	24.5
Patricia Frost, Upsala	So	20	200	32	47	479	24.0
Simone Edwards, FDU-Madison	Sr	25	183	20	206	592	23.7
Brenda Davis, Guilford	Jr	25	238	0	108	584	23.4
Kim Cola, Western New England	So	21	184	44	76	488	23.2

REBOUNDS

	Class	GP	Reb	Avg
Giovanni Licorish, Baruch	Fr	19	317	16.7
Shannon Shaffer, Montclair St	Sr	25	382	15.3
Liza Janssen, Wellesley	Jr	27	407	15.1
Kim Roth, Salisbury St	So	23	340	14.8
Erica Scholl, UC San Diego	Sr	25	368	14.7
Molly Lackman, Immaculata	Jr	25	359	14.4
Wendy Gruenwald, New Jersey Tech	Fr	22	314	14.3
Erin Adamson, Bryn Mawr	Jr	17	242	14.2
Wendy Howard, Utica Tech	Jr	25	354	14.2

ASSISTS

	Class	GP	A	Avg
Karen Barefoot, Chris. Newport	Jr	28	236	8.4
Marlo Foley, Binghamton	Sr	27	211	7.8
Allison Gagnon, Southern Me	Sr	29	221	7.6
Renie Amoss, Goucher	Sr	25	182	7.3
Kristi Schultz, Concordia-M'head	Sr	27	190	7.0
Regina Austin, Buffalo St	Sr	27	188	7.0
Chris Lavery, Immaculata	Jr	23	157	6.8
Leslie Cox, Meredith	So	20	136	6.8
Maureen Andrews, Gettysburg	So	24	162	6.8
Mary Keegan, Loras	So	24	159	6.6

FIELD GOAL PERCENTAGE

	Class	GP	FGA	FG	Pct
Tina Kampa, St Benedict	So	30	231	158	68.4
Lanett Stephan, Franklin	Fr	25	222	147	66.2
Laurie Trow, St Thomas (MN)	Sr	26	413	271	65.6
Sylvia Newman, Meredith	Sr	20	238	149	62.6
Arlene Meinholz, WI-Eau Claire	So	26	313	192	61.3
Jerilyn Johnson, Rhode Isl Col	Sr	23	314	189	60.2
Liza Janssen, Wellesley	Jr	27	357	214	59.9
Audrey Seymour, Adrian	Sr	26	274	163	59.5
Jamie Parrott, Maryville (TN)	Fr	26	245	145	59.2
Jill Coleman, Wesley	Sr	25	384	227	59.1

Note: Minimum 5 made per game.

FREE-THROW PERCENTAGE

	Class	GP	FTA	FT	Pct
Jill Kathman, William Smith	Fr	25	74	66	89.2
Katie Anderson, Luther	Sr	20	65	57	87.7
Jen Olsen, Wellesley	Sr	27	82	70	85.4
Annette Hoffman, Juniata	Sr	22	268	228	85.1
Chris Pagano, Middlebury	Jr	21	93	79	84.9
Tricia Kosenina, Thiel	Sr	24	179	152	84.9
Eileen Horatis, Lake Forest	So	22	73	61	83.6
Heidi Metzger, Elizabethtown	So	24	109	91	83.5
Colleen Tribby, Claremont M-S	Fr	25	113	94	83.2
Pam Porter, Moravian	Jr	24	113	94	83.2
Cindi Neanen, Wilmington (OH)	Fr	24	136	113	83.1

Note: Minimum 2.5 made per game.

Canned

At the NCAA women's basketball regional at Nacogdoches, Texas, a reporter seated at courtside was asked by tournament officials to pour his soft drink, which was in a purple and red Stephen F. Austin State cup, into a container bearing an NCAA logo. At a news conference, Stephen F. Austin coach Gary Blair was asked to do the same with his can of soda. It seems the NCAA doesn't want other entities to get TV exposure at the expense of tournament sponsors.

Meanwhile, Kelvin Davis, a 6' 4" center for Chicago's Mather High, executed his "I'm thirsty" routine in the state high school tournament's slam-dunk contest. After putting a soft drink can—no NCAA requirement here—on the back of the rim, Davis dunked with his right hand, grabbed the rim with his left and the can with his right, made a show of swigging the soda and spiked the can upon landing. Davis was an also-ran in the event, but credit him with being one sly guy. Our sources tell us that he used an empty can and affixed it to the rim with a magnet.

NCAA Division I Men's Championship Results

NCAA Final Four Results

Year	Winner	Score	Runner-up	Third Place	Fourth Place	Winning Coach
1939	Oregon	46-33	Ohio St	*Oklahoma	*Villanova	Howard Hobson
1940	Indiana	60-42	Kansas	*Duquesne	*Southern Cal	Branch McCracken
1941	Wisconsin	39-34	Washington St	*Pittsburgh	*Arkansas	Harold Foster
1942	Stanford	53-38	Dartmouth	*Colorado	*Kentucky	Everett Dean
1943	Wyoming	46-34	Georgetown	*Texas	*DePaul	Everett Shelton
1944	Utah	42-40 (OT)	Dartmouth	*Iowa St	*Ohio St	Vadal Peterson
1945	Oklahoma St	49-45	NYU	*Arkansas	*Ohio St	Hank Iba
1946	Oklahoma St	43-40	N Carolina	Ohio St	California	Hank Iba
1947	Holy Cross	58-47	Oklahoma	Texas	CCNY	Alvin Julian
1948	Kentucky	58-42	Baylor	Holy Cross	Kansas St	Adolph Rupp
1949	Kentucky	46-36	Oklahoma St	Illinois	Oregon St	Adolph Rupp
1950	CCNY	71-68	Bradley	N Carolina St	Baylor	Nat Holman
1951	Kentucky	68-58	Kansas St	Illinois	Oklahoma St	Adolph Rupp
1952	Kansas	80-63	St John's (NY)	Illinois	Santa Clara	Forrest Allen
1953	Indiana	69-68	Kansas	Washington	Louisiana St	Branch McCracken
1954	La Salle	92-76	Bradley	Penn St	Southern Cal	Kenneth Loeffler
1955	San Francisco	77-63	La Salle	Colorado	Iowa	Phil Woolpert
1956	San Francisco	83-71	Iowa	Temple	Southern Meth	Phil Woolpert
1957	N Carolina	54-53†	Kansas	San Francisco	Michigan St	Frank McGuire
1958	Kentucky	84-72	Seattle	Temple	Kansas St	Adolph Rupp
1959	California	71-70	W Virginia	Cincinnati	Louisville	Pete Newell
1960	Ohio St	75-55	California	Cincinnati	NYU	Fred Taylor
1961	Cincinnati	70-65 (OT)	Ohio St	Vacated‡	Utah	Edwin Jucker
1962	Cincinnati	71-59	Ohio St	Wake Forest	UCLA	Edwin Jucker
1963	Loyola (IL)	60-58 (OT)	Cincinnati	Duke	Oregon St	George Ireland
1964	UCLA	98-83	Duke	Michigan	Kansas St	John Wooden
1965	UCLA	91-80	Michigan	Princeton	Wichita St	John Wooden
1966	UTEP	72-65	Kentucky	Duke	Utah	Don Haskins
1967	UCLA	79-64	Dayton	Houston	N Carolina	John Wooden
1968	UCLA	78-55	N Carolina	Ohio St	Houston	John Wooden
1969	UCLA	92-72	Purdue	Drake	N Carolina	John Wooden
1970	UCLA	80-69	Jacksonville	New Mexico St	St Bonaventure	John Wooden
1971	UCLA	68-62	Vacated‡	Vacated‡	Kansas	John Wooden
1972	UCLA	81-76	Florida St	N Carolina	Louisville	John Wooden
1973	UCLA	87-66	Memphis St	Indiana	Providence	John Wooden
1974	N Carolina St	76-64	Marquette	UCLA	Kansas	Norm Sloan
1975	UCLA	92-85	Kentucky	Louisville	Syracuse	John Wooden
1976	Indiana	86-68	Michigan	UCLA	Rutgers	Bob Knight
1977	Marquette	67-59	N Carolina	NV-Las Vegas	NC-Charlotte	Al McGuire
1978	Kentucky	94-88	Duke	Arkansas	Notre Dame	Joe Hall
1979	Michigan St	75-64	Indiana St	DePaul	Penn	Jud Heathcote
1980	Louisville	59-54	Vacated‡	Purdue	Iowa	Denny Crum
1981	Indiana	63-50	N Carolina	Virginia	Louisiana St	Bob Knight
1982	N Carolina	63-62	Georgetown	*Houston	*Louisville	Dean Smith
1983	N Carolina St	54-52	Houston	*Georgia	*Louisville	Jim Valvano
1984	Georgetown	84-75	Houston	*Kentucky	*Virginia	John Thompson
1985	Villanova	66-64	Georgetown	*St John's (NY)	Vacated‡	Rollie Massimino
1986	Louisville	72-69	Duke	*Kansas	*Louisiana St	Denny Crum
1987	Indiana	74-73	Syracuse	*NV-Las Vegas	*Providence	Bob Knight
1988	Kansas	83-79	Oklahoma	*Arizona	*Duke	Larry Brown
1989	Michigan	80-79 (OT)	Seton Hall	*Duke	*Illinois	Steve Fisher
1990	UNLV	103-73	Duke	*Arkansas	*Georgia Tech	Jerry Tarkanian
1991	Duke	72-65	Kansas	*UNLV	*N Carolina	Mike Krzyzewski
1992	Duke	71-51	Michigan	*Cincinnati	*Indiana	Mike Krzyzewski
1993	N Carolina	77-71	Michigan	*Kansas	*Kentucky	Dean Smith

*Tied for third place.

†Three overtimes.

‡Student-athletes representing St Joseph's (PA) in 1961, Villanova in 1971 (runner-up), Western Kentucky in 1971 (third), UCLA (19 80) and Memphis State (1985) were declared ineligible subsequent to the tournament. Under NCAA rules, the teams' and ineligible student-athletes' records were deleted, and the teams' places in the standings were vacated.

NCAA Final Four MVPs

Year	Winner, School	GP	Field Goals		3-Pt FG		Free Throws		Reb	A	Stl	BS	Avg
			FGM	Pct	FGA	FGM	FTM	Pct					
1939	....None selected												
1940	....Marv Huffman, Indiana	2	7	—	—	—	4	—	—	—	—	—	9.0
1941	....John Kotz, Wisconsin	2	8	—	—	—	6	—	—	—	—	—	11.0
1942	....Howard Dallmar, Stanford	2	8	—	—	—	4	66.7	—	—	—	—	10.0
1943	....Ken Sailors, Wyoming	2	10	—	—	—	8	72.7	—	—	—	—	14.0
1944	....Arnie Ferrin, Utah	2	11	—	—	—	6	—	—	—	—	—	14.0
1945	....Bob Kurland, Oklahoma St	2	16	—	—	—	5	—	—	—	—	—	18.5
1946	....Bob Kurland, Oklahoma St	2	21	—	—	—	10	66.7	—	—	—	—	26.0
1947	....George Kaftan, Holy Cross	2	18	—	—	—	12	70.6	—	—	—	—	24.0
1948	....Alex Groza, Kentucky	2	16	—	—	—	5	—	—	—	—	—	18.5
1949	....Alex Groza, Kentucky	2	19	—	—	—	14	—	—	—	—	—	26.0
1950	....Irwin Dambrot, CCNY	2	12	42.9	—	—	4	50.0	—	—	—	—	14.0
1951	....None selected												
1952	....Clyde Lovellette, Kansas	2	24	—	—	—	18	—	—	—	—	—	33.0
1953	....*B.H.Horn, Kansas	2	17	—	—	—	17	—	—	—	—	—	25.5
1954	....Tom Gola, La Salle	2	12	—	—	—	14	—	—	—	—	—	19.0
1955	....Bill Russell, San Francisco	2	19	—	—	—	9	—	—	—	—	—	23.5
1956	....*Hal Lear, Temple	2	32	—	—	—	16	—	—	—	—	—	40.0
1957	....*Wilt Chamberlain, Kansas	2	18	51.4	—	—	19	70.4	25	—	—	—	32.5
1958	....*Elgin Baylor, Seattle	2	18	34.0	—	—	12	75.0	41	—	—	—	24.0
1959	....*Jerry West, West Virginia	2	22	66.7	—	—	22	68.8	25	—	—	—	33.0
1960	....Jerry Lucas, Ohio State	2	16	66.7	—	—	3	100.0	23	—	—	—	17.5
1961	....*Jerry Lucas, Ohio State	2	20	71.4	—	—	16	94.1	25	—	—	—	28.0
1962	....Paul Hogue, Cincinnati	2	23	63.9	—	—	12	63.2	38	—	—	—	29.0
1963	....Art Heyman, Duke	2	18	41.0	—	—	15	68.2	19	—	—	—	25.5
1964	....Walt Hazzard, UCLA	2	11	55.0	—	—	8	66.7	10	—	—	—	15.0
1965	....*Bill Bradley, Princeton	2	34	63.0	—	—	19	95.0	24	—	—	—	43.5
1966	....*Jerry Chambers, Utah	2	25	53.2	—	—	20	83.3	35	—	—	—	35.0
1967	....Lew Alcindor, UCLA	2	14	60.9	—	—	11	45.8	38	—	—	—	19.5
1968	....Lew Alcindor, UCLA	2	22	62.9	—	—	9	90.0	34	—	—	—	26.5
1969	....Lew Alcindor, UCLA	2	23	67.7	—	—	16	64.0	41	—	—	—	31.0
1970	....Sidney Wicks, UCLA	2	15	71.4	—	—	9	60.0	34	—	—	—	19.5
1971	....*Howard Porter, Villanova	2	20	48.8	—	—	7	77.8	24	—	—	—	23.5
1972	....Bill Walton, UCLA	2	20	69.0	—	—	17	73.9	41	—	—	—	28.5
1973	....Bill Walton, UCLA	2	28	82.4	—	—	2	40.0	30	—	—	—	29.0
1974	....David Thompson, NC State	2	19	51.4	—	—	11	78.6	17	—	—	—	24.5
1975	....Richard Washington, UCLA	2	23	54.8	—	—	8	72.7	20	—	—	—	27.0
1976	....Kent Benson, Indiana	2	17	50.0	—	—	7	63.6	18	—	—	1	20.5
1977	....Butch Lee, Marquette	2	11	34.4	—	—	8	100.0	6	2	1	1	15.0
1978	....Jack Givens, Kentucky	2	28	65.1	—	—	8	66.7	17	4	1	3	32.0
1979	....Earvin Johnson, Michigan St	2	17	68.0	—	—	19	86.4	17	3	0	2	26.5
1980	....Darrell Griffith, Louisville	2	23	62.2	—	—	11	68.8	7	15	0	2	28.5
1981	....Isiah Thomas, Indiana	2	14	56.0	—	—	9	81.8	4	9	3	4	18.5
1982	....James Worthy, N Carolina	2	20	74.1	—	—	2	28.6	8	9	2	4	21.0
1983	....*Akeem Olajuwon, Houston	2	16	55.2	—	—	9	64.3	40	3	2	5	20.5
1984	....Patrick Ewing, Georgetown	2	8	57.1	—	—	2	100.0	18	1	15	1	9.0
1985	....Ed Pinckney, Villanova	2	8	57.1	—	—	12	75.0	15	6	3	0	14.0
1986	....Pervis Ellison, Louisville	2	15	60.0	—	—	6	75.0	24	2	3	1	18.0
1987	....Keith Smart, Indiana	2	14	63.6	1	0	7	77.8	7	7	0	2	17.5
1988	....Danny Manning, Kansas	2	25	55.6	1	0	6	66.7	17	4	8	9	28.0
1989	....Glen Rice, Michigan	2	24	49.0	16	7	4	100.0	16	1	0	3	29.5
1990	....Anderson Hunt, UNLV	2	19	61.3	16	9	2	50.0	4	9	1	1	24.5
1991	....Christian Laettner, Duke	2	12	54.5	1	1	21	91.3	17	2	1	2	23.0
1992	....Bobby Hurley, Duke	2	10	41.7	12	7	8	80.0	3	11	0	3	17.5
1993	....Donald Williams, N Carolina	2	15	65.2	14	10	10	100.0	4	2	2	0	25.0

*Not a member of the championship-winning team

Best NCAA Tournament Single-Game Scoring Performances

Player and Team	Year	Round	FG	3FG	FT	TP
Austin Carr, Notre Dame vs Ohio	1970	1st	25	—	11	61
Bill Bradley, Princeton vs Wichita St	1965	C*	22	—	14	58
Oscar Robertson, Cincinnati vs Arkansas	1958	C	21	—	14	56
Austin Carr, Notre Dame vs Kentucky	1970	2nd	22	—	8	52
Austin Car, Notre Dame vs Texas Christian	1971	1st	20	—	12	52
David Robinson, Navy vs Michigan	1987	1st	22	0	6	50
Elvin Hayes, Houston vs Loyola (IL)	1968	1st	20	—	9	49
Hal Lear, Temple vs Southern Meth	1956	C*	17	—	14	48
Austin Carr, Notre Dame vs Houston	1971	C	17	—	13	47
Dave Corzine, DePaul vs Louisville	1978	2nd	18	—	10	46
Bob Houbregs, Washington vs Seattle	1953	2nd	20	—	5	45
Austin Carr, Notre Dame vs Iowa	1970	C	21	—	3	45
Bo Kimble, Loyola Marymount vs New Mexico St	1990	1st	17	5	6	45

C regional third place; C* third-place game.

NIT Championship Results

Year	Winner	Score	Runner-up	Year	Winner	Score	Runner-up
1938	Temple	60-36	Colorado	1966	BYU	97-84	NYU
1939	Long Island U	44-32	Loyola (IL)	1967	Southern Illinois	71-56	Marquette
1940	Colorado	51-40	Duquesne	1968	Dayton	61-48	Kansas
1941	Long Island U	56-42	Ohio U	1969	Temple	89-76	Boston College
1942	W Virginia	47-45	W Kentucky	1970	Marquette	65-53	St John's (NY)
1943	St John's (NY)	48-27	Toledo	1971	N Carolina	84-66	Georgia Tech
1944	St John's (NY)	47-39	DePaul	1972	Maryland	100-69	Niagara
1945	DePaul	71-54	Bowling Green	1973	Virginia Tech	92-91 (OT)	Notre Dame
1946	Kentucky	46-45	Rhode Island	1974	Purdue	97-81	Utah
1947	Utah	49-45	Kentucky	1975	Princeton	80-69	Providence
1948	St Louis	65-52	NYU	1976	Kentucky	71-67	NC-Charlotte
1949	San Francisco	48-47	Loyola (IL)	1977	St Bonaventure	94-91	Houston
1950	CCNY	69-61	Bradley	1978	Texas	101-93	N Carolina St
1951	BYU	62-43	Dayton	1979	Indiana	53-52	Purdue
1952	La Salle	75-64	Dayton	1980	Virginia	58-55	Minnesota
1953	Seton Hall	58-46	St John's (NY)	1981	Tulsa	86-84 (OT)	Syracuse
1954	Holy Cross	71-62	Duquesne	1982	Bradley	67-58	Purdue
1955	Duquesne	70-58	Dayton	1983	Fresno St	69-60	DePaul
1956	Louisville	93-80	Dayton	1984	Michigan	83-63	Notre Dame
1957	Bradley	84-83	Memphis St	1985	UCLA	65-62	Indiana
1958	Xavier (OH)	78-74 (OT)	Dayton	1986	Ohio St	73-63	Wyoming
1959	St John's (NY)	76-71 (OT)	Bradley	1987	Southern Miss	84-80	La Salle
1960	Bradley	88-72	Providence	1988	Connecticut	72-67	Ohio St
1961	Providence	62-59	St Louis	1989	St John's (NY)	73-65	St Louis
1962	Dayton	73-67	St John's (NY)	1990	Vanderbilt	74-72	St Louis
1963	Providence	81-66	Canisius	1991	Stanford	78-72	Oklahoma
1964	Bradley	86-54	New Mexico	1992	Virginia	81-76	Notre Dame
1965	St John's (NY)	55-51	Villanova	1993	Minnesota	62-61	Georgetown

NCAA Division I Men's Season Leaders

Scoring Average

Year	Player and Team	Ht	Class	GP	FG	3FG	FT	Pts	Avg
1948	Murray Wier, Iowa	5-9	Sr	19	152	—	95	399	21.0
1949	Tony Lavelli, Yale	6-3	Sr	30	228	—	215	671	22.4
1950	Paul Arizin, Villanova	6-3	Sr	29	260	—	215	735	25.3
1951	Bill Mlkvy, Temple	6-4	Sr	25	303	—	125	731	29.2
1952	Clyde Lovellette, Kansas	6-9	Sr	28	315	—	165	795	28.4
1953	Frank Selvy, Furman	6-3	Jr	25	272	—	194	738	29.5
1954	Frank Selvy, Furman	6-3	Sr	29	427	—	355	1209	41.7
1955	Darrell Floyd, Furman	6-1	Jr	25	344	—	209	897	35.9
1956	Darrell Floyd, Furman	6-1	Sr	28	339	—	268	946	33.8
1957	Grady Wallace, S Carolina	6-4	Sr	29	336	—	234	906	31.2
1958	Oscar Robertson, Cincinnati	6-5	So	28	352	—	280	984	35.1

Scoring Average (Cont.)

Year	Player and Team	Ht	Class	GP	FG	3FG	FT	Pts	Avg
1959	Oscar Robertson, Cincinnati	6-5	Jr	30	331	—	316	978	32.6
1960	Oscar Robertson, Cincinnati	6-5	Sr	30	369	—	273	1011	33.7
1961	Frank Burgess, Gonzaga	6-1	Sr	26	304	—	234	842	32.4
1962	Billy McGill, Utah	6-9	Sr	26	394	—	221	1009	38.8
1963	Nick Werkman, Seton Hall	6-3	Jr	22	221	—	208	650	29.5
1964	Howard Komives, Bowling Green	6-1	Sr	23	292	—	260	844	36.7
1965	Rick Barry, Miama (FL)	6-7	Sr	26	340	—	293	973	37.4
1966	Dave Schellhase, Purdue	6-4	Sr	24	284	—	213	781	32.5
1967	Jim Walker, Providence	6-3	Sr	28	323	—	205	851	30.4
1968	Pete Maravich, Louisiana St	6-5	So	26	432	—	274	1138	43.8
1969	Pete Maravich, Louisiana St	6-5	Jr	26	433	—	282	1148	44.2
1970	Pete Maravich, Louisiana St	6-5	Sr	31	522	—	337	1381	44.5
1971	Johnny Neumann, Mississippi	6-6	So	23	366	—	191	923	40.1
1972	Dwight Lamar, Southwestern Louisiana	6-1	Jr	29	429	—	196	1054	36.3
1973	William Averitt, Pepperdine	6-1	Sr	25	352	—	144	848	33.9
1974	Larry Fogle, Canisius	6-5	So	25	326	—	183	835	33.4
1975	Bob McCurdy, Richmond	6-7	Sr	26	321	—	213	855	32.9
1976	Marshall Rodgers, TX-Pan American	6-2	Sr	25	361	—	197	919	36.8
1977	Freeman Williams, Portland St	6-4	Jr	26	417	—	176	1010	38.8
1978	Freeman Williams, Portland St	6-4	Sr	27	410	—	149	969	35.9
1979	Lawrence Butler, Idaho St	6-3	Sr	27	310	—	192	812	30.1
1980	Tony Murphy, Southern-BR	6-3	Sr	29	377	—	178	932	32.1
1981	Zam Fredrick, S Carolina	6-2	Sr	27	300	—	181	781	28.9
1982	Harry Kelly, Texas Southern	6-7	Jr	29	336	—	190	862	29.7
1983	Harry Kelly, Texas Southern	6-7	Sr	29	333	—	169	835	28.8
1984	Joe Jakubick, Akron	6-5	Sr	27	304	—	206	814	30.1
1985	Xavier McDaniel, Wichita St	6-8	Sr	31	351	—	142	844	27.2
1986	Terrance Bailey, Wagner	6-2	Jr	29	321	—	212	854	29.4
1987	Kevin Houston, Army	5-11	Sr	29	311	63	268	953	32.9
1988	Hersey Hawkins, Bradley	6-3	Sr	31	377	87	284	1125	36.3
1989	Hank Gathers, Loyola Marymount	6-7	Jr	31	419	0	177	1015	32.7
1990	Bo Kimble, Loyola Marymount	6-5	Sr	32	404	92	231	1131	35.3
1991	Kevin Bradshaw, U.S. Int'l	6-6	Sr	28	358	60	278	1054	37.6
1992	Brett Roberts, Morehead St	6-8	Sr	29	278	66	193	815	28.1
1993	Greg Guy, TX-Pan Amer	6-1	Jr	19	189	67	111	556	29.3

Rebounds

Year	Player and Team	Ht	Class	GP	Reb	Avg
1951	Ernie Beck, Pennsylvania	6-4	So	27	556	20.6
1952	Bill Hannon, Army	6-3	So	17	355	20.9
1953	Ed Conlin, Fordham	6-5	So	26	612	23.5
1954	Art Quimby, Connecticut	6-5	Jr	26	588	22.6
1955	Charlie Slack, Marshall	6-5	Jr	21	538	25.6
1956	Joe Holup, George Washington	6-6	Sr	26	604	†.256
1957	Elgin Baylor, Seattle	6-6	Jr	25	508	†.235
1958	Alex Ellis, Niagara	6-5	Sr	25	536	†.262
1959	Leroy Wright, Pacific	6-8	Jr	26	652	†.238
1960	Leroy Wright, Pacific	6-8	Sr	17	380	†.234
1961	Jerry Lucas, Ohio St	6-8	Jr	27	470	†.198
1962	Jerry Lucas, Ohio St	6-8	Sr	28	499	†.211
1963	Paul Silas, Creighton	6-7	Sr	27	557	20.6
1964	Bob Pelkington, Xavier (OH)	6-7	Sr	26	567	21.8
1965	Toby Kimball, Connecticut	6-8	Sr	23	483	21.0
1966	Jim Ware, Oklahoma City	6-8	Sr	29	607	20.9
1967	Dick Cunningham, Murray St	6-10	Jr	22	479	21.8
1968	Neal Walk, Florida	6-10	Jr	25	494	19.8
1969	Spencer Haywood, Detroit	6-8	So	22	472	21.5
1970	Artis Gilmore, Jacksonville	7-2	Jr	28	621	22.2
1971	Artis Gilmore, Jacksonville	7-2	Sr	26	603	23.2
1972	Kermit Washington, American	6-8	Jr	23	455	19.8
1973	Kermit Washington, American	6-8	Sr	22	439	20.0
1974	Marvin Barnes, Providence	6-9	Sr	32	597	18.7
1975	John Irving, Hofstra	6-9	So	21	323	15.4

Rebounds (Cont.)

Year	Player and Team	Ht	Class	GP	Reb	Avg
1976	Sam Pellom, Buffalo	6-8	So	26	420	16.2
1977	Glenn Mosley, Seton Hall	6-8	Sr	29	473	16.3
1978	Ken Williams, N Texas St	6-7	Sr	28	411	14.7
1979	Monti Davis, Tennessee St	6-7	Jr	26	421	16.2
1980	Larry Smith, Alcorn St	6-8	Sr	26	392	15.1
1981	Darryl Watson, Miss Valley	6-7	Sr	27	379	14.0
1982	LaSalle Thompson, Texas	6-10	Jr	27	365	13.5
1983	Xavier McDaniel, Wichita St	6-7	So	28	403	14.4
1984	Akeem Olajuwon, Houston	7-0	Jr	37	500	13.5
1985	Xavier McDaniel, Wichita St	6-8	Sr	31	460	14.8
1986	David Robinson, Navy	6-11	Jr	35	455	13.0
1987	Jerome Lane, Pittsburgh	6-6	So	33	444	13.5
1988	Kenny Miller, Loyola (IL)	6-9	Fr	29	395	13.6
1989	Hank Gathers, Loyola (CA)	6-7	Jr	31	426	13.7
1990	Anthony Bonner, St Louis	6-8	Sr	33	456	13.8
1991	Shaquille O'Neal, Louisiana St	7-1	So	28	411	14.7
1992	Popeye Jones, Murray St	6-8	Sr	30	431	14.4
1993	Warren Kidd, Middle Tenn St	6-9	Sr	26	386	14.8

†From 1956-1962, title was based on highest individual recoveries out of total by both teams in all games.

Assists

Year	Player and Team	Class	GP	A	Avg
1984	Craig Lathen, IL-Chicago	Jr	29	274	9.45
1985	Rob Weingard, Hofstra	Sr	24	228	9.50
1986	Mark Jackson, St John's (NY)	Jr	36	328	9.11
1987	Avery Johnson, Southern-BR	Jr	31	333	10.74
1988	Avery Johnson, Southern-BR	Sr	30	399	13.30
1989	Glenn Williams, Holy Cross	Sr	28	278	9.93
1990	Todd Lehmann, Drexel	Sr	28	260	9.29
1991	Chris Corchiani, N Carolina St	Sr	31	299	9.65
1992	Van Usher, Tennessee Tech	Sr	29	254	8.76
1993	Sam Crawford, New Mex St	Sr	34	310	9.12

Blocked Shots

Year	Player and Team	Class	GP	BS	Avg
1986	David Robinson, Navy	Jr	35	207	5.91
1987	David Robinson, Navy	Sr	32	144	4.50
1988	Rodney Blake, St Joseph's (PA)	Sr	29	116	4.00
1989	Alonzo Mourning, Georgetown	Fr	34	169	4.97
1990	Kenny Green, Rhode Island	Sr	26	124	4.77
1991	Shawn Bradley, Brigham Young	Fr	34	177	5.21
1992	Shaquille O'Neal, Louisiana St	Jr	30	157	5.23
1993	Theo Ratliff, Wyoming	Jr	28	124	4.43

Steals

Year	Player and Team	Class	GP	S	Avg
1986	Darron Brittman, Chicago St	Sr	28	139	4.96
1987	Tony Fairley, Charleston Sou	Sr	28	114	4.07
1988	Aldwin Ware, Florida A&M	Sr	29	142	4.90
1989	Kenny Robertson, Cleveland St	Jr	28	111	3.96
1990	Ronn McMahon, E Washington	Sr	29	130	4.48
1991	Van Usher, Tennessee Tech	Jr	28	104	3.71
1992	Victor Snipes, NE Illinois	So	25	86	3.44
1993	Jason Kidd, California	Fr	29	110	3.80

Oh, Dad	According to *Newsday*, after Boston College basketball coach Jim O'Brien earned a second technical for berating officials and was ejected from a game against Seton Hall, his 17-year-old daughter, Amy, watching on ESPN, phoned her 18-year-old sister, Erin, who was away at college. "Quick, turn on the television," Amy said. "He got thrown out. He's a lunatic."

Single-Game Records

SCORING HIGHS VS DIVISION I OPPONENT

Pts	Player and Team vs Opponent	Date
72	Kevin Bradshaw, U.S. Int'l vs Loyola Marymount	1-5-91
69	Pete Maravich, Louisiana St vs Alabama	2-7-70
68	Calvin Murphy, Niagara vs Syracuse	12-7-68
66	Jay Handlan, Washington & Lee vs Furman	2-17-51
66	Pete Maravich, Louisiana St vs Tulane	2-10-69
66	Anthony Roberts, Oral Roberts vs N Carolina A&T	2-19-77
65	Anthony Roberts, Oral Roberts vs Oregon	3-9-77
65	Scott Haffner, Evansville vs Dayton	2-18-89
64	Pete Maravich, Louisiana St vs Kentucky	2-21-70
63	Johnny Neumann, Mississippi vs Louisiana St	1-30-71
63	Hersey Hawkins, Bradley vs Detroit	2-22-88

SCORING HIGHS VS NON-DIVISION I OPPONENT

Pts	Player and Team vs Opponent	Date
100	Frank Selvy, Furman vs Newberry	2-13-54
85	Paul Arizin, Villanova vs Philadelphia NAMC	2-12-49
81	Freeman Williams, Portland St vs Rocky Mountain	2-3-78
73	Bill Mlkvy, Temple vs Wilkes	3-3-51
71	Freeman Williams, Portland St vs Southern Oregon	2-9-77

REBOUNDING HIGHS BEFORE 1973

Reb	Player and Team vs Opponent	Date
51	Bill Chambers, William & Mary vs Virginia	2-14-53
43	Charlie Slack, Marshall vs Morris Harvey	1-12-54
42	Tom Heinsohn, Holy Cross vs Boston College	3-1-55
40	Art Quimby, Connecticut vs Boston U	1-11-55
39	Maurice Stokes, St Francis (PA) vs John Carroll	1-28-55
39	Dave DeBusschere, Detroit vs Central Michigan	1-30-60
39	Keith Swagerty, Pacific vs UC-Santa Barbara	3-5-65

REBOUNDING HIGHS SINCE 1973

Reb	Player and Team vs Opponent	Date
34	David Vaughn, Oral Roberts vs Brandeis	1-8-73
33	Robert Parish, Centenary vs Southern Miss	1-22-73
32	Durand Macklin, Louisiana St vs Tulane	11-26-76
31	Jim Bradley, Northern Illinois vs WI-Milwaukee	2-19-73
31	Calvin Natt, Northeast Louisiana vs Georgia Southern	12-29-76

ASSISTS

A	Player and Team vs Opponent	Date
22	Tony Fairley, Baptist vs Armstrong St	2-9-87
22	Avery Johnson, Southern-BR vs Texas Southern	1-25-88
22	Sherman Douglas, Syracuse vs Providence	1-28-89
21	Mark Wade, NV-Las Vegas vs Navy	12-29-86
21	Kelvin Scarborough, New Mexico vs Hawaii	2-13-87
21	Anthony Manuel, Bradley vs UC-Irvine	12-19-87
21	Avery Johnson, Southern-BR vs Alabama St	1-16-88

STEALS

S	Player and Team vs Opponent	Date
13	Mookie Blaylock, Oklahoma vs Centenary	12-12-87
13	Mookie Blaylock, Oklahoma vs Loyola Marymount	12-17-88
12	Kenny Robertson, Cleveland St vs Wagner	12-3-88
12	Terry Evans, Oklahoma vs Florida A&M	1-27-93
11	Darron Brittman, Chicago St vs McKendree	2-24-86
11	Darron Brittman, Chicago St vs St Xavier	2-8-86
11	Marty Johnson, Towson St vs Bucknell	2-17-88
11	Aldwin Ware, Florida A&M vs Tuskegee	2-24-88
11	Mark Macon, Temple vs Notre Dame	1-29-89
11	Carl Thomas, E Michigan vs Chicago St	2-20-91
11	Ron Arnold, St Francis (NY) vs Mt St Mary's (MD)	2-4-93

Single-Game Records *(Cont.)*

BLOCKED SHOTS

BS	Player and Team vs Opponent	Date
14	David Robinson, Navy vs NC-Wilmington	1-4-86
14	Shawn Bradley, Brigham Young vs E Kentucky	12-7-90
13	Kevin Roberson, Vermont vs New Hampshire	1-9-92
13	Jim McIlvaine, Marquette vs Northeastern (IL)	12-9-92
12	David Robinson, Navy vs James Madison	1-9-86
12	Derrick Lewis, Maryland vs James Madison	1-28-87
12	Rodney Blake, St Joseph's (PA) vs Cleveland St	12-2-87
12	Walter Palmer, Dartmouth vs Harvard	1-9-88
12	Alan Ogg, AL-Birmingham vs Florida A&M	12-16-88
12	Dikembe Mutombo, Georgetown vs St John's (NY)	1-23-89
12	Shaquille O'Neal, Louisiana St vs Loyola Marymount	2-3-90
12	Cedric Lewis, Maryland vs S Florida	1-19-91
12	Ervin Johnson, New Orleans vs Texas A&M	12-29-92

Season Records

POINTS

Player and Team	Year	GP	FG	3FG	FT	Pts
Pete Maravich, Louisiana St	1970	31	522	—	337	1381
Elvin Hayes, Houston	1968	33	519	—	176	1214
Frank Selvy, Furman	1954	29	427	—	355	1209
Pete Maravich, Louisiana St	1969	26	433	—	282	1148
Pete Maravich, Lousiana St	1968	26	432	—	274	1138
Bo Kimble, Loyola Marymount	1990	32	404	92	231	1131
Hersey Hawkins, Bradley	1988	31	377	87	284	1125
Austin Carr, Notre Dame	1970	29	444	—	218	1106
Austin Carr, Notre Dame	1971	29	430	—	241	1101
Otis Birdsong, Houston	1977	36	452	—	186	1090

SCORING AVERAGE

Player and Team	Year	GP	FG	FT	Pts	Avg
Pete Maravich, Louisiana St	1970	31	522	337	1381	44.5
Pete Maravich, Louisiana St	1969	26	433	282	1148	44.2
Pete Maravich, Louisiana St	1968	26	432	274	1138	43.8
Frank Selvy, Furman	1954	29	427	355	1209	41.7
Johnny Neumann, Mississippi	1971	23	366	191	923	40.1
Freeman Williams, Portland St	1977	26	417	176	1010	38.8
Billy McGill, Utah	1962	26	394	221	1009	38.8
Calvin Murphy, Niagara	1968	24	337	242	916	38.2
Austin Carr, Notre Dame	1970	29	444	218	1106	38.1
Austin Carr, Notre Dame	1971	29	430	241	1101	38.0
Kevin Bradshaw, U.S. Int'l	1991	28	358	278	1054	37.6

REBOUNDS

Player and Team	Year	GP	Reb	Player and Team	Year	GP	Reb
Walt Dukes, Seton Hall	1953	33	734	Artis Gilmore, Jacksonville	1970	28	621
Leroy Wright, Pacific	1959	26	652	Tom Gola, La Salle	1955	31	618
Tom Gola, La Salle	1954	30	652	Ed Conlin, Fordham	1953	26	612
Charlie Tyra, Louisville	1956	29	645	Art Quimby, Connecticut	1955	25	611
Paul Silas, Creighton	1964	29	631	Bill Russell, San Francisco	1956	29	609
Elvin Hayes, Houston	1968	33	624	Jim Ware, Oklahoma City	1966	29	607

REBOUND AVERAGE BEFORE 1973

Player and Team	Year	GP	Reb	Avg
Charlie Slack, Marshall	1955	21	538	25.6
Leroy Wright, Pacific	1959	26	652	25.1
Art Quimby, Connecticut	1955	25	611	24.4
Charlie Slack, Marshall	1956	22	520	23.6
Ed Conlin, Fordham	1953	26	612	23.5

Season Records *(Cont.)*

REBOUND AVERAGE SINCE 1973

Player and Team	Year	GP	Reb	Avg
Kermit Washington, American	1973	22	439	20.0
Marvin Barnes, Providence	1973	30	571	19.0
Marvin Barnes, Providence	1974	32	597	18.7
Pete Padgett, NV-Reno	1973	26	462	17.8
Jim Bradley, Northern Illinois	1973	24	426	17.8

ASSISTS

Player and Team	Year	GP	A	Player and Team	Year	GP	A
Mark Wade, UNLV	1987	38	406	Sherman Douglas, Syracuse	1989	38	326
Avery Johnson, Southern-BR	1988	30	399	Sam Crawford, N Mex St	1993	34	310
Anthony Manuel, Bradley	1988	31	373	Greg Anthony, UNLV	1991	35	310
Avery Johnson, Southern-BR	1987	31	333	Reid Gettys, Houston	1984	37	309
Mark Jackson, St John's (NY)	1986	32	328	Carl Golston, Loyola (IL)	1985	33	305

ASSIST AVERAGE

Player and Team	Year	GP	A	Avg	Player and Team	Year	GP	A	Avg
Avery Johnson, Southern-BR	1988	30	399	13.3	Chris Corchiani, N Carolina St	1991	31	299	9.6
Anthony Manuel, Bradley	1988	31	373	12.0	Tony Fairley, Baptist	1987	28	270	9.6
Avery Johnson, Southern-BR	1987	31	333	10.7	Tyrone Bogues, Wake Forest	1987	29	276	9.5
Mark Wade, NV-Las Vegas	1987	38	406	10.7	Craig Neal, Georgia Tech	1988	32	303	9.5
Glenn Williams, Holy Cross	1989	28	278	9.9	Ron Weingard, Hofstra	1985	24	228	9.5

FIELD-GOAL PERCENTAGE

Player and Team	Year	GP	FG	FGA	Pct
Steve Johnson, Oregon St	1981	28	235	315	74.6
Dwayne Davis, Florida	1989	33	179	248	72.2
Keith Walker, Utica	1985	27	154	216	71.3
Steve Johnson, Oregon St	1980	30	211	297	71.0
Oliver Miller, Arkansas	1991	38	254	361	70.4
Alan Williams, Princeton	1987	25	163	232	70.3
Mark McNamara, California	1982	27	231	329	70.2
Warren Kidd, Middle Tennessee St	1991	30	173	247	70.0
Pete Freeman, Akron	1991	28	175	250	70.0
Joe Senser, West Chester	1977	25	130	186	69.9
Lee Campbell, SW Missouri St	1990	29	192	275	69.8
Stephen Scheffler, Purdue	1990	30	173	248	69.8

Based on qualifiers for annual championships.

FREE-THROW PERCENTAGE

Player and Team	Year	GP	FT	FTA	Pct
Craig Collins, Penn St	1985	27	94	98	95.9
Rod Foster, UCLA	1982	27	95	100	95.0
Carlos Gibson, Marshall	1978	28	84	89	94.4
Jim Barton, Dartmouth	1986	26	65	69	94.2
Jack Moore, Nebraska	1982	27	123	131	93.9
Rob Robbins, New Mexico	1990	34	101	108	93.5
Tommy Boyer, Arkansas	1962	23	125	134	93.3
Damon Goodwin, Dayton	1986	30	95	102	93.1
Brian Magid, George Washington	1980	26	79	85	92.9
Mike Joseph, Bucknell	1990	29	144	155	92.9

Based on qualifiers for annual championships.

Season Records *(Cont.)*

THREE-POINT FIELD-GOAL PERCENTAGE

Player and Team	Year	GP	3FG	3FGA	Pct
Glenn Tropf, Holy Cross	1988	29	52	82	63.4
Sean Wightman, Western Michigan	1992	30	48	76	63.2
Keith Jennings, E Tennessee St	1991	33	84	142	59.2
Dave Calloway, Monmouth (NJ)	1989	28	48	82	58.5
Steve Kerr, Arizona	1988	38	114	199	57.3
Reginald Jones, Prairie View	1987	28	64	112	57.1
Joel Tribelhorn, Colorado St	1989	33	76	135	56.3
Mike Joseph, Bucknell	1988	28	65	116	56.0
Christian Laettner, Duke	1992	35	54	97	55.7
Reginald Jones, Prairie View	1988	27	85	155	54.8

Based on qualifiers for annual championships.

STEALS

Player and Team	Year	GP	S
Mookie Blaylock, Oklahoma	1988	39	150
Aldwin Ware, Florida A&M	1988	29	142
Darron Brittman, Chicago St	1986	28	139
Nadav Henefeld, Connecticut	1990	37	138
Mookie Blaylock, Oklahoma	1989	35	131

BLOCKED SHOTS

Player and Team	Year	GP	BS
David Robinson, Navy	1986	35	207
Shawn Bradley, BYU	1991	34	177
Alonzo Mourning, Georgetown	1989	34	169
Alonzo Mourning, Georgetown	1992	32	160
Shaquille O'Neal, Louisiana St	1992	30	157

STEAL AVERAGE

Player and Team	Year	GP	S	Avg
Darron Brittman, Chicago St	1986	28	139	4.96
Aldwin Ware, Florida A&M	1988	29	142	4.90
Ronn McMahon, E Washington	1990	29	130	4.48
Jim Paguaga, St Francis (NY)	1986	28	120	4.29
Marty Johnson, Towson St	1988	30	124	4.13

BLOCKED SHOT AVERAGE

Player and Team	Year	GP	BS	Avg
David Robinson, Navy	1986	35	207	5.91
Shaquille O'Neal, Louisiana St	1992	30	157	5.23
Shawn Bradley, BYU	1991	34	177	5.21
Cedric Lewis, Maryland	1991	28	143	5.11
Alonzo Mourning, Georgetown	1992	32	160	5.00

Career Records

POINTS

Player and Team	Ht	Final Year	GP	FG	3FG*	FT	Pts
Pete Maravich, Louisiana St	6-5	1970	83	1387	—	893	3667
Freeman Williams, Portland St	6-4	1978	106	1369	—	511	3249
Lionel Simmons, La Salle	6-7	1990	131	1244	56	673	3217
Alphonso Ford, Mississippi Valley	6-2	1993	109	1121	333	590	3165
Harry Kelly, Texas Southern	6-7	1983	110	1234	—	598	3066
Hersey Hawkins, Bradley	6-3	1988	125	1100	118	690	3008
Oscar Robertson, Cincinnati	6-5	1960	88	1052	—	869	2973
Danny Manning, Kansas	6-10	1988	147	1216	10	509	2951
Alfredrick Hughes, Loyola (IL)	6-5	1985	120	1226	—	462	2914
Elvin Hayes, Houston	6-8	1968	93	1215	—	454	2884
Larry Bird, Indiana St	6-9	1979	94	1154	—	542	2850
Otis Birdsong, Houston	6-4	1977	116	1176	—	480	2832
Kevin Bradshaw, Bethune-Cookman, U.S. Int'l	6-6	1991	111	1027	132	618	2804
Allan Houston, Tennessee	6-6	1993	128	902	346	651	2801
Hank Gathers, Southern Cal, Loyola Marymount	6-7	1990	117	1127	0	469	2723
Reggie Lewis, Northeastern	6-7	1987	122	1043	30 (1)	592	2708
Daren Queenan, Lehigh	6-5	1988	118	1024	29	626	2703
Byron Larkin, Xavier (OH)	6-3	1988	121	1022	51	601	2696
David Robinson, Navy	7-1	1987	127	1032	1	604	2669
Wayman Tisdale, Oklahoma	6-9	1985	104	1077	—	507	2661

*Listed is the number of three-pointers scored since it became the national rule in 1987; the number in the parentheses is number scored prior to 1987—these counted as three points in the game but counted as two-pointers in the national rankings. The three-pointers in the parentheses are not included in total points.

Career Records (Cont.)

SCORING AVERAGE

Player and Team	Final Year	GP	FG	FT	Pts	Avg
Pete Maravich, Louisiana St	1968	83	1387	893	3667	44.2
Austin Carr, Notre Dame	1971	74	1017	526	2560	34.6
Oscar Robertson, Cincinnati	1960	88	1052	869	2973	33.8
Calvin Murphy, Niagara	1970	77	947	654	2548	33.1
Dwight Lamar, Southwestern Louisiana	1973	57	768	326	1862	32.7
Frank Selvy, Furman	1954	78	922	694	2538	32.5
Rick Mount, Purdue	1970	72	910	503	2323	32.3
Darrell Floyd, Furman	1956	71	868	545	2281	32.1
Nick Werkman, Seton Hall	1964	71	812	649	2273	32.0
Willie Humes, Idaho St	1971	48	565	380	1510	31.5
William Averitt, Pepperdine	1973	49	615	311	1541	31.4
Elgin Baylor, Col. of Idaho, Seattle	1958	80	956	588	2500	31.3
Elvin Hayes, Houston	1968	93	1215	454	2884	31.0
Freeman Williams, Portland St	1978	106	1369	511	3249	30.7
Larry Bird, Indiana St	1979	94	1154	542	2850	30.3

REBOUNDS BEFORE 1973

Player and Team	Final Year	GP	Reb
Tom Gola, La Salle	1955	118	2201
Joe Holup, George Washington	1956	104	2030
Charlie Slack, Marshall	1956	88	1916
Ed Conlin, Fordham	1955	102	1884
Dickie Hemric, Wake Forest	1955	104	1802

REBOUNDS FOR CAREERS BEGINNING IN 1973 OR AFTER

Player and Team	Final Year	GP	Reb
Derrick Coleman, Syracuse	1990	143	1537
Ralph Sampson, Virginia	1983	132	1511
Pete Padgett, NV-Reno	1976	104	1464
Lionel Simmons, La Salle	1990	131	1429
Anthony Bonner, St Louis	1990	133	1424

ASSISTS

Player and Team	Final Year	GP	A
Bobby Hurley, Duke	1993	140	1076
Chris Corchiani, N Carolina St	1991	124	1038
Keith Jennings, E Tennessee St	1991	127	983
Sherman Douglas, Syracuse	1989	138	960
Greg Anthony, Portland, UNLV	1991	138	950

FIELD-GOAL PERCENTAGE

Player and Team	Final Year	FG	FGA	Pct
Stephen Scheffler, Purdue	1990	408	596	68.5
Steve Johnson, Oregon St	1981	828	1222	67.8
Murray Brown, Florida St	1980	566	847	66.8
Lee Campbell, SW Missouri St	1990	411	618	66.6
Warren Kidd, Middle Tenn St	1993	496	747	66.4

Note: Minimum 400 field goals.

FREE-THROW PERCENTAGE

Player and Team	Final Year	FT	FTA	Pct
Greg Starrick, Kentucky, Southern Illinois	1972	341	375	90.9
Jack Moore, Nebraska	1982	446	495	90.1
Steve Henson, Kansas St	1990	361	401	90.0
Steve Alford, Indiana	1987	535	596	89.8
Bob Lloyd, Rutgers	1967	543	605	89.8

Note: Minimum 300 free throws.

Career Records (Cont.)

THREE-POINT FIELD GOALS MADE

Player and Team	Final Year	GP	3FG
Doug Day, Radford	1993	117	401
Ronnie Schmitz, MO-Kansas City	1993	112	378
Mark Alberts, Akron	1993	103	375
Jeff Fryer, Loyola Marymount	1990	112	363
Dennis Scott, Georgia Tech	1990	99	351

THREE-POINT FIELD-GOAL PERCENTAGE

Player and Team	Final Year	3FG	3FGA	Pct
Tony Bennett, WI-Green Bay	1992	290	584	49.7
Keith Jennings, E Tennessee St	1991	223	452	49.3
Kirk Manns, Michigan St	1990	212	446	47.5
Tim Locum, Wisconsin	1991	227	481	47.2
David Olson, Eastern Illinois	1992	262	562	46.6

Note: Minimum 200 3-point field goals.

STEALS

Player and Team	Final Year	GP	S
Eric Murdock, Providence	1991	117	376
Michael Anderson, Drexel	1988	115	341
Kenny Robertson, New Mexico, Clev St	1990	119	341
Keith Jennings, E Tennessee St	1991	127	334
Greg Anthony, Portland, UNLV	1991	138	329

BLOCKED SHOTS

Player and Team	Final Year	GP	BS
Alonzo Mourning, Georgetown	1992	120	453
Shaquille O'Neal, Louisiana St	1992	90	412
Kevin Roberson, Vermont	1992	112	409
Rodney Blake, St Joseph's (PA)	1988	116	399
Tim Perry, Temple	1988	130	392

NCAA Division I Team Leaders

Division I Team All-Time Wins

Team	First Year	Yrs	W	L	T
N Carolina	1911	83	1570	564	0
Kentucky	1903	90	1560	506	1
Kansas	1899	95	1513	689	0
St John's (NY)	1908	86	1482	635	0
Duke	1906	88	1435	703	0
Oregon St	1902	92	1413	888	0
Temple	1895	97	1393	761	0
Notre Dame	1898	88	1362	701	1
Pennsylvania	1902	92	1362	785	0
Syracuse	1901	92	1359	644	0
Indiana	1901	93	1329	711	0
Washington	1896	91	1316	821	0
UCLA	1920	74	1294	577	0
Western Kentucky	1915	74	1284	605	0
Princeton	1901	93	1278	810	0

Note: Years in Division I only.

Division I All-Time Winning Percentage

Team	First Year	Yrs	W	L	T	Pct
NV-Las Vegas	1959	33	747	227	0	.767
Kentucky	1903	90	1560	506	1	.755
N Carolina	1911	83	1570	564	0	.736
St Johns (NY)	1908	86	1482	635	0	.700
UCLA	1920	74	1294	577	0	.692
Kansas	1899	95	1513	689	0	.687
Western Kentucky	1915	74	1284	605	0	.680
Syracuse	1901	92	1359	644	0	.679
Duke	1906	88	1435	703	0	.671
DePaul	1924	70	1124	557	0	.669

Note: Minimum of 25 years in Division I only.

NCAA Division I Men's Winning Streaks

Longest—Full Season

Team	Games	Years	Ended by
UCLA	88	1971-74	Notre Dame (71-70)
San Francisco	60	1955-57	Illinois (62-33)
UCLA	47	1966-68	Houston (71-69)
UNLV	45	1990-91	Duke (79-77)
Texas	44	1913-17	Rice (24-18)
Seton Hall	43	1939-41	LIU-Brooklyn (49-26)
LIU-Brooklyn	43	1935-37	Stanford (45-31)
UCLA	41	1968-69	Southern Cal (46-44)
Marquette	39	1970-71	Ohio St (60-59)
Cincinnati	37	1962-63	Wichita St (65-64)
N Carolina	37	1957-58	W Virginia (75-64)

Longest—Home Court

Team	Games	Years
Kentucky	129	1943-55
St Bonaventure	99	1948-61
UCLA	98	1970-76
Cincinnati	86	1957-64
Marquette	81	1967-73
Arizona	81	1945-51
Lamar	80	1978-84
Long Beach St	75	1968-74
NV-Las Vegas	72	1974-78
Arizona	71	1987-92
Cincinnati	68	1972-78

Longest—Regular Season

Team	Games	Years	Ended by
UCLA	76	1971-74	Notre Dame (71-70)
Indiana	57	1975-77	Toledo (59-57)
Marquette	56	1970-72	Detroit (70-49)
Kentucky	54	1952-55	George Tech (59-58)
San Francisco	51	1955-57	Illinois (62-33)
Pennsylvania	48	1970-72	Temple (57-52)
Ohio St	47	1960-62	Wisconsin (86-67)
Texas	44	1913-17	Rice (24-18)
UCLA	43	1966-68	Houston (71-69)
LIU-Brooklyn	43	1935-37	Stanford (45-31)
Seton Hall	42	1939-41	LIU-Brooklyn (49-26)

NCAA Division I Winningest Men's Coaches

Active Coaches

WINS

Coach and Team	W
Dean Smith, N Carolina	774
Don Haskins, UTEP	625
Lefty Driesell, James Madison	621
Bob Knight, Indiana	619
Norm Stewart, Missouri	609
Lou Henson, Illinois	609
Gene Bartow, AL-Birmingham	595
Glenn Wilkes, Stetson	549
Gary Colson, Fresno St	529
Denny Crum Louisville,	518

Note: Minimum 5 years as a Division I head coach; includes record at 4-year colleges only.

WINNING PERCENTAGE

Coach and Team	Yrs	W	L	Pct
Dean Smith, N Carolina	32	774	223	.776
Jim Boeheim, Syracuse	17	410	133	.755
John Chaney, Temple	21	478	156	.754
Bob Knight, Indiana	28	619	214	.743
Nolan Richardson, Arkansas	13	308	109	.739
Ralph Underhill, Wright St	15	316	114	.735
Denny Crum, Louisville	22	518	192	.730
John Thompson, Georgetown	21	481	178	.730
Pete Gillen, Xavier (OH)	8	179	67	.728
Eddie Sutton, Oklahoma St	23	500	189	.726

Note: Minimum 5 years as a Division I head coach; includes record at 4-year colleges only.

All-Time Winningest Division I Men's Coaches

WINS

Coach (Team)	W
Adolph Rupp (Kentucky)	875
Dean Smith (N Carolina)	774
Hank Iba (NW Missouri St, Colorado, Oklahoma St)	767
Ed Diddle (Western Kentucky)	759
Phog Allen (Baker, Kansas, Haskell, Central Missouri St, Kansas)	746
Ray Meyer (DePaul)	724
John Wooden (Indiana St, UCLA)	664
Ralph Miller (Wichita St, Iowa, Oregon St)	657
Marv Harshman (Pacific Lutheran, Washington St, Washington)	642
Norm Sloan (Presbyterian, Citadel, N Carolina St, Florida)	627
Jerry Tarkanian (Long Beach St, UNLV)	625
Cam Henderson (Muskingum, Davis & Elkins, Marshall)	611
Don Haskins (UTEP)	625
Lefty Driesell (Davidson, Maryland, James Madison)	621

Note: Minimum 10 head coaching seasons in Division I.

NCAA Division I Winningest Men's Coaches (Cont.)

WINNING PERCENTAGE

Coach (Team)	Yrs	W	L	Pct
Jerry Tarkanian (Long Beach St 69-73, UNLV 74-92)	24	625	122	.837
Clair Bee (Rider 29-31, LIU-Brooklyn 32-45, 46-51)	21	412	87	.826
Adolph Rupp (Kentucky 31-72)	41	875	190	.822
John Wooden (Indiana St 47-48, UCLA 49-75)	29	664	162	.804
Dean Smith (N Carolina 62-)	32	774	223	.776
Harry Fisher (Columbia 07-16, Army 22-23, 25)	13	147	44	.770
Frank Keaney (Rhode Island 21-48)	27	387	117	.768
George Keogan (St Louis 16, Allegheny 19, Valparaiso 20-21, Notre Dame 24-43)	24	385	117	.767
Jack Ramsay (St Joseph's [PA] 56-66)	11	231	71	.765
Vic Bubas (Duke 60-69)	10	213	67	.761
Jim Boeheim (Syracuse 77-)	17	410	133	.755
John Chaney (Cheyney 73-82, 83-)	21	478	156	.754
Charles "Chick" Davies (Duquesne 25-43, 47-48)	21	314	106	.748
Ray Mears (Wittenberg 57-62, Tennessee 63-77)	21	399	135	.747
Bob Knight (Army 66-71, Indiana 72-)	28	619	214	.743
Phog Allen (Baker 06-08, Kansas 08-09, Haskell 09, C MO St 13-19, Kansas 20-56)	48	746	264	.739
Al McGuire (Belmont Abbey 58-64, Marquette 65-77)	20	405	143	.739
Everett Chase (N Carolina St 47-64)	18	376	133	.739
Nolan Richardson (Tulsa 81-85, Arkansas 86-)	13	308	109	.739
Walter Meanwell (Wisconsin 12-17, 21-34; Missouri 18, 20)	22	280	101	.735

Note: Minimum 10 head coaching seasons in Division I.

NCAA Division I Women's Championship Results

Year	Winner	Score	Runner-up	Winning Coach
1982	Louisiana Tech	76-62	Cheyney	Sonja Hogg
1983	Southern Cal	69-67	Louisiana Tech	Linda Sharp
1984	Southern Cal	72-61	Tennessee	Linda Sharp
1985	Old Dominion	70-65	Georgia	Marianne Stanley
1986	Texas	97-81	Southern Cal	Jody Conradt
1987	Tennessee	67-44	Louisiana Tech	Pat Summitt
1988	Louisiana Tech	56-54	Auburn	Leon Barmore
1989	Tennessee	76-60	Auburn	Pat Summitt
1990	Stanford	88-81	Auburn	Tara VanDerveer
1991	Tennessee	70-67 (OT)	Virginia	Pat Summitt
1992	Stanford	78-62	Western Kentucky	Tara VanDerveer
1993	Texas Tech	84-82	Ohio State	Marsha Sharp

NCAA Division I Women's All-Time Individual Leaders

Single-Game Records

SCORING HIGHS

Pts	Player and Team vs Opponent	Year
60	Cindy Brown, Long Beach St vs San Jose St	1987
58	Kim Perrot, SW Louisiana vs SE Louisiana	1990
58	Lorri Bauman, Drake vs SW Missouri St	1984
55	Patricia Hoskins, Mississippi Valley vs Southern-BR	1989
55	Patricia Hoskins, Mississippi Valley vs Alabama St	1989
54	Wanda Ford, Drake vs SW Missouri St	1986
53	Felisha Edwards, NE Louisiana vs Southern Mississippi	1991
53	Chris Starr, NV-Reno vs Cal St-Sacramento	1983
53	Sheryl Swoopes, Texas Tech vs Texas	1993
52	Sheryl Martin, Georgia St vs Stetson	1983
52	Deborah Temple, Delta St vs Tennessee-Martin	1983
52	Lisa Ingram, NE Louisiana vs Louisiana St	1984

REBOUNDING HIGHS

Reb	Player and Team vs Opponent	Year
40	Deborah Temple, Delta St vs AL-Birmingham	1983
37	Rosina Pearson, Bethune-Cookman vs Florida Memorial	1985
33	Maureen Formico, Pepperdine vs Loyola (CA)	1985

REBOUNDING HIGHS (CONT.)

Reb	Player and Team vs Opponent	Year
31	Darlene Beale, Howard vs S Carolina St	1987
30	Cindy Bonforte, Wagner vs Queens (NY)	1983
29	Gail Norris, Alabama St vs Texas Southern	1992
29	Joy Kellogg, Oklahoma City vs Oklahoma Christian	1984
29	Joy Kellogg, Oklahoma City vs UTEP	1984
28	Tracy Claxton, Kansas vs Pacific Christian	1982
28	Carolyn Thompson, Texas Tech vs Rice	1982
28	Olivia Bradley, W Virginia vs Temple	1985
28	Yvette Larkins, Coppin St vs Charleston Southern	1990
28	Tarcha Hollis, Grambling vs Alcorn St	1991

ASSISTS

A	Player and Team vs Opponent	Year
23	Michelle Burden, Kent St vs Ball St	1991
22	Shawn Monday, Tennessee Tech vs Morehead St	1988
22	Veronica Pettry, Loyola (IL) vs Detroit	1989
22	Tine Freil, Pacific vs Wichita St	1991
21	Tine Freil, Pacific vs Fresno St	1992
21	Amy Bauer, Wisconsin vs Detroit	1989
21	Neacole Hall, Alabama St vs Southern-BR	1989
20	Anja Bordt, St Mary's (CA) vs Loyola (CA)	1991
20	Gaynor O'Donnell, E Carolina vs NC-Asheville	1992
20	Ira Fuquay, Alcorn St vs Grambling	1993

Season Records

POINTS

Player and Team	Year	GP	FG	3FG	FT	Pts
Cindy Brown, Long Beach St	1987	35	362	—	250	974
Genia Miller, Cal St-Fullerton	1991	33	376	0	217	969
Sheryl Swoopes, Texas Tech	1993	34	356	32	211	955
Andrea Congreaves, Mercer	1992	28	353	77	142	925
Wanda Ford, Drake	1986	30	390	—	139	919
Barbara Kennedy, Clemson	1982	31	392	—	124	908
Patricia Hoskins, Mississippi Valley	1989	27	345	13	205	908
LaTaunya Pollard, Long Beach St	1983	31	376	—	155	907
Tina Hutchinson, San Diego St	1984	30	383	—	132	898
Jan Jensen, Drake	1991	30	358	6	166	888

SEASON SCORING AVERAGE

Player and Team	Year	GP	FG	3FG	FT	Pts	Avg
Patricia Hoskins, Mississippi Valley	1989	27	345	13	205	908	33.6
Andrea Congreaves, Mercer	1992	28	353	77	142	925	33.0
Deborah Temple, Delta St	1984	28	373	—	127	873	31.2
Andrea Congreaves, Mercer	1993	26	302	51	150	805	31.0
Wanda Ford, Drake	1986	30	390	—	139	919	30.6
Anucha Browne, Northwestern	1985	28	341	—	173	855	30.5
LeChandra LeDay, Grambling	1988	28	334	36	146	850	30.4
Kim Perrot, Southwestern Louisiana	1990	28	308	95	128	839	30.0
Tina Hutchinson, San Diego St	1984	30	383	—	132	898	29.9
Jan Jensen, Drake	1991	30	358	6	166	888	29.6
Genia Miller, Cal St-Fullerton	1991	33	376	0	217	969	29.4
Barbara Kennedy, Clemson	1982	31	392	—	124	908	29.3
LaTaunya Pollard, Long Beach St	1983	31	376	—	155	907	29.3
Lisa McMullen, Alabama St	1991	28	285	126	119	815	29.1
Tresa Spaulding, BYU	1987	28	347	—	116	810	28.9
Hope Linthicum, Central Conn St	1987	23	282	—	101	665	28.9

Season Records (Cont.)

REBOUNDS

Player and Team	Year	GP	Reb	Player and Team	Year	GP	Reb
Wanda Ford, Drake	1985	30	534	Rosina Pearson, Beth-Cookman	1985	26	480
Wanda Ford, Drake	1986	30	506	Patricia Hoskins, Miss Valley	1987	28	476
Anne Donovan, Old Dominion	1983	35	504	Cheryl Miller, Southern Cal	1985	30	474
Darlene Jones, Miss Valley	1983	31	487	Darlene Beale, Howard	1987	29	459
Melanie Simpson, Okla City	1982	37	481	Olivia Bradley, W Virginia	1985	30	458

REBOUND AVERAGE

Player and Team	Year	GP	Reb	Avg
Rosina Pearson, Bethune-Cookman	1985	26	480	18.5
Wanda Ford, Drake	1985	30	534	17.8
Katie Beck, E Tennessee St	1988	25	441	17.6
Patricia Hoskins, Mississippi Valley	1987	28	476	17.0
Wanda Ford, Drake	1986	30	506	16.9
Patricia Hoskins, Mississippi Valley	1989	27	440	16.3
Joy Kellogg, Oklahoma City	1984	23	373	16.2
Deborah Mitchell, Miss Col	1983	28	447	16.0
Cheryl Miller, Southern Cal	1985	30	474	15.8
Darlene Beale, Howard	1987	29	459	15.8

FIELD-GOAL PERCENTAGE

Player and Team	Year	GP	FG	FGA	Pct
Renay Adams, Tennessee Tech	1991	30	185	258	71.7
Regina Days, Georgia Southern	1986	27	234	332	70.5
Kelly Lyons, Old Dominion	1990	31	308	444	69.4
Trina Roberts, Georgia Southern	1982	31	189	277	68.2
Lidiya Varbanova, Boise St	1991	22	128	188	68.1
Sharon McDowell, NC-Wilmington	1987	28	170	251	67.7
Lidiya Varbanova, Boise St	1992	29	228	338	67.5
Mary Raese, Idaho	1986	31	254	380	66.8
Lydia Sawney, Tennessee Tech	1983	27	167	250	66.8
Michelle Suman, San Diego St	1992	29	156	234	66.7

Based on qualifiers for annual championships.

FREE-THROW PERCENTAGE

Player and Team	Year	GP	FT	FTA	Pct
Ginny Doyle, Richmond	1992	29	96	101	95.0
Linda Cyborski, Delaware	1991	29	74	79	93.7
Keely Feeman, Cincinnati	1986	30	76	82	92.7
Amy Slowikowski, Kent St	1989	27	112	121	92.6
Lea Ann Parsley, Marshall	1990	28	96	104	92.3
Chris Starr, NV-Reno	1986	25	119	129	92.2
DeAnn Craft, Central Florida	1987	24	94	102	92.2
Tracey Sneed, La Salle	1988	30	151	165	91.5
Jana Crosby, Houston	1990	29	84	92	91.3
Lisa Goodin, Eastern Kentucky	1983	27	147	161	91.3

Based on qualifiers for annual championships.

THEY SAID IT

Dale Brown, LSU's voluble basketball coach, on why he dyed his graying hair: "It makes me feel 56 instead of 57."

Career Records

POINTS

Player and Team	Yrs	GP	Pts
Patricia Hoskins, Mississippi Valley	1985-89	110	3122
Lorri Bauman, Drake	1981-84	120	3115
Cheryl Miller, Southern Cal	1983-86	128	3018
Valorie Whiteside, Appalachian St	1984-88	116	2944
Joyce Walker, Louisiana St	1981-84	117	2906
Sandra Hodge, New Orleans	1981-84	107	2860
Andrea Congreaves, Mercer	1989-93	108	2796
Karen Pelphrey, Marshall	1983-86	114	2746
Cindy Brown, Long Beach St	1983-87	128	2696
Carolyn Thompson, Texas Tech	1981-84	121	2655
Sue Wicks, Rutgers	1984-88	125	2655

SCORING AVERAGE

Player and Team	Yrs	GP	FG	3FG	FT	Pts	Avg
Patricia Hoskins, Mississippi Valley	1985-89	110	1196	24	706	3122	28.4
Sandra Hodge, New Orleans	1981-84	107	1194	—	472	2860	26.7
Lorri Bauman, Drake	1981-84	120	1104	—	907	3115	26.0
Andrea Congreaves, Mercer	1989-93	108	1107	153	429	2796	25.9
Valorie Whiteside, Appalachian St	1984-88	116	1153	0	638	2944	25.4
Joyce Walker, Louisiana St	1981-84	117	1259	—	388	2906	24.8
Tarcha Hollis, Grambling	1988-91	85	904	3	247	2058	24.2
Karen Pelphrey, Marshall	1983-86	114	1175	—	396	2746	24.1
Erma Jones, Bethune-Cookman	1982-84	87	961	—	173	2095	24.1
Cheryl Miller, Southern Cal	1983-86	128	1159	—	700	3018	23.6
Chris Starr, Nevada-Reno	1983-86	101	881	—	594	2356	23.3

NCAA Division II Men's Championship Results

Year	Winner	Score	Runner-up	Third Place	Fourth Place
1957	Wheaton (IL)	89-65	Kentucky Wesleyan	Mount St Mary's (MD)	Cal St-Los Angeles
1958	S Dakota	75-53	St Michael's	Evansville	Wheaton (IL)
1959	Evansville	83-67	SW Missouri St	N Carolina A&T	Cal St-Los Angeles
1960	Evansville	90-69	Chapman	Kentucky Wesleyan	Cornell College
1961	Wittenberg	42-38	SE Missouri St	S Dakota St	Mount St Mary's (MD)
1962	Mount St Mary's (MD)	58-57 (OT)	Cal St-Sacramento	Southern Illinois	Nebraska Wesleyan
1963	S Dakota St	44-42	Wittenberg	Oglethorpe	Southern Illinois
1964	Evansville	72-59	Akron	N Carolina A&T	Northern Iowa
1965	Evansville	85-82 (OT)	Southern Illinois	N Dakota	St Michael's
1966	Kentucky Wesleyan	54-51	Southern Illinois	Akron	N Dakota
1967	Winston-Salem	77-74	SW Missouri St	Kentucky Wesleyan	Illinois St
1968	Kentucky Wesleyan	63-52	Indiana St	Trinity (TX)	Ashland
1969	Kentucky Wesleyan	75-71	SW Missouri St	†Vacated	Ashland
1970	Philadelphia Textile	76-65	Tennessee St	UC-Riverside	Buffalo St
1971	Evansville	97-82	Old Dominion	†Vacated	Kentucky Wesleyan
1972	Roanoke	84-72	Akron	Tennessee St	Eastern Mich
1973	Kentucky Wesleyan	78-76 (OT)	Tennessee St	Assumption	Brockport St
1974	Morgan St	67-52	SW Missouri St	Assumption	New Orleans
1975	Old Dominion	76-74	New Orleans	Assumption	TN-Chattanooga
1976	Puget Sound	83-74	TN-Chattanooga	Eastern Illinois	Old Dominion
1977	TN-Chattanooga	71-62	Randolph-Macon	N Alabama	Sacred Heart
1978	Cheyney	47-40	WI-Green Bay	Eastern Illinois	Central Florida
1979	N Alabama	64-50	WI-Green Bay	Cheyney	Bridgeport
1980	Virginia Union	80-74	New York Tech	Florida Southern	N Alabama
1981	Florida Southern	73-68	Mount St Mary's (MD)	Cal Poly-SLO	WI-Green Bay
1982	District of Columbia	73-63	Florida Southern	Kentucky Wesleyan	Cal St-Bakersfield
1983	Wright St	92-73	District of Columbia	*Cal St-Bakersfield	*Morningside
1984	Central Missouri St	81-77	St Augustine's	*Kentucky Wesleyan	*N Alabama
1985	Jacksonville St	74-73	S Dakota St	*Kentucky Wesleyan	*Mount St Mary's (MD)
1986	Sacred Heart	93-87	SE Missouri St	*Cheyney	*Florida Southern
1987	Kentucky Wesleyan	92-74	Gannon	*Delta St	*Eastern Montana

NCAA Division II Men's Championship Results *(Cont.)*

Year	Winner	Score	Runner-up	Third Place	Fourth Place
1988	.......Lowell	75-72	AK-Anchorage	Florida Southern	Troy St
1989	.......N Carolina Central	73-46	SE Missouri St	UC-Riverside	Jacksonville St
1990	.......Kentucky Wesleyan	93-79	Cal St-Bakersfield	N Dakota	Morehouse
1991	.......N Alabama	79-72	Bridgeport (CT)	*Cal St-Bakersfield	*Virginia Union
1992	.......Virginia Union	100-75	Bridgeport (CT)	*Cal St-Bakersfield	*California (PA)
1993	.......Cal St-Bakersfield	85-72	Troy St (AL)	*New Hampshire Coll	*Wayne St (MI)

*Indicates tied for third. †Student-athletes representing American International in 1969 and Southwestern Louisiana in 1971 were declared ineligible subseque nt to the tournament. Under NCAA rules, the teams' and ineligible student-athletes' records were deleted, and the teams' places in t he final standings were vacated.

NCAA Division II Men's All-Time Individual Leaders

SINGLE-GAME SCORING HIGHS

Pts	Player and Team vs Opponent	Date
113	...........................Bevo Francis, Rio Grande vs Hillsdale	1954
84	..............................Bevo Francis, Rio Grande vs Alliance	1954
82	..............................Bevo Francis, Rio Grande vs Bluffton	1954
80	............................Paul Crissman, Southern Cal Col vs Pacific Christian	1966
77	............................William English, Winston-Salem vs Fayetteville St	1968

Season Records

SCORING AVERAGE

Player and Team	Year	GP	FG	FT	Pts	Avg
Bevo Francis, Rio Grande	1954	27	444	367	1255	46.5
Earl Glass, Mississippi Industrial	1963	19	322	171	815	42.9
Earl Monroe, Winston-Salem	1967	32	509	311	1329	41.5
John Rinka, Kenyon	1970	23	354	234	942	41.0
Willie Shaw, Lane	1964	18	303	121	727	40.4

REBOUND AVERAGE

Player and Team	Year	GP	Reb	Avg
Tom Hart, Middlebury	1956	21	620	29.5
Tom Hart, Middlebury	1955	22	649	29.5
Frank Stronczek, American Int'l	1966	26	717	27.6
R.C. Owens, College of Idaho	1954	25	677	27.1
Maurice Stokes, St Francis (PA)	1954	26	689	26.5

ASSISTS

Player and Team	Year	GP	A
Steve Ray, Bridgeport	1989	32	400
Steve Ray, Bridgeport	1990	33	385
Tony Smith, Pfeiffer	1992	35	349
Jim Ferrer, Bentley	1989	31	309
Brian Gregory, Oakland	1989	28	300

ASSIST AVERAGE

Player and Team	Year	GP	A	Avg
Steve Ray, Bridgeport	1989	32	400	12.5
Steve Ray, Bridgeport	1990	33	385	11.7
Demetri Beekman, Assumption	1993	23	264	11.5
Brian Gregory, Oakland	1989	28	300	10.7
Adrian Hutt, Metropolitan St	1991	28	285	10.2

FIELD-GOAL PERCENTAGE

Player and Team	Year	Pct
Todd Linder, Tampa	1987	75.2
Maurice Stafford, N Alabama	1984	75.0
Matthew Cornegay, Tuskegee	1982	74.8
Brian Moten, W Georgia	1992	73.4
Ed Phillips, Alabama A&M	1968	73.3

FREE-THROW PERCENTAGE

Player and Team	Year	Pct
Billy Newton, Morgan St	1976	94.4
Kent Andrews, McNeese St	1968	94.4
Mike Sanders, Northern Colorado	1987	94.3
Joe Cullen, Hartwick	1969	93.2
Charles Byrd, W Texas St	1988	92.9

Career Records

POINTS

Player and Team	Yrs	Pts
Travis Grant, Kentucky St	1969-72	4045
Bob Hopkins, Grambling	1953-56	3759
Tony Smith, Pfeiffer	1989-92	3350
Earnest Lee, Clark Atlanta	1984-87	3298
Joe Miller, Alderson-Broaddus	1954-57	3294

CAREER SCORING AVERAGE

Player and Team	Yrs	GP	Pts	Avg
Travis Grant, Kentucky St	1969-72	121	4045	33.4
John Rinka, Kenyon	1967-70	99	3251	32.8
Florindo Vieira, Quinnipiac	1954-57	69	2263	32.8
Willie Shaw, Lane	1961-64	76	2379	31.3
Mike Davis, Virginia Union	1966-69	89	2758	31.0

REBOUND AVERAGE

Player and Team	Yrs	GP	Reb	Avg
Tom Hart, Middlebury	1953, 55-56	63	1738	27.6
Maurice Stokes, St Francis (PA)	1953-55	72	1812	25.2
Frank Stronczek, American Intl	1965-67	62	1549	25.0
Bill Thieben, Hofstra	1954-56	76	1837	24.2
Hank Brown, Lowell Tech	1965-67	49	1129	23.0

ASSISTS

Player and Team	Yrs	A
Demetri Beekman, Assumption	1990-93	1044
Gallagher Driscoll, St Rose	1989-92	878
Tony Smith, Pfeiffer	1989-92	828
Steve Ray, Bridgeport	1989-90	785
Charles Jordan, Erskine	1989-92	727

ASSIST AVERAGE

Player and Team	Yrs	GP	A	Avg
Steve Ray, Bridgeport	1989-90	65	785	12.1
Demetri Beekman, Assumption	1990-93	119	1044	8.8
Mark Benson, Texas A&I	1989-91	86	674	7.8
Pat Madden, Jacksonville St	1989-91	88	688	7.8

FIELD-GOAL PERCENTAGE

Player and Team	Yrs	Pct
Todd Linder, Tampa	1984-87	70.8
Tom Schurfranz, Bellarmine	1989-92	70.2
Ed Phillips, Alabama, A&M	1968-71	68.9
Otis Evans, Wayne St (MI)	1989-92	67.7
Ulysses Hackett, SC-Spartanburg	1989-92	67.1

FREE-THROW PERCENTAGE

Player and Team	Yrs	Pct
Kent Andrews, McNeese St	1967-69	91.6
Jon Hagen, Mankato St	1963-65	90.0
Dave Reynolds, Davis & Elkins	1986-89	89.3
Terry Gill, New Orleans	1972-74	88.2
Tony Budzik, Mansfield	1989-92	88.2

NCAA Division III Men's Championship Results

Year	Winner	Score	Runner-up	Third Place	Fourth Place
1975	LeMoyne-Owen	57-54	Glassboro St	Augustana (IL)	Brockport St
1976	Scranton	60-57	Wittenberg	Augustana (IL)	Plattsburgh St
1977	Wittenberg	79-66	Oneonta St	Scranton	Hamline
1978	North Park	69-57	Widener	Albion	Stony Brook
1979	North Park	66-62	Potsdam St	Franklin & Marshall	Centre
1980	North Park	83-76	Upsala	Wittenberg	Longwood
1981	Potsdam St	67-65 (OT)	Augustana (IL)	Ursinus	Otterbein
1982	Wabash	83-62	Potsdam St	Brooklyn	Cal St Stanislaus
1983	Scranton	64-63	Wittenberg	Roanoke	WI-Whitewater
1984	WI-Whitewater	103-86	Clark (MA)	DePauw	Upsala
1985	North Park	72-71	Potsdam St	Nebraska Wesleyan	Widener
1986	Potsdam St	76-73	LeMoyne-Owen	Nebraska Wesleyan	Jersey City St
1987	North Park	106-100	Clark (MA)	Wittenberg	Stockton St
1988	Ohio Wesleyan	92-70	Scranton	Nebraska Wesleyan	Hartwick
1989	WI-Whitewater	94-86	Trenton St	Southern Maine	Centre
1990	Rochester	43-42	DePauw	Washington (MD)	Calvin
1991	WI-Platteville	81-74	Franklin & Marshall	Otterbein	Ramapo (NJ)
1992	Calvin	62-49	Rochester	WI-Platteville	Jersey City St
1993	Ohio Northern	71-68	Augustana	Mass-Dartmouth	Rowan

NCAA Division III Men's All-Time Individual Leaders

SINGLE-GAME SCORING HIGHS

Pts	Player and Team vs Opponent	Year
63	Joe DeRoche, Thomas vs St Joseph's (ME)	1988
62	Shannon Lilly, Bishop vs Southwest Assembly of God	1983
61	Steve Honderd, Calvin vs Kalamazoo	1993
61	Dana Wilson, Husson vs Ricker	1974
56	Mark Veenstra, Calvin vs Adrian	1976

Season Records

SCORING AVERAGE

Player and Team	Year	GP	FG	FT	Pts	Avg
Rickey Sutton, Lyndon St	1976	14	207	93	507	36.2
Shannon Lilly, Bishop	1983	26	345	218	908	34.9
Dana Wilson, Husson	1974	20	288	122	698	34.9
Rickey Sutton, Lyndon St	1977	16	223	112	558	34.9
Dwain Govan, Bishop	1975	29	392	179	963	33.2

REBOUND AVERAGE

Player and Team	Year	GP	Reb	Avg
Joe Manley, Bowie St	1976	29	579	20.0
Fred Petty, New Hampshire Col	1974	22	436	19.8
Larry Williams, Pratt	1977	24	457	19.0
Charles Greer, Thomas	1977	17	318	18.7
Larry Parker, Plattsburgh St	1975	23	430	18.7

ASSISTS

Player and Team	Year	GP	A
Robert James, Kean	1989	29	391
Ricky Spicer, WI-Whitewater	1989	31	295
Ron Torgalski, Hamilton	1989	26	275
Albert Kirchner, Mt St Vincent	1990	24	267
Steve Artis, Chris. Newport	1991	29	262

ASSIST AVERAGE

Player and Team	Year	GP	A	Avg
Robert James, Kean	1989	29	391	13.5
Albert Kirchner, Mt St Vincent	1990	24	267	11.1
Ron Torgalski, Hamilton	1989	26	275	10.6
Louis Adams, Rust	1989	22	227	10.3
Eric Johnson, Coe	1991	24	238	9.9

FIELD-GOAL PERCENTAGE

Player and Team	Year	Pct
Pete Metzelaars, Wabash	1982	75.3
Tony Rychlec, Mass Maritime	1981	74.9
Tony Rychlec, Mass Maritime	1982	73.1
Russ Newnan, Menlo	1991	73.0
Ed Owens, Hampden-Sydney	1979	72.9

FREE-THROW PERCENTAGE

Player and Team	Year	Pct
Andy Enfield, Johns Hopkins	1991	95.3
Yudi Teichman, Yeshiva	1989	95.2
Chris Carideo, Widener	1992	95.2
Mike Scheib, Susquehanna	1977	94.1
Jerry Prestier, Baldwin-Wallace	1978	93.3

Career Records

POINTS

Player and Team	Yrs	Pts
Andre Foreman, Salisbury St	1989-92	2940
Dwain Govan, Bishop	1972-75	2796
Dave Russell, Shepherd	1972-75	2761
Lamont Strothers, Chris Newport	1988-91	2709
Matt Hancock, Colby	1987-90	2678

CAREER SCORING AVERAGE

Player and Team	Yrs	GP	Avg
Rickey Sutton, Lyndon St	1976-79	80	29.7
John Atkins, Knoxville	1976-78	70	28.7
Jeff deLaveaga, Cal Lutheran	1989-92	80	28.1
Steve Peknik, Windham	1974-77	76	27.6
Matt Hancock, Colby	1987-90	102	26.3

REBOUND AVERAGE

Player and Team	Yrs	GP	Reb	Avg
Larry Parker, Plattsburgh St	1975-78	85	1482	17.4
Charles Greer, Thomas	1975-77	58	926	16.0
Willie Parr, LeMoyne-Owen	1974-76	76	1182	15.6
Michael Smith, Hamilton	1989-92	107	1632	15.2
Dave Kufeld, Yeshiva	1977-80	81	1222	15.1

ASSIST AVERAGE

Player and Team	Yrs	Avg
Steve Artis, Chris. Newport	1990-93	8.1
Kevin Kevin Root, Eureka	1989-91	7.1
Dennis Jacobi, Bowdoin	1989-92	7.1
Eric Johnson, Coe	1989-92	7.1
Pat Skerry, Tufts	1989-92	6.6

Hockey

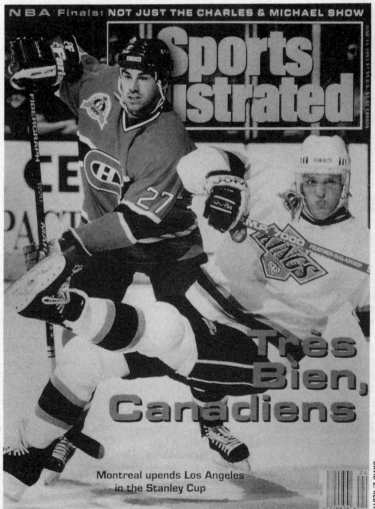

NBA Finals: NOT JUST THE CHARLES & MICHAEL SHOW

Sports Illustrated

JUNE 14, 1993 $2.95 U.S. $3.95 CANADA

Très Bien, Canadiens

Montreal upends Los Angeles
in the Stanley Cup

DAVID E. KLUTHO

A Season Of Shocks

A new leader off the ice and an old champion on it were the highlights of a long, strange season | by JON SCHER

FROM THE HAIL OF PACIFIERS that greeted rookie Eric Lindros in October when he skated onto the ice in Quebec City, to the shower of broken glass that littered the streets of downtown Montreal after the Canadiens won their 24th Stanley Cup in June, the longest season in NHL history often seemed as jarring as a well-placed bodycheck.

In the beginning, aftershocks were still being felt from the 10-day player strike in April 1992, which triggered the ouster of league president John Ziegler. In the end the landscape had been irrevocably rearranged.

The NHL got its first commissioner. Gary Bettman was drafted from the office of the wildly successful NBA, where he had been *consigliere* to the widely respected David Stern. Appointed in December and given broad but unspecified powers, Bettman wasted little time in applying his common sense, a quality that had long been in short supply among hockey's top brass.

Realignment, the knotty problem that brought down former baseball commissioner Fay Vincent in '92, was quickly handled with aplomb. Also, the quaint division and conference names were to be replaced in the fall of '93 by more user-friendly designations (the Patrick, Adams, Norris and Smythe divisions will become the Atlantic, Northeast, Central and Pacific). Expansion plans were executed with precision; the Florida Panthers of Miami and the Mighty Ducks of Anaheim, Calif., were on target to bring membership to a record 26 teams.

On the ice, new rules designed to curtail brawling proved fairly effective. There were fewer fights during the regular season, and almost none in the postseason. During the playoffs an outrageous cheap shot by Dale Hunter of the Washington Capitals on Pierre Turgeon of the New York Islanders was met by Bettman with a 21-game suspension, the stiffest on record. "If this is not a deterrent," said Bettman, 46, who has come

MANNY MILLAN

Appointed the NHL's first commissioner, Bettman vowed to crack down on violence.

out against gratuitous violence but stopped short of calling for an outright ban on fighting in the game, "I'm going to find something that is."

Bettman's former NBA colleagues, who respected him as an attorney, initially were skeptical of his ability to adjust to the new job. "I gave Gary a hockey puck once," joked Pat Williams, general manager of the Orlando Magic, "and he spent the rest of the day trying to open it." But the hockey owners were equally certain that they had the right man. "This," said Washington's Abe Pollin after Bettman was hired, "is a great step forward. No, it's more than a step. It's a leap."

Just as in his first half-season Bettman helped bring the league into the 20th century, he must now face the challenges of the 21st. The NHL remains woefully underexposed in the U.S., particularly on television. Last season a new cable

contract with ESPN led to five Sunday playoff games on ABC, the NHL's first appearance—apart from All-Star games—on a major U.S. network in 13 years. Expanding on that base is, in Bettman's eyes, high on a laundry list of priorities.

With the addition of Anaheim, owned by Disney, and Florida, owned by the Blockbuster Video chain, the NHL has reason to expect that a little pixie dust will rub off on the rest of the league. Either that or Bettman made an idiot of himself for nothing when he stood on a platform at the Anaheim franchise's unveiling and blew duck calls with Disney chairman Michael Eisner. "We made a movie about a hockey team called *The Mighty Ducks*," Eisner earlier quacked. "It did $50 million at the box office. That was our market research."

For the league's two most marketable figures, Wayne Gretzky and Mario Lemieux, the season was a theme-park ride with epic highs and lows. Gretzky missed nearly half the 84-game schedule

DAVID E. KLUTHO

Lemieux won the league scoring title despite sitting out six weeks.

recur. Of course, there is a 5 to 10% chance that it will. His extraordinary career—not to mention his life—hangs in the balance.

The stressed-out Penguins were all too familiar with bad news. In November 1991, 60-year-old Bob Johnson, who that spring had coached Pittsburgh to the first of two consecutive Stanley Cups, died of brain cancer. The year before, goalie Tom Barrasso's daughter, who was two at the time, nearly died during a fight with neuroblastoma, a form of childhood cancer. Both illnesses played havoc with the emotions of the team.

with a herniated disk in his upper back, wondered for a while if he was through, then wound up leading the Los Angeles Kings to the Stanley Cup finals. Lemieux, on the other hand, started out on another planet, scoring in each of the Pittsburgh Penguins' first 12 games and maintaining such a scorching pace through December that Gretzky's single-season scoring record, 215 points, seemed in grave jeopardy.

Then, on Jan. 8, a lump was removed from Super Mario's neck. A week later this very private athlete had to tell the world that he had been diagnosed as having Hodgkin's disease, a form of cancer. "I've faced a lot of battles since I was really young, and I've always come out on top," Lemieux, 28, said matter-of-factly at a somber press conference at Pittsburgh's downtown Hyatt. "I expect that will be the case with this disease."

Medical experts agreed. If, as doctors said, cancer was present only in the one lymph node that was excised from Lemieux's neck, there is a 90 to 95% probability that the disease will not

Now Lemieux? "This was like a kick in the teeth, or some other part of the anatomy," said owner Howard Baldwin. Added power forward Kevin Stevens, who is one of Lemieux's best friends, "It seems like everything bad that happens in hockey happens to our team. It seems as if it just never ends. But we're strong enough to deal with it. And Mario is strong enough to deal with it."

As it turned out, Lemieux was stronger than anyone could have expected. Radiation treatment was prescribed, and the most optimistic forecasts indicated that he could be back on the ice in 10 weeks, just in time for the playoffs. Instead, he returned on March 2, a month ahead of schedule. He was out of the lineup for 24 games, long enough for Buffalo Sabre center Pat LaFontaine to come from 33 points behind to take a 12-point lead in the league scoring race. "I thought about it even during radiation," Lemieux said in his quiet way. "I was determined to come back and regain the lead."

LaFontaine never really had a prayer. Lemieux finished with 160 points in 60 games, winning his fourth scoring title and his second Hart Trophy as the league MVP. As the season wound down, Lemieux said he was drained and sore, but the only outward sign of his mortality was the half-moon-shaped bald patch on the back of his head, where a hunk of his hair had fallen victim to the radiation treatments he had undergone.

Remarkably, the cancer made Lemieux greater than the sum of his parts. After being viewed for years as a major figure in a minor sport, Lemieux finally managed to transcend hockey. At last he was being recognized for what he arguably may be: the world's most dominant pro athlete.

And the three-peat-seeking Penguins nearly proved they were the world's dominant pro team. They entered the playoffs on the biggest roll in hockey history, winning a league-record 17 games in a row before tying the New Jersey Devils on the last night of the season. Their 56-21-7 record and 119 points qualified them for the first time for the President's Trophy, which goes to the

team that finishes with the best record in the regular season. "We're in high gear," said Rick Tocchet, a forward with a seemingly permanent four-stitch cut across the bridge of his nose. "We're ready for the playoffs. And we know that anything less than the Stanley Cup is going to be a failure."

Then it's back to the drawing board. After wiping out the New Jersey Devils in the opening round, the Penguins were stunned in seven games by the up-and-coming New York Islanders.

It was a hugely entertaining postseason, in which a record 28 games went into overtime, and Al Arbour's Islanders seemed to have mastered the art of administering sudden death. The Isles, who barely made the playoffs, snuffed the Washington Capitals 4–2 in the first round, winning three games in overtime. Then they put down the haughty Penguins 4–3 in Game 7, thanks to David Volek's goal 5:16 minutes into OT.

"We never felt we were the Penguins' equal in talent," said Islander forward

Brian Mullen and the upstart Islanders shocked the mighty Penguins in seven.

DAVID E. KLUTHO

Gretzky, great once more, led the Kings to the Stanley Cup finals.

Steve Thomas. "But we felt heart counted for something more than that." After Barrasso's goaltending went sour, after Stevens went down in Game 7 with a horrific facial injury that later required reconstructive surgery, and after Lemieux's bad back forced him to spend his nights in traction, the banner headline in the *Pittsburgh Post-Gazette* pretty much summed up the Penguins' fate: THREE-PEATERED OUT.

With the overwhelming favorite banished to the golf course, the Stanley Cup was up for grabs. Somehow, only the also-rans seemed to understand. In addition to Pittsburgh, the division-winning Boston Bruins, Chicago Blackhawks and Vancouver Canucks quickly fell by the wayside. The four teams that emerged from the divisional playoffs—the Islanders, Canadiens, Toronto Maple Leafs and Kings—each had finished in third place. Which goes to show you: The regular season may have been extended by four games in the settlement of the '92 strike, but its importance continues to dwindle faster than Tipper Gore's waistline. As the Kings' coach, the redoubtable Barry Melrose, said during training camp, "You finish first in the regular season and they give you this big cheese plate. Thanks, but I'd rather win the Stanley Cup."

He nearly pulled it off, dashing a nation's nostalgia-driven hope for an all-Canadian final in the process. The Toronto Maple Leafs, the Islanders of the Campbell Conference, rode a tidal wave of emotion into their semifinal series against the Kings. A patchwork collection of veterans and rookies stitched together by coach Pat Burns around gritty center Doug Gilmour, the erstwhile Maple Loafs briefly brought back memories of the ancient Montreal-Toronto championship rivalry, a battle that hasn't been joined since 1967.

The Leafs threw everything they had at L.A., but the Great One would not be denied. "I've never had as much personal satisfaction," Gretzky said, after his three goals and an assist had lifted the Kings to a 5–4 win in Game 7 at Maple Leaf Gardens. "It took five years of hard work for me to win the Cup with Edmonton. This is my fifth year with the Kings. Maybe it's our time."

It might have been. The Canadiens had won seven consecutive overtime games going into the Stanley Cup finals—having whacked the Islanders twice in OT in the semis—and seemed ready for a fall. They opened flat, losing 4–1 at home, and were trailing Los

DAVID E. KLUTHO

Angeles 2–1 with 1:45 remaining in Game 2.

Desperate times call for desperate measures. The Habs' garrulous coach, Jacques Demers, tapped captain Guy Carbonneau on the shoulder and told him to ask referee Kerry Fraser to measure the curve on the blade of Marty McSorley's stick. Since early in Game 1 the Canadiens had suspected it was illegal, but Demers sat on those suspicions until he felt there was nowhere else to turn. Had he been wrong, the Canadiens would have been penalized for delay of game. But in what was the defining moment in the series, Fraser found the L.A. defenseman's blade was curved more than the legal half inch—a quarter inch more. McSorley received a two-minute penalty.

Thirty-two seconds later, after Demers had raised the stakes by pulling goalie Patrick Roy to gain a two-man advantage, defenseman Eric Desjardins

scored his second goal of the game to make the score 2–2. Desjardins scored again 51 seconds into OT, and the Canadiens celebrated wildly, dancing amid the ghosts of the Forum. The spirits had struck again. Said Gretzky, "We gave them life."

When the finals changed Forums, shifting to L.A. for the first time, the glitterati were out in full bloom. After 26 years it had suddenly become way cool to be a hockey fan in La-La Land. Ronald and Nancy Reagan were ensconced at rinkside, along with Goldie Hawn, John Candy, Michelle Pfeiffer, Andre Agassi, Eisner and a rockin' cast of black-and-silver-clad puckheads.

The atmosphere didn't rattle Roy or the Canadiens. They stole two more games in OT, extending their sudden-life winning streak to an unprecedented 10 in a row. Then they returned home to conquer the Kings, taking Game 5 and the series 4–1. Roy, the playoff MVP, was impenetrable, invincible. Or, as one fan's banner in the Montreal Forum had it: INC-ROY-HAB-LE! Said Demers, a Montreal native who had succeeded Burns as coach and immediately brought the Stanley Cup home for the first time in seven years, "This is the greatest."

Sadly, it was followed by the worst. Hoodlums, only some of whom appeared to be hockey fans, spilled out of the subway station across from the Forum. The celebration in the streets quickly degenerated into a riot. Overmatched police stood and watched as the unruly crowd hurled bottles through store windows, looted a number of businesses and torched cars. Ultimately 115 were arrested, but it was too little, too late. Damage to the city's central business district was estimated at $10 million.

Like the scene in Montreal, the season may have been deplorable at times, but it was almost never dull. Ending a lengthy soap opera, Minnesota North Stars owner Norm Green announced plans to move to Dallas for the 1993–94

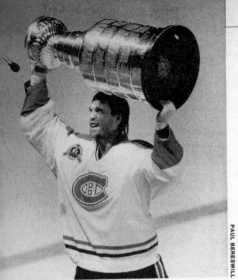

PAUL BERESWILL

disappointed with their child prodigy, who has been all but anointed as the NHL's next superstar. The 19-year-old Lindros scored 41 goals in 61 games, and was undefeated in court (he was acquitted of assault in a tabloid-tingling case in which he had been accused of dumping a beer on a woman in a bar). Even so, the race for the Calder Trophy wasn't a close one; Lindros was beaten out for the Rookie of the Year award by Teemu Selanne of the Winnipeg Jets. The Finnish Flash scored a rookie-record 76 goals.

Seven teams ushered a total of eight coaches to the exit during or after the season, down slightly from the 11 who were scapegoated the previous year. With their ignominious tumble from first to worst in the Patrick Division, the New York Rangers handed pink slips to Roger Neilson and Ron Smith and wound up inflicting hard-nosed Mike Keenan on their underachieving players. Bob Plager resigned in St. Louis and was replaced by Bob Berry; San Jose fired George Kingston and hired Kevin Constantine; New Jersey hired Jacques Lemaire to replace Herb Brooks, who resigned; and Philly fired Bill Dineen and hired Terry Simpson.

After the playoffs the long knives were out in Pittsburgh. The Penguins let coach Scotty Bowman twist in the wind, then tendered a halfhearted offer. Bowman, the most successful bench boss in NHL history, opted to hook on with the Detroit Red Wings, replacing Bryan Murray as coach for $1 million a year (Murray remains the Wings' G.M.).

Meanwhile, the Penguins plucked the losingest coach in their history, Eddie Johnston, out of retirement. Expectations couldn't be higher. Said Johnston, a golfing buddy of Lemieux's, "I feel like I just won the lottery." Not so fast, Eddie. You haven't won anything yet.

season, abandoning the land of 10,000 rinks for the Sun Belt, the land of favorable demographics. There the Dallas Stars will join the incoming Florida Panthers and the surprisingly competitive Tampa Bay Lightning, which earned notoriety in its debut season by inviting female goalie Manon Rheaume to training camp and then stashing her in the minors, where she started one game, stopping 25 of 31 shots.

The Lightning's expansion partners, the Ottawa Senators, were a total embarrassment, finishing 10-70-4. But there was a silver lining: With the No. 1 pick in the June entry draft, the Senators selected center Alexandre Daigle, who's expected to be a franchise player. For hope Ottawa can look to the example set by the Quebec Nordiques, the longtime doormats who went from last place to second in the Adams Division thanks to astute drafting over a period of years (not to mention the '92 deal that brought four players from Philadelphia in exchange for the rights to Lindros, who had infuriated fans in Quebec by sitting out a season rather than play for the Nordiques).

Although the Flyers finished last in the Patrick Division, they were far from

FOR THE RECORD · 1992 - 1993

NHL Final Team Standings

Clarence Campbell Conference

NORRIS DIVISION

	GP	W	L	T	GF	GA	Pts
Chicago	84	47	25	12	279	230	106
Detroit	84	47	28	9	369	280	103
Toronto	84	44	29	11	288	241	99
St Louis	84	37	36	11	282	278	85
Minnesota	84	36	38	10	272	293	82
Tampa Bay	84	23	54	7	245	332	53

SMYTHE DIVISION

	GP	W	L	T	GF	GA	Pts
Vancouver	84	46	29	9	346	278	101
Calgary	84	43	30	11	322	282	97
Los Angeles	84	39	35	10	338	340	88
Winnipeg	84	40	37	7	322	320	87
Edmonton	84	26	50	8	242	337	60
San Jose	84	11	71	2	218	414	24

Prince of Wales Conference

ADAMS DIVISION

	GP	W	L	T	GF	GA	Pts
Boston	84	51	26	7	332	268	109
Quebec	84	47	27	10	351	300	104
Montreal	84	48	30	6	326	280	102
Buffalo	84	38	36	10	335	297	86
Hartford	84	26	52	6	284	369	58
Ottawa	84	10	70	4	202	395	24

PATRICK DIVISION

	GP	W	L	T	GF	GA	Pts
Pittsburgh	84	56	21	7	367	268	119
Washington	84	43	34	7	325	286	93
NY Islanders	84	40	37	7	335	297	87
New Jersey	84	40	37	7	308	299	87
Philadelphia	84	36	37	11	319	319	83
NY Rangers	84	34	39	11	304	308	79

1993 Stanley Cup Playoffs

Stanley Cup Playoff Results

Division Semifinals

ADAMS DIVISION

Apr 18	Buffalo	5	at Boston	4
Apr 20	Buffalo	4	at Boston	0
Apr 22	Boston	3	at Buffalo	4*
Apr 24	Boston	5	at Buffalo	6*

Buffalo won series 4-0

Apr 18	Montreal	2	at Quebec	3*
Apr 20	Montreal	1	at Quebec	4
Apr 22	Quebec	1	at Montreal	2*
Apr 24	Quebec	2	at Montreal	3
Apr 26	Montreal	5	at Quebec	4*
Apr 28	Quebec	2	at Montreal	6

Montreal won series 4-2

Division Semifinals *(Cont.)*

PATRICK DIVISION

Apr 18	New Jersey 3	at Pittsburgh	6
Apr 20	New Jersey 0	at Pittsburgh	7
Apr 22	Pittsburgh 4	at New Jersey	3
Apr 25	Pittsburgh 1	at New Jersey	4
Apr 26	New Jersey 3	at Pittsburgh	5

Pittsburgh won series 4-1

Apr 18	NY Islanders 1	at Washington	3
Apr 20	NY Islanders 5	at Washington	4*
Apr 22	Washington 3	at NY Islanders	4*
Apr 24	Washington 3	at NY Islanders	4*
Apr 26	NY Islanders 4	at Washington	6
Apr 28	Washington 3	at NY Islanders	5

NY Islanders won series 4-2

NORRIS DIVISION

Apr 18	St Louis 4	at Chicago	3
Apr 21	St Louis 2	at Chicago	0
Apr 23	Chicago 0	at St Louis	3
Apr 25	Chicago 3	at St Louis	4*

St Louis won series 4-0

Apr 19	Toronto 3	at Detroit	6
Apr 21	Toronto 2	at Detroit	6
Apr 23	Detroit 2	at Toronto	4
Apr 25	Detroit 2	at Toronto	3
Apr 27	Toronto 5	at Detroit	4*
Apr 29	Detroit 7	at Toronto	3
May 1	Toronto 4	at Detroit	3*

Toronto won series 4-3

SMYTHE DIVISION

Apr 19	Winnipeg 2	at Vancouver	4
Apr 21	Winnipeg 2	at Vancouver	3
Apr 23	Vancouver 4	at Winnipeg	5
Apr 25	Vancouver 3	at Winnipeg	1
Apr 27	Winnipeg 4	at Vancouver	3
Apr 29	Vancouver 4	at Winnipeg	3

Vancouver won series 4-2

Apr 18	Los Angeles 6	at Calgary	3
Apr 21	Los Angeles 4	at Calgary	9
Apr 23	Calgary 5	at Los Angeles	2
Apr 25	Calgary 1	at Los Angeles	3
Apr 27	Los Angeles 9	at Calgary	4
Apr 29	Calgary 6	at Los Angeles	9

Los Angeles won series 4-2.

Division Finals

ADAMS DIVISION

May 2	Buffalo 3	at Montreal	4
May 4	Buffalo 3	at Montreal	4*
May 6	Montreal 4	at Buffalo	3*
May 8	Montreal 4	at Buffalo	3*

Montreal won series 4-0.

PATRICK DIVISION

May 2	NY Islanders 3	at Pittsburgh	2
May 4	NY Islanders 0	at Pittsburgh	3
May 6	Pittsburgh 3	at NY Islanders	1
May 8	Pittsburgh 5	at NY Islanders	6
May 10	NY Islanders 3	at Pittsburgh	6
May 12	Pittsburgh 5	at NY Islanders	7
May 14	NY Islanders 4	at Pittsburgh	3*

NY Islanders won series 4-3

NORRIS DIVISION

May 3	St Louis 1	at Toronto	2*
May 5	St Louis 2	at Toronto	1*
May 7	Toronto 3	at St Louis	4
May 9	Toronto 4	at St Louis	1
May 11	St Louis 1	at Toronto	5
May 13	Toronto 1	at St Louis	2
May 15	St Louis 0	at Toronto	6

Toronto won series 4-3

SMYTHE DIVISION

May 2	Los Angeles 2	at Vancouver	5
May 5	Los Angeles 6	at Vancouver	3
May 7	Vancouver 4	at Los Angeles	7
May 9	Vancouver 7	at Los Angeles	2
May 11	Los Angeles 4	at Vancouver	3*
May 13	Vancouver 3	at Los Angeles	5

Los Angeles won series 4-2.

Wales Final

May 16	NY Islanders 1	at Montreal	4
May 18	NY Islanders 3	at Montreal	4*
May 20	Montreal 2	at NY Islanders	1*
May 24	Montreal 1	at NY Islanders	4
May 24	NY Islaners 2	at Montreal	5

Montreal won series 4-1

Campbell Final

May 17	Los Angeles 1	at Toronto	4
May 19	Los Angeles 3	at Toronto	2
May 21	Toronto 2	at Los Angeles	4
May 23	Toronto 4	at Los Angeles	2
May 25	Los Angeles 2	at Toronto	3*
May 27	Toronto 4	at Los Angeles	5*
May 29	Los Angeles 5	at Toronto	4

Los Angeles won series 4-3.

Stanley Cup Championship

June 1	Los Angeles 4	at Montreal	1
June 3	Los Angeles 2	at Montreal	3*
June 5	Montreal 4	at Los Angeles	3*

June 7	Montreal 3	at Los Angeles	2*
June 9	Los Angeles 1	at Montreal	4

Montreal won series 4-1

*Overtime game.

Stanley Cup Championship Box Scores

Game 1

```
Los Angeles .....1    1    2—4
Montreal .........1    0    0—1
```

FIRST PERIOD

Scoring: 1, LA, Robitaille 7 (p play) (Zhitnik, Gretzky), 3:03.2, Mtl, Ronan 2, 18:09. Penalties: Odelein, Mtl (holding), 2.42; Dionne, Mtl (high-sticking),6:12; Hrudey, LA, served by Donnelly (delay of game), 11:03; Kurri, LA (holding), 15:54.

SECOND PERIOD

Scoring: 3, LA, Robitaille 8 (p play) (Blake, Gretzky), 17:41. Penalties: Granato, LA (interference), 5:08; Taylor, LA (roughing), 6:23; Muller, Mtl (roughing), 6:23; McSorley, LA (unsportsmanlike conduct), 7:16; Odelein, Mtl (unsportsmanlike conduct), 7:16;

Damphousse, Mtl (slashing), 10:23; Millen, LA (high-sticking), 17:23; Desjardins, Mtl (high-sticking), 17:23; Brisebois, Mtl (holding), 17:23; Roy, Mtl, served by LeClair (delay of game), 18:33; Gretzky, LA (hooking), 19:32.

THIRD PERIOD

Scoring: 4, LA, Kurri 9 (Gretzky, Granato), 1:51.5, LA, Gretzky 14 (empty net) (Sandstrom), 18:02. Penalties: Huddy, LA (hooking), 6:41; Daigneault, Mtl (cross-checking), 18:41.

Shots on goal: LA—11-20-7—38. Mtl—11-10-11—32. Power-play opportunities: LA 2-of-6; Mtl 0-of-5. Goalies: LA, Hrudey (32 shots, 31 saves). Mtl, Roy (37 shots, 34 saves). A: 17,959.
Referee: vanHellemond. Linesmen: Gauthier Scapinello.

Game 2

```
Los Angeles .....0    1    1    0—2
Montreal .........1    0    1    1—3
```

FIRST PERIOD

Scoring: 1, Mtl, Desjardins 2 (Damphousse, Lebeau), 18:31. Penalties: Odelein, Mtl (roughing), 5:57; Robitaille, LA (hooking), 6:40; Brisebois, Mtl (interference), 7:05; Blake, LA (tripping), !0:25; Roy, Mtl, served by Bellows (high-sticking), 10:38; Watters, LA (holding stick), 13:01; Muller, Mtl (tripping), 13:01; Sydor, LA (holding), 14:44; Schneider, Mtl (holding stick), 17:02; Granato, LA (holding), 17:53.

SECOND PERIOD

Scoring: 2, LA, Taylor 3 (shorthanded), 5:12. Penalties: Muller, Mtl (cross-checking), :35; Huddy, LA (cross-checking), 4:20; McSorley, LA (roughing), 9:43; Damphousse, Mtl (roughing), 9:43; Robitaille, LA (roughing), 16:02; Dionne, Mtl (roughing), 16:02.

THIRD PERIOD

Scoring: 3, LA, Conacher 6 (Taylor, Granato), 8:32. 4, Mtl, Desjardins 3 (p play) (Damphousse, Schneider), 18:47. Penalties: Brunet, Mtl (slashing), 1:31; Damphousse, Mtl (cross-checking), 2:13; Zhitnik, LA (tripping), 4:17; Taylor, LA (goalie int.), 11:56; Brisebois, Mtl (cross-checking), 13:16; McSorley, LA (illegal stick), 18:15.

OVERTIME

Scoring: 5, Mtl, Desjardins 4 (Brunet, Ronan), :51. Penalties: None.

Shots on goal: LA—5-9-9-1—24. Mtl—16-12-11-2—41. Power-play opportunities: LA 0-of-8; Mtl 1-of-7. Goalies:LA, Hrudey (41 shots, 38 saves). Mtl, Roy (24 shots, 22 saves). A: 17,959.
Referee: Fraser. Linesmen: Collins, Scapinello.

Game 3

```
Montreal .........1    2    0    1—4
Los Angeles .....0    3    0    0—3
```

FIRST PERIOD

Scoring: 1, Mtl, Bellows 6 (p play) (Haller, Muller), 10:26. Penalties: Zhitnik, LA (tripping), 4:23; Bellows, Mtl (cross-checking), 5:21; Desjardins, Mtl (int.), 7:40; Watters, LA (tripping), 10:21; Ronan, Mtl (goalie int.), 13:09; Lebeau, Mtl (slashing), 16:37; Blake, LA (roughing), 19:59.

SECOND PERIOD

Scoring: 2, Mtl, Dionne 6 (Keane, Lebeau), 2:41. 3, Mtl, Schneider 1 (Carbonneau), 3:02. 4, LA, Robitaille 9 (Gretzky, Sandstrom), 7:52. 5, LA, Granato 6,

11:02. 6, LA, Gretzky 15 (Donnelly, Hardy), 17:07. Penalties: Ronan, Mtl (slashing), 11:42; Taylor, LA (slashing), 11:42.

THIRD PERIOD

Scoring: None. Penalties: Lebeau, Mtl (holding), 6:48; Sandstrom, LA (goalie interference), 10:50.

OVERTIME

Scoring: 7, Mtl, LeClair 3 (Muller, Bellows), :34. Penalties: None.

Shots on goal: Mtl—12-9-12-3—36. LA—10-13-10-0—33. Power-play opportunities: Mtl 1-of-4 LA 0-of-5. Goalies: Mtl, Roy (33 shots, 30 saves).LA, Hrudey (36 shots, 32 saves). A: 16,005.
Referee: Gregson. Linesmen: Bonney, Scapinello.

Game 4

```
Montreal ..........1   1   0   1——3
Los Angeles .....0   2   0   0——2
```

FIRST PERIOD

Scoring: 1, Mtl, Muller 9, 10:57. Penalties: Conacher, LA (cross-checking), 1:53; Desjardins, Mtl (high-sticking), 4:24; Granato, LA (roughing), 4:24; Schneider, Mtl (elbowing), 16:50.

SECOND PERIOD

Scoring: 2, Mtl, Damphousse 11 (p play) (Keane, Desjardins), 5:24. 3, LA, Donnelly 6 (Granato), 6:33. 4, LA, McSorley 3 (p play) (Gretzky, Robitaille), 19:55. Penalties: Hardy, LA (holding), 3:32; McSorley, LA (roughing), 12:09;

```
Los Angeles .....0   1       0——1
Montreal ..........1   2       1——4
```

FIRST PERIOD

Scoring: 1, Mtl, DiPietro 7, (Leeman, LeClair), 15:10. Penalties: Schneider, Mtl (tripping), 4:35; Keane, Mtl (charging), 10:46; Granato, LA (tripping), 12:49; Blake, LA (roughing), 19:23; Sandstrom LA (roughing), 19:23; Ronan, Mtl (roughing), 19:23.

SECOND PERIOD

Scoring: 2, LA, McSorley 4 (Carson, Robitaille), 2:40. 3, Mtl, Muller 10 (Damphousse, Odelein), 3:51. 4, Mtl,

Sydor, LA (int.), 15:58; Bellows, Mtl (hooking), 19:10.

THIRD PERIOD

Scoring: None. Penalties: Daigneault, Mtl (cross-checking), 2:42; Schneider, Mtl (roughing), 19:30; Granato, LA (roughing), 19:30.

OVERTIME

Scoring: 5, Mtl, LeClair 4, 14:37. Penalties: None.

Shots on goal: Mtl—13-7-12-7—39. LA—6-11-15-10—42. Power-play opportunities: Mtl 1-of-3; LA 1-of-3. Goalies: Mtl, Roy (42 shots, 40 saves); LA, Hrudey (39 shots, 36 saves). A: 16,005.
Referee: vanHellemond. Linesmen: Bonney, Collins.

Game 5

Lebeau 3 (p play) (Keane, LeClair), 11:31. Penalties: Leeman, Mtl (tripping), 5:32; Damphousse, Mtl (elbowing), 7:40; Hardy, LA (holding stick.), 10:28.

THIRD PERIOD

Scoring: 5, Mtl, DiPietro 8 (Dionne, Odelein), 12:06. Penalties: None.

Shots on goal: LA—7-7-5—19. Mtl—10-12-7—29. Power-play opportunities: LA 0-of-4; Mtl 1-of-3. Goalies: LA, Hrudey (29 shots, 25 saves;); Mtl, Roy (19 shots, 18 saves). A: 17,959.
Referee: Gregson. Linesmen: Scapinello, Bonney.

Individual Playoff Leaders

Scoring

POINTS

Player and Team	GP	G	A	Pts	+/−	PM	Player and Team	GP	G	A	Pts	+/−	PM
Wayne Gretzky, LA	24	15	25	40	6	4	Mario Lemieux, Pitt	11	8	10	18	2	10
Doug Gilmour, Tor	21	10	25	35	16	30	Glenn Anderson, Tor	21	7	11	18	7	31
Tomas Sandstrom, LA	24	8	17	25	-2	12	Kirk Muller, Mtl	20	10	7	17	4	18
V Damphousse, Mtl	20	11	12	23	8	16	Steve Thomas, NYI	18	9	8	17	-1	37
Luc Robitaille, LA	24	9	13	22	-13	28	Jari Kurri, LA	24	9	8	17	2	12
Ray Ferraro, NYI	18	13	7	20	5	18	Ron Francis, Pitt	12	6	11	17	5	19
Wendel Clark, Tor	21	10	10	20	15	51	Tony Granato, LA	24	6	11	17	3	50
Dave Andreychuk, Tor	21	12	7	19	6	35							

GOALS

Player and Team	GP	G
Wayne Gretzky, LA	24	15
Ray Ferraro, NYI	18	13
Dave Andreychuk, Tor	21	12
V Damphousse, Mtl	20	11
Three players tied with 10 goals		

POWER PLAY GOALS

Player and Team	GP	PP
Brett Hull, StL	11	5
Greg Adams, Van	12	5
V Damphousse, Mtl	20	5
Seven players tied with four power play goals		

GAME WINNING GOALS

Player and Team	GP	GW
V Damphousse, Mtl	20	3
John LeClair, Mtl	20	3
Kirk Muller, Mtl	20	3
Dave Andreychuk, Tor	21	3
Wayne Gretzky, LA	24	3

SHORT HANDED GOALS

Player and Team	GP	SH
Benoit Hogue, NYI	18	2
Tom Fitzgerald, NYI	18	2
Dave Taylor, LA	22	2
Jari Kurri, LA	24	2

ASSISTS

Player and Team	GP	A
Doug Gilmour, Tor	21	25
Wayne Gretzky, LA	24	25
Tomas Sandstrom, LA	24	17
Mike Keane, Mtl	19	13
Luc Robitaille, LA	24	13
V Damphousse, Mtl	20	12

PLUS/MINUS

Player and Team	GP	+/−
Doug Gilmour, Tor	21	16
Wendel Clark, Tor	21	15
Matt Schneider, Mtl	11	10
Mike Ramsey, Pitt	12	10
Mike Keane, Mtl	19	10

* Rookie.

Goaltending (Minimum 420 minutes)

GOALS AGAINST AVERAGE

Player and Team	GP	Mins	GA	Avg
Patrick Roy, Mtl	20	1293	46	2.13
Curtis Joseph, StL	11	715	27	2.27
*Felix Potvin, Tor	21	1308	62	2.84
Tom Barrasso, Pitt	12	722	35	2.91
Glenn Healy, NYI	18	1109	59	3.19

SAVE PERCENTAGE

Player and Team	GP	Mins	GA	SA	Pct	W	L
Curtis Joseph, StL	11	715	27	438	.938	7	4
Patrick Roy, Mtl	20	1293	46	647	.929	16	4
Tom Barrasso, Pitt	12	722	35	370	.905	7	5
*Felix Potvin, Tor	21	1308	62	636	.903	11	10
Kelly Hrudey, LA	20	1261	74	656	.887	10	9
Glenn Healy, NYI	18	1109	59	524	.887	9	8

NHL Awards

Award	Player and Team
Hart Trophy (most valuable player)	Mario Lemieux, Pitt
Calder Trophy (rookie of the year)	Teemu Selanne, Winn
Vezina Trophy (top goaltender)	Ed Belfour, Chi
Norris Trophy (top defenseman)	Chris Chelios, Chi
Lady Byng Trophy (for gentlemanly play)	Pierre Turgeon, NYI
Selke Trophy (top defensive forward)	Doug Gilmour, Tor
Adams Award (top coach)	Pat Burns, Tor
Jennings Trophy (best goals against average)	Ed Belfour, Chi
Conn Smythe Trophy (playoff most valuable player)	Patrick Roy, Mtl

NHL Individual Leaders

Scoring

POINTS

Player and Team	GP	G	A	Pts	+/–	PM
Mario Lemieux, Pitt	60	69	91	160	55	38
Pat LaFontaine, Buff	84	53	95	148	11	63
Adam Oates, Bos	84	45	97	142	15	32
Steve Yzerman, Det	84	58	79	137	33	44
*Teemu Selanne, Winn	84	76	56	132	8	45
Pierre Turgeon, NYI	83	58	74	132	1-	26
Alexander Mogilny, Buff	77	76	51	127	7	40
Doug Gilmour, Tor	83	32	95	127	32	100
Luc Robitaille, LA	84	63	62	125	18	100
Mark Recchi, Phil	84	53	70	123	1	95

GOALS

Player and Team	GP	G
Alexander Mogilny, Buff	77	76
*Teemu Selanne, Winn	84	76
Mario Lemieux, Pitt	60	69
Luc Robitaille, LA	84	63
Pavel Bure, Van	83	60

GAME WINNING GOALS

Player and Team	GP	GW
Alexander Mogilny, Buff	77	11
Geof Courtnall, Van	84	11
Adam Oates, Bos	84	11
Mario Lemieux, Pitt	60	10
Mike Ricci, Que	77	10

ASSISTS

Player and Team	GP	A
Adam Oates, Bos	84	97
Doug Gilmour, Tor	83	95
Pat Lafontaine, Buff	84	95
Mario Lemieux, Pitt	60	91
Craig Janney, StL	84	82

POWER PLAY GOALS

Player and Team	GP	PP
D Andreychuk, Buff,Tor	83	32
Brett Hull, StL	80	29
Alexander Mogilny, Buff	77	27
Kevin Stevens, Pitt	72	26
Note: four tied with 24.		

SHORT HANDED GOALS

Player and Team	GP	SHG
Pavel Bure, Van	83	7
Steve Yzerman, Det	84	7
Mario Lemieux, Pitt	60	6
Scott Young, Que	82	6
Dave Reid, Bos	65	5
Dave Poulin, Bos	84	5

PLUS/MINUS

Player and Team	GP	+/–
Mario Lemieux, Pitt	60	55
Larry Murphy, Pitt	83	45
Ray Bourque, Bos	78	38
Ulf Samuelsson, Pitt	77	36
Lyle Odelein, Mtl	83	35
Pavel Bure, Van	83	35

* Rookie.

Goaltending
(Minimum 27 games)

GOALS AGAINST AVERAGE

Player and Team	GP	Mins	GA	Avg
*Felix Potvin, Tor	48	2781	116	2.50
Ed Belfour, Chi	71	4106	177	2.59
Tom Barrasso, Pitt	63	3702	186	3.01
Curtis Joseph, StL	68	3890	196	3.02
Kay Whitmore, Van	31	1817	94	3.10

WINS

Player and Team	GP	Mins	W	L	T
Tom Barrasso, Pitt	63	3702	43	14	5
Ed Belfour, Chi	71	4106	41	18	11
Andy Moog, Bos	55	3194	37	14	3
Tim Cheveldae, Det	67	3880	34	24	7
Bob Essensa, Winn	67	3855	33	26	6

SAVE PERCENTAGE

Player and Team	GP	GA	SA	Pct	W	L
Curtis Joseph, StL	68	196	2202	.911	29	28	9
*Felix Potvin, Tor	48	116	1286	,910	25	15	7
Ed Belfour, Chi	71	177	1880	.906	41	18	11
Tom Barrasso, Pitt	63	186	1885	.901	43	14	5
J Vanbiesbrouck, NYR	48	152	1525	.900	20	18	7

SHUTOUTS

Player and Team	GP	Mins	SO	W	L	T
Ed Belfour, Chi	71	4106	7	41	18	11
*T Soderstrom, Phil	44	2512	5	20	17	6
J Vanbiesbrouck, NYR	48	2757	4	20	18	7
Tom Barrasso, Pitt	63	3702	4	43	14	5
Tim Cheveldae, Det	67	3880	4	34	24	7

NHL Team-by-Team Statistical Leaders

Boston Bruins

SCORING

Player	GP	G	A	Pts	+/-	PM
Adam Oates, C	84	45	97	142	15	32
*Joe Juneau, C	84	32	70	102	23	33
Ray Bourque, D	78	19	63	82	38	40
Dmitri Kvartalnov, L	73	30	42	72	9	16
Stephen Leach, R	79	26	25	51	-6	126
Dave Poulin, C	84	16	33	49	29	62
Vladimir Ruzicka, C	60	19	22	41	-6	38
Dave Reid, L	65	20	16	36	12	10
*Ted Donato, C	82	15	20	35	2	61
Don Sweeney, D	84	7	27	34	34	68
Glen Wesley, D	64	8	25	33	-2	47
*Stephen Heinze, R	73	18	13	31	20	24
David Shaw, D	77	10	14	24	10	108
Cam Neely, R	13	11	7	18	4	25
Gord Murphy, D	49	5	12	17	-13	62
Gordie Roberts, D	65	5	12	17	23	105
*Gregori Pantaleyev, L	39	8	6	14	-6	12
*C.J. Young, R, Cal	28	3	2	5	-7	20
Bos	15	4	5	9	1	12
Total	43	7	7	14	-6	32
Darin Kimble, L	55	7	3	10	4	177
Glen Featherstone, D	34	5	5	10	6	102
Brent Hughes, L	62	5	4	9	-4	191
Peter Douris, R	19	4	4	8	5	4
Tim Sweeney, L	14	1	7	8	1	6
*Glen Murray, R	27	3	4	7	-6	8
Jim Wiemer, D	28	1	6	7	1	48
Stephane Richer, D, TB	3	0	0	0	-3	0
Bos	21	1	4	5	-6	18
Total	24	1	4	5	-9	18

GOALTENDING

Player	GP	Mins	Avg	W	L	T	SO
*Mike Bales	1	25	2.40	0	0	0	0
John Blue	23	1322	2.90	9	8	4	1
Andy Moog	55	3194	3.16	37	14	3	3
Rejean Lemelin	10	542	3.43	5	4	0	0
Team total	84	5095	3.16	51	26	7	4

*Rookie

Buffalo Sabres

SCORING

Player	GP	G	A	Pts	+/-	PM
Pat LaFontaine, C	84	53	95	148	11	63
Alexander Mogilny, R	77	76	51	127	7	40
Dale Hawerchuk, C	81	16	80	96	-17	52
Doug Bodger, D	81	9	45	54	14	87
Bob Sweeney, C, R	80	21	26	47	2	118
Randy Wood, L	82	18	25	43	6	77
Yuri Khmylev, L	68	20	19	39	6	28
Wayne Presley, R	79	15	17	32	5	96
*Richard Smehlik, D	80	4	27	31	9	59
Brad May, L	82	13	13	26	3	242
Petr Svoboda, D	40	2	24	26	3	59
Ken Sutton, D	63	8	14	22	-3	30
Dave Hannan, C	55	5	15	20	8	43
Donald Audette, R	44	12	7	19	-8	51
Bob Errey, L, Pitt	54	8	6	14	-2	76
Buf	8	1	3	4	2	4
Total	62	9	9	18	0	80
Grant Ledyard, D	50	2	14	16	-2	45
Gord Donnelly, R, D	60	3	8	11	5	221
Bob Corkum, R	68	6	4	10	-3	38
*Viktor Gordijuk, R	16	3	8	9	4	0
Randy Moller, D	35	2	7	9	6	83
Bill Houlder, D	15	3	5	8	5	6
Colin Patterson, R	36	4	2	6	-2	22
*Keith Carney, D	30	2	4	6	3	55
Rob Ray, L	68	3	2	5	-3	211

GOALTENDING

Player	GP	Mins	Avg	W	L	T	SO
Dominik Hasek	28	1429	3.15	11	10	4	0
Grant Fuhr, Tor	29	1665	3.14	13	9	4	1
Buf	29	1694	3.47	11	15	2	0
Totals	58	3359	3.31	24	23	6	1
Daren Puppa	24	1306	3.58	11	5	4	0
Tom Draper	11	664	3.70	5	6	0	0
Team total	84	5104	3.49	38	36	10	0

Calgary Flames

SCORING

Player	GP	G	A	Pts	+/–	PM
Theoren Fleury, C.	83	34	66	100	14	88
Robert Reichel, C.	80	40	48	88	25	54
Gary Suter,D	81	23	58	81	-1	112
Gary Roberts, L.	58	38	41	79	32	172
Joe Nieuwendyk, C.	79	38	37	75	9	52
Sergei Makarov, R.	71	18	39	57	0	40
Al Macinnis, D	50	11	43	54	15	61
Joel Otto, C	75	19	33	52	2	150
Paul Ranheim, L.	83	21	22	43	-4	26
Greg Paslawski, R, Phil.	60	14	19	33	0	12
Cal.	13	4	5	9	3	0
Totals	73	18	24	42	3	12
Ronnie Stern, R.	70	10	15	25	4	207
Brent Ashton, L, Bos.	26	2	2	4	0	11
Cal.	32	8	11	19	11	41
Total	58	10	13	23	11	52
*Chris Lindbergh, L.	62	9	12	21	-3	18
Roger Johansson, D	77	4	16	20	13	62
Trent Yawney, D	63	1	16	17	9	67
Frantisek Musil, D.	80	6	10	16	28	131
Brian Skrudland, C, Mtl.	23	5	3	8	1	55
Cal.	16	2	4	6	3	10
Total	39	7	7	14	4	65
Craig Berube, L.	77	4	8	12	-6	209
Michel Petit, D	35	3	9	12	-5	54
Carey Wilson, C	22	4	7	11	10	8
*Kevin Dahl, D.	61	2	9	11	9	56
Chris Dahlquist, D	74	3	7	10	0	66
Alexander Godynyuk,D.	27	3	4	7	6	19
*Todd Harkins, R.	15	2	3	5	-4	22
*Paul Kruse, L	27	2	3	5	2	41

GOALTENDING

Player	GP	Mins	Avg	W	L	T	SO
Jeff Reese	26	1311	3.20	14	4	1	1
Mike Vernon	64	3732	3.26	29	26	9	2
*Andrei Trefilov	1	65	4.62	0	0	1	0
Team Total	84	5119	3.31	43	30	11	3

Chicago Blackhawks

SCORING

Player	GP	G	A	Pts	+/–	PM
Jeremy Roenick, C.	84	50	57	107	15	86
Chris Chelios, D	84	15	58	73	14	282
Steve Larmer, R	84	35	35	70	23	48
Steve Smith, D.	78	10	47	57	12	214
Brent Sutter, C.	65	20	34	54	10	67
Christian Ruuttu, C.	84	17	37	54	14	134
Michel Goulet, L.	63	23	21	44	10	41
Dirk Graham, R	84	20	17	37	0	141
Stephane Matteau, L.	79	15	18	33	6	98
Greg Gilbert, L.	77	13	19	32	5	57
Jocelyn Lemieux, L.	81	10	21	31	5	111
Brian Noonan, R.	63	16	14	30	3	82
Bryan Marchment, D.	78	5	15	20	15	313
Frantisek Kucera, D.	71	5	14	19	7	59
Dave Christian,	60	4	14	18	6	12
Joe Murphy, R.	19	7	10	17	-3	18
Troy Murray,C, Winn	29	3	4	7	-15	34
Chi.	22	1	3	4	0	25
Totals	51	4	7	11	-15	59
Craig Muni, D, Edm.	72	0	11	11	-15	67
Chi.	9	0	0	0	1	8
Totals	81	0	11	11	-14	75
Keith Brown, D.	33	2	6	8	3	39
Rob Brown, R.	15	1	6	7	6	33
Cam Russell, D.	67	2	4	6	5	151
*Karl Dykhuis, D.	12	0	5	5	2	0

GOALTENDING

Player	GP	Mins	Avg	W	L	T	SO
Ed Belfour	71	4106	2.59	41	18	11	7
Jim Waite	20	996	2.95	6	7	1	2
Team total	84	5107	2.70	47	25	12	9

Detroit Red Wings

SCORING

Player	GP	G	A	Pts	+/–	PM
Steve Yzerman, C	84	58	79	137	33	44
Dino Ciccarelli, R	82	41	56	97	12	81
Sergei Fedorov, C	73	34	53	87	33	72
Paul Coffey, D, LA	50	8	49	57	9	50
Det.	30	4	26	30	7	27
Totals	80	12	75	87	16	77
Ray Sheppard, R.	70	32	34	66	7	29
Paul Ysebaert, L.	80	34	28	62	19	42
Steve Chiasson, D.	79	12	50	62	14	155
*Dallas Drake, C.	72	18	26	44	15	93
Bob Probert, R	80	14	29	43	-9	292
Nicklas Lidstrom, D.	84	7	34	41	7	28
Yves Racine, D.	80	9	31	40	10	80
Shawn Burr, L.	80	10	25	35	18	74
Mark Howe, D	60	3	31	34	22	22
Keith Primeau, L.	73	15	17	32	-6	152
Sheldon Kennedy, R	68	19	11	30	-1	46
Gerard Gallant, L	67	10	20	30	20	188

Player	GP	G	A	Pts	+/–	PM
Vlad Konstantinov, D.	82	5	17	22	22	137
*Mike Sillinger, C.	51	4	17	21	0	16
*Jim Hiller, R, LA	40	6	6	12	0	90
Det.	21	2	6	8	7	19
Totals	61	8	12	20	7	109
Steve Konroyd, D, Har	59	3	11	14	-16	63
Det.	6	0	1	1	1	4
Totals	65	3	12	15	-15	67
Brad McCrimmon, D	60	1	14	15	21	71
John Ogrodnick, L	19	6	6	12	-2	2

GOALTENDING

Player	GP	Mins	Avg	W	L	T	S
Vincent Riendeau	22	1193	3.22	13	4	2	0
Tim Cheveldae	67	3880	3.25	34	24	7	4
Team total	84	5088	3.30	47	28	9	4

* Rookie.

Edmonton Oilers

SCORING

Player	GP	G	A	Pts	+/-	PM
Petr Klima, L	68	32	16	48	-15	100
Doug Weight, C, NYR	65	15	25	40	4	55
Edm	13	2	6	8	-2	10
Totals	78	17	31	48	2	65
Shayne Corson, L	80	16	31	47	-19	209
Craig Simpson, L	60	24	22	46	-14	36
Dave Manson, D	83	15	30	45	-28	210
Todd Elik, C, Minn	46	13	18	31	-5	48
Edm	14	1	9	10	1	8
Totals	60	14	27	41	-4	56
Zdeno Ciger, L, NJ	27	4	8	12	-8	2
Edm	37	9	15	24	-5	6
Totals	64	13	23	36	-13	8
Brian Benning, D, Phi	37	9	17	26	0	93
Edm	18	1	7	8	-1	59
Totals	55	10	24	34	-1	152
Scott Mellanby, R	69	15	17	32	-4	147
Kelly Buchberger, L	83	12	18	30	-27	133
Craig MacTavish, C	82	10	20	30	-16	11
Igor Kravchuk, D, Chi	38	6	9	15	11	30
Edm	17	4	8	12	-8	2
Totals	55	10	17	27	3	32
Martin Gelinas, L	65	11	12	23	3	30
Kevin Todd, C, NJ	30	5	5	10	-4	16
Edm	25	4	9	13	-5	10
Totals	55	9	14	23	-9	26
*Shjon Podein, C	40	13	6	19	-2	25
Geoff Smith, D	78	4	14	18	-11	30
Brian Glynn, D	64	4	12	16	-13	60
Luke Richardson, D	82	3	10	13	-18	142
Chris Joseph, D	33	2	10	12	-9	48
*Vladimir Vujtek, L	30	1	10	11	-1	8
Louie Debrusk, L	51	8	2	10	-16	205
*Brad Werenka, D	27	5	3	8	1	24

GOALTENDING

Player	GP	Mins	Avg	W	L	T	SO
Bill Ranford	67	3753	3.84	17	38	6	1
Ron Tugnutt	26	1338	4.17	9	12	2	0
Team total	84	5099	3.97	26	50	8	1

Hartford Whalers

SCORING

Player	GP	G	A	Pts	+/-	PM
Geoff Sanderson, C	82	46	43	89	-21	28
Andrew Cassels, C	84	21	64	85	-11	62
Pat Verbeek, R	84	39	43	82	-7	197
Zarley Zalapski, D	83	14	51	65	-34	94
Terry Yake, C	66	22	31	53	3	46
*Patrick Poulin, L	81	20	31	51	-19	37
Eric Weinrich, D	79	7	29	36	-11	76
*Mikael Nylander, C	59	11	22	33	-7	36
Mark Janssens, C. L	76	12	17	29	-15	237
Nick Kypreos, L	75	17	10	27	-5	325
Robert Kron, L, Van	32	10	11	21	10	14
Har	13	4	2	6	-5	4
Totals	45	14	13	27	5	18
Yvon Corriveau, L, SJ	20	3	7	10	-7	0
Har	37	5	5	10	-13	14
Totals	57	8	12	20	-20	14
Adam Burt, D	65	6	14	20	-11	116
Randy Cunneyworth, L	39	5	4	9	-1	63
*Robert Petrovicky, C	42	3	6	9	-10	45
Jim McKenzie, L	64	3	6	9	-10	202
*Dan Keczmer, D	23	4	4	8	-3	28
Doug Houda, D	60	2	6	8	-19	167
*Mark Greig, R	22	1	7	8	-11	27
*Joe Day, L	24	1	7	8	-8	47
Randy Ladouceur, D	62	2	4	6	-18	109
Tim Kerr, R	22	0	6	6	-11	7
Jamie Leach, R, Pitt	5	0	0	0	-2	2
Har	19	3	2	5	-5	2
Totals	24	3	2	5	-7	4
Allen Pedersen, D	59	1	4	5	0	60

GOALTENDING

Player	GP	Mins	Avg	W	L	T	SO
*Corrie D'Alessio	1	11	.00	0	0	0	0
*Mike Lenarduzzi	3	168	3.21	1	1	0	0
Mario Gosselin	16	867	3.94	5	9	1	0
Sean Burke	50	2656	4.16	16	27	3	0
Frank Pietrangelo	30	1373	4.85	4	15	1	0
Team total	84	5097	4.34	26	52	6	0

Los Angeles Kings

SCORING

Player	GP	G	A	Pts	+/-	PM
Luc Robitaille, L	84	63	62	125	18	100
Jari Kurri, L	82	27	60	87	19	38
Tony Granato, L	81	37	45	82	-1	171
Jimmy Carson, C, Det	52	25	26	51	0	18
LA	34	12	10	22	-2	14
Totals	86	37	36	73	-2	32
Mike Donnelly, L	84	29	40	69	17	45
Wayne Gretzky, C	45	16	49	65	6	6
Rob Blake, D	76	16	43	59	18	152
Tomas Sandstrom, R	39	25	27	52	12	57
*Alexei Zhitnik, D	78	12	36	48	-3	80
Marty McSorley, D	81	15	26	41	1	39
Corey Millen, C	42	23	16	39	16	42
*Darryl Sydor, D	80	6	23	29	-2	63
Charlie Huddy, D	82	2	25	27	16	64
*Lonnie Loach, L, Ott	3	0	0	0	0	0
LA	50	10	13	23	3	27
Totals	53	10	13	23	3	27
Pat Conacher, L	81	9	8	17	-16	20
Dave Taylor, R	48	6	9	15	1	49
Mark Hardy, D, NYR	44	1	10	11	2	85
LA	11	0	3	3	-4	4
Totals	55	1	13	14	-2	89
Warren Rychel, L	70	6	7	13	-15	314
*Gary Shuchuk, C	25	2	4	6	0	16

GOALTENDING

Player	GP	Mins	Avg	W	L	T	SO
*Robb Stauber	31	1735	3.84	15	8	4	0
Kelly Hrudey	50	2718	3.86	18	21	6	2
Rick Knickle	10	532	3.95	6	4	0	0
*Dave Goverde	2	98	7.96	0	2	0	0
Team total	84	5098	4.00	39	35	10	2

* Rookie.

Minnesota North Stars

SCORING

Player	GP	G	A	Pts	+/–	PM
Modano Mike, R	82	33	60	93	-7	83
Russ Courtnall, R	84	36	43	79	1	49
Dave Gagner, C	84	33	43	76	-13	141
Ulf Dahlen, R	83	35	39	74	-20	6
Mark Tinordi, D	69	15	27	42	-1	157
Michael McPhee, L	84	18	22	40	-2	44
Mike Craig, R	70	15	23	38	-11	106
Tommy Sjodin, D	77	7	29	36	-25	30
Neal Broten, C	82	12	21	33	7	22
Gaetan Duchesne, L	84	16	13	29	6	32
*Trent Klatt, R	47	4	19	23	2	38
Jim Johnson, D	79	3	20	23	9	105
Brent Gilchrist, C, Edm	60	10	10	20	-10	47
Minn	8	0	1	1	-2	2
Totals	68	10	11	21	-12	49
Shane Churla, R	73	5	16	21	-8	286
Derian Hatcher, D	67	4	15	19	-27	178
Stewart Gavin, R	63	10	8	18	-4	59
Bobby Smith, C	45	5	7	12	-9	10
Craig Ludwig, D	78	1	10	11	1	153
Brian Propp, L	17	3	3	6	-10	0
*Richard Matvichuk, D	53	2	3	5	-8	26
Mark Osiecki, D, Ott	34	0	4	4	-21	12
Winn	4	1	0	1	1	2
Minn	5	0	0	0	0	5
Totals	43	1	4	5	-20	19

GOALTENDING

Player	GP	Mins	Avg	W	L	T	SO
Jon Casey	60	3476	3.33	26	26	5	3
Darcy Wakaluk	29	1596	3.65	10	12	5	1
Team total	84	5090	3.45	36	38	10	4

Montreal Canadiens

SCORING

Player	GP	G	A	Pts	+/–	PM
Vincent Damphousse, L	84	39	58	97	5	98
Kirk Muller, L	80	37	57	94	8	77
Brian Bellows, L	82	40	48	88	4	44
Stephan Lebeau, C	71	31	49	80	23	20
Mike Keane, R	77	15	45	60	29	95
Denis Savard, C	63	16	34	50	1	90
Gilbert Dionne, L	75	20	28	48	5	63
Eric Desjardins, C	82	13	32	45	20	98
John LeClair, L	72	19	25	44	11	33
Mathieu Schneider, D	60	13	31	44	8	91
Gary Leeman, R, Cal	30	9	5	14	5	10
Mtl	20	6	12	18	9	14
Totals	50	15	17	32	14	24
Patrice Brisebois, D	70	10	21	31	6	79
Kevin Haller, D	73	11	14	25	7	117
Benoit Brunet, L	47	10	15	25	13	19
J.J. Daigneault, D	66	8	10	18	25	57
Rob Ramage, D, TB	66	5	12	17	-21	138
Mtl	8	0	1	1	-3	8
Totals	74	5	13	18	-24	146
Paul DiPietro, C	29	4	13	17	11	14
Guy Carbonneau, C	61	4	13	17	-9	20
Lyle Odelein, D	83	2	14	16	35	205
Todd Ewen, R	75	5	9	14	6	193
*Ed Ronan, R	53	5	7	12	6	20
Mario Roberge, L	50	4	4	8	2	142
*Sean Hill, D	31	2	6	8	-5	54
Jesse Belanger	19	4	2	6	1	4

GOALTENDING

Player	GP	Mins	Avg	W	L	T	SO
*Frederic Chabot	1	40	1.50	0	0	0	0
Patrick Roy	62	3595	3.20	31	25	5	2
Andre Racicot	26	1433	3.39	17	5	1	1
Team total	84	5086	3.30	48	30	6	3

New Jersey Devils

SCORING

Player	GP	G	A	Pts	+/–	PM
Claude Lemieux, R	77	30	51	81	3	155
Alexander Semak, C	82	37	42	79	24	70
Stephane Richer, R	78	38	35	73	-1	44
Valeri Zelepukin	78	23	41	64	19	70
Bernie Nicholls, C, Edm	46	8	32	40	-16	40
NJ	23	5	15	20	3	40
Totals	69	13	47	60	-13	80
Scott Stevens, D	81	12	45	57	14	120
Bruce Driver, D	83	14	40	54	-10	66
John MacLean, R	80	24	24	48	-6	102
Peter Stastny, C	62	17	23	40	-5	22
*Scott Niedermayer, D	80	11	29	40	8	47
Bobby Holik, R	61	20	19	39	-6	76
*Bill Guerin, C	65	14	20	34	14	63
Viacheslav Fetisov, D	76	4	23	27	7	158
Randy McKay, R	73	11	11	22	0	206

* Rookie.

Player	GP	G	A	Pts	+/–	PM
*Scott Pellerin, L	45	10	11	21	-1	41
Tom Chorske, R	50	7	12	19	-1	25
Alexei Kasatonov, D	64	3	14	17	4	57
Dave Barr, R	62	6	8	14	1	61
Janne Ojanen, C	31	4	9	13	-2	14
Ken Daneyko, D	84	2	11	13	4	236
Troy Mallette, C	34	4	3	7	3	56
Tommy Abelin, D	36	1	5	6	0	14
Doug Brown, R	15	0	5	5	3	2

GOALTENDING

Player	GP	Mins	Avg	W	L	T	SO
Chris Terreri	48	2672	3.39	19	21	3	2
Craig Billington	42	2389	3.67	21	16	4	2
Team total	84	5080	3.53	40	37	7	4

New York Islanders

SCORING

Player	GP	G	A	Pts	+/–	PM
Pierre Turgeon, C	83	58	74	132	-1	26
Steve Thomas, L	79	37	50	87	3	111
Derek King, L	77	38	38	76	-3	47
Benoit Hogue, C	70	33	42	75	13	108
Patrick Flatley, L	80	13	47	60	4	63
*Vladimir Malakhov, D	64	14	38	52	14	59
Jeff Norton, D	66	12	38	50	-3	45
Uwe Krupp,D	80	9	29	38	7	67
Tom Kurvers, D	52	8	30	38	8	38
Brian Mullen, R	81	18	14	32	5	28
Brad Dalgarno, R	57	15	17	32	17	62
*Marty McInnis, C	56	10	20	30	7	24
Ray Ferraro, C	46	14	13	27	0	40
Tom Fitzgerald, R	77	9	18	27	-2	34
*Travis Green, R	61	7	18	25	4	43
*Scott LaChance, D	75	7	17	24	-1	67
David Volek, L	56	8	13	21	-1	34
*Darius Kasparaitis, D	79	4	17	21	15	166
Claude Loiselle, C	41	5	3	8	-5	90
Dan Marois, R	28	2	5	7	-3	35
Mick Vukota, R	74	2	5	7	3	216
Dennis Vaske, D	27	1	5	6	9	32
*Ian Fraser, C	7	2	2	4	-1	2
Richard Pilon, D	44	1	3	4	-4	164
Rich Kromm, L	1	1	2	3	3	0

GOALTENDING

Player	GP	Mins	Avg	W	L	T	SO
Glenn Healy	47	2655	3.30	22	20	2	1
Mark Fitzpatrick	39	2253	3.46	17	15	5	0
*Danny Lorenz	4	157	3.82	1	2	0	0
Team total	84	5087	3.50	40	37	7	1

New York Rangers

SCORING

Player	GP	G	A	Pts	+/–	PM
Mark Messier, C	75	25	66	91	-6	72
Tony Amonte, R	83	33	43	76	0	49
Mike Gartner, R	84	45	23	68	-4	59
Adam Graves, C	84	36	29	65	-4	148
Sergei Nemchinov, C	81	23	31	54	15	34
Darren Turcotte, C	71	25	28	53	-3	40
Ed Olczyk, C, Winn	25	8	12	20	-11	26
NYR	46	13	16	29	9	26
Totals	71	21	28	49	-2	52
Esa Tikkanen, L, Edm	66	14	19	33	-11	76
NYR	15	2	5	7	-13	18
Totals	81	16	24	40	-24	94
*Alexei Kovalev	65	20	18	38	-10	79
Brian Leetch, D	36	6	30	36	2	26
*Sergei Zubov, D	49	8	23	31	-1	4
James Patrick, D	60	5	21	26	1	61
Phil Bourque,	55	6	14	20	-9	39
Jeff Beukeboom, D	82	2	17	19	9	153
Jan Erixon, L	45	5	11	16	11	10
Peter Andersson, D	31	4	11	15	4	18
Kevin Lowe, D	49	3	12	15	-2	58
Paul Broten, L	60	5	9	14	-6	48
*Steven King, L	24	7	5	12	4	16
Jay Wells, D	53	1	9	10	-2	107
Joe Cirella, D	55	3	6	9	1	85
Joey Kocur, R	65	3	6	9	-9	131
*Mike Hurlbut, D	23	1	8	9	4	16

GOALTENDING

Player	GP	Mins	Avg	W	L	T	SO
J Vanbiesbrouck	48	2757	3.31	20	18	7	4
*Corey Hirsch	4	224	3.75	1	2	1	0
Mike Richter	38	2105	3.82	13	19	3	1
Team total	84	5107	3.62	34	39	11	5

Ottawa Senators

SCORING

Player	GP	G	A	Pts	+/–	PM
Norm Maciver, D	80	17	46	63	-46	84
Jamie Baker, C	76	19	29	48	-20	54
Sylvain Turgeon, L	72	25	18	43	-29	104
Bob Kudelski, R, LA	15	3	3	6	-3	8
Ott	48	21	14	35	-22	22
Totals	63	24	17	41	-25	30
Brad Shaw, D	81	7	34	41	-47	34
Jody Hull, R	69	13	21	34	-24	14
Mark Lamb, C	71	7	19	26	-40	64
Mike Peluso, L	81	15	10	25	-35	318
Mark Freer, C	63	10	14	24	-35	39
Neil Brady, C	55	7	17	24	-25	57
Andrew McBain, R	59	7	16	23	-37	43
Laurie Boschman, C	70	9	7	16	-26	101
*Darren Rumble, D	69	3	13	16	-24	61
Dave Archibald, C, L	44	9	6	15	-16	32

* Rookie.

Player	GP	G	A	Pts	+/–	PM
Doug Smail, L	51	4	10	14	-34	51
Tomas Jelinek, R	49	7	6	13	-21	52
*Christopher Luongo, D	76	3	9	12	-47	68
Jeff Lazaro, L	26	6	4	10	-8	16
Rob Murphy, C	44	3	7	10	-23	30
*Darcy Loewen, L	79	4	5	9	-26	145
Ken Hammond, D	62	4	4	8	-42	104
Gord Dineen, D	32	2	4	6	-19	30
Brad Marsh, D	59	0	3	3	-29	30

GOALTENDING

Player	GP	Mins	Avg	W	L	T	SO
Daniel Berthiaume	25	1326	4.30	2	17	1	0
Peter Sidorkiewicz	64	3388	4.43	8	46	3	0
*Darrin Madeley	2	90	6.67	0	2	0	0
Steve Weeks	7	249	7.23	0	5	0	0
Team total	84	5097	4.34	26	52	6	0

Philadelphia Flyers

SCORING

Player	GP	G	A	Pts	+/–	PM
Mark Recchi, R	84	53	70	123	1	95
Rod Brind'Amour, C	81	37	49	86	-8	89
*Eric Lindros, C	61	41	34	75	28	147
Kevin Dineen, R	83	35	28	63	14	201
Garry Galley, D	83	13	49	62	18	115
Brent Fedyk, R	74	21	38	59	14	48
Per-Erik Eklund, C	55	11	38	49	12	16
Greg Hawgood, D, Edm	29	5	13	18	-1	35
Phil	40	6	22	28	-7	39
Totals	69	11	35	46	-8	74
Josef Beranek, C, Edm	26	2	6	8	-7	28
Phil	40	13	12	25	-1	50
Totals	66	15	18	33	-8	78
*Dimitri Yushkevich, D	82	5	27	32	12	71
Keith Acton, C	83	8	15	23	-10	51
Doug Evans, L	65	8	13	21	-9	70
Andrei Lomakin, L	51	8	12	20	15	34
Terry Carkner, D	83	3	16	19	18	150
Ric Natress, D	44	7	10	17	1	29
*Vyatcheslav Butsayev, C	52	2	14	16	3	61
*Ryan McGill, D	72	3	10	13	9	238
Dave Snuggerud, L, SJ	25	4	5	9	-3	14
Phil	14	0	2	2	0	0
Totals	39	4	7	11	-3	14
Claude Boivin, L	30	5	4	9	-5	76
Gord Hynes, D	37	3	4	7	-3	16
Allan Conroy, C	21	3	2	5	-1	17

GOALTENDING

Player	GP	Mins	Avg	W	L	T	SO
*T. Soderstrom	44	2512	3.42	20	17	6	5
*Dominic Roussel	34	1769	3.76	13	11	5	1
S Beauregard	16	802	4.41	3	9	0	0
Team total	84	5105	3.75	36	37	11	6

Pittsburgh Penguins

SCORING

Player	GP	G	A	Pts	+/–	PM
Mario Lemieux, C	60	69	91	160	55	38
Kevin Stevens, L	72	55	56	111	17	177
Rick Tocchet, R	80	48	61	109	28	252
Ron Francis, C	84	24	76	100	6	68
Jaromir Jagr, R	81	34	60	94	30	61
Larry Murphy, D	83	22	63	85	45	73
Joe Mullen, R	72	33	37	70	19	14
*Shawn McEachern, C	84	28	33	61	21	46
Ulf Samuelsson, D	77	3	26	29	36	249
Dave Tippett, C	74	6	19	25	5	56
Troy Loney, L	82	5	16	21	1	99
Jim Paek, D	77	3	15	18	13	64
Paul Stanton, D	77	4	12	16	7	97
*Martin Straka, C	42	3	13	16	2	29
Peter Taglianetti, D, TB	61	1	8	9	8	150
Pitt	11	1	4	5	4	34
Totals	72	2	12	14	12	184
*Mike Needham, R	56	8	5	13	-1	14
Mike Stapleton, C	78	4	9	13	-8	10
Mike Ramsey, D, Buf	33	2	8	10	4	20
Pitt	12	1	2	3	13	8
Totals	45	3	10	13	17	28
Jeff Daniels, L	58	5	4	9	-5	14
Kjell Samuelsson, D	63	3	6	9	25	106
Grant Jennings, D	58	0	5	5	6	65
Bryan Fogarty, D	12	0	4	4	-3	4

GOALTENDING

Player	GP	Mins	Avg	W	L	T	SO
Tom Barrasso	63	3702	3.01	43	14	5	4†
Ken Wregget	25	1368	3.42	13	7	2	0
Team total	84	5083	3.16	56	21	7	5

†Tom Barrasso and Ken Wregget shared a shutout vs. Boston, Feb. 8, 1993.

Quebec Nordiques

SCORING

Player	GP	G	A	Pts	+/–	PM
Mats Sundin, R	80	47	67	114	21	96
Joe Sakic, C	78	48	57	105	-3	40
Steve Duchesne, D	82	20	62	82	15	57
Mike Ricci, C	77	27	51	78	8	123
Owen Nolan, R	73	36	41	77	-1	185
*Andrey Kovalenko,	81	27	41	68	13	57
Scott Young, D	82	30	30	60	5	20
*Martin Rucinsky, L	77	18	30	48	16	51
Valeri Kamensky, L	32	15	22	37	13	14
Claude Lapointe, C	74	10	26	36	5	98
Curtis Leschyshyn, D	82	9	23	32	25	61
Mike Hough, L	77	8	22	30	-11	69
Alexei Gusarov, D	79	8	22	30	18	57
Gino Cavallini, L	67	9	15	24	10	34
Kerry Huffman, D	52	4	18	22	0	54
Adam Foote, D	81	4	12	16	6	168
Scott Pearson, L	41	13	1	14	3	95
Steven Finn, D	80	5	9	14	-3	160
*Bill Lindsay, L	44	4	9	13	0	16
Mikhail Tatarinov, D	28	2	6	8	6	28
Craig Wolanin, D	24	1	4	5	9	49

GOALTENDING

Player	GP	Mins	Avg	W	L	T	SO
Stephane Fiset	37	1939	3.40	18	9	4	0
Ron Hextall	54	2988	3.45	29	16	5	0
Jacques Cloutier	3	154	3.90	0	2	1	0
Team total	84	5100	3.53	47	27	10	0

* Rookie.

St Louis Blues

SCORING

Player	GP	G	A	Pts	+/-	PM
Craig Janney, C	84	24	82	106	-4	12
Brett Hull, R	80	54	47	101	-27	41
Brendan Shanahan, R	71	51	43	94	10	174
Jeff Brown, D	71	25	53	78	-6	58
Nelson Emerson, C	82	22	51	73	2	62
Kevin Miller, L, Wash	10	0	3	3	-4	35
StL	72	24	22	46	6	65
Totals	82	24	25	49	2	100
Doug Crossman, D, TB	40	8	21	29	-4	18
StL	19	2	7	9	-3	10
Totals	59	10	28	38	-7	28
Rich Sutter, R	84	13	14	27	-4	100
Ron Sutter, C	59	12	15	27	-11	99
*Igor Korolev, R	74	4	23	27	-1	20
Bob Bassen, C	53	9	10	19	0	63
Ron Wilson, C	78	8	11	19	-8	0
Garth Butcher, D	68	5	15	20	5	189
Rick Zombo, D	71	0	15	15	-2	78
Dave Lowry, L	58	5	8	13	-18	101
*Philippe Bozon, C	54	6	6	12	-3	55
Stephane Quintal, D	75	1	10	11	-6	100
Lee Norwood, D	32	3	7	10	-5	63
Basil McRae, L, TB	14	2	3	5	-3	71
StL	33	1	4	4	-13	98
Totals	47	3	6	9	-16	169
*Brett Hedican, D	42	0	8	8	-2	30
Kelly Chase, R	49	2	5	7	-9	204
*Vitali Prokhorov, L	26	4	1	5	-4	15
Dave Mackey, L	15	1	4	5	-3	23

GOALTENDING

Player	GP	Mins	Avg	W	L	T	SO
Curtis Joseph	68	3890	3.02	29	28	9	1
Guy Hebert	24	1210	3.67	8	8	2	1
Team total	84	5109	3.26	37	36	11	2

San Jose Sharks

SCORING

Player	GP	G	A	Pts	+/-	PM
Kelly Kisio, C	78	26	52	78	-15	90
Johan Garpenlov, L	79	22	44	66	-26	56
*Rob Gaudreau, R	59	23	20	43	-18	18
Dean Evason, C	84	12	19	31	-35	132
Pat Falloon, R	41	14	14	28	-25	12
Jeff Odgers, L	66	12	15	27	-26	253
*Sandis Ozolnich, D	37	7	16	23	-9	40
*Ed Courtenay, R	39	7	13	20	-15	10
*Tom Pederson, D	44	7	13	20	-16	31
Doug Wilson, D	42	3	17	20	-28	40
Mark Pederson, L, Phi	14	3	4	7	-2	6
SJ	27	7	3	10	-20	22
Totals	41	10	7	17	-22	28
John Carter, L	55	7	9	16	-25	81
*Doug Zmolek, D	84	5	10	15	-50	229
Mike Sullivan, C	81	6	8	14	-42	30
David Williams, D	40	1	11	12	-27	49
Jay More, D	73	5	6	11	-35	179
*Ray Whitney, C	26	4	6	10	-14	4
Brian Lawton, C	21	2	8	10	-9	12
David Maley, C, Edm	13	1	1	2	-3	29
SJ	43	1	6	7	-25	126
Totals	56	2	7	9	-28	155

GOALTENDING

Player	GP	Mins	Avg	W	L	T	SO
*Arturs Irbe	36	2074	4.11	7	26	0	1
*Wade Flaherty	1	60	5.00	0	1	0	0
Jeff Hackett	36	2000	5.28	2	30	1	0
Brian Hayward	18	930	5.55	2	14	1	0
Team total	84	5077	4.89	11	71	2	1

Tampa Bay Lightning

SCORING

Player	GP	G	A	Pts	+/-	PM
Brian Bradley, C	80	42	44	86	-24	92
John Tucker, C	78	17	39	56	-12	69
Chris Kontos, C	66	27	24	51	-7	12
*Rob Zamuner, L	84	15	28	43	-25	74
Adam Creighton, C	83	19	20	39	-19	110
Shawn Chambers, D	55	10	29	39	-21	36
Bob Beers, D	64	12	24	36	-25	70
Marc Bureau, C	63	10	21	31	-12	111
Mikael Andersson, L	77	16	11	27	-14	14
Danton Cole, R	67	12	15	27	-2	23
Rob Dimaio, C	54	9	15	24	0	62
*Roman Hamrlik, D	67	6	15	21	-21	71
Steve Maltais, L	63	7	13	20	-20	35
Marc Bergevin, D	78	2	12	14	-16	66
Joe Reekie, D	42	2	11	13	2	69
Steve Kasper, C, Phil	21	1	3	4	-4	2
TB	47	3	4	7	-13	18
Totals	68	4	7	11	-17	20
Ken Hodge, C	25	2	7	9	-6	2
Randy Gilhen, C, NYR	33	3	2	5	-8	8
TB	11	0	2	2	-6	6
Totals	44	3	4	7	-14	14
Jason Lafreniere, C	11	3	3	6	-6	4
Tim Bergland, L	27	3	3	6	-5	11
*Chris Lipuma, D	15	0	5	5	1	34
Matt Hervey, D	17	0	4	4	-6	38

GOALTENDING

Player	GP	Mins	Avg	W	L	T	SO
J.C. Bergeron	21	1163	3.66	8	10	1	0
Wendell Young	31	1591	3.66	7	19	2	0
Pat Jablonski	43	2268	3.97	8	24	4	1
*Dave Littman	1	45	9.33	0	1	0	0
Team total	84	5088	3.92	23	54	7	1

* Rookie.

Toronto Maple Leafs

SCORING

Player	GP	G	A	Pts	+/-	PM
Doug Gilmour, C 83		32	95	127	32	100
D. Andreychuk, L, Buf...52		29	32	61	-8	48
Tor 31		25	13	38	12	8
Totals.........83		54	45	99	4	56
Nikolai Borschevsky, R .78		34	40	74	33	28
Glenn Anderson, R.......76		22	43	65	19	117
John Cullen, C, Har.......19		5	4	9	-15	58
Tor.............47		13	28	41	-8	53
Totals.........66		18	32	50	-23	111
Todd Gill, D 69		11	32	43	4	66
Dave Ellett, D 70		6	34	40	19	46
Mike Krushelnyski, C....84		19	20	39	3	62
Wendel Clark, L......66		17	22	39	2	193
Rob Pearson, R...........78		23	14	37	-2	211
Peter Zezel, C 70		12	23	35	0	24
Dimitri Mironov, D........59		7	24	31	-1	40
Mark Osborne, L 76		12	14	26	-7	89
Bill Berg, L, NYI...........22		6	3	9	4	49
Tor.............58		7	8	15	-1	54
Totals.........80		13	11	24	3	103
*Drake Berehowsky, D..41		4	15	19	1	61
Jamie Macoun, D.......77		4	15	19	3	55
Dave McIlwain, C 66		14	4	18	-18	30
Mike Foligno, R 55		13	5	18	2	84
Bob Rouse, D.............82		3	11	14	7	130
Sylvain Lefebvre, D.....81		2	12	14	8	90
Joe Sacco, L 23		4	4	8	-4	8
*Mike Eastwood, C......12		1	6	7	-2	21

GOALTENDING

Player	GP	Mins	Avg	W	L	T	SO
Darren Puppa, Buf.24		1306	3.58	11	5	4	0
Tor 8		479	2.25	6	2	0	2
Totals.................32		1785	3.20	17	7	4	2
*Felix Potvin..........48		2781	2.50	25	15	7	2
Rick Wamsley........3		160	5.63	0	3	0	0
Team total.............84		5097	2.84	44	29	11	5

Vancouver Canucks

SCORING

Player	GP	G	A	Pts	+/-	PM
Pavel Bure, L................83		60	50	110	35	69
Cliff Ronning, C.............79		29	56	85	19	30
Geoff Courtnall, L........84		31	46	77	27	167
Murray Craven, C, Har..67		25	42	67	-4	20
Van.............10		0	10	10	3	12
Totals.........77		25	52	77	-1	32
Trevor Linden, R...........84		33	39	72	19	64
Petr Nedved, C 84		38	33	71	20	96
Greg Adams, L.............53		25	31	56	31	14
*Dixon Ward, R............70		22	30	52	34	82
Anatoli Semenov, L, TB.13		2	3	5	-5	4
Van.............62		10	34	44	21	28
Totals.........75		12	37	49	16	32
Jyrki Lumme, D 74		8	36	44	30	55
Sergio Momesso, L.....84		18	20	38	11	200
Jim Sandlak, R 59		10	18	28	2	122
Adrien Plavsic, D..........57		6	21	27	28	53
*Jiri Slegr, D 41		4	22	26	16	109
Doug Lidster, D...........71		6	19	25	9	36
Gerald Diduck, D.........80		6	14	20	32	171
Dave Babych, D..........43		3	16	19	6	44
Gino Odjick, L..............75		4	13	17	3	370
Dana Murzyn, D...........79		5	11	16	34	196
Tom Fergus, C.............36		5	9	14	1	20
Garry Valk, L................48		6	7	13	6	77
Tim Hunter, R, Que 48		5	3	8	-4	94
Van.............26		0	4	1	1	99
Totals.........74		5	7	12	-3	193
Robert Dirk, D 69		4	8	12	25	150

GOALTENDING

Player	GP	Mins	Avg	W	L	T	SO
Kay Whitmore.......31		1817	3.10	18	8	4	1
Kirk McLean....54		3261	3.39	28	21	5	3
Team total.............84		5087	3.28	46	29	9	4

Washington Capitals

SCORING

Player	GP	G	A	Pts	+/-	PM
Peter Bondra, R...........83		37	48	85	8	70
Mike Ridley, C..............84		26	56	82	5	44
Kevin Hatcher, D..........83		34	45	79	-7	114
Dale Hunter, C 84		20	59	79	3	198
Michal Pivonka, C 69		21	53	74	14	66
Dimitri Khristich, C 64		31	36	67	29	28
Al Iafrate, D 81		25	41	66	15	169
Pat Elynuik, R..............80		22	35	57	3	66
Sylvain Cote, D............77		21	29	50	28	34
Kelly Miller, L...............84		18	27	45	-2	32
Calle Johansson, D......77		7	38	45	3	56
Bobby Carpenter, L.....68		11	17	28	-16	65
*Keith Jones, R............71		12	14	26	18	124
Todd Krygier, L............77		11	12	23	-13	60
Paul Cavallini, D, StL....11		1	4	5	3	10
Wash.............71		5	8	13	3	46
Totals.........82		6	12	18	6	56
Paul MacDermid, R.......72		9	8	17	-13	80
Alan May, L..................83		6	10	16	1	268
*Steve Konowalchuk, C.36		4	7	11	4	16
Shawn Anderson, D......60		2	6	8	-2	18
*Reggie Savage, C 16		2	3	5	-4	12

GOALTENDING

Player	GP	Mins	Avg	W	L	T	SO
*Byron Dafoe..........1		1	.00	0	0	0	0
R. Tabaracci Winn 19		959	4.38	5	10	0	0
Wash.............6		343	1.75	3	2	0	2
Totals.................25		1302	3.64	8	12	0	2
Don Beaupre........58		3282	3.31	27	23	5	1
*Olaf Kolzig..........1		20	6.00	0	0	0	0
Team total.............84		5085	3.37	43	34	7	3

* Rookie.

Winnipeg Jets

SCORING

Player	GP	G	A	Pts	+/-	PM	Player	GP	G	A	Pts	+/-	PM
*Teemu Selanne, R	84	76	56	132	8	45	Igor Ulanov, D	56	2	14	16	6	124
Phil Housley, D	80	18	79	97	14	52	Tie Domi, R, NYR	12	2	0	2	-1	95
*Alexei Zhamnov, C	68	25	47	72	7	58	Winn	49	3	10	13	2	249
Thomas Steen, C	80	22	50	72	8	75	Totals	61	5	10	15	1	344
Darrin Shannon, L	84	20	40	60	-4	91	Mike Lalor, D	64	1	8	9	-10	76
Fredrik Olausson, D	68	16	41	-4	22	11	Dean Kennedy, D	78	1	7	8	-3	105
*Keith Tkachuk, R	83	28	23	51	-13	201	Bob Essensa, G	67	0	5	5	0	2
*Evgeny Davydov, L, R	79	28	21	49	-2	66	Russ Romaniuk, L	28	3	1	4	0	22
Teppo Numminen, D	66	7	30	37	4	33							
Luciano Borsato, C	67	15	20	35	-1	38							
Mike Eagles, C	84	8	18	26	-1	131							
*Sergei Bautin, D	71	5	18	23	-2	96							
Stu Barnes, C	38	12	10	2	-3	10							
John Druce, R	50	6	14	20	-4	37							
Kris King, L, NYR	30	0	3	3	-1	67							
Winn	48	8	8	16	5	136							
Totals	78	8	11	19	4	203							
Bryan Erickson, R	41	4	12	16	2	14							

* Rookie.

GOALTENDING

Player	GP	Mins	Avg	W	L	T	SO
Bob Essensa	67	3855	3.53	33	26	6	2
Jim Hrivnak Wash.	27	1421	3.50	13	9	2	0
Winn	3	180	4.33	2	1	0	0
Totals	30	1601	3.55	15	10	2	0
*Michael O'Neill	2	73	4.93	0	0	1	0
Team total	84	5082	3.78	40	37	7	2

NHL All-Star Game

	1	2	3	—	Tot
Campbell	0	2	4	—	6
Wales	6	6	4	—	16

First Period: Scoring— 1, Wales, Gartner 1 (Lowe, Oates), 3:15; 2, Wales, Gartner 2 (Oates), 3:37; 3, Wales, Bondra 1 (Oates, Gartner), 4:24; 4, Wales, Mogilny 1 (P-Play) (Bourque), 11:40; 5, Wales, Turgeon 1 (Recchi), 13:05; 6, Wales, Gartner 3 (Oates, Bondra), 13:22. Penalties—Manson, Camp (tripping), 11:12.

Second Period: Scoring—7, Wales, Tocchet 1 (K. Stevense, Recchi), :19; 8, Wales, Gartner 4 (Turgeon), 3:33; 9, Wales, Tocchet 2 (S. Stevens), 4:57; 10, Campbell, Roenick 1 (Selanne), 5:52; 11, Wales, Recchi 1 (Marsh), 9:25; 12, Campbell, Kisio 1 (Roenick, Modano), 10:15; 13, Wales, K. Stevens 1 (Recchi), 14:50; 14, Wales, Turgeon 2 (Sakic, Jagr), 17:56. Penalties—None.

Third Period: Scoring—15, Wales, LaFontaine 1 (Muller, Mogilny), 8:07; 16, Wales, Jagr 1 (Sakic, Turgeon), 9:08; 17, Wales, Marsh 1 (K.Stevens, Recchi), 12:52; 18, Campbell, Gilmour 1 (Coffey), 13:57; 19, Wales, Turgeon 3 (Sakic, S. Stevens), 15:51; 20, Campbell, Selanne 1 (Manson, Kurri), 17:03; 21, Campbell, Bure 1 (Kisio), 18:44; 22, Campbell, Bure 2, 19:32. Penalties—None.

SHOTS ON GOAL

	1	2	3	Tot
Campbell	11	15	14	41
Wales	22	15	12	49

GOALTENDERS

	Time	SA	GA	ENG	Dec
Campbell, Belfour	20:00	22	6	0	L
Campbell, Vernon	20:00	15	6	0	
Campbell, Casey	20:00	12	4	0	
Wales, Roy	20:00	11	0	0	W
Wales, Sidorkiewicz	20:00	16	2	0	
Wales, Billington	20:00	14	4	0	

PP Conversions: Campbell 0 for 0; Wales 1 for 1.
Referee: Marouelle. Linesmen: Bozak, Collins.
Attendance: 17,137 (at the Montreal Forum).
All-Star Game MVP: Mike Gatner (Wales).

1993 NHL Draft

First Round

The opening round of the 1993 NHL draft was held in Quebec on June 26.

	Team	Selection	Position		Team	Selection	Position
1	Ottawa	Alexandre Daigle, Victoriaville	C	14	Quebec	Adam Deadmarsh, Portland	C
2	Hartford	Chris Pronger, Peterborough	D	15	Winnipeg	Mats Lindren, Skelleftea	C
3	Tampa Bay	Chris Gratton, Kingston	C	16	Edmonton	Nick Stajduhar, London	D
4	Anaheim	Paul Kariya, U of Maine	C	17	Washington	Jason Allison, London	C
5	Florida	Rob Niedermayer, Medicine Hat	C	18	Calgary	Jesper Mattson, Malmo	R
6	San Jose	Viktor Kozlov, Moscow Dynamo	C	19	Toronto	Landon Wilson, Dubuque	C
7	Edmonton	Jason Arnott, Oshawa	C	20	Vancouver	Mike Wilson, Sudbury	D
8	NY Rangers	Niklas Sundstrom, MoDo	C	21	Montreal	Saku Koivu, Turku	C
9	Dallas	Todd Harvey, Detroit	C	22	Detroit	Anders Eriksson, MoDo	D
10	Quebec	Jocelyn Thibault, Sherbrooke	G	23	NY Islanders	Todd Bertuzzi, Guelph	C
11	Washington	Brendan Witt, Seattle	D	24	Chicago	Eric Lecompte, Hull	L
12	Toronto	Kenny Jonsson, Rogle	D	25	Boston	Kevyn Adams, Miami (OH)	C
13	New Jersey	Denis Pederson, Prince Albert	C	26	Pittsburgh	Stefan Bergkvist, Leksand	D

FOR THE RECORD·Year by Year

The Stanley Cup

Awarded annually to the team that wins the NHL's best-of-seven final-round playoffs. The Stanley Cup is the oldest trophy competed for by professional athletes in North America. It was donated in 1893 by Frederick Arthur, Lord Stanley of Preston.

Results

WINNERS PRIOR TO FORMATION OF NHL IN 1917

1892-93	Montreal A.A.A.	1904-05	Ottawa Silver Seven
1893-94	Montreal A.A.A.	1905-06	Ottawa Silver Seven (Feb)
1894-95	Montreal Victorias	1905-06	Montreal Wanderers (Mar)
1895-96	Winnipeg Victorias (Feb)	1906-07	Kenora Thistles (Jan)
1895-96	Montreal Victorias (Dec)	1906-07	Montreal Wanderers (Mar)
1896-97	Montreal Victorias	1907-08	Montreal Wanderers
1897-98	Montreal Victorias	1908-09	Ottawa Senators
1898-99	Montreal Victorias (Feb)	1909-10	Montreal Wanderers
1898-99	Montreal Shamrocks (Mar)	1910-11	Ottawa Senators
1899-1900	Montreal Shamrocks	1911-12	Quebec Bulldogs
1900-01	Winnipeg Victorias	1912-13	Quebec Bulldogs
1901-02	Winnipeg Victorias (Jan)	1913-14	Toronto Blueshirts
1901-02	Montreal A.A.A. (Mar)	1914-15	Vancouver Millionaires
1902-03	Montreal A.A.A. (Feb)	1915-16	Montreal Canadiens
1902-03	Ottawa Silver Seven (Mar)	1916-17	Seattle Metropolitans
1903-04	Ottawa Silver Seven		

NHL WINNERS AND FINALISTS

Season	Champion	Finalist	GP in Final
1917-18	Toronto Arenas	Vancouver Millionaires	5
1918-19	No decision*	No decision*	5
1919-20	Ottawa Senators	Seattle Metropolitans	5
1920-21	Ottawa Senators	Vancouver Millionaires	5
1921-22	Toronto St Pats	Vancouver Millionaires	5
1922-23	Ottawa Senators	Vancouver Millionaires, Edmonton	3, 2
1923-24	Montreal Canadiens	Vancouver Millionaires, Calgary	2, 2
1924-25	Victoria Cougars	Montreal Canadiens	4
1925-26	Montreal Maroons	Victoria Cougars	4
1926-27	Ottawa Senators	Boston Bruins	4
1927-28	New York Rangers	Montreal Maroons	5
1928-29	Boston Bruins	New York Rangers	2
1929-30	Montreal Canadiens	Boston Bruins	2
1930-31	Montreal Canadiens	Chicago Blackhawks	5
1931-32	Toronto Maple Leafs	New York Rangers	3
1932-33	New York Rangers	Toronto Maple Leafs	4
1933-34	Chicago Blackhawks	Detroit Red Wings	4
1934-35	Montreal Maroons	Toronto Maple Leafs	3
1935-36	Detroit Red Wings	Toronto Maple Leafs	4
1936-37	Detroit Red Wings	New York Rangers	5
1937-38	Chicago Blackhawks	Toronto Maple Leafs	4
1938-39	Boston Bruins	Toronto Maple Leafs	5
1939-40	New York Rangers	Toronto Maple Leafs	6
1940-41	Boston Bruins	Detroit Red Wings	4
1941-42	Toronto Maple Leafs	Detroit Red Wings	7
1942-43	Detroit Red Wings	Boston Bruins	4
1943-44	Montreal Canadiens	Chicago Blackhawks	4
1944-45	Toronto Maple Leafs	Detroit Red Wings	7
1945-46	Montreal Canadiens	Boston Bruins	5
1946-47	Toronto Maple Leafs	Montreal Canadiens	6
1947-48	Toronto Maple Leafs	Detroit Red Wings	4
1948-49	Toronto Maple Leafs	Detroit Red Wings	4
1949-50	Detroit Red Wings	New York Rangers	7
1950-51	Toronto Maple Leafs	Montreal Canadiens	5

NHL WINNERS AND FINALISTS (Cont.)

Season	Winner	Finalist	Games
1951-52	Detroit Red Wings	Montreal Canadiens	4
1952-53	Montreal Canadiens	Boston Bruins	5
1953-54	Detroit Red Wings	Montreal Canadiens	7
1954-55	Detroit Red Wings	Montreal Canadiens	7
1955-56	Montreal Canadiens	Detroit Red Wings	5
1956-57	Montreal Canadiens	Boston Bruins	5
1957-58	Montreal Canadiens	Boston Bruins	6
1958-59	Montreal Canadiens	Toronto Maple Leafs	5
1959-60	Montreal Canadiens	Toronto Maple Leafs	4
1960-61	Chicago Blackhawks	Detroit Red Wings	6
1961-62	Toronto Maple Leafs	Chicago Blackhawks	6
1962-63	Toronto Maple Leafs	Detroit Red Wings	5
1963-64	Toronto Maple Leafs	Detroit Red Wings	7
1964-65	Montreal Canadiens	Chicago Blackhawks	7
1965-66	Montreal Canadiens	Detroit Red Wings	6
1966-67	Toronto Maple Leafs	Montreal Canadiens	6
1967-68	Montreal Canadiens	St Louis Blues	4
1968-69	Montreal Canadiens	St Louis Blues	4
1969-70	Boston Bruins	St Louis Blues	4
1970-71	Montreal Canadiens	Chicago Blackhawks	7
1971-72	Boston Bruins	New York Rangers	6
1972-73	Montreal Canadiens	Chicago Blackhawks	6
1973-74	Philadelphia Flyers	Boston Bruins	6
1974-75	Philadelphia Flyers	Buffalo Sabres	6
1975-76	Montreal Canadiens	Philadelphia Flyers	4
1976-77	Montreal Canadiens	Boston Bruins	4
1977-78	Montreal Canadiens	Boston Bruins	6
1978-79	Montreal Canadiens	New York Rangers	5
1979-80	New York Islanders	Philadelphia Flyers	6
1980-81	New York Islanders	Minnesota North Stars	5
1981-82	New York Islanders	Vancouver Canucks	4
1982-83	New York Islanders	Edmonton Oilers	4
1983-84	Edmonton Oilers	New York Islanders	5
1984-85	Edmonton Oilers	Philadelphia Flyers	5
1985-86	Montreal Canadiens	Calgary Flames	6
1986-87	Edmonton Oilers	Philadelphia Flyers	7
1987-88	Edmonton Oilers	Boston Bruins	4
1988-89	Calgary Flames	Montreal Canadiens	6
1989-90	Edmonton Oilers	Boston Bruins	5
1990-91	Pittsburgh Penguins	Minnesota North Stars	6
1991-92	Pittsburgh Penguins	Chicago Black Hawks	4
1992-93	Montreal Canadiens	Los Angeles Kings	5

*In the spring of 1919 the Montreal Canadiens traveled to Seattle to meet Seattle, PCHL champions. After 5 games had been played—the teams were tied at 2 wins and 1 tie—the series was called off by the local Department of Health because of the influenza epidemic and the death of Canadian defenseman Joe Hall from influenza.

Conn Smythe Trophy

Awarded to the Most Valuable Player of the Stanley Cup playoffs, as selected by the Professional Hockey Writers Association. The trophy is named after the former coach, general manager, president and owner of the Toronto Maple Leafs.

Year	Player	Year	Player
1965	Jean Beliveau, Mtl	1980	Bryan Trottier, NYI
1966	Roger Crozier, Det	1981	Butch Goring, NYI
1967	Dave Keon, Tor	1982	Mike Bossy, NYI
1968	Glenn Hall, StL	1983	Bill Smith, NYI
1969	Serge Savard, Mtl	1984	Mark Messier, Edm
1970	Bobby Orr, Bos	1985	Wayne Gretzky, Edm
1971	Ken Dryden, Mtl	1986	Patrick Roy, Mtl
1972	Bobby Orr, Bos	1987	Ron Hextall, Phil
1973	Yvan Cournoyer, Mtl	1988	Wayne Gretzky, Edm
1974	Bernie Parent, Phil	1989	Al MacInnis, Calg
1975	Bernie Parent, Phil	1990	Bill Ranford, Edm
1976	Reggie Leach, Phil	1991	Mario Lemieux, Pitt
1977	Guy Lafleur, Mtl	1992	Mario Lemieux, Pitt
1978	Larry Robinson, Mtl	1993	Patrick Roy, Mtl
1979	Bob Gainey, Mtl		

All-Time Stanley Cup Playoff Leaders

Points

	Yrs	GP	G	A	Pts		Yrs	GP	G	A	Pts
*Wayne Gretzky, Edm, LA	14	180	110	236	346	*Larry Robinson, Mtl, LA	20	227	28	116	144
*Mark Messier, Edm, NYR	13	177	87	142	229	Jacques Lemaire, Mtl	11	145	61	78	139
*Jari Kurri, Edm, LA	12	174	102	120	222	Phil Esposito, Chi, Bos, NYR	15	130	61	76	137
*Glenn Anderson, Edm	12	185	88	113	201	*Paul Coffey, Edm, Pitt, LA	10	123	44	92	136
*Bryan Trottier, NYI, Pitt	16	219	71	113	184	Guy Lafleur, Mtlt, NYR	14	128	58	76	134
Jean Beliveau, Mtl	17	162	79	97	176	Bobby Hull, Chi, Hart	14	119	62	67	129
Denis Potvin, NYI	14	185	56	108	164	Henri Richard, Mtlt	18	180	49	80	129
Mike Bossy, NYI	10	129	85	75	160	Yvon Cournoyer, Mtl	12	147	64	63	127
Gordie Howe, Det, Har	20	157	68	92	160	Maurice Richard, Mtl	15	133	82	44	126
*Bobby Smith, Minn, Mtl	13	184	64	96	160	*Ray Bourque, Bos	14	139	31	95	126
*Denis Savard, Chi, Mtl	13	137	58	94	152						
Stan Mikita, Chi	18	155	59	91	150	*Active player.					
*Brian Propp, Phil, Bos, Minn	14	160	64	84	148						

Goals

	Yrs	GP	G
*Wayne Gretzky, Edm, LA	14	180	110
*Jari Kurri, Edm, LA	12	174	102
*Glenn Anderson, Edm	12	185	88
*Mark Messier, Edm, NYR	13	177	87
Mike Bossy, NYI	10	129	85
Maurice Richard, Mtl	15	133	82
Jean Beliveau, Mtl	17	162	79
*Bryan Trottier, NYI, Pitt	16	219	75
Gordie Howe, Det, Hart	20	157	68
Yvon Cournoyer, Mtl	12	147	64
*Brian Propp, Phil, Bos, Minn	14	160	64

*Active player.

Assists

	Yrs	GP	A
*Wayne Gretzky, Edm, LA	14	180	236
*Mark Messier, Edm, NYR	13	177	142
*Jari Kurri, Edm, LA	12	174	120
*Larry Robinson, Mtl, LA	20	227	116
*Bryan Trottier, NYI, Pitt	16	219	113
Denis Potvin, NYI	14	185	108
*Glenn Anderson, Edm	12	185	113
Jean Beliveau, Mtl	17	162	97
*Bobby Smith, Minn, Mtl	13	184	96
*Ray Bourque, Bos	14	139	95

*Active player.

Goaltending

WINS	W	L	Pct	SHUTOUTS	GP	W	SO
Billy Smith	88	36	.709	Clint Benedict	48	25	15
Ken Dryden	80	32	.714	Jacques Plante	112	71	15
*Grant Fuhr	77	36	.681	Turk Broda	101	58	13
Jacques Plante	71	37	.657	Terry Sawchuk	106	54	12
Patrick Roy	67	39	.632	Ken Dryden	112	80	10
Andy Moog	59	41	.590				
Turk Broda	58	42	.580	**GOALS AGAINST AVG**			**Avg**
Terry Sawchuk	54	48	.529	George Hainsworth			1.93
Glenn Hall	49	65	.429	Turk Broda			1.98
Gerry Cheevers	47	35	.573	Jacques Plante			2.17
				Ken Dryden			2.40
				Bernie Parent			2.43

Note: At least 50 games played.

All-Time Stanley Cup Standings

TEAM	W	L	Pct	TEAM	W	L	Pct
Montreal	371	231	.616	Pittsburgh	67	52	.563
Boston	220	227	.492	Calgary	63	75	.457
Toronto	188	204	.480	Buffalo	58	73	.443
Chicago	168	195	.463	Los Angeles	55	87	.387
Detroit	165	178	.481	Washington	42	50	.457
NY Rangers	149	170	.467	Hartford	34	41	.453
NY Islanders	128	86	.598	Quebec	33	41	.446
Edmonton	120	60	.667	Vancouver	33	50	.398
Philadelphia	116	107	.520	New Jersey	20	27	.426
St Louis	93	113	.452	Winnipeg	17	39	.304
Minnesota	80	86	.482				

Stanley Cup Coaching Records

Coach	Team	Yrs	Series	Series W	Series L	Games G	Games W	L	T	Cups	Pct
Toe Blake..................Mtl	Mtl	13	23	18	5	119	82	37	0	8	.689
Glen Sather.................Edm	Edm	11	30	23	7	*142	97	45	0	4	.683
Scott Bowman ....StL, Mtl, Buff, Pitt	StL, Mtl, Buff, Pitt	19	39	26	13	219	137	82	0	6	.626
Hap Day ....Tor	Tor	9	14	10	4	80	49	31	0	5	.613
Al Arbour ....StL, NYI	StL, NYI	15	41	30	11	205	123	82	0	4	.600
Fred Shero................Phil, NYR	Phil, NYR	8	21	15	6	108	61	47	0	2	.565
Mike Keenan...............Phil, Chi	Phil, Chi	8	21	13	8	117	65	52	0	0	.556
Lester Patrick.............NYR	NYR	12	24	14	10	65	31	26	8	2	.538
Tommy Ivan................Det	Det	7	12	8	4	67	36	31	0	3	.537
Dick Irvin.....................Chi, Tor, Mtl	Chi, Tor, Mtl	24	45	25	20	190	100	88	2	4	.532

*Does not include suspended game, May 24, 1988.
Note: Coaches ranked by winning percentage. Minimum: 65 games.

The 10 Longest Overtime Games

Date	Scorer	OT	Results	Series	Series Winner
3-24-36 ....Mud Bruneteau	Mud Bruneteau	116:30	Det 1 vs Mtl M 0	SF	Det
4-3-33 ....Ken Doraty	Ken Doraty	104:46	Tor 1 vs Bos 0	SF	Tor
3-23-43 ....Jack McLean	Jack McLean	70:18	Tor 3 vs Det 2	SF	Det
3-28-30 ....Gus Rivers	Gus Rivers	68:52	Mtl 2 vs NYR 1	SF	Mtl
4-18-87 ....Pat LaFontaine	Pat LaFontaine	68:47	NYI 3 vs Wash 2	DSF	NYI
3-27-51 ....Maurice Richard	Maurice Richard	61:09	Mtl 3 vs Det 2	SF	Mtl
3-26-32 ....Fred Cook	Fred Cook	59:32	NYR 4 vs Mtl 3	SF	NYR
3-21-39 ....Mel Hill	Mel Hill	59:25	Bos 2 vs NYR 1	SF	Bos
5-15-90 ....Petr Klima	Petr Klima	55:13	Edm 3 vs Bos 2	F	Edm
4-9-31 ....Cy Wentworth	Cy Wentworth	53:50	Chi 3 vs Mtl 2	F	Mtl

NHL Awards

Hart Memorial Trophy

Awarded annually "to the player adjudged to be the most valuable to his team." The original trophy was donated by Dr. David A. Hart, father of Cecil Hart, former manager-coach of the Montreal Canadiens. In the decade of the 1980s Wayne Gretzky won the award nine of 10 times.

	Winner	Key Statistics	Runner-Up
1924	Frank Nighbor, Ott	10 goals, 3 assists in 20 games	Sprague Cleghorn, Mtl
1925	Billy Burch, Ham	20 goals, 4 assists in 27 games	Howie Morenz, Mtl
1926	Nels Stewart, Mtl M	42 points in 36 games	Sprague Cleghorn, Mtl
1927	Herb Gardiner, Mtl	12 points in 44 games on defense	Bill Cook, NYR
1928	Howie Morenz, Mtl	33 goals, 18 assists	Roy Worters, Pitt
1929	Roy Worters, NYA	1.21 goals against, 13 shutouts	Ace Bailey, Tor
1930	Nels Stewart, Mtl M	39 games, 16 assists	Lionel Hitchman, Bos
1931	Howie Morenz, Mtl	28 games, 23 assists	Eddie Shore, Bos
1932	Howie Morenz, Mtl	24 games, 25 assists	Ching Johnson, NYR
1933	Eddie Shore, Bos	27 assists in 48 games as defense	Bill Cook, NYR
1934	Aurel Joliat, Mtl	27 points	Lionel Conacher, Chi
1935	Eddie Shore, Bos	26 assists in 48 games as defense	Charlie Conacher, Tor
1936	Eddie Shore, Bos	16 assists in 46 games as defense	Hooley Smith, Mtl M
1937	Babe Siebert, Mtl	28 points	Lionel Conacher, Mtl M
1938	Eddie Shore, Bos	17 points in 47 games as defense	Paul Thompson, Chi
1939	Toe Blake, Mtl	led NHL with 47 points	Syl Apps, Tor
1940	Ebbie Goodfellow, Det	28 points	Syl Apps, Tor
1941	Bill Cowley, Bos	led NHL with 45 assists and 62 points	Dit Clapper, Bos
1942	Tom Anderson, Bos	41 points in his final year	Syl Apps, Tor
1943	Bill Cowley, Bos	led NHL with 45 assists	Doug Bentley, Chi
1944	Babe Pratt, Tor	57 points in 50 games	Bill Cowley, Bos
1945	Elmer Lach, Mtl	led NHL with 54 assists and 80 points	Maurice Richard, Mtl
1946	Max Bentley, Chi	61 points in 47 games	Gaye Stewart, Tor
1947	Maurice Richard, Mtl	45 games, 26 assists	Milt Schmidt, Bos
1948	Buddy O'Connor, NYR	60 points in 60 games	Frank Brimsek, Bos
1949	Sid Abel, Det	28 games, 26 assists	Bill Durnan, Mtl

Hart Memorial Trophy (Cont.)

	Winner	Key Statistics	Runner-Up
1950	Charlie Rayner, NYR	6 shutouts	Ted Kennedy, Tor
1951	Milt Schmidt, Bos	61 points in 62 games	Maurice Richard, Mtl
1952	Gordie Howe, Det	led NHL in games (47) and points (86)	Elmer Lach, Mtl
1953	Gordie Howe, Det	tops in G (49), A (46), PTS (95)	Al Rollins, Chi
1954	Al Rollins, Chi	3960 minutes	Ted Kelly, Det
1955	Ted Kennedy, Tor	52 points	Harry Lumley, Tor
1956	Jean Beliveau, Mtl	led NHL in goals (47) and points (88)	Tod Sloan, Tor
1957	Gordie Howe, Det	led NHL in games (44) and points (89)	Jean Beliveau, Mtl
1959	Andy Bathgate, NYR	40 games, 48 assists	Gordie Howe, Det
1960	Gordie Howe, Det	45 assists, 73 points	Bobby Hull, Chi
1961	Bernie Geoffrion, Mtl	50 games, 95 points	Johnny Bower, Tor
1962	Jacques Plante, Mtl	42 wins, 2.37 goals against	Doug Harvey, NYR
1963	Gordie Howe, Det	47 assists, 73 points	Stan Mikita, Chi
1964	Jean Beliveau, Mtl	50 assists, 78 points	Bobby Hull, Chi
1965	Bobby Hull, Chi	39 goals, 32 assists	Norm Ullman, Det
1966	Bobby Hull, Chi	led NHL with 54 goals, 97 points	Jean Beliveau, Mtl
1967	Stan Mikita, Chi	led NHL with 62 assists, 97 points	Ed Giacomin, NYR
1968	Stan Mikita, Chi	40 goals, 47 assists	Jean Beliveau, Mtl
1969	Phil Esposito, Bos	led NHL with 77 assists, 126 points	Jean Beliveau, Mtl
1970	Bobby Orr, Bos	led NHL with 87 assists, 120 points	Tony Esposito, Chi
1971	Bobby Orr, Bos	102 assists, 139 points	Tony Esposito, Chi
1972	Bobby Orr, Bos	80 assists, 117 points	Ken Dryden, Mtl
1973	Bobby Clarke, Phil	67 assists, 104 points	Phil Esposito, Bos
1974	Phil Esposito, Bos	led NHL with 68 goals, 105 points	Bernie Parent, Phil
1975	Bobby Clarke, Phil	89 assists, 116 points	Rogatien Vachon, LA
1976	Bobby Clarke, Phil	89 assists, 119 points	Denis Potvin, NYI
1977	Guy Lafleur, Mtl	led NHL with 80 assists, 136 points	Bobby Clarke, Phil
1978	Guy Lafleur, Mtl	led NHL with 60 goals, 132 points	Bryan Trottier, NYI
1979	Bryan Trottier, NYI	led NHL with 87 assists, 134 points	Guy Lafleur, Mtl
1980	Wayne Gretzky, Edm	led NHL with 86 assists, 137 points	Marcel Dionne, LA
1981	Wayne Gretzky, Edm	led NHL with 109 assists, 164 points	Mike Liut, StL
1982	Wayne Gretzky, Edm	led NHL in G (71), A (120), PTS (212)	Bryan Trottier, NYI
1983	Wayne Gretzky, Edm	led NHL in G (71), A (125), PTS (196)	Pete Peeters, Bos
1984	Wayne Gretzky, Edm	led NHL in G (87), A (118), PTS (205)	Rod Langway, Was
1985	Wayne Gretzky, Edm	led NHL in G (73), A (135), PTS (208)	Dale Hawerchuk, Win
1986	Wayne Gretzky, Edm	set NHL record in A (163), PTS (215)	Mario Lemieux, Pitt
1987	Wayne Gretzky, Edm	led NHL in G (62), A (121), PTS (183)	Ray Bourque, Bos
1988	Mario Lemieux, Pitt	led NHL in G (70), PTS (168)	Grant Fuhr, Edm
1989	Wayne Gretzky, LA	114 assists, 168 points	Mario Lemieux, Pitt
1990	Mark Messier, Edm	84 assists, 129 points	Ray Bourque, Bos
1991	Brett Hull, StL	86 goals, 131 points	Wayne Gretzky, LA
1992	Mark Messier, NYR	72 assists, 107 points	Patrick Roy, Mtl
1993	Mario Lemieux, Pittsburgh	69 goals, 91 assists in 60 games	Doug Gilmour, Toronto

Art Ross Trophy

Awarded annually "to the player who leads the league in scoring points at the end of the regular season." The trophy was presented to the NHL in 1947 by Arthur Howie Ross, former manager-coach of the Boston Bruins. The tie-breakers, in order, are as follows: (1) player with most goals, (2) player with fewer games played, (3) player scoring first goal of the season. Bobby Orr is the only defenseman in NHL history to win this trophy, and he won it twice (1970 and 1975).

	Winner	Pts		Winner	Pts
1919	Newsy Lalonde, Mtl	44	1927	Bill Cook, NYR	42
1920	Joe Malone, Que	30	1928	Howie Morenz, Mtl	37
1921	Newsy Lalonde, Mtl	48	1929	Ace Bailey, Tor	51
1922	Punch Broadbent, Ott	41	1930	Cooney Weiland, Bos	32
1923	Babe Dye, Tor	46	1931	Howie Morenz, Mtl	73
1924	Cy Denneny, Ott	37	1932	Harvey Jackson, Tor	51
1925	Babe Dye, Tor	23	1933	Bill Cook, NYR	53
1926	Nels Stewart, Mtl M	44	1934	Charlie Conacher, Tor	50

Note: Listing is for scoring leader prior to inception of Art Ross Trophy in 1947-48.

Art Ross Trophy *(Cont.)*

	Winner	Pts		Winner	Pts
1935	Charlie Conacher, Tor	57	1965	Stan Mikita, Chi	87
1936	Sweeney Schriner, NYA	45	1966	Bobby Hull, Chi	97
1937	Sweeney Schriner, NYA	46	1967	Stan Mikita, Chi	97
1938	Gordie Drillon, Tor	52	1968	Stan Mikita, Chi	87
1939	Toe Blake, Mtl	47	1969	Phil Esposito, Bos	126
1940	Milt Schmidt, Bos	52	1970	Bobby Orr, Bos	120
1941	Bill Cowley, Bos	62	1971	Phil Esposito, Bos	152
1942	Bryan Hextall, NYR	56	1972	Phil Esposito, Bos	133
1943	Doug Bentley, Chi	73	1973	Phil Esposito, Bos	130
1944	Herb Cain, Bos	82	1974	Phil Esposito, Bos	145
1945	Elmer Lach, Mtl	80	1975	Bobby Orr, Bos	135
1946	Max Bentley, Chi	61	1976	Guy Lafleur, Mtl	125
1947	*Max Bentley, Chi	72	1977	Guy Lafleur, Mtl	136
1948	Elmer Lach, Mtl	61	1978	Guy Lafleur, Mtl	132
1949	Roy Conacher, Chi	68	1979	Bryan Trottier, NYI	134
1950	Ted Lindsay, Det	78	1980	Marcel Dionne, LA	137
1951	Gordie Howe, Det	86	1981	Wayne Gretzky, Edm	164
1952	Gordie Howe, Det	86	1982	Wayne Gretzky, Edm	212
1953	Gordie Howe, Det	95	1983	Wayne Gretzky, Edm	196
1954	Gordie Howe, Det	81	1984	Wayne Gretzky, Edm	205
1955	Bernie Geoffrion, Mtl	75	1985	Wayne Gretzky, Edm	208
1956	Jean Beliveau, Mtl	88	1986	Wayne Gretzky, Edm	215
1957	Gordie Howe, Det	89	1987	Wayne Gretzky, Edm	183
1958	Dickie Moore, Mtl	84	1988	Mario Lemieux, Pitt	168
1959	Dickie Moore, Mtl	96	1989	Mario Lemieux, Pitt	199
1960	Bobby Hull, Chi	81	1990	Wayne Gretzky, LA	142
1961	Bernie Geoffrion, Mtl	95	1991	Wayne Gretzky, LA	163
1962	Bobby Hull, Chi	84	1992	Mario Lemieux, Pitt	131
1963	Gordie Howe, Det	86	1993	Mario Lemieux, Pitt	160
1964	Stan Mikita, Chi	89			

Lady Byng Memorial Trophy

Awarded annually "to the player adjudged to have exhibited the best type of sportsmanship and gentlemanly conduct combined with a high standard of playing ability." Lady Byng, who first presented the trophy in 1925, was the wife of Canada's Governor-General. She donated a second trophy in 1936 after the first was given permanently to Frank Boucher of the New York Rangers, who won it seven times in eight seasons. Stan Mikita, one of the league's most penalized players during his early years in the NHL, won the trophy twice late in his career (1967 and 1968).

	Winner		Winner		Winner
1925	Frank Nighbor, Ott	1948	Buddy O'Connor, NYR	1971	John Bucyk, Bos
1926	Frank Nighbor, Ott	1949	Bill Quackenbush, Det	1972	Jean Ratelle, NYR
1927	Billy Burch, NYA	1950	Edgar Laprade, NYR	1973	Gilbert Perreault, Buff
1928	Frank Boucher, NYR	1951	Red Kelly, Det	1974	John Bucyk, Bos
1929	Frank Boucher, NYR	1952	Sid Smith, Tor	1975	Marcel Dionne, Det
1930	Frank Boucher, NYR	1953	Red Kelly, Det	1976	Jean Ratelle, NYR-Bos
1931	Frank Boucher, NYR	1954	Red Kelly, Det	1977	Marcel Dionne, LA
1932	Joe Primeau, Tor	1955	Sid Smith, Tor	1978	Butch Goring, LA
1933	Frank Boucher, NYR	1956	Earl Reibel, Det	1979	Bob MacMillan, Atl
1934	Frank Boucher, NYR	1957	Andy Hebenton, NYR	1980	Wayne Gretzky, Edm
1935	Frank Boucher, NYR	1958	Camille Henry, NYR	1981	Rick Kehoe, Pitt
1936	Doc Romnes, Chi	1959	Alex Delvecchio, Det	1982	Rick Middleton, Bos
1937	Marty Barry, Det	1960	Don McKenney, Bos	1983	Mike Bossy, NYI
1938	Gordie Drillon, Tor	1961	Red Kelly, Tor	1984	Mike Bossy, NYI
1939	Clint Smith, NYR	1962	Dave Keon, Tor	1985	Jari Kurri, Edm
1940	Bobby Bauer, Bos	1963	Dave Keon, Tor	1986	Mike Bossy, NYI
1941	Bobby Bauer, Bos	1964	Ken Wharram, Chi	1987	Joe Mullen, Calg
1942	Syl Apps, Tor	1965	Bobby Hull, Chi	1988	Mats Naslund, Mtl
1943	Max Bentley, Chi	1966	Alex Delvecchio, Det	1989	Joe Mullen, Calg
1944	Clint Smith, Chi	1967	Stan Mikita, Chi	1990	Brett Hull, StL
1945	Billy Mosienko, Chi	1968	Stan Mikita, Chi	1991	Wayne Gretzky, LA
1946	Toe Blake, Mont	1969	Alex Delvecchio, Det	1992	Wayne Gretzky, LA
1947	Bobby Bauer, Bos	1970	Phil Goyette, StL	1993	Pierre Turgeon, NYI

James Norris Memorial Trophy

Awarded annually "to the defense player who demonstrates throughout the season the greatest all-around ability in the position." James Norris was the former owner-president of the Detroit Red Wings. Bobby Orr holds the record for most consecutive times winning the award (eight, 1968-1975).

Winner		Winner		Winner	
1954	Red Kelly, Det	1968	Bobby Orr, Bos	1982	Doug Wilson, Chi
1955	Doug Harvey, Mtl	1969	Bobby Orr, Bos	1983	Rod Langway, Wash
1956	Doug Harvey, Mtl	1970	Bobby Orr, Bos	1984	Rod Langway, Wash
1957	Doug Harvey, Mtl	1971	Bobby Orr, Bos	1985	Paul Coffey, Edm
1958	Doug Harvey, Mtl	1972	Bobby Orr, Bos	1986	Paul Coffey, Edm
1959	Tom Johnson, Mtl	1973	Bobby Orr, Bos	1987	Ray Bourque, Bos
1960	Doug Harvey, Mtl	1974	Bobby Orr, Bos	1988	Ray Bourque, Bos
1961	Doug Harvey, Mtl	1975	Bobby Orr, Bos	1989	Chris Chelios, Mtl
1962	Doug Harvey, NYR	1976	Denis Potvin, NYI	1990	Ray Bourque, Bos
1963	Pierre Pilote, Chi	1977	Larry Robinson, Mtl	1991	Ray Bourque, Bos
1964	Pierre Pilote, Chi	1978	Denis Potvin, NYI	1992	Brian Leetch, NYR
1965	Pierre Pilote, Chi	1979	Denis Potvin, NYI	1993	Chris Chelios, Chi
1966	Jacques Laperriere, Mtl	1980	Larry Robinson, Mtl		
1967	Harry Howell, NYR	1981	Randy Carlyle, Pitt		

Calder Memorial Trophy

Awarded annually "to the player selected as the most proficient in his first year of competition in the National Hockey League." Frank Calder was a former NHL president. Sergei Makarov, who won the award in 1989-1990, was the oldest recipient of the trophy, at 31. Players are no longer eligible for the award if they are 26 or older as of September 15th of the season in question.

Winner		Winner		Winner	
1933	Carl Voss, Det	1954	Camille Henry, NYR	1975	Eric Vail, Atl
1934	Russ Blinko, Mtl M	1955	Ed Litzenberger, Chi	1976	Bryan Trottier, NYI
1935	Dave Schriner, NYA	1956	Glenn Hall, Det	1977	Willi Plett, Atl
1936	Mike Karakas, Chi	1957	Larry Regan, Bos	1978	Mike Bossy, NYI
1937	Syl Apps, Tor	1958	Frank Mahovlich, Tor	1979	Bobby Smith, Minn
1938	Cully Dahlstrom, Chi	1959	Ralph Backstrom, Mtl	1980	Ray Bourque, Bos
1939	Frank Brimsek, Bos	1960	Bill Hay, Chi	1981	Peter Stastny, Que
1940	Kilby MacDonald, NYR	1961	Dave Keon, Tor	1982	Dale Hawerchuk, Winn
1941	Johnny Quilty, Mtl	1962	Bobby Rousseau, Mtl	1983	Steve Larmer, Chi
1942	Grant Warwick, NYR	1963	Kent Douglas, Tor	1984	Tom Barrasso, Buff
1943	Gaye Stewart, Tor	1964	Jacques Laperriere, Mtl	1985	Mario Lemieux, Pitt
1944	Gus Bodnar, Tor	1965	Roger Crozier, Det	1986	Gary Suter, Calg
1945	Frank McCool, Tor	1966	Brit Selby, Tor	1987	Luc Robitaille, LA
1946	Edgar Laprade, NYR	1967	Bobby Orr, Bos	1988	Joe Nieuwendyk, Calg
1947	Howie Meeker, Tor	1968	Derek Sanderson, Bos	1989	Brian Leetch, NYR
1948	Jim McFadden, Det	1969	Danny Grant, Minn	1990	Sergei Makarov, Calg
1949	Pentti Lund, NYR	1970	Tony Esposito, Chi	1991	Ed Belfour, Chi
1950	Jack Gelineau, Bos	1971	Gilbert Perreault, Buff	1992	Pavel Bure, Van
1951	Terry Sawchuk, Det	1972	Ken Dryden, Mtl	1993	Teemu Selanne, Winn
1952	Bernie Geoffrion, Mtl	1973	Steve Vickers, NYR		
1953	Gump Worsley, NYR	1974	Denis Potvin, NYI		

Vezina Trophy

Awarded annually "to the goalkeeper adjudged to be the best at his position." The trophy is named after Georges Vezina, an outstanding goalie for the Montreal Canadiens who collapsed during a game on November 28, 1925, and died a few months later of tuberculosis. The general managers of the 21 NHL teams vote on the award.

Winner		Winner		Winner	
1927	George Hainsworth, Mtl	1939	Frank Brimsek, Bos	1951	Al Rollins, Tor
1928	George Hainsworth, Mtl	1940	Dave Kerr, NYR	1952	Terry Sawchuk, Det
1929	George Hainsworth, Mtl	1941	Turk Broda, Tor	1953	Terry Sawchuk, Det
1930	Tiny Thompson, Bos	1942	Frank Brimsek, Bos	1954	Harry Lumley, Tor
1931	Roy Worters, NYA	1943	Johnny Mowers, Det	1955	Terry Sawchuk, Det
1932	Charlie Gardiner, Chi	1944	Bill Durnan, Mtl	1956	Jacques Plante, Mtl
1933	Tiny Thompson, Bos	1945	Bill Durnan, Mtl	1957	Jacques Plante, Mtl
1934	Charlie Gardiner, Chi	1946	Bill Durnan, Mtl	1958	Jacques Plante, Mtl
1935	Lorne Chabot, Chi	1947	Bill Durnan, Mtl	1959	Jacques Plante, Mtl
1936	Tiny Thompson, Bos	1948	Turk Broda, Tor	1960	Jacques Plante, Mtl
1937	Normie Smith, Det	1949	Bill Durnan, Mtl	1961	Johnny Bower, Tor
1938	Tiny Thompson, Bos	1950	Bill Durnan, Mtl	1962	Jacques Plante, Mtl

Vezina Trophy *(Cont.)*

Winner	Winner	Winner
1963 ....Glenn Hall, Chi	1973 ....Ken Dryden, Mtl	1982 ....Bill Smith, NYI
1964 ....Charlie Hodge, Mtl	1974 ....Bernie Parent, Phil (tie)	1983 ....Pete Peeters, Bos
1965 ....Terry Sawchuk, Tor	Tony Esposito, Chi (tie)	1984 ....Tom Barrasso, Buff
.............Johnny Bower, Tor	1975 ....Bernie Parent, Phil	1985 ....Pelle Lindbergh, Phil
1966 ....Gump Worsley, Mtl	1976 ....Ken Dryden, Mtl	1986 ....John Vanbiesbrouck,
.............Charlie Hodge, Mtl	1977 ....Ken Dryden, Mtl	NYR
1967 ....Glenn Hall, Chi	Michel Larocque, Mtl	1987 ....Ron Hextall, Phil
Rogie Vachon, Mtl	1978 ....Ken Dryden, Mtl	1988 ....Grant Fuhr, Edm
1969 ....Jacques Plante, StL	Michel Larocque, Mtl	1989 ....Patrick Roy, Mtl
Glenn Hall, StL	1979 ....Ken Dryden, Mtl	1990 ....Patrick Roy, Mtl
1970 ....Tony Esposito, Chi	Michel Larocque, Mtl	1991 ....Ed Belfour, Chi
1971 ....Ed Giacomin, NYR	1980 ....Bob Sauve, Buff	1992 ....Patrick Roy, Mtl
Gilles Villemure, NYR	Don Edwards, Buff	1993 ....Ed Belfour, Chi
1972 ....Tony Esposito, Chi	1981 ....Richard Sevigny, Mtl	
Gary Smith, Chi	Denis Herron, Mtl	
	Michel Larocque, Mtl	

Selke Trophy

Awarded annually "to the forward who best excels in the defensive aspects of the game." The trophy is named after Frank J. Selke, the architect of the Montreal Canadians dynasty that won five consecutive Stanley Cups in the late '50s. The winner is selected by a vote of the Professional Hockey Writers Association.

Winner	Winner	Winner
1978........Bob Gainey, Mtl	1984........Doug Jarvis, Wash	1990........Rick Meagher, StL
1979........Bob Gainey, Mtl	1985........Craig Ramsay, Buf	1991........Dirk Graham, Chi
1980........Bob Gainey, Mtl	1986........Troy Murray, Chi	1992........Guy Carbonneau, Mtl
1981........Bob Gainey, Mtl	1987........Dave Poulin, Phil	1993........Doug Gilmour, Tor
1982........Steve Kasper, Bos	1988........Guy Carbonneau, Mtl	
1983........Bobby Clarke, Phi	1989........Guy Carbonneau, Mtl	

Adams Award

Awarded annually "to the NHL coach adjudged to have contributed the most to his team's success." The trophy is named in honor of Jack Adams, longtime coach and general manager of the Detroit Red Wings. The winner is selected by a vote of the National Hockey League Broadcasters' Association.

Winner	Winner	Winner
1974 .....Fred Shero, Phil	1981 .....Red Berenson, StL	1988 .....Jacques Demers, Det
1975 .....Bob Pulford, LA	1982 .....Tom Watt, Win	1989 .....Pat Burns, Mtl
1976 .....Don Cherry, Bos	1983 .....Orval Tessier, Chi	1990 .....Bob Murdoch, Winn
1977 .....Scott Bowman, Mtl	1984 .....Bryan Murray, Wash	1991 .....Brian Sutter, StL
1978 .....Bobby Kromm, Det	1985 .....Mike Keenan, Phil	1992 .....Pat Quinn, Van
1979 .....Al Arbour, NYI	1986 .....Glen Sather, Edm	1993 .....Pat Burns, Tor
1980 .....Pat Quinn, Phi	1987 .....Jacques Demers, Det	

The Agony of Victory

In a rampage similar to those that occurred after the Detroit Tigers won the World Series in 1984 and the Chicago Bulls won their first NBA title in '91, Montreal's central business district exploded last June minutes after the Canadiens hoisted the Stanley Cup for the 24th time. For more than two hours crowds that had assembled outside the Forum, ostensibly to celebrate the Habs' victory over the Los Angeles Kings, overturned cars, set fires, smashed windows and heaved rocks and bottles at police. More than 100 people were arrested, and some 50 cops were injured before order was restored. Damage estimates reached $10 million.

With more than one million foreign fans expected to storm U.S. shores in 1994 for the World Cup, authorities in the nine cities where games will be played are worried about possible violence by Europe's notorious soccer hooligans. But as the rash of sports riots in North America sadly suggests, Europe doesn't have a monopoly on thugs.

All-Time Point Leaders

	Player	Yrs	GP	G	A	Pts	Pts/game
1.	*Wayne Gretzky, Edm, LA	14	1044	765	1563	2328	2.230
2.	Gordie Howe, Det, Hart	26	1767	801	1049	1850	1.047
3.	Marcel Dionne, Det, LA, NYR	18	1348	731	1040	1771	1.314
4.	Phil Esposito, Chi, Bos, NYR	18	1282	717	873	1590	1.240
5.	Stan Mikita, Chi	22	1394	541	926	1467	1.052
6.	Bryan Trottier, NYI, Pitt	17	1238	520	890	1410	1.139
7.	John Bucyk, Det, Bos	23	1540	556	813	1369	.889
8.	Guy Lafleur, Mtl, NYR, Que	17	1126	560	793	1353	1.201
9.	Gilbert Perreault, Buff	17	1191	512	814	1326	1.113
10.	Alex Delvecchio, Det	24	1549	456	825	1281	.827
11.	Jean Ratelle, NYR, Bos	21	1281	491	776	1267	.989
12.	*Mark Messier, Edm, NYR	14	1005	452	780	1232	1.226
13.	Norm Ullman, Det, Tor	20	1410	490	739	1229	.872
14.	Jean Beliveau, Mtl	20	1125	507	712	1219	1.084
15.	Bobby Clarke, Phil	15	1144	358	852	1210	1.058

*Active player.

All-Time Goal-Scoring Leaders

	Player	Yrs	GP	G	G/game
1.	Gordie Howe, Det, Hart	26	1767	801	.453
2.	*Wayne Gretzky, Edm, LA	14	1044	765	.733
3.	Marcel Dionne, Det, LA, NYR	18	1348	731	.542
4.	Phil Esposito, Chi, Bos, NYR	18	1282	717	.559
5.	Bobby Hull, Chi, Winn, Hart	16	1063	610	.574
6.	*Mike Gartner, Wash, Minn, NYR	14	1089	583	.535
7.	Mike Bossy, NYI	10	752	573	.762
8.	Guy Lafleur, Mtl, NYR, Que	17	1126	560	.497
9.	John Bucyk, Det, Bos	23	1540	556	.361
10.	Maurice Richard, Mtl	18	978	544	.556

*Active player.

All-Time Assist Leaders

	Player	Yrs	GP	A	A/game
1.	*Wayne Gretzky, Edm, LA	14	1044	1563	1.497
2.	Gordie Howe, Det, Hart	26	1767	1049	.594
3.	Marcel Dionne, Det, LA, NYR	18	1348	1040	.772
4.	Stan Mikita, Chi	22	1394	926	.664
5.	Phil Esposito, Chi, Bos, NYR	18	1282	873	.681
6.	Bryan Trottier, NYI, Pitt	17	1238	890	.719
7.	Bobby Clarke, Phil	15	1144	852	.745
8.	Alex Delvecchio, Det	24	1549	825	.533
9.	Gilbert Perreault, Buff	17	1191	814	.683
10.	John Bucyk, Det, Bos	23	1540	813	.528

*Active player.

All-Time Penalty Minutes Leaders

	Player	Yrs	GP	PIM	Min/game
1.	Dave Williams, 5 teams	13	962	3966	4.12
2.	Chris Nilan, Mtl, NYR, Bos	13	688	3043	4.42
3.	*Dale Hunter, Que, Wash	12	1002	2872	2.87
4.	*Tim Hunter, Cal, Que, Van	12	619	2598	4.20
5.	Willi Plett, 4 teams	12	834	2572	3.08
6.	*Marty McSorley, Edm, LA	9	601	2446	4.07
7.	Dave Schultz, 4 teams	9	535	2294	4.29
8.	*Laurie Boschman, 5 teams	14	1009	2265	2.24
9.	Bryan Watson, 6 teams	16	878	2212	2.52
10.	Terry O'Reilly, Bos	14	891	2095	2.35

*Active player.

Goaltending Records

ALL-TIME WIN LEADERS					ACTIVE GOALTENDING LEADERS				
Goaltender	W	L	T	Pct	Goaltender	W	L	T	Pct
Terry Sawchuk	435	337	188	.551	Andy Moog, Edm, Bos	279	128	57	.663
Jacques Plante	434	246	137	.615	Patrick Roy, Mtl	225	129	48	.619
Tony Esposito	423	307	151	.566	Mike Vernon, Cal	222	138	42	.605
Glenn Hall	407	327	165	.544	Rejean Lemelin, Atl, Cal, Bos	246	152	63	.602
Rogie Vachon	355	291	115	.542	Grant Fuhr, Edm, Tor	275	173	65	.599
Gump Worsley	335	353	150	.489	Rick Wamsley, Mtl, StL, Cal, Tor	204	134	46	.591
Harry Lumley	332	324	143	.505	Tom Barrasso, Buff, Pitt	244	181	55	.566
Billy Smith	305	233	105	.556	Kelly Hrudey, NYI, LA	208	166	59	.549
Turk Broda	302	224	101	.562	Don Beaupre, Minn, Wash	230	205	64	.525
Ed Giacomin	289	206	97	.570					

Note: Ranked by winning percentage; minimum 250 games played.

ALL-TIME SHUTOUT LEADERS

Goaltender	Team	Yrs	GP	SO
Terry Sawchuk	Det, Bos, Tor, LA, NYR	21	971	103
George Hainsworth	Mtl, Tor	11	464	94
Glenn Hall	Det, Chi, StL	18	906	84
Jacques Plante	Mtl, NYR, StL, Tor, Bos	18	837	82
Tiny Thompson	Bos, Det	12	553	81
Alex Connell	Ott, Det, NYA, Mtl M	12	417	81
Tony Esposito	Mtl, Chi	16	886	76
Lorne Chabot	NYR, Tor, Mtl, Chi, Mtl M, NYA	11	411	73
Harry Lumley	Det, NYR, Chi, Tor, Bos	16	804	71
Roy Worters	Pitt Pir, NYA, *Mtl	12	484	66

*Played 1 game for Canadiens in 1929-30, not a shutout.

Coaching Records

Coach	Team	Seasons	W	L	T	Pct*
Scott Bowman	StL, Mtl, Buff, Pitt	1967-87, 91-93	832	380	226	.658
Toe Blake	Mtl	1955-68	500	255	159	.634
Glen Sather	Edm	1979-89	442	241	99	.629
Fred Shero	Phil, NYR	1971-81	390	225	119	.612
Tommy Ivan	Det, Chi	1947-54, 56-58	302	196	112	.587
Emile Francis	NYR, StL	1965-77, 81-83	393	273	112	.577
Bryan Murray	Wash, Det	1981-92	420	309	106	.576
Billy Reay	Tor, Chi	1957-59, 63-77	542	385	175	.571
Al Arbour	StL, NYI	1970-86, 88-93	745	541	236	.567
Dick Irvin	Chi, Tor, Mtl	1930-56	690	521	226	.559

*Percentage arrived at by dividing possible points into actual points.
Note: Minimum 600 regular-season games. Ranked by %.

Single-Season Records

Points per Game

Player	Season	GP	Pts	Avg	Player	Season	GP	Pts	Avg
Wayne Gretzky, Edm	1985-86	80	215	2.69	Wayne Gretzky, LA	1990-91	78	163	2.08
Mario Lemieux, Pitt	1992-93	60	160	2.66	Mario Lemieux, Pitt	1989-90	59	123	2.08
Wayne Gretzky, Edm	1981-82	80	212	2.65	Wayne Gretzky, Edm	1980-81	80	164	2.05
Mario Lemieux, Pitt	1988-89	76	199	2.62	Bill Cowley, Bos	1943-44	36	71	1.97
Wayne Gretzky, Edm	1984-85	80	208	2.60	Phil Esposito, Bos	1970-71	78	152	1.95
Wayne Gretzky, Edm	1982-83	80	196	2.45	Wayne Gretzky, LA	1989-90	73	142	1.95
Wayne Gretzky, Edm	1987-88	64	149	2.33	Steve Yzerman, Det	1988-89	80	155	1.94
Wayne Gretzky, Edm	1986-87	79	183	2.32	Bernie Nicholls, LA	1988-89	79	150	1.90
Mario Lemieux, Pitt	1987-88	77	168	2.18	Phil Esposito, Bos	1973-74	78	145	1.86
Wayne Gretzky, LA	1988-89	78	168	2.15					

Goals per Game

Player	Season	GP	G	Avg
Joe Malone, Mtl	1917-18	20	44	2.20
Cy Denneny, Ott	1917-18	22	36	1.64
Newsy Lalonde, Mtl	1917-18	14	23	1.64
Joe Malone, Que	1919-20	24	39	1.63
Newsy Lalonde, Mtl	1919-20	23	36	1.57
Joe Malone, Ham	1920-21	20	30	1.50
Babe Dye, Ham, Tor	1920-21	24	35	1.46
Cy Denneny, Ott	1920-21	24	34	1.42
Reg Noble, Tor	1917-18	20	28	1.40
Newsy Lalonde, Mtl	1920-21	24	33	1.38

Note: Minimum 20 goals in one season.

Assists per Game

Player	Season	GP	A	Avg
Wayne Gretzky, Edm	1985-86	80	163	2.04
Wayne Gretzky, Edm	1987-88	64	109	1.70
Wayne Gretzky, Edm	1984-85	80	135	1.69
Wayne Gretzky, Edm	1983-84	74	118	1.59
Wayne Gretzky, Edm	1982-83	80	125	1.56
Wayne Gretzky, LA	1990-91	78	122	1.56
Wayne Gretzky, Edm	1986-87	79	121	1.53
Mario Lemieux, Pitt	1992-93	60	91	1.52
Wayne Gretzky, Edm	1981-82	80	120	1.50
Mario Lemieux, Pitt	1988-89	76	114	1.50
Adam Oates, StL	1990-91	60	90	1.50

Shutout Leaders

	Season	SO	Length of Schedule
George Hainsworth, Mtl	1928-29	22	44
Alex Connell, Ott	1925-26	15	36
Alex Connell, Ott	1927-28	15	44
Hal Winkler, Bos	1927-28	15	44
Tony Esposito, Chi	1969-70	15	76
George Hainsworth, Mtl	1926-27	14	44
Clint Benedict, Mtl M	1926-27	13	44
Alex Connell, Ott	1926-27	13	44
George Hainsworth, Mtl	1927-28	13	44
Roy Worters, NYA	1927-28	13	44
John Roach, NYR	1928-29	13	44
Roy Worters, NYA	1928-29	13	44
Harry Lumley, Tor	1953-54	13	70
Tiny Thompson, Bos	1928-29	12	44
Lorne Chabot, Tor	1928-29	12	44
Chuck Gardiner, Chi	1930-31	12	44
Terry Sawchuk, Det	1951-52	12	70
Terry Sawchuk, Det	1953-54	12	70
Terry Sawchuk, Det	1954-55	12	70
Glenn Hall, Det	1955-56	12	70

	Season	SO	Length of Schedule
Bernie Parent, Phil	1973-74	12	78
Bernie Parent, Phil	1974-75	12	80
Lorne Chabot, NYR	1927-28	11	44
Harry Holmes, Det	1927-28	11	44
Clint Benedict, Mtl M	1928-29	11	44
Joe Miller, Pitt Pirates	1928-29	11	44
Tiny Thompson, Bos	1932-33	11	48
Terry Sawchuk, Det	1950-51	11	70
Lorne Chabot, NYR	1926-27	10	44
Roy Worters, Pitt Pirates	1927-28	10	44
Clarence Dolson, Det	1928-29	10	44
John Roach, Det	1932-33	10	48
Chuck Gardiner, Chi	1933-34	10	48
Tiny Thompson, Bos	1935-36	10	48
Frank Brimsek, Bos	1938-39	10	48
Bill Durnan, Mtl	1948-49	10	60
Gerry McNeil, Mtl	1952-53	10	70
Harry Lumley, Tor	1952-53	10	70
Tony Esposito, Chi	1973-74	10	78
Ken Dryden, Mtl	1976-77	10	80

Single-Game Records

Goals

	Date	G
Joe Malone, Que vs Tor	1-31-20	7
Newsy Lalonde, Mtl vs Tor	1-10-20	6
Joe Malone, Que vs Ott	3-10-20	6
Corb Denneny, Tor vs Ham	1-26-21	6
Cy Denneny, Ott vs Ham	3-7-21	6
Syd Howe, Det vs NYR	2-3-44	6
Red Berenson, StL vs Phil	11-7-68	6
Darryl Sittler, Tor vs Bos	2-7-76	6

Assists

	Date	A
Billy Taylor, Det vs Chi	3-16-47	7
Wayne Gretzky, Edm vs Wash	2-15-80	7
Wayne Gretzky, Edm vs Chi	12-11-85	7
Wayne Gretzky, Edm vs Que	2-14-86	7

Note: 19 tied with 6.

Points

	Date	G	A	Pts
Darryl Sittler, Tor vs Bos	2-7-76	6	4	10
Maurice Richard, Mtl vs Det	12-28-44	5	3	8
Bert Olmstead, Mtl vs Chi	1-9-54	4	4	8
Tom Bladon, Phil vs Clev	12-11-77	4	4	8
Bryan Trottier, NYI vs NYR	12-23-78	5	3	8
Peter Stastny, Que vs Wash	2-22-81	4	4	8
Anton Stastny, Que vs Wash	2-22-81	3	5	8
Wayne Gretzky, Edm vs NJ	11-19-83	3	5	8
Wayne Gretzky, Edm vs Minn	1-4-84	4	4	8
Paul Coffey, Edm vs Det	3-14-86	2	6	8
Mario Lemieux, Pitt vs StL	10-15-88	2	6	8
Bernie Nicholls, LA vs Tor	12-1-88	2	6	8
Mario Lemieux, Pitt vs NJ	12-31-88	5	3	8

NHL Season Leaders

Points

Season	Player and Club	Pts	Season	Player and Club	Pts
1917-18	Joe Malone, Mtl	44*	1956-57	Gordie Howe, Det	89
1918-19	Newsy Lalonde, Mtl	30	1957-58	Dickie Moore, Mtl	84
1919-20	Joe Malone, Que	48	1958-59	Dickie Moore, Mtl	96
1920-21	Newsy Lalonde, Mtl	41	1959-60	Bobby Hull, Chi	81
1921-22	Punch Broadbent, Ott	46	1960-61	Bernie Geoffrion, Mtl	95
1922-23	Babe Dye, Tor	37	1961-62	Andy Bathgate, NY	84
1923-24	Cy Denneny, Ott	23		Bobby Hull, Chi	84
1924-25	Babe Dye, Tor	44	1962-63	Gordie Howe, Det	86
1925-26	Nels Stewart, Mtl M	42	1963-64	Stan Mikita, Chi	89
1926-27	Bill Cook, NY	37	1964-65	Stan Mikita, Chi	87
1927-28	Howie Morenz, Mtl	51	1965-66	Bobby Hull, Chi	97
1928-29	Ace Bailey, Tor	32	1966-67	Stan Mikita, Chi	97
1929-30	Cooney Weiland, Bos	73	1967-68	Stan Mikita, Chi	87
1930-31	Howie Morenz, Mtl	51	1968-69	Phil Esposito, Bos	126
1931-32	Harvey Jackson, Tor	53	1969-70	Bobby Orr, Bos	120
1932-33	Bill Cook, NY	50	1970-71	Phil Esposito, Bos	152
1933-34	Charlie Conacher, Tor	52	1971-72	Phil Esposito, Bos	133
1934-35	Charlie Conacher, Tor	57	1972-73	Phil Esposito, Bos	130
1935-36	Sweeney Schriner, NYA	45	1973-74	Phil Esposito, Bos	145
1936-37	Sweeney Schriner, NYA	46	1974-75	Bobby Orr, Bos	135
1937-38	Gord Drillon, Tor	52	1975-76	Guy Lafleur, Mtl	125
1938-39	Hector Blake, Mtl	47	1976-77	Guy Lafleur, Mtl	136
1939-40	Milt Schmidt, Bos	52	1977-78	Guy Lafleur, Mtl	132
1940-41	Bill Cowley, Bos	62	1978-79	Bryan Trottier, NYI	134
1941-42	Bryan Hextall, NY	54	1979-80	Marcel Dionne, LA	137
1942-43	Doug Bentley, Chi	73		Wayne Gretzky, Edm	137
1943-44	Herb Cain, Bos	82	1980-81	Wayne Gretzky, Edm	164
1944-45	Elmer Lach, Mtl	80	1981-82	Wayne Gretzky, Edm	212
1945-46	Max Bentley, Chi	61	1982-83	Wayne Gretzky, Edm	196
1946-47	Max Bentley, Chi	72	1983-84	Wayne Gretzky, Edm	205
1947-48	Elmer Lach, Mtl	61	1984-85	Wayne Gretzky, Edm	208
1948-49	Roy Conacher, Chi	68	1985-86	Wayne Gretzky, Edm	215
1949-50	Ted Lindsay, Det	78	1986-87	Wayne Gretzky, Edm	183
1950-51	Gordie Howe, Det	86	1987-88	Mario Lemieux, Pitt	168
1951-52	Gordie Howe, Det	86	1988-89	Mario Lemieux, Pitt	199
1952-53	Gordie Howe, Det	95	1989-90	Wayne Gretzky, LA	142
1953-54	Gordie Howe, Det	81	1990-91	Wayne Gretzky, LA	163
1954-55	Bernie Geoffrion, Mtl	75	1991-92	Mario Lemieux, Pitt	131
1955-56	Jean Beliveau, Mtl	88	1992-93	Mario Lemieux, Pitt	160

Goals

Season	Player and Club	G	Season	Player and Club	G
1917-18	Joe Malone, Mtl	44	1936-37	Larry Aurie, Det	23
1918-19	Odie Cleghorn, Mtl	23		Nels Stewart, Bos, NYA	23
1919-20	Joe Malone, Que	39	1937-38	Gord Drill, Tor	26
1920-21	Babe Dye, Ham, Tor	35	1938-39	Roy Conacher, Bos	26
1921-22	Punch Broadbent, Ott	32	1939-40	Bryan Hextall, NY	24
1922-23	Babe Dye, Tor	26	1940-41	Bryan Hextall, NY	26
1923-24	Cy Denneny, Ott	22	1941-42	Lynn Patrick, NY	32
1924-25	Babe Dye, Tor	38	1942-43	Doug Bentley, Chi	43
1925-26	Nels Stewart, Mtl M	34	1943-44	Dout Bentley, Chi	38
1926-27	Bill Cook, NY	33	1944-45	Maurice Richard, Mtl	50
1927-28	Howie Morenz, Mtl	33	1945-46	Gaye Stewart, Tor	37
1928-29	Ace Bailey, Tor	22	1946-47	Maurice Richard, Mtl	45
1929-30	Cooney Weiland, Bos	43	1947-48	Ted Lindsay, Det	33
1930-31	Bill Cook, NY	30	1948-49	Sid Abel, Det	28
1931-32	Charlie Conacher, Tor	34	1949-50	Maurice Richard, Mtl	43
	Bill Cook, NY	34	1950-51	Gordie Howe, Det	43
1932-33	Bill Cook, NY	28	1951-52	Gordie Howe, Det	47
1933-34	Charlie Conacher, Tor	32	1952-53	Gordie Howe, Det	49
1934-35	Charlie Conacher, Tor	36	1953-54	Maurice Richard, Mtl	37
1935-36	Charlie Conacher, Tor	23	1954-55	Bernie Geoffrion, Mtl	38
	Bill Thoms, Tor	23		Maurice Richard, Mtl	38

Goals *(Cont.)*

Season	Player and Club	G	Season	Player and Club	G
1955-56	Jean Beliveau, Mtl	47	1975-76	Guy Lafleur, Mtl	56
1956-57	Gordie Howe, Det	44	1976-77	Steve Shutt, Mtl	60
1957-58	Dickie Moore, Mtl	36	1977-78	Guy Lafleur, Mtl	60
1958-59	Jean Beliveau, Mtl	45	1978-79	Mike Bossy, NYI	69
1959-60	Bobby Hull, Chi	39	1979-80	Charlie Simmer, LA	56
	Bronco Horvath, Bos	39		Blaine Stoughton, Hart	56
1960-61	Bernie Geoffrion, Mtl	50	1980-81	Mike Bossy, NYI	68
1961-62	Bobby Hull, Chi	50	1981-82	Wayne Gretzky, Edm	92
1962-63	Gordie Howe, Det	38	1982-83	Wayne Gretzky, Edm	71
1963-64	Bobby Hull, Chi	43	1983-84	Wayne Gretzky, Edm	87
1964-65	Norm Ullman, Det	42	1984-85	Wayne Gretzky, Edm	73
1965-66	Bobby Hull, Chi	54	1985-86	Jari Kurri, Edm	68
1966-67	Bobby Hull, Chi	52	1986-87	Wayne Gretzky, Edm	62
1967-68	Bobby Hull, Chi	44	1987-88	Mario Lemieux, Pitt	70
1968-69	Bobby Hull, Chi	58	1988-89	Mario Lemieux, Pitt	85
1969-70	Phil Esposito, Bos	43	1989-90	Brett Hull, Chi	72
1970-71	Phil Esposito, Bos	76	1990-91	Brett Hull, Chi	78
1971-72	Phil Esposito, Bos	66	1991-92	Brett Hull, Chi	70
1972-73	Phil Esposito, Bos	55	1992-93	Alexander Mogilny, Buff	76
1973-74	Phil Esposito, Bos	68		Teemu Selanne, Winn	
1974-75	Phil Esposito, Bos	61			

Assists

Season	Player and Club	A	Season	Player and Club	A
1917-18	statistic not kept		1957-58	Henri Richard, Mtl	52
1918-19	Newsy Lalonde, Mtl	9	1958-59	Dickie Moore, Mtl	55
1919-20	Corbett Denneny, Tor	12	1959-60	Bobby Hull, Chi	42
1920-21	Louis Berlinquette, Mtl	9	1960-61	Jean Beliveau, Mtl	58
1921-22	Punch Broadbench, Ott	14	1961-62	Andy Bathgate, NY	56
1922-23	Babe Dye, Tor	11	1962-63	Henri Richard, Mtl	50
1923-24	Billy Boucher, Mtl	6	1963-64	Andy Bathgate, NY, Tor	58
1924-25	Cy Denneny, Ott	15	1964-65	Stan Mikita, Chi	59
1925-26	Cy Denneny, Ott	12	1965-66	Stan Mikita, Chi	48
1926-27	Dick Irvin, Chi	18		Bobby Rousseau, Mtl	48
1927-28	Howie Morenz, Mtl	18		Jean Beliveau, Mtl	48
1928-29	Frank Boucher, NY	16	1966-67	Stan Mikita, Chi	62
1929-30	Frank Boucher, NY	36	1967-68	Phil Esposito, Bos	49
1930-31	Joe Primeau, Tor	36	1968-69	Phil Esposito, Bos	77
1931-32	Joe Primeau, Tor	37	1969-70	Bobby Orr, Bos	87
1932-33	Frank Boucher, NY	28	1970-71	Bobby Orr, Bos	102
1933-34	Joe Primeau, Tor	32	1971-72	Bobby Orr, Bos	80
1934-35	Art Chapman, NYA	28	1972-73	Phil Esposito, Bos	75
1935-36	Art Chapman, NYA	28	1973-74	Bobby Orr, Bos	89
1936-37	Syl Apps, Tor	29	1974-75	Bobby Clarke, Phil	89
1937-38	Syl Apps, Tor	29		Bobby Orr, Bos	89
1938-39	Bill Cowley, Bos	34	1975-76	Bobby Clarke, Phil	89
1939-40	Milt Schmidt, Bos	30	1976-77	Guy Lafleur, Mtl	80
1940-41	Bill Cowley, Bos	45	1977-78	Bryan Trottier, NYI	77
1941-42	Phil Watson, NY	37	1978-79	Bryan Trottier, NYI	87
1942-43	Bill Cowley, Bos	45	1979-80	Wayne Gretzky, Edm	86
1943-44	Clint Smith, Chi	49	1980-81	Wayne Gretzky, Edm	109
1944-45	Elmer Lach, Mtl	54	1981-82	Wayne Gretzky, Edm	120
1945-46	Elmer Lach, Mtl	34	1982-83	Wayne Gretzky, Edm	125
1946-47	Billy Taylor, Det	46	1983-84	Wayne Gretzky, Edm	118
1947-48	Doug Bentley, Chi	37	1984-85	Wayne Gretzky, Edm	135
1948-49	Doug Bentley, Chi	43	1985-86	Wayne Gretzky, Edm	163
1949-50	Ted Lindsay, Det	55	1986-87	Wayne Gretzky, Edm	121
1950-51	Gordie Howe, Det	43	1987-88	Wayne Gretzky, Edm	109
	Ted Kennedy, Tor	43	1988-89	Wayne Gretzky, LA	114
1951-52	Elmer Lach, Mtl	50		Mario Lemieux, Pitt	114
1952-53	Gordie Howe, Det	46	1989-90	Wayne Gretzky, LA	102
1953-54	Gordie Howe, Det	48	1990-91	Wayne Gretzky, LA	122
1954-55	Bert Olmstead, Mtl	48	1991-92	Wayne Gretzky, LA	90
1955-56	Bert Olmstead, Mtl	56	1992-93	Adam Oates, Bos	97
1956-57	Ted Lindsay, Det	55			

Goals Against Average

Season	Goaltender and Club	GP	Min	GA	SO	Avg
1917-18	Georges Vezina, Mtl	21	1282	84	1	3.93
1918-19	Clint Benedict, Ott	18	1113	53	2	2.86
1919-20	Clint Benedict, Ott	24	1444	64	5	2.66
1920-21	Clint Benedict, Ott	24	1457	75	2	3.09
1921-22	Clint Benedict, Ott	24	1508	84	2	3.34
1922-23	Clint Benedict, Ott	24	1478	54	4	2.19
1923-24	Georges Vezina, Mtl	24	1459	48	3	1.97
1924-25	Georges Vezina, Mtl	30	1860	56	5	1.81
1925-26	Alex Connell, Ott	36	2251	42	15	1.12
1926-27	Clint Benedict, Mtl M	43	2748	65	13	1.42
1927-28	George Hainsworth, Mtl	44	2730	48	13	1.05
1928-29	George Hainsworth, Mtl	44	2800	43	22	0.92
1929-30	Tiny Thompson, Bos	44	2680	98	3	2.19
1930-31	Roy Worters, NYA	44	2760	74	8	1.61
1931-32	Chuck Gardiner, Chi	48	2989	92	4	1.85
1932-33	Tiny Thompson, Bos	48	3000	88	11	1.76
1933-34	Wilf Cude, Det, Mtl	30	1920	47	5	1.47
1934-35	Lorne Chabot, Chi	48	2940	88	8	1.80
1935-36	Tiny Thompson, Bos	48	2930	82	10	1.68
1936-37	Normie Smith, Det	48	2980	102	6	2.05
1937-38	Tiny Thompson, Bos	48	2970	89	7	1.80
1938-39	Frank Brimsek, Bos	43	2610	68	10	1.56
1939-40	Dave Kerr, NYR	48	3000	77	8	1.54
1940-41	Turk Broda, Tor	48	2970	99	5	2.00
1941-42	Frank Brimsek, Bos	47	2930	115	3	2.35
1942-43	Johnny Mowers, Det	50	3010	124	6	2.47
1943-44	Bill Durnan, Mtl	50	3000	109	2	2.18
1944-45	Bill Durnan, Mtl	50	3000	121	1	2.42
1945-46	Bill Durnan, Mtl	40	2400	104	4	2.60
1946-47	Bill Durnan, Mtl	60	3600	138	4	2.30
1947-48	Turk Broda, Tor	60	3600	143	5	2.38
1948-49	Bill Durnan, Mtl	60	3600	126	10	2.10
1949-50	Bill Durnan, Mtl	64	3840	141	8	2.20
1950-51	Al Rollins, Tor	40	2367	70	5	1.77
1951-52	Terry Sawchuk, Det	70	4200	133	12	1.90
1952-53	Terry Sawchuk, Det	63	3780	120	9	1.90
1953-54	Harry Lumley, Tor	69	4140	128	13	1.86
1954-55	Harry Lumley, Tor	69	4140	134	8	1.94
	Terry Sawchuk, Det	68	4060	132	12	1.94
1955-56	Jacques Plante, Mtl	64	3840	119	7	1.86
1956-57	Jacques Plante, Mtl	61	3660	123	9	2.02
1957-58	Jacques Plante, Mtl	57	3386	119	9	2.11
1958-59	Jacques Plante, Mtl	67	4000	144	9	2.16
1959-60	Jacques Plante, Mtl	69	4140	175	3	2.54
1960-61	Johnny Bower, Tor	58	3480	145	2	2.50
1961-62	Jacques Plante, Mtl	70	4200	166	4	2.37
1962-63	Jacques Plante, Mtl	56	3320	138	5	2.49
1963-64	Johnny Bower, Tor	51	3009	106	5	2.11
1964-65	Johnny Bower, Tor	34	2040	81	3	2.38
1965-66	Johnny Bower, Tor	35	1998	75	3	2.25
1966-67	Glenn Hall, Chi	32	1664	66	2	2.38
1967-68	Gump Worsley, Mtl	40	2213	73	6	1.98
1968-69	Jacques Plante, StL	37	2139	70	5	1.96
1969-70	Ernie Wakely, StL	30	1651	58	4	2.11
1970-71	Jacques Plante Tor	40	2329	73	4	1.88
1971-72	Tony Esposito, Chi	48	2780	82	9	1.77
1972-73	Ken Dryden, Mtl	54	3165	119	6	2.26
1973-74	Bernie Parent, Phil	73	4314	136	12	1.89
1974-75	Bernie Parent, Phil	68	4041	137	12	2.03
1975-76	Ken Dryden, Mtl	62	3580	121	8	2.03
1976-77	Michael Larocque, Mtl	26	1525	53	4	2.09
1977-78	Ken Dryden, Mtl	52	3071	105	5	2.05
1978-79	Ken Dryden, Mtl	47	2814	108	5	2.30
1979-80	Bob Sauve, Buff	32	1880	74	4	2.36
1980-81	Richard Sevigny, Mtl	33	1777	71	2	2.40
1981-82	Denis Herron, Mtl	27	1547	68	3	2.64

Goals Against Average *(Cont.)*

Season	Goaltender and Club	GP	Min	GA	SO	Avg
1982-83	Pete Peeters, Bos	62	3611	142	8	2.36
1983-84	Pat Riggin, Wash	41	2299	102	4	2.66
1984-85	Tom Barrasso, Buff	54	3248	144	5	2.66
1985-86	Bob Froese, Phil	51	2728	116	5	2.55
1986-87	Brian Hayward, Mtl	37	2178	102	1	2.81
1987-88	Pete Peeters, Wash	35	1896	88	2	2.78
1988-89	Patrick Roy, Mtl	48	2744	113	4	2.47
1989-90	Patrick Roy, Mtl	54	3173	134	3	2.53
	Mike Liut, Hart, Wash	37	2161	91	4	2.53
1990-91	Ed Belfour, Chi	74	4127	170	4	2.47
1991-92	Patrick Roy, Mtl	67	3935	155	5	2.36
1992-93	*Felix Potvin, Tor	48	2781	116	2	2.50

*Rookie.

Penalty Minutes

Season	Player and Club	GP	PIM	Season	Player and Club	GP	PIM
1918-19	Joe Hall, Mtl	17	85	1956-57	Gus Mortson, Chi	70	147
1919-20	Cully Wilson, Tor	23	79	1957-58	Lou Fontinato, NYR	70	152
1920-21	Bert Corbeau, Mtl	24	86	1958-59	Ted Lindsay, Chi	70	184
1921-22	S Cleghorn, Mtl	24	63	1959-60	Carl Brewer, Tor	67	150
1922-23	Billy Boucher, Mtl	24	52	1960-61	Pierre Pilote, Chi	70	165
1923-24	Bert Corbeau, Tor	24	55	1961-62	Lou Fontinato, Mtl	54	167
1924-25	Billy Boucher, Mtl	30	92	1962-63	Howie Young, Det	64	273
1925-26	Bert Corbeau, Tor	36	121	1963-64	Vic Hadfield, NYR	69	151
1926-27	Nels Stewart, Mtl M	44	133	1964-65	Carl Brewer, Tor	70	177
1927-28	Eddie Shore, Bos	44	165	1965-66	R Fleming, Bos, NYR	69	166
1928-29	Red Dutton, Mtl M	44	139	1966-67	John Ferguson, Mtl	67	177
1929-30	Joe Lamb, Ott	44	119	1967-68	Barclay Plager, StL	49	153
1930-31	Harvey Rockburn, Det	42	118	1968-69	F Kennedy, Phi, Tor	77	219
1931-32	Red Dutton, NYA	47	107	1969-70	Keith Magnuson, Chi	76	213
1932-33	Red Horner, Tor	48	144	1970-71	Keith Magnuson, Chi	76	291
1933-34	Red Horner, Tor	42	126	1971-72	Brian Watson, Pitt	75	212
1934-35	Red Horner, Tor	46	125	1972-73	Dave Schultz, Phil	76	259
1935-36	Red Horner, Tor	43	167	1973-74	Dave Schultz, Phil	73	348
1936-37	Red Horner, Tor	48	124	1974-75	Dave Schultz, Phil	76	472
1937-38	Red Horner, Tor	47	82	1975-76	S Durbano, Pitt, KC	69	370
1938-39	Red Horner, Tor	48	85	1976-77	Dave Williams, Tor	77	338
1939-40	Red Horner, Tor	30	87	1977-78	Dave Schultz, LA, Pitt	74	405
1940-41	Jimmy Orlando, Det	48	99	1978-79	Dave Williams, Tor	77	298
1941-42	Jimmy Orlando, Det	48	81	1979-80	Jimmy Mann, Winn	72	287
1942-43	Jimmy Orlando, Det	40	89	1980-81	Dave Williams, Van	77	343
1943-44	Mike McMahon, Mtl	42	98	1981-82	Paul Baxter, Pitt	76	409
1944-45	Pat Egan, Bos	48	86	1982-83	Randy Holt, Wash	70	275
1945-46	Jack Stewart, Det	47	73	1983-84	Chris Nilan, Mtl	76	338
1946-47	Gus Mortson, Tor	60	133	1984-85	Chris Nilan, Mtl	77	358
1947-48	Bill Barilko, Tor	57	147	1985-86	Joey Kocur, Det	59	377
1948-49	Bill Ezinicki, Tor	52	145	1986-87	Tim Hunter, Cal	73	361
1949-50	Bill Ezinicki, Tor	67	144	1987-88	Bob Probert, Det	74	398
1950-51	Gus Mortson, Tor	60	142	1988-89	Tim Hunter, Cal	75	375
1951-52	Gus Kyle, Bos	69	127	1989-90	Basil McRae, Minn	66	351
1952-53	Maurice Richard, Mtl	70	112	1990-91	Bob Ray, Buff	66	350
1953-54	Gus Mortson, Chi	68	132	1991-92	Mike Peluso, Chi	63	408
1954-55	Fern Flaman, Bos	70	150	1992-93	Marty McSorley, LA	81	399
1955-56	Lou Fontinato, NYR	70	202				

THEY SAID IT

Edmonton coach Ted Green, when told that rookie center Shaun Van Allen had suffered a concussion and didn't know who he was: "Good. Tell him he's Wayne Gretzky."

NHL All-Star Game

First played in 1947, this game was scheduled before the start of the regular season and used to match the defending Stanley Cup champions against a squad made up of league All-Stars from other teams. In 1966 the games were moved to mid-season, although there was no game that year. The format changed to a conference versus conference showdown in 1969.

Results

Year	Site	Score	MVP	Attendance
1947	Toronto	All-Stars 4, Toronto 3	None named	14,169
1948	Chicago	All-Stars 3, Toronto 1	None named	12,794
1949	Toronto	All-Stars 3, Toronto 1	None named	13,541
1950	Detroit	Detroit 7, All-Stars 1	None named	9,166
1951	Toronto	1st team 2, 2nd team 2	None named	11,469
1952	Detroit	1st team 1, 2nd team 1	None named	10,680
1953	Montreal	All-Stars 3, Montreal 1	None named	14,153
1954	Detroit	All-Stars 2, Detroit 2	None named	10,689
1955	Detroit	Detroit 3, All-Stars 1	None named	10,111
1956	Montreal	All-Stars 1, Montreal 1	None named	13,095
1957	Montreal	All-Stars 5, Montreal 3	None named	13,003
1958	Montreal	Montreal 6, All-Stars 3	None named	13,989
1959	Montreal	Montreal 6, All-Stars 1	None named	13,818
1960	Montreal	All-Stars 2, Montreal 1	None named	13,949
1961	Chicago	All-Stars 3, Chicago 1	None named	14,534
1962	Toronto	Toronto 4, All-Stars 1	Eddie Shack, Tor	14,236
1963	Toronto	All-Stars 3, Toronto 3	Frank Mahovlich, Tor	14,034
1964	Toronto	All-Stars 3, Toronto 2	Jean Beliveau, Mtl	14,232
1965	Montreal	All-Stars 5, Montreal 2	Gordie Howe, Det	13,529
1967	Montreal	Montreal 3, All-Stars 0	Henri Richard, Mtl	14,284
1968	Toronto	Toronto 4, All-Stars 3	Bruce Gamble, Tor	15,753
1969	Montreal	East 3, West 3	Frank Mahovlich, Det	16,260
1970	St Louis	East 4, West 1	Bobby Hull, Chi	16,587
1971	Boston	West 2, East 1	Bobby Hull, Chi	14,790
1972	Minnesota	East 3, West 2	Bobby Orr, Bos	15,423
1973	NY Rangers	East 5, West 4	Greg Polis, Pitt	16,986
1974	Chicago	West 6, East 4	Garry Unger, StL	16,426
1975	Montreal	Wales 7, Campbell 1	Syl Apps Jr, Pitt	16,080
1976	Philadelphia	Wales 7, Campbell 5	Pete Mahovlich, Mtl	16,436
1977	Vancouver	Wales 4, Campbell 3	Rick Martin, Buff	15,607
1978	Buffalo	Wales 3, Campbell 2 (OT)	Billy Smith, NYI	16,433
1980	Detroit	Wales 6, Campbell 3	Reg Leach, Phil	21,002
1981	Los Angeles	Campbell 4, Wales 1	Mike Liut, StL	15,761
1982	Washington	Wales 4, Campbell 2	Mike Bossy, NYI	18,130
1983	NY Islanders	Campbell 9, Wales 3	Wayne Gretzky, Edm	15,230
1984	NJ Devils	Wales 7, Campbell 6	Don Maloney, NYR	18,939
1985	Calgary	Wales 6, Campbell 4	Mario Lemieux, Pitt	16,825
1986	Hartford	Wales 4, Campbell 3 (OT)	Grant Fuhr, Edm	15,100
1988	St Louis	Wales 6, Campbell 5 (OT)	Mario Lemieux, Pitt	17,878
1989	Edmonton	Campbell 9, Wales 5	Wayne Gretzky, LA	17,503
1990	Pittsburgh	Wales 12, Campbell 7	Mario Lemieux, Pitt	16,236
1991	Chicago	Campbell 11, Wales 5	Vince Damphousse, Tor	18,472
1992	Philadelphia	Campbell 10, Wales 6	Brett Hull, StL	17,380
1993	Montreal	Wales 16, Campbell 6	Mike Gartner, NYR	17,137

Note: The Challenge Cup, a series between the NHL All-Stars and the Soviet Union, was played instead of the All-Star Game in 1979. Eight years later, Rendez-Vous '87, a two-game series matching the Soviet Union and the NHL All-Stars, replaced the All-Star Game.

THEY SAID IT

Phil Esposito, general manager of the Tampa Bay Lightning, welcoming the NHL's Miami expansion team: "Now we've got someone our fans can really hate."

Hockey Hall of Fame

Located in Toronto, the Hockey Hall of Fame was officially opened on August 26, 1961. The current president is Ian "Scotty" Morrison, a former NHL referee. There are, at present, 281 members of the Hockey Hall of Fame—192 players, 77 "Builders," and 12 on-ice officials. To be eligible, player and referee/linesman candidates should have been out of the game for three years, but the Hall's Board of Directors can make exceptions.

Players

Sid Abel (1969)
Jack Adams (1959)
Charles "Syl" Apps (1961)
George Armstrong (1975)
Irvine "Ace" Bailey (1975)
Donald H. "Dan" Bain (1945)
Hobey Baker (1945)
Bill Barber (1990)
Marty Barry (1965)
Andy Bathgate (1978)
Jean Beliveau (1972)
Clint Benedict (1965)
Douglas Bentley (1964)
Max Bentley (1966)
Hector "Toe" Blake (1966)
Leo Boivin (1986)
Dickie Boon (1952)
Mike Bossy (1991)
Emile "Butch" Bouchard (1966)
Frank Boucher (1958)
George "Buck" Boucher (1960)
Johnny Bower (1976)
Russell Bowie (1945)
Frank Brimsek (1966)
Harry L. "Punch" Broadbent (1962)
Walter "Turk" Broda (1967)
John Bucyk (1981)
Billy Burch (1974)
Harry Cameron (1962)
Gerry Cheevers (1985)
Francis "King" Clancy (1958)
Aubrey "Dit" Clapper (1947)
Bobby Clarke (1987)
Sprague Cleghorn (1958)
Neil Colville (1967)
Charlie Conacher (1961)
Alex Connell (1958)
Bill Cook (1952)
Arthur Coulter (1974)
Yvan Cournoyer (1982)
Bill Cowley (1968)
Samuel "Rusty" Crawford (1962)
Jack Darragh (1962)
Allan M. "Scotty" Davidson (1950)
Clarence "Hap" Day (1961)
Alex Delvecchio (1977)
Cy Denneny (1959)
Marcel Dionne (1992)
Gordie Drillon (1975)
Charles Drinkwater (1950)
Ken Dryden (1983)

Woody Dumart (1992)
Thomas Dunderdale (1974)
Bill Durnan (1964)
Mervyn A. "Red" Dutton (1958)
Cecil "Babe" Dye (1970)
Phil Esposito (1984)
Tony Esposito (1988)
Arthur F. Farrell (1965)
Ferdinand "Fern" Flaman (1990)
Frank Foyston (1958)
Frank Frederickson (1958)
Bill Gadsby (1970)
Bob Gainey (1992)
Chuck Gardiner (1945)
Herb Gardiner (1958)
Jimmy Gardner (1962)
Bernie "Boom Boom" Geoffrion (1972)
Eddie Gerard (1945)
Ed Giacomin (1987)
Rod Gilbert (1982)
Hamilton "Billy" Gilmour (1962)
Frank "Moose" Goheen (1952)
Ebenezer R. "Ebbie" Goodfellow (1963)
Mike Grant (1950)
Wilfred "Shorty" Green (1962)
Si Griffis (1950)
George Hainsworth (1961)
Glenn Hall (1975)
Joe Hall (1961)
Doug Harvey (1973)
George Hay (1958)
William "Riley" Hern (1962)
Bryan Hextall (1969)
Harry "Hap" Holmes (1972)
Tom Hooper (1962)
George "Red" Horner (1965)
Miles "Tim" Horton (1977)
Gordie Howe (1972)
Syd Howe (1965)
Harry Howell (1979)
Bobby Hull (1983)
John "Bouse" Hutton (1962)
Harry M. Hyland (1962)
James "Dick" Irvin (1958)
Harvey "Busher" Jackson (1971)
Ernest "Moose" Johnson (1952)
Ivan "Ching" Johnson (1958)
Tom Johnson (1970)
Aurel Joliat (1947)

Gordon "Duke" Keats (1958)
Leonard "Red" Kelly (1969)
Ted "Teeder" Kennedy (1966)
Dave Keon (1986)
Elmer Lach (1966)
Guy Lafleur (1988)
Edouard "Newsy" Lalonde (1950)
Jacques Laperriere (1987)
Guy LaPointe (1993)
Edgar Laprade (1993)
Jean "Jack" Laviolette (1962)
Hugh Lehman (1958)
Jacques Lemaire (1984)
Percy LeSueur (1961)
Herbert A. Lewis (1989)
Ted Lindsay (1966)
Harry Lumley (1980)
Lanny McDonald (1992)
Frank McGee (1945)
Billy McGimsie (1962)
George McNamara (1958)
Duncan "Mickey" MacKay (1952)
Frank Mahovlich (1981)
Joe Malone (1950)
Sylvio Mantha (1960)
Jack Marshall (1965)
Fred G. "Steamer" Maxwell (1962)
Stan Mikita (1983)
Dicky Moore (1974)
Patrick "Paddy" Moran (1958)
Howie Morenz (1945)
Billy Mosienko (1965)
Frank Nighbor (1947)
Reg Noble (1962)
Herbert "Buddy" O'Connor (1988)
Harry Oliver (1967)
Bert Olmstead (1985)
Bobby Orr (1979)
Bernie Parent (1984)
Brad Park (1988)
Lester Patrick (1947)
Lynn Patrick (1980)
Gilbert Perreault (1990)
Tommy Phillips (1945)
Pierre Pilote (1975)
Didier "Pit" Pitre (1962)
Jacques Plante (1978)
Denis Potvin (1991)
Walter "Babe" Pratt (1966)

Hockey Hall of Fame *(Cont.)*

Players *(Cont.)*

Joe Primeau (1963)
Marcel Pronovost (1978)
Bob Pulford (1991)
Harvey Pulford (1945)
Hubert "Bill" Quackenbush
  (1976)
Frank Rankin (1961)
Jean Ratelle (1985)
Claude "Chuck" Rayner (1973)
Kenneth Reardon (1966)
Henri Richard (1979)
Maurice "Rocket" Richard
  (1961)
George Richardson (1950)
Gordon Roberts (1971)
Art Ross (1945)
Blair Russel (1965)
Ernest Russell (1965)
Jack Ruttan (1962)
Serge Savard (1986)
Terry Sawchuk (1971)
Fred Scanlan (1965)
Milt Schmidt (1961)
Dave "Sweeney" Schriner
  (1962)
Earl Seibert (1963)
Oliver Seibert (1961)
Eddie Shore (1947)
Steve Shutt (1993)
Albert C. "Babe" Siebert (1964)
Harold "Bullet Joe" Simpson
  (1962)
Daryl Sittler (1989)
Alfred E. Smith (1962)
Billy Smith (1993)
Reginald "Hooley" Smith (1972)
Thomas Smith (1973)
Allan Stanley (1981)
Russell "Barney" Stanley
  (1962)
John "Black Jack" Stewart
  (1964)
Nels Stewart (1962)
Bruce Stuart (1961)
Hod Stuart (1945)
Frederic "Cyclone" (O.B.E.)
  Taylor (1947)
Cecil R. "Tiny" Thompson
  (1959)
Vladislav Tretiak (1989)
Harry J. Trihey (1950)
Norm Ullman (1982)
Georges Vezina (1945)
Jack Walker (1960)
Marty Walsh (1962)
Harry E. Watson (1962)
Ralph "Cooney" Weiland (1971)
Harry Westwick (1962)
Fred Whitcroft (1962)
Gordon "Phat" Wilson (1962)
Lorne "Gump" Worsley (1980)
Roy Worters (1969)

Builders

Charles Adams (1960)
Weston W. Adams (1972)
Thomas "Frank" Ahearn (1962)
John "Bunny" Ahearne (1977)
Montagu Allan (C.V.O.) (1945)
Harold Ballard (1977)
David Bauer (1989)
John Bickell (1978)
Scott Bowman (1991)
George V. Brown (1961)
Walter A. Brown (1962)
Frank Buckland (1975)
Jack Butterfield (1980)
Frank Calder (1947)
Angus D. Campbell (1964)
Clarence Campbell (1966)
Joe Cattarinich (1977)
Joseph "Leo" Dandurand
  (1963)
Francis Dilio (1964)
George S. Dudley (1958)
James A. Dunn (1968)
Alan Eagleson (1989)
Emile Francis (1982)
Jack Gibson (1976)
Tommy Gorman (1963)
Frank Griffiths (1993)
William Hanley (1986)
Charles Hay (1974)
James C. Hendy (1968)
Foster Hewitt (1965)
William Hewitt (1947)
Fred J. Hume (1962)
George "Punch" Imlach (1984)
Tommy Ivan (1974)
William M. Jennings (1975)
Gordon W. Juckes (1979)
John Kilpatrick (1960)
Seymour Knox III (1993)
George Leader (1969)
Robert LeBel (1970)
Thomas F. Lockhart (1965)
Paul Loicq (1961)
Frederic McLaughlin (1963)
John Mariucci (1985)
John "Jake" Milford (1984)
Hartland Molson (1973)
Francis Nelson (1947)
Bruce A. Norris (1969)
James Norris, Sr. (1958)
James D. Norris (1962)
William M. Northey (1947)
John O'Brien (1962)
Frank Patrick (1958)
Fred Page (1993)
Allan W. Pickard (1958)
Rudy Pilous (1985)
Norman "Bud" Poile (1990)
Samuel Pollock (1978)
Donat Raymond (1958)
John Robertson (1947)
Claude C. Robinson (1947)

Builders *(Cont.)*

Philip D. Ross (1976)
Frank J. Selke (1960)
Harry Sinden (1983)
Frank D. Smith (1962)
Conn Smythe (1958)
Edward M. Snider (1988)
Lord Stanley of Preston
  (G.C.B.) (1945)
James T. Sutherland (1947)
Anatoli V. Tarasov (1974)
Lloyd Turner (1958)
William Tutt (1978)
Carl Potter Voss (1974)
Fred C. Waghorn (1961)
Arthur Wirtz (1971)
Bill Wirtz (1976)
John A. Ziegler, Jr. (1987)

Referees/Linesmen

John Ashley (1981)
William L. Chadwick (1964)
John D'Amico (1993)
Chaucer Elliott (1961)
George Hayes (1988)
Robert W. Hewitson (1963)
Fred J. "Mickey" Ion (1961)
Matt Pavelich (1987)
Mike Rodden (1962)
J. Cooper Smeaton (1961)
Roy "Red" Storey (1967)
Frank Udvari (1973)

Note: Year of election to the Hall
of Fame is in parentheses after
the member's name.

Tennis

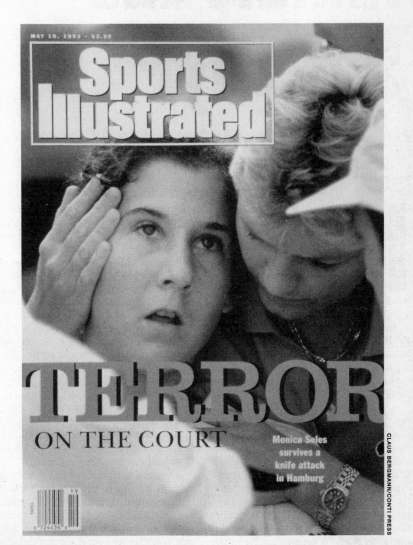

MAY 10, 1993 · $2.95

Sports Illustrated

TERROR
ON THE COURT

Monica Seles
survives a
knife attack
in Hamburg

CLAUS BERGMANN/CONTI PRESS

Tumult and Tragedy

Fine seasons from Pete Sampras and Steffi Graf were overshadowed by offcourt drama | **by SALLY JENKINS**

I T WAS THE YEAR OF THE STALKER IN tennis. Top-ranked Monica Seles was stabbed in the back on a court in Hamburg, Germany. Pete Sampras relentlessly chased the No. 1 ranking. There were tragedies, intrigues, international incidents and affairs. It seemed there had never been such a tumultuous season in a sport, on or off the court.

Andre Agassi dated Barbra Streisand. Boris Becker posed seminude. Martina Navratilova marched on Washington for gay rights. Mary Pierce broke with her abusive father. The only person on either the men's or the women's tour who seemed to be concentrating purely on tennis was Sampras, the 22-year-old who finally fulfilled his promise. Sampras rose to No. 1 in the world by outdueling Jim Courier throughout the season, capturing both the Wimbledon and U.S. Open titles. They were transfiguring events for a player who had struggled with the weight of expectations since he became the youngest U.S. Open champion ever three years ago, at 19, and been called the next great player by no less than Fred Perry and Rod Laver.

But rankings and titles were reduced to silly debates by two tragedies that cast a pall on the year. On Feb. 6, Arthur Ashe died, finally succumbing to complications from AIDS. Ashe almost certainly contracted the disease from a blood transfusion during open-heart surgery in 1983. He had faced the disease with his usual demeanor: academic, analytic, and implacable. He devoted the last year of his life to the public fight against AIDS, just as he had once devoted himself to causes like Artists and Athletes Against Apartheid and the Safe Passage Foundation which guides underprivileged youths towards college. Once of his last acts of public service was to create the Arthur Ashe Foundation for the Defeat of AIDS, which in just three months raised $500,000 toward its goal of $5 million in '93. He was mourned by all throughout the season.

Tennis was again reduced to a mere backdrop one evening in April when a seemingly inconsequential women's match in Germany was interrupted by horrifying reality. Gunter Parche, an unemployed German lathe operator, reached over a spectator barricade and plunged a serrated boning knife into the back of 19-year-old Seles as she sat in her chair during a changeover in a routine match at the Citizen's Cup tournament in Hamburg. Seles leaped to her feet, screamed and then collapsed to the court with a streak of blood visible on her shirt. Parche was immediately subdued by security guards, but he had accomplished his vicious aim: to wound Seles badly enough to deprive her of the No. 1 ranking. Parche, who appeared mentally disturbed, told German police that he "could not bear" the fact that Seles had unseated Steffi Graf, the 24-year-old German idol, as the top-ranked player in the world.

Seles would not strike another ball for the remainder of the season. She suffered muscle and nerve damage from the puncture wound, which barely missed her spinal cord and proved more complicated than anyone could foresee. As she recuperated in virtual seclusion at a clinic in Vail, Colo., it was impossible to say what the cost to her would be either physically or emotionally. Seles finally resurfaced for a brief press conference in New York on the eve of the U.S. Open. She was clearly itching to return, declaring that she hoped to be back on the tour before the 1994 Australian Open. She also displayed a covetous resentment of Graf's No. 1 ranking in her absence, expressing her disappointment that the Women's Tennis Association had not granted her request to freeze her position.

As Seles pointed out, it was a bitter irony that Parche should have so completely achieved his aim. For Graf proceeded to sweep every available title without Seles to challenge her, winning 36 consecutive

The death of Ashe left the tennis world in mourning throughout the season.

In Seles's absence Graf won three majors, including a shaky victory at Wimbledon.

matches and six straight tournaments, including the French Open, Wimbledon and culminating in the U.S. Open. Had it not been for a narrow loss to Seles in the Australian Open in January, Graf would have had a second Grand Slam, reprising her feat of 1988, when she was an unassailable 18-year-old.

Graf, however, drew little satisfaction from her achievements. "Over the years I've said rankings don't mean that much to me, and that's how I feel now," she said. Her Grand Slam victories were shaky, nerve-wracked things haunted by her absent rival. She defeated Mary Joe Fernandez in a hard fought, three-set French final. In the Wimbledon final she all but conceded an upset victory to Jana Novotna, trailing in the third set by two service breaks. But Novotna then

suffered one of the most memorable collapses in history, and Graf prevailed. Only at the U.S. Open was Graf dominant: She lost just one set en route to the final, in which she smothered Helena Sukova 6–3, 6–3. In her speech during the trophy presentation, Graf spoke eloquently and regretfully of Seles's absence.

Graf's grace was a soothing balm in a year of ugly wounds. Seles was not the only victim. Pierce, a willowy 18-year-old with blockbuster talent but little formal training, had risen to No. 14 in the world under the brutal coaching of her father, Jim. In the spring, shortly after reaching legal age, Mary broke with Jim, a convicted felon with a history of mental problems, who was long known for his violent outbursts during tournaments. Tennis officials aided Mary when they banned Jim from the tour after he disrupted the French Open with an outburst.

Jim nevertheless followed Mary as she

traveled, making threats againt her and her mother, Yannick, who had filed for divorce. The two women obtained a series of restraining orders and went public with accusations that he struck and bullied them regularly. At year's end Mary had retained a new coach, Angel Giminez, and had hope of finally becoming known for her tennis ability rather than for her infamous father.

Sampras seemed to restore order and reason wherever he went, both with his play and his persona. He was quiet, conservative, discreet and well mannered. The only disturbance he caused was with his 120 mph serve. His ascendance was the culmination of an organized and grueling yearlong effort. Early in the year he declined to play in the Davis Cup for the U.S., stating that his personal goals of becoming No. 1 and winning Grand Slams would come first.

Unfortunately Courier and Agassi followed suit, which left Davis Cup captain Tom Gorman in dire straits. A team headed by Brad Gilbert lost in the first round to Australia in February. That was a disastrous turn of events, for it meant that the U.S. team, which had won the Davis Cup two of the last three years, was relegated to the qualifying round. Gorman, discouraged by the players' unwillingness to play, later resigned at the U.S. Open, and the USTA began the search for a 1994 captain.

Sampras's singleminded pursuit of the top ranking put considerable pressure on Courier, whose once dominant grip was slipping. Courier once called playing tennis "going to work and clocking in." But the steelworker approach that won him four Grand Slam titles in the previous two years now seemed to be wearing on him. The French Open typified Courier's year. He seemed assured of a third straight French title when he reached the final against Sergi Bruguera of Spain. Instead, Bruguera upset the once indomitable Courier.

Bruguera was a 22-year-old with the unfurling topspin forehand typical of a clay court expert. The son of former Spanish Davis Cup captain, Luis, Bruguera was born into the game and had a command of the clay and of the ebbs and flows of the grueling tournament that Courier did not. Surely Courier had to be the man favored to win once their match reached a fifth set. And when Courier took a 2–0 lead, it seemed all but over. But Bruguera gathered himself to win 18 of 22 points, and Courier was the one to fade in the last moments of their match after nearly four hours. When he won the final point Bruguera fell flat on his back, partly in triumph, but also due to pure exhaustion. He had to be treated afterward for dehydration.

Courier was incensed by the loss and took his simmering anger to Wimbledon. A bludgeoning player without much affinity for grass, he surprised himself by plowing through the draw, along the way arousing the ire of the spectators with his agressive American ways, which included inviting a British sportswriter to step outside. Sampras, too, tangled with the British, who dubbed him a bore and a rube. Sampras and Courier met in ideal circumstances, a Wimbledon final between Nos. 1 and 2 in the world. When Sampras prevailed over four sets of surpassingly elegant play, his whiplash serve untouchable, Courier was forced to concede the mantle of top player. "He won, didn't he?" Courier said.

The back and forth exchanges of the No. 1 ranking dominated a men's season in which not much was heard from Stefan Edberg or Becker, and in which McEnroe and Jimmy Connors faded out apparently once and for all. The 40-year-old Connors was busy launching a seniors tour, and the 34-year-old McEnroe was either perched in a broadcast booth or sorting out his messy divorce from actress Tatum O'Neal.

The so-called middle-aged players, 25-year-old Becker and 24-year-old Edberg, were absent for long stretches in part because they were caught up in personal affairs. Edberg and his wife, Annette, had their first baby in August. Becker withdrew from a variety of events in the spring, alternately suffering from a virus and a case of ennui. He hired and fired two coaches before seeking out McEnroe as a counselor. He dismissed his longtime mentor and manager, Ion Tiriac. He posed seminude for Germany's *Stern* magazine with his fiancée, Barbara Feltus, and went apartment hunting in London and Paris. Following his fourth-round defeat in the U.S. Open, Becker revealed that Feltus was pregnant. By the season's end one had to wonder if the brooding German, who hadn't won a Grand Slam title since the Australian Open in 1991, would ever return to top form.

The personal perils of Agassi should have been played out under a big top. Instead they dominated the sedate confines of the All England Club. Agassi showed up to defend his Wimbledon title grossly overweight and suffering from a case of tendinitis in his right wrist. He admitted that he had played just one hour of tennis in a month. He also showed up missing most of his body hair. When pressed by a tabloid

Sampras and his dominant serve cruised to a straight-set win in the U.S. Open final.

LOU CAPOZZOLA

reporter, he intimated that he shaved it off during a romantic interlude. Agassi's love life then became the focus of the tournament. When Streisand showed up to watch his quarterfinal with Sampras, resplendent in a Donna Karan nautical outfit and cap, fingernails waving adoringly, the match took on an absurdly celluloid quality. When Sampras defeated Agassi over five sets, it begged two questions: What might Agassi have accomplished had he bothered to show up fit, and why did he sabotage himself by creating a three-ring circus with Streisand's presence before his toughest match of the tournament?

Agassi's coach, Nick Bollettieri, asked the same questions. His answer was to resign, tired of the constant uproar surrounding Agassi. Bollettieri's decision caused Agassi to do some reappraising. He responded by hiring Pancho Segura as his new coach, a move designed to help him become a more thoughtful player. Agassi thought himself right out of the U.S. Open, losing in the first round to Thomas Enqvist of Sweden, and so ended one of his most disappointing Grand Slam seasons. Sampras was among those who rightly questioned Agassi's methods. "He's got so many distractions," Sampras said. "Everywhere he goes he's mobbed. Maybe he causes it. Maybe he likes it. I don't know."

When Sampras captured the U.S Open, the year belonged to him completely. Sampras was the man to watch throughout the tournament, as early round upsets felled nearly everybody of note. Seven of the 16 men's seeds were gone by the third round. Courier went down in the round of 16 to Cédric Pioline of France, Sampras's eventual opponent in the final. Pioline was merely a cardboard cutout for Sampras to fire at. His straight-set victory in the final, 6–4, 6–4, 6–3, was more of an occasion for a laurel crowning than an actual match. He accepted his second Grand Slam trophy of the year as his rightful due. "I just play my tennis, sign my autographs and do what I have to do," Sampras said.

Finally, there was a little peace and quiet.

1993 Grand Slam Champions

Australian Open

Men's Singles

	Winner	Finalist	Score
Quarterfinals	Jim Courier (1)	Petr Korda (7)	6-1, 6-0, 6-4
	Michael Stich (14)	Guy Forget (11)	6-4, 6-4, 6-4
	Pete Sampras (3)	Brett Steven	6-3, 6-2, 6-3
	Stefan Edberg (2)	Christian Bergstrom	6-4, 6-4, 6-1
Semifinals	Jim Courier	Michael Stich	7-6, 6-4, 6-2
	Stefan Edberg	Pete Sampras	7-6, 6-3, 7-6
Final	Jim Courier	Stefan Edberg	6-2, 6-1, 2-6, 7-5

Women's Singles

	Winner	Finalist	Score
Quarterfinals	Monica Seles (1)	Julie Halard	6-2, 6-7 (5-7), 6-0
	Gabriela Sabatini (3)	Mary Pierce (10)	4-6, 7-6 (14-12), 6-0
	Arantxa Sanchez Vicario (4)	Mary Joe Fernandez (5)	7-5, 6-4
	Steffi Graf (2)	Jennifer Capriati (7)	7-5, 6-2
Semifinals	Monica Seles	Gabriela Sabatini	6-1, 6-2
	Steffi Graf	Arantxa Sanchez Vicario	7-5, 6-4
Final	Monica Seles	Steffi Graf	4-6, 6-3, 6-2

Doubles

	Winner	Finalist	Score
Men's Final/	Danie Visser/ Laurie Warder (10)	John Fitzgerald/ Anders Jarryd (4)	6-4, 6-3, 6-4
Women's Final	Mary Joe Fernandez/ Natalia Zvereva (1)	Pam Shriver/ Elizabeth Smylie	6-4, 6-3
Mixed Final	Todd Woodbridge/ Arantxa Sanchez Vicario (1)	Zina Garrison-Jackson/ Rick Leach	7-5, 6-4

French Open

Men's Singles

	Winner	Finalist	Score
Quarterfinals	Sergi Bruguera (10)	Pete Sampras (1)	6-3, 4-6, 6-1, 6-4
	Andrei Medvedev (11)	Stefan Edberg (3)	6-0, 6-7 (3-7), 7-5, 6-4
	Richard Krajicek (12)	Karel Novacek (13)	3-6, 6-3, 3-6, 6-3, 6-4
	Jim Courier (2)	Goran Prpic	6-1, 4-6, 6-0, 7-5
Semifinals	Sergi Bruguera	Andrei Medvedev	6-0, 6-4, 6-2
	Jim Courier	Richard Krajicek	6-1, 6-7 (2-7), 7-5, 6-2
Final	Sergi Bruguera	Jim Courier	6-4, 2-6, 6-2, 3-6, 6-3

Women's Singles

	Winner	Finalist	Score
Quarterfinals	Steffi Graf (1)	Jennifer Capriati (6)	6-3, 7-5
	Conchita Martinez (4)	Anke Huber (8)	6-7 (2-7), 6-4, 6-4
	Mary Joe Fernandez (5)	Gabriela Sabatini (3)	1-6, 7-6 (7-4), 10-8
	Arantxa Sanchez Vicario (2)	Jana Novotna (7)	6-2, 7-5
Semifinals	Steffi Graf	Anke Huber	6-1, 6-1
	Mary Joe Fernandez	Arantxa Sanchez Vicario	6-1, 6-1
Final	Steffi Graf	Mary Joe Fernandez	4-6, 6-2, 6-4

Note: Seedings in parentheses.

French Open *(Cont.)*

Doubles

	Winner	Finalist	Score
Men's Final	Luke Jensen/ .... Murphy Jensen	Marc Goellner/ David Prinosil	6-4, 6-7 (4-7), 6-4
Women's Final	Gigi Fernandez/ .... Natalia Zvereva (1)	Larisa Neiland/ Jana Novotna (2)	6-3, 7-5
Mixed Final	Eugenia Maniokova/ .... Andrei Olhovskiy (11)	Elna Reinach/ Danie Visser (9)	6-2, 4-6, 6-4

Wimbledon

Men's Singles

	Winner	Finalist	Score
Quarterfinals	Pete Sampras (1)	Andre Agassi (8)	6-2, 6-2, 3-6, 3-6, 6-4
	Jim Courier (3)	Todd Martin	6-2, 7-6 (7-5), 6-3
	Boris Becker (4)	Michael Stich (6)	7-5, 6-7 (5-7), 6-7 (5-7), 6-2, 6-4
	Stefan Edberg (2)	Cedric Pioline	7-5, 7-5, 6-3
Semifinals	Jim Courier	Stefan Edberg	4-6, 6-4, 6-2, 6-4
	Pete Sampras	Boris Becker	7-6 (7-5), 6-4, 6-4
Final	Pete Sampras	Jim Courier	7-6 (7-3), 7-6 (8-6), 3-6, 6-3

Women's Singles

	Winner	Finalist	Score
Quarterfinals	Steffi Graf (1)	Jennifer Capriati (7)	7-6 (7-3), 6-1
	Conchita Martinez (6)	Helena Sukova (15)	6-1, 6-4
	Jana Novotna (8)	Gabriela Sabatini (4)	6-4, 6-3
	Martina Navratilova (2)	Natalia Zvereva	6-3, 6-1
Semifinals	Steffi Graf	Conchita Martinez	7-6 (7-0), 6-3
	Jana Novotna	Martina Navratilova	6-4, 6-4
Final	Steffi Graf	Jana Novotna	7-6 (8-6), 1-6, 6-4

Doubles

	Winner	Finalist	Score
Men's Final	Todd Woodbridge/ .... Mark Woodforde (1)	Grant Connell/ Patrick Galbraith (5)	7-5, 6-3, 7-6 (7-4)
Women's Final	Gigi Fernandez/ .... Natalia Zvereva (1)	Larisa Neiland/ Jana Novotna (2)	6-4, 6-7 (4-7), 6-4
Mixed Final	Mark Woodforde/ .... Martina Navratilova (3)	Tom Nijssen/ Manon Bollegraf (12)	6-3, 6-4

U.S. Open

Men's Singles

	Winner	Finalist	Score
Quarterfinals	Cédric Pioline (15)	Andrei Medvedev (8)	6-3, 6-1, 3-6, 6-2
	Wally Masur	Magnus Larsson	6-2, 7-5, 7-5
	Alexander Volkov (14)	Thomas Muster (12)	7-6, 6-3, 3-6, 2-6, 7-5
	Pete Sampras (2)	Michael Chang (7)	6-7 (7-0), 7-6 (7-2), 6-1, 6-1
Semifinals	Cédric Pioline	Wally Masur	6-1, 6-7 (3-7), 7-6 (7-2), 6-1
	Pete Sampras	Alexander Volkov	6-4, 6-3, 6-2
Final	Pete Sampras	Cédric Pioline	6-4, 6-4, 6-3

Note: Seedings in parentheses.

Grand Slam Champions *(Cont.)*

U.S. Open *(Cont.)*

Women's Singles

	Winner	Finalist	Score
Quarterfinals	Steffi Graf (1)	Gabriela Sabatini (5)	6-2, 5-7, 6-1
	Manuela Maleeva-Fragniere (11)	Kimiko Date	7-5, 7-5
	Helena Sukova (12)	Katerina Maleeva	6-4, 6-7 (3-7), 6-3
	Arantxa Sanchez Vicario (2)	Natalia Zvereva	3-0 DEF
Semifinals	Steffi Graf	Manuela Maleeva-Fragniere	4-6, 6-1, 6-0
	Helena Sukova	Arantxa Sanchez Vicario	6-7 (9-7), 7-5, 6-2
Final	Steffi Graf	Helena Sukova	6-3, 6-3

Doubles

	Winner	Finalist	Score
Men's Final	Ken Flach/ Rick Leach (12)	Martin Damm/ Karel Novacek	6-7 (5-7), 6-4, 6-2
Women's Final	Helena Sukova/ Arantxa Sanchez-Vicario (3)	Amanda Coetzer/ Ines Gorrochategui (9)	6-4, 6-2
Mixed Final	Mark Woodbridge/ Helena Sukova (1)	Mark Woodforde/ Martina Navratilova (2)	6-3, 7-6 (7-6)

Note: Seedings in parentheses.

Major Tournament Results

Men's Tour (Late 1992)

Date	Tournament	Site	Winner	Finalist	Score
Oct 5-11	Australian Indoor Tennis Championships	Sydney	Goran Ivanisevic	Stefan Edberg	6-4, 6-2, 6-4
Oct 8-12	Seiko Super Tennis	Tokyo	Ivan Lendl	Henrik Holm	7-6 (9-7), 6-4
Oct 20-25	Grand Prix de Tennis	Lyon	Pete Sampras	Cedric Pioline	6-4, 6-2
Oct 26-Nov 1	Stockholm Open	Stockholm	Goran Ivanisevic	Guy Forget	7-6 (7-2), 4-6, 7-6 (7-5), 6-2
Nov 2-8	Open de la Ville de Paris	Paris	Boris Becker	Guy Forget	7-6 (7-5), 6-3, 3-6, 6-3
Nov 16-22	IBM/ATP Tour World Championship	Frankfurt	Boris Becker	Jim Courier	6-4, 6-3, 7-5

Men's Tour (through September 12, 1993)

Date	Tournament	Site	Winner	Finalist	Score
Jan 18-25	Australian Open	Melbourne	Jim Courier	Stefan Edberg	6-2, 6-1, 2-6, 7-5
Feb 1-7	Volvo Tennis Indoor	San Francisco	Andre Agassi	Brad Gilbert	6-2, 6-7 (4-7), 6-2
Feb 8-14	Muratti Time Indoor	Milan	Boris Becker	Sergi Bruguera	6-3, 6-3
Feb 15-21	Eurocard Open	Stuttgart	Michael Stich	Michael Krajicek	4-6, 7-5, 6-7 (4-7), 3-6, 7-5
Mar 1-7	Newsweek Champions Cup	Indian Wells, CA	Jim Courier	Wayne Ferreira	6-3, 6-3, 6-1
Mar 8-21	Lipton Intl Players Championships	Key Biscayne	Pete Sampras	MaliVai Washington	6-3, 6-2
Apr 4-11	Japan Open Tennis Championship	Tokyo	Pete Sampras	Brad Gilbert	6-2, 6-2, 6-2
Apr 21-26	Volvo Monte Carlo Open	Monte Carlo	Sergi Bruguera	Cedric Pioline	7-6 (7-2), 6-0
May 3-9	Panasonic German Open	Hamburg	Michael Stich	Andrei Chesnokov	6-3, 6-7 (1-7), 7-6 (9-7), 6-4
May 10-16	XLX Campionati Intl d'Italia	Rome	Jim Courier	Goran Ivanisevic	6-1, 6-2, 6-2
May 24-31	French Open	Paris	Sergi Bruguera	Jim Courier	6-4, 2-6, 6-2, 3-6, 6-3
June 21-29	Wimbledon Championships	Wimbledon	Pete Sampras	Jim Courier	7-6 (7-3), 7-6 (8-6) 3-6, 6-3

Men's Tour *(Cont.)*

Date	Tournament	Site	Winner	Finalist	Score
July 19-25	Mercedes Cup	Stuttgart	Magnus Gustafsson	Michael Stich	6-3, 6-4, 3-6, 4-6, 6-4
July 26-Aug1	Canadian Open	Montreal	Mikael Pernfors	Todd Martin	
Aug 9-15	Thriftway ATP Championship	Cincinnati	Michael Chang	Stefan Edberg	7-5, 0-6, 6-4
Aug 16-22	RCA/US Men's Hardcourt Championships	Indianapolis	Jim Courier	Boris Becker	7-5, 6-3
Aug 16-22	Volvo Intl Tennis Tournament	New Haven	Andrei Medvedev	Petr Korda	7-5, 6-4
Aug 30-Sep 12	US Open	New York	Pete Sampras	Cédric Pioline	6-4, 6-4, 6-3

Women's Tour (Late 1992)

Date	Tournament	Site	Winner	Finalist	Score
Sep 22-27	Nichirei Intl Championships	Tokyo	Monica Seles	Gabriela Sabatini	6-2, 6-0
Sep 28-Oct 4	Volkswagen Cup	Leipzig	Steffi Graf	Jana Novotna	6-3, 1-6, 6-4
Oct 5-11	European Indoors	Zurich	Steffi Graf	Martina Navratilova	2-6, 7-6, 7-5
Oct 12-18	Porsche Tennis Grand Prix	Filderstadt, Germany	Martina Navratilova	Gabriela Sabatini	7-6 (7-1), 6-3
Oct 20-25	Midland Bank Championships	Brighton, England	Steffi Graf	Jana Novotna	4-6, 6-4, 7-6 (7-3)
Nov 2-8	Bank of the West Classic	Oakland	Monica Seles	Martina Navratilova	6-3, 6-4
Nov 9-15	Virginia Slims of Philadelphia	Philadelphia	Steffi Graf	Arantxa Sanchez Vicario	6-3, 3-6, 6-1
Nov 16-22	Virginia Slims Championships	New York	Monica Seles	Martina Navratilova	7-5, 6-3, 6-1

Women's Tour (through October 3, 1993)

Date	Tournament	Site	Winner	Finalist	Score
Jan 4-10	Danone Australian Hardcourt Championships	Brisbane	Conchita Martinez	Magdalena Maleeva	6-3, 6-4
Jan 11-17	Peters NSW Open	Sydney	Jennifer Capriati	Anke Huber	6-1, 6-4
Jan 18-31	Ford Australian Open	Melbourne	Monica Seles	Steffi Graf	4-6, 6-3, 6-2
Feb 2-7	Toray Pan Pacific Open	Tokyo	Martina Navratilova	Larisa Neiland	7-5, 6-3
Feb 8-14	Virginia Slims of Chicago	Chicago	Monica Seles	Martina Navratilova	3-6, 6-2, 6-1
Feb 15-21	Virginia Slims of Oklahoma	Oklahoma City	Zina Garrison Jackson	Patty Fendick	6-2, 6-2
Mar 1-7	Virginia Slims of Florida	Boca Raton	Steffi Graf	Arantxa Sanchez Vicario	6-4, 6-3
Mar 12-21	Lipton Intl Players Championships	Key Biscayne	Arantxa Sanchez Vicario	Steffi Graf	6-4, 3-6, 6-3
Mar 22-28	Virginia Slims of Houston	Houston	Conchita Martinez	Sabine Hack	6-3, 6-2
Mar 29-Apr 4	Family Circle Magazine Cup	Hilton Head Island, SC	Steffi Graf	Arantxa Sanchez Vicario	7-6 (10-8), 6-1
Apr 5-11	Bausch & Lomb Championships	Amelia Island, FL	Arantxa Sanchez Vicario	Gabriela Sabatini	6-2, 5-7, 6-2
Apr 20-25	International Championships of Spain	Barcelona	Arantxa Sanchez Vicario	Conchita Martinez	6-1, 6-4
Apr 26-May 2	Citizen Cup	Hamburg	Arantxa Sanchez Vicario	Steffi Graf	6-3, 6-3
May 3-9	Italian Open	Rome	Conchita Martinez	Gabriela Sabatini	7-5, 6-1

Women's Tour *(Cont.)*

Date	Tournament	Site	Winner	Finalist	Score
May 10-16	German Open	Berlin	Steffi Graf	Gabriela Sabatini	7-6 (7-3), 2-6, 6-4
May 24-June 6	French Open	Paris	Steffi Graf	Mary Joe Fernandez	4-6, 6-2, 6-4
June 7-13	DFS Classic	Birmingham, England	Lori McNeil	Zina Garrison Jackson	6-4, 2-6, 6-3
June 15-20	Volkswagen Cup	Eastbourne, England	Martina Navratilova	Miriam Oremans	2-6, 6-2, 6-3
June 21-July 4	Wimbledon Championships	Wimbledon	Steffi Graf	Jana Novotna	7-6 (8-6), 1-6, 6-4
July 12-18	Citroen Cup	Kitzbuhel, Austria	Anke Huber	Judith Wiesner	6-3, 6-4
Aug 9-15	Virginia Slims of L.A.	Manhattan Beach	Martina Navratilova	Arantxa Sanchez Vicario	7-5, 7-6 (7-4)
Aug 16-22	Matinee Ltd Canadian Open	Toronto	Steffi Graf	Jennifer Capriati	6-1, 0-6, 6-3
Aug 23-28	OTB International	Schenectady	Larisa Neiland	Natalia Medvedeva	6-3, 6-2
Aug 30-Sep 12	US Open	New York	Steffi Graf	Helena Sukova	6-3, 6-3
Sep 21-26	Nichirei Intl Championships	Tokyo	Amanda Coetzer	Kimiko Date	6-3, 6-2
Sep 27-Oct 3	Volkswagen Cup	Leipzig	Steffi Graf	Jana Novotna	6-2, 6-0

1992 Singles Leaders

Men

Rank	Player	Tournament Wins	Match Record	Earnings ($)
1	Stefan Edberg	3	68–23	2,305,149
2	Jim Courier	5	69–18	2,242,340
3	Boris Becker	5	52–15	2,215,772
4	Pete Sampras	5	70–18	1,533,037
5	Goran Ivanisevic	4	59–18	1,337,405
6	Andre Agassi	3	42–14	989,429
7	Petr Korda	3	61–29	967,191
8	Ivan Lendl	1	50-24	929,701
9	Michael Chang	3	54-22	911,032
10	Richard Krajicek	2	48–22	730,876
11	Guy Forget	1	47–22	642,007
12	Sergi Bruguera	3	46-22	595,283
13	Wayne Ferreira	2	49–24	578,635
14	Carlos Costa	2	40–21	568,947
15	Michael Stich	1	43–21	563,726
16	Emilio Sanchez	1	48–26	506,183
17	MaliVai Washington	2	50–22	505,783
18	Alexander Volkov	0	47–32	445,241
19	Thomas Muster	3	39–23	444,833
20	Karel Novacek	3	42–26	442,751

Note: Compiled by the Association of Tennis Professionals (ATP).

Women

Rank	Player	Tournament Wins	Match Record	Earnings ($)
1	Monica Seles	10	70–5	2,605,852
2	Steffi Graf	8	71–7	1,657,541
4	Gabriela Sabatini	5	65–12	1,201,029
4	Arantxa Sanchez Vicario	2	66–17	1,024,143
5	Martina Navratilova	4	38–8	648,155
6	Mary Joe Fernandez	0	51–17	522,821
7	Conchita Martinez	1	50–19	369,174
8	Lori McNeil	1	39–22	309,553
9	Jennifer Capriati	2	35–11	300,145
10	Manuela Maleeva-Fragniere	1	35–12	283,600
11	Jana Novotna	0	38–19	259,706
13	Zina Garrison Jackson	1	36–20	249,126
14	Helena Sukova	2	45–17	238,703
15	Nathalie Tauziat	0	41–21	237,350
16	Katarina Maleeva	0	31–20	230,276
17	Natalia Zvereva	0	34–20	207,185
18	Amy Frazier	1	33–17	204,343
19	Anke Huber	0	36–16	174,231
20	Magdalena Maleeva	1	31–15	167,757

Note: Compiled by the Women's Tennis Association (WTA).

1992 Davis Cup

FINALS

United States d. Swtizerland 3-1 at Fort Worth, TX
Andre Agassi (US) d. Jakob Hlasek (Swi) 6-1, 6-2, 6-2
Mark Rosset (Swi) d. Jim Courier (US) 6-3, 6-7 (7-9), 3-6, 6-4, 6-4
John McEnroe and Pete Sampras (US) d. Jakob Hlasek and Mark Rosset (Swi) 6-7 (5-7), 6-7 (7-9), 6-1, 6-2
Jim Courier (US) d. Jakob Hlasek (Swi) 6-3, 3-6, 6-3, 6-4

1993 Davis Cup

FIRST ROUND

Australia d. United States 4-1 at Melbourne.
Italy d. Brazil 4-1 at Modena, Italy.
India d. Switzerland 3-2 at Calcutta, India.
France d. Austria 4-1 at Vienna.
The Netherlands d. Spain 3-2 at Barcelona.
Sweden d. Cuba 5-0 at Kalmar, Sweden.
Czech.Slovak Republics d. Denmark 4-1 at Aarhus, Denmark
Germany d. Russia 4-1 at Moscow.

QUARTER FINAL ROUND

Australia d. Italy 3-2 at Florence, Italy.
India d. France 3-2 at Frejus, France.
Sweden d. the Netherlands 4-1 at The Hague.
Germany d. Czech/Slovak Republics 4-1 at Halle, Ger.

SEMIFINALS

Australia d. India 5-0 at Chandigarh, India.
J. Stoltenberg (Aus) .d L. Paes (Ind)
W. Masur (Aus) d. R. Krishnan (Ind)
T. Woodbridge/M. Wodforde (Aus) d. R. Krishnan/L. Paes (Ind)
W. Masur (Aus) d. L. Paes (Ind)
J. Stoltenberg (Aus) d. Z. Ali (Ind)

Germany d. Sweden 5-0 at Borlange, Sweden
M. Stich (Ger) d. M. Gustafsson (Swe)
M. Goellner (Ger) d. S. Edberg (Swe)
P. Kuhnen/Stich (Ger) d. H. Holm/Anders Jarryd (Swe)
M. Stich (Ger) d. S. Edberg (Swe)
Goellner (Ger) d. Holm (Swe)

FINAL: Germany versus Australia to be held Dec. 3–5 in Dusseldorf.

1993 Federation Cup

FIRST ROUND

Spain d. Great Britain 3-0
Indonesia d. Poland 2-1
Latvia d. Belgium 2-1
The Netherlands d. Croatia 3-0
Czechoslovakia d. South Africa 2-1
Italy d. Israel 3-0
Sweden d. Uruguay 3-0
France d. Canada 2-1
United States d. Switzerland 3-0
China d. Peru 2-1
Argentina d. New Zealand 3-0
Bulgaria d. Korea 2-1
Japan d. Colombia 3-0
Finland d. Chile 3-0
Denmark d. Austria 2-1
Australia d. Germany 2-1

SECOND ROUND

Spain d. Indonesia 3-0
The Netherlands d. Latvia 3-0
Czechoslovakia d. Italy 2-1
France d. Sweden 3-0
United States d. China 2-1
Argentina d. Bulgaria 2-1
Finland d. Japan 2-1
Australia d. Denmark 3-0

QUARTERFINALS

Spain d. the Netherlands 3-0
France d. Czechoslovakia 3-0
Argentina d. United States 2-1
Australia d. Finland 3-0

SEMIFINALS

Spain d. France 2-1
Conchita Martinez (Spain) d. J. Halard (France) 6-0, 6-2
Arantxa Sanchez Vicario (Spain) d. N. Tauziat (France) 6-1, 6-4
V. Ruano/C. Torrens (Spain) lost to I. Demongeot/P. Paradis-Magnon (France) 2-1 RET

Australia d. Argentina 2-1
M. Jaggard-Lai (Aus) lost to I. Gorrochategui (Arg) 4-6, 2-6
N. Provis (Aus) d. F. Labat (Arg) 1-6, 6-2, 6-3
E. Sayers-Smylie/R. Stubbs (Aus) d. I. Gorrochategui/P. Tarabini (Arg) 4-6, 6-2, 6-3

FINALS

Spain d. Australia 3-0
Conchita Martinez (Spain) d. Michelle Jaggard-Lai (Australia) 6-0, 6-2
Arantxa Sanchez Vicario (Spain) d. Nicole Provis (Australia) 6-2, 6-3
Arantxa Sanchez Vicario and Conchita Martinez (Spain) d. Elizabeth Smylie and Renae Stubbs (Australia) 3-6, 6-1, 6-3

Note: Held at Frankfurt, Germany, July 17-25, 1993

FOR THE RECORD·Year by Year

Grand Slam Tournaments

MEN

Australian Championships

Year	Winner	Finalist	Score
1905	Rodney Heath	A. H. Curtis	4-6, 6-3, 6-4, 6-4
1906	Tony Wilding	H. A. Parker	6-0, 6-4, 6-4
1907	Horace M. Rice	H. A. Parker	6-3, 6-4, 6-4
1908	Fred Alexander	A. W. Dunlop	3-6, 3-6, 6-0, 6-2, 6-3
1909	Tony Wilding	E. F. Parker	6-1, 7-5, 6-2
1910	Rodney Heath	Horace M. Rice	6-4, 6-3, 6-2
1911	Norman Brookes	Horace M. Rice	6-1, 6-2, 6-3
1912	J. Cecil Parke	A. E. Beamish	3-6, 6-3, 1-6, 6-1, 7-5
1913	E. F. Parker	H. A. Parker	2-6, 6-1, 6-2, 6-3
1914	Pat O'Hara Wood	G. L. Patterson	6-4, 6-3, 5-7, 6-1
1915	Francis G. Lowe	Horace M. Rice	4-6, 6-1, 6-1, 6-4
1916-18	No tournament		
1919	A. R. F. Kingscote	E. O. Pockley	6-4, 6-0, 6-3
1920	Pat O'Hara Wood	Ron Thomas	6-3, 4-6, 6-8, 6-1, 6-3
1921	Rhys H. Gemmell	A. Hedeman	7-5, 6-1, 6-4
1922	Pat O'Hara Wood	Gerald Patterson	6-0, 3-6, 3-6, 6-3, 6-2
1923	Pat O'Hara Wood	C. B. St John	6-1, 6-1, 6-3
1924	James Anderson	R. E. Schlesinger	6-3, 6-4, 3-6, 5-7, 6-3
1925	James Anderson	Gerald Patterson	11-9, 2-6, 6-2, 6-3
1926	John Hawkes	J. Willard	6-1, 6-3, 6-1
1927	Gerald Patterson	John Hawkes	3-6, 6-4, 3-6, 18-16, 6-3
1928	Jean Borotra	R. O. Cummings	6-4, 6-1, 4-6, 5-7, 6-3
1929	John C. Gregory	R. E. Schlesinger	6-2, 6-2, 5-7, 7-5
1930	Gar Moon	Harry C. Hopman	6-3, 6-1, 6-3
1931	Jack Crawford	Harry C. Hopman	6-4, 6-2, 2-6, 6-1
1932	Jack Crawford	Harry C. Hopman	4-6, 6-3, 3-6, 6-3, 6-1
1933	Jack Crawford	Keith Gledhill	2-6, 7-5, 6-3, 6-2
1934	Fred Perry	Jack Crawford	6-3, 7-5, 6-1
1935	Jack Crawford	Fred Perry	2-6, 6-4, 6-4, 6-4
1936	Adrian Quist	Jack Crawford	6-2, 6-3, 4-6, 3-6, 9-7
1937	Vivian B. McGrath	John Bromwich	6-3, 1-6, 6-0, 2-6, 6-1
1938	Don Budge	John Bromwich	6-4, 6-2, 6-1
1939	John Bromwich	Adrian Quist	6-4, 6-1, 6-3
1940	Adrian Quist	Jack Crawford	6-3, 6-1, 6-2
1941-45	No tournament		
1946	John Bromwich	Dinny Pails	5-7, 6-3, 7-5, 3-6, 6-2
1947	Dinny Pails	John Bromwich	4-6, 6-4, 3-6, 7-5, 8-6
1948	Adrian Quist	John Bromwich	6-4, 3-6, 6-3, 2-6, 6-3
1949	Frank Sedgman	Ken McGregor	6-3, 6-3, 6-2
1950	Frank Sedgman	Ken McGregor	6-3, 6-4, 4-6, 6-1
1951	Richard Savitt	Ken McGregor	6-3, 2-6, 6-3, 6-1
1952	Ken McGregor	Frank Sedgman	7-5, 12-10, 2-6, 6-2
1953	Ken Rosewall	Mervyn Rose	6-0, 6-3, 6-4
1954	Mervyn Rose	Rex Hartwig	6-2, 0-6, 6-4, 6-2
1955	Ken Rosewall	Lew Hoad	9-7, 6-4, 6-4
1956	Lew Hoad	Ken Rosewall	6-4, 3-6, 6-4, 7-5
1957	Ashley Cooper	Neale Fraser	6-3, 9-11, 6-4, 6-2
1958	Ashley Cooper	Mal Anderson	7-5, 6-3, 6-4
1959	Alex Olmedo	Neale Fraser	6-1, 6-2, 3-6, 6-3
1960	Rod Laver	Neale Fraser	5-7, 3-6, 6-3, 8-6, 8-6
1961	Roy Emerson	Rod Laver	1-6, 6-3, 7-5, 6-4
1962	Rod Laver	Roy Emerson	8-6, 0-6, 6-4, 6-4
1963	Roy Emerson	Ken Fletcher	6-3, 6-3, 6-1
1964	Roy Emerson	Fred Stolle	6-3, 6-4, 6-2
1965	Roy Emerson	Fred Stolle	7-9, 2-6, 6-4, 7-5, 6-1
1966	Roy Emerson	Arthur Ashe	6-4, 6-8, 6-2, 6-3
1967	Roy Emerson	Arthur Ashe	6-4, 6-1, 6-1
1968	Bill Bowrey	Juan Gisbert	7-5, 2-6, 9-7, 6-4
1969*	Rod Laver	Andres Gimeno	6-3, 6-4, 7-5
1970	Arthur Ashe	Dick Crealy	6-4, 9-7, 6-2

Australian Championships (Cont.)

Year	Winner	Finalist	Score
1971	Ken Rosewall	Arthur Ashe	6-1, 7-5, 6-3
1972	Ken Rosewall	Mal Anderson	7-6, 6-3, 7-5
1973	John Newcombe	Onny Parun	6-3, 6-7, 7-5, 6-1
1974	Jimmy Connors	Phil Dent	7-6, 6-4, 4-6, 6-3
1975	John Newcombe	Jimmy Connors	7-5, 3-6, 6-4, 7-5
1976	Mark Edmondson	John Newcombe	6-7, 6-3, 7-6, 6-1
1977 (Jan)	Roscoe Tanner	Guillermo Vilas	6-3, 6-3, 6-3
1977 (Dec)	Vitas Gerulaitis	John Lloyd	6-3, 7-6, 5-7, 3-6, 6-2
1978	Guillermo Vilas	John Marks	6-4, 6-4, 3-6, 6-3
1979	Guillermo Vilas	John Sadri	7-6, 6-3, 6-2
1980	Brian Teacher	Kim Warwick	7-5, 7-6, 6-3
1981	Johan Kriek	Steve Denton	6-2, 7-6, 6-7, 6-4
1982	Johan Kriek	Steve Denton	6-3, 6-3, 6-2
1983	Mats Wilander	Ivan Lendl	6-1, 6-4, 6-4
1984	Mats Wilander	Kevin Curren	6-7, 6-4, 7-6, 6-2
1985 (Dec)	Stefan Edberg	Mats Wilander	6-4, 6-3, 6-3
1987 (Jan)	Stefan Edberg	Pat Cash	6-3, 6-4, 3-6, 5-7, 6-3
1988	Mats Wilander	Pat Cash	6-3, 6-7, 3-6, 6-1, 8-6
1989	Ivan Lendl	Miloslav Mecir	6-2, 6-2, 6-2
1990	Ivan Lendl	Stefan Edberg	4-6, 7-6, 5-2 ret
1991	Boris Becker	Ivan Lendl	1-6, 6-4, 6-4, 6-4
1992	Jim Courier	Stefan Edberg	6-3, 3-6, 6-4, 6-2
1993	Jim Courier	Stefan Edberg	6-2, 6-1, 2-6, 7-5

*Became Open (amateur and professional) in 1969.

French Championships

Year	Winner	Finalist	Score
1925†	Rene Lacoste	Jean Borotra	7-5, 6-1, 6-4
1926	Henri Cochet	Rene Lacoste	6-2, 6-4, 6-3
1927	Rene Lacoste	Bill Tilden	6-4, 4-6, 5-7, 6-3, 11-9
1928	Henri Cochet	Rene Lacoste	5-7, 6-3, 6-1, 6-3
1929	Rene Lacoste	Jean Borotra	6-3, 2-6, 6-0, 2-6, 8-6
1930	Henri Cochet	Bill Tilden	3-6, 8-6, 6-3, 6-1
1931	Jean Borotra	Claude Boussus	2-6, 6-4, 7-5, 6-4
1932	Henri Cochet	Giorgio de Stefani	6-0, 6-4, 4-6, 6-3
1933	Jack Crawford	Henri Cochet	8-6, 6-1, 6-3
1934	Gottfried von Cramm	Jack Crawford	6-4, 7-9, 3-6, 7-5, 6-3
1935	Fred Perry	Gottfried von Cramm	6-3, 3-6, 6-1, 6-3
1936	Gottfried von Cramm	Fred Perry	6-0, 2-6, 6-2, 2-6, 6-0
1937	Henner Henkel	Henry Austin	6-1, 6-4, 6-3
1938	Don Budge	Roderick Menzel	6-3, 6-2, 6-4
1939	Don McNeill	Bobby Riggs	7-5, 6-0, 6-3
1940	No tournament		
1941‡	Bernard Destremau	n/a	n/a
1942‡	Bernard Destremau	n/a	n/a
1943‡	Yvon Petra	n/a	n/a
1944‡	Yvon Petra	n/a	n/a
1945‡	Yvon Petra	Bernard Destremau	7-5, 6-4, 6-2
1946	Marcel Bernard	Jaroslav Drobny	3-6, 2-6, 6-1, 6-4, 6-3
1947	Joseph Asboth	Eric Sturgess	8-6, 7-5, 6-4
1948	Frank Parker	Jaroslav Drobny	6-4, 7-5, 5-7, 8-6
1949	Frank Parker	Budge Patty	6-3, 1-6, 6-1, 6-4
1950	Budge Patty	Jaroslav Drobny	6-1, 6-2, 3-6, 5-7, 7-5
1951	Jaroslav Drobny	Eric Sturgess	6-3, 6-3, 6-3
1952	Jaroslav Drobny	Frank Sedgman	6-2, 6-0, 3-6, 6-4
1953	Ken Rosewall	Vic Seixas	6-3, 6-4, 1-6, 6-2
1954	Tony Trabert	Arthur Larsen	6-4, 7-5, 6-1
1955	Tony Trabert	Sven Davidson	2-6, 6-1, 6-4, 6-2
1956	Lew Hoad	Sven Davidson	6-4, 8-6, 6-3
1957	Sven Davidson	Herbie Flam	6-3, 6-4, 6-4
1958	Mervyn Rose	Luis Ayala	6-3, 6-4, 6-4
1959	Nicola Pietrangeli	Ian Vermaak	3-6, 6-3, 6-4, 6-1
1960	Nicola Pietrangeli	Luis Ayala	3-6, 6-3, 6-4, 4-6, 6-3
1961	Manuel Santana	Nicola Pietrangeli	4-6, 6-1, 3-6, 6-0, 6-2
1962	Rod Laver	Roy Emerson	3-6, 2-6, 6-3, 9-7, 6-2

French Championships *(Cont.)*

Year	Winner	Finalist	Score
1963	Roy Emerson	Pierre Darmon	3-6, 6-1, 6-4, 6-4
1964	Manuel Santana	Nicola Pietrangeli	6-3, 6-1, 4-6, 7-5
1965	Fred Stolle	Tony Roche	3-6, 6-0, 6-2, 6-3
1966	Tony Roche	Istvan Gulyas	6-1, 6-4, 7-5
1967	Roy Emerson	Tony Roche	6-1, 6-4, 2-6, 6-2
1968*	Ken Rosewall	Rod Laver	6-3, 6-1, 2-6, 6-2
1969	Rod Laver	Ken Rosewall	6-4, 6-3, 6-4
1970	Jan Kodes	Zeljko Franulovic	6-2, 6-4, 6-0
1971	Jan Kodes	Ilie Nastase	8-6, 6-2, 2-6, 7-5
1972	Andres Gimeno	Patrick Proisy	4-6, 6-3, 6-1, 6-1
1973	Ilie Nastase	Nikki Pilic	6-3, 6-3, 6-0
1974	Bjorn Borg	Manuel Orantes	6-7, 6-0, 6-1, 6-1
1975	Bjorn Borg	Guillermo Vilas	6-2, 6-3, 6-4
1976	Adriano Panatta	Harold Solomon	6-1, 6-4, 4-6, 7-6
1977	Guillermo Vilas	Brian Gottfried	6-0, 6-3, 6-0
1978	Bjorn Borg	Guillermo Vilas	6-1, 6-1, 6-3
1979	Bjorn Borg	Victor Pecci	6-3, 6-1, 6-7, 6-4
1980	Bjorn Borg	Vitas Gerulaitis	6-4, 6-1, 6-2
1981	Bjorn Borg	Ivan Lendl	6-1, 4-6, 6-2, 3-6, 6-1
1982	Mats Wilander	Guillermo Vilas	1-6, 7-6, 6-0, 6-4
1983	Yannick Noah	Mats Wilander	6-2, 7-5, 7-6
1984	Ivan Lendl	John McEnroe	3-6, 2-6, 6-4, 7-5, 7-5
1985	Mats Wilander	Ivan Lendl	3-6, 6-4, 6-2, 6-2
1986	Ivan Lendl	Mikael Pernfors	6-3, 6-2, 6-4
1987	Ivan Lendl	Mats Wilander	7-5, 6-2, 3-6, 7-6
1988	Mats Wilander	Henri Leconte	7-5, 6-2, 6-1
1989	Michael Chang	Stefan Edberg	6-1, 3-6, 4-6, 6-4, 6-2
1990	Andres Gomez	Andre Agassi	6-3, 2-6, 6-4, 6-4
1991	Jim Courier	Andre Agassi	3-6, 6-4, 2-6, 6-1, 6-4
1992	Jim Courier	Petr Korda	7-5, 6-2, 6-1
1993	Sergi Bruguera	Jim Courier	6-4, 2-6, 6-2, 3-6, 6-3

†1925 was the first year that entries were accepted from all countries.

‡From 1941 to 1945 the event was called Tournoi de France and was closed to all foreigners.

*Became Open (amateur and professional) in 1968 but closed to contract professionals in 1972.

Wimbledon Championships

Year	Winner	Finalist	Score
1877	Spencer W. Gore	William C. Marshall	6-1, 6-2, 6-4
1878	P. Frank Hadow	Spencer W. Gore	7-5, 6-1, 9-7
1879	John T. Hartley	V. St Leger Gould	6-2, 6-4, 6-2
1880	John T. Hartley	Herbert F. Lawford	6-0, 6-2, 2-6, 6-3
1881	William Renshaw	John T. Hartley	6-0, 6-2, 6-1
1882	William Renshaw	Ernest Renshaw	6-1, 2-6, 4-6, 6-2, 6-2
1883	William Renshaw	Ernest Renshaw	2-6, 6-3, 6-3, 4-6, 6-3
1884	William Renshaw	Herbert F. Lawford	6-0, 6-4, 9-7
1885	William Renshaw	Herbert F. Lawford	7-5, 6-2, 4-6, 7-5
1886	William Renshaw	Herbert F. Lawford	6-0, 5-7, 6-3, 6-4
1887	Herbert F. Lawford	Ernest Renshaw	1-6, 6-3, 3-6, 6-4, 6-4
1888	Ernest Renshaw	Herbert F. Lawford	6-3, 7-5, 6-0
1889	William Renshaw	Ernest Renshaw	6-4, 6-1, 3-6, 6-0
1890	William J. Hamilton	William Renshaw	6-8, 6-2, 3-6, 6-1, 6-1
1891	Wilfred Baddeley	Joshua Pim	6-4, 1-6, 7-5, 6-0
1892	Wilfred Baddeley	Joshua Pim	4-6, 6-3, 6-3, 6-2
1893	Joshua Pim	Wilfred Baddeley	3-6, 6-1, 6-3, 6-2
1894	Joshua Pim	Wilfred Baddeley	10-8, 6-2, 8-6
1895	Wilfred Baddeley	Wilberforce V. Eaves	4-6, 2-6, 8-6, 6-2, 6-3
1896	Harold S. Mahoney	Wilfred Baddeley	6-2, 6-8, 5-7, 8-6, 6-3
1897	Reggie F. Doherty	Harold S. Mahoney	6-4, 6-4, 6-3
1898	Reggie F. Doherty	H. Laurie Doherty	6-3, 6-3, 2-6, 5-7, 6-1
1899	Reggie F. Doherty	Arthur W. Gore	1-6, 4-6, 6-2, 6-3, 6-3
1900	Reggie F. Doherty	Sidney H. Smith	6-8, 6-3, 6-1, 6-2
1901	Arthur W. Gore	Reggie F. Doherty	4-6, 7-5, 6-4, 6-4
1902	H. Laurie Doherty	Arthur W. Gore	6-4, 6-3, 3-6, 6-0

Wimbledon Championship (Cont.)

Year	Winner	Finalist	Score
1903	H. Laurie Doherty	Frank L. Riseley	7-5, 6-3, 6-0
1904	H. Laurie Doherty	Frank L. Riseley	6-1, 7-5, 8-6
1905	H. Laurie Doherty	Norman E. Brookes	8-6, 6-2, 6-4
1906	H. Laurie Doherty	Frank L. Riseley	6-4, 4-6, 6-2, 6-3
1907	Norman E. Brookes	Arthur W. Gore	6-4, 6-2, 6-2
1908	Arthur W. Gore	H. Roper Barrett	6-3, 6-2, 4-6, 3-6, 6-4
1909	Arthur W. Gore	M. J. G. Ritchie	6-8, 1-6, 6-2, 6-2, 6-2
1910	Anthony F. Wilding	Arthur W. Gore	6-4, 7-5, 4-6, 6-2
1911	Anthony F. Wilding	H. Roper Barrett	6-4, 4-6, 2-6, 6-2 ret
1912	Anthony F. Wilding	Arthur W. Gore	6-4, 6-4, 4-6, 6-4
1913	Anthony F. Wilding	Maurice E. McLoughlin	8-6, 6-3, 10-8
1914	Norman E. Brookes	Anthony F. Wilding	6-4, 6-4, 7-5
1915-18	No tournament		
1919	Gerald L. Patterson	Norman E. Brookes	6-3, 7-5, 6-2
1920	Bill Tilden	Gerald L. Patterson	2-6, 6-3, 6-2, 6-4
1921	Bill Tilden	Brian I. C. Norton	4-6, 2-6, 6-1, 6-0, 7-5
1922	Gerald L. Patterson	Randolph Lycett	6-3, 6-4, 6-2
1923	Bill Johnston	Francis T. Hunter	6-0, 6-3, 6-1
1924	Jean Borotra	Rene Lacoste	6-1, 3-6, 6-1, 3-6, 6-4
1925	Rene Lacoste	Jean Borotra	6-3, 6-3, 4-6, 8-6
1926	Jean Borotra	Howard Kinsey	8-6, 6-1, 6-3
1927	Henri Cochet	Jean Borotra	4-6, 4-6, 6-3, 6-4, 7-5
1928	Rene Lacoste	Henri Cochet	6-1, 4-6, 6-4, 6-2
1929	Henri Cochet	Jean Borotra	6-4, 6-3, 6-4
1930	Bill Tilden	Wilmer Allison	6-3, 9-7, 6-4
1931	Sidney B. Wood Jr	Francis X. Shields	walkover
1932	Ellsworth Vines	Henry Austin	6-4, 6-2, 6-0
1933	Jack Crawford	Ellsworth Vines	4-6, 11-9, 6-2, 2-6, 6-4
1934	Fred Perry	Jack Crawford	6-3, 6-0, 7-5
1935	Fred Perry	Gottfried von Cramm	6-2, 6-4, 6-4
1936	Fred Perry	Gottfried von Cramm	6-1, 6-1, 6-0
1937	Don Budge	Gottfried von Cramm	6-3, 6-4, 6-2
1938	Don Budge	Henry Austin	6-1, 6-0, 6-3
1939	Bobby Riggs	Elwood Cooke	2-6, 8-6, 3-6, 6-3, 6-2
1940-45	No tournament		
1946	Yvon Petra	Geoff E. Brown	6-2, 6-4, 7-9, 5-7, 6-4
1947	Jack Kramer	Tom P. Brown	6-1, 6-3, 6-2
1948	Bob Falkenburg	John Bromwich	7-5, 0-6, 6-2, 3-6, 7-5
1949	Ted Schroeder	Jaroslav Drobny	3-6, 6-0, 6-3, 4-6, 6-4
1950	Budge Patty	Frank Sedgman	6-1, 8-10, 6-2, 6-3
1951	Dick Savitt	Ken McGregor	6-4, 6-4, 6-4
1952	Frank Sedgman	Jaroslav Drobny	4-6, 6-3, 6-2, 6-3
1953	Vic Seixas	Kurt Nielsen	9-7, 6-3, 6-4
1954	Jaroslav Drobny	Ken Rosewall	13-11, 4-6, 6-2, 9-7
1955	Tony Trabert	Kurt Nielsen	6-3, 7-5, 6-1
1956	Lew Hoad	Ken Rosewall	6-2, 4-6, 7-5, 6-4
1957	Lew Hoad	Ashley Cooper	6-2, 6-1, 6-2
1958	Ashley Cooper	Neale Fraser	3-6, 6-3, 6-4, 13-11
1959	Alex Olmedo	Rod Laver	6-4, 6-3, 6-4
1960	Neale Fraser	Rod Laver	6-4, 3-6, 9-7, 7-5
1961	Rod Laver	Chuck McKinley	6-3, 6-1, 6-4
1962	Rod Laver	Martin Mulligan	6-2, 6-2, 6-1
1963	Chuck McKinley	Fred Stolle	9-7, 6-1, 6-4
1964	Roy Emerson	Fred Stolle	6-4, 12-10, 4-6, 6-3
1965	Roy Emerson	Fred Stolle	6-2, 6-4, 6-4
1966	Manuel Santana	Dennis Ralston	6-4, 11-9, 6-4
1967	John Newcombe	Wilhelm Bungert	6-3, 6-1, 6-1
1968*	Rod Laver	Tony Roche	6-3, 6-4, 6-2
1969	Rod Laver	John Newcombe	6-4, 5-7, 6-4, 6-4
1970	John Newcombe	Ken Rosewall	5-7, 6-3, 6-2, 3-6, 6-1
1971	John Newcombe	Stan Smith	6-3, 5-7, 2-6, 6-4, 6-4
1972	Stan Smith	Ilie Nastase	4-6, 6-3, 6-3, 4-6, 7-5
1973	Jan Kodes	Alex Metreveli	6-1, 9-8, 6-3
1974	Jimmy Connors	Ken Rosewall	6-1, 6-1, 6-4
1975	Arthur Ashe	Jimmy Connors	6-1, 6-1, 5-7, 6-4
1976	Bjorn Borg	Ilie Nastase	6-4, 6-2, 9-7

Wimbledon Championships (Cont.)

Year	Winner	Finalist	Score
1977	Bjorn Borg	Jimmy Connors	3-6, 6-2, 6-1, 5-7, 6-4
1978	Bjorn Borg	Jimmy Connors	6-2, 6-2, 6-3
1979	Bjorn Borg	Roscoe Tanner	6-7, 6-1, 3-6, 6-3, 6-4
1980	Bjorn Borg	John McEnroe	1-6, 7-5, 6-3, 6-7, 8-6
1981	John McEnroe	Bjorn Borg	4-6, 7-6, 7-6, 6-4
1982	Jimmy Connors	John McEnroe	3-6, 6-3, 6-7, 7-6, 6-4
1983	John McEnroe	Chris Lewis	6-2, 6-2, 6-2
1984	John McEnroe	Jimmy Connors	6-1, 6-1, 6-2
1985	Boris Becker	Kevin Curren	6-3, 6-7, 7-6, 6-4
1986	Boris Becker	Ivan Lendl	6-4, 6-3, 7-5
1987	Pat Cash	Ivan Lendl	7-6, 6-2, 7-5
1988	Stefan Edberg	Boris Becker	4-6, 7-6, 6-4, 6-2
1989	Boris Becker	Stefan Edberg	6-0, 7-6, 6-4
1990	Stefan Edberg	Boris Becker	6-2, 6-2, 3-6, 3-6, 6-4
1991	Michael Stich	Boris Becker	6-4, 7-6, 6-4
1992	Andre Agassi	Goran Ivanisevic	6-7, 6-4, 6-4, 1-6, 6-4
1993	Pete Sampras	Jim Courier	7-6 (7-3), 7-6 (8-6), 3-6, 6-3

*Became Open (amateur and professional) in 1968 but closed to contract professionals in 1972.

Note: Prior to 1922 the tournament was run on a challenge-round system. The previous year's winner "stood out" of an All Comers event, which produced a challenger to play him for the title.

United States Championships

Year	Winner	Finalist	Score
1881	Richard D. Sears	W. E. Glyn	6-0, 6-3, 6-2
1882	Richard D. Sears	C. M. Clark	6-1, 6-4, 6-0
1883	Richard D. Sears	James Dwight	6-2, 6-0, 9-7
1884	Richard D. Sears	H. A. Taylor	6-0, 1-6, 6-0, 6-2
1885	Richard D. Sears	G. M. Brinley	6-3, 4-6, 6-0, 6-3
1886	Richard D. Sears	R. L. Beeckman	4-6, 6-1, 6-3, 6-4
1887	Richard D. Sears	H. W. Slocum Jr	6-1, 6-3, 6-2
1888‡	H. W. Slocum Jr	H. A. Taylor	6-4, 6-1, 6-0
1889	H. W. Slocum Jr	Q. A. Shaw	6-3, 6-1, 4-6, 6-2
1890	Oliver S. Campbell	H. W. Slocum Jr	6-2, 4-6, 6-3, 6-1
1891	Oliver S. Campbell	Clarence Hobart	2-6, 7-5, 7-9, 6-1, 6-2
1892	Oliver S. Campbell	Frederick H. Hovey	7-5, 3-6, 6-3, 7-5
1893‡	Robert D. Wrenn	Frederick H. Hovey	6-4, 3-6, 6-4, 6-4
1894	Robert D. Wrenn	M. F. Goodbody	6-8, 6-1, 6-4, 6-4
1895	Frederick H. Hovey	Robert D. Wrenn	6-3, 6-2, 6-4
1896	Robert D. Wrenn	Frederick H. Hovey	7-5, 3-6, 6-0, 1-6, 6-1
1897	Robert D. Wrenn	Wilberforce V. Eaves	4-6, 8-6, 6-3, 2-6, 6-2
1898‡	Malcolm D. Whitman	Dwight F. Davis	3-6, 6-2, 6-2, 6-1
1899	Malcolm D. Whitman	J. Parmly Paret	6-1, 6-2, 3-6, 7-5
1900	Malcolm D. Whitman	William A. Larned	6-4, 1-6, 6-2, 6-2
1901‡	William A. Larned	Beals C. Wright	6-2, 6-8, 6-4, 6-4
1902	William A. Larned	Reggie F. Doherty	4-6, 6-2, 6-4, 8-6
1903	H. Laurie Doherty	William A. Larned	6-0, 6-3, 10-8
1904‡	Holcombe Ward	William J. Clothier	10-8, 6-4, 9-7
1905	Beals C. Wright	Holcombe Ward	6-2, 6-1, 11-9
1906	William J. Clothier	Beals C. Wright	6-3, 6-0, 6-4
1907‡	William A. Larned	Robert LeRoy	6-2, 6-2, 6-4
1908	William A. Larned	Beals C. Wright	6-1, 6-2, 8-6
1909	William A. Larned	William J. Clothier	6-1, 6-2, 5-7, 1-6, 6-1
1910	William A. Larned	Thomas C. Bundy	6-1, 5-7, 6-0, 6-8, 6-1
1911	William A. Larned	Maurice E. McLoughlin	6-4, 6-4, 6-2
1912†	Maurice E. McLoughlin	Bill Johnson	3-6, 2-6, 6-2, 6-4, 6-2
1913	Maurice E. McLoughlin	Richard N. Williams	6-4, 5-7, 6-3, 6-1
1914	Richard N. Williams	Maurice E. McLoughlin	6-3, 8-6, 10-8
1915	Bill Johnston	Maurice E. McLoughlin	1-6, 6-0, 7-5, 10-8
1916	Richard N. Williams	Bill Johnston	4-6, 6-4, 0-6, 6-2, 6-4
1917#	R. L. Murray	N. W. Niles	5-7, 8-6, 6-3, 6-3
1918	R. L. Murray	Bill Tilden	6-3, 6-1, 7-5
1919	Bill Johnston	Bill Tilden	6-4, 6-4, 6-3
1920	Bill Tilden	Bill Johnston	6-1, 1-6, 7-5, 5-7, 6-3
1921	Bill Tilden	Wallace F. Johnson	6-1, 6-3, 6-1

United States Championships *(Cont.)*

Year	Winner	Finalist	Score
1922	Bill Tilden	Bill Johnston	4-6, 3-6, 6-2, 6-3, 6-4
1923	Bill Tilden	Bill Johnston	6-4, 6-1, 6-4
1924	Bill Tilden	Bill Johnston	6-1, 9-7, 6-2
1925	Bill Tilden	Bill Johnston	4-6, 11-9, 6-3, 4-6, 6-3
1926	Rene Lacoste	Jean Borotra	6-4, 6-0, 6-4
1927	Rene Lacoste	Bill Tilden	11-9, 6-3, 11-9
1928	Henri Cochet	Francis T. Hunter	4-6, 6-4, 3-6, 7-5, 6-3
1929	Bill Tilden	Francis T. Hunter	3-6, 6-3, 4-6, 6-2, 6-4
1930	John H. Doeg	Francis X. Shields	10-8, 1-6, 6-4, 16-14
1931	Ellsworth Vines	George M. Lott Jr	7-9, 6-3, 9-7, 7-5
1932	Ellsworth Vines	Henri Cochet	6-4, 6-4, 6-4
1933	Fred Perry	Jack Crawford	6-3, 11-13, 4-6, 6-0, 6-1
1934	Fred Perry	Wilmer L. Allison	6-4, 6-3, 1-6, 8-6
1935	Wilmer L. Allison	Sidney B. Wood Jr	6-2, 6-2, 6-3
1936	Fred Perry	Don Budge	2-6, 6-2, 8-6, 1-6, 10-8
1937	Don Budge	Gottfried von Cramm	6-1, 7-9, 6-1, 3-6, 6-1
1938	Don Budge	Gene Mako	6-3, 6-8, 6-2, 6-1
1939	Bobby Riggs	Welby van Horn	6-4, 6-2, 6-4
1940	Don McNeill	Bobby Riggs	4-6, 6-8, 6-3, 6-3, 7-5
1941	Bobby Riggs	Francis Kovacs II	5-7, 6-1, 6-3, 6-3
1942	Ted Schroeder	Frank Parker	8-6, 7-5, 3-6, 4-6, 6-2
1943	Joseph R. Hunt	Jack Kramer	6-3, 6-8, 10-8, 6-0
1944	Frank Parker	William F. Talbert	6-4, 3-6, 6-3, 6-3
1945	Frank Parker	William F. Talbert	14-12, 6-1, 6-2
1946	Jack Kramer	Tom P. Brown	9-7, 6-3, 6-0
1947	Jack Kramer	Frank Parker	4-6, 2-6, 6-1, 6-0, 6-3
1948	Pancho Gonzales	Eric W. Sturgess	6-2, 6-3, 14-12
1949	Pancho Gonzales	Ted Schroeder	16-18, 2-6, 6-1, 6-2, 6-4
1950	Arthur Larsen	Herbie Flam	6-3, 4-6, 5-7, 6-4, 6-3
1951	Frank Sedgman	Vic Seixas	6-4, 6-1, 6-1
1952	Frank Sedgman	Gardnar Mulloy	6-1, 6-2, 6-3
1953	Tony Trabert	Vic Seixas	6-3, 6-2, 6-3
1954	Vic Seixas	Rex Hartwig	3-6, 6-2, 6-4, 6-4
1955	Tony Trabert	Ken Rosewall	9-7, 6-3, 6-3
1956	Ken Rosewall	Lew Hoad	4-6, 6-2, 6-3, 6-3
1957	Mal Anderson	Ashley J. Cooper	10-8, 7-5, 6-4
1958	Ashley J. Cooper	Mal Anderson	6-2, 3-6, 4-6, 10-8, 8-6
1959	Neale Fraser	Alex Olmedo	6-3, 5-7, 6-2, 6-4
1960	Neale Fraser	Rod Laver	6-4, 6-4, 9-7
1961	Roy Emerson	Rod Laver	7-5, 6-3, 6-2
1962	Rod Laver	Roy Emerson	6-2, 6-4, 5-7, 6-4
1963	Rafael Osuna	Frank Froehling III	7-5, 6-4, 6-2
1964	Roy Emerson	Fred Stolle	6-4, 6-2, 6-4
1965	Manuel Santana	Cliff Drysdale	6-2, 7-9, 7-5, 6-1
1966	Fred Stolle	John Newcombe	4-6, 12-10, 6-3, 6-4
1967	John Newcombe	Clark Graebner	6-4, 6-4, 8-6
1968**	Arthur Ashe	Bob Lutz	4-6, 6-3, 8-10, 6-0, 6-4
1968*	Arthur Ashe	Tom Okker	14-12, 5-7, 6-3, 3-6, 6-3
1969**	Stan Smith	Bob Lutz	9-7, 6-3, 6-1
1969*	Rod Laver	Tony Roche	7-9, 6-1, 6-3, 6-2
1970	Ken Rosewall	Tony Roche	2-6, 6-4, 7-6, 6-3
1971	Stan Smith	Jan Kodes	3-6, 6-3, 6-2, 7-6
1972	Ilie Nastase	Arthur Ashe	3-6, 6-3, 6-7, 6-4, 6-3
1973	John Newcombe	Jan Kodes	6-4, 1-6, 4-6, 6-2, 6-3
1974	Jimmy Connors	Ken Rosewall	6-1, 6-0, 6-1
1975	Manuel Orantes	Jimmy Connors	6-4, 6-3, 6-3
1976	Jimmy Connors	Bjorn Borg	6-4, 3-6, 7-6, 6-4
1977	Guillermo Vilas	Jimmy Connors	2-6, 6-3, 7-6, 6-0
1978	Jimmy Connors	Bjorn Borg	6-4, 6-2, 6-2
1979	John McEnroe	Vitas Gerulaitis	7-5, 6-3, 6-3
1980	John McEnroe	Bjorn Borg	7-6, 6-1, 6-7, 5-7, 6-4
1981	John McEnroe	Bjorn Borg	4-6, 6-2, 6-4, 6-3
1982	Jimmy Connors	Ivan Lendl	6-3, 6-2, 4-6, 6-4
1983	Jimmy Connors	Ivan Lendl	6-3, 6-7, 7-5, 6-0
1984	John McEnroe	Ivan Lendl	6-3, 6-4, 6-1
1985	Ivan Lendl	John McEnroe	7-6, 6-3, 6-4

United States Championships *(Cont.)*

Year	Winner	Finalist	Score
1986	Ivan Lendl	Miloslav Mecir	6-4, 6-2, 6-0
1987	Ivan Lendl	Mats Wilander	6-7, 6-0, 7-6, 6-4
1988	Mats Wilander	Ivan Lendl	6-4, 4-6, 6-3, 5-7, 6-4
1989	Boris Becker	Ivan Lendl	7-6, 1-6, 6-3, 7-6
1990	Pete Sampras	Andre Agassi	6-4, 6-3, 6-2
1991	Stefan Edberg	Jim Courier	6-2, 6-4, 6-0
1992	Stefan Edberg	Pete Sampras	3-6, 6-4, 7-6, 6-2
1993	Pete Sampras	Cédric Pioline	6-4, 6-4, 6-3

*Became Open (amateur and professional) in 1968.
†Challenge round abolished.
‡No challenge round played.
#National Patriotic Tournament.
**Amateur event held.

WOMEN

Australian Championships

Year	Winner	Finalist	Score
1922	Margaret Molesworth	Esna Boyd	6-3, 10-8
1923	Margaret Molesworth	Esna Boyd	6-1, 7-5
1924	Sylvia Lance	Esna Boyd	6-3, 3-6, 6-4
1925	Daphne Akhurst	Esna Boyd	1-6, 8-6, 6-4
1926	Daphne Akhurst	Esna Boyd	6-1, 6-3
1927	Esna Boyd	Sylvia Harper	5-7, 6-1, 6-2
1928	Daphne Akhurst	Esna Boyd	7-5, 6-2
1929	Daphne Akhurst	Louise Bickerton	6-1, 5-7, 6-2
1930	Daphne Akhurst	Sylvia Harper	10-8, 2-6, 7-5
1931	Coral Buttsworth	Margorie Crawford	1-6, 6-3, 6-4
1932	Coral Buttsworth	Kathrine Le Messurier	9-7, 6-4
1933	Joan Hartigan	Coral Buttsworth	6-4, 6-3
1934	Joan Hartigan	Margaret Molesworth	6-1, 6-4
1935	Dorothy Round	Nancye Wynne Bolton	1-6, 6-1, 6-3
1936	Joan Hartigan	Nancye Wynne Bolton	6-4, 6-4
1937	Nancye Wynne Bolton	Emily Westacott	6-3, 5-7, 6-4
1938	Dorothy Bundy	D. Stevenson	6-3, 6-2
1939	Emily Westacott	Nell Hopman	6-1, 6-2
1940	Nancye Wynne Bolton	Thelma Coyne	5-7, 6-4, 6-0
1941-45	No tournament		
1946	Nancye Wynne Bolton	Joyce Fitch	6-4, 6-4
1947	Nancye Wynne Bolton	Nell Hopman	6-3, 6-2
1948	Nancye Wynne Bolton	Marie Toomey	6-3, 6-1
1949	Doris Hart	Nancye Wynne Bolton	6-3, 6-4
1950	Louise Brough	Doris Hart	6-4, 3-6, 6-4
1951	Nancye Wynne Bolton	Thelma Long	6-1, 7-5
1952	Thelma Long	H. Angwin	6-2, 6-3
1953	Maureen Connolly	Julia Sampson	6-3, 6-2
1954	Thelma Long	J. Staley	6-3, 6-4
1955	Beryl Penrose	Thelma Long	6-4, 6-3
1956	Mary Carter	Thelma Long	3-6, 6-2, 9-7
1957	Shirley Fry	Althea Gibson	6-3, 6-4
1958	Angela Mortimer	Lorraine Coghlan	6-3, 6-4
1959	Mary Carter-Reitano	Renee Schuurman	6-2, 6-3
1960	Margaret Smith	Jan Lehane	7-5, 6-2
1961	Margaret Smith	Jan Lehane	6-1, 6-4
1962	Margaret Smith	Jan Lehane	6-0, 6-2
1963	Margaret Smith	Jan Lehane	6-2, 6-2
1964	Margaret Smith	Lesley Turner	6-3, 6-2
1965	Margaret Smith	Maria Bueno	5-7, 6-4, 5-2 ret
1966	Margaret Smith	Nancy Richey	Default
1967	Nancy Richey	Lesley Turner	6-1, 6-4
1968	Billie Jean King	Margaret Smith	6-1, 6-2
1969*	Margaret Smith Court	Billie Jean King	6-4, 6-1
1970	Margaret Smith Court	Kerry Melville Reid	6-3, 6-1

Australian Championships *(Cont.)*

Year	Winner	Finalist	Score
1971	Margaret Smith Court	Evonne Goolagong	2-6, 7-6, 7-5
1972	Virginia Wade	Evonne Goolagong	6-4, 6-4
1973	Margaret Smith Court	Evonne Goolagong	6-4, 7-5
1974	Evonne Goolagong	Chris Evert	7-6, 4-6, 6-0
1975	Evonne Goolagong	Martina Navratilova	6-3, 6-2
1976	Evonne Goolagong Cawley	Renata Tomanova	6-2, 6-2
1977 (Jan)	Kerry Melville Reid	Dianne Balestrat	7-5, 6-2
1977 (Dec)	Evonne Goolagong Cawley	Helen Gourlay	6-3, 6-0
1978	Chris O'Neil	Betsy Nagelsen	6-3, 7-6
1979	Barbara Jordan	Sharon Walsh	6-3, 6-3
1980	Hana Mandlikova	Wendy Turnbull	6-0, 7-5
1981	Martina Navratilova	Chris Evert Lloyd	6-7, 6-4, 7-5
1982	Chris Evert Lloyd	Martina Navratilova	6-3, 2-6, 6-3
1983	Martina Navratilova	Kathy Jordan	6-2, 7-6
1984	Chris Evert Lloyd	Helena Sukova	6-7, 6-1, 6-3
1985 (Dec)	Martina Navratilova	Chris Evert Lloyd	6-2, 4-6, 6-2
1987 (Jan)	Hana Mandlikova	Martina Navratilova	7-5, 7-6
1988	Steffi Graf	Chris Evert	6-1, 7-6
1989	Steffi Graf	Helena Sukova	6-4, 6-4
1990	Steffi Graf	Mary Joe Fernandez	6-3, 6-4
1991	Monica Seles	Jana Novotna	5-7, 6-3, 6-1
1992	Monica Seles	Mary Joe Fernandez	6-2, 6-3
1993	Monica Seles	Steffi Graf	4-6, 6-3, 6-2

*Became Open (amateur and professional) in 1969.

French Championships

Year	Winner	Finalist	Score
1925†	Suzanne Lenglen	Kathleen McKane	6-1, 6-2
1926	Suzanne Lenglen	Mary K. Browne	6-1, 6-0
1927	Kea Bouman	Irene Peacock	6-2, 6-4
1928	Helen Wills	Eileen Bennett	6-1, 6-2
1929	Helen Wills	Simone Mathieu	6-3, 6-4
1930	Helen Wills Moody	Helen Jacobs	6-2, 6-1
1931	Cilly Aussem	Betty Nuthall	8-6, 6-1
1932	Helen Wills Moody	Simone Mathieu	7-5, 6-1
1933	Margaret Scriven	Simone Mathieu	6-2, 4-6, 6-4
1934	Margaret Scriven	Helen Jacobs	7-5, 4-6, 6-1
1935	Hilde Sperling	Simone Mathieu	6-2, 6-1
1936	Hilde Sperling	Simone Mathieu	6-3, 6-4
1937	Hilde Sperling	Simone Mathieu	6-2, 6-4
1938	Simone Mathieu	Nelly Landry	6-0, 6-3
1939	Simone Mathieu	Jadwiga Jedrzejowska	6-3, 8-6
1940-45	No tournament		
1946	Margaret Osborne	Pauline Betz	1-6, 8-6, 7-5
1947	Patricia Todd	Doris Hart	6-3, 3-6, 6-4
1948	Nelly Landry	Shirley Fry	6-2, 0-6, 6-0
1949	Margaret Osborne duPont	Nelly Adamson	7-5, 6-2
1950	Doris Hart	Patricia Todd	6-4, 4-6, 6-2
1951	Shirley Fry	Doris Hart	6-3, 3-6, 6-3
1952	Doris Hart	Shirley Fry	6-4, 6-4
1953	Maureen Connolly	Doris Hart	6-2, 6-4
1954	Maureen Connolly	Ginette Bucaille	6-4, 6-1
1955	Angela Mortimer	Dorothy Knode	2-6, 7-5, 10-8
1956	Althea Gibson	Angela Mortimer	6-0, 12-10
1957	Shirley Bloomer	Dorothy Knode	6-1, 6-3
1958	Zsuzsi Kormoczi	Shirley Bloomer	6-4, 1-6, 6-2
1959	Christine Truman	Zsuzsi Kormoczi	6-4, 7-5
1960	Darlene Hard	Yola Ramirez	6-3, 6-4
1961	Ann Haydon	Yola Ramirez	6-2, 6-1
1962	Margaret Smith	Lesley Turner	6-3, 3-6, 7-5
1963	Lesley Turner	Ann Haydon Jones	2-6, 6-3, 7-5
1964	Margaret Smith	Maria Bueno	5-7, 6-1, 6-2
1965	Lesley Turner	Margaret Smith	6-3, 6-4
1966	Ann Jones	Nancy Richey	6-3, 6-1

French Championships (Cont.)

Year	Winner	Finalist	Score
1967	Francoise Durr	Lesley Turner	4-6, 6-3, 6-4
1968*	Nancy Richey	Ann Jones	5-7, 6-4, 6-1
1969	Margaret Smith Court	Ann Jones	6-1, 4-6, 6-3
1970	Margaret Smith Court	Helga Niessen	6-2, 6-4
1971	Evonne Goolagong	Helen Gourlay	6-3, 7-5
1972	Billie Jean King	Evonne Goolagong	6-3, 6-3
1973	Margaret Smith Court	Chris Evert	6-7, 7-6, 6-4
1974	Chris Evert	Olga Morozova	6-1, 6-2
1975	Chris Evert	Martina Navratilova	2-6, 6-2, 6-1
1976	Sue Barker	Renata Tomanova	6-2, 0-6, 6-2
1977	Mima Jausovec	Florenza Mihai	6-2, 6-7, 6-1
1978	Virginia Ruzici	Mima Jausovec	6-2, 6-2
1979	Chris Evert Lloyd	Wendy Turnbull	6-2, 6-0
1980	Chris Evert Lloyd	Virginia Ruzici	6-0, 6-3
1981	Hana Mandlikova	Sylvia Hanika	6-2, 6-4
1982	Martina Navratilova	Andrea Jaeger	7-6, 6-1
1983	Chris Evert Lloyd	Mima Jausovec	6-1, 6-2
1984	Martina Navratilova	Chris Evert Lloyd	6-3, 6-1
1985	Chris Evert Lloyd	Martina Navratilova	6-3, 6-7, 7-5
1986	Chris Evert Lloyd	Martina Navratilova	2-6, 6-3, 6-3
1987	Steffi Graf	Martina Navratilova	6-4, 4-6, 8-6
1988	Steffi Graf	Natalia Zvereva	6-0, 6-0
1989	Arantxa Sanchez Vicario	Steffi Graf	7-6, 3-6, 7-5
1990	Monica Seles	Steffi Graf	7-6, 6-4
1991	Monica Seles	Arantxa Sanchez Vicario	6-3, 6-4
1992	Monica Seles	Steffi Graf	6-2, 3-6, 10-8
1993	Steffi Graf	Mary Joe Fernandez	4-6, 6-2, 6-4

*Became Open (amateur and professional) in 1968 but closed to contract professionals in 1972.

†1925 was the first year that entries were accepted from all countries.

Wimbledon Championships

Year	Winner	Finalist	Score
1884	Maud Watson	Lilian Watson	6-8, 6-3, 6-3
1885	Maud Watson	Blanche Bingley	6-1, 7-5
1886	Blanche Bingley	Maud Watson	6-3, 6-3
1887	Charlotte Dod	Blanche Bingley	6-2, 6-0
1888	Charlotte Dod	Blanche Bingley Hillyard	6-3, 6-3
1889	Blanche Bingley Hillyard		
1890	Lena Rice		
1891	Charlotte Dod		
1892	Charlotte Dod	Blanche Bingley Hillyard	6-1, 6-1
1893	Charlotte Dod	Blanche Bingley Hillyard	6-8, 6-1, 6-4
1894	Blanche Bingley Hillyard		
1895	Charlotte Cooper		
1896	Charlotte Cooper	Mrs. W. H. Pickering	6-2, 6-3
1897	Blanche Bingley Hillyard	Charlotte Cooper	5-7, 7-5, 6-2
1898	Charlotte Cooper		
1899	Blanche Bingley Hillyard	Charlotte Cooper	6-2, 6-3
1900	Blanche Bingley Hillyard	Charlotte Cooper	4-6, 6-4, 6-4
1901	Charlotte Cooper Sterry	Blanche Bingley Hillyard	6-2, 6-2
1902	Muriel Robb	Charlotte Cooper Sterry	7-5, 6-1
1903	Dorothea Douglass		
1904	Dorothea Douglass	Charlotte Cooper Sterry	6-0, 6-3
1905	May Sutton	Dorothea Douglass	6-3, 6-4
1906	Dorothea Douglass	May Sutton	6-3, 9-7
1907	May Sutton	Dorothea Douglass Lambert Chambers	6-1, 6-4
1908	Charlotte Cooper Sterry		
1909	Dora Boothby		
1910	Dorothea Douglass Lambert Chambers	Dora Boothby	6-2, 6-2
1911	Dorothea Douglass Lambert Chambers	Dora Boothby	6-0, 6-0
1912	Ethel Larcombe		

Wimbledon Championships (Cont.)

Year	Winner	Finalist	Score
1913	Dorothea Douglass Lambert Chambers		
1914	Dorothea Douglass Lambert Chambers	Ethel Larcombe	7-5, 6-4
1915-18	No tournament		
1919	Suzanne Lenglen	Dorothea Douglass Lambert Chambers	10-8, 4-6, 9-7
1920	Suzanne Lenglen	Dorothea Douglass Lambert Chambers	6-3, 6-0
1921	Suzanne Lenglen	Elizabeth Ryan	6-2, 6-0
1922	Suzanne Lenglen	Molla Mallory	6-2, 6-0
1923	Suzanne Lenglen	Kathleen McKane	6-2, 6-2
1924	Kathleen McKane	Helen Wills	4-6, 6-4, 6-2
1925	Suzanne Lenglen	Joan Fry	6-2, 6-0
1926	Kathleen McKane Godfree	Lili de Alvarez	6-2, 4-6, 6-3
1927	Helen Wills	Lili de Alvarez	6-2, 6-4
1928	Helen Wills	Lili de Alvarez	6-2, 6-3
1929	Helen Wills	Helen Jacobs	6-1, 6-2
1930	Helen Wills Moody	Elizabeth Ryan	6-2, 6-2
1931	Cilly Aussem	Hilde Kranwinkel	7-5, 7-5
1932	Helen Wills Moody	Helen Jacobs	6-3, 6-1
1933	Helen Wills Moody	Dorothy Round	6-4, 6-8, 6-3
1934	Dorothy Round	Helen Jacobs	6-2, 5-7, 6-3
1935	Helen Wills Moody	Helen Jacobs	6-3, 3-6, 7-5
1936	Helen Jacobs	Hilde Kranwinkel Sperling	6-2, 4-6, 7-5
1937	Dorothy Round	Jadwiga Jedrzejowska	6-2, 2-6, 7-5
1938	Helen Wills Moody	Helen Jacobs	6-4, 6-0
1939	Alice Marble	Kay Stammers	6-2, 6-0
1940-45	No tournament		
1946	Pauline Betz	Louise Brough	6-2, 6-4
1947	Margaret Osborne	Doris Hart	6-2, 6-4
1948	Louise Brough	Doris Hart	6-3, 8-6
1949	Louise Brough	Margaret Osborne duPont	10-8, 1-6, 10-8
1950	Louise Brough	Margaret Osborne duPont	6-1, 3-6, 6-1
1951	Doris Hart	Shirley Fry	6-1, 6-0
1952	Maureen Connolly	Louise Brough	6-4, 6-3
1953	Maureen Connolly	Doris Hart	8-6, 7-5
1954	Maureen Connolly	Louise Brough	6-2, 7-5
1955	Louise Brough	Beverly Fleitz	7-5, 8-6
1956	Shirley Fry	Angela Buxton	6-3, 6-1
1957	Althea Gibson	Darlene Hard	6-3, 6-2
1958	Althea Gibson	Angela Mortimer	8-6, 6-2
1959	Maria Bueno	Darlene Hard	6-4, 6-3
1960	Maria Bueno	Sandra Reynolds	8-6, 6-0
1961	Angela Mortimer	Christine Truman	4-6, 6-4, 7-5
1962	Karen Hantze Susman	Vera Sukova	6-4, 6-4
1963	Margaret Smith	Billie Jean Moffitt	6-3, 6-4
1964	Maria Bueno	Margaret Smith	6-4, 7-9, 6-3
1965	Margaret Smith	Maria Bueno	6-4, 7-5
1966	Billie Jean King	Maria Bueno	6-3, 3-6, 6-1
1967	Billie Jean King	Ann Haydon Jones	6-3, 6-4
1968*	Billie Jean King	Judy Tegart	9-7, 7-5
1969	Ann Haydon Jones	Billie Jean King	3-6, 6-3, 6-2
1970	Margaret Smith Court	Billie Jean King	14-12, 11-9
1971	Evonne Goolagong	Margaret Smith Court	6-4, 6-1
1972	Billie Jean King	Evonne Goolagong	6-3, 6-3
1973	Billie Jean King	Chris Evert	6-0, 7-5
1974	Chris Evert	Olga Morozova	6-0, 6-4
1975	Billie Jean King	Evonne Goolagong Cawley	6-0, 6-1
1976	Chris Evert	Evonne Goolagong Cawley	6-3, 4-6, 8-6
1977	Virginia Wade	Betty Stove	4-6, 6-3, 6-1
1978	Martina Navratilova	Chris Evert	2-6, 6-4, 7-5
1979	Martina Navratilova	Chris Evert Lloyd	6-4, 6-4
1980	Evonne Goolagong Cawley	Chris Evert Lloyd	6-1, 7-6
1981	Chris Evert Lloyd	Hana Mandlikova	6-2, 6-2
1982	Martina Navratilova	Chris Evert Lloyd	6-1, 3-6, 6-2

Wimbledon Championships (Cont.)

Year	Winner	Finalist	Score
1983	Martina Navratilova	Andrea Jaeger	6-0, 6-3
1984	Martina Navratilova	Chris Evert Lloyd	7-6, 6-2
1985	Martina Navratilova	Chris Evert Lloyd	4-6, 6-3, 6-2
1986	Martina Navratilova	Hana Mandlikova	7-6, 6-3
1987	Martina Navratilova	Steffi Graf	7-5, 6-3
1988	Steffi Graf	Martina Navratilova	5-7, 6-2, 6-1
1989	Steffi Graf	Martina Navratilova	6-2, 6-7, 6-1
1990	Martina Navratilova	Zina Garrison	6-4, 6-1
1991	Steffi Graf	Gabriela Sabatini	6-4, 3-6, 8-6
1992	Steffi Graf	Monica Seles	6-2, 6-1
1993	Steffi Graf	Jana Novotna	7-6 (8-6), 1-6, 6-4

*Became Open (amateur and professional) in 1968 but closed to contract professionals in 1972.

Note: Prior to 1922 the tournament was run on a challenge round system. The previous year's winner "stood out" of an All Comers event, which produced a challenger to play her for the title.

United States Championships

Year	Winner	Finalist	Score
1887	Ellen Hansell	Laura Knight	6-1, 6-0
1888	Bertha L. Townsend	Ellen Hansell	6-3, 6-5
1889	Bertha L. Townsend	Louise Voorhes	7-5, 6-2
1890	Ellen C. Roosevelt	Bertha L. Townsend	6-2, 6-2
1891	Mabel Cahill	Ellen C. Roosevelt	6-4, 6-1, 4-6, 6-3
1892	Mabel Cahill	Elisabeth Moore	5-7, 6-3, 6-4, 4-6, 6-2
1893	Aline Terry	Alice Schultze	6-1, 6-3
1894	Helen Hellwig	Aline Terry	7-5, 3-6, 6-0, 3-6, 6-3
1895	Juliette Atkinson	Helen Hellwig	6-4, 6-2, 6-1
1896	Elisabeth Moore	Juliette Atkinson	6-4, 4-6, 6-2, 6-2
1897	Juliette Atkinson	Elisabeth Moore	6-3, 6-3, 4-6, 3-6, 6-3
1898	Juliette Atkinson	Marion Jones	6-3, 5-7, 6-4, 2-6, 7-5
1899	Marion Jones	Maud Banks	6-1, 6-1, 7-5
1900	Myrtle McAteer	Edith Parker	6-2, 6-2, 6-0
1901	Elisabeth Moore	Myrtle McAteer	6-4, 3-6, 7-5, 2-6, 6-2
1902**	Marion Jones	Elisabeth Moore	6-1, 1-0 retired
1903	Elisabeth Moore	Marion Jones	7-5, 8-6
1904	May Sutton	Elisabeth Moore	6-1, 6-2
1905	Elisabeth Moore	Helen Homans	6-4, 5-7, 6-1
1906	Helen Homans	Maud Barger-Wallach	6-4, 6-3
1907	Evelyn Sears	Carrie Neely	6-3, 6-2
1908	Maud Barger-Wallach	Evelyn Sears	6-3, 1-6, 6-3
1909	Hazel Hotchkiss	Maud Barger-Wallach	6-0, 6-1
1910	Hazel Hotchkiss	Louise Hammond	6-4, 6-2
1911	Hazel Hotchkiss	Florence Sutton	8-10, 6-1, 9-7
1912†	Mary K. Browne	Eleanora Sears	6-4, 6-2
1913	Mary K. Browne	Dorothy Green	6-2, 7-5
1914	Mary K. Browne	Marie Wagner	6-2, 1-6, 6-1
1915	Molla Bjurstedt	Hazel Hotchkiss Wightman	4-6, 6-2, 6-0
1916	Molla Bjurstedt	Louise Hammond Raymond	6-0, 6-1
1917‡	Molla Bjurstedt	Marion Vanderhoef	4-6, 6-0, 6-2
1918	Molla Bjurstedt	Eleanor Goss	6-4, 6-3
1919	Hazel Hotchkiss Wightman	Marion Zinderstein	6-1, 6-2
1920	Molla Bjurstedt Mallory	Marion Zinderstein	6-3, 6-1
1921	Molla Bjurstedt Mallory	Mary K. Browne	4-6, 6-4, 6-2
1922	Molla Bjurstedt Mallory	Helen Wills	6-3, 6-1
1923	Helen Wills	Molla Bjurstedt Mallory	6-2, 6-1
1924	Helen Wills	Molla Bjurstedt Mallory	6-1, 6-3
1925	Helen Wills	Kathleen McKane	3-6, 6-0, 6-2
1926	Molla Bjurstedt Mallory	Elizabeth Ryan	4-6, 6-4, 9-7
1927	Helen Wills	Betty Nuthall	6-1, 6-4
1928	Helen Wills	Helen Jacobs	6-2, 6-1
1929	Helen Wills	Phoebe Holcroft Watson	6-4, 6-2
1930	Betty Nuthall	Anna McCune Harper	6-1, 6-4
1931	Helen Wills Moody	Eileen Whittingstall	6-4, 6-1
1932	Helen Jacobs	Carolin Babcock	6-2, 6-2
1933	Helen Jacobs	Helen Wills Moody	8-6, 3-6, 3-0 retired

United States Championship *(Cont.)*

Year	Winner	Finalist	Score
1934	Helen Jacobs	Sarah Palfrey	6-1, 6-4
1935	Helen Jacobs	Sarah Palfrey Fabyan	6-2, 6-4
1936	Alice Marble	Helen Jacobs	4-6, 6-3, 6-2
1937	Anita Lizane	Jadwiga Jedrzejowska	6-4, 6-2
1938	Alice Marble	Nancye Wynne	6-0, 6-3
1939	Alice Marble	Helen Jacobs	6-0, 8-10, 6-4
1940	Alice Marble	Helen Jacobs	6-2, 6-3
1941	Sarah Palfrey Cooke	Pauline Betz	7-5, 6-2
1942	Pauline Betz	Louise Brough	4-6, 6-1, 6-4
1943	Pauline Betz	Louise Brough	6-3, 5-7, 6-3
1944	Pauline Betz	Margaret Osborne	6-3, 8-6
1945	Sarah Palfrey Cooke	Pauline Betz	3-6, 8-6, 6-4
1946	Pauline Betz	Patricia Canning	11-9, 6-3
1947	Louise Brough	Margaret Osborne	8-6, 4-6, 6-1
1948	Margaret Osborne duPont	Louise Brough	4-6, 6-4, 15-13
1949	Margaret Osborne duPont	Doris Hart	6-4, 6-1
1950	Margaret Osborne duPont	Doris Hart	6-4, 6-3
1951	Maureen Connolly	Shirley Fry	6-3, 1-6, 6-4
1952	Maureen Connolly	Doris Hart	6-3, 7-5
1953	Maureen Connolly	Doris Hart	6-2, 6-4
1954	Doris Hart	Louise Brough	6-8, 6-1, 8-6
1955	Doris Hart	Patricia Ward	6-4, 6-2
1956	Shirley Fry	Althea Gibson	6-3, 6-4
1957	Althea Gibson	Louise Brough	6-3, 6-2
1958	Althea Gibson	Darlene Hard	3-6, 6-1, 6-2
1959	Maria Bueno	Christine Truman	6-1, 6-4
1960	Darlene Hard	Maria Bueno	6-4, 10-12, 6-4
1961	Darlene Hard	Ann Haydon	6-3, 6-4
1962	Margaret Smith	Darlene Hard	9-7, 6-4
1963	Maria Bueno	Margaret Smith	7-5, 6-4
1964	Maria Bueno	Carole Graebner	6-1, 6-0
1965	Margaret Smith	Billie Jean Moffitt	8-6, 7-5
1966	Maria Bueno	Nancy Richey	6-3, 6-1
1967	Billie Jean King	Ann Haydon Jones	11-9, 6-4
1968*	Virginia Wade	Billie Jean King	6-4, 6-4
1968#	Margaret Smith Court	Maria Bueno	6-2, 6-2
1969*	Margaret Smith Court	Nancy Richey	6-2, 6-2
1969#	Margaret Smith Court	Virginia Wade	4-6, 6-3, 6-0
1970	Margaret Smith Court	Rosie Casals	6-2, 2-6, 6-1
1971	Billie Jean King	Rosie Casals	6-4, 7-6
1972	Billie Jean King	Kerry Melville	6-3, 7-5
1973	Margaret Smith Court	Evonne Goolagong	7-6, 5-7, 6-2
1974	Billie Jean King	Evonne Goolagong	3-6, 6-3, 7-5
1975	Chris Evert	Evonne Goolagong Cawley	5-7, 6-4, 6-2
1976	Chris Evert	Evonne Goolagong Cawley	6-3, 6-0
1977	Chris Evert	Wendy Turnbull	7-6, 6-2
1978	Chris Evert	Pam Shriver	7-6, 6-4
1979	Tracy Austin	Chris Evert Lloyd	6-4, 6-3
1980	Chris Evert Lloyd	Hana Mandlikova	5-7, 6-1, 6-1
1981	Tracy Austin	Martina Navratilova	1-6, 7-6, 7-6
1982	Chris Evert Lloyd	Hana Mandlikova	6-3, 6-1
1983	Martina Navratilova	Chris Evert Lloyd	6-1, 6-3
1984	Martina Navratilova	Chris Evert Lloyd	4-6, 6-4, 6-4
1985	Hana Mandlikova	Martina Navratilova	7-6, 1-6, 7-6
1986	Martina Navratilova	Helena Sukova	6-3, 6-2
1987	Martina Navratilova	Steffi Graf	7-6, 6-1
1988	Steffi Graf	Gabriela Sabatini	6-3, 3-6, 6-1
1989	Steffi Graf	Martina Navratilova	3-6, 6-4, 6-2
1990	Gabriela Sabatini	Steffi Graf	6-2, 7-6
1991	Monica Seles	Martina Navratilova	7-6, 6-1
1992	Monica Seles	Arantxa Sanchez Vicario	6-3, 6-2
1993	Steffi Graf	Helena Sukova	6-3, 6-3

*Became Open (amateur and professional) in 1968. †Challenge round abolished.

‡National Patriotic Tournament. #Amateur event held.

**Five-set final abolished.

Singles

Don Budge, 1938
Maureen Connolly, 1953
Rod Laver, 1962, 1969
Margaret Smith Court, 1970
Steffi Graf, 1988

Doubles

Frank Sedgman and Ken McGregor, 1951
Martina Navratilova and Pam Shriver, 1984
Maria Bueno and two partners: Christine Truman
(Australian), Darlene Hard (French, Wimbledon
and U.S. Championships), 1960

Mixed Doubles

Margaret Smith and Ken Fletcher, 1963
Owen Davidson and two partners: Lesley Turner
(Australian), Billie Jean King (French, Wimbledon
and U.S. Championships), 1967

The All-Time Grand Slam Champions

MEN

Player	Aus. S-D-M	French S-D-M	Wim. S-D-M	U.S. S-D-M	Total
Roy Emerson	6-3-0	2-6-0	2-3-0	2-4-0	28
John Newcombe	2-5-0	0-3-0	3-6-0	2-3-1	25
Frank Sedgman	2-2-2	0-2-2	1-3-2	2-2-2	22
Bill Tilden	*	0-0-1	3-1-0	7-5-4	21
Rod Laver	3-4-0	2-1-1	4-1-2	2-0-0	20
Jean Borotra	1-1-1	2-6-2	2-3-1	0-0-1	20
Fred Stolle	0-3-1	1-2-0	0-2-3	1-3-2	18
Ken Rosewall	4-3-0	2-2-0	0-2-0	2-2-1	18
Neale Fraser	0-3-1	0-3-0	1-2-0	2-3-3	18
Adrian Quist	3-10-0	0-1-0	0-2-0	0-1-0	17
John Bromwich	2-8-1	0-0-0	0-2-2	0-1-1	17
John McEnroe	0-0-0	0-0-1	3-4-0	4-5-0	17
H.L. Doherty	*	*	5-8-0	1-2-0	16
Henri Cochet	*	4-3-2	2-2-0	1-0-1	15
Vic Seixas	0-1-0	0-2-1	1-0-4	1-2-3	15
Jack Crawford	4-4-1	1-1-1	1-1-1	0-0-0	15
Bob Hewitt	0-2-1	0-1-2	0-5-2	0-1-1	15

WOMEN

Player	Aus. S-D-M	French S-D-M	Wim. S-D-M	U.S. S-D-M	Total
Margaret Court	11-8-2	5-4-4	3-2-5	5-5-8	62
Martina Navratilova	3-8-0	2-7-2	9-7-1	4-9-2	54
Billie Jean King	1-0-1	1-1-2	6-10-4	4-5-4	39
Margaret duPont	*	2-3-0	1-5-1	3-13-9	37
Louise Brough	1-1-0	0-3-0	4-5-4	1-12-4	35
Doris Hart	1-1-2	2-5-3	1-4-5	2-4-5	35
Helen Wills Moody	*	4-2-0	8-3-1	7-4-2	30
Elizabeth Ryan	*	0-4-0	0-12-7	0-1-2	26
Suzanne Lenglen	*	6-2-2	6-6-3	0-0-0	25
Pam Shriver	0-7-0	0-4-1	0-5-0	0-5-0	22
Chris Evert	2-0-0	7-2-0	3-1-0	6-0-0	21
Maria Bueno	0-1-0	0-1-1	3-5-0	4-5-0	20
Darlene Hard	*	1-2-2	0-4-3	2-6-0	20
Sarah Palfrey Cooke	*	0-0-1	0-2-0	2-9-4	18
Alice Marble	*	*	1-2-3	4-4-4	18

*Did not compete.

National Team Competition

Davis Cup

Started in 1900 as the International Lawn Tennis Challenge Trophy by America's Dwight Davis, the runner-up in the 1898 U.S. Championships. A Davis Cup meeting between two countries is known as a tie and is a three-day event consisting of two singles matches, followed by one doubles match and then two more singles matches. The United States boasts the greatest number of wins (30), followed by Australia (20).

Year	Winner	Finalist	Site	Score
1900	United States	Great Britain	Boston	3-0
1901	No tournament			
1902	United States	Great Britain	New York	3-2
1903	Great Britain	United States	Boston	4-1
1904	Great Britain	Belgium	Wimbledon	5-0
1905	Great Britain	United States	Wimbledon	5-0
1906	Great Britain	United States	Wimbledon	5-0
1907	Australasia	Great Britain	Wimbledon	3-2
1908	Australasia	United States	Melbourne	3-2
1909	Australasia	United States	Sydney	5-0
1910	No tournament			
1911	Australasia	United States	Christchurch, NZ	5-0
1912	Great Britain	Australasia	Melbourne	3-2
1913	United States	Great Britain	Wimbledon	3-2
1914	Australasia	United States	New York	3-2
1915-18	No tournament			
1919	Australasia	Great Britain	Sydney	4-1
1920	United States	Australasia	Auckland, NZ	5-0
1921	United States	Japan	New York	5-0
1922	United States	Australasia	New York	4-1
1923	United States	Australasia	New York	4-1
1924	United States	Australia	Philadelphia	5-0
1925	United States	France	Philadelphia	5-0
1926	United States	France	Philadelphia	4-1
1927	France	United States	Philadelphia	3-2
1928	France	United States	Paris	4-1
1929	France	United States	Paris	3-2
1930	France	United States	Paris	4-1
1931	France	Great Britain	Paris	3-2
1932	France	United States	Paris	3-2
1933	Great Britain	France	Paris	3-2
1934	Great Britain	United States	Wimbledon	4-1
1935	Great Britain	United States	Wimbledon	5-0
1936	Great Britain	Australia	Wimbledon	3-2
1937	United States	Great Britain	Wimbledon	4-1
1938	United States	Australia	Philadelphia	3-2
1939	Australia	United States	Philadelphia	3-2
1940-45	No tournament			
1946	United States	Australia	Melbourne	5-0
1947	United States	Australia	New York	4-1
1948	United States	Australia	New York	5-0
1949	United States	Australia	New York	4-1
1950	Australia	United States	New York	4-1
1951	Australia	United States	Sydney	3-2
1952	Australia	United States	Adelaide	4-1
1953	Australia	United States	Melbourne	3-2
1954	United States	Australia	Sydney	3-2
1955	Australia	United States	New York	5-0
1956	Australia	United States	Adelaide	5-0
1957	Australia	United States	Melbourne	3-2
1958	United States	Australia	Brisbane	3-2
1959	Australia	United States	New York	3-2
1960	Australia	Italy	Sydney	4-1
1961	Australia	Italy	Melbourne	5-0
1962	Australia	Mexico	Brisbane	5-0
1963	United States	Australia	Adelaide	3-2
1964	Australia	United States	Cleveland	3-2
1965	Australia	Spain	Sydney	4-1
1966	Australia	India	Melbourne	4-1
1967	Australia	Spain	Brisbane	4-1
1968	United States	Australia	Adelaide	4-1

Davis Cup (Cont.)

Year	Winner	Finalist	Site	Score
1969	United States	Romania	Cleveland	5-0
1970	United States	West Germany	Cleveland	5-0
1971	United States	Romania	Charlotte, NC	3-2
1972	United States	Romania	Bucharest	3-2
1973	Australia	United States	Cleveland	5-0
1974	South Africa	India	*	walkover
1975	Sweden	Czechoslovakia	Stockholm	3-2
1976	Italy	Chile	Santiago	4-1
1977	Australia	Italy	Sydney	3-1
1978	United States	Great Britain	Palm Springs	4-1
1979	United States	Italy	San Francisco	5-0
1980	Czechoslovakia	Italy	Prague	4-1
1981	United States	Argentina	Cincinnati	3-1
1982	United States	France	Grenoble	4-1
1983	Australia	Sweden	Melbourne	3-2
1984	Sweden	United States	Gothenburg	4-1
1985	Sweden	West Germany	Munich	3-2
1986	Australia	Sweden	Melbourne	3-2
1987	Sweden	India	Gothenburg	5-0
1988	West Germany	Sweden	Gothenburg	4-1
1989	West Germany	Sweden	Stuttgart	3-2
1990	United States	Australia	St Petersburg	3-2
1991	France	United States	Lyon	3-1
1992	United States	Switzerland	Fort Worth, TX	3-1

*India refused to play the final in protest over South Africa's governmental policy of apartheid.

Note: Prior to 1972 the challenge-round system was in effect, with the previous year's winner "standing out" of the competition until the finals. A straight 16-nation tournament has been held since 1981.

Federation Cup

The women's equivalent of the Davis Cup, this competition was started in 1963 by the International Lawn Tennis Federation (now the ITF). Unlike the Davis Cup, though, all entrants gather at one site at one time for a tournament that is concluded within one week. Matches consist of two singles and one doubles. The United States boasts the greatest number of wins (14), followed by Australia (7).

Year	Winner	Finalist	Site	Score
1963	United States	Australia	London	2-1
1964	Australia	United States	Philadelphia	2-1
1965	Australia	United States	Melbourne	2-1
1966	United States	West Germany	Turin	3-0
1967	United States	Great Britain	West Berlin	2-0
1968	Australia	Netherlands	Paris	3-0
1969	United States	Australia	Athens	2-1
1970	Australia	Great Britain	Freiburg	3-0
1971	Australia	Great Britain	Perth	3-0
1972	South Africa	Great Britain	Johannesburg	2-1
1973	Australia	South Africa	Bad Homburg	3-0
1974	Australia	United States	Naples	2-1
1975	Czechoslovakia	Australia	Aix-en-Provence	3-0
1976	United States	Australia	Philadelphia	2-1
1977	United States	Australia	Eastbourne	2-1
1978	United States	Australia	Melbourne	2-1
1979	United States	Australia	Madrid	3-0
1980	United States	Australia	West Berlin	3-0
1981	United States	Great Britain	Nagoya	3-0
1982	United States	West Germany	Santa Clara	3-0
1983	Czechoslovakia	West Germany	Zurich	2-1
1984	Czechoslovakia	Australia	Sao Paulo	2-1
1985	Czechoslovakia	United States	Tokyo	2-1
1986	United States	Czechoslovakia	Prague	3-0
1987	West Germany	United States	Vancouver	2-1
1988	Czechoslovakia	USSR	Melbourne	2-1
1989	United States	Spain	Tokyo	3-0
1990	United States	USSR	Atlanta	2-1
1991	Spain	United States	Nottingham	2-1
1992	Germany	Spain	Frankfurt	2-1
1993	Spain	Australia	Frankfurt	3-0

ATP Computer Year-End Top 10

1973

Ilie Nastase
John Newcombe
Jimmy Connors
Tom Okker
Stan Smith
Ken Rosewall
Manuel Orantes
Rod Laver
Jan Kodes
Arthur Ashe

1974

Jimmy Connors
John Newcombe
Bjorn Borg
Rod Laver
Guillermo Vilas
Tom Okker
Arthur Ashe
Ken Rosewall
Stan Smith
Ilie Nastase

1975

Jimmy Connors
Guillermo Vilas
Bjorn Borg
Arthur Ashe
Manuel Orantes
Ken Rosewall
Ilie Nastase
John Alexander
Roscoe Tanner
Rod Laver

1976

Jimmy Connors
Bjorn Borg
Ilie Nastase
Manuel Orantes
Raul Ramirez
Guillermo Vilas
Adriano Panatta
Harold Solomon
Eddie Dibbs
Brian Gottfried

1977

Jimmy Connors
Guillermo Vilas
Bjorn Borg
Vitas Gerulaitis
Brian Gottfried
Eddie Dibbs
Manuel Orantes
Raul Ramirez
Ilie Nastase
Dick Stockton

1978

Jimmy Connors
Bjorn Borg
Guillermo Vilas
John McEnroe
Vitas Gerulaitis
Eddie Dibbs
Brian Gottfried
Raul Ramirez
Harold Solomon
Corrado Barazzutti

1979

Bjorn Borg
Jimmy Connors
John McEnroe
Vitas Gerulaitis
Roscoe Tanner
Guillermo Vilas
Arthur Ashe
Harold Solomon
Jose Higueras
Eddie Dibbs

1980

Bjorn Borg
John McEnroe
Jimmy Connors
Gene Mayer
Guillermo Vilas
Ivan Lendl
Harold Solomon
Jose-Luis Clerc
Vitas Gerulaitis
Eliot Teltscher

1981

John McEnroe
Ivan Lendl
Jimmy Connors
Bjorn Borg
Jose-Luis Clerc
Guillermo Vilas
Gene Mayer
Eliot Teltscher
Vitas Gerulaitis
Peter McNamara

1982

John McEnroe
Jimmy Connors
Ivan Lendl
Guillermo Vilas
Vitas Gerulaitis
Jose-Luis Clerc
Mats Wilander
Gene Mayer
Yannick Noah
Peter McNamara

1983

John McEnroe
Ivan Lendl
Jimmy Connors
Mats Wilander
Yannick Noah
Jimmy Arias
Jose Higueras
Jose-Luis Clerc
Kevin Curren
Gene Mayer

1984

John McEnroe
Jimmy Connors
Ivan Lendl
Mats Wilander
Andres Gomez
Anders Jarryd
Henrik Sundstrom
Pat Cash
Eliot Teltscher
Yannick Noah

Kindred Spirits

In his memoir, *Days of Grace*, Arthur Ashe spoke of having "a sense of kinship" with John McEnroe. McEnroe, wrote Ashe, often seemed to be "struggling with his demons," and the two men had some memorable off-court confrontations, most notably when McEnroe played on four of the five U.S. Davis Cup teams that Ashe captained. Nevertheless, it occurred to Ashe that McEnroe served as "a kind of darker angel to my own tightly restrained spirit" and that McEnroe "was expressing my own rage, my own anger, for me, as I never could express it."

For all that, McEnroe might strike some people as a strange choice to run the Safe Passage Foundation, the organization that Ashe created in 1990 to counsel inner-city youngsters. But before he died in February, Ashe made a request: Upon his death, would McEnroe take over? Assuming the job in June, McEnroe echoed Ashe's talk of kinship. "Arthur and I had a closer relationship than most people thought," he said. "Off the court we got along very well."

Speaking enthusiastically about the undertaking, McEnroe says he will bring in top tennis pros to work with some of the 3,160 youngsters who participate in Newark and three other cities. Who knows? Perhaps the new job will help McEnroe harness those demons. Could be that what was what Ashe had in mind all along.

Step Up — A pice led San Diego to a 14-13 win over Cleveland and a surprising 11-5 season.

Charles Haley's sack of Buffalo's Jim Kelly produced a fumble and a TD for Dallas in Super Bowl XXVII.

UCLA crushed Ray Peterson and San Diego State en route to a 35-7 drubbing in September.

STEPHEN DUNN

JOHN BIEVER

...all Alabama needed to insure a 17–0 win

Alonzo Mourning was a true impact rookie, leading Charlotte to its first-ever playoff berth in '93.

Michael Jordan and the Bulls rose to the challenge of Charles Barkley and the Suns in the NBA Finals.

Tough D from Donald Williams and North Carolina helped undo Jalen Rose and Michigan in the First F

Bobby Hurley and Duke defeated Michigan in December, but were upset by Cal in the NCAA tournament.

BOB DONNAN

Cause for celebration: Wayne Gretzky led the Kings past Toronto and into the Stanley Cup final

ictory in the British Open

U.E.I.

APRENDA INGLES

UNITED EDUCATION INSTITUTE

TAESA

RICHARD MACKSON

ir of judges denied

Andre Cason streaked to victory ahead of Carl Lewis in the 100-meter dash at the outdoor nationals

KEN GEIGER

One reason for a Giant resurgence in San Francisco was the acquisition of

The mighty swing of Texas outfielder Juan Gonzales kept him among the home run leaders all season long.

ATP Computer Year-End Top 10 *(Cont.)*

1985

Ivan Lendl
John McEnroe
Mats Wilander
Jimmy Connors
Stefan Edberg
Boris Becker
Yannick Noah
Anders Jarryd
Miloslav Mecir
Kevin Curren

1986

Ivan Lendl
Boris Becker
Mats Wilander
Yannick Noah
Stefan Edberg
Henri Leconte
Joakim Nystrom
Jimmy Connors
Miloslav Mecir
Andres Gomez

1987

Ivan Lendl
Stefan Edberg
Mats Wilander
Jimmy Connors
Boris Becker
Miloslav Mecir
Pat Cash
Yannick Noah
Tim Mayotte
John McEnroe

1988

Mats Wilander
Ivan Lendl
Andre Agassi
Boris Becker
Stefan Edberg
Kent Carlsson
Jimmy Connors
Jakob Hlasek
Henri Leconte
Tim Mayotte

1989

Ivan Lendl
Boris Becker
Stefan Edberg
John McEnroe
Michael Chang
Brad Gilbert
Andre Agassi
Aaron Krickstein
Alberto Mancini
Jay Berger

1990

Stefan Edberg
Boris Becker
Ivan Lendl
Andre Agassi
Pete Sampras
Andres Gomez
Thomas Muster
Emilio Sanchez
Goran Ivanisevic
Brad Gilbert

1991

Stefan Edberg
Jim Courier
Boris Becker
Michael Stich
Ivan Lendl
Pete Sampras
Guy Forget
Karel Novacek
Petr Korda
Andre Agassi

1992

Jim Courier
Stefan Edberg
Pete Sampras
Goran Ivanisevic
Boris Becker
Michael Chang
Petr Korda
Ivan Lendl
Andre Agassi
Richard Krajicek

WTA Computer Year-End Top 10

1973

Margaret Smith Court
Billie Jean King
Evonne Goolagong
Chris Evert
Rosie Casals
Virginia Wade
Kerry Reid
Nancy Gunter
Julie Heldman
Helga Masthoff

1974

Billie Jean King
Evonne Goolagong
Chris Evert
Virginia Wade
Julie Heldman
Rosie Casals
Kerry Reid
Olga Morozova
Lesley Hunt
Francoise Durr

1975

Chris Evert
Billie Jean King
Evonne Goolagong Cawley
Martina Navratilova
Virginia Wade
Margaret Smith Court
Olga Morozova
Nancy Gunter
Francoise Durr
Rosie Casals

1976

Chris Evert
Evonne Goolagong Cawley
Virginia Wade
Martina Navratilova
Sue Barker
Betty Stove
Dianne Balestrat
Mima Jausovec
Rosie Casals
Francoise Durr

1977

Chris Evert
Billie Jean King
Martina Navratilova
Virginia Wade
Sue Barker
Rosie Casals
Betty Stove
Dianne Balestrat
Wendy Turnbull
Kerry Reid

1978

Martina Navratilova
Chris Evert
Evonne Goolagong Cawley
Virginia Wade
Billie Jean King
Tracy Austin
Wendy Turnbull
Kerry Reid
Betty Stove
Dianne Balestrat

WTA Computer Year-End Top 10 (Cont.)

1979	1982	1985
Martina Navratilova	Martina Navratilova	Martina Navratilova
Chris Evert Lloyd	Chris Evert Lloyd	Chris Evert Lloyd
Tracy Austin	Andrea Jaeger	Hana Mandlikova
Evonne Goolagong Cawley	Tracy Austin	Pam Shriver
Billie Jean King	Wendy Turnbull	Claudia Kohde-Kilsch
Dianne Balestrat	Pam Shriver	Steffi Graf
Wendy Turnbull	Hana Mandlikova	Manuela Maleeva
Virginia Wade	Barbara Potter	Zina Garrison
Kerry Reid	Bettina Bunge	Helena Sukova
Sue Barker	Sylvia Hanika	Bonnie Gadusek

1980	1983	1986
Chris Evert Lloyd	Martina Navratilova	Martina Navratilova
Tracy Austin	Chris Evert Lloyd	Chris Evert Lloyd
Martina Navratilova	Andrea Jaeger	Steffi Graf
Hana Mandlikova	Pam Shriver	Hana Mandlikova
Evonne Goolagong Cawley	Sylvia Hanika	Helena Sukova
Billie Jean King	Jo Durie	Pam Shriver
Andrea Jaeger	Bettina Bunge	Claudia Kohde-Kilsch
Wendy Turnbull	Wendy Turnbull	Manuela Maleeva
Pam Shriver	Tracy Austin	Kathy Rinaldi
Greer Stevens	Zina Garrison	Gabriela Sabatini

1981	1984	1987
Chris Evert Lloyd	Martina Navratilova	Steffi Graf
Tracy Austin	Chris Evert Lloyd	Martina Navratilova
Martina Navratilova	Hana Mandlikova	Chris Evert
Andrea Jaeger	Pam Shriver	Pam Shriver
Hana Mandlikova	Wendy Turnbull	Hana Mandlikova
Sylvia Hanika	Manuela Maleeva	Gabriela Sabatini
Pam Shriver	Helena Sukova	Helena Sukova
Wendy Turnbull	Claudia Kohde-Kilsch	Manuela Maleeva
Bettina Bunge	Zina Garrison	Zina Garrison
Barbara Potter	Kathy Jordan	Claudia Kohde-Kilsch

Serve and Volley

In the current climate of the Women's tour, a teenager with a tennis father might consider the Manson family relatively functional, so Lindsay Davenport can count herself lucky. The 17-year old Chadwick High senior from Murrieta, Calif., has a volleyball father: Wink Davenport, a member of the 1968 U.S. Olympic team.

Dad, along with Mom, Ann, who serves on the board of the U.S. Volleyball Association, and sisters Leiann, who played at UC Irvine, and Shannon, who's currently on the team at St. Mary's College of California, all share the same perspective—that an overhead is a spike and a half volley is illegal. All of that's just fine by Lindsay, who upset the 15th-seeded Amanda Coetzer 6–1, 6–2 in the third round of the U.S. Open before losing a hard-fought three-set battle, in which she saved five match points, to No. 5 seed Gabriela Sabatini. "The main thing they do is keep tennis at a distance," Davenport says of her family. "It's been a huge help. We don't really discuss my game at all."

Davenport and another 17-year old, Chanda Rubin, are considered the top U.S. female hopes for the future. Davenport, who won both the singles and doubles titles at last year's U.S. Open Junior Championships, so routinely shut out opponents while playing the junior circuit that she picked up the nickname Bagel. In only her second pro tournament, the Virginia Slims of Florida in March, she upset Sabatini—and celebrated by returning to her hotel room to do some homework. She carried a 4.0 average upon turning pro a week earlier at the Evert Cup in Indian Wells, Calif., and though it has been harder to keep up her studies since then, she's committed to graduating with her class. "Mary Joe Fernandez kind of maintained both lives, and I thought that was really neat," she says. "It's something I'm trying to do."

Davenport's former coach, Robert Lansdorp, is the man who groomed the young Tracy Austin, so it's not surprising that Lindsay has bruising ground strokes. "She likes to hit the ball hard into the corner," says Sabatini. "Very, very hard." But at 6'2" and 150 pounds, Davenport has the ranginess to someday become a serve-and-volleyer. That volley business should at least mean something around the family dinner table.

—ALEXANDER WOLFF

WTA Computer Year-End Top 10 *(Cont.)*

1988

Steffi Graf
Martina Navratilova
Chris Evert
Gabriela Sabatini
Pam Shriver
Manuela Maleeva-Fragniere
Natalia Zvereva
Helena Sukova
Zina Garrison
Barbara Potter

1989

Steffi Graf
Martina Navratilova
Gabriela Sabatini
Zina Garrison
Arantxa Sanchez Vicario
Monica Seles
Conchita Martinez
Helena Sukova
Manuela Maleeva-Fragniere
*Chris Evert

1990

Steffi Graf
Monica Seles
Martina Navratilova
Mary Joe Fernandez
Gabriela Sabatini
Katerina Maleeva
Arantxa Sanchez Vicario
Jennifer Capriati
Manuela Maleeva-Fragniere
Zina Garrison

1991

Monica Seles
Steffi Graf
Gabriela Sabatini
Martina Navratilova
Arantxa Sanchez Vicario
Jennifer Capriati
Jana Novotna
Mary Joe Fernandez
Conchita Martinez
Manuela Maleeva-Fragniere

1992

Monica Seles
Steffi Graf
Gabriela Sabatini
Arantxa Sanchez Vicario
Martina Navratilova
Mary Joe Fernandez
Jennifer Capriati
Conchita Martinez
Manuela Maleeva-Fragniere
Jana Novotna

*When Chris Evert announced her retirement at the 1989 United States Open, she was ranked 4 in the world. That was her last official series tournament.

Prize Money

Top 25 Men's Career Prize Money Leaders

	Earnings ($)
Ivan Lendl	19,516,503
Stefan Edberg	14,279,544
Boris Becker	12,372,481
John McEnroe	12,227,622
Jimmy Connors	8,498,820
Mats Wilander	7,411,283
Jim Courier	6,553,795
Pete Sampras	6,545,750
Andre Agassi	5,759,038
Guillermo Vilas	4,923,452
Anders Jarryd	4,736,194
Emilio Sanchez	4,308,735
Andres Gomez	4,284,725
Brad Gilbert	4,209,709
Guy Forget	3,906,071
Jakob Hlasek	3,743,722
Tomas Smid	3,699,738
Michael Stich	3,655,644
Bjorn Borg	3,651,151
Michael Chang	3,571,910
Goran Ivanisevic	3,331,480
Yannick Noah	3,295,395
Sergi Bruguera	2,969,482
Kevin Curren	2,955,060
John Fitzgerald	2,930,345

Note: From arrival of Open tennis in 1968 through October 1, 1993.

Top 25 Women's Career Prize Money Leaders

	Earnings ($)
Martina Navratilova	19,052,570
Steffi Graf	12,836,510
Chris Evert	8,896,195
Monica Seles	7,408,981
Gabriela Sabatini	6,608,402
Pam Shriver	5,028,325
Helena Sukova	4,942,256
Arantxa Sanchez Vicario	4,658,676
Zina Garrison Jackson	3,845,298
Jana Novotna	3,368,228
Hana Mandlikova	3,340,959
Natalia Zvereva	3,028,529
Manuela Maleeva-Fragniere	2,926,652
Mary Joe Fernandez	2,831,252
Wendy Turnbull	2,769,024
Gigi Fernandez	2,396,702
Lori McNeil	2,309,904
Claudia Kohde-Kilsch	2,225,337
Larisa Neiland	2,018,564
Billie Jean King	1,966,487
Conchita Martinez	1,964,815
Tracy Austin	1,943,928
Katerina Maleeva	1,883,067
Kathy Jordan	1,592,111
Ros Nideffer	1,583,894

Note: From arrival of Open tennis in 1968 through October 1, 1993.

Open Era Overall Wins

Men's Career Leaders—Tournaments Won

The top tournament-winning men from the institution of Open tennis in 1968 through October 1, 1993.

	W		W
Jimmy Connors	109	Arthur Ashe	33
Ivan Lendl	93	Mats Wilander	33
John McEnroe	77	John Newcombe	32
Bjorn Borg	62	Manuel Orantes	32
Guillermo Vilas	62	Ken Rosewall	32
Ilie Nastase	57	Tom Okker	30
Rod Laver	47	Vitas Gerulaitis	27
Stan Smith	39	Jose-Luis Clerc	25
Boris Becker	38	Brian Gottfried	25
Stefan Edberg	37	Yannick Noah	23

Women's Career Leaders—Tournaments Won

The top tournament-winning women from the institution of Open tennis in 1968 through October 1, 1993.

	W		W
Martina Navratilova	165	Hana Mandlikova	27
Chris Evert	157	Nancy Richey	25
Evonne Goolagong Cawley	88	Gabriela Sabatini	25
Margaret Court	79	Kerry Melville Reid	22
Steffi Graf	78	Sue Barker	21
Billie Jean King	71	Pam Shriver	21
Virginia Wade	52	Julie Heldman	20
Helga Masthoff	37	Dianne Fromholtz Balestrat	19
Monica Seles	32	Rosie Casals	18
Olga Morozova	31	Conchita Martinez	18
Tracy Austin	29		

Annual ATP/WTA Champions

Men's ATP Tour—World Championship

Year	Player	Year	Player
1970	Stan Smith	1982	Ivan Lendl
1971	Ilie Nastase	1983	Ivan Lendl
1972	Ilie Nastase	1984	John McEnroe
1073	Ilie Nastase	1985	John McEnroe
1974	Guillermo Vilas	1986	Ivan Lendl
1975	Ilie Nastase	1986	Ivan Lendl
1976	Manuel Orantes	1987	Ivan Lendl
1977	Not held	1988	Boris Becker
1978	Jimmy Connors	1989	Stefan Edberg
1979	John McEnroe	1990	Andre Agassi
1980	Bjorn Borg	1991	Pete Sampras
1981	Bjorn Borg	1992	Boris Becker

Note: Event held twice in 1986.

THEY SAID IT

Jim Courier, paying tribute to James Joyce after being scheduled to play two days in a row at the French Open: "Not in time, place or circumstance, but in the man lies success."

Annual ATP/WTA Champions (Cont.)

Women—Virginia Slims Championship

Year	Player	Year	Player
1972	Chris Evert	1983	Martina Navratilova
1973	Chris Evert	1984	Martina Navratilova
1974	Evonne Goolagong	1985	Martina Navratilova
1975	Chris Evert	1986	Martina Navratilova
1976	Evonne Goolagong	1986	Martina Navratilova
1977	Chris Evert	1987	Steffi Graf
1978	Martina Navratilova	1988	Gabriela Sabatini
1979	Martina Navratilova	1989	Steffi Graf
1980	Tracy Austin	1990	Monica Seles
1981	Martina Navratilova	1991	Monica Seles
1982	Sylvia Hanika	1992	Monica Seles

Note: Virginia Slims Championship held twice in 1986.

Mac the Mouth

Here's the difference between Monica Seles and John McEnroe, two non-starters in 1993's U.S. Open: McEnroe has at least raised a racket of late. He did it with his remark, made on the eve of the event, that women are worse suited than men to comment on men's tennis. McEnroe may be in some vague limbo between playing the tour and full-time retirement, but as he joined USA Network for its coverage of the Open, which he had won four times, his legendary mouth continued to be as active as ever. Colleagues in the broadcast trade promptly responded by accusing him of everything from male chauvinism ("That sounds like he wants women barefoot and pregnant," said Robin Roberts of ESPN) to shallow thinking ("That's like saying Stephen Crane shouldn't have written *The Red Badge of Courage* because he didn't fight in the Civil War," said NBC's Bud Collins).

McEnroe being McEnroe, he stands by his statements. "I think Mary [Carillo of CBS and ESPN] does a great job," he says. "She knows more about tennis than 99 percent of the people out there. But if you don't have the experience, how can you know? I have three children. I was there for the birth of each of them, and being there helped me understand what it must have been like. At the same time, can I say honestly *how that felt*? No way. It's just sports. And here people are acting like I'm David Duke."

McEnroe the analyst wars a blazer with an air of protest, like the the private-school teenager he once was. His hair, graying and in retreat, isn't standard broadcast issue, either. Some TV critics grumbled last spring when he failed to turn up in the strict GQ form for NBC's coverage of the French Open. Instead of taking a shirt off a hanger, he grabbed one from his bag, as tennis players are wont to do. (Better a wrinkled shirt than a stuffed one, of which the sport has quite enough already.)

McEnroe and USA partner Ted Robinson have settled into an easy counterpoint, with Robinson's professional voice setting off Mac's rambles and Long Island intonations. From the booth McEnroe can uncoil a trenchant verbal winner. In the early rounds he picked up Fabrice Santoro's chronic foot-faulting when no linesmen did. He ripped into the glazed-doughnut diet—"[Junk food] sounds good, it looks good in the commercial, but it's not gonna work"—of first-round loser Andre Agassi. And even before officials had to postpone Boris Becker's opening match because of rain, McEnroe had pointed out that forcing Becker to play seven best-of-five-set matches in 11 days to win the tournament would be, more or less, the pits of the world.

He still works out regularly and plays exhibitions—"keeping my options open," as he puts it—but won't return to the tour unless he feels he can win a Grand Slam event. "Once you've set certain standards for yourself, it's not enough to just pick up a paycheck or have your ego boosted for a while," McEnroe says. Then he quotes Connie Hawkins: "The older I get, the better I used to be."

In wardrobe one afternoon last week, moments before going on the air, McEnroe reached into his gym bag and raised from it a checkbook. Then he scratched out a donation from his John McEnroe Foundation for one of many worthy petitioners—in this case a scholarship fund for underprivileged children in East Palo Alto, Calif. "There are 20 other things to worry about besides who commentates," he said before rushing off to the booth.

For years they paid him for his tennis and docked him for his mouth. Now the mouth is earning its keep.

—ALEXANDER WOLFF

International Tennis Hall of Fame

Pauline Betz Addie (1965)
George T. Adee (1964)
Fred B. Alexander (1961)
Wilmer L. Allison (1963)
Manuel Alonso (1977)
Arthur Ashe (1985)
Juliette Atkinson (1974)
Tracy Austin (1992)
Lawrence A. Baker (1975)
Maud Barger-Wallach (1958)
Angela Mortimer Barrett (1993)
Karl Behr (1969)
Bjorn Borg (1987)
Jean Borotra (1976)
Maureen Connolly Brinker(1968)
John Bromwich (1984)
Norman Everard Brookes (1977)
Mary K. Browne (1957)
Jacques Brugnon (1976)
J. Donald Budge (1964)
Maria E. Bueno (1978)
May Sutton Bundy (1956)
Mabel E. Cahill (1976)
Oliver S. Campbell (1955)
Malcom Chace (1961)
Dorothea Douglass Lambert
  Chambers (1981)
Philippe Chatrier (1992)
Louise Brough Clapp (1967)
Clarence Clark (1983)
Joseph S. Clark (1955)
William J. Clothier (1956)
Henri Cochet (1976)
Ashley Cooper (1991)
Margaret Smith Court (1979)
Gottfried von Cramm (1977)
John H. Crawford (1979)
Joseph F. Cullman III (1990)
Allison Danzig (1968)
Sarah Palfrey Danzig (1963)
Dwight F. Davis (1956)
Charlotte Dod (1983)
John H. Doeg (1962)
Laurie Doherty (1980)
Reggie Doherty (1980)
Jaroslav Drobny (1983)
Margaret Osborne duPont
  (1967)
James Dwight (1955)
Roy Emerson (1982)
Pierre Etchebaster (1978)
Robert Falkenburg (1974)
Neale Fraser (1984)
Charles S. Garland (1969)
Althea Gibson (1971)
Kathleen McKane Godfree
  (1978)

Richard A. Gonzales (1968)
Evonne Goolagong Cawley
  (1988)
Bryan M. Grant Jr (1972)
David Gray (1985)
Clarence Griffin (1970)
King Gustaf V of Sweden
  (1980)
Harold H. Hackett (1961)
Ellen Forde Hansell (1965)
Darlene R. Hard (1973)
Doris J. Hart (1969)
Gladys M. Heldman (1979)
W. E. "Slew" Hester Jr (1981)
Bob Hewitt (1992)
Lew Hoad (1980)
Harry Hopman (1978)
Fred Hovey (1974)
Joseph R. Hunt (1966)
Lamar Hunt (1993)
Francis T. Hunter (1961)
Shirley Fry Irvin (1970)
Helen Hull Jacobs (1962)
William Johnston (1958)
Ann Haydon Jones (1985)
Perry Jones (1970)
Billie Jean King (1987)
Jan Kodes (1990)
John A. Kramer (1968)
Rene Lacoste (1976)
Al Laney (1979)
William A. Larned (1956)
Arthur D. Larsen (1969)
Rod G. Laver (1981)
Suzanne Lenglen (1978)
Dorothy Round Little (1986)
George M. Lott Jr (1964)
Chuck McKinley (1986)
Maurice McLoughlin (1957)
Frew McMillan (1992)
W. Donald McNeill (1965)
Gene Mako (1973)
Molla Bjurstedt Mallory (1958)
Alice Marble (1964)
Alastair B. Martin (1973)
William McChesney Martin (1982)
Elisabeth H. Moore (1971)
Gardnar Mulloy (1972)
R. Lindley Murray (1958)
Julian S. Myrick (1963)
Ilie Nastase (1991)
John D. Newcombe (1986)
Arthur C. Nielsen Sr (1971)
Betty Nuthall (1977)
Alex Olmedo (1987)
Rafael Osuna (1979)
Mary Ewing Outerbridge (1981)

Frank A. Parker (1966)
Gerald Patterson (1989)
Budge Patty (1977)
Theodore R. Pell (1967)
Fred Perry (1975)
Tom Pettitt (1982)
Nicola Pietrangeli (1986)
Adrian Quist (1984)
Dennis Ralston (1987)
Ernest Renshaw (1983)
Willie Renshaw (1983)
Vincent Richards (1961)
Robert L. Riggs (1967)
Helen Wills Moody Roark
  (1959)
Anthony D. Roche (1986)
Ellen C. Roosevelt (1975)
Ken Rosewall (1980)
Elizabeth Ryan (1972)
Manuel Santana (1984)
Richard Savitt (1976)
Frederick R. Schroeder (1966)
Eleonora Sears (1968)
Richard D. Sears (1955)
Frank Sedgman (1979)
Pancho Segura (1984)
Vic Seixas Jr (1971)
Francis X. Shields (1964)
Henry W. Slocum Jr (1955)
Stan Smith (1987)
Fred Stolle (1985)
William F. Talbert (1967)
Bill Tilden (1959)
Lance Tingay (1982)
Ted Tinling (1986)
Bertha Townsend Toulmin
  (1974)
Tony Trabert (1970)
James H. Van Alen (1965)
John Van Ryn (1963)
Guillermo Vilas (1991)
Ellsworth Vines (1962)
Virginia Wade (1989)
Marie Wagner (1969)
Holcombe Ward (1956)
Watson Washburn (1965)
Malcolm D. Whitman (1955)
Hazel Hotchkiss Wightman
  (1957)
Anthony Wilding (1978)
Richard Norris Williams II
  (1957)
Sidney B. Wood (1964)
Robert D. Wrenn (1955)
Beals C. Wright (1956)

Note: Years in parentheses are dates of induction.

Golf

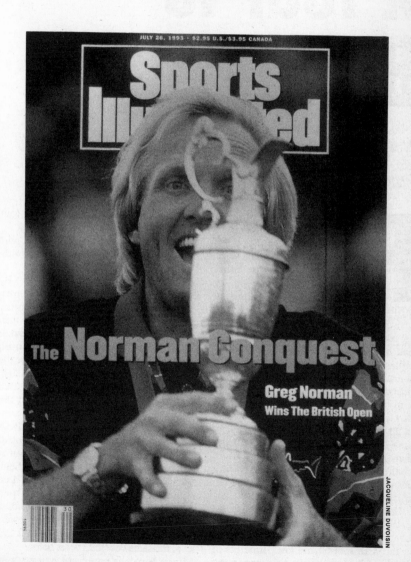

A Year To Bronze

Not since 1986 and the Nicklaus Masters has golf enjoyed such a sterling season | by RICK REILLY

OR ONCE GOLF HAD A YEAR TO bronze. Nineteen hundred and ninety-three was the year golf has waited for for seven years, since Jack Nicklaus won the most memorable Masters ever, in 1986, and disappeared, taking the thrills with him.

In 1993 Greg Norman, the world's greatest place bet, finally achieved what so many had hoped for him. He won the greatest British Open in the last 15 years with a shimmering week of impeccable golf. His final day round of six-under-par 64 not only won the silver claret jug for him at Royal St. George's, it dusted the best Sunday field in 20 years. All five top Sony-ranked players—Nick Faldo, Bernhard Langer, Norman, Nick Price and Fred Couples—had a chance to win the tournament. Had a chance, that is, until Norman woke up the golf god inside himself.

How good was he? This good: Faldo led going into that day, shot 67 and lost by two. Langer, who had won the Masters earlier in the year, shot 67 and lost. Ernie Els of South Africa became the first man in the history of the British Open to shoot four rounds in the 60s. And lost. Tough week.

"I have never had a round like that," the Shark said afterward. "To tell you the truth, I'm in awe of myself right now."

It was an awe-ful kind of year. By autumn records were falling like leaves. How good was it? This good: In the history of major championships, only a dozen men had shot a round of 63. In 1993 three did it: Faldo to take the lead Friday at the British Open, Payne Stewart on the final day at the British and Vijay (Makes His Clubs) Singh, who blistered Toledo's Inverness Golf Club at the sweltering PGA for a 63 and the lead. It was a year when somebody seemingly carved the holes too big. At the PGA Championship alone, 110 shots were holed.

Just a month before, at the U.S. Open at stately Baltusrol Golf Club in Springfield, N.J., a curly-haired moppet named Lee Janzen broke or tied every U.S. Open record there was to break or tie, including lowest 36-hole score, lowest 54 and lowest 72, at eight-under 272, tying Nicklaus's 272 set at the same course 13 years before.

Even Nicklaus could not believe how

terrific golf became in 1993. At both the British Open and the PGA, he shot 144, very near par, and missed both cuts. "Pars aren't good enough anymore in major championship golf," Nicklaus said. Par or cozy to it used to win majors. Some of the most unrelenting par-shooters in history—Hale Irwin, Andy North, Larry Nelson—won eight majors alone since the 1970s shooting not much better than par. Nick Faldo won the 1987 British Open with 18 straight pars. In 1993 that dog definitely wouldn't hunt. Eleven under won the Masters, eight under won the U.S. Open, 13 under won the British and 12 under won the PGA. The dull-as-dishwater-three-

At Royal St. George's the going was rarely rough for Norman, who shot 64 on Sunday.

metal-to-the-fairway-eight-iron-to-the-middle-of-the-green-two-putt-par took gas in 1993.

There was not a cheap winner in the bunch, starting with Langer's runaway win in the Masters in Augusta. Using the Langer Lock, the curious yip-beating putting grip in which he clutches his left forearm with his right hand, Langer ran away from everybody in the field except Chip Beck. Beck, unfortunately, ran away from himself.

Trailing by two shots on the fourth-to-

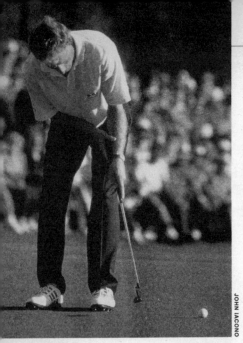

JOHN IACONO

Langer got a grip on his second Masters title, finishing four strokes up on the field.

buzzard's luck. He had the 1986 PGA won until Bob Tway chipped in out of an impossibly deep bunker at Inverness in Toledo. He had the 1987 Masters won until Larry Mize chipped in from an impossibly steep lie at Augusta. He had the 1990 Bay Hill won until Robert Gamez holed out a seven-iron. He had New Orleans won until David Frost holed out a sand wedge. He finished second in five majors. If *Pyschology Today* ever did a golf issue, Norman was sure to be the centerfold.

But then came Royal St. Greg's, where he trailed the great Faldo—the King of the Hill the last seven years—by one shot as the final day started. All he did after that was proceed to hit nearly every tee shot the way he wanted and nearly every iron better than he wanted. "I hit the ball *exactly* where I wanted today," said Norman. Norman was so remarkably straight all day that one pass of the lawnmower per fairway would've done it.

And still Faldo wouldn't budge. Norman made only two errors on this, his greatest day in golf. He came to the sixth hole with the lead and actually *left* his sand shot in the bunker. Then he missed a par putt on the 17th no longer than his shoelace.

Any golf fan knew in the center of his balata heart that a piano would soon fall on Norman. He had a chance to tie Nicklaus that year in 1986 at the Masters until he Federal Expressed a fore!-iron into the crowd on the last hole. He had blown the 1984 U.S. Open at Winged Foot by airmailing the same club on the final hole. He had blown the 1989 British Open at Troon by creaming his drive on the last hole into what most people thought of as an unreachable bunker on the 18th. If he blew this one, he might take that shoelace to his neck.

But this time he simply stepped up to the 18th tee box and hit the most gorgeous drive to the very middlest piece of grass in the fairway and then hit a sublime long iron

last hole, the par-5 15th, Beck decided that going for the green from 236 yards wasn't "worth the risk." He laid up. All around the country, you could hear palms slapping foreheads. "If I were in his shoes, yes, most certainly, I would have gone for it," said Langer. "But I don't mind so much." Beck made bogie. Playing with him, Langer went for the green in two, made birdie and won by four. So much for American ingenuity.

The nature of the contenders was what made Norman's brilliant victory near the white cliffs of Dover worth all the years of missing majors by *thismuch*. It was, at last, an end to a seven-year itch that had nearly cost him his will to play. He had won the British Open that landmark year, 1986, at Turnberry and led the other three majors through three rounds (the Saturday Slam). He was long off the tee, deadly with a putter, handsome, heroic and seemingly born without a nervous system. Holy Sharkbait, how many majors would he win before he was through? Ten? Fifteen? Twenty?

But Norman did not win 20 majors. Or 15. Or 10. Or, in fact, any. Instead, he became the national corporate symbol for

into the middlest of the final green, a position from which a man could two-putt with a wine bottle and a hangover. His four-day total of 267 was the lowest ever for a British Open.

Of the four winners of the majors—Langer, Janzen, Norman and Paul Azinger—only Janzen, 27, was a shock. But Janzen, too, beat the best players to win. He topped short-pantsed star Payne Stewart with an incredible Sunday chip-in on the 16th to sew up a victory. It was not unlike the chip Tom Watson made at the 17th hole at Pebble Beach to snatch the 1972 U.S. Open from Nicklaus. "I remember being a kid and watching that on TV," Janzen recalled after his triumph. "I was on the couch in our family room. When he

The youthful Janzen chipped like an old master, tying Nicklaus' Open record of 272.

made it, I jumped so high in the air, I caught my arm in our ceiling fan."

It was that kind of year, when every loose end tied up nicely, and we all got caught up in fandom. Tom Kite, the defending Open champion, made birdies cheap in winning the Bob Hope Classic at 35-under, an alltime record. Norman brought Doral's Blue Monster past its knees and all the way to its back with a majestic 23-under to win there. It was a year when you barely needed a program. Faldo ran second at the British and third at the PGA. Azinger, the immensely popular American who had won nearly everywhere else, finally won a major despite being so nervous that "flashes were going off in front of my eyes every time my heart beat."

In winning, Azinger gladly dropped the dreaded B.P.N.T.W.A.M (Best Player Never to Win a Major) and handed it firmly to

diminutive Corey Pavin of the U.S., who had his chance at the British but couldn't stay with the varsity. Azinger has a fluky punch swing with a horrific forward press and a backswing you could fit in a K Mart dressing room, but it has served him exceptionally well. "This feels like I always hoped it would," he said afterward. "It's amazing. In 1980 I'd never broken 70 and couldn't break 80 two days in a row."

All of which sounded like tour grinder Lauri Merten, who hadn't won on the tour in nine years and then won the 1993 U.S. Women's Open at storm-ravaged Crooked Stick in Carmel, Ind. Merten, who can always find the gray cloud in a silver lining,

Azinger had to battle his own nerves and a predatory Shark to win his first major.

JOHN BIEVER

ran out of confidence about four rest stops back. Not two years ago a teacher had asked her to rate different aspects of her game—putting, chipping, driving—on a scale of 1 to 10. She never gave herself a score higher than 2. And even when she needed just a 30-inch putt to win at Crooked Stick, she had a wonderfully typically negative thought just before stroking it: *Remember when Scott Hoch missed that 30-incher to lose the Masters?* Despite her worst intentions, it went in.

Crooked Stick is where the legend of Long John Daly was born two years ago. But 1993 was a dull year for Daly. All he did was check into an alcohol recovery center, face charges of spousal abuse, nearly win the Masters (finished sixth), continue to be the biggest draw in golf, become the first man in history to reach the 630-yard par-5 17th hole (your basic LaGuardia runway) at Baltusrol in two, become the first man in history to *drive* the 421-yard 4th hole at Royal St. George's, challenge at the British, file for divorce, gain 20 pounds, lose 30 and easily beat senior Jim Dent for an $80,000 winner-take-all distance contest. Ho-hum.

From the juniors to the seniors, the year was one goosebump piled on the next. Tiger Woods won an unprecedented third straight national junior title in Portland, Ore. Jack Nicklaus won his second Senior Open, this one at Cherry Hills in Denver. An unknown club pro named Tom Wargo won the Senior PGA, then went directly back to his job as greenskeeper-cook-starter at a tiny course in Centralia, Ill. A fortysomething long-suffering ex-pro named John Harris (he was so disgusted with his golf that he gave up the game for three years) won the U.S. Amateur. And nice-guy Tour pro Nick Price looked like he might run away with the Tour money list.

Truth was, golf got so big and good and wonderful that somebody announced plans to start a 24-hour seven-day-a-week cable network known as The Golf Channel.

If they stick to reruns of 1993, the ratings will kill.

Men's Majors

The Masters

Augusta National GC; Augusta, GA
(par 72; 6,905 yds) April 8-11

Player	Score	Earnings ($)
Bernhard Langer	68-70-69-70—277	306,000
Chip Beck	72-67-72-70—281	183,600
Steve Elkington	71-70-71-71—283	81,600
Lanny Wadkins	69-72-71-71—283	81,600
Tom Lehman	67-75-73-68—283	81,600
John Daly	70-71-73-69—283	81,600
Jose M Olazabal	70-72-74-68—284	54,850
Dan Forsman	69-69-73-73—284	54,850
Brad Faxon	71-70-72-72—285	47,600
Payne Stewart	74-70-72-69—285	47,600
Anders Forsbrand	71-74-75-66—286	34,850
Seve Ballesteros	74-70-71-71—286	34,850
Ray Floyd	68-71-74-73—286	34,850
Corey Pavin	67-75-73-71—286	34,850
Scott Simpson	72-71-71-72—286	34,850
Fuzzy Zoeller	75-67-71-73—286	34,850
Jeff Sluman	71-72-71-73—287	24,650
Howard Twitty	70-71-73-73—287	24,650
Ian Woosnam	71-74-73-69—287	24,650
Mark Calcavecchia	71-70-74-72—287	24,650

U.S. Open

Baltusrol GC; Springfield, NJ
(par 70; 7,152 yds) June 17-20

Player	Score	Earnings ($)
Lee Janzen	67-67-69-69—272	290,000
Payne Stewart	70-66-68-70—274	145,000
Craig Parry	66-74-69-68—277	78,556
Paul Azinger	71-68-69-69—277	78,556
Tom Watson	70-66-73-69—278	48,730
Scott Hoch	66-72-72-68—278	48,730
Ernie Els	71-73-68-67—279	35,481
Raymond Floyd	68-73-70-68—279	35,481
Nolan Henke	72-71-67-69—279	35,481
Fred Funk	70-72-67-70—279	35,481
David Edwards	70-72-66-72—280	26,249
Nick Price	71-66-70-73—280	26,249
John Adams	70-70-69-71—280	26,249
Loren Roberts	70-70-71-69—280	26,249
Jeff Sluman	71-71-69-69—280	26,249
Barry Lane	74-68-70-69—281	21,577
Fred Couples	68-71-71-71—281	21,577
Mike Standly	70-69-70-72—281	21,577
Ian Baker-Finch	70-70-70-72—282	18,072
Steve Pate	70-71-71-70—282	18,072
Blaine McCallister	68-73-73-68—282	18,072
Dan Forsman	73-71-70-68—282	18,072
Corey Pavin	68-69-75-70—282	18,072
Tom Lehman	71-70-71-70—282	18,072

British Open

Royal St. George's, Sandwich, England
(par 70; 6,860 yds) July 15-18

Player	Score	Earnings ($)
Greg Norman	66-68-69-64—267	154,000
Nick Faldo	69-63-70-67—269	123,200
Bernhard Langer	67-66-70-67—270	103,180
Peter Senior	66-69-70-67—272	77,770
Corey Pavin	68-66-68-70—272	77,770
Nick Price	68-70-67-69—274	51,077
Paul Lawrie	72-68-69-65—274	51,077
Ernie Els	68-69-69-68—274	51,077
Fred Couples	68-66-72-69—275	39,270
Wayne Grady	74-68-64-69—275	39,270
Scott Simpson	68-70-71-66—275	39,270
Payne Stewart	71-72-70-63—276	33,110
Barry Lane	70-68-71-68—277	31,570
Mark Calcavecchia	66-73-71-68—278	23,430
Tom Kite	72-70-68-68—278	23,430
Mark McNulty	67-71-71-69—278	23,430
Gil Morgan	70-68-70-70—278	23,430
Jose Rivero	68-73-67-70—278	23,430
Fuzzy Zoeller	66-70-71-71—278	23,430
John Daly	71-66-70-71—278	23,430
Peter Baker	70-67-74-68—279	15,400
Jesper Parnevik	68-74-68-69—279	15,400
Howard Clark	67-72-70-70—279	15,400
Rodger Davis	68-71-71-70—280	12,936
David Frost	69-73-70-68—280	12,936
Mark Roe	70-71-73-66—280	12,936

PGA Championship

Inverness Club; Toledo, Ohio
(par 71; 7,024 yds) August 12-15

Player	Score	Earnings ($)
Paul Azinger**	69-66-69-68—272	300,000
Greg Norman	68-68-67-69—272	155,000
Nick Faldo	68-68-69-68—273	105,000
Vijay Singh	68-63-73-70—274	90,000
Tom Watson	69-65-70-72—276	75,000
Bob Estes	69-66-69-73—277	47,812
Hale Irwin	68-69-67-73—277	47,812
Scott Simpson	64-70-71-72—277	47,812
John Cook	72-66-68-71—277	47,812
Dudley Hart	66-68-71-72—277	47,812
Scott Hoch	74-68-68-67—277	47,812
Nolan Henke	72-70-67-68—277	47,812
Phil Mickelson	67-71-69-70—277	47,812
Richard Zokol	66-71-71-70—278	25,000
Steve Elkington	67-66-74-71—278	25,000
Bruce Fleisher	69-74-67-68—278	25,000
Gary Hallberg	70-69-68-71—278	25,000
Lanny Wadkins	65-68-71-74—278	25,000
Brad Faxon	70-70-65-73—278	25,000
Eduardo Romero	67-67-74-71—279	18,500
Jay Haas	69-68-70-72—279	18,500
Lee Janzen	70-68-71-72—281	14,500
Ian Woosnam	70-71-68-72—281	14,500
Greg Twiggs	70-69-70-72—281	14,500
Jim McGovern	69-68-74-70—281	14,500
Frank Nobilo	69-66-74-72—281	14,500
Gene Sauers	68-74-70-69—281	14,500

**Won on second playoff hole

Men's Tour Results

Late 1992 PGA Tour Events

Tournament	Final Round	Winner	Score/ Under Par	Earnings ($)
Buick Southern Open	Sept 29	David Peoples	276/-12	126,000
H.E.B. Texas Open	Oct 6	Blaine McCallister†	269/-11	162,000
Las Vegas Invitational	Oct 13	Andrew Magee†	329/-31	270,000
Walt Disney World-Oldsmobile Classic	Oct 19	Mark O'Meara	267/-21	180,000
Independent Insurance Agent Open	Oct 26	Fulton Allem	273/-15	144,000
TOUR Championship	Nov 3	Craig Stadler†	279/-5	360,000
Kapalua Invitational	Nov 16	Mike Hulbert*	276/-16	150,000
RMCC Invitational	Nov 24	Tom Purtzer/Lanny Wadkins	189/-27	125,000 each
JC Penney Classic	Dec 8	Billy Andrade/Kris Tschetter†	266/-18	110,000 each

1993 PGA Tour Events

Tournament	Final Round	Winner	Score/ Under Par	Earnings ($)
Tournament of Champions	Jan 10	Davis Love III	272/-16	144,000
Hawaiian Open	Jan 17	Howard Twitty	269/-19	216,000
Northern Telecom Open	Jan 24	Larry Mize	271/-17	198,000
Phoenix Open	Jan 31	Lee Janzen	273/-11	180,000
AT & T Pebble Beach National Pro-Am	Feb 7	Brett Ogle	276/-12	225,000
Bob Hope Chrysler Classic	Feb 14	Tom Kite	325/-35	198,000
Buick Invitational	Feb 21	Phil Mickelson	278/-10	180,000
Nissan Los Angeles Open	Feb 28	Tom Kite	206/-7 #	180,000
Doral Ryder Open	Mar 7	Greg Norman	265/-23	252,000
Honda Classic	Mar 14	Fred Couples†	207/-9 #	198,000
Nestle Invitational	Mar 21	Ben Crenshaw	280/-8	180,000
The Players Championship	Mar 28	Nick Price	270/-18	450,000
Freeport-McMoran Classic	Apr 4	Mike Standly	281/-7	180,000
The Masters	Apr 11	Bernhard Langer	277/-11	306,000
MCI Heritage Classic	Apr 18	David Edwards	273/-11	202,500
K Mart Greater Greensboro Open	Apr 25	Rocco Mediate††	281/-7	270,000
Shell Houston Open	May 2	Jim McGovern**	199/-17 #	216,000
BellSouth Atlanta Classic	May 9	Nolan Henke	271/-17	216,000
GTE Byron Nelson Classic	May 16	Scott Simpson	270/-10	216,000
Kemper Open	May 23	Grant Waite	275/-9	234,000
Southwestern Bell Colonial	May 30	Fulton Allem	264/-16	234,000
Memorial Tournament	June 6	Paul Azinger	274/-14	252,000
Buick Classic	June 13	Vijay Singh†	280/-4	180,000
U.S. Open	June 20	Lee Janzen	272/-8	290,000
Greater Hartford Open	June 27	Nick Price	271/-9	180,000
Sprint Western Open	July 4	Nick Price	269/-19	216,000
Anheuser-Busch Classic	July 11	Jim Gallagher	269/-15	198,000
British Open	July 18	Greg Norman	267/-13	154,000
New England Classic	July 25	Paul Azinger	268/-16	180,000
St. Jude Classic	Aug 1	Nick Price	266/-18	198,000
Buick Open	Aug 8	Larry Mize	272/-16	180,000
PGA Championship	Aug 15	Paul Azinger	272/-12	300,000
The International	Aug 22	Phil Mickelson	+45 ‡	234,000
NEC World Series of Golf	Aug 29	Fulton Allem	280/-5	360,000
Greater Milwaukee Open	Sept 5	Billy Mayfair	270/-18	180,000
Canadian Open	Sept 12	David Frost	279/-9	180,000
Hardee's Golf Classic	Sept 19	David Frost	259/-21	180,000
B.C. Open	Sept 26	Blaine McCallister	271/-13	144,000
Buick Southern Open	Oct 3	John Inman**	278/-10	126,000
Walt Disney World/Oldsmobile Classic	Oct 10	Jeff Maggert	197/-19	198,000
H.E.B. Texas Open	Oct 17	Jay Haas**	263/-21	180,000
Las Vegas Invitational	Oct 24	Davis Love III	331/-29	252,000
The TOUR Championship	Oct 31	Jim Gallagher	277/-7	540,000

*Won on 1st playoff hole.
**Won on 2nd playoff hole.
†Won on 3rd playoff hole.
††Won on 4th playoff hole.
‡Revised Stableford scoring
#Tournament shortened by rain

Nabisco Dinah Shore

Mission Hills CC; Rancho Mirage, CA
(par 72; 6,437 yds) March 25-28

Player	Score	Earnings ($)
Helen Alfredsson	69-71-72-72—284	105,000
Amy Benz	72-73-71-70—286	49,901
Tina Barrett	70-73-72-71—286	49,901
Betsy King	71-74-67-74—286	49,901
Hollis Stacy	72-74-71-70—287	25,126
Missie Berteotti	68-74-73-72—287	25,126
Dawn Coe-Jones	72-68-72-75—287	25,126
Nancy Lopez	68-78-72-70—288	15,762
Brandie Burton	73-73-68-74—288	15,762
Trish Johnson	74-68-72-74—288	15,762
Jane Crafter	71-72-70-75—288	15,762
Patty Sheehan	73-70-76-70—289	10,625
Debbie Massey	70-74-74-71—289	10,625
Tammie Green	72-73-72-72—289	10,625
Laura Davies	72-72-73-72—289	10,625
Pamela Wright	74-68-75-72—289	10,625
Pat Bradley	71-69-75-74—289	10,625
Kris Monaghan	76-71-74-69—290	8,806
Donna Andrews	73-74-72-72—291	8,101
Karen Noble	74-72-70-75—291	8,101
Nancy Scranton	73-72-71-75—291	8,101
Michelle McGann	78-70-75-69—292	7,237
Sharon Barrett	69-77-72-74—292	7,237

LPGA Championship

Bethesda CC; Bethesda, MD
(par 71; 6,261 yds) June 10-13

Player	Score	Earnings ($)
Patty Sheehan	68-68-70-69—275	150,000
Lauri Merten	73-70-66-67—276	93,093
Barb Bunkowsky	68-70-69-70—277	67,933
Betsy King	72-66-72-69—279	40,130
Michelle McGann	73-68-68-70—279	40,130
Tammie Green	71-69-69-70—279	40,130
Patti Rizzo	72-69-67-71—279	40,130
Nancy Scranton	74-68-72-66—280	23,651
Trish Johnson	68-73-69-70—280	23,651
C. Johnston-Forbes	68-68-70-74—280	23,651
Terry-Jo Myers	71-69-73-68—281	16,277
Kris Tschetter	73-72-67-69—281	16,277
Joan Pitcock	68-74-70-69—281	16,277
Jan Stephenson	69-69-73-70—281	16,277
Donna Andrews	70-72-68-71—281	16,277
Cindy Rarick	68-67-73-73—281	16,277
Jane Crafter	72-73-70-67—282	11,444
N. Ramsbottom	71-71-72-68—282	11,444
Jane Geddes	76-68-68-70—282	11,444
Elaine Crosby	71-71-70-70—282	11,444
Pamela Wright	68-72-72-70—282	11,444
Beth Daniel	74-67-70-71—282	11,444
Rosie Jones	70-71-69-72—282	11,444
Jenny Lidback	69-67-68-78—282	11,444

U.S. Women's Open

Crooked Stick GC, Carmel, IN
(par 72; 6,311 yds) July 22-25

Player	Score	Earnings ($)
Lauri Merten	71-71-70-68—280	144,000
Donna Andrews	71-70-69-71—281	62,431
Helen Alfredsson	68-70-69-74—281	62,431
Pat Bradley	72-70-68-73—283	29,249
Hiromi Kobayashi	71-67-71-74—283	29,249
Patty Sheehan	73-71-69-71—284	22,379
Betsy King	74-70-72-69—285	17,525
Michelle McGann	70-66-78-71—285	17,525
Nancy Lopez	70-71-70-74—285	17,525
Ayako Okamoto	68-72-71-74—285	17,525
Laura Davies	73-71-69-73—286	13,993
JoAnne Carner	71-69-73-73—286	13,993
Tina Barrett	73-73-70-71—287	11,999
Chris Johnson	71-75-69-72—287	11,999
Sherri Steinhauer	73-67-75-72—287	11,999
Nina Fousi	71-71-71-74—287	11,999
Dottie Mochrie	72-71-74-71—288	9,978
Gail Graham	72-73-70-73—288	9,978
Barb Mucha	75-69-71-73—288	9,978
Kris Tschetter	73-71-69-75—288	9,978
Meg Mallon	73-72-69-75—289	9,061

du Maurier Classic

London Hunt and CC; London, Ontario
(par 72; 6,331 yds) August 26-29

Player	Score	Earnings ($)
Brandie Burton*	71-70-66-70—277	120,000
Betsy King	65-70-71-71—277	74,474
Dawn Coe-Jones	64-74-72-68—278	54,346
Dottie Mochrie	68-69-71-71—279	42,269
Kris Monaghan	72-71-71-66—280	31,198
Vicki Fergon	67-73-68-72—280	31,198
D. Lofland-Dormann	68-68-73-72—281	23,751
Helen Alfredsson	70-70-72-70—282	19,926
Kathy Guadagnino	69-69-70-74—282	19,926
D. Ammacapane	72-72-73-66—283	14,894
Sherri Steinhauer	73-69-71-70—283	14,894
Judy Dickinson	70-71-71-71—283	14,894
Chris Johnson	71-69-72-71—283	14,894
Gail Graham	71-72-72-69—284	11,674
Tammie Green	69-73-72-70—284	11,674
Lori West	72-72-69-71—284	11,674
Tina Barrett	74-72-70-69—285	9,862
Deb Richard	72-74-70-69—285	9,862
Sally Little	72-69-69-75—285	9,862
Beth Daniel	69-70-68-78—285	9,862
Cindy Rarick	73-73-70-70—286	8,302
Nancy Harvey	75-70-71-70—286	8,302
Amy Benz	73-70-71-72—286	8,302
Jenny Lidback	70-73-68-75—286	8,302

*Won on 1st playoff hole

Women's Tour Results

Late 1992 LPGA Tour Events

Tournament	Final Round	Winner	Score/ Under Par	Earnings ($)
MBS LPGA Classic	Sept 29	Pat Bradley	277/–11	52,500
Mazda Japan Classic	Nov 10	Liselotte Neumann	211/–5	82,500
JC Penney Classic	Dec 8	Billy Andrade/Kris Tschetter	266/–18	110,000 each

1993 LPGA Tour Events

Tournament	Final Round	Winner	Score/ Under Par	Earnings ($)
HealthSouth Palm Beach Classic	Feb 7	Tammie Green	208/–8	60,000
Itoki Hawaiian Ladies Open	Feb 20	Lisa Walters	210/–6	67,500
Ping/Welch's Championship	Mar 14	Meg Mallon	272/–16	60,000
Standard Register Ping	Mar 21	Patty Sheehan	275/–17	105,000
Nabisco Dinah Shore	Mar 28	Helen Alfredsson	284/–4	105,000
Las Vegas LPGA International	Apr 4	Trish Johnson	209/–7	67,500
Atlanta Women's Championship	Apr 18	Trish Johnson	282/–6	90,000
Sprint Classic	Apr	Kristi Albers	279/–9	180,000
Sara Lee Classic	May 9	Meg Mallon	205/–11	78,750
McDonald's Championship	May 16	Laura Davies	277/–7	135,000
Lady Keystone Open	May 23	Val Skinner	210/–6	60,000
LPGA Corning Classic	May 30	Kelly Robbins	277/–11	75,000
Oldsmobile Classic	June 6	Jane Geddes	277/–11	82,500
Mazda LPGA Championship	June 13	Patty Sheehan	275/–9	150,000
Rochester International	June 20	Tammie Green	276/–12	75,000
ShopRite LPGA Classic	June 27	Shelley Hamlin	204/–9	67,500
Jamie Farr Toledo Classic	July 4	Brandie Burton	201/–12	67,500
Youngstown-Warren LPGA Classic	July 11	Nancy Lopez	203/–13	75,000
JAL Big Apple Classic	July 18	Hiromi Kobayashi	278/–6	90,000
U.S. Women's Open	July 25	Lauri Merten	280/–8	144,000
Ping/Welch's Championship	Aug 1	Missie Berteotti	276/–12	67,500
Stratton Mountain Classic	Aug 8	Dana Lofland-Dorman	275/–13	75,000
Sun-Times Challenge	Aug 15	Cindy Schreyer	272/–16	71,250
Minnesota LPGA Classic	Aug 22	Hiromi Kobayashi	205/–11	67,500
du Maurier Ltd. Classic	Aug 29	Brandie Burton	277/–11	120,000
State Farm Rail Classic	Sept 6	Helen Dobson	203/–13	75,000
Ping-Cellular One Championship	Sept 12	Donna Andrews	208/–8	67,500
Safeco Classic	Sept 19	Brandie Burton	274/–14	67,500
Kyocera Inamori Classic	Sept 25	Kris Monaghan	275/–13	63,750
World Championship of Women's Golf	Oct 17	Dottie Mochrie	283/–5	102,500

Senior Men's Tour Results

Late 1992 Senior Tour Events

Tournament	Final Round	Winner	Score/ Under Par	Earnings ($)
Vantage Championship	Oct 4	Jim Colbert	132/–12	202,500
Raley's Senior Gold Rush	Oct 11	Bob Charles	201/–15	75,000
Transamerica Senior Golf Championship	Oct 18	Bob Charles	200/–16	75,000
Security Pacific Senior Classic	Oct 25	Raymond Floyd	195/–16	90,000
Kaanapali Classic	Nov 1	Tommy Aaron	198/–15	75,000
Senior TOUR Championship	Dec 13	Raymond Floyd	197/–19	150,000

1993 Senior Tour Events

Tournament	Final Round	Winner	Score/ Under Par	Earnings ($)
Senior Tournament of Champions	Jan 10	Al Geiberger	280/–8	52,500
Royal Caribbean Classic	Feb 7	Jim Colbert	199/–14	112,500
Real Estate Challenge	Feb 14	Mike Hill	202/–14	75,000
Suncoast Classic	Feb 21	Jim Albus	206/–7	75,000
West Classic	Mar 7	Al Geiberger	198/–12	75,000

1993 Senior Tour Events (Cont.)

Tournament	Final Round	Winner	Score/ Under Par	Earnings ($)
Vantage at the Dominion	Mar 14	J.C. Snead	214/-2	97,500
Gulfstream Aerospace Invitational	Mar 21	Ray Floyd	194/-22	82,500
Doug Sanders Celebrity Classic	Mar 28	Bob Charles	208/-8	75,000
Fuji Grandslam	Mar 28	Lee Trevino	207/-9	77,600
The Tradition	Apr 4	Tom Shaw	269/-19	127,500
PGA Seniors Championship	Apr 18	Tom Wargo**	275/-13	110,000
Muratec Reunion Pro-Am	Apr 25	Dave Stockton	211/-5	75,000
Las Vegas Senior Classic	May 2	Gibby Gilbert	204/-12	105,000
Liberty Mutual Legends of Golf	May 9	Harold Henning**	204/-12	250,000
Paine Webber Invitational	May 16	Mike Hill	204/-12	82,500
Bell Atlantic Classic	May 23	Bob Charles	204/-6	92,500
Cadillac NFL Golf Classic	May 30	Lee Trevino	209/-7	127,500
NYNEX Commemorative	June 6	Bob Wynn	203/-7	82,500
Southwestern Bell Classic	June 13	Dave Stockton	204/-6	105,000
Burnet Senior Classic	June 20	Chi Chi Rodriguez	201/-15	157,500
Ford Senior Players Championship	June 27	Jim Colbert	278/-10	180,000
Kroger Senior Classic	July 4	Simon Hobday	202/-11	127,500
U.S. Senior Open	July 11	Jack Nicklaus	278/-6	135,330
Ameritech Senior Open	July 18	George Archer	133/-11	90,000
First of America Classic	July 25	George Archer†	199/-14	82,500
Northville Long Island Classic	Aug 1	Ray Floyd	208/-8	82,500
Bank of Boston Senior Golf Classic	Aug 8	Bob Betley	204/-12	112,500
Franklin Quest Championship	Aug 15	Dave Stockton	197/-19	75,000
GTE Northwest Classic	Aug 22	Dave Stockton	200/-16	75,000
Bruno's Memorial Classic	Aug 29	Bob Murphy	203/-13	127,500
Quicksilver Classic	Sept 5	Bob Charles	207/-9	157,500
GTE North Classic	Sept 12	Bob Murphy	134/-10	75,000
Bank One Senior Classic	Sept 19	Gary Player	202/-14	82,500
Nationwide Championship	Sept 26	Lee Trevino	205/-11	142,500
Vantage Championship	Oct 3	Lee Trevino	198/-18	225,000
The Transamerica	Oct 10	Dave Stockton	203/-13	90,000
Raley's Senior Golf Rush	Oct 17	George Archer	202/-14	90,000
Ralph's Senior Classic	Oct 24	Dale Douglass*	196/-17	97,500

*Won on 1st playoff hole.

**Won on 2nd playoff hole.

†Won on 3rd playoff hole.

Amateur Results

Tournament	Final Round	Winner	Score	Runner-Up
Junior Amateur	July 31	Tiger Woods	19 holes	Ryan Armour
Girls' Junior	Aug 7	Kellee Booth	1-up	Erika Hayashida
Women's Amateur	Aug 14	Jill McGill	1-up	Sarah Ingram
Men's Amateur	Aug 29	John Harris	5 & 3	Danny Ellis
Men's Mid-Amateur	Sep 23	Jeff Thomas	1-up	Joey Ferrari
Women's Mid-Amateur	Sep 16	Sarah Ingram	2 & 1	Mary Burkhardt
Senior Women	Oct 1	Anne Sander	230	Maryann Morrison

International Results

Tournament	Final Round	Winner	Score	Runner-Up
Curtis Cup Matches	June 6	Great Britain/Ireland	10-8	United States
Ryder Cup Matches	Sep 26	United States	15-13	Europe

PGA Tour 1993 Money Leaders

Name	Events	Best Finish	Scoring Average	Money ($)
Nick Price	18	1 (4)	69.11	1,478,557
Paul Azinger	24	1 (3)	69.75	1,458,456
Greg Norman	15	1 (2)	68.90	1,359,653
Jim Gallagher, Jr.	27	1 (2)	71.33	1,078,870
David Frost	22	1 (2)	69.48	1,030,717
Payne Stewart	26	2 (4)	69.82	982,875
Lee Janzen	26	1 (2)	70.91	932,335
Tom Kite	20	1 (2)	69.74	887,811
Fulton Allem	28	1 (2)	71.24	851,345
Fred Couples	19	1	69.85	796,579

LPGA Tour Final 1992 Money Leaders

Name	Events	Best Finish	Scoring Average	Money ($)
Dottie Mochrie	26	1 (4)	70.80	693,335
Betsy King	28	1 (3)	71.50	551,320
Danielle Ammaccapane	27	1 (3)	71.60	513,639
Brandie Burton	24	1	71.30	419,571
Patty Sheehan	22	1 (3)	71.30	418,622
Meg Mallon	24	2 (2)	70.99	400,052
Juli Inkster	24	1	71.43	392,063
Nancy Lopez	21	1 (2)	71.05	382,128
Colleen Walker	26	1 (3)	72.25	368,600
Judy Dickinson	26	1	71.90	351,559

Senior Tour 1992 Money Leaders

Name	Events	Best Finish	Scoring Average	Money ($)
Lee Trevino	28	1 (4)	69.46	1,027,002
George Archer	32	1 (3)	70.04	860,175
Jim Colbert	28	1 (2)	70.33	825,768
Mike Hill	29	1 (3)	69.62	802,423
Chi Chi Rodriguez	32	1	70.16	711,095
Dale Douglass	32	1 (2)	70.40	694,564
Dave Stockton	32	1	70.27	656,458
Gibby Gilbert	30	1 (3)	70.65	603,630
Jim Dent	28	1	70.51	593,979
Bob Charles	28	1 (2)	70.46	473,903

Reality Check

Two members of the women's pro golf tour, Marta Figueras-Dotti and Hollis Stacy, have teed off on men pros who have griped about the prospect of paying higher taxes under President Clinton's economic program. One of their targets, Greg Norman, an Australian who lives in Florida, was so upset by the tax hikes that he criticized Jack Nicklaus for having recently played a round with Clinton. Stacy and Figueras-Dotti also were irked at several U.S. Ryder Cup team members who, after being invited by Clinton to stop off at the White House on their way to England, at first said they wouldn't go; they eventually relented and made the visit.

Figueras-Dotti, a Spaniard, said that the bellyaching pros didn't know how lucky they had it. "Tell them to talk to Seve [Ballesteros]," she said. "In Spain we pay 60 percent taxes and can't get anyone to pick up the garbage." Stacy's comments on the male pros were even tougher. "They don't have a clue about what's fantasy and what's reality," she said, "and that's because most of them have never read a newspaper. They think real life is playing golf all day on perfect golf courses for millions of dollars. Real life is poor peope who can't afford to eat."

Men's Golf

THE MAJOR TOURNAMENTS
The Masters

Year	Winner	Score	Runner-Up
1934	Horton Smith	284	Craig Wood
1935	Gene Sarazen* (144)	282	Craig Wood (149) (only 36-hole playoff)
1936	Horton Smith	285	Harry Cooper
1937	Byron Nelson	283	Ralph Guldahl
1938	Henry Picard	285	Ralph Guldahl, Harry Cooper
1939	Ralph Guldahl	279	Sam Snead
1940	Jimmy Demaret	280	Lloyd Mangrum
1941	Craig Wood	280	Byron Nelson
1942	Byron Nelson* (69)	280	Ben Hogan (70)
1943-45	No tournament		
1946	Herman Keiser	282	Ben Hogan
1947	Jimmy Demaret	281	Byron Nelson, Frank Stranahan
1948	Claude Harmon	279	Cary Middlecoff
1949	Sam Snead	282	Johnny Bulla, Lloyd Mangrum
1950	Jimmy Demaret	283	Jim Ferrier
1951	Ben Hogan	280	Skee Riegel
1952	Sam Snead	286	Jack Burke, Jr
1953	Ben Hogan	274	Ed Oliver, Jr
1954	Sam Snead* (70)	289	Ben Hogan (71)
1955	Cary Middlecoff	279	Ben Hogan
1956	Jack Burke, Jr	289	Ken Venturi
1957	Doug Ford	282	Sam Snead
1958	Arnold Palmer	284	Doug Ford, Fred Hawkins
1959	Art Wall, Jr	284	Cary Middlecoff
1960	Arnold Palmer	282	Ken Venturi
1961	Gary Player	280	Charles R. Coe, Arnold Palmer
1962	Arnold Palmer* (68)	280	Gary Player (71), Dow Finsterwald (77)
1963	Jack Nicklaus	286	Tony Lema
1964	Arnold Palmer	276	Dave Marr, Jack Nicklaus
1965	Jack Nicklaus	271	Arnold Palmer, Gary Player
1966	Jack Nicklaus* (70)	288	Tommy Jacobs (72), Gay Brewer, Jr (78)
1967	Gay Brewer, Jr	280	Bobby Nichols
1968	Bob Goalby	277	Roberto DeVicenzo
1969	George Archer	281	Billy Casper, George Knudson, Tom Weiskopf
1970	Billy Casper* (69)	279	Gene Littler (74)
1971	Charles Coody	279	Johnny Miller, Jack Nicklaus
1972	Jack Nicklaus	286	Bruce Crampton, Bobby Mitchell, Tom Weiskopf
1973	Tommy Aaron	283	J. C. Snead
1974	Gary Player	278	Tom Weiskopf, Dave Stockton
1975	Jack Nicklaus	276	Johnny Miller, Tom Weiskopf
1976	Ray Floyd	271	Ben Crenshaw
1977	Tom Watson	276	Jack Nicklaus
1978	Gary Player	277	Hubert Green, Rod Funseth, Tom Watson
1979†	Fuzzy Zoeller* (4-3)	280	Ed Sneed (4-4), Tom Watson (4-4)
1980	Seve Ballesteros	275	Gibby Gilbert, Jack Newton
1981	Tom Watson	280	Johnny Miller, Jack Nicklaus
1982	Craig Stadler* (4)	284	Dan Pohl (5)
1983	Seve Ballesteros	280	Ben Crenshaw, Tom Kite
1984	Ben Crenshaw	277	Tom Watson
1985	Bernhard Langer	282	Curtis Strange, Seve Ballesteros, Ray Floyd
1986	Jack Nicklaus	279	Greg Norman, Tom Kite
1987	Larry Mize* (4-3)	285	Seve Ballesteros (5), Greg Norman (4-4)
1988	Sandy Lyle	281	Mark Calcavecchia
1989	Nick Faldo* (5-3)	283	Scott Hoch (5-4)
1990	Nick Faldo* (4-4)	278	Ray Floyd (4-x)
1991	Ian Woosnam	277	Jose Maria Olazabal
1992	Fred Couples	275	Ray Floyd
1993	Bernhard Langer	277	Chip Beck

*Winner in playoff. Playoff scores are in parentheses. †Playoff cut from 18 holes to sudden death.

Note: Played at Augusta National Golf Club, Augusta, GA.

United States Open Championship

Year	Winner	Score	Runner-Up	Site
1895	Horace Rawlins	†173	Willie Dunn	Newport GC, Newport, RI
1896	James Foulis	†152	Horace Rawlins	Shinnecock Hills GC, Southampton, NY
1897	Joe Lloyd	†162	Willie Anderson	Chicago GC, Wheaton, IL
1898	Fred Herd	328	Alex Smith	Myopia Hunt Club, Hamilton, MA
1899	Willie Smith	315	George Low	Baltimore CC, Baltimore
			Val Fitzjohn	
			W. H. Way	
1900	Harry Vardon	313	John H. Taylor	Chicago GC, Wheaton, IL
1901	Willie Anderson* (85)	331	Alex Smith (86)	Myopia Hunt Club, Hamilton, MA
1902	Laurie Auchterlonie	307	Stewart Gardner	Garden City GC, Garden City, NY
1903	Willie Anderson* (82)	307	David Brown (84)	Baltusrol GC, Springfield, NJ
1904	Willie Anderson	303	Gil Nicholls	Glen View Club, Golf, IL
1905	Willie Anderson	314	Alex Smith	Myopia Hunt Club, Hamilton, MA
1906	Alex Smith	295	Willie Smith	Onwentsia Club, Lake Forest, IL
1907	Alex Ross	302	Gil Nicholls	Philadelphia Cricket Club, Chestnut Hill, PA
1908	Fred McLeod* (77)	322	Willie Smith (83)	Myopia Hunt Club, Hamilton, MA
1909	George Sargent	290	Tom McNamara	Englewood GC, Englewood, NJ
1910	Alex Smith* (71)	298	John McDermott (75)	Philadelphia Cricket Club, Chestnut Hill, PA
			Macdonald Smith (77)	
1911	John McDermott* (80)	307	Mike Brady (82)	Chicago GC, Wheaton, IL
			George Simpson (85)	
1912	John McDermott	294	Tom McNamara	CC of Buffalo, Buffalo
1913	Francis Ouimet* (72)	304	Harry Vardon (77)	The Country Club, Brookline, MA
			Edward Ray (78)	
1914	Walter Hagen	290	Chick Evans	Midlothian CC, Blue Island, IL
1915	Jerry Travers	297	Tom McNamara	Baltusrol GC, Springfield, NJ
1916	Chick Evans	286	Jock Hutchison	Minikahda Club, Minneapolis
1917-18	No tournament			
1919	Walter Hagen* (77)	301	Mike Brady (78)	Brae Burn CC, West Newton, MA
1920	Edward Ray	295	Harry Vardon	Inverness CC, Toledo
			Jack Burke	
			Leo Diegel	
			Jock Hutchison	
1921	Jim Barnes	289	Walter Hagen	Columbia CC, Chevy Chase, MD
			Fred McLeod	
1922	Gene Sarazen	288	John L. Black	Skokie CC, Glencoe, IL
			Bobby Jones	
1923	Bobby Jones* (76)	296	Bobby Cruickshank (78)	Inwood CC, Inwood, NY
1924	Cyril Walker	297	Bobby Jones	Oakland Hills CC, Birmingham, MI
1925	W. MacFarlane* (75-72)	291	Bobby Jones (75-73)	Worcester CC, Worcester, MA
1926	Bobby Jones	293	Joe Turnesa	Scioto CC, Columbus, OH
1927	Tommy Armour* (76)	301	Harry Cooper (79)	Oakmont CC, Oakmont, PA
1928	Johnny Farrell* (143)	294	Bobby Jones (144)	Olympia Fields CC, Matteson, IL
1929	Bobby Jones* (141)	294	Al Espinosa (164)	Winged Foot GC, Mamaroneck, NY
1930	Bobby Jones	287	Macdonald Smith	Interlachen CC, Hopkins, MN
1931	Billy Burke* (149-148)	292	George Von Elm	Inverness Club, Toledo
			(149-149)	
1932	Gene Sarazen	286	Phil Perkins	Fresh Meadows CC, Flushing, NY
			Bobby Cruickshank	
1933	Johnny Goodman	287	Ralph Guldahl	North Shore CC, Glenview, IL
1934	Olin Dutra	293	Gene Sarazen	Merion Cricket Club, Ardmore, PA
1935	Sam Parks, Jr	299	Jimmy Thompson	Oakmont CC, Oakmont, PA
1936	Tony Manero	282	Harry Cooper	Baltusrol GC (Upper Course), Springfield, NJ
1937	Ralph Guldahl	281	Sam Snead	Oakland Hills CC, Birmingham, MI
1938	Ralph Guldahl	284	Dick Metz	Cherry Hills CC, Denver, CO
1939	Byron Nelson* (68-70)	284	Craig Wood (68-73)	Philadelphia CC, Philadelphia
			Denny Shute (76)	
1940	Lawson Little* (70)	287	Gene Sarazen (73)	Canterbury GC, Cleveland
1941	Craig Wood	284	Denny Shute	Colonial Club, Fort Worth
1942-45	No tournament			
1946	Lloyd Mangrum* (72-72)	284	Vic Ghezzi (72-73)	Canterbury GC, Cleveland
			Byron Nelson (72-73)	
1947	Lew Worsham* (69)	282	Sam Snead (70)	St Louis CC, Clayton, MO
1948	Ben Hogan	276	Jimmy Demaret	Riviera CC, Los Angeles

United States Open Championship (Cont.)

Year	Winner	Score	Runner-Up	Site
1949	Cary Middlecoff	286	Sam Snead Clayton Heafner	Medinah CC, Medinah, IL
1950	Ben Hogan* (69)	287	Lloyd Mangrum (73) George Fazio (75)	Merion GC, Ardmore, PA
1951	Ben Hogan	287	Clayton Heafner	Oakland Hills CC, Birmingham, MI
1952	Julius Boros	281	Ed Oliver	Northwood CC, Dallas
1953	Ben Hogan	283	Sam Snead	Oakmont CC, Oakmont, PA
1954	Ed Furgol	284	Gene Littler	Baltusrol GC (Lower Course), Springfield, NJ
1955	Jack Fleck* (69)	287	Ben Hogan (72)	Olympic Club (Lake Course), San Francisco
1956	Cary Middlecoff	281	Ben Hogan Julius Boros	Oak Hill CC, Rochester, NY
1957	Dick Mayer* (72)	282	Cary Middlecoff (79)	Inverness Club, Toledo
1958	Tommy Bolt	283	Gary Player	Southern Hills CC, Tulsa
1959	Billy Casper	282	Bob Rosburg	Winged Foot GC, Mamaroneck, NY
1960	Arnold Palmer	280	Jack Nicklaus	Cherry Hills CC, Denver
1961	Gene Littler	281	Bob Goalby Doug Sanders	Oakland Hills CC, Birmingham, MI
1962	Jack Nicklaus* (71)	283	Arnold Palmer (74)	Oakmont CC, Oakmont, PA
1963	Julius Boros* (70)	293	Jacky Cupit (73) Arnold Palmer (76)	The Country Club, Brookline, MA
1964	Ken Venturi	278	Tommy Jacobs	Congressional CC, Washington, DC
1965	Gary Player* (71)	282	Kel Nagle (74)	Bellerive CC, St Louis
1966	Billy Casper* (69)	278	Arnold Palmer (73)	Olympic Club (Lake Course), San Francisco
1967	Jack Nicklaus	275	Arnold Palmer	Baltusrol GC (Lower Course), Springfield, NJ
1968	Lee Trevino	275	Jack Nicklaus	Oak Hill CC, Rochester, NY
1969	Orville Moody	281	Deane Beman Al Geiberger Bob Rosburg	Champions GC (Cypress Creek Course), Houston
1970	Tony Jacklin	281	Dave Hill	Hazeltine GC, Chaska, MN
1971	Lee Trevino* (68)	280	Jack Nicklaus (71)	Merion GC (East Course), Ardmore, PA
1972	Jack Nicklaus	290	Bruce Crampton	Pebble Beach GL, Pebble Beach, CA
1973	Johnny Miller	279	John Schlee	Oakmont CC, Oakmont, PA
1974	Hale Irwin	287	Forrest Fezler	Winged Foot GC, Mamaroneck, NY
1975	Lou Graham* (71)	287	John Mahaffey (73)	Medinah CC, Medinah, IL
1976	Jerry Pate	277	Tom Weiskopf Al Geiberger	Atlanta Athletic Club, Duluth, GA
1977	Hubert Green	278	Lou Graham	Southern Hills CC, Tulsa
1978	Andy North	285	Dave Stockton J. C. Snead	Cherry Hills CC, Denver
1979	Hale Irwin	284	Gary Player Jerry Pate	Inverness Club, Toledo
1980	Jack Nicklaus	272	Isao Aoki	Baltusrol GC (Lower Course), Springfield, NJ
1981	David Graham	273	George Burns Bill Rogers	Merion GC, Ardmore, PA
1982	Tom Watson	282	Jack Nicklaus	Pebble Beach GL, Pebble Beach, CA
1983	Larry Nelson	280	Tom Watson	Oakmont CC, Oakmont, PA
1984	Fuzzy Zoeller* (67)	276	Greg Norman (75)	Winged Foot GC, Mamaroneck, NY
1985	Andy North	279	Dave Barr T. C. Chen Denis Watson	Oakland Hills CC, Birmingham, MI
1986	Ray Floyd	279	Lanny Wadkins Chip Beck	Shinnecock Hills GC, Southampton, NY
1987	Scott Simpson	277	Tom Watson	Olympic Club (Lake Course), San Francisco
1988	Curtis Strange* (71)	278	Nick Faldo (75)	The Country Club, Brookline, MA
1989	Curtis Strange	278	Chip Beck Mark McCumber Ian Woosnam	Oak Hill CC, Rochester, NY
1990	Hale Irwin* (74) (3)	280	Mike Donald (74) (4)	Medinah CC, Medinah, IL
1991	Payne Stewart (75)	282	Scott Simpson (77)	Hazeltine GC, Chaska, MN
1992	Tom Kite	285	Jeff Sluman	Pebble Beach GL, Pebble Beach, CA
1993	Lee Janzen	272	Payne Stewart	Baltusrol GC, Springfield, NJ

*Winner in playoff. Playoff scores are in parentheses. The 1990 playoff went to one hole of sudden death after an 18-hole playoff.

†Before 1898, 36 holes. From 1898 on, 72 holes.

British Open

Year	Winner	Score	Runner-Up	Site
1860†	Willie Park	174	Tom Morris, Sr	Prestwick, Scotland
1861‡	Tom Morris, Sr	163	Willie Park	Prestwick, Scotland
1862	Tom Morris, Sr	163	Willie Park	Prestwick, Scotland
1863	Willie Park	168	Tom Morris, Sr	Prestwick, Scotland
1864	Tom Morris, Sr	160	Andrew Strath	Prestwick, Scotland
1865	Andrew Strath	162	Willie Park	Prestwick, Scotland
1866	Willie Park	169	David Park	Prestwick, Scotland
1867	Tom Morris, Sr	170	Willie Park	Prestwick, Scotland
1868	Tom Morris, Jr	154	Tom Morris, Sr	Prestwick, Scotland
1869	Tom Morris, Jr	157	Tom Morris, Sr	Prestwick, Scotland
1870	Tom Morris, Jr	149	David Strath Bob Kirk	Prestwick, Scotland
1871	No tournament			
1872	Tom Morris, Jr	166	David Strath	Prestwick, Scotland
1873	Tom Kidd	179	Jamie Anderson	St Andrews, Scotland
1874	Mungo Park	159	No record	Musselburgh, Scotland
1875	Willie Park	166	Bob Martin	Prestwick, Scotland
1876	#Bob Martin	176	David Strath	St Andrews, Scotland
1877	Jamie Anderson	160	Bob Pringle	Musselburgh, Scotland
1878	Jamie Anderson	157	Robert Kirk	Prestwick, Scotland
1879	Jamie Anderson	169	Andrew Kirkaldy James Allan	St Andrews, Scotland
1880	Robert Ferguson	162	No record	Musselburgh, Scotland
1881	Robert Ferguson	170	Jamie Anderson	Prestwick, Scotland
1882	Robert Ferguson	171	Willie Fernie	St Andrews, Scotland
1883	Willie Fernie*	159	Robert Ferguson	Musselburgh, Scotland
1884	Jack Simpson	160	Douglas Rolland Willie Fernie	Prestwick, Scotland
1885	Bob Martin	171	Archie Simpson	St Andrews, Scotland
1886	David Brown	157	Willie Campbell	Musselburgh, Scotland
1887	Willie Park, Jr	161	Bob Martin	Prestwick, Scotland
1888	Jack Burns	171	Bernard Sayers David Anderson	St Andrews, Scotland
1889	Willie Park, Jr* (158)	155	Andrew Kirkaldy (163)	Musselburgh, Scotland
1890	John Ball	164	Willie Fernie	Prestwick, Scotland
1891	Hugh Kirkaldy	166	Andrew Kirkaldy Willie Fernie	St Andrews, Scotland
1892	Harold Hilton	**305	John Ball Hugh Kirkaldy	Muirfield, Scotland
1893	William Auchterlonie	322	John E. Laidlay	Prestwick, Scotland
1894	John H. Taylor	326	Douglas Rolland	Royal St George's, England
1895	John H. Taylor	322	Alexander Herd	St Andrews, Scotland
1896	Harry Vardon* (157)	316	John H. Taylor (161)	Muirfield, Scotland
1897	Harold Hilton	314	James Braid	Hoylake, England
1898	Harry Vardon	307	Willie Park, Jr	Prestwick, Scotland
1899	Harry Vardon	310	Jack White	Royal St George's, England
1900	John H. Taylor	309	Harry Vardon	St Andrews, Scotland
1901	James Braid	309	Harry Vardon	Muirfield, Scotland
1902	Alexander Herd	307	Harry Vardon	Hoylake, England
1903	Harry Vardon	300	Tom Vardon	Prestwick, Scotland
1904	Jack White	296	John H. Taylor	Royal St George's, England
1905	James Braid	318	John H. Taylor Rolland Jones	St Andrews, Scotland
1906	James Braid	300	John H. Taylor	Muirfield, Scotland
1907	Arnaud Massy	312	John H. Taylor	Hoylake, England
1908	James Braid	291	Tom Ball	Prestwick, Scotland
1909	John H. Taylor	295	James Braid Tom Ball	Deal, England
1910	James Braid	299	Alexander Herd	St Andrews, Scotland
1911	Harry Vardon	303	Arnaud Massy	Royal St George's, England
1912	Ted Ray	295	Harry Vardon	Muirfield, Scotland
1913	John H. Taylor	304	Ted Ray	Hoylake, England
1914	Harry Vardon	306	John H. Taylor	Prestwick, Scotland
1915-19	No tournament			
1920	George Duncan	303	Alexander Herd	Deal, England

British Open (Cont.)

Year	Winner	Score	Runner-Up	Site
1921	Jock Hutchison* (150)	296	Roger Wethered (159)	St Andrews, Scotland
1922	Walter Hagen	300	George Duncan	Royal St George's, England
			Jim Barnes	
1923	Arthur G. Havers	295	Walter Hagen	Troon, Scotland
1924	Walter Hagen	301	Ernest Whitcombe	Hoylake, England
1925	Jim Barnes	300	Archie Compston	Prestwick, Scotland
			Ted Ray	
1926	Bobby Jones	291	Al Watrous	Royal Lytham and St Annes GC, St Annes-on-the-Sea, England
1927	Bobby Jones	285	Aubrey Boomer	St Andrews, Scotland
1928	Walter Hagen	292	Gene Sarazen	Royal St George's, England
1929	Walter Hagen	292	Johnny Farrell	Muirfield, Scotland
1930	Bobby Jones	291	Macdonald Smith	Hoylake, England
			Leo Diegel	
1931	Tommy Armour	296	Jose Jurado	Carnoustie, Scotland
1932	Gene Sarazen	283	Macdonald Smith	Prince's, England
1933	Denny Shute* (149)	292	Craig Wood (154)	St Andrews, Scotland
1934	Henry Cotton	283	Sidney F. Brews	Royal St George's, England
1935	Alfred Perry	283	Alfred Padgham	Muirfield, Scotland
1936	Alfred Padgham	287	James Adams	Hoylake, England
1937	Henry Cotton	290	Reginald A. Whitcombe	Carnoustie, Scotland
1938	Reginald A. Whitcombe	295	James Adams	Royal St George's, England
1939	Richard Burton	290	Johnny Bulla	St Andrews, Scotland
1940-45	No tournament			
1946	Sam Snead	290	Bobby Locke	St Andrews, Scotland
			Johnny Bulla	
1947	Fred Daly	293	Reginald W. Horne	Hoylake, England
			Frank Stranahan	
1948	Henry Cotton	294	Fred Daly	Muirfield, Scotland
1949	Bobby Locke* (135)	283	Harry Bradshaw (147)	Royal St George's, England
1950	Bobby Locke	279	Roberto DeVicenzo	Troon, Scotland
1951	Max Faulkner	285	Tony Cerda	Portrush, Ireland
1952	Bobby Locke	287	Peter Thomson	Royal Lytham, England
1953	Ben Hogan	282	Frank Stranahan	Carnoustie, Scotland
			Dai Rees	
			Peter Thomson	
			Tony Cerda	
1954	Peter Thomson	283	Sidney S. Scott	Royal Birkdale, England
			Dai Rees	
			Bobby Locke	
1955	Peter Thomson	281	John Fallon	St Andrews, Scotland
1956	Peter Thomson	286	Flory Van Donck	Hoylake, England
1957	Bobby Locke	279	Peter Thomson	St Andrews, Scotland
1958	Peter Thomson* (139)	278	Dave Thomas (143)	Royal Lytham, England
1959	Gary Player	284	Fred Bullock	Muirfield, Scotland
			Flory Van Donck	
1960	Kel Nagle	278	Arnold Palmer	St Andrews, Scotland
1961	Arnold Palmer	284	Dai Rees	Royal Birkdale, England
1962	Arnold Palmer	276	Kel Nagle	Troon, Scotland
1963	Bob Charles* (140)	277	Phil Rodgers (148)	Royal Lytham, England
1964	Tony Lema	279	Jack Nicklaus	St Andrews, Scotland
1965	Peter Thomson	285	Brian Huggett	Southport, England
			Christy O'Connor	
1966	Jack Nicklaus	282	Doug Sanders	Muirfield, Scotland
			Dave Thomas	
1967	Robert DeVicenzo	278	Jack Nicklaus	Hoylake, England
1968	Gary Player	289	Jack Nicklaus	Carnoustie, Scotland
			Bob Charles	
1969	Tony Jacklin	280	Bob Charles	Royal Lytham, England
1970	Jack Nicklaus* (72)	283	Doug Sanders (73)	St Andrews, Scotland
1971	Lee Trevino	278	Lu Liang Huan	Royal Birkdale, England
1972	Lee Trevino	278	Jack Nicklaus	Muirfield, Scotland
1973	Tom Weiskopf	276	Johnny Miller	Troon, Scotland
1974	Gary Player	282	Peter Oosterhuis	Royal Lytham, England
1975	Tom Watson* (71)	279	Jack Newton (72)	Carnoustie, Scotland

British Open (Cont.)

Year	Winner	Score	Runner-Up	Site
1976	Johnny Miller	279	Jack Nicklaus	Royal Birkdale, England
			Seve Ballesteros	
1977	Tom Watson	268	Jack Nicklaus	Turnberry, Scotland
1978	Jack Nicklaus	281	Ben Crenshaw	St Andrews, Scotland
			Tom Kite	
			Ray Floyd	
			Simon Owen	
1979	Seve Ballesteros	283	Ben Crenshaw	Royal Lytham, England
			Jack Nicklaus	
1980	Tom Watson	271	Lee Trevino	Muirfield, Scotland
1981	Bill Rogers	276	Bernhard Langer	Royal St George's, England
1982	Tom Watson	284	Nick Price	Royal Troon, Scotland
			Peter Oosterhuis	
1983	Tom Watson	275	Andy Bean	Royal Birkdale, England
1984	Seve Ballesteros	276	Tom Watson	St Andrews, Scotland
			Bernhard Langer	
1985	Sandy Lyle	282	Payne Stewart	Royal St George's, England
1986	Greg Norman	280	Gordon Brand	Turnberry, Scotland
1987	Nick Faldo	279	Paul Azinger	Muirfield, Scotland
			Rodger Davis	
1988	Seve Ballesteros	273	Nick Price	Royal Lytham, England
1989††	Mark Calcavecchia* (4-3-3-3)	275	Wayne Grady (4-4-4-4) Greg Norman (3-3-4-x)	Royal Troon, Scotland
1990	Nick Faldo	270	Payne Stewart	St Andrews, Scotland
			Mark McNulty	
1991	Ian Baker-Finch	272	Mike Harwood	Royal Birkdale, England
1992	Nick Faldo	272	John Cook	Muirfield, Scotland
1993	Greg Norman	267	Nick Faldo	Royal St George's, England

*Winner in playoff. Playoff scores are in parentheses. †The first event was open only to professional golfers.
‡The second annual open was open to amateurs and pros. #Tied, but refused playoff.
**Championship extended from 36 to 72 holes. ††Playoff cut from 18 holes to 4 holes.

PGA Championship

Year	Winner	Score	Runner-Up	Site
1916	Jim Barnes	1 up	Jock Hutchison	Siwanoy CC, Bronxville, NY
1917-18	No tournament			
1919	Jim Barnes	6 & 5	Fred McLeod	Engineers CC, Roslyn, NY
1920	Jock Hutchison	1 up	J. Douglas Edgar	Flossmoor CC, Flossmoor, IL
1921	Walter Hagen	3 & 2	Jim Barnes	Inwood CC, Far Rockaway, NY
1922	Gene Sarazen	4 & 3	Emmet French	Oakmont CC, Oakmont, PA
1923	Gene Sarazen	1 up 38 holes	Walter Hagen	Pelham CC, Pelham, NY
1924	Walter Hagen	2 up	Jim Barnes	French Lick CC, French Lick, IN
1925	Walter Hagen	6 & 5	William Mehlhorn	Olympia Fields CC, Olympia Fields, IL
1926	Walter Hagen	5 & 3	Leo Diegel	Salisbury GC, Westbury, NY
1927	Walter Hagen	1 up	Joe Turnesa	Cedar Crest CC, Dallas
1928	Leo Diegel	6 & 5	Al Espinosa	Five Farms CC, Baltimore
1929	Leo Diegel	6 & 4	Johnny Farrell	Hillcrest CC, Los Angeles
1930	Tommy Armour	1 up	Gene Sarazen	Fresh Meadow CC, Flushing, NY
1931	Tom Creavy	2 & 1	Denny Shute	Wannamoisett CC, Rumford, RI
1932	Olin Dutra	4 & 3	Frank Walsh	Keller GC, St Paul
1933	Gene Sarazen	5 & 4	Willie Goggin	Blue Mound CC, Milwaukee
1934	Paul Runyan	1 up	Craig Wood	Park CC, Williamsville, NY
1935	Johnny Revolta	5 & 4 38 holes	Tommy Armour	Twin Hills CC, Oklahoma City
1936	Denny Shute	3 & 2	Jimmy Thomson	Pinehurst CC, Pinehurst, NC
1937	Denny Shute	1 up 37 holes	Harold McSpaden	Pittsburgh FC, Aspinwall, PA
1938	Paul Runyan	8 & 7	Sam Snead	Shawnee CC, Shawnee-on-Delaware, PA
1939	Henry Picard	1 up 37 holes	Byron Nelson	Pomonok CC, Flushing, NY
1940	Byron Nelson	1 up	Sam Snead	Hershey CC, Hershey, PA

PGA Championship (Cont.)

Year	Winner	Score	Runner-Up	Site
1941	Vic Ghezzi	1 up 38 holes	Byron Nelson	Cherry Hills CC, Denver
1942	Sam Snead	2 & 1	Jim Turnesa	Seaview CC, Atlantic City
1943	No tournament			
1944	Bob Hamilton	1 up	Byron Nelson	Manito G & CC, Spokane, WA
1945	Byron Nelson	4 & 3	Sam Byrd	Morraine CC, Dayton
1946	Ben Hogan	6 & 4	Ed Oliver	Portland GC, Portland, OR
1947	Jim Ferrier	2 & 1	Chick Harbert	Plum Hollow CC, Detroit
1948	Ben Hogan	7 & 6	Mike Turnesa	Norwood Hills CC, St Louis
1949	Sam Snead	3 & 2	Johnny Palmer	Hermitage CC, Richmond
1950	Chandler Harper	4 & 3	Henry Williams, Jr	Scioto CC, Columbus, OH
1951	Sam Snead	7 & 6	Walter Burkemo	Oakmont CC, Oakmont, PA
1952	Jim Turnesa	1 up	Chick Harbert	Big Spring CC, Louisville
1953	Walter Burkemo	2 & 1	Felice Torza	Birmingham CC, Birmingham, MI
1954	Chick Harbert	4 & 3	Walter Burkemo	Keller GC, St Paul
1955	Doug Ford	4 & 3	Cary Middlecoff	Meadowbrook CC, Detroit
1956	Jack Burke	3 & 2	Ted Kroll	Blue Hill CC, Boston
1957	Lionel Hebert	2 & 1	Dow Finsterwald	Miami Valley CC, Dayton
1958	Dow Finsterwald	276	Billy Casper	Llanerch CC, Havertown, PA
1959	Bob Rosburg	277	Jerry Barber Doug Sanders	Minneapolis GC, St Louis Park, MN
1960	Jay Hebert	281	Jim Ferrier	Firestone CC, Akron
1961	Jerry Barber* (67)	277	Don January (68)	Olympia Fields CC, Olympia Fields, IL
1962	Gary Player	278	Bob Goalby	Aronimink GC, Newton Square, PA
1963	Jack Nicklaus	279	Dave Ragan, Jr	Dallas Athletic Club, Dallas
1964	Bobby Nichols	271	Jack Nicklaus Arnold Palmer	Columbus CC, Columbus, OH
1965	Dave Marr	280	Billy Casper Jack Nicklaus	Laurel Valley CC, Ligonier, PA
1966	Al Geiberger	280	Dudley Wysong	Firestone CC, Akron
1967	*Don January (69)	281	Don Massengale (71)	Columbine CC, Littleton, CO
1968	Julius Boros	281	Bob Charles Arnold Palmer	Pecan Valley CC, San Antonio
1969	Ray Floyd	276	Gary Player	NCR CC, Dayton
1970	Dave Stockton	279	Arnold Palmer Bob Murphy	Southern Hills CC, Tulsa
1971	Jack Nicklaus	281	Billy Casper	PGA Natl GC, Palm Beach Gardens, FL
1972	Gary Player	281	Tommy Aaron Jim Jamieson	Oakland Hills CC, Birmingham, MI
1973	Jack Nicklaus	277	Bruce Crampton	Canterbury GC, Cleveland
1974	Lee Trevino	276	Jack Nicklaus	Tanglewood GC, Winston-Salem, NC
1975	Jack Nicklaus	276	Bruce Crampton	Firestone CC, Akron
1976	Dave Stockton	281	Ray Floyd Don January	Congressional CC, Bethesda, MD
1977†	Lanny Wadkins* (4-4-4)	282	Gene Littler (4-4-5)	Pebble Beach GL, Pebble Beach, CA
1978	John Mahaffey* (4-3)	276	Jerry Pate (4-4) Tom Watson (4-5)	Oakmont CC, Oakmont, PA
1979	David Graham* (4-4-2)	272	Ben Crenshaw (4-4-4)	Oakland Hills CC, Birmingham, MI
1980	Jack Nicklaus	274	Andy Bean	Oak Hill CC, Rochester, NY
1981	Larry Nelson	273	Fuzzy Zoeller	Atlanta Athletic Club, Duluth, GA
1982	Raymond Floyd	272	Lanny Wadkins	Southern Hills CC, Tulsa
1983	Hal Sutton	274	Jack Nicklaus	Riviera CC, Pacific Palisades, CA
1984	Lee Trevino	273	Gary Player Lanny Wadkins	Shoal Creek, Birmingham, AL
1985	Hubert Green	278	Lee Trevino	Cherry Hills CC, Denver
1986	Bob Tway	276	Greg Norman	Inverness CC, Toledo
1987	Larry Nelson* (4)	287	Lanny Wadkins (5)	PGA Natl GC, Palm Beach Gardens, FL
1988	Jeff Sluman	272	Paul Azinger	Oak Tree GC, Edmond, OK
1989	Payne Stewart	276	Mike Reid	Kemper Lakes GC, Hawthorn Woods, IL
1990	Wayne Grady	282	Fred Couples	Shoal Creek, Birmingham, AL
1991	John Daly	276	Bruce Lietzke	Crooked Stick GC, Carmel, IN
1992	Nick Price	278	Jim Gallagher Jr	Bellerive CC, St. Louis
1993	Paul Azinger* (4-4)	272	Greg Norman (4-5)	Inverness CC, Toldeo, OH

*Winner in playoff. Playoff scores are in parentheses.

†Playoff changed from 18 holes to sudden death.

THE PGA TOUR
Season Money Leaders

		Earnings ($)			Earnings ($)
1934	Paul Runyan	6,767.00	1965	Jack Nicklaus	140,752.14
1935	Johnny Revolta	9,543.00	1966	Billy Casper	121,944.92
1936	Horton Smith	7,682.00	1967	Jack Nicklaus	188,998.08
1937	Harry Cooper	14,138.69	1968	Billy Casper	205,168.67
1938	Sam Snead	19,534.49	1969	Frank Beard	164,707.11
1939	Henry Picard	10,303.00	1970	Lee Trevino	157,037.63
1940	Ben Hogan	10,655.00	1971	Jack Nicklaus	244,490.50
1941	Ben Hogan	18,358.00	1972	Jack Nicklaus	320,542.26
1942	Ben Hogan	13,143.00	1973	Jack Nicklaus	308,362.10
1943	No statistics compiled		1974	Johnny Miller	353,021.59
1944	Byron Nelson (war bonds)	37,967.69	1975	Jack Nicklaus	298,149.17
1945	Byron Nelson (war bonds)	63,335.66	1976	Jack Nicklaus	266,438.57
1946	Ben Hogan	42,556.16	1977	Tom Watson	310,653.16
1947	Jimmy Demaret	27,936.83	1978	Tom Watson	362,428.93
1948	Ben Hogan	32,112.00	1979	Tom Watson	462,636.00
1949	Sam Snead	31,593.83	1980	Tom Watson	530,808.33
1950	Sam Snead	35,758.83	1981	Tom Kite	375,698.84
1951	Lloyd Mangrum	26,088.83	1982	Craig Stadler	446,462.00
1952	Julius Boros	37,032.97	1983	Hal Sutton	426,668.00
1953	Lew Worsham	34,002.00	1984	Tom Watson	476,260.00
1954	Bob Toski	65,819.81	1985	Curtis Strange	542,321.00
1955	Julius Boros	63,121.55	1986	Greg Norman	653,296.00
1956	Ted Kroll	72,835.83	1987	Curtis Strange	925,941.00
1957	Dick Mayer	65,835.00	1988	Curtis Strange	1,147,644.00
1958	Arnold Palmer	42,607.50	1989	Tom Kite	1,395,278.00
1959	Art Wall	53,167.60	1990	Greg Norman	1,165,477.00
1960	Arnold Palmer	75,262.85	1991	Corey Pavin	979,430.00
1961	Gary Player	64,540.45	1992	Fred Couples	1,344,188.00
1962	Arnold Palmer	81,448.33	1993	Nick Price	1,478,557.00
1963	Arnold Palmer	128,230.00			
1964	Jack Nicklaus	113,284.50			

Note: Total money listed from 1968 through 1974. Official money listed from 1975 on.

Career Money Leaders‡

		Earnings ($)			Earnings ($)
1.	Tom Kite	8,500,729	18. Hale Irwin		4,839,626
2.	Paul Azinger	6,761,306	19. Mark Calcavecchia		4,489,962
3.	Greg Norman	6,607,562	20. David Frost		4,428,831
4.	Payne Stewart	6,377,573	21. Gil Morgan		4,426,178
5.	Tom Watson	6,370,949	22. Davis Love III		4,037,672
6.	Fred Couples	6,263,494	23. Jay Haas		4,011,175
7.	Curtis Strange	6,042,561	24. Wayne Levi		3,990,815
8.	Lanny Wadkins	5,877,256	25. Larry Mize		3,908,681
9.	Ben Crenshaw	5,448,507	26. Scott Hoch		3,868,695
10.	Jack Nicklaus	5,360,662	27. John Cook		3,845,252
11.	Chip Beck	5,304,632	28. Fuzzy Zoeller		3,731,261
12.	Nick Price	5,226,491	29. Scott Simpson		3,665,272
13.	Craig Stadler	5,131,605	30. John Mahaffey		3,606,019
14.	Raymond Floyd	5,033,996	31. Lee Trevino		3,478,449
15.	Mark O'Meara	4,998,267	32. Hal Sutton		3,391,692
16.	Corey Pavin	4,929,138	33. Steve Pate		3,280,181
17.	Bruce Lietzke	4,875,942	34. Peter Jacobsen		3,260,745

35. Joey Sindelar		3,247,940
36. Andy Bean		3,234,265
37. Tim Simpson		3,221,926
38. Mark McCumber		3,215,569
39. Larry Nelson		3,206,418
40. Jim Gallagher Jr		3,200,722
41. Ken Green		3,019,069
42. Jeff Sluman		2,995,571
43. Steve Elkington		2,976,192
44. David Edwards		2,961,573
45. Tom Purtzer		2,942,809
46. Bob Tway		2,914,016
47. Mike Reid		2,874,570
48. D.A. Weibring		2,839,550
49. Jodie Mudd		2,735,887
50. Dan Pohl		2,721,117

Top Single-Season Earnings‡

	Earnings ($)	Year		Earnings ($)	Year
Nick Price	1,478,557	1993	Greg Norman	1,165,477	1990
Paul Azinger	1,458,456	1993	Curtis Strange	1,147,644	1988
Tom Kite	1,395,278	1989	Jim Gallagher, Jr	1,078,870	1993
Greg Norman	1,359,653	1993	David Frost	1,030,717	1993
Fred Couples	1,344,188	1992	Wayne Levi	1,024,647	1990
Payne Stewart	1,201,301	1989	Corey Pavin	979,430	1991

Most Career Wins‡

	Wins		Wins		Wins
Sam Snead	81	Billy Casper	51	Horton Smith	32
Jack Nicklaus	70	Walter Hagen	40	Tom Watson	32
Ben Hogan	63	Cary Middlecoff	40	Harry Cooper	31
Arnold Palmer	60	Gene Sarazen	38	Jimmy Demaret	31
Byron Nelson	52	Lloyd Mangrum	36	Leo Diegel	30

‡Statistics through 11/01/93

Year by Year Statistical Leaders*

SCORING AVERAGE

1980	Lee Trevino	69.73
1981	Tom Kite	69.80
1982	Tom Kite	70.21
1983	Raymond Floyd	70.61
1984	Calvin Peete	70.56
1985	Don Pooley	70.36
1986	Scott Hoch	70.08
1987	David Frost	70.09
1988	Greg Norman	69.38
1989	Payne Stewart	69.485†
1990	Greg Norman	69.10
1991	Fred Couples	69.59
1992	Fred Couples	69.38
1993	Greg Norman	68.90

Note: Scoring average per round, with adjustments made at each round for the field's course scoring average.

DRIVING DISTANCE

		Yds
1980	Dan Pohl	274.3
1981	Dan Pohl	280.1
1982	Bill Calfee	275.3
1983	John McComish	277.4
1984	Bill Glasson	276.5
1985	Andy Bean	278.2
1986	Davis Love III	285.7
1987	John McComish	283.9
1988	Steve Thomas	284.6
1989	Ed Humenik	280.9
1990	Tom Purtzer	279.6
1991	John Daly	288.9
1992	John Daly	283.4
1993	John Daley	288.9

Note: Average computed by charting distance of two tee shots on a predetermined par-four or par-five hole (one on front nine, one on back nine).

DRIVING ACCURACY

1980	Mike Reid	79.5
1981	Calvin Peete	81.9
1982	Calvin Peete	84.6
1983	Calvin Peete	81.3
1984	Calvin Peete	77.5
1985	Calvin Peete	80.6
1986	Calvin Peete	81.7
1987	Calvin Peete	83.0
1988	Calvin Peete	82.5
1989	Calvin Peete	82.6

DRIVING ACCURACY (Cont.)

1990	Calvin Peete	83.7
1991	Hale Irwin	78.3
1992	Doug Tewell	82.3
1993	Doug Tewell	82.5

Note: Percentage of fairways hit on number of par-four and par-five holes played; par-three holes excluded.

GREENS IN REGULATION

1980	Jack Nicklaus	72.1
1981	Calvin Peete	73.1
1982	Calvin Peete	72.4
1983	Calvin Peete	71.4
1984	Andy Bean	72.1
1985	John Mahaffey	71.9
1986	John Mahaffey	72.0
1987	Gil Morgan	73.3
1988	John Adams	73.9
1989	Bruce Lietzke	72.6
1990	Doug Tewell	70.9
1991	Bruce Lietzke	73.3
1992	Tim Simpson	74.0
1993	Fuzzy Zoeller	73.6

Note: Average of greens reached in regulation out of total holes played; hole is considered hit in regulation if any part of the ball rests on the putting surface in two shots less than the hole's par; a par five hit in two shots is one green in regulation.

PUTTING

1980	Jerry Pate	28.81
1981	Alan Tapie	28.70
1982	Ben Crenshaw	28.65
1983	Morris Hatalsky	27.96
1984	Gary McCord	28.57
1985	Craig Stadler	28.627†
1986	Greg Norman	1.736
1987	Ben Crenshaw	1.743
1988	Don Pooley	1.729
1989	Steve Jones	1.734
1990	Larry Rinker	1.7467†
1991	Jay Don Blake	1.7326†
1992	Mark O'Meara	1.731
1993	David Frost	1.739

Note: Average number of putts taken on greens reached in regulation; prior to 1986, based on average number of putts per 18 holes.

ALL-AROUND

1987	Dan Pohl	170
1988	Payne Stewart	170
1989	Paul Azinger	250
1990	Paul Azinger	162
1991	Scott Hoch	283
1992	Fred Couples	256
1993	Gil Morgan	252

Note: Addition of the places of standing from the other nine statistical categories; the player with the number closest to zero leads.

SAND SAVES

1980	Bob Eastwood	65.4
1981	Tom Watson	60.1
1982	Isao Aoki	60.2
1983	Isao Aoki	62.3
1984	Peter Oosterhuis	64.7
1985	Tom Purtzer	60.8
1986	Paul Azinger	63.8
1987	Paul Azinger	63.2
1988	Greg Powers	63.5
1989	Mike Sullivan	66.0
1990	Paul Azinger	67.2
1991	Ben Crenshaw	64.9
1992	Mitch Adcock	66.9
1993	Ken Green	64.4

Note: Percentage of up-and-down efforts from greenside sand traps only; fairway bunkers excluded.

PAR BREAKERS

1980	Tom Watson	.213
1981	Bruce Lietzke	.225
1982	Tom Kite	.2154†
1983	Tom Watson	.211
1984	Craig Stadler	.220
1985	Craig Stadler	.218
1986	Greg Norman	.248
1987	Mark Calcavecchia	.221
1988	Ken Green	.236
1989	Greg Norman	.224
1990	Greg Norman	.219

Note: Average based on total birdies and eagles scored out of total holes played. Discontinued as an official category after 1990.

Year by Year Statistical Leaders* (Cont.)

EAGLES			BIRDIES		
1980	Dave Eichelberger	16	1980	Andy Bean	388
1981	Bruce Lietzke	12	1981	Vance Heafner	388
1982	Tom Weiskopf	10	1982	Andy Bean	392
	J. C. Snead	10	1983	Hal Sutton	399
	Andy Bean	10	1984	Mark O'Meara	419
1983	Chip Beck	15	1985	Joey Sindelar	411
1984	Gary Hallberg	15	1986	Joey Sindelar	415
1985	Larry Rinker	14	1987	Dan Forsman	409
1986	Joey Sindelar	16	1988	Dan Forsman	465
1987	Phil Blackmar	20	1989	Ted Schulz	415
1988	Ken Green	21	1990	Mike Donald	401
1989	Lon Hinkle	14	1991	Scott Hoch	446
	Duffy Waldorf	14	1992	Jeff Sluman	417
1990	Paul Azinger	14	1993	John Huston	426
1991	Andy Bean	15			
1992	Dan Forsman	18			
1993	Davis Love III	15			

Note: Total of eagles scored.

Note: Total of birdies scored.

PGA Player of the Year Award

1948	Ben Hogan	1964	Ken Venturi	1980	Tom Watson
1949	Sam Snead	1965	Dave Marr	1981	Bill Rogers
1950	Ben Hogan	1966	Billy Casper	1982	Tom Watson
1951	Ben Hogan	1967	Jack Nicklaus	1983	Hal Sutton
1952	Julius Boros	1968	Not awarded	1984	Tom Watson
1953	Ben Hogan	1969	Orville Moody	1985	Lanny Wadkins
1954	Ed Furgol	1970	Billy Casper	1986	Bob Tway
1955	Doug Ford	1971	Lee Trevino	1987	Paul Azinger
1956	Jack Burke	1972	Jack Nicklaus	1988	Curtis Strange
1957	Dick Mayer	1973	Jack Nicklaus	1989	Tom Kite
1958	Dow Finsterwald	1974	Johnny Miller	1990	Nick Faldo
1959	Art Wall	1975	Jack Nicklaus	1991	Fred Couples
1960	Arnold Palmer	1976	Jack Nicklaus	1992	Fred Couples
1961	Jerry Barber	1977	Tom Watson		
1962	Arnold Palmer	1978	Tom Watson		
1963	Julius Boros	1979	Tom Watson		

Vardon Trophy: Scoring Average

Year	Winner	Avg	Year	Winner	Avg	Year	Winner	Avg
1937	Harry Cooper	*500	1959	Art Wall	70.35	1977	Tom Watson	70.32
1938	Sam Snead	520	1960	Billy Casper	69.95	1978	Tom Watson	70.16
1939	Byron Nelson	473	1961	Arnold Palmer	69.85	1979	Tom Watson	70.27
1940	Ben Hogan	423	1962	Arnold Palmer	70.27	1980	Lee Trevino	69.73
1941	Ben Hogan	494	1963	Billy Casper	70.58	1981	Tom Kite	69.80
1942-46	No award		1964	Arnold Palmer	70.01	1982	Tom Kite	70.21
1947	Jimmy Demaret	69.90	1965	Billy Casper	70.85	1983	Raymond Floyd	70.61
1948	Ben Hogan	69.30	1966	Billy Casper	70.27	1984	Calvin Peete	70.56
1949	Sam Snead	69.37	1967	Arnold Palmer	70.18	1985	Don Pooley	70.36
1950	Sam Snead	69.23	1968	Billy Casper	69.82	1986	Scott Hoch	70.08
1951	Lloyd Mangrum	70.05	1969	Dave Hill	70.34	1987	Don Pohl	70.25
1952	Jack Burke	70.54	1970	Lee Trevino	70.64	1988	Chip Beck	69.46
1953	Lloyd Mangrum	70.22	1971	Lee Trevino	70.27	1989	Greg Norman	69.49
1954	E. J. Harrison	70.41	1972	Lee Trevino	70.89	1990	Greg Norman	69.10
1955	Sam Snead	69.86	1973	Bruce Crampton	70.57	1991	Fred Couples	69.59
1956	Cary Middlecoff	70.35	1974	Lee Trevino	70.53	1992	Fred Couples	69.38
1957	Dow Finsterwald	70.30	1975	Bruce Crampton	70.51	1993	Nick Price	69.11
1958	Bob Rosburg	70.11	1976	Don January	70.56			

*Point system used, 1937-41.

Note: As of 1988, based on minimum of 60 rounds per year.

All-Time PGA Tour Records*

Scoring

90 HOLES

325—(67-67-64-65-62) by Tom Kite, at four courses, La Quinta, CA, in winning the 1993 Bob Hope Classic (35 under par).

72 HOLES

257—(60-68-64-65) by Mike Souchak, at Brackenridge Park GC, San Antonio, to win 1955 Texas Open (27 under par).

54 HOLES

Opening rounds

191—(66-64-61) by Gay Brewer, at Pensacola CC, Pensacola, FL, in winning the 1967 Pensacola Open.

Consecutive rounds

189—(63-63-63) by Chandler Harper in the last three rounds to win the 1954 Texas Open at Brackenridge Park GC, San Antonio.

36 HOLES

Opening rounds

126—(64-62) by Tommy Bolt, at Cavalier Yacht & CC, Virginia Beach, VA, in 1954 Virginia Beach Open.

126—(64-62) by Paul Azinger, at Oak Hills CC, San Antonio, in 1989 Texas Open.

Consecutive rounds

125—(63-62) by Ron Streck in the last two rounds to win the 1978 Texas Open at Oak Hills CC, San Antonio.

125—(62-63) by Blaine McCallister in the middle two rounds in winning the 1988 Hardee's Golf Classic at Oakwood CC, Coal Valley, IL.

18 HOLES

59—by Al Geiberger, at Colonial Country Club, Memphis, in second round in winning 1977 Memphis Classic.

59—by Chip Beck, at Sunrise Golf Club, Las Vegas, in third round of the 1991 Las Vegas Invitational.

9 HOLES

27—by Mike Souchak, at Brackenridge Park GC, San Antonio, on par-35 second nine of first round in 1955 Texas Open.

27—by Andy North at En-Joie GC, Endicott, NY, on par-34 second nine of first round in 1975 BC Open.

MOST CONSECUTIVE ROUNDS UNDER 70

19—Byron Nelson in 1945.

MOST BIRDIES IN A ROW

8—Bob Goalby at Pasadena GC, St Petersburg, FL, during fourth round in winning the 1961 St Petersburg Open.

8—Fuzzy Zoeller, at Oakwood CC, Coal Valley, IL, during first round of 1976 Quad Cities Open.

8—Dewey Arnette, Warwick Hills GC, Grand Blanc, MI, during first round of the 1987 Buick Open.

Scoring (Cont.)

MOST BIRDIES IN A ROW TO WIN

5—Jack Nicklaus to win 1978 Jackie Gleason Inverrary Classic (last 5 holes).

Wins

MOST CONSECUTIVE YEARS WINNING AT LEAST ONE TOURNAMENT

17—Jack Nicklaus, 1962-78.
17—Arnold Palmer, 1955-71.
16—Billy Casper, 1956-71.

MOST CONSECUTIVE WINS

11—Byron Nelson, from Miami Four Ball, March 8-11, 1945, through Canadian Open, August 2-4, 1945.

MOST WINS IN A SINGLE EVENT

8—Sam Snead, Greater Greensboro Open, 1938, 1946, 1949, 1950, 1955, 1956, 1960, and 1965.

MOST CONSECUTIVE WINS IN A SINGLE EVENT

4—Walter Hagen, PGA Championships, 1924-27.

MOST WINS IN A CALENDAR YEAR

18—Byron Nelson, 1945

MOST YEARS BETWEEN WINS

12—Leonard Thompson, 1977-89.

MOST YEARS FROM FIRST WIN TO LAST

29—Sam Snead, 1936-65.
29—Ray Floyd, 1963-92.

YOUNGEST WINNERS

John McDermott, 19 years and 10 months, 1911 US Open.

OLDEST WINNER

Sam Snead, 52 years and 10 months, 1965 Greater Greensboro Open.

WIDEST WINNING MARGIN: STROKES

16—Bobby Locke, 1948 Chicago Victory National Championship.

Putting

FEWEST PUTTS, ONE ROUND

18—Andy North, at Kingsmill GC, in second round of 1990 Anheuser Busch Golf Classic.

18—Kenny Knox, at Harbour Town GL, in first round of 1989 MCI Heritage Classic.

18—Mike McGee, at Colonial CC, in first round of 1987 Federal Express St Jude Classic.

18—Sam Trahan, at Whitemarsh Valley CC, in final round of 1979 IVB Philadelphia Golf Classic.

FEWEST PUTTS, FOUR ROUNDS

93—Kenny Knox, in 1989 MCI Heritage Classic at Harbour Town GL.

*Through 11/01/93.

THE MAJOR TOURNAMENTS

LPGA Championship

Year	Winner	Score	Runner-Up	Site
1955	Beverly Hanson† (4 and 3)	220	Louise Suggs	Orchard Ridge CC, Ft Wayne, IN
1956	Marlene Hagge* (5)	291	Patty Berg (6)	Forest Lake CC, Detroit
1957	Louise Suggs	285	Wiffi Smith	Churchill Valley CC, Pittsburgh
1958	Mickey Wright	288	Fay Crocker	Churchill Valley CC, Pittsburgh
1959	Betsy Rawls	288	Patty Berg	Sheraton Hotel CC, French Lick, IN
1960	Mickey Wright	292	Louise Suggs	Sheraton Hotel CC, French Lick, IN
1961	Mickey Wright	287	Louise Suggs	Stardust CC, Las Vegas
1962	Judy Kimball	282	Shirley Spork	Stardust CC, Las Vegas
1963	Mickey Wright	294	Mary Lena Faulk Mary Mills Louise Suggs	Stardust CC, Las Vegas
1964	Mary Mills	278	Mickey Wright	Stardust CC, Las Vegas
1965	Sandra Haynie	279	Clifford A. Creed	Stardust CC, Las Vegas
1966	Gloria Ehret	282	Mickey Wright	Stardust CC, Las Vegas
1967	Kathy Whitworth	284	Shirley Englehorn	Pleasant Valley CC, Sutton, MA
1968	Sandra Post* (68)	294	Kathy Whitworth (75)	Pleasant Valley CC, Sutton, MA
1969	Betsy Rawls	293	Susie Berning Carol Mann	Concord GC, Kiameshia Lake, NY
1970	Shirley Englehorn* (74)	285	Kathy Whitworth (78)	Pleasant Valley CC, Sutton, MA
1971	Kathy Whitworth	288	Kathy Ahern	Pleasant Valley CC, Sutton, MA
1972	Kathy Ahern	293	Jane Blalock	Pleasant Valley CC, Sutton, MA
1973	Mary Mills	288	Betty Burfeindt	Pleasant Valley CC, Sutton, MA
1974	Sandra Haynie	288	JoAnne Carner	Pleasant Valley CC, Sutton, MA
1975	Kathy Whitworth	288	Sandra Haynie	Pine Ridge GC, Baltimore
1976	Betty Burfeindt	287	Judy Rankin	Pine Ridge GC, Baltimore
1977	Chako Higuchi	279	Pat Bradley Sandra Post Judy Rankin	Bay Tree Golf Plantation, N. Myrtle Beach, SC
1978	Nancy Lopez	275	Amy Alcott	Jack Nicklaus GC, Kings Island, OH
1979	Donna Caponi	279	Jerilyn Britz	Jack Nicklaus GC, Kings Island, OH
1980	Sally Little	285	Jane Blalock	Jack Nicklaus GC, Kings Island, OH
1981	Donna Caponi	280	Jerilyn Britz Pat Meyers	Jack Nicklaus GC, Kings Island, OH
1982	Jan Stephenson	279	JoAnne Carner	Jack Nicklaus GC, Kings Island, OH
1983	Patty Sheehan	279	Sandra Haynie	Jack Nicklaus GC, Kings Island, OH
1984	Patty Sheehan	272	Beth Daniel Pat Bradley	Jack Nicklaus GC, Kings Island, OH
1985	Nancy Lopez	273	Alice Miller	Jack Nicklaus GC, Kings Island, OH
1986	Pat Bradley	277	Patty Sheehan	Jack Nicklaus GC, Kings Island, OH
1987	Jane Geddes	275	Betsy King	Jack Nicklaus GC, Kings Island, OH
1988	Sherri Turner	281	Amy Alcott	Jack Nicklaus GC, Kings Island, OH
1989	Nancy Lopez	274	Ayako Okamoto	Jack Nicklaus GC, Kings Island, OH
1990	Beth Daniel	280	Rosie Jones	Bethesda CC, Bethesda, MD
1991	Meg Mallon	274	Pat Bradley Ayako Okamoto	Bethesda CC, Bethesda, MD
1992	Betsy King	267	Karen Noble	Bethesda CC, Bethesda, MD
1993	Patty Sheehan	275	Lauri Merten	Bethesda CC, Bethesda, MD

*Won in playoff. Playoff scores are in parentheses. 1956 was sudden death; 1968 and 1970 were 18-hole playoffs.
†Won match play final.

U.S. Women's Open

Year	Winner	Score	Runner-Up	Site
1946	Patty Berg	5&4	Betty Jameson	Spokane CC, Spokane, WA
1947	Betty Jameson	295	Sally Sessions Polly Riley	Starmount Forest CC, Greensboro, NC
1948	Babe Zaharias	300	Betty Hicks	Atlantic City CC, Northfield, NJ
1949	Louise Suggs	291	Babe Zaharias	Prince George's G & CC, Landover, MD
1950	Babe Zaharias	291	Betsy Rawls	Rolling Hills CC, Wichita, KS
1951	Betsy Rawls	293	Louise Suggs	Druid Hills GC, Atlanta

U.S. Women's Open (Cont.)

Year	Winner	Score	Runner-Up	Site
1952	Louise Suggs	284	Marlene Bauer Betty Jameson	Bala GC, Philadelphia
1953	Betsy Rawls* (71)	302	Jackie Pung (77)	CC of Rochester, Rochester, NY
1954	Babe Zaharias	291	Betty Hicks	Salem CC, Peabody, MA
1955	Fay Crocker	299	Mary Lena Faulk Louise Suggs	Wichita CC, Wichita, KS
1956	Kathy Cornelius* (75)	302	Barbara McIntire (82)	Northland CC, Duluth, MN
1957	Betsy Rawls	299	Patty Berg	Winged Foot GC, Mamaroneck, NY
1958	Mickey Wright	290	Louise Suggs	Forest Lake CC, Detroit
1959	Mickey Wright	287	Louise Suggs	Churchill Valley CC, Pittsburgh
1960	Betsy Rawls	292	Joyce Ziske	Worcester CC, Worcester, MA
1961	Mickey Wright	293	Betsy Rawls	Baltusrol GC (Lower Course), Springfield, NJ
1962	Murle Breer	301	Jo Ann Prentice Ruth Jessen	Dunes GC, Myrtle Beach, SC
1963	Mary Mills	289	Sandra Haynie Louise Suggs	Kenwood CC, Cincinnati
1964	Mickey Wright* (70)	290	Ruth Jessen (72)	San Diego CC, Chula Vista, CA
1965	Carol Mann	290	Kathy Cornelius	Atlantic City CC, Northfield, NJ
1966	Sandra Spuzich	297	Carol Mann	Hazeltine Natl GC, Chaska, MN
1967	Catherine LaCoste	294	Susie Berning Beth Stone	Hot Springs GC (Cascades Course), Hot Springs, VA
1968	Susie Berning	289	Mickey Wright	Moslem Springs GC, Fleetwood, PA
1969	Donna Caponi	294	Peggy Wilson	Scenic Hills CC, Pensacola, FL
1970	Donna Caponi	287	Sandra Haynie Sandra Spuzich	Muskogee CC, Muskogee, OK
1971	JoAnne Carner	288	Kathy Whitworth	Kahkwa CC, Erie, PA
1972	Susie Berning	299	Kathy Ahern Pam Barnett Judy Rankin	Winged Foot GC, Mamaroneck, NY
1973	Susie Berning	290	Gloria Ehret Shelley Hamlin	CC of Rochester, Rochester, NY
1974	Sandra Haynie	295	Carol Mann Beth Stone	La Grange CC, La Grange, IL
1975	Sandra Palmer	295	JoAnne Carner Sandra Post Nancy Lopez	Atlantic City CC, Northfield, NJ
1976	JoAnne Carner* (76)	292	Sandra Palmer (78)	Rolling Green CC, Springfield, PA
1977	Hollis Stacy	292	Nancy Lopez	Hazeltine Natl GC, Chaska, MN
1978	Hollis Stacy	289	JoAnne Carner Sally Little	CC of Indianapolis, Indianapolis
1979	Jerilyn Britz	284	Debbie Massey Sandra Palmer	Brooklawn CC, Fairfield, CT
1980	Amy Alcott	280	Hollis Stacy	Richland CC, Nashville
1981	Pat Bradley	279	Beth Daniel	La Grange CC, La Grange, IL
1982	Janet Anderson	283	Beth Daniel Sandra Haynie Donna White JoAnne Carner	Del Paso CC, Sacramento
1983	Jan Stephenson	290	JoAnne Carner Patty Sheehan	Cedar Ridge CC, Tulsa
1984	Hollis Stacy	290	Rosie Jones	Salem CC, Peabody, MA
1985	Kathy Baker	280	Judy Dickinson	Baltusrol GC (Upper Course), Springfield, NJ
1986	Jane Geddes* (71)	287	Sally Little (73)	NCR GC, Dayton
1987	Laura Davies* (71)	285	Ayako Okamoto (73) JoAnne Carner (74)	Plainfield CC, Plainfield, NJ
1988	Liselotte Neumann	277	Patty Sheehan	Baltimore CC, Baltimore
1989	Betsy King	278	Nancy Lopez	Indianwood G & CC, Lake Orion, MI
1990	Betsy King	284	Patty Sheehan	Atlanta Athletic Club, Duluth, GA
1991	Meg Mallon	283	Pat Bradley	Colonial Club, Fort Worth
1992	Patty Sheehan* (72)	280	Juli Inkster	Oakmont CC, Oakmont, PA
1993	Lauri Merten	280	Donna Andrew Helen Alfredsson	Crooked Stick, Carmel, IN

*Winner in playoff. 18-hole playoff scores are in parentheses.

Dinah Shore

Year	Winner	Score	Runner-Up
1972	Jane Blalock	213	Carol Mann, Judy Rankin
1973	Mickey Wright	284	Joyce Kazmierski
1974	Jo Ann Prentice*	289	Jane Blalock, Sandra Haynie
1975	Sandra Palmer	283	Kathy McMullen
1976	Judy Rankin	285	Betty Burfeindt
1977	Kathy Whitworth	289	JoAnne Carner, Sally Little
1978	Sandra Post*	283	Penny Pulz
1979	Sandra Post	276	Nancy Lopez
1980	Donna Caponi	275	Amy Alcott
1981	Nancy Lopez	277	Carolyn Hill
1982	Sally Little	278	Hollis Stacy, Sandra Haynie
1983	Amy Alcott	282	Beth Daniel, Kathy Whitworth
1984	Juli Inkster*	280	Pat Bradley
1985	Alice Miller	275	Jan Stephenson
1986	Pat Bradley	280	Val Skinner
1987	Betsy King*	283	Patty Sheehan
1988	Amy Alcott	274	Colleen Walker
1989	Juli Inkster	279	Tammie Green, JoAnne Carner
1990	Betsy King	283	Kathy Postlewait, Shirley Furlong
1991	Amy Alcott	273	Dottie Mochrie
1992	Dottie Mochrie*	279	Juli Inkster
1993	Helen Alfredsson	284	Amy Benz, Tina Barrett, Betsy King

*Winner in sudden-death playoff.

Note: Designated fourth major in 1983.

Played at Mission Hills CC, Rancho Mirage, CA.

du Maurier Classic

Year	Winner	Score	Runner-Up	Site
1973	Jocelyne Bourassa*	214	Sandra Haynie Judy Rankin	Montreal GC, Montreal
1974	Carole Jo Callison	208	JoAnne Carner	Candiac GC, Montreal
1975	JoAnne Carner*	214	Carol Mann	St George's CC, Toronto
1976	Donna Caponi*	212	Judy Rankin	Cedar Brae G & CC, Toronto
1977	Judy Rankin	214	Pat Meyers Sandra Palmer	Lachute G & CC, Montreal
1978	JoAnne Carner	278	Hollis Stacy	St George's CC, Toronto
1979	Amy Alcott	285	Nancy Lopez	Richelieu Valley CC, Montreal
1980	Pat Bradley	277	JoAnne Carner	St George's CC, Toronto
1981	Jan Stephenson	278	Nancy Lopez Pat Bradley	Summerlea CC, Dorion, Quebec
1982	Sandra Haynie	280	Beth Daniel	St George's CC, Toronto
1983	Hollis Stacy	277	JoAnne Carner Alice Miller	Beaconsfield GC, Montreal
1984	Juli Inkster	279	Ayako Okamoto	St George's G & CC, Toronto
1985	Pat Bradley	278	Jane Geddes	Beaconsfield CC, Montreal
1986	Pat Bradley*	276	Ayako Okamoto	Board of Trade CC, Toronto
1987	Jody Rosenthal	272	Ayako Okamoto	Islesmere GC, Laval, Quebec
1988	Sally Little	279	Laura Davies	Vancouver GC, Coquitlam, British Columbia
1989	Tammie Green	279	Pat Bradley Betsy King	Beaconsfield GC, Montreal
1990	Cathy Johnston	276	Patty Sheehan	Westmount G & CC, Kitchener, Ontario
1991	Nancy Scranton	279	Debbie Massey	Vancouver GC, Coquitlam, British Columbia
1992	Sherri Steinhauer	277	Judy Dickinson	St. Charles CC, Winnipeg, Manitoba
1993	Brandie Burton	277	Betsy King	London Hunt and CC, London, Ontario

*Winner in sudden-death playoff.

Note: Designated third major in 1979.

THE LPGA TOUR

Season Money Leaders

Year	Player	Earnings ($)
1950	Babe Zaharias	14,800
1951	Babe Zaharias	15,087
1952	Betsy Rawls	14,505
1953	Louise Suggs	19,816
1954	Patty Berg	16,011
1955	Patty Berg	16,492
1956	Marlene Hagge	20,235
1957	Patty Berg	16,272
1958	Beverly Hanson	12,639
1959	Betsy Rawls	26,774
1960	Louise Suggs	16,892
1961	Mickey Wright	22,236
1962	Mickey Wright	21,641
1963	Mickey Wright	31,269
1964	Mickey Wright	29,800
1965	Kathy Whitworth	28,658
1966	Kathy Whitworth	33,517
1967	Kathy Whitworth	32,937
1968	Kathy Whitworth	48,379
1969	Carol Mann	49,152
1970	Kathy Whitworth	30,235
1971	Kathy Whitworth	41,181
1972	Kathy Whitworth	65,063
1973	Kathy Whitworth	82,864
1974	JoAnne Carner	87,094
1975	Sandra Palmer	76,374
1976	Judy Rankin	150,734
1977	Judy Rankin	122,890
1978	Nancy Lopez	189,814
1979	Nancy Lopez	197,489
1980	Beth Daniel	231,000
1981	Beth Daniel	206,998
1982	JoAnne Carner	310,400
1983	JoAnne Carner	291,404
1984	Betsy King	266,771
1985	Nancy Lopez	416,472
1986	Pat Bradley	492,021
1987	Ayako Okamoto	466,034
1988	Sherri Turner	350,851
1989	Betsy King	654,132
1990	Beth Daniel	863,578
1991	Pat Bradley	763,118
1992	Dottie Mochrie	693,335

Career Money Leaders*

#	Player	Earnings ($)
1	Pat Bradley	4,347,706.03
2	Betsy King	3,906,642.50
3	Beth Daniel	3,692,664.80
4	Patty Sheehan	3,591,290.01
5	Nancy Lopez	3,562,370.83
6	Amy Alcott	2,850,188.14
7	JoAnne Carner	2,649,641.63
8	Ayako Okamoto	2,621,856.85
9	Jan Stephenson	2,014,186.00
10	Juli Inkster	1,840,006.23
11	Colleen Walker	1,753,739.71
12	Rosie Jones	1,748,401.97
13	Jane Geddes	1,732,505.30
14	Kathy Whitworth	1,722,440.01
15	Hollis Stacy	1,717,706.99
16	Dottie Mochrie	1,670,635.00
17	Judy Dickinson	1,557,611.92
18	Sally Little	1,500,437.80
19	Donna Caponi	1,387,919.73
20	D. Ammaccapane	1,382,010.00
21	Kathy Postlewait	1,332,669.27
22	Sandra Palmer	1,328,663.86
23	Jane Blalock	1,290,943.62
24	Chris Johnson	1,234,411.50
25	Meg Mallon	1,232,383.00
26	Debbie Massey	1,225,889.13
27	Deb Richard	1,194,448.00
28	Cindy Rarick	1,089,378.50
29	Alice Ritzman	1,062,202.32
30	Sandra Haynie	1,055,874.57

*Through 12/31/92.

LPGA Player of the Year

Year	Player
1966	Kathy Whitworth
1967	Kathy Whitworth
1968	Kathy Whitworth
1969	Kathy Whitworth
1970	Sandra Haynie
1971	Kathy Whitworth
1972	Kathy Whitworth
1973	Kathy Whitworth
1974	JoAnne Carner
1975	Sandra Palmer
1976	Judy Rankin
1977	Judy Rankin
1978	Nancy Lopez
1979	Nancy Lopez
1980	Beth Daniel
1981	JoAnne Carner
1982	JoAnne Carner
1983	Patty Sheehan
1984	Betsy King
1985	Nancy Lopez
1986	Pat Bradley
1987	Ayako Okamoto
1988	Nancy Lopez
1989	Betsy King
1990	Beth Daniel
1991	Pat Bradley
1992	Dottie Mochrie

But apart from all that ...

After watching CBS's coverage of the Masters, Ian Woolridge of London's *Daily Mail* made these small criticisms: "Bereft of an original turn of phrase, dispensing cliches like election mailshots, declaiming non sequiturs of prodigious lunacy in the tones of Charlton Heston, polishing one another's egos and generally investing golf with an importance above all other goings on in this violent world, they seem devoid of all original thought and are particularly frantic when it becomes apparent that, for the fifth time in six years, a non-American is about to win the Masters."

Vare Trophy: Best Scoring Average

		Avg				Avg				Avg
1953	Patty Berg	75.00	1967	Kathy Whitworth	72.74	1981	JoAnne Carner	71.75
1954	Babe Zaharias	75.48	1968	Carol Mann	72.04	1982	JoAnne Carner	71.49
1955	Patty Berg	74.47	1969	Kathy Whitworth	72.38	1983	JoAnne Carner	71.41
1956	Patty Berg	74.57	1970	Kathy Whitworth	72.26	1984	Patty Sheehan	71.40
1957	Louise Suggs	74.64	1971	Kathy Whitworth	72.88	1985	Nancy Lopez	70.73
1958	Beverly Hanson	74.92	1972	Kathy Whitworth	72.38	1986	Pat Bradley	71.10
1959	Betsy Rawls	74.03	1973	Judy Rankin	73.08	1987	Betsy King	71.14
1960	Mickey Wright	73.25	1974	JoAnne Carner	72.87	1988	Colleen Walker	71.26
1961	Mickey Wright	73.55	1975	JoAnne Carner	72.40	1989	Beth Daniel	70.38
1962	Mickey Wright	73.67	1976	Judy Rankin	72.25	1990	Beth Daniel	70.54
1963	Mickey Wright	72.81	1977	Judy Rankin	72.16	1991	Pat Bradley	70.76
1964	Mickey Wright	72.46	1978	Nancy Lopez	71.76	1992	Dottie Mochrie	70.80
1965	Kathy Whitworth	72.61	1979	Nancy Lopez	71.20			
1966	Kathy Whitworth	72.60	1980	Amy Alcott	71.51			

Most Career Wins*

	Wins		Wins		Wins
Kathy Whitworth	88	JoAnne Carner	42	Patty Sheehan	29
Mickey Wright	82	Sandra Haynie	42	Amy Alcott	29
Patty Berg	57	Carol Mann	38	Betsy King	28
Betsy Rawls	55	Babe Zaharias	31	Beth Daniel	27
Louise Suggs	50	Pat Bradley	30	Judy Rankin	26
Nancy Lopez	46	Jane Blalock	29	*Through 12/31/92.	

All-Time LPGA Tour Records*

Scoring

72 HOLES

268—(66-67-69-66) by Nancy Lopez to win at the Willow Creek GC, High Point, NC, in the 1985 Henredon Classic (20 under par).

54 HOLES

197—(67-65-65) by Pat Bradley to win at the Rail GC, Springfield, Ill., in the 1991 Rail Charity Golf Classic (19 under par).

36 HOLES

129—(64-65) by Judy Dickinson at Pasadena Yacht & CC, St Petersburg, in the 1985 S&H Golf Classic (15 under par).

18 HOLES

62—by Mickey Wright at Hogan Park GC, Midland, TX, in the first round in winning the 1964 Tall City Open (9 under par).

62—by Vicki Fergon at Almaden G & CC, San Jose, CA, in the second round of the 1984 San Jose Classic (11 under par).

62—by Laura Davies at the Rail Golf Club, Springfield, Ill., in the first round of the 1991 Rail Charity Golf Classic (10 under par).

62—by Hollis Stacy at Meridian Valley Country Club, Seattle, WA, in the second round of the 1992 Safeco Classic (10 under par)

9 HOLES

28—by Mary Beth Zimmerman at Rail GC, 1984 Rail Charity Golf Classic, Springfield, IL (par 36). Zimmerman shot 64.

28—by Pat Bradley at Green Gables CC, Denver, 1984 Columbia Savings Classic (par 35). Bradley shot 65.

Scoring (Cont.)

9 HOLES (Cont.)

28—by Muffin Spencer-Devlin at Knollwood CC, Elmsford, NY, in winning the 1985 MasterCard International Pro-Am (par 35). Spencer-Devlin shot 64.

28—by Peggy Kirsch at Squaw Creek CC, Vienna, OH, in the 1991 Phar-Mor, (7 under par).

MOST CONSECUTIVE ROUNDS UNDER 70

9—Beth Daniel, in 1990.

MOST BIRDIES IN A ROW

8—Mary Beth Zimmerman at Rail GC in Springfield, IL, in the second round of the 1984 Rail Charity Classic. Zimmerman shot 64, (8 under par).

Wins

MOST CONSECUTIVE WINS IN SCHEDULED EVENTS

4—Mickey Wright, in 1962.
4—Mickey Wright, in 1963.
4—Kathy Whitworth, in 1969.

MOST CONSECUTIVE WINS IN ENTERED TOURNAMENTS

5—Nancy Lopez, in 1987.

MOST WINS IN A CALENDAR YEAR

13—Mickey Wright, in 1963.

WIDEST WINNING MARGIN, STROKES

14—Louise Suggs, 1949 US Women's Open.
14—Cindy Mackey, 1986 MasterCard Int'l Pro-Am.
*Through 12/31/92.

U.S. Senior Open

Year	Winner	Score	Runner-Up	Site
1980	Roberto DeVicenzo	285	William C. Campbell	Winged Foot GC, Mamaroneck, NY
1981	*Arnold Palmer (70)	289	Bob Stone (74)	Oakland Hills CC, Birmingham, MI
			Billy Casper (77)	
1982	Miller Barber	282	Gene Littler	Portland GC, Portland, OR
			Dan Sikes, Jr	
1983	*Billy Casper (75) (3)	288	Rod Funseth (75) (4)	Hazeltine GC, Chaska, MN
1984	Miller Barber	286	Arnold Palmer	Oak Hill CC, Rochester, NY
1985	Miller Barber	285	Roberto DeVicenzo	Edgewood Tahoe GC, Stateline, NV
1986	Dale Douglass	279	Gary Player	Scioto CC, Columbus, OH
1987	Gary Player	270	Doug Sanders	Brooklawn CC, Fairfield, CT
1988	*Gary Player (68)	288	Bob Charles (70)	Medinah CC, Medinah, IL
1989	Orville Moody	279	Frank Beard	Laurel Valley GC, Ligonier, PA
1990	Lee Trevino	275	Jack Nicklaus	Ridgewood CC, Paramus, NJ
1991	Jack Nicklaus (65)	282	Chi Chi Rodriguez (69)	Oakland Hills CC, Birmingham, MI
1992	Larry Laoretti	275	Jim Colbert	Saucon Valley CC, Bethlehem, PA

*Winner in playoff. Playoff scores are in parentheses. The 1983 playoff went to one hole of sudden death after an 18-hole playoff.

SENIOR TOUR

Season Money Leaders

Year	Winner	Earnings ($)	Year	Winner	Earnings ($)
1980	Don January	44,100	1987	Chi Chi Rodriguez	509,145
1981	Miller Barber	83,136	1988	Bob Charles	533,929
1982	Miller Barber	106,890	1989	Bob Charles	725,887
1983	Don January	237,571	1990	Lee Trevino	1,190,518
1984	Don January	328,597	1991	Mike Hill	1,065,657
1985	Peter Thomson	386,724	1992	Lee Trevino	1,027,002
1986	Bruce Crampton	454,299			

Career Money Leaders*

	Player	Earnings ($)		Player	Earnings ($)
1.	Chi Chi Rodriguez	3,740,267	17.	Dave Hill	1,836,134
2.	Bob Charles	3,642,545	18.	Walter Zembriski	1,795,698
3.	Mike Hill	3,175,862	19.	Jim Colbert	1,708,517
4.	Bruce Crampton	3,133,913	20.	Jim Ferree	1,581,850
5.	Dale Douglass	3,069,633	21.	Don Bies	1,524,387
6	Lee Trevino	2,949,942	22.	Billy Casper	1,499,659
7.	Miller Barber	2,948,339	23.	Arnold Palmer	1,394,544
8.	Gary Player	2,795,979	24.	Gay Brewer	1,353,680
9.	George Archer	2,671,384	25.	Bobby Nichols	1,324,533
10.	Orville Moody	2,652,269	26.	Lee Elder	1,297,599
11.	Harold Henning	2,501,076	27.	Larry Mowry	1,279,844
12.	Al Geiberger	2,419,454	28.	Butch Baird	1,204,220
13.	Don January	2,404,877	29.	Rocky Thompson	1,194,787
14.	Charles Coody	2,250,751	30.	Ben Smith	1,073,769
15.	Jim Dent	2,154,200			
16.	Gene Littler	1,945,367			

*Through 12/31/92.

Most Career Wins*

Player	Wins	Player	Wins
Miller Barber	25	Lee Trevino	15
Don January	22	Mike Hill	13
Chi Chi Rodriguez	21	George Archer	11
Bruce Crampton	19	Peter Thomson	11
Bob Charles	18	Orville Moody	11
Gary Player	16		

* Through 12/31/92.

MAJOR MEN'S AMATEUR CHAMPIONSHIPS

U.S. Amateur

Year	Winner	Score	Runner-Up	Site
1895	Charles B. Macdonald	12 & 11	Charles E. Sands	Newport GC, Newport, RI
1896	H. J. Whigham	8 & 7	J.G Thorp	Shinnecock Hills GC, Southampton, NY
1897	H. J. Whigham	8 & 6	W. Rossiter Betts	Chicago GC, Wheaton, IL
1898	Findlay S. Douglas	5 & 3	Walter B. Smith	Morris County GC, Morristown, NJ
1899	H. M. Harriman	3 & 2	Findlay S. Douglas	Onwentsia Club, Lake Forest, IL
1900	Walter Travis	2 up	Findlay S. Douglas	Garden City GC, Garden City, NY
1901	Walter Travis	5 & 4	Walter E. Egan	CC of Atlantic City, NJ
1902	Louis N. James	4 & 2	Eben M. Byers	Glen View Club, Golf, Ill.
1903	Walter Travis	5 & 4	Eben M. Byers	Nassau CC, Glen Cove, NY
1904	H. Chandler Egan	8 & 6	Fred Herreshoff	Baltusrol GC, Springfield, NJ
1905	H. Chandler Egan	6 & 5	D.E. Sawyer	Chicago GC, Wheaton, IL
1906	Eben M. Byers	2 up	George S. Lyon	Englewood GC, Englewood, NJ
1907	Jerry Travers	6 & 5	Archibald Graham	Euclid Club, Cleveland, OH
1908	Jerry Travers	8 & 7	Max H. Behr	Garden City GC, Garden City, NY
1909	Robert A. Gardner	4 & 3	H. Chandler Egan	Chicago GC, Wheaton, IL
1910	William C. Fownes, Jr	4 & 3	Warren K. Wood	The Country Club, Brookline, MA
1911	Harold Hilton	1 up	Fred Herreshoff	The Apawamis Club, Rye, NY
1912	Jerry Travers	7 & 6	Charles Evans, Jr.	Chicago GC, Wheaton, IL
1913	Jerry Travers	5 & 4	John G. Anderson	Garden City GC, Garden City, NY
1914	Francis Ouimet	6 & 5	Jerry Travers	Ekwanok CC, Manchester, VT
1915	Robert A. Gardner	5 & 4	John G. Anderson	CC of Detroit, Grosse Pt. Farms, MI
1916	Chick Evans	4 & 3	Robert A. Gardner	Merion Cricket Club,. Haverford, PA
1917-18	No tournament			
1919	S. Davidson Herron	5 & 4	Bobby Jones	Oakmont CC, Oakmont, PA
1920	Chick Evans	7 & 6	Francis Ouimet	Engineers' CC, Roslyn, NY
1921	Jesse P. Guilford	7 & 6	Robert A. Gardner	St. Louis CC, Clayton, MO
1922	Jess W. Sweetser	3 & 2	Chick Evans	The Country Club, Brookline, MA
1923	Max R. Marston	1 up	Jess W. Sweetser	Flossmoor CC, Flossmoor, IL
1924	Bobby Jones	9 & 8	George Von Elm	Merion Cricket Club, Ardmore, PA
1925	Bobby Jones	8 & 7	Watts Gunn	Oakmont CC, Oakmont, PA
1926	George Von Elm	2 & 1	Bobby Jones	Baltusrol GC, Springfield, NJ
1927	Bobby Jones	8 & 7	Chick Evans	Minikahda Club, Minneapolis
1928	Bobby Jones	10 & 9	T. Phillip Perkins	Brae Burn CC, West Newton, MA
1929	Harrison R. Johnston	4 & 3	Dr. O.F. Willing	Del Monte G & CC, Pebble Beach, CA
1930	Bobby Jones	8 & 7	Eugene V. Homans	Merion Cricket Club, Ardmore, PA
1931	Francis Ouimet	6 & 5	Jack Westland	Beverly CC, Chicago, IL
1932	C. Ross Somerville	2 & 1	John Goodman	Baltimore CC, Timonium, MD
1933	George T. Dunlap, Jr	6 & 5	Max R. Marston	Kenwood CC, Cincinnati, OH
1934	Lawson Little	8 & 7	David Goldman	The Country Club, Brookline, MA
1935	Lawson Little	4 & 2	Walter Emery	The Country Club, Cleveland, OH
1936	John W. Fischer	1 up	Jack McLean	Garden City GC, Garden City, NY
1937	John Goodman	2 up	Raymond E. Billows	Alderwood CC, Portland, OR
1938	William P. Turnesa	8 & 7	B. Patrick Abbott	Oakmont CC, Oakmont, PA
1939	Marvin H. Ward	7 & 5	Raymond E. Billows	North Shore CC, Glenview, IL
1940	Richard D. Chapman	11 & 9	W. McCullough, Jr	Winged Foot GC, Mamaroneck, NY
1941	Marvin H. Ward	4 & 3	B. Patrick Abbott	Omaha Field Club, Omaha, NE
1942-45	No tournament			
1946	Ted Bishop	1 up	Smiley L. Quick	Baltusrol GC, Springfield, NJ
1947	Skee Riegel	2 & 1	John W. Dawson	Del Monte G & CC, Pebble Beach, CA
1948	William P. Turnesa	2 & 1	Raymond E. Billows	Memphis CC, Memphis, TN
1949	Charles R. Coe	11 & 10	Rufus King	Oak Hill CC, Rochester, NY
1950	Sam Urzetta	1 up	Frank Stranahan	Minneapolis GC, Minneapolis, MN
1951	Billy Maxwell	4 & 3	Joseph F. Gagliardi	Saucon Valley CC, Bethlehem, PA
1952	Jack Westland	3 & 2	Al Mengert	Seattle GC, Seattle, WA
1953	Gene Littler	1 up	Dale Morey	Oklahoma City G & CC, Oklahoma City
1954	Arnold Palmer	1 up	Robert Sweeny	CC of Detroit, Grosse Pt. Farms, MI
1955	E. Harvie Ward, Jr	9 & 8	Wm. Hyndman III	CC of Virginia, Richmond, VA
1956	E. Harvie Ward, Jr	5 & 4	Charles Kocsis	Knollwood Club, Lake Forest, IL
1957	Hillman Robbins, Jr	5 & 4	Dr. Frank M. Taylor	The Country Club, Brookline, MA
1958	Charles R. Coe	5 & 4	Tommy Aaron	Olympic Club, San Francisco, CA
1959	Jack Nicklaus	1 up	Charles R. Coe	Broadmoor GC, Colorado Springs, CO
1960	Deane Beman	6 & 4	Robert W. Gardner	St. Louis CC, Clayton, MO
1961	Jack Nicklaus	8 & 6	H. Dudley Wysong	Pebble Beach GL, Pebble Beach, CA

U.S. Amateur (Cont.)

Year	Winner	Score	Runner-Up	Site
1962	Labron E. Harris, Jr	1 up	Downing Gray	Pinehurst CC, Pinehurst, NC
1963	Deane Beman	2 & 1	Richard H. Sikes	Wakonda Club, Des Moines, IA
1964	William C. Campbell	1 up	Edgar M. Tutwiler	Canterbury GC, Cleveland, OH
1965	Robert J. Murphy, Jr	291	Robert B. Dickson	Southern Hills, CC, Tulsa, OK
1966	Gary Cowan	285-75	Deane Beman	Merion GC, Ardmore, PA
1967	Robert B. Dickson	285	Marvin Giles III	Broadmoor GC, Colorado Springs, CO
1968	Bruce Fleisher	284	Marvin Giles III	Scioto CC, Columbus, OH
1969	Steven N. Melnyk	286	Marvin Giles III	Oakmont CC, Oakmont, PA
1970	Lanny Wadkins	279	Tom Kite	Waverley CC, Portland, OR
1971	Gary Cowan	280	Eddie Pearce	Wilmington CC, Wilmington DE
1972	Marvin Giles, III	285	two tied	Charlotte CC, Charlotte, NC
1973	Craig Stadler	6 & 5	David Strawn	Inverness Club, Toledo, OH
1974	Jerry Pate	2 & 1	John P. Grace	Ridgewood CC, Ridgewood, NJ
1975	Fred Ridley	2 up	Keith Fergus	CC of Virginia, Richmond, VA
1976	Bill Sander	8 & 6	C. Parker Moore, Jr	Bel Air CC, Los Angeles, CA
1977	John Fought	9 & 8	Doug Fischesser	Aronimink GC, Newton Square, PA
1978	John Cook	5 & 4	Scott Hoch	Plainfield CC, Plainfield, NJ
1979	Mark O'Meara	8 & 7	John Cook	Canterbury GC, Cleveland, OH
1980	Hal Sutton	9 & 8	Bob Lewis	CC of North Carolina, Pinehurst, NC
1981	Nathaniel Crosby	1 up	Brian Lindley	Olympic Club, San Francisco, CA
1982	Jay Sigel	8 & 7	David Tolley	The Country Club, Brookline, MA
1983	Jay Sigel	8 & 7	Chris Perry	North Shore CC, Glenviedw IL
1984	Scott Verplank	4 & 3	Sam Randolph	Oak Tree GC, Edmond, OK
1985	Sam Randolph	1 up	Peter Persons	Montclair GC, West Orange, NJ
1986	Buddy Alexander	5 & 3	Chris Kite	Shoal Creek, Shoal Creek AL
1987	Bill Mayfair	4 & 3	Eric Rebmann	Jupiter Hills Club, Jupiter, FL
1988	Eric Meeks	7 & 6	Danny Yates	Va. Hot Springs G & CC, VA
1989	Chris Patton	3 & 1	Danny Green	Merion GC, Ardmore, PA
1990	Phil Mickelson	5 & 4	Manny Zerman	Cherry Hills CC, Englewood, CO
1991	Mitch Voges	7 & 6	Manny Zerman	The Honors Course, Ooltewah, TN
1992	Justin Leonard	8 & 7	Tom Scherrer	Muirfield Village GC, Dublin, OH
1993	John Harris	5 & 3	Danny Ellis	Champions GC, Houston, TX

Note: All stroke play from 1965 to 1972.

U.S. Junior Amateur

Year	Winner	Year	Winner	Year	Winner
1948	Dean Lind	1964	Johnny Miller	1980	Eric Johnson
1949	Gay Brewer	1965	James Masserio	1981	Scott Erickson
1950	Mason Rudolph	1966	Gary Sanders	1982	Rich Marik
1951	Tommy Jacobs	1967	John Crooks	1983	Tim Straub
1952	Don Bisplinghoff	1968	Eddie Pearce	1984	Doug Martin
1953	Rex Baxter	1969	Aly Trompas	1985	Charles Rymer
1954	Foster Bradley	1970	Gary Koch	1986	Brian Montgomery
1955	William Dunn	1971	Mike Brannan	1987	Brett Quigley
1956	Harlan Stevenson	1972	Bob Byman	1988	Jason Widener
1957	Larry Beck	1973	Jack Renner	1989	David Duval
1958	Buddy Baker	1974	David Nevatt	1990	Mathew Todd
1959	Larry Lee	1975	Brett Mullin	1991	Tiger Woods
1960	Bill Tindall	1976	Madden Hatcher, III	1992	Tiger Woods
1961	Charles McDowell	1977	Willie Wood, Jr	1993	Tiger Woods
1962	Jim Wiechers	1978	Don Hurter		
1963	Gregg McHatton	1979	Jack Larkin		

Note: Event is for amateur golfers younger than 18 years of age.

Mid-Amateur Championship

Year	Winner	Year	Winner	Year	Winner
1981	Jim Holtgrieve	1986	Bill Loeffler	1991	Jim Stuart
1982	William Hoffer	1987	Jay Sigel	1992	Danny Yates
1983	Jay Sigel	1988	David Eger	1993	Jeff Thomas
1984	Mike Podolak	1989	James Taylor		
1985	Jay Sigel	1990	Jim Stuart		

Note: Event is for amateur golfers at least 25 years of age.

British Amateur

1887	H. G. Hutchinson	
1888	John Ball	
1889	J.E. Laidlay	
1890	John Ball	
1891	J.E. Laidlaw	
1892	John Ball	
1893	Peter Anderson	
1894	John Ball	
1895	L.M.B. Melville	
1896	F.G. Tait	
1897	A.J.T. Allan	
1898	F.G. Tait	
1899	John Ball	
1900	H.H. Hilton	
1901	H.H. Hilton	
1902	C. Hutchings	
1903	R. Maxwell	
1904	W.J. Travis	
1905	A.G. Barry	
1906	James Robb	
1907	John Ball	
1908	E.A. Lassen	
1909	R. Maxwell	
1910	John Ball	
1911	H.H. Hilton	
1912	John Ball	
1913	H.H. Hilton	
1914	J.L.C. Jenkins	
1915 to 1919 not played		
1920	C.J.H. Tolley	
1921	W.I. Hunter	
1922	E.W.E. Holderness	
1923	R.H. Wethered	
1924	E.W.E. Holderness	
1925	R. Harris	
1926	Jess Sweetser	
1927	Dr. W. Tweddell	
1928	T.P. Perkins	
1929	C.J.H. Tolley	
1930	Robert T. Jones, Jr.	
1931	E. Martin Smith	
1932	J. DeForest	
1933	M. Scott	
1934	W. Lawson Little	
1935	W. Lawson Little	
1936	H. Thomson	
1937	R. Sweeney, Jr.	
1938	C.R. Yates	
1939	A.T. Kyle	
1940–1945	not held	
1946	J. Bruen	
1947	Willie D. Turnesa	
1948	Frank R. Stranahan	
1949	S.M. McReady	
1950	Frank R. Stranahan	
1951	Richard D. Chapman	
1952	E.H. Ward	
1953	J.B. Carr	
1954	D.W. Bachli	
1955	J.W. Conrad	
1956	J.C. Beharrel	
1957	R. Reid Jack	
1958	J.B. Carr	
1959	Deane Beman	
1960	J.B. Carr	
1961	M. Bonallack	
1962	R. Davies	
1963	M. Lunt	
1964	C. Clark	
1965	M. Bonallack	
1966	C.R. Cole	
1967	R. Dickson	
1968	M. Bonallack	
1969	M. Bonallack	
1970	M. Bonallack	
1971	Steve Melnyk	
1972	Trevor Homer	
1973	R. Siderowf	
1974	Trevor Homer	
1975	M. Giles	
1976	R. Siderowf	
1977	P. McEvoy	
1978	P. McEvoy	
1979	J. Sigel	
1980	D. Evans	
1981	P. Ploujoux	
1982	M. Thompson	
1983	A. Parkin	
1984	J.M. Olozabal	
1985	G. McGimpsey	
1986	D. Curry	
1987	P. Mayo	
1988	C. Hardin	
1989	S. Dodd	
1990	R. Muntz	
1991	G. Wolstenholme	
1992	S. Dundas	
1993	S. Dundas	

Amateur Public Links

1922	Edmund R. Held	
1923	Richard J. Walsh	
1924	Joseph Coble	
1925	Raymond J. McAuliffe	
1926	Lester Bolstad	
1927	Carl F. Kauffmann	
1928	Carl F. Kauffmann	
1929	Carl F. Kauffmann	
1930	Robert E. Wingate	
1931	Charles Ferrera	
1932	R.L. Miller	
1933	Charles Ferrera	
1934	David A. Mitchell	
1935	Frank Strafaci	
1936	B. Patrick Abbott	
1937	Bruce N. McCormick	
1938	Al Leach	
1939	Andrew Szwedko	
1940	Robert C. Clark	
1941	William M. Welch, Jr.	
1942–1945	not held	
1946	Smiley L. Quick	
1947	Wilfred Crossley	
1948	Michael R. Ferentz	
1949	Kenneth J. Towns	
1950	Stanley Bielat	
1951	Dave Stanley	
1952	Omer L. Bogan	
1953	Ted Richards, Jr.	
1954	Gene Andrews	
1955	Sam D. Kocsis	
1956	James H. Buxbaum	
1957	Don Essig III	
1958	Daniel D. Sikes, Jr.	
1959	William A. Wright	
1960	Verne Callison	
1961	Richard H. Sikes	
1962	Richard H. Sikes	
1963	Robert Lunn	
1964	William McDonald	
1965	Arne Dokka	
1966	Lamont Kaser	
1967	Verne Callison	
1968	Gene Towry	
1969	John M. Jackson, Jr.	
1970	Robert Risch	
1971	Fred Haney	
1972	Bob Allard	
1973	Stan Stopa	
1974	Charles Barenaba	
1975	Randy Barenaba	
1976	Eddie Mudd	
1977	Jerry Vidovic	
1978	Dean Prince	
1979	Dennis Walsh	
1980	Jodie Mudd	
1981	Jodie Mudd	
1982	Billy Tuten	
1983	Billy Tuten	
1984	Bill Malley	
1985	Jim Sorenson	
1986	Bill Mayfair	
1987	Kevin Johnson	
1988	Ralph Howe, III	
1989	Tim Hobby	
1990	Michael Combs	
1991	David Berganio, Jr.	
1992	Warren Schulte	
1993	David Berganio, Jr.	

U.S. Senior Golf

1955 ....J. Wood Platt	1968 ....Curtis Person, Sr	1981 ....Ed Updegraff
1956 ....Frederick J. Wright	1969 ....Curtis Person, Sr	1982 ....Alton Duhon
1957 ....J. Clark Espie	1970 ....Gene Andrews	1983 ....William Hyndman, III
1958 ....Thomas C. Robbins	1971 ....Tom Draper	1984 ....Bob Rawlins
1959 ....J. Clark Espie	1972 ....Lewis W. Oehmig	1985 ....Lewis W. Oehmig
1960 ....Michael Cestone	1973 ....William Hyndman, III	1986 ....Bo Williams
1961 ....Dexter H. Daniels	1974 ....Dale Morey	1987 ....John Richardson
1962 ....Merrill L. Carlsmith	1975 ....William F. Colm	1988 ....Clarence Moore
1963 ....Merrill L. Carlsmith	1976 ....Lewis W. Oehmig	1989 ....Bo Williams
1964 ....William D. Higgins	1977 ....Dale Morey	1990 ....Jackie Cummings
1965 ....Robert B. Kiersky	1978 ....K. K. Compton	1991 ....Bill Bosshard
1966 ....Dexter H. Daniels	1979 ....William C. Campbell	1992 ....Clarence Moore
1967 ....Ray Palmer	1980 ....William C. Campbell	1993 ....Joe Ungvary

Event is for golfers at least 55 years of age.

MAJOR WOMEN'S AMATEUR CHAMPIONSHIPS

U.S. Women's Amateur

Year	Winner	Score	Runner-Up	Site
1895 ....Mrs. Charles S. Brown		132	Nellie Sargent	Meadow Brook Club, Hempstead, NY
1896 ....Beatrix Hoyt		2 & 1	Mrs. Arthur Turnure	Morris Couty GC, Morristown, NJ
1897 ....Beatrix Hoyt		5 & 4	Nellie Sargent	Essex County Club, Manchester, MA
1898 ....Beatrix Hoyt		5 &3	Maude Wetmore	Ardsley Club, Ardsley-on-Hudson, NY
1899 ....Ruth Underhill		2 & 1	Margaret Fox	Philadelphia CC, Philadelphia, PA
1900 ....Frances C. Griscom		6 & 5	Margaret Curtis	Shinnecock Hills GC, Shinnecock Hills, NY
1901 ....Genevieve Hecker		5 & 3	Lucy Herron	Baltusrol GC, Springfield, NJ
1902 ....Genevieve Hecker		4 & 3	Louisa A. Wells	The Country Club, Brookline, MA
1903 ....Bessie Anthony		7 & 6	J. Anna Carpenter	Chicago GC, Wheaton, IL
1904 ....Georgianna M. Bishop		5 & 3	Mrs. E.F. Sanford	Merion Cricket Club, Haverford, PA
1905 ....Pauline Mackay		1 up	Margaret Curtis	Morris County GC, Convent, NJ
1906 ....Harriot S. Curtis		2 & 1	Mary B. Adams	Brae Burn CC, West Newton, MA
1907 ....Margaret Curtis		7 & 6	Harriot S. Curtis	Midlothian CC, Blue Island, IL
1908 ....Katherine C. Harley		6 & 5	Mrs. T.H. Polhemus	Chevy Chase Club, Chevy Chase, MD
1909 ....Dorothy I. Campbell		3 & 2	Nonna Barlow	Merion Cricket Club, Haverford, PA
1910 ....Dorothy I. Campbell		2 & 1	Mrs. G.M. Martin	Homewood CC, Flossmoor, IL
1911 ....Margaret Curtis		5 & 3	Lillian B. Hyde	Baltusrol GC, Springfield, NJ
1912 ....Margaret Curtis		3 & 2	Nonna Barlow	Essex County Club, Manchester, MA
1913 ....Gladys Ravenscroft		2 up	Marion Hollins	Wilmington CC, Wilmington, DE
1914 ....Katherine Harley		1 up	Elaine V. Rosenthal	Nassau CC, Glen Cove, NY
1915 ....Florence Vanderbeck		3 & 2	Margaret Gavin	Onwentsia Club, Lake Forest, IL
1916 ....Alexa Stirling		2 & 1	Mildred Caverly	Belmont Springs CC, Waverley, MA
1917-18 ...No tournament				
1919 ....Alexa Stirling		6 & 5	Margaret Gavin	Shawnee CC, Shawnee-on Delaware, PA
1920 ....Alexa Stirling		5 & 4	Dorothy Campbell	Mayfield CC, Cleveland, OH
1921 ....Marion Hollins		5 & 4	Alexa Stirling	Hollywood GC, Deal, NJ
1922 ....Glenna Collett		5 & 4	Margaret Gavin	Greenbriar GC, White Sulphur Springs, W. Va.
1923 ....Edith Cummings		3 & 2	Alexa Stirling	Westchester-Biltmore CC, Rye, NY
1924 ....Dorothy Campbell		7 & 6	Mary K. Browne	Rhode Island CC, Nyatt, RI
1925 ....Glenna Collett		9 & 8	Alexa Stirling	St. Louis CC, Clayton, MO
1926 ....Helen Stetson		3 & 1	Elizabeth Goss	Merion Cricket Club, Ardmore, PA
1927 ....Miiriam Burns Horn		5 & 4	Maureen Orcutt	Cherry Valley Club, Garden City, NY
1928 ....Glenna Collett		13 & 12	Virginia Van Wie	Va. Hot Springs G & TC, Hot Springs, VA
1929 ....Glenna Collett		4 & 3	Leona Pressler	Oakland Hills CC, Birmingham, MI
1930 ....Glenna Collett		6 & 5	Virginia Van Wie	Los Angeles CC, Beverly Hills, CA
1931 ....Helen Hicks		2 & 1	Glenna Collet Vare	CC of Buffalo, Williamsville, NY
1932 ....Virginia Van Wie		10 & 8	Glenna Collet Vare	Salem CC, Peabody, MA
1933 ....Virginia Van Wie		4 & 3	Helen Hicks	Exmoor CC, Highland Park, IL
1934 ....Virginia Van Wie		2 & 1	Dorothy Traung	Whitemarsh Valley CC, Chestnut Hill, PA
1935 ....Glenna Collett Vare		3 & 2	Patty Berg	Interlachen CC, Hopkins, MN
1936 ....Pamela Barton		4 & 3	Maureen Orcutt	Canoe Brook CC, Summit, NJ

U.S. Women's Amateur

Year	Winner	Score	Runner-Up	Site
1937	Estelle Lawson	7 & 6	Patty Berg	Memphis CC, Memphis, TN
1938	Patty Berg	6 & 5	Estelle Lawson	Westmoreland CC, Wilmette, IL
1939	Betty Jameson	3 & 2	Dorothy Kirby	Wee Burn Club, Darien, CT
1940	Betty Jameson	6 & 5	Jane S. Cothran	Del Monte G & CC, Pebble Beach, CA
1941	Elizabeth Hicks	5 & 3	Helen Sigel	The Country Club, Brookline, MA
1942-45	No tournament			
1946	Babe Zaharias	11 & 9	Clara Sherman	Southern Hills CC, Tulsa, OK
1947	Louise Suggs	2 up	Dorothy Kirby	Franklin Hills CC, Franklin, MI
1948	Grace S. Lenczyk	4 & 3	Helen Sigel	Del Monte G & CC, Pebble Beach, CA
1949	Dorothy Porter	3 & 2	Dorothy Kielty	Merion GC, Ardmore, PA
1950	Beverly Hanson	6 & 4	Mae Murray	Atlanta AC, Atlanta, GA
1951	Dorothy Kirby	2 & 1	Claire Doran	Town & CC, St. Paul, MN
1952	Jacqueline Pung	2 & 1	Shirley McFedters	Waverley CC, Portland, OR
1953	Mary Lena Faulk	3 & 2	Polly Riley	Rhode Island CC, West Barrington, RI
1954	Barbara Romack	4 & 2	Miickey Wright	Allegheny CC, Sewickley, PA
1955	Patricia A. Lesser	7 & 6	Jane Nelson	Myers Park CC, Charlotte, NC
1956	Marlene Stewart	2 & 1	JoAnne Gunderson	Meridian Hills CC, Indianapolis, IN
1957	JoAnne Gunderson	8 & 6	Ann Casey Johnstone	Del Paso CC, Sacramento, CA
1958	Anne Quast	3 & 2	Barbara Romack	Wee Burn CC, Darien, CT
1959	Barbara McIntire	4 & 3	Joanne Goodwin	Congressional CC, Washington, D.C.
1960	JoAnne Gunderson	6 & 5	Jean Ashley	Tulsa CC, Tulsa, OK
1961	Anne Quast Sander	14 & 13	Phyllis Preuss	Tacoma G & CC, Tacoma, WA
1962	JoAnne Gunderson	9 & 8	Anne Baker	CC of Rochester, Rochester, NY
1963	Anne Quast Sander	2 & 1	Peggy Conley	Taconic GC, Williamstown, MA
1964	Barbara McIntire	3 & 2	JoAnne Gunderson	Prairie Dunes CC, Hutchinson, KS
1965	Jean Ashley	5 & 4	Anne Quast Sander	Lakewood CC, Denver, CO
1966	JoAnne Gunderson	1 up	Marlene Stewart Streit	Sewickley Heights GC, Sewickley, PA
1967	Mary Lou Dill	5 & 4	Jean Ashley	Annandale GC, Pasadena, CA
1968	JoAnne Gunderson Carner	5 & 4	Anne Quast Sander	Birmingham CC, Birmingham, MI
1969	Catherine Lacoste	3 & 2	Shelley Hamling	Las Colinas CC, Irving, TX
1970	Martha Wilkinson	3 & 2	Cynthia Hall	Wee Burn CC, Darien, CT
1971	Laura Baugh	1 up	Beth Barry	Atlanta CC, Atlanta, GA
1972	Mary Budke	5 & 4	Cynthia Hill	St. Louis CC, St. Louis, MO
1973	Carol Semple	1 up	Anne Quast Sander	Montclair GC, Montclair, NJ
1974	Cynthia Hill	5 & 4	Carol Semple	Broadmoor GC, Seattle, WA
1975	Beth Daniel	3 & 2	Donna Horton	Brae Burn CC, West Newton, MA
1976	Donna Horton	2 & 1	Marianne Bretton	Del Paso CC, Sacramento, CA
1977	Beth Daniel	3 & 1	Cathy Sherk	Cincinnati CC, Cincinnati, OH
1978	Cathy Sherk	4 & 3	Judith Oliver	Sunnybrook GC, Plymouth Meeting, PA
1979	Carolyn Hill	7 & 6	Patty Sheehan	Memphis CC, Memphis, TN
1980	Juli Inkster	2 up	Patti Rizzo	Prairie Dunes CC, Hutchinson, KS
1981	Juli Inkster	1 up	Lindy Goggin	Waverley CC, Portland, OR
1982	Juli Inkster	4 & 3	Cathy Hanlon	Broadmoor GC, Colorado Springs, CO
1983	Joanne Pacillo	2 & 1	Sally Quinlan	Canoe Brook CC, Summit, NJ
1984	Deb Richard	1 up	Kimberly Williams	Broadmoor GC, Seattle, WA
1985	Michiko Hattori	5 & 4	Cheryl Stacy	Fox Chapel CC, Pittsburgh, PA
1986	Kay Cockerill	9 & 7	Kathleen McCarthy	Pasatiempo GC, Santa Cruz, CA
1987	Kay Cockerill	3 & 2	Tracy Kerdyk	Rhode Island CC, Barrington, RI
1988	Pearl Sinn	6 & 5	Karen Noble	Minikahda Club, Miinneapolis, MN
1989	Vicki Goetze	4 & 3	Brandie Burton	Pinehurst CC (No. 2), Pinehurst, NC
1990	Pat Hurst	37 holes	Stephanie Davis	Canoe Brook CC, Summit, NJ
1991	Amy Fruhwirth	5 & 4	Heidi Voorhees	Prairie Dunes CC, Hutchinson, KN
1992	Vicki Goetz	1-up	Annika Sorensteam	Kemper Lakes GC, Hawthorne Hills, IL
1993	Jill McGill	1-up	Sarah Ingram	San Diego CC, Chula Vista, CA

Missing Links

The following poignant advertisement appeared in the Midland (Texas) *Reporter-Telegram*: "Lost: Golfing Husband and Dog—last seen at Ratliff Ranch Golf Links. Reward for Dog."

Girls' Junior Championship

1949	Marlene Bauer
1950	Patricia Lesser
1951	Arlene Brooks
1952	Mickey Wright
1953	Millie Meyerson
1954	Margaret Smith
1955	Carole Jo Kabler
1956	JoAnne Gunderson
1957	Judy Eller
1958	Judy Eller
1959	Judy Rand
1960	Carol Sorenson
1961	Mary Lowell
1962	Mary Lou Daniel
1963	Janis Ferraris
1964	Peggy Conley
1965	Gail Sykes
1966	Claudia Mayhew
1967	Elizabeth Story
1968	Peggy Harmon
1969	Hollis Stacy
1970	Hollis Stacy
1971	Hollis Stacy
1972	Nancy Lopez
1973	Amy Alcott
1974	Nancy Lopez
1975	Dayna Benson
1976	Pilar Dorado
1977	Althea Tome
1978	Lori Castillo
1979	Penny Hammel
1980	Laurie Rinker
1981	Kay Cornelius
1982	Heather Farr
1983	Kim Saiki
1984	Cathy Mockett
1985	Dana Lofland
1986	Pat Hurst
1987	Michelle McGann
1988	Jamille Jose
1989	Brandie Burton
1990	Sandrine Mendiburu
1991	Emilee Klein
1992	Jamie Koizumi
1993	Kellee Booth

British Amateur

1893	Lady Margaret Scott
1894	Lady Margaret Scott
1895	Lady Margaret Scott
1896	Miss Pascoe
1897	Miss E.C. Orr
1898	Miss L. Thomson
1899	Miss M. Hezlet
1900	Miss Adair
1901	Miss Graham
1902	Miss M. Hezlet
1903	Miss Adair
1904	Miss L. Dod
1905	Miss B. Thompson
1906	Mrs. Kennon
1907	Miss M. Hezlet
1908	Miss M. Titterton
1909	Miss D. Campbell
1910	Miss Grant Suttie
1911	Miss D. Campbell
1912	Miss G. Ravenscroft
1913	Miss M. Dodd
1914	Miss C. Leitch
1915–1919	not held
1920	Miss C. Leitch
1921	Miss C. Leitch
1922	Miss J. Wethered
1923	Miss D. Chambers
1924	Miss J. Wethered
1925	Miss J. Wethered
1926	Miss C. Leitch
1927	Miss Thion de la Chaume
1928	Miss N. Le Blan
1929	Miss J. Wethered
1930	Miss D. Fishwick
1931	Miss E. Wilson
1932	Miss E. Wilson
1933	Miss E. Wilson
1934	Mrs. A.M. Holm
1935	Miss W. Morgan
1936	Miss P. Barton
1937	Miss J. Anderson
1938	Mrs. A.M. Holm
1939	Miss P. Barton
1940–45	not held
1946	G.W. Hetherington
1947	B. Zaharias
1948	L. Suggs
1949	F. Stephens
1950	Vicomtesse de Saint Sauveur
1951	P.J. MacCann
1952	M. Paterson
1953	M. Stewart
1954	F. Stephens
1955	J. Valentine
1956	M. Smith
1957	P. Garvey
1958	J. Valentine
1959	E. Price
1960	B. McIntyre
1961	M. Spearman
1962	M. Spearman
1963	B. Varangot
1964	C. Sorenson
1965	B. Varangot
1966	E. Chadwick
1967	E. Chadwick
1968	B. Varangot
1975	C. Lacoste
1976	D. Oxley
1977	A. Uzielli
1978	E. Kennedy
1979	M. Madill
1980	A. Quast
1981	I.C. Robertson
1982	K. Douglas
1983	J. Thornhill
1984	J. Rosenthal
1985	L. Beman
1986	tk McGuire
1987	J. Collingham
1988	J. Furby
1989	H. Dobson
1990	J. Hall
1991	V. Michaud
1992	P. Pedersen
1993	Catriona Lambert

1977	Kelly Fuiks
1978	Kelly Fuiks
1979	Lori Castillo
1980	Lori Castillo
1981	Mary Enright
1982	Nancy Taylor

Amateur Public Links

1983	Kelli Antolock
1984	Heather Farr
1985	Danielle Ammaccapane
1986	Cindy Schreyer
1987	Tracy Kerdyk
1988	Pearl Sinn
1989	Pearl Sinn
1990	Cathy Mockett
1991	Tracy Hanson
1992	Amy Fruhwirth
1993	Connie Masterson

U.S. Senior Women's Amateur

1962 ....Maureen Orcutt	1973 ....Gwen Hibbs	1984 ....Constance Guthrie
1963 ....Sis Choate	1974 ....Justine Cushing	1985 ....Marlene Streit
1964 ....Loma Smith	1975 ....Alberta Bower	1986 ....Connie Guthrie
1965 ....Loma Smith	1976 ....Cecile H. Maclaurin	1987 ....Anne Sander
1966 ....Maureen Orcutt	1977 ....Dorothy Porter	1988 ....Lois Hodge
1967 ....Marge Mason	1978 ....Alice Dye	1989 ....Anne Sander
1968 ....Carolyn Cudone	1979 ....Alice Dye	1990 ....Anne Sander
1969 ....Carolyn Cudone	1980 ....Dorothy Porter	1991 ....Phyllis Preuss
1970 ....Carolyn Cudone	1981 ....Dorothy Porter	1992 ....Rosemary Thompson
1971 ....Carolyn Cudone	1982 ....Edean Ihlanfeldt	1993 ....Anne Sander
1972 ....Carolyn Cudone	1983 ....Dorothy Porter	

Women's Mid-Amateur Championship

1987	Cindy Scholefield
1988	Martha Lang
1989	Robin Weiss
1990	Carol Semple Thompson
1991	Sarah LeBrun Ingram
1992	Marion Mamey-McInerney
1993	Sarah Ingram

International Golf

Ryder Cup Matches

Year	Results	Site
1927	United States 9½, Great Britain 2½	Worcester CC, Worcester, MA
1929	Great Britain 7, United States 5	Moortown GC, Leeds, England
1931	United States 9, Great Britain 3	Scioto CC, Columbus, OH
1933	Great Britain 6½, United States 5½	Southport and Ainsdale Courses, Southport, England
1935	United States 9, Great Britain 3	Ridgewood CC, Ridgewood, NJ
1937	United States 8, Great Britain 4	Southport and Ainsdale Courses, Southport, England
1939-1945	No tournament	
1947	United States 11, Great Britain 1	Portland GC, Portland, OR
1949	United States 7, Great Britain 5	Ganton GC, Scarborough, England
1951	United States 9½, Great Britain 2½	Pinehurst CC, Pinehurst, NC
1953	United States 6½, Great Britain 5½	Wentworth Club, Surrey, England
1955	United States 8, Great Britain 4 ·	Thunderbird Ranch & CC, Palm Springs, CA
1957	Great Britain 7½, United States 4½	Lindrick GC, Yorkshire, England
1959	United States 8½, Great Britain 3½	Eldorado CC, Palm Desert, CA
1961	United States 14½, Great Britain 9½	Royal Lytham & St Anne's GC, St Anne's-on-the-Sea, England
1963	United States 23, Great Britain 9	East Lake CC, Atlanta
1965	United States 19½, Great Britain 12½	Royal Birkdale GC, Southport, England
1967	United States 23½, Great Britain 8½	Champions GC, Houston
1969	United States 16, Great Britain 16	Royal Birkdale GC, Southport, England
1971	United States 18½, Great Britain 13½	Old Warson CC, St Louis
1973	United States 19, Great Britain 13	Hon Co of Edinburgh Golfers, Muirfield, Scotland
1975	United States 21, Great Britain 11	Laurel Valley GC, Ligonier, PA
1977	United States 12½, Great Britain 7½	Royal Lytham & St Anne's GC, St Anne's-on-the-Sea, England
1979	United States 17, Europe 11	Greenbrier, White Sulphur Springs, WV
1981	United States 18½, Europe 9½	Walton Heath GC, Surrey, England
1983	United States 14½, Europe 13½	PGA National GC, Palm Beach Gardens, FL
1985	Europe 16½, United States 11½	Belfry GC, Sutton Coldfield, England
1987	Europe 15, United States 13	Muirfield GC, Dublin, OH
1989	Europe 14, United States 14	Belfry GC, Sutton Coldfield, England
1991	United States 14½, Europe 13½	Ocean Course, Kiawah Island, SC
1993	United States 15, Europe 13	Belfry GC, Sutton Coldfield, England

Team matches held every odd year between US professionals and those of Great Britain/Europe (since 1979, prior to which was US vs GB). Team members selected on basis of finishes in PGA and European tour events.

Walker Cup Matches

Year	Results	Site
1922	United States 8, Great Britain 4	Nat. Golf Links of America, Southampton, NY
1923	United States 6, Great Britain 5	St. Andrews, Scotland
1924	United States 9, Great Britain 3	Garden City GC, Garden City, NY
1926	United States 6, Great Britain 5	St. Andrews, Scotland
1928	United States 11, Great Britain 1	Chicago GC, Wheaton, IL
1930	United States 10, Great Britain 2	Royal St. George GC, Sandwich, England
1932	United States 8, Great Britain 1	The Country Club, Brookline, MA
1934	United States 9, Great Britain 2	St. Andrews, Scotland
1936	United States 9, Great Britain 0	Pine Valley GC, Clementon, NJ
1938	Great Britain 7, United States 4	St. Andrews, Scotland
1940-46	No tournament	
1947	United States 8, Great Britain 4	St. Andrews, Scotland
1949	United States 10, Great Britain 2	Winged Foot GC, Mamaroneck, NY
1951	United States 6, Great Britain 3	Birkdale GC, Southport, England
1953	United States 9, Great Britain 3	The Kittansett Club, Marion, MA
1955	United States 10, Great Britain 2	St. Andrews, Scotland
1957	United States 8, Great Britain 3	Minikahda Club, Minneapolis, MN
1959	United States 9, Great Britain 3	Muirfield, Scotland
1961	United States 11, Great Britain 1	Seattle GC, Seattle, WA
1963	United States 12, Great Britain 8	Ailsa Course, Turnberry, Scotland
1965	Great Britain 11, United States 11	Baltimore CC, Five Farms, Baltimore, MD
1967	United States 13, Great Britain 7	Royal St. George's GC, Sandwich, England
1969	United States 10, Great Britain 8	Milwaukee CC, Milwaukee, WI
1971	Great Britain 13, United States 11	St. Andrews, Scotland
1973	United States 14, Great Britain 10	The Country Club, Brookline, MA
1975	United States 15½, Great Britain 8½	St. Andrews, Scotland
1977	United States 16, Great Britain 8	Shinnecock Hills GC, Southampton, NY
1979	United States 15½, Great Britain 8½	Muirfield, Scotland
1981	United States 15, Great Britain 9	Cypress Point Club, Pebble Beach, CA
1983	United States 13½, Great Britain 10½	Royal Liverpool GC, Hoylake, England
1985	United States 13, Great Britain 11	Pine Valley GC, Pine Valley, NJ
1987	United States 16½, Great Britain 7½	Sunningdale GC, Berkshire, England
1989	Great Britain 12½, United States 11½	Peachtree Golf Club, Atlanta, GA
1991	United States 14, Great Britain 10	Portmarnock GC, Dublin, Ireland
1993	United States 19, Great Britain 5	Interlachen CC, Edina, MN

Men's amateur team competition every other year between United States and Great Britain. US team members selected by USGA.

Curtis Cup Matches

Year	Results	Site
1932	United States 5½, British Isles 3½	Wentworth GC, Wentworth, England
1934	United States 6½, British Isles 2½	Chevy Chase Club, Chevy Chase, MD
1936	United States 4½, British Isles 4½	King's Course, Gleneagles, Scotland
1938	United States 5½, British Isles 3½	Essex CC, Manchester, MA
1940-46	No tournament	
1948	United States 6½, British Isles 2½	Birkdale GC, Southport, England
1950	United States 7½, British Isles 1½	CC of Buffalo, Williamsville, NY
1952	British Isles 5, United States 4	Muirfield, Scotland
1954	United States 6, British Isles 3	Merion GC, Ardmore, PA
1956	British Isles 5, United States 4	Prince's GC, Sandwich Bay, England
1958	British Isles 4½, United States 4½	Brae Burn CC, West Newton, Mass.
1960	United States 6½, British Isles 2½	Lindrick GC, Worksop, England
1962	United States 8, British Isles 1	Broadmoor CG, Colorado Springs,CO
1964	United States 10½, British Isles 7½	Royal Porthcawl GC, Porthcawl, South Wales
1966	United States 13, British Isles 5	Va. Hot Springs G & TC, Hot Springs, VA
1968	United States 10½, British Isles 7½	Royal County Down GC, Newcastle, N. Ire.
1970	United States 11½, British Isles 6½	Brae Burn CC, WEst Newton, MA
1972	United States 10, British Isles 8	Western Gailes, Ayrshire, Scotland
1974	United States 13, British Isles 5	San Francisco GC, San Francisco, CA
1976	United States 11½, British Isles 6½	Royal Lytham & St. Annes GC, England

Curtis Cup Matches (Cont.)

Year	Results	Site
1978	United States 12, British Isles 6	Apawamis Club, Rye, NY
1980	United States 13, British Isles 5	St. Pierre G & CC, Chepstow, Wales
1982	United States 14½, British Isles 3½	Denver CC, Denver, CO
1984	United States 9½, British Isles 8½	Muirfield, Scotland
1986	British Isles 13, United States 5	Prairie Dunes CC, Hutchinson, KS
1988	British Isles 11, United States 7	Royal St. George's GC, Sandwich, England
1990	United States 14, British Isles 4	Somerset Hills CC, Bernardsville, NJ
1992	Great Britain/Ireland 10, United States 8	Royal Liverpool GC, Hoylake, England

Women's amateur team competition every other year between the United States and Great Britain. US team members selected by USGA.

Up from the Ashes

The 18th green at the Doral Resort and Country Club in Miami is just 20 miles from the spot where Raymond Floyd's house once stood. On March 8 the 49-year-old Floyd walked off that green after finishing with a 17–under–par 271 to win the Doral Ryder Open, his 22nd career Tour victory. The title was his first since 1986, and it came 2½ weeks after what Floyd called "the worst thing that ever happened to me."

At 3 a.m. on Feb. 19, when he was in San Diego preparing for the Buick Invitational, the Floyds' six-bedroom house on Indian Creek, an island in Biscayne Bay, caught fire. Floyd's wife, Maria, and their three children escaped unharmed. But the $2.7 million house, which Floyd designed, was destroyed, and most of the mementos from his 31-year pro career and his family's life were lost.

"It's a snapshot or a baby picture or a wedding picture," says Floyd. "Each picture is a 10-minute story. We lost everything. All our picture albums. Two hallways, hundreds of pictures on the wall, with Maria and friends and family. All destroyed." Floyd was so distraught over the fire that he was going to skip the Doral, which he had won twice. "I wasn't going to play, but Maria insisted," Floyd says.

At the Doral, Floyd beat Fred Couples and Keith Clearwater by two strokes, and with the victory he became only the second golfer to win PGA Tour events in four decades (Sam Snead was the first, winning in the 1930s, '40s, '50s and '60s). On Sunday Floyd said, "I've felt all week that this tournament was for Maria and the kids." After pausing, he added, "Maybe adversity is what I need to win, but I sure as hell don't need another fire."

The Floyds are planning to build a new house on the site of the old one. And while some of what they lost is irreplaceable, they now have the first item for a new trophy case.

THEY SAID IT

Irish golfer David Feherty, after being paired with John Daly in the first round of the British Open: "He hits his divots farther than I hit my drives."

Boxing

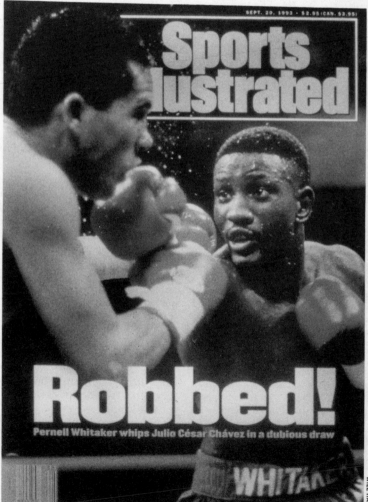

SEPT. 20, 1993 · $2.95 (CAN. $3.95)

Sports Illustrated

Robbed!

Pernell Whitaker whips Julio César Chávez in a dubious draw

WILL HART

Robbery and Lethargy

Too much talking, too little fighting and a horrible decision were the year's lowlights | by RICHARD HOFFER

WELL, HEAVYWEIGHT CHAMP Riddick Bowe finally met Mike Tyson, but it did not make boxing history. Tyson, who was doing Day No. 577 of a six-year sentence for rape at the Indiana Youth Center, told his visiting Brooklyn homeboy that he was not bitter, was much wiser and was not particularly interested in fighting. This was terrific news if you're interested in the rehabilitation of the imprisoned fighter, but it did not do anything to spark excitement in the once electrifying heavyweight division. And does that division need sparking. Year two of Tyson's term—an appeal led by celebrity lawyer Alan Dershowitz failed again—and he still makes more news delivering hard-time homilies than his brethren do delivering jabs.

"Respect the position you have," Bowe said, reporting their conversation. "Don't abuse it like I did."

Good advice, of course. But how many of us wish Tyson had advised him in matters of scheduling, as well. Like, get with this Lennox Lewis, and soon. Say what you will about Tyson; he did, in his youthful and lawless prime, consolidate all those heavyweight titles. Young Bowe's reign, of course, has been distinguished by the division's fragmentation, and as the year drew to a close there was little hope of his performing an immediate unification. Bowe was preparing for a rematch with Evander Holyfield, this after ducking real fighters for a year. And Lewis, who had woken up one morning to find himself the WBC champion, was preparing for fellow Brit Frank Bruno. Nobody figured the fight would be any less dainty than the advertised buildup, which showed the two sluggers sharing afternoon tea. One lump or two, indeed.

Less civilized and considerably more exciting were the lighter weights. Although, in the end, the long-awaited meeting of Pernell (Sweet Pea) Whitaker and Mexican legend Julio César Chávez, was no more conclusive than Bowe's and Tyson's. Yes, it was that kind of year, a year when the two best fighters boxed, and one remained unbeaten and the other remained champion.

The September fight, which took place in San Antonio's Alamodome, offered promoter Don King a nice hook. King, who hasn't been able to make too much money off Tyson these days, had made Chávez, long thought to be the best fighter pound for pound, his Mexican meal ticket. With Chavez as his centerpiece, King staged a four-fight card—"The Grand Slam of Boxing"—in Mexico City in February that drew 136,274. This south-of-the-border interest was enough to motivate King, who has reinvented the English language over the years, to begin his corruption of Spanish—"Spanglish," he was said to be speaking—and its history.

The fight was King-proof, though. It was easily the match of the year or, as Whitaker promised, "the World Series, Super Bowl, NBA Finals." Chávez was clearly the favorite, but still there was suspense. "There comes a night," said Whitaker's co-trainer, Lou Duva, "when a fighter gets old. This may be the night."

King wasn't content to let this bout be just a bout. It was a cultural, historic event.

Whitaker had Chávez in retreat but the judges apparently missed the action.

"Remember the Alamo," he kept bleating, "and this time the Mexicans will win." He was apparently thinking that his Mexican fighter meant to exact revenge. Of course, the Alamo was the fight where General Santa Anna actually won by KO, and hence a Mexican's revenge was largely unnecessary. But the phrase had a nice ring, and King was undeterred. Perhaps King was only thinking that if he had promoted that fight and been able to fly in a few judges of choice, Davey Crockett might have somehow won on points.

Or at least escaped with a majority draw. Because that's what happened to his fighter. Chávez, a five-time world champion and undefeated, was trying to move up in weight to take Whitaker's 147-pound crown. But, by all accounts except his own, he was outboxed and outpunched. Whitaker, who watched videos of Michael Jordan to prepare for the fight and who promised to outfinesse the blood-and-guts fighter,

After defeating Gatti, Norris celebrated with his family—and the ubiquitous King (left).

rained blows on his confused opponent in such profusion that he actually had Chávez in retreat during the fight. It was a stunning development to see Chávez in reverse. It was as if the matador were pursuing the bull.

"Everyone said I might run or something," Whitaker said. Well, hadn't Whitaker said as much? Whitaker, who once circled an opponent and pulled the fighter's trunks down to his ankles, had been among the first to suggest he would spend the night spinning around Chávez. "But I can fight." And, as it turned out, hit. "My middle knuckle hurts from hitting him on the nose so many times," Whitaker said later. It was an amazing performance.

But more amazement was to come. Two of the three judges, picked by the WBC with which King enjoys a cozy relationship, simply could not tell who won. This was surprising, since a punch count showed that Whitaker landed about 100 more than Chávez, and since informal polls of ringsiders indicated an easy decision for Whitaker. But the rare majority draw result meant that Chávez, whom you might call the house fighter in this case, stayed undefeated and that Whitaker kept his welterweight title, and everyone but the fans went home a little richer.

Chávez, a legend in Mexico for his 87 victories going into the fight, would only say, "It was not one of my greatest nights," and retreat to nurse his wounded macho image.

Whitaker, of course, had much more to say, and much more to gain. "This is something that could be the most frustrating night of an athlete's career," he said, "but I'm going to take it like a victory." Most people did.

As for Don King, he was strangely silent, refusing to speak much in any language. All anybody heard him say was, "Let's do it again." Nobody's betting they will. Still, just as he promised, although for all the wrong reasons, it will be a long time before anyone forgets the Alamodome.

With that fight, which drew 65,000 fans to the arena and perhaps another million to pay-per-view shows, Chavez's star certainly dimmed. His near miss against Meldrick Taylor three years earlier—Taylor was well ahead on points, two seconds from an upset decision, when the referee decided he could no longer continue—foreshadowed his troubles as he advanced in age (31) and weight. But had he beaten Whitaker, he might have been able to consolidate his reputation with the casual fan north of the border. As it was, he remained a Mexican sensation taken seriously by aficionados but by few others. His charisma did not cross over.

And with that fight, Whitaker, who had just turned 29, can fairly represent himself as among the best fighters, at least sharing that mythical pound-for-pound title. In March he lifted the WBC welterweight title from Buddy McGirt in a marvelous bout of showboating (even his wife was screaming for him to stop clowning), joining Henry Armstrong, Barney Ross and Roberto Duran as the only men to win titles in the lightweight and welterweight divisions.

If Chávez never returns to his fearsome form, if a rematch never develops, there will be other fighters to challenge Whitaker for boxing's most unofficial title. Super welterweight Terry Norris, despite fighting in an obscure division, continued to impress, dicing up Troy Waters in a June bout and then destroying Joe Gatti in just one round at the Alamodome.

And there is popular junior flyweight champion Michael Carbajal and young lightweight Oscar De La Hoya. Both stars from different Olympics (Carbajal in 1988, De La Hoya the lone standout in 1992), each cruised as they continued their careers. De La Hoya was angling for a title shot at 130 pounds when he aggravated a hand injury, postponing a crown. So his greatness was deferred at least another year.

So was Riddick Bowe's as he indulged in one of the heavyweight champion's most important perks: making money. Following his rousing decision over Holyfield toward the end of 1992, in which he dispelled forever any questions about his heart, Bowe suddenly steered clear of anybody more dangerous than a ring card girl. Talks with Lennox Lewis, the man who beat him in the Seoul Olympics and was the consensus top challenger, were never very serious. In fact, Bowe had to make a hasty show of depositing his WBC belt in a garbage can (literally, not just figuratively) before the WBC trashed him for avoiding the challenger.

For his first defense, in February, the easy payday that is every new champion's right, Bowe chose Michael Dokes, a former champion who had given up drugs but who had otherwise not denied himself much. Bowe, earning a Tyson-like $7 million, demolished the 244-pound Dokes in Round 1. It was not very competitive.

Inasmuch as Bowe had signed a six-fight deal with HBO-TVKO for as much as $100 million, he was in no hurry to take any unnecessary chances. He certainly would not travel to meet Lewis. Instead, he set off on a world tour to meet world leaders and solve hunger (he planned to donate $100,000 during a stop in Somalia). He was especially looking forward to an audience with Pope John Paul II. Asked what they might discuss, Bowe said he planned to say, "Yo, Pope, pray for me."

Jesse Ferguson, a 36-year-old with a 19–9 record, could have used the papal intercession far more than the champion. He was picked for Bowe's next defense when he beat the intended challenger, the far more credible Ray Mercer, in a boxing time-killer. That fight became even more remarkable when the Manhattan district attorney learned that Mercer may have offered Ferguson a bribe *during* their fight. "Want to go down?" the desperate Mercer supposedly asked Ferguson.

That sorry incident was in no way redeemed when Ferguson persisted in that fight to win his shot at Bowe. Because when the two met in May, before a not very hopeful audience of less than 9,000, Ferguson did indeed go down, in just two rounds, whether he wanted to or not.

Unfortunately none of the other heavyweights were doing much to make Bowe ashamed of his career conduct. Holyfield, who had gone into immediate retirement after losing his championship to Bowe, returned in July to fight Alex Stewart. News of a possible rematch between Bowe and Holyfield briefly galvanized the boxing world, but the Stewart fight was so profoundly sleep-inducing it shouldn't have been available without a doctor's prescription. Bowe's manager, Rock Newman, walked from the bout in disgust. "What a joke," he said. "He should go back into retirement." Hardly the kind of talk managers use to drum up interest in money fights. Holyfield's new trainer, Emanuel Steward, tried to save something of the day. He said, "Holyfield's been fighting wars for 10 years. Why can't he have a normal fight?"

And Lewis created no groundswell of support with his defeat of Tony Tucker. "Shameful, amateurlike performance," was Newman's take on that fight. Clearly there was nobody for Bowe to worry about, nothing for him to do. So Bowe repaired to the Maryland countryside to oversee construction of "Bowe Presidential Estate," a 16,000-square-foot compound that was going to feature a four-lane bowling alley, a 16-car garage and a master suite with a 10' by 10' bed and 10 TVs. "You always want to be different," he explained.

The only wild card to emerge in the division was Tommy Morrison, who resurrected his career in a bout with ol' George Foreman. Morrison had been effectively removed from contention in 1991 when the aforementioned Ray Mercer knocked him out. But Morrison had climbed back in the

Bowe's cushy year included a visit with the cast of Broadway's Will Rogers Follies.

heavyweight picture, earned his fight with Big George and, in a modest surprise, sent him packing off to sitcom land. It was not a great fight, but the 12-round decision more or less retired the 44-year-old Foreman, who by then was making more money peddling fried chicken on TV than the young contenders who were fighting in the ring. The word late in the year was that he was finally shedding weight to begin taping of his show called, wouldn't you know it, *George*. If it proves to be anything like his comeback run, it should be plenty of laughs.

However, the outcome of that fight once more exposed the sorry commerce of boxing. Morrison was immediately matched with Lewis, with talk of an $8 million payday, which he deserved for beating Foreman, or maybe for being blond and muscled. But then that fell through, and Lewis agreed to meet Bruno instead, after they share afternoon tea. And Bowe decided to engage Holyfield, after all, no matter that Bowe's own had long since predicted a stinker.

The scenario that all the parties finally agreed upon didn't seem to advance the year in boxing very much at all. It was inconclusive and nonconcussive. Too much maneuvering outside the ring, not enough action within. With that in mind, it's no wonder fight fans know Tyson's remaining sentence, to the day.

FOR THE RECORD·1992-1993

Current Champions

Division	Weight Limit	WBC Champion	WBA Champion	IBF Champion
Heavyweight	None	Lennox Lewis	Riddick Bowe	Riddick Bowe
Cruiserweight	190	Anaclet Wamba	Bobby Czyz	Alfred Cole
Light heavyweight	175	Jeff Harding	Virgil Hill	Henry Maske
Super middleweight	168	Nigel Benn	Michael Nunn	James Toney
Middleweight	160	Gerald McClellan	Reggie Johnson	Roy Jones
Junior middleweight	154	Terry Norris	Julio Cesar Vasquez	Gianfranco Rosi
Welterweight	147	Pernell Whitaker	Crisanto Espana	Felix Trinidad
Junior welterweight	140	Julio César Chávez	Juan M. Coggi	Charles Murray
Lightweight	135	Miguel Gonzalez	Dingaan Thobela	Fred Pendleton
Junior lightweight	130	Azumah Nelson	Genaro Hernandez	Juan Molina
Featherweight	126	Gregorio Vargas	Yong-Kyun Park	Tom Johnson
Junior featherweight	122	Tracy Patterson	Wilfredo Vasquez	Kennedy McKinney
Bantamweight	118	Jung-Il Byun	Jorge Julio	Orlando Canizales
Junior bantamweight	115	Sung-Kil Moon	Katsuya Onizuka	Julio Borboa
Flyweight	112	Yuri Arbachakov	David Griman	Pichit Sithbangprachan
Junior flyweight	108	Michael Carbajal	Myung-Woo Yuh	Michael Carbajal
Strawweight	105	Ricardo Lopez	Chana Porpaoin	Ratanapol Sow Vorapin

Note: WBC = World Boxing Council WBA = World Boxing Association IBF = International Boxing Federation

Championship and Major Fights of 1992 and 1993

Abbreviations: WBC=World Boxing Council WBA= World Boxing Association IBF=International Boxing Federation KO=knockout TKO=technical knockout Dec=decision Split=split decision Disq=disqualification

Heavyweight

Date	Winner	Loser	Result	Title	Site
Nov 13	Riddick Bowe	Evander Holyfield	Dec 12	World	Las Vegas
Feb 6	Riddick Bowe	Michael Dokes	KO 1	WBA, IBF	New York City
May 8	Lennox Lewis	Tony Tucker	Dec 12	WBC	Las Vegas
May 22	Riddick Bowe	Jesse Ferguson	KO 2	WBA	Washington, D.C.

Cruiserweight

Date	Winner	Loser	Result	Title	Site
July 30	Alfred Cole	James Warring	Dec 12	IBF	Stanhope, N.J.
Oct 16	Anaclet Wamba	Andrew Maynard	Dec 12	WBC	Paris
Feb 28	Alfred Cole	Uriah Grant	Dec 12	IBF	Atlantic City, N.J.
Mar 6	Anaclet Wamba	David Vedder	Dec 12	WBC	Perret, France
July 16	Alfred Cole	Glenn McCrory	Dec 12	IBF	Moscow, Russia

Light Heavyweight

Date	Winner	Loser	Result	Title	Site
Sep 29	Virgil Hill	Frank Tate	Dec 12	WBA	Bismarck, N. Dak.
Dec 3	Jeff Harding	David Vedder	Dec 12	WBC	St Jean de Luz, France
Feb 20	Virgil Hill	Adolpho Washington	TKO 11	WBA	Fargo, N. Dak.
Mar 20	Henry Maske	Charles Williams	Dec 12	IBF	Dusseldorf, Germany
April 3	Virgil Hill	Fabrice Tiozzo	Split 12	WBA	Perret, France
Aug 28	Virgil Hill	Sergio Merani	Dec 12	WBA	Bismarck, N. Dak.
Sep 18	Henry Maske	Anthony Hembrick	Dec 12	IBF	Dusseldorf, Germany

Super Middleweight

Date	Winner	Loser	Result	Title	Site
Sep 12	Michael Nunn	Victor Cordova	Split 12	WBA	Las Vegas
Dec 12	Nigel Benn	Nicky Piper	TKO 11	WBC	Muswell Hill, England
Jan 30	Michael Nunn	Victor Cordova	Dec 12	WBA	Memphis, Tennessee
Feb 13	James Toney	Iran Barkley	TKO 9	IBF	Las Vegas
Mar 6	Nigel Benn	Mauro Galvano	Dec 12	WBC	Glasgow, Scotland
Apr 23	Michael Nunn	Crawford Ashley	TKO 6	WBA	Memphis, Tennessee

Middleweight

Date	Winner	Loser	Result	Title	Site
Aug 1	Julian Jackson	Thomas Tate	Dec 12	WBC	Las Vegas
Aug 29	James Toney	Mike McCallum	Dec 12	WBC	Reno
Oct 27	Reggie Johnson	Lamar Parks	Dec 12	WBA	Houston
May 4	Reggie Johnson	Wayne Harris	Dec 12	WBA	Denver, Colorado
May 8	Gerald McClellan	Julian Jackson	TKO 5	WBC	Las Vegas
May 22	Roy Jones	Bernard Hopkins	Dec 12	IBF	Wahington, D.C.
Aug 6	Gerald McClellan	Jay Bell	KO 1	WBC	Bayamon, Puerto Rico

Junior Middleweight (Super Welterweight)

Date	Winner	Loser	Result	Title	Site
Dec 21	Julio C. Vasquez	Hitoshi Kamiyama	KO 1	WBA	Buenos Aires
Jan 20	Gianfranco Rosi	Gilbert Dele	Split 12	IBF	Avoriaz, France
Feb 20	Terry Norris	Maurice Blocker	TKO 2	WBC	Mexico City
Apr 24	Julio C. Vasquez	Javier Castillejos	Dec 12	WBA	Madrid, Spain
Aug 21	Julio C. Vasquez	Aaron Davis	Dec 12	WBA	Monte Carlo, Monaco
Sep 10	Terry Norris	Joe Gatti	TKO 1	WBC	San Antonio, Texas

Welterweight

Date	Winner	Loser	Result	Title	Site
Aug 28	Maurice Blocker	Luis Garcia	Split 12	IBF	Atlantic City
Oct 31	Crisanto Espana	Meldrick Taylor	TKO 8	WBA	London
Jan 12	Buddy McGirt	Genaro Leon	Dec 12	WBC	New York City
Mar 6	Pernell Whitaker	Buddy McGirt	Dec 12	WBC	New York City
May 5	Crisanto Espana	Rodolfo Aguilar	Dec 12	WBA	Belfast, Northern Ireland
Jun 19	Felix Trinidad	Maurice Blocker	KO 2	IBF	San Diego, California
Sep 10	Pernell Whitaker*	Julio César Chávez*	Draw	WBC	San Antonio, Texas

Junior Welterweight (Super Lightweight)

Date	Winner	Loser	Result	Title	Site
Sep 9	Morris East	Akinobu Hiranaka	TKO 11	WBA	Tokyo
Jan 12	Juan Martin Coggi	Morris East	TKO 8	WBA	Mar del Plata, Argentina
Feb 20	Julio César Chávez	Greg Haugen	TKO 5	WBC	Mexico City
May 8	Julio César Chávez	Terrence Alli	TKO 6	WBC	Las Vegas
May 15	Charles Murray	Rodney Moore	Dec 12	IBF	Atlantic City, N.J.
Jun 23	Juan Martin Coggi	Hiroyuki Yoshino	KO 5	WBA	Tokyo, Japan
July 24	Charles Murray	Juan Laporte	Dec 12	IBF	Atlantic City, N.J.
Sep 24	Juan Martin Coggi	Guillermo Cruz	TKO 10	WBA	Rome, Italy

Lightweight

Date	Winner	Loser	Result	Title	Site
Oct 24	Joey Gamache	Tony Lopez	TKO 11	WBA	Portland, Maine
Dec 5	Miguel Gonzalez	Darryl Tyson	Dec 12	WBC	Mexico City
Jan 10	Freddie Pendleton	Tracy Spann	Dec 12	IBF	Atlantic City, N.J.
Feb 12	Tony Lopez	Dingaan Thobela	Dec 12	WBA	Sacramento, California
Apr 26	Miguel Gonzalez	Hector Lopez	Dec 12	WBC	Aguascalientes, Mexico
Jun 26	Dingaan Thobela	Tony Lopez	Dec 12	WBA	Sun City, Bophutsatswana
July 17	Freddie Pendleton	Jorge Paez	Dec 12	IBF	Las Vegas
Aug 13	Miguel Gonzalez	David Sample	Dec 12	WBC	Guadalajara, Mexico

Junior Lightweight (Super Featherweight)

Date	Winner	Loser	Result	Title	Site
Nov 7	Azumah Nelson	Calvin Grove	Dec 12	WBC	Lake Tahoe
Nov 20	Genaro Hernandez	Yuji Watanabe	TKO 6	WBA	Tokyo
Feb 13	Jaun Molina	Francisco Segura	TKO 8	IBF	Bayamon, Puerto Rico
Feb 20	Azumah Nelson	Gabriel Ruelas	Dec 12	WBC	Mexico City
Jun 26	Jaun Molina	Manuel Medina	Dec 12	IBF	Atlantic City, N.J.
Jun 28	Genaro Hernandez	Raul Perez	KO 8	WBA	Inglewood, California

Featherweight

Date	Winner	Loser	Result	Title	Site
Sep 12	Paul Hodkinson	Fabrice Benichou	TKO 10	WBC	Blagriac(ck), France
Oct 23	Manuel Medina	Moussa Sangare	Maj Dec	IBF	Gravelines(ck), France
Dec 19	Yung Kyun-Park	Ever Beleno	Dec 12	WBA	Chun(TK), S Korea
Feb 26	Tom Johnson	Manuel Medina	Split 12	IBF	Melun, France
Apr 28	Gregorio Vargas	Paul Hodkinson	TKO 7	WBC	Dublin
Sep 4	Park Yong-Kyun	Chun Tae-Shik	Dec 12	WBA	Damyong, South Korea
Sep 11	Tom Johnson	Sugar Baby Rojas	Dec 12	IBF	Miami, Florida

Junior Featherweight (Super Bantamweight)

Date	Winner	Loser	Result	Title	Site
Dec 5	Wilfredo Vasquez	Thierry Jacob	TKO 8	WBA	Berck-sur-mer, France
Dec 5	Tracy Patterson	Daniel Zaragoza	Split Draw	WBC	Berck-sur-mer, France
Jun 24	Wilfredo Vasquez	Thierry Jacob	KO 10	WBA	Bordeaux, France
July 17	Kennedy McKinney	Rudy Zavala	TKO 3	IBF	Las Vegas
Sep 25	Tracy Patterson	Daniel Zaragoza	TKO 7	WBC	Poughkeepsie, N.Y.

Bantamweight

Date	Winner	Loser	Result	Title	Site
Sep 17	Victor Rabanales	Joichiro Tatsuyoshi	TKO 9	WBC	Tokyo
Sep 18	Orlando Canizales	Samuel Duran	Dec 12	IBF	Bozeman, Montana
Oct 9	Jorge Julio	Eddie Cook	Dec 12	WBA	Cartagena, Colombia
Mar 28	Jung-Il Byun	Victor Rabanales	Dec 12	WBC	Kyongju, South Korea
Mar 27	Orlando Canizales	Clarence Adams	TKO 11	IBF	Evian les Bains, France
Apr 3	Jorge Julio	Francisco Alvarez	TKO 8	WBA	Cartagena, Colombia

Junior Bantamweight (Super Flyweight)

Date	Winner	Loser	Result	Title	Site
Oct 31	Sung-Kil Moon	Greg Richardson	Split 12	WBC	Seoul
Dec 11	Katsuya Onizuka	Armando Castro	Dec 12	WBA	Tokyo
Jan 16	Julio Borboa	Robert Quiroga	TKO 12	IBF	San Antonio, Texas
May 21	Katsuya Onizuka	Lim Jae-Shin	Split 12	WBA	Tokyo
May 22	Julio Borboa	Joel Zarate	Dec 12	IBF	Naucalpan, Mexico
Jul 3	Sung-Kil Moon	Carlos Salazar	Split 12	WBC	Seoul

Flyweight

Date	Winner	Loser	Result	Title	Site
Oct 20	Yuri Arbachakov	Chin Yun-Un	Dec 12	WBC	Tokyo
Nov 29	Pichit Sithbangprachan	Rodolfo Blanco	KO 3	IBF	Samut Prakar,Thailand
Dec 15	David Griman	Aquiles Guzman	Dec 12	WBA	Caracas, Venezuela
Mar 6	Pichit Sithbangprachan	Antonio Perez	TKO 4	IBF	Uttaradit, Thailand
Mar 20	Yuri Arbachakov	Muangchai Kittikasem	TKO 9	WBC	Lopburi, Thailand
Jun 21	David Griman	Hiroki Ioka	TKO 8	WBA	Osaka

Junior Flyweight (Light Flyweight)

Date	Winner	Loser	Result	Title	Site
Nov 18	Myung-Woo Yuh	Hiroki Ioka	Dec 12	WBA	Osaka
Dec 7	Humberto Gonzalez	Melchor Cob Castro	Dec 12	WBC	Inglewood, California
Dec 12	Michael Carbajal	Robinson Cuasta	TKO 8	IBF	Phoenix, Arizona
Mar 13	Michael Carbajal	Humberto Gonzalez	KO 7	IBF, WBC	Las Vegas
July 17	Michael Carbajal	Kwang-Sun Kim	KO 7	IBF, WBC	Las Vegas

Strawweight (mini flyweight)

Date	Winner	Loser	Result	Title	Site
Oct 11	Ricardo Lopez	Rocky Lim	KO 2	WBC	Tokyo
Oct 14	Hideyuki Ohashi	Choi Hi-Yong	Dec 12	WBA	Tokyo
Dec 10	Ratanapal Sow Voraphin	Manny Melchor	Split 12	IBF	Bangkok
Feb 10	Chana Porpaoin	Hideyuki Ohashi	Dec 12	WBA	Tokyo
Sep 19	Ricardo Lopez	Toto Por Pongsawang	TKO 11	WBC	Bangkok
Sep 26	Ratanapal Sow Voraphin	Dominggus Siwalete	TKO 4	IBF	Bangkok

World Champions

Sanctioning bodies include the National Boxing Association (NBA), the New York State Athletic Commission (NY), the World Boxing Association (WBA), the World Boxing Council (WBC), and the International Boxing Federation (IBF).

Heavyweights
(Weight: Unlimited)

Champion	Reign
John L. Sullivan	1885-92
James J. Corbett	1892-97
Bob Fitzsimmons	1897-99
James J. Jeffries	1899-1905†
Marvin Hart	1905-06
Tommy Burns	1906-08
Jack Johnson	1908-15
Jess Willard	1915-19
Jack Dempsey	1919-26
Gene Tunney	1926-28
Max Schmeling	1930-32
Jack Sharkey	1932-33
Primo Carnera	1933-34
Max Baer	1934-35
James J. Braddock	1935-37
Joe Louis	1937-49†
Ezzard Charles	1949-51
Jersey Joe Walcott	1951-52
Rocky Marciano	1952-56†

Champion	Reign
Floyd Patterson	1956-59
Ingemar Johansson	1959-60
Floyd Patterson	1960-62
Sonny Liston	1962-64
Muhammad Ali (Cassius Clay)	1964-70
Ernie Terrell* WBA	1965-67
Joe Frazier* NY	1968-70
Jimmy Ellis* WBA	1968-70
Joe Frazier	1970-73
George Foreman	1973-74
Muhammad Ali	1974-78
Leon Spinks	1978
Ken Norton* WBC	1978
Larry Holmes* WBC	1978-80
Muhammad Ali	1978-79†
John Tate* WBA	1979-80
Mike Weaver* WBA	1980-82
Larry Holmes	1980-85

Champion	Reign
Michael Dokes* WBA	1982-83
Gerrie Coetzee* WBA	1983-84
Tim Witherspoon* WBC	1984
Pinklon Thomas* WBC	1984-86
Greg Page* WBA	1984-85
Michael Spinks	1985-87
Tim Witherspoon* WBA	1986
Trevor Berbick* WBC	1986
Mike Tyson* WBC	1986-87
James Bonecrusher Smith* WBA	1986-87
Tony Tucker* IBF	1987
Mike Tyson	1987-90
Buster Douglas	1990
Evander Holyfield	1990-92
Lennox Lewis* WBC	1993-
Riddick Bowe	1992-

*Champion not generally recognized.
†Champion retired or relinquished title.

Cruiserweights
(Weight Limit: 190 pounds)

Champion	Reign
Marvin Camel* WBC	1980
Carlos De Leon* WBC	1980-82
Ossie Ocasio* WBA	1982-84
S.T. Gordon* WBC	1982-83
Carlos De Leon* WBC	1983-85
Marvin Camel* IBF	1983-84
Lee Roy Murphy* IBF	1984-86
Piet Crous* WBA	1984-85
Alfonso Ratliff* WBC	1985
Dwight Braxton* WBA	1985-86
Bernard Benton* WBC	1985-86

Champion	Reign
Carlos De Leon* WBC	1986-88
Evander Holyfield * WBA	1986-88
Ricky Parkey* IBF	1986-87
Evander Holyfield * WBA/IBF	1987-88
Evander Holyfield WBA/IBF/WBC	1988†
Toufik Belbouli* WBA	1989
Robert Daniels* WBA	1989-91
Carlos De Leon* WBC	1989-90

Champion	Reign
Glenn McCrory* IBF	1989-90
Jeff Lampkin* IBF	1990
Massimiliano Duran* WBC	1990-91
Bobby Czyz* WBA	1991-
Anaclet Wamba* WBC	1991-
James Pritchard* IBF	1991
James Warring* IBF	1991-92
Alfred Cole* IBF	1992-

*Champion not generally recognized.
†Champion retired or relinquished title.
Note: Division called Junior Heavyweights by the WBA.

Light Heavyweights
(Weight Limit: 175 pounds)

Champion	Reign
Jack Root	1903
George Gardner	1903
Bob Fitzsimmons	1903-05
Philadelphia Jack O'Brien	1905-12†
Jack Dillon	1914-16
Battling Levinsky	1916-20
Georges Carpentier	1920-22
Battling Siki	1922-23
Mike McTigue	1923-25
Paul Berlenbach	1925-26
Jack Delaney	1926-27†
Jimmy Slattery* NBA	1927

Champion	Reign
Tommy Loughran	1927-29
Maxie Rosenbloom	1930-34
George Nichols* NBA	1932
Bob Godwin* NBA	1933
Bob Olin	1934-35
John Henry Lewis	1935-38
Melio Bettina	1939
Billy Conn	1939-40†
Anton Christoforidis	1941
Gus Lesnevich	1941-48
Freddie Mills	1948-50
Joey Maxim	1950-52
Archie Moore	1952-62†

Champion	Reign
Harold Johnson* NBA	1961
Harold Johnson	1962-63
Willie Pastrano	1963-65
Jose Torres	1965-66
Dick Tiger	1966-68
Bob Foster	1968-74†
Vicente Rondon* WBA	1971-72
John Conteh* WBC	1974-77
Victor Galindez* WBA	1974-78
Miguel A. Cuello* WBC	1977-78
Mate Parlov* WBC	1978
Mike Rossman* WBA	1978-79
Marvin Johnson* WBC	1978-79

Light Heavyweights (Cont.)

Champion	Reign
Matthew Saad Muhammad* WBC	1979-81
Marvin Johnson* WBA	1979-80
Eddie Mustapha Muhammad* WBA	1980-81
Michael Spinks* WBA	1981-83
Dwight Muhammad Qawi* WBC	1981-83
Michael Spinks	1983-85†
J. B. Williamson* WBC	1985-86

Champion	Reign
Slobodan Kacar* IBF	1985-86
Marvin Johnson* WBA	1986-87
Dennis Andries* WBC	1986-87
Bobby Czyz* IBF	1986-87
Leslie Stewart* WBA	1987
Virgil Hill* WBA	1987
Prince Charles Williams* IBF	1987-
Thomas Hearns* WBC	1987†
Donny Lalonde* WBC	1987-88

Champion	Reign
Sugar Ray Leonard* WBC	1988
Dennis Andries* WBC	1989
Jeff Harding* WBC	1989-90
Dennis Andries* WBC	1990-91
Thomas Hearns* WBA	1991-92
Jeff Harding* WBC	1991-
Iran Barkley* WBA	1992
Henry Maske* IBF	1993-
Virgil Hill* WBA	1992-

*Champion not generally recognized.
†Champion retired or relinquished title.

Super Middleweights
(Weight Limit: 168 pounds)

Champion	Reign
Murray Sutherland* IBF	1984
Chong-Pal Park* IBF	1984-87
Chong-Pal Park* WBA	1987-88
Graciano Rocchigiani* IBF	1988-89
Fulgencio Obelmejias* WBA	1988-89

Champion	Reign
Sugar Ray Leonard* WBC	1988-90†
In-Chul Baek* WBA	1989-90
Lindell Holmes* IBF	1990-91
Christopher Tiozzo* WBA	1990-91

Champion	Reign
Mauro Galvano* WBC	1990-
Victor Cordova* WBA	1991
Darrin Van Horn* IBF	1991-92
Iran Barkley *WBA	1992-
Nigel Benn* WBC	1992-
James Toney* IBF	1992-
Michael Nunn* WBA	1992-

*Champion not generally recognized.
†Champion retired or relinquished title.

Middleweights
(Weight Limit: 160 pounds)

Champion	Reign
Jack Dempsey	1884-91
Bob Fitzsimmons	1891-97
Kid McCoy	1897-98
Tommy Ryan	1898-1907
Stanley Ketchel	1908
Billy Papke	1908
Stanley Ketchel	1908-10
Frank Klaus	1913
George Chip	1913-14
Al McCoy	1914-17
Mike O'Dowd	1917-20
Johnny Wilson	1920-23
Harry Greb	1923-26
Tiger Flowers	1926
Mickey Walker	1926-31†
Gorilla Jones	1931-32
Marcel Thil	1932-37
Fred Apostoli	1937-39
Al Hostak* NBA	1938
Solly Krieger* NBA	1938-39
Al Hostak* NBA	1939-40
Ceferino Garcia	1939-40
Ken Overlin	1940-41
Tony Zale* NBA	1940-41

Champion	Reign
Billy Soose	1941
Tony Zale	1941-47
Rocky Graziano	1947-48
Tony Zale	1948
Marcel Cerdan	1948-49
Jake La Motta	1949-51
Sugar Ray Robinson	1951
Randy Turpin	1951
Sugar Ray Robinson	1951-52
Bobo Olson	1953-55
Sugar Ray Robinson	1955-57
Gene Fullmer	1957
Sugar Ray Robinson	1957
Carmen Basilio	1957-58
Sugar Ray Robinson	1958-60
Gene Fullmer* NBA	1959-62
Paul Pender	1960-61
Terry Downes	1961-62
Paul Pender	1962-63
Dick Tiger* WBA	1962-63
Dick Tiger	1963
Joey Giardello	1963-65
Dick Tiger	1965-66
Emile Griffith	1966-67

Champion	Reign
Nino Benvenuti	1967
Emile Griffith	1967-68
Nino Benvenuti	1968-70
Carlos Monzon	1970-77†
Rodrigo Valdez* WBC	1974-76
Rodrigo Valdez	1977-78
Hugo Corro	1978-79
Vito Antuofermo	1979-80
Alan Minter	1980
Marvin Hagler	1980-87
Sugar Ray Leonard	1987
Frank Tate* IBF	1987-88
Sumbu Kalambay* WBA	1987-89
Thomas Hearns* WBC	1987-88
Iran Barkley* WBC	1988-89
Michael Nunn* IBF	1988-91
Roberto Duran* WBC	1989-90
Mike McCallum* WBA	1989-91
Julian Jackson* WBC	1990-
James Toney* IBF	1991-
Reggie Johnson* WBA	1992-
Roy Jones* IBF	1993-
Gerald McClellan* WBC	1993-

*Champion not generally recognized.
†Champion retired or relinquished title.

Junior Middleweights
(Weight Limit: 154 pounds)

Champion	Reign	Champion	Reign	Champion	Reign
Emile Griffith (EBU)	1962-63	Eckhard Dagge* WBC	1976-77	Buster Drayton* IBF	1986-87
Dennis Moyer	1962-63	Miguel Angel Castellini	1976-77	Duane Thomas* WBC	1986-87
Ralph Dupas	1963	Eddie Gazo	1977-78	Matthew Hilton* IBF	1987-88
Sandro Mazzinghi	1963-65	Rocky Mattioli* WBC	1977-79	Lupe Aquino* WBC	1987
Nino Benvenuti	1965-66	Masashi Kudo	1978-79	Gianfranco Rosi* WBC	1987-88
Ki-Soo Kim	1966-68	Maurice Hope* WBC	1979-81	Julian Jackson* WBA	1987-90
Sandro Mazzinghi	1968	Ayub Kalule	1979-81	Donald Curry* WBC	1988-89
Freddie Little	1969-70	Wilfred Benitez* WBC	1981-82	Robert Hines* IBF	1988-89
Carmelo Bossi	1970-71	Sugar Ray Leonard	1981-82	Darrin Van Horn* IBF	1989
Koichi Wajima	1971-74	Tadashi Mihara* WBA	1981-82	Rene Jacquot* WBC	1989
Oscar Albarado	1974-75	Davey Moore* WBA	1982-83	John Mugabi* WBC	1989-90
Koichi Wajima	1975	Thomas Hearns* WBC	1982-84	Gianfranco Rosi* IBF	1989-
Miguel de Oliveira* WBC	1975-76	Roberto Duran* WBA	1983-84	Terry Norris* WBC	1990-
Jae-Do Yuh	1975-76	Mark Medal* IBF	1984	Gilbert Dele* WBA	1991
Elisha Obed* WBC	1975-76	Thomas Hearns	1984-86	Vinny Pazienza* WBA	1991-
Koichi Wajima	1976	Mike McCallum* WBA	1984-87	Julio C. Vasquez* WBA	1992-
Jose Duran	1976	Carlos Santos* IBF	1984-86		

*Champion not generally recognized.
Note: ●Division called Super Welterweight by the WBC.

Welterweights
(Weight Limit: 147 pounds)

Champion	Reign	Champion	Reign	Champion	Reign
Paddy Duffy	1888-90	Jackie Fields	1932-33	Hedgemon Lewis* NY	1972-73
Mysterious Billy Smith	1892-94	Young Corbett III	1933	Angel Espada* WBA	1975-76
Tommy Ryan	1894-98	Jimmy McLarnin	1933-34	John H. Stracey*	1975-76
Mysterious Billy Smith	1898-1900	Barney Ross	1934	Carlos Palomino	1976-79
Rube Ferns	1900	Jimmy McLarnin	1934-35	Pipino Cuevas* WBA	1976-80
Matty Matthews	1900-01	Barney Ross	1935-38	Wilfredo Benitez	1979
Rube Ferns	1901	Henry Armstrong	1938-40	Sugar Ray Leonard	1979-80
Joe Walcott	1901-04	Fritzie Zivic	1940-41	Roberto Duran	1980
The Dixie Kid	1904-05	Red Cochrane	1941-46	Thomas Hearns* WBA	1980-81
Honey Mellody	1906-07	Marty Servo	1946	Sugar Ray Leonard	1980-82
Twin Sullivan	1907-08	Sugar Ray Robinson	1946-51†	Donald Curry* WBA	1983-85
Jimmy Gardner	1908	Johnny Bratton	1951	Milton McCrory* WBC	1983-85
Jimmy Clabby	1910-11	Kid Gavilan	1951-54	Donald Curry	1985-86
Waldemar Holberg	1914	Johnny Saxton	1954-55	Lloyd Honeyghan	1986-87
Tom McCormick	1914	Tony DeMarco	1955	Jorge Vaca WBC	1987-88
Matt Wells	1914-15	Carmen Basilio	1955-56	Lloyd Honeyghan WBC	1988-89
Mike Glover	1915	Johnny Saxton	1956	Mark Breland* WBA	1987
Jack Britton	1915	Carmen Basilio	1956-57	Marlon Starling* WBA	1987-88
Ted "Kid" Lewis	1915-16	Virgil Akins	1958	Tomas Molinares* WBA	1988-89
Jack Britton	1916-17	Don Jordan	1958-60	Simon Brown* IBF	1988-91
Ted "Kid" Lewis	1917-19	Kid Paret	1960-61	Mark Breland* WBA	1989-90
Jack Britton	1919-22	Emile Griffith	1961	Marlon Starling* WBC	1989-90
Mickey Walker	1922-26	Kid Paret	1961-62	Aaron Davis* WBA	1990-91
Pete Latzo	1926-27	Emile Griffith	1962-63	Maurice Blocker* WBC	1990-91
Joe Dundee	1927-29	Luis Rodriguez	1963	Meldrick Taylor* WBA	1991-1992
Jackie Fields	1929-30	Emile Griffith	1963-66	Simon Brown* WBC	1991
Young Jack Thompson	1930	Curtis Cokes	1966-69	Buddy McGirt* WBC	1991-1993
Tommy Freeman	1930-31	Jose Napoles	1969-70	Felix Trinidad* IBF	1992-
Young Jack Thompson	1931	Billy Backus	1970-71	Pernell Whitaker WBC	1993-
Lou Brouillard	1931-32	Jose Napoles	1971-75	Crisanto Espana* WBA	1992-

*Champion not generally recognized.
†Champion retired or relinquished title.

World Champions (Cont.)

Junior Welterweight
(Weight Limit: 140 pounds)

Champion	Reign
Pinkey Mitchell	1922-25
Red Herring	1925
Mushy Callahan	1926-30
Jack (Kid) Berg	1930-31
Tony Canzoneri	1931-32
Johnny Jadick	1932-33
Sammy Fuller*	1932-33
Battling Shaw	1933
Tony Canzoneri	1933
Barney Ross	1933-35
Tippy Larkin	1946
Carlos Ortiz	1959-60
Duilio Loi	1960-62
Eddie Perkins	1962
Duilio Loi	1962-63
Roberto Cruz* WBA	1963
Eddie Perkins	1963-65
Carlos Hernandez	1965-66
Sandro Lopopolo	1966-67
Paul Fujii	1967-68
Nicolino Loche	1968-72
Pedro Adigue* WBC	1968-70
Bruno Arcari* WBC	1970-74
Alfonso Frazer	1972

Champion	Reign
Antonio Cervantes	1972-76
Perico Fernandez* WBC	1974-75
Saensak Muangsurin* WBC	1975-76
Wilfred Benitez	1976-79
Miguel Velasquez* WBC	1976
Saensak Muangsurin* WBC	1976-78
Antonio Cervantes* WBA	1977-80
Sang-Hyun Kim* WBC	1978-80
Saoul Mamby* WBC	1980-82
Aaron Pryor* WBA	1980-83
Leroy Haley* WBC	1982-83
Aaron Pryor* IBF	1983-85
Bruce Curry* WBC	1983-84
Johnny Bumphus* WBA	1984
Bill Costello* WBC	1984-
Gene Hatcher* WBA	1984-85
Ubaldo Sacco* WBA	1985-86
Lonnie Smith* WBC	1985-86
Patrizio Oliva* WBA	1986-87

Champion	Reign
Gary Hinton* IBF	1986
Rene Arredondo* WBC	1986
Tsuyoshi Hamada* WBC	1986-87
Joe Louis Manley* IBF	1986-87
Terry Marsh* IBF	1987
Juan Martin Coggi* WBA	1987-90
Rene Arredondo* WBC	1987
Roger Mayweather* WBC	1987-89
James McGirt* IBF	1988
Meldrick Taylor* IBF	1988-90
Julio Cesar Chavez* WBC	1989-
Julio Cesar Chavez* IBF	1990-91
Loreto Garza* WBA	1990-91
Juan Coggi* WBA	1991
Edwin Rosario* WBA	1991-92
Rafael Pineda* IBF	1991-92
Akinobu Hiranaka* WBA	1992-
Pernell Whitaker*† IBF	1992-93
Charles Murray* IBF	1993-

*Champion not generally recognized. †Champion retired or relinquished title. Note: Division called Super Lightweight by the WBC.

Lightweights
(Weight Limit: 135 pounds)

Champion	Reign
Jack McAuliffe	1886-94
Kid Lavigne	1896-99
Frank Erne	1899-1902
Joe Gans	1902-04
Jimmy Britt	1904-05
Battling Nelson	1905-06
Joe Gans	1906-08
Battling Nelson	1908-10
Ad Wolgast	1910-12
Willie Ritchie	1912-14
Freddie Welsh	1915-17
Benny Leonard	1917-25†
Jimmy Goodrich	1925
Rocky Kansas	1925-26
Sammy Mandell	1926-30
Al Singer	1930
Tony Canzoneri	1930-33
Barney Ross	1933-35†
Tony Canzoneri	1935-36
Lou Ambers	1936-38
Henry Armstrong	1938-39
Lou Ambers	1939-40
Sammy Angott* NBA	1940-41
Lew Jenkins	1940-41
Sammy Angott	1941-42†
Beau Jack* NY	1942-43
Bob Montgomery* NY	1943
Sammy Angott* NBA	1943-44
Beau Jack* NY	1943-44
Bob Montgomery* NY	1944-47
Juan Zurita* NBA	1944-45
Ike Williams	1947-51
James Carter	1951-52

Champion	Reign
Lauro Salas	1952
James Carter	1952-54
Paddy DeMarco	1954
James Carter	1954-55
Wallace Smith	1955-56
Joe Brown	1956-62
Carlos Ortiz	1962-65
Ismael Laguna	1965
Carlos Ortiz	1965-68
Carlos Teo Cruz	1968-69
Mando Ramos	1969-70
Ismael Laguna	1970
Ken Buchanan	1970-72
Roberto Duran	1972-79†
Chango Carmona* WBC	1972
Rodolfo Gonzalez* WBC	1972-74
Ishimatsu Suzuki* WBC	1974-76
Esteban DeJesus* WBC	1976-78
Jim Watt* WBC	1979-81
Ernesto Espana* WBA	1979-80
Hilmer Kenty* WBA	1980-81
Sean O'Grady* WBA	1981
Claude Noel* WBA	1981
Alexis Arguello* WBC	1981-82
Arturo Frias* WBA	1981-82
Ray Mancini* WBA	1982-84
Alexis Arguello	1982-83
Edwin Rosario* WBC	1983-84
Choo Choo Brown* IBF	1984

Champion	Reign
Livingstone Bramble* WBA	1984-86
Jose Luis Ramirez* WBC	1984-85
Harry Arroyo* IBF	1984-85
Jimmy Paul* IBF	1985-86
Hector Camacho* WBC	1985-86
Greg Haugen* IBF	1986-87
Edwin Rosario* WBA	1986-87
Julio César Chavez* WBA	1987-88
Jose Luis Ramirez* WBC	1987-88
Julio César Chavez	1988-89
Vinny Pazienza* IBF	1987-88
Greg Haugen* IBF	1988-89
Pernell Whitaker* WBC, IBF	1989-90
Edwin Rosario* WBA	1989-90, 1991-92
Juan Nazario* WBA	1990
Pernell Whitaker* WBA, WBC	1990-92
Pernell Whitaker* IBF	1991-92
Julio César Chavez* IBF	1990-92
Julio César Chavez* WBC	1990-92
Miguel Gonzalez* WBC	1992-
Joey Gamache* WBA	1992-93
Dingaan Thobela* WBA	1993-
Fred Pendleton* IBF	1993-

*Champion not generally recognized. †Champion retired or relinquished title.

Junior Lightweights
(Weight Limit: 130 pounds)

Champion	Reign
Johnny Dundee	1921-23
Jack Bernstein	1923
Johnny Dundee	1923-24
Steve (Kid) Sullivan	1924-25
Mike Ballerino	1925
Tod Morgan	1925-29
Benny Bass	1929-31
Kid Chocolate	1931-33
Frankie Klick	1933-34
Sandy Saddler	1949-50
Harold Gomes	1959-60
Gabriel (Flash) Elorde	1960-67
Yoshiaki Numata	1967
Hiroshi Kobayashi	1967-71
Rene Barrientos* WBC	1969-70
Yoshiaki Numata* WBC	1970-71
Alfredo Marcano	1971-72
Richardo Arredondo* WBC	1971-74

Champion	Reign
Ben Villaflor	1972-73
Kuniaki Shibata	1973
Ben Villaflor	1973-76
Kuniaki Shibata* WBC	1974-75
Alfredo Escalera* WBC	1975-78
Samuel Serrano	1976-80
Alexis Arguello* WBC	1978-80
Yasutsune Uehara	1980-81
Rafael (Bazooka) Limon* WBC	1980-81
Cornelius Boza-Edwards* WBC	1981
Samuel Serrano	1981-83
Rolando Navarrete* WBC	1981-82
Rafael (Bazooka) Limon* WBC	1982
Bobby Chacon* WBC	1982-83
Roger Mayweather	1983-84

Champion	Reign
Hector Camacho* WBC	1983-84
Rocky Lockridge	1984-85
Hwan-Kil Yuh* IBF	1984-85
Julio Cesar Chavez* WBC	1984-87
Lester Ellis* IBF	1985-
Wilfredo Gomez	1985-86
Barry Michael* IBF	1985-87
Alfredo Layne* WBA	1986
Brian Mitchell* WBA	1986-91
Rocky Lockridge* IBF	1987-88
Azumah Nelson* WBC	1988-
Tony Lopez* IBF	1988-89
Juan Molina* IBF	1989-90
Tony Lopez* IBF	1990-91
Joey Gamache, WBA	1991
Brian Mitchell* IBF	1991
Genaro Hernandez* WBA	1991-

*Champion not generally recognized.
Note: Division called Super Featherweight by the WBC.

Featherweights
(Weight Limit: 126 pounds)

Champion	Reign
Torpedo Billy Murphy	1890
Young Griffo	1890-92
George Dixon	1892-97
Solly Smith	1897-98
Dave Sullivan	1898
George Dixon	1898-1900
Terry McGovern	1900-01
Young Corbett II	1901-04
Jimmy Britt	1904
Brooklyn Tommy Sullivan	1904-05
Abe Attell	1906-12
Johnny Kilbane	1912-23
Eugene Criqui	1923
Johnny Dundee	1923-24
Kid, Kaplan	1925-26
Benny Bass	1927-28
Tony Canzoneri	1928
Andre Routis	1928-29
Battling Battalino	1929-32
Tommy Paul* NBA	1932-33
Kid Chocolate* NY	1932-33
Freddie Miller* NBA	1933-36
Mike Beloise* NY	1936-37
Petey Sarron* NBA	1936-37
Maurice Holtzer	1937-38
Henry Armstrong	1937-38
Joey Archibald* NY	1938-39
Leo Rodak* NBA	1938-39
Joey Archibald	1939-40
Petey Scalzo* NBA	1940-41

Champion	Reign
Harry Jeffra	1940-41
Joey Archibald	1941
Richie Lamos* NBA	1941
Chalky Wright	1941-42
Jackie Wilson* NBA	1941-43
Willie Pep	1942-48
Jackie Callura* NBA	1943
Phil Terranova* NBA	1943-44
Sal Bartolo* NBA	1944-46
Sandy Saddler	1948-49
Willie Pep	1949-50
Sandy Saddler	1950-57†
Kid Bassey	1957-59
Davey Moore	1959-63
Sugar Ramos	1963-64
Vicente Saldivar	1964-67†
Paul Rojas* WBA	1968
Jose Legra* WBC	1968-69
Shozo Saijyo* WBA	1968-71
Johnny Famechon* WBC	1969-70
Vicente Saldivar WBC	1970
Kuniaki Shibata WBC	1970-72
Antonio Gomez* WBA	1971-72
Clemente Sanchez WBC	1972
Ernesto Marcel* WBA	1972-74
Jose Legra WBC	1972-73
Eder Jofre WBC	1973-74
Ruben Olivares* WBA	1974
Bobby Chacon* WBC	1974-75

Champion	Reign
Alexis Arguello WBA	1974-76
Ruben Olivares* WBC	1975
Poison Kotey* WBC	1975-76
Danny Lopez WBC	1976-80
Rafael Ortega* WBA	1977
Cecilio Lastra* WBA	1977-78
Eusebio Pedroza* WBA	1978-85
Salvador Sanchez WBC	1980-82
Juan LaPorte* WBC	1982-84
Wilfredo Gomez* WBC	1984
Min-Keun Oh* IBF	1984-85
Azumah Nelson* WBC	1984-88
Barry McGuigan* WBA	1985-86
Ki Young Chung* IBF	1985-86
Steve Cruz* WBA	1986-87
Antonio Rivera* IBF	1986-88
Antonio Esparragoza* WBA	1987-91
Calvin Grove* IBF	1988
Jorge Paez* IBF	1988-91
Jeff Fenech* WBC	1988-90†
Marcos Villasana* WBC	1990-91
Paul Hodkinson* WBC	1991-
Troy Dorsey* IBF	1991
Manuel Medina* IBF	1991-
Yung Kyun Park* WBA	1991-
Gregorio Vargas* WBC	1993-
Tom Johnson* IBF	1993-

*Champion not generally recognized.
†Champion retired or relinquished title.

Junior Featherweights
(Weight Limit: 122 pounds)

Champion	Reign	Champion	Reign	Champion	Reign
Jack (Kid) Wolfe*	1922-23	Seung-Il Suh* IBF	1984-85	Juan Jose	
Carl Duane*	1923-24	Victor Callejas* WBA	1984-86	Estrada* WBA	1988-89
Rigoberto Riasco* WBC	1976	Juan (Kid) Meza* WBC	1984-85	Fabrice Benichou* IBF	1989-90
Royal		Ji-Won Kim* IBF	1985-86	Jesus Salud* WBA	1989-90
Kobayashi* WBC	1976	Lupe Pintor* WBC	1985-86	Welcome Ncita* IBF	1990-
Dong-Kyun Yum* WBC	1976-77	Samart		Paul Banke* WBC	1990
Wilfredo Gomez* WBC	1977-83	Payakaroon* WBC	1986-87	Luis Mendoza* WBA	1990-91
Soo-Hwan Hong* WBA	1977-78	Seung-Hoon Lee* WBC	1987-88	Rual Perez* WBA	1992-
Ricardo Cardona* WBA	1978-80	Louie Espinoza* WBA	1987	Pedro Decima* WBC	1990-91
Leo Randolph* WBA	1980	Jeff Fenech* WBC	1987	Kiyoshi	
Sergio Palma* WBA	1980-82	Julio Gervacio* WBA	1987-88	Hatanaka* WBC	1991
Leonardo Cruz* WBA	1982-84	Daniel Zaragoza* WBC	1988-90	Daniel Zaragoza* WBC	1991-92
Jaime Garza* WBC	1983	Jose Sanabria* IBF	1988-89	Tracy Patterson* WBC	1992-
Bobby Berna* IBF	1983-84	Bernardo		Kennedy McKinney* IBF	1993-
Loris Stecca* WBA	1984	Pinango* WBA	1988	Wilfredo Vasquez *WBA	1992-

*Champion not generally recognized.
Note: Division called Super Bantamweight by the WBC.

Bantamweights
(Weight Limit: 118 pounds)

Champion	Reign	Champion	Reign	Champion	Reign
Spider Kelly	1887	Sixto Escobar* NBA	1935-36	Lupe Pintor* WBC	1979-83
Hughey Boyle	1887-88	Tony Marino	1936	Julian Solis	1980
Spider Kelly	1889	Sixto Escobar	1936-37	Jeff Chandler	1980-84
Chappie Moran	1889-90	Harry Jeffra	1937-38†	Albert Davila* WBC	1983-85
George Dixon	1890-91	Sixto Escobar	1938-39	Richard Sandoval	1984-86
Pedlar Palmer*	1895-99	Georgie Pace NBA	1939-40	Satoshi Shingaki* IBF	1984-85
Terry McGovern	1899-1900	Lou Salica	1940-42	Jeff Fenech* IBF	1985
Harry Harris	1901-2	Manuel Ortiz	1942-47	Daniel Zaragoza* WBC	1985
Harry Forbes	1902-3	Harold Dade	1947	Miguel Lora* WBC	1985-88
Frankie Neil	1903-4	Manuel Ortiz	1947-50	Gaby Canizales	1986
Joe Bowker	1904-5	Vic Toweel	1950-52	Bernardo Pinango	1986-87
Jimmy Walsh	1905-6	Jimmy Carruthers	1952-54†	Wilfredo	
Owen Moran	1907-8	Robert Cohen	1954-56	Vasquez* WBA	1987-88
Monte Attell*	1909-10	Paul Macias* NBA	1955-57	Kevin Seabrooks* IBF	1987-88
Frankie Conley	1910-11	Mario D'Agata	1956-57	Kaokor Galaxy* WBA	1988
Johnny Coulon	1911-14	Alphonse Halimi	1957-59	Moon Sung-Kil* WBA	1988-89
Kid Williams	1914-17	Joe Becerra	1959-60†	Kaokor Galaxy* WBA	1989
Kewpie Ertle*	1915	Eder Jofre	1961-65	Raul Perez* WBC	1988-91
Pete Herman	1917-20	Fighting Harada	1965-68	Orlando	
Joe Lynch	1920-21	Lionel Rose	1968-69	Canizales* IBF	1988-
Pete Herman	1921	Ruben Olivares	1969-70	Luisito Espinosa* WBA	1989-91
Johnny Buff	1921-22	Chucho Castillo	1970-71	Israel Contreras* WBA	1991-92
Joe Lynch	1922-24	Ruben Olivares	1971-72	Eddie Cook* WBA	1992-
Abe Goldstein	1924	Rafael Herrera	1972	Greg	
Cannonball Martin	1924-25	Enrique Pinder	1972-73	Richardson* WBC	1991
Phil Rosenberg	1925-27	Romeo Anaya	1973	Joichiro	
Bud Taylor NBA	1927-28	Rafael Herrera* WBC	1973-74	Tatsuyoshi, WBC	1991-92
Bushy Graham* NY	1928-29	Soo-Hwan Hong	1974-75	Victor Rabanales* WBC	1992-1993
Panama Al Brown	1929-35	Rodolfo Martinez* WBC	1974-76	Jung-Il Byun* WBC	1993-
Sixto Escobar* NBA	1934-35	Alfonso Zamora	1975-77	Jorge Julio, WBA	1993-
Baltazar Sangchilli	1935-36	Carlos Zarate* WBC	1976-79		
Lou Salica* NBA	1935	Jorge Lujan	1977-80		

*Champion not generally recognized. †Champion retired or relinquished title.

Junior Bantamweights
(Weight Limit: 115 pounds)

Champion	Reign	Champion	Reign	Champion	Reign
Rafael Orono* WBC	1980-81	Kaosai Galaxy* WBA	1984	Giberto Roman* WBC	1988-89
Chul-Ho Kim* WBC	1981-82	Ellyas Pical* IBF	1985-86	Juan Polo Perez* IBF	1989-90
Gustavo Ballas* WBA	1981	Cesar Polanco* IBF	1986	Nana Konadu* WBC	1989-90
Rafael Pedroza* WBA	1981-82	Gilberto Roman* WBC	1986-87	Sung-Kil Moon* WBC	1990-
Rafael Orono* WBC	1982-83	Ellyas Pical* IBF	1986	Robert Quiroga* IBF	1990-1993
Payao Poontarat* WBC	1983-84	Santos Laciar* WBC	1987	Julio Borboa* IBF	1993-
Joo-Do Chun* IBF	1983-85	Tae-Il Chang* IBF	1987	Katsuya Onizuka* WBA	1993-
Jiro Watanabe* WBA	1982-84	Sugar Rojas* WBC	1987-88		
Jiro Watanabe	1984-86	Ellyas Pical* IBF	1987-89		

*Champion not generally recognized. Note: Division called Super Flyweight by the WBC.

Flyweights
(Weight Limit: 112 pounds)

Champion	Reign	Champion	Reign	Champion	Reign
Sid Smith	1913	Hiroyuki Ebihara* WBA	1969	Cardona* WBC	1982
Bill Ladbury	1913-14	Bernabe Villacampo* WBA	1969-70	Santos Laciar* WBA	1982-85
Percy Jones	1914	Chartchai Chionoi	1970	Freddie Castillo* WBC	1982
Joe Symonds	1914-16	Berkrerk Chartvanchai* WBA	1970	Eleoncio Mercedes* WBC	1982-83
Jimmy Wilde	1916-23	Masao Ohba* WBA	1970-73	Charlie Magri* WBC	1983
Pancho Villa	1923-25	Erbito Salavarria	1970-73	Frank Cedeno* WBC	1983-84
Fidel LaBarba	1925-27†	Betulio Gonzalez* WBA	1972	Soon-Chun Kwon* IBF	1983-85
Frenchy Belanger NBA	1927-28	Venice Borkorsor* WBC	1972-73	Koji Kobayashi* WBC	1984
Corporal Izzy Schwartz NY	1927-29	Venice Borkorsor	1973	Gabriel Bernal* WBC	1984
Frankie Genaro NBA	1928-29	Chartchai Chionoi* WBA	1973-74	Sot Chitalada* WBC	1984-88
Spider Pladner NBA	1929	Betulio Gonzalez* WBA	1973-74	Hilario Zapate* WBA	1985-87
Frankie Genaro NBA	1929-31	Shoji Oguma* WBC	1974-75	Chong-Kwan Chung* IBF	1985-86
Midget Wolgast* NY	1930-35	Susumu Hanagata* WBA	1974-75	Bi-Won Chung* IBF	1986
Young Perez NBA	1931-32	Miguel Canto* WBC	1975-79	Hi-Sup Shin* IBF	1986-87
Jackie Brown NBA	1932-35	Erbito Salavarria* WBA	1975-76	Dodie Penalosa* IBF	1987
Benny Lynch	1935-38	Alfonso Lopez* WBA	1976	Fidel Bassa* WBA	1987-89
Small Montana* NY	1935-37	Gustavo Espadas* WBA	1976-78	Choi-Chang Ho* IBF	1987-88
Peter Kane	1938-43	Betulio Gonzalez* WBA	1978-79	Rolando Bohol* IBF	1988
Little Dado* NY	1938-40	Chan-Hee Park* WBC	1979-80	Yong-Kang Kim* WBC	1988-89
Jackie Paterson	1943-48	Luis Ibarra* WBA	1979-80	Duke McKenzie* IBF	1988-89
Rinty Monaghan	1948-50	Tae-Shik Kim* WBA	1980	Sot Chitalada* WBC	1989-91
Terry Allen	1950	Shoji Oguma* WBC	1980-81	Dave McAuley* IBF	1989-92
Dado Marino	1950-52	Peter Mathebula* WBA	1980-81	Jesus Rojas* WBA	1989-90
Yoshio Shirai	1953-54	Santos Laciar* WBA	1981	Yul-Woo Lee* WBA	1990
Pascual Perez	1954-60	Antonio Avelar* WBC	1981-82	Leopard Tamakuma* WBA	1990-91
Pone Kingpetch	1960-62	Luis Ibarra* WBA	1981	Muangchai Kittikasem* WBC	1991-92
Masahiko Harada	1962-63	Juan Herrera* WBA	1981-82	Yuri Arbachakov* WBC	1992-
Pone Kingpetch	1963	Prudencio		Yong Kang Kim* WBA	1991-1992
Hiroyuki Ebihara	1963-64			Rodolfo Blanco* IBF	1992-1993
Pone Kingpetch	1964-65			Pichit Sithbangprachan* IBF	1993-
Salvatore Burrini	1965-66			David Griman* WBA	1992-
Horacio Accavallo* WBA	1966-68				
Walter McGowan	1966				
Chartchai Chionoi	1966-69				
Efren Torres	1969-70				

*Champion not generally recognized.
†Champion retired or relinquished title.

Junior Flyweights
(Weight Limit: 108 pounds)

Champion	Reign	Champion	Reign	Champion	Reign
Franco Udella* WBC	1975	Tadashi Tomori* WBC	1982	Humberto	
Jaime Rios* WBA	1975-76	Hilario Zapata* WBC	1982-83	Gonzalez* WBC	1989-90
Luis Estaba* WBC	1975-78	Jung-Koo Chang* WBC	1983-88	Michael Carbajal* IBF	1990-
Juan Guzman* WBA	1976	Lupe Madera* WBA	1983-84	Rolando	
Yoko Gushiken* WBA	1976-81	Dodie Penalosa* IBF	1983-86	Pascua* WBC	1990
Freddy Castillo* WBC	1978	Francisco Quiroz* WBA	1984-85	Melchor Cob	
Netrnoi Vorasingh* WBC	1978	Joey Olivo* WBA	1985	Castro* WBC	1991
Sung-Jun Kim* WBC	1978-80	Myung-Woo Yuh* WBA	1985-91	Humberto	
Shigeo Nakajima* WBC	1980	Jum-Hwan Choi* IBF	1986-88	Gonzalez* WBC	1991-1993
Hilario Zapata* WBC	1980-82	Tacy Macalos* IBF	1988-89	Hirokia Ioka* WBA	1991-1992
Pedro Flores* WBA	1981	German Torres* WBC	1988-89	Michael Carbajal, WBC	1993-
Hwan-Jin Kim* WBA	1981	Yul-Woo Lee* WBC	1989	Myung-Woo Yuh* WBA	1993-
Katsuo Tokashiki* WBA	1981-83	Muangchai			
Amado Urzua* WBC	1982	Kittikasem* IBF	1989-90		

*Champion not generally recognized. Note: Division called Light Flyweight by the WBC.

Strawweights
(Weight Limit: 105 pounds)

Champion	Reign	Champion	Reign	Champion	Reign
Franco Udella* WBC	1975	Amado Urzua* WBC	1982	Muangchai	
Jaime Rios* WBA	1975-76	Tadashi Tomori* WBC	1982	Kittikasem* IBF	1989-90
Luis Estaba* WBC	1975-78	Hilario Zapata* WBC	1982-83	Humberto	
Juan Guzman* WBA	1976	Jung-Koo Chang* WBC	1983-88	Gonzalez* WBC	1989-90
Yoko Gushiken* WBA	1976-81	Lupe Madera* WBA	1983-84	Michael Carbajal* IBF	1990
Freddy Castillo* WBC	1978	Dodie Penalosa* IBF	1983-86	Rolando	
Netrnoi Vorasingh* WBC	1978	Francisco Quiroz* WBA	1984-85	Pascua* WBC	1990
Sung-Jun Kim* WBC	1978-80	Joey Olivo* WBA	1985	Melchor Cob	
Shigeo Nakajima* WBC	1980	Myung-Woo Yuh* WBA	1985-	Castro* WBC	1991
Hilario Zapata* WBC	1980-82	Jum-Hwan Choi* IBF	1986-88	Ricardo Lopez* WBC	1990-
Pedro Flores* WBA	1981	Tacy Macalos* IBF	1988-89	Ratanapol Voraphin* IBF	1992-
Hwan-Jin Kim* WBA	1981	German Torres* WBC	1988-89	Chana Porpaoin* WBA	1993-
Katsuo Tokashiki* WBA	1981-83	Yul-Woo Lee* WBC	1989		

*Champion not generally recognized.
Note: Division called Light Flyweight by the WBC.

All-Time Career Leaders

Most Total Bouts

Name	Years Active	Bouts
Len Wickwar	1928-47	463
Jack Britton	1905-30	350
Johnny Dundee	1910-32	333
Billy Bird	1920-48	318
George Marsden	1928-46	311
Maxie Rosenbloom	1923-39	299
Harry Greb	1913-26	298
Young Stribling	1921-33	286
Battling Levinsky	1910-29	282
Ted (Kid) Lewis	1909-29	279

Note: Based on records in *The Ring Record Book and Boxing Encyclopedia.*

Most Knockouts

Name	Years Active	KOs
Archie Moore	1936-63	130
Young Stribling	1921-33	126
Billy Bird	1920-48	125
George Odwell	1930-45	114
Sugar Ray Robinson	1940-65	110
Sandy Saddler	1944-56	103
Sam Langford	1902-26	102
Henry Armstrong	1931-45	100
Jimmy Wilde	1911-23	98
Len Wickwar	1928-47	93

Note: Based on records in *The Ring Record Book and Boxing Encyclopedia.*

World Heavyweight Championship Fights

Date	Winner	Wgt	Loser	Wgt	Result	Site
Sep 7, 1892	James J. Corbett*	178	John L. Sullivan	212	KO 21	New Orleans
Jan 25, 1894	James J. Corbett	184	Charley Mitchell	158	KO 3	Jacksonville, FL
Mar 17, 1897	Bob Fitzsimmons*	167	James J. Corbett	183	KO 14	Carson City, NV
June 9, 1899	James J. Jeffries*	206	Bob Fitzsimmons	167	KO 11	Coney Island, NY
Nov 3, 1899	James J. Jeffries	215	Tom Sharkey	183	Ref 25	Coney Island, NY
Apr 6, 1900	James J. Jeffries	n/a	Jack Finnegan	n/a	KO 1	Detroit
May 11, 1900	James J. Jeffries	218	James J. Corbett	188	KO 23	Coney Island, NY
Nov 15, 1901	James J. Jeffries	211	Gus Ruhlin	194	TKO 6	San Francisco
July 25, 1902	James J. Jeffries	219	Bob Fitzsimmons	172	KO 8	San Francisco
Aug 14, 1903	James J. Jeffries	220	James J. Corbett	190	KO 10	San Francisco
Aug 25, 1904	James J. Jeffries	219	Jack Munroe	186	TKO 2	San Francisco
July 3, 1905	Marvin Hart*	190	Jack Root	171	KO 12	Reno
Feb 23, 1906	Tommy Burns*	180	Marvin Hart	188	Ref 20	Los Angeles
Oct 2, 1906	Tommy Burns	n/a	Jim Flynn	n/a	KO 15	Los Angeles
Nov 28, 1906	Tommy Burns	172	Philadelphia Jack O'Brien	163½	Draw 20	Los Angeles
May 8, 1907	Tommy Burns	180	Philadelphia Jack O'Brien	167	Ref 20	Los Angeles
Jul 4, 1907	Tommy Burns	181	Bill Squires	180	KO 1	Colma, CA
Dec 2, 1907	Tommy Burns	177	Gunner Moir	204	KO 10	London
Feb 10, 1908	Tommy Burns	n/a	Jack Palmer	n/a	KO 4	London
Mar 17, 1908	Tommy Burns	n/a	Jem Roche	n/a	KO 1	Dublin
Apr 18, 1908	Tommy Burns	n/a	Jewey Smith	n/a	KO 5	Paris
June 13, 1908	Tommy Burns	184	Bill Squires	183	KO 8	Paris
Aug 24, 1908	Tommy Burns	181	Bill Squires	184	KO 13	Sydney
Sep 2, 1908	Tommy Burns	183	Bill Lang	187	KO 6	Melbourne
Dec 26, 1908	Jack Johnson*	192	Tommy Burns	168	TKO 14	Sydney
Mar 10, 1909	Jack Johnson	n/a	Victor McLaglen	n/a	ND 6	Vancouver
May 19, 1909	Jack Johnson	205	Philadelphia Jack O'Brien	161	ND 6	Philadelphia
June 30, 1909	Jack Johnson	207	Tony Ross	214	ND 6	Pittsburgh
Sep 9, 1909	Jack Johnson	209	Al Kaufman	191	ND 10	San Francisco
Oct 16, 1909	Jack Johnson	205½	Stanley Ketchel	170¼	KO 12	Colma, CA
July 4, 1910	Jack Johnson	208	James J. Jeffries	227	KO 15	Reno
July 4, 1912	Jack Johnson	195½	Jim Flynn	175	TKO 9	Las Vegas
Dec 19, 1913	Jack Johnson	n/a	Jim Johnson	n/a	Draw 10	Paris
June 27, 1914	Jack Johnson	221	Frank Moran	203	Ref 20	Paris
Apr 5, 1915	Jess Willard*	230	Jack Johnson	205½	KO 26	Havana
Mar 25, 1916	Jess Willard	225	Frank Moran	203	ND 10	New York
July 4, 1919	Jack Dempsey*	187	Jess Willard	245	TKO 4	Toledo, OH
Sep 6, 1920	Jack Dempsey	185	Billy Miske	187	KO 3	Benton Harbor, MI
Dec 14, 1920	Jack Dempsey	188¼	Bill Brennan	197	KO 12	New York
July 2, 1921	Jack Dempsey	188	Georges Carpentier	172	KO 4	Jersey City
July 4, 1923	Jack Dempsey	188	Tommy Givvons	175½	Ref 15	Shelby, MT
Sep 14, 1923	Jack Dempsey	192½	Luis Firpo	216½	KO 2	New York
Sep 23, 1926	Gene Tunney*	189½	Jack Dempsey	190	UD 10	Philadelphia
Sep 22, 1927	Gene Tunney	189½	Jack Dempsey	192½	UD 10	Chicago
July 26, 1928	Gene Tunney	192	Tom Heeney	203½	TKO 11	New York
June 12, 1930	Max Schmeling*	188	Jack Sharkey	197	Foul 4	New York
July 3, 1931	Max Schmeling	189	Young Stribling	186½	TKO 15	Cleveland
June 21, 1932	Jack Sharkey*	205	Max Schmeling	188	Split 15	Long Island City
June 29, 1933	Primo Carnera*	260½	Jack Sharkey	201	KO 6	Long Island City
Oct 22, 1933	Primo Carnera	259½	Paulino Uzcudun	229¼	UD 15	Rome
Mar 1, 1934	Primo Carnera	270	Tommy Loughran	184	UD 15	Miami
June 14, 1934	Max Baer*	209½	Primo Carnera	263¼	TKO 11	Long Island City
June 13, 1935	James J. Braddock*	193¾	Max Baer	209½	UD 15	Long Island City
June 22, 1937	Joe Louis	197¼	James J. Braddock	197	KO 8	Chicago
Aug 30, 1937	Joe Louis	197	Tommy Farr	204¼	UD 15	New York
Feb 23, 1938	Joe Louis	200	Nathan Mann	193½	KO 3	New York
Apr 1, 1938	Joe Louis	202½	Harry Thomas	196	KO 5	Chicago
June 22, 1938	Joe Louis	198¼	Max Schmeling	193	KO 1	New York
Jan 25, 1939	Joe Louis	200¼	John Henry Lewis	180¾	KO 1	New York
Apr 17, 1939	Joe Louis	201¼	Jack Roper	204¾	KO 1	Los Angeles
June 28, 1939	Joe Louis	200¾	Tony Galento	233¾	TKO 4	New York
Sep 20, 1939	Joe Louis	200	Bob Pastor	183	KO 11	Detroit
Feb 9, 1940	Joe Louis	203	Arturo Godoy	202	Split 15	New York
Mar 29, 1940	Joe Louis	201½	Johnny Paychek	187½	KO 2	New York
June 20, 1940	Joe Louis	199	Arturo Godoy	201¼	TKO 8	New York

World Heavyweight Championship Fights *(Cont.)*

Date	Winner	Wgt	Loser	Wgt	Result	Site
Dec 16, 1940	Joe Louis	202¼	Al McCoy	180¾	TKO 6	Boston
Jan 31, 1941	Joe Louis	202½	Red Burman	188	KO 5	New York
Feb 17, 1941	Joe Louis	203½	Gus Dorazio	193½	KO 2	Philadelphia
Mar 21, 1941	Joe Louis	202	Abe Simon	254½	TKO 13	Detroit
Apr 8, 1941	Joe Louis	203½	Tony Musto	199½	TKO 9	St Louis
May 23, 1941	Joe Louis	201½	Buddy Baer	237½	Disq 7	Washington, DC
June 18, 1941	Joe Louis	199½	Billy Conn	174	KO 13	New York
Sep 29, 1941	Joe Louis	202¼	Lou Nova	202½	TKO 6	New York
Jan 9, 1942	Joe Louis	206¾	Buddy Baer	250	KO 1	New York
Mar 27, 1942	Joe Louis	207½	Abe Simon	255½	KO 6	New York
June 9, 1946	Joe Louis	207	Billy Conn	187	KO 8	New York
Sep 18, 1946	Joe Louis	211	Tami Mauriello	198½	KO 1	New York
Dec 5, 1947	Joe Louis	211½	Jersey Joe Walcott	194½	Split 15	New York
June 25, 1948	Joe Louis	213½	Jersey Joe Walcott	194¾	KO 11	New York
June 22, 1949	Ezzard Charles*	181¾	Jersey Joe Walcott	195½	UD 15	Chicago
Aug 10, 1949	Ezzard Charles	180	Gus Lesnevich	182	TKO 8	New York
Oct 14, 1949	Ezzard Charles	182	Pat Valentino	188½	KO 8	San Francisco
Aug 15, 1950	Ezzard Charles	183¼	Freddie Beshore	184½	TKO 14	Buffalo
Sep 27, 1950	Ezzard Charles	184½	Joe Louis	218	UD 15	New York
Dec 5, 1950	Ezzard Charles	185	Nick Barone	178½	KO 11	Cincinnati
Jan 12, 1951	Ezzard Charles	185	Lee Oma	193	TKO 10	New York
Mar 7, 1951	Ezzard Charles	186	Jersey Joe Walcott	193	UD 15	Detroit
May 30, 1951	Ezzard Charles	182	Joey Maxim	181½	UD 15	Chicago
July 18, 1951	Jersey Joe Walcott*	194	Ezzard Charles	182	KO 7	Pittsburgh
June 5, 1952	Jersey Joe Walcott	196	Ezzard Charles	191½	UD 15	Philadelphia
Sep 23, 1952	Rocky Marciano*	184	Jersey Joe Walcott	196	KO 13	Philadelphia
May 15, 1953	Rocky Marciano	184½	Jersey Joe Walcott	197¾	KO 1	Chicago
Sep 24, 1953	Rocky Marciano	185	Roland LaStarza	184¾	TKO 11	New York
June 17, 1954	Rocky Marciano	187½	Ezzard Charles	185½	UD 15	New York
Sep 17, 1954	Rocky Marciano	187	Ezzard Charles	192½	KO 8	New York
May 16, 1955	Rocky Marciano	189	Don Cockell	205	TKO 9	San Francisco
Sep 21, 1955	Rocky Marciano	188¼	Archie Moore	188	KO 9	New York
Nov 30, 1956	Floyd Patterson*	182¼	Archie Moore	187¾	KO 5	Chicago
July 29, 1957	Floyd Patterson	184	Tommy Jackson	192½	TKO 10	New York
Aug 22, 1957	Floyd Patterson	187¼	Pete Rademacher	202	KO 6	Seattle
Aug 18, 1958	Floyd Patterson	184½	Roy Harris	194	TKO 13	Los Angeles
May 1, 1959	Floyd Patterson	182½	Brian London	206	KO 11	Indianapolis
June 26, 1959	Ingemar Johansson*	196	Floyd Patterson	182	TKO 3	New York
June 20, 1960	Floyd Patterson*	190	Ingemar Johansson	194¾	KO 5	New York
Mar 13, 1961	Floyd Patterson	194¾	Ingemar Johansson	206½	KO 6	Miami Beach
Dec 4, 1961	Floyd Patterson	188½	Tom McNeeley	197	KO 4	Toronto
Sep 25, 1962	Sonny Liston*	214	Floyd Patterson	189	KO 1	Chicago
July 22, 1963	Sonny Liston	215	Floyd Patterson	194½	KO 1	Las Vegas
Feb 25, 1964	Cassius Clay	210½	Sonny Liston	218	TKO 7	Miami Beach
Mar 5, 1965	Ernie Terrell WBA*	199	Eddie Machen	192	UD 15	Chicago
May 25, 1965	Muhammad Ali	206	Sonny Liston	215¼	KO 1	Lewiston, ME
Nov 1, 1965	Ernie Terrell WBA*	206	George Chuvalo	209	UD 15	Toronto
Nov 22, 1965	Muhammad Ali	210	Floyd Patterson	196¾	TKO 12	Las Vegas
Mar 29, 1966	Muhammad Ali	214½	George Chuvalo	216	UD 15	Toronto
May 21, 1966	Muhammad Ali	201½	Henry Cooper	188	TKO 6	London
June 28, 1966	Ernie Terrell WBA*	209½	Doug Jones	187½	UD 15	Houston
Aug 6, 1966	Muhammad Ali	209½	Brian London	201½	KO 3	London
Sep 10, 1966	Muhammad Ali	203½	Karl Mildenberger	194¼	TKO 12	Frankfurt
Nov 14, 1966	Muhammad Ali	212¾	Cleveland Williams	210½	TKO 3	Houston
Feb 6, 1967	Muhammad Ali	212¼	Ernie Terrell WBA	212½	UD 15	Houston
Mar 22, 1967	Muhammad Ali	211½	Zora Folley	202½	KO 7	New York
Mar 4, 1968	Joe Frazier*	204½	Buster Mathis	243½	TKO 11	New York
Apr 27, 1968	Jimmy Ellis*	197	Jerry Quarry	195	Maj 15	Oakland
June 24, 1968	Joe Frazier NY*	203½	Manuel Ramos	208	TKO 2	New York
Aug 14, 1968	Jimmy Ellis WBA*	198	Floyd Patterson	188	Ref 15	Stockholm
Dec 10, 1968	Joe Frazier NY*	203	Oscar Bonavena	207	UD 15	Philadelphia
Apr 22, 1969	Joe Frazier NY*	204½	Dave Zyglewicz	190½	KO 1	Houston
June 23, 1969	Joe Frazier NY*	203½	Jerry Quarry	198½	TKO 8	New York
Feb 16, 1970	Joe Frazier NY*	205	Jimmy Ellis WBA	201	TKO 5	New York
Nov 18, 1970	Joe Frazier*	209	Bob Foster	188	KO 2	Detroit
Mar 8, 1971	Joe Frazier*	205½	Muhammad Ali	215	UD 15	New York
Jan 15, 1972	Joe Frazier	215½	Terry Daniels	195	TKO 4	New Orleans

World Heavyweight Championship Fights *(Cont.)*

Date	Winner	Wgt	Loser	Wgt	Result	Site
May 26, 1972	Joe Frazier	217½	Ron Stander	218	TKO 5	Omaha
Jan 22, 1973	George Foreman*	217½	Joe Frazier	214	TKO 2	Kingston, Jam.
Sep 1, 1973	George Foreman	219½	Jose Roman	196½	KO 1	Tokyo
Mar 26, 1974	George Foreman	224¼	Ken Norton	212¼	TKO 2	Caracas
Oct 30, 1974	Muhammad Ali*	216-½	George Foreman	220	KO 8	Kinshasa, Zaire
Mar 24, 1975	Muhammad Ali	223½	Chuck Wepner	225	TKO 15	Cleveland
May 16, 1975	Muhammad Ali	224½	Ron Lyle	219	TKO 11	Las Vegas
July 1, 1975	Muhammad Ali	224½	Joe Bugner	230	UD 15	Kuala Lumpur, Malaysia
Oct 1, 1975	Muhammad Ali	224½	Joe Frazier	215	TKO 15	Manila
Feb 20, 1976	Muhammad Ali	226	Jean Pierre Coopman	206	KO 5	San Juan
Apr 30, 1976	Muhammad Ali	230	Jimmy Young	209	UD 15	Landover, MD
May 24, 1976	Muhammad Ali	230	Richard Dunn	206½	TKO 5	Munich
Sep 28, 1976	Muhammad Ali	221	Ken Norton	217½	UD 15	New York
May 16, 1977	Muhammad Ali	221¼	Alfredo Evangelista	209¼	UD 15	Landover, MD
Sep 29, 1977	Muhammad Ali	225	Earnie Shavers	211¼	UD 15	New York
Feb 15, 1978	Leon Spinks*	197¼	Muhammad Ali	224¼	Split 15	Las Vegas
June 9, 1978	Larry Holmes*	209	Ken Norton WBC	220	Split 15	Las Vegas
Sep 15, 1978	Muhammad Ali*	221	Leon Spinks	201	UD 15	New Orleans
Nov 10, 1978	Larry Holmes WBC*	214	Alfredo Evangelista	208¼	KO 7	Las Vegas
Mar 23, 1979	Larry Holmes WBC*	214	Osvaldo Ocasio	207	TKO 7	Las Vegas
June 22, 1979	Larry Holmes WBC*	215	Mike Weaver	202	TKO 12	New York
Sep 28, 1979	Larry Holmes WBC*	210	Earnie Shavers	211	TKO 11	Las Vegas
Oct 20, 1979	John Tate*	240	Gerrie Coetzee	222	UD 15	Pretoria
Feb 3, 1980	Larry Holmes WBC*	213½	Lorenzo Zanon	215	TKO 6	Las Vegas
Mar 31, 1980	Mike Weaver*	232	John Tate WBA	232	KO 15	Knoxville
Mar 31, 1980	Larry Holmes WBC*	211	Leroy Jones	254½	TKO 8	Las Vegas
July 7, 1980	Larry Holmes WBC*	214¼	Scott LeDoux	226	TKO 7	Minneapolis
Oct 2, 1980	Larry Holmes WBC*	211¼	Muhammad Ali	217½	TKO 11	Las Vegas
Oct 25, 1980	Mike Weaver WBA*	210	Gerrie Coetzee	226½	KO 13	Sun City, Boph'swana
Apr 11, 1981	Larry Holmes	215	Trevor Berbick	215½	UD 15	Las Vegas
June 12, 1981	Larry Holmes	212¼	Leon Spinks	200¼	TKO 3	Detroit
Oct 3, 1981	Mike Weaver WBA*	215	James Quick Tillis	209	UD 15	Rosemont, IL
Nov 6, 1981	Larry Holmes	213¼	Renaldo Snipes	215¾	TKO 11	Pittsburgh
June 11, 1982	Larry Holmes	212½	Gerry Cooney	225½	TKO 13	Las Vegas
Nov 26, 1982	Larry Holmes	217½	Tex Cobb	234¼	UD 15	Houston
Dec 10, 1982	Michael Dokes*	216	Mike Weaver WBA	209¾	TKO 1	Las Vegas
Mar 27, 1983	Larry Holmes	221	Lucien Rodriguez	209	UD 12	Scranton
May 20, 1983	Michael Dokes WBA*	223	Mike Weaver	218½	Draw 15	Las Vegas
May 20, 1983	Larry Holmes	213	Tim Witherspoon	219½	Split 12	Las Vegas
Sep 10, 1983	Larry Holmes	223	Scott Frank	211¼	TKO 5	Atlantic City
Sep 23, 1983	Gerrie Coetzee*	215	Michael Dokes WBA	217	KO 10	Richfield, OH
Nov 25, 1983	Larry Holmes	219	Marvis Frazier	200	TKO 1	Las Vegas
Mar 9, 1984	Tim Witherspoon	220¼	Greg Page	239½	Maj 12	Las Vegas
Aug 31, 1984	Pinklon Thomas*	216	Tim Witherspoon WBC	217	Maj 12	Las Vegas
Nov 9, 1984	Larry Holmes IBF	221½	James Bonecrusher Smith	227	TKO 12	Las Vegas
Dec 1, 1984	Greg Page*	236½	Gerrie Coetzee WBA	218	KO 8	Sun City, Boph'swana
Mar 15, 1985	Larry Holmes	223½	David Bey	233¼	TKO 10	Las Vegas
Apr 29, 1985	Tony Tubbs*	229	Greg Page WBA	239½	UD 15	Buffalo
May 20, 1985	Larry Holmes	224¼	Carl Williams	215	UD 15	Las Vegas
June 15, 1985	Pinklon Thomas*	220¼	Mike Weaver	221¼	KO 8	Las Vegas
Sep 21, 1985	Michael Spinks*	200	Larry Holmes IBF	221½	UD 15	Las Vegas
Jan 17, 1986	Tim Witherspoon	227	Tony Tubbs WBA	229	Maj 15	Atlanta
Mar 22, 1986	Trevor Berbick*	218½	Pinklon Thomas WBC	222¾	UD 15	Las Vegas
Apr 19, 1986	Michael Spinks	205	Larry Holmes	223	Split 15	Las Vegas
July 19, 1986	Tim Witherspoon*	234¾	Frank Bruno	228	TKO 11	Wembley, England
Sep 6, 1986	Michael Spinks	201	Steffen Tangstad	214¾	TKO 4	Las Vegas
Nov 22, 1986	Mike Tyson*	221¼	Trevor Berbick WBC	218½	TKO 2	Las Vegas
Dec 12, 1986	James Bonecrusher Smith*	228½	Tim Witherspoon WBA	233½	TKO 1	New York
Mar 7, 1987	Mike Tyson WBC*	219	James Bonecrusher Smith WBA	233	UD 12	Las Vegas
May 30, 1987	Mike Tyson*	218¾	Pinklon Thomas	217¾	TKO 6	Las Vegas
May 30, 1987	Tony Tucker	222¼	Buster Douglas	227¼	TKO 10	Las Vegas

Date	Winner	Wgt	Loser	Wgt	Result	Site
June 15, 1987	Michael Spinks	208¾	Gerry Cooney	238	TKO 5	Atlantic City
Aug 1, 1987	Mike Tyson*	221	Tony Tucker IBF	221	UD 12	Las Vegas
Oct 16, 1987	Mike Tyson*	216	Tyrell Biggs	228¾	TKO 7	Atlantic City
Jan 22, 1988	Mike Tyson*	215¾	Larry Holmes	225¾	TKO 4	Atlantic City
Mar 20, 1988	Mike Tyson*	216¼	Tony Tubbs	238¼	KO 2	Tokyo
June 27, 1988	Mike Tyson*	218¼	Michael Spinks	212¼	KO 1	Atlantic City
Feb 25, 1989	Mike Tyson	218	Frank Bruno	228	TKO 5	Las Vegas
July 21, 1989	Mike Tyson	219¼	Carl Williams	218	TKO 1	Atlantic City
Feb 10, 1990	Buster Douglas*	231½	Mike Tyson	220½	KO 10	Tokyo
Oct 25, 1990	Evander Holyfield	208	Buster Douglas	246	KO 3	Las Vegas
Apr 19, 1991	Evander Holyfield	212	George Foreman	257	UD 12	Atlantic City
Nov 23, 1991	Evander Holyfield	210	Bert Cooper	215	TKO 7	Atlanta
June 19, 1992	Evander Holyfield	210	Larry Holmes	233	UD 12	Las Vegas
Nov 13, 1992	Riddick Bowe	235	Evander Holyfield	205	UD 12	Las Vegas
Feb 6, 1993	Riddick Bowe	243	Michael Dokes	244	KO 1	New York City
May 8, 1993	Lennox Lewis	235	Tony Tucker	235	UD 12	Las Vegas
May 22, 1993	Riddick Bowe	244	Jesse Ferguson	224	KO 2	Washington, D.C.

*Champion not generally recognized.

KO=knockout; TKO=technical knockout; UD=unanimous decision; Split=split decision; Ref=referee's decision; Disq=disqualification; ND=no decision.

Ring Magazine Fighter and Fight of the Year

Year	Fighter	Fight	Winner	Site
1928	Gene Tunney	Award not given until 1945		
1929	Tommy Loughran	Award not given until 1945		
1930	Max Schmeling	Award not given until 1945		
1931	Tommy Loughran	Award not given until 1945		
1932	Jack Sharkey	Award not given until 1945		
1933	No award	Award not given until 1945		
1934	Tony Canzoneri	Award not given until 1945		
	Barney Ross	Award not given until 1945		
1935	Barney Ross	Award not given until 1945		
1936	Joe Louis	Award not given until 1945		
1937	Henry Armstrong	Award not given until 1945		
1938	Joe Louis	Award not given until 1945		
1939	Joe Louis	Award not given until 1945		
1940	Billy Conn	Award not given until 1945		
1941	Joe Louis	Award not given until 1945		
1942	Ray Robinson	Award not given until 1945		
1943	Fred Apostoli	Award not given until 1945		
1944	Beau Jack	Award not given until 1945		
1945	Willie Pep	Rocky Graziano-Cochrane	Rocky Graziano	New York City
1946	Tony Zale	Tony Zale-Rocky Graziano	Tony Zale	New York City
1947	Gus Lesnevich	Rocky Graziano-Tony Zale	Rocky Graziano	Chicago
1948	Ike Williams	Marcel Cerdan-Tony Zale	Marcel Cerdan	Jersey City
1949	Ezzard Charles	Willie Pep-Sandy Saddler	Willie Pep	New York City
1950	Ezzard Charles	Jake LaMotta-Laurent Dauthuille	Jake LaMotta	Detroit
1951	Ray Robinson	Jersey Joe Walcott-Ezzard Charles	Jersey Joe Walcott	Pittsburgh
1952	Rocky Marciano	Rocky Marciano-Jersey Joe Walcott	Rocky Marciano	Philadelphia
1953	Carl Olson	Rocky Marciano-Roland LaStarza	Rocky Marciano	New York City
1954	Rocky Marciano	Rocky Marciano-Ezzard Charles	Rocky Marciano	New York City
1955	Rocky Marciano	Carmen Basilio-Tony DeMarco	Carmen Basilio	Boston
1956	Floyd Patterson	Carmen Basilio-Johnny Saxton	Carmen Basilio	Syracuse
1957	Carmen Basilio	Carmen Basilio-Ray Robinson	Carmen Basilio	New York City
1958	Ingemar Johansson	Ray Robinson-Carmen Basilio	Ray Robinson	Chicago
1959	Ingemar Johansson	Gene Fullmer-Carmen Basilio	Gene Fullmer	San Francisco
1960	Floyd Patterson	Floyd Patterson-Ingemar Johansson	Floyd Patterson	New York City
1961	Joe Brown	Joe Brown-Dave Charnley	Joe Brown	London
1962	Dick Tiger	Joey Giardello-Henry Hank	Joey Giardello	Philadelphia
1963	Cassius Clay	Cassius Clay-Doug Jones	Cassius Clay	New York City
1964	Emile Griffith	Cassius Clay-Sonny Liston	Cassius Clay	Miami Beach
1965	Dick Tiger	Floyd Patterson-George Chuvalo	Floyd Patterson	New York City
1966	No award	Jose Torres-Eddie Cotton	Jose Torres	Las Vegas
1967	Joe Frazier	Nino Benvenuti-Emile Griffith	Nino Benvenuti	New York City
1968	Nino Benvenuti	Dick Tiger-Frank DePaula	Dick Tiger	New York City

Year	Fighter	Fight	Winner	Site
1969	Jose Napoles	Joe Frazier-Jerry Quarry	Joe Frazier	New York City
1970	Joe Frazier	Carlos Monzon-Nino Benvenuti	Carlos Monzon	Rome
1971	Joe Frazier	Joe Frazier-Muhammed Ali	Joe Frazier	New York City
1972	Muhammed Ali Carlos Monzon	Bob Foster-Chris Finnegan	Bob Foster	London
1973	George Foreman	George Foreman-Joe Frazier	George Foreman	Kingston, Jam.
1974	Muhammed Ali	Muhammed Ali-George Foreman	Muhammed Ali	Kinshasa
1975	Muhammed Ali	Muhammed Ali-Joe Frazier	Muhammed Ali	Manila
1976	George Foreman	George Foreman-Ron Lyle	George Foreman	Las Vegas
1977	Carlos Zarate	Joe Young-George Foreman	Joe Young	San Juan
1978	Muhammed Ali	Leon Spinks-Muhammed Ali	Leon Spinks	La Vegas
1979	Ray Leonard	Danny Lopez-Tony Ayala	Danny Lopez	San Antonio
1980	Thomas Hearns	Saad Muhammed-Danny Lopez	Saad Muhammed	McAfee, NJ
1981	Ray Leonard Salvador Sanchez	Ray Leonard-Tonny Hearns	Ray Leonard	Las Vegas
1982	Larry Holmes	Bobby Chacon-Rafael Limon	Bobby Chacon	Sacramento
1983	Marvin Hagler	Bobby Chacon-Cornelius Boza-Edwards	Bobby Chacon	Las Vegas
1984	Thomas Hearns	Jose Luis Ramirez-Edwin Rosario	Jose Luis Ramirez	San Juan
1985	Donald Curry Marvin Hagler	Marvin Hagler-Tommy Hearns	Marvin Hagler	Las Vegas
1986	Mike Tyson	Stevie Cruz-Barry McGuigan	Stevie Cruz	Las Vegas
1987	Evander Holyfield	Ray Leonard-Marvin Hagler	Ray Leonard	Las Vegas
1988	Mike Tyson	Tony Lopez-Rocky Lockridge	Tony Lopez	Inglewood, CA
1989	Pernell Whitaker	Roberto Duran-Iran Barkley	Roberto Duran	Atlantic City
1990	Julio César Chávez	Julio César Chávez-Meldrick Taylor	Julio César Chavez	Las Vegas
1991	James Toney	Robert Quiroga-Kid Akeem Anifowoshe	Robert Quiroga	San Antonio
1992	Riddick Bowe	Riddick Bowe-Evander Holyfield	Riddick Bowe	Las Vegas

U.S. Olympic Gold Medalists

LIGHT FLYWEIGHT

1984	Paul Gonzales

FLYWEIGHT

1904	George Finnegan
1920	Frank Di Gennara
1024	Fidel LaBarba
1952	Nathan Brooks
1976	Leo Randolph
1984	Steve McCrory

BANTAMWEIGHT

1904	Oliver Kirk
1988	Kennedy McKinney

FEATHERWEIGHT

1904	Oliver Kirk
1924	John Fields
1984	Meldrick Taylor

LIGHTWEIGHT

1904	Harry Spanger
1920	Samuel Mosberg
1968	Ronald W. Harris
1976	Howard Davis
1984	Pernell Whitaker
1992	Oscar De La Hoya

LIGHT WELTERWEIGHT

1952	Charles Adkins
1972	Ray Seales
1976	Ray Leonard
1984	Jerry Page

WELTERWEIGHT

1904	Albert Young
1932	Edward Flynn
1960	Wilbert McClure
1984	Mark Breland
1984	Frank Tate

MIDDLEWEIGHT

1904	Charles Mayer
1932	Carmen Bath
1952	Floyd Patterson
1960	Edward Crook
1976	Michael Spinks

LIGHT HEAVYWEIGHT

1920	Eddie Eagan
1952	Norvel Lee
1956	James Boyd
1960	Cassius Clay
1976	Leon Spinks
1988	Andrew Maynard

HEAVYWEIGHT

1984	Henry Tillman
1988	Ray Mercer

SUPER HEAVYWEIGHT

1904	Samuel Berger
1952	H. Edward Sanders
1956	T. Peter Rademacher
1964	Joe Frazier
1968	George Foreman
1984	Tyrell Biggs

Horse Racing

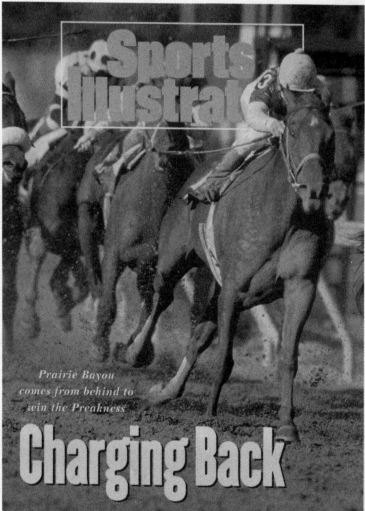

Sports Illustrated

Prairie Bayou comes from behind to win the Preakness

Charging Back

AL TIELEMANS

435

Turmoil at the Track

Julie Krone gave a welcome boost to a sport beset by breakdowns and controversy | **by WILLIAM F. REED**

AS SOON AS MUD-SPLATTERED JOCKEY Julie Krone crossed the finish line aboard Colonial Affair in the Belmont Stakes on June 5, a roar of happiness and approval swept through the crowd at Belmont Park on Long Island. Until that moment, no female rider had ever won a race in the Triple Crown, the lucrative and historic series that virtually every horseman prizes most. For the 29-year-old Krone, the victory filled a glaring hole in her resume and proved to the nation what racetrackers learned long ago—that she's as talented as any rider in the nation. Period.

Yet even as the jubilant Krone was pulling up Colonial Affair so she could jog him back to the winner's circle, a darker tableau had formed on the track's backstretch. Midway through the mile-and-a-half race, Prairie Bayou, the gelding that had won the Preakness only three weeks earlier, had taken a bad step and fractured a front leg. When trainer Tom Bohannon saw jockey Mike Smith tumble off Prairie Bayou's back, he left his clubhouse seat

and began a mad dash through the stands and across the track's vast infield so he could reach his stricken horse's side. Sadly, the injury was irreparable, meaning that Prairie Bayou had to be humanely destroyed.

Those contrasting scenes symbolized one of the most bittersweet years in racing history. On the positive side, the Kentucky Derby was won by what Associated Press writer Ed Schuyler called "the old men and their Sea Hero." Indeed, Sea Hero's victory in the 119th Run for the Roses was the crowning glory in the long and distinguished racing careers of owner Paul Mellon, 85, and trainer Mack Miller, 71. In the Preakness, Prairie Bayou's victory enabled owner John Ed Anthony and trainer Bohannon to become the first repeat winners in the Baltimore classic since 1947. And Krone wasn't the only female to make racing history. By sweeping New York's Acorn, Mother Goose and Coaching Club American Oaks, Sky Beauty became only the eighth winner of the so-called filly Triple Crown. However,

despite these and other wonderful moments, it was mostly a sad, grim year in a sport beset by myriad problems. Even Krone's triumphant year ended in tragedy. She took a violent spill on the final day of the Saratoga racing season and fractured her right ankle so badly that the surgeon who set it compared her injuries to those of a plane crash victim.

The breakdowns and subsequent deaths of Union City in the Preakness and Prairie Bayou in the Belmont caused animal-rights activists and others to call for massive reforms that would ensure greater protection for the horses. While the response of some racetrackers was only that the breakdowns were a tragic, but unavoidable, part of the game, others again were asking the same troublesome questions that have vexed responsible industry leaders for years: Is too much pressure being put on horses as 2-year-olds? Should the Triple Crown races be spread over at least two months instead of five weeks? Doesn't year-round racing inevitably put more horses in jeopardy of breaking down? And,

A muddy but jubilant Krone was all smiles after her stirring victory in the Belmont.

most important, isn't it time that racing cleaned up its medication policies?

Years ago Arthur B. Hancock III, who bred Kentucky Derby winners Gato Del Sol (1982) and Sunday Silence (1989), warned the industry against the disastrous long-term effects of this country's permissive medication policies. As Hancock saw it, the more you allow horses to run with such pain-relieving medications as Lasix and Butazolidin, the more you "deplete the gene pool" and breed infirmities into future generations. Inevitably, as he saw it, there would be a general weakening in thoroughbreds' bones and muscles, which would lead to more unsound horses and more breakdowns.

When Hancock recommended that racing jurisdictions make all medication for racing purposes illegal—as is the case in New York and Europe—his suggestions were dismissed as impractical. Yet Hancock produced statistics indicating that as

Lukas faced severe criticism after the breakdown of Union City in the Preakness.

medication rules have become more lax, the average horse is starting fewer times now than it did 30 years ago.

One of the sadder figures in the breakdown controversy was D. Wayne Lukas, who had spent the 1980s setting national records for victories and earnings that will never be topped. During that heady decade Lukas built an empire that seemed to have a division in every state. He was represented in virtually every major race, and his horses won more than their share of the classics. However, even Lukas wasn't immune to the economic hard times that hit the industry in the latter part of the decade. His major patron, Eugene Klein, got out of the business in 1989 because of bad health (he died in 1990), and Lukas wasn't able to replace him. By the time of the 1993 Triple Crown, you almost couldn't walk through a stable anywhere without hearing rumors that the Lukas empire was crumbling.

Heading into the Kentucky Derby, Lukas told anyone who would listen that Union City, the colt he trained for prominent Kentucky businessman William T. Young, had a great chance to win. After the colt

finished only 15th, Lukas was so puzzled that he decided to give him another chance two weeks later in the Preakness. Remembering how Tank's Prospect had won the 1985 Preakness for him and Klein after finishing only seventh in the Derby, Lukas decided to use the same game plan with Union City that he had used with Tank's Prospect, which meant giving him no serious workouts between the two races. After the colt broke down on the backstretch and had to be destroyed, an emotional Lukas lashed out at writers who questioned whether the colt's lack of training indicated he wasn't completely sound.

"That's ridiculous," Lukas said. "I try to be honest with you people, and I am now. Nobody is immune to this kind of thing. It's happened to Charlie Whittingham, it's happened to Woody Stephens, it's happened to Mack Miller. I do my job. I get up every morning at 3 a.m. That's more than I can say for the —— who are second-guessing me."

By the time of the world's most prestigious thoroughbred auction—the select summer yearling sale in mid-July at Keeneland—Lukas was showing signs of making a comeback. He had just won the training title at the Churchill Downs spring meet. In addition, he had picked up some new clients with pockets deep enough to put him back in action as a yearling buyer, where his keen eye for a future stakes winner is well documented. Nevertheless, Lukas purchased only three yearlings, even though prices at the sale were dramatically lower than during the halcyon days of the 1980s. The sales topper was the $1.05 million paid for a son of Mr. Prospector, far below the world-record of $13.1 million set in 1985.

While Lukas long has been a fixture at the yearling sales, Mack Miller hadn't been to one for years. His boss, Paul Mellon, is one of the last of the old guard, the millionaire owners whose stables consist mainly of horses they breed and raise at their farms instead of ones they buy at public auction. For years Mellon, noted for his art collection and philanthropy, had operated a top-drawer stable that was most known for its success in grass races. He and Miller had never won the Kentucky Derby because they had never really coveted it. However, in recent years Mellon had decided that his racing life wouldn't be complete without a Derby victory. Unfortunately, every time he came up with a promising 2-year-old, the colt would suffer an injury that caused him to be retired.

Because of his age, Mellon ordered that most of his horses be sold. Of the ones he kept, the most promising was Sea Hero, who last year won the prestigious Champagne Stakes for 2-year-olds. He looked like a Derby contender until he ran so poorly in Florida that Miller shipped him to his training center in South Carolina for a rest. When Sea Hero began showing signs of returning to form, Miller sent him to Keeneland, where he finished a respectable fourth in the Blue Grass Stakes. Encouraged, Miller and Mellon decided to give him a crack at the Derby. Sent off at odds of 12–1 by the crowd of 136,817 at Churchill Downs, Sea Hero and jockey Jerry Bailey came through on the rail and held on for a 2½-length victory over Prairie Bayou, the colt that had won the Blue Grass.

The victory proved to be such an elixir for Mellon that he told Miller to come to the Keeneland sale and buy him a couple of yearlings. "He hasn't come down from it yet," said Miller. "Neither have I. People everywhere have been so lovely. I'll be in a store buying something or sitting in the dentist's office, and somebody will say, 'I know you.... You won the Kentucky Derby.' I still can't get it through my thick head."

One of the industry's challenges is to find the Paul Mellons of the future, the deep-pocket owners who will support the game in good times and bad. This has become increasingly difficult in an era when simulcasting, the practice by which one track televises its race card to others, has become racing's double-edged sword. Simulcasting helps a track beef up its pari-mutuel handle, but it also hurts attendance. With smaller crowds, the thrill of victory is diminished for the owner, who expects to be toasted and have his back slapped when he wins.

However, at least simulcasting is a tool that helps racing compete against its many rivals for the gambling dollar. By the end of the year, 36 states had at least one lottery, and many others had approved, or were considering, everything from casinos to riverboats to poker machines. Gambling on Indian reservations continued to burgeon. And, of course, harness racing and dog racing are taking their usual slices of the pie.

At various seminars and conventions, racing leaders wrestled, mostly unsuccessfully, with the question of their sport's future. One of the more outspoken was Tom Meeker, president of the track (Churchill Downs in Louisville) that is home to the sport's grandest prize (the Kentucky Derby). Much to the dismay of some racing traditionalists, Meeker said that racing should concentrate on finding ways to exploit the gambling boom instead of fighting it. To position itself for the future, Churchill bought a harness racing track in Louisville and turned it into a simulcasting outlet that easily could be adapted to casino gambling. In addition, the track entered into an agreement with the conglomerate that owns the Harrah's casinos to study and prepare for riverboat gambling. Asked what he would say if Kentucky approved riverboat gambling, Meeker smiled and snapped off a salute. "Captain Meeker at your service, sir," he said.

Meeker was among the industry leaders who felt that the time had come to appoint a racing "czar" to bring together the industry's diverse factions and formulate a national marketing plan so that racing could face its competition with a unified front. Breeder Arthur Hancock agrees. "We need a commissioner of racing," Hancock said in 1991, adding that such a czar's first priority should be to eliminate medication for racing purposes. "We need desperately to create the perception of credibility, honesty, and absolute integrity."

The game also needs more moments such as Krone's victory in the Belmont. In her 12-year professional career, Krone, who learned to ride while growing up in Eau Claire, Mich., had relentlessly worked her way to the top of the game, winning almost 3,000 races while also capturing riding titles against tough competition in

Bailey acknowledged the crowd after Sea Hero's surprising victory at Churchill Downs.

Florida, New Jersey, and New York. Her Belmont mount, Colonial Affair, hadn't competed in either the Kentucky Derby or Preakness, mainly because trainer Scotty Schulhofer believed he was best suited for the longer Belmont. On the night before the race, Schulhofer told Krone, "They say you can't win the big ones, but this is just another race. Let him relax the first part of it. Be patient. You can do it."

The trainer was right on the money. On a track left muddy by overnight rains, Krone dropped the colt back in the early going, keeping him on the outside so he would have only a minimal amount of mud kicked in his face. When she turned the colt loose in the final turn, he charged powerfully to the lead and then drew off down the stretch for a 2¼-length victory.

As Krone brought the colt back to be unsaddled, former jockey George Martens, who exercises Colonial Affair, was among the crowd waiting to congratulate her.

"Beautiful job, Julie," said Martens.

"How do you stop crying?" asked Krone.

"You don't," Martens said.

For racing, it was a moment of sunshine in a year of dark clouds.

FOR THE RECORD·1992–1993

THOROUGHBRED RACING

The Triple Crown

119th Kentucky Derby

May 1, 1993. Grade I, 3-year-olds; 8th race, Churchill Downs, Louisville. All 126 lbs. Distance: 1¼ miles. Stakes purse: $985,900; Winner: $735,900; Second: $145,000; Third: $70,000; Fourth: $35,000. Track: Cloudy and Fast. Off: 5:34 p.m. Winner: Sea Hero (B c by Polish Navy-Glowing Tribute, by Graustark); Times: 0:22⅘, 0:46⅗, 1:11⅕, 1:36⅘; 2:02⅖. Won: Driving. Breeder: Paul Mellon.

Horse	Finish-PP	Margin	Jockey/Owner
Sea Hero	1-6	2½	Jerry Bailey/Rokeby Stable
Prairie Bayou	2-5	Head	Mike Smith/Loblolly Stable
Wild Gale	3-13	Neck	Shane Sellers/Little Fish Stable
Personal Hope	4-7	¾	Gary Stevens /Debi and Lee Lewis
Diazo	5-18	Head	Kent Desormeaux/Allen E. Paulson
Corby	6-17	¾	Chris McCarron/Allen E. Paulson
Kissin Kris	7-2	2	Jose Santos/John Franks
Silver of Silver	8-9	Nose	Jacinto Vasquez/Chevalier Stable
Ragtime Rebel	9-14	2	Bobby Lester/Ronald J. Childress
Truth of It All	10-3	4	Jorge Velasquez/Alex E. Schmidt
Bull Inthe Heather	11-10	Nose	Wigberto Ramos/Arthur Klein
Dixieland Heat	12-15	Neck	Randy Romero/Leland P. Cook
Wallenda	13-16	2	Pat Day/Dogwood Stable
Mi Cielo	14-12	1¼	Aaron Gryder/Thomas M. Carey
Union City	15-4	1¼	Pat Valenzuela/Overbrook Farm
Storm Tower	16-1	Nose	Rick Wilson/C.J. Hesse-C. Hesse
Rockamundo	17-8	8	Calvin Borel/Mary and Gary West
El Bakan	18-19	1½	Craig Perret/Robert Perez
Tossofthecoin	19-11	—	Laffitt Pincay/Jenny and Sidney Craig

118th Preakness Stakes

May 15, 1993. Grade I, 3-year-olds; 10th race, Pimlico Race Course, Baltimore. All 126 lbs. Distance: 1 3/16 miles; Stakes purse: $725,900; Winner: $471,835; Second: $145,180; Third: $72,590; Fourth: $36,295. Track: Clear&Fast. Off: 5:32 p.m. Winner: Prairie Bayou (Ch g by Little Missouri-Whiffling, by Wavering Monarch); Times: 0:23⅗, 0:46⅘, 1:11⅕, 1:37, 1:56⅗. Won: Driving. Breeder: Loblolly Stable (KY).

Horse	Finish-PP	Margin	Jockey/Owner
Prairie Bayou	1-3	½	Mike Smith/Loblolly Stable
Cherokee Run	2-12	7	Pat Day/Jill E. Robinson
El Bakan	3-2	Neck	Craig Perret/Robert Perez
Personal Hope	4-1	¾	Gary Stevens/Debi and Lee Lewis
Sea Hero	5-9	1¼	Jerry Bailey/Rokeby Stable
Woods of Windsor	6-7	1	Rick Wilson/Mrs. Augustus Riggs
Rockamundo	7-8	¾	Edgar Prado/ Mary and Gary West
Wild Gale	8-10	1	Shane Sellers/Little Fish Stable
Hegar	9-4	6½	Jose C. Ferrer/Huntington Point Stable
Koluctoo Jimmy Al	10-11	7½	Chris McCarron/Basil J. Plasteras
Too Wild	11-5	—	Herb McCauley/William J. Condren
Union City	12-6	Brkdwn	Pat Valenzuela/Overbrook Farm

125th Belmont Stakes

June 5, 1993. Grade I, 3-year-olds; 8th race, Belmont Park, Elmont, NY. All 126 lbs. Distance: 1½ miles. Stakes purse: $740,900; Winner: $444,450; Second: $162,998; Third: $88,908; Fourth: $44,454. Track: Showery. Off: 5:31 p.m. Winner: Colonial Affair (B c, by Pleasant Colony-Snuggle, by Nijinsky II); Times: 0:24, 0:48 4/5, 1:13 2/5, 1:37 2/5, 2:02⅘, 2:29⅘. Won: Driving. Breeder: Rutledge Farm (VA).

Horse	Finish-PP	Margin	Jockey/Owner
Colonial Affair	1-4	2¼	Julie Krone/Centennial Farms
Kissin Kris	2-3	¾	Jose Santos/John Franks
Wild Gale	3-13	2	Shane Sellers/My Littlefish Farm
Silver of Silver	4-11	1	Jacinto Vasquez/Chevalier Stable
Virginia Rapids	5-2	7	Eddie Maple/Middletown Stables
Cherokee Run	6-1	2	Chris Antley/Jill Robinson
Sea Hero	7-10	3½	Jerry Bailey/Paul Mellon
Bull Inthe Heather	8-10	23	Jorge Chavez/Arthur Klein
Antrim Rd	9-12	¾	Richard Migliore/J&A Novogratz
Raglin Road	10-7	7½	Lafitt Pincay/P. Fitzpatrick
Only Alpha	11-9	—	Robbie Davis/Jack Kent Cooke
Arinthod	12-8	Eased	Kent Desormeaux/Sidney Craig
Prairie Bayou	DNF-5	brkdwn	Mike Smith/Loblolly Stable

The American Championship Racing Series

Final points and standings in the 9-race American Championship Racing Series. The 9 races are the Donn Handicap, the Santa Anita Handicap, the Oaklawn Handicap, the Pimlico Special, the Nassau County Handicap, the Hollywood Gold Cup, the Suburban Handicap, the Pacific Classic, and the Iselin Handicap. Points were awarded on a 10-7-5-3-1 basis in each race, and a $1.5 million bonus was split among the top four point leaders.

Horse	Age	Sex	Starts	1	2	3	4	5	Pts.	Bonus ($)
Devil His Due	4	C	6	2	2	0	1	1	38	700,000
Bertrando	4	C	4	2	1	1	0	0	32	225,000
Valley Crossing	5	H	5	1	2	1	0	1	30	125,000
Missionary Ridge	6	H	7	0	2	1	2	2	27	50,000
Pistols and Roses	4	C	5	1	0	2	0	0	20	100,000
Best Pal	5	G	2	1	0	1	0	0	15	
Latin American	5	H	2	1	0	0	0	0	10	
West by West	4	C	2	1	0	0	0	0	10	
Irish Swap	6	H	2	0	1	0	0	1	8	
Offbeat	4	C	2	0	1	0	0	0	7	
Marquetry	6	H	2	0	0	0	2	0	6	
Major Impact	4	C	1	0	0	1	0	0	5	
Memo	6	H	1	0	0	1	0	0	5	
Strike the Gold	5	H	2	0	0	1	0	0	5	
Chief Honcho	6	H	2	0	0	0	1	0	3	
Conte di Savoya	4	C	1	0	0	0	1	0	3	
Scudan	4		1	0	0	0	1	0	3	
Sir Beaufort	6	H	1	0	0	0	1	0	3	
Ibex	6	G	1	0	0	0	0	1	1	
Miner's Mark	3	C	1	0	0	0	0	1	1	
Reign Road	5	H	1	0	0	0	0	1	1	
Stalwars	8		1	0	0	0	0	1	1	

C=Colt; G=Gelding; H=Horse; F=Filly; M=Mare.

Major Stakes Races

Late 1992

Date	Race	Track	Distance	Winner	Jockey/Trainer	Purse ($)
Oct 4	Prix De L'Arc De Triomphe	Longchamp	1½ miles	Subotica	Thierry Jarriet/ Andre Fabre	1,625,200
Oct 10	Champagne Stakes	Belmont	1 mile	Sea Hero	Jerry Bailey/ Mack Miller	500,000
Oct 10	Oak Tree Invitational	Santa Anita	1½ miles	Navarone	Pat Valenzuela/ R. Rash	400,000
Oct 10	Jockey Club Gold Cup	Belmont	1¼ miles	Pleasant Tap	Gary Stevens/ Chris Speckert	850,000
Oct 16	Meadowlands Cup	Meadowlands	1⅛ miles	Sea Cadet	Alex Solis/ Ron McAnally	500,000
Oct 17	Budweiser International	Laurel	1¼ miles	Zoman	Alan Munro/ Paul Cole	750,000
Oct 18	Rothmans International	Woodbine	1½ miles	Snurge	Richard Quinn/ Paul Cole	1,000,000
Oct 24	NYRA Mile	Aqueduct	1 mile	Ibero	Laffit Pincay/ Ron McAnally	500,000
Oct 31	Breeders' Cup Sprint	Gulfstream	6 furlongs	Thirty Slews	Eddie Delahoussaye/Bob Baffert	1,000,000
Oct 31	Breeders' Cup Juvenile Fillies	Gulfstream	1⅟₁₆ miles	Eliza	Pat Valenzuela/ Alex Hassinger	1,000,000
Oct 31	Breeders' Cup Distaff	Gulfstream	1⅛ miles	Paseana	Chris McCarron/ Ron McAnally	1,000,000
Oct 31	Breeders' Cup Mile	Gulfstream	1 mile	Lure	Mike Smith/ Claude McGaughey	1,000,000
Oct 31	Breeders' Cup Juvenile	Gulfstream	1⅟₁₆ miles	Gilded Time	Chris McCarron/ Darrell Vienna	1,000,000

Major Stakes Races (Cont.)

Late 1992 (Cont.)

Date	Race	Track	Distance	Winner	Jockey/Trainer	Purse ($)
Oct 31	Breeders' Cup Turf	Gulfstream	1½ miles	Fraise	Pat Valenzuela/ Bill Mott	2,000,000
Oct 31	Breeders' Cup Classic	Gulfstream	1¼ miles	A.P. Indy	Eddie Delahous-saye/Nell Drysdale	3,000,000
Dec 15	Hollywood Turf Cup	Hollywood Park	1½ miles	Bien Bien	Chris McCarron/ J. Paco Gonzalez	500,000

1993 (Through September 6)

Date	Race	Track	Distance	Winner	Jockey/Trainer	Purse ($)
Feb 7	Charles H. Strub Stakes	Santa Anita	1¼ miles	Siberian Summer	Corey Nakatani/ Ron McAnally	500,000
Feb 20	Donn Handicap	Gulfstream	1⅛ miles	Pistols and Roses	Herberto Castillo/ George Gianos	500,000
Feb 27	Fountain of Youth Stakes	Gulfstream	1$\frac{1}{16}$ miles	Duc d'Sligovil	Julie Krone/ J. McNeill	200,000
Mar 6	Santa Anita Handicap	Santa Anita	1¼ miles	Sir Beaufort	Pat Valenzuela/ Charlie Whittingham	1,000,000
Mar 20	Florida Derby	Gulfstream	1⅛ miles	Bull Inthe Heather	Wigberto Ramos/ Howard Tesher	500,000
Mar 27	Jim Beam Stakes	Turfway	1⅛ miles	Prairie Bayou	Chris McCarron/ Tom Bohannan	600,000
Apr 3	Santa Anita Derby	Santa Anita	1⅛ miles	Personal Hope	Gary Stevens/ Mark Hennig	500,000
Apr 3	Gotham Stakes	Aqueduct	1 mile	As Indicated	Caesar Bisono/ Rick Schosberg	200,000
Apr 10	Blue Grass Stakes	Keeneland	1⅛ miles	Prairie Bayou	Mike Smith/ Tom Bohannan	500,000
Apr 10	Oaklawn Handicap	Oaklawn Park	1⅛ miles	Jovial	Eddie Delahous-saye/James Jackson	750,000
Apr 17	Wood Memorial	Aqueduct	1⅛ miles	Storm Tower	Rick Wilson/ Ben Perkins	500,000
Apr 17	Arkansas Derby	Oakland Park	1⅛ miles	Rock-amundo	Calvin Borel/ O. Glass	500,000
Apr 30	Kentucky Oaks	Churchill Downs	1⅛ miles	Dispute	Jerry Bailey/ Claude McGaughey	250,000
May 1	Kentucky Derby	Churchill Downs	1¼ miles	Sea Hero	Jerry Bailey/ Mack Miller	500,000
May 8	Acorn Stakes	Belmont	1 mile	Sky Beauty	Mike Smith/ Allen Jerkens	150,000
May 14	Black Eyed Susan Stakes	Pimlico	1⅛ miles	Aztec Hill	Mike Smith/ Tom Bohannan	200,000
May 15	Pimlico Special Handicap	Pimlico	1$\frac{3}{16}$ miles	Devil His Due	Herb McCauley/ Allen Jerkens	600,000
May 15	Preakness Stakes	Pimlico	1$\frac{3}{16}$ miles	Prairie Bayou	Mike Smith/ Tom Bohannan	500,000
May 29	Jersey Derby	Garden State	1$\frac{1}{16}$ miles	Llandaff	Julie Krone/ Bill Mott	150,000
May 31	Hollywood Turf Handicap	Hollywood Park	1¼ miles	Bien Bien	Chris McCarron/ P. Gonzalez	500,000
June 2	Ever Ready (Epsom) Derby	Epsom Downs	1½ miles	Commander in Chief	Mick Kinane/ H. Cecil	961,000
June 5	Belmont Stakes	Belmont	1½ miles	Colonial Affair	Julie Krone/ Scotty Schulhofer	500,000
June 6	Mother Goose Stakes	Belmont	1⅛ miles	Sky Beauty	Mike Smith/ Allen Jerkens	200,000
June 27	Budweiser Irish Derby	Curragh	1½ miles	Commander in Chief	Pat Eddery/ H. Cecil	963,900
July 3	Hollywood Gold Cup	Hollywood Park	1¼ miles	Best Pal	Corey Black/ Gary Jones	750,000
July 4	Suburban Handicap	Belmont	1¼ miles	Devil His Due	Herb McCauley/ Allen Jerkens	300,000
July 11	Queen's Plate	Woodbine	1¼ miles	Peteski	Craig Perret/ Roger Attfield	284,654

1993 (Through September 6) (Cont.)

Date	Race	Track	Distance	Winner	Jockey/Trainer	Purse ($)
July 24	Iselin Handicap	Monmouth Park	1⅛ miles	Valley Crossing	Chris Antley/ R. Small	500,000
Aug 1	Haskell Invitational	Monmouth	1⅛ miles	Kissin Kris	Jose Santos/ D. Bell	500,000
Aug 1	Jim Dandy Stakes	Saratoga	1⅛ miles	Miner's Mark	Chris McCarron/ Claude McGaughey	150,000
Aug 14	Alabama Stakes	Saratoga	1¼ miles	Sky Beauty	Mike Smith/ Allen Jerkens	200,000
Aug 21	Travers Stakes	Saratoga	1¼ miles	Sea Hero	Jerry Bailey/ Mack Miller	1,000,000
Aug 28	Whitney Handicap	Saratoga	1⅛ miles	Brunswick	Mike Smith/ Anthony Margotta	250,000
Aug 30	Arlington Million	Arlington	1¼ miles	Star of Cozzene	Jose Santos/ Mark Hennig	1,000,000
Sep 5	Go For Wand Stakes	Belmont	1 mile	TurnBack The Alarm	Chris Antley/ W. Terrill	200,000
Sep 6	Pennsylvania Derby	Philadelphia	1⅛ miles	Wallenda	Herb McCauley/ F. Alexander	200,000

1992 Statistical Leaders

Horses

Horse	Starts	1st	2nd	3rd	Purses ($)	Horse	Starts	1st	2nd	3rd	Purses ($)
A.P. Indy	7	5	0	1	2,622,560	Sky Classic	9	5	3	0	1,655,482
Pine Bluff	6	3	1	1	1,970,896	Fraise	10	5	3	0	1,534,720
Pleasant Tap	10	4	5	0	1,959,914	Paseana-Ar	9	7	1	0	1,518,290
Strike The Gold	13	2	5	1	1,920,176	Mountain Cat	8	6	1	0	1,460,627
Best Pal	5	4	4	0	1,672,000	Sultry Song	8	3	1	1	1,178,700

Jockeys

Jockey	Mounts	1st	2nd	3rd	Purses ($)	Win Pct	$ Pct*
Kent Desormeaux	1,568	361	260	208	14,193,006	.23	53
Chris McCarron	1,150	193	178	177	12,861,946	.17	48
Eddie Delahoussaye	1,366	270	204	188	12,752,971	.20	49
Pat Day	1,213	291	230	162	12,557,077	.24	56
Gary Stevens	1,537	250	254	232	11,201,577	.16	48
Mike Smith	1,613	314	251	233	11,087,541	.20	50
Jerry Bailey	1,101	227	169	128	10,865,789	.21	48
Pat Valenzuela	1,174	219	213	159	10,268,342	.19	50
Julie Krone	1,462	282	245	193	9,220,824	.19	49
Alex Solis	1,635	228	232	228	8,835,192	.14	42

*Percentage in the Money (1st, 2nd, and 3rd)

The Genuine Article

Thousands of thoroughbred foals are born each year, but there is something special about the colt that was delivered at 5:05 p.m., May 15, 1993, near Lexington, Ky. The colt is the first live foal of Genuine Risk, who won the 1980 Kentucky Derby but has had nine failed pregnancies since then. Genuine Risk is one of only three female winners in the history of the Derby. She was bred to Rahy, a young stallion at the Three Chimneys Farm in Midway, Ky. The foal, as yet unnamed, has recovered from minor surgery for an intestinal blockage and will be eligible to run in the 1996 Kentucky Derby.

Trainers

TRainer	Starts	1st	2nd	3rd	Purses ($)	Win Pct	$ Pct*
D. Wayne Lukas	1,349	230	172	162	9,806,436	.17	42
Ron McAnally	641	108	113	83	8,236,051	.17	47
Robert Frankel	341	61	52	54	6,953,238	.18	49
Gary Jones	443	96	62	65	6,018,206	.22	50
William Mott	403	82	73	40	4,837,256	.20	48
James Day	318	67	71	37	4,450,478	.21	55
Nell Drysdale	191	38	31	26	4,224,102	.20	50
Claude McGaughey	238	51	52	43	4,119,832	.21	61
Peter Ferrlola	696	149	139	117	3,728,237	.21	58
Flint Schulhofer	407	76	64	56	3,701,895	.19	48

*Percentage in the Money (1st, 2nd, and 3rd)

Owners

Owner	Starts	1st	2nd	3rd	Purses ($)	Stable Leader
Golden Eagle Farm	592	125	93	64	5,479,484	Best Pal
Juddmonte Farms	204	46	31	31	5,278.037	Defensive Play
Sam-Son Farm	316	67	70	37	4,449,597	Sky Classic
John Franks	1,061	179	146	138	3,690,732	Parisian Flight
Loblolly Stable	228	43	43	38	3,233,281	Pine Bluff
Overbrook Farm	260	49	34	28	3,227,802	Mountain Cat
Buckland Farm	198	25	27	24	3,191,946	Pleasant Tap
Allen E. Paulson	238	52	39	36	2,956,458	Eliza
Jan, Mace & Samantha Siegel	559	111	87	83	2,191,573	Miss Iron Smoke
Sidney Craig II	61	19	2	4	2,112,020	Paseana-Ar

Note: 1992 statistical leaders courtesy of *Daily Racing Form*.

HARNESS RACING

Major Stakes Races (late 1992)

Date	Race	Location	Winner	Driver/Trainer	Purse ($)
Oct 9	Kentucky Futurity	Lexington Red Mile	Armbro Keepsake	John Campbell/ Charles Sylvester	172,000
Oct 9	BC Aged Horse/ Gelding Pace	Mohawk Raceway	Artsplace	John Campbell/ Bob McIntosh	300,000
Oct 9	BC Aged Horse/ Gelding Trot	Mohawk Raceway	No Sex Please	Ron Waples/ Ron Waples Jr.	300,000
Oct 9	BC Aged Mare Pace	Mohawk Raceway	Shady Daisy	Ron Pierce/ Lou Bauslaugh	250,000
Oct 9	BC Aged Mare Trot	Mohawk Raceway	Peace Corps	Torbjorn Jansson/ Torbjorn Jansson	235,500
Oct 23	BC 2-Yr-Old Filly Pace	Pompano Harness	Immortality	John Campbell/ Bruce Nickells	300,000
Oct 23	BC 2-Yr-Old Filly Trot	Pompano Harness	Winky's Goal	Cat Manzi/ Charles Sylvester	300,000
Oct 23	BC 2-Yr-Old Colt Trot	Pompano Harness	Giant Chill	J. Patterson Jr./ Per Eriksson	300,000
Oct 23	BC Three-Year-Old Filly Trot	Pompano Harness	Imperfection	Mike Lachance/ Ron Gurfein	300,000
Oct 23	BC Three-Year-Old Colt Trot	Pompano Harness	Baltic Striker	Mike Lachance/ Ron Gurfein	300,000
Oct 23	BC 2-Yr-Old Colt Pace	Pompano Harness	Village Jiffy	Ron Waples/ Bill Wellwood	300,000
Nov 6	BC Three-Year-Old Filly Pace	Northfield Park	So Fresh	John Campbell/ Bob McIntosh	300,000
Nov 6	BC Three-Year-Old Colt Pace	Northfield Park	Kingsbridge	R. Mayotte/ Kevin Banting	300,000
Nov 21	Governor's Cup	Garden State	Life Sign	John Campbell/ Gene Riegle	537,800

Major Stakes Races (Cont.)

1993 (Through September 23)

Date	Race	Location	Winner	Driver/Trainer	Purse ($)
May 30	Elitlopp	Solvalla (Sweden)	Sea Cove	J. Verbeeck/ Harald Grendel	371,186
June 26	North America Cup	Greenwood Raceway	Presidential Ball	Ron Waples/ Bill Robinson	1,000,000
July 10	Yonkers Trot	Yonkers Raceway	American Winner	Ron Pierce/ Milton Smith	313,699
July 17	Meadowlands Pace	Meadowlands	Presidential Ball	Jack Moiseyev/ Bill Robinson	1,000,000
Aug 3	Peter Haughton Memorial	Meadowlands	Westgate Crown	John Campbell/ Rousell Mackenzie	625,250
Aug 8	Hambletonian	Meadowlands	American Winner	Ron Pierce/ Milton Smith	1,104,000
Aug 11	Sweetheart Pace	Meadowlands	Freedom's Friend	John Campbell/ Bruce Nickells	550,250
Aug 13	Woodrow Wilson Pace	Meadowlands	Magical Mike	John Campbell/ Tom Haughton	747,700
Aug 14	Adios	Ladbroke at the Meadows	Miles McCool	John Campbell/ Tom Haughton	254,160
Aug 28	Cane Pace	Yonkers Raceway	Riyadh	Jim Morrill/ Bill Robinson	432,800
Sept 4	World Trotting Derby	DuQuoin	Pine Chip	John Campbell/ Charles Sylvester	532,000
Sep 11	Messenger Stakes	Rosecraft	Riyadh	Jim Morrill/ Bill Robinson	328,305
Sep 23	Little Brown Jug	Delaware	Life Sign	John Campbell/ Gene Riegle	465,500

Major Races

The Hambletonian

Horse	Driver	PP	¼	½	¾	Stretch	Finish
American Winner	Ron Pierce	2	2	1	1	1-2¾	1-2¾
Pine Chip	John Campbell	5	6	6	6	2-nk	2-1½
Hi Noon Star	Ron Waples	1	3	3	2	3-1	3-1
Toss Out	H. Wewering	3	4	4	4	4-1¾	4-2¼
Giant Chill	John Patterson Jr.	7	1	2	3	5-1¼	5-¾
Capital Star	William O'Donnell	9	9	7	7	8-5	6-nk
King Lavec	J. Takter	4	5	5	5	6-1	7-¾
Dry Wine	Per Henriksen	6	7	8	8	7-hd	8-7¼
Turbo Thrust	D. Rankin	8	8	9	9	9-dis	9-dis
Dylan Lobell	Mickey McNichol	10	10	10	10	10	10

Time: :28.3; :56.4; 1:25.4; 1:53.2; Fast

The Little Brown Jug

Horse	Driver	PP	¼	½	¾	Stretch	Finish
Life Sign	John Campbell	2	4	3	2	2	1-½
Riyadh	Jim Morrill	1	1	1	1	1	2-½
Presidential Ball	Jack Moiseyev	3	2	2	3	3	3-¾
Ready To Rumble	Joe Pavia Jr.	4	3	4	5	4	4-½
Getting Personal	J. Stark	7	7	6	6	6	5-3
Captain Pantastic	Walter Case	6	6	5	4	5	6-4
Native Born	Bill O'Donnell	5	5	7	7	7	7-4¾
Incoreyable Big	K. O'Donnell	8	8	8	8	8	8

Time: :27.0; :56.0; 1:23.4; 1:52.0; Fast

1992 Leading Moneywinners by Age, Sex and Gait

Division	Horse	Starts	1st	2nd	3rd	Earnings ($)
2-Year-Old Pacing Colts and Geldings	Presidential Ball	13	9	1	2	799,197
2-Year-Old Trotting Colts and Geldings	Giant Chill	11	8	1	1	471,585
2-Year-Old Pacing Fillies	Immortality	15	13	2	0	1,033,028
2-Year-Old Trotting Fillies	Suspicious Image	15	9	3	2	447,436
3-Year-Old Pacing Colts and Geldings	Western Hanover	28	19	7	1	1,844,315
3-Year-Old Trotting Colts and Geldings	Alf Palema	16	5	2	1	1,049,167
3-Year-Old Pacing Fillies	So Fresh	19	15	2	0	643,348
3-Year-Old Trotting Fillies	Imperfection	20	11	5	1	633,908
Aged Pacers	Artsplace	16	16	0	0	932,325
Aged Trotters	No Sex Please	22	10	6	2	435,870

Drivers

Driver	Earnings ($)	Driver	Earnings ($)
John Campbell	8,202,108	Doug Brown	4,108,086
Jack Moiseyev	7,675,504	Dave Magee	4,081,149
Michel Lachance	6,551,897	Ron Pierce	4,076,916
Cat Manzi	5,187,292	Walter Case, Jr	3,832,855
Bill Fahy	4,778,282	Herve Filion	3,041,433

Triple Threat?

The deaths of Union City and Prairie Bayou in this year's Preakness and Belmont, respectively, have prompted calls for the overhaul of the Triple Crown. Responding to criticism by animal rights groups and others, officials have discussed shortening the races —for example, cutting the Belmont from 1½ to 1¼ miles—and scheduling the events over eight weeks instead of five. Another suggestion: reducing the weight the horses carry from 126 to 121 pounds for colts and 121 to 116 for fillies.

But SI's racing writer, William Nack, deems such measures precipitate. Nack writes: "Until the Union City and Prairie Bayou mishaps there had not been a fatality in Triple Crown races since Black Hills went down in the 1959 Belmont. There were indications that Union City was unsound and shouldn't have run; if officials are bent on reform, they might subject the horses to more rigorous pre-race physical exams. Apparently Prairie Bayou was injured simply because he took a bad step, as horses will do.

"Run at three distances at three different tracks over a compressed period of time, the Triple Crown is racing's ultimate test of speed and stamina. The sport should not be stampeded into tampering with it."

THEY SAID IT

Jockey Nancy Summers, on two-year-old quarter horse Treacherously: "He tries hard, he's good looking and he's made a lot of money. If he was a man, I'd marry him."

FOR THE RECORD · Year by Year

THOROUGHBRED RACING

Kentucky Derby

Run at Churchill Downs, Louisville, KY, on the first Saturday in May.

Year	Winner (Margin)	Jockey	Second	Third	Time
1875	Aristides (1)	Oliver Lewis	Volcano	Verdigris	2:37¾
1876	Vagrant (2)	Bobby Swim	Creedmoor	Harry Hill	2:38¼
1877	Baden-Baden (2)	William Walker	Leonard	King William	2:38
1878	Day Star (2)	Jimmie Carter	Himyar	Leveler	2:37¼
1879	Lord Murphy (1)	Charlie Shauer	Falsetto	Strathmore	2:37
1880	Fonso (1)	George Lewis	Kimball	Bancroft	2:37½
1881	Hindoo (4)	Jimmy McLaughin	Lelex	Alfambra	2:40
1882	Apollo (½)	Babe Hurd	Runnymede	Bengal	2:40¼
1883	Leonatus (3)	Billy Donohue	Drake Carter	Lord Raglan	2:43
1884	Buchanan (2)	Isaac Murphy	Loftin	Audrain	2:40¼
1885	Joe Cotton (Neck)	Erskine Henderson	Bersan	Ten Booker	2:37¼
1886	Ben Ali (½)	Paul Duffy	Blue Wing	Free Knight	2:36½
1887	Montrose (2)	Isaac Lewis	Jim Gore	Jacobin	2:39¼
1888	MacBeth II (1)	George Covington	Gallifet	White	2:38¼
1889	Spokane (Nose)	Thomas Kiley	Proctor Knott	Once Again	2:34½
1890	Riley (2)	Isaac Murphy	Bill Letcher	Robespierre	2:45
1891	Kingman (1)	Isaac Murphy	Balgowan	High Tariff	2:52¼
1892	Azra (Nose)	Alonzo Clayton	Huron	Phil Dwyer	2:41½
1893	Lookout (5)	Eddie Kunze	Plutus	Boundless	2:39¼
1894	Chant (2)	Frank Goodale	Pearl Song	Sigurd	2:41
1895	Halma (3)	Soup Perkins	Basso	Laureate	2:37½
1896	Ben Brush (Nose)	Willie Simms	Ben Eder	Semper Ego	2:07¾
1897	Typhoon II (Head)	Buttons Garner	Ornament	Dr. Catlett	2:12½
1898	Plaudit (Neck)	Willie Simms	Lieber Karl	Isabey	2:09
1899	Manuel (2)	Fred Taral	Corsini	Mazo	2:12
1900	Lieut. Gibson (4)	Jimmy Boland	Florizar	Thrive	2:06¼
1901	His Eminence (2)	Jimmy Winkfield	Sannazarro	Driscoll	2:07¾
1902	Alan-a-Dale (Nose)	Jimmy Winkfield	Inventor	The Rival	2:08¾
1903	Judge Himes (¾)	Hal Booker	Early	Bourbon	2:09
1904	Elwood (½)	Frankie Prior	Ed Tierney	Brancas	2:08½
1905	Agile (3)	Jack Martin	Ram's Horn	Layson	2:10¾
1906	Sir Huon (2)	Roscoe Troxler	Lady Navarre	James Reddick	2:08 ⅕
1907	Pink Star (2)	Andy Minder	Zal	Ovelando	2:12⅗
1908	Stone Street (1)	Arthur Pickens	Sir Cleges	Dunvegan	2:15⅕
1909	Wintergreen (4)	Vincent Powers	Miami	Dr. Barkley	2:08⅕
1910	Donau (½)	Fred Herbert	Joe Morris	Fighting Bob	2:06⅖
1911	Meridian (¾)	George Archibald	Governor Gray	Colston	2:05
1912	Worth (Neck)	Carroll H. Schilling	Duval	Flamma	2:09⅖
1913	Donerail (½)	Roscoe Goose	Ten Point	Gowell	2:04⅘
1914	Old Rosebud (8)	John McCabe	Hodge	Bronzewing	2:03⅖
1915	Regret (2)	Joe Notter	Pebbles	Sharpshooter	2:05⅖
1916	George Smith (Neck)	Johnny Loftus	Star Hawk	Franklin	2:04
1917	Omar Khayyam (2)	Charles Borel	Ticket	Midway	2:04⅗
1918	Exterminator (1)	William Knapp	Escoba	Viva America	2:10⅘
1919	Sir Barton (5)	Johnny Loftus	Billy Kelly	Under Fire	2:09⅘
1920	Paul Jones (Head)	Ted Rice	Upset	On Watch	2:09
1921	Behave Yourself (Head)	Charles Thompson	Black Servant	Prudery	2:04⅕
1922	Morvich (½)	Albert Johnson	Bet Mosie	John Finn	2:04⅗
1923	Zev (1½)	Earl Sande	Martingale	Vigil	2:05⅖
1924	Black Gold (½)	John Mooney	Chilhowee	Beau Butler	2:05⅕
1925	Flying Ebony (1½)	Earl Sande	Captain Hal	Son of John	2:07⅗
1926	Bubbling Over (5)	Albert Johnson	Bagenbaggage	Rock Man	2:03⅘
1927	Whiskery (Head)	Linus McAtee	Osmond	Jock	2:06
1928	Reigh Count (3)	Chick Lang	Misstep	Toro	2:10⅖
1929	Clyde Van Dusen (2)	Linus McAtee	Naishapur	Panchio	2:10⅘
1930	Gallant Fox (2)	Earl Sande	Gallant Knight	Ned O.	2:07⅗

Kentucky Derby *(Cont.)*

Year	Winner (Margin)	Jockey	Second	Third	Time
1931	Twenty Grand (4)	Charles Kurtsinger	Sweep All	Mate	2:01⅘
1932	Burgoo King (5)	Eugene James	Economic	Stepenfetchit	2:05⅕
1933	Brokers Tip (Nose)	Don Meade	Head Play	Charley O.	2:06⅘
1934	Cavalcade (2½)	Mack Garner	Discovery	Agrarian	2:04
1935	Omaha (1½)	Willie Saunders	Roman Soldier	Whiskolo	2:05
1936	Bold Venture (Head)	Ira Hanford	Brevity	Indian Broom	2:03⅗
1937	War Admiral (1¾)	Charles Kurtsinger	Pompoon	Reaping Reward	2:03⅕
1938	Lawrin (1)	Eddie Arcaro	Dauber	Can't Wait	2:04⅘
1939	Johnstown (8)	James Stout	Challedon	Heather Broom	2:03⅗
1940	Gallahadion (1½)	Carroll Bierman	Bimelech	Dit	2:05
1941	Whirlaway (8)	Eddie Arcaro	Staretor	Market Wise	2:01⅖
1942	Shut Out (2½)	Wayne Wright	Alsab	Valdina Orphan	2:04⅖
1943	Count Fleet (3)	John Longden	Blue Swords	Slide Rule	2:04
1944	Pensive (4½)	Conn McCreary	Broadcloth	Stir Up	2:04⅕
1945	Hoop Jr. (6)	Eddie Arcaro	Pot o' Luck	Darby Dieppe	2:07
1946	Assault (8)	Warren Mehrtens	Spy Song	Hampden	2:06⅗
1947	Jet Pilot (Head)	Eric Guerin	Phalanx	Faultless	2:06⅘
1948	Citation (3½)	Eddie Arcaro	Coaltown	My Request	2:05⅖
1949	Ponder (3)	Steve Brooks	Capot	Palestinian	2:04⅕
1950	Middleground (1¼)	William Boland	Hill Prince	Mr. Trouble	2:01⅗
1951	Count Turf (4)	Conn McCreary	Royal Mustang	Ruhe	2:02⅗
1952	Hill Gail (2)	Eddie Arcaro	Sub Fleet	Blue Man	2:01⅗
1953	Dark Star (Head)	Hank Moreno	Native Dancer	Invigorator	2:02
1954	Determine (1½)	Ray York	Hasty Road	Hasseyampa	2:03
1955	Swaps (1½)	Bill Shoemaker	Nashua	Summer Tan	2:01⅘
1956	Needles (¾)	Dave Erb	Fabius	Come On Red	2:03⅖
1957	Iron Liege (Nose)	Bill Hartack	Gallant Man	Round Table	2:02⅕
1958	Tim Tam (½)	Ismael Valenzuela	Lincoln Road	Noureddin	2:05
1959	Tomy Lee (Nose)	Bill Shoemaker	Sword Dancer	First Landing	2:02⅕
1960	Venetian Way (3½)	Bill Hartack	Bally Ache	Victoria Park	2:02⅖
1961	Carry Back (¾)	John Sellers	Crozier	Bass Clef	2:04
1962	Decidedly (2¼)	Bill Hartack	Roman Line	Ridan	2:00⅖
1963	Chateaugay (1¼)	Braulio Baeza	Never Bend	Candy Spots	2:01⅘
1964	Northern Dancer (Neck)	Bill Hartack	Hill Rise	The Scoundrel	2:00
1965	Lucky Debonair (Neck)	Bill Shoemaker	Dapper Dan	Tom Rolfe	2:01⅕
1966	Kauai King (½)	Don Brumfield	Advocator	Blue Skyer	2:02
1967	Proud Clarion (1)	Bobby Ussery	Barbs Delight	Damascus	2:00⅗
1968	Forward Pass (Disq.)	Ismael Valenzuela	Francie's Hat	T.V. Commercial	2:02⅕
1969	Majestic Prince (Neck)	Bill Hartack	Arts and Letters	Dike	2:01⅘
1970	Dust Commander (5)	Mike Manganello	My Dad George	High Echelon	2:03⅖
1971	Canonero II (3¾)	Gustavo Avila	Jim French	Bold Reason	2:03⅕
1972	Riva Ridge (3¼)	Ron Turcotte	No Le Hace	Hold Your Peace	2:01⅘
1973	Secretariat (2-½)	Ron Turcotte	Sham	Our Native	1:59⅖
1974	Cannonade (2¼)	Angel Cordero Jr	Hudson County	Agitate	2:04
1975	Foolish Pleasure (1¾)	Jacinto Vasquez	Avatar	Diabolo	2:02
1976	Bold Forbes (1)	Angel Cordero Jr	Honest Pleasure	Elocutionist	2:01⅗
1977	Seattle Slew (1¾)	Jean Cruguet	Run Dusty Run	Sanhedrin	2:02⅕
1978	Affirmed (1½)	Steve Cauthen	Alydar	Believe It	2:01⅕
1979	Spectacular Bid (2¾)	Ronald J. Franklin	General Assembly	Golden Act	2:02⅖
1980	Genuine Risk (1)	Jacinto Vasquez	Rumbo	Jaklin Klugman	2:02
1981	Pleasant Colony (¾)	Jorge Velasquez	Woodchopper	Partez	2:02
1982	Gato Del Sol (2½)	Eddie Delahoussaye	Laser Light	Reinvested	2:02⅖
1983	Sunny's Halo (2)	Eddie Delahoussaye	Desert Wine	Caveat	2:02⅕
1984	Swale (3¼)	Laffit Pincay Jr	Coax Me Chad	At the Threshold	2:02⅖
1985	Spend A Buck (5)	Angel Cordero Jr	Stephan's Odyssey	Chief's Crown	2:00⅕
1986	Ferdinand (2¼)	Bill Shoemaker	Bold Arrangement	Broad Brush	2:02⅘
1987	Alysheba (¾)	Chris McCarron	Bet Twice	Avies Copy	2:03⅖
1988	Winning Colors (Neck)	Gary Stevens	Forty Niner	Risen Star	2:02⅕
1989	Sunday Silence (2½)	Pat Valenzuela	Easy Goer	Awe Inspiring	2:05
1990	Unbridled (3½)	Craig Perret	Summer Squall	Pleasant Tap	2:02
1991	Strike the Gold (1¾)	Chris Antley	Best Pal	Mane Minister	2:03
1992	Lil E. Tee (1)	Pat Day	Casual Lies	Dance Floor	2:03
1993	Sea Hero (2½)	Jerry Bailey	Prairie Bayou	Wild Gale	2:02⅖

Note: Distance: 1½ miles (1875-95), 1¼ miles (1896-present).

Preakness

Run at Pimlico Race Course, Baltimore, Md., two weeks after the Kentucky Derby.

Year	Winner (Margin)	Jockey	Second	Third	Time
1873	Survivor (10)	G. Barbee	John Boulger	Artist	2:43
1874	Culpepper (¾)	W. Donohue	King Amadeus	Scratch	2:56½
1875	Tom Ochiltree (2)	L. Hughes	Viator	Bay Final	2:43½
1876	Shirley (4)	G. Barbee	Rappahannock	Algerine	2:44¾
1877	Cloverbrook (4)	C. Holloway	Bombast	Lucifer	2:45½
1878	Duke of Magenta (6)	C. Holloway	Bayard	Albert	2:41¾
1879	Harold (3)	L. Hughes	Jericho	Rochester	2:40½
1880	Grenada (¾)	L. Hughes	Oden	Emily F.	2:40½
1881	Saunterer (½)	T. Costello	Compensation	Baltic	2:40½
1882	Vanguard (Neck)	T. Costello	Heck	Col Watson	2:44½
1883	Jacobus (4)	G. Barbee	Parnell		2:42½
1884	Knight of Ellerslie (2)	S. Fisher	Welcher		2:39½
1885	Tecumseh (2)	Jim McLaughlin	Wickham	John C.	2:49
1886	The Bard (3)	S. Fisher	Eurus	Elkwood	2:45
1887	Dunboyne (1)	W. Donohue	Mahoney	Raymond	2:39½
1888	Refund (3)	F. Littlefield	Judge Murray	Glendale	2:49
1889	Buddhist (8)	W. Anderson	Japhet		2:17½
1890*	Montague (3)	W. Martin	Philosophy	Barrister	2:36¾
1894	Assignee (3)	Fred Taral	Potentate	Ed Kearney	1:49¼
1895	Belmar (1)	Fred Taral	April Fool	Sue Kittie	1:50½
1896	Margrave (1)	H. Griffin	Hamilton II	Intermission	1:51
1897	Paul Kauvar (1½)	C. Thorpe	Elkins	On Deck	1:51¼
1898	Sly Fox (2)	C. W. Simms	The Huguenot	Nuto	1:49⅗
1899	Half Time (1)	R. Clawson	Filigrane	Lackland	1:47
1900	Hindus (Head)	H. Spencer	Sarmation	Ten Candles	1:48⅖
1901	The Parader (2)	F. Landry	Sadie S.	Dr. Barlow	1:47⅕
1902	Old England (Nose)	L. Jackson	Major Daingerfield	Namtor	1:45⅘
1903	Flocarline (½)	W. Gannon	Mackey Dwyer	Rightful	1:44⅘
1904	Bryn Mawr (1)	E. Hildebrand	Wotan	Dolly Spanker	1:44⅕
1905	Cairngorm (Head)	W. Davis	Kiamesha	Coy Maid	1:45⅘
1906	Whimsical (4)	Walter Miller	Content	Larabie	1:45
1907	Don Enrique (1)	G. Mountain	Ethon	Zambesi	1:45⅖
1908	Royal Tourist (4)	E. Dugan	Live Wire	Robert Cooper	1:46⅖
1909	Effendi (1)	Willie Doyle	Fashion Plate	Hilltop	1:39⅗
1910	Layminster (½)	R. Estep	Dalhousie	Sager	1:40⅗
1911	Watervale (1)	E. Dugan	Zeus	The Nigger	1:51
1912	Colonel Holloway (5)	C. Turner	Bwana Tumbo	Tipsand	1:56⅗
1913	Buskin (Neck)	J. Butwell	Kleburne	Barnegat	1:53⅖
1914	Holiday (¾)	A. Schuttinger	Brave Cunarder	Defendum	1:53⅘
1915	Rhine Maiden (1½)	Douglas Hoffman	Half Rock	Runes	1:58
1916	Damrosch (1½)	Linus McAtee	Greenwood	Achievement	1:54⅘
1917	Kalitan (2)	E. Haynes	Al M. Dick	Kentucky Boy	1:54⅖
1918	War Cloud (¾)	Johnny Loftus	Sunny Slope	Lanius	1:53⅗
1918	Jack Hare, Jr (2)	C. Peak	The Porter	Kate Bright	1:53⅖
1919	Sir Barton (4)	Johnny Loftus	Eternal	Sweep On	1:53
1920	Man o' War (1½)	Clarence Kummer	Upset	Wildair	1:51⅗
1921	Broomspun (¾)	F. Coltiletti	Polly Ann	Jeg	1:54⅕
1922	Pillory (Head)	L. Morris	Hea	June Grass	1:51⅗
1923	Vigil (1¼)	B. Marinelli	General Thatcher	Rialto	1:53⅗
1924	Nellie Morse (1½)	J. Merimee	Transmute	Mad Play	1:57⅕
1925	Coventry (4)	Clarence Kummer	Backbone	Almadel	1:59
1926	Display (Head)	J. Maiben	Blondin	Mars	1:59⅘
1927	Bostonian (½)	A. Abel	Sir Harry	Whiskery	2:01⅗
1928	Victorian (Nose)	Sonny Workman	Toro	Solace	2:00⅕
1929	Dr. Freeland (1)	Louis Schaefer	Minotaur	African	2:01⅗
1930	Gallant Fox (¾)	Earl Sande	Crack Brigade	Snowflake	2:00⅗
1931	Mate (1½)	G. Ellis	Twenty Grand	Ladder	1:59
1932	Burgoo King (Head)	E. James	Tick On	Boatswain	1:59⅘
1933	Head Play (4)	Charles Kurtsinger	Ladysman	Utopian	2:02
1934	High Quest (Nose)	R. Jones	Cavalcade	Discovery	1:58⅕
1935	Omaha (6)	Willie Saunders	Firethorn	Psychic Bid	1:58⅖
1936	Bold Venture (Nose)	George Woolf	Granville	Jean Bart	1:59

Preakness (Cont.)

Year	Winner (Margin)	Jockey	Second	Third	Time
1937	War Admiral (Head)	Charles Kurtsinger	Pompoon	Flying Scot	1:58⅖
1938	Dauber (7)	M. Peters	Cravat	Menow	1:59⅘
1939	Challedon (1¼)	George Seabo	Gilded Knight	Volitant	1:59⅘
1940	Bimelech (3)	F. A. Smith	Mioland	Gallahadion	1:58⅗
1941	Whirlaway (5½)	Eddie Arcaro	King Cole	Our Boots	1:58⅘
1942	Alsab (1)	B. James	Requested Sun Again	(dead heat for second)	1:57
1943	Count Fleet (8)	Johnny Longden	Blue Swords	Vincentive	1:57⅖
1944	Pensive (¾)	Conn McCreary	Platter	Stir Up	1:59⅕
1945	Polynesian (2½)	W. D. Wright	Hoop Jr	Darby Dieppe	1:58⅘
1946	Assault (Neck)	Warren Mehrtens	Lord Boswell	Hampden	2:01⅖
1947	Faultless (1¼)	Doug Dodson	On Trust	Phalanx	1:59
1948	Citation (5½)	Eddie Arcaro	Vulcan's Forge	Boyard	2:02⅖
1949	Capot (Head)	Ted Atkinson	Palestinian	Noble Impulse	1:56
1950	Hill Prince (5)	Eddie Arcaro	Middleground	Dooley	1:59⅕
1951	Bold (7)	Eddie Arcaro	Counterpoint	Alerted	1:56⅖
1952	Blue Man (3½)	Conn McCreary	Jampol	One Count	1:57⅖
1953	Native Dancer (Neck)	Eric Guerin	Jamie K.	Royal Bay Gem	1:57⅘
1954	Hasty Road (Neck)	Johnny Adams	Correlation	Hasseyampa	1:57⅖
1955	Nashua (1)	Eddie Arcaro	Saratoga	Traffic Judge	1:54⅗
1956	Fabius (¾)	Bill Hartack	Needles	No Regrets	1:58⅖
1957	Bold Ruler (2)	Eddie Arcaro	Iron Liege	Inside Tract	1:56⅕
1958	Tim Tam (1½)	I. Valenzuela	Lincoln Road	Gone Fishin'	1:57⅕
1959	Royal Orbit (4)	William Harmatz	Sword Dancer	Dunce	1:57
1960	Bally Ache (4)	Bobby Ussery	Victoria Park	Celtic Ash	1:57⅗
1961	Carry Back (¾)	Johnny Sellers	Globemaster	Crozier	1:57⅗
1962	Greek Money (Nose)	John Rotz	Ridan	Roman Line	1:56⅕
1963	Candy Spots (3½)	Bill Shoemaker	Chateaugay	Never Bend	1:56⅕
1964	Northern Dancer (2¼)	Bill Hartack	The Scoundrel	Hill Rise	1:56⅘
1965	Tom Rolfe (Neck)	Ron Turcotte	Dapper Dan	Hail to All	1:56⅕
1966	Kauai King (1¾)	Don Brumfield	Stupendous	Amberoid	1:55⅖
1967	Damascus (2¼)	Bill Shoemaker	In Reality	Proud Clarion	1:55⅕
1968	Forward Pass (6)	I. Valenzuela	Out of the Way	Nodouble	1:56⅘
1969	Majestic Prince (Head)	Bill Hartack	Arts and Letters	Jay Ray	1:55⅗
1970	Personality (Neck)	Eddie Belmonte	My Dad George	Silent Screen	1:56⅕
1971	Canonero II (1½)	Gustavo Avila	Eastern Fleet	Jim French	1:54
1972	Bee Bee Bee (1¼)	Eldon Nelson	No Le Hace	Key to the Mint	1:55⅗
1973	Secretariat (2½)	Ron Turcotte	Sham	Our Native	1:54⅖
1974	Little Current (7)	Miguel Rivera	Neapolitan Way	Cannonade	1:54⅗
1975	Master Derby (1)	Darrel McHargue	Foolish Pleasure	Diabolo	1:56⅖
1976	Elocutionist (3)	John Lively	Play the Red	Bold Forbes	1:55
1977	Seattle Slew (1½)	Jean Cruguet	Iron Constitution	Run Dusty Run	1:54⅖
1978	Affirmed (Neck)	Steve Cauthen	Alydar	Believe It	1:54⅖
1979	Spectacular Bid (5½)	Ron Franklin	Golden Act	Screen King	1:54⅕
1980	Codex (4¾)	Angel Cordero Jr	Genuine Risk	Colonel Moran	1:54⅕
1981	Pleasant Colony (1)	Jorge Velasquez	Bold Ego	Paristo	1:54⅗
1982	Aloma's Ruler (½)	Jack Kaenel	Linkage	Cut Away	1:55⅖
1983	Deputed Testamony (2¾)	Donald Miller Jr	Desert Wine	High Honors	1:55⅖
1984	Gate Dancer (1½)	Angel Cordero Jr	Play On	Fight Over	1:53⅗
1985	Tank's Prospect (Head)	Pat Day	Chief's Crown	Eternal Prince	1:53⅖
1986	Snow Chief (4)	Alex Solis	Ferdinand	Broad Brush	1:54⅘
1987	Alysheba (½)	Chris McCarron	Bet Twice	Cryptoclearance	1:55⅘
1988	Risen Star (1¼)	E. Delahoussaye	Brian's Time	Winning Colors	1:56⅕
1989	Sunday Silence (Nose)	Pat Valenzuela	Easy Goer	Rock Point	1:53⅘
1990	Summer Squall (2¼)	Pat Day	Unbridled	Mister Frisky	1:53⅗
1991	Hansel (Head)	Jerry Bailey	Corporate Report	Mane Minister	1:54
1992	Pine Bluff (¾)	Chris McCarron	Alydeed	Casual Lies	1:55⅗
1993	Prairie Bayou (½)	Mike Smith	Cherokee Run	El Bakan	1:56⅗

*Preakness was not run 1891—1893. In 1918, it was run in two divisions.

Note: Distance: 1½ miles (1873—88), 1¼ miles (1889), 1½ miles (1890), 1¹⁄₁₆ miles (1894—1900), 1 mile and 70 yards (1901—1907), 1¹⁄₁₆ miles (1908), 1 mile (1909—10), 1⅛ miles (1911—24), 1³⁄₁₆ miles (1925—present).

Belmont

Run at Belmont Park, Elmont, NY, three weeks after the Preakness Stakes. Held previously at two locations in the Bronx, NY: Jerome Park (1867—1889) and Morris Park (1890—1904).

Year	Winner (Margin)	Jockey	Second	Third	Time
1867	Ruthless (Head)	J. Gilpatrick	De Courcy	Rivoli	3:05
1868	General Duke (2)	R. Swim	Northumberland	Fannie Ludlow	3:02
1869	Fenian (Unknown)	C. Miller	Glenelg	Invercauld	3:04¼
1870	Kingfisher (½)	E. Brown	Foster	Midday	2:59½
1871	Harry Bassett (3)	W. Miller	Stockwood	By-the-Sea	2:56
1872	Joe Daniels (¾)	James Rowe	Meteor	Shylock	2:58¼
1873	Springbok (4)	James Rowe	Count d'Orsay	Strachino	3:01¾
1874	Saxon (Neck)	G. Barbee	Grinstead	Aaron Pennington	2:39½
1875	Calvin (2)	R. Swim	Aristides	Milner	2:40¼
1876	Algerine (Head)	W. Donahue	Fiddlestick	Barricade	2:40½
1877	Cloverbrook (1)	C. Holloway	Loiterer	Baden-Baden	2:46
1878	Duke of Magenta (2)	L. Hughes	Bramble	Sparta	2:43½
1879	Spendthrift (5)	S. Evans	Monitor	Jericho	2:42¾
1880	Grenada (½)	L. Hughes	Ferncliffe	Turenne	2:47
1881	Saunterer (Neck)	T. Costello	Eole	Baltic	2:47
1882	Forester (5)	James McLaughlin	Babcock	Wyoming	2:43
1883	George Kinney (2)	James McLaughlin	Trombone	Renegade	2:42½
1884	Panique (½)	James McLaughlin	Knight of Ellerslie	Himalaya	2:42
1885	Tyrant (3½)	Paul Duffy	St Augustine	Tecumseh	2:43
1886	Inspector B (1)	James McLaughlin	The Bard	Linden	2:41
1887	Hanover (28-32)	James McLaughlin	Oneko		2:43½
1888	Sir Dixon (12)	James McLaughlin	Prince Royal		2:40¼
1889	Eric (Head)	W. Hayward	Diable	Zephyrus	2:47
1890	Burlington (1)	S. Barnes	Devotee	Padishah	2:07¾
1891	Foxford (Neck)	E. Garrison	Montana	Laurestan	2:08¾
1892	Patron (Unknown)	W. Hayward	Shellbark		2:17
1893	Comanche (Head)(21)	Willie Simms	Dr. Rice	Rainbow	1:53¼
1894	Henry of Navarre (2-4)	Willie Simms	Prig	Assignee	1:56½
1895	Belmar (Head)	Fred Taral	Counter Tenor	Nanki Pooh	2:11½
1896	Hastings (Neck)	H. Griffin	Handspring	Hamilton II	2:24½
1897	Scottish Chieftain (1)	J. Scherrer	On Deck	Octagon	2:23¼
1898	Bowling Brook (8)	P. Littlefield	Previous	Hamburg	2:32
1899	Jean Bereaud (Head)	R. R. Clawson	Half Time	Glengar	2:23
1900	Ildrim (Head)	N. Turner	Petrucio	Missionary	2:21½
1901	Commando (½)	H. Spencer	The Parader	All Green	2:21
1902	Masterman (2)	John Bullmann	Ranald	King Hanover	2:22½
1903	Africander (2)	John Bullmann	Whorler	Red Knight	2:23⅕
1904	Delhi (3½)	George Odom	Graziallo	Rapid Water	2:06⅗
1905	Tanya (1/2)	E. Hildebrand	Blandy	Hot Shot	2:08
1906	Burgomaster (4)	L. Lyne	The Quail	Accountant	2:20
1907	Peter Pan (1)	G. Mountain	Superman	Frank Gill	Unknown
1908	Colin (Head)	Joe Notter	Fair Play	King James	Unknown
1909	Joe Madden (8)	E. Dugan	Wise Mason	Donald MacDonald	2:21⅗
1910*	Sweep (6)	J. Butwell	Duke of Ormonde		2:22
1913	Prince Eugene (½)	Roscoe Troxler	Rock View	Flying Fairy	2:18
1914	Luke McLuke (8)	M. Buxton	Gainer	Charlestonian	2:20
1915	The Finn (4)	G. Byrne	Half Rock	Pebbles	2:18⅖
1916	Friar Rock (3)	E. Haynes	Spur	Churchill	2:22
1917	Hourless (10)	J. Butwell	Skeptic	Wonderful	2:17⅘
1918	Johren (2)	Frank Robinson	War Cloud	Cum Sah	2:20⅖
1919	Sir Barton (5)	Johnny Loftus	Sweep On	Natural Bridge	2:17⅖
1920	Man o' War (20)	Clarence Kummer	Donnacona		2:14⅕
1921	Grey Lag (3)	Earl Sande	Sporting Blood	Leonardo II	2:16⅘
1922	Pillory (2)	C. H. Miller	Snob II	Hea	2:18⅘
1923	Zev (1½)	Earl Sande	Chickvale	Rialto	2:19
1924	Mad Play (2)	Earl Sande	Mr. Mutt	Modest	2:18⅘
1925	American Flag (8)	Albert Johnson	Dangerous	Swope	2:16⅘
1926	Crusader (1)	Albert Johnson	Espino	Haste	2:32⅕
1927	Chance Shot (1½)	Earl Sande	Bois de Rose	Flambino	2:32⅖

Belmont (Cont.)

Year	Winner (Margin)	Jockey	Second	Third	Time
1928	Vito (3)	Clarence Kummer	Genie	Diavolo	2:33⅕
1929	Blue Larkspur (¾)	Mack Garner	African	Jack High	2:32⅘
1930	Gallant Fox (3)	Earl Sande	Whichone	Questionnaire	2:31⅗
1931	Twenty Grand (10)	Charles Kurtsinger	Sun Meadow	Jamestown	2:29⅗
1932	Faireno (1½)	T. Malley	Osculator	Flag Pole	2:32⅘
1933	Hurryoff (1½)	Mack Garner	Nimbus	Union	2:32⅗
1934	Peace Chance (6)	W. D. Wright	High Quest	Good Goods	2:29⅕
1935	Omaha (1½)	Willie Saunders	Firethorn	Rosemont	2:30⅗
1936	Granville (Nose)	James Stout	Mr. Bones	Hollyrood	2:30
1937	War Admiral (3)	Charles Kurtsinger	Sceneshifter	Vamoose	2:28⅗
1938	Pasteurized (Neck)	James Stout	Dauber	Cravat	2:29⅖
1939	Johnstown (5)	James Stout	Belay	Gilded Knight	2:29⅗
1940	Bimelech (¾)	F. A. Smith	Your Chance	Andy K	2:29⅗
1941	Whirlaway (2½)	Eddie Arcaro	Robert Morris	Yankee Chance	2:31
1942	Shut Out (2)	Eddie Arcaro	Alsab	Lochinvar	2:29⅕
1943	Count Fleet (25)	Johnny Longden	Fairy Manhurst	Deseronto	2:28⅕
1944	Bounding Home (½)	G. L. Smith	Pensive	Bull Dandy	2:32⅕
1945	Pavot (5)	Eddie Arcaro	Wildlife	Jeep	2:30⅕
1946	Assault (3)	Warren Mehrtens	Natchez	Cable	2:30⅘
1947	Phalanx (5)	R. Donoso	Tide Rips	Tailspin	2:29⅖
1948	Citation (8)	Eddie Arcaro	Better Self	Escadru	2:28⅕
1949	Capot (½)	Ted Atkinson	Ponder	Palestinian	2:30⅕
1950	Middleground (1)	William Boland	Lights Up	Mr. Trouble	2:28⅗
1951	Counterpoint (4)	D. Gorman	Battlefield	Battle Morn	2:29
1952	One Count (2½)	Eddie Arcaro	Blue Man	Armageddon	2:30⅕
1953	Native Dancer (Neck)	Eric Guerin	Jamie K.	Royal Bay Gem	2:38⅗
1954	High Gun (Neck)	Eric Guerin	Fisherman	Limelight	2:30⅘
1955	Nashua (9)	Eddie Arcaro	Blazing Count	Portersville	2:29
1956	Needles (Neck)	David Erb	Career Boy	Fabius	2:29⅘
1957	Gallant Man (8)	Bill Shoemaker	Inside Tract	Bold Ruler	2:26⅗
1958	Cavan (6)	Pete Anderson	Tim Tam	Flamingo	2:30⅕
1959	Sword Dancer (¾)	Bill Shoemaker	Bagdad	Royal Orbit	2:28⅖
1960	Celtic Ash (5½)	Bill Hartack	Venetian Way	Disperse	2:29⅗
1961	Sherluck (2¼)	Braulio Baeza	Globemaster	Guadalcanal	2:29⅕
1962	Jaipur (Nose)	Bill Shoemaker	Admiral's Voyage	Crimson Satan	2:28⅘
1963	Chateaugay (2½)	Braulio Baeza	Candy Spots	Choker	2:30⅕
1964	Quadrangle (2)	Manuel Ycaza	Roman Brother	Northern Dancer	2:28⅖
1965	Hail to All (Neck)	John Sellers	Tom Rolfe	First Family	2:28⅖
1966	Amberold (2½)	William Boland	Buffle	Advocator	2:29⅗
1967	Damascus (2½)	Bill Shoemaker	Cool Reception	Gentleman James	2:28⅘
1968	Stage Door Johnny (1¼)	Hellodoro Gustines	Forward Pass	Call Me Prince	2:27⅕
1969	Arts and Letters (5½)	Braulio Baeza	Majestic Prince	Dike	2:28⅘
1970	High Echelon (¾)	John L. Rotz	Needles N Pins	Naskra	2:34
1971	Pass Catcher (¾)	Walter Blum	Jim French	Bold Reason	2:30⅖
1972	Riva Ridge (7)	Ron Turcotte	Ruritania	Cloudy Dawn	2:28
1973	Secretariat (31)	Ron Turcotte	Twice a Prince	My Gallant	2:24
1974	Little Current (7)	Miguel A. Rivera	Jolly Johu	Cannonade	2:29⅕
1975	Avatar (Neck)	Bill Shoemaker	Foolish Pleasure	Master Derby	2:28⅕
1976	Bold Forbes (Neck)	Angel Cordero Jr	McKenzie Bridge	Great Contractor	2:29
1977	Seattle Slew (4)	Jean Cruguet	Run Dusty Run	Sanhedrin	2:29⅗
1978	Affirmed (Head)	Ruben Hernandez	Alydar	Darby Creek Road	2:26⅘
1979	Coastal (3¼)	Ruben Hernandez	Golden Act	Spectacular Bid	2:28⅗
1980	Temperence Hill (2)	Eddie Maple	Genuine Risk	Rockhill Native	2:29⅘
1981	Summing (Neck)	George Martens	Highland Blade	Pleasant Colony	2:29
1982	Conquistador Cielo (14½)	Laffit Pincay, Jr	Gato Del Sol	Illuminate	2:28⅕
1983	Caveat (3½)	Laffit Pincay, Jr	Slew o'Gold	Barberstown	2:27⅘
1984	Swale (4)	Laffit Pincay, Jr	Pine Circle	Morning Bob	2:27⅕
1985	Creme Fraiche (½)	Eddie Maple	Stephan's Odyssey	Chief's Crown	2:27
1986	Danzig Connection (1¼)	Chris McCarron	Johns Treasure	Ferdinand	2:29⅘

Belmont *(Cont.)*

Year	Winner (Margin)	Jockey	Second	Third	Time
1987	Bet Twice (14)	Craig Perret	Cryptoclearance	Gulch	2:28⅕
1988	Risen Star (14¾)	Eddie Delahoussaye	Kingpost	Brian's Time	2:26⅖
1989	Easy Goer (8)	Pat Day	Sunday Silence	Le Voyageur	2:26
1990	Go and Go (8¼)	Michael Kinane	Thirty Six Red	Baron de Vaux	2:27⅕
1991	Hansel (Head)	Jerry Bailey	Strike the Gold	Mane Minister	2:28
1992	A.P. Indy (¾)	Eddie Delahoussaye	My Memoirs	Pine Bluff	2:26
1993	Colonial Affair	Julie Krone	Kissin Kris	Wild Gale	2:29⅘

*Race not held in 1911-1912.

Note: Distance: 1 mile 5 furlongs (1867-89), 1¼ miles (1890-1905), 1⅜ miles (1906-25), 1½ miles (1926-present).

Triple Crown Winners

Year	Horse	Jockey	Owner	Trainer
1919	Sir Barton	John Loftus	J. K. L. Ross	H. G. Bedwell
1930	Gallant Fox	Earle Sande	Belair Stud	James Fitzsimmons
1935	Omaha	William Saunders	Belair Stud	James Fitzsimmons
1937	War Admiral	Charles Kurtsinger	Samuel D. Riddle	George Conway
1941	Whirlaway	Eddie Arcaro	Calumet Farm	Ben Jones
1943	Count Fleet	John Longden	Mrs J. D. Hertz	Don Cameron
1946	Assault	Warren Mehrtens	King Ranch	Max Hirsch
1948	Citation	Eddie Arcaro	Calumet Farm	Jimmy Jones
1973	Secretariat	Ron Turcotte	Meadow Stable	Lucien Laurin
1977	Seattle Slew	Jean Cruguet	Karen L. Taylor	William H. Turner Jr
1978	Affirmed	Steve Cauthen	Harbor View Farm	Laz Barrera

Blundering Hooves

The Grand National, held April 3, 1993, in Aintree, England, was a fiasco. The race was declared void, forcing the return of $115 million in wagers, after a horribly botched start resulted in eight horses' unofficially completing the 4½ miles while nine horses waited at the start and others in the field of 40 wandered aimlessly around the course. But then misadventure and the National, the world's most prestigious steeplchase, have been stablemates throughout the event's 156-year history.

In 1885 one of the favorites, Zoedone, collapsed during the National , and it was determined that she had been poisoned. The 1948 winner, Sheila's Cottage, celebrated by biting off the finger of her jockey, Arthur Thompson. In 1956 the Queen Mother's horse, Devon Loch, was leading when, 50 yards from the finish, he went down, legs splayed; the reason for Devon Loch's contretemps remains a mystery, which is fitting, since his jockey was Dick Francis, now the author of best-selling horse racing whodunits. In 1967 a horse named Popham Down balked at a fence, causing the pileup of more than 20 horses and allowing a 445-1 shot, Foinavon, to come from far back to win.

Then there was the 1951 National, which became a shambles when the starter began the race before most of the field was set. There were so many spills that only three of the 36 horses finished. Of that foul-up, Vian Smith wrote in his 1969 book, ***The Grand National: A History of the World's Greatest Steeplechase***: "There was a feeling among those in the sport and outside it that such a mess couldn't have happened elsewhere. Blunder and confusion became associated with Aintree from that day." The debacle of April 3, 1993 only strengthens that association.

Awards

Horse of the Year

Year	Horse	Owner	Trainer	Breeder
1936	Granville	Belair Stud	James Fitzsimmons	Belair Stud
1937	War Admiral	Samuel D. Riddle	George Conway	Mrs. Samuel D. Riddle
1938	Seabiscuit	Charles S. Howard	Tom Smith	Wheatley Stable
1939	Challedon	William L. Brann	Louis J. Schaefer	Branncastle Farm
1940	Challedon	William L. Brann	Louis J. Schaefer	Branncastle Farm
1941	Whirlaway	Calumet Farm	Ben Jones	Calumet Farm
1942	Whirlaway	Calumet Farm	Ben Jones	Calumet Farm
1943	Count Fleet	Mrs. John D. Hertz	Don Cameron	Mrs. John D. Hertz
1944	Twilight Tear	Calumet Farm	Ben Jones	Calumet Farm
1945	Busher	Louis B. Mayer	George Odom	Idle Hour Stock Farm
1946	Assault	King Ranch	Max Hirsch	King Ranch
1947	Armed	Calumet Farm	Jimmy Jones	Calumet Farm
1948	Citation	Calumet Farm	Jimmy Jones	Calumet Farm
1949	Capot	Greentree Stable	John M. Gaver Sr	Greentree Stable
1950	Hill Prince	C. T. Chenery	Casey Hayes	C. T. Chenery
1951	Counterpoint	C. V. Whitney	Syl Veitch	C. V. Whitney
1952	One Count	Mrs. W. M. Jeffords	O. White	W. M. Jeffords
1953	Tom Fool	Greentree Stable	John M. Gaver Sr	D. A. Headley
1954	Native Dancer	A. G. Vanderbilt	Bill Winfrey	A. G. Vanderbilt
1955	Nashua	Belair Stud	James Fitzsimmons	Belair Stud
1956	Swaps	Ellsworth-Galbreath	Mesh Tenney	R. Ellsworth
1957	Bold Ruler	Wheatley Stable	James Fitzsimmons	Wheatley Stable
1958	Round Table	Kerr Stables	Willy Molter	Claiborne Farm
1959	Sword Dancer	Brookmeade Stable	Elliott Burch	Brookmeade Stable
1960	Kelso	Bohemia Stable	C. Hanford	Mrs. R. C. duPont
1961	Kelso	Bohemia Stable	C. Hanford	Mrs. R. C. duPont
1962	Kelso	Bohemia Stable	C. Hanford	Mrs. R. C. duPont
1963	Kelso	Bohemia Stable	C. Hanford	Mrs. R. C. duPont
1964	Kelso	Bohemia Stable	C. Hanford	Mrs. R. C. duPont
1965	Roman Brother	Harbor View Stable	Burley Parke	Ocala Stud
1966	Buckpasser	Ogden Phipps	Eddie Neloy	Ogden Phipps
1967	Damascus	Mrs. E. W. Bancroft	Frank Y. Whiteley Jr	Mrs. E. W. Bancroft
1968	Dr. Fager	Tartan Stable	John A. Nerud	Tartan Farms
1969	Arts and Letters	Rokeby Stable	Elliott Burch	Paul Mellon
1970	Fort Marcy	Rokeby Stable	Elliott Burch	Paul Mellon
1971	Ack Ack	E. E. Fogelson	Charlie Whittingham	H. F. Guggenheim
1972	Secretariat	Meadow Stable	Lucien Laurin	Meadow Stud
1973	Secretariat	Meadow Stable	Lucien Laurin	Meadow Stud
1974	Forego	Lazy F Ranch	Sherrill W. Ward	Lazy F Ranch
1975	Forego	Lazy F Ranch	Sherrill W. Ward	Lazy F Ranch
1976	Forego	Lazy F Ranch	Frank Y. Whiteley Jr	Lazy F Ranch
1977	Seattle Slew	Karen L. Taylor	Billy Turner Jr	B. S. Castleman
1978	Affirmed	Harbor View Farm	Laz Barrera	Harbor View Farm
1979	Affirmed	Harbor View Farm	Laz Barrera	Harbor View Farm
1980	Spectacular Bid	Hawksworth Farm	Bud Delp	Mmes. Gilmore and Jason
1981	John Henry	Dotsam Stable	Ron McAnally and Lefty Nickerson	Golden Chance Farm
1982	Conquistador Cielo	H. de Kwiatkowski	Woody Stephens	L. E. Landoli
1983	All Along	Daniel Wildenstein	P. L. Biancone	Dayton

A Sure Thing

On June 16, 1993, at Boston's Suffolk Downs, bettors got to lay down their money on a sure thing when the wagering system was accidentally opened up after the third race was over. According to the track and tote company, human error was the cause. The winning horse paid $20.60 and the perfecta—the first two horses in exact order—paid $84.60 on a $2 bet. However, a built-in security system activated after only a few bets were placed.

Horse of the Year (Cont.)

Year	Horse	Owner	Trainer	Breeder
1984	John Henry	Dotsam Stable	Ron McAnally	Golden Chance Farm
1985	Spend a Buck	Hunter Farm	Cam Gambolati	Irish Hill Farm & R. W. Harper
1986	Lady's Secret	Mr. & Mrs. Eugene Klein	D. Wayne Lukas	R. H. Spreen
1987	Ferdinand	Mrs. H. B. Keck	Charlie Whittingham	H. B. Keck
1988	Alysheba	D. & P. Scharbauer	Jack Van Berg	Preston Madden
1989	Sunday Silence	Gaillard, Hancock, & Whittingham	Charlie Whittingham	Oak Cliff Thoroughbreds
1990	Criminal Type	Calumet Farm	D. Wayne Lukas	Calumet Farm
1991	Black Tie Affair	Jeffrey Sullivan	Ernie Poulos	Stephen D. Peskoff
1992	A.P. Indy	Tomonori Tsurumaki	Neil Drysdale	W.S. Farish & W.S. Kilroy

Note: From 1936 to 1970, the *Daily Racing Form* annually selected a "Horse of the Year." In 1971 the *Daily Racing Form*, with the Thoroughbred Racing Associations and the National Turf Writers Association, jointly created the Eclipse Awards.

Eclipse Award Winners

2-YEAR-OLD COLT

1971	Riva Ridge
1972	Secretariat
1973	Protagonist
1974	Foolish Pleasure
1975	Honest Pleasure
1976	Seattle Slew
1977	Affirmed
1978	Spectacular Bid
1979	Rockhill Native
1980	Lord Avie
1981	Deputy Minister
1982	Roving Boy
1983	Devil's Bag
1984	Chief's Crown
1985	Tasso
1986	Capote
1987	Forty Niner
1988	Easy Goer
1989	Rhythm
1990	Fly So Free
1991	Arazi
1992	Gilded Time

2-YEAR-OLD FILLY

1971	Numbered Account
1972	La Prevoyante
1973	Talking Picture
1974	Ruffian
1975	Dearly Precious
1976	Sensational
1977	Lakeville Miss
1978	Candy Eclair
	It's in the Air
1979	Smart Angle
1980	Heavenly Cause
1981	Before Dawn
1982	Landaluce
1983	Althea
1984	Outstandingly
1985	Family Style
1986	Brave Raj
1987	Epitome
1988	Open Mind
1989	Go for Wand
1990	Meadow Star
1991	Pleasant Stage
1992	Eliza

3-YEAR-OLD COLT

1971	Canonero II
1972	Key to the Mint
1973	Secretariat
1974	Little Currant
1975	Wajima
1976	Bold Forbes
1977	Seattle Slew
1978	Affirmed
1979	Spectacular Bid
1980	Temperence Hill
1981	Pleasant Colony
1982	Conquistador Cielo
1983	Slew o' Gold
1984	Swale
1985	Spend A Buck
1986	Snow Chief
1987	Alysheba
1988	Risen Star
1989	Sunday Silence
1990	Unbridled
1991	Hansel
1992	A.P. Indy

3-YEAR-OLD FILLY

1971	Turkish Trousers
1972	Susan's Girl
1973	Desert Vixen
1974	Chris Evert
1975	Ruffian
1976	Revidere
1977	Our Mims
1978	Tempest Queen
1979	Davona Dale
1980	Genuine Risk
1981	Wayward Lass
1982	Christmas Past
1983	Heartlight No. One
1984	Life's Magic
1985	Mom's Command
1986	Tiffany Lass
1987	Sacahuista
1988	Winning Colors
1989	Open Mind
1990	Go for Wand
1991	Dance Smartly
1992	Saratoga Dew

Mazel tov

The harness horse Son of Account celebrated his 13th birthday on Sunday, May 23, 1993, in the Jewish tradition. He was bar mitzvahed. The ceremony took place in Monticello, N.Y. and was performed by Sherry Skramstad, a schoolteacher from Fallsburg, N.Y. who is also a publicist for the Goshen Historic Track. Assisting her was 8-year-old Hebrew student Isaiah First, who read the appropriate text while Ms. Skramstad pinned a yarmulke over the horse's ears and draped a prayer shawl over his neck. The horse's stall was adorned with a computer-printed sign reading: "Today, I am a mensch."

Eclipse Awards (Cont.)

OLDER COLT, HORSE OR GELDING

1971.....Ack Ack (5)
1972.....Autobiography (4)
1973.....Riva Ridge (4)
1974.....Forego (4)
1975.....Forego (5)
1976.....Forego (6)
1977.....Forego (7)
1978.....Seattle Slew (4)
1979.....Affirmed (4)
1980.....Spectacular Bid (4)
1981.....John Henry (6)
1982.....Lemhi Gold (4)
1983.....Bates Motel (4)
1984.....Slew o'Gold (4)
1985.....Vanlandingham (4)
1986.....Turkoman (4)
1987.....Ferdinand (4)
1988.....Alysheba (4)
1989.....Blushing John (4)
1990.....Criminal Type (5)
1991.....Black Tie Affair (5)
1992.....Pleasant Tap

CHAMPION TURF HORSE

1971.....Run the Gantlet (3)
1972.....Cougar II (6)
1973.....Secretariat (3)
1974.....Dahlia (4)
1975.....Snow Knight (4)
1976.....Youth (3)
1977.....Johnny D (3)
1978.....Mac Diarmida (3)

STEEPLECHASE OR HURDLE HORSE

1971.....Shadow Brook (7)
1972.....Soothsayer (5)
1973.....Athenian Idol (5)
1974.....Gran Kan (8)
1975.....Life's Illusion (4)
1976.....Straight & True (6)
1977.....Cafe Prince (7)
1978.....Cafe Prince (8)
1979.....Martie's Anger (4)
1980.....Zaccio (4)
1981.....Zaccio (5)
1982.....Zaccio (6)
1983.....Flatterer (4)
1984.....Flatterer (5)
1985.....Flatterer (6)
1986.....Flatterer (7)
1987.....Inlander (6)
1988.....Jimmy Lorenzo (6)
1989.....Highland Bud (4)
1990.....Morley Street (7)
1991.....Morley Street (8)
1992.....Lonesome Glory

OLDER FILLY OR MARE

1971.....Shuvee (5)
1972.....Typecast (6)
1973.....Susan's Girl (4)
1974.....Desert Vixen (4)
1975.....Susan's Girl (6)
1976.....Proud Delta (4)
1977.....Cascapedia (4)
1978.....Late Bloomer (4)
1979.....Waya (5)
1980.....Glorious Song (4)
1981.....Relaxing (5)
1982.....Track Robbery (6)
1983.....Ambassador of Luck (4)
1984.....Princess Rooney (4)
1985.....Life's Magic (4)
1986.....Lady's Secret (4)
1987.....North Sider (5)
1988.....Personal Ensign (4)
1989.....Bayakoa (5)
1990.....Bayakoa (6)
1991.....Queena (5)
1992.....Paseana

CHAMPION MALE TURF HORSE

1979.....Bowl Game (5)
1980.....John Henry (5)
1981.....John Henry (6)
1982.....Perrault (5)
1983.....John Henry (8)
1984.....John Henry (9)
1985.....Cozzene (4)
1986.....Manila (3)
1987.....Theatrical (5)
1988.....Sunshine Forever (3)
1989.....Steinlen (6)
1990.....Itsallgreektome (3)
1991.....Tight Spot (4)
1992.....Sky Classic

OUTSTANDING OWNER

1971.....Mr. & Mrs. E. E. Fogleson
1974.....Dan Lasater
1975.....Dan Lasater
1976.....Dan Lasater
1977.....Maxwell Gluck
1978.....Harbor View Farm
1979.....Harbor View Farm
1980.....Mr. & Mrs. Bertram Firestone
1981.....Dotsam Stable
1982.....Viola Sommer
1983.....John Franks
1984.....John Franks
1985.....Mr. & Mrs. Eugene Klein
1986.....Mr. & Mrs. Eugene Klein
1987.....Mr. & Mrs. Eugene Klein
1988.....Ogden Phipps
1989.....Ogden Phipps
1990.....Frances Genter
1991.....Sam-Son Farm
1992.....Juddmonte Farms

SPRINTER

1971.....Ack Ack (5)
1972.....Chou Croute (4)
1973.....Shecky Greene (3)
1974.....Forego (4)
1975.....Gallant Bob (3)
1976.....My Juliet (4)
1977.....What a Summer (4)
1978.....Dr. Patches (4)
J. O. Tobin (4)
1979.....Star de Naskra (4)
1980.....Plugged Nickel (3)
1981.....Guilty Conscience (5)
1982.....Gold Beauty (3)
1983.....Chinook Pass (4)
1984.....Eillo (4)
1985.....Precisionist (4)
1986.....Smile (4)
1987.....Groovy (4)
1988.....Gulch (4)
1989.....Safely Kept (3)
1990.....Housebuster (3)
1991.....Housebuster (4)
1992.....Rubiano

CHAMPION FEMALE TURF HORSE

1979.....Trillion (5)
1980.....Just a Game II (4)
1981.....De La Rose (3)
1982.....April Run (4)
1983.....All Along (4)
1984.....Royal Heroine (4)
1985.....Pebbles (4)
1986.....Estrapade (6)
1987.....Miesque (3)
1988.....Miesque (4)
1989.....Brown Bess (7)
1990.....Laugh and Be Merry (5)
1991.....Miss Alleged (4)
1992.....Flawlessly

OUTSTANDING TRAINER

1971.....Charlie Whittingham
1972.....Lucien Laurin
1973.....H. Allen Jerkens
1974.....Sherrill Ward
1975.....Steve DiMauro
1976.....Lazaro Barrera
1977.....Lazaro Barrera
1978.....Lazaro Barrera
1979.....Lazaro Barrera
1980.....Bud Delp
1981.....Ron McAnally
1982.....Charlie Whittingham
1983.....Woody Stephens
1984.....Jack Van Berg
1985.....D. Wayne Lukas
1986.....D. Wayne Lukas
1987.....D. Wayne Lukas
1988.....Claude R. McGaughey III
1989.....Charlie Whittingham
1990.....Carl Nafzger
1991.....Ron McAnally
1992.....Ron McAnally

Note: Number in parentheses is horse's age.

Awards (Cont.)

Eclipse Awards (Cont.)

OUTSTANDING JOCKEY

1971.....Laffit Pincay Jr
1972.....Braulio Baeza
1973.....Laffit Pincay Jr
1974.....Laffit Pincay Jr
1975.....Braulio Baeza
1976.....Sandy Hawley
1977.....Steve Cauthen
1978.....Darrel McHargue
1979.....Laffit Pincay Jr
1980.....Chris McCarron
1981.....Bill Shoemaker
1982.....Angel Cordero Jr
1983.....Angel Cordero Jr
1984.....Pat Day
1985.....Laffit Pincay Jr
1986.....Pat Day
1987.....Pat Day
1988.....Jose Santos
1989.....Kent Desormeaux
1990.....Craig Perret
1991.....Pat Day
1992.....Kent Desormeaux

OUTSTANDING APPRENTICE JOCKEY

1971.....Gene St. Leon
1972.....Thomas Wallis
1973.....Steve Valdez
1974.....Chris McCarron
1975.....Jimmy Edwards
1976.....George Martens
1977.....Steve Cauthen

OUTSTANDING APPRENTICE JOCKEY *(Cont.)*

1978.....Ron Franklin
1979.....Cash Asmussen
1980.....Frank Lovato Jr
1981.....Richard Migliore
1982.....Alberto Delgado
1983.....Declan Murphy
1984.....Wesley Ward
1985.....Art Madrid Jr
1986.....Allen Stacy
1987.....Kent Desormeaux
1988.....Steve Capanas
1989.....Michael Luzzi
1990.....Mark Johnston
1991.....Mickey Walls
1992.....Jesus A. Bracho

SPECIAL AWARD

1971.....Robert J. Kleberg
1974.....Charles Hatton
1976.....Bill Shoemaker
1980.....John T. Landry
Pierre E. Bellocq (Peb)
1984.....C. V. Whitney
1985.....Arlington Park
1987.....Anheuser-Busch
1988.....Edward J. DeBartolo Sr
1989.....Richard Duchossois

Note: Not presented annually. For long-term and/or outstanding service to the industry.

OUTSTANDING BREEDER

1974.....John W. Galbreath
1975.....Fred W. Hooper
1976.....Nelson Bunker Hunt
1977.....Edward Plunket Taylor
1978.....Harbor View Farm
1979.....Claiborne Farm
1980.....Mrs. Henry D. Paxson
1981.....Golden Chance Farm
1982.....Fred W. Hooper
1983.....Edward Plunket Taylor
1984.....Claiborne Farm
1985.....Nelson Bunker Hunt
1986.....Paul Mellon
1987.....Nelson Bunker Hunt
1988.....Ogden Phipps
1989.....North Ridge Farm
1990.....Calumet Farm
1991.....John and Betty Mabee
1992.....William S. Farish III

AWARD OF MERIT

1976.....Jack J. Dreyfus
1977.....Steve Cauthen
1978.....Ogden Phipps
1979.....Frank E. Kilroe
1980.....John D. Schapiro
1981.....Bill Shoemaker
1984.....John Gaines
1985.....Keene Daingerfield
1986.....Herman Cohen
1987.....J. B. Faulconer
1988.....John Forsythe
1989.....Michael P. Sandler
1991.....Fred W. Hooper

Breeders' Cup

Location: Hollywood Park (CA) 1984, 1987; Aqueduct Racetrack (NY) 1985; Santa Anita Park (CA) 1986; Churchill Downs (KY) 1988, 1991; Gulfstream Park (FL) 1989, 1992; Belmont Park (NY) 1990.

Juveniles

Year	Winner (Margin)	Jockey	Second	Third	Time
1984	Chief's Crown (¾)	Don MacBeth	Tank's Prospect	Spend a Buck	1:36⅕
1985	Tasso (Nose)	Laffit Pincay Jr	Storm Cat	Scat Dancer	1:36⅕
1986	Capote (1¼)	Laffit Pincay Jr	Qualify	Alysheba	1:43⅘
1987	Success Express (1¾)	Jose Santos	Regal Classic	Tejano	1:35⅕
1988	Is It True (1¼)	Laffit Pincay Jr	Easy Goer	Tagel	1:46⅗
1989	Rhythm (2)	Craig Perret	Grand Canyon	Slavic	1:43⅗
1990	Fly So Free (3)	Jose Santos	Take Me Out	Lost Mountain	1:43⅖
1991	Arazi (4¾)	Pat Valenzuela	Bertrando	Snappy Landing	1:44⅗
1992	Gilded Time (¾)	Chris McCarron	It'sali'lknownfact	River Special	1:43⅖

Note: One mile (1984—85, 87); 1¹⁄₁₆ miles (1986 and since 1988).

Juvenile Fillies

Year	Winner (Margin)	Jockey	Second	Third	Time
1984	Outstandingly*	Walter Guerra	Dusty Heart	Fine Spirit	1:37⅘
1985	Twilight Ridge (1)	Jorge Velasquez	Family Style	Steal a Kiss	1:35⅘
1986	Brave Raj (5½)	Pat Valenzuela	Tappiano	Saros Brig	1:43⅕
1987	Epitome (Nose)	Pat Day	Jeanne Jones	Dream Team	1:36⅖
1988	Open Mind (1¾)	Angel Cordero Jr	Darby Shuffle	Lea Lucinda	1:46⅗
1989	Go for Wand (2¾)	Randy Romero	Sweet Roberta	Stella Madrid	1:44⅕
1990	Meadow Star (5)	Jose Santos	Private Treasure	Dance Smartly	1:44

Breeders' Cup *(Cont.)*

Juvenile Fillies *(Cont.)*

Year	Winner (Margin)	Jockey	Second	Third	Time
1991	Pleasant Stage (Neck)	Eddie Delahoussaye	La Spia	Cadillac Women	1:46⅖
1992	Eliza (1½)	Pat Valenzuela	Educated Risk	Boots 'n Jackie	1:42⅘

*In 1984, winner Fran's Valentine was disqualified for interference in the stretch and placed 10th.
Note: One mile (1984—85, 87); 1 1/16 miles (1986 and since 1988).

Sprint

Year	Winner (Margin)	Jockey	Second	Third	Time
1984	Eillo (Nose)	Craig Perret	Commemorate	Fighting Fit	1:10⅕
1985	Precisionist (¾)	Chris McCarron	Smile	Mt. Livermore	1:08⅖
1986	Smile (1¼)	Jacinto Vasquez	Pine Tree Lane	Bedside Promise	1:08⅖
1987	Very Subtle (4)	Pat Valenzuela	Groovy	Exclusive Enough	1:08⅘
1988	Gulch (¾)	Angel Cordero Jr	Play the King	Afleet	1:10⅖
1989	Dancing Spree (Neck)	Angel Cordero Jr	Safely Kept	Dispersal	1:09
1990	Safely Kept (Neck)	Craig Perret	Dayjur	Black Tie Affair	1:09⅗
1991	Sheikh Albadou (Neck)	Pat Eddery	Pleasant Tap	Robyn Dancer	1:09⅕
1992	Thirty Slews (Neck)	Eddie Delahoussaye	Meafara	Rubiano	1:08⅕

Note: Six furlongs (since 1984).

Mile

Year	Winner (Margin)	Jockey	Second	Third	Time
1984	Royal Heroine (1½)	Fernando Toro	Star Choice	Cozzene	1:32⅗
1985	Cozzene (2¼)	Walter Guerra	Al Mamoon*	Shadeed	1:35
1986	Last Tycoon (Head)	Yves St-Martin	Palace Music	Fred Astaire	1:35⅕
1987	Miesque (3½)	Freddie Head	Show Dancer	Sonic Lady	1:32⅘
1988	Miesque (4)	Freddie Head	Steinlen	Simply Majestic	1:38⅗
1989	Steinlen (¾)	Jose Santos	Sabona	Most Welcome	1:37⅕
1990	Royal Academy (Neck)	Lester Piggott	Itsallgreektome	Priolo	1:35⅕
1991	Opening Verse (2¼)	Pat Valenzuela	Val de Bois	Star of Cozzene	1:37⅖
1992	Lure (3)	Mike Smith	Paradise Creek	Brief Truce	1:32⅘

*2nd place finisher Palace Music was disqualified for interference and placed 9th.

Distaff

Year	Winner (Margin)	Jockey	Second	Third	Time
1984	Princess Rooney (7)	Eddie Delahoussaye	Life's Magic	Adored	2:02⅖
1985	Life's Magic (6¼)	Angel Cordero Jr	Lady's Secret	Dontstop Themusic	2:02
1986	Lady's Secret (2½)	Pat Day	Fran's Valentine	Outstandingly	2:01⅕
1987	Sacahuista (2¼)	Randy Romero	Clabber Girl	Oueee Bebe	2:02⅘
1988	Personal Ensign (Nose)	Randy Romero	Winning Colors	Goodbye Halo	1:52
1989	Bayakoa (1½)	Laffit Pincay Jr	Gorgeous	Open Mind	1:47⅖
1990	Bayakoa (6¾)	Laffit Pincay Jr	Colonial Waters	Valay Maid	1:49⅕
1991	Dance Smarty (½)	Pat Day	Versailles Treaty	Brought to Mind	1:50⅘
1992	Paseana (4)	Chris McCarron	Versailles Treaty	Magical Maiden	1:48

Note: 1¼ miles (1984-87); 1⅛ miles (since 1988).

Turf

Year	Winner (Margin)	Jockey	Second	Third	Time
1984	Lashkari (Neck)	Yves St-Martin	All Along	Raami	2:25⅕
1985	Pebbles (Neck)	Pat Eddery	Strawberry Rd II	Mourjane	2:27
1986	Manila (Neck)	Jose Santos	Theatrical	Estrapade	2:25⅖
1987	Theatrical (½)	Pat Day	Trempolino	Village Star II	2:24⅖
1988	Great Communicator (½)	Ray Sibille	Sunshine Forever	Indian Skimmer	2:35⅕
1989	Prized (Head)	Eddie Delahoussaye	Sierra Roberta	Star Lift	2:28
1990	In the Wings (½)	Gary Stevens	With Approval	El Senor	2:29⅗
1991	Miss Alleged (2)	Eric Legrix	Itsallgreektome	Quest for Fame	2:30⅘
1992	Fraise (Nose)	Pat Valenzuela	Sky Classic	Quest For Fame	2:24

Note: 1½ miles.

Breeders' Cup *(Cont.)*

Classic

Year	Winner (Margin)	Jockey	Second	Third	Time
1984	Wild Again (Head)	Pat Day	Slew o' Gold*	Gate Dancer	2:03⅖
1985	Proud Truth (Head)	Jorge Velasquez	Gate Dancer	Turkoman	2:00⅘
1986	Skywalker (1-1/4)	Laffit Pincay Jr	Turkoman	Precisionist	2:00⅖
1987	Ferdinand (Nose)	Bill Shoemaker	Alysheba	Judge Angelucci	2:01⅖
1988	Alysheba (Nose)	Chris McCarron	Seeking the Gold	Waquoit	2:04⅘
1989	Sunday Silence (1/2)	Chris McCarron	Easy Goer	Blushing John	2:00⅕
1990	Unbridled (1)	Pat Day	Ibn Bey	Thirty Six Red	2:02⅕
1991	Black Tie Affair	Jerry Bailey	Twilight Agenda	Unbridled	2:02⅘
1992	A.P. Indy (2)	Eddie Delahoussaye	Pleasant Tap	Jolypha	2:00⅕

*2nd place finisher Gate Dancer was disqualified for interference and placed 3rd.
Note: 1¼ miles.

England's Triple Crown Winners

England's Triple Crown consists of the Two Thousand Guineas, held at Newmarket; the Epsom Derby, held at Epsom Downs; and the St. Leger Stakes, held at Doncaster.

Year	Horse	Owner
1853	West Australian	Mr. Bowes
1865	Gladiateur	F. DeLagrange
1866	Lord Lyon	R. Sutton
1886	*Ormonde	Duke of Westminster
1891	Common	†F. Johnstone
1893	Isinglass	H. McCalmont
1897	Galtee More	J. Gubbins
1899	Flying Fox	Duke of Westminster
1900	Diamond Jubilee	Prince of Wales
1903	*Rock Sand	J. Miller
1915	Pommern	S. Joel
1917	Gay Crusader	Mr. Fairie
1918	Gainsborough	Lady James Douglas
1935	*Bahram	Aga Khan
1970	‡Nijinsky II	C. W. Engelhard

*Imported into United States. †Raced in name of Lord Alington in Two Thousand Guineas. ‡Canadian-bred.

Annual Leaders

Horse—Money Won

Year	Horse	Age	Starts	1st	2nd	3rd	Winnings ($)
1919	Sir Barton	3	13	8	3	2	88,250
1920	Man o'War	3	11	11	0	0	166,140
1921	Morvich	2	11	11	0	0	115,234
1922	Pillory	3	7	4	1	1	95,654
1923	Zev	3	14	12	1	0	272,008
1924	Sarzen	3	12	8	1	1	95,640
1925	Pompey	2	10	7	2	0	121,630
1926	Crusader	3	15	9	4	0	166,033
1927	Anita Peabody	2	7	6	0	1	111,905
1928	High Strung	2	6	5	0	0	153,590
1929	Blue Larkspur	3	6	4	1	0	153,450
1930	Gallant Fox	3	10	9	1	0	308,275
1931	Gallant Flight	2	7	7	0	0	219,000
1932	Gusto	3	16	4	3	2	145,940
1933	Singing Wood	2	9	3	2	2	88,050
1934	Cavalcade	3	7	6	1	0	111,235
1935	Omaha	3	9	6	1	2	142,255
1936	Granville	3	11	7	3	0	110,295
1937	Seabiscuit	4	15	11	2	2	168,580
1938	Stagehand	3	15	8	2	3	189,710
1939	Challedon	3	15	9	2	3	184,535
1940	Bimelech	3	7	4	2	1	110,005
1941	Whirlaway	3	20	13	5	2	272,386
1942	Shut Out	3	12	8	2	0	238,872
1943	Count Fleet	3	6	6	0	0	174,055
1944	Pavot	2	8	8	0	0	179,040
1945	Busher	3	13	10	2	1	273,735
1946	Assault	3	15	8	2	3	424,195

Note: Annual leaders on pages 460-465 courtesy of *The American Racing Manual*, a publication of Daily Racing Form, Inc.

Horse—Money Won (Cont.)

Year	Horse	Age	Starts	1st	2nd	3rd	Winnings ($)
1947	Armed	6	17	11	4	1	376,325
1948	Citation	3	20	19	1	0	709,470
1949	Ponder	3	21	9	5	2	321,825
1950	Noor	5	12	7	4	1	346,940
1951	Counterpoint	3	15	7	2	1	250,525
1952	Crafty Admiral	4	16	9	4	1	277,225
1953	Native Dancer	3	10	9	1	0	513,425
1954	Determine	3	15	10	3	2	328,700
1955	Nashua	3	12	10	1	1	752,550
1956	Needles	3	8	4	2	0	440,850
1957	Round Table	3	22	15	1	3	600,383
1958	Round Table	4	20	14	4	0	662,780
1959	Sword Dancer	3	13	8	4	0	537,004
1960	Bally Ache	3	15	10	3	1	445,045
1961	Carry Back	3	16	9	1	3	565,349
1962	Never Bend	2	10	7	1	2	402,969
1963	Candy Spots	3	12	7	2	1	604,481
1964	Gun Bow	4	16	8	4	2	580,100
1965	Buckpasser	2	11	9	1	0	568,096
1966	Buckpasser	3	14	13	1	0	669,078
1967	Damascus	3	16	12	3	1	817,941
1968	Forward Pass	3	13	7	2	0	546,674
1969	Arts and Letters	3	14	8	5	1	555,604
1970	Personality	3	18	8	2	1	444,049
1971	Riva Ridge	2	9	7	0	0	503,263
1972	Droll Role	4	19	7	3	4	471,633
1973	Secretariat	3	12	9	2	1	860,404
1974	Chris Evert	3	8	5	1	2	551,063
1975	Foolish Pleasure	3	11	5	4	1	716,278
1976	Forego	6	8	6	1	1	401,701
1977	Seattle Slew	3	7	6	0	1	641,370
1978	Affirmed	3	11	8	2	0	901,541
1979	Spectacular Bid	3	12	10	1	1	1,279,334
1980	Temperence Hill	3	17	8	3	1	1,130,452
1981	John Henry	6	10	8	0	0	1,798,030
1982	Perrault	5	8	4	1	2	1,197,400
1983	All Along	4	7	4	1	1	2,138,963
1984	Slew o'Gold	4	6	5	1	0	2,627,944
1985	Spend A Buck	3	7	5	1	1	3,552,704
1986	Snow Chief	3	9	6	1	1	1,875,200
1987	Alysheba	3	10	3	3	1	2,511,156
1988	Alysheba	4	9	7	1	0	3,808,600
1989	Sunday Silence	3	9	7	2	0	4,578,454
1990	Unbridled	3	11	4	3	2	3,718,149
1991	Dance Smartly	3	8	8	0	0	2,876,821
1992	A.P. Indy	3	7	5	0	1	2,622,560

Trainer—Money Won

Year	Trainer	Wins	Winnings ($)	Year	Trainer	Wins	Winnings ($)
1908	James Rowe, Sr	50	284,335	1924	Sam Hildreth	77	255,608
1909	Sam Hildreth	73	123,942	1925	G. R. Tompkins	30	199,245
1910	Sam Hildreth	84	148,010	1926	Scott P. Harlan	21	205,681
1911	Sam Hildreth	67	49,418	1927	W. H. Bringloe	63	216,563
1912	John F. Schorr	63	58,110	1928	John F. Schorr	65	258,425
1913	James Rowe, Sr	18	45,936	1929	James Rowe, Jr	25	314,881
1914	R. C. Benson	45	59,315	1930	Sunny Jim Fitzsimmons	47	397,355
1915	James Rowe, Sr	19	75,596	1931	Big Jim Healey	33	297,300
1916	Sam Hildreth	39	70,950	1932	Sunny Jim Fitzsimmons	68	266,650
1917	Sam Hildreth	23	61,698	1933	Humming Bob Smith	53	135,720
1918	H. Guy Bedwell	53	80,296	1934	Humming Bob Smith	43	249,938
1919	H. Guy Bedwell	63	208,728	1935	Bud Stotler	87	303,005
1920	L. Feustal	22	186,087	1936	Sunny Jim Fitzsimmons	42	193,415
1921	Sam Hildreth	85	262,768	1937	Robert McGarvey	46	209,925
1922	Sam Hildreth	74	247,014	1938	Earl Sande	15	226,495
1923	Sam Hildreth	75	392,124	1939	Sunny Jim Fitzsimmons	45	266,205

Trainer—Money Won *(Cont.)*

Year	Trainer	Wins	Winnings ($)	Year	Trainer	Wins	Winnings ($)
1940	Silent Tom Smith	14	269,200	1967	Eddie Neloy	72	1,776,089
1941	Plain Ben Jones	70	475,318	1968	Eddie Neloy	52	1,233,101
1942	John M. Gaver Sr	48	406,547	1969	Elliott Burch	26	1,067,936
1943	Plain Ben Jones	73	267,915	1970	Charlie Whittingham	82	1,302,354
1944	Plain Ben Jones	60	601,660	1971	Charlie Whittingham	77	1,737,115
1945	Silent Tom Smith	52	510,655	1972	Charlie Whittingham	79	1,734,020
1946	Hirsch Jacobs	99	560,077	1973	Charlie Whittingham	85	1,865,385
1947	Jimmy Jones	85	1,334,805	1974	Pancho Martin	166	2,408,419
1948	Jimmy Jones	81	1,118,670	1975	Charlie Whittingham	93	2,437,244
1949	Jimmy Jones	76	978,587	1976	Jack Van Berg	496	2,976,196
1950	Preston Burch	96	637,754	1977	Laz Barrera	127	2,715,848
1951	John M. Gaver Sr	42	616,392	1978	Laz Barrera	100	3,307,164
1952	Plain Ben Jones	29	662,137	1979	Laz Barrera	98	3,608,517
1953	Harry Trotsek	54	1,028,873	1980	Laz Barrera	99	2,969,151
1954	Willie Molter	136	1,107,860	1981	Charlie Whittingham	74	3,993,302
1955	Sunny Jim Fitzsimmons	66	1,270,055	1982	Charlie Whittingham	63	4,587,457
1956	Willie Molter	142	1,227,402	1983	D. Wayne Lukas	78	4,267,261
1957	Jimmy Jones	70	1,150,910	1984	D. Wayne Lukas	131	5,835,921
1958	Willie Molter	69	1,116,544	1985	D. Wayne Lukas	218	11,155,188
1959	Willie Molter	71	847,290	1986	D. Wayne Lukas	259	12,345,180
1960	Hirsch Jacobs	97	748,349	1987	D. Wayne Lukas	343	17,502,110
1961	Jimmy Jones	62	759,856	1988	D. Wayne Lukas	318	17,842,358
1962	Mesh Tenney	58	1,099,474	1989	D. Wayne Lukas	305	16,103,998
1963	Mesh Tenney	40	860,703	1990	D. Wayne Lukas	267	14,508,871
1964	Bill Winfrey	61	1,350,534	1991	D. Wayne Lukas	289	15,942,223
1965	Hirsch Jacobs	91	1,331,628	1992	D. Wayne Lukas	230	9,806,436
1966	Eddie Neloy	93	2,456,250				

Jockey—Money Won

Year	Jockey	Mts	1st	2nd	3rd	Pct	Winnings ($)
1919	John Loftus	177	65	36	24	.37	252,707
1920	Clarence Kummer	353	87	79	48	.25	292,376
1921	Earl Sande	340	112	69	59	.33	263,043
1922	Albert Johnson	297	43	57	40	.14	345,054
1923	Earl Sande	430	122	89	79	.28	569,394
1924	Ivan Parke	844	205	175	121	.24	290,395
1925	Laverne Fator	315	81	54	44	.26	305,775
1926	Laverne Fator	511	143	90	86	.28	361,435
1927	Earl Sande	179	49	33	19	.27	277,877
1928	Pony McAtee	235	55	43	25	.23	301,295
1929	Mack Garner	274	57	39	33	.21	314,975
1930	Sonny Workman	571	152	88	79	.27	420,438
1931	Charles Kurtsinger	519	93	82	79	.18	392,095
1932	Sonny Workman	378	87	48	55	.23	385,070
1933	Robert Jones	471	63	57	70	.13	226,285
1934	Wayne D. Wright	919	174	154	114	.19	287,185
1935	Silvio Coucci	749	141	125	103	.19	319,760
1936	Wayne D. Wright	670	100	102	73	.15	264,000
1937	Charles Kurtsinger	765	120	94	106	.16	384,202
1938	Nick Wall	658	97	94	82	.15	385,161
1939	Basil James	904	191	165	105	.21	353,333
1940	Eddie Arcaro	783	132	143	112	.17	343,661
1941	Don Meade	1164	210	185	158	.18	398,627
1942	Eddie Arcaro	687	123	97	89	.18	481,949
1943	John Longden	871	173	140	121	.20	573,276
1944	Ted Atkinson	1539	287	231	213	.19	899,101
1945	John Longden	778	180	112	100	.23	981,977
1946	Ted Atkinson	1377	233	213	173	.17	1,036,825
1947	Douglas Dodson	646	141	100	75	.22	1,429,949
1948	Eddie Arcaro	726	188	108	98	.26	1,686,230
1949	Steve Brooks	906	209	172	110	.23	1,316,817
1950	Eddie Arcaro	888	195	153	144	.22	1,410,160
1951	Bill Shoemaker	1161	257	197	161	.22	1,329,890
1952	Eddie Arcaro	807	188	122	109	.23	1,859,591
1953	Bill Shoemaker	1683	485	302	210	.29	1,784,187

Jockey—Money Won (Cont.)

Year	Jockey	Mts	1st	2nd	3rd	Pct	Winnings ($)
1954	Bill Shoemaker	1251	380	221	142	.30	1,876,760
1955	Eddie Arcaro	820	158	126	108	.19	1,864,796
1956	Bill Hartack	1387	347	252	184	.25	2,343,955
1957	Bill Hartack	1238	341	208	178	.28	3,060,501
1958	Bill Shoemaker	1133	300	185	137	.26	2,961,693
1959	Bill Shoemaker	1285	347	230	159	.27	2,843,133
1960	Bill Shoemaker	1227	274	196	158	.22	2,123,961
1961	Bill Shoemaker	1256	304	186	175	.24	2,690,819
1962	Bill Shoemaker	1126	311	156	128	.28	2,916,844
1963	Bill Shoemaker	1203	271	193	137	.22	2,526,925
1964	Bill Shoemaker	1056	246	147	133	.23	2,649,553
1965	Braulio Baeza	1245	270	200	201	.22	2,582,702
1966	Braulio Baeza	1341	298	222	190	.22	2,951,022
1967	Braulio Baeza	1064	256	184	127	.24	3,088,888
1968	Braulio Baeza	1089	201	184	145	.18	2,835,108
1969	Jorge Velasquez	1442	258	230	204	.18	2,542,315
1970	Laffit Pincay Jr	1328	269	208	187	.20	2,626,526
1971	Laffit Pincay Jr	1627	380	288	214	.23	3,784,377
1972	Laffit Pincay Jr	1388	289	215	205	.21	3,225,827
1973	Laffit Pincay Jr	1444	350	254	209	.24	4,093,492
1974	Laffit Pincay Jr	1278	341	227	180	.27	4,251,060
1975	Braulio Baeza	1190	196	208	180	.16	3,674,398
1976	Angel Cordero Jr	1534	274	273	235	.18	4,709,500
1977	Steve Cauthen	2075	487	345	304	.23	6,151,750
1978	Darrel McHargue	1762	375	294	263	.21	6,188,353
1979	Laffit Pincay Jr	1708	420	302	261	.25	8,183,535
1980	Chris McCarron	1964	405	318	282	.20	7,666,100
1981	Chris McCarron	1494	326	251	207	.22	8,397,604
1982	Angel Cordero Jr	1838	397	338	227	.22	9,702,520
1983	Angel Cordero Jr	1792	362	296	237	.20	10,116,807
1984	Chris McCarron	1565	356	276	218	.23	12,038,213
1985	Laffit Pincay Jr	1409	289	246	183	.21	13,415,049
1986	Jose Santos	1636	329	237	222	.20	11,329,297
1987	Jose Santos	1639	305	268	208	.19	12,407,355
1988	Jose Santos	1867	370	287	265	.20	14,877,298
1989	Jose Santos	1459	285	238	220	.20	13,847,003
1990	Gary Stevens	1504	283	245	202	.19	13,881,198
1991	Chris McCarron	1440	265	228	206	.18	14,441,083
1992	Kent Desormeaux	1568	361	260	208	.23	14,193,006

Jockey—Races Won

Year	Jockey	Mts	1st	2nd	3rd	Pct
1895	J. Perkins	762	192	177	129	.25
1896	J. Scherrer	1093	271	227	172	.24
1897	H. Martin	803	173	152	116	.21
1898	T. Burns	973	277	213	149	.28
1899	T. Burns	1064	273	173	266	.26
1900	C. Mitchell	874	195	140	139	.23
1901	W. O'Connor	1047	253	221	192	.24
1902	J. Ranch	1069	276	205	181	.26
1903	G.C. Fuller	918	229	152	122	.25
1904	E. Hildebrand	1169	297	230	171	.25
1905	D. Nicol	861	221	143	136	.26
1906	W. Miller	1384	388	300	199	.28
1907	W. Miller	1194	334	226	170	.28
1908	V. Powers	1260	324	204	185	.26
1909	V. Powers	704	173	121	114	.25
1910	G. Garner	947	200	188	153	.20
1911	T. Koerner	813	162	133	112	.20
1912	P. Hill	967	168	141	129	.17
1913	M. Buxton	887	146	131	136	.16
1914	J. McTaggart	787	157	132	106	.20
1915	M. Garner	775	151	118	90	.19

Jockey—Races Won *(Cont.)*

Year	Jockey	Mts	1st	2nd	3rd	Pct
1916	F. Robinson	791	178	131	124	.23
1917	W. Crump	803	151	140	101	.19
1918	F. Robinson	864	185	140	108	.21
1919	C. Robinson	896	190	140	126	.21
1920	J. Butwell	721	152	129	139	.21
1921	C. Lang	696	135	110	105	.19
1922	M. Fator	859	188	153	116	.22
1923	I. Parke	718	173	105	95	.24
1924	I. Parke	844	205	175	121	.24
1925	A. Mortensen	987	187	145	138	.19
1926	R. Jones	1172	190	163	152	.16
1927	L. Hardy	1130	207	192	151	.18
1928	J. Inzelone, J.	1052	155	152	135	.15
1929	M. Knight	871	149	132	133	.17
1930	H.R. Riley	861	177	145	123	.21
1931	H. Roble	1174	173	173	155	.15
1932	J. Gilbert	1050	212	144	160	.20
1933	J. Westrope	1224	301	235	166	.25
1934	M. Peters	1045	221	179	147	.21
1935	C. Stevenson	1099	206	169	146	.19
1936	B. James	1106	245	195	161	.22
1937	J. Adams	1265	260	186	177	.21
1938	J. Longden	1150	236	168	171	.21
1939	D. Meade	1284	255	221	180	.20
1940	E. Dew	1377	287	201	180	.21
1941	D. Meade	1164	210	185	158	.18
1942	J. Adams	1120	245	185	150	.22
1943	J. Adams	1069	228	159	171	.21
1944	T. Atkinson	1539	287	231	213	.19
1945	J.D. Jessop	1085	290	182	168	.27
1946	T. Atkinson	1377	233	213	173	.17
1947	J. Longden	1327	316	250	195	.24
1948	J. Longden	1197	319	233	161	.27
1949	G. Glisson	1347	270	217	181	.20
1950	W. Shoemaker	1640	388	266	230	.24
1951	C. Burr, C.	1319	310	232	192	.24
1952	A. DeSpirito	1482	390	247	212	.26
1953	W. Shoemaker	1683	485	302	210	.29
1954	W. Shoemaker	1251	380	221	142	.30
1955	W. Hartack	1702	417	298	215	.25
1956	W. Hartack	1387	347	252	184	.25
1957	W. Hartack	1238	341	208	178	.28
1958	W. Shoemaker	1133	300	185	137	.26
1959	W. Shoemaker	1285	347	230	159	.27
1960	W. Hartack	1402	307	247	190	.22
1961	J. Sellers	1394	328	212	227	.24
1962	R. Ferraro	1755	352	252	226	.20
1963	W. Blum	1704	360	286	215	.21
1964	W. Blum	1577	324	274	170	.21
1965	J. Davidson	1582	319	228	190	.20
1966	A. Gomez	996	318	173	142	.32
1967	J. Velasquez	1939	438	315	270	.23
1968	A. Cordero Jr.	1662	345	278	219	.21
1969	L. Snyder	1645	352	290	243	.21
1970	S. Hawley	1908	452	313	265	.24
1971	L Pincay Jr.	1627	380	288	214	.23
1972	S. Hawley	1381	367	269	200	.27
1973	S. Hawley	1925	515	336	292	.27
1974	C.J. McCarron	2199	546	392	297	.25
1975	C.J. McCarron	2194	458	389	305	.21
1976	S. Hawley	1637	413	245	201	.25
1977	S. Cauthen	2075	487	345	304	.23
1978	E. Delahoussaye	1666	384	285	238	.23
1979	D. Gall	2146	479	396	326	.22
1980	C.J. McCarron	1964	405	318	282	.20

Jockey—Races Won (Cont.)

Year	Jockey	Mts	1st	2nd	3rd	Pct
1981	D. Gall.	1917	376	305	297	.20
1982	P. Day	1870	399	326	255	.21
1983	P. Day	1725	454	321	251	.26
1984	P. Day	1694	399	296	259	.24
1985	C.W. Antley	2335	469	371	288	.20
1986	P. Day	1417	429	246	202	.30
1987	K. Desormeaux	2207	450	370	294	.28
1988	K. Desormeaux	1897	474	295	276	.25
1989	K. Desormeaux	2312	598	385	309	.25
1990	P. Day	1421	364	265	222	.26
1991	P. Day	1405	430	256	213	.31
1992	R.A. Baze	1691	433	296	237	.25

Leading Jockeys—Career Records Through 1992

Jockey	Years Riding	Mts	1st	2nd	3rd	Win Pct	Winnings ($)
Shoemaker, W. (1990)	42	40,350	8,833	6,136	4,987	.219	123,375,524
Pincay, L. Jr.	27	37,464	7,888	6,207	5,174	.211	170,325,931
Cordero, A. Jr.	31	38,646	7,057	6,136	6,359	.183	164,526,217
Velasquez, J.	30	38,588	6,570	5,907	5,474	.170	119,978,481
Snyder, L.	33	34,614	6,276	4,914	3,320	.182	45,829,977
Gall, D.	36	33,568	6,185	5,331	4,991	.176	18,096,208
Gambardella, C.	37	37,655	6,104	5,728	5,170	.162	27,501,884
Longden, J. (1966)	40	32,413	6,032	4,914	4,273	.186	24,665,800
Hawley, S.	26	28,661	6,008	4,442	3,779	.210	77,888,807
McCarron, C. J.	18	27,131	5,762	4,483	3,689	.212	155,143,763
Day, P.	20	26,397	5,727	4,429	3,656	.217	126,252,384
E. Fires	28	36,227	5,340	4,520	4,328	.147	59,307,881
Vasquez, J.	33	35,742	5,080	4,554	4,342	.142	77,169,893
Delahoussaye, E.	23	30,430	4,963	4,364	4,188	.163	119,170,122
Arcaro E. (1961)	31	24,092	4,779	3,807	3,302	.198	30,039,543
Brumfield, D. (1989)	37	33,223	4,573	4,076	3,758	.138	48,567,861
Brooks, S. (1975)	34	30,330	4,451	4,219	3,658	.147	18,239,817
Blum, W. (1975)	22	28,673	4,382	3,913	3,350	.153	26,497,189
Hartack, W. (1974)	22	21,535	4,272	3,370	2,871	.198	26,466,758
Gomez, A. (1980)	34	17,028	4,081	2,947	2,405	.240	11,777,297
Maple, E.	25	30,593	4,047	4,064	3,938	.132	91,422,137
Dittfach, H. (1989)	33	33,905	4,000	4,092	6,113	.118	13,506,052
Baze, R. A.	19	22,610	3,924	3,396	3,074	.174	58,101,367
Atkinson, D. (1959)	22	23,661	3,795	3,300	2,913	.160	17,449,360
Whited, D. E.	35	27,927	3,784	3,592	3,355	.135	25,065,166

Note: Records include available statistics for races ridden in foreign countries. Figures in parentheses after jockey's name indicate last year in which he rode.

Leading jockeys courtesy of *The American Racing Manual*, a publication of Daily Racing Form, Inc.

National Museum of Racing Hall of Fame

HORSES

Ack Ack (1986, 1966)
Affectionately (1989, 1960)
Affirmed (1980, 1975)
All Along (1990, 1979)
Alsab (1976, 1939)
Alydar (1989, 1975)
American Eclipse (1970, 1814)
Armed (1963, 1941)
Artful (1956, 1902)

Assault (1964, 1943)
Battleship (1969, 1927)
Bed o'Roses (1976, 1947)
Beldame (1956, 1901)
Ben Brush (1955, 1893)
Bewitch (1977, 1945)
Bimelech (1990, 1937)
Black Gold (1989, 1921)
Black Helen (1991, 1932)

Blue Larkspur (1957, 1926)
Bold Ruler (1973, 1954)
Bon Nouvel (1976, 1960)
Boston (1955, 1833)
Broomstick (1956, 1901)
Buckpasser (1970, 1963)
Busher (1964, 1942)
Bushranger (1967, 1930)
Cafe Prince (1985, 1970)

HORSES (Cont.)

Carry Back (1975, 1958)
Challedon (1977, 1936)
Chris Evert (1988, 1971)
Cicada (1967, 1959)
Citation (1959, 1945)
Coaltown (1983, 1945)
Colin (1956, 1905)
Commando (1956, 1898)
Count Fleet (1961, 1940)
Dahlia (1981, 1970)
Damascus (1974, 1964)
Dark Mirage (1974, 1965)
Davona Dale (1985, 1976)
Desert Vixen (1979, 1970)
Devil Diver (1980, 1939)
Discovery (1969, 1931)
Domino (1955, 1891)
Dr. Fager (1971, 1964)
Elkridge (1966, 1938)
Emperor of Norfolk (1988, 1885)
Equipoise (1957, 1928)
Exterminator (1957, 1915)
Fairmount (1985, 1921)
Fair Play (1956, 1905)
Fashion (1980, 1837)
Firenze (1981, 1884)
Forego (1979, 1970)
Gallant Bloom (1977, 1966)
Gallant Fox (1957, 1927)
Gallant Man (1987, 1954)
Gallorette (1962, 1942)
Gamely (1980, 1964)
Genuine Risk (1986, 1977)
Good and Plenty (1956, 1900)
Grey Lag (1957, 1918)
Hamburg (1986, 1895)

Hanover (1955, 1884)
Henry of Navarre (1985, 1891)
Hill Prince (1991, 1947)
Hindoo (1955, 1878)
Imp (1965, 1894)
Jay Trump (1971, 1957)
John Henry (1990, 1975)
Johnstown (1992, 1982)
Jolly Roger (1965, 1922)
Kelso (1967, 1957)
Kentucky (1983, 1861)
Kingston (1955, 1884)
Lady's Secret (1992, 1982)
L'Escargot (1977, 1963)
Lexington (1955, 1850)
Longfellow (1971, 1867)
Luke Blackburn (1956, 1877)
Majestic Prince (1988, 1966)
Man o'War (1957, 1917)
Miss Woodford (1967, 1880)
Myrtlewood (1979, 1932)
Nashua (1965, 1952)
Native Dancer (1963, 1950)
Native Diver (1978, 1959)
Neji (1966, 1950)
Northern Dancer (1976, 1961)
Oedipus (1978, 1946)
Old Rosebud (1968, 1911)
Omaha (1965, 1932)
Pan Zareta (1972, 1910)
Parole (1984, 1879)
Peter Pan (1956, 1904)
Princess Doreen (1982, 1921)
Princess Rooney (1991, 1980)
Real Delight (1987, 1949)
Regret (1957, 1912)

Reigh Count (1978, 1925)
Roamer (1981, 1911)
Roseben (1956, 1901)
Round Table (1972, 1954)
Ruffian (1976, 1972)
Ruthless (1975, 1864)
Salvator (1955, 1886)
Sarazen (1957, 1921)
Seabiscuit (1958, 1933)
Searching (1978, 1952)
Seattle Slew (1981, 1974)
Secretariat (1974, 1970)
Shuvee (1975, 1966)
Silver Spoon (1978, 1956)
Sir Archy (1955, 1805)
Sir Barton (1957, 1916)
Slew o' Gold (1992, 1980)
Spectacular Bid (1982, 1976)
Stymie (1975, 1941)
Susan's Girl (1976, 1969)
Swaps (1966, 1952)
Sword Dancer (1977, 1956)
Sysonby (1956, 1902)
Ten Broeck (1982, 1872)
Tim Tam (1985, 1955)
Tom Fool (1960, 1949)
Top Flight (1966, 1929)
Tosmah (1984, 1961)
Twenty Grand (1957, 1928)
Twilight Tear (1963, 1941)
Two Lea (1982, 1946)
War Admiral (1958, 1934)
Whirlaway (1959, 1938)
Whisk Broom II (1979, 1907)
Zev (1983, 1920)

Note: Years of election and foaling in parentheses.

Vested for Life

When jockey Julie Krone was thrown off her mount during a race in August, the crowd at Saratoga held its collective breath until word was passed that the feisty 30-year-old Krone, winner of the 1993 Belmont aboard Colonial Affair, would be all right. A flesh wound to her elbow and a severely broken ankle that would eventually require two plates and 14 screws to properly secure appeared to be the extent of her injuries. Krone would miss six months of racing and be back as good as new.

What was not revealed until her first press conference nearly a month later was just how life-threatening Krone's accident actually was. It seems that when the aptly named Two Is Trouble, all 1,200 pounds of him, ran over Krone, he kicked her in the chest for good measure, resulting in a cardiac contusion that would have been far, far worse had Krone not been wearing a two-pound Kevlar vest for protection.

Both Krone and her doctor, Dr. Frank Ariosta, the director of orthopedic surgery at Staten Island University Hospital, believe that the vests, now worn by only a handful of jockeys, should be mandatory attire for all of them. "I knew I was going to get hit as soon as I went down, and boom! It took my breath away," Krone said at her press conference. "But at the same time, I could feel that the vest proteced me. It was the most incredible force. I feel like if I didn't have my vest on, I can't imagine what kind of shape I'd be in."

And what persuaded Krone to wear the vest in the first place? "I do it because Jerry Bailey does it," she said. "He's older and he's smart and I do what he does."

HARNESS RACING

Major Races

Hambletonian

Year	Winner	Driver	Year	Winner	Driver
1926	Guy McKinney	Nat Ray	1961	Harlan Dean	James Arthur
1927	Iosola's Worthy	Marvin Childs	1962	A. C.'s Viking	Sanders Russell
1928	Spenser	W. H. Leese	1963	Speedy Scot	Ralph Baldwin
1929	Walter Dear	Walter Cox	1964	Ayres	J. Simpson, Sr
1930	Hanover's Bertha	Tom Berry	1965	Egyptian Candor	Del Cameron
1931	Calumet Butler	R. D. McMahon	1966	Kerry Way	Frank Ervin
1932	The Marchioness	William Caton	1967	Speedy Streak	Del Cameron
1933	Mary Reynolds	Ben White	1968	Nevele Pride	Stanley Dancer
1934	Lord Jim	Doc Parshall	1969	Lindy's Pride	H. Beissinger
1935	Greyhound	Sep Palin	1970	Timothy T.	J. Simpson, Jr
1936	Rosalind	Ben White	1971	Speedy Crown	H. Beissinger
1937	Shirley Hanover	Henry Thomas	1972	Super Bowl	Stanley Dancer
1938	McLin Hanover	Henry Thomas	1973	Flirth	Ralph Baldwin
1939	Peter Astra	Doc Parshall	1974	Christopher T.	Bill Haughton
1940	Spencer Scott	Fred Egan	1975	Bonefish	Stanley Dancer
1941	Bill Gallon	Lee Smith	1976	Steve Lobell	Bill Haughton
1942	The Ambassador	Ben White	1977	Green Speed	Bill Haughton
1943	Volo Song	Ben White	1978	Speedy Somolli	H. Beissinger
1944	Yankee Maid	Henry Thomas	1979	Legend Hanover	George Sholty
1945	Titan Hanover	H. Pownall Sr	1980	Burgomeister	Bill Haughton
1946	Chestertown	Thomas Berry	1981	Shiaway St. Pat	Ray Remmen
1947	Hoot Mon	Sep Palin	1982	Speed Bowl	Tom Haughton
1948	Demon Hanover	Harrison Hoyt	1983	Duenna	Stanley Dancer
1949	Miss Tilly	Fred Egan	1984	Historic Freight	Ben Webster
1950	Lusty Song	Del Miller	1985	Prakas	Bill O'Donnell
1951	Mainliner	Guy Crippen	1986	Nuclear Kosmos	Ulf Thoresen
1952	Sharp Note	Bion Shively	1987	Mack Lobell	John Campbell
1953	Helicopter	Harry Harvey	1988	Armbro Goal	John Campbell
1954	Newport Dream	Del Cameron	1989	Park Avenue Joe*	Ron Waples
1955	Scott Frost	Joe O'Brien		Probe*	Bill Fahy
1956	The Intruder	Ned Bower	1990	Harmonious	John Campbell
1957	Hickory Smoke	J. Simpson Sr	1991	Giant Victory	Jack Moiseyev
1958	Emily's Pride	Flave Nipe	1992	Alf Palema	Mickey McNichol
1959	Diller Hanover	Frank Ervin	1993	American Winner	Ron Pierce
1960	Blaze Hanover	Joe O'Brien			

*Park Avenue Joe and Probe dead-heated for win. Park Avenue Joe finished first in the summary 2-1-1 to Probe's 1-9-1 finish.

Note: Run at 1 mile since 1947.

Little Brown Jug

Year	Winner	Driver	Year	Winner	Driver
1946	Ensign Hanover	Wayne Smart	1968	Rum Customer	Bill Haughton
1947	Forbes Chief	Del Cameron	1969	Laverne Hanover	Bill Haughton
1948	Knight Dream	Frank Safford	1970	Most Happy Fella	Stanley Dancer
1949	Good Time	Frank Ervin	1971	Nansemond	Herve Filion
1950	Dudley Hanover	Del Miller	1972	Strike Out	Keith Waples
1951	Tar Heel	Del Cameron	1973	Melvin's Woe	Joe O'Brien
1952	Meadow Rice	Wayne Smart	1974	Armbro Omaha	Bill Haughton
1953	Keystoner	Frank Ervin	1975	Seatrain	Ben Webster
1954	Adios Harry	Morris MacDonald	1976	Keystone Ore	Stanley Dancer
1955	Quick Chief	Bill Haughton	1977	Governor Skipper	John Chapman
1956	Noble Adios	John Simpson Sr	1978	Happy Escort	William Popfinger
1957	Torpid	John Simpso Sr	1979	Hot Hitter	Herve Filion
1958	Shadow Wave	Joe O'Brien	1980	Niatross	Clint Galbraith
1959	Adios Butler	Clint Hodgins	1981	Fan Hanover	Glen Garnsey
1960	Bullet Hanover	John Simpson Sr	1982	Merger	John Campbell
1961	Henry T. Adios	Stanley Dancer	1983	Ralph Hanover	Ron Waples
1962	Lehigh Hanover	Stanley Dancer	1984	Colt Fortysix	Chris Boring
1963	Overtrick	John Patterson	1985	Nihilator	Bill O'Donnell
1964	Vicar Hanover	Bill Haughton	1986	Barberry Spur	Bill O'Donnell
1965	Bret Hanover	Frank Ervin	1987	Jaguar Spur	Dick Stillings
1966	Romeo Hanover	George Sholty	1988	B. J. Scoot	Michel Lachance
1967	Best of All	James Hackett	1989	Goalie Jeff	Michel Lachance

Little Brown Jug (Cont.)

Year	Winner	Driver	Year	Winner	Driver
1990	Beach Towel	Ray Remmen	1992	Fake Left	Ron Waples
1991	Precious Bunny	Jack Moiseye	1993	Life Sign	John Campbell

Breeders' Crown

1984

Div	Winner	Driver
2PC	Dragon's Lair	Jeff Mallet
2PF	Amneris	John Campbell
3PC	Troublemaker	Bill O'Donnell
3PF	Naughty But Nice	Tommy Haughton
2TC	Workaholic	Berndt Lindstedt
2TF	Conifer	George Sholty
3TC	Baltic Speed	Jan Nordin
3TF	Fancy Crown	Bill O'Donnell

1985

Div	Winner	Driver
2PC	Robust Hanover	John Campbell
2PF	Caressable	Herve Filion
3PC	Nihilator	Bill O'Donnell
3PF	Stienam	Buddy Gilmour
2TC	Express Ride	John Campbell
2TF	JEF's Spice	Mickey McNichol
3TC	Prakas	John Campbell
3TF	Armbro Devona	Bill O'Donnell
AP	Division Street	Michel Lachance
AT	Sandy Bowl	John Campbell

1986

Div	Winner	Driver
2PC	Sunset Warrior	Bill Gale
2PF	Halcyon	Ray Remmen
3PC	Masquerade	Richard Silverman
3PF	Glow Softly	Ron Waples
2TC	Mack Lobell	John Campbell
2TF	Super Flora	Ron Waples
3TC	Sugarcane Hanover	Ron Waples
3TF	JEF's Spice	Bill O'Donnell
APM	Samshu Bluegrass	Michel Lachance
ATM	Grades Singing	Herve Filion
APH	Forrest Skipper	Lucien Fontaine
ATH	Nearly Perfect	Mickey McNichol

1987

Div	Winner	Driver
2PC	Camtastic	Bill O'Donnell
2PF	Leah Almahurst	Bill Fahy
3PC	Call For Rain	Clint Galbraith
3PF	Pacific	Tom Harmer
2TC	Defiant One	Howard Beissinger
2TF	Nan's Catch	Berndt Lindstedt
3TC	Mack Lobell	John Campbell
3TF	Armbro Fling	George Sholty
APM	Follow My Star	John Campbell
ATM	Grades Singing	Olle Goop
APH	Armbro Emerson	Walter Whelan
ATH	Sugarcane Hanover	Ron Waples

1988

Div	Winner	Driver
2PC	Kentucky Spur	Dick Stillings
2PF	Central Park West	John Campbell
3PC	Camtastic	Bill O'Donnell
3PF	Sweet Reflection	Bill O'Donnell
2TC	Valley Victory	Bill O'Donnell
2TF	Peace Corps	John Campbell
3TC	Firm Tribute	Mark O'Mara
3TF	Nalda Hanover	Mickey McNichol
APM	Anniecrombie	Dave Magee
ATM	Armbro Flori	Larry Walker
APH	Call For Rain	Clint Galbraith
ATH	Mack Lobell	John Campbell

1989

Div	Winner	Driver
2PC	Till We Meet Again	Mickey McNichol
2PF	Town Pro	Doug Brown
3PC	Goalie Jeff	Michel Lachance
3PF	Cheery Hello	John Campbell
2TC	Royal Troubador	Carl Allen
2TF	Delphi's Lobell	Ron Waples
3TC	Esquire Spur	Dick Stillings
3TF	Pace Corps	John Campbell
APM	Armbro Feather	John Kopas
ATM	Grades Singing	Olle Goop
APH	Matt's Scooter	Michel Lachance
ATH	Delray Lobell	John Campbell

1990

Div	Winner	Driver
2PC	Artsplace	John Campbell
2PF	Miss Easy	John Campbell
3PC	Beach Towel	Ray Remmen
3PF	Town Pro	Doug Brown
2TC	Crysta's Best	Dick Richardson Jr
2TF	Jean Bi	Jan Nordin
3TC	Embassy Lobell	Michel Lachance
3TF	Me Maggie	Berndt Lindstedt
APM	Caesar's Jackpot	Bill Fahy
ATM	Peace Corps	Stig Johansson
APH	Bay's Fella	Paul MacDonell
ATH	No Sex Please	Ron Waples

1991

Div	Winner	Driver
2PC	Digger Almahurst	Doug Brown
2PF	Hazleton Kay	John Campbell
3PC	Three Wizzards	Bill Gale
3PF	Miss Easy	John Campbell
2TC	King Conch	Bill Gale
2TF	Armbro Keepsake	John Campbell
3TC	Giant Victory	Ron Pierce
3TF	Twelve Speed	Ron Waples
APM	Delinquent Account	Bill O'Donnell

Note: 2=Two-year-old; T=Trotter; C=Colt; 3=Three-year-old; P=Pacer; F=Filly; A=Aged; H=Horse; M=Mare.

Major Races (Cont.)

Breeders' Crown (Cont.)

1991 (Cont.)

Div	Winner	Driver
ATM	Me Maggie	Berndt Lindstedt
APH	Camluck	Michel Lachance
ATH	Billyjojimbob	Paul MacDonell

1992

Div	Winner	Driver
2PC	Village Jiffy	Ron Waples
2PF	Immortality	John Campbell
3PC	Kingsbridge	Roger Mayotte

1992 (Cont.)

Div	Winner	Driver
3PF	So Fresh	John Campbell
2TC	Giant Chill	John Patterson, Jr
2TF	Winky's Goal	Cat Manzi
3TC	Baltic Striker	Michel Lachance
3TF	Imperfection	Michel Lachance
APM	Shady Daisy	Ron Pierce
ATM	Peace Corps	Torbjorn Jansson
APH	Artsplace	John Campbell
ATH	No Sex Please	Ron Waples

Note: 2=Two-year-old; T=Trotter; C=Colt; 3=Three-year-old; P=Pacer; F=Filly; A=Aged; H=Horse; M=Mare.

Triple Crown Winners

Trotting

Trotting's Triple Crown consists of the Hambletonian (first run in 1926), the Kentucky Futurity (first run in 1893), and the Yonkers Trot (known as the Yonkers Futurity when it began in 1955).

Year	Horse	Owner	Breeder	Trainer & Driver
1955	Scott Frost	S.A. Camp Farms	Est of W. N. Reynolds	Joe O'Brien
1963	Speedy Scot	Castleton Farms	Castleton Farms	Ralph Baldwin
1964	Ayres	Charlotte Sheppard	Charlotte Sheppard	John Simpson Sr
1968	Nevele Pride	Nevele Acres & Lou Resnick	Mr & Mrs E. C. Quin	Stanley Dancer
1969	Lindy's Pride	Lindy Farm	Hanover Shoe Farms	Howard Beissinger
1972	Super Bowl	Rachel Dancer & Rose Hild Breeding Farm	Stoner Creek Stud	Stanley Dancer

Pacing

Pacing's Triple Crown consists of the Cane Pace (called the Cane Futurity when it began in 1955), the Little Brown Jug (first run in 1946), and the Messenger Stake (first run in 1956).

Year	Horse	Owner	Breeder	Trainer/Driver
1959	Adios Butler	Paige West & Angelo Pellillo	R. C. Carpenter	Paige West/Clint Hodgins
1965	Bret Hanover	Richard Downing	Hanover Shoe Farms	Frank Ervin
1966	Romeo Hanover	Lucky Star Stables & Morton Finder	Hanover Shoe Farms	Jerry Silverman/ William Meyer (Cane) & George Sholty (Jug & Messenger)
1968	Rum Customer	Kennilworth Farms & L. C. Mancuso	Mr. & Mrs. R. C. Larkin	Bill Haughton
1970	Most Happy Fella	Egyptian Acres Stable	Stoner Creek Stud	Stanley Dancer
1980	Niatross	Niagara Acres, C. Galbraith & Niatross Stables	Niagara Acres	Clint Galbraith
1983	Ralph Hanover	Waples Stable, Pointsetta Stable, Grant's Direct Stable & P. J. Baugh	Hanover Shoe Farms	Stew Firlotte/Ron Waples

Awards

Horse of the Year

Year	Horse	Gait	Owner	Year	Horse	Gait	Owner
1947	Victory Song	T	Castleton Farm	1952	Good Time	P	William Cane
1948	Rodney	T	R. H. Johnston	1953	Hi Lo's Forbes	P	Mr. and Mrs. Earl Wagner
1949	Good Time	P	William Cane	1954	Stenographer	T	Max Hempt
1950	Proximity	T	Ralph and Gordon Verhurst	1955	Scott Frost	T	S. A. Camp Farms
1951	Pronto Don	T	Hayes Fair Acres Stable	1956	Scott Frost	T	S. A. Camp Farms
				1957	Torpid	P	Sherwood Farm

Horse of the Year (Cont.)

Year	Horse	Gait	Owner
1958	Emily's Pride	T	Walnut Hall and Castleton Farms
1959	Bye Bye Byrd	P	Mr. and Mrs. Rex Larkin
1960	Adios Butler	P	Adios Butler Syndicate
1961	Adios Butler	P	Adios Butler Syndicate
1962	Su Mac Lad	T	I. W. Berkemeyer
1963	Speedy Scot	T	Castleton Farm
1964	Bret Hanover	P	Richard Downing
1965	Bret Hanover	P	Richard Downing
1966	Bret Hanover	P	Richard Downing
1967	Nevele Pride	T	Nevele Acres
1968	Nevele Pride	T	Nevele Acres, Louis Resnick
1969	Nevele Pride	T	Nevele Acres, Louis Resnick
1970	Fresh Yankee	T	Duncan MacDonald
1971	Albatross	P	Albatross Stable
1972	Albatross	P	Amicable Stable
1973	Sir Dalrae	P	A La Carte Racing Stable
1974	Delmonica Hanover	T	Delvin Miller, W. Arnold Hanger
1975	Savoir	T	Allwood Stable
1976	Keystone Ore	P	Mr. and Mrs. Stanley Dancer, Rose Hild Farms, Robert Jones
1977	Green Speed	T	Beverly Lloyds
1978	Abercrombie	P	Shirley Mitchell, L. Keith Bulen
1979	Niatross	P	Niagara Acres, Clint Galbraith
1980	Niatross	P	Niatross Syndicate, Niagara Acres, Clint Galbraith
1981	Fan Hanover	P	Dr. J. Glen Brown
1982	Cam Fella	P	Norm Clements, Norm Faulkner
1983	Cam Fella	P	JEF's Standardbred, Norm Clements, Norm Faulkner
1984	Fancy Crown	T	Fancy Crown Stable
1985	Nihilator	P	Wall Street-Nihilator Syndicate
1986	Forrest Skipper	P	Forrest L. Bartlett
1987	Mack Lobell	T	One More Time Stable and Fair Wind Farm
1988	Mack Lobell	T	John Erik Magnusson
1989	Matt's Scooter	P	Gordon and Illa Rumpel, Charles Jurasvinski
1990	Beach Towel	P	Uptown Stables
1991	Precious Bunny	P	R. Peter Heffering
1992	Artsplace	P	George Segal

Note: Balloting is conducted by the U.S Trotting Association and U.S. Harness Writers Association.

Leading Drivers—Money Won

Year	Driver	Winnings ($)	Year	Driver	Winnings ($)
1946	Thomas Berry	121,933	1970	Herve Filion	1,647,837
1947	H. C. Fitzpatrick	133,675	1971	Herve Filion	1,915,945
1948	Ralph Baldwin	153,222	1972	Herve Filion	2,473,265
1949	Clint Hodgins	184,108	1973	Herve Filion	2,233,303
1950	Del Miller	306,813	1974	Herve Filion	3,474,315
1951	John Simpson Sr	333,316	1975	Carmine Abbatiello	2,275,093
1952	Bill Haughton	311,728	1976	Herve Filion	2,278,634
1953	Bill Haughton	374,527	1977	Herve Filion	2,551,058
1954	Bill Haughton	415,577	1978	Carmine Abbatiello	3,344,457
1955	Bill Haughton	599,455	1979	John Campbell	3,308,984
1956	Bill Haughton	572,945	1980	John Campbell	3,732,306
1957	Bill Haughton	586,950	1981	Bill O'Donnell	4,065,608
1958	Bill Haughton	816,659	1982	Bill O'Donnell	5,755,067
1959	Bill Haughton	771,435	1983	John Campbell	6,104,082
1960	Del Miller	567,282	1984	Bill O'Donnell	9,059,184
1961	Stanley Dancer	674,723	1985	Bill O'Donnell	10,207,372
1962	Stanley Dancer	760,343	1986	John Campbell	9,515,055
1963	Bill Haughton	790,086	1987	John Campbell	10,186,495
1964	Stanley Dancer	1,051,538	1988	John Campbell	11,148,565
1965	Bill Haughton	889,943	1989	John Campbell	9,738,460
1966	Stanley Dancer	1,218,403	1990	John Campbell	11,620,878
1967	Bill Haughton	1,305,773	1991	Jack Moiseyev	9,568,468
1968	Bill Haughton	1,654,463	1992	John Campbell	8,202,108
1969	Del Insko	1,635,463			

Motor Sports

SPORTS Illustrated

GOODYEAR

Marlboro

KING
of the
ROAD

Emerson Fittipaldi
celebrates his second
victory in the Indy 500

GEORGE TIEDEMANN

Dreadful Days

A pair of tragic deaths and a series of racing setbacks produced a dismal year for U.S. drivers | by ED HINTON

IN U.S. MOTOR RACING HISTORY, 1993 will be remembered almost solely for the bad: the tragedies and the humiliation. NASCAR lost two of its brightest and most popular young drivers, Alan Kulwicki and Davey Allison, to death in private aircraft crashes. And Michael Andretti, who at season's outset was America's great hope to compete internationally on the Formula One Grand Prix tour, flopped worldwide.

Doubly crushing to the United States' world racing prestige was the fact that Englishman Nigel Mansell, the 1992 Formula One world champion, bolted from Europe, stepped into Andretti's old Indy Car spot and made a virtual cakewalk of his first U.S. driving season.

Two of America's greatest racing names, Richard Petty and A.J. Foyt, were missing from the starting lineups of the races they made famous. In February, Petty, who retired after the '92 season, stood in the pits at the Daytona 500 only as a car owner. In May, Foyt finally officially hung it up, aborting his attempt to qualify for the Indianapo-

lis 500, and like Petty stepped into a full-time car owner's role.

Kulwicki, 38, the soft-spoken diminutive Polish-American from Wisconsin, had been the dark horse winner of the '92 Winston Cup season championship and had flowered into one of NASCAR's most popular champions ever. He touched the public's heartstrings with his work ethic and his long-shot success in an era when much of the nation's faith in the American dream was fading.

In modern-day NASCAR, conventional wisdom demanded that a driver work for someone else, a separate car owner who would take care of sponsorship deals and hire the mechanics to build and maintain the cars. Kulwicki insisted on being his own boss, against all odds and advice: Twice he turned down job offers from the legendary car owner Junior Johnson in order to push ahead stubbornly with his own Kulwicki Racing Team. And so he came to the Daytona 500, the season-opening race of 1993, as NASCAR's refreshing new champion and the sudden darling of U.S. race fans.

The Daytona 500 produced another dark-horse winner, Dale Jarrett, driving for the team of former Washington Redskin coach Joe Gibbs. Jarrett's father, Ned, a former Winston Cup champion turned color analyst for CBS television, called the final laps of his son's duel with Dale Earnhardt. Ned's play-by-play turned into de facto coaching. Though the younger Jarrett couldn't actually hear his father, he did exactly what Ned wanted him to do. He tucked in close behind Earnhardt, aerodynamically loosening Earnhardt's car, and passed Earnhardt on the last lap to win. That left Earnhardt, NASCAR's most dominant driver overall, an amazing 0 for 15 in Daytona 500 starts.

Next on the agenda of U.S. race fans was the settling of a long-running dispute with Europeans and South Americans over who produced the best open-wheel race drivers—the U.S. or the international set. The '93 season promised to be an ongoing showdown for the bragging rights. Andretti, the 1991 Indy Car champion, who dominated that circuit in recent years, moved to For-

mula One to drive for the storied McLaren team. Meanwhile, Mansell, after a split with the Williams-Renault F/1 team following his '92 championship, replaced Andretti with the Newman-Haas Indy Car team.

The international driver exchange wasn't exactly a fair contest, in that Andretti went to Europe in an off-year for McLaren, which had lost its engine supply deal with once dominant Honda and had to settle in '93 for less powerful Cosworth Ford engines. Mansell, though, stepped into the best seat on the Indy Car tour. The Newman-Haas Lola was powered by a turbocharged Ford Cosworth quite different from the company's normally aspirated F/1 engines, and was the most powerful in Indy Car racing.

Mansell had won the '92 world championship in a Williams FW-14 with computer-controlled "active ride" suspension, which did much of a driver's thinking and work for

Allison's gravesite was surrounded by tokens of the racing world's esteem.

JIM GUND

him on the track. Further, the Williams carried a semiautomatic gearbox so that Mansell didn't have to take his hands off the wheel to shift gears. Mansell might find much tougher going, observers believed, when he climbed into a relatively crude Indy Car, which still had to be shifted manually and whose suspension had to be adjusted in the pits. Meanwhile Andretti's talent was expected to carry him at least to respectable finishes in Formula One.

Then the bottom fell out of all those arguments, all around. In the season-opening Grand Prix of South Africa, at Kyalami on March 14, Andretti stalled on the starting grid and failed even to get off with the rest of the field from the standing start. His mechanics blamed a clutch problem; still, it was an enormously embarrassing scene on live worldwide television.

A week later Mansell won the Indy Car season opener at Surfer's Paradise, Australia—the only Indy Car race outside North America—by merrily manhandling the Lola-Ford roughly but quickly through the street circuit. He would roar on to win four of the first 11 Indy Car races of the season and log a respectable third-place finish and Rookie of the Year honors in the Indianapolis 500, his first-ever oval-track race.

Then on March 28, at the Brazilian Grand Prix near São Paulo, Andretti crashed on the first turn of the first lap. And then, in the third F/1 race, the Grand Prix of Europe at Donington, England, Andretti again crashed on the first lap, and a headline in London's *Daily Mail* said it best for him: ANOTHER RACE, ANOTHER NIGHTMARE.

On April 1 the U.S. racing nightmare of 1993 came home, and came hard. Kulwicki, gladly mingling with the public, which now worshipped him, detoured to Knoxville, Tenn., for an autograph session with fans before continuing on to Bristol, Tenn., for that weekend's NASCAR race. After the session he and three other people boarded a private plane owned by his sponsor, Hooter's restaurants, for the 90-mile hop to Bristol. On the approach to the airport, the plane crashed. All aboard were killed.

The Bristol race that ensued was a bleak gathering, and after Rusty Wallace won, he mourned Kulwicki publicly with a "Polish victory lap," as Kulwicki used to call it when he would drive around the track backward after he won a race.

By the Indianapolis 500 in May, the international hoopla over American shortcomings in motor racing had reached fever pitch. Even *The Economist*, Britain's staid, 150-year-old news magazine, which had hardly noticed U.S. motor racing since Henry Ford retired from competition, gloated over the Indy results in a full-page story headlined THE INTERNATIONAL 500. The magazine charted the final standings in the '93 500 as follows: "1. Emerson Fittipaldi, Brazil; 2. Arie Luyendyk, Holland; 3. Nigel Mansell, Britain; 4. Raul Boesel, Brazil." And in the unkindest cut of all, *The Economist* listed, "5. Mario Andretti, Italy." That, according to the most respected British news authority in print, left unknown Scott Brayton as the highest-finishing American at Indy, sixth.

Unmentioned was the fact that Fittipaldi lives most of each year in Miami, that Luyendyk lives near Phoenix, that Mansell has moved to Clearwater, Fla., and that Mario Andretti, Michael's father, sailed past the Statue of Liberty at the age of 15 and has considered himself American ever since. But none of this mattered at the crest of subtle U.S. driver–bashing worldwide. Mario was the last American to win the Formula One world championship, in 1978, and 15 years later Europeans were still claiming him as Italian.

Such was the luck of U.S. drivers in '93 that Bobby Rahal of Dublin, Ohio, the 1986 Indy 500 winner and the '92 PPG Indy Car season champion, failed even to qualify at Indianapolis.

Thoroughly unfazed by the Michael Andretti for Nigel Mansell exchange was England's Frank Williams, the quadriplegic and indomitable owner of Williams Grand Prix Engineering, whose cars continued to be the class of Formula One, whatever the names of the drivers he

GEORGE TIEDEMANN

Mansell's third place finish in his first Indy earned him Rookie of the Year honors.

employed. After his one-two finish in the world championship of '92 with Mansell and Riccardo Patrese, Williams lost both drivers in the off-season. But for '93 he brought three-time world champion Alain Prost of France out of retirement, and Prost immediately set his sights on a fourth title. As his second driver Williams hired an English sentimental favorite, Damon Hill, son of the late two-time world champion Graham Hill.

Williams-Renault's only real hindrance in '93 was the ever maddening bureaucracy of the Federation Internationale du Sport Automobile (FISA), whose legislation became even more outrageous under English president Max Mosley than it had been under the highly controversial Frenchman Jean-Marie Balestre. In February '93, FISA announced that all computerized suspensions and traction controls would be banned for '94—which would negate years of Williams research and development. By July, Mosley's regime suddenly ruled that no further victories of cars with active suspensions would be allowed, even for the remainder of '93. The reasoning was that active suspensions not only automatically adjust themselves so that cars don't lean in corners, squat on acceleration or dive on deceleration, they also automatically adjust a car's aerodynamics, which was already illegal in Formula One.

Under vehement protests from the top three teams—Williams, McLaren and Benetton, all of whom used some version of active suspension and might have dropped out for the remainder of the season had the rule been enforced—FISA backed off the ruling until 1994.

By July, U.S. race fans were resigned to Michael Andretti's dismal showing in Europe and were still in mourning over the sudden loss of Kulwicki. Then, just when it seemed matters couldn't get any worse, they got much worse.

Stock car racing's popular Allison family of Hueytown, Ala., had already suffered enough tragedy in the past five years to devastate any family for a generation. Patriarch Bobby Allison had suffered a career-ending brain injury in a crash in 1988 at Pocono International Raceway in Pennsylvania. Then in August 1991, Clifford Allison, 27, the younger of Bobby's two sons, was killed in a crash during a practice run at Michigan International Speedway. Davey Allison, Bobby's elder son, had become by 1993 a national example of resilience in the face of family tragedy and personal setbacks. Twice in '92 Davey had been injured—suffering

Andretti emerged unhurt from a crash in Brazil but his season was a wreck of another sort.

broken ribs at Charlotte in May in the Winston bonus race, then suffering a broken left arm and concussion in a horrific-looking, 11-flip crash at Pocono in July. With all that, he battled back and was in strong contention for the '92 championship until, in the last race of the season, in Atlanta, he was caught up in a crash that wasn't his fault, and lost the championship to Kulwicki. Still he pressed on enthusiastically in '93.

Then on July 12, 1993, Davey was piloting a helicopter he had recently bought. He and old family friend Red Farmer were less than one foot from touching down in a parking lot at Talladega Superspeedway, the Allisons' "home track," which lay a short 60-mile hop from Hueytown on the other side of Birmingham. Within inches of touchdown, according to witnesses, the helicopter began oscillating left and right, then suddenly rose 25 feet, began spinning, rolled and crashed. Farmer, who'd had time to brace himself, escaped with a broken collarbone and ribs. Davey, who'd been trying to regain control right up until impact, was unable to brace himself. He suffered massive head injuries and was transported to a Birmingham hospital by medical helicopter.

At 7 a.m. on July 13, Davey was pronounced dead by attending physicians, and a U.S. motor racing public still stunned by Kulwicki's death now fell into further disbelief. The NASCAR community was heartsick. At Pocono the following Sunday, Dale Earnhardt won the race and carried out a doubly mournful victory ceremony, not only driving a Kulwicki-style "Polish victory lap" backward around Pocono, but also flying from his window a black flag bearing Davey Allison's car number, 28.

The Pocono victory took the iron-willed Earnhardt to a commanding lead in the '93 Winston Cup point standings. Earnhardt's sixth championship would put him within one Winston Cup title of tying the alltime career record for season championships, Richard Petty's seven.

But only in NASCAR, thoroughly populated by U.S. drivers, would an American win a major championship in '93. The PPG Indy Car season championship would come down to an international parade of England's Mansell, Brazil's Fittipaldi, and Canada's Paul Tracy.

Nothing in the all-American NASCAR Winston Cup Series could redeem 1993 from being a black chapter in the record books. And nothing, it seemed, could get U.S. open-wheel racers going against international competition. It was, for the Yanks, a simply dreadful year.

FOR THE RECORD·1992-1993

CART Racing

Indianapolis 500

Results of the 77th running of the Indianapolis 500 and 4th round of the 1993 IndyCar season. Held Sunday, May 30, at the 2.5-mile Indianapolis Motor Speedway in Speedway, IN.

Distance, 500 miles; starters, 33; time of race, 3:10:50; average speed, 157.207 mph; margin of victory, 2.862 seconds; caution flags, 8 for 33 laps; lead changes, 24 among 12 drivers; attendance, 450,000.

TOP 10 FINISHERS

Pos	Driver (start pos.)	Car	Qual. Speed	Laps	Status
1	Emerson Fittipaldi (9)	Penske-Chevy	220.150	200	157.207
2	Arie Luyendyk (1)	Ford-Cosworth	223.967	200	157.168
3	Nigel Mansell (8)	Ford-Cosworth	220.255	200	157.149
4	Raul Boesel (3)	Ford-Cosworth	222.379	200	157.142
5	Mario Andretti (2)	Ford-Cosworth	223.414	200	157.133
6	Scott Brayton (11)	Ford-Cosworth	219.637	200	157.117
7	Scott Goodyear (4)	Ford-Coswroth	222.344	200	157.099
8	Al Unser Jr (5)	L93-Chevy	221.773	200	157.070
9	Teo Fabio (17)	L93-Chevy	220.514	200	156.968
10	John Andretti (24)	Ford-Cosworth	221.746	200	156.964

1993 Indy Car Results

Date	Track/Distance	Winner (start pos.)	Car	Avg Speed
Mar 21	Australian Grand Prix	Nigel Mansell (1)	Ford-Cosworth	97.284
Apr 4	Phoenix 200	Mario Andretti (2)	Ford-Cosworth	123.847
Apr 12	Long Beach Grand Prix	Paul Tracy (2)	Penske-Chevy	93.089
May 30	Indianapolis 500	Emerson Fittipaldi (9)	Penske-Chevy	157.207
June 6	Miller Genuine Draft 200	Nigel Mansell (7)	Ford-Cosworth	110.970
June 13	Detroit Grand Prix	Danny Sullivan (10)	L93-Chevy	83.116
June 27	Portland 200	Emerson Fittipaldi (2)	Penske-Chevy	96.312
July 11	Cleveland Grand Prix	Paul Tracy (1)	Penske-Chevy	127.913
July 19	Indy Toronto	Paul Tracy (2)	Penske-Chevy	95.510
Aug 1	Michigan 500	Nigel Mansell (2)	Ford-Cosworth	188.203
Aug 8	New England 200	Nigel Mansell (1)	Ford-Cosworth	130.148
Aug 22	Wisconsin 200	Paul Tracy (1)	Penske-Chevy	118.408
Aug 29	Indy Vancouver	Al Unser Jr (5)	L93-Chevy	91.794
Sept 12	Mid-Ohio	Emerson Fittipaldi (3)	Penske-Chevy	102.217
Sept 19	Nazareth	Nigel Mansell (1)	Ford-Cosworth	158.686
Oct 3	Monterey Grand Prix	Paul Tracy (2)	Penske-Chevy	106.303

Note: Distances are in miles.

Championship Standings

Driver	Starts	Wins	Pts
Nigel Mansell	15	5	191
Emerson Fittipaldi	16	3	183
Paul Tracy	16	5	157
Bobby Rahal	15	0	133
Raul Boesel	16	0	132
Mario Andretti	16	1	117
Al Unser Jr	16	1	100
Arie Luyendyk	16	0	90
Scott Goodyear	16	0	86
Robby Gordon	15	0	84

Daytona 500

Results of the opening round of the 1993 Winston Cup series. Held Sunday, February 14, at the 2.5-mile high-banked Daytona International Speedway.

Distance, 500 miles; starters, 41; time of race, 3:13:35; average speed, 154.972 mph; margin of victory, .16 second; caution flags, 7 for 30 laps; lead changes, 38 among 13 drivers; attendance, 120,000.

TOP 10 FINISHERS

Pos	Driver (start pos.)	Car	Laps	Winnings ($)
1	Dale Jarrett (2)	Chevrolet	200	238,200
2	Dale Earnhardt (4)	Ford	200	181,825
3	Geoff Bodine (6)	Ford	200	141,450
4	Hut Stricklin(18)	Ford	200	95,950
5	Jeff Gordon (3)	Chevrolet	200	111,150
6	Mark Martin (23)	Ford	200	74,625
7	Morgan Shepherd(32)	Ford	200	62,350
8	Ken Schrader (7)	Chevrolet	200	64,025
9	Sterling Marlin (14)	Ford	200	54,225
10	Wally Dallenbach, Jr (22)	Ford	200	49,125

Late 1992 NASCAR Results

Date	Track/Distance	Winner (start pos.)	Car	Avg Speed	Winnings ($)
Oct 5	N Wilkesboro 400*	Geoff Bodine (3)	Ford	107.360	71,625
Oct 11	Charlotte 500	Mark Martin (1)	Ford	153.537	101,500
Oct 25	Rockingham 500	Kyle Petty (1)	Pontiac	130.748	153,100
Nov 1	Phoenix 500	Davey Allison (12)	Ford	103.885	65,285
Nov 15	Atlanta 500	Bill Elliott (11)	Ford	133.322	93,600

Note: Distances are in miles unless followed by * (laps) or K (kilometers).

1993 NASCAR Results (through October 10)

Date	Track/Distance	Winner (start pos.)	Car	Avg Speed	Winnings ($)
Feb 14	Daytona 500	Dale Jarrett (2)	Chevrolet	154.972	238,200
Feb 28	Rockingham 500	Rusty Wallace (10)	Pontiac	124.486	42,735
Mar 7	Richmond 400*	Davey Allison (14)	Ford	107.709	70,125
Mar 20	Atlanta 500	Morgan Shepherd (7)	Ford	150.442	70,350
Mar 28	Darlington 500	Dale Earnhart (1)	Chevrolet	139.958	64,815
Apr 4	Bristol 500*	Rusty Wallace (1)	Pontiac	84.730	107,610
Apr 18	N Wilkesboro 400*	Rusty Wallace (9)	Pontiac	92.602	43,535
Apr 25	Martinsville 500*	Rusty Wallace (5)	Pontiac	79.078	45,175
May 2	Talladega 500	Ernie Irvan (16)	Chevrolet	155.412	85,875
May 16	Sonoma 300K	Geoff Bodine(3)	Ford	77.013	66,510
May 30	Charlotte 600	Dale Earnhardt (14)	Chevrolet	145.504	156,650
June 6	Dover Downs 500	Dale Earnhardt (8)	Chevrolet	105.600	68,030
June 13	Pocono 500	Kyle Petty (8)	Pontiac	138.005	44,960
June 20	Michigan 400	Ricky Rudd (2)	Chevrolet	148.484	77,890
July 3	Daytona 400	Dale Earnhardt (5)	Chevrolet	151.755	75,940
July 11	New Hampshire 300	Rusty Wallace (8)	Pontiac	105.947	77,500
July 18	Pocono 500	Dale Earnhardt	Chevrolet	133.343	66,795
July 25	Talladega 500	Dale Earnhardt (11)	Chevrolet	153.858	87,315
Aug 8	Watkins Glen 90*	Mark Martin (1)	Ford	84.771	166,110
Aug 15	Michigan 400	Mark Martin (12)	Ford	144.564	76,645
Aug 28	Bristol 500*	Mark Martin (1)	Ford	88.172	80,125
Sep 5	Darlington 500	Mark Martin (4)	Ford	137.932	67,765
Sept 11	Richmond 400	Rusty Wallace (3)	Pontiac	99.917	49,415
Sept 19	Dover Downs 500	Rusty Wallace (1)	Pontiac	100.334	77,645
Sept 26	Martinsville 500	Ernie Irvan (1)	Ford	74.102	75,300
Oct 3	N Wilkesboro 400*	Rusty Wallace (11)	Pontiac	96.920	46,260
Oct 10	Charlotte 500	Ernie Irvan (2)	Ford	154.537	147,450

*Distance in laps.

Note: Distances are in miles unless followed by K (kilometers)

1992 Winston Cup Standings

Driver	Car	Starts	Wins	Pts
Alan Kulwicki	Ford	29	2	4078
Bill Elliott	Ford	29	5	4068
Davey Allison	Ford	29	5	4015
Harry Gant	Olds	29	2	3955
Kyle Petty	Pontiac	29	2	3945
Mark Martin	Ford	29	2	3887
Ricky Rudd	Chevy	29	1	3735
Terry Labonte	Chevy	29	0	3674
Darrell Waltrip	Chevy	29	3	3659
Sterling Marlin	Ford	29	0	3603

1992 Winston Cup Driver Winnings

Driver	Winnings ($)
Alan Kulwicki	2,322,561
Bill Elliott	1,692,381
Davey Allison	1,955,628
Harry Gant	1,122,776
Kyle Petty	1,107,063
Mark Martin	1,000,571
Ernie Irvan	996,885
Dale Earnhardt	915,463
Darrell Waltrip	876,492
Ricky Rudd	793,903

Formula One/Grand Prix Racing

1993 Formula One Results (through September 26)

Date	Grand Prix	Winner	Car	Distance
Mar 14	South Africa	Alain Prost	Williams-Renault	190.6 mi
Mar 28	Brazil	Ayrton Senna	McLaren-Ford	190.8 mi
Apr 11	Europe	Ayrton Senna	McLaren-Ford	189.9 mi
Apr 25	San Marino	Alain Prost	Williams-Renault	191.0 mi
May 9	Spain	Alain Prost	Williams-Renault	191.7 mi
May 23	Monaco	Ayrton Senna	McLaren-Honda	161.2 mi
June 13	Canada	Alain Prost	Williams-Renault	189.9 mi
July 4	France	Alain Prost	Williams-Renault	193 mi
July 11	Britain	Alain Prost	Williams-Renault	191.5 mi
July 24	Germany	Alain Prost	Williams-Renault	189.9 mi
Aug 15	Hungary	Damon Hill	Williams-Renault	189.8 mi
Aug 29	Belgium	Damon Hill	Williams-Renault	190.6 mi
Sept 12	Italy	Damon Hill	Williams-Renault	191 mi
Sept 26	Portugal	Michael Schumacher	Bennetton-Ford	191.91 mi

1992 World Championship Standings

Drivers compete in Grand Prix races for the title of World Driving Champion. Below are the top 10 results from the 1992 season. Points are awarded for places 1-6 as follows: 10-6-4-3-2-1.

Driver, Country	Starts	Wins	Car	Pts
Nigell Mansell, Great Britain*	16	9	Williams-Renault	108
Riccardo Patrese, Italy	16	1	Williams-Renault	56
Michael Schumacher, Germany	16	1	Benetton-Ford	53
Ayrton Senna, Brazil	16	3	McLaren-Honda	50
Gerhard Bergher, Austria	16	1	McLaren-Honda	49
Martin Brundle, Great Britain	16	0	Benetton-Ford	38
Jean Alesi, France	16	0	Ferrari	18
Mika Hakkinen, Finland	16	0	Lotus-Ford	11
Andrea de Cesaris, Italy	16	0	Tyrrell-Ilmor	8
Michele Alboreto, Italy	16	0	Mugen-Honda	6

*Left Formula One for Indy Car circuit in1993.

IMSA Racing

The 24 Hours of Daytona

Held at the Daytona International Speedway on January 30-31, 1993, the 24 Hours of Daytona annually serves as the opening round for the International Motor Sports Association sports car season.

Place	Drivers	Car	Distance
1	P.J. Jones, Mark Dismore, Rocky Moran	Toyota Eagle MK III	698 laps (103.537 mph)
2	Tom Kendall, Wally Dallenbach, Robby Gordon, Robbie Buhl	Ford Mustang	688 laps
3	Jim Stevens, Mark Martin, John Fergus	Ford Mustang	686 laps
4	Steve Millen, Johnny O'Connell, John Morton	Nissan 300ZX	668 laps
5	Robert Dyson, James Weaver, Price Cobb, Elliott Forbes-Robinson	Porsche 962C	655 laps

Late 1992 GTP Results

Date	Race	Winner	Car	Avg Speed
Oct 11	San Diego	P.J. Jones	Toyota Eagle MKIII	90.397

1993 GTP Results

Date	Race	Winner(s)	Car	Avg Speed
Jan 30-31	24 Hours of Daytona	Jones/Dismore/Moran/	Toyota Eagle MKIII	103.537
Feb 20-21	Miami GP	Juan Fangio II	Toyota Eagle MKIII	88.631
Mar 20	12 Hours of Sebring	Juan Fangio II/ Andy Wallace	Toyota Eagle MKIII	70.699
Apr 18	Atlanta GP	Juan Fangio II	Toyota Eagle	118.08
May 31	Lime Rock GP	Juan Fangio II	Toyota Eagle MKIII	87.900
June 13	Ohio GP	Juan Fangio II	Toyota Eagle MKIII	108.59
June 27	Watkins Glen	Juan Fangio II	Toyota Eagle MKIII	77.770
July 11	Road America GP	John Winter/Manuel Reuter	Porsche 962C	106.23
July 25	Laguna Seca	P.J. Jones	Toyota Eagle	99.823
Aug 1	Portland GP	Juan Fangio II	Toyota Eagle MKIII	105.90
Oct 2	Phoenix	P.J. Jones	Toyota Eagle MKIII	95.165

1993 IMSA GTP Championship Standings

Driver	Pts
Juan Fangio II	183
P.J. Jones	168
Gianpiero Moretti	98
Derek Bell	88
John Paul, Jr	81
Manuel Reuter	74
John Winter	50
David Tennyson	49
Price Cobb	47
Andy Evans	43

FIA World Sports Car Racing

The 24 Hours of LeMans

Held at LeMans, France, on June 19-20, 1993, the 24 Hours of LeMans is the most prestigious event in the FIA World Sports Car Championship.

Place	Drivers	Car	Distance
1	Geoff Brabham, Christophe Bouchut, Eric Helary	Peugeot 905	375 laps (132.495 mph)
2	Yannick Dalmas, Thierry Boutsen, Teo Fabi	Peugeot 905	374 laps
3	Phillippe Alliot, Marco Baldi, Jean-Pierre Jabouille	Peugeot 905	367 laps

The 24 Hours of LeMans (Cont.)

Place	Drivers	Car	Distance
4	Masanori Sekiya, T. Suzuki, Eddie Irvine	Toyota TS010	364 laps
5	Roland Ratzenberger, N. Nagasaka, M. Martini	Y's Toyota	363 laps
6	George Fouche, Steven Andskar, Eje Elgh	Nisso Toyota	358 laps
7	J. Oppermann, L. Kessel, Otto Altenbach	Porsche 962C	355 laps
8	Geoff Lees, Jan Lammers, Juan Fangio	Toyota TS010	353 laps
9	R. Meixner, Robert Wollek, Henri Pescarolo	Porsche 962C	351 laps
10	Derek Bell, P. Fabre, L. Robert	Porsche 962C	347 laps

1992 FIA Results*

Date	Track	Drivers	Car	Avg Speed (KMH)
April 26	Monza	Lees/Ogawa	Toyota TS010	221.460
May 10	Silverstone	Derek Warwick, Yannick Dalmas	Peugeot 905B	192.405
June 20-21	LeMans	Derek Warwick, Yannick Dalmas	Peugeot 905B	199.340
July 19	Donington	Mauro Baldi/Philippe Alliot	Peugeot 905B	173.341
Aug 30	Suzuka	Derek Warwick/Yannick Dalmas	Peugeot 905B	182.228

1992 FIA Championship Standings*

Driver	Pts
Derek Warwick	90
Yannick Dalmas	90
Mauro Baldi	64
Philippe Alliot	64
Geoff Lees	59

*No Sports Car World Championship in 1993

Drag Racing

National Hot Rod Association

1993 Results (through Oct 3)

Race locations are the same for both Top Fuel and Funny Car drag races and are listed here with the Top Fuel events.

TOP FUEL

Date	Race, Site	Winner	Time	Speed
Feb 7	Winternationals, Pomona, CA	Joe Amato	4.918	294.02
Feb 21	Arizona Nationals, Phoenix	Eddie Hill	4.924	290.04
March 7	Supernationals, Houston	Ed McCulloch	4.907	285.44
March 21	Gatornationals, Gainesville, FL	Eddie Hill	4.879	286.07
April 4	Winston Invit., Rockingham, NC	Scott Kalitta	4.995	294.02
April 25	Southern Nationals, Atlanta	Eddie Hill	4.875	293.63
May 16	Mid-South Nationals, Memphis	Joe Amato	4.971	293.92
May 23	Mopar Nationals, Englishtown N.J.	Kenny Bernstein	4.876	297.02
June 13	Springnationals, Columbus, OH	Doug Herbert	4.933	295.56
June 27	W Auto Nationals, Topeka, KS	Eddie Hill	5.019	283.55
July 25	Mile-High Nationals, Denver	Mike Dunn	5.140	271.82
Aug 1	California Nationals, Sonoma, CA	Eddie Hill	4.961	287.90
Aug 8	Northwest Nationals, Seattle	Tommy Johnson, Jr	4.988	278.37
Aug 22	NorthStar Nationals, Brainerd, MN	Eddie Hill	5.072	291.07
Sept 6	US Nationals, Indianapolis	Pat Austin	7.164	155.70
Sept 19	Keystone Nationals, Reading, PA	Shelly Anderson	4.984	281.42
Oct 3	Topeka Nationals, Topeka, KS	Scott Kalitta	4.914	292.23

FUNNY CAR

Date	Race, Site	Winner	Time	Speed
Feb 7	Winternationals, Pomona, CA	John Force	5.216	288.00
Feb 21	Arizona Nationals, Phoenix	Cruz Pedregon	5.219	263.31
March 7	Supernationals, Houston	John Force	5.057	289.66
March 21	Gatornationals, Gainesville, FL	John Force	5.218	257.28
April 4	Winston Invit., Rockingham, NC	Al Hofmann	5.260	278.63

Drag Racing

National Hot Rod Association

FUNNY CAR (Cont.)

Date	Race, Site	Winner	Time	Speed
April 25	Southern Nationals, Atlanta	John Force	5.301	284.90
May 16	Mid-South Nationals, Memphis	John Force	5.219	283.82
May 23	Mopar Nationals, Englishtown N.J.	John Force	5.146	290.88
June 13	Springnationals, Columbus, OH	Gordie Bonin	5.605	194.34
June 27	W Auto Nationals, Topeka, KS	John Force	5.254	283.91
July 25	Mile-High Nationals, Denver	Cruz Pedregon	5.489	263.38
Aug 1	California Nationals, Sonoma, CA	Tom Hoover	5.408	268.01
Aug 8	Northwest Nationals, Seattle	John Force	5.171	287.72
Aug 22	NorthStar Nationals, Brainerd, MN	Chuck Etchells	5.297	281.07
Sept 6	US Nationals, Indianapolis	John Force	5.102	289.29
Sept 19	Keystone Nationals, Reading, PA	John Force	5.102	291.63
Oct 3	Topeka Nationals	Chuch Etchells	4.987	296.73

PRO STOCK

Date	Race, Site	Winner	Time	Speed
Feb 7	Winternationals, Pomona, CA	Warren Johnson	7.164	194.04
Feb 21	Arizona Nationals, Phoenix	Mark Pawuk	7.169	192.20
March 7	Supernationals, Houston	Bob Glidden	7.134	193.34
March 21	Gatornationals, Gainesville, FL	Warren Johnson	7.148	193.17
April 4	Winston Invit., Rockingham, NC	Warren Johnson	7.097	195.05
April 25	Southern Nationals, Atlanta	Warren Johnson	7.179	193.05
May 16	Mid-South Nationals, Memphis	Scott Geoffrion	7.211	191.08
May 23	Mopar Nationals, Englishtown N.J.	Warren Johnson	7.153	194.38
June 13	Springnationals, Columbus, OH	Warren Johnson	7.238	192.10
June 27	W Auto Nationals, Topeka, KS	Warren Johnson	7.312	189.79
July 25	Mile-High Nationals, Denver	Bob Glidden	7.685	179.14
Aug 1	California Nationals, Sonoma, CA	Rickie Smith	7.398	188.00
Aug 8	Northwest Nationals, Seattle	Kurt Johnson	7.159	193.05
Aug 22	NorthStar Nationals, Brainerd, MN	Warren Johnson	7.244	190.83
Sept 6	US Nationals, Indianapolis	Warren Johnson	7.165	193.29
Sept 19	Keystone Nationals, Reading, PA	Kurt Johnson	7.060	194.34
Oct 3	Topeka Nationals, Topeka, KS	Larry Morgan	7.194	193.67

1992 Standings

TOP FUEL

Driver	Wins	Pts
Joe Amato	3	12,232
Cory McClenathan	2	12,140
Kenny Bernstein	4	11,980
Eddie Hill	1	11,712
Ed McCullough	3	11,536
Don Prudhomme	3	10,386
Pat Austin	1	9,588
Michael Brotherton	1	9,568
Doug Herbert	0	9,000
Dannielle DePorter	0	5,296

FUNNY CAR

Driver	Wins	Pts
Cruz Pedregon	6	15,246
John Force	4	14,008
Al Hofmann	3	12,510
Del Worsham	0	10,566
Chuck Etchells	3	10,256

FUNNY CAR (CONT.)

Driver	Wins	Pts
Tom Hoover	1	8,622
Mark Oswald	0	7,986
Gordon Mineo	0	7,354
Whit Bazemore	0	7,162
Gary Bolger	0	7,036

PRO STOCK

Driver	Wins	Pts
Warren Johnson	8	15,818
Scott Geoffrion	0	12,696
Jerry Eckman	3	12,090
Don Beverly	2	10,998
Bob Glidden	2	10,044
Larry Morgan	0	9,354
Mark Pawuk	2	9,094
Bruce Allen	1	9,044
Jim Yates	0	8,148
Rickie Smith	0	7,592

FOR THE RECORD · Year to Year

Indianapolis 500

First held in 1911, the Indy 500—200 laps of the 2.5-mile Indianapolis Motor Speedway Track (called the Brickyard in honor of its original pavement)—has grown to become the most famous auto race in the world. Held on Memorial Day weekend, it annually draws the largest crowd of any sporting event in the world.

Year	Winner (Start Position)	Car	Avg MPH	Pole Winner	MPH
1911	Ray Harroun (28)	Marmon Wasp	74.590	Lewis Strang	Awarded pole
1912	Joe Dawson (7)	National	78.720	Gil Anderson	Drew pole
1913	Jules Goux (7)	Peugeot	75.930	Caleb Bragg	Drew pole
1914	Rene Thomas (15)	Delage	82.470	Jean Chassagne	Drew pole
1915	Ralph DePalma (2)	Mercedes	89.840	Howard Wilcox	98.90
1916	Dario Resta (4)	Peugeot	84.000	John Aitken	96.69
1917-18	No race				
1919	Howard Wilcox (2)	Peugeot	88.050	Rene Thomas	104.78
1920	Gaston Chevrolet (6)	Monroe	88.620	Ralph DePalma	99.15
1921	Tommy Milton (20)	Frontenac	89.620	Ralph DePalma	100.75
1922	Jimmy Murphy (1)	Murphy Special	94.480	Jimmy Murphy	100.50
1923	Tommy Milton (1)	H.C.S. Special	90.950	Tommy Milton	108.17
1924	L. L. Corum Joe Boyer (21)	Duesenberg Special	98.230	Jimmy Murphy	108.037
1925	Peter DePaolo (2)	Duesenberg Special	101.130	Leon Duray	113.196
1926	Frank Lockhart (20)	Miller Special	95.904	Earl Cooper	111.735
1927	George Souders (22)	Duesenberg	97.545	Frank Lockhart	120.100
1928	Louis Meyer (13)	Miller Special	99.482	Leon Duray	122.391
1929	Ray Keech (6)	Simplex Piston Ring Special	97.585	Cliff Woodbury	120.599
1930	Billy Arnold (1)	Miller Hartz Special	100.448	Billy Arnold	113.268
1931	Louis Schneider (13)	Bowes Seal-Fast Special	96.629	Russ Snowberger	112.796
1932	Fred Frame (27)	Miller Hartz Special	104.144	Lou Moore	117.363
1933	Louis Meyer (6)	Tydol Special	104.162	Bill Cummings	118.524
1934	Bill Cummings (10)	Boyle Products Special	104.863	Kelly Petillo	119.329
1935	Kelly Petillo (22)	Gilmore Speedway Special	106.240	Rex Mays	120.736
1936	Louis Meyer (28)	Ring-Free Special	109.069	Rex Mays	119.664
1937	Wilbur Shaw (2)	Shaw-Gilmore Special	113.580	Bill Cummings	123.343
1938	Floyd Roberts (1)	Burd Piston Ring Special	117.200	Floyd Roberts	125.681
1939	Wilbur Shaw (3)	Boyle Special	115.035	Jimmy Snyder	130.138
1940	Wilbur Shaw (2)	Boyle Special	114.277	Rex Mays	127.850
1941	Floyd Davis Mauri Rose (17)	Noc-Out Hose Clamp Special	115.117	Mauri Rose	128.691
1942-45	No race				
1946	George Robson (15)	Thorne Engineering Special	114.820	Cliff Bergere	126.471
1947	Mauri Rose (3)	Blue Crown Spark Plug Special	116.338	Ted Horn	126.564
1948	Mauri Rose (3)	Blue Crown Spark Plug Special	119.814	Rex Mays	130.577
1949	Bill Holland (4)	Blue Crown Spark Plug Special	121.327	Duke Nalon	132.939
1950	Johnnie Parsons (5)	Wynn's Friction Proofing	124.002	Walt Faulkner	134.343
1951	Lee Wallard (2)	Belanger Special	126.244	Duke Nalon	136.498
1952	Troy Ruttman (7)	Agajanian Special	128.922	Fred Agabashian	138.010
1953	Bill Vukovich (1)	Fuel Injection Special	128.740	Bill Vukovich	138.392
1954	Bill Vukovich (19)	Fuel Injection Special	130.840	Jack McGrath	141.033
1955	Bob Sweikert (14)	John Zink Special	128.209	Jerry Hoyt	140.045
1956	Pat Flaherty (1)	John Zink Special	128.490	Pat Flaherty	145.596
1957	Sam Hanks (13)	Belond Exhaust Special	135.601	Pat O'Connor	143.948
1958	Jim Bryan (7)	Belond AP Parts Special	133.791	Dick Rathmann	145.974
1959	Rodger Ward (6)	Leader Card 500 Roadster	135.857	Johnny Thomson	145.908
1960	Jim Rathmann (2)	Ken-Paul Special	138.767	Eddie Sachs	146.592
1961	A. J. Foyt (7)	Bowes Seal-Fast Special	139.130	Eddie Sachs	147.481
1962	Rodger Ward (2)	Leader Card 500 Roadster	140.293	Parnelli Jones	150.370
1963	Parnelli Jones (1)	Agajanian-Willard Special	143.137	Parnelli Jones	151.153
1964	A. J. Foyt (5)	Sheraton-Thompson Special	147.350	Jim Clark	158.828
1965	Jim Clark (2)	Lotus Ford	150.686	A. J. Foyt	161.233
1966	Graham Hill (15)	American Red Ball Special	144.317	Mario Andretti	165.899
1967	A. J. Foyt (4)	Sheraton-Thompson Special	151.207	Mario Andretti	168.982
1968	Bobby Unser (3)	Rislone Special	152.882	Joe Leonard	171.559
1969	Mario Andretti (2)	STP Oil Treatment Special	156.867	A. J. Foyt	170.568
1970	Al Unser (1)	Johnny Lightning 500 Special	155.749	Al Unser	170.221

Indianapolis 500 (Cont.)

Year	Winner (Start Position)	Car	Avg MPH	Pole Winner	MPH
1971	Al Unser (5)	Johnny Lightning Special	157.735	Peter Revson	178.696
1972	Mark Donohue (3)	Sunoco McLaren	162.962	Bobby Unser	195.940
1973	Gordon Johncock (11)	STP Double Oil Filters	159.036	Johnny Rutherford	198.413
1974	Johnny Rutherford (25)	McLaren	158.589	A. J. Foyt	191.632
1975	Bobby Unser (3)	Jorgensen Eagle	149.213	A. J. Foyt	193.976
1976	Johnny Rutherford (1)	Hy-Gain McLaren/Goodyear	148.725	Johnny Rutherford	188.957
1977	A. J. Foyt (4)	Gilmore Racing Team	161.331	Tom Sneva	198.884
1978	Al Unser (5)	FNCTC Chaparral Lola	161.361	Tom Sneva	202.156
1979	Rick Mears (1)	The Gould Charge	158.899	Rick Mears	193.736
1980	Johnny Rutherford (1)	Pennzoil Chaparral	142.862	Johnny Rutherford	192.256
1981	Bobby Unser (1)	Norton Spirit Penske PC-9B	139.084	Bobby Unser	200.546
1982	Gordon Johncock (5)	STP Oil Treatment	162.026	Rick Mears	207.004
1983	Tom Sneva (4)	Texaco Star	162.117	Teo Fabi	207.395
1984	Rick Mears (3)	Pennzoil Z-7	163.612	Tom Sneva	210.029
1985	Danny Sullivan (8)	Miller American Special	152.982	Pancho Carter	212.583
1986	Bobby Rahal (4)	Budweiser/Truesports/March	170.722	Rick Mears	216.828
1987	Al Unser (20)	Cummins Holset Turbo	162.175	Mario Andretti	215.390
1988	Rick Mears (1)	Penske-Chevrolet	144.809	Rick Mears	219.198
1989	Emerson Fittipaldi (3)	Penske-Chevrolet	167.581	Rick Mears	223.885
1990	Arie Luyendyk (3)	Domino's Pizza Chevrolet	185.981*	Emerson Fittipaldi	225.301†
1991	Rick Mears (1)	Penske-Chevrolet	176.457	Rick Mears	224.113
1992	Al Unser Jr (12)	G92-Chevrolet	134.477	Roberto Guerrero	232.482
1993	Emerson Fittipaldi (9)	Penske-Chevrolet	157.207	Arie Luyendyk	223.967

*Track record, winning time.
†Track record, qualifying time.

Indianapolis 500 Rookie of the Year Award

1952	Art Cross	1967	Denis Hulme	1982	Jim Hickman
1953	Jimmy Daywalt	1968	Billy Vukovich	1983	Teo Fabi
1954	Larry Crockett	1969	Mark Donohue*	1984	Michael Andretti
1955	Al Herman	1970	Donnie Allison		Roberto Guerrero
1956	Bob Veith	1971	Denny Zimmerman	1985	Arie Luyendyk
1957	Don Edmunds	1972	Mike Hiss	1986	Randy Lanier
1958	George Amick	1973	Graham McRae	1987	Fabrizio Barbazza
1959	Bobby Grim	1974	Pancho Carter	1988	Billy Vukovich III
1960	Jim Hurtubise	1975	Bill Puterbaugh	1989	Bernard Jourdain
1961	Parnelli Jones*	1976	Vern Schuppan		Scott Pruett
	Bobby Marshman	1977	Jerry Sneva	1990	Eddie Cheever
1962	Jimmy McElreath	1978	Rick Mears*	1991	Jeff Andretti
1963	Jim Clark*		Larry Rice	1992	Lyn St. James
1964	Johnny White	1979	Howdy Holmes	1993	Nigel Mansell
1965	Mario Andretti*	1980	Tim Richmond		
1966	Jackie Stewart	1981	Josele Garza		

*Future winner of Indy 500.

Indy Car Champions

From 1909 to 1955, this championship was awarded by the American Automobile Association (AAA), and from 1956 to 1979 by United States Auto Club (USAC). Since 1979, Championship Auto Racing Teams (CART) has conducted the championship.

1909	George Robertson	1925	Peter DePaolo	1941	Rex Mays
1910	Ray Harroun	1926	Harry Hartz	1942-45	No racing
1911	Ralph Mulford	1927	Peter DePaolo	1946	Ted Horn
1912	Ralph DePalma	1928	Louis Meyer	1947	Ted Horn
1913	Earl Cooper	1929	Louis Meyer	1948	Ted Horn
1914	Ralph DePalma	1930	Billy Arnold	1949	Johnnie Parsons
1915	Earl Cooper	1931	Louis Schneider	1950	Henry Banks
1916	Dario Resta	1932	Bob Carey	1951	Tony Bettenhausen
1917	Earl Cooper	1933	Louis Meyer	1952	Chuck Stevenson
1918	Ralph Mulford	1934	Bill Cummings	1953	Sam Hanks
1919	Howard Wilcox	1935	Kelly Petillo	1954	Jimmy Bryan
1920	Tommy Milton	1936	Mauri Rose	1955	Bob Sweikert
1921	Tommy Milton	1937	Wilbur Shaw	1956	Jimmy Bryan
1922	Jimmy Murphy	1938	Floyd Roberts	1957	Jimmy Bryan
1923	Eddie Hearne	1939	Wilbur Shaw	1958	Tony Bettenhausen
1924	Jimmy Murphy	1940	Rex Mays	1959	Rodger Ward

Indy Car Champions (Cont.)

1960	A. J. Foyt	1972	Joe Leonard	1983	Al Unser
1961	A. J. Foyt	1973	Roger McCluskey	1984	Mario Andretti
1962	Rodger Ward	1974	Bobby Unser	1985	Al Unser
1963	A. J. Foyt	1975	A. J. Foyt	1986	Bobby Rahal
1964	A. J. Foyt	1976	Gordon Johncock	1987	Bobby Rahal
1965	Mario Andretti	1977	Tom Sneva	1988	Danny Sullivan
1966	Mario Andretti	1978	Tom Sneva	1989	Emerson Fittipaldi
1967	A. J. Foyt	1979	A. J. Foyt	1990	Al Unser Jr
1968	Bobby Unser	1979	Rick Mears	1991	Michael Andretti
1969	Mario Andretti	1980	Johnny Rutherford	1992	Bobby Rahal
1970	Al Unser	1981	Rick Mears	1993	Nigel Mansell
1971	Joe Leonard	1982	Rick Mears		

All-Time Indy Car Leaders

WINS

A. J. Foyt*	67
Mario Andretti*	52
Al Unser*	39
Bobby Unser	35
Rick Mears*	29
Johnny Rutherford	27
Michael Andretti*	27
Rodger Ward	26
Gordon Johncock	25
Ralph DePalma	24
Bobby Rahal*	24
Tommy Milton	23
Tony Bettenhausen	21
Earl Cooper	21
Emerson Fittipaldi*	20
Jimmy Murphy	19
Jimmy Bryan	19
Al Unser Jr*	19
Ralph Mulford	17
Danny Sullivan*	17

*Active driver.

Note: Leaders through 1993 season.

WINNINGS ($)

Bobby Rahal*	12,024,828
Emerson Fittipaldi*	11,668,712
Al Unser Jr*	11,644,093
Rick Mears*	11,050,807
Mario Andretti*	10,887,392
Michael Andretti*	10,197,503
Danny Sullivan*	8,254,673
Al Unser*	6,740,843
Arie Luyendyk*	6,503,359
A. J. Foyt*	5,357,589
Tom Sneva*	4,392,993
Raul Boesel*	4,391,972
Scott Brayton*	4,323,599
Johnny Rutherford*	4,209,232
Roberto Guerrero*	4,131,251
Scott Goodyear*	3,488,236
Gordon Johncock*	3,431,414
Kevin Cogan*	3,202,106
Teo Fabi*	3,115,465
John Andretti*	2,983,624

POLE POSITIONS

Mario Andretti*	67
A. J. Foyt*	53
Bobby Unser	49
Rick Mears	39
Al Unser*	39
Johnny Rutherford	23
Michael Andretti*	24
Gordon Johncock	20
Danny Sullivan*	19
Rex Mays	19
Bobby Rahal*	18
Emerson Fittipaldi*	17
Don Branson	15
Tom Sneva*	14
Tony Bettenhausen	14
Parnelli Jones	12
Danny Ongais	11
Rodger Ward	11
Johnny Thomson	10
Dan Gurney	10

NASCAR Racing

Stock Car Racing's Major Events

Winston offers a $1 million bonus to any driver to win 3 of NASCAR's top 4 events in the same season. These races are the richest (Daytona 500), the fastest (Winston 500 at Talladega), the longest (Coca-Cola 600 at Charlotte) and the oldest (Heinz Southern 500 at Darlington). These events form the backbone of NASCAR racing. Only 3 drivers, LeeRoy Yarbrough (1969), David Pearson (1976) and Bill Elliott (1985), have scored the 3-track hat trick.

Daytona 500

Year	Winner	Car	Avg MPH	Pole Winner	MPH
1959	Lee Petty	Oldsmobile	135.520	Cotton Owens	143.198
1960	Junior Johnson	Chevrolet	124.740	Fireball Roberts	151.556
1961	Marvin Panch	Pontiac	149.601	Fireball Roberts	155.709
1962	Fireball Roberts	Pontiac	152.529	Fireball Roberts	156.995
1963	Tiny Lund	Ford	151.566	Johnny Rutherford	165.183
1964	Richard Petty	Plymouth	154.345	Paul Goldsmith	174.910
1965	Fred Lorenzen	Ford	141.539	Darel Dieringer	171.151
1966	Richard Petty	Plymouth	160.627	Richard Petty	175.165
1967	Mario Andretti	Ford	149.926	Curtis Turner	180.831
1968	Cale Yarborough	Mercury	143.251	Cale Yarborough	189.222
1969	LeeRoy Yarbrough	Ford	157.950	David Pearson	190.029
1970	Pete Hamilton	Plymouth	149.601	Cale Yarborough	194.015

Daytona 500 (Cont.)

Year	Winner	Car	Avg MPH	Pole Winner	MPH
1971	Richard Petty	Plymouth	144.462	A. J. Foyt	182.744
1972	A. J. Foyt	Mercury	161.550	Bobby Isaac	186.632
1973	Richard Petty	Dodge	157.205	Buddy Baker	185.662
1974	Richard Petty	Dodge	140.894	David Pearson	185.017
1975	Benny Parsons	Chevrolet	153.649	Donnie Allison	185.827
1976	David Pearson	Mercury	152.181	A. J. Foyt	185.943
1977	Cale Yarborough	Chevrolet	153.218	Donnie Allison	188.048
1978	Bobby Allison	Ford	159.730	Cale Yarborough	187.536
1979	Richard Petty	Oldsmobile	143.977	Buddy Baker	196.049
1980	Buddy Baker	Oldsmobile	177.602*	A. J. Foyt	195.020
1981	Richard Petty	Buick	169.651	Bobby Allison	194.624
1982	Bobby Allison	Buick	153.991	Benny Parsons	196.317
1983	Cale Yarborough	Pontiac	155.979	Ricky Rudd	198.864
1984	Cale Yarborough	Chevrolet	150.994	Cale Yarborough	201.848
1985	Bill Elliott	Ford	172.265	Bill Elliott	205.114
1986	Geoff Bodine	Chevrolet	148.124	Bill Elliott	205.039
1987	Bill Elliott	Ford	176.263	Bill Elliott	210.364†
1988	Bobby Allison	Buick	137.531	Ken Schrader	193.823
1989	Darrell Waltrip	Chevrolet	148.466	Ken Schrader	196.996
1990	Derrike Cope	Chevrolet	165.761	Ken Schrader	196.515
1991	Earnie Irvan	Chevrolet	148.148	Davey Allison	195.955
1992	Davey Allison	Ford	160.256	Sterling Marlin	192.213
1993	Dale Jarrett	Chevrolet	154.972	Kyle Petty	189.426

*Track record, winning time. †Track record, qualifying time.

Note: The Daytona 500, held annually in February, now opens the NASCAR season with 200 laps around the high-banked Daytona, FL, superspeedway.

World 600

Year	Winner	Car	Avg MPH	Pole Winner
1960	Joe Lee Johnson	Chevy	107.752	J.L. Johnson
1961	David Pearson	Pontiac	111.634	Richard Petty
1962	Nelson Stacy	Ford	125.552	Fireball Roberts
1963	Fred Lorenzen	Ford	132.418	Junior Johnson
1964	Jim Paschal	Plymouth	125.772	Junior Johnson
1965	Fred Lorenzen	Ford	121.772	Fred Lorenzon
1966	Marvin Panch	Plymouth	135.042	Paul Goldsmith
1967	Jim Paschal	Plymouth	135.832	Cale Yarborough
1968	Buddy Baker	Dodge	104.207	Donnie Allison
1969	Lee Yarbrough	Mercury	134.631	Donnie Allison
1970	Donnie Allison	Ford	129.680	Bobby Isaac
1971	Bobby Allison	Mercury	140.442	Charlie Glotzbach
1972	Buddy Baker	Dodge	142.255	Bobby Allison
1973	Buddy Baker	Dodge	134.890	Buddy Baker
1974	David Pearson	Mercury	135.720	David Pearson
1975	Richard Petty	Dodge	145.327	David Pearson
1976	David Pearson	Mercury	137.352	David Pearson
1977	Richard Petty	Dodge	137.636	David Pearson
1978	Darrell Waltrip	Chevy	138.355	David Pearson
1979	Darrell Waltrip	Chevy	136.674	Neil Bonnet
1980	Benny Parsons	Chevy	119.265	Cale Yarborough
1981	Bobby Allison	Buick	129.326	Neil Bonnet
1982	Neil Bonnet	Ford	130.508	David Pearson
1983	Neil Bonnett	Chevy	140.406	Buddy Baker
1984	Bobby Allison	Buick	129.233	Harry Gant
1985	Darrell Waltrip	Chevy	141.807	Bill Elliott
1986	Dale Earnhardt	Chevy	140.406	Geoff Bodine
1987	Kyle Petty	Ford	131.483	Bill Elliott
1988	Darrell Waltrip	Chevy	124.460	Davey Allison
1989	Darrell Waltrip	Chevy	144.077	Alan Kulwicki
1990	Rusty Wallace	Pontiac	137.650	Ken Schrader
1991	Davey Allison	Ford	138.951	Mark Martin
1992	Dale Earnhardt	Chevy	132.980	Bill Elliott
1993	Dale Earnhardt	Chevy	145.504	Ken Schrader

Note: Held at the 1.5-mile Charlotte, NC, Motor Speedway on Memorial Day weekend.

Talladega 500

Year	Winner	Car	Avg MPH	Pole Winner	MPH
1969	Richard Brickhouse	Dodge	153.778	Charlie Glotzbach	199.466
1970	Pete Hamilton	Plymouth	158.517	Bobby Isaac	186.834
1971	Bobby Allison	Mercury	145.945	Davey Allison	187.323
1972	James Hylton	Mercury	148.728	Bobby Isaac	190.677
1973	Dick Brooks	Plymouth	145.454	Bobby Allison	187.064
1974	Richard Petty	Dodge	148.637	David Pearson	184.926
1975	Buddy Baker	Ford	130.892	Dave Marcis	191.340
1976	Dave Marcis	Dodge	157.547	Dave Marcis	190.651
1977	Davey Allison	Chevy	162.524	Benny Parsons	192.682
1978	Lennie Pond	Olds	174.700	Cale Yarborough	192.917
1979	Darrell Waltrip	Olds	161.229	Neil Bonnet	193.600
1980	Neil Bonnet	Mercury	166.894	Buddy Baker	198.545
1981	Ron Bouchard	Buick	156.737	Harry Gant	195.897
1982	Darrell Waltrip	Buick	168.157	Geoff Bodine	199.400
1983	Dale Earnhardt	Ford	170.611	Cale Yarborough	201.744
1984	Dale Earnhardt	Chevy	155.485	Cale Yarborough	202.474
1985	Cale Yarborough	Ford	148.772	Bill Elliott	207.578
1986	Bobby Hillin	Buick	151.552	Bill Elliott	209.005
1987	Bill Elliott	Ford	171.293	Bill Elliott	203.827
1988	Ken Schrader	Chevy	154.505	Darrell Waltrip	196.274
1989	Terry Labonte	Ford	157.354	Mark Martin	194.800
1990	Dale Earnhardt	Chevy	174.430	Dale Earnhardt	192.513
1991	Harry Gant	Olds	165.620	Sterling Marlin	192.085
1992	Ernie Irvan	Chevy	176.309	Sterling Marlin	190.586
1993	Dale Earnhardt	Chevy	153.858	Bill Elliott	192.397

Note: Held at the 2.66-mile high-banked Talladega, AL, Superspeedway on the last weekend in July.

Southern 500

Year	Winner	Car	Avg MPH	Pole Winner
1950	Johnny Mantz	Plymouth	76.260	Wally Campbell
1951	Herb Thomas	Hudson	76.900	Marshall Teague
1952	Fonty Flock	Olds	74.510	Dick Rathman
1953	Buck Baker	Olds	92.780	Fonty Flock
1954	Herb Thomas	Hudson	94.930	Buck Baker
1955	Herb Thomas	Chevy	92.281	Tim Flock
1956	Curtis Turner	Ford	95.067	Buck Baker
1957	Speedy Thompson	Chevy	100.100	Paul Goldsmith
1958	Fireball Roberts	Chevy	102.590	Fireball Roberts
1959	Jim Reed	Chevy	111.836	Fireball Roberts
1960	Buck Baker	Pontiac	105.901	Cotton Owens
1961	Nelson Stacy	Ford	117.880	Fireball Roberts
1962	Larry Frank	Ford	117.965	Fireball Roberts
1963	Fireball Roberts	Ford	129.784	Fireball Roberts
1964	Buck Baker	Dodge	117.757	Richard Petty
1965	Ned Jarrett	Ford	115.924	Junior Johnson
1966	Darel Dieringer	Mercury	114.830	Lee Yarborough
1967	Richard Petty	Plymouth	131.933	David Pearson
1968	Cale Yarborough	Mercury	126.132	Charlie Glotzbach
1969	Lee Yarbrough	Ford	105.612	Cale Yarborough
1970	Buddy Baker	Dodge	128.817	David Pearson
1971	Bobby Allison	Mercury	131.398	Bobby Allison
1972	Bobby Allison	Chevy	128.124	David Pearson
1973	Cale Yarborough	Chevy	134.033	David Pearson
1974	Cale Yarborough	Chevy	111.075	Richard Petty
1975	Bobby Allison	Matador	116.825	David Pearson
1976	David Pearson	Mercury	120.534	David Pearson
1977	David Pearson	Mercury	106.797	Darrell Waltrip
1978	Cale Yarborough	Olds	116.828	David Pearson
1979	David Pearson	Chevy	126.259	Bobby Allison
1980	Terry Labonte	Chevy	115.210	Darrell Waltrip
1981	Neil Bonnett	Ford	126.410	Harry Gant
1982	Cale Yarborough	Buick	126.703	David Pearson
1983	Bobby Allison	Buick	123.343	Neil Bonnett
1984	Harry Gant	Chevy	128.270	Harry Gant

Southern 500

Year	Winner	Car	Avg MPH	Pole Winner
1985	Bill Elliott	Ford	121.254	Bill Elliott
1986	Tim Richmond	Chevy	121.068	Tim Richmond
1987	Dale Earnhardt	tChevy	115.520	Davey Allison
1988	Bill Elliott	Ford	128.297	Bill Elliott
1989	Dale Earnhardt	Chevy	135.462	Alan Kulwicki
1990	Dale Earnhardt	Chevy	123.141	Dale Earnhardt
1991	Harry Gant	Olds	133.508	Davey Allison
1992	Darrell Waltrip	Chevy	129.114	Sterling Marlin
1993	Mark Martin	Ford	137.932	Ken Schrader

Note: Held at the 1.366-mile Darlington, SC, International Raceway on Labor Day weekend.

Winston Cup NASCAR Champions

Year	Driver	Car	Wins	Poles	Winnings ($)
1949	Red Byron	Oldsmobile	2	0	5,800
1950	Bill Rexford	Oldsmobile	1	0	6,175
1951	Herb Thomas	Hudson	7	4	18,200
1952	Tim Flock	Hudson	8	4	20,210
1953	Herb Thomas	Hudson	11	10	27,300
1954	Lee Petty	Dodge	7	3	26,706
1955	Tim Flock	Chrysler	18	19	33,750
1956	Buck Baker	Chrysler	14	12	29,790
1957	Buck Baker	Chevy	10	5	24,712
1958	Lee Petty	Olds	7	4	20,600
1959	Lee Petty	Plymouth	10	2	45,570
1960	Rex White	Chevy	6	3	45,260
1961	Ned Jarrett	Chevy	1	4	27,285
1962	Joe Weatherly	Pontiac	9	6	56,110
1963	Joe Weatherly	Mercury	3	6	58,110
1964	Richard Petty	Plymouth	9	8	98,810
1965	Ned Jarrett	Ford	13	9	77,966
1966	David Pearson	Dodge	14	7	59,205
1967	Richard Petty	Plymouth	27	18	130,275
1968	David Pearson	Ford	16	12	118,824
1969	David Pearson	Ford	11	14	183,700
1970	Bobby Isaac	Dodge	11	13	121,470
1971	Richard Petty	Plymouth	21	9	309,225
1972	Richard Petty	Plymouth	8	3	227,015
1973	Benny Parsons	Chevy	1	0	114,345
1974	Richard Petty	Dodge	10	7	299,175
1975	Richard Petty	Dodge	13	3	378,865
1976	Cale Yarborough	Chevy	9	2	387,173
1977	Cale Yarborough	Chevy	9	3	477,499
1978	Cale Yarborough	Oldsmobile	10	8	530,751
1979	Richard Petty	Chevy	5	1	531,292
1980	Dale Earnhardt	Chevy	5	0	588,926
1981	Darrell Waltrip	Buick	12	11	693,342
1982	Darrell Waltrip	Buick	12	7	873,118
1983	Bobby Allison	Buick	6	0	828,355
1984	Terry Labonte	Chevy	2	2	713,010
1985	Darrell Waltrip	Chevy	3	4	1,318,735
1986	Dale Earnhardt	Chevy	5	1	1,783,880
1987	Dale Earnhardt	Chevy	11	1	2,099,243
1988	Bill Elliott	Ford	6	6	1,574,639
1989	Rusty Wallace	Pontiac	6	4	2,247,950
1990	Dale Earnhardt	Chevy	9	4	3,083,056
1991	Dale Earnhardt	Chevy	4	0	2,396,685
1992	Alan Kulwicki	Ford	2	6	2,322,561

All-Time NASCAR Leaders

WINS

Richard Petty	200
David Pearson	105
Bobby Allison	84
Darrell Waltrip*	84
Cale Yarborough	83
Dale Earnhardt*	59
Lee Petty	54
Junior Johnson	50
Ned Jarrett	50
Herb Thomas	48
Buck Baker	46
Tim Flock	40
Bill Elliott*	39
Bobby Isaac	37
Fireball Roberts	32
Rex White	26

WINNINGS ($)

Dale Earnhardt*	17,207,349
Bill Elliott*	12,783,084
Darrell Waltrip*	12,396356
Rusty Wallace*	8,037,082
Richard Petty	7,680,789
Terry Labonte*	7,384,501
Harry Gant*	7,106,741
Bobby Allison	7,102,233
Ricky Rudd*	7,010,881
Geoff Bodine*	6,554,242
Davey Allison	6,142,971
Mark Martin*	5,364,264
Ken Schrader*	5,104,038
Cale Yarborough	5,003,716
Kyle Petty*	4,755,702
Benny Parsons	3,926,539

POLE POSITIONS

Richard Petty	127
David Pearson	113
Cale Yarborough	70
Darrell Waltrip*	59
Bobby Allison	57
Bobby Isaac	51
Junior Johnson	47
Bill Elliott*	43
Buck Baker	40
Herb Thomas	38
Tim Flock	37
Fireball Roberts	37
Ned Jarrett	36
Rex White	36
Fred Lorenzen	33
Fonty Flock	30

*Active drivers.

Note: NASCAR Leaders through Sept 11, 1993.

Formula One/Grand Prix Racing

World Driving Champions

Year	Winner	Car	Year	Winner	Car
1950	Guiseppe Farina, Italy	Alfa Romeo	1969	Jackie Stewart, Scotland	Matra-Ford
1951	Juan-Manuel Fangio, Argentina	Alfa Romeo	1970	Jochen Rindt, Austria*	Lotus-Ford
			1971	Jackie Stewart, Scotland	Tyrell-Ford
1952	Alberto Ascari, Italy	Ferrari	1972	Emerson Fittipaldi, Brazil	Lotus-Ford
1953	Alberto Ascari, Italy	Ferrari	1973	Jackie Stewart, Scotland	Tyrell-Ford
1954	Juan-Manuel Fangio, Argentina	Maserati/ Mercedes	1974	Emerson Fittipaldi, Brazil	McLaren-Ford
			1975	Niki Lauda, Austria	Ferrari
1955	Juan-Manuel Fangio, Argentina	Mercedes	1976	James Hunt, England	McLaren-Ford
			1977	Niki Lauda, Austria	Ferrari
1956	Juan-Manuel Fangio, Argentina	Ferrari	1978	Mario Andretti, U.S.	Lotus-Ford
			1979	Jody Scheckter, S Africa	Ferrari
1957	Juan-Manuel Fangio, Argentina	Maserati	1980	Alan Jones, Australia	Williams-Ford
			1981	Nelson Piquet, Brazil	Brabham-Ford
1958	Mike Hawthorne, England	Ferrari	1982	Keke Rosberg, Finland	Williams-Ford
1959	Jack Brabham, Australia	Cooper-Climax	1983	Nelson Piquet, Brazil	Brabham-BMW
1960	Jack Brabham, Australia	Cooper-Climax	1984	Niki Lauda, Austria	McLaren-Porsche
1961	Phil Hill, United States	Ferrari	1985	Alain Prost, France	McLaren-Porsche
1962	Graham Hill, England	BRM	1986	Alain Prost, France	McLaren-Porsche
1963	Jim Clark, Scotland	Lotus-Climax	1987	Nelson Piquet, Brazil	Williams-Honda
1964	John Surtees, England	Ferrari	1988	Ayrton Senna, Brazil	McLaren-Honda
1965	Jim Clark, Scotland	Lotus-Climax	1989	Alain Prost, France	McLaren-Honda
1966	Jack Brabham, Australia	Brabham-Climax	1990	Ayrton Senna, Brazil	McLaren-Honda
1967	Denis Hulme, New Zealand	Brabham-Repco	1991	Ayrton Senna, Brazil	McLaren-Honda
			1992	Nigel Mansell, Britain	Williams-Renault
1968	Graham Hill, England	Lotus-Ford	1993	Alain Prost, France	Williams-Renault

*The championship was awarded after Rindt was killed in practice for the Italian Grand Prix.

All-Time Grand Prix Winners

Driver	Wins	Driver	Wins
Alain Prost, France*	51	Juan-Manuel Fangio, Argentina	24
Ayrton Senna, Brazil*	38	Nelson Piquet, Brazil*	20
Jackie Stewart, Scotland	27	Stirling Moss, England	16
Nigel Mansell, England*	28	Jack Brabham, Australia	14
Jim Clark, Scotland	25	Graham Hill, England	14
Niki Lauda, Austria	25	Emerson Fittipaldi, Brazil*	14

*Active driver.

Note: Grand Prix Winners through September 26, 1993.

All-Time Grand Prix Pole Winners

Driver	Poles	Driver	Poles
Ayrton Senna, Brazil*	62	Mario Andretti, United States*	18
Jim Clark, Scotland	33	Jackie Stewart, Scotland	17
Juan-Manuel Fangio, Argentina	28	Stirling Moss, England	16
Alain Prost, France*	28	Alberto Ascari, Italy	14
Niki Lauda, Austria	24	Ronnie Peterson, Sweden	14
Nelson Piquet, Brazil*	24	James Hunt, England	14

*Active driver. Note: Pole Winners through 1992 season.

IMSA Racing

The 24 Hours of Daytona

Year	Winner	Car	Avg Speed	Distance
1962	Dan Gurney	Lotus 19-Class SP11	104.101 mph	3 hrs (312.42 mi)
1963	Pedro Rodriguez	Ferrari-Class 12	102.074 mph	3 hrs (308.61 mi)
1964	Pedro Rodriguez/Phil Hill	Ferrari 250 LM	98.230 mph	2,000 km
1965	Ken Miles/Lloyd Ruby	Ford	99.944 mph	2,000 km
1966	Ken Miles/Lloyd Ruby	Ford Mark II	108.020 mph	24 hrs (2,570.63 mi)
1967	Lorenzo Bandini/Chris Amon	Ferrari 330 P4	105.688 mph	24 hrs (2,537.46 mi)
1968	Vic Elford/Jochen Neerpasch	Porsche 907	106.697 mph	24 hrs (2,565.69 mi)
1969	Mark Donohue/Chuck Parsons	Chevy Lola	99.268 mph	24 hrs (2,383.75 mi)
1970	Pedro Rodriguez/Leo Kinnunen	Porsche 917	114.866 mph	24 hrs (2,758.44 mi)
1971	Pedro Rodriguez/Jackie Oliver	Porsche 917K	109.203 mph	24 hrs (2,621.28 mi)
1972*	Mario Andretti/Jacky Ickx	Ferrari 312/P	122.573 mph	6 hrs (738.24 mi)
1973	Peter Gregg/Hurley Haywood	Porsche Carrera	106.225 mph	24 hrs (2,552.7 mi)
1974	(No race)			
1975	Peter Gregg/Hurley Haywood	Porsche Carrera	108.531 mph	24 hrs (2,606.04 mi)
1976†	Peter Gregg/Brian Redman/ John Fitzpatrick	BMW CSL	104.040 mph	24 hrs (2,092.8 mi)
1977	John Graves/Hurley Haywood/ Dave Helmick	Porsche Carrera	108.801 mph	24 hrs (2,615 mi)
1978	Rolf Stommelen/ Antoine Hezemans/Peter Gregg	Porsche Turbo	108.743 mph	24 hrs (2,611.2 mi)
1979	Ted Field/Danny Ongais/ Hurley Haywood	Porsche Turbo	109.249 mph	24 hrs (2,626.56 mi)
1980	Volkert Meri/Rolf Stommelen/ Reinhold Joest	Porsche Turbo	114.303 mph	24 hrs
1981	Bob Garretson/Bobby Rahal/ Brian Redman	Porsche Turbo	113.153 mph	24 hrs
1982	John Paul, Jr/John Paul, Sr/ Rolf Stommelen	Porsche Turbo	114.794 mph	24 hrs
1983	Preston Henn/Bob Wollek/ Claude Ballot-Lena/A. J. Foyt	Porsche Turbo	98.781 mph	24 hrs
1984	Sarel van der Merwe/ Graham Duxbury/Tony Martin	Porsche March	103.119 mph	24 hrs (2,476.8 mi)
1985	A. J. Foyt/Bob Wollek/ Al Unser, Sr/Thierry Boutsen	Porsche 962	104.162 mph	24 hrs (2,502.68 mi)
1986	Al Holbert/Derek Bell/Al Unser Jr	Porsche 962	105.484 mph	24 hrs (2,534.72 mi)
1987	Chip Robinson/Derek Bell/ Al Holbert/Al Unser Jr	Porsche 962	111.599 mph	24 hrs (2,680.68 mi)
1988	Martin Brundle/John Nielsen/ Raul Boesel	Jaguar XJR-9	107.943 mph	24 hrs (2,591.68 mi)
1989	John Andretti/Derek Bell/ Bob Wollek	Porsche 962	92.009 mph	24 hrs (2,210.76 mi)
1990	Davy Jones/Jan Lammers/ Andy Wallace	Jaguar XJR-12	112.857 mph	24 hrs (2,709.16 mi)
1991	Hurley Haywood/John Winter/ Frank Jelinski/Henri Pescarolo/ Bob Wollek	Porsche 962C	106.633 mph	24 hrs (2,559.64 mi)
1992	Massahiro Hasemi/ Kazuoyshi Hoshino/Toshio Suzuki/Anders Olofsson	Nissan R91CP	112.987	24 hrs (2,712.72 mi)
1993	P.J. Jones/Mark Dismore/ Rocky Moran	Toyota Eagle MK III	103.537	24 hrs (2,484.88 mi)

*Race shortened due to fuel crisis.
†Course lengthened from 3.81 miles to 3.84 miles.

World Champions

Year	Winner	Car	Year	Winner	Car
1971	Peter Gregg/	Porsche 914	1982	John Paul Jr	Chevy Lola
	Hurley Haywood		1983	Al Holbert	Chevy March
1972	Hurley Haywood	Porsche 911	1984	Randy Lanier	Chevy March
1973	Peter Gregg	Porsche Carrera	1985	Al Holbert	Porsche 962
1974	Peter Gregg	Porsche Carrera	1986	Al Holbert	Porsche 962
1975	Peter Gregg	Porsche Carrera	1987	Chip Robinson	Porsche 962
1976	Al Holbert	Chevy Monza	1988	Geoff Brabham	Nissan GTP
1977	Al Holbert	Chevy Monza	1989	Geoff Brabham	Nissan GTP
1978	Peter Gregg	Porsche 935	1990	Geoff Brabham	Nissan GTP
1979	Peter Gregg	Porsche 935	1991	Geoff Brabham	Nissan NPT
1980	John Fitzpatrick	Porsche 935	1992	Juan Fangio II	Toyota EGL MKIII
1981	Brian Redman	Chevy Lola	1993	Juan Fangio II	Toyota EGL MKIII

All-Time IMSA Leaders

WINS

Al Holbert	49
Peter Gregg	41
Hurley Haywood	28
Geoff Brabham	26
Gene Felton	25
Irv Hoerr	25
Don Devendorf	22
Jim Downing	22
Jack Baldwin	21
Tommy Riggins	21
Amos Johnson	20
Bob Earl	20

FASTEST QUALIFIERS

Peter Gregg	37
Al Holbert	27
Geoff Brabham	26
John Paul Jr	19
John Fitzpatrick	12
Sarel Van der Merwe	11
Chip Robinson	11
Davy Jones	10
Danny Ongais	10
David Hobbs	9
Klaus Ludwig	9
John Greenwood	8
Hans Stuck	8
Bill Whittington	7

Note: Leaders through 1993 season.

FIA World Sports Car Racing

The 24 Hours of LeMans

Year	Winning Drivers	Car
1923	André Lagache/René Léonard	Chenard & Walker
1924	John Duff/Francis Clement	Bentley 3-litre
1925	Gérard de Courcelles/André Rossignol	La Lorraine
1926	Robert Bloch/André Rossignol	La Lorraine
1927	J. Dudley Benjafield/Sammy Davis	Bentley 3-litre
1928	Woolf Barnato/Bernard Rubin	Bentley 4½
1929	Woolf Barnato/Sir Henry Birkin	Bentley Speed Six
1930	Woolf Barnato/Glen Kidston	Bentley Speed Six
1931	Earl Howe/Sir Henry Birkin	Alfa Romeo 8C-2300 sc
1932	Raymond Sommer/Luigi Chinetti	Alfa Romeo 8C-2300 sc
1933	Raymond Sommer/Tazio Nuvolari	Alfa Romeo 8C-2300 sc
1934	Luigi Chinetti/Philippe Etancelin	Alfa Romeo 8C-2300 sc

The 24 Hours of LeMans (Cont.)

Year	Winning Drivers	Car
1935	John Hindmarsh/Louis Fontés	Lagonda M45R
1936	Race cancelled	
1937	Jean-Pierre Wimille/Robert Benoist	Bugatti 57G sc
1938	Eugene Chaboud/Jean Tremoulet	Delahaye 135M
1939	Jean-Pierre Wimille/Pierre Veyron	Bugatti 57G sc
1940-48	Races cancelled	
1949	Luigi Chinetti/Lord Selsdon	Ferrari 166MM
1950	Louis Rosier/Jean-Louis Rosier	Talbot-Lago
1951	Peter Walker/Peter Whitehead	Jaguar C
1952	Hermann Lang/Fritz Reiss	Mercedes-Benz 300 SL
1953	Tony Rolt/Duncan Hamilton	Jaguar C
1954	Froilan Gonzales/Maurice Trintignant	Ferrari 375
1955	Mike Hawthorn/Ivor Bueb	Jaguar D
1956	Ron Flockhart/Ninian Sanderson	Jaguar D
1957	Ron Flockhart/Ivor Buab	Jaguar D
1958	Olivier Gendebien/Phil Hill	Ferrari 250 TR58
1959	Carroll Shelby/Roy Salvadori	Aston Martin DBR1
1960	Olivier Gendebien/Paul Fräre	Ferrari 250 TR59/60
1961	Olivier Gendebien/Phil Hill	Ferrari 250 TR61
1962	Olivier Gendebien/Phil Hill	Ferrari 250P
1963	Lodovico Scarfiotti/Lorenzo Bandini	Ferrari 250P
1964	Jean Guichel/Nino Vaccarella	Ferrari 275P
1965	Jochen Rindt/Masten Gregory	Ferrari 250LM
1966	Chris Amon/Bruce McLaren	Ford Mk2
1967	Dan Gurney/A. J. Foyt	Ford Mk4
1968	Pedro Rodriguez/Lucien Bianchi	Ford GT40
1969	Jacky Ickx/Jackie Oliver	Ford GT40
1970	Hans Herrmann/Richard Attwood	Porsche 917
1971	Helmut Marko/Gijs van Lennep	Porsche 917
1972	Henri Pescarolo/Graham Hill	Matra-Simca MS670
1973	Henri Pescarolo/Gérard Larrousse	Matra-Simca MS670B
1974	Henri Pescarolo/Gérard Larrousse	Matra-Simca MS670B
1975	Jacky Ickx/Derek Bell	Mirage-Ford MB
1976	Jacky Ickx/Gijs van Lennep	Porsche 936
1977	Jacky Ickx/Jurgen Barth/Hurley Haywood	Porsche 936
1978	Jean-Pierre Jaussaud/Didier Pironi	Renault-Alpine A442
1979	Klaus Ludwig/Bill Whttington/Don Whittington	Porsche 935
1980	Jean-Pierre Jaussaud/Jean Rondeau	Rondeau-Ford M379B
1981	Jacky Ickx/Derek Bell	Porsche 936-81
1982	Jacky Ickx/Derek Bell	Porsche 956
1983	Vern Schuppan/Hurley Haywood/Al Holbert	Porsche 956-83
1984	Klaus Ludwig/Henri Pescarolo	Porsche 956B
1985	Klaus Ludwig/Paolo Barilla/John Winter	Porsche 956B
1986	Derek Bell/Hans-Joachim Stuck/Al Holbert	Porsche 962C
1987	Derek Bell/Hans-Joachim Stuck/Al Holbert	Porsche 962C
1988	Jan Lammers/Johnny Dumfries/Andy Wallace	Jaguar XJR9LM
1989	Jochen Mass/Manuel Reuter/Stanley Dickens	Sauber-Mercedes C9-88
1990	John Nielsen/Price Cobb/Martin Brundle	TWR Jaguar XJR-12
1991	Volker Weidler/Johnny Herbert/Bertrand Gachof	Mazda 787B
1992	Derek Warwick/Yannick Dalmas/Mark Blundell	Peugeot 905B
1993	Geoff Brabham/Christophe Bouchut/Eric Helary	Peugeot 905

THEY SAID IT

*Richard Petty, after a fiery crash put
him out of 1992's Hooters 500, the
final race of his 35-year NASCAR
career: "I guess you're supposed to
go out in a blaze of glory, but
I didn't mean to do it this way."*

Drag Racing: Milestone Performances

Top Fuel

ELAPSED TIME

9.00....................Jack Chrisman	Feb 18, 1961	Pomona, CA
8.97....................Jack Chrisman	May 20, 1961	Empona, VA
7.96....................Bobby Vodnick	May 16, 1964	Bayview, MD
6.97....................Don Johnson	May 7, 1967	Carlsbad, CA
5.97....................Mike Snively	Nov 17, 1972	Ontario, CA
5.78....................Don Garlits	Nov 18, 1973	Ontario, CA
5.698..................Gary Beck	Oct 10, 1975	Ontario, CA
5.636..................Don Garlits	Oct 10, 1975	Ontario, CA
5.573..................Gary Beck	Oct 18, 1981	Irvine, CA
5.484..................Gary Beck	Sep 6, 1982	Clermont, IN
5.391..................Gary Beck	Oct 1, 1983	Fremont, CA
5.280..................Darrell Gwynn	Sep 25, 1986	Ennis, TX
5.176..................Darrell Gwynn	April 4, 1987	Ennis, TX
5.090..................Joe Amato	Oct 1, 1987	Ennis, TX
4.990..................Eddie Hill	April 9, 1988	Ennis, TX
4.936..................Eddie Hill	Oct 9, 1988	Baytown, TX
4.919..................Gary Ormsby	Oct 7, 1989	Ennis, TX
4.881..................Gary Ormsby	Sep 29, 1990	Topeka, KS
4.801..................Eddie Hill	March 22, 1992	Gainesville, FL

SPEED

180.36..............Connie Kalitta	Sep 3, 1962	Clermont, IN
190.26..............Don Garlits	Sep 21, 1963	East Haddam, CT
201.34..............Don Garlits	Aug 1, 1964	Great Meadows, NJ
226.12..............John Edmunds	May 7, 1967	Carlsbad, CA
232.55..............Larry Hendrickson	July 11, 1970	Vancouver, WA
243.24..............Don Garlits	March 18, 1973	Gainesville, FL
250.69..............Don Garlits	Oct 11, 1975	Ontario, CA
260.11..............Joe Amato	March 18, 1984	Gainesville, FL
272.56..............Don Garlits	March 23, 1986	Gainesville, FL
282.13..............Joe Amato	Sep 5, 1987	Clermont, IN
291.54..............Connie Kalitta	Feb 11, 1989	Pomona, CA
294.88..............Michael Brotherton	Oct 7, 1989	Ennis, TX
294.88..............Gary Ormsby	Oct 8, 1989	Ennis, TX
296.05..............Gary Ormsby	Sep 29, 1990	Topeka, KS
297.12..............Mike Dunn	March 8, 1992	Baytown, TX
301.70..............Kenny Bernstein	March 20, 1992	Gainesville, FL
303.6................Pat Austin	April 25, 1993	Atlanta., GA

Funny Car

ELAPSED TIME

6.92....................Leroy Goldstein	Sep 3, 1970	Clermont, IN
5.987..................Don Prudhomme	Oct 12, 1975	Ontario, CA
5.868..................Raymond Beadle	July 16, 1981	Englishtown, NJ
5.799..................Tom Anderson	Sep 3, 1982	Clermont, IN
5.637..................Don Prudhomme	Sep 4, 1982	Clermont, IN
5.588..................Rick Johnson	Feb 3, 1985	Pomona, CA
5.425..................Kenny Bernstein	Sep 26, 1986	Ennis, TX
5.397..................Kenny Bernstein	April 5, 1987	Ennis, TX
5.255..................Ed McCulloch	April 17, 1988	Ennis, TX
5.193..................Don Prudhomme	March 2, 1989	Baytown, TX
5.132..................Ed McCulloch	Oct 7, 1989	Ennis, TX
5.102..................Cruz Pedregon	March 8, 1992	Baytown, TX

SPEED

200.44..............Gene Snow	August, 1968	Houston, TX
250.00..............Don Prudhomme	May 23, 1982	Erwinville, LA
260.11..............Kenny Bernstein	March 18, 1984	Gainesville, FL

Funny Car (Cont.)

SPEED (Cont.)

271.41	Kenny Bernstein	Aug 30, 1986	Clermont, IN
280.72	Mike Dunn	Oct 2, 1987	Ennis, TX
283.28	Mark Oswald	Oct 29, 1989	Pomona, CA
284.18	Mark Oswald	Oct 11, 1990	Ennis, TX
289.94	Jim White	Sept 15, 1991	Mohnton, PA
290.13	Jim White	Oct 11, 1991	Ennis TX
291.82	Jim White	Oct 25, 1991	Pomona, CA
300.40	Jim Epler	Oct 3, 1993	Topeka, KS

Pro Stock

ELAPSED TIME

7.778	Lee Shepherd	March 12, 1982	Gainesville, FL
7.655	Lee Shepherd	Oct 1, 1982	Fremont, CA
7.557	Bob Glidden	Feb 2, 1985	Pomona, CA
7.497	Bob Glidden	Sep 13, 1985	Maple Grove, PA
7.377	Bob Glidden	Aug 28, 1986	Clermont, IN
7.294	Frank Sanchez	Oct 7, 1988	Baytown, TX
7.256	Bob Glidden	March 11, 1989	Baytown, TX
7.184	Darrell Alderman	Oct 12, 1990	Ennis, TX
7.127	Warren Johnson	July 31, 1992	Sonoma, CA

SPEED

181.08	Warren Johnson	Oct 1, 1982	Fremont, CA
190.07	Warren Johnson	Aug 29, 1986	Clermont, IN
191.32	Bob Glidden	Sep 4, 1987	Clermont, IN
192.18	Warren Johnson	Oct 13, 1990	Ennis, TX
193.21	Bob Glidden	July 28, 1991	Sonoma, CA
194.46	Warren Johnson	March 20, 1992	Gainesville, FL
194.51	Warren Johnson	July 31, 1992	Sonoma, CA

All-Time Drag Racing Leaders

NATIONAL EVENT WINS

Bob Glidden	84
Don Prudhomme	46
Warren Johnson	42
Kenny Bernstein	41
Don Garlits	35
Joe Amato	33
John Force	31
Darrell Gwynn	28
Lee Shepherd	26
David Schultz/Terry Vance	24

BEST WON-LOST RECORD (WINNING PCT)

John Myers	128-28 (821)
Bob Glidden	761-171 (.817)
David Schultz	161-42 (.793)
Joe Amato	333-131 (.703)
Warren Johnson	370-165 (.693)
John Force	314-147 (.681)
Kenny Bernstein	343-163 (.678)
Cruz Pedregon	74-36 (.673)
Don Prudhomme	357-184 (.659)
Mark Oswald	245-149 (.623)

Note: Drag Racing Leaders through Oct 3, 1993.

THEY SAID IT

*Ken Squier, television commentator,
offering advice to colleagues
working the NASCAR Charlotte 600
for Russian and Ukrainian TV:
"There are only two things you
really have to grasp. You have to be
able to say, 'There they go' and
'What a wreck!'"*

Bowling

Sports Illustrated

Strike Season

Anne Marie Duggan
dominates the
women's bowling tour

Lord of the Lanes

Horseshoe star Walter Ray Williams Jr. dominated the PBA tour like no one had since Mark Roth | **by KELLI ANDERSON**

IF THE TABLOIDS GAVE PROFESSIONAL bowling its due, we might have seen some fine headlines in 1993, including this one: LORD OF RINGERS NOW PIN KING. That was the story of Walter Ray Williams Jr., a five-time men's and three-time junior world horseshoe champion who dominated the Professional Bowlers Association tour like no one had in 15 years. By the end of the Summer Tour—with four fall tournaments still to go—Williams had banked $259,310, averaged 223.79 and won seven tournaments, putting several major PBA records in serious jeopardy, including Mark Roth's estimable 1978 record of eight season victories.

That Labor Day would find Williams in reach of Roth would have seemed absurd on Memorial Day. In fact, Williams, the 1986 PBA Player of the Year, didn't even begin his assault on the PBA record books in earnest until late May. Coming off a disappointing '92 campaign, in which he won no tournaments and ranked 13th in earn-

ings, Williams picked up his first '93 victory in March at the Flagship City Open in Erie, Pa. He was runner-up twice before he got his second win, in San Antonio on May 22. "That win," says Williams, "was the start of the big finishes. All I did was step it up a notch." Within a month he had taken back-to-back titles in Kennewick, Wash., and Portland, Ore. By early July he had brought his win total to five. If this was a notch, what would two notches produce? The bowling world would have to wait to find out. After his fifth win, in Tucson, at the peak of his red-hot streak, Williams skipped two of the next three PBA dates so he could make his 24th consecutive appearance at the World Horseshoe Tournament, in Spearfish, N. Dak. Nothing, not even the prospect of bowling immortality, could stand in the way of the premier event of the sport Williams loves best. "Horseshoes means a lot to me," says Williams, who earned the name Deadeye in his first World Horseshoe appearance at the age of 10. Unfortunately, Williams's hot hand on the lanes didn't

Williams had more luck pitching strikes than horseshoes in '93.

BILL FRAKES

carry over into the pits at Spearfish: He placed a dismal 12th, his worst finish ever.

Likewise, his bad luck in horseshoes didn't rub off on his bowling. Williams won the very next PBA tournament, in Grand Rapids on Aug. 12, bringing his win total to six. In the qualifying rounds for the Greater Harrisburg (Pa.) Open the next week, Williams rolled four perfect games, breaking the PBA record of three and tying the PBA record of seven 300s in one year, set by Amleto Monacelli in 1989. But Williams's first bid for his seventh title, which would tie Earl Anthony's 1975 total, fell short in the championship match when tour novice Brian Davis, 21, decided to make some history of his own, throwing a 299 to Williams's 267. Davis was only the second player to win a PBA title in his first tour event.

It took Williams only a week to secure his seventh crown. Recognizing at last the rare ride he was on, he reluctantly bowed out of a commitment to pitch horseshoes at the Ohio State Fair in Columbus and showed up instead at the rebuilt Paula Carter's Pro Bowl in Homestead, Fla. Nearly a year to the day after Hurricane Andrew leveled the original facility, the new center hosted its first major event, and Williams made it an emotional occasion with a 248–215 win over Joe Firpo. Said Williams, "I guess I'm glad I decided not to pitch horseshoes after all."

Besides Tornado Walter Ray, 1993 had a few other historic moments. George Branham III became the first black to win a Triple Crown event by capturing the last Firestone Tournament of Champions, which will hereafter be known as the General Tire Tournament of Champions. In a more dubious achievement, David Ozio recorded the PBA's highest ever *losing* score in a championship match, at the Wichita Open. His 279

couldn't beat Mike Aulby's perfect game, but it was a significant contribution to the highest-scoring televised PBA match ever.

Just months after making an unsuccessful bid to bowl in a PBA tournament, Anne Marie Duggan, the Ladies Pro Bowlers Tour's 1993 leader in wins (two) and earnings ($40,300), bowled back-to-back 300 games and broke the women's world record for a three-game series, with an 865, in a LPBT regional event in July. Tish Johnson bowled five perfect games on the year, setting a new LPBT record. Lisa Wagner became the first LPBT member to reach the half million career earnings mark, and she added another title to her career total of 27.

Ground was broken on the National Bowling Stadium in Reno. The stadium, which is scheduled to open in early 1995, will feature 80 lanes in line and a seating capacity of 1,800, making it the biggest little bowling arena in the world.

Finally, Washington welcomed its biggest bowling buff since Richard Nixon. Bill Clinton, whose average remains a White House secret, has even promised to refurbish the one-lane facility that Nixon built in 1973. Said Clinton before he moved in in January, "Now I have an excuse to buy my own bowling shoes." Before he got a chance, a pair was donated: size 13, specially designed for those who roll to the left.

The Majors

MEN

Firestone Tournament of Champions

CHAMPIONSHIP ROUND

Bowler	Games	Total	Earnings ($)
George Branham III	1	227	60,000
Parker Bohn III	3	728	33,000
Dave Ferraro	1	209	24,000
Dave Husted	1	183	18,000

Playoff Results: Bohn III def. Husted, 266-183; Bohn III def. Ferraro 258-209; Branham III def. Bohn III 227-2†4.

Held at Riviera Lanes, Fairlawn, Ohio, April 20-24, 1993.

BPAA United States Open

CHAMPIONSHIP ROUND

Bowler	Games	Total	Earnings ($)
Dell Ballard, Jr	2	505	40,000
Walter Ray Williams, Jr	1	193	22,000
Tony Westlake	2	445	12,000
Ted Hannahs	1	202	8,000

Playoff Results: Westlake def. Hannahs, 245-202; Ballard, Jr def. Westlake 268-200; Ballard, Jr def. Williams, Jr 237-193.

Held at Roseland Bowl, Canandaigua, NY, April 4-10, 1993.

PBA National Championship

CHAMPIONSHIP ROUND

Bowler	Games	Total	Earnings ($)
Ron Palombi, Jr	1	237	55,000
Eugene McCune	3	684	28,000
Phillip Ringener	1	204	15,000
Adam Apo	1	214	10,000

Playoff Results: McCune def. Apo, 245-214; McCune def. Ringener, 215-204; Palombi def. McCune 237-224.

Held at Imperial Lanes, Toledo, Ohio, Feb 21-27, 1993.

ABC Masters Tournament

CHAMPIONSHIP ROUND

Bowler	Games	Total	Earnings ($)
Phil Ware	1	238	35,000
Frankie May	3	752	21,000
Robert McDonald	1	170	15,000
Shell Wilson	2	436	10,000
John Handegard	1	194	6.000

Playoff Results: Wilson def. Handegard, 223-194; May def. Wilson, 236-213; May def. McDonald, 279-170; Ware def. May, 238-237.

Held at Bayfront Plaza Convention Center, Corpus Christi, Texas, March 13-18, 1993.

WOMEN

Sam's Town Invitational

CHAMPIONSHIP ROUND

Bowler	Games	Total	Earnings ($)
Tish Johnson	1	279	20,000
Robin Romeo	3	660	10,000
Aleta Sill	1	233	5,000
Diana Teeters	2	391	4,500
Carol Gianotti	1	165	4,000

Playoff Results: Teeters def. Gianotti, 199-165; Romeo def. Teeters, 237-192; Romeo def. Sill, 234-233; Johnson def. Romeo, 279-189.

Held at Sam's Town Bowling Center, Las Vegas, NV, Nov. 15-21, 1992.

BPAA United States Open

CHAMPIONSHIP ROUND

Bowler	Games	Total	Earnings ($)
Dede Davidson	1	213	18,000
Dana Miller-Mackie	2	408	9,000
Sandra Jo Shiery	2	461	7,000
Anne Marie Duggan	2	394	5,000
Stacy Rider	1	192	4,000

Playoff Results: Duggan def. Rider, 215-192; Shiery def. Duggan, 259-179; Miller-Mackie def. Shiery, 214-202; Davidson def. Miller-Mackie, 213-194.

Held at Showplace Lanes, Garland, TX, May 22-29, 1993.

WIBC Queens

CHAMPIONSHIP ROUND

Bowler	Games	Total	Earnings ($)
Jan Schmidt	1	201	13,245
Pat Costello	4	815	8,410
Jeanne Naccarato	1	172	5,185
Wendy Macpherson	1	179	5,080
Linda Kelly	1	202	3,755

Playoff Results: Costello def. Kelly, 227-202; Costello def. Macpherson, 202-179; Costello def. Naccarato, 223-172; Schmidt def. Costello, 201-163.

Held at Don Carter All Star Lanes, Baton Rouge, LA, May 9-13, 1993.

Moonlighting

Bruce Hamilton is the PBA Tour's resident rocket scientist. He joined the Tour in 1990 and won his first title in '92, at the True Value Open, but Hamilton's distinction derives from his pursuit of a unique double life. He is a computer software specialist by night and a pro bowler by day. This self-described "garage-nerd, computer-type" has developed software for NASA's Ambient Temperature Recorder, a small computer-controlled thermometer for NASA's space shuttle, and the STEP (Stratospheric/Tropospheric Exchange Programs) Radon instrument. "It's a nice marriage," says Hamilton, 32, of his occupational duality. "I take my work on the road, and it's a bridge for some of the dead time and gets my mind off bowling."

He works about twenty hours a week on his computer career, mostly evenings, after PBA tournaments. In 1992, he competed well enough in those tournaments to rank 23rd on the money list with $61,690 in earnings. He faltered somewhat in 1993, dropping out of the top 50 ranked players. "I'm far from being a top professional," admits Hamilton, "I've put in the time to be good, but it takes a lot more than people think to be world class."

Hamilton forged his careers to make his most significant contribution to the game: he developed the computer power rankings that the PBA began using in March of '93. Players are ranked weekly based on their earnings and placings. "It's nice for fans to have some gauge for players, and it's nice for guys to have something to strive for to be No. 1."

PBA Tour Results

1992 Fall Tour

Date	Event	Winner	Earnings	Runner-Up
Oct 8-11	Oronamin C Japan Cup	Parker Bohn III	18,500	T. Tsukahara
Oct 16-21	Bud Light Touring Players Championship	Peter Weber	27,000	Harry Sullins
Oct 24-28	Rochester Open	Marc McDowell	23,000	Randy Pederson
Oct 30-31	Taylor Lanes Open	Amleto Monacelli	23,000	Chris Warren
Nov 5-11	Brunswick Memorial World Open	Jeff Lizzi	39,000	Amleto Monacelli

1993 Winter Tour

Date	Event	Winner	Earnings	Runner-Up
Jan 5-9	AC-Delco Classic	Ron Williams	42,000	Mark Williams
Jan 12-16	Phoenix Open	Parker Bohn III	24,000	Amleto Monacelli
Jan 17-23	Showboat Invitational	Mike Aulby	35,000	Parker Bohn III
Jan 26-30	Quaker State Open	Steve Hoskins	41,000	Ron Williams
Feb 2-6	True Value Open	John Mazza	42,000	Norm Duke
Feb 9-13	Bud Light Hall of Fame Championship	Bob Learn, Jr	54,000	Ray Edwards
Feb 16-20	Cleveland Open	Ron Williams	23,000	Jeff Morin
Feb 21-27	Bud Light PBA National Championship	Ron Palombi	55,000	Eugene McCune
Mar 2-6	Flagship City Open	Walter Ray Williams, Jr	30,000	John Mazza
Mar 9-13	Baltimore Open	George Branham III	24,000	Brian Voss
Mar 16-20	Johnny Petraglia Open	Ricky Ward	34,000	Kelly Coffman
Mar 23-27	Leisure's Long Island	Dave Arnold	30,000	Walter Ray Williams, Jr
Mar 30-Apr 3	Tums Classic	Jason Couch	34,000	Brian Voss
Apr 4-10	BPAA U.S. Open	Del Ballard, Jr	40,000	Walter Ray Williams, Jr
Apr 13-17	IOF Foresters Bowling for Miracles	Pete Weber	43,000	Jim Lewis
Apr 20-24	Firestone Tournament of Champions	George Branham III	60,000	Parker Bohn III

1993 Spring/Summer Tour

Date	Event	Winner	Earnings	Runner-Up
May 11-15	Touring Pro/Senior Doubles	Rich Abboud/Teata Semiz	30,000	Dick Weber/Justin Hromek
May 18-22	Columbia 300 Open	Walter Ray Williams	27,000	Butch Super
May 25-29	Fresno Open	Randy Pederson	18,000	David Ozio
June 8-12	Seattle Open	Steve Fields	21,000	Bill Oakes
June 15-19	Northwest Classic	Walter Ray Williams	18,000	Bryan Goebel
June 22-26	PBA Oregon Open	Walter Ray Williams	23,000	Brian Voss
June 29-July 3	Active West Open	Brian Voss	18,000	Kelly Coffman
July 6-10	Tucson Open	Walter Ray Williams	20,000	D. D'Entremont
July 13-17	El Paso Open	Bob Benoit	20,000	Robert Lawrence
July 27-31	Wichita Open	Mike Aulby	23,000	Parker Bohn III
Aug 2-7	Choice Hotels Summer Classic	Steve Jaros	38,000	Kevin McGerr
Aug 8-12	Greater Grand Rapids Open	Walter Ray Williams	18,000	Bob Learn, Jr
Aug 14-19	Greater Harrisburg Open	Brian Davis	20,000	W. Ray Williams
Aug 21-26	Paula Carter's Homestead Classic	Walter Ray Williams	18,000	Joe Firpo

1992 Senior Fall Tour

Date	Event	Winner	Earnings	Runner-Up
Aug 23-29	Ebonite PBA Senior Championships	Gene Stus	20,000	Teata Semiz
Sept 1-5	Canadian Senior Open	Tommy Evans	5,000	Jim Lewis
Sept 26-30	Don Carter PBA Senior Classic	Les Zikes	5,000	J. Handegard
Oct 3-7	Hammer Naples Senior Open	John Hricsina	8,000	Jerry Brunette
Oct 10-14	Pinellas Suncoast Senior PBA Open	Robert Gibbs	8,000	Gene Stus

1993 Senior Tour (through Aug 11)

Date	Event	Winner	Earnings	Runner-Up
June 24-29	Showboat PBA Senior Invitational	Gary Dickinson	24,000	Gene Stus
June 28-July 2	Pacific Cal Bowl PBA Senior Open	John Handegard	18,000	Gene Stus
Aug 8-11	Springfield Senior Open	Darrel Curtis	6,000	Barry Gurney

LPBT Tour Results

1992 Fall Tour

Date	Event	Winner	Earnings	Runner-Up
Oct 2-7	Columbia 300 Delaware Open	Carol Gianotti	13,500	Dede Davidson
Oct 9-14	Hammer Eastern Open	Leanne Barrette	9,000	Carol Gianotti
Oct 20-25	Three Rivers Open	Carol Norman	5,000	Carol Gianotti
Oct 27-Nov 1	Hammer Midwest Open	Carol Gianotti	9,000	Wendy Macpherson
Nov 4-8	Ebonite Fall Classic	Carol Gianotti	9,000	Cindy Coburn-Carroll
Nov 15-21	Bud Light Sam's Town Invitational	Tish Johnson	20,000	Robin Romeo

1993 Winter Tour

Date	Event	Winner	Earnings	Runner-Up
Feb 3-7	Claremore Classic	Anne Marie Duggan	5,000	Lisa Wagner
Feb 10-13	Las Vegas Western Open	Wendy Macpherson	5,000	Anne Marie Duggan
Feb 17-21	Santa Maria Classic	Lisa Wagner	5,000	Cheryl Daniels
Feb 24-28	Nu Generation Classix	Jeanne Naccarato	5,000	Tish Johnson
Mar 3-7	New Reno Open	Anne Marie Duggan	5,000	Cheryl Daniels

1993 Spring Tour

Date	Event	Winner	Earnings	Runner-Up
Apr 25-29	Athens Open	Dana Miller-Mackie	5,000	Aleta Sill
May 2-6	New Orleans Classic	Jill Albrecht	5,000	Tish Johnson
May 9-13	WIBC Queens	Jan Schmidt	13,245	Pat Costello
May 16-20	Alexandria Louisiana Open	Kim Couture	5,000	Patty Ann
May 22-29	BPAA U.S. Open	Dede Davidson	18,000	Dana Miller Mackie

No Fooling

LPBT star Dede Davidson was a prodigy from an early age, bowling her first frame at the age of eight. At 11, she bowled an incredible 299, a record that still stands for bantam-class girls. Then, on April 1, 1983, at the age of 16, she returned home from the Lucky Lanes in San Pablo, Calif., claiming to have rolled a 300. "That's right Dede, April Fool," Lori Davidson, Dede's mother, responded. Despite the date, young Dede was not fooling.

PBA

MONEY LEADERS

Name	Titles	Tournaments	Earnings ($)
Marc McDowell	3	31	174,215
Eric Forkel	2	33	169,350
Amleto Monacelli	2	28	162,030
Dave Ferraro	2	28	141,535
Bob Vespi	2	31	131,890

AVERAGE

Name	Games	Pinfall	Average
Dave Ferraro	1038	228,051	219.702
Amleto Monacelli	896	195,847	218.579
Eric Forkel	1011	220,199	217.803
Parker Bohn III	934	202,873	217.209
Ron Williams	913	198,294	217.189

Seniors

MONEY LEADERS

Name	Titles	Tournaments	Earnings ($)
Gene Stus	2	10	62,725
John Handegard	1	12	38,325
John Hricsina	1	12	29,695
Dick Weber	1	12	26,180
Teata Semiz	0	11	24,050

AVERAGE

Name	Games	Pinfall	Average
John Handegard	499	110,190	220.78
Gene Stus	425	93,301	219.53
John Hricsina	429	93,858	218.78
Ron Winger	384	83,931	218.57
Dave Davis	392	85,503	218.12

LPBT

MONEY LEADERS

Name	Titles	Tournaments	Earnings ($)
Tish Johnson	4	21	96,872.00
Carol Gianotti	4	20	85,135.00
Leanne Barrette	1	21	56,250.00
Anne Marie Duggan	2	21	56,060.00
Robin Romeo	1	21	44,727.00

AVERAGE

Name	Games	Pinfall	Average
Leanne Barrette	800	169,088	211.36
Tish Johnson	804	169,893	211.31
Aleta Sill	452	95,006	210.19
Carol Gianotti	755	158,392	209.79
Anne Marie Duggan	778	162,532	208.91

FOR THE RECORD·Year by Year

Men's Majors

BPAA United States Open

Year	Winner	Score	Runner-Up	Site
1942	John Crimmins	265.09-262.33	Joe Norris	Chicago
1943	Connie Schwoegler	not available	Frank Benkovic	Chicago
1944	Ned Day	315.21-298.21	Paul Krumske	Chicago
1945	Buddy Bomar	304.46-296.16	Joe Wilman	Chicago
1946	Joe Wilman	310.27-305.37	Therman Gibson	Chicago
1947	Andy Varipapa	314.16-308.04	Allie Brandt	Chicago
1948	Andy Varipapa	309.23-309.06	Joe Wilman	Chicago
1949	Connie Schwoegler	312.31-307.27	Andy Varipapa	Chicago
1950	Junie McMahon	318.37-307.17	Ralph Smith	Chicago
1951	Dick Hoover	305.29-304.07	Lee Jouglard	Chicago
1952	Junie McMahon	309.29-305.41	Bill Lillard	Chicago
1953	Don Carter	304.17-297.36	Ed Lubanski	Chicago
1954	Don Carter	308.02-307.25	Bill Lillard	Chicago
1955	Steve Nagy	307.17-303.34	Ed Lubanski	Chicago
1956	Bill Lillard	304.30-304.22	Joe Wilman	Chicago
1957	Don Carter	308.49-305.45	Dick Weber	Chicago
1958	Don Carter	311.03-308.09	Buzz Fazio	Minneapolis
1959	Billy Welu	311.48-310.26	Ray Bluth	Buffalo
1960	Harry Smith	312.24-308.12	Bob Chase	Omaha
1961	Bill Tucker	318.49-309.11	Dick Weber	San Bernadino
1962	Dick Weber	299.34-297.38	Roy Lown	Miami Beach
1963	Dick Weber	642-591	Billy Welu	Kansas City, MO
1964	Bob Strampe	714-616	Tommy Tuttle	Dallas
1965	Dick Weber	608-586	Jim St. John	Philadelphia
1966	Dick Weber	684-681	Nelson Burton Jr	Lansing, MI
1967	Les Schissler	613-610	Pete Tountas	St. Ann, MO
1968	Jim Stefanich	12,401-12,104	Billy Hardwick	Garden City, NY
1969	Billy Hardwick	12,585-11,463	Dick Weber	Miami
1970	Bobby Cooper	12,936-12,307	Billy Hardwick	Northbrook, IL
1971	Mike Limongello	397 (2 games)	Teata Semiz	St. Paul, MN
1972	Don Johnson	233 (1 game)	George Pappas	New York City
1973	Mike McGrath	712 (3 games)	Earl Anthony	New York City
1974	Larry Laub	749 (3 games)	Dave Davis	New York City
1975	Steve Neff	279 (1 game)	Paul Colwell	Grand Prairie, TX
1976	Paul Moser	226 (1 game)	Jim Frazier	Grand Prairie, TX
1977	Johnny Petraglia	279 (1 game)	Bill Spigner	Greensboro, NC
1978	Nelson Burton Jr	873 (4 games)	Jeff Mattingly	Greensboro, NC
1979	Joe Berardi	445 (2 games)	Earl Anthony	Windsor Locks, CT
1980	Steve Martin	930 (4 games)	Earl Anthony	Windsor Locks, CT
1981	Marshall Holman	684 (3 games)	Mark Roth	Houston, TX
1982	Dave Husted	1011 (4 games)	Gil Sliker	Houston, TX
1983	Gary Dickinson	214 (1 game)	Steve Neff	Oak Lawn, IL
1984	Mark Roth	244 (1 game)	Guppy Troup	Oak Hill, IL
1985	Marshall Holman	233 (1 game)	Wayne Webb	Venice, FL
1986	Steve Cook	467 (2 games)	Frank Ellenburg	Venice, FL
1987	Del Ballard Jr	525 (2 games)	Pete Weber	Tacoma, WA
1988	Pete Weber	929 (4 games)	Marshall Holman	Atlantic City, NJ
1989	Mike Aulby	429 (2 games)	Jim Pencak	Edmond, OK
1990	Ron Palombi Jr	269 (1 game)	Amleto Monacelli	Indianapolis, IN
1991	Pete Weber	956 (4 games)	Mark Thayer	Indianapolis, IN
1992	Robert Lawrence	667 (3 games)	Scott Devers	Canandaigua, NY
1993	Del Ballard, Jr	505 (2 games)	Walter Ray Williams,	Canandaigua, NY

Note: From 1942 to 1970, the tournament was called the BPAA All-Star. Peterson scoring was used from 1942 through 1962. Under this system, the winner of an individual match game gets one point, plus one point for each 50 pins knocked down. From 1963 through 1967, a three-game championship was held between the two top qualifiers. From 1968 through 1970 total pinfall determined the winner. From 1971 to the present, five qualifiers compete for the championship.

PBA National Championship

Year	Winner	Score	Runner-Up	Site
1960	Don Carter	6512 (30 games)	Ronnie Gaudern	Memphis, TN
1961	Dave Soutar	5792 (27 games)	Morrie Oppenheim	Cleveland, OH
1962	Carmen Salvino	5369 (25 games)	Don Carter	Philadelphia, PA

PBA National Championship (Cont.)

Year	Winner	Score	Runner-Up	Site
1963	Billy Hardwick	13,541 (61 games)	Ray Bluth	Long Island, NY
1964	Bob Strampe	13,979 (61 games)	Ray Bluth	Long Island, NY
1965	Dave Davis	13,895 (61 games)	Jerry McCoy	Detroit, MI
1966	Wayne Zahn	14,006 (61 games)	Nelson Burton Jr	Long Island, NY
1967	Dave Davis	421 (2 games)	Pete Tountas	New York City
1968	Wayne Zahn	14,182 (60 games)	Nelson Burton Jr	New York City
1969	Mike McGrath	13,670 (60 games)	Bill Allen	Garden City, NY
1970	Mike McGrath	660 (3 games)	Dave Davis	Garden City, NY
1971	Mike Limongello	911 (4 games)	Dave Davis	Paramus, NJ
1972	Johnny Guenther	12,986 (56 games)	Dick Ritger	Rochester, NY
1973	Earl Anthony	212 (1 game)	Sam Flanagan	Oklahoma City, OK
1974	Earl Anthony	218 (1 game)	Mark Roth	Downey, CA
1975	Earl Anthony	245 (1 game)	Jim Frazier	Downey, CA
1976	Paul Colwell	191 (1 game)	Dave Davis	Seattle, WA
1977	Tommy Hudson	206 (1 game)	Jay Robinson	Seattle, WA
1978	Warren Nelson	453 (2 games)	Joseph Groskind	Reno, NV
1979	Mike Aulby	727 (3 games)	Earl Anthony	Las Vegas, NV
1980	Johnny Petraglia	235 (1 game)	Gary Dickinson	Sterling Heights, MI
1981	Earl Anthony	242 (1 game)	Ernie Schlegel	Toledo, OH
1982	Earl Anthony	233 (1 game)	Charlie Tapp	Toledo, OH
1983	Earl Anthony	210 (1 game)	Mike Durbin	Toledo, OH
1984	Bob Chamberlain	961 (4 games)	Dan Eberl	Toledo, OH
1985	Mike Aulby	476 (2 games)	Steve Cook	Toledo, OH
1986	Tom Crites	190 (1 game)	Mike Aulby	Toledo, OH
1987	Randy Pedersen	759 (3 games)	Amleto Monacelli	Toledo, OH
1988	Brian Voss	246 (1 game)	Todd Thompson	Toledo, OH
1989	Pete Weber	221 (1 game)	Dave Ferraro	Toledo, OH
1990	Jim Pencak	900 (4 games)	Chris Warren	Toledo, OH
1991	Mike Miller	450 (2 games)	Norm Duke	Toledo, OH
1992	Eric Forkel	833 (4 games)	Bob Vespi	Toledo, OH
1993	Ron Palombi Jr	237 (1 game)	Eugene McCune	Toledo, OH

Note: Totals from 1963-66, 1968-69 and 1972 include bonus pins

Firestone Tournament of Champions

Year	Winner	Score	Runner-Up	Site
1965	Billy Hardwick	484 (2 games)	Dick Weber	Akron, OH
1966	Wayne Zahn	595 (3 games)	Dick Weber	Akron, OH
1967	Jim Stefanich	227 (1 game)	Don Johnson	Akron, OH
1968	Dave Davis	213 (1 game)	Don Johnson	Akron, OH
1969	Jim Godman	266 (1 game)	Jim Stefanich	Akron, OH
1970	Don Johnson	299 (1 game)	Dick Ritger	Akron, OH
1971	Johnny Petraglia	245 (1 game)	Don Johnson	Akron, OH
1972	Mike Durbin	775 (3 games)	Tim Harahan	Akron, OH
1973	Jim Godman	451 (2 games)	Barry Asher	Akron, OH
1974	Earl Anthony	679 (3 games)	Johnny Petraglia	Akron, OH
1975	Dave Davis	448 (2 games)	Barry Asher	Akron, OH
1976	Marshall Holman	441 (2 games)	Billy Hardwick	Akron, OH
1977	Mike Berlin	434 (2 games)	Mike Durbin	Akron, OH
1978	Earl Anthony	237 (1 game)	Teata Semiz	Akron, OH
1979	George Pappas	224 (1 game)	Dick Ritger	Akron, OH
1980	Wayne Webb	750 (3 games)	Gary Dickinson	Akron, OH
1981	Steve Cook	287 (1 game)	Pete Couture	Akron, OH
1982	Mike Durbin	448 (2 games)	Steve Cook	Akron, OH
1983	Joe Berardi	865 (4 games)	Henry Gonzalez	Akron, OH
1984	Mike Durbin	950 (4 games)	Mike Aulby	Akron, OH
1985	Mark Williams	616 (3 games)	Bob Handley	Akron, OH
1986	Marshall Holman	233 (1 game)	Mark Baker	Akron, OH
1987	Pete Weber	928 (4 games)	Jim Murtishaw	Akron, OH
1988	Mark Williams	237 (1 game)	Tony Westlake	Fairlawn, OH
1989	Del Ballard Jr	490 (2 games)	Walter Ray Williams Jr	Fairlawn, OH
1990	Dave Ferraro	226 (1 game)	Tony Westlake	Fairlawn, OH
1991	David Ozio	476 (2 games)	Amleto Monacelli	Fairlawn, OH
1992	Marc McDowell	471 (2 games)	Don Genalo	Fairlawn, OH
1993	George Branham III	227 (1 game)	Parker Bohn III	Fairlawn, OH

ABC Masters Tournament

Year	Winner	Scoring Avg	Runner-Up	Site
1951	Lee Jouglard	201.8	Joe Wilman	St. Paul, MN
1952	Willard Taylor	200.32	Andy Varipapa	Milwaukee, WI
1953	Rudy Habetler	200.13	Ed Brosius	Chicago, IL
1954	Eugene Elkins	205.19	W. Taylor	Seattle, WA
1955	Buzz Fazio	204.13	Joe Kristof	Ft. Wayne, IN
1956	Dick Hoover	209.9	Ray Bluth	Rochester, NY
1957	Dick Hoover	216.39	Bill Lillard	Ft. Worth, TX
1958	Tom Hennessy	209.15	Lou Frantz	Syracuse, NY
1959	Ray Bluth	214.26	Billy Golembiewski	St. Louis, MO
1960	Billy Golembiewski	206.13	Steve Nagy	Toledo, OH
1961	Don Carter	211.18	Dick Hoover	Detroit, MI
1962	Billy Golembiewski	223.12	Ron Winger	Des Moines, IA
1963	Harry Smith	219.3	Bobby Meadows	Buffalo, NY
1964	Billy Welu	227	Harry Smith	Oakland, CA
1965	Billy Welu	202.12	Don Ellis	St. Paul, MN
1966	Bob Strampe	219.80	Al Thompson	Rochester, NY
1967	Lou Scalia	216.9	Bill Johnson	Miami Beach, FL
1968	Pete Tountas	220.15	Buzz Fazio	Cincinnati, OH
1969	Jim Chestney	223.2	Barry Asher	Madison, WI
1970	Don Glover	215.10	Bob Strampe	Knoxville, TN
1971	Jim Godman	229.8	Don Johnson	Detroit, MI
1972	Bill Beach	220.27	Jim Godman	Long Beach, CA
1973	Dave Soutar	218.61	Dick Ritger	Syracuse, NY
1974	Paul Colwell	234.17	Steve Neff	Indianapolis, IN
1975	Eddie Ressler	213.51	Sam Flanagan	Dayton, OH
1976	Nelson Burton Jr	220.79	Steve Carson	Oklahoma City
1977	Earl Anthony	218.21	Jim Godman	Reno, NV
1978	Frank Ellenburg	200.61	Earl Anthony	St. Louis, MO
1979	Doug Myers	202.9	Bill Spigner	Tampa, FL
1980	Neil Burton	206.69	Mark Roth	Louisville, KY
1981	Randy Lightfoot	218.3	Skip Tucker	Memphis, TN
1982	Joe Berardi	207.12	Ted Hannahs	Baltimore, MD
1983	Mike Lastowski	212.65	Pete Weber	Niagara Falls, NY
1984	Earl Anthony	212.5	Gil Sliker	Reno, NV
1985	Steve Wunderlich	210.4	Tommy Kress	Tulsa, OK
1986	Mark Fahy	206.5	Del Ballard Jr	Las Vegas, NV
1987	Rick Steelsmith	210.7	Brad Snell	Niagara Falls, NY
1988	Del Ballard Jr	219.1	Keith Smith	Jacksonville, FL
1989	Mike Aulby	218.5	Mike Edwards	Wichita, KS
1990	Chris Warren	231.6	David Ozio	Reno, NV
1991	Doug Kent	226.8	George Branham III	Toledo, OH
1992	Ken Johnson	230.0	Dave D'Entremont	Corpus Christi, TX
1993	Phil Ware	238.0	Frankie May	Tulsa, OK

Women's Majors

BPAA United States Open

Year	Winner	Score	Runner-Up	Site
1949	Marion Ladewig	113.26-104.26	Catherine Burling	Chicago
1950	Marion Ladewig	151.46-146.06	Stephanie Balogh	Chicago
1951	Marion Ladewig	159.17-148.03	Sylvia Wene	Chicago
1952	Marion Ladewig	154.39-142.05	Shirley Garms	Chicago
1953	Not held			
1954	Marion Ladewig	148.29-143.01	Sylvia Wene	Chicago
1955	Sylvia Wene	142.30-141.11	Sylvia Fanta	Chicago
1955	Anita Cantaline	144.40-144.13	Doris Porter	Chicago
1956	Marion Ladewig	150.16-145.41	Marge Merrick	Chicago
1957	Not held			
1958	Merle Matthews	145.09-143.14	Marion Ladewig	Minneapolis
1959	Marion Ladewig	149.33-143.00	Donna Zimmerman	Buffalo
1960	Sylvia Wene	144.14-143.26	Marion Ladewig	Omaha
1961	Phyllis Notaro	144.13-143.12	Hope Riccilli	San Bernadino

BPAA United States Open (Cont.)

Year	Winner	Score	Runner-Up	Site
1962	Shirley Garms	138.44-135.49	Joy Abel	Miami Beach
1963	Marion Ladewig	586-578	Bobbie Shaler	Kansas City, MO
1964	LaVerne Carter	683-609	Evelyn Teal	Dallas
1965	Ann Slattery	597-550	Sandy Hooper	Philadelphia
1966	Joy Abel	593-538	Bette Rockwell	Lansing, MI
1967	Gloria Bouvia	578-516	Shirley Garms	St. Ann, MO
1968	Dotty Fothergill	9,000-8,187	Doris Coburn	Garden City, NY
1969	Dotty Fothergill	8,284-8,258	Kayoka Suda	Miami
1970	Mary Baker	8,730-8,465	Judy Cook	Northbrook, IL
1971	Paula Carter	5,660-5,650	June Llewellyn	Kansas City, MO
1972	Lorrie Nichols	5,272-5,189	Mary Baker	Denver
1973	Millie Martorella	5,553-5,294	Patty Costello	Garden City, NY
1974	Patty Costello	219-216	Betty Morris	Irving, TX
1975	Paula Carter	6,500-6,352	Lorrie Nichols	Toledo, OH
1976	Patty Costello	11,341-11,281	Betty Morris	Tulsa, OK
1977	Betty Morris	10,511-10,358	Virginia Norton	Milwaukee, WI
1978	Donna Adamek	236-202	Vesma Grinfelds	Miami
1979	Diana Silva	11,775-11,718	Bev Ortner	Phoenix
1980	Pat Costello	223-199	Shinobu Saitoh	Rockford, IL
1981	Donna Adamek	201-190	Nikki Gianulias	Rockford, IL
1982	Shinobu Saitoh	12,184-12,028	Robin Romeo	Hendersonville, TN
1983	Dana Miller-Mackie	247-200	Aleta Sill	St. Louis
1984	Karen Ellingsworth	236-217	Lorrie Nichols	St. Louis
1985	Pat Mercatani	214-178	Nikki Gianulias	Topeka, KS
1986	Wendy Macpherson	265-179	Lisa Wagner	Topeka, KS
1987	Carol Norman	206-179	Cindy Coburn	Mentor, OH
1988	Lisa Wagner	226-218	Lorrie Nichols	Winston-Salem, NC
1989	Robin Romeo	187-163	Michelle Mullen	Addison, IL
1990	Dana Miller-Mackie	190-189	Tish Johnson	Dearborn Heights, MI
1991	Anne Marie Duggan	196-185	Leanne Barrette	Fountain Valley, CA
1992	Tish Johnson	216-213	Aleta Sill	Fountain Valley, CA
1993	Dede Davidson	213-194	Dana Miller-Mackie	Garland, TX

Note: From 1942 to 1970, the tournament was called the BPAA All-Star. Peterson scoring was used from 1949 through 1962. Under this system, the winner of an individual match game gets one point, plus one point for each 50 pins knocked down. From 1963 through 1967, a three-game championship was held between the two top qualifiers. From 1968 through 1973, 1975-77, 1979 and 1982, total pinfall determined the winner. In the other years, five qualifiers competed in a playoff for the championship, with the final match listed above.

WIBC Queens

Year	Winner	Score	Runner-Up	Site
1961	Janet Harman	794-776	Eula Touchette	Fort Wayne, IN
1962	Dorothy Wilkinson	799-794	Marion Ladewig	Phoenix, AZ
1963	Irene Monterosso	852-803	Georgette DeRosa	Memphis, TN
1964	D. D. Jacobson	740-682	Shirley Garms	Minneapolis, MN
1965	Betty Kuczynski	772-739	LaVerne Carter	Portland, OR
1966	Judy Lee	771-742	Nancy Peterson	New Orleans, LA
1967	Millie Ignizio	840-809	Phyllis Massey	Rochester, NY
1968	Phyllis Massey	884-853	Marian Spencer	San Antonio, TX
1969	Ann Feigel	832-765	Millie Ignizio	San Diego, CA
1970	Millie Ignizio	807-797	Joan Holm	Tulsa, OK
1971	Millie Ignizio	809-778	Katherine Brown	Atlanta, GA
1972	Dotty Fothergill	890-841	Maureen Harris	Kansas City, MO
1973	Dotty Fothergill	804-791	Judy Soutar	Las Vegas, NV
1974	Judy Soutar	939-705	Betty Morris	Houston, TX
1975	Cindy Powell	758-674	Patty Costello	Indianapolis, IN
1976	Pam Buckner	214-178	Shirley Sjostrom	Denver, CO
1977	Dana Stewart	175-167	Vesma Grinfelds	Milwaukee, WI
1978	Loa Boxberger	197-176	Cora Fiebig	Miami, FL
1979	Donna Adamek	216-181	Shinobu Saitoh	Tucson, AZ
1980	Donna Adamek	213-165	Cheryl Robinson	Seattle, WA
1981	Katsuko Sugimoto	166-158	Virginia Norton	Baltimore, MD
1982	Katsuko Sugimoto	160-137	Nikki Gianulias	St. Louis, MO
1983	Aleta Sill	214-188	Dana Miller-Mackie	Las Vegas, NV
1984	Kazue Inahashi	248-222	Aleta Sill	Niagara Falls, NY

WIBC Queens (Cont.)

Year	Winner	Score	Runner-Up	Site
1985	Aleta Sill	279-192	Linda Graham	Toledo, OH
1986	Cora Fiebig	223-177	Barbara Thorberg	Orange County, CA
1987	Cathy Almeida	850-817	Lorrie Nichols	Hartford, CT
1988	Wendy Macpherson	213-199	Leanne Barrette	Reno/Carson City, NV
1989	Carol Gianotti	207-177	Sandra Jo Shiery	Bismarck-Mandan, ND
1990	Patty Ann	207-173	Vesma Grinfelds	Tampa, FL
1991	Dede Davidson	231-159	Jeanne Maiden	Cedar Rapids, IA
1992	Cindy Coburn-Carroll	184-170	Dana Miller-Mackie	Lansing, MI
1993	Jan Schmidt	201-163	Pat Costello	Baton Rouge, LA

Sam's Town Invitational

Year	Winner	Score	Runner-Up	Site
1984	Aleta Sill	238 (1 game)	Cheryl Daniels	Las Vegas, NV
1985	Patty Costello	236 (1 game)	Robin Romeo	Las Vegas, NV
1986	Aleta Sill	238 (1 game)	Dina Wheeler	Las Vegas, NV
1987	Debbie Bennett	880 (4 games)	Lorrie Nichols	Las Vegas, NV
1988	Donna Adamek	634 (3 games)	Robin Romeo	Las Vegas, NV
1989	Tish Johnson	210 (1 game)	Dede Davidson	Las Vegas, NV
1990	Wendy Macpherson	900 (4 games)	Jeanne Maiden	Las Vegas, NV
1991	Lorrie Nichols	469 (2 games)	Dana Miller-Mackie	Las Vegas, NV
1992	Tish Johnson	279 (1 game)	Robin Romeo	Las Vegas, NV

PWBA Championships

1960	Marion Ladewig	1971	Patty Costello
1961	Shirley Garms	1972	Patty Costello
1962	Stephanie Balogh	1973	Betty Morris
1963	Janet Harman	1974	Pat Costello
1964	Betty Kuczynski	1975	Pam Buckner
1965	Helen Duval	1976	Patty Costello
1966	Joy Abel	1977	Vesma Grinfelds
1967	Betty Mivalez	1978	Toni Gillard
1968	Dotty Fothergill	1979	Cindy Coburn
1969	Dotty Fothergill	1980	Donna Adamek
1970	Bobbe North		

Men's Awards

BWAA Bowler of the Year

1942 Johnny Crimmins	1960 Don Carter	1976 Earl Anthony
1943 Ned Day	1961 Dick Weber	1977 Mark Roth
1944 Ned Day	1962 Don Carter	1978 Mark Roth
1945 Buddy Bomar	1963 Dick Weber,	1979 Mark Roth
1946 Joe Wilman	Billy Hardwick (PBA)*	1980 Wayne Webb
1947 Buddy Bomar	1964 Billy Hardwick,	1981 Earl Anthony
1948 Andy Varipapa	Bob Strampe (PBA)*	1982 Earl Anthony
1949 Connie Schwoegler	1965 Dick Weber	1983 Earl Anthony
1950 Junie McMahon	1966 Wayne Zahn	1984 Mark Roth
1951 Lee Jouglard	1967 Dave Davis	1985 Mike Aulby
1952 Steve Nagy	1968 Jim Stefanich	1986 Walter Ray Williams Jr
1953 Don Carter	1969 Billy Hardwick	1987 Marshall Holman
1954 Don Carter	1970 Nelson Burton Jr	1988 Brian Voss
1955 Steve Nagy	1971 Don Johnson	1989 Mike Aulby,
1956 Bill Lillard	1972 Don Johnson	Amleto Monacelli (PBA)*
1957 Don Carter	1973 Don McCune	1990 Amleto Monacelli
1958 Don Carter	1974 Earl Anthony	1991 David Ozio
1959 Ed Lubanski	1975 Earl Anthony	1992 Dave Ferraro

*The PBA began selecting a player of the year in 1963. Its selection has been the same as the BWAA's in all but three years.

Women's Awards

BWAA Bowler of the Year

1948 ....Val Mikiel	1964 ....LaVerne Carter	1980 ....Donna Adamek
1949 ....Val Mikiel	1965 ....Betty Kuczynski	1981 ....Donna Adamek
1950 ....Marion Ladewig	1966 ....Joy Abel	1982 ....Nikki Gianulias
1951 ....Marion Ladewig	1967 ....Millie Martorella	1983 ....Lisa Wagner
1952 ....Marion Ladewig	1968 ....Dotty Fothergill	1984 ....Aleta Sill
1953 ....Marion Ladewig	1969 ....Dotty Fothergill	1985 ....Aleta Sill,
1954 ....Marion Ladewig	1970 ....Mary Baker	Patty Costello (LPBT)*
1955 ....Marion Ladewig	1971 ....Paula Sperber Carter	1986 ....Lisa Wagner,
1956 ....Sylvia Martin	1972 ....Patty Costello	Jeanne Madden (LPBT)*
1957 ....Anita Cantaline	1973 ....Judy Soutar	1987 ....Betty Morris
1958 ....Marion Ladewig	1974 ....Betty Morris	1988 ....Lisa Wagner
1959 ....Marion Ladewig	1975 ....Judy Soutar	1989 ....Robin Romeo
1960 ....Sylvia Martin	1976 ....Patty Costello	1990 ....Tish Johnson,
1961 ....Shirley Garms	1977 ....Betty Morris	Leanne Barrette (LPBT)*
1962 ....Shirley Garms	1978 ....Donna Adamek	1991 ....Leanne Barrette
1963 ....Marion Ladewig	1979 ....Donna Adamek	1992 ....Tish Johnson

*The LPBT began selecting a player of the year in 1983. Its selection has been the same as the BWAA's in all but three years.

Career Leaders

Earnings

MEN		WOMEN	
Marshall Holman	$1,555,851	Lisa Wagner	$515,989
Mark Roth	$1,400,881	Donna Adamek	$494,384
Earl Anthony	$1,361,931	Aleta Sill	$488,061
Pete Weber	$1,319,142	Nikki Gianulias	$463,026
Mike Aulby	$1,316,230	Lorrie Nichols	$444,781
Note: Through Dec 31, 1992.		Note: Through Dec 31, 1992.	

Titles

MEN		WOMEN	
Earl Anthony	41	Lisa Wagner	27
Mark Roth	33	Patty Costello	25
Don Johnson	26	Tish Johnson	21
Dick Weber	26	Donna Adamek	19
Marshall Holman	21	Nikkie Gianulias	19
Note: Through Dec 31, 1992.		Note: Through Dec 31, 1992.	

Boy King

Ricky Ward, a 24-year-old Florida native and the 1991 PBA rookie of the year, won his first title on March 20, 1993 at the Johnny Petraglia Open in North Brunswick, N.J. After taking the $34,000 tournament, Ward beat Walter Ray Williams Jr in the weekly King of the Hill match to earn an additional $5,000. Entering the final frame, Ward and Williams were tied at 219. Williams rolled a strike and a spare while Ward closed with three strikes.

THEY SAID IT

PBA Official Eddie Elias, on General Tires replacing Firestone as the Tournament of Champions sponsor: "It was not easy to replace Firestone. The name is synonymous with the tournament ... but Firestone is in a different era from when we started 29 years ago."

Soccer

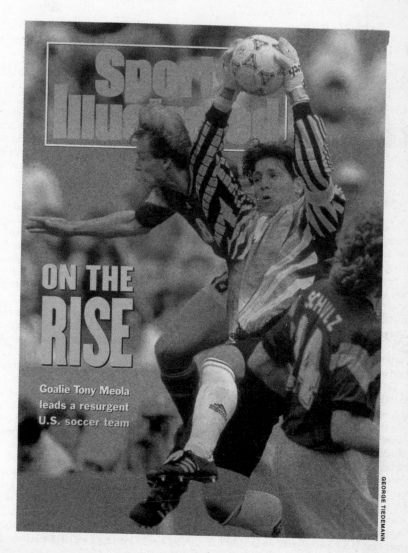

ON THE RISE

Goalie Tony Meola leads a resurgent U.S. soccer team

GEORGE TIEDEMANN

A World Away

As the World Cup approached, the U.S. team showed how far it has come—and how far it must go | by HANK HERSCH

"THE END OF THE WORLD." THAT was the apocalyptic spin one newspaper in England put on the events of June 9, 1993, at Foxboro Stadium in Foxboro, Mass. For on that evening, before a crowd of 36,652, across a soggy pitch that normally serves a more colonial brand of football, the U.S. national soccer team dominated England's finest 2–0 in the 1993 U.S. Cup tournament. It was an outcome doubly unexpected: The Brits have long held a reputation as an international power, while the Yanks had been struggling to manufacture goals, let alone victories, all year. And yet there was the U.S., some 25 miles and 200 years removed from a memorable Tea Party with the Crown, toppling mighty England once again with unimaginable ease.

Tab Ramos set up both goals, the first in the 43rd minute on a cross to Thomas Dooley, whose header beat goalkeeper Chris Woods. Ramos, a midfielder in the Spanish second division, and Dooley, a veteran of the Bundesliga in Germany, were two of the five Americans suiting up professionally in Europe who had come home to start in the match, lifting the U.S. squad to full strength for the first time all season. A corner kick by Ramos set up goal number two, in the 72nd minute, when reserve defender Alexi Lalas, one of the U.S.-based players, nodded the ball

in from the far post. Upon scoring, the red-headed Lalas raced toward midfield, skidded on his knees and wound up writhing in cele-bratory spasms right in front of the England bench. "I did?" Lalas said later. "I had no idea where I was."

It was just that sort of victory, one that put the U.S. in a place where it had no seeming right to belong. And while the double-header win would prove to be a rare highlight in the national team's disappointing season, it *did* fit nicely in the pocketful of large triumphs by U.S. soccer over the years, right behind the 1–0 upset of England in the 1950 World Cup. U.S. keeper Tony Meola, who had been brilliant on at least half of his 15 saves, said afterward, "I'm sure this result has shocked people all over the world."

The world, still spinning but appropriately shocked, was also pleasantly suprised by the scope of the U.S. Cup, a fortnight-long series among four teams at five sites which served as a dry run for the 1994 World Cup to be held here one year later. The tournament started to the strains of a samba at the Yale Bowl in New Haven, Conn., where the U.S. fell to dazzling Brazil 2–0; it passed through Washington, where the Brazilians had their hotel rooms looted and then a victory swiped away by the Germans in a 3–3 tie at RFK Stadium; it headed to Soldier Field in Chicago, where ABC aired Germany's wild 4–3 win over the

After finding the England goal with a header, Lalas (22) joyously lost his head.

U.S., marking the inaugural live network broadcast of the national team; and it climaxed at the Silverdome in Pontiac, Mich., where England bowed 2–1 to Germany in the first international match held indoors.

Some 1,800 hexagonal slabs of specially grown sod were stitched together for the Silverdome's experimental turf—a "field of seams," one wag called it—and they held together brilliantly. "It's a magnificent facility," said Berti Vogts, coach of the German team. "The pitch is something of a miracle." And though striker Juergen Klinsmann, the MVP for the victorious German squad, was put off by the dome's humidity, he did rather enjoy its "taste of popcorn" in the air.

More important to the local organizers, the U.S. Cup had the feel of coin and the sound of clicking turnstiles. The six games raised some $2 million and drew an average of 47,793 fans. "This is the most important step in the history of soccer in this country," said Guido Tognoni, a spokesman for the Federation Internationale de Football Association (FIFA), soccer's ruling body. "Nowhere else in the world could you average 47,000 fans for such matches. No one should say the Americans don't like soccer."

There was other evidence of that fondness as well. World Cup USA 1994 Inc., the event's organizing body, set aside 450,000 of the 1.7 million tickets in an initial sale for longtime supporters of the sport. That allotment was snapped up at such a furious pace that Cup '94 had to make another 150,000 tickets available. With the Cup on the way to being sold out, its organizers were projecting a $25 million surplus that would help to fund the growth of the sport. One matter less often raised by the powers in U.S. soccer, however, was their plan for a topflight pro league, which FIFA demanded be up and running by 1995. By the fall of '93, no blueprint had been accepted.

The Cup's 24-team field was also up in the air. The U.S., as host of the monthlong tournament, had secured a spot; Germany, as defending champ, was also in and guaranteed a top seeding. Mexico was the first team to make it through the qualifying competition, led by the left-footed brilliance of striker Zaguinho (Little Zig Zag). Under the coaching of Alkis Panagoulias, a U.S. citizen for the past 25 years and the one time coach of the U.S. team, his native Greece qualified for the first time. Russia, too, joined the field, while hardy perennials Italy, the Netherlands and, yes, England were pushed to the brink of elimination.

In South America, Brazil also struggled but made the field. A surprise entry was Bolivia, which would be playing in its first Cup in 44 years. "In a country like Bolivia, where so many people are poor, there are very few times the country as a whole can feel pride and joy," said Guido Loayza, the president of the nation's soccer federation. "This is one of those times." Even more shocking was the play of another qualifier, Colombia, which first snapped Argentina's 31-match winning streak 2–1 in Barranquilla, then journeyed to Buenos Aires and humiliated the Argentines 5–0 before 60,000 fans there, setting off bloody rioting back home that left 20 dead.

For Argentina, one of the Cup favorites, the losses to Colombia forced it to face Australia in a two-game playoff for a berth. As the Argentines tried to hit stride, so too did their most fabled player, 33-year-old Diego Maradona, who in June decided to retire after Seville of the Spanish League alleged he had made regular visits to the city's red-light district and terminated his $4 million contract. But two months later Maradona un-retired and signed to play for Newell's Old Boys in Buenos Aires. Still, his future with the national team was up in the air, and charges of cocaine trafficking remained against him on the docket in Italy.

Scandal of other sorts rocked the soccer world in '93, with match-fixing investigations ongoing in Poland, Turkey and Israel. The most lurid tale involved Olympique Marseilles, which beat superpower AC Milan of Italy 1–0 in the final to become the first French team to win the prestigious European Champions Cup. According to a player from Valenciennes, an official from Olympique Marseilles had offered him and two of his teammates 250,000 francs each (or $43,800) to go easy in a May 20 league match, thereby allowing Marseilles to save its energy for the Cup time six days later. The charges marked the seventh time Marseilles owner, Bernard Tapie, a parlimentarian, had been accused of dirty-dealing. With the backing of FIFA, the Union of European Football Associations announced it was barring Marseilles from defending its Cup championship.

But beyond the pratfalls of English football, the trials of Maradona and the malfeasance of Marseilles, there was tragedy in Zambia. There, April 28, 1993, did almost seem like the end of the world: A 20-year-old military plane carrying 16 members of the national soccer team to a qualifying match against Senegal crashed into the Atlantic Ocean and exploded, killing all 30 passengers aboard. Somehow, though, under the direction of coach Freddie Mwilia and with an almost entirely new squad, Zambia went 2-0-1 in early qualifying games and kept its chances alive for a World Cup debut until October when a 1–0 loss to Morocco eliminated the team from contention.

And on the day the World Cup would begin—June 17, 1994—what sort of hope would the U.S. team have of advancing on its own soil? Like most things in '93, the answer was very unclear. Until the victory over England, the U.S. had gone 1-5-9 in international play; until Dooley's header, it had played 389 minutes without a goal. But by beating England and then battling from behind against the prepotent Germans in the U.S. Cup, the team brightened hopes that it might be capable of something inspirational next summer, especially with its expatriate corps in uniform.

Besides Ramos and Dooley, the Americans abroad included John Harkes, the tenacious midfielder from Kearny, N.J., who in May had

become the first American to appear in England's FA Cup final. Playing for runner-up Sheffield Wednesday, Harkes had two assists—one in a tie and one in a loss to Arsenal. There was striker Eric (Waldo) Wynalda, from Westlake Village, Calif., who had transferred to FC Saarbruecken of the Bundesliga and taken Germany by *Sturm* with a blizzard of early-season goals. And there was Roy Wegerle, born in Pretoria, South Africa, and educated at South Florida, a 29-year-old veteran of the English first division, whose creativity with the ball seemed to expand the field and lift his teammates to another level.

But while the U.S. had rarely achieved such stunning soccer success, its overall results were disturbingly uneven. After the U.S. Cup, the team traveled to Ecuador for the Copa America and lost its first two games, to Uruguay and Ecuador, without scoring. Up 3-0 against Venezuela in its next match with a chance to advance to the second round, the Yanks then let in three second-half goals and were sent packing. "I don't know what I have to do," said coach Bora Milutinovic, "but I know I have to do something."

The Gold Cup in late July provided Bora's Boys a shot at redemption. In 1991 the U.S.

Old World players were delighted with innovations like the Silverdome's Field of Seams.

went undefeated in the eight-nation tournament, which marks the championship of the Caribbean and Central America. Once again, the U.S. reached the finals without a loss. But before 120,000 fans—the largest to watch the U.S. team play—at Azteca Stadium in Mexico City, a more poised and skillful Mexico team crushed the U.S. 4–0. While players offered excuses—the smog, the noise, the altitude and the absence of Ramos, who had been yellow-carded in the semis—Bora could only face the result. "You lose, you need to accept," he said. "They played much better than we played."

From 1983 to '86 Bora had coached the Mexican national team, and he keeps a townhouse in Mexico City. After the loss he invited the players and press to his home, where a mariachi band performed. Lalas, a bass player in a rock group called the Gypsies, borrowed one of the band's guitars and sang a few tunes. He ended with "Ain't That America." For the world of soccer, America—and the U.S. team—was a year away from being discovered.

World Cup Qualifying

Final Qualifiers

ASIA

Country	GP	W	D	L	G	GA	Pts
Saudi Arabia	5	2	3	0	8	6	7
S Korea	5	2	2	1	9	4	6

SOUTH AMERICA—GROUP A

Country	GP	W	D	L	G	GA	Pts
Colombia	6	5	2	0	13	2	10

SOUTH AMERICA—GROUP B

Country	GP	W	D	L	G	GA	Pts
Brazil	8	5	2	1	20	4	12
Bolivia	8	5	1	2	22	12	11

CENTRAL AMERICA, CARIBBEAN, NORTH AMERICA

Country	GP	W	D	L	G	GA	Pts
Mexico	6	4	1	1	22	3	9

AFRICA—GROUP A

Country	GP	W	D	L	G	GA	Pts
Nigeria	4	2	1	1	10	5	5

AFRICA—GROUP B

Country	GP	W	D	L	G	GA	Pts
Morocco	4	3	0	1	5	4	6

AFRICA—GROUP C

Country	GP	W	D	L	G	GA	Pts
Cameroon	4	3	0	1	7	3	6

EUROPE—GROUP 5

Country	GP	W	D	L	G	GA	Pts
Russia	7	5	2	0	15	3	12
Greece	7	5	2	0	9	2	12

Automatic Qualifiers: Germany (defending champions); U.S. (host).

Qualifying Still in Progress as of November 1, 1993

EUROPE—GROUP 1

Country	GP	W	D	L	G	GA	Pts
Italy	9	6	2	1	21	7	14
Switzerland	9	5	3	1	19	6	13
Portugal	8	5	2	1	15	4	12
Scotland	9	3	3	3	12	13	9
Malta	9	1	1	7	3	21	3
Estonia	8	0	1	7	1	20	1

EUROPE—GROUP 2

Country	GP	W	D	L	G	GA	Pts
Norway*	9	7	2	0	24	3	16
Netherlands	9	5	3	1	26	8	13
England	9	4	3	2	19	8	11
Poland	8	3	2	3	8	10	8
Turkey	8	1	1	6	7	17	3
San Marino	9	0	1	8	1	39	1

EUROPE—GROUP 3

Country	GP	W	D	L	G	GA	Pts
Denmark	11	7	4	0	15	1	18
Spain	11	7	3	1	26	4	17
Ireland	11	7	3	1	18	5	17
N Ireland	11	5	2	4	13	12	12
Lithuania	12	2	3	7	8	21	7
Latvia	12	0	5	7	4	21	5
Albania	12	1	2	9	6	26	4

EUROPE—GROUP 4

Country	GP	W	D	L	G	GA	Pts
Belgium	9	7	0	2	16	5	14
Romania	9	6	1	2	27	11	13
Wales	9	5	2	2	18	10	12
RCS†	8	3	4	1	18	9	10
Cyprus	9	2	1	6	8	15	5
Farow Isl.	10	0	0	10	1	38	0

EUROPE—GROUP 6

Country	GP	W	D	L	G	GA	Pts
Sweden*	9	6	2	1	18	8	14
France	9	6	1	2	16	8	13
Bulgaria	9	5	2	2	17	9	12
Austria	8	3	0	5	13	14	6
Israel	8	1	2	5	8	23	4
Finland	9	1	1	7	6	17	3

*Clinched a World Cup berth.

†RCS=Representation of Czechs and Slovaks.

U.S. Men's National Team Results

Date	Opponent	Site	Result	U.S. Goals
Jan 30	Denmark	Tempe	2-2 T	Murray, Moore
Feb. 6	Romania	Santa Barbara	1-1 T	Kinnear
Feb. 9	F.C. Zurich	Mission Viejo	2-1 W	Henderson, Jones
Feb. 13	Russia	Orlando	1-0 L	none
Feb. 22	Russia	Palo Alto	0-0 T	none
March 3	Canada	Costa Mesa	2-2 T	Kinnear, Murray
March 9	Hungary	Nagoya	0-0 T	none
March 14	Japan	Tokyo	3-1 L	Perez
March 23	El Salvador	San Salvador	2-2 T	Allnutt, Jones
March 25	Honduras	Tegucigalpa	4-1 L	Allnutt
April 9	Saudi Arabia	Riyadh	2-0 W	Moore, Michallik
April 17	Iceland	Costa Mesa	1-1 T	Vernes
April 22	Kedah	Mission Viejo	3-0 W	Moore, Kinnear, Harbor
May 8	Colombia	Miami	2-1 L	Lalas
May 23	Bolivia	Fullerton	0-0 T	none
May 26	Peru	Mission Viejo	0-0 T	none
June 6	Brazil	New Haven	2-0 L	none
June 9	England	Foxboro	2-0 W	Dooley, Lalas
June 13	Germany	Chicago	4-3 L	Dooley 2, Stewart
June 16	Uruguay	Ambata	1-0 L	none
June 19	Ecuador	Quito	2-0 L	none
June 22	Venezuela	Quito	3-3 T	Henderson, Vernes, Kinnear
July 10	Jamaica	Dallas	1-0 W	Wynalda
July 14	Panama	Dallas	2-1 W	Wynalda, Dooley
July 17	Honduras	Dallas	1-0 W	Lalas
July 21	Costa Rica	Dallas	1-0 W	Kooiman
July 26	Mexico	Mexico City	4-0 L	none

U.S. Women's National Team

Date	Opponent	Site	Result	U.S. Goals
March 11	Denmark	Chicago	2-0 W	Hamm, Akers-Stahl
March 12	Norway	Chicago	1-0 L	none
March 14	Germany	Chicago	1-0 L	none
April 7	Germany	Oakford (PA)	2-1 L	Fawcett
April 10	Germany	Atlanta	3-0 W	Venturini, Lilly 2
June 12	Canada	Cincinnati	7-0 W	Lilly, Fawcett, Akers-Stahl 2, Gabarra, Rafanelli, Milbrett
June 15	Italy	Mansfield (OH)	5-0 W	Venturini, Gabarra, Hamm 2, Lilly
June 19	Italy	Columbus (OH)	1-0 W	Hamm
June 21	Canada	Detroit	3-0 W	Fawcett 2, Akers-Stahl
August 4	New Zealand	Long Island	3-0 W	Lilly, Rafanelli, Gabarra
August 6	Trinidad&Tobago	Long Island	9-0 W	Akers-Stahl 2, Lilly, Fawcett, Foudy Venturini, Rafanelli, Gabarra, Kaufman
August 8	Canada	Long Island	1-0 W	Fawcett

New Rule a No Go

At the Under-17 World Cup last summer in Japan, FIFA, soccer's world governing body, experimented with a radical rule change: 'kick-ins'. Instead of throwing the ball—overhead, with two hands—back into play when it crossed the touchline, the new rule allowed for a kick to restart. The idea was that, with players now able to put the ball in front of the oponent's net from almost anywhere on the field, there would be more scoring chances. The new rule was not well-received as it slanted play toward the long-ball, traditionally British or Irish style, and favored the taller player. As the coach of Ghana said: "This is not football."

1992 Toyota Cup Final

Competition between winners of European Cup and Libertadores Cup

TOKYO: DEC 12, 1992

| Sao Paulo (Brazil) ....1 | 1 —2 |
| Barcelona (Spain) ....1 | 0 —1 |

Goals: Rai (27, 79); Stoichkov (12)

Att: 60,000

Sao Paulo: Zetti, Vitor, Ronaldo, Ronaldo Luiz, Cafu, Adilson, Pintado, Cerezo, Rai, Muller, Palhinha.

Barcelona: Zubizarretta, Ferrer, Guardiola, Koeman, Eusebio, Bakero (Goikoetxea), Amor, Barticciotto, Pizarro, Yanez, Martinez (60 Rubio).

European Cup

League champions of the countries belonging to UEFA (Union of European Football Associations).

MUNICH: MAY 26, 1993

| Olympique Marseille (Fr) 1 | 0 —1 |
| A.C. Milan (Italy) ....0 | 0 —0 |

Goals: Boli (44).

Att: 64,400

Marseille: Barthez, Angloma (Durand 62) Di Meco, Boli, Sauzee, Desailly, Eydelle, Boksic, Voeller (Thomas 79), Pele, Deschamps.

A.C. Milan: Rossi, Tassotti, Maldini, Albertini, Costacurta, Baresi, Lentini, Rijkaard, Van Basten (Eranio 85), Donadoni (Papin 55), Massaro.

European Cup-Winners' Cup

Cup winners of countries belonging to UEFA.

LONDON: MAY 12, 1993

| Parma (Italy) ....2 | 1 —3 |
| Antwerp (Belgium) ....1 | 0 —1 |

Goals: Minotti (9), Melli (30), Coughi (85); Severeyns (12)

Att: 37,393

Parma: Ballotta, Benarrivo, Di Chiara, Monotti, Appollini, Grun, Melli, Zoratto (Pin 26), Osio (Pizzi 68), Coughi, Brolin.

Antwerp: Stojanovic, Kiekens, Broeckaert, Taeymans, Smidts, Jakovijevic (Van Veirdeghem 56), Van Rethy, Segers (Moukrim 80), Severeyns, Lehnhoff, Czerniatynski

UEFA Cup

Competition between teams other than league champions and cup-winners from UEFA.

(SECOND LEG) TURIN: MAY 19, 1993

| Juventus (Italy) ....2 | 1 —3 |
| Borussia Dortmund (Gr)..0 | 0 —0 |

Goals: Baggio (5, 40); Moeller (65) (aggregate: 6–1)

Att: 60,000

Juventus: Perruzzi, Carrera, Torricelli (Di Canio 65),De Marchi, Kohler, Julio Cesar, Galia, D. Baggio, Vialli (Ravanelli 75), R. Baggio, Moeller.

Bor Dortmund: Kios, Reinhardt, Schmidt, Schulz, Zelic, Poschner, Reuter (Lusch 65), Karl, Sippel, Rumenigge (Franck 40), Mill.

Libertadores Cup

Competition between champion clubs and runners-up of 10 South American National Associations.

(FIRST LEG) SAO PAULO: MAY 19, 1993

| Sao Paulo (Brazil) ....2 | 3 —5 |
| Univ. Catolica (Chile)......0 | 1 —1 |

Goals: own (31), Vitor (41), Gilmar (55), Rai (60) Muller (65); Almada, PK, (80) (Sao Paulo wins 5–3 on aggregate)

Att: 94,629

Sao Paulo: Zetti, Vitor, Valber, Gilmar, Ronaldo, Luis (Andre), Cafu, Rai, Pintado, Dinho, Palhinha, Muller.

Univ. Catolica: Wirth,Romero, Vazquez, Lopez (Barrera), Contreras, Parraguaz, Lepe, Tupper, Lunari, Almada, Perez (Reinoso).

National Club Champions—Europe

Country	League Champion	League Scoring Leader, Club	Cup Winner
Albania ....Partizani		Dosti, Partizani	Partizani
Austria ....FK Austria		Danek, Tirol	Tirol
Belgium ....Anderlecht		Weber, Cercle Brugge	Standard Liege
Bulgaria ....Levski Sofia		Guetov, Levski Sofia	CSKA Sofia
Belarus ....Dynamo Minsk		Baranouski, Dynamo Minsk	Neman Grodno
		Romachenko, Dnepr	
Croatia ....Zagreb Croatia		Vlaovic, C. Zagreb	Hajduk Split
Cyprus ....Omonia		Scepovic, Apollon	Apoel Nicosia
Denmark ....FC Copenhagen		Moller, Aalborg	Odense BK
England ....Manchester United		Sheringham, Tottenham	Arsenal
Estonia...................Norma Tallinn		Bragin, Norma Tallinn	Nikol Tallinn
Faroe Isles ....B68 Tofta		Justinssen, GI	HB Havnar
Finland...................HJK Helsinki		Antonio, Jazz Pori	My Pa
France ....Olympique Marseille		Boksix, Marseille	Paris St. Germaine

Club Competition (Cont.)

National Club Champions—Europe (Cont.)

Country	League Champion	League Scoring Leader, Club	Cup Winner
Georgia	Dynamo Tbilisi	Melgreladze, Samgurali	Dynamo Tbilisi
Germany	Werder Bremen	Yeboah, Eintracht Frankfurt	Leverkusen
Greece	AEK Athens	Dimitriadis, AEK Athens	Panathinaikos
Holland	Feyenoord	Bergkamp, Ajax Amsterdam	Ajax Amsterdam
Hungary	Honved Kispest	Rapasi, Vac	Ferencuaros
Iceland	IA Akranes	Gunnlauggson, IA Akranes	Valur
Ireland	Cork City	Morley, Cork City	Shelbourne
Italy	AC Milan	Signori, Lazio	Torino
Latvia	Skonto Riga	Jevnerovich, VEF	RAF Jelgava
Lithuania	Ekranas	Shlekis, Ekranas	Zal Vilnius
Luxembourg	Union	Krings, Avenir Beggen	Avenir Beggen
Malta	Floriana	Zacchau, Hibernians	Floriana
Northern Ireland	Linfield	Cowans, Portadown	Bangor
Norway	Rosenborg	Kaasa, Kongsvinger	Rosenborg
Poland	Leggia Warsaw	Podbrozny, Lech Poznan	Katowice
		Sliwowski, Liggia Warsaw	
Portugal	FC Porto	Cadete, Sporting	Benefica
Romania	Stegua Bucharest	Dumitrescu, Stegua Bucharest	Uni Craiova
Russia	Spartak Moscow	Kasumov, Spartak Moscow	Torpedo Moscow
San Marino	Tre Fiori	Bernardini, Libertas	Tre Fiori
Scotland	Rangers	McCoist, Rangers	Rangers
Slovenia	Olimpija Ljubljana	Udovic, Slovan Mavrica	Olimpija Ljubljana
Spain	Barcelona	Bebeto, La Coruna	Real Madrid
Sweden	IAK Stockholm	Eklund, Osters	Degefors
Switzerland	Aarau	Anderson, Sion	Lugano
Turkey	Galatasaray	Tanju, Fenerbahce	Galatasaray
Ukraine	Dynamo Kiev	Gusev, Chernomorets	Dynamo Kiev
Wales	Cwmbran Town	Woods, Ebbw Vale	Cardiff City
Yugoslavia	Partizan Belgrade	Mihajlovic, Vojvodina	Red Star Belgrade
		Drobrnjak, Red Star Belgrade	

National Professional Soccer League

Final Standings

American	W	L	Pct	GB	PF	PA	National	W	L	Pct	GB	PF	PA
Baltimore	27	13	.675	—	582	488	Wichita	27	13	.675	—	587	435
Cleveland	25	15	.625	2.0	702	563	Kansas City	26	14	.650	1.0	657	555
Buffalo	23	17	.575	4.0	570	503	Chicago	22	18	.550	5.0	483	514
Harrisburg	22	18	.550	5.0	597	556	St Louis	19	21	.475	8.0	582	610
Dayton	20	20	.500	7.0	562	584	Milwaukee	17	23	.425	10.0	513	509
Detroit	16	24	.400	11.0	566	666	Denver	3	37	.075	24.0	439	752
Canton	13	27	.325	14.0	519	634							

Playoff Results (Semi-Finals)

HARRISBURG VS CLEVELAND

Date	Results	Attendance
Apr 10	Cleveland 16 vs Harrisburg 15	4,744
Apr 11	Harrisburg 20 vs Cleveland 18 (OT)	5,911
Apr 14	Cleveland 16 vs Harrisburg 7	6,901
	(Cleveland wins series 2–1)	

ST LOUIS VS KANSAS CITY

Date	Results	Attendance
Apr 8	Kansas City 21 vs St Louis 17	9,525
Apr 9	St Louis 15 vs Kansas City 4	4,713
Apr 11	Kansas City 16 vs St Louis 14 (OT)	3,817
	(Kansas City wins series 2–1)	

CHAMPIONSHIP SERIES

Date	Results	Attendance
Apr 16	Kansas City 18 vs Cleveland 6	10,313
Apr 18	Kansas City 12 vs Cleveland 8	6,767
Apr 23	Cleveland 17 vs Kansas City 12	10,317
Apr 25	Cleveland 19 vs Kansas City 16	9,276
Apr 30	Kansas City 19 vs Cleveland 7	12,134
	(Kansas City wins series 3–2)	

Statistical Leaders

SCORING

Rank	Player	3PG	2PG	1PG	Assists	Points
1	Hector Marinaro, Cle	12	74	14	50	248
2	Zoran Karic, Cle	6	60	12	72	222
3	Gino DiFlorio, Can	2	65	14	28	178
4	Rudy Pikuzinski, Buf	1	60	6	36	165
5	Jon Parry, KC	4	60	2	27	161

THREE-POINT GOALS

Player	Team	Games	3PG
1 Hector Marinaro	Clev	38	12
2 Randy Prescott	Det	40	7

Several players tied at 6

ASSISTS

Player	Team	Games	Assists
1 Zoran Karic	Clev	33	72
2 Pato Margetic	Chi	37	65
2 Franklin McIntosh	Har	40	51
4 Tony Bono	Day	40	50
4 Kevin Koetters	KC	40	50
4 Hector Marinaro	Cle	38	50

GOALKEEPING LEADERS (Minimum 1410 minutes)

Player	Team	GP	Min	Shots	Svs	GA	PAA	W	L
1 Kris Peat	Wich	32	1772:26	524	365	159	10.36	22	8
2 Cris Vaccaro	Balt	37	1993:46	697	500	197	11.22	23	11
3 Victor Nogueira	Mil	30	1691:49	584	415	169	11.42	15	15
4 Jamie Swanner	Buf	39	2293:00	850	609	241	12.27	22	16
5 Otto Orf	Clev	38	2031:36	790	570	220	12.58	25	9

American Professional Soccer League

Final Standings

	W	L	GF	GA	Pts	Home	Road
Vancouver Eighty-Sixers	15	9	43	35	126	9-3	6-6
Colorado Foxes	15	9	40	34	121	8-4	7-5
Tampa Bay Rowdies	12	12	53	47	118	6-6	6-6
Los Angeles Salsa	12	12	41	37	109	8-4	4-8
Toronto Blizzard	10	14	35	41	96	9-3	1-11
Ft Lauderdale Strikers	9	15	39	52	93	6-6	3-9
Montreal Impact	11	13	28	33	90	7-5	4-8

Point system—six points for each victory in regulation or overtime; four points for a Shootout win; two points for a Shootout loss; one bonus point for each goal in regulation up to a maximun of three (regardless of whether team wins or loses

Playoff Results: Four teams—Vancouver, Colorado, Tampa Bay, and Los Angeles—qualified for the playoffs. Los Angeles beat Vancouver 3–2, Colorado defeated Tampa Bay 1–0, in the Semis; Colorado defeated Los Angeles 3–1 in the finals for the APSL championship.

SCORING LEADERS

Paulinho, Los Angeles	37
Paul Wright, Los Angeles	33
Paul Dougherty, Tampa Bay	27
Zico Doe, Ft Lauderdale	26
Hector Marinaro, Toronto	26

ASSISTS LEADERS

Hector Marinaro, Toronto	12
Paul Dougherty, Tampa Bay	11
Ivor Evans, Vancouver	8
Dale Mitchell, Vancouver	8
Four tied with seven	

GOALS LEADERS

Paulinho, Los Angeles	15
Paul Wright, Los Angeles	13
Zico Doe, Ft Lauderdale	12
Scott Benedetti, Colorado	10
Taifour Diane, Colorado	10
Domenic Mobilio, Vancouver	10

GOALS-AGAINST-AVERAGE LEADERS

Jim St Andre, Colorado	1.19
Pat Harrington, Montreal	1.35
Brett Phillips, Tampa Bay	1.39
Ian Feuer, Los Angeles	1.40
Paul Dolan, Vancouver	1.42

FOR THE RECORD·Year by Year

The World Cup

Results

Year	Champion	Score	Runner-Up	Winning Coach
1930	Uruguay	4-2	Argentina	Alberto Supicci
1934	Italy	2-1	Czechoslovakia	Vittorio Pozzo
1938	Italy	4-2	Hungary	Vittorio Pozzo
1950	Uruguay	2-1	Brazil	Juan Lopez
1954	West Germany	3-2	Hungary	Sepp Herberger
1958	Brazil	5-2	Sweden	Vicente Feola
1962	Brazil	3-1	Czechoslovakia	Aymore Moreira
1966	England	4-2	West Germany	Alf Ramsey
1970	Brazil	4-1	Italy	Mario Zagalo
1974	West Germany	2-1	Netherlands	Helmut Schoen
1978	Argentina	3-1	Netherlands	Cesar Menotti
1982	Italy	3-1	West Germany	Enzo Bearzot
1986	Argentina	3-2	West Germany	Carlos Bilardo
1990	West Germany	1-0	Argentina	Franz Beckenbauer

Alltime World Cup Participation

Of the 55 nations which have taken part in the World Cup, only Brazil has competed in each of the 13 tournaments held to date. West Germany has played in 12 World Cups, including the 1934 and 1938 editions when the team represented an undivided Germany.

	Matches	Wins	Ties	Losses	Goals For	Goals Against
Brazil	66	44	11	11	148	65
*West Germany	68	39	15	14	145	90
Italy	54	31	12	11	89	54
Argentina	48	24	9	15	82	59
England	41	18	12	11	55	38
Uruguay	37	15	8	14	61	52
USSR	31	15	6	10	53	34
France	34	15	5	14	71	56
Yugoslavia	33	15	5	13	55	42
Hungary	32	15	3	14	87	57
Spain	32	13	7	12	43	38
Poland	25	13	5	7	39	29
Sweden	31	11	6	14	51	52
Czechoslovakia	30	11	5	14	44	45
Austria	26	12	2	12	40	43
Holland	20	8	6	6	35	23
Belgium	25	7	4	14	33	49
Mexico	29	6	6	17	27	64
Chile	21	7	3	11	26	32
Scotland	20	4	6	10	23	35
Portugal	9	6	0	3	19	12
Switzerland	18	5	2	11	28	44
Northern Ireland	13	3	5	5	13	23
Peru	15	4	3	8	19	31
Paraguay	11	3	4	4	16	25
Rumania	12	3	3	6	16	20
Cameroon	8	3	3	2	8	10
Denmark	4	3	0	1	10	6
East Germany	6	2	2	2	5	5
USA	10	3	0	7	14	29
Bulgaria	16	0	6	10	11	35
Wales	5	1	3	1	4	4
Algeria	6	2	1	3	6	10
Morocco	7	1	3	3	5	8
Republic of Ireland	5	0	4	1	2	3
Costa Rica	4	2	0	2	4	6
Colombia	7	1	2	4	9	15
Tunisia	3	1	1	1	3	2
North Korea	4	1	1	2	5	9
Cuba	3	1	1	1	5	12
Turkey	3	1	0	2	10	11
Honduras	3	0	2	1	2	3
Israel	3	1	0	2	1	3
Egypt	4	0	2	2	3	6
Kuwait	3	0	1	2	2	6
Australia	3	0	1	2	0	5
Iran	3	0	1	2	2	8
South Korea	8	0	1	7	5	29
Norway	1	0	0	1	1	2
Dutch East Indies	1	0	0	1	0	6
Iraq	3	0	0	3	1	4
Canada	3	0	0	3	0	5
United Arab Emirates	3	0	0	3	2	11
New Zealand	3	0	0	3	2	12
Haiti	3	0	0	3	2	14
Zaire	3	0	0	3	0	14
Bolivia	3	0	0	3	0	16
El Salvador	6	0	0	6	1	22

*Includes Germany 1930-38.
Note: Matches decided by penalty kicks are shown as drawn games.

Foxes in the Hunt

July's Four Nations Cup in Denver was another sign that U.S. soccer is catching up to the world's best. The Colorado Foxes, 1992 and '93 APSL champs, held their own in games against FC Kaiserslautern, a top German club, and Norwich City, third place finishers in the English premier league. They lost to the Germans but beat the brits, both by 3-2 scores. Said Kaiserslautern coach Friedel Rausch: "The Americans have come a long way, there are players on the Foxes' team who could definitely play in the Bundesliga."

The World Cup *(Cont.)*

World Cup Final Box Scores

URUGUAY 1930

| Uruguay | ....1 | 3 — 4 |
| Argentina | ....2 | 0 — 2 |

FIRST HALF

Scoring: 1, Uruguay, Dorado (12); 2, Argentina, Peucelle (20); 3, Argentina, Stabile (37).

SECOND HALF

Scoring: 4, Uruguay, Cea (57); 5, Uruguay, Iriarte (68); 6, Uruguay, Castro (89).

Argentina: Botosso; Della Toree, Paternoster, Evaristo, J., Monti, Suarez, Peucelle, Varallo, Stabile, Ferreira, Evaristo, M.

Uruguay: Ballesteros; Nasazzi, Mascheroni, Andrade, Fernandez, Gestido, Dorado, Scarone, Castro, Cea, Iriarte.

Referee: Langenus (Belgium)

FRANCE 1938

| Italy | ....3 | 1 — 4 |
| Hungary | ....1 | 1 — 2 |

FIRST HALF

Scoring: 1, Italy, Colaussi (5); 2, Hungary, Titkos (7); Italy Piola (16); 4, Italy, Piola (35).

SECOND HALF

Scoring: 5, Hungary, Sarosi (70); 6, Italy, Colaussi (82).

Italy: Olivieri, Foni, Rava, Serantoni, Andreolo, Locatelli, Biavati, Meazza, Piola, Ferrari, Colaussi.

Hungary: Szabo; Polger, Biro, Szalay, Szucs, Lazar, Sas, Vincze, Sarosi, Zsengeller, Titkos.

Referee: Capdeville (France)

SWITZERLAND 1954

| W Germany | ......2 | 1 — 3 |
| Hungary | ....2 | 0 — 2 |

FIRST HALF

Scoring: 1, Hungary, Puskas (6); 2, Hungary, Czibor (8); 3, W Germ, Morlock (10); 4, W Germ, Rahn (18).

SECOND HALF

Scoring: 5, W Germ, Rahn (84).

West Germany: Turek; Posipal, Kohlmeyer, Eckel, Liebrich, Mai, Rahn, Morlock, Walter, O., Walter, F., Schaefer.

Hungary: Grosics; Buzansky, Lantos, Bozsik, Lorant, Zakarias, Czibor, Kocsis, Hidegkuti, Puskas, Toth

Referee: Ling (England)

ITALY 1934

| Italy | ....0 | 1 | 1 — 2 |
| Czechoslovakia | ..0 | 1 | 0 — 1 |

SECOND HALF

Scoring: 1, Czech., Puc (70); 2, Italy, Orsi (80).

OVERTIME

Scoring: 3, Italy, Schiavio (95).

Italy: Combi; Monzeglio, Allemandi, Ferraris Monti, Monti, Bertolini, Guaita, Meazza, Schiavio, Ferrari, Orsi

Czecholslovakia: Planicka, Zenisek, Ctyroky, Kostalek, Cambal, Cambal, Krcil, Junek, Svoboda, Sobotka, Nejedly, Puc.

Referee: Eklind (Sweden).

BRAZIL 1950

| Uruguay | ....0 | 2 — 2 |
| Brazil | ....0 | 1 — 1 |

SECOND HALF

Scoring: 1, Brazil, Friaca (47); 2, Uruguay, Schiaffino (66); 3, Uruguay Ghiggia (79).

Uruguay: Maspoli, Gonzales, Tejera, Gambretta, Varela, Andrade, Ghiggia, Perez, Miguez, Schiffiano, Moran

Brazil: Barbosa, Augusto, Juvenal, Bauer, Banilo, Bigode, Friaca, Zizinho, Ademir, Jair, Chico

Referee: Reader (England)

SWEDEN 1958

| Brazil | ....2 | 3 — 5 |
| Sweden | ....1 | 1 — 2 |

FIRST HALF

Scoring:1, Sweden, Liedholm (3); 2, Brazil, Vava (9); 3, Brazil, Vava (32).

SECOND HALF

Scoring: 4, Brazil, Pele (55); 5, Brazil, Zagalo (68); 6, Sweden Simonsson (80); 7, Brazil, Pele (90).

Brazil: Glymar, Santos, D., Santos, N., Zito, Bellini, Orlando, Garrincha, Didi, Vava, Pele, Zagalo.

Sweden: Svensson, Bergmark, Axbom, Boerjesson, Gustavsson, Parling, Hamrin, Gren, Simonsson, Liedholm, Skoglund

Referee: Guigue (France).

CHILE 1962

| Brazil | ....1 | 2 — 3 |
| Czechoslovakia | ....1 | 0 — 1 |

FIRST HALF

Scoring: 1, Czech, Masopust (15); 2, Brazil, Amarildo (17).

SECOND HALF

Scoring: 3, Brazil, Zito (68); 4, Brazil, Vava (77).

Brazil: Glymar; Santos, D., Santos, N., Zito, Mauro, Zozimo, Garrincha, Didi, Vava, Amarildo, Zagalo

Czechoslovakia: Schroiff, Tichy, Novak, Pluskal, Popluhar, Masopust, Pospichal, Scherer, Kvasnak, Kadraba, Jelinek.

Referee: Latychev (USSR)

World Cup Final Box Scores (Cont.)

ENGLAND 1966

England	1	1	2—4
W. Germany	1	1	0—2

FIRST HALF

Scoring: 1, Germany, Haller (12); 2, England, Hurst, (18).

SECOND HALF

Scoring: 3, England, Peters (78); 4, Germany, Weber (90).

OVERTIME

Scoring: 5, England, Hurst (101); 6, England, Hurst (120).

England: Banks, Cohen, Wilson, Stiles, Charlton, J., Moore, Ball, Hurst, Hunt, Charlton, R., Peters.

W. Germnay: Tilkowski, Hottges, Schmellinger, Beckenbauer, Schulz, Weber, Held, Haller, Seeler, Overath, Emmerich.

Referee: Dienst (Switzerland).

W. GERMANY 1974

W. Germany	2	0 —2
Netherlands	1	0 —1

FIRST HALF

Scoring: 1, The Netherlands, Neeskens, PK, (1) 2, W. Germany, Breitner, PK, (26); 3, W. Germany, Muller, (44).

W. Germany: Maier, Vogts, Beckenbauer, Schwarzenbeck, Breitner, Hoeness, Bonhof, Overath, Grabowski, Muller, Holzenbein

The Netherlands: Jongbloed, Suurbier, Rijsbergen (de Jong), Haan, Krol, Jansen, Neeskens, van Hanagem, Cruyff, Rensenbrink (van der Kerkhof)

Referee: Taylor (England).

ITALY 1982

Italy	0	3 —3
W. Germany	0	1 —1

SECOND HALF

Scoring: 1, Italy, Rossi (57); 2, Italy, Tardelli (68); 3, Italy, Altobelli (81); 4, Germany, Breitner (83).

Italy: Zoff, Bergomi, Scirea, Collovati, Cabrini, Oriali, Gentile, Tardelli, Conti, Rossi, Graziani (Altobelli, Causio)
W. Germany: Schumacher, Kaltz, Stielike, Foerster, K., Foerster, B., Dremmler (Hrubesch), Breitner, Briegel, Rummenigge (Mueller), Fischcer (Littbrarski)

Referee: Coelho (Brazil).

ITALY 1990

W. Germany	0	1 —1
Argentina	0	0 —0

SECOND HALF

Scoring: 1, W. Germany, Brehme, PK, (84).

W. Germany: Illgner, Brehme, Kohler, Augenthaler, Buchwald, Berthold (Reuter), Littbarski, Haessler, Mattaeus, Voeller, Klinsmann

MEXICO 1970

Brazil	1	3 —4
Italy	1	0 —1

FIRST HALF

Scoring: 1, Brazil, Pele (18); 2, Italy, Boninsegna (32).

SECOND HALF

Scoring: 3, Brazil, Gerson (65); 4, Brazil, Jairzinho (70); 5, Brazil, Alberto (86).

Brazil: Feliz, Alberto, Brito, Wilson, Piazza, Everaldo, Clodoaldo, Gerson, Jairzinho, Tostao, Pele, Rivelino.

Italy: Albertosi, Burgnich, Cera, Rosato, Facchetti, Bertini (Juliano), Mazzola, De Sisti, Domenghini, Boninsegna (Rivera), Riva.

Referee: Glockner (E. Germany)

ARGENTINA 1978

Argentina	1	0	2—3
Netherlands	0	1	0—1

FIRST HALF

Scoring: 1, Argentina, Kempes (38).

SECOND HALF

Scoring: 2, The Netherlands , Nanninga (81).

OVERTIME

Scoring: 3, Arg., Kempes (104); 4, Arg., Bertoni (114).

Argentina: Fillol, Olguin, Galvan, Passarella, Tarantini, Ardiles (Larrosa), Gallego, Kempes, Bertoni, Luque, Ortiz (Houseman)

The Netherlands: Jongbloed, Jansen (Suurbier), Krol, Brandts, Poortvliet, Neeskens, Haan, van der Kerkhoff, W., van der Kerkhoff, R., Rep (Nanninga), Rensenbrink

Referee: Gonella (Italy)

MEXICO 1986

Argentina	1	2 —3
W. Germany	0	2 —2

FIRST HALF

Scoring: 1, Argentina, Brown (22).

SECOND HALF

Scoring: 2, Arg., Valdano (55); 3, W. Germ., Rummenigge (73) 4, W. Germ., Voller (81); 5, Arg., Burruchaga (83).

Argentina: Pumpido, Brown, Cuciuffo, Ruggeri, Olarticoecha, Bastista, Giusti, Burruchaga (90, Trobbiani), Enrique, Maradona, Valdona
W. Germany: Schumacher, Jakobs, Forster, Eder, Brehme, Matthaus, Berthold, Magath (62 Hoeness), Briegel, Rummenigge, Allofs (46 Voller)Referee: Coelho (Brazil).

Referee: Filho (Brazil)

Argentina: Goychoechea, Lorenzo, Serrizuela, Sensini, Ruggeri (Monzon), Simon, Basualdo, Burruchag (Calderon), Maradona, Troglio, Dezottir, Briegel, Rummenigge (Mueller), Fischch (Littbrarski)
Referee: Coelho (Brazil).

All-Time Leaders

GOALS

Player, Nation	Tournaments	Goals Scored
Gerd Muller, West Germany	1970, 1974	14
Just Fontaine, France	1958	13
Pele, Brazil	1958, 1962, 1966, 1970	12
Sandor Kocsis, Hungary	1954	11
Teofilo Cubillas, Peru	1970, 1978	10
Gregorz Lato, Poland	1974, 1978, 1982	10
Helmut Rahn, West Germany	1954, 1958	10
Gary Lineker, England	1986, 1990	10
Ademir, Brazil	1950	9
Eusebio, Portugal	1966	9
Jairzinho, Brazil	1970, 1974	9
Paolo Rossi, Italy	1982, 1986	9
Karl-Heinz Rummenigge, W. Germany	1978, 1982, 1986	9
Uwe Seeler, West Germany	1958, 1962, 1966, 1970	9
Vava, Brazil	1958, 1962	9

LEADING SCORER, CUP BY CUP

Year	Player/Nation	Goals	Year	Player/Nation	Goals
1930	Guillermo Stabile, Argentina	8	1962	Leonel Sanchez, Chile	4
1934	Oldrich Nejedly, Czechoslovakia	5		Vava, Brazil	
1938	Leonidas da Silva, Brazil	8	1966	Eusebio Ferreira, Portugal	9
1950	Ademir de Menezes, Brazil	9	1970	Gerd Mueller, West Germany	10
1954	Sandor Kocsis, Hungary	11	1974	Gregorz Lato, Poland	7
1958	Just Fontaine, France	13	1978	Mario Kempes, Argentina	6
1962	Florian Albert, Hungary	4	1982	Paolo Rossi, Italy	6
	Valentin Ivanov, USSR		1986	Gary Lineker, England	6
	Garrincha, Brazil		1990	Salvatore Schillaci, Italy	6
	Drazan Jerkovic, Yugoslavia				

Most Goals, Individual, One Game

Goals	Player, Nation	Score	Date
4	Leonidas, Brazil	Brazil-Poland, 6-5	6-5-38
4	Ernest Willimowski, Poland	Brazil-Poland, 6-5	6-5-38
4	Gustav Wetterstrm, Sweden	Sweden-Cuba, 8-0	6-12-38
4	Juan Alberto Schiaffino, Uruguay	Uruguay-Bolivia, 8-0	7-2-50
4	Ademir, Brazil	Brazil-Sweden, 7-1	7-9-50
4	Sandor Kocsis, Hungary	Hungary-West Germany, 8-3	6-20-54
4	Just Fontaine, France	France-West Germany, 6-3	6-28-58
4	Eusebio, Portugal	Portugal-No. Korea, 5-3	7-23-66
4	Emilio Butragueño, Spain	Spain-Denmark, 5-1	6-18-86

Note: 30 players have scored 31 World Cup hat tricks. Gerd Mueller of West Germany is the only man to have two World Cup hat tricks, both in 1970. The last hat tricks were 6-23-90, Tomas Skuhravy (Czech) vs. Costa Rica and Michel (Spain) vs. So. Korea, 6-17-90.

Attendance and Goal Scoring, Year by Year

Year	Site	No. of Games	Goals	Goals/Game	Attendance	Avg Att
1930	Uruguay	18	70	3.89	434,500	24,139
1934	Italy	17	70	4.12	395,000	23,235
1938	France	18	84	4.67	483,000	26,833
1950	Brazil	22	88	4.00	1,337,000	60,773
1954	Switzerland	26	140	5.38	943,000	36,269
1958	Sweden	35	126	3.60	868,000	24,800
1962	Chile	32	89	2.78	776,000	24,250
1966	England	32	89	2.78	1,614,677	50,459
1970	Mexico	32	95	2.97	1,673,975	52,312
1974	West Germany	38	97	2.55	1,774,022	46,685
1978	Argentina	38	102	2.68	1,610,215	42,374
1982	Spain	52	146	2.80	1,856,277	35,698
1986	Mexico	52	132	2.54	2,441,731	46,956
1990	Italy	52	115	2.21	2,514,443	48,354
	Totals	412	1328	3.22		

The United States in the World Cup

URUGUAY 1930: FINAL COMPETITION

Date	Opponent	Result	Scoring
7-13-30	Belgium	3-0 W	US: McGhee 2, Patenaude
7-17-30	Paraguay	3-0 W	US: Patenaude 2, Florie
7-26-30	Argentina	1-6 L	ARG: Monti 2, Scopelli 2, Stabile 2 US: Brown.

BRAZIL 1950: FINAL COMPETITION

Date	Opponent	Result	Scoring
6-25-50	Spain	1-3 L	US: Pariani SPN: Igoa, Basora, Zarra
6-29-50	England	1-0 W	US: Gaetjens.
7-2-50	Chile	2-5 L	US: Wallace, Maca CHL: Robledo, Cremaschi 3, Prieto

ITALY 1934: FINAL COMPETITION

Date	Opponent	Result	Scoring
5-27-34	Italy	1-7 L	US: Donelli ITA: Schiavio 3, Orsi 2, Meazza, Ferrari

ITALY 1990: FINAL COMPETITION

Date	Opponent	Result	Scoring
6-10-90	Czechoslovakia	1-5 L	US: Caligiuri Czech: Skuhravy 2, Hasek, Bilek, Luhovy
6-14-90	Italy	0-1 L	Italy: Giannini
6-19-90	Austria	1-2 L	US: Murray Austria: Rodax, Ogris

International Competition

Under-20 World Championship

Year	Host	Champion	Runner-Up
1977	Tunisia	USSR	Mexico
1979	Japan	Argentina	USSR
1981	Australia	W. Germany	Qatar
1983	Mexico	Brazil	Argentina
1985	USSR	Brazil	Spain
1987	Chile	Yugoslavia	W. Germany
1989	Saudi Arabia	Portugal	Nigeria
1991	Portugal	Portugal	Brazil
1993	Australia	Brazil	Ghana

Under-17 World Championship

1985	Nigeria
1987	USSR
1989	Saudi Arabia

Under-17 (Cont.)

1991	Ghana
1993	Nigeria

Pan American Games

1951	Argentina
1955	Argentina
1959	Argentina
1963	Brazil
1967	Mexico
1971	Argentina
1975	Brazil-Mexico (tie)
1979	Brazil
1983	Uruguay
1987	Brazil
1991	United States

European Championship

Official name: the European Football Championship. Held every four years since 1960.

Year	Champion	Score	Runner-up	Year	Champion	Score	Runner-up
1960	USSR	2-1	Yugoslavia	1980	West Germany	2-1	Belgium
1964	Spain	2-1	USSR	1984	France	2-0	Spain
1968	Italy	2-0	Yugoslavia	1988	Holland	2-0	USSR
1972	West Germany	3-0	USSR	1992	Denmark	2-0	Germany
1976	Czechoslovakia*	2-2	West Germany				

*Won on penalty kicks.

South American Championship (Copa America)

Year	Champion	Host	Year	Champion	Host
1916	Uruguay	Argentina	1927	Argentina	Peru
1917	Uruguay	Uruguay	1929	Argentina	Argentina
1919	Brazil	Brazil	1935	Uruguay	Peru
1920	Uruguay	Chile	1937	Argentina	Argentina
1921	Argentina	Argentina	1939	Peru	Peru
1922	Brazil	Brazil	1941	Argentina	Chile
1923	Uruguay	Uruguay	1942	Uruguay	Uruguay
1924	Uruguay	Uruguay	1945	Argentina	Chile
1925	Argentina	Argentina	1946	Argentina	Argentina
1926	Uruguay	Chile	1947	Argentina	Ecuador

South American Championship (Copa America) *(Cont.)*

Year	Champion	Host	Year	Champion	Host
1949	Brazil	Brazil	1975	Peru	—
1953	Paraguay	Peru	1979	Paraguay	—
1955	Argentina	Chile	1983	Uruguay	—
1956	Uruguay	Uruguay	1987	Uruguay	Argentina
1957	Argentina	Peru	1989	Brazil	Brazil
1958	Argentina	Argentina	1990	Brazil	Argentina
1959	Uruguay	Ecuador	1991	Argentina	Chile
1963	Bolivia	Bolivia	1993	Argentina	Ecuador
1967	Uruguay	Uruguay			

Awards

European Footballer of the Year

Year	Player	Team	Year	Player	Team
1956	Stanley Matthews	Blackpool	1976	Franz Beckenbauer	Bayern Munich
1957	Alfredo Di Stefano	Real Madrid	1977	Allan Simonsen	Borussia Moenchengladbach
1958	Raymond Kopa	Real Madrid			
1959	Alfredo Di Stefano	Real Madrid	1978	Kevin Keegan	SV Hamburg
1960	Luis Suarez	Barcelona	1979	Kevin Keegan	SV Hamburg
1961	Omar Sivori	Juventus	1980	Karl-Heinz Rummenigge	Bayern Munich
1962	Josef Masopust	Dukla Prague			
1963	Lev Yashin	Moscow Dynamo	1981	Karl-Heinz Rummenigge	Bayern Munich
1964	Denis Law	Manchester United			
1965	Eusebio	Benfica	1982	Paolo Rossi	Juventus
1966	Bobby Charlton	Manchester United	1983	Michel Platini	Juventus
1967	Florian Albert	Ferencvaros	1984	Michel Platini	Juventus
1968	George Best	Manchester United	1985	Michel Platini	Juventus
1969	Gianni Rivera	AC Milan	1986	Igor Belanov	Dynamo Kiev
1970	Gerd Mueller	Bayern Munich	1987	Ruud Gullit	AC Milan
1971	Johan Cruyff	Ajax	1988	Marco Van Basten	AC Milan
1972	Franz Beckenbauer	Bayern Munich	1989	Marco Van Basten	AC Milan
1973	Johan Cruyff	Barcelona	1990	Lothar Matthaeus	Inter Milan
1974	Johan Cruyff	Barcelona	1991	Jean-Pierre Papin	Olympique Marseille
1975	Oleg Blokhin	Dynamo Kiev	1992	Marco Van Basten	AC Milan

South American Player of the Year

Year	Player	Team	Year	Player	Team
1971	Tostao	Cruzeiro	1982	Zico	Flamengo
1972	Teofilo Cubillas	Alianza Lima	1983	Socrates	Corinthians
1973	Pelé	Santos	1984	Enzo Francescoli	River Plate
1974	Elias Figueroa	Internacional	1985	Julio Cesar Romero	Fluminense
1975	Elias Figueroa	Internacional	1986	Antonio Alzamendi	River Plate
1976	Elias Figueroa	Internacional	1987	Carlos Valderrama	Deportivo Cali
1977	Zico	Flamengo	1988	Ruben Paz	Racing Buenos Aires
1978	Mario Kempes	Valencia	1989	Bebeto	Vasco da Gama
1979	Diego Maradona	Argentinos Juniors	1990	Raul Amarilla	Olimpia
1980	Diego Maradona	Boca Juniors	1991	Oscar Ruggeri	Velez Sarsfield
1981	Zico	Flamengo	1992	Rai	Sao Paulo

African Footballer of the Year

Year	Player	Team	Year	Player	Team
1970	Salif Keita	Mali	1982	Thomas Nkono	Cameroon
1971	Ibrahim Sunday	Ghana	1983	Mahmoud Al-Khatib	Egypt
1972	Chérif Souleyman	Guinea	1984	ThÇophile Abega	Cameroon
1973	Tshimimu Bwanga	Zaire	1985	Mohamed Timoumi	Morocco
1974	Paul Moukila	Congo	1986	Badou Zaki	Morocco
1975	Ahmed Faras	Morocco	1987	Rabah Madjer	Algeria
1976	Roger Milla	Cameroon	1988	Kalusha Bwalya	Zambia
1977	Dhiab Tarak	Tunisia	1989	George Weah	Liberia
1978	Abdul Razak	Ghana	1990	Roger Milla	Cameroon
1979	Thomas Nkono	Cameroon	1991	Abedi Pele	Ghana
1980	Jean Manga Onguene	Cameroon	1992	Abedi Pele	Ghana
1981	Lakhdar Belloumi	Algeria			

Selected by *France Football.*

Club Competition

Toyota Cup

Competition between winners of European Champion Clubs' Cup and Libertadores Cup.

1960...Real Madrid, Spain	1972...Ajax, Holland	1984...Independiente, Argentina
1961...Penarol, Uruguay	1973...Independiente, Argentina	1985...Juventus, Italy
1962...Santos, Brazil	1974...Atletico de Madrid, Spain	1986...River Plate, Argentina
1963...Santos, Brazil	1975...No tournament	1987...Porto, Portugal
1964...Inter, Italy	1976...Bayern Munich	1988...Nacional, Uruguay
1965...Inter, Italy	1977...Boca Juniors, Argentina	1989...Milan, Italy
1966...Penarol, Uruguay	1978...No tournament	1990...Milan, Italy
1967...Racing Club, Argentina	1979...Olimpia, Paraguay	1991...Red Star Belgrade,
1968...Estudiantes, Argentina	1980...Nacional, Uruguay	Yugoslavia
1969...Milan, Italy	1981...Flamengo, Brazil	1992 Sao Paulo, Brazil
1970...Feyenoord, Netherlands	1982...Penarol, Uruguay	
1971...Nacional, Uruguay	1983...Gremio, Brazil	

Note: Until 1968 a best-of-three-games format decided the winner. After that a two-game/total-goal format was used until Toyota became the sponsor in 1980, moved the game to Tokyo, and switched the format to a one game championship. The European Cup runner-up substituted for the winner in 1971, 1973, 1974, and 1979.

European Cup

1956...Real Madrid, Spain	1972...Ajax Amsterdam,	1983...SV Hamburg,
1957...Real Madrid, Spain	Netherlands	West Germany
1958...Real Madrid, Spain	1973...Ajax Amsterdam,	1984...Liverpool, England
1959...Real Madrid, Spain	Netherlands	1985...Juventus, Italy
1960...Real Madrid, Spain	1974...Bayern Munich,	1986...Steaua Bucharest,
1961...Benfica, Portugal	West Germany	Romania
1962...Benfica, Portugal	1975...Bayern Munich,	1987...Porto, Portugal
1963...A.C. Milan, Italy	West Germany	1988...P.S.V. Eindhoven,
1964...Inter-Milan, Italy	1976...Bayern Munich,	Netherlands
1965...Inter-Milan, Italy	West Germany	1989...A.C. Milan, Italy
1966...Real Madrid, Spain	1977...Liverpool, England	1990...A.C. Milan, Italy
1967...Celtic, Scotland	1978...Liverpool, England	1991...Red Star, Belgrade
1968...Manchester United,	1979...Nottingham Forest,	1992...Barcelona, Spain
England	England	1993...Olympique Marseille, France
1969...A.C. Milan, Italy	1980...Nottingham Forest,	
1970...Feyenoord, Netherlands	England	
1971...Ajax Amsterdam,	1981...Liverpool, England	
Netherlands	1982...Aston Villa, England	

On four occasions the European Cup winner has refused to play in the Intercontinental Cup (now Toyota Cup) and has been replaced by the runner-up: Panathinaikos (Greece) in 1971, Juventus (Italy) in 1973, Atletico Madrid (Spain) in 1974, and Malmo (Sweden) in 1979.

Libertadores Cup

Competition between champion clubs and runners-up of 10 South American National Associations.

1960...Penarol, Uruguay	1972...Independiente, Argentina	1984...Independiente, Argentina
1961...Penarol, Uruguay	1973...Independiente, Argentina	1985...Argentinos Juniors,
1962...Santos, Brazil	1974...Independiente, Argentina	Argentina
1963...Santos, Brazil	1975...Independiente, Argentina	1986...River Plate, Argentina
1964...Independiente, Argentina	1976...Cruzeiro, Brazil	1987...Penarol, Uruguay
1965...Independiente, Argentina	1977...Boca Juniors, Argentina	1988...Nacional, Uruguay
1966...Penarol, Uruguay	1978...Boca Juniors, Argentina	1989...Atletico Nacional,
1967...Racing Club, Argentina	1979...Olimpia, Paraguay	Colombia
1968...Estudiantes, Argentina	1980...Nacional, Uruguay	1990...Olimpia, Paraguay
1969...Estudiantes, Argentina	1981...Flamengo, Brazil	1991...Colo Colo, Chile
1970...Estudiantes, Argentina	1982...Penarol, Uruguay	1992...Sao Paulo, Brazil
1971...Nacional, Uruguay	1983...Gremio, Brazil	1993...Sao Paulo, Brazil

UEFA Cup

Competition between teams other than league champions and cup winners from the Union of European Football Associations.

1958...Barcelona, Spain
1959...No tournament
1960...Barcelona, Spain
1961...AS Roma, Italy
1962...Valencia, Spain
1963...Valencia, Spain
1964...Real Zaragoza, Spain
1965...Ferencvaros, Hungary
1966...Barcelona, Spain
1967...Dynamo Zagreb, Yugoslavia
1968...Leeds United, England
1969...Newcastle United, England
1970...Arsenal, England
1971...Leeds United, England

1972...Tottenham Hotspur, England
1973...Liverpool, England
1974...Feyenoord, Netherlands
1975...Borussia Moenchengladbach, West Germany
1976...Liverpool, England
1977...Juventus, Italy
1978...P.S.V. Eindhoven, Netherlands
1979...Borussia Moenchengladbach, West Germany
1980...Eintracht Frankfurt, West Germany
1981...Ipswich Town, England

1982...I.F.K. Gothenburg, Sweden
1983...Anderlecht, Belgium
1984...Tottenham Hotspur, England
1985...Real Madrid, Spain
1986...Real Madrid, Spain
1987...I.F.K. Gothenburg, Sweden
1988...Bayer Leverkusen, West Germany
1989...Naples, Italy
1990...Juventus, Italy
1991...Inter-Milan, Italy
1992...Torino, Italy
1993...Juventus, Italy

European Cup-Winners' Cup

Competition between cup winners of countries belonging to UEFA.

1961...A.C. Fiorentina, Italy
1962...Atletico Madrid, Spain
1963...Tottenham Hotspur, England
1964...Sporting Lisbon, Portugal
1965...West Ham United, England
1966...Borussia Dortmund, West Germany
1967...Bayern Munich, West Germany
1968...A.C. Milan, Italy
1969...Slovan Bratislava, Czechoslovakia
1970...Manchester City, England

1971...Chelsea, England
1972...Glasgow Rangers, Scotland
1973...A.C. Milan, Italy
1974...Magdeburg, East Germany
1975...Dynamo Kiev, USSR
1976...Anderlecht, Belgium
1977...S.V. Hamburg, West Germany
1978...Anderlecht, Belgium
1979...Barcelona, Spain
1980...Valencia, Spain
1981...Dynamo Tbilisi, USSR
1982...Barcelona, Spain

1983...Aberdeen, Scotland
1984...Juventus, Italy
1985...Everton, England
1986...Dynamo Kiev, USSR
1987...Ajax Amsterdam, Netherlands
1988...Mechelen, Belgium
1989...Barcelona, Spain
1990...Sampdoria, Italy
1991...Manchester United, England
1992...Werder Bremen, Germany
1993...Parma, Italy

Major Soccer League

Results

Called the Major Indoor Soccer League from 1979-90.

	Champion	Series	Runner-Up	Championship Series Most Valuable Player
1979	NY Arrows	2-0	Philadelphia	Shep Messing, NY
1980	NY Arrows	7-4	Houston	Steve Zungul, NY
1981	NY Arrows	6-5	St Louis	Steve Zungul, NY
1982	NY Arrows	3-2	St Louis	Steve Zungul, NY
1983	San Diego	3-2	Baltimore	Juli Veee, SD
1984	Baltimore	4-1	St Louis	Scott Manning, Balt
1985	San Diego	4-1	Baltimore	Steve Zungul, SD
1986	San Diego	4-3	Minnesota	Brian Quinn, SD
1987	Dallas	4-3	Tacoma	Tatu, Dall
1988	San Diego	4-0	Cleveland	Hugo Perez, SD
1989	San Diego	4-3	Baltimore	Victor Nogueira, SD
1990	San Diego	4-2	Baltimore	Brian Quinn, SD
1991	San Diego	4-2	Cleveland	Ben Collins, SD
1992	San Diego	4-2	Dallas	Thomas Usiyan, SD

Championship format: 1979, best-of-three-games series; 1980-81, one-game championship; 1982-83, best-of-five-games series; 1984 to present, best-of-seven-games series.

Statistical Leaders

SCORING

Year	Player/Team	Points
1978-79	Fred Grgurev, Phil	74
1979-80	Steve Zungul, NY	136
1980-81	Steve Zungul, NY	152
1981-82	Steve Zungul, NY	163
1982-83	Steve Zungul, NY	122
1983-84	Stan Stamenkovic, Balt	97
1984-85	Steve Zungul, SD	136
1985-86	Steve Zungul, Tac	115
1986-87	Tatu, Dall	111
1987-88	Erik Rasmussen, Wich	112
1988-89	Preci, Tac	104
1989-90	Tatu, Dall	113
1990-91	Tatu, Dall	144
1991-92	Zoran Karic, Clev	102

GOALS

Year	Player/Team	Goals
1978-79	Fred Grgurev, Phil	46
1979-80	Steve Zungul, NY	90
1980-81	Steve Zungul, NY	108
1981-82	Steve Zungul, NY/GB	103
1982-83	Steve Zungul, NY/GB	75
1983-84	Mark Liveric, NY	58
1984-85	Steve Zungul, SD	68
1985-86	Erik Rasmussen, Wich	67
1986-87	Tatu, Dall	73
1987-88	Hector Marinaro, Minn	58
1988-89	Preki, Tac	51
1989-90	Tatu, Dall	64
1990-91	Tatu, Dall	78
1991-92	Hector Marinaro, Clev	53

ASSISTS

Year	Player/Team	Assists
1978-79	Fred Grgurev, Phil	28
1979-80	Steve Zungul, NY	46
1980-81	Jorgen Kristensen, Wich	52
1981-82	Steve Zungul, NY	60
1982-83	Stan Stamenkovic, Mem	65
1983-84	Stan Stamenkovic, Balt	63
1984-85	Steve Zungul, SD	68
1985-86	Steve Zungul, Tac	60
1986-87	Kai Haaskivi, Clev	55
1987-88	Preki, Tac	58
1988-89	Preki, Tac	53
1989-90	Jan Goossens, KC	55
1990-91	Tatu, Dall	66
1991-92	Zoran Karic, Clev	63

TOP GOALKEEPERS

Year	Player/Team	Goals Agst Avg
1978-79	Paul Hammond, Hous	4.16
1979-80	Sepp Gantenhammer, Hous	4.42
1980-81	Enzo DiPede, Chi	4.06
1981-82	Slobo Liljevski, StL	3.85*
1982-83	Zoltan Toth, NY	4.01
1983-84	Slobo Liljevski, StL	3.67
1984-85	Scott Manning, Balt	3.89
1985-86	Keith Van Eron, Balt	3.66
1986-87	Tino Lettieri, Minn	3.38
1987-88	Zoltan Toth, SD	2.94
1988-89	Victor Nogueira, SD	2.86
1989-90	Joe Papaleo, Dall	3.34
1990-91	Victor Nogueira, SD	4.37
1991-92	Victor Nogueira, SD	4.60

North American Soccer League

Formed in 1968 by the merger of the National Professional Soccer League and the USA League, both of which had begun operations a year earlier. The NPSL's lone champion was the Oakland Clippers. The USA, which brought entire teams in from Europe, was won in 1967 by the LA Wolves, who were the English League's Wolverhampton Wanderers.

Year	Champion	Score	Runner-Up	Regular Season MVP
1968	Atlanta	0-0,3-0	San Diego	John Kowalik, Chi
1969	Kansas City	No game	Atlanta	Cirilio Fernandez, KC
1970	Rochester	3-0,1-3	Washington	Carlos Metidieri, Roch
1971	Dallas	1-2, 4-1, 2-0	Atlanta	Carlos Metidieri, Roch
1972	NY	2-1	St Louis	Randy Horton, NY
1973	Philadelphia	2-0	Dallas	Warren Archibald, Mia
1974	Los Angeles	4-3*	Miami	Peter Silvester, Balt
1975	Tampa Bay	2-0	Portland	Steve David, Miami
1976	Toronto	3-0	Minnesota	Pelé, NY
1977	NY	2-1	Seattle	Franz Beckenbauer, NY
1978	NY	3-1	Tampa Bay	Mike Flanagan, NE
1979	Vancouver	2-1	Tampa Bay	Johan Cruyff, LA
1980	NY	3-0	Ft Lauderdale	Roger Davies, Sea
1981	Chicago	1-0*	NY	Giorgio Chinaglia, NY
1982	NY	1-0	Seattle	Peter Ward, Sea
1983	Tulsa	2-0	Toronto	Roberto Cabanas, NY
1984	Chicago	2-1, 3-2	Toronto	Steve Zungul, SJ

*Shootout.

Championship Format: 1968 & 1970: Two games/total goals. 1971 & 1984: Best-of-three game series. 1972-1983: One game championship. Title in 1969 went to the regular season champion.

North American Soccer League *(Cont.)*

Statistical Leaders

SCORING

Year	Player/Team	Pts	Year	Player/Team	Pts
1968	John Kowalik, Chi	69	1977	Steven David, LA	58
1969	Kaiser Motaung, Atl	36	1978	Giorgio Chinaglia, NY	79
1970	Kirk Apostolidis, Dall	35	1979	Oscar Fabbiani, Tampa Bay	58
1971	Carlos Metidieri, Roch	46	1980	Giorgio Chinaglia, NY	77
1972	Randy Horton, NY	22	1981	Giorgio Chinaglia, NY	74
1973	Kyle Rote, Dall	30	1982	Giorgio Chinaglia, NY	55
1974	Paul Child, San Jose	36	1983	Roberto Cabanas, NY	66
1975	Steven David, Miami	52	1984	Slavisa Zungul, Golden Bay	50
1976	Giorgio Chinaglia, NY	49			

American Professional Soccer League

Year	Champion	Score	Runner-Up	Regular Season MVP
1991	San Francisco	1-3,2-0 (1-0 on penalty kicks)	Albany	Jean Harbor, MD
1992	Colorado	1-0	Tampa Bay	Taifour Diane, CO
1993	Colorado	3-1(OT)	Los Angeles	Taifour Diane, CO

Outfoxing the French

In 1991, at age 18, Taifour Diane was already a soccer supertstar in his native Guinea. With hopes of playing in the French First Division like many of his french-speaking countrymen, Diane applied for a visa to France. His request was denied. One year later, he left Guinea to visit his brother and uncle who were attending school in New York City. He began playing with a Jamican club on weekends in Brooklyn. One club member had played on the Jamaican national team with Colorado Foxes assistant coach Lorne Donaldson. The Foxes were opening camp, and the teammate suggested to Donaldson that he have a look at Diane. Through this circuitous route Diane arrived on the U.S. soccer scene and ended up taking the APSL by storm. He was league MVP and Rookie of the Year in 1992, and MVP in '93 as well, with 10 goals and five assists in 24 games. In the '93 title game he set up one goal and scored the game-winner in overtime to lead the Foxes to their second straight championship, a 3–1 victory over Los Angeles. Look for him to be earning handsome sums competing in Europe before too long.

NCAA Sports

Bully Bears

Jim Montgomery leads Maine to the NCAA title

JOHN BIEVER

Child's Play

A trio of talented underclassmen led the way to NCAA titles in soccer, hockey and baseball | by **HANK HERSCH**

I F THE 1992–93 NCAA CHAMPIONSHIPS proved one thing, it was that youth isn't always wasted on the young. In recent years, as more college athletes have opted to turn professional before their senior seasons, the opportunities for underclassmen to step forward have become greater as well. And so three of them did. In December sophomore midfielder Claudio Reyna guided Virginia to its second consecutive soccer championship. In April freshman Paul Kariya spearheaded Maine's first-ever NCAA title in hockey. And in June, Brett Laxton, a fireballing freshman, hurled Louisiana State to its second baseball championship in three years.

SOCCER

Reyna has the look of a young man just awakened from a fitful sleep. He has a tousled crop of black hair, droopy brown eyes and dark stubble dotting his jawline. By all appearances Reyna would not know how to hurry if he wanted to, which, on the soccer field, he seldom does. Or at least he didn't on Dec. 6 in Davidson, N.C., where Reyna dictated the tempo and the outcome of the NCAA title game, a 2–0 throttling of the University of San Diego that gave top-ranked Virginia a place among the elite in

college soccer history. "The other thing I'm proud of is we played with some style, some elegance," said Cavalier coach Bruce Arena.

Those traits clearly belonged to Reyna, a 19-year-old from Springfield, N.J. He is 5'10" and 160 pounds of thigh and calf, and in Davidson he sported a diamond stud in his right earlobe, a silver loop in his left. Settling the ball and then stroking it forward with a variety of precision passes, Reyna kept Virginia's opponents off-balance all season while serving as the hub of their ball-possession attack. Essentially Arena gave him the freedom to run the game as he saw fit. "Claudio has a 38-year-old's brain in a 19-year-old's body," said Jack Writer, who coached Cornell from 1976 to '88.

But for someone so gifted at sizing up situations, Reyna found himself at sea in Spain last July. After his first Olympic appearance, Reyna, the youngest member of the U.S. team, was approached by a well-dressed gent who introduced himself as Josep Nuñez, the president of FC Barcelona, the European club champion. Nunez had a proposition for Reyna: a four-year contract worth $35,000 to $100,000 annually and a $50,000 signing bonus.

There was more: Upon signing, Reyna would be whisked off by limo and then flown to Holland, where he would train with the team's top 22 players under the legendary Johan Cruyff.

As word of the offer spread, Spaniards hailed Reyna on the street and cheered his every touch on the field. Meanwhile, he weighed the conflicting counsel of his parents and his teammates, wavering and wondering: Was he ready? "One day I wanted to do it, the next day I was coming back to school," Reyna said. "But in the end I just didn't want to regret the decision, and I knew that coming back wasn't a decision I'd regret."

Any bit of uncertainty for Reyna evaporated at the Final Four, where a cozy hamlet of 3,254 finally provided the big-time flavor the event had long needed. As first-time host, wee Davidson College (enrollment 1,500) spent more than $150,000 to outfit Richardson Field with a new scoreboard, lights and auxiliary stands and to expand the press box. That Davidson was one of the semifinalists helped heighten interest, though the Wildcats lost their semi 3–2 to San Diego while Virginia was drubbing Duke 3–0. Still, sellouts both days set an attendance record of 16,300, and $15 tickets were being scalped for—rumor had it—$300. Said Davidson coach Charlie Slagle, "This is what college soccer should be like."

The past two finals had been what college soccer should *not* be like: conservative affairs ending up in scoreless ties and decided on penalty kicks. The Toreros provided ample firepower, with 6' 5" forward Chugger Adair and leftwinger Guillermo Jara. Arena had even promised that if no goals were scored, he would jump in frigid Lake Norman. His risk of hypothermia was finally averted in the 70th minute, when reserve forward Nate Friends floated in his own rebound off a sliding save by San Diego goalkeeper Scott Garlick, thereby ending a scoreless drought of 435 minutes in the last four finals. Eight minutes later defender Erik Imler headed in a cross to seal Virginia's victory.

While Reyna did not score a goal himself—he assisted on the Cavaliers' second—he directed a multi-directional attack that outshot the Toreros 17–5 and was named the tournament's MVP. Having earned a co-championship with Santa Clara in 1989 to go along with their back-to-back outright titles, the Cavaliers (21-2-1) joined the dynastic reigns of St. Louis (the 1960s and early '70s), San Francisco (late '70s) and Indiana (early '80s). But in the early '90s, the Cavs bestride an era of more—and more competitive—teams. "In this game, you're only as good as your competition allows you to be," said San Diego coach Seamus McFadden, "and they were the better team today. That's the bottom line."

Not long after turning down FC Barcelona, Reyna turned up the heat on the Toreros.

MANNY MILLAN

HOCKEY

On April 3, with 20 minutes remaining in the championship game at the Bradley Center in Milwaukee, Maine trailed Lake Superior State 4–2, and a season of amazing grace seemed poised to end on a sour note. No matter that the Black Bears came into the game with a 41-1-2 record, their sole loss coming to Boston University in overtime, 7–6. No matter that for the 138th straight time they had sold out Alford Arena in remote Orono with 5,200 Mainiacs sporting lobster hats. No matter that coach Shawn Walsh's depth made Maine the envy of the nation. Said Lake State coach Jeff Jackson before the final, "It's got to go down as one of the greatest teams in hockey history."

No matter, too, that left wing Paul Kariya, an 18-year-old freshman from North Vancouver, B.C., had set an NCAA record for scoring average with 2.6 points per game, a feat that earned him college hockey's Heisman, the Hobey Baker Award. In scoring 25 goals and setting up 75, he was nothing short of dominant. With senior center Jim Montgomery (95 points) and 5'4" right wing Cal Ingraham (a nation-leading 46 goals), Kariya had helped to establish the most potent line in the country. "When those guys come at you at 100 miles an hour," Jackson said, "there's not a lot you can do."

Entering the final period against Lake State, Kariya knew it was time to get up to speed; assistant coach Red Gendron told him so. "If you keep your feet moving along the boards," he said, "then you'll beat your guy." With slightly more than four minutes gone, Kariya, feet moving, swiped the puck from defenseman Keith Aldridge along the boards behind the Laker net. In a flash he pirouetted around Aldridge to free himself and from the right circle slipped the puck across the goalmouth to Montgomery, who batted it past goalie Blaine Lacher. The score was 4–3, and suddenly a dream ending to

JOHN BIEVER

Kariya, Maine's sensational frosh, left a trail of bewildered defensemen in his wake.

Maine's dream season seemed possible again.

At 7:40 Montgomery struck again, scoring the 300th point of his career with a rebound shot. Kariya had instigated the all-out assault on the Lakers' goal, but he had help from his own net. After the second period Walsh had replaced starter Mike Dunham with Garth Snow, a gifted puck-handler and passer, who helped counter Lake State's dump-and-chase strategy while creating transition opportunities for the Black Bears. "He's the best offensive goalie in hockey," Walsh said. Snow's also cool: About an hour before the game he had a hot dog and soda and was buying

souvenir T-shirts and caps around the arena.

In the end, with 8:54 gone, it would be Montgomery, the son of a Canadian Olympic boxer, who delivered the knockout blow. He combined, naturally, with Kariya, who carried the puck in from the blue line to the left corner and then fed it gently to Montgomery in the slot for a tap-in at the right post. Maine led 5–4. Lake State, the defending champ, took its best shot with a minute left, but freshman winger Sean Tallaire hit the crossbar. "I heard a ping," said Snow, who was sprawled out on the ice at the time. "Sometimes pings are good, and sometimes pings aren't good. The puck can bounce in as well as out."

This time, it bounced out. By winning, Maine thwarted Lake State's bid to be the first repeat titlist since Boston University 21 years ago. Victory just seemed Kariya's due. He had been announced as the Baker award winner on April 2, to a deafening roar from 250 Maine fans who had gathered in the Hyatt Regency ballroom. One day later he proved himself a most deserving choice. "When you think about [the award] you think about the myth of the individual and the legend he created," Montgomery said. "And when you look at Paul, you see a legend out there."

BASEBALL

Entering the College World Series championship game, LSU was on not so much a roll as a rollercoaster. In their three previous games the Tigers had come back from a 7–2 deficit to defeat Texas A&M 13–8, blown an 8–6 lead in the eighth inning to lose to Long Beach State 10–8 and then

Laxton went the distance in the Series finale, stunning the Shockers with his fastball.

avenged their loss to the 49ers by rallying for three runs in the bottom of the ninth and a 6–5 victory. So when righthander Brett Laxton took the mound to start the title game against Wichita State on June 13 at Rosenblatt Stadium in Omaha, he figured every pitch would be especially precious. "Those comebacks were in the back of my mind," he said. "As we've all seen, anything can happen."

For Laxton some very special things did. He became the first pitcher to go the distance in a World Series finale in 32 years. He surrendered only three singles against a powerhouse club that had racked up 21 runs in its last three games. He whiffed 16 Shockers to set a championship game record. In sum, to conclude a tournament that saw 10 come-from-behind victories in 13 games, Laxton turned the climax into an anticlimax, an 8–0 trouncing by the Tigers. "Brett's performance was one of the greatest I've ever seen here," said LSU coach Skip Bertman. And, he added, with a shake of his head to popular opinion, "It *was* exciting."

Laxton might well have been in the minor league system of the Padres rather than finishing his freshman season 12–1 with a 1.98 ERA. A two-time all-state pitcher at Audubon (N.J.) High, he was San Diego's fourth-round pick in the '92 amateur draft, but he turned down a signing bonus of $150,000 to play at Baton Rouge. His father, Bill, had spent parts of five seasons in the big leagues with five different teams during the 1970s, going 3–10 in 121 games. "He got drafted right out of high school, and he signed," Brett said. "He played for 14 years, and he didn't have anything to fall back on…. He's never pushed me into this game. He's let me follow my own path."

In the last eight championship games, the eventual winner has been the first to score. For LSU, All-America second baseman Todd Walker supplied the necessary offensive punch. With a .395 average, 22 homers and 102 RBIs, Walker nearly won the Southeastern Conference triple crown, but he struggled early in the CWS, going 1 for 11. Then he finished strong, going 6 for 9, and started the Tigers with a bang against Wichita State, launching a two-run shot in the first and singling home another run in the second. By the end of three, Laxton had been staked to a 7–0 lead.

By the end of the game, two sights were recurring with amazing regularity: LSU catcher Adrian Antonini flashing his right index finger and Wichita State batters taking their lumber back to the bench. There was a correlation. Laxton relied essentially on his 90-mph fastball that dips and darts and proved sufficiently elusive to fan every Shocker in the lineup. "It's been a long time since anybody's beat us like that with one pitch, and that is basically what he had," Wichita State coach Gene Stephenson said. "He threw some curveballs, but we were looking fastball the entire game. We got a truckload of them and couldn't do anything with them."

Bertman acknowledged that the '93 champs, who set a school record with 125 errors in 71 games, were not as talented as his '91 team. "But there is no question these kids have great heart," he said. "They are tremendous competitors." And in Laxton, they had a 16-K gem.

NCAA Team Champions

Fall 1992

Cross-Country

MEN

	Champion	Runner-Up
Division I:	Arkansas	Wisconsin
Division II:	Adams St	Western St
Division III:	North Central	Rochester

WOMEN

	Champion	Runner-Up
Division I:	Villanova	Arkansas
Division II:	Adams St	Western St
Division III:	Cortland St	Calvin

Field Hockey

WOMEN

	Champion	Runner-Up
Division I:	Old Dominion	Iowa
Division II	Lock Haven	Bloomsburg
Division III:	William Smith	Trenton St

Football

MEN

	Champion	Runner-Up
Division I-A:	Alabama	
Division I-AA:	Marshall	Youngstown St
Division II:	Jacksonville St	Pittsburg St
Division III:	WI-LaCrosse	Washington and Jefferson

Soccer

MEN

	Champion	Runner-Up
Division I:	Virginia	University of San Diego
Division II:	Southern Connecticut St	Tampa
Division III:	Kean	Ohio Wesleyan

WOMEN

	Champion	Runner-Up
Division I:	N Carolina	Duke
Division II:	Barry	Adelphi
Division III:	Cortland St	Mass-Dartmouth

Volleyball

WOMEN

	Champion	Runner-Up
Division I:	Stanford	UCLA
Division II:	Portland St	Northern Michigan
Division III:	Washington (MO)	UC-San Diego

Water Polo

MEN

Champion	Runner-Up
California	Stanford

Winter 1992-1993

Basketball

MEN

	Champion	Runner-Up
Division I:	N Carolina	Michigan
Division II:	Cal St-Bakersfield	Troy St (AL)
Division III:	Ohio Northern	Augustana

WOMEN

	Champion	Runner-Up
Division I:	Texas Tech	Ohio State
Division II:	N Dakota St	Delta St
Division III:	Central (IA)	Capital (OH)

Fencing

Champion	Runner-Up
Columbia/Columbia-Barnard	Penn St

Gymnastics

MEN

Champion	Runner-Up
Stanford	Nebraska

WOMEN

Georgia	Alabama

Ice Hockey

MEN

	Champion	Runner-Up
Division I:	Maine	Lake Superior St
Division II:	Bemidji St	Mercyhurst
Division III:	WI-Stevens Point	WI-River Falls

Rifle

Champion	Runner-Up
West Virginia	AK-Fairbanks

Skiing

Champion	Runner-Up
Utah	Vermont

Swimming and Diving

MEN

	Champion	Runner-Up
Division I:	Stanford	Michigan
Division II:	Cal St-Bakersfield	Oakland
Division III:	Kenyon	UC-San Diego

WOMEN

	Champion	Runner-Up
Division I:	Stanford	Florida
Division II:	Oakland	Clarion
Division III:	Kenyon	UC-San Diego

Wrestling

MEN

	Champion	Runner-Up
Division I:	Iowa	Penn State
Division II:	Central Oklahoma	Nebraska-Omaha
Division III:	Augsburg	Wartburg

Winter 1992-1993 (Cont.)

Indoor Track

MEN

	Champion	Runner-Up
Division I:	Arkansas	Clemson
Division II:	Abilene Christian	St Augustine's
Division III:	WI-La Crosse	Lincoln (PA)

WOMEN

Division I:	Louisiana St	Wisconsin
Division II:	Abilene Christian	Norfolk St
Division III:	Lincoln (PA)	WI-La Crosse

Spring 1993

Baseball

MEN

	Champion	Runner-Up
Division I:	Louisiana St	Wichita State
Division II:	Tampa	Cal Poly-San Luis Obispo
Division III:	Montclair St	WI-Oshkosh

Golf

MEN

	Champion	Runner-Up
Division I:	Florida	Georgia Tech
Division II:	Abilene Christian	Columbus
Division III:	UC-San Diego	Ohio Wesleyan

WOMEN

	Arizona St	Texas

Lacrosse

MEN

	Champion	Runner-Up
Division I:	Syracuse	N Carolina
Division III:	Hobart	Ohio Wesleyan

WOMEN

Division I:	Virginia	Princeton
Division III:	Trenton St	William Smith

Softball

WOMEN

	Champion	Runner-Up
Division I:	Arizona	UCLA
Division II:	Florida Southern	Augustana (SD)
Division III:	Central (IA)	Trenton St

Tennis

MEN

	Champion	Runner-Up
Division I:	Southern Cal	Georgia
Division II:	Lander (SC)	Hampton
Division III:	Kalamazoo	UC-Santa Cruz

WOMEN

Division I:	Texas	Stanford
Division II:	UC-Davis	Cal Poly-San Luis Obispo
Division III:	Kenyon	Gustavus Adolphus

Spring 1993 (Cont.)

Outdoor Track

MEN

	Champion	Runner-Up
Division I:	Arkansas	Louisiana St & Ohio St
Division II:	St Augustine's	Abilene Christian
Division III:	WI-La Crosse	Lincoln (PA)

WOMEN

	Champion	Runner-Up
Division I:	Louisiana St	Wisconsin
Division II:	Alabama A&M	Abilene Christian
Division III:	Lincoln (PA)	WI-La Crosse

Volleyball

MEN

Champion	Runner-Up
UCLA	Cal St-Northridge

NCAA Division I Individual Champions

Fall 1992

Cross-Country

MEN

Champion	Runner-Up
Bob Kennedy, Indiana	Gary Stolz, Stanford

WOMEN

Champion	Runner-Up
Carole Zajac, Villanova	Deena Drossin, Arkansas

Winter 1992-1993

Fencing

MEN

	Champion	Runner-Up
Sabre	Thomas Strzalkowski, Penn St	George Kalmar, Pennsylvania
Foil	Nick Bravin, Stanford	Andy Gearhart, Penn St
Épée	Ben Atkins, Columbia	Christopher Klaus, Princeton

WOMEN

	Champion	Runner-Up
Foil	Olga Kalinovskaya, Penn St	Olga Chernyak, Penn St

Gymnastics

MEN

	Champion	Runner-Up
All-around	John Roethlisberger, Minn	Chainey Umphrey, UCLA
Vault	Steve Wiegel, New Mexico	Brad Hayashi, UCLA
		Chad Babcock, W Michigan
Parallel bars	Jair Lynch, Stanford	Josh Saegert, Nebraska
Horizontal bar	Steve McCain, UCLA	Che Bowers, Nebraska
Floor exercise	Richard Grace, Nebraska	Daniel Stover, Oklahoma
		Tim Hess, Air Force
Pommel horse	John Roethlisberger, Minn	Jing-Wei Liang, Stanford
Rings	Chris LaMorte, New Mexico	Brian Kobylinski, Illinois

Gymnastics (Cont.)

WOMEN

	Champion	Runner-Up
All-around	Jenny Hansen, Kentucky	Dee Foster, Alabama
Balance beam	Dana Dobransky, Alabama	Jenny Hansen, Kentucky
		Hope Spivey-Sheeley, Georgia
Uneven bars	Agina Simpkins, Georgia	Jenny Hansen, Kentucky
	Beth Wymer, Michigan	Lori Strong, Georgia
Floor exercise	Heather Stepp, Georgia	Aimee Trepanier, Utah
	Tammy Marshall, U Mass	Dee Foster, Alabama
	Amy Durham, Oregon St	Hope Spivey-Sheeley, Georgia
Vault	Heather Stepp, Georgia	Jenny Hansen, Kentucky

Skiing

MEN

	Champion	Runner-Up
Slalom	Mark Bonnell, Utah	Atle Hovi, Denver
Giant slalom	Sean Ramaden, Colorado	Per Johansson, Utah
Freestyle cross country	Peter Vordenberg, N. Mich	Marcus Nash, Utah
Diagonal cross country	Luke Bodensteiner, Utah	Jeff Heusevelt, AK-Anchorage

WOMEN

	Champion	Runner-Up
Slalom	Gibson LaFountaine, Vermont	Andreja Rojs, Colorado
Giant slalom	Karianne Ericksen, Utah	Sally Knight, Vermont
Freestyle cross country	Ivana Radlova, N Mexico	Anette Skjolden, Colorado
Diagonal cross country	Anette Skjolden, Colorado	Kristin Vestgren, Utah

Wrestling

	Champion	Runner-Up
118 lb	Sam Henson, Clemson	Chad Zaputil, Iowa
126 lb	Tony Purler, Nebraska	Shawn Charles, Arizona St
134 lb	T.J. Jaworsky, N Carolina	Cary Kolat, Penn St
142 lb	Lincoln McIlravy, Iowa	Gerry Abas, Fresno St
150 lb	Terry Steiner, Iowa	Troy Sunderland, Penn St
158 lb	Markus Mollica, Arizona St	Josh Robbins, Penn St
167 lb	Ray Miller, Arizona St	Shaon Fry, Missouri
177 lb	Kevin Randleman, Ohio St	Corey Olson, Nebraska
190 lb	Rex Holman, Ohio St	Joel Sharratt, Iowa
Heavyweight	Sylvester Terkay, NC State	Don Whipp, Michigan St

Swimming

MEN

	Champion	Time	Runner-Up	Time
50-yard freestyle	David Fox, N Carolina St	19.14*	Brian Kurza, UCLA	19.35
100-yard freestyle	Gustavo Borges, Michigan	42.91	David Fox, N Carolina St	43.07
200-yard freestyle	Josh Davis, Texas	1:34.25	Joe Hudepohl, Stanford	1:34.31
500-yard freestyle	Marcel Wouda, Michigan	4:15.55	Matt Hooper, Texas	4:15.95
1650-yard freestyle	Marcel Wouda, Michigan	14:46.16	Matt Hooper, Texas	14:47.80
100-yard backstroke	Derek Weatherford, Stanford	47.10	Tripp Schwenk, Tennessee	47.34
200-yard backstroke	Tripp Schwenk, Tennessee	1:42.06	Derek Weatherford, Stanford	1:42.21
100-yard breaststroke	Tyler Mayfield, Stanford	53.07	Eric Wunderlich, Michigan	53.63
200-yard breaststroke	Eric Wunderlich, Michigan	1:55.55	Tyler Mayfield, Stanford	1:56.87
100-yard butterfly	Seth Pepper, Arizona	46.51	Trip Zedlitz, Stanford	47.72
200-yard butterfly	Ray Carey, Stanford	1:44.01	Brian Gunn, Michigan	1:44.85
200-yard IM	Greg Burgess, Florida	1:43.52*	Trip Zedlitz, Stanford	1:45.50
400-yard IM	Greg Burgess, Florida	3:41.54*	Marcel Wouda, Michigan	3:44.32

	Champion	Pts	Runner-Up	Pts
1-meter diving†	Dean Panaro, Miami (FL)	590.05	Yoshihiro Sakata, Ohio St	561.35
3-meter diving†	Dean Panaro, Miami (FL)	647.95	Pat Bogart, Minnesota	594.45
Platform†	Pat Bogart, Minnesota	752.65	Dean Panaro, Miami (FL)	730.10

*Meet Record.

†Scoring based on 22 dives

Swimming (Cont.)

WOMEN

	Champion	Time	Runner-Up	Time
50-yard freestyle	Jenny Thompson, Stanford	22.16	Amy Van Dyken, Arizona	22.60
100-yard freestyle	Jenny Thompson, Stanford	48.03	Nicole Haislett, Florida	48.29
200-yard freestyle	Nicole Haislett, Florida	1:43.98	Jenny Thompson, Stanford	1:44.13
500-yard freestyle	Lisa Jacob, Stanford	4:45.79	Sandra Cam, SMU	4:46.14
1650-yard freestyle	Mimosa McNerney, Florida	16:14.28	Tobie Smith, Texas	16:15.22
100-yard backstroke	Lea Loveless, Stanford	52.98	Janie Wagstaff, Texas	54.12
200-yard backstroke	Lea Loveless, Stanford	1:53.67	Whitney Hedgepeth, Texas	1:55.89
100-yard breaststroke	Lara Hooiveld, Michigan	1:00.47*	Beata Kaszuba, Arizona St	1:01.44
200-yard breaststroke	Lara Hooiveld, Michigan	2:12.71	Lydia Morrow, Texas	2:12.74
100-yard butterfly	Janel Jorgensen, Stanford	53.19	Kristie Krueger, Auburn	53.43
200-yard butterfly	Janel Jorgensen, Stanford	1:57.43	Janie Wagstaff, Florida	1:57.57
200-yard IM	Nicole Haislett, Florida	1:57.15	Janel Jorgenson, Stanford	1:57.69
400-yard IM	Mindy Gehrs, Michigan	4:11.39	Kendra Thayer, Stanford	4:15.68

	Champion	Pts	Runner-Up	Pts
1-meter diving#	Marina Smith, Auburn	433.60	Vanessa Thelin, BYU	430.35
3-meter diving†	Eileen Richetelli, Stanford	528.75	Robin Carter, Texas	518.25
Platform†	Eileen Richetelli, Stanford	530.95	Cinnamon Woods, Michigan	523.20

*Meet Record
#Scoring based on 20 dives
†Scoring based on 22 dives

Indoor Track

MEN

	Champion	Mark	Runner-Up	Mark
55-meter dash	Michael Green, Clemson	6.15	Marlon Thomas, Auburn	6.26
55-meter hurdles	Glenn Terry, Indiana	7.13	Allen Johnson, N Carolina	7.22
200-meter dash	Chris Nelloms, Ohio St	20.93	Andrew Tynes, UTEP	21.07
400-meter dash	Wesley Russell, Clemson	45.92	Calvin Davis, Arkansas	46.16
800-meter run	Marko Koers, Illinois	1:48.39	Jose Parrilla, Tennessee	1:49.75
Mile run	Niall Bruton, Arkansas	4:00.05	Andy Keith, Providence	4:00.27
3000-meter run	David Morris, Montana	8:04.17	Ray Appenheimer, Colgate	8:04.76
5000-meter run	Jonah Koech, Iowa St	13:47.18	Frank Hanley, Arkansas	13:48.08
High jump	Percell Gaskins, Kansas St	7 ft 5¼ in	Chris Murrell, Minnesota	7 ft 4¼ in
Long jump	Erick Walder, Arkansas	27 ft 4 in	Roland McGhee, M Tenn St	26 ft 11 in
Triple jump	Erick Walder, Arkansas	55 ft 3¾ in	Tyrell Taitt, N Carolina St	54 ft 6½ in
Shot put	Kevin Coleman, Nebraska	63 ft 9 in	Courtney Ireland, SMU	63 ft 2¾ in
Pole vault	Martin Eriksson, Minnesota	18 ft ½ in	Lawrence Johnson, Tenn	18 ft ½ in
35-pound wt throw	Marko Wahlman, UTEP	71 ft 8 in	Ron Willis, S Carolina	71 ft 5¼ in

WOMEN

	Champion	Mark	Runner-Up	Mark
55-meter dash	Holli Hyche, Indiana St	6.76	Cheryl Taplin, LSU	6.78
55-meter hurdles	Monifa Taylor, Florida	7.53	Tonja Buford, Illinois	7.60
200-meter dash	Holli Hyche, Indiana St	22.98	Juliet Campbell, Auburn	23.11
400-meter dash	Shanelle Porter, Nebraska	52.82	Crystal Irving, UNLV	52.84
800-meter run	Amy Wickus, Wisconsin	2:04.80	Vicky Lynch, Alabama	2:05.65
Mile run	Clare Eichner, Wisconsin	4:38.64	Cheri Goddard, Villanova	4:40.01
3000-meter run	Clare Eichner, Wisconsin	9:09.66	Kay Gooch, Oklahoma	9:12.53
5000-meter run	Tracy Dahl Morris, Iowa	15:49.52	Deena Drossin, Arkansas	15:52.80
High jump	J.C. Broughton, Arizona	6 ft 3½ in*	Gwen Wentland, Kansas St	6 ft 2¼ in
Long jump	Daphnie Saunders, LSU	21 ft 2¾ in	Shana Williams, Seton Hall	21 ft
Triple jump	Telisa Young, Texas	43 ft 3¼ in	Leah Kirklin, Florida	42 ft 9 in
Shot put	Danyel Mitchell, LSU	55 ft 5¾ in	Eileen Vanisi, Texas	55 ft 3½ in

Rifle

	Champion	Pts	Runner-Up	Pts
Smallbore	Eric Uptagrafft, W Virginia	1174	Jason Parker, Xavier (OH)	1168
Air rifle	Trevor Gathman, W Virginia	390	Katherine Kelemen, Murray St	390

Golf

MEN

Champion	Score	Runner-Up	Score
Todd Demsey, Arizona St	278	David Duval, Georgia Tech	279

WOMEN

Charlotta Sorenstam, Texas	287	Angela Buzminski, Indiana	289

Outdoor Track

MEN

	Champion	Mark	Runner-Up	Mark
100-meter dash	Michael Green, Clemson	10.09	Glenroy Gilbert, Louisiana St	10.18
200-meter dash	Chris Nelloms, Ohio St	20.27	Oluyemi Koyade, BYU	20.35
400-meter dash	Calvin Davis, Arkansas	45.04	Anthuan Maybank, Iowa	45.04
800-meter run	Jose Parilla, Tennessee	1:46.51	Scott Peters, Florida	1:47.04
1,500-meter run	Marko Koers, Illinois	3:38.50	Andy Keith, Providence	3:39.06
3,000-met. steeplech.	Donovan Bergstrom, Wisc	8:29.08	Jim Svenoy, UTEP	8:29.18
5,000-meter run	Jon Dennis, South Florida	13:59.00	David Welsh, Arkansas	13:59.25
10,000-meter run	Jonah Koech, Iowa St	28:28.67	Pablo Sierra, Mississippi	29:07.88
110-meter hurdles	Glenn Terry, Indiana	13.43	Allen Johnson, N Carolina	13.47
400-meter hurdles	Bryan Bronson, Rice	49.07	Jordan Gray, Ohio St	49.10
High jump	Randy Jenkins, Tennessee	7 ft 5¾ in	Ray Doakes, Arkansas	7 ft 4½ in
Pole vault	Mark Buse, Indiana	18 ft 4½ in	Adam Smith, Tennessee	18 4½ in
Long jump	Erick Walder, Arkansas	28 ft*	Dion Bentley, Florida	27 ft 6½ in
Triple jump	Tyrell Taitt, N Carolina St	55 ft 5¾ in	Reggie Jones, Louisiana St	55 ft 5½ in
Shot put	Brent Noon, Georgia	66 ft 11½ in	John Godina, UCLA	65 ft 8¾ in
Discus throw	Brian Milne, Penn St	200 ft 5 in	Ramon Jimenez-Gaona, Cal	200 ft
Hammer throw	Balazs Kiss, Southern Cal	246 ft 10 in	Mika Laaksonen, UTEP	233 ft 7 in
Javelin throw	Eric Smith, Tennessee	259 ft 10 in	Derek Trafas, Florida	240 ft 11 in
Decathlon	Chris Huffins, Cal	8007	Ron Blums, Iowa St	7918

WOMEN

	Champion	Mark	Runner-Up	Mark
100-meter dash	Holli Hyche, Indiana St	11.14	Beverly McDonald, TCU	11.25
200-meter dash	Holli Hyche, Indiana St	22.34	Beverly McDonald, TCU	22.69
400-meter dash	Juliet Campbell, Auburn	50.58	Nelrae Pasha, Georgia Tech	51.58
800-meter run	Kim Sherman, Wisconsin	2:02.99	Amy Wickus, Wisconsin	2:03.00
1,500-meter run	Clare Eichner, Wisconsin	4:20.12	Aaronda Watson, Georgetown	4:21.95
3,000-meter run	Clare Eichner, Wisconsin	9:03.06	Fran Ten Bensel, Nebraska	9:07.39
5,000-meter run	Kay Gooch, Oklahoma	16:31.02	Molly McClimon, Michigan	16:33.38
10,000-meter run	Carole Zajac, Villanova	34:18.14	Caryn Landau, Georgetown	34:21.71
100-meter hurdles	Gillian Russell, Miami (FL)	13.02	Ime Akpan, Arizona St	13.10
400-meter hurdles	Debbie Ann Parris, LSU	56.37	Tonja Buford, Illinois	56.91
High jump	Tanya Hughes, Arizona	6 ft 3½ in	Gwen Wentland, Kansas St	6 ft 3½ in
Long jump	Daphnie Saunders, LSU	22 ft 2½ in	Dedra Davis, Tennessee	21 ft 9 in
Triple jump	Claudia Haywood, Rice	44 ft 5¼ in	Roshanda Glenn, UCLA	43 ft 9¾ in
Shot put	Dawn Dumble, UCLA	56 ft 4 in	Stevanie Wadsworth, TCU	55 ft 6½ in
Discus throw	Danyel Mitchell, LSU	186 ft 6 in	Dawn Dumble, UCLA	183 ft 2 in
Javelin throw	Ashley Selman, Oregon	188 ft 5 in	Vallerie Tulloch, Rice	185 ft 7 in
Heptathlon	Kelly Blair, Oregon	6038	Sharon Jaklofsky, LSU	5892

Tennis

MEN

	Champion	Score	Runner-Up
Singles	Chris Woodruff, Tennessee	(6-3, 6-1)	Wade McGuire, Georgia
Doubles	David Blair & Mark Merklein, Florida	(5-7, 6-2, 6-1)	Chris Cocotos & Michael Flanagan, Stanford

WOMEN

	Champion	Score	Runner-Up
Singles	Lisa Raymond, Florida	(6-3, 6-1)	Cinda Gurney, N Carolina
Doubles	Alix Creek & Michelle Oldham, Arizona	(default)	Susan Gilchrist & Vickie Paynter, Texas

CHAMPIONSHIP RESULTS

Baseball

Men

DIVISION I

Year	Champion	Coach	Score	Runner-Up	Most Outstanding Player
1947	California*	Clint Evans	8-7	Yale	No award
1948	Southern Cal	Sam Barry	9-2	Yale	No award
1949	Texas*	Bibb Falk	10-3	Wake Forest	Charles Teague, Wake Forest, 2B
1950	Texas	Bibb Falk	3-0	Washington St	Ray VanCleef, Rutgers, CF
1951	Oklahoma*	Jack Baer	3-2	Tennnessee	Sidney Hatfield, Tennessee, P-1B
1952	Holy Cross	Jack Barry	8-4	Missouri	James O'Neill, Holy Cross, P
1953	Michigan	Ray Fisher	7-5	Texas	J. L. Smith, Texas, P
1954	Missouri	John "Hi" Simmons	4-1	Rollins	Tom Yewcic, Michigan St, C
1955	Wake Forest	Taylor Sanford	7-6	Western Michigan	Tom Borland, Oklahoma St, P
1956	Minnesota	Dick Siebert	12-1	Arizona	Jerry Thomas, Minnesota, P
1957	California*	George Wolfman	1-0	Penn St	Cal Emery, Penn St, P-1B
1958	Southern Cal	Rod Dedeaux	8-7†	Missouri	Bill Thom, Southern Cal, P
1959	Oklahoma St	Toby Greene	5-3	Arizona	Jim Dobson, Oklahoma St, 3B
1960	Minnesota	Dick Siebert	2-1‡	Southern Cal	John Erickson, Minnesota, 2B
1961	Southern Cal*	Rod Dedeaux	1-0	Oklahoma St	Littleton Fowler, Oklahoma St, P
1962	Michigan	Don Lund	5-4	Santa Clara	Bob Garibaldi, Santa Clara, P
1963	Southern Cal	Rod Dedeaux	5-2	Arizona	Bud Hollowell, Southern Cal, C
1964	Minnesota	Dick Siebert	5-1	Missouri	Joe Ferris, Maine, P
1965	Arizona St	Bobby Winkles	2-1#	Ohio St	Sal Bando, Arizona St, 3B
1966	Ohio St	Marty Karow	8-2	Oklahoma St	Steve Arlin, Ohio St, P
1967	Arizona St	Bobby Winkles	11-2	Houston	Ron Davini, Arizona St, C
1968	Southern Cal*	Rod Dedeaux	4-3	Southern Illinois	Bill Seinsoth, Southern Cal, 1B
1969	Arizona St	Bobby Winkles	10-1	Tulsa	John Dolinsek, Arizona St, LF
1970	Southern Cal	Rod Dedeaux	2-1	Florida St	Gene Ammann, Florida St, P
1971	Southern Cal	Rod Dedeaux	7-2	Southern Illinois	Jerry Tabb, Tulsa, 1B
1972	Southern Cal	Rod Dedeaux	1-0	Arizona St	Russ McQueen, Southern Cal, P
1973	Southern Cal*	Rod Dedeaux	4-3	Arizona St	Dave Winfield, Minnesota, P-OF
1974	Southern Cal	Rod Dedeaux	7-3	Miami (FL)	George Milke, Southern Cal, P
1975	Texas	Cliff Gustafson	5-1	S Carolina	Mickey Reichenbach, Texas, 1B
1976	Arizona	Jerry Kindall	7-1	Eastern Michigan	Steve Powers, Arizona, P-DH
1977	Arizona St	Jim Brock	2-1	S Carolina	Bob Horner, Arizona St, 3B
1978	Southern Cal*	Rod Dedeaux	10-3	Arizona St	Rod Boxberger, Southern Cal, P
1979	Cal St-Fullerton	Augie Garrido	2-1	Arkansas	Tony Hudson, Cal St-Fullerton, P
1980	Arizona	Jerry Kindall	5-3	Hawaii	Terry Francona, Arizona, LF
1981	Arizona St	Jim Brock	7-4	Oklahoma St	Stan Holmes, Arizona St, LF
1982	Miami (FL)*	Ron Fraser	9-3	Wichita St	Dan Smith, Miami (FL), P
1983	Texas*	Cliff Gustafson	4-3	Alabama	Calvin Schiraldi, Texas, P
1984	Cal St-Fullerton	Augie Garrido	3-1	Texas	John Fishel, Cal St-Fullerton, LF
1985	Miami (FL)	Ron Fraser	10-6	Texas	Greg Ellena, Miami (FL), DH
1986	Arizona	Jerry Kindall	10-2	Florida St	Mike Senne, Arizona, LF
1987	Stanford	Mark Marquess	9-5	Oklahoma St	Paul Carey, Stanford, RF
1988	Stanford	Mark Marquess	9-4	Arizona St	Lee Plemel, Stanford, P
1989	Wichita St	Gene Stephenson	5-3	Texas	Greg Brummett, Wichita St, P
1990	Georgia	Steve Webber	2-1	Oklahoma St	Mike Rebhan, Georgia, P
1991	Louisiana St	Skip Bertman	6-3	Wichita St	Gary Hymel, Louisiana St, C
1992	Pepperdine	Andy Lopez	3-2	Cal St-Fullerton	Phil Nevin, Cal St-Fullerton, 3B
1993	Louisiana St	Skip Bertman	8-0	Wichita St	Todd Walker, Louisiana St, 2B

*Undefeated teams in College World Series play. †12 innings. ‡10 innings. #15 innings.

DIVISION II

Year	Champion	Year	Champion	Year	Champion	Year	Champion
1968	Chapman*	1975	Florida Southern	1982	UC-Riverside*	1989	Cal Poly-SLO
1969	Illinois St*	1976	Cal Poly-Pomona	1983	Cal Poly-Pomona*	1990	Jacksonville St
1970	Cal St-Northridge	1977	UC-Riverside	1984	Cal St-Northridge	1991	Jacksonville St
1971	Florida Southern	1978	Florida Southern	1985	Florida Southern*	1992	Tampa*
1972	Florida Southern	1979	Valdosta St	1986	Troy St	1993	Tampa
1973	UC-Irvine*	1980	Cal Poly-Pomona*	1987	Troy St*		
1974	UC-Irvine	1981	Florida Southern*	1988	Florida Southern*		

*Undefeated teams.

DIVISION III

Year	Champion	Year	Champion	Year	Champion
1976	Cal St-Stanislaus	1982	Eastern Connecticut St	1988	Ithaca
1977	Cal St-Stanislaus	1983	Marietta	1989	NC Wesleyan
1978	Glassboro St	1984	Ramapo	1990	Eastern Connecticut St
1979	Glassboro St	1985	WI-Oshkosh	1991	Southern Maine
1980	Ithaca	1986	Marietta	1992	William Patterson
1981	Marietta	1987	Montclair St	1993	Montclair St

Cross-Country

Men

DIVISION I

Year	Champion	Coach	Pts	Runner-Up	Pts	Individual Champion	Time
1938	Indiana	Earle Hayes	51	Notre Dame	61	Greg Rice, Notre Dame	20:12.9
1939	Michigan St	Lauren Brown	54	Wisconsin	57	Walter Mehl, Wisconsin	20:30.9
1940	Indiana	Earle Hayes	65	Eastern Michigan	68	Gilbert Dodds, Ashland	20:30.2
1941	Rhode Island	Fred Tootell	83	Penn St	110	Fred Wilt, Indiana	20:30.1
1942	Indiana	Earle Hayes	57			Oliver Hunter, Notre Dame	20:18.0
	Penn St	Charles Werner	57				
1943	No meet						
1944	Drake	Bill Easton	25	Notre Dame	64	Fred Feiler, Drake	21:04.2
1945	Drake	Bill Easton	50	Notre Dame	65	Fred Feiler, Drake	21:14.2
1946	Drake	Bill Easton	42	NYU	98	Quentin Brelsford, Ohio Wesleyan	20:22.9
1947	Penn St	Charles Werner	60	Syracuse	72	Jack Milne, N Carolina	20:41.1
1948	Michigan St	Karl Schlademan	41	Wisconsin	69	Robert Black, Rhode Island	19:52.3
1949	Michigan St	Karl Schlademan	59	Syracuse	81	Robert Black, Rhode Island	20:25.7
1950	Penn St	Charles Werner	53	Michigan St	55	Herb Semper Jr, Kansas	20:31.7
1951	Syracuse	Robert Grieve	80	Kansas	118	Herb Semper Jr, Kansas	20:09.5
1952	Michigan St	Karl Schlademan	65	Indiana	68	Charles Capozzoli, Georgetown	19:36.7
1953	Kansas	Bill Easton	70	Indiana	82	Wes Santee, Kansas	19:43.5
1954	Oklahoma St	Ralph Higgins	61	Syracuse	118	Allen Frame, Kansas	19:54.2
1955	Michigan St	Karl Schlademan	46	Kansas	68	Charles Jones, Iowa	19:57.4
1956	Michigan St	Karl Schlademan	28	Kansas	88	Walter McNew, Texas	19:55.7
1957	Notre Dame	Alex Wilson	121	Michigan St	127	Max Truex, Southern Cal	19:12.3
1958	Michigan St	Francis Dittrich	79	Western Michigan	104	Crawford Kennedy, Michigan State	20:07.1
1959	Michigan St	Francis Dittrich	44	Houston	120	Al Lawrence, Houston	20:35.7
1960	Houston	John Morriss	54	Michigan St	80	Al Lawrence, Houston	19:28.2
1961	Oregon St	Sam Bell	68	San Jose St	82	Dale Story, Oregon St	19:46.6
1962	San Jose St	Dean Miller	58	Villanova	69	Tom O'Hara, Loyola (IL)	19:20.3
1963	San Jose St	Dean Miller	53	Oregon	68	Victor Zwolak, Villanova	19:35.0
1964	Western Miichigan	George Dales	86	Oregon	116	Elmore Banton, Ohio	20:07.5
1965	Western Miichigan	George Dales	81	Northwestern	114	John Lawson, Kansas	29:24.0
1966	Villanova	James Elliott	79	Kansas St	155	Gerry Lindgren, Washington St	29:01.4
1967	Villanova	James Elliott	91	Air Force	96	Gerry Lindgren, Washington St	30:45.6
1968	Villanova	James Elliott	78	Stanford	100	Michael Ryan, Air Force	29:16.8
1969	UTEP	Wayne Vandenburg	74	Villanova	88	Gerry Lindgren, Washington St	28:59.2
1970	Villanova	James Elliott	85	Oregon	86	Steve Prefontaine, Oregon	28:00.2
1971	Oregon	Bill Dellinger	83	Washington St	122	Steve Prefontaine, Oregon	29:14.0
1972	Tennessee	Stan Huntsman	134	E Tennessee St	148	Neil Cusack, E Tennessee St	28:23.0
1973	Oregon	Bill Dellinger	89	UTEP	157	Steve Prefontaine, Oregon	28:14.0
1974	Oregon	Bill Dellinger	77	Western Kentucky	110	Nick Rose, Western Kentucky	29:22.0
1975	UTEP	Ted Banks	88	Washington St	92	Craig Virgin, Illinois	28:23.3

Cross Country (Cont.)

Men (Cont.)

Year	Champion	Coach	Pts	Runner-Up	Pts	Individual Champion	Time
1976	UTEP	Ted Banks	62	Oregon	117	Henry Rono, Washington St	28:06.6
1977	Oregon	Bill Dellinger	100	UTEP	105	Henry Rono, Washington St	28:33.5
1978	UTEP	Ted Banks	56	Oregon	72	Alberto Salazar, Oregon	29:29.7
1979	UTEP	Ted Banks	86	Oregon	93	Henry Rono, Washington St	28:19.6
1980	UTEP	Ted Banks	58	Arkansas	152	Suleiman Nyambui, UTEP	29:04.0
1981	UTEP	Ted Banks	17	Providence	109	Mathews Motshwarateu, UTEP	28:45.6
1982	Wisconsin	Dan McClimon	59	Providence	138	Mark Scrutton, Colorado	30:12.6
1983	Vacated			Wisconsin	164	Zakarie Barie, UTEP	29:20.0
1984	Arkansas	John McDonnell	101	Arizona	111	Ed Eyestone, Brigham Young	29:28.8
1985	Wisconsin	Martin Smith	67	Arkansas	104	Timothy Hacker, Wisconsin	29:17.88
1986	Arkansas	John McDonnell	69	Dartmouth	141	Aaron Ramirez, Arizona	30:27.53
1987	Arkansas	John McDonnell	87	Dartmouth	119	Joe Falcon, Arkansas	29:14.97
1988	Wisconsin	Martin Smith	105	Northern Arizona	160	Robert Kennedy, Indiana	29:20.0
1989	Iowa St	Bill Bergan	54	Oregon	72	John Nuttall, Iowa St	29:30.55
1990	Arkansas	John McDonnell	68	Iowa St	96	Jonah Koech, Iowa St	29:05.0
1991	Arkansas	John McDonnell	52	Iowa St	114	Sean Dollman, Western Ky	30:17.1
1992	Arkansas	John McDonnell	46	Wisconsin	87	Bob Kennedy, Indiana	30:15.3

Division II

Year	Champion	Year	Champion
1958	Northern Illinois	1976	UC-Irvine
1959	S Dakota St	1977	Eastern Illinois
1960	Central St (OH)	1978	Cal Poly-SLO
1961	Southern Illinois	1979	Cal Poly-SLO
1962	Central St (OH)	1980	Humboldt St
1963	Emporia St	1981	Millersville
1964	Kentucky St	1982	Eastern Washington
1965	San Diego St	1983	Cal Poly-Pomona
1966	San Diego St	1984	SE Missouri St
1967	San Diego St	1985	S Dakota St
1968	Eastern Illinois	1986	Edinboro
1969	Eastern Illinois	1987	Edinboro
1970	Eastern Michigan	1988	Edinboro, Mankato St
1971	Cal St-Fullerton	1989	S Dakota St
1972	N Dakota St	1990	Edinboro
1973	S Dakota St	1991	MA-Lowell
1974	SW Missouri St	1992	Adams St
1975	UC-Irvine		

Division III

Year	Champion	Year	Champion
1973	Ashland	1983	Brandeis
1974	Mount Union	1984	St Thomas (MN)
1975	North Central	1985	Luther
1976	North Central	1986	St Thomas (MN)
1977	Occidental	1987	North Central
1978	North Central	1988	WI-Oshkosh
1979	North Central	1989	WI-Oshkosh
1980	Carleton	1990	WI-Oshkosh
1981	North Central	1991	Rochester
1982	North Central	1992	North Central

Women
DIVISION I

Year	Champion	Coach	Pts	Runner-Up	Pts	Individual Champion	Time
1981	Virginia	John Vasvary	36	Oregon	83	Betty Springs, N Carolina St	16:19.0
1982	Virginia	Martin Smith	48	Stanford	91	Lesley Welch, Virginia	16:39.7
1983	Oregon	Tom Heinonen	95	Stanford	98	Betty Springs, N Carolina St	16:30.7
1984	Wisconsin	Peter Tegen	63	Stanford	89	Cathy Branta, Wisconsin	16:15.6
1985	Wisconsin	Peter Tegen	58	Iowa St	98	Suzie Tuffey, N Carolina St	16:22.53

Women (Cont.)
DIVISION I (CONT.)

1986 ....Texas	Terry Crawford	62	Wisconsin	64	Angela Chalmers, Northern Arizona	16:55.49
1987 ....Oregon	Tom Heinonen	97	N Carolina St	99	Kimberly Betz, Indiana	16:10.85
1988 ....Kentucky	Don Weber	75	Oregon	128	Michelle Dekkers, Indiana	16:30.0
1989 ......Villanova	Marty Stern	99	Kentucky	168	Vicki Huber, Villanova	15:59.86
1990 ......Villanova	Marty Stern	82	Providence	172	Sonia O'Sullivan, Villanova	16:06.0
1991 ......Villanova	Marty Stern	85	Arkansas	168	Sonia O'Sullivan, Villanova	16:30.3
1992 .....Villanova	Marty Stern	123	Arkansas	130	Carole Zajac, Villanova	17:01.9

DIVISION II

Year	Champion	Year	Champion	Year	Champion
1981	S Dakota St	1985	Cal Poly-SLO	1989	Cal Poly-SLO
1982	Cal Poly-SLO	1986	Cal Poly-SLO	1990	Cal Poly-SLO
1983	Cal Poly-SLO	1987	Cal Poly-SLO	1991	Cal Poly-SLO
1984	Cal Poly-SLO	1988	Cal Poly-SLO	1992	Adams St

DIVISION III

Year	Champion	Year	Champion	Year	Champion
1981	Central (IA)	1986	St Thomas (MN)	1990	Cortland St
1982	St Thomas (MN)	1987	St Thomas (MN)	1991	WI-Oshkosh
1983	WI-La Crosse		WI-Oshkosh	1992	Cortland St
1984	St Thomas (MN)	1988	WI-Oshkosh		
1985	Franklin & Marshall	1989	Cortland St		

Fencing

Men
TEAM CHAMPIONS

Year	Champion	Coach	Pts	Runner-Up	Pts
1941	Northwestern	Henry Zettleman	28½	Illinois	27
1942	Ohio St	Frank Riebel	34	St John's (NY)	33½
1943-1946	No tournament				
1947	NYU	Martinez Castello	72	Chicago	50½
1948	CCNY	James Montague	30	Navy	28
1949	Army	Servando Velarde	63		
	Rutgers	Donald Cetrulo	63		
1950	Navy	Joseph Fiems	67½	NYU	66½
				Rutgers	66½
1951	Columbia	Servando Velarde	69	Pennsylvania	64
1952	Columbia	Servando Velarde	71	NYU	69
1953	Pennsylvania	Lajos Csiszar	94	Navy	86
1954	Columbia	Irving DeKoff	61		
	NYU	Hugo Castello	61		
1955	Columbia	Irving DeKoff	62	Cornell	57
1956	Illinois	Maxwell Garret	90	Columbia	88
1957	NYU	Hugo Castello	65	Columbia	64
1958	Illinois	Maxwell Garret	47	Columbia	43
1959	Navy	Andre Deladrier	72	NYU	65
1960	NYU	Hugo Castello	65	Navy	57
1961	NYU	Hugo Castello	79	Princeton	68
1962	Navy	Andre Deladrier	76	NYU	74
1963	Columbia	Irving DeKoff	55	Navy	50
1964	Princeton	Stan Sieja	81	NYU	79
1965	Columbia	Irving DeKoff	76	NYU	74
1966	NYU	Hugo Castello	5-0	Army	5-2
1967	NYU	Hugo Castello	72	Pennsylvania	64
1968	Columbia	Louis Bankuti	92	NYU	87
1969	Pennsylvania	Lajos Csiszar	54	Harvard	43
1970	NYU	Hugo Castello	71	Columbia	63
1971	NYU	Hugo Castello	68		
	Columbia	Louis Bankuti	68		

Fencing (Cont.)

TEAM CHAMPIONS (Cont.)

Year	Champion	Coach	Pts	Runner-Up	Pts
1972	Detroit	Richard Perry	73	NYU	70
1973	NYU	Hugo Castello	76	Pennsylvania	71
1974	NYU	Hugo Castello	92	Wayne St (MI)	87
1975	Wayne St (MI)	Istvan Danosi	89	Cornell	83
1976	NYU	Herbert Cohen	79	Wayne St (MI)	77
1977	Notre Dame	Michael DeCicco	114*	NYU	114
1978	Notre Dame	Michael DeCicco	121	Pennsylvania	110
1979	Wayne St (MI)	Istvan Danosi	119	Notre Dame	108
1980	Wayne St (MI)	Istvan Danosi	111	Pennsylvania	106
				MIT	106
1981	Pennsylvania	Dave Micahnik	113	Wayne St (MI)	111
1982	Wayne St (MI)	Istvan Danosi	85	Clemson	77
1983	Wayne St (MI)	Aladar Kogler	86	Notre Dame	80
1984	Wayne St (MI)	Gil Pezza	69	Penn St	50
1985	Wayne St (MI)	Gil Pezza	141	Notre Dame	140
1986	Notre Dame	Michael DeCicco	151	Columbia	141
1987	Columbia	George Kolombatovich	86	Pennsylvania	78
1988	Columbia	George Kolombatovich Aladar Kogler	90	Notre Dame	83
1989	Columbia	George Kolombatovich Aladar Kogler	88	Penn St	85
1990	Penn St	Emmanuil Kaidanov	36	Columbia-Barnard	35
1991	Penn St	Emmanuil Kaidanov	4700	Columbia/Columbia-Barnard	4200
1992	Columbia/Columbia-Barnard	George Kolombatovich/Aladar Kogler	4150	Penn St	3646
1993	Columbia/Columbia-Barnard	George Kolumbatovich/Aladar Kogler	4525	Penn St	4500

*Tie broken by a fence-off.
Note: Beginning in 1990, men's and women's combined teams competed for the national championship.

INDIVIDUAL CHAMPIONS

	Foil	Sabre	Épée
1941	Edward McNamara, Northwestern	William Meyer, Dartmouth	G. H. Boland, Illinois
1942	Byron Kreiger, Wayne St (MI)	Andre Deladrier, St John's (NY)	Ben Burtt, Ohio St
1947	Abraham Balk, NYU	Oscar Parsons, Temple	Abraham Balk, NYU
1948	Albert Axelrod, CCNY	James Day, Navy	William Bryan, Navy
1949	Ralph Tedeschi, Rutgers	Alex Treves, Rutgers	Richard C. Bowman, Army
1950	Robert Nielsen, Columbia	Alex Treves, Rutgers	Thomas Stuart, Navy
1951	Robert Nielsen, Columbia	Chamberless Johnston, Princeton	Daniel Chafetz, Columbia
1952	Harold Goldsmith, CCNY	Frank Zimolzak, Navy	James Wallner, NYU
1953	Ed Nober, Brooklyn	Robert Parmacek, Pennsylvania	Jack Tori, Pennsylvania
1954	Robert Goldman, Pennsylvania	Steve Sobel, Columbia	Henry Kolowrat, Princeton
1955	Herman Velasco, Illinois	Barry Pariser, Columbia	Donald Tadrawski, Notre Dame
1956	Ralph DeMarco, Columbia	Gerald Kaufman, Columbia	Kinmont Hoitsma, Princeton
1957	Bruce Davis, Wayne St (MI)	Bernie Balaban, NYU	James Margolis, Columbia
1958	Bruce Davis, Wayne St (MI)	Art Schankin, Illinois	Roland Wommack, Navy
1959	Joe Paletta, Navy	Al Morales, Navy	Roland Wommack, Navy
1960	Gene Glazer, NYU	Mike Desaro, NYU	Gil Eisner, NYU
1961	Herbert Cohen, NYU	Israel Colon, NYU	Jerry Halpern, NYU
1962	Herbert Cohen, NYU	Barton Nisonson, Columbia	Thane Hawkins, Navy
1963	Jay Lustig, Columbia	Bela Szentivanyi, Wayne St (MI)	Larry Crum, Navy
1964	Bill Hicks, Princeton	Craig Bell, Illinois	Paul Pesthy, Rutgers
1965	Joe Nalven, Columbia	Howard Goodman, NYU	Paul Pesthy, Rutgers
1966	Al Davis, NYU	Paul Apostol, NYU	Bernhardt Hermann, Iowa
1967	Mike Gaylor, NYU	Todd Makler, Pennsylvania	George Masin, NYU
1968	Gerard Esponda, San Francisco	Todd Makler, Pennsylvania	Don Sieja, Cornell
1969	Anthony Kestler, Columbia	Norman Braslow, Pennsylvania	James Wetzler, Pennsylvania
1970	Walter Krause, NYU	Bruce Soriano, Columbia	John Nadas, Case Reserve

INDIVIDUAL CHAMPIONS (Cont.)

	Foil	Sabre	Épée
1971	Tyrone Simmons, Detroit	Bruce Soriano, Columbia	George Szunyogh, NYU
1972	Tyrone Simmons, Detroit	Bruce Soriano, Columbia	Ernesto Fernandez, Pennsylvania
1973	Brooke Makler, Pennsylvania	Peter Westbrock, NYU	Risto Hurme, NYU
1974	Greg Benko, Wayne St (MI)	Steve Danosi, Wayne St (MI)	Risto Hurme, NYU
1975	Greg Benko, Wayne St (MI)	Yuri Rabinovich, Wayne St (MI)	Risto Hurme, NYU
1976	Greg Benko, Wayne St (MI)	Brian Smith, Columbia	Randy Eggleton, Pennsylvania
1977	Pat Gerard, Notre Dame	Mike Sullivan, Notre Dame	Hans Wieselgren, NYU
1978	Ernest Simon, Wayne St (MI)	Mike Sullivan, Notre Dame	Bjorne Vaggo, Notre Dame
1979	Andrew Bonk, Notre Dame	Yuri Rabinovich, Wayne St (MI)	Carlos Songini, Cleveland St
1980	Ernest Simon, Wayne St (MI)	Paul Friedberg, Pennsylvania	Gil Pezza, Wayne St (MI)
1981	Ernest Simon, Wayne St (MI)	Paul Friedberg, Pennsylvania	Gil Pezza, Wayne St (MI)
1982	Alexander Flom, George Mason	Neil Hick, Wayne St (MI)	Peter Schifrin, San Jose St
1983	Demetrios Valsamis, NYU	John Friedberg, North Carolina	Ola Harstrom, Notre Dame
1984	Charles Higgs-Coulthard, Notre Dame	Michael Lofton, NYU	Ettore Bianchi, Wayne St (MI)
1985	Stephan Chauvel, Wayne St (MI)	Michael Lofton, NYU	Ettore Bianchi, Wayne St (MI)
1986	Adam Feldman, Penn St	Michael Lofton, NYU	Chris O'Loughlin, Pennsylvania
1987	William Mindel, Columbia	Michael Lofton, NYU	James O'Neill, Harvard
1988	Marc Kent, Columbia	Robert Cottingham, Columbia	Jon Normile, Columbia
1989	Edward Mufel, Penn St	Peter Cox, Penn St	Jon Normile, Columbia
1990	Nick Bravin, Stanford	David Mandell, Columbia	Jubba Beshin, Notre Dame
1991	Ben Atkins, Columbia	Vitali Nazlimov, Penn St	Marc Oshima, Columbia
1992	Nick Bravin, Stanford	Tom Strzalkowski, Penn St	Harald Bauder, Wayne St
1993	Nick Bravin, Stanford	Tom Strzalkowski, Penn St	Ben Atkins, Columbia

Women

TEAM CHAMPIONS

Year	Champion	Coach	Rec	Runner-Up	Rec
1982	Wayne St (MI)	Istvan Danosi	7-0	San Jose St	6-1
1983	Penn St	Beth Alphin	5-0	Wayne St (MI)	3-2
1984	Yale	Henry Harutunian	3-0	Penn St	2-1
1985	Yale	Henry Harutunian	3-0	Pennsylvania	2-1
1986	Pennsylvania	David Micahnik	3-0	Notre Dame	2-1
1987	Notre Dame	Yves Auriol	3-0	Temple	2-1
1988	Wayne St (MI)	Gil Pezza	3-0	Notre Dame	2-1
1989	Wayne St (MI)	Gil Pezza	3-0	Columbia-Barnard	2-1

Note: Beginning in 1990, men's and women's combined teams competed for the national championship.

INDIVIDUAL CHAMPIONS

1982	Joy Ellingson, San Jose St	1988	Molly Sullivan, Notre Dame
1983	Jana Angelakis, Penn St	1989	Yasemin Topcu, Wayne St (MI)
1984	Mary Jane O'Neill, Pennsylvania	1990	Tzu Moy, Columbia-Barnard
1985	Caitlin Bilodeaux, Columbia-Barnard	1991	Heidi Piper, Notre Dame
1986	Molly Sullivan, Notre Dame	1992	Olga Cheryak, Penn St
1987	Caitlin Bilodeaux, Columbia-Barnard	1993	Olga Kalinovskaya, Penn St

Field Hockey

Women

DIVISION I

Year	Champion	Coach	Score	Runner-Up
1981	Connecticut	Diane Wright	4-1	Massachusetts
1982	Old Dominion	Beth Anders	3-2	Connecticut
1983	Old Dominion	Beth Anders	3-1 (3 OT)	Connecticut
1984	Old Dominion	Beth Anders	5-1	Iowa
1985	Connecticut	Diane Wright	3-2	Old Dominion
1986	Iowa	Judith Davidson	2-1 (2 OT)	New Hampshire
1987	Maryland	Sue Tyler	2-1 (OT)	N Carolina
1988	Old Dominion	Beth Anders	2-1	Iowa

DIVISION I (Cont.)

Year	Champion	Coach	Score	Runner-Up
1989	N Carolina	Karen Shelton	2-1 (3 OT)*	Old Dominion
1990	Old Dominion	Beth Anders	5-0	N Carolina
1991	Old Dominion	Beth Anders	2-0	N Carolina
1992	Old Dominion	Beth Anders	4-0	Iowa

*Penalty strokes.

DIVISION II *(DISCONTINUED, THEN RENEWED)*

Year	Champion	Coach	Score	Runner-Up
1981	Pfeiffer	Ellen Briggs	5-3	Bentley
1982	Lock Haven	Sharon E. Taylor	4-1	Bloomsburg
1983	Bloomsburg	Jan Hutchinson	1-0	Lock Haven
1992	Lock Haven	Sharon E. Taylor	3-1	Bloomsburg

DIVISION III

Year	Champion	Year	Champion
1981	Trenton St	1987	Bloomsburg
1982	Ithaca	1988	Trenton St
1983	Trenton St	1989	Lock Haven
1984	Bloomsburg	1990	Trenton St
1985	Trenton St	1991	Trenton St
1986	Salisbury St	1992	William Smith

Golf

Men

DIVISION I

Results, 1897-1938

Year	Champion	Site	Individual Champion
1897	Yale	Ardsley Casino	Louis Bayard Jr, Princeton
1898	Harvard (spring)		John Reid Jr, Yale
1898	Yale (fall)		James Curtis, Harvard
1899	Harvard		Percy Pyne, Princeton
1900	No tournament		
1901	Harvard	Atlantic City	H. Lindsley, Harvard
1902	Yale (spring)	Garden City	Charles Hitchcock Jr, Yale
1902	Harvard (fall)	Morris County	Chandler Egan, Harvard
1903	Harvard	Garden City	F. O. Reinhart, Princeton
1904	Harvard	Myopia	A. L. White, Harvard
1905	Yale	Garden City	Robert Abbott, Yale
1906	Yale	Garden City	W. E. Clow Jr, Yale
1907	Yale	Nassau	Ellis Knowles, Yale
1908	Yale	Brae Burn	H. H. Wilder, Harvard
1909	Yale	Apawamis	Albert Seckel, Princeton
1910	Yale	Essex County	Robert Hunter, Yale
1911	Yale	Baltusrol	George Stanley, Yale
1912	Yale	Ekwanok	F. C. Davison, Harvard
1913	Yale	Huntingdon Valley	Nathaniel Wheeler, Yale
1914	Princeton	Garden City	Edward Allis, Harvard
1915	Yale	Greenwich	Francis Blossom, Yale
1916	Princeton	Oakmont	J. W. Hubbell, Harvard
1917-18	No tournament		
1919	Princeton	Merion	A. L. Walker Jr, Columbia
1920	Princeton	Nassau	Jess Sweetster, Yale
1921	Dartmouth	Greenwich	Simpson Dean, Princeton
1922	Princeton	Garden City	Pollack Boyd, Dartmouth
1923	Princeton	Siwanoy	Dexter Cummings, Yale
1924	Yale	Greenwich	Dexter Cummings, Yale
1925	Yale	Montclair	Fred Lamprecht, Tulane
1926	Yale	Merion	Fred Lamprecht, Tulane
1927	Princeton	Garden City	Watts Gunn, Georgia Tech

Men (Cont.)
Results, 1897-1938 (Cont.)

Year	Champion	Site	Individual Champion
1928	Princeton	Apawamis	Maurice McCarthy, Georgetown
1929	Princeton	Hollywood	Tom Aycock, Yale
1930	Princeton	Oakmont	G. T. Dunlap Jr, Princeton
1931	Yale	Olympia Fields	G. T. Dunlap Jr, Princeton
1932	Yale	Hot Springs	J. W. Fischer, Michigan
1933	Yale	Buffalo	Walter Emery, Oklahoma
1934	Michigan	Cleveland	Charles Yates, Georgia Tech
1935	Michigan	Congressional	Ed White, Texas
1936	Yale	North Shore	Charles Kocsis, Michigan
1937	Princeton	Oakmont	Fred Haas Jr, Louisiana St
1938	Stanford	Louisville	John Burke, Georgetown

Results, 1939-1993

Year	Champion	Coach	Score	Runner-Up	Score	Host or Site	Individual Champion
1939	Stanford	Eddie Twiggs	612	Northwestern	614	Wakonda	Vincent D'Antoni, Tulane
				Princeton	614		
1940	Princeton	Walter Bourne	601			Ekwanok	Dixon Brooke, Virginia
	Louisiana St	Mike Donahue	601				
1941	Stanford	Eddie Twiggs	580	Louisiana St	599	Ohio St	Earl Stewart, Louisiana St
1942	Louisiana St	Mike Donahue	590			Notre Dame	Frank Tatum Jr
	Stanford	Eddie Twiggs	590				
1943	Yale	William Neale Jr	614	Michigan	618	Olympia Fields	Wallace Ulrich, Carleton
1944	Notre Dame	George Holderith	311	Minnesota	312	Inverness	Louis Lick, Minnesota
1945	Ohio St	Robert Kepler	602	Northwestern	621	Ohio St	John Lorms, Ohio St
1946	Stanford	Eddie Twiggs	619	Michigan	624	Princeton	George Hamer, Georgia
1947	Louisiana St	T. P. Heard	606	Duke	614	Michigan	Dave Barclay, Michigan
1948	San Jose St	Wilbur Hubbard	579	Louisiana St	588	Stanford	Bob Harris, San Jose St
1949	N Texas	Fred Cobb	590	Purdue	600	Iowa St	Harvie Ward, N Carolina
				Texas	600		
1950	N Texas	Fred Cobb	573	Purdue	577	New Mexico	Fred Wampler, Purdue
1951	N Texas	Fred Cobb	588	Ohio St	589	Ohio St	Tom Nieporte, Ohio St
1952	N Texas	Fred Cobb	587	Michigan	593	Purdue	Jim Vickers, Oklahoma
1953	Stanford	Charles Finger	578	N Carolina	580	Broadmoor	Earl Moeller, Oklahoma St
1954	Southern Meth	Graham Ross	572	N Texas	573	Houston, Rice	Hillman Robbins, Memphis St
1955	Louisiana St	Mike Barbato	574	N Texas	583	Tennessee	Joe Campbell, Purdue
1956	Houston	Dave Williams	601	N Texas	602	Ohio St	Rick Jones, Ohio St
				Purdue	602		
1957	Houston	Dave Williams	602	Stanford	603	Broadmoor	Rex Baxter Jr, Houston
1958	Houston	Dave Williams	570	Oklahoma St	582	Williams	Phil Rodgers, Houston
1959	Houston	Dave Williams	561	Purdue	571	Oregon	Dick Crawford, Houston
1960	Houston	Dave Williams	603	Purdue	607	Broadmoor	Dick Crawford, Houston
				Oklahoma St	607		
1961	Purdue	Sam Voinoff	584	Arizona St	595	Lafayette	Jack Nicklaus, Ohio St
1962	Houston	Dave Williams	588	Oklahoma St	598	Duke	Kermit Zarley, Houston
1963	Oklahoma St	Labron Harris	581	Houston	582	Wichita St	R. H. Sikes, Ark.

Men (Cont.)
Results, 1939-1991 (Cont.)

Year	Champion	Coach	Score	Runner-Up	Score	Host or Site	Individual Champion
1964	Houston	Dave Williams	580	Oklahoma St	587	Broadmoor	Terry Small, San Jose St
1965 ....Houston	Dave Williams	577	Cal St-LA	587	Tennessee	Marty Fleckman, Houston
1966 ....Houston	Dave Williams	582	San Jose St	586	Stanford	Bob Murphy, Florida
1967 ....Houston	Dave Williams	585	Florida	588	Shawnee, PA	Hale Irwin, Colorado
1968 ....Florida	Buster Bishop	1154	Houston	1156	New Mexico St	Grier Jones, Oklahoma St
1969 ....Houston	Dave Williams	1223	Wake Forest	1232	Broadmoor	Bob Clark, Cal St-LA
1970	Houston	Dave Williams	1172	Wake Forest	1182	Ohio St	John Mahaffey, Houston
1971 ....Texas	George Hannon	1144	Houston	1151	Arizona	Ben Crenshaw, Texas
1972 ....Texas	George Hannon	1146	Houston	1159	Cape Coral	Ben Crenshaw, Texas; Tom Kite, Texas
1973 ....Florida	Buster Bishop	1149	Oklahoma St	1159	Oklahoma St	Ben Crenshaw, Texas
1974 ....Wake Forest	Jess Haddock	1158	Florida	1160	San Diego St	Curtis Strange, Wake Forest
1975 ....Wake Forest	Jess Haddock	1156	Oklahoma St	1189	Ohio St	Jay Haas, Wake Forest
1976 ....Oklahoma St	Mike Holder	1166	Brigham Young	1173	New Mexico	Scott Simpson, Southern Cal
1977 ....Houston	Dave Williams	1197	Oklahoma St	1205	Colgate	Scott Simpson, Southern Cal
1978 ....Oklahoma St	Mike Holder	1140	Georgia	1157	Oregon	David Edwards, Oklahoma St
1979 ....Ohio St	James Brown	1189	Oklahoma St	1191	Wake Forest	Gary Hallberg, Wake Forest
1980 ....Oklahoma St	Mike Holder	1173	Brigham Young	1177	Ohio St	Jay Don Blake, Utah St
1981 ....Brigham Young	Karl Tucker	1161	Oral Roberts	1163	Stanford	Ron Commans, Southern Cal
1982 ....Houston	Dave Williams	1141	Oklahoma St	1151	Pinehurst	Billy Ray Brown, Houston
1983 ....Oklahoma St	Mike Holder	1161	Texas	1168	Fresno St	Jim Carter, Arizona St
1984 ....Houston	Dave Williams	1145	Oklahoma St	1146	Houston	John Inman, N Carolina
1985 ....Houston	Dave Williams	1172	Oklahoma St	1175	Florida	Clark Burroughs, Ohio St
1986 ....Wake Forest	Jess Haddock	1156	Oklahoma St	1160	Wake Forest	Scott Verplank, Oklahoma St
1987 ....Oklahoma St	Mike Holder	1160	Wake Forest	1176	Ohio St	Brian Watts, Oklahoma St
1988 ....UCLA	Eddie Merrins	1176	UTEP; Oklahoma; Oklahoma St	1179; 1179; 1179	Southern Cal	E. J. Pfister, Oklahoma St
1989 ....Oklahoma	Gregg Grost	1139	Texas	1158	Oklahoma; Oklahoma St	Phil Mickelson, Arizona St
1990 ....Arizona St	Steve Loy	1155	Florida	1157	Florida	Phil Mickelson, Arizona St
1991 ....Oklahoma St	Mike Holder	1161	N Carolina	1168	San Jose St	Warren Schutte, UNLV
1992 ....Arizona	Rick LaRose	1129	Arizona St	1136	New Mexico	Phil Mickelson, Arizona St
1993 ....Florida	Buddy Alexander	1145	Georgia Tech	1146	Kenutcky	Todd Demsey, Arizona St

Notes: Match play, 1897-1964; par-70 tournaments held in 1969, 1973 and 1989; par-71 tournaments held in 1968, 1981 and 1988; all other championships par-72 tournaments. Scores are based on 4 rounds instead of 2 after 1967.

Men (Cont.)

DIVISION II

Year	Champion
1963	SW Missouri St
1964	Southern Illinois
1965	Middle Tennessee St
1966	Cal St-Chico
1967	Lamar
1968	Lamar
1969	Cal St-Northridge
1970	Rollins
1971	New Orleans
1972	New Orleans
1973	Cal St-Northridge
1974	Cal St-Northridge
1975	UC-Irvine
1976	Troy St
1977	Troy St
1978	Columbus
1979	UC-Davis
1980	Columbus
1981	Florida Southern
1982	Florida Southern
1983	SW Texas St
1984	Troy St
1985	Florida Southern
1986	Florida Southern
1987	Tampa
1988	Tampa
1989	Columbus
1990	Florida Southern
1991	Florida Southern
1992	Columbus
1993	Abilene Christian

DIVISION III

Year	Champion
1975	Wooster
1976	Cal St-Stanislaus
1977	Cal St-Stanislaus
1978	Cal St-Stanislaus
1979	Cal St-Stanislaus
1980	Cal St-Stanislaus
1981	Cal St-Stanislaus
1982	Ramapo
1983	Allegheny
1984	Cal St-Stanislaus
1985	Cal St-Stanislaus
1986	Cal St-Stanislaus
1987	Cal St-Stanislaus
1988	Cal St-Stanislaus
1989	Cal St-Stanislaus
1990	Methodist (NC)
1991	Methodist (NC)
1992	Methodist (NC)
1993	UC-San Diego

Note: All championships par-72 except for 1986 and 1988, which were par-71; fourth round of 1975 championships canceled as a result of bad weather, first round of 1988 championships canceled as a result of rain.

Women

Year	Champion	Coach	Score	Runner-Up	Score	Individual Champion
1982	Tulsa	Dale McNamara	1191	Texas Christian	1227	Kathy Baker, Tulsa
1983	Texas Christian	Fred Warren	1193	Tulsa	1196	Penny Hammel, Miami (FL)
1984	Miami (FL)	Lela Cannon	1214	Arizona St	1221	Cindy Schreyer, Georgia
1985	Florida	Mimi Ryan	1218	Tulsa	1233	Danielle Ammaccapane, Arizona St
1986	Florida	Mimi Ryan	1180	Miami (FL)	1188	Page Dunlap, Florida
1987	San Jose St	Mark Gale	1187	Furman	1188	Caroline Keggi, New Mexico
1988	Tulsa	Dale McNamara	1175	Georgia	1182	Melissa McNamara, Tulsa
				Arizona	1182	
1989	San Jose St	Mark Gale	1208	Tulsa	1209	Pat Hurst, San Jose St
1990	Arizona St	Linda Vollstedt	1206	UCLA	1222	Susan Slaughter, Arizona
1991	UCLA*	Jackie Steinmann	1197	San Jose St	1197	Annika Sorenstam, Arizona
1992	San Jose St	Mark Gale	1171	Arizona	1175	Vicki Goetze, Georgia
1993	Arizona St	Linda Vollstedt	1187	Texas	1189	Charlotta Sorenstam, Texas

*Won sudden death playoff. Note: Par-74 tournaments held in 1983 and 1988; par-72 tournament held in 1990; all other championships par-73 tournaments.

Buckeye Bonanza

When it comes to Division III athletic success, all roads lead to Ohio. First and foremost, of course, there is mighty Kenyon College in Gambier, the champion in both men's and women's swimming, for the 14th and tenth consecutive seasons respectively. As if that isn't enough, Kenyon added a national title in women's tennis as well, its first ever. But Kenyon isn't the only Division III power in the Buckeye state. Ohio Wesleyan in Delaware was the runner-up in three sports—soccer, lacrosse and golf—while Ohio Northern in Ada was the national champion in men's basketball and Capital University in Columbus was the national runner-up in women's basketball.

Gymnastics

Men
Team Champions

Year	Champion	Coach	Pts	Runner-Up	Pts
1938	Chicago	Dan Hoffer	22	Illinois	18
1939	Illinois	Hartley Price	21	Army	17
1940	Illinois	Hartley Price	20	Navy	17
1941	Illinois	Hartley Price	68.5	Minnesota	52.5
1942	Illinois	Hartley Price	39	Penn St	30
1943-47	No tournament				
1948	Penn St	Gene Wettstone	55	Temple	34.5
1949	Temple	Max Younger	28	Minnesota	18
1950	Illinois	Charley Pond	26	Temple	25
1951	Florida St	Hartley Price	26	Illinois	23.5
				Southern Cal	23.5
1952	Florida St	Hartley Price	89.5	Southern Cal	75
1953	Penn St	Gene Wettstone	91.5	Illinois	68
1954	Penn St	Gene Wettstone	137	Illinois	68
1955	Illinois	Charley Pond	82	Penn St	69
1956	Illinois	Charley Pond	123.5	Penn St	67.5
1957	Penn St	Gene Wettstone	88.5	Illinois	80
1958	Michigan St	George Szypula	79		
	Illinois	Charley Pond	79		
1959	Penn St	Gene Wettstone	152	Illinois	87.5
1960	Penn St	Gene Wettstone	112.5	Southern Cal	65.5
1961	Penn St	Gene Wettstone	88.5	Southern Illinois	80.5
1962	Southern Cal	Jack Beckner	95.5	Southern Illinois	75
1963	Michigan	Newton Loken	129	Southern Illinois	73
1964	Southern Illinois	Bill Meade	84.5	Southern Cal	69.5
1965	Penn St	Gene Wettstone	68.5	Washington	51.5
1966	Southern Illinois	Bill Meade	187.200	California	185.100
1967	Southern Illinois	Bill Meade	189.550	Michigan	187.400
1968	California	Hal Frey	188.250	Southern Illinois	188.150
1969	Iowa	Mike Jacobson	161.175	Penn St	160.450
	Michigan*	Newton Loken		Colorado St	
1970	Michigan	Newton Loken	164.150	Iowa St	164.050
				New Mexico St	
1971	Iowa St	Ed Gagnier	319.075	Southern Illinois	316.650
1972	Southern Illinois	Bill Meade	315.925	Iowa St	312.325
1973	Iowa St	Ed Gagnier	325.150	Penn St	323.025
1974	Iowa St	Ed Gagnier	326.100	Arizona St	322.050
1975	California	Hal Frey	437.325	Louisiana St	433.700
1976	Penn St	Gene Wettstone	432.075	Louisiana St	425.125
1977	Indiana St	Roger Counsil	434.475		
	Oklahoma	Paul Ziert	434.475		
1978	Oklahoma	Paul Ziert	439.350	Arizona St	437.075
1979	Nebraska	Francis Allen	448.275	Oklahoma	446.625
1980	Nebraska	Francis Allen	563.300	Iowa St	557.650
1981	Nebraska	Francis Allen	284.600	Oklahoma	281.950
1982	Nebraska	Francis Allen	285.500	UCLA	281.050
1983	Nebraska	Francis Allen	287.800	UCLA	283.900
1984	UCLA	Art Shurlock	287.300	Penn St	281.250
1985	Ohio St	Michael Willson	285.350	Nebraska	284.550
1986	Arizona St	Don Robinson	283.900	Nebraska	283.600
1987	UCLA	Art Shurlock	285.300	Nebraska	284.750
1988	Nebraska	Francis Allen	288.150	Illinois	287.150
1989	Illinois	Yoshi Hayasaki	283.400	Nebraska	282.300
1990	Nebraska	Francis Allen	287.400	Minnesota	287.300
1991	Oklahoma	Greg Buwick	288.025	Penn St	285.500
1992	Stanford	Sadao Hamada	289.575	Nebraska	288.950
1993	Stanford	Sadao Hamada	276.500	Nebraska	275.500

*Trampoline.

Men (Cont.)
Individual Champions

ALL-AROUND

1938.....Joe Giallombardo, Illinois
1939.....Joe Giallombardo, Illinois
1940.....Joe Giallombardo, Illinois
          Paul Fina, Illinois
1941.....Courtney Shanken, Chicago
1942.....Newt Loken, Minnesota
1948.....Ray Sorenson, Penn St
1949.....Joe Kotys, Kent
1950.....Joe Kotys, Kent
1951.....Bill Roetzheim, Florida St
1952.....Jack Beckner, Southern Cal
1953.....Jean Cronstedt, Penn St
1954.....Jean Cronstedt, Penn St
1955.....Karl Schwenzfeier, Penn St
1956.....Don Tonry, Illinois
1957.....Armando Vega, Penn St
1958.....Abie Grossfeld, Illinois
1959.....Armando Vega, Penn St
1960.....Jay Werner, Penn St
1961.....Gregor Weiss, Penn St
1962.....Robert Lynn, Southern Cal
1963.....Gil Larose, Michigan
1964.....Ron Barak, Southern Cal
1965.....Mike Jacobson, Penn St
1966.....Steve Cohen, Penn St
1967.....Steve Cohen, Penn St
1968.....Makoto Sakamoto, USC
1969.....Mauno Nissinen, Wash
1970.....Yoshi Hayasaki, Wash
1971.....Yoshi Hayasaki, Wash
1972.....Steve Hug, Stanford
1973.....Steve Hug, Stanford
          Marshall Avener, Penn St.
1974.....Steve Hug, Stanford
1975.....Wayne Young, BYU
1976   Peter Kormann, Southern
          Conn St
1977.....Kurt Thomas, Indiana St
1978.....Bart Conner, Oklahoma
1979.....Kurt Thomas, Indiana St
1980.....Jim Hartung, Nebraska
1981.....Jim Hartung, Nebraska
1982.....Peter Vidmar, UCLA
1983.....Peter Vidmar, UCLA
1984.....Mitch Gaylord, UCLA
1985.....Wes Suter, Nebraska
1986.....Jon Louis, Stanford
1987......Tom Schlesinger, Nebraska
1988.....Vacated†
1989.....Patrick Kirsey, Nebraska
1990.....Mike Racanelli, Ohio St
1991.....John Roethlisberger, Minn
1992.....John Roethlisberger, Minn
1993.....John Roethlisberger, Minn

HORIZONTAL BAR

1938.....Bob Sears, Army
1939.....Adam Walters, Temple
1940.....Norm Boardman, Temple
1941.....Newt Loken, Minnesota
1942.....Norm Boardman, Temple
1948.....Joe Calvetti, Illinois
1949.....Bob Stout, Temple

1950.....Joe Kotys, Kent
1951.....Bill Roetzheim, Florida St
1952.....Charles Simms, USC
1953.....Hal Lewis, Navy
1954.....Jean Cronstedt, Penn St
1955.....Carlton Rintz, Michigan St
1956.....Ronnie Amster, Florida St
1957.....Abie Grossfeld, Illinois
1958.....Abie Grossfeld, Illinois
1959.....Stanley Tarshis, Mich St
1960.....Stanley Tarshis, Mich St
1961.....Bruno Klaus, Southern Ill
1962.....Robert Lynn, USC
1963.....Gil Larose, Michigan
1964.....Ron Barak, USC
1965.....Jim Curzi, Michigan St
          Mike Jacobsen, Penn St
1966.....Rusty Rock, Cal St-
          Northridge
1967.....Rich Grigsby, Cal St-
          Northridge
1968.....Makoto Sakamoto, USC
1969.....Bob Manna, New Mexico
1970.....Yoshi Hayasaki, Wash
1971.....Brent Simmons, Iowa St
1972.....Tom Lindner, Southern Ill
1973.....Jon Aitken, New Mexico
1974.....Rick Banley, Indiana St
1975.....Rich Larsen, Iowa St
1976.....Tom Beach, California
1977.....John Hart, UCLA
1978.....Mel Cooley, Washington
1979.....Kurt Thomas, Indiana St
1980.....Philip Cahoy, Nebraska
1981.....Philip Cahoy, Nebraska
1982.....Peter Vidmar, UCLA
1983.....Scott Johnson, Nebraska
1984.....Charles Lakes, Illinois
1985.....Dan Hayden, Arizona St
............Wes Suter, Nebraska
1986.....Dan Hayden, Arizona St
1987.....David Moriel, UCLA
1988.....Vacated†
1989.....Vacated†
1990.....Chris Waller, UCLA
1991.....Luis Lopez, New Mexico
1992.....Jair Lynch, Stanford
1993.....Steve McCain, UCLA

PARALLEL BARS

1938.....Erwin Beyer, Chicago
1939.....Bob Sears, Army
1940.....Bob Hanning, Minnesota
1941.....Caton Cobb, Illinois
1942.....Hal Zimmerman, Penn St
1948.....Ray Sorenson, Penn St
1949.....Joe Kotys, Kent
          Mel Stout, Michigan St
1950.....Joe Kotys, Kent
1951.....Jack Beckner, USC
1952.....Jack Beckner, USC
1953.....Jean Cronstedt, Penn St
1954.....Jean Cronstedt, Penn St
1955.....Carlton Rintz, Michigan St
1956.....Armando Vega, Penn St

1957.....Armando Vega, Penn St
1958.....Tad Muzyczko, Mich St
1959.....Armando Vega, Penn St
1960.....Robert Lynn, Southern Cal
1961.....Fred Tijerina, Southern Ill
          Jeff Cardinalli, Springfield
1962.....Robert Lynn, Southern Cal
1963.....Arno Lascari, Michigan
1964.....Ron Barak, Southern Cal
1965.....Jim Curzi, Michigan St
1966.....Jim Curzi, Michigan St
1967.....Makoto Sakamoto, USC
1968.....Makoto Sakamoto, USC
1969.....Ron Rapper, Michigan
1970.....Ron Rapper, Michigan
1971.....Brent Simmons, Iowa St
          Tom Dunn, Penn St
1972.....Dennis Mazur, Iowa St
1973.....Steve Hug, Stanford
1974.....Steve Hug, Stanford
1975.....Yoichi Tomita, Long
          Beach St
1976.....Gene Whelan, Penn St
1977.....Kurt Thomas, Indiana St
1978.....John Corritore, Michigan
1979.....Kurt Thomas, Indiana St
1980.....Philip Cahoy, Nebraska
1981.....Philip Cahoy, Nebraska
          Peter Vidmar, UCLA
          Jim Hartung, Nebraska
1982.....Jim Hartung, Nebraska
1983.....Scott Johnson, Nebraska
1984.....Tim Daggett, UCLA
1985.....Dan Hayden, Arizona St
          Noah Riskin, Ohio St
          Seth Riskin, Ohio St
1986.....Dan Hayden, Arizona St
1987.....Kevin Davis, Nebraska
          Tom Schlesinger, Nebraska
1988.....Kevin Davis, Nebraska
1989.....Vacated†
1990.....Patrick Kirksey, Nebraska
1991.....Scott Keswick, UCLA
          John Roethlisberger, Minn
1992.....Dom Minicucci, Temple
1993.....Jair Lynch, Stanford

LONG HORSE VAULT

1938.....Erwin Beyer, Chicago
1939.....Marv Forman, Illinois
1940.....Earl Shanken, Chicago
1941.....Earl Shanken, Chicago
1942.....Earl Shanken, Chicago
1948.....Jim Peterson, Minnesota
1962.....Bruno Klaus, Southern Ill
1963.....Gil Larose, Michigan
1964.....Sidney Oglesby, Syracuse
1965.....Dan Millman, California
1966.....Frank Schmitz, S Illinois
1967.....Paul Mayer, S Illinois
1968.....Bruce Colter, Cal St-Los
          Angeles
1969.....Dan Bowles, California
          Jack McCarthy, Illinois
1970.....Doug Boger, Arizona

Men (Cont.)
Individual Champions (Cont.)

1971.....Pat Mahoney, Cal St-
Northridge
1972.....Gary Morava, Southern Ill
1973.....John Crosby, S Conn St
1974.....Greg Goodhue, Oklahoma
1975.....Tom Beach, California
1976.....Sam Shaw, Cal St-
Fullerton
1977.....Steve Wejmar, Wash
1978......Ron Galimore, Louisiana St
1979.....Leslie Moore, Oklahoma
1980.....Ron Galimore, Iowa St
1981.....Ron Galimore, Iowa St
1982.....Randall Wickstrom, Cal
Steve Elliott, Nebraska
1983.....Chris Riegel, Nebraska
Mark Oates, Oklahoma
1984.....Chris Riegel, Nebraska
1985.....Derrick Cornelius,
Cortland St
1986.....Chad Fox, New Mexico
1987.....Chad Fox, New Mexico
1988.....Chad Fox, New Mexico
1989.....Chad Fox, New Mexico
1990.....Brad Hayashi, UCLA
1991.....Adam Carton, Penn St
1992.....Jason Hebert, Syracuse
1993.....Steve Wiegel, N Mexico

SIDE HORSE

1938.....Erwin Beyer, Chicago
1939.....Erwin Beyer, Chicago
1940.....Harry Koehnemann, Illinois
1941.....Caton Cobb, Illinois
1942.....Caton Cobb, Illinois
1948.....Steve Greene, Penn St
1949.....Joe Berenato, Temple
1950.....Gene Rabbitt, Syracuse
1951.....Joe Kotys, Kent
1952.....Frank Bare, Illinois
1953.....Carlton Rintz, Michigan St
1954.....Robert Lawrence, Penn St
1955.....Carlton Rintz, Michigan St
1956.....James Brown, Cal St-
Los Angeles
1957.....John Davis, Illinois
1958.....Bill Buck, Iowa
1959.....Art Shurlock, California
1960.....James Fairchild, California
1961.....James Fairchild, California
1962.....Mike Aufrecht, Illinois
1963.....Russ Mills, Yale
1964.....Russ Mills, Yale
1965.....Bob Elsinger, Springfield
1966.....Gary Hoskins, Cal St-
Los Angeles
1967.....Keith McCanless, Iowa
1968.....Jack Ryan, Colorado
1969.....Keith McCanless, Iowa
1970.....Russ Hoffman, Iowa St
John Russo, Wisconsin
1971.....Russ Hoffman, Iowa St

1972.....Russ Hoffman, Iowa St
1973.....Ed Slezak, Indiana St
1974.....Ted Marcy, Stanford
1975.....Ted Marcy, Stanford
1976.....Ted Marcy, Stanford
1977.....Chuck Walter, New Mexico
1978.....Mike Burke, Northern Ill
1979.....Mike Burke, Northern Ill
1980.....David Stoldt, Illinois
1981.....Mark Bergman, California
Steve Jennings, New Mexico
1982.....Peter Vidmar, UCLA
Steve Jennings, New Mexico
1983.....Doug Kieso, Northern Ill
1984.....Tim Daggett, UCLA
1985.....Tony Pineda, UCLA
1986.....Curtis Holdsworth, UCLA
1987.....Li Xiao Ping, Cal St-
Fullerton
1988.....Vacated†
Mark Sohn, Penn St
1989.....Mark Sohn, Penn St
Chris Waller, UCLA
1990.....Mark Sohn, Penn St
1991.....Mark Sohn, Penn St
1992.....Che Bowers, Nebraska
1993.....John Roethlisberger, Minn

FLOOR EXERCISE

1941.....Lou Fina, Illinois
1953.....Bob Sullivan, Illinois
1954.....Jean Cronstedt, Penn St
1955.....Don Faber, UCLA
1956.....Jamile Ashmore, Florida St
1957.....Norman Marks, Cal St-
Los Angeles
1958.....Abie Grossfeld, Illinois
1959.....Don Tonry, Illinois
1960.....Ray Hadley, Illinois
1961.....Robert Lynn, Southern Cal
1962.....Robert Lynn, Southern Cal
1963.....Tom Seward, Penn St
Mike Henderson, Michigan
1964.....Rusty Mitchell, S Illinois
1965.....Frank Schmitz, S Illinois
1966.....Frank Schmitz, S Illinois
1967.....Dave Jacobs, Michigan
1968.....Toby Towson, Michigan St
1969.....Toby Towson, Michigan St
1970.....Tom Proulx, Colorado St
1971.....Stormy Eaton, New Mexico
1972.....Odessa Lovin, Oklahoma
1973.....Odessa Lovin, Oklahoma
1974.....Doug Fitzjarrell, Iowa St
1975.....Kent Brown, Arizona St
1976.....Bob Robbins, Colorado St
1977.....Ron Galimore, Louisiana St
1978.....Curt Austin, Iowa St
1979.....Mike Wilson, Oklahoma
Bart Conner, Oklahoma
1980.....Steve Elliott, Nebraska
1981......James Yuhashi, Oregon

1982.....Steve Elliott, Nebraska
1983.....Scott Johnson, Nebraska
David Branch, Arizona St
Donnie Hinton, Arizona St
1984.....Kevin Ekburg, Northern Ill
1985.....Wes Suter, Nebraska
1986.....Jerry Burrell, Arizona St
Brian Ginsberg, UCLA
1987.....Chad Fox, New Mexico
1988.....Chris Wyatt, Temple
1989.....Jody Newman, Arizona St
1990.....Mike Racanelli, Ohio St
1991.....Brad Hayashi, UCLA
1992.....Brian Winkler, Michigan
1993.....Richard Grace, Nebraska

RINGS

1959.....Armando Vega, Penn St
1960.....Sam Garcia, Southern Cal
1961.....Fred Orlofsky, Southern Ill
1962.....Dale Cooper, Michigan St
1963.....Dale Cooper, Michigan St
1964.....Chris Evans, Arizona St
1965.....Glenn Gailis, Iowa
1966.....Ed Gunny, Michigan St
1967.....Josh Robison, California
1968.....Pat Arnold, Arizona
1969.....Paul Vexler, Penn St
Ward Maythaler, Iowa St
1970.....Dave Seal, Indiana St
1971.....Charles Ropiequet, S Illinois
1972.....Dave Seal, Indiana St
1973.....Bob Mahorney, Indiana St
1974.....Keith Heaver, Iowa St
1975.....Keith Heaver, Iowa St
1976.....Doug Wood, Iowa St
1977.....Doug Wood, Iowa St
1978.....Scott McEldowney, Oregon
1979.....Kirk Mango, Northern Ill
1980.....Jim Hartung, Nebraska
1981.....Jim Hartung, Nebraska
1982.....Jim Hartung, Nebraska
1983.....Alex Schwartz, UCLA
1984.....Tim Daggett, UCLA
1985.....Mark Diab, Iowa St
1986.....Mark Diab, Iowa St
1987.....Paul O'Neill, Houst Baptist
1988.....Paul O'Neill, New Mexico
1989.....Vacated†
Paul O'Neill, New Mexico
1990.....Wayne Cowden, Penn St
1991.....Adam Carton, Penn St
1992.....Scott Keswick, UCLA
1993.....Chris LaMorte, N Mexico

† Championships won by Miguel
Rubio (All Around, 1988; Horizontal
Bar, 1988-89) and Alfonso Rodriguez
(Pommel Horse, 1988; Rings, 1989;
Parallel Bars, 1989) were vacated by
action of the NCAA Committee on
Infractions

Gymnastics (Cont.)

Men (Cont.)

DIVISION II (DISCONTINUED)

Year	Champion	Coach	Pts	Runner-Up	Pts
1968	Cal St-Northridge	Bill Vincent	179.400	Springfield	178.050
1969	Cal St-Northridge	Bill Vincent	151.800	Southern Connecticut St	145.075
1970	Northwestern Louisiana	Armando Vega	160.250	Southern Connecticut St	159.300
1971	Cal St-Fullerton	Dick Wolfe	158.150	Springfield	156.987
1972	Cal St-Fullerton	Dick Wolfe	160.550	Southern Connecticut St	153.050
1973	Southern Connecticut St	Abe Grossfeld	160.750	Cal St-Northridge	158.700
1974	Cal St-Fullerton	Dick Wolfe	309.800	Southern Connecticut St	309.400
1975	Southern Connecticut St	Abe Grossfeld	411.650	IL-Chicago	398.800
1976	Southern Connecticut St	Abe Grossfeld	419.200	IL-Chicago	388.850
1977	Springfield	Frank Wolcott	395.950	Cal St-Northridge	381.250
1978	IL-Chicago	Clarence Johnson Arnold Gentile	406.850	Cal St-Northridge	400.400
1979	IL-Chicago	Clarence Johnson	418.550	WI-Oshkosh	385.650
1980	WI-Oshkosh	Ken Allen	260.550	Cal St-Chico	256.050
1981	WI-Oshkosh	Ken Allen	209.500	Springfield	201.550
1982	WI-Oshkosh	Ken Allen	216.050	East Stroudsburg	211.200
1983	East Stroudsburg	Bruno Klaus	258.650	WI-Oshkosh	257.850
1984	East Stroudsburg	Bruno Klaus	270.800	Cortland St	246.350

Women
Team Champions

Year	Champion	Coach	Pts	Runner-Up	Pts
1982	Utah	Greg Marsden	148.60	Cal St-Fullerton	144.10
1983	Utah	Greg Marsden	184.65	Arizona St	183.30
1984	Utah	Greg Marsden	186.05	UCLA	185.55
1985	Utah	Greg Marsden	188.35	Arizona St	186.60
1986	Utah	Greg Marsden	186.95	Arizona St	186.70
1987	Georgia	Suzanne Yoculan	187.90	Utah	187.55
1988	Alabama	Sarah Patterson	190.05	Utah	189.50
1989	Georgia	Suzanne Yoculan	192.65	UCLA	192.60
1990	Utah	Greg Marsden	194.900	Alabama	194.575
1991	Alabama	Sarah Patterson	195.125	Utah	194.375
1992	Utah	Greg Marsden	195.650	Georgia	194.600
1993	Georgia	Suzanne Yoculan	198.000	Alabama	196.825

Individual Champions

ALL-AROUND

1982	Sue Stednitz, Utah
1983	Megan McCunniff, Utah
1984	Megan McCunniff-Marsden, Utah
1985	Penney Hauschild, Alabama
1986	Penney Hauschild, Alabama
	Jackie Brummer, Arizona St
1987	Kelly Garrison-Steves, Oklahoma
1988	Kelly Garrison-Steves, Oklahoma
1989	Corrinne Wright, Georgia
1990	Dee Dee Foster, Alabama
1991	Hope Spivey, Georgia
1992	Missy Marlowe, Utah
1993	Jenny Hansen, Kentucky

VAULT

1982	Elaine Alfano, Utah
1983	Elaine Alfano, Utah
1984	Megan Marsden, Utah
1985	Elaine Alfano, Utah
1986	Kim Neal, Arizona St
	Pam Loree, Penn St
1987	Yumi Mordre, Washington
1988	Jill Andrews, UCLA
1989	Kim Hamilton, UCLA
1990	Michele Bryant, Nebraska
1991	Anna Basaldva, Arizona

1992	Tammy Marshall, Massachusetts
	Heather Stepp, Georgia
	Kristein Kenoyer, Utah
1993	Heather Stepp, Georgia

BALANCE BEAM

1982	Sue Stednitz, Utah
1983	Julie Goewey, Cal St-Fullerton
1984	Heidi Anderson, Oregon St
1985	Lisa Zeis, Arizona St
1986	Jackie Brummer, Arizona St
1987	Yumi Mordre, Washington
1988	Kelly Garrison-Steves, Oklahoma
1989	Jill Andrews, UCLA
	Joy Selig, Oregon St
1990	Joy Selig, Oregon St
1991	Missy Marlowe, Utah
1992	Missy Marlowe, Utah
	Dana Dobransky, Alabama
1993	Dana Dobransky, Alabama

FLOOR EXERCISE

1982	Mary Ayotte-Law, Oregon St
1983	Kim Neal, Arizona St
1984	Maria Anz, Florida
1985	Lisa Mitzel, Utah
1986	Lisa Zeis, Arizona St
	Penney Hauschild, Alabama

Gymnastics (Cont.)

Women (Cont.)
Individual Champions (Cont.)

1987 ....Kim Hamilton, UCLA
1988 ....Kim Hamilton, UCLA
1989 ....Corrinne Wright, Georgia
                Kim Hamilton, UCLA
1990 ....Joy Selig, Oregon St
1991 ....Hope Spivey, Georgia
1992 ....Missy Marlowe, Utah
1993 ....Heather Stepp, Georgia
                Tammy Marshall, Massachusetts
                Amy Durham, Oregon St

1983 ....Jeri Cameron, Arizona St
1984 ....Jackie Brummer, Arizona St
1985 ....Penney Hauschild, Alabama
1986 ....Lucy Wener, Georgia
1987 ....Lucy Wener, Georgia
1988 ....Kelly Garrison-Steves, Oklahoma
1989 ....Lucy Wener, Georgia
1990 ....Marie Roethlisberger, Minnesota
1991 ....Kelly Macy, Georgia
1992 ....Missy Marlowe, Utah
1993 ....Agina Simpkins, Georgia
                Beth Wymer, Michigan

UNEVEN BARS

1982 ....Lisa Shirk, Pittsburgh

DIVISION II (DISCONTINUED)

Year	Champion	Coach	Pts	Runner-Up	Pts
1982	Cal St-Northridge	Donna Stuart	138.10	Jacksonville St	134.05
1983	Denver	Dan Garcia	174.80	Cal St-Northridge	174.35
1984	Jacksonville St	Robert Dillard	173.40	SE Missouri St	171.45
1985	Jacksonville St	Robert Dillard	176.85	SE Missouri St	173.95
1986	Seattle Pacific	Laurel Tindall	175.80	Jacksonville St	175.15

Ice Hockey

DIVISION I

Year	Champion	Coach	Score	Runner-Up	Most Outstanding Player
1948	Michigan	Vic Heyliger	8-4	Dartmouth	Joe Riley, Dartmouth, F
1949	Boston Col	John Kelley	4-3	Dartmouth	Dick Desmond, Dartmouth, G
1950	Colorado Col	Cheddy Thompson	13-4	Boston U	Ralph Bevins, Boston U, G
1951	Michigan	Vic Heyliger	7-1	Brown	Ed Whiston, Brown, G
1952	Michigan	Vic Heyliger	4-1	Colorado Col	Kenneth Kinsley, Colorado Col, G
1953	Michigan	Vic Heyliger	7-3	Minnesota	John Matchefts, Michigan, F
1954	Rensselaer	Ned Harkness	5-4 (OT)	Minnesota	Abbie Moore, Rensselaer, F
1955	Michigan	Vic Heyliger	5-3	Colorado Col	Philip Hilton, Colorado Col, Def
1956	Michigan	Vic Heyliger	7-5	Michigan Tech	Lorne Howes, Michigan, G
1957	Colorado Col	Thomas Bedecki	13-6	Michigan	Bob McCusker, Colorado Col, F
1958	Denver	Murray Armstrong	6-2	N Dakota	Murray Massier, Denver, F
1959	N Dakota	Bob May	4-3 (OT)	Michigan St	Reg Morelli, N Dakota, F
1960	Denver	Murray Armstrong	5-3	Michigan Tech	Bob Marquis, Boston U, F
1961	Denver	Murray Armstrong	12-2	St Lawrence	Barry Urbanski, Boston U, G
1962	Michigan Tech	John MacInnes	7-1	Clarkson	Louis Angotti, Michigan Tech, F
1963	N Dakota	Barney Thorndycraft	6-5	Denver	Al McLean, N Dakota, F
1964	Michigan	Allen Renfrew	6-3	Denver	Bob Gray, Michigan, G
1965	Michigan Tech	John MacInnes	8-2	Boston Col	Gary Milroy, Michigan Tech, F
1966	Michigan St	Amo Bessone	6-1	Clarkson	Gaye Cooley, Michigan St, G
1967	Cornell	Ned Harkness	4-1	Boston U	Walt Stanowski, Cornell, Def
1968	Denver	Murray Armstrong	4-0	N Dakota	Gerry Powers, Denver, G
1969	Denver	Murray Armstrong	4-3	Cornell	Keith Magnuson, Denver, Def
1970	Cornell	Ned Harkness	6-4	Clarkson	Daniel Lodboa, Cornell, Def
1971	Boston U	Jack Kelley	4-2	Minnesota	Dan Brady, Boston U, G
1972	Boston U	Jack Kelley	4-0	Cornell	Tim Regan, Boston U, G
1973	Wisconsin	Bob Johnson	4-2	Vacated	Dean Talafous, Wisconsin, F
1974	Minnesota	Herb Brooks	4-2	Michigan Tech	Brad Shelstad, Minnesota, G
1975	Michigan Tech	John MacInnes	6-1	Minnesota	Jim Warden, Michigan Tech, G
1976	Minnesota	Herb Brooks	6-4	Michigan Tech	Tom Vanelli, Minnesota, F
1977	Wisconsin	Bob Johnson	6-5 (OT)	Michigan	Julian Baretta, Wisconsin, G
1978	Boston U	Jack Parker	5-3	Boston Col	Jack O'Callahan, Boston U, Def
1979	Minnesota	Herb Brooks	4-3	N Dakota	Steve Janaszak, Minnesota, G
1980	N Dakota	John Gasparini	5-2	Northern Michigan	Doug Smail, N Dakota, F
1981	Wisconsin	Bob Johnson	6-3	Minnesota	Marc Behrend, Wisconsin, G
1982	N Dakota	John Gasparini	5-2	Wisconsin	Phil Sykes, N Dakota, F
1983	Wisconsin	Jeff Sauer	6-2	Harvard	Marc Behrend, Wisconsin, G
1984	Bowling Green	Jerry York	5-4 (OT)	MN-Duluth	Gary Kruzich, Bowling Green, G
1985	Rensselaer	Mike Addesa	2-1	Providence	Chris Terreri, Providence, G
1986	Michigan St	Ron Mason	6-5	Harvard	Mike Donnelly, Michigan St, F
1987	N Dakota	John Gasparini	5-3	Michigan St	Tony Hrkac, N Dakota, F

Ice Hockey (Cont.)

DIVISION I (CONT.)

Year	Champion	Coach	Score	Runner-Up	Most Outstanding Player
1988	Lake Superior St	Frank Anzalone	4-3 (OT)	St Lawrence	Bruce Hoffort, Lake Superior St, G
1989	Harvard	Bill Cleary	4-3 (OT)	Minnesota	Ted Donato, Harvard, F
1990	Wisconsin	Jeff Sauer	7-3	Colgate	Chris Tancill, Wisconsin, F
1991	Northern Michigan	Rick Comley	8-7 (3OT)	Boston U	Scott Beattie, Northern Michigan, F
1992	Lake Superior St	Jeff Jackson	4-2	Wisconsin	Paul Constantin, Lake Superior St, F
1993	Maine	Shawn Walsh	5-4	Lake Superior St	Jim Montgomery, Maine

DIVISION II (DISCONTINUED, THEN RENEWED)

Year	Champion	Coach	Score	Runner-Up
1978	Merrimack	Thom Lawler	12-2	Lake Forest
1979	Lowell	Bill Riley Jr	6-4	Mankato St
1980	Mankato St	Don Brose	5-2	Elmira
1981	Lowell	Bill Riley Jr	5-4	Plattsburgh St
1982	Lowell	Bill Riley Jr	6-1	Plattsburgh St
1983	Rochester Inst	Brian Mason	4-2	Bemidji St
1984	Bemidji St	R.H. (Bob) Peters	14-4*	Merrimack
1993	Bemidji St	R.H. (Bob) Peters	15-6*	Mercyhurst

*Two-game, total-goal series.

DIVISION III

Year	Champion	Coach	Score	Runner-Up
1984	Babson	Bob Riley	8-0	Union (NY)
1985	Rochester Inst	Bruce Delventhal	5-1	Bemidji St
1986	Bemidji St	R.H. (Bob) Peters	8-5	Vacated
1987	Vacated			Oswego St
1988	WI-River Falls	Rick Kozuback	7-1, 3-5, 3-0	Elmira
1989	WI-Stevens Point	Mark Mazzoleni	3-3, 3-2	Rochester Inst
1990	WI-Stevens Point	Mark Mazzoleni	10-1, 3-6, 1-0	Plattsburgh St
1991	WI-Stevens Point	Mark Mazzoleni	6-2	Mankato St
1992	Plattsburgh St	Bob Emery	7-3	WI-Stevens Point
1993	WI-Stevens Point	Joe Baldarotta	4-3	WI-River Falls

Lacrosse

Men

DIVISION I

Year	Champion	Coach	Score	Runner-Up
1971	Cornell	Richie Moran	12-6	Maryland
1972	Virginia	Glenn Thiel	13-12	Johns Hopkins
1973	Maryland	Bud Beardmore	10-9 (2 OT)	Johns Hopkins
1974	Johns Hopkins	Bob Scott	17-12	Maryland
1975	Maryland	Bud Beardmore	20-13	Navy
1976	Cornell	Richie Moran	16-13 (OT)	Maryland
1977	Cornell	Richie Moran	16-8	Johns Hopkins
1978	Johns Hopkins	Henry Ciccarone	13-8	Cornell
1979	Johns Hopkins	Henry Ciccarone	15-9	Maryland
1980	Johns Hopkins	Henry Ciccarone	9-8 (2 OT)	Virginia
1981	N Carolina	Willie Scroggs	14-13	Johns Hopkins
1982	N Carolina	Willie Scroggs	7-5	Johns Hopkins
1983	Syracuse	Roy Simmons Jr	17-16	Johns Hopkins
1984	Johns Hopkins	Don Zimmerman	13-10	Syracuse
1985	Johns Hopkins	Don Zimmerman	11-4	Syracuse
1986	N Carolina	Willie Scroggs	10-9 (OT)	Virginia
1987	Johns Hopkins	Don Zimmerman	11-10	Cornell
1988	Syracuse	Roy Simmons Jr	13-8	Cornell
1989	Syracuse	Roy Simmons Jr	13-12	Johns Hopkins
1990	Syracuse	Roy Simmons Jr	21-9	Loyola (MD)
1991	N Carolina	Dave Klarmann	18-13	Towson St
1992	Princeton	Bill Tierney	10-9	Syracuse
1993	Syracuse	Roy Simmons Jr	13-12	N Carolina

Men (Cont.)

DIVISION II (DISCONTINUED, THEN RENEWED)

Year	Champion	Coach	Score	Runner-Up
1974	Towson St	Carl Runk	18-17 (OT)	Hobart
1975	Cortland St	Chuck Winters	12-11	Hobart
1976	Hobart	Jerry Schmidt	18-9	Adelphi
1977	Hobart	Jerry Schmidt	23-13	Washington (MD)
1978	Roanoke	Paul Griffin	14-13	Hobart
1979	Adelphi	Paul Doherty	17-12	MD-Baltimore County
1980	MD-Baltimore County	Dick Watts	23-14	Adelphi
1981	Adelphi	Paul Doherty	17-14	Loyola (MD)
1993	Adelphi	Kevin Sheehan	11-7	LIU-C.W. Post

DIVISION III

Year	Champion	Coach	Score	Runner-Up
1980	Hobart	Dave Urick	11-8	Cortland St
1981	Hobart	Dave Urick	10-8	Cortland St
1982	Hobart	Dave Urick	9-8 (OT)	Washington (MD)
1983	Hobart	Dave Urick	13-9	Roanoke
1984	Hobart	Dave Urick	12-5	Washington (MD)
1985	Hobart	Dave Urick	15-8	Washington (MD)
1986	Hobart	Dave Urick	13-10	Washington (MD)
1987	Hobart	Dave Urick	9-5	Ohio Wesleyan
1988	Hobart	Dave Urick	18-9	Ohio Wesleyan
1989	Hobart	Dave Urick	11-8	Ohio Wesleyan
1990	Hobart	B. J. O'Hara	18-6	Washington (MD)
1991	Hobart	B. J. O'Hara	12-11	Salisbury St
1992	Nazareth (NY)	Scott Nelson	13-12	Hobart
1993	Hobart	B.J. O'Hara	16-10	Ohio Wesleyan

Women

DIVISION I

Year	Champion	Coach	Score	Runner-Up
1982	Massachusetts	Pamela Hixon	9-6	Trenton St
1983	Delaware	Janet Smith	10-7	Temple
1984	Temple	Tina Sloan Green	6-4	Maryland
1985	New Hampshire	Marisa Didio	6-5	Maryland
1986	Maryland	Sue Tyler	11-10	Penn St
1987	Penn St	Susan Scheetz	7-6	Temple
1988	Temple	Tina Sloan Green	15-7	Penn St
1989	Penn St	Susan Scheetz	7-6	Harvard
1990	Harvard	Carole Kleinfelder	8-7	Maryland
1991	Virginia	Jane Miller	8-6	Maryland
1992	Maryland	Cindy Timchal	11-10	Harvard
1993	Virginia	Jane Miller	8-6 (OT)	Princeton

DIVISION III

Year	Champion	Score	Runner-Up	Year	Champion	Score	Runner-Up
1985	Trenton St	7-4	Ursinus	1990	Ursinus	7-6	St Lawrence
1986	Ursinus	12-10	Trenton St	1991	Trenton St	7-6	Ursinus
1987	Trenton St	8-7 (OT)	Ursinus	1992	Trenton St	5-3	William Smith
1988	Trenton St	14-11	William Smith	1993	Trenton St	10-9	William Smith
1989	Ursinus	8-6	Trenton St				

Rifle

Men's and Women's Combined

Year	Champion	Coach	Score	Runner-Up	Score	Individual Champion Air Rifle	Smallbore
1980	Tennessee Tech	James Newkirk	6201	W Virginia	6150	Rod Fitz-Randolph, Tennessee Tech	Rod Fitz-Randolph, Tennessee Tech
1981	Tennessee Tech	James Newkirk	6139	W Virginia	6136	John Rost, W Virginia	Kurt Fitz-Randolph, Tennessee Tech
1982	Tennessee Tech	James Newkirk	6138	W Virginia	6136	John Rost, W Virginia	Kurt Fitz-Randolph, Tennessee Tech

Men's and Women's Combined (Cont.)

Year	Champion	Coach	Score	Runner-Up	Score	Individual Champion Air Rifle	Smallbore
1983	W Virginia	Edward Etzel	6166	Tennessee Tech	6148	Ray Slonena, Tennessee Tech	David Johnson, W Virginia
1984	W Virginia	Edward Etzel	6206	East Tennessee St	6142	Pat Spurgin, Murray St	Bob Broughton, W Virginia
1985	Murray St	Elvis Green	6150	W Virginia	6149	Christian Heller, W Virginia	Pat Spurgin, Murray St
1986	W Virginia	Edward Etzel	6229	Murray St	6163	Marianne Wallace, Murray St	Mike Anti, W Virginia
1987	Murray St	Elvis Green	6205	W Virginia	6203	Rob Harbison, TN-Martin	Web Wright, W Virginia
1988	W Virginia	Greg Perrine	6192	Murray St	6183	Deena Wigger, Murray St	Web Wright, W Virginia
1989	W Virginia	Edward Etzel	6234	S Florida	6180	Michelle Scarborough, S Florida	Deb Sinclair, AK-Fairbanks
1990	W Virginia	Marsha Beasley	6205	Navy	6101	Gary Hardy, W Virginia	Michelle Scarborough, S Florida
1991	W Virginia	Marsha Beasley	6171	Alaska-Fairbanks	6110	Ann Pfiffner, W Virginia	Soma Dutta, UTEP
1991	W Virginia	Marsha Beasley	6171	Alaska-Fairbanks	6110	Ann Pfiffner, W Virginia	Soma Dutta, UTEP
1992	W Virginia	Marsha Beasley	6214	Alaska-Fairbanks	6166	Ann Pfiffner, W Virginia	Tim Manges, W Virginia
1993	W Virginia	Marsha Beasley	6179	Alaska-Fairbanks	6169	Trevor Gathman, W Virginia	Eric Uptagrafft, W Virginia

Skiing

Men's and Women's Combined

Year	Champion	Coach	Pts	Runner-Up	Pts	Host or Site
1954	Denver	Willy Schaeffler	384.0	Seattle	349.6	NV-Reno
1955	Denver	Willy Schaeffler	567.05	Dartmouth	558.935	Norwich
1956	Denver	Willy Schaeffler	582.01	Dartmouth	541.77	Winter Park
1957	Denver	Willy Schaeffler	577.95	Colorado	545.29	Ogden Snow Basin
1958	Dartmouth	Al Merrill	561.2	Denver	550.6	Dartmouth
1959	Colorado	Bob Beattie	549.4	Denver	543.6	Winter Park
1960	Colorado	Bob Beattie	571.4	Denver	568.6	Bridger Bowl
1961	Denver	Willy Schaeffler	376.19	Middlebury	366.94	Middlebury
1962	Denver	Willy Schaeffler	390.08	Colorado	374.30	Squaw Valley
1963	Denver	Willy Schaeffler	384.6	Colorado	381.6	Solitude
1964	Denver	Willy Schaeffler	370.2	Dartmouth	368.8	Franconia Notch
1965	Denver	Willy Schaeffler	380.5	Utah	378.,4	Crystal Mountain
1966	Denver	Willy Schaeffler	381.02	Western Colorado	365.92	Crested Butte
1967	Denver	Willy Schaeffler	376.7	Wyoming	375.9	Sugarloaf Mountain
1968	Wyoming	John Cress	383.9	Denver	376.2	Mount Werner
1969	Denver	Willy Schaeffler	388.6	Dartmouth	372.0	Mount Werner
1970	Denver	Willy Schaeffler	386.6	Dartmouth	378.8	Cannon Mountain
1971	Denver	Peder Pytte	394.7	Colorado	373.1	Terry Peak
1972	Colorado	Bill Marolt	385.3	Denver	380.1	Winter Park
1973	Colorado	Bill Marolt	381.89	Wyoming	377.83	Middlebury
1974	Colorado	Bill Marolt	176	Wyoming	162	Jackson Hole
1975	Colorado	Bill Marolt	183	Vermont	115	Fort Lewis
1976	Colorado	Bill Marolt	112			Bates
	Dartmouth	Jim Page	112			
1977	Colorado	Bill Marolt	179	Wyoming	154.5	Winter Park
1978	Colorado	Bill Marolt	152.5	Wyoming	121.5	Cannon Mountain
1979	Colorado	Tim Hinderman	153	Utah	130	Steamboat Springs
1980	Vermont	Chip LaCasse	171	Utah	151	Lake Placid and Stowe
1981	Utah	Pat Miller	183	Vermont	172	Park City
1982	Colorado	Tim Hinderman	461	Vermont	436.5	Lake Placid
1983	Utah	Pat Miller	696	Vermont	650	Bozeman

Men's and Women's Combined

Year	Champion	Coach	Pts	Runner-Up	Pts	Host or Site
1984	Utah	Pat Miller	750.5	Vermont	684	New Hampshire
1985	Wyoming	Tim Ameel	764	Utah	744	Bozeman
1986	Utah	Pat Miller	612	Vermont	602	Vermont
1987	Utah	Pat Miller	710	Vermont	627	Anchorage
1988	Utah	Pat Miller	651	Vermont	614	Middlebury
1989	Vermont	Chip LaCasse	672	Utah	668	Jackson Hole
1990	Vermont	Chip LaCasse	671	Utah	571	Vermont
1991	Colorado	Richard Rokos	713	Vermont	682	Park City
1992	Vermont	Chip LaCasse	693.5	New Mexico	642.5	New Hampshire
1993	Utah	Pat Miller	783	Vermont	700.5	Steamboat Springs

Soccer

Men

DIVISION I

Year	Champion	Coach	Score	Runner-Up
1959	St Louis	Bob Guelker	5-2	Bridgeport
1960	St Louis	Bob Guelker	3-2	Maryland
1961	West Chester	Mel Lorback	2-0	St Louis
1962	St Louis	Bob Guelker	4-3	Maryland
1963	St Louis	Bob Guelker	3-0	Navy
1964	Navy	F. H. Warner	1-0	Michigan St
1965	St Louis	Bob Guelker	1-0	Michigan St
1966	San Francisco	Steve Negoesco	5-2	LIU-Brooklyn
1967	Michigan St	Gene Kenney	0-0	Game called
	St Louis	Harry Keough		due to inclement weather
1968	Maryland	Doyle Royal	2-2 (2 OT)	
	Michigan St	Gene Kenney		
1969	St Louis	Harry Keough	4-0	San Francisco
1970	St Louis	Harry Keough	1-0	UCLA
1971	Vacated		3-2	St Louis
1972	St Louis	Harry Keough	4-2	UCLA
1973	St Louis	Harry Keough	2-1 (OT)	UCLA
1974	Howard	Lincoln Phillips	2-1 (4 OT)	St Louis
1975	San Francisco	Steve Negoesco	4-0	SIU-Edwardsville
1976	San Francisco	Steve Negoesco	1-0	Indiana
1977	Hartwick	Jim Lennox	2-1	San Francisco
1978	Vacated		2-0	Indiana
1979	SIU-Edwardsville	Bob Guelker	3-2	Clemson
1980	San Francisco	Steve Negoesco	4-3 (OT)	Indiana
1981	Connecticut	Joe Morrone	2-1 (OT)	Alabama A&M
1982	Indiana	Jerry Yeagley	2-1 (8 OT)	Duke
1983	Indiana	Jerry Yeagley	1-0 (2 OT)	Columbia
1984	Clemson	I. M. Ibrahim	2-1	Indiana
1985	UCLA	Sigi Schmid	1-0 (8 OT)	American
1986	Duke	John Rennie	1-0	Akron
1987	Clemson	I. M. Ibrahim	2-0	San Diego St
1988	Indiana	Jerry Yeagley	1-0	Howard
1989	Santa Clara	Steve Sampson	1-1 (2 OT)	
	Virginia	Bruce Arena		
1990	UCLA	Sigi Schmid	1-0 (OT)	Rutgers
1991	Virginia	Bruce Arena	0-0*	Santa Clara
1992	Virginia	Bruce Arena	2-0	San Diego

*Under a rule passed in 1991, the NCAA determined that when a score is tied after regulation and overtime, and the championship is determined by penalty kicks, the official score will be 0-0.

DIVISION II

Year	Champion	Year	Champion
1972	SIU-Edwardsville	1976	Loyola (MD)
1973	MO-St Louis	1977	Alabama A&M
1974	Adelphi	1978	Seattle Pacific
1975	Baltimore	1979	Alabama A&M

Men's (Cont.)

DIVISION II (CONT.)

Year	Champion
1980	Lock Haven
1981	Tampa
1982	Florida Intl
1983	Seattle Pacific
1984	Florida Intl
1985	Seattle Pacific
1986	Seattle Pacific

Year	Champion
1987	Southern Connecticut St
1988	Florida Tech
1989	New Hampshire Col
1990	Southern Connecticut St
1991	Florida Tech
1992	Southern Connecticut St

DIVISION III

Year	Champion
1974	Brockport St
1975	Babson
1976	Brandeis
1977	Lock Haven
1978	Lock Haven
1979	Babson
1980	Babson
1981	Glassboro St
1982	NC-Greensboro
1983	NC-Greensboro

Year	Champion
1984	Wheaton (IL)
1985	NC-Greensboro
1986	NC-Greensboro
1987	NC-Greensboro
1988	UC-San Diego
1989	Elizabethtown
1990	Glassboro St
1991	UC-San Diego
1992	Kean

Women

DIVISION I

Year	Champion	Coach	Score	Runner-Up
1982	N Carolina	Anson Dorrance	2-0	Central Florida
1983	N Carolina	Anson Dorrance	4-0	George Mason
1984	N Carolina	Anson Dorrance	2-0	Connecticut
1985	George Mason	Hank Leung	2-0	N Carolina
1986	N Carolina	Anson Dorrance	2-0	Colorado Col
1987	N Carolina	Anson Dorrance	1-0	Massachusetts
1988	N Carolina	Anson Dorrance	4-1	N Carolina St
1989	N Carolina	Anson Dorrance	2-0	Colorado Col
1990	N Carolina	Anson Dorrance	6-0	Connecticut
1991	N Carolina	Anson Dorrance	3-1	Wisconsin
1992	N Carolina	Anson Dorrance	9-1	Duke

DIVISION II

Year	Champion
1988	Cal St-Hayward
1989	Barry
1990	Sonoma St
1991	Cal St-Dominguez Hills
1992	Barry

DIVISION III

Year	Champion
1986	Rochester
1987	Rochester
1988	William Smith
1989	UC-San Diego
1990	Ithaca
1991	Ithaca
1992	Cortland St

Softball

Women

DIVISION I

Year	Champion	Coach	Score	Runner-Up
1982	UCLA*	Sharron Backus	2-0†	Fresno St
1983	Texas A&M	Bob Brock	2-0‡	Cal St-Fullerton
1984	UCLA	Sharron Backus	1-0#	Texas A&M
1985	UCLA	Sharron Backus	2-1**	Nebraska
1986	Cal St-Fullerton*	Judi Garman	3-0	Texas A&M
1987	Texas A&M	Bob Brock	4-1	UCLA
1988	UCLA	Sharron Backus	3-0	Fresno St
1989	UCLA*	Sharron Backus	1-0	Fresno St
1990	UCLA	Sharron Backus	2-0	Fresno St
1991	Arizona	Mike Candrea	5-1	UCLA

Women (Cont.)

DIVISION I (CONT.)

Year	Champion	Coach	Score	Runner-Up
1992	UCLA*	Sharron Backus	2-0	Arizona
1993	Arizona	Mike Candrea	1-0	UCLA

*Undefeated teams in final series. †8 innings. ‡12 innings. #13 innings. **9 innings.

DIVISION II

Year	Champion
1982	Sam Houston St
1983	Cal St-Northridge
1984	Cal St-Northridge
1985	Cal St-Northridge
1986	SF Austin St
1987	Cal St-Northridge
1988	Cal St-Bakersfield
1989	Cal St-Bakersfield
1990	Cal St-Bakersfield
1991	Augustana (SD)
1992	Missouri Southern
1993	Florida Southern

DIVISION III

Year	Champion
1982	Eastern Connecticut St*
1983	Trenton St
1984	Buena Vista*
1985	Eastern Connecticut St
1986	Eastern Connecticut St
1987	Trenton St*
1988	Central (IA)
1989	Trenton St*
1990	Eastern Connecticut St
1991	Central (IA)
1992	Trenton St
1993	Central (IA)

*Undefeated teams in final series.

Swimming

Men

DIVISION I

Year	Champion	Coach	Pts	Runner-Up	Pts
1937	Michigan	Matt Mann	75	Ohio St	39
1938	Michigan	Matt Mann	46	Ohio St	45
1939	Michigan	Matt Mann	65	Ohio St	58
1940	Michigan	Matt Mann	45	Yale	42
1941	Michigan	Matt Mann	61	Yale	58
1942	Yale	Robert J. H. Kiphuth	71	Michigan	39
1943	Ohio St	Mike Peppe	81	Michigan	47
1944	Yale	Robert J. H. Kiphuth	39	Michigan	38
1945	Ohio St	Mike Peppe	56	Michigan	48
1946	Ohio St	Mike Peppe	61	Michigan	37
1947	Ohio St	Mike Peppe	66	Michigan	39
1948	Michigan	Matt Mann	44	Ohio St	41
1949	Ohio St	Mike Peppe	49	Iowa	35
1950	Ohio St	Mike Peppe	64	Yale	43
1951	Yale	Robert J. H. Kiphuth	81	Michigan St	60
1952	Ohio St	Mike Peppe	94	Yale	81
1953	Yale	Robert J. H. Kiphuth	96½	Ohio St	73½
1954	Ohio St	Mike Peppe	94	Michigan	67
1955	Ohio St	Mike Peppe	90	Yale	51
				Michigan	51
1956	Ohio St	Mike Peppe	68	Yale	54
1957	Michigan	Gus Stager	69	Yale	61
1958	Michigan	Gus Stager	72	Yale	63
1959	Michigan	Gus Stager	137½	Ohio St	44
1960	Southern Cal	Peter Daland	87	Michigan	73
1961	Michigan	Gus Stager	85	Southern Cal	62
1962	Ohio St	Mike Peppe	92	Southern Cal	46
1963	Southern Cal	Peter Daland	81	Yale	77
1964	Southern Cal	Peter Daland	96	Indiana	91
1965	Southern Cal	Peter Daland	285	Indiana	278½
1966	Southern Cal	Peter Daland	302	Indiana	286
1967	Stanford	Jim Gaughran	275	Southern Cal	260
1968	Indiana	James Counsilman	346	Yale	253
1969	Indiana	James Counsilman	427	Southern Cal	306
1970	Indiana	James Counsilman	332	Southern Cal	235
1971	Indiana	James Counsilman	351	Southern Cal	260
1972	Indiana	James Counsilman	390	Southern Cal	371

Men (Cont.)
DIVISION I (CONT.)

Year	Champion	Coach	Pts	Runner-Up	Pts
1973	Indiana	James Counsilman	358	Tennessee	294
1974	Southern Cal	Peter Daland	339	Indiana	338
1975	Southern Cal	Peter Daland	344	Indiana	274
1976	Southern Cal	Peter Daland	398	Tennessee	237
1977	Southern Cal	Peter Daland	385	Alabama	204
1978	Tennessee	Ray Bussard	307	Auburn	185
1979	California	Nort Thornton	287	Southern Cal	227
1980	California	Nort Thornton	234	Texas	220
1981	Texas	Eddie Reese	259	UCLA	189
1982	UCLA	Ron Ballatore	219	Texas	210
1983	Florida	Randy Reese	238	Southern Meth	227
1984	Florida	Randy Reese	287½	Texas	277
1985	Stanford	Skip Kenney	403½	Florida	302
1986	Stanford	Skip Kenney	404	California	335
1987	Stanford	Skip Kenney	374	Southern Cal	296
1988	Texas	Eddie Reese	424	Southern Cal	369½
1989	Texas	Eddie Reese	475	Stanford	396
1990	Texas	Eddie Reese	506	Southern Cal	423
1991	Texas	Eddie Reese	476	Stanford	420
1992	Stanford	Skip Kenney	632	Texas	356
1993	Stanford	Skip Kenney	520½	Michigan	396

DIVISION II

Year	Champion	Year	Champion
1964	Bucknell	1979	Cal St-Northridge
1965	San Diego St	1980	Oakland
1966	San Diego St	1981	Cal St-Northridge
1967	UC-Santa Barbara	1982	Cal St-Northridge
1968	Long Beach St	1983	Cal St-Northridge
1969	UC-Irvine	1984	Cal St-Northridge
1970	UC-Irvine	1985	Cal St-Northridge
1971	UC-Irvine	1986	Cal St-Bakersfield
1972	Eastern Michigan	1987	Cal St-Bakersfield
1973	Cal St-Chico	1988	Cal St-Bakersfield
1974	Cal St-Chico	1989	Cal St-Bakersfield
1975	Cal St-Northridge	1990	Cal St-Bakersfield
1976	Cal St-Chico	1991	Cal St-Bakersfield
1977	Cal St-Northridge	1992	Cal St-Bakersfield
1978	Cal St-Northridge	1993	Cal St-Bakersfield

DIVISION III

Year	Champion	Year	Champion
1975	Cal St-Chico	1985	Kenyon
1976	St Lawrence	1986	Kenyon
1977	Johns Hopkins	1987	Kenyon
1978	Johns Hopkins	1988	Kenyon
1979	Johns Hopkins	1989	Kenyon
1980	Kenyon	1990	Kenyon
1981	Kenyon	1991	Kenyon
1982	Kenyon	1992	Kenyon
1983	Kenyon	1993	Kenyon
1984	Kenyon		

Women
DIVISION I

Year	Champion	Coach	Pts	Runner-Up	Pts
1982	Florida	Randy Reese	505	Stanford	383
1983	Stanford	George Haines	418½	Florida	389½
1984	Texas	Richard Quick	392	Stanford	324
1985	Texas	Richard Quick	643	Florida	400
1986	Texas	Richard Quick	633	Florida	586
1987	Texas	Richard Quick	648½	Stanford	631½
1988	Texas	Richard Quick	661	Florida	542½
1989	Stanford	Richard Quick	610½	Texas	547
1990	Texas	Mark Schubert	632	Stanford	622½

Women (Cont.)
DIVISION I (CONT.)

Year	Champion	Coach	Pts	Runner-Up	Pts
1991	Texas	Mark Schubert	746	Stanford	653
1992	Stanford	Richard Quick	735½	Texas	651
1993	Stanford	Richard Quick	649½	Florida	421

DIVISION II

Year	Champion
1982	Cal St-Northridge
1983	Clarion
1984	Clarion
1985	S Florida
1986	Clarion
1987	Cal St-Northridge
1988	Cal St-Northridge
1989	Cal St-Northridge
1990	Oakland (MI)
1991	Oakland (MI)
1992	Oakland (MI)
1993	Oakland (MI)

DIVISION III

Year	Champion
1982	Williams
1983	Williams
1984	Kenyon
1985	Kenyon
1986	Kenyon
1987	Kenyon
1988	Kenyon
1989	Kenyon
1990	Kenyon
1991	Kenyon
1992	Kenyon
1993	Kenyon

Tennis

Men
DIVISION I

Year	Champion	Coach	Pts	Runner-Up	Pts	Individual Champion
1946	Southern Cal	William Moyle	9	William & Mary	6	Robert Falkenburg, Southern Cal
1947	William & Mary	Sharvey G. Umbeck	10	Rice	4	Gardner Larned, William & Mary
1948	William & Mary	Sharvey G. Umbeck	6	San Francisco	5	Harry Likas, San Francisco
1949	San Francisco	Norman Brooks	7	Rollins	4	Jack Tuero, Tulane
				Tulane	4	
				Washington	4	
1950	UCLA	William Ackerman	11	California	5	Herbert Flam, UCLA
				Southern Cal	5	
1951	Southern Cal	Louis Wheeler	9	Cincinnati	7	Tony Trabert, Cincinnati
1952	UCLA	J. D. Morgan	11	California	5	Hugh Stewart, Southern Cal
				Southern Cal	5	
1953	UCLA	J. D. Morgan	11	California	6	Hamilton Richardson, Tulane
1954	UCLA	J. D. Morgan	15	Southern Cal	10	Hamilton Richardson, Tulane
1955	Southern Cal	George Toley	12	Texas	7	Jose Aguero, Tulane
1956	UCLA	J. D. Morgan	15	Southern Cal	14	Alejandro Olmedo, Southern Cal
1957	Michigan	William Murphy	10	Tulane	9	Barry MacKay, Michigan
1958	Southern Cal	George Toley	13	Stanford	9	Alejandro Olmedo, Southern Cal
1959	Notre Dame	Thomas Fallon	8			Whitney Reed, San Jose St
	Tulane	Emmet Pare	8			
1960	UCLA	J. D. Morgan	18	Southern Cal	8	Larry Nagler, UCLA
1961	UCLA	J. D. Morgan	17	Southern Cal	16	Allen Fox, UCLA
1962	Southern Cal	George Toley	22	UCLA	12	Rafael Osuna, Southern Cal
1963	Southern Cal	George Toley	27	UCLA	19	Dennis Ralston, Southern Cal
1964	Southern Cal	George Toley	26	UCLA	25	Dennis Ralston, Southern Cal
1965	UCLA	J. D. Morgan	31	Miami (FL)	13	Arthur Ashe, UCLA
1966	Southern Cal	George Toley	27	UCLA	23	Charles Pasarell, UCLA
1967	Southern Cal	George Toley	28	UCLA	23	Bob Lutz, Southern Cal
1968	Southern Cal	George Toley	31	Rice	23	Stan Smith, Southern Cal
1969	Southern Cal	George Toley	35	UCLA	23	Joaquin Loyo-Mayo, Southern Cal
1970	UCLA	Glenn Bassett	26	Trinity (TX)	22	Jeff Borowiak, UCLA
				Rice	22	
1971	UCLA	Glenn Bassett	35	Trinity (TX)	27	Jimmy Connors, UCLA
1972	Trinity (TX)	Clarence Mabry	36	Stanford	30	Dick Stockton, Trinity (TX)
1973	Stanford	Dick Gould	33	Southern Cal	28	Alex Mayer, Stanford
1974	Stanford	Dick Gould	30	Southern Cal	25	John Whitlinger, Stanford
1975	UCLA	Glenn Bassett	27	Miami (FL)	20	Bill Martin, UCLA
1976	Southern Cal	George Toley	21			Bill Scanlon, Trinity (TX)
	UCLA	Glenn Bassett	21			

Men (Cont.)
DIVISION I (CONT.)

Year	Champion	Coach	Runner-Up	Individual Champion
1977	....Stanford	Dick Gould	Trinity (TX)	Matt Mitchell, Stanford
1978	....Stanford	Dick Gould	UCLA	John McEnroe, Stanford
1979	....UCLA	Glenn Bassett	Trinity (TX)	Kevin Curren, Texas
1980	....Stanford	Dick Gould	California	Robert Van't Hof, Southern Cal
1981	....Stanford	Dick Gould	UCLA	Tim Mayotte, Stanford
1982	....UCLA	Glenn Bassett	Pepperdine	Mike Leach, Michigan
1983	....Stanford	Dick Gould	Southern Meth	Greg Holmes, Utah
1984	....UCLA	Glenn Bassett	Stanford	Mikael Pernfors, Georgia
1985	....Georgia	Dan Magill	UCLA	Mikael Pernfors, Georgia
1986	....Stanford	Dick Gould	Pepperdine	Dan Goldie, Stanford
1987	....Georgia	Dan Magill	UCLA	Andrew Burrow, Miami (FL)
1988	....Stanford	Dick Gould	Louisiana St	Robby Weiss, Pepperdine
1989	....Stanford	Dick Gould	Georgia	Donni Leaycraft, Louisiana St
1990	....Stanford	Dick Gould	Tennessee	Steve Bryan, Texas
1991	....Southern Cal	Dick Leach	Georgia	Jared Palmer, Stanford
1992	....Stanford	Dick Gould	Notre Dame	Alex O'Brien, Stanford
1993	....Southern Cal	Dick Leach	Georgia	Chris Woodruff, Tennessee

Note: Prior to 1977, individual wins counted in the team's total points. In 1977, a dual-match single-elimination team championship was initiated, eliminating the point system.

INDIVIDUAL CHAMPIONS 1883-1945

Year	Champion	Year	Champion
1883	Joesph Clark, Harvard (spring)	1914	George Church, Princeton
1883	Howard Taylor, Harvard (fall)	1915	Richard Williams II, Harvard
1884	W. P. Knapp, Yale	1916	G. Colket Caner, Harvard
1885	W. P. Knapp, Yale	1917-18	No tournament
1886	G. M. Brinley, Trinity (CT)	1919	Charles Garland, Yale
1887	P. S. Sears, Harvard	1920	Lascelles Banks, Yale
1888	P. S. Sears, Harvard	1921	Philip Neer, Stanford
1889	R. P. Huntington, Jr, Yale	1922	Lucien Williams, Yale
1890	Fred Hovey, Harvard	1923	Carl Fischer, Philadelphia Osteo
1891	Fred Hovey, Harvard	1924	Wallace Scott, Washington
1892	William Larned, Cornell	1925	Edward Chandler, California
1893	Malcolm Chace, Brown	1926	Edward Chandler, California
1894	Malcolm Chace, Yale	1927	Wilmer Allison, Texas
1895	Malcolm Chace, Yale	1928	Julius Seligson, Lehigh
1896	Malcolm Whitman, Harvard	1929	Berkeley Bell, Texas
1897	S. G. Thompson, Princeton	1930	Clifford Sutter, Tulane
1898	Leo Ware, Harvard	1931	Keith Gledhill, Stanford
1899	Dwight Davis, Harvard	1932	Clifford Sutter, Tulane
1900	Raymond Little, Princeton	1933	Jack Tidball, UCLA
1901	Fred Alexander, Princeton	1934	Gene Mako, Southern Cal
1902	William Clothier, Harvard	1935	Wilbur Hess, Rice
1903	E. B. Dewhurst, Pennsylvania	1936	Ernest Sutter, Tulane
1904	Robert LeRoy, Columbia	1937	Ernest Sutter, Tulane
1905	E. B. Dewhurst, Pennsylvania	1938	Frank Guernsey, Rice
1906	Robert LeRoy, Columbia	1939	Frank Guernsey, Rice
1907	G. Peabody Gardner, Jr, Harvard	1940	Donald McNeil, Kenyon
1908	Nat Niles, Harvard	1941	Joseph Hunt, Navy
1909	Wallace Johnson, Pennsylvania	1942	Frederick Schroeder, Jr, Stanford
1910	R. A. Holden, Jr, Yale	1943	Pancho Segura, Miami (FL)
1911	E. H. Whitney, Harvard	1944	Pancho Segura, Miami (FL)
1912	George Church, Princeton	1945	Pancho Segura, Miami (FL)
1913	Richard Williams II, Harvard		

DIVISION II

Year	Champion	Year	Champion
1963	Cal St-LA	1970	UC-Irvine
1964	Cal St-LA	1971	UC-Irvine
	Southern Illinois	1972	UC-Irvine
1965	Cal St-LA		Rollins
1966	Rollins	1973	UC-Irvine
1967	Long Beach St	1974	San Diego
1968	Fresno St	1975	UC-Irvine
1969	Cal St-Northridge		San Diego

Men (Cont.)

DIVISION II (CONT.)

Year	Champion	Year	Champion
1976	Hampton	1985	Chapman
1977	UC-Irvine	1986	Cal Poly-SLO
1978	SIU-Edwardsville	1987	Chapman
1979	SIU-Edwardsville	1988	Chapman
1980	SIU-Edwardsville	1989	Hampton
1981	SIU-Edwardsville	1990	Cal Poly-SLO
1982	SIU-Edwardsville	1991	Rollins
1983	SIU-Edwardsville	1992	UC-Davis
1984	SIU-Edwardsville	1993	Lander (SC)

DIVISION III

Year	Champion	Year	Champion
1976	Kalamazoo	1985	Swarthmore
1977	Swarthmore	1986	Kalamazoo
1978	Kalamazoo	1987	Kalamazoo
1979	Redlands	1988	Washington & Lee
1980	Gustavus Adolphus	1989	UC-Santa Cruz
1981	Claremont-M-S Swarthmore	1990	Swarthmore
1982	Gustavus Adolphus	1991	Kalamazoo
1983	Redlands	1992	Kalamazoo
1984	Redlands	1993	Kalamazoo

Women

DIVISION I

Year	Champion	Coach	Runner-Up	Individual Champion
1982	Stanford	Frank Brennan	UCLA	Alycia Moulton, Stanford
1983	Southern Cal	Dave Borelli	Trinity (TX)	Beth Herr, Southern Cal
1984	Stanford	Frank Brennan	Southern Cal	Lisa Spain, Georgia
1985	Southern Cal	Dave Borelli	Miami (FL)	Linda Gates, Stanford
1986	Stanford	Frank Brennan	Southern Cal	Patty Fendick, Stanford
1987	Stanford	Frank Brennan	Georgia	Patty Fendick, Stanford
1988	Stanford	Frank Brennan	Florida	Shaun Stafford, Florida
1989	Stanford	Frank Brennan	UCLA	Sandra Birch, Stanford
1990	Stanford	Frank Brennan	Florida	Debbie Graham, Stanford
1991	Stanford	Frank Brennan	UCLA	Sandra Birch, Stanford
1992	Florida	Andy Brandi	Texas	Lisa Raymond, Florida
1993	Texas	Jeff Moore	Stanford	Lisa Raymond, Florida

DIVISION II

Year	Champion
1982	Cal St-Northridge
1983	TN-Chattanooga
1984	TN-Chattanooga
1985	TN-Chattanooga
1986	SIU-Edwardsville
1987	SIU-Edwardsville
1988	SIU-Edwardsville
1989	SIU-Edwardsville
1990	UC-Davis
1991	Cal Poly-Pomona
1992	Cal Poly-Pomona
1993	UC-Davis

DIVISION III

Year	Champion
1982	Occidental
1983	Principia
1984	Davidson
1985	UC-San Diego
1986	Trenton St
1987	UC-San Diego
1988	Mary Washington
1989	UC-San Diego
1990	Gustavus Adolphus
1991	Mary Washington
1992	Pomona-Pitzer
1993	Kenyon

Indoor Track and Field

Men
DIVISION I

Year	Champion	Coach	Pts	Runner-Up	Pts
1965	Missouri	Tom Botts	14	Oklahoma St	12
1966	Kansas	Bob Timmons	14	Southern Cal	13

Men (Cont.)

DIVISION I (CONT.)

Year	Champion	Coach	Pts	Runner-Up	Pts
1967	Southern Cal	Vern Wolfe	26	Oklahoma	17
1968	Villanova	Jim Elliott	35	Southern Cal	25
1969	Kansas	Bob Timmons	41½	Villanova	33
1970	Kansas	Bob Timmons	27½	Villanova	26
1971	Villanova	Jim Elliott	22	UTEP	19¼
1972	Southern Cal	Vern Wolfe	19	Bowling Green/ Mich St	18
1973	Manhattan	Fred Dwyer	18	Kansas/Kent St/UTEP	12
1974	UTEP	Ted Banks	19	Colorado	18
1975	UTEP	Ted Banks	36	Kansas	17½
1976	UTEP	Ted Banks	23	Villanova	15
1977	Washington St	John Chaplin	25½	UTEP	25
1978	UTEP	Ted Banks	44	Auburn	38
1979	Villanova	Jim Elliott	52	UTEP	51
1980	UTEP	Ted Banks	76	Villanova	42
1981	UTEP	Ted Banks	76	Southern Meth	51
1982	UTEP	John Wedel	67	Arkansas	30
1983	Southern Meth	Ted McLaughlin	43	Villanova	32
1984	Arkansas	John McDonnell	38	Washington St	28
1985	Arkansas	John McDonnell	70	Tennessee	29
1986	Arkansas	John McDonnell	49	Villanova	22
1987	Arkansas	John McDonnell	39	Southern Meth	31
1988	Arkansas	John McDonnell	34	Illinois	29
1989	Arkansas	John McDonnell	34	Florida	31
1990	Arkansas	John McDonnell	44	Texas A&M	36
1991	Arkansas	John McDonnell	34	Georgetown	27
1992	Arkansas	John McDonnell	53	Clemson	46
1993	Arkansas	John McDonnell	66	Clemson	30

DIVISION II

Year	Champion
1985	SE Missouri St
1987	St Augustine's
1988	Abilene Christian
	St Augustine's
1989	St Augustine's
1990	St Augustine's
1991	St Augustine's
1992	St Augustine's
1993	Abilene Christian

DIVISION III

Year	Champion
1985	St Thomas (MN)
1986	Frostburg St
1987	WI-La Crosse
1988	WI-La Crosse
1989	North Central
1990	Lincoln (PA)
1991	WI-La Crosse
1992	WI-La Crosse
1993	WI-La Crosse

Women

DIVISION I

Year	Champion	Coach	Pts	Runner-Up	Pts
1983	Nebraska	Gary Pepin	47	Tennessee	44
1984	Nebraska	Gary Pepin	59	Tennessee	48
1985	Florida St	Gary Winckler	34	Texas	32
1986	Texas	Terry Crawford	31	Southern Cal	26
1987	Louisiana St	Loren Seagrave	49	Tennessee	30
1988	Texas	Terry Crawford	71	Villanova	52
1989	Louisiana St	Pat Henry	61	Villanova	34
1990	Texas	Terry Crawford	50	Wisconsin	26
1991	Louisiana St	Pat Henry	48	Texas	39
1992	Florida	Bev Kearney	50	Stanford	26
1993	Louisiana St	Pat Henry	49	Wisconsin	44

DIVISION II

Year	Champion
1985	St Augustine's
1987	St Augustine's
1988	Abilene Christian
1989	Abilene Christian
1990	Abilene Christian
1991	Abilene Christian
1992	Alabama A&M
1993	Abilene Christian

DIVISION III

Year	Champion
1985	MA-Boston
1986	MA-Boston
1987	MA-Boston
1988	Christopher Newport
1989	Christopher Newport
1990	Christopher Newport
1991	Cortland St
1992	Christopher Newport
1993	Lincoln (PA)

Outdoor Track and Field

Men

DIVISION I

Year	Champion	Coach	Pts	Runner-Up	Pts
1921	Illinois	Harry Gill	20†	Notre Dame	16†
1922	California	Walter Christie	28†	Penn St	19†
1923	Michigan	Stephen Farrell	29†	Mississippi St	16
1924	No meet				
1925	Stanford*	R. L. Templeton	31†		
1926	Southern Cal*	Dean Cromwell	27†		
1927	Illinois*	Harry Gill	35†		
1928	Stanford	R. L. Templeton	72	Ohio St	31
1929	Ohio St	Frank Castleman	50	Washington	42
1930	Southern Cal	Dean Cromwell	55†	Washington	40
1931	Southern Cal	Dean Cromwell	77†	Ohio St	31†
1932	Indiana	Billy Hayes	56	Ohio St	49†
1933	Louisiana St	Bernie Moore	58	Southern Cal	54
1934	Stanford	R. L. Templeton	63	Southern Cal	54†
1935	Southern Cal	Dean Cromwell	74†	Ohio St	40†
1936	Southern Cal	Dean Cromwell	103†	Ohio St	73
1937	Southern Cal	Dean Cromwell	62	Stanford	50
1938	Southern Cal	Dean Cromwell	67†	Stanford	38
1939	Southern Cal	Dean Cromwell	86	Stanford	44†
1940	Southern Cal	Dean Cromwell	47	Stanford	28†
1941	Southern Cal	Dean Cromwell	81†	Indiana	50
1942	Southern Cal	Dean Cromwell	85†	Ohio St	44†
1943	Southern Cal	Dean Cromwell	46	California	39
1944	Illinois	Leo Johnson	79	Notre Dame	43
1945	Navy	E. J. Thomson	62	Illinois	48†
1946	Illinois	Leo Johnson	78	Southern Cal	42†
1947	Illinois	Leo Johnson	59†	Southern Cal	34†
1948	Minnesota	James Kelly	46	Southern Cal	41†
1949	Southern Cal	Jess Hill	55†	UCLA	31
1950	Southern Cal	Jess Hill	49†	Stanford	28
1951	Southern Cal	Jess Mortenson	56	Cornell	40
1952	Southern Cal	Jess Mortenson	66†	San Jose St	24†
1953	Southern Cal	Jess Mortenson	80	Illinois	41
1954	Southern Cal	Jess Mortenson	66†	Illinois	31†
1955	Southern Cal	Jess Mortenson	42	UCLA	34
1956	UCLA	Elvin Drake	55†	Kansas	51
1957	Villanova	James Elliott	47	California	32
1958	Southern Cal	Jess Mortenson	48†	Kansas	40†
1959	Kansas	Bill Easton	73	San Jose St	48
1960	Kansas	Bill Easton	50	Southern Cal	37
1961	Southern Cal	Jess Mortenson	65	Oregon	47
1962	Oregon	William Bowerman	85	Villanova	40†
1963	Southern Cal	Vern Wolfe	61	Stanford	42
1964	Oregon	William Bowerman	70	San Jose St	40
1965	Oregon	William Bowerman	32		
	Southern Cal	Vern Wolfe	32		
1966	UCLA	Jim Bush	81	Brigham Young	33
1967	Southern Cal	Vern Wolfe	86	Oregon	40
1968	Southern Cal	Vern Wolfe	58	Washington St	57
1969	San Jose St	Bud Winter	48	Kansas	45
1970	Brigham Young	Clarence Robison	35		
	Kansas	Bob Timmons	35		
	Oregon	William Bowerman	35		
1971	UCLA	Jim Bush	52	Southern Cal	41
1972	UCLA	Jim Bush	82	Southern Cal	49
1973	UCLA	Jim Bush	56	Oregon	31
1974	Tennessee	Stan Huntsman	60	UCLA	56
1975	UTEP	Ted Banks	55	UCLA	42
1976	Southern Cal	Vern Wolfe	64	UTEP	44
1977	Arizona St	Senon Castillo	64	UTEP	50
1978	UCLA/UTEP	Jim Bush/Ted Banks	50		
1979	UTEP	Ted Banks	64	Villanova	48
1980	UTEP	Ted Banks	69	UCLA	46
1981	UTEP	Ted Banks	70	Southern Meth	57
1982	UTEP	John Wedel	105	Tennessee	94

Men *(Cont.)*

DIVISION I *(CONT.)*

Year	Champion	Coach	Pts	Runner-Up	Pts
1983	Southern Meth	Ted McLaughlin	104	Tennessee	102
1984	Oregon	Bill Dellinger	113	Washington St	94½
1985	Arkansas	John McDonnell	61	Washington St	46
1986	Southern Meth	Ted McLaughlin	53	Washington St	52
1987	UCLA	Bob Larsen	81	Texas	28
1988	UCLA	Bob Larsen	82	Texas	41
1989	Louisiana St	Pat Henry	53	Texas A&M	51
1990	Louisiana St	Pat Henry	44	Arkansas	36
1991	Tennessee	Doug Brown	51	Washington St	42
1992	Arkansas	John McDonnell	60	Tennessee	46½
1993	Arkansas	John McDonnell	69	LSU/Ohio St	45

*Unofficial championship. †Fraction of a point.

DIVISION II

Year	Champion	Year	Champion	Year	Champion
1963	MD-Eastern Shore	1974	Eastern Illinois	1984	Abilene Christian
1964	Fresno St		Norfolk St	1985	Abilene Christian
1965	San Diego St	1975	Cal St-Northridge	1986	Abilene Christian
1966	San Diego St	1976	UC-Irvine	1987	Abilene Christian
1967	Long Beach St	1977	Cal St-Hayward	1988	Abilene Christian
1968	Cal Poly-SLO	1978	Cal St-LA	1989	St Augustine's
1969	Cal Poly-SLO	1979	Cal Poly-SLO	1990	St Augustine's
1970	Cal Poly-SLO	1980	Cal Poly-SLO	1991	St Augustine's
1971	Kentucky St	1981	Cal Poly-SLO	1992	St Augustine's
1972	Eastern Michigan	1982	Abilene Christian	1993	St Augustine's
1973	Norfolk St	1983	Abilene Christian		

DIVISION III

Year	Champion	Year	Champion	Year	Champion
1974	Ashland	1981	Glassboro St	1988	WI-La Crosse
1975	Southern-N Orleans	1982	Glassboro St	1989	North Central
1976	Southern-N Orleans	1983	Glassboro St	1990	Lincoln (PA)
1977	Southern-N Orleans	1984	Glassboro St	1991	WI-La Crosse
1978	Occidental	1985	Lincoln (PA)	1992	WI-La Crosse
1979	Slippery Rock	1986	Frostburg St	1993	WI-La Crosse
1980	Glassboro St	1987	Frostburg St		

Women

DIVISION I

Year	Champion	Coach	Pts	Runner-Up	Pts
1982	UCLA	Scott Chisam	153	Tennessee	126
1983	UCLA	Scott Chisam	116-1/2	Florida St	108
1984	Florida St	Gary Winckler	145	Tennessee	124
1985	Oregon	Tom Heinonen	52	Florida St/LSU	46
1986	Texas	Terry Crawford	65	Alabama	55
1987	Louisiana St	Loren Seagrave	62	Alabama	53
1988	Louisiana St	Loren Seagrave	61	UCLA	58
1989	Louisiana St	Pat Henry	86	UCLA	47
1990	Louisiana St	Pat Henry	53	UCLA	46
1991	Louisiana St	Pat Henry	78	Texas	67
1992	Louisiana St	Pat Henry	87	Florida	81
1993	Louisiana St	Pat Henry	93	Wisconsin	44

DIVISION II

Year	Champion	Year	Champion	Year	Champion
1982	Cal Poly-SLO	1986	Abilene Christian	1990	Cal Poly-SLO
1983	Cal Poly-SLO	1987	Abilene Christian	1991	Cal Poly-SLO
1984	Cal Poly-SLO	1988	Abilene Christian	1992	Alabama A&M
1985	Abilene Christian	1989	Cal Poly-SLO	1993	Alabama A&M

DIVISION III

Year	Champion	Year	Champion	Year	Champion
1982	Central (IA)	1986	MA-Boston	1990	WI-Oshkosh
1983	WI-La Crosse	1987	Chris. Newport	1991	WI-Oshkosh
1984	WI-La Crosse	1988	Chris. Newport	1992	Chris. Newport
1985	Cortland St	1989	Chris. Newport	1993	Lincoln (PA)

Volleyball

Men

Year	Champion	Coach	Score	Runner-Up	Most Outstanding Player
1970	UCLA	Al Scates	3-0	Long Beach St	Dane Holtzman, UCLA
1971	UCLA	Al Scates	3-0	UC-Santa Barbara	Kirk Kilgore, UCLA Tim Bonynge, UC-Santa Barbara
1972	UCLA	Al Scates	3-2	San Diego St	Dick Irvin, UCLA
1973	San Diego St	Jack Henn	3-1	Long Beach St	Duncan McFarland, San Diego St
1974	UCLA	Al Scates	3-2	UC-Santa Barbara	Bob Leonard, UCLA
1975	UCLA	Al Scates	3-1	UC-Santa Barbara	John Bekins, UCLA
1976	UCLA	Al Scates	3-0	Pepperdine	Joe Mika, UCLA
1977	Southern Cal	Ernie Hix	3-1	Ohio St	Celso Kalache, Southern Cal
1978	Pepperdine	Marv Dunphy	3-2	UCLA	Mike Blanchard, Pepperdine
1979	UCLA	Al Scates	3-1	Southern Cal	Sinjin Smith, UCLA
1980	Southern Cal	Ernie Hix	3-1	UCLA	Dusty Dvorak, Southern Cal
1981	UCLA	Al Scates	3-2	Southern Cal	Karch Kiraly, UCLA
1982	UCLA	Al Scates	3-0	Penn St	Karch Kiraly, UCLA
1983	UCLA	Al Scates	3-0	Pepperdine	Ricci Luyties, UCLA
1984	UCLA	Al Scates	3-1	Pepperdine	Ricci Luyties, UCLA
1985	Pepperdine	Marv Dunphy	3-1	Southern Cal	Bob Ctvrtlik, Pepperdine
1986	Pepperdine	Rod Wilde	3-2	Southern Cal	Steve Friedman, Pepperdine
1987	UCLA	Al Scates	3-0	Southern Cal	Ozzie Volstad, UCLA
1988	Southern Cal	Bob Yoder	3-2	UC-Santa Barbara	Jen-Kai Liu, Southern Cal
1989	UCLA	Al Scates	3-1	Stanford	Matt Sonnichsen, UCLA
1990	Southern Cal	Jim McLaughlin	3-1	Long Beach St	Bryan Ivie, Southern Cal
1991	Long Beach St	Ray Ratelle	3-1	Southern Cal	Brent Hilliard, Long Beach St
1992	Pepperdine	Marv Dunphy	3-0	Stanford	Alon Grinberg, Pepperdine
1993	UCLA	Al Skates	3-0	Cal St-Northridge	Mike Sealy/Jeff Nygaard, UCLA

Women

DIVISION I

Year	Champion	Coach	Score	Runner-Up
1981	Southern Cal	Chuck Erbe	3-2	UCLA
1982	Hawaii	Dave Shoji	3-2	Southern Cal
1983	Hawaii	Dave Shoji	3-0	UCLA
1984	UCLA	Andy Banachowski	3-2	Stanford
1985	Pacific	John Dunning	3-1	Stanford
1986	Pacific	John Dunning	3-0	Nebraska
1987	Hawaii	Dave Shoji	3-1	Stanford
1988	Texas	Mick Haley	3-0	Hawaii
1989	Long Beach St	Brian Gimmillaro	3-0	Nebraska
1990	UCLA	Andy Banachowski	3-0	Pacific
1991	UCLA	Andy Banachowski	3-2	Long Beach St
1992	Stanford	Don Shaw	3-1	UCLA

DIVISION II

Year	Champion
1981	Cal St-Sacramento
1982	UC-Riverside
1983	Cal St-Northridge
1984	Portland St
1985	Portland St
1986	UC-Riverside
1987	Cal St-Northridge
1988	Portland St
1989	Cal St-Bakersfield
1990	West Texas St
1991	West Texas St
1992	Portland St

DIVISION III

Year	Champion
1981	UC-San Diego
1982	La Verne
1983	Elmhurst
1984	UC-San Diego
1985	Elmhurst
1986	UC-San Diego
1987	UC-San Diego
1988	UC-San Diego
1989	Washington (MO)
1990	UC-San Diego
1991	Washington (MO)
1992	Washington (MO)

Water Polo

Men

Year	Champion	Coach	Score	Runner-Up
1969	UCLA	Bob Horn	5-2	California
1970	UC-Irvine	Ed Newland	7-6 (3 OT)	UCLA
1971	UCLA	Bob Horn	5-3	San Jose St
1972	UCLA	Bob Horn	10-5	UC-Irvine
1973	California	Pete Cutino	8-4	UC-Irvine
1974	California	Pete Cutino	7-6	UC-Irvine
1975	California	Pete Cutino	9-8	UC-Irvine
1976	Stanford	Art Lambert	13-12	UCLA
1977	California	Pete Cutino	8-6	UC-Irvine
1978	Stanford	Dante Dettamanti	7-6 (3 OT)	California
1979	UC-Santa Barbara	Pete Snyder	11-3	UCLA
1980	Stanford	Dante Dettamanti	8-6	California
1981	Stanford	Dante Dettamanti	17-6	Long Beach St
1982	UC-Irvine	Ed Newland	7-4	Stanford
1983	California	Pete Cutino	10-7	Southern Cal
1984	California	Pete Cutino	9-8	Stanford
1985	Stanford	Dante Dettamanti	12-11 (2 OT)	UC-Irvine
1986	Stanford	Dante Dettamanti	9-6	California
1987	California	Pete Cutino	9-8 (OT)	Southern Cal
1988	California	Pete Cutino	14-11	UCLA
1989	UC-Irvine	Ed Newland	9-8	California
1990	California	Steve Heaston	8-7	Stanford
1991	California	Steve Heaston	7-6	UCLA
1992	California	Steve Heaston	12-11	Stanford

Wrestling

Division I

Year	Champion	Coach	Pts	Runner-Up	Pts	Most Outstanding Wrestler
1928	Oklahoma St*	E. C. Gallagher				
1929	Oklahoma St	E. C. Gallagher	26	Michigan	18	
1930	Oklahoma St*	E. C. Gallagher	27	Illinois	14	
1931	Oklahoma St*	E. C. Gallagher		Michigan		
1932	Indiana*	W. H. Thom		Oklahoma St		Edwin Belshaw, Indiana
1933	Oklahoma St*	E. C. Gallagher				Allan Kelley, Oklahoma St
	Iowa St*	Hugo Otopalik				Pat Johnson, Harvard
1934	Oklahoma St	E. C. Gallagher	29	Indiana	19	Ben Bishop, Lehigh
1935	Oklahoma St	E. C. Gallagher	36	Oklahoma	18	Ross Flood, Oklahoma St
1936	Oklahoma	Paul Keen	14	Central St (OK)	10	Wayne Martin, Oklahoma
				Oklahoma St	10	
1937	Oklahoma St	E. C. Gallagher	31	Oklahoma	13	Stanley Henson, Oklahoma St
1938	Oklahoma St	E. C. Gallagher	19	Illinois	15	Joe McDaniels, Oklahoma St
1939	Oklahoma St	E. C. Gallagher	33	Lehigh	12	Dale Hanson, Minnesota
1940	Oklahoma St	E. C. Gallagher	24	Indiana	14	Don Nichols, Michigan
1941	Oklahoma St	Art Griffith	37	Michigan St	26	Al Whitehurst, Oklahoma St
1942	Oklahoma St	Art Griffith	31	Michigan St	26	David Arndt, Oklahoma St
1943-45	No tournament					
1946	Oklahoma St	Art Griffith	25	Northern Iowa	24	Gerald Leeman, Northern Iowa
1947	Cornell	Paul Scott	32	Northern Iowa	19	William Koll, Northern Iowa
1948	Oklahoma St	Art Griffith	33	Michigan St	28	William Koll, Northern Iowa
1949	Oklahoma St	Art Griffith	32	Northern Iowa	27	Charles Hetrick, Oklahoma St
1950	Northern Iowa	David McCuskey	30	Purdue	16	Anthony Gizoni, Waynesburg
1951	Oklahoma	Port Robertson	24	Oklahoma St	23	Walter Romanowski, Cornell
1952	Oklahoma	Port Robertson	22	Northern Iowa	21	Tommy Evans, Oklahoma
1953	Penn St	Charles Speidel	21	Oklahoma	15	Frank Bettucci, Cornell
1954	Oklahoma St	Art Griffith	32	Pittsburgh	17	Tommy Evans, Oklahoma
1955	Oklahoma St	Art Griffith	40	Penn St	31	Edward Eichelberger, Lehigh
1956	Oklahoma St	Art Griffith	65	Oklahoma	62	Dan Hodge, Oklahoma
1957	Oklahoma	Port Robertson	73	Pittsburgh	66	Dan Hodge, Oklahoma
1958	Oklahoma St	Myron Roderick	77	Iowa St	62	Dick Delgado, Oklahoma
1959	Oklahoma St	Myron Roderick	73	Iowa St	51	Ron Gray, Iowa St
1960	Oklahoma	Thomas Evans	59	Iowa St	40	Dave Auble, Cornell

Wrestling (Cont.)

DIVISION I (Cont.)

Year	Champion	Coach	Pts	Runner-Up	Pts	Most Outstanding Wrestler
1961	Oklahoma St	Myron Roderick	82	Oklahoma	63	E. Gray Simons, Lock Haven
1962	Oklahoma St	Myron Roderick	82	Oklahoma	45	E. Gray Simons, Lock Haven
1963	Oklahoma	Thomas Evans	48	Iowa St	45	Mickey Martin, Oklahoma
1964	Oklahoma St	Myron Roderick	87	Oklahoma	58	Dean Lahr, Colorado
1965	Iowa St	Harold Nichols	87	Oklahoma St	86	Yojiro Uetake, Oklahoma St
1966	Oklahoma St	Myron Roderick	79	Iowa St	70	Yojiro Uetake, Oklahoma St
1967	Michigan St	Grady Peninger	74	Michigan	63	Rich Sanders, Portland St
1968	Oklahoma St	Myron Roderick	81	Iowa St	78	Dwayne Keller, Oklahoma St
1969	Iowa St	Harold Nichols	104	Oklahoma	69	Dan Gable, Iowa St
1970	Iowa St	Harold Nichols	99	Michigan St	84	Larry Owings, Washington
1971	Oklahoma St	Tommy Chesbro	94	Iowa St	66	Darrell Keller, Oklahoma St
1972	Iowa St	Harold Nichols	103	Michigan St	72½	Wade Schalles, Clarion
1973	Iowa St	Harold Nichols	85	Oregon St	72½	Greg Strobel, Oregon St
1974	Oklahoma	Stan Abel	69½	Michigan	67	Floyd Hitchcock, Bloomsburg
1975	Iowa	Gary Kurdelmeier	102	Oklahoma	77	Mike Frick, Lehigh
1976	Iowa	Gary Kurdelmeier	123½	Iowa St	85¾	Chuch Yagla, Iowa
1977	Iowa St	Harold Nichols	95½	Oklahoma St	88¾	Nick Gallo, Hofstra
1978	Iowa	Dan Gable	94½	Iowa St	94	Mark Churella, Michigan
1979	Iowa	Dan Gable	122½	Iowa St	88	Bruce Kinseth, Iowa
1980	Iowa	Dan Gable	110¾	Oklahoma St	87	Howard Harris, Oregon St
1981	Iowa	Dan Gable	129¾	Oklahoma	100¼	Gene Mills, Syracuse
1982	Iowa	Dan Gable	131¾	Iowa St	111	Mark Schultz, Oklahoma
1983	Iowa	Dan Gable	155	Oklahoma St	102	Mike Sheets, Oklahoma St
1984	Iowa	Dan Gable	123¾	Oklahoma St	98	Jim Zalesky, Iowa
1985	Iowa	Dan Gable	145¼	Oklahoma	98½	Barry Davis, Iowa
1986	Iowa	Dan Gable	158	Oklahoma	84¼	Marty Kistler, Iowa
1987	Iowa St	Jim Gibbons	133	Iowa	108	John Smith, Oklahoma St
1988	Arizona St	Bobby Douglas	93	Iowa	85½	Scott Turner, N Carolina St
1989	Oklahoma St	Joe Seay	91¼	Arizona St	70½	Tim Krieger, Iowa St
1990	Oklahoma St	Joe Seay	117¾	Arizona St	104¾	Chris Barnes, Oklahoma St
1991	Iowa	Dan Gable	157	Oklahoma St	108¾	Jeff Prescott, Penn St
1992	Iowa	Dan Gable	149	Oklahoma St	100½	Tom Brands, Iowa
1993	Iowa	Dan Gable	123¾	Penn St	87½	Terry Steiner, Iowa

*Unofficial champions.

DIVISION II

Year	Champion	Year	Champion
1963	Western St (CO)	1979	Cal St-Bakersfield
1964	Western St (CO)	1980	Cal St-Bakersfield
1965	Mankato St	1981	Cal St-Bakersfield
1966	Cal Poly-SLO	1982	Cal St-Bakersfield
1967	Portland St	1983	Cal St-Bakersfield
1968	Cal Poly-SLO	1984	SIU-Edwardsville
1969	Cal Poly-SLO	1985	SIU-Edwardsville
1970	Cal Poly-SLO	1986	SIU-Edwardsville
1971	Cal Poly-SLO	1987	Cal St-Bakersfield
1972	Cal Poly-SLO	1988	N Dakota St
1973	Cal Poly-SLO	1989	Portland St
1974	Cal Poly-SLO	1990	Portland St
1975	Northern Iowa	1991	NE-Omaha
1976	Cal St-Bakersfield	1992	Central Oklahoma
1977	Cal St-Bakersfield	1993	Central Oklahoma
1978	Northern Iowa		

DIVISION III

Year	Champion	Year	Champion
1974	Wilkes	1984	Trenton St
1975	John Carroll	1985	Trenton St
1976	Montclair St	1986	Montclair St
1977	Brockport St	1987	Trenton St
1978	Buffalo	1988	St Lawrence
1979	Trenton St	1989	Ithaca
1980	Brockport St	1990	Ithaca
1981	Trenton St	1991	Augsburg
1982	Brockport St	1992	Brockport
1983	Brockport St	1993	Augsburg

INDIVIDUAL CHAMPIONSHIP
RECORDS

Swimming and Diving

Men

Event	Time	Record Holder	Date
50-yard freestyle	19.14	David Fox, N Carolina St	3-25-93
100-yard freestyle	41.80	Matt Biondi, California	4-4-87
200-yard freestyle	1:33.03	Matt Biondi, California	4-3-87
500-yard freestyle	4:12.24	Artur Wojdat, Iowa	3-30-89
1650-yard freestyle	14:37.87	Jeff Kostoff, Stanford	4-5-86
100-yard backstroke	46.12	Jeff Rouse, Stanford	3-28-92
200-yard backstroke	1:40.64	Jeff Rouse, Stanford	3-28-92
100-yard breaststroke	52.48	Steve Lundquist, Southern Meth	3-25-83
200-yard breaststroke	1:53.77	Mike Barrowman, Michigan	3-24-90
100-yard butterfly	46.26	Pablo.Morales, Stanford	4-4-86
200-yard butterfly	1:41.78	Melvin Stewart, Tennessee	3-30-91
200-yard individual medley	1:43.52	Greg Burgess, Florida	3-25-93
400-yard individual medley	3:41.54	Greg Burgess, Florida	3-26-93

Women

Event	Time	Record Holder	Date
50-yard freestyle	21.92	Leigh Ann Fetter, Texas	3-16-90
100-yard freestyle	47.61	Jenny Thompson, Stanford	3-21-92
200-yard freestyle	1:43.28	Nicole Haislett, Florida	3-20-92
500-yard freestyle	4:34.39	Janet Evans, Stanford	3-15-90
1650-yard freestyle	15:39.14	Janet Evans, Stanford	3-17-90
100-yard backstroke	53.98	Betsy Mitchell, Texas	3-21-92
200-yard backstroke	1:52.98	Whitney Hedgepeth, Texas	3-21-87
100-yard breaststroke	1:00.47	Lara Hooiveld, Michigan	3-19-93
200-yard breaststroke	2:11.54	Dorsey Tierney, Texas	3-23-91
100-yard butterfly	51.75	Crissy Ahmann-Leighton, Arizona	3-20-92
200-yard butterfly	1:53.42	Summer Sanders, Stanford	3-21-92
200-yard individual medley	1:55.54	Summer Sanders, Stanford	3-20-92
400-yard individual medley	4:02.28	Summer Sanders, Stanford	3-20-92

Indoor Track and Field

Men

Event	Mark	Record Holder	Date
55-meter dash	6.00	Lee McRae, Pittsburgh	3-14-86
55-meter hurdles	7.07	Allen Johnson, N Carolina	3-13-92
200-meter dash	20.59	Michael Johnson, Baylor	3-10-89
400-meter dash	45.79	Gabriel Luke, Rice	3-10-90
500-meter run	59.82	Roddie Haley, Arkansas	3-15-86
800-meter run	1:46.19	George Kersh, Mississippi	3-9-91
1000-meter run	2:18.74	Freddie Williams, Abilene Christian	3-15-86
1500-meter run	3:43.48	Paul Donovan, Arkansas	3-9-85
3000-meter run	7:50.00	Reuben Reina, Arkansas	3-9-91
5000-meter run	13:37.94	Jonah Koech, Iowa St	3-9-90
High jump	7 ft 9¼ in	Hollis Conway, Southwestern Louisiana	3-11-89
Pole vault	18 ft 6½ in	Dean Starkey, Illinois	3-11-89
		Istvan Bagyula, George Mason	3-10-90
Long jump	27 ft 10 in	Carl Lewis, Houston	3-13-81
Triple jump	56 ft 9½ in	Keith Connor, Southern Meth	3-13-81
Shot put	69 ft 8½ in	Michael Carter, Southern Meth	3-13-81
		Soren Tallhem, Brigham Young	3-9-85
35-pound weight throw	76 ft 5½ in	Robert Weir, Southern Meth	3-11-83

Indoor Track and Field *(Cont.)*

Women

Event	Mark	Record Holder	Date
55-meter dash	6.56	Gwen Torrence, Georgia	3-14-87
55-meter hurdles	7.44	Lynda Tolbert, Arizona St	3-9-90
200-meter dash	22.96	Dawn Sowell, Louisiana St	3-10-89
400-meter dash	51.05	Maicel Malone, Arizona St	3-9-91
500-meter run	1:08.89	Linetta Wilson, Nebraska	3-14-87
800-meter run	2:02.77	Meredith Rainey, Harvard	3-10-90
1000-meter run	2:41.08	Trena Hull, NV-Las Vegas	3-14-87
1500-meter run	4:17.85	Tina Krebs, Clemson	3-9-85
3000-meter run	8:54.98	Stephanie Herbst, Wisconsin	3-15-86
5000-meter run	15:48.17	Valerie McGovern, Kentucky	3-9-90
High jump	6 ft 3½ in	J.C. Broughton, Arizona	3-14-93
Long jump	21 ft 10¼ in	Angela Thacker, Nebraska	3-10-84
Triple jump	45 ft 9 in	Sheila Hudson, California	3-10-90
Shot put	57 ft 11¾ in	Regina Cavanaugh, Rice	3-14-86

Outdoor Track and Field

Men

Event	Mark	Record Holder	Date
100-meter dash	10.03	Stanley Floyd, Houston	6-5-82
		Joe DeLoach, Houston	6-4-88
200-meter dash	19.87	Lorenzo Daniel, Mississippi St	6-3-88
400-meter dash	44.00	Quincy Watts, Southern Cal	6-6-92
800-meter run	1:44.70	Mark Everett, Florida	6-1-90
1500-meter run	3:35.30	Sydney Maree, Villanova	6-6-81
3000-meter steeplechase	8:12.39	Henry Rono, Washington St	6-1-78
5000-meter run	13:20.63	Sydney Maree, Villanova	6-2-79
10000-meter run	28:01.30	Suleiman Nyambui, UTEP	6-1-79
110-meter high hurdles	13.22	Greg Foster, UCLA	6-2-78
400-meter intermediate hurdles	47.85	Kevin Young, UCLA	6-3-88
High jump	7 ft 9¾ in	Hollis Conway, Southwestern Louisiana	6-3-89
Pole vault	19 ft ¼ in	Istvan Bagyula, George Mason	5-31-91
Long jump	28 ft	Erick Walder, Arkansas	6-3-93
Triple jump	57 ft 7¾ in	Keith Connor, Southern Meth	6-5-82
Shot put	71 ft 11 in	John Brenner, UCLA	6-2-84
Discus throw	220 ft	Kamy Keshmiri, Nevada	6-5-92
Hammer throw	257 ft 0 in	Ken Flax, Oregon	6-6-86
Javelin throw	295 ft 2 in	Einar Vilhjalmsson, Texas	6-2-83
Decathlon	8279 pts	Tito Steiner, Brigham Young	6-2/3-81

Women

Event	Mark	Record Holder	Date
100-meter dash	10.78	Dawn Sowell, Louisiana St	6-3-89
200-meter dash	22.04	Dawn Sowell, Louisiana St	6-2-89
400-meter dash	50.18	Pauline Davis, Alabama	6-3-89
800-meter run	1:59.11	Suzy Favor, Wisconsin	6-1-90
1500-meter run	4:08.26	Suzy Favor, Wisconsin	6-2-90
3000-meter run	8:47.35	Vicki Huber, Villanova	6-3-88
5000-meter run	15:38.47	Annette Hand, Oregon	6-4-88
10000-meter run	32:28.57	Sylvia Mosqueda, Cal St-LA	6-1-88
100-meter hurdles	12.70	Tananjalyn Stanley, Louisiana St	6-3-89
400-meter hurdles	54.64	Latanya Sheffield, San Diego St	5-31-85
High jump	6 ft 4¼ in	Katrena Johnson, Arizona	6-1-85
Long jump	22 ft 9¼ in	Sheila Echols, Louisiana St	6-5-87
Triple jump	46 ft ¾ in	Sheila Hudson, California	6-2-90
Shot put	57 ft 6 ½ in	Regina Cavanaugh, Rice	6-4-86
Discus throw	209 ft 10 in	Leslie Deniz, Arizona St	6-4-83
Javelin throw	206 ft 9 in	Karin Smith, Cal Poly-SLO	6-4-82
Heptathlon	6365 pts	Jackie Joyner, UCLA	5-30/31-83

Olympics

Sports Illustrated

12

Lillehammer braces for the
arrival of the Olympics

Waiting
for the
World

Omnipresent Olympics

The Games, now scheduled every other year, seemed to be everywhere in evidence

by WILLIAM OSCAR JOHNSON

IT USED TO BE THE BETTER PART OF four long, comfortable years between one Olympiad and the next, a kind of elegant interlude which lent the Games an aura of majesty and uniqueness that placed them in quite another galaxy from all the world's other games, which are spelled with a *g* instead of a *G*. But now with the Winter and Summer Olympics staggered one after another on a biennial basis, the Games suddenly seem to be coming on us with alarming frequency. Indeed when the opening ceremonies unveil the Winter Games of '94 on Feb. 12 in Lillehammer, Norway, a bare 18 months will have passed since the closing ceremonies wrapped up the Barcelona Games on Aug. 9, 1992.

Is this a good thing? No one knows yet. The new two-year cycle was strictly a commercial move. It was the brainchild of American TV networks, the theory being that both networks and corporate sponsors would find it easier to operate if they could spread their Olympic cash flow over two separate Games every other year rather than having to come up with a huge

double-Olympic lump sum in a single year. Whether the split Games actually produce more money or better TV ratings won't be known for a while. The world might find an Olympics every two years to be too much of a good thing, TV ratings would fall, sponsors' money would diminish, and there would be nothing to do but return to the quadrennial rhythms. Or, in the wildest of all scenarios, the public appetite for more and more Olympics could prove to be so wildly voracious (and therefore so obscenely profitable) that the International Olympic Committee would have no choice but to put on Games every year by creating—what else?—a Spring Olympics and a Fall Olympics.

Neither extreme is likely. For now, the first two split Olympics—Winter in Lillehammer in February 1994 and Summer in Atlanta in July and August 1996—are both moving nicely toward their separate goals. Lillehammer, a snug, slow lakeside town 95 miles north of Oslo, with a population of just 22,000, was a stunning dark horse winner in 1988. No one was more surprised—and more alarmed—than the local

CARL YARBROUGH

Lillehammer citizenry when their town got the prize. They began to ask immediately, "Is there any way we can get out of this? Can we give it back?" As Ivar Odegaard, executive editor of the local newspaper, put it, "The people were a little bit proud and a little bit curious, but above all they were very, very frightened."

The fright changed to efficiency almost at once, and by March '93, a full 11 months before the Games were to begin, 100% of the permanent Olympic facilities had been finished. Better yet, each was getting generally rave reviews from athletes and coaches after a series of world-class competitions in events including Alpine skiing, ski jumping, speed skating, bobsledding and cross-country skiing. And even better, all of Lillehammer's Olympic construction had been accomplished under environmental standards so strict and yet so practical that the IOC is thinking of requiring organizing committees in the future to conform to the same high standards.

These were supposed to be a "compact" Olympics, basically confined to Lillehammer's environs, but as it turns out, the

Fright turned to efficiency as Lillehammer accepted its place in the Olympic spotlight.

venues are scattered over a 72-mile stretch along the hills of Lake Mjosa, Norway's largest inland body of water, and up the Gudbrandsdalen Valley, with Lillehammer approximately in the middle. The one compact centerpiece facility is Olympic Park, on a mountainside in the town, which includes a 10,500-seat hockey arena and a freestyle skiing course, plus a ski jump arena that seats 10,000 with room for another 47,000 standing spectators. The latter will also be used for opening and closing ceremonies, with room for a further 33,000 standing-room spectators. Several miles north of town are the bob and luge runs, as well as the men's and women's Alpine runs.

The bob and luge track is 1,760 meters long and winds through deep woods. The U.S.'s Brian Shimer, winner of two World Cup titles last year, labeled it a fine, testing course on which "any little mistake shows throughout your whole trip." As for the Alpine ski venues, the superstar of them all

JOEY IVANSCO

Payne weathered his share of storms in Atlanta.

hammer's Olympic structures is the 5,500-seat hockey arena, called Mountain Hall, in the town of Gjovik, 25 miles southwest of Lillehammer. Billed by its builders as "the world's largest in-mountain coliseum," this is a vast, man-made cavern about half the size of Madison Square Garden. From the outside the mountain is essentially unblemished by construction except for a low, bunkerlike entrance to the arena. It cost $20 million and required the removal of 141,000 cubic meters of rock. Even though it cost more than a normal arena, says assistant project manager Steinar Simonsen, "it will be cheaper in the future—no windows to wash, no outside walls to paint, no roof to repair. And it costs about half as much to heat as a regular building."

So the preparations for the Lillehammer Games were pretty impressive. Yet editor Odegaard reports that not all of the small-town fears have evaporated: "You know, for 16 days we will have 100,000 people per day moving in and out of this little place, a trainful of people arriving every 10 minutes from Oslo. We get readers' questions such as, 'Shall we buy bread and milk for the whole period before it starts? Can we get to the hospital here, or will we have to go to Oslo?' They are not negative. They are just a little bit anxious."

Anxiety has been the operative emotion in Atlanta, too, in the past year. And there has been plenty of negativism besides. Billy Payne, president and CEO of the Atlanta Committee for the Olympic Games (ACOG), has come to refer to the '96 Games as "the greatest peacetime event in the 20th century." However, for a long time the atmosphere around ACOG could only be described as warlike. One point of sharp conflict occurred in the fall of '92 when Payne declared that ACOG wanted to add

was the men's downhill, which delighted racers labeled a certifiably great run— "among the top courses in the world, just behind Kitzbühel," said the U.S.'s AJ Kitt. In contrast, the women's downhill, on a different mountain, was so insultingly flat and easy that organizers responded to fierce complaints from racers by promising to redesign it completely before the Games begin.

Far down Lake Mjosa were the remaining venues, all for ice sports. The speed skating arena was in Hamar, 20 miles from Lillehammer, a stunning structure meant to resemble the hull of an overturned Viking ship. When the world speed skating championships were held there in February '93, Falko Zandstra of the Netherlands, the all-around titlist, burbled, "Oh, what a hall! It must have been expensive, but the ice is perfect!" Figure skating will be held in a nondescript 6,000-seat arena in Hamar, too, but the least nondescript of all Lille-

golf to the '96 Games (the first time since 1904) and that the competition would be held at the fabled Augusta National Golf Club—a segregated institution for white men that has but one token black member (admitted in 1990) and no women at all. The idea offended blacks and women everywhere. Michael Lomax, a black Fulton County commissioner, declared coldly, "Giving the venue to Augusta would be an embarrassment to Atlanta. It would ignore everything we have achieved here." In January, Juan Antonio Samaranch, president of the IOC, cut the racial tension by declaring that there would be no golf in the '96 Games—at Augusta or anywhere else.

ACOG remained under attack for other perceived transgressions. An organization called the Atlanta Olympic Conscience Coalition was formed as a kind of all-around moral watchdog for a variety of social causes—labor unions, the homeless, civil liberties, neighborhood protection. Coalition co-chairman Timothy McDonald, a black clergyman, was in a sharply militant mood early in the year, particularly in regard to the $207 million Olympic Stadium to be built in Summerhill, a historic black neighborhood. "Atlanta has a history of displacing poor people when it builds major structures," said McDonald back in January. "In the past, developers did not use neighborhood people to do the work. There were even illegal aliens. The Olympic people have given no guarantee on what level they will use union labor. The day they break ground [for the stadium], we will have a tent city there, and we will not go away. We'll take every chance we get to embarrass the Olympic organizers." When Payne was asked about McDonald's remarks, the ACOG CEO said, "I will not honor him by mentioning his name."

Groundbreaking for the stadium was scheduled for late April, but nothing happened until late July, when workmen began the very preliminary process of nailing up a plywood fence around the site. Were there tent cities full of angry coalition demonstrators? No. By this time, the Atlanta Olympic machine had begun to purr instead of growl. A surprisingly amicable deal had been struck between ACOG and local labor unions regarding Olympic construction work, and there have been positive negotiations on protecting the rights of the homeless and of the neighborhoods. Indeed, the formerly hostile Reverend McDonald said of ACOG in July, "They've gotten a lot more friendly, and they listen better than they did a year or two ago. I don't sense the same degree of tension, although we're definitely not bedfellows."

Early in 1993, Atlanta had seemed to be facing a drastic shortfall in raising the $1.47 billion it had budgeted for the Games. The $40 million price tag for each major sponsor seemed outrageously high. The economy was in doubt. A few deep-dyed pessimists even predicted that Atlanta might wind up facing a financial debacle similar to that which left Montreal reeling after the Games of 1976, stuck with a $1 billion debt that irritated citizens are still paying off to this day. But, as the months passed, a few big sponsors signed deals, and more were in the offing. In late July, NBC bid the decent sum of $456 million for U.S. TV rights. This was less than ACOG wanted, but with the $250 million that European TV had anted up earlier, it pretty much guaranteed that a respectable Olympics can be produced—and paid for—in Atlanta beginning on July 20, 1996.

The biggest Olympic news of the year was the choice of the city to host the millenium Olympics in 2000. There were six candidates: Sydney, Beijing, Berlin, Manchester, Istanbul and Brasilia. Each had plenty of pluses in their Olympic dossiers, but it was the minuses that they feared would turn the tide when the IOC voted on Sept. 23 in Monaco. From the start Sydney was the front-runner, with everything going for it—particularly its exotic Southern Hemisphere location (the only non–Northern Hemisphere host city ever was Melbourne in 1956). So intense was Sydney's desire to leave not the slightest negative impression

China's festive demonstrations failed to win the day for Beijing's Olympic bid.

among visiting IOC members that the city council of a suburb adjacent to a majority of Olympic venues (including the main stadium, pool and athletes' village) ordered residents of high-rise apartments to desist from hanging laundry on their balconies because the practice was "degrading and unsightly" and could hurt the city's Olympic bid.

Other cities had far larger problems. Berlin's bid was constantly being undermined by violent left-wing demonstrators who wanted Olympic money spent for unemployed eastern Germans. Istanbul was seen as an Islam city of volatile politics and misunderstood religious practices. Beijing had the biggest problem of all—a horrendous world reputation for gross violations of human rights, dating back most explicitly to the massacre of a thousand dissidents in Tiananmen Square on June 3 and 4, 1989. The Chinese seemed coldly unrepentant: Amazingly enough, the man named to chair the bid committee, Chen Xitong, had been the mayor of Beijing in 1989 and had formally authorized the declaration of martial law that triggered the mass murders. The IOC seemed equally unmoved by the atrocities. When Samaranch visited Beijing, he was asked if he

thought China's human rights policies should affect its bid, and he said, "For me, Beijing is a candidate as the others. And also in the IOC, we have the mind that the People's Republic of China is an important member of the Olympic family." In midsummer, the U.S. House of Representatives passed a resolution opposing Beijing's bid, and New Jersey senator Bill Bradley, winner of a gold medal in Olympic basketball in 1964, wrote to Samaranch declaring "strong opposition" to it. The protests provoked cries of "interference" from China and the IOC.

In July an official IOC report that discussed each city's various technical merits—specifically not including human rights records—was leaked to a German newspaper. Intended as an advisory for IOC members, the report did not actually rank the candidates, but its findings indicated that Sydney was clearly No. 1, followed approximately in order by Berlin, Manchester and Beijing. It savaged Brasilia and Istanbul as polluted, potentially dangerous and lacking sadly in infrastructure. IOC members have a reputation for voting their own often squirrelly mindsets in these matters. Whether the disappearance of drying laundry from apartment balconies tipped the balance, no one knows, but this time they went with the obvious best choice: Sydney on the fourth ballot.

FOR THE RECORD·1992 Games

TRACK AND FIELD

Men

100 METERS

1. ..Linford Christie, Great Britain   9.96
2. ..Frank Fredericks, Namibia   10.02
3. ..Dennis Mitchell, United States   10.04

200 METERS

1. ..Mike Marsh, United States   20.01
2. ..Frank Fredericks, Namibia   20.13
3. ..Michael Bates, United States   20.38

400 METERS

1. ..Quincy Watts, United States   43.50OR
2. ..Steve Lewis, United States   44.21
3. ..Samson Kitur, Kenya   44.24

800 METERS

1. ..William Tanui, Kenya   1:43.66
2. ..Nixon Kiprotich, Kenya   1:43.70
3. ..Johnny Gray, United States   1:43.97

1500 METERS

1. ..Fermin Cacho, Spain   3:40.12
2. ..Rachid El-Basir, Morocco   3:40.62
3. ..Mohamed Ahmed Sulaiman, Qatar   3:40.69

5000 METERS

1. ..Dieter Baumann, Germany   13:12.52
2. ..Paul Bitok, Kenya   13:12.71
3. ..Fita Bayisa, Ethiopia   13:13.03

10,000 METERS

1. ..Khalid Skah, Morocco   27:46.70
2. ..Richard Chelimo, Kenya   27:47.72
3. ..Addis Abebe, Ethiopia   28.00.07

MARATHON

1. ..Hwang Young-Cho, South Korea   2:13:23
2. ..Koichi Morishita, Japan   2:13:45
3. ..Stephan Freigang, Germany   2:14:00

110-METER HURDLES

1. ..Mark McKoy, Canada   13.12
2. ..Tony Dees, United States   13.24
3. ..Jack Pierce, United States   13.26

400-METER HURDLES

1. ..Kevin Young, United States   46.78WR
2. ..Winthrop Graham, Jamaica   47.66
3. ..Kriss Akabusi, Great Britain   47.82

Note: OR=Olympic record. WR=world record

EOR=equals Olympic record

EWR=equals world record

3000-METER STEEPLECHASE

1. ..Mathew Birir, Kenya   8:08.84
2. ..Patrick Sang, Kenya   8:09.55
3. ..William Mutwol, Kenya   8:10.74

4 X 100 METER RELAY

1. ..United States: Mike Marsh,   37.40WR
   Leroy Burrell,
   Dennis Mitchell,
   Carl Lewis
2. ..Nigeria   37.98
3. ..Cuba   38.00

4 X 400 METER RELAY

1. ..United States: Andrew Valmon,   2:55.74WR
   Quincy Watts, Michael Johnson,
   Steve Lewis
2. ..Cuba   2:59.51
3. ..Great Britain   2:59.73

20-KILOMETER WALK

1. ..Daniel Plaza, Spain   1:21:45
2. ..Guillaume Leblanc, France   1:22:25
3. ..Giovanni De Benedictis, Italy   1:23:11

50-KILOMETER WALK

1. ..Andrey Perlov, Unified Team   3:50:13
2. ..Carlos Mercenario, Mexico   3:52:09
3. ..Ronald Weigel, Germany   3:53:45

HIGH JUMP

1. ..Javier Sotomayor, Cuba   7 ft 8 in
2. ..Patrik Sjoberg, Sweden   7 ft 8 in
3. ..Artur Partyka, Poland   7 ft 8 in
3. ..Timothy Forsythe, Australia   7 ft 8 in
3. ..Hollis Conway, United States   7 ft 8 in

POLE VAULT

1. ..Maksim Tarasov, Unified Team   19 ft ¼ in
2. ..Igor Trandenkov, Unified Team   19 ft ¼ in
3. ..Javier Garcia, Spain   18 ft 10¼ in

LONG JUMP

1. ..Carl Lewis, United States   28 ft 5½ in
2. ..Mike Powell, United States   28 ft 4¼ in
3. ..Joe Greene, United States   27 ft 4½in

TRIPLE JUMP

1. ..Mike Conley, United States   59 ft 7½ in
2. ..Charles Simpkins, United States   57 ft 9 in
3. ..Frank Rutherford, Bahamas   56 ft 11½in

SHOT PUT

1. ..Mike Stulce, United States   71 ft 2½in
2. ..Jim Doehring, United States   68 ft 9¼ in
3. ..Vyacheslav Lykho, Unified Team   68 ft 8½in

TRACK AND FIELD (Cont.)

Men (Cont.)

DISCUS THROW

1. ..Romas Ubartas, Lithuania	213 ft 8 in
2. ..Jürgen Schult, Germany	213 ft 1 in
3. ..Roberto Moya, Cuba	210 ft 4 in

HAMMER THROW

1. ..Andrey Abduvaliyev, Unified Team	270 ft 9 in
2. ..Igor Astapkovich, Unified Team	268 ft 11 in
3. ..Igor Nikulin, Unified Team	267 ft

JAVELIN

1. ..Jan Zelezny, Czechoslovakia	294 ft 2 in OR
2. ..Seppo Räty, Finland	284 ft 1 in
3. ..Steve Backley, Great Britain	273 ft 7 in

DECATHLON

	Pts
1. ..Robert Zmelik, Czechoslovakia	8611
2. ..Antonio Peñalver, Spain	8412
3. ..Dave Johnson, United States	8309

Women

100 METERS

1. ..Gail Devers, United States	10.82
2. ..Juliet Cuthbert, Jamaica	10.83
3. ..Irina Privalova, Unified Team	10.84

200 METERS

1. ..Gwen Torrence, United States	21.81
2. ..Juliet Cuthbert, Jamaica	22.02
3. ..Merlene Ottey, Jamaica	22.09

400 METERS

1. ..Marie-Jose Péréc, France	48.83
2. ..Olga Bryzgina, Unified Team	49.05
3. ..Ximena Restrepo, Colombia	49.64

800 METERS

1. ..Ellen Van Langen, The Netherlands	1:55.54
2. ..Lilia Nurutdinova, Unified Team	1:55.99
3. ..Ana Fidelia Quirot, Cuba	1:56.80

1500 METERS

1. ..Hassiba Boulmerka, Algeria	3:55.30
2. ..Lyudmila Rogacheva, Unified Team	3:56.91
3. ..Qu Yunxia, China	3:57.08

3000 METERS

1. ..Elena Romanova, Unified Team	8:46.04
2. ..Tatiana Dorovskikh, Unified Team	8:46.85
3. ..Angela Chalmers, Canada	8:47.22

10,000 METERS

1. ..Derartu Tulu, Ethiopia	31:06.02
2. ..Elana Meyer, South Africa	31:11.75
3. ..Lynn Jennings, United States	31:19.89

MARATHON

1. ..Valentina Yegorova, Unified Team	2:32:41
2. ..Yuko Arimori, Japan	2:32:49
3. ..Lorraine Moller, New Zealand	2:33:59

100-METER HURDLES

1. ..Paraskevi Patoulidou, Greece	12.64
2. ..LaVonna Martin, United States	12.69
3. ..Yordanka Donkova, Bulgaria	12.70

400-METER HURDLES

1. ..Sally Gunnell, Great Britain	53.23
2. ..Sandra Farmer-Patrick, United States	53.69
3. ..Janeene Vickers, United States	54.31

4 X 100 METER RELAY

1. ..United States: Evelyn Ashford, Esther Jones, Carlette Guidry, Gwen Torrence	42.11
2. ..Unified Team	42.16
3. ..Nigeria	42.81

4 X 400 METER RELAY

1. ..Unified Team: Yelena Ruzina, Lioudmila Dzhigalova, Olga Nazarova, Olga Bryzgina	3:20.20
2. ..United States: Natasha Kaiser, Gwen Torrence, Jearl Miles, Rochelle Stevens	3:20.92
3. ..Great Britain	3:24.2c

HIGH JUMP

1. ..Heike Henkel, Germany	6 ft 7½ in
2. ..Galina Astafei, Romania	6 ft 6¾ in
3. ..Joanet Quintero, Cuba	6 ft 5½ in

LONG JUMP

1. ..Heike Drechsler, Germany	23 ft 5¼ in
2. ..Inessa Kravets, Unified Team	23 ft 4½ in
3. ..Jackie Joyner-Kersee, United States	23 ft 2½ in

SHOT PUT

1. ..Svetlana Kriveleva, Unified Team	69 ft 1¼ in
2. ..Huang Zhihong, China	67 ft 2 in
3. ..Kathrin Neimke, Germany	64 ft 10¾ in

DISCUS THROW

1. ..Maritza Martén, Cuba	229 ft 10 in
2. ..Tzvetanka Mintcheva Khristova, Unified Team	222 ft 4 in
3. ..Daniela Costian, Australia	217 ft 4 in

Note: OR=Olympic record. WR=world record

TRACK AND FIELD (Cont.)

Women (Cont.)

JAVELIN

1. ..Silke Renk, Germany — 224 ft 2 in
2. ..Natalia Shikolenka, Unified Team — 223 ft 11 in
3. ..Karen Forkel, Germany — 219 ft 4 in

Note: OR=Olympic record. WR=world record.
EOR=equals Olympic record.

EWR=equals world record

HEPTATHLON

	Pts
1. ..Jackie Joyner-Kersee, United States	7044
2. ..Irina Belova, Unified Team	6845
3. ..Sabine Braun, Germany	6649

BASKETBALL

Men

Final: United States 117, Croatia 85
Lithuania (3rd)
United States: Christian Laettner, David Robinson, Patrick Ewing, Larry Bird, Scottie Pippen, Michael Jordan, Clyde Drexler, Karl Malone, John Stockton, Chris Mullin, Charles Barkley, Earvin Johnson

Women

Final: Unified Team 76, China 66
United States (3rd):
Teresa Edwards, Daedra Charles, Clarissa Davis, Tammy Jackson, Teresa Weatherspoon, Vickie Orr, Victoria Bullett, Carolyn Jones, Katrina McClain, Medina Dixon, Cynthia Cooper, Suzanne McConnell

BOXING

LIGHT FLYWEIGHT (106 LB)

1. ....Rogelio Marcelo, Cuba
2. ....Daniel Bojinov, Bulgaria
3. ....Jan Quast, Germany
3. ....Roel Velasco, Philippines

FLYWEIGHT (112 LB)

1. ....Su Choi Choi, North Korea
2. ....Raul Gonzalez, Cuba
3. ....Timothy Austin, United States
3. ....Istvan Kovacs, Hungary

BANTAMWEIGHT (119 LB)

1. ....Joel Casamayor, Cuba
2. ....Wayne McCullough, Ireland
3. ....Li Gwang Sik, North Korea
3. ....Mohamed Achik, Morocco

FEATHERWEIGHT (125 LB)

1. ....Andreas Tews, Germany
2. ....Faustino Reyes, Spain
3. ....Hocine Soltani, Algeria
3. ....Ramazi Paliani, Unified Team

LIGHTWEIGHT (132 LB)

1. ....Oscar De La Hoya, United States
2. ....Marco Rudolph, Germany
3. ....Hong Sung Sik, North Korea
3. ....Namjil Bayarsaikhan, Mongolia

LIGHT WELTERWEIGHT (139 LB)

1. ....Hector Vinent, Cuba
2. ....Mark Leduc, Canada
3. ....Jyri Kjall, Finland
3. ....Leonard Doroftei, Romania

WELTERWEIGHT (147 LB)

1. ....Michael Carruth, Ireland
2. ....Juan Hernandez, Cuba
3. ....Aniibal Acevedo Santiago, Puerto Rico
3. ....Arkom Chenglai, Thailand

LIGHT MIDDLEWEIGHT (156 LB)

1. ....Juan Lemus, Cuba
2. ....Orhan Delibas, Netherlands
3. ....Gyorgy Mizsei, Hungary
3. ....Robin Reid, Great Britain

MIDDLEWEIGHT (165 LB)

1. ....Ariel Hernandez, Cuba
2. ....Chris Byrd, United States
3. ....Chris Johnson, Canada
3. ....Lee Seung Bae, South Korea

LIGHT HEAVYWEIGHT (178 LB)

1. ....Torsten May, Germany
2. ....Rostislav Zaoulitchnyi, Unified Team
3. ....Zoltan Beres, Hungary
3. ....Wojciech Bartnik, Poland

HEAVYWEIGHT (201 LB)

1. ....Felix Savon, Cuba
2. ....David Izonritei, Nigeria
3. ....Arnold Van Der Lijde, The Netherlands
3. ....David Tua, New Zealand

SUPERHEAVYWEIGHT (201+ LB)

1. ....Roberto Balado, Cuba
2. ....Richard Igbineghu, Nigeria
3. ....Brian Nielsen, Denmark
3. ....Svilen Roussinov, Bulgaria

GYMNASTICS

Men

ALL-AROUND

		Pts
1.	Vitaly Scherbo, Unified Team	59.025
2.	Grigory Misiutin, Unified Team	58.925
3.	Valery Belenki, Unified Team	58.625

HORIZONTAL BAR

		Pts
1.	Trent Dimas, United States	9.875
1.	Grigory Misiutin, Unified Team	9.837
3.	Andreas Wecker, Germany	9.837

PARALLEL BARS

		Pts
1.	Vitaly Scherbo, Unified Team	9.900
2.	Li Jing, China	9.812
3.	Guo Linyao, China	9.800
3.	Igor Korobchinski, Unified Team	9.800
3.	Masayuki Matsunaga, Japan	9.800

VAULT

		Pts
1.	Vitaly Scherbo, Unified Team	9.856
2.	Grigory Misiutin, Unified Team	9.781
3.	Yoo Ok Ryul, South Korea	9.762

POMMEL HORSE

		Pts
1.	Vitaly Scherbo, Unified Team	9.925
1.	Pae Gil Su, North Korea	9.925
3.	Andreas Wecker, Germany	9.887

RINGS

		Pts
1.	Vitaly Scherbo, Unified Team	9.937
1.	Li Jing, China	9.875
3.	Li Xiaosahuang, China	9.862
3.	Andreas Wecker, Germany	9.862

FLOOR EXERCISE

		Pts
1.	Li Xizosahuang, China	9.925
2.	Grigory Misiutin, Unified Team	9.787
2.	Yukio Iketani, Japan	9.787

TEAM COMBINED EXERCISES

		Pts
1.	Unified Team	585.450
2.	China	580.375
3.	Japan	578.250

Women

ALL-AROUND

		Pts
1.	Tatiana Gutsu, Unified Team	39.737
2.	Shannon Miller, United States	39.725
3.	Lavinia Milosovici, Romania	39.687

VAULT

		Pts
1.	Henrietta Onodi, Hungary	9.925
1.	Lavinia Milosovici, Romania	9.925
3.	Tatiana Lisenko, Unified Team	9.912

UNEVEN BARS

		Pts
1.	Lu Li, China	10.000
2.	Tatiana Gutsu, Unified Team	9.975
3.	Shannon Miller, United States	9.962

BALANCE BEAM

		Pts
1.	Tatiana Lisenko, Unified Team	9.975
2.	Lu Li, China	9.912
2.	Shannon Miller, United States	9.912

FLOOR EXERCISE

		Pts
1.	Lavinia Milosovici, Romania	10.000
2.	Henrietta Onodi, Hungary	9.950
3.	Shannon Miller, United States	9.912
3.	Cristina Bontas, Romania	9.912
3.	Tatiana Gutsu, Unified Team	9.912

TEAM COMBINED EXERCISES

		Pts
1.	Unified Team	395.666
2.	Romania	395.079
3.	United States	394.704

RHYTHMIC ALL-AROUND

		Pts
1.	Aleksandra Timoshenko, Unified Team	59.037
2.	Carolina Pascual Gracia, Spain	58.100
3.	Oksana Skaldina, Unified Team	57.912

THEY SAID IT

Kevin Young, Olympic 400-meter hurdles champ, when asked what it was like to run for years in the shadow of Edwin Moses: "Nice and cool."

SWIMMING

Men

50-METER FREESTYLE

1. ..Aleksandr Popov, Unified Team   21.91 OR
2. ..Matt Biondi, United States   22.09
3. ..Tom Jager, Unifed States   22.30

100-METER FREESTYLE

1. ..Aleksandr Popov, Unified Team   49.02
2. ..Gustavo Borges, Brazil   49.43
3. ..Stephan Caron, France   49.50

200-METER FREESTYLE

1. ..Evgueni Sadovyi, Unified Team   1:46.70 OR
2. ..Anders Holmertz, Sweden   1:46.86
3. ..Antti Kasvio, Finland   1:47.63

400-METER FREESTYLE

1. ..Evgueni Sadovyi, Unified Team   3:45.00 WR
2. ..Kieren Perkins, Australia   3:45.16
3. ..Anders Holmertz, Sweden   3:46.77

1500-METER FREESTYLE

1. ..Kieren Perkins, Australia   14:43.48 WR
2. ..Glen Housman, Australia   14:55.29
3. ..Jörg Hoffmann, Germany   15:02.29

100-METER BACKSTROKE

1. ..Mark Tewksbury, Canada   53.98 WR
2. ..Jeff Rouse, United States   54.04
3. ..David Berkoff, United States   54.78

200-METER BACKSTROKE

1. ..Martin Zubero-Lopez, Spain   1:58.47 OR
2. ..Vladimir Selkov, Unified Team   1:58.87
3. ..Stefano Battistelli, Italy   1:59.40

100-METER BREASTSTROKE

1. ..Nelson Diebel, United States   1:01.50 OR
2. ..Norbert Rozsa, Hungary   1:01.68
3. ..Philip Rogers, Australia   1:01.76

200-METER BREASTSTROKE

1. ..Mike Barrowman, United States   2:10.16 WR
2. ..Norbert Rozsa, Hungary   2:11.23
3. ..Nick Gillingham, Great Britain   2:11.29

100-METER BUTTERFLY

1. ..Pablo Morales, United States   53.32
2. ..Rafal Szukala, Poland   53.35
3. ..Anthony Nesty, Surinam   53.41

200-METER BUTTERFLY

1. ..Melvin Stewart, United States   1:56.26
2. ..Danyon Loader, New Zealand   1:57.93
3. ..Franck Esposito, France   1:58.51

200-METER INDIVIDUAL MEDLEY

1. ..Tamas Darnyi, Hungary   2:00.76
2. ..Greg Burgess, United States   2:00.97
3. ..Attila Czene, Hungary   2:01.00

400-METER INDIVIDUAL MEDLEY

1. ..Tamas Darnyi, Hungary   4:14.23 OR
2. ..Eric Namesnik, United States   4:15.57
3. ..Luca Sacchi, Italy   4:16.34

4 X 100 METER MEDLEY RELAY

1. ..United States: Jeff Rouse,   3:36.93 WR
   Nelson Diebel, Pablo Morales,
   Jon Olsen
2. ..Unified Team   3:38.56
3. ..Canada   3:39.66

4 X 100 METER FREESTYLE RELAY

1. ..United States: Joe Hudepohl,   3:16.74
   Matt Biondi, Tom Jager,
   Jon Olsen
2. ..Unified Team   3:17.56
3. ..Germany   3:17.90

4 X 200 METER FREESTYLE RELAY

1. ..Unified Team: Dimitri Lepikov,   7:11.95 WR
   Vladimir Pychenko, Veniamin Taianovitch,
   Evgueni Sadovyi
2. ..Sweden   7:15.51
3. ..United States   7:16.23

Note: OR=Olympic record. WR=world record.

EOR=equals Olympic record.

EWR=equals world record.

Women

50-METER FREESTYLE

1. ..Yang Wenyi, China   24.79 WR
2. ..Zhuang Yong, China   25.08
3. ..Angel Martino, United States   25.23

100-METER FREESTYLE

1. ..Zhuang Yong, China   54.64 OR
2. ..Jenny Thompson, United States   54.84
3. ..Franziska Van Almsick, Germany   54.94

SWIMMING (Cont.)

Women (Cont.)

200-METER FREESTYLE

1.	Nicole Haislett, United States	1:57.90
2.	Franziska Van Almsick, Germany	1:58.00
3.	Kerstin Kielgass, Germany	1:59.67

400-METER FREESTLYE

1.	Dagmar Hase, Germany	4:07.18
2.	Janet Evans, United States	4:07.37
3.	Hayley Lewis, Australia	4:11.22

800-METER FREESTYLE

1.	Janet Evans, United States	8:25.52
2.	Hayley Lewis, Australia	8:30.34
3.	Jana Henke, Germany	8:30.99

100-METER BACKSTROKE

1.	Krisztina Egerszegi, Hungary	1:00.68 OR
2.	Tunde Szabo, Hungary	1:01.14
3.	Lea Loveless, United States	1:01.43

200-METER BACKSTROKE

1.	Krisztina Egerszegi, Hungary	2:07.06
2.	Dagmar Hase, Germany	2:09.46
3.	Nicole Stevenson, Australia	2:10.20

100-METER BREASTSTROKE

1.	Elena Roudkovskaia, Unified Team	1:08.00
2.	Anita Nall, United States	1:08.17
3.	Samantha Riley, Australia	1:09.25

200-METER BREASTSTROKE

1.	Kyoko Iwasaki, Japan	2:26.65 OR
2.	Lin Li, China	2:26.85
3.	Anita Nall, United States	2:26.88

Note: OR=Olympic record. WR=world record.

EOR=equals Olympic record.

EWR=equals world record.

100-METER BUTTERFLY

1.	Qian Hong, China	58.62 OR
2.	Crissy Ahmann-Leighton, United States	58.74
3.	Catherine Plewinski, France	59.01

200-METER BUTTERFLY

1.	Summer Sanders, United States	2:08.67
2.	Wang Ziaohong, China	2:09.01
3.	Susan O'Neill, Australia	2:09.03

200-METER INDIVIDUAL MEDLEY

1.	Lin Li, China	2:11.65 WR
2.	Summer Sanders, United States	2:11.91
3.	Daniela Hunger, Germany	2:13.92

400-METER INDIVIDUAL MEDLEY

1.	Krisztina Egerszegi, Hungary	4:36.54
2.	Lin Li, China	4:36.73
3.	Summer Sanders, United States	4:37.58

4 X 100 METER MEDLEY RELAY

1.	United States: Lea Loveless, Anita Nall, Crissy Ahmann-Leighton, Jenny Thompson	4:02.54 WR
2.	Germany	4:05.19
3.	Unified Team	4:06.44

4 X 100 METER FREESTYLE RELAY

1.	United States: Nicole Haislett, Dara Torres, Angel Martino, Jenny Thompson	3:39.46 WR
2.	China	3:40.12
3.	Germany	3:41.60

DIVING

Men
SPRINGBOARD

		Pts
1.	Mark Lenzi, United States	676.53
2.	Tan Liangde, China	645.57
3.	Dmitri Saoutine, Unified Team	627.78

PLATFORM

		Pts
1.	Sun Shuwei, China	677.31
2.	Scott Donie, United States	633.63
3.	Xiong Ni, China	600.15

Women
SPRINGBOARD

		Pts
1.	Gao Min, China	572.40
2.	Irina Lachko, Unified Team	514.14
3.	Brita Pia Baldus, Germany	503.07

PLATFORM

		Pts
1.	Fu Mingxia, China	461.43
2.	Yelena Mirochina, Unified Team	411.63
3.	Mary Ellen Clark, United States	401.91

INDIVIDUAL ARCHERY

Men

1. ....Sebastien Flute, France
2. ....Chung Jae Hun, South Korea
3. ....Simon Terry, Great Britain

Women

1. ....Cho Youn Jeong, South Korea
2. ....Kim Soo Nyung, South Korea
3. ....Natalia Valeeva, Unified Team

CYCLING

Men

100 KM TEAM TIME TRIAL

1. ..Germany: Bernd Dittert, Christian Meyer, Uwe Peschel, Michael Rich — 2:01:39
2. ..Italy — 2:02:39
3. ..France — 2:05:25

1 KM TIME TRIAL

1. ..Jose Moreno, Spain — 1:03.342 OR
2. ..Shane Kelly, Australia — 1:04.288
3. ..Erin Hartwell, United States — 1:04.753

4000 METER INDIVIDUAL PURSUIT

1. ..Chris Boardman, Great Britain
2. ..Jens Lehmann, Germany
3. ..Gary Anderson, New Zealand

4000 METER TEAM PURSUIT

1. ..Germany: M. Gloeckner, Jens Lehmann, Stefan Steinweg, Guido Fulst — 4:08.791
2. ..Australia — 4:10.218
3. ..Denmark — 4:15.860

POINTS RACE

1. ..Giovanni Lombardi, Italy — 44
2. ..Leon Van Bon, The Netherlands — 43
3. ..Cedric Mathy, Belgium — 41

INDIVIDUAL ROAD RACE

1. ..Fabio Casartelli, Italy — 4:35.21
2. ..Erik Dekker, The Netherlands — 4:35.22
3. ..Dainis Ozols, Latvia — 4:35.24

Women

SPRINT

1. ......Erika Saloumiae, Estonia
2. ......Annett Neumann, Germany
3. ......Ingrid Haringa, The Netherlands

ROAD RACE

1. ..Kathryn Watt, Australia — 2:04.42
2. ..Jeannie Longo-Ciprelli, France — 2:05.02
3. ..Monique Knol, The Netherlands — 2:05.03

EQUESTRIAN

3-DAY TEAM

1. ......Australia: David Green, Gillian Rolton, Andrew Hoy Matthew Ryan — 288.60
2. ......New Zealand — 290.80
3. ......Germany — 300.30

3-DAY INDIVIDUAL

1. ......Matthew Ryan, Australia — 70.00
2. ......Herbert Blocker, Germany — 81.30
3. ......Blyth Tait, New Zealand — 87.60

TEAM DRESSAGE

1. ......Germany: Isabelle Werth, Klaus Balkenhol, Monica Theodorescu, Nicole Uphoff — 5224
2. ......The Netherlands — 4742
3. ......United States — 4643

INDIVIDUAL DRESSAGE

1. ......Nicole Uphoff, Germany — 1768
2. ......Isabelle Werth, Germany — 1762
3. ......Klaus Balkenhol, Germany — 1694

TEAM JUMPING

1. ......The Netherlands: Piet Raymakers, Bert Romp, Jan Tops, Jos Lansink — 12.00
2. ......Austria — 16.75
3. ......France — 24.75

INDIVIDUAL JUMPING

1. ......Ludger Beerbaum, Germany — 0.00
2. ......Piet Raymakers, The Netherlands — .25
3. ......Norman Dello Joio, United States — 4.75

INDIVIDUAL FENCING

Men

FOIL

1. ....Philippe Omnes, France
2. ....Sergei Goloubitski, Unified Team
3. ....Elvis Gregory Gil, Cuba

SABRE

1. ....Bence Szabo, Hungary
2. ....Marco Marin, Italy
3. ....Jean-Francois Lamour, France

EPEE

1. ....Eric Srecki, France
2. ....Pavel Kolobkov, Unified Team
3. ....Jean-Michel Henry, France

Women

FOIL

1. ....Giovanna Trillini, Italy
2. ....Wang Huifeng, China
3. ....Tatiana Sadovskaia, Unified Team

FIELD HOCKEY

Men

1. ....Germany
2. ....Australia
3. ....Pakistan

Women

1. ....Spain
2. ....Germany
3. ....Great Britain

TEAM HANDBALL

Men

1. ....Unified Team
2. ....Sweden
3. ....France

Women

1. ....South Korea
2. ....Norway
3. ....Unified Team

JUDO

EXTRA-LIGHTWEIGHT

1. ....Nazim Guseinov, Unified Team
2. ....Yoon Hyun, South Korea
3. ....Tadanori Koshino, Japan
3. ....Richard Trautmann, Germany

HALF-LIGHTWEIGHT

1. ....Rogerio Sampaio Cardoso, Brazil
2. ....Josef Czak, Hungary
3. ....Udo Quellmalz, Germany
3. ....Israel Hernandez Planas, Cuba

LIGHTWEIGHT

1. ....Toshihiko Koga, Japan
2. ....Bertalan Hajtos, Hungary
3. ....Chung Hoon, South Korea
3. ....Shay Oren Smadga, Israel

HALF-MIDDLEWEIGHT

1. ....Hidehiko Yoshida, Japan
2. ....Jason Morris, United States
3. ....Bertrand Domaisin, France
3. ....Kim Byung Joo, South Korea

MIDDLEWEIGHT

1. ....Waldemar Legien, Poland
2. ....Pascal Tayot, France
3. ....Hirotaka Okada, Japan
3. ....Nicolas Gill, Canada

HALF-HEAVYWEIGHT

1. ....Antal Kovacs, Hungary
2. ....Raymond Stevens, Great Britain
3. ....Dmitri Sergeev, Unified Team
3. ....Theo Meijer, The Netherlands

HEAVYWEIGHT

1. ....David Khakaleshvili, Unified Team
2. ....Naoya Ogowa, Japan
3. ....David Douillet, France
3. ....Imre Csosz, Hungary

MODERN PENTATHLON

TEAM	INDIVIDUAL
1. ....Poland	1. ....Arkadiusz Skrzypaszek, Poland
2. ....Unified Team	2. ....Attila Mizser, Hungary
3. ....Italy	3. ....Eduard Zenovka, Unified Team

ROWING

Men

SINGLE SCULLS

1. ..Thomas Lange, Germany	6:51.40	
2. ..Vaclav Chalupa, Czechoslovakia	6:52.93	
3. ..Kajetan Broniewski, Poland	6:56.82	

COXED PAIR

1. ..Great Britain	6:49.83
2. ..Italy	6:50.98
3. ..Romania	6:51.58

DOUBLE SCULLS

1. ..Australia	6:17.32
2. ..Austria	6:18.42
3. ..The Netherlands	6:22.82

QUADRUPLE SCULLS

1. ..Germany	5:45.17
2. ..Norway	5:47.09
3. ..Italy	5:47.33

COXLESS PAIR

1. ..Great Britain	6:27.72
2. ..Germany	6:32.68
3. ..Slovenia	6:33.43

COXLESS FOUR

1. ..Australia	5:55.04
2. ..United States	5:56.68
3. ..Slovenia	5:58.24

COXED FOUR

1. ..Romania	5:59.37
2. ..Germany	6:00.34
3. ..Poland	6:03.27

EIGHT-OARS

1. ..Canada	5:29.53
2. ..Romania	5:29.67
3. ..Germany	5:31.00

Women

SINGLE SCULLS

1. ..Elisabeta Lipa, Romania	7:25.54
2. ..Annelies Bredael, Belgium	7:26.64
3. ..Silken Suzette Laumann, Canada	7:28.85

COXLESS FOUR

1. ..Canada	6:30.85
2. ..United States	6:31.86
3. ..Germany	6:32.34

DOUBLE SCULLS

1. ..Germany	6:49.00
2. ..Romania	6:51.47
3. ..China	6:55.16

QUADRUPLE SCULLS

1. ..Germany	6:20.18
2. ..Romania	6:24.34
3. ..Unified Team	6:25.07

COXLESS PAIR

1. ..Canada	7:06.22
2. ..Germany	7:07.96
3. ..United States	7:08.12

EIGHT-OARS

1. ..Canada	6:02.62
2. ..Romania	6:06.26
3. ..Germany	6:07.80

SOCCER

1. ....Spain
2. ....Poland
3. ....Ghana

SYNCHRONIZED SWIMMING

SOLO

	Pts
1. ....Kristen Babb-Sprague, United States	191.848
2. ....Sylvie Frechette, Canada	191.717
3. ....Fumiko Okuno, Japan	187.056

DUET

	Pts
1. ....Karen & Sarah Josephson, United States	192.175
2. ....Penny & Vicky Vilagos, Canada	189.394
3. ....Fumiko Okuno & Aki Takayama, Japan	186.868

TABLE TENNIS

Men

SINGLES

1. ....Jan-Ove Waldner, Sweden
2. ....Jean Gatien, France
3. ....Kim Taek Soo, South Korea
3. ....Ma Wenge, China

DOUBLES

1. ....Lu Lin & Wang Tao, China
2. ....Steffan Fetzner & Jorg Rosskopf, Germany
3. ....Kang Hee Chan & Lee Chul Seung, South Korea
3. ....Kim Taek Soo & Yoo Nam Kyu, South Korea

Women

SINGLES

1. ....Deng Yaping, China
2. ....Qiao Hong, China
3. ....Hyun Jung Hwa, South Korea
3. ....Li Bun Hui, North Korea

DOUBLES

1. ....Deng Yaping & Qiao Hong, China
2. ....Chen Zihe & Gao Jun, China
3. ....Li Bun Hui & Yu Sun Bok, North Korea
3. ....Hong Cha Ok & Hyun Jung Hwa, South Korea

TENNIS

Men

SINGLES

1. ....Marc Rosset, Switzerland
2. ....Jordi Arrese, Spain
3. ....Goran Ivanisevic, Croatia
3. ....Andrei Cherkasov, Unified Team

DOUBLES

1. ....Boris Becker & Michael Stich, Germany
2. ....Wayne Ferreira & Piet Norval, South Africa
3. ....Goran Ivanisevic & Goran Prpic, Croatia
3. ....Javier Frana & Christian Carlos Miniussi, Argentina

Women

SINGLES

1. ....Jennifer Capriati, United States
2. ....Steffi Graf, Germany
3. ....Aranxta Sanchez Vicario, Spain
3. ....Mary Joe Fernandez, United States

DOUBLES

1. ....Gigi Fernandez & Mary Joe Fernandez, United States
2. ....Conchita Martinez & Aranxta Sanchez Vicario, Spain
3. ....Natalya Zvereva & Leila Meskhi, Unified Team
3. ....Rachel McQuillan & Nicole Provis, Australia

VOLLEYBALL

Men

1. ....Brazil
2. ....The Netherlands
3. ....United States: Bob Ctvrtlik, Doug Partie, Steve Timmons, Scott Fortune, Jeff Stork Eric Sato, Dan Hanan, Dan Greenbaum, Uvaldo Acosta, Bryan Ivie, Bob Samuelson, Javier Gaspar, Trevor Schirman, Carlos Briceno, Nick Becker, Brent Hilliard, Mark Arnold, Allen Allen

Women

1. ....Cuba
2. ....Unified Team
3. ....United States: Tee Sanders, Yoko Zetterlund, Ann Schirman, Kim Oden, Lori Endicott, Paula Weishoff, Caren Kemner, Tammy Liley, Elaina Oden, Daiva Tomkus, Deitre Collins, Janet Cobbs, Tara Battle, Liane Sato, Ruth Lawanson, Bev Oden

WATER POLO

1. ....Italy
2. ....Spain
3. ....Unified Team

Centennial Slap

The selection of Atlanta to host the 1996 Summer Games was a bitter blow to Athens, which as the site of the first modern Olympics, in 1896, had also bid to stage the centennial Games. Now, without a trace of irony, Atlanta organizers have expressed their intention to have the '96 gold medal Olympic soccer game played in Athens—Georgia, that is.

WEIGHTLIFTING

114 POUNDS

1. ....Ivan Ivanov, Bulgaria   584 lb
2. ....Lin Qisheng, China   579 lb
3. ....Traian Ciharean, Romania   557 lb

123 POUNDS

1. ....Chun Byun Kwan, South Korea   634 lb
2. ....Liu Shoubin, China   612 lb
3. ....Luo Jianming, China   612 lb

132 POUNDS

1. ....Naim Suleymanoglu, Turkey   705 lb
2. ....Nikolai Peshalov, Unified Team   672 lb
3. ....He Yingqiang, China   650 lb

148.5 POUNDS

1. ....Israel Militossian, Unified Team   744 lb
2. ....Yoto Yotov, Bulgaria   722 lb
3. ....Andreas Behm, Germany   706 lb

165 POUNDS

1. ....Fedor Kassapu, Unified Team   788 lb
2. ....Pablo Lara Rodriguez, Cuba   788 lb
3. ....Kim Myong Nam, North Korea   777 lb

181.5 POUNDS

1. ....Pyrros Dimas, Greece   816 lb
2. ....Krzysztof Siemion, Poland   816 lb
3. ....Ibragim Samadov, Unified Team   816 lb

198 POUNDS

1. ....Kakhi Kakhiachveili,   910 lb OR
       Unified Team
2. ....Sergei Sirtsov, Unified Team   910 lb OR
3. ....Sergivsz Wolczanjecki, Poland   865 lb

220 POUNDS

1. ....Victor Tregoubov, Unified Team   904 lb
2. ....Timour Taimazov, Unified Team   887 lb
3. ....Waldemar Malak, Poland   882 lb

243 POUNDS

1. ....Ronny Weller, Germany   953 lb
2. ....Artur Akoev, Unified Team   948 lb
3. ....Stefan Botev, Bulgaria   920 lb

243+ POUNDS

1. ....Aleksandr Kurlovich,   992 lb
       Unified Team
2. ....Leonid Taranenko, Unified Team   937 lb
3. ....Manfred Nerlinger, Germany   909 lb

FREESTYLE WRESTLING

106 POUNDS

1. ....Kim Il, North Korea
2. ....Kim Jong, South Korea
3. ....Vougar Oroudjov, Unified Team

115 POUNDS

1. ....Li Hak Son, North Korea
2. ....Zeke Jones, United States
3. ....Valentin Jordanov, Bulgaria

126 POUNDS

1. ....Alejandro Puerto Diaz, Cuba
2. ....Serguei Smal, Unified Team
3. ....Kim Yong Sik, North Korea

137 POUNDS

1. ....John Smith, United States
2. ....Asgari Mohammadian, Iran
3. ....Lazaro Reinoso, Cuba

150 POUNDS

1. ....Arsen Fadzaev, Unified Team
2. ....Valentin Getzov, Bulgaria
3. ....Kosei Akaishi, Japan

163 POUNDS

1. ....Park Jang-Soon, South Korea
2. ....Kenny Monday, United States
3. ....Amir Khadem, Iran

181 POUNDS

1. ....Kevin Jackson, United States
2. ....Elmadi Jabraijlov, Unified Team
3. ....Rasul Khadem, Iran

198 POUNDS

1. ....Makharbek Khadartsev, Unified Team
2. ....Kenan Simsek, Turkey
3. ....Chris Campbell, United States

220 POUNDS

1. ....Leri Khabelov, Unified Team
2. ....Heiko Balz, Germany
3. ....Ali Kayali, Turkey

286 POUNDS

1. ....Bruce Baumgartner, United States
2. ....Jeffrey Thue, Canada
3. ....David Gobedjichvili, Unified Team

Note: OR=Olympic Record; WR=World Record
EOR=Equals Olympic Record;
EWR=Equals World Record.WB=World Best.

GRECO-ROMAN WRESTLING

106 POUNDS

1. Oleg Koutcherenko, Unified Team
2. Vincenzo Maenza, Italy
3. Wilber Sanchez, Cuba

115 POUNDS

1. Jon Ronningen, Norway
2. Alfred Ter-Mkrtychan, Unified Team
3. Min Kyung, South Korea

126 POUNDS

1. An Han-Bong, South Korea
2. Rifat Yildiz, Germany
3. Sheng Zetian, China

137 POUNDS

1. Akif Pirim, Turkey
2. Sergei Martynov, Unified Team
3. Juan Maren, Cuba

150 POUNDS

1. Attila Repka, Hungary
2. Islam Duguchiev, Unified Team
3. Rodney Smith, United States

163 POUNDS

1. Mnatsakan Iskandarian, Unified Team
2. Josef Tracz, Poland
3. Torbjoern Korbakk, Sweden

181 POUNDS

1. Peter Farkas, Hungary
2. Piotr Stepien, Poland
3. Daulet Tourlykhanov, Unified Team

198 POUNDS

1. Maik Bullmann, Germany
2. Hakki Basar, Turkey
3. Gogi Kogouachvili, Unified Team

220 POUNDS

1. Hector Millian, Cuba
2. Dennis Koslowski, United States
3. Sergei Demyashkevich, Unified Team

286 POUNDS

1. Aleksandr Karelin, Unified Team
2. Tomas Johansson, Sweden
3. Ioan Grigoras, Romania

YACHTING

SOLING CLASS

1. Denmark
2. United States
3. Great Britain

STAR CLASS

1. United States
2. New Zealand
3. Canada

FLYING DUTCHMAN CLASS

1. Spain
2. United States
3. Denmark

FINN CLASS

1. Jose Van Der Ploeg, Spain
2. Brian Ledbetter, United States
3. Craig Monk, New Zealand

TORNADO CLASS

1. France
2. United States
3. Australia

EUROPE CLASS

1. Linda Andersen, Norway
2. Natalia Via Dufresne, Spain
3. Julia Trotman, United States

MEN'S .470 CLASS

1. Spain
2. United States
3. Estonia

WOMEN'S 470 CLASS

1. Spain
2. New Zealand
3. United States

Paddling Panhandler

U.S. Olympic kayaker Eric Jackson took his cause to the people this past May. Literally. In need of roughly $1,200 to continue his career, Jackson hauled his kayak to a busy Washington, D.C. intersection, pulled on his Olympic warmups and panhandled passersby for rent money and travel costs. According to U.S. coach Bill Endicott, the campaign was successful and enabled Jackson and his family to travel to the U.S. trials in Colorado. En route, they slept in their van. Says Endicott: "To him, this is not a joke."

BIATHLON

Men
10 KILOMETERS
1. ..Mark Kirchner, Germany — 26:02.3
2. ..Ricco Gross, Germany — 26:18.0
3. ..Harri Eloranta, Finland — 26:26.6

20 KILOMETERS
1. ..Evgueni Redkine, Unified Team — 57:34.4
2. ..Mark Kirchner, Germany — 57:40.8
3. ..Mikael Lofgren, Sweden — 57:59.4

4 X 7.5 KILOMETER RELAY
1. ....Germany — 1:24:43.5
2. ....Unified Team — 1:25:06.3
3. ....Sweden — 1:25:38.2

Women
7.5 KILOMETERS
1. ..Antissa Restzova, Unified Team — 24:29.2
2. ..Antje Misersky, Germany — 24:45.1
3. ..Elena Belova, Unified Team — 24:50.8

15 KILOMETERS
1. ..Antje Misersky, Germany — 51:47.2
2. ..Svetlana Pecherskaia, Unified Team — 51:58.5
3. ..Myriam Bedard, Canada — 52:15.0

3 X 7.5 KILOMETER RELAY
1. ....France — 1:15:55.6
2. ....Germany — 1:16:18.4
3. ....Unified Team — 1:16:54.6

BOBSLED

4-MAN BOB
1. ....Austria — 3:53.90
2. ....Germany — 3:53.92
3. ....Switzerland — 3:54.13

2-MAN BOB
1. ....Switzerland — 4:03.26
2. ....Germany — 4:03.55
3. ....Germany II — 4:03.63

ICE HOCKEY
1. ....Unified Team
2. ....Canada
3. ....Czechoslovakia

LUGE

Men
SINGLES
1. ....Georg Hackl, Germany — 3:02.363
2. ....Markus Prock, Austria — 3:02.669
3. ....Markus Schmidt, Austria — 3:02.942

PAIRS
1. ....Germany — 1:32.053
2. ....Germany — 1:32.239
3. ....Italy — 1:32.298

Women
SINGLES
1. ....Doris Neuner, Austria — 3:06.696
2. ....Angelica Neuner, Austria — 3:06.769
3. ....Susi Erdmann, Germany — 3:07.115

FIGURE SKATING

Men
1. ....Victor Petrenko, Unified Team
2. ....Paul Wylie, United States
3. ....Petr Barna, Czechoslovakia

Women
1. ....Kristi Yamaguchi, United States
2. ....Midori Ito, Japan
3. ....Nancy Kerrigan, United States

Pairs
1. ..Natalia Michkouteniok & Artour Dmitriev, Unified Team
2. ..Elena Betchke & Denis Petrov, Unified Team
3. ..Isabelle Brasseur & Lloyd Eisler, Canada

Ice Dancing
1. ..Marina Klimova & Sergei Ponomarekno, Unified Team
2. ..Isabelle Duchesnay-Dean & Paul Duchesnay, France
3. ..Maia Usova & Alexander Zhulin, Unified Team

SPEED SKATING

Men

500 METERS

1. ..Uwe-Jens Mey, Germany	37.14
2. ..Toshiyuki Kuroiwa, Japan	37.18
3. ..Junichi Inoue, Japan	37.26

1000 METERS

1. ...Olaf Zinke, Germany	1:14.85
2. ...Kim Yoon Man, South Korea	1:14.86
3. ...Yukinori Miyabe, Japan	1:14.92

1500 METERS

1. ..Johann Koss, Norway	1:54.81
2. ..Adne Sondral, Norway	1:54.85
3. ..Leo Visser, The Netherlands	1:54.90

5000 METERS

1. ..Geir Karlstad, Norway	6:59.97
2. ..Falco Zanstra, The Netherlands	7:02.28
3. ..Leo Visser, The Netherlands	7:04.96

10,000 METERS

1. ..Bart Veldkamp, The Netherlands	14:12.12
2. ..Johann Koss, Norway	14:14.58
3. ..Geir Karlstad, Norway	14:18.13

Women

500 METERS

1. ..Bonnie Blair, United States	40.33
2. ..Ye Qiaobo, China	40.51
3. ..Christa Luding, Germany	50.57

1000 METERS

1. ..Bonnie Blair, United States	1:21.90
2. ..Ye Qiaobo, China	1:21.92
3. ..Monique Garbrecht, Germany	1:22.10

1500 METERS

1. ..Jacqueline Boerner, Germany	2:05.87
2. ..Gunda Niemann, Germany	2:05.92
3. ..Seiko Hashimoto, Japan	2:06.88

3000 METERS

1. ..Gunda Niemann, Germany	4:19.90
2. ..Heike Warnicke, Germany	4:22.88
3. ..Emese Hunyady, Austria	4:24.64

5000 METERS

1. ..Gunda Niemann, Germany	7:31.57
2. ..Heike Warnicke, Germany	7:37.59
3. ..Claudia Pechstein, Germany	7:39.80

SHORT TRACK SPEED SKATING

Men

1000 METERS

1. ..Kim Ki-Hoon, South Korea	1:30.76 WR
2. ..Fredric Blackburn, Canada	1:31.11
3. ..Lee Joon-Ho, South Korea	1:31.16

5000-METER RELAY

1. ...South Korea	7:14.02 WR
2. ...Canada	7:14.06
3. ...Japan	7:18.18

Women

500 METERS

1. ..Cathy Turner, United States	47.04
2. ..Li Yan, China	47.08
3. ..Hwang Ok Sil, North Korea	47.23

3000-METER RELAY

1. ..Canada	4:36.62
2. ..United States	4:37.85
3. ..Unified Team	4:42.69

ALPINE SKIING

Men

DOWNHILL

1. ..Patrick Ortlieb, Austria	1:50.37
2. ..Franck Piccard, France	1:50.42
3. ..Guenther Mader, Austria	1:50.47

SUPER GIANT SLALOM

1. ..Kjetil Andre Aamodt, Norway	1:13.04
2. ..Marc Girardelli, Luxembourg	1:13.77
3. ..Jan Einer Thorsen, Norway	1:13.83

GIANT SLALOM

1. ..Alberto Tomba, Italy	2:06.98
2. ..Marc Giarardelli, Luxembourg	2:07.30
3. ..Kjetil Andre Aamodt, Norway	2:07.82

SLALOM

1. ..Finn Christian Jagge, Norway	1:44.39
2. ..Alberto Tomba, Italy	1:44.67
3. ..Michael Tritscher, Austria	1:44.85

COMBINED

	Pts
1. ..Josef Polig, Italy	14.58
2. ..Gianfranco Martin, Italy	14.90
3. ..Steve Locher, Switzerland	18.16

Note: OR=Olympic Record; WR=World Record; EOR=Equals Olympic Record; EWR=Equals World Record; WB=World Best.

ALPINE SKIING (Cont.)

Women

DOWNHILL

1. ..Kerrin Lee-Gartner, Canada   1:52.55
2. ..Hilary Lindh, United States   1:52.61
3. ..Veronika Wallinger, Austria   1:52.64

SUPER GIANT SLALOM

1. ..Deborah Compagnoni, Italy   1:21.22
2. ..Carole Merle, France   1:22.63
3. ..Katja Seizinger, Germany   1:23.19

GIANT SLALOM

1. ..Pernilla Wiberg, Sweden   2:12.74
2. ..Diann Roffe, United States   2:13.71
2. ..Anita Wachter, Austria   2:13.71

SLALOM

1. ..Petra Kronberger, Austria   1:32.68
2. ..Annelise Coberger, New Zealand   1:33.10
3. ..Blanca Fernandez-Ochoa, Spain   1:33.35

COMBINED

	Pts
1. ..Petra Kronberger, Austria	2.55
2. ..Anita Wachter, Austria	19.39
3. ..Florence Masnada, France	21.38

FREESTYLE SKIING

Men
MOGUL

	Pts
1. ..Edgar Grospiron, France	25.81
2. ..Olivier Allamand, France	24.87
3. ..Nelson Carmichael, United States	24.82

Women
MOGUL

	Pts
1. ..Donna Weinbrecht, United States	23.69
2. ..Elizaveta Kojevnikova, Unified Team	23.50
3. ..Stine Hattestad, Unified Team	23.04

Bonus-Plus

The U.S. Olympic Committee is to be commended for increasing the bonus money it awards Americans who win Olympic medals. Although the sums—$15,000 for gold, $10,000 for silver and $7,500 for bronze—pale next to the loot paid out in other countries (for example, each of Spain's 13 gold medalists in Barcelona got an $80,000 bonus from the national sports federation and a $1 million pension from a bank), they represent a big leap forward for the USOC, which previously gave $2,500 to those who placed in the top eight at the Games.

One cavil: The USOC's largesse doesn't benefit college athletes, who are barred by NCAA rules from accepting money; it's time the NCAA relaxed its rigid stance and allowed collegians to put Olympic bonuses into trust funds. Another: USOC officials are fretting about the p.r. fallout of paying bonuses to Dream Teamers, tennis pros and other well-heeled Olympians. They should lighten up. One expects that the Michael Jordans and Jennifer Capriatis will be savvy enough to give their 15 grand to charity without any coaxing.

NORDIC SKIING

Men

10 KILOMETERS (CLASSICAL)

1. ..Vegard Ulvang, Norway	27:36.0
2. ..Marco Albarello, Italy	27:55.2
3. ..Christer Majback, Sweden	27:56.4

30 KILOMETERS (CLASSICAL)

1. ..Vegard Ulvang, Norway	1:22:27.8
2. ..Bjorn Dählie, Norway	1:23:14.0
3. ..Terje Langli, Norway	1:23:42.5

50 KILOMETERS (FREESTYLE)

1. ..Bjorn Dählie, Norway	2:03:41.5
2. ..Maurilio De Zolt, Italy	2:04:39.1
3. ..Giorgio Vanzetta, Italy	2:06:42.1

15 KILOMETERS (FREESTYLE)

1. ..Bjorn Dählie, Norway	1:05:37.9
2. ..Vegard Ulvang, Norway	1:06:31.3
3. ..Giorgio Vanzetta, Italy	1:06:32.3

4 X 10 KILOMETER RELAY (MIXED)

1.................Norway	1:39:26.0
2.................Italy	1:40:52.7
3.................Finland	1:41:22.9

SKI JUMPING (NORMAL HILL)

	Pts
1. ..Ernst Vettori, Austria	222.8
2. ..Martin Hollworth, Austria	218.1
3. ..Toni Nieminen, Finland	217.0

SKI JUMPING (LARGE HILL)

	Pts
1. ..Toni Nieminen, Finland	239.5
2. ..Martin Hollworth, Austria	227.3
3. ..Heinz Kuttin, Austria	214.8

TEAM SKI JUMPING

	Pts
1.................Finland	644.4
2.................Austria	642.9
3.................Czechoslovakia	620.1

NORDIC COMBINED

1.................Fabrice Guy, France	
2.................Sylvain Guillaume, France	
3.................Klaus Sulzenbacher, Austria	

TEAM COMBINED

1.................Japan	
2.................Norway	
3.................Austria	

Women

5 KILOMETERS (CLASSICAL)

1. ..Marjut Lukkarinen, Finland	14:13.8
2. ..Lyubov Egorova, Unified Team	14:14.7
3. ..Elena Valbe, Unified Team	14:22.7

15 KILOMETERS (CLASSICAL)

1. ..Lyubov Egorova, Unified Team	42:20.8
2. ..Marjut Lukkarinen, Finland	43:29.9
3. ..Elena Valbe, Unified Team	43:42.3

10 KILOMETERS (FREESTYLE)

1. ..Lyubov Egorova, Unified Team	40:07.7
2. ..Stefania Belmondo, Italy	40:31.8
3. ..Elena Valbe, Unified Team	40:51.7

30 KILOMETERS (FREESTYLE)

1. ..Stefania Belmondo, Italy	1:22:30.1
2. ..Lyubov Egorova, Unified Team	1:22:52.0
3. ..Elena Valbe, Unified Team	1:24:13.9

4 X 5 KILOMETER RELAY (MIXED)

1. ....Unified Team	59:34.8
2. ....Norway	59:56.4
3. ....Italy	1:00:25.9

THEY SAID IT

Decathlon world-record holder Dan O'Brien, when asked what he plans to do when he retires from the sport: "I always said I wanted to be like Bruce Jenner and talk about the record the rest of my life."

Summer

	Year	Site	Dates	Competitors Men	Women	Nations	Most Medals	US Medals
I	1896	Athens, Greece	Apr 6-15	311	0	13	Greece (10-19-18—47)	11-6-2—19 (2nd)
II	1900	Paris, France	May 20-Oct 28	1319	11	22	France (29-41-32—102)	20-14-19—53 (2nd)
III	1904	St Louis, United States	July 1-Nov 23	681	6	12	United States (80-86-72—238)	
—	1906	Athens, Greece	Apr 22-May 28	77	7	20	France (15-9-16—40)	12-6-5—23 (4th)
IV	1908	London, Great Britain	Apr 27-Oct 31	1999	36	23	Britain (56-50-39—145)	23-12-12—47 (2nd)
V	1912	Stockholm, Sweden	May 5-July 22	2490	57	28	Sweden (24-24-17—65)	23-19-19—61 (2nd)
VI	1916	Berlin, Germany	Cancelled because of war					
VII	1920	Antwerp, Belgium	Apr 20-Sep 12	2543	64	29	United States (41-27-28—96)	
VIII	1924	Paris, France	May 4-July 27	2956	136	44	United States (45-27-27—99)	
IX	1928	Amsterdam, Netherlands	May 17-Aug 12	2724	290	46	United States (22-18-16—56)	
X	1932	Los Angeles, United States	July 30-Aug 14	1281	127	37	United States (41-32-31—104)	
XI	1936	Berlin, Germany	Aug 1-16	3738	328	49	Germany (33-26-30—89)	24-20-12—56 (2nd)
XII	1940	Tokyo, Japan	Cancelled because of war					
XIII	1944	London, Great Britain	Cancelled because of war					
XIV	1948	London, Great Britain	July 29-Aug 14	3714	385	59	United States (38-27-19—84)	
XV	1952	Helsinki, Finland	July 19-Aug 3	4407	518	69	United States (40-19-17—76)	
XVI	1956	Melbourne, Australia*	Nov 22-Dec 8	2958	384	67	USSR (37-29-32—98)	32-25-17—74 (2nd)
XVII	1960	Rome, Italy	Aug 25-Sep 11	4738	610	83	USSR (43-29-31—103)	34-21-16—71 (2nd)
XVIII	1964	Tokyo, Japan	Oct 10-24	4457	683	93	United States (36-26-28—90)	
XIX	1968	Mexico City, Mexico	Oct 12-27	4750	781	112	United States (45-28-34—107)	
XX	1972	Munich, West Germany	Aug 26-Sep 10	5848	1299	122	USSR (50-27-22—99)	33-31-30—94 (2nd)
XXI	1976	Montreal, Canada	July 17-Aug 1	4834	1251	92†	USSR (49-41-35—125)	34-35-25—94 (3rd)
XXII	1980	Moscow, USSR	July 19-Aug 3	4265	1088	81‡	USSR (80-69-46—195)	Did not compete
XXIII	1984	Los Angeles, United States	July 28-Aug 12	5458	1620	141#	United States (83-61-30—174)	
XXIV	1988	Seoul, South Korea	Sep 17-Oct 2	7105	2476	160	USSR (55-31-46—132)	36-31-27—94 (3rd)
XXV	1992	Barcelona, Spain	July 25-Aug. 9	7555	3008	172	Unified Team (45-38-29—112)	37-34-37—108 (2nd)

*The equestrian events were held in Stockholm, Sweden, June 10-17, 1956.

†This figure includes Cameroon, Egypt, Morocco, and Tunisia, countries that boycotted the 1976 Olympics after some of their athletes had already competed.

‡The US was among 65 countries that refused to participate in the 1980 Summer Games in Moscow.

#The USSR, East Germany, and 14 other countries skipped the Summer Games in Los Angeles.

Winter

	Year	Site	Dates	Competitors Men	Women	Nations	Most Medals	US Medals
I	1924	Chamonix, France	Jan 25-Feb 4	281	13	16	Norway (4-7-6—17)	1-2-1—4 (3rd)
II	1928	St Moritz, Switzerland	Feb 11-19	468	27	25	Norway (6-4-5—15)	2-2-2—6 (2nd)
III	1932	Lake Placid, United States	Feb 4-15	274	32	17	United States (6-4-2—12)	
IV	1936	Garmisch-Partenkirchen, Germany	Feb 6-16	675	80	28	Norway (7-5-3—15)	1-0-3—4 (T-5th)
—	1940	Garmisch-Partenkirchen, Germany	Cancelled because of war					
—	1944	Cortina d'Ampezzo, Italy	Cancelled because of war					
V	1948	St Moritz, Switzerland	Jan 30-Feb 8	636	77	28	Norway (4-3-3—10) Sweden (4-3-3—10) Switzerland (3-4-3—10)	3-4-2—9 (4th)
VI	1952	Oslo, Norway	Feb 14-25	623	109	30	Norway (7-3-6—16)	4-6-1—11 (2nd)
VII	1956	Cortina d'Ampezzo, Italy	Jan 26-Feb 5	686	132	32	USSR (7-3-6—16)	2-3-2—7 (T-4th)
VIII	1960	Squaw Valley, United States	Feb 18-28	521	144	30	USSR (7-5-9—21)	3-4-3—10 (2nd)
IX	1964	Innsbruck, Austria	Jan 29-Feb 9	986	200	36	USSR (11-8-6—25)	1-2-3—6 (7th)
X	1968	Grenoble, France	Feb 6-18	1081	212	37	Norway (6-6-2—14)	1-5-1—7 (T-7th)
XI	1972	Sapporo, Japan	Feb 3-13	1015	217	35	USSR (8-5-3—16)	3-2-3—8 (6th)
XII	1976	Innsbruck, Austria	Feb 4-15	900	228	37	USSR (13-6-8—27)	3-3-4—10 (T-3rd)
XIII	1980	Lake Placid, United States	Feb 14-23	833	234	37	USSR (10-6-6—22)	6-4-2—12 (3rd)
XIV	1984	Sarajevo, Yugoslavia	Feb 7-19	1002	276	49	USSR (6-10-9—25)	4-4-0—8 (T-5th)
XV	1988	Calgary, Canada	Feb 13-28	1128	317	57	USSR (11-9-9—29)	2-1-3—6 (T-8th)
XVI	1992	Albertville, France	Feb 8-23	1318	490	65	Germany (10-10-6—26)	5-4-2—11 (6th)

Summer Games Champions

TRACK AND FIELD

Men

100 METERS

1896....Thomas Burke, United States	12.0	
1900....Frank Jarvis, United States	11.0	
1904....Archie Hahn, United States	11.0	
1906....Archie Hahn, United States	11.2	
1908....Reginald Walker, South Africa	10.8 OR	
1912....Ralph Craig, United States	10.8	
1920....Charles Paddock, United States	10.8	
1924....Harold Abrahams, Great Britain	10.6 OR	
1928....Percy Williams, Canada	10.8	
1932....Eddie Tolan, United States	10.3 OR	
1936....Jesse Owens, United States	10.3	
1948....Harrison Dillard, United States	10.3	
1952....Lindy Remigino, United States	10.4	
1956....Bobby Morrow, United States	10.5	
1960....Armin Hary, West Germany	10.2 OR	
1964....Bob Hayes, United States	10.0 EWR	
1968....Jim Hines, United States	9.95 WR	
1972....Valery Borzov, USSR	10.14	
1976....Hasely Crawford, Trinidad	10.06	
1980....Allan Wells, Great Britain	10.25	
1984....Carl Lewis, United States	9.99	
1988....Carl Lewis, United States*	9.92 WR	
1992....Linford Christie, Great Britain	9.96	

*Ben Johnson, Canada, disqualified.

TRACK AND FIELD (Cont.)

Men (Cont.)

200 METERS

1900	John Walter Tewksbury, United States	22.2
1904	Archie Hahn, United States	21.6 OR
1906	Not held	
1908	Robert Kerr, Canada	22.6
1912	Ralph Craig, United States	21.7
1920	Allen Woodring, United States	22.0
1924	Jackson Scholz, United States	21.6
1928	Percy Williams, Canada	21.8
1932	Eddie Tolan, United States	21.2 OR
1936	Jesse Owens, United States	20.7 OR
1948	Mel Patton, United States	21.1
1952	Andrew Stanfield, United States	20.7
1956	Bobby Morrow, United States	20.6 OR
1960	Livio Berruti, Italy	20.5 EWR
1964	Henry Carr, United States	20.3 OR
1968	Tommie Smith, United States	19.83 WR
1972	Valery Borzov, USSR	20.00
1976	Donald Quarrie, Jamaica	20.23
1980	Pietro Mennea, Italy	20.19
1984	Carl Lewis, United States	19.80 OR
1988	Joe DeLoach, United States	19.75 OR
1992	Mike Marsh, United States	20.01

400 METERS

1896	Thomas Burke, United States	54.2
1900	Maxey Long, United States	49.4 OR
1904	Harry Hillman, United States	49.2 OR
1906	Paul Pilgrim, United States	53.2
1908	Wyndham Halswelle, Great Britain	50.0
1912	Charles Reidpath, United States	48.2 OR
1920	Bevil Rudd, South Africa	49.6
1924	Eric Liddell, Great Britain	47.6 OR
1928	Ray Barbuti, United States	47.8
1932	William Carr, United States	46.2 WR
1936	Archie Williams, United States	46.5
1948	Arthur Wint, Jamaica	46.2
1952	George Rhoden, Jamaica	45.9
1956	Charles Jenkins, United States	46.7
1960	Otis Davis, United States	44.9 WR
1964	Michael Larrabee, United States	45.1
1968	Lee Evans, United States	43.86 WR
1972	Vincent Matthews, United States	44.66
1976	Alberto Juantorena, Cuba	44.26
1980	Viktor Markin, USSR	44.60
1984	Alonzo Babers, United States	44.27
1988	Steve Lewis, United States	43.87
1992	Quincy Watts, United States	43.50 OR

800 METERS

1896	Edwin Flack, Australia	2:11
1900	Alfred Tysoe, Great Britain	2:01.2
1904	James Lightbody, United States	1:56 OR
1906	Paul Pilgrim, United States	2:01.5
1908	Mel Sheppard, United States	1:52.8 WR
1912	James Meredith, United States	1:51.9 WR
1920	Albert Hill, Great Britain	1:53.4
1924	Douglas Lowe, Great Britain	1:52.4
1928	Douglas Lowe, Great Britain	1:51.8 OR

800 METERS (Cont.)

1932	Thomas Hampson, Great Britain	1:49.8 WR
1936	John Woodruff, United States	1:52.9
1948	Mal Whitfield, United States	1:49.2 OR
1952	Mal Whitfield, United States	1:49.2 EOR
1956	Thomas Courtney, United States	1:47.7 OR
1960	Peter Snell, New Zealand	1:46.3 OR
1964	Peter Snell, New Zealand	1:45.1 OR
1968	Ralph Doubell, Australia	1:44.3 EWR
1972	Dave Wottle, United States	1:45.9
1976	Alberto Juantorena, Cuba	1:43.50 WR
1980	Steve Ovett, Great Britain	1:45.40
1984	Joaquim Cruz, Brazil	1:43.00 OR
1988	Paul Ereng, Kenya	1:43.45
1992	William Tanui, Kenya	1:43.66

1500 METERS

1896	Edwin Flack, Australia	4:33.2
1900	Charles Bennett, Great Britain	4:06.2 WR
1904	James Lightbody, United States	4:05.4 WR
1906	James Lightbody, United States	4:12.0
1908	Mel Sheppard, United States	4:03.4 OR
1912	Arnold Jackson, Great Britain	3:56.8 OR
1920	Albert Hill, Great Britain	4:01.8
1924	Paavo Nurmi, Finland	3:53.6 OR
1928	Harry Larva, Finland	3:53.2 OR
1932	Luigi Beccali, Italy	3:51.2 OR
1936	Jack Lovelock, New Zealand	3:47.8 WR
1948	Henri Eriksson, Sweden	3:49.8
1952	Josef Barthel, Luxemburg	3:45.1 OR
1956	Ron Delany, Ireland	3:41.2 OR
1960	Herb Elliott, Australia	3:35.6 WR
1964	Peter Snell, New Zealand	3:38.1
1968	Kipchoge Keino, Kenya	3:34.9 OR
1972	Pekkha Vasala, Finland	3:36.3
1976	John Walker, New Zealand	3:39.17
1980	Sebastian Coe, Great Britain	3:38.4
1984	Sebastian Coe, Great Britain	3:32.53 OR
1988	Peter Rono, Kenya	3:35.96
1992	Fermin Cacho, Spain	3:40.12

5000 METERS

1912	Hannes Kolehmainen, Finland	14:36.6 WR
1920	Joseph Guillemot, France	14:55.6
1924	Paavo Nurmi, Finland	14:31.2 OR
1928	Villie Ritola, Finland	14:38
1932	Lauri Lehtinen, Finland	14:30 OR
1936	Gunnar Höckert, Finland	14:22.2 OR
1948	Gaston Reiff, Belgium	14:17.6 OR
1952	Emil Zatopek, Czechoslovakia	14:06.6 OR
1956	Vladimir Kuts, USSR	13:39.6 WR
1960	Murray Halberg, New Zealand	13:43.4
1964	Bob Schul, United States	13:48.8
1968	Mohamed Gammoudi, Tunisia	14:05.0
1972	Lasse Viren, Finland	13:26.4 OR
1976	Lasse Viren, Finland	13:24.76
1980	Miruts Yifter, Ethiopia	13:21.0
1984	Said Aouita, Morocco	13:05.59 OR
1988	John Ngugi, Kenya	13:11.70
1992	Dieter Baumann, Germany	13:12.52

Note: OR=Olympic Record; WR=World Record; EOR=Equals Olympic Record; EWR=Equals World Record; WB=World Best.

TRACK AND FIELD (Cont.)

Men (Cont.)

10,000 METERS

1912	Hannes Kolehmainen, Finland	31:20.8
1920	Paavo Nurmi, Finland	31:45.8
1924	Vilho (Ville) Ritola, Finland	30:23.2 WR
1928	Paavo Nurmi, Finland	30:18.8 OR
1932	Janusz Kusocinski, Poland	30:11.4 OR
1936	Ilmari Salminen, Finland	30:15.4
1948	Emil Zatopek, Czechoslovakia	29:59.6 OR
1952	Emil Zatopek, Czechoslovakia	29:17.0 OR
1956	Vladimir Kuts, USSR	28:45.6 OR
1960	Pyotr Bolotnikov, USSR	28:32.2 OR
1964	Billy Mills, United States	28:24.4 OR
1968	Naftali Temu, Kenya	29:27.4
1972	Lasse Viren, Finland	27:38.4 WR
1976	Lasse Viren, Finland	27:40.38
1980	Miruts Yifter, Ethiopia	27:42.7
1984	Alberto Cova, Italy	27:47.54
1988	Brahim Boutaib, Morocco	27:21.46 OR
1992	Khalid Skah, Morocco	27:46.70

MARATHON

1896	Spiridon Louis, Greece	2:58:50
1900	Michel Theato, France	2:59:45
1904	Thomas Hicks, United States	3:28:53
1906	William Sherring, Canada	2:51:23.6
1908	John Hayes, United States	2:55:18.4 OR
1912	Kenneth McArthur, South Africa	2:36:54.8
1920	Hannes Kolehmainen, Finland	2:32:35.8 WB
1924	Albin Stenroos, Finland	2:41:22.6
1928	Boughera El Ouafi, France	2:32:57
1932	Juan Zabala, Argentina	2:31:36 OR
1936	Kijung Son, Japan (Korea)	2:29:19.2 OR
1948	Delfo Cabrera, Argentina	2:34:51.6
1952	Emil Zatopek, Czechoslovakia	2:23:03.2 OR
1956	Alain Mimoun O'Kacha, France	2:25:00.0
1960	Abebe Bikila, Ethiopia	2:15:16.2 WB
1964	Abebe Bikila, Ethiopia	2:12:11.2 WB
1968	Mamo Wolde, Ethiopia	2:20:26.4
1972	Frank Shorter, United States	2:12:19.8
1976	Waldemar Cierpinski, East Germany	2:09:55 OR
1980	Waldemar Cierpinski, East Germany	2:11:03.0
1984	Carlos Lopes, Portugal	2:09:21.0 OR
1988	Gelindo Bordin, Italy	2:10:32
1992	Hwang Young-Cho, S Korea	2:13:23

Note: Marathon distances: 1896, 1904—40,000 meters; 1900—40,260 meters; 1906—41,860 meters; 1912—40,200 meters; 1920—42,750 meters; 1908 and since 1924—42,195 meters (26 miles, 385 yards).

110-METER HURDLES

1896	Thomas Curtis, United States	17.6
1900	Alvin Kraenzlein, United States	15.4 OR
1904	Frederick Schule, United States	16.0
1906	Robert Leavitt, United States	16.2
1908	Forrest Smithson, United States	15.0 WR
1912	Frederick Kelly, United States	15.1
1920	Earl Thomson, Canada	14.8 WR
1924	Daniel Kinsey, United States	15.0
1928	Sydney Atkinson, South Africa	14.8
1932	George Saling, United States	14.6
1936	Forrest Towns, United States	14.2
1948	William Porter, United States	13.9 OR
1952	Harrison Dillard, United States	13.7 OR
1956	Lee Calhoun, United States	13.5 OR
1960	Lee Calhoun, United States	13.8
1964	Hayes Jones, United States	13.6
1968	Willie Davenport, United States	13.3 OR
1972	Rod Milburn, United States	13.24 EWR
1976	Guy Drut, France	13.30
1980	Thomas Munkelt, East Germany	13.39
1984	Roger Kingdom, United States	13.20 OR
1988	Roger Kingdom, United States	12.98 OR
1992	Mark McKoy, Canada	13.12

400-METER HURDLES

1900	John Walter Tewksbury, United States	57.6
1904	Harry Hillman, United States	53.0
1906	Not held	
1908	Charles Bacon, United States	55.0 WR
1912	Not held	
1920	Frank Loomis, United States	54.0 WR
1924	F. Morgan Taylor, United States	52.6
1928	David Burghley, Great Britain	53.4 OR
1932	Robert Tisdall, Ireland	51.7
1936	Glenn Hardin, United States	52.4
1948	Roy Cochran, United States	51.1 OR
1952	Charles Moore, United States	50.8 OR
1956	Glenn Davis, United States	50.1 EOR
1960	Glenn Davis, United States	49.3 EOR
1964	Rex Cawley, United States	49.6
1968	Dave Hemery, Great Britain	48.12 WR
1972	John Akii-Bua, Uganda	47.82 WR
1976	Edwin Moses, United States	47.64 WR
1980	Volker Beck, East Germany	48.70
1984	Edwin Moses, United States	47.75
1988	Andre Phillips, United States	47.19 OR
1992	Kevin Young, United States	46.78 WR

Some Advantage

Bob Keino, who attends Ridgewood (N.J.) High and is a son of Kenyan Olympic hero Kip Keino, says he came to the U.S. in quest of stronger academics. But the New Jersey State Interscholastic Association says he "transferred for athletic advantage" and late last year stripped him of the state cross-country title he won in 1992. In Kenya, Bob could have attended St. Patrick's, a school 14 miles from his home. St. Patrick's has produced 15 Olympic runners, Ridgewood none.

TRACK AND FIELD (Cont.)

Men (Cont.)

3000-METER STEEPLECHASE

1920	Percy Hodge, Great Britain	10:00.4 OR
1924	Vilho (Ville) Ritola, Finland	9:33.6 OR
1928	Toivo Loukola, Finland	9:21.8 WR
1932	Volmari Iso-Hollo, Finland	10:33.4*
1936	Volmari Iso-Hollo, Finland	9:03.8 WR
1948	Thore Sjöstrand, Sweden	9:04.6
1952	Horace Ashenfelter, United States	8:45.4 WR
1956	Chris Brasher, Great Britain	8:41.2 OR
1960	Zdzislaw Krzyszkowiak, Poland	8:34.2 OR
1964	Gaston Roelants, Belgium	8:30.8 OR
1968	Amos Biwott, Kenya	8:51
1972	Kipchoge Keino, Kenya	8:23.6 OR
1976	Anders Gärderud, Sweden	8:08.2 WR
1980	Bronislaw Malinowski, Poland	8:09.7
1984	Julius Korir, Kenya	8:11.8
1988	Julius Kariuki, Kenya	8:05.51 OR
1992	Mathew Birir, Kenya	8:08.84

*About 3450 meters; extra lap by error.

4 X 100-METER RELAY

1912	Great Britain	42.4 OR
1920	United States	42.2 WR
1924	United States	41.0 EWR
1928	United States	41.0 EWR
1932	United States	40.0 EWR
1936	United States	39.8 WR
1948	United States	40.6
1952	United States	40.1
1956	United States	39.5 WR
1960	West Germany	39.5 EWR
1964	United States	39.0 WR
1968	United States	38.2 WR
1972	United States	38.19 EWR
1976	United States	38.33
1980	USSR	38.26
1984	United States	37.83 WR
1988	USSR	38.19
1992	United States	37.40 WR

4 X 400-METER RELAY

1908	United States	3:29.4
1912	United States	3:16.6 WR
1920	Great Britain	3:22.2
1924	United States	3:16.0 WR
1928	United States	3:14.2 WR
1932	United States	3:08.2 WR
1936	Great Britain	3:09.0
1948	United States	3:10.4 WR
1952	Jamaica	3:03.9 WR
1956	United States	3:04.8
1960	United States	3:02.2 WR
1964	United States	3:00.7 WR
1968	United States	2:56.16 WR
1972	Kenya	2:59.8
1976	United States	2:58.65
1980	USSR	3:01.1
1984	United States	2:57.91
1988	United States	2:56.16 EWR
1992	United States	2:55.74 WR

20-KILOMETER WALK

1956	Leonid Spirin, USSR	1:31:27.4
1960	Vladimir Golubnichiy, USSR	1:33:07.2
1964	Kenneth Mathews, Great Britain	1:29:34.0 OR
1968	Vladimir Golubnichiy, USSR	1:33:58.4
1972	Peter Frenkel, East Germany	1:26:42.4 OR
1976	Daniel Bautista, Mexico	1:24:40.6 OR
1980	Maurizio Damilano, Italy	1:23:35.5 OR
1984	Ernesto Canto, Mexico	1:23:13.0 OR
1988	Jozef Pribilinec, Czechoslovakia	1:19:57.0 OR
1992	Daniel Plaza, Spain	1:21:45.0

50-KILOMETER WALK

1932	Thomas Green, Great Britain	4:50:10
1936	Harold Whitlock, Great Britain	4:30:41.4 OR
1948	John Ljunggren, Sweden	4:41:52
1952	Giuseppe Dordoni, Italy	4:28:07.8 OR
1956	Norman Read, New Zealand	4:30:42.8
1960	Donald Thompson, Great Britain	4:25:30 OR
1964	Abdon Parnich, Italy	4:11:12.4 OR
1968	Christoph Höhne, East Germany	4:20:13.6
1972	Bernd Kannenberg, West Germany	3:56:11.6 OR
1980	Hartwig Gauder, East Germany	3:49:24.0 OR
1984	Raul Gonzalez, Mexico	3:47:26.0 OR
1988	Viacheslav Ivanenko, USSR	3:38:29.0 OR
1992	Andrey Perlov, Unified Team	3:50:13

HIGH JUMP

1896	Ellery Clark, United States	5 ft 11¼ in
1900	Irving Baxter, United States	6 ft 2¾ in OR
1904	Samuel Jones, United States	5 ft 11 in
1906	Cornelius Leahy, Great Britain/Ireland	5 ft 10 in
1908	Harry Porter, United States	6 ft 3 in OR
1912	Alma Richards, United States	6 ft 4 in OR
1920	Richmond Landon, United States	6 ft 4 in OR
1924	Harold Osborn, United States	6 ft 6 in OR
1928	Robert W. King, United States	6 ft 4½ in
1932	Duncan McNaughton, Canada	6 ft 5½ in
1936	Cornelius Johnson, United States	6 ft 8 in OR
1948	John L. Winter, Australia	6 ft 6 in
1952	Walter Davis, United States	6 ft 8½ in OR
1956	Charles Dumas, United States	6 ft 11½ in OR
1960	Robert Shavlakadze, USSR	7 ft 1 in
1964	Valery Brumel, USSR	7 ft 1¾ in OR
1968	Dick Fosbury, United States	7 ft 4¼ in OR
1972	Yuri Tarmak, USSR	7 ft 3¾ in
1976	Jacek Wszola, Poland	7 ft 4½ in OR
1980	Gerd Wessig, East Germany	7 ft 8¾ in WR
1984	Dietmar Mögenburg, West Germany	7 ft 8½ in
1988	Gennadiy Avdeyenko, USSR	7 ft 9¾ in OR
1992	Javier Sotomayor, Cuba	7 ft 8 in.

Note: OR=Olympic Record; WR=World Record; EOR=Equals Olympic Record; EWR=Equals World Record; WB=World Best.

TRACK AND FIELD (Cont.)

Men (Cont.)

POLE VAULT

1896	William Hoyt, United States	10 ft 10 in
1900	Irving Baxter, United States	10 ft 10 in
1904	Charles Dvorak, United States	11 ft 5¾ in
1906	Fernand Gonder, France	11 ft 5¾ in
1908	Alfred Gilbert, United States	12 ft 2 in OR
	Edward Cooke, Jr, United States	
1912	Harry Babcock, United States	12 ft 11½ in OR
1920	Frank Foss, United States	13 ft 5 in WR
1924	Lee Barnes, United States	12 ft 11½ in
1928	Sabin Carr, United States	13 ft 9¼ in OR
1932	William Miller, United States	14 ft 1¾ in OR
1936	Earle Meadows, United States	14 ft 3¼ in OR
1948	Guinn Smith, United States	14 ft 1¼ in
1952	Robert Richards, United States	14 ft 11 in OR
1956	Robert Richards, United States	14 ft 11½ in OR
1960	Don Bragg, United States	15 ft 5 in OR
1964	Fred Hansen, United States	16 ft 8¾ in OR
1968	Bob Seagren, United States	17 ft 8½ in OR
1972	Wolfgang Nordwig, East Germany	18 ft ½ in OR
1976	Tadeusz Slusarski, Poland	18 ft ½ in EOR
1980	Wladyslaw Kozakiewicz, Poland	18 ft 11½ in WR
1984	Pierre Quinon, France	18 ft 10¼ in
1988	Sergei Bubka, USSR	19 ft 9¼ in OR
1992	Maksim Tarasov, Unified Team	19 ft ¼ in

LONG JUMP

1896	Ellery Clark, United States	20 ft 10 in
1900	Alvin Kraenzlein, United States	23 ft 6¾ in OR
1904	Meyer Prinstein, United States	24 ft 1 in OR
1906	Meyer Prinstein, United States	23 ft 7½ in
1908	Frank Irons, United States	24 ft 6½ in OR
1912	Albert Gutterson, United States	24 ft 11¼ in OR
1920	William Petersson, Sweden	23 ft 5½ in
1924	DeHart Hubbard, United States	24 ft 5 in
1928	Edward B. Hamm, United States	25 ft 4½ in OR
1932	Edward Gordon, United States	25 ft ¾ in
1936	Jesse Owens, United States	26 ft 5½ in OR
1948	William Steele, United States	25 ft 8 in
1952	Jerome Biffle, United States	24 ft 10 in
1956	Gregory Bell, United States	25 ft 8¼ in
1960	Ralph Boston, United States	26 ft 7¾ in OR
1964	Lynn Davies, Great Britain	26 ft 5¾ in
1968	Bob Beamon, United States	29 ft 2½ in WR

LONG JUMP (Cont.)

1972	Randy Williams, United States	27 ft ½ in
1976	Arnie Robinson, United States	27 ft 4¾ in
1980	Lutz Dombrowski, East Germany	28 ft ¼ in
1984	Carl Lewis, United States	28 ft ¼ in
1988	Carl Lewis, United States	28 ft 7½ in
1992	Carl Lewis, United States	28 ft 5½ in

TRIPLE JUMP

1896	James Connolly, United States	44 ft 11¾ in
1900	Meyer Prinstein, United States	47 ft 5¾ in OR
1904	Meyer Prinstein, United States	47 ft 1 in
1906	Peter O'Connor, Great Britain/Ireland	46 ft 2¼ in
1908	Timothy Ahearne, Great Britain/Ireland	48 ft 11¼ in OR
1912	Gustaf Lindblom, Sweden	48 ft 5¼ in
1920	Vilho Tuulos, Finland	47 ft 7 in
1924	Anthony Winter, Australia	50 ft 11¼ in WR
1928	Mikio Oda, Japan	49 ft 11 in
1932	Chuhei Nambu, Japan	51 ft 7 in WR
1936	Naoto Tajima, Japan	52 ft 6 in WR
1948	Arne Ahman, Sweden	50 ft 6¼ in
1952	Adhemar da Silva, Brazil	53 ft 2¾ in WR
1956	Adhemar da Silva, Brazil	53 ft 7¾ in OR
1960	Jozef Schmidt, Poland	55 ft 2 in
1964	Jozef Schmidt, Poland	55 ft 3½ in OR
1968	Viktor Saneyev, USSR	57 ft ¾ in WR
1972	Viktor Saneyev, USSR	56 ft 11¾ in
1976	Viktor Saneyev, USSR	56 ft 8¾ in
1980	Jaak Uudmae, USSR	56 ft 11¼ in
1984	Al Joyner, United States	56 ft 7½ in
1988	Khristo Markov, Bulgaria	57 ft 9½ in OR
1992	Mike Conley, United States	59 ft 7½ in

SHOT PUT

1896	Robert Garrett, United States	36 ft 9¾ in
1900	Richard Sheldon, United States	46 ft 3¼ in OR
1904	Ralph Rose, United States	48 ft 7 in WR
1906	Martin Sheridan, United States	40 ft 5¼ in
1908	Ralph Rose, United States	46 ft 7½ in
1912	Pat McDonald, United States	50 ft 4 in OR
1920	Ville Porhola, Finland	48 ft 7¼ in
1924	Clarence Houser, United States	49 ft 2¼ in
1928	John Kuck, United States	52 ft ¾ in WR
1932	Leo Sexton, United States	52 ft 6 in OR
1936	Hans Woellke, Germany	53 ft 1¾ in OR
1948	Wilbur Thompson, United States	56 ft 2 in OR
1952	Parry O'Brien, United States	57 ft ½ in OR
1956	Parry O'Brien, United States	60 ft 11¼ in OR
1960	William Nieder, United States	64 ft 6¾ in OR

TRACK AND FIELD (Cont.)

Men (Cont.)

SHOT PUT (Cont.)

1964	Dallas Long, United States	66 ft 8½ in OR
1968	Randy Matson, United States	67 ft 4¾ in
1972	Wladyslaw Komar, Poland	69 ft 6 in OR
1976	Udo Beyer, East Germany	69 ft ¾ in
1980	Vladimir Kiselyov, USSR	70 ft ½ in OR
1984	Alessandro Andrei, Italy	69 ft 9 in
1988	Ulf Timmermann, East Germany	73 ft 8¾ in OR
1992	Mike Stulce, United States	71 ft 2½ in

DISCUS THROW

1896	Robert Garrett, United States	95 ft 7½ in
1900	Rudolf Bauer, Hungary	118 ft 3 in OR
1904	Martin Sheridan, United States	128 ft 10½ in OR
1906	Martin Sheridan, United States	136 ft
1908	Martin Sheridan, United States	134 ft 2 in OR
1912	Armas Taipele, Finland	148 ft 3 in OR
1920	Elmer Niklander, Finland	146 ft 7 in
1924	Clarence Houser, United States	151 ft 4 in OR
1928	Clarence Houser, United States	155 ft 3 in OR
1932	John Anderson, United States	162 ft 4 in OR
1936	Ken Carpenter, United States	165 ft 7 in OR
1948	Adolfo Consolini, Italy	173 ft 2 in OR
1952	Sim Iness, United States	180 ft 6 in OR
1956	Al Oerter, United States	184 ft 11 in OR
1960	Al Oerter, United States	194 ft 2 in OR
1964	Al Oerter, United States	200 ft 1 in OR
1968	Al Oerter, United States	212 ft 6 in OR
1972	Ludvik Danek, Czechoslovakia	211 ft 3 in
1976	Mac Wilkins, United States	221 ft 5 in OR
1980	Viktor Rashchupkin, USSR	218 ft 8 in
1984	Rolf Dannenberg, West Germany	218 ft 6 in
1988	Jürgen Schult, East Germany	225 ft 9 in OR
1992	Romas Ubartas, Lithuania	213 ft 8 in

HAMMER THROW

1900	John Flanagan, United States	163 ft 1 in
1904	John Flanagan, United States	168 ft 1 in OR
1906	Not held	
1908	John Flanagan, United States	170 ft 4 in OR
1912	Matt McGrath, United States	179 ft 7 in OR
1920	Pat Ryan, United States	173 ft 5 in
1924	Fred Tootell, United States	174 ft 10 in
1928	Patrick O'Callaghan, Ireland	168 ft 7 in
1932	Patrick O'Callaghan, Ireland	176 ft 11 in
1936	Karl Hein, Germany	185 ft 4 in OR
1948	Imre Nemeth, Hungary	183 ft 11 in
1952	Jozsef Csermak, Hungary	197 ft 11 in WR
1956	Harold Connolly, United States	207 ft 3 in OR
1960	Vasily Rudenkov, USSR	220 ft 2 in OR

HAMMER THROW (Cont.)

1964	Romuald Klim, USSR	228 ft 10 in OR
1968	Gyula Zsivotsky, Hungary	240 ft 8 in OR
1972	Anatoli Bondarchuk, USSR	247 ft 8 in OR
1976	Yuri Sedykh, USSR	254 ft 4 in OR
1980	Yuri Sedykh, USSR	268 ft 4 in WR
1984	Juha Tiainen, Finland	256 ft 2 in
1988	Sergei Litvinov, USSR	278 ft 2 in OR
1992	Andrey Abduvaliyev, Unified Team	270 ft 9 in

JAVELIN

1908	Erik Lemming, Sweden	179 ft 10 in
1912	Erik Lemming, Sweden	198 ft 11 in WR
1920	Jonni Myyrä, Finland	215 ft 10 in OR
1924	Jonni Myyrä, Finland	206 ft 6 in
1928	Eric Lundkvist, Sweden	218 ft 6 in OR
1932	Matti Jarvinen, Finland	238 ft 6 in OR
1936	Gerhard Stöck, Germany	235 ft 8 in
1948	Kai Rautavaara, Finland	228 ft 10½ in
1952	Cy Young, United States	242 ft 1 in OR
1956	Egil Danielson, Norway	281 ft 2¼ in WR
1960	Viktor Tsibulenko, USSR	277 ft 8 in
1964	Pauli Nevala, Finland	271 ft 2 in
1968	Janis Lusis, USSR	295 ft 7 in OR
1972	Klaus Wolfermann, West Germany	296 ft 10 in OR
1976	Miklos Nemeth, Hungary	310 ft 4 in WR
1980	Dainis Kuta, USSR	299 ft 2⅜ in
1984	Arto Härkönen, Finland	284 ft 8 in
1988	Tapio Korjus, Finland	276 ft 6 in
1992	Jan Zelezny, Czechoslovakia	294 ft 2 in OR

DECATHLON

		Pts
1904	Thomas Kiely, Ireland	6036
1912	Jim Thorpe, United States*	8412 WR
1920	Helge Lövland, Norway	6803
1924	Harold Osborn, United States	7711 WR
1928	Paavo Yrjölä, Finland	8053.29 WR
1932	James Bausch, United States	8462 WR
1936	Glenn Morris, United States	7900 WR
1948	Robert Mathias, United States	7139
1952	Robert Mathias, United States	7887 WR
1956	Milton Campbell, United States	7937 OR
1960	Rafer Johnson, United States	8392 OR
1964	Willi Holdorf, West Germany	7887
1968	Bill Toomey, United States	8193 OR
1972	Nikolai Avilov, USSR	8454 WR
1976	Bruce Jenner, United States	8617 WR
1980	Daley Thompson, Great Britain	8495
1984	Daley Thompson, Great Britain	8798 EWR
1988	Christian Schenk, East Germany	8488
1992	Robert Zmelik, Czechoslovakia	8611

*In 1913, Thorpe was disqualified for having played professional baseball in 1910. His record was restored in 1982.

Note: OR=Olympic Record; WR=World Record;

EOR=Equals Olympic Record; EWR=Equals World Record; WB=World Best.

Women

100 METERS

1928	Elizabeth Robinson, United States	12.2 EWR
1932	Stella Walsh, Poland	11.9 EWR
1936	Helen Stephens, United States	11.5
1948	Francina Blankers-Koen, Netherlands	11.9
1952	Marjorie Jackson, Australia	11.5 EWR
1956	Betty Cuthbert, Australia	11.5 EWR
1960	Wilma Rudolph, United States	11.0
1964	Wyomia Tyus, United States	11.4
1968	Wyomia Tyus, United States	11.0 WR
1972	Renate Stecher, East Germany	11.07
1976	Annegret Richter, West Germany	11.08
1980	Lyudmila Kondratyeva, USSR	11.06
1984	Evelyn Ashford, United States	10.97 OR
1988	Florence Griffith Joyner, United States	10.54
1992	Gail Devers, United States	10.82

200 METERS

1948	Francina Blankers-Koen, Netherlands	24.4
1952	Marjorie Jackson, Australia	23.7
1956	Betty Cuthbert, Australia	23.4 EOR
1960	Wilma Rudolph, United States	24.0
1964	Edith McGuire, United States	23.0 OR
1968	Irena Szewinska, Poland	22.5 WR
1972	Renate Stecher, East Germany	22.40 EWR
1976	Bärbel Eckert, East Germany	22.37 OR
1980	Bärbel Wöckel (Eckert), East Germany	22.03 OR
1984	Valerie Brisco-Hooks, United States	21.81 OR
1988	Florence Griffith Joyner, United States	21.34 WR
1992	Gwen Torrence, United States	21.81

400 METERS

1964	Betty Cuthbert, Australia	52.0 OR
1968	Colette Besson, France	52.0 EOR
1972	Monika Zehrt, East Germany	51.08 OR
1976	Irena Szewinska, Poland	49.29 WR
1980	Marita Koch, East Germany	48.88 OR
1984	Valerie Brisco-Hooks, United States	48.83 OR
1988	Olga Bryzgina, USSR	48.65 OR
1992	Marie-José Pérec, France	48.83

800 METERS

1928	Lina Radke, Germany	2:16.8 WR
1932	Not held 1932-1956	
1960	Lyudmila Shevtsova, USSR	2:04.3 EWR
1964	Ann Packer, Great Britain	2:01.1 OR
1968	Madeline Manning, United States	2:00.9 OR
1972	Hildegard Falck, West Germany	1:58.55 OR
1976	Tatyana Kazankina, USSR	1:54.94 WR
1980	Nadezhda Olizarenko, USSR	1:53.42 WR
1984	Doina Melinte, Romania	1:57.6
1988	Sigrun Wodars, East Germany	1:56.10
1992	Ellen Van Langen, the Netherlands	1:55.54

1500 METERS

1972	Lyudmila Bragina, USSR	4:01.4 WR
1976	Tatyana Kazankina, USSR	4:05.48
1980	Tatyana Kazankina, USSR	3:56.6 OR
1984	Gabriella Dorio, Italy	4:03.25

1500 METERS *(Cont.)*

1988	Paula Ivan, Romania	3:53.96 OR
1992	Hassiba Boulmerka, Algeria	3:55.30

3000 METERS

1984	Maricica Puica, Romania	8:35.96 OR
1988	Tatyana Samolenko, USSR	8:26.53 OR
1992	Elena Romanova, Unified Team	8:46.04

10,000 METERS

1988	Olga Bondarenko, USSR	31:05.21 OR
1992	Derartu Tulu, Ethiopia	31:06.02

MARATHON

1984	Joan Benoit, United States	2:24:52
1988	Rosa Mota, Portugal	2:25:40
1992	Valentin Yegorova, Unified Team	2:32:41

80-METER HURDLES

1932	Babe Didrikson, United States	11.7 WR
1936	Trebisonda Valla, Italy	11.7
1948	Francina Blankers-Koen, Netherlands	11.2 WR
1952	Shirley Strickland, Australia	10.9 WR
1956	Shirley Strickland, Australia	10.7 OR
1960	Irina Press, USSR	10.8
1964	Karin Balzer, East Germany	10.5
1968	Maureen Caird, Australia	10.3 OR

100-METER HURDLES

1972	Annelie Ehrhardt, East Germany	12.59 WR
1976	Johanna Schaller, East Germany	12.77
1980	Vera Komisova, USSR	12.56 OR
1984	Benita Fitzgerald-Brown, United States	12.84
1988	Yordanka Donkova, Bulgaria	12.38 OR
1992	Paraskevi Patoulidou, Greece	12.64

400-METER HURDLES

1984	Nawal el Moutawakel, Morocco	54.61 OR
1988	Debra Flintoff-King, Australia	53.17 OR
1992	Sally Gunnell, Great Britain	53.23

4 X 100-METER RELAY

1928	Canada	48.4 WR
1932	United States	46.9 WR
1936	United States	46.9
1948	Netherlands	47.5
1952	United States	45.9 WR
1956	Australia	44.5 WR
1960	United States	44.5
1964	Poland	43.6
1968	United States	42.8 WR
1972	West Germany	42.81 EWR
1976	East Germany	42.55 OR
1980	East Germany	41.60 WR
1984	United States	41.65
1988	United States	41.98
1992	United States	42.11

Note: OR=Olympic Record; WR=World Record;
EOR=Equals Olympic Record; EWR=Equals World Record;
WB=World Best.

TRACK AND FIELD (Cont.)

Women (Cont.)

4 X 400-METER RELAY

1972	East Germany	3:23 WR
1976	East Germany	3:19.23 WR
1980	USSR	3:20.02
1984	United States	3:18.29 OR
1988	USSR	3:15.18 WR
1992	Unified Team	3:20.20

HIGH JUMP

1928	Ethel Catherwood, Canada	5 ft 2½ in
1932	Jean Shiley, United States	5 ft 5¼ in WR
1936	Ibolya Csak, Hungary	5 ft 3 in
1948	Alice Coachman, United States	5 ft 6 in OR
1952	Esther Brand, South Africa	5 ft 5¾ in
1956	Mildred L. McDaniel, United States	5 ft 9¼ in WR
1960	Iolanda Balas, Romania	6 ft ¾ in OR
1964	Iolanda Balas, Romania	6 ft 2¾ in OR
1968	Miloslava Reskova, Czechoslovakia	5 ft 11½ in
1972	Ulrike Meyfarth, West Germany	6 ft 3½ in EWR
1976	Rosemarie Ackermann, East Germany	6 ft 4 in OR
1980	Sara Simeoni, Italy	6 ft 5½ in OR
1984	Ulrike Meyfarth, West Germany	6 ft 7½ in OR
1988	Louise Ritter, United States	6 ft 8 in OR
1992	Heike Henkel, Germany	6 ft 7½ in

LONG JUMP

1948	Olga Gyarmati, Hungary	18 ft 8¼ in
1952	Yvette Williams, New Zealand	20 ft 5¾ in OR
1956	Elzbieta Krzeskinska, Poland	20 ft 10 in EWR
1960	Vyera Krepkina, USSR	20 ft 10¾ in OR
1964	Mary Rand, Great Britain	22 ft 2¼ in WR
1968	Viorica Viscopoleanu, Romania	22 ft 4½ in WR
1972	Heidemarie Rosendahl, West Germany	22 ft 3 in
1976	Angela Voigt, East Germany	22 ft ¾ in
1980	Tatyana Kolpakova, USSR	23 ft 2 in OR
1984	Anisoara Stanciu, Romania	22 ft 10 in
1988	Jackie Joyner-Kersee, United States	24 ft 3½ in OR
1992	Heike Drechsler, Germany	23 ft 5¼ in

SHOT PUT

1948	Micheline Ostermeyer, France	45 ft 1½ in
1952	Galina Zybina, USSR	50 ft 1¾ in WR
1956	Tamara Tyshkevich, USSR	54 ft 5 in OR
1960	Tamara Press, USSR	56 ft 10 in OR
1964	Tamara Press, USSR	59 ft 6¼ in OR
1968	Margitta Gummel, East Germany	64 ft 4 in WR
1972	Nadezhda Chizhova, USSR	69 ft WR
1976	Ivanka Hristova, Bulgaria	69 ft 5¼ in OR
1980	Ilona Slupianek, East Germany	73 ft 6¼ in
1984	Claudia Losch, West Germany	67 ft 2¼ in

SHOT PUT (Cont.)

1988	Natalya Lisovskaya, USSR	72 ft 11¾ in
1992	Svetlana Kriveleva, Unified Team	69 ft 1¼ in

DISCUS THROW

1928	Helena Konopacka, Poland	129 ft 11¾ in WR
1932	Lillian Copeland, United States	133 ft 2 in OR
1936	Gisela Mauermayer, Germany	156 ft 3 in OR
1948	Micheline Ostermeyer, France	137 ft 6 in
1952	Nina Romaschkova, USSR	168 ft 8 in OR
1956	Olga Fikotova, Czechoslovakia	176 ft 1 in OR
1960	Nina Ponomaryeva, USSR	180 ft 9 in OR
1964	Tamara Press, USSR	187 ft 10 in OR
1968	Lia Manoliu, Romania	191 ft 2 in OR
1972	Faina Melnik, USSR	218 ft 7 in OR
1976	Evelin Schlaak, East Germany	226 ft 4 in OR
1980	Evelin Jahl (Schlaak), East Germany	229 ft 6 in OR
1984	Ria Stalman, Netherlands	214 ft 5 in
1988	Martina Hellmann, East Germany	237 ft 2 in OR
1992	Maritza Martén, Cuba	229 ft 10 in

JAVELIN THROW

1932	Babe Didrikson, United States	143 ft 4 in OR
1936	Tilly Fleischer, Germany	148 ft 3 in OR
1948	Herma Bauma, Austria	149 ft 6 in
1952	Dana Zatopkova, Czechoslovakia	165 ft 7 in
1956	Inese Jaunzeme, USSR	176 ft 8 in
1960	Elvira Ozolina, USSR	183 ft 8 in OR
1964	Mihaela Penes, Romania	198 ft 7 in
1968	Angela Nemeth, Hungary	198 ft
1972	Ruth Fuchs, East Germany	209 ft 7 in OR
1976	Ruth Fuchs, East Germany	216 ft 4 in OR
1980	Maria Colon, Cuba	224 ft 5 in OR
1984	Tessa Sanderson, Great Britain	228 ft 2 in OR
1988	Petra Felke, East Germany	245 ft OR
1992	Silke Renk, Germany	224 ft 2 in

PENTATHLON

Year		Pts
1964	Irina Press, USSR	5246 WR
1968	Ingrid Becker, West Germany	5098
1972	Mary Peters, Great Britain	4801 WR*
1976	Siegrun Siegl, East Germany	4745
1980	Nadezhda Tkachenko, USSR	5083 WR

*In 1971, 100-meter hurdles replaced 80-meter hurdles, necessitating a change in scoring tables.

HEPTATHLON

Year		Pts
1984	Glynis Nunn, Australia	6390 OR
1988	Jackie Joyner-Kersee, United States	7291 WR
1992	Jackie Joyner-Kersee, United States	7044

BASKETBALL

Men

1936
Final: United States 19, Canada 8
United States: Ralph Bishop, Joe Fortenberry, Carl Knowles, Jack Ragland, Carl Shy, William Wheatley, Francis Johnson, Samuel Balter, John Gibbons, Frank Lubin, Arthur Mollner, Donald Piper, Duane Swanson, Willard Schmidt

1948
Final: United States 65, France 21
United States: Cliff Barker, Don Barksdale, Ralph Beard, Lewis Beck, Vince Boryla, Gordon Carpenter, Alex Groza, Wallace Jones, Bob Kurland, Ray Lumpp, Robert Pitts, Jesse Renick, Bob Robinson, Ken Rollins

1952
Final: United States 36, USSR 25
United States: Charles Hoag, Bill Hougland, Melvin Dean Kelley, Bob Kenney, Clyde Lovellette, Marcus Freiberger, Victor Wayne Glasgow, Frank McCabe, Daniel Pippen, Howard Williams, Ronald Bontemps, Bob Kurland, William Lienhard, John Keller

1956
Final: United States 89, USSR 55
United States: Carl Cain, Bill Hougland, K. C. Jones, Bill Russell, James Walsh, William Evans, Burdette Haldorson, Ron Tomsic, Dick Boushka, Gilbert Ford, Bob Jeangerard, Charles Darling

1960
Final: United States 90, Brazil 63
United States: Jay Arnette, Walt Bellamy, Bob Boozer, Terry Dischinger, Jerry Lucas, Oscar Robertson, Adrian Smith, Burdette Haldorson, Darrall Imhoff, Allen Kelley, Lester Lane, Jerry West

1964
Final: United States 73, USSR 59
United States: Jim Barnes, Bill Bradley, Larry Brown, Joe Caldwell, Mel Counts, Richard Davies, Walt Hazzard, Lucius Jackson, John McCaffrey, Jeff Mullins, Jerry Shipp, George Wilson

1968
Final: United States 65, Yugoslavia 50
United States: John Clawson, Ken Spain, Jo-Jo White, Michael Barrett, Spencer Haywood, Charles Scott, William Hosket, Calvin Fowler, Michael Silliman, Glynn Saulters, James King, Donald Dee

1972
Final: USSR 51, United States 50
United States: Kenneth Davis, Doug Collins, Thomas Henderson, Mike Bantom, Bobby Jones, Dwight Jones, James Forbes, James Brewer, Tom Burleson, Tom McMillen, Kevin Joyce, Ed Ratleff

1976
Final: United States 95, Yugoslavia 74
United States: Phil Ford, Steve Sheppard, Adrian Dantley, Walter Davis, Quinn Buckner, Ernie Grunfeld, Kenny Carr, Scott May, Michel Armstrong, Tom La Garde, Phil Hubbard, Mitch Kupchak

1980
Final: Yugoslavia 86, Italy 77
U.S. participated in boycott.

1984
Final: United States 96, Spain 65
United States: Steve Alford, Leon Wood, Patrick Ewing, Vern Fleming, Alvin Robertson, Michael Jordan, Joe Kleine, Jon Koncak, Wayman Tisdale, Chris Mullin, Sam Perkins, Jeff Turner

1988
Final: USSR 76, Yugoslavia 63
United States (3rd): Mitch Richmond, Charles E. Smith, IV, Vernell Coles, Hersey Hawkins, Jeff Grayer, Charles D. Smith, Willie Anderson, Stacey Augmon, Dan Majerle, Danny Manning, J. R. Reid, David Robinson

1992
Final: United States 117, Croatia 85
United States: David Robinson, Christian Laettner, Patrick Ewing, Larry Bird, Scottie Pippen, Michael Jordan, Clyde Drexler, Karl Malone, John Stockton, Chris Mullin, Charles Barkley, Earvin Johnson

Women

1976
Gold USSR; Silver, United States*
United States: Cindy Brogdon, Susan Rojcewicz, Ann Meyers, Lusia Harris, Nancy Dunkle, Charlotte Lewis, Nancy Lieberman, Gail Marquis, Patricia Roberts, Mary Anne O'Connor, Patricia Head, Julienne Simpson

*In 1976 the women played a round-robin tournament, with the gold medal going to the team with the best record. The USSR won with a 5-0 record, and the USA, with a 3-2 record, was given the silver by virtue of a 95-79 victory over Bulgaria, which was also 3-2.

1980
Final: USSR 104, Bulgaria 73
U.S. participated in boycott.

1984
Final: United States 85, Korea 55
United States: Teresa Edwards, Lea Henry, Lynette Woodard, Anne Donovan, Cathy Boswell, Cheryl Miller, Janice Lawrence, Cindy Noble, Kim Mulkey, Denise Curry, Pamela McGee, Carol Menken-Schaudt

BASKETBALL (Cont.)

Women (Cont.)

1988

Final: United States 77, Yugoslavia 70
United States: Teresa Edwards, Mary Ethridge, Cynthia Brown, Anne Donovan, Teresa Weatherspoon, Bridgette Gordon, Victoria Bullett, Andrea Lloyd, Katrina McClain, Jennifer Gillom, Cynthia Cooper, Suzanne McConnell

1992

Final: Unified Team 76, China 66
United States (3rd): Teresa Edwards, Teresa Weatherspoon, Victoria Bullett, Katrina McClain, Cynthia Cooper, Suzanne McConnell, Daedra Charles, Clarissa Davis, Tammy Jackson, Vickie Orr, Carolyn Jones, Medina Dixon

BOXING

LIGHT FLYWEIGHT (106 LB)

1968	Francisco Rodriguez, Venezuela
1972	Gyorgy Gedo, Hungary
1976	Jorge Hernandez, Cuba
1980	Shamil Sabyrov, USSR
1984	Paul Gonzalez, United States
1988	Ivailo Hristov, Bulgaria
1992	Rogelio Marcelo, Cuba

FLYWEIGHT (112 LB)

1904	George Finnegan, United States
1906-1912	Not held
1920	Frank Di Gennara, United States
1924	Fidel LaBarba, United States
1928	Antal Kocsis, Hungary
1932	Istvan Enekes, Hungary
1936	Willi Kaiser, Germany
1948	Pascual Perez, Argentina
1952	Nathan Brooks, United States
1956	Terence Spinks, Great Britain
1960	Gyula Torok, Hungary
1964	Fernando Atzori, Italy
1968	Ricardo Delgado, Mexico
1972	Georgi Kostadinov, Bulgaria
1976	Leo Randolph, United States
1980	Peter Lessov, Bulgaria
1984	Steve McCrory, United States
1988	Kim Kwang Sun, South Korea
1992	Su Choi Chol, North Korea

BANTAMWEIGHT (119 LB)

1904	Oliver Kirk, United States
1906	Not held
1908	A. Henry Thomas, Great Britain
1912	Not held
1920	Clarence Walker, South Africa
1924	William Smith, South Africa
1928	Vittorio Tamagnini, Italy
1932	Horace Gwynne, Canada
1936	Ulderico Sergo, Italy
1948	Tibor Csik, Hungary
1952	Pentti Hamalainen, Finland
1956	Wolfgang Behrendt, East Germany
1960	Oleg Grigoryev, USSR
1964	Takao Sakurai, Japan
1968	Valery Sokolov, USSR
1972	Orlando Martinez, Cuba
1976	Yong Jo Gu, North Korea
1980	Juan Hernandez, Cuba
1984	Maurizio Stecca, Italy
1988	Kennedy McKinney, United States
1992	Joel Casamayor, Cuba

FEATHERWEIGHT (125 LB)

1904	Oliver Kirk, United States
1906	Not held
1908	Richard Gunn, Great Britain
1912	Not held
1920	Paul Fritsch, France
1924	John Fields, United States
1928	Lambertus van Klaveren, Netherlands
1932	Carmelo Robledo, Argentina
1936	Oscar Casanovas, Argentina
1948	Ernesto Formenti, Italy
1952	Jan Zachara, Czechoslovakia
1956	Vladimir Safronov, USSR
1960	Francesco Musso, Italy
1964	Stanislav Stephashkin, USSR
1968	Antonio Roldan, Mexico
1972	Boris Kousnetsov, USSR
1976	Angel Herrera, Cuba
1980	Rudi Fink, East Germany
1984	Meldrick Taylor, United States
1988	Giovanni Parisi, Italy
1992	Andreas Tews, Germany

LIGHTWEIGHT (132 LB)

1904	Harry Spanger, United States
1906	Not held
1908	Frederick Grace, Great Britain
1912	Not held
1920	Samuel Mosberg, United States
1924	Hans Nielsen, Denmark
1928	Carlo Orlandi, Italy
1932	Lawrence Stevens, South Africa
1936	Imre Harangi, Hungary
1948	Gerald Dreyer, South Africa
1952	Aureliano Bolognesi, Italy
1956	Richard McTaggart, Great Britain
1960	Kazimierz Pazdzior, Poland
1964	Jozef Grudzien, Poland
1968	Ronald Harris, United States
1972	Jan Szczepanski, Poland
1976	Howard Davis, United States
1980	Angel Herrera, Cuba
1984	Pernell Whitaker, United States
1988	Andreas Zuelow, East Germany
1992	Oscar De La Hoya, United States

LIGHT WELTERWEIGHT (139 LB)

1952	Charles Adkins, United States
1956	Vladimir Yengibaryan, USSR
1960	Bohumil Nemecek, Czechoslovakia
1964	Jerzy Kulej, Poland
1968	Jerzy Kulej, Poland
1972	Ray Seales, United States
1976	Ray Leonard, United States

BOXING (Cont.)

LIGHT WELTERWEIGHT (Cont.)

1980 ....Patrizio Oliva, Italy
1984 ....Jerry Page, United States
1988 ....Viatcheslav Janovski, USSR
1992 ....Hector Vinent, Cuba

WELTERWEIGHT (147 LB)

1904 ....Albert Young, United States
1906-1912 ......Not held
1920 ....Albert Schneider, Canada
1924 ....Jean Delarge, Belgium
1928 ....Edward Morgan, New Zealand
1932 ....Edward Flynn, United States
1936 ....Sten Suvio, Finland
1948 ....Julius Torma, Czechoslovakia
1952 ....Zygmunt Chychla, Poland
1956 ....Nicolae Linca, Romania
1960 ....Giovanni Benvenuti, Italy
1964 ....Marian Kasprzyk, Poland
1968 ....Manfred Wolke, East Germany
1972 ....Emilio Correa, Cuba
1976 ....Jochen Bachfeld, East Germany
1980 ....Andres Aldama, Cuba
1984 ....Mark Breland, United States
1988 ....Robert Wangila, Kenya
1992 ....Michael Carruth, Ireland

LIGHT MIDDLEWEIGHT (156 LB)

1952 ....Laszlo Papp, Hungary
1956 ....Laszlo Papp, Hungary
1960 ....Wilbert McClure, United States
1964 ....Boris Lagutin, USSR
1968 ....Boris Lagutin, USSR
1972 ....Dieter Kottysch, West Germany
1976 ....Jerzy Rybicki, Poland
1980 ....Armando Martinez, Cuba
1984 ....Frank Tate, United States
1988 ....Park Si-Hun, South Korea
1992 ....Juan Lemus, Cuba

MIDDLEWEIGHT (165 LB)

1904 ....Charles Mayer, United States
1908 ....John Douglas, Great Britain
1912 ....Not held
1920 ....Harry Mallin, Great Britain
1924 ....Harry Mallin, Great Britain
1928 ....Piero Toscani, Italy
1932 ....Carmen Barth, United States
1936 ....Jean Despeaux, France
1948 ....Laszlo Papp, Hungary
1952 ....Floyd Patterson, United States
1956 ....Gennady Schatkov, USSR
1960 ....Edward Crook, United States
1964 ....Valery Popenchenko, USSR
1968 ....Christopher Finnegan, Great Britain
1972 ....Vyacheslav Lemechev, USSR
1976 ....Michael Spinks, United States

MIDDLEWEIGHT (Cont.)

1980 ....Jose Gomez, Cuba
1984 ....Shin Joon Sup, South Korea
1988 ....Henry Maske, East Germany
1992 ....Ariel Hernandez, Cuba

LIGHT HEAVYWEIGHT (178 LB)

1920 ....Edward Eagan, United States
1924 ....Harry Mitchell, Great Britain
1928 ....Victor Avendano, Argentina
1932 ....David Carstens, South Africa
1936 ....Roger Michelot, France
1948 ....George Hunter, South Africa
1952 ....Norvel Lee, United States
1956 ....James Boyd, United States
1960 ....Cassius Clay, United States
1964 ....Cosimo Pinto, Italy
1968 ....Dan Poznyak, USSR
1972 ....Mate Parlov, Yugoslavia
1976 ....Leon Spinks, United States
1980 ....Slobodan Kacer, Yugoslavia
1984 ....Anton Josipovic, Yugoslavia
1988 ....Andrew Maynard, United States
1992 ....Torsten May, Germany

HEAVYWEIGHT (OVER 201 LB)

1904 ....Samuel Berger, United States
1906 ....Not held
1908 ....Albert Oldham, Great Britain
1912 ....Not held
1920 ....Ronald Rawson, Great Britain
1924 ....Otto von Porat, Norway
1928 ....Arturo Rodriguez Jurado, Argentina
1932 ....Santiago Lovell, Argentina
1936 ....Herbert Runge, Germany
1948 ....Rafael Inglesias, Argentina
1952 ....H. Edward Sanders, United States
1956 ....T. Peter Rademacher, United States
1960 ....Franco De Piccoli, Italy
1964 ....Joe Frazier, United States
1968 ....George Foreman, United States
1972 ....Teofilo Stevenson, Cuba
1976 ....Teofilo Stevenson, Cuba
1980 ....Teofilo Stevenson, Cuba

HEAVYWEIGHT (201* LB)

1984 ....Henry Tillman, United States
1988 ....Ray Mercer, United States
1992 ....Felix Savon, Cuba

SUPER HEAVYWEIGHT (UNLIMITED)

1984 ....Tyrell Biggs, United States
1988 ....Lennox Lewis, Canada
1992 ....Roberto Balado, Cuba

*Until 1984 the heavyweight division was unlimited. With the addition of the super heavyweight division, a limit of 201 pounds was imposed.

SWIMMING

Men

50-METER FREESTYLE

1904....Zoltan Halmay, Hungary (50 yds) 28.0
1988....Matt Biondi, United States 22.14 WR
1992....Aleksandr Popov, Unified Team 22.30

100-METER FREESTLYE

1896....Alfred Hajos, Hungary 1:22.2 OR
1904.....Zoltan Halmay, Hungary (100 yds) 1:02.8
1906....Charles Daniels, United States 1:13.4
1908....Charles Daniels, United States 1:05.6 WR
1912.....Duke Kahanamoku, United States 1:03.4
1920.....Duke Kahanamoku, United States 1:00.4 WR
1924....John Weissmuller, United States 59.0 OR
1928....John Weissmuller, United States 58.6 OR
1932....Yasuji Miyazaki, Japan 58.2
1936....Ferenc Csik, Hungary 57.6
1948....Wally Ris, United States 57.3 OR
1952....Clarke Scholes, United States 57.4
1956....Jon Henricks, Australia 55.4 OR
1960....John Devitt, Australia 55.2 OR
1964....Don Schollander, United States 53.4 OR
1968....Mike Wenden, Australia 52.2 WR
1972....Mark Spitz, United States 51.22 WR
1976....Jim Montgomery, United States 49.99 WR
1980....Jörg Woithe, East Germany 50.40
1984....Rowdy Gaines, United States 49.80 OR
1988....Matt Biondi, United States 48.63 OR
1992....Aleksandr Popov, Unified Team 49.02

200-METER FREESTYLE

1900....Frederick Lane, Australia 2:25.2 OR
1904....Charles Daniels, United States 2:44.2
1906....Not held 1906-1964
1968....Michael Wenden, Australia 1:55.2 OR
1972....Mark Spitz, United States 1:52.78 WR
1976....Bruce Furniss, United States 1:50.29 WR
1980....Sergei Kopliakov, USSR 1:49.81 OR
1984....Michael Gross, West Germany 1:47.44 WR
1988....Duncan Armstrong, Australia 1:47.25 WR
1992....Evgueni Sadovyi, Unified Team 1:46.70

400-METER FREESTYLE

1896 ....Paul Neumann, Austria (500 yds) 8:12.6
1904....Charles Daniels, U.S. (440 yds) 6:16.2
1906....Otto Scheff, Austria (440 yds) 6:23.8
1908....Henry Taylor, Great Britain 5:36.8
1912....George Hodgson, Canada 5:24.4
1920....Norman Ross, United States 5:26.8
1924....John Weissmuller, United States 5:04.2 OR
1928....Albert Zorilla, Argentina 5:01.6 OR
1932....Buster Crabbe, United States 4:48.4 OR
1936....Jack Medica, United States 4:44.5 OR
1948....William Smith, United States 4:41.0 OR
1952....Jean Boiteux, France 4:30.7 OR
1956....Murray Rose, Australia 4:27.3 OR
1960....Murray Rose, Australia 4:18.3 OR
1964....Don Schollander, United States 4:12.2 WR
1968....Mike Burton, United States 4:09.0 OR
1972....Brad Cooper, Australia 4:00.27 OR
1976....Brian Goodell, United States 3:51.93 WR
1980....Vladimir Salnikov, USSR 3:51.31 OR
1984....George DiCarlo, United States 3:51.23 OR
1988....Uwe Dassler, East Germany 3:46.95 WR
1992....Evgueni Sadovyi, Unified Team 3:45.00 WR

1500-METER FREESTYLE

1908....Henry Taylor, Great Britain 22:48.4 WR
1912....George Hodgson, Canada 22:00.0 WR
1920....Norman Ross, United States 22:23.2
1924....Andrew Charlton, Australia 20:06.6 WR
1928....Arne Borg, Sweden 19:51.8 OR
1932....Kusuo Kitamura, Japan 19:12.4 OR
1936....Noboru Terada, Japan 19:13.7
1948....James McLane, United States 19:18.5
1952....Ford Konno, United States 18:30.3 OR
1956....Murray Rose, Australia 17:58.9
1960....John Konrads, Australia 17:19.6 OR
1964....Robert Windle, Australia 17:01.7 OR
1968....Mike Burton, United States 16:38.9 OR
1972....Mike Burton, United States 15:52.58 OR
1976....Brian Goodell, United States 15:02.40 WR
1980....Vladimir Salnikov, USSR 14:58.27 WR
1984....Michael O'Brien, United States 15:05.20
1988....Vladimir Salnikov, USSR 15:00.40
1992.....Kieren Perkins, Australia 14:43.48 WR

100-METER BACKSTROKE

1904....Walter Brack, Germany (100 yds) 1:16.8
1908....Arno Bieberstein, Germany 1:24.6 WR
1912....Harry Hebner, United States 1:21.2
1920....Warren Kealoha, United States 1:15.2
1924....Warren Kealoha, United States 1:13.2 OR
1928....George Kojac, United States 1:08.2 WR
1932....Masaji Kiyokawa, Japan 1:08.6
1936....Adolph Kiefer, United States 1:05.9 OR
1948....Allen Stack, United States 1:06.4
1952....Yoshi Oyakawa, United States 1:05.4 OR
1956....David Thiele, Australia 1:02.2 OR
1960....David Thiele, Australia 1:01.9 OR
1964....Not held
1968....Roland Matthes, East Germany 58.7 OR
1972....Roland Matthes, East Germany 56.58 OR
1976....John Naber, United States 55.49 WR
1980....Bengt Baron, Sweden 56.33
1984....Rick Carey, United States 55.79
1988....Daichi Suzuki, Japan 55.05
1992....Mark Tewksbury, Canada 53.98 WR

200-METER BACKSTROKE

1900....Ernst Hoppenberg, Germany 2:47.0
1904....Not held 1904-1960
1964....Jed Graef, United States 2:10.3 WR
1968....Roland Matthes, East Germany 2:09.6 OR
1972.....Roland Matthes, East Germany 2:02.82 EWR
1976....John Naber, United States 1:59.19 WR
1980....Sandor Wladar, Hungary 2:01.93
1984....Rick Carey, United States 2:00.23
1988....Igor Polianski, USSR 1:59.37
1992....Martin Lopez-Zubero, Spain 1:58.47 OR

100-METER BREASTSTROKE

1968....Don McKenzie, United States 1:07.7 OR
1972....Nobutaka Taguchi, Japan 1:04.94 WR
1976....John Hencken, United States 1:03.11 WR
1980....Duncan Goodhew, Great Britain 1:03.44
1984....Steve Lundquist, United States 1:01.65 WR
1988....Adrian Moorhouse, Great Britain 1:02.04
1992....Nelson Diebel, United States 1:01.50 OR

SWIMMING *(Cont.)*

Men *(Cont.)*

200-METER BREASTSTROKE

1908	Frederick Holman, Great Britain	3:09.2 WR
1912	Walter Bathe, Germany	3:01.8 OR
1920	Haken Malmroth, Sweden	3:04.4
1924	Robert Skelton, United States	2:56.6
1928	Yoshiyuki Tsuruta, Japan	2:48.8 OR
1932	Yoshiyuki Tsuruta, Japan	2:45.4
1936	Tetsuo Hamuro, Japan	2:41.5 OR
1948	Joseph Verdeur, United States	2:39.3 OR
1952	John Davies, Australia	2:34.4 OR
1956	Masura Furukawa, Japan	2:34.7 OR
1960	William Mulliken, United States	2:37.4
1964	Ian O'Brien, Australia	2:27.8 WR
1968	Felipe Munoz, Mexico	2:28.7
1972	John Hencken, United States	2:21.55 WR
1976	David Wilkie, Great Britain	2:15.11 WR
1980	Robertas Zhulpa, USSR	2:15.85
1984	Victor Davis, Canada	2:13.34 WR
1988	Jozsef Szabo, Hungary	2:13.52
1992	Mike Barrowman, United States	2:10.16 WR

100-METER BUTTERFLY

1968	Doug Russell, United States	55.9 OR
1972	Mark Spitz, United States	54.27 WR
1976	Matt Vogel, United States	54.35
1980	Pär Arvidsson, Sweden	54.92
1984	Michael Gross, West Germany	53.08 WR
1988	Anthony Nesty, Suriname	53.00 OR
1992	Pablo Morales, United States	53.32

200-METER BUTTERFLY

1956	William Yorzyk, United States	2:19.3 OR
1960	Michael Troy, United States	2:12.8 WR
1964	Kevin Berry, Australia	2:06.6 WR
1968	Carl Robie, United States	2:08.7
1972	Mark Spitz, United States	2:00.70 WR
1976	Mike Bruner, United States	1:59.23 WR
1980	Sergei Fesenko, USSR	1:59.76
1984	Jon Sieben, Australia	1:57.04 WR
1988	Michael Gross, West Germany	1:56.94 OR
1992	Melvin Stewart, United States	1:56.26 OR

200-METER INDIVIDUAL MEDLEY

1968	Charles Hickcox, United States	2:12.0 OR
1972	Gunnar Larsson, Sweden	2:07.17 WR
1984	Alex Baumann, Canada	2:01.42 WR
1988	Tamas Darnyi, Hungary	2:00.17 WR
1992	Tamas Darnyi, Hungary	2:00.76

400-METER INDIVIDUAL MEDLEY

1964	Richard Roth, United States	4:45.4 WR
1968	Charles Hickcox, United States	4:48.4
1972	Gunnar Larsson, Sweden	4:31.98 OR
1976	Rod Strachan, United States	4:23.68 WR
1980	Aleksandr Sidorenko, USSR	4:22.89 OR
1984	Alex Baumann, Canada	4:17.41 WR
1988	Tamas Darnyi, Hungary	4:14.75 WR
1992	Tamas Darnyi, Hungary	4:14.23 OR

4 X 100-METER MEDLEY RELAY

1960	United States	4:05.4 WR
1964	United States	3:58.4 WR
1968	United States	3:54.9 WR
1972	United States	3:48.16 WR
1976	United States	3:42.22 WR
1980	Australia	3:45.70
1984	United States	3:39.30 WR
1988	United States	3:36.93 WR
1992	United States	3:36.93 EWR

4 X 100-METER FREESTYLE RELAY

1964	United States	3:32.2 WR
1968	United States	3:31.7 WR
1972	United States	3:26.42 WR
1976-1980	Not held	
1984	United States	3:19.03 WR
1988	United States	3:16.53 WR
1992	United States	3:16.74

4 X 200-METER FREESTYLE RELAY

1906	Hungary (1000 m)	16:52.4
1908	Great Britain	10:55.6
1912	Australia/New Zealand	10:11.6 WR
1920	United States	10:04.4 WR
1924	United States	9:53.4 WR
1928	United States	9:36.2 WR
1932	Japan	8:58.4 WR
1936	Japan	8:51.5 WR
1948	United States	8:46.0 WR
1952	United States	8:31.1 OR
1956	Australia	8:23.6 WR
1960	United States	8:10.2 WR
1964	United States	7:52.1 WR
1968	United States	7:52.33
1972	United States	7:35.78 WR
1976	United States	7:23.22 WR
1980	USSR	7:23.50
1984	United States	7:15.69 WR
1988	United States	7:12.51 WR
1992	Unified Team	7:11.95 WR

Women

50-METER FREESTYLE

1988	Kristin Otto, East Germany	25.49 OR
1992	Yang Wenyi, China	24.79 WR

100-METER FREESTYLE

1912	Fanny Durack, Australia	1:22.2
1920	Ethelda Bleibtrey, United States	1:13.6 WR
1924	Ethel Lackie, United States	1:12.4
1928	Albina Osipowich, United States	1:11.0 OR

100-METER FREESTYLE *(Cont.)*

1932	Helene Madison, United States	1:06.8 OR
1936	Hendrika Mastenbroek, Netherlands	1:05.9 OR
1948	Greta Andersen, Denmark	1:06.3
1952	Katalin Szöke, Hungary	1:06.8
1956	Dawn Fraser, Australia	1:02.0 WR
1960	Dawn Fraser, Australia	1:01.2 OR
1964	Dawn Fraser, Australia	59.5 OR
1968	Jan Henne, United States	1:00.0

SWIMMING (Cont.)

Women (Cont.)

100-METER FREESTYLE (Cont.)

1972	Sandra Neilson, United States	58.59 OR
1976	Kornelia Ender, East Germany	55.65 WR
1980	Barbara Krause, East Germany	54.79 WR
1984	Carrie Steinseifer, United States	55.92
	Nancy Hogshead, United States	55.92
1988	Kristin Otto, East Germany	54.93
1992	Zhuang Yong, China	54.64 OR

200-METER FREESTYLE

1968	Debbie Meyer, United States	2:10.5 OR
1972	Shane Gould, Australia	2:03.56 WR
1976	Kornelia Ender, East Germany	1:59.26 WR
1980	Barbara Krause, East Germany	1:58.33 OR
1984	Mary Wayte, United States	1:59.23
1988	Heike Friedrich, East Germany	1:57.65 OR
1992	Nicole Haislett, United States	1:57.90

400-METER FREESTYLE

1924	Martha Norelius, United States	6:02.2 OR
1928	Martha Norelius, United States	5:42.8 WR
1932	Helene Madison, United States	5:28.5 WR
1936	Hendrika Mastenbroek, Netherlands	5:26.4 OR
1948	Ann Curtis, United States	5:17.8 OR
1952	Valeria Gyenge, Hungary	5:12.1 OR
1956	Lorraine Crapp, Australia	4:54.6 OR
1960	Chris von Saltza, United States	4:50.6 OR
1964	Virginia Duenkel, United States	4:43.3 OR
1968	Debbie Meyer, United States	4:31.8 OR
1972	Shane Gould, Australia	4:19.44 WR
1976	Petra Thümer, East Germany	4:09.89 WR
1980	Ines Diers, East Germany	4:08.76 WR
1984	Tiffany Cohen, United States	4:07.10 OR
1988	Janet Evans, United States	4:03.85 WR
1992	Dagmar Hase, Germany	4:07.18

800-METER FREESTYLE

1968	Debbie Meyer, United States	9:24.0 OR
1972	Keena Rothhammer, United States	8:53.68 WR
1976	Petra Thümer, East Germany	8:37.14 WR
1980	Michelle Ford, Australia	8:28.90 OR
1984	Tiffany Cohen, United States	8:24.95 OR
1988	Janet Evans, United States	8:20.20 OR
1992	Janet Evans, United States	8:25.52

100-METER BACKSTROKE

1924	Sybil Bauer, United States	1:23.2 OR
1928	Marie Braun, Netherlands	1:22.0
1932	Eleanor Holm, United States	1:19.4
1936	Dina Senff, Netherlands	1:18.9
1948	Karen Harup, Denmark	1:14.4 OR
1952	Joan Harrison, South Africa	1:14.3
1956	Judy Grinham, Great Britain	1:12.9 OR
1960	Lynn Burke, United States	1:09.3 OR
1964	Cathy Ferguson, United States	1:07.7 WR
1968	Kaye Hall, United States	1:06.2 WR
1972	Melissa Belote, United States	1:05.78 OR
1976	Ulrike Richter, East Germany	1:01.83 OR
1980	Rica Reinisch, East Germany	1:00.86 WR
1984	Theresa Andrews, United States	1:02.55
1988	Kristin Otto, East Germany	1:00.89
1992	Krisztina Egerszegi, Hungary	1:00.68 OR

200-METER BACKSTROKE

1968	Pokey Watson, United States	2:24.8 OR
1972	Melissa Belote, United States	2:19.19 WR
1976	Ulrike Richter, East Germany	2:13.43 OR
1980	Rica Reinisch, East Germany	2:11.77 WR
1984	Jolanda De Rover, Netherlands	2:12.38
1988	Krisztina Egerszegi, Hungary	2:09.29 OR
1992	Krisztina Egerszegi, Hungary	2:07.06

100-METER BREASTSTROKE

1968	Djurdjica Bjedov, Yugoslavia	1:15.8 OR
1972	Catherine Carr, United States	1:13.58 WR
1976	Hannelore Anke, East Germany	1:11.16
1980	Ute Geweniger, East Germany	1:10.22
1984	Petra Van Staveren, Netherlands	1:09.88 OR
1988	Tania Dangalakova, Bulgaria	1:07.95 OR
1992	Elena Roudkovskaia, Unified Team	1:08.00

200-METER BREASTSTROKE

1924	Lucy Morton, Great Britain	3:33.2 OR
1928	Hilde Schrader, Germany	3:12.6
1932	Clare Dennis, Australia	3:06.3 OR
1936	Hideko Maehata, Japan	3:03.6
1948	Petronella Van Vliet, Netherlands	2:57.2
1952	Eva Szekely, Hungary	2:51.7 OR
1956	Ursula Happe, West Germany	2:53.1 OR
1960	Anita Lonsbrough, Great Britain	2:49.5 WR
1964	Galina Prozumenshikova, USSR	2:46.4 OR
1968	Sharon Wichman, United States	2:44.4 OR
1972	Beverly Whitfield, Australia	2:41.71 OR
1976	Marina Koshevaia, USSR	2:33.35 WR
1980	Lina Kaciusyte, USSR	2:29.54 OR
1984	Anne Ottenbrite, Canada	2:30.38
1988	Silke Hoerner, East Germany	2:26.71 WR
1992	Kyoko Iwasaki, Japan	2:26.65 OR

100-METER BUTTERFLY

1956	Shelley Mann, United States	1:11.0 OR
1960	Carolyn Schuler, United States	1:09.5 OR
1964	Sharon Stouder, United States	1:04.7 WR
1968	Lynn McClements, Australia	1:05.5
1972	Mayumi Aoki, Japan	1:03.34 WR
1976	Kornelia Ender, East Germany	1:00.13 EWR
1980	Caren Metschuck, East Germany	1:00.42
1984	Mary T. Meagher, United States	59.26
1988	Kristin Otto, East Germany	59.00 OR
1992	Qian Hong, China	58.62 OR

200-METER BUTTERFLY

1968	Ada Kok, Netherlands	2:24.7 OR
1972	Karen Moe, United States	2:15.57 WR
1976	Andrea Pollack, East Germany	2:11.41 OR
1980	Ines Geissler, East Germany	2:10.44 OR
1984	Mary T. Meagher, United States	2:06.90 OR
1988	Kathleen Nord, East Germany	2:09.51
1992	Summer Sanders, United States	2:08.67

200-METER INDIVIDUAL MEDLEY

1968	Claudia Kolb, United States	2:24.7 OR
1972	Shane Gould, Australia	2:23.07 WR
1976	Not held 1976-1980	
1984	Tracy Caulkins, United States	2:12.64 OR

SWIMMING (Cont.)

Women (Cont.)

200-METER INDIVIDUAL MEDLEY (Cont.)

1988	Daniela Hunger, East Germany	2:12.59 OR
1992	Lin Li, China	2:11.65 WR

400-METER INDIVIDUAL MEDLEY

1964	Donna de Varona, United States	5:18.7 OR
1968	Claudia Kolb, United States	5:08.5 OR
1972	Gail Neall, Australia	5:02.97 WR
1976	Ulrike Tauber, East Germany	4:42.77 WR
1980	Petra Schneider, East Germany	4:36.29 WR
1984	Tracy Caulkins, United States	4:39.24
1988	Janet Evans, United States	4:37.76
1992	Krisztina Egerszegi, Hungary	4:36.54

4 X 100-METER MEDLEY RELAY

1960	United States	4:41.1 WR
1964	United States	4:33.9 WR
1968	United States	4:28.3 OR
1972	United States	4:20.75 WR
1976	East Germany	4:07.95 WR
1980	East Germany	4:06.67 WR
1984	United States	4:08.34
1988	East Germany	4:03.74 OR
1992	United States	4:02.54 WR

4 X 100-METER FREESTYLE RELAY

1912	Great Britain	5:52.8 WR
1920	United States	5:11.6 WR
1924	United States	4:58.8 WR
1928	United States	4:47.6 WR
1932	United States	4:38.0 WR
1936	Netherlands	4:36.0 OR
1948	United States	4:29.2 OR
1952	Hungary	4:24.4 WR
1956	Australia	4:17.1 WR
1960	United States	4:08.9 WR
1964	United States	4:03.8 WR
1968	United States	4:02.5 OR
1972	United States	3:55.19 WR
1976	United States	3:44.82 WR
1980	East Germany	3:42.71 WR
1984	United States	3:43.43
1988	East Germany	3:40.63 OR
1992	United States	3:39.46 WR

DIVING

Men

SPRINGBOARD

		Pts
1908	Albert Zürner, Germany	85.5
1912	Paul Günther, Germany	79.23
1920	Louis Kuehn, United States	675.40
1924	Albert White, United States	97.46
1928	Pete DesJardins, United States	185.04
1932	Michael Galitzen, United States	161.38
1936	Richard Degener, United States	163.57
1948	Bruce Harlan, United States	163.64
1952	David Browning, United States	205.29
1956	Robert Clotworthy, United States	159.56
1960	Gary Tobian, United States	170.00
1964	Kenneth Sitzberger, United States	159.90
1968	Bernie Wrightson, United States	170.15
1972	Vladimir Vasin, USSR	594.09
1976	Phil Boggs, United States	619.05
1980	Aleksandr Portnov, USSR	905.02
1984	Greg Louganis, United States	754.41
1988	Greg Louganis, United States	730.80
1992	Mark Lenzi, United States	676.53

PLATFORM

		Pts
1904	George Sheldon, United States	12.66
1906	Gottlob Walz, Germany	156.0
1908	Hjalmar Johansson, Sweden	83.75
1912	Erik Adlerz, Sweden	73.94
1920	Clarence Pinkston, United States	100.67
1924	Albert White, United States	97.46
1928	Pete DesJardins, United States	98.74
1932	Harold Smith, United States	124.80
1936	Marshall Wayne, United States	113.58
1948	Sammy Lee, United States	130.05
1952	Sammy Lee, United States	156.28
1956	Joaquin Capilla, Mexico	152.44
1960	Robert Webster, United States	165.56
1964	Robert Webster, United States	148.58
1968	Klaus Dibiasi, Italy	164.18
1972	Klaus Dibiasi, Italy	504.12
1976	Klaus Dibiasi, Italy	600.51
1980	Falk Hoffmann, East Germany	835.65
1984	Greg Louganis, United States	710.91
1988	Greg Louganis, United States	638.61
1992	Sun Shuwei, China	677.31

Women

SPRINGBOARD

		Pts
1920	Aileen Riggin, United States	539.90
1924	Elizabeth Becker, United States	474.50
1928	Helen Meany, United States	78.62
1932	Georgia Coleman, United States	87.52
1936	Marjorie Gestring, United States	89.27
1948	Victoria Draves, United States	108.74

SPRINGBOARD (Cont.)

		Pts
1952	Patricia McCormick, United States	147.30
1956	Patricia McCormick, United States	142.36
1960	Ingrid Krämer, East Germany	155.81
1964	Ingrid Engel Krämer, East Germany	145.00
1968	Sue Gossick, United States	150.77

DIVING (Cont.)

Women (Cont.)

SPRINGBOARD (Cont.)

		Pts
1972	Micki King, United States	450.03
1976	Jennifer Chandler, United States	506.19
1980	Irina Kalinina, USSR	725.91
1984	Sylvie Bernier, Canada	530.70
1988	Gao Min, China	580.23
1992	Gao Min, China	572.40

PLATFORM

		Pts
1912	Greta Johansson, Sweden	39.90
1920	Stefani Fryland-Clausen, Denmark	34.60
1924	Caroline Smith, United States	33.20
1928	Elizabeth B. Pinkston, United States	31.60

PLATFORM (CONT.)

		Pts
1932	Dorothy Poynton, United States	40.26
1936	Dorothy Poynton Hill, United States	33.93
1948	Victoria Draves, United States	68.87
1952	Patricia McCormick, United States	79.37
1956	Patricia McCormick, United States	84.85
1960	Ingrid Krämer, East Germany	91.28
1964	Lesley Bush, United States	99.80
1968	Milena Duchkova, Czechoslovakia	109.59
1972	Ulrika Knape, Sweden	390.00
1976	Elena Vaytsekhovskaya, USSR	406.59
1980	Martina Jäschke, East Germany	596.25
1984	Zhou Jihong, China	435.51
1988	Xu Yanmei, China	445.20
1992	Fu Mingxia, China	461.43

GYMNASTICS

Men

ALL-AROUND

		Pts
1900	Gustave Sandras, France	302
1904	Julius Lenhart, Austria	69.80
1906	Pierre Paysse, France	97
1908	Alberto Braglia, Italy	317.0
1912	Alberto Braglia, Italy	135.0
1920	Giorgio Zampori, Italy	88.35
1924	Leon Stukelj, Yugoslavia	110.340
1928	Georges Miez, Switzerland	247.500
1932	Romeo Neri, Italy	140.625
1936	Alfred Schwarzmann, Germany	113.100
1948	Veikko Huhtanen, Finland	229.70
1952	Viktor Chukarin, USSR	115.70
1956	Viktor Chukarin, USSR	114.25
1960	Boris Shakhlin, USSR	115.95
1964	Yukio Endo, Japan	115.95
1968	Sawao Kato, Japan	115.90
1972	Sawao Kato, Japan	114.65
1976	Nikolai Andrianov, USSR	116.65
1980	Aleksandr Dityatin, USSR	118.65
1984	Koji Gushiken, Japan	118.70
1988	Vladimir Artemov, USSR	119.125
1992	Vitaly Scherbo, Unified Team	59.025

HORIZONTAL BAR

		Pts
1896	Hermann Weingärtner, Germany	—
1900	Not held	
1904	Anton Heida, United States	40
1908-20	Not held	
1924	Leon Stukelj, Yugoslavia	19.73
1928	Georges Miez, Switzerland	19.17
1932	Dallas Bixler, United States	18.33
1936	Aleksanteri Saarvala, Finland	19.367
1948	Josef Stafler, Switzerland	19.85
1952	Jack Günthard, Switzerland	19.55
1956	Takashi Ono, Japan	19.60
1960	Takashi Ono, Japan	19.60
1964	Boris Shakhlin, USSR	19.625
1968	Akinori Nakayama, Japan	19.55
1972	Mitsuo Tsukahara, Japan	19.725

HORIZONTAL BAR (Cont.)

		Pts
1976	Mitsuo Tsukahara, Japan	19.675
1980	Stoyan Deltchev, Bulgaria	19.825
1984	Shinji Morisue, Japan	20.00
1988	Vladimir Artemov, USSR	19.90
1992	Trent Dimas, United States	9.875

PARALLEL BARS

		Pts
1896	Alfred Flatow, Germany	—
1900	Not held	
1904	George Eyser, United States	44
1908-20	Not held	
1924	August Güttinger, Switzerland	21.63
1928	Ladislav Vacha, Czechoslovakia	18.83
1932	Romeo Neri, Italy	18.97
1936	Konrad Frey, Germany	19.067
1948	Michael Reusch, Switzerland	19.75
1952	Hans Eugster, Switzerland	19.65
1956	Viktor Chukarin, USSR	19.20
1960	Boris Shakhlin, USSR	19.40
1964	Yukio Endo, Japan	19.675
1968	Akinori Nakayama, Japan	19.475
1972	Sawao Kato, Japan	19.475
1976	Sawao Kato, Japan	19.675
1980	Aleksandr Tkachyov, USSR	19.775
1984	Bart Conner, United States	19.95
1988	Vladimir Artemov, USSR	19.925
1992	Vitaly Scherbo, Unified Team	9.900

LONG HORSE VAULT

		Pts
1896	Karl Schumann, Germany	—
1900	Not held	
1904	George Eyser, United States	36
1908-20	Not held	
1924	Frank Kriz, United States	9.98
1928	Eugen Mack, Switzerland	9.58
1932	Savino Guglielmetti, Italy	18.03
1936	Alfred Schwarzmann, Germany	19.20
1948	Paavo Aaltonen, Finland	19.55

GYMNASTICS (Cont.)

Men (Cont.)

LONG HORSE VAULT (Cont.)

	Pts
1952 .....Viktor Chukarin, USSR	19.20
1956 .....Helmut Bantz, Germany	18.85
1960 .....Takashi Ono, Japan	19.35
1964 .....Haruhiro Yamashita, Japan	19.60
1968 .....Mikhail Voronin, USSR	19.00
1972 .....Klaus Köste, East Germany	18.85
1976 .....Nikolai Andrianov, USSR	19.45
1980 .....Nikolai Andrianov, USSR	19.825
1984 .....Lou Yun, China	19.95
1988 .....Lou Yun, China	19.875
1992 .....Vitaly Scherbo, Unified Team	9.856

SIDE HORSE

	Pts
1896 .....Louis Zutter, Switzerland	—
1900 .....Not held	
1904 .....Anton Heida, United States	42
1908-20.Not held	
1924 .....Josef Wilhelm, Switzerland	21.23
1928 .....Hermann Hänggi, Switzerland	19.75
1932 .....Istvan Pelle, Hungary	19.07
1936 .....Konrad Frey, Germany	19.333
1948 .....Paavo Aaltonen, Finland	19.35
1952 .....Viktor Chukarin, USSR	19.50
1956 .....Boris Shakhlin, USSR	19.25
1960 .....Eugen Ekman, Finland	19.375
1964 .....Miroslav Cerar, Yugoslavia	19.525
1968 .....Miroslav Cerar, Yugoslavia	19.325
1972 .....Viktor Klimenko, USSR	19.125
1976 .....Zoltan Magyar, Hungary	19.70
1980 .....Zoltan Magyar, Hungary	19.925
1984 .....Li Ning, China	19.95
1988 .....Dmitri Bilozerchev, USSR	19.95
1992 .....Vitaly Scherbo, Unified Team	9.925

RINGS

	Pts
1896 .....Ioannis Mitropoulos, Greece	—
1900 .....Not held	
1904 .....Hermann Glass, United States	45
1908-20.Not held	
1924 .....Francesco Martino, Italy	21.553
1928 .....Leon Stukelj, Yugoslavia	19.25
1932 .....George Gulack, United States	18.97
1936 .....Alois Hudec, Czechoslovakia	19.433
1948 .....Karl Frei, Switzerland	19.80
1952 .....Grant Shaginyan, USSR	19.75
1956 .....Albert Azaryan, USSR	19.35
1960 .....Albert Azaryan, USSR	19.725
1964 .....Takuji Haytta, Japan	19.475
1968 .....Akinori Nakayama, Japan	19.45

RINGS (Cont.)

	Pts
1972 .....Akinori Nakayama, Japan	19.35
1976 .....Nikolai Andrianov, USSR	19.65
1980 .....Aleksandr Dityatin, USSR	19.875
1984 .....Koji Gushiken, Japan	19.85
1988 .....Holger Behrendt, East Germany	19.925
1992 .....Vitaly Scherbo, Unified Team	9.937

FLOOR EXERCISES

	Pts
1896-28.Not held	
1932 .....Istvan Pelle, Hungary	9.60
1936 .....Georges Miez, Switzerland	18.666
1948 .....Ferenc Pataki, Hungary	19.35
1952 .....K. William Thoresson, Sweden	19.25
1956 .....Valentin Muratov, USSR	19.20
1960 .....Nobuyuki Aihara, Japan	19.45
1964 .....Franco Menichelli, Italy	19.45
1968 .....Sawao Kato, Japan	19.475
1972 .....Nikolai Andrianov, USSR	19.175
1976 .....Nikolai Andrianov, USSR	19.45
1980 .....Roland Brückner, East Germany	19.75
1984 .....Li Ning, China	19.925
1988 .....Sergei Kharkov, USSR	19.925
1992 .....Li Xiaosahuang, China	9.925

TEAM COMBINED EXERCISES

	Pts
1896-00..Not held	
1904 .....Turngemeinde Philadelphia	374.43
1906 .....Norway	19.00
1908 .....Sweden	438
1912 .....Italy	265.75
1920 .....Italy	359.855
1924 .....Italy	839.058
1928 .....Switzerland	1718.625
1932 .....Italy	541.850
1936 .....Germany	657.430
1948 .....Finland	1358.30
1952 .....USSR	574.40
1956 .....USSR	568.25
1960 .....Japan	575.20
1964 .....Japan	577.95
1968 .....Japan	575.90
1972 .....Japan	571.25
1976 .....Japan	576.85
1980 .....USSR	598.60
1984 .....United States	591.40
1988 .....USSR	593.35
1992 .....Unified Team	585.450

GYMNASTICS (Cont.)

Women

ALL-AROUND

		Pts
1952	Maria Gorokhovskaya, USSR	76.78
1956	Larissa Latynina, USSR	74.933
1960	Larissa Latynina, USSR	77.031
1964	Vera Caslavska, Czechoslovakia	77.564
1968	Vera Caslavska, Czechoslovakia	78.25
1972	Lyudmila Tousischeva, USSR	77.025
1976	Nadia Comaneci, Romania	79.275
1980	Yelena Davydova, USSR	79.15
1984	Mary Lou Retton, United States	79.175
1988	Yelena Shushunova, USSR	79.662
1992	Tatiana Gutsu, Unified Team	39.737

SIDE HORSE VAULT

		Pts
1952	Yekaterina Kalinchuk, USSR	19.20
1956	Larissa Latynina, USSR	18.833
1960	Margarita Nikolayeva, USSR	19.316
1964	Vera Caslavska, Czechoslovakia	19.483
1968	Vera Caslavska, Czechoslovakia	19.775
1972	Karin Janz, East Germany	19.525
1976	Nelli Kim, USSR	19.80
1980	Natalya Shaposhnikova, USSR	19.725
1984	Ecaterina Szabo, Romania	19.875
1988	Svetlana Boginskaya, USSR	19.905
1992	Henrietta Onodi, Hungary	9.925
	Lavinia Milosovici, Romania	9.925

UNEVEN BARS

		Pts
1952	Margit Korondi, Hungary	19.40
1956	Agnes Keleti, Hungary	18.966
1960	Polina Astakhova, USSR	19.616
1964	Polina Astakhova, USSR	19.332
1968	Vera Caslavska, Czechoslovakia	19.65
1972	Karin Janz, East Germany	19.675
1976	Nadia Comaneci, Romania	20.00
1980	Maxi Gnauck, East Germany	19.875
1984	Ma Yanhong, China	19.95
1988	Daniela Silivas, Romania	20.00
1992	Lu Li, China	10.00

BALANCE BEAM

		Pts
1952	Nina Bocharova, USSR	19.22
1956	Agnes Keleti, Hungary	18.80
1960	Eva Bosakova, Czechoslovakia	19.283

BALANCE BEAM (Cont.)

		Pts
1964	Vera Caslavska, Czechoslovakia	19.449
1968	Natalya Kuchinskaya, USSR	19.65
1972	Olga Korbut, USSR	19.40
1976	Nadia Comaneci, Romania	19.95
1980	Nadia Comaneci, Romania	19.80
1984	Simona Pauca, Romania	19.80
1988	Daniela Silivas, Romania	19.924
1992	Tatiana Lisenko, Unified Team	9.975

FLOOR EXERCISES

		Pts
1952	Agnes Keleti, Hungary	19.36
1956	Agnes Keleti, Hungary	18.733
1960	Larissa Latynina, USSR	19.583
1964	Larissa Latynina, USSR	19.599
1968	Vera Caslavska, Czechoslovakia	19.675
1972	Olga Korbut, USSR	19.575
1976	Nelli Kim, USSR	19.85
1980	Nadia Comaneci, Romania	19.875
1984	Ecaterina Szabo, Romania	19.975
1988	Daniela Silivas, Romania	19.937
1992	Lavinia Milosovici, Romania	10.00

TEAM COMBINED EXERCISES

		Pts
1928	Holland	316.75
1932	Not held	
1936	Germany	506.50
1948	Czechoslovakia	445.45
1952	USSR	527.03
1956	USSR	444.800
1960	USSR	382.320
1964	USSR	280.890
1968	USSR	382.85
1972	USSR	380.50
1976	USSR	466.00
1980	USSR	394.90
1984	Romania	392.02
1988	USSR	395.475
1992	Unified Team	395.666

RHYTHMIC ALL-AROUND

		Pts
1984	Lori Fung, Canada	57.95
1988	Marina Lobach, USSR	60.00
1992	Aleksandra Timoshenko, UTeam	59.037

A Bumpy Ride

The U.S. bobsled team was hopeful that a new bobsled financed by 1986 Daytona 500 winner Geoff Bodine and designed by race-car builder Robert Cuneo would glide its way to a medal at the Winter Games in Lillehammer next year. Then, much to the consternation of the team and its supporters, the sled was banned from its first World Cup race in March due to its unusual bodywork.

Before the sled was banned, however, it was among the five fastest in practice and its chassis, which Cuneo asserts contains most of its advantages, was given written approval by officials. He is confident that a redesigned version of the sled, with new bodywork but still including the speedy chassis, will be ready in time for the Olympic competition in Lillehammer in 1994.

BIATHLON

Men

10 KILOMETERS

1980	Frank Ullrich, East Germany	32:10.69
1984	Eirik Kvalfoss, Norway	30:53.8
1988	Frank-Peter Rötsch, W Germany	25:08.1
1992	Mark Kirchner, Germany	26:02.3

20 KILOMETERS

1960	Klas Lestander, Sweden	1:33:21.6
1964	Vladimir Melyanin, Soviet Union	1:20:26.8
1968	Magnar Solberg, Norway	1:13:45.9
1972	Magnar Solberg, Norway	1:15:55.5
1976	Nikolay Kruglov, Soviet Union	1:14:12.26
1980	Anatoliy Alyabiev, Soviet Union	1:08:16.31

20 KILOMETERS *(Cont.)*

1984	Peter Angerer, W Germany	1:11:52.7
1988	Frank-Peter Rötsch, W Germany	56:33.3
1992	Evgueni Redkine, Unified Team	57:34.4

4 X 7.5-KILOMETER RELAY

1968	Soviet Union	2:13:02.4
1972	Soviet Union	1:51:44.92
1976	Soviet Union	1:57:55.64
1980	Soviet Union	1:34:03.27
1984	Soviet Union	1:38:51.7
1988	Soviet Union	1:22:30.0
1992	Germany	1:24:43.5

Women

7.5 KILOMETERS

1992	Antissa Restzova, Unified Team	24.29.2

15 KILOMETERS

1992	Antje Misersky, Germany	51:47.2

3 X 7.5-KILOMETER RELAY

1992	France	1:15:55.6

BOBSLED

4-MAN BOB

1924	Switzerland (Eduard Scherrer)	5:45.54
1928	United States (William Fiske) (5-man)	3:20.50
1932	United States (William Fiske)	7:53.68
1936	Switzerland (Pierre Musy)	5:19.85
1948	United States (Francis Tyler)	5:20.10
1952	Germany (Andreas Ostler)	5:07.84
1956	Switzerland (Franz Kapus)	5:10.44
1960	Not held	
1964	Canada (Victor Emery)	4:14.46
1968	Italy (Eugenio Monti) (2 runs)	2:17.39
1972	Switzerland (Jean Wicki)	4:43.07
1976	East Germany (Meinhard Nehmer)	3:40.43
1980	East Germany (Meinhard Nehmer)	3:59.92
1984	East Germany (Wolfgang Hoppe)	3:20.22
1988	Switzerland (Ekkehard Fasser)	3:47.51
1992	Austria (Ingo Appelt)	3:53.90

Note: Driver in parentheses.

2-MAN BOB

1932	United States (Hubert Stevens)	8:14.74
1936	United States (Ivan Brown)	5:29.29
1948	Switzerland (Felix Endrich)	5:29.20
1952	Germany (Andreas Ostler)	5:24.54
1956	Italy (Lamberto Dalla Costa)	5:30.14
1960	Not held	
1964	Great Britain (Anthony Nash)	4:21.90
1968	Italy (Eugenio Monti)	4:41.54
1972	West Germany (Wolfgang Zimmerer)	4:57.07
1976	East Germany (Meinhard Nehmer)	3:44.42
1980	Switzerland (Erich Schärer)	4:09.36
1984	East Germany (Wolfgang Hoppe)	3:25.56
1988	USSR (Janis Kipours)	3:53.48
1992	Switzerland (Gustav Weder)	4:03.26

Note: Driver in parentheses.

ICE HOCKEY

1920*	Canada, United States, Czechoslovakia
1924	Canada, United States, Great Britain
1928	Canada, Sweden, Switzerland
1932	Canada, United States, Germany
1936	Great Britain, Canada, United States
1948	Canada, Czechoslovakia, Switzerland
1952	Canada, United States, Sweden
1956	USSR, United States, Canada
1960	United States, Canada, USSR
1964	USSR, Sweden, Czechoslovakia
1968	USSR, Czechoslovakia, Canada
1972	USSR, United States, Czechoslovakia
1976	USSR, Czechoslovakia, West Germany
1980	United States, USSR, Sweden
1984	USSR, Czechoslovakia, Sweden
1988	USSR, Finland, Sweden
1992	Unified Team, Canada, Czechoslovakia

*Competition held at summer games in Antwerp.
Note: Gold, silver, and bronze medals.

LUGE

Men

SINGLES			DOUBLES		
1964	Thomas Köhler, East Germany	3:26.77	1964	Austria	1:41.62
1968	Manfred Schmid, Austria	2:52.48	1968	East Germany	1:35.85
1972	Wolfgang Scheidel, W Germany	3:27.58	1972	East Germany	1:28.35
1976	Detlef Guenther, West Germany	3:27.688	1976	East Germany	1:25.604
1980	Bernhard Glass, West Germany	2:54.796	1980	East Germany	1:19.331
1984	Paul Hildgartner, Italy	3:04.258	1984	West Germany	1:23.620
1988	Jens Müller, West Germany	3:05.548	1988	East Germany	1:31.940
1992	Georg Hackl, Germany	3:02.363	1992	Germany	1:32.053

Women

SINGLES			SINGLES (Cont.)		
1964	Ortrun Enderlein, Germany	3:24.67	1980	Vera Zozulya, USSR	2:36.537
1968	Erica Lechner, Italy	2:28.66	1984	Steffi Martin, East Germany	2:46.570
1972	Anna-Maria Müller, East Germany	2:59.18	1988	Steffi Walter (Martin) E Germany	3:03.973
1976	Margit Schumann, East Germany	2:50.621	1992	Doris Neuner, Austria	3:06.696

FIGURE SKATING

Men

SINGLES		SINGLES (Cont.)	
1908*	Ulrich Salchow, Sweden	1964	Manfred Schnelldorfer, West Germany
1920†	Gillis Grafström, Sweden	1968	Wolfgang Schwarz, Austria
1924	Gillis Grafström, Sweden	1972	Ondrej Nepela, Czechoslovakia
1928	Gillis Grafström, Sweden	1976	John Curry, Great Britain
1932	Karl Schäfer, Austria	1980	Robin Cousins, Great Britain
1936	Karl Schäfer, Austria	1984	Scott Hamilton, United States
1948	Dick Button, United States	1988	Brian Boitano, United States
1952	Dick Button, United States	1992	Victor Petrenko, Unified Team
1956	Hayes Alan Jenkins, United States		
1960	David Jenkins, United States		

*Competition held at summer games in London
†Competition held at summer games in Antwerp

Women

SINGLES		SINGLES (Cont.)	
1908*	Madge Syers, Great Britain	1964	Sjoukje Dijkstra, Netherlands
1920†	Magda Julin, Sweden	1968	Peggy Fleming, United States
1924	Herma Szabo-Planck, Austria	1972	Beatrix Schuba, Austria
1928	Sonja Henie, Norway	1976	Dorothy Hamill, United States
1932	Sonja Henie, Norway	1980	Anett Pötzsch, East Germany
1936	Sonja Henie, Norway	1984	Katarina Witt, East Germany
1948	Barbara Ann Scott, Canada	1988	Katarina Witt, East Germany
1952	Jeanette Altwegg, Great Britain	1992	Kristi Yamaguchi, United States
1956	Tenley Albright, United States		
1960	Carol Heiss, United States		

*Competition held at summer games in London
†Competition held at summer games in Antwerp

FIGURE SKATING (Cont.)

Mixed

PAIRS

1908* ..Anna Hübler & Heinrich Burger, Germany
1920#..Ludovika & Walter Jakobsson, Finland
1924....Helene Engelmann & Alfred Berger, Austria
1928....Andree Joly & Pierre Brunet, France
1932....Andree Brunet (Joly) & Pierre Brunet, France
1936....Maxi Herber & Ernst Baier, Germany
1948....Micheline Lannoy & Pierre Baugniet, Belgium
1952....Ria Falk and Paul Falk, West Germany
1956....Elisabeth Schwartz & Kurt Oppelt, Austria
1960....Barbara Wagner & Robert Paul, Canada
1964....Lyudmila Beloussova & Oleg Protopopov, USSR
1968....Lyudmila Beloussova & Oleg Protopopov, USSR
1972....Irina Rodnina & Alexei Ulanov, USSR
1976....Irina Rodnina & Aleksandr Zaitzev, USSR

PAIRS (Cont.)

1980....Irina Rodnina & Aleksandr Zaitzev, USSR
1984....Elena Valova & Oleg Vasiliev, USSR
1988....Ekaterina Gordeeva & Sergei Grinkov, USSR
1992....Natalia Michkouteniok & Artour Dmitriev, Unified Team

ICE DANCING

1976....Lyudmila Pakhomova & Aleksandr Gorshkov, USSR
1980....Natalia Linichuk & Gennadi Karponosov, USSR
1984....Jayne Torvill & Christopher Dean, Great Britain
1988....Natalia Bestemianova & Andrei Bukin, USSR
1992....Marina Klimova & Sergei Ponomarenko, Unified Team

*Competition held at summer games in London.
#Competition held at summer games in Antwerp.

SPEED SKATING

Men

500 METERS

1924	Charles Jewtraw, United States	44.0
1928	Clas Thunberg, Finland	43.4 OR
	Bernt Evensen, Norway	43.4 OR
1932	John Shea, United States	43.4 EOR
1936	Ivar Ballangrud, Norway	43.4 EOR
1948	Finn Helgesen, Norway	43.1 OR
1952	Kenneth Henry, United States	43.2
1956	Yevgeny Grishin, USSR	40.2 EWR
1960	Yevgeny Grishin, USSR	40.2 EWR
1964	Terry McDermott, United States	40.1 OR
1968	Erhard Keller, West Germany	40.3
1972	Erhard Keller, West Germany	39.44 OR
1976	Yevgeny Kulikov, USSR	39.17 OR
1980	Eric Heiden, United States	38.03 OR
1984	Sergei Fokichev, USSR	38.19
1988	Uwe-Jens Mey, East Germany	36.45 WR
1992	Uwe-Jens Mey, East Germany	37.14

1000 METERS

1976	Peter Mueller, United States	1:19.32
1980	Eric Heiden, United States	1:15.18 OR
1984	Gaetan Boucher, Canada	1:15.80
1988	Nikolai Gulyaev, USSR	1:13.03 OR
1992	Olaf Zinke, Germany	1:14.85

1500 METERS

1924	Clas Thunberg, Finland	2:20.8
1928	Clas Thunberg, Finland	2:21.1
1932	John Shea, United States	2:57.5
1936	Charles Mathisen, Norway	2:19.2 OR
1948	Sverre Farstad, Norway	2:17.6 OR

1500 METERS (Cont.)

1952	Hjalmar Andersen, Norway	2:20.4
1956	Yevgeny Grishin, USSR	2:08.6 WR
	Yuri Mikhailov, USSR	2:08.6 WR
1960	Roald Aas, Norway	2:10.4
	Yevgeny Grishin, USSR	2:10.4
1964	Ants Anston, USSR	2:10.3
1968	Cornelis Verkerk, Netherlands	2:03.4 OR
1972	Ard Schenk, Netherlands	2:02.96 OR
1976	Jan Egil Storholt, Norway	1:59.38 OR
1980	Eric Heiden, United States	1:55.44 OR
1984	Gaetan Boucher, Canada	1:58.36
1988	Andre Hoffmann, East Germany	1:52.06 WR
1992	Johann Koss, Norway	1:54.81

5000 METERS

1924	Clas Thunberg, Finland	8:39.0
1928	Ivar Ballangrud, Norway	8:50.5
1932	Irving Jaffee, United States	9:40.8
1936	Ivar Ballangrud, Norway	8:19.6 OR
1948	Reidar Liaklev, Norway	8:29.4
1952	Hjalmar Andersen, Norway	8:10.6 OR
1956	Boris Shilkov, USSR	7:48.7 OR
1960	Viktor Kosichkin, USSR	7:51.3
1964	Knut Johannesen, Norway	7:38.4 OR
1968	Fred Anton Maier, Norway	7:22.4 WR
1972	Ard Schenk, Netherlands	7:23.61
1976	Sten Stensen, Norway	7:24.48
1980	Eric Heiden, United States	7:02.29 OR
1984	Sven Tomas Gustafson, Sweden	7:12.28
1988	Tomas Gustafson, Sweden	6:44.63 WR
1992	Geir Karlstad, Norway	6:59.97

SPEED SKATING (Cont.)

Men (Cont.)

10,000 METERS

1924	Julius Skutnabb, Finland	18:04.8
1928	Not held, thawing of ice	
1932	Irving Jaffee, United States	19:13.6
1936	Ivar Ballangrud, Norway	17:24.3 OR
1948	Ake Seyffarth, Sweden	17:26.3
1952	Hjalmar Andersen, Norway	16:45.8 OR
1956	Sigvard Ericsson, Sweden	16:35.9 OR
1960	Knut Johannesen, Norway	15:46.6 WR

10,000 METERS (Cont.)

1964	Jonny Nilsson, Sweden	15:50.1
1968	Johnny Höglin, Sweden	15:23.6 OR
1972	Ard Schenk, Netherlands	15:01.35 OR
1976	Piet Kleine, Netherlands	14:50.59 OR
1980	Eric Heiden, United States	14:28.13 WR
1984	Igor Malkov, USSR	14:39.90
1988	Tomas Gustafson, Sweden	13:48.20 WR
1992	Bart Veldkamp, The Netherlands	14:12.12

Women

500 METERS

1960	Helga Haase, East Germany	45.9
1964	Lydia Skoblikova, USSR	45.0 OR
1968	Lyudmila Titova, USSR	46.1
1972	Anne Henning, United States	43.33 OR
1976	Sheila Young, United States	42.76 OR
1980	Karin Enke, East Germany	41.78 OR
1984	Christa Rothenburger, East Germany	41.02 OR
1988	Bonnie Blair, United States	39.10 WR
1992	Bonnie Blair, United States	40.33

1000 METERS

1960	Klara Guseva, USSR	1:34.1
1964	Lydia Skoblikova, USSR	1:33.2 OR
1968	Carolina Geijssen, Netherlands	1:32.6 OR
1972	Monika Pflug, West Germany	1:31.40 OR
1976	Tatiana Averina, USSR	1:28.43 OR
1980	Natalya Petruseva, USSR	1:24.10 OR
1984	Karin Enke, East Germany	1:21.61 OR
1988	Christa Rothenburger, East Germany	1:17.65 WR
1992	Bonnie Blair, United States	1:21.90

1500 METERS

1960	Lydia Skoblikova, USSR	2:25.2 WR
1964	Lydia Skoblikova, USSR	2:22.6 OR

1500 METERS (Cont.)

1968	Kaija Mustonen, Finland	2:22.4 OR
1972	Dianne Holum, United States	2:20.85 OR
1976	Galina Stepanskaya, USSR	2:16.58 OR
1980	Anne Borckink, Netherlands	2:10.95 OR
1984	Karin Enke, East Germany	2:03.42 WR
1988	Yvonne van Gennip, Netherlands	2:00.68 OR
1992	Jacqueline Boerner, Germany	2:05.87

3000 METERS

1960	Lydia Skoblikova, USSR	5:14.3
1964	Lydia Skoblikova, USSR	5:14.9
1968	Johanna Schut, Netherlands	4:56.2 OR
1972	Christina Baas-Kaiser, Netherlands	4:52.14 OR
1976	Tatiana Averina, USSR	4:45.19 OR
1980	Bjorg Eva Jensen, Norway	4:32.13 OR
1984	Andrea Schöne, East Germany	4:24.79 OR
1988	Yvonne van Gennip, Netherlands	4:11.94 WR
1992	Gunda Niemann, Germany	4:19.90

5000 METERS

1988	Yvonne van Gennip, Netherlands	7:14.13 WR
1992	Gunda Niemann, Germany	7:31.57

SHORT TRACK SPEED SKATING

Men

1000 METERS

1992	Kim Ki-Hoon, South Korea	1:30.76 WR

5000-METER RELAY

1992	Korea	7:14.02 WR

Women

500 METERS

1992	Cathy Turner, United States	47.04

3000-METER RELAY

1992	Canada	4:36.62

ALPINE SKIING

Men

DOWNHILL

1948	Henri Oreiller, France	2:55.0
1952	Zeno Colo, Italy	2:30.8
1956	Anton Sailer, Austria	2:52.2
1960	Jean Vuarnet, France	2:06.0
1964	Egon Zimmermann, Austria	2:18.16
1968	Jean-Claude Killy, France	1:59.85
1972	Bernhard Russi, Switzerland	1:51.43
1976	Franz Klammer, Austria	1:45.73
1980	Leonhard Stock, Austria	1:45.50
1984	Bill Johnson, United States	1:45.59
1988	Pirmin Zurbriggen, Switzerland	1:59.63
1992	Patrick Ortlieb, Austria	1:50.37

SUPER GIANT SLALOM

1988	Franck Piccard, France	1:39.66
1992	Kjetil Andre Aamodt, Norway	1:13.04

GIANT SLALOM

1952	Stein Eriksen, Norway	2:25.0
1956	Anton Sailer, Austria	3:00.1
1960	Roger Staub, Switzerland	1:48.3
1964	Francois Bonlieu, France	1:46.71
1968	Jean-Claude Killy, France	3:29.28
1972	Gustav Thöni, Italy	3:09.62
1976	Heini Hemmi, Switzerland	3:26.97
1980	Ingemar Stenmark, Sweden	2:40.74
1984	Max Julen, Switzerland	2:41.18
1988	Alberto Tomba, Italy	2:06.37
1992	Alberto Tomba, Italy	2:06.98

SLALOM

1948	Edi Reinalter, Switzerland	2:10.3
1952	Othmar Schneider, Austria	2:00.0
1956	Anton Sailer, Austria	3:14.7
1960	Ernst Hinterseer, Austria	2:08.9
1964	Josef Stiegler, Austria	2:11.13
1968	Jean-Claude Killy, France	1:39.73
1972	Francisco Fernandez Ochoa, Spain	1:49.27
1976	Piero Gros, Italy	2:03.29
1980	Ingemar Stenmark, Sweden	1:44.26
1984	Phil Mahre, United States	1:39.41
1988	Alberto Tomba, Italy	1:39.47
1992	Finn Christian Jagge, Norway	1:44.39

COMBINED

		Pts
1936	Franz Pfnür, Germany	99.25
1948	Henri Oreiller, France	3.27
1988	Hubert Strolz, Austria	36.55
1992	Josef Polig, Italy	14.58

Women

DOWNHILL

1948	Hedy Schlunegger, Switzerland	2:28.3
1952	Trude Jochum-Beiser, Austria	1:47.1
1956	Madeleine Berthod, Switzerland	1:40.7
1960	Heidi Biebl, West Germany	1:37.6
1964	Christl Haas, Austria	1:55.39
1968	Olga Pall, Austria	1:40.87
1972	Marie-Theres Nadig, Switzerland	1:36.68
1976	Rosi Mittermaier, West Germany	1:46.16
1980	Annemarie Moser-Pröll, Austria	1:37.52
1984	Michela Figini, Switzerland	1:13.36
1988	Marina Kiehl, West Germany	1:25.86
1992	Kerrin Lee-Gartner, Canada	1:52.55

SUPER GIANT SLALOM

1988	Sigrid Wolf, Austria	1:19.03
1992	Deborah Compagnoni, Italy	1:21.22

GIANT SLALOM

1952	Andrea Mead Lawrence, United States	2:06.8
1956	Ossi Reichert, West Germany	1:56.5
1960	Yvonne Rüegg, Switzerland	1:39.9
1964	Marielle Goitschel, France	1:52.24
1968	Nancy Greene, Canada	1:51.97
1972	Marie-Theres Nadig, Switzerland	1:29.90
1976	Kathy Kreiner, Canada	1:29.13
1980	Hanni Wenzel, Liechtenstein (2 runs)	2:41.66
1984	Debbie Armstrong, United States	2:20.98
1988	Vreni Schneider, Switzerland	2:06.49
1992	Pernilla Wiberg, Sweden	2:12.74

SLALOM

1948	Gretchen Fraser, United States	1:57.2
1952	Andrea Mead Lawrence, United States	2:10.6
1956	Renee Colliard, Switzerland	1:52.3
1960	Anne Heggtveigt, Canada	1:49.6
1964	Christine Goitschel, France	1:29.86
1968	Marielle Goitschel, France	1:25.86
1972	Barbara Cochran, United States	1:31.24
1976	Rosi Mittermaier, West Germany	1:30.54
1980	Hanni Wenzel, Liechtenstein	1:25.09
1984	Paoletta Magoni, Italy	1:36.47
1988	Vreni Schneider, Switzerland	1:36.69
1992	Petra Kronberger, Austria	1:32.68

COMBINED

		Pts
1988	Anita Wachter, Austria	29.25
1992	Petra Kronberger, Austria	2.55

NORDIC SKIING

Men

15 KILOMETERS (CLASSICAL)

*1924	..Thorlief Haug, Norway	1:14:31.0
†1928	..Johan Gröttumsbraaten, Norway	1:37:01.0
‡1932	..Sven Utterström, Sweden	1:23:07.0
*1936	..Erik-August Larsson, Sweden	14:38.0
*1948	..Martin Lundström, Sweden	13:50.0
*1952	..Hallgeir Brenden, Norway	1:34.0
1956	....Hallgeir Brenden, Norway	49:39.0
1960	....Haakon Brusveen, Norway	51:55.5
1964	....Eero Mantyränta, Finland	50:54.1
1968	....Harald Grönningen, Norway	47:54.2
1972	....Sven-Ake Lundback, Sweden	45:28.24
1976	....Nikolay Bajukov, Unified Team	43:58.47
1980	....Thomas Wassberg, Sweden	41:57.63
1984	....Gunde Swan, Sweden	41:25.6
1988	....Michael Deviatyarov, USSR	41:18.9
**1992	.Vegard Ulvang, Norway	27:36.0

*distance was 18 km; †distance was 19.7 km.;
‡distance was 18.2 km; **distance was 10 km.

30 KILOMETERS (CLASSICAL)

1956	....Veikko Hakulinen, Finland	1:44:06.0
1960	....Sixten Jernberg, Sweden	1:51:03.9
1964	....Eero Mantyränta, Finland	1:30:50.7
1968	....Franco Nones, Italy	1:35:39.2
1972	....Viaceslav Vedenine, USSR	1:36:31.2
1976	....Sergei Savelyev, USSR	1:30:29.38
1980	....Nikolai Simyatov, USSR	1:27:02.80
1984	....Nikolai Simyatov, USSR	1:28:56.3
1988	....Alexey Prokororov, USSR	1:24:26.3
1992	....Vegard Ulvang, Norway	1:22:27.8

50 KILOMETERS (FREESTYLE)

1924	....Thorlief Haug, Norway	3:44:32.0
1928	....Per Erik Hedlund, Sweden	4:52:03.0
1932	....Veli Saarinen, Finland	4:28:00.0
1936	....Elis Wiklund, Sweden	3:30:11.0
1948	....Nils Karlsson, Sweden	3:47:48.0
1952	....Veikko Hakulinen, Finland	3:33:33.0
1956	....Sixten Jernberg, Sweden	2:50:27.0
1960	....Kalevi Hämäläinen, Finland	2:59:06.3
1964	....Sixten Jernberg, Sweden	2:43:52.6
1968	....Olle Ellefsaeter, Norway	2:28:45.8
1972	....Paal Tyldrum, Norway	2:43:14.75
1976	....Ivar Formo, Norway	2:37:30.50
1980	....Nikolai Simyatov, USSR	2:27:24.60
1984	....Thomas Wassberg, Sweden	2:15:55.8
1988	....Gunde Swan, Sweden	2:04:30.9
1992	....Bjorn Dählie, Norway	2:03:41.5

15 KILOMETERS (FREESTYLE)

1992	....Bjorn Daehlie, Norway	1:05.37.9

4 X 10 KILOMETER RELAY

1936	....................Finland	2:41:33.0
1948	....................Sweden	2:32:80.0
1952	....................Finland	2:20:16.0
1956	....................USSR	2:15:30.0

4 X 10 KILOMETER RELAY (Cont.)

1960	....................Finland	2:18:45.6
1964	....................Sweden	2:18:34.6
1968	....................Norway	2:08:33.5
1972	....................USSR	2:04:47.94
1976	....................Finland	2:07:59.72
1980	....................USSR	1:57:03.46
1984	....................Sweden	1:55:06.3
1988	....................Sweden	1:43:58.6
1992	....................Norway	1:39:26.0

SKI JUMPING (NORMAL HILL)

1964	....Veikko Kankkonen, Finland	229.90
1968	....Jiri Raska, Czechoslovakia	216.5
1972	....Yukio Kasaya, Japan	244.2
1976	....Hans-Georg Aschenbach, East Germany	252.0
1980	....Toni Innauer, Austria	266.3
1984	....Jens Weissflog, East Germany	215.2
1988	....Matti Nykänen, Finland	229.1
1992	....Ernst Vettori, Austria	222.8

SKI JUMPING (LARGE HILL)

1924	....Jacob Tullin Thams, Norway	18.960
1928	....Alf Andersen, Norway	19.208
1932	....Birger Ruud, Norway	228.1
1936	....Birger Ruud, Norway	232.0
1948	....Petter Hugsted, Norway	228.1
1952	....Arnfinn Bergmann, Norway	226.0
1956	....Antti Hyvärinen, Finland	227.0
1960	....Helmut Recknagel, East Germany	227.2
1964	....Toralf Engan, Norway	230.70
1968	....Vladimir Beloussov, USSR	231.3
1972	....Wojciech Fortuna, Poland	219.9
1976	....Karl Schnabl, Austria	234.8
1980	....Jouko Tormanen, Finland	271.0
1984	....Matti Nykänen, Finland	231.2
1988	....Matti Nykänen, Finland	224.0
1992	....Toni Nieminen, Finland	239.5

TEAM SKI JUMPING

1988	....Finland	634.4
1992	....Finland	644.4

NORDIC COMBINED

*1924	..Thorleif Haug, Norway	
*1928	..Johan Gröttumsbraaten, Norway	
1932	....Joan Gröttumsbraaten, Norway	446.0
1936	....Oddbjörn Hagen, Norway	430.30
1948	....Heikki Hasu, Finland	448.80
1952	....Simon Slattvik, Norway	451.621
1956	....Sverre Stenersen, Norway	455.0
1960	....Georg Thoma, West Germany	457.952
1964	....Tormod Knutsen, Norway	469.28
1968	....Frantz Keller, West Germany	449.04
1972	....Ulrich Wehling, East Germany	413.34
1976	....Ulrich Wehling, East Germany	423.39
1980	....Ulrich Wehling, East Germany	432.20

NORDIC SKIING (Cont.)

Men (Cont.)

NORDIC COMBINED (Cont.)

1984	Tom Sandberg, Norway	422.595
1988	Hippolyt Kempf, Switzerland	432.230
1992	Fabrice Guy, France	426.47

*Different scoring system; 1924-1952 distance was 18 km

TEAM NORDIC COMBINED

1988	West Germany
1992	Japan

Women

5 KILOMETERS (CLASSICAL)

1964	Klaudia Boyarskikh, USSR	17:50.5
1968	Toini Gustafsson, Sweden	16:45.2
1972	Galina Kulakova, USSR	17:00.50
1976	Helena Takalo, Finland	15:48.69
1980	Raisa Smetanina, USSR	15:06.92
1984	Marja-Liisa Hamalainen, Finland	17:04.0
1988	Marjo Matikainen, Finland	15:04.0
1992	Marjut Lukkarinen, Finland	14:13.8

10 KILOMETERS (CLASSICAL)

1952	Lydia Widemen, Finland	41:40.0
1956	Lyubov Kosyryeva, USSR	38:11.0
1960	Maria Gusakova, USSR	39:46.6
1964	Klaudia Boyarskikh, USSR	40:24.3
1968	Toini Gustafsson, Sweden	36:46.5
1972	Galina Kulakova, USSR	34:17.8
1976	Raisa Smetanina, USSR	30:13.41
1980	Barbara Petzold, East Germany	30:31.54
1984	Marja-Lissa Hamalainen, Finland	31:44.2
1988	Vida Ventsene, USSR	30:08.3
1992*	Lyubov Egorova, Unified Team	42:20.8

*distance changed to 15 kilometers

20 KILOMETERS (FREESTYLE)

1984	Marja-Liisa Hamalainen, Finland	1:01:45.0
1988	Tamara Tikhonova, USSR	55:53.6
1992†	Stefania Belmondo, Italy	1:22:30.1

†distance changed to 30 kilometers

10 KILOMETERS FREESTYLE PURSUIT

1992	Lyubov Egorova, Unified Team	40:07.7

4 X 5-KILOMETER RELAY

1956	Finland	1:9:01.0
1960	Sweden	1:4:21.4
1964	USSR	59:20.0
1968	Norway	57:30.0
1972	USSR	48:46.15
1976	USSR	1:07:49.75
1980	East Germany	1:02:11.10
1984	Norway	1:06:49.7
1988	USSR	59:51.1
1992	Unified Team	59:34.8

THEY SAID IT

Chris Nelloms, the Ohio State sprinter who survived a random shooting near his home in Dayton in August of 1992 and came back to win the 200-meter dash at the NCAA championships the following summer, on his plans to become an embalmer: "It's a nice future," he says. "You're always going to be born, and you're always going to die."

Track and Field

FASTEST!

Linford Christie defeats Carl Lewis to claim the title of world's speediest human

Changing Times

Records fell all season long, but so did the fortunes of track's alltime great, Carl Lewis | **by MERRELL NODEN**

SPRINTERS AREN'T SUPPOSED TO get faster with age. Until this year 32-year-old Carl Lewis's career had been a repudiation of that rule. While Lewis may surprise us yet, 1993 could go down as the year when the greatest athlete in track and field history finally began to show his age.

Lewis went to the fourth IAAF World Track and Field Championships, held from August 14 to 22, in Stuttgart, Germany, eager to add to his collection of 16 world championship or Olympic gold medals. But it was Great Britain's Linford Christie, Lewis's senior by 15 months, who seemed hungriest in the 100, exploding powerfully from the blocks. "By the *b* in 'bang' I was out," he said. His time, 9.87, was just .01 off Lewis's world record. U.S. champion Andre Cason ran 9.92 in second, with Lewis fourth, in 10.02. Basking in the glow of the fastest race of his life, even the sometimes prickly Christie sounded mellow. "I'm on the way out," he said. "There will be youngsters like Andre coming in next year. It

means a lot to me to do this now, at the end of an era."

Whether or not Christie is right, and this is the end of the Lewis era, remains to be seen. Lewis has had years when he ran slower than he did in 1993, but never when it really counted, as it did in Stuttgart. Lewis did not win a 100 all year and took home from Stuttgart a single bronze medal, in the 200. And due to a chronic back problem exacerbated by a car accident in February, Lewis did not long jump once. In his absence Mike Powell dominated the event, winning the world title by the unheard of margin of 17 inches.

This year's world championships were the first to be held on a biennial basis. Some cognoscenti had grumbled that adding another major meet to each Olympiad would dilute the glory and overextend the athletes. The rapturous crowds who filled Stuttgart's Nickar Stadion would disagree. They were treated to a carnival of historic performances, close races and controversy. World records fell to Colin Jackson and Sally Gunnell, both of Great Britain, in the

110 (12.91) and the 400 hurdles (52.74), respectively, and to Ana Biryukova of Russia in the triple jump (49' 6¼").

Certainly some of the sport's biggest names were grateful to find so grand a stage so soon after a disappointing Olympic year. Pole vaulter Sergei Bubka, who no-heighted in Barcelona, won his fourth world outdoor title, making the 29-year-old Ukrainian the only athlete with a perfect record at the four world championships. Nourredine Morceli, seventh in the Olympic 1,500, ran away from the field to win the 1,500 in 3:34.24. Gail Devers pulled off the rare double she had missed in Barcelona, edging Merlene Ottey in the 100 (both timed in 10.82) and then dominating the 100 hurdles in 12.46. No one had won a dash–hurdle double in a major championship since Fanny Blankers-Koen did it at the 1948 Olympics. And Dan O'Brien, who failed to make the U.S. Olympic team, defended his world decathlon title, with 8,817 points.

But the athlete who found sweetest redemption in Stuttgart was sprinter Michael Johnson. Favored to win the Olympic 200, Johnson had not even reached the final, the victim, it turned out, of severe food poisoning. This year, forced by a hamstring strain to concentrate on the less familiar of his two events, the 400, Johnson was sensational. He won the U.S. title in 43.74 and the world championship in 43.65. Even more satisfying, Johnson anchored the U.S. 4 x 400 team to a stunning world record of 2:54.29, his 42.97 anchor standing as the fastest in history.

With the business of winning a world title out of the way, athletes turned their attention to records. Shining brightest of all was Morceli who after failing three times to break Steve Cram's world mile record, finally got it in Rieti, Italy, on Sept. 5. Morceli ran a stunning 3:44.39 mile, lopping nearly two seconds off Cram's eight-year-old record. Earlier, at the Bislett Games in Oslo, Yobes Ondieki of Kenya made history by running 10,000 meters in 26:58.38, the first time anyone has broken 27 minutes.

But Ondieki's was not the most amazing

RICHARD MACKSON

Morceli breezed through the semis en route to a world title in the 1,500 in Stuttgart.

10,000 record set in 1993. That honor went to China's Wang Junxia, 20, from the mountainous province of Liaoning. In Stuttgart she and her teammates became the subject of widespread innuendo after they swept the distance golds with devastating ease. Those suspicions were reinforced when, on Sept. 8, in the National Games in Beijing, Wang clocked 29:31.78 for the 10,000, lopping almost 42 seconds off Ingrid Kristiansen's record for the distance.

Something seemed very fishy, and it wasn't just the diet of turtles and worms and caterpillar fungi that Wang's coach, Zunren Ma, claims she thrives on. The doubts grew over the next five days as Wang went on the greatest distance-record spree in history, breaking the listed world records for both the 1,500 (clocking 3:51.92, but finishing second to countrywoman Qu Yunxia, who ran 3:50.46) and the 3,000 (8:12.19 in the heats and 8:06.11 in the finals). Can Wang satisfy her doubters by duplicating those times outside of China? That may well be the story of 1994.

U.S. Outdoor Track and Field Championships

Eugene, Ore., June 15-19, 1993

Men

100 METERS

1.	Andre Cason, Goldwin TC	9.85w
2.	Dennis Mitchell, Mazda TC	9.85
3.	Carl Lewis, Santa Monica TC	9.90

200 METERS

1.	Mike Marsh, Santa Monica TC	19.97w
2.	Carl Lewis, Santa Monica TC	20.07
3.	Jason Hendrix, Blinn College	20.35

400 METERS

1.	Michael Johnson, Nike Intl TC	43.74*
2.	Butch Reynolds, Foot Locker AC	44.12
3.	Quincy Watts, Nike Intl-LA	44.24

800 METERS

1.	Mark Everett, Nike Intl TC	1:44.43
2.	Johnny Gray, Santa Monica TC	1:44.67
3.	Jose Parrilla, U. of Tennessee	1:45.13

1500 METERS

1.	Bill Burke, NYAC	3:42.74
2.	Mark Dailey, NYAC	3:42.92
3.	Jim Spivey, Asics International	3:42.92

STEEPLECHASE

1.	Marc Davis, Nike Intl TC	8:20.93
2.	Mark Croghan, Nike TC	8:21.37
3.	Brian Diemer, Nike Intl TC	8:22.41

5000 METERS

1.	Matt Giusto, Foot Locker AC	13:23.60
2.	Bob Kennedy, Nike Indiana TC	13:25.51
3.	Ken Martin, Reebok RC	13:44.68

10,000 METERS

1.	Todd Williams, Team adidas	28:02.05
2.	Steve Plasencia, Asics Intl TC	28:02.41
3.	Dan Nelson, Nike RR	28:02.44

110-METER HURDLES

1.	Jack Pierce, Mizuno TC	13.19
2.	Tony Dees, Nike Intl TC	13.21
3.	Mark Crear, Nike Intl-LA	13.33

400-METER HURDLES

1.	Kevin Young, Nike Intl TC	47.69
2.	Derrick Adkins, Reebok RC	48.69
3.	David Patrick, Reebok RC	48.95

*Meet record. w=wind aided.

20-KILOMETER WALK

1.	Allen James, Athletes in Action	1:29:09
2.	Jonathan Matthews, GG Walkers	1:30:45
3.	Doug Fournier, unatt	1:31:25

HIGH JUMP

1.	Hollis Conway, Nike Intl TC	7 ft 7 in
2T.	Tony Barton, Nike TC	7 ft 4½ in
2T.	Rick Noji, Stars & Stripes TC	7 ft 4½ in

POLE VAULT

1.	Scott Huffman, Mizuno TC	18 ft 8¼ in
2.	Dean Starkey, Reebok RC	18 ft 8¼ in
3.	Mike Holloway, Miz.-Hou TC	18 ft 6½ in

LONG JUMP

1.	Mike Powell, Foot Locker AC	28 ft 0 inw
2.	Erick Walder, U. of Arkansas	27 ft 9¼ inw
3.	Joe Greene, Mazda TC	27 ft 4 in

TRIPLE JUMP

1.	Mike Conley, Foot Locker AC	58 ft ½ inw
2.	Kenny Harrison, Mizuno TC	56 ft 8 in
3.	Reggie Jones, LSU	55 ft 11 inw

SHOT PUT

1.	Randy Barnes, unatt	69 ft 9¾ in
2.	Mike Stulce, unatt	69 ft 4¼ in
3.	Kevin Toth, Nike TC	66 ft 7¼ in

DISCUS THROW

1.	Anthony Washington, Mazda	207 ft 6 in
2.	Mike Buncic, unatt	202 ft 6 in
3.	Michael Gravelle, unatt	200 ft 6 in

HAMMER THROW

1.	Lance Deal, NYAC	256 ft 3 in
2.	Jim Driscoll, unatt	235 ft 4 in
3.	Kevin McMahon, unatt	225 ft 11 in

JAVELIN THROW

1.	Tom Pukstys, NYAC	272 ft 6 in*
2.	Art Skipper, Nike Oregon	251 ft 4 in
3.	Ed Kaminski, SSTC	239 ft 11 in

DECATHLON

1.	Dan O'Brien, Reebok	8331
2.	Steve Fritz, Accusplit SC	8176w
3.	Rob Muzzio, VISA TC	8057

Women

100 METERS

1. ....Gail Devers, Nike Intl TC   10.82w
2. ....Gwen Torrence, Mazda TC   11.03
3. ....Michelle Finn, Santa Monica TC   11.07

200 METERS

1. ....Gwen Torrence, Mazda TC   22.57w
2. ....Dannette Young, Reebok RC   22.68
3. ....Michelle Finn, Santa Monica TC   22.81

400 METERS

1. ....Jearl Miles, Reebok RC   50.43
2. ....Natasha Kaiser-Brown, Cheetahs   50.93
3. ....Michele Collins, unatt   51.77

800 METERS

1. ....Joetta Clark, Foot Locker AC   2:01.47
2. ....Amy Wickus, U. of Wisconsin   2:02.22
3. ....Julie Jenkins-Donley, Reebok RC   2:02.23

1500 METERS

1. ....Annette Peters, Nike TC   4:11.53
2. ....Alisa Hill, Foot Locker AC   4:12.43
3. ....Gina Procaccio, Sallie Mae TC   4:12.51

3,000 METERS

1. ....Annette Peters, Nike TC   8:48.59
2. ....Shelly Steely, Mizuno TC   8:52.99
3. ....Sheila Carrozza, Run-Texas RT   8:55.03

10,000 METERS

1. ....Lynn Jennings, Nike Intl TC   31:57.83*
2. ....Anne Marie Letko, Nike RR   32:00.37
3. ....Elaine Van Blunk, Nike RR   32:07.19

10,000 METER WALK

1. ....Debbi Lawrence, Natural Sport   45:55
2. ....Teresa Vaill, unatt   46:04
3. ....Sara Standley, unatt   48:16

100-METER HURDLES

1. ....Lynda Tolbert, Nike TC   12.72w
2. ....Gail Devers, Nike Intl TC   12.73
3. ....Dawn Bowles, Foot Locker AC   12.89

*Meet record. w=wind aided

400-METER HURDLES

1. ....Sandra Farmer-Patrick, Reebok RC 53.96
2. ....Kim Batten, Reebok RC   54.57
3. ....Tonja Buford, Mazda TC   54.63

HIGH JUMP

1. ....Tanya Hughes, Nike Coast TC   6 ft 2¾ in
2. ....Connie Teaberry, Goldwin TC   6 ft 2¼ in
3. ....Sue Rembao, Reebok RC   6 ft 2¼ in

LONG JUMP

1. ....Jackie Joyner-Kersee, unatt   23 ft ½ in
2. ....Sheila Echols, unatt   21 ft 10 inw
3. ....Sharon Couch, Asics Intl TC   21 ft 6¾ inw

TRIPLE JUMP

1. ....Claudia Haywood, AIA   45 ft 5¾ inw
2. ....Sheila Hudson, Mizuno TC   44 ft 9¾ inw
3. ....Cynthea Rhodes, unatt   44 ft 2¾ inw

SHOT PUT

1. ....Connie Price-Smith, Nike Coast TC   62 ft 5 in
2. ....Ramona Pagel, unatt   58 ft 1¼ in
3. ....Stevanie Wadsworth, TCU   56 ft 3 in

DISCUS THROW

1. ....Connie Price-Smith, Nike Coast 208 ft 5 in
2. ....Kristin Kuehl, unatt   197 ft 4 in
3. ....Carla Garrett, Nike Coast TC   193 ft 4 in

JAVELIN

1. ....Donna Mayhew, Nike Coast TC   206 ft 7 in
2. ....Heather Berlin, unatt   182 ft 8 in
3. ....Erica Wheeler, Mizuno TC   181 ft 1 in

HEPTATHLON

1. ....Jackie Joyner Kersee, unatt   6770 points
2. ....Kym Carter, unatt   6038 points
3. ....DeDe Nathan, Nike Indiana   6038 points

Kiss, Kiss

"Never, never. He can live 200 years." That's what Primo Nebiolo, president of the IAAF, the world governing body for track and field, said in July of U.S. sprinter Butch Reynolds's chances of getting any of the 27.3 million he was awarded by a U.S. court for damages related to the IAAF's improper handling of a Reynolds drug suspension. Reynolds still has 171 years to go—he's a mere 29—but on August 27 a U.S. magistrate in Alexandria, Va., attached $691,667 that a U.S. company, Mobil, owes the London-based IAAF under a support contract and ordered that the money be put in escrow for Reynolds. Reynolds won't get the loot until all appeals are exhausted, but because other U.S. companies also make payments to the IAAF, he stands to wind up with a lot more money.

Two weeks ago, in a peace offering of sorts, Nebiolo kissed Reynolds on both cheeks during an awards ceremony at the World Championships. You might say Reynolds gave him a smack in return.

IAAF World Track and Field Championships

Stuttgart, Germany, August 14-22, 1993

Men

100 METERS

1. ....Linford Christie, Great Britain   9.87
2. ....Andre Cason, United States   9.92
3. ....Dennis Mitchell, United States   9.99

200 METERS

1. ....Frank Fredericks, Namibia   19.85*
2. ....John Regis, Great Britain   19.94
3. ....Carl Lewis, United States   19.99

400 METERS

1. ....Michael Johnson, United States   43.65*
2. ....Butch Reynolds, United States   44.13
3. ....Samson Kitur, Kenya   44.54

800 METERS

1. ....Paul Ruto, Kenya   1:44.71
2. ....Guiseppie D'Urso, Italy   1:44.86
3. ....Billy Konchellah, Kenya   1:44.89

1,500 METERS

1. ....Nourredine Morceli, Algeria   3:34.24
2. ....Fermin Cacho, Spain   3:35.56
3. ....Abdi Bile, Somalia   3:35.96

STEEPLECHASE

1. ....Moses Kiptanui, Kenya   8:06.36*
2. ....Patrick Sang, Kenya   8:07.53
3. ....Alesandro Lambruschini, Italy   8:08.78

5,000 METERS

1. ....Ismael Kirui, Kenya   13:02.75*
2. ....Haile Gebresilasie, Ethiopia   13:03.17
3. ....Fita Bayesa, Ethiopia   13:05.40

10,000 METERS

1. ....Haile Gebresilasie, Ethiopia   27:46.02
2. ....Moses Tanui, Kenya   27:46.54
3. ....Richard Chelimo, Kenya   28:06.02

MARATHON

1. ....Mark Plaatjes, United States   2:13:57
2. ....Lucketz Swartbooi, Namibia   2:14:11
3. ....Bert Van Vlaanderen, Holland   2:15:12

110-METER HURDLES

1. ....Colin Jackson, Great Britain   12.91†
2. ....Tony Jarrett, Great Britain   13.00
3. ....Jack Pierce, United States   13.06

400-METER HURDLES

1. ....Kevin Young, United States   47.18*
2. ....Samuel Matete, Zambia   47.60
3. ....Winthrop Graham, Jamaica   47.62

20-KILOMETER WALK

1. ....Valentin Massana, Spain   1:22:31
2. ....Giovanni De Benedictis, Italy   1:23:06
3. ....Danie Plaza, Spain   1:23:18

50-KILOMETER WALK

1. ....Jesus Angel Garcia, Spain   3:41:41
2. ....Valentin Kononen, Finland   3:42:02
3. ....Valery Spitsyn, Russia   3:42:50

4 X 100 METER RELAY

1. ....United States   37.48
2. ....Great Britain   37.77
3. ....Canada   37.83

4 X 400 METER RELAY

1. ....United States   2:54.29†
2. ....Kenya   2:59.82
3. ....Germany   2:59.99

HIGH JUMP

1. ....Javier Sotomayor, Cuba   7 ft 10½ in
2. ....Artur Partyka, Poland   7 ft 9¼ in
3. ....Steve Smith, Great Britain   7 ft 9¼ in

POLE VAULT

1. ....Sergei Bubka, Ukraine   19 ft 8¼ in*
2. ....Grigoriy Yegerov, Kazakhstan   19 ft 4½ in
3. ....Maksim Tarasov, Russia   19 ft ½ in

LONG JUMP

1. ....Mike Powell, United States   28 ft 2¼ in
2. ....Stanislav Tarasenko, Russia   26 ft 9¼ in
3. ....Vitaliy Kirilenko, Ukraine   26 ft 9 in

TRIPLE JUMP

1. ....Mike Conley, United States   58 ft 7¼ in
2. ....Leonid Voloshin, Russia   57 ft 11 in
3. ....Jonathan Edwards, Gr Britain   57 ft 2¾ in

SHOT PUT

1. ....Werner Guenthor, Switzerland   72 ft 1 in
2. ....Randy Barnes, United States   71 ft 6¼ in
3. ....Mike Stulce, United States   68 ft 8½ in

DISCUS

1. ....Lars Reidel, Germany   222 ft 2 in
2. ....Dmitry Shevchenko, Russia   219 ft 6 in
3. ....Juergen Schult, Germany   216 ft 11 in

HAMMER

1. ....Andrey Abduvaliyev, Tad.   267 ft 10 in
2. ....Igor Astapkovich, Belarus   262 ft 1 in
3. ....Tibor Gecsek, Hungary   260 ft 11 in

JAVELIN

1. ....Jan Zelezny, Czech Republic   282 ft 1 in
2. ....Kimmo Kinnunen, Finland   278 ft 2 in
3. ....Dmitriy Polyunin, Uzbekistan   273 ft 7 in

DECATHLON

1. ....Dan O'Brien, United States   8817 pts
2. ....Eduard Hamalainen, Belarus   8724 pts
3. ....Paul Meier, Germany   8548 pts

*Meet record. †World record

Stuttgart, Germany, August 14-22, 1993

Women

100 METERS

1.	Gail Devers, United States	10.82*
2.	Merlene Ottey, Jamaica	10.82
3.	Gwen Torrence, United States	10.89

200 METERS

1.	Merlene Ottey, Jamaica	21.98
2.	Gwen Torrence, United States	22.00
3.	Irina Privalova, Russia	22.13

400 METERS

1.	Jearl Miles, United States	49.82
2.	Natasha Kaiser-Brown, U.S.	50.17
3.	Sandie Richards, Jamaica	50.44

800 METERS

1.	Maria Mutola, Mozambique	1:55.43
2.	Lyubov Gurina, Russia	1:57.10
3.	Ella Kovacs, Romania	1:57.92

1,500 METERS

1.	Dong Liu, China	4:00.50
2.	Sonia O'Sullivan, Ireland	4:03.48
3.	Hassiba Boulmerka, Algeria	4:04.29

3,000 METERS

1.	Yunxia Qu, China	8:28.71*
2.	Linli Zhang, China	8:29.25
3.	Liron Zhang, China	8:31.95

10,000 METERS

1.	Wang Junxia, China	30:49.30*
2.	Huandi Zhong, China	31:12.55
3.	Tecla Lorupe, Kenya	31:29.91

MARATHON

1.	Junko Asari, Japan	2:30:03
2.	Manuela Machado, Portugal	2:30:54
3.	Tomoe Abe, Japan	2:31:01

100-METER HURDLES

1.	Gail Devers, United States	12.46**
2.	Marina Azyabina, Russia	12.60
3.	Lynda Tolbert, United States	12.67

400-METER HURDLES

1.	Sally Gunnell, Great Britain	52.74†
2.	Sandra Farmer-Patrick, U.S.	52.79**
3.	Margarita Ponomaryova, Russia	53.48

10-KILOMETER WALK

1.	Sari Essayah, Finland	42:59
2.	Ileana Salvador, Italy	43:08
3.	Encamacion Granados, Spain	43:26

4 X 100 METER RELAY

1.	Russia	41.49
2.	United States	41.49
3.	Jamaica	41.94

4 X 400 METER RELAY

1.	United States	3:16.71
2.	Russia	3:18.38
3.	Great Britain	3:23.41

HIGH JUMP

1.	Ioamnet Quintero, Cuba	6 ft 6¼ in
2.	Silvia Costa, Cuba	6 ft 5½ in
3.	Sigrid Kirchmann, Austria	6 ft 5½ in

LONG JUMP

1.	Heike Drechsler, Germany	23 ft 4 in
2.	Larisa Berezhnaya, Ukraine	22 ft 10¾ in
3.	Renata Nielsen, Denmark	22 ft 2¼ in

TRIPLE JUMP

1.	Ana Biryukova, Russia	49 ft 6¼ in†
2.	Yolanda Chen, Russia	48 ft 2¾ in
3.	Iva Prandzheva, Bulgaria	46 ft 8¼ in

SHOT PUT

1.	Zhihong Huang, China	67 ft 6 in
2.	Svetlana Krivelyova, Russia	65 ft 6¼ in
3.	Kathrin Neimke, Germany	64 ft 8 in

DISCUS

1.	Olga Burova, Russia	221 ft 1 in
2.	Daniela Costian, Australia	214 ft 5 in
3.	Chunfeng Min, China	214 ft 1 in

JAVELIN

1.	Trine Hattestad, Finland	227 ft 0 in
2.	Karen Forkel, Germany	215 ft 10 in
3.	Natalya Shikolenko, Belarus	215 ft 4 in

HEPTATHLON

1.	Jackie Joyner-Kersee, U.S.	6837 pts
2.	Sabine Braun, Germany	6797 pts
3.	Svetlana Buraga, Belarus	6635 pts

*Meet record. **American record. †World record.

Mercy Killing

For all their recent successes in cross country, road running and long distance races on the European circuit's spacious 400-meter tracks, Kenya's fabulous distance runners have not had much success on the tight, banked turns of Madison Square Garden's wooden track. After an especially frustrating race last winter, Moses Kiptanui, the world record holder in the steeplechase, approached American miler Jim Spivey and beseeched him, "Jim, if you ever see us Kenyans here again, shoot us."

IAAF World Cross-Country Championships

Amorebieta, Spain, March 28, 1993

MEN (12,000 METERS; 7.45 MILES)		WOMEN (6,000 METERS; 3.72 MILES)	
1. ....William Sigei, Kenya	32:51	1. ....Albertina Dias, Portugal	20:00
2. ....Dominic Kirui, Kenya	32:56	2. ....Catherina McKiernan, Ireland	20:09
3. ....Ismael Kirui, Kenya	32:59	3. ....Lynn Jennings, U.S.	20:09

Major Marathons

New York City: November 1, 1992

MEN

1. ....Willie Mtolo, South Africa	2:09:29
2. ....Andres Espinosa, Mexico	2:10:53
3. ....Kim Wan-gi, South Korea	2:10:54

WOMEN

1. ....Lisa Ondieki, Australia	2:24:40
2. ....Olga Markova, Russia	2:26:38
3. ....Yoshiko Yamamoto, Japan	2:29:58

Tokyo: November 15, 1992

WOMEN ONLY

1. ....Liz McColgan, Great Britain	2:27:38
2. ....Katrin Dörre, Germany	2:30:05
3. ....Ramilya Burangulova, Russia	2:30:34

Fukuoka, Japan: December 6, 1992

MEN ONLY

1. ....Tena Negere, Ethopia	2:09:04
2. ....Lawrence Peu, South Africa	2:10:29
3. ....Diego Garcia, Spain	2:10:30

Honolulu: December 13, 1992

MEN

1. ....Benson Masya, Kenya	2:14:19
2. ....Cosmas N'Deti, Kenya	2:14:28
3. ....David Tsebe, South Africa	2:16:45

WOMEN

1. ....Carla Beurskens, Holland	2:32:13
2. ....Lisa Weidenbach, United States	2:38:58
3. ....Ritva Lemettinen, Finland	2:39:21

Los Angeles: March 7, 1993

MEN

1. ....Joseildo Rocha, Brazil	2:14:29
2. ....Jose Santana, Brazil	2:15:00
3. ....Gumercindo Olmedo, Mexico	2:15:40

WOMEN

1. ....Lyubov Klochko, Ukraine	2:39:49
2. ....Carole Rouillard, Canada	2:41:09
3. ....Lyutsia Belayeva, Ukraine	2:44:26

Rotterdam: April 18, 1993

MEN

1. ....Dionicio Ceron, Mexico	2:11:06
2. ....Simon Robert Naali, Tanzania	2:11:44
3. ....Harri Hanninen, Finland	2:11:58

WOMEN

1. ....Anne van Schuppen, Holland	2:34:15
2. ....Wilma van Onna, Holland	2:34:28
3. ....Siska Maton, Belgium	2:39:24

London: April 18, 1993

MEN

1. ....Eamonn Martin, Great Britain	2:10:50
2. ....Isidro Rico, Mexico	2:10:53
3. ....Grzegorz Gajdus, Poland	2:11:07

WOMEN

1. ....Katrin Dörre, Germany	2:27:09
2. ....Lisa Ondieki, Australia	2:27:27
3. ....Liz McColgan, Great Britain	2:29:37

Boston: April 19, 1993

MEN

1. ....Cosmas N'Deti, Kenya	2:09:33
2. ....Kim Jae-Yong, South Korea	2:09:43
3. ....Lucketz Swartbooi, Namibia	2:09:57

WOMEN

1. ....Olga Markova, Russia	2:25:27
2. ....Kim Jones, United States	2:30:00
3. ....Carmen de Oliveira, Brazil	2:31:18

THEY SAID IT

Former world 10,000-meter record holder Ingrid Kristiansen on the 26 miles per day of training done by China's Wang Junxia, whose time of 29:31.78 shattered Kristiansen's record by almost 42 seconds: "You can't do all that on oatmeal."

World Records

As of September 20, 1993. World outdoor records are recognized by the International Amateur Athletics Federation (IAAF).

Men

Event	Mark	Record Holder	Date	Site
100 meters	9.86	Carl Lewis, United States	8-25-91	Tokyo
200 meters	19.72	Pietro Mennea, Italy	9-12-79	Mexico City
400 meters	43.29	Butch Reynolds, United States	8-17-88	Zurich
800 meters	1:41.73	Sebastian Coe, Great Britain	6-10-81	Florence
1,000 meters	2:12.18	Sebastian Coe, Great Britain	7-11-81	Oslo
1,500 meters	3:28.86	Noureddine Morceli, Algeria	9-6-92	Rieti, Italy
Mile	3:44.39	Noureddine Morceli, Algeria	9-5-93	Rieti, Italy
2,000 meters	4:50.81	Said Aouita, Morocco	7-16-87	Paris
3,000 meters	7:28.96	Moses Kiptanui, Kenya	8-16-92	Cologne
Steeplechase	8:02.08	Moses Kiptanui, Kenya	8-19-92	Zurich
5,000 meters	12:58.39	Said Aouita, Morocco	7-22-87	Rome
10,000 meters	26:58.38	Yobes Ondieki, Kenya	7-10-93	Oslo
20,000 meters	56:55.6	Arturo Barrios, Mexico	3-30-91	La Flâche, France
Hour	21,101 meters	Arturo Barrios, Mexico	3-30-91	La Flâche, France
25,000 meters	1:13:55.8	Toshihiko Seko, Japan	3-22-81	Christchurch, New Zealand
30,000 meters	1:29:18.8	Toshihiko Seko, Japan	3-22-81	Christchurch, New Zealand
Marathon	2:06:50	Belayneh Densimo, Ethiopia	4-17-88	Rotterdam
110-meter hurdles	12.91	Colin Jackson, Great Britain	8-20-93	Stuttgart, Germany
400-meter hurdles	46.78	Kevin Young, United States	8-6-92	Barcelona
20 kilometer walk	1:18:35.2	Stefan Johansson, Sweden	5-15-92	Fana, Norway
30 kilometer walk	2:01:44.1	Maurizio Damilano, Italy	10-3-92	Cuneo, Italy
50 kilometer walk	3:41:38.4	Raul Gonzalez, Mexico	5-25-79	Bergen, Norway
4x100-meter relay	37.40	United States (Mike Marsh, Leroy Burrell, Dennis Mitchell, Carl Lewis)	8-8-92	Barcelona
		United States (Jon Drummond, Andre Cason, Dennis Mitchell, Leroy Burrell)	8-22-93	Stuttgart, Germany
4x200-meter relay	1:19.11	Santa Monica TC (Mike Marsh, Leroy Burrell, Floyd Heard, Carl Lewis)	4-25-92	Philadelphia
4x400-meter relay	2:54.29	United States (Andrew Valmon, Quincy Watts, Butch Reynolds, Michael Johnson)	8-22-93	Barcelona
4x800-meter relay	7:03.89	Great Britain (Peter Elliott, Garry Cook, Steve Cram, Sebastian Coe)	8-30-82	London
4x1500-meter relay	14:38.8	West Germany (Thomas Wessinghage, Harald Hudak, Michael Lederer, Karl Fleschen)	8-17-77	Cologne
High jump	8 ft ½ in	Javier Sotomayor, Cuba	7-27-93	Salamanca, Spain
Pole vault	20 ft 1½ in	Sergei Bubka, CIS	9-19-92	Tokyo
Long jump	29 ft 4½ in	Mike Powell, United States	8-30-91	Tokyo
Triple jump	58 ft 11½ in	Willie Banks, United States	6-16-85	Indianapolis
Shot put	75 ft 10¼ in	Randy Barnes, United States	5-20-90	Westwood, CA
Discus throw	243 ft 0 in	Jurgen Schult, East Germany	6-6-86	Neubrandenburg, Germany
Hammer throw	284 ft 7 in	Yuri Syedikh, USSR	8-30-86	Stuttgart
Javelin throw	313 ft 10 in	Jan Zelezny, Czech Republic	8-29-93	Sheffield, England
Decathlon	8891 pts	Dan O'Brien, United States	9/4-5/92	Talence, France

Note: The decathlon consists of 10 events—the 100 meters, long jump, shot put, high jump and 400 meters on the first day; the 110-meter hurdles, discus, pole vault, javelin and 1500 meters on the second.

Women

Event	Mark	Record Holder	Date	Site
100 meters	10.49	Florence Griffith Joyner, United States	7-16-88	Indianapolis
200 meters	21.34	Florence Griffith Joyner, United States	9-29-88	Seoul
400 meters	47.60	Marita Koch, East Germany	10-6-85	Canberra, Australia
800 meters	1:53.28	Jarmila Kratochvilova, Czechoslovakia	7-26-83	Munich
1,500 meters	3:50.46	Qu Yunxia, China	9-11-93	Beijing
Mile	4:15.61	Paula Ivan, Romania	7-10-89	Nice
2,000 meters	5:28.69	Maricica Puica, Romania	7-11-86	London
3,000 meters	8:06.11	Wang Junxia, China	9-13-93	Beijing
5,000 meters	14:37.33	Ingrid Kristiansen, Norway	8-5-86	Stockholm
10,000 meters	29:31.78	Wang Junxia, China	9-8-93	Beijing
25,000 meters	1:29:29.2	Karolina Szab¢, Hungary	4-22-88	Budapest
30,000 meters	1:49:05.6	Karolina Szab¢, Hungary	4-22-88	Budapest
Marathon	2:21:06	Ingrid Kristiansen, Norway	4-21-85	London
100-meter hurdles	12.21	Yordanka Donkova, Bulgaria	8-20-88	Stara Zagora, Bulgaria
400-meter hurdles	52.74	Sally Gunnell, Great Britain	8-19-93	Stuttgart, Germany
5-kilometer walk	20:07.52	Beate Anders, East Germany	6-23-90	Rostock, Germany
10-kilometer walk	41:56.23	Nadezhda Ryashkina, USSR	7-24-90	Seattle
4x100-meter relay	41.37	East Germany (Silke Gladisch, Sabine Rieger, Ingrid Auerswald, Marlies Göhr)	10-6-85	Canberra, Australia
4x200-meter relay	1:28.15	East Germany (Marlies Göhr, Romy Müller, Bärbel Wöckel, Marita Koch)	8-9-80	Jena, East Germany
4x400-meter relay	3:15.17	USSR (Tatyana Ledovskaya, Olga Nazarova, Maria Pinigina, Olga Bryzgina)	10-1-88	Seoul
4x800-meter relay	7:50.17	USSR (Nadezhda Olizarenko, Lyubov Gurina, Lyudmila Borisova, Irina Podyalovskaya)	8-5-84	Moscow
High jump	6 ft 10¼ in	Stefka Kostadinova, Bulgaria	8-30-87	Rome
Long jump	24 ft 8¼ in	Galina Chistyakova, USSR	6-11-88	Leningrad
Triple Jump	49 ft 6¼ in	Ana Biryukova, Russia	8-21-93	Stuttgart, Germany
Shot put	74 ft 3 in	Natalya Lisovskaya, USSR	6-7-87	Moscow
Discus throw	252 ft 0 in	Gabriele Reinsch, East Germany	7-9-88	Neubrandenburg, Germany
Javelin throw	262 ft 5 in	Petra Felke, East Germany	9-9-88	Berlin
Heptathlon	7291 pts	Jackie Joyner-Kersee, United States	9-23/24-88	Seoul

Note: The heptathlon consists of 7 events—the 100-meter hurdles, high jump, shot put and 200 meters on the first day; the long jump, javelin and 800 meters on the second.

Ben Again

The news on March 5 that sprinter Ben Johnson had again tested positive for a banned substance—testosterone this time—was numbing and sad. So was what followed: The IAAF's doping commission voted to ban Johnson from the sport for life. Johnson, whose positive sample came from a Jan. 17 indoor meet in Montreal, said he won't appeal the suspension.

Since January 1991, when he returned from his two-year ban for having tested positive for steroids at the '88 Olympics in Seoul, Johnson had run no better than 10.16 seconds for 100 meters—a time that placed him 22nd on the world list for '92—and last summer he failed to make the 100 final at the Barcelona Games. Johnson, 31, who at his peak was virtually unbeatable and enjoyed six-figure paydays, had become an also-ran. That status changed, however, on the indoor circuit this winter. Last month in Grenoble, France, he ran 5.65 for 50 meters, only .04 off his own world record. Then came the results of the Montreal test.

Perhaps the best measure of how much drugs boosted Johnson's performance comes from Carl Lewis's coach, Tom Tellez. Two years ago Tellez noted that, while Lewis still had room to improve, he could never match the 9.79 Johnson ran in Seoul. If Lewis—the most gifted sprinter of our time—cannot run that fast, what chance do other runners have?

Track and field athletes often see themselves in an adversarial relationship with the sport's drug-testing system. That must change. The athletes have to acknowledge that drug use leaves the next generation with a terrible choice: Either settle for a lower level of performance or use drugs to attain a higher one. That choice ruined Johnson.

As of September 20, 1993. American outdoor records are recognized by USA Track and Field (USATF). WR=world record.

Men

Event	Mark	Record Holder	Date	Site
100 meters	9.86 WR	Carl Lewis	8-25-91	Tokyo
200 meters	19.73	Mike Marsh	8-5-92	Barcelona
400 meters	43.29 WR	Butch Reynolds	8-17-88	Zurich
800 meters	1:42.60	Johnny Gray	8-28-85	Koblenz, Germany
1,000 meters	2:13.9	Rick Wohlhuter	7-30-74	Oslo
1,500 meters	3:29.77	Sydney Maree	8-25-85	Cologne
Mile	3:47.69	Steve Scott	7-7-82	Oslo
2,000 meters	4:52.44	Jim Spivey	9-15-87	Lausanne
3,000 meters	7:35.84	Doug Padilla	7-9-83	Oslo
Steeplechase	8:09.17	Henry Marsh	8-28-85	Koblenz, Germany
5,000 meters	13:01.15	Sydney Maree	7-27-85	Oslo
10,000 meters	27:20.56	Mark Nenow	9-5-86	Brussels
20,000 meters	58:25.0	Bill Rodgers	8-9-77	Boston
Hour	20,547 meters	Bill Rodgers	8-9-77	Boston
25,000 meters	1:14:11.8	Bill Rodgers	2-21-79	Saratoga, CA
30,000 meters	1:31:49	Bill Rodgers	2-21-79	Saratoga, CA
Marathon	2:10:04	Pat Petersen	4-23-89	London
110-meter hurdles	12.92	Roger Kingdom	8-16-89	Zurich
400-meter hurdles	46.78 WR	Kevin Young	8-6-92	Barcelona
20-kilometer walk	1:24:50	Tim Lewis	5-7-88	Seattle
30-kilometer walk	2:23:14.0	Goetz Klopfer	11-15-70	Seattle
50-kilometer walk	4:04:23.8	Herm Nelson	10-29-89	Seattle
4x100-meter relay	37.40 WR	United States (Mike Marsh, Leroy Burrell, Dennis Mitchell, Carl Lewis)	8-8-92	Barcelona
		United States (Jon Drummond, Andre Cason, Dennis Mitchell, Leroy Burrell)	8-22-93	Stuttgart, Germany
4x200-meter relay	1:19.11 WR	Santa Monica Track Club (Mike Marsh, Leroy Burrell, Floyd Heard, Carl Lewis)	4-24-92	Philadelphia
4x400-meter relay	2:54.29 WR	United States (Andrew Valmon, Quincy Watts, Butch Reynolds, Michael Johnson)	8-22-93	Stuttgart, Germany
4x800-meter relay	7:06.5	Santa Monica Track Club (James Robinson, David Mack, Earl Jones, Johnny Gray)	4-26-86	Walnut, CA
4x1500-meter relay	14:46.3	National Team (Dan Aldredge, Andy Clifford, Todd Harbour, Tom Duits)	6-24-79	Bourges, France
High jump	7 ft 10½ in	Charles Austin	8-15-91	Zurich
Pole vault	19 ft 6½ in	Joe Dial	6-18-87	Norman, OK
Long jump	29 ft 4½ in WR	Mike Powell	8-30-91	Tokyo
Triple jump	58 ft 11½ in WR	Willie Banks	6-16-85	Indianapolis
Shot put	75 ft 10¼ in WR	Randy Barnes	5-20-90	Westwood, CA
Discus throw	237 ft 4 in	Ben Plucknett	7-7-81	Stockholm
Hammer throw	268 ft 8 in	Jud Logan	4-22-88	University Park, PA
Javelin throw	281 ft 2 in	Tom Pukstys	6-26-93	Kuortane, Finland
Decathlon	8891 pts WR	Dan O'Brien	9-4/5-92	Talence, France

Women

Event	Mark	Record Holder	Date	Site
100 meters	10.49 WR	Florence Griffith Joyner	7-16-88	Indianapolis
200 meters	21.34 WR	Florence Griffith Joyner	9-29-88	Seoul
400 meters	48.83	Valerie Brisco-Hooks	8-6-84	Los Angeles
800 meters	1:56.90	Mary Slaney	8-16-85	Bern, Switzerland
1,500 meters	3:57.12	Mary Slaney	7-26-83	Stockholm
Mile	4:16.71	Mary Slaney	8-21-85	Zurich
2,000 meters	5:32.7	Mary Slaney	8-3-84	Eugene, Ore.
3,000 meters	8:25.83	Mary Slaney	9-7-85	Rome
5,000 meters	14:56.07	Annette Peters	8-27-93	Berlin
10,000 meters	31:19.89	Lynn Jennings	8-7-92	Barcelona
Marathon	2:21:21	Joan Samuelson	10-20-85	Chicago
100-meter hurdles	12.46	Gail Devers	8-20-93	Stuttgart, Germany
400-meter hurdles	52.79	Sandra Farmer-Patrick	8-19-93	Stuttgart, Germany
5,000 meter walk	21:32	Debbi Lawrence	4-25-92	Philadelphia
10,000 meter walk	45:28.4	Debbi Lawrence	7-19-91	Westwood, Calif.
10-kilometer walk road	44:42	Debbi Lawrence	5-16-92	Kenosha, Wisconsin
4x100-meter relay	41.55	National Team (Alice Brown, Diane Williams, Florence Griffith, Pam Marshall)	8-21-87	Berlin
4x200-meter relay	1:32.57	Louisiana State (Tananjalyn Stanley, Sylvia Brydson, Esther Jones, Dawn Sowell)	4-28-89	Des Moines
4x400-meter relay	3:15.51	Olympic Team (Denean Howard, Diane Dixon, Valerie Brisco, Florence Griffith Joyner)	10-1-88	Seoul
4x800-meter relay	8:17.09	Athletics West (Sue Addison, Lee Arbogast, Mary Decker, Chris Mullen)	4-24-83	Walnut, Calif.
High jump	6 ft 8 in	Louise Ritter	7-8-88	Austin
		Louise Ritter	9-30-88	Seoul
Long jump	24 ft 5½ in	Jackie Joyner-Kersee	8-13-87	Indianapolis
Triple jump	46 ft 8¼ in	Sheila Hudson	6-20-92	New Orleans
Shot put	66 ft 2½ in	Ramona Pagel	6-25-88	San Diego
Discus throw	216 ft 10 in	Carol Cady	5-31-86	San Jose
Javelin throw	227 ft 5 in	Kate Schmidt	9-10-77	Fürth, West Germany
Heptathlon	7291 pts WR	Jackie Joyner-Kersee	9-23/24-88	Seoul

World and American Indoor Records

As of September 20, 1993. American indoor records are recognized by USA Track and Field. World Indoor records are recognized by the International Amateur Athletics Federation (IAAF).

Men

Event	Mark	Record Holder	Date	Site
50 meters	5.61	Manfred Kokot, East Germany (W)	2-4-73	Berlin
	5.61	James Sanford (W, A)	2-20-81	San Diego
55 meters*	6.00	Lee McRae (A)	3-14-86	Oklahoma City
60 meters	6.41	Andre Cason (W, A)	2-14-92	Madrid
200 meters	20.36	Bruno Marie-Rose, France (W)	2-22-72	Liévin, France
	20.55	Michael Johnson (A)	1-26-91	Liévin, France
400 meters	45.02	Danny Everett (W, A)	2-2-92	Stuttgart
800 meters	1:44.84	Paul Ereng, Kenya (W)	3-4-89	Budapest
	1:45.00	Johnny Gray (A)	3-8-92	Sindelfingen, Germany
1,000 meters	2:15.26	Noureddine Morceli, Algeria (W)	2-22-92	Birmingham, England
	2:18.19	Ocky Clark (A)	2-12-89	Stuttgart
1,500 meters	3:34.16	Noureddine Morceli, Algeria (W)	2-28-91	Seville
	3:38.12	Jeff Atkinson (A)	3-5-89	Budapest
Mile	3:49.78	Eamonn Coughlan, Ireland (W)	2-27-83	East Rutherford, NJ
	3:51.8	Steve Scott (A)	2-20-81	San Diego

Men (Cont.)

Event	Mark	Record Holder	Date	Site
3,000 meters	7:37.31	Moses Kiptanui, Kenya (W)	2-20-92	Seville
	7:39.94	Steve Scott (A)	2-10-89	East Rutherford, NJ
5,000 meters	13:20.4	Suleiman Nyambui, Tanzania (W)	2-6-81	New York City
	13:20.55	Doug Padilla (A)	2-12-82	Rosemont, Illinois
50-meter hurdles	6.25	Mark McKoy, Canada (W)	3-3-86	Kobe, Japan
	6.35	Greg Foster (A)	1-27-85	Rosemont, Illinois
55-meter hurdles*	6.35	Greg Foster (A)	1-31-87	Ottawa, Ontario
	6.89	Renaldo Nehemiah (A)	1-20-79	New York City
60-meter hurdles	7.36	Greg Foster (W, A)	1-16-87	Los Angeles
5,000-meter walk	18:15.25	Grigori Kornev, CIS	2-7-92	Karlsruhe, Germany
4x200-meter relay	1:22.11	Great Britain (W) (Linford Christie, Darren Braithwaite, Ade Mafe, John Regis)	3-3-91	Glasgow
	1:22.71	National Team (Thomas Jefferson, Raymond Pierre, Antonio McKay Kevin Little)	3-3-91	Glasgow
4x400-meter relay	3:03.05	Germany (W) (Rico Lieder, Jens Carlowitz, Klaus Just, Thomas Schönlebe)	3-10-91	Seville
	3:03.24	National Team (A) (Raymond Pierre, Chip Jenkins, Andrew Valmon, Antonio McKay)	3-10-91	Seville
4x800-meter relay	7:17.8	Soviet Union (W) (Valeriy Taratynov, Stanislav Meshcherskikh, Aleksey Taranov, Viktor Semyashkin)	3-14-71	Sofia
	7:18.23	University of Florida (A) (Dedric Jones, Lewis Lacy, Stephen Adderly, Scott Peters)	3-14-92	Sindelfingen, Germany
High jump	7 ft 11½ in	Javier Sotomayor, Cuba (W)	3-4-89	Budapest
	7 ft 10½ in	Hollis Conway (A)	3-10-91	Seville
Pole vault	20 ft 2 in	Sergei Bubka, Ukraine (W)	2-21-93	Donetsk, Ukraine
	19 ft 3¾ in	Billy Olsen (A)	1-25-86	Albuquerque
Long jump	28 ft 10¼ in	Carl Lewis (W, A)	1-27-84	New York City
Triple jump	58 ft 3¾ in	Mike Conley (W, A)	2-27-87	New York City
Shot put	74 ft 4¼ in	Randy Barnes (W, A)	1-20-89	Los Angeles
Weight Throw*	81 ft 6 in	Lance Deal (A)	2-26-93	Princeton, N.J.
Pentathlon	4440 pts	Christian Plaziat, France (W)	2-25-90	Toronto
	4399 pts	Bruce Reid (A)	2-25-89	Baton Rouge
Heptathlon	6476 pts	Dan O'Brien (W, A)	3-13/14-93	Toronto

*No world record.

Sidetracked

In May, after months of fruitless negotiations with dozens of potential sponsors, the New York Road Runners Club announced that Reebok had agreed to bankroll the New York Games only hours before the May 22 event was to be scratched. Founded in 1989, the track meet lost its main sponsor last fall when Mita, the copy machine company, pulled out. With Reebok's help, the meet went on at Columbia's Wien Stadium as scheduled.

Obviously, that's good news. But one wonders how the New York City meet ever got so close to extinction. After all, it's one of only two Grand Prix events in North America—the other is the Bruce Jenner Classic, in San Jose, which was held a week later—and it has consistently drawn such top athletes as Leroy Burrell, Jackie Joyner-Kersee, Roger Kingdom and Carl Lewis. Yet attendance has been disappointing.

But then, track and field is having its troubles generally, especially in New York. USA Track and Field announced in May that starting next year, the USA/Mobil indoor championship will move to the Georgia Dome, in Atlanta. The meet has been held in Madison Square Garden almost continuously since 1888, but lately attendance has declined and performances have been hampered by the Garden's narrow, 160-yard board track. The Georgia Dome will offer a state-of-the-art 200-meter track, and it is hoped that the Mobil meet can capitalize on increasing interest in track and field in Atlanta as the 1996 Summer Olympics draw closer.

Women

Event	Mark	Record Holder	Date	Site
50 meters	6.00	Irina Privalova, Russia (W)	2-2-93	Moscow
	6.10	Gail Devers (A)	2-20-93	Los Angeles
55 meters*	6.56	Gwen Torrence (A)	3-14-87	Oklahoma City
60 meters	6.92	Irina Privalova, Russia (W)	2-11-93	Madrid
	6.95	Gail Devers (A)	3-12-93	Toronto
200 meters	21.87	Merlene Ottey, Jamaica (W)	2-13-93	Lievin, France
	22.85	Gwen Torrence (A)	3-2-93	San Sebastian, Spain
400 meters	49.59	Jarmila Kratochvilová, Czech.	3-7-82	Milan
	50.64	Diane Dixon (A)	3-10-91	Seville
800 meters	1:56.40	Christine Wachtel, E Germany (W)	2-14-88	Vienna
	1:58.9	Mary Slaney (A)	2-22-80	San Diego
1,000 meters	2:34.67	Lilia Nurutdinova, CIS (W)	2-7-92	Moscow
	2:34.67	Lyubov Kremlyova, Russia (W)	2-13-93	Lievin, France
	2:37.60	Mary Slaney (A)	1-21-89	Portland
1,500 meters	4:00.27	Doina Melinte, Romania (W)	2-9-90	East Rutherford, NJ
	4:00.80	Mary Slaney (A)	2-8-80	New York City
Mile	4:17.14	Doina Melinte, Romania (W)	2-9-90	East Rutherford, NJ
	4:20.5	Mary Slaney (A)	2-19-82	San Diego
3,000 meters	8:33.82	Elly van Hulst, Netherlands (W)	3-4-89	Budapest
	8:40.45	Lynn Jennings (A)	2-23-90	New York City
5,000 meters	15:03.17	Liz McColgan, Scotland (W)	2-22-92	Birmingham, England
	15:22.64	Lynn Jennings (A)	1-7-90	Hanover, NH
50-meter hurdles	6.58	Comelia Oschkenat, E Germany (W)	2-20-88	Berlin
	6.84	Kim McKenzie (A)	1-20-89	Ottaway
	6.84	Jackie Joyner-Kersee (A)	2-20-93	Los Angeles
55-meter hurdles*	7.37	Jackie Joyner-Kersee (A)	2-3-89	New York City
60-meter hurdles	7.63	Lyudmila Narozhilenko, Russia (W)	2-4-93	Seville, Spain
	7.81	Jackie Joyner-Kersee (A)	2-5-89	Fairfax, Virginia
3,000 meter walk	11:44.00	Yelena Ivanova, CIS (W)	2-7-92	Moscow
	12:20.42	Debbi Lawrence (A)	3-12-93	Toronto
4x200-meter relay	1:32.55	SC Eintracht Hamm, W Gemany (W) (Helga Arendt, Silke-Beate Knoll, Mechthild Kluth, Gisela Kinzel)	2-20-88	Dortmund, W Germany
	1:34.97	National Team (A) (Wenda Vereen, Kim Graham, Angela Williams, Terri Dendy)	2-13-93	Birmingham, England
4x400-meter relay	3:27.22	Germany (W) (Sandra Seuser, Annett Hesselbarth, Katrin Schreiter, Grit Breuer)	3-10-91	Seville
	3:29.00	National Team (A) (Terri Dendy, Lillie Leatherwood, Jearl Miles, Diane Dixon)	3-10-91	Seville
4x800-meter relay	8:25.5	Villanova (W, A) (Gina Procaccio, Debbie Grant, Michelle DiMuro, Celeste Halliday)	2-27-87	Gainesville, Florida
High jump	6 ft 9½ in	Heike Henkel, Germany (W)	2-8-92	Karlsruhe, Germany
	6 ft 6¾ in	Coleen Sommer (A)	2-13-82	Ottawa
Long jump	24 ft 2¼ in	Heike Drechsler, E Germany (W)	2-14-88	Vienna
	23 ft 1¼ in	Jackie Joyner-Kersee (A)	3-7-92	Yokohama, Japan
Triple jump	47 ft 5 ¾ in	Inessa Kravets, Ukraine (W)	3-14-93	Toronto
	45 ft 9 in	Sheila Hudson (A)	3-10-90	Indianapolis
Shot put	73 ft 10 in	Helena Fibingerová, Czech.	2-19-77	Jablonec, Czech.
	65 ft ¾ in	Ramona Pagel (A)	2-20-87	Inglewood, California
Weight Throw*	62 ft 10 in	Sonja Fitts (unatt)	2-28-92	Princeton, N.J.
Pentathlon	4991 pts	Irina Byelova, CIS (W)	2-14/15-92	Berlin
	4566 pts	Kym Carter (A)	3-12-93	Toronto

World Track and Field Championships

Historically, the Olympics have served as the outdoor world championships for track and field. In 1983 the International Amateur Athletic Federation (IAAF) instituted a separate World Championship meet, to be held every 4 years between the Olympics. The first was held in Helsinki in 1983, the second in Rome in 1987, the third in Tokyo in 1991. In 1993 the IAAF began to hold the meet on a biennial basis.

HELSINKI 1983

Men

TRACK EVENTS

Event	Winner	Time
100 meters	Carl Lewis, United States	10.07
200 meters	Calvin Smith, United States	20.14
400 meters	Bert Cameron, Jamaica	45.05
800 meters	Willi Wulbeck, West Germany	1:43.65
1,500 meters	Steve Cram, Great Britain	3:41.59
Steeplechase	Patriz Ilg, West Germany	8:15.06
5,000 meters	Eamonn Coghlan, Ireland	13:28.53
10,000 meters	Alberto Cova, Italy	28:01.04
Marathon	Rob de Castella, Australia	2:10:03
110-meter hurdles	Greg Foster, United States	13.42
400-meter hurdles	Edwin Moses, United States	47.50
20 kilometer walk	Ernesto Canto, Mexico	1:20:49
50 kilometer walk	Ronald Weigel, East Germany	3:43:08
4x100 meter relay	United States (Emmit King, Willie Gault, Calvin Smith, Carl Lewis)	37.86
4x400 meters	USSR (Sergei Lovachev, Alecksandr Troschilo, Nikolay Chernyetski, Viktor Markin)	3:00.79

FIELD EVENTS

Event	Winner	Mark
High jump	Gennadi Avdeyenko, USSR	7 ft 7¼ in
Pole vault	Sergei Bubka, USSR	18 ft 8¼ in
Long jump	Carl Lewis, United States	28 ft 3/4 in
Triple jump	Zdzislaw Hoffmann, Poland	57 ft 2 in
Shot put	Edward Sarul, Poland	70 ft 2¼ in
Discus throw	Imrich Bugar, Czechoslovakia	222 ft 2 in
Hammer throw	Sergei Litvinov, USSR	271 ft 3 in
Javelin throw	Detlef Michel, East Germany	293 ft 7 in

DECATHLON

Event	Winner	Pts
Decathlon	Daley Thompson, Great Britain	8666 pts.

Women

TRACK EVENTS

Event	Winner	Time
100 meters	Marlies Gohr, East Germany	10.97
200 meters	Marita Koch, East Germany	22.13
400 meters	Jarmila Kratochvilova, Czechoslovakia	47.99
800 meters	Jarmila Kratochvilova, Czechoslovakia	1:54.68
1,500 meters	Mary Slaney, United States	4:00.90
3,000 meters	Mary Slaney, United States	8:34.62
Marathon	Grete Waitz, Norway	2:28:09
100-meter hurdles	Bettine Jahn, East Germany	12.35
400-meter hurdles	Yekaterina Fesenko, USSR	54.14
4x100 meter relay	East Germany (Silke Gladisch, Marita Koch, Averswald, Marlies Gohr)	41.76
4x400 meter relay	East Germany (Kerstin Walther, Sabine Busch, Marita Koch, Dagmar Rubsam)	3:19.73

FIELD EVENTS

Event	Winner	Mark
High jump	Tamara Bykova, USSR	6 ft 7 in
Long jump	Heike Daute, East Germany	23 ft 10¼ in
Shot put	Helena Fibingerova, Czechoslovakia	69 ft ¾ in
Discus throw	Martina Opitz, East Germany	226 ft 2 in
Javelin throw	Tiina Lillak, Finland	232 ft 4 in

HEPTATHLON

Event	Winner	Pts
Heptathlon	Ramona Neubert, East Germany	6714

ROME 1987

Men

TRACK EVENTS

Event	Winner	Time
100 meters*	Carl Lewis, United States	9.93WR
200 meters	Calvin Smith, United States	20.16
400 meters	Thomas Schoenlebe, East Germany	44.33
800 meters	Billy Konchellah, Kenya	1:43.06
1,500 meters	Abdi Bile, Somalia	3:36.80
Steeplechase	Francesco Panetta, Italy	8:08.57
5,000 meters	Said Aouita, Morocco	13:26.44
10,000 meters	Paul Kipkoech, Kenya	27:38.63
Marathon	Douglas Wakiihuri, Kenya	2:11:48
110-meter hurdles	Greg Foster, United States	13.21
400-meter hurdles	Edwin Moses, United States	47.46
20 kilometer walk	Maurizio Damilano, Italy	1:20:45
50 kilometer walk	Hartwig Gauder, East Germany	3:40:53
4x100 meter relay	United States (Lee McRae, Lee McNeil, Harvey Glance, Carl Lewis)	37.90
4x400 meter relay	United States (Danny Everett, Rod Haley, Antonio McKay, Butch Reynolds)	2:57.29

FIELD EVENTS

Event	Winner	Mark
High jump	Patrik Sjoberg, Sweden	7 ft 9¾ in
Pole vault	Sergei Bubka, USSR	19 ft 2¼ in
Long jump	Carl Lewis, United States	28 ft 5¼ in
Triple jump	Khristo Markov, Bulgaria	58 ft 9½ in
Shot put	Werner Gunthor, Switzerland	72 ft 11¼ in
Discus throw	Juergen Schult, East Germany	225 ft 6 in
Hammer throw	Sergei Litvinov, USSR	272 ft 6 in
Javelin throw	Seppo Räty, Finland	274 ft 1 in

DECATHLON

Event	Winner	Pts
Decathlon	Torsten Voss, East Germany	8680

Women

TRACK EVENTS

Event	Winner	Time
100 meters	Silke Gladisch, East Germany	10.90
200 meters	Silke Gladisch, East Germany	21.74
400 meters	Olga Bryzgina, USSR	49.38
800 meters	Sigrun Wodars, East Germany	1:55.26
1,500 meters	Tatyana Samolenko, USSR	3:58.56
3,000 meters	Tatyana Samolenko, USSR	8:38.73
10,000 meters	Ingrid Kristiansen, Norway	31:05.85
Marathon	Rosa Mota, Portugal	2:25:17
100-meter hurdles	Ginka Zagorcheva, Bulgaria	12.34
400-meter hurdles	Sabine Busch, East Germany	53.62
10 kilometer walk	Irina Strakhova, USSR	44:12
4x100 meter relay	United States (Alice Brown, Diane Williams, Florence Griffith, Pam Marshall)	41.58
4x400 meter relay	East Germany (Dagmar Neubauer, Kirsten Emmelmann, Petra Müller, Sabine Busch)	3:18.63

FIELD EVENTS

Event	Winner	Mark
High jump	Stefka Kostadinova, Bulgaria	6 ft 10¼ in
Long jump	Jackie Joyner-Kersee, United States	24 ft 1¾ in
Shot put	Natalya Lisovskaya, USSR	69 ft 8¼ in
Discus throw	Martina Hellmann, East Germany	235 ft 0 in
Javelin throw	Fatima Whitbread, Great Britain	251 ft 5 in

HEPTATHLON

Event	Winner	Pts
Heptathlon	Jackie Joyner-Kersee, United States	7128

WR=World record.

*Ben Johnson, Canada, disqualified

TOKYO 1991

Men

TRACK EVENTS

Event	Winner	Time
100 meters	Carl Lewis, US	9.86 WR
200 meters	Michael Johnson, US	20.01
400 meters	Antonio Pettigrew, US	44.57
800 meters	Billy Konchellah, Kenya	1:43.99
1,500 meters	Noureddine Morceli, Algeria	3:32.84
Steeplechase	Moses Kiptanui, Kenya	8:12.59
5,000 meters	Yobes Ondieki, Kenya	13:14.45
10,000 meters	Moses Tanui, Kenya	27:38.74
Marathon	Hiromi Taniguchi, Japan	2:14:57
110-meter hurdles	Greg Foster, US	13.06
400-meter hurdles	Samuel Matete, Zambia	47.64
20-kilometer walk	Maurizio Damilano, Italy	1:19:37
50-kilometer walk	Aleksandr Potashov, USSR	3:53:09
4x100-meter relay	United States (Andre Cason, Leroy Burrell, Dennis Mitchell, Carl Lewis)	37.50 WR
4x400-meter relay	Great Britain (Roger Black Derek Redmond, John Regis, Kriss Akabusi)	2:57.53

FIELD EVENTS

Event	Winner	Mark
High jump	Charles Austin, United States	7 ft 9¾ in
Pole vault	Sergei Bubka, USSR	19 ft 6¼ in
Long jump	Mike Powell, United States	29 ft 4 ½ in WR
Triple jump	Kenny Harrison, United States	58 ft 4 in
Shot put	Werner Gunthor, Switzerland	71 ft 1¼ in
Discus	Lars Riedel, Germany	217 ft 2 in
Hammer	Yuriy Sedykh, USSR	268 ft
Javelin	Kimmo Kinnunen, Finland	297 ft 11 in

DECATHLON

Event	Winner	Pts
Decathlon	Dan O'Brien, US	8812

Women

TRACK EVENTS

Event	Winner	Time
100 meters	Katrin Krabbe, Germany	10.99
200 meters	Katrin Krabbe, Germany	22.09
400 meters	Marie-Jose Perec, France	49.13
800 meters	Lilia Nurutdinova, USSR	1:57.50
1,500 meters	Hassiba Boulmerka, Algeria	4:02.21
3,000 meters	Tatyana Dorovskikh, USSR	8:35.82
10,000 meters	Liz McColgan, Great Britain	31:14.31
Marathon	Wanda Panfil, Poland	2:29:53
100-meter hurdles	Lyudmila Narozhilenko, USSR	12.59
400-meter hurdles	Tatyana Ledovskaya, USSR	53.11
10-kilometer walk	Alina Ivanova, USSR	42:57
4x100-meter relay	Jamaica (Dahlia Duhaney, Juliet Cuthbert, Beverley McDonald, Merlene Ottey)	41.94
4x400-meter relay	USSR (Tatyana Ledovskaya, Lyudmila Dzhigalova, Olga Nazarova, Olga Bryzgina)	3:18.43

WR=World record.

FIELD EVENTS

Event	Winner	Mark
High jump	Heike Henkel, Germany	6 ft 8¾ in
Long jump	Jackie Joyner-Kersee, United States	24 ft ¼ in
Shot put	Zhihong Huang, China	68 ft 4¼ in
Discus	Tsvetanka Khristova, Bulgaria	233 ft
Javelin	Demei Xu, China	225 ft 8 in

HEPTATHLON

Event	Winner	Pts
Heptathlon	Sabine Braun, Germany	6672 pts

Track & Field News Athlete of the Year

Each year (since 1959 for men and since 1974 for women) Track & Field News has chosen the outstanding athlete in the sport.

Men

Year	Athlete	Event
1959	Martin Lauer, West Germany	110-meter hurdles/Decathlon
1960	Rafer Johnson, United States	Decathlon
1961	Ralph Boston, United States	Long jump
1962	Peter Snell, New Zealand	800/1500 meters
1963	C. K. Yang, Taiwan	Decathlon/Pole vault
1964	Peter Snell, New Zealand	800/1500 meters
1965	Ron Clarke, Australia	5,000/10,000 meters
1966	Jim Ryun, United States	800/1500 meters
1967	Jim Ryun, United States	1500 meters
1968	Bob Beamon, United States	Long jump
1969	Bill Toomey, United States	Decathlon
1970	Randy Matson, United States	Shot put
1971	Rod Milburn, United States	110-meter hurdles
1972	Lasse Viren, Finland	5,000/10,000 meters
1973	Ben Jipcho, Kenya	1500/5000 meters/Steeplechase
1974	Rick Wohlhuter, United States	800/1500 meters
1975	John Walker, New Zealand	800/1500 meters
1976	Alberto Juantorena, Cuba	400/800 meters
1977	Alberto Juantorena, Cuba	400/800 meters
1978	Henry Rono, Kenya	5,000/10,000 meters/Steeplechase
1979	Sebastian Coe, Great Britain	800/1500 meters
1980	Edwin Moses, United States	400-meter hurdles
1981	Sebastian Coe, Great Britain	800/1500 meters
1982	Carl Lewis, United States	100/200 meters/Long jump
1983	Carl Lewis, United States	100/200 meters/Long jump
1984	Carl Lewis, United States	100/200 meters/Long jump
1985	Said Aouita, Morocco	1500/5000 meters
1986	Yuri Syedikh, USSR	Hammer throw
1987	Ben Johnson, Canada	100 meters
1988	Sergei Bubka, USSR	Pole vault
1989	Roger Kingdom, United States	110-meter hurdles
1990	Michael Johnson, United States	200/400 meters
1991	Sergei Bubka, CIS	Pole vault
1992	Kevin Young, U.S.	400-meter hurdles

Women

Year	Athlete	Event
1974	Irena Szewinska, Poland	100/200/400 meters
1975	Faina Melnik, USSR	Shot put/Discus
1976	Tatyana Kazankina, USSR	800/1500 meters
1977	Rosemarie Ackermann, East Germany	High jump
1978	Marita Koch, East Germany	100/200/400 meters
1979	Marita Koch, East Germany	100/200/400 meters
1980	Ilona Briesenick, East Germany	Shot put
1981	Evelyn Ashford, United States	100/200 meters
1982	Marita Koch, East Germany	100/200/400 meters
1983	Jarmila Kratochvilova, Czechoslovakia	200/400/800 meters
1984	Evelyn Ashford, United States	100 meters
1985	Marita Koch, East Germany	100/200/400 meters
1986	Jackie Joyner-Kersee, United States	Long jump/Heptathlon
1987	Jackie Joyner-Kersee, United States	100-meter hurdles/Long jump/Heptathlon
1988	Florence Griffith Joyner, United States	100/200 meters
1989	Ana Quirot, Cuba	400/800 meters
1990	Merlene Ottey, Jamaica	100/200 meters
1991	Heike Henkel, Germany	High jump
1992	Heike Drechsler, Germany	Long Jump

MARATHON

World Record Progression

Men

Record Holder	Time	Date	Site
John Hayes, United States	2:55:18.4	7-24-08	Shepherd's Bush, London
Robert Fowler, United States	2:52:45.4	1-1-09	Yonkers, NY
James Clark, United States	2:46:52.6	2-12-09	New York City
Albert Raines, United States	2:46:04.6	5-8-09	New York City
Frederick Barrett, Great Britain	2:42:31	5-26-09	Shepherd's Bush, London
Harry Green, Great Britain	2:38:16.2	5-12-13	Shepherd's Bush, London
Alexis Ahlgren, Sweden	2:36:06.6	5-31-13	Shepherd's Bush, London
Johannes Kolehmainen, Finland	2:32:35.8	8-22-20	Antwerp, Belgium
Albert Michelsen, United States	2:29:01.8	10-12-25	Port Chester, NY
Fusashige Suzuki, Japan	2:27:49	3-31-35	Tokyo
Yasuo Ikenaka, Japan	2:26:44	4-3-35	Tokyo
Kitei Son, Japan	2:26:42	11-3-35	Tokyo
Yun Bok Suh, Korea	2:25:39	4-19-47	Boston
James Peters, Great Britain	2:20:42.2	6-14-52	Chiswick, England
James Peters, Great Britain	2:18:40.2	6-13-53	Chiswick, England
James Peters, Great Britain	2:18:34.8	10-4-53	Turku, Finland
James Peters, Great Britain	2:17:39.4	6-26-54	Chiswick, England
Sergei Popov, USSR	2:15:17	8-24-58	Stockholm
Abebe Bikila, Ethiopia	2:15:16.2	9-10-60	Rome
Toru Terasawa, Japan	2:15:15.8	2-17-63	Beppu, Japan
Leonard Edelen, United States	2:14:28	6-15-63	Chiswick, England
Basil Heatley, Great Britain	2:13:55	6-13-64	Chiswick, England
Abebe Bikila, Ethiopia	2:12:11.2	6-21-64	Tokyo
Morio Shigematsu, Japan	2:12:00	6-12-65	Chiswick, England
Derek Clayton, Australia	2:09:36.4	12-3-67	Fukuoka, Japan
Derek Clayton, Australia	2:08:33.6	5-30-69	Antwerp, Belgium
Rob de Castella, Australia	2:08:18	12-6-81	Fukuoka, Japan
Steve Jones, Great Britain	2:08:05	10-21-84	Chicago
Carlos Lopes, Portugal	2:07:12	4-20-85	Rotterdam, Netherlands
Belayneh Densimo, Ethiopia	2:06:50	4-17-88	Rotterdam, Netherlands

Women

Record Holder	Time	Date	Site
Dale Greig, Great Britain	3:27:45	5-23-64	Ryde, England
Mildred Simpson, New Zealand	3:19:33	7-21-64	Auckland, New Zealand
Maureen Wilton, Canada	3:15:22	5-6-67	Toronto
Anni Pede-Erdkamp, West Germany	3:07:26	9-16-67	Waldniel, West Germany
Caroline Walker, United States	3:02:53	2-28-70	Seaside, OR
Elizabeth Bonner, United States	3:01:42	5-9-71	Philadelphia
Adrienne Beames, Australia	2:46:30	8-31-71	Werribee, Australia
Chantal Langlace, France	2:46:24	10-27-74	Neuf Brisach, France
Jacqueline Hansen, United States	2:43:54.5	12-1-74	Culver City, CA
Liane Winter, West Germany	2:42:24	4-21-75	Boston
Christa Vahlensieck, West Germany	2:40:15.8	5-3-75	Dülmen, West Germany
Jacqueline Hansen, United States	2:38:19	10-12-75	Eugene, OR
Chantal Langlace, France	2:35:15.4	5-1-77	Oyarzun, France
Christa Vahlensieck, West Germany	2:34:47.5	9-10-77	West Berlin, West Germany
Grete Waitz, Norway	2:32:29.9	10-22-78	New York City
Grete Waitz, Norway	2:27:32.6	10-21-79	New York City
Grete Waitz, Norway	2:25:41.3	10-26-80	New York City
Grete Waitz, Norway	2:25:29	4-17-83	London
Joan Benoit Samuelson, United States	2:22:43	4-18-83	Boston
Ingrid Kristiansen, Norway	2:21:06	4-21-85	London

Boston Marathon

The Boston Marathon began in 1897 as a local Patriot's Day event. Run every year but 1918 since then, it has grown into one of the world's premier marathons.

Men

Year	Winner	Time	Year	Winner	Time
1897	John J. McDermott, United States	2:55:10	1946	Stylianos Kyriakides, Greece	2:29:27
1898	Ronald J. McDonald, United States	2:42:00	1947	Yun Bok Suh, Korea	2:25:39
1899	Lawrence J. Brignolia, United States	2:54:38	1948	Gerard Cote, Canada	2:31:02
1900	James J. Caffrey, Canada	2:39:44	1949	Karl Gosta Leandersson, Sweden	2:31:50
1901	James J. Caffrey, Canada	2:29:23	1950	Kee Yong Ham, Korea	2:32:39
1902	Sammy Mellor, United States	2:43:12	1951	Shigeki Tanaka, Japan	2:27:45
1903	John C. Lorden, United States	2:41:29	1952	Doroteo Flores, Guatemala	2:31:53
1904	Michael Spring, United States	2:38:04	1953	Keizo Yamada, Japan	2:18:51
1905	Fred Lorz, United States	2:38:25	1954	Veikko Karvonen, Finland	2:20:39
1906	Timothy Ford, United States	2:45:45	1955	Hideo Hamamura, Japan	2:18:22
1907	Tom Longboat, Canada	2:24:24	1956	Antti Viskari, Finland	2:14:14
1908	Thomas Morrissey, United States	2:25:43	1957	John J. Kelley, United States	2:20:05
1909	Henri Renaud, United States	2:53:36	1958	Franjo Mihalic, Yugoslavia	2:25:54
1910	Fred Cameron, United States	2:28:52	1959	Eino Oksanen, Finland	2:22:42
1911	Clarence H. DeMar, United States	2:21:39	1960	Paavo Kotila, Finland	2:20:54
1912	Mike Ryan, United States	2:21:18	1961	Eino Oksanen, Finland	2:23:39
1913	Fritz Carlson, United States	2:25:14	1962	Eino Oksanen, Finland	2:23:48
1914	James Duffy, Canada	2:25:01	1963	Aurele Vandendriessche, Belgium	2:18:58
1915	Edouard Fabre, Canada	2:31:41	1964	Aurele Vandendriessche, Belgium	2:19:59
1916	Arthur Roth, United States	2:27:16	1965	Morio Shigematsu, Japan	2:16:33
1917	Bill Kennedy, United States	2:28:37	1966	Kenji Kimihara, Japan	2:17:11
1918	No race		1967	David McKenzie, New Zealand	2:15:45
1919	Carl Linder, United States	2:29:13	1968	Amby Burfoot, United States	2:22:17
1920	Peter Trivoulidas, Greece	2:29:31	1969	Yoshiaki Unetani, Japan	2:13:49
1921	Frank Zuna, United States	2:18:57	1970	Ron Hill, England	2:10:30
1922	Clarence H. DeMar, United States	2:18:10	1971	Alvaro Mejia, Colombia	2:18:45
1923	Clarence H. DeMar, United States	2:23:37	1972	Olavi Suomalainen, Finland	2:15:39
1924	Clarence H. DeMar, United States	2:29:40	1973	Jon Anderson, United States	2:16:03
1925	Chuck Mellor, United States	2:33:00	1974	Neil Cusack, Ireland	2:13:39
1926	John C. Miles, Canada	2:25:40	1975	Bill Rodgers, United States	2:09:55
1927	Clarence H. DeMar, United States	2:40:22	1976	Jack Fultz, United States	2:20:19
1928	Clarence H. DeMar, United States	2:37:07	1977	Jerome Drayton, Canada	2:14:46
1929	John C. Miles, Canada	2:33:08	1978	Bill Rodgers, United States	2:10:13
1930	Clarence H. DeMar, United States	2:34:48	1979	Bill Rodgers, United States	2:09:27
1931	James "Hinky" Henigan, United States	2:46:45	1980	Bill Rodgers, United States	2:12:11
1932	Paul de Bruyn, Germany	2:33:36	1981	Toshihiko Seko, Japan	2:09:26
1933	Leslie Pawson, United States	2:31:01	1982	Alberto Salazar, United States	2:08:52
1934	Dave Komonen, Canada	2:32:53	1983	Gregory A. Meyer, United States	2:09:00
1935	John A. Kelley, United States	2:32:07	1984	Geoff Smith, England	2:10:34
1936	Ellison M. "Tarzan" Brown, United States	2:33:40	1985	Geoff Smith, England	2:14:05
1937	Walter Young, Canada	2:33:20	1986	Rob de Castella, Australia	2:07:51
1938	Leslie Pawson, United States	2:35:34	1987	Toshihiko Seko, Japan	2:11:50
1939	Ellison M. "Tarzan" Brown, United States	2:28:51	1988	Ibrahim Hussein, Kenya	2:08:43
1940	Gerard Cote, Canada	2:28:28	1989	Abebe Mekonnen, Ethiopia	2:09:06
1941	Leslie Pawson, United States	2:30:38	1990	Gelindo Bordin, Italy	2:08:19
1942	Bernard Joseph Smith, United States	2:26:51	1991	Ibrahim Hussein, Kenya	2:11:06
1943	Gerard Cote, Canada	2:28:25	1992	Ibrahim Hussein, Kenya	2:08:14
1944	Gerard Cote, Canada	2:31:50	1993	Cosmas N'Deti, Kenya	2:09:33
1945	John A. Kelley, United States	2:30:40			

Women

Year	Winner	Time	Year	Winner	Time
1966	Roberta Gibb, United States	3:21:40*	1976	Kim Merritt, United States	2:47:10
1967	Roberta Gibb, United States	3:27:17*	1977	Miki Gorman, United States	2:48:33
1968	Roberta Gibb, United States	3:30:00*	1978	Gayle Barron, United States	2:44:52
1969	Sara Mae Berman, United States	3:22:46*	1979	Joan Benoit, United States	2:35:15
1970	Sara Mae Berman, United States	3:05:07*	1980	Jacqueline Gareau, Canada	2:34:28
1971	Sara Mae Berman, United States	3:08:30*	1981	Allison Roe, New Zealand	2:26:46
1972	Nina Kuscsik, United States	3:10:36	1982	Charlotte Teske, West Germany	2:29:33
1973	Jacqueline A. Hansen, United States	3:05:59	1983	Joan Benoit, United States	2:22:43
1974	Miki Gorman, United States	2:47:11	1984	Lorraine Moller, New Zealand	2:29:28
1975	Liane Winter, West Germany	2:42:24	1985	Lisa Larsen Weidenbach, United States	2:34:06

Boston Marathon (Cont.)

Women (Cont.)

Year	Winner	Time	Year	Winner	Time
1986...Ingrid Kristiansen, Norway		2:24:55	1990...Rosa Mota, Portugal		2:25:24
1987...Rosa Mota, Portugal		2:25:21	1991...Wanda Panfil, Poland		2:24:18
1988...Rosa Mota, Portugal		2:24:30	1992...Olga Markova, Russia		2:23:43
1989...Ingrid Kristiansen, Norway		2:24:33	1993...Olga Markova, Russia		2:25:27

*Unofficial.

Note: Over the years the Boston course has varied in length. The distances have been 24 miles, 1232 yards (1897-1923); 26 miles, 209 yards (1924-1926); 26 miles 385 yards (1927-1952); and 25 miles, 958 yards (1953-1956). Since 1957, the course has been certified to be the standard marathon distance of 26 miles, 385 yards.

New York City Marathon

From 1970 through 1975 the New York City Marathon was a small local race run in the city's Central Park. In 1976 it was moved to the streets of New York's 5 boroughs. It has since become one of the biggest and most prestigious marathons in the world.

Men

Year	Winner	Time	Year	Winner	Time
1970...Gary Muhrcke, United States		2:31:38	1982...Alberto Salazar, United States		2:09:29
1971...Norman Higgins, United States		2:22:54	1983...Rod Dixon, New Zealand		2:08:59
1972...Sheldon Karlin, United States		2:27:52	1984...Orlando Pizzolato, Italy		2:14:53
1973...Tom Fleming, United States		2:21:54	1985...Orlando Pizzolato, Italy		2:11:34
1974...Norbert Sander, United States		2:26:30	1986...Gianni Poli, Italy		2:11:06
1975...Tom Fleming, United States		2:19:27	1987...Ibrahim Hussein, Kenya		2:11:01
1976...Bill Rodgers, United States		2:10:10	1988...Steve Jones, Great Britain		2:08:20
1977...Bill Rodgers, United States		2:11:28	1989...Juma Ikangaa, Tanzania		2:08:01
1978...Bill Rodgers, United States		2:12:12	1990...Douglas Wakiihuri, Kenya		2:12:39
1979...Bill Rodgers, United States		2:11:42	1991...Salvador Garcia, Mexico		2:09:28
1980...Alberto Salazar, United States		2:09:41	1992...Willie Mtolo, South Africa		2:09:29
1981...Alberto Salazar, United States		2:08:13			

Women

Year	Winner	Time	Year	Winner	Time
1970...No finisher			1982...Grete Waitz, Norway		2:27:14
1971...Beth Bonner, United States		2:55:22	1983...Grete Waitz, Norway		2:27:00
1972...Nina Kuscsik, United States		3:08:41	1984...Grete Waitz, Norway		2:29:30
1973...Nina Kuscsik, United States		2:57:07	1985...Grete Waitz, Norway		2:28:34
1974...Katherine Switzer, United States		3:07:29	1986...Grete Waitz, Norway		2:28:06
1975...Kim Merritt, United States		2:46:14	1987...Priscilla Welch, Great Britain		2:30:17
1976...Miki Gorman, United States		2:39:11	1988...Grete Waitz, Norway		2:28:07
1977...Miki Gorman, United States		2:43:10	1989...Ingrid Kristiansen, Norway		2:25:30
1978...Grete Waitz, Norway		2:32:30	1990...Wanda Panfiil, Poland		2:30:45
1979...Grete Waitz, Norway		2:27:33	1991...Liz McColgan, Scotland		2:27:23
1980...Grete Waitz, Norway		2:25:41	1992...Lisa Ondieki, Australia		2:24:40
1981...Allison Roe, New Zealand		2:25:29			

CROSS COUNTRY

World Cross-Country Championships

Conducted by the International Amateur Athletic Federation (IAAF), this meet annually brings together the best runners in the world at every distance from the mile to the marathon to compete in the same cross-country race.

Men

Year	Winner	Winning Team	Year	Winner	Winning Team
1973.....Pekka Paivarinta, Finland		Belgium	1977.....Leon Schots, Belgium		Belgium
1974.....Eric DeBeck, Belgium		Belgium	1978.....John Treacy, Ireland		France
1975.....Ian Stewart, Scotland		New Zealand	1979.....John Treacy, Ireland		England
1976.....Carlos Lopes, Portugal		England	1980.....Craig Virgin, United States		England

Men (Cont.)

Year	Winner	Winning Team	Year	Winner	Winning Team
1981	Craig Virgin, United States	Ethiopia	1988	John Ngugi, Kenya	Kenya
1982	Mohammed Kedir, Ethiopia	Ethiopia	1989	John Ngugi, Kenya	Kenya
1983	Bekele Debele, Ethiopia	Ethiopia	1990	Khalid Skah, Morocco	Kenya
1984	Carlos Lopes, Portugal	Ethiopia	1991	Khalid Skah, Morocco	Kenya
1985	Carlos Lopes, Portugal	Ethiopia	1992	John Ngugi, Kenya	Kenya
1986	John Ngugi, Kenya	Kenya	1993	William Sigei, Kenya	Kenya
1987	John Ngugi, Kenya	Kenya			

Women

Year	Winner	Winning Team	Year	Winner	Winning Team
1973	Paola Cacchi, Italy	England	1984	Maricica Puica, Romania	United States
1974	Paola Cacchi, Italy	England	1985	Zola Budd, England	United States
1975	Julie Brown, United States	United States	1986	Zola Budd, England	England
1976	Carmen Valero, Spain	USSR	1987	Annette Sergent, France	United States
1977	Carmen Valero, Spain	USSR	1988	Ingrid Kristiansen, Norway	USSR
1978	Grete Waitz, Norway	Romania	1989	Annette Sergent, France	USSR
1979	Grete Waitz, Norway	United States	1990	Lynn Jennings, United States	USSR
1980	Grete Waitz, Norway	USSR	1991	Lynn Jennings, United States	Kenya
1981	Grete Waitz, Norway	USSR	1992	Lynn Jennings, United States	Kenya
1982	Maricica Puica, Romania	USSR	1993	Albertina Dias, Portugal	Kenya
1983	Grete Waitz, Norway	United States			

Notable Achievements

Longest Winning Streaks

MEN

Event	Name and Nationality	Streak	Years
100-meter dash	Bob Hayes, United States	49	1962-64
200-meter dash	Manfred Gemar, Germany	41	1956-60
400-meter run	Ardalion Ignatyev, USSR	29	1952-56
800-meter run	Mal Whitfield, United States	40	1951-54
1500-meter run	Josy Barthel, Luxembourg	17	1952
1500-meter run/mile	Steve Ovett, Great Britain	45	1977-80
Mile	Herb Elliott, Australia	35	1957-60
Steeplechase	Gaston Roelants, Belgium	45	1961-66
5000-meter run	Emil Zátopek, Czechoslovakia	48	1949-52
10,000-meter run	Emil Zátopek, Czechoslovakia	38	1948-54
Marathon	Frank Shorter, United States	6	1971-73
110-meter hurdles	Jack Davis, United States	44	1952-55
400-meter hurdles	Edwin Moses, United States	107	1977-87
High Jump	Ernie Shelton, United States	46	1953-55
Pole Vault	Bob Richards, United States	50	1950-52
Long Jump	Carl Lewis, United States	65	1981-91
Triple Jump	Adhemar da Silva, Brazil	60	1950-56
Shot Put	Parry O'Brien, United States	116	1952-56
Discus Throw	Ricky Bruch, Sweden	54	1972-73
Hammer Throw	Imre Nemeth, Hungary	73	1946-50
Javelin Throw	Janis Lusis, USSR	41	1967-70
Decathlon	Bob Mathias, United States	11	1948-56

WOMEN

Event	Name and Nationality	Streak	Years
100-meter dash	Merlene Ottey, Jamaica	56	1987-91
200-meter dash	Irena Szewinska, Poland	38	1973-75
400-meter run	Irena Szewinska, Poland	36	1973-78
800-meter run	Ana Fidelia Quirot, Cuba	36	1987-90
1500-meter run	Paula Ivan, Romania	15	1988-91
1500-meter run/mile	Paula Ivan, Romania	19	1988-90
3000-meter run	Mary Slaney, United States	10	1982-84
10,000-meter run	Ingrid Kristiansen, Norway	5	1985-87

Longest Winning Streaks (Cont.)

WOMEN (Cont.)

Event	Name and Nationality	Streak	Years
Marathon	Katrin Dörre, East Germany	10	1982-86
100-meter hurdles	Annelie Ernhardt, East Germany	44	1972-75
400-meter hurdles	Ann-Louise Skoglund, Sweden	18	1981-83
High Jump	Iolanda Balas, Romania	140	1956-67
Long Jump	Tatyana Shchelkanova, USSR	19	1964-66
Shot Put	Nadezhda Chizhova, USSR	57	1969-73
Discus Throw	Gisela Mauermeyer, Germany	65	1935-42
Javelin Throw	Ruth Fuchs, East Germany	30	1972-73
Multi	Heide Rosendahl, West Germany	15	1969-72

Most Consecutive Years Ranked No. 1 in the World

MEN

No.	Name and Nationality	Event	Years
9	Victor Saneyev, USSR	Triple Jump	1968-76
8	Bob Richards, United States	Pole Vault	1949-56
8	Ralph Boston, United States	Long Jump	1960-67
7	Emil Zátopek (Czech)	10,000-meter run	1948-54

WOMEN

No.	Name and Nationality	Event	Years
9	Iolanda Balas, Romania	High Jump	1958-66
8	Ruth Fuchs, East Germany	Javelin Throw	1972-79
7	Faina Melnick, USSR	Discus Throw	1971-77

Major Barrier Breakers

MEN

Event	Mark	Name and Nationality	Date	Site
sub 10-second 100-meter dash	9.95	Jim Hines, United States	Oct. 14, 1968	Mexico City
sub 20-second 200-meter dash	19.83	Tommie Smith, United States	Oct. 16, 1968	Mexico City
sub 45-second 400-meter run	44.9	Otis Davis, United States	Sept. 6, 1960	Rome.
sub 1:45 800-meter run	1:44.3	Peter Snell, New Zealand	Feb. 3, 1962	Christchurch, New Zealand
sub four minute mile	3:59.4	Roger Bannister, Great Britain	May 6, 1954	Oxford
sub 3:50 mile	3:49.4	John Walker, New Zealand	Aug. 12, 1975	Goteborg
sub 13-minute 5,000-meter run	12:58.39	Said Aouita, Morocco	July 22, 1986	Rome
sub 28:00 10,000-meter run	27:39.4	Ron Clarke, Australia	July 14, 1965	Oslo
sub 13-second 110-meter hurdles	12.93	Renaldo Nehemiah, United States	Aug. 19, 1981	Zurich
sub 50-second 400-meter hurdles	49.5	Glenn Davis, United States	June 29, 1956	Los Angeles
7' high jump	7' ⅝"	Charles Dumas, United States	June 29, 1956	Los Angeles
8' high jump	8	Javier Sotomayor, Cuba	July 29, 1989	San Juan
20' pole vault	20'	Sergei Bubka, USSR	March 15, 1991	San Sebastian, Spain
70' shot put	70' 7¼"	Randy Matson, United States	May 5, 1965	College Station, Texas
200' discus throw	200' 5"	Al Oerter, United States	May 18, 1962	Los Angeles
300' (new) javelin	300' 1"	Steve Backley, Great Britain	Jan. 25, 1992	Auckland, New Zealand

WOMEN

Event	Mark	Name and Nationality	Date	Site
sub 11-second 100-meter dash	10.88	Marlies Oelsner, East Germany	July 1, 1977	Dresden
sub 22-second 200-meter dash	21.71	Marita Koch, East Germany	June 10, 1979	Karl Marx Stadt
sub 50-second 400-meter run	49.9	Irena Szewinska, Poland	June 22, 1974	Warsaw
sub 2:00 800-meter run	1:59.1	Shin Geum Dan, North Korea	Nov. 12, 1963	Djakarta
sub 4:00 1500-meter run	3:56.0	Tatyana Kazankina, USSR	June 28, 1976	Podolsk, USSR

Major Barrier Breakers *(Cont.)*

WOMEN *(Cont.)*

Event	Mark	Name and Nationality	Date	Site
sub 4:20 mile	4:17.55	Mary Decker, United States	Feb. 16, 1980	Houston
sub 15:00 5,000-meter run	14:58.89	Ingrid Kristiansen, Norway	June 28, 1984	Oslo
sub 30:00 10,000-meter run	29:31.78	Wang Junxia, China	Sept. 8, 1993	Beijing
sub 2:30 marathon	2:27:33	Grete Waitz, Norway	Oct. 21, 1979	New York City
sub 13-second 100-meter hurdles	12.9	Karin Balzer, East Germany	Sept. 5, 1969	Berlin
6' high jump	6'	Iolanda Balas, Romania	Oct. 18, 1958	Budapest
70' shot put	70' 4½'	Nadyezhda Chizhova, USSR	Sept. 29, 1973	Varna, Bulgaria
200' discus throw	201'	Liesel Westermann, West Germany	Nov. 5, 1967	Sao Paulo
200' javelin throw	201' 4''	Elvira Ozolina, USSR	Aug. 27, 1964	Kiev
first 7,000-point heptathlon	7,148	Jackie Joyner-Kersee, United States	July 6-7, 1986	Moscow

Olympic Accomplishments

Oldest Olympic gold medalist—Patrick (Babe) McDonald, United States, 42 years, 26 days, 56-pound weight throw, 1920
Oldest Olympic medalist—Tebbs Lloyd Johnson, Great Britain, 48 years, 115 days, 1948 (bronze), 50K walk
Youngest Olympic gold medalist—Barbara Jones, United States, 15 years 123 days, 1952, 4 x 100 relay
Youngest gold medalist in individual event—Ulrike Meyfarth, West Germany, 16 years, 123 days, 1972, high jump

World Record Accomplishments*

Most world records equaled or set in a day—6, Jesse Owens, United States, 5/25/35, (9.4 100-yard dash; 26' 8¼' long jump; 20.3 200-meter dash and 220-yard dash; and 22.6 220-yard hurdles and 200-meter hurdles
Most records in a year—10, Gunder Hägg, Sweden, 1941-42, 1500 to 5,000 meters
Most records in a career—34, Sergei Bubka, 1983-93, pole vault indoors and out
Longest span of record setting—11 years, 20 days, Irena Szewinska, Poland, 1965-76, 200-meter dash
Youngest person to set a set world record—Carolina Gisolf, Holland, 15 years, 5 days, 1928, high jump , 5' 3⅜''
Youngest man to set a world record—John Thomas, United States, 17 years, 355 days, 1959, high jump, 7' 1¼''
Oldest person to set world record—Carlos Lopes, Portugal, 38 years, 59 days, marathon, 2:07:12
Greatest percentage improvement—6.59, Bob Beamon, United States, 1968, long jump
Longest lasting record—long jump, 26' 8¼'', Jesse Owens, United States, 25 years, 79 days (1935-60)
Highest clearance over head, men—23¼'', Franklin Jacobs United States (5' 8''), 1978
Highest over head by a woman—12¾'', Yolanda Henry, United States (5' 6''), 1990

*Marks sanctioned by the IAAF

1-800-94-TRACK

It hasn't been easy of late to obtain up-to-date track and field results from the usual sources, such as newspapers and television. So Vic Holchak, a lifelong track devotee who covers sports for National Public Radio, the BBC and ABC, decided last summer to provide his own results service.

With backing from a group of concerned track fans, all of them European, Holchak created 1-800-94-TRACK, a phone service that allowed callers to hear, tollfree, daily reports from the European circuit and from the world championships in August. "[My sponsors] see track and field dying in this country," says Holchak. "So do I. The sport is going to get a boost from the Atlanta Olympics, but we can't wait that long."

The caller response surprised even Holchak. Over the month the service ran, it received 93,000 calls. On the final day of the world championships, more than 16,000 calls came in. Virtually all of the callers who chose to leave Holchak a message were ecstatic to have found such a service.

Holchak is more than just another mellifluous voice. He was still in high school when he began working as a sports reporter for the *Los Angeles Examiner*. The first track meet Holchak covered was the Melbourne Olympics, in 1956. In the mid '60s Holchak changed careers. After studying at the Royal Academy of Dramatic Art in London, he acted in Shakespeare and Chekov in Europe and then came back to L.A. where he worked on numerous TV series. He played Howard Hughes in the movie *Hughes and Harlow: Angels in Hell* and for four years was a regular on *Days of Our Lives*. But in 1983, with the Olympics scheduled for his hometown, Holchak decided to return to his original calling, sports journalism. Everyone who dialed 1-800-94-TRACK last summer was happy he did.

Swimming

Sports Illustrated

MAKING A SPLASH

JENNY THOMPSON: THE LATEST U.S. SWIMMING SENSATION

BILL FRAKES

Repeating and Retreating

While swimming's superstars pondered their futures, a
speedy new crop was growing up fast | by KELLI ANDERSON

T IS THE YEAR AFTER WHAT WAS arguably the most fabulous Olympics ever. The spotlights on the world's swimming pools have dimmed, and the media, like four-year locusts, have retreated into dormancy. International competitions are few and far between. Further Olympic glory is a grueling three years away. What does an Olympic swimming superstar do?

If you are freestyle sprint legend Matt Biondi, you take your 11 Olympic medals and your 100-free world record and announce that you are "riding off into the sunset," adding that from now on, swimming for you will consist of floating on your back, blowing bubbles.

If you are Pablo Morales, you complete the stunning comeback that produced a gold medal in Barcelona with a final stab at your 1986 100-butterfly world record. But even you cannot break the oldest men's record on the books. At the age of 28, you retire again and return to Cornell law school.

If you are Melvin Stewart, you keep train-ing enough to win the 200 fly at the outdoor nationals, and in your spare time you become swim coach to the stars. You even convince swim student/actor Dolph Lundgren to give you a part in his next movie.

If you are Janet Evans, you change programs again, start swimming with the men at USC and return to speeds that caught the world's attention in Seoul five years ago. At the nationals in Austin in July, you win your 36th national title (only Tracy Caulkins, with 48, has more), with a 15:59.44 in the 1,500 free. You remain the only female to beat 16:00, and you've now done it three times.

If you are Jenny Thompson, you look forward to the Pan Pacific Swimming Championships in Kobe, Japan, where you'll finally get a rematch against Zhuang Yong, the Chinese woman who beat you in the 100 freestyle at Barcelona.

If you are the Chinese team, you don't show up in Kobe.

That was the kind of year 1993 was—a little redirecting, a little retrenching, a little repeating, a little retreating. Thompson

SIMON BRUTY/ALLSPORT

won a record six gold medals at the Pan Pacifics without the benefit of competition from the Chinese, who stayed away to prepare for their own national games. Lost in the hoopla surrounding the incredible world-record-breaking performances of the Chinese women runners at their nationals were the almost as dramatic accomplishments of their sister swimmers.

In a meet that echoed East Germany's sudden rise to supremacy in the early '70s, the Chinese displayed surprising depth in nearly all the women's events. Although no world records were broken, legions of swimmers came close. In the 100 butterfly alone, seven Chinese women broke a minute, a feat which only 19 women had ever accomplished. Three swimmers came within a half second of Thompson's world record of 54.48 in the 100 free.

As China sowed the seeds of future dominance in women's swimming, the last vestige of the former East German juggernaut was blossoming. Franziska van Almsick, a 15-year-old Berlin schoolgirl who at 14 had won an Olympic silver medal in the 200 free and a bronze in the 100 free, hauled in five gold medals and one silver at the European Championships. Barcelona triple-gold medalist Krisztina Egerszegi of Hungary won four individual golds.

At the Pan Pacifics, the only international competition for the U.S., just 30% of the American team were Olympic veterans,

Van Almsick grabbed a silver in the 100-fly to go with her five golds at the Europeans.

which is a good indicator of how callow the U.S. will be at the next Olympics. "Our colors in Atlanta are going to be red, white and *green*," says former U.S. Swimming p.r. director Jeff Dimond. Greenhorns on the rise include USC freshman-to-be Kristine Quance, who won the 400 IM in Kobe, and 15-year-old Allison Wagner, who took the 200 IM in 2:12.54, the second-fastest U.S. women's performance ever.

Some of Barcelona's unsung swimmers claimed Pan Pacific titles as well. Royce Sharp, a Michigan freshman who holds the American record in the 200 back, bounced back from a disappointing 11th place in Barcelona to victory in Kobe. And Jon Olsen, who anchored the world-record-breaking 4 x 100 medley and the gold medal 4 x 100 freestyle relays in Barcelona, won the 50 and 100 free titles.

Although it was an altogether promising year for U.S. swimmers, there was alarming news on the collegiate front. In an attempt to save money, UCLA dropped its men's swimming program. It was not the first major NCAA Division I swimming program to go under, and it likely won't be the last. But when southern California, the very cradle of America's aquatic ascendancy, begins to drain its pools, the future of U.S. swimming becomes awash in uncertainty.

FOR THE RECORD·1992-1993

1993 Major Competitions

Men

US INDOOR CHAMPIONSHIPS
Nashville, Tennessee, March 31-April 5

50 free	Raimundas Majuolis, Ft. Lauderdale, 22.57
100 free	Raimundas Majuolis, Ft. Lauderdale, 49.80
200 free	Jon Sakovich, Florida Aquatics, 1:51.49
400 free	Jon Sakovich, Florida Aquatics, 3:56.31
800 free	Chad Carvin, UNA/Arizona, 8:10.70
1500 free	Carlton Bruner, UNA/Florida, 15:28.08
100 back	Jeff Rouse, Stanford University, 54.87
200 back	Royce Sharp, Michigan, 2:00.80
100 breast	Seth VanNeerden, Ft. Lauderdale, 1:02.46
200 breast	Seth VanNeerden, Ft. Lauderdale, 2:14.82
100 fly	Brian Alderman, Santa Barbara, 54.11
200 fly	Ugur Taner, UNA-Chinook, 2:01.51
200 IM	Sergey Mariniuk, Santa Clara, 2:03.17
400 IM	Eric Namesnik, Michigan, 4:17.13
400 m relay	Ft. Lauderdale "A", 3:47.21
400 f relay	Ft. Lauderdale "A", 3:24.76
800 f relay	Syracuse Univ. "A", 7:40.41
1-m spgbd**	1. Dean Panaro, Miami, 593.13
	2. Russ Bertram, FLD, 561.66
3-m spgbd**	1. Mark Bradshaw, Ohio St, 651.99
	2. Mark Lenzi, Kimball Divers, 646.95
Platform**	1. Russ Bertram, FLD, 567.42
	2. Pat Evans, Cincinnati, 556.17

**Held in Austin, April 20-24.

EUROPEAN CHAMPIONSHIPS
Sheffield, England, July 31-August 8

50 free	Alexander Popov, Russia, 22.27*
100 free	Alexander Popov, Russia, 49.15*
200 free	Antii Kasvio, Finland, 1:47.11
400 free	Antii Kasvio, Finland, 3:47.81
800 free	not held
1500 free	Jorg Hoffmann, Germany, 15:13.31
100 back	Martin Lopez-Zubero, Spain, 55.03*
200 back	Vladimir Selkov, Russia, 1:58.09*
100 breast	Karoly Guttler, Hungary, 1:01.04
200 breast	Nick Gillingham, Great Britain, 2:12.49*
100 fly	Rafal Szukula, Poland, 53.41*
200 fly	Denis Pankratov, Russia, 1:56.25*
200 IM	Jani Sievinen, Finland, 1:59.50*
400 IM	Tamas Darnyi, Hungary, 4:15.24*
400 m relay	Russia, 3:38.90*
400 f relay	Russia, 3:18.80*
800 f relay	Russia, 7:15.84

US OUTDOOR CHAMPIONSHIPS
Austin, Texas, July 26-30

David Fox, Ft. Lauderdale, 22.49
Jon Olsen, Santa Clara, 49.33
Joe Hudepohl, Stanford, 1:49.22
Chad Carvin, Hilldenbrand, 3:50.89
Peter Wright, Jersey Wahoos, 7:58.90
Carlton Bruner, Florida Aquatics, 15:16.21
Jeff Rouse, Stanford, 54.21
Royce Sharp, Florida Aquatics, 1:58.81
Tyler Mayfield, Stanford, 1:02.31
Eric Wunderlich, Club Wolverine, 2:14.45
Mark Henderson, Curl-Burke, 53.62
Melvin Stewart, Team Bruin, 1:58.11
Greg Burgess, Florida Aquatic, 2:00.84
Eric Namesnik, Club Wolverine, 4:14.50 #
Stanford "A", 3:39.26
Ft. Lauderdale "A", 3:22.46
Stanford, 7:28.09
Mark Lenzi, Kimball Divers, 618.66 ‡
Dean Panaro, University of Miami, 605.82
Mark Bradshaw, Ohio State Diving, 648.06 ‡
Mark Lenzi, Kimball Divers, 626.31
Patrick Jeffrey, Fort Lauderdale DT, 565.02‡
Dave Pichler, Fort Lauderdale DT, 559.29

‡Held in Los Angeles, Aug 11-15.

PAN PACIFIC CHAMPIONSHIPS
Kobe, Japan, August 12-15

Jon Olsen, United States, 22.68
Jon Olsen, United States, 49.73
Josh Davis, United States 1:48.50
Kieren Perkins, Australia, 3:49.43*
Kieren Perkins, Australia, 7:50.51*
Kieren Perkins, Australia, 14:55.92*
Jeff Rouse, United States, 54.85*
Royce Sharp, United States, 1:59.21*
Philip Rogers, Australia, 1:01.56*
Philip Rogers, Australia, 2:13.50
Mark Henderson, United States, 53.91
Danyon Loader, New Zealand, 1:58.30
Michael Dunn, Australia, 2:01.52
Matthew Dunn, Australia, 4:19.05
United States, 3:59.52
United States, 3:17.50
United States, 7:18.66

*Meet record. #American record

WORLD UNIVERSITY GAMES
Buffalo, NY; July 9-15

50 free	David Fox, United States, 22.30
100 free	David Fox, United States, 50.18
200 free	Yann deFrabrique, France, 1:51.24
400 free	Turlough O'Hara, Canada, 3:55.01
800 free	Turlough O'Hara, Canada, 8:04.80
1500 free	Rob Darzynkiewicz, U.S., 15:33.96
100 back	R. Palcon Cabrera, Cuba, 55.60
200 back	R. Palcon Cabrera, Cuba, 1:59.90
100 breast	Jud Crawford, United States, 1:02.76
200 breast	Mario Gonzalez, Cuba, 2:16.24
100 fly	Martin Roberts, Australia, 54.14

U.S. OLYMPIC FESTIVAL
San Antonio, Texas, July 24-27

Scott Claypool, South, 23.50
Scott Jones, West, 50.94
Scott Tucker, North, 1:51.61
Jay Telford, West, 3:59.34
not held
Jay Telford, West, 15:47.00
Tate Blahnik, East, 58.18
Tate Blahnik, East, 2:01.81
Anthony Attiah, North, 1:04.85
Christian Claytor, East, 2:18.01
John Hargis, South, 55.40

Men (Cont.)

WORLD UNIVERSITY GAMES *(Cont.)*

200 fly	Martin Roberts, Australia, 2:00.91
200 IM	Fraser Walker, Great Britain, 2:04.48
400 IM	Ian Mull, United States, 4:24.08
400 m relay	United States, 3:43.20
400 f relay	United States, 3:21.28
800 f relay	United States, 7:25.90
1-m spgbd	1. Chen Sheng, China, 380.52
	2. Fernando Platas, Mexico, 377.52
3-m spgbd	1. Xiong Ni, China, 433.77
	2. Fernando Platas, Mexico, 427.20
Platform	1. Xiong Ni, China, 659.52
	2. Ying Gui, China, 621.30

WORLD DIVING CUP

Beijing, China, May 28-June 1

1-m spgbd	1. Lan Wei, China, 366.48
	2. Wang Yijie, China, 344.52
3-m spgbd	1. Yu Zhuocheng, China, 427.83
	2. Wang Tianling, China, 404.52
Platform	1. Xiong Ni, China, 458.40
	2. Dmitry Sautin, Russia, 433.71

U.S. OLYMPIC FESTIVAL *(Cont.)*

Ben Mercier, East, 2:03.81
Shawn McNew, West, 2:06.22
Rob Iglinski, West, 4:27.76
East "A", 3:49.02
West "B", 3:27.26
West "A", 7:34.54
Mark Lenzi, North, 405.27
John Sharkey, South, 332.40
Mark Lenzi, North, 704.31
Mark Bradshaw, North, 687.09
P.J. Bogart, West, 589.59
Russ Bertram, East, 560.07

ALAMO INTERNATIONAL

Ft. Lauderdale, Florida, May 6-9

Wang Yijie, China, 375.54
Patrick Jeffrey, United States, 360.66
Lan Wei, China, 704.16
Mark Bradshaw, United States, 637.41
Vladimir Timoshinin, Russia, 587.58
Scott Donie, United States, 572.52

*Meet record.

Women

U.S. INDOOR CHAMPIONSHIPS

Nashville, March 31-April 5

50 free	Jenny Thompson, UNA/Seacoast, 25.72
100 free	Jenny Thompson, UNA/Seacoast, 55.63
200 free	Angie Wester-Krieg, Stanford, 2:03.84
400 free	Janet Evans, Trojan Swimming, 4:11.01
800 free	Janet Evans, Trojan Swimming, 8:34.99
1500 free	Janet Evans, Trojan Swimming, 16:16.38
100 back	Jenny Thompson, UNA/Seacoast, 1:03.24
200 back	Rachel Joseph, Eugene City, 2:14.05
100 breast	Megan Kleine, Wildcat Aquatics, 1:09.80
200 breast	Anita Nall, North Baltimore, 2:28.58
100 fly	Summer Sanders, California Capital, 59.83
200 fly	Angie Wester-Krieg, Stanford, 2:13.26
200 IM	Kristine Quance, CLASS Aquatics, 2:16.30
400 IM	Kristine Quance, CLASS Aquatics, 4:42.08
400 m relay	Bolles "A", 4:22.10
400 f relay	Ft. Lauderdale "A", 3:54.62
800 f relay	Bolles School, 8:24.84
1-m spgbd**	1. Carrie Zarse, Unat., 438.39
	2. Mary Ellen Clark, FLD, 425.01
3-m spgbd**	1. Veronica Ribot-Canales, Univ. of Miami, 475.89
	2. Sherry Wigginton, Texas, 462.99
Platform**	1. Mary Ellen Clark, FLD, 412.26
	2. Jenny Keim, FLD, 401.40

**Held in Austin, April 20-24

EUROPEAN CHAMPIONSHIPS

Sheffield, England, July 31-August 8

50 free	Franziska van Almsick, Germany, 25.53
100 free	Franziska van Almsick, Germany, 54.57*
200 free	Franziska van Almsick, Germany, 1:57.97*
400 free	Dagmar Hase, Germany, 4:10.47
800 free	Jana Henke, Germany, 8:32.47
1500 free	not held
100 back	Krisztina Egerszegi, Hungary, 1:00.83
200 back	Krisztina Egerszegi, Hungary, 2:09.12

US OUTDOOR CHAMPIONSHIPS

Austin, Texas, July 26-30

Angel Martino, Americus Blue Tide, 25.63
Jenny Thompson, Seacoast, 55.34
Nicole Haislett, St. Petersburg, 1:59.38
Janet Evans, Trojan, 4:05.85
Janet Evans, Trojan, 8:23.61
Janet Evans, Trojan, 15:59.44
B.J. Bedford, Florida Aquatics, 1:01.58
Lea Loveless, Badger, 2:11.69
Anita Nall, North Baltimore, 1:09.65
Anita Nall, North Baltimore, 2:27.79
Jenny Thompson, Seacoast, 59.49
Paige Wilson, Athens Bulldogs, 2:12.89
Allison Wagner, Florida Aquatics, 2:14.34
Allison Wagner, Florida Aquatics, 4:41.93
Ft. Lauderdale Swim Team "A", 4:12.80
Ft. Lauderdale Swim Team "A", 3:48.54
Badger Dolphins, 8:20.08
Carrie Zarse, Kimball Divers, 430.41‡
Doris Glenn Easterly, Fort Lauderdale DT, 420.09
Eileen Richetelli, Stanford Diving, 476.82 ‡
Veronica Ribot-Canales, Univ. of Miami, 470.25
Mary Ellen Clark, Fort Lauderdale DT, 412.38 ‡
Eileen Richetelli, Stanford Diving,. 384.30

‡Held in Los Angeles, August 11-15

PAN PACIFIC CHAMPIONSHIPS

August 12-15, Kobe, Japan

Jenny Thompson, United States, 25.60*
Jenny Thompson, United States, 55.25
Claudia Poll, Costa Rica, 1:58.85*
Janet Evans, United States, 4:07.47
Janet Evans, United States, 8:23.72
Hayley Lewis, Australia, 16:04.84*
Lea Loveless, United States, 1:01.35
Barbara Bedford, United States, 2:10.97

Women *(Cont.)*

EUROPEAN CHAMPIONSHIPS *(Cont.)*

100 breast	...Sylvia Gerasch, Germany, 1:10.05
200 breast	...Brigitte Becue, Belgium, 2:31.18
100 fly	.........Catherine Plewinski, France, 1:00.13
200 fly	.........Krisztina Egerszegi, Hungary, 2:10.71
200 IM	........Daniela Hunger, Germany, 2:15.33
400 IM	........Krisztina Egerszegi, Hungary, 4:39.55
400 m relay	.Germany, 4:06.91
400 f relay	...Germany, 3:41.69
800 f relay	...not held

*Meet record.

WORLD UNIVERSITY GAMES
Buffalo, NY; July 9–15

50 free	.........Jingyi Le, China, 25.17
100 free	.......Jingyi Le, China, 55.16
200 free	.......Heike Luenenschloss, Germany, 2:03.18
400 free	.......Sandra Cam, Belgium, 4:18.21
800 free	.......not held
1500 free	....Christine Stephenson, U.S., 16:41.75
100 back	.....Barbara Bedford, United States, 1:01.60
200 back	.....Whitney Hedgepeth, U.S., 2:11.31
100 breast	...Guylaine Cloutier, Canada, 1:10.91
200 breast	...S. Bondarenko, Ukraine, 2:31.41
100 fly	.........Yoko Kando, Japan, 1:01.59
200 fly	.........Yoko Kando, Japan, 2:14.45
200 IM	........Marianne Limpert, Canada, 2:15.46
400 IM	........Nancy Sweatnam, Canada, 4:46.91
400 m relay	.United States, 4:12.55
400 f relay	...United States, 3:17.83
800 f relay	...Canada, 8:18.00
1-m spgbd	..1. Yu Xiaoling, China, 275.28
	2. Anne Pelletier, Canada, 258.57
3-m spgbd	..1. Brita Baldus, Germany, 295.56
	2. Paige Gordon, Canada, 292.68
Platform	.......1. Anne Montminy, Canada, 407.79
	2. Yang Yan, China, 403.32

WORLD DIVING CUP
Beijing, China, May 28–June 1

1-m spgbd	..1. Tan Shuping, China, 271.20
	2. Irina Lashko, Russia, 264.12
3-m spgbd	..1. Tan Shuping, China, 315.21
	2. Irina Lashko, Russia, 301.86
Platform	.......1. Chi Bin, China, 259.59
	2. Svetlana Khokhova, Russia, 257.94

PAN PACIFIC CHAMPIONSHIPS *(Cont.)*

Anita Nall, United States, 1:09.11*
Anita Nall, United States, 2:28.40
Jenny Thompson, United States, 59.33
Rie Shito, Japan, 2:10.36
Allison Wagner, United States, 2:12.54*
Kristine Quance, United States, 4:39.25*
United States, 4:04.90*
United States, 3:42.56*
United States, 8:06.28

U.S. OLYMPIC FESTIVAL
San Antonio, Texas; July 24–27

Liesl Pimentel, South, 26.68
Catherine Fox, South, 57.09
Emily Peters, East, 2:03.85
Emily Peters, East, 4:18.27
Sara Nichols, East, 8:48.38
not held
Rachel Joseph, West, 1:03.58
Rachel Joseph, West, 2:13.42
Cathy O'Neill, West, 1:12.10
Cathy O'Neill, West 2:33.50
Michelle Collins, North, 1:02.67
Kerri Hale, South, 2:14.99
Rachel Joseph, West, 2:19.89
Cathy O'Neill, West, 4:51.44
West "A", 4:18.00
North "A", 3:53.64
West "A", 8:23.15
Carrie Zarse, North, 274.74
Jane Lautenschlager, West, 252.54
Mary Ellen Clark, East, 481.32
Reyne Borup, East, 455.64
Mary Ellen Clark, East, 427.17
Paige Weiskittel, South, 390.03

*Meet record.

ALAMO INTERNATIONAL
Ft. Lauderdale, Florida, May 6-9

Simona Koch, Germany, 245.58
Melisa Moses, United States, 244.02
Irina Lashko, Russia, 510.51
Paige Gordon, Canada, 483.03
Svetlana Khokhlova, Russia, 417.30
Xiong Min, China, 414.18

World and American Records set in 1992-1993

Men

Event	Mark	Record Holder	Date	Site
100 breast	1:00.95	Karoly Guttler, Hungary (W)	8-5-93	Sheffield, England
400 IM	4:14.50	Eric Namesnik (A)	7-28-93	Austin, TX

World and American Records Through Sept. 29, 1993

MEN

Freestyle

Event	Time	Record Holder	Date	Site
50 meters	21.81	Tom Jager (W,A)	3-24-90	Nashville
100 meters	48.42	Matt Biondi (W,A)	8-10-88	Austin
200 meters	1:46.69	Giorgio Lamberti, Italy (W)	8-15-89	Bonn
	1:47.72	Matt Biondi (A)	8-8-88	Austin
400 meters	3:45.00	Yevgeny Sadovyi, EUN (W)	7-29-92	Barcelona
	3:48.06	Matt Cetlinski (A)	8-11-88	Austin
800 meters	7:46.60	Kieren Perkins, Australia (W)	2-14-92	Sydney
	7:52.45	Sean Killion (A)	7-27-87	Clovis, CA
1500 meters	14:43.48	Kieren Perkins, Australia (W)	7-31-92	Barcelona
	15:01.51	George DiCarlo (A)	6-30-84	Indianapolis

Backstroke

Event	Time	Record Holder	Date	Site
100 meters	53.86*	Jeff Rouse (W,A)	7-31-92	Barcelona
200 meters	1:56.57	Martin Zubero, Spain (W)	11-23-91	Tuscaloosa
	1:58.66	Royce Sharp (A)	3-3-92	Indianapolis

*Set on first leg of relay.

Breaststroke

Event	Time	Record Holder	Date	Site
100 meters	1:00.95	Karoly Guttler, Hungary (W)	8-5-93	Sheffield, England
	1:01.40	Nelson Diebel (A)	3-1-92	Indianapolis
200 meters	2:10.16	Mike Barrowman (W,A)	7-29-92	Barcelona

Butterfly

Event	Time	Record Holder	Date	Site
100 meters	52.84	Pablo Morales (W,A)	6-23-86	Orlando, FL
200 meters	1:55.69	Melvin Stewart (W,A)	1-12-91	Perth, Australia

Individual Medley

Event	Time	Record Holder	Date	Site
200 meters	1:59.36	Tamás Darnyi, Hungary (W)	1-13-91	Perth, Australia
	2:00.11	Dave Wharton (A)	8-20-89	Tokyo
400 meters	4:12.36	Tamás Darnyi, Hungary (W)	1-8-91	Perth, Australia
	4:15.21	Eric Namesnik (A)	1-8-91	Perth, Australia

Relays

Event	Time	Record Holder	Date	Site
400-meter medley	3:36.93	United States (David Berkoff, Rich Schroeder, Matt Biondi, Chris Jacobs) (W,A)	9-23-88	Seoul
	3:36.93	United States (Jeff Rouse, Nelson Diebel, Pablo Morales, Jon Olsen), (W, A)	7-31-92	Barcelona
400-meter freestyle	3:16.53	United States (Chris Jacobs, Troy Dalbey, Tom Jager, Matt Biondi) (W,A)	9-23-88	Seoul
800-meter freestyle	7:11.95	EUN (Dmitri Lepikov, Vladimir Taianovitch Veniamin Taianovitch, Yevgeny Sadovyi) (W)	7-27-92	Barcelona
	7:12.51	United States (Troy Dalbey, Matt Cetlinski, Doug Gjertsen, Matt Biondi) (A)	9-21-88	Seoul

WOMEN

Freestyle

Event	Time	Record Holder	Date	Site
50 meters	24.79	Yang Wenyi, China (W)	7-31-92	Barcelona
	25.20	Jenny Thompson, (A)	3-6-92	Indianapolis
100 meters	54.48	Jenny Thompson, USA (W, A)	3-1-92	Indianapolis
200 meters	1:57.55	Heike Friedrich, East Germany (W)	6-18-86	Berlin
	1:57.90	Nicole Haislett (A)	7-27-92	Barcelona
400 meters	4:03.85	Janet Evans (W,A)	9-22-88	Seoul
800 meters	8:16.22	Janet Evans (W,A)	8-20-89	Tokyo
1500 meters	15:52.10	Janet Evans (W,A)	3-26-88	Orlando, FL

Backstroke

Event	Time	Record Holder	Date	Site
100 meters	1:00.31	Krisztina Egerszegi, Hungary (W)	8-20-91	Athens, Greece
	1:00.82*	Lea Loveless (A)	7-30-92	Barcelona
200 meters	2:06.62	Krisztina Egerszegi, Hungary (W)	8-26-91	Athens, Greece
	2:08.60	Betsy Mitchell (A)	6-27-86	Orlando, FL

Breaststroke

Event	Time	Record Holder	Date	Site
100 meters	1:07.91	Silke Hoerner, East Germany (W)	8-21-87	Strasbourg, France
	1:08.17	Anita Nall (A)	7-29-92	Barcelona
200 meters	2:25.35	Anita Nall, (W, A)	3-2-92	Indianapolis

Butterfly

Event	Time	Record Holder	Date	Site
100 meters	57.93	Mary T. Meagher (W,A)	8-16-81	Brown Deer, WI
200 meters	2:05.96	Mary T. Meagher (W,A)	8-13-81	Brown Deer, WI

Individual Medley

Event	Time	Record Holder	Date	Site
200 meters	2:11.65	Lin Li, China (W)	7-30-92	Barcelona
	2:11.91	Summer Sanders (A)	7-30-92	Barcelona
400 meters	4:36.10	Petra Schneider, East Germany (W)	8-1-82	Guayaquil, Ecuador
	4:37.58	Summer Sanders, (A)	7-26-92	Barcelona

Relays

Event	Time	Record Holder	Date	Site
400-meter medley	4:02.54	United States (Lea Loveless, Anita Nall, Crissy Ahmann-Leighton, Jenny Thompson) (W, A)	7-30-92	Barcelona
400-meter freestyle	3:39.46	United States (Nicole Haislett, Dara Torres, Angel Martino, Jenny Thompson) (W, A)	7-28-92	Barcelona
800-meter freestyle	7:55.47	East Germany (Manuela Stellmach, Astrid Strauss, Anke Mohring, Heike Friedrich) (W)	8-18-87	Strasbourg, France
	8:02.12	United States (Betsy Mitchell, Mary T. Meagher, Kim Brown, Mary Wayte) (A)	8-22-86	Madrid

Championship venues: Belgrade, Yugoslavia, Sep 4-9, 1973; Cali, Colombia, July 18-27, 1975; West Berlin, Aug 20-28, 1978; Guayaquil, Equador, Aug 1-7, 1982; Madrid, Aug 17-22, 1986; Perth, Australia, Jan 7-13, 1991.

MEN

50-meter Freestyle

1986	Tom Jager, United States	22.49‡
1991	Tom Jager, United States	22.16‡

100-meter Freestyle

1973	Jim Montgomery, United States	51.70
1975	Andy Coan, United States	51.25
1978	David McCagg, United States	50.24
1982	Jorg Woithe, East Germany	50.18
1986	Matt Biondi, United States	48.94
1991	Matt Biondi, United States	49.18

200-meter Freestyle

1973	Jim Montgomery, United States	1:53.02
1975	Tim Shaw, United States	1:52.04‡
1978	Billy Forrester, United States	1:51.02‡
1982	Michael Gross, West Germany	1:49.84
1986	Michael Gross, West Germany	1:47.92
1991	Giorgio Lamberti, Italy	1:47.27‡

400-meter Freestyle

1973	Rick DeMont, United States	3:58.18‡
1975	Tim Shaw, United States	3:54.88‡
1978	Vladimir Salnikov, USSR	3:51.94‡
1982	Vladimir Salnikov, USSR	3:51.30‡
1986	Rainer Henkel, West Germany	3:50.05
1991	Joerg Hoffman, Germany	3:48.04‡

1500-meter Freestyle

1973	Stephen Holland, Australia	15:31.85
1975	Tim Shaw, United States	15:28.92‡
1978	Vladimir Salnikov, USSR	15:03.99‡
1982	Vladimir Salnikov, USSR	15:01.77‡
1986	Rainer Henkel, West Germany	15:05.31
1991	Joerg Hoffman, Germany	14:50.36*

100-meter Backstroke

1973	Roland Matthes, East Germany	57.47
1975	Roland Matthes, East Germany	58.15
1978	Bob Jackson, United States	56.36‡
1982	Dirk Richter, East Germany	55.95
1986	Igor Polianski, USSR	55.58‡
1991	Jeff Rouse, United States	55.23‡

200-meter Backstroke

1973	Roland Matthes, East Germany	2:01.87†
1975	Zoltan Varraszto, Hungary	2:05.05
1978	Jesse Vassallo, United States	2:02.16
1982	Rick Carey, United States	2:00.82‡
1986	Igor Polianski, USSR	1:58.78‡
1991	Martin Zubero, Spain	1:59.52

* World record.

†National record.

‡World championship record.

100-meter Breaststroke

1973	John Hencken, United States	1:04.02†
1975	David Wilkie, Great Britain	1:04.26‡
1978	Walter Kusch, West Germany	1:03.56‡
1982	Steve Lundquist, United States	1:02.75‡
1986	Victor Davis, Canada	1:02.71
1991	Norbert Rozsa, Hungary	1:01.45*

200-meter Breaststroke

1973	David Wilkie, Great Britain	2:19.28‡
1975	David Wilkie, Great Britain	2:18.23‡
1978	Nick Nevid, United States	2:18.37
1982	Victor Davis, Canada	2:14.77*
1986	Jozsef Szabo, Hungary	2:14.27‡
1991	Mike Barrowman, United States	2:11.23*

100-meter Butterfly

1973	Bruce Robertson, Canada	55.69
1975	Greg Jagenburg, United States	55.63
1978	Joe Bottom, United States	54.30
1982	Matt Gribble, United States	53.88‡
1986	Pablo Morales, United States	53.54‡
1991	Anthony Nesty, Surinam	53.29‡

200-meter Butterfly

1973	Robin Backhaus, United States	2:03.32
1975	Bill Forrester, United States	2:01.95‡
1978	Mike Bruner, United States	1:59.38‡
1982	Michael Gross, East Germany	1:58.85‡
1986	Michael Gross, East Germany	1:56.53‡
1991	Melvin Stewart, United States	1:55.69*

200-meter Individual Medley

1973	Gunnar Larsson, Sweden	2:08.36
1975	Andras Hargitay, Hungary	2:07.72
1978	Graham Smith, Canada	2:03.65*
1982	Alexander Sidorenko, USSR	2:03.30‡
1986	Tamás Darnyi, Hungary	2:01.57‡
1991	Tamás Darnyi, Hungary	1:59.36*

400-meter Individual Medley

1973	Andras Hargitay, Hungary	4:31.11
1975	Andras Hargitay, Hungary	4:32.57
1978	Jesse Vassallo, United States	4:20.05*
1982	Ricardo Prado, Brazil	4:19.78*
1986	Tamás Darnyi, Hungary	4:18.98†‡
1991	Tamás Darnyi, Hungary	4:12.36*

MEN (Cont.)

400-meter Medley Relay

1973.....United States (Mike Stamm,   3:49.49
John Hencken, Joe Bottom,
Jim Montgomery)
1975.....United States (John Murphy,   3:49.00
Rick Colella, Greg Jagenburg,
Andy Coan)
1978.....United States (Robert Jackson,   3:44.63
Nick Nevid, Joe Bottom,
David McCagg)
1982.....United States (Rick Carey,   3:40.84*
Steve Lundquist, Matt Gribble,
Rowdy Gaines)
1986.....United States (Dan Veatch,   3:41.25
David Lundberg, Pablo Morales,
Matt Biondi)
1991.....United States (Jeff Rouse,   3:39.66‡
Eric Wunderlich, Mark Henderson
Matt Biondi)

400-meter Freestyle Relay

1973.....United States (Mel Nash,   3:27.18
Joe Bottom, Jim Montgomery,
John Murphy)
1975.....United States (Bruce Furniss,   3:24.85
Jim Montgomery, Andy Coan,
John Murphy)
1978.....United States (Jack Babashoff,   3:19.74
Rowdy Gaines, Jim Montgomery,
David McCagg)
1982.....United States (Chris Cavanaugh,   3:19.26*
Robin Leamy, David McCagg,
Rowdy Gaines)
1986.....United States (Tom Jager,   3:19.89
Mike Heath, Paul Wallace,
Matt Biondi)
1991.....United States (Tom Jager,   3:17.15‡
Brent Lang, Doug Gjertsen,
Matt Biondi)

800-meter Freestyle Relay

1973.....United States (Kurt Krumpholz,   7:33.22*
Robin Backhaus, Rick Klatt,
Jim Montgomery)
1975.....West Germany (Klaus Steinbach,   7:39.44
Werner Lampe,
Hans Joachim Geisler, Peter Nocke)
1978.....United States (Bruce Furniss,   7:20.82
Billy Forrester, Bobby Hackett,
Rowdy Gaines)

1982.....United States (Rich Saeger,   7:21.09
Jeff Float, Kyle Miller,
Rowdy Gaines)
1986.....East Germany (Lars Hinneburg,   7:15.91††‡
Thomas Flemming, Dirk Richter,
Sven Lodziewski)
1991.....Germany (Peter Sitt,   7:13.50‡
Steffan Zesner, Stefan Pfeiffer,
Michael Gross)

WOMEN

50-meter Freestyle

1986....Tamara Costache, Romania   25.28*
1991....Zhuang Yong, China   25.47

100-meter Freestyle

1973....Kornelia Ender, East Germany   57.54†
1975....Kornelia Ender, East Germany   56.50†
1978....Barbara Krause, East Germany   55.68‡
1982....Birgit Meineke, East Germany   55.79
1986....Kristin Otto, East Germany   55.05‡
1991....Nicole Haislett, United States   55.17†

200-meter Freestyle

1973....Keena Rothhammer, United States   2:04.99
1975....Shirley Babashoff, United States   2:02.50
1978....Cynthia Woodhead, United States   1:58.53*
1982....Annemarie Verstappen,   1:59.53†
Netherlands
1986....Heike Friedrich, East Germany   1:58.26‡
1991....Hayley Lewis, Australia   2:00.48

400-meter Freestyle

1973.....Heather Greenwood, United States   4:20.28
1975....Shirley Babashoff, United States   4:22.70
1978....Tracey Wickham, Australia   4:06.28*
1982....Carmela Schmidt, East Germany   4:08.98
1986....Heike Friedrich, East Germany   4:07.45
1991....Janet Evans, United States   4:08.63

800-meter Freestyle

1973....Novella Calligaris, Italy   8:52.97
1975....Jenny Turrall, Australia   8:44.75‡
1978....Tracey Wickham, Australia   8:24.94‡
1982....Kim Linehan, United States   8:27.48
1986....Astrid Strauss, East Germany   8:28.24
1991....Janet Evans, United States   8:24.05‡

* World record.

†National record.

‡World championship record.

WOMEN (Cont.)

100-meter Backstroke

1973	Ulrike Richter, East Germany	1:05.42†
1975	Ulrike Richter, East Germany	1:03.30‡
1978	Linda Jezek, United States	1:02.55†‡
1982	Kristin Otto, East Germany	1:01.30‡
1986	Betsy Mitchell, United States	1:01.74
1991	Krisztina Egerszegi, Hungary	1:01.78

200-meter Backstroke

1973	Melissa Belote, United States	2:20.52
1975	Birgit Treiber, East Germany	2:15.46*
1978	Linda Jezek, United States	2:11.93*
1982	Cornelia Sirch, East Germany	2:09.91*
1986	Cornelia Sirch, East Germany	2:11.37
1991	Krisztina Egerszegi, Hungary	2:09.15‡

100-meter Breaststroke

1973	Renate Vogel, East Germany	1:13.74
1975	Hannalore Anke, East Germany	1:12.72
1978	Julia Bogdanova, USSR	1:10.31*
1982	Ute Geweniger, East Germany	1:09.14‡
1986	Sylvia Gerasch, East Germany	1:08.11*
1991	Linley Frame, Australia	1:08.81

200-meter Breaststroke

1973	Renate Vogel, East Germany	2:40.01
1975	Hannalore Anke, East Germany	2:37.25‡
1978	Lina Kachushite, USSR	2:31.42*
1982	Svetlana Varganova, USSR	2:28.82‡
1986	Silke Hoerner, East Germany	2:27.40*
1991	Elena Volkova, USSR	2:29.53

100-meter Butterfly

1973	Kornelia Ender, East Germany	1:02.53
1975	Kornelia Ender, East Germany	1:01.24*
1978	Joan Pennington, United States	1:00.20†‡
1982	Mary T. Meagher, United States	59.41‡
1986	Kornelia Gressler, East Germany	59.51
1991	Qian Hong, China	59.68

200-meter Butterfly

1973	Rosemarie Kother, East Germany	2:13.76†
1975	Rosemarie Kother, East Germany	2:15.92
1978	Tracy Caulkins, United States	2:09.87*
1982	Ines Geissler, East Germany	2:08.66‡
1986	Mary T. Meagher, United States	2:08.41‡
1991	Summer Sanders, United States	2:09.24

200-meter Individual Medley

1973	Andrea Huebner, East Germany	2:20.51
1975	Kathy Heddy, United States	2:19.80
1978	Tracy Caulkins, United States	2:14.07*
1982	Petra Schneider, East Germany	2:11.79
1986	Kristin Otto, East Germany	2:15.56
1991	Lin Li, China	2:13.40

400-meter Individual Medley

1973	Gudrun Wegner, East Germany	4:57.71†
1975	Ulrike Tauber, East Germany	4:52.76‡
1978	Tracy Caulkins, United States	4:40.83*
1982	Petra Schneider, East Germany	4:36.10*
1986	Kathleen Nord, East Germany	4:43.75
1991	Lin Li, China	4:41.45

400-meter Medley Relay

1973	East Germany (Ulrike Richter, Renate Vogel, Rosemarie Kother, Kornelia Ender)	4:16.84
1975	East Germany (Ulrike Richter, Hannelore Anke, Rosemarie Kother, Kornelia Ender)	4:14.74
1978	United States (Linda Jezek, Tracy Caulkins, Joan Pennington, Cynthia Woodhead)	4:08.21†‡
1982	East Germany (Kristin Otto, Ute Gewinger, Ines Geissler, Birgit Meineke)	4:05.8*
1986	East Germany (Kathrin Zimmermann, Sylvia Gerasch, Kornelia Gressler, Kristin Otto)	4:04.82
1991	United States (Janie Wagstaff, Tracey McFarlane, Crissy Ahmann-Leighton, Nicole Haislett)	4:06.51†

400-meter Freestyle Relay

1973	East Germany (Kornelia Ender, Andrea Eife, Andrea Huebner, Sylvia Eichner)	3:52.45†
1975	East Germany (Kornelia Ender, Barbara Krause, Claudia Hempel, Ute Bruckner)	3:49.37
1978	United States (Tracy Caulkins, Stephanie Elkins, Joan Pennington, Cynthia Woodhead)	3:43.43*
1982	East Germany (Birgit Meineke, Susanne Link, Kristin Otto, Caren Metschuk)	3:43.97
1986	East Germany (Kristin Otto, Manuela Stellmach, Sabine Schulze, Heike Friedrich)	3:40.57*
1991	United States (Nicole Haislett, Julie Cooper, Whitney Hedgepeth, Jenny Thompson)	3:43.26†

800-meter Freestyle Relay

1986	East Germany (Manuela Stellmach, Astrid Strauss, Nadja Bergknecht, Heike Friedrich)	7:59.33*
1991	Germany (Kerstin Kielgass, Manuela Stellmach, Dagmar Hase, Stephanie Ortwig)	8:02.56

* World record.

†National record.

‡World championship record.

World Diving Championships

MEN

1-meter Springboard

		Pts
1991	Edwin Jongejans, Holland	588.51

3-meter Springboard

		Pts
1973	Phil Boggs, United States	618.57
1975	Phil Boggs, United States	597.12
1978	Phil Boggs, United States	913.95
1982	Greg Louganis, United States	752.67
1986	Greg Louganis, United States	750.06
1991	Kent Ferguson, United States	650.25

Platform

		Pts
1973	Klaus Dibiasi, Italy	559.53
1975	Klaus Dibiasi, Italy	547.98
1978	Greg Louganis, United States	844.11
1982	Greg Louganis, United States	634.26
1986	Greg Louganis, United States	668.58
1991	Sun Shuwei, China	626.79

WOMEN

1-meter Springboard

		Pts
1991	Gao Min, China	478.26

3-meter Springboard

		Pts
1973	Christa Koehler, East Germany	442.17
1975	Irina Kalinina, USSR	489.81
1978	Irina Kalinina, USSR	691.43
1982	Megan Neyer, United States	501.03
1986	Gao Min, China	582.90
1991	Gao Min, China	539.01

Platform

		Pts
1973	Ulrike Knape, Sweden	406.77
1975	Janet Ely, United States	403.89
1978	Irina Kalinina, USSR	412.71
1982	Wendy Wyland, United States	438.79
1986	Chen Lin, China	449.67
1991	Fu Mingxia, China	426.51

When Madame Butterfly Flew

The old saw notwithstanding, there are a handful of records that seem to have been made *not* to be broken. Some of them, like Bob Beamon's 29'2½" long jump at the Mexico City Olympics, owe their longevity at least partially to the unusual conditions in which they were set—to altitude, in the case of Beamon's jump. And of course Beamon's mark was eventually broken—by Mike Powell, who jumped 29'4½" in 1991.

Other records owe their durability to fundamental changes in the way a game is played. It's hard to imagine anyone ever approaching Cy Young's total of 511 career wins because pitchers are no longer called upon to work as often as their predecessors were.

But neither of those explanations begins to make sense of what Mary T. Meagher did over four days in August of 1981 at the U.S. long course swimming championships in Brown Deer, Wisconsin. First, on August 13, she swam 2:05.96 for the 200 fly, breaking her own world record for the event by .41 seconds. Three days later she smashed her own world record for the 100 fly by 1.33 seconds, touching in 57.93.

More than a dozen years have passed since Meagher swam those magical, mystery times, and they seem as remote now as they did in 1981. In the 200 fly no one but Meagher herself has come close. The second woman on the alltime list—after 10 Meagher swims—is Cornelia Polit of Germany, who swam 2:07.82 in 1983. Summer Sanders's winning time at the Barcelona Olympics was 2:08.67. And in the 100 no one would break 59 seconds until 1990, when Xiao Hong Wang of China swam 58.87. The winning time at the Barcelona Games was 58.62, in swimming a veritable ocean behind the great Mary T.

In 1990, when *Sports Illustrated's* Jack McCallum ranked the 10 greatest single event records ever, he put Meagher's 2:05.96 fifth, behind Wilt Chamberlain's 100 point game; Secretariat's time of 2:24 at the 1973 Belmont Stakes; Beamon's jump; and Norm Van Brocklin's 554-yard passing game in 1951.

Last summer Phillips Petroleum and U.S. Swimming honored Meagher by naming her the swimmer with the greatest overall performance in 20 years of senior nationals. Meagher, who was also inducted into the Women's Sports Foundation's Hall of Fame on October 4, 1993, won three gold medals at the 1984 Olympics, in the two flys and in the 400 medley relay. But what she is best remembered for are two records that may never be broken.

U.S. Olympic Champions

Men

50-METER FREESTYLE

1988	Matt Biondi	22.14 WR

100-METER FREESTLYE

1906	Charles Daniels	1:13.4
1908	Charles Daniels	1:05.6 WR
1912	Duke Kahanamoku	1:03.4
1920	Duke Kahanamoku	1:00.4
1924	John Weissmuller	59.0 OR
1928	John Weissmuller	58.6 OR
1948	Wally Ris	57.3 OR
1952	Clarke Scholes	57.4
1964	Don Schollander	53.4 OR
1972	Mark Spitz	51.22 WR
1976	Jim Montgomery	49.99 WR
1984	Rowdy Gaines	49.80 OR
1988	Matt Biondi	48.63 OR

200-METER FREESTYLE

1904	Charles Daniels	2:44.2
1906	Not held 1906-1964	
1972	Mark Spitz	1:52.78 WR
1976	Bruce Furniss	1:50.29 WR

400-METER FREESTYLE

1904	Charles Daniels (440 yds)	6:16.2
1920	Norman Ross	5:26.8
1924	John Weissmuller	5:04.2 OR
1932	Buster Crabbe	4:48.4 OR
1936	Jack Medica	4:44.5 OR
1948	William Smith	4:41.0 OR
1964	Don Schollander	4:12.2 WR
1968	Mike Burton	4:09.0 OR
1976	Brian Goodell	3:51.93 WR
1984	George DiCarlo	3:51.23 OR

1500-METER FREESTYLE

1920	Norman Ross	22:23.2
1948	James McLane	19:18.5
1952	Ford Konno	18:30.3 OR
1968	Mike Burton	16:38.9 OR
1972	Mike Burton	15:52.58 OR
1976	Brian Goodell	15:02.40 WR
1984	Michael O'Brien	15:05.20

100-METER BACKSTROKE

1912	Harry Hebner	1:21.2
1920	Warren Kealoha	1:15.2
1924	Warren Kealoha	1:13.2 OR
1928	George Kojac	1:08.2 WR
1936	Adolph Kiefer	1:05.9 OR
1948	Allen Stack	1:06.4
1952	Yoshi Oyakawa	1:05.4 OR
1976	John Naber	55.49 WR
1984	Rick Carey	55.79

200-METER BACKSTROKE

1964	Jed Graef	2:10.3 WR
1976	John Naber	1:59.19 WR
1984	Rick Carey	2:00.23

100-METER BREASTSTROKE

1968	Donald McKenzie	1:07.7 OR

100-METER BREASTSTROKE (Cont.)

1976	John Hencken	1:03.11 WR
1984	Steve Lundquist	1:01.65 WR
1992	Nelson Diebel	1:01.50 OR

200-METER BREASTSTROKE

1924	Robert Skelton	2:56.6
1948	Joseph Verdeur	2:39.3 OR
1960	William Mulliken	2:37.4
1972	John Hencken	2:21.55
1992	Mike Barrowman	2:10.16 WR

100-METER BUTTERFLY

1968	Douglas Russell	55.9 OR
1972	Mark Spitz	54.27 WR
1976	Matt Vogel	54.35
1992	Pablo Morales	53.32

200-METER BUTTERFLY

1956	William Yorzyk	2:19.3 OR
1960	Michael Troy	2:12.8 WR
1968	Carl Robie	2:08.7
1972	Mark Spitz	2:00.70 WR
1976	Mike Bruner	1:59.23 WR
1992	Melvin Stewart	1:56.26

200-METER INDIVIDUAL MEDLEY

1968	Charles Hickcox	2:12.0 OR

400-METER INDIVIDUAL MEDLEY

1964	Richard Roth	4:45.4 WR
1968	Charles Hickcox	4:48.4
1976	Rod Strachan	4:23.68 WR

3-METER SPRINGBOARD DIVING

1920	Louis Kuehn	675.4 points
1924	Albert White	696.4
1928	Pete Desjardins	185.04
1932	Michael Galitzen	161.38
1936	Richard Degener	163.57
1948	Bruce Harlan	163.64
1952	David Browning	205.29
1956	Robert Clotworthy	159.56
1960	Gary Tobian	170.00
1964	Kenneth Sitzberger	159.90
1968	Bernard Wrightson	170.15
1976	Philip Boggs	619.05
1984	Greg Louganis	754.41
1988	Greg Louganis	730.80

PLATFORM DIVING

1904	George Sheldon	12.66
1920	Clarence Pinkston	100.67
1924	Albert White	97.46
1928	Pete Desjardins	98.74
1932	Harold Smith	124.80
1936	Marshall Wayne	113.58
1948	Sammy Lee	130.05
1952	Sammy Lee	156.28
1960	Robert Webster	165.56
1964	Robert Webster	148.58
1984	Greg Louganis	576.99
1988	Greg Louganis	638.61

Women

100-METER FREESTLYE

1920	Ethelda Bleibtrey	1:13.6 WR
1924	Ethel Lackie	1:12.4
1928	Albina Osipowich	1:11.0 OR
1932	Helene Madison	1:06.8 OR
1968	Jan Henne	1:00.0
1972	Sandra Neilson	58.59 OR
1984	Carrie Steinseifer	55.92
	Nancy Hogshead	55.92

200-METER FREESTYLE

1968	Debbie Meyer	2:10.5 OR
1984	Mary Wayte	1:59.23
1992	Nicole Haislett	1:57.90

400-METER FREESTYLE

1924	Martha Norelius	6:02.2 OR
1928	Martha Norelius	5:42.8 WR
1932	Helene Madison	5:28.5 WR
1948	Ann Curtis	5:17.8 OR
1960	Chris von Saltza	4:50.6
1964	Virginia Duenkel	4:43.3 OR
1968	Debbie Meyer	4:31.8 OR
1984	Tiffany Cohen	4:07.10 OR
1988	Janet Evans	4:03.85 WR

800-METER FREESTYLE

1968	Debbie Meyer	9:24.0 OR
1972	Keena Rothhammer	8:53.86 WR
1984	Tiffany Cohen	8:24.95 OR
1988	Janet Evans	8:20.20 OR
1992	Janet Evans	8:25.52

100-METER BACKSTROKE

1924	Sybil Bauer	1:23.2 OR
1932	Eleanor Holm	1:19.4
1960	Lynn Burke	1:09.3 OR
1964	Cathy Ferguson	1:07.7 WR
1968	Kaye Hall	1:06.2 WR
1972	Melissa Belote	1:05.78 OR
1984	Theresa Andrews	1:02.55

200-METER BACKSTROKE

1968	Pokey Watson	2:24.8 OR
1972	Melissa Belote	2:19.19 WR

100-METER BREASTSTROKE

1972	Catherine Carr	1:13.58 WR

200-METER BREASTSTROKE

1968	Sharon Wichman	2:44.4 OR

100-METER BUTTERFLY

1956	Shelley Mann	1:11.0 OR
1960	Carolyn Schuler	1:09.5 OR
1964	Sharon Stouder	1:04.7 WR
1984	Mary T. Meagher	59.26

200-METER BUTTERFLY

1972	Karen Moe	2:15.57 WR
1984	Mary T. Meagher	2:06.90 OR
1992	Summer Sanders	2:08.67

200-METER INDIVIDUAL MEDLEY

1968	Sharon Wichman	2:44.4 OR
1984	Tracy Caulkins	2:12.64 OR

400-METER INDIVIDUAL MEDLEY

1964	Donna De Varona	5:18.7 OR
1968	Claudia Kolb	5:08.5 OR
1984	Tracy Caulkins	4:39.24
1988	Janet Evans	4:37.76

3-METER SPRINGBOARD DIVING

1920	Aileen Riggin	539.9 points
1924	Elizabeth Becker	474.5
1928	Helen Meany	78.62
1932	Georgia Coleman	87.52
1936	Marjorie Gestring	89.27
1948	Victoria Draves	108.74
1952	Patricia McCormick	147.30
1956	Patricia McCormick	142.36
1968	Sue Gossick	150.77
1972	Micki King	450.03
1976	Jennifer Chandler	506.19

PLATFORM DIVING

1924	Caroline Smith	33.2
1928	Elizabeth Becker Pinkston	31.6
1932	Dorothy Poynton	40.26
1936	Dorothy Poynton Hill	33.93
1948	Victoria Draves	68.87
1952	Patricia McCormick	79.37
1956	Patricia McCormick	84.85
1964	Lesley Bush	99.80

Notable Achievements

Barrier Breakers

MEN

Event	Barrier	Athlete and Nation	Time	Date
100 Freestyle	1:00	Johnny Weissmuller, United States	58.6	7-9-22
100 Freestyle	:50	James Montgomery, United States	49.99	7-25-76
200 Freestyle	2:00	Don Schollander, United States	1:58.8	7-27-63
200 Freestyle	1:50	Sergei Kopliakov, USSR	1:49.83	4-7-79
400 Freestyle	4:00	Rick DeMont, United States	3:58.18	9-6-73
400 Freestyle	3:50	Vladimir Salnikov, USSR	3:49.57	3-12-82
800 Freestyle	8:00	Vladimir Salnikov, USSR	7:56.49	3-23-79
1500 Freestyle	15:00	Vladimir Salnikov, USSR	14:58.27	7-22-80
100 Backstroke	1:00	Thompson Mann, United States	59.6	10-16-64
200 Backstroke	2:00	John Naber, United States	1:59.19	7-24-76
200 Breaststroke	2:30	Chester Jastremski, United States	2:29.6	8-19-61
100 Butterfly	1:00	Lance Larson, United States	59.0	6-29-60
200 Butterfly	2:00	Roger Pyttel, East Germany	1:59.63	6-3-76

WOMEN

Event	Barrier	Athlete and Nation	Time	Date
100 Freestyle	1:00	Dawn Fraser, Australia	59.9	10-27-62
200 Freestyle	2:00	Kornelia Ender, East Germany	1:59.78	6-2-76
400 Freestyle	4:30	Debbie Meyer, United States	4:29.0	8-18-67
800 Freestyle	10:00	Jane Cederqvist, Sweden	9:55.6	8-17-60
800 Freestyle	9:00	Ann Simmons, United States	8:59.4	9-10-71
1500 Freestyle	20:00	Ilsa Konrads, Australia	19:25.7	1-14-60
	16:00	Janet Evans, United States	15:52.10	3-26-88
200 Backstroke	2:30	Satoko Tanaka, Japan	2:29.6	2-10-63
100 Butterfly	1:00	Christiane Knacke, East Germany	59.78	8-28-77
400 Individual Medley	5:00	Gudrun Wegner, East Germany	4:57.51	9-6-73

Olympic Achievements

MOST INDIVIDUAL GOLDS IN SINGLE OLYMPICS

MEN

No.	Athlete and Nation	Olympic Year	Events
4	Mark Spitz, United States	1972	100, 200 Free; 100, 200 Fly

WOMEN

No.	Athlete and Nation	Olympic Year	Events
4	Kristin Otto, East Germany	1988	50, 100 Free; 100 Back; 100 Fly
3	Debbie Meyer, United States	1968	200, 400, 800 Free
3	Shane Gould, Australia	1972	200, 400 Free; 200 IM
3	Kornelia Ender, East Germany	1976	100, 200 Free; 100 Fly
3	Janet Evans, United States	1988	400, 800 Free; 400 IM
3	Krisztina Egerszegi, Hungary	1992	100, 200 Back; 400 IM

Olympic Achievements *(Cont.)*

MOST INDIVIDUAL OLYMPIC GOLD MEDALS, CAREER

MEN

No.	Athlete and Nation	Olympic Years and Events
4	Charles Meldrum Daniels, United States	1904 (220, 440 Free); 1906 (100 Free,) 1908 (100 Free)
4	Roland Matthes, East Germany	1968 (100, 200 Back); 1972 (100, 200 Back)
4	Mark Spitz, United States	1972 (100, 200 Free; 100, 200 Fly)

WOMEN

4	Kristin Otto, East Germany	1988 (50 Free; 100 Free, Back and Fly)

Most Olympic Gold Medals in a Single Olympics, Men—7, Mark Spitz, United States, 1972, 100, 200 Free; 100, 200 Fly; 4 x 100, 4 x 200 Free Relays; 4 x 100 Medley

Most Olympic Gold Medals in a Single Olympics, Women—6, Kristin Otto, East Germany, 1988, 50, 100 Free; 100 Back; 100 Fly; 4 x 100 Free Relay; 4 x 100 Medley Relay

Most Olympic Medals in a Career, Men—
11, Matt Biondi, United States:1984 (one gold), '88 (five gold, one silver, one bronze), 92 (two gold, one silver)
11, Mark Spitz, United States: 1968 (two gold, one silver, one bronze), 1972 (seven gold)

Most Olympic Medals in Career, Women—
8, Dawn Fraser, Australia: 1956 (two gold, one silver), '60 (one gold, two silvers), '64 (one gold, one silver)
8, Kornelia Ender, East Germany: 1972 (three silver), '76 (four gold, one silver)
8, Shirley Babashoff, United States: 1972 (one gold, two silver), '76 (one gold, four silver)

Winner, Same Event, Three Consecutive Olympics—Dawn Fraser, Australia, 100 Freestyle, 1956, '60, '64.

Youngest Person to Win an Olympic Diving Gold—Marjorie Gestring, United States, 1936, 13 years, 9 months, springboard diving

Youngest Person to Win Olympic Swimming Gold—Krisztina Egerszegi, Hungary, 1988, 14 years,

World Record Achievements

one month, 200 backstroke

Most World Records, Career, Women—42 Ragnhild Hveger, Denmark, 1936-42

Most World Records , Career, Men—32 Arne Borg, Sweden, 1921-29

Most Freestyle Records Held Concurrently—
5, Helene Madison, United States, 1931-33.
5, Shane Gould, Australia, 1972.

Most Consecutive Lowerings of a Record—10, Kornelia Ender, East Germany, 100 Freestyle, 7-13-73 to 7-19-76.

Longest Duration of World Record—19 years, 359 days, 1:04.6 in 100 Free, Willy den Ouden , the Netherlands

Skiing

Snow Star

World Cup ski queen Katja Seizinger of Germany

Bad News, Bad Vibes

An ill wind blew through the World Cup circuit, leaving a trail of disgruntled skiers | by WILLIAM OSCAR JOHNSON

THE 1992–93 ALPINE SKI RACING season had far more than its fair share of bad news, bad luck, bad vibes and bad weather. It began when the best all-around woman skier since the 1970s, Austria's Petra Kronberger, 23, retired abruptly before the season was a month old, saying she was skiing so badly that she was frightened she would seriously injure herself.

Then the best male slalomist in history, Italy's Alberto Tomba, 26, turned in his worst season since he was a teenager: He won but one race and finished completely out of the medals in the world championships in Morioka-Shizukuishi, Japan—a failure he has repeated so consistently since 1987, when he won a bronze, that he wondered in Japan if he was "haunted."

The best American woman skier, Julie Parisien, 22, won the first World Cup slalom of the year in Park City, Utah, and seemed bound for a magnificent year. She never finished first again all season—due, in part, to a profound and crushing personal tragedy in December, when her brother, Jean-Paul, 24, died in a hit-and-run accident in rural Maine. Julie did rebound in the Morioka-Shizukuishi championships to get the silver medal in the slalom, but her season was mediocre for her.

Then there was the case of AJ Kitt, 23, the best American downhiller since Olympic gold medalist Bill Johnson in 1984. Kitt finished first in two World Cup downhills—and didn't get credit for a victory in either of them. In Val d'Isère, France, in early December in the first World Cup downhill of the year, Kitt was standing a strong No. 1 after 23 skiers when suddenly fog and falling snow cut down visibility. Officials debated, waited, then finally canceled the race—and AJ's win. Three months later, competing in early March in "America's Downhill" in Aspen, Colo., Kitt

was in first place after 16 skiers by an insurmountable .96 of a second. Suddenly two European officials ruled that the race had to be halted due to an ostensible deterioration of the course due to warm weather. American coaches objected strenuously. But the ruling stood, and even though Kitt was given the $30,000 prize for first place, the race was officially canceled—along with Kitt's second World Cup win of the year.

Following that fiasco, in mid-March there were two more bitter controversies on the World Cup circuit. One occurred when the women went to Lillehammer, Norway, site of the 1994 Winter Olympics, for their first look at their Olympic downhill course in nearby Hafjell. They were so disgusted by the flat, boring terrain that 12 of the top 15 racers boycotted a training run and made their feelings public during a ferocious press conference. Kerrin Lee-Gartner, gold medalist in the 1992 Olympic downhill, complained that "there is no

After a strong World Cup start, Parisien was slowed by the tragic death of her brother.

place to take a chance or a risk," and Germany's Katja Seizinger, the 1993 World Cup downhill and Super G winner, simply called the course "demeaning." Stunned by the women's rage, Olympic organizers agreed to consider moving from the too-tame Hafjell course to the men's Olympic course in nearby Kvetfjell, which male racers judged a thoroughly world-class course during a pair of races in March.

But the male racers, too, had risen up in protest over the condition of a race course—this one being the slalom run in Sierra Nevada, Spain, which is to hold the 1995 FIS world championships. This revolt, led by Tomba himself, was over the very poor preparation of a slalom course compared to the very good preparation on the downhill run. Tomba charged that slalomists were treated like "the spare tire" for the downhillers, and the brightest new World Cup superstar, Norway's Kjetil André Aamodt, 21, who won the 1993 World Cups for the giant slalom and Super G, complained: "The downhill course is always given priority, and slalom is treated as a side discipline. We're not against Spain or against the course. It's like a revolution—you can't prepare for it, it just explodes." In the end FIS officials had to cancel the Sierra Nevada slalom, and the revolution of the racers against the authorities seemed likely to keep exploding for some time.

But of all the bad vibes and dissent that dogged the regular World Cup schedule, the worst of times occurred during the world championships in Morioka-Shizukuishi. It was a 12-day bad-weather nightmare in which gale force winds combined with torrential rain, blinding snow, impenetrable fog and even a 6.6 Richter-scale earthquake to raise so much havoc with events that, in the end, not one race was held on the day it was originally scheduled.

Still, whenever the racers were able to perform, it was as if the sun had come out. No one shone brighter than the acrobatic Aamodt, who won two golds (slalom and

Aamodt battled the elements in Japan and came away with a pair of golds and a silver.

giant slalom) and a silver (combined). The men's Super G was canceled due to insane weather, but if it had been run, the hands-down favorite was Aamodt—who won the gold in that event in Albertville last year. Aamodt didn't enter the Morioka-Shizukuishi downhill, but it was a point of dissent, too, for being too easy. Marc Girardelli, 29, the legendary Luxembourger who finished this year by winning a record-breaking fifth overall World Cup, refused even to enter the downhill, saying the course was designed for "development racers and restaurant workers." The downhill winner was an unknown Swiss, Urs Lehmann, while another of Aamodt's Norwegian mates, Atle Skaardal won the silver, giving Norway a stunning total of three golds and two silvers, which bodes awfully well for their hometown Olympics next year. Happily enough the bronze was won by AJ Kitt, giving him at least one bright spot in a dark year. Another American, the feisty Picabo Street, 21, won a silver medal in the combined, giving the U.S. its best championship performance since 1985.

Despite these few points of light, most everyone in World Cup ski racing had good reason to view this entire season just as Tomba viewed his performance in the world championships—haunted.

FOR THE RECORD·1992-1993

World Cup Season Race Results

Men

Date	Event	Site	Winner
11-29-92	Slalom	Sestriere, Italy	Fabrizio Tescari, Italy
12-3-92	Slalom	Sestriere, Italy	Tomas Fogdoe, Sweden
12-5-92	Super G	Val d'Isere, France	Jan Einar Thorsen, Norway
12-6-92	Slalom	Val d'Isere, France	Tomas Fogdoe, Sweden
12-11-92	Downhill	Gardens-Groeden, Italy	William Besse, Switzerland
12-12-92	Downhill	Gardens-Groeden, Italy	Leonard Stock, Austria
12-13-92	Giant slalom	Alta Badia, Italy	Marc Girardelli, Luxembourg
12-15-92	Slalom	Madonna di Campiglio, Italy	Patrice Bianchi, France
12-19-92	Slalom	Kranjska Gora, Slovenia	Tomas Fogdoe, Sweden
12-20-92	Giant Slalom	Kranjska Gora, Slovenia	Marc Girardelli, Luxembourg
12-22-92	Super G	Bad Kleinkirchheim, Austria	Armin Assinger, Austria
1-9-93	Slalom	Garmisch-Partenkirchen, Germany	Alberto Tomba, Italy
1-11-93	Downhill	Garmisch-Partenkirchen, Germany	Daniel Mahrer, Switzerland
1-12-93	Super G	St Anton, Austria	Marc Girardelli, Luxembourg
1-16-93	Downhill	St Anton, Austria	Franz Heinzer, Switzerland
1-17-93	Slalom	Lech, Austria	Tomas Fogdoe, Sweden
1-19-93	Giant Slalom	Veysonnaz, Switzerland	Michael Von Gruenigen, Switz.
1-23-93	Downhill	Veysonnaz, Switzerland	Franz Heinzer, Switzerland
1-24-93	Slalom	Veysonnaz, Switzerland	Thomas Stangassinger, Austria
2-27-93	Downhill	Whistler Mountain, Canada	Atle Skaardal, Norway
2-28-93	Super G	Whistler Mountain, Canada	Guenther Mader, Austria
3-7-93	Super G	Aspen, USA	Kjetil André Aamodt, Norway
3-15-93	Downhill	Sierra Nevada, Spain	Armin Assinger, Austria
3-20-93	Downhill	Kvitfjell, Norway	Armin Assinger, Austria
3-21-93	Super G	Kvitfjell, Norway	Kjetil André Aamodt, Norway
3-23-93	Giant Slalom	Oppdal, Norway	Kjetil André Aamodt, Norway
3-27-93	Giant Slalom	Are, Sweden	Kjetil André Aamodt, Norway

Women

Date	Event	Site	Winner
11-28-92	Giant Slalom	Park City, Utah	Ulrike Maier, Austria
11-29-92	Slalom	Park City, Utah	Julie Parisien, U.S.
12-5-92	Giant Slalom	Steamboat Springs, Colorado	Anita Wachter, Austria
12-6-92	Slalom	Steamboat Springs, Colorado	Pernilla Wiberg, Sweden
12-12-92	Downhill	Vail, Colorado	Miriam Vogt, Germany
12-13-92	Super G	Vail, Colorado	Ulrike Maier, Austria
12-19-92	Downhill	Lake Louise, Canada	Chantal Bournissen, Switzerland
12-20-92	Super G	Lake Louise, Canada	Katja Seizinger, Germany
1-5-93	Giant Slalom	Maribor, Slovenia	Carole Merle, France
1-6-93	Slalom	Maribor, Slovenia	Vreni Schneider, Switzerland
1-8-93	Downhill	Cortina d'Ampezzo, Italy	Regina Haeusl, Germany
1-9-93	Downhill	Cortina d'Ampezzo, Italy	Katje Seizinger, Germany
1-16-93	Super G	Cortina d'Ampezzo, Italy	Ulrike Maier, Austria
1-17-93	Slalom	Cortina d'Ampezzo, Italy	Vreni Schneider, Switzerland
1-22-93	Downhill	Haus, Austria	Chantal Bournissen, Switzerland
1-24-93	Slalom	Haus, Austria	Patricia Chauvet, France
2-26-93	Downhill	Veysonnaz, Switzerland	Katje Seizinger, Germany
2-27-93	Downhill	Veysonnaz, Switzerland	Anja Haas, Austria
2-28-93	Super G	Whistler Mountain, Canada	Carole Merle, France
3-6-93	Downhill	Morzino, France	Katje Seizinger, Germany
3-13-93	Downhill	Hafjell, Norway	Kate Pace, Canada
3-14-93	Slalom	Hafjell, Norway	Renate Goetschl, Austria
2-15-93	Giant Slalom	Hafjell, Norway	Christina Meier, Germany
3-19-93	Slalom	Kloevsjoe-Verndalen, Sweden	Vreni Schneider, Switzerland
3-20-93	Giant Slalom	Kloevsjoe-Verndalen, Sweden	Katja Seizinger, Germany
3-27-93	Giant Slalom	Are, Sweden	Carole Merle, France

World Cup Standings

Men

OVERALL

	Pts
Marc Girardelli, Luxembourg	1379
Kjetil-André Aamodt, Norway	1347
Franz Heinzer, Switzerland	828
Günther Mader, Austria	826
Alberto Tomba, Italy	817
Atle Skaardal, Norway	596
Patrick Ortlieb, Austria	560
Daniel Mahrer, Switzerland	556

DOWNHILL

	Pts
Franz Heinzer, Switzerland	527
Atle Skaardal, Norway	427
William Besse, Switzerland	366
Armin Assinger, Austria	360
Daniel Mahrer, Switzerland	343
Marc Girardelli, Luxembourg	331
Patrick Ortlieb, Austria	272
Hannes Trinkl, Austria	264

SLALOM

	Pts
Tomas Fogdof, Sweden	545
Alberto Tomba, Italy	436
Thomas Stangassinger, Austria	362
Bernhard Gstrein, Austria	276
Kjetil-André Aamodt, Norway	267
Jure Kosir, Slovenia	251
Thomas Sykora, Austria	238
Peter Roth, Germany	202

GIANT SLALOM

	Pts
Kjetil-André Aamodt, Norway	410
Alberto Tomba, Italy	381
Marc Girardelli, Luxembourg	372
Lasse Kjus, Norway	254
Fredrik Nyberg, Sweden	250
Michael Von Gruenigen, Switzerland	236
Johan Wallner, Sweden	208
Paul Accola, Switzerland	168
Alain Feutrier, France	148

SUPER G

	Pts
Kjetil-André Aamodt, Norway	420
Günther Mader, Austria	307
Franz Heinzer, Switzerland	301
Jan Einar Thorsen, Norway	294
Marc Girardelli, Luxembourg	216
Daniel Mahrer, Switzerland	213
Patrick Ortlieb, Austria	190
Luigi Colturi, Italy	181

Women

OVERALL

	Pts
Anita Wachter, Austria	1286
Katja Seizinger, Germany	1266
Carole Merle, France	1086
Miriam Vogt, Germany	699
Ulrike Meier, Austria	696
Vreni Schneider, Switzerland	626
Martina Ertl, Germany	605
Heidi Zeller, Switzerland	599

DOWNHILL

	Pts
Katja Seizinger, Germany	604
Regina Haeusl, Germany	323
Kerrin Lee-Gartner, Canada	294
Anja Haas, Austria	291
Kate Pace, Canada	285
Miriam Vogt, Germany	283
Regine Cavagnoud, France	271
Chantal Bournissen, Switzerland	258

SLALOM

	Pts
Vreni Schneider, Switzerland	490
Annelise Coberger, New Zealand	484
Patricia Chauvet, France	402
Anita Wachter, Austria	272
Kristina Andersson, Sweden	261
Morena Gallizio, Italy	256
Julie Parisien, United States	230
Elfi Eder, Austria	207

GIANT SLALOM

	Pts
Carole Merle, France	480
Anita Wachter, Austria	396
Martina Eril, Germany	278
Ulrike Maier, Austria	252
Heidi Zeller, Switzerland	245
Sabina Panzanini, Italy	238
Katja Seizinger, Germany	234
Deborah Compagnoni, Italy	200

SUPER G

	Pts
Katja Seizinger, Germany	371
Ulrike Maier, Austria	356
Carole Merle, France	326
Anita Wachter, Austria	313
Sylvia Eder, Austria	263
Deborah Compagnoni, Italy	230
Kerrin Lee-Gartner, Canada	199
Regina Haeusl, Germany	181

Event Descriptions

Downhill: A speed event entailing a single run on a course with a minimum vertical drop of 500 meters (800 for Men's World Cup) and very few control gates.
Slalom: A technical event in which times for runs on 2 courses are totaled to determine the winner. Skiers must make many quick, short turns through a combination of gates (55-75 gates for men, 40-60 for women) over a short course (140-220-meter vertical drop for men, 120-180 for women).

Giant Slalom: A faster technical event with fewer, more broadly spaced gates than in the slalom. Times for runs on 2 courses with vertical drops of 250-400 meters (250-300 for women) are combined to determine the winner.
Super G: A speed event that is a cross between the downhill and the giant slalom.
Combined: An event in which scores from designated slalom and downhill races are combined to determine finish order.

FIS World Championships

Sites

1931 ....Mürren, Switzerland	1936 ....Innsbruck, Austria
1932 ....Cortina d'Ampezzo, Italy	1937 ....Chamonix, France
1933 ....Innsbruck, Austria	1938 ....Engelberg, Switzerland
1934 ....St Moritz, Switzerland	1939 ....Zakopane, Poland
1935 ....Mürren, Switzerland	

Men

DOWNHILL

1931............Walter Prager, Switzerland	1936............Rudolf Rominger, Switzerland
1932............Gustav Lantschner, Austria	1937............Émile Allais, France
1933............Walter Prager, Switzerland	1938............James Couttet, France
1934............David Zogg, Switzerland	1939............Hans Lantschner, Germany
1935............Franz Zingerle, Austria	

SLALOM

1931............David Zogg, Switzerland	1936............Rudi Matt, Austria
1932............Friedrich Dauber, Germany	1937............Émile Allais, France
1933............Anton Seelos, Austria	1938............Rudolf Rominger, Switzerland
1934............Franz Pfnür, Germany	1939............Rudolf Rominger, Switzerland
1935............Anton Seelos, Austria	

Women

DOWNHILL

1931 ....Esme Mackinnon, Great Britain	1936 ....Evie Pinching, Great Britain
1932 ....Paola Wiesinger, Italy	1937 ....Christel Cranz, Germany
1933 ....Inge Wersin-Lantschner, Austria	1938 ....Lisa Resch, Germany
1934 ....Anni Rüegg, Switzerland	1939 ....Christel Cranz, Germany
1935 ....Christel Cranz, Germany	

SLALOM

1931 ....Esme Mackinnon, Great Britain	1936 ....Gerda Paumgarten, Austria
1932 ....Rösli Streiff, Switzerland	1937 ....Christel Cranz, Germany
1933 ....Inge Wersin-Lantschner, Austria	1938 ....Christel Cranz, Germany
1934 ....Christel Cranz, Germany	1939 ....Christel Cranz, Germany
1935 ....Anni Rüegg, Switzerland	

FIS World Alpine Ski Championships

Sites

1950............Aspen, Colorado	1978............Garmisch-Partenkirchen, West Germany
1954............Are, Sweden	1982............Schladming, Austria
1958............Badgastein, Austria	1985............Bormio, Italy
1962............Chamonix, France	1987............Crans-Montana, Switzerland
1966............Portillo, Chile	1989............Vail, Colorado
1970............Val Gardena, Italy	1991............Saalbach-Hinterglemm, Austria
1974............St Moritz, Switzerland	1993............Morioka-Shizukuishi, Japan

Men

DOWNHILL

1950............Zeno Colo, Italy	1978............Josef Walcher, Austria
1954............Christian Pravda, Austria	1982............Harti Weirather, Austria
1958............Toni Sailer, Austria	1985............Pirmin Zurbriggen, Switzerland
1962............Karl Schranz, Austria	1987............Peter Müller, Switzerland
1966............Jean-Claude Killy, France	1989............Hansjörg Tauscher, West Germany
1970............Bernard Russi, Switzerland	1991............Franz Heinzer, Switzerland
1974............David Zwilling, Austria	1993............Urs Lehmann, Switzerland

SLALOM

1950............Georges Schneider, Switzerland	1978............Ingemar Stenmark, Sweden
1954............Stein Eriksen, Norway	1982............Ingemar Stenmark, Sweden
1958............Josl Rieder, Austria	1985............Jonas Nilsson, Sweden
1962............Charles Bozon, France	1987............Frank Wörndl, West Germany
1966............Carlo Senoner, Italy	1989............Rudolf Nierlich, Austria
1970............Jean-Noël Augert, France	1991............Marc Girardelli, Luxembourg
1974............Gustavo Thoeni, Italy	1993............Kjetil-André Aamodt, Norway

GIANT SLALOM

1950............Zeno Colo, Italy	1978............Ingemar Stenmark, Sweden
1954............Stein Eriksen, Norway	1982............Steve Mahre, United States
1958............Toni Sailer, Austria	1985............Markus Wasmaier, West Germany
1962............Egon Zimmermann, Austria	1987............Pirmin Zurbriggen, Switzerland
1966............Guy Périllat, France	1989............Rudolf Nierlich, Austria
1970............Karl Schranz, Austria	1991............Rudolf Nierlich, Austria
1974............Gustavo Thoeni, Italy	1993............Kjetil-André Aamodt, Norway

COMBINED

1982............Michel Vion, France	1989............Marc Girardelli, Luxembourg
1985............Pirmin Zurbriggen, Switzerland	1991............Stefan Eberharter, Austria
1987............Marc Girardelli, Luxembourg	1993............Lasse Kjus, Norway

SUPER G

1987............Pirmin Zurbriggen, Switzerland	1991............Stefan Eberharter, Austria
1989............Martin Hangl, Switzerland	1993............Cancelled due to weather

Women

DOWNHILL

1950............Trude Beiser-Jochum, Austria	1978............Annemarie Moser-Pröll, Austria
1954............Ida Schopfer, Switzerland	1982............Gerry Sorensen, Canada
1958............Lucile Wheeler, Canada	1985............Michela Figini, Switzerland
1962............Christl Haas, Austria	1987............Maria Walliser, Switzerland
1966............Erika Schinegger, Austria	1989............Maria Walliser, Switzerland
1970............Annerösli Zryd, Switzerland	1991............Petra Kronberger, Austria
1974............Annemarie Moser-Pröll, Austria	1993............Kate Pace, Canada

SLALOM

1950............Dagmar Rom, Austria	1978............Lea Sölkner, Austria
1954............Trude Klecker, Austria	1982............Erika Hess, Switzerland
1958............Inger Bjornbakken, Norway	1985............Perrine Pelen, France
1962............Marianne Jahn, Austria	1987............Erika Hess, Switzerland
1966............Annie Famose, France	1989............Mateja Svet, Yugoslavia
1970............Ingrid Lafforgue, France	1991............Vreni Schneider, Switzerland
1974............Hanni Wenzel, Liechtenstein	1993............Karin Buder, Austria

Women (Cont.)

GIANT SLALOM

1950	Dagmar Rom, Austria	1978	Maria Epple, West Germany
1954	Lucienne Schmith-Couttet, France	1982	Erika Hess, Switzerland
1958	Lucile Wheeler, Canada	1985	Diann Roffe, United States
1962	Marianne Jahn, Austria	1987	Vreni Schneider, Switzerland
1966	Marielle Goitschel, France	1989	Vreni Schneider, Switzerland
1970	Betsy Clifford, Canada	1991	Pernilla Wiberg, Sweden
1974	Fabienne Serrat, France	1993	Carole Merle, France

COMBINED

1982	Erika Hess, Switzerland	1989	Tamara McKinney, United States
1985	Erika Hess, Switzerland	1991	Chantal Bournissen, Switzerland
1987	Erika Hess, Switzerland	1993	Miriam Vogt, Germany

SUPER G

1987	Maria Walliser, Switzerland	1991	Ulrike Maier, Austria
1989	Ulrike Maier, Austria	1993	Katja Seizinger, Germany

World Cup Season Title Holders

Men
OVERALL

1967	Jean-Claude Killy, France	1981	Phil Mahre, United States
1968	Jean-Claude Killy, France	1982	Phil Mahre, United States
1969	Karl Schranz, Austria	1983	Phil Mahre, United States
1970	Karl Schranz, Austria	1984	Pirmin Zurbriggen, Switzerland
1971	Gustavo Thoeni, Italy	1985	Marc Girardelli, Luxembourg
1972	Gustavo Thoeni, Italy	1986	Marc Girardelli, Luxembourg
1973	Gustavo Thoeni, Italy	1987	Pirmin Zurbriggen, Switzerland
1974	Piero Gros, Italy	1988	Pirmin Zurbriggen, Switzerland
1975	Gustavo Thoeni, Italy	1989	Marc Girardelli, Luxembourg
1976	Ingemar Stenmark, Sweden	1990	Pirmin Zurbriggen, Switzerland
1977	Ingemar Stenmark, Sweden	1991	Marc Girardelli, Luxembourg
1978	Ingemar Stenmark, Sweden	1992	Paul Accola, Switzerland
1979	Peter Lüscher, Switzerland	1993	Marc Girardelli, Luxembourg
1980	Andreas Wenzel, Liechtenstein		

DOWNHILL

1967	Jean-Claude Killy, France	1981	Harti Weirather, Austria
1968	Gerhard Nenning, Austria	1982	Steve Podborski, Canada
1969	Karl Schranz, Austria		Peter Müller, Switzerland
1970	Karl Schranz, Austria	1983	Franz Klammer, Austria
	Karl Cordin, Austria	1984	Urs Raber, Switzerland
1971	Bernhard Russi, Switzerland	1985	Helmut Höflehner, Austria
1972	Bernhard Russi, Switzerland	1986	Peter Wirnsberger, Austria
1973	Roland Collumbin, Switzerland	1987	Pirmin Zurbriggen, Switzerland
1974	Roland Collumbin, Switzerland	1988	Pirmin Zurbriggen, Switzerland
1975	Franz Klammer, Austria	1989	Marc Girardelli, Luxembourg
1976	Franz Klammer, Austria	1990	Helmut Höflehner, Austria
1977	Franz Klammer, Austria	1991	Franz Heinzer, Switzerland
1978	Franz Klammer, Austria	1992	Franz Heinzer, Switzerland
1979	Peter Müller, Switzerland	1993	Franz Heinzer, Switzerland
1980	Peter Müller, Switzerland		

Men *(Cont.)*

SLALOM

1967 ....Jean-Claude Killy, France	1980 ....Ingemar Stenmark, Sweden
1968 ....Domeng Giovanoli, Switzerland	1981 ....Ingemar Stenmark, Sweden
1969 ....Jean-Noël Augert, France	1982 ....Phil Mahre, United States
1970 ....Patrick Russel, France	1983 ....Ingemar Stenmark, Sweden
Alain Penz, France	1984 ....Marc Girardelli, Luxembourg
1971 ....Jean-Noël Augert, France	1985 ....Marc Girardelli, Luxembourg
1972 ....Jean-Noël Augert, France	1986 ....Rok Petrovic, Yugoslavia
1973 ....Gustavo Thoeni, Italy	1987 ....Bojan Krizaj, Yugoslavia
1974 ....Gustavo Thoeni, Italy	1988 ....Alberto Tomba, Italy
1975 ....Ingemar Stenmark, Sweden	1989 ....Armin Bittner, West Germany
1976 ....Ingemar Stenmark, Sweden	1990 ....Armin Bittner, West Germany
1977 ....Ingemar Stenmark, Sweden	1991 ....Marc Girardelli, Luxembourg
1978 ....Ingemar Stenmark, Sweden	1992 ....Alberto Tomba, Italy
1979 ....Ingemar Stenmark, Sweden	1993 ....Tomas Fogdof, Sweden

GIANT SLALOM

1967 ....Jean-Claude Killy, France	1982 ....Phil Mahre, United States
1968 ....Jean-Claude Killy, France	1983 ....Phil Mahre, United States
1969 ....Karl Schranz, Austria	1984 ....Ingemar Stenmark, Sweden
1970 ....Gustavo Thoeni, Italy	Pirmin Zurbriggen, Switzerland
1971 ....Patrick Russel, France	1985 ....Marc Girardelli, Luxembourg
1972 ....Gustavo Thoeni, Italy	1986 ....Joël Gaspoz, Switzerland
1973 ....Hans Hinterseer, Austria	1987 ....Joël Gaspoz, Switzerland
1974 ....Piero Gros, Italy	Pirmin Zurbriggen, Switzerland
1975 ....Ingemar Stenmark, Sweden	1988 ....Alberto Tomba, Italy
1976 ....Ingemar Stenmark, Sweden	1989 ....Pirmin Zurbriggen, Switzerland
1977 ....Heini Hemmi, Switzerland	1990 ....Ole-Cristian Furuseth, Norway
Ingemar Stenmark, Sweden	Günther Mader, Austria
1978 ....Ingemar Stenmark, Sweden	1991 ....Alberto Tomba, Italy
1979 ....Ingemar Stenmark, Sweden	1992 ....Alberto Tomba, Italy
1980 ....Ingemar Stenmark, Sweden	1993 ....Kjetil-André Aamodt, Norway
1981 ....Ingemar Stenmark, Sweden	

SUPER G

1986 ....Markus Wasmeier, West Germany	1990 ....Pirmin Zurbriggen, Switzerland
1987 ....Pirmin Zurbriggen, Switzerland	1991 ....Franz Heinzer, Switzerland
1988 ....Pirmin Zurbriggen, Switzerland	1992 ....Paul Accola, Switzerland
1989 ....Pirmin Zurbriggen, Switzerland	1993 ....Kjetil-André Aamodt, Norway

COMBINED

1979 ....Andreas Wenzel, Liechtenstein	1987 ....Pirmin Zurbriggen, Switzerland
1980 ....Andreas Wenzel, Liechtenstein	1988 ....Hubert Strolz, Austria
1981 ....Phil Mahre, United States	1989 ....Marc Girardelli, Luxembourg
1982 ....Phil Mahre, United States	1990 ....Pirmin Zurbriggen, Switzerland
1983 ....Phil Mahre, United States	1991 ....Marc Girardelli, Luxembourg
1984 ....Andreas Wenzel, Liechtenstein	1992 ....Paul Accola, Switzerland
1985 ....Andreas Wenzel, Liechtenstein	1993 ....Marc Girardelli, Luxembourg
1986 ....Markus Wasmaier, West Germany	

Women

OVERALL

1967 ....Nancy Greene, Canada	1981 ....Marie-Thérèse Nadig, Switzerland
1968 ....Nancy Greene, Canada	1982 ....Erika Hess, Switzerland
1969 ....Gertrud Gabl, Austria	1983 ....Tamara McKinney, United States
1970 ....Michèle Jacot, France	1984 ....Erika Hess, Switzerland
1971 ....Annemarie Pröll, Austria	1985 ....Michela Figini, Switzerland
1972 ....Annemarie Pröll, Austria	1986 ....Maria Walliser, Switzerland
1973 ....Annemarie Pröll, Austria	1987 ....Maria Walliser, Switzerland
1974 ....Annemarie Moser-Pröll, Austria	1988 ....Michela Figini, Switzerland
1975 ....Annemarie Moser-Pröll, Austria	1989 ....Vreni Schneider, Switzerland
1976 ....Rosi Mitermaier, West Germany	1990 ....Petra Kronberger, Austria
1977 ....Lise-Marie Morerod, Switzerland	1991 ....Petra Kronberger, Austria
1978 ....Hanni Wenzel, Liechtenstein	1992 ....Petra Kronberger, Austria
1979 ....Annemarie Moser-Pröll, Austria	1993 ....Anita Wachter, Austria
1980 ....Hanni Wenzel, Liechtenstein	

Women (Cont.)

DOWNHILL

1967 ....Marielle Goitschel, France	1980 ....Marie-Thérèse Nadig, Switzerland
1968 ....Isabelle Mir, France	1981 ....Marie-Thérèse Nadig, Switzerland
Olga Pall, Austria	1982 ....Marie-Cecile Gros-Gaudenier, France
1969 ....Wiltrud Drexel, Austria	1983 ....Doris De Agostini, Switzerland
1970 ....Isabelle Mir, France	1984 ....Maria Walliser, Switzerland
1971 ....Annemarie Pröll, Austria	1985 ....Michela Figini, Switzerland
1972 ....Annemarie Pröll, Austria	1986 ....Maria Walliser, Switzerland
1973 ....Annemarie Pröll, Austria	1987 ....Michela Figini, Switzerland
1974 ....Annemarie Moser-Pröll, Austria	1988 ....Michela Figini, Switzerland
1975 ....Annemarie Moser-Pröll, Austria	1989 ....Michela Figini, Switzerland
1976 ....Brigitte Totschnig, Austria	1990 ....Katrin Gutensohn-Knopf, Germany
1977 ....Brigitte Totschnig-Habersatter, Austria	1991 ....Chantal Bournissen, Switzerland
1978 ....Annemarie Moser-Pröll, Austria	1992 ....Katja Seizinger, Germany
1979 ....Annemarie Moser-Pröll, Austria	1993 ....Katja Seizinger, Germany

SLALOM

1967 ....Marielle Goitschel, France	1981 ....Erika Hess, Switzerland
1968 ....Marielle Goitschel, France	1982 ....Erika Hess, Switzerland
1969 ....Gertrud Gabl, Austria	1983 ....Erika Hess, Switzerland
1970 ....Ingrid Lafforgue, France	1984 ....Tamara McKinney, United States
1971 ....Britt Lafforgue, France	1985 ....Erika Hess, Switzerland
1972 ....Britt Lafforgue, France	1986 ....Roswitha Steiner, Austria
1973 ....Patricia Emonet, France	Erika Hess, Switzerland
1974 ....Christa Zechmeister, West Germany	1987 ....Corrine Schmidhauser, Switzerland
1975 ....Lise-Marie Morerod, Switzerland	1988 ....Roswitha Steiner, Austria
1976 ....Rosi Mittermaier, West Germany	1989 ....Vreni Schneider, Switzerland
1977 ....Lise-Marie Morerod, Switzerland	1990 ....Vreni Schneider, Switzerland
1978 ....Hanni Wenzel, Liechtenstein	1991 ....Petra Kronberger, Austria
1979 ....Regina Sackl, Austria	1992 ....Vreni Schneider, Switzerland
1980 ....Perrine Pelen, France	1993 ....Vreni Schneider, Switzerland

GIANT SLALOM

1967 ....Nancy Greene, Canada	1981 ....Marie-Thérèse Nadig, Switzerland
1968 ....Nancy Greene, Canada	1982 ....Irene Epple, West Germany
1969 ....Marilyn Cochran, United States	1983 ....Tamara McKinney, United States
1970 ....Michèle Jacot, France	1984 ....Erika Hess, Switzerland
Françoise Macchi, France	1985 ....Maria Keihl, West Germany
1971 ....Annemarie Pröll, Austria	Michela Figini, Switzerland
1972 ....Annemarie Pröll, Austria	1986 ....Vreni Schneider, Switzerland
1973 ....Monika Kaserer, Austria	1987 ....Vreni Schneider, Switzerland
1974 ....Hanni Wenzel, Liechtenstein	Maria Walliser, Switzerland
1975 ....Annemarie Moser-Pröll, Austria	1988 ....Mateja Svet, Yugoslavia
1976 ....Lise-Marie Morerod, France	1989 ....Vreni Schneider, Switzerland
1977 ....Lise-Marie Morerod, France	1990 ....Anita Wachter, Austria
1978 ....Lise-Marie Morerod, France	1991 ....Vreni Schneider, Switzerland
1979 ....Christa Kinshofer, West Germany	1992 ....Carole Merle, France
1980 ....Hanni Wenzel, Liechtenstein	1993 ....Carole Merle, France

SUPER G

1986 ....Maria Kiehl, West Germany	1990 ....Carole Merle, France
1987 ....Maria Walliser, Switzerland	1991 ....Carole Merle, France
1988 ....Michela Figini, Switzerland	1992 ....Carole Merle, France
1989 ....Carole Merle, France	1993 ....Katja Seizinger, Germany

COMBINED

1979 ....Annemarie Moser-Pröll, Austria	1986 ....Maria Walliser, Switzerland
Hanni Wenzel, Liechtenstein	1987 ....Brigitte Oertli, Switzerland
1980 ....Hanni Wenzel, Liechtenstein	1988 ....Brigitte Oertli, Switzerland
1981 ....Marie-Thérèse Nadig, Switzerland	1989 ....Brigitte Oertli, Switzerland
1982 ....Irene Epple, West Germany	1990 ....Anita Wachter, Austria
1983 ....Hanni Wenzel, Liechtenstein	1991 ....Sabine Ginther, Austria
1984 ....Erika Hess, Switzerland	1992 ....Sabine Ginther, Austria
1985 ....Brigitte Oertli, Switzerland	1993 ....Anita Wachter, Austria

World Cup Career Victories

Men

DOWNHILL

25	Franz Klammer, Austria
19	Peter Müller, Switzerland
14	Franz Heinzer, Switzerland*

SLALOM

37	Ingemar Stenmark, Sweden
17	Marc Girardelli, Luxembourg*
16	Alberto Tomba, Italy*

GIANT SLALOM

44	Ingemar Stenmark, Sweden
11	Pirmin Zurbriggen, Switzerland
10	Gustavo Thoeni, Italy
	Alberto Tomba, Italy*

SUPER G

6	Markus Wasmeier, Germany*
6	Marc Girardelli, Luxembourg*
4	Pirmin Zurbriggen, Switzerland

COMBINED

11	Phil Mahre, United States
8	Pirmin Zurbriggen, Switzerland
5	Marc Girardelli, Luxembourg*
	Andreas Wenzel, Lichtenstein

Women

DOWNHILL

33	Annemarie Moser-Pröll, Austria
17	Michela Figini, Switzerland
14	Maria Walliser, Switzerland

SLALOM

21	Erika Hess, Switzerland
21	Vreni Schneider, Switzerland*
14	Perrine Pelen, France

GIANT SLALOM

19	Vreni Schneider, Switzerland*
16	Annemarie Moser-Pröll, Austria
12	Hanni Wenzel, Lichtenstein

SUPER G

12	Carole Merle, France*
3	Maria Kiehl, Germany
	Maria Walliser, Switzerland
	Sigrid Wolf, Austria

COMBINED

8	Hanni Wenzel, Lichtenstein
7	Annemarie Moser-Pröll, Austria
6	Brigitte Oertli, Switzerland

*still active

U.S. Olympic Gold Medalists

Men

Year	Winner	Event
1980	Phil Mahre	Combined
1984	Bill Johnson	Downhill
1984	Phil Mahre	Slalom

Women

Year	Winner	Event
1948	Gretchen Fraser	Slalom
1952	Andrea Mead Lawrence	Slalom
1952	Andrea Mead Lawrence	Giant Slalom
1972	Barbara Ann Cochran	Slalom
1984	Debbie Armstrong	Giant Slalom

Figure Skating

THE
ICE
MAN

Canada's Kurt Browning
wins the world figure
skating title in Prague

Sonja Redux

A 15-year-old sprite won the ladies title and revived memories of a star named Henie | by E.M. SWIFT

SO WHAT IF SHE HAD NEVER heard of Sonja Henie, the 10-time world and three-time Olympic champion, or seen one of that Norwegian beauty's vintage Hollywood films? They were kindred spirits, she and Henie, precocious and engaging, two skaters who seemed to light up from the inside, firefly-like, in front of an audience. Natural showpeople, whose skating was so infectiously appealing that their admirers cut right across international borders. Her name? Oksana Baiul, a 15-year-old from out of nowhere by way of Dnepropetrovsk, Ukraine. Nineteen ninety-three, in figure skating, should be remembered as the year Baiul, the bedazzler with the heartbreaking past, replaced Henie as the youngest ladies' world champion ever.

Oh, there were other things the year could be remembered by. The flame-out in the international arena by the U.S. figure skaters, for example, who failed to win a single medal at the Prague world championships—the first time that has happened since 1964. Particularly disappointing was Nancy Kerrigan, the U.S. ladies' champion, who in 1992 had won

the silver at the worlds and the bronze at the Albertville Olympics. Kerrigan, it was thought, would assume the top spot vacated by Kristi Yamaguchi. But the pressure proved too much for the elegant 23-year-old from Stoneham, Mass., cited by *People* magazine as one of 1993's 50 most beautiful people in the world. In Prague, to the theme song from Disney's *Beauty and the Beast*, Kerrigan skated the part of the water buffalo. "I wish I could die," she said through her tears after finishing fifth.

In Canada the year might well be remembered for the return of the world championships to Prague. In 1962, the last time the worlds were held in that magical, architecturally timeless city, the Canadians had their most successful showing ever—two golds, a silver and a bronze. In '93 they nearly matched it, capturing two golds and a silver. Lloyd Eisler from Seaforth, Ont., and Isabelle Brasseur from St. Jean-sur-Richelieu, Que., won their first world pairs title, breaking an eight-year reign by pairs skaters from the former Soviet Union. It vindicated Eisler and Brasseur's decision to remain amateur after finishing a disappointing third in both the worlds and Olympics in '92. Canada's other two medals were won in the men's competition, in which Kurt Browning and Elvis Stojko finished one-two. Browning, a three-time world champ who bombed to sixth last year in Albertville, displayed a surer artistic sense than judges had seen from him previously. His new freeskating program, in which Browning manages to strut languidly on skates and generally assumes the persona of a modern-day Rick from *Casablanca*—at one point he pauses at center-ice, pretending to light a cigarette—was immediately hailed as a classic.

In ice dancing the year's big news was bad news for the West. Three Russian couples swept 1-2-3, led by Maya Usova and Alexander Zhulin, who waltzed to their first world title. All told, six of the top 10 placements went to ice dancers representing former Soviet republics.

Since her mother's death when Baiul was 13, her family has been the skating world.

MANNY MILLAN

Nineteen ninety-three might also be remembered as the first year the International Skating Union (ISU) allowed professionals to be reinstated as amateurs, provided they put their income from skating into a trust fund. The new policy will enable former pros to come back and compete in the Olympics, and a number of the sport's biggest names declared their intentions to do just that. Brian Boitano and Victor Petrenko, the 1988 and '92 gold medalists, respectively, applied for reinstatement so they could compete in Lillehammer, where they will provide Browning with his sternest opposition. Ice dancing legends Jayne Torville and Christopher Dean, gold medalists in '84, will attempt to end the Russian stranglehold on that event. In pairs, Ekaterina Gordeeva and Sergei Grinkov, and Natalia Michkouteniok and Artur Dmitriev, gold medalists in the last two Winter Games, were reinstated as amateurs so they could challenge Eisler and Brasseur. And in the ladies' competition, two-time gold medalist Katarina Witt surprised the figure skating world by announcing that she, too, would attempt a comeback. As for Yamaguchi, she disappointed her fans and U.S. skating officials by deciding in April she would remain on the sidelines as a professional.

The emergence of Baiul might have had something to do with Yamaguchi's decision. Virtually unknown until she finished second in the European championships in Helsinki in January, Baiul was recognized as the real thing. She is stunningly lithe, musical, athletic and poised beyond her years. Life has made her pay for these gifts. Baiul's father disappeared when she was two; her mother died two years ago, at 36, of cancer. Baiul still cries when she speaks of her. Orphaned at 13, Baiul now lives with her coach, Galina Zmievskaya, in Odessa. "God has taken away her family, " says Zmievskaya. "But the skating world is now her family."

And her oyster, if 1993 presages what lies in store for Oksana Baiul.

FIGURE SKATING**677**

FOR THE RECORD·1992-1993

World Champions

Prague, Czechoslovakia, March 9—14

Women

1. ....Oksana Baiul, Ukraine
2. ....Surya Bonaly, France
3. ....Chen Lu, China

Men

1. ....Kurt Browning, Canada
2. ....Elvis Stojko, Canada
3. ....Alexei Urmanov, Russia

Pairs

1 ....Isabelle Brasseur and Lloyd Eisler, Canada
2. ......Mandy Wötzel and Ingo Steuer, Germany
3. ......Evgenia Shishkova and Vadim Naumov, Rus

Dance

1. ..Maya Usova and Alexandr Zhulin, Russia
2. ..Oksana Gritschuk and Evgeny Platov, Russia
3. ..Anjelika Krylova and Vladimir Fedorov, Russia

World Figure Skating Championships Medal Table

Country	Gold	Silver	Bronze	Total
Russia	1	1	3	5
Canada	2	1	0	3
Ukraine	1	0	0	1
Germany	0	1	0	1
France	0	1	0	1
China	0	0	1	1

Champions of the United States

Phoenix, Arizona, January 17—24

Women

1. ....Nancy Kerrigan, Colonial FSC
2. ....Lisa Ervin, Winterhurst FSC
3. ....Tonia Kwiatkowski, Winterhurst FSC

Men

1. ....Scott Davis, Broadmoor SC
2. ....Mark Mitchell, SC of Hartford
3. ....Michael Chack, SC of Rockland, NY

Pairs

1. ....Calla Urbanski and Rocky Marval,
U of Delaware FSC/SC of New York
2. ....Jenni Meno and Todd Sand,
Winterhurst FSC/Los Angeles FSC
3. ....Karen Courtland and Todd
Reynolds, U of Delaware
FSC/Houston FSC

Dance

1. ....Renee Roca and Gorsha Sur,
Broadmoor SC/Broadmoor SC
2. ....Susan Wynne and Russ Witherby,
Phila SC & HS/SC of Wilmington
3. ....Elizabeth Punsalan and Jerod Swallow,
Broadmoor SC/Detroit SC

Special Achievements

Women successfully landing a triple Axel in competition:
Midori Ito, Japan, 1988 free-skating competition at Aichi, Japan.
Tonya Harding, United States, 1991 U.S. Figure Skating Championship.

On Thin Ice

The news that Katarina Witt was planning to seek reinstatement as an amateur received a low score from *USA Today*, which in an editorial entitled "The Geezer Olympics?" questioned whether the Games were "losing the zest of youth." The editorial appeared under a masthead bearing the names of *USA Today* founder Allen H. Neuharth, editor Peter S. Prichard, editorial page editor Karen Jurgensen and publisher Tom Curley, who are 68, 48, 43 and 44, respectively. Witt, a two-time Olympic figure skating gold medalist who wants to compete in the '94 Winter Games, is all of 27.

Skating Terminology*

Basic Skating Terms

Edges: The two sides of the skating blade, on either side of the grooved center. There is an inside edge, on the inner side of the leg; and an outside edge, on the outer side of the leg.

Free Foot, Hip, Knee, Side, Etc.: The foot a skater is not skating on at any one time is the free foot; everything on that side of the body is then called "free." (See also "skating foot.")

Free Skating (Freestyle): A 4- or 5-minute competition program of free-skating components, choreographed to music, with no set elements. Skating moves include jumps, spins, steps and other linking movements.

Skating Foot, Hip, Knee, Side, Etc.: Opposite of the free foot, hip, knee, side, etc. The foot a skater is skating on at any one time is the skating foot; everything on that side of the body is then called "skating."

Toe Picks (Toe Rakes): The teeth at the front of the skate blade, used primarily for certain jumps and spins.

Trace, Tracing: The line left on the ice by the skater's blade.

Jumps

Waltz: A beginner's jump, involving half a revolution in the air, taken from a forward outside edge and landed on the back outside edge of the other foot.

Toe Loop: A one-revolution jump taken off from and landed on the same back outside edge. This jump is similar to the loop jump except that the skater kicks the toe pick of the free leg into the ice upon takeoff, providing added power.

Toe Walley: A jump similar to the toe loop, except that the takeoff is from the inside edge.

Flip: A jump taken off with the toe pick of the free leg from a back inside edge and landed on a back outside edge, with one in-air revolution.

Lutz: A toe jump similar to the flip, taken off with the toe pick of the free leg from a backwrd outside edge. The skater enters the jump skating in one direction, and concludes the jump skating in the opposite direction. Usually performed in the corners of the rink. Named after founder Alois Lutz, who first completed the jump in Vienna, 1918.

Salchow: A one-, two- or three-revolution jump. The skater takes off from the back inside edge of one foot and lands backwards on the outside edge of the right foot, the opposite foot from which the skater took off. Named for its originator and first Olympic champion (1908), Sweden's Ulrich Salchow.

Axel: A combination of the waltz and loop jumps, including one-and-a-half revolutions. The only jump begun from a forward outside edge, the axel is landed on the back outside edge of the opposite foot. Named for its inventor, Norway's Axel Paulsen.

Spins

Spin: The rotation of the body in one place on the ice. Various spins are the back, fast or scratch, sit, camel, butterfly and layback.

Camel Spin: A spin with the skater in an arabesque position (the free leg at right angles to the leg on the ice).

Flying Camel Spin: A jump spin ending in the camel-spin position.

Flying Sit Spin: A jump spin in which the skater leaps off the ice, assumes a sitting position at the peak of the jump, lands and spins in a similar sitting position.

Pair Movements/Techniques

Death Spiral: One of the most dramatic moves in figure skating. The man, acting as the center of a circle, holds tightly to the land of his partner and pulls her around him. The woman, gliding on one foot, achieves a position almost horizontal to the ice.

Lifts: The most spectacular moves in pairs skating. They involve any maneuver in which the man lifts the woman off the ice. The man often holds his partner above his head with one hand.

Throws: The man lifts the woman into the air and throws her away from him. She spins in the air and lands on one foot.

Twist: The man throws the woman into the air. She spins in the air (either a double- or triple-twist), and he catches her at the landing.

*Compiled by the United States Figure Skating Assocation.

World Champions

Women

1906	Madge Sayers-Cave, Great Britain
1907	Madge Sayers-Cave, Great Britain
1908	Lily Kronberger, Hungary
1909	Lily Kronberger, Hungary
1910	Lily Kronberger, Hungary
1911	Lily Kronberger, Hungary
1912	Opika von Meray Horvath, Hungary
1913	Opika von Meray Horvath, Hungary
1914	Opika von Meray Horvath, Hungary
1915-21	No competition
1922	Herma Plank-Szabo, Austria
1923	Herma Plank-Szabo, Austria
1924	Herma Plank-Szabo, Austria
1925	Herma Jaross-Szabo, Austria
1926	Herma Jaross-Szabo, Austria
1927	Sonja Henie, Norway
1928	Sonja Henie, Norway
1929	Sonja Henie, Norway
1930	Sonja Henie, Norway
1931	Sonja Henie, Norway
1932	Sonja Henie, Norway
1933	Sonja Henie, Norway
1934	Sonja Henie, Norway
1935	Sonja Henie, Norway
1936	Sonja Henie, Norway
1937	Cecilia Colledge, Great Britain
1938	Megan Taylor, Great Britain
1939	Megan Taylor, Great Britain
1940-46	No competition
1947	Barbara Ann Scott, Canada
1948	Barbara Ann Scott, Canada
1949	Alena Vrzanova, Czechoslovakia
1950	Alena Vrzanova, Czechoslovakia
1951	Jeannette Altwegg, Great Britain

Women (Cont.)

1952	Jacqueline duBief, France
1953	Tenley Albright, United States
1954	Gundi Busch, West Germany
1955	Tenley Albright, United States
1956	Carol Heiss, United States
1957	Carol Heiss, United States
1958	Carol Heiss, United States
1959	Carol Heiss, United States
1960	Carol Heiss, United States
1961	No competition
1962	Sjoukje Dijkstra, Netherlands
1963	Sjoukje Dijkstra, Netherlands
1964	Sjoukje Dijkstra, Netherlands
1965	Petra Burka, Canada
1966	Peggy Fleming, United States
1967	Peggy Fleming, United States
1968	Peggy Fleming, United States
1969	Gabriele Seyfert, East Germany
1970	Gabriele Seyfert, East Germany
1971	Beatrix Schuba, Austria
1972	Beatrix Schuba, Austria
1973	Karen Magnussen, Canada
1974	Christine Errath, East Germany
1975	Dianne DeLeeuw, Netherlands
1976	Dorothy Hamill, United States
1977	Linda Fratianne, United States
1978	Annett Poetzsch, East Germany
1979	Linda Fratianne, United States
1980	Annett Poetzsch, East Germany
1981	Denise Biellmann, Switzerland
1982	Elaine Zayak, United States
1983	Rosalynn Sumners, United States
1984	Katarina Witt, East Germany
1985	Katarina Witt, East Germany
1986	Debi Thomas, United States
1987	Katarina Witt, East Germany
1988	Katarina Witt, East Germany
1989	Midori Ito, Japan
1990	Jill Trenary, United States
1991	Kristi Yamaguchi, United States
1992	Kristi Yamaguchi, United States
1993	Oksana Baiul, Ukraine

Men

1896	Gilbert Fuchs, Germany
1897	Gustav Hugel, Austria
1898	Henning Grenander, Sweden
1899	Gustav Hugel, Austria
1900	Gustav Hugel, Austria
1901	Ulrich Salchow, Sweden
1902	Ulrich Salchow, Sweden
1903	Ulrich Salchow, Sweden
1904	Ulrich Salchow, Sweden
1905	Ulrich Salchow, Sweden
1906	Gilbert Fuchs, Germany
1907	Ulrich Salchow, Sweden
1908	Ulrich Salchow, Sweden
1909	Ulrich Salchow, Sweden
1910	Ulrich Salchow, Sweden
1911	Ulrich Salchow, Sweden
1912	Fritz Kachler, Austria
1913	Fritz Kachler, Austria
1914	Gosta Sandhal, Sweden
1915-21	No competition
1922	Gillis Grafstrom, Sweden
1923	Fritz Kachler, Austria
1924	Gillis Grafstrom, Sweden
1925	Willy Bockl, Austria
1926	Willy Bockl, Austria
1927	Willy Bockl, Austria
1928	Willy Bockl, Austria
1929	Gillis Grafstrom, Sweden
1930	Karl Schafer, Austria
1931	Karl Schafer, Austria
1932	Karl Schafer, Austria
1933	Karl Schafer, Austria
1934	Karl Schafer, Austria
1935	Karl Schafer, Austria
1936	Karl Schafer, Austria
1937	Felix Kaspar, Austria
1938	Felix Kaspar, Austria
1939	Graham Sharp, Great Britain
1940-46	No competition
1947	Hans Gerschwiler, Switzerland
1948	Dick Button, United States
1949	Dick Button, United States
1950	Dick Button, United States
1951	Dick Button, United States
1952	Dick Button, United States
1953	Hayes Alan Jenkins, United States
1954	Hayes Alan Jenkins, United States
1955	Hayes Alan Jenkins, United States
1956	Hayes Alan Jenkins, United States
1957	David W. Jenkins, United States
1958	David W. Jenkins, United States
1959	David W. Jenkins, United States
1960	Alan Giletti, France
1961	No competition
1962	Donald Jackson, Canada
1963	Donald McPherson, Canada
1964	Manfred Schneldorfer, W Germany
1965	Alain Calmat, France
1966	Emmerich Danzer, Austria
1967	Emmerich Danzer, Austria
1968	Emmerich Danzer, Austria
1969	Tim Wood, United States
1970	Tim Wood, United States
1971	Andrej Nepela, Czechoslovakia
1972	Andrej Nepela, Czechoslovakia
1973	Andrej Nepela, Czechoslovakia
1974	Jan Hoffmann, East Germany
1975	Sergei Volkov, USSR
1976	John Curry, Great Britain
1977	Vladimir Kovalev, USSR
1978	Charles Tickner, United States
1979	Vladimir Kovalev, USSR
1980	Jan Hoffmann, East Germany
1981	Scott Hamilton, United States
1982	Scott Hamilton, United States
1983	Scott Hamilton, United States
1984	Scott Hamilton, United States
1985	Aleksandr Fadeev, USSR
1986	Brian Boitano, United States
1987	Brian Orser, Canada
1988	Brian Boitano, United States
1989	Kurt Browning, Canada
1990	Kurt Browning, Canada
1991	Kurt Browning, Canada
1992	Viktor Petrenko, CIS
1993	Kurt Browning, Canada

Pairs

1908	Anna Hubler, Heinrich Burger, Germany
1909	Phyllis Johnson, James H. Johnson, Great Britain
1910	Anna Hubler, Heinrich Burger, Germany
1911	Ludowika Eilers, Walter Jakobsson, Germany/Finland
1912	Phyllis Johnson, James H. Johnson, Great Britain
1913	Helene Engelmann, Karl Majstrik, Germany
1914	Ludowika Jakobsson-Eilers, Walter Jakobsson-Eilers, Finland
1915-21	No competition
1922	Helene Engelmann, Alfred Berger, Germany
1923	Ludowika Jakobsson-Eilers, Walter Jakobsson-Eilers, Finland
1924	Helene Engelmann, Alfred Berger, Germany
1925	Herma Jaross-Szabo, Ludwig Wrede, Austria
1926	Andree Joly, Pierre Brunet, France
1927	Herma Jaross-Szabo, Ludwig Wrede, Austria
1928	Andree Joly, Pierre Brunet, France
1929	Lilly Scholz, Otto Kaiser, Austria
1930	Andree Brunet-Joly, Pierre Brunet-Joly, France
1931	Emilie Rotter, Laszlo Szollas, Hungary
1932	Andree Brunet-Joly, Pierre Brunet-Joly, France
1933	Emilie Rotter, Laszlo Szollas, Hungary
1934	Emilie Rotter, Laszlo Szollas, Hungary
1935	Emilie Rotter, Laszlo Szollas, Hungary
1936	Maxi Herber, Ernst Bajer, Germany
1937	Maxi Herber, Ernst Bajer, Germany
1938	Maxi Herber, Ernst Bajer, Germany
1939	Maxi Herber, Ernst Bajer, Germany
1940-46	No competition
1947	Micheline Lannoy, Pierre Baugniet, Belgium
1948	Micheline Lannoy, Pierre Baugniet, Belgium
1949	Andrea Kekessy, Ede Kiraly, Hungary
1950	Karol Kennedy, Peter Kennedy, United States
1951	Ria Baran, Paul Falk, West Germany
1952	Ria Baran Falk, Paul Falk, West Germany
1953	Jennifer Nicks, John Nicks, Great Britain
1954	Frances Dafoe, Norris Bowden, Canada
1955	Frances Dafoe, Norris Bowden, Canada
1956	Sissy Schwarz, Kurt Oppelt, Austria
1957	Barbara Wagner, Robert Paul, Canada
1958	Barbara Wagner, Robert Paul, Canada
1959	Barbara Wagner, Robert Paul, Canada
1960	Barbara Wagner, Robert Paul, Canada
1961	No competition
1962	Maria Jelinek, Otto Jelinek, Canada
1963	Marika Kilius, Hans-Jurgen Baumler, West Germany
1964	Marika Kilius, Hans-Jurgen Baumler, West Germany
1965	Ljudmila Protopopov, Oleg Protopopov, USSR
1966	Ljudmila Protopopov, Oleg Protopopov, USSR
1967	Ljudmila Protopopov, Oleg Protopopov, USSR
1968	Ljudmila Protopopov, Oleg Protopopov, USSR
1969	Irina Rodnina, Alexsei Ulanov, USSR
1970	Irina Rodnina, Alexsei Ulanov, USSR
1971	Irina Rodnina, Sergei Ulanov, USSR
1972	Irina Rodnina, Sergei Ulanov, USSR
1973	Irina Rodnina, Aleksandr Zaitsev, USSR
1974	Irina Rodnina, Aleksandr Zaitsev, USSR
1975	Irina Rodnina, Aleksandr Zaitsev, USSR
1976	Irina Rodnina, Aleksandr Zaitsev, USSR
1977	Irina Rodnina, Aleksandr Zaitsev, USSR
1978	Irina Rodnina, Aleksandr Zaitsev, USSR
1979	Tai Babilonia, Randy Gardner, United States
1980	Maria Cherkasova, Sergei Shakhrai, USSR
1981	Irina Vorobieva, Igor Lisovsky, USSR
1982	Sabine Baess, Tassilio Thierbach, East Germany
1983	Elena Valova, Oleg Vasiliev, USSR
1984	Barbara Underhill, Paul Martini, Canada
1985	Elena Valova, Oleg Vasiliev, USSR
1986	Yekaterina Gordeeva, Sergei Grinkov, USSR
1987	Yekaterina Gordeeva, Sergei Grinkov, USSR
1988	Elena Valova, Oleg Vasiliev, USSR
1989	Yekaterina Gordeeva, Sergei Grinkov, USSR
1990	Yekaterina Gordeeva, Sergei Grinkov, USSR
1991	Natalia Mishkutienok, Artur Dmitriev, USSR
1992	Natalia Mishkutienok, Artur Dmitriev CIS
1993	Isabelle Brasseur, Lloyd Eisler, Canada

Dance

1950..................Lois Waring, Michael McGean, U.S.
1951..................Jean Westwood, Lawrence Demmy, Great Britain
1952..................Jean Westwood, Lawrence Demmy, Great Britain
1953..................Jean Westwood, Lawrence Demmy, Great Britain
1954..................Jean Westwood, Lawrence Demmy, Great Britain
1955..................Jean Westwood, Lawrence Demmy, Great Britain
1956..................Pamela Wieght, Paul Thomas, Great Britain
1957..................June Markham, Courtney Jones, Great Britain
1958..................June Markham, Courtney Jones, Great Britain
1959..................Doreen D. Denny, Courtney Jones, Great Britain
1960..................Doreen D. Denny, Courtney Jones, Great Britain
1961..................No competition
1962..................Eva Romanova, Pavel Roman, Czechoslovakia
1963..................Eva Romanova, Pavel Roman, Czechoslovakia
1964..................Eva Romanova, Pavel Roman, Czechoslovakia
1965..................Eva Romanova, Pavel Roman, Czechoslovakia
1966..................Diane Towler, Bernard Ford, Great Britain
1967..................Diane Towler, Bernard Ford, Great Britain
1968..................Diane Towler, Bernard Ford, Great Britain
1969..................Diane Towler, Bernard Ford, Great Britain
1970..................Ljudmila Pakhomova, Aleksandr Gorshkov, USSR
1971..................Ljudmila Pakhomova, Aleksandr Gorshkov, USSR
1972..................Ljudmila Pakhomova, Aleksandr Gorshkov, USSR

1973..................Ljudmila Pakhomova, Aleksandr Gorshkov, USSR
1974..................Ljudmila Pakhomova, Aleksandr Gorshkov, USSR
1975..................Irina Moiseeva, Andreij Minenkov, USSR
1976..................Ljudmila Pakhomova, Aleksandr Gorshkov, USSR
1977..................Irina Moiseeva, Andreij Minenkov, USSR
1978..................Natalia Linichuk, Gennadi Karponosov, USSR
1979..................Natalia Linichuk, Gennadi Karponosov, USSR
1980..................Krisztina Regoeczy, Andras Sallai, Hungary
1981..................Jayne Torvill, Christopher Dean, Great Britain
1982..................Jayne Torvill, Christopher Dean, Great Britain
1983..................Jayne Torvill, Christopher Dean, Great Britain
1984..................Jayne Torvill, Christopher Dean, Great Britain
1985..................Natalia Bestemianova, Andrei Bukin, USSR
1986..................Natalia Bestemianova, Andrei Bukin, USSR
1987..................Natalia Bestemianova, Andrei Bukin, USSR
1988..................Natalia Bestemianova, Andrei Bukin, USSR
1989..................Marina Klimova, Sergei Ponomarenko, USSR
1990..................Marina Klimova, Sergei Ponomarenko, USSR
1991..................Isabelle Duchesnay, Paul Duchesnay, France
1992..................Marina Klimova, Sergei Ponomarenko , CIS
1993..................Renee Roca, Gorsha Sur, Broadmoor SC

Champions of the United States

The championships held in 1914, 1918, 1920 and 1921 under the auspices of the International Skating Union of America were open to Canadians, although they were considered to be United States championships. Beginning in 1922, the championships have been held under the auspices of the United States Figure Skating Association.

Women

1914 ....Theresa Weld, SC of Boston
1915-17 ......No competition
1918..........Rosemary S. Beresford, New York SC
1919 ....No competition
1920 ....Theresa Weld, SC of Boston
1921 ....Theresa Weld Blanchard, SC of Boston
1922 ....Theresa Weld Blanchard, SC of Boston
1923 ....Theresa Weld Blanchard, SC of Boston
1924 ....Theresa Weld Blanchard, SC of Boston
1925 ....Beatrix Loughran, New York SC
1926 ....Beatrix Loughran, New York SC
1927 ....Beatrix Loughran, New York SC

1928 ....Maribel Y. Vinson, SC of Boston
1929 ....Maribel Y. Vinson, SC of Boston
1930 ....Maribel Y. Vinson, SC of Boston
1931 ....Maribel Y. Vinson, SC of Boston
1932 ....Maribel Y. Vinson, SC of Boston
1933 ....Maribel Y. Vinson, SC of Boston
1934 ....Suzanne Davis, SC of Boston
1935 ....Maribel Y. Vinson, SC of Boston
1936 ....Maribel Y. Vinson, SC of Boston
1937 ....Maribel Y. Vinson, SC of Boston
1938 ....Joan Tozzer, SC of Boston
1939 ....Joan Tozzer, SC of Boston

Women *(Cont.)*

1940 ....Joan Tozzer, SC of Boston
1941 ....Jane Vaughn, Philadelphia SC & HS
1942 ....Jane Vaughn Sullivan,
         Philadelphia SC & HS
1943...........Gretchen Van Zandt Merrill, SC of Boston
1944...........Gretchen Van Zandt Merrill, SC of Boston
1945...........Gretchen Van Zandt Merrill, SC of Boston
1946...........Gretchen Van Zandt Merrill, SC of Boston
1947...........Gretchen Van Zandt Merrill, SC of Boston
1948...........Gretchen Van Zandt Merrill, SC of Boston
1949 ....Yvonne Claire Sherman, SC of New York
1950 ....Yvonne Claire Sherman, SC of New York
1951 ....Sonya Klopfer, Junior SC of New York
1952 ....Tenley E. Albright, SC of Boston
1953 ....Tenley E. Albright, SC of Boston
1954 ....Tenley E. Albright, SC of Boston
1955 ....Tenley E. Albright, SC of Boston
1956 ....Tenley E. Albright, SC of Boston
1957 ....Carol E. Heiss, SC of New York
1958 ....Carol E. Heiss, SC of New York
1959 ....Carol E. Heiss, SC of New York
1960 ....Carol E. Heiss, SC of New York
1961 ....Laurence R. Owen, SC of Boston
1962 ....Barbara Roles Pursley,
         Arctic Blades FSC
1963 ....Lorraine G. Hanlon, SC of Boston
1964 ....Peggy Fleming, Arctic Blades FSC
1965 ....Peggy Fleming, Arctic Blades FSC

1966 ....Peggy Fleming, City of Colorado Springs
1967 ....Peggy Fleming, Broadmoor SC
1968 ....Peggy Fleming, Broadmoor SC
1969 ....Janet Lynn, Wagon Wheel FSC
1970 ....Janet Lynn, Wagon Wheel FSC
1971 ....Janet Lynn, Wagon Wheel FSC
1972 ....Janet Lynn, Wagon Wheel FSC
1973 ....Janet Lynn, Wagon Wheel FSC
1974 ....Dorothy Hamill, SC of New York
1975 ....Dorothy Hamill, SC of New York
1976 ....Dorothy Hamill, SC of New York
1977 ....Linda Fratianne, Los Angeles FSC
1978 ....Linda Fratianne, Los Angeles FSC
1979 ....Linda Fratianne, Los Angeles FSC
1980 ....Linda Fratianne, Los Angeles FSC
1981 ....Elaine Zayak, SC of New York
1982 ....Rosalynn Sumners, Seattle SC
1983 ....Rosalynn Sumners, Seattle SC
1984 ....Rosalynn Sumners, Seattle SC
1985 ....Tiffany Chin, San Diego FSC
1986 ....Debi Thomas, Los Angeles FSC
1987 ....Jill Trenary, Broadmoor SC
1988 ....Debi Thomas, Los Angeles FSC
1989 ....Jill Trenary, Broadmoor SC
1990 ....Jill Trenary, Broadmoor SC
1991 ....Tonya Harding, Carousel FSC
1992 ....Kristi Yamaguchi, St Moritz ISC
1993 ....Nancy Kerrigan, Colonial FSC

Men

1914 ....Norman M. Scott, WC of Montreal
1915-17 ......No competition
1918 ....Nathaniel W. Niles, SC of Boston
1919 ....No competition
1920 ....Sherwin C. Badger, SC of Boston
1921 ....Sherwin C. Badger, SC of Boston
1922 ....Sherwin C. Badger, SC of Boston
1923 ....Sherwin C. Badger, SC of Boston
1924 ....Sherwin C. Badger, SC of Boston
1925 ....Nathaniel W. Niles, SC of Boston
1926 ....Chris I. Christenson, Twin City FSC
1927 ....Nathaniel W. Niles, SC of Boston
1928 ....Roger F. Turner, SC of Boston
1929 ....Roger F. Turner, SC of Boston
1930 ....Roger F. Turner, SC of Boston
1931 ....Roger F. Turner, SC of Boston
1932 ....Roger F. Turner, SC of Boston
1933 ....Roger F. Turner, SC of Boston
1934 ....Roger F. Turner, SC of Boston
1935 ....Robin H. Lee, SC, New York
1936 ....Robin H. Lee, SC, New York
1937 ....Robin H. Lee, SC, New York
1938 ....Robin H. Lee, Chicago FSC
1939 ....Robin H. Lee, St Paul FSC
1940 ....Eugene Turner, Los Angeles FSC
1941 ....Eugene Turner, Los Angeles FSC
1942 ....Robert Specht, Chicago FSC
1943 ....Arthur R. Vaughn, Jr,
         Philadelphia SC & HS
1944-45 ......No competition
1946 ....Dick Button, Philadelphia SC & HS
1947 ....Dick Button, Philadelphia SC & HS
1948 ....Dick Button, Philadelphia SC & HS
1949 ....Dick Button, Philadelphia SC & HS
1950 ....Dick Button, SC of Boston

1951 ......Dick Button, SC of Boston
1952 ......Dick Button, SC of Boston
1953 ......Hayes Alan Jenkins, Cleveland SC
1954 ......Hayes Alan Jenkins, Broadmoor SC
1955 ......Hayes Alan Jenkins, Broadmoor SC
1956 ......Hayes Alan Jenkins, Broadmoor SC
1957 ......David Jenkins, Broadmoor SC
1958 ......David Jenkins, Broadmoor SC
1959 ......David Jenkins, Broadmoor SC
1960 ......David Jenkins, Broadmoor SC
1961 ......Bradley R. Lord, SC of Boston
1962 ......Monty Hoyt, Broadmoor SC
1963 ......Thomas Litz, Hershey FSC
1964 ......Scott Ethan Allen, SC of New York
1965 ......Gary C. Visconti, Detroit SC
1966 ......Scott Ethan Allen, SC of New York
1967 ......Gary C. Visconti, Detroit SC
1968 ......Tim Wood, Detroit SC
1969 ......Tim Wood, Detroit SC
1970 ......Tim Wood, City of Colorado Springs
1971 ......John Misha Petkevich, Great Falls FSC
1972 ......Kenneth Shelley, Arctic Blades FSC
1973 ......Gordon McKellen, Jr, SC of Lake Placid
1974 ......Gordon McKellen, Jr, SC of Lake Placid
1975 ......Gordon McKellen, Jr, SC of Lake Placid
1976 ......Terry Kubicka, Arctic Blades FSC
1977 ......Charles Tickner, Denver FSC
1978 ......Charles Tickner, Denver FSC
1979 ......Charles Tickner, Denver FSC
1980 ......Charles Tickner, Denver FSC
1981 ......Scott Hamilton, Philadelphia SC & HS
1982 ......Scott Hamilton, Philadelphia SC & HS
1983 ......Scott Hamilton, Philadelphia SC & HS
1984 ......Scott Hamilton, Philadelphia SC & HS
1985 ......Brian Boitano, Peninsula FSC

Men *(Cont.)*

1986 ......Brian Boitano, Peninsula FSC
1987 ......Brian Boitano, Peninsula FSC
1988 ......Brian Boitano, Peninsula FSC
1989 ......Christopher Bowman, Los Angeles FSC

1990 ......Todd Eldredge, Los Angeles FSC
1991 ......Todd Eldredge, Los Angeles FSC
1992 ......Christopher Bowman, Los Angeles FSC
1993 ......Scott Davis, Broadmoor SC

Pairs

1914 ......Jeanne Chevalier, Norman M. Scott,
WC of Montreal
1915-17 .No competition
1918 ......Theresa Weld, Nathaniel W. Niles,
SC of Boston
1919 ......No competition
1920 ......Theresa Weld, Nathaniel W. Niles,
SC of Boston
1921 ......Theresa Weld Blanchard, Nathaniel W.
Niles,SC of Boston
1922 ......Theresa Weld Blanchard, Nathaniel W.
Niles, SC of Boston
1923 ......Theresa Weld Blanchard, Nathaniel W.
Niles, SC of Boston
1924 ......Theresa Weld Blanchard, Nathaniel W.
Niles, SC of Boston
1925 ......Theresa Weld Blanchard, Nathaniel W.
Niles, SC of Boston
1926 ......Theresa Weld Blanchard, Nathaniel W. Niles
SC of Boston
1927 ......Theresa Weld Blanchard, Nathaniel W.
Niles, SC of Boston
1928 ......Maribel Y. Vinson, Thornton L. Coolidge,
SC of Boston
1929 ......Maribel Y. Vinson, Thornton L. Coolidge,
SC of Boston
1930 ......Beatrix Loughran, Sherwin C. Badger,
SC of New York
1931 ......Beatrix Loughran, Sherwin C. Badger,
SC of New York
1932 ......Beatrix Loughran, Sherwin C. Badger,
SC of New York
1933 ......Maribel Y. Vinson, George E. B. Hill,
SC of Boston
1934 ......Grace E. Madden, James L. Madden,
SC of Boston
1935 ......Maribel Y. Vinson, George E. B. Hill,
SC of Boston
1936 ......Maribel Y. Vinson, George E. B. Hill,
SC of Boston
1937 ......Maribel Y. Vinson, George E. B. Hill,
SC of Boston
1938 ......Joan Tozzer, M. Bernard Fox,
SC of Boston
1939 ......Joan Tozzer, M. Bernard Fox,
SC of Boston
1940 ......Joan Tozzer, M. Bernard Fox,
SC of Boston
1941 ......Donna Atwood, Eugene Turner, Mercury
FSC/Los Angeles FSC
1942 ......Doris Schubach, Walter Noffke,
Springfield Ice Birds
1943 ......Doris Schubach, Walter Noffke,
Springfield Ice Birds
1944 ......Doris Schubach, Walter Noffke,
Springfield Ice Birds
1945 ......Donna Jeanne Pospisil, Jean-Pierre Brunet,
SC of New York
1946 ......Donna Jeanne Pospisil, Jean-Pierre Brunet,
SC of New York

1947 ......Yvonne Claire Sherman, Robert J.
Swenning, SC of New York
1948 ......Karol Kennedy, Peter Kennedy,
Seattle SC
1949 ......Karol Kennedy, Peter Kennedy,
Seattle SC
1950 ......Karol Kennedy, Peter Kennedy,
Broadmoor SC
1951 ......Karol Kennedy, Peter Kennedy,
Broadmoor SC
1952 ......Karol Kennedy, Peter Kennedy,
Broadmoor SC
1953 ......Carole Ann Ormaca, Robin Greiner,
SC of Fresno
1954 ......Carole Ann Ormaca, Robin Greiner,
SC of Fresno
1955 ......Carole Ann Ormaca, Robin Greiner,
St Moritz ISC
1956 ......Carole Ann Ormaca, Robin Greiner,
St Moritz ISC
1957 ......Nancy Rouillard Ludington, Ronald
Ludington, Commonwealth FSC/
SC of Boston
1958 ......Nancy Rouillard Ludington, Ronald
Ludington, Commonwealth FSC/
SC of Boston
1959 ......Nancy Rouillard Ludington, Ronald
Ludington, Commonwealth FSC
1960 ......Nancy Rouillard Ludington, Ronald
Ludington, Commonwealth FSC
1961 ......Maribel Y. Owen, Dudley S. Richards,
SC of Boston
1962 ......Dorothyann Nelson, Pieter Kollen,
Village of Lake Placid
1963 ......Judianne Fotheringill, Jerry J. Fotheringill,
Broadmoor SC
1964 ......Judianne Fotheringill, Jerry J. Fotheringill,
Broadmoor SC
1965 ......Vivian Joseph, Ronald Joseph,
Chicago FSC
1966 ......Cynthia Kauffman, Ronald Kauffman,
Seattle SC
1967 ......Cynthia Kauffman, Ronald Kauffman,
Seattle SC
1968 ......Cynthia Kauffman, Ronald Kauffman,
Seattle SC
1969 ......Cynthia Kauffman, Ronald Kauffman,
Seattle SC
1970 ......Jo Jo Starbuck, Kenneth Shelley,
Arctic Blades FSC
1971 ......Jo Jo Starbuck, Kenneth Shelley,
Arctic Blades FSC
1972 ......Jo Jo Starbuck, Kenneth Shelley,
Arctic Blades FSC
1973 ......Melissa Militano, Mark Militano,
SC of New York
1974 ......Melissa Militano, Johnny Johns,
SC of New York/Detroit SC
1975 ......Melissa Militano, Johnny Johns,
SC of New York/Detroit SC

1976 ......Tai Babilonia, Randy Gardner,
          Los Angeles FSC
1977 ......Tai Babilonia, Randy Gardner,
          Los Angeles FSC
1978 ......Tai Babilonia, Randy Gardner,
          Los Angeles FSC/Santa Monica FSC
1979 ......Tai Babilonia, Randy Gardner,
          Los Angeles FSC/Santa Monica FSC
1980 ......Tai Babilonia, Randy Gardner,
          Los Angeles FSC/Santa Monica FSC
1981 ......Caitlin Carruthers, Peter Carruthers,
          SC of Wilmington
1982 ......Caitlin Carruthers, Peter Carruthers,
          SC of Wilmington
1983 ......Caitlin Carruthers, Peter Carruthers,
          SC of Wilmington
1984 ......Caitlin Carruthers, Peter Carruthers,
          SC of Wilmington

1985 ......Jill Watson, Peter Oppegard,
          Los Angeles FSC
1986 ......Gillian Wachsman, Todd Waggoner,
          SC of Wilmington
1987 ......Jill Watson, Peter Oppegard,
          Los Angeles FSC
1988 ......Jill Watson, Peter Oppegard,
          Los Angeles FSC
1989 ......Kristi Yamaguchi, Rudi Galindo,
          St Moritz ISC
1990 ......Kristi Yamaguchi, Rudi Galindo,
          St Moritz ISC
1991 ......Natasha Kuchiki, Todd Sand,
          Los Angeles FSC
1992 ......Calla Urbanski, Rocky Marval,
          U of Delaware FSC/SC of New York
1993 ......Calla Urbanski, Rocky Marval,
          U of Delaware FSC/SC of New York

Dance

1914 ......Waltz
          Theresa Weld, Nathaniel W. Niles,
          SC of Boston
1915-19.No competition
1920 ......Waltz
          Theresa Weld, Nathaniel W. Niles
          SC of Boston
          Fourteenstep
          Gertrude Cheever Porter, Irving Brokaw,
          New York SC
1921 ......Waltz and Fourteenstep
          Theresa Weld Blanchard, Nathaniel W.
          Niles, SC of Boston
1922 ......Waltz
          Beatrix Loughran, Edward M. Howland,
          New York SC/SC of Boston
          Fourteenstep
          Theresa Weld Blanchard, Nathaniel W.
          Niles, SC of Boston
1923 ......Waltz
          Mr. & Mrs. Henry W. Howe, New York SC
          Fourteenstep
          Sydney Goode, James B. Greene,
          New York SC
1924 ......Waltz
          Rosaline Dunn, Frederick Gabel
          New York SC
          Fourteenstep
          Sydney Goode, James B. Greene,
          New York SC
1925 ......Waltz and Fourteenstep
          Virginia Slattery, Ferrier T. Martin,
          New York SC
1926 ......Waltz
          Rosaline Dunn, Joseph K. Savage,
          New York SC
          Fourteenstep
          Sydney Goode, James B. Greene,
          New York SC
1927 ......Waltz and Fourteenstep
          Rosaline Dunn, Joseph K. Savage,
          New York SC
1928 ......Waltz
          Rosaline Dunn, Joseph K. Savage,
          New York SC
          Fourteenstep
          Ada Bauman Kelly, George T. Braakman,
          New York SC

1929 ......Waltz and Original Dance combined
          Edith C. Secord, Joseph K. Savage,
          SC of New York
1930 ......Waltz
          Edith C. Secord, Joseph K. Savage,
          SC of New York
          Original
          Clara Rotch Frothingham, George E. B. Hill,
          SC of Boston
1931 ......Waltz
          Edith C. Secord, Ferrier T. Martin,
          SC of New York
          Original
          Theresa Weld Blanchard, Nathaniel W.
          Niles, SC of Boston
1932 ......Waltz
          Edith C. Secord, Joseph K. Savage,
          SC of New York
          Original
          Clara Rotch Frothingham, George E. B. Hill,
          SC of Boston
1933 ......Waltz
          Ilse Twaroschk, Frederick F. Fleishmann,
          Brooklyn FSC
          Original
          Suzanne Davis, Frederick Goodridge,
          SC of Boston
1934 ......Waltz
          Nettie C. Prantel, Roy Hunt, SC of New York
          Original
          Suzanne Davis, Frederick Goodridge,
          SC of Boston
1935 ......Waltz
          Nettie C. Prantel, Roy Hunt, SC of New York
1936 ......Marjorie Parker, Joseph K. Savage,
          SC of New York
1937 ......Nettie C. Prantel, Harold Hartshorne,
          SC of New York
1938 ......Nettie C. Prantel, Harold Hartshorne,
          SC, of New York
1939 ......Sandy Macdonald, Harold Hartshorne,
          SC of New York
1940 ......Sandy Macdonald, Harold Hartshorne,
          SC of New York
1941 ......Sandy Macdonald, Harold Hartshorne,
          SC of New York

Dance *(Cont.)*

1942 .....Edith B. Whetstone, Alfred N. Richards, Jr,
Philadelphia SC & HS

1943 .....Marcella May, James Lochead, Jr,
Skate & Ski Club

1944 .....Marcella May, James Lochead, Jr,
Skate & Ski Club

1945 .....Kathe Mehl Williams, Robert J. Swenning,
SC of New York

1946 .....Anne Davies, Carleton C. Hoffner, Jr,
Washington FSC

1947 .....Lois Waring, Walter H. Bainbridge, Jr,
Baltimore FSC/Washigton FSC

1948 .....Lois Waring, Walter H. Bainbridge, Jr,
Baltimore FSC/Washington FSC

1949 .....Lois Waring, Walter H. Bainbridge, Jr,
Baltimore FSC/Washington FSC

1950 .....Lois Waring, Michael McGean,
Baltimore FSC

1951 .....Carmel Bodel, Edward L. Bodel,
St Moritz ISC

1952 .....Lois Waring, Michael McGean,
Baltimore FSC

1953 .....Carol Ann Peters, Daniel C. Ryan,
Washington FSC

1954 .....Carmel Bodel, Edward L. Bodel,
St Moritz ISC

1955 .....Carmel Bodel, Edward L. Bodel,
St Moritz ISC

1956 .....Joan Zamboni, Roland Junso,
Arctic Blades FSC

1957 .....Sharon McKenzie, Bert Wright,
Los Angeles FSC

1958 .....Andree Anderson, Donald Jacoby,
Buffalo SC

1959 .....Andree Anderson Jacoby, Donald Jacoby,
Buffalo SC

1960 .....Margie Ackles, Charles W. Phillips, Jr,
Los Angeles FSC/Arctic Blades FSC

1961 .....Diane C. Sherbloom, Larry Pierce,
Los Angeles FSC/WC of Indianapolis

1962 .....Yvonne N. Littlefield, Peter F. Betts,
Arctic Blades FSC/ Paramount, CA

1963 .....Sally Schantz, Stanley Urban,
SC of Boston/Buffalo SC

1964 .....Darlene Streich, Charles D. Fetter, Jr,
WC of Indianapolis

1965 .....Kristin Fortune, Dennis Sveum,
Los Angeles FSC

1966 .....Kristin Fortune, Dennis Sveum,
Los Angeles FSC

1967 .....Lorna Dyer, John Carrell, Broadmoor SC

1968 .....Judy Schwomeyer, James Sladky,
WC of Indianapolis/Genesee FSC

1969 .....Judy Schwomeyer, James Sladky,
WC of Indianapolis/Genesee FSC

1970 .....Judy Schwomeyer, James Sladky,
WC of Indianapolis/Genesee FSC

1971 .....Judy Schwomeyer, James Sladky,
WC of Indianapolis/Genesee FSC

1972 .....Judy Schwomeyer, James Sladky,
WC of Indianapolis/Genesee FSC

1973 .....Mary Karen Campbell, Johnny Johns,
Lansing SC/Detroit SC

1974 .....Colleen O'Connor, Jim Millns,
Broadmoor SC/City of Colorado Springs

1975 .....Colleen O'Connor, Jim Millns,
Broadmoor SC

1976 .....Colleen O'Connor, Jim Millns,
Broadmoor SC

1977 .....Judy Genovesi, Kent Weigle,
SC of Hartford/Charter Oak FSC

1978 .....Stacey Smith, John Summers,
SC of Wilmington

1979 .....Stacey Smith, John Summers,
SC of Wilmington

1980 .....Stacey Smith, John Summers,
SC of Wilmington

1981 .....Judy Blumberg, Michael Seibert,
Broadmoor SC/ISC of Indianapolis

1982 .....Judy Blumberg, Michael Seibert,
Broadmoor SC/ISC of Indianapolis

1983 .....Judy Blumberg, Michael Seibert,
Pittsburgh FSC

1984 .....Judy Blumberg, Michael Seibert,
Pittsburgh FSC

1985 .....Judy Blumberg, Michael Seibert,
Pittsburgh FSC

1986 .....Renee Roca, Donald Adair,
Genesee FSC/Academy FSC

1987 .....Suzanne Semanick, Scott Gregory,
U of Delaware SC

1988 .....Suzanne Semanick, Scott Gregory,
U of Delaware SC

1989 .....Susan Wynne, Joseph Druar,
Broadmoor SC/Seattle SC

1990 .....Susan Wynne, Joseph Druar,
Broadmoor SC/Seattle SC

1991 .....Elizabeth Punsalan, Jerod Swallow,
Broadmoor SC

1992 .....April Sargent, Russ Witherby,
Ogdensburg FSC/U of Delaware FSC

1993 .....Renee Roca, Gorsha Sur, Broadmoor SC

U.S. Olympic Gold Medalists

Women

1956	Tenley Albright	1976	Dorothy Hamill
1960	Carol Heiss	1992	Kristi Yamaguchi
1968	Peggy Fleming		

Men

1948	Richard Button	1960	David W. Jenkins
1952	Richard Button	1984	Scott Hamilton
1956	Hayes Alan Jenkins	1988	Brian Boitano

Miscellaneous Sports

Sports Illustrated

PEDAL PRINCE

Lance Amstrong establishes
himself as the heir
apparent to Greg LeMond

A New Star in the West

Miguel Induráin won his third Tour, but young Lance Armstrong beat him at the Worlds | by ALEXANDER WOLFF

WITH EIGHT YEARS HAVING passed since a Frenchman last won the world's greatest bicycle race, the Tour de France might now be officially declared a misnomer. Only once during this year's edition did a Frenchman cross a finish line first. Indeed, in 1993 a Dane, a Swiss, a German, an Italian, a Pole, a Belgian, a Colombian, even an Uzbek won stages in the race—as did a 21-year-old American with the irresistible name of Lance Armstrong. And for the third consecutive year Miguel Induráin of Spain took cycling's top prize to the far side of the Pyrenees.

If Induráin weren't so inoffensive a young man, the French might be gnashing their *dents* even more. The 29-year-old rider for the Banesto team is unfailingly modest and obliging. He's a good soldier who aged slowly into championship form, waiting seven seasons before winning his first marquee stage race. He outdistanced Tony Rominger of Switzerland by nearly five minutes over the 21 days of this year's

race, receiving his only real scare from a dog that nearly upended him on the way into Montpellier. Now he's poised to match the record, shared by France's Jacques Anquetil and Belgium's Eddy Merckx, of four Tour wins in a row. (That mark, rather than British amateur Chris Boardman's hour record of 52.270 kilometers, which was set in Bordeaux the morning this year's Tour rolled through, is the target that intrigues the Induráin camp most.)

The American presence in the Tour, so acute during the late 1980s when Greg LeMond lorded over the Continental scene, seemed ready to disappear in 1993. First Motorola, the sponsor of Armstrong's team, announced it would bail out of its sponsorship of the only U.S.-based contingent in the race. Then LeMond decided not to enter the Tour, the event he had won three times previously, after an immune system deficiency flared up and forced him to abandon three stage races early in the season. But within a few days in July, Motorola reversed its decision, and

Armstrong, racing in his first Tour de France, outsprinted his elders to win the eighth stage, into Verdun. He became the Tour's youngest stage winner in almost 90 years.

But Armstrong's eye-opening summer wasn't over yet. On Aug. 29 he won the pro road race at the World Cycling Championships in Hamar, Norway, despite crashing twice. He finished the 160-mile course in six hours, 17 minutes and 10 seconds, 19 seconds ahead of Induráin. Armstrong's U.S. teammate Rebecca Twigg also claimed a gold medal, winning the 3,000-meter pursuit.

European cyclists tend to be working-class heroes, willing to spend long, painful hours in the saddle for the promise of a better life— most analogous to inner-city boxers and basketballers Stateside. Their American counterparts, by contrast, tend to come from comfort, to be Boulder-based fanciers of tofu burgers and esoteric music. Armstrong has borrowed from both traditions, to good effect. He has an upper-middle-class panache and public confidence that's just this side of arrogance. (He stole a few extra kisses from the girls on the podium after his stage win.) But his hardscrabble upbringing in a broken home gives him more in common socioeconomically with those who race as if their lives depend on it.

In the spring, after finishing a loud second in the Tour DuPont, Armstrong won the Thrift Drug Classic in Pittsburgh in a sprint on a hilly course. A week later he went on to win the six-day West Virginia K-Mart Classic. So it was that, in the Core States Championship in Philadelphia,

Induráin won his third consecutive Tour by a comfortable five minutes.

several laps from the finish, he could be seen blowing a kiss to his mother, Linda. They both knew he was on the verge of pocketing a $1 million prize for winning American pro cycling's Triple Crown. Lance and Linda, who scrimped and scraped to get Lance his start as a teenage triathlete back in Plano, Texas, figured to appreciate a purse like that more than most.

As LeMond fades, Armstrong comes into focus. But there is still only one sharper image in cycling. He can be found neither in the United States, nor among the feckless French, but just outside Pamplona, where Induráin stables his bike.

DE MARTIGNAC/PRESSE SPORTS

Archery

National Men's Champions

1879 ......Will H. Thompson	1916 ......Dr. Robert Elmer	1959 ......Wilbert Vetrovsky
1880 ......L. L. Pedinghaus	1919 ......Dr. Robert Elmer	1960 ......Robert Kadlec
1881 ......F. H. Walworth	1920 ......Dr. Robert Elmer	1961 ......Clayton Sherman
1882 ......D. H. Nash	1921 ......James Jiles	1962 ......Charles Sandlin
1883 ......Col. Robert Williams	1922 ......Dr. Robert Elmer	1963 ......Dave Keaggy, Jr.
1884 ......Col. Robert Williams	1923 ......Bill Palmer	1964 ......Dave Keaggy, Jr.
1885 ......Col. Robert Williams	1924 ......James Jiles	1965 ......George Slinzer
1886 ......W. A. Clark	1925 ......Dr. Paul Crouch	1966 ......Hardy Ward
1887 ......W. A. Clark	1926 ......Stanley Spencer	1967 ......Ray Rogers
1888 ......Lewis Maxson	1927 ......Dr. Paul Crouch	1968 ......Hardy Ward
1889 ......Lewis Maxson	1928 ......Bill Palmer	1969 ......Ray Rogers
1890 ......Lewis Maxson	1929 ......Dr. E. K. Roberts	1970 ......Joe Thornton
1891 ......Lewis Maxson	1930 ......Russ Hoogerhyde	1971 ......John Williams
1892 ......Lewis Maxson	1931 ......Russ Hoogerhyde	1972 ......Kevin Erlandson
1893 ......Lewis Maxson	1932 ......Russ Hoogerhyde	1973 ......Darrell Pace
1894 ......Lewis Maxson	1933 ......Ralph Miller	1974 ......Darrell Pace
1895 ......W. B. Robinson	1934 ......Russ Hoogerhyde	1975 ......Darrell Pace
1896 ......Lewis Maxson	1935 ......Gilman Keasey	1976 ......Darrell Pace
1897 ......W. A. Clark	1936 ......Gilman Keasey	1977 ......Rick McKinney
1898 ......Lewis Maxson	1937 ......Russ Hoogerhyde	1978 ......Darrell Pace
1899 ......M. C. Howell	1938 ......Pat Chambers	1979 ......Rick McKinney
1900 ......A. R. Clark	1939 ......Pat Chambers	1980 ......Rick McKinney
1901 ......Will H. Thompson	1940 ......Russ Hoogerhyde	1981 ......Rick McKinney
1902 ......Will H. Thompson	1941 ......Larry Hughes	1982 ......Rick McKinney
1903 ......Will H. Thompson	1946 ......Wayne Thompson	1983 ......Rick McKinney
1904 ......George Bryant	1947 ......Jack Wilson	1984 ......Darrell Pace
1905 ......George Bryant	1948 ......Larry Hughes	1985 ......Rick McKinney
1906 ......Henry Richardson	1949 ......Russ Reynolds	1986 ......Rick McKinney
1907 ......Henry Richardson	1950 ......Stan Overby	1987 ......Rick McKinney
1908 ......Will H. Thompson	1951 ......Russ Reynolds	1988 ......Jay Barrs
1909 ......Geroge Bryant	1952 ......Robert Larson	1989 ......Ed Eliason
1910 ......Henry Richardson	1953 ......Bill Glackin	1990 ......Ed Eliason
1911 ......Dr. Robert Elmer	1954 ......Robert Rhode	1991 ......Ed Eliason
1912 ......George Bryant	1955 ......Joe Fries	1992 ......Alan Rasor
1913 ......George Bryant	1956 ......Joe Fries	1993 ......Jay Barrs
1914 ......Dr. Robert Elmer	1957 ......Joe Fries	
1915 ......Dr. Robert Elmer	1958 ......Robert Bitner	

National Women's Champions

1879 ......Mrs. S. Brown	1903 ......Mrs. M. C. Howell	1929 ......Audrey Grubbs
1880 ......Mrs. T. Davies	1904 ......Mrs. M. C. Howell	1930 ......Audrey Grubbs
1881 ......Mrs. Gibbes	1905 ......Mrs. M. C. Howell	1931 ......Doroth Cummings
1882 ......Mrs. A. H. Gibbes	1906 ......Mrs. E. C. Cook	1932 ......Ilda Hanchette
1883 ......Mrs. M. C. Howell	1907 ......Mrs. M. C. Howell	1933 ......Madelaine Taylor
1884 ......Mrs. H. Hall	1908 ......Harriet Case	1934 ......Desales Mudd
1885 ......Mrs. M. C. Howell	1909 ......Harriet Case	1935 ......Ruth Hodgert
1886 ......Mrs. M. C. Howell	1910 ......J. V. Sullivan	1936 ......Gladys Hammer
1887 ......Mrs. A. M. Phillips	1911 ......Mrs. J. S. Taylor	1937 ......Gladys Hammer
1888 ......Mrs. A. M. Phillips	1912 ......Mrs. Witwer Tayler	1938 ......Jean Tenney
1889 ......Mrs. A. M. Phillips	1913 ......Mrs. P. Fletcher	1939 ......Belvia Carter
1890 ......Mrs. M. C. Howell	1914 ......Mrs. B. P. Gray	1940 ......Ann Weber
1891 ......Mrs. M. C. Howell	1915 ......Cynthia Wesson	1941 ......Ree Dillinger
1892 ......Mrs. M. C. Howell	1916 ......Cynthia Wesson	1946 ......Ann Weber
1893 ......Mrs. M. C. Howell	1919 ......Dorothy Smith	1947 ......Ann Weber
1894 ......Mrs. Albert Kern	1920 ......Cynthia Wesson	1948 ......Jean Lee
1895 ......Mrs. M. C. Howell	1921 ......Mrs. L. C. Smith	1949 ......Jean Lee
1896 ......Mrs. M. C. Howell	1922 ......Dorothy Smith	1950 ......Jean Lee
1897 ......Mrs. J. S. Baker	1923 ......Norma Pierce	1951 ......Jean Lee
1898 ......Mrs. M. C. Howell	1924 ......Dorothy Smith	1952 ......Ann Weber
1899 ......Mrs. M. C. Howell	1925 ......Dorothy Smith	1953 ......Ann Weber
1900 ......Mrs. M. C. Howell	1926 ......Dorothy Smith	1954 ......Luarette Young
1901 ......Mrs. C. E. Woodruff	1927 ......Mrs. R. Johnson	1955 ......Ann Clark
1902 ......Mrs. M. C. Howell	1928 ......Beatrice Hodgson	1956 ......Carole Meinhart

Archery (Cont.)

National Women's Champions (Cont.)

1957 .....Carole Meinhart	1970 .....Nancy Myrick	1983 .....Nancy Myrick
1958 .....Carole Meinhart	1971 .....Doreen Wilber	1984 .....Ruth Rowe
1959 .....Carole Meinhart	1972 .....Ruth Rowe	1985 .....Terri Pesho
1960 .....Ann Clark	1973 .....Doreen Wilber	1986 .....Debra Ochs
1961 .....Victoria Cook	1974 .....Doreen Wilber	1987 .....Terry Quinn
1962 .....Nancy Vonderheide	1975 .....Irene Lorensen	1988 .....Debra Ochs
1963 .....Nancy Vonderheide	1976 .....Luann Ryon	1989 .....Debra Ochs
1964 .....Victoria Cook	1977 .....Luann Ryon	1990 .....Denise Parker
1965 .....Nancy Pfeiffer	1978 .....Luann Ryon	1991 .....Denise Parker
1966 .....Helen Thornton	1979 .....Lynette Johnson	1992 .....Sherry Block
1967 .....Ardelle Mills	1980 .....Judi Adams	1993 .....Denise Parker
1968 .....Victoria Cook	1981 .....Debra Metzger	
1969 .....Doreen Wilber	1982 .....Luann Ryon	

Chess

World Champions

1866-94....................Wilhelm Steinitz, Austria	1960-61....................Mikhail Tal, USSR
1894-1921...............Emanuel Lasker, Germany	1961-63....................Mikhail Botvinnik, USSR
1921-27....................Jose Capablanca, Cuba	1963-69....................Tigran Petrosian, USSR
1927-35....................Alexander Alekhine, France	1969-72....................Boris Spassky, USSR
1935-37....................Max Euwe, Holland	1972-75....................Bobby Fischer, United States
1937-46....................Alexander Alekhine, France	1975-85....................Anatoly Karpov, USSR
1948-57....................Mikhail Botvinnik, USSR	1985-93....................*Garry Kasparov, USSR
1957-58....................Vassily Smyslov, USSR	1993-.........................vacant
1958-59....................Mikhail Botvinnik, USSR	*Kasparov stripped of title by FIDE in 1993

United States Champions

1857-71....................Paul Morphy	1969-72....................Samuel Reshevsky
1871-76....................George Mackenzie	1972-73....................Robert Byrne
1876-80....................James Mason	1973-74....................Lubomir Kavalek
1880-89....................George Mackenzie	....................John Grefe
1889-90....................Samuel Lipschutz	1974-77....................Walter Browne
1890.........................Jackson Showalter	1978-80....................Lubomir Kavalek
1890-91....................Max Judd	1980-81....................Larry Evans
1891-92....................Jackson Showalter	....................Larry Christiansen
1892-94....................Samuel Lipschutz	....................Walter Browne
1894.........................Jackson Showalter	1981-83....................Walter Browne
1894-95....................Albert Hodges	....................Yasser Seirawan
1895-97....................Jackson Showalter	1983.........................Roman Dzindzichashvili
1897-1906...............Harry Pillsbury	....................Larry Christiansen
1906-09....................Vacant	....................Walter Browne
1909-36....................Frank Marshall	1984-85....................Lev Alburt
1936-44....................Samuel Reshevsky	1986.........................Yasser Seirawan
1944-46....................Arnold Denker	1987.........................Joel Benjamin
1946-48....................Samuel Reshevsky	....................Nick DeFirmian
1948-51....................Herman Steiner	1988.........................Michael Wilder
1951-54....................Larry Evans	1989-.........................Roman Dzindzichashvili
1954-57....................Arthur Bisguier	....................Stuart Rachels
1957-61....................Bobby Fischer	....................Yasser Seirawan
1961-62....................Larry Evans	1990.........................Lev Alburt
1962-68....................Bobby Fischer	1991.........................Gata Kamski
1968-69....................Larry Evans	1992.........................Patrick Wolf

Curling

World Champions

Year	Country, Skip	Year	Country, Skip
1972.....................Canada, Crest Melesnuk		1977.....................Sweden, Ragnar Kamp	
1973.....................Sweden, Kjell Oscarius		1978.....................United States, Bob Nichols	
1974.....................United States, Bud Somerville		1979.....................Norway, Kristian Soerum	
1975.....................Switzerland, Otto Danieli		1980.....................Canada, Rich Folk	
1976.....................United States, Bruce Roberts		1981.....................Switzerland, Jurg Tanner	

World Champions (Cont.)

Year	Country, Skip	Year	Country, Skip
1982	Canada, Al Hackner	1988	Norway, Eigil Ramsfjell
1983	Canada, Ed Werenich	1989	Canada, Pat Ryan
1984	Norway, Eigil Ramsfjell	1990	Canada, Ed Werenich
1985	Canada, Al Hackner	1991	Scotland, David Smith
1986	Canada, Ed Luckowich	1992	Switzerland, Markus Eggler
1987	Canada, Russ Howard	1993	Canada, Russ Howard

U.S. Men's Champions

Year	Site	Winning Club	Skip
1957	Chicago, IL	Hibbing, MN	Harold Lauber
1958	Milwaukee, WI	Detroit, MI	Douglas Fisk
1959	Green Bay, WI	Hibbing, MN	Fran Kleffman
1960	Chicago, IL	Grafton, ND	Orvil Gilleshammer
1961	Grand Forks, ND	Seattle, WA	Frank Crealock
1962	Detroit, MI	Hibbing, MN	Fran Kleffman
1963	Duluth, MN	Detroit, MI	Mike Slyziuk
1964	Utica, NY	Duluth, MN	Robert Magle, Jr.
1965	Seattle, WA	Superior, WI	Bud Somerville
1966	Hibbing, MN	Fargo, ND	Joe Zbacnik
1967	Winchester, MA	Seattle, WA	Bruce Roberts
1968	Madison, WI	Superior, WI	Bud Somerville
1969	Grand Forks, ND	Superior, WI	Bud Somerville
1970	Ardsley, NY	Grafton, ND	Art Tallackson
1971	Duluth, MN	Edmore, ND	Dale Dalziel
1972	Wilmette, IL	Grafton, ND	Robert Labonte
1973	Colorado Springs, CO	Winchester, MA	Charles Reeves
1974	Schenectady, NY	Superior, WI	Bud Somerville
1975	Detroit, MI	Seattle, WA	Ed Risling
1976	Wausau, WI	Hibbing, MN	Bruce Roberts
1977	Northbrook, IL	Hibbing, MN	Bruce Roberts
1978	Utica, NY	Superior, WI	Bob Nichols
1979	Superior, WI	Bemidji, MN	Scott Baird
1980	Bemidji, MN	Hibbing, MN	Paul Pustovar
1981	Fairbanks, AK	Superior, WI	Bob Nichols
1982	Brookline, MA	Madison, WI	Steve Brown
1983	Colorado Springs, CO	Colorado Springs, CO	Don Cooper
1984	Hibbing, MN	Hibbing, MN	Bruce Roberts
1985	Mequon, WI	Wilmette, IL	Tim Wright
1986	Seattle, WA	Madison, WI	Steve Brown
1987	Lake Placid, NY	Seattle, WA	Jim Vukich
1988	St. Paul, MN	Seattle, WA	Doug Jones
1989	Detroit, MI	Seattle, WA	Jim Vukich
1990	Superior, WI	Seattle, WA	Doug Jones
1991	Utica, NY	Madison, WI	Steve Brown
1992	Grafton, ND	Seattle	Doug Jones
1993	St Paul, MN	Bemidji, MN	Scott Baird

U.S. Women's Champions

Year	Site	Winning Club	Skip
1977	Wilmette, IL	Hastings, NY	Margaret Smith
1978	Duluth, MN	Wausau, WI	Sandy Robarge
1979	Winchester, MA	Seattle, WA	Nancy Langley
1980	Seattle, WA	Seattle, WA	Sharon Kozal
1981	Kettle Moraine, WI	Seattle, WA	Nancy Langley
1982	Bowling Green, OH	Oak Park, IL	Ruth Schwenker
1983	Grafton, ND	Seattle, WA	Nancy Langley
1984	Wauwatosa, WI	Duluth, MN	Amy Hatten
1985	Hershey, PA	Fairbanks, AK	Bev Birklid
1986	Chicago, IL	St. Paul, MN	Gerri Tilden
1987	St. Paul, MN	Seattle, WA	Sharon Good
1988	Darien, CT	Seattle, WA	Nancy Langley
1989	Detroit, MI	Rolla, ND	Jan Lagasse
1990	Superior, WI	Denver, CO	Bev Behnke

U.S. Women's Champions *(Cont.)*

1991 ....Utica, NY	Houston, TX	Maymar Gemmell
1992 ....Grafton, ND	Madison, WI	Lisa Schoeneberg
1993 ....St Paul, MN	Denver, CO	Bev Behnke

Cycling

Professional Road Race World Champions

1927 ....Alfred Binda, Italy
1928 ....George Ronsse, Belgium
1929 ....George Ronsse, Belgium
1930 ....Alfred Binda, Italy
1931 ....Learco Guerra, Italy
1932 ....Alfred Binda, Italy
1933 ....George Speicher, France
1934 ....Karel Kaers, Belgium
1935 ....Jean Aerts, Belgium
1936 ....Antonio Magne, France
1937 ....Elio Meulenberg, Belgium
1938 ....Marcel Kint, Belgium
1939 ....No competition
1940 ....No competition
1941 ....No competition
1942 ....No competition
1943 ....No competition
1944 ....No competition
1945 ....No competition
1946 ....Hans Knecht, Switzerland
1947 ....Theo. Middelkamp, Holland
1948 ....Alberic Schotte, Belgium
1949 ....Henri Van Steenbergen, Belgium
1950 ....Alberic Schotte, Belgium

1951 ....Ferdinand Kubler, Switzerland
1952 ....Heinz Mueller, Germany
1953 ....Fausto Coppi, Italy
1954 ....Louison Bobet, France
1955 ....Stan Ockers, Belgium
1956 ....Rik Van Steenbergen, Belgium
1957 ....Rik Van Steenbergen, Belgium
1958 ....Ercole Baldini, Italy
1959 ....Andre Darrigade, France
1960 ....Rik van Looy, Belgium
1961 ....Rik van Looy, Belgium
1962 ....Jean Stablenski, France
1963 ....Bennoni Beheyt, Belgium
1964 ....Jan Janssen, Holland
1965 ....Tommy Simpson, England
1966 ....Rudi Altig, West Germany
1967 ....Eddy Merckx, Belgium
1968 ....Vittorio Adorni, Italy
1969 ....Harm Ottenbros, Netherlands
1970 ....J.P. Monseré, Belgium
1971 ....Eddy Merckx, Belgium

1972 ....Marino Basso, Italy
1973 ....Felice Gimondi, Italy
1974 ....Eddy Merckx, Belgium
1975 ....Hennie Kuiper, Holland
1976 ....Freddy Maertens, Belgium
1977 ....Francesco Moser, Italy
1978 ....Gerri Knetemann, Holland
1979 ....Jan Raas, Holland
1980 ....Bernard Hinault, France
1981 ....Freddy Maertens, Belgium
1982 ....Giuseppe Saronni, Italy
1983 ....Greg LeMond, United States
1984 ....Claude Criquielion, Belgium
1985 ....Joop Zoetemelk, Holland
1986 ....Moreno Argentin, Italy
1987 ....Stephen Roche, Ireland
1988 ....Maurizio Fondriest, Italy
1989 ....Greg LeMond, United States
1990 ....Rudy Dhaenene, Belgium
1991 ....Gianni Bugno, Italy
1992 ....Gianni Bugno, Italy
1993 ....Lance Armstrong, United States

Tour DuPont Winners

Year	Winner	Time
1989	Dag Otto Lauritzen, Norway	33 hrs, 28 min, 48 sec
1990	Raul Alcala, Mexico	45 hrs, 20 min, 9 sec
1991	Erik Breukink, Holland	48 hrs, 56 min, 53 sec
1992	Greg LeMond, United States	44 hrs, 27 min, 43 sec
1993	Raul Alcala, Mexico	46 hrs, 42 min, 52 sec

Tour de France Winners

Year	Winner	Time
1903	Maurice Garin, France	94 hrs, 33 min
1904	Henri Cornet, France	96 hrs, 5 min, 56 sec
1905	Louis Trousselier, France	110 hrs, 26 min, 58 sec
1906	Rene Pottier, France	Not available
1907	Lucien Petit-Breton, France	158 hrs, 54 min, 5 sec
1908	Lucien Petit-Breton, France	Not available
1909	Francois Faber, Luxembourg	157 hrs, 1 min, 22 sec
1910	Octave Lapize, France	162 hrs, 41 min, 30 sec
1911	Gustave Garrigou, France	195 hrs, 37 min
1912	Odile Defraye, Belgium	190 hrs, 30 min, 28 sec
1913	Philippe Thys, Belgium	197 hrs, 54 min
1914	Philippe Thys, Belgium	200 hrs, 28 min, 48 sec
1915-18	No race	
1919	Firmin Lambot, Belgium	231 hrs, 7 min, 15 sec
1920	Philippe Thys, Belgium	228 hrs, 36 min, 13 sec
1921	Leon Scieur, Belgium	221 hrs, 50 min, 26 sec
1922	Firmin Lambot, Belgium	222 hrs, 8 min, 6 sec
1923	Henri Pelissier, France	222 hrs, 15 min, 30 sec
1924	Ottavio Bottechia, Italy	226 hrs, 18 min, 21 sec
1925	Ottavio Bottechia, Italy	219 hrs, 10 min, 18 sec

Tour de France Winners (Cont.)

Year	Winner	Time
1926	Lucien Buysse, Belgium	238 hrs, 44 min, 25 sec
1927	Nicolas Frantz, Luxembourg	198 hrs, 16 min, 42 sec
1928	Nicolas Frantz, Luxembourg	192 hrs, 48 min, 58 sec
1929	Maurice Dewaele, Belgium	186 hrs, 39 min, 16 sec
1930	Andre Leducq, France	172 hrs, 12 min, 16 sec
1931	Antonin Magne, France	177 hrs, 10 min, 3 sec
1932	Andre Leducq, France	154 hrs, 12 min, 49 sec
1933	Georges Speicher, France	147 hrs, 51 min, 37 sec
1934	Antonin Magne, France	147 hrs, 13 min, 58 sec
1935	Romain Maes, Belgium	141 hrs, 32 min
1936	Sylvere Maes, Belgium	142 hrs, 47 min, 32 sec
1937	Roger Lapebie, France	138 hrs, 58 min, 31 sec
1938	Gino Bartali, Italy	148 hrs, 29 min, 12 sec
1939	Sylvere Maes, Belgium	132 hrs, 3 min, 17 sec
1940-46	No race	
1947	Jean Robic, France	148 hrs, 11 min, 25 sec
1948	Gino Bartali, Italy	147 hrs, 10 min, 36 sec
1949	Fausto Coppi, Italy	149 hrs, 40 min, 49 sec
1950	Ferdi Kubler, Switzerland	145 hrs, 36 min, 56 sec
1951	Hugo Koblet, Switzerland	142 hrs, 20 min, 14 sec
1952	Fausto Coppi, Italy	151 hrs, 57 min, 20 sec
1953	Louison Bobet, France	129 hrs, 23 min, 25 sec
1954	Louison Bobet, France	140 hrs, 6 min, 5 sec
1955	Louison Bobet, France	130 hrs, 29 min, 26 sec
1956	Roger Walkowiak, France	124 hrs, 1 min, 16 sec
1957	Jacques Anquetil, France	129 hrs, 46 min, 11 sec
1958	Charly Gaul, Luxembourg	116 hrs, 59 min, 5 sec
1959	Federico Bahamontes, Spain	123 hrs, 46 min, 45 sec
1960	Gastone Nencini, Italy	112 hrs, 8 min, 42 sec
1961	Jacques Anquetil, France	122 hrs, 1 min, 33 sec
1962	Jacques Anquetil, France	114 hrs, 31 min, 54 sec
1963	Jacques Anquetil, France	113 hrs, 30 min, 5 sec
1964	Jacques Anquetil, France	127 hrs, 9 min, 44 sec
1965	Felice Gimondi, Italy	116 hrs, 42 min, 6 sec
1966	Lucien Aimar, France	117 hrs, 34 min, 21 sec
1967	Roger Pingeon, France	136 hrs, 53 min, 50 sec
1968	Jan Janssen, Netherlands	133 hrs, 49 min, 32 sec
1969	Eddy Merckx, Belgium	116 hrs, 16 min, 2 sec
1970	Eddy Merckx, Belgium	119 hrs, 31 min, 49 sec
1971	Eddy Merckx, Belgium	96 hrs, 45 min, 14 sec
1972	Eddy Merckx, Belgium	108 hrs, 17 min, 18 sec
1973	Luis Ocana, Spain	122 hrs, 25 min, 34 sec
1974	Eddy Merckx, Belgium	116 hrs, 16 min, 58 sec
1975	Bernard Thevenet, France	114 hrs, 35 min, 31 sec
1976	Lucien Van Impe, Belgium	116 hrs, 22 min, 23 sec
1977	Bernard Thevenet, France	115 hrs, 38 min, 30 sec
1978	Bernard Hinault, France	108 hrs, 18 min
1979	Bernard Hinault, France	103 hrs, 6 min, 50 sec
1980	Joop Zoetemelk, Netherlands	109 hrs, 19 min, 14 sec
1981	Bernard Hinault, France	96 hrs, 19 min, 38 sec
1982	Bernard Hinault, France	92 hrs, 8 min, 46 sec
1983	Laurent Fignon, France	105 hrs, 7 min, 52 sec
1984	Laurent Fignon, France	112 hrs, 3 min, 40 sec
1985	Bernard Hinault, France	113 hrs, 24 min, 23 sec
1986	Greg LeMond, United States	110 hrs, 35 min, 19 sec
1987	Stephen Roche, Ireland	115 hrs, 27 min, 42 sec
1988	Pedro Delgado, Spain	84 hrs, 27 min, 53 sec
1989	Greg LeMond, United States	87 hrs, 38 min, 35 sec
1990	Greg LeMond, United States	90 hrs, 43 min, 20 sec
1991	Miguel Induráin, Spain	101 hrs, 1 min, 20 sec
1992	Miguel Induráin, Spain	100 hrs, 49 min, 30 sec
1993	Miguel Induráin, Spain	95 hrs, 57 min, 9 sec

Sled Dog Racing

Iditarod

Year	Winner	Time	Year	Winner	Time
1973	Dick Wilmarth	20 days, 00:49:41	1984	Dean Osmar	12 days, 15:07:33
1974	Carl Huntington	20 days, 15:02:07	1985	Libby Riddles	18 days, 00:20:17
1975	Emmitt Peters	14 days, 14:43:45	1986	Susan Butcher	11 days, 15:06:00
1976	Gerald Riley	18 days, 22:58:17	1987	Susan Butcher	11 days, 02:05:13
1977	Rick Swenson	16 days, 16:27:13	1988	Susan Butcher	11 days, 11:41:40
1978	Dick Mackey	14 days, 18:52:24	1989	Joe Runyan	11 days, 05:24:34
1979	Rick Swenson	15 days, 10:37:47	1990	Susan Butcher	11 days, 01:53:23
1980	Joe May	14 days, 07:11:51	1991	Rick Swenson	12 days, 16:34:39
1981	Rick Swenson	12 days, 08:45:02	1992	Martin Buser	10 days, 19:17:15
1982	Rick Swenson	16 days, 04:40:10	1993	Jeff King	10 days, 15:38:15
1983	Dick Mackey	12 days, 14:10:44			

Fishing

Saltwater Fishing Records

Species	Weight	Where Caught	Date	Angler
Albacore	88 lb 2 oz	Port Mogan, Canary Islands	Nov 19, 1977	Siegfried Dickemann
Amberjack, greater	155 lb 10 oz	Challenger Bank, Bermuda	June 24, 1981	Joseph Dawson
Amberjack, Pacific	104 lb	Baja California, Mexico	July 4, 1984	Richard Cresswell
Barracuda, great	85 lb	Christmas Island, Kiribati	April 11, 1992	John W. Helfrich
Barracuda, Mexican	21 lb	Phantom Isle, Costa Rica	Mar 27, 1987	E. Greg Kent
Barracuda, pickhandle	17 lb 4 oz	Sitra Channel, Bahrain	Nov 21, 1985	Roger Cranswick
Bass, barred sand	13 lb 3 oz	Huntington Beach, CA	Aug 29, 1988	Robert Halaj
Bass, black sea	9 lb 8 oz	Virginia Beach, VA	Jan 9, 1987	Joe Mizelle, Jr
Bass, European	20 lb 11 oz	Stes Maries de la Mer, France	May 6, 1986	Jean Baptiste Bayle
Bass, giant sea	563 lb 8 oz	Anacapa Island, CA	Aug 20, 1968	James D. McAdam, Jr
Bass, striped	78 lb 8 oz	Atlantic City, NJ	Sep 21, 1982	Albert McReynolds
Bluefish	31 lb 12 oz	Hatteras Inlet, NC	Jan 30, 1972	James M. Hussey
Bonefish	19 lb	Zululand, South Africa	May 26, 1962	Brian W. Batchelor
Bonito, Atlantic	18 lb 14 oz	Fayal Island, Azores	July 8, 1953	D. G. Higgs
Bonito, Pacific	14 lb 12 oz	Baja California, Mexico	Oct. 12, 1980	Jerome H. Rilling
Cabezon	23 lb	Juan De Fuca Strait, WA	Aug 4, 1990	Wesley Hunter
Cobia	135 lb 9 oz	Shark Bay, Australia	July 9, 1985	Peter W. Goulding
Cod, Atlantic	98 lb 12 oz	Isle of Shoals, NH	June 8, 1969	Alphonse Bielevich
Cod, Pacific	30 lb	Andrew Bay, AK	June 7, 1984	Donald Vaughn
Conger	110 lb 8 oz	Plymouth, England	Aug. 20, 1991	Hans C. Clausen
Dolphin	87 lb	Papagallo Gulf, Costa Rica	Sep 25, 1976	Manual Salazar
Drum, black	113 lb 1 oz	Lewes, DE	Sep 15, 1975	Gerald Townsend
Drum, red	94 lb 2 oz	Avon, NC	Nov 7, 1984	David Deuel
Eel, African mottled	36 lb 1 oz	Durban, South Africa	June 10, 1984	Ferdie van Nooten
Eel, American	8 lb 8 oz	Brewster, MA	May 17, 1992	Gerald G. Lapierre, Sr
Flounder, southern	20 lb 9 oz	Nassau Sound, FL	Dec 23, 1983	Larenza Mungin
Flounder, summer	22 lb 7 oz	Montauk, NY	Sep 15, 1975	Charles Nappi
Grouper, Warsaw	436 lb 12 oz	Destin, FL	Dec 22, 1985	Steve Haeusler
Halibut, Atlantic	255 lb 4 oz	Gloucester, MA	July 28, 1989	Sonny Manley
Halibut, California	53 lb 4 oz	Santa Rosa Island, CA	July 7, 1988	Russell Harmon
Halibut, Pacific	368 lb	Gustavus, AK	July 5, 1991	Celia H. Dueitt
Jack, crevalle	54 lb 7 oz	Port Michel, Gabon	Jan 15, 1982	Thomas Gibson, Jr
Jack, horse-eye	24 lb 8 oz	Miami, FL	Dec 20, 1982	Tilo Schnau
Jack, Pacific, crevalle	26 lb. 12 oz	Golfito, Costa Rica	Aug. 2, 1992	Dr. J. N. Matthews
Jewfish	680 lb	Fernandina Beach, FL	May 20, 1961	Lynn Joyner
Kawakawa	29 lb	NSW, Australia	Dec 17, 1986	Ronald Nakamura
Lingcod	69 lb	Langara Island, B.C.	June 16, 1992	Murray M. Romer
Mackerel, cero	17 lb 2 oz	Islamorada, FL	Apr 5, 1986	G. Michael Mills
Mackerel, king	90 lb	Key West, FL	Feb 16, 1976	Norton Thomton
Mackerel, Spanish	13 lb	Ocracoke Inlet, NC	Nov 4, 1987	Robert Cranton
Marlin, Atlantic blue	1402 lb	Vitoria, Brazil	Feb. 29, 1992	Paulo R.A. Amorim
Marlin, black	1560 lb	Cabo Blanco, Peru	Aug 4, 1953	A. C. Glassell, Jr
Marlin, Pacific blue	1376 lb	Kaaiwa Point, HI	May 31, 1982	J. W. deBeaubien
Marlin, striped	494 lb	Tutukaka, New Zealand	Jan 16, 1986	Bill Boniface
Marlin, white	181 lb 14 oz	Vitoria, Brazil	Dec 8, 1979	Evandro Luiz Caser
Permit	51 lb 8 oz	Lake Worth, FL	Apr 28, 1978	William M. Kenney
Pollock	46 lb 10 oz	Ogunquit, ME	Oct. 24, 1990	Linda Paul

Saltwater Fishing Records (Cont.)

Species	Weight	Where Caught	Date	Angler
Pompano, African	50 lb 8 oz	Daytona Beach, FL	Apr 21, 1990	Tom Sargent
Roosterfish	114 lb	La Paz, Mexico	June 1, 1960	Abe Sackheim
Runner, blue	8 lb 4 oz	Bimini, Bahamas	Sep 9, 1990	Brent Rowland
Runner, rainbow	37 lb 9 oz	Isla Clarion, Mexico	Nov. 21, 1991	Tom Pfleger
Sailfish, Atlantic	135 lb 5 oz	Lagos, Nigeria	Nov. 10, 1991	Ron King
Sailfish, Pacific	221 lb	Santa Cruz Island, Ecuador	Feb 12, 1947	C. W. Stewart
Seabass, white	83 lb 12 oz	San Felipe, Mexico	Mar 31, 1953	L. C. Baumgardner
Seatrout, spotted	16 lb	Mason's Beach, VA	May 28, 1977	William Katko
Shark, blue	437 lb	Catherine Bay, NSW, Australia	Oct 2, 1976	Peter Hyde
Shark, Greenland	1708 lb 9 oz	Trondheim, Norway	Oct 18, 1987	Terje Nordtvedt
Shark, hammerhead	991 lb	Sarasota, FL	May 30, 1982	Allen Ogle
Shark, man-eater or white	2664 lb	Ceduna, Australia	Apr 21, 1959	Alfred Dean
Shark, mako	1115 lb	Black River, Mauritius	Nov 16, 1988	Patrick Guillanton
Shark, porbeagle	465 lb	Cornwall, England	July 23, 1976	Jorge Potier
Shark, thresher	802 lb	Tutukaka, New Zealand	Feb 8, 1981	Dianne North
Shark, tiger	1780 lb	Cherry Grove, SC	June 14, 1964	Walter Maxwell
Skipjack, black	26 lb	Baja California, Mexico	Oct. 23, 1991	Clifford K. Hamaishi
Snapper, cubera	121 lb 8 oz	Cameron, LA	July 5, 1982	Mike Hebert
Snook	53 lb 10 oz	Costa Rica	Oct 18, 1978	Gilbert Ponzi
Spearfish	90 lb 13 oz	Madeira Island, Portugal	June 2, 1980	Joseph Larkin
Swordfish	1182 lb	Iquique, Chile	May 7, 1953	L. Marron
Tanguigue	99 lb	Natal, South Africa	Mar 14, 1982	Michael J. Wilkinson
Tarpon	283 lb 4 oz	Sherbor Island, Sierre Leone	April 16, 1991	Yvon Victor Sebag
Tautog	24 lb	Wachapreagee, VA	Aug 25, 1987	Gregory Bell
Tope	72 lb 12 oz	Parengarenga Harbor, New Zealand	Dec 19, 1986	Melanie Feldman
Trevally, bigeye	15 lb 8 oz	Waianae, HI	Mar 6, 1992	Darryl R. Bailey
Trevally, giant	145 lb 8 oz	Maui, HI	Mar 28, 1991	Russell Mori
Tuna, Atlantic bigeye	375 lb 8 oz	Ocean City, MD	Aug 26, 1977	Cecil Browne
Tuna, blackfin	42 lb	Bermuda	June 2, 1978	Alan J. Card
Tuna, bluefin	1496 lb	Aulds Cove, Nova Scotia	Oct 26, 1979	Ken Fraser
Tuna, longtail	79 lb 2 oz	Montague Island, NSW, Australia	Apr 12, 1982	Tim Simpson
Tuna, Pacific bigeye	435 lb	Cabo Blanco, Peru	Apr 17, 1957	Russel Lee
Tuna, skipjack	41 lb 14 oz	Mauritius	Nov 12, 1985	Edmund Heinzen
Tuna, southern bluefin	348 lb 5 oz	Whakatane, New Zealand	Jan 16, 1981	Rex Wood
Tuna, yellowfin	388 lb 12 oz	San Benedicto Is, Mexico	Apr 1, 1977	Curt Wiesenhutter
Tunny, little	35 lb 2 oz	Cape de Garde, Algeria	Dec 14, 1988	Jean Yves Chatard
Wahoo	155 lb 8 oz	San Salvador, Bahamas	Apr 3, 1990	William Bourne
Weakfish	19 lb 2 oz	Jones Beach Inlet, NY	Oct 11, 1984	Dennis Rooney
Yellowtail, California	79 lb 4 oz	Baja California, Mexico	July 2, 1991	Robert I. Welker
Yellowtail, southern	114 lb 10 oz	Tauranga, New Zealand	Feb 5, 1984	Mike Godfrey

Freshwater Fishing Records

Species	Weight	Where Caught	Date	Angler
Barramundi	63 lb 2 oz	Queensland, Australia	April 28, 1991	Scott Barnsley
Bass, largemouth	22 lb 4 oz	Montgomery Lake, GA	June 2, 1932	George W. Perry
Bass, peacock	26 lb 8 oz	Matevini River, Colombia	Jan 26, 1982	Rod Neubert
Bass, redeye	8 lb 3 oz	Flint River, GA	Oct 23, 1977	David A. Hubbard
Bass, rock	3 lb	York River, Ontario	Aug 1, 1974	Peter Gulgin
Bass, smallmouth	11 lb 15 oz	Dale Hollow Lake, KY	July 9, 1955	David L. Hayes
Bass, Suwannee	3 lb 14 oz	Suwannee River, FL	Mar 2, 1985	Ronnie Everett
Bass, white	6 lb 13 oz	Orange, VA	July 31, 1989	Ronald Sprouse
Bass, whiterock	24 lb 3 oz	Leesville Lake, VA	May 12, 1989	David Lambert
Bass, yellow	2 lb 4 oz	Lake Monroe, IN	Mar 27, 1977	Donald L. Stalker
Bluegill	4 lb 12 oz	Ketona Lake, AL	Apr 9, 1950	T. S. Hudson
Bowfin	21 lb 8 oz	Florence, SC	Jan 29, 1980	Robert Harmon
Buffalo, bigmouth	70 lb 5 oz	Bastrop, LA	Apr 21, 1980	Delbert Sisk
Buffalo, black	55 lb 8 oz	Cherokee Lake, TN	May 3, 1984	Edward McLain
Buffalo, smallmouth	68 lb 8 oz	Lake Hamilton, AR	May 16, 1984	Jerry Dolezal
Bullhead, brown	5 lb 8 oz	Veal Pond, GA	May 22, 1975	Jimmy Andrews
Bullhead, yellow	4 lb 4 oz	Mormon Lake, AZ	May 11, 1984	Emily Williams
Burbot	18 lb 4 oz	Pickford, MI	Jan 31, 1980	Thomas Courtemanche

Freshwater Fishing Records *(Cont.)*

Species	Weight	Where Caught	Date	Angler
Carp	75 lb 11 oz	Lac de St Cassien, France	May 21, 1987	Leo van der Gugten
Catfish, blue	109 lb 4 oz	Moncks Corner, SC	Mar 14, 1991	George A. Lijewski
Catfish, channel	58 lb	Santee-Cooper Reservoir, SC	July 7, 1964	W. B. Whaley
Catfish, flathead	91 lb 4 oz	Lake Lewisville, TX	Mar 28, 1982	Mike Rogers
Catfish, white	18 lb 14 oz	Inverness, FL	Sept. 21, 1991	Jim Miller
Char, Arctic	32 lb 9 oz	Tree River, Canada	July 30, 1981	Jeffrey Ward
Crappie, white	5 lb 3 oz	Enid Dam, MS	July 31, 1957	Fred L. Bright
Dolly Varden	16 lb 12 oz	Mashutuk River, AK	July 21, 1991	Gary (Butch) King, Jr.
Dorado	51 lb 5 oz	Corrientes, Argentina	Sep 27, 1984	Armando Giudice
Drum, freshwater	54 lb 8 oz	Nickajack Lake, TN	Apr 20, 1972	Benny E. Hull
Gar, alligator	279 lb	Rio Grande River, TX	Dec 2, 1951	Bill Valverde
Gar, Florida	21 lb 3 oz	Boca Raton, FL	June 3, 1981	Jeff Sabol
Gar, longnose	50 lb 5 oz	Trinity River, TX	July 30, 1954	Townsend Miller
Gar, shortnose	5 lb	Sally Jones Lake, OK	Apr 26, 1985	Buddy Croslin
Gar, spotted	8 lb 12 oz	Tennessee River, AL	Aug 26, 1987	Winston Baker
Grayling, Arctic	5 lb 15 oz	Katseyedie River, Northwest Territories	Aug 16, 1967	Jeanne P. Branson
Inconnu	53 lb	Pah River, AK	Aug 20, 1986	Lawrence Hudnall
Kokanee	9 lb 6 oz	Okanagan Lake, Vernon, BC	June 18, 1988	Norm Kuhn
Muskellunge	65 lb	Lake Huron	Oct 15, 1988	Ken J. O'Brien
Muskellunge, tiger	51 lb 3 oz	Lac Vieux-Desert, WI, MI	July 16, 1919	John Knobla
Perch, Nile	191 lb 8 oz	Lake Victoria, Kenya	Sept. 5, 1991	Andy Davison
Perch, white	4 lb 12 oz	Messalonskee Lake, ME	June 4, 1949	Mrs Earl Small
Perch, yellow	4 lb 3 oz	Bordentown, NJ	May 1865	C. C. Abbot
Pickerel, chain	9 lb 6 oz	Homerville, GA	Feb 17, 1961	Baxley McQuaig, Jr
Pike, northern	55 lb 1 oz	Lake of Grefeern, West Germany	Oct 16, 1986	Lothar Louis
Redhorse, greater	9 lb 3 oz	Salmon River, Pulaski, NY	May 11, 1985	Jason Wilson
Redhorse, silver	11 lb 7 oz	Plum Creek, WI	May 29, 1985	Neal Long
Salmon, Atlantic	79 lb 2 oz	Tana River, Norway	1928	Henrik Henriksen
Salmon, chinook	97 lb 4 oz	Kenai River, AK	May 17, 1985	Les Anderson
Salmon, chum	32 lb	Behm Canal, AK	June 7, 1985	Fredrick Thynes
Salmon, coho	33 lb 4 oz	Pulaski, NY	Sept 27, 1989	Jerry Lifton
Salmon, pink	13 lb 1 oz	Ontario, Canada	Sept. 23, 1992	Ray Higaki
Salmon, sockeye	15 lb 3 oz	Kenai River, AK	Aug 9, 1987	Stan Roach
Sauger	8 lb 12 oz	Lake Sakakawea, ND	Oct 6, 1971	Mike Fischer
Shad, American	11 lb 4 oz	Connecticut River, MA	May 19, 1986	Bob Thibodo
Sturgeon, white	468 lb	Benicia, CA	July 9, 1983	Joey Pallotta III
Sunfish, green	2 lb 2 oz	Stockton Lake, MO	June 18, 1971	Paul M. Dilley
Sunfish, redbreast	1 lb 12 oz	Suwannee River, FL	May 29, 1984	Alvin Buchanan
Sunfish, redear	4 lb 13 oz	Marianna, FL	Mar 13, 1986	Joey Floyd
Tigerfish, giant	97 lb	Zaire River, Kinshasa, Zaire	July 9, 1988	Raymond Houtmans
Tilapia	6 lb	Clewiston, FL	June 24, 1989	Joseph Tucker
Trout, Apache	5 lb 3 oz	Apache Reservation, AZ	May 29, 1991	John Baldwin
Trout, brook	14 lb 8 oz	Nipigon River, Ontario	July 1916	W. J. Cook
Trout, brown	40 lb 4 oz	Heber Springs, AR	May 9, 1992	Howard L. Collins
Trout, bull	32 lb	Lake Pend Oreille, ID	Oct 27, 1949	N. L. Higgins
Trout, cutthroat	41 lb	Pyramid Lake, NV	Dec 1925	J. Skimmerhorn
Trout, golden	11 lb	Cook's Lake, WY	Aug 5, 1948	Charles S. Reed
Trout, lake	66 lb 8 oz	Great Bear Lake, Northwest Territories	July 19, 1991	Rodney Harback
Trout, rainbow	42 lb 2 oz	Bell Island, AK	June 22, 1970	David Robert White
Trout, tiger	20 lb 13 oz	Lake Michigan, WI	Aug 12, 1978	Pete Friedland
Walleye	25 lb	Old Hickory Lake, TN	Aug 1, 1960	Mabry Harper
Warmouth	2 lb 7 oz	Yellow River, Holt, FL	Oct 19, 1985	Tony D. Dempsey
Whitefish, lake	14 lb 6 oz	Meaford, Ontario	May 21, 1984	Dennis Laycock
Whitefish, mountain	5 lb 6 oz	Rioh River, Saskatchewan, Canada	June 15, 1988	John Bell
Whitefish, river	11 lb 2 oz	Nymoua, Sweden	Dec 9, 1984	Jorgen Larsson
Whitefish, round	6 lb	Putahow River, Manitoba	June 14, 1984	Allen Ristori
Zander	25 lb 2 oz	Trosa, Sweden	June 12, 1986	Harry Lee Tennison

Greyhound Racing

Annual Greyhound Race of Champions Winners

Year	Winner (Sex)	Affiliation/Owner	Year	Winner	Affiliation/Owner
1982	DD's Jackie (F)	Wonderland Park/R.H. Walters, Jr.	1988	BB's Old Yellow (M)	Supplemental (Southland)/ Margie Bonita Hyers
1983	Comin' Attraction (F)	Rocky Mt Greyhound Park/ Bob Riggin	1989	Osh Kosh Juliet (F)	Tampa Greyhound Track/ William F. Pollard
1984	Fallon (F)	Tampa Greyhound Track/ E.J. Alderson	1990	Daring Don (M)	Interstate Kennel Club/ Perry Padrta
1985	Lady Delight (F)	Lincoln Greyhound Park/ Julian A. Gay	1991	Mo Kick (M)	Flagler Greyhound Track/ Eric M. Kennon
1986	Ben G Speedboat (M)	Multnomah Kennel Club/ Louis Bennett	1992	Dicky Vallie (M)	Dairyland Greyhound Track/ George Benjamin
1987	ET's Pesky (F)	Supplemental (Flagler)/ Emil Tanis			

Gymnastics

World Champions

MEN

All-Around

Year	Champion and Nation	Year	Champion and Nation
1903	Joseph Martinez, France	1958	Boris Shaklin, Soviet Union
1905	Marcel Lalue, France	1962	Yuri Titov, Soviet Union
1907	Joseph Czada, Czechoslovakia	1966	Mikhail Voronin, Soviet Union
1909	Marcos Torres, France	1970	Eizo Kenmotsu, Japan
1911	Ferdinand Steiner, Czechoslovakia	1974	Shigeru Kasamatsu, Japan
1913	Marcos Torres, France	1978	Nikolai Andrianov, Soviet Union
1922	Peter Sumi, Yugoslavia	1979	Alexander Ditiatin, Soviet Union
	Frantisek Pechacek, Czech	1981	Yuri Korolev, Soviet Union
1926	Peter Sumi, Yugoslavia	1983	Dimitri Bilozertchev, Soviet Union
1930	Josip Primozic, Yugoslavia	1985	Yuri Korolev, Soviet Union
1934	Eugene Mack, Switzerland	1987	Dimitri Bilozertchev, Soviet Union
1938	Jan Gajdos, Czechoslovakia	1989	Igor Korobchinsky, Soviet Union
1950	Walter Lehmann, Switzerland	1991	Grigori Misutin, CIS
1954	Valentin Mouratov, Soviet Union	1993	Vitaly Scherbo, Belarus
	Victor Chukarin, Soviet Union		

Pommel Horse

Year	Champion and Nation	Year	Champion and Nation
1930	Josip Primozic, Yugoslavia	1981	Michael Mikolai, East Germany
1934	Eugene Mack, Switzerland		Li Xiaoping, China
1938	Michael Reusch, Switzerland	1983	Dmitri Bilozertchev, Soviet Union
1950	Josef Stalder, Switzerland	1985	Valentin Moguilny, Soviet Union
1954	Grant Chaguinjan, Soviet Union	1987	Zsolt Borkai, Hungary
1958	Boris Shaklin, Soviet Union		Dmitri Bilozertchev, Soviet Union
1962	Miroslav Cerar, Yugoslavia	1989	Valentin Moguilny, Soviet Union
1966	Miroslav Cerar, Yugoslavia	1991	Valeri Belenki, Soviet Union
1970	Miroslav Cerar, Yugoslavia	1992	Pae Gil Su, North Korea
1974	Zoltan Magyar, Hungary		Vitaly Scherbo, CIS
1978	Zoltan Magyar, Hungary		Li Jing, China
1979	Zoltan Magyar, Hungary	1993	Pae Gil Su, North Korea

Floor Exercise

Year	Champion and Nation	Year	Champion and Nation
1930	Josip Primozic, Yugoslavia	1970	Akinori Nakayama, Japan
1934	Georges Miesz, Switzerland	1974	Shigeru Kasamatsu, Japan
1938	Jan Gajdos, Czechoslovakia	1978	Kurt Thomas, United States
1950	Josef Stalder, Switzerland	1979	Kurt Thomas, United States
1954	Valentin Mouratov, Soviet Union		Roland Brucker, GDR, tk
	Masao Takemoto, Japan	1981	Yuri Korolev, Soviet Union
1958	Masao Takemoto, Japan		Li Yuejui, China
1962	Nobuyuki Aihara, Japan	1983	Tong Fei, China
	Yukio Endo, Japan	1985	Tong Fei, China
1966	Akinori Nakayama, Japan	1987	Lou Yun, China

World Champions (Cont.)

MEN (Cont.)

Floor Exercise (Cont.)

Year	Champion and Nation	Year	Champion and Nation
1989	Igor Korobchinsky, Soviet Union	1992	Igor Korobchinsky, CIS
1991	Igor Korobchinsky, Soviet Union	1993	Grigori Misutin, Ukraine

Rings

Year	Champion and Nation	Year	Champion and Nation
1930	Emanuel Loffler, Czechoslovakia	1978	Nikolai Andrianov, Soviet Union
1934	Alois Hudec, Czechoslovakia	1979	Alexander Ditiatin, Soviet Union
1938	Alois Hudec, Czechoslovakia	1981	Alexander Ditiatin, Soviet Union
1950	Walter Lehmann, Switzerland	1983	Dimitri Bilozertchev, Soviet Union
1954	Albert Azarian, Soviet Union	1985	Li Ning, China
1958	Albert Azarian, Soviet Union		Yuri Korolev, Soviet Union
1962	Yuri Titov, Soviet Union	1987	Yuri Korolev, Soviet Union
1966	Mikhail Voronin, Soviet Union	1989	Andreas Aguilar, West Germany
1970	Akinori Nakayama, Japan	1991	Grigory Misutin, Soviet Union
1974	Nikolai Andrianov, Soviet Union	1992	Vitaly Scherbo, CIS
	Danut Grecu, Romania	1993	Yuri Chechi, Italy

Parallel Bars

Year	Champion and Nation	Year	Champion and Nation
1930	Josip Primozic, Yugoslavia	1983	Vladimir Artemov, Soviet Union
1934	Eugene Mack, Switzerland		Lou Yun, China
1938	Michael Reusch, Switzerland	1985	Sylvio Kroll, East Germany
1950	Hans Eugster, Switzerland		Valentin Moguilny, Soviet Union
1954	Victor Chukarin, Soviet Union	1987	Vladimir Artemov, Soviet Union
1958	Boris Shaklin, Soviet Union	1989	Li Jing, China
1962	Miroslav Cerar, Yugoslavia		Vladimir Artemov, Soviet Union
1966	Sergei Diamidov, Soviet Union	1991	Li Jing, China
1970	Akinori Nakayama, Japan	1992	Li Jin, China
1974	Eizo Kenmotsu, Japan		Alexei Voropaev. CIS
1978	Eizo Kenmotsu, Japan	1993	Vitaly Scherbo, Belarus
1979	Bart Conner, United States		
1981	Koji Gushiken, Japan		
	Alexandr Ditiatin, Soviet Union		

High Bar

Year	Champion and Nation	Year	Champion and Nation
1930	Istvan Pelle, Hungary	1978	Shigeru Kasamatsu, Japan
1934	Ernst Winter, Germany	1979	Kurt Thomas, United States
1938	Michael Reusch, Switzerland	1981	Alexander Takchev, Soviet Union
1950	Paavo Aaltonen, Finland	1983	Dimitri Bilozertchev, Soviet Union
1954	Valentin Mouratov, Soviet Union	1985	Tong Fei, China
1958	Boris Shaklin, Soviet Union	1987	Dimitri Bilozertchev, Soviet Union
1962	Takashi Ono, Japan	1989	Li Chunyang, China
1966	Akinori Nakayama, Japan	1991	Li Chunyang, China
1970	Eizo Kenmotsu, Japan		Ralf Buechner, Germany
1974	Eberhard Gienger, West Germany	1992	Grigori Misutin, CIS
		1993	Sergei Kharkov, Russia

Vault

Year	Champion and Nation	Year	Champion and Nation
1934	Eugene Mack, Switzerland	1979	Alexander Ditiatin, Soviet Union
1938	Eugene Mack, Switzerland	1981	Ralf-Peter Hemmann, East Germany
1950	Ernst Gebendinger, Switzerland	1983	Arthur Akopian, Soviet Union
1954	Leo Sotornik, Czechoslovakia	1985	Yuri Korolev, Soviet Union
1958	Yuri Titov, Soviet Union	1987	Lou Yun, China
1962	Premysel Krbec, Czechoslovakia		Sylvio Kroll, East Germany
1966	Haruhiro Yamashita, Japan	1989	Joreg Behrend, East Germany
1970	Mitsuo Tsukahara, Japan	1991	Yoo Ok Youl, South Korea
1974	Shigeru Kasamatsu, Japan	1992	Yoo Ok Youl, South Korea
1978	Junichi Shimizu, Japan	1993	Vitaly Scherbo, Belarus

World Champions *(Cont.)*

WOMEN

All-Around

Year	Champion and Nation	Year	Champion and Nation
1934	Vlasta Dekanova, Czechoslovakia	1979	Nelli Kim, Soviet Union
1938	Vlasta Dekanova, Czechoslovakia	1981	Olga Bicherova, Soviet Union
1950	Helena Rakoczy, Poland	1983	Natalia Yurchenko, Soviet Union
1954	Galina Roudiko, Soviet Union	1985	Elena Shoushounova, Soviet Union
1958	Larissa Latynina, Soviet Union		Oksana Omeliantchik, Soviet Union
1962	Larissa Latynina, Soviet Union	1987	Aurelia Dobre, Romania
1966	Vera Caslavska, Czechoslovakia	1989	Svetlana Bouguinskaia, Soviet Union
1970	Ludmilla Tourischeva, Soviet Union	1991	Kim Zmeskal, United States
1974	Ludmilla Tourischeva, Soviet Union	1993	Shannon Miller, United States
1978	Elena Mukhina, Soviet Union		

Floor Exercise

Year	Champion and Nation	Year	Champion and Nation
1950	Helena Rakoczy, Poland	1983	Ecaterina Szabo, Romania
1954	Tamara Manina, Soviet Union	1985	Oksana Omeliantchik, Soviet Union
1958	Eva Bosakava, Czechoclovakia	1987	Elena Shoushounova, Soviet Union
1962	Larissa Latynina, Soviet Union		Daniela Silivas, Romania
1966	Natalia Kuchinskaya, Soviet Union	1989	Svetlana Bouguinskaia, Soviet Union
1970	Ludmilla Tourischeva, Soviet Union		Daniela Silivas, Romania
1974	Ludmilla Tourischeva, Soviet Union	1991	Cristina Bontas, Romania
1978	Nelli Kim, Soviet Union		Oksana Tchusovitina, Soviet Union
	Elena Mukhina, Soviet Union	1992	Kim Zmeskal, United States
1979	Emilia Eberle, Romania	1993	Shannon Miller, United States
1981	Natalia Ilenko, Soviet Union		

Uneven Bars

Year	Champion and Nation	Year	Champion and Nation
1950	Gertchen Kolar, Austria	1981	Maxi Gnauck, East Germany
	Anna Pettersson, Sweden	1983	Maxi Gnauck, East Germany
1954	Agnes Keleti, Hungary	1985	Gabriele Fahrnich, East Germany
1958	Larissa Latynina, Soviet Union	1987	Daniela Silivas, Romania
1962	Irina Pervuschina, Soviet Union		Doerte Thuemmler, East Germany
1966	Natalia Kuchinskaya, Soviet Union	1989	Fan Di, China
1970	Karin Janz, East Germany		Daniela Silivas, Romania
1974	Annelore Zinke, East Germany	1991	Gwang Suk Kim, North Korea
1978	Marcia Frederick, United States	1992	Lavinia Milosivici, Romania
1979	Ma Yanhong, China	1993	Shannon Miller, United States
	Maxi Gnauck, East Germany		

Balance Beam

Year	Champion and Nation	Year	Champion and Nation
1950	Helena Rakoczy, Poland	1981	Maxi Gnauck, East Germany
1954	Keiko Tanaka, Japan	1983	Olga Mostepanova, Soviet Union
1958	Larissa Latynina, Soviet Union	1985	Daniela Silivas, Romania
1962	Eva Bosakova, Czechoslovakia	1987	Aurelia Dobre, Romania
1966	Natalia Kuchinskaya, Soviet Union	1989	Daniela Silivas, Romania
1970	Erika Zuchold, East Germany	1991	Svetlana Boguinskaia, Soviet Union
1974	Ludmilla Tourischeva, Soviet Union	1992	Kim Zmeskal, United States
1978	Nadia Comaneci, Romania	1993	Lavinia Milosivici, Romania
1979	Vera Cerna, Czechoslovakia		

Vault

Year	Champion and Nation	Year	Champion and Nation
1950	Helena Rakoczy, Poland	1979	Dumitrita Turner, Romania
1954	Tamara Manina, Soviet Union	1981	Maxi Gnauck, East Germany
	Anna Pettersson, Sweden	1983	Boriana Stoyanova, Bulgaria
1958	Larissa Latynina, Soviet Union	1985	Elena Shoushounova, Soviet Union
1962	Vera Caslavska, Czechoslovakia	1987	Elena Shoushounova, Soviet Union
1966	Vera Caslavska, Czechoslovakia	1989	Olesia Durnik, Soviet Union
1970	Erika Zuchold, East Germany	1991	Lavinia Milosivici, Romania
1974	Olga Korbut, Soviet Union	1992	Henrietta Onodi, Hungary
1978	Nelli Kim, Soviet Union	1993	Elena Piskun, Belarus

National Champions

MEN

All-Around

Year	Champion
1963	Art Shurlock
1964	Rusty Mitchell
1965	Rusty Mitchell
1966	Rusty Mitchell
1967	Katsuzoki Kanzaki
1968	Yoshi Hayasaki
1969	Steve Hug
1970	Makoto Sakamoto
	Mas Watanabe
1971	Yoshi Takei
1972	Yoshi Takei

Year	Champion
1973	Marshall Avener
1974	John Crosby
1975	Tom Beach
	Bart Conner
1976	Kurt Thomas
1977	Kurt Thomas
1978	Kurt Thomas
1979	Bart Conner
1980	Peter Vidmar
1981	Jim Hartung
1982	Peter Vidmar

Year	Champion
1983	Mitch Gaylord
1984	Mitch Gaylord
1985	Brian Babcock
1986	Tim Daggett
1987	Scott Johnson
1988	Dan Hayden
1989	Tim Ryan
1990	John Roethlisberger
1991	Chris Waller
1992	John Roethlisberger
1993	John Roethlisberger

Floor Exercise

Year	Champion
1963	Tom Seward
1964	Rusty Mitchell
1965	Rusty Mitchell
1966	Dan Millman
1967	Katsuzoki Kanzaki
	Ron Aure
1968	Katsuzoki Kanzaki
1969	Steve Hug
	Dave Thor
1970	Makoto Sakamoto
1971	John Crosby

Year	Champion
1972	Yoshi Takei
1973	John Crosby
1974	John Crosby
1975	Peter Korman
1977	Ron Galimore
1978	Kurt Thomas
1979	Ron Galimore
1980	Ron Galimore
1981	Jim Hartung
1982	Jim Hartung
1983	Mitch Gaylord

Year	Champion
1984	Peter Vidmar
1985	Mark Oates
1986	Robert Sundstrom
1987	John Sweeney
1988	Mark Oates
	Charles Lakes
1989	Mike Racanelli
1990	Bob Stelter
1991	Mike Racanelli
1992	Gregg Curtis
1993	Kerry Huston

Pommel Horse

Year	Champion
1963	Larry Spiegel
1964	Sam Bailie
1965	Jack Ryan
1966	Jack Ryan
1967	Paul Mayer
	Dave Doty
1968	Katsuoki Kanzaki
1969	Dave Thor
1970	Mas Watanabe
1971	Leonard Caling
1972	Sadao Hamada

Year	Champion
1973	Marshall Avener
1974	Marshall Avener
1975	Bart Conner
1977	Gene Whelan
1978	Jim Hartung
1979	Bart Conner
1980	Jim Hartung
1981	Jim Hartung
1982	Jim Hartung
1983	Bart Conner
1984	Tim Daggett

Year	Champion
1985	Phil Cahoy
1986	Phil Cahoy
1987	Tim Daggett
1988	Kevin Davis
1989	Kevin Davis
1990	Patrick Kirksey
1991	Chris Waller
1992	Chris Waller
1993	Chris Waller

Rings

Year	Champion
1963	Art Shurlock
1964	Glen Gailis
1965	Glen Gailis
1966	Glen Gailis
1967	Fred Dennis
	Don Hatch
1968	Yoshi Hayasaki
1969	Fred Dennis
	Bob Emery
1970	Makoto Sakamoto
1971	Yoshi Takei

Year	Champion
1972	Yoshi Takei
1973	Jim Ivicek
1974	Tom Weeden
1975	Tom Beach
1977	Kurt Thomas
1978	Mike Silverstein
1979	Bart Conner
1980	Jim Hartung
1981	Jim Hartung
1982	Jim Hartung
	Peter Vidmar

Year	Champion
1983	Mitch Gaylord
1984	Jim Hartung
1985	Dan Hayden
1986	Dan Hayden
1987	Scott Johnson
1988	Dan Hayden
1989	Scott Keswick
1990	Scott Keswick
1991	Scott Keswick
1992	Tim Ryan
1993	John Roethlisberger

National Champions *(Cont.)*

MEN *(Cont.)*

Vault

Year	Champion	Year	Champion	Year	Champion
1963	Art Shurlock	1974	John Crosby	1985	Scott Johnson
1964	Gary Hery	1975	Tom Beach		Mark Oates
1965	Brent Williams	1977	Ron Galimore	1986	Scott Wilbanks
1966	Dan Millman	1978	Jim Hartung	1987	John Sweeney
1967	Jack Kenan	1979	Ron Galimore	1988	John Sweeney
	Sid Jensen	1980	Ron Galimore		Bill Paul
1968	Rich Scorza	1981	Ron Galimore	1989	Bill Roth
1969	Dave Butzman	1982	Jim Hartung	1990	Lance Ringnald
1970	Makoto Sakamoto		Jim Mikus	1991	Scott Keswick
1971	Gary Morava	1983	Chris Reigel	1992	Trent Dimas
1972	Mike Kelley	1984	Chris Reigel	1993	Bill Roth
1973	Gary Morava				

Parallel Bars

Year	Champion	Year	Champion	Year	Champion
1963	Tom Seward	1975	Bart Conner	1985	Tim Daggett
1964	Rusty Mitchell	1977	Kurt Thomas	1986	Tim Daggett
1965	Glen Gailis	1978	Bart Conner	1987	Scott Johnson
1966	Ray Hadley	1979	Bart Conner	1988	Dan Hayden
1967	Katsuzoki Kanzaki	1980	Phil Cahoy		Kevin Davis
	Tom Goldsborough		Larry Gerard	1989	Conrad Voorsanger
1968	Yoshi Hayasaki	1981	Bart Conner	1990	Trent Dimas
1969	Steve Hug	1982	Peter Vidmar	1991	Scott Keswick
1970	Makoto Sakamoto	1983	Mitch Gaylord	1992	Jair Lynch
1971	Brent Simmons	1984	Peter Vidmar	1993	Chainey Umphrey
1972	Yoshi Takei		Mitch Gaylord		
1973	Marshall Avener		Tim Daggett		
1974	Jim Ivicek				

High Bars

Year	Champion	Year	Champion	Year	Champion
1963	Art Shurlock	1974	Brent Simmons	1985	Dan Hayden
1964	Glen Gailis	1975	Tom Beach	1986	Dan Hayden
1965	Rusty Mitchell	1977	Kurt Thomas		David Moriel
1966	Katsuzoki Kanzaki	1978	Kurt Thomas	1987	David Moriel
1967	Katsuzoki Kanzaki	1979	Yoichi Tomita	1988	Dan Hayden
	Jerry Fontana	1980	Jim Hartung	1989	Tim Ryan
1968	Yoshi Hayasaki	1981	Bart Conner	1990	Trent Dimas
1969	Rich Grisby	1982	Mitch Gaylord		Lance Ringnald
1970	Makoto Sakamoto	1983	Mario McCutcheon	1991	Lance Ringnald
1971	Yoshi Takei	1984	Peter Vidmar	1992	Jair Lynch
1972	Tom Lindner		Tim Daggett	1993	Steve McCain
1973	John Crosby		Mitch Gaylord		

WOMEN

All-Around

Year	Champion	Year	Champion	Year	Champion
1963	Donna Schanezer	1973	Joan Moore Gnat	1985	Sabrina Mar
1965	Gail Daley	1974	Joan Moore Gnat	1986	Jennifer Sey
1966	Donna Schanezer	1975	Tammy Manville	1987	Kristie Phillips
1968	Linda Scott	1976	Denise Cheshire	1988	Phoebe Mills
1969	Joyce Tanac	1977	Donna Turnbow	1989	Brandy Johnson
	Schroeder	1978	Kathy Johnson	1990	Kim Zmeskal
1970	Cathy Rigby McCoy	1979	Leslie Pyfer	1991	Kim Zmeskal
1971	Joan Moore Gnat	1980	Julianne McNamara	1992	Kim Zmeskal
	Linda Metheny	1981	Tracee Talavera	1993	Shannon Miller
	Mulvihill	1982	Tracee Talavera		
1972	Joan Moore Gnat	1983	Dianne Durham		
	Cathy Rigby McCoy	1984	Mary Lou Retton		

National Champions (Cont.)

WOMEN (Cont.)

Vault

Year	Champion	Year	Champion	Year	Champion
1963	Donna Schanezer	1974	Dianne Dunbar	1985	Yolanda Mavity
1965	Gail Daley	1975	Kolleen Casey	1986	Joyce Wilborn
1966	Donna Schanezer	1976	Debbie Wilcox	1987	Rhonda Faehn
1968	Terry Spencer	1977	Lisa Cawthron	1988	Rhonda Faehn
1969	Joyce Tanac Schroeder	1978	Rhonda Schwandt Sharon Shapiro	1989	Brandy Johnson
	Cleo Carver	1979	Christa Canary	1990	Brandy Johnson
1970	Cathy Rigby McCoy	1980	Julianne McNamara	1991	Kerri Strug
1971	Joan Moore Gnat		Beth Kline	1992	Kerri Strug
	Adele Gleaves	1981	Kim Neal	1993	Dominique Dawes
1972	Cindy Eastwood	1982	Yumi Mordre		
1973	Roxanne Pierce Mancha	1983	Dianne Durham		
		1984	Mary Lou Retton		

Uneven Bars

Year	Champion	Year	Champion	Year	Champion
1963	Donna Schanezer	1973	Roxanne Pierce Mancha	1983	Julianne McNamara
1965	Irene Haworth	1974	Diane Dunbar	1984	Julianne McNamara
1966	Donna Schanezer	1975	Leslie Wolfsberger	1985	Sabrina Mar
1968	Linda Scott	1976	Leslie Wolfsberger	1986	Marie Roethlisberger
1969	Joyce Tanac Schroeder	1977	Donna Turnbow	1987	Melissa Marlowe
	Lisa Nelson	1978	Marcia Frederick	1988	Chelle Stack
1970	Roxanne Pierce Mancha	1979	Marcia Frederick	1989	Chelle Stack
		1980	Marcia Frederick	1990	Sandy Woolsey
1971	Joan Moore Gnat	1981	Julianne McNamara	1991	Elisabeth Crandall
1972	Cathy Rigby McCoy	1982	Marie Roethlisberger	1992	Dominique Dawes
				1993	Shannon Miller

Balance Beam

Year	Champion	Year	Champion	Year	Champion
1963	Leissa Krol	1974	Joan Moore Gnat	1985	Kelly Garrison-Steves
1965	Gail Daley	1975	Kyle Gayner	1986	Angie Denkins
1966	Irene Haworth	1976	Carrie Englert	1987	Kristie Phillips
	Linda Scott	1977	Donna Turnbow	1988	Kelly Garrison-Steves
1968	Linda Scott	1978	Christa Canary	1989	Brandy Johnson
1969	Lonna Woodward	1979	Heidi Anderson	1990	Betty Okino
1970	Joyce Tanac Schroeder	1980	Kelly Garrison-Steves	1991	Shannon Miller
1971	Linda Metheny Mulvihill	1981	Tracee Talavera	1992	Kerri Strug
		1982	Julianne McNamara		Kim Zmeskal
1972	Kim Chace	1983	Dianne Durham	1993	Dominique Dawes
1973	Nancy Thies Marshall	1984	Pam Bileck Tracee Talavera		

Floor Exercise

Year	Champion	Year	Champion	Year	Champion
1963	Donna Schanezer	1975	Kathy Howard	1986	Yolanda Mavity
1965	Gail Daley	1976	Carrie Englert	1987	Kristie Phillips
1966	Donna Schanezer	1977	Kathy Johnson	1988	Phoebe Mills
1968	Linda Scott	1978	Kathy Johnson	1989	Brandy Johnson
1970	Cathy Rigby McCoy	1979	Heidi Anderson	1990	Brandy Johnson
1971	Joan Moore Gnat	1980	Beth Kline	1991	Kim Zmeskal
	Linda Metheny Mulvihill	1981	Michelle Goodwin		Dominique Dawes
1972	Joan Moore Gnat	1982	Amy Koopman	1992	Kim Zmeskal
1973	Joan Moore Gnat	1983	Dianne Durham	1993	Shannon Miller
1974	Joan Moore Gnat	1984	Mary Lou Retton		
		1985	Sabrina Mar		

Handball

National Four-Wall Champions

1919 .....Bill Ranft	1938 .....Joe Platak	1957 .....Jimmy Jacobs	1976 .....Fred Lewis
1920 .....Max Gold	1939 .....Joe Platak	1958 .....John Sloan	1977 .....Naty Alvarado
1921 .....Carl Haedge	1940 .....Joe Platak	1959 .....John Sloan	1978 .....Fred Lewis
1922 .....Art Shinners	1941 .....Joe Platak	1960 .....Jimmy Jacobs	1979 .....Naty Alvarado
1923 .....Joe Murray	1942 .....Jack Clemente	1961 .....John Sloan	1980 .....Naty Alvarado
1924 .....Maynard Lasw	1943 .....Joe Platak	1962 .....Oscar Obert	1981 .....Fred Lewis
1925 .....Maynard Lasw	1944 .....Frank Coyle	1963 .....Oscar Obert	1982 .....Naty Alvarado
1926 .....Maynard Laswe	1945 .....Joe Platak	1964 .....Jimmy Jacobs	1983 .....Naty Alvarado
1927 .....George Nelson	1946 .....Angelo Trutio	1965 .....Jimmy Jacobs	1984 .....Naty Alvarado
1928 .....Joe Griffin	1947 .....Gus Lewis	1966 .....Paul Haber	1985 .....Naty Alvarado
1919 .....Al Banuet	1948 .....Gus Lewis	1967 .....Paul Haber	1986 .....Naty Alvarado
1930 .....Al Banuet	1949 .....Vic Hershkowitz	1968 .....Stuffy Singer	1987 .....Naty Alvarado
1931 .....Al Banuet	1950 .....Ken Schneider	1969 .....Paul Haber	1988 .....Naty Alvarado
1932 .....Angelo Trutio	1951 .....Walter Plakan	1970 .....Paul Haber	1989 .....Poncho Monreal
1933 .....Sam Atcheson	1952 .....Vic Hershkowitz	1971 .....Paul Haber	1990 .....Naty Alvarado
1934 .....Sam Atcheson	1953 .....Bob Brady	1972 .....Fred Lewis	1991 .....John Bike
1935 .....Joe Platak	1954 .....Vic Hershkowitz	1973 .....Terry Muck	1992 .....Octavio Silveyra
1936 .....Joe Platak	1955 .....Jimmy Jacobs	1974 .....Fred Lewis Pro	1993 .....David Chapman
1937 .....Joe Platak	1956 .....Jimmy Jacobs	1975 .....Fred Lewis	

National Three-Wall Champions

1950 .....Vic Hershkowitz	1961 .....Jimmy Jacobs	1972 .....Lou Russo	1983 .....Naty Alvarado
1951 .....Vic Hershkowitz	1962 .....Oscar Obert	1973 .....Paul Haber	1984 .....Naty Alvarado
1952 .....Vic Hershkowitz	1963 .....Marty Decatur	1974 .....Fred Lewis	1985 .....Vern Roberts
1953 .....Vic Herskkowitz	1964 .....Marty Decatur	1975 .....Lou Russo	1986 .....Vern Roberts
1954 .....Vic Hershkowitz	1965 .....Carl Obert	1976 .....Lou Russo	1987 .....Vern Roberts
1955 .....Vic Hershkowitz	1966 .....Marty Decatur	1977 .....Fred Lewis	1988 .....Jon Kendler
1956 .....Vic Hershkowitz	1967 .....Carl Obert	1978 .....Fred Lewis	1989 .....John Bike
1957 .....Vic Hershkowitz	1968 .....Marty Decatur	1979 .....Naty Alvarado	1990 .....Vince Munoz
1958 .....Vic Hershkowitz	1969 .....Marty Decatur	1980 .....Lou Russo	1991 .....John Bike
1959 .....Jimmy Jacobs	1970 .....Steve August	1981 .....Naty Alvarado	1992 .....John Bike
1960 .....Jimmy Jacobs	1971 .....Lou Russo	1982 .....Naty Alvarado	1993 .....Eric Klarman

World Four-Wall Champions

1984 ....Merv Deckert, Canada	1988 ....Naty Alvarado, United States
1986 ....Vern Roberts, United States	1991 ....Pancho Monreal, United States

Lacrosse

United States Club Lacrosse Association Champions

1960....................Mt Washington Club	1977....................Mt Washington Club
1961....................Baltimore Lacrosse Club	1978....................Long Island Athletic Club
1962....................Mt Washington Club	1979....................Maryland Lacrosse Club
1963....................University Club	1980....................Long Island Athletic Club
1964....................Mt Washington Club	1981....................Long Island Athletic Club
1965....................Mt Washington Club	1982....................Maryland Lacrosse Club
1966....................Mt Washington Club	1983....................Maryland Lacrosse Club
1967....................Mt Washington Club	1984....................Maryland Lacrosse Club
1968....................Long Island Athletic Club	1985....................Long Island-Hofstra Lacrosse Club
1969....................Long Island Athletic Club	1986....................Long Island-Hofstra Lacrosse Club
1970....................Long Island Athletic Club	1987....................Long Island-Hofstra Lacrosse Club
1971....................Long Island Athletic Club	1988....................Maryland Lacrosse Club
1972....................Carling	1989....................Long Island-Hofstra Lacrosse Club
1973....................Long Island Athletic Club	1990....................Mt Washington Club
1974....................Long Island Athletic Club	1991....................Mt Washington Club
1975....................Mt Washington Club	1992....................Maryland Lacrosse Club
1976....................Mt Washington Club	1993....................Mt Washington Club

Little League Baseball

Little League World Series Champions

Year	Champion	Runner-Up	Score	Year	Champion	Runner-Up	Score
1947	Williamsport, PA.	Lock Haven, PA.	16-7	1971	Tainan, Taiwan	Gary, IN	12-3
1948	Lock Haven, PA	St. Petersburg, FL	6-5	1972	Taipei, Taiwan	Hammond, IN	6-0
1949	Hammonton, NJ	Pensacola, FL	5-0	1973	Tainan City, Taiwan	Tucson, AZ	12-0
1950	Houston, TX	Bridgeport, CT	2-1	1974	Kao Hsiung, Taiwan	El Cajun, CA	7-2
1951	Stamford, CT	Austin, TX	3-0	1975	Lakewood, NJ	Tampa, FL	4-3
1952	Norwalk, CT	Monongahela, PA	4-3	1976	Tokyo, Japan	Campbell, CA	10-3
1953	Birmingham, AL	Schenectady, NY	1-0	1977	Kao Hsiung, Taiwan	El Cajun, CA	7-2
1954	Schenectady, NY	Colton, CA	7-5	1978	Pin-Tung, Taiwan	Danville, CA	11-1
1955	Morrisville, PA	Merchantville, NJ	4-3	1979	Hsien, Taiwan	Campbell, CA	2-1
1956	Roswell, NM	Merchantville, NJ	3-1	1980	Hua Lian, Taiwan	Tampa, FL	4-3
1957	Monterrrey, Mex.	LaMesa, CA	4-0	1981	Tai-Chung, Taiwan	Tampa, FL	4-2
1958	Monterrey, Mex.	Kankakee, IL	10-1	1982	Kirkland, WA	Hsien, Taiwan	6-0
1959	Hamtramck, MI	Auburn, CA	12-0	1983	Marietta, GA	Barahona, D.Rep.	3-1
1960	Levittown, PA	Ft. Worth, TX	5-0	1984	Seoul, S. Korea	Altamonte Sgs, FL	6-2
1961	El Cajon, CA	El Campo, TX	4-2	1985	Seoul, S. Korea	Mexicali, Mex.	7-1
1962	San Jose, CA	Kankakee, IL	3-0	1986	Tainan Park, Taiwan	Tucson, AZ	12-0
1963	Granada Hills, CA	Stratford, CT	2-1	1987	Hua Lian, Taiwan	Irvine, CA	21-1
1964	Staten Island, NY	Monterrey, Mex.	4-0	1988	Tai-Chung, Taiwan	Pearl City, HI	10-0
1965	Windsor Locks, CT	Stoney Creek, Can.	3-1	1989	Trumbull, CT	Kaohsiung, Taiwan	5-2
1966	Houston, TX	W.New York, NJ	8-2	1990	Taipei, Taiwan	Shippensburg, PA	9-0
1967	West Tokyo, Japan	Chicago, IL	4-1	1991	Tai-Chung, Taiwan	San Ramon Vly, CA	11-0
1968	Osaka, Japan	Richmond, VA	1-0	1992*	Long Beach, CA	Zamboanga, Phil.	6-0
1969	Taipei, Taiwan	Santa Clara, CA	5-0	1993	Long Beach, CA	David Chiriqui, Pan.	3-2
1970	Wayne, NJ	Campbell, CA	2-0				

*Long Beach declared a 6-0 winner after the international tournament committee determined that Zamboanga City had used players that were not within its city limits.

Motor Boat Racing

American Power Boat Association Gold Cup Champions

Year	Boat	Driver	Avg MPH	Year	Boat	Driver	Avg MPH
1904	Standard (June)	Carl Riotte	23.160	1930	Hotsy Totsy	Vic Kliesrath	52.673
1904	Vingt-et-Un II (Sep)	W. Sharpe Kilmer	24.900	1931	Hotsy Totsy	Vic Kliesrath	53.602
1905	Chip I	J. Wainwright	15.000	1932	Delphine IV	Bill Horn	57.775
1906	Chip II	J. Wainwright	25.000	1933	El Lagarto	George Reis	56.260
1907	Chip II	J. Wainwright	23.903	1934	El Lagarto	George Reis	55.000
1908	Dixie II	E. J. Schroeder	29.938	1935	El Lagarto	George Reis	55.056
1909	Dixie II	E. J. Schroeder	29.590	1936	Impshi	Kaye Don	45.735
1910	Dixie III	F. K. Burnham	32.473	1937	Notre Dame	Clell Perry	63.675
1911	MIT II	J. H. Hayden	37.000	1938	Alagi	Theo Rossi	64.340
1912	P.D.Q. II	A. G. Miles	39.462	1939	My Sin	Z. G. Simmons, Jr	66.133
1913	Ankle Deep	Cas Mankowski	42.779	1940	Hotsy Totsy III	Sidney Allen	48.295
1914	Baby Speed Demon II	Jim Blackton & Bob Edgren	48.458	1941	My Sin	Z. G. Simmons, Jr	52.509
1915	Miss Detroit	Johnny Milot & Jack Beebe	37.656	1942-45	No race		
				1946	Tempo VI	Guy Lombardo	68.132
1916	Miss Minneapolis	Bernard Smith	48.860	1947	Miss Peps V	Danny Foster	57.000
1917	Miss Detroit II	Gar Wood	54.410	1948	Miss Great Lakes	Danny Foster	46.845
1918	Miss Detroit II	Gar Wood	51.619	1949	My Sweetie	Bill Cantrell	73.612
1919	Miss Detroit III	Gar Wood	42.748	1950	Slo-Mo-Shun IV	Ted Jones	78.216
1920	Miss America I	Gar Wood	62.022	1951	Slo-Mo-Shun V	Lou Fageol	90.871
1921	Miss America I	Gar Wood	52.825	1952	Slo-Mo-Shun IV	Stan Dollar	79.923
1922	Packard Chriscraft	J. G. Vincent	40.253	1953	Slo-Mo-Shun IV	Joe Taggart & Lou Fageol	99.108
1923	Packard Chriscraft	Caleb Bragg	43.867				
1924	Baby Bootlegger	Caleb Bragg	45.302	1954	Slo-Mo-Shun IV	Joe Taggart & Lou Fageol	92.613
1925	Baby Bootlegger	Caleb Bragg	47.240				
1926	Greenwich Folly	George Townsend	47.984	1955	Gale V	Lee Schoenith	99.552
				1956	Miss Thriftaway	Bill Muncey	96.552
1927	Greenwich Folly	George Townsend	47.662	1957	Miss Thriftaway	Bill Muncey	101.787
				1958	Hawaii Kai III	Jack Regas	103.000
1928	No race			1959	Maverick	Bill Stead	104.481
1929	Imp	Richard Hoyt	48.662	1960	No race		
				1961	Miss Century 21	Bill Muncey	99.678

American Power Boat Association Gold Cup Champions (Cont.)

Year	Boat	Driver	Avg MPH	Year	Boat	Driver	Avg MPH
1962	Miss Century 21	Bill Muncey	100.710	1979	Atlas Van Lines	Bill Muncey	100.765
1963	Miss Bardahl	Ron Musson	105.124	1980	Miss Budweiser	Dean Chenoweth	106.932
1964	Miss Bardahl	Ron Musson	103.433	1981	Miss Budweiser	Dean Chenoweth	116.932
1965	Miss Bardahl	Ron Musson	103.132	1982	Atlas Van Lines	Chip Hanauer	120.050
1966	Tahoe Miss	Mira Slovak	93.019	1983	Atlas Van Lines	Chip Hanauer	118.507
1967	Miss Bardahl	Bill Shumacher	101.484	1984	Atlas Van Lines	Chip Hanauer	130.175
1968	Miss Bardahl	Bill Shumacher	108.173	1985	Miller American	Chip Hanauer	120.643
1969	Miss Budweiser	Bill Sterett	98.504	1986	Miller American	Chip Hanauer	116.523
1970	Miss Budweiser	Dean Chenoweth	99.562	1987	Miller American	Chip Hanauer	127.620
1971	Miss Madison	Jim McCormick	98.043	1988	Miss Circus Circus	Chip Hanauer & Jim Prevost	123.756
1972	Atlas Van Lines	Bill Muncey	104.277	1989	Miss Budweiser	Tom D'Eath	131.209
1973	Miss Budweiser	Dean Chenoweth	99.043	1990	Miss Budweiser	Tom D'Eath	143.176
1974	Pay 'n Pak	George Henley	104.428	1991	Winston Eagle	Mark Tate	137.771
1975	Pay 'n Pak	George Henley	108.921	1992	Miss Budweiser	Chip Hanauer	136.282
1976	Miss U.S.	Tom D'Eath	100.412	1993	Miss Budweiser	Chip Hanauer	141.195
1977	Atlas Van Lines	Bill Muncey	111.822				
1978	Atlas Van Lines	Bill Muncey	111.412				

American Power Boat Association Annual Champion Drivers

Year	Driver	Boats	Wins	Year	Driver	Boats	Wins
1947	Danny Foster	Miss Peps V	6	1971	Dean Chenoweth	Miss Budweiser	2
1948	Dan Arena	Such Crust	2	1972	Bill Muncey	Atlas Van Lines	6
1949	Bill Cantrell	My Sweetie	7	1973	Mickey Remund	Pay 'n Pack	4
1950	Dan Foster	Such Crust/DaphneX	2	1974	George Henley	Pay 'n Pack	7
1951	Chuck Thompson	Miss Pepsi	5	1975	Billy Schumacher	Weisfield's	2
1952	Chuck Thompson	Miss Pepsi	3	1976	Bill Muncey	Atlas/Mt. Everelt	5
1953	Lee Schoenith	Gale II	1	1977	Mickey Remund	Miss Budweiser	3
1954	Lee Schoenith	Gale V	4	1978	Bill Muncey	Atlast Van Lines	6
1955	Lee Schoenith	Gale V/Wha Hoppen	1	1979	Bill Muncey	Atlas Van Lines	7
1956	Russ Schleeh	Shanty I	3	1980	Dean Chenoweth	Mlss Budweiser	5
1957	Jack Regas	Hawaii Kai III	5	1981	Dean Chenoweth	Miss Budweiser	6
1958	Mira Slovak	Bardah/Miss Buren	3	1982	Chip Hanauer	Atlas Van Lines	5
1959	Bill Stead	Maverick	5	1983	Chip Hanauer	Atlas Van Lines	3
1960	Bill Muncey	Miss Thriftway	4	1984	Jim Kropfeld	Miss Budweiser	6
1961	Bill Muncey	Miss Century 21	4	1985	Chip Hanauer	Miller American	5
1962	Bill Muncey	Miss Century 21	5	1986	Jim Kropfeld	Miss Budweiser	3
1963	Bill Cantrell	Gale V	0	1987	Jim Kropfeld	Miss Budweiser	5
1964	Ron Musson	Miss Bardahl	4	1988	Tom D'Eath	Miss Budweiser	4
1965	Ron Musson	Miss Bardahl	4	1989	Chip Hanauer	Miss Circus Circus	5
1966	Mira Slovak	Tahoe Miss	4	1990	Chip Hanauer	Miss Circus Circus	6
1967	Billy Schumacher	Miss Bardahl	6	1991	Mark Tate	Winston/Oberto	3
1968	Billy Schumacher	Miss Bardahl	4	1992	Chip Hanauer	Miss Budweiser	7
1969	Bill Sterett, Sr.	Miss Budweiser	4				
1970	Dean Chenoweth	Miss Budweiser	4				

American Power Boat Association Annual Champion Boats

Year	Boat	Owner	Wins	Year	Boat	Owner	Wins
1970	Miss Budweiser	Little-Friedkin	4	1982	Atlas Van Lines	Fran Muncey	5
1971	Miss Budweiser	Little-Friedkin	2	1983	Atlas Van Lines	Muncey-Lucero	3
1972	Atlas Van Lines	Joe Schoenith	6	1984	Miss Budweiser	Bernie Little	6
1973	Pay 'n Pak	Dave Heerensperger	4	1985	Miller American	Muncey-Lucero	5
1974	Pay 'n Pak	Dave Heerensperger	7	1986	Miss Budweiser	Bernie Little	3
1975	Pay 'n Pak	Dave Heerensperger	5	1987	Miss Budweiser	Bernie Little	5
1976	Atlas Van Lines	Bill Muncey	5	1988	Miss Budweiser	Bernie Little	4
1977	Miss Budweiser	Bernie Little	3	1989	Miss Budweiser	Bernie Little	4
1978	Atlas Van Lines	Bill Muncey	6	1990	Circus Circus	Bill Bennett	6
1979	Atlas Van Lines	Bill Muncey	7	1991	Miss Budweiser	Bernie Little	4
1980	Miss Budweiser	Bernie Little	5	1992	Miss Budweiser	Bernie Little	7
1981	Miss Budweiser	Bernie Little	6				

Polo

United States Open Polo Champions

1904	Wanderers	1937	Old Westbury	1967	Bunntyco—Oak Brook
1905-09	Not contested	1938	Old Westbury	1968	Midland
1910	Ranelagh	1939	Bostwick Field	1969	Tulsa Greenhill
1911	Not contested	1940	Aknusti	1970	Tulsa Greenhill
1912	Cooperstown	1941	Gulf Stream	1971	Oak Brook
1913	Cooperstown	1942-45	Not played for	1972	Milwaukee
1914	Meadow Brook Magpies	1946	Mexico	1973	Oak Brook
1915	Not contested	1947	Old Westbury	1974	Milwaukee
1916	Meadow Brook	1948	Hurricanes	1975	Milwaukee
1917-18	Not contested	1949	Hurricanes	1976	Willow Bend
1919	Meadow Brook	1950	Bostwick	1977	Retama
1920	Meadow Brook	1951	Milwaukee	1978	Abercrombie & Kent
1921	Great Neck	1952	Beverly Hills	1979	Retama
1922	Argentine	1953	Meadow Brook	1980	Southern Hills
1923	Meadow Brook	1954	C.C.C.—Meadow Brook	1981	Rolex A & K
1924	Midwick	1955	C.C.C.	1982	Retama
1925	Orange County	1956	Brandywine	1983	Ft. Lauderdale
1926	Hurricanes	1957	Detroit	1984	Retama
1927	Sands Point	1958	Dallas	1985	Carter Ranch
1928	Meadow Brook	1959	Circle F	1986	Retama II
1929	Hurricanes	1960	Oak Brook C.C.C.	1987	Aloha
1930	Hurricanes	1961	Milwaukee	1988	Les Diables Bleus
1931	Santa Paula	1962	Santa Barbara	1989	Les Diables Bleus
1932	Templeton	1963	Tulsa	1990	Les Diables Bleus
1933	Aurora	1964	Concar Oak Brook	1991	Grant's Farm Manor
1934	Templeton	1965	Oak Brook—Santa Barbara	1992	Hanalei Bay
1935	Greentree	1966	Tulsa		
1936	Greentree				

Top-Ranked Players

The United States Polo Association ranks its registered players from minus 2 to plus 10 goals, with 10 Goal players being the game's best. At present, the USPA recognizes ten 10-Goal and seven 9-Goal players:

10-GOAL

Adolfo Cambiaso (Palm Beach)
Carlos Gracida (San Antonio)
Guillermo Gracida Jr (Palm Beach)
Batista Heguy (Palm Beach)
Eduardo Heguy (Palm Beach)
Marcos Heguy (Palm Beach)
Christian LaPrida (Palm Beach)
Alfonso Pieres (Palm Beach)
Owen R. Rinehart (Palm Beach)
Ernesto Trotz (Palm Beach)

9-GOAL

Mariano Aguerre (Greenwich)
Benjamin Araya (Palm Beach)
Santiago Araya (Palm Beach)
Michael Vincen Azzaro (San Antonio)
Hector Juni Crotto (Palm Beach)
Esteban Panelo (Hidden Pond)
Martin Zubia (Palm Beach)

Rodeo

All-Around

1929	Earl Thode	1947	Todd Whatley	1963	Dean Oliver	1979	Tom Ferguson
1930	Clay Carr	1948	Gerald Roberts	1964	Dean Oliver	1980	Paul Tierney
1931	John Schneider	1949	Jim Shoulders	1965	Dean Oliver	1981	Jimmie Cooper
1932	Donald Nesbit	1950	Bill Linderman	1966	Larry Mahan	1982	Chris Lybbert
1933	Clay Carr	1951	Casey Tibbs	1967	Larry Mahan	1983	Roy Cooper
1934	Leonard Ward	1952	Harry Tompkins	1968	Larry Mahan	1984	Dee Picket
1935	Everett Bowman	1953	Bill Linderman	1969	Larry Mahan	1985	Lewis Feild
1936	John Bowman	1954	Buck Rutherford	1970	Larry Mahan	1986	Lewis Feild
1937	Everett Bowman	1955	Casey Tibbs	1971	Phil Lyne	1987	Lewis Feild
1938	Burel Mulkey	1956	Jim Shoulders	1972	Phil Lyne	1988	Dave Appleton
1939	Paul Carney	1957	Jim Shoulders	1973	Larry Mahan	1989	Ty Murray
1940	Fritz Truan	1958	Jim Shoulders	1974	Tom Ferguson	1990	Ty Murray
1941	Homer Pettigrew	1959	Jim Shoulders	1975	Tom Ferguson	1991	Ty Murray
1942	Gerald Roberts	1960	Harry Tompkins	1976	Tom Ferguson	1992	Ty Murray
1943	Louis Brooks	1961	Benny Reynolds	1977	Tom Ferguson		
1944	Louis Brooks	1962	Tom Nesmith	1978	Tom Ferguson		

Rodeo Champions

Saddle Bronc Riding

1929....Earl Thode	1947....Carl Olson	1963....Guy Weeks	1979....Bobby Berger
1930....Clay Carr	1948....Gene Pruett	1964....Marty Wood	1980....Clint Johnson
1931....Earl Thode	1949....Casey Tibbs	1965....Shawn Davis	1981....B. Gjermundson
1932....Peter Knight	1950....Bill Linderman	1966....Marty Wood	1982....Monty Henson
1933....Peter Knight	1951....Casey Tibbs	1967....Shawn Davis	1983....B. Gjermundson
1934....Leonard Ward	1952....Casey Tibbs	1968....Shawn Davis	1984....B. Gjermundson
1935....Peter Knight	1953....Casey Tibbs	1969....Bill Smith	1985....B. Gjermundson
1936....Peter Knight	1954....Casey Tibbs	1970....Dennis Reiners	1986....Bud Munroe
1937....Burel Mulkey	1955....DebCopenhaver	1971....Bill Smith	1987....Clint Johnson
1938....Burel Mulkey	1956....DebCopenhaver	1972....Mel Hyland	1988....Clint Johnson
1939....Fritz Truan	1957....Alvin Nelson	1973....Bill Smith	1989....Clint Johnson
1940....Fritz Truan	1958....Marty Wood	1974....John McBeth	1990....Robert Etbauer
1941....Doff Aber	1959....Casey Tibbs	1975....Monty Henson	1991....Robert Etbauer
1942....Doff Aber	1960....Enoch Walker	1976....Monty Henson	1992....Billy Etbauer
1943....Louis Brooks	1961....Winston Bruce	1977....Bobby Berger	
1944....Louis Brooks	1962....Kenny McLean	1978....Joe Marvel	

Bareback Riding

1929....No bareback	1947....Larry Finley	1963....John Hawkins	1979....Bruce Ford
1930....champions	1948....Sonny Tureman	1964....Jim Houston	1980....Bruce Ford
1931....until 1932	1949....Jack Buschbom	1965....Jim Houston	1981....J.C. Trujillo
1932....Smoky Snyder	1950....Jim Shoulders	1966....Paul Mayo	1982....Bruce Ford
1933....Nate Waldrum	1951....Casey Tibbs	1967....Clyde Vamvoras	1983....Bruce Ford
1934....Leonard Ward	1952....Harry Tompkins	1968....Clyde Vamvoras	1984....Larry Peabody
1935....Frank Schneider	1953....Eddy Akridge	1969....Gary Tucker	1985....Lewis Feild
1936....Smoky Snyder	1954....Eddy Akridge	1970....Paul Mayo	1986....Lewis Feild
1937....Paul Carney	1955....Eddy Adridge	1971....Joe Alexander	1987....Bruce Ford
1938....Pete Grubb	1956....Jim Shoulders	1972....Joe Alexander	1988....Marvin Garrett
1939....Paul Carney	1957....Jim Shoulders	1973....Joe Alexander	1989....Marvin Garrett
1940....Carl Dossey	1958....Jim Shoulders	1974....Joe Alexander	1990....Chuck Logue
1941....George Mills	1959....Jack Buschbom	1975....Joe Alexander	1991....Clint Corey
1942....Louis Brooks	1960....Jack Buschbom	1976....Joe Alexander	1992....Wayne Herman
1943....Bill Linderman	1961....Eddy Akridge	1977....Joe Alexander	
1944....Louis Brooks	1962....Ralph Buell	1978....Bruce Ford	

Bull Riding

1929....John Schneider	1943....Ken Roberts	1961....Ronnie Rossen	1977....Don Gay
1930....John Schneider	1944....Ken Roberts	1962....Freckles Brown	1978....Don Gay
1931....Smokey Snyder	1947....Wag Blessing	1963....Bill Kornell	1979....Don Gay
1932....John Schneider	1948....Harry Tompkins	1964....Bob Wegner	1980....Don Gay
1932....Smokey Snyder	1949....Harry Tompkins	1965....Larry Mahan	1981....Don Gay
John Schneider	1950....Harry Tompkins	1966....Ronnie Rossen	1982....Charles Sampson
1933....Frank Schneider	1951....Jim Shoulders	1967....Larry Mahan	1983....Cody Snyder
1934....Frank Schneider	1952....Harry Tompkins	1968....George Paul	1984....Don Gay
1935....Smokey Snyder	1953....Todd Whatley	1969....Doug Brown	1985....Ted Nuce
1936....Smokey Snyder	1954....Jim Shoulders	1970....Gary Leffew	1986....Tuff Hedeman
1937....Smokey Snyder	1955....Jim Shoulders	1971....Bill Nelson	1987....Lane Frost
1938....Kid Fletcher	1956....Jim Shoulders	1972....John Quintana	1988....Jim Sharp
1939....Dick Griffith	1957....Jim Shoulders	1973....Bobby Steiner	1989....Tuff Hedeman
1940....Dick Griffith	1958....Jim Shoulders	1974....Don Gay	1990....Jim Sharp
1941....Dick Griffith	1959....Jim Shoulders	1975....Don Gay	1991....Tuff Hedeman
1942....Dick Griffith	1960....Harry Tompkins	1976....Don Gay	1992....Cody Custer

Calf Roping

1929....Everett Bowman	1939....Toots Mansfield	1950....Toots Mansfield	1960....Dean Oliver
1930....Jake McClure	1940....Toots Mansfield	1951....Don McLaughlin	1961....Dean Oliver
1931....Herb Meyers	1941....Toots Mansfield	1952....Don McLaughlin	1962....Dean Oliver
1932....Richard Merchant	1942....Clyde Burk	1953....Don McLaughlin	1963....Dean Oliver
1933....Bill McFarlane	1943....Toots Mansfield	1954....Don McLaughlin	1964....Dean Oliver
1934....Irby Mundy	1944....Clyde Burk	1955....Dean Oliver	1965....Glen Franklin
1935....Everett Bowman	1945-46 No champ.	1956....Ray Wharton	1966....Junior Garrison
1936....Clyde Burk	1947....Troy Fort	1957....Don McLaughlin	1967....Glen Franklin
1937....Everett Bowman	1948....Toots Mansfield	1958....Dean Oliver	1968....Glen Franklin
1938....Burel Mulkey	1949....Troy Fort	1959....Jim Bob Altizer	1969....Dean Oliver

Calf Roping *(Cont.)*

1970....Junior Garrison	1976....Roy Cooper	1982....Roy Cooper	1988....Joe Beaver
1971....Phil Lyne	1977....Roy Cooper	1983....Roy Cooper	1989....Rabe Rabon
1972....Phil Lyne	1978....Roy Cooper	1984....Roy Cooper	1990....Troy Pruitt
1973....Ernie Taylor	1979....Paul Tierney	1985....Joe Beaver	1991....Fred Whitfield
1974....Tom Ferguson	1980....Roy Cooper	1986....Chris Lybbert	1992....Joe Beaver
1975....Jeff copenhaver	1981....Roy Cooper	1987....Joe Beaver	

Steer Wrestling

1929....Gene Ross	1945-46 No champ.	1962....Tom Nesmith	1978....Byron Walker
1930....Everett Bowman	1947....Todd Whatley	1963....Jim Bynum	1979....Stan Williamson
1931....Gene Ross	1948....Homer Pettigrew	1964....C.R. Boucher	1980....Butch Myers
1932....Hugh Bennett	1949....Bill McGuire	1965....Harley May	1981....Byron Walker
1933....Everett Bowman	1950....Bill Linderman	1966....Jack Roddy	1982....Stan Williamson
1934....Shorty Ricker	1951....Dub Phillips	1967....Roy Duvall	1983....Joel Edmondson
1935....Everett Bowman	1952....Harley May	1968....Jack Roddy	1984....John W. Jones
1936....Jack Kerschner	1953....Ross Dollarhide	1969....Roy Duvall	1985....Ote Berry
1937....Gene Ross	1954....James Bynum	1970....John W. Jones	1986....Steve Duhon
1938....Everett Bowman	1955....Benny Combs	1971....Billy Hale	1987....Steve Duhon
1939....Harry Hart	1956....Harley May	1972....Roy Duvall	1988....John W. Jones
1940....Homer Pettigrew	1957....Clark McEntire	1973....Bob Marshall	1989....John W. Jones
1941....Hub Whiteman	1958....James Bynum	1974....Tommy Puryear	1990....Ote Berry
1942....Homer Pettigrew	1959....Harry Charters	1975....F. Shepperson	1991....Ote Berry
1943....Homer Pettigrew	1960....Bob A. Robinson	1976....Tom Ferguson	1992....Mark Roy
1944....Homer Pettigrew	1961....Jim Bynum	1977....Larry Ferguson	

Team Roping

1929....Charles Maggini	1944....Murphy Chaney	1963....Les Hirdes	1980....Tee Woolman
1930....Norman Cowan	1947....Jim Brister	1964....Bill Hamilton	1981....Walt Woodard
1931....Arthur Beloat	1948 Joe Glenn	1965....Jim RodriguezJr.	1982....Tee Woolman
1932....Ace Gardner	1949....Ed Yanez	1966....Ken Luman	1983....Leo Camarillo
1933....Roy Adams	1950....Buck Sorrels	1967....Joe Glenn	1984....Dee Pickett
1934....Andy Jauregui	1951....Olan Sims	1968....Art Arnold	1985....Jake Barnes
1935....Lawrence Conltk	1952....Asbury Schell	1969....Jerold Camarillo	1986....Clay O. Cooper
1936....John Rhodes	1953....Ben Johnson	1970....John Miller	1987....Clay O. Cooper
1937....Asbury Schell	1954....Eddie Schell	1971....John Miller	1988....Jake Barnes
1938....John Rhodes	1955....Vern Castro	1972....Leo Camarillo	1989....Jake Barnes
1939....Asbury Schell	1956....Dale Smith	1973....Leo Camarillo	1990....Allen Bach
1940....Pete Grubb	1957....Dale Smith	1974....H.P. Evetts	1991....Bob Harris
1941....Jim Hudson	1958....Ted Ashworth	1975....Leo Camarillo	1992....Clay O. Cooper
1942....Verne Castro	1959....Jim RodriguezJr.	1976....Leo Camarillo	
Vic Castro	1960....Jim RodriguezJr.	1977....Jerold Camarillo	
1943....Mark Hull	1961....Al Hooper	1978....Doyle Gellerman	
Leonard Block	1962....Jim RodriguezJr.	1979....Allen Bach	

Steer Roping

1929....Charles Maggini	1945....Everett Shaw	1961....Clark McEntire	1977....Buddy Cockrell
1930....Clay Carr	1946....Everett Shaw	1962....Everett Shaw	1978....Sonny Worrell
1931....Andy Jauregui	1947....Ike Rude	1963....Don McLaughlin	1979....Gary Good
1932....George Weir	1948....Everett Shaw	1964....Sonny Davis	1980....Guy Allen
1933....John Bowman	1949....Shoat Webster	1965....Sonny Wright	1981....Arnold Felts
1934....John McEntire	1950....Shoat Webster	1966....Sonny Davis	1982....Guy Allen
1935....Richard Merchant	1951....Everett Shaw	1967....Jim Bob Altizer	1983....Roy Cooper
1936....John Bowman	1952....Buddy Neal	1968....Sonny Davis	1984....Guy Allen
1937....Everett Bowman	1953....Ike Rude	1969....Walter Arnold	1985....Jim Davis
1938....Hugh Bennett	1954....Shoat Webster	1970....Don McLaughlin	1986....Jim Davis
1939....Dick Truitt	1955....Shoat Webster	1971....Olin Young	1987....Shaun Burchett
1940....Clay Carr	1956....Jim Snively	1972....Allen Keller	1988....Shaun Burchett
1941....Ike Rude	1957....Clark McEntire	1973....Roy Thompson	1989....Guy Allen
1942....King Merrit	1958....Clark McEntire	1974....Olin Young	1990....Phil Lyne
1943....Tom Rhodes	1959....Everett Shaw	1975....Roy Thompson	1991....Guy Allen
1944....Tom Rhodes	1960....Don McLaughlin	1976....Marvin Cantrell	1992....Guy Allen

Rowing

National Collegiate Rowing Champions
MEN'S EIGHT

1982	Yale	1986	Wisconsin	1990	Wisconsin
1983	Harvard	1987	Harvard	1991	Pennsylvania
1984	Washington	1988	Harvard	1992	Harvard
1985	Harvard	1989	Harvard	1993	Brown

WOMEN'S EIGHT

1979	Yale	1984	Washington	1989	Cornell
1980	California	1985	Washington	1990	Princeton
1981	Washington	1986	Wisconsin	1991	Boston University
1982	Washington	1987	Washington	1992	Boston University
1983	Washington	1988	Washington	1993	Princeton

Rugby

National Men's Club Championship

Year	Winner	Runner-Up	Year	Winner	Runner-Up
1979	Old Blues (Calif.)	St Louis Falcons	1987	Old Blues (Calif.)	Pittsburgh
1980	Old Blues (Calif.)	St. Louis Falcons	1988	Old Mission Beach AC	Milwaukee
1981	Old Blues (Calif.)	Old Blue (NY)	1989	Old Mission Beach AC	Philly/Whitemarsh
1982	Old Blues (Calif.)	Denver Barbos	1990	Denver Barbos	Old Blues (CA)
1983	Old Blues (Calif.)	Dallas Harlequins	1991	Old Mission Beach AC	Washington
1984	Dallas Harlequins	Los Angeles	1992	Old Blues (Calif.)	Mystic River (MA)
1985	Milwaukee	Denver Barbos	1993	Old Mission Beach AC	Milwaukee
1986	Old Blues (Calif.)	Old Blue (NY)			

National Men's Collegiate Championship

Year	Winner	Runner-Up	Year	Winner	Runner-Up
1980	California	Air Force	1987	San Diego State	Air Force
1981	California	Harvard	1988	California	Dartmouth
1982	California	Life College	1989	Air Force	Long Beach
1983	California	Air Force	1990	Air Force	Army
1984	Harvard	Colorado	1991	California	Army
1985	California	Maryland	1992	California	Army
1986	California	Dartmouth	1993	California	Air Force

World Cup Championship

Year	Winner	Runner-Up	Year	Winner	Runner-Up
1987	New Zealand	France	1991	Australia	England

Sailing

America's Cup Champions
SCHOONERS AND J-CLASS BOATS

Year	Winner	Skipper	Series	Loser	Skipper
1851	America	Richard Brown			
1870	Magic	Andrew Comstock	1-0	Cambria, Great Britain	J. Tannock
1871	Columbia (2-1)	Nelson Comstock	4-1	Livonia, Great Britain	J. R. Woods
	Sappho (2-0)	Sam Greenwood			
1876	Madeleine	Josephus Williams	2-0	Countess of Dufferin, Canada	J. E. Ellsworth
1881	Mischief	Nathanael Clock	2-0	Atalanta, Canada	Alexander Cuthbert
1885	Puritan	Aubrey Crocker	2-0	Genesta, Great Britain	John Carter
1886	Mayflower	Martin Stone	2-0	Galatea, Great Britain	Dan Bradford
1887	Volunteer	Henry Haff	2-0	Thistle, Great Britain	John Barr
1893	Vigilant	William Hansen	3-0	Valkyrie II, Great Britain	William Granfield
1895	Defender	Henry Haff	3-0	Valkyrie III, Great Britain	William Granfield
1899	Columbia	Charles Barr	3-0	Shamrock I, Great Britain	Archie Hogarth
1901	Columbia	Charles Barr	3-0	Shamrock II, Great Britain	E. A. Sycamore
1903	Reliance	Charles Barr	3-0	Shamrock III, Great Britain	Bob Wringe

America's Cup Champions *(Cont.)*

SCHOONERS AND J-CLASS BOATS (Cont.)

Year	Winner	Skipper	Series	Loser	Skipper
1920	Resolute	Charles F. Adams	3-2	Shamrock IV, Great Britain	William Burton
1930	Enterprise	Harold Vanderbilt	4-0	Shamrock V, Great Britain	Ned Heard
1934	Rainbow	Harold Vanderbilt	4-2	Endeavour, Great Britain	T. O. M. Sopwith
1937	Ranger	Harold Vanderbilt	4-0	Endeavour II, Great Britain	T. O. M. Sopwith

12-METER BOATS

Year	Winner	Skipper	Series	Loser	Skipper
1958	Columbia	Briggs Cunningham	4-0	Sceptre, Great Britain	Graham Mann
1962	Weatherly	Bus Mosbacher	4-1	Gretel, Australia	Jock Sturrock
1964	Constellation	Bob Bavier & Eric Ridder	4-0	Sovereign, Australia	Peter Scott
1967	Intrepid	Bus Mosbacher	4-0	Dame Pattie, Australia	Jock Sturrock
1970	Intrepid	Bill Ficker	4-1	Gretel II, Australia	Jim Hardy
1974	Courageous	Ted Hood	4-0	Southern Cross, Australia	John Cuneo
1977	Courageous	Ted Turner	4-0	Australia	Noel Robins
1980	Freedom	Dennis Conner	4-1	Australia	Jim Hardy
1983	Australia II	John Bertrand	4-3	Liberty, United States	Dennis Conner
1987	Stars & Stripes	Dennis Conner	4-0	Kookaburra III, Australia	Iain Murray

60-FOOT CATAMARAN VS 133-FOOT MONOHULL

Year	Winner	Skipper	Series	Loser	Skipper
1988	Stars & Stripes	Dennis Conner	2-0	New Zealand	David Barnes

75-FOOT MONOHULL (IACC)

Year	Winner	Skipper	Series	Loser	Skipper
1992	America[3]	Bill Koch	4-1	Il Moro di Vinezia, Italy	Paul Cayard

Note: Winning entry was from the United States every year but 1983, when an Australian vessel won.

Shooting World Champions

Men

50M FREE RIFLE PRONE

1947 .....O. Sannes, Norway
1949 .....A.C. Jackson,
  United States
1952 .....A.C. Jackson,
  United States
1954 .....G. Boa, Canada
1958 .....M. Nordquist
1962 .....K. Wenk, West Germany
1966 .....D. Boyd, United States
1970 .....M. Fiess, S. Africa
1974 .....K. Bulan, Czech.
1978 .....A. Allan, Great Britain
1982 .....V. Danilschenko,
  Soviet Uniom
1986 .....S. Bereczky, Hungary
1990 .....V. Bochkarev,
  Soviet Union

AIR RIFLE

1966 .....G. Kümmet, W. Germany
1970 .....G. Kusterman, W. Germ.
1974 .....E. Pedzisz, Poland
1978 .....O. Schlipf, W. Germany
1979 .....K. Hillenbrand
1981 .....F. Bessy, France
1982 .....F. Rettkowski, E. Germ.
1983 .....P. Heberle, France
1985 .....P. Heberle, France
1986 .....H. Riederer, W. Germany

AIR RIFLE *(Cont.)*

1987 .....K. Ivanov, Soviet Union
1989 .....J. P. Amet, France
1990 .....H. Riederer, W. Germany

MEN'S TRAP

1929 .....De Lumniczer, Hungary
1930 .....M. Arie, United States
1931 .....Kiszkurno, Poland
1933 .....De Lumniczer, Hungary
1934 .....A. Montagh, Hungary
1935 .....R. Sack, W. Germany
1936 .....Kiszkurno, Poland
1937 .....K. Huber, Finland
1938 .....I. Strassburger, Hungary
1939 .....De Lumniczer, Hungary
1947 .....H. Liljedahl, Sweden
1949 .....F. Rocchi, Argentina
1950 .....C. Sala, Italy
1952 .....P.J. Grossi, Argentina
1954 .....C. Merlo, Italy
1958 .....F. Eisenlauer,
  United States
1959 .....H. Badravi, Egypt
1961 .....E. Mattarelli, Italy
1962 .....W. Zimenko, Soviet Union
1965 .....J.E. Lire, Chile
1966 .....K. Jones, United States
1967 .....G. Rennard, Belgium
1969 .....E. Mattarelli, Italy

MEN'S TRAP *(Cont.)*

1970 .....M. Carrega, France
1971 .....M. Carrega, France
1973 .....A. Andrushkin,
  Soviet Union
1974 .....M. Carrega, France
1975 .....J. Primrose, Canada
1977 .....E. Azkue, Spain
1978 .....E. Vallduvi, Spain
1979 .....M. Carrega, France
1981 .....A. Asanov, Soviet Union
1982 .....L. Giovonnetti, Italy
1983 .....J. Primrose, Canada
1985 .....M. Bednarik, Czech.
1986 .....M. Benarik, Czech.
1987 .....D. Monakov, Soviet Union
1989 .....M. Venturini, Italy
1990 .....J. Damne, E. Germany

50M FREE RIFLE STANDING

1929 .....O. Ericsson, Sweden
1930 .....Petersen, Denmark
1931 .....Amundson; Norway
1933 .....De Lisle, France
1935 .....Leskinnen, Finland
1937 .....Mazoyer, France
1939 .....Steigelmann, Germany
1947 .....I. H. Erben, Sweden
1949 .....P. Janhonen, Finland
1952 .....Kongshaug, Norway

Men *(Cont.)*

50M FREE RIFLE STAND. *(Cont.)*

1954 ....A. Bugdanov,
      Soviet Union
1958 .....Itkis, Soviet Union
1962 ....G. Anderson,
      United States

50M FREE RIFLE STAND. *(Cont.)*

1966 .....G. Anderson,
      United States
1970 .....Parkhimovitch,
      Soviet Union
1974 .....L. Wigger, United States

50M FREE RIFLE STAND. *(Cont.)*

1978 ....E. Svensson, Sweden
1982 .....K. Ivanov, Soviet Union
1986 .....P. Heinz, W. Germany
1990 .....E. C. Lee, S. Korea

Women

STANDARD RIFLE

1966 .....M. Thompson,
      United States
1970 .....M. Thompson Murdock,
      United States
1974 ....A. Pelova, Bulgaria
1978 ....W. Oliver, United States
1982 ....M. Helbig, E. Germany
1986 ....V. Letcheva, Bulgaria
1990 ....V. Letcheva, Bulgaria

AIR RIFLE

1970 ....V. Cherkasque, Soviet Union
1974 ....T. Ratkinova, Soviet Union
1978 ....W. Oliver, United States
1979 ....K. Monez, United States
1981 ....S. Romaristova,
      Soviet Union
1982 ....S. Lang, W. Germany

AIR RIFLE *(Cont.)*

1983 .....M. Helbig, E. Germany
1985 .....E. Forian, Hungary
1986 .....V. Letcheva, Bulgaria
1987 .....V. Letcheva, Bulgaria
1989 .....V. Letcheva, Bulgaria
1990 .....E.Joc, Hungary

SPORT PISTOL

1966 .....N. Rasskazova,
      Soviet Union
1970 .....N. Stoljarova, Soviet Union
1974.....N. Stoljarova, Soviet Union
1978 .....K. Dyer, United States
1982 .....P. Balogh, Hungary
1986 .....M. Dobrantcheva,
      Soviet Union
1990 .....M. Logvinenko,
      Soviet Union

AIR PISTOL

1970 .....S. Carroll, United States
1974 ....Z. Simonian, Soviet Union
1978 ....K. Hansson, Sweden
1979 ....R. Fox, United States
1981 ....N. Kalinina, Soviet Union
1982 ....M. Dobrantcheva,
      Soviet Union
1983 ....K. Bodin, Sweden
1985 ....M. Dobrantcheva,
      Soviet Union
1986 ....A. Völker, E. Germany
1987 ....J. Brajkovic, Yugoslavia
1989 ....N. Salukvadse,
      Soviet Union
1990 .....J. Sekaric, Yugoslavia

Softball

Men

MAJOR FAST PITCH

1933.................J. L. Gill Boosters, Chicago
1934.................Ke-Nash-A, Kenosha, WI
1935.................Crimson Coaches, Toledo, OH
1936.................Kodak Park, Rochester, NY
1937.................Briggs Body Team, Detroit
1938.................The Pohlers, Cincinnati
1939.................Carr's Boosters, Covington, KY
1940.................Kodak Park, Rochester, NY
1941.................Bendix Brakes, South Bend, IN
1942.................Deep Rock Oilers, Tulsa
1943.................Hammer Air Field, Fresno
1944.................Hammer Air Field, Fresno
1945.................Zollner Pistons, Fort Wayne, IN
1946.................Zollner Pistons, Fort Wayne, IN
1947.................Zollner Pistons, Fort Wayne, IN
1948.................Briggs Beautyware, Detroit
1949.................Tip Top Tailors, Toronto
1950.................Clearwater (FL) Bombers
1951.................Dow Chemical, Midland, MI
1952.................Briggs Beautyware, Detroit
1953.................Briggs Beautyware, Detroit
1954.................Clearwater (FL) Bombers
1955.................Raybestos Cardinals, Stratford, CT
1956.................Clearwater (FL) Bombers
1957.................Clearwater (FL) Bombers
1958.................Raybestos Cardinals, Stratford, CT
1959.................Sealmasters, Aurora, IL
1960.................Clearwater (FL) Bombers
1961.................Sealmasters, Aurora, IL
1962.................Clearwater (FL) Bombers
1963.................Clearwater (FL) Bombers

1964.................Burch Tool, Detroit
1965.................Sealmasters, Aurora, IL
1966.................Clearwater (FL) Bombers
1967.................Sealmasters, Aurora, IL
1968.................Clearwater (FL) Bombers
1969.................Raybestos Cardinals, Stratford, CT
1970.................Raybestos Cardinals, Stratford, CT
1971.................Welty Way, Cedar Rapids, IA
1972.................Raybestos Cardinals, Stratford, CT
1973.................Clearwater (FL) Bombers
1974.................Gianella Bros, Santa Rosa, CA
1975.................Rising Sun Hotel, Reading, PA
1976.................Raybestos Cardinals, Stratford, CT
1977.................Billard Barbell, Reading, PA
1978.................Billard Barbell, Reading, PA
1979.................McArdle Pontiac/Cadillac, Midland, MI
1980.................Peterbilt Western, Seattle
1981.................Archer Daniels Midland, Decatur, IL
1982.................Peterbilt Western, Seattle
1983.................Franklin Cardinals, Stratford, CT
1984.................California Kings, Merced, CA
1985.................Pay'n Pak, Seattle
1986.................Pay'n Pak, Seattle
1987.................Pay'n Pak, Seattle
1988.................TransAire, Elkhart, IN
1989.................Penn Corp, Sioux City, IA
1990.................Penn Corp, Sioux City, IA
1991.................Guanella Brothers, Rohnert Park, CA
1992.................Natl Health Care Disc, Sioux City, IA
1993.................Natl Health Care Disc, Sioux City, IA

Softball

Men (Cont.)

SUPER SLOW PITCH

1981 ....Howard's/Western Steer, Denver, NC	1988 ....Starpath, Monticello, KY
1982 ....Jerry's Catering, Miami	1989 ....Ritch's Salvage, Harrisburg, NC
1983 ....Howard's/Western Steer, Denver, NC	1990 ....Steele's Silver Bullets, Grafton, OH
1984 ....Howard's/Western Steer, Denver, NC	1991 ....Sunbelt/Worth, Centerville, GA
1985 ....Steele's Sports, Grafton, OH	1992 ....Ritch's/Superior, Windsor Locks, CT
1986 ....Steele's Sports, Grafton, OH	1993 ....Ritch's/Superior, Windsor Locks, CT
1987 ....Steele's Sports, Grafton, OH	

MAJOR SLOW PITCH

1953 ....Shields Construction, Newport, KY	1974 ....Howard's Furniture, Denver, NC
1954 ....Waldneck's Tavern, Cincinnati	1975 ....Pyramid Cafe, Lakewood, OH
1955 ....Lang Pet Shop, Covington, KY	1976 ....Warren Motors, Jacksonville, FL
1956 ....Gatliff Auto Sales, Newport, KY	1977 ....Nelson Painting, Oklahoma City
1957 ....Gatliff Auto Sales, Newport, KY	1978 ....Campbell Carpets, Concord, CA
1958 ....East Side Sports, Detroit	1979 ....Nelco Mfg Co, Oklahoma City
1959 ....Yorkshire Restaurant, Newport, KY	1980 ....Campbell Carpets, Concord, CA
1960 ....Hamilton Tailoring, Cincinnati	1981 ....Elite Coating, Gordon, CA
1961 ....Hamilton Tailoring, Cincinnati	1982 ....Triangle Sports, Minneapolis
1962 ....Skip Hogan A.C., Pittsburgh	1983 ....No. 1 Electric & Heating, Gastonia, NC
1963 ....Gatliff Auto Sales, Newport, KY	1984 ....Lilly Air Systems, Chicago
1964 ....Skip Hogan A.C., Pittsburgh	1985 ....Blanton's, Fayetteville, NC
1965 ....Skip Hogan A.C., Pittsburgh	1986 ....Non-Ferrous Metals, Cleveland
1966 ....Michael's Lounge, Detroit	1987 ....Starpath, Monticello, KY
1967 ....Jim's Sport Shop, Pittsburgh	1988 ....Bell Corp/FAF, Tampa, FL
1968 ....County Sports, Levittown, NY	1989 ....Ritch's Salvage, Harrisburg, NC
1969 ....Copper Hearth, Milwaukee	1990 ....New Construction, Shelbyville, IN
1970 ....Little Caesar's, Southgate, MI	1991 ....Riverside Paving, Louisville, KY
1971 ....Pile Drivers, Virginia Beach, VA	1992 ....Vernon's, Jacksonville, FL
1972 ....Jiffy Club, Louisville, KY	1993 ....Back Porch/Destin Roofing, Destin, FL
1973 ....Howard's Furniture, Denver, NC	

Women

MAJOR FAST PITCH

1933 ....Great Northerns, Chicago	1964 ....Erv Lind Florists, Portland, OR
1934 ....Hart Motors, Chicago	1965 ....Orange (CA) Lionettes
1935 ....Bloomer Girls, Cleveland	1966 ....Raybestos Brakettes, Stratford, CT
1936 ....Nat'l Screw & Mfg, Cleveland	1967 ....Raybestos Brakettes, Stratford, CT
1937 ....Nat'l Screw & Mfg, Cleveland	1968 ....Raybestos Brakettes, Stratford, CT
1938 ....J. J. Krieg's, Alameda, CA	1969 ....Orange (CA) Lionettes
1939 ....J. J. Krieg's, Alameda, CA	1970 ....Orange (CA) Lionettes
1940 ....Arizona Ramblers, Phoenix	1971 ....Raybestos Brakettes, Stratford, CT
1941 ....Higgins Midgets, Tulsa	1972 ....Raybestos Brakettes, Stratford, CT
1942 ....Jax Maids, New Orleans	1973 ....Raybestos Brakettes, Stratford, CT
1943 ....Jax Maids, New Orleans	1974 ....Raybestos Brakettes, Stratford, CT
1944 ....Lind & Pomeroy, Portland, OR	1975 ....Raybestos Brakettes, Stratford, CT
1945 ....Jax Maids, New Orleans	1976 ....Raybestos Brakettes, Stratford, CT
1946 ....Jax Maids, New Orleans	1977 ....Raybestos Brakettes, Stratford, CT
1947 ....Jax Maids, New Orleans	1978 ....Raybestos Brakettes, Stratford, CT
1948 ....Arizona Ramblers, Phoenix	1979 ....Sun City (AZ) Saints
1949 ....Arizona Ramblers, Phoenix	1980 ....Raybestos Brakettes, Stratford, CT
1950 ....Orange (CA) Lionettes	1981 ....Orlando (FL) Rebels
1951 ....Orange (CA) Lionettes	1982 ....Raybestos Brakettes, Stratford, CT
1952 ....Orange (CA) Lionettes	1983 ....Raybestos Brakettes, Stratford, CT
1953 ....Betsy Ross Rockets, Fresno	1984 ....Los Angeles Diamonds
1954 ....Leach Motor Rockets, Fresno	1985 ....Hi-Ho Brakettes, Stratford, CT
1955 ....Orange (CA) Lionettes	1986 ....Southern California Invasion, Los Angeles
1956 ....Orange (CA) Lionettes	1987 ....Orange County Majestics, Anaheim, CA
1957 ....Hacienda Rockets, Fresno	1988 ....Hi-Ho Brakettes, Stratford, CT
1958 ....Raybestos Brakettes, Stratford, CT	1989 ....Whittier (CA) Raiders
1959 ....Raybestos Brakettes, Stratford, CT	1990 ....Raybestos Brakettes, Stratford, CT
1960 ....Raybestos Brakettes, Stratford, CT	1991 ....Raybestos Brakettes, Stratford, CT
1961 ....Gold Sox, Whittier, CA	1992 ....Raybestos Brakettes, Stratford, CT
1962 ....Orange (CA) Lionettes	1993 ....Redding Rebels, Redding, CA
1963 ....Raybestos Brakettes, Stratford, CT	

Women *(Cont.)*
MAJOR SLOW PITCH

1959..........Pearl Laundry, Richmond, VA	1977..........Fox Valley Lassies, St Charles, IL
1960..........Carolina Rockets, High Pt, NC	1978..........Bob Hoffman's Dots, Miami
1961..........Dairy Cottage, Covington, KY	1979..........Bob Hoffman's Dots, Miami
1962..........Dana Gardens, Cincinnati	1980..........Howard's Rubi-Otts, Graham, NC
1963..........Dana Gardens, Cincinnati	1981..........Tifton (GA) Tomboys
1964..........Dana Gardens, Cincinnati	1982..........Richmond (VA) Stompers
1965..........Art's Acres, Omaha	1983..........Spooks, Anoka, MN
1966..........Dana Gardens, Cincinnati	1984..........Spooks, Anoka, MN
1967..........Ridge Maintenance, Cleveland	1985..........Key Ford Mustangs, Pensacola, FL
1968..........Escue Pontiac, Cincinnati	1986..........Sur-Way Tomboys, Tifton, GA
1969..........Converse Dots, Hialeah, FL	1987..........Key Ford Mustangs, Pensacola, FL
1970..........Rutenschruder Floral, Cincinnati	1988..........Spooks, Anoka, MN
1971..........Gators, Ft Lauderdale, FL	1989..........Canaan's Illusions, Houston
1972..........Riverside Ford, Cincinnati	1990..........Spooks, Anoka, MN
1973..........Sweeney Chevrolet, Cincinnati	1991..........Kannan's Illusions, San Antonio, TX
1974..........Marks Brothers Dots, Miami	1992..........Universal Plastics, Cookeville, TN
1975..........Marks Brothers Dots, Miami	1993..........Universal Plastics, Cookeville, TN
1976..........Sorrento's Pizza, Cincinnati	

Speedskating

All World Champions
MEN

1891.....Joseph F. Donoghue, US	1932.....Ivar Ballangrud, Norway	1967.....Kees Verkerk, Holland
1893.....Jaap Eden, Holland	1933.....Hans Engnestangen, Nor.	1968.....Fred Anton Maier, Nor.
1895.....Jaap Eden, Holland	1934.....Bernt Evensen,.Norway	1969.....Dag Fornaes, Norway
1896.....Jaap Eden, Holland	1935.....Michael Staksrud, Nor.	1970.....Ard Schenk, Holland
1897.....Jack K. McCulloch, Can.	1936.....Ivar Ballangrud, Norway	1971.....Ard Schenk, Holland
1898.....Peder Ostlund, Norway	1937.....Michael Staksrud, Nor.	1972.....Ard Schenk, Holland
1899.....Peder Ostlund, Norway	1938.....Ivar Ballangrud, Norway	1973.....Göran Claeson, Sweden
1900.....Edvard Engelsaas, Nor.	1939.....Birger Wasenius, Finland	1974.....Sten Stensen, Norway
1901.....Franz F. Wathan, Finland	1947.....Lassi Parkkinen, Finland	1975.....Harm Kuipers, Holland
1904.....Sigurd Mathisen, Norway	1948.....Odd Lundberg, Norway	1976.....Piet Kleine,.Holland
1905.....C. Coen de Koning, Holl.	1949.....Kornel Pajor, Hungary	1977.....Eric Heiden, USA
1908.....Oscar Mathisen, Norway	1950.....Hjalmar Andersen, Nor.	1978.....Eric Heiden, USA
1909.....Oscar Mathisen, Norway	1951.....Hjalmar Andersen, Nor.	1979.....Eric Heiden, USA
1910.....Nikolai Strunnikov, Russia	1952.....Hjalmar Andersen, Nor.	1980.....Hilbert van der Duin, Holl.
1911.....Nikolai Strunnikov, Russia	1953.....Oleg Goncharenko, Sov U	1981.....Amund Sjobrand, Norway
1912.....Oscar Mathisen, Norway	1954.....Boris Shilkov, Sov U	1982.....Hilbert van der Duin, Holl
1913.....Oscar Mathisen, Norway	1955.....Sigvard Ericsson, Swe.	1983.....Rolf Falk-Larssen, Nor.
1914.....Oscar Mathisen, Norway	1956.....Oleg Goncharenko, Sov U	1984.....Oleg Bozhev, Sov U
1922.....Harald Strom, Norway	1957.....Knut Johannesen, Nor.	1985.....Hein Vergeer, Holland
1923.....Klas Thunberg, Finland	1958.....Oleg Goncharenko, Sov U	1986.....Hein Vergeer, Holland
1924.....Roald Larsen, Norway	1959.....Juhani Järvinen, Finland	1987.....Nikolai Guliaev, Sov U
1925.....Klas Thunberg, Finland	1960.....Boris Stenin, Sov U	1988.....Eric Flaim, USA
1926.....Ivar Ballangrud, Norway	1961.....Henk van der Grift, Holl.	1989.....Leo Visser, Holland
1927.....Bernt Evensen, Norway	1962.....Viktor Kosichkin, Sov U	1990.....Johann Olav Koss, Nor.
1928.....Klas Thunberg, Finland	1963.....Jonny Nilsson, Sweden	1991.....Johann Olav Koss, Nor.
1929.....Klas Thunberg, Finland	1964.....Knut Johannesen, Nor.	1992.....Roberto Sighel, Italy
1930.....Michael Staksrud, Nor.	1965.....Per Ivar Moe, Norway	1993.....Falko Zandstra, Holland
1931.....Klas Thunberg, Finland	1966.....Kees Verkerk, Holland	

WOMEN

1936.....Kit Klein, USA	1953.....Khalida Shchegoleeva, Soviet Union	1962.....Inga Artamonova, Sov U
1937.....Laila Schou Nilsen, Nor.	1954.....Lidia Selikhova, Sov U	1963.....Lidia Skoblikova, Sov U
1938.....Laila Schou Nilsen, Nor.	1955.....Rimma Zhukova, Sov U	1964.....Lidia Skoblikova, Sov U
1939.....Verné Lesche, Finland	1956.....Sofia Kondakova, Sov U	1965.....Inga Artamonova, Sov U
1947.....Verné Lesche, Finland	1957.....Inga Artamonova, Sov U	1966.....Valentina Stenina, Sov U
1948.....Maria Isakova, Sov U	1958.....Inga Artamonova, Sov U	1967.....Stien Kaiser, Holland
1949.....Maria Isakova, Sov U	1959.....Tamara Rylova, Sov U	1968.....Stien Kaiser, Holland
1950.....Maria Isakova, Sov U	1960.....Valentina Stenina, Sov U	1969.....Lasma Kauniste, Sov U
1951.....Eevi Huttunen, Finland	1961.....Valentina Stenina, Sov U	1970.....Atje Keulen-Deelstra, Holl.
1952.....Lidia Selikhova, Sov U		1971.....Nina Statkevich, Sov U

All World Champions *(Cont.)*

WOMEN

Year	Champion	Year	Champion	Year	Champion
1972	Atje Keulen-Deelstra, Holl.	1980	Natalia Petruseva, Sov U	1988	Karin Kania, GDR
1973	Atje Keulen-Deelstra, Holl.	1981	Natalia Petruseva, Sov U	1989	Constanze Moser, GDR
1974	Atje Keulen-Deelstra, Holl.	1982	Karin Busch, GDR	1990	Jacqueline Börner, GDR
1975	Karin Kessow, GDR	1983	Andrea Schöne,.GDR	1991	Gunda Kleemann, Ger.
1976	Sylvia Burka, Canada	1984	Karin Enke-Busch, GDR	1992	Gunda Niemann-Kleemann, Germany
1977	Vera Bryndzej, Sov U	1985	Andrea Schöne, GDR	1993	Gunda Niemann, Germany
1978	Tatiana Averina, Sov U	1986	Karin Kania-Enke, GDR		
1979	Beth Heiden, USA	1987	Karin Kania, GDR		

Squash

National Men's Champions

Year	Champion, Hometown	Year	Champion, Hometown
1907	John A. Miskey, Philadelphia	1952	Harry B. Conlon, Buffalo
1908	John A. Miskey, Philadelphia	1953	Ernest Howard, Toronto
1909	William L. Freeland, Philadelphia	1954	G. Diehl Mateer Jr., Philadelphia
1910	John A. Miskey, Philadelphia	1955	Henri R. Salaun, Hartford, CT
1911	Francis S. White, Philadelphia	1956	G. Diehl Mateer Jr., Philadelphia
1912	Constantine Hutchins, Boston	1957	Henri R. Salaun, Boston
1913	Morton L. Newhall, Philadelphia	1958	Henri R. Salaun, Boston
1914	Constantine Hutchins, Boston	1959	Benjamin H. Heckscher, Philadelphia
1915	Stanley W. Pearson, Philadelphia	1960	G. Diehl Mateer Jr., Philadelphia
1916	Stanley W. Pearson, Philadelphia	1961	Henri R. Salaun, Hartford, CT
1917	Stanley W. Pearson, Philadelphia	1962	Samuel P. Howe III, Philadelphia
1918-19	No tournament	1963	Benjamin H. Heckscher, Philadelphia
1920	Charles C. Peabody, Boston	1964	Ralph E. Howe, New York
1921	Stanley W. Pearson, Philadelphia	1965	Stephen T. Vehslage, New York
1922	Stanley W. Pearson, Philadelphia	1966	Victor Niederhoffer, Chicago
1923	Stanley W. Pearson, Philadelphia	1967	Samuel P. Howe III, Philadelphia
1924	Gerald Roberts, England	1968	Colin Adair, Montreal
1925	W. Palmer Dixon, New York	1969	Anil Nayar, Boston
1926	W. Palmer Dixon, New York	1970	Anil Nayar, Boston
1927	Myles Baker, Boston	1971	Colin Adair, Montreal
1928	Herbert N. Rawlins Jr., New York	1972	Victor Niederhoffer, New York
1929	J. Lawrence Pool New York	1973	Victor Niederhoffer, New York
1930	Herbert N. Rawlins Jr., New York	1974	Victor Niederhoffer, New York
1931	J. Lawrence Pool, New York	1975	Victor Niederhoffer, New York
1932	Beckman H. Pool, New York	1976	Peter Briggs, New York
1933	Beckman H. Pool, New York	1977	Thomas E. Page, Philadelphia
1934	Neil J. Sullivan II, Philadelphia	1978	Michael Desaulniers, Montreal
1935	Donald Strachan, Philadelphia	1979	Mario Sanchez, Mexico
1936	Germain G. Glidden, New York	1980	Michael Desaulniers, Montreal
1937	Germain G. Glidden, New York	1981	Mark Alger, Tacoma, WA
1938	Germain G. Glidden, New York	1982	John Nimick, Narberth, PA
1939	Donald Strachan, Philadelphia	1983	Kenton Jernigan, Newport, RI
1940	A. Willing Patterson, Philadelphia	1984	Kenton Jernigan, Newport, RI
1941	Charles M. P. Britton, Philadelphia	1985	Kenton Jernigan, Newport, RI
1942	Charles M. P. Britton, Philadelphia	1986	Hugh LaBossier, Seattle
1943-45	No tournament	1987	Frank J. Stanley IV, Princeton, NJ
1946	Charles M. P. Britton, Philadelphia	1988	Scott Dulmage, Toronto
1947	Charles M. P. Britton, Philadelphia	1989	Rodolfo Rodriquez, Mexico
1948	Stanley W. Pearson Jr., Philadelphia	1990	Hector Barragan, Mexico
1949	H. Hunter Lott Jr., Philadelphia	1991	Hector Barragan, Mexico
1950	Edward J. Hahn, Detroit	1992	Hector Barragan, Mexico
1951	Edward J. Hahn, Detroit	1993	Hector Barragan, Mexico

Squash (Cont.)

National Women's Champions

Year	Champion, Hometown	Year	Champion, Hometown
1928	Eleanora Sears, Boston	1963	Margaret Varner, Wilmington, DE
1929	Margaret Howe, Boston	1964	Ann Wetzel, Philadelphia
1930	Hazel Wightman, Boston	1965	Joyce Davenport, Philadelphia
1931	Ruth Banks, Philadelphia	1966	Betty Meade, Philadelphia
1932	Margaret Howe, Boston	1967	Betty Meade, Philadelphia
1933	Susan Noel, England	1968	Betty Meade, Philadelphia
1934	Margaret Howe, Boston	1969	Joyce Davenport, Philadelphia
1935	Margot Lumb, England	1970	Nina Moyer, Princeton, NJ
1936	Anne Page, Philadelphia	1971	Carol Thesieres, Philadelphia
1937	Anne Page, Philadelphia	1972	Nina Moyer, Princeton, NJ
1938	Cecile Bowes, Philadelphia	1973	Gretchen Spruance, Wilmington, DE
1939	Anne Page, Philadelphia	1974	Gretchen Spruance, Wilmington, DE
1940	Cecile Bowes, Philadelphia	1975	Ginny Akabane, Rochester, NY
1941	Cecile Bowes, Philadelphia	1976	Gretchen Spruance, Wilmington, DE
1942-46	No tournament	1977	Gretchen Spruance, Wilmington, DE
1947	Anne Page Homer, Philadelphia	1978	Gretchen Spruance, Wilmington, DE
1948	Cecile Bowes, Philadelphia	1979	Heather McKay, Toronto
1949	Janet Morgan, England	1980	Barbara Maltby, Philadelphia
1950	Betty Howe, New Haven, CT	1981	Barbara Maltby, Philadelphia
1951	Jane Austin, Philadelphia	1982	Alicia McConnell, New York
1952	Margaret Howe, Boston	1983	Alicia McConnell, New York
1953	Margaret Howe, Boston	1984	Alicia McConnell, New York
1954	Lois Dilks, Philadelphia	1985	Alicia McConnell, New York
1955	Janet Morgan, England	1986	Alicia McConnell, Bala Cynwyd, PA
1956	Betty Howe Constable, Princeton, NJ	1987	Alicia McConnell, New York
1957	Betty Howe Constable, Princeton, NJ	1988	Alicia McConnell, New York
1958	Betty Howe Constable, Princeton, NJ	1989	Demer Holleran, Hanover, NH
1959	Betty Howe Constable, Princeton, NJ	1990	Demer Holleran, Hanover, NH
1960	Margaret Varner, Wilmington, DE	1991	Demer Holleran, Hanover, NH
1961	Margaret Varner, Wilmington, DE	1992	Demer Holleran, Hanover, NH
1962	Margaret Varner, Wilmington, DE	1993	Demer Holleran, Hanover, NH

Triathlon

Ironman Championship

MEN

Date	Winner	Time	Site
1978	Gordon Haller	11:46	Waikiki Beach
1979	Tom Warren	11:15:56	Waikiki Beach
1980	Dave Scott	9:24:33	Ala Moana Park
1981	John Howard	9:38:29	Kailua-Kona
1982	Scott Tinley	9:19:41	Kailua-Kona
1982	Dave Scott	9:08:23	Kailua-Kona
1983	Dave Scott	9:05:57	Kailua-Kona
1984	Dave Scott	8:54:20	Kailua-Kona
1985	Scott Tinley	8:50:54	Kailua-Kona
1986	Dave Scott	8:28:37	Kailua-Kona
1987	Dave Scott	8:34:13	Kailua-Kona
1988	Scott Molina	8:31:00	Kailua-Kona
1989	Mark Allen	8:09:15	Kailua-Kona
1990	Mark Allen	8:28:17	Kailua-Kona
1991	Mark Allen	8:18:32	Kailua-Kona
1992	Mark Allen	8:09:09	Kailua-Kona

WOMEN

Date	Winner	Time	Site
1978	No finishers		
1979	Lyn Lemaire	12:55	Waikiki Beach
1980	Robin Beck	11:21:24	Ala Moana Park
1981	Linda Sweeney	12:00:32	Kailua-Kona
1982	Kathleen McCartney	11:09:40	Kailua-Kona
1982	Julie Leach	10:54:08	Kailua-Kona

Ironman Championship *(Cont.)*

WOMEN *(Cont.)*

Date	Winner	Time	Site
1983	Sylviane Puntous	10:43:36	Kailua-Kona
1984	Sylviane Puntous	10:25:13	Kailua-Kona
1985	Joanne Ernst	10:25:22	Kailua-Kona
1986	Paula Newby-Fraser	9:49:14	Kailua-Kona
1987	Erin Baker	9:35:25	Kailua-Kona
1988	Paula Newby-Fraser	9:01:01	Kailua-Kona
1989	Paula Newby-Fraser	9:00:56	Kailua-Kona
1990	Erin Baker	9:13:42	Kailua-Kona
1991	Paula Newby-Fraser	9:07:52	Kailua-Kona
1992	Paula Newby-Fraser	8:55:29	Kailua-Kona

Note: The Ironman Championship was contested twice in 1982.

Volleyball

World Champions

MEN

Year	Winner	Runnerup	Site
1949	Soviet Union	Czechoslovakia	Prague, Czechoslovakia
1952	Soviet Union	Czechoslovakia	Moscow, Soviet Union
1956	Czechoslovakia	Soviet Union	Paris, France
1960	Soviet Union	Czechoslovakia	Rio de Janeiro, Brazil
1962	Soviet Union	Czechoslovakia	Moscow, Soviet Union
1966	Czechoslovakia	Romania	Prague, Czechoslovakia
1970	East Germany	Bulgaria	Sofia, Bulgaria
1974	Poland	Soviet Union	Mexico City
1978	Soviet Union	Italy	Rome, Italy
1982	Soviet Union	Brazil	Buenos Aires, Argentina
1986	United States	Soviet Union	Paris, France
1990	Italy	Cuba	Rio de Janeiro, Brazil

WOMEN

Year	Winner	Runnerup	Site
1952	Soviet Union	Poland	Moscow, Soviet Union
1956	Soviet Union	Romania	Paris, France
1960	Soviet Union	Japan	Rio de Janeiro, Brazil
1962	Japan	Soviet Union	Moscow, Soviet Union
1966	Japan	United States	Prague, Czechoslovakia
1970	Soviet Union	Japan	Sofia, Bulgaria
1974	Japan	Soviet Union	Mexico City
1978	Cuba	Japan	Rome, Italy
1982	China	Peru	Lima, Peru
1986	China	Cuba	Prague, Czechoslovakia
1990	Soviet Union	China	Beijing, China

U.S. Men's Open Champions—Gold Division

Year	Champion	Year	Champion
1928	Germantown, PA YMCA	1943-44	No Championships
1929	Hyde Park YMCA, IL	1945	North Ave. YMCA, IL
1930	Hyde Park YMCA, IL	1946	Pasadena, CA YMCA
1931	San Antonio, TX YMCA	1947	North Ave. YMCA, IL
1932	San Antonio, TX YMCA	1948	Hollywood, CA YMCA
1933	Houston, TX YMCA	1949	Downtown YMCA, CA
1934	Houston, TX YMCA	1950	Long Beach, CA YMCA
1935	Houston, TX YMCA	1951	Hollywood, CA YMCA
1936	Houston, TX YMCA	1952	Hollywood, CA YMCA
1937	Duncan YMCA, IL	1953	Hollywood, CA YMCA
1938	Houston, TX YMCA	1954	Stockton, CA YMCA
1939	Houston, TX YMCA	1955	Stockton, CA YMCA
1940	Los Angeles AC, CA	1956	Hollywood, CA YMCA Stars
1941	North Ave. YMCA, IL	1957	Hollywood, CA YMCA Stars
1942	North Ave. YMCA, IL	1958	Hollywood, CA YMCA Stars

U.S. Men's Open Champions—Gold Division *(Cont.)*

1959	Hollywood, CA YMCA Stars	1977	Chuck's, Santa Barbara
1960	Westside JCC, CA	1978	Chuck's, Los Angeles
1961	Hollywood, CA YMCA	1979	Nautilus, Long Beach
1962	Hollywood, CA YMCA	1980	Olympic Club, San Francisco
1963	Hollywood, CA YMCA	1981	Nautilus, Long Beach
1964	Hollywood, CA YMCA Stars	1982	Chuck's, Los Angeles
1965	Westside JCC, CA	1983	Nautilus Pacifica, CA
1966	Sand & Sea Club, CA	1984	Nautilus Pacifica, CA
1967	Fresno, CA VBC	1985	Molten/SSI Torrance, CA
1968	Westside JCC, L.A., CA	1986	Molten, Torrance, CA
1969	Los Angeles, CA YMCA	1987	Molten, Torrance, CA
1970	Chart House, San Diego	1988	Molten, Torrance, CA
1971	Santa Monica, CA YMCA	1989	Not held
1972	Chart House, San Diego	1990	Nike, Carson, CA
1973	Chuck's Steak, L.A., CA	1991	Offshore, Woodland Hills, CA
1974	Un of CA Santa Barbara	1992	Creole Six Pack, Elmhurst, NY
1975	Chart House, San Diego	1993	Asics, Huntington Beach, CA
1976	Maliabu, L.A., CA		

U.S. Women's Open Champions—Gold Division

1949	Eagles, Houston TX	1972	E Pluribus Unum, Houston
1950	Voit #1, Santa Monica, CA	1973	E Pluribus Unum, Houston
1951	Eagles, Houston, TX	1974	Renegades, Los Angeles, CA
1952	Voit #1, Santa Monica, CA	1975	Adidas, Norwalk, CA
1953	Voit #1, Los Angeles, CA	1976	Pasadena, TX
1954	Houstonettes, Houston, TX	1977	Spoilers, Hermosa, CA
1955	Mariners, Santa Monica, CA	1978	Nick's, Los Angeles, CA
1956	Mariners, Santa Monica, CA	1979	Mavericks, Los Angeles, CA
1957	Mariners, Santa Monica, CA	1980	NAVA, Fountain Valley, CA
1958	Mariners, Santa Monica, CA	1981	Utah State, Logan, UT
1959	Mariners, Santa Monica, CA	1982	Monarchs, Hilo, HI
1960	Mariners, Santa Monica, CA	1983	Syntex, Stockton, CA
1961	Breakers, Long Beach, CA	1984	Chrysler, Palo Alto, CA
1962	Shamrocks, Long Beach, CA	1985	Merrill Lynch, Arizona
1963	Shamrocks, Long Beach, CA	1986	Merrill Lynch, Arizona
1964	Shamrocks, Long Beach, CA	1987	Chrysler, Pleasanton, CA
1965	Shamrocks, Long Beach, CA	1988	Chrysler, Hayward, CA
1966	Renegades, Los Angeles, CA	1989	Plymouth, Hayward, CA
1967	Shamrocks, Long Beach, CA	1990	Plymouth, Hayward, CA
1968	Shamrocks, Long Beach, CA	1991	Fitness, Champaign, IL
1969	Shamrocks, Long Beach, CA	1992	Nick's Kronies, Chicago, IL
1970	Shamrocks, Long Beach, CA	1993	Nick's Fishmarket/Gold's Gym, Chicago, IL
1971	Renegades, Los Angeles, CA		

Wrestling

United States National Champions

1983

FREESTYLE			GRECO-ROMAN	
105.5	Rich Salamone	105.5	T. J. Jones
114.5	Joe Gonzales	114.5	Mark Fuller
125.5	Joe Corso	125.5	Rob Hermann
136.5	Rich Dellagatta*	136.5	Dan Mello
149.5	Bill Hugent	149.5	Jim Martinez
163	Lee Kemp	163	James Andre
180.5	Chris Campbell	180.5	Steve Goss
198	Pete Bush	198	Steve Fraser*
220	Greg Gibson	220	Dennis Koslowski
Hvy	Bruce Baumgartner	Hvy	No champion
Team	Sunkist Kids	Team	Minnesota Wrestling Club

*Outstanding wrestler

United States National Champions

1984

FREESTYLE		GRECO-ROMAN	
105.5	Rich Salamone	105.5	T. J. Jones
114.5	Charlie Heard	114.5	Mark Fuller
125.5	Joe Corso	125.5	Frank Famiano
136.5	Rick Dellagatta	136.5	Dan Mello
149.5	Andre Metzger	149.5	Jim Martinez*
163	Dave Schultz*	163	John Matthews
180.5	Mark Schultz	180.5	Tom Press
198	Steve Fraser	198	Mike Houck
220	Harold Smith	220	No champion
Hvy	Bruce Baumgartner	Hvy	No champion
Team	Sunkist Kids	Team	Adirondack Three-Style, WA

1985

105.5	Tim Vanni	105.5	T. J. Jones
114.5	Jim Martin	114.5	Mark Fuller
125.5	Charlie Heard	125.5	Eric Seward*
136.5	Darryl Burley	136.5	Buddy Lee
149.5	Bill Nugent*	149.5	Jim Martinez
163	Kenny Monday	163	David Butler
180.5	Mike Sheets	180.5	Chris Catallo
198	Mark Schultz	198	Mike Houck
220	Greg Gibson	220	Greg Gibson
286	Bruce Baumgartner	286	Dennis Koslowski
Team	Sunkist Kids	Team	U.S. Marine Corps

1986

105.5	Rich Salamone	105.5	Eric Wetzel
114.5	Joe Gonzales	114.5	Shawn Sheldon
125.5	Kevin Darkus	125.5	Anthony Amado
136.5	John Smith	136.5	Frank Famiano
149.5	Andre Metzger*	149.5	Jim Martinez
163	Dave Schultz	163	David Butler*
180.5	Mark Schultz	180.5	Darryl Gholar
198	Jim Scherr	198	Derrick Waldroup
220	Dan Severn	220	Dennis Koslowski
286	Bruce Baumgartner	286	Duane Koslowski
Team	Sunkist Kids (Div. I)	Team	U.S. Marine Corps (Div. I)
	Hawkeye Wrestling Club (Div. II)		U.S. Navy (Div. II)

1987

105.5	Takashi Irie	105.5	Eric Wetzel
114.5	Mitsuru Sato	114.5	Shawn Sheldon
125.5	Barry Davis	125.5	Eric Seward
136.5	Takumi Adachi	136.5	Frank Famiano
149.5	Andre Metzger	149.5	Jim Martinez
163	Dave Schultz*	163	David Butler
180.5	Mark Schultz	180.5	Chris Catallo
198	Jim Scherr	198	Derrick Waldroup*
220	Bill Scherr	220	Dennis Koslowski
286	Bruce Baumgartner	286	Duane Koslowski
Team	Sunkist Kids (Div. I)	Team	U.S. Marine Corp (Div. I)
	Team Foxcatcher (Div. II)		U.S. Army (Div. II)

1988

105.5	Tim Vanni	105.5	T. J. Jones
114.5	Joe Gonzales	114.5	Shawn Sheldon
125.5	Kevin Darkus	125.5	Gogi Parseghian*
136.5	John Smith*	136.5	Dalen Wasmund
149.5	Nate Carr	149.5	Craig Pollard
163	Kenny Monday	163	Tony Thomas
180.5	Dave Schultz	180.5	Darryl Gholar
198	Melvin Douglas III	198	Mike Carolan
220	Bill Scherr	220	Dennis Koslowski
286	Bruce Baumgartner	286	Duane Koslowski
Team	Sunkist Kids (Div. I)	Team	U.S. Marine Corps (Div. I)
	Team Foxcatcher (Div. II)		Sunkist Kids (Div. II)

FREESTYLE

1989

105.5	Tim Vanni
114.5	Zeke Jones
125.5	Brad Penrith
136.5	John Smith
149.5	Nate Carr
163	Rob Koll
180.5	Rico Chiapparelli
198	Jim Scherr*
220	Bill Scherr
286	Bruce Baumgartner
Team	Sunkist Kids (Div. I)
	Team Foxcatcher (Div. II)

1990

105.5	Rob Eiter
114.5	Zeke Jones
125.5	Joe Melchiore
136.5	John Smith
149.5	Nate Carr
163	Rob Koll
180.5	Royce Alger
198	Chris Campbell*
220	Bill Scherr
286	Bruce Baumgartner
Team	Sunkist Kids (Div. I)
	Team Foxcatcher (Div. II)

1991

105.5	Tim Vanni
114.5	Zeke Jones
125.5	Brad Penrith
136.5	John Smith*
149.5	Townsend Saunders
163	Kenny Monday
180.5	Kevin Jackson
198	Chris Campbell
220	Mark Coleman
286	Bruce Baumgartner
Team	Sunkist Kids (Div. I)
	Jets USA (Div. II)

1992

105.5	Rob Elter
114.5	Jack Griffin
125.5	Kendall Cross*
136.5	John Fisher
149.5	Matt Demaray
163	Greg Elinsky
180.5	Royce Alger
198	Dan Chaid
220	Bill Scherr
286	Bruce Baumgartner
Team	Sunkist Kids (Div. I)
	Team Foxcatcher (Div. II)

1993

105.5	Rob Elter
114.5	Zeke Jones
125.5	Brad Penrith
136.5	Tom Brands
149.5	Matt Demaray
163	Dave Schultz*
180.5	Kevin Jackson
198	Melvin Douglas
220	Kirk Trost
286	Bruce Baumgartner
Team	Sunkist Kids (Div. I)
	Team Foxcatcher (Div. II)

*Outstanding wrestler

GRECO-ROMAN

1989

105.5	Lew Dorrance
114.5	Mark Fuller
125.5	Gogi Parseghian
136.5	Isaac Anderson
149.5	Andy Seras*
163	David Butler
180.5	John Morgan
198	Michial Foy
220	Steve Lawson
286	Craig Pittman
Team	U.S. Marine Corps (Div. I)
	Jets USA (Div. II)

1990

105.5	Lew Dorrance
114.5	Sam Henson
125.5	Mark Pustelnik
136.5	Isaac Anderson
149.5	Andy Seras
163	David Butler
180.5	Derrick Waldroup
198	Randy Coutre*
220	Chris Tironi
286	Matt Ghaffari
Team	Jets USA (Div. I)
	California Jets (Div. II)

1991

105.5	Eric Wetzel
114.5	Shawn Sheldon
125.5	Frank Famiano
136.5	Buddy Lee
149.5	Andy Seras
163	Gordy Morgan
180.5	John Morgan*
198	Michial Foy
220	Dennis Koslowski
286	Craig Pittman
Team	Jets USA (Div. I)
	Sunkist Kids (Div. II)

1992

105.5	Eric Wetzel
114.5	Mark Fuller
125.5	Dennis Hall
136.5	Buddy Lee*
149.5	Rodney Smith
163	Travis West
180.5	John Morgan
198	Michial Foy
220	Dennis Koslowski
286	Matt Ghaffari
Team	NY Athletic Club (Div. I)
	Sunkist Kids (Div. II)

1993

105.5	Eric Wetzel
114.5	Shawn Sheldon
125.5	Dennis Hall*
136.5	Shon Lewis
149.5	Andy Seras
163	Gordy Morgan
180.5	Dan Henderson
198	Randy Couture
220	James Johnson
286	Matt Ghaffari
Team	NY Athletic Club (Div. I)
	Sunkist Kids (Div. II)

Sports Market

How this man turned a tiny sneaker company into the most powerful force in sports

AUGUST 16, 1993 · $2.95 (CAN. $3.85)

Sports Illustrated

Nike
Boss
Phil
Knight

BURK UZZLE

Dollars and Sense

New faces, new teams and new deals abounded as sports struggled to keep the money flowing | by JOHN STEINBREDER

I N MANY WAYS IT WAS BUSINESS AS usual in the sports market last year as athletes signed monster contracts, owners padded huge bank accounts, and franchise values soared higher than a big league pop-up. But 1993 was also a time of great change. Free agency finally arrived in the National Football League. Sound thinking finally came to the commissioner's office of the National Hockey League. And baseball decided to add a couple of wild cards to its playoff scheme.

Nowhere did the winds of change blow more strongly than in the NFL. After six years of court battles, the owners and players agreed to a new labor pact that shortened the college draft to eight rounds, put a cap on rookie salaries and gave players the right to become free agents after five years in the league. The effects of those moves were felt almost immediately. More than 100 players changed teams before training camps opened last summer, including big names such as Reggie White (four years, $18 million from the Green Bay Packers) and Gary Clark (three years, $6 million

from the Phoenix Cardinals). And the average annual NFL salary soared 33%, to $643,000. When the last collective bargaining agreement expired in 1987, that figure had stood at just over $200,000.

But don't worry about the owners suddenly having to scrounge for money. They will soon begin splitting $280 million in franchise fees from the two of the five cities—Baltimore, Charlotte, Jacksonville, Memphis and St. Louis—that win the right to field NFL teams in 1995. They are also likely to institute a salary cap next year (projected at $31 million to $35 million per team) for all their players, a move that may actually *reduce* the average annual salary because more than half of all NFL teams already have payrolls above the cap projections. And in a step that should lessen many of their tax burdens, the owners have agreed to permit franchises to be part of privately held corporations, giving them the ability to deduct any losses their teams may incur from profits in their other enterprises.

The developments in hockey were almost as dramatic, thanks to the election

of Gary Bettman as NHL commissioner. A longtime deputy to National Basketball Association head David Stern, Bettman learned how to run a professional sports league "at the feet of the master," as he described work with his former boss, and he brings energy, intellect and much-needed new perspective to the job. His strong grasp of marketing and his keen understanding of the importance of television should pay big dividends to a league that has never lived up to its potential.

The early returns on the Bettman regime are good. Already the new commissioner has assumed control of the league's anemic merchandise-licensing operations and signed on heavyweight corporate sponsors such as Gillette and Kellogg's. In addition, he has led a realignment of all NHL divisions and

A newly affluent White (92) met Randall Cunningham and his former team in September.

renamed its conferences, dropping the often confusing Wales and Campbell in favor of the pedestrian but universally understood East and West. And he has dumped the old divisional playoff system, which sometimes forced good teams from strong divisions to sit out postseason play, in favor of a more sensible format featuring the top eight teams in each conference, à la the NBA.

But perhaps Bettman's most important move was bringing two marketing and entertainment tours de force—Blockbuster Video and the Disney Co.—into the league as owners. The Florida Panthers (Blockbuster) and the Mighty Ducks of Anaheim (Disney) began play in 1993, and while their arrival

If needed, Eisner and the Mighty Ducks can call on the services of a mighty mouse.

threatens to dilute an already shallow talent pool, the addition of those two companies and their brilliant chief executives Wayne Huizenga and Michael Eisner gives the NHL added financial muscle and marketing know-how.

Alas, every rink must have its share of ruts. Canadian developer Norman Green, a.k.a Norman Greed, moved the Minnesota North Stars to Dallas, where they're now known simply as the Stars. And it was revealed last summer that the management of the expansion Ottawa Senators, specifically its former owner and NHL governor Bruce Firestone, had considered tanking a game at the end of last season to clinch the No. 1 draft pick. Fortunately that never happened, but the NHL may have to borrow yet another page from the NBA's book and implement a lottery for their player draft to ensure that no one even contemplates throwing a game again.

The big change in basketball last year came in the form of an innovative TV contract that the league signed with NBC

Sports. The four-year, $750 million pact, which takes effect at the start of the 1994–95 season, calls for the two entities to share revenues equally once NBC attains $1.06 billion in gross advertising sales. The new deal also transfers the rights to all NBA games to NBC, a move that effectively bars the two superstations—WGN of Chicago and WTBS of Atlanta—from showing NBA games on national cable and ends a longstanding dispute between the league offices and some owners. But it won't interfere with NBA games being shown on TNT. In fact, last September, TNT inked a new four-year deal with the league for the rights to televise 45 regular-season games and 35 playoff contests each season. Total cost: $352 million. And there's a revenue-sharing provision in that contract, as well; it kicks in once TNT surpasses $350 million in net advertising sales.

The NBA also announced plans last year to expand north of the border and add a franchise in Toronto for the 1995–96 season. The heavily financed investor group in Toronto won out over a second group that included Magic Johnson, who has been looking to fulfill his dream of owning an NBA franchise.

Speaking of the former Laker star, 1993 was the year the NBA discovered that life without Magic (and Larry Bird) might not be so bad after all. That's because Shaquille O'Neal came into the league. The imposing man-child from Louisiana State wooed fans, players and advertisers alike during his rookie season. He filled arenas everywhere, was named a starter to the All-Star team and snagged more than $30 million in advertising and marketing deals.

Major League Baseball had a mixed year. On the bright side, the expansion Colorado Rockies and Florida Marlins turned in stellar performances at the box office. The Rockies broke the single-season major league attendance record—4.02 million set last year by the Toronto Blue Jays—in mid-September, and the Marlins drew more than three million fans, something only seven teams had done before the 1993 season. And while the young franchises may have been walkovers on the field, they were superstars in licensing, with the Rockies leading all major league teams in terms of merchandise sales and the Marlins coming in a close third.

But by season's end baseball still didn't have a commissioner, and Bud Selig of the Milwaukee Brewers continued to lead the cabal of owners that ran the game. They spent much of the year trying to work out a revenue-sharing agreement among themselves, even traveling to a Kohler, Wis., retreat in mid-August for intensive meetings. But while they agreed there would be no lockout in spring training of 1994 and no change in free agency or salary arbitration rules next winter, the owners still didn't accomplish what they had set out to do: bridge the economic gap between the big- and small-market teams.

Other problems jumped up quicker than a catcher fielding a bunt. The owners blocked the sale of the San Francisco Giants last spring to a group that wanted to move the team to Tampa/St. Petersburg, and that so angered some members of Congress that they began taking steps to rescind baseball's antitrust exemption. Then it was reported that Anheuser-Busch, the game's biggest advertiser, had been cutting back on baseball sponsorships. Five years ago the brewer spent $100 million on advertising, but its 1993 budget called for only $75 million. Some of the company's marketing executives openly fretted about the slump in TV ratings and indications that the game's appeal, especially to the young, has been slipping. And, of course, there were the cry-poor Padres, who quickly went from division title contender to last-place laughingstock as owner Tom Werner and his crew unloaded one All-Star player after another in an effort to meet a bare bones budget. Outraged fans called for some sort of league intervention, but there was none because there was no commissioner.

In other developments the owners voted

The NBA is hoping that O'Neal can fill the void left by the recent superstar exodus.

to divide baseball into six divisions and add an extra round of playoffs by including a wild-card team from each league. The move irked traditionalists, but at least it put teams in more geographically reasonable spots. The owners also negotiated a six-year joint television venture with ABC and NBC to replace the lucrative four-year, $1.06 billion deal they had struck with CBS in 1990. The new agreement doesn't call for any money up front and includes a revenue-sharing scheme and the regionalization of postseason TV coverage. All playoff and World Series games will be aired during prime time, and Major League Baseball will be responsible for selling the advertising. It's a far cry from the old pact and will probably generate only half the annual revenues. But given the tremendous losses CBS had racked up under the current agreement, no network was going to offer baseball that type of money again.

There didn't seem to be any shortage of cash when it came time to bid on the 1996 Summer Olympics in Atlanta, and NBC carried the day by agreeing to pay a record $456 million for the television rights. The move surprised many observers because the Peacock Network was still smarting from an estimated $100 million in losses from the 1992 Games in Barcelona. But executives at NBC said the Atlanta Games were a much more valuable event, pointing out that the 1996 Olympics will include extensive live prime-time coverage, unlike Barcelona, which was carried largely on tape delay. In

MICHAEL LEWIS/RICH CLARKSON & ASSOCIATES

travel, hotels and equipment; and finally, by not having the ill-fated Triplecast option, which produced nothing but losses.

No one knows what the television fees for the 2000 Summer Games will be, but we do know the cameras will be rolling in Sydney, Australia, which won the right to host the first Olympics of the new millennium by edging Beijing in a close vote. It was Australia's third stab at an Olympics in recent years—Brisbane lost a bid for the 1988 Games and Melbourne fell short for 1996—and the victory brings the Games back to Oceania for the first time since 1956. Beijing had led the first three rounds of balloting but was eliminated on the fourth vote when the other candidates—Instanbul, Berlin and Manchester, England—dropped out. The Chinese came close, but theirs was a controversial bid that drew widespread criticism because of the numerous human rights violations there.

And, finally, there was the Internal Revenue Service. It was revealed two years ago that the IRS was auditing the nonprofit groups that put on college bowl games to determine whether the big bucks that corporate sponsors give those events should be taxed. Agents were arguing that the sponsorship fees the organizers received were taxable because they weren't "substantially related" to the nonprofit educational purposes of the organizers. In other words, the IRS believed that when a company contributes money to get its logo plastered all over a stadium and the TV screen, it is employing the bowl as an advertising vehicle.

Not surprisingly, the news rattled the college bowl groups and a whole slew of other sports organizations who rely on corporate sponsors to put on their events. But after a couple of years on the case, the IRS backed off and said it wouldn't pursue the bowl organizers for taxes, demonstrating that even the IRS can make a rational move every now and again.

Now that was certainly a change.

addition, that year for the first time the Summer Games will not be competing for advertising dollars and viewers' attention with a Winter Olympics, because they are now held in off years.

NBC Sports head Dick Ebersol likes the setup so much he is confidently predicting a profit. How will he pull it off? First, by possibly taking on a cable TV partner; second, by advancing the opening ceremonies from Saturday afternoon to Friday night and making Saturday the first full day of competition, which will enable NBC to sell commercials for a prime-time opening night and an extra weekend day of action; third, by raising ad rates and attracting new sponsors who are suckers for an American Olympics; fourth, by saving at least $20 million on

Baseball Directory

Major League Baseball
Address: 350 Park Avenue
           New York, NY 10022
Telephone: (212) 339-7800
Commissioner: TBA
Chairmam of the Executive Council: Bud Selig
Ass't Chairman of the Executive Council: Dick Wagner

Major League Baseball Players Association
Address: 12 East 49th Street 24th Floor
           New York, NY 10017
Telephone: (212) 826-0808
Executive Director: Donald Fehr
Director of Marketing: Judy Heeter

American League

American League Office
Address: 350 Park Avenue
           New York, NY 10022
Telephone: (212) 339-7600
President: Dr. Bobby Brown
Director of Public Relations: Phyllis Merhige

Baltimore Orioles
Address: Oriole Park at Camden Yards
           333 W Camden Street
           Baltimore, MD 21201
Telephone: (410) 685-9800
Stadium (Capacity): Camden Yards (48,071)
Chairman: Peter G. Angelos
General Manager: Roland Hemond
Manager: John Oates
Director of Media and Community Relations: Rick Vaughn

Boston Red Sox
Address: 4 Yawkey Way
           Fenway Park
           Boston, MA 02215
Telephone: (617) 267-9440
Stadium (Capacity): Fenway Park (33,925)
Majority Owner and Chairman of the Board: John Harrington
General Manager: Lou Gorman
Manager: Butch Hobson
Vice President, Public Relations: Dick Bresciani

California Angels
Address: P.O. Box 2000
           Anaheim Stadium
           Anaheim, CA 92803
Telephone: (714) 937-7200 or (213) 625-1123
Stadium (Capacity): Anaheim Stadium (64,573)
Chairman of the Board: Gene Autry
General Manager: Whitey Herzog
Manager: Buck Rodgers
Assistant VP of Media Relations: Tim Mead

Chicago White Sox
Address: Comiskey Park
           Chicago, IL 60616
Telephone: (312) 924-1000
Stadium (Capacity): Comiskey Park (44,229)
Chairman: Jerry Reinsdorf
General Manager: Ron Schueler
Manager: Gene Lamont
Director of Publc Relations: Doug Abel

Cleveland Indians
Address: Cleveland Stadium
           Cleveland, OH 44114
Telephone: (216) 861-1200
Stadium (Capacity): Cleveland Stadium (74,483)
Chairman of the Board and Chief Executive Officer: Richard Jacobs
Executive VP and General Manager: John Hart
Manager: Mike Hargrove
Vice President, Public Relations: Bob DiBiasio

Detroit Tigers
Address: 2121 Trumbull
           Tiger Stadium
           Detroit, MI 48216
Telephone: (313) 962-4000
Stadium (Capacity): Tiger Stadium (52,416)
Owner: Mike Ilitch
President and Chief Operating Officer: TBA
Manager: Sparky Anderson
Vice President, Media and Public Relations: Dan Ewald

Kansas City Royals
Address: P.O. Box 419969
           Kansas City, MO 64141
Telephone: (816) 921-2200
Stadium (Capacity): Royals Stadium (40,625)
Chairman of the Board and CEO: David D. Glass
General Manager: Herk Robinson
Manager: Hal McRae
Vice President, Public Relations: Dean Vogelaar

Milwaukee Brewers
Address: Milwaukee County Stadium
           Milwaukee, WI 53214
Telephone: (414) 933-4114
Stadium (Capacity): Milwaukee County Stadium (53,192)
President and Chief Executive Officer: Bud Selig
Senior VP, Baseball Operations: Sal Bando
Manager: Phil Garner
Director of Publicity: Tom Skibosh

Minnesota Twins
Address: 501 Chicago Avenue South
           Hubert H. Humphrey Metrodome
           Minneapolis, MN 55415
Telephone: (612) 375-1366
Stadium (Capacity): Hubert H. Humphrey Metrodome (55,883)
Owner: Carl Pohlad
General Manager: Andy MacPhail
Manager: Tom Kelly
Director of Media Relations: Rob Antony

New York Yankees
Address: Yankee Stadium
           Bronx, NY 10451
Telephone: (718) 293-4300
Stadium (Capacity): Yankee Stadium (57,545)
Majority Owner: George Steinbrenner
Managing General Partner: Joseph Molloy
General Manager: Gene Michael
Manager: Buck Showalter
Director of Media Relations and Publicity: Rob Butcher

American League *(Cont.)*

Oakland Athletics
Address: Oakland-Alameda County Coliseum
            Oakland, CA 94621
Telephone: (510) 638-4900
Stadium (Capacity): Oakland-Alameda County
Coliseum (47,313)
Owner/Managing General Partner: Walter Haas
President and General Manager: Sandy Alderson
Manager: Tony LaRussa
Director of Baseball Information: Jay Alves

Seattle Mariners
Address: P.O. Box 4100
            Seattle, WA 98104
Telephone: (206) 628-3555
Stadium (Capacity): The Kingdome (58,879)
Chairman: John Ellis
General Manager: Woody Woodward
Manager: Lou Piniella
Director of Public Relations: Dave Aust

Texas Rangers
Address: P.O. Box 90111
            Arlington, TX 76004
Telephone: (817) 273-5222
Stadium (Capacity): Arlington Stadium (43,508)
General Partners: George W. Bush, Rusty Rose
General Manager: Tom Grieve
Manager: Kevin Kennedy
Vice President, Public Relations: John Blake

Toronto Blue Jays
Address: SkyDome
            1 Blue Jays Way, Suite 3200
            Toronto, Ontario, Canada M5V 1J1
Telephone: (416) 341-1000
Stadium (Capacity): SkyDome (50,516)
Chairman of the Board: Peter N.T. Widdrington
President and CEO: Paul Beeston
Executive VP of Baseball Operations: Pat Gillick
Manager: Cito Gaston
Director of Public Relations: Howard Starkman

National League

National League Office
Address: 350 Park Avenue
            New York, NY 10022
Telephone: (212) 339-7700
President: Bill White
Director of Public Relations: Katy Feeney

Atlanta Braves
Address: P.O. Box 4064
            Atlanta, GA 30302
Telephone: (404) 522-7630
Stadium (Capacity): Atlanta-Fulton County Stadium
(52,007)
Owner: Ted Turner
General Manager: John Schuerholz
Manager: Bobby Cox
Director of Public Relations: Jim Schultz

Chicago Cubs
Address: 1061 West Addison
            Wrigley Field
            Chicago, IL 60613
Telephone: (312) 404-2827
Stadium (Capacity): Wrigley Field (38,756)
Chairman of the Board: Stanton R. Cook
Executive VP of Baseball Operations: Larry Himes
Manager: Tom Trebelhorn
Director of Media Relations: Sharon Panozzo

Cincinnati Reds
Address: 100 Riverfront Stadium
            Cincinnati, OH 45202
Telephone: (513) 421-4510
Stadium (Capacity): Riverfront Stadium (52,392)
General Partner: Marge Schott
General Manager: James G. Bowden
Manager: Davey Johnson
Publicity Director: Jon Braude

Colorado Rockies
Address: 1700 Broadway, Suite 2100
            Denver, CO 80290
Telephone: (303) 292-0200
Stadium (Capacity): Mile High Stadium (76,100)
President: Steve Ehrhart
Executive VP of Baseball Operations: John McHale
Manager: Don Baylor
Director of Public Relations: Mike Swanson

Florida Marlins
Address: 100 N.E. 3rd Avenue
            Fort Lauderdale, FL 33301
Telephone: (305) 626-7400
Stadium (Capacity): Joe Robbie Stadium (45,706)
Owner: Wayne Huizenga
Vice President and General Manager: David
Dombrowski
Manager: Rene Lachemann
Director of Media Relations: Chuck Pool

Houston Astros
Address: P.O. Box 288
            Houston, TX 77001
Telephone: (713) 799-9500
Stadium (Capacity): Astrodome (54,223)
Chairman: Drayton McLane Jr.
General Manager: Bob Watson
Manager: TBA
Director of Media Relations: Rob Matwick

Los Angeles Dodgers
Address: Dodger Stadium
            Los Angeles, CA 90012
Telephone: (213) 224-1500
Stadium (Capacity): Dodger Stadium (56,000)
President: Peter O'Malley
Executive Vice President: Fred Claire
Manager: Tom Lasorda
Director of Publicity: Jay Lucas

Montreal Expos
Address: P.O. Box 500
            Station M
            Montreal
            Quebec, Canada H1V 3P2
Telephone: (514) 253-3434
Stadium (Capacity): Olympic Stadium (46,500)
President: Claude Brochu
General Manager: Dan Duquette
Manager: Felipe Alou
Director, Media Relations: Rich Griffin

National League (Cont.)

New York Mets
Address: Shea Stadium
              Flushing, NY 11368
Telephone: (718) 507-6387
Stadium (Capacity): Shea Stadium (55,601)
Chairman: Nelson Doubleday
President: Fred Wilpon
Executive VP of Baseball Operations: Joe McIlvaine
Manager: Dallas Green
Director of Public Relations: Jay Horwitz

Philadelphia Phillies
Address: P.O. Box 7575
              Philadelphia, PA 19101
Telephone: (215) 463-6000
Stadium (Capacity): Veterans Stadium (62,382)
President: Bill Giles
General Manager: Lee Thomas
Manager: Jim Fregosi
Vice President, Public Relations: Larry Shenk

Pittsburgh Pirates
Address: P.O. Box 7000
              Pittsburgh, PA 15212
Telephone: (412) 323-5000
Stadium (Capacity): Three Rivers Stadium (58,729)
Chairman: Doug Danforth
General Manager: Cam Bonifay
Manager: Jim Leyland
Director of Media Relations: Jim Trdinich

St. Louis Cardinals
Address: 250 Stadium Plaza
              Busch Stadium
              St. Louis, MO 63102
Telephone: (314) 421-3060
Stadium (Capacity): Busch Stadium (57,001)
Chairman of the Board: August A. Busch III
General Manager: Dal Maxvill
Manager: Joe Torre
Director of Public Relations: Jeff Wehling

San Diego Padres
Address: P.O. Box 2000
              San Diego, CA 92112
Telephone: (619) 283-7294
Stadium (Capacity): San Diego/Jack Murphy Stadium (60,000)
Chairman: Tom Werner
General Manager: Randy Smith
Manager: Jim Riggleman
Director of Media Relations: Jim Ferguson

San Francisco Giants
Address: Candlestick Park
              San Francisco, CA 94124
Telephone: (415) 468-3700
Stadium (Capacity): Candlestick Park (58,000)
Chairman: Peter Magowan
General Manager: Bob Quinn
Manager: Dusty Baker
Vice President, Public Relations: Bob Rose

Pro Football Directory

National Football League
Address: 410 Park Avenue
              New York, New York 10022
Telephone: (212) 758-1500
Commissioner: Paul Tagliabue
Director of Communications: Greg Aiello

National Football League Players Association
Address: 2021 L Street, N.W.
              Washington, D.C. 20036
Telephone: (202) 463-2200
Executive Director: Gene Upshaw
Director, Public Relations: Frank Woschitz

National Conference

Atlanta Falcons
Address: I-85 and Suwanee Road
              Suwanee, GA 30174
Telephone: (404) 945-1111
Stadium (Capacity): Georgia Dome (71,500)
Chairman of the Board: Rankin M. Smith
President: Taylor W. Smith
Director of Player Personnel: Ken Herock
Coach: Jerry Glanville
Publicity Director: Charlie Taylor

Chicago Bears
Address: 250 N. Washington Road
              Lake Forest, IL 60045
Telephone: (708) 295-6600
Stadium (Capacity): Soldier Field (66,946)
President: Michael McCaskey
General Manager: Bill Tobin
Coach: Dave Wannstedt
Director of Public Relations: Bryan Harlan

Dallas Cowboys
Address: One Cowboys Parkway
              Irving, TX 75063
Telephone: (214) 556-9900
Stadium (Capacity): Texas Stadium (65,024)
Owner, President, and General Manager: Jerry Jones
Coach: Jimmy Johnson
Public Relations Director: Rich Dalrymple

Detroit Lions
Address: 1200 Featherstone Road
              Pontiac, MI 48342
Telephone: (313) 335-4131
Stadium (Capacity): Pontiac Silverdome (80,500)
President and Owner: William Clay Ford
Executive VP/CEO: Chuck Schmidt
Coach: Wayne Fontes
Media Relations Director: Mike Murray

National Conference *(Cont.)*

Green Bay Packers
Address: 1265 Lombardi Avenue
         Green Bay, WI 54307-0628
Telephone: (414) 496-5700
Stadium (Capacity): Lambeau Field (59,543),
Milwaukee County Stadium (56,051)
President: Bob Harlan
General Manager: Ron Wolf
Coach: Mike Holmgren
Public Relations Director: Lee Remmel

Los Angeles Rams
Address: 2327 W. Lincoln Avenue
         Anaheim, CA 92801
Telephone: (714) 535-7267
Stadium (Capacity): Anaheim Stadium (69,008)
President: Georgia Frontiere
Executive VP: John Shaw
Vice President and Coach: Chuck Knox
Director of Public Relations: Rick Smith

Minnesota Vikings
Address: 9520 Viking Drive
         Eden Prairie, MN 55344
Telephone: (612) 828-6500
Stadium (Capacity): HHH Metrodome (63,000)
President: Roger L. Hendrick
General Manager: Jeff Diamond
Coach: Dennis Green
Public Relations Director: David Pelletier

New Orleans Saints
Address: 1500 Poydras Street
         New Orleans, LA 70112
Telephone: (504) 733-0255
Stadium (Capacity): Louisiana Superdome (69,065)
Owner: Tom Benson
President and General Manager: Jim Finks
Coach: Jim Mora
Director of Media Relations: Rusty Kasmiersky

New York Giants
Address: Giants Stadium
         East Rutherford, NJ 07073
Telephone: (201) 935-8111
Stadium (Capacity): Giants Stadium (77,311)
President and co-CEO: Wellington T. Mara
Chairman and co-CEO: Preston Robert Tisch
General Manager: George Young
Coach: Dan Reeves
Director of Public Relations: Pat Hanlon

Philadelphia Eagles
Address: Veterans Stadium
         Broad Street and Pattison Avenue
         Philadelphia, PA 19148
Telephone: (215) 463-2500
Stadium (Capacity): Veterans Stadium (65,356)
Owner: Norman Braman
President/CEO: Harry Gamble
Coach: Rich Kotite
Director of Public Relations: Ron Howard

Phoenix Cardinals
Address: P.O. Box 888
         Phoenix, AZ 85001-0888
Telephone: (602) 379-0101
Stadium (Capacity): Sun Devil Stadium (73,473)
President: Bill Bidwill
General Manager: Larry Wilson
Coach: Joe Bugel
Director of Public Relations: Paul Jensen

San Francisco 49ers
Address: 4949 Centennial Boulevard
         Santa Clara, CA 95054
Telephone: (408) 562-4949
Stadium (Capacity): Candlestick Park (66,455)
Owner: Edward J. DeBartolo Jr.
General Manager: John McVay
Coach: George Seifert
Public Relations Director: Rodney Knox

Tampa Bay Buccaneers
Address: One Buccaneer Place
         Tampa, FL 33607
Telephone: (813) 870-2700
Stadium (Capacity): Tampa Stadium (74,296)
Owner: Hugh F. Culverhouse
Director of Football Operations and Coach: Sam
 Wyche
Director of Public Relations: Rick Odioso

Washington Redskins
Address: Redskin Park Drive,
         Ashburn, VA 22011
Telephone: (703) 478-8900
Stadium (Capacity): RFK Memorial Stadium (55,683)
Owner: Jack Kent Cooke
General Manager: Charley Casserly
Coach: Richie Petitbon
Vice President of Communications: Charlie Dayton

American Conference

Buffalo Bills
Address: One Bills Drive
         Orchard Park, NY 14127
Telephone: (716) 648-1800
Stadium (Capacity): Rich Stadium (80,290)
President: Ralph C. Wilson Jr.
General Manager: John Butler
Coach: Marv Levy
Manager of Media Relations: Scott Berchtold

Cincinnati Bengals
Address: 200 Riverfront Stadium
         Cincinnati, OH 45202
Telephone: (513) 621-3550
Stadium (Capacity): Riverfront Stadium (60,389)
President: John Sawyer
General Manager: Mike Brown
Coach: Dave Shula
Director of Public Relations: Allan Heim

American Conference *(Cont.)*

Cleveland Browns
Address: 80 First Street
           Berea, OH 44017
Telephone: (216) 891-5000
Stadium (Capacity): Cleveland Stadium (78,512)
President: Art Modell
Coach: Bill Belichick
VP and Director of Public Relations: Kevin Byrne

Denver Broncos
Address: 13665 Broncos Parkway
           Englewood, CO 80112
Telephone: (303) 649-9000
Stadium (Capacity): Mile High Stadium (76,273)
President: Pat Bowlen
General Manager: John Beake
Coach: Wade Phillips
Director of Media Relations: Jim Saccomano

Houston Oilers
Address: 6910 Fannin Street
           Houston, TX 77030
Telephone: (713) 797-9111
Stadium (Capacity): Astrodome (62,021)
President: K. S. (Bud) Adams Jr.
General Manager: Mike Holovak
Coach: Jack Pardee
Director of Media Relations: Chip Namias

Indianapolis Colts
Address: P.O. Box 535000
           Indianapolis, IN 46253
Telephone: (317) 297-2658
Stadium (Capacity): Hoosier Dome (60,129)
Owner: Robert Irsay
VP and General Manager: Jim Irsay
Coach: Ted Marchibroda
Public Relations Director: Craig Kelley

Kansas City Chiefs
Address: One Arrowhead Drive
           Kansas City, MO 64129
Telephone: (816) 924-9300
Stadium (Capacity): Arrowhead Stadium (77,622)
Founder: Lamar Hunt
President and General Manager: Carl Peterson
Coach: Marty Schottenheimer
Public Relations Director: Bob Moore

Los Angeles Raiders
Address: 332 Center Street
           El Segundo, CA 90245
Telephone: (310) 322-3451
Stadium (Capacity): Los Angeles Memorial Coliseum
  (92,516)
Managing General Partner: Al Davis
Coach: Art Shell
Executive Assistant: Al LoCasale

Miami Dolphins
Address: Joe Robbie Stadium
           2269 N.W. 199th Street
           Miami, FL 33056
Telephone: (305) 620-5000
Stadium (Capacity): Joe Robbie Stadium (74,916)
President: Timothy J. Robbie
Coach: Don Shula
Director of Publicity: Harvey Greene

New England Patriots
Address: Foxboro Stadium
           Route 1
           Foxboro, MA 02035
Telephone: (508) 543-8200
Stadium (Capacity): Foxboro Stadium (60,794)
Owner: James B. Orthwein
President: Francis Murray
Executive VP of Football Operations: Patrick Forté
Coach: Bill Parcells
Director of Public Relations: Mike Hanson

New York Jets
Address: 1000 Fulton Avenue
           Hempstead, NY 11550
Telephone: (516) 538-6600
Stadium (Capacity): Giants Stadium (76,891)
Chairman of the Board: Leon Hess
General Manager: Dick Steinberg
Coach: Bruce Coslet
Director of Public Relations: Frank Ramos

Pittsburgh Steelers
Address: Three Rivers Stadium
           300 Stadium Circle
           Pittsburgh, PA 15212
Telephone: (412) 323-1200
Stadium (Capacity): Three Rivers Stadium (59,600)
President: Dan Rooney
Coach: Bill Cowher
Public Relations Director: Dan Edwards

San Diego Chargers
Address: San Diego Jack Murphy Stadium
           P.O. Box 609609
           San Diego, CA 92160
Telephone: (619) 280-2111
Stadium (Capacity): San Diego Jack Murphy Stadium
  (61,863)
President: Alex G. Spanos
General Manager: Bobby Beathard
Coach: Bobby Ross
Director of Public Relations: Bill Johnston

Seattle Seahawks
Address: 11220 N.E. 53rd Street
           Kirkland, WA 98033
Telephone: (206) 827-9777
Stadium (Capacity): The Kingdome (66,400)
Owner: Ken Behring
President: Dave Behring
GM and Coach: Tom Flores
VP of Administration and Public Relations: Gary Wright

Other Leagues

Canadian Football League
Address: 110 Eglinton Avenue West, 5th floor
Toronto, Ontario M4R 1A3, Canada
Telephone: (416) 322-9650
Commissioner: Larry Smith
Communications Director: Michael Murray

World League of American Football
Address: 540 Madison Avenue
New York, NY 10022
Telephone: (212) 758-1500
Chief Operating Officer: Tom Spock

Pro Basketball Directory

National Basketball Association
Address: 645 Fifth Avenue
New York, NY 10022
Telephone: (212) 826-7000
Commissioner: David Stern
Deputy Commissioner: Russell Granik
Vice President, Public Relations: Brian McIntyre

National Basketball Association Players Association
Address: 1775 Broadway
Suite 2401
New York, NY 10019
Telephone: (212) 333-7510
Executive Director: Charles Grantham

Atlanta Hawks
Address: One CNN Center, South Tower
Suite 405
Atlanta, GA 30303
Telephone: (404) 827-3800
Arena (Capacity): The Omni (16,510)
Owner: Ted Turner
President: Stan Kasten
General Manager: Pete Babcock
Coach: Lenny Wilkens
Director of Public Relations: Arthur Triche

Boston Celtics
Address: 151 Merrimac Street
Boston, MA 02114
Telephone: (617) 523-6050
Arena (Capacity): Boston Garden (14,890)
Owner and Chairman of the Board: Paul Gaston
President: Arnold (Red) Auerbach
Senior Executive Vice President: David Gavitt
General Manager: Jan Volk
Coach: Chris Ford
Director of Public Relations: R. Jeffrey Twiss

Charlotte Hornets
Address: One Hive Drive
Charlotte, NC 28217
Telephone: (704) 357-0252
Arena (Capacity): Charlotte Coliseum (23,698)
Owner: George Shinn
President: Spencer Stolpen
Coach: Allan Bristow
Director of Media Relations: Harold Kaufman

Chicago Bulls
Address: 980 N. Michigan Avenue
Suite 1600
Chicago, IL 60611
Telephone: (312) 943-5800
Arena (Capacity): Chicago Stadium (17,339)
Chairman: Jerry Reinsdorf
General Manager: Jerry Krause
Coach: Phil Jackson
Director of Media Services: Tim Hallam

Cleveland Cavaliers
Address: The Coliseum, 2923 Streetsboro Road
Richfield, OH 44286
Telephone: (216) 659-9100
Arena (Capacity): The Coliseum (20,273)
Chairman of the Board: Gordon Gund
Vice President and General Manager: Wayne Embry
Coach: Mike Fratello
Director of Public Relations: Bob Price

Dallas Mavericks
Address: Reunion Arena
777 Sports Street
Dallas, TX 75207
Telephone: (214) 748-1808
Arena (Capacity): Reunion Arena (17,502)
Owner and President: Donald Carter
General Manager: Norm Sonju
Coach: Quinn Buckner
Director of Public Relations: Kevin Sullivan

Denver Nuggets
Address: McNichols Sports Arena
1635 Clay Street
Denver, CO 80204
Telephone: (303) 893-6700
Arena (Capacity): McNichols Sports Arena (17,171)
Owners: Peter Bynoe and Robert Wussler
General Manager: Bernie Bickerstaff
Coach: Dan Issel
Media Relations Director: Jay Clark

Detroit Pistons
Address: The Palace of Auburn Hills
Two Championship Drive
Auburn Hills, MI 48326
Telephone: (313) 377-0100
Arena (Capacity): The Palace of Auburn Hills
(21,454)
Owner: William M. Davidson
Director of Player Personnel: Bill McKinney
Coach: Don Chaney
Director of Public Relations: Matt Dobek

Golden State Warriors
Address: 7000 Coliseum Way
Oakland Coliseum Arena
Oakland, CA 94621
Telephone: (510) 638-6300
Arena (Capacity): Oakland Coliseum Arena (15,025)
Chairman: James F. Fitzgerald
Coach and General Manager: Don Nelson
Media Relations Director: Julie Marvel

Houston Rockets
Address: The Summit
Ten Greenway Plaza
Houston, TX 77046
Telephone: (713) 627-0600
Arena (Capacity): The Summit (16,279)
Owner: Leslie Alexander
President: Todd Leiweke
General Manager: Steve Patterson
Coach: Rudy Tomjanovich
Director of Media Information: Jay Goldberg

Indiana Pacers
Address: 300 E. Market Street
Indianapolis, IN 46204
Telephone: (317) 263-2100
Arena (Capacity): Market Square Arena (16,530)
Owners: Melvin Simon and Herbert Simon
President: Donnie Walsh
Coach: Larry Brown
Media Relations Director: Dale Ratermann

Los Angeles Clippers
Address: L.A. Memorial Sports Arena
3939 S. Figueroa Street
Los Angeles, CA 90037
Telephone: (213) 748-8000
Arena (Capacity): L.A. Memorial Sports Arena (16,500)
Owner: Donald T. Sterling
General Manager: Elgin Baylor
Coach: Bob Weiss
VP of Communications: Joe Safety

Los Angeles Lakers
Address: Great Western Forum
3900 West Manchester Boulevard
Inglewood, CA 90306
Telephone: (310) 419-3100
Arena (Capacity): The Great Western Forum (17,505)
Owner: Dr. Jerry Buss
General Manager: Jerry West
Coach: Randy Pfund
Director of Public Relations: John Black

Miami Heat
Address: The Miami Arena
Miami, FL 33136
Telephone: (305) 577-4328
Arena (Capacity): Miami Arena (15,008)
Managing Partner: Lewis Schaffel
Executive VP: Pauline Winick
Coach: Kevin Loughery
Director of Public Relations: Mark Pray

Milwaukee Bucks
Address: The Bradley Center
1001 N. Fourth Street
Milwaukee, WI 53203
Telephone: (414) 227-0500
Arena (Capacity): The Bradley Center (18,633)
Owner: Herb Kohl
Coach and VP of Bask. Operations: Mike Dunleavy
Public Relations Director: Bill King II

Minnesota Timberwolves
Address: 600 First Avenue North
Minneapolis, MN 55403
Telephone: (612) 673-1600
Arena (Capacity): Timberwolves Arena (19,006)
Owners: Harvey Ratner and Marv Wolfenson
General Manager and Director of Player Personnel:
Jack McCloskey
Coach: Sidney Lowe
Director of Media Relations: Kent Wipf

New Jersey Nets
Address: Meadowlands Arena
East Rutherford, NJ 07073
Telephone: (201) 935-8888
Arena (Capacity): Meadowlands Arena (20,029)
Chairman/CEO: Alan L. Aufzien
General Manager: Willis Reed
Coach: Chuck Daly
Director of Public Relations: John Mertz

New York Knickerbockers
Address: Madison Square Garden
Two Pennsylvania Plaza
New York, NY 10121
Telephone: (212) 465-6499
Arena (Capacity): Madison Square Garden (19,763)
Owner: Paramount Communications, Inc.
President: David Checketts
General Manager: Ernie Grunfeld
Coach: Pat Riley
Vice President, Public Relations: John Cirillo

Orlando Magic
Address: One Magic Place
Orlando Arena
Orlando, FL 32801
Telephone: (407) 649-3200
Arena (Capacity): Orlando Arena (15,151)
Owner: Rich DeVos
General Manager: Pat Williams
Coach: Brian Hill
Director of Publicity/Media Relations: Alex Martins

Philadelphia 76ers
Address: Veterans Stadium
P.O. Box 25040
Broad Street and Pattison Avenue
Philadelphia, PA 19147
Telephone: (215) 339-7600
Arena (Capacity): The Spectrum (18,168)
Owner and President: Harold Katz
General Manager: Jim Lynam
Coach: Fred Carter
Public Relations Director: Joe Favorito

Phoenix Suns
Address: P.O. Box 1369
Phoenix, AZ 85001
Telephone: (602) 379-7867
Arena (Capacity): America West Arena (19,023)
Owner: Jerry Colangelo
Coach: Paul Westphal
Media Relations Director: Julie Fie

Pro Basketball Directory (Cont.)

Portland Trail Blazers
Address: 700 N.E. Multnomah Street
            Suite 600
            Portland, OR 97232
Telephone: (503) 234-9291
Arena (Capacity): Memorial Coliseum (12,888)
Chairman of the Board: Paul Allen
Senior VP, Operations: Geoff Petrie
Coach: Rick Adelman
Director of Media Services: John Lashway

Sacramento Kings
Address: One Sports Parkway
            Sacramento, CA 95834
Telephone: (916) 928-0000
Arena (Capacity): ARCO Arena (17,014)
Managing General Partner: Jim Thomas
General Manager: Jerry Reynolds
Coach: Garry St. Jean
Director of Public Relations: Travis Stanley

San Antonio Spurs
Address: 600 E. Market Street
            Suite 102
            San Antonio, TX 78205
Telephone: (210) 554-7787
Arena (Capacity): HemisFair Arena (16,057)
Owner and Chairman: Red McCombs
President: Gary Woods
Coach: John Lucas
Director of Public Relations: Dave Senko

Seattle Supersonics
Address: 190 Queen Anne Avenue North
            Suite 200
            Seattle, WA 98109
Telephone: (206) 281-5800
Arena (Capacity): The Coliseum (14,252)
Owner: Barry Ackerley
President: Bob Whitsitt
Coach: George Karl
Director of Public/Media Relations: Cheri White

Utah Jazz
Address: 301 West So. Temple
            Salt Lake City, UT 84180
Telephone: (801) 575-7800
Arena (Capacity): Delta Center (19,911)
Owner: Larry H. Miller
General Manager: R. Tim Howells
Coach: Jerry Sloan
Director of Media Services/Special Events: Kim Turner

Washington Bullets
Address: One Harry S. Truman Drive
            Landover, MD 20785
Telephone: (301) 773-2255
Arena (Capacity): USAir Arena (18,756)
Owner: Abe Pollin
General Manager: John Nash
Coach: Wes Unseld
Director of Public Relations and Communications:
  Matt Williams

Other League

Continental Basketball Association
Address: 425 South Cherry Street, Suite 230
            Denver, CO 80222
Telephone: (303) 331-0404
Commissioner: TBA
Director of Media Relations: Greg Anderson

Hockey Directory

National Hockey League
Address: 650 Fifth Avenue
            33rd floor
            New York, NY 10019
Telephone: (212) 398-1100
Commissioner and President: Gary Bettman
Senior VP and Chief Operating Officer: Steven Solomon
Vice President, Public Relations: Arthur Pincus

National Hockey League Players Association
Address: One Dundas Street West
            Suite 2406
            Toronto, Ontario
            Canada M5G 1Z3
Telephone: (416) 408-4040
Executive Director: Bob Goodenow

Mighty Ducks of Anaheim
Address: 2695 Katella Avenue
            P.O. Box 61077
            Anaheim, CA 92803
Telephone: (714) 704-2700
Arena (Capacity): Arrowhead Pond of Anaheim (17,174)
Owner: Disney Sports Enterprises
General Manager: Jack Ferreira
Coach: Ron Wilson
Director of Media Relations: Bill Robertson

Boston Bruins
Address: Boston Garden
            150 Causeway Street
            Boston, MA 02114
Telephone: (617) 227-3206
Arena (Capacity): Boston Garden (14,448)
Owner and Governor: Jeremey M. Jacobs
Alternative Governor, President and General
  Manager: Harry Sinden
Coach: Brian Sutter
Director of Media Relations: Heidi Holland

Buffalo Sabres
Address: Memorial Auditorium
            Buffalo, NY 14202
Telephone: (716) 856-7300
Arena (Capacity): Memorial Auditorium (16,325)
Chairman of the Board and President: Seymour H.
  Knox III
General Manager and Coach: John Muckler
Director of Public Relations: Steve Rossi

Calgary Flames
Address: Olympic Saddledome
P.O. Box 1540, Station M
Calgary, Alberta T2P 3B9
Telephone: (403) 261-0475
Arena (Capacity): Olympic Saddledome (20,230)
Owners: Harley N. Hotchkiss, Norman L. Kwong,
Sonia Scurfield, Byron J. Seaman, and
Daryl K. Seaman
President and Governor: William Hay
Director of Hockey Operations: Al MacNeil
General Manager: Doug Risebrough
Coach: Dave King
Director of Public Relations: Rick Skaggs

Chicago Blackhawks
Address: 1800 W. Madison Street
Chicago, IL 60612
Telephone: (312) 733-5300
Arena (Capacity): Chicago Stadium (17,317)
President: William W. Wirtz
General Manager: Robert Pulford
Coach: Darryl Sutter
Public Relations Director: Jim DeMaria

Dallas Stars
Address: 901 Main Street
Suite 2301
Dallas, TX 75202
Telephone: (214) 712-2890
Arena (Capacity): Reunion Arena (16,914)
Owner: Norman N. Green
General Manager and Coach: Bob Gainey
Director of Public Relations: Larry Kelly

Detroit Red Wings
Address: Joe Louis Sports Arena
600 Civic Center Drive
Detroit, MI 48226
Telephone: (313) 396-7544
Arena (Capacity): Joe Louis Sports Arena (19,275)
Owner and President: Michael Ilitch
General Manager: Bryan Murray
Coach: Scotty Bowman
Director of Public Relations: Bill Jamieson

Edmonton Oilers
Address: Northlands Coliseum
Edmonton, Alberta T5B 4M9
Telephone: (403) 474-8561
Arena (Capacity): Northlands Coliseum
(17,313; standing: 190)
Owner and Governor: Peter Pocklington
General Manager: Glen Sather
Coach: Ted Green
Director of Public Relations: Bill Tuele

Florida Panthers
Address: 100 Northeast Third Avenue, 10th floor
Fort Lauderdale, FL 33301
Telephone: (305) 768-1900
Arena (Capacity): Miami Arena (14,500)
Owner: H. Wayne Huizenga
General Manager: Bob Clarke
Coach: Roger Neilson
Director of Media Relations: Greg Bouris

Hartford Whalers
Address: 242 Trumbull Street, 8th floor
Hartford, CT 06103
Telephone: (203) 728-3366
Arena (Capacity): Hartford Civic Center Coliseum
(15,635)
Managing General Partner and Owner: Richard Gordon
General Manager and Coach: Paul Holmgren
Assistant General Manager: Pierre McGuire
Director of Public Relations: Mark Mancini

Los Angeles Kings
Address: The Great Western Forum
3900 West Manchester Boulevard
P.O. Box 17013
Inglewood, CA 90308
Telephone: (310) 419-3160
Arena (Capacity): The Great Western Forum (16,005)
Governor: Bruce McNall
General Manager: Nick Beverley
Coach: Barry Melrose
Media Relations: Rick Minch

Montreal Canadiens
Address: Montreal Forum
2313 St. Catherine Street West
Montreal, Quebec H3H 1N2
Telephone: (514) 932-2582
Arena (Capacity): Montreal Forum (16,197)
Chairman of the Board, President and Governor:
Ronald Corey
General Manager: Serge A. Savard
Coach: Jacques Demers
Director of Public Relations: Claude Mouton

New Jersey Devils
Address: Byrne Meadowlands Arena
P.O. Box 504
East Rutherford, NJ 07073
Telephone: (201) 935-6050
Arena (Capacity): Byrne Meadowlands Arena
(19,040)
Chairman: John J. McMullen
President and General Manager: Lou Lamoriello
Coach: Jacques Lemaire
Publicity Director: Dave Freed

New York Islanders
Address: Nassau Veterans' Memorial Coliseum
Uniondale, NY 11553
Telephone: (516) 794-4100
Arena (Capacity): Nassau Veterans' Memorial
Coliseum (16,297)
Co-Chairmen: Robert Rosenthal, Stephen Walsh
General Manager: Don Maloney
Coach: Al Arbour
Media Relations Director: Ginger Killian

New York Rangers
Address: Madison Square Garden
4 Pennsylvania Plaza
New York, NY 10001
Telephone: (212) 465-6000
Arena (Capacity): Madison Square Garden (18,200)
Owner: Paramount Communications, Inc.
President and General Manager: Neil Smith
Coach: Mike Keenan
Director of Communications: Barry Watkins

Ottawa Senators

Address: 301 Moodie Drive
Suite 200
Nepean, Ontario K2H 9C4
Telephone: (613) 721-0115
Arena (Capacity): Ottawa Civic Centre (10,500)
Founder: Bruce M. Firestone
Chairman and Governor: Rod Bryden
General Manager: Randy Sexton
Coach: Rick Bowness
Director, Media Relations: Laurent Benoit

Philadelphia Flyers

Address: The Spectrum
Pattison Place
Philadelphia, PA 19148
Telephone: (215) 465-4500
Arena (Capacity): The Spectrum (17,380)
Majority Owners: Ed Snider and family
Limited Partners: Sylvan and Fran Tobin
General Manager: Russ Farwell
Coach: Terry Simpson
Director of Public Relations: Mark Piazza

Pittsburgh Penguins

Address: Civic Arena
300 Auditorium Place
Pittsburgh, PA 15219
Telephone: (412) 642-1800
Arena (Capacity): Civic Arena (17,537)
Ownership: Howard Baldwin, Morris Belzberg,
Thomas Ruta
General Manager: Craig Patrick
Coach: Eddie Johnston
Director of Press Relations: Cindy Himes

Quebec Nordiques

Address: Colisée de Québec
2205 Ave de Colisée
Quebec City, Quebec G1L 4W7
Telephone: (418) 529-8441
Arena (Capacity): Colisée de Québec (15,399)
President and Governor: Marcel Aubut
Coach and General Manager: Pierre Pagé
Director of Press Relations: Jean Martineau

St. Louis Blues

Address: St. Louis Arena
5700 Oakland Avenue
St. Louis, MO 63110
Telephone: (314) 781-5300
Arena (Capacity): St. Louis Arena (17,188)
Chairman: Michael F. Shanahan
General Manager: Ron Caron
Coach: Bob Berry
Director, Public Relations: Susie Mathieu

San Jose Sharks

Address: 525 West Santa Clara Street
San Jose, CA 95113
Telephone: (408) 287-7070
Arena (Capacity): San Jose Arena (17,190)
Owner: George and Gordon Gund
VP and Director of Hockey Operations: Dean
Lombardi
Coach: George Kingston
Director of Media Relations: Kevin Constantine

Tampa Bay Lightning

Address: 501 East Kennedy Boulvard
Suite 175
Tampa, FL 33602
Telephone: (813) 229-2658
Arena (Capacity): The Thunderdome (27,000)
President: Yoshio Nakamura
General Manager: Phil Esposito
Coach: Terry Crisp
Media Relations Manager: Gerry Helper

Toronto Maple Leafs

Address: Maple Leaf Gardens
60 Carlton Street
Toronto, Ontario M5B 1L1
Telephone: (416) 977-1641
Arena (Capacity): Maple Leaf Gardens (16,182;
standing: 200)
Chairman: Steve A. Stavro
General Manager: Cliff Fletcher
Coach: Pat Burns
Director of Business Operations and Communications:
Bob Stellick

Vancouver Canucks

Address: Pacific Coliseum
100 North Renfrew Street
Vancouver, B.C. V5K 3N7
Telephone: (604) 254-5141
Arena (Capacity): Pacific Coliseum (16,123)
Board of Directors: (Northwest Sports Enterprises
Ltd.) J. Lawrence Dampier, Arthur R. Griffiths,
Frank A. Griffiths, F. W. Griffiths, Coleman E. Hall,
Senator E. M. Lawson, W. L. McEwen, David S.
Owen, Senator Ray Perrault, J. Raymond Peters,
Peter Paul Saunders, Andrew E. Saxton, Peter W.
Webster, Sydney W. Welsh, D. A. Williams, D.
Alexander Farac (Sec.)
Coach, President, and General Manager: Pat Quinn
Director of Public and Media Relations:
Steve Tambellini

Washington Capitals

Address: Capital Centre
Landover, MD 20785
Telephone: (301) 386-7000
Arena (Capacity): USAir Arena (18,130)
Board of Directors: Abe Pollin, David P. Binderman,
Stewart L. Binderman, James E. Cafritz, A. James
Clark, Albert Cohen, J. Martin Irving, James T.
Lewis, R. Robert Linowes, Arthur K. Mason, Dr.
Jack Meshel, David M. Osnos, Richard M. Patrick
VP and General Manager: Dave Poile
Coach: Terry Murray
VP of Communications: Ed Quinlan

Winnipeg Jets

Address: Winnipeg Arena
15–1430 Maroons Road
Winnipeg, Manitoba R3G 0L5
Telephone: (204) 982-5387
Arena (Capacity): Winnipeg Arena (15,393)
Board of Directors: Barry L. Shenkarow, Jerry Kruk,
Bob Chapman, Marvin Shenkarow, Don Binda,
Steve Bannatyne, Harvey Secter, Bill Davis
General Manager: Mike Smith
Coach: John Paddock
Director of Communications: Mike O'Hearn

NATIONAL COLLEGIATE ATHLETIC ASSOCIATION (NCAA)
Address: 6201 College Boulevard
               Overland Park, KS 66211
Telephone: (913) 339-1906
Executive Director: TBA
Director of Communications: Jim Marchiony

ATLANTIC COAST CONFERENCE
Address: P.O. Drawer ACC
               Greensboro, NC 27419
Telephone: (919) 854-8787
Commissioner: Eugene F. Corrigan
Director of Media Relations: Brian Morrison

Clemson University
Address: Clemson, SC 29633
Nickname: Tigers
Telephone: (803) 656-2101
Football Stadium (Capacity): Clemson Memorial Stadium (79,854)
Basketball Arena (Capacity): Littlejohn Coliseum (11,020)
President: Dr. Max Lennon
Athletic Director: Bobby Robinson
Football Coach: Ken Hatfield
Basketball Coach: Cliff Ellis
Sports Information Director: Tim Bourret

Duke University
Address: Durham, NC 27708
Nickname: Blue Devils
Telephone: (919) 684-8111
Football Stadium (Capacity): Wallace Wade Stadium (33,941)
Basketball Arena (Capacity): Cameron Indoor Stadium (9,314)
President: Nan Keohane
Athletic Director: Tom Butters
Football Coach: Barry Wilson
Basketball Coach: Mike Krzyzewski
Sports Information Director: Mike Cragg

Florida State University
Address: P.O. Box 2195
               Tallahassee, FL 32316
Nickname: Seminoles
Telephone: (904) 644-1403
Football Stadium (Capacity): Doak S. Campbell Stadium (72,589)
Basketball Arena (Capacity): Leon County Civic Center (12,500)
Interim President: Bernie Sliger
Athletic Director: Bob Goin
Football Coach: Bobby Bowden
Basketball Coach: Pat Kennedy
Sports Information Director: Wayne Hogan

Georgia Tech
Address: 150 Bobby Dodd Way
               Atlanta, GA 30332
Nickname: Yellow Jackets
Telephone: (404) 894-2000
Football Stadium (Capacity): Bobby Dodd Stadium (46,000)
Basketball Arena (Capacity): Alexander Memorial Coliseum (10,000)
President: Dr. John P. Crecine
Athletic Director: Dr. Homer Rice
Football Coach: Bill Lewis
Basketball Coach: Bobby Cremins
Sports Information Director: Mike Finn

University of Maryland
Address: P.O. Box 295
               College Park, MD 20740
Nickname: Terrapins
Telephone: (301) 314-3131
Football Stadium (Capacity): Byrd Stadium (45,000)
Basketball Arena (Capacity): Cole Fieldhouse (14,500)
President: Dr. William E. Kirnan
Athletic Director: Andy Geiger
Football Coach: Mark Duffner
Basketball Coach: Gary Williams
Sports Information Director: Herb Hartnett

University of North Carolina
Address: P.O. Box 2126
               Chapel Hill, NC 27514
Nickname: Tar Heels
Telephone: (919) 962-2211
Football Stadium (Capacity): Kenan Memorial Stadium (52,000)
Basketball Arena (Capacity): Dean E. Smith Center (21,572)
Chancellor: Paul Hardin
Athletic Director: John Swofford
Football Coach: Mack Brown
Basketball Coach: Dean Smith
Sports Information Director: Rick Brewer

North Carolina State University
Address: Box 8501
               Raleigh, NC 27695
Nickname: Wolfpack
Telephone: (919) 515-2102
Football Stadium (Capacity): Carter-Finley Stadium (51,500)
Basketball Arena (Capacity): Reynolds Coliseum (12,400)
Chancellor: Dr. Larry K. Monteith
Athletic Director: Todd Turner
Football Coach: Mike O'Cain
Basketball Coach: Les Robinson
Sports Information Director: Mark Bockelman

University of Virginia
Address: P.O. Box 3785
               Charlottesville, VA 22903
Nickname: Cavaliers
Telephone: (804) 982-5151
Football Stadium (Capacity): Scott Stadium (42,000)
Basketball Arena (Capacity): University Hall (8,500)
President: John Casteen III
Athletic Director: Jim Copeland, Jr.
Football Coach: George Welsh
Basketball Coach: Jeff Jones
Sports Information Director: Rich Murray

Wake Forest University
Address: P.O. Box 7426
               Winston-Salem, NC 27109
Nickname: Demon Deacons
Telephone: (919) 759-5640
Football Stadium (Capacity): Groves Stadium (31,500)
Basketball Arena (Capacity): Lawrence Joel Memorial Coliseum (14,407)
President: Dr. Thomas K. Hearn Jr.
Athletic Director: Ron Wellman
Football Coach: Jim Caldwell
Basketball Coach: Dave Odom
Sports Information Director: John Justus

College Sports Directory (Cont.)

BIG EAST CONFERENCE
Address: 56 Exchange Terrace, fifth floor
              Providence, RI 02903
Telephone: (401) 272-9108
Commissioner: Michael A. Tranghese
Publicity Director: John Paquette

Boston College
Address: Chestnut Hill, MA 02167
Nickname: Eagles
Telephone: (617) 552-2628
Football Stadium (Capacity): Alumni Stadium (33,500)
Basketball Arena (Capacity): Silvio O. Conte Forum
  (8,604)
President: Rev. J. Donald Monan, S.J.
Athletic Director: Chet Gladchuk
Football Coach: Tom Coughlin
Basketball Coach: Jim O'Brien
Sports Information Director: Reid Oslin

University of Connecticut
Address: 2095 Hillside Road
              Storrs, CT 06269
Nickname: Huskies
Telephone: (203) 486-2725
Football Stadium (Capacity): Memorial Stadium
  (16,200)
Basketball Arena (Capacity): Gampel Pavilion (8,241)
President: Dr. Harry J. Hartley
Athletic Director: Lew Perkins
Football Coach: Tom Jackson
Basketball Coach: Jim Calhoun
Sports Information Director: Tim Tolokan

Note: Division I-AA football

Georgetown University
Address: 37th & O Street, NW
              Washington, DC 20057
Nickname: Hoyas
Telephone: (202) 687-2435
Football Stadium (Capacity): Kehoe Field (2,000)
Basketball Arena (Capacity): USAir Arena (19,035)
President: Rev. Leo J. O'Donovan, S.J.
Athletic Director: Francis X. Rienzo
Football Coach: Robert Benson
Basketball Coach: John Thompson
Sports Information Director: Bill Shapland (basketball),
  Bill Hurd

Note: Division I-AA football

University of Miami
Address: One Hurricane Drive
              Coral Gables, FL 33146
Nickname: Hurricanes
Telephone: (305) 284-3244
Football Stadium (Capacity): Orange Bowl (74,712)
Basketball Arena (Capacity): Miami Arena (16,500)
President: Edward Foote II
Athletic Director: Paul T. Dee
Football Coach: Dennis Erickson
Basketball Coach: Leonard Hamilton
Sports Information Director: Linda Venzon

University of Pittsburgh
Address: Dept. of Athletics, P.O. Box 7436
              Pittsburgh, PA 15213
Nickname: Panthers
Telephone: (412) 648-8240
Football Stadium (Capacity): Pitt Stadium (56,500)
Basketball Arena (Capacity): Fitzgerald Field House
(6,798), Pittsburgh Civic Arena (16,798)
Chancellor: J. Dennis O'Connor
Athletic Director: Oval Jaynes
Football Coach: Johnny Majors
Basketball Coach: Paul Evans
Sports Information Director: Larry Eldridge

Providence College
Address: River Avenue
              Providence, RI 02918
Nickname: Friars
Telephone: (401) 865-2265
Basketball Arena (Capacity): Providence Civic Center
  (13,410)
President: Rev. John Cunningham, O.P.
Athletic Director: John Marinatto
Basketball Coach: Rick Barnes
Sports Information Director: Gregg Burke

Note: No football program

Rutgers University
Address: New Brunswick, NJ 08093
Nickname: Scarlet Knights
Telephone: (908) 932-4200
Football Stadium (Capacity): Rutgers Stadium
  (42,000), Giants Stadium (76,000)
Basketball Arena (Capacity): Louis Brown Athletic
  Center (9,000)
President: Dr. Francis L. Lawrence
Athletic Director: Frederick Gruninger
Football Coach: Doug Graber
Basketball Coach: Bob Wenzel
Sports Information Director: Peter Kowalski

Note: Plays football in Big East, basketball in Atlantic 10
Conference.

St. John's University
Address: 8000 Utopia Parkway
              Jamaica, NY 11439
Nickname: Redmen
Telephone: (718) 990-6367
Football Stadium (Capacity): St. John's Stadium (3,000)
Basketball Arena (Capacity): Alumni Hall (6,008),
Madison Square Garden (19,576)
President: Very Rev. Donald J. Harrington, C.M.
Athletic Director: John W. Kaiser
Football Coach: Bob Ricca
Basketball Coach: Brian Mahoney
Sports Information Director: Frank Racaniello

Note: Division I-AA football

Seton Hall University
Address: 400 South Orange Avenue
              South Orange, NJ 07079
Nickname: Pirates
Telephone: (201) 761-9497
Basketball Arena (Capacity): Walsh Auditorium
(3,200), The Meadowlands (20,029)
President: Rev. Thomas R. Peterson
Athletic Director: Larry Keating
Basketball Coach: P. J. Carlesimo
Sports Information Director: John Wooding

Note: No football program.

Syracuse University
Address: Manley Field House
Syracuse, NY 13244
Nickname: Orangemen
Telephone: (315) 443-2384
Football Stadium (Capacity): Carrier Dome (50,000)
Basketball Arena (Capacity): Carrier Dome (33,000)
Chancellor: Dr. Kenneth Shaw
Athletic Director: Jake Crouthamel
Football Coach: Paul Pasqualoni
Basketball Coach: Jim Boeheim
Sports Information Director: Larry Kimball

Temple University
Address: McGonigle Hall
Philadelphia, PA 19122
Nickname: Owls
Telephone: (215) 204-7000
Football Stadium (Capacity): Veterans Stadium
(66,592)
Basketball Arena (Capacity): McGonigle Hall (3,900)
President: Peter Liacouras
Acting Athletic Director: Jim Brown
Football Coach: Ron Dickerson
Basketball Coach: John Chaney
Sports Information Director: Al Shrier

Note: Plays football in Big East, basketball in Atlantic 10
Conference.

Villanova University
Address: Lancaster Avenue
Villanova, PA 19085
Nickname: Wildcats
Telephone: (215) 519-4110
Football Stadium (Capacity): Villanova Stadium (13,400)
Basketball Arena (Capacity): duPont Pavilion (6,500),
The Spectrum (18,497)
President: Rev. Edmund Dobbin, O.S.A.
Athletic Director: Gene DeFilippo
Football Coach: Andy Talley
Basketball Coach: Steve Lappas
Sports Information Director: Jim DeLorenzo

Note: Division I-AA football

Virginia Tech
Address: Jamerson Athletic Center
Blacksburg, VA 24061
Nickname: Hokies
Telephone: (703) 231-6726
Football Stadium (Capacity): Lane Stadium/Worsham
Field (51,000)
Basketball Arena (Capacity): Cassell Coliseum (9,971)
President: TBA
Athletic Director: Dave Braine
Football Coach: Frank Beamer
Basketball Coach: Bill Foster
Sports Information Director: Dave Smith

Note: Plays football in Big East, basketball in Metro
Conference.

West Virginia University
Address: P.O. Box 877
Morgantown, WV 26507
Nickname: Mountaineers
Telephone: (304) 293-2821
Football Stadium (Capacity): Mountaineer Field
(63,500)
Basketball Arena (Capacity): WVU Coliseum (14,000)
President: Dr. Neil Bucklew
Athletic Director: Ed Pastilong
Football Coach: Don Nehlen
Basketball Coach: Gale Catlett
Sports Information Director: Shelley Poe

Note: Plays football in Big East, basketball in Atlantic 10
Conference.

BIG EIGHT CONFERENCE
Address: 104 West Ninth Street, Suite 408
Kansas City, MO 64105
Telephone: (816) 471-5088
Commissioner: Carl C. James
Publicity Director: Jeff Bollig

University of Colorado
Address: Campus Box 357
Boulder, CO 80309
Nickname: Buffaloes
Telephone: (303) 492-5626
Football Stadium (Capacity): Folsom Field (51,748)
Basketball Arena (Capacity): Coors Event Center
(11,199)
President: Dr. Judith Albino
Athletic Director: Bill Marolt
Football Coach: Bill McCartney
Basketball Coach: Joe Harrington
Sports Information Director: David Plati

Iowa State University
Address: Olsen Building
Ames, IA 50011
Nickname: Cyclones
Telephone: (515) 294-3372
Football Stadium (Capacity): Cyclone Stadium-Trice
Field (50,000)
Basketball Arena (Capacity): Hilton Coliseum
(14,020)
President: Dr. Martin C. Jischke
Athletic Director: Gene Smith
Football Coach: Jim Walden
Basketball Coach: Johnny Orr
Sports Information Director: Dave Starr

University of Kansas
Address: Allen Field House
Lawrence, KS 66045
Nickname: Jayhawks
Telephone: (913) 864-3417
Football Stadium (Capacity): Memorial Stadium
(50,250)
Basketball Arena (Capacity): Allen Field House
(15,800)
Chancellor: Dr. Gene Budig
Athletic Director: Dr. Bob Fredrick
Football Coach: Glen Mason
Basketball Coach: Roy Williams
Sports Information Director: Doug Vance

Kansas State University

Address: Manhattan, KS 66502
Nickname: Wildcats
Telephone: (913) 532-6011
Football Stadium (Capacity): KSU Stadium (45,000)
Basketball Arena (Capacity): Bramlage Coliseum
(13,500)
President: Dr. Jon Wefald
Athletic Director: Max Urick
Football Coach: Bill Snyder
Basketball Coach: Dana Altman
Sports Information Director: Ben Boyle

University of Missouri

Address: P.O. Box 677
Columbia, MO 65205
Nickname: Tigers
Telephone: (314) 882-3241
Football Stadium (Capacity): Faurot Field (62,000)
Basketball Arena (Capacity): Hearnes Center (13,349)
Chancellor: Dr. Charles Kiesler
Athletic Director: Dan Devine
Football Coach: Bob Stull
Basketball Coach: Norm Stewart
Sports Information Director: Bob Brendel

University of Nebraska

Address: 116 South Stadium
Lincoln, NE 68588
Nickname: Cornhuskers
Telephone: (402) 472-7211
Football Stadium (Capacity): Memorial Stadium
(73,650)
Basketball Arena (Capacity): Bob Devaney Sports
Center (14,302)
President: Dr. Martin Massengale
Athletic Director: Bill Byrne
Football Coach: Tom Osborne
Basketball Coach: Danny Nee
Sports Information Director: Chris Anderson

University of Oklahoma

Address: 180 W. Brooks, Room 235
Norman, OK 73019
Nickname: Sooners
Telephone: (405) 325-8231
Football Stadium (Capacity): Owen Field (74,993)
Basketball Arena (Capacity): Lloyd Noble Center
(10,861)
President: Dr. Richard Van Horn
Athletic Director: Donnie Duncan
Football Coach: Gary Gibbs
Basketball Coach: Billy Tubbs
Sports Information Director: Mike Prusinski

Oklahoma State University

Address: 202 Gallagher-Iba Arena
Stillwater, OK 74078
Nickname: Cowboys
Telephone: (405) 744-5749
Football Stadium (Capacity): Lewis Field (50,614)
Basketball Arena (Capacity): Gallagher-Iba Arena
(6,381)
Interim President: Dr. Ray Bowen
Interim Athletic Director: Dave Martin
Football Coach: Pat Jones
Basketball Coach: Eddie Sutton
Sports Information Director: Steve Buzzard

BIG TEN CONFERENCE

Address: 1500 West Higgins Road
Park Ridge, IL 60068
Telephone: (708) 696-1010
Commissioner: James E. Delany
Assistant Commissioner: Mark Rudner

University of Illinois

Address: 1817 S. Neil Street, Suite 201
Champaign, IL 61820
Nickname: Fighting Illini
Telephone: (217) 333-1390
Football Stadium (Capacity): Memorial Stadium (72,292)
Basketball Arena (Capacity): Assembly Hall (16,153)
President: Stanley O. Ikenberry
Athletic Director: Ronald Guenther
Football Coach: Lou Tepper
Basketball Coach: Lou Henson
Sports Information Director: Mike Pearson

Indiana University

Address: 17th Street and Fee Lane/Assembly Hall
Bloomington, IN 47405
Nickname: Hoosiers
Telephone: (812) 855-4848
Football Stadium (Capacity): Memorial Stadium
52,354)
Basketball Arena (Capacity): Assembly Hall (17,357)
President: Thomas Ehrlich
Athletic Director: Clarence Doninger
Football Coach: Bill Mallory
Basketball Coach: Bob Knight
Sports Information Director: Kit Klingelhoffer

University of Iowa

Address: 205 Carver-Hawkeye Arena
Iowa City, IA 52242
Nickname: Hawkeyes
Telephone: (319) 335-9411
Football Stadium (Capacity): Kinnick Stadium (70,397)
Basketball Arena (Capacity): Carver-Hawkeye Arena
(15,500)
President: Hunter Rawlings III
Athletic Director: Robert Bowlsby
Football Coach: Hayden Fry
Basketball Coach: Tom Davis
Sports Information Director: Phil Haddy

University of Michigan

Address: 1000 S. State Street
Ann Arbor, MI 48109
Nickname: Wolverines
Telephone: (313) 763-4423
Football Stadium (Capacity): Michigan Stadium
(102,501)
Basketball Arena (Capacity): Crisler Arena (13,562)
President: James Duderstadt
Athletic Director: Jack Weidenbach
Football Coach: Gary Moeller
Basketball Coach: Steve Fisher
Sports Information Director: Bruce Madej

Michigan State University

Address: East Lansing, MI 48824
Nickname: Spartans
Telephone: (517) 355-2271
Football Stadium (Capacity): Spartan Stadium (76,000)
Basketball Arena (Capacity): Jack Breslin Student
  Events Center (15,138)
President: M. Peter McPherson
Athletic Director: Merrily Dean Baker
Football Coach: George Perles
Basketball Coach: Jud Heathcote
Sports Information Director: Ken Hoffman

University of Minnesota

Address: 516 15th Avenue S.E.
             Minneapolis, MN 55455
Nickname: Golden Gophers
Telephone: (612) 625-4090
Football Stadium (Capacity): Hubert H. Humphrey
  Metrodome (63,699)
Basketball Arena (Capacity): Williams Arena (14,300)
President: Nils Hasselmo
Athletic Director: McKinley Boston
Football Coach: Jim Wacker
Basketball Coach: Clem Haskins
Interim Sports Information Director: Marc Ryan

Northwestern University

Address: 1501 Central Street
             Evanston, IL 60208
Nickname: Wildcats
Telephone: (708) 491-3205
Football Stadium (Capacity): Dyche Stadium (49,256)
Basketball Arena (Capacity): McGaw Hall (8,117)
President: Arnold Weber
Acting Athletic Director: Ken Kraft
Football Coach: Gary Barnett
Basketball Coach: Ricky Birdsong
Director of Media Services: Greg Shea

Ohio State University

Address: 410 Woody Hayes Drive
             Columbus, OH 43210
Nickname: Buckeyes
Telephone: (614) 292-6861
Football Stadium (Capacity): Ohio Stadium (91,470)
Basketball Arena (Capacity): St. John Arena (13,276)
President: Dr. E. Gordon Gee
Athletic Director: Jim Jones
Football Coach: John Cooper
Basketball Coach: Randy Ayers
Sports Information Director: Steve Snapp

Penn State University

Address: Recreation Building
             University Park, PA 16802
Nickname: Nittany Lions
Telephone: (814) 865-1757
Football Stadium (Capacity): Beaver Stadium (93,967)
Basketball Arena (Capacity): Recreation Hall (6,846)
President: Dr. Joab Thomas
Athletic Director: Jim Tarman
Football Coach: Joe Paterno
Basketball Coach: Bruce Parkhill
Sports Information Director: Budd Thalman

Note: Plays 1992 football season as independent.

Purdue University

Address: Mackey Arena
             West Lafayette, IN 47907
Nickname: Boilermakers
Telephone: (317) 494-3200
Football Stadium (Capacity): Ross-Ade Stadium
  (67,861)
Basketball Arena (Capacity): Mackey Arena (14,123)
President: Dr. Steven C. Beering
Athletic Director: Morgan Burke
Football Coach: Jim Colletto
Basketball Coach: Gene Keady
Sports Information Director: Mark Adams

University of Wisconsin

Address: 1440 Monroe Street
             Madison, WI 53711
Nickname: Badgers
Telephone: (608) 262-1811
Football Stadium (Capacity): Camp Randall Stadium
  (77,745)
Basketball Arena (Capacity): UW Fieldhouse (11,895)
Chancellor: David Ward
Athletic Director: Pat Richter
Football Coach: Barry Alvarez
Basketball Coach: Stu Jackson
Sports Information Director: Steve Malchow

BIG WEST CONFERENCE

Address: 2 Corporate Park
             Suite 206
             Irvine, CA 92714
Telephone: (714) 261-2525
Commissioner: Dennis Farrell
Publicity Director: Dennis Bickmeyer

California State University–Fullerton

Address: 800 North State College Boulevard
             P.O. Box 34080
             Fullerton, CA 92634-9480
Nickname: Titans
Telephone: (714) 773-2677
Basketball Arena (Capacity): Titan Gym (4,000)
President: Dr. Milton A. Gordon
Athletic Director: Bill Shumard
Basketball Coach:Brad Holland
Sports Information Director: Mel Franks

Note: No football program in 1993

Fresno State University

Address: 5305 N. Campus Drive
             Fresno, CA 93740-0027
Nickname: Bulldogs
Telephone: (209) 278-2643
Football Stadium (Capacity): Bulldog Stadium
  (41,041)
Basketball Arena (Capacity): Selland Arena (10,159)
President: Dr. John Welty
Athletic Director: Dr. Gary Cunningham
Football Coach: Jim Sweeney
Basketball Coach: Gary Colson
Sports Information Director: Scott Johnson

Long Beach State University
Address: 1250 Bellflower Boulevard
             Long Beach, CA 90840
Nickname: 49ers .
Telephone: (310) 985-4655
Basketball Arena (Capacity): The Gold Mine (2,000)
President: Karl W.E. Anatol
Acting Athletic Director: David O'Brien
Basketball Coach: Seth Greenberg
Sports Information Director: Scott Cathcart

University of Nevada at Las Vegas
Address: 4505 Maryland Parkway
             Las Vegas, NV 89154
Nickname: Runnin' Rebels
Telephone: (702) 895-3207
Football Stadium (Capacity): Silver Bowl (32,000)
Basketball Arena (Capacity): Thomas Mack Center
 (18,500)
President: Dr. Robert C. Maxson
Athletic Director: Jim Weaver
Football Coach: Jim Strong
Basketball Coach: Rollie Massimino
Sports Information Director: Tommy Sheppard

New Mexico State University
Address: Box 3145
             Las Cruces, NM 88003
Nickname: Aggies
Telephone: (505) 646-4126
Football Stadium (Capacity): Aggie Memorial Stadium
 (30,343)
Basketball Arena (Capacity): Pan American Center
 (13,007)
President: James Halligan
Athletic Director: Al Gonzales
Football Coach: Jim Hess
Basketball Coach: Neil McCarthy
Sports Information Director: Steve Shutt

University of the Pacific
Address: 3601 Pacific Avenue
             Stockton, CA 95211
Nickname: Tigers
Telephone: (209) 946-2479
Football Stadium (Capacity): Amos Alonzo Stagg
 Memorial Stadium (30,000)
Basketball Arena (Capacity): A.G. Spanos Center
 (6,150)
President: Dr. Bill Atchley
Athletic Director: Bob Lee
Football Coach: Chuck Shelton
Basketball Coach: Bob Thomason
Sports Information Director: Kevin Messenger

San Jose State University
Address: One Washgton Square
             San Jose, CA 95192-0062
Nickname: Spartans
Telephone: (408) 924-1200
Football Stadium (Capacity): Spartan Stadium
 (31,218)
Basketball Arena (Capacity): Event Center (4,600)
President: J. Handel Evans
Athletic Director: Dr. Tom Brennan
Football Coach: John Ralston
Basketball Coach: Stan Morrison
Sports Information Director: Lawrence Fan

Utah State University
Address: UMC 7400
             Logan, UT 84322-7400
Nickname: Aggies
Telephone: (801) 750-1850
Football Stadium (Capacity): Romney Stadium
 (30,000)
Basketball Arena (Capacity): The Smith Spectrum
 (10,200)
President: George Emert
Athletic Director: Chuck Bell
Football Coach: Charlie Weatherbie
Basketball Coach: Larry Eustachy
Sports Information Director: John Lewandowski

IVY LEAGUE
Address: 120 Alexander Street
             Princeton, NJ 08544
Telephone: (609) 258-6426
Commissioner: Jeff Orleans
Publicity Director: Chuck Yrigoyen

Brown University
Address: Hope Street
             Providence, RI 02912
Nickname: Bears
Telephone: (401) 863-2211
Football Stadium (Capacity): Brown Stadium (20,000)
Basketball Arena (Capacity): Paul Bailey Pizzitola
 Memorial Sports Center (2,500)
President: Vartan Gregorian
Athletic Director: David Roach
Football Coach: Mickey Kwiatkowski
Basketball Coach: Franklin Dobbs
Sports Information Director: Christopher Humm

Columbia University
Address: Dodge Physical Fitness Center
             New York, NY 10027
Nickname: Lions
Telephone: (212) 854-2538
Football Stadium (Capacity): Lawrence A. Wien
 Stadium at Baker Field (17,000)
Basketball Arena (Capacity): Levien Gymnasium
 (3,400)
President: Dr. George Rupp
Athletic Director: Dr. John Reeves
Football Coach: Ray Tellier
Basketball Coach: Jack Rohan
Sports Information Director: William C. Steinman

Cornell University
Address: Teagle Hall, Campus Road
             Ithaca, NY 14853
Nickname: Big Red
Telephone: (607) 255-5220
Football Stadium (Capacity): Schoellkopf Field (27,000)
Basketball Arena (Capacity): Alberding Fieldhouse
 (4,750)
President: Frank Rhodes
Athletic Director: Laing Kennedy
Football Coach: Jim Hofher
Basketball Coach: Al Walker
Sports Information Director: Dave Wohlhueter

Dartmouth College
Address: 6083 Alumni Gym
                    Hanover, NH 03755
Nickname: Big Green
Telephone: (603) 646-2465
Football Stadium (Capacity): Memorial Field (20,416)
Basketball Arena (Capacity): Leede Arena (2,100)
President: James Freedman
Athletic Director: Richard G. Jaeger
Football Coach: John Lyons
Basketball Coach: Dave Faucher
Sports Information Director: Kathy Slattery

Harvard University
Address: 60 John F. Kennedy St.
                    Cambridge, MA 02138
Nickname: Crimson
Telephone: (617) 495-2204
Football Stadium (Capacity): Harvard Stadium (37,967)
Basketball Arena (Capacity): Briggs Athletic Center (3,000)
President: Neil L. Rudentsine
Athletic Director: William J. Cleary, Jr. '56
Football Coach: Joe Restic
Basketball Coach: Frank Sullivan
Sports Information Director: John Veneziano

University of Pennsylvania
Address: Weightman Hall N
                    Philadelphia, PA 19104-6322
Nickname: Quakers
Telephone: (215)898-6121
Football Stadium (Capacity): Franklin Field (60,546)
Basketball Arena (Capacity): Palestra Arena (8,700)
Interim President: Claire Fagan
Athletic Director: Paul Rubincam
Football Coach: Al Bagnoli
Basketball Coach: Fran Dunphy
Co-Sports Information Director: Gail Stasvlli
Co-Sports Information Director: Brad Hurlbut

Princeton University
Address: P.O. Box 71
                    Jadwin Gym
                    Princeton, NJ 08544
Nickname: Tigers
Telephone: (609) 258-3568
Football Stadium (Capacity): Palmer Stadium (45,725)
Basketball Arena (Capacity): Jadwin Gym (7,550)
President: Harold Shapiro
Athletic Director: Robert J. Myslik
Football Coach: Steve Tosches
Basketball Coach: Pete Carril
Sports Information Director: Kurt Kehl

Yale University
Address: Box 208216
                    New Haven, CT 06520
Nickname: Bulldogs, Elis
Telephone: (203) 432-1456
Football Stadium (Capacity): Yale Bowl (70,896)
Basketball Arena (Capacity): Payne Whitney Gym (3,100)
President: Richard C. Levin
Athletic Director: Harold E. Woodsum, Jr.
Football Coach: Carmen Cozza
Basketball Coach: Dick Kuchen
Sports Information Director: Steve Conn

MID-AMERICAN CONFERENCE
Address: Four Seagate, Suite 102
                    Toledo, OH 43604
Telephone: (419) 249-7177
Commissioner: Karl Benson
Publicity Director: Sue Wagner

Ball State University
Address: 2000 University Avenue
                    Muncie, IN 47306
Nickname: Cardinals
Telephone: (317) 285-8225
Football Stadium (Capacity): Ball State University Stadium (16,319)
Basketball Arena (Capacity): Ball State University Arena (11,500)
President: Dr. John E. Worthen
Athletic Director: Don Purvis
Football Coach: TBA
Basketball Coach: Dick Hunsaker
Sports Information Director: Joe Hernandez

Bowling Green University
Address: Bowling Green, OH 43403
Nickname: Falcons
Telephone: (419) 372-2401
Football Stadium (Capacity): Doyt L. Perry Stadium (30,599)
Basketball Arena (Capacity): Anderson Arena (5,000)
President: Dr. Paul Olscamp
Athletic Director: Jack C. Gregory
Football Coach: Gary Blackney
Basketball Coach: Jim Larranga
Sports Information Director: Steve Barr

Central Michigan University
Address: Rose Center
                    Mount Pleasant, MI 48859
Nickname: Chippewas
Telephone: (517) 774-3041
Football Stadium (Capacity): Kelly/Shorts Stadium (20,083)
Basketball Arena (Capacity): Rose Arena (6,000)
President: Leonare Plachta
Athletic Director: Dave Keilitz
Football Coach: Herb Deromedi
Basketball Coach: Keith Dambrot
Sports Information Director: Fred Stabley, Jr.

Eastern Michigan University
Address: Bowen Fieldhouse
                    Ypsilanti, MI 48197
Nickname: Eagles
Telephone: (313) 487-1050
Football Stadium (Capacity): Rynearson Stadium (30,200)
Basketball Arena (Capacity): Bowen Arena (5,600)
President: Dr. William Shelton
Athletic Director: Tim Weiser
Football Coach: Ron Cooper
Basketball Coach: Ben Braum
Sports Information Director: James Streeter

Kent University

Address: Kent, OH 44242
Nickname: Golden Flashes
Telephone: (216) 672-3120
Football Stadium (Capacity): Dix Stadium (30,520)
Basketball Arena (Capacity): Memorial Athletic and
  Convocation Center (6,034)
President: Dr. Carol A. Cartwright
Athletic Director: Paul Amodio
Football Coach: Pete Cordelli
Basketball Coach: Dave Grube
Sports Information Director: Dale Gallagher

Miami University

Address: Millett Hall
             Oxford, OH 45056
Nickname: Redskins
Telephone: (513) 529-3113
Football Stadium (Capacity): Yager Stadium (25,183)
Basketball Arena (Capacity): Millett Hall (9,200)
President: Dr. Paul G. Risser
Athletic Director: R.C. Johnson
Football Coach: Randy Walker
Basketball Coach: Herb Sendek
Sports Information Director: Brian Teter

Ohio University

Address: P.O. Box 689
             Convocation Center
             Athens, OH 45701-2979
Nickname: Bobcats
Telephone: (614) 593-1174
Football Stadium (Capacity): Don Peden Stadium
  (20,000)
Basketball Arena (Capacity): Convocation Center
  (13,000)
President: Dr. Charles Ping
Athletic Director: Harold McElhaney
Football Coach: Tom Lichtenberg
Basketball Coach: Larry Hunter
Associate Media Relations Director: Pam Fronko

University of Toledo

Address: 2801 W. Bancroft St.
             Toledo, OH 43606
Nickname: Rockets
Telephone: (419) 537-4184
Football Stadium (Capacity): Glass Bowl (26,248)
Basketball Arena (Capacity): Savage Hall (9,000)
President: Dr. Frank E. Horton
Athletic Director: Dr. Allen R. Bohl
Football Coach: Gary Pinkel
Basketball Coach: Larry Gipson
Sports Information Director: Rod Brandt

Western Michigan University

Address: Kalamazoo, MI 49008
Nickname: Broncos
Telephone: (616) 387-4104
Football Stadium (Capacity): Waldo Stadium (30,062)
Basketball Arena (Capacity): Read Fieldhouse (8,250)
President: Dr. D. H. Haenicke
Athletic Director: Dan Meinert
Football Coach: Al Molde
Basketball Coach: Bob Donewald
Sports Information Director: John Beatty

PACIFIC-10 CONFERENCE

Address: 800 S. Broadway, Suite 400
             Walnut Creek, CA 94596
Telephone: (510) 932-4411
Commissioner: Thomas C. Hansen
Publicity Director: Jim Muldoon

University of Arizona

Address: McHale Center
             Tuscon, AZ 85721
Nickname: Wildcats
Telephone: (602) 621-2211
Football Stadium (Capacity): Arizona Stadium (56,167)
Basketball Arena (Capacity): McHale Center (13,447)
President: Dr. Manuel Pacheco
Athletic Director: Dr. Cedric Dempsey
Football Coach: Dick Tomey
Basketball Coach: Lute Olson
Sports Information Director: Butch Henry

Arizona State University

Address: Tempe, AZ 85287
Nickname: Sun Devils
Telephone: (602) 965-6592
Football Stadium (Capacity): Sun Devil Stadium (74,865)
Basketball Arena (Capacity): University Activity
  Center (14,287)
President: Lattie Coor
Athletic Director: Charles Harris
Football Coach: Bruce Snyder
Basketball Coach: Bill Frieder
Sports Information Director: Mark Brand

University of California

Address: Berkeley, CA 94720
Nickname: Golden Bears
Telephone: (510) 642-5363
Football Stadium (Capacity): Memorial Stadium (76,700)
Basketball Arena (Capacity): Harmon Gym (6,600)
Chancellor: Chang-Lin Tien
Athletic Director: TBA
Football Coach: Keith Gilbertson
Basketball Coach: Todd Bozeman
Sports Information Director: Kevin Reneau

University of California at Los Angeles

Address: 405 Hilgard Avenue
             Los Angeles, CA 90024
Nickname: Bruins
Telephone: (310) 206-6831
Football Stadium (Capacity): Rose Bowl (102,083)
Basketball Arena (Capacity): Pauley Pavilion (12,819)
Chancellor: Dr. Charles Young
Athletic Director: Peter T. Dalis
Football Coach: Terry Donahue
Basketball Coach: Jim Harrick
Sports Information Director: Marc Dellins

University of Oregon

Address: Len Casanova Athletic Center
             2727 Leo Harris Parkway
             Eugene, OR 97401
Nickname: Ducks
Telephone: (503) 346-4481
Football Stadium (Capacity): Autzen Stadium (41,698)
Basketball Arena (Capacity): McArthur Court (10,063)
President: Myles Brand
Athletic Director and Football Coach: Rich Brooks
Basketball Coach: Jerry Green
Sports Information Director: Steve Hellyer

Oregon State University
Address: Gill Coliseum
             Corvallis, OR 97331
Nickname: Beavers
Telephone: (503) 737-3720
Football Stadium (Capacity): Parker Stadium (36,345)
Basketball Arena (Capacity): Gill Coliseum (10,400)
President: Dr. John V. Bryne
Athletic Director: Dutch Baughman
Football Coach: Jerry Pettibone
Basketball Coach: Jim Anderson
Sports Information Director: Hal Cowan

University of Southern California
Address: Los Angeles, CA 90089
Nickname: Trojans
Telephone: (213) 740-8480
Football Stadium (Capacity): Los Angeles Memorial
  Coliseum (92,516)
Basketball Arena (Capacity): Los Angeles Memorial
  Sports Arena (15,509)
President: Dr. Steven Sample
Athletic Director: Mike Garrett
Football Coach: John Robinson
Basketball Coach: George Raveling
Sports Information Director: Tim Tessalone

Stanford University
Address: Stanford, CA 94305
Nickname: Cardinal
Telephone: (415) 723-4418
Football Stadium (Capacity): Stanford Stadium (86,019)
Basketball Arena (Capacity): Maples Pavilion (7,500)
President: Gerhard Casper
Athletic Director: Dr. Ted Leland
Football Coach: Bill Walsh
Basketball Coach: Mike Montgomery
Sports Information Director: Gary Migdol

University of Washington
Address: 202 Graves Building
             Seattle, WA 98195
Nickname: Huskies
Telephone: (206) 543-2230
Football Stadium (Capacity): Husky Stadium (72,500)
Basketball Arena (Capacity): Hec Edmundson
  Pavilion (8,000)
President: Dr. William P. Gerberding
Athletic Director: Barbara Hedges
Football Coach: Jim Lambright
Basketball Coach: Bob Bender
Sports Information Director: Jim Daves

Washington State University
Address: 107 Bohler Gym
             Pullman, WA 99164
Nickname: Cougars
Telephone: (509) 335-0311
Football Stadium (Capacity): Martin Stadium (40,000)
Basketball Arena (Capacity): Friel Court (12,058)
President: Dr. Samuel H. Smith
Athletic Director: Jim Livengood
Football Coach: Mike Price
Basketball Coach: Kelvin Sampson
Sports Information Director: Rod Commons

SOUTHEASTERN CONFERENCE
Address: 2201 Civic Center Boulevard
             Birmingham, AL 35203
Telephone: (205) 458-3000
Commissioner: Roy Kramer
Publicity Director: Mark Whitworth

University of Alabama
Address: P.O. Box 870323
             Paul Bryant Drive
             Tuscaloosa, AL 35487
Nickname: Crimson Tide
Telephone: (205) 348-3600
Football Stadium (Capacity): Bryant-Denny Stadium
  (70,123)
Basketball Arena (Capacity): Coleman Coliseum
  (15,043)
President: Dr. Roger Sayers
Athletic Director: Cecil (Hootie) Ingram
Football Coach: Gene Stallings
Basketball Coach: David Hobbs
Sports Information Director: Larry White

University of Arkansas
Address: Broyles Athletic Center
             Fayetteville, AR 72701
Nickname: Razorbacks
Telephone: (501) 575-2751
Football Stadium (Capacity): Razorback Stadium
  (52,968)
Basketball Arena (Capacity): Bud Walton Arena
  (18,600)
Chancellor: Dr. Dan Ferritor
Athletic Director: Frank Broyles
Football Coach: Danny Ford
Basketball Coach: Nolan Richardson
Sports Information Director: Rick Schaeffer

Auburn University
Address: P.O. Box 351
             Auburn, AL 36831-0351
Nickname: Tigers
Telephone: (205) 844-9800
Football Stadium (Capacity): Jordan Hare Stadium
  (85,214)
Basketball Arena (Capacity): Beard-Eaves Memorial
  Coliseum (13,500)
President: Dr. William V. Muse
Athletic Director: Mike Lude
Football Coach: Terry Bowden
Basketball Coach: Tommy Joe Eagles
Sports Information Director: David Housel

University of Florida
Address: P.O. Box 14485
             Gainesville, FL 32604
Nickname: Gators
Telephone: (904) 375-4683
Football Stadium (Capacity): Florida Field (83,000)
Basketball Arena (Capacity): Stephen C. O'Connell
  Center (12,000)
President: Dr. John Lombardi
Athletic Director: Jeremy Foley
Football Coach: Steve Spurrier
Basketball Coach: Lon Kruger
Sports Information Director: John Humenik

University of Georgia
Address: P.O. Box 1472
             Athens, GA 30613
Nickname: Bulldogs
Telephone: (706) 542-1621
Football Stadium (Capacity): Sanford Stadium (85,434)
Basketball Arena (Capacity): The Coliseum (10,512)
President: Dr. Charles Knapp
Athletic Director: Vince Dooley
Football Coach: Ray Goff
Basketball Coach: Hugh Durham
Sports Information Director: Claude Felton

University of Kentucky
Address: Memorial Coliseum
             Lexington, KY 40506
Nickname: Wildcats
Telephone: (606) 257-3838
Football Stadium (Capacity): Commonwealth Stadium
(57,800)
Basketball Arena (Capacity): Rupp Arena (23,000)
President: Dr. Charles Wethington Jr.
Athletic Director: C. M. Newton
Football Coach: Bill Curry
Basketball Coach: Rick Pitino
Sports Information Director: Rena Vicini

Louisiana State University
Address: Baton Rouge, LA 70894
Nickname: Fighting Tigers
Telephone: (504) 388-8226
Football Stadium (Capacity): Tiger Stadium (80,150)
Basketball Arena (Capacity): Pete Maravich
Assembly Center (14,164)
Chancellor: Dr. William E. Davis
Athletic Director: Joe Dean
Football Coach: Curley Hallman
Basketball Coach: Dale Brown
Sports Information Director: Herb Vincent

University of Mississippi
Address: P.O. Box 217
             University, MS 38677
Nickname: Rebels
Telephone: (601) 232-7522
Football Stadium (Capacity): Vaught-Hemingway
Stadium (42,577)
Basketball Arena (Capacity): C. M. (Tad) Smith
Coliseum (8,135)
Chancellor: Dr. R. Gerald Turner
Athletic Director: Warner Alford
Football Coach: Billy Brewer
Basketball Coach: Robert Evans
Sports Information Director: Langston Rogers

Mississippi State University
Address: P.O. Drawer 5308
             Mississippi St., MS 39762
Nickname: Bulldogs
Telephone: (601) 325-2703
Football Stadium (Capacity): Scott Field (41,200)
Basketball Arena (Capacity): Humphrey Coliseum
(10,000)
President: Dr. Donald Zacharias
Athletic Director: Larry Templeton
Football Coach: Jackie Sherrill
Basketball Coach: Richard Williams
Sports Information Director: Mike Nemeth

University of South Carolina
Address: Rex Enright Athletic Center
             Rosewood Drive
             Columbia, SC 29208
Nickname: Gamecocks
Telephone: (803) 777-5204
Football Stadium (Capacity): Williams-Brice Stadium
(72,400)
Basketball Arena (Capacity): Frank McGuire Arena
(12,401)
President: Dr. John Palms
Athletic Director: Dr. Mike McGee
Football Coach: Sparky Woods
Basketball Coach: Eddie Fogler
Sports Information Director: Kerry Tharp

University of Tennessee
Address: P.O. Box 15016
             Knoxville, TN 37901
Nickname: Volunteers
Telephone: (615) 974-1212
Football Stadium (Capacity): Neyland Stadium
(91,902)
Basketball Arena (Capacity): Thompson Boling Arena
and Assembly Center (24,535)
President: Dr. Joseph E. Johnson
Athletic Director: Doug Dickey
Football Coach: Phillip Fulmer
Basketball Coach: Wade Houston
Sports Information Director: Bud Ford

Vanderbilt University
Address: P.O. Box 120158
             Nashville, TN 37212
Nickname: Commodores
Telephone: (615) 322-4121
Football Stadium (Capacity): Vanderbilt Stadium
(41,000)
Basketball Arena (Capacity): Memorial Gym (15,378)
Chancellor: Joe B. Wyatt
Athletic Director: Paul Hoolahan
Football Coach: Gerry DiNardo
Basketball Coach: Jan Van Breda Kolff
Sports Information Director: Tony Neely

SOUTHWEST ATHLETIC CONFERENCE
Address: P.O. Box 569420
             Dallas, TX 75356
Telephone: (214) 634-7353
Commissioner and Sports Information Director: Steve
Hatchell

Baylor University
Address: 3031 Dutton
             Waco, TX 76711
Nickname: Bears
Telephone: (817) 755-1234
Football Stadium (Capacity): Floyd Casey Stadium
(48,500)
Basketball Arena (Capacity): Ferrell Center (10,080)
President: Dr. Herbert H. Reynolds
Athletic Director: Dr. Dick Ellis
Football Coach: Chuck Reedy
Basketball Coach: Darrel Johnson
Sports Information Director: Maxey Parrish

College Sports Directory (Cont.)

University of Houston
Address: 3855 Holman
Houston, TX 77204-5121
Nickname: Cougars
Telephone: (713) 743-9370
Football Stadium (Capacity): Astrodome (65,000)
Basketball Arena (Capacity): Hofheinz Pavilion (10,060)
President: Dr. James Pickering
Athletic Director: William C. Carr
Football Coach: Kim Helton
Basketball Coach: Alvin Brooks
Sports Information Director: Ted Nance

Rice University
Address: P.O. Box 1892
Houston, TX 77251
Nickname: Owls
Telephone: (713) 527-4034
Football Stadium (Capacity): Rice Stadium (70,000)
Basketball Arena (Capacity): Autry Court (5,000)
President: Malcolm Gillis
Athletic Director: Bobby May
Football Coach: Fred Goldsmith
Basketball Coach: Willis Wilson
Sports Information Director: Bill Cousins

Southern Methodist University
Address: SMU Box 216
Dallas, TX 75275
Nickname: Mustangs
Telephone: (214) 768-2883
Football Stadium (Capacity): Ownby Stadium (23,783)
Basketball Arena (Capacity): Moody Coliseum (9,007)
President: A. Kenneth Pye
Athletic Director: Forrest Gregg
Football Coach: Tom Rossley
Basketball Coach: John Shumate
Sports Information Director: Ed Wisneski

University of Texas
Address: P.O. Box 7399
Austin, TX 78713
Nickname: Longhorns
Telephone: (512) 471-7437
Football Stadium (Capacity): Memorial Stadium (77,809)
Basketball Arena (Capacity): Erwin Special Events Center (16,231)
Chancellor: Dr. William Cunningham
Athletic Director: DeLoss Dodds
Football Coach: John Mackovic
Basketball Coach: Tom Penders
Sports Information Director: Bill Little

Texas A&M University
Address: Room 222, Student Services Building
College Station, TX 77843
Nickname: Aggies
Telephone: (409) 845-3218
Football Stadium (Capacity): Kyle Field (72,387)
Basketball Arena (Capacity): G. Rollie White Coliseum (7,800)
Interim President: Dr. E. Dean Gage
Athletic Director: Wally Groff
Football Coach: R. C. Slocum
Basketball Coach: Tony Barone
Sports Information Director: Alan Cannon

Texas Christian University
Address: P.O. Box 32924
Fort Worth, TX 76129
Nickname: Horned Frogs
Telephone: (817) 921-7969
Football Stadium (Capacity): Amon G. Carter Stadium (46,000)
Basketball Arena (Capacity): Daniel-Meyer Coliseum (7,166)
Chancellor: Dr. William E. Tucker
Athletic Director: Frank Windegger
Football Coach: Pat Sullivan
Basketball Coach: Moe Iba
Sports Information Director: Glen Stone

Texas Tech University
Address: P.O. Box 43021
Lubbock, TX 79409
Nickname: Red Raiders
Telephone: (806) 742-2770
Football Stadium (Capacity): Jones Stadium (50,500)
Basketball Arena (Capacity): Lubbock Municipal Coliseum (8,196)
President: Dr. Robert Lawless
Athletic Director: Bob Bockrath
Football Coach: Spike Dykes
Basketball Coach: James Dickey
Sports Information Director: Joe Hornaday

WESTERN ATHLETIC CONFERENCE
Address: 14 West Dry Creek Circle
Littleton, CO 80120
Telephone: (303) 795-1962
Commissioner: Dr. Joe Kearney
Publicity Director: Jeff Hurd

Air Force
Address: Colorado Springs, CO 80840-5461
Nickname: Falcons
Telephone: (719) 472-4008
Football Stadium (Capacity): Falcon Stadium (52,153)
Basketball Arena (Capacity): Cadet Field House (6,007)
President: Lt. Gen. Bradley C. Hosmer
Athletic Director: Col. Kenneth L. Schweitzer
Football Coach: Fisher DeBerry
Basketball Coach: Reggie Minton
Sports Information Director: David Kellogg

Brigham Young University
Address: Smith Field House
Provo, UT 84602
Nickname: Cougars
Telephone: (801) 378-4911
Football Stadium (Capacity): Cougar Stadium (65,000)
Basketball Arena (Capacity): Marriott Center (23,000)
President: Rex Lee
Athletic Director: Clayne Jensen
Football Coach: LaVell Edwards
Basketball Coach: Roger Reid
Sports Information Director: Ralph Zobell

Colorado State University

Address: Moby Arena
             Fort Collins, CO 80523
Nickname: Rams
Telephone: (303) 491-5300
Football Stadium (Capacity): Hughes Stadium (30,000)
Basketball Arena (Capacity): Moby Arena (9,001)
President: Dr. Albert C. Yates
Interim Athletic Director: Dr. David Ames
Football Coach: Sonny Lubick
Basketball Coach: Stew Morrill
Sports Information Director: Gary Ozello

University of Hawaii

Address: 1337 Lower Campus Road
             Honolulu, HI 96822-2370
Nickname: Rainbow Warriors
Telephone: (808) 956-8111
Football Stadium (Capacity): Aloha Stadium (50,000)
Basketball Arena (Capacity): Neal Blaisedell Center Arena (7,575)
President: Dr. Kenneth Mortimer
Athletic Director: Hugh Yoshida
Football Coach: Bob Wagner
Basketball Coach: Riley Wallace
Sports Information Director: Ed Inouye

University of New Mexico

Address: 1414 University S.E.
             Albuquerque, NM 87131
Nickname: Lobos
Telephone: (505) 277-6375
Football Stadium (Capacity): University Stadium (30,646)
Basketball Arena (Capacity): University Arena—The Pit (18,100)
President: Dr. Richard Peck
Athletic Director: Rudy Davalos
Football Coach: Dennis Franchione
Basketball Coach: Dave Bliss
Sports Information Director: Greg Remington

San Diego State University

Address: San Diego, CA 92182
Nickname: Aztecs
Telephone: (619) 594-5163
Football Stadium (Capacity): San Diego Jack Murphy Stadium (61,104)
Basketball Arena (Capacity): Peterson Gym (3,668)
President: Dr. Thomas B. Day
Athletic Director: Dr. Fred Miller
Football Coach: Al Luginbill
Basketball Coach: Tony Fuller
Sports Information Director: John Rosenthal

University of Texas at El Paso

Address: 500 West University Avenue
             El Paso, TX 79968
Nickname: Miners
Telephone: (915) 747-5347
Football Stadium (Capacity): Sun Bowl (53,000)
Basketball Arena (Capacity): Special Events Center (12,222)
President: Dr. Diana Natalicio
Athletic Director: John Thompson
Football Coach: Charlie Bailey
Basketball Coach: Don Haskins
Sports Information Director: Eddie Mullens

University of Utah

Address: Huntsman Center
             Salt Lake City, UT 84112
Nickname: Utes
Telephone: (801) 581-8171
Football Stadium (Capacity): Rice Stadium (35,000)
Basketball Arena (Capacity): Huntsman Center (15,000)
President: Dr. Arthur K. Smith
Athletic Director: Dr. Chris Hill
Football Coach: Ron McBride
Basketball Coach: Rick Majerus
Sports Information Director: Bruce Woodbury

University of Wyoming

Address: P.O. Box 3414
             Laramie, WY 82071-3414
Nickname: Cowboys
Telephone: (307) 766-2292
Football Stadium (Capacity): War Memorial Stadium (33,500)
Basketball Arena (Capacity): Arena-Auditorium (15,028)
President: Dr. Terry Roark
Athletic Director: Paul Roach
Football Coach: Joe Tiller
Basketball Coach: Joby Wright
Sports Information Director: Kevin McKinney

INDEPENDENTS

Army

Address: West Point, NY 10996
Nickname: Cadets/Black Knights
Telephone: (914) 938-3303
Football Stadium (Capacity): Michie Stadium (39,929)
Basketball Arena (Capacity): Cristl Arena (5,043)
Superintendent: Lt. Gen. Howard D. Graves
Athletic Director: Al Vanderbush
Football Coach: Bob Sutton
Basketball Coach: Dino Gaudio
Sports Information Director: Bob Kinney

Note: Plays football as independent, basketball in Patriot League.

University of Cincinnati

Address: Cincinnati, OH 45221-0021
Nickname: Bearcats
Telephone: (513) 556-5601
Football Stadium (Capacity): Nippert Stadium (35,500)
Basketball Arena (Capacity): Myrl Shoemaker Center (13,176)
President: Dr. Joseph A. Steger
Athletic Director: Rick Taylor
Football Coach: Tim Murphy
Basketball Coach: Bob Huggins
Sports Information Director: Tom Hathaway

Note: Plays football as independent, basketball in Great Midwest Conference.

East Carolina University

Address: Greenville, NC 27858-4353
Nickname: Pirates
Telephone: (919) 757-4600
Football Stadium (Capacity): Ficklen Stadium (35,000)
Basketball Arena (Capacity): Minges Coliseum (6,500)
Chancellor: Dr. Richard R. Eakin
Athletic Director: David R. Hart, Jr.
Football Coach: Steve Logan
Basketball Coach: Eddie Payne
Sports Information Director: Charles Bloom

University of Louisville

Address: Louisville, KY 40292
Nickname: Cardinals
Telephone: (502) 588-5732
Football Stadium (Capacity): Cardinal Stadium (37,500)
Basketball Arena (Capacity): Freedom Hall (19,000)
President: Dr. Donald Swain
Athletic Director: William Olsen
Football Coach: Howard Schnellenberger
Basketball Coach: Denny Crum
Sports Information Director: Kenny Klein

Note: Plays football as independent, basketball in Metro Conference.

Memphis State University

Address: Memphis, TN 38152
Nickname: Tigers
Telephone: (901) 678-2337
Football Stadium (Capacity): Liberty Bowl Memorial Stadium/Rex Dockery Field (62,380)
Basketball Arena (Capacity): The Pyramid (20,142)
President: Dr. V. Lane Rawlins
Athletic Director: Charles Cavagnaro
Football Coach: Chuck Stobart
Basketball Coach: Larry Finch
Sports Information Director: Bob Winn

Navy

Address: 566 Brownson Road
Ricketts Hall
Annapolis, MD 21402
Nickname: Midshipmen
Telephone: (410) 268-6220
Football Stadium (Capacity): Navy-Marine Corps Memorial Stadium (30,000)
Basketball Arena (Capacity): Alumni Hall (5,710)
Superintendent: Rear Adm. Thomas C. Lynch, USN
Athletic Director: Jack Lengyel
Football Coach: George Chaump
Basketball Coach: Don DeVoe
Sports Information Director: Thomas Bates

Note: Plays football as independent, basketball in the Patriot League.

University of Notre Dame

Address: Notre Dame, IN 46556
Nickname: Fighting Irish
Telephone: (219) 631-6107
Football Stadium (Capacity): Notre Dame Stadium (59,075)
Basketball Arena (Capacity): Joyce Athletic and Convocation Center (11,418)
President: Rev. Edward A. Malloy, CSC
Athletic Director: Richard Rosenthal
Football Coach: Lou Holtz
Basketball Coach: John MacLeod
Sports Information Director: John Heisler

University of Southern Mississippi

Address: Box 5017
Hattiesburg, MS 39406
Nickname: Golden Eagles
Telephone: (601) 266-4503
Football Stadium (Capacity): M. M. Roberts Stadium (33,000)
Basketball Arena (Capacity): Green Coliseum (8,095)
President: Dr. Aubrey K. Lucas
Athletic Director: Bill McLellan
Football Coach: Jeff Bower
Basketball Coach: M. K. Turk
Sports Information Director: Regiel Napier

Note: Plays football as independent, basketball in Metro Conference.

Tulane University

Address: James Wilson Jr. Center for Intercollegiate Athletics
New Orleans, LA 70118
Nickname: Green Wave
Telephone: (504) 865-5501
Football Stadium (Capacity): Louisiana Superdome (71,000)
Basketball Arena (Capacity): Fogelman Arena (5,000)
President: Dr. Eamon Kelly
Athletic Director: Dr. Kevin White
Football Coach: Eugene (Buddy) Teevens
Basketball Coach: Perry Clark
Sports Information Director: Lenny Vangilder

Note: Plays football as independent, basketball in Metro Conference.

University of Tulsa

Address: 600 S. College
Tulsa, OK 74104
Nickname: Golden Hurricane
Telephone: (918) 631-2395
Football Stadium (Capacity): Skelley Stadium (40,385)
Basketball Arena (Capacity): Tulsa Convention Center (8,659)
President: Dr. Robert H. Donaldson
Athletic Director: Rick Dickson
Football Coach: Dave Rader
Basketball Coach: Orlando (Tubby) Smith
Sports Information Director: Don Tomkalski

THEY SAID IT

Jimmy Soto, University of Utah basketball guard on why he gave up baseball, even though he's better in that sport: "I got bored standing around chewing sunflower seeds"

Olympic Sports Directory

United States Olympic Committee
Address: Olympic House
        1 Olympic Plaza
        Colorado Springs, CO 80909
Telephone: (719) 632-5551
Executive Director: Dr. Harvey Schiller
Director of Plans and Programs: Jeff Cravens
Assistant Director of Plans and Programs: Gayle
  Plant

U.S. Olympic Training Center
Address: 1 Olympic Plaza
        Colorado Springs, CO 80909
Telephone: (719) 578-4500
Director: Charles Davis

U.S. Olympic Training Center
Address: 421 Old Military Road
        Lake Placid, NY 12946
Telephone: (518) 523-2600
Director: Gloria Chadwick

International Olympic Committee
Address: Chateau de Vidy
        CH-1007 Lausanne
        Switzerland
Telephone: (41.21) 25 3271/3272
President: Juan Antonio Samaranch
Director General: Francois Carrard
Public Relations Officer: Michele Verdier

Lillehammer Olympic Organizing Committee
Address: Storgatan 95
        P.O. Box 106
        N-2601 Lillehammer, Norway
Telephone: (47.62) 57455
President: Gerhard Heiberg
Director of Planning: Osmund Uelaud
Director of Communication: Aage Enghaug
(XVIIth Olympic Winter Games; February 12—27, 1994)

Atlanta Olympic Organizing Committee
Address: Suite 3450, One Atlantic Center
        1201 West Peachtree Street
        Atlanta, GA 30309
Telephone: (404) 874-1996
Chairman: Hon. Andrew Young
President: William Porter Payne
Executive Director: Doug Gatlin
(Games of the XXVIth Olympiad; Tentative Dates:
July 20—August 4, 1996)

U.S. Olympic Organizations

Archery

National Archery Association (NAA)
Address: 1 Olympic Plaza
        Colorado Springs, CO 80909
Telephone: (719) 578-4576
President: Don A. Marcure
Executive Director: Christine McCartney

Athletics (Track & Field)

USA Track & Field (formerly TAC)
Address: P.O. Box 120
        Indianapolis, IN 46206
Telephone: (317) 261-0500
President: Larry Ellis
Executive Director: Ollan Cassell
Press Information Director: Pete Cava

Badminton

U.S. Badminton Association (USBA)
Address: 1 Olympic Plaza
        Colorado Springs, CO 80909
Telephone: (719) 578-4808
President: Cynthia Kelly
Executive Director: Jim Hadley

Baseball

U.S. Baseball Federation (USBF)
Address: 2160 Greenwood Avenue
        Trenton, NJ 08609
Telephone: (609) 586-2381
President: Mark Marquess
Executive Director: Richard Case
Acting Communications Director: Mike Lantz

Basketball

USA Basketball
Address: 1 Olympic Plaza
        Colorado Springs, CO 80909
Telephone: (719) 632-7687
President: C.M. Newton
Executive Director: Warren Brown
Assistant Executive Director for Public Relations:
  Craig Miller

Biathlon

U.S. Biathlon Association (USBA)
Address: 421 Old Military Road
        Lake Placid, NY 12946
Telephone: (518) 523-3836
President: Ed Williams
Executive Director: Dusty Johnstone

Bobsled

U.S. Bobsled and Skeleton Federation
Address: P.O. Box 828
            Lake Placid, NY 12946
Telephone: (518) 523-1842
President: Jim Morris
Executive Director: Matt Roy
Marketing and Communications Director: Terry Kent

Bowling

U.S. Tenpin Bowling Federation
Address: 5301 South 76th Street
            Greendale, WI 53129
Telephone: (414) 421-9008
President: Joyce Dietch
Executive Director: Gerald Koenig
Public Relations Coordinator: Maureen Boyle

Boxing

USA Boxing
Address: 1 Olympic Plaza
            Colorado Springs, CO 80909
Telephone: (719) 578-4506
President: Jerry Dusenberry
Acting Executive Director: Bruce Mathis
Director of Communications: Jay Miller

Canoe/Kayak

U.S. Canoe and Kayak Team
Address: Pan American Plaza, Suite 610
            201 South Capitol Avenue
            Indianapolis, IN 46225
Telephone: (317) 237-5690
Chairman: Eric Haught
Executive Director: Chuck Wielgus
Communications Director: Craig Bohnert

Cycling

U.S. Cycling Federation (USCF)
Address: 1 Olympic Plaza
            Colorado Springs, CO 80909
Telephone: (719) 578-4581
President: Richard DeGarmo
Executive Director: Lisa Voight
Media and Public Relations Director: Steve Penny

Diving

United States Diving, Inc. (USD)
Address: Pan American Plaza, Suite 430
            201 South Capitol Avenue
            Indianapolis, IN 46225
Telephone: (317) 237-5252
President: Micki King
Executive Director: Todd Smith
Director of Communications: Dave Shatkowski

Equestrian

U.S. Equestrian Team (USET)
Address: Gladstone, NJ 07934
Telephone: (908) 234-0155
Chairman of the Board and President: Robert C.
  Standish
Director of Public Relations: Marty Bauman

Fencing

U.S. Fencing Association (USFA)
Address: 1 Olympic Plaza
            Colorado Springs, CO 80909
Telephone: (719) 578-4511
President: Stephen Sobel
Executive Director: Carla-Mae Richards
Media Relations Director: Colleen Walker-Mar

Field Hockey

**U.S. Field Hockey Association (USFHA)
(Women)**
Address: 1 Olympic Plaza
            Colorado Springs, CO 80909
Telephone: (719) 578-4567
President: Jenepher Shillingford
Executive Director: Carrie Haag
Director of Public Relations: Noreen Landis-Tyson

Figure Skating

U.S. Figure Skating Association (USFSA)
Address: 20 First Street
            Colorado Springs, CO 80906
Telephone: (719) 635-5200
President: Claire Ferguson
Executive Director: Jerry Lace
Communications Director: Kristin Matta

Gymnastics

U.S. Gymnastics Federation (USGF)
Address: Pan American Plaza, Suite 300
            201 South Capitol Avenue
            Indianapolis, IN 46225
Telephone: (317) 237-5050
Chairman of the Board: Sandy Knapp
Executive Director: TBA
Director of Public Relations: Luan Peszek

Hockey

USA Hockey
Address: 4965 North 30th Street
            Colorado Springs, CO 80919
Telephone: (719) 599-5500
President: Walter Bush
Executive Director: Dave Ogrean
Public Relations Coordinator: Darryl Sibel

Judo

United States Judo, Inc. (USJ)
Address: P.O. Box 10013
            El Paso, TX 79991
Telephone: (915) 565-8754
President and Media Contact: Frank Fullerton

Luge

U.S. Luge Association (USLA)
Address:　P.O. Box 651
　　　　　Lake Placid, NY 12946
Telephone: (518) 523-2071
President: Dwight Bell
Executive Director: Ron Rossi
Public Relations and Media Coordinator:
　Dmitri Feld

Modern Pentathlon

U.S. Modern Pentathlon Association (USMPA)
Address:　530 McCullough Avenue, Suite 1010
　　　　　San Antonio, TX 78215
Telephone: (210) 246-3000
President: Daniel Steinman
Executive Director: Michael J. Cermele

Racquetball

American Amateur Racquetball Association (AARA)
Address:　1685 West Uintah
　　　　　Colorado Springs, CO 80904
Telephone: (719) 635-5396
President: Keith Calkins
Executive Director: Luke St. Onge
Public Relations Director: Linda Mojer

Roller Skating

U.S. Amateur Confederation of Roller Skating (USAC/RS)
Address:　4730 South Street
　　　　　P.O. Box 6579
　　　　　Lincoln, NE 68506
Telephone: (402) 483-7551
President: Charles Wahlig
Executive Director: George H. Pickard
Sports Information Director: Kirk Spellman

Rowing

U.S. Rowing Association (USRA)
Address:　Pan American Plaza, Suite 400
　　　　　201 South Capitol Avenue
　　　　　Indianapolis, IN 46225
Telephone: (317) 237-5656
President: Frank Coyle
Executive Director: Sandra Hughes
Director of Communications: Maureen Merhoff

Shooting

U.S. Shooting Association
Address:　1 Olympic Plaza
　　　　　Colorado Springs, CO 80909
Telephone: (719) 578-4670
Chairman, International Competition Committee: Col.
William Deneke
Acting Executive Director: Dr. Henry Cross III
Director of Public Relations: Karen Mutka

Skiing

U.S. Skiing
Address:　P.O. Box 100
　　　　　Park City, UT 84060
Telephone: (801) 649-9090
Chairman: Thomas Weisel
President and CEO: Mike Jacki
Vice-Chairman: Serge Lussi
President, U.S. Ski Educational Foundation:
　Vinton Sommerville
Director of Communications: Tom Kelly
News Bureau Coordinator: Ron Goch
Press Officer: Jolene Aubel

Soccer

U.S. Soccer Federation (USSF)
Address:　1801-1811 South Prairie Avenue
　　　　　Chicago, IL 60616
Telephone: (312) 808-1300
President: Alan Rothenberg
Executive Director: Hank Steinbrecher
Director of Marketing: Terry Weekes
Director of Communications: Tom Lang

Softball

Amateur Softball Association (ASA)
Address:　2801 N.E. 50th Street
　　　　　Oklahoma City, OK 73111
Telephone: (405) 424-5266
President: Jack Aaron
Executive Director: Don Porter
Director of Communications: Bill Plummer

Speedskating

U.S. International Speedskating Association (USISA)
Address:　P.O. Box 16157
　　　　　Rocky River, OH 44116
Telephone: (216) 226-5052
President: Bill Cushman
Program Director: Katie Class
Media Contact: Susan Polakoff-Shaw

Swimming

U.S. Swimming, Inc. (USS)
Address:　1 Olympic Plaza
　　　　　Colorado Springs, CO 80909
Telephone: (719) 578-4578
President: Bill Maxson
Executive Director: Ray Essick
Communication Director: Charlie Snyder

Synchronized Swimming

U.S. Synchronized Swimming, Inc. (USSS)
Address:　Pan American Plaza, Suite 510
　　　　　201 South Capitol Avenue
　　　　　Indianapolis, IN 46225
Telephone: (317) 237-5700
President: Nancy Wichtman
Executive Director: Betty Watanabe
Membership and Communications: Laura LaMarca

Table Tennis

U.S. Table Tennis Association (USTTA)
Address: 1 Olympic Plaza
              Colorado Springs, CO 80909
Telephone: (719) 578-4583
Executive Director: Kae Rader
President: Dan Seemiller
Office Manager: Linda Gleeson

Taekwondo

U.S. Taekwondo Union (USTU)
Address: 1 Olympic Plaza, Suite 405
              Colorado Springs, CO 80909
Telephone: (719) 578-4632
President: Hwa Chong
Executive Director: Robert Fujimura

Team Handball

U.S. Team Handball Federation (USTHF)
Address: 1 Olympic Plaza
              Colorado Springs, CO 80909
Telephone: (719) 578-4582
President: Dr. Peter Buehning
Executive Director: Michael D. Cavanaugh
Media Contact: Evelyn Anderson

Tennis

U.S. Tennis Association
Address: 70 West Red Oak Lane
              White Plains, NY 10604
Telephone: (914) 696-7000
President: Jay Howard Frazier
Executive Director: M. Marshall Happer III
Director of Communications: Page Crosland

Volleyball

U.S. Volleyball Association (USVBA)
Address: 3595 East Fountain Boulevard, Suite I-2
              Colorado Springs, CO 80909-1740
Telephone: (719) 637-8300
President: Jerry Sherman
Executive Director: John Carroll
Media Relations and Publications: Rich Wanninger
Media Relations Telephone: (619) 692-4162

Water Polo

United States Water Polo (USWP)
Address: Pan American Plaza, Suite 520
              201 South Capitol Avenue
              Indianapolis, IN 46225
Telephone: (317) 237-5599
President: Richard Foster
Executive Director: Bruce J. Wigo
Director of Media and Public Relations: Eileen Sexton

Weightlifting

U.S. Weightlifting Federation (USWF)
Address: 1 Olympic Plaza
              Colorado Springs, CO 80909
Telephone: (719) 578-4508
President: Jim Schmitz
Executive Director: George Greenway
Communications Director: John Halpin

Wrestling

USA Wrestling
Address: 6155 Lehman
              Colorado Springs, CO 80918
Telephone: (719) 598-8181
President: Arthur Martoni
Executive Director: Jim Scherr
Director of Communications: Gary Abbott

Yachting

U.S. Yacht Racing Union (USYRU)
Address: P.O. Box 209
              Newport, RI 02840
Telephone: (401) 849-5200
President: Bob Hobbs
Executive Director: John B. Bonds
Communications Director: Dana Marane
Olympic Yachting Director: Jonathan R. Harley

Affiliated Sports Organizations

Amateur Athletic Union (AAU)
Address: 3400 West 86th Street
              P.O. Box 68207
              Indianapolis, IN 46268
Telephone: (317) 872-2900
President: Bobby Dodd
Executive Director: Dr. Lou Marciani

Curling

U.S. Curling Association (USCA)
Address: 1100 Center Point Drive
              Box 866
              Stevens Point, WI 54481
Telephone: (715) 344-1199
President: Evelyn Nostrand
Executive Director: David Garber

Affiliated Sports Organizations (Cont.)

Karate

USA Karate Federation
Address: 1300 Kenmore Boulevard
             Akron, OH 44314
Telephone: (216) 753-3114
President: George Anderson

Orienteering

U.S. Orienteering Federation
Address: P.O. Box 1444
             Forest Park, GA 30051
Telephone: (404) 363-2110
President: Larry Pedersen
Executive Director: Robin Shannonhouse
Media and Publicity Contact: John Nash
Publicity telephone: (914) 941-0896

Squash

U.S. Squash Racquets Association
Address: 23 Cynwyd Road
             P.O. Box 1216
             Bala Cynwyd, PA 19004
Telephone: (215) 667-4006
President: Alan Fox
Executive Director: Craig Brand

Trampoline and Tumbling

American Trampoline and Tumbling Association
Address: 1610 East Cardwell
             or P.O. Box 306
             Brownfield, TX 79316
Telephone: (806) 637-8670
President: Connie Mara
Executive Director: Ann Sims

Triathlon

Triathlon Federation USA
Address: 3595 East Fountain Boulevard, Suite F-1
             Colorado Springs, CO 80910
Telephone: (719) 597-9090
President and Executive Director: Steve Locke
Deputy Director and Media Contact: Tim Yount

Underwater Swimming

Underwater Society of America
Address: 849 West Orange Avenue
             No. 1002
             South San Francisco, CA 94080
Telephone: (415) 583-8492
President: George Rose

Water Skiing

American Water Ski Association
Address: 799 Overlook Drive, S.E.
             Winter Haven, FL 33884
Telephone: (813) 324-4341
President: Harold Hill
Executive Director: Duke Cullimore
Public Relations Manager: Don Cullimore

Miscellaneous Sports Directory

American Professional Soccer League
Address: 122 C Street NW, Suite 810
             Washington, D.C. 20001
Telephone: (202) 638-0022
Chairman of the Board: Dr. William De La Peña
Commissioner: TBA
Director of Operations: Emily Ballus

Continental Indoor Soccer League
Address: 16027 Ventura Boulevard, Suite 605
             Encino, CA 91436
Telephone: (818) 906-7627
Commissioner: Ron Weinstein
Director of Public Relations: Dan Courtemanchi

National Professional Soccer League
Address: 229 Third Street NW
             Canton, OH 44702
Telephone: (216) 455-4625
Commissioner: Steve Paxos
Director of Public Relations: Paul Luchowski

Ladies Professional Golf Association
Address: 2570 W International Speedway
             Boulevard, Suite B
             Daytona Beach, FL 32114
Telephone: (904) 254-8800
Commissioner: Charles S. Mechem Jr.
Director of Communications: Elaine Scott

Professional Golfers Association
Address: Sawgrass, 112 TPC Boulevard
             Ponte Vedra, FL 32082
Telephone: (904) 285-3700
Commissioner: Deane R. Beman
Director of Public Relations: Sid Wilson

United States Golf Association
Address: P.O. Box 708, Golf House
             Liberty Corner Road
             Far Hills, NJ 07931-0708
Telephone: (908) 234-2300
President: Stuart F. Bloch

Association of Tennis Professionals Tour

Address: 200 ATP Tour Boulevard
            Ponte Vedra Beach, FL 32082
Telephone: (904) 285-8000
Chief Executive Officer: Mark Miles
Director of Communications: Pete Alfano

Women's Tennis Association

Address: 133 First Street N.E.
            St. Petersburg, FL 33701
Telephone: (813) 895-5000
Executive Director: Gerard Smith
President: Pam Shriver
Director of Public Relations: Ana Leaird

United States Tennis Association

Address: 70 West Red Oak Lane
            White Plains, NY 10604
Telephone: (914) 696-7000
President: Jay Howard Frazier
Executive Director: M. Marshall Happer III
Director of Communications: Page Crosland

National Association for Stock Car Auto Racing (NASCAR)

Address: P.O. Box 2875, 1801 W International
            Speedway Boulevard
            Daytona Beach, FL 32120
Telephone: (904) 253-0611
President: Bill France Jr.
Manager of Public Relations: Andy Hall

Championship Auto Racing Teams (CART)

Address: 390 Enterprise Court
            Bloomfield Hills, MI 48302
Telephone: (313) 334-8500
Executive Vice President: TBA
Director of Publicity: Dave Elshoff

National Hot Rod Association

Address: 2035 East Financial Way
            Glendora, CA 91741
Telephone: (818) 914-4761
President: Dallas Gardner
Director of Communications: Denny Darnell

International Motor Sports Association

Address: 3502 Henderson Boulevard
            Tampa, FL 33609
Telephone: (813) 877-4672
President: Dan Greenwood
Media Director: Lynn Myfelt

Professional Rodeo Cowboys Association

Address: 101 Pro Rodeo Drive
            Colorado Springs, CO 80919
Telephone: (719) 593-8840
Commissioner: Lewis Cryer
Director of Communications: Steve Fleming

Thoroughbred Racing Associations of America

Address: 420 Fair Hill Drive, Suite 1
            Elkton, MD 21921
Telephone: (410) 392-9200
President: Christoph Scherf
Director of Service Bureau: Conrad Sobkoviak

Thoroughbred Racing Communications, Inc.

Address: 40 East 52nd Street
            New York, NY 10022
Telephone: (212) 371-5910
Executive Director: Tom Merritt
Director of Media Relations and Development:
  Bob Curran

Breeders' Cup Limited

Address: 2525 Harrodsburg Road
            Lexington, KY 40504-3359
Telephone: (606) 223-5444
President: James Bassett
Media Relations Directors: James Gluckson and
  Ben Metzger

The Jockeys' Guild, Inc.

Address: 250 West Main Street
            Lexington, KY 40507
Telephone: (606) 259-3211
President: Jerry Bailey
National Manager/Secretary: John Giovanni

United States Trotting Association

Address: 750 Michigan Avenue
            Columbus, OH 43215
Telephone: (614) 224-2291
President: Corwin Nixon
Publicity Department: John Pawlak

Professional Bowlers Association

Address: 1720 Merriman Road, P.O. Box 5118
            Akron, OH 44334-0118
Telephone: (216) 836-5568
Commissioner: Michael Connor
Public Relations Director: Kevin Shippy

Ladies Pro Bowlers Tour

Address: 7171 Cherryvale Boulevard
            Rockford, IL 61112
Telephone: (815) 332-5756
Executive Director: Tom Shimeck
Media Director: Linda Thomas

Women's International Bowling Congress

Address: 5301 South 76th Street
            Greendale, WI 53129-1191
Telephone: (414) 421-9000
President: Joyce Deitch
Public Relations Manager: Karen Sytsma

American Bowling Congress

Address: 5301 South 76th Street
            Greendale, WI 53129
Telephone: (414) 421-6400
President: Ted Melonis
Communications Executive: Steve James

Association of Volleyball Professionals

Address: 100 Corporate Pointe, #160
            Culver City, CA 90230
Telephone: (310) 337-4842
President: Jon Stevenson
Public Relations: Debbie Rubio

U.S. Chess Federation
Address: 186 Route 9W
             New Windsor, NY 12553
Telephone: (914) 562-8350
Director: Al Lawrence
Assistant Director: Russ Garber

Iditarod Trail Committee
Address: P.O. Box 870800
             Wasilla, AK 99687
Telephone: (907) 376-5155
Executive Director: Stan Hooley
Race Director: Joanne Potts

International Game Fish Association
Address: 1301 East Atlantic Boulevard
             Pompano Beach, FL 33060
Telephone: (305) 941-3474
President: Mike Leech

American Greyhound Track Operators Association
Address: 1065 Northeast 125th Street, Suite 219
             North Miami, FL 33161
Telephone: (305) 893-2101
President: Fred Havenick
Secretary/Executive Director: George D. Johnson Jr.

U.S. Handball Association
Address: 2333 North Tucson Boulevard
             Tucson, AZ 85716
Telephone: (602) 795-0434
Executive Director: Vern Roberts
Director of Public Relations: Cheri Morden

U.S. Club Lacrosse Association
Address: c/o Lacrosse Foundation
             113 W University Parkway
             Baltimore, MD 21210
Telephone: (410) 235-6882
Executive Director: Steven B. Stenersen

Little League Baseball, Inc.
Address: P.O. Box 3485
             Williamsport, PA 17701
Telephone: (717) 326-1921
President: Dr. Creighton Hale
Communications Director: Dennis Sullivan

American Powerboating Association
Address: P.O. Box 377
             East Pointe, MI 48021
Telephone: (313) 773-9700
Executive Administrator: Gloria Urbin

U.S. Polo Association
Address: 4059 Iron Works Pike
             Lexington, KY 40511
Telephone: (606) 255-0593
Executive Director: Allan D. Scherer

U.S. Rugby Football Union
Address: 3595 East Fountain Boulevard
             Colorado Springs, CO 80910
Telephone: (719) 637-1022
Director of Administration: Karen Kast

World Cup USA 1994, Inc.
XV FIFA World Cup Organizing Committee
Address: 1270 Avenue of the Americas
             Suite 220
             New York, NY 10020
Telephone: (212) 332-1994
Chairman: Alan Rothenberg

MINOR LEAGUES

Baseball (AAA)

American Association
Address: 410 East McMillan, Suite 250
             Cincinnati, OH 45206
Telephone: (513) 281-8100
President: Branch Rickey

International League
Address: 55 South High Street, Suite 202
             Dublin, OH 43017
Telephone: (614) 791-9300
President: Randy Mobley

Mexican League
Address: Angela Pola #16
             Col. Periodista, C.P. 11220
             Mexico D.F.
Telephone: (905) 587-10-07
President: Petro Cisneros

Pacific Coast League
Address: 2101 East Broadway, Suite 35
             Tempe, AZ 85282
Telephone: (602) 838-2171
President: Bill Cutler

Hockey

American Hockey League
Address: 425 Union Street
             West Springfield, MA 01089
Telephone: (413) 781-2030
President: Jack Butterfield
Vice-President: Gordon Anziano

International Hockey League
Address: 3850 Priority Way, Suite 100
             Indianapolis, IN 46240
Telephone: (317) 573-3888
Commissioner: N. Thomas Berry Jr.
Director of Public Relations: Andrew J. McGowan

Hall of Fame Directory

National Baseball Hall of Fame And Museum
Address: P.O. Box 590
                Cooperstown, NY 13326
Telephone: (607) 547-9114
President: Donald Marr
Director of Public Relations: Bill Guilfoile

Naismith Memorial Basketball Hall of Fame
Address: 1150 West Columbus Avenue
                Springfield, Mass. 01101
Telephone: (413) 781-6500
President: Joseph O'Brien
Director of Public Relations: Robin Deutsch

National Bowling Hall of Fame And Museum
Address: 111 Stadium Plaza
                St Louis, MO 63102
Telephone: (314) 231-6340
Executive Director: Gerald Baltz
Director of Marketing: RoseAnne Gruchala

National Boxing Hall of Fame
Address: 1 Hall of Fame Drive
                Canastota, NY 13032
Telephone: (315) 697-7095
President: Donald Ackerman
Executive Director: Edward Brophy

Professional Football Hall of Fame
Address: 2121 George Halas Drive NW
                Canton, OH 44708
Telephone: (216) 456-8207
Executive Director: Pete Elliott
Vice President, Public Relations: Don Smith

LPGA Hall of Fame
Address: 2750 West International Speedway
Boulevard, Suite B
                Daytona Beach, FL 32114
Telephone: (904) 254-880
Commissioner: Charles S. Mechem
Communications Director: Elaine Scott

Note: PGA Hall of Fame is closed until at least 1995.

Professional Hockey Hall of Fame
Address: 30 Young Street BCE Place
                Toronto, Ontario Canada M5E 1X8
Telephone: (416) 360-7735
President: David Taylor
Director of Marketing: Phil Denyes

National Museum of Racing and Hall of Fame
Address: Union Avenue
                Saratoga Springs, NY 12866
Telephone: (518) 584-0400
Executive Director: Peter Hammell
Assistant Director: Catherine Maguire

National Soccer Hall of Fame
Address: 5-11 Ford Avenue
                Oneonta, N.Y. 13820
Telephone: (607) 432-3351
Executive Director: Albert Colone
External Affairs: Will Lunn

International Swimming Hall of Fame
Address: 1 Hall of Fame Drive
                Fort Lauderdale, FL 33316
Telephone: (305) 462-6536
President: Dr. Samuel J. Freas
Director of Marketing: Michelle Mitchell-Rocha

International Tennis Hall of Fame
Address: 194 Bellevue Avenue
                Newport, R.I. 02840
Telephone: (401) 849-3990
Executive Director: Mark Stenning
Director of Public Relations: Linda Johnson

National Track & Field Hall of Fame
Address: P.O. Box 120
                Indianapolis, IN 46206
Telephone: (317) 261-0500
Curator: Marty Weiss
Director of Media Relations: Pete Cava

Awards

DEC. 21, 1992 - $2.95

Sports Illustrated

SPORTSMAN OF THE YEAR

Arthur Ashe

MICHAEL O'NEILL

FOR THE RECORD · Year by Year

Athlete Awards

Sports Illustrated Sportsman of the Year

1954	Roger Bannister, Track
1955	Johnny Podres, Baseball
1956	Bobby Morrow, Track
1957	Stan Musial, Baseball
1958	Rafer Johnson, Track
1959	Ingemar Johansson, Boxing
1960	Arnold Palmer, Golf
1961	Jerry Lucas, Basketball
1962	Terry Baker, Football
1963	Pete Rozelle, Pro Football
1964	Ken Venturi, Golf
1965	Sandy Koufax, Baseball
1966	Jim Ryun, Track
1967	Carl Yastrzemski, Baseball
1968	Bill Russell, Pro Basketball
1969	Tom Seaver, Baseball
1970	Bobby Orr, Hockey
1971	Lee Trevino, Golf
1972	Billie Jean King, Tennis
	John Wooden, Basketball
1973	Jackie Stewart, Auto Racing
1974	Muhammad Ali, Boxing
1975	Pete Rose, Baseball
1976	Chris Evert, Tennis
1977	Steve Cauthen, Horse Racing
1978	Jack Nicklaus, Golf
1979	Terry Bradshaw, Pro Football
	Willie Stargell, Baseball
1980	US Olympic Hockey Team
1981	Sugar Ray Leonard, Boxing
1982	Wayne Gretzky, Hockey
1983	Mary Decker, Track
1984	Mary Lou Retton, Gymnastics
	Edwin Moses, Track
1985	Kareem Abdul-Jabbar, Pro Basketball
1986	Joe Paterno, Football
1987	Athletes Who Care
	Bob Bourne, Hockey
	Kip Keino, Track
	Judi Brown King, Track
	Dale Murphy, Baseball
	Chip Rives, Football
	Patty Sheehan, Golf
	Rory Sparrow, Pro Basketball
	Reggie Williams, Pro Football
1988	Orel Hershiser, Baseball
1989	Greg LeMond, Cycling
1990	Joe Montana, Pro Football
1991	Michael Jordan, Pro Basketball
1992	Arthur Ashe

Associated Press Athletes of the Year

	MEN	WOMEN
1931	Pepper Martin, Baseball	Helene Madison, Swimming
1932	Gene Sarazen, Golf	Babe Didrikson, Track
1933	Carl Hubbell, Baseball	Helen Jacobs, Tennis
1934	Dizzy Dean, Baseball	Virginia Van Wie, Golf
1935	Joe Louis, Boxing	Helen Wills Moody, Tennis
1936	Jesse Owens, Track	Helen Stephens, Track
1937	Don Budge, Tennis	Katherine Rawls, Swimming
1938	Don Budge, Tennis	Patty Berg, Golf
1939	Nile Kinnick, Football	Alice Marble, Tennis
1940	Tom Harmon, Football	Alice Marble, Tennis
1941	Joe DiMaggio, Baseball	Betty Hicks Newell, Golf
1942	Frank Sinkwich, Football	Gloria Callen, Swimming
1943	Gunder Haegg, Track	Patty Berg, Golf
1944	Byron Nelson, Golf	Ann Curtis, Swimming
1945	Bryon Nelson, Golf	Babe Didrikson Zaharias, Golf
1946	Glenn Davis, Football	Babe Didrikson Zaharias, Golf
1947	Johnny Lujack, Football	Babe Didrikson Zaharias, Golf
1948	Lou Boudreau, Baseball	Fanny Blankers-Koen, Track
1949	Leon Hart, Football	Marlene Bauer, Golf
1950	Jim Konstanty, Baseball	Babe Didrikson Zaharias, Golf
1951	Dick Kazmaier, Football	Maureen Connolly, Tennis
1952	Bob Mathias, Track	Maureen Connolly, Tennis
1953	Ben Hogan, Golf	Maureen Connolly, Tennis
1954	Willie Mays, Baseball	Babe Didrikson Zaharias, Golf
1955	Hopalong Cassidy, Football	Patty Berg, Golf
1956	Mickey Mantle, Baseball	Pat McCormick, Diving
1957	Ted Williams, Baseball	Althea Gibson, Tennis
1958	Herb Elliott, Track	Althea Gibson, Tennis
1959	Ingemar Johansson, Boxing	Maria Bueno, Tennis
1960	Rafer Johnson, Track	Wilma Rudolph, Track
1961	Roger Maris, Baseball	Wilma Rudolph, Track
1962	Maury Wills, Baseball	Dawn Fraser, Swimming
1963	Sandy Koufax, Baseball	Mickey Wright, Golf
1964	Don Schollander, Swimming	Mickey Wright, Golf

Associated Press Athletes of the Year (Cont.)

	MEN	WOMEN
1965	Sandy Koufax, Baseball	Kathy Whitworth, Golf
1966	Frank Robinson, Baseball	Kathy Whitworth, Golf
1967	Carl Yastrzemski, Baseball	Billie Jean King, Tennis
1968	Denny McLain, Baseball	Peggy Fleming, Skating
1969	Tom Seaver, Baseball	Debbie Meyer, Swimming
1970	George Blanda, Pro Football	Chi Cheng, Track
1971	Lee Trevino, Golf	Evonne Goolagong, Tennis
1972	Mark Spitz, Swimming	Olga Korbut, Gymnastics
1973	O. J. Simpson, Pro Football	Billie Jean King, Tennis
1974	Muhammad Ali, Boxing	Chris Evert, Tennis
1975	Fred Lynn, Baseball	Chris Evert, Tennis
1976	Bruce Jenner, Track	Nadia Comaneci, Gymnastics
1977	Steve Cauthen, Horse Racing	Chris Evert, Tennis
1978	Ron Guidry, Baseball	Nancy Lopez, Golf
1979	Willie Stargell, Baseball	Tracy Austin, Tennis
1980	US Olympic Hockey Team	Chris Evert Lloyd, Tennis
1981	John McEnroe, Tennis	Tracy Austin, Tennis
1982	Wayne Gretzky, Hockey	Mary Decker, Track
1983	Carl Lewis, Track	Martina Navratilova, Tennis
1984	Carl Lewis, Track	Mary Lou Retton, Gymnastics
1985	Dwight Gooden, Baseball	Nancy Lopez, Golf
1986	Larry Bird, Pro Basketball	Martina Navratilova, Tennis
1987	Ben Johnson, Track	Jackie Joyner-Kersee, Track
1988	Orel Hershiser, Baseball	Florence Griffith Joyner, Track
1989	Joe Montana, Pro Football	Steffi Graf, Tennis
1990	Joe Montana, Pro Football	Beth Daniel, Golf
1991	Michael Jordan, Pro Basketball	Monica Seles, Tennis
1992	Michael Jordan, Pro Basketball	Monica Seles, Tennis

James E. Sullivan Award

Presented annually by the Amateur Athletic Union to the athlete who "by his or her performance, example and influence as an amateur, has done the most during the year to advance the cause of sportsmanship."

1930	Bobby Jones, Golf	1962	Jim Beatty, Track
1931	Barney Berlinger, Track	1963	John Pennel, Track
1932	Jim Bausch, Track	1964	Don Schollander, Swimming
1933	Glenn Cunningham, Track	1965	Bill Bradley, Basketball
1934	Bill Bonthron, Track	1966	Jim Ryun, Track
1935	Lawson Little, Golf	1967	Randy Matson, Track
1936	Glenn Morris, Track	1968	Debbie Meyer, Swimming
1937	Don Budge, Tennis	1969	Bill Toomey, Track
1938	Don Lash, Track	1970	John Kinsella, Swimming
1939	Joe Burk, Rowing	1971	Mark Spitz, Swimming
1940	Greg Rice, Track	1972	Frank Shorter, Track
1941	Leslie MacMitchell, Track	1973	Bill Walton, Basketball
1942	Cornelius Warmerdam, Track	1974	Rich Wohlhuter, Track
1943	Gilbert Dodds, Track	1975	Tim Shaw, Swimming
1944	Ann Curtis, Swimming	1976	Bruce Jenner, Track
1945	Doc Blanchard, Football	1977	John Naber, Swimming
1946	Arnold Tucker, Football	1978	Tracy Caulkins, Swimming
1947	John B. Kelly, Jr, Rowing	1979	Kurt Thomas, Gymnastics
1948	Bob Mathias, Track	1980	Eric Heiden, Speed Skating
1949	Dick Button, Skating	1981	Carl Lewis, Track
1950	Fred Wilt, Track	1982	Mary Decker, Track
1951	Bob Richards, Track	1983	Edwin Moses, Track
1952	Horace Ashenfelter, Track	1984	Greg Louganis, Diving
1953	Sammy Lee, Diving	1985	Joan B. Samuelson, Track
1954	Mal Whitfield, Track	1986	Jackie Joyner-Kersee, Track
1955	Harrison Dillard, Track	1987	Jim Abbott, Baseball
1956	Pat McCormick, Diving	1988	Florence Griffith Joyner, Track
1957	Bobby Morrow, Track	1989	Janet Evans, Swimming
1958	Glenn Davis, Track	1990	John Smith, Wrestling
1959	Parry O'Brien, Track	1991	Mike Powell, Track
1960	Rafer Johnson, Track	1992	Bonnie Blair, Speed Skating
1961	Wilma Rudolph, Track		

The Sporting News Man of the Year

1968 ....Denny McLain, Baseball	1981 ....Wayne Gretzky, Hockey
1969 ....Tom Seaver, Baseball	1982 ....Whitey Herzog, Baseball
1970 ....John Wooden, Basketball	1983 ....Bowie Kuhn, Baseball
1971 ....Lee Trevino, Golf	1984 ....Peter Ueberroth, LA Olympics
1972 ....Charles O. Finley, Baseball	1985 ....Pete Rose, Baseball
1973 ....O. J. Simpson, Pro Football	1986 ....Larry Bird, Pro Basketball
1974 ....Lou Brock, Baseball	1987 ....No award
1975 ....Archie Griffin, Football	1988 ....Jackie Joyner-Kersee, Track
1976 ....Larry O'Brien, Pro Basketball	1989 ....Joe Montana, Pro Football
1977 ....Steve Cauthen, Horse Racing	1990 ....Nolan Ryan, Baseball
1978 ....Ron Guidry, Baseball	1991 ....Michael Jordan, Pro Basketball
1979 ....Willie Stargell, Baseball	1992 ....Mike Krzyzewski,
1980 ....George Brett, Baseball	College Basketball Coach

United Press International Male and Female Athlete of the Year

	MEN	WOMEN
1974	Muhammad Ali, Boxing	Irena Szewinska, Track and Field
1975	Joao Oliveira, Track and Field	Nadia Comaneci, Gymnastics
1976	Alberto Juantorena, Track and Field	Nadia Comaneci, Gymnastics
1977	Alberto Juantorena, Track and Field	Rosie Ackermann, Track and Field
1978	Henry Rono, Track and Field	Tracy Caulkins, Swimming
1979	Sebastian Coe, Track and Field	Marita Koch, Track and Field
1980	Eric Heiden, Speed Skating	Hanni Wenzel, Alpine Skiing
1981	Sebastian Coe, Track and Field	Chris Evert Lloyd, Tennis
1982	Daley Thompson, Track and Field	Marita Koch, Track and Field
1983	Carl Lewis, Track and Field	Jarmila Kratochvilova, Track and Field
1984	Carl Lewis, Track and Field	Martina Navratilova, Tennis
1985	Steve Cram, Track and Field	Mary Decker Slaney, Track and Field
1986	Diego Maradona, Soccer	Heike Drechsler, Track and Field
1987	Ben Johnson, Track and Field	Steffi Graf, Tennis
1988	Matt Biondi, Swimming	Florence Griffith Joyner, Track and Field
1989	Boris Becker, Tennis	Steffi Graf, Tennis
1990	Stefan Edberg, Tennis	Merlene Ottey, Track and Field
1991	Michael Jordan, Pro Basketball	Monica Seles, Tennis
1992	Mario Lemieux, Hockey	Monica Seles, Tennis

Dial Award

Presented annually by the Dial Corporation to the male and female national high schooll athlete/scholar of the year.

	MEN	WOMEN
1979	Herschel Walker, Football	No award
1980	Bill Fralic, Football	Carol Lewis, Track
1981	Kevin Willhite, Football	Cheryl Miller, Basketball
1982	Mike Smith, Basketball	Elaine Zayak, Skating
1983	Chris Spielman, Football	Melanie Buddemeyer, Swimming
1984	Hart Lee Dykes, Football	Nora Lewis, Basketball
1985	Jeff George, Football	Gea Johnson, Track
1986	Scott Schaffner, Football	Mya Johnson, Track
1987	Todd Marinovich, Football	Kristi Overton, Water Skiing
1988	Carlton Gray, Football	Courtney Cox, Basketball
1989	Robert Smith, Football	Lisa Leslie, Basketball
1990	Derrick Brooks, Football	Vicki Goetze, Golf
1991	Jeff Buckey, Football, Track	Katie Smith, Basketball, Volleyball, Track
1992	Jacque Vaughn, Basketball	Amanda White, Track, Swimming

Profiles

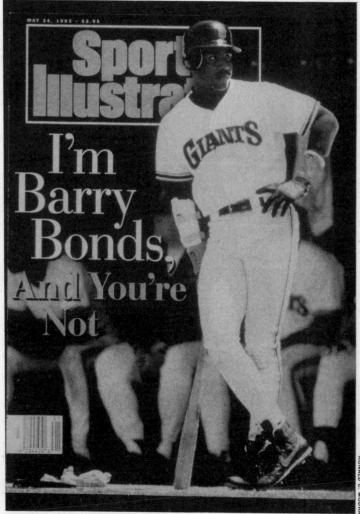

Henry Aaron (b. 2-5-34): Baseball OF. "Hammerin' Hank." Alltime leader in HR (755) and RBI (2,297); third in hits (3,771). 1957 MVP. Led league in HR and RBI 4 times each, runs scored 3 times, hits and batting average 2 times. No. 44, he had 44 homers 4 times. Had 40+ HR 8 times; 100+ RBI 11 times; .300+ average 14 times. 24-time All-Star. Career span 1954–76; jersey number retired by Atlanta and Milwaukee.

Kareem Abdul-Jabbar (b. 4-16-47): Born Lew Alcindor. Basketball C. All-time leader points scored (38,387), field goals attempted (28,307), field goals made (15,837), blocked shots (3,189), games played (1,560), and years played (20); third all-time rebounds (17,440). Won 6 MVP awards (1971–72, 1974, 1976–77, 1980). Career scoring average was 24.6, rebounding average 11.2. Led league in blocks 4 times, scoring 2 times, rebounding and field goal percentage 1 time each. Averaged 30+ points 4 times, 20+ points 13 other times. 10-time All-Star, All-Defensive team 5 times. 1970 Rookie of the Year. Played on 6 championship teams; was playoff MVP in 1971, 1985. Career span 1969–88 with Milwaukee, Los Angeles. Also played on 3 NCAA championship teams with UCLA; tournament MVP 1967–69; Player of the Year 2 times.

Affirmed (b. 2-21-75): Thoroughbred race horse. Triple Crown winner in 1978 with jockey Steve Cauthen aboard. Trained by Laz Barrera.

Troy Aikman (b. 11-21-66): Football QB. MVP of Super Bowl XXVII, in which he completed 22 of 30 passes for 273 yards and four TDs with no interceptions. Career span since 1989 with Dallas Cowboys.

Tenley Albright (b. 7-18-35): Figure skater. Gold medalist at 1956 Olympics, silver medalist at 1952 Olympics. World champion 2 times (1953, 1955) and U.S. champion 5 consecutive years (1952–56).

Grover Cleveland Alexander (b. 2-26-1887, d. 11-4-50): Baseball RHP. Third alltime most wins (373), second most shutouts (90). Won 30+ games 3 times, 20+ games 6 other times. Set rookie record with 28 wins in 1911. Career span 1911–30 with Philadelphia (NL), Chicago (NL), St Louis (NL).

Vasili Alexeyev (b. 1942): Soviet weightlifter. Gold medalist at 2 consecutive Olympics in 1972, 1976. World champion 8 times.

Muhammad Ali (b. 1-17-42): Born Cassius Clay. Boxer. Heavyweight champion 3 times (1964–67, 1974–78, 1978–79). Stripped of title in 1967 because he refused to serve in the Vietnam War. Career record 56–5 with 37 KOs. Defended title 19 times. Also light heavyweight gold medalist at 1960 Olympics.

Phog Allen (b. 11-18-1885, d. 9-16-74): College basketball coach. Fourth alltime most wins (746); .739 career winning percentage. Won 1952 NCAA championship. Most of career, 1920–56, with Kansas.

Bobby Allison (b. 12-3-37): Auto racer. Third all-time in NASCAR victories (84). Won Daytona 500 3 times (1978, 1982, 1988). Also NASCAR champion in 1983.

Naty Alvarado (b. 7-25-55): Mexican-born handball player. "El Gato (The Cat)." Won a record 11 U.S. pro four-wall handball titles starting in 1977.

Lance Alworth (b. 8-3-40): Football TE. "Bambi" led

NFL in receiving in 1966, '68 and '69. 200+ yards in a game 5 times in career, a record. Gained 100+ yards in game 41 times. In 1965 gained 1,602 yards, still second highest seasonal yardage ever. Career span 1962–70 with San Diego and 1971–72 with Dallas. Electdd to Pro Football Hall of Fame 1978.

Sparky Anderson (b. 2-22-34): Baseball manager. Only manager to win World Series in both leagues (Detroit, 1984, Cincinnati, 1975–76); only manager to win 100 games in both leagues. .552 career winning percentage since 1970.

Willie Anderson (b. 1880, d. 1910): Scottish golfer. Won U.S. Open 4 times (1901 and an unmatched three straight, 1903–05). Also won 4 Western Opens between 1902 and 1909.

Mario Andretti (b. 2-28-40): Auto racer. The only driver in history to win Daytona 500 (1967), Indy 500 (1969): and Formula One world championship (1978). Second alltime in CART victories (52 as of 10/1/93). Also 12 career Formula One victories. USAC/CART champion 4 times (consecutively 1965–66, 1969, 1984). Named Indy 500 Rookie of the Year in 1965.

Earl Anthony (b. 4-27-38): Bowler. Won PBA National Championship 6 times, more than any other bowler (consecutively 1973–75, 1981–83) and Tournament of Champions 2 times (1974, 1978). First bowler to top $1 million in career earnings. Bowler of the Year 6 times (consecutively 1974–76, 1981–83). Has won 45 career PBA titles since 1970.

Said Aouita (b. 11-2-60): Track and field. Moroccan holds world record in 2,000 meters (4:50.81 set in 1987), and 5,000 meters (12:58.39 set in 1987). 1984 Olympic champion in 5,000; 1988 Olympic third place in 800.

Al Arbour (b. 11-1-32): Hockey D-coach. Led NY Islanders to 4 consecutive Stanley Cup championships (1980–83). Also played on 3 Stanley Cup champions: Detroit, Chicago and Toronto, from 1953 to 1971.

Eddie Arcaro (b. 2-19-16): Horse racing jockey. The only jockey to win the Triple Crown 2 times (aboard Whirlaway in 1941, Citation in 1948). Rode Preakness Stakes winner (1941, 1948, consecutively 1950–51, 1955, 1957) and Belmont Stakes winner (consecutively 1941–42, 1945, 1948, 1952, 1955) 6 times each and Kentucky Derby winner 5 times (1938, 1941, 1945, 1948, 1952). 4,779 career wins.

Nate Archibald (b. 9-2-48): Basketball player. "Tiny" only by NBA standards at 6' 1", 160 pounds. Drafted by Cincinnati in 1970. Averaged 34 points per game for K.C.-Omaha in 1972–73. Led NBA in scoring (34.0) and assists (910) in 1972–73. First team, all-NBA in 1973, '75 and '76. MVP of NBA All Star game in 1981. Retired in 1984.

Alexis Arguello (b. 4-19-52): Nicaraguan Boxer. Won world titles in three weight classes—featherweight, super featherweight and lightweight. Won first title, WBA featherweight, on 11-23-74 when he KO'd Ruben Olivares in 13. Won last title, vacant WBC lightweight, on 5-22-82 when he KO'd Andrew Ganigan in 5. Career record: 86 bouts; won 65 by KO, 15 by decision; lost 6, three by KO.

Henry Armstrong (b. 12-12-12): Boxer. Champion in 3 different weight classes: featherweight (1937—relinquished 1938), welterweight (1938–40) and lightweight (1938–39). Career record 145–20–9 with 98 KOs (27 consecutively, 1937–38) from 1931 to 1945.

Arthur Ashe (b. 7-10-43; d. 2-6-93): Tennis player. First black man to win U.S. Open (1968, as an amateur), Australian Open (1970) and Wimbledon singles titles (1975). 33 career tournament victories. Member of Davis Cup team 1963–78; captain 1980–85. Died of AIDS-related pneumonia.

Assault (b. 1943): Thoroughbred race horse. Horse of the Year for 1946 won Triple Crown that year. Won Kentucky Derby by 8 lengths; Preakness by a neck over Lord Boswell; and the Belmont by 3 lengths from Natchez. Trained by Max Hirsch.

Red Auerbach (b. 9-20-17): Basketball coach-executive. All-time leader in wins (938). Coached Boston from 1946 to 1965, winning 9 championships, 8 consecutively. Had .662 career winning percentage, with 50+ wins 8 consecutive seasons. Also won 7 championships as general manager.

Hobey Baker (b. 1-15-1892, d. 12-21-18): Sportsman. Member of both college football and hockey Halls of Fame. College hockey and football star with Princeton, 1911–14. Fighter pilot in World War I, died in plane crash. College hockey Player of the Year award named in his honor.

Seve Ballesteros (b. 4-9-57): Spanish golfer. Notorious scrambler. Won British Opens in 1979, '84 and '88. Won Masters in 1980 and '83.

Ernie Banks (b. 1-31-31): Baseball SS-1B. "Mr. Cub." Won 2 consecutive MVP awards, in 1958–59. 512 career HR. League leader in HR, RBI 2 times each; career batting average of .274; 40+ HR 5 times; 100+ RBI 8 times. Most HR by a shortstop with 47 in 1958. Career span 1953–71 with Chicago.

Roger Bannister (b. 3-23-29): Track and field. British runner broke the 4-minute mile barrier, running 3:59.4 on May 6, 1954.

Red Barber (b. 2-17-08, d. 10-22-92): Sportscaster. TV-radio baseball announcer was the voice of Cincinnati, Brooklyn and NY Yankees. His expressions, such as "sitting in the catbird seat," "pea patch" and "rhubarb" captivated audiences from 1934 to 1966.

Charles Barkley (b. 2-20-63): Basketball F. Five-time first-team All-Star. All-Star MVP, 1991. All-Rookie team, 1985. Led NBA in rebounding, 1987. Has averaged 20+ points in seven of 8 seasons with Philadelphia. 1992 Olympic team leading scorer. Traded to Phoenix before 1992-93 season. League MVP for 1992-93 season, during which he averaged 25.6 points and 12.2 rebounds a game and led the Suns into the NBA finals.

Rick Barry (b. 3-28-44): Basketball F. Only player in history to win scoring titles in NBA (San Francisco, 1967) and ABA (Oakland, 1969). Second alltime highest free throw percentage (.900). Career scoring average 23.2. Led league in free throw percentage 6 times, steals and scoring 1 time each. Averaged 30+ points 2 times, 20+ points 6 other times. 5-time All-Star. 1975 playoff MVP with Golden State. 1966 Rookie of the Year. Career span 1967–79.

Carmen Basilio (b. 4-2-27): Boxer. Won titles in two weight classes, welter and middle. Lost first welter title bid to Kid Gavilan on 9-18-53. Won world welter title by TKO of Tony DeMarco in 12 rounds on 6-10-55. Lost, regained and retained welter title in three fights with Johnny Saxton. Won and then lost middleweight title in

two 15 round fights with Ray Robinson. Made three unsuccessful bids to regain middle title. *The Ring* Fighter of the Year for 1957. Career record: 78 bouts; won 26 by KO and 29 by decision; drew 7; lost 16, two by KO. Elected to Boxing Hall of Fame in 1969.

Sammy Baugh (b. 3-17-14): Football QB-P. Set records by leading league in passing 6 times and punting 4 times. Also holds record for highest career punting average (45.1) and highest season average (51.0 in 1940). Career span 1937–52 with Washington. Also All-America with Texas Christian 3 consecutive seasons.

Elgin Baylor (b. 9-16-34): Basketball F. Third alltime highest scoring average (27.4), 10th alltime most points scored (23,149). Averaged 30+ points 3 consecutive seasons, 20+ points 8 other times. 10-time All-Star. 1962 Rookie of the Year. Played in 8 finals without winning championship. Career span 1958–71 with Los Angeles. Also 1958 MVP in NCAA tournament with Seattle.

Bob Beamon (b. 8-29-46): Track and field. Gold medalist in long jump at 1968 Olympics with world record jump of 29' 2½" that stood until 1991.

Franz Beckenbauer (b. 1945): West German soccer player. Captain of 1974 World Cup champions and coach of 1990 champions. Also played for NY Cosmos from 1977 to 1980.

Boris Becker (b. 11-22-67): German tennis player. The youngest male player to win a Wimbledon singles title at age 17 in 1985. Has won 3 Wimbledon titles (consecutively 1985–86, 1989), 1 U.S. Open (1989) and 1 Australian Open title (1991). Led West Germany to 2 consecutive Davis Cup victories (1988–89).

Chuck Bednarik (b. 5-1-25): Football C-LB. Last of the great two-way players, was named All-Pro at both center and linebacker. Missed only 3 games in 14 seasons with Philadelphia from 1949–62. Also All-America 2 times at Pennsylvania.

Clair Bee (b. 3-2-1896, d. 5-20-83): Basketball coach. Originated 1-3-1 defense, helped develop three-second rule, 24-second clock. Won 82.7 percent of games as coach for Rider College and Long Island University. Coach Baltimore Bullets, 1952–54. Author, 23-volume Chip Hilton series for children, 21 nonfiction sports books.

Jean Beliveau (b. 8-31-31): Hockey C. Won MVP award 2 times (1956, 1964), playoff MVP in 1965. Led league in assists 3 times, goals 2 times and points 1 time. 507 career goals, 712 assists. All-Star 6 times. Played on 10 Stanley Cup champions with Montreal from 1950 to 1971.

Bert Bell (b. 2-25-1895, d. 10-11-59): Football executive. Second NFL commissioner (1946–59). Also owner of Philadelphia (1933–40) and Pittsburgh (1941–46). Proposed the first college draft in 1936.

James "Cool Papa" Bell (b. 5-17-03): Baseball OF. Legendary foot speed—according to Satchel Paige could flip light switch before in bed before room was dark. Hit .392 in games against white major leaguers. Career span 1922–46 with many teams of the Negro Leagues, including the Pittsburgh Crawfords and the Homestead Grays. Inducted in the Hall of Fame in 1974.

Lyudmila Belousova/Oleg Protopov (no dates of birth available): Soviet figure skaters. Won Olympic gold medal in pairs competition in 1964 and 1968. Won four consecutive World and European championships (1965–68) and eight consecutive Soviet titles (1961–68).

Deane Beman (b. 4-22-38): Commissioner of the PGA Tour since 1974. Won British Amateur title in 1959 and U.S. Amateur titles in 1960 and 1963.

Johnny Bench (b. 12-7-47): Baseball C. MVP in 1970, 1972; World Series MVP in 1976; Rookie of the Year in 1968. 389 career HR. League leader in HR 2 times, RBI 3 times. Career span 1967–83 with Cincinnati.

Patty Berg (b. 2-13-18): Golfer. Alltime women's leader in major championships (16), third alltime in career wins (57). Won Titleholders Championship (1937–39, 1948, 1953–54, 1957) and Western Open (1941, 1943, 1948, 1951, 1955, 1957–58) 7 times each, the most of any golfer. Also won U.S. Women's Amateur (1938) and U.S. Women's Open (1946).

Yogi Berra (b. 5-12-25): Baseball C. Played on 10 World Series winners. All-time Series leader in games, at bats, hits and doubles. MVP in 1951 and consecutively 1954–55. 358 career HR. Career span 1946–65. Also managed pennant-winning Yankees (1964) and NY Mets (1973).

Jay Berwanger (b. 3-19-14): College football RB. Won the first Heisman Trophy and named All-America with Chicago in 1935.

Raymond Berry (b. 2-27-33): Football E. Led NFL in receiving 1958–60. In 13-season career, caught 631 passes, 68 for TDs. Career span 1955–67, all with Baltimore Colts. Later coached New England Patriots from 1984–89 with 51–41 record.

George Best (b. 5-22-46): Irish soccer player. Led Manchester United to European Cup title in 1968. Named England's and Europe's Player of the Year in 1968. Played in North American Soccer League for Los Angeles (1976–78), Fort Lauderdale (1978–79) and San Jose (1980–81). Suspended from San Jose in 1982 for failure to report to two matches. Frequent troubles with alcohol and gambling overshadowed career.

Abebe Bikila (b. 8-7-32, d. 10-25-73): Track and field. Ethiopian barefoot runner won consecutive gold medals in the marathon at Olympics, in 1960 and 1964.

Fred Biletnikoff (b. 2-23-43): Football WR. In 14 pro seasons caught 589 passes for 8,974 yards and 76 TDs. In 1961 led NFL receivers with 61 catches; in '62 led AFC with 58. Career span 1965–78, all with Raiders. Elected to Pro Football Hall of Fame in 1988.

Dmitri Bilozerchev (b. 12-22-66): Soviet gymnast. Won 3 gold medals at 1988 Olympics. Made comeback after shattering his left leg into 44 pieces in 1985. Two-time world champion (1983, 1987). At 16, became youngest to win all-around world championship title in 1983.

Dave Bing (b. 11-24-43): Basketball G. Averaged 24.8 points a game in four years at Syracuse. NBA Rookie of Year in 1967. Led NBA in scoring (27.1) in 1968. MVP NBA All Star game in 1976. In 12 year career from 1967–78, most of it with Detroit Pistons, averaged 20.3 points.

Matt Biondi (b. 10-8-65): Swimmer. Winner of 5 gold medals, 1 silver medal and 1 bronze medal at 1988 Olympics. Won one gold and one silver at 1992 Olympics.

Larry Bird (b. 12-7-56): Basketball F. Won 3 consecutive MVP awards (1984–86) and 2 playoff MVP awards (1984, 1986). Also Rookie of the Year (1980) and All-Star 9 consecutive seasons. Has led league in free throw percentage 4 times. Averaged 20+ points 10 times. Career span since 1979-1992 with Boston. Also named Player of the Year in 1979 with Indiana State.

Bonnie Blair (b. 3-18-64): Speed skater. Won gold medal in 500 meters and bronze medal in 1,000 meters at 1988 Olympics and gold medals in both events in 1992. Also 1989 World Sprint champion. Winner of 1992 Sullivan Award.

Toe Blake (b. 8-21-12): Hockey LW and coach. Second alltime highest winning percentage (.640): and fifth in wins (582). Led Montreal to 8 Stanley Cup championships from 1955 to 1968 (consecutively 1956–60, 1965–66, 1968). Also MVP and scoring leader in 1939. Played on 2 Stanley Cup champions with Montreal from 1932 to 1948.

Doc Blanchard (b. 12-11-24): College football FB. "Mr. Inside." Teamed with Glenn Davis to lead Army to 3 consecutive undefeated seasons (1944–46) and 2 consecutive national championships (1944–45). Won Heisman Trophy and Sullivan Award in 1945. Also All-America 3 times.

George Blanda (b. 9-17-27): Football QB-K. Alltime leader in seasons played (26), games played (340), points scored (2,002), points after touchdown (943); second in field goals (335). Also passed for 26,920 career yards and 236 touchdowns. Tied record with 7 touchdown passes on Nov. 19, 1961. Player of the Year 2 times (1961, 1970). Retired at age 48, the oldest to ever play. Career span 1949–75 with Chicago, Houston, Oakland.

Fanny Blankers-Koen (b. 4-26-18): Track and field. Dutch athlete won four gold medals at 1948 Olympics, in 100-meters; 200 meters; 80-meter hurdles; and 400-meter relay. Versatile, she also set world records in high jump (5' 7-1/4" in 1943), long jump (20' 6" in 1943) and pentathlon (4,692 points in 1951).

Wade Boggs (b. 6-15-58): Baseball 3B. Won 5 batting titles (1983, consecutively 1985–88); has had .350+ average 5 times, 200+ hits 7 times. Career span 1982–92 with Boston, 1993 with New York Yankees.

Nick Bolletieri (b. 7-31-31): Tennis coach. Since 1976, has run Nick Bolletieri Tennis Academy in Bradenton, Fla. Former residents of the academy include Andre Agassi, Monica Seles and Jim Courier.

Barry Bonds (b. 7-24-64): Baseball OF. Three-time National League MVP (1990, '92, '93); Career span 1986 to '92, with Pirates; 1993 with Giants.

Bjorn Borg (b. 6-6-56): Swedish tennis player. Second alltime men's leader in Grand Slam singles titles (11—tied with Rod Laver). Set modern record by winning 5 consecutive Wimbledon titles (1976–80). Won 6 French Open titles (consecutively 1974–75, 1978–81). Reached U.S. Open final 4 times, but title eluded him. 65 career tournament victories. Led Sweden to Davis Cup win in 1975.

Julius Boros (b. 3-3-20): Golfer. Won US. Opens in 1952 at Northwood CC in Dallas and in 1963 at The Country Club in Brookline, Mass. Also won 1968 PGA Championship at Pecan Valley CC, San Antonio, when 48 years old, making him oldest winner of a major ever. Led PGA money list in 1952 and '55.

Mike Bossy (b. 1-22-57): Hockey RW. In 1978 set

NHL rookie scoring record of 54 goals, broken in 1993. Scored 50 or more each of first nine seasons, totaling 573 goals and 1,126 points in 10 seasons (1977–78 through 1986–87) with New York Islanders. Elected to Hall of Fame in 1991.

Ralph Boston (b. 5-9-39): Track and field. Long jumper won medals at 3 consecutive Olympics; gold in 1960, silver in 1964, bronze in 1968.

Ray Bourque (b. 12-28-60): Hockey D. Won Norris Trophy as NHL's top defenseman four times. Career span 1979–80 through 1993, all with Boston Bruins.

Scotty Bowman (b. 9-18-33): Hockey coach. Entered 1993–94 season with Detroit as alltime leader in regular season wins (832) and in regular season winning percentage (.658). Also alltime leader in playoff wins (137). Led Montreal to 5 Stanley Cups, and has also coached St Louis and Buffalo. Won Jack Adams Award, Coach of the Year, 1976–77.

Bill Bradley (b. 7-28-43): Basketball F. Played on 2 NBA championship teams with New York from 1967 to 1977. Player of the Year and NCAA tournament MVP in 1965 with Princeton; All-America 3 times; Sullivan Award winner in 1965. Rhodes scholar. U.S. Senator (D-NJ) since 1979.

Terry Bradshaw (b. 9-2-48): Football QB. Played on 4 Super Bowl champions (consecutively 1974–75, 1978–79); named Super Bowl MVP 2 consecutive seasons (1978–79). 212 career touchdown passes; 27,989 yards passing. Player of the Year in 1978. Career span 1970–83 with Pittsburgh.

George Brett (b. 5-15-53): Baseball 3B-1B. MVP in 1980 with .390 batting average; 3 batting titles, in 1976, 1980, 1990; and .300+ mark. Led league in hits and triples 3 times. Reached 3,000-hit mark in 1992. Career span 1973–93, with Kansas City. Career totals: 3,153 hits; 317 HR; 1,595 RBIs; batting average .305.

Bret Hanover (b. 5-19-62): Horse. Son of Adios. Won 62 of 68 harness races and earned $922,616. Undefeated as two-year-old. From total of 1,694 foals, he sired winners of $61 million and 511 horses which have recorded sub-2:00 performances.

Lou Brock (b. 6-18-39): Baseball OF. Second alltime most stolen bases (938); second most season steals (118). Led league in steals 8 times, with 50+ steals 12 consecutive seasons. Alltime World Series leader in steals (14—tied with Eddie Collins); second in Series batting average (.391). 3,023 career hits. Career span 1961–79 with St Louis.

Jim Brown (b. 2-17-36): Football FB. Alltime leader in touchdowns (126): and third in yards rushing (12,312). Led league in rushing a record 8 times. His 5.22-yards per carry average is also the best ever. Player of the Year 4 times (consecutively 1957–58, 1963, 1965) and Rookie of the Year in 1957. Rushed for 1,000+ yards in 7 seasons, 200+ yards in 4 games, 100+ yards in 54 other games. Career span 1957–65 with Cleveland; never missed a game. Also All-America with Syracuse.

Paul Brown (b. 9-7-08, d. 8-5-91): Football coach. Led Cleveland to 10 consecutive championship games. Won 4 consecutive AAFC titles (1946–49) and 3 NFL titles (1950, consecutively 1954–55). Coached Cleveland from 1946 to 1962; became first coach of Cincinnati, 1968–75, and then general manager. Career coaching record 222–113–9. Also won national championship with Ohio State in 1942.

Avery Brundage (b. 9-28-1887, d. 5-5-75): Amateur sports executive. President of International Olympic Committee 1952–72. Served as president of U.S. Olympic Committee 1929–53. Also president of Amateur Athletic Union 1928–35. Member of 1912 U.S. Olympic track and field team.

Paul "Bear" Bryant (b. 9-11-13, d. 1-26-83): College football coach. Alltime Division I-A leader in wins (323). Won 6 national championships (1961, consecutively 1964–65, 1973, consecutively 1978–79) with Alabama. Career record 323–85–17, including 4 undefeated seasons. Also won 15 bowl games. Career span 1945–82 with Maryland, Kentucky, Texas A&M, Alabama.

Sergei Bubka (b. 12-4-63): Track and field. Ukrainian pole vaulter won gold medalist at 1988 Olympics. Only four-time world outdoor champion in any event (1983, 1987, 1991, 1993). First man to vault 20 feet, set world indoor record of 20' 2" on 2-21-93 and world outdoor record of 20' 1½", set on 9-20-92.

Buck Buchanan (b. 9-10-40): Football DT. Career span 1963–75 with Kansas City Chiefs. Elected to Pro Football Hall of Fame 1990.

Don Budge (b. 6-13-15): Tennis player. First player to achieve the Grand Slam, in 1938. Won 2 consecutive Wimbledon and U.S. singles titles (1937–38), 1 French and 1 Australian title (1938).

Dick Butkus (b. 12-9-42): Football LB. Recovered 25 opponents' fumbles, second most in history. Selected for Pro Bowl 8 times. Career span 1965–73 with Chicago. Also All-America 2 times with Illinois. Award recognizing the outstanding college linebacker named in his honor.

Dick Button (b. 7-18-29): Figure skater. Gold medalist at 2 consecutive Olympics in 1948, 1952. World champion 5 consecutive years (1948–52) and U.S. champion 7 consecutive years (1946–52). Sullivan Award winner in 1949.

Walter Byers (b. 3-13-22): Amateur sports executive. First executive director of NCAA, served from 1952 to 1987.

Frank Calder (b. 11-17-1877, d. 2-4-43): Hockey executive. First commissioner of NHL, served from 1917 to 1943. Rookie of the Year award named in his honor.

Walter Camp (b. 4-7-1859, d. 3-14-25): Football pioneer. Played for Yale in its first football game vs. Harvard on Nov. 17, 1876. Proposed rules such as 11 men per side, scrimmage line, center snap, yards and downs. Founded the All-America selections in 1889.

Roy Campanella (b. 11-19-21; d. 6-26-93): Baseball C. Career span 1948–57, ended when paralyzed in car crash. MVP in 1951, 1953, 1955. Played on 5 pennant winners; 1955 World Series winner with Brooklyn Dodgers.

Earl Campbell (b. 3-29-55): Football RB. Ninth alltime yards rushing (9,407); third alltime season yards rushing (1,934 in 1980) and touchdowns rushing (19 in 1979). Led league in rushing 3 consecutive seasons. Rushed for 1,000+ yards in 5 seasons, 100+ yards in 40 games, 200+ yards in 4 other games. Scored 74 career touchdowns. Player of the Year 2 consecutive seasons (1978–79). Rookie of the Year in 1978. Career span 1978–85 with Houston, New Orleans. Won Heisman Trophy with Texas in 1977.

John Campbell (b. 4-8-55): Canadian harness racing driver. Alltime leading money winner with over

$100 million in earnings. Leading money winner 1986–90. Has more than 5,500 career wins.

Billy Cannon (b. 2-8-37): Football RB. Led Louisiana State to national championship in 1958 and won Heisman Trophy in 1959. Signed contract in both NFL (Los Angeles) and AFL (Houston). Houston won lawsuit for his services. Played in 6 AFL championship games with Houston, Oakland, Kansas City. Career span 1960–70. Served three-year jail term for 1983 conviction on counterfeiting charges.

Jose Canseco (b. 7-2-64): Baseball OF. Only player to top 40 homers (42) and 40 (40) steals in same season (1988). AL MVP in 1988, when he also batted .307 with 124 RBIs. Career span 1985–1992 with Oakland and since1992 with Texas Rangers.

Harry Caray (b. 3-1-17): Sportscaster. TV-radio baseball announcer since 1945 with St Louis (NL), Oakland, Chicago (AL) and Chicago (NL). Achieved celebrity status on Cubs' superstation WGN by singing "Take Me Out to the Ballgame" with Wrigley Field fans.

Rod Carew (b. 10-1-45): Baseball 2B-1B. Won 7 batting titles (1969, consecutively 1972–75, 1977–78). Had .328 career average, 3,053 career hits, and .300+ average 16 times. 1977 MVP; 1967 Rookie of the Year. Career span 1967–85; jersey number (29) retired by Minnesota and California.

Steve Carlton (b. 12-22-44): Baseball LHP. Second alltime most strikeouts (4,136). 4 Cy Young awards (1972, 1977, 1980, 1982). 329 career wins; won 20+ games 6 times. League leader in wins 4 times, innings pitched and strikeouts 5 times each. Struck out 19 batters in 1 game in 1969. Career span 1965–88 with St. Louis, Philadelphia and four other teams in last two years.

JoAnne Carner (b. 4-21-39): Golfer. Won 42 titles, including US Women's Opens in 1971 and '76 and du Maurier Classic in 1975 and '78. LPGA top earner in 1974 and 1982–83. LPGA Player of the Year in 1974 and 1981–82. Won five Vare Trophies (1974–75 and 1981–83).

Joe Carr (b. 10-22-80; d. 5-20-39): Football administrator. Instrumental in forming American Professional Football Association in 1920. President of AAFA from 1922 to '39.

Don Carter (b. 7-29-26): Bowler. Won All-Star Tournament 4 times (1952, 1954, 1956, 1958) and PBA National Championship in 1960. Voted Bowler of the Year 6 times (consecutively 1953–54, 1957–58, 1960, 1962).

Alexander Cartwright (b. 4-17-1820, d. 7-12-1892): Baseball pioneer. Organized the first baseball game on June 19, 1846, and set the basic rules of bases 90 feet apart, 9 men per side, 3 strikes per out and 3 outs per inning. In that first game his New York Knickerbockers lost to the New York Nine 23–1 at Elysian Fields in Hoboken, NJ.

Billy Casper (b. 6-24-31): Golfer. Famed putter. Won 51 PGA tournaments. PGA Player of the Year in both 1966 and '70. Won Vardon Trophy in 1960, '63, '64, '65 and '68. Won the US Open twice, in 1959 at Winged Foot in Mamaroneck, New York, and in 1966 in 18-hole playoff over Arnold Palmer at Olympic Club, San Francisco. Beat Gene Littler in 18 hole playoff to win 1970 Masters.

Tracy Caulkins (b. 1-11-63): Swimmer. Won 3 gold medals at 1984 Olympics. Won 48 U.S. national titles,

more than any other swimmer, from 1978 to 1984. Also won Sullivan Award in 1978.

Steve Cauthen (b. 5-1-60): Jockey. In 1978 became youngest jockey to win Triple Crown, aboard Affirmed. First jockey to top $6 million in season earnings (1977). *Sports Illustrated* Sportsman of Year for 1977. Moved to England in 1979. Among the 1,389 winners he had ridden in England through end of 1990 were two winners of Epsom Derby—Slip Anchor in 1985 and Reference Point in 1987.

Evonne Goolagong Cawley (b. 7-31-51): Tennis. Won 4 Australian Open titles from 1974 through '77; won '71 French Open; Wimbledon in 1971 and '80, Runnerup four straight years at US Open (1973–76) which she never won.

Bill Chadwick (b. 10-10-15): Hockey referee. Spent 16 years as a referee despite vision in only one eye. Developed hand signals to signify penalties. Also former television announcer for the New York Rangers.

Wilt Chamberlain (b. 8-21-36): Basketball C. Alltime leader in rebounds (23,924) and rebounding average (22.9). Alltime season leader in points scored (4,029 in 1962), scoring average (50.4 in 1962), rebounding average (27.2 in 1961) and field goal percentage (.727 in 1973). Alltime single-game most points scored (100 in 1962) and most rebounds (55 in 1960). Second alltime most points scored (31,419) and most field goals made (12,681). 4 MVP awards (1960, consecutively 1966–68); playoff MVP in 1972 and 1960 Rookie of the Year. 7-time All-Star. 30.1 career scoring average. Led league in rebounding 11 times, field goal percentage 9 times, scoring 7 consecutive seasons, assists 1 time. Averaged 50+ points and 40+ points 1 time each; 30+ points and 20+ points 5 other times each. Career span 1959–72 with Philadelphia, Los Angeles. Also named College Player of the Year in 1957 at Kansas.

Colin Chapman (b. 1928, d. 12-16-83): Auto racing engineer. Founded Lotus race and street cars, designing the first Lotus racer in 1948. Introduced the monocoque design for Formula One cars in 1962 and ground effects in 1978. Four of his drivers, including Mario Andretti, won Formula One world championships.

Julio Cesar Chavez (b. 7-12-62): Boxer. Through 10-1-93 the current WBC junior welterweight champion has a career record of 87-0-1. But many thought he lost fight against Pernell Whitaker on 9-10-93 in Alamodome which ended officially as a "majority draw". Also won titles as super featherweight (1984–87) and lightweight (1987–89).

Gerry Cheevers (b. 12-7-40): Hockey goalie. Goaltender for Stanley Cup-winning Boston Bruins teams of 1970 and '72. In 12 seasons with Boston had 230-94-74 record with a goals against average of 2.89. Also coached Bruins from 1980–84, with 204-126-46 record. Elected to Hall of Fame 1985.

Citation (b. 4-11-45, d. 8-8-70): Thoroughbred race horse. Triple Crown winner in 1948 with jockey Eddie Arcaro aboard. Trained by Ben A. Jones.

King Clancy (b. 2-25-03, d. 11-6-86): Hockey D. Four-time All-Star. Coach, Montreal Maroons, Toronto. Referee. Trophy named in his honor, recognizing leadership qualities and contribution to community.

Jim Clark (b. 3-4-36, d. 4-7-68): Scottish auto racer. Third alltime in Formula 1 victories (25—tied with Niki Lauda). Formula 1 champion 2 times (1963, 1965).

Won Indy 500 1 time (1965). Named Indy 500 Rookie of the Year in 1963. Killed during competition in 1968 at age 32.

Bobby Clarke (b. 8-13-49): Hockey C. Won MVP award 3 times (1973, consecutively 1975–76). 358 career goals, 852 assists. Led league in assists 2 consecutive seasons and scored 100+ points 3 times. Played on 2 consecutive Stanley Cup champions (1974–75) with Philadelphia. Career span 1969 to 1984. Also general manager with Philadelphia from 1984 to 1990 and Minnesota since 1991.

Roger Clemens (b. 8-4-62): Baseball RHP. Record 20 strikeouts in 1 game. Won 2 consecutive Cy Young Awards in 1986, 1987. Also 1986 MVP. League leader in ERA 4 times, wins and strikeouts 2 times each. Career span since 1984 with Boston.

Roberto Clemente (b. 8-18-34, d. 12-31-72): Baseball OF. Killed in plane crash while still an active player. Had 3,000 career hits and .317 career average. 4 batting titles; .300+ average 13 times. 1966 MVP; 1971 World Series MVP. 12 consecutive Gold Gloves; led league in assists 5 times. Career span 1955–72 with Pittsburgh.

Ty Cobb (b. 12-18-1886, d. 7-17-61): Baseball OF. Alltime leader in batting average (.367) and runs scored (2,245); second most hits (4,191); third most stolen bases (892). 1911 MVP and 1909 Triple Crown winner. 12 batting titles. Had .400+ average 3 times, .350+ average 13 other times; 200+ hits 9 times. Led league in hits 7 times, steals 6 times and runs scored 5 times. Career span 1905–28 with Detroit.

Mickey Cochrane (b. 4-6-03, d. 6-28-62): Baseball C. Alltime highest career batting average among catchers (.320). MVP in 1928, 1934. Had .300+ average 8 times. Career span 1925–37 with Philadelphia, Detroit.

Sebastian Coe (b. 9-29-56): Track and field. British runner was gold medalist in 1,500 meters and silver medalist in 800 meters at 2 consecutive Olympics in 1980, 1984. World record holder in 800 meters (1:41.73 set in 1981) and 1,000 meters (2:12.18 set in 1981). Now a member of parliament.

Eddie Collins (b. 5-2-1887, d. 3-25-51): Baseball 2B. Alltime leader among 2nd basemen in games, chances and assists; led league in fielding 9 times. 3,311 career hits; .333 career average; .330+ average 12 times. Fourth alltime most stolen bases (743); alltime most World Series steals (14—tied with Lou Brock); alltime leader in single-game steals (6, twice). 1914 MVP. Career span 1906–30 with Philadelphia, Chicago.

Nadia Comaneci (b. 11-12-61): Romanian gymnast. First ever to score a perfect 10 at Olympics (on uneven parallel bars in 1976). Won 3 gold, 2 silver and 1 bronze medal at 1976 Olympics. Also won 2 gold and 2 silver medals at 1980 Olympics.

Dennis Conner (b. 9-16-42): Sailing. Captain of America's Cup winner 2 times (1980, 1987).

Maureen Connolly (b. 9-17-34, d. 6-21-69): Tennis player. "Little Mo" first woman to achieve the Grand Slam, in 1953. Won the U.S. singles title in 1951 at age 16. Thereafter lost only 4 matches before retiring in 1954 because of a broken leg caused by a riding accident. Was never beaten in singles at Wimbledon, winning 3 consecutive titles (1952–54). Won 3 consecutive U.S. singles titles (1951–53) and 2 consecutive French titles (1953–54). Also won 1 Australian title (1953).

Jimmy Connors (b. 9-2-52): Tennis player. Alltime men's leader in tournament victories (109). Held men's #1 ranking a record 159 consecutive weeks, July 29, 1974 through Aug. 16, 1977. Won 5 U.S. Open singles titles on 3 different surfaces (grass 1974, clay 1976, hard 1978, consecutively 1982–83). Won 2 Wimbledon singles titles (1974, 1982) farther apart than anyone since Bill Tilden. Also won 1974 Australian Open title. Reached Grand Slam final 7 other times.

Jim Corbett (b. 9-1-66; d. 2-18-33): Boxer. "Gentleman Jim". Invented jab. Fight with Australian Peter Jackson on 5-21-91 ruled no contest when neither could continue into 62nd round. Won heavyweight title on 9-7-92 with a KO of John Sullivan in 21 rounds; it was first heavyweight title fight using gloves. Retained title with KO of British champ Charley Mitchell. Lost title when KO'd by Bob Fitzsimmons in 14 on 3-17-97, then lost two bids to regain it against Jim Jeffries. Career record: 19 fights; won 7 by KO and 4 by decision; drew 2; lost 4; 2 no decision. Elected to Boxing Hall of Fame in 1954.

Angel Cordero (b. 11-8-42): Jockey. At end of 1992 third alltime in wins (7,057) and earnings (164,526,217). Led yearly earnings three times, in 1976 and 1982–83, winning Eclipse Awards in the last two years.

Howard Cosell (b. 3-25-18): Sportscaster. Lawyer turned TV-radio sports commentator in 1953. Best known for his work on "Monday Night Football." His nasal voice and "tell it like it is" approach made him a controversial figure.

James "Doc" Counsilman (b. 12-28-20): Swimming coach. Coached Indiana from 1957 to 1990. Won 6 consecutive NCAA championships (1968–73). Career record 287–36–1. Coached U.S. men's team at Olympics in 1964, 1976. Also oldest person to swim English Channel (58 in 1979).

Count Fleet (b. 3-24-40, d. 12-3-73): Thoroughbred race horse. Triple Crown winner in 1943 with jockey Johnny Longden aboard. Trained by Don Cameron.

Yvan Cournoyer (b. 11-22-43): Hockey RW. "The Roadrunner" had 428 goals and 435 assists during his 15 season career with the Montreal Canadiens. Had 25 or more goals in 12 straight seasons. Played on 10 Stanley Cup championship teams. Elected to Hall of Fame in 1982.

Margaret Smith Court (b. 7-16-42): Australian tennis player. Alltime leader in Grand Slam singles titles (26) and total Grand Slam titles (66). Achieved Grand Slam in 1970 and mixed doubles Grand Slam in 1963 with Ken Fletcher. Won 11 Australian singles titles (consecutively 1960–66, 1969–71, 1973), 5 French titles (1962, 1964, consecutively 1969–70, 1973), 5 U.S. titles (1962, 1965, consecutively 1969–70, 1973) and 3 Wimbledon titles (1963, 1965, 1970). Also won 19 Grand Slam doubles titles and 19 mixed doubles titles.

Bob Cousy (b. 8-9-28): Basketball G. Seventh alltime most assists (6,955), second alltime most assists in a game (28 in 1958). League leader in assists 8 consecutive seasons. Averaged 18+ points and named to All-Star team 10 consecutive seasons. 1957 MVP. Played on 6 championship teams with Boston from 1950 to 1969. Also played on NCAA championship team in 1947 with Holy Cross.

Dave Cowens (b. 10-25-48): Basketball C. After college career at Florida State, NBA co-Rookie of Year in 1971. NBA MVP for 1973. All-Star game MVP in

1973. Career span 1970–71 through 1982–83, all but the last year with the Boston Celtics. Elected to Hall of Fame in 1991.

Ben Crenshaw (b. 1-11-52): Golfer. Legendary putter. Won 1984 Masters.

Larry Csonka (b. 12-25-46): Football RB. In 11 seasons rushed 1,891 times for 8,081 yards (4.3 per carry) and 64 TDs. MVP of Super Bowl VIII, when he rushed 33 times for a Super Bowl record 145 yards in Miami's 24–7 defeat of Minnesota. Career span 1968–74, 1979 with Miami Dolphins; 1976–78 with New York Giants. Elected to Hall of Fame in 1987.

Billy Cunningham (b. 6-3-43): Basketball player and coach. Averaged 24.8 points a game at North Carolina. In nine seasons (1965–66 through 1975–76) with Philadelphia 76ers, averaged 20.8 points per game. All NBA first team 1969, '70 and '71. In 8 seasons as Sixer coach went 454–196 in season, 66–39 in playoffs and won NBA title in 1983. Elected to Hall of Fame in 1985.

Chuck Daly (b. 7-20-30): Basketball coach. Won 2 consecutive championships with Detroit (1989–90). Won 50+ games 4 consecutive seasons. Coach of 1992 Olympic team. Career span as pro coach 1983–92 with Pistons; 1992 to present with New Jersey Nets.

Damascus (b. 1964): Thoroughbred race horse. After finishing 3rd in 1967 Kentucky Derby, won the Preakness, the Belmont, the Dwyer, the American Derby, the Travers, the Woodward and others—12 of 16 starts. Unanimous Horse of the Year for 1967.

Stanley Dancer (b. 7-25-27): Harness racing driver. Only driver to win the Trotting Triple Crown 2 times (Nevele Pride in 1968, Super Bowl in 1972). Also won Pacing Triple Crown driving Most Happy Fella in 1970. Won The Hambletonian 4 times (1968, 1972, 1975, 1983). Driver of the Year in 1968.

Tamas Darnyi (b. 6-3-67): Hungarian swimmer. Gold medalist in 200-meter and 400-meter individual medleys at 1988 and 1992 Olympics. Also won both events at World Championships in 1986 and 1991. Set world record in these events at 1991 Championships (1:59.36 and 4:12.36).

Al Davis (b. 7-4-29): Football executive. Owner and general manager of Oakland-LA Raiders since 1963. Built winningest franchise in sports history (294–179-11—a .619 winning percentage entering the 1993 season). Team has won 3 Super Bowl championships (1976, 1980, 1983). Also served as AFL commissioner in 1966, helped negotiate AFL–NFL merger.

Ernie Davis (b. 12-14-39, d. 5-18-63): Football RB. Won Heisman Trophy in 1961, the first black man to win the award. All-America 3 times at Syracuse. First selection in 1962 NFL draft, but became fatally ill with leukemia and never played professionally.

Glenn Davis (b. 12-26-24): College football HB. "Mr. Outside." Teamed with Doc Blanchard to lead Army to 3 consecutive undefeated seasons (1944–46) and 2 consecutive national championships (1944–45). Won Heisman Trophy in 1946. Also named All-America 3 times.

John Davis (b. 1-12-21, d. 7-13-84): Weightlifter. Gold medalist at 2 consecutive Olympics in 1948, 1952. World champion 6 times.

Pete Dawkins (b. 3-8-38): Football RB. Starred at Army 1956–58. Won Heisman Trophy 1958. Was first

captain of cadets, class president, top 5 percent of class academically, and football team captain; first man to do all four at West Point. Did not play pro football. Attended Oxford on Rhodes scholarship, won two Bronze Stars in Vietnam, rose to brigadier general before leaving Army to become investment banker. Made unsuccessful run for Senate from New Jersey in 1988.

Len Dawson (b. 6-20-35): Football QB. Completed 2,136 of 3,741 pass attempts with 239 TDs. In first Super Bowl threw for one TD in 35–10 loss to Green Bay. MVP of Super Bowl IV, which Kansas City won 23–7 over Minnesota. Career span 1957–75, the last 13 seasons with Kansas City Chiefs. Elected to Hall of Fame in 1987.

Dizzy Dean (b. 1-16-11, d. 7-17-74): Baseball RHP. 1934 MVP with 30 wins. League leader in strikeouts, complete games 4 times each. 150 career wins. Arm trouble shortened career after 134 wins by age 26. Career span 1930–41 and 1947 with St Louis and Chicago Cubs.

Dave DeBusschere (b. 10-16-40): Basketball F. NBA First Team Defense six straight seasons, 1969–74. Member of NBA champion New York Knicks in 1970 and '73. Career span 1962–63 through middle of 1968–69 season with Detroit Pistons; through 1973–74 with Knicks. Youngest coach (24) in NBA history. Elected to NBA Hall of Fame in 1982.

Pierre de Coubertin (b. 1-1-1863, d. 9-2-37): Frenchman called the father of the Modern Olympics. President of International Olympic Committee from 1896 to 1925.

Jack Dempsey (b. 6-24-1895, d. 5-31-83): Boxer. Heavyweight champion (1919–26), lost title to Gene Tunney and rematch in the famous "long count" bout in 1927. Career record 62–6–10 with 49 KOs from 1914 to 1928.

Gail Devers (b. 11-19-66): Track and field sprinter/hurdler. Won 100 at 1992 Olympics; leading 100 hurdles when she tripped over final hurdle and finished fifth. Successfully completed same double at 1993 World Championships, winning 100 in 10.82 and 100 hurdles in American record 12.46. Also won world indoor title in 60 (6.95). Battled Graves Disease.

Klaus Dibiasi (b. 10-6-47): Italian diver. Gold medalist in platform at 3 consecutive Olympics (1968, 1972, 1976) and silver medalist at 1964 Olympics.

Eric Dickerson (b. 9-2-60): Football RB. Alltime season leader in yards rushing (2,105 in 1984), second alltime most career yards rushing (13,168 entering 1992 season). Rushed for 1,000+ yards a record 7 consecutive seasons; 100+ yards in 61 games, including a record 12 times in 1984. Led league in rushing 4 times. Rookie of the Year in 1983. Career span since 1983 with Los Angeles Rams, Indianapolis, L.A. Raiders and Atlanta Falcons.

Bill Dickey (b. 6-6-07): Baseball C. Lifetime average .313. Hit 202 career home runs. Played on 11 AL All-Star teams. In eight World Series, hit five homers and 24 RBIs. Career span 1928–43 and 1946, all with the New York Yankees. Inducted into Hall of Fame 1954.

Harrison Dillard (b. 7-8-23): Track and field. Only man to win Olympic gold medal in sprint (100 meters in 1948) and hurdles (110 meters in 1952). Sullivan Award winner in 1955.

Joe DiMaggio (b. 11-25-14): Baseball OF. Voted

baseball's greatest living player. Record 56-game hitting streak in 1941. MVP in 1939, 1941, 1947. Had .325 career batting average; .300+ average 11 times; 100+ RBI 9 times. League leader in batting average, HR, and RBI 2 times each. Played on 10 World Series winners with NY Yankees. Career span 1936–51.

Mike Ditka (b. 10-18-39): Football TE. NFL Rookie of the Year in 1961. Named to Pro Bowl five times. Made 427 catches for 5,812 yards and 43 TDs. Career span 1961 to 72 with Bears, Eagles and Cowboys. Coach of Bears from 1982–92 with 112–68 overall record. Coach of Bear team that won Super Bowl XX, 46–10 over New England. Elected to Hall of Fame 1988.

Tony Dorsett (b. 4-7-54): Football RB. Third alltime in yards rushing (12,739), third in attempts (2,936). Rushed for 1,000+ yards in 8 seasons. Set record for longest run from scrimmage with 99-yard touchdown run on January 3, 1983. Scored 91 career touchdowns. Named Rookie of the Year in 1977. Career span 1977–88 with Dallas, Denver. Also won Heisman Trophy in 1976, leading Pittsburgh to national championship. Alltime NCAA leader in yards rushing and only man to break 6,000-yard barrier (6,082).

Abner Doubleday (b. 6-26-1819, d. 1-26-1893): Civil War hero incorrectly credited as the inventor of baseball in Cooperstown, New York, in 1839. More recent research calls Alexander Cartwright the true father of the game.

Clyde Drexler (b. 6-22-62): Basketball G. "The Glide" for his smooth play. Member of U.S. "Dream Team" that won 1992 Olympic gold medal. Career span since 1984 with Portland Trail Blazers.

Don Drysdale (b. 7-23-36, d. 7-3-93): Baseball RHP. Led NL three times in strikeouts (1959, '60, '62) and once in wins (1962). Won 1962 Cy Young Award with 25–9 mark. In 1968 pitched six straight shutouts en route to major league record—broken in 1988 by Orel Hershiser—of 58 consecutive scoreless innings. Career record of 209–166, with 2,484 K's and ERA of 2.95. Career span 1956–69, all with Dodgers. Inducted into Hall of Fame 1984.

Ken Dryden (b. 8-8-47): Hockey G. Goaltender of the Year 5 times (1973, consecutively 1976–79). Playoff MVP as a rookie in 1971, maintained rookie status and named Rookie of the Year in 1972. Led league in goals against average 5 times, wins and shutouts 4 times each. Career record 258–57–74, including 46 shutouts. Career 2.24 goals against average is the modern record. Second alltime in playoff wins (80). Tied record of 4 playoff shutouts in 1977. Played on 6 Stanley Cup champions with Montreal from 1970 to 1979.

Roberto Duran (b. 6-16-51): Panamanian boxer. Champion in 3 different weight classes: lightweight (1972–79), welterweight (1980, lost rematch to Sugar Ray Leonard in famous "no mas" bout) and junior middleweight (1983–84). Career record 90–9 with 62 KOs since 1967.

Leo Durocher (b. 7-27-05, d. 10-7-91): Baseball manager. "Leo the Lip." Said "Nice guys finish last." Managed 3 pennant winners and 1954 World Series winner. Won 2,008 games in 24 years. Led Brooklyn 1939–48; New York 1948–55; Chicago 1966–72; and Houston 1972–73.

Eddie Eagan (b. 4-26-1898, d. 6-14-67): Only American athlete to win gold medal at Summer and Winter Olympic Games (boxing 1920, bobsled 1932).

Alan Eagleson (b. 4-24-33): Hockey labor leader.

Founder of NHL Players' Association and its executive director since 1967.

Dale Earnhardt (b. 4-29-52): Auto racer. NASCAR champion 5 times (1980, 1986–87, 1990–91). 59 career NASCAR victories through 10-1-93.

Stefan Edberg (b. 1-19-66): Swedish tennis player. Has won 2 Wimbledon singles titles (1988, 1990), 2 Australian Open titles (1985, 1987) and 2 U.S. Open titles (1991-92). Led Sweden to 3 Davis Cup victories (consecutively 1984–85, 1987).

Gertrude Ederle (b. 10-23-06): Swimmer. First woman to swim the English Channel, in 1926. Swam 21 miles from France to England in 14:39. Also won 3 medals at the 1924 Olympics.

Herb Elliott (b. 2-25-38): Track and field. Australian runner was gold medalist in 1960 Olympic 1,500 meters in world record 3:35.6. Also set world mile record of 3:54.5 in 1958. Undefeated at 1500 meters/mile in international competition. Retired at 21.

John Elway (b. 6-28-60): Football QB. First player taken in 1983 NFL draft. Topped 3,000 yards every season from 1985–91. Through '92 season had thrown for 30,216 yards 158 TDs. Famous for last minute drives, 24 of which won game in fourth quarter. Career span since 1983 with Denver Broncos.

Roy Emerson (b. 11-3-36): Australian tennis player. Alltime men's leader in Grand Slam singles titles (12). Won 6 Australian titles, 5 consecutively (1961, 1963–67), 2 consecutive Wimbledon titles (1964–65), 2 U.S. titles (1961, 1964); and 2 French titles (1963, 1967). Also won 13 Grand Slam doubles titles.

Kornelia Ender (b. 10-25-58): East German swimmer. Won 4 gold medals at 1976 Olympics and 3 silver medals at 1972 Olympics.

Julius Erving (b. 2-22-50): "Dr. J." Basketball F. Third alltime most points scored for combined ABA and NBA career (30,026). 24.2 scoring average. Averaged 20+ points 14 consecutive seasons. 4 MVP awards, consecutively 1974–76, 1981; playoff MVP 1974, 1976. All-Star 9 times. Led league in scoring 3 times. Played on 3 championship teams, with New York (ABA) and Philadelphia (NBA). Career span 1971 to 1986.

Phil Esposito (b. 2-20-42): Hockey C. "Espo." First to break the 100-point barrier (126 in 1969). Fourth alltime in points (1,590) and goals (717), fifth in assists (873). Led league in goals 6 consecutive seasons, points 5 times and assists 3 times. Won MVP award 2 times (1969, 1974). Scored 30+ goals 13 consecutive seasons and 100+ points 6 times. All-Star 6 times. Career span 1963–81 with Chicago, Boston, NY Rangers. Also general manager of NY Rangers from 1986 to 1989. Currently general manager of Tampa Bay. Brother Tony was Goaltender of the Year 3 times.

Tony Esposito (b. 4-23-43): Hockey goalie. Brother of Phil. A five-time All Star during 16-season NHL career, almost all of it with the Chicago Blackhawks. In 886 games gave up 2,563 goals, an average of 2.92 per game. Won or shared Vezina Trophy three times. Elected to Hall of Fame in 1988.

Janet Evans (b. 8-28-71): Swimmer. Won 3 gold medals at 1988 Olympics and 1 at 1992 Olympics. Holds world record in 400-meter freestyle (4:03.85 set in 1988), 800-meter freestyle (8:16.22 set in 1989) and 1,500-meter freestyle (15:52.10 set in 1988). Sullivan Award winner in 1989.

Lee Evans (b. 2-25-47): Track and field. Gold

medalist in 400 meters at 1968 Olympics with world record time of 43.86 that stood until 1988.

Chris Evert (b. 12-21-54): Also Chris Evert Lloyd. Tennis player. Alltime leader in tournament victories (157). Third all-time in women's Grand Slam singles titles (18—tied with Martina Navratilova). Won at least 1 Grand Slam singles title every year from 1974 to 1986. Won 7 French Open titles (1974–75, 1979–1980, 1983, 1985–86), 6 U.S. Open titles (1975–77, 1978, 1980, 1982), 3 Wimbledon titles (1974, 1976, 1981) and 2 Australian Open titles (1982, 1984). Reached Grand Slam finals 16 other times. Reached semifinals at 52 of her last 56 Grand Slam tournaments.

Weeb Ewbank (b. 5-6-07): Football coach. Only coach to win titles in both the NFL and AFL. Coached Baltimore Colts to classic overtime defeat of New York Giants in 1958 and New York Jets to their stunning 16–7 win over Baltimore in Super Bowl III. Career record of 134-130-7. Career span 1954–62 with Colts and 1963–73 with Jets. Elected to Hall of Fame in 1978.

Patrick Ewing (b. 8-5-62): Basketball C. 1986 Rookie of the Year with New York. 20+ points average in all 8 seasons with Knicks. All-NBA first team 1990. Eight-season scoring average of 23.7 through start of 1993–94 season. Played on 3 NCAA final teams with Georgetown (1982, 1984–85); tournament MVP in 1984. All-America 3 times.

Nick Faldo (b. 7-18-57): British golfer. Winner of the Masters 2 consecutive years (1989–90) and British Open 3 times (1987, 1990, 1992).

Juan Manuel Fangio (b. 6-24-11): Argentinian auto racer. Fourth all-time in Formula 1 victories (24, but in just 51 starts). Formula 1 champion 5 times, the most of any driver (1951, consecutively 1954–57). Retired in 1958.

Bob Feller (b. 11-3-18): Baseball RHP. League leader in wins 6 times, strikeouts 7 times, innings pitched 5 times. Pitched 3 no-hitters and 12 one-hitters. 266 career wins; 2,581 career strikeouts. Won 20+ games 6 times. Served 4 years in military during career. Career span 1936–41, 1945–56 with Cleveland.

Tom Ferguson (b. 12-20-50): Rodeo. First to top $1 million in career earnings. All-Around champion 6 consecutive years (1974–79).

Enzo Ferrari (b. 2-8-1898, d. 8-14-88): Auto racing engineer. Team owner since 1929, he built first Ferrari race car in Italy in 1947 and continued to preside over Ferrari race and street cars until his death. In 61 years of competition, Ferrari's cars have won over 5,000 races.

Mark Fidrych (b. 8-14-54): Baseball RHP. "The Bird." Rookie of the Year in 1976 with Detroit. Had 19–9 record with league-best 2.39 ERA and 24 complete games. Habit of talking to the ball on the mound made him a cult hero. Arm injuries curtailed career.

Cecil Fielder (b. 9-21-63): Baseball 1B. The last man to hit 50+ HR (51 in 1990). Has led the major leagues in HR twice and RBI 3 consecutive seasons (1990–92) after spending 1989 season in Japanese league. Career span since 1985 with Toronto, Detroit.

Herve Filion (b. 2-1-40): Harness racing driver. Alltime leader in career wins (more than 13,000). Driver of the Year 10 times, more than any other driver (consecutively 1969–74, 1978, 1981, 1989).

Rollie Fingers (b. 8-25-46): Baseball RHP. Alltime leader in saves (341); third in relief wins (107); fourth in

appearances (944). 1981 Cy Young and MVP winner; 1974 World Series MVP. Alltime Series leader in saves (6). Career span 1968–85 with Oakland, San Diego, Milwaukee.

Bobby Fischer (b. 3-9-43): Chess. World champion from 1972 to 1975, the only American to hold title. Never played competitive chess during his reign. Forfeited title to Anatoly Karpov by refusing to play him.

Carlton Fisk (b. 12-26-47): Baseball C. Career ended on 6-28-93. Alltime HR leader among catchers (352) and second in games caught (2,226). 376 career HR, including a record 75 after age 40. Rookie of the Year in 1972 and All-Star 11 times. Hit dramatic 12th-inning HR to win Game 6 of 1975 World Series. Career span 1969-1993 with Boston, Chicago (AL).

Emerson Fittipaldi (b. 12-12-46): Brazilian auto racer. Won Indy 500 in 1989 and '93. Won CART championship in 1989. Currently 16 career CART victories and 14 career Formula 1 victories. Formula 1 champion 2 times (1972, 1974).

James Fitzsimmons (b. 7-23-1874, d. 3-11-66): Horse racing trainer. "Sunny Jim." Trained Triple Crown winner 2 times (Gallant Fox in 1930, Omaha in 1935). Trained Belmont Stakes winner 6 times (1930, 1932, consecutively 1935–36, 1939, 1955), Preakness Stakes winner 4 times (1930, 1935, 1955, 1957) and Kentucky Derby winner 3 times (1930, 1935, 1939).

Peggy Fleming (b. 7-27-48): Figure skater. Gold medalist at 1968 Olympics. World champion 3 consecutive years (1966–68) and U.S. champion 5 consecutive years (1964–68).

Curt Flood (b. 1-18-38): Baseball OF. Won 7 consecutive Gold Gloves from 1963 to 1969. Career batting average of .293. Refused to be traded after 1969 season, challenging baseball's reserve clause. Supreme Court rejected his plea, but baseball was eventually forced to adopt free agency system. Career span 1956–69 with St. Louis.

Whitey Ford (b. 10-21-26): Baseball LHP. All-time World Series leader in wins, losses, games started, innings pitched, hits allowed, walks and strikeouts. 236 career wins, 2.75 ERA. Third alltime best career winning percentage (.690). Led league in wins and winning percentage 3 times each; ERA, shutouts, innings pitched 2 times each. 1961 Cy Young winner and World Series MVP. Career span 1950, 1953–67 with New York Yankees.

Forego (b. 1970): Thoroughbred race horse. Horse of the Year in 1974 (won 8 of 13 starts); '75 (won 6 of 9); and '76 (won 6 of 8). Finished fourth in 1973 Kentucky Derby. Over six years won 34 of 57 starts and $1,938,957.

George Foreman (b. 1-22-48): Boxer. Heavyweight champion (1973–74). Retired in 1977, but returned to the ring in 1987. Lost 12–round decision to champion Evander Holyfield in 1991. Retired after losing to Tommy Morrison 6-7-93. Career record 72–4 with 67 KOs since 1969. Also heavyweight gold medalist at 1968 Olympics.

Dick Fosbury (b. 3-6-47): Track and field. Gold medalist in high jump at 1968 Olympics. Introduced back-to-the-bar style of high jumping, called the "Fosbury Flop."

Jimmie Foxx (b. 10-22-07, d. 7-21-67): Baseball 1B. Won 3 MVP awards, consecutively 1932–33, 1938. Fourth alltime highest slugging average (.609), with 534 career HR; hit 30+ HR 12 consecutive seasons, 100+ RBI 13 consecutive seasons. Won Triple Crown in 1933. Led league in HR 4 times, batting average 2 times. Career span 1925–45 with Philadelphia, Boston.

A. J. Foyt (b. 1-16-35): Auto racer. Alltime leader in Indy Car victories (67). Won Indy 500 4 times (1961, 1964, 1967, 1977), Daytona 500 1 time (1972), 24 Hours of Daytona 2 times (1983, 1985) and 24 Hours of LeMans 1 time (1967). USAC champion 7 times, more than any other driver (consecutively 1960–61, 1963–64, 1967, 1975, 1979).

William H. G. France (b. 9-26-09): Auto racing executive. Founder of NASCAR and president from 1948 to 1972, succeeded by his son Bill Jr. Builder of Daytona and Talladega speedways.

Dawn Fraser (b. 9-4-37): Australian swimmer. Only swimmer to win gold medal in same event at 3 consecutive Olympics (100-meter freestyle in 1956, 1960, 1964). First woman to break the 1-minute barrier at 100 meters (59.9 in 1962).

Joe Frazier (b. 1-12-44): Boxer. "Smokin' Joe." Heavyweight champion (1970–73). Best known for his 3 epic bouts with Muhammad Ali. Career record 32–4–1 with 27 KOs from 1965 to 1976. Also heavyweight gold medalist at 1964 Olympics.

Walt Frazier (b. 3-29-45): Basketball G. Point guard on championship Knick teams of 1970 and '73. First team All Star in 1970, '72, '74 and '75. First team All Defense every year from 1969–1975. Averaged 18.9 points per game in 13-season NBA career. Elected to Hall of Fame in 1986.

Frankie Frisch (b. 9-9-98, d. 3-12-73): Baseball IN. "The Fordham Flash." Led NL in hits in 1923 (223). Hit over .300 13 seasons. Scored 100+ runs 7 times. Drove in 100+ runs three times. Career .316 batting average. Career span 1919–26 with New York Giants and 1927–37 with St. Louis Cardinals "Gashouse Gang." NL MVP in 1931. Elected to Hall of Fame in 1947.

Dan Gable (b. 10-25-48): Wrestler. Gold medalist in 149–pound division at 1972 Olympics. Also NCAA champion 2 times (in 1968 at 130 pounds, in 1969 at 137 pounds). Career record 118–1. Coached Iowa to NCAA championship 12 years (consecutively 1978–86 and 1991–93).

Clarence Gaines (b. 5-21-23): College basketball coach. "Bighouse." Entering 1993–94 season with 822 career wins in 46 seasons at Division II Winston-Salem State since 1947.

John Galbreath (b. 8-10-1897, d. 7-20-88): Horse racing owner. Owner of Darby Dan Farms from 1935 until his death and of baseball's Pittsburgh Pirates from 1946 to 1985. Only man to breed and own winners of both the Kentucky Derby (Chateaugay in 1963 and Proud Clarion in 1967) and the Epsom Derby (Roberto in 1972).

Gallant Fox (b. 3-23-27, d. 11-13-54): Thoroughbred race horse. Triple Crown winner in 1930 with jockey Earle Sande aboard. Trained by James Fitzsimmons. The only Triple Crown winner to sire another Triple Crown winner (Omaha in 1935).

Don Garlits (b. 1-14-32): Auto racer. "Big Daddy." Has won 35 National Hot Rod Association top fuel events. Fifth on alltime NHRA national event win list. Won 3 NHRA top fuel points titles (1975, 1985–86). First top fuel driver to surpass 190 mph (1963), 200 mph

(1964), 240 mph (1973), 250 mph (1975) and 270 mph (1986). Credited with developing rear engine dragster.

Lou Gehrig (b. 6-19-03, d. 6-2-41): Baseball 1B. "The Iron Horse." All-time leader in consecutive games played (2,130) and grand slam HR (23), third in RBI (1,990) and slugging average (.632). MVP in 1927, 1936; won Triple Crown in 1934. .340 career average; 493 career HR. 100+ RBI 13 consecutive seasons. Led league in RBI 5 times and HR 3 times. Played on 7 World Series winners with New York Yankees. Died of disease since named for him. Career span 1923–39.

Bernie Geoffrion (b. 2-16-31): Hockey RW. "Boom Boom" for his powerful slapshot. Won Hart Memorial Trophy for 1960–61. Scored 393 goals and 429 assists in 16 seasons (1950–51 through 1967–68), the first 14 with the Montreal Canadiens, the final two with the New York Rangers. Elected to Hall of Fame 1972.

Eddie Giacomin (b. 6-6-39): Hockey goalie. "Fast Eddie" led NHL goalies in games won for three straight seasons. Shared Vezina Trophy for 1970–71. In 610 games gave up 1,675 goals, a goals against average of 2.82. Career span 1965–75 with the New York Rangers and 1975–78 with Detroit Red Wings.

Althea Gibson (b. 8-25-27): Tennis player. Won 2 consecutive Wimbledon and U.S. singles titles (1957–58), the first black player to win these tournaments. Also won 1 French title (1956).

Bob Gibson (b. 11-9-35): Baseball RHP. 1968 Cy Young and MVP award winner, with alltime National League best in ERA (1.12): and second most shutouts (13). Also 1970 Cy Young award winner. Record holder for most strikeouts in a World Series game (17); Series MVP in 1964, 1967. Won 20+ games 5 times. 251 career wins; 3,117 strikeouts. Pitched no-hitter in 1971. Career span 1959–75 with St. Louis.

Josh Gibson (b. 12-21-11, d. 1-20-47): Baseball C in Negro leagues. "The Black Babe Ruth." Couldn't play in major leagues because of color. Credited with 950 HR (75 in 1931, 69 in 1934) and .350 batting average. Had .400+ average 2 times. Career span 1930–46 with Homestead Grays, Pittsburgh Crawfords.

Kirk Gibson (b. 5-28-57): Baseball OF. Played on 2 World Series champions (Detroit in 1984 and Los Angeles in 1988). Hit dramatic pinch-hit HR in 9th inning to win Game 1 of 1988 series. MVP in 1988. Career span since 1979, currently with Pittsburgh. Also starred in baseball and football with Michigan State.

Frank Gifford (b. 8-16-30): Football RB. NFL Player of Year in 1956 when he rushed for 819 yards and caught 51 passes. Played in seven Pro Bowls. Retired for one season after ferocious hit by Chuck Bednarik. Career span 1952–60 and 1962–64, all with New York Giants. Elected to Hall of Fame in 1977.

Rod Gilbert (b. 7-1-41): Hockey RW. Played 16 seasons, all with the New York Rangers (1960–61 through 1977–78), and had 406 goals and 615 assists. Elected to Hall of Fame 1982.

Sid Gillman (b. 10-26-11): Football coach. Developed wide-open, pass-oriented style of offense, introduced techniques for situational player substitutions and the study of game films. Won one division title with Los Angeles Rams and five division titles and one AFL championship (1963) with Los Angeles/San Diego Chargers. Career span 1955–59 Los Angeles Rams; 1960 Los Angeles Chargers; 1961–69 San Diego; 1973–74 Houston. Lifetime record 124–101–7. Also general manager in San Diego and Houston.

Pancho Gonzales (b. 5-9-28): Tennis player. Won 2 consecutive U.S. singles titles (1948–49). In 1969, at age 41, beat Charlie Pasarell 22–24, 1–6, 16–14, 6–3, 11–9 in longest Wimbledon match ever (5:12).

Shane Gould (b. 11-23-56): Australian swimmer. Won 3 gold medals, 1 silver and 1 bronze medal at 1972 Olympics. Set 11 world records over 23-month period beginning in 1971. Held world record in 5 freestyle distances ranging from 100 meters to 1,500 meters in late 1971 and 1972. Retired at age 16.

Steffi Graf (b. 6-14-69): German tennis player. Achieved the Grand Slam in 1988. Has won 3 Australian Open singles titles (1988–90), 5 Wimbledon titles (1988–89, 1991–93), 3 French Open titles (1987–88 and '93) and 3 U.S. Open titles (1988–89 and '93). Held the #1 ranking a record 186 weeks; Aug. 17, 1987 through March 10, 1991. Also, gold medalist at 1988 Olympics.

Otto Graham (b. 12-6-21): Football QB. Led Cleveland to 10 championship games in his 10-year career. Played on 4 consecutive AAFC champions (1946–49) and 3 NFL champions (1950, consecutively 1954–55). Combined league totals: 23,584 yards passing, 174 touchdown passes. Player of the Year 2 times (1953, 1955). Led league in passing 6 times. Career span 1946–55.

Red Grange (b. 6-13-03, d. 1-28-91): Football HB. "The Galloping Ghost." All-America 3 consecutive seasons with Illinois (1923–25), scoring 31 touchdowns in 20–game collegiate career. Signed by George Halas of Chicago in 1925, attracted sellout crowds across the country. Established the first AFL with manager C. C. Pyle in 1926, but league folded after 1 year. Career span 1925–34 with Chicago, New York.

Rocky Graziano (b. 6-7-22, d. 5-22-90): Boxer. Middleweight champion from 1947 to 1948. Career record 67–13. Endured 3 brutal title fights against Tony Zale, with Zale winning by KO in 1946 and 1948, and Graziano winning by KO in 1947.

Hank Greenberg (b. 1-1-11, d. 9-4-86): Baseball 1B. 331 career HR (58 in 1938). MVP in 1935, 1940. League leader in HR and RBI 4 times each. Fifth highest slugging average (.605). 100+ RBI 7 times. Career span 1933–41, 1945–47 with Detroit, Pittsburgh.

Joe Greene (b. 9-24-46): Football DT. "Mean Joe." Anchored Pittsburgh's famed "Steel Curtain" defense. Selected to Pro Bowl 10 times. Played on 4 Super Bowl champions (consecutively 1974-75, 1978-79). Career span 1969 to 1981.

Forrest Gregg (b. 10-18-33): Football OT/G. Played in then-record 188 straight games from 1956 through 1971. Named all-NFL eight straight years starting in 1960. Career span 1956–71, most of it with Green Bay Packers. Played on winning Packer team in first two Super Bowls. Inducted into Hall of Fame in 1977.

Wayne Gretzky (b. 1-26-61): Hockey C. "The Great One." Most dominant player in history. Alltime scoring leader in points (2,328) and assists (1,563), third in goals (765) through 1992-93 season. Alltime season scoring leader in points (215 in 1986), goals (92 in 1982) and assists (163 in 1986). Has won MVP award 9 times, more than any other player (consecutively 1980-87, 1989). Led league in assists 13 times, scoring 10 times, goals 5 times. Scored 200+ points 4 times, 100+ points 8 other times; 70+ goals 4 consecutive seasons; 50+ goals 5 other times; 100+ assists 11 consecutive seasons. Also alltime playoff scoring leader in points

(346), goals (110) and assists (236). Playoff MVP 2 times (1985, 1988). All-Star 8 times. Played on 5 Stanley Cup champions with Edmonton from 1978 to 1988. Traded to Los Angeles on Aug. 9, 1988.

Bob Griese (b. 2-3-45): Football QB. Career span 1967–80 with Miami Dolphins. Played in three straight Super Bowls, 1971–73. Quarterback of 1972 Dolphin team that went 17–0. Won Super Bowl VII and VIII. In 14 seasons completed 1,926 passes for 25,092 yards and 192 TDs. Elected to Hall of Fame in 1990.

Archie Griffin (b. 8-21-54): College football RB. Only player to win the Heisman Trophy 2 times (consecutively 1974-75), with Ohio State. Fourth alltime NCAA most yards rushing (5,177), his 6.13 yards per carry is the collegiate record. Professional career span 1976-83 with Cincinnati; totaled 2,808 yards rushing and 192 receptions.

Lefty Grove (b. 3-6-00, d. 5-22-75): Baseball LHP. 300 career wins and fifth alltime highest winning percentage (.680). League leader in ERA 9 times, strikeouts 7 consecutive seasons. Won 20+ games 8 times. 1931 MVP. Career span 1925-41 with Philadelphia, Boston.

Tony Gwynn (b. 5-9-60): Baseball OF. 4 batting titles (1984, consecutively 1987-89). League leader in hits 4 times, with .300+ average 10 times, 200+ hits 4 times. Career span since 1982 with San Diego.

Walter Hagen (b. 12-21-1892, d. 10-5-69): Golfer. Third alltime leader in major championships (11). Won PGA Championship 5 times (1921, consecutively 1924-27), British Open 4 times (1922, 1924, consecutively 1928-29) and U.S. Open 2 times (1914, 1919). Won 40 career tournaments.

Marvin Hagler (b. 5-23-54): Boxer. "Marvelous." Middleweight champion (1980-87). Career record 62-3-2 with 52 KOs from 1973 to 1987. Defended title 13 times.

George Halas (b. 2-2-1895, d. 10-31-83): Football owner and coach. "Papa Bear." Alltime leader in seasons coaching (40) and wins (324). Career record 324-151-31 intermittently from 1920 to 1967. Remained as owner until his death. Chicago won a record 7 NFL championships during his tenure.

Glenn Hall (b. 10-3-31): Hockey goalie. "Mr. Goalie" was an All Star goalie in 11 of his 18 seasons. Set record for consecutive games by a goaltender, with 502, and ended career with goals against average of 2.51. Won or shared Vezina Trophy three times. Career span 1952-53 through 1970-71.

Arthur B. "Bull" Hancock (b. 1-24-10, d. 9-14-72): Horse racing owner. Owner of Claiborne Farm and arguably the greatest breeder in history. For 15 straight years, from 1955 to 1969, a Claiborne stallion led the sire list. Foaled at Claiborne Farm were 4 Horses of the Year (Kelso, Round Table, Bold Ruler and Nashua).

Tom Harmon (b. 9-28-19, d. 3-17-90): Football RB. Won Heisman Trophy in 1940 with Michigan. Triple-threat back led nation in scoring and named All-America 2 consecutive seasons (1939-40). Awarded Silver Star and Purple Heart in World War II. Played in NFL with Los Angeles (1946-47).

Franco Harris (b. 3-7-50): Football RB. Fifth alltime most rushing yards (12,120) and fourth in rushing touchdowns (91). Rushed for 1,000+ yards in 8 seasons, 100+ yards in 47 games. Scored 100 career touchdowns. Selected for Pro Bowl 9 times. Rookie of the Year in 1972. Played on 4 Super Bowl champions (consecutively 1974-75, 1978-79) with Pittsburgh. Super Bowl MVP in 1974. Holds Super Bowl record for most rushing yards (354) and most rushing touchdowns (4). Made the "Immaculate Reception" to win 1972 playoff game against Oakland. Career span 1972-83 with Pittsburgh.

Leon Hart (b. 11-2-28): Football DE. Won Heisman Trophy in 1949, the last lineman to win the award. Played on 3 national champions with Notre Dame (consecutively 1946–47, 1949) and the Irish went undefeated during his 4 years (36-0-2). Also played on 3 NFL champions with Detroit. Career span 1950-57.

Bill Hartack (b. 12-9-32): Horse racing jockey. Rode Kentucky Derby winner 5 times (1957, 1960, 1962, 1964, 1969), Preakness Stakes winner 3 times (1956, 1964, 1969) and Belmont Stakes winner 1 time (1960).

Doug Harvey (b. 12-19-24, d. 12-26-90): Hockey D. Defensive Player of the Year 7 times (consecutively 1954-57, 1959-61). Led league in assists in 1954. All-Star 10 times. Played on 6 Stanley Cup champions with Montreal from 1947 to 1968.

Billy Haughton (b. 11-2-23, d. 7-15-86): Harness racing driver. Won the Pacing Triple Crown driving Rum Customer in 1968. Won The Hambletonian 4 times (1974, consecutively 1976-77, 1980).

John Havlicek (b. 4-8-40): Basketball F/G. Member of Ohio State team that won 1960 NCAA title. "Hondo" averaged 20.8 points per game over 16-season NBA career, all with Boston. First team NBA All Star in 1971, '72, '73 and '74. Member of eight Celtic teams that won NBA title. Playoff MVP 1974. Elected to Hall of Fame in 1983.

Elvin Hayes (b. 11-17-45): Basketball C. 1968 *Sporting News* College Player of Year as Houston senior. Averaged 21.0 points over 16-season NBA career. Led NBA in scoring (28.4) in 1969 and in rebounding in 1970 (16.9 per game) and '74 (18.1). First team All NBA in 1975, '77 and '79. Elected to Hall of Fame in 1989.

Woody Hayes (b. 2-14-13, d. 3-12-87): College football coach. Fifth alltime in wins (238). Won national championship 3 times (1954, 1957, 1968) and Rose Bowl 4 times. Career record 238-72-10, including 4 undefeated seasons, with Ohio State from 1951 to 1978. Forced to resign after striking an opposing player during 1978 Gator Bowl.

Marques Haynes (b. 10-3-26): Basketball G. Known as "The World's Greatest Dribbler." Since 1946 has barnstormed more than 4 million miles throughout 97 countries for the Harlem Globetrotters, Harlem Magicians, Meadowlark Lemon's Bucketeers, Harlem Wizards.

Thomas Hearns (b. 10-18-58): Boxer. "Hit Man." Champion in 5 different weight classes: junior middleweight, light heavyweight, middleweight, super middleweight, and light heavyweight.

Eric Heiden (b. 6-14-58): Speed skater. Won 5 gold medals at 1980 Olympics. World champion 3 consecutive years (1977-79). Also won Sullivan Award in 1980.

Carol Heiss (b. 1-20-40): Figure skater. Gold medalist at 1960 Olympics, silver medalist at 1956 Olympics. World champion 5 consecutive years (1956-60) and U.S. champion 4 consecutive years (1957-60). Married 1956 gold medalist Hayes Jenkins.

Rickey Henderson (b. 12-25-57): Baseball OF. Alltime career stolen base leader (1095); alltime season stolen base record holder (130) in 1982. Led league in steals 11 times. Scored 100+ runs 11 times. 1990 MVP. All-time most HR leading off game. Career span since 1979 with Oakland, New York and Toronto.

Sonja Henie (b. 4-8-12, d. 10-12-69): Norwegian figure skater. Gold medalist at 3 consecutive Olympics (1928, 1932, 1936). World champion 10 consecutive years (1927-36).

Orel Hershiser (b. 9-16-58): Baseball RHP. Alltime leader most consecutive scoreless innings pitched (59 in 1988). Cy Young Award winner in 1988 and World Series MVP. Career span since 1983 with Los Angeles.

Foster Hewitt (b. 11-21-02, d. 4-22-85): Hockey sportscaster. In 1923, aired one of hockey's first radio broadcasts. Became the voice of hockey in Canada on radio and later television. Famous for the phrase, "He shoots ... he scores!"

Tommy Hitchcock (b. 2-11-00, d. 4-19-44): Polo. 10-goal rating 18 times in his 19-year career from 1922 to 1940. Killed in plane crash in World War II.

Lew Hoad (b. 11-23-34): Australian tennis player. Won 2 consecutive Wimbledon singles titles (1956-57). Also won French title and Australian title in 1956, but failed to achieve the Grand Slam when defeated at Forest Hills by countryman Ken Rosewall.

Ben Hogan (b. 8-13-12): Golfer. Third alltime in career wins (63). Won U.S. Open 4 times (1948, consecutively 1950-51, 1953), the Masters (1951, 1953) and PGA Championship (1946, 1948) 2 times each and British Open once (1953). PGA Player of the Year 4 times (1948, consecutively 1950-51, 1953).

Marshall Holman (b. 9-29-54): Bowler. Won 21 PBA titles between 1975 and 1988. Had leading average in 1987 (213.54) and was named PBA Bowler of the Year.

Nat Holman (b. 10-18-1896): College basketball coach. Only coach in history to win NCAA and NIT championships in same season in 1950 with CCNY. 423 career wins, a .689 winning percentage.

Larry Holmes (b. 11-3-49): Boxer. Heavyweight champion (1978-85). Career record 53-3 with 37 KOs from 1973 to 1991. Defended title 21 times.

Lou Holtz (b. 1-6-37): Football coach. Coached Notre Dame to national championship in 1988 with 12–0 record and a 34–21 win over West Virginia in Fiesta Bowl. At start of '93 season had 182-83-6 career record. 9-6-2 career record in bowl games. Career span 1969–71 at William & Mary (13–20); 1972–75 at N.C. State (33-12-3); 1977–83 at Arkansas (60-21-2); 1984–85 at Minnesota 10–12); and 1986–92 at Notre Dame (66-18-1).

Evander Holyfield (b. 10-19-62): Boxer. Undefeated heavyweight champion since Oct. 25, 1990 when he beat James "Buster" Douglas in Las Vegas. Lost title to Riddick Bowe in Las Vegas on 11-13-92. That is only loss of Holyfield's career.

Red Holzman (b. 8-10-20): Basketball coach. Led New York Knicks to NBA title in 1970 and '73. NBA coach of the Year in 1970. Member of Rochester team that won NBA title in both 1946 (in NBL) and '51. After two-year coaching stints with Milwaukee and St. Louis, coached New York Knicks from 1968-82. Elected to Hall of Fame in 1985.

Harry Hopman (b. 8-12-06, d. 12-27-85): Australian

tennis coach. As nonplaying captain, led Australia to 15 Davis Cup titles between 1950 and 1969. Mentor to Lew Hoad, Ken Rosewall, Rod Laver and John Newcombe.

Willie Hoppe (b. 10-11-1887, d. 2-1-59): Billiards. Won 51 world championship matches from 1904 to 1952.

Rogers Hornsby (b. 4-27-1896, d. 1-5-63): Baseball 2B. Second all-time highest career batting average (.358) and 7 batting titles, including .424 average in 1924. 200+ hits 7 times; .400+ average 3 times and .300+ average 12 other times. Led league in slugging average 9 times. Triple Crown winner in 1922, 1925; MVP award winner in 1925, 1929. Career span 1915-37 with St Louis (NL), New York (NL), Boston, Chicago (NL).

Paul Hornung (b. 12-23-35): Football RB-K. Led league in scoring 3 consecutive seasons, including a record 176 points in 1960 (15 touchdowns, 15 field goals, 41 extra points). Player of the Year in 1961. Career span 1957-66 with Green Bay. Suspended for 1963 season by Pete Rozelle for gambling. Also won Heisman Trophy in 1956 with Notre Dame.

Gordie Howe (b. 3-31-28): Hockey RW. Alltime leader in goals (801), years played (26) and games (1,767). Second alltime scoring leader in points (1,850) and assists (1,049). Won MVP award 6 times (consecutively 1952-53, 1957-58, 1960, 1963). Led league in scoring 6 times, goals 5 times and assists 3 times. Scored 40+ goals 5 times, 30+ goals 13 other times, 100+ points 3 times. All-Star 12 times. Played on 4 Stanley Cup champions with Detroit from 1946 to 1971. Teamed with sons Mark and Marty in the WHA with Houston and New England from 1973 to 1979, in NHL with Hartford in 1980.

Carl Hubbell (b. 6-22-03, d. 11-21-88): Baseball LHP. 253 career wins. MVP in 1933, 1936. League leader in wins and ERA 3 times each. Won 24 consecutive games from 1936 to 1937. Struck out Ruth, Gehrig, Foxx, Simmons and Cronin consecutively in 1934 All-Star game. Pitched no-hitter in 1929. Career span 1928-43 with New York.

Sam Huff (b. 10-4-34): Football LB. Made 30 interceptions. Career span 1956-69 with New York Giants and Washington Redskins. Elected to Hall of Fame in 1982.

Bobby Hull (b. 1-3-39): Hockey LW. "The Golden Jet." Fifth all-time in goals scored (610). Led league in goals 7 times and points 3 times. Scored 50+ goals 5 times, 30+ goals 8 other times. Won MVP award 2 consecutive seasons (1965-66). Son Brett won MVP award in 1991, the only father and son to be so honored. All-Star 10 times. Career span 1957-72 with Chicago, 1973-80 with Winnipeg of WHA.

Brett Hull (b. 8-9-64): Hockey RW. Son of Bobby Hull. Won Hart Memorial Trophy for 1990-91 season. Career span 1986-87 with Calgary Flames; since 1987 with St. Louis Blues.

Jim "Catfish" Hunter (b. 4-8-46): Baseball RHP. 1974 Cy Young award winner. Won 20+ games 5 consecutive seasons. Led league in wins and winning percentage 2 times each, ERA 1 time. 250+ innings pitched 8 times. Pitched perfect game in 1968. Member of 5 World Series champions for Oakland and New York Yankees. Career span 1965-79.

Don Hutson (b. 1-31-13): Football WR. Third alltime in touchdown receptions (99). Led league in pass

receptions 8 times, receiving yards 7 times and scoring 5 consecutive seasons. Caught at least 1 pass in 95 consecutive games. Player of the Year 2 consecutive seasons (1941-42). Career span 1935-45 with Green Bay.

Hank Iba (b. 8-6-04; d. 1-15-93): College basketball coach. Coached Oklahoma A&M (which became Oklahoma State) from 1934 to 1970. Team won NCAA titles in 1945 and '46. 767 career wins is second alltime to Adolph Rupp.

Jackie Ickx (b. 1-1-45): Belgian auto racer. Won the 24 Hours of LeMans a record six times (1969, consecutively 1975-77, 1981-82) before retiring in 1985.

Punch Imlach (b. 3-15-18, d. 12-1-87): Hockey coach. Seventh alltime in wins (467). With Toronto from 1958 to 1969. Won 4 Stanley Cup championships (consecutively 1962-64, 1967).

Bo Jackson (b. 11-30-62): Baseball OF and Football RB. Only person in history to be named to baseball All-Star game and football Pro Bowl game. 1985 Heisman Trophy winner at Auburn. First pick in 1986 NFL draft by Tampa Bay, but opted to play baseball at Kansas City. 1989 All-Star game MVP. Signed with football's LA Raiders in 1988. Sustained football injury in 1990, released from baseball contract by KC, signed by Chicago and returned from injury in early September 1991, but comeback failed at first. Had hip replacement surgery and hit homer in first at bat.

Joe Jackson (b. 7-16-1889, d. 12-5-51): Baseball OF. "Shoeless Joe." Third alltime highest career batting average (.356), with .300+ average 11 times. One of the "8 men out" banned from baseball for throwing 1919 World Series. Career span 1908-20 with Cleveland, Chicago.

Reggie Jackson (b. 5-18-46): Baseball OF. "Mr. October." Alltime leader in World Series slugging average (.755). 1977 Series MVP, hit 3 HR in final game on 3 consecutive pitches. 563 career HR total is sixth best all-time. Led league in HR 4 times. 1973 MVP. Alltime strikeout leader (2,597). In a 12-year period played on 10 first-place teams, 5 World Series winners. Career span 1967-87 with Oakland, New York, California. Inducted to baseball Hall of Fame in 1993.

Bruce Jenner (b. 10-28-49): Track and Field. Set world decathlon record (8,634) in winning gold medal at 1976 Olympics. Sullivan Award winner in 1976.

John Henry (b. 1975): Thoroughbred race horse. Sold as yearling for $1,100, the gelding was Horse of the Year in 1981 and in 1984 and retired with then-record $6,597,947 in winnings.

Ben Johnson (b. 12-30-61): Track and field. Canadian sprinter set world record in 100 meters (9.83 in 1987). Won event at 1988 Olympics in 9.79, but gold medal revoked for failing drug test. Both world records revoked for steroid usage. Suspended for life after testing positive for elevated testosterone level at an indoor meet in Montreal on 1-17-93.

Earvin "Magic" Johnson (b. 8-14-59): Basketball G. Sat out the 1991-92 season after being diagnosed with AIDS. Alltime leader in assists (9,921); alltime playoff leader in assists (2,320) and steals (358). MVP award 3 times (1987, consecutively 1989-90) and playoff MVP 1980, 1982, 1987. Played on 5 championship teams with Los Angeles since 1979. All-Star 8 consecutive seasons. League leader in assists 4 times, steals 2 times, free throw percentage 1 time. Also won NCAA championship and named tournament MVP in 1979 with Michigan State.

Jack Johnson (b. 3-31-1878, d. 6-10-46): Boxer. First black heavyweight champion (1908-15). Career record 78-8-12 with 45 KOs from 1897 to 1928.

Jimmy Johnson (b. 7-16-43): Football coach. Led the Cowboys from 1–15 in 1989, his first season in Dallas, to a 52–17 win over the Buffalo Bills in the Super Bowl XXVII just four seasons later. Head coach at Oklahoma State from 1979–83 and Univ. of Miami 1984–88 with career collegiate record of 81-34-3. Johnson's Hurricanes won national championship in 1987.

Michael Johnson (b. 9-13-67): Track and field sprinter. Only person ever to break 44 seconds for 400 (best of 43.65) and 20 seconds for 200 (19.79). Won 200 at 1991 World Championships and at 1993 World Championships. Anchored US 4 x 400 team at 1993 World Championship to world record of 2:54.29 with fastest ever relay carry of 42.97.

Walter Johnson (b. 11-6-1887, d. 12-10-46): Baseball RHP. "Big Train." Alltime leader in shutouts (110), second in wins (416), fourth in losses (279) and innings pitched (5,923). His 2.17 career ERA and 3,508 career strikeouts are seventh best alltime. MVP in 1913, 1924. Won 20+ games 12 times. League leader in strikeouts 12 times, ERA 5 times, wins 6 times. Pitched no-hitter in 1920. Career span 1907-27 with Washington.

Ben A. Jones (b. 12-31-1882, d. 6-13-61): Horse racing trainer. Trained Triple Crown winner 2 times (Whirlaway in 1941, Citation in 1948). Trained Kentucky Derby winner 6 times, more than any other trainer (1938, 1941, 1944, consecutively 1948-49, 1952), Preakness Stakes winner 2 times (1941, 1944) and Belmont Stakes winner 1 time (1941).

Bobby Jones (b. 3-17-02, d. 12-18-71): Golfer. Achieved golf's only recognized Grand Slam in 1930. Second alltime in major championships (13). Won U.S. Amateur 5 times, more than any golfer (consecutively 1924-25, 1927-28, 1930), U.S. Open 4 times (1923, 1926, consecutively 1929-30), British Open 3 times (consecutively 1926-27, 1930) and British Amateur (1930). Also designed Augusta National course, site of the Masters, and founded the tournament. Winner of Sullivan Award in 1930.

K.C. Jones (b. 5-25-32): Basketball G-coach. Member of 8 straight NBA-championship Boston Celtic teams in his nine season career from 1958–59 through 1966–67. Averaged 7.4 points and 4.3 assists per game. Coached Celtics from 1983–84 through 1987–88, with 308–102 regular season record and 65–37 playoff record with NBA titles in 1984 and '86.

Robert Trent Jones (b. 6-20-06): English-born golf course architect designed or remodelled over 400 courses, including Baltusrol, Hazeltine, Oak Hill and Winged Foot. In the mid-60s five straight U.S. Opens were played on courses designed or remodelled by Jones.

Sam Jones (b. 6-24-33): Basketball G. Played 12 seasons with Boston Celtics (1958–69) and made the playoffs every year, winning NBA title every year from 1959–66 plus 1968 and '69. Averaged 17.7 points per game for career. Elected to Hall of Fame in 1983.

Michael Jordan (b. 2-17-63): Basketball G. "Air." After 1992-93 season, alltime highest regular season scoring average (32.3) and most points scored in a playoff game (63 in 1986). Has led league in scoring 7 consecutive seasons, steals 3 times. MVP in 1988, 1991-92; playoff MVP in 1991-93; Rookie of the Year in 1985. All-Star team 6 consecutive seasons, All-Defensive team 5 consecutive seasons. Career span since 1984–93 with Chicago. Announced retirement on 10-6-93. Also College Player of the Year in 1984. Played on NCAA championship team with North Carolina in 1982. Member of gold medal-winning 1984 and '92 Olympic teams.

Florence Griffith Joyner (b. 12-21-59): Track and field. Won 3 gold medals (100 meters, 200 meters, 4x100-meter relay) at 1988 Olympics; silver medalist at 1984 Olympics. Women's world record holder in 100 meters (10.49 set in 1988) and 200 meters (21.34 set at 1988 Olympics). Sullivan Award winner in 1988.

Jackie Joyner-Kersee (b. 3-3-62): Track and field. Gold medalist in heptathlon and long jump at 1988 Olympics and in the former at the 1992 Olympics. Heptathlon world record holder (7,291 points set at 1988 Olympics). Also won silver medal in heptathlon at 1984 Olympics and bronze in long jump at 1992 Olympics. Sullivan Award winner in 1986.

Alberto Juantorena (b. 3-12-51): Track and field. Cuban was gold medalist in 400 meters and 800 meters at 1976 Olympics.

Sonny Jurgensen (b. 8-23-34): Football QB. In 18 seasons completed 2,433 of 4,262 pass attempts for 32,224 yards and 255 TDs. Led NFL in passing both 1967 and '69. Career span 1957–1974 with Philadelphia Eagles and Washington Redskins. Elected to Hall of Fame in 1983.

Duke Kahanamoku (b. 8-24-1890, d. 1-22- 68): Swimmer. Won a total of 5 medals (3 gold and 2 silver) at 3 Olympics in 1912, 1920, 1924. Introduced the crawl stroke to America. Surfing pioneer and water polo player. Later sheriff of Honolulu.

Al Kaline (b. 12-19-34): Baseball OF. 3,007 career hits and 399 career HR. Youngest player to win batting title with .340 average as a 20-year-old in 1955. Had .300+ average 9 times. Played in 18 All-Star games. Career span 1953-74 with Detroit.

Anatoly Karpov (b. 5-23-61): Soviet chess player. First world champion to receive title by default, in 1975, when Bobby Fischer chose not to defend his crown. Champion until 1985 when beaten by Gary Kasparov.

Gary Kasparov (b. 4-13-63): Born Harry Weinstein. Chess player. World champion since 1985.

Kip Keino (b. 1-17-40): Track and field. Kenyan was gold medalist in 1,500 meters at 1968 Olympics and in steeplechase at 1972 Olympics.

Jim Kelly (b. 2-14-60): Football QB. Led NFL in passing in 1990 (219 of 346 for 2,829 yards and 24 TDs). Led AFC in passing in 1991. In seven seasons through '92 completed 1,824 of 3,024 attempts for 23,031 yars and 161 TDs. Career span 1983–85 with New Jersey Generals of USFL, 1986–93 with Buffalo Bills.

Kelso (b. 1957, d. 1983): Thoroughbred race horse. Gelding was Horse of the Year 5 straight years (1960-64). Finished in the money in 53 of 63 races. Career earnings $1,977,896.

Harmon Killebrew (b. 6-29-36): Baseball 3B-1B. 573 career HR total is fifth most alltime. 100+ RBI 9 times, 40+ HR 8 times. League leader in HR 6 times and RBI 4 times. 1969 MVP. 100+ walks and strikeouts 7 times each. Career span 1954-75 with Washington, Minnesota.

Jean Claude Killy (b. 8-30-43): French skier. Won 3 gold medals at 1968 Olympics. World Cup overall champion 2 consecutive years (1967-68).

Ralph Kiner (b. 10-27-22): Baseball OF. Second to Babe Ruth in alltime HR frequency (7.1 HR every 100 at bats). 369 career HR. Led league in HR 7 consecutive seasons, with 50+ HR 2 times; 100+ RBI and runs scored in same season 6 times; 100+ walks 6 times. Career span 1946-55 with Pittsburgh.

Billie Jean King (b. 11-22-43): Tennis player. Won a record 20 Wimbledon titles, including 6 singles titles (consecutively 1966-68, 1972-73, 1975). Won 4 U.S. singles titles (1967, consecutively 1971-72, 1974), and singles titles at Australian Open (1968) and French Open (1972). Won 27 Grand Slam doubles titles—total of 39 Grand Slam titles is third alltime. Helped found the women's pro tour in 1970, serving as president of the Women's Tennis Association 2 times. Helped form Team Tennis. Also won the "Battle of the Sexes" match against Bobby Riggs in straight sets on Sept. 20, 1973, at the Houston Astrodome.

Nile Kinnick (b. 7-9-18, d. 6-2-43): College football RB. Won the Heisman Trophy in 1939 with Iowa. Premier runner, passer and punter was killed in plane crash during routine Navy training flight. Stadium in Iowa City named for his honor.

Tom Kite (b. 12-9-49): Golfer. PGA alltime money leader, with $6,258,893 through end of '92 season. Led PGA in scoring average in 1981 (69.80) and '82 (70.21). PGA Player of Year in 1989, when he won a record $1,395,278. Shook reputation for failing to win the big ones by winning 1992 US Open at windy Pebble Beach.

Franz Klammer (b. 12-3-54): Austrian alpine skier. Greatest downhiller ever. Gold medalist in downhill at 1976 Olympics. Also won four World Cup downhill titles (1975-78).

Bob Knight (b. 10-25-40): College basketball coach. Won 3 NCAA championships with Indiana in 1976, 1981, 1987. Coached U.S. Olympic team to gold medal in 1984. 588 career wins and .737 career winning percentage entering 1992-93 season. Career span since 1966.

Olga Korbut (b. 5-16-55): Soviet gymnast. First ever to complete backward somersault on balance beam. Won 3 gold medals at 1972 Olympics.

Sandy Koufax (b. 12-30-35): Baseball LHP. Cy Young Award winner 3 times (1963, consecutively 1965-66); and MVP in 1963; World Series MVP in 1963, 1965. Pitched 1 perfect game, 3 no-hitters. League leader in ERA 5 consecutive seasons, strikeouts 4 times. Won 25+ games 3 times. Career record 165-87, with 2.76 ERA. Career span 1955-66 with Brooklyn/Los Angeles.

Jack Kramer (b. 8-1-21): Tennis player. Won 2 consecutive U.S. singles titles (1946-47) and 1 Wimbledon title (1947). Also won 6 Grand Slam doubles titles. Served as executive director of Association of Tennis Professionals from 1972 to 1975.

Ingrid Kristiansen (b. 3-21-56): Track and field. Norwegian runner is only person—male or female—to hold world records in 5,000 meters (14:37.33 set in 1986), 10,000 meters (30:13.74 set in 1986) and marathon (2:21:06 set in 1985). Also won Boston Marathon 2 times (1986, 1989).

Bob Kurland (b. 12-23-24): College basketball player. 6' 10¼" center on Oklahoma A&M teams that won NCAA titles in 1945 and '46. Consensus All America and NCAA tournament MVP in both 1945 and '46. Led nation in scoring in '46. His habit of swatting shots off rim led to creation of goaltending rule in 1945. Won gold medals in both 1948 and '52 Olympics. Turned down lucrative pro offers, playing instead for Phillips 66 Oilers AAU team.

Rene Lacoste (b. 7-2-05): French tennis player. "The Crocodile." One of France's "Four Musketeers" of the 1920s. Won 3 French singles titles (1925, 1927, 1929), 2 consecutive U.S. titles (1926-27) and 2 Wimbledon titles (1925, 1928). Also designed casual shirt with embroidered crocodile that bears his name.

Marion Ladewig (b. 10-30-14): Bowler. Won All-Star Tournament 8 times (consecutively 1949-52, 1954, 1956, 1959, 1963) and WPBA National Championship once (1960). Also voted Bowler of the Year 9 times, more than any other bowler (consecutively 1950-54, 1957-59, 1963).

Guy Lafleur (b. 9-20-51): Hockey RW. Won MVP award 2 consecutive seasons (1977-78), playoff MVP in 1977. Scored 50+ goals and 100+ points 6 consecutive seasons. Led league in points scored 3 consecutive seasons, goals and assists 1 time each. 560 career goals, 793 assists. Played on 5 Stanley Cup champions with Montreal from 1971 to 1985.

Curly Lambeau (b. 4-9-98; d. 6-1-65): Football Q and coach. Quarterback for Packer team in early 20's. Went 212-106-21 in his 29 seasons (1921–49) as Packer coach, winning three NFL titles in 1929–31.

Jack Lambert (b. 7-8-52): Football LB. Anchored Pittsburgh's famed "Steel Curtain" defense. Selected for Pro Bowl 9 times. Played on 4 Super Bowl champions (consecutively 1974-75, 1978-79) with Pittsburgh from 1974 to 1984.

Jake LaMotta (b. 7-10-21): Boxer. "The Bronx Bull." Subject of *Raging Bull*, movie by Martin Scorcese, starring Robert DeNiro. Won middleweight title by knocking out Marcel Cerdan in 10 on 6-16-49. Lost title to Ray Robinson, who KO'd him in 13 on 2-13-51. Career record: 106 bouts; won 30 by KO and 53 by decision; drew 4; and lost 19, 4 by KO.

Kenesaw Mountain Landis (b. 11-20-1866, d. 11-25-44): Baseball's first and most powerful commissioner from 1920 to 1944. By banning the 8 Black Sox he restored public confidence in the integrity of baseball.

Tom Landry (b. 9-11-24): Football coach. Third alltime in wins (270). The first coach in Dallas history, from 1960 to 1988. Led team to 13 division titles, 7 championship games and 5 Super Bowls. Won 2 Super Bowl championships (1971, 1977). Career record 270-178-6.

Dick "Night Train" Lane (b. 4-16-28): Football DB. Third alltime in interceptions (68) and second in interception yardage (1,207). Set record with 14 interceptions as a rookie in 1952. Career span 1952-65 with Los Angeles, Chicago Cardinals, Detroit.

Joe Lapchick (b. 4-12-00, d. 8-10-70): Basketball C-coach. One of the first big men in basketball, member of New York's Original Celtics. Coached St. John's (1936-47, 1956-65) winning four NIT Tournaments. Coached New York Knicks, 1947-56.

Steve Largent (b. 9-28-54): Football WR. Second alltime in pass receptions (819) and TD receptions (100), and all-time leader in consecutive games with reception (177), seasons with 50+ receptions (10), and seasons with 1,000+ yards receiving (8). Career span 1976-89 with Seattle.

Don Larsen (b. 8-7-29): Baseball RHP. Pitched only perfect game in World Series history for the NY Yankees on Oct. 8, 1956, beating the Dodgers 2-0; named World Series MVP. Career span 1953-67 for many teams.

Tommy Lasorda (b. 9-22-27): Baseball manager. Has spent nearly his entire minor and major league career in Dodgers organization as a pitcher, coach and manager. Has managed Dodgers since 1977, winning 4 pennants and 2 World Series (1981, 1988).

Rod Laver (b. 8-9-38): Australian tennis player. "Rocket." Only player to achieve the Grand Slam twice (as an amateur in 1962 and as a pro in 1969). Second alltime in men's Grand Slam singles titles (11—tied with Bjorn Borg). Won 4 Wimbledon titles (consecutively 1961-62, 1968-69), 3 Australian titles (1960, 1962, 1969), 2 U.S. titles (1962, 69) and 2 French titles (1962, 1969). Also won 8 Grand Slam doubles titles. First player to earn $1 million in prize money. 47 career tournament victories. Member of undefeated Australian Davis Cup team from 1959 to 1962.

Andrea Mead Lawrence (b. 4-19-32): Skier. Gold medalist in slalom and giant slalom at 1952 Olympics.

Bobby Layne (b. 12-19-26; d. 12-1-86): Football QB. Led Detroit Lions to NFL championships in both 1952 and '53. In 1952 led NFL in every passing category. Career span 1948-62, most with the Detroit Lions. Elected to Hall of Fame in 1967.

Sammy Lee (b. 8-1-20): Diver. Gold medalist at 2 consecutive Olympics (highboard in 1948, 1952); bronze medalist in springboard at 1948 Olympics. Won the 1953 Sullivan Award. Also 1960 U.S. Olympic diving coach.

Jacques Lemaire (b. 9-7-45): Hockey C. As center for Montreal Canadiens from 1967-68 through 1978-79 was part of eight Stanley Cup winning teams. Over 12 seasons, all with Montreal, scored 366 goals and had 469 assists. Elected to Hall of Fame in 1984.

Mario Lemieux (b. 10-5-65): Hockey C. Won MVP award in 1988, playoff MVP in 1991. Led league in most points and goals scored 2 consecutive seasons, assists 1 season. Scored 40+ goals and 100+ points 6 consecutive seasons, including 85 goals and 199 points in 1989. Rookie of the Year in 1985. Tied playoff game record for points (8) and goals (5) on April 25, 1989. Career span since 1984 with Pittsburgh.

Greg LeMond (b. 6-26-61): Cyclist. Only American to win Tour de France; won event 3 times (1986, consecutively 1989-90). Recovered from hunting accident to win in 1989.

Ivan Lendl (b. 3-7-60): Tennis player. Second alltime men's most career tournament victories (93). Won 3 consecutive U.S. Open singles titles (1985-87) and 3 French Open titles (1984, consecutively 1985-86). Also won 2 consecutive Australian Open titles (1989-90). Reached Grand Slam final 9 other times. Alltime leader in prize money, with more than $19 million.

Suzanne Lenglen (b. 5-24-1899, d. 7-4-38): French tennis player. Lost only 1 match from 1919 to her retirement in 1926. Won 6 Wimbledon singles and doubles titles (consecutively 1919-23, 1925). Won 6 French singles and doubles titles (consecutively 1920-23, 1925-26).

Sugar Ray Leonard (b. 5-17-56): Boxer. Champion in 5 different weight classes: welterweight, junior middleweight, middleweight, light heavyweight and super middleweight. Career record 36-2-1 with 25 KOs from 1977 to 1991. Also light welterweight gold medalist at 1976 Olympics.

Carl Lewis (b. 7-1-61): Track and field. Set world record for 100 meters (9.86) on 8-25-91 at World Championships in Tokyo. Duplicated Jesse Owens's feat by winning 4 gold medals at 1984 Olympics (100 and 200 meters, 4x100-meter relay and long jump). Also won 2 gold medals (100 meters, long jump) and 1 silver (200 meters) at 1988 Olympics and two gold medals (long jump, 4x100 relay) at 1992 Olympics. Sullivan Award winner in 1981.

Nancy Lieberman (b. 7-1-58): Basketball G. Three-time All-America at Old Dominion. Player of the Year (1979, 1980). Olympian, 1976, and selected for 1980 team, but quit because of Moscow boycott. Promoter of women's basketball, played in WPBL, WABA. First woman to play basketball in a men's professional league (USBL) in 1986.

Bob Lilly (b. 7-26-39): Football DT. Dallas Cowboys' first ever draft pick, first Pro Bowl player and first all-NFL choice. Made all-NFL eight times. Career span 1961-74, all with Cowboys. Elected to Hall of Fame in 1980.

Sonny Liston (b. 5-8-32, d. 12-30-70): Boxer. Heavyweight champion from 1962 to 1964. Won title by KO of Floyd Patterson on 9-25-62. Lost title when TKO'd by Cassius Clay (Muhammad Ali) on 2-25-64 and then lost rematch on 5-25-65 when KO'd in first round. Career record: 54 fights; won 39 by KO and 11 by decision; lost 4, three by KO.

Vince Lombardi (b. 6-11-13, d. 9-3-70): Football coach. Alltime highest winning percentage (.736). Career record 105-35-6. Won 5 NFL championships and 2 consecutive Super Bowl titles with Green Bay from 1959 to 1967. Coached Washington in 1969. Super Bowl trophy named in his honor.

Johnny Longden (b. 2-14-07): Horse racing jockey. Rode Triple Crown winner Count Fleet in 1943. Eighth alltime most wins (6,032).

Nancy Lopez (b. 1-6-57): Golfer. LPGA Player of the Year 4 times (consecutively 1978-79, 1985, 1988). Winner of LPGA Championship 3 times (1978, 1985, 1989). Youngest member of the LPGA Hall of Fame.

Greg Louganis (b. 1-29-60): Diver. Gold medalist in platform and springboard at 2 consecutive Olympics in 1984, 1988. World champion 5 times (platform in 1978, 1982, 1986; springboard in 1982, 1986). Also Sullivan Award winner in 1984.

Joe Louis (b. 5-13-14, d. 4-12-81): Boxer. "The Brown Bomber." Longest title reign of any heavyweight champion (11 years, 9 months) from June 1937 through March 1949. Career record 63-3 with 49 KOs from 1934 to 1951. Defended title 25 times.

Jerry Lucas (b. 3-30-40): Basketball F. Star at Ohio State. *Sporting News* College Player of Year in both 1961 and '62. In 1960 member of both NCAA championship team and gold-medal winning U.S. Olympic team. Averaged over 20 points and 20 rebounds a game for college career. NBA First Team All Star in 1965, '66 and '68. NBA Rookie of Year in 1964. In 11 NBA seasons averaged 17 points a game. Elected to Hall of Fame in 1979.

Sid Luckman (b. 11-21-16): Football QB. Played on

4 NFL champions (consecutively 1940-41, 1943, 1946) with Chicago. Player of the Year in 1943. Tied record with 7 touchdown passes on Nov. 14, 1943. All-Pro 6 times. 137 career touchdown passes. Career span 1939-50. Also All-America with Columbia.

Jon Lugbill (b. 5-27-61): White water canoe racer. Won 5 world singles titles from 1979 to 1989.

Hank Luisetti (b. 6-16-16): Basketball F. The first player to use the one-handed shot. All-America at Stanford 3 consecutive years from 1936-38.

D. Wayne Lukas (b. 9-2-35): Horse racing trainer. Former college basketball coach and quarter horse trainer takes mass production approach with stables at most major tracks around country. Trained two Horses of the Year, Lady's Secret in 1986 and Criminal Type in 1990. Won 1988 Kentucky Derby with a filly, Winning Colors.

Connie Mack (b. 2-22-1862, d. 2-8-56): Born Cornelius McGillicuddy. Baseball manager. Managed Philadelphia for 50 years (1901-50) until age 87. All-time leader in games (7,755), wins (3,731) and losses (3,948). Won 9 pennants and 5 World Series (1910-11, 1913, 1929-30).

Larry Mahan (b. 11-21-43): Rodeo. All-Around champion 6 times (consecutively 1966-70, 1973).

Frank Mahovlich (b. 1-10-38): Hockey LW. Winner of Calder Trophy for top rookie for 1957-58 season. In 18 NHL seasons with Toronto Maple Leafs, Detroit Red Wings and Montreal Canadiens, had 533 goals and 570 assists. Played for six Stanley Cup winners. Elected to Hall of Fame 1981.

Phil Mahre (b. 5-10-57): Skier. Gold medalist in slalom at 1984 Olympics (twin brother Steve won silver medal). World Cup champion 3 consecutive years (1981-83).

Joe Malone (b. 2-28-1890, d. 5-15-69): Hockey F. "Phantom Joe." Led the NHL in its first season, 1917-18, with 44 goals in 20 games with Montreal. Led league in scoring 2 times (1918, 1920). Holds NHL record with most goals scored, single game (7) in 1920.

Karl Malone (b. 7-24-63): Basketball F. "The Mailman." Four-time first-team All-Star. All-Star MVP, 1989. All-Rookie team, 1986. Scored 20+ points in six of seven seasons with Utah. Member of 1992 Olympic team. Career span since 1987 with Utah.

Moses Malone (b. 3-23-55): Basketball C. Entering 1993-94 season alltime leader free throws made (8,419), fifth in rebounds (15,940) and fourth in points scored (27,066). 3 MVP awards in 1979, consecutively 1982-83; playoff MVP in 1983. 4-time All-Star. Led league in rebounding 6 times, 5 consecutively. Career span since 1976 with Houston, Philadelphia, Washington, Atlanta, Milwaukee.

Man o' War (b. 1917, d. 1947): Thoroughbred race horse. Won 20 of 21 races from 1919 to 1920. Only loss was in 1919 in Sanford Stakes to Upset. Passed up Derby but won both Preakness and Belmont. Winner of $249,465. Sire of War Admiral, 1937 Triple Crown winner.

Mickey Mantle (b. 10-20-31): Baseball OF. Won 3 MVP awards, consecutively 1956-57 and 1962; won Triple Crown in 1956. 536 career HR. Led league in runs scored 6 times, HR and slugging average 4 times. 50+ HR 2 times, 30+ HR 7 other times. Led league in walks and strikeouts 5 times each. Greatest switch

hitter in history. Played in 20 All-Star games. Alltime World Series leader in HR (18), RBI (40) and runs scored (42). No. 7 was a member of 7 World Series winners with NY Yankees. Career span 1951-68.

Diego Maradona (b. 10-30-60): Argentinian soccer player. Led Argentina to 1986 World Cup victory and to 1990 World Cup finals. Led Naples to Italian League titles (1987, 1990), Italian Cup (1987) and to European Champion Clubs' Cup title (1989). Throughout 1980s often acknowledged as best player in the world. Tested positive for cocaine and suspended by FIFA and Italian Soccer Federation for 15 months in March 1991.

Pete Maravich (b. 6-22-47, d. 1-5-88): Basketball G. "Pistol Pete." Alltime NCAA leader in points scored (3,667), scoring average (44.2) and games scoring 50+ points (28, including then Division I record 69 points in 1970). Alltime season leader in points scored (1,381) and scoring average (44.5) in 1970. College Player of the Year in 1970. NCAA scoring leader and All-America 3 consecutive seasons from 1968 to 1970 with Louisiana State. Also led NBA in scoring in 1977. Averaged 20+ points 8 times. All-Star 2 times. Career span 1970-79 with Atlanta, New Orleans/Utah, Boston.

Gino Marchetti (b. 1-2-27): Football DE. Played in Pro Bowl every year from 1955 to '65, except 1958 when he broke right ankle tackling Frank Gifford in Colts' 23–17 win over the Giants. Career span 1952–66, almost all with Baltimore Colts. Inducted into Hall of Fame in 1972.

Rocky Marciano (b. 9-1-23, d. 8-31-69): Boxer. Heavyweight champion (1952-56). Career record 49-0 with 43 KOs from 1947 to 1956. Retired as undefeated champion.

Juan Marichal (b. 10-24-37): Baseball RHP. 243 career wins, 2.89 career ERA. Won 20+ games 6 times; 250+ innings pitched 8 times; 200+ strikeouts 6 times. Pitched no-hitter in 1963. Career span 1960-75, mostly with San Francisco.

Dan Marino (b. 9-15-61): Football QB. Set all-time season record for yards passing (5,084) and touchdown passes (48) in 1984. Prior to 1993 season had passed for 4,000+ yards 4 other seasons and 400+ yards a record 10 games. Player of the Year in 1984. Career totals: 39,502 yards passing, 290 touchdown passes. Career span since 1983 with Miami.

Roger Maris (b. 9-10-34, d. 12-14-85): Baseball OF. Broke Babe Ruth's alltime season HR record with 61 in 1961. Won consecutive MVP awards and led league in RBI 1960-61. Career span 1957-68 with Kansas City, New York (AL), St Louis.

Billy Martin (b. 5-16-28, d. 12-25-89): Baseball 2B-manager. Volatile manager was hired and fired by Minnesota, Detroit, Texas, New York Yankees (5 times!) and Oakland from 1969 to 1988. Won World Series with Yankees as manager in 1977 and as player 4 times.

Eddie Mathews (b. 10-13-31): Baseball 3B. 512 career HR and 30+ HR 9 consecutive seasons. League leader in HR 2 times, walks 4 times. Career span 1952-68 with Milwaukee.

Christy Mathewson (b. 8-12-1880, d. 10-7-25): Baseball RHP. Third alltime most wins (373) and shutouts (80); fifth alltime best ERA (2.13). Led league in wins 5 times; won 30+ games 4 times and 20+ games 9 other times. Led league in ERA and strikeouts

5 times each. 300+ innings pitched 11 times. Pitched 2 no-hitters. Pitched 3 shutouts in 1905 World Series. Career span 1900-16 with New York.

Bob Mathias (b. 11-17-30): Track and field. At age 17, youngest to win gold medal in decathlon at 1948 Olympics. First decathlete to win gold medal at consecutive Olympics (1948, 1952). Also won Sullivan Award in 1948.

Ollie Matson (b. 5-1-30): Football RB. Versatile runner totalled 12,884 combined yards rushing, receiving and kick returning. His 9 touchdowns on punt and kickoff returns is an NFL record. Scored 73 career touchdowns, including a 105-yard kickoff return on Oct. 14, 1956, the second longest ever. Career span 1952-66 with Chicago Cardinals, Los Angeles, Detroit, Philadelphia. Also won bronze medal in 400-meters at 1952 Olympics.

Roland Matthes (b. 11-17-50): German swimmer. Gold medalist in 100-meter and 200-meter backstroke at 2 consecutive Olympics (1968, 1972). Set 16 world records from 1967 to 1973.

Don Maynard (b. 1-25-37): Football WR. Retired in 1973 as the NFL's alltime leading receiver. In 15 seasons, 10 with the New York Jets, caught 633 passes for 11,834 yards and 88 TDs. Averaged 18.7 yards per catch for career. In 1967 and '68 led AFL with average of 20.2 and 22.8 yards per catch. Elected to Hall of Fame in 1987.

Willie Mays (b. 5-6-31): Baseball OF. "Say Hey Kid." MVP in 1954, 1965; Rookie of the Year in 1951. Third alltime most HR (660), with 50+ HR 2 times, 30+ HR 9 other times. Led league in HR 4 times. 100+ RBI 10 times; 100+ runs scored 12 consecutive seasons. 3,283 career hits. Led league in stolen bases 4 consecutive seasons. 30 HR and 30 steals in same season 2 times and first man in history to hit 300+ HR and steal 300+ bases. Won 11 consecutive Gold Gloves; set record for career putouts by an outfielder and league record for total chances. His catch in the 1954 World Series off the bat of Vic Wertz called the greatest ever. Career span 1951-73 with New York and San Francisco Giants, New York Mets.

Bill Mazeroski (b. 9-5-36): Baseball 2B. Hit dramatic 9th-inning home run in Game 7 to win 1960 World Series, one of only two Series' to end on a home run. Also a great fielder, won Gold Glove 8 times. Led league in assists 9 times, double plays 8 times and putouts 5 times.

Joe McCarthy (b. 4-21-1887, d. 1-3-78): Baseball manager. Alltime highest winning percentage among managers for regular season (.615) and World Series (.763). First manager to win pennants in both leagues (Chicago (NL), 1929, New York (AL), 1932). From 1926 to 1950 his teams won 7 World Series and 9 pennants.

Mark McCormack (b. 11-6-30): Sports marketing agent. Founded International Management Group in 1962. Also author of best-selling business advice books.

Pat McCormick (b. 5-12-30): Diver. Gold medalist in platform and springboard at 2 consecutive Olympics (1952, 1956). Also won Sullivan Award in 1956.

Willie McCovey (b. 1-10-38): Baseball 1B. Led NL in homer three times (1963, '68, '69) and in RBIs twice (1968-69). 521 career homers. .270 career batting average. Hit 18 grand slams, a NL record. Rookie of Year 1959. NL MVP in 1969. Career span 1959-73 and 1977-80 with San Francisco Giants, 1974-76 with San

Diego Padres and 1976 with Oakland A's. Elected to Hall of Fame in 1986.

John McEnroe (b. 2-26-59): Tennis player. Has won 4 U.S. Open singles titles (consecutively 1979-81, 1984) and 3 Wimbledon titles (1981, consecutively 1983-84). Also won 8 Grand Slam doubles titles. Third alltime men's most career tournament victories (77). Led U.S. to 5 Davis Cup victories (1978-79, 1981-82, 1992).

John McGraw (b. 4-7-1873, d. 2-25-34): Baseball manager. Second alltime most games (4,801) and wins (2,784). Guided New York Giants to 3 World Series titles and 10 pennants from 1902 to 1932.

Denny McLain (b. 3-29-44): Baseball RHP. Last pitcher to win 30+ games in a season (Detroit, 1968); won 20+ games 2 other times. Won 2 consecutive Cy Young Awards (1968-69). Led league in innings pitched 2 times. Served 2½-year jail term for 1985 conviction of extortion, racketeering and drug possession. Career span 1963-72.

Mary T. Meagher (b. 10-27-64): Swimmer. "Madame Butterfly." Won 3 gold medals at 1984 Olympics (100-meter butterfly, 200-meter butterfly and 400-medley relay). World record holder in 100-meter butterfly (57.93 set in 1981) and 200-meter butterfly (2:05.96 set in 1981).

Rick Mears (b. 12-3-51): Auto racer. Has won Indy 500 4 times (1979, 1984, 1988, 1991). Fifth all-time in CART victories (29 as of 10-1-93) and CART champion 3 times (1979, consecutively 1981-82). Named Indy 500 Rookie of the Year in 1978.

Cary Middlecoff (b. 1-6-21): Golfer. Also a dentist. Won 40 PGA tournaments, including 1955 Masters and US Opens in 1949 and '56. Won 1956 Vardon Trophy.

George Mikan (b. 6-18-24): Basketball C. Averaged 20+ points and named to All-Star team 6 consecutive seasons. Led league in scoring 3 times, rebounding 1 time. Played on 5 championship teams in 6 years (1949-54) with Minneapolis. Also played on 1945 NIT championship team with DePaul. All-America 3 times. Served as ABA Commissioner from 1968 to 1969.

Stan Mikita (b. 5-20-40): Hockey C. Won MVP award 2 consecutive seasons (1967-68). Fourth alltime in assists (926); fifth alltime in points (1,467). Led league in assists 4 consecutive seasons and points 4 times. 541 career goals. All-Star 6 times. Career span 1958-80 with Chicago.

Del Miller (b. 7-5-13): Harness racing driver. Has raced in 8 decades since 1929, the longest career of any athlete. Won The Hambletonian in 1950. As of 8-13-91 has won 2,435 career races.

Marvin Miller (b. 4-14-17): Labor negotiator. Union chief of Major League Baseball Players Association from 1966 to 1984. Led strikes in 1972 and 1981. Negotiated 5 labor contracts with owners that increased minimum salary and pension fund, allowed for agents and arbitration, and brought about the end of the reserve clause and the beginning of free agency.

Art Monk (b. 12-5-57): Football WR. Caught more passes than anyone in NFL history (847 for 11,628 and 63 TDs through end of 1992 season). 106 catches in 1984 was NFL single season record. Twice caught 13 passes in single game. Career span 1980-93, all with Redskins.

Earl Monroe (b. 11-21-44): Basketball G. "The Pearl" played 13 seasons (1968-80) with the Baltimore Bullets and New York Knicks. NBA Rookie of Year in 1968. Member of 1973 NBA championship Knicks team. Averaged 18.8 points a game. Elected to Hall of Fame 1989.

Joe Montana (b. 6-11-56): Football QB. Entering 1993 season alltime highest-rated passer (93.5), third in completions (2,929), fifth in passing yards (35,124) and sixth in touchdown passes (244). Has won 4 Super Bowl championships (1981, 1984, consecutively 1988-89) with San Francisco since 1979. Named Super Bowl MVP 3 times (1981, 1984, 1989). Player of the Year in 1989. Also led Notre Dame to national championship in 1977. Traded to Kansas City in 1993.

Carlos Monzon (b. 8-7-42): Argentinian boxer. Longest title reign of any middleweight champion (6 years, 9 months) from Nov. 1970 through Aug. 1977. Career record 89-3-9 with 61 KOs from 1963 to 1977. Won 82 consecutive bouts from 1964 to 1977. Defended title 14 times. Retired as champion.

Helen Wills Moody (b. 10-6-05): Tennis player. Second alltime most women's Grand Slam singles titles (19). Her 8 Wimbledon titles are second most alltime (consecutively 1927-30, 1932-33, 1935, 1938). Won 7 U.S. titles (consecutively 1923-25, 1927-29, 1931) and 4 French titles (consecutively 1928-30, 1932). Also won 12 Grand Slam doubles titles.

Archie Moore (b. 12-13-16): Boxer. Longest title reign of any light heavyweight champion (9 years, 1 month) from Dec. 1952 through Feb. 1962. Career record 199-26-8 with an alltime record 145 KOs from 1935 to 1965. Retired at age 52.

Davey Moore (b. 11-1-33; d. 3-23-63): Boxer. Won featherweight title by KO of Kid Bassey in 13 on 3-18-59. Five successful defenses of title, before losing it on 3-21-63 to Sugar Ramos who KO'd him in 10. Died two days after fight of brain damage suffered during fight. Career record: 67 bouts; won 30 by KO, 28 by decision, 1 because of foul; drew 1; lost 7, two by KO.

Noureddine Morceli (b. 2-20-70). Algerian track and field middle distance runner. Set world record for mile (3:44.39) in Rieti, Italy, on 9-5-93. Set world record for 1,500 (3:28.86) on 9-5-92. World champion at 1,500 in both 1991 and '93. Finished a shocking seventh at 1992 Olympics. Only man ever to rank first in the world at 1,500/mile four straight years (1990-93).

Joe Morgan (b. 9-19-43): Baseball 2B. Won 2 consecutive MVP awards in 1975-76. Third alltime most walks (1,865), tenth most stolen bases (689). Led league in walks 4 times. 100+ walks and runs scored 8 times each; 40+ stolen bases 9 times. Won 5 Gold Gloves. Second alltime most games played by 2nd baseman (2,527). Career span 1963-84 with Houston, Cincinnati.

Willie Mosconi (b. 6-27-13; d. 9-16-93): Pocket billiards player. Won world title a record 15 straight times between 1941 and 1957. Once pocketed 526 balls without a miss.

Edwin Moses (b. 8-31-55): Track and field. Gold medalist in 400-meter hurdles at 2 Olympics, in 1976, 1984 (U.S. boycotted 1980 Games); bronze medalist at 1988 Olympics. Set four world records in 400-meter hurdles (best of 47.02 set on 8-31-83). Now second alltime in 400 hurdles to Kevin Young's world record 46.78. Also won 122 consecutive races from 1977 to 1987. Won Sullivan Award in 1983.

Marion Motley (b. 6-5-20): Football FB. All-time AAFC leader in yards rushing (3,024). Also led NFL in rushing 1 time. Combined league totals: 4,712 yards rushing, 39 touchdowns. Played on 4 consecutive AAFC champions (1946-49), 1 NFL champion (1950) with Cleveland from 1946 to 1953.

Shirley Muldowney (b. 6-19-40): Drag racer. First woman to win the Top Fuel championship, which she won 3 times (1977, 1980, 1982).

Anthony Munoz (b. 8-19-58): Football OT. Probably the greatest tackle ever. Made Pro Bowl a record-tying 11 times. Career span 1980-92 with the Cincinnati Bengals.

Isaac Murphy (b. 4-16-1861, d. 2-12-1896): Horse racing jockey. Top jockey of his era, Murphy, who was black, won 3 Kentucky Derbys (aboard Buchanan in 1884, Riley in 1890 and Kingman in 1891).

Eddie Murray (b. 2-24-56): Baseball 1B. 100+ RBIs 6 seasons and 30+ HRs five seasons. Through '93 season had 2,820 hits, 441 HRs and 1,662 RBIs. Alltime leader in RBIs by switch hitter. Career span 1977-88 with Baltimore Orioles; 1989-91 with LA Dodgers; and 1992-93 with New York Mets.

Jim Murray (b. 12-29-19): Sportswriter. Won Pulitzer Prize in 1990. Named Sportswriter of the Year 14 times. Columnist for *Los Angeles Times* since 1961.

Ty Murray (b. 10-11-69): Rodeo cowboy. All-Around world champion, 1989-92. Set single-season earnings record, 1990 ($213,771). Rookie of the Year, 1988. At 20 in 1989, became youngest man ever to win national all-around title.

Stan Musial (b. 11-21-20): Baseball OF-1B. "Stan the Man." Had .331 career batting average and 475 career HR. MVP award winner 1943, 1946, 1948. Fourth alltime in hits (3,630) and third in doubles (725). Won 7 batting titles. Led league in hits 6 times, slugging average 5 times, doubles 8 times. Had .300+ batting average 17 times, 200+ hits 6 times, 100+ RBI 10 times, and 100+ runs scored 11 times. 24-time All-Star. Career span 1941-63 with St. Louis.

John Naber (b. 1-20-56): Swimmer. Won 4 gold medals and 1 silver medal at 1976 Olympics. Sullivan Award winner in 1977.

Bronko Nagurski (b. 11-3-08, d. 1-7-90): Football FB. Punishing runner played on 3 NFL champions (consecutively 1932-33, 1943) with Bears. Rushed for 2,778 career yards, 1930-37 and 1943 with Chicago. Also All-America with Minnesota.

James Naismith (b. 11-6-1861, d. 11-28-39): Invented basketball in 1891 while an instructor at YMCA Training School in Springfield, Mass. Refined the game while a professor at Kansas from 1898 to 1937. Hall of Fame is named in his honor.

Joe Namath (b. 5-31-43): Football QB. "Broadway Joe." Super Bowl MVP in 1968 after he guaranteed victory for AFL. 173 career touchdown passes. Led league in yards passing 3 times, including 4,007 yards in 1967. Player of the Year in 1968, Rookie of the Year in 1965. Career span 1965-77 with NY Jets, LA Rams.

Ilie Nastase (b. 7-19-46): Romanian tennis player. "Nasty" for his unruly deportment on court. Beat Arthur Ashe to win 1972 US Open title. Won 1973 French Open. Twice Wimbledon runnerup (to Stan Smith in 1972 and Bjorn Borg in '76).

Martina Navratilova (b. 10-18-56): Tennis player. Third alltime most women's Grand Slam singles titles (18—tied with Chris Evert). Won a record 9 Wimbledon titles, including 6 consecutively (1978-79, 1982-87, 1990). Won 4 U.S. Open titles (consecutively 1983-84, 1986-87), 3 Australian Open titles (1981, 1983, 1985) and 2 French Open titles (1982, 1984). Reached Grand Slam final 12 other times. Also won 36 Grand Slam doubles titles. Her total of 54 Grand Slam titles is second alltime to Margaret Court's. Completed a non-calendar year Grand Slam in 1984-85. Set mark for longest winning streak with 74 matches in 1984. Also won the doubles Grand Slam in 1984 with Pam Shriver. Won 109 consecutive matches with Shriver from 1983 to 1985.

Byron Nelson (b. 2-14-12): Golfer. Won the Masters (1937, 1942) and PGA Championship (1940, 1945) 2 times each and U.S. Open once (1939). Won 52 career tournaments, including 11 consecutively in 1945.

Ernie Nevers (b. 6-11-03, d. 5-3-76): Football FB. Set alltime pro single game record for points scored (40) and touchdowns (6) on Nov. 28, 1929. Career span 1926-31 with Duluth, Chicago. Also a pitcher with St. Louis, surrendered 2 of Babe Ruth's 60 HR in 1927. All-America at Stanford, earned 11 letters in 4 sports.

John Newcombe (b. 5-23-44): Australian tennis player. Won 3 Wimbledon singles titles (1967, consecutively 1970-71), 2 U.S. titles (1967, 1973) and 2 Australian Open titles (1973, 1975). Also won 17 Grand Slam doubles titles.

Pete Newell (b. 8-31-15): College basketball coach. Despite coaching only 13 seasons, 1947 through 1960, was first coach to win NIT, NCAA and Olympic crowns. Led Univ. of San Francisco to 1949 NIT title, Cal to 1959 NCAA title, and the 1960 U.S. Olympic basketball team that included Jerry Lucas, Oscar Robertson and Jerry West to gold medal. Overall collegiate coaching record of 234–123.

Jack Nicklaus (b. 1-21-40): Golfer. "The Golden Bear." Alltime leader in major championships (20). Second alltime in career wins (70). Winner of the Masters 6 times, more than any golfer (1963, consecutively 1965-66, 1972, 1975, 1986—at age 46, the oldest player to win event), PGA Championship 5 times (1963, 1971, 1973, 1975, 1980), U.S. Open 4 times (1962, 1967, 1972, 1980), British Open 3 times (1966, 1970, 1978) and U.S. Amateur 2 times (1959, 1961). PGA Player of the Year 5 times (1967, consecutively 1972-73, 1975-76). Also NCAA champion with Ohio State in 1961.

Ray Nitschke (b. 12-29-36): Football LB. Defensive signal caller for the great Packer teams of the 60's. Voted Packer MVP by teammates after 1967 season. MVP of the 1962 NFL title game. Career span 1958–72 with Green Bay Packers.

Greg Norman (b. 2-10-55): Golfer. "The Shark" led PGA in winnings in 1986 and '90. Won Vardon Trophy twice, 1989–90. Won two British Opens—in 1986 at Turnberry and in '93 at Royal St. George's—but is almost as famous for his heartbreaking misses. Beaten at the 1986 PGA when Bob Tway holed out a sand shot and at the 1987 Masters when Larry Mize chipped in from a tough downhill lie.

James D. Norris (b. 11-6-06, d. 2-25-66): Hockey executive. Owner of Detroit from 1933 to 1943 and Chicago from 1946 to 1966. Teams won 4 Stanley Cup championships (consecutively 1936-37, 1943, 1961). Defensive Player of the Year award named in his honor. Also a boxing promoter, operated International Boxing Club from 1949 to 1958.

Paavo Nurmi (b. 6-13-1897, d. 10-2-73): Track and field. Finnish middle- and long-distance runner won a total of 9 gold medals at 3 Olympics in 1920, 1924, 1928

Matti Nykänen (b. 7-17-63): Finnish ski jumper. Three-time Olympic gold medalist. Won 90-meter jump (1984, 1988) and 70-meter jump (1988). World champion on 90-meter jump in 1982. Won four World Cups (1983, 1985, 1986, 1988).

Dan O'Brien (b. 7-18-66): Track and field decathlete. Won world decathlon title in 1991 and 1993. Set world decathlon record of 8,891 in Talence, France, on 9-4 and 5-92. Heavily favored to win 1992 Olympic decathlon but missed making U.S. team when he no heighted in pole vault at US Olympic Trials.

Parry O'Brien (b. 1-28-32): Track and field. Shot putter who revolutionized the event with his "glide" technique and won Olympic gold medals in 1952 and 1956, silver in 1960. Set 10 world records from 1953 to 1959, topped by a put of 63' 4" in 1959. Sullivan Award winner in 1959.

Al Oerter (b. 8-19-36): Track and field. Gold medalist in discus at 4 consecutive Olympics (1956, 1960, 1964, 1968), setting Olympic record each time. First to break the 200-foot barrier, throwing 200' 5" in 1962.

Sadaharu Oh (b. 5-20-40): Baseball 1B in Japanese league. 868 career HR in 22 seasons for the Tokyo Giants. Led league in HR 15 times, RBI 13 times, batting 5 times and runs 13 consecutive seasons. Awarded MVP 9 times; won 2 consecutive Triple Crowns and 9 Gold Gloves.

Hakeem Olajuwon (b. 1-21-63): Basketball C. From Nigeria. As part of the University of Houston's "Phi Slamma Jamma" his senior year led NCAA in field goal percentage, rebounding and blocked shots in 1984. NBA First Team 1987, '88, '89. Led NBA in rebounding in both 1989 (13.5 per game) and '90 (14.0), and in blocked shots in '90 (4.59) and '91 (3.95). Career span 1985–93, all with Houston Rockets.

Merlin Olsen (b. 9-15-40): Fooball DT. Part of L.A. Rams "Fearsome Foursome" defensive line. Named to Pro Bowl 14 straight times. Career span 1962–76, all with L.A. Rams. Elected to Hall of Fame 1982.

Omaha (b. 1932): Thoroughbred race horse. In 1935 third horse to win Triple Crown. Won Kentucky Derby by 1½ lengths over Roman Soldier; Preakness by 6 over Firethorn; and the Belmont by 1½ from Firethorn. Trained by Sunny Jim Fitzsimmons.

Shaquille O'Neal (b. 3-6-72): Basketball C. As LSU junior led NCAA in blocked shots in 1992, with 5.23 a game, and averaged 4.58 over his 90-game, three-year career. Top pick of Orlando Magic in 1992 NBA draft. Almost unanimous NBA Rookie of the Year 1993. Averaged 23.4 points, 13.9 rebounds and 3.5 blocked shots in first NBA season.

Bobby Orr (b. 3-20-48): Hockey D. Defensive Player of the Year more than any other player, 8 consecutive seasons (1968-75). Won MVP award 3 consecutive seasons (1970-72), playoff MVP 2 times (1970, 1972). Also Rookie of the Year in 1967. Led league in assists 5 times and scoring 2 times. Career span 1966-77 with Boston.

Mel Ott (b. 3-2-09, d. 11-21-58): Baseball OF. 511 career HR, 1,861 RBI, .304 batting average. League leader in HR and walks 6 times each. 100+ RBI 9 times and 100+ walks 10 times. Career span 1926-47 with New York.

Jim Otto (b. 1-5-38): Football C. Number 00 started every game (308) in his 15 year career (1960–74) with the Oakland Raiders. Inducted to Hall of Fame in 1980.

Kristin Otto (b. 1966): German swimmer. Won 6 gold medals for East Germany at 1988 Olympics.

Jesse Owens (b. 9-12-13, d. 3-31-80): Track and field. Gold medalist in 4 events (100 meters and 200 meters; 4x100-meter relay and long jump) at 1936 Olympics. At the 1935 Big 10 championship set or equaled 4 world record in 70 minutes, including 100 yards, long jump, 220-yard low hurdles and 220 dash.

Alan Page (b. 8-7-45): Football DT. First defensive player to be named NFL Player of the Year, in 1972. Career span 1967–78 with Minnesota Vikings and 1978–81 with Chicago Bears. Now sits on Minnesota Supreme Court.

Satchel Paige (b. 7-7-06, d. 6-8-82): Baseball RHP. Alltime greatest black pitcher, didn't pitch in major leagues until 1948 at age 42 with Cleveland. Oldest pitcher in major league history at age 59 with Kansas City in 1965. Pitched in the Negro leagues from 1926 to 1950 with Birmingham Black Barons, Pittsburgh Crawfords and Kansas City Monarchs. Estimated career record is 2,000 wins, 250 shutouts, 30,000 strikeouts, 45 no-hitters. Said "Don't look back. Something may be gaining on you."

Arnold Palmer (b. 9-10-29): Golfer. Fourth all-time in career wins (60). Won the Masters 4 times (1958, 1960, 1962, 1964), British Open 2 consecutive years (1961-62) and U.S. Open (1960) and U.S. Amateur (1954) once each. PGA Player of the Year 2 times (1960, 1962). The first golfer to surpass $1 million in career earnings. Also won Seniors Championship 2 times (1980, 1984) and U.S. Senior Open once (1981). 10 career seniors titles as of 10-1-93.

Jim Palmer (b. 10-15-45): Baseball RHP. 268 career wins, 2.86 ERA. Won 3 Cy Young Awards (1973, consecutively 1975-76). Won 20+ games 8 times. Led league in wins 3 times, innings pitched 4 times, ERA 2 times. Never allowed a grand slam HR. Pitched on 6 World Series teams with Baltimore, including shutout at 20 years old in 1966. Pitched no-hitter in 1969. Jockey underwear pitchman. Career span 1965-84.

Bernie Parent (b. 4-3-45): Hockey G. Alltime leader for wins in a season (47 in 1974). Goaltender of the Year, playoff MVP, league leader in wins, goals against average and shutouts 2 consecutive seasons (1974-75). Career record 270-197-121, including 55 shutouts. Career 2.55 goals against average. Tied record of 4 playoff shutouts in 1975. Played on 2 consecutive Stanley Cup champions (1974-75). Career span 1965 to 1979 with Philadelphia. Also the first NHL player to sign with the WHA in 1972, with Philadelphia.

Brad Park (b. 7-6-48): Hockey D. Seven-time All Star. In 17 seasons with the New York Rangers, Boston Bruins and Detroit Red Wings (1968–69 through 1984–85) scored 213 goals and had 683 assists. Elected to Hall of Fame 1988.

Jim Parker (b. 4-3-34): Football T/G. Winner of 1956 Outland Trophy as Ohio State senior. Blocked for Johnyy Unitas. All-NFL four times at guard, four times at tackle. Career span 1957-67, all with Baltimore Colts. Inducted into Hall of Fame in 1973.

Joe Paterno (b. 12-21-26): College football coach. Fourth alltime in wins in Division I-A (247—the most of any active coach at that level). Has won 2 national championships (1982, 1986) with Penn State since

1966. Career record 247-67-3, including 4 undefeated seasons. Has also won 14 bowl games.

Lester Patrick (b. 12-30-1883, d. 6-1-60): Hockey coach. Led NY Rangers to only Stanley Cup championships (1928, 1933, 1940). Originated the NHL's farm system and developed playoff format.

Floyd Patterson (b. 1-4-35): Boxer. Heavyweight champion 2 times (1956-59, 1960-62). First heavyweight to regain title, in rematch with Ingemar Johansson. Career record 55-8-1 with 40 KOs from 1952 to 1972. Also middleweight gold medalist at 1952 Olympics.

Walter Payton (b. 7-25-54): Football RB. Alltime leader in yards rushing (16,726), rushing attempts (3,838), games gaining 100+ yards rushing (77), seasons gaining 1,000+ yards rushing (10) and rushing touchdowns (110). His 125 total touchdowns rank second. Rushed for a record 275 yards on Nov. 20, 1977. Selected for Pro Bowl 9 times. Player of the Year 2 times (1977, 1985). Led league in rushing 5 consecutive seasons. Career span 1975-87 with Chicago.

Pele (b. 10-23-40): Born Edson Arantes do Nascimento. Brazilian soccer player. Soccer's great ambassador. Played on 3 World Cup winners with Brazil (1958, 1962, 1970). Helped promote soccer in U.S. by playing with NY Cosmos from 1975 to 1977. Scored 1,281 goals in 22 years.

Willie Pep (b. 9-19-22): Boxer. Featherweight champion 2 times (1942-48, 1949-50). Lost title to Sandy Saddler, won it back in rematch, then lost it to Saddler again. Career record 230-11-1 with 65 KOs from 1940 to 1966. Won 73 consecutive bouts from 1940 to 1943. Defended title 9 times.

Gil Perreault (b. 11-13-50): Hockey C. Won Calder Trophy as NHL's top rookie for 1970–71 season. Played 17 seasons (1970–71 through 1986–87), all with Buffalo Sabres. Scored 512 goals and had 814 assists in career. Elected to Hall of Fame in 1990.

Fred Perry (b. 5-18-09): British tennis player. Won 3 consecutive Wimbledon singles titles (1934-36), the last British man to win the tournament. Also won 3 U.S. titles (consecutively 1933-34, 1936), 1 French title (1935) and 1 Australian title (1934).

Gaylord Perry (b. 9-15-38): Baseball RHP. Only pitcher to win Cy Young Award in both leagues (Cleveland 1972, San Diego 1978). 314 career wins, 3,534 strikeouts. 20+ wins 5 times; 200+ strikeouts 8 times; 250+ innings pitched 12 times. Pitched no-hitter in 1968. Admitted to throwing a spitter. Career span 1962-83 with San Francisco, Cleveland, San Diego.

Bob Pettit (b. 12-12-32): Basketball F. First player in history to break 20,000-point barrier (20,880 career points scored). Sixth alltime highest scoring average (26.4) and seventh most free throws made (6,182). Also grabbed 12,849 rebounds for 16.2 average. MVP in 1956, 1959; Rookie of the Year in 1955. All-Star 10 consecutive seasons. Led league in scoring 2 times, rebounding 1 time. Career span 1954-64 with St Louis.

Richard Petty (b. 7-2-37): Auto racer. Alltime leader in NASCAR victories (currently 200). Daytona 500 winner (1964, 1966, 1971, consecutively 1973-74, 1979, 1981) and NASCAR champion (1964, 1967, consecutively 1971-72, 1974-75, 1979) 7 times each, the most of any driver. First stock car racer to reach $1 million in earnings. Son of Lee Petty, 3-time NASCAR champion (1954, consecutively 1958-59).

Laffit Pincay Jr. (b. 12-29-46): Jockey. Through 1992 had won more money than any other jockey ($170,325,931) and was second only to Bill Shoemaker in wins, with 7,888. Won 5 Eclipse Awards as outstanding jockey. Rode 3 Kentucky Derby winners; 2 Preakness winners; and 1 Belmont winner.

Jacques Plante (b. 1-17-29, d. 2-27-86): Hockey G. First goalie to wear a mask. Second alltime in wins (434) and second lowest modern goals against average (2.38). Goaltender of the Year 7 times, more than any other goalie (consecutively 1955-59, 1961, 1968). Won MVP award in 1961. Led league in goals against average 8 times, wins 6 times and shutouts 4 times. Was on 6 Stanley Cup champions with Montreal from 1952 to 1962 and played for 4 other teams until retirement in 1972.

Gary Player (b. 11-1-35): South African golfer. Won the Masters (1961, 1974, 1978) and British Open (1959, 1968, 1974) 3 times each, PGA Championship 2 times (1962, 1972) and U.S. Open (1965). Also won Seniors Championship 3 times (1986, 1988, 1990) and U.S. Senior Open 2 consecutive years (1987-88).

Sam Pollock (b. 12-15-25): Hockey executive. As general manager of Montreal from 1964 to 1978 won 9 Stanley Cup championships (1965-66, 1968-69, 1971, 1973, 1976-78).

Denis Potvin (b. 10-29-53): Hockey D. Seven time All Star during 15 season career (1973–74 through 1987–88), all with New York Islanders. Won Calder Trophy for 1973–74 season. Won Norris Trophy three times. Captained Islanders to four Stanley Cup championships. Elected to Hall of Fame in 1991.

Mike Powell (b. 11-10-63): Track and field. Long jumper broke Bob Beamon's 23-year-old world record at 1991 World Championships in Tokyo with a jump of 29' 4½".

Annemarie Moser-Pröll (b. 3-27-53): Austrian skier. Gold medalist in downhill at 1980 Olympics. World Cup overall champion 6 times, more than any other skier (consecutively 1971-75, 1979).

Alain Prost (b. 2-24-55): French auto racer. Alltime leader in Formula 1 victories. Formula 1 champion 4 times (consecutively 1985-86, 1989, 1993).

Jack Ramsay (b. 2-21-25): Basketball coach. Never played in NBA. Coached 11 seasons at St. Joseph's University, with 234–72 record. Overall record of 864–783 as NBA coach. Coach of NBA champion 1977 Portland Trail Blazers. Elected to Hall of Fame 1992.

Jean Ratelle (b. 10-3-40): Hockey C. In 21 season career (1960–61 through 1980–81) with the New York Rangers and Boston Bruins, scored 491 goals and had 776 assists. Twice won Lady Bing Trophy. Elected to Hall of Fame in 1985.

Willis Reed (b. 6-25-42): Basketball C. Played 10 seasons (1965–74), all with the New York Knicks. Career average of 18.7 points a game. NBA Rookie of Year in 1965. Playoff MVP of both Knick championship teams, in 1970 and '73. NBA MVP in 1970. Elected to Hall of Fame in 1970.

Harold Henry "Pee Wee" Reese (b. 7-23-18): Baseball SS. Played for 7 pennant-winning Dodger teams. Led NL in runs scored in 1949, with 132. Elected to Hall of Fame in 1984.

Mary Lou Retton (b. 1-24-68): Gymnast. Won 1 gold, 1 silver and 2 bronze medals at 1984 Olympics.

Grantland Rice (b. 11-1-1880, d. 7-13-54): Sportswriter. Legendary figure during sport's Golden Age of the 1920s. Wrote "When the Last Great Scorer comes / To mark against your name, / He'll write not 'won' or 'lost' / But how you played the game." Also named the 1924-25 Notre Dame backfield the "Four Horsemen."

Jerry Rice (b. 10-13-62): Football WR. Alltime leader in touchdown receptions (103) and in consecutive games with a TD reception (13 in 1988). Player of the Year in 1987 and led league in scoring (138 points on 23 touchdowns). Super Bowl MVP in 1989 with record 215 receiving yards on 11 catches. Also set Super Bowl record with 3 touchdown receptions in 1990. Career span since 1985 with San Francisco 49ers.

Henri Richard (b. 2-29-36): Hockey C. "The Pocket Rocket." Played on 11 Stanley Cup champions with Montreal. Four-time All-Star. Career span from 1955 to 1975.

Maurice Richard (b. 8-4-21): Hockey RW. "The Rocket." First player ever to score 50 goals in a season, in 1945. Led league in goals 5 times. 544 career goals. Won MVP award in 1947. All-Star 8 times. Tied playoff game record for most goals (5 on March 23, 1944). Played on 8 Stanley Cup champions with Montreal from 1942 to 1959.

Bob Richards (b. 2-2-26): Track and field. The only pole vaulter to win gold medal at 2 consecutive Olympics (1952, 1956). Also won Sullivan Award in 1951.

Branch Rickey (b. 12-20-1881, d. 12-9-65): Baseball executive. Integrated major league baseball in 1947 by signing Jackie Robinson to contract with Brooklyn Dodgers. Conceived minor league farm system in 1919 at St Louis; instituted batting cage and sliding pit.

Pat Riley (b. 3-20-45): Basketball coach. Going into 1993-94 season most playoff wins (117). Coached Los Angeles to 4 championships, 2 consecutively, from 1981 to 1989. 60+ wins 6 times (4 times consecutively), 50+ wins 4 other times. Currently coaching New York Knicks.

Cal Ripken Jr (b. 8-24-60): Baseball SS. Ended 1993 season with second longest consecutive game streak (1,897 since May 29, 1982). Set record for consecutive errorless games by a shortstop (95 in 1990). MVP in 1983 and Rookie of the Year in 1982. Has hit 20+ HRs in 11 consecutive seasons and started in 10 consecutive All-Star games.

Glenn "Fireball" Roberts (b. 1-20-31, d. 7-2-64): Auto racer. Won 34 NASCAR races. Died as a result of fiery accident in World 600 at Charlotte Motor Speedway in May 1964. At time of his death had won more major races than any other driver in NASCAR history.

Oscar Robertson (b. 11-24-38): Basketball G. "The Big O." Second alltime most assists (9,887) and free throws made (7,694), fifth most points scored (26,710), sixth most field goals made (9,508) and ninth highest scoring average (25.7). MVP in 1964, All-Star 9 consecutive seasons and 1961 Rookie of the Year. Led league in assists 6 times, free throw percentage 2 times. Averaged 30+ points 6 times in 7 seasons, 20+ points 4 other times. Only player in history to average a season triple-double (1961). Career span 1960-72 with Cincinnati, Milwaukee. Also College Player of the Year, All-America and NCAA scoring leader 3 consecutive seasons from 1958 to 1960 with Cincinnati. Third all-time NCAA highest scoring average (33.8); sixth most points scored (2,973).

Brooks Robinson (b. 5-18-37): Baseball 3B. Alltime leader in assists, putouts, double plays and fielding average among 3rd baseman. Won 16 consecutive Gold Gloves. Led league in fielding average a record 11 times. MVP in 1964—led league in RBIs—and MVP in 1970 World Series. Career span 1955-77 with Baltimore.

David Robinson (b. 8-6-65): Basketball C. *Sporting News* Player of the Year for 1987. Led college players in 1986 in both rebounding (13.0) and blocked shots (5.91, a record that still stands). NBA Rookie of Year in 1990. Led NBA in rebounding 1991 (13.0) and in blocked shots in 1992, when he was named Defensive Player of the Year.

Eddie Robinson (b. 2-13-19): College football coach. Has had alltime college record 381 career wins at Division I-AA Grambling State since 1941.

Frank Robinson (b. 8-31-35): Baseball OF-manager. Only player to win MVP awards in both leagues (Cincinnati, 1961, Baltimore, 1966). Won Triple Crown and World Series MVP in 1966. Rookie of the Year in 1956. Fourth alltime most HR (586). 30+ HR 11 times; 100+ RBI 6 times; 100+ runs scored 8 times (led league 3 times). Had .300+ batting average 9 times. Became first black manager in major leagues, with Cleveland in 1975. Career span as player 1956-76. Career span as manager 1975-77 with Cleveland; 1981-84 with San Francisco; 1988-91 with Baltimore.

Jackie Robinson (b. 1-13-19, d. 10-24-72): Baseball 2B. Broke the color barrier as first black player in major leagues in 1947 with Brooklyn Dodgers. 1947 Rookie of the Year; 1949 MVP with .342 batting average to lead league. Had .311 career batting average. Led league in stolen bases 2 times; stole home 19 times. Played on 6 pennant winners in 10 years with Brooklyn.

Larry Robinson (b. 6-2-51): Hockey D. Twice won Norris Trophy as NHL's top defenseman. Career span 1972-73 through 1991-92, all but the last three with the Montreal Canadiens. Member of six Montreal teams that won Stanley Cup. Awarded Conn Smythe Trophy as MVP of 1978 Stanley Cup.

Sugar Ray Robinson (b. 5-3-21, d. 4-12-89): Born Walker Smith, Jr. Boxer. Called best pound-for-pound boxer in history. Welterweight champion (1946-51) and middleweight champion 5 times. Career record 174-19-6 with 109 KOs from 1940 to 1965. Won 91 consecutive bouts from 1943 to 1951. 15 of his 19 losses came after age 35. Retired at age 45.

Knute Rockne (b. 3-4-1888, d. 3-31-31): College football coach. Won national championship 3 times (1924, consecutively 1929-30). Alltime highest winning percentage (.881). Career record 105-12-5, including 5 undefeated seasons, with Notre Dame from 1918 to 1930.

Bill Rodgers (b. 12-23-47): Track and field. Won the Boston and New York City marathons 4 times each between 1975 and 1980.

Chi Chi Rodriguez (b. 10-23-35): Golfer. Puerto Rican had won 21 Senior tour events through 1992 season. Led senior money list for 1987 ($509,145). Won 8 events during PGA career that began in 1960.

Art Rooney (b. 1-27-01; d. 8-25-88): Owner of Pittsburgh Steelers. Bought team in 1933 and ran it until his death in 1988. Elected to Hall of Fame in 1964.

Murray Rose (b. 1-6-39) Australian swimmer. Won 3 gold medals (including 400- and 1500-meter freestyle) at 1956 Olympics. Also won 1 gold, 1 silver and 1 bronze medal at 1960 Olympics.

Pete Rose (b. 4-14-41): Baseball OF-IF. "Charlie Hustle." Alltime leader in hits (4,256), games played (3,562) and at bats (14,053); second in doubles (746); fourth in runs scored (2,165). Had .303 career average and won 3 batting titles. Averaged .300+ 15 times, 200+ hits and 100+ runs scored each 10 times. Led league in hits 7 times, runs scored 4 times, doubles 5 times. 1963 Rookie of the Year; 1973 MVP; 1975 World Series MVP. Had 44-game hitting streak in 1978. Played in 17 All-Star games, starting at 5 different positions. Career span 1963-86 with Cincinnati, Philadelphia. Manager of Cincinnati from 1984 to 1989. Banned from baseball for life by Commissioner Bart Giamatti in 1989 for betting activities. Served 5-month jail term for tax evasion in 1990. Ineligible for Hall of Fame.

Ken Rosewall (b. 11-2-34): Australian tennis player. Won Grand Slam singles titles at ages 18 and 35. Won 4 Australian titles (1953, 1955, consecutively 1971-72), 2 French titles (1953, 1968) and 2 U.S. titles (1956, 1970). Reached 4 Wimbledon finals, but title eluded him.

Art Ross (b. 1-13-1886, d. 8-5-64): Hockey D-coach. Improved design of puck and goal net. Manager-coach of Boston, 1924-45, won Stanley Cup, 1938-39. The Art Ross Trophy is awarded to the NHL scoring champion.

Donald Ross (b. 1873, d. 4-26-48): Scottish-born golf course architect. Trained at St. Andrews under Old Tom Morris. Designed over 500 courses, including Pinehurst No. 2 course and Oakland Hills.

Patrick Roy (b. 10-5-65): Hockey G. Won Vezina Trophy as NHL's top goalie three times. Won Conn Smythe Trophy as MVP of 1993 Stanley Cup. Career span 1984–85 through 1993 with Montreal.

Pete Rozelle (b. 3-1-26): Football executive. Fourth NFL commissioner, served from 1960 to 1989. During his term, league expanded from 12 to 28 teams. Created Super Bowl in 1966 and negotiated merger with AFL. Devised plan for revenue sharing of lucrative TV monies among owners. Presided during players' strikes of 1982, 1987.

Wilma Rudolph (b. 6-23-40): Track and field. Gold medalist in 3 events (100-, 200- and 4x100-meter relay) at 1960 Olympics. Also won Sullivan Award in 1961.

Adolph Rupp (b. 9-2-01, d. 12-10-77): College basketball coach. Alltime NCAA leader in wins (875) and third highest winning percentage (.822). Won 4 NCAA championships: consecutively 1948-49, 1951, 1958. Career span 1930-72 with Kentucky.

Amos Rusie (b. 5-3-1871, d. 12-6-42): Baseball RHP. Fastball was so intimidating that in 1893 the pitching mound was moved back 5' 6" to its present distance of 60' 6". Led league in strikeouts and walks 5 times each. Career record 246-174, 3.07 ERA with New York (NL) from 1889-1901.

Bill Russell (b. 2-12-34): Basketball C. Won MVP award 5 times (1958, consecutively 1961-63, 1965). Played on 11 championship teams, 8 consecutively, with Boston (1957, 1959-66, 1968-69). Player-coach 1968-69 (league's first black coach). Second all-time most rebounds (21,620) and second highest rebounding average (22.5); second most rebounds in a game (51 in 1960). Led league in rebounding 4 times. Also played on 2 consecutive NCAA championship teams with San Francisco in 1955-56; tournament MVP in 1955. Member of gold medal-winning 1956 Olympic team.

Babe Ruth (b. 2-6-1895, d. 8-16-48): Given name George Herman Ruth. Baseball P-OF. Most dominant player in history. Alltime leader in slugging average (.690), HR frequency (8.5 HR every 100 at bats) and walks (2,056); second alltime most HR (714), RBI (2,211) and runs scored (2,174). Holds season record for most walks (170 in 1923) and highest slugging average (.847 in 1920). 1923 MVP. League leader in slugging average 13 times, HR 12 times, walks 11 times, runs scored 8 times and RBI 6 times. 1 batting title. Had .342 career batting average and 2,873 hits. 60 HR in 1927, 50+ HR 3 other times and 40+ HR 7 other times; 100+ RBI and 100+ walks 13 times each; 100+ runs scored 12 times. Second alltime most World Series HR (15), including his "called shot" off Charlie Root in 1932. Began career as a pitcher for Boston Red Sox: 94 career wins and 2.28 ERA. Won 20+ games 2 times; ERA leader in 1916. Played on 10 pennant winners, 7 World Series winners (3 with Boston, 4 with New York). Sold to Yankees in 1920 (Boston hasn't won World Series since). Career span 1914-35.

Nolan Ryan (b. 1-31-47): Baseball RHP. Pitched record 7th no hitter on May 1, 1991. Alltime leader in strikeouts (5,714), walks (2,795). League leader in strikeouts 11 times, walks 8 times, shutouts 3 times, ERA 2 times. 300+ strikeouts 6 times, including season record of 383 in 1973. 324 career wins. Career span 1966–93 with New York (NL), California, Houston, Texas.

Jim Ryun (b. 4-29-47): Track and field. Youngest ever to run under four minutes for the mile (3:59.0 at 17 years, 37 days). Set two world records in mile (3:51.3 in 1966 and 3:51.1 in 1967) and one in 1,500 (3:33.1 in 1967). Plagued by bad luck at Olympics; won silver medal in 1968 1,500 meters despite mononucleosis; was bumped and fell in 1972. Won Sullivan Award in 1967.

Toni Sailer (b. 11-17-35): Austrian skier. Won gold medals in 1956 Olympics in slalom, giant slalom and downhill, the first skier to accomplish the feat.

Juan Antonio Samaranch (b. 7-17-20): Amateur sports executive. Spaniard served as president of International Olympic Committee from 1980-1993.

Joan Benoit Samuelson (b. 5-16-57): Track and field. Gold medalist in first ever women's Olympic marathon (1984). Won Boston Marathon 2 times (1979, 1983). Sullivan Award winner in 1985.

Barry Sanders (b. 7-16-68): Football RB. Alltime NCAA season leader in yards rushing (2,628 in 1988). Won Heisman Trophy in 1988 at Oklahoma State. Entered NFL in 1989 with Detroit and named Rookie of the Year. Gained 1,000+ yards rushing and named to Pro Bowl each of his first 4 seasons. Led league in rushing in 1990.

Gene Sarazen (b. 2-27-02): Golfer. Won PGA Championship 3 times (consecutively 1922-23, 1933), U.S. Open 2 times (1922, 1932), British Open once (1932) and the Masters once (1935). His win at the Masters included golf's most famous shot, a double eagle on the 15th hole of the final round to tie Craig Wood (Sarazen then won the playoff). Won 38 career tournaments. Also won Seniors Championship 2 times (1954, 1958). Pioneered the sand wedge in 1930.

Glen Sather (b. 9-2-43): Hockey coach and general manager. As coach, third alltime highest winning percentage (.634) and sixth in regular season wins (542). Led Edmonton to 4 Stanley Cup championships (consecutively 1984-85, 1987-88) from 1979 to 1989. Relinquished coaching duties in 1989. Also played for 6 teams from 1966 to 1976.

Terry Sawchuk (b. 12-28-29): Hockey G. All-time leader in wins (435) and shutouts (103). Career 2.52 goals against average. Goaltender of the Year 4 times (consecutively 1951-52, 1954, 1964). Led league in wins and shutouts 3 times and goals against average 2 times. Rookie of the Year in 1950. Tied record of 4 playoff shutouts in 1952. Played on 4 Stanley Cup champions with Detroit and Toronto from 1949 to 1969.

Gale Sayers (b. 5-30-43): Football RB. Alltime leader in kickoff return average (30.6). Scored 56 career touchdowns, including a rookie record 22 in 1965. Led league in rushing and gained 1,000+ yards rushing 2 times. Averaged 5 yards per carry, third best in history. Rookie of the Year in 1965. Tied record with 6 rushing touchdowns on Dec. 12, 1965. Career span 1965-71 with Chicago cut short due to knee injury. Also All-America 2 times with Kansas.

Dolph Schayes (b. 5-19-28): Basketball player. College star at NYU. In 1960 became first NBA player to reach 15,000 career points. Also first NBA player to play in 1,000 games. Led NBA in free throw percentage three times, and averaged .843 for his career. Over stretch of 10 years played in 706 consecutive games. Elected to Hall of Fame 1972.

Bo Schembechler (b. 4-1-29): Football coach. In 21 seasons at Michigan from 1969–89, had a 194-48-5 record. Overall college coaching record 234-65-8.

Mike Schmidt (b. 9-27-49): Baseball 3B. Won 3 MVP awards (consecutively 1980-81, 1986). 548 career HR. Led league in HR 8 times, slugging average 5 times and RBI, walks and strikeouts 4 times each. 40+ HR 3 times, 30+ HR 10 other times; 100+ RBI 9 times, 100+ runs scored 7 times, 100+ strikeouts 12 times and third alltime most strikeouts (1,883). 100+ walks 7 times. Won 10 Gold Gloves. Career span 1972-89 with Philadelphia.

Don Schollander (b. 4-30-46): Swimmer. Won 4 gold medals (including 100- and 400-meter freestyle) at 1964 Olympics; won 1 gold and 1 silver medal at 1968 Olympics. Also won Sullivan Award in 1964.

Dick Schultz (b. 9-5-29): Amateur sports executive. Second executive director of the NCAA, served from 1987 to '93. Also served as athletic director at Cornell (1976-81) and Virginia (1981-87).

Seattle Slew (b. 1974): Thoroughbred race horse. Horse of the Year for 1977, when he won the Triple Crown, winning the Kentucky Derby by 1¾ lengths; the Preakness by 1½; and the Belmont by 4. In three year career from 1976–78, won 14 of 17 starts.

Tom Seaver (b. 11-17-44): Baseball RHP. "Tom Terrific." 311 career wins. 2.86 ERA. Cy Young Award winner 3 times (1969, 1973, 1975) and Rookie of the Year 1967. Fourth alltime most strikeouts (3,640). Led league in strikeouts 5 times, winning percentage 4 times and wins and ERA 3 times each. Won 20+ games 5 times; 200+ strikeouts 10 times. Struck out 19 batters in 1 game in 1970, including the final 10 in succession. Pitched no-hitter in 1978. Career span 1967-86 with New York (NL), Cincinnati, Chicago (AL), Boston.

Secretariat (b. 3-30-70, d. 10-4-89): Thoroughbred race horse. Triple Crown winner in 1973 with jockey Ron Turcotte aboard. Trained by Lucien Laurin.

Monica Seles (b. 12-2-73): Tennis player. Has won 3 consecutive French Open singles titles (1990-92), 3 Australian Open titles (1991-93) and 2 U.S. Open titles (1991-92). Seles' 1993 season ended on 4-30 when she was stabbed in the back by Gunther Parche while seated during a change over in a tournament in Hamburg, Germany.

Bill Sharman (b. 5-25-26): Basketball G. First team All Star four straight years 1956-59. Led NBA in free throw percentage every year from 1953-57, and in 1959 and '61. All Star Game MVP in 1955. NBA Coach of the Year in 1972, when his Lakers won NBA title. Elected to Hall of Fame in 1974.

Wilbur Shaw (b. 10-31-02, d. 10-30-54): Auto racer. Won Indy 500 3 times in 4 years (1937, consecutively 1939-40). AAA champion 2 times (1937, 1939). Also pioneered the use of the crash helmet after suffering skull fracture in 1923 crash.

Patty Sheehan (b. 10-27-57): Golfer. Won back-to-back LPGA championships, 1983–84. Won 1992 US Women's Open. 1983 LPGA Player of Year. Vare Trophy winner in 1984. Through '92 season, 29 career wins on LPGA tour; fourth alltime in earnings, with $3,562,370.01.

Fred Shero (b. 10-23-25, d. 11-24-90): Hockey coach. Fourth all-time highest winning percentage (.612, regular season). Led Philadelphia to 2 Stanley Cup championships (1974-75). Also coached NY Rangers. Played defense for NY Rangers, 1947-50.

Bill Shoemaker (b. 8-19-31): Horse racing jockey. Alltime leader in wins (8,833). Rode Belmont Stakes winner 5 times (1957, 1959, 1962, 1967, 1975), Kentucky Derby winner 4 times (1955, 1959, 1965, 1986–at age 54, the oldest jockey to win Derby) and Preakness Stakes winner 2 times (1963, 1967). Also won Eclipse Award in 1981.

Eddie Shore (b. 11-25-02, d. 3-16-85): Hockey D. Won MVP award 4 times (1933, consecutively 1935-36, 1938). All-Star 7 times. Played on 2 Stanley Cup champions with Boston from 1926 to 1940.

Frank Shorter (b. 10-31-47): Track and field. Gold medalist in marathon at 1972 Olympics, the first American to win the event since 1908. Olympic silver medalist in 1976 marathon. Sullivan Award winner in 1972.

Jim Shoulders (b. 5-13-28): Rodeo. All-time leader in career titles (16). All-Around champion 5 times (1949, consecutively 1956-59).

Don Shula (b. 1-4-30): Football coach. Second alltime in wins (318, the most of any active coach). Won 2 consecutive Super Bowl championships (1972-73) with Miami, including NFL's only undefeated season in 1972. Also reached Super Bowl 4 other times. Career span since 1963 with Baltimore and Miami.

Al Simmons (b. 5-22-02; d. 5-26-56): Baseball OF. "Bucketfoot Al" for hitting stance. Named AL MVP for 1929, when he led league 157 RBIs. Led league in batting average in 1930 (.381) and '31 (.390). Lifetime average of .334 with 307 homers. Career span 1924–44 with a variety of teams, but mostly Philadelphia A's. Elected to Hall of Fame in 1953.

O. J. Simpson (b. 7-9-47): Given name Orenthal James. Football RB. Seventh alltime in yards rushing (11,236). Gained 1,000+ yards rushing 5 consecutive seasons, including then-record 2,003 yards in 1973. Player of the Year 3 times (consecutively 1972-73, 1975). Led league in rushing 4 times. Gained 200+ yards rushing in a game a record 6 times, including 273 yards on Nov. 25, 1976. Scored 61 career touchdowns, including 23 in 1975. Also won Heisman Trophy with USC in 1968.

Sir Barton (b. 1916): Thoroughbred race horse. In 1919, before they were linked as the Triple Crown, became first horse to win the Kentucky Derby, the Preakness and the Belmont Stakes. Won 8 of 13 starts as 3-year-old.

George Sisler (b. 3-24-1893, d. 3-26-73): Baseball 1B. Alltime most hits in a season (257 in 1920). League leader in hits 2 times, with 200+ hits 6 times. Won 2 batting titles, including .420 average in 1922; averaged .400+ 2 times and .300+ 11 other times. Had 2,812 career hits and .340 average. Career span 1915-30 with St Louis.

Mary Decker Slaney (b. 8-4-58): Track and field. American record holder in 5 events ranging from 800 to 3,000 meters. Won 1,500 and 3,000 meters at World Championships in 1983. Lost chance for medal at 1984 Olympics when she tripped and fell after contact with Zola Budd. Won Sullivan Award in 1982.

Dean Smith (b. 2-28-31): College basketball coach. Entered 1993-94 season fifth alltime in wins (740), the most among active coaches; fifth alltime highest winning percentage (.772). Alltime most NCAA tournament appearances (23), reached Final Four 9 times. Won NCAA championship in 1982 and '93. Coached 1976 Olympic team to gold medal. Career span since 1962 with North Carolina.

Emmitt Smith (b. 5-15-69): Football RB. Led NFL in rushing in 1991 (1,563 yards) and '92 (1,713 and 18 TDs). Rushed for 108 yards in 52–17 Cowboy win over Bills in Super Bowl XXVI. Career span 1990–93 with Dallas Cowboys.

Ozzie Smith (b. 12-26-54): Baseball SS. "The Wizard of Oz." May be the best defensive shortstop in history. Holds alltime record for most assists in a season among shortstops (621 in 1980). 10 consecutive starts in All-Star game. Entered 1993 with 13 consecutive Gold Gloves. Career span since 1978 with San Diego, St Louis.

Red Smith (b. 9-25-05, d. 1-15-82): Sportswriter. Won Pulitzer Prize in 1976. After Grantland Rice, the most widely syndicated sports columnist. His literate essays appeared in the NY Herald Tribune from 1945 to 1971 and the NY Times from 1971 to 1982.

Stan Smith (b. 12-14-46): Tennis. Won 39 tournaments in career, including 1972 Wimbledon in 5 sets over Ilie Nastase. Won 1971 US Open over Jan Kodes and amateur version of US Open in 1969. 1970 won inaugural Grand Prix Masters. Inducted to Tennis Hall of Fame in 1987.

Tommy Smith (b. 6-5-44): Track and field. Sprinter won 1968 Olympic 200 meters in world record of 19.83, then was expelled from Olympic Village, along with bronze medalist John Carlos, for raising black-gloved fist and bowing head during playing of national anthem to protest racism in U.S.

Conn Smythe (b. 2-1-1895, d. 11-18-80): Hockey executive. As general manager with Toronto from 1929 to 1961 won 7 Stanley Cup championships (1932, 1942, 1945, consecutively 1947-49, 1951). Award for playoff MVP named in his honor.

Sam Snead (b. 5-27-12): Golfer. Alltime leader in career wins (81). Won the Masters (1949, 1952, 1954) and PGA Championship (1942, 1949, 1951) 3 times each and British Open (1946). Runner-up at U.S. Open 4 times, but title eluded him. PGA Player of the Year in 1949. Won Seniors Championship 6 times, more than any golfer (1964-65, 1967, 1970, 1972-73).

Peter Snell (b. 12-17-38): Track and field. New Zealand runner was gold medalist in 800 meters at 2 consecutive Olympics in 1960, 1964. Also gold medalist in 1,500 meters at 1964 Olympics. Twice broke world mile record; broke world 800 record once.

Duke Snider (b. 9-19-26): Baseball OF. Career .295 average, 407 HR and 1,333 RBIs. Hit 40+ HR 5 consecutive seasons and 100+ RBIs 6 times. Also led league in runs scored 3 consecutive seasons. Played on 6 pennant winners with the Brooklyn Dodgers. World Series total of 11 HR and 26 RBIs are NL best. Career span from 1947-64.

Javier Sotomayor (b. 10-13-67): Track and field. Cuban high jumper broke the 8-foot barrier with world record jump of 8' 0" in 1989. Set current record of 8' ½" in 7-27-93 in Salamanca, Spain.

Warren Spahn (b. 4-23-21): Baseball LHP. Alltime leader in games won for a lefthander (363): 20+ wins 13 times. League leader in wins 8 times (5 seasons consecutively), complete games 9 times (7 seasons consecutively), strikeouts 4 consecutive seasons, innings pitched 4 times and ERA 3 times. 1957 Cy Young award. 63 career shutouts. Pitched 2 no-hitters after age 39. Career span 1942-65, all but last year with Boston (NL), Milwaukee.

Tris Speaker (b. 4-4-1888, d. 12-8-58): Baseball OF. Alltime leader in doubles (792), fifth in hits (3,514) and fifth in batting average (.345). 1 batting title (.386 in 1916), but .375+ average 6 times and .300+ average 12 other times. League leader in doubles 8 times, hits 2 times and HR and RBI 1 time each. 200+ hits 4 times, 40+ doubles 10 times and 100+ runs scored 7 times. MVP in 1912. Alltime leader among outfielders in assists and double plays, second in putouts. Career span 1907-28 with Boston, Cleveland.

Michael Spinks (b. 7-13-56): Boxer. 1976 Olympic middleweight champion. Brother Leon was heavyweight champ. Won world light heavyweight title by decision over Mustafa Muhammad on 7-18-81. Defended it 5 times and then consolidated light heavy titles with decision over Dwight Braxton on 3-18-83. Defended four more times. Won heavyweight title on 9-22-85 in decision over Larry Holmes. Lost title to Mike Tyson in 91 seconds on 6-27-88.

Mark Spitz (b. 2-10-50): Swimmer. Won a record 7 gold medals (2 in freestyle, 2 in butterfly, 3 in relays) at 1972 Olympics, setting world record in each event. Also won 2 gold medals and 1 silver and 1 bronze medal at 1968 Olympics. Sullivan Award winner in 1971.

Amos Alonzo Stagg (b. 8-16-1862, d. 3-17-65): College football coach. Second alltime in wins (314). Won national championship with Chicago in 1905. Coach of the Year with Pacific in 1943 at age 81. Career record 314-199-35, including 5 undefeated seasons, from 1892 to 1946. Only person elected to both college football and basketball Halls of Fame. Played in the first basketball game in 1891.

Willie Stargell (b. 3-6-40): Baseball OF/1B. "Pops" achieved a 1979 MVP triple crown, winning NL regular season, playoff and World Series MVP awards. Led NL in homers in 1971 and '73. Only person to hit ball out of Dodger Stadium and he did it twice. Hit 475 career homers. Drove in 1,540 runs. Had .282 career batting average. Played all 21 seasons with the Pirates. Elected to Hall of Fame in 1988.

Bart Starr (b. 1-9-34): Football QB. Played on 3 NFL champions (consecutively 1961-62, 1965) and first two Super Bowl champions (1966-67) with Green Bay. Also named MVP of first two Super Bowls. Player of the Year in 1966. Led league in passing 3 times. Also coached Green Bay to 53-77-3 record from 1975 to 1983.

Roger Staubach (b. 2-5-42): Football QB. Won Heisman Trophy with Navy as a junior in 1963. Served 4-year military obligation before turning pro. Led Dallas to 6 NFC Championships, 4 Super Bowls and 2 Super Bowl titles (1971, 1977). Player of the Year and Super Bowl MVP in 1971. Also led league in passing 4 times. Career span 1969-79.

Jan Stenerud (b. 11-26-42): Football K. Second to George Blanda on NFL scoring list, with 1,699 points. Converted an NFL record 373 field goals in 558 attempts. Career span 1967–79 with Kansas City Chiefs, 1980–83 with Green Bay Packers and 1984–85 with Minnesota Vikings. First pure kicker inducted to Hall of Fame 1991.

Casey Stengel (b. 7-30-1890, d. 9-29-75): Baseball manager. "The Ol' Perfesser." Managed New York Yankees to 10 pennants and 7 World Series titles (5 consecutively) in 12 years from 1949 to 1960. Alltime leader in World Series games (63) and wins (37), second in winning percentage (.587) and losses (26). Platoon system was his trademark strategy, Stengelese his trademark language ("You could look it up"). Managed New York Mets from 1962 to 1965. Jersey number (37) retired by Yankees and Mets.

Ingemar Stenmark (b. 3-18-56): Swedish skier. Gold medalist in slalom and giant slalom at 1980 Olympics. World Cup overall champion 3 consecutive years (1976-78).

Woody Stephens (b. 9-1-13): Horse racing trainer. Trained 2 Kentucky Derby winners (Cannonade, who won the 100th Derby in 1974 and Swale in 1984) and an incredible 5 straight Belmont winners from 1982-86, starting with 1982 Horse of the Year Conquistador Cielo.

David Stern (b. 9-22-42): Fourth NBA commissioner. Served since 1984. Average worth of a franchise has tripled from $20 million to $65 million. Owners rewarded him with 5-year, $27.5 million contract extension in 1990.

Jackie Stewart (b. 6-11-39): Scottish auto racer. Third alltime in Formula 1 victories (27); Formula 1 champion 3 times (1969, 1971, 1973). Also Indy 500 Rookie of the Year in 1966. Retired in 1973.

John L. Sullivan (b. 10-15-1858, d. 2-2-18): Boxer. Last bare knuckle champion. Heavyweight title holder (1882-92), lost to Jim Corbett. Career record 38-1-3 with 33 KOs from 1878 to 1892.

Paul Tagliabue (b. 11-24-40): Football executive. Fifth NFL commissioner, has served since 1989.

Anatoli Tarasov (b. 1918): Hockey coach. Orchestrated Soviet Union's emergence as a hockey power. Won 9 consecutive world amateur championships (1963-71) and 3 Olympic gold medals in 1964, 1968, 1972.

Fran Tarkenton (b. 2-3-40): Football QB. Alltime

leader in touchdown passes (342), yards passing (47,003), pass attempts (6,467) and pass completions (3,686). Player of the Year in 1975. Career span 1961-78 with Minnesota, NY Giants.

Lawrence Taylor (b. 2-4-59): Football LB. Revolutionized the linebacker position. Entered 1993 season as the alltime leader in sacks. Also named to Pro Bowl a record 10 consecutive seasons. Player of the Year in 1986. Has played on 2 Super Bowl champions with New York Giants (1986, 1990). Career span since 1981 with Giants.

Isiah Thomas (b. 4-30-61): Basketball G. Member of Indiana University team that won 1981 NCAA title. Point guard for Detroit Pistons since 1982. All-NBA First Team 1984, '85 and '86. NBA All Star Game MVP both 1984 and '86. Led NBA in assists (13.9) in 1984–85. Third alltime in assists (8,662). Member of Piston team that won NBA title in both 1989 and '90.

Thurman Thomas (b. 5-15-66): Football RB. Led AFC in rushing both 1990 (1,297 yards) and '91 (1,407). Career span since 1988 with Buffalo Bills.

Daley Thompson (b. 7-30-58): Track and field. British decathlete was gold medalist at 2 consecutive Olympics in 1980, 1984. At 1984 Olympics set world record (8,847 points) that lasted eight years.

John Thompson (b. 9-2-41): College basketball coach. From 1973 to present, head coach at Georgetown, where he taught Patrick Ewing, Alonzo Mourning and Dikembe Mutombo to play center. Won NCAA title in 1984, beating Houston 84–75. NCAA runnerup in 1982 and '85. Overall record in 21 years as college coach 484–178.

Bobby Thomson (b. 10-25-23): Baseball OF. Hit dramatic 9th-inning playoff home run to win NL pennant for New York Giants on Oct. 3, 1951. The Giants came from 13½ games behind the Brooklyn Dodgers on Aug. 11 to win the pennant on Thomson's 3-run homer off Ralph Branca in the final game of the 3-game playoff.

Jim Thorpe (b. 5-28-1888, d. 3-28-53): Sportsman. Gold medalist in decathlon and pentathlon at 1912 Olympics. Played pro baseball with New York (NL) and Cincinnati from 1913 to 1919, and pro football with several teams from 1919 to 1926. Also All-America 2 times with Carlisle.

Dick Tiger (b. 8-14-29; d. 12-14-71): Nigerian Boxer. Born Richard Ihetu. Won middleweight title by decision over Gene Fullmer on 10-23-62. Lost middle title to Joey Giardello on 12-7-63, then regained it from Giardello on 10-21-65. Lost middle title to Emile Griffith on 4-25-65. Won world light heavyweight title by decision over Jose Torres on 12-16-66, then lost it when KO'd by Bob Foster in 4 on 5-24-68. *The Ring* Fighter of the Year for 1962 and '65. Career record: 81 bouts; won 26 by KO, 35 by decision; drew 3; lost 17, 2 by KO. Elected to Boxing Hall of Fame 1974.

Bill Tilden (b. 2-10-1893, d. 6-5-53): Tennis player. "Big Bill." Won 7 U.S. singles titles, 6 consecutively (1920-25, 1929) and 3 Wimbledon titles (consecutively 1920-21, 1930). Also won 6 Grand Slam doubles titles. Led U.S. to 7 consecutive Davis Cup victories (1920-26).

Ted Tinling (b. 6-23-10, d. 5-23-90): British tennis couturier. The premier source on women's tennis from Suzanne Lenglen to Steffi Graf. Also designed tennis clothes, most notably the frilled lace panties worn by Gorgeous Gussy Moran at Wimbledon in 1949.

Y.A. Tittle (b. 10-24-26): Football QB. Threw 33 TD passes in 1962 and in '63 led league in passing, completing 221 of 367 attempts for 3,145 yards and 36 TDs. Career span 1948–64, mostly with San Francisco 49ers and New York Giants. Inducted into Hall of Fame 1971.

Jayne Torvil/Christopher Dean (b. 10-7-57/ b. 7-27-58): British figure skaters. Won 4 consecutive ice dancing world championships (1981-84) and Olympic ice dancing gold medal (1984). Won world professional championships in 1985.

Vladislav Tretiak (b. 4-25-52): Hockey G. Led Soviet Union to 3 gold medals at Olympics in 1972, 1976, 1984. Played on 13 world amateur champions from 1970 to 1984.

Lee Trevino (b. 12-1-39): Golfer. Won U.S. Open (1968, 1971), British Open (consecutively 1971-72) and PGA Championship (1974, 1984) 2 times each. PGA Player of the Year in 1971. Also won U.S. Senior Open in 1990. First Senior $1 million season.

Emlen Tunnell (b. 3-29-25, d. 7-23-75): Football S. Alltime leader in interception yardage (1,282) and second in interceptions (79). All-Pro 9 times. Career span 1948-61 with New York Giants and Green Bay.

Gene Tunney (b. 5-25-1897, d. 11-7-78): Boxer. Heavyweight champion (1926-28). Defeated Jack Dempsey 2 times, including famous "long count" bout. Career record 65-2-1 with 43 KOs from 1915 to 1928. Retired as champion.

Ted Turner (b. 11-19-38): Sportsman. Skipper who successfully defended the America's Cup in 1977. Also owner of the Atlanta Braves since 1976 and Hawks since 1977. Founded the Goodwill Games in 1986.

Mike Tyson (b. 6-30-66): Boxer. Youngest heavyweight champion at 19 years old in 1986. Held title until knocked out by James "Buster" Douglas in Tokyo on Feb. 10, 1990. Career record as of 10-1-93 41–1 with 36 KOs since 1985. Convicted of rape in 1992, currently serving sentence.

Johnny Unitas (b. 5-7-33): Football QB. Alltime leader for consecutive games throwing touchdown pass (47, 1956-60), tied for second alltime touchdown passes (290), third alltime yards passing (40,239). Led league in touchdown passes a record 4 consecutive seasons. Player of the Year 3 times (1959, 1964, 1967). Career span 1956-72 with Baltimore, San Diego.

Al Unser Sr (b. 5-29-39): Auto racer. Won Indy 500 4 times (consecutively 1970-71, 1978, 1987). Third alltime in CART victories (39). USAC/CART champion 3 times (1970, 1983, 1985). Brother of Bobby.

Bobby Unser (b. 2-20-34): Auto racer. Won Indy 500 3 times (1968, 1975, 1981). Fourth alltime in CART victories (35). USAC champion 2 times (1968, 1974). Brother of Al, Sr.

Harold S. Vanderbilt (b. 7-6-1884, d. 7-4-70): Sailer. Owner and skipper who successfully defended the America's Cup 3 consecutive times (1930, 1934, 1937).

Glenna Collett Vare (b. 6-20-03, d. 2-2-89): Golfer. Won U.S. Women's Amateur 6 times, more than any golfer (1922, 1925, consecutively 1928-30, 1935).

Bill Veeck (b. 2-9-14, d. 1-2-86): Baseball owner. From 1946 to 1980, owned ballclubs in Cleveland, St Louis (AL), Chicago (AL). In 1948, Cleveland became baseball's first team to draw 2 million in attendance.

That year Veeck integrated AL by signing Larry Doby and then Satchel Paige. A brilliant promoter, Veeck sent midget Eddie Gaedel up to bat for St Louis in 1951. Brought exploding scoreboard to stadiums and put players' names on uniforms.

Guillermo Vilas (b. 8-17-52): Tennis. Argentine won 50 straight matches in 1977. In '77 won French Open, where he beat Brian Gottfried, and the US Open, where he beat Jimmy Connors. Also won Australian Open twice, 1978–79.

Lasse Viren (b. 7-22-49): Track and field. Finnish runner was gold medalist in 5,000 and 10,000 meters at 2 consecutive Olympics (1972, 1976).

Virginia Wade (b. 7-10-45): Tennis. Beloved in Britain, Wade won four major titles, most notably Wimbledon in 1977, its centenary year, where she triumphed over Betty Stove. Also won 1968 US Open and '72 Australian Open.

Honus Wagner (b. 2-24-1874, d. 12-6-55): Baseball SS. Had .327 career batting average, 3,415 hits and 8 batting titles. Averaged .300+ 15 consecutive seasons. Led league in RBI 4 times, with 100+ RBI 9 times. Third alltime in triples (252) and league leader in doubles 8 times. Ninth alltime in stolen bases (722) and league leader 5 times. Career span 1897-1917 with Pittsburgh.

Grete Waitz (b. 10-1-53): Track and field. Norwegian runner has won New York City Marathon a record 9 times (consecutively 1978-80, 1982-86, 1988). Won the women's marathon at the 1983 World Championship.

Jersey Joe Walcott (b. 10-31-14): Boxer. Heavyweight champion from 1951 to 1952. Won title at age 37 on fifth attempt before surrendering it to Rocky Marciano. Later became sheriff of Camden, NJ.

Doak Walker (b. 1-1-27): Football HB. Led league in scoring 2 times, his first and final seasons. All-Pro 5 times. Played on 2 consecutive NFL champions (1952-53) with Detroit. Career span 1950 to 1955. Also won Heisman Trophy as a junior in 1948. All-America 3 consecutive seasons with SMU.

Herschel Walker (b. 3-3-62): Football RB. Won Heisman Trophy in 1982 with Georgia. Turned pro by entering USFL with New Jersey. Gained 7,000+ rushing yards and scored 61 touchdowns in 3 seasons before league folded. Entered NFL in 1986 with Dallas and led league in rushing yards (1,606 in 1987). Currently with Philadelphia.

Bill Walsh (b. 11-30-31): Football coach. Led the San Francisco 49ers to four Super Bowl wins, after the 1981, '84, '88 and '89 seasons. Career record with 49ers 102-63-1. Developed short-passing game. Returned to Stanford University for 1992 season.

Bill Walton (b. 11-5-52): Basketball C. MVP in 1978, playoff MVP in 1977. Led league in rebounding and blocks in 1977. Career span 1974-86 with Portland, San Diego, Boston. Also College Player of the Year 3 consecutive seasons (1972-74). Played on 2 consecutive NCAA championship teams (1972-73) with UCLA; tournament MVP twice (1972-73). Sullivan Award winner in 1973.

Junxia Wang (b. 1963): Chinese distance runner. Broke four existing world records over six days in Sept. 1993. Broke 10,000 (29:31.78) on 9-8; ran 1500 in 3:51.92 in finishing second to countrywoman Qu Yunxia's world record of 3:50.46 on 9-11; ran 3,000 record of 8:12.19 in heats on 9-12 and lowered it to 8:06.11 on 9-13.

War Admiral (b. 1934): Thoroughbred race horse. A son of Man o' War won Triple Crown and Horse of the Year honors in 1937.

Paul Warfield (b. 11-28-42): Football WR. Caught 427 passes for 8,565 yards and 85 TDs. Played on two Super Bowl-winning Miami Dolphin teams. Career span 1964–77, all with Cleveland Browns except for 1970–74 with Miami Dolphins. Inducted to Hall of Fame 1983.

Glenn "Pop" Warner (b. 4-5-1871, d. 9-7-54): College football coach. Third alltime in wins (313). Won 3 national championships with Pittsburgh (1916, 1918) and Stanford (1926). Career record 313-106-32 with 6 teams from 1896 to 1938.

Tom Watson (b. 9-4-49): Golfer. Winner of British Open 5 times (1975, 1977, 1980, consecutively 1982-83), the Masters 2 times (1977, 1981) and U.S. Open once (1982). PGA Player of the Year 6 times, more than any golfer (consecutively 1977-80, 1982, 1984).

Dick Weber (b. 12-23-29): Bowler. Won All-Star Tournament 4 times (consecutively 1962-63, 1965-66). Voted Bowler of the Year 3 times (1961, 1963, 1965). Won 31 career PBA titles.

Johnny Weissmuller (b. 6-2-04, d. 1-21-84): Swimmer. Won 3 gold medals (including 100- and 400-meter freestyle) at 1924 Olympics and 2 gold medals at 1928 Olympics. Also played Tarzan in the movies.

Jerry West (b. 5-28-38): Basketball G. 10 time All-Star; All-Defensive Team 4 times; 1969 playoff MVP. Set season record for most free throws made (840 in 1966). Led league in assists and scoring 1 time each. Career span 1960-72 with Los Angeles. Currently general manager. Also NCAA tournament MVP in 1959. All-America 2 times with West Virginia. Played on 1960 gold medal-winning Olympic team.

Whirlaway (b. 4-2-38, d. 4-6-53): Thoroughbred race horse. Triple Crown winner in 1941 with jockey Eddie Arcaro aboard. Trained by Ben A. Jones.

Byron "Whizzer" White (b. 6-8-17): Football RB. Led NFL in rushing 2 times (Pittsburgh in 1938, Detroit in 1940). Led NCAA in scoring and rushing with Colorado in 1937; named All-America. Supreme Court justice from 1962 to '93.

Reggie White (b. 12-19-62): Football DE. Entering the 1993 season only player to have more sacks (124) than games (121). Winner in new era of free agency, signed with Packers for $17 million over four years. Career span: 1984 with Memphis Showboats, 1985–92 with Philadelphia Eagles and since 1993 with Green Bay.

Charles Whittingham (b. 4-13-13): Thoroughbred race horse trainer. "Bald Eagle" after losing hair to tropical disease in World War II. In 1986 became the oldest trainer to win Kentucky Derby, with Ferdinand. Led yearly earnings list for trainers from 1970–73 c onsecutively; in 1975; and in 1981–82 consecutively. Won three Eclipse Awards and trained two Horses of the Year (Ack Ack in 1971 and Ferdinand in 1987).

Kathy Whitworth (b. 9-27-39): Golfer. Alltime LPGA leader with 88 tour victories, including six majors. Won LPGA Championship in 1967, '71 and '75. Won 1977 Dinah Shore. Won Titleholders Championship (extinct major) in 1965 and '66. Won Western Open (extinct major) in 1967. Won Vare Trophy every year from 1965–72, except 1968. LPGA Player of Year from 1966–69 and 1971–73.

Hoyt Wilhelm (b. 7-26-23): Baseball RHP. Only relief

pitcher in Hall of Fame. Threw knuckleball until age 48. Alltime pitching leader in games (1,070) and relief wins (124). Career record: 143-122, 2.52 ERA, 227 saves. Hit home run in his first at bat (never hit another) and pitched no-hitter in 1958. Career span with 9 teams from 1952-72.

Bud Wilkinson (b. 4-23-15): Football coach. Alltime NCAA leader in consecutive wins (47, 1953-57). Won 3 national championships (1950, consecutively 1955-56) with Oklahoma, where he coached from 1947 to 1963. Won Orange Bowl 4 times and Sugar Bowl 2 times. Career record 145-29-4, including 4 undefeated seasons. Also coached with St Louis of NFL in 1978-79.

Billy Williams (b. 6-15-38): Baseball OF. Nicknamed "Sweet Swinging". NL Rookie of the Year for 1961. Hit 426 career home runs. Drove in 1,475 runs. Lifetime averge of .290. Named to six NL All Star teams. Career span 1959-74 with Chicago Cubs, 19775-76 with Oakland A's. Elected to Hall of Fame in 1987.

Ted Williams (b. 8-30-18): Baseball OF. "The Splendid Splinter." Last player to hit .400 (.406 in 1941). MVP in 1946, 1949 and Triple Crown winner in 1942, 1947. Sixth alltime highest batting average (.344), second most walks (2,019) and second highest slugging average (.634). Tied for tenth career HR (521); 11th in career RBI (1,839). League leader in batting average and runs scored 6 times each, RBI and HR 4 times each, walks 8 times and doubles 2 times. Had .300+ average 15 consecutive seasons; 100+ RBI and runs scored 9 times each; 30+ HR 8 times; and 100+ walks 11 times. Lost nearly 5 seasons to military service. Career span 1939-42 and 1946-60 with Boston.

Hack Wilson (b. 4-26-00; d. 11-23-48): Baseball OF. Stood 5' 6" but weighed 210. Had five incredible seasons 1926-30. Best was 1930 when he hit .356, scored 146 runs, hit a NL record 56 homers and drove in 191, which is still the major league record. Declined through drinking. Career span 1923-34 with several teams. Elected to Hall of Fame in 1979.

Dave Winfield (b. 10-3-51): Baseball OF. Also drafted out of Univ. of Minnesota for both pro basketball and football. Led NL in RBIs in 1979 (118). In 1992, first 40-year-old to get 100+ RBIs, with 108. Had clutch double to win 1992 World Series. Got 3,000th hit, off Dennis Eckersley, on 9-16-93. Career span 1973-80 with San Diego; 1981-90 with Yankees; 1990-91 with California; 1992 with Toronto; and since 1993 with Minnesota.

Major W. C. Wingfield (b. 19-16-1833, d. 4-18-12): British tennis pioneer. Credited with inventing the game of tennis, which he called "Sphairistike" or "sticky" and patented in February 1874.

Colonel Matt Winn (b. 6-30-1861, d. 10-6-49): As general manager of Churchill Downs from 1904 until his death, promoted the Kentucky Derby into the premier race in the country.

Katarina Witt (b. 12-3-65): East German figure skater. Gold medalist at 2 consecutive Olympics in 1984, 1988. Also world champion 4 times (consecutively 1984-85, 1987-88).

John Wooden (b. 10-14-10): College basketball coach. Only member of basketball Hall of Fame as coach and player. Coached UCLA to 10 NCAA championships in 12 years (consecutively 1964-65, 1967-73, 1975). Alltime winning streak 88 games (1971-74). 664 career wins and fourth alltime highest

winning percentage (.804). Career span 1949-75 with UCLA. Also 1932 College Player of the Year at Purdue.

Mickey Wright (b. 2-14-35): Golfer. Second alltime in career wins (82) and major championships (13—tied with Louise Suggs). Won U.S. Open 4 times (consecutively 1958-59, 1961, 1964), LPGA Championship 4 times, more than any other golfer (1958, consecutively 1960-61, 1963), Western Open 3 times (consecutively 1962-63, 1966) and Titleholders Championship twice (1961-62).

Cale Yarborough (b. 3-27-40): Auto racer. Won Daytona 500 4 times (1968, 1977, consecutively 1983-84). Fifth alltime in NASCAR victories (83). Also NASCAR champion 3 consecutive years (1976-78).

Carl Yastrzemski (b. 8-22-39): Baseball OF. "Yaz." 3,419 career hits, 452 HR. 1967 MVP and Triple Crown winner. 3 batting titles, including .301 in 1968, the lowest ever to win. Second alltime in games played (3,308) and fourth in walks (1,845). Led league in slugging average, runs scored and doubles 3 times each, hits and walks 2 times each. Holds league record for most times intentionally walked (190) and seasons leading in outfield assists (6). Career span 1961-83 with Boston.

Cy Young (b. 3-29-1867, d. 11-4-55): Baseball RHP. Alltime leader in wins (511), losses (315), innings pitched (7,354.2) and complete games (749); fourth in shutouts (76). Had 2.63 career ERA. Led league in shutouts 7 times; wins 4 times; complete games 3 times; and ERA, innings pitched and strikeouts 2 times each. 30+ wins 5 times, 20+ wins 10 other times; 400+ innings pitched 5 times, 300+ innings pitched 11 other times. Pitched 3 no-hitters, including a perfect game in 1904. Pitching award named in his honor. Career span 1890-1911 with Cleveland, Boston.

Robin Yount (b. 9-16-55):Baseball OF/SS. Became Brewer shortstop at 18. Landslide winner of 1982 AL MVP in 1982 when he hit .331 with 29 homers. Hit .414 in Brewers' 1982 Series loss to Cardinals. Shoulder injury made Yount move to outfield in 1984. Career span since 1974 with the Brewers.

Babe Didrikson Zaharias (b. 6-26-14, d. 9-27-56): Sportswoman. The greatest female athlete. Gold medalist in 80-meter hurdles and javelin throw at 1932 Olympics; also won silver medal in high jump (her gold medal jump was disallowed for using the then-illegal western roll). Became a golfer in 1935 and won 12 major titles, including U.S. Open 3 times (1948, 1950, 1954—a year after cancer surgery). Also helped found the LPGA in 1949.

Tony Zale (b. 5-29-13): Boxer. Born Anthony Zaleski. "The Man of Steel." Won vacant middleweight title by decision over Georgie Abrams on 11-28-41. Lost title to Billy Conn on 2-13-42. Spent almost 4 years in Navy. In sensational 3 fight series with Rocky Graziano, retained title with KO in 6 on 9-27-46; lost it to Graziano by KO in 6 on 7-17-47; and then reclaimed it by KOing Graziano in 3 on 6-10-48. Lost title to Marcel Cerdan, who KO'd him in 12 on 9-21-48. Career record: 88 bouts; won 46 by KO and 24 by decision; drew 2; lost 16, 4 by KO. Elected to Boxing Hall of Fame 1958.

Emil Zatopek (b. 9-19-22): Track and field. Czechoslovakian runner became only athlete to win gold medal in 5,000 and 10,000 meters and marathon, at 1952 Olympics. Also gold medalist in 10,000 meters at 1948 Olympics.

Obituaries

Davey Allison, 32, auto racer. A member of one of the most accomplished yet tragic families in racing history, Allison was enjoying one of his most successful seasons at the time of his death. Ed Hinton writes:

"Two years ago Davey Allison turned to a journalist acquaintance of his and said, in a calm and thoughtful manner, 'If I get killed in a race car, I'm gonna die with a smile on my face.' That statement summed up his family's acceptance of what it calls the 'occupational hazard' of stock car racing. But Davey Allison was not granted that kind of end. After a horrific collapse of fortune, the Allisons of Hueytown, Ala., are now, surely, the most tragic family in American motor racing.

"Davey Allison, 32, died on July 13 of massive head injuries he had sustained 16 hours earlier in the crash of a helicopter he was piloting; he was attempting to land in a parking lot in the infield of Talladega (Ala.) Superspeedway. That his NASCAR career had seemingly not yet peaked—he had 19 Winston Cup Series wins, including the 1992 Daytona 500—was just one of the reasons the nation's racers and fans were so shocked by his death. That he, above all other NASCAR drivers, delighted and influenced children and teenagers with his warm personality and devout life was another reason for mourning.

"Davey was the second of the two sons of former NASCAR star Bobby Allison to die in an accident in the space of 11 months. Last August, Clifford Allison, 27, was killed in a stock car crash during practice at the Michigan International Speedway. The deaths of Bobby Allison's sons came as Bobby, 55, was continuing his own agonizing recovery from a near-fatal, career-ending brain injury suffered in a crash at Pocono (Pa.) International Raceway in 1988. And Bobby's younger brother Donnie, 53, who is now retired, raced only sporadically after suffering life-threatening injuries in Charlotte in 1981. During the past year Davey had re-evaluated his priorities, especially after a very close call at Pocono last July, when his car flipped 11 times. He escaped with a broken arm and collarbone and a fractured and dislocated wrist, then raced again the next Sunday at his beloved 'home track,' Talladega....

"Ever since his father's critical injury in 1988, Davey had been the de facto head of the family. On that Sunday evening in Pennsylvania it was Davey who influenced the decision by his mother, Judy, to allow the brain surgery that would could either have left Bobby in a permanent vegetative state or given him the tiniest chance at recovery. Bobby, who was unconscious, had for years expressed his wish never to be kept on life support. But Davey persuaded Judy to sign the papers approving the operation. "We've got to take the chance," he told her, and then prayed for a miracle. He got it. By the day of Davey's helicopter crash, his father was walking and talking almost normally.

"So Davey's death not only left behind his wife, Liz, and their children, Krista, 3, and Robert, 1, but it also left the larger Allison family without its central pillar. Scarcely an hour after he died, Robert Yates, his car owner, said, "God has asked an awful lot of this family.""

Arthur Ashe, 49, tennis player. The first black man to win the U.S. Open (1968), the Australian Open (1970) and the Wimbledon singles title (1975), Ashe won 33 tournaments during a career distinguished as much by his humanitarian work as his play on the court. Kenny Moore writes:

"Why, when we knew Arthur Ashe's health was precarious, did the news of his death from pneumonia hit us like a ball peen hammer between the eyes? Why did the announcement of this gentle man's passing force even the raucous Madison Square Garden crowd at the Riddick Bowe–Michael Dokes fight into unwonted reflection, never to quite return to the fray?

"In part, surely, we reel because, even with AIDS and a history of heart attacks, Ashe didn't seem to be sick. He, of all men, hid things well. His gentility shielded us from appreciating his risk.

"In greater part, Ashe's illness had made us take stock. His 49 years of achievement in tennis, philanthropy and human rights led this magazine to name him its Sportsman of the Year for 1992. As all of us reflected on the magnitude of those achievements, it now seems, we were measuring our loss, calculating the blow. Ashe, with his usual luck, is the first SI Sportsman to pass from this green and clamorous world. His life's merit is now felt in its sudden blinding absence.

"He lay in state in Virginia's capitol, at his Richmond birthplace, the Richmond where his father taught him to help others and where his coach, Dr. Robert Johnson, taught him the exquisite manners and unshakable calm. I know what Ashe would ask. He would ask that we keep this occasion in perspective.

"He was almost comical, last November, in his insistence that he had gotten his life in such order, had provided so well for his wife, Jeanne, and his daughter, Camera, had given such clear direction to his many foundations, that if he were to be taken unexpectedly, 'it won't cause disruption.' He was not trying to dismiss the emotional cavern he would leave, just straining to be practical. He had done all he could do.

"Perhaps the man he was, an independent soul, not given to idolatry, could never fully understand how he could have been taken into so many hearts, so many minds, so many social consciences. Perhaps he could never fully realize what he meant to us. So, now it feels like the thing to do is to tell him....

"So at his best he was a wonderful paradox. Compared with the antics of his racket-throwing, blaspheming opponents, Ashe's blithe shrugging off of errors and injustices seemed almost lackadaisical, as if he didn't care. Yet his was the truer picture of focus. He cut his losses and moved on, unharmed by them.

"That rational practice shaped his life. He pointedly noted the dearth of trophies in his apartment. You had to hunt to find mementos of his 1968 U.S. Open and 1975 Wimbledon singles championships. 'I want to look forward, and trophies draw you back,' he said in November. 'And I don't want my daughter to think her daddy was just an athlete.'...

"In sporting deportment, Ashe was a contemporary of Joe DiMaggio, just barely tipping his cap to acknowledge the crowd after a home run, or of Jim Brown, calmly handing the ball to the official in the end zone, a trail of writhing, would-be tacklers sufficient testimony to his work well done. Ashe was of a time when the core of the American athlete was a sense of fair play. He believed he had control of his own behavior and therefore responsibility for his character.

"In this crucial sense he played the game quite opposite to how he lived. He played serve-and-volley tennis, attacking and reacting, hitting or missing on instinct. Yet off the court, even a single second away from furious, frustrating exchanges, his replies were always considered, always balanced. Enlightened disinterest is rare. To find it in a champion athlete is almost beyond what is given to human nature.

"Ashe, of course, was given to self-possession as a child, and then had it hardened by his father and coach into carbon-steel control because he was a pioneer, America's first great black male tennis player....

"He was offhand to the end. He had gone into New York Hospital for two weeks in early January for pneumonia, had recovered well and was resting at home. He made his last public appearance on Feb. 2, and the next day became ill with a fever. Pneumonia, unopposed by his AIDS-weakened immune system, progressed rapidly for 48 hours. During his last day he was without his voice because he was on a ventilator, but he scribbled notes to his doctors, to Jeanne and to his lawyer and friend of 25 years, Donald Dell. He dies with equanimity at 3:13 in the afternoon, Feb. 6, bearing onward a list of questions he very much wants answered.

"'He fought hard, and as in his tennis days, it was always how he played the game,' said Jeanne, getting it exactly right....

"Adrift, I find myself staring at a photograph Jeanne took to accompany the Sportsman profile. Arthur is standing on expensively groomed greensward, helping Camera swing a golf club, perhaps a nine-iron, at a bright-orange fold ball. A foot behind the ball there is a divot, and a foot to one side there is another. Eighteen inches beyond there is a third. In the clear, hilarious story of those divots is the essence of Ashe. Camera had torn up the turf *here* and *there* and then back *there*, while her father stayed patiently above her, knowing each wild miss was necessary for the child to learn. The effect is that the viewer becomes the child and feels the comfort, the blessing of being so gently guided, so loosely loved."

In New York, of AIDS-related pneumonia, February 6.

Don Barksdale, 69, basketball player. The third black player to sign an NBA contract, in 1951, Barksdale played two seasons for the Baltimore Bullets and two for the Boston Celtics, averaging 11 points and 8.0 rebounds. In 1953, he was selected to the All-Star Game, becoming the first black to be so honored. Prior to his pro career, Barksdale had played college basketball for UCLA and had been a member of the U.S. Olympic basketball team that won a gold medal at the 1948 Games in London. In Oakland, of cancer, March 8.

Alfred Butts, 93, game inventor. After Butts spent 20 years trying to sell a word-oriented board game that awarded premium points for inventive words, a vacationing Macy's executive saw the game being played at a resort and decided to buy it for his national chain of stores. The game exploded in popularity and soon Scrabble sets could be found in almost every home around the country. An architect by trade, Butts invented the game while out of work during the depression. In Rhinebeck, N.Y., of natural causes, April 4.

Roy Campanella, 71, baseball player. Among the most popular players in baseball during his career as a catcher for the Brooklyn Dodgers, Campanella remained a beloved figure in ballparks around the league after an auto accident left him a quadriplegic in 1958. Ron Fimrite writes:

"Roy Campanella liked to portray himself as just another old ballplayer who loved the game and enjoyed playing and watching it and talking about it. The sociopolitical side, the serious stuff about breaking baseball's color barrier, he gladly left to his more renowned teammate, Jackie Robinson. 'I never felt like a pioneer,' Campy would say in his later years, 'just a ballplayer.'

"That, at least, was his pose. In fact, Campanella was acutely aware of his place in history, and I can think of few athletes who demonstrated a keener sense of responsibility to their sport. In every regard Campy was baseball's best ambassador of goodwill. He was such a presence at the annual Hall of Fame celebrations at Cooperstown that he gave the impression he was either the mayor of the town or the curator of the Hall. He was equally impressive at Dodger Stadium, tirelessly entertaining an endless succession of visitors in his aerie above aisle 201. And he was a buoyant confidant in the clubhouse, able to communicate to modern players, as few old-timers have done, a sense of the game's rich history, of his own involvement in a revolutionary time.

"Yet life was never very fair to Campanella. The son of an Italian father and a black mother, he was 26 and had already played nine years in the Negro leagues when he finally made it to the majors, with the Brooklyn Dodgers, in 1948, joining Robinson, who had been called up the year before. Campy was a finished product by then, crafty and powerful, a brilliant catcher who had benefited from the tutelage of his manager with the Baltimore Elite Giants, Biz Mackey. Given his chance he quickly made up for lost time, thrice winning the National League's MVP award. In 1953 he became the first catcher to hit more than 40 homers in a season, and he led the league with 142 RBIs that same year.

And then, with terrible finality, it was all over. On a January night in 1958, Campy was driving from his liquor store in Harlem to his house on the North Shore of Long Island when his car hit an icy patch, spun out of control and after glancing off a telephone pole, rolled over. Campy suffered spinal injuries that left him paralyzed—except for minimal movement of his hands—from the shoulders down....

"'When they put me in that wheelchair,' said Campy. 'I accepted it.' And that was that. It was time to get on with the rest of his life. Doctors said it wouldn't be a long life; they gave him probably 10, maybe 20 years to live. And there would be much suffering. Somehow he prevailed over pneumonia, gallbladder surgery, diabetes and a tracheotomy to correct a severe respiratory problem. Always he endured bedsores, some so virulent they required skin grafts. But he still made it to the ball park. And he put in his time with Dodgers' community relations department, working there with his old batterymate Don Newcombe. He also gave encouragement to the handicapped, visiting hospitals and private homes, corresponding with patients all over the world. 'He's the toughest s.o.b. I've ever known,' Newcombe once said.

"It was my privilege to spend some weeks with this extraordinary man three years ago. He was still experiencing some difficulty breathing after the tracheotomy, but, using his words sparingly, he told entertaining stories about his days with those wonderful Dodger teams of the 1950s, and of growing up in Philadelphia and playing in the Negro leagues. I was astonished when he made it all the way from Los Angeles to Cooperstown for the Hall of Fame ceremonies that year. Of course, he hadn't missed an induction there since his own in 1969.

"Last Saturday night Roy Campanella died of a heart attack at his home in the Los Angeles suburb of Woodland Hills. He was 71 and had lived 35 years after his accident, surviving, as his wife, Roxie, observed, all of the doctors who forecast his early demise. He had been a great ballplayer, one of the best ever at his position. But in the final analysis, he was an even better human being. That it should be his heart that finally gave out comes as no surprise, for it was that part of him that he gave of so freely all these years. May he rest at last in peace."

Ben Chapman, 84, baseball player. Outfield mate to Babe Ruth, Chapman had a batting average of .302 in 15 seasons. In 1933 he hit .312 and was the first batter up in the first All-Star game on July 6 at Comiskey Park. In Hoover, Ala., of natural causes, July 7.

Freddie (Red) Cochrane, 77, boxer. The world welterweight champion for five years, Cochrane won the title with a 15-round decision over Freddie Zivic in July 1941. He lost the title when Marty Servo knocked him out in the fourth round in February 1946. Cochrane's professional record was 72-35-9, with 26 knockouts. In Lyons, New Jersey, of complications from Alzheimer's Disease, on January 16.

Billy Conn, 75, boxer. After two years as the light-heavyweight champion, Conn decided to fight as a heavyweight, thereby setting the stage for his unforgettable bout with heavyweight champion Joe Louis in 1941. Leading by a wide margin entering the thirteenth round, the ever brash Conn chose to slug it out with Louis instead of cruising to the easy decision. The result was a knockout by Louis and a defeat that would haunt Conn for the rest of his life. In a boxing career that ran from 1935 to 1948, Conn won 63 fights, lost 11 and had one draw. A popular figure, particularly in his native Pittsburgh area, Conn enhanced his reputation in 1990 by scuffling with a would-be robber in a convenience store after the man had punched the store's manager. "You always go with your best punch—a straight left," the then 72-year-old Conn said afterward. "I think I interrupted his plans." In Pittsburgh, of pneumonia, May 29.

Don Drysdale, 56, baseball player. Possessed of overpowering stuff, Drysdale combined with Dodgers teammate Sandy Koufax to create perhaps the most potent one-two pitching punch in baseball history. Ron Fimrite writes:

"He was one of the most-feared pitchers in baseball history, an imperious 6'5" figure whose smoking sidearm fastball seemed to be aimed directly at a right-handed batter's rib cage. And sometimes it was, for Don Drysdale held a belief common to pitchers of his day that the inside part of the plate was his domain and that trespassers must be summarily punished. It was no picnic batting against Big D.

The righthanded Drysdale and the southpaw Sandy Koufax gave the Los Angeles Dodgers of the 1960s a one-two pitching punch unequaled in modern times. In 1965 the two combined for 49 wins and 592 strikeouts. Koufax's earned run average that year was 2.04, Drysdale's 2.78. But while Koufax's numbers were generally more spectacular, Drysdale had the longer and more consistent career. He broke in with the Brooklyn Dodgers as a 19-year-old in '56 and was the staff ace the next year with 17 wins, at a time when Koufax was still trying to harness his enormous talent. And it was Drysdale who pitched six straight shutouts and a then record 58⅔ scoreless innings in '68, two years after Koufax had retired.

As with so many other fierce competitors, Drysdale was as charming and approachable off the field as he was intimidating on it. He retired as a player in 1969 and started a baseball announcing career that took him to Montreal, Texas, Anaheim and Chicago before he came home to work Dodger games in 1988.

"On July 3, one week after his old batterymate and fellow Hall of Famer, Roy Campanella, died, Drysdale was found dead of a heart attack in his hotel room in Montreal, where he had traveled with the Dodgers. Capanella's death was not unexpected, since, as former Dodger general manager buzzy Bavasi has said, he had "been living on borrowed time [since his 1958 auto accident] for 35 years." But the 56-year-old Drysdale, despite some heart problems, had seemed to be in the prime of life. He leaves his wife, former basketball star Ann Meyers, and four children.

"Baseball and, particularly, the Dodgers do not deserve any more such shocks."

Reuben Fine, 79, chess player. Along with Bobby Fischer perhaps this country's most brilliant chess genius, Fine chose to retire from competitive play after a brilliant victory at the AVRO tournament in the Netherlands in 1938, but before he could fulfill his international promise. Fine went on to become a successful psychologist and analyst and the author of many classic chess texts as well as a variety of books on psychology and the psychology of chess. In New York, of pneumonia, March 26.

Charlie Gehringer, 89, baseball player. The second baseman on pennant-winning Detroit Tiger teams in 1934, '35 and '40, Gehringer was consistency personified throughout his 19-year career, collecting at least 200 hits and 100 rbi in seven seasons and finishing his career with a lifetime batting average of .320. In 1929 he led the American League in runs, hits, doubles, triples and stolen bases; he was the AL Most Valuable Player in 1937 when he led the league with a .371 batting average. He was elected to the Hall of Fame in 1949 after a career that included 2,839 hits, 1,427 rbi and 1,774 runs. In Bloomfield Hills, Mich., after a stroke, on January 21.

Eric Guerin, 68, jockey. Best known as the jockey who lost the Kentucky Derby aboard Native Dancer in 1953, Guerin went on to ride the colt to victory in the Preakness and Belmont Stakes. In fact, the Derby loss was Native Dancer's only defeat in 22 career starts. Guerin rode to victory in his first Derby, in 1947, aboard Jet Pilot, ahead of Phalanx and Eddie Arcaro. He would go on to ride 2,712 winners and amass $17 million in purse earnings before his retirement in 1975. He was voted into the Racing Hall of Fame in 1972. In Plantation, Fla., following a lengthy illness, March 21.

Henry (Hank) Iba, 88, basketball coach. One of college basketball's most revered coaches, Iba—known throughout the coaching fraternity simply as Mr. Iba—spawned an entire generation of coaches influenced by his defensive, ball-control style of play. It was a philosophy that enabled Iba to compile a career record of 767–338, making him the second-winningest coach in college history. Most of his career was spent at Oklahoma A&M (now known as Oklahoma State), where Iba coached from 1934 until 1970, leading the Cowboys to 14 league titles and a pair of NCAA championships. The only blemish on his record was a shocking loss suffered by the Iba-coached U.S. team at the hands of the Soviet Union during the 1972 Olympics, a loss which remains controversial to this day. "He was perhaps the greatest coach of all time," said North Carolina's Dean Smith after Iba's death. "Whether he realized it or not, he has touched every coach's philosophy on the game." In Stillwater, Okla., of heart failure, January 15.

Ewing Kauffman, 76, baseball owner. Founder of the Kansas City Royals baseball club in 1969, Kauffman opened Royals Stadium four years later. During his ownership, the Royals won six division titles, two AL pennants, and one World Series. In Kansas City, of bone cancer , August 1.

Mark Koenig, 88, baseball player. The last living member of the 1927 New York Yankees' legendary Murderer's Row, Koenig was a switch-hitting shortstop with surprising power; he drove in 62 runs in '27. In his 12-season career Koenig hit .279 and scored 572 runs. In Willow, Calif., of cancer, April 22.

Ron Kostelnik, 53, football player. A member of the Green Bay Packer team that won two Super Bowls in the 1960s, Kostelnick was a ferocious presence at defensive tackle, his finest game coming in the 1966 NFL Championship Game played in the Cotton Bowl. Kostelnik made 14 tackles in the 34–27 Packer victory that earned the team a trip to the first Super Bowl. Kostelnik was killed when his car ran off the interstate highway between Cincinnati and Lexington, Ky., and overturned several times before coming to rest. It was later determined that he had suffered a heart attack before the accident. In Georgetown, Ky., January 29.

Alan Kulwicki, 38, Auto Racer. A self-made NASCAR driver, Kulwicki was killed in a plane crash in April, sending shock waves through the racing circuit that had quickly grown fond of the small, quiet Polish-American who carried his briefcase through even the boisterous garage areas. Ed Hinton writes:

"Alan Kulwicki went south in 1985 to pursue his NASCAR dream when a dream was all he had. He had sold most of his belongings back home in Greenfield, Wis., and two days before he set out for Charlotte, an electrical short ignited a fire that burned up his truck and trailer—and all the possessions he had retained. Struggling on his first NASCAR tour that year, he was a source of amusement to the veterans. He was a mechanical engineer out of the University of Wisconsin at Milwaukee in a sport in which most of his competitors had made it only through high school. The good ol' boys snickered, but he was unobtrusive, so they let him alone.

"Then they began to watch him work. The big-name drivers, who rarely dirtied their hands, had a dozen crewmen swarming around their cars; Kulwicki was doing the same amount of work by himself with maybe two or three partially skilled volunteers.

"In 1988 Kulwicki did the impossible: He won a Winston Cup race, at Phoenix. He took what he called "my Polish victory lap," driving around the track backward. And the good ol' boys cheered. Dale Earnhardt, the toughest veteran on the tour, warmed to him and began calling him Kwik, which evolved into the nickname that stuck, Kwikie.

"As his fortunes improved, he began to get offers from major teams. Twice he rebuffed legendary team owner Junior Johnson. The good ol' boys thought that Kwikie's stubborn streak would be his undoing, but he wanted to win the Winston Cup by driving for a team that he also owned.

"In 1992 he at last realized his dream. He won the Winston Cup, edging Bill Elliott and Davey Allison in the season point totals. Suddenly Kulwicki was one of the most popular drivers in the sport. Fans respected his "I did it my way" approach, and he would sit for hours signing autographs.

On Thursday, April 1,after just such an autograph session in Knoxville, Tenn., Kulwicki, and three other people, including the pilot, boarded a private plane for the short flight to Bristol, Tenn., where that weekend's NASCAR race was to be held. As the twin-engine Merlin made its final approach to the airport near Blountville, it suddenly began spiraling downward, nose-first, and crashed into a hill. Everyone on board died, and all were believed to have been killed on impact.

"But, briefly, Alan Kulwicki knew that he'd done it his way."

Reggie Lewis, 27, basketball player. When Boston Celtic captain Reggie Lewis collapsed and died on July 27 while shooting baskets at Brandeis University, all of New England mourned. That included Boston resident Leigh Montville, who wrote:

"The telephone calls do not stop. It is a warm summer night, and I have my car radio tuned to the station that features talk about sports. These are not the usual sad souls on the line, suggesting trades that never can be made—'I think the Red Sox can win the pennant, Jimmy, if they just trade Carlos Quintana for Ken Griffey Jr.'—or speaking just to speak, finding a paid listener when no other listener can be found. These are calls from ordinary, yet brokenhearted people.

"'I worked two basketball games tonight, Jimmy,' says Paul, a former NBA referee. 'These games were in the city. Kids, they all think they're going to the NBA, but they'll never come close because they're wise guys. They'll never do anything. But tonight? Tonight these wise guys all showed up with number 35 on their jerseys. It got to me, you know? They say they're all dedicating their season to Reggie They're wearing his number on their jerseys for the rest of their season…'

"'I have a poem,' an obviously young girl says. 'Is it O.K. if I read my poem, Jimmy?' She begins to read in a sad little voice.

"I have never heard anything like this. Never. Reggie Lewis is dead, 27 years old, the captain of the Boston Celtics, felled by a faulty heart. There is a great swirl of controversy about the particulars, about what the doctors told him and about the decisions he made, about his shooting baskets out at Brandeis University, about the legal and ethical ramifications of his death. The calls mostly are not about these things. These are calls about grief. A window to the soul has been opened by this event. How much hurt do how many people feel?…

"'The hard times are yet to come,' Rita from Newton says. 'There is all this attention now, but soon there will be quiet. This woman will have to raise Reggie Jr. and the child that will be born. I just want to say that my heart goes out to them…'

"The stories in the newspapers also do not stop. How good was this guy? How—for the lack of a better word—nice? The stories about the turkeys are an obvious beginning. For three years, Lewis gave out turkeys two days before Thanksgiving to needy people in Boston. No one asked him to do this. He felt a need and responded from his heart. The photos had become almost a local cliché: Reggie Lewis at his alma mater, Northeastern University, handing out 550 turkeys with a smile, signing autographs, shaking hands.…

The death of any athlete is a shock. If the best of us, the fittest of our breed, are vulnerable, what does this say about the rest of us? The good nature of this athlete seemed to double the stakes. I think about my own dealing with him, friendly yet businesslike. I remember most a tournament when he was in college. He was easily named the most valuable player, but at the award presentation he called a kid named Andre LaFleur to the microphone. LaFleur was an ordinary guy in a college program. Lewis gave him the trophy, just like that.

"'This is Joe from Watertown,' a voice on the radio says. 'I'd like to talk about Reggie.'

"Joe from Watertown? I know this voice. I know the guy. Maybe 15 years ago, maybe longer, I was at a party at his house. His kids went to the local library where my wife was the children's librarian. I know the things that have happened in his life since then.

"'My own son died of a heart problem, Jimmy,' Joe says. 'He was a hockey player, 17 years old. He died on the ice. There is a parallel with Reggie. He was the captain of his team too. I know the heartbreak that is involved here.'

"The announcer is a guy named Jimmy Myers, another person I know. He was one of Lewis's best friends and biggest advocates. He always called Lewis 'His Reggieness' and championed Lewis as the next great Celtic. Myers, in fact, broke the news to Lewis's wife, Donna, that her husband had been stricken at Brandeis. He says that his show is going to be a record, a tape for Lewis's children to listen to in the future, a testimony to the affection people had for their father. Myers is very nice with Joe. He is nice with everyone.

"'One more thing,' Joe says. 'I want everyone to know, Jimmy, that Children's Hospital has a very good "grief" center. You just go there, and there are people who will help you. They are very good.'

"'I've been there, Joe,' Jimmy says. 'Thank you for letting people know.'

"I am alone in my car, listening to the radio. Tears come down my face. I suppose I am crying for Reggie Lewis, the tragedy at hand. I also suppose I am crying for all of us."

In Boston, of heart failure, July 27.

Roger McCluskey, 63, Auto Racer. Starting in his hometown of Tucson, Ariz., in 1947, McCluskey had a competitive career that lasted 32 years. He entered 17 Indianapolis 500s, finishing third in 1973. In 1979, after winning the Milwaukee 200, he retired to work for the United States Auto Club. He became vice president and chief operating officer of the USAC. In Indianapolis, of cancer, August 29.

Johnny Mize, 80, baseball player. Known as the Big Cat, Johnny Mize was a feared batter. Steve Wulf recalls the gentle slugger:

"Mize was not called the Big Cat because of his feline grace as a first baseman. He was given the nickname by New York Giant teammate Bill Rigney, who saw him sprawled in the sun one day at the Polo Grounds and said, 'Look at him. He looks just like a big cat.'

"In fact, Mize was not much of a fielder. When Ralph Houk, who played with Mize on the New York Yankees in the early 1950s and who later became a manager, was asked recently to name the ideal designated hitter, he replied without hesitation, 'Johnny Mize.' Mize could sure hit. He is the only player to have hit 50 or more homers and to have struck out 50 or fewer times in the same season—1947, when he had 51 homers and only 42 whiffs. Over his 15-year career with the St. Louis Cardinals, the Giants and the Yankees, he had a slugging percentage of .563, the eighth highest of all time. He led the National League in batting once, home runs four times and RBIs three times. Late in his career his hitting inspired the famous lines from sportswriter Dan Parker:

> Your arm is gone, your legs likewise,
> But not your eyes, Mize, not your eyes.

"Mize was a gentle giant with a Georgia drawl. After his overdue election to the Hall of Fame in 1981, he and his wife, Marjorie, were frequent, delightful guests in Cooperstown. During one induction weekend, David Eisenhower, the grandson of one president and the son-in-law of another, was introduced to Mize. It was all the star-struck Eisenhower could do to mutter, "Not your eyes, Mize, not your eyes."

Bobby Moore, 51, soccer player. Fullback and captain on England's national team that won the World Cup in 1966, Moore was known for his tackling skills, his unflappable style of play and his lack of ego. For most of his career, he played for the London team West Ham United; he was known by the team's fans as "the people's captain." Perhaps the greatest tribute to his ability was voiced by Brazilian star Pele, who said that Moore could have played on any Brazilian team in any time period. In London, of cancer, February 24.

Willie Mosconi, 80, Pool Player. One of billiards' greatest, Mosconi could run a table—could run *successive* tables—with deadly efficiency and grand flair. Steve Rushin writes:

"He always wore a pocket square, say that for Willie Mosconi: The man could fill a pocket with style.

"The (under)world of pocket billiards was once peopled by stylish legends, cartoonish men like Alvin (Titanic Thompson) Thomas. His eye was so sharp, it was said, that he could pitch a key into a lock from across a room and shoot bullets through washers flung into the sky. When not shooting pool, Rudolph (Minnesota Fats) Wanderone engaged in eating contests. Fats, it was said, began one contest by swallowing an entire ham and telling his opponent that he wouldn't count it toward his total. That's what they say: *Fats spotted the man a ham.*

"Such impossible stories were told of Willie Mosconi as well, but with Mosconi there was a difference—the stories were true. Mosconi really did win the world championship of straight pool 15 times, between 1941 and '57. He really did run 526 consecutive balls in a straight-pool exhibition in Springfield, Ohio, calling the ball and pocket before every shot. 'I never did miss,' Mosconi said. 'I just got tired and quit.' Mosconi left this world on September 17, suffering a heart attack at age 80 in his New Jersey home. He took with him one more remnant of that Runyonesque era around Broadway, commemorated *on* broadway in the musical *Guys and Dolls.* Is it a surprise that the show's composer, Frank Loesser, was Mosconi's Army bunkmate?

"Mosconi learned to play pool (elegantly, he always called the game 'pocket billiards') in a South Philadelphia dance academy run by an uncle. At the age of six, Willie was playing exhibitions at the Friars Club in New York City, performing for its members, including his cousins Charlie and Louie, vaudevillians in the Ziegfeld Follies who had once headlined at the Palace. Mosconi's own most memorable Broadway performance came in 1948. At the Strand Theatre his match with 13-time world champion Ralph Greenleaf was to begin at 8 p.m. Trouble was, Mosconi had tickets to *Abie's Irish Rose* across Times Square that night, and curtain time was 8:30. So after Greenleaf broke the rack, Mosconi rose from his chair, chalked and ran off 125 points *and* 10 trick shots in 17 minutes. When the curtain rose on *Rose,* Mosconi was in the audience, reading his playbill.

"Minnesota Fats always called the game's great players 'legendaries.' Pool lost a legendary last September. Runyon is gone. Gleason is gone. And now, gone as well, is Mosconi.

"He didn't die. He just got tired and quit."

Johnny Most, 69, basketball announcer. The radio voice of the Boston Celtics from 1952 to 1990, Most was a beloved New England fixture, whose immediately recognizable voice was inevitably described as "gravelly." Most's most famous call was his description of the steal by Celtics guard John Havlicek that preserved a win for the Celtics over the Philadelphia 76ers in the Eastern Conference Finals of the NBA playoffs in 1965 "Havlicek stole the ball! Havlicek stole the ball!" Most screamed, over and over again. Most retired in October 1990 after a series of debilitating illnesses. He was given a night at Boston Garden two months later and his microphone was retired. In Hyannis, Mass, of a heart attack, January 3.

Pat Nappi, 75, boxing coach. The U.S. Olympic boxing coach in 1976 and '84, Nappi's teams won five gold medals, one silver and one bronze in '76 and nine golds—an Olympic record—two silvers and one bronze for an Olympic-record total of 12 medals overall in '84. Among the boxers who fought in the Olympics under Nappi's tutelage were Sugar Ray Leonard, Leon and Michael Spinks, Mark Breland, Pernell Whitaker and former heavyweight champion Evander Holyfield. In Syracuse, of cancer, February 27.

John Pennel, 53, pole vaulter. The first man to clear 17 feet in the pole vault, Pennel was a dominant figure in pole vaulting throughout the 1960s, when the fiberglass pole made its first sanctioned appearance. In an incredible string of performances in 1963, Pennel added more than nine inches to the pre-1963 world record, finally going over the 17-foot mark with a vault of 17' ¾" at the Gold Coast meet at the University of Miami on August 24. Pennel went on to win the Sullivan Award as the nation's top amateur athlete that year but was hampered by injuries at the 1964 Olympics and failed to win a medal. Throughout the rest of the decade, he battled for preeminence with fellow U.S. vaulter Bob Seagren, whose path to the gold medal at the 1968 Olympics in Mexico City was cleared by Pennel's elimination from contention when his pole fell under the bar on a successful vault that would have guaranteed him the bronze and put him in a battle with Seagren for the gold. Pennel set his eighth and last world record in 1969, clearing 17' 10¾". In Santa Monica, Calif., of cancer, September 24.

Drazen Petrovic, 28, basketball player. Underrated and improving each year, New Jersey Nets star Petrovic was cruelly cut down in his prime. Alex Wolff writes:

"'IMPOSSIBLE!' keened the headline in a Croatian newspaper, bearing word that one of that troubled land's favorite sons, 28-year-old New Jersey Net Star Drazen Petrovic, had been killed in a car accident on a rain-slicked German autobahn. But the news was crushingly true.

"Petrovic played with an intensity that belied his slacked-jawed expression on the court. 'You play correct, or we will fight!' he once snapped at Utah Jazz forward Blue Edwards, who had fixed him with an elbow. In time Edwards and the rest of the NBA came to play Drazen correct.

"Petrovic had a passionate belief in his abilities, a conviction that didn't waver even when he rode the bench for his first NBA club, the Portland Trail Blazers. In 1991 Portland obliged his request for a trade, sending him to New Jersey. Over his first off-season with the Nets he worked out zealously, adding 20 pounds to his bony frame and demonstrating a discipline many had doubted he had. Only once all

summer did he take time off, to visit his brother Aleksandr in Florida—or so he told his agent and the Nets. In fact, he had sneaked off for three days to visit family and friends in war-torn Croatia. 'I'm playing basketball," he said, "and my friends are getting killed.'

"At age 20 Petrovic scored 112 points in a game in the Yugoslav league, and at 22 he was recognized as the finest player in Europe. He was also a provocateur who spat at referees, taunted opposing fans and once emptied a bottle of mineral water over the head of a courtside official. That mix of talent and ferocity helped Petrovic excel not only in the NBA but also at the Barcelona Olympics, where he outshone celebrated teammate Toni Kukoc in leading Croatia to the silver medal, behind the Dream Team.

"Petrovic believed that xenophobia kept him off the NBA All-Star Team the past two years, during which he helped lead New Jersey back to respectability. The slight was particularly galling last season when he averaged 22.3 points a game and was third in the NBA in three-point shooting. He would have become an unrestricted free agent on July 1, 1993 and he vowed to play next season in Europe, where he felt he would receive the respect he deserved. Despite his bitterness, the onetime Trail Blazer remained a trailblazer, a man whose career will be an inspiration to the next generation of European stars."

Near Munich, Germany, of injuries sustained in a car crash, June 7.

Jim Pollard, 70, basketball player. Born in Oakland, Pollard attended Stanford University, where he was a member of The Cardinal's 1942 NCAA championship team. After playing for amateur teams in the Bay Area, Pollard signed with the Minneapolis Lakers in 1948, the team's first year of existence. He became captain of the Lakers and won six titles with the club. At 6'5" and possessed of tremendous leaping ability, he was nicknamed the Kangaroo Kid. In Stockton, CA., of natural causes, January 22.

Roy Riegels, 84, football player. An All-America center at the University of California, Riegels is far better known as Wrong-Way Riegels, the man who picked up a loose fumble and ran 69 yards in the wrong direction in the 1929 Rose Bowl. In the second quarter Cal's Benny Lom tackled Georgia Tech's Stumpy Thomason, resulting in a fumble that Riegels picked up at the Tech 30-yard line. As the entire stadium watched in stunned amazement, Riegels began in the right direction, then in eluding a would-be tackler got spun in the wrong direction and began speeding toward his own end zone. Lom tracked him down and got him turned back in the right direction at the Cal three-yard line but a group of Tech players arrived to tackle Riegels before he could correct his mistake. A safety was the eventual result of the gaffe and it proved to be the margin of victory in the 8–7 Georgia Tech victory. In Woodland, Calif., of complications from Parkinson's Disease, March 26.

Andre (The Giant) Rousimoff, 46, professional wrestler. Born with acromegaly, a disorder marked by progressive enlargement of the head, face, hands feet and chest, Rousimoff grew to the enormous size of 7' 4", 520 pounds, taking on the moniker Andre the Giant when he decided to take advantage of his size with a career in the professional wrestling ring. Rousimoff also used his bulk to good effect in his brief movie career, appearing as Fezzick the gentle giant in the Rob Reiner film *The Princess Bride*. In Paris, of an apparent heart attack, January 28.

n Schwartzwalder, 83, football coach. After winning a total of nine games over the previous four seasons, Syracuse turned to Schwartzwalder to revive the team's flagging football fortunes in 1949. Despite having just three seasons of coaching experience under his belt—and that at tiny Muhlenberg College in Allentown, Pa.—Schwartzwalder quickly turned the team around, going on to record 22 winning seasons out of his 25 at the school and compiling a won-lost record of 153-91-3, making him the winningest coach in Syracuse history. His trademark running offenses were built around a series of spectacular running backs, including Jim Brown, Ernie Davis, Floyd Little and Larry Csonka. In 1959 the Orangemen were the consensus national champions after going 11-0 and finishing the season with a 23-14 win over Texas in the Cotton Bowl. In St. Petersburg, Fla., of a heart attack, April 28.

Chris Street, 21, college basketball player. As a player and as a young man, Street touched people throughout Iowa and the college basketball world. Phil Taylor writes:

"Both the women's and men's basketball teams at Iowa are ranked in the Top 20, but no matter how successful they are on the court, their memories of the 1992-93 season will be forever shrouded in black. On Thanksgiving Day Bill Stringer, the 47-year-old husband of women's coach Vivian Stringer and an exercise physiologist with the school's athletic department, died of a heart attack. Then on Jan. 19 Chris Street, a 6'8" junior forward on the men's team, was killed in an auto accident. 'These kinds of things tear the guts out of an organization,' says athletic director Bob Bowlsby.

The grief has extended throughout the state. The Iowa House of Representatives observed a moment of silence for Street, and the flags in Indianola, Iowa, his hometown, flew at half staff. Several players from rival Iowa State wrote Street's uniform number, 40, on the backs of their sneakers, and the entire Cyclone team wore black ribbons or armbands in his memory. Iowa State forward Morgan Wheat, who played against Street in high school, changed his number from 00 to 40 before the Cyclones' 81-74 upset of Oklahoma.

"Street, who was averaging 14.5 points and was one of the top rebounders in the Big Ten, was driving back to campus with his girlfriend Kimberly Sue Vinton, after a team meal, when his car crashed into a snowplow. Vinton was released from the hospital on Sunday. Street was buried wearing his gold Hawkeye uniform, the one reserved for special games, and his warmup suit."

Jim Valvano, 47, college basketball coach. Leader of the 1983 NCAA champion North Carolina State Wolfpack, Valvano waged a public battle with cancer over the last year of his life. Gary Smith writes:

"Why just one Wig? Jim Valvano was sitting in front of a few hundred hairpieces one day last summer, his head freshly shaved because he didn't want to wait for chemotherapy to make him bald, his mind mulling one of the great existential questions: Why just one wig?

" 'One of the wigs had hair down to the shoulders, like a rock star's,' he recalled a few months later. 'One was a crew cut, another one had a ponytail, another one made me look like the Beatles. I thought, God, wouldn't it be great? People could turn on their TV's one night and I'd be Steven Seagal, with the ponytail, The next night they'd turn it on and I'd be a Marine sergeant. The next I'd be a rocker, and the night after that, I wouldn't wear one at all and be Sigourney Weaver in Alien 3, and then...'

"He wanted to be everything, to try on everyone's life

for size. That was Jimmy Vee's glory and, some said, his sin. Until he faced cancer, he saw no boundaries in life. When you sat and talked with him, you laughed a lot and you forgot about your own boundaries, too.

"I was nervous before I met him for the first time last fall. How could I ask a total stranger questions about his impending death? But Vee didn't flinch. He put both arms around what he felt at midnight—when he was awake, alone, terrified of what was happening—and he handed it to me. He wasn't afraid to do that.

"When he was diagnosed with metastatic adenocarcinoma in June of '92, many people still saw him as the scandal-scarred basketball coach who had been drummed out of NC State in 1990. By the time he died at age 47, on April 28, 1993 at Duke University Medical Center, most everyone saw him as something else. The two images that were played over and over on the TV news—the mop-haired Vee ricocheting all over the court in search of someone to hug after his Wolfpack had shocked Houston to win the '83 NCAA championship and the gaunt Vee peering down the podium at ESPN's American Sports Awards roaring that 'Cancer can take away all my physical abilities, but it cannot touch my mind, it cannot touch my heart, and it cannot touch my soul'—were so powerful that the scandal that had occurred between those events was eclipsed. In an odd way, just as Valvano used to take risks at the end of a close game to ensure that his team would get the last shot, so he had control at the end of his life.

"He achieved that by dying a public death. During his last few months as a basketball analyst for ESPN and ABC, his family and colleagues would shake their heads in disbelief as he squirmed incessantly in a chair, trying to find some position in which the pain wouldn't overwhelm him, then hobbled in front of camera, took a deep breath…and came alive, sparkling with all his old wit and intelligence, making everyone watching forget how sick he was.

"He had hoped to attend the Final Four in March and to accept a personal invitation from Bill Clinton to visit the White House in late April. He was going to go in a wheelchair, wearing a small plastic container that would pump morphine into his his veins a few times a minute. But his body wouldn't let him, and he died in the Duke hospital, with his wife, Pam, and his three daughters, Nicole, Jamie and Lee Ann, at his side.

"Last spring, when he was in Frankfurt, Germany, for ABC's coverage of a World League football game and he first began feeling the pain of his disease, he saw something he had never seen before, in the stadium parking lot. People were donning Velcro-covered clothing, running as fast and leaping as high as they could to stick themselves to a wall. 'Forget the pain, gotta do it,' Valvano remembered telling himself. 'Can't go all the way to Frankfurt and not jump and stick to a wall.'

"He clenched his teeth. He ran. He jumped. He stuck. That's what everyone will always remember about him. Vee stuck."

In Durham, North Carolina, of cancer, April 28.

David Waymer, 34, football player. A durable defensive back who played for the New Orleans Saints, the San Francisco 49ers and the Los Angeles Raiders, Waymer never missed a regular season game during a 13-year career that included an appearance in the Pro Bowl in 1987. Waymer collapsed and died of heart failure at his home in Mooresville, N.C. on April 30. An autopsy revealed that Waymer had recently ingested cocaine and it was later determined that the drug was a major contributor to his death.